FEDERAL TAX PRACTICE AND PROCEDURE
CASES, MATERIALS AND PROBLEMS

Second Edition

■ ■ ■

By

Camilla E. Watson
Professor of Law
University of Georgia, School of Law

Brookes D. Billman, Jr.
Professor of Law
New York University, School of Law

AMERICAN CASEBOOK SERIES®

WEST®

A Thomson Reuters business

Mat #41169600

© West, a Thomson business, 2005
© 2012 Thomson Reuters
   610 Opperman Drive
   St. Paul, MN 55123
   1–800–313–9378
Printed in the United States of America

ISBN: 978–0–314–27643–8

Dedication

To BJ, with grateful appreciation
for everything you do
                              CEW

To MGB, HGB, and AGB
                              BDB

*

PREFACE TO THE SECOND EDITION

A Federal Tax Practice and Procedure course should be a basic component of any tax curriculum. The issues it presents pertain mostly to compliance (e.g., filing returns, paying the tax, collections) and the problems arising from compliance (e.g., overpayments, tax controversies and litigation) or noncompliance (e.g., penalties and criminal prosecution). Federal tax practice and procedure is divided into two general components: civil and criminal. This casebook introduces students to both components and is designed to be used in a variety of two or three credit hour courses or seminars at both the J.D. and LL.M. levels. These include courses in civil tax practice and procedure, ethics of tax practice, tax litigation, and tax crimes. The casebook contains questions and problems throughout to test students' comprehension of the material and to provoke further thought about the issues presented. While a limited background in substantive federal tax is useful, it is not required. Therefore, students may take these courses without first taking Federal Income Taxation. It is recommended (although not required) that students take Criminal Law or Criminal Procedure prior to taking Tax Crimes.

This second edition is updated through September 2011. Between the first and second editions, there have been numerous cases and tax legislation that made significant changes to the practice and procedure area. We took the liberty in this new edition to change the structure of the first chapter to make it shorter and more of a basic introductory chapter. Some of the material in the original version of Chapter 1 relating to the United States Tax Court has been moved to Chapter 8 in which the subject of litigation in that court is fully considered. Otherwise, the organization of this edition follows the basic organization of the first edition. In some chapters, however, new material has been added and some old material may have been deleted. As one example, Chapter 7 now contains a new section focusing upon Collection Due Process. This reflects the large volume of cases, primarily in the United States Tax Court, in which taxpayers have exercised their rights to have their collection issues reviewed first by the Internal Revenue Service and then by a court of law.

We have edited most of the cases and other materials in an attempt to keep the book at a manageable length. Deleted material has been marked with asterisks (* * *), although footnotes, citations, and dissenting opinions may have been deleted without indication. Footnotes retain their numbering from the original sources.

This edition has benefitted greatly from the advice and suggestions of Carlton M. Smith, Clinical Associate Professor of Law and Director of the Tax Clinic, Benjamin M. Cardozo School of Law. We are deeply grateful for his assistance.

As always, we encourage any questions, comments and suggestions.

*

CAMILLA E. WATSON
BROOKES D. BILLMAN

October, 2011

SUMMARY OF CONTENTS

	Page
PREFACE	v
TABLE OF CASES	xxxiii
TABLE OF INTERNAL REVENUE CODE SECTIONS	xxxix
TABLE OF OTHER U.S. CODE SECTIONS	xlv
TABLE OF TREASURY REGULATIONS	xlvii
TABLE OF CIRCULAR 230 SECTIONS	xlix
TABLE OF REVENUE RULINGS	li
TABLE OF REVENUE PROCEDURES	liii
TABLE OF MISCELLANEOUS RULINGS	lv
TABLE OF INTERNAL REVENUE MANUAL SECTIONS	lvii
TABLE OF TAX COURT RULES	lix
TABLE OF SECONDARY AUTHORITIES	lxi

Chapter 1. Introduction to Federal Tax Practice and Procedure ... 1

I. The Legislative Process	2
II. The Administrative Process	5
A. The Restructured IRS	6
B. Administrative Interpretation of the Tax Laws	10
III. The Judicial Process – An Overview	63
A. The United States Tax Court	63
B. The United States District Courts	65
C. The United States Court of Federal Claims	67
D. The United States Bankruptcy Courts	67

Chapter 2. Practice Before the Internal Revenue Service ... 70

I. Introduction	70
A. What Constitutes Practice Before the IRS and Who is Eligible to Practice?	70
B. The Uneasy Professional Alliance Between Lawyers and Accountants	72
II. Standards of Practice	79
A. Statutory Standards – Civil Penalties	79
B. Statutory Standards – Criminal Penalties	114
C. Injunctions Against Preparers	115

D. Professional Standards 123
E. Administrative Standards – Circular 230 143
III. The Government's Conflicting Duties of Disclosure and
      Confidentiality 155
    A. Freedom of Information Act 155
    B. Disclosure under the IRC 170
    C. The Privacy Act 171
    D. The Government's Duty of Confidentiality 173
IV. The Government's Access to Taxpayer Information 194
    A. Federally Authorized Tax Practitioners 195
    B. The Attorney-Client Privilege 195
    C. The Work Product Doctrine 207

Chapter 3. Taxpayer Compliance and Administrative
       Review of Returns **234**

I. Compliance 234
    A. Returns 234
    B. Payment 253
II. Examination of Returns 255
    A. In General 255
    B. Access to Taxpayers' Books and Records 262
    C. Specialized Audits 276
III. Representing the Audited Taxpayer 299
    A. Pre-Audit Preparation 300
    B. The Taxpayer Bill of Rights 303
    C. Conducting the Examination 306
    D. Concluding the Audit 308
IV. The Appeals Process 311
    A. The Protest 313
    B. Docketed Cases 314
    C. Request for Technical Advice 315
    D. Alternative Dispute Resolution 316
    E. Settlement Agreements 316

Chapter 4. The Notice of Deficiency and Administrative
       Appeals **319**

I. Assessment Procedure 319
    A. Validity of a Notice of Deficiency 319
    B. Waiver of Restrictions on Assessment 334
    C. Jeopardy and Termination Assessments 346
II. Statutes of Limitations for Assessment 347
    A. Substantial Omissions of Income – § 6501(e)(1) 348

B. Amended Returns 366
C. Extensions by Agreement 374

Chapter 5. Overpayments – Refunds, Credits, Abatements and Judicial Determinations **388**
I. The Refund Claim 388
   A. Overpayment 388
   B. Formal Claims and Waivers of Claims 402
   C. Informal Claims 407
   D. Substantial Variance 411
   E. Filing the Claim 419
II. Statute of Limitations 429
   A. Internal Revenue Code § 6511 430
   B. Payment 432
   C. Timing of the Claim 446
   D. Tolling the Statute of Limitations 450
   E. Remedies to Absolve the Harshness of the Statute of
      Limitations 456
III. Administrative Review of the Claim 482
   A. Abatement 483
   B. Joint Committee Review 485
IV. Refund Litigation 485
   A. Full Payment 486
   B. The Divisible Tax Principle 497
   C. Limitations Periods on Refund Suits 498
   D. Pleadings 503
   E. Burden of Proof 504

Chapter 6. Civil Penalties and Interest **509**
I. Delinquency Penalties 509
   A. Failure to File 510
   B. Failure to Pay Tax Shown on Return 516
   C. Failure to Pay After Notice and Demand 522
   D. Reasonable Cause 522
II. Accuracy-Related Penalties 533
   A. Negligence or Disregard of Rules and Regulations 534
   B. Substantial Understatement of Income Tax 548
   C. Substantial Valuation Misstatements 600
III. The Civil Fraud Penalty 617
   A. Recognizing Fraud 618
   B. Calculating the Fraud Penalty 623
   C. Collateral Estoppel 631

IV. Miscellaneous Penalties   639
    A. Frivolous Returns   639
    B. Estimated Tax Penalty   646
V. Interest   647
    A. Underpayments   648
    B. Overpayments   653
    C. Netting of Overpayments and Underpayments   668
VI. Abatement of Penalties and Interest   670
    A. Erroneous IRS Advice   670
    B. Insufficient IRS Notice   671
    C. Judicial Review of Abatement Decisions   672

Chapter 7.   The Collection Process **679**
I. The Summary Collection Process: Liens, Levies,
          and Distraint   679
    A. The Notice and Demand for Payment   680
    B. The Tax Lien   693
    C. Collection Due Process   738
    D   Enforcement of the Lien   768
II. Collection Actions in Bankruptcy Proceedings   827
    A. The Automatic Stay   827
    B. The Bankruptcy Estate   837
III. Collection from Third Parties   859
    A. Innocent Spouses   859
    B. Transferee and Fiduciary Liability   889
    C. Trust Fund Taxes   904
IV. Alternative Collection   936
    A. Installment Payment Arrangements   937
    B. Offers in Compromise   939

Chapter 8.   Tax Court Litigation **950**
I. The Tax Court   950
    A. Tribunal or Court?   950
    B. Appeals   960
II. Deficiency Litigation   963
    A. Tax Court Jurisdiction   964
    B. Case Designation   982
    C. Pleadings   987
    D. Discovery   988
    E. Pre-Trial Proceedings   1008
    F. Trial   1021
    G. Post-Trial Proceedings   1044

II. Recovery of Costs 1055
   A. Limitations on the Right to Recover Costs 1055
   B. Appealing a Denial of Costs 1099

Chapter 9.   Federal Tax Crimes **1100**
I. Criminal Offenses Under the Internal Revenue Code
          (Title 26) 1101
   A. Most Commonly Prosecuted Offenses 1101
   B. Miscellaneous Offenses 1195
   C. Defenses 1197
II. General Criminal Offenses Under Title 18 of the
          U.S. Code 1218
   A. Conspiracy – 18 U.S.C. § 371 1218
   B. False Statements – 18 U.S.C. § 1001 1239
   C. Mail Fraud, Wire Fraud and Bank Fraud 1248
   D. RICO – Title 18 U.S.C. §§ 1961-1968 1254
III. Currency Transaction Offenses 1268
   A. Money Laundering – Title 18 U.S.C. §§ 1956
          and 1957 1268
   B. Currency Transaction Reporting – Title 26 U.S.C.
          § 6050I 1296
   C. The Bank Secrecy Act 1303
IV. Federal Sentencing Guidelines in Tax Offenses 1319
   A. Determination of Tax Loss 1319
   B. Sentencing Under the Guidelines 1325

**Chapter 10.   Criminal Tax Investigation and
          Prosecution** **1342**
I. Initiation of a Criminal Investigation 1342
   A. The Interface of Civil and Criminal Investigations ... 1343
   B. Methods of Investigation 1355
   C. Voluntary Disclosure 1380
   D. Investigative Techniques 1386
II. Prosecution of a Criminal Tax Case 1388
   A. Venue 1388
   B. Third Party Witnesses 1395
   C. Defense Challenges 1410

INDEX 1503

*

TABLE OF CONTENTS

Page

PREFACE v
TABLE OF CASES xxxiii
TABLE OF INTERNAL REVENUE CODE SECTIONS xxxix
TABLE OF OTHER U.S. CODE SECTIONS xlv
TABLE OF TREASURY REGULATIONS xlvii
TABLE OF CIRCULAR 230 SECTIONS xlix
TABLE OF REVENUE RULINGS li
TABLE OF REVENUE PROCEDURES liii
TABLE OF MISCELLANEOUS RULINGS lv
TABLE OF INTERNAL REVENUE MANUAL SECTIONS lvii
TABLE OF TAX COURT RULES lix
TABLE OF SECONDARY AUTHORITIES lxi

**Chapter 1. Introduction to Federal Tax Practice
and Procedure** 1
I. The Legislative Process 2
   Notes and Questions 4
II. The Administrative Process 5
   A. The Restructured IRS 6
      Notes 9
   B. Administrative Interpretation of the Tax Laws 10
      1. Treasury Regulations 10
         a. Promulgation 10
         b. Effective Date 12
         c. Judicial Review of Regulations 12
            *1) Interpretive and Legislative
               Regulations* 13
            Mayo Foundation for Medical Education
               and Research v. United States 14
               Notes and Questions 23
            2) Procedural Regulations 25
      2. Public and Private Rulings 26
         a. Revenue Rulings 26
            1) Retroactivity 27
            William L. Becker v. Commissioner 27

Notes and Questions 32
   2) *Scope of Judicial Review* 33
      United States v. Mead Corporation 34
      Notes and Questions 49
   b. *Letter Rulings* 50
   1) *Consistency in Treatment of Taxpayers* 50
      Bookwalter v. Brecklein 50
      Notes and Questions 56
   2) *Requesting a Ruling* 56
      Question 57
   3. Other IRS Rulings and Publications 57
      a. *Revenue Procedures* 57
         Vosters v. United States 57
         Note and Question 58
      b. *Chief Counsel Advice* 59
         Notes 60
      c. *Closing Agreements* 60
      d. *Determination Letters* 61
      e. *Information Letters* 61
      f. *Actions on Decisions and Acquiescences* 62
      g. *Internal Revenue Manual* 63
III. The Judicial Process – An Overview 63
   A. The United States Tax Court 63
   B. The United States District Courts 65
      Question 67
   C. The United States Court of Federal Claims 67
   D. The United States Bankruptcy Courts 67
      Question 69

**Chapter 2. Practice Before the Internal Revenue
   Service** **70**
I. Introduction 70
   A. What Constitutes Practice Before the IRS and
      Who is Eligible to Practice 70
      Questions 72
   B. The Uneasy Professional Alliance Between
      Lawyers and Accountants 72
   Notes and Questions 78
II. Standards of Practice 79
   A. Statutory Standards – Civil Penalties 79
   1. Return Preparer Penalty for Substantial
      Understatement of Tax Liability – § 6694(a) 79

        a. *Who is a Preparer?* 80
            Goulding v. United States 80
            Notes and Questions 87
            Problem 88
        b. *Substantial Authority* 89
            Questions 90
        c. *Reasonable Basis* 90
        d. *Adequate Disclosure* 90
            Question 91
        e. *Reasonable Cause* 91
            Question 92
    2. Penalty for Understatement Due to Willful,
        Reckless or Intentional Conduct – § 6694(b) 92
    3. Other Preparer Penalties Under § 6695 92
        Question 93
    4. Promoting Abusive Tax Shelters – § 6700 93
        In Re Tax Refund Litigation v. United States 93
        Notes and Questions 104
    5. Aiding and Abetting Understatement of
        Tax Liability – § 6701 106
        Berger v. United States 106
        Notes and Questions 112
        Lea v. United States 112
B. Statutory Standards – Criminal Penalties 114
C. Injunctions Against Preparers 115
    United States v. Gleason 115
    Notes 123
D. Professional Standards 123
    1. General Standards of Practice – Lawyers 124
        ABA Model Rule 3.3 124
        ABA Formal Opinion 314 124
        ABA Formal Opinion 85-352 126
        Questions 129
    2. Tax Shelter Opinions – Lawyers' Standards 129
        ABA Formal Opinion 346 (Revised) 130
        Questions 139
    3. Standards of Practice – CPAs 139
        Question 143
E. Administrative Standards – Circular 230 143
    1. General Standards Applicable to Practitioners 143
        Harary v. United States 145
        Notes and Questions 148

2. Tax Shelter Opinions 148
   a. Covered Opinions 151
   b. Other Written Advice 153
   Notes and Questions 154
III. The Government's Conflicting Duties of Disclosure and
   Confidentiality 155
   A. Freedom of Information Act 155
   U.S. Department of Justice v. Tax Analysts 158
   Notes and Questions 170
   B. Disclosure under the IRC 170
   C. The Privacy Act 171
   D. The Government's Duty of Confidentiality 173
   Johnson v. Sawyer 174
   Notes and Questions 192
IV. The Government's Access to Taxpayer Information 194
   A. Federally Authorized Tax Practitioners 195
   Questions 195
   B. The Attorney-Client Privilege 195
   United States v. El Paso Company 196
   Notes and Questions 206
   C. The Work Product Doctrine 207
   United States v. Textron, Inc. 208
   Notes and Questions 233

Chapter 3. Taxpayer Compliance and Administrative
   Review of Returns 234
I. Compliance 234
   A. Returns 234
      1. What Constitutes a Return? 235
      Williams v. Commissioner 235
      Notes and Questions 240
      2. Filing the Return 242
         a. Electronic Filing 243
         b. Extensions of Time to File 244
         Natalie Holdings, Ltd. v. United States 245
         Notes and Problems 248
      3. Amended Returns 249
         Goldstone v. Commissioner 250
         Notes 253
   B. Payment 253
      Questions 254
II. Examination of Returns 255

A. In General 255
   Questions 256
   1. Methods of Return Selection 256
      Note and Question 258
   2. General Methods of Conducting Audits 259
   3. Nonfilers 260
      Notes and Question 262
B. Access to Taxpayers' Books and Records 262
   United States v. Powell 263
   Notes and Question 270
   1. Third Party Contacts 271
   2. Prohibition Against Subsequent Inspections 271
      United States v. Crespo 272
      Notes and Questions 275
C. Specialized Audits 276
   1. TEFRA Partnership Audit Procedure 277
      Notes 278
      a. *Partnership Items* 279
      b. *The Tax Matters Partner* 280
        Notes 282
      c. *Administrative Proceedings* 282
      d. *Statute of Limitations on Assessment* 286
      e. *The* Munro *Problem and Its Solution* 287
      f. *Requests for Administrative Adjustment* 289
        Question 290
   2. Employment Tax Examination Program 290
      IRS Watch: Focus on Bridging the
        Employment Tax Gap 292
        Notes and Questions 297
   3. Coordinated Examination Program 298
III. Representing the Audited Taxpayer 299
  A. Pre-Audit Preparation 300
     Questions 303
  B. The Taxpayer Bill of Rights 303
     Salman v. Swanson 304
     Notes and Question 306
  C. Conducting the Examination 306
     Question 308
  D. Concluding the Audit 308
    1. Agreed Cases 308
    2. Unagreed Cases 309

a. *Preliminary Notice of Deficiency (the "30-Day Letter")* 309
b. *Responses to the 30-Day Letter* 310
IV. The Appeals Process 311
   A. The Protest 313
     Questions 314
   B. Docketed Cases 314
   C. Request for Technical Advice 315
   D. Alternative Dispute Resolution 316
   E. Settlement Agreements 316
     1. Appeals Office Special Purpose Waiver 317
     2. Closing Agreements 317
     3. Collateral Agreement 318

Chapter 4. The Notice of Deficiency and Assessment Procedure **319**
I. Assessment 319
   A. Validity of a Notice of Deficiency 319
     Mulvania v. Commissioner 320
     Notes and Questions 325
     Armstrong v. Commissioner 326
     Notes and Questions 332
   B. Waiver of Restrictions on Assessment 334
     1. The Consequences of Signing a Form 870 334
       Webster and Herlach v. Commissioner 334
       Question 337
     2. Offer to Waive Restrictions on Assessment and Collection of Deficiency 337
       Whitney v. United States 337
       Notes and Questions 344
   C. Jeopardy and Terminations Assessments 346
II. Statute of Limitations For Assessment 347
   Notes 348
   A. Substantial Omissions of Income – § 6501(e)(1) 348
     The Colony, Inc. v. Commissioner 348
     Notes and Question 351
     Home Concrete and Supply v. Commissioner 353
     Notes 365
   B. Amended Returns 366
     Badaracco v. Commissioner 366
     Questions 374
   C. Extensions by Agreement 374

1. The Nature of the Agreement 375
Hubert v. Internal Revenue Service 375
Notes 378
2. Termination of an Open-Ended Extension 378
Holof v. Commissioner 378
Notes and Question 387

**Chapter 5. Overpayments – Refunds, Credits,
Abatements and Judicial Determinations** 388
I. The Refund Claim 388
A. Overpayment 388
Internal Revenue Code § 6401 389
Internal Revenue Code § 6402 389
Internal Revenue Code § 6514 389
Lewis v. Reynolds 390
Notes and Questions 391
Pacific Gas and Electric Co. v. United States 392
Notes 402
B. Formal Claims and Waivers of Claims 402
Kikalos v. United States 403
Notes 406
C. Informal Claims 407
Ebert v. United States 407
Notes and Questions 410
D. Substantial Variance 411
Ottawa Silica Co. v. United States 411
Notes and Questions 418
E. Filing the Claim 419
1. In General 419
2. Proper Parties 419
a. *Non-Taxpayer Third Parties* 419
Munaco v. United Statess 419
Notes and Questions 426
b. *The Anti-Assignment Statute* 426
R & L Refunds, Inc. v. United States 426
Questions 429
II. Statute of Limitations 429
A. Internal Revenue Code § 6511 430
Problem 431
Questions 432
B. Payment 432
Deaton v. Commissioner 432

        Notes and Questions 443
        Problem 445
    C. Timing of the Claim 446
        Omohundro v. United States 446
        Notes and Question 449
        Problems 450
    D. Tolling the Statute of Limitations 450
        Doe v. KPMG 450
        Notes and Questions 455
    E. Remedies to Absolve the Harshness of the Statute of
            Limitations 456
      1. Statutory Mitigation 456
        First National Bank of Omaha v. United States . . . 456
        Notes and Questions 470
      2. Equitable Recoupment 471
        Menard, Inc. v. Commissioner 471
        Notes and Questions 482
III. Administrative Review of the Claim 482
    A. Abatement 483
    B. Joint Committee Review 485
IV. Refund Litigation 485
    A. Full Payment 486
        Flora v. United States 486
        Notes and Question 496
        Problem 496
    B. The Divisible Tax Principle 497
        Steele v. United States 497
        Notes and Question 498
    C. Limitation Periods on Refund Suits 498
        Notes and Questions 499
      1. Suits on Account Stated 500
      2. Tax Court Claims 500
        Questions 503
    D. Pleadings 503
      1. The Complaint 503
      2. The Answer 503
    E. Burden of Proof 504
        Knudsen v. Commissioner 504
        Notes and Questions 508

Chapter 6. Civil Penalties and Interest **509**
I. Delinquency Penalties 509

A. Failure to File 510
Estate of Forgey 511
Notes and Questions 515
B. Failure to Pay Tax Shown on Return 516
Cabirac v. Commissioner 517
Notes and Question 520
Problems 521
C. Failure to Pay After Notice and Demand 522
D. Reasonable Cause 522
United States v. Boyle 523
Notes and Questions 532
II. Accuracy-Related Penalties 533
A. Negligence or Disregard of Rules 534
1. The Negligence Penalty 535
Wallis v. Commissioner 536
Notes and Questions 541
2. The "Disregard" Penalty 542
Drucker v. Commissioner 542
Notes and Questions 547
B. Substantial Understatement of Income Tax 548
Woods, II v. Commissioner 548
Notes 555
1. Substantial Authority 555
Peerless Industries, Inc. v. United States 556
Notes and Questions 565
Estate of Kluener v. Commissioner 567
Notes and Question 577
2. Adequate Disclosure 577
Henry v. Commissioner 578
Notes 581
Problems 581
3. Reasonable Cause 582
NPR Investments, LLC v. United States 582
Notes and Question 597
4. Tax Shelters/Reportable Transactions 597
Notes and Question 600
C. Substantial Valuation Misstatements 600
1. Determining When an Underpayment is
Attributable to a Valuation Overstatement 601
Donahue v. Commissioner 601
Notes 606
Problem 607

2. Reasonable Cause 608
Jacobson v. Commissioner 608
Notes and Questions 616
III. The Civil Fraud Penalty 617
A. Recognizing Fraud 618
Nelon v. Commissioner 618
Notes and Questions 622
B. Calculating the Fraud Penalty 623
Levinson v. United States 623
Notes and Question 630
Problems 630
C. Collateral Estoppel 631
Wright v. Commissioner 631
Notes and Questions 638
IV. Miscellaneous Penalties 639
A. Frivolous Returns 639
Ganz v. United States 640
Notes and Questions 645
B. Estimated Tax Penalty 646
Notes 648
V. Interest 648
A. Underpayments 649
1. Exceptions to the General Rule of Interest
Accrual 649
a. *Suspension of Interest* 649
b. *Deposits Against* Interest 650
Notes and Questions 652
2. Effect of Carrybacks 652
Question 653
B. Overpayments 653
1. Claim for Refund 653
Problems 654
2. Crediting of Overpayments 655
a. *Earlier Arising Underpayment* 655
Problems 655
b. *Later Arising Underpayment* 656
Marsh & McLennan Companies v.
United States 656
Questions 667
3. Erroneous Refunds 667
Note 669
C. Netting of Overpayments and Underpayments 668

Notes 669
VI. Abatement of Penalties and Interest 670
  A. Erroneous IRS Advice 670
  B. Insufficient IRS Notice 671
    Notes and Problems 672
  C. Judicial Review of Abatement Decisions 672
    Hinck v. United States 672
    Notes 678

Chapter 7. The Collection Process **679**
I. The Summary Collection Process: Liens, Levies,
    and Distraint 679
  A. The Notice and Demand for Payment 680
    Planned Investments, Inc. v. United States 680
    Notes and Questions 686
    Blackston v. United States 687
    Notes and Questions 692
  B. The Tax Lien 693
    1. Scope of the Lien 694
      United States v. Craft 694
      Notes and Questions 706
    2. Duration of the Lien 707
      Questions 709
    3. Priority of Claims 709
      a. Statutory Priorities and inchoate Claims 710
      Valley Bank of Nevada v. City of Henderson 710
      Notes and Questions 715
      b. Superpriorities 716
      United States v. Ripa 717
      Notes and Questions 723
      Problem 724
      c. Claims Arising in Insolvency Outside of
        Bankruptcy 724
      United States v. Estate of Romani 724
      Notes and Questions 735
    4. Releasing the Lien 736
      Question 737
      Problems 737
  C. Collection Due Process 738
    1. Tax Court Review 739
      a. Abuse of Discretion 739
      Venatieri v. Commissioner 739

    Notes 748
   b. *Scope of the Record* 748
    Robinette v. Commissioner 748
    Notes 758
  2. Statute of Limitations 759
   Problems 760
  3. Equivalent Hearing 761
   Craig v. Commissioner 761
   Notes 768
 D. Enforcement of the Lien 768
  1. Judicial Enforcement 768
   United States v. Barr 768
   Notes and Questions 779
  2. Administrative Enforcement 780
   United States v. National Bank of Commerce 780
   Notes and Questions 794
   American Trust v. United States 795
   Notes and Question 798
   a. *Sale of Seized Property* 799
    Grable & Sons Metal Products Inc. v.
     Darue Engineering Co. 801
    Question 807
   b. *Civil Damages for Wrongful Collection* 808
    Johnson v. United States 808
    Notes 813
   c. *Restraining Collection* 813
    Sokolow v. United States 813
    Notes and Questions 815
  3. Statute of Limitations 815
   United States v. Weintraub 816
   Notes and Questions 826
II. Collection Actions in Bankruptcy Proceedings 827
 A. The Automatic Stay 827
  In Re Hunt 828
  Notes and Questions 837
 B. The Bankruptcy Estate 837
  Begier v. IRS 838
  Notes and Questions 846
  1. Priority of Tax Claims in Bankruptcy 848
   Problems 850
  2. Discharge of Liabilities 850
   Young v. United States 852

Notes 858
III. Collection from Third Parties 859
  A. Innocent Spouses 859
    1. Requirements for Relief 860
      Cheshire v. Commissioner 860
      Notes and Questions . . . . : 870
    2. Tax Court Jurisdiction (Stand Alone Cases) 871
      Commissioner v. Neal 871
  B. Transferee and Fiduciary Liability 889
    Stanko v. Commissioner 890
    Notes and Questions 897
    Grieb v. Commissioner 898
    Notes and Questions 903
  C. Trust Fund Taxes 904
    1. The Nature of the Tax 904
      Mortenson v. National Union Fire Insurance
        Company 904
      Notes and Question 909
    2. The Responsible Person 910
      Davis v. United States 910
      Notes and Questions 921
    3. Joint and Several Liability 922
      McCray v. United States 922
      Notes 924
    4. Allocation of Partial Payment 925
      Muntwyler v. United States 925
      Notes and Question 929
    5. Lenders and Sureties 930
      United States v. Security Pacific Business
        Credit, Inc. 931
      Notes and Questions 935
IV. Alternative Collection 936
  A. Installment Payment Arrangements 937
    Notes 939
  B. Offers in Compromise 939
    Fowler v. Commissioner 940
    Notes and Questions 947

Chapter 8. Tax Court Litigation **950**
I. The Tax Court 950
  A. Tribunal or Court? 950
    Freytag v. Commissioner 950

Notes 959
B. Appeals 960
Lawrence v. Commissioner 960
Golsen v. Commissioner 961
Notes and Questions 963
II. Deficiency Litigation 963
A. Tax Court Jurisdiction 964
1. Exclusivity of Tax Court Jurisdiction 965
Wagner v. Commissioner 965
Notes and Question 968
2. Requirements for Jurisdiction 968
a. *Sufficiency of the Notice of Deficiency* 968
Estate of Rickman v. Commissioner 969
Notes 975
b. *Proper Parties* 975
Fletcher Plastics, Inc. v. Commissioner 976
Notes 980
Problems 980
c. *Timely Petition* 981
Correia v. Commissioner 981
Notes 982
B. Case Designation 982
Dressler v. Commissioner 983
Notes and Questions 986
C. Pleadings 987
D. Discovery 988
1. The Informal Discovery Process 989
The Branerton Corporation v. Commissioner 989
Notes and Questions 990
2. Methods of Discovery 991
a. *Interrogatories* 991
Pleier v. Commissioner 991
Notes 993
b. *Requests for Productions of Documents* 994
Melea Limited v. Commissioner 994
Notes and Question 1001
c. *Depositions* 1001
3. Sanctions for Failure to Comply 1002
Johnson v. Commissioner 1003
Notes 1008
E. Pre-Trial Proceedings 1008
1. Settlement Procedures 1008

Question 1010
2. Admissions and Stipulations 1010
Bakare v. Commissioner 1011
Notes and Question 1014
3. Test Case Procedures 1015
4. Alternative Dispute Resolution (ADR) 1015
Notes and Question 1016
5. Protective Orders 1016
Anonymous v. Commissioner 1016
F. Trial 1021
Estate of Sels v. Commissioner 1022
Notes 1023
1. Burden of Proof 1023
a. *Shift of the Burden to the Service
under § 7491* 1024
Higbee v. Commissioner 1024
Notes and Questions 1032
b. *New Matters* 1032
Abatti v. Commissioner 1033
Notes and Questions 1038
2. Evidence 1038
Lukens v. Commissioner 1040
Notes 1043
G. Post-Trial Proceedings 1044
1. Appellate Review 1046
a. *Interlocutory Appeals* 1047
Kovens v. Commissioner 1047
Notes 1052
b. *Appeals Procedure* 1053
c. *Venue* 1053
2. Finality of Tax Court Decisions and Restrictions
on Assessment and Collection 1054
II. Recovery of Costs 1055
A. Limitations on the Right to Recover Costs 1055
1. Exhaustion of Administrative Remedies 1056
Allen v. Commissioner 1056
Notes 1068
2. No Unreasonable Protraction of the Proceedings .. 1069
Nordvik v. Commissioner 1069
Notes and Question 1072
3. Reasonable Costs 1073
a. *Administrative Costs* 1074

         b.   *Litigation Costs* 1074
         c.   *Attorney's Fees* 1074
            Action on Decision 2002-06 1075
            Notes and Questions 1076
      4.   The Taxpayer Must Be the Prevailing Party 1077
         Culpepper-Smith v. United States 1077
         Notes and Questions 1086
         a.   *Substantial Justification* 1086
            Cleveland Golden Gloves Assoc. v.
                United States 1086
            Notes and Questions 1088
         b.   *Qualified Offers* 1089
            Gladden v. Commissioner 1089
            Notes 1093
         c.   *Net Worth Requirement* 1094
            Christoph v. United States 1094
            Notes 1098
    B.   Appealing a Denial of Costs 1099
      Notes 1099

Chapter 9.   Federal Tax Crimes **1100**
I.   Criminal Offenses Under the Internal Revenue Code
      (Title 26) 1101
    A.   Most Commonly Prosecuted Offenses 1101
      1.   Evasion – § 7201 1101
         a.   *Deficiency Due and Owing* 1102
            Boulware v. United States 1102
            Notes and Questions 1112
            1) Methods of Proof 1114
            2) Contrasting the Direct and Indirect
                Methods of Proof 1115
            United States v. Black 1115
            Notes and Questions 1120
         b.   *Attempt to Evade* 1121
            1) Distinction Between Misdemeanor and
                Felony Offenses 1121
            Spies v. United States 1121
            Notes and Questions 1125
            2) Acts of Evasion 1126
            United States v. McGill 1126
            Notes and Questions 1138
         c.   *Willfulness* 1139

Cheek v. United States 1139
Notes and Questions 1151
United States v. McGill 1152
Notes 1154
2. Willful Failure to Collect or Pay Over Tax –
§ 7202 1155
United States v. Easterday 1155
Notes and Questions 1167
3. Willful Failure to File, Supply Information or
Pay the Tax – § 7203 1167
United States v. Kimball 1168
Notes and Questions 1170
4. Fraud and False Statements – § 7206 1171
a. *False Statements – § 7206(1)* 1172
United States v. Borman 1172
Notes and Question 1174
1) *Materiality* 1175
United States v. Luiz Ben Zvi 1175
Notes and Questions 1177
2) *Willfulness* 1179
b. *Aiding and Assisting – § 7206(2)* 1179
United States v. Hooks 1180
Notes and Questions 1186
5. Delivery or Disclosure of Fraudulent Statements
and Returns – § 7207 1188
Sansone v. United States 1188
Notes and Questions 1194
B. Miscellaneous Offenses 1195
1. Fraudulent Withholding Information – § 7205 1195
2. Interference With the Administration of the
Internal Revenue Laws – § 7212(a) 1195
3. Unauthorized Disclosure and Unauthorized
Browsing – §§ 7213 and 7213A 1196
4. Preparer Disclosure of Unauthorized Return
Information – § 7216 1197
C. Defenses 1197
1. Third Party Reliance 1198
United States v. Cheek 1198
Questions 1202
2. Lack of Notice of Illegality 1202
United States v. Harris 1202
Questions 1210

3. Mental Incompetence 1211
   United States v. McCaffrey 1211
   Notes and Questions 1214
4. Statute of Limitations 1214
   United States v. Habig 1215
   Notes and Questions 1217
II. General Criminal Offenses Under Title 18 of the
    U.S. Code 1218
    A. Criminal Conspiracy – 18 U.S.C. § 371 1218
       1. *Klein* Conspiracy 1219
          United States v. Gricco 1219
          Notes and Questions 1227
       2. Defenses 1227
          United States v. Mann 1228
          Notes and Questions 1238
    B. False Statements – Title 18 U.S.C. § 1001 1239
       United States v. Fern 1240
       Notes and Questions 1247
    C. Mail Fraud, Wire Fraud and Bank Fraud 1248
       Neder v. United States 1248
       Notes and Questions 1253
    D. RICO – Title 18 U.S.C. §§ 1961-1968 1254
       United States v. Zichettello 1255
       Notes 1259
       United States v. Busher 1259
       Notes 1267
III. Currency Transaction Offenses 1268
     A. Money Laundering – Title 18 U.S.C. §§ 1956
        and 1957 1268
        1. Commingled Funds 1268
           United States v. Braxtonbrown-Smith 1269
           Notes and Questions 1275
        2. Criminal Forfeiture 1275
           a. *Burden of Proof and Tracing of Forfeitable
              Funds* 1276
              United States v. Voight 1276
              Notes and Questions 1288
           b. *Third Party Transferees* 1288
              United States v. Saccoccia 1288
              Notes and Questions 1294
     B. Currency Transaction Reporting – Title 26 U.S.C.
        § 6050I 1296

United States v. McLamb 1297

Notes and Question 1302

C. The Bank Secrecy Act 1303

United States v. Eisenstein 1303

Notes and Question 1310

United States v. Reguer 1311

Notes and Question 1318

IV. Federal Sentencing Guidelines in Tax Offenses 1319

A. Determination of Tax Loss 1319

United States v. Delfino 1320

Notes and Questions 1323

B. Sentencing Under the Guidelines 1325

United States v. Sedore 1325

Notes 1341

Chapter 10. Criminal Tax Investigation and Prosecution **1342**

I. Initiation of a Criminal Investigation 1342

A. The Interface of Civil and Criminal Investigations 1343

United States v. Rutherford 1343

Notes and Questions 1354

B. Methods of Investigation 1355

1. Administrative Summons 1356

Jones v. United States 1356

Notes and Questions 1358

2. Grand Jury Investigations 1361

a. *Exculpatory Evidence* 1362

United States v. Williams 1362

Question 1373

b. *Grand Jury Secrecy* 1373

United States v. Dynavac 1373

Notes and Questions 1379

C. Voluntary Disclosure 1380

United States v. Hebel 1380

Notes and Questions 1385

D. Investigative Techniques 1386

II. Prosecution of a Criminal Tax Case 1388

A. Venue 1388

United States v. Melvan 1388

Notes 1395

B. Third Party Witnesses 1395

1. Expert Testimony 1396

United States v. Monus 1396
Notes 1397
2. Conflicts in Representation 1398
Wheat v. United States 1398
Notes and Question 1409
C. Defense Challenges 1410
1. Fourth Amendment 1410
a. *Standing* 1410
United States v. Payner 1410
Notes and Question 1424
b. *Particularity* 1425
Vonderahe v. Howland 1425
Notes and Questions 1433
c. *Reasonableness* 1434
United States v. Caceres 1434
Notes and Questions 1440
2. Fifth Amendment 1441
a. *Privilege Against Self-Incrimination* 1441
1) *Failure to File* 1441
Garner v. United States 1441
Notes and Question 1451
United States v. Carlson 1452
Note and Question 1456
United States v. Neff 1456
Questions 1460
2) *Document Production* 1460
United States v. Hubbell 1460
Notes and Question 1470
b. *Double Jeopardy* 1471
Louis v. Commissioner 1471
Notes and Questions 1475
3. Sixth Amendment Right to Counsel 1476
United States v. Jeffrey Stein 1476
Notes and Questions 1500

INDEX 1503

*

TABLE OF CASES

The principal cases are in bold type. Cases cited or discussed in the text are in roman type. References are to Pages. Cases cited in principal cases and within other quoted materials are not included.

———

Abatti v. Comm'r., 630
Abatti v. Comm'r., 1033, 1038
Abbate v. U.S., 1126
Abeles v. Comm'r., 981
Addison International, Inc. v. Comm'r., 33
AD Global Fund, LLC v. U.S., 286 n.55
Adler & Drobny, Ltd. v. U.S, 87
Akmakjian, U.S. v., 1218
Alcocer v. Superior Court, 1410
Allen v. Comm'r., (T.C. 2002), 1056
Allen v. Comm'r. (T.C. 1992), 450
American Trust v. U.S., 795
Anastasato v. Comm'r., 333
Anaya v. U.S., 1359-1360
Anderson v. U.S., 248
Andresen v. Maryland, 1425
Andrews , U.S. v., 406
Angelus Milling Co. v. Comm'r., 406
Anonymous v. Comm'r., 1016
Antonides v. Comm'r., 566
Apprendi v. New Jersey, 1319
Armstrong v. Comm'r. (10th Cir. 1994), 326, 333
Armstrong, U.S. v., (E.D. Va. 1997), 1196
Arthur Young & Co., U.S. v., 233
Associates Commercial Corp., U.S. v., 693
Atchison, Topeka & Santa Fe Railway v. Pena, 25

Badaracco v. Comm'r., 366, 1324
Bajakajian, U.S. v., 1288
Bakare v. Comm'r., 1011
Baker v. U.S., 32
Bakersfield Energy Partners v. Comm'r., 252
Ballard, U.S. v., 1248
Bankers Life and Casualty Co. v. U.S., 14
Baral v. U.S., 449
Barr, U.S. v., 768
Barrett v. U.S., 194
Bartkus v. U.S., 1126
Bauer v. Foley, 687
Baxter v. U.S., 1500-1501
Beard v. Comm'r., 352, 365
Becker v. Comm'r. (T.C. 1985), 32

Becker, William L. v. Comm'r (3rd Cir. 1984), 27, 32
Begier v. IRS, 838, 847, 930
Benes v. U.S., 1218
Benton, U.S. v., 1475
Ben Zvi, Luis, U.S. v. , 1175, 1178, 1179
Berger v. U.S., 106
Berhnoft, U.S. v., 1359
Bioff v. Comm'r., 968
Black, U.S. v., 1115
Blackston v. U.S., 687, 692
Blakely v. Washington, 1319
Blakeney, U.S. v., 1434
Blockburger v. U.S., 1475, 1476
BMC Bankcorp., Inc. v. U.S., 248
Bok, U.S. v., 1247
Bond v. U.S., 104
Bonwit Teller & Co. v. U.S., 499
Booker, U.S. v., 1319
Bookwalter v. Brecklein, 50, 56
Borman, U.S. v., 1172
Botany Worsted Mills v. U.S., 345
Boulware v. U.S., 1102
Boyle, U.S. v., 523, 532, 533, 541, 1202
Brandon Ridge Partners v. U.S., 352
Branerton Corp. v. Comm'r., 989, 1008
Brast v. Winding Gulf Colliery Co., 1015
Braxtonbrown-Smith, U.S. v., 1269, 1275
Brewery, Inc. v. U.S., 532
Brogan v. U.S., 1247-1248
Bronx Reptiles, U.S. v., 1170
Brown v. U.S., 922
Bruce v. U.S., 426
Bryan v. U.S., 1151
Bucey, U.S. v., 1253, 1318
Burks v. U.S., 23, 24, 365
Busher, U.S. v., (9th Cir. 1987), 1259, 1267
Busher, U.S. v., (9th Cir. 1989), 1267

Cabirac v. Comm'r., 517
Caceres, U.S. v., 58, 1434, 1440
Calandra, U.S. v., 1434
California v. Greenwood, 1387

Campbell, U.S. v., 105
Campfield v. Comm'r., 623
Canal Corporation v. Comm'r., 597
Caplin & Drysdale v. U.S., 1295-1296
Carlson, U.S. v., 1451, **1452**, 1456, 1460
Carroll v. Comm'r., 248
Catholic Diocese of Wilmington, Inc. (In Re), 847
CC&F Western Operations Ltd Partnership v. Comm'r., 352
Cellura v. U.S., 922
Cencast Services v. U.S., 91 Fed. Cl. 496 (2010), 61
Cheek v. IRS (7th Cir 1983), 193
Cheek v. U.S. (S.Ct. 1991), 1139, 1151, 1152, 1171, 1456
Cheek, U.S. v., (3rd Cir. 1993), 1198
Cheshire v. Comm'r., 860, 870
Chevron USA, Inc. v. Natural Resources Defense Council, Inc., 2, 12, 13, 23, 24, 25, 33, 49, 352
Chicago Title Ins. Co. v. Kern, 723
Chila, U.S. v., 692
Christoph v. U.S., 1094
Church of Scientology of California v. I.R.S., 157, n.12
Cindy's Inc. v. U.S., 426
Cleveland Golden Gloves Assoc. v. U.S., 1086
Cleveland Indians Baseball Co., U.S. v., 49
Clinton v. City of N.Y., 4 n.6
Colamatteo, U.S. v., 708
Coleman v. Comm'r., 541
Colestock v. Comm'r., 351
Colony, Inc. v. Comm'r., 348, 351, 352, 365
Commissioner v. (see name of party)
Computer Programs Lambda, Ltd. v. Comm'r., 282
Cooper v. U.S., 418
Correia v. Comm'r., 981
Cortese v. U.S., 1361
Cote, U.S. v., 207
Council of British Societies v. U.S., 275
Craig v. Comm'r., 761, 768
Craft v. U.S., (6th Cir. 1998), 706
Craft, U.S. v., (S.Ct. 2002), 694, 706, 707
Creamer, U.S. v., 1217
Crespo, U.S. v., 272, 276
Crittendon v. Comm'r., 533
Cross v. U.S., 345
Crum, U.S. v., 1186
Crystal v. U.S., 1385
Cuevas, U.S. v., 1310
Culpepper-Smith v. U.S., 1072, **1077**
CWT Farms v. Comm'r., 33

Davidson v. Brady, 193

Davis v. U.S., (9th Cir. 1992), 910
Davis, U.S. v., (5th Cir. 2000), 248, 1275
Deaton v. Comm'r., 432, 444
Delfino, U.S. v., 1320, 1324
Delorean Motor Co., In Re, 123
Desimone v. State of Nevada, 1476
Dhillion v. Comm'r., 278
DiRezza, Estate of v. Comm'r., 515
DiRico, U.S. v., 1177, 1179
Doe v. KPMG, 450
Donahue v. Comm'r., 601, 606, 607
Douglas Oil Co. v. Petrol Stops Northwest, 1379
Dressler v. Comm'r., 983
Drucker v. Comm'r., 542
Duberstein v. Comm'r., 980
Dubuque Packing Co. v. U.S., 445
Duncan v. Comm'r., 909
Dynavac, U.S. v., 1373, 1380

Eaken, U.S. v., 1155
East Wind Industries, Inc. v. U.S., 532
Easterday, U.S. v., 1155
Ebert v. U.S., 407, 410
Eisenstein, U.S. v., 1303
Elbo Coals, Inc. v. U.S., 345
Elmore v. Comm'r., 630
El Paso Company, U.S. v., 196, 207
Enochs v. Williams Packing & Navigation Co., 815
Ernst & Whinney, U.S. v., 270
Estate of ____, (see name of party).

Factory Storage Corp. v. U.S., 426
FDIC v. Ernst & Whinney, 1379
Feldman, U.S. v., 1217
Fern, U.S. v., 1240, 1247
Finkelstein v. U.S., 499
Finlen v. U.S., 654
First National Bank v. U.S., 426
First National Bank of Omaha v. U.S., 456
Fleming v. U.S., 1388
Fletcher Plastics, Inc. v. Comm'r., 976
Flora v. U.S., 486
Forgey, Estate of v. Comm'r., 510, 515
Founding Church of Scientology v. Smith, 170
Fountain v. U.S., 1254
Fowler v. Comm'r., 940, 949
FPL Group, Inc. v. Comm'r., 1039
Fran Corp. v. U.S., 532
Franchi, U.S. v., 123
Freytag v. Comm'r., 827, 837, **950**, 959
Friendship Materials, Inc. v. Michigan Brick, Inc., 123
Fuchs, U.S. v., 1218
Fuller v. U.S., 1170

Gainer v. Comm'r., 607
Gall v. U.S., 1341
Galuska v. Comm'r., 450
Ganz v. U.S., 640, 645
Garber, U.S. v., 1179
Gardner v. U.S., 707
Garner v. U.S., 1441, 1451
Gates v. U.S., 104
Gaudin, U.S. v., 1177, 1178, 1247
Gehl Co. v. Comm'r., 33
Geiger v. U.S., 922
Germantown Trust Co. v. Comm'r., 242
Gilmore, U.S. v., 859
Gladden v. Comm'r., 1089
Gleason, United States v., 115
G.M. Leasing Corp. v. U.S., 794
Godfrey v. U.S., 654
Goldstone v. Comm'r., 250
Golsen v. Comm'r., 961, 1054
Goodstein v. Comm'r., 50
Goulding v. U.S., (7th Cir. 1992), 80, 87, 88
Grable & Sons Metal Products, Inc. v. U.S., 801
Graham, U.S. v., 123, 1187
Grand Jury Subpoena, In Re, 207
Grapevine Imports, Ltd. v. U.S., 286 n.55
Gray v. Comm'r., 678
Green, U.S. v., 1398
Greenberg, U.S. v., 1179
Gricco, U.S. v., 1219
Grieb v. Comm'r., 898
Griffin v. Comm'r., 1032
Grunewald v. U.S., 1228, 1238
Gustin v. U.S., 922
Guterman v. Scanlon, 1015
Guzzino v. F.B.I., 157, n.13

Habig, U.S. v., 1215
Haddad, U.S. v., 1275
Hall v. U.S., 471
Halper, U.S. v., 1476
Halprin, In Re, 716
Harary v. U.S., 145
Harlow v. Fitzgerald, 193
Harper v. Virginia Dept. of Taxation, 706
Harris, U.S. v., (7th Cir. 1991), 1202
Harrison, U.S. v., 241
Hartford-Connecticut Trust Fund Co. v. Eaton, 242
Hatchett v. U.S., 706
Hayman v. Comm'r., 871
Heasley v. Comm'r., 607
Hebel, U.S. v., 1380, 1385, 1386
Helmsley, U.S. v., (2d Cir. 1991), 1112-1113
Helvering v. Mitchell, 617, 631
Henderson, U.S. v., 1253, 1254
Henry v. Comm'r., 578

Hersch v. U.S., 104
Herzig v. U.S., 924
Higbee v. Comm'r., 1024
Hillman v. Comm'r., 1015
Hinck v. U.S., 672
Hindenlang, U.S. v., 241
H.J. Inc. v. Northwestern Bell Telephone Co., 1255
Hodes, U.S. v., 708
Hoffman v. U.S., 847
Holland v. U.S., 1120-1121
Holof v. Comm'r., 378
Home Concrete & Supply Co. v. U.S., 24, 353, 365, 366
Hooks, U.S. v., 1180, 1186, 1187
Hoskins, U.S. v., 1324
Hotel Conquistador, Inc. v. U.S., 426
Hotel Equities Corp. v. Comm'r., 348
Hubbell, U.S. v., 1460
Hubert v. I.R.S., 375
Hunt, In Re, 828

Illes v. Comm'r., 607
In Re _____ (*See* Name of Party)
Intermountain Insurance Service of Vail v. Comm'r., 352, 355
Israel v. U.S., 444

Jaben v. U.S., 1218
Jacobson v. Comm'r., 608, 617
Janis, U.S. v., 333, 1433
Jersey Shore State Bank, U.S. v., 693
Johnson v. Comm'r. (7th Cir. 2002), 1003, 1008
Johnson v. Sawyer (5th Cir. 1997), 174, 192, 194
Johnson v. U.S., (N.D. Ga. 1999), 808
Johnston v. Comm'r., (T.C. 2004), 1093
Jones v. U.S., (E.D. Ark. 1992), 1356
Jones, U.S. v., (W.D. Mo. 1986), 708
Joyce v. Gentsch, 345
Judish v. U.S., 88

Kallich v. Comm'r., 987
Kassouf, U.S. v., 1196
Kikalos v. U.S., 403
Killingsworth v. U.S., 499
Kimball, U.S. v., 1168, 1170, 1171
Klausner, U.S. v., 1178, 1179
Kluener, Estate of v. Comm'r., 567
Knapp, U.S. v., 1178
Knetsch v. U.S., 50
Kontny, U.S. v., 1354
Korobkin v. U.S., 498
Kovens v. Comm'r., 1047
Kretchmar v. U.S., 345

Lankford, U.S. v., 1152

LaSalle National Bank, U.S. v., 1360, 1361
Lawless, U.S. v., 207
Lawrence v. Comm'r., 960
Le v. Comm'r., 980
Lea v. U.S., 112
Lehigh, U.S. v., 687
Leon, U.S. v., 1433
LeSavoy Foundation v. Comm'r., 33
Levinson v. U.S., 623
Lewis v. Reynolds, 345, **390**, 391, 392
Lewis v. U.S., 692
Long, U.S. v., 1170
Long Island Care at Home, Ltd. v. Coke, 24
Louis v. Comm'r., 1471
Luhring v. Glotzbach, 25, 275
Lukens v. Comm'r., 1040
Lundy, Comm,r. v., 501-502

Mal, U.S. v., 1139
Malinowski, U.S. v., 1195
Mallas v. U.S., 194
Mandel, U.S. v., 708
Manhattan General Equip. Co. v. Comm'r,
    12
Mann, U.S. v., 1228
Marre v. U.S., 1076
**Marsh & McLennan Companies v. U.S.,
656**
Massengill v. Comm'r., 607
**Mayo Foundation for Medical Education
    and Research v. U.S.**, 12, 13, 14, **23**,
    25, 33
McAllister, State v., 1425
McCaffrey, U.S. v., 1211
McCray v. U.S., 922
McDonald v. U.S., 193
McGill, U.S. v., 1126, 1139, **1152**, 1194-
    1195
McGuire, U.S. v., 1178
McLamb, U.S. v., 1297, 1302
McNally v. U.S., 1253
McPherson, U.S. v., 1077
Mead Corporation, U.S. v., 25, 33, **34**, 49
Melea Limited v. Comm'r., 994
Melvan, U.S. v., 1388, 1395
Menard, Inc. v. Comm'r., 471
Mercer, U.S. v., 1323
Miller v. U.S., (6th Cir. 1986), 248
Miller, U.S. v., (N.D.N.Y. 1998), 1254
Mills v. U.S., 411
Minneapolis Community Development
    Agency v. Buchanan, 1267
Mobil Corp., U.S. v., 270
Monday v. U.S., 924
Monus, U.S. v., 1396
Moore, U.S. v., (7th Cir. 1980), 1170
Moore, U.S. v., (4th Cir. 1994), 1275
Morgan v. U.S., 922

**Mortenson v. Nat'l. Union Fire Ins. Co.,
904**
Mosel, U.S. v., 1170
Mousley, U.S. v., 1217
Mulvania v. Comm'r., 320
Munaco v. U.S., 419, 426
Munro v. Comm'r., 287, 288
Muntwyler v. U.S., 925

Natalie Holdings, Ltc. v. U.S., 245
Nathanson, U.S. v., 1395
National Bank of Commerce, U.S. v., 780
National Cable & Telecommunications
    Assoc'n v. Brand X Internet Services, 24
National Muffler Dealers Assn v. U.S., 13,
    23-24
Neal, Comm'r., v., 871
Neder v. U.S., 1178, 1179, 1247, **1248**
Neff, U.S. v., 1456, 1460
Nelon v. Comm'r., 618, 622, 623
New York Life Ins. Co. v. U.S., 445
Nguyen v. Comm'r., 1072
Niedringhaus v. Comm'r., 622, 623
Night Hawk Leasing Co. v. U.S., 411
Nipper, U.S. v., 1460
Nordvik v. Comm'r., 1069
Norfolk Southern Corp. v. Comm'r., 49
North Carolina v. Pearce, 1475
NPR Investments, LLC v. U.S., 582, 597

O'Connor v. U.S., 193
Ohio Bell Telephone Co, U.S. v., 270
Olsen v. Helvering, 975
Omohundro v. U.S., 446
OPR, Director v. Sykes, 149
Ottawa Silica Co. v. U.S., 411, 419
Overman, U.S. v., 708

Pacific Gas and Electric Co. v. U.S., 392,
    402, 668
Palmer, In Re, 859
Patronik-Holder v. Comm'r., 516
Payne, U.S. v., 1139
Payner, U.S. v., 1410, 1424, 1425
Peerless Industries, Inc. v. U.S., 556, 566
Pennsylvania Board of Probation and Parole
    v. Scott, 1433-1434
Pepperman, U.S. v., 909
Phillips-Jones Corp. v. Parmley, 897
Pietro v. Comm'r., 1076
Pinkerton v. U.S., 1227
Planned Investments, Inc. v. U.S., 680,
    687
Pleier v. Comm'r., 991
Podde, U.S. v., 1318
Ponsford v. U.S., 1359 n.2
Powell v. Comm'r. (5th Cir. 1986), 1055
Powell, U.S. v., 263, 270, 1359, 1360

Proctor & Gamble, U.S. v., 1379

Randazzo v. U.S. Dept. of Treasury, 1099
Ratzlaf v. U.S., 1151-1152, 1310
Reddock v. Comm'r., 325
Regan, U.S. v., (S.D.N.Y. 1989), 1253
Reguer, U.S. v., (E.D.N.Y. 1995), 1311
Reguer, U.S. v., (E.D.N.Y. 1995), 1318
Rickman, Estate of v. Comm'r., 969
Rickman, U.S. v., 1170
Ripa, U.S. v., 717
Ritchie, U.S. v., 1359
R&L Refunds, Inc. v. U.S., 426
Robinette v. Comm'r., 748
Rochelle v. Comm'r., 333
Rodgers v. Hyatt, 194
Rodgers, U.S. v., 794
Romani, Estate of, U.S. v., 724, 735
Rosario v. Comm'r., 1088
Rowley v. U.S., 194
Rutgard, U.S. v., 1275
Rutherford, U.S. v., 1343, 1355

Saac, U.S. v., 1341
Saccoccia, U.S. v., 1288
St. Joseph Lease Capital Corp. v. Comm'r.,
    325
Salinitro, Estate of v. Comm'r., 968
Salman v. Swanson, 304, 306
Salman Ranch Ltd. v. U.S., 352, 353, 355
Sansone v. U.S., 1188
Sassak, U.S. v., 1186, 1187
Scar v. Comm'r., 975
Schlegel, U.S. v., 207
Scholbe, U.S. v., 1361
Schering-Plough v. U.S., 60
Schumacher Trading Partners v. U.S., 286
    n.55
Schuster v. Comm'r., 12
Schwartz, U.S. v., 276
Scotty's Contracting and Stone, Inc. v. U.S.,
    1358
Searan, U.S. v., 1186
Security Pacific Business Credit, Inc.,
    U.S. v., 930
Security Trust & Savings Bank, U.S. v., 716
Sedore, U.S. v., 1325
Seebold v. Comm'r., 630
Sels, Estate of v. Comm'r., 1022, 1023
Shapiro, U.S. v. (S.Ct. 1947), 207
Shapiro, Comm'r. v., (S.Ct. 1976), 815
Shaw, U.S. v., 1341
Shea v. Comm'r., 1038
Shore v. U.S., 497
Shorter, U.S. v., 1139, 1214
Silverman v. Comm'r., 387
Sinicki v. U.D. Dept. Of Treasury, 193
Skidmore v. Swift & Co., 13, 33

Smith v. Comm'r., 768
Sokolow v. U.S., (9th Cir. 1999), 813
Sokolow, U.S. v., (3d Cir. 1996), 1275
Sorenson v. Sec. of the Treasury, 444
Sotelo, U.S. v., 909
Sotir v. U.S., 929-930
Spies v. U.S., 623, 1121
Stair v. U.S., 345
Standefer v. U.S., 1186
Stanko v. Comm'r., 890, 897
Steele v. U.S., 497
Stein, U.S. v., 1476
Stephens ex rel R.E. v. Astrue, 1086
Sternberg, In Re, 851
Stewart v. Comm'r., 630
Stone v. Powell, 1424
Stoval, U.S. v., 1295
Straus v. U.S., 736
Stringer v. U.S., 1359 n.2
Swan, U.S. v., 1267
Swanson v. Comm'r., 533

Tank Truck Rentals v. Comm'r., 909
Tax Analysts v. I.R.S., 61
Tax Refund Litigation, In Re v. U.S., 93
Taylor v. U.S., 193
Textron, United States v., 208, 233
Thomas v. Mercantile Nat'l. Bank, 445
Tidewater Finance Co. v. Williams, 859
Tirado v. Comm'r., 1433
Todd v. Comm'r., 601, 607
Tota, U.S. v., 1318
Trafficant v. Comm'r., 631
Transpac Drilling Venture v. U.S., 282
Tucker v. Comm'r., 959-960
Tunnell v. Comm'r., 639

Uchimura, U.S. v., (9th Cir. 1997), 1178
Uchimura, U.S. v., (9th Cir. 1997, substituted
    opinion), 1178
Upjohn Co. v. U.S., 206
Upton, U.S., v., 1238
Union Pacific Railroad v. U.S., 392
Unita Livestock Corp. v. U.S., 345
U.S. v. _____, (see name of party)
U.S. Department of Justice v. Tax
    Analysts, 158, 170

Valley Bank of Nevada v. City of
    Henderson, 710, 716
Vander Heide v. Comm'r., 281 n.24
Verive, State v., 1475
Vinatieri v. Comm'r., 739, 748
Vogt, U.S. v., 779
Voight, U.S. v., 1276, 1288
Vonderahe v. Howland, 1425, 1434
Vosters v. U.S., 57, 58

Wagner v. Comm'r, 965
Wallis v. Comm'r, 536, 541
Walters v. U.S., 1218
Ward v. U.S., 193
Washton v. U.S., 248
Weatherspoon, U.S. v., 1254
Webster and Herlach v. Comm'r, 334
Weintraub, U.S. v., 816, 826, 827
Weisbart v. U.S Dept. of Treasury, 432
Weiss v. Comm'r, 1088
Wheat v. U.S., 1398, 1409
Wheeler, U.S. v., 1126
Whitney v. U.S., 337, 344
Williams v. Comm'r, (T.C. 2000), 235, 241
Williams, U.S. v., (5th Cir. 1991), 1138-1139
Williams, U.S. v., (S.Ct. 1992), 1362
Williams, U.S. v. (S.Ct. 1995), 326

Wood, Estate of v. Comm'r, (8th Cir. 1990), 248
Wood v. U.S., (5th Cir. 1987), 922
Woods, II v. Comm'r, (T.C. 1988), 548, 555
Wright, U.S. v., (5th Cir. 2000), 1113
Wright v. Comm'r, (T.C. 1985), 631, 639
Wright v. Comm'r, (T.C. 1994), 541

Young v. U.S., 852, 858-859

Zallerbach Paper Co. v. Helvering, 241
Zfass v. Comm'r, 607
Zichetello, U.S. v., 1255

*

TABLE OF
INTERNAL REVENUE CODE SECTIONS

UNITED STATES

UNITED STATES CODE ANNOTATED
26 U.S.C.A. – Internal Revenue Code

Sec.	This Work Page
§ 1017	10
§ 1311	456
§ 1312	456, 471
§ 1313	456
§ 1313(a)	456
§ 1314	456
§ 1502	13
§ 3102	921
§ 3111	921
§ 3121	291 n.81
§ 3202	921
§ 3301	921
§ 3306	291 n.81
§ 3401	291 n.81, 921
§ 3402	921
§ 3505	935
§ 3505(a)	930, 935
§ 3505(b)	930
§ 3508	291 n.81
§ 6001	262, 270
§ 6011	597, 598, 599
§ 6012	598
§ 6013(e)	859
§ 6015	860, 871
§ 6015(e)	761, 889, 964, 1054
§ 6020	241
§ 6020(b)	261, 515, 516
§ 6037(c)(1)	277 n.8
§ 6037(c)(2)	277 n.8
§ 6050I	1170, 1296, 1303
§ 6050I(f)	1296, 1302
§ 6072	242
§ 6075	242
§ 6081	244
§ 6081(a)	245
§ 6091	242
§ 6103	60, 173, 193, 194, 1197
§ 6110	59, 60, 155, 170

UNITED STATES CODE ANNOTATED
26 U.S.C.A. – Internal Revenue Code

Sec.	This Work Page
§ 6110(a)	60
§ 6110(f)	1089
§ 6110(i)	59, 60
§ 6110(j)(2)	171
§ 6110(k)(3)	50, 59
§ 6111(b)(2)	599
§ 6112	600
§ 6151	253
§ 6155	1038
§ 6159	521
§ 6159(a)	254, 937, 949
§ 6159(b)(3)	939
§ 6159(c)	937
§ 6159(d)	949
§ 6161(b)(3)	254
§ 6201(a)(1)	255
§ 6203	255, 319
§ 6211	319, 1113
§ 6211(a)	555, 964
§ 6212	815, 837, 964, 975, 1038
§ 6212(a)	325, 975
§ 6212(b)	325
§ 6213	319, 982
§ 6213(a)	680, 964, 975, 1054
§ 6213(d)	334
§ 6213(f)	68, 828
§ 6214	964
§ 6214(b)	471, 964
§ 6221	278 n.9
§ 6222(b)(1)	278 n.16
§ 6223	281 n.18
§ 6223(a)(1)	283 n.30 & 31
§ 6223(a)(2)	284 n.39
§ 6223(b)	283 n.31
§ 6223(d)(1)	284 n.40
§ 6223 (e)(2)	283 n.33
§ 6223 (e)(3)	283 n.32
§ 6223(g)	281 n.22
§ 6224	283 n.35
§ 6224(b)(2)	284 n.36
§ 6224(c)(3)	282 n.26, 283 n.37
§ 6225(a)	284 n.41, 286 n.53

UNITED STATES CODE ANNOTATED

26 U.S.C.A. – Internal Revenue Code

Sec.	This Work Page
§ 6225(c)	286 n.54
§ 6226(a)	282 n.27, 285 n.42 & 43
§ 6226(b)	285 n.48 & 49
§ 6226 (d)	286 n.51
§ 6226(e)(1)	285 n.44
§ 6226(e)(3)	285 n.45
§ 6226(f)	286 n.52
§ 6226(g)	282 n.28
§ 6227	289 n.73 & 74, 290 n. 75 and 76
§ 6228	290 n. 77-80
§ 6229	353
§ 6229(a)	286 n.55
§ 6229 (b)	287 n.58
§ 6229(b)(1)(B)	281 n.25
§ 6229(c)	286 n.55, 351, 352
§ 6229(d)	286 n.56
§ 6229(g)	287 n.57
§ 6229(h)	286 n.55
§ 6230(f)	281 n.23, 284 n.38
§ 6231(a)	278 n.12
§ 6231(a)(3)	279 n.13
§ 6231(a)(4)	279 n.14
§ 6231(a)(7)	281 n.19 & 21
§ 6231(a)(8)	281 n.18
§ 6231(b)	279 n.14, 284 n.38
§ 6231(c)	279 n.14
§ 6233	278 n.9
§ 6234	278
§ 6234(a)	288 n.61 & 62
§ 6234(b)	288 n.60
§ 6234(c)	288 n.63, 289 n.69
§ 6234(d)	289 n.70 & 71
§ 6234(e)	288 n.62 & 64
§ 6234(g)	288 n.66, 289 n.68
§ 6241	277 n.8
§ 6244	277 n.8
§ 6255	278 n.10
§ 6301	679
§ 6303	680, 693, 1038
§ 6303(a)	680
§ 6320	680, 738, 759
§ 6321	679, 693, 707
§ 6322	693, 707, 826
§ 6323	716
§ 6323(b)	716, 723
§ 6323(e)	723
§ 6323(g)	709
§ 6323(j)	737
§ 6323(j)(2)	737
§ 6324(a)	707
§ 6325(a)(1)	736
§ 6325(b)	737
§ 6325(d)(1)	737
§ 6325(e)	736

UNITED STATES CODE ANNOTATED

26 U.S.C.A. – Internal Revenue Code

Sec.	This Work Page
§ 6326	736
§ 6326(b)	736
§ 6329	794
§ 6330	680, 738, 759, 768, 794, 1054
§ 6330(c)(3)	759
§ 6330(d)	499
§ 6330(e)	759
§ 6330(e)(1)	760
§ 6331	780, 815
§ 6331(a)	680, 780
§ 6331(b)	794
§ 6331(c)	794
§ 6331(d)	521, 738
§ 6331(f)	799
§ 6331(h)	798, 799
§ 6331(i)(3)	938
§ 6331(j)	799
§ 6331(k)	938
§ 6334	780, 798, 847
§ 6334(a)(9)	798
§ 6334(f)	798
§ 6335	799
§ 6335(d)	799
§ 6335(f)	800
§ 6336	800
§ 6339	794
§ 6343(b)	779
§ 6401	347, 389
§ 6401(c)	445
§ 6402	389
§ 6402(a)	419
§ 6404	672, 1054
§ 6404(b)	483
§ 6404(c)	483
§ 6404(e)	483, 484
§ 6404(f)	306, 484, 533, 670
§ 6404(g)	485, 671, 672
§ 6404(h)	678
§ 6405(a)	2 n.3
§ 6434(e)	936
§ 6501	288 n.62
§ 6501(a)	286 n. 55, 347
§ 6501(b)(1)	242, 347, 348
§ 6501(c)	347
§ 6501(c)(1)	345
§ 6501(c)(4)	348, 374, 430
§ 6501(c)(4)(B)	378, 948
§ 6501(c)(10)	351, 352
§ 6501(e)	24, 345, 347, 351, 353, 365, 366
§ 6501(e)(1)	348
§ 6501(e)(1)(A)	351, 352, 355
§ 6502	707, 759, 815, 826, 948
§ 6502(a)(2)	709, 826, 948
§ 6503	708

UNITED STATES CODE ANNOTATED

26 U.S.C.A. – Internal Revenue Code

Sec.	This Work Page
§ 6503(a)	347, 708
§ 6503(a)(1)	325, 347
§ 6503(b)	347
§ 6503(h)	68
§ 6503(j)	347
§ 6511	430, 455, 500, 501
§ 6511(a)	432, 449, 502
§ 6511(b)(1)	402
§ 6511(b)(2)	501, 502
§ 6511(b)(2)(A)	432, 444
§ 6511(c)	430
§ 6512	500
§ 6512(b)	964
§ 6512(b)(1)	500
§ 6512(b)(3)	500, 502
§ 6512(b)(3)(B)	501, 502, 503
§ 6512(b)(3)(C)	501
§ 6513(b)	444
§ 6514	389, 402
§ 6514(b)	391
§ 6531	759, 1214, 1217
§ 6532	499, 759
§ 6532(a)	499
§ 6532(a)(1)	498, 499
§ 6631	649
§ 6601(a)	649
§ 6601(b)(1)	244
§ 6601(b)(3)	651
§ 6601(c)	649
§ 6601(e)	1113
§ 6601(e)(2)(B)	535
§ 6601(e)(3)	650
§ 6601(f)	669
§ 6602	402
§ 6603	443, 444, 445, 650, 651, 652, 669
§ 6603(d)(2)(A)	443
§ 6603(d)(2)(B)	443
§ 6611(b)(1)	656, 667
§ 6611(b)(2)	653, 654
§ 6611(b)(3)	653
§ 6611(e)(1)	653
§ 6611(e)(2)	654
§ 6611(e)(3)	654
§ 6611(f)	654, 655
§ 6621	647, 653
§ 6621(a)(1)	648, 669
§ 6621(c)	669
§ 6621(d)	668, 669
§ 6631	648
§ 6651	509, 520, 521, 671
§ 6651(a)	509, 510
§ 6651(a)(1)	285 n.45, 510, 515, 516, 522
§ 6651(a)(2)	254, 515, 516, 522, 938
§ 6651(a)(3)	522, 693

UNITED STATES CODE ANNOTATED

26 U.S.C.A. – Internal Revenue Code

Sec.	This Work Page
§ 6651(b)	521
§ 6651(b)(1)	510
§ 6651(b)(2)	285 n.45
§ 6651(c)	521
§ 6651(d)	521
§ 6651(e)	255
§ 6651(f)	515, 618
§ 6651(g)	515, 516
§ 6651(h)	521, 938
§ 6653	534
§ 6654	521, 646
§ 6654(b)(1)	647
§ 6654(b)(2)	647
§ 6654(e)	647
§ 6655	521, 648
§ 6658(a)	521
§ 6659	601
§ 6662	56, 89, 90, 91, 139, 534, 535, 548, 618
§ 6662(a)	555
§ 6662(b)(1)	534, 535, 542
§ 6662(b)(2)	534
§ 6662(b)(3)	534, 600
§ 6662(b)(4)	534
§ 6662(b)(5)	534
§ 6662(b)(6)	534, 541, 548, 565, 566, 599, 600
§ 6662(b)(7)	534
§ 6662(c)	535
§ 6662(d)	548
§ 6662(d)(2)(B)	555, 577
§ 6662(d)(2)(C)	597, 598
§ 6662(e)	600, 607
§ 6662(h)	534, 600
§ 6662(i)(1)	534
§ 6662A(a)	599
§ 6662A(c)	599
§ 6663	617
§ 6663(b)	623
§ 6663(c)	623
§ 6664	535, 555, 577
§ 6664(c)	151, 510, 598, 599, 616
§ 6664(d)	599
§ 6672	904, 909, 921, 930
§ 6672(d)	922
§ 6672(e)	921
§ 6673	1003
§ 6694	79, 80, 87, 88, 90, 93, 112, 115, 143, 548, 1069
§ 6694(a)	92
§ 6694(b)	92
§ 6695	92, 93, 115
§ 6695(b)	92
§ 6700	93, 104, 105, 112, 498

UNITED STATES CODE ANNOTATED

26 U.S.C.A. – Internal Revenue Code

Sec.	This Work Page
§ 6700(b)(2)	105
§ 6700(c)	105
§ 6701	106, 112
§ 6701(c)	112
§ 6702	639, 645, 1170, 1171
§ 6702(b)	1170
§ 6702(c)	645
§ 6703	105, 112, 645, 1023, 1069
§ 6707A	599
§ 6713	115
§ 6721	347
§ 6851	346, 347
§ 6861	346, 347
§ 6863	346
§ 6863(b)(3)	347
§ 6867	347
§ 6901	889, 921
§ 6901(c)	897
§ 6902(a)	1023
§ 7121	61, 317, 345
§ 7121(b)	317
§ 7122	317 n.86
§ 7122(c)	948
§ 7123	1016
§ 7201	638, 639, 1101, 1113, 1125, 1154 1167, 1170, 1174, 1187 1188, 1195, 1196, 1214
§ 7202	1155, 1167, 1214
§ 7203	521, 639, 1101, 1167, 1170 1171, 1174, 1195, 1196 1214, 1239, 1302
§ 7205	1195, 1196
§ 7206	1101, 1171, 1179, 1214, 1247
§ 7206(1)	1171, 1172, 1174 1178, 1188, 1239
§ 7206(2)	112, 114, 1171, 1178, 1179 1186, 1187, 1323
§ 7207	1101, 1188, 1195, 1247
§ 7212	1195, 1196
§ 7212(a)	1195, 1196, 1214, 1323
§ 7213	193, 1196
§ 7213A	195, 1196, 1197
§ 7213A(b)(2)	1197
§ 7216	114, 115, 1197
§ 7403	768, 779, 794
§ 7407	115
§ 7404(c)	123
§ 7408	105
§ 7421	794
§ 7422	485
§ 7426	706, 794
§ 7427	1023
§ 7429	346
§ 7429(a)	346

UNITED STATES CODE ANNOTATED

26 U.S.C.A. – Internal Revenue Code

Sec.	This Work Page
§ 7429(b)(1)(B)	1068
§ 7429(f)	1099
§ 7429(g)	1023
§ 7430	837, 964, 1054, 1055, 1056 1073, 1086, 1094
§ 7430(a)(1)	837
§ 7430(b)(1)	312, 1068
§ 7430(c)	1074
§ 7430(c)(1)(B)	1074
§ 7430(c)(2)	1074
§ 7430(c)(3)(A)	1074
§ 7430(c)(4)	1077
§ 7430(c)(4)(A)	1086
§ 7430(c)(4)(A)(ii)	678
§ 7430(c)(4)(B)	1086
§ 7430(c)(4)(D)	1098
§ 7430(c)(4)(E)	1089
§ 7430(c)(7)	1088
§ 7430(f)(1)	1099
§ 7430(f)(2)	1099
§ 7430(g)(1)	1089
§ 7430(g)(2)	1089
§ 7431	193, 1197
§ 7431(b)	193
§ 7431(c)	194
§ 7433	808
§ 7433(a)	808
§ 7433(b)	808
§ 7433(d)(1)	808
§ 7433(d)(2)	808
§ 7433(d)(3)	808
§ 7433(e)	813
§ 7436	964
§ 7453	1038
§ 7454(a)	1023
§ 7459	1044
§ 7459(c)	1045
§ 7460	1045
§ 7463(a)(1)	982
§ 7463(b)	982
§ 7463(d)	983
§ 7481	1054
§ 7481(c)	964
§ 7482	1046
§ 7482(a)(2)(A)	1052
§ 7482(a)(2)(C)	1053
§ 7482(b)(1)	1046, 1053, 1054
§ 7482(b)(2)	1008
§ 7483	1053
§ 7485	1054, 1055
§ 7491	504, 1024, 1032, 1038
§ 7491(a)(2)	1032
§ 7491 (a)(2)(B)	262
§ 7491(c)	508, 1024

UNITED STATES CODE ANNOTATED

26 U.S.C.A. – Internal Revenue Code

Sec.	This Work Page
§ 7502	242, 248, 348, 649, 1053
§ 7502(f)	249
§ 7503	242, 649
§ 7521(a)	306
§ 7521(c)	300 n.83
§ 7522	1038
§ 7524	686
§ 7525	195, 207, 302
§ 7525(a)	195
§ 7602	194, 195, 263, 270, 1356 1358, 1359, 1395
§ 7602 (c)	271
§ 7602(c)(3)	271
§ 7602(e)	258
§ 7604	1356
§ 7603	270
§ 7605(b)	271, 276
§ 7609	1068, 1359, 1360, 1396
§ 7609(a)	271
§ 7609(b)	1359 n.2
§ 7609(c)(2)	1396

UNITED STATES CODE ANNOTATED

26 U.S.C.A. – Internal Revenue Code

Sec.	This Work Page
§ 7609(f)	1359
§ 7610	270
§ 7623	1054
§ 7623(a)	257
§ 7701(a)(1)	1126
§ 7701(a)(11)(B)	1 n.2
§ 7701(a)(12)	1 n.2
§ 7701(a)(36)	115
§ 7701(o)	541, 566, 599
§ 7802(b)	8
§ 7802(b)(3)	8
§ 7802(d)(3)	8
§ 7803(a)(2)	7
§ 7803(b)	7
§ 7803(c)(4)(A)	9
§ 7805(a)	1 n.2, 10, 13
§ 7805(b)	12, 25, 315
§ 7805(b)(8)	28
§ 7805(e)	12
§ 7811	9
§ 8022	2, n.3

*

TABLE OF OTHER U.S. CODE SECTIONS

UNITED STATES

UNITED STATES CODE ANNOTATED

Sec.	This Work Page
5 USC § 500	71 n.4
5 USC § 551	11 n.11 & 12
5 USC § 552	170
5 USC § 552(a)(1)	156
5 USC § 552(b)	157, n.11
5 USC § 552(b)(2)	170
5 USC § 552a(a)(1)	172
5 USC § 552a(a)(5)	172
5 USC § 552a(b)	172
5 USC § 552a(d)(2)(B)	172
5 USC § 552a(j)	173
5 USC § 552a(k)	173
5 USC § 553	11 n.13
5 USC § 553(b)(3)(B)	11
11 USC § 362	813
11 USC § 362(a)(6)	68, 826
11 USC § 362(a)(8)	826
11 USC § 362(b)	827
11 USC § 362(b)(9)	827
11 USC § 362(h)	837
11 USC § 502(f)	848
11 USC § 505(b)	69
11 USC § 507(a)	848, 849
11 USC § 507(a)(1)	848
11 USC § 507(a)(2)	848, 851
11 USC § 507(a)(8)	848, 851, 859
11 USC § 522(b)	847
11 USC § 523(a)(1)	851
11 USC § 524	813
11 USC § 541(a)	68, 827, 837
11 USC § 545	849
11 USC § 547(b)	847

UNITED STATES CODE ANNOTATED

Sec.	This Work Page
11 USC § 549	849
11 USC § 724(b)	849
11 USC § 726(a)	850
11USC § 727(a)(8)	859
18 USC § 2	1126, 1186, 1187
18 USC § 371	1126, 1187, 1218, 1227
18 USC § 924(a)(1)(D)	1151
18 USC § 981	1276
18 USC § 982	1276
18 USC § 982(a)(6)(B)	1295
18 USC § 1001	1239, 1247, 1318
18 USC § 1956	1238, 1239, 1268, 1269, 1275
18 USC § 1957	1238, 1239, 1268, 1275
18 USC § 1961	1254
18 USC § 1962	1254
18 USC § 1963(a)(3)	1259
18 USC §§ 1961-1968	1254
18 USC § 2517(l)	1388
18 USC § 3553(a)	1341
18 USC §§ 6001-6005	1470-1471
21 USC § 853	1295
21 USC § 853(a)	1295
21 USC § 853(c)	1295, 1296
21 USC § 853(e)(1)	1294
28 USC § 1346(a)	485
28 USC § 2401	499, 500
28 USC § 2501	499, 500
28 USC § 3201	707
31 USC § 3713	724, 725, 735, 736
31 USC § 3727	426
31 USC § 5313	1318
31 USC § 5322-5324	1151
31 USC § 5322(a)	1318
31 USC § 5324	1310, 1311
31 USC § 5328	1318

*

TABLE OF TREASURY REGULATIONS

TREASURY REGULATIONS

Sec.	This Work Page
§ 1.170A-17	617
§ 1.1313(a)-4	456
§ 1.6011-4(b)(2)	152, 599
§ 1.6011-4T(b)(2)	233
§ 1.6050I-1(c)(7)	1302
§ 1.6081-1(a)	244, 245
§ 1.6081-4(a)(5)	245
§ 1.6161-1	254, 532
§ 1.6601-1(c)(3)	651
§ 1.6662-1	547
§ 1.6662-3(b)	535, 548
§ 1.6662-3(c)	547
§ 1.6662-4(b)(1)	541
§ 1.6662-4(c)(2)	555
§ 1.6662-4(d)(2)	535
§ 1.6662-4(d)(3)(i)	566
§ 1.6662-4(d)(3)(iii)	56, 89, 90, 566
§ 1.6662-4(d)(3)((iv)	565
§ 1.6662-4(e)(2)	577
§ 1.6662-4(f)(3)	581
§ 1.6662-4(g)(1)	598
§ 1.6662-5(c)(1)	607
§ 1.6662-5(f)	608
§ 1.6662-5(g)	607
§ 1.6664-2(c)(2)	630
§ 1.6664-2(d)	555
§ 1.6664-2(d)(2)	90
§ 1.6664-3	631
§ 1.6694-3(c)(2)	92
§ 1.6664-4(b)	617
§ 1.6694-4(f)(2)	92
§ 1.6694-2	90, 91
§ 1.6694-2(b)(2)	90
§ 1.6694-2(d)	91
§ 31.3102-1(c)	297
§ 301.6011-3(a)	243
§ 301.6011-3(c)	243
§ 301.6011-3(d)(1)	243
§ 301.6020-1(a)(2)	241
§ 301.6110-2(d)	50
§ 301.6211-1(a)	366
§ 301.6213(b)(3)	334
§ 301.6222(a)-1T	279 n.15, 280
§ 301.6222(b)-2	280 n.16
§ 301.6223(h)-1	283 n.31
§ 301.6226(e)-1T	285 n.45 & 46
§ 301.6231(a)(1)-1	278 n.12
§ 301.6231(a)(5)-1	280 n.17
§ 301.6303-1	692
§ 301.6311-2T	254

TREASURY REGULATIONS

Sec.	This Work Page
§ 301.6320-1(e)(3)	739
§ 301.6320-1(f)(2)	759
§ 301.6320-1(g)(2)	760
§ 301.6325-1(b)(5)	736
§ 301.6326-1(b)	736
§ 301.6231(a)(7)-1	281 n.20 and 21
§ 301.6330-1(g)(1)	760
§ 301.6330-1(i)	761
§ 301.6331-2(b)	799
§ 301.6335-1(b) and (c)	799
§ 301.6335-1(c)(5)(iii)	800
§ 301.6402-3(a)	403
§ 301.6404-2(b)	484
§ 301.6404-3(b)	670
§ 301.6501(b)-1(a)	347
§ 301.6532-1(c)	500
§ 301.6611-1(h)(2)(iv)	655
§ 301.6651-1(c)	532
§ 301.6651-1(c)(3)	254, 255, 521
§ 301.7122-1(b)(3)	949
§ 301.7122-1(d)(5)	939
§ 301.7122-1(i)(1)	948
§ 301.7216-2(b)	115
§ 301.7430-1(b)(1)	312
§ 301.7430-1(d)(1)	1068
§ 301.7430-1(d)(2)	1068
§ 301.7430-1(f)	1069
§ 301.7430-2(d)	1073
§ 301.7430-3(a)	1072
§ 301.7430-4(b)(3)(iii)(B)	1074
§ 301.7430-5(f)(2)	1099
§ 301.7430-7(c)(6)	1094
§ 301.7433-1(d)(1)	808
§ 301.7701-15(a)(7)(v)	88

PROCEDURAL TREASURY REGULATIONS

Sec.	This Work Page
§ 601.106	311
§ 601.201(a)(6)	26
§ 601.601(d)(2)	50

PROPOSED TREASURY REGULATIONS

Sec.	This Work Page
Reg. § 301.7430-1(b)(4)	1068

TABLE OF CIRCULAR 230 SECTIONS

**CIRCULAR 230
31 C.F.R. PART 10**

Sec.	This Work Page
§ 10.2(e)	71 n.2
§ 10.3	71 n.5
§ 10.7	71 n.3 & 7
§ 10.21	149
§ 10.22	148
§ 10.24	144
§ 10.27	149
§ 10.33 (a)(1)	151, n.9
§ 10.33 (a)(5)	151
§ 10.33 (b)(1)	151, n.8
§ 10.33 (b)(4)	151, n.8
§ 10.33 (c)(3)	374
§ 10.33 (c)(4)	150, n.7

**CIRCULAR 230
31 C.F.R. PART 10**

Sec.	This Work Page
§ 10.34	374
§ 10.34 (a)(3)	144
§ 10.35(b)(2)	152
§ 10.35(b)(3)	152
§ 10.35(b)(10)	152
§ 10.35(c)	153
§ 10.35(e)(1)	153
§ 10.35(e)(4)	153
§ 10.37	153
§ 10.50	144
§ 10.51(a)(11)	144
§ 10.52	144
§ 10.80	144

*

TABLE OF REVENUE RULINGS

REVENUE RULINGS

Sec.	This Work Page
Rev. Rul. 56-381, 1956-2 C.B. 953	499
Rev. Rul. 76-74, 1976 WL 36429	654
Rev. Rul. 80-112, 1980-1 C.B. 306	735
Rev. Ru. 83-36, 1983-1 C.B. 358	366
Rev. Rul. 84-58, 1984-2 C.B. 501	650
Rev. Rul. 85-187, 1985-2 C.B. 338	88

REVENUE RULINGS

Sec.	This Work Page
Rev. Rul. 85-189, 1985-2 C.B. 339	88
Rev. Ru. 87-41, 1987-1 C.B. 296	291
Rev. Rul. 87-53, 1987-1 C.B. 348	651
Rev. Rul. 2003-41, 2003-17 I.R.B. 814 .	450
Rev. Rul. 2005-18, I.R.B. 2005-13 .	650, 651

*

TABLE OF REVENUE PROCEDURES

REVENUE PROCEDURES

| | This Work |
| Sec. | Page |
| Rev. Proc. 72-40, 1972-2 C.B. 819 ..... 275 |
| Rev. Proc. 79-7, 1979-1 C.B. 336 .... 93 |
| Rev. Proc. 87-24, 1987-1 C.B. 720 .... 1009 |
| Rev. Proc. 94-68, 1994-2 C.B. 803 ..... 275 |
| Rev. Proc. 99-41, 1999-2 C.B. 566 ..... 581 |
| Rev. Proc. 2001-2, 2001-1 C.B. 79 ..... 316 |
| Rev. Proc. 2000-25, 2000-1 C.B. 1033 .. 243 |
| Rev. Proc. 2000-43, 2000-2 C.B. 404 ... 312 |

REVENUE PROCEDURES

| | This Work |
| Sec. | Page |
| Rev. Proc. 2002-26, 2002-1 C.B. 746 .... 925 |
| Rev. Proc. 2005-18 .... 443, 445 |
| Rev. Proc. 2005-32, 2005-1 C.B. 1206 .. 275 |
| Rev. Proc. 2010-1, 2010-1 I.R.B. 1 .... 56 |
| Rev. Proc. 2010-3, 2010-1 I.R.B. 110 ..... 56 |
| Rev. Proc. 2010-7. 2010-1 I.R.B. 231 ..... 56 |
| Rev. Proc. 2010-16, 2010-19 I.R.B. 664 .. 332 |

*

TABLE OF MISCELLANEOUS RULINGS

MISCELLANEOUS RULINGS

Sec.	This Work Page
AOD-2002-06 .... **1075**	
AOD 200602 402	
PLR 8341018 735	

MISCELLANEOUS RULINGS

Sec.	This Work Page
Notice 97-26, 1997-1 C.B. 413 249	
Notice 2004-83, 2004-2 C.B. 1030 249	
Notice 2009-55, I.R.B. 2009-31 599	
Notice 2010-33, I.R.B. 2010-17 645	
Notice 2010-62, 2010 WL 3529402 600	

*

TABLE OF INTERNAL REVENUE MANUAL SECTIONS

Internal Revenue Manual

Sec.	This Work Page
I.R.M. 4.14.17	276
I.R.M. 4.15.1.2	346
I.R.M. § 4.18.7.3	318
I.R.M. § 4.19.17.1	261 n.6
I.R.M. 5.7.6.1.3	921
I.R.M. 5.7.7	925
I.R.M. 5.8.7.5	939
I.R.M. 5.16.1	936
I.R.M. § 8.1.1.1	311
I.R.M. § 8.6.1.1.4	312
I.R.M. § 9.4	1355

Internal Revenue Manual

Sec.	This Work Page
I.R.M. § 9.4.5.6.4.3	1354
I.R.M. § 9.4.5.11.3	1354
I.R.M. § 9.4.9.2	1387, 1410
I.R.M. § 9.5.2.2	1362
I.R.M. § 20.1.1.2	509
I.R.M. § 20.1.1.3.2	533
I.R.M. § 20.1.1.3.2.2	533
I.R.M. § 20.1.2.1.2	521
I.R.M.§ 20.1.5.7.1	623
I.R.M. § 20.1.5.12.2	623

*

TABLE OF TAX COURT RULES

Tax Court Rules

Sec.	This Work Page
Tax Court Rule 25(a)(1)	982
Tax Court Rule 31(a)	987
Tax Court Rule 33(b)	987
Tax Court Rule 34(b)(1)	980
Tax Court Rule 36	987
Tax Court Rule 37	988
Tax Court Rule 39	988
Tax Court Rule 60	975
Tax Court Rules 70-76	988
Tax Court Rule 71(c)	991
Tax Court Rule 71(d)	993
Tax Court Rule 71(e)	993
Tax Court Rule 72	994
Tax Court Rule 72(a)(1)	994
Tax Court Rule 73	994
Tax Court Rule 74(e)	1001
Tax Court Rule 75(b)	1001
Tax Court Rule 76	1002
Tax Court Rule 76(e)	1002
Tax Court Rule 81	1001
Tax Court Rule 81(b)(1)	1002
Tax Court Rule 91	990 n.1
Tax Court Rule 91(a)	1010

Tax Court Rules

Sec.	This Work Page
Tax Court Rule 91(b)	1010
Tax Court Rule 91(c)	1010
Tax Court Rule 91(f)	1014, 1015
Tax Court Rule 103	990, 1001, 1003, 1016
Tax Court Rule 104	1003
Tax Court Rule 104(c)	1003
Tax Court Rule 110	1008
Tax Court Rule 122	1010
Tax Court Rule 124	1015, 1016
Tax Court Rule 131	1021
Tax Court Rule 133	1021
Tax Court Rule 142(a)	1023, 1033
Tax Court Rule 143	1038
Tax Court Rule 143(b)	1038
Tax Court Rule 143(c)	1038
Tax Court Rule 143(d)	1038
Tax Court Rule 143(f)	1002, 1039
Tax Court Rule 155	1045, 1046
Tax Court Rule 155(a)	1046
Tax Court Rule 190(a)	1053
Tax Court Rule 250(a)	282
Tax Court Rule 290	964
Tax Court Rule 320	964

*

TABLE OF SECONDARY AUTHORITIES

References are to Pages

Abel, "Why Does the ABA Promulgate Ethical Rules?," 59 Tex. L. Rev. 666 (1981), 79

Adams and Matheson, "Law Firms On the Big Board?: A Proposal For Nonlawyer Investment In Law Firms," 86 Calif. L. Rev. 1 (1998), 79

Allison, Mark, "The New Battle In An Old War: Omissions From Gross Income," 126 Tax Notes 1227 (Mar. 8, 2010), 353

Baker, Hanson and Smith, "The Uneasy Professional Alliance Between Lawyers and Accountants," 62 Practical Tax Strategies 30-39 (May 1999), 72

Bamberg, "A Different Point of Venue: The Plainer Meaning of Section 7482(b)(1)," 61 Tax Law. 445 (Winter 2008), 65

Boelter, Arthur, REPRESENTATION BEFORE THE APPEALS DIVISION OF THE IRS 17-3.10 (West Publ Co. 1999), 282

Brown and Dugan, "Sad Account: Andersen's Fall From Grace Is A Tale of Greed and Miscues," Wall St. J., June 2, 2002, at A1, 78

Buch, Ronald L., "The Touch and Feel of Work Product," 124 Tax Notes 915, 917 (Aug. 31, 2009), 233

Clark, Kenneth B., "A Different View of *Textron*," 125 Tax Notes 1197 (Dec. 14, 2009), 233

Coder, Jeremiah D., "IRS Undeterred After Tax Court's *Intermountain* Decision," 127 Tax Notes 729 (May 17, 2010), 353

Cohen and Harrington, "Is the Internal Revenue Service Bound By Its Own Regulations and Rulings?," 51 Tax Law. 675 (1998), 33

Cunningham and Repetti, "Textualism and Tax Shelters," 24 Va. Tax. Rev. 1 (2004), 2

Dorocak, John R., "Potential Penalties and Ethical Problems In Filing An Amended Return: the Case of the Repentant Sports/Entertainment Figure's Legal Expenses Deduction," 52 Maine Law Rev. 1, 15 (2000), 253

Falk, Theodore C., "Tax Ethics, Legal Ethics and Real Ethics: A Critique of ABA Formal Opinion 85-352," 39 Tax Law. 643, 647-49 (1986), 143

Handleman, Gwen Thayer, "Constraining Aggressive Return Advice," 9 Va. Tax Rev. 77, 95 (1989), 143

Hickman, "Coloring Outside the Lines: Examining Treasury's (Lack of) Compliance With Administrative Procedure Act Rulemaking Requirements," 82 Notre Dame L. Rev. 1727, 1730 (2007), 23

Holden, James P., "New Professional Standards in the Tax Marketplace: Opinions 314, 346 and Circular 230," 4 Va. Tax Rev. 209, 218 (1985), 139, 150

Horowitz, "Supreme Court Opts For *Chevron* Analysis of Treasury Regulations, Discarding the Traditional *National Muffler Dealers* Analysis," Tax Appellate Blog, Jan 11, 2011, http://appellatetax.com/2011/01/11, 24

Petronchak, Keenan & Lagun, "IRS Watch: Focus on Bridging the Employment Tax Gap," J. Tax Pract. & Proc. 9 (Feb.-Mar. 2010), 292

Pietruszkiewicz, "Does the Internal Revenue Service Have A Duty to Treat Similarly Situated Taxpayers Similarly?," 74 U. Cinn. L. Rev. 531 (2005), 56

Pollack, "A New Dynamics of Tax Policy?," 12 Am. J. Tax Pol. 61 (1995), 5

Povich, "Vote For Respect/Congress Passes IRS Overhaul Bill to Add Taxpayer Rights," A05, Newsday (NY), July 10, 1998, 6

Raby and Raby, "Still Another Half Truth—Postmark Date Is Filing Date," 73 Tax Notes 827 (Nov. 16, 1996), 248

Robinson, Toni, "'To Be Or Not To Be': A Worker May Not Know For Many Years," 97 Tax Notes 1611 (1998), 297

Schenk, Deborah H., "The Circular 230 Amendments: Time to Throw Them Out and Start Over," 110 Tax Notes 1311 (2006), 154

Slaughter, D. French III, "The Empire Strikes Back: Injunctions of Abusive Tax Shelters After TEFRA," 3 Va. Tax Rev. 1, 2 (1983), 149

Smith, "The Deliberative Stylings of Leading Tax Law Scholars," 61 Tax Law. 1 (2007), 2

Smith, "*Brand X* and Omissions From Gross Income," 126 Tax Notes 665 (Feb. 1, 2010), 24

Spellmann, "Taxation Without Notice: Due Process and Other Notice Shortcomings With the Partnership Audit Rules," 52 Tax Law. 133 (1998), 281 n.24

Stratton, "Ernst and Young to End Alliance With McKee Nelson," 104 Tax Notes 122, 124 (July 12, 2004), 78

Stratton, "Former Commissioners See Challenges Facing the Tax System," 94 Tax Notes 693, 694 (Feb. 11, 2002), 7 n.10

Sugarman, Federal Tax Rulings Procedure, 10 Tax L. Rev. 1, 37 (1954), 26 n.17

Sutherland, "Supreme Court Resolves 'Hot Button' Tax Issue – Holds *Chevron* Deference Inapplicable to 'Interpretive' Regulations," Jan. 20, 2011, www.sutherland.com/files/News/b1fb40f4-c98f-4290-bd50-573f62bfee51/Presentation/NewsAttachment/1f52abb5-d463-4fec-b282-58dc40aa, 24

Yablon, "As Certain As Death–Quotations About Taxes," 102 Tax Notes 99, 117 (Jan. 5, 2004), 1 n.1, 70 n.1, 234 n.1, 319 n.1, 388 n.1

*

FEDERAL TAX PRACTICE AND PROCEDURE

CASES, MATERIALS AND PROBLEMS

Second Edition

CHAPTER 1

INTRODUCTION TO FEDERAL TAX PRACTICE AND PROCEDURE

> They [the members of Congress] have established a system remarkable for its complexity and vexatiousness. They have rendered taxation as mischievous and depressing as a perverted ingenuity could make it.
>
> – – The New York Times[1]

Federal tax practice is a multifaceted area that focuses on taxpayer compliance with the federal tax laws; controversies (both civil and criminal) between taxpayers and the government; and representation of taxpayers by attorneys, accountants, and enrolled agents. In each of these facets, taxpayers and their representatives must interact with the Internal Revenue Service ("the IRS" or "the Service"), the largest agency of the Treasury Department. The IRS is authorized by Congress to administer and enforce the tax laws and to collect revenue that funds most of the operating budget of the federal government.

The federal tax laws are very complex statutory provisions enacted by Congress pursuant to constitutional authority and codified at 26 U.S.C. §§ 1 *et seq*. Often, these provisions are ambiguous and must be interpreted. The Treasury Department and the IRS have general authority to promulgate "all needful rules and regulations for enforcement" of the laws.[2] Pursuant to this congressional grant of authority, the government has promulgated regulations that accompany most of the provisions of the tax code ("the Code"). These regulations interpret the law, implement specific provisions, or delineate IRS policy, practice, or procedure. Unlike the Code provisions, regulations are not law, although they are entitled to judicial deference. See § II.B.1., below.

The Service also issues rulings that further interpret the Code provisions. Rulings fall into several categories, and the extent to which taxpayers may rely on them, as well as the judicial deference they are given, varies according to the type of ruling. See further discussion of rulings in § II.B.2, below.

---

1. Jeffery L. Yablon, As Certain As Death–Quotations About Taxes (2004 Edition), 102 TAX NOTES 99, 117 (Jan. 5, 2004).

2. IRC §§ 7805(a), 7701(a)(11)(B), 7701(a)(12). In addition, specific authority may be found throughout the Code.

If the Service and the taxpayer disagree over an interpretation of a Code provision, the issue may be resolved by a court of law, although the courts must give deference to an interpretation of the Service if the interpretation falls within the *Chevron* standard. See further discussion, § II.B.1, below. More broadly, the general debate about the proper methods of statutory interpretation continues to have a significant impact on interpretation of the Code. Textualists maintain generally that statutory interpretation should focus on the plain meaning of the text without resort to the legislative history. "Purposivists" and "intentionalists" believe that an ambiguous Code provision should be interpreted according to the purpose or intent of Congress and that this purpose or intent can be gleaned through an examination of a variety of sources, including the legislative history of the provision. For a discussion of this debate in the tax area, see Andre L. Smith, "The Deliberative Stylings of Leading Tax Law Scholars," 61 Tax Lawyer 1 (2007); Noel B. Cunningham and James R Repetti, "Textualism and Tax Shelters," 24 Virginia Tax Review 1 (2004). See further discussion, § II.B. Regardless of the theory to which one subscribes, a well-rounded tax student should understand the legislative process through which tax laws are enacted.

I. THE LEGISLATIVE PROCESS

The United States Constitution, Article I, Section 7, mandates that tax bills originate in the House of Representatives. The tax committee of the House with primary jurisdiction over revenue bills is the Ways and Means (W&M) Committee, which consists of six subcommittees, composed of members of both political parties in a ratio reflecting the balance of Democrats and Republicans in the House. A revenue bill originates as a proposal which is forwarded to the W&M Committee for consideration. Proposals generally come from the Treasury Department or from the W&M Committee itself, although they also may emanate from executive communications from the President, a cabinet member, or an agency head. The Assistant Secretary of the Treasury for Tax Policy prepares the proposal, with the help of staff attorneys and economists, and forwards it to the Speaker of the House or to the Chair of the W&M Committee.

The Joint Committee on Taxation, composed of the ranking members of the W&M Committee and the Senate Finance Committee, prepares a description of both the current law and the proposal.[3] The W&M

---

3. The Joint Committee serves as an overseer of the Service in its administration and enforcement of the revenue laws. See IRC § 8022. It also may publish a description and general explanation of enacted tax legislation. This publication is commonly referred to as the "Blue Book." In addition to its role in the legislative process, the Joint Committee must review refunds in excess of $2 million ($1 million prior to 2000). IRC § 6405(a).

Committee then holds public hearings to determine the extent to which legislation is needed to address the problem areas identified in the proposal.[4] This is accomplished through the use of witnesses who appear before the Committee to provide a summary of their previously submitted written statements. The first witness is usually the member of Congress who proposed the legislation, or the Secretary of the Treasury, if the legislation was proposed by the Administration. Statistics and other data often are presented at this point. Then other Administration witnesses, such as IRS and Treasury staffs may follow. Finally, repre-sentatives from various private interest groups, and on occasion, even individual taxpayers, may appear. The hearings often expose areas of tension between the government and the private sector.

After the hearings have concluded, the W&M Committee meets in mark-up sessions to outline the policy aspects of the legislation it plans to report. This is translated into bill form by the House Legislative Counsel, whose job is to draft important legislation originating in the House. The Legislative Counsel is assisted by technical advisors from the Staff of the W&M Committee, the Treasury Department, the IRS, and the Joint Committee on Taxation. The Joint Committee then prepares a Committee Report, which sets out the justification for the legislation, and summarizes and defines the issues for debate. If both the bill and the report are approved by the W&M Committee, they are reported to the full House and debated. Both the Joint Committee Report and the testimony presented during the W&M Committee hearings are published and become part of the legislative history if the bill is enacted into law.

The House debates, along with the votes on the bill, are recorded in the Congressional Record. The voting may be done under a "closed rule" procedure, which allows only members of the W&M Committee to amend the bill. This ensures that if the bill passes the House,[5] it will be in the form reported by the W&M Committee, although if the bill is not approved by the House, it may be remanded back to the W&M Committee for modification.

The bill can die in the House or it can be approved, with or without modification, and sent to the Senate, where it usually is referred to the Committee on Finance for consideration. The process in the Senate is much the same as in the House, with the Finance Committee holding hearings, preparing the legislation, and reporting the bill to the full Senate for further consideration, although the Finance Committee may

---

4. The Committee may hold hearings not only on proposals, but also on bills that may be pending before it.

5. In 1995, the House adopted a resolution requiring a "supermajority" (3/5) vote to pass a tax increase.

hold hearings and prepare the legislation simultaneously while the bill is working its way through the House. When the bill is reported to the Senate, it is accompanied by a Senate Finance Committee Report. The bill either may be the same version as the House bill, or it may be substantially amended.

When the Senate debates the bill, there is no "closed rule" procedure as there is in the House; thus, any Senator may propose an amendment. This provides an opportunity for a political action committee or other private interest group to attempt to influence the legislation by persuading a Senator to propose an amendment in accordance with its objectives. After the debates, the members of the Senate vote on the bill. Both the floor debates and the votes are recorded in the Congressional Record.

If the Senate approves the House bill without amendment (which seldom happens), the bill is sent to the President for final action. If the Senate does not accept the House bill, but chooses instead to draft its own version, the two bills then go to a Committee of Conference of the House and Senate, composed of the ranking members of the House W&M Committee and the Senate Finance Committee, to work out a compromise before the bill is sent to the President. The Conference Committee may issue a Conference Report, explaining its actions and changes. Both the House and the Senate must approve the Conference Report, and afterward, the approved bill is sent to the President for signature.

If the President signs, the bill becomes law.[6] If the President vetoes the bill, it still may become law if two-thirds of the House and Senate vote to override the Presidential veto. If the President does not take action on a bill within ten days of receiving it, the bill becomes law without his signature. Once the bill becomes law, it may become effective immediately, or it may take effect either retroactively or prospectively, as designated in the bill itself. The effective date of new tax legislation is often an important issue in tax planning.

Notes and Questions

The complexity of the tax laws is a recurring complaint among both taxpayers and tax professionals. While there are various reasons for the complexity, much of the blame lies in the legislative process itself. Under the U.S. Constitution tax legislation must originate in the House, but in recent years the Senate, on occasion, has flagrantly defied the Constitution

---

6. In 1997, Congress authorized a line item veto that allowed the President to cancel a limited tax benefit, in whole or in part, after a bill had been signed into law. See Line Item Veto Act, Pub. L. No. 104-130, 110 Stat. 1200, codified at 2 U.S.C. § 691 et seq. But the Supreme Court declared this Act an unconstitutional violation of the Presentment Clause in Clinton v. City of New York, 524 U.S. 417 (1998).

and has introduced its own revenue bills without waiting for legislation to be reported to or approved by the House. This may result in two very different bills being reported to the Conference Committee, which then can select provisions from each bill. In addition, the Conference Committee may add provisions of its own that were not contained in either the House bill or the Senate bill. When this happens, the legislation has bypassed the stage of public hearings and committee deliberations, and thus has lost the benefit of the critical examination and consideration that it otherwise would have had.

In addition, there are several stages in the legislative process in which the legislation may be influenced by special interest groups, and often such influence is brought to bear on the process. For an interesting view of the various factors that have played a significant role in the shaping of tax policy over the years, see Sheldon D. Pollack, A New Dynamics of Tax Policy?, 12 Am. J. Tax Pol'y 61 (1995).

Another factor contributing to the complexity of the tax laws is the policy of revenue neutrality, which requires the overall effect of tax legislation to be revenue neutral, so that no new revenue is raised. Under this policy, provisions that result in increased revenue must be accompanied by provisions that decrease revenue by the same amount. This often has been accomplished in a manner that not only compounds the complexity of the Internal Revenue Code, but also contravenes coherent tax policy.

1. When might a tax professional find it helpful to examine legislative history?

2. What is the significance of the committee reports?

3. Are some committee reports considered more important than others? If so, which ones?

II. THE ADMINISTRATIVE PROCESS

The Sixteenth Amendment of the Constitution authorizes Congress to "lay and collect taxes on income from whatever source derived * * * ." Once a bill has been enacted into law, the law is administered and enforced by the Treasury Department through its agency, the IRS, originally called the "Bureau of Internal Revenue." Today, the IRS has more than 115,000 employees and processes over 200 million returns annually. The importance of the agency is underscored by the fact that it collects revenues in the trillions of dollars that, in turn, fund 95 percent of the activities of the federal government.

Despite its importance, however, the organization of the IRS remained relatively unchanged for over 45 years, as did the IRS's view of itself as primarily a tax collection agency. Under its former structure, the IRS was organized into four geographical regions, under the control of the National Office, located in Washington, D.C., headed by the Commissioner of Internal Revenue. Each geographical region was headed by a Regional Commissioner who oversaw the operating field offices, known as District Offices, within his area.[7] District Offices were the offices with which taxpayers had contact if they failed to file a return or if a problem developed after a return was filed.

A. THE RESTRUCTURED IRS

In the summer of 1997, the Senate began holding hearings on alleged IRS abuses. The extraordinary stories that emerged from these hearings eventually overwhelmed even the staunchest opponents to IRS reform. At the conclusion of the hearings, Senator Pete Domenici (R-N.M.) remarked: "There is little doubt that the IRS needs reforming when one out of two Americans say they would rather be mugged than be audited by the IRS."[8]

The result was the IRS Restructuring and Reform Act of 1998,[9] signed into law by President Clinton on July 22, 1998. This Act mandated a complete overhaul of the structure and management of the IRS, and called for an about-face in its culture from tax collection to an emphasis on taxpayer service.

Under the reorganization, the National Office generally remains unchanged, although it has been streamlined. It retains responsibility for issuing rulings and regulations, formulating national policy and programs for the administration of tax laws and regulations, providing executive direction, and controlling statistical standards. As before, it is headed by the Commissioner of Internal Revenue who is appointed by the President with the advice and consent of the Senate, and who answers to the Secretary of the Treasury. In formulating national policy, the Commissioner is assisted by the Assistant Treasury Secretary for Tax Policy.

In an effort to provide greater continuity and to minimize political interference, the 1998 Act extends the Commissioner's term from four years to five years, with the possibility of an extension for another five-year term. Thus, whenever a new President takes office, the Commis-

---

7. From 1952 until 1995, the Service was divided according to seven geographical regions, which were further divided into 63 districts. In 1995, this structure was condensed to four regions with 33 districts.

8. Elaine S. Povich, Vote For Respect/Congress Passes IRS Overhaul Bill to Add Taxpayer Rights, A05, Newsday (NY), July 10, 1998.

9. Pub. L. No. 105-206, 112 Stat. 685 (1998) (codified in scattered sections of the I.R.C.).

sioner will have a slightly greater degree of job security. It also allows the Commissioner more time to absorb the organization and operations of the agency, and to master the mammoth requirements of the job.

In the past, the duties of the Commissioner were left to the discretion of the Treasury Secretary and were not clearly defined. The 1998 Restructuring and Reform Act, however, provides specific duties, such as (1) to administer, manage, direct and supervise the execution and application of the tax laws and tax treaty provisions, and (2) to recommend to the President candidates for the position of Chief Counsel when a vacancy in that position occurs, and to recommend the removal of the Chief Counsel, if needed. IRC § 7803(a)(2). The Chief Counsel acts as legal advisor to the Commissioner and represents the Commissioner before the United States Tax Court. See IRC § 7803(b). It has been noted that the Chief Counsel's job becomes even more important when the Commissioner is not a lawyer.[10]

The biggest change made to the organization of the IRS under the 1998 Reform Act was the replacement of the geographical structure with four operating divisions organized according to taxpayers with similar needs. These four divisions are: (1) the Wage and Investment Division, which serves individual taxpayers and joint filers who report only wage and investment income, (2) the Small Business and Self-Employed Division, which serves self-employed and partially self-employed individuals, and small business entities, including corporations with assets less than $10 million, (3) the Large Business and International Division (formerly the Large and Mid-Sized Business Division), which serves corporations, subchapter S corporations and partnerships with assets over $10 million, as well as handling international tax compliance issues and (4) the Tax-Exempt and Government Entities Division, which serves pension plans, state governments and other tax-exempt organizations.

There are also four functional divisions that handle specific issues and cases.   These are: (1) the Chief Counsel, (2) Appeals, (3) Criminal Investigation, and (4) the National Taxpayer Advocate. In addition to the duties noted above, the Chief Counsel is responsible for furnishing legal advice to IRS personnel, issuing rulings and Technical Advice Memoranda, and recommending to the Justice Department which civil cases should be litigated. The Appeals Division reviews issues and cases in controversy, providing a fresh perspective when the taxpayer and the government cannot reach an agreement.   The Criminal Investigation Division investigates criminal tax violations and financial crimes. The National Taxpayer Advocate is responsible for assisting taxpayers in resolving

---

10. Sheryl Stratton, Former Commissioners See Challenges Facing the Tax System, 94 Tax Notes 693, 694 (Feb. 11, 2002)(Statement of former Commissioner Fred Goldberg, Jr.).

problems with the IRS, issuing Taxpayer Assistance Orders, overseeing local advocate offices, and identifying changes both in the law and in the IRS's administrative practice that might make the problem resolution process between taxpayers and the IRS a smoother one. The National Taxpayer Advocate is appointed by the Secretary of the Treasury, and is required under the 1998 Restructuring and Reform Act to have a background in customer service, as well as experience in representing individual taxpayers. Moreover, in order to be eligible for the position, the individual must not have been an officer or employee of the IRS during the preceding two years, and must agree not to accept any employment with the IRS for at least five years after leaving the position. In one of its most controversial provisions, the 1998 Restructuring and Reform Act established a nine member Oversight Board with broad authority to oversee IRS management and policies, and to ensure that taxpayers are treated fairly in their dealings with the IRS. The nine members consist of the Commissioner of Internal Revenue, the Secretary of the Treasury (or Deputy Treasury Secretary), a full-time federal employee or employee representative, and six "private life" members, one of whom serves as chair. The employee representative and the private life members are appointed for five-year staggered terms by the President with the advice and consent of the Senate, without regard to the members' political affiliations. See IRC § 7802(b).

The Board has the authority to review the budget of the IRS, recommend candidates to fill high level IRS positions, and review and approve IRS strategic plans. It also has oversight responsibilities for IRS law enforcement and collection activities, and it is required to make an annual report to the President and Congress. In the exercise of its duties, it is required to maintain confidentiality. IRC § 7802 (c)(1). The members of the Board must adhere to other ethical standards as well, such as restricted post-employment opportunities, certain conflict of interest rules, and annual public financial disclosure reports. IRC § 7802 (b)(3).

In addition, there are restrictions on the Board's powers to ensure its impartiality and to maintain its accountability. For instance, it may not develop or formulate tax policy, it cannot interfere with specific IRS law enforcement activities, it cannot take part in any procurement activities of the IRS, and it cannot be involved in specific personnel actions, with the exception of those actions concerning the Commissioner and certain senior executives granted to it by statute. See IRC § 7802(d)(3). It also cannot receive confidential return information.

Returns are processed either at one of three central computing centers or one of ten service centers (now called "campuses") scattered across the country. The central computing centers process electronically filed returns and payments, maintain taxpayer data, and provide on-line access to the data to users at other IRS sites. The service centers process returns (currently both paper and electronic), and forward data to the computing centers to be analyzed and posted to taxpayers' accounts. The IRS anticipates that in the immediate future, these ten service centers will be reduced to five and will receive only paper returns.

Taxpayers needing assistance in resolving problems with the Service may contact a local office of the National Taxpayer Advocate. There is at least one local office in each state and they operate independently of any other IRS office. In order to encourage taxpayers to use this resource and to inspire taxpayer confidence in the voluntary compliance system, the local taxpayer advocates have discretion not to disclose taxpayer information to the IRS or even the fact that the taxpayer has contacted the local office. See IRC § 7803(c)(4)(A). If the problem involves a potentially significant hardship to the taxpayer because of expense, delay, or threat of adverse action by the Service, the taxpayer advocate has authority to issue a Taxpayer Assistance Order (TAO) to help relieve the hardship. A TAO may require the Service to take action or refrain from acting, provided the case does not involve an ongoing criminal investigation and provided the Service is not required to act or refrain from acting in a manner that would circumvent Code provisions. See IRC § 7811.

In a further effort to improve customer service, the IRS maintains 24 customer service sites across the country to provide telephone assistance to taxpayers.

Notes

Another controversial provision of the 1998 Restructuring and Reform Act is the list of ten infractions, the violation of any one of which will result in the mandatory dismissal of an IRS employee. This list has come to be known as "the Ten Deadly Sins." One of the most draconian of the provisions requires the automatic dismissal of any IRS employee who files a late tax return, even though the return is one day late and the employee is entitled to a refund. While IRS officials admit that their employees should be held to stricter standards in order to set examples for the taxpaying public, they protest the unfairness of this provision, which can result in job loss for a minor infraction. Officials argue that these rules have resulted in lowered moral and "an atmosphere of anxiety in the workplace." IRS Employees Seek Partial Absolution for 'Ten Deadly Sins,' 2001 Tax Notes Today 39-H (Feb. 27, 2001).

B. ADMINISTRATIVE INTERPRETATION OF THE TAX LAWS

When a revenue bill is enacted into law, it is codified under Title 26 of the United States Code. The collective tax laws under Title 26 are referred to as "the Internal Revenue Code." The first tax code was enacted in 1939, when Congress repealed all internal revenue laws then in effect and reenacted them in codified form. In 1954, there was a major revision of the internal revenue laws, resulting in congressional approval of the Internal Revenue Code of 1954. In 1986, there was another wholesale revision of the revenue laws under the Tax Reform Act of 1986, and as a result, the 1954 Code was redesignated the Internal Revenue Code of 1986. This Code, with many revisions, remains in effect today.

Tax laws are complex and frequently ambiguous. Fortunately, there are a variety of tools available to aid in interpreting these laws such as regulations, rulings and cases.

1. Treasury Regulations

Congress has authorized the Treasury Department, and through it the IRS, to promulgate regulations (often referred to as Treasury Regulations) to interpretation Code provisions. Regulations fall into three general categories: interpretive, legislative, and procedural. Interpretive regulations are the most numerous, and are promulgated under a general congressional delegation of authority to the Secretary of the Treasury to "prescribe all needful rules and regulations for the enforcement" of the Code. IRC § 7805(a). These regulations provide guidance in interpreting the Code provisions they accompany. In some cases, however, Congress specifically defers its legislative authority to the Treasury Secretary. See, e.g., IRC § 1017. In these cases, the Treasury Department is not limited to merely interpreting the Code; instead, it can go beyond the Code and make the rules. Regulations promulgated under this specific delegation of authority are called legislative regulations. Finally, the IRS may issue procedural regulations describing its own rules of practice and procedure.

a. Promulgation

The Office of the Tax Legislative Counsel is responsible for drafting regulations. The Assistant Secretary of the Treasury for Tax Policy oversees the process, although the initial drafting usually is done by the Office of the Chief Counsel, Legislative and Regulations Division. When the Chief Counsel and the Commissioner have approved the draft, it then goes to the Assistant Secretary of the Treasury for Tax Policy, as delegate for the Secretary of the Treasury, for final approval.

Treasury regulations are considered "rules" under the Administrative Procedure Act (APA),[11] which applies to administrative agencies that have formal rule making authority.[12] Since the IRS is considered an administrative agency, its rule making authority is subject to regulation under the APA. Thus, new regulations are required to be published in the Federal Register[13] not less than 30 days before their effective date. The purpose of this requirement is to give notice to the public of the proposed rule and to provide an opportunity for comments.

Usually, regulations are published first in proposed form. If there are substantial adverse comments from the public, the proposed regulations may be withdrawn and amended. If substantial amendments are made, the final regulations must be republished in order to give the public adequate notice and opportunity to comment. In the alternative, the proposed regulations may not be republished but instead may languish indefinitely as proposed regulations, particularly if there is internal disagreement within the IRS or the Treasury Department over the regulation in question. If there are minor amendments to the proposed regulations, or if no amendments are made, final regulations may be issued after the expiration of the 30-day period with the signatures of the Commissioner and the Assistant Secretary of the Treasury for Tax Policy.

Under the APA, the Treasury Department has the option of bypassing the notice and comment procedures if there is a finding of "good cause" that the procedures are "impracticable, unnecessary, or contrary to the public interest." 5 U.S.C. § 553(b)(3)(B). This option may be exercised when new legislation has been enacted and the Treasury Department believes it to be in the best interest of the public for regulations to be issued immediately. These regulations will be issued as "temporary regulations," to provide guidance until final regulations are issued.

---

11. 5 U.S.C. § 551 et seq. This provision defines a "rule" in a poorly drafted sentence as "the whole or a part of an agency statement of general or particular applicability and future effect designed to implement, interpret, or prescribe law or policy or describing the organization, procedure, or practice requirements of an agency and includes the approval or prescription for the future of rates, wages, corporate or financial structures or reorganizations thereof, prices, facilities, appliances, services or allowances therefor or of valuation, costs, or accounting, or practices bearing on any of the foregoing." Id. at § 551(4).

12. Under the APA, "rule making" means the "agency process for formulating, amending, or repealing a rule." Id. at § 551(5).

13. There are several exceptions to the publication requirement: It does not apply (1) to interpretative rules, general statements of policy, or rules of agency organization, procedure, or practice; (2) when the regulation states that there has been a finding of "good cause" that the procedures are "impracticable, unnecessary, or contrary to the public interest; (3) where the rule is a substantive one that grants or recognizes an exemption or relieves a restriction. Id. at § 553 (b) and (d).

Temporary regulations frequently use a question and answer format to address salient issues that may arise in the new legislation. These regulations expire three years after their date of issuance, and before they become final they must be issued as proposed regulations in order to allow public comment.[14] IRC § 7805(e).

b. *Effective Date*

The APA provides that rules or regulations should have prospective effect. Under former § 7805(b) of the Code, however, many regulations had retroactive effect because of the "relation back doctrine," under which the regulation related back to the effective date of the Code provision it interpreted. This caused problems for many taxpayers, who found it difficult to structure transactions or properly report items when there was a significant lapse of time between the effective date of a statutory provision and the promulgation of regulations. Another thorny issue was whether an amendment of a regulation related back to the effective date of the statute or whether it had prospective effect only. What if taxpayers had relied on the prior regulation? Compare Manhattan General Equipment Co. v. Commissioner, 297 U.S. 129 (1936), rehg denied 297 U.S. 728 (1936) with Schuster v. Commissioner, 312 F.2d 311 (9th Cir. 1962), affg. 32 T.C. 998 (1959).

Under the Taxpayers' Bill of Rights 2, enacted in 1996, § 7805(b) was amended to provide that regulations must have prospective effect except for certain narrow exceptions, such as when the regulation is promulgated within 18 months of the enactment of the statute it interprets.

c. *Judicial Review of Regulations*

While regulations are not law, they are entitled to considerable judicial deference, because they are promulgated under congressional grants of authority. The extent of that deference, particularly to Treasury regulations, had been an evolving issue since the United States Supreme Court's decision in Chevron U.S.A., Inc. v. Natural Resource Defense Council, Inc., 467 U.S. 837, 104 S.Ct. 2778 (1984). This issue, in general, has been clarified by Mayo Foundation For Medical Education and Research v. United States, 562 U.S. ____, 131 S. Ct. 704 (2011), reproduced below.

---

14. This applies only to regulations issued after November 20, 1988. Those issued prior to that date may languish indefinitely as "temporary" regulations. See Technical and Miscellaneous Revenue Act of 1988, Pub. L. No. 100-647, § 6232(b), 102 Stat. 3342, 3735 (1988).

1) Interpretive and Legislative Regulations

The vast majority of Treasury regulations are promulgated under the general authority of IRC § 7805(a). These are known as "interpretive" or "general authority" regulations. Under some specific statutory provisions, however, Congress may grant further authority to the Treasury Department to promulgate regulations. See, e.g., IRC § 1017(b)(1) (reduction in basis for discharge of indebtedness); § 1502 (consolidated returns). These are referred to as "legislative" or "specific authority" regulations, and since Congress has specifically granted its authority to the Treasury Department under these statutory provisions, the Treasury may go beyond mere interpretation of the statute to establish new rules and duties.

Traditionally, the highest level of judicial deference was given to legislative regulations because of their specific grant of congressional authority. These regulations were given the force and effect of law unless they were arbitrary or capricious, conflicted with the statute, exceeded the scope of authority granted, or were not issued in accordance with proper procedure.

Until recently, the deference due interpretive regulations was not as clearly established, and in fact had varied widely among the courts. The question generally was whether a court could impose its own interpretation or position over that of the regulation if the regulation was not inconsistent with the statute and was not unreasonable in its interpretation, but in the view of the court, its own interpretation was more reasonable.

Historically in the federal judicial system, courts had been viewed as the primary interpreters of statutory text. In determining the proper interpretation of a statute, courts have looked to the tests espoused by the Supreme Court in Skidmore v. Swift & Co., 323 U.S. 134 (1944), a lower standard of review in which the agency's interpretation is entitled to "appropriate weight" and National Muffler Dealers Association v. United States, 440 U.S. 472 (1979), discussed in *Mayo*, in which courts could rely upon various factors in determining whether regulations had the "power to persuade."

In 1984, the United States Supreme Court again addressed the extent to which regulations are entitled to judicial deference in the case of Chevron U.S.A., Inc. v. Natural Resources Defense Council, Inc., 467 U.S. 837, 104 S. Ct. 2778 (1984). *Chevron* involved a regulation promul-gated by the Environmental Protection Agency under the Clean Air Act, but its analysis is equally applicable to Treasury regulations. If *Chevron* applies, the court's role is more limited, because the regulation is entitled to deference as long as it is a "permissible construction of the statute."

But the application of *Chevron* to Treasury regulations remained unclear. In particular, questions arose as to whether and to what extent general authority regulations were entitled to judicial deference. For a discussion of the conflicts among the courts that followed in the wake of *Chevron*, see Bankers Life and Casualty Co. v. United States, 142 F.3d 973 (7th Cir. 1998), cert. denied, 525 U.S. 961. After years of mixed messages, the Supreme Court finally resolved this issue in 2011.

MAYO FOUNDATION FOR MEDICAL EDUCATION AND RESEARCH V. UNITED STATES
United States Supreme Court, 2011
562 U.S. ____, 131 S.Ct. 704.

CHIEF JUSTICE ROBERTS delivered the opinion of the Court.

Nearly all Americans who work for wages pay taxes on those wages under the Federal Insurance Contributions Act (FICA), which Congress enacted to collect funds for Social Security. The question presented in this case is whether doctors who serve as medical residents are properly viewed as "student[s]" whose service Congress has exempted from FICA taxes under 26 U.S.C. § 3121(b)(10).

I

A

Most doctors who graduate from medical school in the United States pursue additional education in a specialty to become board certified to practice in that field. Petitioners Mayo Foundation for Medical Education and Research, Mayo Clinic, and the Regents of the University of Minnesota (collectively Mayo) offer medical residency programs that provide such instruction. Mayo's residency programs, which usually last three to five years, train doctors primarily through hands-on experience. Residents often spend between 50 and 80 hours a week caring for patients, typically examining and diagnosing them, prescribing medication, recommending plans of care, and performing certain procedures. Residents are generally supervised in this work by more senior residents and by faculty members known as attending physicians. In 2005, Mayo paid its residents annual "stipends" ranging between $41,000 and $56,000 and provided them with health insurance, malpractice insurance, and paid vacation time.

Mayo residents also take part in "a formal and structured educational program." Residents are assigned textbooks and journal articles to read and are expected to attend weekly lectures and other conferences. Residents also take written exams and are evaluated by the attending faculty physicians. But the parties do not dispute that the bulk of residents' time is spent caring for patients.

B

Through the Social Security Act and related legislation, Congress has created a comprehensive national insurance system that provides benefits for retired workers, disabled workers, unemployed workers, and their families. Congress funds Social Security by taxing both employers and employees under FICA on the wages employees earn. See 26 U.S.C. § 3101(a) (tax on employees); § 3111(a) (tax on employers). Congress has defined "wages" broadly, to encompass "all remuneration for employment." § 3121(a) (2006 ed. and Supp. III). The term "employment" has a similarly broad reach, extending to "any service, of whatever nature, performed . . . by an employee for the person employing him." § 3121(b).

Congress has, however, exempted certain categories of service and individuals from FICA's demands. As relevant here, Congress has excluded from taxation "service performed in the employ of ... a school, college, or university . . . if such service is performed by a student who is enrolled and regularly attending classes at such school, college, or university." § 3121(b)(10) (2006 ed.). The Social Security Act, which governs workers' eligibility for benefits, contains a corresponding student exception materially identical to § 3121(b)(10). 42 U.S.C. § 410(a)(10).

Since 1951, the Treasury Department has applied the student exception to exempt from taxation students who work for their schools "as an incident to and for the purpose of pursuing a course of study" there. 16 Fed.Reg. 12474 (adopting Treas. Regs. 127, § 408.219(c)); see Treas. Reg. § 31.3121(b)(10)-2(d) * * *. Until 2005, the Department determined whether an individual's work was "incident to" his studies by performing a case-by-case analysis. The primary considerations in that analysis were the number of hours worked and the course load taken.

For its part, the Social Security Administration (SSA) also articulated in its regulations a case-by-case approach to the corresponding student exception in the Social Security Act. See 20 CFR § 404.1028(c) (1998). The SSA has, however, "always held that resident physicians are not students." SSR 78-3, 1978 Cum. Bull. 55-56. In 1998, the Court of Appeals for the Eighth Circuit held that the SSA could not categorically exclude residents from student status, given that its regulations provided for a case-by-case approach. See Minnesota v. Apfel, 151 F.3d 742, 747-748. Following that decision, the Internal Revenue Service received more than 7,000 claims seeking FICA tax refunds on the ground that medical residents qualified as students under § 3121(b)(10) of the Internal Revenue Code. 568 F.3d 675, 677 (C.A.8 2009).

Facing that flood of claims, the Treasury Department "determined that it [wa]s necessary to provide additional clarification of the ter[m]" "student" as used in § 3121(b)(10), particularly with respect to individuals who perform "services that are in the nature of on the job training." 69 Fed.Reg. 8605 (2004). The Department proposed an amended rule for comment and held a public hearing on it.

On December 21, 2004, the Department adopted an amended rule prescribing that an employee's service is "incident" to his studies only when "[t]he educational aspect of the relationship between the employer and the employee, as compared to the service aspect of the relationship, [is] predominant." * * * Treas. Reg. § 31.3121(b)(10)-2(d)(3)(I) * * * (2005). The rule categorically provides that "[t]he services of a full-time employee"-as defined by the employer's policies, but in any event including any employee normally scheduled to work 40 hours or more per week-"are not incident to and for the purpose of pursuing a course of study." * * * Treas. Reg. § 31.3121(b)(10)-2(d)(3)(iii) * * * (the full-time employee rule). The amended provision clarifies that the Department's analysis "is not affected by the fact that the services performed . . . may have an educational, instructional, or training aspect." Ibid. The rule also includes as an example the case of "Employee E," who is employed by "University V" as a medical resident. * * * Treas. Reg. § 31.3121(b)(10) -2(e) * * * (Example 4). Because Employee E's "normal work schedule calls for [him] to perform services 40 or more hours per week," the rule provides that his service is "not incident to and for the purpose of pursuing a course of study," and he accordingly is not an exempt "student" under § 3121(b)(10). * * * Treas. Reg. § 31.3121(b)(10)-2(e) * * *.

C

After the Department promulgated the full-time employee rule, Mayo filed suit seeking a refund of the money it had withheld and paid on its residents' stipends during the second quarter of 2005. * * * Mayo asserted that its residents were exempt under § 3121(b)(10) and that the Treasury Department's full-time employee rule was invalid.

The District Court granted Mayo's motion for summary judgment. The court held that the full-time employee rule is inconsistent with the unambiguous text of § 3121, which the court understood to dictate that "an employee is a 'student' so long as the educational aspect of his service predominates over the service aspect of the relationship with his employer." * * * The court also determined that the factors governing this Court's analysis of regulations set forth in National Muffler Dealers Assn., Inc. v. United States, 440 U.S. 472, 99 S.Ct. 1304, 59 L.Ed.2d 519 (1979), "indicate that the full-time employee exception is invalid." * * *

The Government appealed, and the Court of Appeals reversed. 568 F.3d 675. Applying our opinion in Chevron U.S.A. Inc. v. Natural Resources Defense Council, Inc., 467 U.S. 837, 104 S.Ct. 2778, 81 L.Ed.2d 694 (1984), the Court of Appeals concluded that "the statute is silent or ambiguous on the question whether a medical resident working for the school full-time is a 'student' " for purposes of § 3121(b)(10), and that the Department's amended regulation "is a permissible interpretation of the statut[e]." 568 F.3d, at 679-680, 683.

We granted Mayo's petition for certiorari. * * *

II
A

We begin our analysis with the first step of the two-part framework announced in *Chevron, supra,* * * * and ask whether Congress has "directly addressed the precise question at issue." We agree with the Court of Appeals that Congress has not done so. The statute does not define the term "student," and does not otherwise attend to the precise question whether medical residents are subject to FICA. See 26 U.S.C. § 3121(b)(10).

Mayo nonetheless contends that the Treasury Department's full-time employee rule must be rejected under *Chevron* step one. Mayo argues that the dictionary definition of "student"-one "who engages in 'study' by applying the mind 'to the acquisition of learning, whether by means of books, observation, or experiment' "-plainly encompasses residents. Brief for Petitioners 22 (quoting Oxford Universal Dictionary 2049-2050 (3d ed.1955)). And, Mayo adds, residents are not excluded from that category by the only limitation on students Congress has imposed under the statute-that they "be 'enrolled and regularly attending classes at [a] school' " Brief for Petitioners 22 (quoting 26 U.S.C. § 3121(b)(10)).

Mayo's reading does not eliminate the statute's ambiguity as applied to working professionals. In its reply brief, Mayo acknowledges that a full-time professor taking evening classes-a person who presumably would satisfy the statute's class-enrollment requirement and apply his mind to learning-could be excluded from the exemption and taxed because he is not "'predominant[ly]'" a student. Medical residents might likewise be excluded on the same basis; the statute itself does not resolve the ambiguity.

The District Court interpreted § 3121(b)(10) as unambiguously foreclosing the Department's rule by mandating that an employee be deemed "a 'student' so long as the educational aspect of his service predominates over the service aspect of the relationship with his employer." * * * We do not think it possible to glean so much from the little that § 3121 provides. In any event, the statutory text still would offer no insight into how Congress intended predominance to be determined or whether Congress thought that medical residents would satisfy the requirement.

To the extent Congress has specifically addressed medical residents in § 3121, moreover, it has expressly excluded these doctors from exemptions they might otherwise invoke. See 26 U.S.C. §§ 3121(b)(6)(B), (7)(C)(ii) (excluding medical residents from exemptions available to employees of the District of Columbia and the United States). That choice casts doubt on any claim that Congress specifically intended to insulate medical residents from FICA's reach in the first place.

In sum, neither the plain text of the statute nor the District Court's interpretation of the exemption "speak[s] with the precision necessary to say definitively whether [the statute] applies to" medical residents. United States v. Eurodif S.A.* * *.

B

In the typical case, such an ambiguity would lead us inexorably to *Chevron* step two, under which we may not disturb an agency rule unless it is " 'arbitrary or capricious in substance, or manifestly contrary to the statute.' " Household Credit Services, Inc. v. Pfennig * * * (quoting United States v. Mead Corp., * * *). In this case, however, the parties disagree over the proper framework for evaluating an ambiguous provision of the Internal Revenue Code.

Mayo asks us to apply the multi-factor analysis we used to review a tax regulation in National Muffler * * *. There we explained:

> "A regulation may have particular force if it is a substantially contemporaneous construction of the statute by those presumed to have been aware of congressional intent. If the regulation dates from a later period, the manner in which it evolved merits inquiry. Other relevant considerations are the length of time the regulation has been in effect, the reliance placed on it, the consistency of the Commissioner's interpretation, and the degree of scrutiny Congress has devoted to the regulation during subsequent re-enactments of the statute." * * *

The Government, on the other hand, contends that the *National Muffler* standard has been superseded by *Chevron*. The sole question for the Court at step two under the *Chevron* analysis is "whether the agency's answer is based on a permissible construction of the statute." * * *

Since deciding *Chevron*, we have cited both *National Muffler* and *Chevron* in our review of Treasury Department regulations. See, e.g., United States v. Cleveland Indians Baseball Co., * * * (citing *National Muffler*); Cottage Savings Assn. v. Commissioner, * * * (same); United States v. Boyle, * * * (citing *Chevron*); see also Atlantic Mut. Ins. Co. v. Commissioner, * * * (citing *Chevron* and *Cottage Savings*).

Although we have not thus far distinguished between *National Muffler* and *Chevron*, they call for different analyses of an ambiguous statute. Under *National Muffler*, for example, a court might view an agency's interpretation of a statute with heightened skepticism when it has not been consistent over time, when it was promulgated years after the relevant statute was enacted, or because of the way in which the regulation evolved. * * * The District Court in this case cited each of these factors in rejecting the Treasury Department's rule, noting in particular that the regulation had been promulgated after an adverse judicial decision. * * *

Under *Chevron*, in contrast, deference to an agency's interpretation of an ambiguous statute does not turn on such considerations. We have repeatedly held that "[a]gency inconsistency is not a basis for declining to analyze the agency's interpretation under the *Chevron* framework." National Cable & Telecommunications Assn. v. Brand X Internet Services * * * ; *accord*, Eurodif S. A., *supra* * * *. We have instructed that "neither antiquity nor contemporaneity with [a] statute is a condition of [a regulation's] validity." Smiley v. Citibank (South Dakota) * * *. And we have found it immaterial to our analysis that a "regulation was prompted by litigation." Id. * * *. Indeed, in United Dominion Industries, Inc. v. United States * * *, we expressly invited the Treasury Department to "amend its regulations" if troubled by the consequences of our resolution of the case.

Aside from our past citation of *National Muffler*, Mayo has not advanced any justification for applying a less deferential standard of review to Treasury Department regulations than we apply to the rules of any other agency. In the absence of such justification, we are not inclined to carve out an approach to administrative review good for tax law only. To the contrary, we have expressly "[r]ecogniz[ed] the importance of maintaining a uniform approach to judicial review of administrative action." Dickinson v. Zurko * * *. See, e.g., Skinner v. Mid-America Pipeline Co.,* * * (declining to apply "a different and stricter nondelegation doctrine in cases where Congress delegates discretionary authority to the Executive under its taxing power").

The principles underlying our decision in *Chevron* apply with full force in the tax context. *Chevron* recognized that "[t]he power of an administrative agency to administer a congressionally created . . . program necessarily requires the formulation of policy and the making of rules to fill any gap left, implicitly or explicitly, by Congress." * * * It acknowledged that the formulation of that policy might require "more than ordinary knowledge respecting the matters subjected to agency regulations." * * * Filling gaps in the Internal Revenue Code plainly requires the Treasury Department to make interpretive choices for statutory implementation at least as complex as the ones other agencies must make in administering their statutes. Cf. Bob Jones Univ. v. United States * * * ("[I]n an area as complex as the tax system, the agency Congress vests with administrative responsibility must be able to exercise its authority to meet changing conditions and new problems"). We see no reason why our review of tax regulations should not be guided by agency expertise pursuant to *Chevron* to the same extent as our review of other regulations.

As one of Mayo's amici points out, however, both the full-time employee rule and the rule at issue in *National Muffler* were promulgated pursuant to the Treasury Department's general authority under 26 U.S.C. § 7805(a) to "prescribe all needful rules and regulations for the enforcement" of the Internal Revenue Code. See Brief for Carlton M. Smith 4-7. In two decisions predating *Chevron*, this Court stated that "we owe the [Treasury Department's] interpretation less deference" when it is contained in a rule adopted under that "general authority" than when it is "issued under a specific grant of authority to define a statutory term or prescribe a method of executing a statutory provision." Rowan Cos. v. United States * * *; United States v. Vogel Fertilizer Co.* * * (quoting Rowan).

Since *Rowan* and *Vogel* were decided, however, the administrative landscape has changed significantly. We have held that *Chevron* deference is appropriate "when it appears that Congress delegated authority to the agency generally to make rules carrying the force of law, and that the agency interpretation claiming deference was promulgated in the exercise of that authority." *Mead* * * *. Our inquiry in that regard does not turn on whether Congress's delegation of authority was general or specific. For example, in *National Cable & Telecommunications Assn.*, *supra*, we held that the Federal Communications Commission was delegated "the authority to promulgate binding legal rules" entitled to *Chevron* deference under statutes that gave the Commission "the authority to 'execute and enforce,' " and "to 'prescribe such rules and regulations as may be necessary in the public interest to carry out the provisions' of," the Communications Act of 1934. * * * (quoting 47 U.S.C. §§ 151, 201(b)). See also Sullivan v. Everhart * * * (applying *Chevron* deference to rule promulgated pursuant to delegation of "general authority to 'make rules and regulations and to establish procedures, not inconsistent with the provisions of this subchapter, which are necessary or appropriate to carry out such provisions' " (quoting 42 U.S.C. § 405(a) (1982 ed.))).

We believe *Chevron* and *Mead*, rather than *National Muffler* and *Rowan*, provide the appropriate framework for evaluating the full-time employee rule. The Department issued the full-time employee rule pursuant to the explicit authorization to "prescribe all needful rules and regulations for the enforcement" of the Internal Revenue Code. 26 U.S.C. § 7805(a). We have found such "express congressional authorizations to engage in the process of rulemaking" to be "a very good indicator of delegation meriting *Chevron* treatment." *Mead, supra* * * *. The Department issued the full-time employee rule only after notice-and-comment procedures, 69 Fed.Reg. 76405, again a consideration identified in our precedents as a "significant" sign that a rule merits *Chevron* deference. *Mead, supra* * * *; see, e.g., Long Island Care at Home, Ltd. v. Coke * * *.

We have explained that "the ultimate question is whether Congress would have intended, and expected, courts to treat [the regulation] as within, or outside, its delegation to the agency of 'gap-filling' authority." * * * In the *Long Island Care* case, we found that *Chevron* provided the appropriate standard of review "[w]here an agency rule sets forth important individual rights and duties, where the agency focuses fully and directly upon the issue, where the agency uses full notice-and-comment procedures to promulgate a rule, [and] where the resulting rule falls within the statutory grant of authority." * * * These same considerations point to the same result here. This case falls squarely within the bounds of, and is properly analyzed under, *Chevron* and *Mead*.

C

The full-time employee rule easily satisfies the second step of *Chevron*, which asks whether the Department's rule is a "reasonable interpretation" of the enacted text. * * * To begin, Mayo accepts that "the 'educational aspect of the relationship between the employer and the employee, as compared to the service aspect of the relationship, [must] be predominant' " in order for an individual to qualify for the exemption. Reply Brief for Petitioners 6-7 (quoting Treas. Reg. § 31.3121(b)(10)-2(d)(3)(I) * * *). Mayo objects, however, to the Department's conclusion that residents who work more than 40 hours per week categorically cannot satisfy that requirement. Because residents' employment is itself educational, Mayo argues, the hours a resident spends working make him "more of a student, not less of one." Mayo contends that the Treasury Department should be required to engage in a case-by-case inquiry into "what [each] employee does [in his service] and why " he does it. Mayo also objects that the Department has drawn an arbitrary distinction between "hands-on training" and "class-room instruction."

We disagree. Regulation, like legislation, often requires drawing lines. Mayo does not dispute that the Treasury Department reasonably sought a way to distinguish between workers who study and students who work, see IRS Letter Ruling 9332005 (May 3, 1993). Focusing on the hours an individual works and the hours he spends in studies is a perfectly sensible way of accomplishing that goal. The Department explained that an individual's service and his "course of study are separate and distinct activities" in "the vast majority of cases," and reasoned that "[e]mployees who are working enough hours to be considered full-time employees ... have filled the conventional measure of available time with work, and not study." 69 Fed.Reg. 8607. The Department thus did not distinguish classroom education from clinical training but rather education from service. The Department reasonably concluded that its full-time employee rule would "improve administrability," id., at 76405, and it thereby "has avoided the wasteful litigation and continuing uncertainty that would inevitably accompany any purely case-by-case approach" like the one Mayo advocates, United States v. Correll * * *.

As the Treasury Department has explained, moreover, the full-time employee rule has more to recommend it than administrative convenience. The Department reasonably determined that taxing residents under FICA would further the purpose of the Social Security Act and comport with this Court's precedent. As the Treasury Department appreciated, this Court has understood the terms of the Social Security Act to " 'import a breadth of coverage,' " 69 Fed.Reg. 8605 (quoting Social Security Bd. v. Nierotko, * * *), and we have instructed that "exemptions from taxation are to be construed narrowly," Bingler v. Johnson * * *. Although Mayo contends that medical residents have not yet begun their "working lives" because they are not "fully trained," the Department certainly did not act irrationally in concluding that these doctors-"who work long hours, serve as highly skilled professionals, and typically share some or all of the terms of employment of career employees"-are the kind of workers that Congress intended to both contribute to and benefit from the Social Security system.

The Department's rule takes into account the SSA's concern that exempting residents from FICA would deprive residents and their families of vital disability and survivorship benefits that Social Security provides. Mayo wonders whether the full-time employee rule will result in residents being taxed under FICA but denied coverage by the SSA. The Government informs us, however, that the SSA continues to adhere to its longstanding position that medical residents are not students and thus remain eligible for coverage. * * *

We do not doubt that Mayo's residents are engaged in a valuable educational pursuit or that they are students of their craft. The question whether they are "students" for purposes of § 3121, however, is a different matter. Because it is one to which Congress has not directly spoken, and because the Treasury Department's rule is a reasonable construction of what Congress has said, the judgment of the Court of Appeals must be affirmed.

It is so ordered.

Notes and Questions

While *Mayo* resolved the deference issues that had divided the lower courts since *Chevron*, nevertheless some questions remain. For instance, how important is notice and comment? Some tax regulations, such as temporary regulations, are issued without notice and comment. Under *Mayo*, are such regulations entitled to *Chevron* deference or should they be evaluated under *National Muffler*? Professor Kristin Hickman has noted that in promulgating regulations, "Treasury often fails to adhere to APA rulemaking requirements and thus leaves many of its regulations, including some of its most complex and controversial efforts, open to legal challenge on that basis." Hickman, Coloring Outside the Lines: Examining Treasury's (Lack of) Compliance with Administrative Procedure Act Rulemaking Requirements, 82 Notre Dame L. Rev. 1727, 1730 (2007). See also Burks v. United States, 633 F.3d 347 (5th Cir. 2011), n. 9 (questioning whether temporary regulations that do not receive notice and comment are entitled to *Chevron* deference).

Another question is whether the application of *Chevron* would differ from that of *National Muffler* in the case of a regulation issued contemporaneously with a new statutory provision. But the most interesting question after *Mayo* is whether *Chevron* deference applies to less formal guidance such as revenue rulings, general counsel advice and IRS announcements. See further discussion § 2.a.2 and *Mead* below.

A final question is whether there is any difference in the deference afforded interpretive regulations versus legislative regulations. The Court in *Mayo* specifically stated that *Chevron* applies to both, but it was not specific in explaining how *Chevron* applies. In step two of the *Chevron* analysis, the Court stated that a court "may not disturb an agency rule unless it is 'arbitrary or capricious in substance' . . . ." Later, it referred to the second step of *Chevron* as asking whether the agency's rule is a *reasonable interpretation* of the statute. Although traditionally, the arbitrary and capricious standard has sometimes been viewed as a different standard than the reasonable interpretation standard, the Court in *Chevron* itself cited both standards in describing the judicial deference due agency interpretations. Some have suggested that the arbitrary and capricious standard applies to legislative regulations while the reasonable interpretation standard applies to interpretive regulations in the second step of *Chevron*. See "Supreme Court Resolves 'Hot Button' Tax Issue–Holds Chevron Deference Applicable to 'Interpretive' Regulations," Jan. 20, 2011, www.sutherland.com/files/News/b1fb40f4-c98f-4290-bd50-573f62bfee51/Presentation/NewsAttachment/1f52abb5-d463-4fec-b282-58dc40aa.

Concern had been expressed after *Mayo* that the Treasury Department would be emboldened to issue regulations to give itself a litigation advantage in pending cases or to overturn results in which it had lost in court on statutory interpretation grounds. See Alan Horowitz, "Supreme Court Opts for Chevron Analysis of Treasury Regulations, Discarding the Traditional National Muffler Dealers Analysis," Tax Appellate Blog, Jan. 11, 2011, http://appellatetax.com/2011/01/11. Cases addressing this concern are now winding their way through the courts. See, e.g., Burks v. United States, 633 F.3d 347 (5th Cir. 2011) (addressing recent regulations interpreting § 6501(e)); Home Concrete & Supply Co., LLC v. United States, 634 F.3d 249 (4th Cir. 2011) (same). See further discussion in Chapter 4.

In *National Cable & Telecommunications Association v. Brand X Internet Services,* 545 U.S. 967 (2005) the Supreme Court addressed the interesting question of whether a court's prior construction of a statute would prevail over a contrary agency construction or whether *Chevron* deference would cause the agency construction to prevail. The Ninth Circuit had adhered to its precedent under the principal of *stare decisis,* but the Supreme Court overturned the decision in favor of *Chevron* deference. The Court stated: "A court's prior construction of a statute trumps an agency construction otherwise entitled to *Chevron* deference only if the prior court decision holds that its construction follows from the unambiguous terms of the statute and thus leaves no room for agency discretion." *Id.,* at 982. Thus, the principle established by *Brand X* is that a prior determination of a court can be overruled by a subsequent contrary interpretation of an agency, provided the agency's interpretation is otherwise permissible and reasonable. *See* Patrick J. Smith, Brand X and Omissions From Gross Income, 126 Tax Notes 665 (Feb. 1, 2010) (arguing that the temporary and proposed Treasury regulations under § 6501(e)(1)(A) were issued under a mistaken construction of *Brand X*). See further discussion of these regulations in Chapter 4 at § II.B.

1. The Court mentions the importance of the notice and comment process in Long Island Care at Home, Ltd. v. Coke, 551 U.S. 158, 173-174

(2007) (cited in *Mayo*), in *Mead* (below in § 2.a.2), and in *Mayo*. Why is this process important to the standard of deference? See also Atchison, Topeka and Santa Fe Railway v. Pena, 44 F.3d 437 (7th Cir. 1994) (en banc), aff'd. without discussion, Brotherhood of Locomotive Engineers v. Atchison, Topeka and Santa Fe Railway, 516 U.S. 152, 116 S.Ct. 595, 133 L.Ed.2d 535 (1996).

2. Since *Chevron* shifts the focus from the courts to the agencies in interpreting statutory ambiguities, what are the pros and cons of this shift?

3. Will it be possible for a taxpayer to succeed in the challenge of a regulation after *Mayo*? If so, under what circumstances?

4. Does an analysis of legislative history retain any importance after *Mayo*?

2) *Procedural Regulations*

Procedural regulations address internal management and operating procedures of the IRS. They are promulgated by the IRS alone, and not by the Treasury Department.[15] They differ in three respects from interpretive and legislative regulations: (1) they are not subject to the notice and comment requirements of the APA, (2) they are not subject to the prohibition on retroactivity under § 7805(b) (see IRC § 7805(b)(5)), and (3) they generally do not bind the Service.

Procedural regulations must be distinguished from interpretive regulations that address procedural aspects of the tax laws, such as filing returns and furnishing required information, which occasionally are referred to as procedural regulations.[16] The latter regulations are subject to the publication requirements of the APA, as well as the prohibition on retroactivity, while the former are not.

Usually, true procedural regulations are regarded as "directory" rather than "mandatory." Thus, courts often have held that the Service is not bound by these regulations unless the taxpayer can show that she relied to her detriment on the regulation, and that a relatively important right would be contravened if the regulation is not upheld. Without such a showing, it will be difficult for a taxpayer to succeed in the challenge of a procedural regulation. See Luhring v. Glotzbach, 304 F.2d 560 (4th Cir. 1962).

---

15. In specific, they are promulgated as "Statements of Procedural Rules" and designated with the prefix "601" because they are contained in 26 CFR Part 601.

16. These regulations may be designated with the prefix "301," such as Reg. § 301.6011.

2. Public and Private Rulings

In its administrative capacity, the Service may act as a quasi-judicial body, issuing rulings or statements applying the law to a specific set of facts. A taxpayer may apply for an advance ruling, and if one is issued, the ruling essentially will serve as an insurance policy to guarantee that the Service will apply the law as stated in the ruling.

In the distant past, these rulings were privately issued by the Service and were unpublished. In time, however, criticism of the practice began to grow because of the perception that the unpublished rulings permitted favoritism, encouraged the use of influence, and gave some revenue agents an unfair advantage in disputes with taxpayers.[17] In 1953, in response to mounting criticism from Congress and the tax bar, the Service established its revenue rulings program under which it regularly publishes its opinions on a variety of substantive tax issues to promote uniform application of the tax laws and to assist taxpayers in attaining maximum voluntary compliance.

When the issue is one that is likely to be of general interest to the public, the Service may release the ruling as a public ruling, also called a revenue ruling. Such a ruling may be relied upon and cited as precedent in any case in which the facts are substantially similar to those of the ruling.

If a ruling is intended to apply only to the specific taxpayer who requests it, the Service will issue the ruling as a private letter ruling (PLR). These may not be cited as precedent by other taxpayers, but they may be of general interest to the public since they indicate how the Service is likely to rule under similar facts.

a. Revenue Rulings

Revenue rulings are formally issued by the Treasury Department, but are drafted by the offices of the Associate Chief Counsels in the National Office of the IRS in Washington, D.C. They are published initially in the Internal Revenue Bulletin, and later in permanent form in the Cumulative Bulletin. Rulings are subject to review by the Commissioner and the Assistant Secretary for Tax Policy, who approve them for publication. Unlike regulations, revenue rulings are not subject to the APA procedures. The Service defines revenue rulings as "official interpretations" of the revenue laws, related treaties, and regulations. The Service considers revenue rulings to be binding until they are revoked or superceded. Treas. Reg. § 601.201(a)(6)(as amended in 2002). Until then, they may be cited

---

17. Norman A. Sugarman, Federal Tax Rulings Procedure, 10 Tax L. Rev. 1, 37 (1954).

as precedent and relied upon by taxpayers in general, but only if the facts in issue are substantially the same as those of the ruling. Thus, revenue rulings are very helpful to taxpayers in structuring transactions and in determining how to report items. Given the complexity of the tax laws and the frequency with which Congress amends these laws, the rulings program has become an important part of tax practice.

1) Retroactivity

Revenue rulings are not subject to the prohibition on retroactivity, (see IRC § 7805(b)(8)), although they usually have prospective effect, as do any amendments or revocations. The Commissioner has discretion, however, to determine when revenue rulings (or revocations or amendments of rulings) will have retroactive effect.

WILLIAM L. BECKER v. COMMISSIONER
United States Court of Appeals, Third Circuit, 1984.

751 F.2d 146.

Opinion of the Court

SEITZ, CIRCUIT JUDGE.

I.

William L. Becker (taxpayer) appeals from a decision of the United States Tax Court retroactively disallowing his deduction, as a business expense, of the full cost of a commercial flight training course for which he also had received a tax-exempt educational assistance allowance equal to 90 percent of his expenditures from the Veterans' Administration.

II.　Facts

The facts of the case were stipulated at trial by the parties. Taxpayer is a veteran of the U.S. armed forces. During 1976 and 1977 he was employed as a DC-9 pilot for Eastern Airlines. To maintain and improve his aviation skills, he enrolled in a Lear jet flight training course offered by Midwest Aviation. The total cost of the tuition and fees for the course was $12,250. Taxpayer paid $6,150 of this amount in 1976 and the remaining $6,100 in 1977. Because of his previous military service taxpayer was eligible to receive an educational assistance allowance from the Veterans' Administration for flight training necessary for the attainment of a recognized vocational objective. The Veterans' Administration approved taxpayer's application for a tax-exempt allowance equal to 90 percent of the tuition expenses as provided under 38 U.S.C. § 1677

(1976) (repealed 1981).[1] He subsequently received $5,535 in 1976 and $5,490 in 1977 from the Veterans' Administration as direct reimbursement for expenditures related to the course. Taxpayer's out-of-pocket expenses for the flight training, therefore, equaled $615 in 1976 and $610 in 1977.

On his 1976 and 1977 federal income tax returns, taxpayer excluded the Veterans' Administration payments from income under 38 U.S.C. § 3101(a)(1976). He also claimed "employee business expense" deductions of $6,150 and $6,100 respectively under I.R.C. § 162(a)(1976).

At the time taxpayer filed his income tax returns, Internal Revenue Service ("I.R.S.") Revenue Ruling 62-213 and I.R.S. Publication No. 17, entitled "Your Federal Income Tax," stated that deductions for educational expenses incurred by veterans need not be reduced by the amount of any nontaxable educational benefits received during the taxable year from the Veterans' Administration. Rev. Rul. 62-213, 1962-2 Cum. Bull. 59, revoked by Rev. Rul. 83-3, 1983-1 Cum. Bull. 72; 1977 I.R.S. Publication No. 17. Taxpayer claims that he relied on the 1962 Revenue Ruling and the 1977 I.R.S. pamphlet when preparing his returns.

I.R.S. agents audited taxpayer's 1976 and 1977 returns twice, once in New Jersey and later in Texas where the taxpayer's real estate interests were located. Referring to the second audit, taxpayer averred that "after one month of investigation, [he] received written notice that the expenses were valid, and the case was again closed."

In 1980, the I.R.S. issued Revenue Ruling 80-173 which purported to "distinguish and clarify" Revenue Ruling 62-213. Revenue Ruling 80-173, 1980-2 Cum. Bull. 60. In the 1980 ruling the I.R.S. announced that flight training expenses for which veterans are reimbursed under 38 U.S.C. § 1677 (1976) are not also deductible because "the taxpayer suffers no economic detriment and incurs no expense in making the expenditure to the extent of the reimbursement."

As a result of the retroactive application of the 1980 ruling pursuant to I.R.C. § 7805(b) (1976),[4] taxpayer's returns were audited for the third time and the I.R.S. assessed a deficiency against him in the amounts of $2,578 and $2,884 for the years 1976 and 1977.

Representing himself, taxpayer challenged the deficiency in the Tax Court. He claimed that the I.R.S., having twice allowed the deductions,

---

1.   38 U.S.C. § 1677 (1976) permitted eligible veterans to receive an educational assistance allowance for a portion of the expenses incurred for approved flight training courses related to the veteran's vocation. Id. It was repealed in 1981 by the Omnibus Budget Reconciliation Act. § 2003, P.L. 97-35, 95 Stat. 357, 782.

4.   I.R.C. § 7805(b) (1976) states that "The Secretary or his delegate may prescribe the extent, if any, to which any ruling or regulation, relating to the internal revenue laws, shall be applied without retroactive effect." Id.

was estopped from "changing the rules after the game has been played." To support this claim he alleged that he relied to his detriment on the 1962 Revenue Ruling then still in effect and took the course expecting that "the cost of the training would be a legitimate deduction."

Citing Manocchio v. Commissioner, 78 T.C. 989 (1982), aff'd 710 F.2d 1400 (9th Cir. 1983), the Tax Court upheld the determination of the I.R.S. that I.R.C. § 265(1) (1976)[5] prohibited the deduction of the reimbursed portion of the flight training expenditures. Although the Tax Court appreciated taxpayer's frustration at being assessed a deficiency after I.R.S. agents had examined his returns and permitted him to claim the deductions, it nevertheless found that the I.R.S. was not estopped from retroactively disallowing the deductions. The taxpayer appealed.

We begin by noting the appropriate standard of review. The Commissioner's decision whether or not to give retroactive effect to a regulation or ruling relating to internal revenue laws is reviewable for abuse of discretion. Dixon v. U.S., 381 U.S. 68, 75 (1965); Automobile Club of Michigan v. Commissioner, 353 U.S. 180, 184 (1957). The taxpayer bears the ultimate burden of proving, by the preponderance of the evidence, that a particular assessment is erroneous. Helvering v. Taylor, 293 U.S. 507, 515 (1935). In addition *pro se* complaints are held to less stringent standards than formal pleadings drafted by lawyers and the allegations contained therein are to be liberally construed.

III.

We first address taxpayer's argument that the Commissioner should be estopped from giving retroactive effect to Revenue Ruling 80-173, adopted pursuant to I.R.C. § 7805(b). Taxpayer concedes that while the I.R.S. has the power to apply revenue rulings retroactively, the agency should be estopped from doing so with respect to flight training deductions because the scale of equities tips so heavily in his favor. He claims that the I.R.S.'s initial allowance of the business deductions, its sudden repudiation in 1980 of a longstanding policy embodied in a well-publicized 1962 revenue ruling, and its disregard for its own operating procedures all work to estop the retroactive assessment of a tax deficiency against him.

The I.R.S. defines a revenue ruling as "an official interpretation by the Service which has been published in the Internal Revenue Bulletin." Rev. Proc. 67-1, 1967-1 Cum. Bull. 544-555. The introduction to each issue of the Internal Revenue Bulletin states that "Revenue Rulings and Revenue Procedures do not have the force and effect of Treasury Department

---

5.   I.R.C. § 265(1) (1976) prohibits the deductions of expenses allocable to tax exempt income. Id.

Regulations * * * but are published to provide precedents to be used in the disposition of other cases and may be cited and relied upon for that purpose." The Supreme Court has held that such rulings are administrative in nature and do not have the force of law although they may be useful in discerning precedent and in interpreting the Internal Revenue Code and regulations. Dixon v. U.S., 381 U.S. 68, 73 (1965).

To encourage taxpayers to "rely upon such rulings in determining the rule applicable to their own transactions" the I.R.S. has reassured taxpayers that "Revenue Rulings published in the Internal Revenue Bulletin ordinarily are not revoked or modified retroactively." Id. The I.R.S. Revenue Procedures, however, caution that a ruling may be modified or revoked retroactively "at any time" unless "the Commissioner or his delegate exercises the discretionary power under section 7805(b) of the Code to limit the retroactive application of the ruling." Rev. Proc. 67-1, 1967-1 Cum. Bull. At 552-553.

Although Revenue Ruling 80-173 does not expressly state whether it is to have retroactive effect, in the absence of limitations imposed by statute or the I.R.S., such rulings generally are entitled to retroactive application. The language of I.R.C. § 7805(b) presumes that these agency rulings will be given retroactive effect unless otherwise specified.

The Supreme Court has upheld the retroactive application of revenue rulings on the ground that the I.R.S. should not be estopped from correcting a "mistake of law," Automobile Club of Michigan v. Commissioner, 353 U.S. 180, 183 (1957), even though a taxpayer may have relied to his detriment on a prior agency ruling. This position reflects the fact that Congress, not the I.R.S., is charged with promulgating the tax laws. The Commissioner of the I.R.S. is simply a delegate of the Secretary of the Treasury whose function is to implement the law.

In the case of disallowing deductions for flight training taken by veterans receiving tuition reimbursement, the Commissioner corrected his past error. Section 265(1) of the Internal Revenue Code embodies the established policy forbidding the deduction of any business expense (otherwise allowable as a deduction) which is allocable to a class of tax-exempt income other than interest. The very fact that a class of income (in this case a direct cash reimbursement) is nontaxable disqualifies its deduction as a business expense.

* * * There is nothing in the language or legislative history of [the] veterans' benefits statutes to indicate that Congress intended to create an exception to existing tax law by permitting veterans to have both a tax exemption and a tax deduction for reimbursed education expenses. Indeed, Congress clearly signaled its concern that the legislation not burden the treasury by authorizing double benefits.

Revenue Ruling 62-213 interpreted Section 1.162-5 of the Income Tax Regulations to mean that veterans who properly deduct educational expenses on their federal income tax returns need not reduce or offset the deduction by the amount of any nontaxable cash payments directly allocable as reimbursement from the Veterans' Administration. This reading of the tax law contravenes Congress's express intention to prevent veteran/taxpayers from realizing double benefits. Revenue Ruling 80-173 which disallowed deductions for veterans enrolled in flight training courses rectified the Commissioner's earlier mistaken interpretation of the law.

Notwithstanding taxpayer's reasonable reliance on the Commissioner's prior position, the I.R.S. clearly is not estopped from nullifying a prior ruling, based on a mistake of law, by means of a new ruling having retroactive effect.

IV.

The taxpayer contends, however, that the Commissioner should be estopped from applying Revenue Ruling 80-173 to his particular case. The facts involved in Manocchio v. Commissioner, supra, cited by the Tax Court, are similar although not identical to the facts in the case before us. In *Manocchio* the taxpayer, an airline pilot and Air Force veteran, attended a flight training course in 1977. Like the taxpayer in our case, he was reimbursed for 90 percent of the cost of the classes by the Veterans' Administration. Relying on Revenue Ruling 62-213 he deducted the entire cost of the flight training course on his income tax returns. The I.R.S. retroactively disallowed the deduction of the reimbursed portion of the course fees and assessed a tax deficiency against him in the amount of $ 924.

The Tax Court upheld the deficiency determination. It found that the taxpayer could point to no extraordinary injury suffered as a result of his reliance on the 1962 ruling:

> He can hardly be heard to complain, for example, that he would not have taken the flight training course had he known the deduction was not available, because (1) the VA provided tax-free reimbursement for 90 percent of the costs, (2) his out-of-pocket cost on the remaining 10 percent was partially offset by the tax benefit attributable to the deduction of such costs, and (3) the education maintained and improved skills required in his trade or business. Nor was it a sufficient injury that petitioner must now disgorge the windfall tax benefit he received and compensate the Government for the use of its money during the intervening period. To hold otherwise would

effectively strip respondent of the authority vested in him by section 7805(b).

Manocchio v. Commissioner, 78 T.C. at 1002.

In the case before us the deficiency assessed against the taxpayer amounts to more than $5,000, not an inconsiderable sum. The taxpayer does not claim, however, that he is financially unable to satisfy the judgment nor does he indicate that repaying the government would so severely burden him or his family as to result in a miscarriage of justice. See Lesavoy Foundation v. Commissioner, 238 F.2d 589 (3d Cir. 1956).

We conclude that the Commissioner was not estopped from applying the Revenue Ruling retroactively. * * *

Notes and Questions

The Eleventh Circuit, in Baker v. United States, 748 F.2d 1465 (11th Cir. 1984), *acq.* 1995-33 I.R.B. 4, considered the retroactive revocation of the same ruling that was at issue in *Becker*, and reached the opposite conclusion of the Third Circuit. The Eleventh Circuit held that the Service could not retroactively revoke the flight training expense ruling because it had prospectively revoked a similar ruling permitting a deduction of general educational expenses that were allowed to be offset by veterans' benefits. Thus, the Eleventh Circuit held that the Commissioner had abused his discretion by treating the two groups of taxpayers inconsistently.

The Third Circuit remanded the *Becker* case to the Tax Court to address the issue of fairness and the right of the taxpayer to expect equal treatment in the enforcement of the tax laws. The Tax Court ultimately decided that the Commissioner had not abused his discretion in retroactively revoking the ruling because the expenses at issue in the two rulings were different and this was reflected in their computation. Thus, according to the court, since the Commissioner could demonstrate a rational basis for distinguishing between the two expenses, the retroactive revocation of the flight training expense ruling constituted a valid exercise of his discretion. See Becker v. Commissioner, 85 T.C. 291 (1985).

Consider, however, the dissent of Judge Goffe in the remanded Tax Court case:

If the Commissioner wants to encourage taxpayers to voluntarily comply with the tax law, which indeed all of us who are concerned with the administration of the tax laws should want, he should accord greater weight to that factor than the relatively insignificant loss of revenue occasioned by prospective revocation. The perception of the taxpayers who have appeared before me in these cases is that they have received unfair treatment by the Commissioner, and I find it difficult to argue with their logic. These taxpayers attempted to file correct income tax returns in abiding by a ruling published by the Commissioner, only to find several years later that the Commissioner changed his mind. Such action by the Commissioner requires that the taxpayers either concede or litigate the point and pay not only the tax but accrued interest as well. I agree with the taxpayers that this is unfair treatment, and I fail to see how it promotes the avowed objective of voluntary compliance as enunciated by the Commissioner * * *.

Id. at 299-300.

Although the Commissioner has discretion to amend or revoke a ruling retroactively in order to correct a mistake of law, a retroactive amendment or revocation is less compelling when the "mistake" arises from "an arguable question of law," where the taxpayer was honest in its disclosure to the government, and where the retroactive revocation was detrimental to the taxpayer. See Lesavoy Foundation v. Commissioner, 238 F.2d 589 (3rd Cir. 1956); see also Benjamin J. Cohen and Catherine A. Harrington, "Is the Internal Revenue Service Bound By Its Own Regulations and Rulings?" 51 TAX LAW. 675 (1998).

In addition to the revenue ruling, William Becker had relied on an unofficial IRS publication. To what extent is the Service bound by representations it makes in unofficial publications? Compare CWT Farms v. Commissioner 755 F.2d 790 (11th Cir. 1985) with Addison International, Inc. v. Commissioner, 887 F.2d 660 (6th Cir. 1989) and Gehl Co. v. Commissioner, 795 F.2d 1324 (7th Cir. 1986).

If you were a sitting judge hearing a case in which the Service is seeking to retroactively revoke a revenue ruling, what factors, other than those mentioned above, might you consider? The next section considers the scope of deference that courts have given revenue rulings.

2) Scope of Judicial Review

While *Mayo* resolved the general issue of deference to regulations, it did not address the deference that less formal guidance such as revenue rulings should receive. After *Chevron*, there was much confusion among the lower courts as to whether agency rulings (as opposed to regulations) were entitled to deference, and if so, what degree of deference they should receive. There also was confusion about whether *Skidmore* deference remained viable. Which of these issues did the Court address in *Mead* and what did the Court decide?

UNITED STATES v. MEAD CORPORATION
United States Supreme Court, 2001.
533 U.S. 218, 121 S.Ct. 2164, 150 L.Ed.2d 292.

JUSTICE SOUTER delivered the opinion of the Court.

The question is whether a tariff classification ruling by the United States Customs Service deserves judicial deference. The Federal Circuit rejected Customs's invocation of Chevron U.S.A. Inc. v. Natural Resources Defense Council, Inc., 467 U.S. 837 (1984), in support of such a ruling, to which it gave no deference. We agree that a tariff classification has no claim to judicial deference under *Chevron*, there being no indication that Congress intended such a ruling to carry the force of law, but we hold that under Skidmore v. Swift & Co., 323 U.S. 134 (1944), the ruling is eligible to claim respect according to its persuasiveness.

I.

A.

Imports are taxed under the Harmonized Tariff Schedule of the United States (HTSUS), 19 U.S.C. § 1202. Title 19 U.S.C. § 1500(b) provides that Customs "shall, under rules and regulations prescribed by the Secretary [of the Treasury] * * * fix the final classification and rate of duty applicable to * * * merchandise" under the HTSUS. Section 1502(a) provides that the Secretary of the Treasury shall establish and promulgate such rules and regulations not inconsistent with the law (including regulations establishing procedures for the issuance of binding rulings prior to the entry of the merchandise concerned), and may disseminate such information as may be necessary to secure a just, impartial, and uniform appraisement of imported merchandise and the classification and assessment of duties thereon at the various ports of entry.[1]

The Secretary provides for tariff rulings before the entry of goods by regulations authorizing "ruling letters" setting tariff classifications for particular imports. A ruling letter represents the official position of the Customs Service with respect to the particular transaction or issue described therein and is binding on all Customs Service personnel in accordance with the provisions of his section until modified or revoked. In the absence of a change of practice or other modification or revocation which affects the principle of the ruling set forth in the ruling letter, that principle may be cited as authority in the disposition of transactions involving the same circumstances. § 177.9(a).

---

1.   The statutory term "ruling " is defined by regulation as "a written statement * * * that interprets and applies the provisions of the Customs and related laws to a specific set of facts." 19 CFR §177.1(d)(1)(2000).

After the transaction that gives it birth, a ruling letter is to "be applied only with respect to transactions involving articles identical to the sample submitted with the ruling request or to articles whose description is identical to the description set forth in the ruling letter." § 177.9(b)(2). As a general matter, such a letter is "subject to modification or revocation without notice to any person, except the person to whom the letter was addressed," § 177.9(c), and the regulations consequently provide that "no other person should rely on the ruling letter or assume that the principles of that ruling will be applied in connection with any transaction other than the one described in the letter," ibid. Since ruling letters respond to transactions of the moment, they are not subject to notice and comment before being issued, may be published but need only be made "available for public inspection," 19 U.S.C. § 1625(a), and, at the time this action arose, could be modified without notice and comment under most circumstances.
* * *

B.

Respondent, the Mead Corporation, imports "day planners," three-ring binders with pages having room for notes of daily schedules and phone numbers and addresses, together with a calendar and suchlike. * * *[Eds: From 1989 until 1993, Customs classified the day planners under a HTSUS subheading that was duty-free. In January 1993, Customs changed its position and issued a Headquarters ruling letter classifying the day planners as "Diaries" subject to a 4 percent tariff. Mead protested the reclassification and Customs Headquarters issued a new, more carefully reasoned letter rejecting Mead's protest. Mead filed a protest to the second letter].

Customs rejected Mead's further protest of the second Headquarters ruling letter, and Mead filed suit in the Court of International Trade (CIT). The CIT granted the Government's motion for summary judgment, adopting Customs's reasoning without saying anything about deference. 17 F.Supp. 2d 1004 (1998).

Mead then went to the United States Court of Appeals for the Federal Circuit. While the case was pending there this Court decided United States v. Haggar Apparel Co., 526 U.S. 380 (1999), holding that Customs regulations receive the deference described in Chevron U.S.A. Inc. v. Natural Resources Defense Council, Inc., 467 U.S. 837 (1984). The Appeals court requested briefing on the impact of *Haggar*, and the Government argued that classification rulings, like Customs regulations, deserve *Chevron* deference.

The Federal Circuit, however, reversed the CIT and held that Customs classification rulings should not get *Chevron* deference, owing to differences from the regulations at issue in *Haggar*. Rulings are not preceded by notice and comment as under the Administrative Procedure Act (APA), 5 U.S.C. § 553, they "do not carry the force of law and are not, like regulations, intended to clarify the rights and obligations of importers beyond the specific case under review." 185 F.3d at 1307. The appeals court thought classification rulings had a weaker *Chevron* claim even than Internal Revenue Service interpretive rulings, to which that court gives no deference; unlike rulings by the IRS, Customs rulings issue from many locations and need not be published. 185 F.3d at 1307-1308.

The Court of Appeals accordingly gave no deference at all to the ruling classifying the Mead day planners and rejected the agency's reasoning * * *. It thought that planners were not diaries because they had no space for "relatively extensive notations about events, observations, feelings, or thoughts" in the past. * * *

We granted certiorari, 530 U.S. 1202 (2000), in order to consider the limits of *Chevron* deference owed to administrative practice in applying a statute. We hold that administrative implementation of a particular statutory provision qualifies for *Chevron* deference when it appears that Congress delegated authority to the agency generally to make rules carrying the force of law, and that the agency interpretation claiming deference was promulgated in the exercise of that authority. Delegation of such authority may be shown in a variety of ways, as by an agency's power to engage in adjudication or notice-and-comment rulemaking, or by some other indication of a comparable congressional intent. The Custom ruling at issue here fails to qualify, although the possibility that it deserves some deference under *Skidmore* leads us to vacate and remand.

II.

A.

When Congress has "explicitly left a gap for an agency to fill, there is an express delegation of authority to the agency to elucidate a specific provision of the statute by regulation," *Chevron*, 467 U.S. at 843-844, and any ensuing regulation is binding in the courts unless procedurally defective, arbitrary or capricious in substance, or manifestly contrary to the statute. But whether or not they enjoy any express delegation of authority on a particular question, agencies charged with applying a statute necessarily make all sorts of interpretive choices, and while not all of those choices bind judges to follow them, they certainly may influence courts facing questions the agencies have already answered. "The well-reasoned views of the agencies implementing a statute 'constitute a body of experience and informed judgment to which courts and litigants may properly resort for guidance," and "we have long recognized that considerable weight should be accorded to an executive department's construction of a statutory scheme it is entrusted to administer * * * ." *Chevron, supra,* at 844. The fair measure of deference to an agency administering its own statute has been understood to vary with circumstances, and courts have looked to the degree of the agency's care, its consistency, formality, and relative expertness, and to the persuasiveness of the agency's position. The approach has produced a spectrum of judicial responses, from great respect at one end, to near indifference at the other * * * . Justice Jackson summed things up in Skidmore v. Swift & Co:

> "The weight [accorded to an administrative] judgment in a particular case will depend upon the thoroughness evident in its consideration, the validity of its reasoning, its consistency with earlier and later pronouncements, and all those factors which give it power to persuade, if lacking power to control." 323 U.S. at 140.

Since 1984, we have identified a category of interpretive choices distinguished by an additional reason for judicial deference. This Court in *Chevron* recognized that Congress not only engages in express delegation of specific interpretive authority, but that "sometimes the legislative delegation to an agency on a particular question is implicit." 467 U.S. at 844. Congress, that is, may not have expressly delegated authority or responsibility to implement a particular provision or fill a particular gap. Yet it can still be apparent from the agency's generally conferred authority and other statutory circumstances that Congress would expect the agency to be able to speak with the force of law when it addresses ambiguity in the statute or fills a space in the enacted law, even one about which "Congress did not actually have an intent" as to a particular result. Id., at 845. When circumstances implying such an expectation exist, a reviewing court has no business rejecting an agency's exercise of its generally conferred authority to resolve a particular statutory ambiguity simply because the agency's chosen resolution seems unwise, but is obliged to accept the agency's position if Congress has not previously spoken to the point at issue and the agency's interpretation is reasonable, see id., at 842-845; cf. 5 U.S.C. § 706(2) (a reviewing court shall set aside agency action, findings, and conclusions found to be "arbitrary, capricious, an abuse of discretion, or otherwise not in accordance with law").

We have recognized a very good indicator of delegation meriting *Chevron* treatment in express congressional authorizations to engage in the process of rulemaking or adjudication that produces regulations or rulings for which deference is claimed. It is fair to assume generally that Congress contemplates administrative action with the effect of law when it provides for a relatively formal administrative procedure tending to foster the fairness and deliberation that should underlie a pronouncement of such force.[11] Thus, the overwhelming number of our cases applying *Chevron* deference have reviewed the fruits of notice-and-comment rulemaking or formal adjudication. That said, and as significant as notice-and-comment is in pointing to *Chevron* authority, the want of that procedure here does not decide the case, for we have sometimes found reasons for *Chevron* deference even when no such administrative formality was required and none was afforded. The fact that the tariff classification here was not a product of such formal process does not alone, therefore, bar the application of *Chevron*.

There are, nonetheless, ample reasons to deny *Chevron* deference here. The authorization for classification rulings, and Customs's practice in making them, present a case far removed not only from notice-and-comment process, but from any other circumstances reasonably suggesting that Congress ever thought of classification rulings as deserving the deference claimed for them here.

B.

No matter which angle we choose for viewing the Customs ruling letter in this case, it fails to qualify under *Chevron*. On the face of the statute, to begin with, the terms of the congressional delegation give no indication that Congress meant to delegate authority to Customs to issue classification rulings with the force of law. We are not, of course, here making any global statement about Customs's authority, for it is true that the general rulemaking power conferred on Customs, authorizes some regulation with the force of law, or "legal norms," as we put it in *Haggar,* 526 U.S. at 391. It is true as well that Congress had classification rulings in mind when it explicitly authorized, in a parenthetical, the issuance of "regulations establishing procedures for the issuance of binding rulings prior to the entry of the merchandise concerned," 19 U.S.C. § 1502(a).[15] The reference to binding classifications does not, however, bespeak the legislative type of activity that would naturally bind more than the parties to the ruling, once the goods classified are admitted into this country. And though the statute's direction to disseminate "information" necessary to "secure" uniformity, 19 U.S.C. § 1502(a), seems to assume that a ruling may be precedent in later transactions, precedential value alone does not add up

---

11. See Merrill & Hickman, *Chevron's* Domain, 89 Geo. L.J. 833, 872 (2001)("If *Chevron* rests on a presumption about congressional intent, then *Chevron* should apply only where Congress would want *Chevron* to apply. In delineating the types of delegations of agency authority that trigger *Chevron* deference, it is therefore important to determine whether a plausible case can be made that Congress would want such a delegation to mean that agencies enjoy primary interpretational authority").

15. The ruling in question here, however, does not fall within that category.

to *Chevron* entitlement; interpretive rules may sometimes function as precedents, and they enjoy no *Chevron* status as a class. In any event, any precedential claim of a classification ruling is counterbalanced by the provision for independent review of Customs classifications by the CIT, see 28 U.S.C. §§ 2638-2640; the scheme for CIT review includes a provision that treats classification rulings on a par with the Secretary's rulings on "valuation, rate of duty, marking, restricted merchandise, entry requirements, drawbacks, vessel repairs, or similar matters. It is hard to imagine a congressional understanding more at odds with the *Chevron* regime.[16]

It is difficult, in fact, to see in the agency practice itself any indication that Customs ever set out with a lawmaking pretense in mind when it undertook to make classifications like these. Customs does not generally engage in notice-and-comment practice when issuing them, and their treatment by the agency makes it clear that a letter's binding character as a ruling stops short of third parties; Customs has regarded a classification as conclusive only as between itself and the importer to whom it was issued, and even then only until Customs has given advance notice of intended change. Other importers are in fact warned against assuming any right of detrimental reliance.

Indeed, to claim that classifications have legal force is to ignore the reality that 46 different Customs offices issue 10,000 to 15,000 of them each year. Any suggestion that rulings intended to have the force of law are being churned out at a rate of 10,000 a year at an agency's 46 scattered offices is simply self-refuting. Although the circumstances are less startling here, with a Headquarters letter in issue, none of the relevant statutes recognizes this category of rulings as separate or different from others; there is thus no indication that a more potent delegation might have been understood as going to Headquarters even when Headquarters provides developed reasoning, as it did in this instance.

* * *

In sum, classification rulings are best treated like "interpretations contained in policy statements, agency manuals, and enforcement guidelines." They are beyond the *Chevron* pale.

C.

To agree with the Court of Appeals that Customs ruling letters do not fall within *Chevron* is not, however, to place them outside the pale of any deference whatever. *Chevron* did nothing to eliminate *Skidmore's* holding

---

16. Although Customs's decision "is presumed to be correct" on review, 28 U.S.C. § 2639(a)(1), the CIT "may consider any new ground" even if not raised below, § 2638, and "shall make its determinations upon the basis of the record made before the court," rather than that developed by Customs, § 2640(a); see generally *Haggar Apparel,* 526 U.S. at 391.

that an agency's interpretation may merit some deference whatever its form, given the "specialized experience and broader investigations and information" available to the agency, 323 U.S. at 139, and given the value of uniformity in its administrative and judicial understandings of what a national law requires.

There is room at least to raise a *Skidmore* claim here, where the regulatory scheme is highly detailed, and Customs can bring the benefit of specialized experience to bear on the subtle questions in this case: whether the daily planner with room for brief daily entries falls under "diaries," when diaries are grouped with "notebooks and address books, bound; memorandum pads, letter pads and similar articles," * * * . A classification ruling in this situation may therefore at least seek a respect proportional to its "power to persuade," *Skidmore,* supra, at 140. Such a ruling may surely claim the merit of its writer's thoroughness, logic and expertness, its fit with prior interpretations, and any other sources of weight.

D.

Underlying the position we take here, like the position expressed by Justice Scalia in dissent, is a choice about the best way to deal with an inescapable feature of the body of congressional legislation authorizing administrative action. That feature is the great variety of ways in which the laws invest the Government's administrative arms with discretion, and with procedures for exercising it, in giving meaning to Acts of Congress. Implementation of a statute may occur in formal adjudication or the choice to defend against judicial challenge; it may occur in a central board or office or in dozens of enforcement agencies dotted across the country; its institutional lawmaking may be confined to the resolution of minute detail or extend to legislative rulemaking on matters intentionally left by Congress to be worked out at the agency level.

Although we all accept the position that the Judiciary should defer to at least some of this multifarious administrative action, we have to decide how to take account of the great range of its variety. If the primary objective is to simplify the judicial process of giving or withholding deference, then the diversity of statutes authorizing discretionary administrative action must be declared irrelevant or minimized. If, on the other hand, it is simply implausible that Congress intended such a broad range of statutory authority to produce only two varieties of administrative action, demanding either *Chevron* deference or none at all, then the breadth of the spectrum of possible agency action must be taken into account. Justice Scalia's first priority over the years has been to limit and simplify. The Court's choice has been to tailor deference to variety. This acceptance of the range of statutory variation has led the Court to recognize more than one variety of judicial deference, just as the Court has recognized a variety of indicators that Congress would expect *Chevron* deference.[18]

Our respective choices are repeated today. Justice Scalia would pose the question of deference as an either-or choice. On his view that *Chevron* rendered *Skidmore* anachronistic, when courts owe any deference it is *Chevron* deference that they owe. Whether courts do owe deference in a given case turns, for him, on whether the agency action (if reasonable) is "authoritative." The character of the authority derives, in turn, not from breadth of delegation or the agency's procedure in implementing it, but is defined as the "official" position of an agency, and may ultimately be a function of administrative persistence alone.

The Court, on the other hand, said nothing in *Chevron* to eliminate *Skidmore's* recognition of various justifications for deference depending on statutory circumstances and agency action; *Chevron* was simply a case recognizing that even without express authority to fill a specific statutory gap, circumstances pointing to implicit congressional delegation present a particularly insistent call for deference. Indeed, in holding here that *Chevron* left *Skidmore* intact and applicable where statutory circumstances indicate no intent to delegate general authority to make rules with force of law, or where such authority was not revoked, we hold nothing more than we said last Term in response to the particular statutory circumstances in *Christensen,* to which Justice Scalia then took exception, just as he does again today.

We think, in sum, that Justice Scalia's efforts to simplify ultimately run afoul of Congress's indications that different statutes present different reasons for considering respect for the exercise of administrative authority or deference to it. Without being at odds with congressional intent much of the time, we believe that judicial responses to administrative action must continue to differentiate between *Chevron* and *Skidmore,* and that continued recognition of *Skidmore* is necessary for just the reasons Justice Jackson gave when that case was decided.[19]

---

18. It is, of course, true that the limit of *Chevron* deference is not marked by a hard-edged rule. But *Chevron* itself is a good example showing when *Chevron* deference is warranted, while this is a good case showing when it is not. Judges in other, perhaps harder, cases will make reasoned choices between the two examples, the way courts have always done.

19. Surely Justice Jackson's practical criteria, along with *Chevron's* concern with congressional understanding, provide more reliable guideposts than conclusory references to the "authoritative" or "official." Even if those terms provided a true criterion, there would have to be something wrong with a standard that accorded the status of substantive law to every one of 10,000 "official" customs classifications rulings turned out each year from over 46 offices placed around the country at the Nation's entryways. Justice Scalia tries to avoid that result by limiting what is "authoritative" or "official" to a pronouncement that expresses the "judgment of central agency management, approved

Since the *Skidmore* assessment called for here ought to be made in the first instance by the Court of Appeals for the Federal Circuit or the Court of International Trade, we go no further than to vacate the judgment and remand the case for further proceedings consistent with this opinion.

It is so ordered.

JUSTICE SCALIA, dissenting.

* * *

I.

Only five years ago, the Court described the *Chevron* doctrine as follows: "We accord deference to agencies under *Chevron* * * * because of a presumption that Congress, when it left ambiguity in a statute meant for implementation by an agency, understood that the ambiguity would be resolved, first and foremost, by the agency, and desired the agency (rather than the courts) to possess whatever degree of discretion the ambiguity allows." Today the Court collapses this doctrine, announcing instead a presumption that agency discretion does not exist unless the statute, expressly or impliedly, says so. While the Court disclaims any hard-and-fast rule for determining the existence of discretion-conferring intent, it asserts that "a very good indicator [is] express congressional authorizations to engage in the process of rulemaking or adjudication that produces regulations or rulings for which deference is claimed. Only when agencies act through "adjudication[,] notice-and-comment rulemaking, or * * * some other [procedure] indicating comparable congressional intent [whatever that means]" is *Chevron* deference applicable – because these "relatively formal administrative procedures [designed] to foster * * * fairness and deliberation" bespeak (according to the Court) congressional willingness to have the agency, rather than the courts, resolve statutory ambiguities. Once it is determined that *Chevron* deference is not in order, the uncertainty is not at an end – and indeed is just beginning. Litigants cannot then assume that the statutory question is one for the courts to determine, according to traditional interpretive principles and by their own judicial lights. No, the Court now resurrects, in full force, the pre-*Chevron* doctrine of *Skidmore* deference, whereby "the fair measure of deference to

---

at the highest level," as distinct from the pronouncements of "underlings." But that analysis would not entitle a Headquarters ruling to *Chevron* deference; the "highest level" at Customs is the source of the regulation at issue in *Haggar,* the Commissioner of Customs, with the approval of the Secretary of the Treasury. 526 U.S. at 386. The Commissioner did not issue the Headquarters ruling. What Justice Scalia has in mind here is that because the Secretary approved the Government's position in its brief to this Court, *Chevron* deference is due. But if that is so, *Chevron* deference was not called for until sometime after the litigation began, when central management at the highest level decided to defend the ruling, and the deference is not to the classification ruling as such but to the brief. This explains why the Court has not accepted Justice Scalia's position.

an agency administering its own statute * * * varies with circumstances," including "the degree of the agency's care, its consistency, formality, and relative expertness, and * * * the persuasiveness of the agency's position." The Court has largely replaced *Chevron*, in other words, with that test most beloved by a court unwilling to be held to rules (and most feared by litigants who want to know what to expect): th' ol' "totality of the circumstances" test.

The Court's new doctrine is neither sound in principle nor sustainable in practice.

A.

As to principle: The doctrine of *Chevron* – that all *authoritative* agency interpretations of statutes they are charged with administering deserve deference – was rooted in a legal presumption of congressional intent, important to the division of powers between the Second and Third Branches. When, *Chevron* said, Congress leaves an ambiguity in a statute that is to be administered by an executive agency, it is presumed that Congress meant to give the agency discretion, within the limits of reasonable interpretation, as to how the ambiguity is to be resolved. By committing enforcement of the statute to an agency rather than the courts, Congress committed its initial and primary interpretation to that branch as well.

* * *

Statutory ambiguities, in other words, were left to reasonable resolution by the Executive.

The basis in principle for today's new doctrine can be described as follows: The background rule is that ambiguity in legislative instructions to agencies is to be resolved not by the agencies but by the judges. Specific congressional intent to depart from this rule must be found – and while there is no single touchstone for such intent it can generally be found when Congress has authorized the agency to act through (what the Court says is) relatively formal procedures such as informal rulemaking and formal (and informal?) adjudication, and when the agency in fact employs such procedures. The Court's background rule is contradicted by the origins of judicial review of administrative action. But in addition, the Court's principal criterion of congressional intent to supplant its background rule seems to me quite implausible. There is no necessary connection between the formality of procedure and the power of the entity administering the procedure to resolve authoritatively questions of law. The most formal of the procedures the Court refers to – formal adjudication – is modeled after the process used in trial courts, which of course are not generally accorded deference on questions of law. The purpose of such a procedure is to produce a closed record for determination and review of the facts – which implies nothing about the power of the agency subjected to the procedure to resolve authoritatively questions of law.

As for informal rulemaking: While formal adjudication procedures are *prescribed* (either by statute or by the Constitution), informal rulemaking is more typically *authorized* but not required.   Agencies with such authority are free to give guidance through rulemaking, but they may proceed to administer their statute case-by-case, "making law" as they implement their program (not necessarily through formal adjudication). Is it likely – or indeed even plausible – that Congress meant, when such an agency chooses rulemaking, to accord the administrators of that agency, *and their successors,* the flexibility of interpreting the ambiguous statute now one way, and later another, but when such an agency chooses case-by-case administration, to eliminate all future agency discretion by having that same ambiguity resolved authoritatively (and forever) by the courts? Surely that makes no sense. It is also the case that certain significant categories of rules – those involving grant and benefit programs, for example, are exempt from the requirements of informal rulemaking.   Under the Court's novel theory, when an agency takes advantage of that exemption its rules will be deprived of *Chevron* deference, i.e., authoritative effect. Was this either the plausible intent of the APA rulemaking exemption, or the plausible intent of the Congress that established the grant or benefit program?

Some decisions that are neither informal rulemaking nor formal adjudication are required to be made personally by a Cabinet Secretary, without any prescribed procedures.   Is it conceivable that decisions specifically committed to these high-level officers are meant to be accorded no deference, while decisions by an administrative law judge left in place without further discretionary agency review are authoritative? This seems to me quite absurd, and not at all in accord with any plausible actual intent of Congress.

B.

As for the practical effects of the new rule:

(1) The principal effect will be protracted confusion. As noted above, the one test for *Chevron* deference that the Court enunciates is wonderfully imprecise: whether "Congress delegated authority to the agency generally to make rules carrying the force of law, * * * as by * * * adjudication[,] notice-and-comment rulemaking, or * * * some other [procedure] indicating comparable congressional intent." But even this description does not do justice to the utter flabbiness of the Court's criterion, since, in order to maintain the fiction that the new test is really

just the old one, applied consistently throughout our case law, the Court must make a virtually open-ended exception to its already imprecise guidance: In the present case, it tells us, the absence of notice-and-comment rulemaking (and "[who knows?] [of] some other [procedure] indicating comparable congressional intent") is not enough to decide the question of *Chevron* deference, "for we have sometimes found reasons for *Chevron* deference even when no such administrative formality was required and none was afforded." The opinion then goes on to consider a grab bag of other factors – including the factor that used to be the sole criterion for *Chevron* deference: whether the interpretation represented the *authoritative* position of the agency. It is hard to know what the lower courts are to make of today's guidance.

(2) Another practical effect of today's opinion will be an artificially induced increase in informal rulemaking. Buy stock in the GPO. Since informal rulemaking and formal adjudication are the only more-or-less safe harbors from the storm that the Court has unleashed; and since formal adjudication is not an option but must be mandated by statute or constitutional command; informal rulemaking – which the Court was once careful to make voluntary unless required by statute – will now become a virtual necessity. As I have described, the Court's safe harbor requires not merely that the agency have been given rulemaking authority, but also that the agency have *employed* rulemaking as the means of resolving the statutory ambiguity. (It is hard to understand why that should be so. Surely the mere *conferral* of rulemaking authority demonstrates – if one accepts the Court's logic – a congressional intent to allow the agency to resolve ambiguities. And given that intent, what difference does it make that the agency chooses instead to use another perfectly permissible means for that purpose?). Moreover, the majority's approach will have a perverse effect on the rules that do emerge, given the principle (which the Court leaves untouched today) that judges must defer to reasonable agency interpretations of their own regulations. Agencies will now have high incentive to rush out barebones, ambiguous rules construing statutory ambiguities, which they can then in turn further clarify through informal rulings entitled to judicial respect.

(3) Worst of all, the majority's approach will lead to the ossification of large portions of our statutory law. Where *Chevron* applies, statutory ambiguities remain ambiguities subject to the agency's ongoing clarification. They create a space, so to speak, for the exercise of continuing agency discretion. * * * For the indeterminately large number of statutes taken out of *Chevron* by today's decision, however, ambiguity (and hence flexibility) will cease with the first judicial resolution. *Skidmore* deference gives the agency's current position some vague and uncertain amount of respect, but it does not, like *Chevron*, leave the matter within the control

of the Executive Branch for the future. Once the court has spoken, it becomes *unlawful* for the agency to take a contradictory position; the statute now *says* what the court has prescribed. It will be bad enough when this ossification occurs as a result of judicial determination (under today's new principles) that there is no affirmative indication of congressional intent to "delegate"; but it will be positively bizarre when it occurs simply because of an agency's failure to act by rulemaking (rather than informal adjudication) before the issue is presented to the courts.

One might respond that such ossification would not result if the agency were simply to readopt its interpretation, after a court reviewing it under *Skidmore* had rejected it, by repromulgating it through one of the *Chevron*-eligible procedural formats approved by the Court today. Approving this procedure would be a landmark abdication of judicial power. It is worlds apart from *Chevron* proper, where the court does not *purport* to give the statute a judicial interpretation – except in identifying the scope of the statutory ambiguity, as to which the court's judgment is final and irreversible. (Under *Chevron* proper, when the agency's authoritative interpretation comes within the scope of that ambiguity – and the court therefore approves it – the agency will not be "overruling " the court's decision when it later decides that a different interpretation (still within the scope of the ambiguity) is preferable). By contrast, under this view, the reviewing court will not be holding the agency's authoritative interpretation within the scope of the ambiguity; but will be holding that the agency has not used the "delegation-conferring" procedures, and that the court must therefore *interpret the statute on its own* – but subject to reversal if and when the agency uses the proper procedures.

* * *

There is, in short, no way to avoid the ossification of federal law that today's opinion sets in motion. What a court says is the law after according *Skidmore* deference will be the law forever, beyond the power of the agency to change even through rulemaking.

(4) And finally, the majority's approach compounds the confusion it creates by breathing new life into the anachronism of *Skidmore*, which sets forth a sliding scale of deference owed an agency's interpretation of a statute that is dependent "upon the thoroughness evident in [the agency's] consideration, the validity of its reasoning, its consistency with earlier and later pronouncements, and all those factors which give it power to persuade, if lacking power to control;" in this way, the appropriate measure of deference will be accorded the "body of experience and informed judgment" that such interpretations often embody. [The] rule of *Skidmore* deference is an empty truism and a trifling statement of the obvious: A judge should take into account the well-considered views of expert observers.

It was possible to live with the indeterminacy of *Skidmore* deference in earlier times. But in an era when federal statutory law administered by federal agencies is pervasive, and when the ambiguities (intended or unintended) that those statutes contain are innumerable, totality-of-the-circumstances *Skidmore* deference is a recipe for uncertainty, unpredictability, and endless litigation. To condemn a vast body of agency action to that regime (all except rulemaking, formal (and informal?) adjudication, and whatever else might now and then be included within today's intentionally vague formulation of affirmative congressional intent to "delegate") is irresponsible.

* * *

III.

To decide the present case, I would adhere to the original formulation of *Chevron*. "'The power of an administrative agency to administer a congressionally created * * * program necessarily requires the formulation of policy and the making of rules to fill any gap left, implicitly or explicitly, by Congress,'" 467 U.S. at 843 (quoting Morton v. Ruiz, 415 U.S. 199 (1974)). We accordingly presume – and our precedents have made clear to Congress that we presume – that, absent some clear textual indication to the contrary, "Congress, when it left ambiguity in a statute meant for implementation by an agency understood that the ambiguity would be resolved, first and foremost, by the agency, and desired the agency (rather than the courts) to possess whatever degree of discretion the ambiguity allows," *Smiley*, 517 U.S. at 740-41 (citing *Chevron,* supra, at 843-44). *Chevron* sets forth an across-the-board presumption, which operates as a background rule of law against which Congress legislates: Ambiguity means Congress intended agency discretion. Any resolution of the ambiguity by the administering agency that is authoritative – that represents the official position of the agency – must be accepted by the courts if it is reasonable.

Nothing in the statute at issue here displays an intent to modify the background presumption on which *Chevron* deference is based. The Court points to 28 U.S.C. § 2640(a), which provides that, in reviewing the ruling by the Customs Service, the Court of International Trade (CIT) "shall make its determinations upon the basis of the record made before the court." But records are made to determine the facts, not the law. All this provision means is that new evidence may be introduced at the CIT stage; it says nothing about whether the CIT must respect the Customs Service's authoritative interpretation of the law. More significant than § 2640(a), insofar as the CIR's obligation to defer to the Customs Service's legal interpretations is concerned, is § 2639(a)(1), which requires the CIT to accord a "presum[ption of] correctness" to the Customs Service's decision.

Another provision cited by the Court, is § 2638, which provides that the CIT "by rule, may consider any new ground in support" of the challenge to the Customs Service's ruling. Once again, it is impossible to see how this has any connection to the degree of deference the CIT must accord the Customs Service's interpretation of its statute. Such "new grounds" may be intervening or newly discovered facts, or some intervening law or regulation that might render the Customs Service's ruling unsound.

There is no doubt that the Customs Service's interpretation represents the authoritative view of the agency. Although the actual ruling letter was signed by only the Director of the Commercial Rulings Branch of Customs Headquarters' Office of Regulations and Rulings, the Solicitor General of the United States has filed a brief, cosigned by the General Counsel of the Department of the Treasury, that represents the position set forth in the ruling letter to be the official position of the Customs Service. No one contends that it is merely a "post hoc rationalization" or an "agency litigating position wholly unsupported by regulations, rulings, or administrative practice," Bowen v. Georgetown Univ. Hospital, 488 U.S. 204 (1988).[6]

There is also no doubt that the Customs Service's interpretation is a reasonable one, whether or not judges would consider it the best. I will not belabor this point, since the Court evidently agrees: An interpretation

---

6.   The Court's parting shot, that "there would have to be something wrong with a standard that accorded the status of substantive law to every one of 10,000 'official' customs classifications rulings turned out each year from over 46 offices placed around the country at the Nation's entryways," misses the mark. I do not disagree. The "authoritativeness" of an agency interpretation does not turn upon whether it has been enunciated by someone who is actually employed by the agency. It must represent the judgment of central agency management, approved at the highest levels. I would find that condition to have been satisfied when, a ruling having been attacked in court, the general counsel of the agency has determined that it should be defended. If one thinks that that does not impart sufficient authoritativeness, then surely the line has been crossed when, as here, the General Counsel of the agency and the Solicitor General of the United States have assured this Court that the position represents the agency's authoritative view. (Contrary to the Court's suggestion, there would be nothing bizarre about the fact that this latter approach would entitle the ruling to deference here, though it would not have been entitled to deference in the lower courts. Affirmation of the official agency position before this court – if that is thought necessary – is no different from the agency's issuing a new rule after the Court of Appeals determination. It establishes a new legal basis for the decision, which this Court must take into account (or remand for that purpose), even though the Court of Appeals could not. See Thorpe v. Housing Authority of Durham, 393 U.S. 268 (1969); see also United States v. Schooner Peggy, 5 U.S. 103, 1 Cranch 103 (1801).

The *authoritativeness* of the agency ruling may not be a bright-line standard – but it is infinitely brighter than the line the Court asks us to draw today, between a statute such as the one at issue in *NationsBank* [eds: Nationsbank of N.C., N.A. v. Variable Annuity Life Ins. Co., 513 U.S. 251 (1995)]that (according to the Court) *does* display an "affirmative intent" to "delegate" interpretive authority, and innumerable indistinguishable statutes that (according to the Court) do *not*. And, most important of all, it is a line that focuses attention on the right question: not whether Congress "affirmatively intended" to delegate interpretive authority (if it entrusted administration of the statue to an agency, it did, because that is how our system works); but whether it is truly the agency's considered view, or just the opinions of some underlings, that are at issue.

that was unreasonable would not merit the remand that the Court decrees for consideration of *Skidmore* deference.

IV.
* * *

For the reasons stated, I respectfully dissent from the Court's judgment. I would uphold the Customs Service's construction of * * * the Harmonized Tariff Schedule, and would reverse the contrary decision of the Court of Appeals. I dissent even more vigorously from the reasoning that produces the Court's judgment, and that makes today's decision one of the most significant opinions ever rendered by the Court dealing with the judicial review of administrative action. Its consequences will be enormous, and almost uniformly bad.

Notes and Questions

The Court left many questions unresolved in *Mead*. For instance, the Court concluded that notice and comment is but *one* of the factors to be considered in determining whether Congress intended to delegate rule-making authority to the agency. Thus, after *Mead*, regulations issued without notice and comment conceivably can receive *Chevron* deference, although this is not entirely clear. The Court could have established a bright line test if it had held instead that where an agency has the authority to speak with the force and effect of law, and that agency issues rulings through the notice-and-comment procedure of the APA, the rulings are entitled to *Chevron* deference. The Court chose not to establish such a test, however.

1. Does *Chevron* deference apply to revenue rulings? See United States v. Cleveland Indians Baseball Co., 532 U.S. 200 (2001).

2. Should the deference afforded revenue rulings vary according to whether the Service or the taxpayer is challenging the ruling?

3. The Tax Court refuses to give revenue rulings *Chevron* deference on the ground that revenue rulings " * * * do not have the force of law and are merely statements of the Commissioner's litigating and administrative position." Norfolk Southern Corp. v. Commissioner, 104 T.C. 13, 46 (1995), modified on reconsideration, 104 T.C. 417 (1995). Do you agree with the Tax Court's position?

4. If Justice Scalia had prevailed and the Court had adopted his position, how if at all, would this position have affected the tax law? What effect, if any, would such a position have on the second tier analysis of *Chevron* in which the court must determine the reasonableness of the ruling?

b. Letter Rulings

Letter rulings (also called private letter rulings) are issued by the Chief Counsel's Office to taxpayers or taxpayers' representatives, in response to specific requests for guidance. A letter ruling generally recites the relevant facts, sets forth the applicable provisions of law, and applies the law to the facts. Reg. § 301.6110-2(d). If the transaction deviates from the stated facts, the taxpayer is no longer entitled to rely on the ruling.

Although letter rulings apply only to the taxpayers to whom they are issued, the rulings are available to the public under the Freedom of Information Act (see Chapter 2), with any identifying data redacted. Since the rulings are private, they are not published by the government, but instead are published by commercial tax publishers and also are available on-line. While revenue rulings may be relied upon by the taxpaying public and cited as precedent, private letter rulings may not be similarly cited since they apply only to the taxpayers who requested them. See IRC § 6110(k)(3); Reg. § 601.601(d)(2); K.F. Knetsch v. United States, 348 F.2d 932 (Ct. Cl. 1965); E.D. Goodstein v. Commissioner, 267 F.2d 127 (1st Cir. 1959). They will be of interest to other taxpayers, however, because they indicate how the Service is likely to rule under similar facts and circumstances. Since the Service must treat all taxpayers fairly, taxpayers who are similarly situated have the right to expect consistent treatment. If so, then why can taxpayers not rely upon or cite as precedent letter rulings issued to other taxpayers? To what extent does the Service have a duty of consistency?

1) Consistency in Treatment of Taxpayers

BOOKWALTER v. BRECKLEIN
United States Court of Appeals, Eighth Circuit, 1966.
357 F.2d 78.

VOGEL, CIRCUIT JUDGE.

The question in this case is whether the taxpayer, plaintiff-appellee herein, is entitled to refunds for tax deductions not previously taken by him in 1957, the taxable year involved, on the grounds that private letter rulings issued to other taxpayers in 1958 erroneously allowed such other taxpayers to take similar deductions. The said letter rulings were eventually revoked but were revoked prospectively rather than retroactively. The District Court, * * * allowed appellee to recover for years prior to the time the private letter rulings were revoked. We reverse.

* * *

In 1958 the City of Bismarck, North Dakota, sought a ruling relating to the deductibility for income tax purposes of special assessments levied by that city against some 500 property owners with land located in and benefitted by parking improvement districts in Bismarck's central business area. Such deductions were made permissible in a May 21, 1958, letter sent to the Commissioners of the City of Bismarck by Dan J. Ferris, the Acting Director of the Tax Rulings Division (this will hereafter be referred to as the Bismarck letter). * * *

* * *

The Bismarck letter was never published in the Internal Revenue Bulletin but it was picked up and published by the Commerce Clearing House, a private tax service. The Bismarck letter was revoked prospectively in an April 4, 1960, letter from Dana Latham, the Commissioner of Internal Revenue, to the Bismarck Commissioners.

* * *

The revocation of the Bismarck letter was published in the Internal Revenue Bulletin as Rev. Rul. 60-327, 1960-2, Cum. Bull. 65.

After the issuance, but before the revocation, of the Bismarck letter, a Bismarck type of ruling was sought by a partnership owning business rental property known as the Wirthman Building in Kansas City, Missouri. The Wirthman Building partners sought to deduct payments being made by them on their obligation under the same special assessment (for the proposed offstreet parking improvement) as was levied against the appellee herein. The Wirthman partners, however, had elected to pay the assessment in annual payments rather than in one lump sum payment, as was true with appellee. The first installment paid during the 1958 fiscal year was capitalized by the Wirthman partners. In response to their request, the Wirthman partners were informed in a letter dated June 18, 1959 * * * (hereinafter this will be referred to as the Wirthman determination letter) that in the future a deduction for the assessment payments would be allowed.

* * *

For the fiscal years ending in 1959 and 1960, the Wirthman partners deducted the installments paid as ordinary and necessary business expenses pursuant to the Wirthman determination letter. However, the Wirthman determination letter was revoked "henceforth" in a letter, dated January 12, 1961, sent to the Wirthman partners * * * .

Following the prospective repudiations of the Bismarck letter and the Wirthman determination letter, appellee, on March 23, 1961, filed suit to recover an overpayment of taxes for 1957 resulting from a failure to deduct the benefit district assessments paid by him in one lump sum in 1957. After an evidentiary hearing, the District Court entered judgment for appellee, holding * * * that the taxpayer was

* * * entitled as a matter of law to equality of treatment with the 500 Bismarck taxpayers, the Wirthman partners, and any others who were accorded the benefit of the Commissioner's modification provision of no retroactive application of the modification ruling of April 4, 1960. * * *

Appellee argues that: "The unlawful discrimination between similarly-situated taxpayers, as found by the district court, was such that the judgment of the district court was not erroneous."

We do not agree. Ordinarily, the Commissioner of Internal Revenue or his duly authorized subordinates act within their power when revoking an erroneous private ruling with or without retroactive effect. The evidence does not show that the appellee herein is being treated any worse or any differently from other taxpayers in his position who did not request or receive private letter rulings. Taxpayers without rulings are entitled only to be taxed the same as other taxpayers without rulings.

The fact that the private Bismarck letter was published by the Commerce Clearing House is not of decisive consequence. In [Goodstein v. Commissioner, 267 F.2d 127 (1st Cir. 1959)], the taxpayer had seen other private but officially unpublished rulings and this factor was not enough to allow him (and, inferentially, all other taxpayers in his position) to rely on the said private rulings. As a practical matter, officials of the Internal Revenue Service are themselves not bound for precedent purposes by rulings or decisions not officially published. This fact is not unknown to the public since the policy of the Internal Revenue Service is set out in the introduction to the Internal Revenue Bulletins. In any event, the appellee did not rely either on the Bismarck letter or the Wirthman determination letter for he had paid his taxes on the assessment prior to when those letters were issued. There is no showing that appellee ever incurred expense or arranged his affairs in reliance on the Bismarck or Wirthman determinations. Even if such reliance had been shown, this is not necessarily decisive.

Certain cases relied on by the court below and by the appellee in his brief are inapposite to the instant situation. Each case must be viewed on its facts to determine if the Commissioner has abused his discretion under 26 U.S.C.A. § 7805(b). * * *

International Business Machines Corp. v. United States, 343 F.2d 914 (Ct. Cl. 1965) (hereafter referred to as the I.B.M. case), a three to one decision, involved two competitors, I.B.M. and Remington Rand, in the manufacturing, selling and leasing of large electronic computer systems. On April 13, 1955, Remington requested a ruling from the Commissioner of Internal Revenue to permit it to avoid existing tax liabilities arising out of the sale and rental of its computers. A favorable ruling was issued by the Commissioner in a telegram sent to Remington on April 15, 1955. On July 13, 1955, I.B.M., having learned of the Remington ruling, sought a similar ruling on its sale and leasing of comparable computers. I.B.M.'s letter to the Commissioner was marked "Urgent! Please Expedite" and closed as follows: "In view of the extreme urgency of this matter, your immediate ruling, wire collect, is respectfully requested." 343 F.2d at 916.

I.B.M.'s request was not acted upon for over two years, and then in a negative manner. Both I.B.M. (On July 29, 1955) and Remington (in September 1955) also sought refunds for taxes paid on the sale and leasing of computers in the past. I.B.M.'s claim covered the period from June 1, 1951, to May 31, 1955, and Remington's from January 1, 1952, to April 30, 1955. Remington's refund was allowed in July of 1956. I.B.M.'s refund claim, however, was rejected. The favorable tax ruling as to Remington was finally revoked prospectively as of February 1, 1958. In other words, Remington enjoyed six years of paying no tax on the selling and leasing of its computers, while I.B.M. did not share in such advantages for the selling and leasing of an almost identical product, even though both companies made similar requests of the Commissioner. This amounted to a comparative loss of over $13,000,000 to I.B.M. The Court of Claims allowed I.B.M. to recover the taxes paid by it on income derived from the rental and sale of computers for the period that Remington was not subjected to the tax.

Clearly, the facts of the *I.B.M.* case are entirely different from those in the instant situation. In *I.B.M.* there are clear and uncontradicted indications that the Commissioner abused his discretion in granting Remington tax-free treatment to the detriment of I.B.M. Unlike the instant appeal, the *I.B.M.* case involved a situation where one competitor was being favored unjustifiably over the only other competitor in the computer industry. Thus, the only members of the only logical class therein – the computer industry – were being treated in exactly opposite ways to the great detriment of I.B.M. Herein the situation is entirely different since appellee was treated no differently from many other similarly situated taxpayers who also had not sought rulings. In *I.B.M.* no reason was shown as to why Remington was not taxed retroactively. Here rational explanations were set forth as to why the Wirthman partners were not taxed retroactively – e.g., Mr. Jack U. Hiatt, a group supervisor for the Field Audit Branch of the Internal Revenue Service, testified that it was not feasible to collect a relatively small tax liability from a large number of taxpayers (the 22 members of the Wirthman partnership) located in different collection districts. There is a great contrast between the relatively small amounts involved herein and the $13,000,000 involved in *I.B.M.* Furthermore, there was a much greater reliance factor in *I.B.M.* since I.B.M. was, at the time it was paying the disputed taxes, aware of the ruling made to Remington and within three months after the private ruling to Remington had made an urgent request for a similar ruling. Herein appellee paid his assessment *before* either the Bismarck or Wirthman determination letters were issued.

In *I.B.M.* Judge Davis, writing for the three-man majority, stated in 343 F.2d at 920, 921 and 923:

> Implicit, too, in the Congressional award of discretion to the [Internal Revenue] Service, through Section 7805(b), is the power as well as the *obligation to consider the totality of the circumstances surrounding the handing down of a ruling – including the comparative or differential effect on the other taxpayers in the same class. 'The Commissioner cannot tax one and not tax another without some rational basis for the difference.'* United States v. Kaiser, 363 U.S. 299, 308 (1960) (Frankfurter, J., concurring). This factor has come to be recognized as central to the administration of the section. Equality of treatment is so dominant in our understanding of justice that discretion, where it is allowed a role, must pay the strictest heed.
>
> * * *
>
> * * * *When we examine the agreed facts,* we cannot escape holding that there was a clear abuse, that the circumstances compelled the Service to confine its ruling (when it was finally given) to the future period for which Remington Rand's computers were to be held taxable. * * *
>
> * * *
>
> *This history* exposes a manifest and unjustifiable discrimination against the taxpayer. (Emphasis supplied).

As is apparent from the italicized portions of the above quotation, the Court of Claims was limiting itself in *I.B.M.* to the "totality of the circumstances" there involved. That *I.B.M.* was not intended to be a blanket ruling is clearly evidenced in two later case decided by the Court of Claims. Those decisions are Knetsch v. United States, 348 F.2d 932 (Ct. Cl. 1965), and Bornstein v. United States, 345 F.2d 558 (Ct. Cl. 1965). In *Knetsch,* that court stated in fn. 14 at page 940 of 348 F.2d:

> As the court pointed out in *Bornstein,* supra, *our decision in International Business Machines Corp. v. United States,* Ct. Cl. 343 F.2d 914, decided April 16, 1965, rested in section 7805(b) of the Internal Revenue Code, of 1954, and *was based on the court's evaluation of the particular circumstances in that case.* (Emphasis supplied).

In *Bornstein* the Court of Claims stated in fn. 2 at page 564 of 345 F.2d:

> There are also controlling factual differences between these cases [*Bornstein*] and International Business Machines Corp. v. United States. In that case the court applied section 7805(b) of the Internal Revenue Code of 1954 in behalf of a taxpayer who had made prompt

application to obtain a private ruling to the same effect as a ruling issued to another taxpayer, which manufactured and sold business machines that were similar in all material respects to the machines manufactured by plaintiff. *In these cases, none of the taxpayers nor the corporations in which they are shareholders asked for rulings.* (Emphasis supplied).

Herein, as in *Bornstein*, the appellee had not requested a ruling prior to paying his assessment and was clearly not discriminated against in the manner that I.B.M. was in the *I.B.M.* case. In *I.B.M.* the evidence was very strong that the Commissioner abused his discretion under 26 U.S.C.A. § 7805(b) but, under the facts of the instant case, the evidence is at least just as strong that there was no abuse of administrative discretion in prospectively withdrawing the Bismarck and Wirthman letters.

* * *

We would not be remiss to point out that a favorable ruling to appellee herein could open the proverbial floodgates of litigation as suits could feasibly be brought by all other similarly situated taxpayers who did not deduct special assessments from their returns during the years in question. Not allowing the Commissioner some proper discretion in prospectively or retroactively revoking private rulings could cause the elimination of private letter rulings and any and all benefits to be derived therefrom. Private letter rulings are issued to certain private parties and are not intended to be relied on by the general public as a whole. It is only when the Commissioner abuses his discretion under 26 U.S.C.A. § 7805(b) that remedial action should be taken. The instant case is no such situation.

We also note that to allow appellee to recover herein would arguably prejudice other taxpayers – e.g., the Wirthman partners – since appellee could deduct his entire assessment, whereas other taxpayers could deduct only that portion paid prior to the revocation of the private letter rulings. The shoe would then be on the other foot and appellee would have a windfall merely because he chose to pay his entire assessment in one lump sum. This could give rise to even more undesirable litigation. In the absence of cogent reasons to the contrary, no court should overturn a discretionary ruling by the Commissioner under 26 U.S.C.A. § 7805(b) which could lead to wholesale and time-consuming litigation. As already noted, such cogent reasons are not present herein.

We reverse and remand for further proceedings not inconsistent with the foregoing.

Notes and Questions

Since letter rulings may used as an indication of the Service's ruling position, even though they may not be cited as precedent, the Service now accepts letter rulings as substantial authority, sufficient to avoid the imposition of an accuracy-related penalty under IRC § 6662. See Reg. § 1.6662-4(d)(3)(iii). (Accuracy-related penalties are discussed in Chapter 6).

1. The general rule is that a letter ruling cannot be relied upon except by the taxpayer who requests the ruling. Why did the taxpayer in *Bookwalter* think that he was entitled to rely on the ruling requested by the Bismarck and Wirthman groups?

2. Do you think *Bookwalter* was correctly and fairly decided?

3. After the *Bookwalter* decision, does the Service have a duty of consistency? See Christopher M. Pietruszkiewicz, "Does the Internal Revenue Service Have A Duty To Treat Similarly Situated Taxpayers Similarly?" 74 U. Cinn. L. Rev. 531 (2005).

4. The court in *Bookwalter* held that the taxpayer could not obtain favorable tax treatment because he had not requested a ruling and thus he was not entitled to rely on the ruling obtained by the other taxpayers. Is this really a significant distinction? If so, how do you reconcile the *I.B.M.* decision?

2) *Requesting a Ruling*

Guidelines for structuring and submitting a request for a letter ruling are provided by the Service in the first Rev. Proc. issued each year (for example, see Rev. Proc. 2010-1, 2010-1 C..B. 1). The Service will not issue rulings in response to oral requests. Although oral requests for advice may be made in preparing a return or report (as long as the issue is not "under examination, in appeals, or in litigation"), the Service regards such advice as advisory only and nonbinding. Note that the Service charges a user fee for issuing a ruling and several years ago, it drastically increased these fees to reflect the actual processing costs. These fees currently range from $275 to $14,000, depending on the type of ruling requested, the complexity of the issues and the income level of the taxpayer. If the taxpayer fails to remit the full amount of the user fee when requesting the ruling, the Service has discretion to return the request to the taxpayer or to request that the taxpayer remit the full amount.

There are certain areas in which the Service will not issue rulings. These are listed in Rev. Proc. 2010-3, 2010-1 C.B. 110 (domestic) and Rev. Proc. 2010-7, 2010-1 C.B. 231 (international). If the Service declines to rule on all the issues for which the ruling was requested, the taxpayer may be entitled to a full or partial refund of the user fee.

Question

What are the pros and cons of requesting a letter ruling?

3. Other IRS Rulings and Publications

a. Revenue Procedures

Revenue procedures are statements of IRS practice and procedure that are issued for the guidance of the taxpaying public. They are published in the Internal Revenue Bulletin and later in final form in the Cumulative Bulletin, along with revenue rulings. Revenue procedures usually are effective prospectively unless they state otherwise.

Failure to follow a revenue procedure can result in delay for the taxpayer and may precipitate an audit. From the other side of the coin, to what extent is a taxpayer entitled to rely on a revenue procedure?

VOSTERS v. UNITED STATES
United States District Court, Northern District of California, 1989.
89-1 USTC ¶ 9387.

In this action, plaintiff seeks to invalidate a 100% tax penalty assessed against him, pursuant to the Internal Revenue Code 26 U.S.C. § 6672, on the ground that the Internal Revenue Service (IRS) failed to follow the procedures published in Revenue Procedures 61-27, 1961-2 CB 563.[1] Specifically, an IRS representative allegedly told plaintiff that plaintiff's oral request for an Appellant Hearing was sufficient, however, the procedural rules require plaintiff to file a written protest letter in order to obtain an Appellant Hearing. Plaintiff was never granted or offered an Appellant Hearing. Plaintiff alleges that he was denied his right to appeal the proposed assessment of the penalty as provided in Revenue Procedure 61-27, 1961-2 CB 563.

The question presented is whether the IRS's failure to follow the procedures published in the Revenue Procedures does not invalidate plaintiff's tax assessment, as a matter of law. The Ninth Circuit has not yet considered this issue. However, several other circuits have held that such procedural rules do not grant plaintiff a substantive right for which

---

1.   The 100% penalty was assessed against plaintiff because he willfully failed to collect and pay-over employment taxes from the wages of employees of LAV Enterprises, Inc.

a violation of such rule could effect the validity of a deficiency determination.

In Luhring v. Glotzback, 304 F.2d 560, 565 (4th Cir. 1962), the taxpayers were deprived of the right to an informal conference provided by 26 C.F.R. § 601.105. Plaintiff argued that this denial voided their notice of deficiency. The court held that the rules were directory rather than mandatory and failure to allow the taxpayer to attend an informal conference did not curtail the power of the Commissioner to send a notice of deficiency.

In Cleveland Trust Company v. United States, 421 F.2d 475 (6th Cir. 1970), it was argued that the IRS's failure to follow the Revenue Procedures prevented the IRS from rejecting an informal agreement and did not affect the right of the IRS to assert a deficiency. The court held that "[i]t is clear that the * * * Revenue Procedure is directory, not mandatory, and the IRS's alleged failure to [follow the procedure] cannot affect its right to assert a deficiency against the estate." Id. at 481-482.

Similarly, in Rosenberg v. Commissioner, 450 F.2d 529 (10th Cir. 1971), the taxpayer argued that the Tax Court's deficiency determination was invalid because the IRS violated its own procedural rules by denying the taxpayer an administrative hearing before the Appellant Review Division. The court considered the effect of the IRS's failure to follow the adopted procedures. The court expressly followed *Luhring* and *Cleveland Trust* and held that the procedures were "directory rather than mandatory." Id. at 533.

The court is cognizant of the inequitable circumstances of plaintiff's allegations. However, the court is compelled to follow the other circuits which have held that such procedural rules are directory rather than mandatory. Thus, as a matter of law, the IRS's failure to follow Revenue Procedure 61-27 does not invalidate plaintiff's civil tax assessment.

Note and Question

In United States v. Caceres, 440 U.S. 741 (1979), (see case and discussion, Chapter 10), a criminal case, the Supreme Court decided that the Service's failure to follow its own procedures set forth in the Internal Revenue Manual was an insufficient ground to allow the suppression of evidence obtained as a result of that failure. But the Court did not conclude that the Service was not bound by its procedural rules, and on occasion, courts have required the Service to comply with these rules. Generally, such cases have involved rules that impacted important taxpayer rights where the taxpayers had relied on the rules to their detriment. Does this reasoning apply in *Vosters*?

b. Chief Counsel Advice

Section 6110(i) defines Chief Counsel advice as "written advice or instruction" prepared by the Office of the Chief Counsel "issued to field or service center employees * * * or regional or district employees of the Office of Chief Counsel" which "conveys (I) any legal interpretation of a revenue provision, (II) any IRS * * * position or policy concerning a revenue provision; or (III) any legal interpretation * * * relating to the assessment or collection of any liability under a revenue provision." IRC § 6110(i)(1)(A).

Most of this advice is issued as Technical Advice Memoranda (TAMs) and is furnished by the National Office on the request of a district director or an appeals officer when a technical or procedural question arises during (1) the examination of a taxpayer's return, (2) the consideration of a taxpayer's claim for refund or credit, (3) any matter under examination or in appeals pertaining to tax-exempt bonds or mortgage credit certificates, and (4) any other matter involving a specific taxpayer under the jurisdiction of the chief of the examination division, or the chief of the appeals office. Technical advice generally is requested when the question is unusual or complex, or when there is a lack of uniformity on the resolution of the question. (See Chapter 4 for a further discussion of TAMs in the context of administrative appeals).

Like letter rulings, a TAM applies only to the taxpayer in question and may not be used as precedent by any other taxpayer. IRC § 6110(k)(3). Because the request for technical advice can be made only with respect to closed transactions, the advice (whether favorable or unfavorable) usually applies retroactively unless the Chief Counsel exercises his discretion to apply the advice prospectively.

The Chief Counsel formerly issued field service advice memoranda (FSAs) in response to requests by field personnel (revenue agents, appeals officers, and staff attorneys) for legal advice with respect to a particular taxpayer. FSAs were advisory only and did not constitute a final case determination. The IRS office with primary jurisdiction over the case had discretion to decide what weight to give the FSA. Although the Chief Counsel's office continues to provide written legal advice to the field, it no longer issues FSAs. See CC-2004-012.

Under the IRS Restructuring and Reform Act of 1998, Congress amended the disclosure provision of the Code so that Chief Counsel advice falls within the definition of "written determination" under § 6110(a). See IRC § 6110(i). Thus, Chief Counsel advice is available to the public exclusively through § 6110, and not through the FOIA. Before disclosure, however, the document must be "sanitized" by deleting any identifying taxpayer data. Advice that does not fall within the § 6110(i) definition remains subject to disclosure under FOIA. See Chapter 2 for a further discussion and comparison of § 6110 and the FOIA. If the technical advice relates to an ongoing civil fraud or criminal investigation, or to an ongoing jeopardy or termination assessment (see discussion of jeopardy and termination assessments, Chapter 4), it is not subject to public inspection until the investigation (or proceedings) have been completed.

Notes

The Service formerly took the position that some of the advice issued by the Chief Counsel's office constituted return information which could not be disclosed under the confidentiality shield of § 6103, the attorney/client privilege, and the work product doctrine. In 1997, however, the United States Court of Appeals for the District of Columbia Circuit concluded that the advice in question (field service advice memoranda) constituted agency records that fell under no exception to or exemption from the Freedom of Information Act (FOIA) and therefore was subject to disclosure. See Tax Analysts v. I.R.S., 117 F.3d 607 (D.C. Cir. 1997). Other courts, however, have declined to follow the lead of the D.C. Circuit and have held that confidential communications between agency personnel and agency attorneys may be privileged, even if the underlying information is not confidential in nature. See Cencast Services v. U.S., 91 Fed. Cl. 496 (2010)(concluding that the Federal Circuit has not adopted the approach of the D.C. Circuit).

The Service's lack of success in defending against disclosure of letter rulings and Chief Counsel advice has had (and will continue to have) a profound effect on taxpayer reliance. Although taxpayers are not entitled to rely on these documents, the Service's duty of consistency and fairness transcends the prohibition on reliance. Thus, while these rulings may not be used as the *sine qua non* of the taxpayer's case, taxpayers and their attorneys rely on these documents as an indication of how the Service is likely to rule in a factually similar situation. But note that the Service does not recognize this "duty" as a cognizable cause of action. In addition, there are many limitations on the Service's duty of consistency. See Schering-Plough v. United States, 100 AFTR2d 2007-5522 (unpublished opinion) for a discussion of these limitations.

c. *Closing Agreements*

A closing agreement is a binding agreement between the Service and the taxpayer on a specific issue or liability. Closing agreements are authorized under § 7121 and are final, absent a showing of fraud, malfeasance, or misrepresentation of a material fact. A taxpayer may be asked to enter into a closing agreement as a condition to the issuance of a letter ruling. See the discussion of closing agreements in Chapter 7.

d. Determination Letters

A determination letter is a written statement issued by an Area Director for the appropriate Operating Division in response to an inquiry by a taxpayer in which the principles and precedents previously announced by the National Office are applied to a specific set of facts. Determination letters are based on clearly established rules of the statutes, tax treaties, or regulations, or on conclusions in revenue rulings, IRS opinions, or court decisions that specifically address the facts presented. Determination letters have the same force and effect as private letter rulings. Unlike private letter rulings, however, determination letters are issued only in response to completed transactions. Determination letters are requested primarily by pension plans and charitable (tax exempt) organizations in order to ensure their special tax status. These taxpayers will be assured of favorable tax treatment as long as their actual facts correspond to those on which the ruling was based.

e. Information Letters

Information letters are issued either by the Chief Counsel's Office or by an Area Director. They resemble determination letters because they call attention to well-established principles of tax law. They differ from determination letters, though, in that they are not issued in response to specific sets of facts and they do not bind the Service. Thus, an information letter is advisory only, and is issued when the taxpayer requests a ruling and indicates a need for general information, or when the Service on its own motion determines that the taxpayer could benefit from such information.

The Service does not categorize information letters as "written determinations." Thus, it takes the position that it is not required to make these available to the public under IRC § 6110. In an effort to increase public confidence in the tax system, however, the government has chosen to publish voluntarily information letters issued by the Chief Counsel's Office after January 1, 2000 and to make those available to the public. Information letters issued by Area Directors will not be made available to the public, probably because information letters issued by Area Directors are not reviewed by the Chief Counsel's Office.

f. Actions on Decisions and Acquiescences

When the Service loses a case in the Tax Court, Federal District Court, United States Court of Federal Claims, or the United States Court of Appeals, the attorney in the Office of the Associate Chief Counsel (Litigation) responsible for review of the case will prepare a formal recommendation to the Justice Department as to whether the case should be appealed. At the same time, the attorney will prepare an Action On Decision (AOD) that will be sent to the Office of the Assistant Commissioner (Technical) for review. The AOD is a legal memorandum setting forth (1) the issue that was decided against the government, (2) a brief discussion of the facts, (3) the attorney's reasoning behind the recommendation to appeal or not, and (4) if the case is not appealed, the attorney's recommendation that the Commissioner either "acquiesce" or "nonacquiesce" in the adverse decision of the court.

An acquiescence means that the Service will follow an adverse decision and will not appeal. This gives the taxpayer an idea of how the Service is likely to view a transaction with facts closely analogous to those of the case in question. But the taxpayer must be cautious because there are different types of acquiescences. An acquiescence in the decision means that while the Service accepts the conclusion reached in the case, it does not necessarily accept all of the reasons behind the decision. An acquiescence "in result only" means that the Commissioner expressly disagrees with some or all of the reasoning of the decision. Thus, a taxpayer is on notice that it may be perilous to rely on the acquiescence. In addition, an acquiescence is discretionary with the Service and may be withdrawn retroactively in order to correct a mistake of law.

A nonacquiescence means that the Service will not follow the decision and may appeal, although if the Service decides not to appeal it does not affect the nonacquiescence. Thus, a nonacquiescence is a caveat to the taxpayer that the Service intends to litigate cases with similar facts. A nonacquiescence to a circuit court decision means that while the Service is bound to follow the decision in the rendering circuit, it will not follow it in other circuits.

If the Technical Commissioner agrees with the Associate Chief Counsel's recommendation, the AOD is published and made available to the public under the FOIA. It also is distributed to the National Office and to field personnel to be used as guidance and a research tool for the brief writers in the Office of the Chief Counsel.

g. *Internal Revenue Manual*

Service personnel rely heavily on the Internal Revenue Manual in the performance of their duties. The Manual provides an overview of the structure of the Service, and contains policies and operating procedures of the various divisions, as well as industry audit guidelines for various industries. It also contains handbooks designated for particular categories of IRS personnel.

Most of the Manual is available to the public under the FOIA. Taxpayers may not rely on the Manual, however, since it is intended only as a tool for Service personnel. In general, the Manual does not bind the Service, since most courts consider it directive, rather than mandatory. But with respect to matters of procedure, the Service must follow its own guidelines. Thus, if a taxpayer can establish that a revenue agent has not followed the proper operating procedure of the Manual, this could be a strategic advantage for the taxpayer, particularly if the noncompliance may subject the agent to an internal sanction.

III. THE JUDICIAL PROCESS – AN OVERVIEW

If taxpayers cannot resolve their differences administratively with the Service, they may choose to litigate in one of three fora available to federal tax litigants: the United States Tax Court, the federal district courts, or the United States Court of Federal Claims. Increasingly, however, tax issues are being resolved in the United States Bankruptcy Courts, which are becoming known as the fourth tax forum.

The choice of forum should be made after careful consideration because the courts differ in jurisdictional requirements, level of judicial expertise, opportunity for a jury trial, and body of precedent. In some cases, these differences can be outcome determinative.

A. THE UNITED STATES TAX COURT

The United States Tax Court was created under the Revenue Act of 1924 as the Board of Tax Appeals, an independent agency of the Executive Branch. In 1942, the Board became the Tax Court of the United States, although it remained an independent agency within the Executive Branch with no substantive change in its jurisdiction. In 1969, it became an Article I (United States Constitution, Article I, § 8) legislative court of record within the federal judicial system, redesignated the United States Tax Court.

The court is headquartered in Washington, D.C. and its judicial officers travel to approximately 70 cities around the country to conduct trials. It has exclusive jurisdiction and hears only tax cases (income, estate, gift, windfall profits, some employment tax claims, and certain excise tax cases). Thus, the level of judicial expertise in the intricacies of tax law is likely to be greatest in the Tax Court than in any of the other federal tax fora. The Tax Court has deficiency jurisdiction, which means that it is the only court in which a litigant may be heard without first paying the tax in question (a sue-first-pay-later forum). A prerequisite to Tax Court jurisdiction is a timely filed petition with a notice of deficiency attached. The mailing of a notice of deficiency to the taxpayer is a statutory requirement the Service must meet before it can assess (record) a deficiency. It is important to note that the Service can raise additional deficiencies after a petition is filed in the Tax Court, because the filing of the Tax Court petition tolls the statute of limitations on assessment. (Assessment, the notice of deficiency, and the statute of limitations on assessment are discussed further in Chapter 4). In addition, the Tax Court may hear some non-deficiency cases such as those involving innocent spouse relief and denials of collection due process.

The taxpayer is always the plaintiff in the Tax Court, while the government is always the defendant/respondent. The government is represented in the Tax Court by attorneys from the Division Counsel of the IRS, who work in conjunction with the Appeals Division. The case is heard by a single judge, sitting without a jury. The Tax Court has its own court rules and the rules of evidence generally are more lenient there than in the other federal tax fora. Thus, evidence often is admitted more easily in the Tax Court than it would be in the federal district courts.

Unlike the other federal courts, the Tax Court allows taxpayers to be represented by individuals who are not attorneys. Accountants, enrolled agents, and others may qualify to practice before the Tax Court after passing an examination administered by the court. There are generally more *pro se* cases in the Tax Court than in the other federal courts. Over half of all cases and most small tax cases (about 90 percent) are filed by taxpayers who are not represented by counsel of record.[18]

There are two general types of cases in the Tax Court: regular cases and "S" cases. S cases are small cases in which the amount in issue does not exceed $50,000 for each tax year and in which special simplified procedures apply with no right of appeal. S status must be elected by the taxpayer. They generally are less formal cases that result in more

---

18. Cohen, How to Handle a Tax Controversy at the Restructured IRS and in Court, 2002 Houston Bus. & Tax Law J. 443.

expedited dispositions than the regular cases. Since most taxpayers represent themselves in small cases, this is an attractive alternative.

There are four types of opinions: a division opinion, published in the Tax Court reports; a reviewed opinion, which has been reviewed by the full court; memorandum opinions, which are not published by the court and are not intended for use as precedent; and summary opinions issued for S cases – these may not be used as precedent or cited as authority and the Court discourages their publication, even by commercial publishers. The Chief Judge decides in which category the cases, other than S cases, fall.

There are nineteen presidentially appointed judges who sit on the bench of the Tax Court. In addition, there are senior judges who may be recalled to hear cases, and there are special trial judges appointed by the Chief Judge. Special trial judges hear S cases, regular cases to which they are appointed by the Chief Judge in which the amount in issue does not exceed $50,000, declaratory judgment actions, lien and levy actions, and whistleblower actions. Tax Court judges are Article I judges, appointed under Congress's general legislative power to "constitute tribunals inferior to the Supreme Court." They do not have life tenure, but instead are appointed for 15-year terms, which are frequently renewed upon expiration.

Appeals from the Tax Court generally are to the federal court of appeals for the circuit in which the taxpayer resides. But see James Bamberg, A Different Point of Venue: The Plainer Meaning of Section 7482(b)(1), 61 Tax Law. 445 (Winter 2008)(pointing out common venue misconception under § 7482(b)) and further discussion, Chapter 8. An adverse appellate decision may be appealed further to the United States Supreme Court.

B. THE UNITED STATES DISTRICT COURTS

The federal district courts are constitutional courts, created by Congress pursuant to the authority granted to it under Article III, § 1 of the Constitution to "create such inferior courts as Congress may from time to time ordain and establish." Federal district court judges have life tenure (holding their offices during good behavior), and are entitled to compensation "which shall not be diminished during their continuance in office." Id.

There are several important differences between the Tax Court and the federal district courts. First, the federal district courts have refund jurisdiction. Thus, taxpayers must pay the full amount of the tax first, and file a claim for refund with the Service before they are eligible to be heard in the federal district courts. Second, the federal district court is the only tax forum that offers a jury trial. A taxpayer may have a better chance of prevailing if the case is heard by a jury of her peers. Third, the judges in the Tax Court and the Court of Federal Claims are based in Washington, D.C., whereas federal district court judges generally reside in or near the districts in which they sit. This means that district court judges are likely to be more "in touch" with the local community and thus better able to determine the facts, and to judge the competency of any expert witnesses. Fourth, the filing of a complaint in the federal district court does not toll the statute of limitations on assessment, so if the statute has run, the Service will not be able to raise new adjustments except by way of setoff in defending against the amount of the claimed refund. (See Chapter 5 for a discussion of setoff and statutes of limitation). Thus, if the taxpayer is fearful of further issues being raised by the Service, she would be well advised to avoid bringing suit in the Tax Court. Fifth, the dockets of the federal district courts tend to be more crowded than those of the Tax Court. Therefore, the case is likely to be more timely adjudicated in the Tax Court. Sixth, a federal district court case is likely to be more expensive for the taxpayer than a Tax Court case. This is because, unlike the Tax Court, the federal district court does not allow a taxpayer to be represented by a non-lawyer. Although the taxpayer may appear *pro se* in the federal district courts, it is not advisable, because the rules of evidence and procedure in the federal district courts are more complex and more strictly construed than in the Tax Court. The district courts strictly adhere to both the Federal Rules of Evidence and the Federal Rules of Civil Procedure. In addition, the discovery process is used more liberally in the federal district courts. In the Tax Court, the parties are expected to stipulate to issues before trial. Seventh, the taxpayer should be concerned about the settlement potential of each court. In general, the potential to settle will be greater in the district court than in the Tax Court because in the district court the government is represented by attorneys from the Tax Division of the Department of Justice. Their focus generally leans toward settlement of the case, if at all possible, rather than on the collection of taxes, which is more likely to be the focus of the IRS attorneys from the Division Counsel's office. Finally, in the Tax Court, the taxpayer brings the suit and is refuting the Service's proposed adjustment/deficiency. Thus, the Tax Court case centers around whether the taxpayer actually owes this amount. The Service bears the burden of proving the additional amount owed. (See Chapter 8 for a discussion of the burden of proof in the Tax Court). In the district court, the taxpayer is asking for a refund and thus bears the burden of proving the correct amount of tax owed and the amount to be refunded.

The district courts will apply the body of precedent applicable in the relevant circuits. For further discussion of district court jurisdiction, see

Chapter 5. Appeals from district court decisions are to the courts of appeal for the circuits in which the district courts are located. Further appeals are to the United States Supreme Court.

Question

What other rationale(s) may support the greater settlement potential in the federal district courts than in the Tax Court?   .

C. THE UNITED STATES COURT OF FEDERAL CLAIMS

The United States Court of Federal Claims, formerly the United States Claims Court, shares some similarities with both the Tax Court and the federal district courts. Like the Tax Court, the Court of Federal Claims is an Article I court of limited jurisdiction based in Washington, D.C., and its judges travel around the country to hear cases. Also like the Tax Court, there is no jury trial available in the Court of Federal Claims. Since the jurisdiction of both the Tax Court and the Court of Federal Claims is more limited than that of the federal district courts, the federal tax expertise of the judges in those courts is likely to be greater than that of the federal district court judges.

Like the federal district courts, though, the Court of Federal Claims has refund jurisdiction. Thus, it is a pay-first-sue-later forum. It has concurrent jurisdiction with the federal district courts over federal tax cases and its jurisdictional requirements are similar to those of the federal district courts. (See discussion, Chapter 5). In addition, the Court of Federal Claims hears intellectual property cases, money claims, and other constitutional and statutory claims against the United States.

In choosing a forum, a taxpayer should consider the body of precedent to which the court would have to adhere, as well as the path of appeal in the event of an adverse decision. Appeals from the United States Court of Federal Claims are to the Court of Appeals for the Federal Circuit. In this respect, the Court of Federal Claims differs from both the Tax Court and the federal district courts. The Court of Federal Claims is bound by its own precedents, as well as by the precedents of its forerunners, the United States Claims Court and the United States Court of Claims, as well as by the United States Supreme Court and the Court of Appeals for the Federal Circuit.

D. THE UNITED STATES BANKRUPTCY COURTS

The amount of a proposed tax bill, including penalties and interest, may be large enough to push an otherwise over-extended taxpayer into

Bankruptcy Court. The filing of a bankruptcy petition immediately does two things: (1) it creates a bankruptcy estate, consisting of all the assets of the debtor, which will be under the control of the Bankruptcy Court (11 U.S.C. § 541(a)), and (2) it automatically enjoins or stays all creditors, including the government, from taking any further collection action against the debtor (11 U.S.C. § 362(a)(6)).

The Service is not precluded from issuing a notice of deficiency to the debtor/taxpayer, however, and if it does so, the Bankruptcy Court is faced with two choices. It either may lift the stay to allow the taxpayer to petition the Tax Court or it may determine the tax liability itself. The Bankruptcy Court has concurrent jurisdiction with the Tax Court over unadjudicated determinations of liability for tax deficiencies, including penalties and interest. Increasingly, complex issues of substantive and procedural tax law are being decided in the Bankruptcy Courts.

If a bankruptcy petition has been filed, and a notice of deficiency is issued subsequently to the debtor/taxpayer (either pre-bankruptcy petition or post-petition), the Bankruptcy Court will determine whether the case will be heard in the Tax Court or in the Bankruptcy Court, unless the case involves a tax that is not within the jurisdiction of the Tax Court, such as employment taxes. In that event, only the Bankruptcy Court will have jurisdiction over the controversy.

If a notice of deficiency is sent to the taxpayer and the taxpayer files a petition in the Tax Court prior to the filing of the bankruptcy petition, the automatic stay prevents the Tax Court from taking any further action without the approval of the Bankruptcy Court, whether or not the Tax Court proceedings have begun. If the Tax Court has decided the case, though, the decision is final and the Bankruptcy Court will not have jurisdiction over the matter. If the Tax Court has not decided the case, and the Bankruptcy Court does not lift the automatic stay, but decides the case itself, all relevant parties are bound by the decision of the Bankruptcy Court. The doctrine of res judicata prevents the taxpayer from relitigating the deficiency in any other court.

Both the statute of limitations on assessment and the limitations period for filing a Tax Court petition are tolled for the length of time the stay is in effect, plus 60 days thereafter. IRC §§ 6213(f), 6503(h). If the taxes are imposed on the bankruptcy estate, rather than on the debtor/taxpayer, the statute of limitations is not tolled and the Service may immediately assess the tax without having to follow the normal procedural rules of sending a notice of deficiency and waiting 90 days. 11 U.S.C. § 505(b). (See the further discussion of the assessment procedure in Chapter 4).

The Bankruptcy Court also has jurisdiction over refund claims. If a debtor has overpaid her tax liability and is entitled to a refund, the trustee of the bankruptcy estate succeeds to the debtor's claim. If the refund claim has not been filed with the Service, the trustee may file on behalf of the estate. If the Service denies the claim or if there is no response from the Service within 120 days after the claim is filed, the Bankruptcy Court has jurisdiction to determine the claim.

Appeals from the Bankruptcy Court are heard by the federal district courts and in some circuits, by the Bankruptcy Appellate Panel. See further discussion of the Bankruptcy Court in Chapter 7.

Question

What restrictions or considerations might narrow a taxpayer's choice of forum?

CHAPTER 2

PRACTICE BEFORE THE
INTERNAL REVENUE SERVICE

[R]elying on the legal and accounting professionals to prescribe appropriate
standards of practitioner conduct * * * is an idea whose time has surely passed.
— — Michael J. Graetz[1]

I. INTRODUCTION

Federal tax practice differs in two important respects from other
areas of law practice. First, the opposing party is always the federal
government through its agency, the IRS. But the IRS is not like any
other opponent, because it assumes a variety of roles with respect to
those professionals authorized to practice before it. For instance, it
assumes a regulatory role in processing and examining taxpayers'
returns, and in promulgating and enforcing ethical standards for the
various professional groups it authorizes to practice. It also assumes a
police role in enforcing the revenue laws, and a quasi-judicial role in
issuing rulings, hearing appeals from assertions of deficiencies, and
deciding claims for refund. Second, tax practice is a multi-professional
practice of lawyers and nonlawyers, which raises the problem of uniform
standards of professional responsibility.

A. WHAT CONSTITUTES PRACTICE BEFORE
THE IRS AND WHO IS ELIGIBLE TO PRACTICE?

Practice before the IRS is governed by Treasury Department
regulations commonly referred to as Circular 230. These regulations are
administered by the IRS Director of Practice, who reports directly to the
Commissioner and who is appointed by the Secretary of the Treasury.
Circular 230 lists a variety of activities that constitutes practice before
the Service, such as preparing and filing certain documents; correspond-

---

1. Jeffery L. Yablon, As Certain As Death – Quotations About Taxes (2004 Edition), 102 TAX
NOTES 99, 147 (Jan. 5, 2004).

ing and communicating with the Service; and representing clients at conferences, hearings and meetings.[2] It also lists some activities that are not considered practice, such as preparing a tax return, appearing as a witness for the taxpayer, and furnishing information at the request of the Service.[3]

There are four general groups of practitioners eligible to practice before the Service: attorneys, certified public accountants (CPAs), enrolled agents, and enrolled actuaries. Under federal statute, attorneys and CPAs are granted an automatic right to practice upon filing a declaration statement attesting that they are duly licensed and qualified in their respective professions, and that they are authorized to represent the clients on whose behalf they are acting.[4] Under Circular 230, the attorney or CPA also must be in good standing with the Service.[5]

Enrolled agents generally consist of noncertified accountants and former federal employees with a minimum of five years experience with the Service. They may practice before the Service after demonstrating their competence in tax law by passing a written examination administered by the Service, and by not engaging in any conduct that otherwise would disqualify an attorney or a CPA from practicing in their professions.

An individual enrolled as an actuary by the Joint Board for the Enrollment of Actuaries may engage in limited practice before the IRS without further enrollment, provided the individual files a written declaration stating that she is currently qualified as an enrolled actuary and that she is authorized to represent the client on whose behalf she is acting.

In addition to these four groups of practitioners, taxpayers may appear on their own behalf (*pro se*), and under very limited circumstances, an individual who is not otherwise authorized to practice before the Service may represent a third party with whom the individual has the familial or professional relationship specified in Circular 230.[6]

---

2.   Circular 230, 31 C.F.R. Part 10, § 10.2(e).

3.   Id. at § 10.7(e).

4.   See 5 U.S.C. § 500 (1982). The form on which this statement is filed is a Form 2848, Power of Attorney and Declaration of Representative. If the representative is authorized to receive tax information, a Form 8821, Tax Information Authorization also must be filed. These forms are available at http://www.irs.gov/pub/irs-fill/f2848 and http://www.irs.gov/pub/irs-fill/f8821.pdf.

5.   Circular 230, 31 C.F.R. Part 10, § 10.3(a) and (b).

6.   See Circular 230, § 10.7.

Questions

1. Circular 230 requires attorneys, CPAs, and enrolled actuaries to file written authorization statements with the Service. Why does Circular 230 not require an enrolled agent to file a similar statement as a condition of enrollment?

2. Does a taxpayer have any recourse if the Service does not permit that person to be represented by a third party who is not an attorney, CPA, enrolled agent, enrolled actuary or related party under Circular 230? See Salman v. Swanson, 1980 WL 1616 (D. Nev. 1980), reproduced in Chapter 3 at III.B.

B. THE UNEASY PROFESSIONAL ALLIANCE BETWEEN LAWYERS AND ACCOUNTANTS

PROFESSIONS CLASH ON WHAT IS "THE PRACTICE OF LAW", JACK BAKER, RANDALL K. HANSON, AND JAMES K. SMITH
62 Practical Tax Strategies 30-39 (May 1999). *

Attorneys and CPAs have long held an uneasy truce regarding the boundary between the practice of law and accounting in the tax area. The truce is evidenced by a 1981 agreement between the American Institute of Certified Public Accountants (AICPA) and the American Bar Association (ABA), which provides general guidelines for each profession's role in the tax area. Recently this truce has begun to unravel as accounting firms expand their practice into areas previously considered the private domain of attorneys. The ABA believes the 1981 agreement is being breached and, as a result, has set up the Commission on Multidisciplinary Practice to investigate the expansion of accounting firms into the practice of law. CPAs, on the other hand, believe the boundaries suggested by the legal profession are self-serving and artificial.

The disagreement between attorneys and CPAs is fueled by the dual nature of tax practice. The accounting and legal functions required to complete a tax return are hopelessly entangled. Producing the numbers and financial statements needed in a tax return are clearly an account-

---

ing task, but it is impossible to complete even an average tax return without an understanding of the applicable tax laws. For some matters extensive research and interpretation of the law is needed. While attorneys have conceded the right to do tax research to accountants, they appear to be drawing the line in other areas of tax practice.

For example, an administrative complaint was filed in June 1997 with the Texas Supreme Court charging the "Big Five" accounting firm Arthur Andersen LLP with the unauthorized practice of law (UPL). The complaint was mainly motivated by Arthur Andersen's decision to file Tax Court petitions on behalf of clients, but accused the accounting firm of a number of other UPL violations. Possibly as a result of the complaint's dismissal in July 1998, two other Big Five accounting firms (KPMG LLP and Ernst & Young LLP) have since decided to begin representing clients in Tax Court.

Federal statutes clearly give CPAs the right to represent clients in disputes before the IRS and Tax Court. These statutes appear to preempt state UPL statutes as a result of a U.S. Supreme Court decision.[1] Despite this clarity, attorneys have raised various concerns regarding the abilities of accountants to adequately represent clients. Many of the concerns are premised on limitations accountants face in representing taxpayers in disputes, such as conflict of interest, choice of forum limitation, and audit independence.

Accountants may be able to circumvent some of their UPL limitations by hiring attorneys to do the work for them, and this is probably a greater concern for attorneys. Public accounting firms have done little to allay this fear by hiring a record number of attorneys and openly practicing law in Europe. Attorneys are understandably concerned by these developments and are currently organizing efforts to stop accounting firms from becoming one-stop providers of professional services. The primary weapon attorneys may use to stop accounting firms from employing attorneys to practice law is ABA Model Rule of Professional Conduct 5.4 [Eds: prohibiting a lawyer or law firm from sharing legal fees with a nonlawyer]. This rule has been adopted by almost every state and prevents attorneys from forming partnerships with accountants to render legal services.

* * *

Significant decisions. The early case law dealing with the unauthorized practice of law struggled with the concept of when tax accountants cross the threshold into the practice of law. The courts developed theories in an attempt to define the practice of law within the setting of

---

1.   Sperry v. Florida, 373 U.S. 379 (1963).

a tax practice, but they all tended to be overly subjective. The volume of case law in this area dropped significantly in the mid-1960's as a result of two significant events:

(1) In 1963, the U.S. Supreme Court held, in *Sperry v. Florida* that a federal statute admitting nonattorneys to practice before federal agencies took precedence over state regulations.

(2) In 1965, Congress changed the law to allow CPAs to practice before the IRS.

As a result of these events, most commentators agree that federal statutes expanding the role of CPAs in the tax area preempt the conflicting state UPL statutes.

* * *

While the UPL clash between attorneys and CPAs may ebb and flow, the one constant is the difficulty in defining the practice of law. Despite the many attempts by attorneys to define the practice of law, the definition remains hazy and elusive. The difficulty in defining the practice of law is particularly keen in the tax area, where questions of law and accounting are often inextricably intertwined. An income tax return requires the calculation of income, which is clearly an accounting task, but also requires the interpretation of statutes, which may be construed as a legal task. This issue is further clouded by federal statutes, giving accountants the right to practice in areas that otherwise might be construed as the practice of law. While the federal statutes have not provided a definition of the practice of law within a tax setting, they have increased CPAs' certainty of their rights in the tax area.

The right of accountants to engage in tax compliance and the necessary tax research has never been in much dispute. Other areas of tax practice are more controversial, including conflict resolution with the IRS, writing opinion letters, the preparation of legal documents, and the formation of legal entities. Much of the controversy in these areas has been cleared up by federal statutes, which give CPAs the right to practice in previously untouched areas of tax. Federal statutes now allow CPAs a number of expanded tax duties, including the right to practice before the IRS, to represent clients in U.S. Tax Court, and to prepare and present pension plans for IRS approval. Of course, the federal statutes are only effective if they preempt the state unauthorized practice of law statutes, which appears to be the case as a result of the *Sperry* decision.

* * *

Representing clients. CPAs, and other nonattorneys, are also allowed to practice before the U.S. Tax Court as a result of § 7452. The Code provision states that no person is to be denied admission to practice before the Tax Court because of failure to be a member of a particular profession (i.e., an attorney). The provision gives the Tax Court the right to make the rules regarding practice before the court. Tax Court Rule 200(a)(3) allows nonattorneys to practice before the court by passing a written examination.

As a result, accountants are allowed to act as a taxpayer's advocate in Tax Court, a task that previously would be construed as the practice of law. In a further expansion of CPAs' rights, the Employee Retirement Income Security Act of 1974 (ERISA) and the Code have been held to give CPAs the right to prepare and present pension plans for IRS approval.

NET EFFECT

The combination of *Sperry* and federal statutes expanding CPAs' rights in the tax area have had a chilling effect on UPL efforts by attorneys. This is particularly true in the area relating to practice before the IRS. Circular 230's definition of practice before the IRS is both broad and vague, creating an uncertainty that hinders UPL efforts against CPAs. Despite this uncertainty, there are still limitations on what CPAs are entitled to do in the tax area.

Although CPAs' duties in the tax area have greatly expanded in the last 30 years, they still face limitations. Many of the tasks required to fully service clients in the tax area continue to be considered the practice of law. Examples include:

— Formation of legal entities.

— Preparation of certain legal documents (e.g., contracts).

— Representing taxpayers in courts other than the Tax Court.

Offending CPAs may be sanctioned through state UPL statutes or, when they attempt to represent a client in court, through contempt of court. Despite the threat of sanctions, many in the legal profession provide anecdotal evidence of CPAs violating these restrictions by preparing legal documents for the signature of clients or their independent attorneys.

Even if CPAs were legally entitled to provide legal services to clients, bar associations claim they would be ineffective due to the limitations they face. For example, they contend that CPAs do not have the same attorney-client and work-product privileges as attorneys. The attorney-client privilege protects written and oral communication between an attorney and a client that is soliciting legal advice. The argument regarding the attorney-client privilege limitation has been essentially deflated by the IRS Restructuring and Reform Act of 1998, which extends the attorney-client privilege to any individual authorized to practice before the IRS (e.g, CPAs, enrolled agents, and enrolled actuaries). The advantage attorneys held in this area might have been overstated, in any event, because the privilege does not apply to communications between an attorney and client in the context of tax return preparation and business advice.

The work-product doctrine protects all written communications prepared in anticipation of litigation. CPAs are quick to point out that the work-product doctrine does not apply to only attorneys. CPAs preparing documents in anticipation of litigation may also invoke the work-product doctrine. Despite the inroads made by CPAs in the privilege area, attorneys still claim to have an advantage by questioning whether the new tax advisor privilege is as broad as the attorney-client privilege.

Attorneys also highlight the choice-of-forum limitation CPAs face in litigating tax cases. While CPAs are entitled to represent clients in Tax Court, they are unable to do the same in U.S. District Court or the U.S. Court of Federal Claims. These alternative tax trial courts sometimes offer advantages that are not available in Tax Court, such as jury trials or more favorable legal precedent. Attorneys argue that CPAs may unconsciously steer clients towards Tax Court despite the advantages offered by the other trial courts. A related limitation is the inability of CPAs to represent clients in appellate court.

Ethical concerns represent another limitation for CPAs in the legal area. For example, some attorneys argue that CPAs have a conflict of interest if they represent a client in Tax Court after preparing the tax return. More important ethical issues for accounting firms providing legal advice may be audit independence and potential violations of Securities and Exchange Commission (SEC) rules. The SEC has indicated in a January 1999 letter to the ABA's MDP Committee that "it would consider a firm's independence from an SEC registrant to be impaired if that firm also provides legal advice to the registrant." KPMG and Ernst & Young have responded to this concern by publicly announcing they will not file petitions in Tax Court on behalf of audit clients.

Accounting firms may attempt to evade many of the limitations they face in legal-related tax matters by hiring attorneys to perform the work they are unable or unqualified to do. For example, attorneys working for accounting firms might potentially draft legal documents, form legal entities, or file petitions for tax cases in courts other than the Tax Court. While there is not direct evidence that accounting firms are currently engaged in these types of activities, the legal profession is still concerned. This concern is driven by recent developments, such as the Big Five accounting firms' decision to litigate in Tax Court and to openly practice law in Europe and Australia. As a result, attorneys are organizing efforts to prevent this trend from becoming a fact of life. The primary weapon available to attorneys in this effort is the ABA Model Rule of Professional Conduct (MRPC) 5.4.

MRPC 5.4 prevents attorneys from sharing legal fees with nonattorneys, forming partnerships with nonattorneys to render legal services, or rendering legal services under the direction of a nonattorney employer. Sanctions for violations may be brought directly against the offending attorneys and may lead to disbarment. The MRPC have been adopted in some form by most states and appears to be a strong deterrent to public accounting firms. Nevertheless, there are weaknesses in the MRPC 5.4 approach. The biggest weakness may be that attorneys are back to square one in trying to define when accounting firm attorneys are practicing law. The definition of the practice of law in this context is just as elusive and difficult as it is with accountants.

The greater fear of the legal community is that MRPC 5.4 may violate some type of federal or international law. Although there is surprisingly little precedence in this area, there are due process and first amendment concerns for any type of UPL statute.[2]

* * *

[T]he Department of Justice [has] criticized a narrow ABA ruling on attorneys working for accounting firms as unnecessarily hindering competition and urged the Department of Treasury to adopt regulations recognizing attorneys' rights to practice before the IRS, regardless of the type of firm they work for. A final concern for enforcement efforts by attorneys in this area is the GATT treaty, which governs international trade matters and has historically been biased against self-interested regulation.

The hiring of attorneys by accounting firms may create more questions than answers regarding the unauthorized practice of law. If attorney groups are successful in enforcing MRPC 5.4, attorneys working for accounting firms will be unable to do anything more in the tax area than accountants. If enforcement efforts are slack or ineffective, on the other hand, attorneys working for accounting firms may ultimately provide legal services to accounting firm clients. This raises additional, as-yet-unanswered questions. For instance, does the attorney-client privilege apply to legal advice provided by accounting firm attorneys, or does the new tax advisor privilege apply?

---

2. See Rhode, Policing the Professional Monopoly: A Constitutional and Empirical Analysis of Unauthorized Practice Prohibitions, 34 Stanford L. Rev. 1 (November 1981).

Accounting firms are currently expanding their services beyond the traditional boundaries of accounting practice, and the legal profession has taken note. The ABA is concerned enough about the intentions of public accounting firms to form the MDP Commission to investigate the pros and cons of multidisciplinary practice. The legal profession is faced with the dilemma of forming a strategy on how to deal with the expanding accounting firms. Past efforts at enforcing state UPL statutes have been unsatisfactory for several reasons. First, Congress has granted CPAs expanded roles in the tax area and recently extended the attorney-client privilege to them. Second, the definition of the UPL has always been a difficult and elusive concept making the UPL statutes difficult to enforce. This is particularly true in the tax area, where the legal and accounting tasks are difficult to separate. Third, accounting firms are now hiring a record number of attorneys with the knowledge and possibly the right to perform legal work. Bar associations wishing to prevent accounting firm attorneys from practicing law are most likely to use MRPC 5.4, which disallows attorneys from sharing fees with CPAs. There are no guarantees that MRPC 5.4 will work, and this strategy requires a costly state-by-state campaign.

* * *

Notes and Questions

Arthur Andersen was one of the oldest and most venerable of the big accounting firms, but its involvement in the marketing of highly questionable tax avoidance schemes to such large clients as Enron in the late 1990's, led to its downfall. After the Enron debacle, the "Big Five" accounting firms became the "Final Four," without Andersen. See Ken Brown and Ianthe Jeanne Dugan, "Sad Account: Andersen's Fall from Grace Is a Tale of Greed and Miscues," Wall St. J., June 2, 2002, at A1 (chronicling the rise and fall of Andersen).

Enron and other corporate accounting scandals, combined with the passage of the Sarbanes-Oxley corporate governance reform, and the ongoing criminal investigations against big accounting firms (and some law firms) because of their involvement in creating and promoting abusive tax shelters, have heralded the end of MDPs. As one observer has noted, though: " * * * we may have closed the MDP chapter in the book, but we haven't yet turned the page of the next chapter." Sheryl Stratton, "Ernst and Young to End Alliance With McKee Nelson," 104 Tax Notes 122, 124 (July 12, 2004) (quoting Steve Salch of Fulbright & Jaworski). Currently, the issue is being considered by the Ethics Commission of the ABA.

1. What is the rationale behind the prohibition of fee-splitting between lawyers and nonlawyers? Do you think this rationale is valid? See Edward S. Adams and John H. Matheson, Law Firms On the Big Board?: A Proposal For Nonlawyer Investment In Law Firms, 86 Calif. L. Rev. 1 (1998); Richard Abel, Why Does the ABA Promulgate Ethical Rules?, 59 Tex. L. Rev. 666 (1981).

2. Are lawyers who are employed by public accounting firms subject to the ABA Model Rules if the state bar associations of the states in which they are licensed to practice have adopted these rules?

II. STANDARDS OF PRACTICE

The two primary professional groups that practice before the IRS– attorneys and accountants–each have their own discrete rules of professional ethics. But because tax practice is a multidisciplinary practice, there is a need for a more uniform regulation of the standards of practice. There are two ways in which this need is met. One is through the civil and criminal penalty provisions of the Internal Revenue Code, which provide preparer penalties for violations of minimum standards of conduct. The other is through Circular 230, which establishes uniform standards of practice and imposes disciplinary sanctions for violations of these standards.

A. STATUTORY STANDARDS – CIVIL PENALTIES

1. Return Preparer Penalty for Substantial Understatement of Tax Liability – § 6694(a)

Section 6694(a) of the Internal Revenue Code imposes a penalty on return preparers who understate tax liability on a return or refund claim by recommending an unreasonable position. The Small Business Tax Act of 2007 and the Emergency Economic Stabilization Act of 2008 made substantial changes to the penalties applicable to return preparers under § 6694. These changes apply to returns filed after May 25, 2007. First, the scope of return preparers who are subject to the substantial understatement penalties was broadened to include not only preparers of income tax returns but also preparers of estate and gift tax, employment tax, excise tax, and exempt organization returns. Second, the definition of "unreasonable position" was changed and the standards for imposition of the penalty were raised. Third, the amount of the penalties was increased. In the case of the § 6694(a) penalty, the amount was increased from $250 per return or claim to the greater of $1,000 or 50%

of the income derived or to be derived from the position. The increased penalty also applies per return or claim.

a.   Who is a Preparer?

Since the § 6694 penalties apply to return preparers, a threshold question that must be answered in determining whether the penalties apply is who is a return preparer? This question currently assumes greater importance since the § 6694 penalties have been substantially increased.

GOULDING v. UNITED STATES
United States Court of Appeals, Seventh Circuit, 1992.
957 F.2d 1420.

RIPPLE, CIRCUIT JUDGE.

* * *

II.

ANALYSIS
* * *

A.   Statutory and Regulatory Scheme

1.   Statute

Section 6694 of the Internal Revenue Code penalizes income tax preparers for understatements of taxpayer's liability which result from negligent disregard of rules and regulations by the return preparer or from wilful attempts by the return preparer to understate the tax due.[3] Section 6694 was included in the Tax Reform Act of 1976 as part of a package of provisions designed to regulate income tax preparers and to deter improper conduct by them. These provisions were enacted in response to abuses by tax return preparers. In addition to the § 6694 penalties, the provisions included penalties for failing to provide the taxpayer with a copy of the return, to sign the return as preparer, to furnish an identifying number and to retain a copy or list of returns prepared. See 26 U.S.C. § 6695.

---

3.   Section 6694 states in pertinent part:(a) negligent or intentional disregard of rules and regulations. – If any part of any understatement of liability with respect to any return or claim for refund is due to the negligent or intentional disregard of rules and regulations by any person who is an income tax return preparer with respect to such return or claim, such person shall pay a penalty of $100 with respect to such return or claim.

Section 6694(a) was amended in 1989 to apply to "understatements due to unrealistic positions." The amended version applies to documents prepared after December 31, 1989.

Before the 1976 Tax Reform Act, tax return forms required the preparer to sign the form, but there was no penalty for failing to do so. Tax return preparers were subject to criminal liability for wilfully aiding or assisting in the preparation of false or fraudulent tax returns under § 7206. They were not subject to civil fraud penalties or negligence penalties of the sort individual taxpayers could incur. Thus, under the pre-1976 Code, it was difficult for the IRS to determine if a preparer or the taxpayer himself was responsible for a return. Moreover, if the IRS found an incorrect return prepared by a professional or commercial preparer, it was difficult to trace other returns prepared by the same preparer. Even if the IRS could trace the improper preparation of returns to an individual tax return preparer, the criminal penalties available under the pre-1976 Code were "often inappropriate, cumbersome, and ineffective deterrents because of the costs and length of time involved in trying these cases in court." H.R. Rep. No. 68, 94th Cong., 2d Sess. 274, reprinted in 1976 U.S.C.C.A.N. 2897, 3170.

The difficulties in regulating tax return preparers became acute with the "substantial increase in the number of persons whose business is to prepare income tax returns for individuals and families of average income." Id. at 3169. Nonetheless, the provisions were not aimed solely at commercial preparers preparing large numbers of relatively simple returns for average income taxpayers, but were intended also to apply to professional preparers – lawyers and accountants – preparing more complex returns.

Along with the penalty provisions, the 1976 Act provided a statutory definition of "income tax return preparer."[4] The definition was intended to limit application of the penalty provisions to professional and commercial preparers, and to exclude those preparing returns for employers, friends and relatives. Another purpose of the definition was to ensure that the person who makes the decisions and calculations involved in preparing a particular return will be considered the preparer

---

4.   Section 7701(a)(36) defines income tax return preparer as

(A) In general. – The term "income tax return preparer" means any person who prepares for compensation, or who employs one or more persons to prepare for compensation, any return of tax imposed by subtitle A or any claim for refund of tax imposed by subtitle A. For purposes of the preceding sentence, the preparation of a substantial portion of a return or claim for refund shall be treated as if it were the preparation of such return or claim for refund.

(B) Exceptions. – A person shall not be an "income tax return preparer" merely because such person – (i) furnishes typing, reproducing, or other mechanical assistance, (ii) prepares a return or claim for refund of the employer (or of an officer or employee of the employer) by whom he is regularly and continuously employed, (iii) prepares as a fiduciary a return or claim for refund for any person, or * * * (iv) prepares a claim for refund for a taxpayer in response to any notice of deficiency issued to such taxpayer or in response to any waiver of restriction or another taxpayer if a determination in such audit of such other taxpayer directly or indirectly affects the tax liability of such taxpayer.

of that return, even if that person "does not actually place the figures on the lines of the taxpayer's final tax return." H.R.Rep. No. 658, 94th Cong., 2d Sess. 275, reprinted in 1976 U.S.C.C.A.N. 3171. Thus, furnishing of advice can make one a preparer, while mechanical assistance in preparing the return does not:

> A person who supplies to a taxpayer sufficient information and advice so that filling out the final tax return becomes merely a mechanical or clerical matter is to be considered an income tax return preparer. However, an individual who gives advice on particular issues of law or IRS policy relating to particular deductions or items of income will not have prepared a return with respect to those issues if the advice does not directly relate to any specific amounts which are to be placed on the return of the taxpayer.

Id. Where more than one person makes substantive contributions to the return, the definition of preparer limits liability to those who prepare a "substantial portion" of the return.

2. Regulation

Pursuant to his statutory authority, see 26 U.S.C. § 7805, the Commissioner promulgated a regulation elucidating the definition of "income tax return preparer." This regulation, Treasury Regulation § 1.301.7701-15, was adopted in 1977 and thus is a "substantially contemporaneous construction of the statute," which was passed in 1976. Subparagraph (b)(3) of the regulation defines the circumstances in which the preparer of one return may be deemed the preparer of another which directly reflects an entry (or entries) of the return actually prepared:

> A preparer of a return is not considered a preparer of another return merely because an entry or entries reported on the return may affect an entry reported on the other return, unless the entry or entries reported on the prepared return are directly reflected on the other return and constitute a substantial portion of the other return.

The subparagraph gives the example of the preparer of a partnership return:

> For example, the sole preparer of a partnership return of income or a small business corporation income tax return is considered a preparer of a partner's or a shareholder's return if the entry or entries on the partnership or small business corporation return reportable on the partner's or shareholder's return constitutes a substantial portion of the partner's or shareholder's return.

Both the regulation quoted above and the statutory definition of preparer state that a person is not the preparer of a return unless one is responsible for a "substantial portion" of it. Treasury Regulation 301.7701-15(b)(1) sets forth what constitutes substantial preparation:

(b) *Substantial preparation.* – (1) Only a person (or persons acting in concert) who prepares all or a substantial portion of a return or claim for refund shall be considered to be a preparer (or preparers) of the return or claim for refund. A person who renders advice which is directly relevant to the determination of the existence, characterization, or amount of an entry on a return or claim for refund, will be regarded as having prepared that entry. Whether a schedule, entry, or other portion of a return or claim for refund is a substantial portion is determined by comparing the length and complexity of, and the tax liability or refund involved in, that portion to the length and complexity of, and tax liability or refund involved in, the return or claim for refund as a whole.

B. Application of Statutory and Regulatory Scheme to the Case

1. Contentions of the parties

Mr. Goulding challenges the validity of Treasury Regulation § 301.7701-15(b)(3), in accordance with which he was deemed the preparer of the partners' returns and penalized for the understatements in them. As the sole preparer of the partnership return, Mr. Goulding provided copies of the partnership K-1 forms to the individual partners, who then entered (or whose own return preparers then entered) a single number (a deduction) on their own tax returns. Mr. Goulding argues that he cannot have "prepared" returns he never saw or touched, that he did not give advice to partners he never met or spoke with, and that in any case, he cannot be considered as having prepared a "substantial portion" of returns on which he is responsible for a single entry. Mr. Goulding also argues that he was not "compensated" by the partners, as required by the statutory definition of preparer.

Mr. Goulding contends that in deeming him the preparer of the partners' returns, the regulation is contrary to the statutory definition of preparer, to the Commissioner's own regulation defining "substantial portion," and to the intent of Congress as revealed in the legislative history. Under the statutory definition of preparer, Mr. Goulding cannot be the preparer of these returns unless he prepared a "substantial portion" of the returns. According to Mr. Goulding, the single entry on the partnership returns cannot constitute a "substantial portion." He argues that in promulgating a regulation which transforms a single entry into a "substantial portion," the Commissioner has exceeded his authority. In this regard, Mr. Goulding relies primarily on a passage from the legislative history which explains the intent behind the "substantial portion" language of the statute:

> Whether or not a portion of a return constitutes a substantial portion is to be determined by examining both the length and complexity of that particular portion of the return and the amount of tax liability involved. In a normal case, the filling out of a single schedule of a tax return would not be considered a substantial portion of that return unless that particular schedule was the dominant portion of the entire tax return.

H.R. Rep. No. 658, 94th Cong., 2d Sess. 275, reprinted in 1976 U.S.C.C.-A.N. 3171. As noted above, the regulation defining substantial preparation also directs that length and complexity be taken into consideration. Mr. Goulding maintains that the single entry on a partner's return which reflects information from the partnership return cannot be considered a substantial portion of the partner's return under the "length and complexity" standard.

Mr. Goulding also points to the House Report's statement that "an individual who gives advice on particular issues of law or IRS policy relating to particular deductions or items of income will not have prepared a return with respect to those issues if the advice does not directly relate to any specific amounts which are to be placed on the return of the taxpayer." Id. Because "issues," "deductions," "items," and "amounts" are plural, Mr. Goulding argues that Congress did not intend that giving advice relating to a single amount or deduction [would] result in preparer status. Moreover, Mr. Goulding argues that, in providing copies of the K-1 forms to the partners, he did not "give advice" to them; in most cases he never spoke with them or even met them.

Finally, Mr. Goulding suggests that the regulation is in conflict with other provisions of the Internal Revenue Code. He argues that the other provisions regarding preparers cannot possibly apply to him. For example, he could not be required to sign the partners' returns or retain copies of them. A consistent construction of the definition of preparer, he argues, would exclude him from liability under § 6694 as well.[5]

---

5. Mr. Goulding also contends that K-1 Schedules are similar to forms W-2, forms 1099, and other informational forms. Mr. Goulding claims that the same logic which makes him the preparer of the partners' returns would make every employer the preparer of his employees' returns, and every bank the preparer of its depositors' returns. Here we note, however, that the Secretary's regulations specifically provide that a return of tax does not include "an informational statement on Form 990, any Form 1099 or similar form." § 301.7701-15(c)(ii). * * *

The government argues that the legislative history makes clear that a person who supplies substantive information and advice relating to specific entries on a return may be treated as a preparer of that return even though someone else fills it out. The Regulations "apply that principle to a person in appellant's position, treating the preparer of a partnership return as the preparer of a partner's return if the information on the partnership return is directly reflected on, and constitutes a substantial portion of, the partner's return." The objective of the statutory scheme is to impose the penalty on the person who is responsible as a substantive matter for the way in which a return is prepared. Because the partnership pays no taxes itself, the purpose of the partnership tax return and the Schedules K-1 is to figure out the deductions or income that each partner may state on his return. Therefore, argues the IRS, appellant is directly responsible as a substantive matter for the partners' returns. Moreover, the IRS points out, there would be very little deterrent effect in penalizing the preparer of the partnership return for that return alone. Therefore, the regulations are a reasonable method of carrying out the intent of Congress to deter improper preparation.

2. Analysis

In evaluating these contentions, we believe that one point must be central to our analysis. In drafting and in enforcing the regulation, the Commissioner has a duty to apply the intent of the Congress to a myriad of financial relationships and transactions. In each instance, the relationship of the preparer and the taxpayer necessarily will differ. But the policy objective remains the same: to deter negligent conduct on the part of a person who prepares an analysis of financial data upon which the taxpayer will rely in stating a substantial part of his tax liability.

Here the government's position reflects both the congressional intent and the realities of the limited partnership relationship. Partnerships are hybrids – for some purposes they are entities separate from the partners, for other purposes they are aggregates of the individual partners. Under the Internal Revenue Code, partnerships are not taxpayers or taxable entities. When a partnership receives income, the partners record their share of that income on their individual returns and are taxed on it, whether or not that income is actually distributed to them. Partners also deduct partnership losses on their individual returns. Partnerships are "entities for purposes of calculating and filing informational returns;" otherwise they "are conduits through which the taxpaying obligation passes to the individual partners in accord with their distributive shares." This arrangement means that "the calculation of income at the partner-ship level is nothing more than 'a method of centralizing a host of decisions that must be made uniformly for all partners, such as whether particular items received by the partnership constitute income or the return of capital, whether expenditures qualify as ordinary or necessary expenses of conducting the firm's business, and so on.'" Estate of Newman v. C.I.R., 934 F.2d 426, 432-33 (2d Cir. 1991) (quoting 3 B. Bittker & L. Lokken, Federal Taxation of Income, Estates and Gifts, ¶ 86.1.1 (2d ed. 1991)).

As the partnership is both entity and aggregate, the tax preparer's relationship to the partnership is necessarily dual – he is dealing with the partnership both as entity and as aggregate of partners. Appellant was retained to analyze the partnership operation; however, the analysis of the partnership operation was a making of decisions and calculations for all the individual partners, to whom the tax liability or deductions would flow through the partnership. These decisions and calculations were directly reflected on the returns of the partners; all the individual partners depended upon Mr. Goulding's analysis. Thus while appellant was retained by the partnership and compensated by the partnership, in reality his work was for all the partners.

True, Mr. Goulding's work boiled down to one entry on each partner's return, but it represented a far more complicated analysis of partnership earnings – an analysis upon which the limited partners necessarily relied. Thus, Mr. Goulding's comparison of the Schedules K-1 to other informational forms is unconvincing. As appellee points out, normally it is "just a question of fact how much a taxpayer has earned from wages or interest; a bookkeeper can prepare a Form W-2 or 1099 and the taxpayer who receives the form can check it against his own records." This is not true of Schedules K-1; because of the often complicated nature of a partnership return and partnership transactions, a partner cannot readily verify the information and calculations on the partnership return. Moreover, the Internal Revenue Code requires, as a general rule, that tax treatment of partnership items be determined at the partnership level, see 26 U.S.C. § 6221, and that an individual partner, on his own return, treat a partnership item in a manner which is consistent with the treatment of the item on the partnership return. See 26 U.S.C. § 6222.

Because appellant's analysis of the partnership's financial operations was in essence an analysis of income directly taxable to the partners and losses directly deductible by them, the regulation making him the preparer of their returns reflects the real relationship between Mr. Goulding and the partners. The compensation Mr. Goulding received for his legal service to the partnership is, given the relationship of the partners to the partnership, really from the partners. His relationship to the partnership and its members was very much the one Congress had in mind in its regulation of income tax return preparers.

We note, moreover, that under the regulation, only a "preparer" of a return – a person who meets the statutory definition of preparer with respect to a return – may be deemed to be the preparer of another return. If Mr. Goulding were the employee of the partnership, or had not received compensation for the partnership return, or had merely furnished mechanical assistance in the preparation of the partnership return, see 26 U.S.C. § 7701(a)(36), he could not, under the regulation, be deemed the preparer of the partners' return. The regulation thus preserves the congressional intention to distinguish between professional or commercial preparers on the one hand and employees, friends or relatives on the other.

Finally, we cannot accept Mr. Goulding's contention that, by deeming him the preparer of the partners' returns, the regulation is inconsistent with other uses of the term "income tax return preparer" in the Internal Revenue Code. None of the other statutory provisions governing the conduct of income tax return preparers applies in blanket fashion to all preparers. Rather, in each case application is expressly limited to those specified in regulations prescribed by the Secretary. Thus, the statutory scheme reflects recognition of the fact that more than one person may be a preparer in respect to one return, and that not all provisions imposing duties on preparers will apply to all preparers.

In short, we conclude that the regulation "harmonizes with the plain language of the statute, its origin, and its purpose." National Muffler Dealers Ass'n v. United States, 440 U.S. 472, 477, 99 S. Ct. 1304, 1307, 59 L.Ed.2d 519 (1979). It was well within the Commissioner's authority to promulgate the regulation in question, and under the terms of that regulation, Mr. Goulding is properly considered the preparer of the limited partners' returns.

Notes and Questions

For a further discussion of what constitutes substantial preparation of a return, see Adler & Drobny, Ltd. v. United States, 9 F.3d 627 (7th Cir. 1993). The *Goulding* case involved an infraction that occurred prior to 1989, the year that § 6694 was amended by the Improved Penalty Administration and Compliance Tax Act of 1989 (IMPACT), thus the provision at issue in *Goulding* was former § 6694, which applied to understatements attributable to negligence, as well as to those attributable to willfulness. Under this former provision, it was determined that a preparer could be liable for both the negligence penalty under former § 6694(a), as well as the penalty based on willful conduct under former § 6694(b). See Judish v. United States, 755 F.2d 823 (11th Cir. 1985). Under current law, both penalties may apply, but if so, the willful understatement penalty under § 6694(b) is reduced by the amount of the negligence penalty under § 6694(a). See § 6694(b)(3).

Low income taxpayer clinics that qualify for federal grants are not considered preparers, no matter how extensive their services or advice in preparing returns, provided the advice is directly related to a controversy with the Service for which the clinic is providing assistance, and provided the clinic does not charge more than a nominal fee for its services. Reg. § 301.7701-15(a)(7)(v).

1. Under *Goulding*, will the preparer of a partnership return always be considered the preparer of the partners' returns? Who bears the burden of proving the status of "preparer?"

2. Can a company that prepares and markets computer software programs for practitioners be subject to a preparer penalty under § 6694 if it does not sign the return as a preparer and does not deal directly with the public? See Rev. Rul. 85-187, 1985-2 C.B. 338; Rev. Rul. 85-189, 1985-2 C.B. 339.

3. Can a bookkeeper or an in-house accountant who prepares a tax return for an employer be held liable under § 6694?

4. Goulding argued that he should not be considered a return preparer because he neither saw the final returns nor met the limited partners. Yet he was held liable as a preparer, nonetheless. What effect, if any, would the current changes to § 6694 have if Mr. Goulding were arguing his case today?

Problem

Accountant A seeks an opinion from lawyer B, a partner in a law firm, on a matter material to a tax return of A's client. The matter will constitute a substantial portion of the client's return. B seeks the advice of associate C in her law firm, who ultimately advises B on the matter. B, in turn advises A in accordance with the advice B received from C. The position is not disclosed on the return. If it is ultimately determined that the position lacks substantial authority, which of the parties will be liable as a preparer and what will be the extent of that party's liability?

b. Substantial Authority

In order for liability to be imposed, a preparer must have known (or reasonably should have known) that the return position that caused the understatement was due to an unreasonable position. Whether or not a position is unreasonable depends upon two factors: (1) whether the position relates to a tax shelter or a reportable transaction and (2) whether the position was disclosed or not. The highest standard applies to tax shelters and reportable transactions. This position will be considered reasonable only if it is disclosed and it is more likely than not that the position will be sustained on its merits. Thus, there must be a greater than 50% chance that the position will succeed if challenged. If the position does not relate to a tax shelter or a reportable transaction, it will be considered reasonable if it is based on substantial authority, regardless of whether it is disclosed. If there is no substantial authority for the position but it has a reasonable basis, it will be considered reasonable only if it is disclosed. Substantial authority has the same meaning for this purpose as it does for purposes of the substantial understatement accuracy related penalty that applies to the taxpayer under § 6662. See discussion of accuracy related penalties, Chapter 6. In determining substantial authority, all authorities relevant to the tax treatment of an item, including the authorities contrary to the treatment, are taken into account. The authority supporting the position must be substantial in relation to the weight of authorities supporting contrary treatment. The weight of authorities is determined in light of the pertinent facts and circumstances. There may be substantial authority for more than one position with respect to the same item. Because the substantial authority standard is an objective standard, the taxpayer's belief that there is substantial authority for the tax treatment of an item is not relevant in determining whether there is substantial authority for that treatment.

The preparer may rely on the authorities listed in Reg. §1.6662-4(d)(3)(iii), which include the Internal Revenue Code and regulations (including proposed and temporary regulations), revenue rulings and revenue procedures, tax treaties, court cases, congressional committee reports and pre-enactment floor statements made by a bill's manager, the Blue Book (issued by the Joint Committee on Taxation), private letter rulings and technical advice memoranda, and other current IRS notices, announcements, memoranda, information and press releases. If an authority listed in the regulation has been overruled or modified, it is no longer valid authority.

Under the regulations, however, the preparer may not rely on certain types of authorities regularly relied upon by tax practitioners, such as tax treatises, legal periodicals, and opinions of attorneys or other tax professionals.   Treas. Reg. § 1.6694-2(b)(2); Treas. Reg. § 1.6662-4(d)(3)(iii). A particular concern to practitioners is that these materials may be the only authority available when the law is unclear and/or there is no issued guidance.

Question

Would a position that advocates a modification or reversal of existing law ever be considered substantial? Why or why not?

c. Reasonable Basis

A preparer may avoid a § 6694 penalty if the return position has a reasonable basis and is adequately disclosed. Reasonable basis for this purpose has the same meaning as under § 6662. The standard is not satisfied by a return position that is merely arguable or a claim that is merely colorable. But if a return position is reasonably based on one or more of the authorities listed in Reg. §1.6662-4(d)(3)(iii) (taking into account the relevance and persuasiveness of the authorities, and subsequent developments), applicable for purposes of the substantial authority standard for undisclosed positions, the return position generally will satisfy the reasonable basis standard.

The regulations provide that for purposes of determining whether the preparer has a reasonable basis for a position, the preparer may rely in good faith, without verification, on information furnished by the taxpayer and information and advice furnished by another advisor, another preparer, or other party, including another advisor or another preparer in the same firm. Reg. §1.6694-2(d)(2)).

d. Adequate Disclosure

Adequate disclosure means generally that the position must be disclosed either on a Form 8275 (Disclosure Statement or on a Form 8275-R if the position is contrary to a regulation) attached to the return, or on the return itself in accordance with the applicable forms and instructions. Thus, the disclosure must be sufficient to alert the Service to the position being taken. But what happens in the case of a nonsigning preparer? The regulations at Reg. § 1.6694-2 allow the preparer to meet this standard by advising the taxpayer of any opportunity to avoid penalties by disclosure and of the requirements for disclosure. If the preparer's advice was in writing, the statement must be in writing. If the advice was oral, the statement also can be given orally but the preparer must contemporaneously prepare documentation for her files to prove that the advice was given to the taxpayer or to another return preparer.

Question

What happens if a preparer advises a client to disclose but the client refuses? See Reg. § 1.6694-2.

e. Reasonable Cause

The third opportunity to avoid the substantial understatement penalty is through proof that the position has a reasonable basis, and that the preparer has acted with reasonable cause and in good faith, even though there is no substantial authority for the position and no disclosure has been made. Under the regulations, reasonable cause is a facts and circumstances determination made on a case by case basis. Some of the factors the Service will consider include the complexity of the error, whether the error was an isolated occurrence, whether the understatement was of a relatively immaterial amount in relation to the correct tax liability, and whether the preparer in good faith relied on the advice of another preparer. Generally, the preparer may rely without verification on advice and information furnished by the taxpayer or another preparer or other party. However, if the preparer has reason to question the advice or information, the preparer must verify the information. The Service also examines the preparer's normal office practice and considers the likelihood of the occurrence of such an error. If the indications are that such an error would rarely occur, the Service then determines whether the preparer's normal office practice was followed. Treas. Reg. § 1.6694-2(d).

The Service also will consider the educational level and expertise of the individual preparer. The higher the level of education or sophistication of the preparer, the higher the threshold of reasonable cause. Thus, attorneys and CPAs may have a more difficult time establishing reasonable cause than commercial tax return preparers who are not attorneys or CPAs.

Question

A taxpayer may avoid an understatement penalty under § 6662 by establishing that she acted with reasonable cause and in good faith. Reliance on the advice of a professional advisor may constitute reasonable cause. Could such a defense create any problems for the advisor?

2. Penalty for Understatement Due to Willful, Reckless or Intentional Conduct – § 6694(b)

Section 6694(b) provides a penalty of the greater of $5,000 or 50% of the income derived or to be derived from the return for any return preparer who willfully attempts to understate tax liability on a return or claim for refund, or who recklessly or intentionally disregards IRS rules and regulations. This penalty was increased from its former level of $1,000 per return or claim. Unlike the §6694(a) penalty, the § 6694(b) penalty is not excused for reasonable cause. Since the § 6694(a) penalty and the § 6694(b) penalty are likely to overlap, the amount of the § 6694(b) penalty is reduced by the amount of any § 6694(a) penalty that applies to the same conduct.

If the preparer makes little or no effort to determine whether a rule or regulation exists, the preparer will be considered reckless. If the position has substantial authority, the preparer will not be subject to the penalty, provided the position does not relate to a tax shelter or a reportable transaction. Any challenge to a regulation must be made in good faith and the specific regulation must be clearly identified. See Reg. § 1.6694-3(c)(2). If the position has a reasonable basis and is adequately disclosed, the penalty does not apply. However, adequate disclosure means disclosure on Forms 8275 or 8275-R. It does not include disclosure on the return without the disclosure statement. See Reg. § 1.6694-4(f)(2).

If the preparer willfully disregards information furnished by the taxpayer or other persons with the objective of reducing the taxpayer's tax liability, the preparer will be subject to the § 6694(b) penalty.

3. Other Preparer Penalties Under § 6695

A paid return preparer is required to sign the return disclosing that she has been paid to prepare the return. IRC § 6695. The purpose of this requirement is to enable the Service to identify and monitor returns of a single preparer. Thus, the Code imposes a civil penalty for failure to sign the return as a preparer. IRC § 6695(b). There are also a variety of other civil penalties under § 6695 that apply to preparers, such as failure to furnish a copy of the return to the taxpayer, and failure to keep copies or lists of returns prepared. These penalties apply in addition to the § 6694 penalty.

Question

Are there any circumstances under which a preparer may refuse to sign a return? See Rev. Proc. 79-7, 1979-1 C.B. 336.

4.　Promoting Abusive Tax Shelters – § 6700

An individual who organizes, promotes or assists in the sale of any interest in a tax shelter who makes or furnishes (or causes another to make or furnish) a false or fraudulent statement or a valuation over-statement on a material matter in connection with the tax shelter is subject to a penalty of $1,000 (or 100% of the income derived or to be derived from the activity, if less). In the case of a false or fraudulent statement concerning the allowance of tax benefits in connection with the shelter, the penalty is increased to 50% of the gross income derived or to be derived from the activity. The latter penalty was imposed under the American Jobs Creation Act of 2004 and applies to activities after October 22, 2004.

IN RE TAX REFUND LITIGATION v. UNITED STATES
United States Court of Appeals, Second Circuit, 1993.
989 F.2d 1290, cert. denied sub nom Madison Library, Inc. v. U.S., 510 U.S. 964 (1993).

WINTER, CIRCUIT JUDGE.
＊　＊　＊
BACKGROUND

1.　The Parties

Central to the tax shelters at issue were three individuals--appellants Robert Gold and Paul Belloff, and Irving Cohen, who is not a party to the instant action. Gold, Belloff, and Cohen, or some combination of the three, were the shareholders, corporate officers, or general partners of each of the organizations responsible for promoting and organizing the tax shelters.

Irving Cohen founded and served as the president and director of appellant Madison Library, Inc. ("Madison"), a Nevada corporation with its principal place of business in Las Vegas. All of Madison's stock is directly or indirectly owned by, or held in trust for, Cohen's children. Madison, in turn, is the corporate parent of appellants Geoffrey Townsend, Ltd. ("Townsend") and Universal Publishing Resources, Ltd. ("Universal"), also Nevada corporations with their principal place of business in Las Vegas. Cohen is the chief executive officer and president of Townsend and Universal, whose stock is also held in trust for Cohen's children.

Appellant Barrister Associates is a New York general partnership established in 1981 by Belloff and Gold, who serve as general partners. It was formed to organize and act as general partner of, inter alia, the ninety-five limited partnerships relevant to the instant matter – Barrister Equipment Associates Series 81 through 167, 171 through 175, 201, 301, and 302.

Appellant Parliament Securities Corp., formally known as Chadwick Investment Co. ("Chadwick"), is a New York subchapter S corporation. At most pertinent times, Gold, Belloff, and Ronald Cohen (not related to Irving Cohen) each owned one-third of Chadwick's outstanding stock. Chadwick was responsible for marketing the Barrister Equipment Associates limited partnerships to investors.

2. The Transactions and Their Tax Consequences

The tax shelters promoted by appellants involved the 1982 and 1983 purchase and subsequent leasing of certain properties, i.e., metallic plates, lithographic films, and other equipment used in the printing of soft and hard cover books, and unencrypted master computer discs used in the manufacturing of computer software (the "Properties"). Townsend and Universal, through their president and CEO Irving Cohen, negotiated with a number of different publishers to purchase the Properties.

The transfer of each of the Properties was effectuated by an acquisition agreement, executed by the purchaser (Townsend or Universal) and the publisher. The terms of each purchase were essentially identical – Townsend or Universal made a small down payment, usually representing two to three percent of the purchase price, and executed a recourse promissory obligation for the remainder. * * * A chattel mortgage on the Properties secured each of the promissory notes. These notes matured approximately twelve years after execution and bore interest at a rate of nine percent per annum. No payments (interest or principal) were due during the intervening twelve years except to the extent the works produced from the transferred Properties realized net revenues. After twelve years, Townsend and Universal were obligated to make balloon payments of all remaining unpaid interest and principal.

* * *

The Properties were purchased for widely varying amounts--from a minimum of about $100,000 to well over $1,000,000. According to Gold's testimony, Townsend and Universal purchased 3,774 Properties during 1982 and 1983. Because they made only a small down payment and executed a promissory agreement for the balance, Townsend and Universal took on large debt obligations pursuant to their 1982 and 1983 purchases. Townsend, the purchasing entity for 1982, owed $627,155,989 at the end of that year (excluding any interest). Universal, which was responsible for the 1983 purchases, had an outstanding debt of $1,313,061,699 (again excluding any interest). Putting aside any cash down payments, the 3,774 Properties purchased by Townsend and Universal during 1982 and 1983 cost, on average, over $500,000 per Property.

* * *

After purchasing the Properties, Townsend and Universal leased a bundle of diverse Properties representing about forty works (books or software) to each of the ninety-five Barrister Equipment Associates limited partnerships. (Townsend acted as lessor for the thirty-five limited partnerships established in 1982, Universal for the sixty established in 1983.) The terms of the leases were formalized in lease agreements, executed by Townsend or Universal and the relevant Barrister Equipment Associates limited partnership. The leases remained in effect for approximately eight years after the Properties were delivered and obligated the limited partnerships, as lessees, to make annual rent payments to either Townsend or Universal.

Under I.R.C. §§ 38 and 46(a)(2)(B), Townsend and Universal were allowed, disregarding other possibly relevant tax rules, a credit against their federal income taxes. This was ten percent of the value of the purchased Properties during 1982, and eight percent during 1983, even though only a small fraction of the purchase price had been paid. The lessors – Townsend or Universal – then made a pass-through election pursuant to I.R.C. § 48(d). The § 48(d) election designated the limited partnerships as the beneficiaries of this credit as to all Properties each partnership leased.

A partnership, however, is generally not a taxable entity, see I.R.C. § 701, and this investment tax credit was enjoyed by the individual partners of the limited partnerships. Each partner acquired a proportionate share of the credit, based on his or her capital interest in the partnership, and each was allowed to take advantage of this share when filing his or her personal income tax return.

Additionally, each of the partners took a tax deduction based on his or her proportionate share of the operational expenses of the partnership. In combination, this credit and deduction produced attractive tax consequences for wealthy investors. A brochure used to market one of the limited partnerships – Barrister Equipment Associates Series 115 – indicated that, in return for a $50,000 investment, an investment tax credit of $50,600 ($43,100 in 1983 and $7,500 in 1984), as well as tax deductions of $15,000 for 1983 and $35,000 for 1984, would become available. Assuming an investor was in the fifty-percent income tax bracket, the brochure advised that the total tax savings in return for a $50,000 investment would be $50,600 in 1983 and $25,000 in 1984.

None of the limited partnerships engaged or risked capital in the actual printing, manufacturing, or distribution of any books or software. Instead, the limited partnerships retained entities known as service contractors to perform these tasks and to bear the concomitant costs. Service agreements for the Properties were executed by the limited partnerships and the service contractors. These agreements were negotiated by Irving Cohen, usually in connection with the acquisition of the Properties covered by a particular service agreement. In fact, the service contractor for a particular Property was generally affiliated with the publisher from whom that Property had been purchased. Partially as a result of this connection between the selling publisher and the service contractor, the limited partnerships never obtained physical control over any of the Properties.

The service agreements specified both an "anticipated initial printing" and a "minimum additional printing(s)" for every Property. A service contractor was obligated to print, bind, and distribute the number of copies called for in the initial printing. If requested by the limited partnership, the service contractor also had to make available additional copies up to the number specified by the minimum additional printing term of the agreement. Notably, the number of copies specified in the "minimum additional printing(s)" category, i.e., the maximum number of copies the service contractor was obliged to print after the initial print order, bore no relationship to the number of copies from additional printings that Cohen and the publisher assumed would be printed when they negotiated the purchase price.

In return for this work, the service contractors collected fees from the limited partnerships – typically a portion of the sales price of each book or piece of software printed and distributed. However, the contractors received these fees only to the extent any books or software were actually sold. In addition, the contractors were reimbursed for printing, binding and distribution fees, but again only to the extent revenues actually were generated by the sale of books and software.

Chadwick acted as the placement agent for the limited partnerships and was thus responsible for finding sophisticated investors interested in participating in the tax shelter program. Chadwick received from the limited partnerships, in return for its efforts in selling partnership units, a sales commission of $5,000 per unit sold. Between thirty and forty partnership units were available in each of the ninety-five Barrister Equipment Associates limited partnerships, at a price of $50,000 per unit. This $50,000 payment was due in three installments over the course of two years--$5,000 at the closing, $20,000 sometime later in the year of the purchase, and $25,000 sometime during the year following the purchase. Barrister Associates, the general partner of the limited partnerships, invested $25,000 in each limited partnership and received a general partner's fee of approximately $62,500 from each.

3. Procedural History

In 1986, the IRS determined that the transactions described above constituted the promotion of an abusive tax shelter, in violation of I.R.C. § 6700, * * *.

* * *

On July 11, 1990, the jury returned a special verdict, finding that appellants were liable for a § 6700 penalty.

* * *

DISCUSSION
* * *

1. Appellants' Liability Under Section 6700

The version of § 6700 of the Internal Revenue Code in effect at the time of the pertinent transactions imposed a penalty on:

Any person who--

(1)(A) organizes (or assists in the organization of)-- (i) a partnership or other entity, (ii) any investment plan or arrangement, or (iii) any other plan or arrangement, or (B) participates in the sale of any interest in an entity or plan or arrangement referred to in subparagraph (A), and

(2) makes or furnishes (in connection with such organization or sale)-- (A) a statement with respect to the allowability of any deduction or credit, the excludability of any income, or the securing of any other tax benefit by reason of holding an interest in the entity

or participating in the plan or arrangement which the person knows or has reason to known [sic] is false or fraudulent as to any material matter, or (B) a gross valuation overstatement as to any material matter* * *.

I.R.C. § 6700(a).

The jury returned a special verdict, which found that appellants, in their organization and promotion of the representative Barrister Equipment Associates limited partnerships, had made: (i) gross valuation overstatements with regard to each of the Properties leased by the six representative limited partnerships and (ii) false or fraudulent statements with respect to tax benefits that might be available to those who purchased an interest in one of the limited partnerships. Appellants contest both findings. Before turning to the specifics of their arguments, we note that because the § 6700 penalty applies to either gross valuation overstatements or false or fraudulent statements, the penalty must be affirmed unless we reverse both jury findings. Because we affirm the finding regarding gross valuation overstatements, we do not reach the jury's finding regarding false or fraudulent statements.

A gross valuation overstatement is "any statement as to the value of any property or services if * * * the value so stated exceeds 200 percent of the amount determined to be the correct valuation." I.R.C. § 6700(b)(1). Whether such a gross valuation overstatement has been made is a question of fact, upon which the government bears the burden of proof. I.R.C. § 6703(a). The government introduced at trial the reports and testimony of four different appraisers, who together valued the Properties leased by the six representative limited partnerships as worth considerably less than one-half of their declared values.

The value of a piece of property must be established in order to determine whether an individual has made a gross valuation overstatement with respect to that property. See I.R.C. § 6700(b)(1). Generally, the correct or fair market value of a good is defined as the price at which a willing buyer would purchase the good from a willing seller. A price arrived at through arm's length negotiations is usually the most reliable evidence of fair market value, although it is not invariably conclusive. It does not apply, for example, "where a transaction is based upon 'peculiar circumstances' which influence the purchaser to agree to a price in excess of the property's fair market value." *Bixby v. Commissioner*, 58 T.C. 757, 776, 1972 WL 2458 (1972).

* * *

In the instant matter, the jury was free to find, and found, that the negotiations were not arm's-length. The special verdict sheet in the instant matter properly instructed the jury to consider whether there had been any gross valuation overstatements only after determining that the transactions were not at arm's length. The jury thus specifically found that the purchases of the Properties were not the result of arm's-length negotiations. This finding flowed logically from the totality of the evidence offered by the government, including the testimony and reports of the appraisers and the evidence concerning the various relationships and transactions.

An arm's-length transaction between a buyer and seller is one untainted by motives other than the desire of each to obtain the best price. The facts concerning this tax shelter, and inferences to be drawn from them, indicate that the purchases were dominated by other motives. Irving Cohen, in negotiating the purchase of the Properties, had strong incentives to agree to inflated prices in order to increase the tax benefits available to the limited partnerships. The acquisition agreements provided for small down payments and relatively massive promissory notes. By labeling the notes recourse, Cohen insured that these debts would be included in computing the investment tax credit. In reality, however, the promissory notes were functionally identical to nonrecourse obligations. The Properties purchased with the notes were pledged as security but, until twelve years after their execution, no payments were due on the notes except to the extent the Properties purchased realized net revenues. At the end of twelve years, the publishers could look only to the corporate assets of Townsend and Universal to collect amounts still owed on the notes. A trier could thus easily find that by then the corporate cupboards would be bare.

By structuring the purchases of the Properties in this fashion, Cohen created the appearance of substantial capital investments without a genuine risk of loss beyond the down payments and the nonexistent assets of Townsend and Universal. The notes thus look like nonrecourse debt. Once the transactions were so understood by the jury, its conclusion that Cohen wanted to inflate the size of the promissory obligations--the larger the obligation, the greater the resulting investment tax credit--was inexorable. And, of course, the publishers had no incentive to resist such arrangements. The acquisition agreements guaranteed that any net revenues realized through the sale of the works produced from the Properties would eventually flow to the publishers, either immediately, or through payments to the service contractors. The publishers thus had absolutely nothing to lose as a result of these agreements. In sum, the transactions here were based upon the sort of "peculiar circumstances" that defeat any presumption that the purchase prices reflected the fair market values of each of the Properties.

* * *

2. Amount of the Penalty

Under the version of § 6700 in effect at the time of the relevant transactions, a person found liable for organizing or promoting abusive tax shelters had to "pay a penalty equal to the greater of $1,000 or 10 percent of the gross income derived or to be derived by such person from such activity." I.R.C. § 6700. * * *

a. Assessment on an Annualized Basis

Appellants Barrister Associates, Chadwick, Belloff, Gold, Universal, and Townsend argue that the government must assess the § 6700 penalty with reference to a discrete taxable year and only on income actually earned during that year. For simplicity, we will examine the specifics of this argument with regard to Barrister Associates, although our conclusions apply to all appellants.

* * *

In assessing the penalty against Barrister Associates, the government assigned to a particular year all of the income attributable to the limited partnerships promoted during that year, whether or not the income was actually earned in that year. The district court approved this technique. Barrister Associates argues that this violates I.R.C. § 6671(a), which provides that "penalties and liabilities provided by this subchapter [which includes I.R.C.§ 6700] * * * shall be   assessed and collected in the same manner as taxes." Taxes, Barrister Associates correctly notes, are assessed annually, with reference to a particular calendar period. Barrister Associates concludes that the § 6700 penalty must also be assessed with reference to a taxable period.

In determining the penalty owed for 1982, Barrister Associates argues, the government should have looked only to the limited partnership fees (and other income) Barrister Associates actually received in 1982. Money earned in later years could be considered only when (and if) the government assessed a penalty for those years. Under the rule suggested by Barrister Associates, therefore, the government would have to divide a § 6700 penalty assessment into discrete taxable periods, and, in computing the penalty for each period, consider only gross income actually earned during that period. We disagree. [2]

---

2.   As a practical matter, the resolution of this issue might have no real effect except perhaps to complicate IRS efforts to penalize organizers and promoters of abusive tax shelters. No statute of limitation applies to the government's assessment of a § 6700 penalty, and the government is thus free to assess a penalty against a promoter of an abusive tax shelter at any time.

If we agreed that an assessment may only be made with regard to income earned during a discrete taxable period, we would have to remand the instant matter with directions to eliminate

The plain language of the statute is contrary to Barrister Associates' argument. In enacting § 6700, Congress expressly authorized the IRS to assess a penalty on future income, that is, on income "to be derived" from the promotion of an abusive tax shelter. I.R.C. § 6700; see S.Rep. No. 494, 97th Cong., 2d Sess. 248 (1982), reprinted in 1982 U.S.C.C.A.N. 781, 1015 ("In determining the penalty with respect to the amount of gross income *yet to be derived from an activity*, the Secretary may look only to unrealized amounts which the promoter or other person may reasonably expect to realize.") (emphasis added). A holding that the government could assess a penalty only on income actually earned would disregard Congress's unambiguous direction that the penalty be imposed on future earnings. We cannot ignore their unambiguous language. The Internal Revenue Code thus does not obligate the IRS to assess § 6700 penalties only on income actually earned during discrete taxable periods. Unlike the assessment of, for example, a tax deficiency, see I.R.C. §§ 6211-6216, which is directly tied to the payment of a particular tax owed in a particular taxable period, the assessment of a § 6700 penalty turns on income earned from specific conduct – the organization or promotion of an abusive tax shelter – that may occur at times different from those in which income is actually realized. This is in contrast to other Internal Revenue Code penalties, which depend on whether, and how often, an individual avoids certain tax obligations arising in a particular taxable period. See, e.g., I.R.C. § 6704 (civil penalty for failing to keep certain records; penalty "for any calendar year shall be $50, multiplied by the number of individuals with respect to whom such failure occurs in such year"); I.R.C. § 6723 (person who fails to include correct information on an information return shall pay a penalty for each failure). Other circuits have similarly found that § 6700 penalties need not be assessed with reference to a discrete taxable period. See Sage v. United States, 908 F.2d 18, 22 (5th Cir.1990); Planned Invs. Inc. v. United States, 881 F.2d 340, 344 (6th Cir.1989); Gates v. United States, 874 F.2d 584, 588 (8th Cir.1989). But see Bond v. United States, 872 F.2d 898, 901 (9th Cir.1989) (dicta that § 6700 penalties should be assessed on an annualized basis).

---

from the penalties assessed amounts not attributable to money earned during 1982 or 1983. The government could then assess an additional penalty against Barrister Asso-ciates based on income earned after 1983. In the end, Barrister Associates might have to pay at least the same total penalty already reflected in the district court's judgment. In fact, because of a 1984 amendment to § 6700, which increased the penalty to twenty percent of gross income, see Tax Reform Act of 1984, Pub.L. No. 98-369; § 143(a), 98 Stat. 494, 682 (1984); see also *Gang v. United States*, 783 F.Supp. 376, 379-81 (N.D.Ill.1992) (holding that twenty-percent penalty applies to all income earned after effective date of 1984 amendment), Barrister Associates could potentially be liable for a larger penalty than the one already assessed, depending on when it actually received its post-1983 income.

Barrister Associates argues, however, that, because the practical difficulties in assessing the penalty without reference to discrete taxable periods are so great, this construction of § 6700 "reads [the section] out of the Internal Revenue Code." The argument underlying this bit of hyperbole is that: income, whether subject to a tax or a penalty, can only be measured by reference to some time period. If this "temporal dimension" is ignored, it becomes impossible to measure and tax or penalize income in any rational manner. The government thus collects taxes on an annual and retrospective basis because of the intractable problem of predicting with accuracy the individual future incomes of millions of taxpayers.

However, the instant matter raises issues of a less intractable dimension. For purposes of calculating a § 6700 penalty, the government is concerned only with gross income to be derived from a particular, well-defined activity. With regard to such an activity, it is far less daunting to predict future earnings, at least those earnings that a person "may reasonably expect to realize." We therefore see no practical obstacles to assessing the penalty on income expected in later years.

b. Inclusion of Earnings Expected but Never Received in Gross Income Base

Barrister Associates argues that the district court should not have allowed the government to consider, in assessing the penalty against Barrister Associates, limited partners' fees never actually paid to Barrister Associates by certain of the limited partnerships. Again, we disagree.

Section 6700 allows the government to assess a penalty on "gross income derived or to be derived" from the tax shelter activity. As noted, this language contemplates assessments on earnings to be derived in the future from the promotion of an abusive tax shelter. But "[i]n determining the penalty with respect to the amount of gross income yet to be derived from an activity, the [government] may look only to unrealized amounts which the promoter or other person may reasonably expect to realize." S.Rep. No. 494 at 267, 1982 U.S.C.C.A.N. at 1015.

In the instant matter, the only income Barrister Associates earned from the tax shelter promotion was the one-time general partner's fees owed it by each of the limited partnerships. With the exception of $28,750 still owed by three of the limited partnerships, Barrister Associates had received all of these fees by 1986. Thus, at issue is whether this $28,750 was unrealized income that Barrister Associates could have "reasonably expect[ed] to realize" when the government first assessed the penalty in 1986.[3] We believe that the answer is yes.

As the district court noted, at the time of the first assessment, Barrister Associates could have brought suit to recover the unpaid fees from the defaulting limited partnerships. While, with the benefit of hindsight, we now know (and indeed the government knew in 1989) that a lawsuit to recover those fees was necessary but never pursued, this fact does not make consideration of the $28,750 improper. The burden was on appellants to show that the fees would not have been recoverable through such a lawsuit. Absent such a showing, the government was entitled to take the $28,750 into account.

* * *

e. Imposition of a Penalty On Both a Partnership and Its Partners

The district court excluded earnings Belloff and Gold had received from Barrister Associates from the gross income base of the assessments against them. Chief Judge Platt reasoned that Belloff and Gold were the general partners of Barrister Associates, and they were personally liable under New York law for the Section 6700 penalty assessed against the partnership. N.Y. Partnership Law §§ 24, 26 (McKinney 1988). Moreover, Barrister Associates was liable for any penalty assessed against Belloff or Gold as a result of actions taken within the scope of their authority as general partners, including the promotion of the tax shelter program at issue here. Chief Judge Platt concluded that imposing a penalty on Belloff and Gold based on gross income they derived from Barrister Associates, and, at the same time, imposing a

---

3.   When the government first assessed a penalty on Barrister Associates in 1986, it assessed the penalty on a $1000 per each separate tax shelter transaction basis. In granting the motion for partial summary judgment, the district court held that this method was improper and that the $1000 penalty is to be used only when ten percent of the gross income from all transactions is less than $1000. *In re Tax Refund Litigation*, 698 F.Supp. at 443. Because ten percent of Barrister Associates' income from the tax shelter promotion exceeded $1000, the district court ordered the government to reassess the penalty using the gross income method. Thus, it was only in the subsequent 1989 assessment that Barrister Associates' gross income became relevant. However, for purposes of determining the proper amount of that assessment, the government had to evaluate Barrister Associates' actual and expected gross income as if it were still 1986. In other words, in computing the penalty, the government could consider the full amount of any income already received as of 1986, and the 1986 present value of any income expected to be realized after 1986. This is because interest on the unpaid portion of the 1989 assessment accrued from the time of the first assessment in 1986, at least to the extent the amount of the 1989 assessment was less then or equal to the amount of the 1986 assessment. And, therefore, if the government were permitted to make its assessment using the full value of all income Barrister Associates realized as of 1989, and it were also allowed to calculate interest on this assessment from 1986, Barrister Associates would pay double interest on post-1986 income. Of course, to the extent any income actually received by 1989 could not have been anticipated in 1986, the government could issue a new assessment against Barrister Associates, but interest would accrue only from the date of this new assessment.

penalty on Barrister Associates based on that same income, would constitute a double tax not authorized by Congress.

In its cross-appeal, the government argues that this was error. It points out that a § 6700 penalty may be assessed against "any person" who promotes or organizes an abusive tax shelter. I.R.C. § 6700. A partnership and its individual partners are both persons for purposes of the Internal Revenue Code. See I.R.C. § 7701(a)(1) (definition of "person"). Had a non-partner of the partnership engaged in conduct within the scope of his or her authority that violated § 6700, both the agent and the partnership could be penalized on any income earned as a result of that conduct. The government thus argues that, because the jury found that Gold, Belloff, and Barrister Associates had engaged in conduct subject to a penalty under § 6700, all three should be held accountable to the full extent of any income derived from their tax shelter activity. The question is a close one, but we disagree.

The government's agent scenario is different from the situation here. It is true that an agent who promotes abusive tax shelters on behalf of a partnership is subject to a penalty based on the agent's earnings derived from that conduct, as is the partnership. Unlike the instant case, however, income to the partnership is not income to the agent, and an agent of the partnership has no obligation to pay the partnership's penalty. The agent is thus not double-taxed by a penalty. On the other hand, debts of the partnership are debts of the partners, and income to the partnership is income to the partners. Indeed, partnerships and individual proprietorships are generally not taxable entities, see I.R.C. § 701, presumably to avoid double taxation of owners who do not have unlimited liability. Absent a clear direction from the Congress, we follow that logic here and agree with Chief Judge Platt.

* * *

Affirmed on the appeal, affirmed in part and reversed in part on the cross-appeal.

Notes and Questions

Prior to IMPACT, there were differing interpretations of the § 6700 penalty computation. See Hersch v. United States, 685 F. Supp. 325 (DC N.Y. 1988) (rejecting government's attempt to impose a separate penalty for each activity); Bond v. United States, 872 F.2d 898 (9th Cir. 1989) ("Congress clearly intended the use of a percentage penalty unless it would result in a fine of less than $1,000); Gates v. United States, 874 F.2d 584 (8th Cir. 1989) (holding that the penalty should be assessed on the basis of the overall duration of the abusive scheme and not on the individual sales). These inconsistencies led to the amendment of § 6700 by IMPACT in 1989, which clarified that the penalty is the lesser of $1,000 per activity or 100% of the gross income derived (or to be derived) by such person from such activity. The burden of establishing the amount of gross income is on the person subject to the penalty.

The § 6700 penalty may be "stacked" – i.e., imposed in addition to any other penalty provided by law. IRC § 6700(c). Because the amount of the § 6700 penalty alone can be significant, Congress has granted the Service discretion to waive all or a part of the penalty with respect to a gross valuation overstatement upon a showing by the taxpayer that there was reasonable cause for the valuation and that it was made in good faith. IRC § 6700(b)(2).

In addition, § 6703 allows the promoter to pay 15 percent of the penalty within 30 days of the notice and demand, and to file a claim for refund with the Service. If this claim is denied, the promoter then may file in the federal district court to contest the liability. The Service is prohibited from engaging in further collection actions until the suit is concluded.

The government may enjoin promoters of abusive tax shelters and those aiding or abetting others in understating tax liabilities from further engaging in such activity. IRC § 7408. Suit for injunction may be brought in the federal district court for the district in which the individual resides.

1. In order to determine whether there has been a gross valuation overstatement, the correct valuation first must be established. In determining the correct valuation, the government may present its own appraisers to refute the valuation set by the parties. When this happens, there is less emphasis placed on arm's length negotiation between the parties. Is this consistent with the general rule? What is the rationale for this position? See United States v. Campbell, 897 F.2d 1317 (5th Cir. 1990).

2. Does § 6703 change the burden of proof with respect to the § 6700 penalty?

5. Aiding and Abetting Understatement of Tax Liability – § 6701

BERGER v. UNITED STATES
United States District Court, District of Connecticut, 1997.
1997 WL 375319.

COVELLO, DISTRICT JUDGE.

* * *

FACTS
* * *

The plaintiff is an attorney licensed to practice law in the state of New York and he specializes in the field of pension and profit sharing. During 1987 and 1988, the plaintiff's clients included twenty-three corporate employers with employee pension plans. On behalf of each of these corporate employers, the plaintiff prepared applications for determination of employee benefit plans, otherwise known as forms 5300.

A form 5300 provides information to the IRS about a corporation's pension plan and requests that the IRS issue a determination that the plan is "qualified" for federal taxation purposes, as "qualified pension plans receive preferential treatment under the Internal Revenue Code." "Specifically, a qualified plan is exempt from taxation under IRC § 501(a); a plan beneficiary is not taxed on contributions when made to the plan on his behalf * * *; and an employer maintaining such a plan may deduct his contributions to the plan from his taxable income pursuant to § 404(a)."

Congress amended the qualifications for qualified pension plans in the 1980s. As a result of these amendments, the plaintiff's clients would have to amend their pension plans in order for the plans to remain qualified. The applicable statutes set forth specific dates by which the plans would have to be amended in order to be retroactively qualified for the tax years 1984 and 1985.

The plaintiff submitted forms 5300 on behalf of his clients which indicated that the plans had been amended prior to the applicable compliance date of June 30, 1986. The IRS, however, "detected several irregularities" in the forms and concluded that the documents were "prepared after the compliance date and backdated."[4] On May 21, 1993,

---

4.   Specifically, the IRS noted several peculiarities in the documents submitted in connection with the requests for determination, including the following facts: 1) the plan documents contained language which was verbatim from Treasury Regulations issued after the documents were adopted; 2) the "Application for Determination for Defined Benefit Plan" was signed prior to the preprinted revision date on the form; and 3) a gap of approximately 2 years between the time the plan sponsors signed the tax form 2848 ("Power of Attorney and Declaration of Representative") and the time when

the IRS issued a "Notice of Penalty Charge and Demand for Payment" to the plaintiff for aiding and abetting the understatement of tax liability. The IRS determined that the plaintiff used the forms 5300 for the purpose of understating the tax liability of the 23 corporate entities,[5] and assessed a penalty of $700,000, pursuant to 26 U.S.C. § 6701. The IRS assessed a $10,000 penalty[6] for each "tax year affected" with respect to each corporation.

* * *

On June 17, 1993, less than 30 days after the assessment of the tax penalty, the plaintiff challenged the IRS determination. Pursuant to 26 U.S.C. § 6703(c)(1), the plaintiff paid fifteen percent of the assessed penalty, $105,000, and filed a claim for a refund with the IRS.[8]

The IRS did not take action on the plaintiff's claim for six months. On January 13, 1994, pursuant to the provisions of 26 U.S.C. § 6703(c)(2), the plaintiff instituted the instant action.

Subsequently, on January 31, 1994, the IRS determined that with respect to certain of the plaintiff's corporate clients, no penalties were due and the IRS reduced the assessed penalty to $540,000.

* * *

DISCUSSION

In his motion for partial summary judgment, the plaintiff argues that, assuming the validity of the factual basis for the imposition of the penalty, the IRS improperly imposed multiple penalties in violation of 26 U.S.C. § 6701(a) and the case law interpreting that statute. Mattingly v. United States, 924 F.2d 785 (8th Cir. 1991); Emanuel v. United States, 705 F. Supp. 434 (N.D. Ill. 1989). The defendant responds that the IRS properly imposed multiple penalties upon the plaintiff with respect to each corporation for which he filed a form 5300 and for each tax year affected.

---

the plaintiff appeared to have signed the form. The IRS concluded that these observations created doubts as to the authenticity of the plan sponsors' signatures on the documents.

5. Based upon its determination that the plans had been amended after the applicable compliance date, the IRS concluded that each corporate pension plan had lost "qualified" status for several years. Because the corporations had allegedly taken a deduction in those years, for their contributions to the plans, they had understated their tax liability.

6. The "corporate penalty provision" of section 6701(b)(2) imposes a $10,000 penalty "[i]f the return, affidavit, claim, or other document relates to the tax liability of a corporation." 26 U.S.C. § 6701(b)(2).

8. In his claim for a refund, the plaintiff disputed the IRS findings with respect to the forms 5300 and the alleged resultant understatement of tax liability.

Section 6701(a) provides that any person:

(1) who aids or assists in, procures, or advises with respect to, the preparation or presentation of any portion of a return, affidavit, claim, or other document,

(2) who knows (or has reason to believe) that such portion will be used in connection with any material matter arising under the internal revenue laws, and

(3) who knows that such portion (if so used) would result in an understatement of the liability for tax of another person, shall pay a penalty with respect to each such document in the amount determined under [§ 6701(b)].

On appeal, the second circuit held that "the forms 5300 'relate to' the corporate tax liability of the sponsors of the pension plans within the meaning of § 6701(b)(2), and 'would result in an understatement of the tax liability' of those sponsors within the meaning of § 6701(a)(3)." The court did not address the issue of multiple penalties under § 6701.[10]

In Mattingly v. United States, 924 F.2d 785 (8th Cir. 1991), a tax preparer appealed assessment of a penalty based upon the fact that the tax preparer supplied valuation overstatements in tax returns. The court recognized that § 6701 "clearly states that separate penalties may be imposed for violations involving different taxpayers in the same year." Further, the court noted that, "[i]t is also clear that separate penalties may not be imposed for violations involving different taxpayers in the same year." Further, the court noted that, "[i]t is also clear that separate penalties may not be imposed for multiple documents in the same year involving the same taxpayer." What the court found "unclear" was the "relating to" language of the following provision of § 6701(b):

(3) Only 1 penalty per person per period. If any person is subject to a penalty under subsection (a) with respect to any document relating to any taxpayer for any taxable period (or where there is no taxable period, any taxable event), such person shall not be subject to a penalty under subsection (a) with respect to any other document relating to such taxpayer for such taxable period (or event).

---

10. The second circuit noted that, "[a]s In Re Mitchell, 977 F.2d 1318 (9th Cir. 1992)) points out, '§ 6701(a)'s broad language – 'a penalty with respect to each such document' – could impose entirely disproportionate liability.' Accordingly, in pointing out that each erroneous Form 5300 could impact upon the tax liability of both plan sponsors and plan beneficiaries (and in each case for multiple tax periods), we do not wish to be understood as deciding, or even addressing, the question whether separate penalties may be imposed as to each such taxpayer and taxable period. Cf. Mattingly v. United States, 924 F.2d 785, 792-93 (8th Cir. 1991) (imposing § 6701 penalties as to taxable year to which valuation overstatements directly pertained, but precluding tax penalties for carryforward and carryback of resulting tax credits to other taxable years)." Berger v. United States, Docket No. 95-6202 (2d Cir. June 25, 1996), slip op. at 5396-97.

26 U.S.C. § 6701(b)(3). The court concluded that "[t]here is simply no clear indication as to the scope of the "relating to" language," and held that "when a § 6701 penalty is imposed with respect to an understatement document in one tax period, another penalty may not be imposed on a carryover document of the same taxpayer, based on the same original understatement." Id.

In Emanuel v. United States, 705 F.Supp. 434 (N.D.Ill. 1989), the plaintiff, an accountant, helped in the preparation of sixty investors' income tax returns, forms 1040, as well as the investors' applications for a tentative refund, forms 1045. The IRS assessed a § 6701 penalty against the plaintiff for each investor's form 1040 and one or more penalties for the forms 1045.

The court held that the forms 1045 related to the 1982 tax period with respect to which a penalty was imposed for the forms 1040 and, therefore, the government improperly included penalties for the forms 1045 in computing the § 6701 penalty. Emanuel v. United States, 705 F.Supp. 434, 438 (N.D.Ill.1989).[12]

The plaintiff, citing *Mattingly* and *Emanuel*, argues that the IRS wrongfully imposed a penalty for each of the effected tax years as the understatements in these years relate to and arise from the forms 5300 submitted in 1987 and 1988. The plaintiff argues that the penalties should only apply to the years in which the forms 5300 were prepared, 1987 and 1988, and not to the previous years in which the various corporate tax returns were filed.

The defendant responds that it properly determined that penalties should be assessed with respect to each tax year affected. Specifically, the defendant argues that the understatements with respect to each corporate tax return were independent of each other and not, as in *Mattingly,* a carryover from a prior or subsequent year. The defendant also argues that "it is not solely the number of documents prepared, but the effect of those documents which determines the amount of the penalty imposed," and cites Kuchan v. United States, 679 F.Supp. 764 (N.D.Ill. 1988).

In *Kuchan*, the plaintiff accountant prepared three letters, indicating that an enclosed schedule C represented deductible business expenses, attached Schedule Cs and mailed the duplicated letters with attached

---

12. The court cited the following legislative history to § 6701:

The penalty can however be imposed only for any taxable period (or taxable event) with respect to the taxpayer's actions in assisting any one person. Thus, someone who assists two individuals in preparing false documents would be liable for a $2,000 penalty whereas the penalty would only be $1,000 if he had advised in the preparation of two false documents for the same tax year.

Schedule Cs to 191 investors. The court first held that although the plaintiff had only prepared three letters, the IRS properly assessed penalties based upon the number of schedules mailed. The court also concluded that the penalties were properly imposed as to the year in which the prohibited conduct occurred as opposed to the "year for which the underlying tax document was prepared." The court noted as follows:

> simple logic dictates that the penalty should relate to the year in which the prohibited conduct occurs rather than the year for which the underlying tax document was prepared. The penalty is triggered by 'any person's' *act of aiding, assisting, procuring, or advising, not by the taxpayer's act of filing an understated return.*

Kuchan v. United States, 679 F.Supp. 764, 767 (N.D. Ill. 1988) (emphasis added).

The defendant also cites In Re Mitchell, 977 F.2d 1318 (9th Cir. 1992), in which the Ninth Circuit addressed whether a debtor who organized tax shelters and supplied information for an S corporation return and related forms K-1 could be liable for § 6701 penalties based upon the preparation of the form K-1 that aided and abetted in the understatement of tax liability. The court noted that § 6701(a) requires that the court first identify the documents that relate to an understatement of tax liability. "Having identified the documents that provide a basis for imposing a penalty," the court must "look to subsection (b) to determine the amount of the penalty for each such document."[13] Subsection (b) provides, in relevant part, as follows:

> (2) Corporations. If the return, affidavit, claim, or other document relates to the tax liability of a corporation, the amount of the penalty imposed by subsection (a) shall be $10,000.

"Statutory construction always starts with the language of the statute itself." Where the statutory language itself is clear and unambiguous, this court will not look to the legislative history of the statute. Conn. Nat'l Bank v. Germain, 503 U.S. 249 (1992). Further, "[p]articular phrases must be construed in light of the overall purpose and structure of the whole statutory scheme."

The statute at issue imposes a penalty upon a person "who aids or assists in * * * the preparation or presentation of any portion of a return * * * or other document * * *." 26 U.S.C. § 6701(a)(1). Section 6701 goes on to provide that the aider or abettor "shall pay a penalty *with respect*

---

13. The court also noted that "[t]he statute's limiting language is found in the interplay between the last clause of § 6701(a) and § 6701(b)(3). The IRS may seek only one penalty per abetted taxpayer per taxable period, no matter how many § 6701(a) documents relate to that taxpayer." In Re Mitchell, 977 F.2d 1318, 1322 (9th Cir. 1992). The court found the terms of the statute clear and unambiguous and, therefore, found no need to look to the legislative history for interpretation.

to each such document in the amount determined under subsection (b)."[14] 26 U.S.C. § 6701(a) (emphasis added). The express provisions of the statute, therefore, provide a penalty based upon the plaintiff's preparation of the forms 5300.

The courts have recognized that "[t]he penalty is triggered by 'any person's' *act of aiding, assisting, procuring, or advising, not by the taxpayer's act of filing an understated return.*" Kuchan v. United States, 679 F.Supp. 764, 767 (N.D. Ill. 1988) (emphasis added). Further, the statute focuses on the act of aiding or assisting in the preparation of a document with knowledge that the document will be used to understate a tax liability. There is no reference to the imposition of a penalty with respect to each tax year affected by the taxpayer's conduct.[15] Rather, the statute plainly imposes a penalty as to each document through which the plaintiff aided or assisted in the understatement of a tax liability. In this case, the documents which allegedly provide a basis for imposition of a § 6701 penalty are the forms 5300.

Assuming, without deciding, that the plaintiff prepared documents in violation of § 6701, he did so with respect to each form 5300. Although the forms 5300 may have resulted in an understatement of tax liability for previous tax years as to each of the plaintiff's corporate clients, the conduct allegedly warranting imposition of a § 6701 penalty was the plaintiff's alleged falsification of the forms 5300. The court concludes that based upon the language of § 6701 and the relevant case law interpreting the statute, the IRS improperly imposed multiple penalties upon the plaintiff based upon each of the "tax years affected." If the defendant proves that the plaintiff is liable pursuant to § 6701, penalties may be properly imposed only for the years in which the plaintiff prepared the forms 5300 for each corporation and not for each affected year in which a corporate return was filed.

CONCLUSION

For the foregoing reasons, the plaintiff's motion for partial summary judgment is granted and the defendant's motion is denied.

It is so ordered.

---

14. Subsection (b) refers to the "document" through which the plaintiff aided or assisted in the understatement of a tax liability and imposes a $10,000 penalty based upon that document.

15. Indeed, the defendant cites no case specifically interpreting the statute to require the imposition of a penalty for each tax year affected.

Notes and Questions

The taxpayer whose tax liability is understated need not have knowledge of or have consented to the understatement. Thus, the preparer alone may be liable for the penalty, even though no penalty applies to the taxpayer. The § 6701 penalty also may apply to persons other than preparers, such as a supervisor who does nothing to prevent the understatement of tax on a return when he has knowledge of an act by a subordinate that would result in such an understatement. IRC § 6701(c).

1. Review IRC § 6694. Would liability under § 6701 automatically subject a preparer to liability under § 6694 as well?

2. What statute of limitations applies to the § 6700 and § 6701 penalties? Does § 6703 have any effect on the statute of limitations?

Section 7206(2) provides a criminal penalty for aiding and abetting an understatment of tax. See Chapter 9 and § B, below. The next case explores the relationship between the civil and criminal preparer penalties.

LEA v. UNITED STATES

United States District Court, Western District of Tennessee, 1995.
882 F. Supp. 687.

ORDER GRANTING UNITED STATES' MOTION FOR SUMMARY JUDGMENT

TODD, DISTRICT JUDGE. This is a civil action brought by the Plaintiff, William M. Lea, pursuant to 28 U.S.C. § 1346(a)(1), for refund of a civil penalty allegedly erroneously assessed and collected by the Internal Revenue Service ("IRS") under 26 U.S.C. § 6701. Before the court is a motion for summary judgment on behalf of the United States. Plaintiff has responded to the motion.

On August 12, 1987, in the United States District Court for the Western District of Tennessee, Plaintiff, an accountant, was convicted of seven counts of violating 26 U.S.C. § 7206(2), aiding and assisting in the preparation of false tax returns. Plaintiff was sentenced to one year and one day imprisonment, and fined $1,000 on each of the seven counts. On March 26, 1990, the IRS assessed a civil penalty against the Plaintiff, pursuant to 26 U.S.C. § 6701, in the amount of $34,000.[1]

---

1. The penalty was $10,000 for each of three corporate taxable years and $1,000 for each of four individual taxable years.

In his complaint, Plaintiff alleges that the assessment of the § 6701 penalty is barred by the statute of limitations, and that the penalty constitutes a second punishment for the same offense, in violation of the Double Jeopardy Clause of the Fifth Amendment. The United States contends that there are no genuine issues of material fact, and that it is entitled to judgment as a matter of law.

Plaintiff first contends that the assessment of the civil penalty is barred by the statutes of limitation found in either 28 U.S.C. § 2462 (5 years) or 26 U.S.C. § 6501 (3 years), or by "other applicable principles of law." Plaintiff's position, however, was squarely rejected by the Court of Appeals for the Sixth Circuit in Mullikin v. United States, 952 F.2d 920, 925-29 (6th Cir. 1991). The Court of Appeals held that it was Congress' intent that no statute of limitations apply to the initial assessment of civil penalties under 26 U.S.C. § 6701. Id. at 925-29. Thus, such assessments may be made at any time. Once an assessment is made, however, then the ten-year statute of limitations on the collection of assessed taxes applies. 26 U.S.C. § 6502. Therefore, as the penalty in this case was assessed on March 26, 1990, the IRS would have had until March 26, 2000, in which to collect the penalty.

Plaintiff also contends that the civil penalty assessed by the IRS constitutes a punishment that is barred by the Double Jeopardy Clause of the Fifth Amendment. Plaintiff relies on the decision of the United States Supreme Court in United States v. Halper, 490 U.S. 435 (1989). The United States asserts that the civil penalty is not punitive, but remedial, and thus does not run afoul of the Double Jeopardy Clause.

In *Halper,* the Supreme Court stated:

> [T]he determination whether a given civil sanction constitutes punishment in the relevant sense requires a particularized assessment of the penalty imposed and the purposes that the penalty may fairly be said to serve * * *.

> * * * We therefore hold that under the Double Jeopardy Clause a defendant who already has been punished in a criminal prosecution may not be subjected to an additional civil sanction to the extent that the second sanction may not fairly be characterized as remedial, but only as a deterrent or retribution.

490 U.S. at 448-49. The Court further recognized that:

> [T]his inquiry will not be an exact pursuit * * * the precise amount of the Government's damages and costs may prove to be difficult, if not impossible, to ascertain. Similarly, it would be difficult if not impossible in many cases for a court to determine the precise dollar figure at which a civil sanction has accomplished its remedial

purpose of making the Government whole, but beyond which the sanction takes on the quality of punishment. In other words, * * * the process * * * inevitably involves an element of rough justice * * *.

> * * * What we announce now is a rule for the rare case, * * * where a fixed-penalty provision subjects [the offender] to a sanction overwhelmingly disproportionate to the damages he has caused. The rule is one of reason: Where a defendant previously has sustained a criminal penalty and the civil penalty sought in the subsequent proceeding bears no rational relation to the goal of compensating the Government for its loss, but rather appears to qualify as "punishment" in the plain meaning of the word, then the defendant is entitled to an accounting of the Government's damages and costs to determine if the penalty sought in fact constitutes a second punishment.

Id. at 449-50.

In this case, it is clear that the civil penalty is remedial in nature rather than punitive, serving the purpose of compensating the United States for its losses. The tax losses which the Plaintiff helped cause amounted to over $160,000. In addition, evidence submitted by the United States shows that the case required months of investigation by government agents and weeks of preparation for trial by the Assistant United States Attorney, plus the eight days of the trial itself. Under these circumstances, a civil penalty of $22,000 is by no means "overwhelmingly disproportionate" to the damage caused.

The United States' motion for summary judgment is GRANTED.

IT IS SO ORDERED.

B. STATUTORY STANDARDS – CRIMINAL PENALTIES

There are several criminal tax penalties to which return preparers may be subject. Section 7206(2) provides that any person who willfully aids or assists in the filing of a false or fraudulent return, claim or affidavit shall be guilty of a felony. This penalty is discussed in more depth in Chapter 9.

Section 7216 provides a criminal penalty for unauthorized disclosure of return information by preparers who knowingly and recklessly reveal such information. For this purpose, those furnishing auxiliary services in connection with return preparation will be considered return preparers. Thus, a secretary to a tax return preparer who merely types or otherwise has access to returns will be considered a return preparer.

(Note the contrast to § 7701(a)(36), under which secretaries are not considered preparers for purposes of the preparer penalty under § 6694).

There are some limited exceptions to liability found under the regulations. These include disclosure pursuant to provisions of the Internal Revenue Code, disclosure to related parties where the information is necessary to the preparation of the related party's return, disclosure pursuant to a court order or to a federal or state agency, disclosure for use in revenue investigations and court proceedings, disclosure to a return processor, etc. See Reg. § 301.7216-2(b). There is also a related civil penalty for improper disclosure by return preparers under § 6713. The exceptions under § 7216 also are applicable to § 6713.

C. INJUNCTIONS AGAINST PREPARERS

The Service may enjoin a preparer from further preparing federal tax returns if it determines that such relief is appropriate to prevent the recurrence of conduct subject to penalty under §§ 6694 or 6695, or under any criminal tax provision. See IRC § 7407. Other conduct that might elicit an injunction includes misrepresentation to the Service of eligibility to practice; misrepresentation of experience or education as an income tax preparer; guaranteeing the payment of any tax refund or the allowance of any tax credit; or engaging in fraudulent or deceptive conduct that substantially interferes with the proper administration of the Internal Revenue laws. The Service also may obtain an injunction against a preparer who consistently files frivolous returns.

Suits for injunctive relief are brought in the federal district court for the district in which the preparer resides. The court may exercise jurisdiction over the injunction action separate and apart from any other action that may be brought by the government against the preparer. Injunctive relief may be temporary or permanent, but the relief sought must be commensurate with the conduct that led to the suit.

UNITED STATES v. GLEASON

United States Court of Appeals, Sixth Circuit, 2005.

432 F.3d 678.

MERRITT, CIRCUIT JUDGE:

"Every day can be a new deduction if you structure your life right," defendant Daniel J. Gleason promised potential customers of his "Tax Toolbox." Mr. Gleason's aggressive tax strategies attracted the attention of the Internal Revenue Service (IRS) and prompted the District Court to enjoin him, pursuant to 26 U.S.C. § 6700 and 26 U.S.C. § 7408, from selling the Tax Toolbox, a collection of pamphlets, record-keeping aids, a CD-Rom, and other information, and from providing services to Tax Toolbox customers. Mr. Gleason appeals that permanent injunction on two grounds. First, he claims that the materials comprising the Tax Toolbox were never introduced into evidence at the hearing on the injunction. Second, he argues that the bar on providing services to Tax Toolbox customers unduly restricts his ability to earn a living. Because the record reflects more than ample evidence to support the District Court's findings, including relevant portions and descriptions of the Tax Toolbox, and because the injunction's scope is appropriately tailored and does not unduly burden his livelihood, we affirm.

I. FACTUAL BACKGROUND

For over fifteen years, Mr. Gleason has provided tax preparation and representation services individually and through Tax Toolbox, Inc., and My Tax Man, Inc. In 2000, Mr. Gleason, the President and CEO of My Tax Man, Inc., created the Tax Toolbox that, in the charitable words of the District Court, "aggressively promoted tax saving through home-based businesses."

In "no more than a couple of minutes a day," Mr. Gleason's materials asserted, "you transform your non-deductible personal expenses into legal and audit-proof business deductions" by following his tax strategies. A new business can "magically" erase taxes by purportedly creating deductions for weddings, college, "travel, meals, and golf, and cars and medical expenses, kids [sic] allowances, every day household expenses and much more."

According to Mr. Gleason, executing the Tax Toolbox's employment agreement between spouses and children eliminates many of life's more expensive costs. To deduct medical expenses, "[a]ll it takes is a business that you have, or can start, and a spouse who can become an employee .... Medical expenses that are usually subject to a 7.5% of income floor limitation are moved over to your business returns and become 100% deductible! " Get a head start on a college or wedding fund by turning a child's "weekly allowance into a pay check and it's a business deduction for you." With the Tax Toolbox's promissory agreement form, the children "loan" the money back to their parents without money actually changing hands. Mr. Gleason called his methods "audit-proof" and provided a "100% Accuracy Guarantee" that promised to pay any "penalties or interest from our mistake," but not the underlying tax resulting from using the Tax Toolbox.

Mr. Gleason's misrepresentations about tax deductions rival his generous resume embellishments to induce purchases of the Tax Toolbox. His promotional materials boasted that he was an attorney when he was neither licensed to practice in any state nor a graduate of an accredited law school, that he was an enrolled agent with the IRS when that status had lapsed, and that he was an adjunct professor of business law and federal taxation when he could not provide one name of a person to corroborate his claim. The District Court found further fabrications from the self-proclaimed tax expert:

a. falsely claiming to be . . . an editor and a reviewer of articles for Newsweek . . .;

b. falsely claiming that all of his tax coaches were CPAs and IRS Enrolled Agents;

c. falsely claiming that he is such a good attorney that the government pays his fees, when he is not an attorney and has been awarded fees in only one case, for the relatively minor sum of $318.75;

d. falsely claiming that he has never "lost a case in tax court" when Gleason admits that he has never even tried a case in Tax Court;

[e.] disingenuously claiming that he has "never lost a tax court dispute to date" and that he "has a 100% success record in tax court" when Gleason is referring to cases he has *conceded* and defines "loss" to mean that he has never had a client receive a decision that they did not agree to;

[f.] falsely claiming that over 50% of his audits result in *refunds*, when this figure includes audits resulting in "no changes" to the taxpayer's return;

[g.] falsely claiming that customers would have "free Form 1040 preparation," when in reality the cost to Gleason's customers varies based on the number of schedules attached to the return;

[h.] falsely presenting "customer testimonials" in promotional materials, including that of "A.M.," who was not a customer but one of Gleason's own salespersons, Alexander Mandossian;

[i.] misleading customers by referring them to only certain IRS publications, but not IRS Publication 4035, which expressly warns taxpayers of the potential dangers of home-based business scams, claiming he need not do so on the specious ground that this publication was not "relevant" to his home-based business customers.

United States v. Gleason, No. 3:03-0311, 2004 WL 2483220, at *2 (M.D.Tenn. Aug.25, 2004) (emphasis in original).

On April 10, 2003, the United States sued Mr. Gleason individually and d/b/a Tax Toolbox, Inc., and My Tax Man, Inc., seeking permanent injunctions under 26 U.S.C. §§ 7407-08. In spite of Mr. Gleason's continuing assertions of the Tax Toolbox's legitimacy, he stopped selling it in late 2003. On February 23, 2004, pursuant to 26 U.S.C. § 7407, the District Court permanently enjoined him from misrepresenting his eligibility to practice before the IRS and his experience or education as an income tax preparer, and from guaranteeing the payment of any tax refund or the allowance of any tax credit. Mr. Gleason did not appeal that injunction. On June 22, 2004, the District Court denied the Government's motion to enjoin Mr. Gleason permanently from acting as a federal income tax preparer, stating that "Mr. Gleason's primary business and livelihood is tax preparation and a total ban on his livelihood should not be undertaken lightly." The Government has withdrawn its appeal of that denial.

On August 25, 2004, the District Court issued a permanent injunction under 26 U.S.C. § 7408, prohibiting Mr. Gleason from selling or promoting the Tax Toolbox and from providing services to Tax Toolbox customers. It is from this injunction that Mr. Gleason now appeals.

II. ANALYSIS
A. Standard of Review

We review a district court's grant of a permanent injunction for abuse of discretion. "The district court abuses its discretion if it 'applies the wrong legal standard, misapplies the correct legal standard, or relies on clearly erroneous findings of fact.' "

B. The District Court Did Not Abuse Its Discretion in Issuing a Permanent Injunction

Section 7408 of the Internal Revenue Code empowers a district court to grant an injunction when (1) the defendant has engaged in conduct subject to penalty under 26 U.S.C. § 6700, and (2) injunctive relief is appropriate to prevent recurrence of such conduct.[2] See United States v.

---

2.   Section 7408 provides in pertinent part:

(b) Adjudication and decree.–In any action under subsection (a), if the court finds--

(1) that the person has engaged in any specified conduct, and

(2) that injunctive relief is appropriate to prevent recurrence of such conduct, the court may enjoin such person from engaging in such conduct or in any other activity subject to

Bell, 414 F.3d 474, 477 n. 2 (3d Cir.2005); United States v. Schiff, 379 F.3d 621, 625 (9th Cir.2004); United States v. Buttorff, 761 F.2d 1056, 1059 (5th Cir.1985). Because section 7408 expressly authorizes the issuance of an injunction, the traditional requirements for equitable relief need not be satisfied. Estate Pres. Servs., 202 F.3d at 1098.

1.   Mr. Gleason's Conduct Subject to Penalty Under 26 U.S.C. § 6700

A person is subject to penalty under section 6700 when (1) he organized or participated in the sale of an entity, plan, or arrangement, (2) he made false or fraudulent statements regarding specified tax matters, including deductions, in connection with that organization or sale, (3) he knew or had reason to know that his statements were false or fraudulent, and (4) the statements pertained to a material matter.[3] See Estate Pres. Servs., 202 F.3d at 1098.

First, the parties do not dispute that Mr. Gleason created the Tax Toolbox, that he participated in its sale, and that it is an "entity, plan or arrangement" within the meaning of section 6700(a)(1)(A). See United States v. Raymond, 228 F.3d 804, 811-12 (7th Cir.2000) (describing the broad scope of section 6700(a)(1)(A)).

Second, the District Court is not clearly erroneous in finding that Mr. Gleason made false statements about the purported home-based business deductions that can be derived from using the Tax Toolbox. Mr. Gleason did not properly qualify his assertions about the deductibility of weddings, college, travel, meals, golf, cars, and everyday household expenses by stating that business expenses must be "ordinary and

---

penalty under this title.

(c) Specified conduct.–For purposes of this section, the term "specified conduct" means any action, or failure to take action, which is–

(1) subject to penalty under section 6700 . . . .

3.   Section 6700 provides in pertinent part:

(a) Imposition of penalty.–Any person who–

(1)(A) organizes (or assists in the organization of)–

(i) a partnership or other entity,

(ii) any investment plan or arrangement, or

(iii) any other plan or arrangement, or

(B) participates (directly or indirectly) in the sale of any interest in an entity or plan or arrangement referred to in subparagraph (A), and

(2) makes or furnishes or causes another person to make or furnish (in connection with such organization or sale)–

(A) a statement with respect to the allowability of any deduction or credit, the excludability of any income, or the securing of any other tax benefit by reason of holding an interest in the entity or participating in the plan or arrangement which the person knows or has reason to know is false or fraudulent as to any material matter . . . .

necessary" to the business, 26 U.S.C. § 162(a) (2005); Commissioner v. Groetzinger, 480 U.S. 23, 27- 36, 107 S.Ct. 980, 94 L.Ed.2d 25 (1987), and that personal consumption expenditures must be "inextricably linked to the production of income," Buttorff, 761 F.2d at 1060 (quoting Schulz v. Commissioner, 686 F.2d 490, 493 (7th Cir.1982)). See also Estate Pres. Servs., 202 F.3d at 1101 (disallowing deduction of expenses related to ownership of a personal residence); Grimes v. Commissioner, 806 F.2d 1451, 1453-54 (9th Cir.1986) (per curiam) (precluding deduction of personal expenditures to achieve the "American Standard of 'good living'"); Kasun v. United States, 671 F.2d 1059, 1061-63 (7th Cir.1982) (disallowing deduction of commuting expense). Mr. Gleason also failed to warn customers that the notion of deducting wages and all medical expenses through executing employment contracts with family members is subject to close scrutiny and has been rejected in similar abusive tax shelter cases. His claim that his methods are "audit-proof" misleads customers because no tax arrangement is immune from IRS scrutiny, and in fact the IRS has begun auditing many Tax Toolbox customers. Furthermore, many of his statements to induce customers to purchase the Tax Toolbox, including those regarding his education and experience, were flagrantly false.

Third, the District Court is not clearly erroneous in concluding that Mr. Gleason knew or had reason to know that his statements were false. Factors relevant to this inquiry include: "(1) the extent of the defendant's reliance upon knowledgeable professionals; (2) the defendant's level of sophistication and education; and (3) the defendant's familiarity with tax matters." Estate Pres. Servs., 202 F.3d at 1103. Mr. Gleason has not claimed to have relied upon knowledgeable professionals, but instead has promoted himself as a nationally recognized tax expert. Although neither attorney nor law professor, Mr. Gleason has been involved in tax preparation for over fifteen years. Moreover, in his deposition, Mr. Gleason conceded the complexity of Internal Revenue rules governing deductions for employment of family members and admitted knowledge of numerous cases where deductions for payments to children have been disallowed.

Fourth, the District Court's conclusion that Mr. Gleason's false statements pertained to a material matter is not clearly erroneous. Statements with a "substantial impact" on the decision to purchase a tax package pertain to a material matter. Mr. Gleason's exaggerations and misstatements about himself, his company, and the tax benefits of home-based businesses undoubtedly influenced individuals deciding whether to purchase the Tax Toolbox.

2. The Injunction Was Appropriate to Prevent Recurrence

Other Courts of Appeals have set out various factors for consideration in determining the need for an injunction to prevent future violations of section 6700, including:

> (1) the gravity of the harm caused by the offense; (2) the extent of the defendant's participation; (3) the defendant's degree of scienter; (4) the isolated or recurrent nature of the infraction; (5) the defendant's recognition (or non-recognition) of his own culpability; and (6) the likelihood that defendant's occupation would place him in a position where future violations could be anticipated.

Estate Pres. Servs., 202 F.3d at 1105; see also United States v. Kaun, 827 F.2d 1144, 1149-50 (7th Cir.1987). These factors strongly support the District Court's issuance of an injunction. Adherence to Mr. Gleason's tax strategies by his apparently large number of clients, which he advertised as over 250,000, indicates the possibility of significant harm to the federal treasury. Mr. Gleason's participation in this scheme was pervasive and central. Morever, he maintained at the injunction hearing that the Tax Toolbox offers legitimate advice. Furthermore, his continued tax practice places him in a position where future violations could be anticipated.

* * *

D. The Injunction Does Not Unduly Burden Mr. Gleason's Livelihood

Mr. Gleason challenges the scope of the injunction as an overly burdensome restriction on his ability to earn a living. As the District Court rightly remarked "a total ban on his livelihood should not be undertaken lightly." However, permanently enjoining him from providing services to Tax Toolbox customers is far from a total ban on his livelihood and is fully warranted in light of his egregious misrepresentations about tax deductions, his company, and his resume.

At the injunction hearing, Mr. Gleason and his counsel indicated that the Tax Toolbox constituted a relatively small portion of his overall tax practice and was, as the District Court described Mr. Gleason's position, "an unfortunate offshoot" of his primary business, My Tax Man, Inc. Mr. Gleason testified that he sold the Tax Toolbox for only three of his roughly fifteen years of tax preparation and that such sales were limited only to those who were already operating small businesses. Moreover, towards the end of the injunction hearing, Mr. Gleason's counsel asserted that, despite the Tax Toolbox's demise, Mr. Gleason still "provides services to a lot of entities." Based on these representations, the injunction will not overly restrict Mr. Gleason's ability to continue conducting his primary tax practice.

Even if the injunction encroaches on more of Mr. Gleason's livelihood than the transcript reflects, the injunction comports with applicable case law. Some courts have gone so far as issuing a lifetime ban on acting as an income tax preparer in the face of extreme misconduct. See United States v. Nordbrock, 38 F.3d 440, 447 (9th Cir.1994) (finding no error in lifetime injunction prohibiting preparation of tax returns pursuant to 26 U.S.C. § 7407(b)); United States v. Bailey, 789 F.Supp. 788, 819 (N.D.Tex.1992) (permanently enjoining individuals from acting as income tax preparers pursuant to 26 U.S.C. § 7407(b)). Others have enjoined a range of tax-related conduct pursuant to 26 U.S.C. § 7408 where, as in this case, violations of 26 U.S.C. § 6700 occurred. See, e.g., United States v. Bell, 414 F.3d 474, 477 n. 3 (3d Cir.2005) (permanent injunction); Estate Pres. Servs., 202 F.3d at 1097 n. 3 (preliminary injunction); Kaun, 827 F.2d at 1146 n. 1 (permanent injunction); United States v. Stephenson, 313 F.Supp.2d 1054, 1061- 62 (W.D.Wash.2004) (preliminary injunction).

In the instant case, the District Court's permanent injunction aligns with these cases and their applications of sections 7408 and 6700, and is especially appropriate to avert a serious conflict of interest. Allowing Mr. Gleason to continue providing services to Tax Toolbox customers would foster his direct financial interest in peddling further faulty tax advice to Tax Toolbox customers and in obstructing IRS audits to avoid malpractice liability for his abusive tax scheme embodied in the Tax Toolbox.

III. CONCLUSION

Through the Tax Toolbox, Mr. Gleason systematically overstated the tax benefits of a home-based business without warning of well-established limitations in the tax code. Although, as Judge Learned Hand wrote, an individual "is not bound to choose that pattern which will best pay the Treasury," Helvering v. Gregory, 69 F.2d 809, 810 (2d Cir.1934), the tax code does not grant deductions for sham home-based businesses and a few minutes of daily paperwork. Nor does the tax code tolerate Mr. Gleason's outright lies to induce purchases of his tax preparation product. For the foregoing reasons, we affirm the decision of the District Court.

Notes

Section 7407(c) previously allowed the preparer to avoid the injunction by posting bond in the amount of $50,000. This provision was repealed, however, under the Omnibus Budget Reconciliation Act of 1989. Pub. L. No. 101-239, § 7738(a).

The factors the court mentions are not necessarily prerequisites to injunctive relief. Instead, they are considered "balancing factors" which the court should consider (i.e., balance) against each other in determining whether to grant the extraordinary remedy of injunctive relief. See, e.g., In re Delorean Motor Co., 755 F.2d 1223 (6th Cir. 1985); Friendship Materials, Inc. v. Michigan Brick, Inc., 679 F.2d 100 (6th Cir. 1982). Other factors that courts have considered include (1) the threat of irreparable harm, (2) the balance between any irreparable harm and the injury to the enjoined tax preparer, (3) the probability of success on the merits, and (4) the public interest. United States v. Franchi, 756 F. Supp. 889 (W.D.Pa. 1991). The federal district court for the Southern District of Ohio has noted: "as the strength of showing as to irreparable harm increases, the necessity of showing a likelihood of success on the merits decreases." United States v. Graham, 2003 WL 23169851, p. 6 (S.D. Ohio 2003) (unreported opinion).

D. PROFESSIONAL STANDARDS

The bar and the accounting profession both have standards of professional conduct that apply to their various constituents. Lawyers are regulated by the state bar associations of the jurisdictions to which they are admitted to practice and by the courts in which they appear. In addition, the American Bar Association (ABA) influences the ethics rules of both the state bar associations and the courts. For instance, most states have adopted the ABA's Model Rules of Professional Conduct, either in whole or in part, and the United States Tax Court has adopted the Model Rules in their entirety. The ABA also has issued formal opinions on a variety of subjects, some of which are specific to tax practice.

The accounting profession has adopted the American Institute of Certified Public Accountants' Statements on Standards for Tax Services (available on the AICPA home site at http://taxsites.com/aicpa.html).

1. General Standards of Practice – Lawyers

ABA Model Rule 3.3 CANDOR TOWARD THE TRIBUNAL[*]

(a) A lawyer shall not knowingly:

(1) make a false statement of material fact or law to a tribunal;

(2) fail to disclose a material fact to a tribunal when disclosure is necessary to avoid assisting a criminal or fraudulent act by the client;

(3) ail to disclose to the tribunal legal authority in the controlling jurisdiction known to the lawyer to be directly adverse to the position of the client and not disclosed by opposing counsel; or

(4) offer evidence that the lawyer knows to be false. If a lawyer has offered material evidence and comes to know of its falsity, the lawyer shall take reasonable remedial measures.

(b) The duties stated in paragraph (a) continue to the conclusion of the proceeding, and apply even if compliance requires disclosure of information otherwise protected * * *.

(c) A lawyer may refuse to offer evidence that the lawyer reasonably believes is false.

(d) In an *ex parte* proceeding, a lawyer shall inform the tribunal of all material facts known to the lawyer which will enable the tribunal to make an informed decision, whether or not the facts are adverse.

ABA FORMAL OPINION 314
(April 27, 1965) *

In practice before the Internal Revenue Service, which is itself an adversary party rather than a judicial tribunal, the lawyer is under a duty not to mislead the Service, either by misstatement, silence, or through his client, but is under no duty to disclose the weaknesses of his client's case. He must be candid and fair, and his defense of his client must be exercised within the bounds of the law and without resort to any manner of fraud or chicane.

*   *   *

The Internal Revenue Service is neither a true tribunal, nor even a quasi-judicial institution. It has no machinery or procedure for adversary proceedings before impartial judges or arbiters, involving the weighing of conflicting testimony of witnesses examined and cross-examined by opposing counsel and the consideration of arguments of counsel for both sides of a dispute. While its procedures provide for "fresh looks" through departmental reviews and informal and formal conferences procedures, few will contend that the Service provides any truly dispassionate and unbiased consideration to the taxpayer. Although willing to listen to taxpayers and their representatives and obviously intending to be fair, the Service is not designed and does not purport to be unprejudiced and unbiased in the judicial sense.

It by no means follows that a lawyer is relieved of all ethical responsibility when he practices before this agency. There are certain things which he clearly cannot do, and they are set forth explicitly in the canons of ethics.

*   *   *

[A] lawyer who is asked to advise his client in the course of the preparation of the client's tax returns may freely urge the statement of positions most favorable to the client just as long as there is reasonable basis for those positions. Thus where the lawyer believes there is a reasonable basis for a position that a particular transaction does not result in taxable income, or that certain expenditures are properly deductible as expenses, the lawyer has no duty to advise that riders be attached to the client's tax return explaining the circumstances surrounding the transaction or the expenditures.

The foregoing principle necessarily relates to the lawyer's ethical obligations – what he is *required* to do. Prudence may recommend procedures not required by ethical considerations. Thus, even where the lawyer believes that there is no obligation to reflect a transaction in or with his client's return, nevertheless he *may*, as a tactical matter, advise his client to disclose the transaction in reasonable detail by way of a rider to the return. This occurs when it is to the client's advantage to be free from either a *claim* of fraud (albeit unfounded) or to have the protection of a shorter statute of limitations (which might be available by the full disclosure of such a transaction in detail by way of a rider to the return).

In all cases, with regard both to the preparation of returns and negotiating administrative settlements, the lawyer is under a duty not to mislead the Internal Revenue Service deliberately and affirmatively, either by misstatements or by silence or by permitting his client to mislead. The difficult problem arises where the client has in fact misled but without the lawyer's knowledge or participation. In that situation, upon discovery of the misrepresentation, the lawyer must advise the client to correct the statement; if the client refuses, the lawyer's obligation depends on all the circumstances.

Fundamentally, subject to the restrictions of the attorney-client privilege * * *, the lawyer may have the duty to withdraw from the matter. If for example, under all the circumstances, the lawyer believes that the Service relies on him as corroborating statements of his client which he knows to be false, then he is under a duty to disassociate himself from any such reliance unless it is obvious that the very act of disassociation would have the effect of violating [an ethical rule]. Even then, however, if a direct question is put to the lawyer, he must at least advise the Service that he is not in a position to answer.

But as an advocate before a Service which itself represents the adversary point of view, where his client's case is fairly arguable, a lawyer is under no duty to disclose its weaknesses, any more than he would be to make such a disclosure to a brother lawyer.

* * *

So long as a [lawyer's] duty is "performed within and not without the bounds of the law," he "owes 'entire devotion to the interest of the client, warm zeal in the maintenance and defense of his rights and the exertion of his utmost learning and ability,' to the end that nothing be taken or be withheld from him, save by the rules of law, legally applied" in his practice before the Internal Revenue Service, as elsewhere.

FORMAL OPINION 85-352
(July 7, 1985) *

Tax Return Advice; Reconsideration of Formal Opinion 314

Opinion 314 was issued in response to a number of specific inquiries regarding the ethical relationship between the Internal Revenue Service and lawyers practicing before it. The opinion formulated general principles governing this relationship including the following: "[A] lawyer

---

who is asked to advise his client in the course of the preparation of the client's tax returns may freely urge the statement of positions most favorable to the client just as long as there is a *reasonable basis* for this position."

The Committee is informed that the standard of 'reasonable basis" has been construed by many lawyers to support the use of any colorable claim on a tax return to justify exploitation of the lottery of the tax return audit selection process.* * * This view is not universally held, and the Committee does not believe that the reasonable basis standard, properly interpreted and applied, permits this construction.

However, the Committee is persuaded that as a result of serious controversy over this standard and its persistent criticism by distinguished members of the tax bar, IRS officials and members of Congress, sufficient doubt has been created regarding the validity of the standard so as to erode its effectiveness as an ethical guideline. For this reason, the Committee has concluded that it should be restated. Another reason for restating the standard is that since publication of Opinion 314, the ABA has adopted in succession the Model Code of Professional Responsibility and the Model Rules of Professional Conduct. Both the Model Code and the Model Rules directly address the duty of a lawyer in presenting or arguing positions for a client in language that does not refer to "reasonable basis." It is therefore appropriate to conform the standard of Opinion 314 to the language of the new rules.

The ethical standards governing the conduct of a lawyer in advising a client on positions that can be taken in a tax return are no different from those governing a lawyer's conduct in advising or taking positions for a client in other civil matters. Although the Model Rules distinguish between the roles of advisor and advocate, both roles are involved here, and the ethical standards applicable to them provide relevant guidance. In many cases a lawyer must realistically anticipate that the filing of the tax return may be the first step in a process that may result in an adversary relationship between the client and the IRS. This normally occurs in situations when a lawyer advises an aggressive position on a tax return, not when the position taken is a safe or conservative one that is unlikely to be challenged by the IRS.

Rule 3.1 of the Model Rules, which is in essence a restatement of DR 7-102(A)(2) of the Model Code, (DR 7-102(A)(2) states: "In his representation of a client, a lawyer shall not: * * * (2) Knowingly advance a claim or defense that is unwarranted under existing law, except that he may advance such claim or defense if it can be supported by good faith argument for an extension, modification or reversal of existing law.") states in pertinent part: "A lawyer shall not bring or defend a proceeding, or assert or controvert an issue therein, unless there is a basis for doing so that is not frivolous, which includes a good faith argument for an extension, modification or reversal of existing law." Rule 1.2(d), which applies to representation generally, states: "A lawyer shall not counsel a client to engage, or assist a client, in conduct that the lawyer knows is criminal or fraudulent, but a lawyer may discuss the legal consequences of any proposed course of conduct with a client and may counsel or assist a client to make a good faith effort to determine the validity, scope, meaning or application of the law."

On the basis of these rules and analogous provisions of the Model Code, a lawyer, in representing a client in the course of the preparation of the client's tax return, may advise the statement of positions most favorable to the client if the lawyer has a good faith belief that those positions are warranted in existing law or can be supported by a good faith argument for an extension, modification or reversal of existing law. A lawyer can have a good faith belief in this context even if the lawyer believes the client's position probably will not prevail. However, good faith requires that there be some realistic possibility of success if the matter is litigated.

This formulation of the lawyer's duty in the situation addressed by this opinion is consistent with the basic duty of the lawyer to a client, recognized in ethical standards since the ABA Canons of Professional Ethics, and in the opinions of this Committee: zealously and loyally to represent the interests of the client within the bounds of the law.

Thus, where a lawyer has a good faith belief in the validity of a position in accordance with the standard stated above that a particular transaction does not result in taxable income or that certain expenditures are properly deductible as expenses, the lawyer has no duty to require as a condition of his or her continued representation that riders be attached to the client's tax return explaining the circumstances surrounding the transaction or the expenditures.

In the role of advisor, the lawyer should counsel the client as to whether the position is likely to be sustained by a court if challenged by the IRS, as well as of the potential penalty consequences to the client if the position is taken on the tax return without disclosure. [The] Internal Revenue Code imposes a penalty for substantial understatement of tax liability which can be avoided if the facts are adequately disclosed or if there is or was substantial authority for the position taken by the taxpayer. Competent representation of the client would require the lawyer to advise the client fully as to whether there is or was substantial authority for the position taken in the tax return. If the lawyer is unable to conclude that the position is supported by substantial authority, the lawyer should advise the client of the penalty the client may suffer and of the opportunity to avoid such penalty by adequately disclosing the facts in the return or in a statement attached to the return. If after receiving such advice the client decides to risk the penalty by making no disclosure and to take the position initially advised by the lawyer in accordance with the standard stated above, the lawyer has met his or her ethical responsibility with respect to the advice.

In all cases, however, with regard both to the preparation of returns and negotiating administrative settlements, the lawyer is under a duty not to mislead the Internal Revenue Service deliberately, either by misstatements or by silence or by permitting the client to mislead. Rules 4.1 and 8.4(c); DRs 1-102(A)(4), 7-102(A)(3) and (5).

In summary, a lawyer may advise reporting a position on a return even where the lawyer believes the position probably will not prevail, there is no "substantial authority" in support of the position, and there will be no disclosure of the position in the return. However, the position to be asserted must be one which the lawyer in good faith believes is warranted in existing law or can be supported by a good faith argument for an extension, modification or reversal of existing law. This requires that there is some realistic possibility of success if the matter is litigated. In addition, in his role as advisor, the lawyer should refer to potential penalties and other legal consequences should the client take the position advised.

Questions

1. Do you agree with the ABA's position in Formal Opinion 85-382 that the "lawyer must realistically anticipate that the filing of the tax return may be the first step in a process that may result in an adversary relationship between the client and the IRS?"

2. Does Formal Opinion 85-352 conflict with either Circular 230 or the Internal Revenue Code? If so, which should control?

2. Tax Shelter Opinions – Lawyers' Standards

In response to the Treasury Department's 1980 proposed amendments to Circular 230, the ABA Standing Committee on Ethics and Professional Responsibility issued Formal Ethics Opinion 346. This Opinion, issued on June 1, 1981, proposed ethical standards for attorneys issuing tax shelter opinions. Under this Opinion, a lawyer was prohibited from issuing a negative opinion (i.e., an opinion that concluded that the proposed benefits from a tax shelter were not likely to survive challenge by the Service). Numerous concerns were raised about this provision, and on January 29, 1982, the Opinion was revised to reflect these concerns.

GENERAL ABA FORMAL OPINION 346 (REVISED)
January 29, 1982 *

Tax Law Opinions In Tax Shelter Investment Offerings

An opinion by a lawyer analyzing the tax effects of a tax shelter investment is frequently of substantial importance in a tax shelter offering.[1] The promoter of the offering may depend upon the recommendations of the lawyer in structuring the venture and often publishes the opinion with the offering materials or uses the lawyer's name in connection with sales promotion efforts. The offerees may be expected to rely upon the tax shelter opinion in determining whether to invest in the venture. It is often uneconomic for the individual offeree to pay for a separate tax analysis of the offering because of the relatively small sum each offeree may invest.

Because the successful marketing of tax shelters frequently involves tax opinions issued by lawyers, concerns have been expressed by the organized bar, regulatory agencies and others over the need to articulate ethical standards applicable to a lawyer who issues an opinion which the lawyer knows will be included among the tax shelter offering materials and relied upon by offerees.[2]

---

1. (A "tax shelter," as the term is used in this Opinion, is an investment which has as a significant feature for federal income or excise tax purposes either or both of the following attributes: (1) deductions in excess of income from the investment being available in any year to reduce income from other sources in that year, and (2) credits in excess of the tax attributable to the income from the investment being available in any year to offset taxes on income from other sources in that year. Excluded from the term are investments such as, but not limited to, the following: municipal bonds; annuities; family trusts; qualified retirement plans; individual retirement accounts; stock option plans; securities issued in a corporate reorganization; mineral development ventures, if the only tax benefit would be percentage depletion; and real estate where it is anticipated that deductions are unlikely to exceed gross income from the investment in any year, and that any tax credits are unlikely to exceed the tax on the income from that source in any year).

2. (The U.S. Treasury Department proposed a rule which would require lawyers who provide tax opinions to comply with standards of due diligence, disclosure and judgmental determinations. Proposed Rule adding to 31 C.F.R., Subtitle A, Part 10, a new Section 10.33 and amending Sections

* * *

A "tax shelter opinion," as the term is used in this Opinion, is advice by a lawyer concerning the federal tax law applicable to a tax shelter if the advice is referred to either in offering materials or in connection with sales promotion efforts directed to persons other than the client who engages the lawyer to give the advice. The term includes the tax aspects or tax risks portion of the offering materials prepared by the lawyer whether or not a separate opinion letter is issued. The term does not, however, include rendering advice solely to the offeror or reviewing parts of the offering materials, so long as neither the name of the lawyer nor the fact that a lawyer has rendered advice concerning the tax aspects is referred to at all in the offering materials or in connection with sales promotion efforts. In this case the lawyer has the ethical responsibility of assuring that in the offering materials and in connection with sales promotion efforts there is no reference to the lawyer's name or to the fact that a lawyer has rendered tax advice. The term also does not include the case where a small group of investors negotiate the terms of the arrangement directly with the offeror of securities and depend for tax advice concerning the investment entirely upon advisors other than the lawyer engaged to represent the offeror.

Disciplinary Standards

A false opinion is one which ignores or minimizes serious legal risks or misstates the facts or the law, knowingly or through gross incompetence. The lawyer who gives a false opinion, including one which is intentionally or recklessly misleading, violates the Disciplinary Rules of the Model Code of Professional Responsibility. Quite clearly, the lawyer exceeds the duty to represent the client zealously within the bounds of the law. See DR 7-101; EC 7-10. Knowingly misstating facts or law violates DR 7-102(A)(5) and is "conduct involving dishonesty, fraud, deceit, or misrepresentation," a violation of DR 1-102(A)(4). The lawyer also violates DR 7-102(A)(7) by counseling or assisting the offeror "in conduct that the lawyer knows to be illegal or fraudulent." In addition, the lawyer's conduct may involve the concealment or knowing

---

10.51 and 10.52, relating to standards for providing opinions regard-ing tax shelters, 45 Fed. Reg. 58,594 (1980). See also Sax, Lawyer Responsibility in Tax Shelter Opinions, 34 Tax Law. 5 (1980); Lewis, Lawyer's Ethical Responsibilities in Render-ing Opinions on Tax Shelter Promotions, Tax Notes (April 13, 1981) at 795. For general discussions of the legal and ethical responsibilities of lawyers who write tax shelter opinions, see Sax, supra; Lewis, supra; Kennedy, Problems Faced by the Tax Adviser in Registration of Tax Shelter Securities with the SEC, 33 N.Y.U. Tax Inst. 1365, 1389-1395 (1975); Watts, Professional Standards in Tax Practice: Conflicts of Interest, Disclosure Problems under Regulatory Agency Rules, Potential Liabilities, 33 N.Y.U. Tax. Inst. 649 (1975)).

nondisclosure of matters which the lawyer is required by law to reveal, a violation of DR 7-102(A)(3).

The lawyer who accepts as true the facts which the promoter tells him, when the lawyer should know that a further inquiry would disclose that these facts are untrue, also gives a false opinion. It has been said that lawyers cannot "escape criminal liability on a plea of ignorance when they have shut their eyes to what was plainly to be seen." United States v. Benjamin, 328 F.2d 854, 863 (2d Cir. 1964). Recklessly and consciously disregarding information strongly indicating that material facts expressed in the tax shelter opinion are false or misleading involves dishonesty as does assisting the offeror in conduct the lawyer knows to be fraudulent. Such conduct violates DR 1-102(A)(4) and DR 7-102(A). We equate the minimum extent of the knowledge required for the lawyer's conduct to have violated these Disciplinary Rules with the knowledge required to sustain a Rule 10b-5 recovery, see Ernst & Ernst v. Hochfelder, 425 U.S. 185 (1976), rather than the lesser negligence standard. Compare SEC v. Coven, 581 F.2d 1020, 1025 (2d Cir.1978), cert. denied, 441 U.S. 928 (1979); Rolf v. Blyth, Eastman Dillon & Co., 570 F.2d 38, 44-47 (2d Cir.), cert. denied, 439 U.S. 1039 (1978); Sharp v. Coopers & Lybrand, 457 F. Supp. 879 (E.D. Pa. 1978).

But even if the lawyer lacks the knowledge required to sustain a recovery under the *Hochfelder* standard, the lawyer's conduct nevertheless may involve gross incompetence, or indifference, inadequate preparation under the circumstances and consistent failure to perform obligations to the client. If so, the lawyer will have violated DR 6-101(A). ABA Informal Opinion 1273 (1973).

Ethical Considerations

Beyond the requirements of the Disciplinary Rules, the lawyer who issues a tax shelter opinion should follow the Canons and the Ethical Considerations of the Model Code.[3] Although not constituting absolute requirements, the violation of which may result in sanctions, these Canons and Ethical Considerations constitute a body of principles which provide guidance in the application of the lawyer's professional responsibility to specific situations, such as the rendering of tax shelter opinions. The guidelines developed here are to be applied to each specific situation reasonably and in a practical fashion.

---

3. (Canon 1 says "[a] lawyer should assist in maintaining the integrity and competence of the legal profession." Canon 6 says "[a] lawyer should represent a client competently." * * *).

Lawyer as Advisor

EC 7-22 says "a litigant or his lawyer may, in good faith and within the framework of the law, take steps to test the correctness of a ruling of a tribunal." Principles similar to these are applied where the lawyer represents a client in adversarial proceedings before the Internal Revenue Service. In that case the lawyer has duties not to mislead the Service by any misstatement, not to further any misrepresentations made by the client, and to deal candidly and fairly. ABA Formal Opinion 314 (1965); see also Watts, supra note 2 at 651-653.

The lawyer rendering a tax shelter opinion which he knows will be relied upon by third persons, however, functions more as an advisor than as an advocate. Since the Model Code was adopted in 1969, the differing functions of the advisor and advocate have become more widely recognized.[4]

The Proposed Model Rules specifically recognize the ethical considerations applicable where a lawyer undertakes an evaluation for the use of third persons other than a client. These third persons have an interest in the integrity of the evaluation. The legal duty of the lawyer therefore "goes beyond the obligations a lawyer normally has to third persons." Proposed Model Rules, supra note 3 at 117; see also ABA Formal Opinion 335 (1974). Because third persons may rely on the advice of the lawyer who gives a tax shelter opinion, the principles announced in ABA Formal Opinion 314 have little, if any, applicability.

Establishing Lawyer's Relationship

The lawyer should establish the terms of the relationship with the offeror-client at the time the lawyer is engaged to work on the tax shelter offering. See Proposed Model Rules, supra note 3, Rule 2.3. This includes making it clear that the lawyer requires from the client a full disclosure of the structure and intended operations of the venture and complete access to all relevant information.

---

4.   (See Watts, supra note 2 at 655-658; Wolfman & Holden, Ethical Problems in Federal Tax Practice (Michie, Bobbs-Merrill 1981) at 1-2, 100-121; see also Proposed Model Rules, supra note 3, Preamble at 1: "As advisor, a lawyer provides a client with an informed understanding of the client's legal rights and obligations and explains their practical implications. As advocate, a lawyer asserts the client's position under the rules of the adversary system.")

Making Factual Inquiry

ABA Formal Opinion 335 (1974) establishes guidelines which a lawyer should follow when furnishing an assumed facts opinion in connection with the sale of unregistered securities. The same guidelines describe the extent to which a lawyer should verify the facts presented to him as the basis for a tax shelter opinion:

"[T]he lawyer should, in the first instance, make inquiry of his client as to the relevant facts and receive answers. If any of the alleged facts, or the alleged facts taken as a whole, are incomplete in a material respect; or are suspect; or are inconsistent; or either on their face or on the basis of other known facts are open to question, the lawyer should make further inquiry. The extent of this inquiry will depend in each case upon the circumstances; for example, it would be less where the lawyer's past relationship with the client is sufficient to give him a basis for trusting the client's probity than where the client has recently engaged the lawyer, and less where the lawyer's inquiries are answered fully than when there appears a reluctance to disclose information.

"Where the lawyer concludes that further inquiry of a reasonable nature would not give him sufficient confidence as to all the relevant facts, or for any other reasons he does not make the appropriate further inquiries, he should refuse to give an opinion. However, assuming that the alleged facts are not incomplete in a material respect, or suspect, or in any way inherently inconsistent, or on their face or on the basis of other known facts open to question, the lawyer may properly assume that the facts as related to him by his client, and checked by him by reviewing such appropriate documents as are available, are accurate * * *.

"The essence of this opinion * * * is that, while a lawyer should make adequate preparation including inquiry into the relevant facts that is consistent with the above guidelines, and while he should not accept as true that which he should not reasonably believe to be true, he does not have the responsibility to 'audit' the affairs of his client or to assume, without reasonable cause, that a client's statement of the facts cannot be relied upon." ABA Formal Opinion 335 at 3, 5-6.

For instance, where essential underlying information, such as an appraisal or financial projection, makes little common sense, or where the reputation or expertise of the person who has prepared the appraisal or projection is dubious, further inquiry clearly is required. Indeed, failure to make further inquiry may result in a false opinion. If further inquiry reveals that the appraisal or projection is reasonably well supported and complete, the lawyer is justified in relying upon the material facts which the underlying information supports.

Relating Law to Facts

In discussing the legal issues in a tax shelter opinion, the lawyer should relate the law to the actual facts to the extent the facts are ascertainable when the offering materials are being circulated. A lawyer should not issue a tax shelter opinion which disclaims responsibility for inquiring as to the accuracy of the facts, fails to analyze the critical facts or discusses purely hypothetical facts. It is proper, however, to assume facts which are not currently ascertainable, such as the method of conducting future operations of the venture, so long as the factual assumptions are clearly identified as such in the offering materials, and are reasonable and complete.

Non-Tax Legal Issues

Although the lawyer rendering the tax shelter opinion may not be asked to address the non-tax legal issues, the lawyer should make reasonable inquiries to ascertain that a good faith effort has been expended to comply with laws other than tax laws. Tax counsel need not reexamine the conclusions of other counsel rendering opinions in other specialized areas of law, such as the exemption of the transaction or securities from registration or the validity of a patent. Tax counsel, never-theless, should be satisfied that competent professional advice on these and similar matters has been obtained where relevant to the offering.

Material Tax Issues

A "material" tax issue for purposes of this Opinion is any income or excise tax issue relating to the tax shelter that would have a significant effect in sheltering from federal taxes income from other sources by providing deductions in excess of the income from the tax shelter investment in any year or tax credits which will offset tax liabilities in excess of the tax attributable to the tax shelter investment in any year. The determination of what is material is to be made in good faith by the lawyer based on the information which is available at the time the offering materials are being circulated.

The lawyer should satisfy himself that either he or another competent professional has considered all material tax issues. In addition, the tax shelter opinion should fully and fairly address each material tax issue respecting which there is a reasonable possibility that the Internal Revenue Service will challenge the tax effect proposed in the offering materials.[5]

Where some material tax issues are being considered by other competent professionals, the lawyer should review their written advice and make inquiries of the client and the other professionals to assure that the division of responsibility is clear and to reasonably assure that all material tax issues will be considered, either by the lawyer or by the other tax professional, in accordance with the standards developed in this Opinion. If, as a result of review of the written advice of another profes-sional or otherwise, the lawyer believes there is a reasonable possibility that the Internal Revenue Service will challenge the proposed tax effect respecting any material tax issue considered by the other professional, and the issue is not fully addressed in the offering materials, the lawyer has ethical responsibilities to so advise the client and the other professional and to refuse to provide an opinion unless the matter is addressed adequately in the offering materials. The lawyer also should assure that his own opinion identifies clearly its limited nature, if the lawyer is not retained to consider all of the material tax issues.

Opinion as to Outcome – Material Tax Issues

Since the term "opinion" connotes a lawyer's conclusion as to the likely outcome of an issue if challenged and litigated, the lawyer should, if possible, state the lawyer's opinion of the probable outcome on the merits of each material tax issue. However, if the lawyer determines in good faith that it is not possible to make a judgment as to the outcome of a material tax issue, the lawyer should so state and give the reasons for this conclusion.

A tax shelter opinion may question the validity of a Revenue Ruling or the reasoning in a lower court opinion which the lawyer believes is wrong. But there must also be a complete explanation to the offerees, including what position the Service is likely to take on the issue and a summary of why this position is considered to be wrong. The opinion also should set forth the risks of an adversarial proceeding if one is likely to occur.

---

5. (It is not necessary that these material tax issues be discussed in a separate opinion letter, so long as the issues are fully and fairly addressed in the offering materials in accordance with the standards expressed in this Opinion).

Overall Evaluation of Realization of Tax Benefits

The clear disclosure of the tax risks in the offering materials should include an opinion by the lawyer or by another professional providing an overall evaluation of the extent to which the tax benefits, in the aggregate, which are a significant feature of the investment to the typical investor are likely to be realized as contemplated by the offering materials. In making this evaluation, the lawyer should state that the significant tax benefits, in the aggregate, probably will be realized or probably will not be realized, or that the probabilities of realization and nonrealization of the significant tax benefits are evenly divided.

In rare instances, the lawyer may conclude in good faith that it is not possible to make a judgment of the extent to which the significant tax benefits are likely to be realized. This impossibility may occur where, for example, the most significant tax benefits are predicated upon a newly enacted Code provision when there are no regulations and the legislative history is obscure. In these circumstances, the lawyer should fully explain why the judgment cannot be made and assure full disclosure in the offering materials of the assumptions and risks which the investors must evaluate.

The Committee does not accept the view that it is always ethically improper to issue an opinion which concludes that the significant tax benefits in the aggregate probably will not be utilized. However, full disclosure requires that the negative conclusion be clearly stated and prominently noted in the offering materials.

If another professional is providing the overall evaluation, the lawyer should nonetheless satisfy himself that the evaluation meets the standards set forth above.

Accuracy of Offering Materials

In all cases, the lawyer who issues a tax shelter opinion, especially an opinion which does not contain a prediction of a favorable outcome, should assure that the offerees will not be misled as a result of mischaracterizations of the extent of the opinion in the offering materials or in connection with sales promotion efforts. In addition, the lawyer always should review the offering materials to assure that the standards set forth in this Opinion are met and that the offering materials, taken as a whole, make it clear the lawyer's opinion is not a prediction of a favorable outcome of the tax issues concerning which no favorable prediction is made. The risks and uncertainties of the tax issues should be referred to in a summary statement at the very outset of the opinion or the tax aspects or tax risks section of the offering materials.

If the lawyer disagrees with the client over the extent of disclosure made in the offering materials or over other matters necessary to satisfy the lawyer's ethical responsibilities as expressed in this Opinion, and the disagreement cannot be resolved, the lawyer should withdraw from the employment and not issue an opinion.

Summary of Ethical Considerations

The general ethical guidelines to be followed by the lawyer who issues a tax shelter opinion are briefly summarized below. However, *reference to this summary must not be substituted for a review of the more complete statement of ethical standards contained in this Opinion.*

1.　Establish in the beginning the lawyer's relationship with the offeror-client, making clear that in order to issue the opinion, the lawyer requires from that client a full disclosure of the structure and intended operations of the venture and complete access to all relevant information.

2.　Make inquiry as to the relevant facts and, consistent with the standards developed in ABA Formal Opinion 335, be satisfied that the material facts are accurately and completely stated in the offering materials, and that the representations as to intended future activities are clearly identified, reasonable and complete.

3.　Relate the law to the actual facts to the extent ascertainable and, when addressing issues based on future activities, clearly identify what facts are assumed.

4.　Make inquiries to ascertain that a good faith effort has been made to address legal issues other than those to be addressed in the tax shelter opinion.

5.　Take reasonable steps to assure that all material federal income and excise tax issues have been considered and that all of those issues which involve the reasonable possibility of a challenge by the Internal Revenue Service have been fully and fairly addressed in the offering materials.

6.　Where possible, provide an opinion as to the likely outcome on the merits of the material tax issues addressed in the offering materials.

7.　Where possible, provide an overall evaluation of the extent to which the tax benefts in the aggregate are likely to be realized.

8.　Assure that the offering materials correctly represent the nature and extent of the tax shelter opinion.

Questions

1. It has been noted that Formal Opinion 346 at the time it was issued "reflect[ed] much of the content of the proposed Circular 230 amendments." James P. Holden, New Professional Standards In the Tax Marketplace: Opinions 314, 346 and Circular 230, 4 Va. Tax Rev. 209, 218 (1985). Why would the ABA bother to issue an opinion after the proposed amendments to Circular 230?

2. Since there was much overlap between Formal Opinion 346 and the then proposed amendments to Circular 230, why did the Treasury Department not withdraw the proposed amendments?

3. Both Circular 230 and ABA Formal Opinion 346 permit a lawyer to issue a "negative opinion," in which the opinion must clearly state that the material tax benefits specified in the offering probably will not be allowable by the IRS. If an investor disregards the opinion and claims these benefits on a return, does the investor have any defense to a substantial understatement penalty under § 6662?

4. What is the significance of the following passage from Formal Opinion 346?

> The Proposed Model Rules specifically recognize the ethical considerations applicable where a lawyer undertakes an evaluation for the use of third persons other than a client. These third persons have an interest in the integrity of the evaluation. The legal duty of the lawyer therefore "goes beyond the obligations a lawyer normally has to third persons."

3. Standards of Practice – CPAs

The American Institute of Certified Public Accountants (AICPA) has issued Statements on Standards for Tax Services to provide guidance to its members. The AICPA Statements differ from the ABA Opinions in that the AICPA takes the position that the realistic possibility standard cannot be expressed in terms of a percentage. It notes that "the realistic possibility standard is less stringent that the 'substantial authority' and the 'more likely than not' standards that apply under the Internal Revenue Code to substantial understatements of liability by taxpayers. But it is more strict than the 'reasonable basis' standard * * *." See Statement On Standards for Tax Services Interpretation No. 1-1 Issued August 2000, § 7.

The AICPA also is more thoughtful in its attitude to the realistic possibility standard than is the ABA. Compare the following:

ABA Formal Opinion 85-382 – * * * a lawyer may advise reporting a position on a return even where the lawyer believes the position probably will not prevail, there is no 'substantial authority' in support of the position, and there will be no disclosure of the position in the return. However, the position to be asserted must be one which the lawyer in good faith believes is warranted in existing law or can be supported by a good faith argument for an extension, modification or reversal of existing law. This requires that there is some realistic possibility of success if the matter is litigated. In addition, in his role as advisor, the lawyer should refer to potential penalties and other legal consequences should the client take the position advised.

AICPA Statement on Standards for Tax Services No. 1, Tax Return Positions *

1. This statement sets forth the applicable standards for members when recommending tax return positions, or preparing or signing tax returns (including amended returns, claims for refund, and information returns) filed with any taxing authority. For purposes of these standards,

     a. a *tax return position* is (i) a position reflected on a tax return on which a member has specifically advised a taxpayer or (ii) a position about which a member has knowledge of all material facts and, on the basis of those facts, has concluded whether the position is appropriate.

     * * *

2. This statement also addresses a member's obligation to advise a taxpayer of relevant tax return disclosure responsibilities and potential penalties.

3. In addition to the AICPA, various taxing authorities, at the federal, state, and local levels, may impose specific reporting and disclosure standards with regard to recommending tax return positions or preparing or signing tax returns.[1] These standards can vary between taxing authorities and by type of tax.

---

     *   AICPA Statement on Standards for Tax Services No. 1, Tax Return Positions Copyright © 2009. American Institute of Certified Public Accountants, Inc. All rights reserved. Used with permission.

     1.   A member should refer to the current version of Internal Revenue Code § 6694, Understatement of taxpayer's liability by tax return preparer, and other relevant federal, state, and jurisdictional authorities to determine the reporting and disclosure standards that are applicable to preparers of tax returns.

4. A member should determine and comply with the standards, if any, that are imposed by the applicable taxing authority with respect to recommending a tax return position, or preparing or signing a tax return.

5. If the applicable taxing authority has no written standards with respect to recommending a tax return position or preparing or signing a tax return, or if its standards are lower than the standards set forth in this paragraph, the following standards will apply:

a. A member shall not recommend a tax return position or prepare or sign a tax return taking a position unless the member has a good-faith belief that the position has at least a realistic possibility of being sustained administratively or judicially on its merits if challenged.

b. Notwithstanding paragraph 5(a), a member may *recommend a tax return position* if the member (i) concludes that there is a reasonable basis for the position and (ii) advises the taxpayer to appropriately disclose that position. Notwithstanding paragraph 5(a), a member may *prepare or sign a tax return* that reflects a position if (I) the member concludes that there is a reasonable basis for the position and (ii) the position is appropriately disclosed.

6. When recommending a tax return position or when preparing or signing a tax return on which a position is taken, a member should, when relevant, advise the taxpayer regarding potential penalty consequences of such tax return position and the opportunity, if any, to avoid such penalties through disclosure.

7. A member should not recommend a tax return position or prepare or sign a tax return reflecting a position that the member knows

a. exploits the audit selection process of a taxing authority, or

b. serves as a mere arguing position advanced solely to obtain leverage in a negotiation with a taxing authority.

8. When recommending a tax return position, a member has both the right and the responsibility to be an advocate for the taxpayer with respect to any position satisfying the aforementioned standards.

9. The AICPA and various taxing authorities impose specific reporting and disclosure standards with respect to tax return positions and preparing or signing tax returns. In a given situation, the standards, if any, imposed by the applicable taxing authority may be higher or lower than the standards set forth in paragraph 5. A member is to comply with the standards, if any, of the applicable

taxing authority; if the applicable taxing authority has no standards or if its standards are lower than the standards set forth in paragraph 5, the standards set forth in paragraph 5 will apply.

10. Our self-assessment tax system can function effectively only if taxpayers file tax returns that are true, correct, and complete. A tax return is prepared based on a taxpayer's representation of facts, and the taxpayer has the final responsibility for positions taken on the return. The standards that apply to a taxpayer may differ from the standards that apply to a member.

11. In addition to a duty to the taxpayer, a member has a duty to the tax system. However, it is well established that a taxpayer has no obligation to pay more taxes than are legally owed, and a member has a duty to the taxpayer to assist in achieving that result. The standards contained in paragraphs 4-8 recognize a member's responsibilities to both the taxpayer and the tax system.

12. In reaching a conclusion concerning whether a given standard in paragraph 4 or 5 has been satisfied, a member may consider a well-reasoned construction of the applicable statute, well-reasoned articles or treatises, or pronouncements issued by the applicable taxing authority, regardless of whether such sources would be treated as *authority* by Internal Revenue Code § 6662, *Imposition of accuracy-related penalty on underpayments*, and the regulations thereunder. A position would not fail to meet these standards merely because it is later abandoned for practical or procedural considerations during an administrative hearing or in the litigation process.

13. If a member has a good-faith belief that more than one tax return position meets the standards set forth in paragraphs 4-5, a member's advice concerning alternative acceptable positions may include a discussion of the likelihood that each such position might or might not cause the taxpayer's tax return to be examined and whether the position would be challenged in an examination. In such circumstances, such advice is not a violation of paragraph 7.

14. A member's determination of whether information is appropriately disclosed by the taxpayer should be based on the facts and circumstances of the particular case and the disclosure requirements of the applicable taxing authority. If a member recommending a position, but not engaged to prepare or sign the related tax return, advises the taxpayer concerning appropriate disclosure of the position, then the member shall be deemed to meet the disclosure requirements of these standards.

15. If particular facts and circumstances lead a member to

believe that a taxpayer penalty might be asserted, the member should so advise the taxpayer and should discuss with the taxpayer the opportunity, if any, to avoid such penalty by disclosing the position on the tax return. Although the member should advise the taxpayer with respect to disclosure, it is the taxpayer's responsibility to decide whether or how to disclose.

16. For purposes of this statement, preparation of a tax return includes giving advice on events that have occurred at the time the advice is given if the advice is directly relevant to determining the existence, character, or amount of a schedule, entry, or other portion of a tax return.

Question

ABA Formal Opinion 85-352 has been criticized for inviting exploitation of the audit lottery. See Theodore C. Falk, Tax Ethics, Legal Ethics, and Real Ethics: A Critique of ABA Formal Opinion 85-352, 39 Tax Law. 643, 647-49 (1986); Gwen Thayer Handleman, Constraining Aggressive Return Advice, 9 Va. Tax Rev. 77, 95 (1989). Do you see any other differences between the positions of the ABA and the AICPA?

E. ADMINISTRATIVE STANDARDS –
CIRCULAR 230

1. General Standards Applicable to Practitioners

Prior to the amendments to § 6694 in 2007 and 2008, Circular 230 contained language similar to that of § 6694, which prohibited a tax practitioner from signing a return as a preparer if the return contained a position that did not have a realistic possibility of being sustained on the merits. Since the amendments to § 6694, however, the language of the preparer penalty provision is no longer in sync with Circular 230. Recall that under § 6694, the practitioner may sign as a preparer without fear of penalty provided any aggressive return positions have a reasonable basis and are adequately disclosed. The standard under Circular 230 is lower than the standard under the revised penalty provision. Under Circular 230, a practitioner may not advise a client to take a position in any submission to the IRS unless the position is not frivolous. Circular 230 goes one step farther than the penalty provision, though, in providing that the practitioner must inform the client of the penalties that are reasonably likely to apply if the client fails to disclose an aggressive position, even though the practitioner is not subject to a preparer penalty.

In advising a client to take a position on a return, or in preparing the return, or in signing as a preparer, the practitioner may rely without verification upon information furnished by the client. Circ. 230, § 10.34 (a)(3). But the practitioner may not ignore implications of this information and must make reasonable inquiries if the information appears to be incorrect, inconsistent, or incomplete. Id. Query whether the practitioner has a greater duty of inquiry if the client chooses not to disclose a return position contrary to the advice of the practitioner?

Violations of Circular 230 that are the result of willful or reckless conduct, or gross incompetence will subject the practitioner to suspension or disbarment from practice before the Service. Circ. 230, §§ 10.52 and 10.50). A pattern of conduct may establish or aid in establishing willfulness, recklessness, or gross incompetence. Conviction of a criminal offense, or of any offense involving dishonesty or breach of trust, is also grounds for disbarment.

Disbarment raises a host of problems for the practitioner beyond the obvious one of no longer being able to practice before the Service. If the practitioner is a lawyer or an accountant, the Office of Professional Responsibility will notify any other interested departments and agencies of the federal government, as well as the proper state authorities, of the disbarment. See Circ. 230, § 10.80. This, in turn, could lead to the disbarment of the lawyer or accountant from the practice of law or accountancy. If it does not lead to state disbarment proceedings, so that the practitioner may continue to practice in that state, a further problem for the practitioner is that under Circular 230, knowingly aiding and abetting a person who has been suspended or disbarred from practicing before the Service, or maintaining a professional partnership with such a person, will be considered disreputable conduct subject to sanction. Circ. 230, § 10.24 and § 10.51(a)(11).

Circular 230 places the civil return preparer penalty under § 6694(a) in a different perspective. While the nonwillful, nonreckless understatement penalty is currently a more meaningful penalty since it has been increased from $250 per return to the greater of 50% of the fee or $1,000 per return, it also may establish a pattern of misconduct that, at best, could subject the practitioner to higher scrutiny by the Service and at worst, could subject the practitioner to disciplinary action under Circular 230.

HARARY v. UNITED STATES
United States Court of Appeals, Second Circuit, 1977.
555 F.2d 1113.

OAKES, CIRCUIT JUDGE.

Appellant, a certified public accountant, seeks by this appeal to avoid "disbarment" from practice before the Internal Revenue Service (IRS). He was disbarred in an administrative disciplinary proceeding before the Secretary of the Treasury, pursuant to 31 U.S.C. § 1026 and regulations thereunder, and sought review of the administrative decision in the United States District Court for the Southern District of New York* * *. Assuming jurisdiction, the district court granted summary judgment for the Secretary. We affirm.

I.

Appellant's disbarment arose out of a prior criminal proceeding in which he was charged with bribing and conspiring to bribe a special agent of the IRS in violation of 18 U.S.C. §§ 201(b), 371, and with paying the agent a gratuity in violation of 18 U.S.C. § 201(f). He admitted that he had paid the agent the sum of $1,250 on behalf of his client, that he had told the client that the agent wanted $2,000 and that he (appellant) had kept the $750 difference.

Appellant was tried before a jury and was acquitted of the conspiracy and bribery charges, but was convicted of the gratuity charge. On appeal this court reversed the conviction on the gratuity charge and ordered that count of the indictment dismissed. United States v. Harary, 457 F.2d 471 (2d Cir. 1972). The court held that the district court had erred in submitting the lesser included gratuity offense to the jury, because there was no disputed factual element that would have allowed the jury rationally to conclude that appellant was guilty of the lesser offense but not of the greater offense of bribery. Id., at 477-78.

Subsequently, Treasury Department officials filed an administrative complaint, pursuant to 31 C.F.R. § 10.54, seeking appellant's disbarment from practice before the IRS. The grounds alleged included appellant's attempt to influence an agent in the conduct of an audit of appellant's client and appellant's overstating to his client the amount of the payment that the agent had agreed to accept. Following a hearing, at which the parties jointly offered in evidence the transcript from appellant's criminal trial, an administrative law judge (ALJ) found that appellant had committed the acts charged and ordered appellant disbarred. Appellant's appeal to the Secretary of the Treasury resulted in an opinion by the Department's General Counsel, acting on behalf of the Secretary, affirming the ALJ's decision in all respects. Appellant then sought relief in the district court and from that court's order took the instant appeal.

II.

In support of appellant's contention that the disbarment decision should be overturned, the principal argument is that collateral estoppel prevents his being disbarred for bribery and conspiracy to bribe, since he was acquitted of those charges at his prior criminal trial. This acquittal, appellant reasons, "definitely" establishes that he was entrapped by the IRS into paying the bribe, because at his trial appellant admitted the payment and relied wholly on an entrapment defense. Appellant's legal premise, however, is clearly wrong. The standard of proof in a criminal trial is guilt beyond a reasonable doubt. An acquittal in such a trial, under such a standard, cannot control a subsequent disbarment proceeding, in which a lower standard of proof is required. Moreover, the issue in a disbarment proceeding is essentially fitness to practice, rather than the criminality of the acts involved. See Bar Association v. Anonymous Attorneys, 45 U.S.L.W. 2478 (N.Y. Ct. App. Apr. 5, 1977) (per curiam).

Even were appellant's legal premise correct, however, his factual premise that the jury's verdict constituted a finding of entrapment is clearly incorrect in the circumstances of this case. As noted above, the jury at appellant's trial, while acquitting him of the bribery charges, found him guilty of giving the IRS agent a gratuity. This court later stated that the jury's verdict amounted to "a compromise." *United States v. Harary, supra,* 457 F.2d at 479. The jury, in the court's view, could not rationally have concluded that appellant had been entrapped by the IRS into giving a bribe but not entrapped into giving a gratuity. Id. at 478. From such a compromise verdict it cannot be said that the question of entrapment was "necessarily determined" against the Government, as is required to support a later holding of collateral estoppel, see United States v. Kramer, 289 F.2d 909, 916 (2d Cir. 1961); 2 C. Wright, Federal Practice and Procedure § 468, at 263 (1969), nor can it be said that a finding of entrapment was the only one consistent with the evidence and the verdict. Under these circumstances, when it is uncertain exactly what the jury decided on a particular issue in a prior criminal action, the issue may be litigated in a later, noncriminal action. See United States v. Davis, 460 F.2d 792, 799 (4th Cir. 1972).

III.

As a separate ground for disbarring appellant, a ground unrelated to his prior criminal trial, the Secretary held that appellant had willfully deceived his client.[3] As stated above, appellant told his client that the IRS agent had to be paid $2,000, but appellant in fact paid the agent $1,250, pocketing the $750 difference for himself. The Secretary held that his conduct violated 31 C.F.R. § 10.22(c), which requires that each attorney, certified public accountant or enrolled agent "exercise due diligence * * * [i]n determining the correctness of oral or written representations made by him to clients with reference to any matter administered by the Internal Revenue Service." Appellant argues that this regulation has not been violated or, in the alternative, that the regulation is unconstitutionally vague.

With regard to the first point, appellant's position is that 31 C.F.R § 10.22(c) was not meant to apply to conduct of the type here involved. A requirement that practitioners before the IRS make correct representations to clients with regard to illegal courses of conduct, appellant reasons, would encourage illegality by practitioners in situations in which it could otherwise be avoided. He cites the hypothetical example of an IRS agent soliciting a bribe from an accountant and argues that, under the Secretary's interpretation of the regulation, the accountant could be disbarred for failing truthfully to communicate the criminal overture to his client. We need not determine the correctness of appellant's resolution of the hypothetical, for, even if he were correct that the overture had to be reported to the client, the accountant would also have an obligation to advise his client against participation and to report the entire matter to the proper officials of the IRS. See 31 C.F.R. § 10.51(d), (f). Hence there would be no fostering of illegality unless the accountant were already so disposed.

The regulation at issue, 31 C.F.R. § 10.22(c), requires, quite simply, that a representative be honest with his client in connection with all IRS-related matters. While the phrasing of the regulation ("due diligence in determining correctness") suggests a principal concern with making

---

3.   The Secretary argues that this ground was "independent" of the bribery ground, thereby implying that we could uphold appellant's disbarment solely on the basis of his deception of the client. Neither the General Counsel's nor the ALJ's opinion, however, definitively states that the sanction of permanent disbarment would have been ordered had this deception been the only misconduct alleged against appellant. Neither the statute nor [the] regulation makes disbarment mandatory in such circumstances. The administrative complaint sought suspension as an alternative to disbarment. See also 31 U.S.C. § 1026; 31 C.F.R. §§ 10.50, 10.52. Accordingly, if we are to uphold appellant's disbarment without a remand, we must determine both the bribery and client deception issues in favor of the Secretary.

representatives accountable for negligence, nothing in the regulation limits it to cases of negligence. The term "diligence" carries connotations of loyalty and devotion as well as care and prudence. A deliberate conveying of misinformation is certainly more opprobrious conduct than a careless misrepresentation. Appellant does not dispute the fact that he was deliberately dishonest with his client and, since the dishonesty related to an IRS agent's audit, it was plainly a representation "with reference to [a] matter administered by the [IRS]." Appellant accordingly violated 31 C.F.R. § 10.22(c).

In view of our construction of the regulation, appellant's vagueness argument is rejected. He contends that the words of the regulation did not give notice that a misrepresentation to a client in connection with an audit could lead to disbarment. Apart from the fact that every professional knows or should know that cheating a client can lead to disbarment, the regulation here gave quite specific notice that representations to clients must be correct with regard to a wide but clearly defined range of matters.

Judgment affirmed.

Notes and Question

In 2009, an Administrative Law Judge dismissed a complaint brought by the OPR against a prominent tax attorney for purported violation of the due diligence requirements under § 10.22. The OPR sought to suspend the attorney from practicing before the IRS for one year because of several short-form tax opinions the attorney had written on leasing transactions later challenged by the IRS as abusive tax shelter transactions. The OPR alleged that the attorney had engaged in disreputable conduct by failing to adequately analyze the relevant law and facts in writing the opinions. The Administrative Law Judge held in favor of the attorney, concluding that the short-form opinions were standard practice at the time they were written and that the OPR had failed to prove by clear and convincing evidence that the attorney had acted unreasonably or that he had failed to use due diligence.

Interestingly, one of the attorney's witnesses was Larry Langdon, former Commissioner of the Large and Midsized Business Division of the IRS who had been involved in drafting the IRS guidelines for practitioners. He testified that it was "typical and an accepted practice for outside counsel to use the short form."

This begs the question of why the case was brought in the first place. The answer to this may be found in footnote 10 of the decision: "Respondent has repeatedly questioned OPR's good faith in bringing this proceeding. However, it appears that if he had been more forthcoming during OPR's investigation of his conduct in preparing the basis opinions, this complaint might not have been issued." See Director, OPR v. Sykes, No. 2006-1, Doc. 2009-11345(Jan. 29, 2009).

1. Can a practitioner be disbarred by the Service solely for misleading a client?

2. What is a practitioner's duty when she discovers that there is an error or omission on a client's filed return? See Circular 230, § 10.21.

3. Section 10.27 reflects a softening of the Service's position prohibiting contingent fees. The amended provision allows such fees under three limited circumstances: (1) in connection with the Service's examination or challenge to an original return; or an amended return or refund claim filed within 120 days of the taxpayer's receiving written notice of the examination or challenge to the original return, (2) in connection with a claim for credit or refund filed for the determination of statutory interest or penalties assessed by the IRS, and (3) for services rendered in connection with any judicial proceeding arising under the Code. What is the policy in general behind the Service's change of position and what is the reason for the exceptions?

2. Tax Shelter Opinions

The high tax rates of the 1970's led to the mass-marketing of tax shelters to middle class Americans, who enthusiastically embraced the notion that solid investments could generate tax preferences many times greater than the initial investment. Thus, the investments would cost them little or nothing in the long run because of the tax savings they would enjoy. Promoters were quick to recognize the opportunities presented to them, and they began to market tax shelter investments at prices and credit terms geared to the smaller investor.

By the late 1970's, there was a proliferation of tax shelters, many of them perceived by the Service as abusive. Abusive shelters are those in which the tax benefits are overstated due to overvaluation of the underlying property and/or other mischaracterization of the investment. Because of these abusive tax shelters, the Treasury Department lost vast amounts of revenue. In the words of one commentator, "tax shelters have created a crisis in federal tax administration of unprecedented proportions." D. French Slaughter, III, The Empire Strikes Back: Injunctions of Abusive Tax Shelters After TEFRA, 3 Va. Tax Rev. 1, 2 (1983).

The crisis was fueled by the issuance of misleading tax shelter opinions by attorneys, which facilitated the marketing of abusive shelters. These opinions, through a variety of means, appeared to sanction the promoted tax benefits, when in fact the benefits were not allowable. Since most smaller investors lacked the sophistication to decipher the tax opinion letters, they were deceived into making what they thought was a legitimate investment. See James P. Holden, New Professional Standards In The Tax Marketplace: Opinions 314, 346 and Circular 230, 4 Va. Tax Rev. 209, 212-18 (1985).

As part of its campaign to curb abusive tax shelters, the Treasury Department warned that it would severely discipline attorneys who issued misleading opinions to promote such shelters, unless the organized bar accepted its responsibility by regulating these attorneys. The bar was slow to act, however, and on September 3, 1980, the Treasury Department carried out its threat by issuing proposed amendments to Circular 230, establishing stricter standards of conduct for practitioners who provide tax shelter opinions.

Under the proposed amendments, a tax practitioner issuing a tax shelter opinion was required to exercise due diligence in fully disclosing and describing the facts and legal issues; to exercise due diligence in ascertaining that the offering materials accurately described the practitioner's opinion; and to refrain from issuing a negative opinion in which the practitioner concluded that the tax benefits of the shelter probably would not be allowed if challenged by the IRS.

In 1984, the amendments were issued in final form and they applied to *any* tax shelter, whether abusive or not. Under these amendments, the realistic possibility standard of conduct generally applicable to practitioners was increased for tax shelter opinions.[7] The applicable standard was that the material tax benefits would "more likely than not" be realized. This meant that the practitioner must believe in good faith that there is a greater than 50 percent chance that the material tax

---

7.   A tax shelter was defined as an investment in which the tax benefits are expected to exceed the income generated by the activity. A tax shelter opinion was defined as advice concerning the federal tax aspects of a tax shelter either referred to or appearing in the offering materials, or used or referred to in connection with sales promotion efforts, and directed to persons other than the client who engaged the practitioner. Circ. 230, § 10.33(c)(3)(1984).

benefits[8] will be realized if challenged by the Service. Circ. 230, § 10.33(a)(5).[9]

In the late 1990's, it became clear that the earlier efforts to curb abusive tax shelters had not been successful. Instead, the transactions became more sophisticated and were marketed, often under conditions of confidentiality, by unscrupulous accountants and attorneys to corporations and other business entities, as well as to wealthy individuals. The linchpin of these transactions was the tax opinion letter. This letter was used to market the transactions and also was used by investors as an insurance policy to establish "reasonable cause" under § 6664(c) to avoid penalties in the event the tax benefits of the shelter were disallowed.

In 2005, Treasury issued new regulations under Circular 230 to prevent the "rush to the bottom" and to restore confidence in the tax system. These regulations pertain to tax opinions and they establish more stringent standards for tax professionals. These standards govern three aspects of tax advice: (1) an inspirational standard called "best practices" that practitioners should seek to attain but which do not carry sanctions for failure to comply, (2) a mandatory standard for "covered opinions" and (3) a mandatory standard for "other written advice" that is not a covered opinion.

a. Covered Opinions

A covered opinion is written advice, including electronic communication, on federal tax issues arising from (1) a "listed" transaction, (2) a partnership or other entity, plan or arrangement, the principal purpose of which is the avoidance or evasion of federal tax, or (3) a partnership

---

8. Material benefits are those flowing from a tax shelter (1) offering deductions in excess of the income from the investment, or tax credits offsetting liabilities in excess of the tax attributable to the shelter investment in any taxable year, (2) that reasonably could be expected to have a significant impact on a shelter investor, and (3) which may subject the investor to penalties, interest, or additions to tax with respect to the tax shelter. Id., at § 10.33(b)(4). In determining whether or not there is a greater than 50 percent chance of material tax benefits being realized, the practitioner may rely on the advice of another practitioner, provided the practitioner being relied upon is competent and there is no reason to believe that this practitioner has not complied with the proper standards. Id., at § 10.33(b)(1).

9. The final amendments also provided that a practitioner rendering a tax shelter opinion has a greater duty of inquiry and cannot rely on unverified information, including any appraisals or financial information, furnished by the client if the practitioner should have any reason to question the information, based on her knowledge or background. The practitioner may rely on such information, however, if it is reasonable on its face, made by a competent person, and based on a definition of fair market value that is in accordance with federal tax provisions. Circ. 230, § 10.33(a)(1)(1984).

or other entity, or a plan or arrangement, a significant purpose of which is the avoidance or evasion of federal tax, if the written advice is (a) a reliance opinion, (b) a marketed opinion, (c) subject to conditions of confidentiality, or (d) subject to contractual protection. 31 C.F.R § 10.35(b)(2). Excluded from the definition is written advice provided by a practitioner who is reasonably expected to provide subsequent written advice that meets the covered opinion standard. Also excluded is written advice concerning the qualification of a qualified plan, a state or local bond opinion, or documents required to be filed with the Securities and Exchange Commission.

A listed transaction is any transaction the IRS identifies in published guidelines under Treas. Reg. § 1.6011-4(b)(2) and transactions that are "substantially similar" to an identified transaction.

A partnership or other entity, plan or arrangement has a principal purpose to avoid or evade federal tax if this purpose exceeds any other purpose. If tax benefits are claimed in a manner consistent with the Code or Congressional intent, this does not constitute a principal purpose to avoid or evade tax. *Id.* at § 10.35(b)(10). A partnership, entity, plan or arrangement may have a significant purpose of avoidance or evasion without having a principal purpose of avoidance or evasion. *Id.*

A reliance opinion is written advice that concludes that the tax benefits at issue will more likely than not be sustained. A written opinion that prominently discloses that the taxpayer cannot use the opinion for purposes of avoiding penalties is not considered a reliance opinion.

A federal tax issue is significant if the IRS has a reasonable basis for challenging the position and the resolution could have a significant impact on the tax treatment of the transaction addressed in the opinion. *Id.* at § 10.35(b)(3).

A marketed opinion is written advice that will be used, either directly or indirectly, in the promotion, marketing or recommendation of a plan or investment. A practitioner may issue a marketed opinion only if she concludes that it is more likely than not that the taxpayer will prevail on each of the significant federal tax issues in the opinion. In addition, the opinion must disclose the relationship between the promoter and the practitioner, including the compensation arrangement. An opinion will not be considered a marketed opinion if it prominently discloses that it was provided to support the promotion or marketing of the transaction, that it cannot be used to avoid penalties and that the taxpayer should seek independent tax advice.

An opinion is subject to confidentiality if the practitioner imposes limitations on the disclosure of the tax treatment or tax structure of the transaction or the tax strategies of the practitioner.

A written opinion has contractual protection if the taxpayer has a right to a refund of fees if the transaction does not result in a reduction of the taxpayer's taxes.

A practitioner who gives a covered opinion must adhere to certain strict due diligence requirements under Circular 230. These include considering and specifically identifying all relevant facts without basing any part of the opinion on unreasonable factual assumptions or representations; relating the applicable law to the facts; considering all significant federal tax issues and making a conclusion as to the likelihood of the taxpayer's succeeding on the merits with respect to each of those issues; and providing an overall conclusion as to the likelihood that the federal tax treatment of the transaction will be upheld. *See id.* at § 10.35(c). In addition, the opinion must prominently disclose the relationship between the promoter and practitioner, including any compensation arrangement and any referral agreement between the parties. *Id.* at § 10.35(e)(1).

Circular 230 permits limited scope opinions that address less than all of the federal tax issues, provided the attorney and client explicitly agree to a limited scope opinion, the opinion is clear is that is limited in scope and that it may not be used to avoid penalties with respect to significant tax issues outside the scope of the opinion. If the opinion does not conclude that the tax benefits will more likely than not be realized, it must prominently disclose that fact and must state that with respect to those issues, the opinion was not written and cannot be used by the taxpayer for purposes of avoiding penalties. *Id.* at § 10.35(e)(4).

b. *Other Written Advice*

Written advice, including electronic communications, that does not fall into the covered opinion category is considered "other written advice." This advice is subject to less stringent requirements than covered opinions. The practitioner must not base the advice on unreasonable factual or legal assumptions, or unreasonably rely on representations, statements, findings or agreements of the taxpayer or any other person. The practitioner must consider all relevant facts that she knows or should know but may not take into account the possibility of the return not being audited, that an issue will not be raised on audit, or the likelihood of an issue being resolved through settlement if raised. *Id.* at § 10.37. There is a heightened standard applicable in the case of an opinion that the practitioner knows or has reason to know will be used or referred to in the promotion, marketing or recommendation of a partnership or other entity, investment plan or arrangement a significant purpose of which is the avoidance or evasion of federal tax.

Notes and Question

There has been much criticism of the tax opinion standards because the term "covered opinion" goes beyond tax shelter opinion letters and is broadly defined to cover routine tax advice, while the sanctions are severe. If a practitioner fails to comply with the requirements of Circular 230, the Secretary of the Treasury is authorized to censure, suspend or disbar the practitioner from practice before the IRS. The Secretary also may impose a monetary penalty in addition to or in lieu of the other sanctions.

While disbarment under Circular 230 prevents a practitioner from practicing only before the IRS, this is a very serious penalty because the practitioner also will be prohibited from filing returns on behalf of clients and other practitioners will be prohibited from accepting assistance, either directly or indirectly, from a disbarred individual. Thus, this sanction essentially brings to an end the practitioner's ability to practice in the tax area, at least as far as appearing before the IRS, submitting documents to the IRS and working as a tax advisor with a law firm or accounting firm.

1. The disclaimer commonly seen on emails and other informal communications that any opinion expressed therein may not be used to avoid penalties is an attempt to avoid the covered opinion requirements of Circular 230. Under what circumstances will the disclaimer be successful in enabling the practitioner to avoid the regulatory requirements and under what circumstances will it not be successful?

2. Are there any other circumstances under which a disclaimer will be successful in avoiding the regulatory requirements?

3. What is the difference between a covered opinion and other written advice?

4. What problems, if any, do the covered opinion requirements present? See Deborah H. Schenk, *The Circular 230 Amendments: Time to Throw Them Out and Start Over*, 110 Tax Notes 1311 (2006).

5. The Circular 230 amendments require more stringent standards for tax practitioners than the ABA standards. What does this mean for tax practitioners?

III. THE GOVERNMENT'S CONFLICTING DUTIES OF DISCLOSURE AND CONFIDENTIALITY

A. FREEDOM OF INFORMATION ACT

The Freedom of Information Act (FOIA), enacted in 1966, amended the public disclosure section of the Administrative Procedure Act to establish a statutory right of access to virtually every federal agency record, unless such record (or portion thereof) is protected from disclosure by one of the nine exemptions or by one of three special law enforcement record exclusions under the Act. The policy behind the Act was summarized by President Clinton in 1993:

> For more than a quarter century now, the Freedom of Information Act has played a unique role in strengthening our democratic form of government. The statute was enacted based upon the fundamental principle that an informed citizenry is essential to the democratic process and that the more the American people know about their government the better they will be governed. Openness in government is essential to accountability and the Act has become an integral part of that process.[10]

It was through the FOIA that the IRS Manual, letter rulings, and technical advice memoranda initially were made available to the public, although requests for rulings, technical advice memoranda and other related materials currently must be made available in accordance with the Code under § 6110, instead of the FOIA. The release of the IRS materials has had a dramatic effect on tax practice, because it has helped to level the playing field for taxpayers in dealing with the Service. This material can provide an indication to taxpayers of how they are being treated by the Service relative to other taxpayers, it can provide an indication of whether the Service is following its own procedural rules in particular cases, and it can help taxpayers apply the law to their particular sets of facts. These taxpayers now have access to the data used by the Service in their cases and thus they are better able to challenge positions they believe are improper or unfair.

The public's right to know, however, must be balanced against the government's interest in prudent use of its limited fiscal resources and in the preservation of confidentiality of sensitive information. FOIA maintains this balance by delineating certain categories of information

---

10. President's Memorandum for Heads of Departments and Agencies regarding the Free-dom of Information Act, 29 Weekly Comp. Pres. Doc. 1999 (Oct. 4, 1993), reprinted in FOIA Update, Summer/Fall 1993, at 3, and in Justin D. Franklin and Robert F. Bouchard, GUIDE-BOOK TO THE FREEDOM OF INFORMATION AND PRIVACY ACTS 1-17 (2d ed. 1997).

that must be disclosed automatically by federal agencies and other categories in which the agencies may withhold information in their discretion. There is also a middle category under the FOIA in which information may be disclosed upon receipt of a proper access request.

There are two types of information that fall within the automatic release category. The first type consists of descriptions of agency organization, statements and rules of procedure, substantive rules of general applicability, and statements of policy. This information is considered of wide interest to the general public, and must be published in the Federal Register. If the agency fails to publish the information in the required manner, the FOIA provides that no person may be adversely affected by this failure. 5 U.S.C. § 552(a)(1). The second category consists of court decisions, staff manuals, and certain policy statements, all of which are of general interest to the public. This information must be made available in "reading rooms" (including electronic reading rooms available on the World Wide Web) for public inspection and copying. If an agency fails to make its required information available, it is precluded from relying on or citing the information as authority.

There are nine categories of information that are exempted from disclosure. These are (1) matters classified as secret by Executive Order that are in the interest of national defense or foreign policy, (2) agency internal personnel rules and practices, (3) materials specifically exempted from disclosure by statute, (4) trade secrets and privileged or confidential information obtained from a person, (5) internal agency memoranda or other communications which are not otherwise available by law except to another agency in a litigation context, (6) personnel and medical files, the release of which would constitute an unwarranted invasion of personal privacy, (7) certain records or information compiled for law enforcement purposes, (8) material contained in the reports of an agency responsible for the regulation or supervision of financial institutions, and (9) geological and geophysical information and data, including maps, concerning wells.

There are three categories under exemption seven for investigatory records compiled for law enforcement purposes. These categories of exclusion are designed to protect the integrity of an ongoing criminal investigation, to protect the safety of an informant, or to protect national security. The Service has invoked these exemptions to prevent release of confidential information that could compromise the integrity of ongoing fraud investigations.

Any reasonably described agency records and information that are not exempted or excluded by the FOIA must be made available to any person who submits a proper access request to the agency. The term "person" under the FOIA includes individuals, partnerships, corporations, associations and foreign or domestic governments.

The fact that a record contains some exempt material does not necessarily preclude the release of the record. The FOIA provides that "any reasonably segregable portion of a record shall be provided to any person requesting such record after deletion of the portions which are exempt under this subsection." [11] The United States Supreme Court has held that tax return information has statutory protection and can be released only if it is part of a composite statistical study or report, and then only if no identifying material is included. [12]

The FOIA permits the agency to charge reasonable fees to comply with an access request. There are three levels of fees authorized under the FOIA and these vary according to the requester and the use to be made of the requested information. When the request is made for commercial use, the requester can be charged for the time spent looking for the material, even if the search is ultimately unsuccessful. [13] Also included within this level of fees is the time spent in perusing the document to ascertain whether an exemption or exclusion applies to prohibit disclosure, and the direct costs of reproducing the material and preparing it for release. When the purpose of the request is scientific or scholarly research, and the requester is an educational or noncommercial scientific institution or member of the news media, the search and review fees do not apply, and the requester will be charged only for the direct costs. The third level applies to requesters who do not fall within either of the other two categories. This level includes attorneys and accountants representing clients. The fees that may be charged at this level include reasonable charges for document searches, and direct costs of duplication and mailing. For all requesters except commercial enterprises, the agency must provide the first 100 pages of duplication and the first two hours of document search time at no cost to the requester.

If a request for access is denied, the person requesting the information may seek redress in the federal district courts, where jurisdiction is contingent upon a showing that the agency has (1) improperly (2) withheld (3) agency records. The burden is on the agency to establish that the requested material falls under one of the exemptions or exclusions. If the agency fails to carry this burden, the information must be made available to the requesting party.

---

11. 5 U.S.C. § 552(b)(1994), as amended by Pub. L. No. 104-231 (1996).

12. Church of Scientology of California v. I.R.S., 484 U.S. 9 (1987).

13. See Guzzino v. F.B.I., 1997 WL 22886 (D. DC. 1997).

U.S. DEPARTMENT OF JUSTICE v. TAX ANALYSTS
Supreme Court of the United States, 1989.
492 U.S. 136, 109 S.Ct. 2841, 106 L.Ed.2d 112.

JUSTICE MARSHALL delivered the opinion of the Court.

The question presented is whether the Freedom of Information Act (FOIA or Act), 5 U.S.C. § 552 (1982 ed. and Supp. V), requires the United States Department of Justice (Department) to make available copies of district court decisions that it receives in the course of litigating tax cases on behalf of the Federal Government. We hold that it does.

I.

The Department's Tax Division represents the Federal Government in nearly all civil tax cases in the district courts, the courts of appeals, and the Claims Court. Because it represents a party in litigation, the Tax Division receives copies of all opinions and orders issued by these courts in such cases. Copies of these decisions are made for the Tax Division's staff attorneys. The original documents are sent to the official files kept by the Department.

* * *

Respondent Tax Analysts publishes a weekly magazine, Tax Notes, which reports on legislative, judicial, and regulatory developments in the field of federal taxation to a readership largely composed of tax attorneys, accountants, and economists. As one of its regular features, Tax Notes provides summaries of recent federal-court decisions on tax issues. To supplement the magazine, Tax Analysts provides full texts of these decisions in microfiche form. Tax Analysts also publishes Tax Notes Today, a daily electronic data base that includes summaries and full texts of recent federal-court tax decisions.

In late July 1979, Tax Analysts filed a FOIA request in which it asked the Department to make available all district court tax opinions and final orders received by the Tax Division earlier that month. The Department denied the request on the ground that these decisions were not Tax Division records. Tax Analysts then appealed this denial adminis-tratively. While the appeal was pending, Tax Analysts agreed to with-draw its request in return for access to the Tax Divisions's weekly log of tax cases decided by the federal courts. These logs list the name and date of a case, the docket number, the names of counsel, the nature of the case, and its disposition.

Since gaining access to the weekly logs, Tax Analysts' practice has been to examine the logs and to request copies of the decisions noted therein from the clerks of the 90 or so district courts around the country and from participating attorneys. In most instances, Tax Analysts procures copies reasonably promptly, but this method of acquisition has proven unsatisfactory approximately 25% of the time. Some court clerks ignore Tax Analysts' requests for copies of decisions, and others respond slowly, sometimes only after Tax Analysts has forwarded postage and copying fees. Because the Federal Government is required to appeal tax cases within 60 days, Tax Analysts frequently fails to obtain copies of district court decisions before appeals are taken.

Frustrated with this process, Tax Analysts initiated a series of new FOIA requests in 1984. Beginning in November 1984, and continuing approximately once a week until May 1985, Tax Analysts asked the Department to make available copies of all district court tax opinions and final orders identified in the Tax Division's weekly logs. The Department denied these requests and Tax Analysts appealed administratively. When the Department sustained the denial, Tax Analysts filed the instant suit in the United States District Court for the District of Columbia, seeking to compel the Department to provide it with access to district court decisions received by the Tax Division.

The District Court granted the Department's motion to dismiss the complaint, holding that 5 U.S.C. §552(a)(4)(B), which confers jurisdiction in the district courts when "agency records" have been "improperly withheld,"[2] had not been satisfied. 643 F. Supp. 740, 742 (1986). The court reasoned that the district court decisions at issue had not been "improperly withheld" because they "already are available from their primary sources, the District Courts," id., at 743, and thus were "on the public record." Id., at 744. The court did not address whether the district court decisions are "agency records." Id., at 742.

The Court of Appeals for the District of Columbia Circuit reversed. 269 U.S. App. D.C. 315, 845 F.2d 1060 (1988). It first held that the district court decisions were "improperly withheld." An agency ordinarily may refuse to make available documents in its control only if it proves that the documents fall within one of the nine disclosure exemptions set forth in § 552(b), the court noted, and in this instance, "[n]o exemption

_____

2.   Section 552(a)(4)(B) provides:

"On complaint, the district court of the United States in the district in which the complainant resides, or has his principal place of business, or in which the agency records are situated, or in the District of Columbia, has jurisdiction to enjoin the agency from withholding agency records and to order the production of any agency records improperly withheld from the complainant. In such a case the court shall determine the matter de novo, and may examine the contents of such agency records in camera to determine whether such records or any part thereof shall be withheld under any of the exemptions set forth in subsection (b) of this section, and the burden is on the agency to sustain its action."

applies to the district court opinions." Id., at 319, 845 F.2d, at 1064. As for the Department's contention that the district court decisions are publicly available at their source, the court observed that "no court * * * has denied access to * * * documents on the ground that they are available elsewhere, and several have assumed that such documents must still be produced by the agency unless expressly exempted by the Act." Id., at 321, 845 F.2d, at 1066.

The Court of Appeals next held that the district court decisions sought by Tax Analysts are "agency records" for purposes of the FOIA. The court acknowledged that the district court decisions had originated in a part of the Government not covered by the FOIA, but concluded that the documents nonetheless constituted "agency records" because the Department has the discretion to use the decisions as it sees fit, because the Department routinely uses the decisions in performing its official duties, and because the decisions are integrated into the Department's official case files. The court therefore remanded the case to the District Court with instructions to enter an order directing the Department "to provide some reasonable form of access" to the decisions sought by Tax Analysts. Id., at 317, 845 F.2d, at 1062.

We granted certiorari, 488 U.S. 1003 (1989), and now affirm.

II.

In enacting the FOIA 23 years ago, Congress sought "'to open agency action to the light of public scrutiny.'" Department of Justice v. Reporters Committee for Freedom of Press, 489 U.S. 749, 772 (1989), quoting Department of Air Force v. Rose, 425 U.S. 352, 372 (1976). Congress did so by requiring agencies to adhere to "'a general philosophy of full agency disclosure.'" Id., at 360, quoting S. Rep. No. 813, 89th Cong., 1st Sess., 3 (1965). Congress believed that this philosophy, put into practice, would help "ensure an informed citizenry, vital to the functioning of a democratic society." NLRB v. Robbins Tire & Rubber Co., 437 U.S. 214, 242 (1978).

The FOIA confers jurisdiction on the district courts "to enjoin the agency from withholding agency records and to order the production of any agency records improperly withheld." § 552(a)(4)(B). Under this provision, "federal jurisdiction is dependent on a showing that an agency has (1) 'improperly' (2) 'withheld' (3) 'agency records.'" Kissinger v. Reporters Committee for Freedom of Press, 445 U.S. 136, 150 (1980). Unless each of these criteria is met, a district court lacks jurisdiction to devise remedies to force an agency to comply with the FOIA's disclosure requirements.[3]

In this case, all three jurisdictional terms are at issue. Although these terms are defined neither in the Act nor in its legislative history, we do not write on a clean slate. Nine Terms ago we decided three cases that explicated the meanings of these partially overlapping terms. Kissinger v. Reporters Committee for Freedom of Press, supra; Forsham v. Harris, 445 U.S. 169 (1980); GTE Sylvania, Inc. v. Consumers Union of United States, Inc., 445 U.S. 375 (1980). These decisions form the basis of our analysis of Tax Analysts' requests.

A.

We consider first whether the district court decisions at issue are "agency records," a term elaborated upon both in Kissinger and in *Forsham*. * * *

* * *

Two requirements emerge from *Kissinger* and *Forsham*, each of which must be satisfied for requested materials to qualify as "agency records." First, an agency must "either create or obtain" the requested materials "as a prerequisite to its becoming an 'agency record' within the meaning of the FOIA." Id., at 182. In performing their official duties, agencies routinely avail themselves of studies, trade journal reports, and other materials produced outside the agencies both by private and governmental organizations. To restrict the term "agency records" to materials generated internally would frustrate Congress' desire to put within public reach the information available to an agency in its decision-making processes. As we noted in *Forsham,* "The legislative history of the FOIA abounds with * * * references to records *acquired* by an agency." 445 U.S., at 184 (emphasis added).[4]

Second, the agency must be in control of the requested materials at the time the FOIA request is made. By control we mean that the mater-

---

3. The burden is on the agency to demonstrate, not the requester to disprove, that the materials sought are not "agency records" or have not been "improperly" "withheld." See S.Rep. No 813, 89th Cong., 1st Sess., 8 (1965) ("Placing the burden of proof upon the agency puts the task of justifying the withholding on the only party able to explain it"); H.R. Rep. No. 1497, 89th Cong., 2d Sess., 9 (1966) (same); cf. Federal Open Market Committee v. Merrill, 443 U.S. 340, 352 (1979).

4. Title 5 U.S.C. § 552(b)(4), which exempts from disclosure trade secrets and commercial or financial information "obtained from a person," provides further support for the principle that the term "agency records" includes materials received by an agency. See *Forsham*, 445 U.S., at 184-185; see also id., at 183-184 (noting that the definition of "records" in the Records Disposal Act, 44 U.S.C. § 3301, and in the Presidential Records Act of 1978, 44 U.S.C. § 2201(2), encompassed materials "received" by an agency).

ials have come into the agency's possession in the legitimate conduct of its official duties. This requirement accords with *Kissinger's* teaching that the term "agency records" is not so broad as to include personal materials in an employee's possession, even though the materials may be physically located at the agency. This requirement is suggested by *Forsham* as well, where we looked to the definition of agency records in the Records Disposal Act, 44 U.S.C. § 3301. Under that definition, agency records include "all books, papers, maps, photographs, machine readable materials, or other documentary materials, regardless of physical form or characteristics, made or received by an agency of the United States Government *under Federal law or in connection with the transaction of public business* * * *." Ibid. (emphasis added).[5] Furthermore, the requirement that the materials be in the agency's control at the time the request is made accords with our statement in *Forsham* that the FOIA does not cover "information in the abstract." 445 U.S., at 185.[6]

Applying these requirements here, we conclude that the requested district court decisions constitute "agency records." First, it is undisputed that the Department has obtained these documents from the district courts. This is not a case like *Forsham*, where the materials never in fact had been received by the agency. The Department contends that a district court is not an "agency" under the FOIA, but this truism is beside the point. The relevant issue is whether an agency covered by the FOIA has "create[d] or obtaine[d]" the materials sought, not whether

---

5.   In GTE Sylvania, Inc. v. Consumers Union of United States, Inc., 445 U.S. 375, 385 (1980), we noted that Congress intended the FOIA to prevent agencies from refusing to disclose, among other things, agency telephone directories and the names of agency employees. We are confident, however, that requests for documents of this type will be relatively infrequent. Common sense suggests that a person seeking such documents or materials housed in an agency library typically will find it easier to repair to the Library of Congress, or to the nearest public library, rather than to invoke the FOIA's disclosure mechanisms. Cf. Department of Justice v. Reporters Committee for Freedom of Press, 489 U.S. 749, 764 (1989) ("[I]f the [requested materials] were 'freely available,' there would not be reason to invoke the FOIA to obtain access"). To the extent such requests are made, the fact that the FOIA allows agencies to recoup the costs of processing requests from the requester may discourage recourse to the FOIA where materials are readily available elsewhere. See 5 U.S.C. § 552 (a)(4)(A).

6.   Because requested materials ordinarily will be in the agency's possession at the time the FOIA request is made, disputes over control should be infrequent. In some circumstances, however, requested materials might be on loan to another agency, "purposefully routed * * * out of agency possession in order to circumvent [an impending] FOIA request," or "wrongfully removed by an individual after a request is filed." Kissinger v. Reporters Committee for Feedom of Press, 445 U.S. 136, 155, n.9 (1980). We leave consideration of these issues to another day.

the organization from which the documents originated is itself covered by the FOIA.[7]

Second, the Department clearly controls the district court decisions that Tax Analysts seeks. Each of Tax Analysts' FOIA requests referred to district court decisions in the agency's possession at the time the requests were made. This is evident from the fact that Tax Analysts based its weekly requests on the Tax Division's logs, which compile information on decisions the Tax Division recently had received and placed in official case files. Furthermore, the court decisions at issue are obviously not personal papers of agency employees. The Department counters that it does not control these decisions because the district courts retain authority to modify the decisions even after they are released, but this argument, too, is beside the point. The control inquiry focuses on an agency's possession of the requested materials, not on its power to alter the content of the materials it receives. Agencies generally are not at liberty to alter the content of the materials that they receive from outside parties. An authorship-control requirement thus would sharply limit "agency records" essentially to documents generated by the agencies themselves. This result is incompatible with the FOIA's goal of giving the public access to all nonexempt information received by an agency as it carries out its mandate.

The Department also urges us to limit "agency records," at least where materials originating outside the agency are concerned, "to those documents 'prepared substantially to be relied upon in agency decision-making.'" This limitation disposes of Tax Analysts' requests, the Department argues, because district court judges do not write their decisions primarily with an eye toward agency decisionmaking. This argument, however, makes the determination of "agency records" turn on the intent of the creator of a document relied upon by an agency. Such a *mens rea* requirement is nowhere to be found in the Act.[8] Moreover, discerning the intent of the drafters of a document may often prove an elusive endeavor, particularly if the document was created years earlier or by a large number of people for whom it is difficult to divine a common intent.

---

7.   This point is implicit in Department of Justice v. Julian, 486 U.S. 1, 7, and n.6 (1988), where it was uncontroverted that presentence reports, which had been prepared under district court auspices and turned over to the Department and the Parole Commission, constituted "agency records."

8.   Nonpersonal materials in an agency's possession may be subject to certain disclosure restrictions. This fact, however, does not bear on whether the materials are in the agency's control, but rather on the subsequent question whether they are exempted from disclosure under § 552(b)(3).

B.

We turn next to the term "withheld," which we discussed in *Kissinger*. Two of the requests in that case – for summaries of all the telephone conversations in which Kissinger had engaged while serving as National Security Adviser and as Secretary of State – implicated that term. These summaries were initially stored in Kissinger's personal files at the State Department. Near the end of his tenure as Secretary of State, Kissinger transferred the summaries first to a private residence and then to the Library of Congress. Significantly, the two requests for these summaries were made only after the summaries had been physically delivered to the Library. We found this fact dispositive, concluding that Congress did not believe that an agency "withholds a document which has been removed from the possession of the agency prior to the filing of the FOIA request. In such a case, the agency has neither the custody nor control necessary to enable it to withhold." 445 U.S., at 150-151.[9] We accordingly refused to order the State Department to institute a retrieval action against the Library. As we explained, such a course "would have us read the 'hold' out of 'withhold * * *. A refusal to resort to legal remedies to obtain possession is simply not conduct subsumed by the verb withhold.'" Id., at 151.

The construction of "withholding" adopted in *Kissinger* readily encompasses Tax Analysts' requests. There is no claim here that Tax Analysts filed its requests for copies of recent district court tax decisions received by the Tax Division after these decisions had been transferred out of the Department. On the contrary, the decisions were on the Department's premises and otherwise in the Department's control, when the requests were made. Thus, when the Department refused to comply with Tax Analysts' requests, it "withheld" the district court decisions for purposes of § 552 (a)(4)(B).

The Department's counter argument is that, because the district court decisions sought by Tax Analysts are publicly available as soon as they are issued and thus may be inspected and copied by the public at any time, the Department cannot be said to have "withheld" them. The Department notes that the weekly logs it provides to Tax Analysts contain sufficient information to direct Tax Analysts to the "original source of the requested documents." It is not clear from the Department's brief whether this argument is based on the term "withheld" or

---

9. Although a control inquiry for "withheld" replicates part of the test for "agency records," the FOIA's structure and legislative history make clear that agency control over requested materials is a "prerequisite to triggering *any* duties under the FOIA." *Kissinger*, 445 U.S., at 151 (emphasis added); see also id., at 152-153; Forsham v. Harris, 445 U.S. 169, 185 (1980).

the term "improperly."[11] But, to the extent the Department relies on the former term, its argument is without merit. Congress used the word "withheld" only "in its usual sense." When the Department refused to grant Tax Analysts' requests for the district court decisions in its files, it undoubtedly "withheld" these decisions in any reasonable sense of that term. Nothing in the history or purposes of the FOIA counsels contorting this word beyond its usual meaning. We therefore reject the Department's argument that an agency has not "withheld" a document under its control when, in denying an otherwise valid request, it directs the requester to a place outside of the agency where the document may be publicly available.

C.

The Department is left to argue, finally, that the district court decisions were not "improperly" withheld because of their public availability. The term "improperly," like "agency records" and "withheld," is not defined by the Act. We explained in *GTE Sylvania*, however, that Congress' use of the word "improperly" reflected its dissatisfaction with § 3 of the Administrative Procedure Act, 5 U.S.C. § 1002 (1964 ed.), which "had failed to provide the desired access to information relied upon in Government decisionmaking, and in fact had become 'the major statutory excuse for withholding Government records from public view.'" 445 U.S., at 384, quoting H.R. Rep. No. 1497, 89th Cong., 2d Sess., 3 (1966). Under § 3, we explained, agencies had "broad discretion * * * in deciding what information to disclose, and that discretion was often abused." 445 U.S., at 385.

In enacting the FOIA, Congress intended "to curb this apparently unbridled discretion" by "clos[ing] the 'loopholes which allow agencies to deny legitimate information to the public.'" Ibid. Toward this end, Congress formulated a system of clearly defined exemptions to the FOIA's otherwise mandatory disclosure requirements. An agency must disclose agency records to any person under § 552(a), "unless they may be withheld pursuant to one of the nine enumerated exemptions listed in § 552(b)." Consistent with the Act's goal of broad disclosure, these exemptions have been consistently given a narrow compass. See, e.g., FBI v. Abramson, 456 U.S. 615, 630 (1982). More important for present purposes, the exemptions are "explicitly exclusive." As JUSTICE

---

11. The Court of Appeals believed that the Department was arguing "that it need not affirmatively make [the district court decisions] available to Tax Analysts because the documents have not been *withheld* to begin with." 269 U.S. App. D.C. 315, 319-320, 845 F.2d 1060, 1064-1065 (1988) (emphasis in original).

O'CONNOR has explained, Congress sought "to insulate its product from judicial tampering and to preserve the emphasis on disclosure by admonishing that the 'availability of records to the public' is not limited, 'except as *specifically* stated.'" *Abramson*, supra, at 642 (dissenting opinion) (emphasis in original), quoting § 552(c) (now codified at § 552(d)). It follows from the exclusive nature of the § 552(b) exemption scheme that agency records which do not fall within one of the exemptions are "improperly" withheld.[12]

The Department does not contend here that any exemption enumerated in § 552(b) protects the district court decisions sought by Tax Analysts. The Department claims nonetheless that there is nothing "improper" in directing a requester "to the principal, public source of records." The Department advances three somewhat related arguments in support of this proposition. We consider them in turn.

First, the Department contends that the structure of the Act evinces Congress' desire to avoid redundant disclosures. An understanding of this argument requires a brief survey of the disclosure provisions of § 552(a). Under subsection (a)(1), an agency must "currently publish in the Federal Register" specific materials, such as descriptions of the agency, statements of its general functions, and the agency's rules of procedure. Under subsection (a)(2), an agency must "make available for public inspection and copying "its final opinions, policy statements, and administrative staff manuals, "unless the materials are promptly published and copies offered for sale." Under subsection (a)(3), the general provision covering the disclosure of agency records, an agency need not make available those materials that have already been disclosed under subsections (a)(1) and (a)(2). Taken together, the Department argues, these provisions demonstrate the inapplicability of the FOIA's disclosure requirements to previously disclosed, publicly available materials. "*A fortiori,* a judicial record that is a public document should not be subject to a FOIA request." Id., at 29.

The Department's argument proves too much. The disclosure requirements set out in subsections (a)(1) and (a)(2) are carefully limited to situations in which the requested materials have been previously published or made available by the *agency itself.* It is one thing to say that an agency need not disclose materials that it has previously

---

12. Even when an agency does not deny a FOIA request outright, the requesting party may still be able to claim "improper" withholding by alleging that the agency has responded in an inadequate manner. Cf. § 552(a)(6)(C); Kissinger v. Reporters Committee for Freedom of Press, 445 U.S., at 166 (STEVENS, J., concurring in part and dissenting in part). No such claim is made in this case. Indeed, Tax Analysts does not dispute the Court of Appeals' conclusion that the Department could satisfy its duty of disclosure simply by making the relevant district court opinions available for copying in the public reference facility that it maintains.

released; it is quite another to say that an agency need not disclose materials that some other person or group may have previously released. Congress undoubtedly was aware of the redundancies that might exist when requested materials have been previously made available. It chose to deal with that problem by crafting only narrow categories of materials which need not be, in effect, disclosed twice *by the agency*. If Congress had wished to codify an exemption for all publicly available materials, it knew perfectly well how to do so. It is not for us to add or detract from Congress' comprehensive scheme, which already "balances, and protects all interests" implicated by Executive Branch disclosure.[13]

It is not surprising, moreover, that Congress declined to exempt all publicly available materials from the FOIA's disclosure requirements. In the first place, such an exemption would engender intractable fights over precisely what constitutes public availability, unless the term were defined with precision. In some sense, nearly all of the information that comes within an agency's control can be characterized as publicly available. Although the form in which this material comes to an agency – i.e., a report or testimony – may not be generally available, the information included in that report or testimony may very well be. Even if there were some agreement over what constitutes publicly available materials, Congress surely did not envision agencies satisfying their disclosure obligations under the FOIA simply by handing requesters a map and sending them on scavenger expeditions throughout the Nation. Without some express indication in the Act's text or legislative history that Congress intended such a result, we decline to adopt this reading of the statute.

The Department's next argument rests on the fact that the disclosure of district court decisions is partially governed by other statutes, in particular 28 U.S.C. § 1914, and by rules set by the Judicial Conference of the United States. The FOIA does not compel disclosure of district court decisions, the Department contends, because these other provisions are "more precisely drawn to govern the provision of court records to the general public." We disagree. As with the Department's first argument, this theory requires us to read into the FOIA a disclosure exemption that Congress did not itself provide. This we decline to do. That Congress knew that other statutes created overlapping disclosure requirements is evident from § 552(b)(3), which authorizes an agency to refuse a FOIA

---

13. The obligations imposed under subsections (a)(1) and (a)(2) are not properly viewed as additions to the disclosure exemptions set out in subsection (b). If an agency refuses to disclose agency records that indisputably fall within one of the subsection (b) exemptions, the agency has "withheld" the records, albeit not "improperly" given the legislative authorization to do so. By contrast, once an agency has complied with the subsection (a)(1) and (a)(2) obligations, it can no longer be charged with "withholding" the relevant records.

request when the materials sought are expressly exempted from disclosure by another statute. If Congress had intended to enact the converse proposition – that an agency may refuse to provide disclosure of materials whose disclosure is *mandated* by another statute – it was free to do so. Congress, however, did not take such a step.

The Department's last argument is derived from *GTE Sylvania,* where we held that agency records sought from the Consumer Products Safety Commission were not "improperly" withheld even though the records did not fall within one of subsection (b)'s enumerated exemptions. The Commission had not released the records in question because a district court, in the course of an unrelated lawsuit, had enjoined the Commission from doing so. In these circumstances, we held, "[t]he concerns underlying the Freedom of Information Act [were] inapplicable, for the agency * * * made no effort to avoid disclosure." 445 U.S., at 386. We therefore approved the Commission's compliance with the injunction, noting that when Congress passed the FOIA, it had not "intended to require an agency to commit contempt of court in order to release documents. Indeed, Congress viewed the federal courts as the necessary protectors of the public's right to know." Id., at 387.

Although the Department is correct in asserting that *GTE Sylvania* represents a departure from the FOIA's self-contained exemption scheme, this departure was a slight one at best, and was necessary in order to serve a critical goal independent of the FOIA – the enforcement of a court order. As we emphasized, *GTE Sylvania* arose in "a distinctly different context" than the typical FOIA case where the agency decides for itself whether to comply with a request for agency records. In such a case, the agency cannot contend that it has "no discretion * * * to exercise."

The present dispute is clearly akin to those typical FOIA cases. No claim has been made that the Department was powerless to comply with Tax Analysts' requests. On the contrary, it was the Department's decision, and the Department's decision alone, not to make the court decisions available. We reject the Department's suggestion that *GTE Sylvania* invites courts in every case to engage in balancing, based on public availability and other factors, to determine whether there has been an unjustified denial of information. The FOIA invests courts neither with the authority nor the tools to make such determinations.

III.

For the reasons stated, the Department improperly withheld agency records when it refused Tax Analysts' requests for copies of the district court tax decisions in its files.[15] Accordingly, the judgment of the Court of Appeals is *Affirmed*.

JUSTICE WHITE concurs in the judgment.

JUSTICE BLACKMUN, dissenting.

The Court in this case has examined once again the Freedom of Information Act (FOIA), 5 U.S.C. § 552. It now determines that under the Act the Department of Justice on request must make available copies of federal district court orders and opinions it receives in the course of its litigation of tax cases on behalf of the Federal Government. The majority holds that these qualify as agency records, within the meaning of § 552(a)(4)(B), and that they were improperly withheld by the Department when respondent asked for their production. The Court's analysis, I suppose, could be regarded as a fairly routine one.

I do not join the Court's opinion, however, because it seems to me that the language of the statute is not that clear or conclusive on the issue and, more important, because the result the Court reaches cannot be one that was within the intent of Congress when the FOIA was enacted.

Respondent Tax Analysts, although apparently a nonprofit organization for federal income tax purposes, is in business and in that sense is a commercial enterprise. It sells summaries of these opinions and supplies full texts to major electronic data bases. The result of its now-successful effort in this litigation is to impose the cost of obtaining the court orders and opinions upon the Government and thus upon taxpayers generally. There is no question that this material is available elsewhere. But it is quicker and more convenient, and less "frustrat[ing]," for respondent to have the Department do the work and search its files and produce the items than it is to apply to the respective court clerks.

This, I feel, is almost a gross misuse of the FOIA. What respondent demands, and what the Court permits, adds nothing whatsoever to public knowledge of Government operations. That, I had thought, and the majority acknowledges, was the real purpose of the FOIA and the spirit in which the statute has been interpreted thus far. I also sense, I believe not unwarrantedly, a distinct lack of enthusiasm on the part of the majority for the result it reaches in this case.

---

15. On appeal, Tax Analysts limited its requests to the approximately 25% of the district court decisions that it was unable to procure from court clerks or other sources. See 269 U.S. App. D.C., at 318, n. 5, 845 F.2d, at 1963, n. 5 The Court of Appeals' remand thus was limited to these decisions, as is our affirmance. However, the reasoning we have employed applies equally to all of the district court decisions initially sought by Tax Analysts.

If, as I surmise, the Court's decision today is outside the intent of Congress in enacting the statute, Congress perhaps will rectify the decision forthwith and will give everyone concerned needed guidelines for the administration and interpretation of this somewhat opaque statute.

Notes and Questions

Prior to 1966, the burden was on the requester to show there was a right to access with respect to the requested document. After the FOIA was enacted in 1966, the right to access generally has been presumed, and the burden has shifted to the government to establish that there is an applicable exception to disclosure.

1. Do you think the dissenting view of Justice Blackmun has any credence? Do you see any problems with Justice Blackmun's view?

2. The second exemption from mandatory disclosure under the FOIA applies to "matters that are – related solely to the internal personnel rules and practices of an agency. 5 U.S.C. § 552(b)(2)(1994), as amended by Electronic Freedom of Information Act Amendments of 1996, 5 U.S.C. § 552 (1997). At first blush, this appears to have no bearing on the court records at issue in *Tax Analysts*. But the legislative history of the FOIA contains conflicting language as to what specifically is covered under this exemption, which creates confusion as to its parameters. Cf. S. Rep. No. 89-813, at 8 (1965) and H. Rep. No. 89-1497, at 10 (1966). The District of Columbia Circuit Court has held in Founding Church of Scientology v. Smith, 721 F.2d 828 (D.C. Cir. 1983), that the exemption is automatic if the material falls "within the terms of the statutory language as a personnel rule or internal practice of the agency" and where the "material relates to trivial administrative matters of no genuine public interest." 721 F.2d 830-31, n. 4. Would the district court opinions at issue in *Tax Analysts* fit within this exemption? Why or why not?

B. DISCLOSURE UNDER THE IRC

All IRS rulings, determination letters, technical advice memoranda, and the accompanying background file documents must be available for public inspection under the authority of § 6110 of the Internal Revenue Code. Any identifying information must be deleted in order to encourage taxpayers to continue to request rulings from the Service. A background file document includes any request for a written determination, written material submitted in support of the request, and any communication (oral or written) between the Service and persons outside the Service in connection with the written determination. There are seven exemptions from disclosure: (1) identifying data, (2) information classified as secret in the interest of national security or foreign policy, (3) information exempted by statute, (4) trade secrets and commercial or financial information, (5) information that would constitute an unwarranted invasion of privacy, (6) information prepared by, on behalf of, or for the use of an agency engaged in regulation or supervision of financial institutions, and (7) geological and geophysical information and data.

If identifying data is not redacted from released documents, the taxpayer whose rights have been violated under this provision may bring suit in the United States Court of Federal Claims. In the case of a willful or intentional failure to delete the identifying information, the taxpayer may recover actual damages of no less than $1,000, plus costs of the action, including reasonable attorney's fees. IRC § 6110(j)(2).

C. THE PRIVACY ACT

When the first income tax was introduced in the United States in 1861, there was a policy of liberal access to return information. In those days, the prevailing view was that public inspection of tax returns would discourage fraud – "sunlight is said to be the best of disinfectants."[14] Thus, anyone could examine the tax lists simply by making a request to do so. This policy carried over to the Revenue Act of 1913, which provided that tax returns were public records. Over the years, tax return information was liberally shared with a broad range of governmental institutions on a need-to-know basis. Public concern over this policy reached a zenith, however, during the Watergate era of the early 1970's when it was learned that the Nixon Administration was using such information to harass and intimidate political opponents. Also during this time, there was increasing concern over the computerization of government data banks, because these data banks contained information that the federal government had been gathering for decades on law abiding citizens, and computerization meant that this material would be easier than ever to collect and disseminate.

Congress responded to the public's concern by enacting the Privacy Act of 1974. The Privacy Act, in general, guarantees a right to individual privacy and provides for access by individuals to records pertaining to them. The Privacy Act provides that "[n]o agency shall disclose any record which is contained in a system of records by any means of communication to any person, or to another agency, except pursuant to a written request by, or with the prior written consent of, the individual

---

14. Louis D. Brandeis, Other People's Money 92 (1913).

to whom the record pertains * * *." 5 U.S.C. § 552a(b). The term "individual" is defined as a "citizen of the United States or an alien lawfully admitted for permanent residence." 5 U.S.C. § 552a(a)(1). Thus, the scope of the Privacy Act is narrower than that of the FOIA.

Corporations, partnerships, businesses and nonresident aliens are excluded from coverage under the Act because of legitimate government interests in regulating commerce, and because of national security and foreign policy concerns. The term "agency" is defined as it is under the FOIA. Thus only federal agencies, not private agencies or companies or individual employees, can be held liable for violations of the Act.

The term "record" is defined broadly as:

* * * any item, collection, or grouping of information about an individual that is maintained by an agency, including, but not limited to his education, financial transactions, medical history, and criminal or employment history, and that contains his name, or the identifying number, symbol, or other identifying particular assigned to the individual, such as a finger or voice print or a photograph.

The term "system of records" is defined as "a group of any records under the control of any agency from which information is retrieved by the name of the individual or by some identifying number, symbol, or other identifying particular assigned to the individual." 5 U.S.C. § 522a (a)(5). The rationale underlying this formulation is administrative convenience – it becomes burdensome for agencies to search through files that *might* pertain to an individual when those files are not accessible through use of the requester's name or identifying number. Information that is not maintained in a system of records and thus is not accessible under the Privacy Act may be reachable nonetheless under the FOIA, which operates in conjunction with the Privacy Act.

The Privacy Act requires the agency to make corrections if the requester believes these are necessary to insure that the record is accurate, relevant, timely, or complete. 5 U.S.C. § 522a (d)(2)(B). The Act further provides that information gathered for one purpose cannot be used for another purpose without the notification and consent of the individual(s) affected by the disclosure. There are civil remedies available to individuals whose rights have been violated under the Act.

Under the Privacy Act, an individual can obtain access to records pertaining to himself, even though the record may contain other material or pertain to other individuals. The Act covers only tangible records, not oral statements or opinions.

Like the FOIA, the Privacy Act is subject to a number of exceptions, some general and some more specific. The general exceptions apply to all records maintained by the Central Intelligence Agency and to any agency whose principal function is criminal law enforcement, to the extent the record identifies a particular individual. 5 U.S.C. § 552a (j). But even if a general exception applies, portions of the record may be available under the FOIA.

There are 7 specific exemptions: (1) information classified as secret in the interest of national defense or foreign policy, (2) investigatory material compiled for law enforcement purposes other than material covered by the general law enforcement exemption, (3) records maintained in connection with providing protective services to the President of the United States or other individuals who receive protection from the Secret Service, (4) statistical records, (5) investigatory material compiled solely to determine suitability, eligibility, or qualifications for Federal civilian employment, military service, Federal contracts, or access to classified information, to the extent that such information would reveal the identity of a confidential source who provided information under a promise of confidentiality, (6) testing or examination material used solely to determine individual qualifications for appointment or promotion in Federal service when disclosure would compromise the objectivity or fairness of the testing or examination process, and (7) evaluation material used to determine potential for promotion in the armed services, to the extent the information would identify a confidential source who provided information under a promise of confidentiality. 5 U.S.C. § 552a(k).

D. THE GOVERNMENT'S DUTY OF CONFIDENTIALITY

In order to ensure the integrity of the voluntary compliance system, Congress enacted § 6103 of the Internal Revenue Code two years after the Privacy Act was passed. Section 6103 prevents the government from releasing confidential tax return information except in certain specified circumstances, such as to state tax officials, state and local law enforcement agencies, federal officers and employees for purposes of tax administration, or pursuant to a court order. Return information may also be released in a judicial or administrative proceeding in which a federal criminal statute is at issue, and in which the United States or a federal agency is a party. What is not currently clear, however, is the extent to which information released at trial, or otherwise in the public domain, loses its status as confidential return information.

JOHNSON v. SAWYER
United States Court of Appeals, Fifth Circuit, 1997.
120 F.3d 1307.

RHESA HAWKINS BARKSDALE, CIRCUIT JUDGE:

* * *

I.

In 1981, Johnson was an executive with American National Insurance Company (ANICO) and was employed at its headquarters in Galveston, Texas. Johnson began in 1951 with ANICO as an agent in Springfield, Missouri. Because of his success, he was transferred to Galveston in 1971. By 1976, he had become executive vice-president and a member of the board of directors. He and Orson Clay, ANICO's president, reported directly to the board. In an intra-company circular, Clay described Johnson as "the most successful field man and home office executive in [ANICO's] history."

In 1976, the IRS began auditing ANICO and its key executives, including Johnson and his wife. Upon discovering discrepancies, the examining agent referred the matter to the IRS Criminal Investigation Division (CID), which assigned the case to appellant Robert G. Stone, a Special Agent with the CID.

Following an investigation, the CID referred the case to the Department of Justice to prosecute Johnson and his wife for tax evasion for the years 1974 and 1975. The case was assigned to Assistant United States Attorney James L. Powers. In February 1981, Powers advised Johnson's attorney, Robert I. White, that he planned to seek an indictment of both Johnson and his wife; but, if Johnson pled guilty to a one-count criminal information that he underpaid his 1975 taxes (by approximately $3,500), the Government would not prosecute his wife for either 1974 or 1975, would not prosecute Johnson for 1974, and would recommend a probated sentence.

According to Johnson, he kept ANICO's executive committee, president (Clay), and counsel fully apprised of the situation. Evidently, White and Johnson were reassured that, even if Johnson pled guilty to a crime, as long as there was no publicity that would embarrass ANICO, Johnson could continue with ANICO as executive vice-president. White therefore determined to ensure that Johnson's identity would never be disclosed – that if someone looked at the district court file, he could not associate Johnson with ANICO.

White notified Powers that publicity of a conviction would be extremely damaging, and Powers evidently agreed, as he had with White on other occasions for other defendants, to preserve Johnson's relative anonymity. Powers agreed to let White seek the district court's authorization to have the presentence investigation performed before charges were filed. The completed presentence investigation report was delivered to the court on 2 April 1981. Johnson's case was to be heard on Friday, 10 April, at 4:00 p.m. in the Galveston courthouse. White requested that the criminal information be filed at the time of the hearing, along with Johnson's waiver of indictment and the plea bargain agreement; and that the "Defendant's Information" sheet give White's office address for Johnson's address. Powers agreed to these precautions and agreed that no press release would be issued concerning Johnson. But, Powers did not advise the IRS of this "no publicity" agreement.

At approximately 4:00 p.m. on 10 April, proceedings on the record commenced. White had ensured that the district judge (Judge Gibson) had no other business that Friday afternoon, and Powers had agreed to that time to minimize the risk of publicity. White and Johnson searched the Galveston courthouse for members of the press and found none, so the only people present for the hearing were Johnson, White, Powers, the district judge, and court personnel. Johnson signed and filed a waiver of indictment.

The "Defendant Information" sheet, identifying Johnson as "Elvis Johnson" of "1100 Milam St., 28th Floor, Houston, Texas 77002," was also filed. In fact, although Johnson's full name is Elvis E. Johnson, he was known as "Johnny" Johnson by friends, ANICO executives and employees, and business acquaintances; he signed all correspondence as "Johnny." In addition, Johnson's home address was 25 Adler Circle, in Galveston.

A criminal information, charging Johnson with tax evasion for 1975 in the amount of $3,474.97, was filed; and he signed and swore to a written "Plea of Guilty." After a Fed. R. Crim. P. 11 hearing, the court sentenced Johnson to six months confinement, suspended, and one-year of supervised probation. None of the documents filed on 10 April mentioned Johnson's employment. (As discussed infra, properly excluded from evidence was the transcript of the plea hearing; it reflects that the district judge did make reference to Johnson being "an executive with American National Insurance Company"). The following Monday, 13 April, a judgment of conviction and sentence was filed.

According to Johnson, when returning from court on 10 April, he notified ANICO's president (Clay) about what transpired, and Clay responded favorably that the IRS matter was over and that he (Johnson) should move forward because he was important to ANICO. By the end of business of Tuesday, 14 April, Johnson informed other members of ANICO's executive committee that he had pled guilty to a tax crime and put the matter behind him. Johnson testified that he was not asked to resign; instead, he was told the "best interest of the company is served by keeping you exactly where you are."

The day before, however, Monday, 13 April, appellant Sally Sassen, an IRS Public Affairs Officer, had prepared the following press release about Johnson's conviction, entitled "Insurance Executive Pleads Guilty in Tax Case:"

GALVESTON, TEXAS– In U.S. District Court here, Apr. 10, Elvis E. Johnson, 59, plead [sic] guilty to a charge of federal tax evasion. Judge Hugh Gibson sentenced Johnson, of 25 Adler Circle, to a six-month suspended prison term and one year supervised probation.

Johnson, an executive vice-president for the American National Insurance Corporation, was charged in a criminal information with claiming false business deductions and altering documents involving his 1974 and 1975 income tax returns.

In addition to the sentence, Johnson will be required to pay back taxes, plus penalties and interest.

Sassen had prepared the release with the help of Special Agent Stone, relying, with one exception (the paragraph regarding back taxes, penalties and interest), solely on information she received from him. She testified that she did not ask Stone about the source of that information, although she knew Stone had not been in the courtroom for Johnson's hearing on 10 April. As noted, the last paragraph of the release (penalty portion) was not based on information received from Stone. It was boilerplate language in the form Sassen used.

According to Stone, he learned of the conviction from Powers on either Friday, 10 April, or Monday, 13 April. Stone testified that, based on that conversation, he prepared on Monday, 13 April, the following internal "Report of Legal Action:"

On [10 April 1981] AUSA JIM POWERS filed a criminal information charging JOHNSON with tax evasion under 26 USC 7201 for the years 1974 and 1975. JOHNSON plead [sic] guilty on the same day to one count of 7201 for 1975 and the 1974 count was dismissed. Judge GIBSON sentenced JOHNSON to 6 months to serve with this 6 months being suspended and placed him on 1 years supervised preparation [sic]. No fine was assessed and no appeal is expected. This legal action occurred in Galveston.

In addition to not attending Johnson's hearing, neither Sassen nor Stone had any of the court documents. Stone, who was in Houston, was not advised by Powers about either the plea agreement or the hearing in Galveston until approximately two hours before the hearing, when

Powers was leaving his Houston office to travel to Galveston for the hearing. Because of such short notice, another matter prevented Stone from attending the hearing. Stone, however, did not check the public record before giving the information to Sassen.

Sassen prepared the release in conformance with a District Director's Memorandum (DDM), directing her, following guilty pleas, to prepare press releases based on information furnished by the investigating special agent (Stone). Pursuant to the DDM, Stone was to provide the taxpayer's age, occupation, home address, and other facts to the Public Affairs Officer (Sassen) and was to obtain the information from the IRS investigatory file for that taxpayer. The DDM did not require inquiry as to whether information taken from the file had been disclosed in the criminal proceeding. The DDM did, however, state that "the DPAO [Sassen] will coordinate all CID releases with the Branch Chief, Criminal Investigation Division, and the prosecuting U.S. Attorney."

After preparing a draft of the release, Sassen telephoned Stone and read it to him (this was pre-FAX). Stone testified that he copied it verbatim. According to Stone, he telephoned Powers and read the release to him; but, Powers testified that he remembered neither this telephone call nor basically anything else about the case. Stone then contacted Sassen and told her that Powers had approved the release.

Sassen also called appellant Michael Orth, a CID supervisory employee, and read the release to him. IRS procedures then in effect (1981) required that such releases be cleared at the supervisory level. After Orth approved the release, Sassen mailed it on 13 April to 21 media outlets in the Galveston area.

On 15 April, a Galveston journalist telephoned ANICO to inquire about Johnson's conviction. Johnson learned of the press release and contacted White, who immediately contacted Powers. In a telephone conversation surreptitiously recorded by White, Powers denied any knowledge of the release and assumed the IRS was responsible. Powers told White, "If they damaged your client in some way, sue the hell out of them as far as I'm concerned."

White also telephoned and wrote to the IRS about the release. Among others, he spoke with appellant Dale V. Braun, who was Acting District Director of the IRS Austin, Texas, District on that day (15 April). It was then that the IRS realized that the release contained erroneous information: that Johnson had been charged only for 1975; and that the criminal information did not charge him with claiming false business deductions or altering documents.

Braun contacted appellant Robert C. Sawyer, the Chief of the CID in the Austin District, and Harold Friedman, the IRS Austin District Counsel, and all agreed to withdraw the release. Sassen informed the media outlets that the release might contain errors and asked that it not be publicized.

The IRS then obtained a copy of the criminal information to which Johnson had pled guilty and, following discussion on 16 April among Sawyer, Sassen, Orth, Braun, and other IRS personnel, decided to issue a revised release. IRS Counsel Friedman strongly advised against issuing a second release because it would only compound their potential liability. The revised release was identical to the 13 April release, except for the following italicized portion of the second (middle) paragraph:

> Johnson, an executive vice-president for the American National Insurance Corporation, was charged in a criminal information with *willful evasion of federal tax by filing a false and fraudulent tax return for 1975.* (Emphasis added).

Powers evidently participated in the process resulting in this second release. An IRS special agent testified that, on 16 April, as instructed by Orth, he took a copy of the proposed revised release to Powers, who was participating in a trial; that, during a recess, he gave it to Powers for his review and approval; and that Powers approved it. Consistent with his other testimony, Powers did not recall the incident; he only recalled discussing this issue with some lawyer some years ago about a correction of the press release. I don't remember a second press release. Maybe there was one.

The IRS special agent then gave the proposed release to a secretary with the comment that "Powers said this was okay;" the secretary relayed that information to the Austin office. This second release was issued on 17 April to the 21 media outlets that received the first.

According to Johnson, he informed ANICO president Clay and two executive committee board members of the first release on 15 April and provided Clay with a copy of the release that same day. On learning from White that the IRS would not withdraw the 13 April release and planned to issue a second, Johnson told Clay that all ANICO board members should be informed. Clay advised Johnson that he (Clay) would contact the entire board. On Saturday, 18 April, and Monday, 20 April, Clay asked Johnson to resign from his positions as executive vice-president and board member.

On the one hand, Clay testified that he was unaware of the press release when he asked Johnson for his resignation. According to Clay, the ANICO board decided that someone with a felony conviction could not hold a high position within the corporation. But, Johnson presented evidence that the "real problem" was the publicity surrounding his conviction, not the fact of the conviction. (Obviously, the jury accepted Johnson's version). Johnson resigned on 20 April 1981.

Johnson was reassigned to ANICO's office in Springfield, Missouri (where he began in 1951), as an associate regional director. He served there at considerably diminished compensation until 1986, when he reached the mandatory retirement age (65). He then worked for ANICO as an agent, his starting position with it.

In 1983, Johnson filed this action against Sawyer, Braun, Sassen, and other IRS employees for wrongful disclosure of tax return information, in violation of 26 U.S.C. § 6103. That section provides:

(a) General Rule. – Returns and return information shall be confidential, and except as authorized by this title–(1) no officer or employee of the United States, shall disclose any *return or return information* obtained by him in any manner in connection with his service as such an officer or an employee or otherwise or under the provisions of this section * * *.

(b) Definitions.– For purposes of this section–(2) * * * The term "return information" means – (A) *a taxpayer's identity*, the nature, *source*, or amount of his income, payments, receipts, deductions, exemptions, credits, assets, liabilities, net worth, *tax liability*, tax withheld, deficiencies, overassessments, or tax payments, whether the taxpayer's return was, is being, or will be examined or subject to other investigation or processing, or any other data, received by, recorded by, prepared by, furnished to, or collected by the Secretary with respect to a return or with respect to the determination of the existence, or possible existence, of liability (or the amount thereof) of any person under this title for any tax, penalty, interest, fine, forfeiture, or other imposition, or offense * * *.

Id. § 6103(a)(1), (b)(2)(A) (emphasis added).

Johnson sought recovery under 26 U.S.C. § 7217(a), which permits an action for damages against "any person" who knowingly or negligently discloses a return or return information (collectively, "tax return information") in violation of § 6103. No liability attaches if the disclosure "resulted from a good faith, but erroneous, interpretation of section 6103." Id. § 7217(b). * * *

Pursuant to § 7217, a plaintiff is entitled to his actual damages sustained as a result of an unauthorized disclosure (including punitive damages for willful or grossly negligent disclosures) or to liquidated damages of $1,000 per such disclosure, whichever is greater, as well as the costs of the action. 26 U.S.C. § 7217(c). It bears repeating that an individual who discloses as the result of a "good faith, but erroneous, interpretation" of § 6103 cannot incur liability. Id. § 7217(b).

* * *

In 1986, the district court (Chief Judge Singleton) ruled on the cross-motions, concluding that, as a matter of law, "issuing the [releases] violated § 6103." *Johnson v. Sawyer*, 640 F. Supp. 1126, 1133 (S.D. Tex. 1986). The court determined that the releases "disclosed" tax return information within the meaning of § 6103 and that none of the statutory exceptions to the rule against disclosure applied. Id. at 1131-32 & n. 16.

Along a similar line, the Appellants had urged the court to create a judicial exception for disclosure of material in which Johnson "had no reasonable expectation of privacy * * * because those items were incidental to information already in the public record." Id. at 1132. The court rejected that suggestion, explaining that "Congress made the language of § 6103 quite clear: any disclosure of return information is illegal' except as authorized *by this title*.'" Id. (quoting § 6103(a))(emphasis added by district court).

Consequently, Johnson's motion for partial summary judgment was granted on that issue. Id. at 1139. * * *

The claims against the individual defendants were severed, and a bench trial was held on the FTCA claim in 1990. Johnson was awarded approximately $10 million. *Johnson,* 760 F. Supp. 1216, 1233 (S.D. Tex. 1991). Initially, our court affirmed the judgment, Johnson v. Sawyer, 980 F.2d 1490 (5th Cir. 1992) and 4 F.3d 369 (5th Cir. 1993), but our *en banc* court reversed and remanded with directions to dismiss the FTCA claim. *Johnson,* 47 F.3d at 738.

While the case was on appeal, Chief Judge Singleton retired. The case was reassigned to Judge Hoyt. On remand, Johnson filed a third amended complaint, discarding the FTCA claim and adding a claim that "identifying" him constituted a sixth item of wrongful disclosure.

A hotly, if not bitterly, contested jury trial was held in 1996. The jury found for Johnson, awarding $6 million in actual, and $3 million in punitive, damages. The court awarded pre-judgment interest at 6% per annum on $6 million commencing 4 August 1986, post-judgment interest on all sums awarded at 5.6% per annum, attorneys' fees of $1.2 million (20% of $6 million), and costs of approximately $54,000.

II.

* * *

b.

Because Appellants contend that the challenged instruction failed to distinguish between information in the releases that was wrongfully disclosed and information that was not wrongfully disclosed, we must first determine the § 6103 violation in the releases. This requires us to answer a question explicitly left open in our *en banc* opinion – namely, "whether to follow the rule of Lampert v. United States, 854 F.2d 335, 338 (9th Cir. 1988), that § 6103(a) does not bar disclosure of matters of public record." *Johnson,* 47 F.3d at 737 n. 46.

i.

Section 6103 establishes a general, salutary rule that "returns" and "return information" shall be confidential. Disclosure by a government employee is prohibited unless a specific statutory exception provides for it. 26 U.S.C. § 6103 (forbidding disclosure "except as authorized by *this title*")(emphasis added). Although there are a number of exceptions, none includes the issuance of press releases by the IRS.

One exception, however, authorizes disclosure of tax return information in a judicial proceeding to determine a taxpayer's civil or criminal tax liability. 26 U.S.C. § 6103(h)(4)(A). Citing *Lampert,* Appellants contend that once tax return information is lawfully disclosed in such proceedings, it loses its confidentiality, rendering § 6103's prohibition moot. Johnson, citing Rodgers v. Hyatt, 697 F.2d 899 (10th Cir. 1983), and Mallas v. United States, 993 F.2d 1111 (4th Cir. 1993), counters that § 6103 prohibits disclosure despite prior publication of the information in court. In the alternative, Johnson maintains that, under the reasoning of *Thomas v. United States,* liability under § 6103 is premised on the source of the information, not its "public" status (if any).

Lampert involved press releases issued by the United States Attorney's office and the IRS that summarized tax evasion charges against three individuals. *Lampert,* 854 F.2d at 336. The Ninth Circuit began its analysis by explaining that the releases disclosed "return information" as defined by § 6103. Id. at 335-37 (citing Barrett v. United States, 795 F.2d 446,449 (5th Cir. 1986)). Contra *Johnson,* 47 F.3d at 732 n. 34 ("Language, which on its face purports only to describe the content of [a] criminal information, is not return information under § 6103(a)"). It then determined that, although § 6103 contained no exception authorizing this disclosure, giving effect to that language would frustrate the statute's purpose – to prohibit the disclosure of confidential return information. * * * The court determined that, once tax return information is made a part of the public domain, a taxpayer "may no longer claim a right of privacy in that information." Id. Therefore, when such information is lawfully disclosed in a court proceeding, subsequent disclosure does not violate § 6103.

The Ninth Circuit reaffirmed *Lampert* in Schrambling Accountancy Corp. v. United States, 937 F.2d 1485, 1489-90 (9th Cir. 1991), when it held that tax return information included in notices of federal tax liens and a bankruptcy petition lost their confidentiality and "[could] be disclosed again without regard to § 6103." As the court explained, "The relevant inquiry should focus on whether the prior authorized disclosure * * * destroys the confidential nature of the information." Id. at 1488-89. Because tax liens are filed in the county recorder's office and are open for public inspection, the information in them is exposed to even greater publicity than in a judicial proceeding.

In Rowley v. United States, 76 F.3d 796 (6th Cir. 1996), the Sixth Circuit recently adopted the Ninth Circuit's approach. *Rowley* involved IRS disclosure of information (via newspaper ad) that, like the information in *Schrambling,* had previously been disclosed in a publicly recorded tax lien. The Sixth Circuit concluded that the prior, authorized, disclosure placed the information in the public domain, stripping it of its confidentiality. The court did make an effort to distinguish cases where the prior disclosure occurred in a judicial proceeding, explaining that "the recording of a federal tax lien * * * is designed to provide public notice and is thus qualitatively different from disclosures made in judicial proceedings, which are only incidentally made public." Id.

The Fourth and Tenth Circuits, however, have rejected the Ninth Circuit's analysis. *Rodgers v. Hyatt,* from the Tenth Circuit, involved disclosure of tax return information by an IRS agent who had previously and lawfully disclosed that information in testimony in open court, see 26 U.S.C. § 6103(h)(4)(A). *Rodgers,* 697 F.2d at 899-900. However, the se-cond, challenged, disclosure was not governed by any of § 6103's exceptions. The Tenth Circuit explained that the issue in a § 6103 case is not confidentiality but rather, whether an unauthorized disclosure of return information occurred. The court noted that "even assuming the loss of confidentiality in the content of the statements," the disclosure was "clearly unauthorized" because it lacked express statutory authorization. Id.

In *Mallas v. United States*, the Fourth Circuit followed the Tenth Circuit. There, the IRS issued a series of revenue agent reports to investors in a tax shelter, describing the convictions (later reversed) and "financing scheme" of the two individuals who set up the shelter. *Mallas,* 993 F.2d at 1114-15. Noting that § 6103 contained no exception permitting disclosure of information "within the public domain," the Fourth Circuit declined the Government's "invitation to usurp the legislative function by adding a judicially created exception to those set forth by Congress." Id. at 1120. The court rejected the Government's contention that the Ninth Circuit's approach struck a better balance between taxpayer interests in privacy and the Government's interest in disclosing tax return information to administer the tax laws: "It is for Congress * * * not this court, to 'strike a balance' between these interests. Congress has done so in § 6103, without articulating the exception advanced by the Government * * * and adopted by the Ninth Circuit * * *." Id. at 1121.

The Seventh Circuit took a slightly different approach to § 6103 in *Thomas v. United States*, in which a taxpayer contested an assessment of taxes and lost in the United States Tax Court. *Thomas,* 890 F.2d at 19. The IRS then prepared a press release and mailed it to the taxpayer's hometown newspaper. The Seventh Circuit explained that it refused to "retreat" from its earlier statement that § 6103 is a "general prohibition against the disclosure of tax return information unless expressly authorized by an exception." Id. at 21 (quoting *Wiemerslage v. United States,* 838 F.2d 899, 902 (7th Cir. 1988)). However, it also refused to "take sides" in the conflict over whether disclsoure of tax return information in a public record "bars the taxpayer from complaining about any subsequent disclosure." Id. at 20.

Instead, in ruling for the Government, the Seventh Circuit reasoned: "The information disclosed in the press release did not come from [the taxpayer's] tax return – not directly, at any rate. It came from the Tax Court's opinion." Id. at 20. For that reason, the Government was not disclosing tax return information within the meaning of § 6103, because "a return, or some internal document based on a return" was not the immediate source of the information. When the source of the information is a public document, the definition of return information simply does not come into play, and there is no § 6103 violation. A contrary holding, the court noted, would have serious First Amendment implications. Id. (citing Cox Broadcasting Corp. v. Cohn, 420 U.S. 469, 43 L.Ed. 2d 328, 95 S. Ct. 1029 (1975)).

Consistent with the district court's summary judgment in 1986, we decline to follow the Ninth and Sixth Circuits and judicially create an exception to § 6103 for tax return information disclosed in "public records." Our analysis of the text of § 6103, the legislative history, and the pertinent case law compels us to conclude that there is simply no basis for creating such an exception. Instead, we follow the approach of the Fourth and Tenth Circuits, modified by the Seventh Circuit's "source" analysis in *Thomas.* If the immediate source of the information claimed to be wrongfully disclosed is tax return information ("return" or "return information" pursuant to § 6103), the disclosure violates § 6103, regardless of whether that information has been previously disclosed (lawfully) in a judicial proceeding and has therefore arguably lost its taxpayer "confidentiality."

Section 6103, * * * enumerates 13 separate (and quite detailed) exceptions to § 6103, providing for disclosure to various federal and state agencies and employees for a variety of purposes. Despite this elaborate structure, it is undisputed that the plain text of § 6103 contains no express exceptions permitting disclosure of tax return information that has arguably lost its confidentiality because it has been made available to the public via disclosure in open court. The circuits concur on this point, including the Ninth Circuit. See *Lampert,* 854 F.2d at 338. ("[A] strict, technical reading of the statute supports the taxpayers' position [that for a government employee to disclose any return information, confidential or not, there must exist an applicable exception to § 6103(a)]."); *Mallas,* 993 F.2d at 1120; *Rodgers,* 697 F.2d at 906; cf. *Thomas,* 890 F.2d at 20 ("[Section 6103] makes federal tax returns confidential with exceptions that do not include the issuance of press releases by the [IRS].").

As the Supreme Court stated, "When we find the terms of a statute unambiguous, judicial inquiry is complete except in rare and exceptional circumstances * * * [such as] where the application of the statute as written will produce a result 'demonstrably at odds with the intentions of its drafters.'"

Restated, we follow the plain meaning of a statute unless it would lead to a result "so bizarre that Congress 'could not have intended' it." *Demarest,* 498 U.S. at 191 (quoting *Griffin,* 458 U.S. at 575).

At first – even second, third, or fourth – glance, it appears that, to find a violation of § 6103 for disclosure of tax return information that was in most, if not all, respects previously disclosed in a court proceeding, is to reach an absurd result. But, in applying this rule of statutory construction, we must apply a reasoned, objective method for determining whether a result is actually "absurd" or whether, instead, it is simply personally disagreeable. In general, courts look to two sources to make this call – other provisions of the statute and legislative history.

* * *

Turning to § 6103, we note that immediately following the express disclosure exceptions (§ 6103(c)-(o)) is a provision that explains the procedures by which disclosure requests are made to the IRS. 26 U.S.C. § 6103(p). Part of that provision is a list of "Safeguards," requiring that certain federal agencies to which the IRS may lawfully disclose return information must, inter alia: (1) establish a system of records to keep track of all disclosure requests, the date of request, and the reason for the request; (2) establish a secure area in which to store the information; and (3) restrict the access of persons to that information. Id. § 6103(p)(4)(A)-(F). However, these record-keeping/security requirements "shall cease to apply with respect to any return or return information if, and to the extent that, such return or return information is disclosed in the course of any judicial or administrative proceeding and made a part of the public record thereof." Id. § 6103(p)(4).

For example, if the IRS discloses tax return information to the Department of Commerce (DOC) for statistical use, id. § 6103(j)(1), the DOC does not have to comply with § 6103(p)(4) safeguards if the information has already been disclosed publicly in a judicial proceeding. However, the fact that the DOC does not have to be as vigilant about the information does not mean that it (or the IRS, for that matter) can disclose that information in, for example, a press release. That information is still subject to § 6103(a)'s general rule of non-disclosure; § 6103(p)(4) does not create an exception to that rule.

Section 6103(p)(4) does, however, indicate that, when Congress drafted § 6103, it considered the possibility that some tax return information might be otherwise available to the public – e.g., in court records, because it had been disclosed in a judicial proceeding. For that reason, Congress deemed it unnecessary for those federal agencies to follow the safeguards in § 6103(p)(4) for keeping the documents in a safe place and ensuring that access to them was restricted. That, however, is the only provision Congress chose to make in § 6103 regarding this "publicized" tax return information. Under the reasoning of *Demarest* and *GTE Sylvania*, then, it is difficult to conclude that Congress' failure to include an exception for "public record" tax return information in the exceptions to § 6103 was unintentional. * * * it is difficult to conclude that Congress' failure to include an exception for "public record" tax return information in the exceptions to § 6103 was unintentional.[1]

---

1.   Of course, in describing this proposed exception to § 6103 as an exception for "publicized" or "public record" tax return information, we are not holding that the IRS, or any other federal agency, is prohibited from publishing the contents of a public record, such as a judicial opinion, see *Thomas*, 890 F.2d at 20-21, *provided it is the public record that is the immediate source.* Rather, as we explain infra, we simply hold that the fact that tax return information is *otherwise available* in the public record-and therefore arguably has lost its confidentiality-does not remove § 6103's proscription against improper disclosure of tax return information.

In addition, although Appellant's contention is that tax return information disclosed in a

More generally, § 6103(m) indicates that Congress also considered the possibility that the IRS would need to disclose tax return information to the news media in certain circumstances. One of § 6103's exceptions, subsection (m), permits disclosure of taxpayer identity information to, *inter alia*, "the press and other media for purposes of identifying persons entitled to tax refunds when the Secretary, after reasonable effort and lapse of time, has been unable to locate such persons." 26 U.S.C. § 6103(m)(1). We note that this exception does not allow the IRS to disclose tax return information to identify individuals convicted of tax offenses (e.g., Johnson) or, more broadly, individuals who appear in court concerning civil or criminal tax liability. Again, we cannot conclude that Congress' failure to include in § 6103 the exception Appellants press upon us was unintentional. Hence, applying the plain meaning of the statute leads to neither an absurd result nor one that is demonstrably at odds with congressional intent.

Furthermore, * * * the legislative history supports the conclusion that Congress considered the relationship between § 6103 and "public record" tax return information. In discussing the § 6103(p)(4) safeguard procedure, the Senate Finance Committee noted: "The *record-keeping requirements* would not apply in certain situations, including disclosure of returns and return information open to the public generally." S. REP. NO. 94-938, at 343 (1976), reprinted in 1976 U.S.C.C.A.N. 3439, 3773 (emphasis added). Importantly, the committee did *not* say that the rule of nondisclosure does not apply where the information is open to the public generally.

In addition, Congress considered a taxpayer's privacy interest in tax return information when enumerating the exceptions to § 6103. In evaluating the areas in which tax return information was formerly subject to disclosure and deciding whether to maintain such disclosure provision, the committee "balanced the particular office or agency's need for the information involved with the citizen's right to privacy and the related impact of the disclosure upon the continuation of compliance with our country's voluntary assessment system." Id. at 318, 1976 U.S.C.C.A.N. at 3747. In spite of this consideration, however, Congress chose not to create an exception for "public record" tax return information.

---

judicial proceeding has lost its confidentiality and, therefore, the protection of § 6103, we refer more broadly to this proposed exception as one for "public record" tax return information. It seems that the logical implication of Appellants' position is that any tax return information otherwise available to the public – whether it be in court records or real estate filings – would likewise have lost its confidentiality and the protection of § 6103.

In judicially creating that exception, the Sixth Circuit explained: "The approach we adopt today strikes the proper balance between a taxpayer's reasonable expectation of privacy and the government's legitimate interest in disclosing tax return information to the extent necessary for tax administration functions." *Rowley,* 76 F.3d at 802. We, however, agree with the Fourth Circuit: "It is for Congress * * * to 'strike a balance' between these interests [and it] has done so in section 6103, without articulating [this] exception." *Mallas,* 993 F.2d at 1121. We are a federal appellate court, not a super-legislature; we are not vested with plenary authority to re-evaluate the policy choices made by our elected representatives.

Section 6103 provides blanket protection to tax return information. If we recognized an exception for "public record" tax return information, as the Ninth and Sixth Circuits have, we would be concluding that § 6103 distinguishes between confidential (private) and non-confidential (public) tax return information. See *Lampert,* 854 F.2d at 338 ("Once tax return information is made a part of the public domain, the taxpayer may no longer claim a right of privacy in that information "); see also *Rowley,* 76 F.3d at 801-02 (information in public domain loses confidentiality and protection of § 6103). Appellants ask us to hold that § 6103 makes that distinction.

But, again, this flies in the face of § 6103. It states that "returns and return information *shall be confidential,* and except as authorized by this title * * * shall [not be] disclosed"; not that "[confidential] returns and return information * * * shall [not be] disclosed". (Emphasis added.) This is a critical, indeed dispositive, difference.[2]

We recognized in our en banc opinion that § 6103 protects more than simply "confidential" or "private" return information:

> Section 6103 is a regulation of the conduct of those who in the course of their duties as government employees or contractors glean information from tax returns. The regulation is prophylactic, proscribing disclosure by such an individual of any such information so obtained by him. Plainly, Congress was not determining that all the information on a tax return would always be truly private and

---

2. Before the Tax Reform Act of 1976, all returns were described as "public records," although they were open to inspection only under regulations approved by the President, or under Presidential order. See S. REP. NO. 94-938, at 315, 318, 1976 U.S.C.C.A.N. at 3744, 3747. Despite that limitation, Congress decided that, under the new law, "returns and return information should generally be *treated* as confidential." Id. at 318, 1976 U.S.C.C.A.N. at 3747 (emphasis added). In other words, § 6103(a)'s description of tax return information as "confidential" does not represent a congressional conclusion that all such information is, in fact, confidential or private. Rather, it is simply a directive to treat that information as if it is confidential – i.e., not to disclose it unless authorized by exception.

intimate or embarrassing. Rather, it was simply determining that since much of the information on tax returns does fall within that category, it was better to proscribe disclosure of all return information, rather than rely on ad hoc determinations by those with official access to returns as to whether particular items were or were not private, intimate or embarrassing. Because such determinations would inevitably sometimes err, ultimately a broad prophylactic proscription would result in less disclosure by return handlers of such sensitive matters than would a more precisely tailored enactment.

* * *

Thus, § 6103's protection does not disappear simply because tax return information has been disclosed in the public record and has therefore arguably lost its confidentiality.[3] In enacting § 6103 as a prophylactic ban, Congress was determining that a taxpayer has a statutorily created "privacy" interest in all his tax return information, despite the fact that some of it is not entirely "secret."[4] * * *

That interest is furthered by a construction of § 6103 that premises a violation on the source of the information claimed to be wrongfully disclosed, not its public or non-confidential status. Again, our en banc court has already interpreted § 6103 as having precisely that focus. In comparing § 6103 and the Texas tort of public disclosure of embarrassing private facts, our court noted:

Unlike § 6103(a), the Texas tort * * * is not concerned with the identity of the party making the disclosure, or his sources, but merely with whether the information disclosed is both private and intimate or embarrassing, and also not of public concern, none of which factors are relevant under the terms of § 6103(a). The Texas tort and § 6103(a) address totally distinct subject matters and impose distinctly

---

3.We say "arguably" because, as the Seventh Circuit has noted, it is a legal fiction that "every item of information contained in a public document is known to the whole world, so that further dissemination can do no additional harm to privacy." *Thomas,* 890 F.2d at 21. Like the Seventh Circuit, we eschew the idea that "only secrets [can] be confidences." Id.

4. The brand new Taxpayer Browsing Protection Act, H.R. 1226 (5 Aug. 1997) (to be codified at 26 U.S.C. §§ 7213A and 7431) is further proof of this. This law makes it unlawful for any federal employee "willfully to inspect, except as authorized in this title, any return or return information". Id. § 2(a). In addition, a taxpayer may sue the United States under § 7431 for civil damages for an unauthorized inspection. Id. § 3(a).

That Congress deemed simply browsing through a tax return, even if no tax return information is ultimately disclosed, to be serious enough to merit criminal and civil penalties strengthens our interpretation of § 6103, which recognizes that all tax return information is protected, not simply the "private" or "confidential" portions. In addition, although we hesitate to infer too much from this new law, we note that, on its face, it too does not distinguish between "public" and "private" tax return information. Hence, a federal employee may be subject to criminal and civil liability even if he only browses through portions of a return or return information, and even though that data is otherwise available in public records.

different duties: the latter, applicable only to certain individuals who in connection with their government-related duties obtain tax return information, enjoins them not to disclose any of it so obtained, even though it is not private and not intimate or embarrassing and is of public concern * * *.

Johnson, 47 F.3d at 735-36. Therefore, if tax return information is the immediate source for the information claimed to be wrongfully disclosed, it makes no difference that the information is neither "private" nor "confidential."

For this reason, we find unpersuasive Appellants' contention that this construction of § 6103 raises First Amendment concerns.* * *

* * *

* * * Government employees – e.g., IRS agents – are not members of the media and therefore have no First Amendment responsibility to report on criminal proceedings or other government operations. * * *

In addition, the Court noted that accurate reports of judicial proceedings have special protection under the First Amendment. But, as noted above, that protection arises only when the *source* of those reports is *public records* or personal observation of the events in court: "What transpires in the court room is public property * * *. *Those who see and hear what transpired* can report it with impunity." Id. at 492, 95 S.Ct. at 1044 (quoting Craig v. Harney, 331 U.S. 367, 374, 91 L.Ed. 1546, 67 S. Ct. 1249 (1947)) (emphasis added).

* * *

[U]nder our analysis, § 6103 is violated only when tax return information – which is not a public record open to public inspection – is the immediate source of the information claimed to be wrongfully disclosed * * *.

ii.

Given this interpretation of § 6103, we must decide what tax return information was wrongfully disclosed in the releases. At the beginning of the 1996 trial, Johnson claimed six items: his age; his home address; the fact that he was executive vice-president of ANICO; the statement that he was charged with false business deductions and altering documents on his 1974 and 1975 returns; the statement that he would be required to pay back taxes plus penalties and interest; and his middle initial.

But, our en banc opinion had already concluded that the statements about altering documents (charge portion) and about the penalties for Johnson's conviction (penalty portion) were not "return information" within the meaning of § 6103. *Johnson,* 47 F.3d at 732 n.34 (for charge portion: "language, which on its face purports only to describe the content of the criminal information, is not return information under § 6103(a)"; for penalty portion: "[it] in substance merely describes the known, universally applicable legal consequences of willfully and knowingly filing a false and fraudulent income tax return understating the tax due by several thousand dollars"). Because neither of these two portions were tax return information, their inclusion in the press releases did not violate § 6103.

In addition, Appellants have conceded in this appeal – for the first time during this case – that Johnson's age, home address, and the word "vice-president" were wrongfully disclosed.[6] Appellants maintain that the district judge who sentenced Johnson in 1981 (Judge Gibson) referred to him as an "executive with American National Insurance Company"; therefore, they could disclose Johnson's affiliation with ANICO to that extent. Under their view, because Johnson's specific job title, vice-president, was not mentioned in open court, it could not be disclosed.

Neither Stone nor Sassen, however, attended the court proceedings at which Johnson pled guilty. Nor, prior to the release, did they examine the official transcript. Moreover, they could not have seen the transcript; it did not exist when the releases were issued. (The court reporter did not transcribe his notes and file the transcript until July 1981, over three months *after* the releases were issued).

In fact, Stone admitted that *all* of the identifying information given to Sassen that is at issue in this case – age, middle initial, home address, and occupation (executive vice president of ANICO) – came either from Johnson's return file or from information "in his [Stone's] head" (that is, information that Stone had gathered during the course of investigating Johnson). Stone testified that *all* information gathered about a tax-payer, including data learned in the course of an investigation that is not actually present in a return or the return file, is protected by § 6103. Because neither public (court) records nor knowledge of the open court reference was the source for Johnson's occupation, *any* disclosure of his affiliation with ANICO, and not simply the word "vice-president", was a violation of § 6103.

---

6.   For this reason, Appellants conceded at oral argument that the public record exception they urge (and which we reject) would not apply to these three items and that, therefore, Johnson is entitled, at a minimum, to statutory liquidated damages of $1,000 per disclosure for the wrongful disclosure of these three items. See 26 U.S.C. § 7217(c)(1) (repealed). In its 1986 summary judgment, the district court held that, under § 7217(c)(1), Johnson would be entitled to $21,000 because Sassen sent the release to 21 news outlets. *Johnson,* 640 F. Supp. at 1135-36, 1139. Neither party has contested that aspect of the summary judgment ruling. Accordingly, it is law of the case.

As for Johnson's middle initial (E), there is a dispute, *outside this record*, over whether it was previously disclosed in public on the docket sheet for the 1981 criminal proceeding.[7] However, because a § 6103 violation is premised on the *source* of the information claimed to be wrongfully disclosed, we need not determine whether the middle initial is in the public record, because it is not relevant to the question of whether § 6103 was violated. As noted above, in providing Sassen with the identifying information in the releases, Stone relied on Johnson's return file or information he had otherwise gathered about Johnson, not on any public (court) document. Therefore, the middle initial disclosure was a violation of § 6103.

In sum, four items in the releases were wrongfully disclosed: Johnson's middle initial (E), his age (59), his home address (25 Adler Circle), and his occupation (executive vice-president for the American National Insurance Corporation). The rest of the information in the releases was not wrongfully disclosed; this includes the two statements (charge and penalty portions) that our en banc court previously held were not § 6103 return information. *Johnson,* 47 F.3d at 732, n.34.

* * *

2.

The court instructed that the Appellants could be liable under § 7217 for "negligently or knowingly * * * disclosing or *permitting the disclosure of* tax return information." (Emphasis added). Asserting that only Sassen made a "disclosure" within the meaning of § 6103, the other Appellants maintain that persons who *permit* disclosures or who *negligently supervise* others who make disclosures cannot be held liable under § 7217.

* * *

We find no error. "Disclosure" is defined by § 6103 as "the making known to any person *in any manner whatever* a return or return information." 26 U.S.C. § 6103(b)(8) (emphasis added). We agree with Johnson that, under the plain meaning of the statute, IRS agents like Stone and IRS supervisors like Orth, Braun, and Sawyer can "make known" return information in "some manner" without actually putting their names on a press release and mailing it to a news outlet. In this regard, we are informed by Chandler v. United States, 687 F. Supp. 1515

---

7.   Appellants contend, for the first time on appeal, that a criminal docket sheet obtained from the district court by the Department of Justice's Office of Professional Responsibility includes Johnson's middle initial. That initial does not appear on the sheet entered in evidence by Johnson. * * *

(C.D. Utah 1988), aff'd, 887 F.2d 1397 (10th Cir. 1989). (There is a dearth of law on this point).

In *Chandler,* an IRS teller received a penalty check that failed to contain a taxpayer identification number (TIN). The teller accessed the taxpayer account via computer but mistakenly transcribed the number onto the check. Consequently, the taxpayer's account was not credited with those funds, and an IRS revenue officer mailed a notice of levy to the taxpayer's place of employment to collect the penalty. The taxpayer brought suit against the United States under 26 U.S.C. § 7431. See supra (§ 7217 and § 7431 contain the same definition of disclosure and same predicate for liability).

Because the Government conceded that the notice of levy disclosed tax return information, the issue was whether the disclosure was the result of negligence (or willfulness). The court concluded that several IRS officers were negligent, including the teller. The court reached this conclusion despite the fact that it was the *revenue officer* who actually mailed the notice of levy and despite the fact that the teller's only contribution to that action was in transcribing the TIN incorrectly. Id. Nevertheless, the negligent conduct of the teller was actionable under § 7431.

We agree with *Chandler* that § 7217 expands the universe of liability beyond the federal employee who actually "publishes" tax return information. Other individuals in the chain of causation who contribute to a wrongful disclosure (either by acting or by failing to act) are proper party-defendants in a § 7217 action. Stone, who supplied the tax return information to Sassen for the first release, and supervisors Orth, Braun, and Sawyer, who approved and/or were personally involved in the first or second release are equally as subject to liability under § 7217 as Sassen, who distributed both releases. Therefore, it was not error to instruct the jury in that regard.

* * *

The judgment of the district court is VACATED and this matter is REMANDED for further proceedings consistent with this opinion. On remand, both § 7217 liability and damages are in issue.

Notes and Question

The *Johnson* case wound its way through the courts for approximately 15 years. Finally, on January 23, 1998, shortly before the new trial was to begin, Johnson reached a settlement with the government under which he would receive $3.5 million.

Statutory Damages. Section 7431 applies to each unauthorized disclosure, rather than to each dissemination. Thus, where the unauthorized return information is released to a newspaper with thousands of subscribers, statutory damages apply only to the one media release, rather than to the multiple releases to the subscribers. See Ward v. United States, 973 F.Supp. 996 (D. Colo. 1997).

Exclusive Remedy. There is a split among the circuits as to whether § 6103 overrides the Privacy Act to provide an exclusive remedy for disclosures of tax return information. The majority view is that § 6103 provides the exclusive remedy and overrides the broader Privacy Act. See, e.g., Cheek v. IRS, 703 F.2d 271 (7th Cir. 1983) (holding that §§ 6103/7431 provide the exclusive remedy); O'Connor v. United States, 669 F. Supp. 317, 323 (D. Nev. 1987), aff'd. 935 F.2d 275 (9th Cir. 1991) (same). A minority of courts have held that the Privacy Act continues to apply where there are no irreconcilable conflicts between it and the Internal Revenue Code. See Taylor v. United States, 106 F.3d 833 (8th Cir. 1997) (where district court applied Privacy Act). The split among the courts is highlighted and discussed in Sinicki v. United States Dept. of Treasury, 1998 WL 80188 (S.D.N.Y. Feb. 24, 1998) (§ 6103 implicitly repeals the Privacy Act to the extent of any inconsistency).

Burden of Proof. No liability for an unauthorized disclosure will arise where the disclosure is made from a good faith, but erroneous interpretation of § 6103. IRC § 7431(b). The standard of good faith is that the agent must not "violate clearly established statutory or constitutional rights of which a reasonable person would have known." Harlow v. Fitzgerald, 457 U.S. 800, 818 (1982). It is not clearly settled, however, which party has the burden of proof. See McDonald v. United States, 102 F.3d 1009 (9th Cir. 1996) (good faith is an affirmative defense which the government must prove); Davidson v. Brady, 732 F.2d 552 (6th Cir. 1984) (burden is on taxpayer to show bad faith on the part of the government).

Damages. A violation of § 6103 can carry both criminal penalties (§ 7213) and civil penalties (§ 7431) under the Code. Under § 7431, damages recoverable for unauthorized inspection of returns or unauthorized disclosure of return information consist of costs of the action (including attorney's fees) plus the greater of (1) $1,000 for each unauthorized inspection or disclosure, or (2) actual damages (which includes emotional distress) plus punitive damages, if the taxpayer establishes that the unauthorized inspection or disclosure was attributable to willfulness or gross negligence.

There is currently a split among the courts whether punitive damages are recoverable under § 7431 in the absence of actual damages.

See Mallas v. United States, 993 F.2d 1111 (4th Cir. 1993) (holding that the absence of actual damages does not preclude an award of punitive damages if the punitive damages are greater than the statutory damages); Barrett v. United States, 917 F. Supp. 493, 504 (SD Tex. 1995) ("clear statutory language of Section 7431(c) precludes the award of punitive damages in a case in which actual damages have not been shown.).

1. As *Johnson v. Sawyer* notes, there is a split among the circuits as to the extent of § 6103 protection against unauthorized disclosure by the government. In Rowley v. United States, 76 F.3d 796 (6th Cir. 1996), the Sixth Circuit distinguished information released in the filing and recording of a tax lien from the release of information that had been previously disclosed in the context of a public trial. As the court noted, "* * * the type of previous disclosure involved here (i.e., the recording of a federal tax lien in a County Register of Deeds' office) is designed to provide public notice and is thus qualitatively different from disclosures made in judicial proceedings, which are only incidentally made public." Do you agree with this statement?

2. In Rodgers v. Hyatt, 697 F.2d 899 (10th Cir. 1983), the IRS sought to enforce a summons against a bank to obtain records regarding a taxpayer who was believed to have underreported income. During the hearing to enforce the summons, taxpayer called the chief of the district division of the Criminal Investigation Division (CID) as a witness. On the stand, this witness testified that the IRS was investigating the correctness of income tax due and owing to the United States by the taxpayer for certain years. He stated that the IRS suspected that the taxpayer's returns were not correct based upon certain allegations that all of the income received by him had not been reported and tax paid thereon. He further stated that there were allegations, based upon information from the Sheriff's Department and the FBI, that the taxpayer was dealing in stolen oil and was not reporting all income received from the sale of that oil. A short time later, the CID Chief was investigating another case when he remarked that the taxpayer was rumored to be involved in stealing oil. The taxpayer in question brought suit seeking damages for violation of § 6103. What result? Cf. Rowley v. United States, 76 F.3d 796 (6th Cir. 1996).

IV. THE GOVERNMENT'S ACCESS TO TAXPAYER INFORMATION

The Service is authorized under § 7602 to examine books, records, and other documents, and to subpoena witnesses to determine the correctness of any return and amount of tax liability owed by the taxpayer. Thus, the Service has a right of inspection. On the other hand, the anti-browsing provision prohibits Service employees, § 7213A, and other federal and state employees from willfully inspecting any return or return information, except as authorized under § 7602.

The extent to which the government may obtain taxpayer information from a third party representative, however, depends upon who the party is and what type of information is involved.

A. FEDERALLY AUTHORIZED TAX PRACTITIONERS

In 1998, Congress granted to federally authorized tax practitioners ("FATPs") (i.e., CPAs, enrolled agents, and enrolled actuaries authorized to practice before the IRS) "the same common law protections of confidentiality" previously applicable to attorney-client communications. IRC § 7525. Thus, communications between a client and a FATP are considered privileged "to the extent that the communication would be considered a privileged communication if it were between a taxpayer and an attorney." IRC § 7525(a).

The privilege is subject to a number of exceptions, however. Under § 7525, the privilege applies only to communications with respect to tax advice and only to the extent the attorney-client privilege would otherwise apply; it does not apply to criminal proceedings, either before the Service or in the federal courts; and it does not apply to written communications in connection with the promotion of any tax shelter.

Questions

1. Several commentators have noted that the FATP privilege creates more problems than it solves. What problems, if any, do you see with the privilege?

2. Section 7525 states that the privilege applies to the extent the "common law protections of confidentiality" would have applied "to a communication between a taxpayer and an attorney." How does the privilege apply to nonlawyers?

B. THE ATTORNEY-CLIENT PRIVILEGE

The FATP privilege is based on the attorney-client privilege, so the first step in determining whether the FATP privilege applies is to determine the extent to which the attorney-client privilege applies. The attorney-client privilege does not apply to business or accounting advice;

instead it applies only to legal advice rendered by an attorney to the client. Sometimes, however, the distinction between business/accounting advice and legal advice is a difficult one to draw. This distinction is at issue in the *El Paso* case, although bear in mind that this case arose prior to the FATP privilege.

UNITED STATES v. EL PASO COMPANY
United States Court of Appeals, Fifth Circuit, 1982.
682 F.2d 530, *cert. denied* 466 U.S. 944, 104 S.Ct. 1927, 80 L.Ed.2d 473 (1984).

JERRE S. WILLIAMS, CIRCUIT JUDGE.

The United States and two agents of the Internal Revenue Service (IRS) petitioned the district court to enforce two summonses issued to the El Paso Company (El Paso) with regard to a tax audit. One summons sought El Paso's "tax-pool analysis" – a summary of El Paso's contingent liability for additional taxes should it ultimately be determined that El Paso owed more taxes than indicated on its return. After a hearing, the district court enforced the tax pool analysis summons and El Paso brought this appeal. We affirm.

I.

El Paso is the holding company for several large corporations, including 67 subsidiaries. The principal operations in the El Paso conglomerate are the El Paso Natural Gas Company, the El Paso Products Company, and the El Paso LNG Company. All are based in Texas. Because of the size and variety of El Paso's business, the calculation of El Paso's tax liability is an immense task. To prepare a return for a single year, El Paso's in-house staff expends over 10,000 hours.

The IRS, as it does with most giant corporations, annually audits El Paso and has been doing so since the 1940s. To perform the audit, the IRS assembles a team of revenue agents. Even with a team specifically assigned to El Paso, however, the IRS has time to review and inspect only a small sample of the documents that underlie El Paso's returns. The audit of El Paso that triggered the summons in this case was not conducted on suspicion of fraud; rather, it was a routine audit occasioned by the amount of taxes at stake.

Each audit of El Paso covers several years of tax returns. The relevant cycle in this case includes the years 1976, 1977, and 1978. Early in the audit of the 1976-1978 cycle, the IRS team coordinator delivered a document request to El Paso for "all analyses prepared by the

El Paso Company regarding potential tax liabilities and tax problems" for the years covered by the cycle. Five days later, Jack McCarthy, the head of El Paso's tax department, returned the request form marked "refused."

Shortly after receiving El Paso's refusal to respond to the potential tax-liabilities document request, the IRS issued a summons to McCarthy covering "any document, memorandum, letter, or work papers which identify potential tax liabilities or tax problems for the period beginning January 1, 1976 and ending December 31, 1978, inclusive." McCarthy also declined to comply with the summons, stating his reasons in a letter written to the case manager of the El Paso audit.

On May 27, 1981, the IRS filed its petition to enforce the summons under 26 U.S.C. § 7604.[2] El Paso defended against enforcement on grounds of burdensomeness, relevance, attorney-client privilege, and work product doctrine. After a hearing at which both sides were permitted to call and cross-examine witnesses, the district court rejected El Paso's defenses and concluded that El Paso must comply with the summons.

El Paso appealed and sought a stay of the district court's judgment from this Court. Because of the importance and the novelty of the issues raised with respect to the IRS's summons powers, we granted the stay pending our resolution of the case.

II.

This appeal is centrally concerned with documents known to the accounting profession under various names – the noncurrent tax account, the tax accrual work papers, and the tax pool analysis. Because the nomenclature is not standardized, the IRS chose to request El Paso's version of these documents under a loose descriptive label – documents analyzing potential tax liabilities or tax problems. No matter what alias is used, however, the documents are of similar nature. It is useful to explain what these documents are before proceeding to determine whether the IRS may have access to them.

The income tax laws, as every citizen knows, are far from a model of clarity. Written to accommodate a multitude of competing policies and differing situations, the Internal Revenue Code is a sprawling tapestry

---

2.   Section 7604(a) provides:

If any person is summoned under the Internal Revenue laws to appear, testify, or to produce books, papers, records, or other data, the United States District Court for the district in which such person resides or is found shall have jurisdiction by appropriate process to compel such attendance, testimony, or production of books, papers, records, or other data.

of almost infinite complexity. Its details and intricate provisions have fostered a wealth of interpretations. To thread one's way through this maze, the business or wealthy taxpayer needs the mind of a Talmudist and the patience of Job.

Even endowed with these qualities, however, no taxpayer completes a return with the certainty that the IRS will agree with the bottom line, or the many steps taken to get there. There is no tax oracle one may consult to learn how a return will fare under the scrutiny of the revenue agents and the courts. The Code, after all, is a finite system of rules designed to apply flexibility to an infinite variety of situations. There are many "gray areas" in the tax world, twilight zones in which one may only dimly perceive how properly to treat a given accretion to wealth or given expenditure of funds.

When a large corporation like El Paso completes its return, the number of decisions in the gray areas is enormous. To characterize a sale as ordinary income or capital gain, to depreciate equipment over ten years or twenty, to attribute a transaction to this year or to the next: these decisions recur over and over in a course of preparing a return and guarantee that a large corporation has many opportunities to choose in good faith an interpretation of the tax code that leans toward lessening its taxes. The return is filed with the understanding, however, that the IRS may challenge some of these questionable positions and, through settlement or litigation, the corporation may end up owing more taxes than it initially acknowledged.

Business reality compels corporations to recognize on their financial sheets that the return as filed is not the last word in determining the taxes owed. Public companies subject to the securities laws must file financial statements with the Securities and Exchange Commission (SEC), 15 U.S.C. § 78l. SEC regulations require that independent accountants verify these financial statements in accord with Generally Accepted Auditing Principles. To demonstrate to the accountant that a balance sheet does not portray an overly-rosy view of a corporation's financial health, the balance sheet must provide for contingent future tax liabilities. In short, the corporation must set aside an account to cover additional taxes that it may become liable to pay above and beyond the amount indicated on the initial return.

To comply with the securities laws, therefore, companies such as El Paso *must* prepare in-house or have prepared by outside auditors an analysis of their contingent tax liabilities.[3] The analysis pinpoints the

3. El Paso also informs us that the New York Stock Exchange requires that a corporation whose stock is traded on the Exchange have its books audited in accord with Generally Accepted Auditing Principles. Moreover, banks that lend to public companies may also demand that a

soft spots on the corporation's tax returns and indicates those areas in which the taxpayer has taken a position that may, upon challenge, negotiation, or litigation, require the payment of more taxes. The analysis is known in the trade as the tax pool analysis, the noncurrent tax account, or tax accrual work papers.

Several points are worth noting about the tax pool analysis. First, it is not prepared to assist in filling out a tax return. The tax pool analysis is undertaken only after the return is filed. Although the same corporate employees or outside auditors may prepare both the return and the tax pool analysis, there is no necessary connection between the two jobs.

Second, the tax pool analysis may be performed either in house or by outside accountants. El Paso happens to prepare its own tax pool analysis, but many firms retain outside accountants to accomplish that task. See United States v. Arthur Young & Co., 677 F.2d 211 (2d Cir. 1982). It is not essential to consult an attorney to prepare the tax pool analysis.

Finally, * * * [w]hile the analysis must forecast the cumulative results of IRS audit, settlement, and litigation, the tax pool analysis itself is not prepared to respond to a specific charge by the IRS or to any pending or impending lawsuit. The tax pool analysis is undertaken solely to insure that the corporation sets aside on its balance sheet a sufficient amount to cover contingent tax liability.

* * *

V.

We now turn to El Paso's contention that the tax pool analysis is shielded by the attorney-client privilege. El Paso carries the burden of establishing this defense to the enforcement of the summons.

In Upjohn Co. v. United States, 449 U.S. 383, 101 S.Ct. 677, 66 L.Ed.2d 584 (1981), the Supreme Court delineated the purpose of the attorney-client privilege.[8]

The attorney-client privilege is the oldest of the privileges for confidential communications known to the common law. Its purpose

---

corporation maintain an account for contingent tax liabilities.

8.   In *Upjohn* the IRS summoned the files of a corporate taxpayer's general counsel on the counsel's investigation of illegal foreign payments made by the corporation. The court held that the attorney-client privilege protected the files whether or not the client communications therein were made by the corporation's "control group." Because the purpose of the attorney-client privilege is to promote the flow of information to the attorney to enable him to give informed legal advice, communications from lower echelon employees were within the privilege as long as the communications were made to the attorney to assist him in giving legal advice to the client corporation. 101 S.Ct. at 682-86.

is to encourage full and frank communication between attorneys and their clients and thereby promote broader public interests in the observance of law and administration of justice. The privilege recognizes that sound legal advice or advocacy serves public ends and that such advice or advocacy depends upon the lawyer being fully informed by the client. As we stated last term in Trammel v. United States, 445 U.S. 40, 51, 100 S.Ct. 906, 913, 63 L.Ed.2d 186 (1980), "the attorney-client privilege rests on the need for the advocating counselor to know all that relates to the client's reasons for seeking representation if the professional mission is to be carried out." And in Fisher v. United States, 425 U.S. 391, 403, 96 S.Ct. 1569, 1577, 48 L.Ed.2d 39 (1976), we recognized the purpose of the privilege to be "to encourage clients to make full disclosures to their attorneys."

Id. 101 S.Ct. at 682.

The scope of the attorney-client privilege is shaped by its purposes. While the elements of the privilege have been comprehensively restated elsewhere,[9] it is sufficient here to note that "[w]hat is vital to the privilege is that the communication be made *in confidence* for the purpose of obtaining *legal* advice *from the lawyer.*" United States v. Kovel, 296 F.2d 918, 922 (2d Cir. 1961) (emphasis in original). Moreover, "disclosure of any significant portion of a confidential communication waives the privilege as to the whole." United States v. Davis, 636 at 1043 n.18.[10] Finally, we have made clear that the attorney-client privilege may not be tossed as a blanket over an undifferentiated group of documents. United States v. Davis, 636 F.2d at 1044 n.20; United States v. Roundtree, 420 F.2d 845, 852 (5th Cir. 1969). The privilege must be specifically asserted with respect to particular documents.

---

9. See 8 J. Wigmore Evidence § 2292 at 554 (J. McNaughton rev. 1961):

(1) Where legal advice of any kind is sought; (2) from a professional legal advisor in his capacity as such; (3) the communications relating to that purpose; (4) made in confidence; (5) by the client; (6) are at his instance permanently protected; (7) from disclosure by himself or by the legal advisor; (8) except the protection be waived.

See generally Petersen, Attorney Client Privilege and Internal Revenue Service Investigations, 54 Minn.L.Rev. 67 (1969).

10. The Sixth Circuit might take a different view of disclosure, see United States v. Upjohn Co., 600 F.2d 1223, 1227 n.12 (6th Cir. 1979) ("the corporation's voluntary disclosure to the SEC amounts to a waiver of the privilege only with respect to the facts actually disclosed"), rev'd, 449 U.S. 383, 101 S.Ct. 677, 66 L.Ed.2d 584 (1981). The Supreme Court in *Upjohn* noted the Sixth Circuit's treatment of the waiver issue but did not discuss or decide it, see 101 S.Ct. at 682.

The revelations to the SEC made in *Upjohn* were facts concerning foreign payments. The attorney-client privilege does not protect against discovery of underlying facts from their source merely because those facts have been communicated to an attorney. 101 S.Ct. at 685-86. The public disclosure of those facts, moreover, does not destroy the privilege with respect to attorney-client communications about those facts. Thus, it is not clear that the Sixth Circuit was concerned in *Upjohn* with a potential divulgence of a confidential communication.

The IRS argues that El Paso has failed to prove any of the elements of the attorney-client privilege. In its broadest theory, the IRS urges that preparing the tax pool analysis is not legal work and that El Paso's attorneys in performing it are not giving legal advice. In the IRS's view the tax pool analysis is a business document, drawn up solely to bring the company's financial statements in line with generally accepted auditing principles. Because the tax pool analysis simply supports a record of the corporation's finances, the IRS sees it as business work rather than legal work.

The line between accounting work and legal work in the giving of tax advice is extremely difficult to draw. See Kenderdine, The Internal Revenue Service Summons to Produce Documents: Powers, Procedures & Taxpayer Defenses, 64 Minn.L.Rev. 73, 100-01 (1979). We have held that the preparation of tax returns is generally not legal advice within the scope of the privilege. United States v. Davis, 636 F.2d at 1043. *Davis* withheld the privilege from communications made to an attorney to prepare a tax return because such work is primarily an accounting service. The tax pool analysis may also be considered an accounting service since it is often performed by accountants. Nevertheless, we would be reluctant to hold that a lawyer's analysis of the soft spots in a tax return and his judgments on the outcome of litigation on it are not legal advice. We need not decide this issue, however, because we believe that El Paso's attempt to claim the privilege fails on other grounds.

To retain the attorney-client privilege, the confidentiality surrounding the communications made in that relationship must be preserved. The purpose of the privilege is to foster full client disclosure to the lawyer; the privilege exists to assure the client that his private disclosures will not become common knowledge. The need to cloak these communications with secrecy, however, ends when the secrets pass through the client's lips to others. Thus, a breach of confidentiality forfeits the client's right to claim the privilege. As Justice Holmes wrote when a member of the Massachusetts Supreme Court,

> [T]he privacy for the sake of which the privilege was created was gone by the appellant's own consent, and the privilege does not remain in such circumstances for the mere sake of giving the client an additional weapon to use or not at his choice.

Green v. Crapo, 181 Mass. 55, 62 N.E. 956, 959 (1902).

The district court found in this case that El Paso discussed "some of the information and many of the potential tax liability issues" in its tax pool analysis with the independent auditors who certify the corporation's books. This finding is not clearly erroneous. The evidence showed that in the course of the audit, the accountants determine whether the company has set aside an adequate reserve for contingent taxes. This task carries the auditors into the tax pool analysis and into at least some of the supporting memoranda. Confidentiality as to these documents is neither expected nor preserved, for they are created with the knowledge that independent accountants may need access to them to complete the audit.

El Paso generates the tax pool analysis to portray its financial condition accurately. As the securities laws require, independent accountants then verify the financial statements by probing the corporation's reasons for allocating a given amount to its noncurrent tax account.[12] In El Paso's case, the tax pool analysis is revealed to the independent accountants as part of their audit. Our Circuit does not recognize an accountant-client communications privilege, and, as the Supreme Court has acknowledged, neither does any other federal court. Couch v. United States, 409 U.S. 322, 335, 93 S.Ct. 611, 619, 34 L.Ed.2d 548 (1973) ("* * * we note that no confidential accountant client privilege exists under federal law, and no state created privilege has been recognized in federal cases * * *."). Under these circumstances, El Paso's disclosure of the tax pool analysis to the auditors destroys confidentiality with respect to it. With the destruction of confidentiality goes as well the right to claim the attorney-client privilege.

We recognize that the Second Circuit has denied enforcement of IRS summons to the taxpayer's accountant seeking tax accrual workpapers that the accountant has prepared. United States v. Arthur Young & Co., supra. The logic of *Arthur Young* implies that the taxpayer's revelation of tax accrual workpapers to an accountant should be considered a communication in confidence.[13] *Arthur Young* does not persuade us,

---

12. The *Arthur Young* court gave the following description of the auditing process:

[G]enerally accepted auditing standards require an auditor to determine whether his client has put aside enough reserves to cover the contingency that upon audit it will owe the government more taxes than originally remitted. To make this assessment, the auditor must determine not only how the taxpayer treated his income and expenses in his tax return; he must also decide whether that treatment comports favorably with the Internal Revenue Code, the regulations, and the case law. In areas where the law is unclear, he must predict the chances that the taxpayer's position will be upheld by the courts – a judgment based on his knowledge of the law and his opinion of where the law is headed. The auditor must also take into account the likelihood that the client will settle the dispute – a judgment based on the auditor's confidential and intimate knowledge of the client.

677 F.2d at 217.

13. The *Arthur Young* court reasoned that if the IRS could reach tax accrual workpapers prepared by accountants, taxpayers might conceal their tax vulnerabilities from the accountants. The concealment, in turn, would impair the accuracy of financial statements and the ability of investors to rely on them. In the Second Circuit's view, this result would run counter to the policy of the securities laws to guard investors against flawed financial information. Accordingly, the

however, that El Paso's disclosure of its tax pool analysis to its independent accountants is consistent with the confidentiality required to assert the attorney-client privilege. To extend *Arthur Young* to this case would, in effect, create an accountant-client communications privilege. No such privilege exists under federal law, however, as we noted above. In the absence of a contrary rule established by law, we cannot view El Paso's discussions with its auditors as confidential. The attorney-client privilege is, therefore, waived.

We believe that El Paso may not withdraw behind the shield of the attorney-client privilege for an additional reason. El Paso failed to particularize its assertion of the privilege and prove its case with respect to any specific document. El Paso made only a blanket assertion of the privilege as to all documents in, or backing up, its tax pool analysis. Such a showing is simply inadequte.

In *United States v. Davis,* we reiterated the unacceptability of blanket assertions of the attorney-client privilege. 636 F.2d at 1044 n.20. Such assertions disable the court and the adversary party from testing the merits of the claim of privilege. In *Davis* we relaxed the rule because of confusion about when the attorney-client privilege should be raised in a tax summons enforcement proceeding. We cautioned, however, that "future litigants who make only blanket assertions of privilege at enforcement proceedings should not expect such grace." Id. El Paso had fair notice of the obligation to make its privilege claim precise.[14] We cannot excuse its failure to do so.

The reasons for refusing to tolerate blanket assertions of the privilege apply fully to this case. El Paso's tax department employs eighty accountants and ten attorneys. The tax department as a whole has responsibility for preparing the various memoranda that underpin the tax pool analysis. Both the head of the tax department and the general counsel testified at the enforcement hearing, but neither witness had reviewed the backup memoranda prior to testifying. As a result, neither

---

Second Circuit fashioned an accountant's work-product rule for tax accrual workpapers. 677 F.2d at 221.

To the extent that the Second Circuit wished to encourage companies to reveal freely their tax vulnerabilities to independent accountants, the *Arthur Young* rule implicitly strives to shelter the confidentiality of the taxpayer's communications to the accountant about the noncurrent tax account. See *Arthur Young,* 677 F.2d at 223 n.5 (dissenting opinion observing that the *Arthur Young* holding is grounded on policies more germane to a client-communications confidentiality rule than an accountant's work-product rule). Thus, if we were to adopt the reasoning of *Arthur Young,* a question would arise whether the El Paso's communications to its accountants were confidential, and, therefore, not in breach of the confidentiality necessary to assert the attorney-client privilege.

14. *United States v. Davis* was decided on February 12, 1981; the government filed its enforcement petition in this case on May 27, 1981.

was able to state how many or which memoranda were prepared by attorneys rather than by accountants.

El Paso's failure to prove which documents were prepared by attorneys considerably undermines its claim to the attorney-client privilege. Because the privilege does not attach to tax work prepared by accountants unless the accountant is translating complex tax terms into a form intelligible to a lawyer at the lawyer's behest, United States v. Kovel, 296 F.2d at 922, the memoranda prepared by accountants do not qualify for the privilege. We cannot say that any single memorandum in the El Paso's tax department is stamped with an attorney's seal. A general claim that the tax department funnels tax work through its attorneys will not do, and El Paso's proof amounted to little more.

We hold, therefore, that El Paso has breached the confidentiality needed to shield its attorney-client communications, and in any event, has failed to meet its burden to assert the privilege specifically. The attorney-client privilege does not protect El Paso against disclosing the documents that the IRS seeks.

* * *

GARWOOD, CIRCUIT JUDGE, dissenting.

I respectfully dissent.

* * *

I agree with the majority that "El Paso failed to particularize its assertion of the (attorney-client) privilege and prove its case with respect to any specific document," and with so much of the majority opinion as concerns the denial on this ground of El Paso's attempt to defeat the summonses by invoking the attorney-client privilege. I also believe that essentially the same reasoning dictates denial of El Paso's attempt to invoke blanket work product protection against these summonses.

I am concerned, however, with the majority's holding that El Paso *waived* any possible attorney-client privilege. Not only is this holding unnecessary to the result reached, but this case presents a particularly unfortunate context within which to make such a determination of waiver. Because we really have no information whatever respecting any asserted attorney-client communication, determining whether the privilege in regard thereto has been waived is virtually impossible (which is another good reason to deny blanket assertions of the privilege).

The majority bases its waiver holding on the district court's finding that El Paso "*discussed 'some* of the information and *many* of the potential tax liability issues' in the tax pool analysis with the independent auditors." (Emphasis added). The majority then asserts that the auditors' task "carries" them "into the tax pool analysis and into at least *some* of the supporting memoranda," which are not confidential since "they are created with the knowledge that independent accountants *may need* access to them." (Emphasis added).

But what of the supporting memoranda and items in the tax pool analysis that are *not* discussed with or shown to the auditors? (The evidence and findings below indicate such items exist, and indeed that a substantial number of the "subject files" fell into this category). Moreover, even regarding a subject file or tax pool item that has been "discussed" with the auditors, the scope of the waiver would appear to depend on the scope of the discussion. Surely not every discussion relating to a topic included in a file mandates a waiver of the entirety of every item in that file.[15] Footnote 18 in United States v. Davis, 636 F.2d 1028, 1043 (5th Cir. 1981), is far too slender a reed to bear the full weight of such an extensive holding.[16] Nor does United States v. Pipkins, 528 F.2d 559, 563 (5th Cir.1976), provide significant guidance in this setting.[17]

Moreover, in my view substantial concerns argue in favor of holding that the attorney-client privilege is not waived by confidential disclosures to the client's independent auditors. Of course, as to information which the client intends the auditors to disclose to others or can anticipate a substantial possibility that such disclosure may be made in the proper fulfillment of the auditors' engagement, no such protection should exist. In a practical, operational sense the corporation and its outside auditor regard the information which the latter acquires in the course of its work, especially that within the scope of the attorney-client privilege, as fully confidential except insofar as the nature of the engagement contemplates the actual or likely disclosure of same to third parties. The reality of the matter is that for publicly held companies very little

---

15. See, e.g., United States v. Upjohn Co., 600 F.2d 1223, 1227 n.12 (6th Cir. 1979), rev'd on other grounds, 449 U.S. 383, 101S.Ct. 677, 66 L.Ed.2d 584 (1981); United States v. Lipshy, 492 F.Supp. 35, 44 (N.D.Tex.1979) (employee communications made to attorney in connection with preparing report for corporate client on corporate wrongdoing; held that disclosure of the report to the IRS and of portions of it to the SEC did not waive the privilege as to "all details underlying the statement").

16. For example, a young man informs his mother that he was at the convenience store which was held up earlier in the evening. At her suggestion he sees Lawyer Jones, and on returning home his mother asks, "Did you tell Lawyer Jones you were at the store when it was held up?" He acknowledges that he did so. Has he thereby waived the privilege as to his entire conversation with Lawyer Jones respecting the occurrence at the store?

17. *Pipkins* involved handwriting samples the client gave a handwriting expert retained by his attorney. This Court rejected a claim of privilege, pointing out that Pipkins had "already voluntarily disclosed his handwriting style to the government," 528 F.2d at 563, and that "one's style of handwriting, readily observable by anyone, [is] not subject to the attorney-client privilege," 528 F.2d at 563 n.2.

information can properly be held entirely confidential from independent auditors. If we do not take these realities into account in developing and applying theories of waiver of the attorney-client privilege in these situations, there is a substantial danger that the attorney-client privilege for publicly held corporations, so recently reaffirmed in Upjohn Co. v. United States, 449 U.S. 383, 101 S.Ct. 677, 66 L.Ed.2d 584 (1981), will become nothing but an empty theory. This danger is especially acute if courts broadly apply the concept of waiver of the entirety of a communication by the disclosure of any significant portion of it. Though informed by some of the same considerations, the suggestion here made does not create a new privilege or cover anywhere near as wide a range of communications as the rule adopted in *Arthur Young & Co.* Moreover, the restrictions on waiver hypothesized here are considerably narrower, and more in keeping with the concept of expected confidentiality, than the limited waiver approved in Diversified Industries, Inc. v. Meredith, 572 F.2d 596, 611 (8th Cir. 1977) (en banc), involving material disclosed to a public body.[18] And, there is no reason to believe that the courts will be any less able to control abuse of the privilege in this context than they have been in others.

For these reasons I cannot accept the majority's blanket and unnecessary invocation of waiver of the attorney-client privilege in the context of this case.

* * *

Notes and Questions

When the client is a corporation, the question arises as to who can represent the corporate entity in order to claim the privilege. Is it only the "control group" of senior management, or does it extend more broadly? In Upjohn Co. v. United States, 449 U.S. 385 (1980), the Supreme Court addressed this issue and discarded the control group test. In *Upjohn,* the Court concluded that communications between the company's attorney and any employee could result in a privileged communication. The Court reasoned that the control group test was too narrowly construed, because many times the management group will have to consult with the middle management group, and often with rank and file employees as well, in order to properly determine the facts that led to the claim of privilege. The Court also reasoned that the control

---

18. Under the *Meredith* limited-waiver approach, of course, the privilege does not extend to the governmental unit to which disclosure was made. Cf. United States v. Miller, 660 F.2d 563 (5th Cir. 1981) (in a criminal tax fraud case the attorney-client privilege was waived with respect to ledger books previously turned over to the IRS during its civil investigation respecting the taxes in issue). The *Meredith* limited-waiver theory was rejected in Permian Corp. v. United States, 665 F.2d 1214 (D.C.Cir. 1981).

group test was too uncertain and that the attorney-client privilege, in order to be workable, must be certain because "an uncertain privilege, or one which purports to be certain but results in widely varying applications by the courts, is little better than no privilege at all." Id. at 393. Thus, as long as all the elements of the attorney-client privilege are met, the privilege can apply to the corporation without regard to the control group test.

1. Does the enactment of § 7525 have any effect on the *El Paso* decision?

2. Clearly, information included in a tax return is not privileged. But the underlying rationale as to why divides along two lines. First, the attorney-client privilege applies only to legal advice; the preparation of tax returns is considered an accounting service, rather than legal advice. Second, communications that are disclosed or intended to be disclosed to third parties lose the benefit of the privilege. United States v. Lawless, 709 F.2d 485, 488 (1983). Because a tax return is intended to be filed with the government, the privilege is waived. But does the waiver apply only to the information ultimately sent to the government or does it also apply to the underlying data and peripheral communications between the lawyer or accountant and the client? See United States v. Schlegel, 313 F.Supp. 177 (D. Neb. 1970); United States v. Cote, 456 F.2d 142 (8th Cir. 1972); United States v. Shapiro, 335 U.S. 1 (1947); In Re Grand Jury Subpoena Dated March 24, 1983, 566 F.Supp. 883 (S.D.N.Y. 1983).

3. Is there likely to be a greater problem with waiver of the privilege in the Tax Court than in the federal district court? If so, why?

C. THE WORK PRODUCT DOCTRINE

Another protection against compelled disclosure is the work product doctrine. This doctrine is closely related to the attorney-client privilege, but where the attorney-client privilege belongs to the client and can be waived only by the client or by the attorney with the client's permission, work-product protection belongs to the attorney or other professional advisor or consultant working directly with the client.

The work product doctrine is embodied in Rule 26(b)(3) of the Federal Rules of Civil Procedure, which provides that "a party may obtain discovery of documents and tangible things otherwise discoverable . . . and prepared in anticipation of litigation or for trial by or for another party or by or for that other party's representative (including the other party's attorney, consultant, surety, indemnitor, insurer, or agent) only upon a showing that the party seeking discovery has substantial need of the materials in the preparation of the party's case and that the party is unable without undue hardship to obtain the substantial equivalent of the materials by other means."

Problems have arisen, however, when the document in question is prepared for a dual purpose, i.e., it is prepared for a business purpose but may be used in litigation.

UNITED STATES v. TEXTRON INC.
First Circuit Court of Appeals (en banc), 2009
577 F.3d 21, cert. denied, ___ U.S. ___, 130 S.Ct. 3320, 2010

BOUDIN, CIRCUIT JUDGE.

The question for the en banc court is whether the attorney work product doctrine shields from an IRS summons "tax accrual work papers" prepared by lawyers and others in Textron's Tax Department to support Textron's calculation of tax reserves for its audited corporate financial statements. Textron is a major aerospace and defense conglomerate, with well over a hundred subsidiaries, whose consolidated tax return is audited by the IRS on a regular basis. To understand the dispute, some background is required concerning financial statements, contingent tax reserves and tax audit work papers.

As a publicly traded corporation, Textron is required by federal securities law to have public financial statements certified by an independent auditor. To prepare such financial statements, Textron must calculate reserves to be entered on the company books to account for contingent tax liabilities. Such liabilities, which affect the portrayal of assets and earnings, include estimates of potential liability if the IRS decides to challenge debatable positions taken by the taxpayer in its return.

The calculation of such reserves entails preparing work papers describing Textron's potential liabilities for further taxes; these underpin the tax reserve entries in its financial statement and explain the figures chosen to the independent auditor who certifies that statement as correct. By examining the work papers the accountant discharges its own duty to determine "the adequacy and reasonableness of the corporation's reserve account for contingent tax liabilities." United States v. Arthur Young & Co., 465 U.S. 805, 812, 104 S.Ct. 1495, 79 L.Ed.2d 826 (1984) (rejecting claim of accountant work product privilege protecting such work papers). The work papers are thus one step in a process whose outcome is a certified financial statement for the company.

In Textron's case, its Tax Department lists items in the tax return that, if identified and challenged by the IRS, could result in additional taxes being assessed. The final spreadsheets list each debatable item, including in each instance the dollar amount subject to possible dispute and a percentage estimate of the IRS' chances of success. Multiplying the amount by the percentage fixes the reserve entered on the books for that item. The spreadsheets reflecting these calculations may be supported by backup emails or notes.

A company's published financial statements do not normally identify the specific tax items on the return that may be debatable but incorporate or reflect only the total reserve figure. As the Supreme Court explained in *Arthur Young*, tax accrual work papers provide a resource for the IRS, if the IRS can get access to them, by "pinpoint[ing] the 'soft spots' on a corporation's tax return by highlighting those areas in which the corporate taxpayer has taken a position that may, at some later date, require the payment of additional taxes" and providing "an item-by-item analysis of the corporation's potential exposure to additional liability." 465 U.S. at 813, 104 S.Ct. 1495.

The IRS does not automatically request tax accrual work papers from taxpayers; rather, in the wake of Enron and other corporate scandals, the IRS began to seek companies' tax accrual work papers only where it concluded that the taxpayer had engaged in certain listed transactions "that [are] the same as or substantially similar to one of the types of transactions that the [IRS] has determined to be a tax avoidance transaction." Only a limited number of transactions are so designated.

The present case began with a 2003 IRS audit of Textron's corporate income tax liability for the years 1998-2001. In reviewing Textron's 2001 return, the IRS determined that a Textron subsidiary-Textron Financial Corp. ("Textron Financial")-had engaged in nine listed transactions. In each of the nine instances, Textron Financial had purchased equipment from a foreign utility or transit operator and leased it back to the seller on the same day. Although such transactions can be legitimate, the IRS determined that they were sale-in, lease-out ("SILO") transactions, which are listed as a potential tax shelter subject to abuse by taxpayers.

* * *

Textron had shown the spreadsheets to its outside accountant, Ernst & Young, but refused to show them to the IRS. The IRS issued an administrative summons pursuant to 26 U.S.C. § 7602 (2006), which allows the IRS, in determining the accuracy of any return, to "examine any books, papers, records, or other data which may be relevant or material to such inquiry." Id. § 7602(a)(1). According to IRS policy, where the taxpayer claims benefits from only a single listed transaction, the IRS seeks only the workpapers for that transaction; but where (as in Textron's case) the taxpayer claims benefits from multiple listed transactions, the IRS seeks all of the workpapers for the tax year in question. I.R.S. The summons also sought related work papers created by Ernst & Young in determining the adequacy of Textron's reserves that Textron might possess or could obtain. Textron again refused.

The IRS brought an enforcement action in federal district court in Rhode Island. See 26 U.S.C. § 7604(a) (2006). Textron challenged the summons as lacking legitimate purpose and also asserted, as bars to the demand, the attorney-client and tax practitioner privileges and the qualified privilege available for litigation materials under the work product doctrine. The IRS contested all of the privilege claims. Both the IRS and Textron filed affidavits and, in addition, the district court heard witnesses from both sides.

Textron agreed that it usually settled disputes with the IRS through negotiation or concession or at worst through the formal IRS administrative process; but it testified that sometimes it had litigated disputed tax issues in federal court. Its evidence also showed that the estimates for tax reserves and the supporting work papers were generated within its Tax Department but that tax lawyers in that department were centrally involved in their preparation and that Textron Financial also used an outside counsel to advise it on tax reserve requirements.

Textron described generically the contents of the work papers in question: these included (1) summary spreadsheets showing for each disputable item the amount in controversy, estimated probability of a successful challenge by the IRS, and resulting reserve amounts; and (2) back up e-mail and notes. In some instances the spreadsheet entries estimated the probability of IRS success at 100 percent. Textron said that the spreadsheets had been shown to and discussed with its independent auditor but physically retained by Textron.

Neither side disputed that the immediate purpose of the work papers was to establish and support the tax reserve figures for the audited financial statements. Textron's evidence was to the effect that litigation over specific items was always a possibility; the IRS did not deny that in certain cases litigation could result although it said that this was often unlikely. Whether Textron's evidence is materially different than that of the IRS remains to be considered.

Ultimately, the district court denied the petition for enforcement. United States v. Textron Inc., 507 F.Supp.2d 138, 150, 155 (D.R.I.2007). The court agreed with the IRS that the agency had a legitimate purpose for seeking the work papers. Id. at 145. It also ruled that insofar as the Textron-prepared work papers might otherwise be protected by attorney-client privilege, or the counterpart tax practitioner privilege for non-lawyers engaged in tax practice, see 26 U.S.C. § 7525 (2006), those privileges had been waived when Textron disclosed the work papers' content to Ernst & Young. Id. at 152.

However, the district court concluded that the papers were protected by the work product privilege, which derived from Hickman v. Taylor, 329 U.S. 495, 67 S.Ct. 385, 91 L.Ed. 451 (1947), and is now embodied in Rule 26(b)(3) of the Federal Rules of Civil Procedure. This privilege, the district court held, had not been waived by disclosure of the work papers to the accountant. Textron, 507 F.Supp.2d at 152-53. The district court's decision that the work papers were protected work product involved both a description of factual premises and a legal interpretation of applicable doctrine.

The district court first said (paraphrasing a Textron witness) the work papers were prepared to assure that Textron was "adequately reserved with respect to any potential disputes or litigation" over its returns; the court also said that, by fair inference, the work papers served "to satisfy an independent auditor that Textron's reserve for contingent liabilities satisfied the requirements of generally accepted accounting principles (GAAP) so that a 'clean' opinion would be given" for Textron financial statements. Textron, 507 F.Supp.2d at 143.

Then, in its discussion of legal doctrine, the district court stated:

As the IRS correctly observes, the work product privilege does not apply to " 'documents that are prepared in the ordinary course of business or that would have been created in essentially similar form irrespective of the litigation.' " Maine, 298 F.3d at 70 (quoting [United States v. Adlman, 134 F.3d 1194, 1202 (2d Cir.1998)]). However, it is clear that the opinions of Textron's counsel and accountants regarding items that might be challenged by the IRS, their estimated hazards of litigation percentages and their calculation of tax reserve amounts would not have been prepared at all "but for" the fact that Textron anticipated the possibility of litigation with the IRS .... Thus, while it may be accurate to say that the workpapers helped Textron determine what amount should be reserved to cover any potential tax liabilities and that the workpapers were useful in obtaining a "clean" opinion from E & Y regarding the adequacy of the reserve amount, there would have been no need to create a reserve in the first place, if Textron had not anticipated a dispute with the IRS that was likely to result in litigation or some other adversarial proceeding.

Textron, 507 F.Supp.2d at 150.

The court concluded that the work papers were therefore prepared "because of" the prospect of litigation, Textron, 507 F.Supp.2d at 150, a phrase used in Maine v. United States Dep't of Interior, 298 F.3d 60, 68 (1st Cir.2002). The court rejected the IRS' reliance on a Fifth Circuit decision rejecting work product protection for tax accrual work papers on the ground that the Fifth Circuit followed a different "primary purpose" test for work protect. Textron, 507 F.Supp.2d at 150 (discussing United States v. El Paso Co., 682 F.2d 530, 543 (5th Cir.1982), cert. denied, 466 U.S. 944, 104 S.Ct. 1927, 80 L.Ed.2d 473 (1984)).

On appeal, a divided panel upheld the district court's decision. The en banc court then granted the government's petition for rehearing en banc, vacated the panel decision, and obtained additional briefs from the parties and interested amici. We now conclude that under our own prior *Maine* precedent-which we reaffirm en banc-the Textron work papers were independently required by statutory and audit requirements and that the work product privilege does not apply.

The case presents two difficulties. One, which can readily be dispelled, stems from the mutability of language used in the governing rules and a confusion between issues of fact and issues of legal characterization. The other problem is more basic: how far work product protection extends turns on a balancing of policy concerns rather than application of abstract logic; here, two circuits have addressed tax accrual work papers in the work product context, but, apart from whatever light is cast by *Arthur Young*, the Supreme Court has not ruled on the issue before us, namely, one in which a document is not in any way prepared "for" litigation but relates to a subject that might or might not occasion litigation.

In origin, the work product privilege derives from the Supreme Court's decision in *Hickman v. Taylor*, 329 U.S. at 510-11, 67 S.Ct. 385, and focused at the outset on the materials that lawyers typically prepare for the purpose of litigating cases. *Hickman v. Taylor* concerned ongoing litigation in which one side filed interrogatories seeking from opposing counsel memoranda recording witness interviews that the latter had conducted after receiving notice of possible claims. Often such material and other items designed for use at trial (*e.g.*, draft briefs, outlines of cross examination) are not obtained from or shared with clients and are unprotected by the traditional attorney-client privilege.

Hickman v. Taylor addressed "the extent to which a party may inquire into oral and written statements of witnesses, or other information, secured by an adverse party's counsel in the course of preparation for possible litigation after a claim has arisen." 329 U.S. at 497, 67 S.Ct. 385. The Court cited a privilege in English courts protecting

> [a]ll documents which are called into existence for the purpose-but not necessarily the sole purpose-of assisting the deponent or

his legal advisers in any actual or anticipated litigation . . . . Reports . . . if made in the ordinary course of routine, are not privileged . . . .

Id. at 510 n. 9, 67 S.Ct. 385.

This history led the Court to practical considerations:

Proper preparation of a client's case demands that he assemble information, sift what he considers to be the relevant from the irrelevant facts, prepare his legal theories and plan his strategy without undue and needless interference .... This work is reflected, of course, in interviews, statements, memoranda, correspondence, briefs, mental impressions, personal beliefs, and countless other tangible and intangible ways-aptly though roughly termed ... as the "work product of the lawyer."

Id. at 511, 67 S.Ct. 385.

On this basis the Court declared that the interrogatories, which sought witness interviews conducted by opponent counsel in preparation for litigation, were protected by a qualified privilege. See id. at 511-12, 67 S.Ct. 385. When in 1970 the Supreme Court through the rule-making process codified the work product privilege in Rule 26(b)(3), it described the privilege as extending to documents and other tangible things that "are prepared in anticipation of litigation or for trial." This phrase, as illuminated by *Hickman v. Taylor's* reasoning, is the one to be applied in this case.

Turning back to the present case, the IRS is unquestionably right that the immediate motive of Textron in preparing the tax accrual work papers was to fix the amount of the tax reserve on Textron's books and to obtain a clean financial opinion from its auditor. And Textron may be correct that unless the IRS might dispute an item in the return, no reserve for that item might be necessary, so perhaps some of the items might be litigated. But in saying that Textron wanted to be "adequately reserved," the district judge did not say that the work papers were prepared for use in possible litigation-only that the reserves would cover liabilities that might be determined in litigation. If the judge had made a "for use" finding-which he did not-that finding would have been clearly erroneous.

That the purpose of the work papers was to make book entries, prepare financial statements and obtain a clean audit cannot be disputed. * * *

* * *

As the IRS expert stated, even if litigation were "remote," the company would still have to prepare work papers to support its judgment. Textron's own witness acknowledged that it would "have to include in its ... tax accrual work papers any new transactions that the company entered into that year that there might be some tax exposure on" regardless of whether it anticipated likely litigation. Judged by Textron's own experience, most-certainly those with high percentage estimates of IRS success-would never be litigated.

To complete the story, we note one suggestion by one Textron witness that, if litigation did occur, the work papers could be useful to Textron in that litigation. This assertion was not supported by any detailed explanation, was not adopted by the district judge and is more than dubious: the main aim of audit work papers is to estimate the amount potentially in dispute and the percentage chance of winning or losing. Even an academic supporter of Textron's legal position conceded that "it is doubtful that tax accrual workpapers, which typically just identify and quantify vulnerable return positions, would be useful in the litigation anticipated with respect to those positions." Pease-Wingenter, The Application of the Attorney-Client Privilege to Tax Accrual Workpapers: The Real Legacy of United States v. Textron, 8 Houston Bus. & Tax L.J. 337, 346 (2008).

Any experienced litigator would describe the tax accrual work papers as tax documents and not as case preparation materials. Whether work product protection should apply to such documents is a legal question informed by the language of rules and Supreme Court doctrine, direct precedent, and policy judgments. The first of these sources-Supreme Court doctrine and the wording of the rules-is helpful to the IRS; direct circuit precedent and the underlying policy of the doctrine and other prudential considerations are more helpful still. Legal commentators can be found on each side; the most persuasive of them favors the IRS.

From the outset, the focus of work product protection has been on materials prepared for use in litigation, whether the litigation was underway or merely anticipated. Thus, *Hickman v. Taylor* addressed "the extent to which a party may inquire into oral and written statements of witnesses, or other information, secured by an adverse party's counsel in the course of preparation for possible litigation after a claim has arisen." 329 U.S. at 497, 67 S.Ct. 385 (emphasis added). Similarly, the English privilege, invoked by *Hickman v. Taylor*, privileged "documents which are called into existence for the purpose-but not necessarily the sole purpose-of assisting the deponent or his legal advisers in any actual or anticipated litigation." Id. at 510 n. 9, 67 S.Ct. 385 (emphasis added).

The phrase used in the codified rule–"prepared in anticipation of litigation or for trial" did not, in the reference to anticipation, mean prepared for some purpose other than litigation: it meant only that the work might be done for litigation but in advance of its institution. The

English precedent, doubtless the source of the language in Rule 26, specified the purpose "of assisting the deponent or his legal advisers in any actual or anticipated litigation ...." The Advisory Committee's Note cited with approval a decision denying work product protection to a driver's accident report, made pursuant to Interstate Commerce Commission rules, even though it might well have become the subject of litigation. Fed.R.Civ.P. 26 advisory committee's note (1970).[7]

It is not enough to trigger work product protection that the subject matter of a document relates to a subject that might conceivably be litigated. Rather, as the Supreme Court explained, "the literal language of [Rule 26(b)(3)] protects materials prepared for any litigation or trial as long as they were prepared by or for a party to the subsequent litigation." Federal Trade Commission v. Grolier Inc., 462 U.S. 19, 25, 103 S.Ct. 2209, 76 L.Ed.2d 387 (1983) (emphasis added). This distinction is well established in the case law. See, e.g., NLRB v. Sears, Roebuck & Co., 421 U.S. 132, 138, 95 S.Ct. 1504, 44 L.Ed.2d 29 (1975).

Nor is it enough that the materials were prepared by lawyers or represent legal thinking. Much corporate material prepared in law offices or reviewed by lawyers falls in that vast category. It is only work done in anticipation of or for trial that is protected. Even if prepared by lawyers and reflecting legal thinking, "[m]aterials assembled in the ordinary course of business, or pursuant to public requirements unrelated to litigation, or for other nonlitigation purposes are not under the qualified immunity provided by this subdivision." Fed.R.Civ.P. 26 advisory committee's note (1970). Accord Hickman v. Taylor, 329 U.S. at 510 n. 9, 67 S.Ct. 385 (quoting English precedent that "[r]eports ... if made in the ordinary course of routine, are not privileged").

Every lawyer who tries cases knows the touch and feel of materials prepared for a current or possible (i.e., "in anticipation of") law suit. They are the very materials catalogued in Hickman v. Taylor and the English precedent with which the decision began. No one with experience of law suits would talk about tax accrual work papers in those terms. A set of tax reserve figures, calculated for purposes of accurately stating a company's financial figures, has in ordinary parlance only that purpose: to support a financial statement and the independent audit of it.

Focusing next on direct precedent, work product protection for tax audit work papers has been squarely addressed only in two circuits: this

---

7. Goosman v. A. Duie Pyle, Inc., 320 F.2d 45 (4th Cir.1963). In *Goosman*, the Fourth Circuit denied work product protection to reports a truck driver made to the lessee and owner of the truck following an accident. The court explained that the reports "were made in the ordinary course of business under ICC regulations and do not represent the lawyer's work product within the holding in *Hickman v. Taylor*." Id. at 52. See also, e.g., Calabro v. Stone, 225 F.R.D. 96, 99 (E.D.N.Y.2004); In re Raytheon Securities Litigation, 218 F.R.D. 354, 359 (D.Mass.2003).

one and the Fifth. In Maine, we said that work product protection does not extend to "documents that are prepared in the ordinary course of business or that would have been created in essentially similar form irrespective of the litigation." Maine, 298 F.3d at 70 (quoting United States v. Adlman, 134 F.3d 1194, 1202 (2d Cir.1998)). *Maine* applies straightforwardly to Textron's tax audit work papers-which were prepared in the ordinary course of business-and it supports the IRS position.

Similarly, the Fifth Circuit in *El Paso* denied protection for the work papers because the court recognized that the company in question was conducting the relevant analysis because of a need to "bring its financial books into conformity with generally accepted auditing principles." 682 F.2d at 543. The Fifth Circuit, which employs a "primary purpose" test, found that the work papers' "sole function" was to back up financial statements. Id. at 543-44. Here, too, the only purpose of Textron's papers was to prepare financial statements.

Other circuits have not passed on tax audit work papers and some might take a different view. But many of the debatable cases affording work product protection involve documents unquestionably prepared for potential use in litigation if and when it should arise.[9] There is no evidence in this case that the work papers were prepared for such a use or would in fact serve any useful purpose for Textron in conducting litigation if it arose.

Finally, the underlying prudential considerations squarely support the IRS' position in this case, and such considerations have special force because *Hickman v. Taylor* was the child of such considerations, as the quotations above make clear. The privilege aimed centrally at protecting the litigation process, Coastal States Gas Corp. v. Department of Energy, 617 F.2d 854, 864 (D.C.Cir.1980), specifically, work done by counsel to help him or her in litigating a case. It is not a privilege designed to help the lawyer prepare corporate documents or other materials prepared in the ordinary course of business. Where the rationale for a rule stops, so ordinarily does the rule.

Nor is there present here the concern that *Hickman v. Taylor* stressed about discouraging sound preparation for a law suit. That danger may exist in other kinds of cases, but it cannot be present where, as here, there is in substance a legal obligation to prepare such papers:

---

9.   See, e.g., Delaney, Migdail & Young, Chartered v. IRS, 826 F.2d 124, 127 (D.C.Cir.1987) (protection for "attorneys' assessment of . . . legal vulnerabilities in order to make sure it does not miss anything in crafting its legal case"); see also In re Sealed Case, 146 F.3d 881, 885 (D.C.Cir.1998) (protection for documents to "protect the client from future litigation about a particular transaction").

the tax audit work papers not only have a different purpose but have to be prepared by exchange-listed companies to comply with the securities laws and accounting principles for certified financial statements. *Arthur Young* made this point in refusing to create an accountant's work product privilege for tax audit papers:

> [T]he auditor is ethically and professionally obligated to ascertain for himself as far as possible whether the corporation's contingent tax liabilities have been accurately stated.... Responsible corporate management would not risk a qualified evaluation of a corporate taxpayer's financial posture to afford cover for questionable positions reflected in a prior tax return.

465 U.S. at 818-19, 104 S.Ct. 1495; *see also* Johnson, supra, at 160-61.

Textron apparently thinks it is "unfair" for the government to have access to its spreadsheets, but tax collection is not a game. Underpaying taxes threatens the essential public interest in revenue collection. If a blueprint to Textron's possible improper deductions can be found in Textron's files, it is properly available to the government unless privileged. Virtually all discovery against a party aims at securing information that may assist an opponent in uncovering the truth. Unprivileged IRS information is equally subject to discovery.

The practical problems confronting the IRS in discovering under-reporting of corporate taxes, which is likely endemic, are serious. Textron's return is massive-constituting more than 4,000 pages-and the IRS requested the work papers only after finding a specific type of transaction that had been shown to be abused by taxpayers. It is because the collection of revenues is essential to government that administrative discovery, along with many other comparatively unusual tools, are furnished to the IRS.

As Bentham explained, all privileges limit access to the truth in aid of other objectives, 8 Wigmore, Evidence § 2291 (McNaughton Rev. 1961), but virtually all privileges are restricted-either (as here) by definition or (in many cases) through explicit exceptions-by countervailing limitations. The Fifth Amendment privilege against self-incrimination is qualified, among other doctrines, by the required records exception, see Grosso v. United States, 390 U.S. 62, 67-68, 88 S.Ct. 709, 19 L.Ed.2d 906 (1968), and the attorney client privilege, along with other limitations, by the crime-fraud exception, see Clark v. United States, 289 U.S. 1, 15, 53 S.Ct. 465, 77 L.Ed. 993 (1933).

To sum up, the work product privilege is aimed at protecting work done for litigation, not in preparing financial statements. Textron's work papers were prepared to support financial filings and gain auditor

approval; the compulsion of the securities laws and auditing requirements assure that they will be carefully prepared, in their present form,
even though not protected; and IRS access serves the legitimate, and
important, function of detecting and disallowing abusive tax shelters.

The judgment of the district court is vacated and the case is remanded for further proceedings consistent with this decision. It is so
ordered.

TORRUELLA, CIRCUIT JUDGE, with whom LIPEZ, CIRCUIT JUDGE, joins,
Dissenting.

To assist the IRS in its quest to compel taxpayers to reveal their own
assessments of their tax returns, the majority abandons our "because of"
test, which asks whether " 'in light of the nature of the document and the
factual situation in the particular case, the document can be fairly said
to have been prepared or obtained because of the prospect of litigation.'
" Maine v. United States Dep't of the Interior, 298 F.3d 60, 68 (1st
Cir.2002) (emphasis in original) (quoting United States v. Adlman, 134
F.3d 1194, 1202 (2d Cir.1998)). The majority purports to follow this test,
but never even cites it. Rather, in its place, the majority imposes a
"prepared for" test, asking if the documents were "prepared for use in
possible litigation." Maj. Op. at 27. This test is an even narrower variant
of the widely rejected "primary motivating purpose" test used in the Fifth
Circuit and specifically repudiated by this court. In adopting its test, the
majority ignores a tome of precedents from the circuit courts and
contravenes much of the principles underlying the work-product doctrine.
It also brushes aside the actual text of Rule 26(b)(3), which "[n]owhere
. . . state[s] that a document must have been prepared to aid in the
conduct of litigation in order to constitute work product." *Adlman*, 134
F.3d at 1198. Further, the majority misrepresents and ignores the
findings of the district court. All while purporting to do just the opposite
of what it actually does.

I. The Majority Quietly Rejects Circuit Precedent

The majority claims allegiance to our prior decision in *Maine*, 298
F.3d at 70. Specifically, the majority seizes upon a single line from that
decision: "the 'because of' standard does not protect from disclosure
'documents that are prepared in the ordinary course of business or that
would have been created in essentially similar form irrespective of the
litigation.' " Id. (quoting *Adlman*, 134 F.3d at 1202). This qualification is
important to be sure, and I will address it infra, Section III.B.2. But I

must start by addressing the rest of the *Maine* decision, which the majority is careful to ignore.

In that decision, Maine sought documents prepared by the Department of the Interior regarding its decision, made during pending related litigation, to classify salmon as a protected species. Id. at 64. The district court found some of these administrative documents unprotected as the Department had not shown that litigation preparation was " 'the primary motivating factor for the preparation of the documents.' " Id. at 66-67. This formulation of the test for "anticipation of litigation" was based on the Fifth Circuit rule that the work-product doctrine did not protect documents that were "not primarily motivated to assist in future litigation." United States v. El Paso, 682 F.2d 530, 542-43 (5th Cir.1982) (emphasis added) (citing United States v. Davis, 636 F.2d 1028, 1040 (5th Cir.1981)). On appeal in *Maine*, we specifically repudiated this test and adopted the broader "because of" test, which had been thoughtfully and carefully explained by Judge Leval in the Second Circuit decision in *Adlman*, 134 F.3d at 1202-03. See *Maine*, 298 F.3d at 68 ("In light of the decisions of the Supreme Court, we therefore agree with the formulation of the work-product rule adopted in *Adlman* and by five other courts of appeals.").

In the present case, the majority purports to follow *Maine*, but really conducts a new analysis of the history of the work-product doctrine and concludes that documents must be " ' prepared for any litigation or trial.' " Maj. Op. at 29 (emphasis in original) (quoting FTC v. Grolier Inc., 462 U.S. 19, 25, 103 S.Ct. 2209, 76 L.Ed.2d 387 (1983)). Similarly, at another point, the majority suggests that documents must be "for use" in litigation in order to be protected. Id. at 13. *Grolier* did not establish such a test and the majority can point to no court that has so ruled.[11] Rather, the majority of circuit courts, led by the Second Circuit's decision in *Adlman*, have rejected such a rule.

---

11. To support its conclusion, the majority commits a plain logical error. The majority states that work-product protection must not be judged solely on its subject matter, but rather whether the documents's purpose is for use in litigation. In support of this proposition, the majority cites a number of cases that propound the uncontroversial proposition that a document must be judged according to its purpose, not solely its content. Maj. Op. at 29 n. 8. But those cases do not establish the majority's rule that the documents' purpose must be limited to use in litigation. Rather,one of the cases the majority cites adopts the test that the document must have been created "because of" litigation, which, as *Adlman* describes, is antithetical to the majority's new requirement. United States v. Roxworthy, 457 F.3d 590, 593-94 (6th Cir.2006) (adopting *Adlman*'s "because of" test). Another of the majority's citations is from the D.C. Circuit, which has also since adopted the "because of" test. Senate of Puerto Rico v. United States Dep't of Justice, 823 F.2d 574, 587 n. 42 (D.C.Cir.1987). The final decision cited by the majority, from the Northern District of California, deals with the deliberative process privilege, not the work-product doctrine. Church of Scientology Int'l v. IRS, 845 F.Supp. 714, 723 (C.D.Cal.1993). In any event, the Ninth Circuit also applies the "because of" test. In re Grand Jury Subpoena, 357 F.3d 900, 907-08 (9th Cir.2004) (praising and following *Adlman*).

Adlman's articulation of the "because of" test is fatal to the majority's position. In that case, Judge Leval discussed the application of the work-product doctrine "to a litigation analysis prepared by a party or its representative in order to inform a business decision which turns on the party's assessment of the likely outcome of litigation expected to result from the transaction." *Adlman*, 134 F.3d at 1197. In other words, *Adlman* asked whether the work-product doctrine applies where a dual purpose exists for preparing the legal analysis, that is, where the dual purpose of anticipating litigation and a business purpose co-exist. To answer that question, the *Adlman* court examined and rejected the "primary purpose" test adopted by the Fifth Circuit in *El Paso*, 682 F.2d at 542-43, which only grants work-product immunity to workpapers prepared "primarily motivated to assist in future litigation over the return," id. at 543:

> [Protection] is less clear, however, as to documents which, although prepared because of expected litigation, are intended to inform a business decision influenced by the prospects of the litigation. The formulation applied by some courts in determining whether documents are protected by work-product privilege is whether they are prepared "primarily or exclusively to assist in litigation"-a formulation that would potentially exclude documents containing analysis of expected litigation, if their primary, ultimate, or exclusive purpose is to assist in making the business decision. Others ask whether the documents were prepared "because of" existing or expected litigation-a formulation that would include such documents, despite the fact that their purpose is not to "assist in" litigation. Because we believe that protection of documents of this type is more consistent with both the literal terms and the purposes of the Rule, we adopt the latter formulation.

Adlman, 134 F.3d at 1197-98, quoted in part in *Maine*, 298 F.3d at 68. And if it needs to be spelled out any more clearly, *Adlman* makes it explicitly clear that the broader "because of" formulation is not limited to documents prepared for use in litigation:

> We believe that a requirement that documents be produced primarily or exclusively to assist in litigation in order to be protected is at odds with the text and the policies of the Rule. Nowhere does Rule 26(b)(3) state that a document must have been prepared to aid in the conduct of litigation in order to constitute work product, much less primarily or exclusively to aid in litigation. Preparing a document "in anticipation of litigation" is sufficient.

> The text of Rule 26(b)(3) does not limit its protection to materials prepared to assist at trial. To the contrary, the text of the Rule

clearly sweeps more broadly. It expressly states that work-product privilege applies not only to documents "prepared ... for trial" but also to those prepared "in anticipation of litigation." If the drafters of the Rule intended to limit its protection to documents made to assist in preparation for litigation, this would have been adequately conveyed by the phrase "prepared ... for trial." The fact that documents prepared "in anticipation of litigation" were also included confirms that the drafters considered this to be a different, and broader category. Nothing in the Rule states or suggests that documents prepared "in anticipation of litigation" with the purpose of assisting in the making of a business decision do not fall within its scope.

Id. at 1198-99 (emphasis and alterations in original). Rather than confront this language, the majority resorts to simplistic generalizations. Using its novel "prepared for" test, the majority unhelpfully explains that "[e]very lawyer who tries cases knows the touch and feel of materials prepared for a current or possible ... law suit." Once the majority ignores decades of controlling precedent, the matter becomes so clear that "[n]o one with experience of law suits" could disagree. Id.

I need say little else; the majority's new "prepared for" rule is blatantly contrary to *Adlman*, a leading case interpreting the work-product doctrine that we specifically adopted in *Maine*. The majority's opinion is simply stunning in its failure to even acknowledge this language and its suggestion that it is respecting rather than overruling *Maine*.

II. The Majority Announces a Bad Rule

The majority acts as if it is left to this court to draw a line from *Hickman* to the present case. In so doing, the majority ignores a host of cases which grapple with tough work product questions that go beyond the stuff that "[e]very lawyer who tries cases" would know is work product. Lower courts deserve more guidance than a simple reassurance that a bare majority of the en banc court knows work product when it sees it.[12] Of course, since this is an en banc proceeding, the majority is free to create a new rule for the circuit-though it would be better if it

---

12. This test is reminiscent of Justice Stewart's famously unhelpful test for identifying obscenity:

> [C]riminal laws in this area are constitutionally limited to hard-core pornography. I shall not today attempt further to define the kinds of material I understand to be embraced within that shorthand description; and perhaps I could never succeed in intelligibly doing so. But I know it when I see it, and the motion picture involved in this case is not that.

Jacobellis v. Ohio, 378 U.S. 184, 197, 84 S.Ct. 1676, 12 L.Ed.2d 793 (1964) (Stewart, J., concurring).

admitted that it was doing so. But our new circuit rule is not even a good rule.

First, as Judge Leval observed in *Adlman*, a "prepared for" requirement is not consistent with the plain language of Federal Rule of Civil Procedure 26, which provides protection for documents "prepared in anticipation of litigation or for trial." Fed.R.Civ.P. 26(b)(3)(A) (emphasis added); see also *Adlman*, 134 F.3d at 1198-99. There is no reason to believe that "anticipation of litigation" was meant as a synonym for "for trial." Claudine Pease-Wingenter, Prophetic or Misguided? The Fifth Circuit's (Increasingly) Unpopular Approach to the Work Product Doctrine, 29 Rev. Litig. (forthcoming 2009) (analyzing and rejecting many of the arguments advanced by the majority in favor of a narrow construction of the phrase "anticipation of litigation"). Since the terms are not synonymous, the term "anticipation of litigation" should not be read out of the rule by requiring a showing that documents be prepared for trial. See Carcieri v. Salazar, --- U.S. ----, 129 S.Ct. 1058, 1066, 172 L.Ed.2d 791 (2009) (discussing the basic principle that statutes should be construed to give effect to each word).

Second, though the majority goes into some depth describing the foundational case of Hickman v. Taylor, 329 U.S. 495, 67 S.Ct. 385, 91 L.Ed. 451 (1947), it misses the fundamental concern of that decision with protecting an attorney's "privacy, free from unnecessary intrusion by opposing parties and their counsel." Id. at 510, 67 S.Ct. 385. Without such privacy, litigants would seek unfair advantage by free-riding off another's work, thus reducing lawyers' ability to write down their thoughts:

> Were the attorney's work accessible to an adversary, the *Hickman* court cautioned, "much of what is now put down in writing would remain unwritten" for fear that the attorney's work would redound to the benefit of the opposing party. Legal advice might be marred by "inefficiency, unfairness and sharp practices," and the "effect on the legal profession would be demoralizing." Neither the interests of clients nor the cause of justice would be served, the court observed, if work product were freely discoverable.

Adlman, 134 F.3d at 1197 (quoting *Hickman*, 329 U.S. at 511, 67 S.Ct. 385). The majority posits that these rationales do not apply to documents containing a lawyer's legal analysis of a potential litigation, if that analysis was prepared for a business purpose. This is both unpersuasive and directly contrary to the policy analysis in *Adlman*, which we adopted in *Maine*. *Adlman* identified an example of a protected document:

> A business entity prepares financial statements to assist its executives, stockholders, prospective investors, business partners,

> and others in evaluating future courses of action. Financial statements include reserves for projected litigation. The company's independent auditor requests a memorandum prepared by the company's attorneys estimating the likelihood of success in litigation and an accompanying analysis of the company's legal strategies and options to assist it in estimating what should be reserved for litigation losses.

Adlman, 134 F.3d at 1200. Discussing this example, the court concluded that in this scenario "the company involved would require legal analysis that falls squarely within *Hickman*'s area of primary concern-analysis that candidly discusses the attorney's litigation strategies, appraisal of likelihood of success, and perhaps the feasibility of reasonable settlement." Id. Further, there is "no basis for adopting a test under which an attorney's assessment of the likely outcome of litigation is freely available to his litigation adversary merely because the document was created for a business purpose rather than for litigation assistance." Id. In other words,

> [i]n addition to the plain language of the Rule, the policies underlying the work-product doctrine suggest strongly that work-product protection should not be denied to a document that analyzes expected litigation merely because it is prepared to assist in a business decision. Framing the inquiry as whether the primary or exclusive purpose of the document was to assist in litigation threatens to deny protection to documents that implicate key concerns underlying the work-product doctrine.

Id. at 1199; see also Roxworthy, 457 F.3d at 595 (stating "the IRS would appear to obtain an unfair advantage by gaining access to KPMG's detailed legal analysis of the strengths and weaknesses of [the taxpayer's] position. This factor weighs in favor of recognizing the documents as privileged.").

The majority offers no response to this sound policy analysis and no reason to doubt that inefficiency and "sharp practices" will result from its new rule allowing discovery of such dual purpose documents, which contain confidential assessments of litigation strategies and chances. Instead of addressing these concerns, the majority's policy analysis relies instead on case-specific rationales-namely the need to assist the IRS in its difficult task of reviewing Textron's complex return. Such outcome determinative reasoning is plainly unacceptable. Thus, properly framed, it is clear that the rationales underlying the work-product doctrine apply to documents prepared in anticipation of litigation, even if they are not also for use at trial.[13]

And these policy rationales are squarely implicated in this case. First, Textron's litigation hazard percentages contain exactly the sort of mental impressions about the case that *Hickman* sought to protect. In fact, these percentages contain counsel's ultimate impression of the value of the case. Revealing such impressions would have clear free-riding consequences. With this information, the IRS will be able to immediately identify weak spots and know exactly how much Textron should be willing to spend to settle each item. Indeed, the IRS explicitly admits that this is its purpose in seeking the documents.

Second, as argued to us by amici, the Chamber of Commerce of the United States and the Association of Corporate Counsel, if attorneys who identify good faith questions and uncertainties in their clients' tax returns know that putting such information in writing will result in discovery by the IRS, they will be more likely to avoid putting it in writing, thus diminishing the quality of representation. The majority dismisses such concerns, concluding that tax accrual workpapers are required by law. But the majority fails to cite the record for this conclusion, likely because the majority is simply wrong. As the majority opinion earlier admits, id. at 22–23, the law only requires that Textron prepare audited financial statements reporting total reserves based on contingent tax liabilities. Accounting standards require some evidential support before such statements can be certified, but do not explicitly require the form and detail of the documents prepared here by Textron's attorneys with respect to each potentially challenged tax item. See also Michelle M. Henkel, Textron: The Debate Continues as to Whether Auditor Transparency Waives the Work Product Privilege, 50 Tax Management Memorandum 251, 260 (2009) (distinguishing auditor's workpapers and corporate workpapers and explaining that the latter are not mandatory but serve to evaluate a company's litigation risks). Rather, all that must be actually reported is the final tax reserve liability amount. Thus, as amicii worry, the majority's new rule will have ramifications that will affect the form and detail of documents attorneys prepare when working to convince auditors of the soundness of a corporation's reserves.

---

13. Perhaps because of these very same concerns about privacy and fairness, the IRS itself argued for the protection of its documents prepared for the dual purposes of helping the IRS understand the litigation risks that might result if the IRS made the administrative decision to adopt a new program. Delaney, Migdail & Young, Chartered v. IRS, 826 F.2d 124 (D.C.Cir.1987). This point was also noted by the *Adlman* court when it observed that "the IRS successfully argued against the very position it here advocates." *Adlman*, 134 F.3d at 1201.

These concerns are even more clearly implicated in this case because the majority's decision will remove protection for Textron's "backup materials" as well as its actual workpapers. The district court found that these materials included "notes and memoranda written by Textron's in-house tax attorneys reflecting their opinions as to which items should be included on the spreadsheet and the hazard of litigation percentage that should apply to each item." United States v. Textron Inc., 507 F.Supp.2d 138, 143 (D.R.I.2007). Thus, these documents thus go beyond the numbers used to compute a total reserve. Rather, they explain the legal rationale underpinning Textron's views of its litigation chances. The majority fails to acknowledge this subtlety, explain why it views such documents as required by regulatory rules, or explain why such mental impressions should go unprotected. Exposing such documentation to discovery is a significant expansion of the IRS's power and will likely reveal information far beyond the basic numbers that the IRS could discover through production of Textron's auditor's workpapers.

But more important are the ramifications beyond this case and beyond even the case of tax accrual workpapers in general. The scope of the work-product doctrine should not depend on what party is asserting it. Rather, the rule announced in this case will, if applied fairly, have wide ramifications that the majority fails to address.

For example, as the IRS explicitly conceded at oral argument, under the majority's rule one party in a litigation will be able to discover an opposing party's analysis of the business risks of the instant litigation, including the amount of money set aside in a litigation reserve fund, created in accordance with similar requirements as Textron's tax reserve fund. Though this consequence was a major concern of the argument in this case, the majority does not even consider this "sharp practice," which its new rule will surely permit.

And there are plenty more examples. Under the majority's rule, there is no protection for the kind of documents at issue in *Adlman*, namely "documents analyzing anticipated litigation, but prepared to assist in a business decision rather than to assist in the conduct of the litigation." 134 F.3d at 1201-02. Nearly every major business decision by a public company has a legal dimension that will require such analysis. Corporate attorneys preparing such analyses should now be aware that their work product is not protected in this circuit.

III. The Workpapers Are Protected Under the Right Test

Applying the "because of" test thoughtfully adopted in *Adlman* and *Maine*, the majority should have concluded that Textron's workpapers are protected by the work-product doctrine. The proper starting point in reaching this legal conclusion should be the factual findings of the district court, which held an evidentiary hearing to understand the nature of the documents sought here by the IRS.

A. Factual findings

After considering affidavits and testimony, the district court found that the tax accrual workpapers * * * d[id] not contain any facts about the transactions that concerned the IRS.

The district court also found,[that]Textron's ultimate purpose in preparing the tax accrual workpapers was to ensure that Textron was 'adequately reserved with respect to any potential disputes or litigation that would happen in the future.' " Further, "there would have been no need to create a reserve in the first place, if Textron had not anticipated a dispute with the IRS that was likely to result in litigation or some other adversarial proceeding."

In addition to recognizing these litigation purposes, the district court also recognized the dual purposes driving the creation of these documents and found that the workpapers' creation "also was prompted, in part" by the need to satisfy Textron's auditors and get a "clean" opinion letter. Id. at 143. The district court later clarified:

Thus, while it may be accurate to say that the workpapers helped Textron determine what amount should be reserved to cover any potential tax liabilities and that the workpapers were useful in obtaining a "clean" opinion from [the auditor] regarding the adequacy of the reserve amount, there would have been no need to create a reserve in the first place, if Textron had not anticipated a dispute with the IRS that was likely to result in litigation or some other adversarial proceeding.

Id. at 150. Relatedly, the district court found that anticipation of litigation was the "but for" cause of the documents' creation. Id. Thus, the district court clearly found two purposes leading to the creation of the workpapers.

The majority makes no effort to reject these factual findings, but simply recharacterizes the facts as suits its purposes. For example, the majority declares, without reference to the district court's more nuanced findings, that the "the IRS is unquestionably right that the immediate motive of Textron in preparing the tax accrual work papers was to fix the amount of the tax reserve on Textron's books and to obtain a clean financial opinion from its auditor." Maj. Op. at 27. At another point, the majority boldly pronounces, "the only purpose of Textron's papers was to prepare financial statements." Id. at 30. Of course, as explained above, the district court's factual findings about Textron's "ultimate purpose" were directly contrary to these pronouncements. Discarding a district court's factual finding on causation without any demonstration of clear error is not within this court's proper appellate function. See Fed.R.Civ.P. 52(a) ("Findings of fact, whether based on oral or other evidence, must not be set aside unless clearly erroneous, and the reviewing court must give due regard to the trial court's opportunity to judge the witnesses' credibility."); see also Constructora Maza, Inc. v. Banco de Ponce, 616 F.2d 573, 576 (1st Cir.1980) (noting that clear error review applies even when "much of the evidence is documentary and the challenged findings are factual inferences drawn from undisputed facts").

Instead, the majority exalts in the fact that the district court made no finding that the documents were " for use in possible litigation." Maj. Op. at 30. That proposition is true. But, as described above, "for use" (i.e. "prepared for") is not and has never been the law of this circuit.

The majority does suggest that the documents business purpose "cannot be disputed." Id. This is also uncontroversial. The district court found both a litigation and a business purpose. But, in straining to ignore the documents' litigation purposes, the majority proceeds to rely heavily on the IRS's expert. In so doing, the majority makes no effort to explain why the district court should have been required to adopt the view that the workpapers existed only for a non-litigation purpose. The majority claims that Textron's witnesses agreed with the IRS expert, but the majority fails to reconcile this proclamation with the competing view of Textron's witnesses, which the district court explicitly relied upon in its factual findings regarding Textron's "ultimate purpose." Textron, 507 F.Supp.2d at 143. This is another corruption of the proper role of an appellate court. See Anderson v. Bessemer City, 470 U.S. 564, 574, 105 S.Ct. 1504, 84 L.Ed.2d 518 (1985) ("Where there are two permissible views of the evidence, the factfinder's choice between them cannot be clearly erroneous.").

The majority does suggest that the district court's findings regarding the cause of the workpapers' creation was only stated in its legal analysis section. But the actual purpose of the documents' creators, or, in the words of the district court, "but-for" causation, is a factual issue, and the majority makes no effort to explain why such issue should be reviewed as a legal conclusion.

The majority also proclaims, without record support, that "[a]ny experienced litigator would describe the tax accrual work papers as tax documents and not as case preparation materials." Id. at 28. As described above, this conclusion reverses, without any finding of clear error, the

district court's factual findings. Further, this language dangerously
suggests that this court can, from its general knowledge, offer an expert
opinion as to how such documents are always seen by "experienced
litigators." Another of the many errors of this approach is revealed by
reference to undisputed record testimony. Namely, the majority's
assumption that tax accrual workpapers are a uniform class from
corporation to corporation is simply wrong. When the district court
carefully and specifically defined what documents were actually at issue
in this case, it explained that "there is no immutable definition of the
term 'tax accrual papers,' " and that their content varies from case to
case, Textron, 507 F.Supp.2d at 142, a conclusion that is consonant with
the testimony of the government's expert. Id. at 142 n. 2. Thus, even
were it not our rule that we defer to the district court's factfinding, such
a rule would make good sense in handling the wide range of workpapers
likely to confront district courts in the future as the IRS increasingly
seeks their discovery.

Even if we looked at the purpose of tax accrual workpapers as a
general matter, the district court's conclusion that Textron's anticipation
of litigation drove its reporting obligations is not so outrageous as to
leave us with a firm conviction of error. Rather, other courts reviewing
similar kinds of documents have reached similar conclusions. Regions
Fin. Corp. & Subsidiaries v. United States, No. 2:06-CV-00895-RDP,
2008 WL 2139008, at(N.D.Ala. May 8, 2008) (concluding, in examining
another company's workpapers that "[w]ere it not for anticipated
litigation, Regions would not have to worry about contingent liabilities
and would have no need to elicit opinions regarding the likely results of
litigation"); Comm'r of Revenue v. Comcast Corp., 453 Mass. 293, 901
N.E.2d 1185, 1191, 1205 (2009) (affirming a finding of work-product
protection for a business memorandum analyzing the "pros and cons of
the various planning opportunities and the attendant litigation risks"
since the author "had 'the prospect of litigation in mind when it directed
the preparation of the memorandum' " and would not have been prepared
irrespective of that litigation (quoting Adlman, 134 F.3d at 1204)).

B. Analysis

This court should accept the district court's factual conclusion that
Textron created these documents for the purpose of assessing its chances
of prevailing in potential litigation over its tax return in order to assess
risks and reserve funds. Under these facts, work-product protection
should apply.

1. The "because of" test

First, the majority does not develop any analysis contesting the proposition that disputes with the IRS in an audit can constitute litigation, within the meaning of Fed.R.Civ.P. 26(b)(3)(A). Indeed, such a conclusion is clear. For these purposes, the touchstone of "litigation" is that it is adversarial. Though the initial stages of a tax audit may not be adversarial, the disputes themselves are essentially adversarial; the subject of these disputes will become the subject of litigation unless the dispute is resolved.

Applying the "because of" test as articulated in *Adlman* and *Maine*, the workpapers are protected. Under these precedents, a document is protected if, " 'in light of the nature of the document and the factual situation in the particular case, the document can be fairly said to have been prepared or obtained because of the prospect of litigation.' " *Maine*, 298 F.3d at 68 (emphasis in original) (quoting *Adlman*, 134 F.3d at 1202). The "because of" test "really turns on whether [the document] would have been prepared irrespective of *41 the expected litigation with the IRS." *Adlman*, 134 F.3d at 1204. As the district court found, the driving force behind the preparation of the documents was the need to reserve money in anticipation of disputes with the IRS. Textron, 507 F.Supp.2d at 143. Though other business needs also contributed to Textron's need to create the documents, those needs depended on Textron's anticipating litigation with the IRS. In other words, without the anticipation of litigation, there would be no need to estimate a reserve to fund payment of tax disputes. Id. at 150. In this way, the dual purposes leading to the documents' creation were intertwined, and work-product protection should apply.

The majority simply refuses to accept the district court's finding that the documents would not exist but for Textron's need to anticipate litigation. This rejection is essential to the majority's erroneous conclusion. Accepting the district court's findings regarding purpose compels a finding of work-product protection, since the precedents are clear that under the "because of" test, dual purpose documents are protected. In fact, that is one of the very reasons some courts have adopted the test. 8 Charles Alan Wright, Arthur R. Miller & Richard L. Marcus, Federal Practice and Procedure, § 2024 (2d ed. 2009) (" 'Dual purpose' documents created because of the prospect of litigation are protected even though they were also prepared for a business purpose."); see also Roxworthy, 457 F.3d at 598-99 ("[D]ocuments do not lose their work product privilege 'merely because [they were] created in order to assist with a business decision,' unless the documents 'would have been created in essentially similar form irrespective of the litigation.' " (quoting Adlman, 134 F.3d at 1202)); In re Grand Jury Subpoena, 357 F.3d at 907 (adopting Wright and Miller's "because of" test in order to handle "dual purpose" documents); Maine, 298 F.3d at 68 (adopting Adlman after recounting the distinction between the "because of" test and the "primary purpose" test in their handling of dual purpose documents); Adlman, 134 F.3d at 1197-98, 1202 ("Where a document is created because of the prospect of litigation, analyzing the likely outcome of that litigation, it does not lose protection under this formulation merely because it is created in order to assist with a business decision."); In re Special Sept. 1978 Grand Jury (II), 640 F.2d 49, 61 (7th Cir.1980) ("We conclude that the materials ... were indeed prepared in anticipation of litigation, even though they were prepared as well for the filing of the Board of Elections reports.").

2.   The exception to the "because of" test

The majority reads too much into one sentence from *Maine* and *Adlman*. Specifically, it is true that "the 'because of' standard does not protect from disclosure'documents that are prepared in the ordinary course of business or that would have been created in essentially similar form irrespective of the litigation.' " Maine, 298 F.3d at 70 (quoting Adlman, 134 F.3d at 1202). This proviso relates to the advisory notes to the rule, which excludes from protection "[m]aterials assembled in the ordinary course of business, or pursuant to public requirements unrelated to litigation, or for other nonlitigation purposes." Fed.R.Civ.P. 26 advisory committee's note (1970). Understood in light of the fact that the "because of" test unequivocally protects "dual purpose" documents, this proviso does not strip protection for dual purpose documents that have one business or regulatory purpose. Rather, the best reading of the advisory committee's note is simply that preparation for business or for public requirements is preparation for a nonlitigation purpose insufficient in itself to warrant protection. The note states that there is no protection for documents created for business, regulatory, or "other nonlitigation purposes." This language suggests the note is considering business and regulatory purposes as nonlitigation purposes, but does not suggest that the presence of such a purpose should somehow override a litigation purpose, should one exist. Thus, correctly formulated, this exception should be understood as simply clarifying the rule that dual purpose documents are protected, though "there is no work-product immunity for documents prepared in the regular course of business rather than for purposes of the litigation." Charles A. Wright & Arthur R. Miller, supra, § 2024 (emphasis added); see also Roxworthy, 457 F.3d at 599 ("[A] document can be created for both use in the ordinary course of business and in anticipation of litigation without losing its work-product privilege."). Under the majority's interpretation, the exception swallows the rule protecting dual purpose documents.

So understood, the exception does not control this case. After citing this exception, the district court concluded that the documents were not created irrespective of litigation because Textron would not have prepared the documents but for the anticipation of litigation. Textron, 507 F.Supp.2d at 150. The majority makes no effort to label this finding clearly erroneous. To the contrary, the finding is correct. The tax accrual workpapers identify specific tax line items, and then anticipate the likelihood that litigation over those items will result in Textron having to pay the IRS more money. That Textron will not ultimately litigate each position does not change the fact that when it prepared the documents, Textron was acting to anticipate and analyze the consequences of possible litigation, just like the memorandum example in Adlman, 134 F.3d at 1200. The documents would not be the same at all had Textron not anticipated litigation. So, under the "because of" test, as applied in Adlman and the many circuit courts that have followed it, these documents were not prepared "irrespective" of the prospect of litigation. They should be protected.

3. *Arthur Young* and *El Paso* do not control

Neither the Supreme Court's decision in United States v. Arthur Young & Co., 465 U.S. 805, 104 S.Ct. 1495, 79 L.Ed.2d 826 (1984), nor the Fifth Circuit's decision in El Paso, 682 F.2d at 530, support a different result.

In *Arthur Young*, the Court declined to recognize an accountant's work-product doctrine, thus holding that tax accrual workpapers created by an independent auditor were not protected. Arthur Young, 465 U.S. at 815-21, 104 S.Ct. 1495. But unlike the Court in *Arthur Young*, we are not now confronted with the question of whether to recognize a new privilege. Here, the doctrinal decision we face is how to apply existing work-product doctrine to the present facts, in other words whether the "because of" test protects dual purpose documents, as the *Maine* and *Adlman* courts so held. This question was not at all presented in *Arthur Young*.

On the other hand, *El Paso* is clearly factually on point-there the Fifth circuit rejected work-product protection for similar tax accrual workpapers. El Paso, 682 F.2d at 542. But, as explained above, that court applied a different definition of the work-product doctrine, asking whether the "primary motivating purpose behind the creation of the document was to aid in possible future litigation." Id. at 542-44 (concluding that the document should not be protected as it "carries much more the aura of daily business than it does of courtroom combat"). Finding Textron's workpapers protected would not create a circuit split, but be merely an application of a widely acknowledged existing difference between our law and the law of the Fifth Circuit. It is precisely in these "dual purpose" situations that the "because of" test used in this circuit is meant to distinguish itself from the "primary purpose" test used in the Fifth Circuit. Maine, 298 F.3d at 68 (citing Adlman for the proposition that the primary purpose test "is at odds with the text and the policies of Rule 26 because nothing in it suggests that documents prepared for dual purposes of litigation and business or agency decisions do not fall within its scope"). Thus, unlike the Fifth Circuit, we need not assess whether the tax accrual workpapers carry more of one "aura" than another.

IV. Conclusion

The majority's decision may please the IRS and some tax scholars who understandably see discovery of tax accrual workpapers as an important tool in combating fraud. But this decision will be viewed as a dangerous aberration in the law of a well-established and important evidentiary doctrine. Whatever else one may think about this case, the majority's assertion that it is following *Maine* is plainly erroneous. Rather, the majority's "prepared for" test is directly contrary to *Adlman*, a decision we explicitly adopted in Maine.

In straining to craft a rule favorable to the IRS as a matter of tax law, the majority has thrown the law of work-product protection into disarray. Circuits have already split interpreting the meaning of "anticipation of litigation," between the "primary purpose" and "because of" tests. Now this court has proceeded to further the split by purporting to apply the "because of" test while rejecting that test's protection for dual purpose documents. In reality, the majority applied a new test that requires that documents be actually "prepared for" use in litigation. The time is ripe for the Supreme Court to intervene and set the circuits straight on this issue which is essential to the daily practice of litigators across the country.

The correct test is that spelled out in *Adlman*, and adopted by most circuit courts. Applying that test to the facts actually found by the district court, these tax accrual workpapers should be protected. For these reasons, I respectfully dissent.

Notes and Questions

The Supreme Court denied certiorari in *Textron*, __ U.S.__, 130 S.Ct. 3320 (2010), thus declining to resolve the conflict among the circuits and to clarify the correct test for work product protection.

Ronald L. Buch, in an article in Tax Notes, criticizes the statement of the *en banc* majority that "Every lawyer who tries cases knows the touch and feel of materials prepared for a current or possible (i.e., "in anticipation of") law suit." He argues that the issue is not nearly as clear as the majority claims. He makes the interesting point that seven experienced jurists considered the case but a minority determined the outcome. The other four judges, who had a combined experience of 114 years on the bench, with 71 of those years spent in trial courts, would have upheld work product protection for Textron's documents. See Ronald L. Buch, "The Touch and Feel of Work Product," 124 TAX NOTES 915, 917 (Aug. 31, 2009).

In U.S. v. Arthur Young & Co., 465 U.S. 805 (1984), the Supreme Court noted that work product immunity would apply to a taxpayer's accountant. However, the Court held in favor of the IRS and reasoned that the IRS should have access to any documents that might "shed light" on the preparation of a return. In the wake of the *Arthur Young* decision, the IRS announced that it would follow a policy of restraint in requesting tax accrual workpapers. However, in 2002, the IRS announced that it would request such workpapers if the taxpayer engaged in any listed transaction (defined as tax avoidance transactions under Reg. § 1.6011-4T(b)(2)). In general, the request would be confined to the listed transaction disclosed in the return, but *all* tax accrual workpapers would be requested if (1) the listed transaction was not disclosed, (2) the taxpayer claimed tax benefits from multiple investments, or (3) financial reporting irregularities are present. See Announcement 2002-63, 2002-2 C.B. 72.

1.   How does work product protection differ from the attorney-client privilege?

2.   What tests have been used to determine work product protection? What test does the majority employ in *Textron* and how, if at all, does it differ from the other tests?

3.   Does *Textron* foreclose work product protection for all documents generated in connection with tax reserves? See Kenneth B. Clark, "A Different View of *Textron*," 125 TAX NOTES 1197 (Dec. 14, 2009).

4.   Are there any steps that a taxpayer might take to strengthen a work product claim after *Textron*?

CHAPTER 3

TAXPAYER COMPLIANCE AND ADMINISTRATIVE REVIEW OF RETURNS

There is hardly an American citizen above the poverty level whose tax conscience is so completely clear that he isn't scared of being audited.

–– "Diogenes" (nom de plume of an IRS agent)[1]

I. COMPLIANCE

The average taxpayer has relatively little contact with the Service other than through filing tax returns and paying the tax. Occasionally, the taxpayer's return may be examined (administratively reviewed) and if the Service determines that the taxpayer owes an additional amount, the taxpayer may be subject to collection action. If the taxpayer disagrees with the Service's determination, the taxpayer may resort to the administrative appeals process to attempt to resolve the difference of agreement, and if that is not successful, the taxpayer may litigate the issue. Sometimes, the taxpayer may choose to litigate without having used the administrative appeals process. See § IV, below for a discussion of the administrative appeals process, and Chapters 7 and 8 for a discussion of the collection and litigation processes.

A. RETURNS

The federal income tax system functions as a system of self-assessment because taxpayers must determine their tax liability, file their returns, and pay their tax without initial government involvement. The integrity of tax returns is of pivotal importance because it is through these returns that the government monitors the level of voluntary compliance with the internal revenue laws, and in turn, maintains the integrity of the federal tax system. In order to process the tremendous volume of income tax returns the government receives each year (between 100 and 200 million), the returns must adhere to a uniform standard.

---

1.   Jeffery L. Yablon, As Certain As Death–Quotations About Taxes (2004 Edition), 102 TAX NOTES 99, 149 (Jan. 5, 2004).

1. What Constitutes a Return?

WILLIAMS v. COMMISSIONER
Tax Court of the United States, 2000.
114 T.C. 136.

VASQUEZ, JUDGE:

* * *

BACKGROUND

During 1991, petitioner was employed as a veterinarian by Stephen W. Williams, P.C., an S corporation (Williams P.C.). Petitioner received extensions of time for filing his 1991 income tax return until October 15, 1992.

On October 1, 1994, petitioner mailed a Form 1040 for 1991 to the Internal Revenue Service (IRS). Petitioner altered the Form 1040 (altered 1040) by marking through the captions on lines 7 and 18 and typing his own caption, "Non Taxable Compensation." Petitioner reported income of $20,500 and $135,861 on lines 7 and 18, respectively. Next, petitioner whited out the captions on lines 24a and b and typed in "Non Taxable Compensation Eisner v. Macomber 252 U.S. 189, 64 L. Ed. 521, 40 S. Ct. 189." Petitioner reported a deduction of $156,861 on line 24a, which brought his adjusted gross income to $0. Petitioner did not sign the altered 1040.

The IRS treated the altered 1040 as a frivolous return under § 6702 and fined petitioner $500. Petitioner stipulated that the altered 1040 was a frivolous return and not a return within the meaning of § 6501(a).

On November 21, 1996, petitioner mailed another Form 1040 (disclaimer 1040) for 1991 to the IRS. On the disclaimer 1040, petitioner reported adjusted gross income of $150,852 consisting of wages of $20,500, taxable interest income of $14, a capital loss of ($2,986), and rents and partnership income of $133,324. Petitioner reported a total tax of $41,586 and an amount owed of $36,621. Petitioner, this time, did not strike or change any language on the form. Instead, beside the amount owed reported on line 64, petitioner placed an asterisk. At the bottom of the page, petitioner stated that the asterisk denoted "The admitted liability is zero. See attached Disclaimer Statement." The attached disclaimer statement (the disclaimer) read in part:

> The above named taxpayer respectfully declines to volunteer concerning assessment and payment of any tax balance due on the return or any redetermination of said tax. Be it known that the

above said taxpayer, therefore, denies tax liability and does not admit that the stated amount of tax on return is due and collectable.

Petitioner signed the disclaimer 1040.

Except for the altered 1040 and the disclaimer 1040, petitioner did not mail to or file with the IRS any other Forms 1040 for 1991.

During 1991, petitioner received income and incurred losses as follows:

Wages from Williams P.C.	$ 20,500
Interest from Vista Properties (Vista)	$ 14
Interest from Charles Schwab	$ 3
Net short term capital loss	($ 2,986)
Rents from Williams P.C.	$ 29,000
Nonpassive loss from Vista	($ 1,637)
Nonpassive income from Williams P.C.	$105,961
Rents from Summit Outdoor Advertising (Summit)	$ 900

DISCUSSION

I. DEFICIENCY LIABILITY

Petitioner does not challenge either the facts on which respondent's determination is based or respondent's calculation of tax. In fact, respondent based the computation of the deficiency on the amounts reported by petitioner on the altered 1040 and the disclaimer 1040. Petitioner, nevertheless, contends he is not liable for the deficiency. Petitioner claims that (1) he did not volunteer to self–assess or pay his taxes, and he therefore cannot be held liable for any deficiency; (2) his income is not from any of the sources listed in § 1.861-8(a), Income Tax Regs., and thus is not taxable; and (3) the notice of deficiency was improperly issued because petitioner disclaimed the tax liability shown on the return.

Petitioner's arguments are reminiscent of tax-protestor rhetoric that has been universally rejected by this and other courts. We shall not painstakingly address petitioner's assertions "with somber reasoning and copious citation of precedent; to do so might suggest that these arguments have some colorable merit." Crain v. Commissioner, 737 F.2d 1417, 1417 (5th Cir. 1984). Accordingly, we conclude that petitioner is liable for the deficiency determined by respondent.

II. ACCURACY-RELATED PENALTY

Respondent determined that petitioner is liable for an accuracy-related penalty pursuant to § 6662(a) for his underpayment of tax attributable to negligence or disregard of rules or regulations. The penalty under § 6662(a) applies only where a return has been filed. See § 6664(b). We therefore must determine whether the disclaimer 1040 constitutes a valid return.

Generally, pursuant to § 6011(a), taxpayers are required to file returns that conform to the forms and regulations prescribed by the Secretary. See § 1.6011-1(a), Income Tax Regs. The Form 1040 is the form prescribed by the Secretary for use by individual taxpayers in filing returns.

Section 6065 requires returns to contain or be verified by a written declaration that they are made under the penalties of perjury. To facilitate a taxpayer's compliance with this requirement, the Form 1040 contains a preprinted jurat.[3] By signing the jurat included within the Form 1040, a taxpayer satisfies the requirement that his return be executed under penalty of perjury. See Sloan v. Commissioner, 102 T.C. 137, 146-147 (1994), aff'd. 53 F.3d 799 (7th Cir. 1995).

The U.S. Supreme Court has also held that certain documents drafted by taxpayers that do not comply with the forms prescribed by the Secretary will nevertheless be treated as valid returns, for purposes of the statute of limitations, if they contain certain elements. See Badaracco v. Commissioner, 464 U.S. 386, 78 L.Ed2d 549, 104 S.Ct. 756 (1984); Commissioner v. Lane-Wells Co., 321 U.S. 219, 88 L.Ed. 684, 64 S.Ct. 511 (1944).*** In Beard v. Commissioner, 82 T.C. 766, 777 (1984), affd. 793 F.2d 139 (6th Cir. 1986), we summarized the Supreme Court's test for a valid return as follows:

> First, there must be sufficient data to calculate [the] tax liability; second, the document must purport to be a return; third, there must be an honest and reasonable attempt to satisfy the requirements of the tax law; and fourth, the taxpayer must execute the return under penalties of perjury.

The fourth requirement is the same requirement found in § 6065 and can be satisfied by signing the jurat on the Form 1040.

In *Beard*, we applied the Supreme Court's test in our analysis of whether the document at issue was a tax return for purposes of §

---

3. The jurat is the portion of the Form 1040 which reads: "Under penalties of perjury, I declare that I have examined this return and accompanying schedules and statements, and to the best of my knowledge and belief, they are true, correct, and complete."

6651(a)(1). We see no reason why the same test should not apply in determining whether a document constitutes a tax return for purposes of § 6662(a).

We first determine whether the disclaimer 1040 complies with the form prescribed by the Secretary. Although petitioner used a Form 1040, petitioner added the disclaimer to the form. Respondent contends that the addition of the disclaimer to the Form 1040 vitiated petitioner's signature under the jurat.

In the past, we have analyzed the effect of tax protesters' alterations to the Form 1040, and in particular to the jurat, and determined whether the altered Form 1040 constituted a valid return. In the beginning, tax protesters simply crossed out the entire text of the jurat, and we held that the Forms 1040 were not valid returns. See Cupp v. Commissioner, 65 T.C. 68, 78-79, affd. without published opinion 559 F.2d 1207 (3rd Cir. 1977); see also Mosher v. Internal Revenue Service, 775 F.2d 1292, 1294 (5th Cir. 1985)(per curiam). Next, tax protesters deleted particular words from the jurat such as "under penalties of perjury" and/or "true, correct, and complete." In those cases, we held that the Forms 1040 did not constitute valid returns.

Recently, tax protesters have begun to add to rather than strike out the text of the jurat. We have generally found that the addition of language to the jurat invalidated the Form 1040 as a return.[4] See Andrews v. Commissioner, T.C. Memo. 1999-281; Hodge v. Commissioner, T.C. Memo. 1998-561. For example, in *Sloan v. Commissioner*, supra 102 T.C. at 141, immediately following the preprinted text of the jurat and immediately above the taxpayer's signature (i.e., within the jurat box), the taxpayer wrote "Denial and Disclaimer attached as part of this Form." The following statement was attached to the Form 1040:

---

4. We note that some courts have found that the addition of protest language to the Form 1040 will not invalidate the form as a return. In McCormick v. Peterson, 73 A.F.T.R.2d (RIA) 94-597, 94-1 U.S.T.C. (CCH) ¶ 50,026 (E.D.N.Y. 1993), the court held that the addition of the words "under protest" to the jurat did not alter the meaning of the jurat and thus did not invalidate the Form 1040 as a return; see also Berger v. Commissioner, T.C. Memo. 1996-76 (holding the addition of a disclaimer statement which declared that the return was signed "under duress by court order" did not alter the jurat in such a way as to invalidate the return); Todd v. United States, 849 F.2d 365, 367 (9th Cir. 1988) (holding that the addition of the words "signed involuntarily under penalty of statutory punishment" below the jurat did not make the Form 1040 a frivolous return under § 6702). But see In re Schmitt v. United States, 140 B.R. 571, 572 (Bankr. W.D. Okla. 1992) (holding the addition of the words "signed under duress see statement attached" to the jurat invalidated the return).

DENIAL AND DISCLAIMER OF LORIN G. SLOAN FOR THE YEAR

I submit this "Denial and Disclaimer" as an attachment to the IRS Form 1040 for the year stated above. I deny that I am liable or made liable for any "1040 income tax" for the above stated year. I claim all of my rights and waive none of them merely for exercising my right to work. I submit the 1040 form to prevent the further theft of my property and loss of my liberty. My signature on the form is not an admission of jurisdiction or submission to subject status. I "disclaim liability" for any tax shown on the form.

[102 T.C. at 141].

We stated in *Sloan* that the above "Denial and Disclaimer" statement [raised] serious questions about whether petitioner [was] 'denying' the accuracy of the information contained in the return, 'disclaiming' the jurat altogether, or simply protesting the tax laws." Id. at 145. We held that, by adding the disclaimer to the jurat, the return was invalidated.

In affirming our decision in *Sloan*, the U.S. Court of Appeals for the Seventh Circuit stated in part:

It is a close question whether the "Denial & Disclaimer" should be interpreted in this light–that is, as an attempt to retract or qualify the jurat. * * * But we think that the Internal Revenue Service should be entitled to construe alterations of the jurat against the taxpayer, at least when there is any doubt. * * * The government receives tens of millions of tax returns and if taxpayers start embellishing the jurat the staggering task of processing all these returns may become entirely unmanageable. [*Sloan v. Commissioner*, 53 F.3d at 800].

Against the foregoing backdrop, we consider for the first time whether disclaimer language added outside the jurat box invalidates the Form 1040 as a return because it fails to comply with the form prescribed by the Secretary. Petitioner argues that his disclaimer is "nowhere near the jurat;" therefore, he executed a valid return.

It is true that petitioner has carefully avoided adding language within the jurat box. We, however, believe that this is just another attempt by a taxpayer to alter the essence of the jurat and the Form 1040 without actually tampering with the preprinted form. While not physically deleting, altering, or adding words to the jurat, the disclaimer negated the meaning of the jurat. The jurat states that the signatory declares, under penalties of perjury, that the return is true, correct, and complete. The disclaimer at a minimum calls into question the veracity, accuracy, and completeness of the disclaimer 1040 and can be construed as a denial of the jurat altogether. Although petitioner physically signed the return below the jurat, his disclaimer, in effect, vitiated his verification of the truthfulness of the return as required by the regulations prescribed by the Secretary and by § 6065.

We have previously stated that the acceptance of documents which vary from the form prescribed by the Secretary

> adversely affects the form's usability by respondent. The tampered form, * * * , must be handled by special procedures and must be withdrawn from normal processing channels. * * *, it substantially impedes the Commissioner's physical task of handling and verifying tax returns. * * * [*Beard v. Commissioner*, 82 T.C. at 776-777].

We refuse to require respondent to engage in guessing games to determine what disclaimers like this one mean. To require such would drastically hinder the Commissioner's ability to process returns effectively and efficiently. We find that the disclaimer 1040 does not comport with the form prescribed by the Secretary.

The disclaimer 1040 may, nevertheless, be treated as a valid return if it contains the four elements outlined in the Supreme Court's test. Under the Supreme Court's test, in order for a document to be a valid return, a taxpayer must execute the document under penalties of perjury. As we found above, by his disclaimer, petitioner altered the meaning of the jurat to the extent that it cannot be said that petitioner executed the document under penalties of perjury.

Additionally, under the Supreme Court's test, there must be an honest and reasonable attempt to satisfy the requirements of the tax laws. The disclaimer contained tax protester legal gibberish that has been consistently rejected by courts. Petitioner's denial of tax liability and refusal to self-assess does not evidence a reasonable attempt to satisfy his obligation to file a return under the tax laws. We find that petitioner has not filed a valid return under the Supreme Court's test.

We conclude that the disclaimer 1040 does not constitute a valid return; therefore, petitioner is not liable for the penalty pursuant to § 6662(a).

* * *

Notes and Questions

The validity of a tax return is important for a number of reasons, chief among them is that the filing of a valid return marks the commencement of the statute of limitations on assessment and collection. If a valid return has not been filed, the statute does not begin to run and a tax deficiency, plus additions to tax may be assessed at any time. See discussion of statutes of limitation on assessment, Chapter 4. Also, various penalties may apply to the failure to file a return. See discussion of delinquency and civil fraud penalties in Chapter 6. Moreover, the bankruptcy laws prohibit the discharge of a tax deficiency if the debtor has not filed a valid return. See United States v. Hindenlang, 164 F.3d 1029 (6th Cir. 1999); see also Chapter 7 for a discussion of discharges in bankruptcy.

If a taxpayer fails to file a return, § 6020 authorizes the Service to prepare a substitute return, with or without the taxpayer's assistance. If the return is prepared with the taxpayer's assistance and signed by the taxpayer, it is considered a valid return for all purposes. The taxpayer remains responsible for the correctness of the return as though it had not been prepared by the Service. Reg. § 301.6020-1(a)(2). If, however, the Service prepares a return without the taxpayer's assistance, using data supplied by third-party payers and/or through testimony and other means, such a return is considered merely an administrative device for assessing deficiencies and imposing penalties. It does not relieve the taxpayer of the obligation to file a return, nor will it have any effect on the running of the statute of limitations on assessment and collection. Furthermore, it will not protect the delinquent taxpayer from the imposition of criminal penalties for failure to file. See United States v. Harrison, 1972 WL 3127 (EDNY 1972), aff'd. 486 F.2d 1397 (2d Cir. 1972), cert. denied 411 U.S. 965 (1973).

Given the complexity of the tax laws, the question is where does one draw the line in determining the validity of a return in a case that does not involve what the Tax Court in *Williams* refers to as "tax protester legal gibberish that has been consistently rejected by courts?" In Zellerbach Paper Co. v. Helvering, 293 U.S. 172, 55 S.Ct. 127, 79 L.Ed. 264 (1934), Justice Cardozo, writing for the majority, noted:

> Perfect accuracy or completeness is not necessary to rescue a return from nullity, if it purports to be a return, is sworn to as such * * * and evinces an honest and genuine endeavor to satisfy the law. This is so even though at the time of filing the omissions or inaccuracies are such as to make amendment necessary. Even more clearly is it so when the return is full and accurate in the beginning under the statutes then in force, but is made inaccurate or incomplete by supervening changes of the law, unforeseen and unforeseeable. Supplement and correction in such circumstances will not take from a taxpayer, free from personal fault, the protection of a term of limitation already running for his benefit.

Id. at 180.

If a taxpayer files the correct tax information on the wrong form, has the taxpayer filed a valid return? See Germantown Trust Co. v. Commissioner, 309 U.S. 304 (1940); Hartford-Connecticut Trust Fund Co. v. Eaton, 34 F.2d 128 (2d Cir. 1929).

2. Filing the Return

In general, returns are required to be filed with the IRS Service Center in the internal revenue district in which the taxpayer is located. IRC § 6091. The due date of the return depends upon the type of return being filed. Individual taxpayers must file their income tax returns by the fifteenth day of the fourth month following the close of the taxable year. Since most individual taxpayers use the calendar year as their taxable year, their returns must be filed by April 15th of the year following the close of their taxable year. IRC § 6072(a). Corporations must file their income tax returns by the fifteenth day of the third month following the close of their taxable years (IRC § 6072(b)); estates must file within nine months of the date of the decedent's death (IRC § 6075). Regardless of the type of return, if the due date falls on a Saturday, Sunday, or legal holiday, the due date is extended to the next business day. IRC § 7503.

The filing date of the return is procedurally significant because it determines the starting point of the commencement of the statute of limitations on assessment (see Chapter 4) and it also may determine the starting point of the statute of limitations on refund claims (see Chapter 5). Under § 6501(b)(1), a return received by the Service before the due date (without regard to extensions of time to file) is considered filed on the due date. A delinquency penalty will accrue if the return is filed after the due date, with regard to extensions of time to file. See Chapter 6 for a discussion of delinquency penalties.

In general, a return is considered timely filed if it is received before the end of the last day of the filing period, including any extensions of time to file. But if the return, claim or other document is mailed before the expiration of the due date and it is in an envelope or wrapper properly addressed to the appropriate IRS office with the correct amount of postage prepaid, the postmarked date will be deemed the filing date if the return is received by the Service after the due date. IRC § 7502. This timely-mailed-is-timely-filed rule is commonly known as "the mailbox rule." See Chapter 4 for a further discussion of the mailbox rule and its effect on the statute of limitations.

The mailbox rule does not apply, however, if the return, claim or payment is filed after the due date, including extensions of time to file.

Thus, a document postmarked after the due date is considered filed on the date it is received by the Service.

a. Electronic Filing

The processing of paper returns is a cumbersome and inefficient use of government resources. Thus, the IRS Restructuring and Reform Act of 1998[2] mandated a policy of encouraging paperless filing of federal tax and information returns. While the government had hoped that 80% of filers would be filing electronically by 2007, this goal was not realized. As of 2010, about two-third of returns were filed electronically, but the Service continues to provide incentives to encourage electronic filing, such as free filing for lower and lower-middle income taxpayers, and faster refunds.

Some taxpayers, such as large partnerships (more than 100 partners) and taxpayers filing 250 or more information returns, are required to file returns on magnetic media. Reg. § 301.6011-3(a); Rev. Proc. 2000-25, 2000-1 C.B. 1033. Magnetic media includes magnetic tape, tape cartridge, diskette, and other media such as electronic filing. Reg. § 301.6011-3(d)(1). The filing requirement may be waived in cases of hardship, such as equipment breakdowns and unreasonable incremental costs. Otherwise, penalties apply to taxpayers who file paper returns when required to file on magnetic media. Reg. § 301.6011-3(c).

There are distinct advantages to electronic filing, such as faster refunds, fewer mistakes, and lower processing costs. The Service will notify the taxpayer within 48 hours whether the return is accepted as filed or whether corrections are needed. Because the calculations are done by computer, the error rate is significantly lower than with paper returns. Thus any refund to which the taxpayer may be entitled is accelerated and can be deposited directly to the taxpayer's checking or savings account. In fact, about half of the individual returns that were filed electronically were done to take advantage of refund anticipation loans offered by some financial institutions, that were tied to the expedited refunds.

When the taxpayer receives confirmation that the return has been accepted, the taxpayer then must mail any Forms W-2, along with any supporting documentation accompanied by a Form 8453 (U.S. Individual Income Tax Transmittal for an IRS *e-file* Return).[3] The return may be

---

2.   IRS Restructuring and Reform Act of 1998, H.R. 2676, 105th Cong., 2d Sess. § 2001.

3.   Available online at http://www.irs.gov/pub/irs-pdf/f8453.pdf

signed electronically with a personal identification number (PIN) or by signing the Form 8453. If any additional tax is due, it must be paid by the due date. The taxpayer has the option of paying any tax due with a credit card, or with a direct debit (electronic funds withdrawal) from a checking or savings account.

There are some disadvantages to electronic filing, however, such as cost and security concerns. For lower income taxpayers, the government provides free e-filing but for others, e-filed forms must be submitted either by a tax professional or through special software that must be purchased and updated annually. The General Accounting Office (GAO) raised concerns in a 2009 report about the lack of a clear system to monitor the tax software industry's compliance with established security and privacy standards. Moreover, e-filing is not always as simple and easy as it seems, because if all required data is not entered correctly, the Service will reject the return. The error(s), even if very minor, must be corrected and the return must be resubmitted. A significant number of returns have been rejected by the IRS computers, whereas a paper return with the same errors may have been accepted as filed.

b. *Extensions of Time to File*

The Code authorizes an extension of time to file a return. IRC § 6081. An individual taxpayer may obtain an automatic six-month filing extension simply by filing a Form 4868 (Application for Automatic Extension of Time to File U.S. Individual Income Tax Return)[4] on or before the due date of the return.[5] No signature is required on the Form 4868.

Since the obligation to file a tax return and the obligation to pay the tax are separate and distinct obligations, the automatic extension of time to file does not extend the due date of the payment, unless so specified in the extension. In order to obtain an extension of time to file, the taxpayer first will have to make a bona fide, reasonable estimate of the amount of tax liability due for the year. Reg. § 1.6081-1(a). The tax liability must be paid on or before the original due date in order to avoid late payment penalties and interest. Interest runs from the due date of the return, without regard to the extension, until the tax is paid. IRC § 6601(b)(1); see Chapter 6 for a discussion of interest.

---

4.   Available online at http://www.irs.gov/pub/irs-pdf/f4868.pdf

5.   In the case of a taxpayer who is out of the country, an automatic 6-month filing extension may be obtained.

Under normal circumstances, a six-month extension from the due date of the return is the maximum amount of time that an extension that can be granted. See I.R.C. § 6081(a) and Treas. Reg. § 1.6081-1(a). However, longer extensions can be obtained by business taxpayers and by individuals living abroad. A request filed after the expiration of the original due date of the return will not be valid. Reg. § 1.6081-4(a)(5).

If a taxpayer requests an extension of time to file, and the return is mailed and received by the Service before the extended due date, does the mailbox rule apply to determine the running of the statute of limitations on assessment? This question is addressed in the following case.

NATALIE HOLDINGS, LTC. v. UNITED STATES
United States District Court for the Western District of Texas, San Antonio Division, 2003.
91 A.F.T.R.2d 616.

OPINION BY: EDWARD C. PRADO

* * *

Nature of the Case

* * *

DAVMY is a Texas corporation owned by Amy and David Perez, who each own 50% of the corporation. Natalie is a Texas limited partnership. DAVMY holds a one percent interest in Natalie and is the sole general partner of NATALIE. NATALIE deposited its 1997 tax returns in the mail in an envelope, certified postage prepaid, and addressed to the IRS Service Center in Philadelphia, Pennsylvania on September 3, 1998.[2] The IRS received the NATALIE return on September 10, 1998.

In March 2001, the IRS alerted various IRS executives, agents and managers of an emerging potentially abusive tax shelter. In April 2001, the IRS requested a list of shelter investors from the Seattle based firm involved in the promotion of the shelter. This list was forwarded to the IRS, Office of Tax Shelter Analysis (OTSA), the focal point for IRS investigations of abusive corporate tax shelter issues. Using the list, OTSA retrieved information from the IRS's Integrated Document Retrieval System to order tax returns for the tax shelter participants. In July 2001, an IRS agent with OTSA, an IRS manager and a tax shelter coordinator for this tax shelter reviewed the information and prepared an investor list and determined that entities on the list were involved in a Foreign Leverage Investment Program (FLIP).

---

2.   NATALIE received two valid extensions, one to August 15, 1998 and the second to October 15, 1998.

In July 2001, IRS agents, financial products specialists and an economist attended a training session in Washington D.C. regarding the examination of this tax shelter program. Using their expertise and training, upon analyzing the available information, the IRS decided to assign a group of experts to examine Natalie's tax liabilities. The group examined the tax returns for all entities involved in the FLIP except for Natalie's and one other entity's, which were unavailable. After hours of analysis, the group was able to develop an organizational chart showing the ownership of the various entities and the flow through of the various tax attributes of the shelter. Based upon this analysis and advice of IRS counsel, the IRS manager assigned to this case decided to issue an FPAA [eds: Notice of Final Partnership Administrative Adjustment] to Plaintiffs based upon the correct determination of Natalie's participation in the tax shelter under review.

The IRS mailed the FPAA to Plaintiff on September 7, 2001 disallowing $ 5,002,941 in capital losses. Plaintiff filed a petition in this Court to contest the FPAA as provided in 26 U.S.C. § 6226(a)(2).

* * *

Statute of Limitations

Plaintiff argues it is entitled to summary judgment because the IRS issued the FPAA after the governing statute of limitations expired. The statute of limitations for issuing an FPAA expires three years after the later of (i) the date on which the partnership return for such taxable year was filed or (ii) the last day for filing such return for such year, without regard to extensions. 26 U.S.C. § 6229(a). Here, the Natalie return was mailed on September 3, 1998 by certified mail and received by the IRS on September 10, 1998. The resolution of this issue turns on whether the Natalie return was "filed" on the date it was postmarked or the date it was received where it was both timely mailed and timely received.

Normally, a return is considered "filed" with the IRS on the date that it is received by the appropriate office of the IRS. Here, Plaintiff's returns were due on October 15, 1998. The returns were received by the IRS on September 10, 1998. The statute of limitations thus began to run on September 10, 1998. The FPAA was mailed on September 7, 2001, within the three-year statute of limitations under 26 U.S.C. § 6229(a).

Plaintiff argues that under 26 U.S.C. § 7502 the postage date of a timely mailed return is the date of filing and that here, the statute of limitations began to run on September 3, 1998 and thus the FPAA mailed on September 7, 2001 was time-barred by the three-year statute of limitations. Section 7502 states in relevant part:

(a) General rule. –

(1) Date of delivery. – If any return, claim, statement, or other document required to be filed, or any payment required to be made, within a prescribed period or on or before a prescribed date under authority of any provision of the internal revenue laws is, after such period or such date, delivered by United States mail to the agency, officer, or office with which such return, claim, statement, or other document is required to be filed, or to which such payment is required to be made, the date of the United States postmark stamped on the cover in which such return, claim, statement, or other document, or payment, is mailed shall be deemed to be the date of delivery or the date of payment, as the case may be.

(2) Mailing requirements. – This subsection shall apply only if – (A) the postmark date falls within the prescribed period or on or before the prescribed date – (I) for the filing (including any extension granted for such filing) of the return, claim, statement, or other document, or

* * *

26 U.S.C. § 7502. The plain language of the statute states that § 7502 only applies to situations where a return is timely mailed but *delivered to the IRS after a prescribed date.* Interpreting this provision, the United States Court of Appeals for the Sixth Circuit has held:

Section 7502 was enacted as a remedial provision to alleviate inequities arising from differences in mail delivery from one part of the country to another * * *. This "mailbox rule," both by its terms and as revealed in the legislative history, applies only in cases where the document is actually received by the I.R.S. after the statutory period.

Miller v. United States, 784 F.2d 728, 730. In this case, Plaintiff wants to avail itself of the postage date equals filing date rule in § 7502. The problem is, however, that Plaintiff's return was timely mailed and timely received. There is no reason for the Court to depart from the general rule that delivery date equals filing date and apply the exceptions in § 7502 to the facts here. If timely mailing equals filing even when the return is timely delivered, there would be no need for § 7502 since all returns that were timely mailed would be considered timely filed on the date of postage, not delivery.

Plaintiff relies on Emmons v. Comm'r, 898 F.2d 50 (5th Cir. 1990), for the proposition that the filing date of a timely filed return is the date of mailing. Plaintiff cites the language, "We decline to ignore the statute's plain words. Thus, all timely [mailed] returns are considered filed as of the postmark date and all late [mailed] returns are considered filed as of the date of delivery." *Emmons,* 898 F.2d at 51. The facts in *Emmons,* however, involve returns that were mailed late and received late. The issue in *Emmons* is on what date, post date or receipt date, did the statute of limitations run. The court simply noted that timely mailed and late received returns get the benefit of the mailing equals filing rule of § 7502 while late mailed and late received returns are determined by the general rule that delivery equals filing. In both instances the *Emmons* court referred to late received returns. This Court will not ignore the statute's plain words, "* * * *after such period or date, delivered* * * *" and finds that § 7502 is inapplicable to these facts since the FPAA in this case was timely delivered. The Court finds that the Natalie returns were delivered to the IRS on September 10, 1998, that they were due on October 15, 1998 and thus the filing date is September 10, 1998. As such, the FPAA mailed on September 7, 2001 was mailed within the three-year statute of limitations as prescribed by 26 U.S.C. § 6229(a). As a result, Plaintiff is not entitled to summary judgment on the grounds of limitations.

* * *

Notes and Problems

If a taxpayer files a return or claim for refund or credit by certified or registered mail, the sender's receipt is prima facie evidence of delivery, provided the receipt contains a postmark. But in the absence of a certified or registered mail receipt, there is a split among the circuits as to whether the mailing date can be established through other circumstantial evidence when the return or claim does not reach its destination. The Eighth and Ninth Circuits have held that other credible proof is acceptable to establish that the return was mailed when the Service claims that the return was not delivered. See Anderson v. United States, 966 F.2d 487 (9th Cir. 1992); Estate of Wood v. Commissioner, 909 F.2d 1155 (8th Cir. 1990). The Second and Sixth Circuits, and the Court of Federal Claims, however, have held that the only acceptable proof of mailing is the registered or certified mail receipts, because I.R.C. § 7502 specifically provides that these constitute prima facie evidence of filing. See Washton v. United States, 13 F.3d 49 (2d Cir. 1993)(per curiam); Carroll v. Commissioner, 71 F.3d 1228 (6th Cir. 1995); BMC Bankcorp., Inc. v. United States, 59 F.3d 170 (6th Cir. 1995); Miller v. United States, 784 F.2d 728 (6th Cir. 1986); Davis v. U.S., 43 Fed. Cl. 92 (1999). See also Raby and Raby, Still Another Half Truth – Postmark Date Is Filing Date, 73 Tax Notes 827 (Nov. 16, 1996).

The Service has designated several private delivery services that it deems reliable for purposes of the mailbox rule. IRC § 7502(f); see Notice 2004-83, 2004-2 C.B. 1030 for a list of these services. If, however, the return is sent by privately metered mail, the mailbox rule will apply only if the postmark bears a timely date and the return is received by the Service within the time period it would have been received if it had been mailed through the United States Postal Service on the same date. If the return is not received within that time period, there is a rebuttable presumption that the return was not timely mailed. The taxpayer bears the burden of rebutting this presumption, which can be a difficult burden for the taxpayer to overcome. Notice 97-26, 1997-1 C.B. 413.

1. John Smith is an individual taxpayer who uses the calendar year method of tax accounting. The due date of his federal income tax return is April 15. If John mails his return on March 28 by regular mail (through the United States Postal Service), and the return is received by the Service on April 1, when is the return filed?

2. When is John's return filed if he mails his return by regular mail on April 14 and it is received by the Service on April 17?

3. Suppose instead that John files a Form 4868, Application For Automatic Extension of Time To File U.S. Individual Income Tax Return, and automatically obtains a six-month filing extension. His extended due date is October 15, and he mails the return by regular mail on October 1, along with a check for $1,200 (the remaining tax liability that he owes). The return and the payment are received by the Service on October 3. When is the return filed?

4. In question 3, on what date is John's return filed if he mails the return by regular mail on October 14, and it is received by the Service on October 17?

3. Amended Returns

In order to allow taxpayers an opportunity to file supplemental information after a return has been filed, the Service has a long-established administrative policy of permitting taxpayers to file amended returns. If an amended return is filed, it relates back to the original return and becomes a part of that return for purposes of determining a deficiency (see further discussion, Chapter 4).

There are two general reasons why taxpayers file amended returns: (1) to correct errors in a previously filed return and (2) to claim a refund or credit of overpaid taxes after an original return has been filed.

GOLDSTONE v. COMMISSIONER

United States Tax Court, 1975.
65 T.C. 113.

OPINION

STERRETT, JUDGE:

* * *

Petitioners Jack R. and Ursula Goldstone, husband and wife, were residents of San Francisco, Calif., at the time they filed their petition herein. Petitioners filed joint Federal income tax returns for the calendar years 1967, 1969, and 1970 with the Director, Internal Revenue Service Center, Ogden, Utah.

On their return for 1967, petitioners properly claimed an investment credit under § 38 in the amount of $1,400 for certain property they purchased in that year. Hereinafter, this property will be referred to as the credit property.

On October 1, 1967, Golden Gate Fashions, Inc. (hereinafter Fashions), was incorporated under the laws of the State of California. During October 1967 petitioners transferred various assets of a gift shop business, including the credit property, to Fashions in exchange for all of the capital stock thereof. This transfer met the statutory requirements for nonrecognition of gain or loss under § 351.

Fashions disposed of the credit property during petitioners' 1970 taxable year. As a result of this disposition the parties have agreed that petitioners were required to recapture the investment credit of $1,400 claimed on their 1967 return.

On or about July 1, 1971, petitioners mailed an amended 1967 joint Federal income tax return to the Internal Revenue Service Center, Fresno, Calif.

On or about December 1, 1972, petitioners mailed an amendment to the aforementioned amended return. On both the amended return and amendment thereto, petitioners claimed a refund of $4,596.61 and attempted to delete the investment credit as claimed on their original 1967 return stating, "The $1,400 Investment Credit Claimed on the original return has not been considered in the preparation of the amended return. This means that the credit is recaptured by the IRS thru the 1967 Amended Tax Return Adjustment."

Respondent denied petitioners' refund claims for 1967 in two letters, both dated November 1, 1973, and made no direct comment in either letter on petitioners' statement on the investment credit. Implicit in his action on the refund claims was a nonacceptance of the purported changed treatment of the credit by petitioners. In a statutory notice of deficiency for 1970 respondent increased petitioners' 1970 tax liability as follows:

> Investment credit in the amount of $1,400.00 which was deducted by you on your 1967 income tax return has been recaptured on your 1970 income tax return as the assets, from which the investment credit was computed in 1967 were disposed of during 1970.

We must decide the correctness of respondent's determination.

Respondent argues that the acceptance or rejection of an amended return is discretionary with the Internal Revenue Service. He contends that since both petitioners' amended returns were appropriately rejected, petitioners' initial return for 1967 on which the investment credit was claimed remains their effective return for that year. Consequently, the investment credit must be recaptured in 1970, the year of disposition of the credit property, pursuant to the express terms of § 47(a)(1).[3]

Petitioners advance the argument that the Internal Revenue Code grants them the right to file an amended return. They argue that the effect of exercising this right and deleting the investment credit on their amended returns is the same as if the credit had never been claimed. They urge, therefore, that there is no credit to be recaptured in 1970 and that § 47(a)(1) is inapplicable in the present context.

Petitioners have cited no authority in support of their arguments and we have found none. Rather, we conclude that the instant case is within the ambit of the Supreme Court's decision in Pacific National Co. v. Welch, 304 U.S. 191 (1938). There the issue was whether the taxpayer, having filed a return on which he employed the deferred payment method, was entitled to file a claim for refund 2 years later utilizing the installment method to compute the profit on the sales. In holding that the taxpayer was bound by his original method of reporting the gain from the sales the Supreme Court stated:

> Change from one method to the other, as petitioner seeks, would require recomputation and readjustment of tax liability for subsequent years and impose burdensome uncertainties upon the

---

3.　SEC. 47. CERTAIN DISPOSITIONS, ETC., OF SECTION 38 PROPERTY.

　　(a) GENERAL RULE.-- Under regulations prescribed by the Secretary or his delegate-- (1) EARLY DISPOSITION, ETC.-- IF during any taxable year any property is disposed of, or otherwise ceases to be § 38 property with respect to the taxpayer, before the close of the useful life which was taken into account in computing the credit under § 38, then the tax under this chapter for such taxable year shall be increased by an amount equal to the aggregate decrease in the credits allowed under § 38 for all prior taxable years which would have resulted solely from substituting, in determining qualified investment, for such useful life the period beginning with the time such property was placed in service by the taxpayer and ending with the time such property ceased to be § 38 property.

administration of the revenue laws. It would operate to enlarge the statutory period for filing returns (sec. 53(a)) to include the period allowed for recovering overpayments (sec. 322(b)). There is nothing to suggest that Congress intended to permit a taxpayer, after expiration of the time within which return is to be made, to have his tax liability computed and settled according to the other method.

* * * (*Pacific National Co. v. Welch*, supra at 194.)

The rationale of *Pacific National Co. v. Welch*, is clearly applicable to the case before us. Petitioners correctly claimed an investment credit on their initial 1967 tax return. Should they be allowed to change their tax treatment of the credit both problems envisioned by the Supreme Court in *Pacific National Co.* would surface. Such change would obviously impose uncertainty in the administration of § 47 as a taxpayer would have at his disposal the option to file an amended return deleting an investment credit rather than have the recapture provisions of § 47 apply. As is clear in the instant case, such change would also bear on a taxpayer's liability for a subsequent year, the year of disposition. Hence, we hold that petitioners must recapture the investment credit in 1970, the year of disposition of the credit property.

In so holding we are aware that cases in a myriad of factual settings have upheld the validity of amended returns. See, e.g., Haggar Co. v. Helvering, 308 U.S. 389 (1940); Mamula v. Commissioner, 346 F.2d 1016 (9th Cir. 1965), revg. 41 T.C. 572 (1964); John P. Reaver, 42 T.C. 72 (1964); Robert M. Foley, 56 T.C. 765 (1971). However, such cases fall within one of the following factual contexts: (1) The amended return was filed prior to the date prescribed for filing a return; (2) the taxpayer's treatment of the contested item in the amended return was not inconsistent with his treatment of that item in his original return; or (3) the taxpayer's treatment of the item in the original return was improper and the taxpayer elected one of several allowable alternatives in the amended return.

It is obvious that the factual setting before us falls within none of the aforenoted contexts. Petitioners' treatment of the investment credit on their 1967 return was entirely correct, and the treatment accorded it on the amended returns, filed long after the period for filing a return for 1967 had expired, is manifestly inconsistent with the initial treatment thereof.

Furthermore, we note that the plain, unambiguous language of § 47(a) requires that the investment credit be recaptured in the year of disposition. To sanction the course of action petitioners seek to pursue would enable petitioners to contravene the clear statutory language and would constitute a usurpation of the legislative function by this Court. Petitioners must, pursuant to § 47, recapture the investment credit in 1970.

Notes

There is no legal requirement that a taxpayer file an amended return, although if an original return contains errors or omissions, the filing of an amended return may reduce the penalties and interest that otherwise might apply. If the return preparer advises the taxpayer to file an amended return to correct noncompliance, errors or omissions and the taxpayer fails to do so, there is a chance that the Service might instigate a fraud investigation. On the other hand, there are some disadvantages to filing an amended return, such as a risk of increased scrutiny of the original return by the Service, perhaps triggering an audit. See § II..A.1, below. Also, if the original return was false or fraudulent, the amended return may raise Fifth Amendment problems of self-incrimination. See John R. Dorocak, Potential Penalties and Ethical Problems in Filing an Amended Return: the Case of the Repentant Sports/Entertainment Figure's Legal Expenses Deduction, 52 Maine Law Review 1, 15 (2000). For a discussion of potential ethical problems raised by advising taxpayers to file amended returns, see Chapter 4.

B. PAYMENT

Income taxes are paid quarterly through employer withholding on wages and other income, or through estimated tax payments made by the taxpayer on payments not subject to withholding. Income tax returns report taxpayers' financial transactions that occurred during the taxable year, and reconcile the quarterly payments that were made. The quarterly payments of withheld or estimated tax offset the tax liability on the return as a credit. Any remaining balance of the tax liability must be paid by the due date of the return, determined without regard to extensions of time to file. IRC § 6151. The taxpayer must remit the tax to the IRS Service Center where the return is filed, without waiting for the government to assess the tax due or send a notice and demand for payment.

Extensions of time to pay may be granted for periods of up to six months (twelve months in the case of an estate tax return). Unlike extensions of time to file, extensions of time to pay are not automatic. Prior to the due date of the return, the taxpayer must file a timely application for extension of time to pay. The taxpayer must submit a balance sheet and financial statement for the preceding three months, plus must make a showing of undue hardship if the payment is required to be remitted by the due date. Reg. § 1.6161-1(b) and (c). According to the regulations, an "undue hardship" means more than a mere inconvenience to the taxpayer. An example of such a hardship is a substantial financial loss from the sale of property at a sacrifice price if payment is required to be made by the due date. Id. The Service will not grant the taxpayer a payment extension if there is a tax deficiency due to taxpayer negligence, intentional disregard of the rules and regulations, or fraud. IRC § 6161(b)(3).

A taxpayer who cannot pay the full tax liability may be eligible to submit an offer in compromise or to enter into an installment agreement with the Service to make payments according to an agreed schedule (see Chapter 7 for a discussion of offers in compromise and installment agreements). IRC § 6159(a).

If the full amount of the tax is not paid by the due date, and no payment agreement or other extension of time to pay has been granted, the taxpayer will be liable for penalties and interest on the unpaid tax after the due date. If a payment extension is granted, the taxpayer will be relieved of liability for penalties, but not of the obligation to pay interest. Thus, for purposes of interest, the due date for payment of the tax remains fixed and unchanged by the extension of time to pay.

The late payment penalty may be avoided by a showing of "reasonable cause." IRC § 6651(a)(2); see discussion of delinquency penalties and defenses, Chapter 6. According to the regulations, a taxpayer who receives an automatic extension of time to file and who pays at least 90 percent of the balance of the tax by the original due date, will be eligible for a safe harbor avoidance of a delinquency penalty. See Reg. § 301.6651-1(c)(3).

Payments may be made by check or money order, or by debit, credit or charge card, although certain restrictions apply to the use of cards. See Temp. Reg. § 301.6311-2T. Electronic funds transfers may be made through the Electronic Federal Tax Payment System (EFTPS).

Questions

1. A taxpayer whose return is due April 15 requests an extension of time to file and is granted a six-month automatic extension. She does not request an extension of time to pay. Discuss the consequences if she mails her return on October 15, paying her remaining tax liability at that time (which amounts to 30 percent of her total tax liability), and the

return and payment are received by the Service on October 19. See IRC § 6651(e); Reg. § 301.6651-1(c)(3).

2. As you will see in Chapter 6, the civil penalty for late filing of a return is ten times greater than the comparable penalty for late payment. Why is late filing considered a more serious offense than late payment?

II. EXAMINATION OF RETURNS

A. IN GENERAL

When a taxpayer files a return, the amount of tax shown on the return is assessed by the government. Assessment is the recording of the tax liability in the government's summary assessment roll along with the taxpayer's name, identifying number, taxable period and type of tax, in accordance with the requirements of §§ 6201(a)(1) and 6203. Since the government merely records the amount of tax shown on the return filed by the taxpayer, this amount has been "self-assessed" by the taxpayer.

In order to ensure the integrity of the self-assessment/voluntary compliance system, the government periodically examines (audits) returns to determine the level of taxpayer compliance with the internal revenue laws. The fact that a return is audited does not mean that the taxpayer has underpaid the tax liability. In fact, many audits result in no changes to the return and some result in refunds to the taxpayer. A taxpayer's chance of being audited varies according to the classification of the taxpayer, the amount of income involved, and the type of audit. But in general, the risk of being audited remains low, ranging from slightly more than one-half of one percent to just under three percent for most individual taxpayers. This low audit rate is often referred to as the "audit lottery."

Some taxpayers, however, are more at risk of audit than others. Individual taxpayers are more likely to be audited if they file a Schedule C (self-employed income) or if they have gross income levels above $200,000. Generally, corporations with assets of greater than $5 million are more at risk of audit than other taxpayers. But the taxpayers with the greatest audit risk are the larger corporations with assets greater than $250 million – nearly half of this group is audited. The high audit risk potential of larger corporations is reinforced by the fact that the majority of these audits result in the assessment of additional tax.

Questions

1. What purpose(s) do tax audits serve?
2. Is it ethical for a lawyer to inform a client about the audit lottery?

1. Methods of Return Selection

Returns are processed at the ten IRS Campuses (formerly called "Service Centers") scattered across the country. The Campuses select returns for audit based on National Office examination guidelines. Most returns selected for audit (approximately two-thirds) are selected by IRS computers in Martinsburg, West Virginia, under a top-secret formula called "discriminant information function," or DIF, designed to select returns that have the highest potential for adjustment. Under this system, returns are scored using a mathematical system that assigns numerical weights to entries on the returns – the higher the score, the greater the potential for adjustment. Returns selected by the computer are then reviewed manually to determine their audit potential.

A second general method of return selection is through the matching of information returns with tax returns. This is referred to as an information reporting program (IRP) audit. The IRP audit has become more efficient as more businesses have been required to file information returns electronically, because the data from electronic returns can be fed directly into the IRS computers.

A third method in which returns are selected for examination is through the project audit, in which the Service attempts to address a specific problem of noncompliance by auditing returns of taxpayers within a particular group. An example of this is the Return Preparer Program, in which the tax returns prepared by a particular firm or individual preparer are selected for audit because other returns prepared by that firm or individual have been subject to penalties for negligence or fraud.

A fourth, and controversial, method of return selection was the Taxpayer Compliance Measurement Program (TCMP) audit, in which returns were selected at random for an intensive audit of every item of income, deduction, and credit on the return. TCMP audits had the dual purpose of providing data used in programming the DIF criteria and identifying areas of noncompliance that the Service otherwise might not have discovered through routine methods.

After the TCMP audits began, the effectiveness of the DIF audits increased dramatically. But the TCMP audits were very invasive, expensive, and time consuming for taxpayers. They often targeted small business owners (Schedule C filers) who were more likely to have under-reported income, overstated expenses, or deducted personal expenses as business expenses. Because of congressional concern over constituents' complaints about the TCMP audits, the Service indefinitely suspended these audits in 1995.

A significant percentage of the enforcement audits (close to 25 percent) conducted by the Service resulted in no changes being made to the returns. This was regarded as an inefficient use of its audit resources, so the Service designed a new audit method, referred to as the National Research Program (NRP) audit. This is a general calibration audit similar to the TCMP audits, but supposedly less intrusive and burdensome to taxpayers. Returns are selected randomly for examination with the purpose of generating compliance data that in turn will be used in programming the IRS computers for DIF and other enforcement audits. Many of the returns selected under the NRP audit are examined without further taxpayer contact. Others are selected for a line-by-line examination similar to the former TCMP audits, although compared to the old TCMP audits, very few returns are selected for this more intrusive phase. NRP audits are conducted every few years.

There are several other methods in which returns may be selected for examination, such as through the taxpayer's filing a claim for refund, or making a request for a ruling or determination letter, because this usually involves a manual examination of the original return to determine whether the claim or request is warranted. Thus, the original return receives greater scrutiny than it might have received otherwise. Returns also may be selected through referrals by state and local governments, or through referrals by other branches of the federal government. Another method of selection is through related returns in which one return may taint or "infect" other returns. For example, the audit of a partnership may lead to an audit of the returns of the individual partners, or two or more related taxpayers may take inconsistent positions, such as divorced spouses, both claiming dependency exemptions for the same dependent. Finally, some returns are selected as a result of information received from unrelated third parties, such as informants – former employees, jealous colleagues, and ex-spouses – and from the media, where the report of a drug bust or an embezzlement conviction involving large sums of money that might not have been reported to the government may cause the return to be selected for examination. Some of these informants may receive compensation for their information under certain circumstances. See whistleblower legislation at IRC § 7623(a).

Another controversial type of audit is the "economic reality" or "financial status" audit, which focuses on the underground economy and is designed to detect unreported income. Because underground transactions usually are conducted with cash, or bartered with property or services, there is no paper trail or information reporting system to allow the government to link financial transactions to the return. Thus, unreported income from these transactions is very difficult for the government to detect. Economic reality audits address this particular difficulty by examining taxpayers' spending patterns, rather than the income reported on the returns. This requires different audit techniques that typically are more aggressive than those used in routine audits. For instance, a revenue agent may request a tour of the taxpayer's business and may interview the taxpayer's clients or customers. The agent also may ask personal questions that ordinarily would be beyond the bounds of a routine audit, such as: what major assets do you own, what is their value, where are they located, are they subject to any loans or mortgages, and if so, what is the amount of your payment(s)?

Both taxpayers and the tax bar have expressed great concern over the intrusiveness of these audits and their resemblance to criminal investigations. A particular concern is that the Service may find it tempting to use these audits as "fishing expeditions" to uncover criminal activity where there otherwise may be no reason to suspect noncompliance. Since the audits are civil, rather than criminal in nature, taxpayers are not entitled to the constitutional safeguards to which they would be entitled in a criminal investigation. (See discussion of criminal investigations, Chapter 10). Because of these concerns, Congress enacted § 7602(e) in 1998, which prohibits the use of financial status or economic reality audits "to determine the existence of unreported income of any taxpayer unless the Secretary has reasonable indication that there is likelihood of such unreported income." Thus, such an audit would be inappropriate in the case of a taxpayer whose income consists entirely of wage and investment income subject to reporting through information returns.

Note and Question

Another successful audit technique for measuring taxpayer compliance is the Market Segment Specialization Program. A market segment is a group of taxpayers with similar characteristics, such as foreign controlled corporations, manufacturers, and sports franchises. If the Service determines that a particular group has a high level of noncompliance, or that there is uncertainty in the law pertaining to one or more groups, the audit penetration within that group may be increased. What advantages do you think the Market Segment Specialization Program will offer?

2. General Methods of Conducting Audits

Returns selected for examination are classified according to the type of audit to be conducted, which in turn is determined by the nature and complexity of the issues involved. There are three general types of audits: correspondence audits, office audits, and field audits. A correspondence audit is conducted by mail and is limited to individual returns. It is a very efficient type of audit, usually involving simple issues with minor adjustments. Returns are typically selected by computer based on high DIF scores, indicating that the issues are appropriate for correspondence audit. Returns with mathematical errors, missing schedules, mismatching of income with information returns, and unsigned returns generally trigger a correspondence audit. Occasionally, taxpayers are asked to verify the accuracy of deductions, exemptions, and/or credits, and to respond by mail within a designated time period, usually 30 days. If a return contains issues that fall within an ongoing project audit, the return may be classified for an office audit instead of a correspondence audit.

Office audits of most individual income tax returns are conducted at an IRS office by personnel of the Examination Division of the IRS Campuses. Business returns are generally examined at the district offices. An office audit usually involves a verification of the claimed deductions, exemptions, and credits. It also typically involves tax returns of under $100,000 of total positive income ("TPI"), which for individual income tax returns is the sum of the positive income figures on the return with the deductions and losses calculated at zero. Thus, TPI will always be equal to or greater than adjusted gross income. Generally, the Service defines the issues in advance so the taxpayer can prepare for the audit. If the examiner determines that a field examination is necessary, the examiner may order such an audit.

A field audit is a more complex and thorough audit, generally imposing greater burdens on the taxpayer. These audits usually are confined to high income individuals and businesses, both corporate and noncorporate, and are conducted at the taxpayer's home or place of business. A field audit usually involves an examination of the complete tax return for a particular taxable year, and an extensive examination of the taxpayer's books and records. Field audits generally are conducted by revenue agents, who are more highly educated and experienced than office auditors, and who are trained to search for unreported income. Usually, at the outset of a field audit, the agent does not inform the taxpayer of the issues to be examined, although the agent may identify the taxable year or years at issue. Thus, there is a high probability of new issues being raised during the audit.

Most audits, regardless of type, are conducted on an informal basis where everything on the return is potentially subject to examination, and therefore to substantiation both in law and in fact. In a routine audit, however, the revenue agent usually focuses on a few items. For instance, in an office audit, the agent ordinarily will examine unusually large items of deduction on the return such as casualties and other losses, charitable contributions (especially contributions in kind, such as art objects), and travel and entertainment expenses. In a field audit, issues that typically arise are frequent bank deposits, accounting methods, gains and losses on sales and exchanges of property, and losses arising from the abandonment, exhaustion, or obsolescence of business or investment property

3. Nonfilers

The government estimates that the gross tax gap (the difference between what is owed and what is paid) is $345 billion, of which $290 billion will remain unpaid after late payments and enforcement actions. It is further estimated that approximately eight percent of the gross tax gap is attributable to nonfilers, with the remainder attributable to underreporters (those who fail to report the full amount owed on a timely filed return) and underpayers (those who fail to timely pay the full amount owed).

There are several reasons why people fail to file their tax returns. One is because of a failure to comprehend their filing obligation. An offshoot of this problem is the mistaken belief that if a person cannot afford to pay the tax liability, that person should not file a return. Two is through procrastination that may arise through hardship (death, divorce, bankruptcy) or through simple inaction with the intent to file later. Three is through willful evasion.

In the past, it was very difficult for the IRS to identify and locate nonfilers but recently, the IRS technology budget has been increased and as a result, the IRS has increased its efforts to bring non-compliant taxpayers back into the fold through a national non-filer strategy. The Service has identified the nonfiler problem as "one of the most significant compliance issues facing our system of taxation."[6] This is because non-filers often are difficult to detect and over time they undermine the voluntary compliance system of taxation.

The Non-Filer Program employs several tactics to deal with the serious problem of noncompliance. First, non-filers are encouraged to voluntarily file their delinquent returns. If they come forward voluntarily, have only legal source income, file an accurate return and pay their tax (or make bona fide arrangements to pay), they will not be prosecuted for willful failure to file. Second, the campus examination branches will coordinate with other functional areas to conduct non-filer investigations and to implement an effective outreach program. The Information Reporting System (IRS) is an important tool in the non-filer (and underreporting of income) investigation. This system matches information documents such as W-2s and 1099s to information reported by the taxpayer.

When the government identifies a potential non-filer, it sends a series of notices to that individual or business to encourage the filing of a return or to establish some communication with the taxpayer about the return. If the taxpayer is uncooperative, stronger notices are sent and telephone calls may be made by a member of the automated collection system staff. If these efforts fail, the case usually then becomes a collection action and is turned over to the field collection staff.

If the taxpayer refuses to voluntarily file a return or if the taxpayer cannot be located, the IRS may prepare its own Substitute for Return (SFR) on behalf of the taxpayer based on available data. The IRS is authorized by IRC § 6020(b) to prepare such returns and to initiate collection action on those returns. Without the SFR, however, the IRS has no legal ground to begin a collection action, such as placing a lien on property or seizing the taxpayer's assets to collect any outstanding tax owed. The SFR also creates a powerful incentive for the taxpayer to file a return because the created return makes assumptions most favorable to the government, such single filing status, zero dependents, and no offsetting deductions or credits. As a result, the taxpayer ultimately may be liable for more than he actually owes.

In addition, the IRS has partnered with the states in several joint initiatives to target abusive tax avoidance schemes. One of these initiatives, the State Income Tax Reverse Filing Match, is designed specifically to identify potential non-filers and those underreporting income. Under this initiative, the states share income tax filing data

---

6.   Internal Revenue Manual, § 4.19.17.1 (Non-Filer Program).

with the IRS which then matches this data against its own to identify discrepancies and improve compliance.

With a growing deficit and worsening economy, a focus on non-filers and other tax cheats is likely to be viewed by the public much more favorably than a tax increase, although the two are by no means mutually exclusive.

Notes and Question

An important point is that non-filers do not all fit within the same category. For instance, not all cases of non-filing are potential criminal cases or attributable to willful conduct. Moreover, pursuing non-filers is a resource intensive effort and at the end of the effort, there may be very little tax liability to be collected. In some cases, a refund may be owed to the taxpayer. In other cases, the non-filer may not agree with the IRS on the amount of tax liability owed. What will happen if a nonfiler refuses to file because she and the IRS do not agree on the amount of tax liability owed?

B. ACCESS TO TAXPAYERS' BOOKS AND RECORDS

Under the Internal Revenue Code, a taxpayer is required to keep books and records documenting items of income, deductions, or credits that are required to be reported on a return. IRC § 6001. Generally, taxpayers are required to maintain these documents for at least as long as the applicable statute of limitations remains open. See Chapter 4 for a discussion of the statute of limitations. If the records relate to property, they should be kept until the expiration of the statute of limitations for the year in which the property is disposed of in a taxable transction.

A taxpayer will be subject to penalties if she fails to produce the required books, records, and other materials. See Chapter 6 for a discussion of civil penalties. There could be further problems for the taxpayer as well. For instance, a failure to produce books or records when requested to do so by an examining officer or revenue agent is likely to result in a lack of trust in the taxpayer by the officer or agent. This could cause the officer or agent to question items that otherwise might not have been questioned, and to resolve any doubts against the taxpayer. Failure to produce books and records is also an indication of fraud. Further, if the case is litigated, and the taxpayer has not produced the requested books and records, the burden of proof which normally would shift to the Service under § 7491(a)(2)(B) will not do so, but instead will remain with the taxpayer. See discussion of the burden of proof in court proceedings in Chapter 8. Note that under normal conditions, the burden of proof shifts only if the case goes to court. During the time the taxpayer is engaged in an administrative proceeding with the Service, the burden of proof falls on the taxpayer. Thus, the taxpayer has the burden of proving the correctness of the return at the audit or administrative level.

The Service has broad power under § 7602 to examine books, records, and other materials, and to compel the production of these documents. In addition, § 7602 gives the Service authority to compel the sworn testimony of any person deemed relevant or material to the determination or collection of proper tax liability. This authority is often referred to as "summons power," and because the power is broad, there are checks to insure that the government does not abuse its discretion.

UNITED STATES v. POWELL
Supreme Court of the United States, 1964.
379 U.S. 48, 85 S.Ct. 248, 13 L.Ed.2d 112.

MR. JUSTICE HARLAN delivered the opinion of the Court.

In March 1963, the Internal Revenue Service, pursuant to powers afforded the Commissioner by § 7602(2) of the Internal Revenue Code of 1954, summoned respondent Powell to appear before Special Agent Tiberino to give testimony and produce records relating to the 1958 and 1959 returns of the William Penn Laundry (the taxpayer), of which Powell was president. Powell appeared before the agent but refused to produce the records. Because the taxpayer's returns had been once previously examined, and because the three-year statute of limitations barred assessment of additional deficiencies for those years[1] except in cases of fraud (the asserted basis for this summons),[2] Powell contended that before he could be forced to produce the records the Service had to indicate some grounds for its belief that a fraud had been committed. The agent declined to give any such indication and the meeting terminated.

Thereafter the Service petitioned the District Court for the Eastern District of Pennsylvania for enforcement of the administrative summons. With this petition the agent filed an affidavit stating that he had been investigating the taxpayer's returns for 1958 and 1959; that based on this investigation the Regional Commissioner of the Service had

---

1. I.R.C. § 6501(a).

2. I.R.C., § 6501(c)(1), which in relevant part provides: 'In the case of a false or fraudulent return with the intent to evade tax, the tax may be assessed, or a proceeding in court for collection of such tax may be begun without assessment, at any time.'

determined an additional examination of the taxpayer's records for those years to be necessary and had sent Powell a letter to that effect; and that the agent had reason to suspect that the taxpayer had fraudulently falsified its 1958 and 1959 returns by overstating expenses. At the court hearing Powell again stated his objections to producing the records and asked the Service to show some basis for its suspicion of fraud. The Service chose to stand on the petition and the agent's affidavit, and, after argument, the District Court ruled that the agent be given one hour in which to re-examine the records.[3]

The Court of Appeals reversed, 325 F.2d 914. It reasoned that since the returns in question could only be reopened for fraud, re-examination of the taxpayer's records must be barred by the prohibition of § 7605(b) of the Code against 'unnecessary examination' unless the Service possessed information 'which might cause a reasonable man to suspect that there has been fraud in the return for the otherwise closed year';[5] and whether this standard has been met is to be decided 'on the basis of the showing made in the normal course of an adversary proceeding * * *.[6] The court concluded that the affidavit in itself was not sufficient to satisfy its test of probable cause.[7] Consequently, enforcement of the summons was withheld.

Because of the differing views in the circuits on the standards the Internal Revenue Service must meet to obtain judicial enforcement of its orders,[8] we granted certiorari, 377 U.S. 929, 84 S.Ct. 1334, 12 L.Ed.2d 294.

We reverse, and hold that the Government need make no showing of probable cause to suspect fraud unless the taxpayer raises a substantial question that judicial enforcement of the administrative summons would be an abusive use of the court's process, predicated on more than the fact

---

3. The parties subsequently agreed that if the Government was upheld in its claim of right to examine without showing probable cause, the one-hour time limitation would be removed.

5. 325 F.2d 914, 915-916.

6. Id., at 916.

7. 'Probable cause' as used in this opinion is meant to include the full range of formulations offered by lower courts.

8. Compare Foster v. United States, 265 F.2d 183 (C.A.2d Cir. 1959); United States v. Ryan, 320 F.2d 500 (C.A.6th Cir. 1963), affirmed today, 379 U.S. 61, 85 S.Ct. 232, with O'Connor v. O'Connell, 253 F.2d 365 (C.A.1st Cir. 1958), followed in Lash v. Nighosian, 273 F.2d 185 (C.A.1st Cir. 1959); Globe Construction Co. v. Humphrey, 229 F.2d 148 (C.A.5th Cir. 1956); De Masters v. Arend, 313 F.2d 79 (C.A.9th Cir. 1963).

of re-examination and the running of the statute of limitations on ordinary tax liability.

* * *

II.

Respondent primarily relies on § 7605(b) to show that the Government must establish probable cause for suspecting fraud, and that the existence of probable cause is subject to challenge by the taxpayer at the hearing.[11] That section provides:

> 'No taxpayer shall be subjected to unnecessary examination or investigations, and only one inspection of a taxpayer's books of account shall be made for each taxable year unless the taxpayer requests otherwise or unless the Secretary or his delegate, after investigation, notifies the taxpayer in writing that an additional inspection is necessary.'

We do not equate necessity as contemplated by this provision with probable cause or any like notion. If a taxpayer has filed fraudulent returns, a tax liability exists without regard to any period of limitations. Section 7602 authorizes the Commissioner to investigate any such liability.[12] If, in order to determine the existence or nonexistence of fraud in the taxpayer's returns, information in the taxpayer's records is needed which is not already in the Commissioner's possession, we think the examination is not 'unnecessary' within the meaning of § 7605(b). Although a more stringent interpretation is possible, one which would require some showing of cause for suspecting fraud, we reject such an interpretation because it might seriously hamper the Commissioner in carrying out investigations he thinks warranted, forcing him to litigate and prosecute appeals on the very subject which he desires to investigate, and because the legislative history of § 7605(b) indicates that no severe restriction was intended.

---

11. See n. 18, infra.

12. Section 7602 provides:'For the purpose of ascertaining the correctness of any return, making a return where none has been made, determining the liability of any person for any internal revenue tax or the liability at law or in equity of any transferee or fiduciary of any person in respect of any internal revenue tax, or collecting any such liability, the Secretary or his delegate is authorized-'(1) To examine any books, papers, records, or other data which may be relevant or material to such inquiry;'(2) To summon the person liable for tax or required to perform the act, or any officer or employee of such person, or any person having possession, custody, or care of books of account containing entries relating to the business of the person liable for tax or required to perform the act, or any other person the Secretary or his delegate may deem proper, to appear before the Secretary or his delegate at a time and place named in the summons and to produce such books, papers, records, or other data, and to give such testimony, under oath, as may be relevant or material to such inquiry; and'(3) To take such testimony of the person concerned, under oath, as may be relevant or material to such inquiry.'

Section 7605(b) first appeared as § 1309 of the Revenue Act of 1921, 42 Stat. 310. Its purpose and operation were explained by the manager of the bill, Senator Penrose, on the Senate floor:

'Mr. PENROSE. Mr. President, the provision is entirely in the interest of the taxpayer and for his relief from unnecessary annoyance. Since these income taxes and direct taxes have been in force very general complaint has been made, especially in the large centers of wealth and accumulation of money, at the repeated visits of tax examiners, who perhaps are overzealous or do not use the best of judgment in the exercise of their functions. I know that from many of the cities of the country very bitter complaints have reached me and have reached the department of unnecessary visits and inquisitions after a thorough examination is supposed to have been had. This section is purely in the interest of quieting all this trouble and in the interest of the peace of mind of the honest taxpayer.

'Mr. WALSH. * * * So that up to the present time an inspector could visit the office of an individual or corporation and inspect the books as many times as he chose?

'Mr. PENROSE. And he often did so.

'Mr. WALSH. * * * And this provision of the Senate committee seeks to limit the inspection to one visit unless the commissioner indicates that there is necessity for further examination?

'Mr. PENROSE. That is the purpose of the amendment.

'Mr. WALSH. * * * I heartily agree with the beneficial results that the amendment will produce to the taxpayer.

'Mr. PENROSE. I knew the Senator would agree to the amendment, and it will go a long way toward relieving petty annoyances on the part of honest taxpayers.' 61 Cong.Rec. 5855 (Sept. 28, 1921).[13]

---

13. Other relevant legislative history to like effect may be found in H.R.Rep. No. 350, 67th Cong., 1st Sess., 16 (1921); S.Rep. No. 275, 67th Cong., 1st Sess., 31 (1921); 61 Cong.Rec. 5202 (Aug. 18, 1921), remarks of Mr. Hawley. The provision was re-enacted in 1926. In the Senate, a substitute measure was adopted which would have limited the Commissioner to two examinations appertaining to returns of any one year. Senator Reed's objection to the original provision was: 'By merely claiming fraud the Government at any time can make examination after examination, subject only to one limitation, that it must give notice that it is going to make the examination. That, in ordinary course, is done by the mere writing of a letter,' 67 Cong.Rec. 3856 (Feb. 12, 1926). There is no indication in the discussion that the courts were thought to play any significant limiting role. The Senate substitute was ultimately deleted by the Conference Committee and the original provision resubstituted. H.R.Rep. No. 356, 69th Cong., 1st Sess., 55. The section was re-enacted in 1939 and 1954 without substantial change and without further elaboration of the congressional intent. Respondent contends that in re-enacting the provision, Congress must have been aware of, and acquiesced in, decisions of lower courts that a showing of probable cause is required. In re Andrews' Tax Liability, 18 F.Supp. 804 (1937); Zimmermann v. Wilson, 105 F.2d 583 (C.A.3d Cir. 1939); In re

Congress recognized a need for a curb on the investigating powers of low-echelon revenue agents, and considered that it met this need simply and fully by requiring such agents to clear any repetitive examination with a superior. For us to import a probable cause standard to be enforced by the courts would substantially overshoot the goal which the legislators sought to attain. There is no intimation in the legislative history that Congress intended the courts to oversee the Commissioner's determinations to investigate. No mention was made of the statute of limitations[14] and the exception for fraud.

We are asked to read § 7605(b) together with the limitations sections in such a way as to impose a probable cause standard upon the Commissioner from the expiration date of the ordinary limitations period forward. Without some solid indication in the legislative history that such a gloss was intended, we find it unacceptable.[15] Our reading of the statute is said to render the first clause of § 7605(b) surplusage to a large extent, for, as interpreted, the clause adds little beyond the relevance and materiality requirements of § 7602. That clause does appear to require that the information sought is not already within the Commissioner's possession, but we think its primary purpose was no more than to emphasize the responsibility of agents to exercise prudent judgment in wielding the extensive powers granted to them by the Internal Revenue Code.[16]

This view of the statute is reinforced by the general rejection of probable cause requirements in like circumstances involving other agencies. In Oklahoma Press Pub. Co. v. Walling, 327 U.S. 186, 216, 66 S.Ct. 494, 509, 90 L.Ed. 614, in reference to the Administrator's subpoena power under the Fair Labor Standards Act, the Court said 'his investigative function, in searching out violations with a view to securing enforcement of the Act, is essentially the same as the grand jury's, or the

---

Brooklyn Pawnbrokers, 39 F.Supp. 304 (1941); Martin v. Chandis Securities Co., 128 F.2d 731 (C.A.9th Cir. 1942). These cases represent neither a settled judicial construction, see In re Keegan, 18 F.Supp. 746 (1937), nor one which we sould be justified in presuming Congress, by its silence, impliedly approved. Compare Shapiro v. United States, 335 U.S. 1, 68 S.Ct. 1375, 92 L.Ed. 1787.

14. Revenue Act of 1921, s 250(d), 42 Stat. 265, provided a four-year period of limitation on ordinary tax liability.

15. The contrary view derives no support from the characterization of the limitations provision as a 'statute of response.' The present three-year limitation on assessment of ordinary deficiencies relieves the taxpayer of concern for further assessments of that type, but it by no means follows that it limits the right of the Government to investigate with respect to deficiencies for which no statute of limitations is imposed.

16. The Court of Appeals appears to have been led astray by the fact that the Government argued its case on the premise that § 7604(b) was the governing statute.

court's in issuing other pretrial orders for the discovery of evidence, and is governed by the same limitations,' and accordingly applied the view that inquiry must not be "limited * * * by * * * forecasts of the probable result of the investigation." In United States v. Morton Salt Co., 338 U.S. 632, 642-643, 70 S.Ct. 357, 364, 94 L.Ed. 401, the Court said of the Federal Trade Commission, 'It has a power of inquisition, if one chooses to call it that, which is not derived from the judicial function. It is more analogous to the Grand Jury, which does not depend on a case or controversy for power to get evidence but can investigate merely on suspicion that the law is being violated, or even just because it wants assurance that it is not.' While the power of the Commissioner of Internal Revenue derives from a different body of statutes, we do not think the analogies to other agency situations are without force when the scope of the Commissioner's power is called in question.

III.

Reading the statutes as we do, the Commissioner need not meet any standard of probable cause to obtain enforcement of his summons, either before or after the three-year statute of limitations on ordinary tax liabilities has expired. He must show that the investigation will be conducted pursuant to a legitimate purpose, that the inquiry may be relevant to the purpose, that the information sought is not already within the Commissioner's possession, and that the administrative steps required by the Code have been followed – in particular, that the "Secretary or his delegate," after investigation, has determined the further examination to be necessary and has notified the taxpayer in writing to that effect. This does not make meaningless the adversary hearing to which the taxpayer is entitled before enforcement is ordered. At the hearing he "may challenge the summons on any appropriate ground," Reisman v. Caplin, 374 U.S. 440, at 449. Nor does our reading of the statutes mean that under no circumstances may the court inquire into the underlying reasons for the examination. It is the court's process which is invoked to enforce the administrative summons and a court may not permit its process to be abused. Such an abuse would take place if the summons had been issued for an improper purpose, such as to harass the taxpayer or to put pressure on him to settle a collateral dispute, or for any other purpose reflecting on the good faith of the particular investigation. The burden of showing an abuse of the court's process is on the taxpayer, and it is not met by a mere showing, as was made in this case, that the statute of limitations for ordinary deficiencies has run or that the records in question have already been once examined.

The judgment of the Court of Appeals is reversed, and the case is remanded for further proceedings consistent with this opinion.

It is so ordered

MR. JUSTICE DOUGLAS, with whom MR. JUSTICE STEWART and MR. JUSTICE GOLDBERG concur, dissenting.

Congress, by the three-year statute of limitations that bars assessments of tax deficiencies except (so far as relevant here) in case of fraud, 26 U.S.C. §§ 6501(a) and (c), has brought into being a 'statute of repose' that I would respect more highly than my Brethren. I would respect it by requiring the District Court to be satisfied that the Service is not acting capriciously in reopening the closed tax period. Since the agency must go to the court for process to compel the production of the records for the closed tax period, I would insist that the District Court act in a judicial capacity, free to disagree with the administrative decision unless that minimum standard is met.[2]

Oklahoma Press Pub. Co. v. Walling, 327 U.S. 186, 66 S.Ct. 494, 90 L.Ed. 614, does not seem to me to be relevant. It dealt with the usual investigative powers of administrative agencies; and as the Court said in that case, Congress set no standards for administrative action which the judiciary first had to weigh and appraise.[3] Id., 215-216, 66 S.Ct. 508-509. Here we have a congressional 'statute of repose' embodied in the three-year statute of limitations. I would make it meaningful by protecting it from invasion by mere administrative fiat. Where the limitations period has expired, an examination is presumptively 'unnecessary' within the meaning of § 7605(b)-a presumption the Service must overcome. That is to say, a re-examination of the taxpayer's records after the three-year period is 'unnecessary' within the meaning of § 7605(b), unless the District Court is shown something more than mere caprice for believing fraud was practiced on the revenue. Without that minimum safeguard the statutory status of repose becomes rather meaningless.

---

2.   The First Circuit requires the Commissioner to show that 'a reasonable basis exists for a suspicion of fraud,' O'Connor v. O'Connell, 253 F.2d 365, 370; the Ninth Circuit requires that the decision to investigate for fraud appear as 'a matter of rational judgment based on the circumstances of the particular case,' De Masters v. Arend, 313 F.2d 79, 90; the Third Circuit requires that the agent's suspicion of fraud be 'reasonable' in the eyes of the District Court. 325 F.2d 914, 916.

3.   The case is more like United States v. Morton Salt Co., 338 U.S. 632, 70 S.Ct. 357, where, as respects the power of the Federal Trade Commission to require issuance of 'special' reports, the Court reserved the right to prevent the 'arbitrary' exercise of that administrative power. Id., at 654, 70 S.Ct. at 369.

Notes and Question

Courts have allowed the Service broad latitude in determining what is a legitimate purpose and what is a relevant inquiry. While the Service bears the burden of meeting the *Powell* factors, the burden is not heavy. Once the Service has made its prima facie case, the burden then shifts to the taxpayer to contest the summons by specific proof.

There are conflicting opinions about whether § 6001 permits the government to compel the production of books and records without a summons, or whether it must follow the summons procedures under § 7602. Section 6001 requires only that the taxpayer *make and keep* books and records. It does not address the production of these materials. But in United States v. Ohio Bell Telephone Co, 475 F. Supp. 697 (N.D. Ohio 1978), the district court held that § 6001 implicitly allows the Service to require the production of records for investigation. The Fifth Circuit, however, in United States v. Mobil Corp., 543 F. Supp. 507 (N.D. Tex. 1981), rejected the reasoning of *Ohio Bell* and held there is no implicit authority under § 6001 for the Service to compel a taxpayer to make such materials available for inspection without the issuance of a summons. The Fifth Circuit based its decision on the fact that Congress had authorized the inspection of documents under other statutory provisions, such as the summons procedures under § 7602 (and other such procedures under §§ 7603-7610), and has required an administrative warrant or its equivalent for those inspections. The court also reasoned that if § 6001 is construed to imply a unilateral right of inspection, this would frustrate the purpose of the administrative summons and would raise a serious constitutional question of whether such an implied authority would violate the Fourth Amendment's prohibition against compulsory searches. Id. at 517; see also United States v. Ernst & Whinney, 735 F.2d 1296, 1300 (11th Cir. 1984) (approving the *Mobil* holding in dictum, but disagreeing on other grounds), cert denied 470 U.S. 1050 (1985).

The records at issue in *Mobil* contained personnel information unrelated to the employees' tax liability. Thus, the company was reluctant to turn the records over to the government. On the other hand, if the records had contained information solely relevant to the employees' tax liability, there would have been no reason for the company to refuse to comply with the Service's request. Nor would it have been in the company's best interest for it to have refused to comply, because a failure to keep adequate books and records (and thus, to refuse to comply with a request to produce them) is an indication of fraud.

What other factors should a taxpayer take into account in considering whether or not to refuse an IRS request for production of records?

1. Third Party Contacts

In examining the taxpayer's return, the Service usually deals directly with the taxpayer or the taxpayer's representative. But occasionally, it may seek the aid of third parties to obtain information the taxpayer has been unable or unwilling to provide, or to verify information it has received. For instance, either the Service or the taxpayer may call upon third parties who have knowledge of the taxpayer's books, records, or returns. For the purpose of appearing as a witness, the third party does not have to qualify to practice before the Service. The government may solicit information from governmental agencies and financial institutions as well. Such contact is authorized under § 7602(c). If the third party refuses to cooperate, the Service may issue a summons to compel the party to produce the required information.

In order to protect the rights of taxpayers under investigation, the Service first must give reasonable advance notice to the taxpayer before any third parties are contacted. In addition, the Service periodically must provide a record of third party contacts to the taxpayer or upon request. If a third party is summoned to appear before the IRS during a civil investigation, the taxpayer must be notified of the contact within three days of the date of the service of the summons. IRC § 7609(a). A taxpayer under criminal investigation is not entitled to notification. The Service also is not required to notify the taxpayer of third party contacts where the taxpayer has authorized the contact, or where the Service determines that the notice would jeopardize collection of any tax, or involve reprisal against any person. IRC § 7602(c)(3). Generally, the Service takes the word of the third party that reprisal is a distinct possibility. Under proposed regulations, an employee acting within the scope of his or her employment is not considered a third party. For an overview of the administrative summons in a criminal investigation, see Chapter 10.

2. Prohibition Against Subsequent Inspections

Section § 7605(b), protects taxpayers from unwarranted inspection of their books and records. As you will see, however, this provision is not a blanket prohibition against subsequent inspections.

UNITED STATES v. CRESPO

United States District Court for the District of Maryland, 1968.
281 F. Supp. 928.

OPINION by THOMSEN, CHIEF JUDGE.

* * *

Section 7605(b) provides:

"(b) Restrictions on examination of taxpayer. – No taxpayer shall be subjected to unnecessary examination or investigations, and only one inspection of a taxpayer's books of account shall be made for each taxable year unless the taxpayer requests otherwise or unless the Secretary or his delegate, after investigation, notifies the taxpayer in writing that an additional inspection is necessary."

* * *

Discussion

Respondents contend that the IRS has already conducted one inspection for the tax years in question, so that § 7605(b) prohibits another inspection in the absence of notice from the Secretary. Respondents argue that § 7605(b), quoted above, contains two separate restrictions: first, "[n]o taxpayer shall be subjected to unnecessary examination or investigations"; second, "only one inspection of a taxpayer's books of account shall be made for each taxable year unless the taxpayer requests otherwise or unless the Secretary or his delegate, after investigation, notifies the taxpayer in writing that an additional inspection is necessary."

Respondents do not contend that taxpayer is being subjected to "unnecessary examinations or investigations." Such an argument would be without merit. Respondents rely only on the absence of a notice from the Secretary or his delegate.

The government argues that the intent and meaning of § 7605(b) is that such a notice is necessary only when the investigation, including a sufficient inspection of the taxpayer's books and records, has been completed and a determination of the tax liability for the year or years in question has been made. The government's position is given effect in Revenue Procedure 64-40, Cumulative Bulletin 1964-2, p. 971, 26 C.F.R. 601.105, the pertinent parts of which are set out in note 7 in the margin.[7]

---

7.   Revenue Procedure 64-40 reads in pertinent part:

Section 1. *Purpose.* The purpose of this revenue procedure is to restate and supersede Revenue procedure 63-9, C.B. 1963-1, 488, which sets forth the conditions under which cases closed by examination in the office of District Director of Internal Revenue may be reopened.

Section 2. *Scope.*

Both sides cite portions of the legislative history to support their respective contentions.[8] However, neither the legislative history nor the few court decisions referring to § 7605(b) which have been cited or found are conclusive of the issue. Most of the cases involved factual situations quite different from that presented in the instant case.[9]

Respondents cited In re Paramount Jewelry Co., 80 F.Supp. 375 (S.D.N.Y. 1948), in which the court held that an investigation that had involved an examination of the taxpayer's books three or four times during the past two years should not be halted as unnecessary by vacating a direction that books and records be produced but that, if the taxpayer insisted, it was entitled to receive a notice that an additional inspection was necessary before being required to produce the taxpayer's books for a fourth or fifth time. That case has apparently been cited only once, in Application of Magnus, 196 F.Supp. 127, 128 (S.D.N.Y. 1961), where it was summarized substantially as set out above in an opinion dealing with a different question. On appeal in the *Magnus* case, the Second Circuit did not cite the *Paramount Jewelry* case, but noted that an investigation "often requires a long period of time. There may be many ramifications which lead into many areas. Each new clue investigated is not a new investigation in a Section 7605(b) sense." 299 F.2d 335, at 337 (2d Cir. 1962). Similarly, the fact that a revenue agent

---

.01   For the purpose of this procedure, a case is considered closed when a taxpayer has been notified in writing of an adjustment to his tax liability or the acceptance of the return as filed.

.02   This procedure does not include any action pertaining to the reopening of cases or issues under the jurisdiction of the offices of the Appellate Division or the Regional counsel.

Section 3. *Conditions for Reopening.*

.01   It is the administrative practice of the Internal Revenue Service not to reopen cases previously closed by the District Director, unless–

1.   There is evidence of fraud, malfeasance, collusion, concealment or the misrepresentation of material fact; or

2.   The prior closing involved a substantial error; or

3.   Other circumstances indicate that failure to reopen would be a serious administrative omission."   * * *

A Policy Statement contained in Internal Revenue Manual, section P-4020-2, approved September 14, 1962, adds: "Reopenings resulting from post-review action must have the approval of the Assistant Regional Commissioner (Audit). Reopenings at the District level must have the approval of the District Director."

8.   61 Cong. Rec. 5202 (1921); Sen. Rep. No. 275, 67th Cong., 1st Sess., p. 31; H.Rep. No. 337, 67th Cong., 1st Sess., p. 16; 8A Mertens, Law of Federal Income Taxation, § 47.48, p. 140.

9.   United States v. Powell, 379 U.S. 48, 85 S.Ct. 248, 13 L.Ed.2d 112 (1964); United States v. Howard, 360 F.2d 373 (3rd Cir. 1966); Reineman v. United States, 301 F.2d 267 (7th Cir. 1962); National Plate & Window Glass company, Inc. v. United States, 254 F.2d 92 (2nd Cir. 1958); Norda Essential Oil & Chemical Co., Inc. v. United States, 253 F.2d 700 (2d Cir. 1958); United States v. United Distillers Products Corporation, 156 F.2d 872, 873 (2d Cir. 1946).

has seen a cash book, journal or ledger once does not mean that he may not need to see it again for a different purpose.

This Court does not accept the government's position that a notice from the Secretary is never needed unless the investigation, including a sufficient inspection of the taxpayer's books and records, has been completed and a determination made of the tax liability for the year or years in question.[10] When the investigation has not been completed, the question whether a further examination of the books and records would constitute a second "inspection " within the meaning of § 7605(b) depends on the circumstances. If such examination of the books and records is part of a continuing investigation, made necessary by the discovery of invoices, correspondence, or other material which requires the agent to look at the books again, such examination is not a second "inspection" within the meaning of § 7605(b).

The taxpayers and other people of the United States have an interest in seeing that income tax returns are carefully audited, and that revenue agents investigate leads which indicate that a taxpayer has understated his taxable income, intentionally or unintentionally. But taxpayers and other people also have an interest in requiring that the work be done as promptly as is practicable, and that they are not harassed by investigations which are prolonged beyond any reasonable need, or by repeated examinations of their books and records unless such further examinations are required by the discovery or development of new leads.

The Courts are not in a position to require that all agents operate with the same efficiency, or to pass on what individual books and records an agent may re-examine as the result of a new lead. But the Courts should intervene when taxpayers are able to show that agents have abused their discretion in wielding the extensive powers granted to them by the Internal Revenue Code.

In the present case respondents Crespo and Smith did not testify themselves, but rested on the testimony of the two agents. From the evidence the Court finds that by March 1967 Revenue Agent Weider had made a sufficient examination of the corporate taxpayer's books and records for the fiscal year ending March 31, 1963, to be able to complete his report for that year. On the other hand, Revenue Agent Weider has not yet completed his report for the years ending March 31, 1964 and March 31, 1965. He has examined some of the taxpayer's records for those years, but has not seen other items, e.g., correspondence with M.C. Ramos, Commercial Envelope Co. and Standard Register Co., nor the

---

10. Certainly, such a notice is needed under those circumstances, and would have been needed here if the government were seeking to examine the books and records for the year ending March 31, 1963.

purchase invoices of the latter two concerns. He desires, and the evidence shows that he needs, further information with respect to those items, because of various questions which have arisen as to the propriety of certain claimed deductions relating to those transactions.

This Court concludes that the original investigation of the corporation's tax liabilities for the years ending March 31, 1964, and March 31, 1965 is continuing and that the production of the books and records for those taxable years would not amount to a second inspection within the meaning of § 7605(b). Therefore, notice from the Secretary or his delegate to examine taxpayer's books and records for the taxable years ending March 31, 1964 and March 31, 1965 is not required.

Notes and Questions

The Service has stated that it will not reopen any case that has been closed after an examination to make an adjustment unfavorable to the taxpayer unless "(1) there is evidence of fraud, malfeasance, collusion, concealment, or misrepresentation of a material fact; or (2) the prior closing involved a clearly defined substantial error based on an established Service position existing at the time of the previous examination; or (3) other circumstances exist that indicate failure to reopen would be a serious administrative omission." Rev. Proc. 2005-32, 2005-1 C.B. 1206, superceding Rev. Proc. 94-68, 1994-2 C.B. 803.

A case is considered closed when the taxpayer is notified in writing either that adjustments to tax liability are required or that the return is accepted without change. If an additional examination is necessary, the taxpayer must be given notice properly signed by the official in charge of the division that conducted the examination.

A California district court, in an unreported case, has held that the Service's internal procedural provisions such as Rev. Proc. 72-40, 1972-2 C.B. 819 (ultimately superceded by Rev. Proc. 94-68, 1994-2 C.B. 803) are merely directory and not mandatory. Thus, the Service is not required to comply with them. Therefore, if the Service closes a case then reopens it in the absence of any of the factors mentioned in Rev. Proc. 94-68, a subsequent notice of deficiency is valid. See Council of British Societies In Southern California v. United States, 1978 WL 4584 (C.D. Calif. 1978), citing Luhring v. Glotzbach, 304 F.2d 560 (4th Cir. 1962).

Not all taxpayer contacts are considered examinations. For instance, a correction of mathematical or clerical errors, a verification or adjustment of a discrepancy between the taxpayer's return and an information return, and a verification of the accuracy of, or the need for, a Tax Shelter Registration number are considered cursory reviews and not examinations. Thus, they do not trigger the prohibition against subsequent inspections. Note, however, that if the inquiry goes beyond the face of the return (whether initial return, amended return or information return), an examination will result and the reopening criteria will apply. An example of such an inquiry is medical payments to a doctor, where it may be necessary to examine the income received from individual patients and other sources because otherwise it may not be possible to determine whether the payments were included in gross receipts. I.R.M. 4(14)17, Part IV.

1. Since a prohibited reopening can be "cured" by providing the taxpayer with the required written notice, does § 7605(b) provide any real benefit or protection to the taxpayer?

2. In United States v. Schwartz, 332 F. Supp. 820 (N.D. Ga. 1971), the federal district court held in favor of the taxpayer in refusing to allow the government to make a subsequent inspection of the taxpayer's returns. The court stated that the *Crespo* court had not applied the correct standard because it had focused on the "continuing investigation" rather than on the "continuing inspection" of the books and records. Do you agree with this statement?

C. SPECIALIZED AUDITS

In order to ensure uniformity and efficiency, the Service has specialized audit procedures for certain groups of taxpayers who present special audit problems, such as large partnerships with many partners scattered across the country. Partnerships in general, and large partnerships in particular, present coordination problems in examining the returns of the individual partners and the partnership. Thus, there is a special partnership audit procedure that applies to these taxpayers.

Employee classification historically has presented tax problems for employers, because if employees are misclassified as independent contractors, the result can be devastating to the employer's financial stability, and can have adverse consequences to any qualified retirement plans of the employer, which, in turn, can affect the employees as well as the employer. The Service has addressed these issues in the Employment Tax Examination Program, discussed below.

Finally, large corporate taxpayers (those with assets of more than $250 million) that may have several subsidiaries are audited under the Coordinated Examination Program (CEP), also called the Large Case Program. Under this program, corporations within a controlled group are treated as one unit and are coordinated so that other IRS offices are prevented from auditing any entity within the group. Issues are coordinated for purposes of appeal as well, thus audits involving Appeals Coordinated Issues cannot be settled without the approval of the national coordinator.

1. TEFRA Partnership Audit Procedure

The early 1980's witnessed a proliferation of tax shelters, most of which were in the form of large limited partnerships. But the procedure for auditing these large partnerships was cumbersome and inefficient, thus making it difficult for the Service to address the spread of abusive shelters. The crux of the problem lay in the relationship between the partnership and its partners. A partnership is a tax-reporting, but not a tax-paying, entity. The amount, timing and characterization of items of income, deductions and credits are determined by the partnership, but are reported on the returns of the individual partners according to their distributive shares of partnership profits and losses. An audit of a partnership could not result in an adjustment of any individual partner's tax liability without a corresponding audit of that partner. In the case of a large partnership, the partners could be scattered across the country and beyond. Prior to 1982, there was little to no coordination between the partnership and the individual partners with respect to audits of returns, administrative appeals, and litigation of unsettled cases. Thus, the audit of a single partnership could result in multiple audits of the individual partners, leading to cumbersome multiple appeals and court cases.

The Tax Equity and Fiscal Responsibility Act of 1982 (TEFRA),[7] attempted to address the problem by unifying the partnership audit process so that items of income, deductions and credits are determined through unified administrative and judicial proceedings at the partnership level, while the tax liability is imposed at the partner level.[8]

---

7.   Tax Equity and Fiscal Responsibility Act of 1982, Pub. L. No. 97-248, § 402.

8.   Also in 1982, the Subchapter S Revision Act enacted similar provisions that applied to S corporations. These provisions were repealed by the Small Business Job Protection Act of 1996, Pub. L. No. 104-88, 104th Cong., 2d Sess. § 1307(c)(1), applicable to tax yeas beginning after December 31, 1996. Thus, the TEFRA audit procedure is applicable to S corporations in taxable years beginning after September 3, 1982 and before January 1, 1997. Similar consistency provisions continue to apply to S corporations, however, under I.R.C. §§ 6037(c)(1) and 6037(c)(2), as amended by the Small Business Job Protection Act of 1996, id. at § 1307(c)(2). (The inconsistency notification exception applicable to TEFRA partnerships does not apply to S corporations). See also IRC § 6241 (tax treatment of items determined at corporate level, not the shareholder level); § 6244 (rules applicable to unified partnerships also generally apply to S corporations).

This specialized type of audit is known as the "TEFRA partnership audit procedure" or the "unified partnership audit procedure."[9]

The TEFRA procedure applies to all partnerships required to file tax returns,[10] unless the small partnership exception applies. Under the exception, small partnerships with 10 or fewer partners at any one time during the partnership taxable year (where each of the partners is a natural person, and not a nonresident alien or estate), are not subject automatically to the TEFRA procedure.[11] But such a partnership may elect to have the unified rules apply if all the partners agree.[12]

Notes

The TEFRA partnership provisions also apply to limited liability companies (LLCs) in the same manner in which they apply to partnerships.

In Dhillion v. Commissioner, 1999-214 T.C. Memo (July 1, 1999), a partnership with less than 10 partners received a statutory notice of deficiency (90-day letter) from the Service (see Chapter 4 for a discussion of the significance of a statutory notice of deficiency) after failing to reach a settlement agreement. The partners filed a Tax Court petition one day after the expiration of the 90-day filing deadline. The partners argued that the TEFRA provisions gave them an extended 150-day limit in which to file the petition and thus the petition was timely filed. The Tax Court held, however, that since the partnership had less than 10 partners, the TEFRA provisions did not apply automatically. Since the partners had failed to elect the provisions, the petition was not timely filed and the case was dismissed for lack of jurisdiction.

The classification of an entity as a partnership is important for purposes of determining whether or not a partner may bring an individual action. If an entity is determined to be a partnership, any

---

9.   See IRC §§ 6221 through 6233. The procedure was significantly modified by the Taxpayer Relief Act of 1997, Pub. L. No. 105-34, which added IRC § 6234, effective for partnership taxable years ending after August 5, 1997.

10.   Those partnerships with at least 100 partners during the preceding taxable year may elect to be treated under special TEFRA rules applicable to large partnerships. See IRC § 775(a), incorporated by reference in IRC § 6255(a)(1), added by the Taxpayer Relief Act of 1997, § 122(a), effective for partnership taxable years ending on or after December 31, 1997.

11.   For partnership taxable years ending after August 5, 1997, a small partnership with a C corporation partner continues to be subject to the exception.

12.   IRC § 6231(a)(1)(B); Treas. Reg. § 301.6231(a)(1)-1. For this purpose, a husband and wife (and their estates) are considered one person. Treas. Reg. § 301.6231(a)(1)-1(a)(1).

judicial action pending with respect to any of the partners must be dismissed because the court does not have jurisdiction over the individual partner with respect to the partnership items. Instead, suit must be filed under the unified partnership procedure. Similarly, any administrative examination of the partner's return must be conducted under the TEFRA unified procedure to the extent of partnership items on the return.

Under the Taxpayer Relief Act of 1997, if the Service reasonably but erroneously determines that an entity is a partnership, the TEFRA rules apply to the partnership and its partners for that taxable year, despite the error. Conversely, if the Service determines that the entity is not a partnership, the TEFRA rules do not apply to the entity for that taxable year, even if the determination is in error. IRC § 6231(g)(1) and (g)(2).

a.   *Partnership Items*

The TEFRA procedure applies to partnership items, which are items required to be taken into account for the partnership's taxable year, to the extent the regulations provide that such items are more appropriately determined at the partnership level than at the partner level.[13] These items cannot be changed without a partnership-level proceeding. Items not classified as partnership items are "nonpartnership items," to which the unified audit procedure does not apply.[14]

Under the TEFRA procedure, the partners generally must treat partnership items consistently with the way they are treated by the partnership. For example, B is a partner of Partnership P. Both B and P use the calendar year as the taxable year. In December 2010, P receives an advance payment for services to be performed in 2011, and P reports this amount as income for calendar year 2010. However, B reports B's distributive share of this amount on B's income tax return for 2011, and not on B's return for 2010. B's treatment of this partnership item is inconsistent with the treatment of the item by P.[15]

If the partners conform to the rule of consistency in reporting items of income, deduction, and credit in accordance with the partnership, the

---

13.   I.R.C. § 6231(a)(3).

14.   Id. at § 6231(a)(4). Under some circumstances, a partnership item may be treated as a nonpartnership item, either with respect to the entire partnership (IRC § 6231(c)(2)) or with respect to a particular partner (id. at § 6231(b)).

15.   Prop. Reg. §301.6222(a)-1T(c), Ex. (1).

Service generally may not adjust partnership items on the partners' returns without making a partnership-level adjustment. Treas. Reg. § 301.6221-1T(a). A partner may treat a partnership item inconsistently if the partner notifies the Service of the inconsistency by filing a statement with her tax return.[16]

As a practical matter, the notice statement is an open invitation to an audit. Thus, it is only worthwhile for a partner to treat a partnership item inconsistently and to file such a notice in the case of fraud or error at the partnership level.

If a partner treats a partnership item on her return inconsistently with the partnership treatment of that item without notifying the Service, the Service may make a computational adjustment to conform the partner's treatment of the item to that of the partnership. Such an adjustment may affect other items on the partner's return, even though those other items are not related to the partnership items. These items are known as "affected items." For example, if the computational adjustment to a partnership item affects the amount of the partner's adjusted gross income, this in turn could affect the threshold limit for a medical expense deduction under § 213[17] or a charitable contribution deduction under § 170. Any addition to tax attributable to the affected item is also considered an affected item that is included in the computational adjustment.

b. *The Tax Matters Partner*

Each partnership must designate a tax matters partner (TMP) to represent the partnership in the unified partnership-level administrative and judicial proceedings. The TMP serves as a liaison between the partners and the Service or the courts. When a partnership-level administrative proceeding is initiated, the Service must notify both the

---

16. IRC § 6222(b)(1). Notice is given by filing a completed Form 8082 with the IRS Service Centers where the partner files her returns. If proper notice is given, the Service may not make a computational adjustment with respect to the item at issue without first conducting a partnership-level proceeding or treating the item as a nonpartnership item. Prop. Reg. § 301.6222(b)-(2)(a). Note that this applies only to those items that were reported inconsistently. Any other partnership items treated inconsistently that were not reported on the statement will not be subject to the protection against computational adjustment. Id. at § 301.6222(b)-2(b).

17. Treas. Reg. § 301.6231(a)(5)-1.

TMP and the partners who are entitled to notice.[18] The TMP then must notify those partners not entitled to notice from the Service.

The TMP is usually a general partner designated by the partnership. In the absence of a designation, the general partner with the largest profits interest in the partnership at the close of the taxable year becomes the TMP.[19] If the partnership fails to designate a TMP or if the status of the TMP has been terminated without designation,[20] and the Service determines that it is impractical to follow the statutory designation, the Service then may appoint any partner to serve as TMP, including a limited partner.[21]

The TMP has a fiduciary obligation to provide notice of partnership-level administrative and judicial proceedings to all other partners.[22] If the TMP fails to notify the partners, however, it does not affect the validity of the unified procedure.[23] Thus, any adjustments will be binding on the partners, regardless of notice.[24]

The designation of the TMP is important because the TMP may bind the partnership in certain circumstances. For instance, the TMP may extend the statute of limitations for assessment of tax on any partnership item or affected item,[25] she may enter into a settlement

---

18. See IRC § 6231(a)(8); IRC § 6223. In general, all partners whose names and addresses have been furnished to the IRS are entitled to notice. Special rules apply, however, to partners with a less than one percent interest in a partnership with more than 100 partners, and to indirect partners – i.e., those who hold interests in passthrough entities such as partnerships, estates, trust, S Corporations.

19. IRC § 6231(a)(7).

20. See Treas. Reg. § 301.6231(a)(7)-1(j) through (l) for a discussion of how the status of TMP may be revoked or terminated.

21. See id. at § 301.6231(a)(7)-1(m) through (q) for a discussion of the selection of the TMP by the Service when no designation is made by the partnership. Under the Internal Revenue Service Restructuring and Reform Act of 1998, § 3507(a), amending IRC § 6231(a)(7), effective for selections after July 22, 1998, the Service must notify all partners required to receive notice of the name and address of the TMP selected.

22. IRC § 6223(g).

23. IRC § 6230(f). Actual notice by the Service to the TMP is considered constructive notice to the non-notice partners.

24. Vander Heide v. Comm'r., 1996-74 T.C. Memo (February 22, 1996). For a discussion of notice problems with the TEFRA rules, see Spellmann, Taxation Without Notice: Due Process and Other Notice Shortcomings With The Partnership Audit Rules, 52 TAX. LAW. 133 (1998).

25. IRC § 6229(b)(1)(B).

agreement with the Service that expressly binds some of the partners,[26] she has the initial right to select the forum of the judicial review,[27] and she may appeal a decision of the Tax Court, district court, or Court of Federal Claims regarding a final partnership administrative adjustment (FPAA).[28] Thus, the partnership should designate its own TMP, rather than allow the Service to appoint one, and care should be taken to choose a responsible, fair-minded person, preferably one who has a significant stake in the eventual outcome of any partnership-level proceedings.

Notes

If no general partner is eligible to serve and the Service fails to designate a TMP, it remains unclear who becomes the TMP and how that person is chosen. This situation may occur when a final partnership administrative adjustment (FPAA) has been issued by the Service. The Tax Court held in Computer Programs Lambda, Ltd. v. Commissioner., 89 TC 198 (1987) that the limited partners may designate a limited partner as the TMP. Moreover, Tax Court Rule 250(a) requires the court to take action necessary to identify or facilitate the selection of a TMP if one has not been designated by the partnership nor chosen by the Service at the time the Tax Court petition is filed. A different result was reached by the Court of Federal Claims, however, in Transpac Drilling Venture v. United States, 92-2 USTC ¶ 50,486, aff'g 16 F3d 383 (CA Fed. 1994), cert. denied 115 S. Ct. 79 (1994), where the court held that a limited partner may not serve as the TMP. This effectively means that such a partnership is precluded from appealing judicially in the Court of Federal Claims.[29]

c. Administrative Proceedings

The examination of the partnership return and the concomitant administrative proceedings usually progress in the standard manner beginning with a field audit of the partnership return, possible issuance of a 30-day letter, and the filing of an administrative appeal if the partnership files a protest. The administrative proceeding is commenced

---

26. IRC § 6224(c)(3).

27. IRC § 6226(a).

28. IRC § 6226(g).

29. This issue is raised by Arthur Boelter in REPRESENTATION BEFORE THE APPEALS DIVISION OF THE IRS 17-3.10 (West Publ. Co. 1999).

when the Service notifies the partnership of its intent to conduct a partnership-level examination.[30] This notice must be sent to the TMP, if known, and to all partners entitled to receive notice.[31] If the Service fails to give proper notice of a partnership-level proceeding to a notice partner, the partner has three choices: (1) she can become a party to the proceeding, (2) she can elect to accept a settlement agreement between the Service and another partner, or (3) she can elect to have her partnership items for the year converted to nonpartnership items as of the date the late notice was mailed to her.[32] If the proceeding has concluded, she may either elect to have the adjustment, settlement agreement, or decision apply to her, or if no election is made, the partnership items on her return will be treated as nonpartnership items.[33]

Any partner may participate in the partnership-level administrative proceedings. At any time, a partner may waive any right that partner has or any restriction on action by the Service.[34] Any of the partners may agree at any time to a settlement with the Service on the treatment of partnership items for the partnership taxable year. The Service must notify all notice partners of the settlement and it also must offer consistent settlement terms to any partner who requests them.[35] Partners may enter into a consistent settlement agreement only under

---

30. IRC § 6223(a)(1).

31. IRC § 6223(a)(1). Partners entitled to notice are those whom the partnership has identified to the Service as notice partners, and whose names and addresses have been furnished to the Service. Id. In a partnership of less than 100 partners, this essentially is everyone. Partners with a less than one percent interest in the profits of a partnership with more than 100 partners are not entitled to notice unless they form a notice group. The notice group will be entitled to notice provided certain requirements are met: (1) the group, in the aggregate must have at least a five percent profits interest, (2) the group must request notice, and (3) one member of the group must be designated to receive the notice. Id. at § 6223(b).

A special rule applies to indirect partners. An indirect partner is a person who owns a partnership interest through one or more "pass-thru partners." A pass-thru partner is another partnership, estate, trust, nominee, corporation or similar person through whom other persons hold an interest in the partnership. An indirect partner may become a direct, notice partner if that person's interest is large enough and her name, address, and taxpayer identifying number are furnished to the Service as a notice partner. Otherwise, indirect partners receive notice through the pass-thru partner who must forward notice to the indirect partners within 30 days of receiving such notice. Prop. Reg. § 301.6223(h)-1.

32. IRC § 6223(e)(3).

33. Id. at § 6223(e)(2).

34. Id.

35. IRC § 6224.

certain conditions. First, the terms of the original agreement must have been entered into before the notice of FPAA was sent to the TMP, and the partner must have requested the consistent settlement within 150 days after the mailing of an FPAA.[36] Once an agreement is reached, it is binding on both the Service and the partner(s) who requested the settlement.[37] The partnership items that were the subject of the settlement agreement become nonpartnership items as of the date of the agreement[38] and the settling partner then no longer has an interest in the TEFRA proceeding. The Service can then make a computational adjustment to the tax liability of the partner reflecting the settlement of the partnership item.

At the conclusion of the examination, if there are issues that have not been resolved in the partnership-level administrative proceeding, an FPAA will be issued reflecting the Service's proposed adjustment of the partnership items in question.[39] The mailing of the notice of commencement of administrative proceedings to each notice partner is a prerequisite to the issuance of an FPAA, which may not be mailed to the TMP until 120 days after the mailing of the notice of commencement.[40] The FPAA, in turn, is a prerequisite to the assessment of a partnership-level deficiency because the earliest date on which a deficiency may be assessed is the close of the 150th day following the day on which the FPAA was mailed to the TMP.[41]

The FPAA is also a jurisdictional prerequisite for judicial review in the Tax Court. During the first 90 days after the mailing of the FPAA, the TMP has the exclusive power to petition the court to contest the

---

36. IRC § 6224(b)(2).

37. A settlement between the Service and the TMP is not binding on notice partners. But note that some partners may be bound by settlement agreements they have not entered into themselves. An indirect partner, for instance, may be bound by an agreement entered into by a pass-thru partner. Similarly, a partner who is not a notice or notice-group member is bound by an agreement entered into by the TMP. IRC § 6224(c)(3)(A). The partner may avoid this dilemma by filing a statement with the IRS that the TMP does not have authority to bind her. IRC § 6224 (c)(3)(B).

38. IRC § 6231(b)(1)(C). The government has one year from the date the settlement agreement is signed to assess a deficiency on those items and on any affected items, such as penalties. Id. at § 6229(f).

39. IRC § 6223(a)(2). The Service may also issue an FPAA when the statute of limitations is nearing expiration.

40. IRC § 6223(d)(1).

41. IRC § 6225(a)(1). If a Tax Court petition is filed during the 150-day period, however, the restriction on assessment and collection continues until the Tax Court decision becomes final. Id. at § 6225(a)(2).

proposed adjustment, thus the choice of forum lies with the TMP.[42] If the TMP chooses to file a petition in the Tax Court, the Service is barred from assessing a deficiency until a final determination has been rendered in the Tax Court proceeding.[43] If the TMP chooses a refund forum (federal district court or the Claims Court), she must deposit with the court the amount by which her tax liability would be increased if the treatment of the partnership items on her return were made consistent with the treatment of partnership items as adjusted by the FPAA.[44] Thus, the full amount of the partnership liability is not required to be deposited.

The deposit is considered a payment only with respect to interest.[45] Thus, the deposit will halt the running of interest during the period of the deposit.   For all other purposes, however, the deposit is not considered a payment. Thus, the Service may assess a deficiency against the depositor attributable to nonpartnership items without regard to the deposit.[46] If the restrictions on assessment of a deficiency against partnership items have lapsed and an assessment is made against the depositor, the amount of the deposit will be applied to offset the amount of the deficiency.[47]

If the TMP fails to seek judicial review, any notice partner may do so by filing within 60 days after the expiration of the 90-day period.[48] In order to avoid multiple proceedings in the various courts, the first petition filed in the Tax Court will be given priority, and any other action that may have been filed in the district court or the Court of Federal Claims will be dismissed, and the partner's deposit refunded without interest.[49] If no petition is filed in the Tax Court, then the first petition

---

42. IRC § 6226(a).

43. IRC § 6225(a)(2).

44. IRC § 6226(e)(1).

45. IRC § 6226(e)(3); Temp. Reg. § 301.6226(e)-1T. The deposit also is considered a payment that will stop the running of the failure to pay penalty under IRC § 6651(a)(2) or (b)(2). Id.

46. Temp. Reg. § 301.6226(e)-1T.

47. Id. It is unclear whether the Service will assess the entire deficiency against the partnership while an FPAA is being contested in a refund forum.

48. IRC § 6226(b)(1).

49. Id. at § 6226(b).

filed in one of the refund forums is given priority.[50] All partners with an interest in the outcome are parties and are entitled to participate in the judicial proceeding.[51] The reviewing court has jurisdiction to determine all partnership items for the taxable year covered by the FPAA, the proper allocation of these items among the partners, and the amount of any penalty or other addition to tax.[52]

During the 150-day filing period, the Service is barred from assessing a deficiency against partnership items. If a Tax Court petition is filed during this time, the Service is further barred from assessing until the Tax Court decision becomes final.[53] If no Tax Court petition is filed by any of the partners during the 150-day period, the Service may assess a deficiency against any partner with respect to the adjustments proposed in the FPAA, but the amount of the assessment with respect to the partnership items cannot exceed the amount of the proposed adjustment in the FPAA.[54]

d. Statute of Limitations on Assessment

The statute of limitations on assessment of a tax liability against a partner is three years from the later of (1) the date on which the partnership return for the year was filed or (2) the due date of the partnership return (determined without regard to extensions).[55] This period is suspended from the date of the mailing of an FPAA to the TMP until one year after the expiration of the period for filing a petition for judicial review (and if a petition is filed, the limitations period includes the period from the filing of the petition until the time the decision of the court becomes final).[56] Penalties are determined at the partnership level

---

50. Id.

51. Id. at § 6226(d).

52. Id. at § 6226(f).

53. I.R.C. § 6225(a)(1).

54. IRC § 6225(c).

55. IRC § 6229(a). Special limitations provisions apply to bankruptcy, fraud, substantial omissions of income, failure to file, and returns executed by the Service. Id. at § 6229(c) and (h). Several cases have held that § 6229(a) does not provide a separate statute of limitations on partnership items but instead it extends the statutory period under § 6501(a). See, e.g., Schumacher Trading Partners v. U.S., 72 Fed.Cl. 95 (2006); AD Global Fund, LLC v. U.S., 481 F.3d 1351 (Fed.Cir. 2007); Grapevine Imports, Ltd.. v. U.S., 71 Fed.Cl. 324 (2006).

56. Id. at § 6229(d).

and the three-year statute of limitations applies to them as well.[57] A partner may agree with the IRS to extend the statute as to herself only, or the TMP may agree to an extension for the entire partnership.[58]

The statutory period is applied to the partnership rather than to the individual partners. Thus, a partner may have different limitation periods for partnership items and nonpartnership items on her return. This has presented problems for the government.

e. The Munro *Problem and Its Solution*

Prior to 1997, if the return of an individual partner was audited, any TEFRA partnership items on that return generally were not subject to adjustment until the conclusion of the TEFRA partnership proceeding. In examining the partner's return, the Service would assume that all TEFRA partnership items were correctly reported. In some cases, however, the amount of the partnership loss claimed by the partner would exceed the amount of adjustments to nonpartnership items that otherwise would have produced a deficiency. Thus, the partnership loss would eliminate the deficiency on the individual partner's return.

If the offsetting loss was subsequently disallowed in the TEFRA partnership proceeding, the Service would be unable to assess the resulting deficiency against the partner if the statute of limitations on assessment of the partner's deficiency had expired. In the case of *Munro v. Commissioner*,[59] the Service tried to protect itself by issuing a notice of deficiency on nonpartnership items that had been determined by disallowing, for computational purposes only, the partnership loss the partners had claimed. This resulted in the problem being shifted from the government to the taxpayer, because the taxpayer/partner would have to pay an artificially high deficiency if some or all of the partnership loss was allowed in the TEFRA proceeding. The taxpayer in *Munro* protested this treatment by bringing suit in the Tax Court. The Tax Court held that partnership items (whether income, deduction, or credit) must be ignored in determining whether a deficiency exists with respect to non-TEFRA items.

In order to remedy the problem, the Taxpayer Relief Act of 1997 adopted the Service's former practice of assuming the TEFRA partnership items on the partner's return are correctly reported. In

---

57. Id. at § 6229(g).

58. Id. at § 6229(b).

59. Munro v. Commissioner, 92 T.C. 71 (1989).

addition, the act addresses the *Munro* problem by providing a new declaratory judgment procedure in the Tax Court for "oversheltered returns." An oversheltered return is defined as a return that shows no taxable income and a net loss from a TEFRA partnership.[60] Under the new procedure, if the Service makes a determination with respect to the tax treatment of nonpartnership items on the return and the adjustments that result from this determination do not give rise to a deficiency, but would have done so if there had not been a net loss from the TEFRA partnership items, the Service is authorized to send a notice of adjustment reflecting this determination with respect to the non-TEFRA items.[61]

The notice must be sent by certified or registered mail prior to the expiration of the statutory period for assessment of deficiencies.[62] The taxpayer then has 90 days (150 days if notice is addressed to a person outside the United States) to contest the proposed adjustment by filing a petition in the Tax Court.[63] During this 90-day period, the statute of limitations on assessment is tolled and the Service is barred from making an assessment.[64] If a Tax Court petition is filed, the Service is further barred from assessing any deficiency until the decision of the Tax Court becomes final.[65] The Tax Court has jurisdiction to determine the correctness of the adjustment with respect to non-TEFRA items.

If after the notice of adjustment is mailed, but before the 90-day filing period expires or a Tax Court decision becomes final, the TEFRA partnership items either are finally determined or cease to be partnership items, and the Service determines that a deficiency exists, the notice of adjustment will be treated as a notice of deficiency.[66] Any Tax Court petition subsequently filed will be treated as a petition for a regular deficiency proceeding, rather than a petition for a declaratory judgment proceeding.[67]

---

60. IRC § 6234(b).

61. Id. at § 6234(a)(3).

62. See IRC §§ 6501, 6234(a)(3) and (e)(1).

63. IRC § 6234(c).

64. Id. at § 6234(e)(3).

65. Id.

66. Id. at § 6234(g)(3).

67. Id.

If the final determination in the TEFRA partnership proceeding reduces the partner's loss or otherwise eliminates the excess shelter from the partnership item, the Service will have preserved its ability to collect tax on any deficiency attributable to the nonpartnership items. The declaratory judgment on nonpartnership items must be considered in determining the amount of any computational adjustments made in connection with any partnership proceeding.[68]

No tax is immediately due upon the Tax Court's determination, although the determination is treated as final, and either the taxpayer or the Service may appeal the decision.[69] If the taxpayer does not contest the notice of adjustment within the 90-day period, the Service's determination is deemed correct.[70] After the TEFRA partnership items are finally determined, however, the taxpayer has the right to file a refund claim for the tax attributable to the items adjusted, despite the taxpayer's default on the notice of adjustment.[71] While the claim is pending, the items in the notice of adjustment are presumed correct for purposes of determining the amount of any computational adjustment in connection with a TEFRA partnership proceeding or in a nonpartnership deficiency proceeding.[72]

f. Requests for Administrative Adjustment

If the partnership wishes to make a change in its partnership information return after the return has been filed and before an FPAA has been issued, the TMP may, within the applicable limitations period,[73] make a request for administrative adjustment (RAA) that the partnership items be treated as described in the request, rather than as reported on the partnership return.[74] The RAA is comparable to an amended return in that it can serve either as a substitute return for the

---

68. IRC § 6234(g)(1).

69. Id. at § 6234(c).

70. Id. at § 6234(d)(1).

71. Id. at § 6234(d)(2).

72. Id.

73. This period is within three years from the later of the date the partnership return was filed for the year in question or the date the return was due, without regard to extensions. IRC § 6227(a)(1).

74. IRC § 6227(a).

original partnership return or as a refund claim, or both. If the TMP does not file such a request, then any partner may file on her own behalf.[75] If a partner files such a request, the Service has four options: (1) it may treat the request as a claim for refund or credit of nonpartnership items, (2) it may assess any additional tax that might result from the requested adjustments, (3) it may treat all partnership items of that partner for that taxable year as nonpartnership items, or (4) it may conduct a partnership-level proceeding.[76]

If the Service rejects the partnership RAA or fails to act on it within six months, the TMP may seek judicial confirmation of the adjusted items by filing a petition in either the Tax Court, the district court, or the Court of Federal Claims.[77] Such a petition must be filed no later than two years after the filing of the RAA.[78] No petition may be filed, however, after the Service mails a notice of commencement of administrative proceeding with respect to the partnership taxable year in question.[79] But if such a notice is mailed within the two-year period, and the Service fails to send a FPAA before the expiration of the statutory period for assessment, the two-year filing bar no longer applies, despite the issuance of the notice of commencement of administrative proceeding. The TMP then will have an additional six months after the expiration of the assessment period to file the petition.[80]

Question

Have the TEFRA partnership audit provisions effectively solved the problems they were designed to address?

2. Employment Tax Examination Program

An employer is required to withhold federal, state, and local income taxes from the wages of its employees. In addition, the employer is required to remit FICA taxes (Federal Insurance Contributions Act), for

---

75. Id. at § 6227(c) and (d).

76. IRC § 6227(d).

77. IRC § 6228(a)(1).

78. IRC § 6228(a)(2). This period may be extended by agreement between the TMP and the Service. Id. at § 6228(a)(2)(D).

79. Id. at § 6228(a)(2)(B).

80. Id. at § 6228(a)(2)(C).

which the employer and the employee share responsibility. The employer must withhold the employee's portion and must remit that, along with the employer's portion, to the government. The employer also must pay FUTA taxes (Federal Unemployment Tax Act), which are entirely the responsibility of the employer. These various taxes are collectively referred to as "employment taxes" and the employer generally must deposit them on a quarterly basis with the government.

If the worker is classified as an independent contractor, the employer does not have to remit the employment taxes. Instead, they are the responsibility of the independent contractor. If the worker is misclassified as an independent contractor, the tax bill that can result from a subsequent assessment of delinquent employment taxes and additions to tax can be staggering. In some cases, it can be a financial death knell, particularly for a small business or one that is struggling financially.

But the distinction between an employee and an independent contractor is often a difficult one to draw. The Internal Revenue Code defers to the common law rules in determining who is an employee.[81] The Service has delineated 20 common-law factors in Revenue Ruling 87-41, 1987-1 CB 296 to determine whether a worker is an employee. The problem of determining employee status is far from resolved, though, because the importance of each of the factors is case specific. For instance, some of the factors may have no importance in a particular occupation. In other cases, even though more than half of the factors apply, it may not mean that the worker is in fact an employee. Thus, the distinction between the categories remains complex.

In the past, concerns were raised that the Service was pursuing its employment tax enforcement efforts too aggressively, without giving proper deference to the complexity of the determination. Indeed, in many cases it was alleged that the revenue agents had an inherent bias in favor of employee status.

---

81. IRC § 3121(d), 3306(i), and 3401(c). The Code classifies some workers as "employees" for FICA purposes. This group consists of an officer of a corporation; full-time life insurance salesmen; home workers whose work is directed by the person for whom they are working, where that person also furnishes the materials or goods which the worker uses; traveling or city salesmen; agent-drivers or commission drivers; any person who is considered an employee under the common law rules. Id. at § 3121(d). These employees are also called "statutory employees." An employer does not have to withhold income taxes on remunerations paid to statutory employees who otherwise would not be considered employees under the common law test. There also is a group of statutory "nonemployees" under § 3508 consisting of licensed real estate agents and "direct sellers" who are engaged in selling consumer products in the home or otherwise than in a permanent retail establishment. IRC § 3508(b).

In response to these concerns, Congress enacted § 530 under the Revenue Act of 1978[82] to provide interim relief for businesses while Congress considered what to do about the classification problems in the employment tax area. The Service, in turn, suspended most of its employment tax examination efforts from 1978 to 1984. By the late 1980's, however, Congress had not dealt with the problem, so the Service began to resume its aggressive employment tax examinations. In deference to the concerns of employers, the Service has given additional training to its agents handling employment tax matters, and it has implemented both a classification settlement program and a procedure for an expedited appeal. The crux of the problem, however, continues to be the distinction between an independent contractor and an employee.

IRS Watch: Focus on Bridging the Employment Tax Gap
by Kathy Petronchak, John Keenan and Julia Lagun
J. of Tax Practice & Procedure 9 (February-March 2010) *

The Employment Tax Gap

The annual tax gap from noncompliance is estimated at $345 billion. Approximately $54 billion of this amount is estimated to be attributable to employment tax underreporting.[1] Of this $54 billion, $15 billion is estimated to be attributable [to] the underreporting of Federal Insurance Contribution Act (FICA) and Federal Unemployment Tax Act (FUTA) taxes reported on Form 941, *Employer's Quarterly Federal Tax Return*. The IRS has not completed a comprehensive study on employment taxes and worker misclassification since 1984.

The IRS updates these figures from audits conducted under the National Research Project (NRP). The project measures tax compliance and helps the IRS prioritize the use of its resources in addressing tax compliance. The time has come for this employment tax update to take place and taxpayers will be contacted soon for examinations in this regard. It has been reported that these examinations are expected to focus on four areas: (i) worker classification, (ii) fringe benefits, (iii) backup withholding, and (iv) executive compensation.

---

82. Although § 530 was originally slated to expire on December 31, 1979, it was extended indefinitely by the Tax Equity and Fairness Reform Act of 1982.

.* "IRS Watch: Focus on Bridging the Employment Tax Gap," Kathy Petronchak, John Keenan, and Julia Lagun, J. of Tax Practice & Procedure 9 (Feb.-Mar. 2010). Copyright © 2010 CCH. All rights reserved. Reprinted with permission.

1. Treasury Inspector General for Tax Administration (TIGTA) Report issued February 4, 2009 (2009-30-035).

Current IRS Enforcement Efforts

The IRS has several enforcement and education efforts that focus on employee misclassification. The IRS primarily identifies employers to examine for potential employee misclassification through four sources: (i) the Determination of Worker Status (Form SS-8) Program, (ii) the Employment Tax Examination Program (ETEP), (iii) general employment tax examinations, and (iv) the Questionable Employment Tax Practices (QETP) program.

As part of the Determination of Worker Status Program, workers or employers request the IRS determine whether a specific worker is an employee or an independent contractor for purposes of federal employment tax and income tax withholding by submitting Form SS-8, *Determination of Worker Status for Purposes of Employment Taxes and Income Tax Withholding.* The ETEP program is used by the IRS to select employers that have a high likelihood of misclassifying employees for examination. The QETP program is one in which the IRS and various states share information on worker classification-related examinations and other questionable employment tax issues, which allows the IRS to focus its examinations on employers determined to have misclassified employees.

According to the GAO report, the IRS's Small Business/Self Employed Division (SB/SE) conducts the majority of the IRS's misclassification-related examinations. During the 2008 fiscal year, it assessed taxes and penalties in 71 percent of examinations, resulting in a total of almost $64 million in assessments.

After reviewing the IRS's current enforcement efforts, TIGTA recommended conducting a formal National Research program compliance study to measure the impact of worker misclassification on the employment tax gap.[2] One of the objectives outlined in the IRS Strategic Plan for 2009-2013 focused on using data research across the organization to make informed decisions and improve resource allocation in order to combat noncompliance.[3]

---

2. *Id.*

3. IRS Strategic Plan 2009-2013, available at www.irs.gov/pub/irs-pdf/p3744.pdf. See Kathy Petronchak, IRS Watch: Where the IRS Plans to Go: IRS Strategic Plan 2009-2013, J. TAX PRACTICE & PROCEDURE, June-July 2009, at 9, for additional discussion of the IRS Strategic Plan.

National Research Program

The goal of the National Research Program (NRP) is "to design and implement a successful strategy to collect data that will be used to measure payment, filing and reporting compliance and to deliver the data to the Business Operation Divisions to meet a wide range of needs including support for the development of strategic plans and improvements in workload identification."

In September of 2009, the IRS announced plans to examine a randomly selected sample of employers' tax returns for tax years 2008 to 2010 as part of the NRP. The NRP will result in the IRS examining a total of 6,000 business organizations including corporations, partnerships, LLCs and S corporations over the three years. The program will include taxpayers from each of the IRS Operating Divisions. Each year, the IRS will randomly select 2,000 Forms 941, *Employer's Quarterly Federal Tax Return*, for the program. The NRP will cover employment taxes, which include (i) Social Security tax, (ii) Medicare tax, (iii) Federal Unemployment Insurance Tax (FUTA), and (iv) personal income tax withholding.

According to IRS Chief of Employment Tax Operations John Tyzynski, the IRS is training almost 200 examiners for the program.[4] The program will focus on four employment tax initiatives in 2010: (i) worker classification, (ii) tip reporting compensation, (iii) officer compensation, and (iv) fringe benefits.

Worker Classification

There are a number of issues that contribute to the employment tax gap, including worker misclassification. According to the Employee Misclassification report (the report) issued by the U.S. Government Accountability Office (GAO),[5] the current extent of the misclassification is unknown. In the IRS's efforts to close the tax gap, employee misclassification has been resurrected as a key issue.

The worker classification initiative will focus on whether workers are properly classified as employees or independent contractors. This is significant because an employer generally must withhold income taxes, withhold and pay Social Security and Medicare taxes, and pay unemployment tax on wages paid to an employee. However, these

---

4.   2009 TNT 183-4.

5.   GAO-09-717.

withholding and payment requirements generally do not apply with respect to independent contractors. If an employer is unsure of the proper classification, it can file a Form SS-8, *Determination of Worker Status for Purposes of Employment Taxes and Income Tax Withholding*, and the IRS will determine the worker's status.

In 1984, the IRS estimated that approximately 15 percent of employers misclassified 3.4 million employees as independent contractors, resulting in an estimated revenue loss of approximately $1.6 billion.[6] According to the GAO report, approximately 60 percent of the revenue loss was attributable to individuals failing to report and pay income taxes on compensation they received as misclassified independent contractors. The remaining 40 percent of the revenue loss resulting from the failure of employers and misclassified independent contractors to pay Social Security and Medicare taxes and from the failure of employers to pay federal unemployment taxes. Furthermore, according to the report, a study commissioned by the Department of Labor (DOL) in 2000 found that the number of firms that misclassified employees as independent contractors was somewhere in the range of 10 to 30 percent.

In 1978 Congress enacted Section 530 of the Revenue Act of 1978 in an effort to provide some objective guidance and protection for taxpayers faced with employee classification issues. Section 530 created a "safe harbor" for taxpayers classifying individuals as independent contractors for employment tax purposes if certain requirements are met. The safe harbor provision of Section 530 prevents the IRS from retroactively reclassifying "independent contractors" as employees and subjecting the principal to federal employment taxes, penalties and interest for such misclassification. To be eligible for Section 530 relief, an employer must meet three requirements: (i) the employer must have a reasonable basis for not treating the workers as employees; (ii) the employer must meet the substantive consistency test by having treated the workers, and any similar workers, as independent contractors; and (iii) the employer must meet the reporting consistency test by having filed all required federal tax returns (including information returns) consistent with its treatment of each worker as not being an employee, including filing Forms 1099-MISC for the independent contractors as required.

Tip Reporting Compensation

The IRS continues to focus on increasing tax compliance among individuals receiving tip income. In 2006 the IRS released formal

---

6.   The estimated $1.6 billion loss is in 1984 dollars.

guidance on the Attributed Tip Income Program (ATIP), a voluntary program in which employers use a formula approach to report the tip income of employees. The goal of ATIP was to reduce industry recordkeeping burdens and to promote reporting tips on federal income tax returns.

Officer Compensation

The officer compensation initiative relates to compensation of S corporation officers. This area has been a focus of the IRS because S corporations may be underreporting employment taxes by compensating their officers through dividends, which are not subject to employment taxes, rather than salary.

Generally, S corporations should treat payments for services to officers as wages and not as distributions of cash and property or loans to shareholders. If cash or property is distributed to an officer, a salary amount must be determined and the level of salary must be reasonable and appropriate. Since there are no specific guidelines for reasonable compensation, it is determined based on the facts and circumstances of each case.

Fringe Benefits

The fringe benefits initiative will include a focus on company cars, frequent flyer miles, club memberships, personal use of corporate owned vacation properties, etc. The audits will also focus on Section 409A deferred compensation because it is considered a fringe benefit.

Additionally, according to Mary C. Gorman, assistant division counsel (pre-filing) at the IRS SB/SE division, mandatory audit items will include backup withholding and Forms 1099.[7]

What Employers Can Expect Next

On January 22, 2010, an IRS officiation announced that cases have been selected for the first round of the NRP audits. Businesses that have been selected for examination will be notified by Letter 3850-B from the IRS beginning in February or March of 2010.

It is important that employers are prepared for these audits. The IRS provides employers with guidance on employment tax recordkeeping requirements. According to the IRS, employers must keep all records of

---

7.   2010 TNT 15-8.

employment taxes for at least four years after filing the fourth quarter for the year. These records should be available for IRS review and should include (i) employer identification number; (ii) amounts and dates of all wage, annuity and pension payments; (iii) amount of tips reported; (iv) the fair market value of in-kind wages paid; (v) names, addresses, Social Security numbers and occupations of employees and recipients; (vi) any employee copies of Form W-2 that are returned as undeliverable; (vii) dates of employment; (viii) periods for which employees and recipients were paid while absent due to sickness or injury and the amount and weekly rate of payments made to them; (ix) copies of employees' and recipients' income tax withholding allowance certificates (Forms W-4, W-4P, W-4S and W-4V); (x) dates and amounts of tax deposits made; (xi) copies of returns filed; (xii) records of allocated tips; and (xiii) records of fringe benefits provided, including substantiation.

Notes and Questions

Section 530, the "safe harbor," has no effect on the rights, liabilities, and status of the workers. Those workers who are considered employees under the common law rules will remain employees, even though classified by the employer as independent contractors under § 530. But under § 530, the employee will be liable for its share of the employment taxes that otherwise would have been withheld by the employer. Treas. Reg. § 31.3102-1(c). Thus the effect of § 530 is to shift the liability for the employment taxes from the employer to the employee.

In the event the employer is not entitled to relief under any of the provisions discussed above, it has been suggested that Congress should amend the code to allow mitigation of the statute of limitations for those employees who, by virtue of being misclassified as independent contractors, have overpaid self-employment taxes. Otherwise, the greatest penalty for mischaracterization may fall on the most innocent of the parties involved." Toni Robinson, To Be Or Not To Be: A Worker May Not Know For Many Years, 79 Tax Notes 1611 (1998). See Chapter 5 for a discussion of statutory mitigation and its effect on the statute of limitations.

Prior to 1996, an employer was required to establish by a preponderance of the evidence that it was eligible for § 530 treatment. The Small Business Jobs protection Act of 1996, Pub. L. No. 104-188, provides, however, that if an employer makes a prima facie case that § 530 applies, the burden will shift to the Service to prove that § 530 should not apply.

The Taxpayer Relief Act of 1997 expanded Tax Court jurisdiction to encompass employment status determinations and whether the employer is entitled to relief under § 530. There are limitations, however, on this expanded jurisdiction. First, there must be an actual controversy between the employer and the Service. Second, a Tax Court petition may be filed only by the person for whom the services were performed, and the petition must be filed within 90 days of notification by the Service that it has made a determination. See IRS Notice 2002-5, 2002-1 C.B. 320, Updated procedures for Processing Tax Cases Involving Worker Classification and Section 530 of the Revenue Act of 1978 Under Section 7436 of the IRC.

1.   What result if a worker signs an agreement with an employer that he/she is an independent contractor and will be responsible for all income, FICA, and FUTA taxes on remunerations paid by the employer?

2.   Why should the Tax Court, which normally does not have jurisdiction over employment tax matters, be given expanded jurisdiction to cover worker classification disputes?

3.   Why do employment tax issues continue to rank high on the government's list of compliance problems?

3.   Coordinated Examination Program

Large corporations with gross assets greater than $250 million are audited under a special procedure called the Coordinated Examination Program (CEP). Under this procedure, a corporation and all of its controlled affiliates are coordinated and treated as one unit for purposes of the audit. The audit is also coordinated within the Service, so that other IRS offices will not independently audit any member of the affiliated group.

The CEP audits are the most efficient of the Service's audits. CEP auditors generate about two-thirds of the tax recommended from all audits, while using only about 20 percent of the government's audit resources. There are several explanations for this efficiency. First, under the CEP procedure, a team of revenue agents and specialist revenue agents, such as international examiners, computer audit specialists, economists, etc., conduct the examination under the auspices of a case manager who operates in accordance with a written plan. The team conducts audits of a given corporation for every taxable year, usually in three-year cycles. The National Office monitors the progress of the cases and develops uniform national CEP standards in conjunction with the case managers. Second, the case managers have coordinated settlement authority. This allows them to reach an efficient and consistent settlement with a related taxpayer on an issue that has previously been resolved by the IRS Appeals Division with respect to another entity within the coordinated group, provided the settlement is consistent with the decision of the Appeals Division. Third, the CEP procedure allows the taxpayer to obtain a pre-filing determination where the taxpayer and the examining team agree on the tax treatment of a completed transaction before the return reporting that transaction is filed. This serves the same purpose as a ruling obtained by an ordinary taxpayer – i.e., it serves as an insurance policy of how the transaction will be viewed by the Service. It also takes the determination issue off the board for purposes of the audit. Fourth, CEP cases can be expedited under a procedure that allows an issue on which the taxpayer and the examination team cannot agree (unagreed issue) to be heard by the Appeals Division while other issues remain under examination by the CEP team.

A similar program exists for nationwide coordination among specific industries. This program is called the Industry Specialization Program (ISP) and, like the CEP, the ISP is designed for greater audit efficiency in various specified industries. The industries are grouped by National Industry Coordinators who work with Industry Specialists in identifying issues common to the group, such as bookkeeping and accounting methods, tax issues, and other business and economic issues. Those issues of importance to the group as a whole may be coordinated by the National Industry Coordinators and the Industry Specialists, who in turn advise the case managers who are conducting audits of the specific businesses. This provides uniform treatment in the resolution of audit issues within the industry.

III. REPRESENTING THE AUDITED TAXPAYER

A tax audit can be a trying event for a taxpayer, and most taxpayers will want to conclude the audit as quickly and painlessly as possible. Although the examining officer or revenue agent normally shares the taxpayer's interest in bringing the examination to an end as quickly as practicable, nevertheless, the goals of the taxpayer and the examiner usually are adverse. The taxpayer will be interested primarily in limiting the exposure to any additional tax liability, including time-sensitive penalties and interest. These time-sensitive additions to tax run from the date the payment was due (usually the due date of the return), rather than from the date of the assessment, or the date of the notice and demand for payment. See further discussion of these additions to tax, Chapter 6. The revenue agent, on the other hand, in a field or office audit generally has several aims: (1) to identify items that might require adjustment, (2) to verify the accuracy of reported amounts by examining books and records, and (3) to analyze transactions to determine whether the taxpayer has complied with the applicable law. The agent ultimately is concerned with determining the correct amount of the taxpayer's tax liability. Note that in any IRS administrative proceeding, the taxpayer has the burden of proof.

Under the Taxpayer Bill of Rights I, enacted in 1988, taxpayers have a right to be represented during all stages of the administrative process.[83] The representative, however, must meet two requirements: (1) she must be an attorney, a certified public accountant, an enrolled agent, an enrolled actuary, or any other person permitted to represent the taxpayer before the Service and who is not disbarred or suspended from practice before the Service, and (2) she must have a written power of attorney (Form 2848)[84] executed by the taxpayer on file with the Service, authorizing the representative to represent the taxpayer for the types of tax (i.e., individual, corporate, estate, gift, excise) and taxable periods in question. Until a validly executed power of attorney has been filed with the Service employee in charge of the case, the Service is prohibited under the Privacy Act from discussing the taxpayer's case with the third-party representative.

A. PRE-AUDIT PREPARATION

The representative should meet with the taxpayer as soon as possible to obtain the facts, identify and organize any documents that may be required, identify issues in which the representative may be required to serve as an advocate for the taxpayer, and discuss the audit strategy (i.e., whether the taxpayer is willing to settle a particular issue, whether there are any other issues that might expose the taxpayer to liability, etc.). The representative should examine all returns and records in question, plus any correspondence the taxpayer may have had with the Service.

The representative should take note of the applicable statute of limitations to ensure that the examination is valid. If the taxpayer has failed to file a return or if fraud is involved, there is no statute of limitations on assessment, so those issues remain open indefinitely. See the discussion of the statute of limitations on assessment in Chapter 4.

---

83.   Technical Corrections and Miscellaneous Revenue Act of 1988, § 6228, adding I.R.C. § 7520(c), and subsequently redesignated § 7521(c) by Pub. L. No. 101-239, § 7816(u)(1).

84.   Available online at http://www.irs.gov/pub/irs-pdf/f4868.pdf

The representative also should have a preliminary meeting with the revenue agent to set the parameters for the audit – i.e., where it will occur and when, and whether the taxpayer will be required to be present. Unless it is a criminal investigation, the Service may not compel the taxpayer to attend the audit without the issuance of a formal summons. At the preliminary meeting, the representative should try to determine what information the agent is seeking, and whether, when, and how the taxpayer can accommodate the agent. The representative should try to narrow the scope of the examination to specific issues, if possible, by asking the agent to submit a written list of proposed adjustments. This list serves two purposes: (1) it clearly defines the issues to be examined, thus allowing the representative to better defend the taxpayer's position, and (2) it makes it less likely that the agent will propose other adjustments.

If it appears that the agent is likely to make multiple requests for information, the taxpayer may ask the agent to list these requests in writing in an information document request ("IDR"). The preliminary meeting also provides the opportunity for the taxpayer's representative to negotiate the scope of the information request(s), thus lessening the burden on the taxpayer. In addition, the meeting provides the opportunity for the taxpayer to attempt to establish a timetable for the audit.

The Service regards the initial interview with the taxpayer as a very important stage in the audit process. It is through this interview that the agent attempts to assess the taxpayer's economic circumstances – i.e., standard of living and potential for unreported income. Thus, it is generally advisable for the representative to meet with the agent alone and to request that the audit be conducted at the representative's office, rather than at the taxpayer's place of business.

The most difficult issue for a representative to address in preparing for an audit is fraud. For instance, if the representative discovers income that was intentionally unreported or false deductions that were taken intentionally, the taxpayer may be subject to civil and criminal fraud sanctions. For a discussion of the fraud penalties, see Chapters 6 (civil) and 9 (criminal). If fraud is suspected, the representative should determine early in the examination process whether the agent is from the Examination Division or the Criminal Investigation Division of the Service.

The taxpayer's strategy in terms of the degree of cooperation with the agent depends upon whether the examination is routine or criminal in nature. (But see § C, below). If the examination is routine, the taxpayer should cooperate fully with the agent while not volunteering more information than the agent has requested, unless there is information that is favorable to the taxpayer. If the examination is criminal, the representative must insure that the procedural safeguards are observed, and that the taxpayer does not make statements or present evidence that would advance the government's case. If the representative is not present, the taxpayer should immediately request that the examination proceed no further until she has had a chance to notify her attorney. If the representative is not an attorney or federally authorized tax practitioner (IRC § 7525), no privilege will apply to make communications between the taxpayer and the representative confidential. If the representative is a federally authorized tax practitioner but is not an attorney, the privilege is limited in non-criminal cases and does not apply at all in a criminal proceeding. Because of the high risk of criminal liability in a fraud case, the taxpayer is well-advised to seek the advice of an attorney, preferably one with experience in the area of tax fraud.

After the initial meeting with the agent, either the taxpayer (if unrepresented) or the representative should send the agent a confirming letter stating the taxpayer's understanding of any oral commitments made by either party (e.g., a commitment by the agent to use best efforts to conclude the audit by a certain date, and the taxpayer's commitment to submit certain information or documents relevant to a particular issue). Any document submissions should be accompanied by a transmittal letter. The taxpayer should retain copies of the documents submitted, as well as copies of the transmittal letters.

Any documents not requested in advance, but which may be required during the audit, should be photocopied and ready to submit to the agent when the need arises. These include supporting authority for any deductions that are likely to be questioned by the agent, and any other authority relied upon by the taxpayer. Any required documentation should be organized according to the order in which it will be needed and if a large number of documents are involved, a document summary should be prepared. Note, however, that the taxpayer/representative must be careful not to overcompensate by providing more documentation than is required by the scope of the audit. This could provide a tempting opportunity for the auditor to expand the audit.

If the representative discovers that the taxpayer cannot comply with the IDR because there are missing documents or records, the representative should inform the agent immediately of this fact, and should offer to try to meet the agent's request in some other way, for instance by reconstructing the missing documents or records.

Before the representative complies with any request for production of records and documents, however, the representative should ensure that the material does not contain privileged information. If a privileged document is removed from a file and that document is responsive to the agent's request, a privilege log must be prepared to notify the government that a privileged document has been removed. The log also must identify the document. It is always best to prevent the agent from having free access to the taxpayer's files because if the agent is allowed to go through the files at will, the agent may discover other issues that require examination, and thus the scope of the audit may be expanded.

Questions

1. Is it ever to the taxpayer's advantage to delay an audit, if possible? If so, when?

2. If you are representing a client who has received a notice of audit and you believe the client might be the target of a potential criminal investigation, what strategy should you consider?

B. THE TAXPAYER BILL OF RIGHTS

Safeguards for audited taxpayers are provided under two Taxpayers' Bills of Rights: the Omnibus Taxpayers' Bill of Rights, enacted in 1988, and the Taxpayers' Bill of Rights II, enacted in 1996.[85] Under the Omnibus Taxpayers' Bill of Rights, examinations must be conducted at a reasonable time and place, and the Service must furnish an explanation of both the examination process and the taxpayer's rights in the process. If at any time during the examination the taxpayer states that she wishes to consult an attorney or accountant, the examination must be suspended until the taxpayer has had time to do so.

If the taxpayer has not received an IRS summons, the taxpayer may elect not to attend the examination but instead may be represented by an authorized representative. Either the taxpayer or the Service, upon advance notice, may make an audio recording of the audit interview at the requester's expense. If the Service makes the recording, the taxpayer may request and receive, at her expense, either a transcript or a copy of the recording.

---

85. There is a third Taxpayer Bill of Rights (TBOR), enacted in 1998, but this one has less important safeguards for the audited taxpayer. Instead, this TBOR focuses on collection issues, such as innocent spouses, offers in compromise, installment agreements, and the Taxpayer Advocate.

SALMAN v. SWANSON
United States District Court, District of Nevada, 1980.
80-2 U.S.T.C. ¶ 9574.

REED, DISTRICT JUDGE: The four defendants, although sued individually, are all employees of the Internal Revenue Service. The plaintiff has asked damages for deprivation of due process rights, in that he has been refused permission both to bring a tape recorder to an administrative appeal conference and to be represented at such conference by an individual who is not an attorney or certified public accountant or otherwise authorized to represent a taxpayer in Internal Revenue Service proceedings.

An examination by the IRS of the plaintiff's income tax returns for 1976 and 1977 gave rise to a 30-day letter advising the plaintiff of a possible deficiency by reason of his failure to report tip income and improper deduction for employee business expense. The letter offered an opportunity for a conference within the district wherein the areas of disagreement might be discussed informally.

The plaintiff asked for such a conference. In a letter dated August 21, 1979, he informed the IRS, among other things, that:

At this proposed hearing I will be represented by counsel of choice who is not an attorney, a certified public accountant or an individual enrolled to practice before the I.R.S. Our meeting will be attended by witnesses. I will also tape record the meeting. At our proposed meeting I will not provide any papers that are private for according to Senate investigations of the I.R.S. taxpayers are not legally required to provide private papers."

The IRS advised the plaintiff of the rules governing authority to practice before it and informed him that tape recording of an administrative appeal conference is not permitted. Further, the IRS wrote to the plaintiff that his refusal to present any papers necessary to resolve tax controversies had led to a decision to process the case based on the information already in IRS's files.

The plaintiff then commenced this lawsuit. The defendants have moved to dismiss the complaint, with prejudice, because: (1) the Court lacks jurisdiction over the subject matter by reason of sovereign immunity; (2) the complaint fails to state a claim upon which relief can be granted, in that the allegations therein do not constitute a violation of constitutional rights; and (3) the Court lacks jurisdiction over the subject matter because the Anti-Injunction Act, 26 USC § 7421(a) prohibits a suit for damages against an official of the U.S. engaged in the assessment or collection of taxes.

It is now clear that a federal official may be sued for damages if he has violated the constitutional rights of the plaintiff. Thus, if the plaintiff herein has alleged in his complaint facts constituting a denial of due process, the complaint will state a claim for relief.

Due process does not require a hearing at any particular time, but only before substantial rights are affected. An administrative appeal conference provides the taxpayer with an opportunity to question the preliminary determinations made during an audit by the IRS. The taxpayer may not be compelled to attend such a conference. It is a voluntary, informal meeting. No order adverse to the taxpayer is entered by reason of the conference. It is an attempt to achieve agreement by virtue of the taxpayer explaining his view of the contested issues. Substantial rights of the plaintiff are not adversely affected thereby.

A governmental agency may extend to a disgruntled party a hearing, even though there is no legal entitlement to such a hearing. However, such an act of courtesy does not generate any duty to afford the party a full panoply of rights, as is due in a formal due process hearing involving a livelihood or a liberty interest. In order to be entitled to a due process hearing, either a property or liberty interest of the party must be subject to loss as a result of the hearing. A property interest is not created by the Constitution, but must stem from an independent source. The administrative appeal conference here involved would have afforded the plaintiff an opportunity to persuade the IRS that his tax returns were not erroneous. The conference could not have resulted in a greater tax liability or other loss of a property interest of the plaintiff.

The Internal Revenue Manual declares that, as a general rule, neither IRS representatives nor taxpayers shall be permitted to make their own tape or other verbatim recordings of meetings. The reasoning is that recordation would adversely affect the informal setting and inhibit the free exchange of information and opinions. Only where special circumstances exist so that both sides desire a recording is provision made for waiver of the rule.

The plaintiff has not specified any particular reason why he insisted upon making a recording of the conference. He merely claims that denial violated his Fifth Amendment due process rights. A few courts have considered this question and have found there is no such constitutional right. Plaintiff cites *United States v. Duval*, in United States District Court for the Eastern District of Washington in support of his position. However, in *Duval* the hearing was mandatory, resulting from an IRS summons. Here, appearance at the conference would have been voluntary. The IRS has no authority to summon the taxpayer to an administrative appeal conference.

The limitation of representation of a taxpayer to attorneys, certified public accountants and enrolled agents is supported by 5 U.S.C. § 500. Both sides have an interest in making sure only qualified individuals represent taxpayers in IRS proceedings. The enrolled agents have passed an examination which demonstrates their proficiency in tax matters. In the absence of federal law authorizing representation by qualified non-lawyers in proceedings before a government agency, such representation could well constitute an unauthorized practice of law. See Sperry v. Florida, 373 U.S. 379 (1963).

From the foregoing it can be seen that the plaintiff's complaint fails to state a claim upon which relief can be granted. First, the nature of the conference involved does not call for the type of due process formalities demanded by the plaintiff. Second, there is no constitutional right in the taxpayer at such a conference to make a tape recording. Third, the limitation on representation is reasonable and valid.

IT IS, THEREFORE, HEREBY ORDERED that the plaintiff's complaint be, and the same hereby is, dismissed with prejudice.

Notes and Question

A portion of the result in *Salman* has been changed by § 7521(a), enacted under the Taxpayer Bill of Rights I, which allows either the Service or the taxpayer to record any in-person interview concerning the determination and collection of any tax. Do you think the court's argument in *Salman* is valid that recording the proceeding could destroy the informality of the interview?

If an IRS agent, acting in an official capacity, responds to a taxpayer in writing, the taxpayer may rely upon the writing and the Service must abate any portion of any penalty or addition to tax attributable to any erroneous advice. The abatement is granted only if the written advice was reasonably relied upon by the taxpayer, was in response to a specific written request by the taxpayer, and a portion of the penalty or addition to tax did not result from the taxpayer's failure to provide adequate or accurate information. IRC § 6404(f); see also discussion of this issue in Chapter 6.

C. CONDUCTING THE EXAMINATION

A correspondence audit generally involves less preparation than either an office audit or a field audit because the issues are clearly stated and usually can be addressed simply by sending a written response to the Service. The taxpayer must document her position, however, so copies of cancelled checks, billing statements, etc. must be sent along with the response.

In the case of an office audit or a field audit, the taxpayer or the taxpayer's representative has face-to-face contact with an examining agent or a revenue agent. Nevertheless, the audit is conducted on an informal basis. There is no sworn testimony and no rules of evidence apply. Thus, the taxpayer or the representative has great flexibility in presenting the case. It is important for the taxpayer and the representative to demonstrate a willingness to cooperate with the agent, because the agent has the discretion to raise new issues, to determine the weight to be given to the taxpayer's unsubstantiated statements, and to determine the standard of proof to be afforded evidence presented by the taxpayer. The agent also has discretion to determine whether the facts and circumstances indicate fraud. Thus, if either the taxpayer or the representative do not interact well with the agent, the audit is not likely to go smoothly for the taxpayer. The importance of the personal interaction between the taxpayer/representative and the agent cannot be over-emphasized. On the other hand, the taxpayer must bear in mind that her interests and the interests of the agent may be adverse.

Since it is in the taxpayer's interest to end the audit as quickly and as inexpensively as possible, the representative should try to settle the case, after establishing the parameters of the settlement agreement with the taxpayer. If the case involves a tax shelter, the settlement range will be limited to a standard settlement, generally consisting of relief from some penalties and a deduction limited to the taxpayer's actual expenditures. If the case does not fall within the Service's standard settlement policy, there is a wide range of settlement possibilities. For instance, the Service may concede one issue if the taxpayer concedes another. The most common example is a concession of penalties by the Service in return for the taxpayer's concession of an item of adjustment.

It is important to note that in a routine audit, the taxpayer can stop the examination process at any time simply by paying the additional tax liability. (This is not the case in a criminal investigation, however). If the taxpayer pays the amount of the proposed adjustment but does not believe she owes this additional amount, she may file a refund claim with the Service. If the claim is denied, she then may file suit to recover the refund in the federal district court. See Chapter 5 for a discussion of the jurisdictional requirements for refund suits.

In general, the taxpayer is well-advised not to attend the audit because there is a risk that she may volunteer information that may not be in her best interest to disclose. The taxpayer should be available by telephone, however, in order to respond to any questions that may arise that the representative cannot answer. If the representative does not have complete knowledge of the relevant facts, documents, and other records, the agent may issue an administrative summons to compel the taxpayer's appearance. In this case, the taxpayer must attend the audit. This underscores the importance of adequate preparation by the representative.

Question

If the taxpayer does not think she owes the additional amount, why might it be advantageous nonetheless for her to consider paying the contested tax liability and to later file a refund claim for this amount?

D. CONCLUDING THE AUDIT

At the conclusion of the audit, there may be no changes made to the return. The revenue agent then will issue a "no change" letter. If, however, there are proposed adjustments, the agent will explain these to the taxpayer. Unless the issue in question is one in which the representative thinks the taxpayer should prevail as a matter of right, the taxpayer should be open to a discussion of a possible settlement. Generally, it is in the taxpayer's best interest to settle the case at the examination level, if possible, because of the expenditures of time and money, as well as the emotional toll on the taxpayer as the case winds its way through the Appeals Division and subsequently through the courts.

Revenue agents have limited settlement authority. In general, the chances of reaching a settlement at the audit level are much greater if the issue is one of fact, rather than law. If the issue involves a question of law, the agent will be bound by the position of the Service, whether it is a formal position in a regulation or revenue ruling, or an informal position in the Internal Revenue Manual. In some cases, there are standard settlements from which the agent may not deviate, such as in the tax shelter cases mentioned previously.

1. Agreed Cases

Most tax cases are settled through agreements between the revenue agent and the taxpayer, although the settlements may take several forms. First, the taxpayer may concede the entire adjustment. This will bring the examination to a close, and the taxpayer will be asked to sign a Form 870 (Waiver of Restrictions on Assessment and Collection of Deficiency in Tax), which lifts the restrictions on assessment and allows the Service to immediately assess the amount of the agreed upon tax liability, plus interest and penalties. (See Chapter 4 for a further discussion of the Form 870 and the restrictions on assessment). Second, both parties may concede some issues. For instance, the taxpayer may concede the substantive issue(s) and the Service may concede the penalties. Third, each side may concede a percentage of the adjustment, or they may reach an agreement on a specific amount of tax liability without a percentage.

Whether or not an agreement is reached at the conclusion of the examination, the agent must prepare a detailed, written report of the examination referred to as a "Revenue Agent's Report (RAR)." The taxpayer will receive a copy of the RAR, as will the Appeals Officer if no agreement is reached between the taxpayer and the revenue agent.

2. Unagreed Cases

At the conclusion of the audit, the taxpayer and the agent may not be able to agree on a satisfactory resolution of some or all of the issues under examination. If that is the case, the taxpayer usually has several alternatives available. First, the taxpayer may use the Appeals process within the Service, in which the parties may reach a binding settlement agreement. If the Appeals process is not successful or if the taxpayer wishes to bypass the Appeals process altogether, another alternative is to use one of the methods of alternative dispute resolution offered by the Service, in which the parties may reach either a binding or a nonbinding agreement. If the taxpayer believes no compromise can be reached and she wishes to litigate the issues, a third alternative is to request an immediate issuance of a notice of deficiency, which is required before the taxpayer can file a petition in the Tax Court. A fourth alternative is to concede the issues and pay the tax, then file a claim for refund, and later bring suit in one of the refund fora. The taxpayer should consider this alternative if she believes no compromise can be reached, and she wants to litigate, but also wants to maintain control over the timing of the litigation in order to stop the running of penalties and interest, and to bring the audit to a speedy end.

a. *Preliminary Notice of Deficiency (the "30-Day Letter")*

If the examination is conducted as an office audit, the taxpayer will be informed of her appeal rights and if she orally requests an appeal, the case will be forwarded to the Appeals Division of the Service. If the examination is a correspondence audit or a field audit, however, the taxpayer will be sent a 30-day letter or Preliminary Notice of Deficiency, which will contain a summary of the agent's report and will advise the taxpayer of her right to appeal. A preliminary notice of deficiency also may be sent to the taxpayer without any prior correspondence or contact from the Service.

The preliminary notice of deficiency, also known as a "30-day letter" is an administrative device used by the Service to give taxpayers the chance to resolve informally any differences of opinion prior to the formal assessment procedure. The preliminary notice of deficiency gives the taxpayer 30 days to respond, although the Service often will grant an additional 30-day extension upon request. There are several alternative responses that a taxpayer may make to a preliminary notice of deficiency, which the taxpayer should consider carefully, because the choice could affect the disposition of the case.

b. *Responses to the 30-Day Letter*

First, the taxpayer could concede the issues and accept the adjustment proposed in the RAR. The taxpayer then either would make an immediate payment or sign a Form 870, "Consent to Assessment and Collection," (usually enclosed with the preliminary notice of deficiency) and the Service will immediately assess the amount of the proposed adjustment, plus interest. This will prevent the taxpayer from bringing suit in the Tax Court because a jurisdictional prerequisite for Tax Court jurisdiction is a notice of deficiency. If the taxpayer signs the Form 870, a notice of deficiency will not be issued. This would mean that the taxpayer would have to pay the tax, file a claim for refund, then file suit in one of the refund fora if she wished to contest the adjustment.

Alternatively, the taxpayer could ignore the 30-day letter. In this case, after 30 days the Service will process the case on the basis of the adjustment proposed in the RAR and the taxpayer will receive a notice of deficiency. This will give the taxpayer the opportunity to file a petition with the Tax Court to contest the proposed deficiency.

If the taxpayer does not agree with the conclusions of the revenue agent, the taxpayer may submit additional information (usually within a 15-day period) and/or request an informal conference to discuss the agent's findings. If no agreement is reached at the end of the conference, the taxpayer may orally request an appeal, or the taxpayer and the agent may "agree to disagree." In that case, the taxpayer would request a notice of deficiency, the agent would issue his report, and the taxpayer would receive a notice of deficiency entitling her to bring suit in the Tax Court.

The final response to a 30-day letter is to bypass the informal conference and proceed directly to the Appeals Division. This can be accomplished in several ways. First, the taxpayer may make an oral request to transfer the case to Appeals if the audit is either an office examination or a field audit and the proposed tax is less than $2500. In the case of a field audit in which the amount at issue (including penalties) is greater than $2500 but less than $10,000, a brief statement of the disputed issues and a request to transfer the case to the Appeals Division is required. In other cases in which the amount in controversy is greater than $2500, (and in field audit cases in which the amount is greater than $10,000) the taxpayer must file a formal written protest. 26 C.F.R. § 601.106.

IV. THE APPEALS PROCESS

The administrative appeals process affords taxpayers an opportunity to try to settle their differences with the Service administratively, although the Appeals Division also may consider cases in which there is no disputed tax liability for the period under consideration. Examples that fall into this category include employee benefit plan determinations; adjustments to a return that result in a deficiency or an overassessment that is counterbalanced in full by a net operating loss (NOL) carryback; and adjustments that result in an NOL carryforward where the carryforward year has not been examined.

The Appeals Division is the tribunal of last resort within the IRS, so the taxpayer has no further administrative recourse after the conclusion of the appeal. If a taxpayer is permitted to use the appeals process (most requests for Appeals conferences are granted) the process is informal; there is no sworn testimony, and the Federal Rules of Evidence do not apply. The stated mission of the Appeals Division is "to resolve tax controversies, without litigation, on a basis which is fair and impartial to both the Government and the taxpayer and in a manner that will enhance voluntary compliance and public confidence in the integrity and efficiency of the Service." Internal Revenue Manual § 8.1.1.1 (10-23-2007).

Congress has had concerns about the impartiality and independence of the Appeals Division, so under the Internal Revenue Restructuring and Reform Act of 1998, the Service is required to establish an independent Appeals Office within its structure as part of its reorganization plan. This plan also prohibits ex parte communications "to the extent such communications appear to compromise the independence" of the appeals process. Rev. Proc. 2000-43, 2000-2 C.B. 404. Thus, the Appeals Office must avoid the appearance of impropriety.

The Appeals Office has the authority to negotiate a binding settlement with the taxpayer, and usually the appeals process is a feasible alternative for the taxpayer because it saves the taxpayer time and expense. It also provides flexibility to both parties because the government and the taxpayer are free to negotiate a settlement within their own time parameters without being pressured by the court. The appeals process also gives the taxpayer more time to consider the advantages and disadvantages of litigation, and there is the possibility that in the interim, there may be favorable changes in the law. If the government's position is ultimately found to be unjustified, the taxpayer will not be eligible to recover attorneys fees and costs unless the administrative remedies available within the Internal Revenue Service have been exhausted. This includes an Appeals conference. IRC § 7430(b)(1); Reg. § 301.7430-1(b)(1)(i)(A).

The Appeals Office has jurisdiction over four types of cases: (1) preassessment cases, (2) postassessment cases, (3) employee plan and exempt organization (EP/EO) cases, and (4) collection cases. The process usually begins with the filing of a protest by the taxpayer. A protest is a statement of disagreement with the adjustments proposed by the Service. Upon receiving the protest, the Appeals Office staff will review it to decide whether the case can be disposed of without appellate review. If so, it will be returned to the Examination Division. If not, the Appeals staff will then determine whether the case can proceed as is, or whether it should be referred back to the Examination Division to resolve issues that can be addressed better there. If the protest lacks sufficient information, it may be returned to the taxpayer with a request to supply the required information.

There are two general categories of cases the Appeals Office hears: nondocketed and docketed. Nondocketed cases are those in which a petition has not been filed in the Tax Court, while a docketed case is one in which the taxpayer has petitioned the Tax Court and the case has been placed on the trial docket. The appeals procedure may vary according to whether the case is docketed or nondocketed.

The government has many more controversies than it can litigate. Therefore, even in nondocketed cases the Appeals officer must consider the hazards of litigation by evaluating the strength of the taxpayer's case based upon applicable rulings, regulations, and case law. The result of this consideration is a settlement rate of approximately 85 to 95 percent.

A. THE PROTEST

Although a protest is not required in every case, it generally is required when the amount in controversy (proposed tax, penalties and interest) exceeds $25,000. Internal Revenue Manual § 8.6.1.1.4. Some cases, however, require a protest even though they involve lesser amounts. These include all cases involving employee benefit plans and exempt organizations. Cases involving lesser amounts that do not fall within this special category can be handled under the small case procedure, which requires a written request for an appeal to be filed, in which the taxpayer must state any disagreement with the Service and give reasons for the disagreement. If the amount in controversy is not greater than $2,500, a telephone request for an Appeals conference will suffice, although the taxpayer often is well advised to file a written protest regardless.

If a protest is required, it must be filed with the Service within 30 days of the date (not the receipt) of the 30-day letter. The Service requires the protest to contain certain information such as (1) the taxpayer's name, address, taxpayer identification number (TIN), and daytime phone number, (2) a copy of the letter proposing adjustments (or the date and symbols from the letter), (3) a statement that the taxpayer wishes to appeal the findings of the revenue agent to the Appeals Division, (4) identification of the tax periods or years involved, (5) an itemized list of the proposed adjustments with which the taxpayer disagrees and a statement of why the taxpayer disagrees, (6) a statement of facts supporting the taxpayer's position, (7) a statement outlining the law or other authority on which the taxpayer relies, and (8) a declaration under penalties of perjury that the statements made in the protest are true and complete to the best of the taxpayer's knowledge. IRS Pub. No. 5 (Dept. of Treasury). If the protest is filed by the taxpayer's representative, a power of attorney also must be enclosed.

A full protest carefully develops the facts of the taxpayer's case, clearly states the issues and the legal arguments, and conveys the supporting authority in an organized, clear manner. Any supporting documents should be attached. The protest should convey to the Appeals Officer that the taxpayer is organized, serious about her position, ready to discuss the issues with the Appeals Division, and to go to trial, if necessary.

The purpose of the protest is to get the case admitted to Appeals and not to try to win the case at this stage. Thus, there are several theories of how to write a protest. Remember that most protests are filed in response to 30-day letters, so the taxpayer has a limited time to prepare and submit the protest. The mailbox rule does not apply to protests. Therefore, the protest must be received by the Service before the expiration of the 30-day period.

If time is short (i.e., the taxpayer has not sought the advice of the tax advisor until close to the end of the 30-day period), and the advisor does not have time to develop the facts and applicable law, there are two strategies available. First, the advisor may request an extension of time to file the protest, which usually will be granted if the taxpayer can demonstrate that reasonable circumstances warrant such an extension. A second strategy is to submit a skeletal protest that merely reiterates the revenue agent's findings and denies them, and gives the taxpayer's explanation of why a more complete protest is not being filed (e.g., illness, injury, complexity of facts or issues, retention of new representative, unavailability of the taxpayer). This protest also must contain a statement assuring the Service that a more complete memorandum will be filed prior to the Appeals conference.

A minimal protest is one in which the facts have been developed (because the tax advisor has had time to meet with the taxpayer), but the protest contains only a bare outline of the law, such as a list of cases with a brief statement of how they support the taxpayer's position. This protest also should contain a statement that a more comprehensive memorandum of laws will be submitted prior to the Appeals conference.

At the Appeals level, the taxpayer has the burden of proving that the proposed adjustments are incorrect or inappropriate. Although experts disagree over which type of protest is most strategically advantageous, there is a general belief that a full protest is more advantageous because it best meets the taxpayer's burden of proof.

Questions

1. What factors should be considered in deciding whether or not to file a protest in a case in which a protest is not required?

2. What advantages and disadvantages do you see with respect to the various theories of how to write a protest?

B. DOCKETED CASES

If a taxpayer does not file a response to the 30-day letter, the District Director usually will issue a 90-day letter (statutory notice of deficiency). See further discussion, Chapter 4. If the taxpayer files a petition with the Tax Court during the 90-day period following the issuance of the 90-

day letter, the case will be docketed for hearing by the Tax Court. At that point, the case usually will be referred to Appeals for settlement consideration, unless the District Counsel determines that the chances of a settlement are unlikely. If the case involves a deficiency of more than $10,000 (including tax and penalties), Appeals will return the case to the District Counsel (1) if no satisfactory progress toward settlement is being made or (2) when the case appears on the Tax Court's trial calendar. If the case involves a deficiency of less than $10,000 (tax and penalties), Appeals will consider the case (1) for a period of six months or (2) until shortly before the call of the trial calendar, depending on the status of the case by the Tax Court.

The Appeals Office hearing the appeal has sole settlement authority over the case. If the District Counsel requests the case in order to prepare for trial, Appeals can retain settlement authority with the agreement of the District Counsel. If the case is settled, the written stipulation of the parties becomes the judgment of the Tax Court and must be accepted, signed, and filed by a Tax Court judge.

C. REQUEST FOR TECHNICAL ADVICE

If during the appeal (or during the initial examination of a taxpayer's return), a technical or procedural question arises that turns on the proper application of tax law, tax treaties, regulations, revenue rulings, notices, or other precedents to a specific set of facts, either the taxpayer or the Appeals Officer or the Examination Officer may request a technical advice memorandum from the National Office. Technical advice helps the Service close cases and maintain consistency. It applies only to completed transactions and is sought when there is a lack of uniformity, or when the case presents an unusual or complex issue.

Technical advice applies only to the taxpayer who requests the advice or for whom the advice was requested. Although the technical advice procedure is slow and costly, if the technical advice memorandum (TAM) is favorable to the taxpayer, the Appeals Office is bound by it and the advice usually is applied retroactively. If the advice is not favorable to the taxpayer, the Appeals Office may decide to disregard the TAM and settle the case under the existing authority. On the other hand, the Appeals Office may decide to apply the unfavorable advice retroactively. If the unfavorable advice modifies or revokes a prior TAM, the advice generally is not applied retroactively for the period in which the taxpayer relied on the prior holding. Under some circumstances, the taxpayer may make a § 7805(b) request to limit the retroactive effect of a TAM.

See Rev. Proc. 2001-2, 2001-1 C.B. 79, superceding Rev. Proc. 2000-2, 2000-1 C.B. 73.

D. ALTERNATIVE DISPUTE RESOLUTION

In some cases, the parties may fail to negotiate a settlement in the normal appeals process, or efforts to enter into a closing agreement or compromise may prove unsuccessful. If the case has not been docketed in any court, the parties may elect to enter into nonbinding mediation in which a neutral third party, either from outside the Service or from another Appeals Office, will attempt to negotiate a settlement. Under the IRS Restructuring and Reform Act of 1998, mediation is available for resolution of factual issues such as transfer pricing, reasonable compensation, and valuation, but it is not available in cases in which an Industry Specialization Issue or an Appeals Coordinated Issue is involved. Mediation may be used to resolve problems in areas such as collection, offers in compromise, installment agreements, and collection due process. It is a quicker and less expensive process than litigation, and it allows taxpayers another bite at the apple, because if they are unhappy with the result of the mediation, they can go to court.

In the alternative, the parties may agree to enter into a binding arbitration. Under this alternative, the parties must agree not only to the arbitration itself, but also to the specific terms of the arbitration. Only factual issues are arbitrable, so the parties must agree on the applicable law to be applied to the case. The parties will each submit a summary of their positions to the arbitrator and the arbitration agreement will control what evidence and witnesses the arbitrator may consider. The parties also must agree on the arbitrator, who like the mediator, may come from inside or outside the Service. If the arbitrator is an Appeals Officer or staff member, the taxpayer will be required to waive the obvious conflict of interest. At the conclusion of the process, the arbitrator will issue a finding of fact, having no precedential value unless the parties agree otherwise. The decision of the arbitrator is binding and not subject to appeal, either within the Service or to any court.

E. SETTLEMENT AGREEMENTS

At the conclusion of an appeal of a nondocketed case, if the taxpayer and the government have reached an agreement, the settlement may be finalized on any of four forms, depending on the type of agreement reached. These forms are (1) a waiver of restrictions on assessment,

Form 870 (discussed in Chapter 4), (2) an Appeals Office waiver, Form 870-AD, (3) a closing agreement, and (4) a collateral agreement.

1. Appeals Office Special Purpose Waiver

The Form 870-AD, Offer to Waiver Restrictions on Assessment and Collection of Tax Deficiency and to Accept Overassessment, reflects an agreement made as a result of mutual compromise and concession. The agreement becomes effective only when a Form 870-AD is accepted by or on behalf of the Commissioner. Under the language of the form, the taxpayer promises that no claim for refund will be filed and the Service promises that the case will not be reopened absent certain specific conditions. This waiver is discussed in Chapter 4.

2. Closing Agreements

The only settlement agreement that is binding statutorily on the parties is the closing agreement authorized under § 7121 of the Code.[86] If a closing agreement is executed, the Service may not reopen the case without a showing of fraud, malfeasance or misrepresentation of a material fact, nor may the taxpayer rescind the agreement or challenge it in any legal proceeding. IRC § 7121(b).

The closing agreement applies only to the matters expressly stated within the agreement itself (i.e., it does not by implication affect unstated items). Because of its binding nature, the Service is cautious about entering into closing agreements, and will do so only when it has good and sufficient reasons, and where it will sustain no disadvantage. A closing agreement is valid only when it has been accepted and signed by or on behalf of the Service.

The Service generally uses two forms for closing agreements. A Form 866 (Agreement as to Final Determination of Tax Liability) is used when the tax liability and type of tax for the period in question have been finally determined. Typically, this form is used in the case of a liquidating corporation or a fiduciary in discharging her obligations. A Form 906 (Closing Agreement on Final Determination Covering Specific Matters) is used when the parties have been unable to agree on an unqualified tax liability figure and instead agree on separate issues affecting tax liability, such as the determination of taxable income, basis, or depreciation. Because these agreements often do not fully resolve all the inherent tax issues that may have an effect on the taxable year at

---

86. There is a compromise agreement authorized under § 7122 that also is binding on the parties, but it is used more often in collection cases and thus is discussed in Chapter 7.

issue or on another taxable year, the Service also uses a combined agreement that establishes the parties' understanding with respect to both tax liability and separate issues.

3. Collateral Agreement

A collateral agreement is an administrative device not provided for under the Code. It is a non-binding agreement executed to resolve a matter that is not directly in issue but is related to the disposition of the case, such as valuation for purposes of depreciation. Since there is some question as to whether any of the parties can be bound by a collateral agreement, it is not used as frequently as the other agreements. Collateral agreements may be used, however, as additional consideration for the acceptance of an offer in compromise, because the agreements may provide for " * * * payments from future income; reduction in basis of assets for computing depreciation, and gain or loss for tax purposes; waiver of net operating loss or unused investment credit carrybacks or carryovers; and waiver of bad debt loss or other deductions." IRM § 4.18.7.3.

CHAPTER 4

THE NOTICE OF DEFICIENCY
AND ADMINISTRATIVE APPEALS

Death and taxes and childbirth. There's never any convenient time for any of them.

— Margaret Mitchell[1]

I. ASSESSMENT PROCEDURE

The assessment of a deficiency is the starting point of the collection process. Under the normal rules, the Service is prohibited from collecting a deficiency until there has been an assessment, which is the recording of a deficiency in the summary records of the Service. IRC § 6203. Section 6211 defines a deficiency as the amount by which the tax imposed exceeds the excess of (1) the sum of (A) the amount shown as tax on the return, plus (B) the amounts previously assessed (or collected without assessment) as a deficiency, over (2) the amount of any rebates (abatements, credits, refunds or other payments). Thus, the amount of tax shown on the return, and any amounts previously assessed, even though not paid, are not considered deficiencies.

A. VALIDITY OF A NOTICE OF DEFICIENCY

A deficiency may not be assessed until the Service has mailed a notice of deficiency to the taxpayer's last known address. IRC § 6213. The notice of deficiency, also referred to as a "90-day letter," gives the taxpayer 90 days to contest the proposed deficiency administratively with the Service or judicially by filing a petition in the Tax Court. After mailing a notice of deficiency, the Service must wait the requisite 90 days (150 days if the notice is mailed to an address outside the United States) before it can assess the deficiency. Because the Service is prohibited from assessing during this 90-day period, the notice of deficiency tolls the statute of limitations to preserve the Service's right to assess when the 90-day period expires.

---

1. Jeffery L. Yablon, As Certain As Death—Quotations About Taxes (2004 Edition), 102 Tax Notes 99 (Jan. 5, 2004).

MULVANIA v. COMMISSIONER
United States Court of Appeals, Ninth Circuit, 1985.
769 F.2d 1376.

GOODWIN, CIRCUIT JUDGE.

The Commissioner of the Internal Revenue Service appeals a decision of the Tax Court that it lacked jurisdiction to assess a deficiency against taxpayer, Richard L. Mulvania, because he did not receive a valid notice of deficiency within the three-year statute of limitations on assessments. We affirm.

Mulvania timely filed an income tax return for 1977 showing his address as 57 Linda Isle Drive, Newport Beach, California. The return was prepared by Gerald F. Simonis Accountants, Inc. On June 13, 1979, the IRS sent a letter to Mulvania setting forth proposed adjustments to his 1974 and 1977 income tax. A copy of that letter was also forwarded to Simonis, who held a power of attorney requesting that copies of all documents sent to Mulvania also be sent to him. Mulvania received the letter.

On December 31, 1980, the IRS sent a letter to Mulvania requesting an extension of the limitations period for assessing Mulvania's 1977 tax liability, which was never executed. On April 15, 1981, the last day of the three-year statutory period in which the IRS could assess a tax deficiency, the IRS sent Mulvania a notice of deficiency with respect to the tax year 1977. The notice was sent by certified mail, addressed as "St. Linda Isle Drive," rather than "57 Linda Isle Drive," Mulvania's correct address. The postal service returned the notice to the IRS on April 21, 1981, marked "Not deliverable as addressed." The IRS placed the returned notice in Mulvania's file and, because the statutory period had expired, did not attempt to remail it.

On the same date that the misaddressed notice of deficiency was mailed to Mulvania, the IRS sent a copy of the notice by ordinary mail to Simonis, who received it on or about April 17, 1981. Expecting that Mulvania would soon call him about the notice, Simonis filed the notice and made a note to follow up. About June 1, 1981, when Simonis called Mulvania to discuss the notice of deficiency, he found out that Mulvania had never received the notice. There is no evidence in the record that Simonis discussed the contents of the notice with Mulvania.

On or about June 15, 1981, after Simonis (who is not a lawyer) advised Mulvania that Simonis' notice was not a valid notice of deficiency for 1977, Mulvania decided not to file a petition in the Tax Court for a redetermination of assessment of deficiency. Mulvania changed his mind, however, and, on April 1, 1983, filed a petition in the Tax Court requesting a redetermination of the deficiency for 1977.

Both parties then filed cross-motions to dismiss for lack of jurisdiction. The Commissioner argued that Mulvania's petition, which was filed almost two years after the notice of deficiency was mailed, was untimely pursuant to 26 U.S.C. § 6123(a).[1] Mulvania claimed the Tax Court lacked jurisdiction to assess a deficiency for 1977 because the three-year statute of limitations had run, and Mulvania had never received a valid notice of deficiency which would have tolled the statute of limitations as provided in 26 U.S.C. § 6503(a).[2]

The Tax Court granted Mulvania's motion to dismiss for lack of jurisdiction and denied the Commissioner's motion to dismiss. This appeal followed.

Section 6501(a)[3] provides that the amount of any deficiency in income tax shall be assessed within three years after the return is filed. Section 6503(a) provides, however, that the running of the three-year limitation period is suspended by "the mailing of a notice under section 6212(a)."[4] Section 6212(a) authorizes the Commissioner, upon determining that there is a deficiency in income tax, to send a notice of deficiency to the

---

1.   § 6213. Restrictions applicable to deficiencies; petition to Tax Court

(a) Time for filing petition and restriction on assessment.–Within 90 days, or 150 days if the notice is addressed to a person outside the United States, after the notice of deficiency authorized in section 6212 is mailed (not counting Saturday, Sunday, or a legal holiday in the District of Columbia as the last day), the taxpayer may file a petition with the Tax Court for a redetermination of the deficiency * * *.

2.   § 6503. Suspension of running of period of limitation

(a) Issuance of statutory notice of deficiency.–

(1) General rule.–The running of the period of limitations provided in section 6501 or 6502 on the making of assessments or the collection by levy or a proceeding in court, in respect of any deficiency * * *, shall (after the mailing of a notice under section 6212(a)) be suspended for the period during which the Secretary or his delegate is prohibited from making the assessment or from collecting by levy or a proceeding in court * * *, and for 60 days thereafter.

3.   § 6501. Limitations on assessment and collection

(a) General rule.–Except as otherwise provided in this section, the amount of any tax imposed by this title shall be assessed within 3 years after the return was filed (whether or not such return was filed on or after the date prescribed) or, if the tax is payable by stamp, at any time after such tax became due and before the expiration of 3 years after the date on which any part of such tax was paid, and no proceeding in court without assessment for the collection of such tax shall be begun after the expiration of such period.

4.   § 6212. Notice of deficiency

(a) In general.–If the Secretary determines that there is a deficiency in respect of any tax imposed by subtitles A or B or chapters 41, 42, 43, 44, or 45, he is authorized to send notice of such deficiency to the taxpayer by certified mail or registered mail.

taxpayer by certified mail or registered mail. Section $6212(b)(1)^5$ provides that a notice of income tax deficiency shall be sufficient if it is mailed to the taxpayer at his last known address. Section 6213(a) permits a tax-payer to whom a notice of deficiency is mailed to file a petition in the Tax Court within 90 days after the notice is mailed.

Cases interpreting the interplay of these sections have fallen into three broad categories.

First, a notice of deficiency actually, physically received by a taxpayer is valid under § 6212(a) if it is received in sufficient time to permit the taxpayer, without prejudice, to file a petition in the Tax Court even though the notice is erroneously addressed.

Second, a notice of deficiency mailed to a taxpayer's last known address is valid under § 6212(b)(1) regardless of when the taxpayer eventually receives it.

Third, an erroneously addressed and undelivered registered notice of deficiency is not valid under either § 6212(a) or 6212(b)(1) even if the Commissioner also sends a copy of the notice by regular mail to the taxpayer's attorney.

In this case the actual notice of deficiency which was mailed to Mulvania became null and void when it was returned to the IRS; at that time, the IRS then knew that the notice had been misaddressed and had not been received. This is not a case in which the notice was improperly addressed, but the postal authorities nonetheless delivered the letter to the taxpayer. Mulvania has never physically received a notice of deficiency.

The Commissioner argues that because Mulvania's accountant received a courtesy copy of the notice and called Mulvania before the 90 days had expired, Mulvania therefore received valid notice and now lacks a basis for a petition in the Tax Court. Mulvania argues that a courtesy copy of a notice of deficiency cannot be transformed into a valid notice of deficiency simply because the accountant called and told the taxpayer about the notice.

With a broad power of attorney, registered notice to the attorney or accountant may also serve as notice to the taxpayer under the law of principal and agent if the taxpayer himself received some notification in

---

5.   § 6212. Notice of Deficiency

(b) Address for notice of deficiency.–

(1) Income and gift taxes and certain excise taxes.–In the absence of notice to the Secretary under section 6903 of the existence of a fiduciary relationship, notice of a deficiency in respect of a tax * * * if mailed to the taxpayer at his last known address, shall be sufficient ** even if such taxpayer is deceased, or is under a legal disability, or, in the case of a corporation, has terminated its existence.

time to file a petition before the tax court. But see *D'Andrea*, 263 F.2d at 907-08 (copy sent by ordinary mail insufficient where there was no evidence that taxpayer seasonably received the information contained in the notice to his attorney). A taxpayer may also designate the address of his representative as that to which any deficiency notice should be sent.

Because Simonis did not have a broad power of attorney, however, the law of principal and agent does not apply. Mulvania had only granted him a power of attorney which requests that courtesy copies of all communication be sent to his representative. The IRS clearly knew that Simonis was not to be the addressee of the official notice of deficiency; it sent him only a copy and only by ordinary, unregistered, uncertified mail.

The Commissioner relies on two Tax Court cases for the proposition that the copy of the notice sent to Simonis sufficed to toll the three-year statute of limitations. In Lifter v. Commissioner, 59 T.C. 818 (1973), the notice of deficiency was sent to the taxpayers' last known address but was returned undelivered. The Commissioner then sent a copy of the notice to the taxpayers' attorney who had been appointed to handle their federal income tax matters. The taxpayers learned of the notice before the running of the statute of limitations and timely filed a petition with the Tax Court. The notice of deficiency was held valid.

Lifter may be distinguished from this case in three respects. First, the IRS sent the notice to what was reasonably believed to be petitioners' last known address, and a notice of deficiency mailed to a taxpayer's last known address is valid even if the taxpayer does not receive it. Second, taxpayers invoked the jurisdiction of the Tax Court by filing a timely petition. By timely invoking Tax Court jurisdiction, taxpayers effectively waived any objection to the notice of deficiency. Finally, the attorney to whom a copy of the notice was sent apparently had a broad power of attorney, beyond mere receipt of copies of notices sent to taxpayers. The Commissioner in *Lifter* could have sent the original notice to the attorney alone.

In Whiting v. Commissioner, T.C. Memo 1984-142 (1984), the notice was sent to taxpayers' previous address although the IRS had been informed of the change of address. The notice was returned undelivered. A copy of the notice was also sent to their attorney who eventually informed them of the notice. The taxpayers filed a timely petition with the Tax Court. They challenged the validity of the notice, but the Tax Court held it was valid because the petitioners became aware that the notice had been issued and timely filed a petition.

Whiting and this case differ in two critical respects. First, in *Whiting* the notice was sent to the wrong address, even after the IRS had been informed of the change of address. Here the notice was misaddressed because of a typographical error. Second, in *Whiting*, petitioners chose to invoke jurisdiction of the Tax Court after learning of the notice from their attorney. As in *Lifter*, by timely invoking Tax Court jurisdiction, taxpayers essentially acknowledged notice; the purpose of § 6212 had been satisfied. Here, Mulvania has never acknowledged notice by invoking Tax Court jurisdiction in a timely manner.

In *Whiting*, the Tax Court engaged in a cursory analysis of the validity of the notice, concluding that an error in the address to which the notice of deficiency is mailed does not render the notice invalid when the petition is timely filed, citing *Mulvania*, 81 T.C. at 68. In *Mulvania*, however, the taxpayer received the actual, physical notice of deficiency although it had been mailed to his former address and had later been hand delivered by his child.

The resolution of this issue is a "least-worse" result. Mulvania argues that he never received the actual written notice of deficiency because it was misaddressed. The IRS sent the notice on the last day of the statutory period, making it impossible for the Commissioner to remail the notice within the prescribed time once the error was discovered. To decide for the Commissioner would relieve the IRS of its cumulative errors, and create uncertainty in the law. The IRS argues, however, that this is a mobile society, clerical mistakes do happen, and the taxpayer had actual knowledge of the notice even if not its contents.

The Tax Court was understandably concerned that a decision in the Commissioner's favor would result in an uncertain rule depending upon whether the tax adviser happened to be a lawyer. As a lawyer, a tax adviser's call to Mulvania regarding the notice would have been privileged. The Tax Court correctly believed that a decision for the Commissioner would result in an uncertain rule, subject to manipulation by taxpayers who authorize copies to be sent to their accountant or lawyer, or by taxpayers with the most sophisticated tax advisers.

It is better for the government to lose some revenue as the result of its clerical error than to create uncertainty. If Simonis, either intentionally or unintentionally, had not informed Mulvania of the receipt of the copy of the notice of deficiency, then Mulvania would not have received any notification of the deficiency. Tax law requires more solid footings than the happenstance of a tax adviser telephoning a client to tell him of a letter from the IRS.

We conclude that, where a notice of deficiency has been misaddressed to the taxpayer or sent only to an adviser who is merely authorized to receive a copy of such a notice, actual notice is necessary but not sufficient to make the notice valid. The IRS is not forgiven for its clerical errors or for mailing notice to the wrong party unless the taxpayer, through his own actions, renders the Commissioner's errors harmless. In this case, the notice of deficiency became null and void when it was returned to the IRS undelivered. Regardless of the coincidence by which Mulvania later came to know of its existence, the taxpayer's actual knowledge did not transform the void notice into a valid one.

Had Mulvania timely petitioned the Tax Court for a redetermination of deficiency, the IRS error might have fallen into the line of harmless error cases where the taxpayer suffered no ill effects for the Commissioner's inadvertence. Such is not the case here.

Affirmed.

Notes and Questions

There is dicta in St. Joseph Lease Capital Corp. v. Commissioner, 235 F.3d 886 (4th Cir. 2000), aff'g T.C. Memo 1996-256, 1996 WL 289096, that a misaddressed notice of deficiency is sufficient to toll the statute of limitations, regardless of whether the taxpayer receives actual notice. The taxpayer in *St . Joseph* received actual notice after the expiration of the three-year statute of limitations, but in time to petition the Tax Court. The Fourth Circuit relied on the language of § 6503(a)(1), which provides for the suspension of the three-year limitations period on assessment "after the mailing of a notice under § 6212(a)." Id. at 888-889. The court noted, though, that § 6212(a) only addresses the mailing of a notice of deficiency by certified or registered mail, and the notification to the taxpayer of the right to contact a local office of the National Taxpayer Advocate; it does not require that the notice be mailed to the taxpayer's last known address. Instead, this requirement is found at § 6212(b). This issue is currently unresolved.

1.   What is the significance of a notice of deficiency?

2.   What result if the Service mails a notice of deficiency to the wrong address, it is not received by the taxpayer, and after the three-year statute of limitations on assessment has run, the Service remails the notice? Compare Reddock v. Commissioner, 72 T.C. 21 (1979) with St. Joseph Lease Capital Corp. v. Commissioner, 235 F.3d 886 (4th Cir. 2000).

The following case addresses the validity of a notice of deficiency following the taxpayer's failure to aid the Service in determining the last known address.

ARMSTRONG v. COMMISSIONER
United States Court of Appeals, Tenth Circuit, 1994.
15 F.3d 970.

BALDOCK, CIRCUIT JUDGE.

* * *

On March 2, 1990, the Internal Revenue Service ("IRS") sent by certified mail a notice of deficiency to Petitioner for his individual tax liability for the 1985 and 1986 tax years. The notice was addressed to P.O. Box 35343, Tulsa, Oklahoma, the address the IRS determined was Petitioner's "last known address" within the meaning of I.R.C. § 6212(b)(1). On March 22, 1990, after leaving two certified mail notices in this post office box, the post office returned the certified letter to the IRS marked "unclaimed."

The facts leading up to the IRS's mailing of the deficiency notice to Petitioner are essentially undisputed. At all times from December 30, 1988, through the time of the hearing in this matter, Petitioner had been registered as the renter of P.O. Box 35343, Tulsa, Oklahoma. The record reveals that from the years 1985 through 1989, Petitioner used the following addresses on his Federal income tax returns:

Year	Address
1985	P.O. Box 35343
1986	P.O. Box 35343
1987	4150 S. 100th E. Avenue Ste. 308
1988	P.O. Box 74153
1989	P.O. Box 35343

In connection with the audit of Petitioner's 1985 and 1986 tax returns, Revenue Agent Terri Marino mailed correspondence to Petitioner at the 4150 S.100th E. Avenue address. This address was the address of Terry Cumbey, Petitioner's tax preparer for his 1987 tax return. In a telephone call on February 8, 1989, Mr. Cumbey informed Agent Marino that the 4150 S.100th E. Avenue address was his own business address and that he no longer represented Petitioner. Mr. Cumbey also informed Agent Marino that Petitioner's current mailing address was P.O. Box 35343. Thereafter, the IRS forwarded a Form 872 (Consent to Extend Time to Assess Tax) to Petitioner at the P.O. Box 35343 address. Petitioner received the form, signed it, and returned it to the IRS together with a Form 2848 naming R. Paul Cecil as his attorney representative. Both documents reflected Petitioner's current address as P.O. Box 35343. The Form 872 also stated after the P.O. Box 35343 address: "[f]ormerly of 4150 S. 100th E. Ave." Thereafter, on August 2, 1989, the IRS mailed further correspondence to Petitioner at the P.O. Box 35343 address, which evidence before the Tax Court indicates Petitioner received.

On December 12, 1989, Mr. Cecil called Agent Marino and informed her that he was no longer representing Petitioner. Mr. Cecil also informed Agent Marino that Petitioner could be reached at 417 W.7th Street, and he provided her a telephone number. After receiving this information from Mr. Cecil, Agent Marino attempted to contact Petitioner, leaving a message on Petitioner's answering machine. Petitioner never returned her call. On December 15, 1989, and January 23, 1990, the IRS mailed additional Forms 872 to Petitioner at the P.O. Box 35343 address. These correspondences were returned marked "unclaimed."

On January 31, 1990, the IRS initiated a separate audit of Petitioner's 1987 tax return. Revenue Agent Linda Burgess handled this audit and made an entry in her file that Petitioner's address appeared to be the same as that listed in the Tulsa business telephone directory, 417 W. 7th Street, Tulsa, Oklahoma. She was later able to confirm this address through contact with an attorney, Mr. Doss, and through Petitioner himself.

IRS employee Janet Shell was responsible for preparing Petitioner's notices of deficiency for the 1985 and 1986 tax years. Pursuant to routine procedure, Ms. Shell generated a computer printout on February 7, 1990, which showed Petitioner's address as P.O. Box 74153, Tulsa, Oklahoma 74153–the address given on Petitioner's most recently filed return.[1] Suspecting a mistake in the address because the post office box number and the zip code were identical, Ms. Shell checked the zip code directory and discovered that there was no such post office box within the 74153 zip code. Ms. Shell then reviewed all the information in Petitioner's file and concluded that P.O. Box 35343 was the correct address. On March 2, 1990, the IRS mailed the notice of deficiency at issue in this case to the P.O. Box 35343 address, and, after two certified notices were left in the post office box, the deficiency notice was returned on March 22, 1990 marked "unclaimed."

On August 29, 1991, Petitioner filed a petition in the Tax Court seeking redetermination of the tax deficiency assessed against him for

---

1.   The IRS did not receive Petitioner's 1989 tax return bearing the P.O. Box 35343 address until October 15, 1990.

the 1985 and 1986 tax years. The Commissioner filed a motion to dismiss the petition as untimely because it was not filed within ninety days of the mailing of the notice of deficiency as required by I.R.C. § 6213(a). Petitioner objected to the Commissioner's motion to dismiss claiming that the IRS's notice of deficiency was insufficient because it was not sent to his last known address, as required by I.R.C. § 6212(b)(1). Petitioner claimed that his last known address on March 2, 1990, was P.O. Box 74153, Tulsa, Oklahoma, 74153, the address on his 1988 tax return. Petitioner further claimed that the IRS knew of two additional addresses to which to direct correspondence to him: (1) the address shown on his 1987 return, and (2) an address the IRS used to send Petitioner a letter involving the audit of his 1987 return. Petitioner claimed that these correspondences proved that the IRS had been given "clear and concise notification" of several different addresses to which, in the exercise of reasonable diligence, the IRS should have sent the notice of deficiency.

After a hearing on the matter, the Tax Court dismissed Petitioner's petition for lack of jurisdiction because the petition was filed more than ninety days after March 2, 1990. The court found that the address to which the IRS mailed Petitioner's notice of deficiency was a correct address when mailed and remained an address of Petitioner's through the time of the hearing before the Tax Court. The court further found that Petitioner was not a credible witness, and concluded that Petitioner had refused to take receipt of the notice of deficiency. The court finally concluded that in light of all the surrounding circumstances, the Commissioner reasonably believed that Petitioner wished correspondence in this case to be mailed to P.O. Box 35343, Tulsa, Oklahoma, making this address Petitioner's last known address within the meaning of I.R.C. § 6212(b)(1).

Petitioner appeals claiming that the Tax Court erred in concluding that the IRS mailed the notice of deficiency to Petitioner's last known address. Petitioner argues that the IRS had clear and concise notice that Petitioner's last known address was 417 W. 7th Street, and the IRS failed to exercise reasonable diligence in mailing the notice of deficiency to Petitioner.

We first must determine our standard of review. The historical facts and legal standard governing the last known address determination are undisputed. The issue centers on the Tax Court's ultimate conclusion that the Commissioner mailed the notice of deficiency to Petitioner's last known address within the meaning of I.R.C. § 6212(b)(1). As such, the issue is a mixed question of law and fact. See Pullman-Standard v. Swint, 456 U.S. 273, 289 n. 19, 102 S.Ct. 1781, 1790 n. 19, 72 L.Ed.2d 66

(1982) (mixed questions are "questions in which the historical facts are admitted or established, the rule of law is undisputed, and the issue is whether the facts satisfy the statutory standard"). We review mixed questions under the clearly erroneous or de novo standard, depending on whether the mixed question involves primarily a factual inquiry or the consideration of legal principles. We have held that the last known address determination involves primarily a factual inquiry, see Cyclone Drilling, Inc. v. Kelley, 769 F.2d 662, 664 (10th Cir.1985); as a result, clearly erroneous review is appropriate.

Petitioner's first claim is that the IRS failed to mail the notice of deficiency to his last known address because it had clear and concise notice that Petitioner's last known address was 417 W.7th Street. We disagree.

The IRS must give notice to the taxpayer before it may assess or collect any tax deficiency. I.R.C. § 6213(a). A notice of deficiency is valid, even if it is not received by the taxpayer, if it is mailed to the taxpayer's "last known address." I.R.C. § 6212(b)(1). The term "last known address" has been defined by case law to mean "that address to which the IRS reasonably believes the taxpayer wishes the notice sent." Cyclone Drilling, 769 F.2d at 664. The IRS is entitled to rely on the address shown on the taxpayer's tax return for the year in question unless the taxpayer satisfies his burden to provide clear and concise notice of his current address to the IRS. Id. "*Clear and concise notice is notice by which the taxpayer indicates to the IRS that he wishes the new address to replace all old addresses in subsequent communication.*" Id. (emphasis in original). A subsequent tax return bearing a new address provides the IRS with clear and concise notice; therefore, the address on the taxpayer's most recent tax return is ordinarily deemed to be his last known address. Id.

If the notice of deficiency is sufficient, the taxpayer has ninety days in which to file a petition for redetermination of the deficiency. I.R.C. § 6213(a). If the taxpayer fails to file a petition within this ninety-day period, the Tax Court lacks jurisdiction to entertain the case. Even so, the taxpayer is not without an avenue of redress; rather, he is entitled to pay the full tax and then bring an action in federal district court to challenge the assessment. See I.R.C. § 7422.

At the time the IRS mailed Petitioner's notice of deficiency for the 1985 and 1986 tax years, Petitioner's most recent tax return, the 1988 tax return, contained the address P.O. Box 741537, Tulsa, Oklahoma 741537. This address, however, as the revenue agent alertly discovered, was nonexistent. Furthermore, correspondence to the 4150 S.100th E. Avenue Ste. 308 address contained on Petitioner's1987 tax return, revealed that it was the address of an accountant who no longer represented Petitioner. In the face of such information, the IRS could not reasonably conclude that either address on Petitioner's 1987 or 1988 tax return constituted clear and concise notice of Petitioner's current address. As a result, the IRS was entitled to rely on the address shown on Petitioner's 1985 and 1986 tax return (P.O. Box 35343), as those tax returns were the subject of the audit, unless Petitioner, in some other fashion, provided clear and concise notice to the IRS that he wished a new address to replace the P.O. Box 35343 address.

We conclude the Tax Court's determination that Petitioner has failed his burden of showing that he provided the IRS with clear and concise notice that his last known address was 417 W. 7th Street is not clearly erroneous. The only knowledge the revenue agent handling Petitioner's 1985 and 1986 audit had of the 417 W. 7th Street address came from Mr. Cecil who, after disclosing that he no longer represented Petitioner, informed the agent that Petitioner could be reached at this address and gave her a phone number. Mr. Cecil at no time informed the agent that Petitioner intended the 417 W. 7th Street address to replace all of Petitioner's addresses for the purposes of future correspondence, and given Mr. Cecil's withdrawal from representation of Petitioner, it is unclear whether he even had the authority to do so. Further, although the revenue agent left a message for Petitioner at the phone number given her by Mr. Cecil, Petitioner never responded, thereby casting some doubt on Mr. Cecil's information.

Petitioner also claims the IRS failed to exercise reasonable diligence in mailing the notice of deficiency to the P.O. Box 35343 address, because it failed to send duplicate notices to all known addresses, it failed to look to outside sources to determine Petitioner's address, and it failed to conduct further research to ascertain the 417 W. 7th Street address, once the notice was returned marked "unclaimed."

In a last known address determination, the focus is on the information available to the IRS at the time it issued the notice of deficiency, rather than what may in fact be the taxpayer's correct address. The IRS is required to use reasonable diligence in attempting to ascertain the taxpayer's correct address. In discharging its burden of reasonable diligence, the IRS is entitled to rely on those documents which are submitted by the taxpayer. It is the taxpayer's responsibility to notify the IRS of any changes in address, and the burden rests with the taxpayer to show that the IRS failed to exercise reasonable diligence in ascertaining the last known address. *Cyclone Drilling*, 769 F.2d at 664.

We conclude the Tax Court's finding that the IRS exercised reasonable diligence in ascertaining Petitioner's last known address is not clearly erroneous. Contrary to Petitioner's assertion, reasonable diligence does not require that the IRS send duplicate notices to every address of which it has knowledge. Petitioner relies on the IRS manual which directs an agent to send duplicate notices "if there is any doubt as to what constitutes the last known address of the taxpayer." "It is well-settled, however, that the provisions of the manual are directory rather than mandatory * * * and clearly do not have the force and effect of law." *Marks*, 947 F.2d at 986 n. 1; see also *Pomeroy*, 864 F.2d at 1194-95. Furthermore, under the facts of this case, the revenue agent reasonably did not doubt that P.O. Box 35343 was Petitioner's last known address. In reviewing Petitioner's file, the agent determined that the last correspondence received from Petitioner bore the P.O. Box 35343 address and that there had been successful communication with Petitioner through the use of this address. Moreover, although two correspondences mailed to this address were subsequently returned, they were not returned marked "undeliverable;" instead, they were merely unclaimed.

Likewise, the IRS's failure to look to outside sources to determine Petitioner's address does not indicate that the IRS failed to exercise reasonable diligence. The fact of the matter is that P.O. Box 35343 was a current and correct address of Petitioner at the time the notice of deficiency was mailed, and any research of outside sources would merely have confirmed this.[3] That the agent conducting the audit of Petitioner's 1987 tax return located the 417 W. 7th Street address in the business telephone directory does not signify that the agent conducting the audit of the 1985 and 1986 returns failed to exercise reasonable diligence. The only reason the agent conducting the 1987 audit could rely on the 417 W. 7th Street address was because Petitioner returned this agent's telephone call and confirmed the address change. He did not do so, however, until March 19, 1990, making this information unavailable to the agent responsible for mailing the March 2, 1990 notice of deficiency. Furthermore, Petitioner had been contacted earlier by the agent conducting the 1985 and 1986 audit, and he failed to return her call, thereby avoiding an opportunity to alert the agent to an address change. Given that the IRS is entitled to rely on information provided by Petitioner, and Petitioner did not notify the IRS prior to the mailing of the notice that he wished to replace the P.O. Box 35343 address, the IRS, in the exercise of reasonable diligence, mailed the notice to the P.O. Box 35343 address.

---

3.   Indeed, Petitioner again used P.O. Box 35343 as his address on his 1989 tax return.

Finally, we reject Petitioner's argument that the IRS failed to exercise reasonable diligence because it failed to conduct further research to ascertain the 417 W. 7th Street address, once the notice of deficiency was returned marked "unclaimed." We agree with the Fifth, Seventh, and Ninth Circuits, as well as the Tax Court, that the IRS's duty to exercise reasonable diligence in ascertaining a taxpayer's last known address extends only to the point in time when the deficiency notice is mailed.

As the Third Circuit explained in Delman v. Commissioner, 384 F.2d 929, 932-33 (3d Cir.1967), Congress enacted I.R.C.§ 6212(b)(1) to protect the Commissioner in those circumstances where the deficiency notice was not received for some unforeseeable reason on the part of the issuing agent. Thus, § 6212(b)(1) explicitly states that a notice of deficiency is valid "*if mailed to the taxpayer at his last known address.*" Id. (emphasis added). As a result, the validity of a notice of deficiency turns on whether the IRS used the last known address when the notice was mailed, regardless of whether it is ever received. A notice which is mailed in conformity with § 6212(b)(1) is valid, and "[n]othing in the statute suggests that the IRS is obligated to take additional steps to effectuate delivery if the notice is returned." *King*, 857 F.2d at 681. Consequently, because the IRS mailed the notice to Petitioner's last known address, it had no further obligations of reasonable diligence after the notice was returned unclaimed.

AFFIRMED.

Notes and Questions

In Rev. Proc. 2010-16, 2010-19 I.R.B. 664, the Service states that the last known address is the address on the most recently filed, properly processed return, unless it has received "clear and concise notification of a different address." Form 8822[2] may be used to provide clear and concise notification of a change of address prior to the filing of a tax return. Note that the Rev. Proc. states that Form 4868, Application For Automatic Extension of Time To File U.S. Individual Income Tax Return, will not be considered clear and concise notification of a change of address.

After a return is filed, it will not be considered properly processed to provide notification of an address change until 45 days after the date of receipt by the Service, unless the return is filed before the due date, in which case the 45-day period will run from the due date. If the return

---

2.   Available online at http://www.irs.gov/pub/irs-pdf/f8822.pdf

contains an error that delays the processing, the 45-day period will begin after the error is corrected.

1. In *Armstrong*, both the taxpayer and the government asked the Tax Court to dismiss the petition. If the parties both agree that the case should not be heard by the Tax Court, should the grounds for dismissal make any difference to them?

2. Since both parties in *Armstrong* requested a dismissal for lack of jurisdiction, whose claim should the Tax Court consider first? Why?

The IRS Restructuring and Reform Act of 1998 provided that in the 90-day letter the Service should give the last date on which the taxpayer could file a petition in the tax court. In Rochelle v. Commissioner, 116 T.C. 356 (2001), *aff'd* 293 F.3d 740 (5th Cir. 2002), the taxpayer, a practicing attorney, received a 90-day letter that left the filing date blank. He filed a petition in the Tax Court 56 days after the expiration of the 90-day period and argued that his notice of deficiency was defective because of the lack of a filing date. The Tax Court, however, refused to invalidate the notice. The court noted that the 90-day letter had stated clearly that the petition must be filed within 90 days of the date of the letter and the taxpayer had the sophistication to comprehend and calculate the filing date. Judge Beghe, in his concurrence noted that the case might have been decided differently if the taxpayer had been "suffering from cognitive deficit, dyscalculia, or other disability." 116 T.C. at 366.

The Service's determination of deficiency is afforded the "presumption of correctness," which means that the burden of proof shifts to the taxpayer to produce evidence to rebut the presumption by establishing that the determination is arbitrary and erroneous. See United States v. Janis, 428 U.S. 433, 49 L.Ed.2d 1046, 96 S.Ct. 3021 (1976). If the determination is based on alleged unreported income – usually illegal income – the Service cannot make a "naked assessment" (i.e., a determination that lacks foundation), because the taxpayer then would be in the untenable position of having to prove a negative (i.e., nonreceipt of the income). Thus, in order to make its prima facie case, the Service must produce some evidence linking the taxpayer to the income-generating activity. If it does, the burden then will shift to the taxpayer to show that the determination is arbitrary and erroneous. See Anastasato v. Commissioner, 794 F.2d 884 (3rd Cir. 1986).

B. WAIVER OF RESTRICTIONS ON ASSESSMENT

Section 6213(d) provides that a taxpayer shall have the right to file a waiver of restrictions on assessment and collection at any time "whether or not a notice of deficiency has been issued." If the tax is paid before a deficiency notice is mailed, the payment of the tax operates as a waiver of the restrictions on assessment and collection. Reg. § 301.6213(b)(3). Otherwise, the taxpayer may waive the restrictions by signing a Form 870.

The filing of a Form 870 (Waiver of Restrictions on Assessment and Collection of Deficiency in Tax and Acceptance of Overassessment) does not preclude the taxpayer from suing for a refund, nor does it preclude the government from asserting a further deficiency. The taxpayer should realize, however, that signing the waiver may have irreversible consequences.

1. The Consequences of Signing a Form 870

WEBSTER AND HERLACH v. COMMISSIONER
United States Tax Court (Memorandum Decision), 1992.
64 TCM 724.

* * *

Petitioner G. Marshall Webster, a dentist, untimely filed his Federal income tax returns for tax years 1983 and 1984. * * * Petitioner claims to have entrusted the filing of his income tax returns to his return preparer, Terry Baer, whom he believed to be a certified public accountant, and to have been unaware that the returns for 1983 and 1984 were never filed. He learned otherwise when respondent began an examination of his returns beginning in September 1990. Petitioner and his wife, Lisa R. Herlach, filed Form 2848, Power of Attorney, designating Terry Baer as their representative.

At approximately that time, petitioner signed blank returns for tax years 1983 and 1984, and allowed Terry Baer to file them without examining them himself. For 1983 and 1984, petitioner, again on Terry Baer's advice, signed Form 870, Waiver of Restrictions on Assessment and Collection; petitioner and his wife similarly signed Forms 870 for tax years 1985 and 1986, and 1987 and 1988. After the returns were filed, respondent made assessments for the liabilities shown on the returns.

Petitioners subsequently learned that Terry Baer's certification was suspended in April 1989. Petitioners contend that Terry Baer was not entitled to represent them and that consequently the waivers they signed are invalid. Petitioners further maintain that the returns for 1983 and 1984 are not accurate and report too much tax due.

* * *

II. Tax Years 1985 through 1988

For tax years 1985 through 1988, petitioners filed joint returns, and respondent, after examination of the returns, proposed a deficiency for each year on the basis of certain adjustments to income.   When petitioners learned of the examination of their tax returns, they designated their return preparer as their representative, and, on his advice, executed Forms 870, Waiver of Restrictions on Assessment and Collection, for all years under examination. For tax years 1985 though 1988, respondent proceeded to levy on petitioners' bank account on the basis of the assessment made for these years pursuant to the waivers which petitioners had signed.

Petitioners now ask the Court to declare their waivers void, as in signing them they placed excessive reliance upon the advice of their return preparer. For the reason stated below, we reject petitioners' argument and uphold the validity of the waivers.

Section 6213 provides for restrictions on assessment and collection for the period during which a taxpayer may file a petition with this Court for a redetermination of a deficiency and, if a petition has been filed, until the decision of the Tax Court becomes final. § 6213(a). Section 6213(d) provides, however, that a taxpayer shall have the right at any time to file a written and signed waiver of the restrictions provided in subsection (a) on the assessment and collection of the whole or any part of the deficiency. It is a long-established principle that a taxpayer may sign a waiver at any time, and respondent may proceed with immediate assessment and collection, though no notice of deficiency has been issued. United States v. Price, 361 U.S. 304 (1960).

"After such waiver has been acted upon by the district director and the assessment has been made in accordance with its terms, the waiver cannot be withdrawn." § 301.6213-1(d), Proced. & Admin. Regs. Assessments have subsequently been made in accordance with the terms of the waivers, and, under the regulations, the waivers may not now be withdrawn.

The signing of a waiver is not a contract, but rather a unilateral waiver of a defense by the taxpayer. Contract principles are significant, however, in a case in which it is necessary to interpret a written agreement, as an agreement is a manifestation of mutual assent.

Petitioners claim as their defense the existence of a unilateral mistake, that they did not "knowingly and willfully" sign the waivers. They feel they were ill advised to have signed such waivers and did not fully understand the consequences.

We know of no authority supporting the voiding of an agreement on the basis of unilateral mistake. The Form 870 was clear on its face: "I understand that by signing this waiver, I will not be able to contest these years in the United States Tax Court, unless additional deficiencies are determined for these years." Petitioners do not plead that they were not capable of reading and understanding the waiver. Nor do they claim they were induced to sign it by fraud or duress, circumstances under which a contract with respondent might be void or voidable. Quigley v. Internal Revenue Service, 289 F.2d 878, 880 (D.C. Cir. 1960) (holding that Form 870, which the taxpayer signed believing it to be Form 872, was not voidable: taxpayer could read and write and was familiar with tax matters); accord Monge v. Smyth, 229 F.2d 361 (9th Cir. 1956) (holding that reliance on the advice of a disloyal attorney was not grounds for voiding a waiver); cf. Slawek v. Commissioner, T.C. Memo. 1991-338, affd. 972 F.2d 1332 (3d Cir. 1992) (holding unilateral mistake not a ground for rescinding a stipulation). Because of their waiver the taxpayers have no further right to and cannot invoke the jurisdiction of the Tax Court.

Petitioners' position here is no different from that of any other taxpayer who believes he is the recipient of bad advice. When a taxpayer relies on the advice of an accountant or attorney concerning a matter of tax law, such as whether a liability exists, it is reasonable for the taxpayer to rely on that advice. Even so, reliance on an adviser does not insulate the taxpayer from the correct application of the law, but only under certain circumstances from certain additions. Woodbury v. Commissioner, 49 T.C. 180, 200 (1967). The choice of an adviser, however, is not a technical matter, but one calling for ordinary human wisdom and careful deliberation: to use a medical metaphor, "Therein the patient must minister to himself."[3]

The waivers of the restrictions on assessment and collection which they executed for tax years 1985 through 1988 are valid. Consequently, we have no authority to grant petitioners the relief they seek. As to tax years 1985 through 1988, petitioners' motion to restrain assessment and collection must be denied.

* * *

---

3. Shakespeare, "Macbeth" V, iii.

Question

What effect will the court's decision have on these taxpayers?

2. Offer to Waive Restrictions on Assessment and Collection of Deficiency

The Offer to Waive Restrictions on Assessment and Collection of Tax Deficiency and to Accept Overassessment (Form 870-AD), differs from the waiver of restrictions on assessment and collection (Form 870) in that the Form 870-AD represents an agreement between the Service and the taxpayer reached as a result of mutual compromise and concession. As a result, the taxpayer promises that no claim for refund will be filed and the Service promises that the case will not be reopened absent "fraud, malfeasance, concealment or misrepresentation of a material fact, an important mistake in mathematical calculation, or excessive tentative allowances of [net operating loss] carrybacks."

Therefore, there is some degree of finality with a Form 870-AD agreement that is not present with a Form-870 waiver. Since neither is a closing agreement, however, the question is how much finality does a Form-870-AD provide?

WHITNEY v. UNITED STATES
United States Court of Appeals, Ninth Circuit, 1987.
826 F.2d 896.

J. BLAINE ANDERSON, CIRCUIT JUDGE:

William and Barbara Whitney (Whitneys) are farmers in the Salinas Valley of Monterey County, California. In this regard they lease farm land from other landowners and produce crops from it. In 1975 the Whitneys sold a portion of their farming operation to Melvin and Neil Bassetti (Bassettis). A partnership was formed to purchase the farming operation. Melvin and Neil Bassetti each held a forty-nine percent interest in the partnership while the Whitneys held a two percent interest. The Bassettis paid for the farm by a $1,124,876.00 promissory note. The purchase included $206,048.00 in prepaid rent for farm land leased for 1974 and $287,116.00 for land leased for 1975. The Whitneys deducted the prepaid rent as a business expense on their 1974 and 1975 tax returns.[1] On its 1975 return, the partnership itself also claimed a

---

1. The Whitneys filed joint income tax returns so they are treated as one taxpayer.

deduction for prepaid rent. After an audit, the Internal Revenue Service (IRS) disallowed these deductions.

Edward Singleton (Singleton), an accountant, reviewed the deductions taken by the Whitneys, the partnership and the Bassettis, and asked the IRS to allow the deductions to each of them. The IRS sent Singleton a Form 870-AD ("Offer of Waiver of Restrictions on Assessment and Collection of Deficiency in Tax and of Acceptance of Overassessment") and indicated that the prepaid rent was not deductible, but that the partnership could deduct a portion of the promissory note as a business expense.

The Whitneys and the Bassettis executed Form 870-AD and returned it to the IRS. The IRS understood execution of the Form 870-AD to mean that the nondeductibility of the prepaid rent was being conceded in exchange for the deduction granted to the partnership. Less than one month after the executed Form 870-AD was accepted by the IRS, this court decided Zaninovich v. Commissioner, 616 F.2d 429 (9th Cir.1980), which held that prepaid rent (such as that deducted by the Whitneys) was a business expense which was deductible in the year of payment. The Whitneys then filed a refund claim for the deductibility of the 1974 prepaid rent based on *Zaninovich.* The IRS denied the claim on the basis of the Form 870-AD, stating that it was a binding settlement agreement.

The Whitneys then filed this suit in district court to seek their refund. They, along with Singleton, alleged Form 870-AD was understood to be simply a suggestion by the IRS as to what the law was with respect to prepaid rent rather than a "package settlement" agreement between them, the partnership and the IRS. The IRS cried foul and moved for summary judgment. The district court granted summary judgment for the government on the ground that the Whitneys were equitably estopped from receiving a refund because they signed the Form 870-AD and the IRS detrimentally relied upon it. The Whitneys appeal the grant of summary judgment against them. We reverse and remand for further proceedings.

The government argues the language of Form 870-AD conclusively determines that those signing it are barred from seeking a refund.[2] Alternatively, the government contends that the Whitneys are equitably

---

2.   Form 870-AD in part states:

If this offer is accepted for the Commissioner, the case shall not be reopened in the absence of fraud, malfeasance, concealment or misrepresentation of material fact, an important mistake in mathematical calculation, or excessive tentative allowances of carrybacks provided by law; and no claim for refund or credit shall be filed or prosecuted for the year(s) stated above other than for amounts attributed to carrybacks provided by law.

However, Form 870-AD also states: "NOTE – The execution and filing of this offer * * * will not, however, constitute a closing agreement under section 7121 of the Internal Revenue Code."

estopped from claiming a refund since it relied on their representations in signing Form 870-AD by letting the statute of limitations run on additional assessments against the partnership.

In this circuit, we have not squarely decided whether Form 870-AD *standing alone* estops the executing taxpayers from later seeking a refund. Initially, in Monge v. Smyth, 229 F.2d 361 (9th Cir.1956), we peripherally indicated that a Form 870-TS (the predecessor to Form 870-AD), executed prior to a notice of deficiency, was a bilateral agreement when accepted by the IRS and constituted a final determination on a tax deficiency. Id. at 367. Later, in United States v. Price, 263 F.2d 382 (9th Cir.1959) (en banc), we appropriately ruled that the language in *Monge* concerning the validity of the waiver (Form 870-AD) was dictum.

Other circuit courts addressing the Form 870-AD question have taken divergent views. Those finding Form 870-AD binds a taxpayer do so largely on grounds of equitable estoppel. See, e.g., Flynn v. United States, 786 F.2d 586, 591 (3d Cir.1986) (dicta) (also applying contract principles); Elbo Coals, Inc. v. United States, 763 F.2d 818, 821 (6th Cir.1985); General Split Corp. v. United States, 500 F.2d 998, 1004 (7th Cir.1974); Cain v. United States, 255 F.2d 193, 199 (8th Cir.1958). Courts holding Form 870-AD does not in itself preclude a taxpayer from seeking a refund find their authority in the theory that a binding settlement agreement under section 7121 of the Internal Revenue Code is the exclusive means whereby tax disputes can be settled. See Arch Engineering Co., Inc. v. United States, 783 F.2d 190, 192 (Fed.Cir.1986) (dicta); Lignos v. United States, 439 F.2d 1365, 1367 (2d Cir.1971); Uinta Livestock Corp. v. United States, 355 F.2d 761 (10th Cir.1966); cf. Cain v. United States, 255 F.2d 193, 199 (8th Cir.1958) (Van Oosterhout, J., dissenting). In light of these divergent cases, it is clear the question is not easily answered. The decisions turn on the intricacies of the facts involved

After reviewing these cases of tax gamesmanship, we believe the nonbinding position is the more logical view consistent with general principles in this area. The language in Form 870-AD is contradictory. As such it should be construed against the drafter. Form 870-AD purports to prevent taxpayers from reopening a disputed tax case without being a settlement agreement under I.R.C. § 7121.[4] Since it is

---

4.   Under I.R.C. § 7121, a closing agreement is authorized as follows:
CLOSING AGREEMENTS.

    (a) AUTHORIZATION--The Secretary is authorized to enter into an agreement in writing with any person relating to the liability of such person (or of the person or estate for whom he acts) in respect of any internal revenue tax for any taxable period.

not a valid compromise of a tax deficiency, standing alone it should not estop the executing taxpayer from seeking a refund.

Having found that Form 870-AD standing alone does not control, we arrive at the next question. Should the Whitneys be estopped from seeking a refund because the IRS decided not to seek other assessments against the partnership and allowed the statute of limitations to run against it? We cannot answer this question on the record before us. The district court granted the government summary judgment. Whether equitable estoppel should apply against the Whitneys involves questions of fact and credibility determinations which must be resolved. Chief among these is why the Whitneys would enter into a "package settlement" with the partnership in which they received nothing in return. Also, what was actually said by, and what was the intent of, the parties during the negotiations? If the government believed this was a "package settlement," why didn't it state that in its negotiations with Singleton and the Whitneys? On the record before us, the government can point to no false representations (since Form 870-AD alone will not suffice) by the Whitneys which would justify application of the doctrine of equitable estoppel.[5]

Since a determination of these questions and possibly others requires review by a trier of fact, the district court improperly granted summary judgment.

Reversed and Remanded.

Cynthia Holcomb Hall, Circuit Judge, dissenting:

I agree with the majority's conclusion that the Form 870-AD is not a binding settlement agreement. The government does not dispute this.[1]

(b) FINALITY--If such agreement is approved by the Secretary (within such time as may be stated in such agreement, or later agreed to) such agreement shall be final and conclusive, and, except upon a showing of fraud or malfeasance, or misrepresentation of a material fact-- (1) the case shall not be reopened as to the matters agreed upon or the agreement modified by any officer, employee, or agent of the United States, and (2) in any suit, action, or proceeding, such agreement, or any determination, assessment, collection, payment, abatement, refund, or credit made in accordance therewith, shall not be annulled, modified, set aside, or disregarded.

5. For equitable estoppel to be applied:

(1) there must be false representation or wrongful misleading silence; (2) the error must originate in a statement of fact, not in an opinion or a statement of law; (3) the one claiming the benefits of estoppel must not know the true facts; and (4) that same person must be adversely affected by the acts or statements of the one against whom an estoppel is claimed.

Lignos, 439 F.2d at 1368.

1. The majority states that the "government argues the language of Form 870-AD conclusively determines that those signing it are barred from seeking a refund." Supra at 897. This is not the case. In its brief on appeal, the government consistently argues only that "[Forms 870-AD] are

I vigorously disagree, however, with the majority's conclusion that on the record before us, it cannot decide whether the Whitneys are estopped from seeking a refund. The district court correctly determined that the uncontroverted facts show that the Whitneys are estopped.

The majority outlines the factual questions to be determined on remand: Did the Whitneys make any false representation, required for equitable estoppel? Why did the Whitneys enter into a package settlement with the partnership in which they received "nothing in return"? Why did the parties enter into the settlement negotiations? During the negotiations, why didn't the government state that it viewed the settlement as a package settlement?

These questions are definitively answered on the facts before us. These facts are dispositive despite the majority's decision to ignore them.

First, the majority states that the Whitneys apparently made no false representation. The majority believes that a false representation is a requirement of equitable estoppel. Under the circumstances presented here, I believe that the appropriate test for estoppel does not require a *false* representation. In Robinson v. Commissioner, 100 F.2d 847, 849 (6th Cir. 1939), the court set out these requirements:

> The taxpayer, by his conduct, which includes language, acts or silence knowingly makes a representation or conceals material facts which he intends or expects will be acted upon by taxing officials in determining his tax, and the true or concealed material facts are unknown to the taxing officials or they lack equal means of knowledge with the taxpayer, and act on his representation or concealment and to retrace their steps on a different state of facts would cause the loss of taxes to the Government.

This test is particularly appropriate in the "package deal" context before us.

The Second Circuit has itself expressly rejected the applicability of the *Lignos* test, which the majority utilizes, to the circumstances of this case. In Stair v. United States, 516 F.2d 560 (2d Cir.1975), the Second Circuit explains that estoppel is available in circumstances similar to those here. The court explained that the *Lignos* requirement of a false representation was not applicable where it is clear that the Commissioner has been adversely affected, particularly by the running of the statute of limitations.

In *Stair,* the court found that there were grounds for estoppel where the taxpayer misrepresented his position by failing to say, at the time of

---

binding on a taxpayer if the IRS changes its position in reliance on his representation * * *."

settlement, that his agreement not to file for a refund was conditional upon the relevant tax law remaining static. The court explained:

> It requires little elaboration to demonstrate that a contrary outcome would arm the taxpayer with both a shield and a sword, and permit him to enter the lists with no chance of losing. The Stairs, if allowed to proceed, would fare no worse than the compromise they have already succeeded in negotiating. If victorious on the merits, they would be freed even from the obligation of sustaining their half of that bargain. Given such a state of affairs, it would be an imprudent taxpayer indeed who did not resort to litigation even after compromise. We see little purpose in straining *Botany Mills* to the breaking point in order to accommodate such a result.

Id. at 565.

In this case, the Whitneys represented that they would not sue for a refund, the Commissioner reasonably relied on that representation, and there exists a detriment to the Commissioner, i.e., the expiration of the statute of limitations period for the related parties prevented the Commissioner from recouping concessions made in the package settlement. This detriment cannot be rectified other than by estoppel of the Whitneys. Where there is a settlement with one taxpayer regarding multiple issues, the Commissioner may litigate issues conceded by a settlement even though the statute of limitations has run. However, where, as here, the statute has run and a multiple taxpayer settlement is involved, the Commissioner "cannot set off deficiencies of other taxpayers against the claims of the plaintiff taxpayers." "False representations" therefore should not be required.

The remaining questions allegedly left unanswered for the majority relate to the benefits and existence of a package settlement. The facts clearly demonstrate that the close relationship between the Whitneys, the Bissettis, and the partnership shows that a package settlement was intended, the Whitneys benefited from it, and the Commissioner suffered a detriment from it. It is absurd for the Whitneys to claim that there was no relationship between them and the Bissettis. Not only were they seller and buyer, but they were also partners in the new business.

The deductions taken by the taxpayers are also closely linked. The Whitneys incurred $1,124,376 of expenses in planting and growing crops prior to the March 1, 1975 sale of the business to the partnership. These expenses were deducted on their 1974 and 1975 returns. On the other hand, the profits from the crops when harvested were not reported by the

Whitneys (except for 2% flow through to them from the partnership)[2] but were reported by the partnership in 1975 (and 98% flowed through to the Bissettis).

The partnership also claimed the $1,124,376 expense of planting and growing the crops as a deduction on its 1975 return. Ninety-eight percent of the benefit of the deduction flowed through the partnership to the Bissettis and was reported on their 1975 return and 2% was reported on the Whitney's 1975 return (resulting in a double deduction of this 2% on the Whitney's return). The basis of this deduction was the Bissettis' note, which was not paid in 1975. The partnership had not originally claimed this deduction on its return.

Part of the cost of planting and growing crops represented prepaid rent, namely, $206,048 in 1974 and $287,116 in 1975. The Commissioner contended that these prepaid rental expenses were not deductible by the Whitneys in 1974 and 1975. The conferee denied the partnership deduction for the amount of the unpaid note and for the amount of prepaid rent, explaining that a cash basis taxpayer cannot deduct the note until paid and cannot deduct prepaid rent. This presented the partnership with the dilemma of receiving the income from the sale of the crops grown but getting no deductions to offset that income. On the other hand, the Whitneys claimed the deductions for the expenses but reported none of the income. The compromise settlement gave both the Whitneys and the partnership the deductions for the cost of planting and growing the crops, except for prepaid rent.

The relationship between the partnership, the Whitneys, and the Bissettis raised questions regarding the propriety of the deductions. First, there was the question of which taxpayers may claim the deductions and for which years. The second question was which taxpayer must report the income from the sale of the crops.

The Commissioner could have resolved these issues in numerous ways. As a matter of accounting, the Commissioner could have attempted to match the expenses and the income and attributed both to one taxpayer or the other. Under section 482 of the Internal Revenue Code, the Commissioner could have allocated the income among the related entities on the basis of which taxpayer's work and money gave rise to the income. 26 U.S.C. § 482. Under the tax benefit rule, the Commissioner could have denied the deductions to the entity that did not report the income. Therefore, under the settlement, the Commissioner

---

2. A partnership return is solely an information return and all income and deductions flow through to the partners and are reported on the partners' individual returns.

relinquished all these possible resolutions of the issues, and the partnership thereby benefited.

The Whitneys further benefited from the settlement because of the disparate financial circumstances of the two groups of taxpayers. Because the Whitneys were high income taxpayers, the deductions were more valuable to the Whitneys than to the Bissettis who could not use all their deductions in 1975 or in the three-year carryback years and the five-year forward years. The income was more valuable to the Bissettis.

The close relationship between the Whitneys and Bissettis and the "package" nature of the settlement are further illustrated by the fact that both groups were represented by one public accountant. This public accountant had a Power of Attorney from each of them, and the entire matter was handled by one district conferee and was later handled by one appellate conferee. The single settlement agreement related to all the parties, although, as is customary, separate Forms 870-AD were sent to each taxpayer. It was only after *all* Forms 870-AD were signed and returned by the taxpayers that the Commissioner signed them. In light of the entanglement of the parties and their deductions, there is no doubt that the Commissioner would not have settled with the taxpayers separately.

I therefore believe that the Whitneys are estopped from seeking a refund. The majority applies an estoppel test which courts have held inappropriate in circumstances similar if not identical to those here. The close relationship between the Whitneys, Bissettis and the partnership shows that a package deal was intended and the Whitneys benefited therefrom. The Commissioner relied on their representations in signing the Form 870-AD by allowing the statute of limitations to run on additional assessments against the related parties. The facts established in the record are sufficient to uphold the summary judgment granted by the district court.

Notes and Questions

Why should the Service need an agreement that is less formal and less binding than a closing agreement?

Courts have struggled with cases in which a taxpayer signs a Form 870-AD, pays the agreed upon tax, and later files a refund claim in contravention of the agreement, particularly in cases like *Whitney*, where the refund claim was based upon a subsequent change in the case law. As the Ninth Circuit noted in *Whitney*, several courts have held that the Form 870-AD does not preclude the taxpayer from filing a refund claim because the Form 870-AD does not constitute a binding agreement, and that if the Service had intended to be bound by the agreement, it should have executed a § 7121 closing agreement. See, e.g., Botany Worsted Mills v. United States, 278 U.S. 282, 49 S.Ct. 129 (1929); Unita Livestock Corp. v. United States, 355 F.2d 761 (10th Cir. 1966); Joyce v. Gentsch, 141 F.2d 891 (6th Cir. 1944).

Other courts have used principles of equitable estoppel to uphold the validity of the Form 870-AD, even though the agreement itself is not considered binding. See Elbo Coals, Inc. v. United States, 763 F.2d 818 (6th Cir. 1985); Stair v. United States, 516 F.2d 560 (2d Cir. 1975). Some of these decisions have been based on the taxpayer's silence as misrepresentation in waiting until the statute of limitations for assessment has expired before filing the refund suit. Other courts have held that detrimental reliance applied in favor of the Service to prevent the taxpayer from filing a refund suit after the statute of limitations on assessment had expired. See Kretchmar v. United States, 9 Ct. Cl. 191 (1985). In *Kretchmar,* the taxpayer argued that the Service was not prejudiced by the running of the three-year statute of limitations on assessment because the Service could continue to assess a deficiency after the running of the general statute in cases of fraud or substantial omissions of income. IRC §§ 6501(c)(1) and (e). The court, however, dismissed this argument on the ground that proving fraud or a substantial omission of income is a heavy burden for the Service; thus, the Service was prejudiced by the running of the three-year statute of limitations on assessment.

The burden of establishing that a Form 870-AD has been properly executed and is controlling rests on the Service. But where the agreement itself could not be produced, the Service has been allowed to establish the signed form by means of circumstantial evidence. In Cross v. United States, 149 F.3d 1190 (10th Cir. 1998), the circumstantial evidence consisted of affidavits of revenue agents that the negotiations could not have progressed without the signed form. Since the taxpayer was unable to dispute this claim, the Service prevailed.

1.   Under the principle of Lewis v. Reynolds, 284 U.S. 281 (1932), the Service may set off an otherwise barred deficiency claim against a valid refund claim, provided both arise in the same taxable year (see discussion of *Lewis v. Reynolds* in Chapter 5). See also Joyce v. Gentsch, 141 F.2d 891 (6th Cir. 1944). In light of this principle, can it be said that the Service is prejudiced if the Form 870-AD is disregarded? Is this a more valid argument for the taxpayer?

2.   If the taxpayer intends to file a subsequent refund claim, is the taxpayer ever justified in signing a Form 870-AD or is this considered a misrepresentation?

C. JEOPARDY AND TERMINATION ASSESSMENTS

Jeopardy and termination assessments are extraordinary collection devices that allow the IRS to bypass the normal assessment procedure and to make an immediate assessment if it determines that collection of the tax might be jeopardized by delay. The jeopardy and termination assessment procedures are found at §§ 6851 and 6861 of the tax code. The normal assessment procedure is reversed with a jeopardy and termination assessment because the assessment and notice and demand for payment occurs before the notice of deficiency. The Service also can immediately levy on the taxpayer's property without waiting the requisite ten days if the taxpayer does not promptly pay the tax after the notice and demand. See discussion of the collection process and the notice and demand for payment, Chapter 7.

In a jeopardy assessment, the IRS must send a notice of deficiency within 60 days of the assessment. In a termination assessment, the Service must mail the notice of deficiency for the full taxable year within 60 days of the later of the due date of the return or the date the return is filed.

According to the Internal Revenue Manual, "jeopardy/termination assessments of tax are to be used sparingly. They are to be reasonable, appropriate and limited to amounts which can be expected to protect the government." IRM 4.15.1.2 (6-30-99). Nevertheless, the potential for the Service to abuse taxpayers is great in jeopardy or termination assessments. Before 1998, no prior approval was required for a jeopardy or termination assessment. But the IRS Restructuring and Reform Act of 1998 amended § 7429(a) to require the Chief Counsel or his delegate to personally approve in writing all jeopardy and termination levies prior to assessment. Because of the potentially devastating effect of a jeopardy or termination assessment, the taxpayer is entitled to an expedited administrative and judicial post-assessment hearing under § 7429. Notice of the right to appeal a jeopardy or termination assessment must be given to the taxpayer within five days of the assessment under § 7429.

Section 6863 provides that the taxpayer may post a bond to stay the sale of any seized property. If such a bond is posted, the sale is stayed until the decision of the court becomes final, or until the expiration of the time for requesting administrative review, or until the time for filing a civil suit has expired. The property may be sold, regardless of the bond, if the taxpayer consents to the sale, or if the Service determines that the expenses of conservation and maintenance will greatly decrease the net proceeds, or if the property consists of perishable goods that will greatly decline in value. I.R.C. § 6863(b)(3).

In addition to the jeopardy and termination assessments, there is a third type of jeopardy assessment found at § 6867. This provision allows the Service to make a jeopardy or termination assessment when an individual is found in possession of a large amount of cash (over $10,000) which the individual alleges does not belong to him or to any third person whose identity is readily verifiable.

1. What is the difference between a jeopardy assessment (§ 6851) and a termination assessment (§ 6861)?

2. What protections are available to the taxpayer in a jeopardy or termination assessment?

3. What steps must the taxpayer follow in order to obtain an expedited judicial review of the jeopardy or termination assessment?

II. STATUTE OF LIMITATIONS FOR ASSESSMENT

The general statute of limitations for assessment of a deficiency is three years from the later of the due date of the return or the date the return is filed. IRC § 6501(a) and (b)(1). For administrative convenience, the Code provides for purposes of the statute of limitations, a return filed prior to the due date is treated as filed on the due date, without regard to extensions. IRC § 6501(b)(1); Reg. § 301.6501(b)-1(a).

Once the statutory period has run, the Service may not legally assess a deficiency unless the taxpayer has agreed either to an extension or a waiver of the limitations period. IRC § 6401. There are several exceptions to the general rule, however. First, some penalties may be collected without assessment, such as the penalty for failure to file information returns. See IRC § 6721. Second, some events may temporarily suspend the statute, such as the issuance of a statutory Notice of Deficiency (IRC § 6503(a)(1)), the filing of a bankruptcy petition (IRC § 6503(b)), the filing of a lawsuit to issue or enforce an administrative summons (IRC § 6503(j)), and where the taxpayer is out of the country for an extended period of time (IRC § 6503(a)). Third, an inadvertent error or a willful action of the taxpayer may result in a lengthening of the statutory period. These include a 25 percent or greater omission of an item from gross income, which will extend the statutory period from three years to six years (IRC § 6501(e)), and a fraudulent or willful attempt to evade tax, which will extend the statute indefinitely and will allow the Service to assess the tax at any time (IRC § 6501(c)). Fourth, the statute may be extended by agreement between the taxpayer and the Service, provided the agreement is made before the expiration of the statute of limitations or before the expiration of a period previously agreed upon. IRC § 6501(c)(4).

Notes

The date the return is filed generally determines the starting point of the statute of limitations. Review the rules in Chapter 3 for determining when a return is considered filed. The first day of the statutory period is the day after the return is filed. Thus, the first day of the statute of limitations on a return deemed filed on April 15 under the early return rule of § 6501(b)(1) will be April 16. See Hotel Equities Corp. v. Commissioner, 546 F.2d 725 (7th Cir. 1976) (discussing application of § 7502 and § 6501(b)(1)).

A. SUBSTANTIAL OMISSIONS OF INCOME – § 6501(e)(1)

THE COLONY, INC. v. COMMISSIONER
Supreme Court of the United States, 1958.
357 U.S. 28, 78 S.Ct. 1033, 2 L.Ed.2d 11.

MR. JUSTICE HARLAN delivered the opinion of the Court.

The sole question in this case is whether assessments by the Commissioner of two asserted tax deficiencies were barred by the three-year statute of limitations provided in the Internal Revenue Code of 1939.

* * *

The Commissioner assessed deficiencies in the taxpayer's income taxes for each of the fiscal years ending October 31, 1946, and 1947, within the extended period provided in waivers which were executed by the taxpayer more than three but less than five years [currently six years] after the returns were filed. There was no claim that the taxpayer had inaccurately reported its gross receipts. Instead, the deficiencies were based upon the Commissioner's determination that the taxpayer had understated the gross profits on the sales of certain lots of land for residential purposes as a result of having overstated the "basis" of such lots by erroneously including in their cost certain unallowable items of development expense. There was no claim that the returns were fraudulent.

The Tax Court sustained the Commissioner. It held that substantial portions of the development costs were properly disallowed, and that these errors by the taxpayer had resulted in the understatement of the taxpayer's total gross income by 77.2% and 30.7%, respectively, of the amounts reported for the taxable years 1946 and 1947. In addition, the Tax Court held that in these circumstances the [six-year] period of limitation provided for in [the Code] was applicable. It took the view that the statutory language, "omits from gross income an amount properly includible therein," embraced not merely the omission from a return of an item of income received by or accruing to a taxpayer, but also an understatement of gross income resulting from a taxpayer's miscalculation of profits through the erroneous inclusion of an excessive item of cost.

* * *

In determining the correct interpretation of [§ 6501(e)] we start with the critical statutory language, "omits from gross income an amount properly includible therein." The Commissioner states that the draftsman's use of the word "amount" (instead of, for example, "item") suggests a concentration on the quantitative aspect of the error – that is, whether or not gross income was understated by as much as 25%. This view is somewhat reinforced if, in reading the above-quoted phrase, one touches lightly on the word "omits" and bears down hard on the words "gross income," for where a cost item is overstated, as in the case before us, gross income is affected to the same degree as when a gross-receipt item of the same amount is completely omitted from a tax return.

On the other hand, the taxpayer contends that the Commissioner's reading fails to take full account of the word "omits," which Congress selected when it could have chosen another verb such as "reduces" or "understates," either of which would have pointed significantly in the Commissioner's direction. The taxpayer also points out that normally "statutory words are presumed to be used in their ordinary and usual sense, and with the meaning commonly attributable to them." "Omit" is defined in Webster's New International Dictionary as "to leave out or unmentioned; not to insert, include, or name," * * *. Relying on this definition, the taxpayer says that the statute is limited to situations in which specific receipts or accruals of income items are *left out* of the computation of gross income. * * *

Although we are inclined to think that the statute on its face lends itself more plausibly to the taxpayer's interpretation, it cannot be said that the language is unambiguous. In these circumstances we turn to the legislative history of [§ 6501(e)]. We find in that history persuasive evidence that Congress was addressing itself to the specific situation where a taxpayer actually omitted some income receipt or accrual in his computation of gross income, and not more generally to errors in that computation arising from other causes.

* * *

[Eds: The House Ways and Means Committee bill proposed an unlimited statute of limitations where a taxpayer fails to report an amount of gross income in excess of 25% of the amount of the gross income stated in the return].

The Senate Finance Committee approved of the intended coverage and language of the bill, except that it believed the statute of limitations should not be kept open indefinitely in the case of an honest but negligent taxpayer. Its report stated:

"* * * Your committee is in general accord with the policy expressed in this section of the House bill. However, it is believed that in the case of a taxpayer who makes an honest mistake, it would be unfair to keep the statute open indefinitely. For instance, a case might arise where a taxpayer failed to report a dividend because he was erroneously advised by the officers of the corporation that it was paid out of capital or he might report as income for one year an item of income which properly belonged in another year. Accordingly, your committee has provided for a 5-year [now six-year] statute in such cases." S. Rep. No. 558, 73d Cong., 2d Sess. 43-44.

* * *

The Commissioner * * * suggests that in enacting [§ 6501(e)] Congress was primarily concerned with providing for a longer period of limitations where returns contained relatively large errors adversely affecting the Treasury, and that effect can be given this purpose only by adopting the Government's broad construction of the statute. But this theory does not persuade us. For if the mere size of the error had been the principal concern of Congress, one might have expected to find the statute cast in terms of errors in the total tax due or in total taxable net income. We have been unable to find any solid support for the Government's theory in the legislative history. Instead, * * * this history shows to our satisfaction that the Congress intended an exception to the usual three-year statute of limitations only in the restricted type of situation already described.

We think that in enacting [§ 6501(e)] Congress manifested no broader purpose than to give the Commissioner an additional two years to investigate tax returns in cases where, because of a taxpayer's omission to report some taxable item, the Commissioner is at a special disadvantage in detecting errors. In such instances the return on its face provides no clue to the existence of the omitted item. On the other hand, when, as here, the understatement of a tax arises from an error in reporting an item disclosed on the face of the return the Commissioner is at no such disadvantage. And this would seem to be so whether the error be one affecting "gross income" or one, such as overstated deductions, affecting other parts of the return.   To accept the Commissioner's interpretation and to impose a [six-year] limitation when such errors affect "gross income," but a three-year limitation when they do not, not only would be to read [§ 6501(e)] more broadly than is justified by the evident reason for its enactment, but also to create a patent incongruity in the tax law.

* * * And without doing more than noting the speculative debate between the parties as to whether Congress manifested an intention to clarify or change the 1939 Code, we observe that the conclusion we reach is in harmony with the unambiguous language of § 6501(a)(1)(A) of the Internal Revenue Code of 1954.

We hold that both tax assessments before us were barred by the statute of limitations.

Reversed.

Notes and Question

If § 6501(e) applies, is the statute of limitations extended on all items on the return or only on the understated item(s)? See Colestock v. Commissioner, 102 T.C. 380 (1994).

Unfortunately, *The Colony* left many questions unanswered, such as what does the term "to omit" really mean? What is an "amount" of gross income and what does the term "gross income" really mean? These are not esoteric questions because they have become center stage in a battle between the government on one side and the courts and tax practitioners on the other. The problem has arisen recently in the context of tax shelter litigation and the central question is whether an overstatement of basis constitutes an omission of gross income under § 6501(e)(1)(A) and its companion section, § 6229(c)(2), which applies to substantial omissions from gross income by a partnership. Since many of the tax shelter transactions, such as the infamous Son-of-Boss, involved an overstatement of basis, the question is an important one for the government. In addition, the American Jobs Creation Act of 2004 (the "Jobs Act") added new § 6501(c)(10), which extends the statute of limitations for listed transactions until one year after the earlier of the date on which either the taxpayer or the material adviser discloses the required information regarding the transaction. See Chapter 2, § II.E.2 for a discussion of listed transactions. The problem, however, is that § 6501(c)(10) is effective only for those taxable years in which the statute of limitations on assessment had not expired prior to October 22, 2004, the effective date of the Jobs Act. For pre-October 22, 2004 transactions with an expired statute of limitations, § 6501(c)(10) does not revive the statute. Thus, the operation of § 6501(e)(1)(A) remains important.

The Service has argued that *The Colony* does not apply outside of the trade or business context of § 6501(e)(1)(A)(i) because that was the provision before the Supreme Court in *The Colony* (or so the Service speculates). In that provision, basis is not important because gross income is determined by gross receipts. Some courts have agreed with the Service. *See, e.g.,* CC&F Western Operations Ltd Partnership v. Commissioner, 273 F.3d 402, 406 n.2 (1st Cir. 2002) (the "arguable implication"is that the *Colony* does not apply to income other than that derived from the sale of goods and services); Brandon Ridge Partners v. United States, 2007 WL 2209129 (M.D. Fla.) (unreported) (concluding that an overstatement of basis constitutes an omission from gross income). Other courts, most notably the Tax Court, have disagreed with the Service's argument, holding that an overstatement of basis was not an omission from gross income and did not trigger the extended statute of limitations under § 6501(e)(1)(A). *See, e.g.,* Intermountain Insurance Service of Vail v. Commissioner, T.C. Memo. 2009-195, n.5 ("We are unpersuaded by respondent's attempt to distinguish and diminish the Supreme Court's holding in [*Colony*]."); Beard v. Commissioner, T.C. Memo. 2009-184 ("The principles of *Colony* apply where a taxpayer overstates his basis."). *See also* Salman Ranch Ltd. v. United States, 573 F.3d 1362 (Fed. Cir. 2009), *rev'g* 79 Fed. Cl. 189 (2007)(concluding that the *Colony* was not limited to the trade or business context); Bakersfield Energy Partners v. Commissioner, 568 F.3d 767, 778 (9th Cir. 2009)(noting that there is "no ground for suggesting that the Court intended . . . [its holding] . . . to apply differently to taxpayers in a trade or business than to other taxpayers.")

On September 24, 2009, shortly after the adverse decisions in *Intermountain* and *Salman Ranch*, Treasury issued new proposed and temporary regulations under §§ 6501(e)(1)(A) and 6229(c)(2) to "clarify" the meaning of the term "gross income" outside the trade or business context. These regulations specify that "an understated amount of gross income resulting from an overstatement of unrecovered cost or other basis constitutes an omission from gross income for purposes of § 6501(e)(1)(A)."

The IRS asked the Tax Court to vacate its decision in *Intermountain* and to reconsider it in light of the new regulations. The Tax Court refused, reasoning that under the legislative history, the statute was unambiguous and thus the regulations did not overturn the result in the *Colony* and were not entitled to *Chevron* deference. See Chapter 1, §

II.B.1.c. for a discussion of deference due regulations. The Justice Department similarly asked the Federal Circuit to reconsider its decision in *Salman Ranch* but the Federal Circuit also refused.

The IRS has refused to back down, however, and the battle lines have been clearly drawn. The courts (i.e., the Tax Court, the Ninth Circuit and the Federal Circuit) are standing firmly by their position while the IRS has stated that it will not change its position because the regulations are based on its "longstanding position" under §§ 6501(e) and 6229. One commentator has suggested that such obstinance and aggressiveness "may damage the IRS's credibility and hurt its relationship with the taxpayer community." Mark Allison, "The New Battle In An Old War: Omissions From Gross Income," 126 Tax Notes 1227, 1240 (Mar. 8, 2010). See also Jeremiah Coder, "IRS Undeterred After Tax Court's *Intermountain* Decision," 127 Tax Notes 729 (May 17, 2010).

The following case is one of the most recent decisions in the battle over the new regulations.

HOME CONCRETE AND SUPPLY, LLC v. UNITED STATES
United States Court of Appeals, Fourth Circuit, 2011.
634 F.3d 249, cert.granted 2011 WL 3322358 (2011).

WYNN, CIRCUIT JUDGE:

In *Colony, Inc. v. Commissioner of Internal Revenue*, the United States Supreme Court held that an overstatement of basis in assets resulting in an understatement of reported gross income does not constitute an "omission" from gross income for purposes of extending the general three-year statute of limitations for tax assessments. 357 U.S. 28, 78 S.Ct. 1033, 2 L.Ed.2d 1119 (1958). Because *Colony* squarely applies to this case, and because we will not defer to Treasury Regulation § 301.6501(e)-1(e), which was promulgated during this litigation and, by its own terms, does not apply to the tax year at issue, we reverse and hold that the tax assessments at issue here were untimely.

I.

In 1999, plaintiffs Stephen R. Chandler and Robert L. Pierce were the sole shareholders of plaintiff Home Oil and Coal Company, Incorporated ("Home Oil"). Mr. Pierce contemplated selling his interest in Home Oil and sought professional financial planning advice in anticipation of the transaction. This financial advice, rendered by several financial planning firms, included proposals to minimize the tax liability generated by Mr.

Pierce's sale of his interest in Home Oil. The ensuing transactions form the grounds of this dispute.

Plaintiff Home Concrete & Supply, LLC ("Home Concrete"), a pass-through entity for tax purposes, was formed on April 15, 1999. Its partners were Mr. Chandler, Mr. Pierce, Home Oil, and two trusts established for the benefit of Mr. Pierce's children (collectively "the taxpayers").

On May 13, 1999, each of the taxpayers initiated short sales[1] of United States Treasury Bonds. In the aggregate, the taxpayers received $7,472,405 in short sale proceeds. Four days later, the taxpayers transferred the short sale proceeds and margin cash to Home Concrete as capital contributions. By transferring the short sale proceeds to Home Concrete as capital contributions, the taxpayers created "outside basis" equal to the amount of the proceeds contributed.[2] The next day, May 18, 1999, Home Concrete closed the short sales by purchasing and returning essentially identical Treasury Bonds on the open market at an aggregate purchase price of $7,359,043.

On June 11, 1999, Home Oil transferred substantially all of its business assets to Home Concrete as a capital contribution. Three days later, the taxpayers (except Home Oil) transferred percentages of their respective partnership interests in Home Concrete to Home Oil as capital contributions to Home Oil. On August 31, 1999, Home Concrete sold substantially all of its assets to a third-party purchaser for $10,623,348.

In April 2000, Home Concrete and the taxpayers timely filed their tax returns for the 1999 tax year. Home Concrete elected to adjust, or "step-up," its inside basis under 26 U.S.C. ("I.R.C.") § 754 to equal the taxpayers' outside bases. See I.R.C. § 743(b)(1). Home Concrete then adjusted its inside basis to $10,527,350.53, including the amount of short sale proceeds earlier contributed by the taxpayers. As a result, Home Concrete reported a modest $69,125 .08 gain from the sale of its assets.

Home Concrete's 1999 tax return reported the basic components of the transactions. Its § 754 election form gave, for each partnership asset,

---

1.   A "short sale" is a "sale of a security that the seller does not own or has not contracted for at the time of sale, and that the seller must borrow to make delivery." Black's Law Dictionary 1456 (9th ed.2009). To close the short sale, " '[t]he short seller is obligated . . . to buy an equivalent number of shares [or substantially identical security] in order to return the borrowed [property]. In theory, the short seller makes this covering purchase using the funds he received from selling the borrowed [property].' " Kornman & Assocs., Inc. v. United States, 527 F.3d 443, 450 (5th Cir.2008) (quoting Zlotnick v. TIE Commc'ns, 836 F.2d 818, 820 (3d Cir.1988)).

2.   A partner's basis in her partnership interest is called "outside basis," and a partnership's basis in its assets is referred to as its "inside basis." Kornman, 527 F.3d at 456 n .12; see also 26 U.S.C. §§ 722-23.

an itemized accounting of the partnership's inside basis, the amount of the basis adjustment, and the post-election basis. The sum of the post-election bases is indicated at the end of the form. On its face, Home Concrete's return also showed a "Sale of U.S. Treasury Bonds" acquired on May 18, 1999 at a cost of $7,359,043, and a sale of those Bonds on May 19, 1999 for $7,472,405. The return also reported the resulting gain of $113,362. Similarly, the taxpayers' individual returns showed that "during the year the proceeds of a short sale not closed by the taxpayer in this tax year were received."

Notwithstanding these disclosures, the Internal Revenue Service ("IRS") did not investigate the taxpayers' transactions until June 2003. The IRS issued a summons to Jenkins & Gilchrist, P.C., the law firm that assisted the taxpayers with the transactions, on June 19, 2003. The parties agree that substantial compliance with the IRS summons did not occur until at least May 17, 2004.

As a result of the investigation, on September 7, 2006 the IRS issued a Final Partnership Administrative Adjustment ("FPAA"), decreasing to zero the taxpayers' reported outside bases in Home Concrete and thereby substantially increasing the taxpayers' taxable income. Specifically, the IRS reasoned that

> the purported partnership was formed and availed of solely for purposes of tax avoidance by artificially overstating basis in the partnership interests of its purported partners. . . . [T]he acquisition of any interest in the purported partnership by the purported partner, short sales of Treasury Notes, the transfer of proceeds from short sales of Treasury Notes or other assets to a partnership in return for a partnership interest, the purchase or disposition of assets by the partnership, and the distribution of those assets or proceeds from the disposition of those assets to the purported partners, and the subsequent sale of those assets to generate a loss, all within a period of 8 months, had no business purpose other than tax avoidance, lacked economic substance, and, in fact and substance, constitutes an economic sham for federal income tax purposes. Accordingly, the partnership and the transactions described above shall be disregarded in full and (1) any purported losses resulting from these transactions are not allowable as deductions; and (2) increases in basis of assets are not allowed to eliminate gain for federal income tax purposes.

Accordingly, Home Concrete deposited $1,392,118 with the IRS and sued in the District Court for the Eastern District of North Carolina to recover that amount, alleging that the FPAA was barred by the general three-year limitations period in I.R.C. § 6501(a).

In response, the IRS contended that the FPAA was timely under the six-year limitations period in § 6501(e)(1)(A). The IRS invoked the extended statute of limitations arguing that Home Concrete "omit[ted] from gross income an amount properly includable therein" and which exceeded 25% of the amount of gross income stated in Home Concrete's 1999 tax return. Home Concrete & Supply, LLC v. United States, 599 F.Supp.2d 678, 683 (E.D.N.C.2008). There was no dispute that if an amount had been omitted from Home Concrete's return, that amount exceeded the 25% threshold. Likewise, there was no dispute that the FPAA would have been timely under the six-year statute of limitations, which would have been tolled beginning six months after the date the summons issued to the date of compliance. Id. at 681 n. 5; see also I.R.C. § 7609(e)(2). By the district court's calculation, "the limitations period for the 1999 tax returns was suspended from December 20, 2003, until May 17, 2004. . . . Thus, a six-year statute, tolled, would not have run even under this most restrictive interpretation of the record until" September 14, 2006. Home Concrete & Supply, 599 F.Supp.2d at 681 n. 5.

On the other hand, the taxpayers argued that the six-year statute of limitations was inapplicable because Home Concrete's allegedly overstated basis did not constitute an omission from gross income. And even if it had been an omission, the taxpayers argued, their tax returns collectively made adequate disclosure of the transactions such that they were entitled to the safe harbor of the three-year statute of limitations under § 6501(e)(1)(B)(ii) (hereafter "safe harbor provision"). Id. at 683.

Thereafter, the district court granted partial summary judgment in the IRS's favor, ruling that "where a taxpayer overstates basis and, as a result, leaves an amount out of gross income, the taxpayer 'omits from gross income an amount properly includible therein' for purposes of § 6501(e)(1)(A)." Id. at 687. The court ordered further briefing on, among other issues, whether the taxpayers adequately disclosed any omitted amount such that the safe harbor provision applied.

After considering the supplemental briefs,[3] the district court ruled that the taxpayers failed to make adequate disclosure and therefore could not invoke the safe harbor provision. Accordingly, the district court concluded that the FPAA was timely under the six-year statute of limitations in § 6501(e)(1)(A). Home Concrete and the taxpayers appealed.

---

3. In their supplemental brief to the district court, the taxpayers stipulated "for purposes of resolving the [cross-motions for summary judgment] only, that 'they overstated the tax basis of the assets that [Home Concrete] sold in 1999 resulting in an omission [ ] from gross income in excess of 25 percent of the stated gross income amount.' "

II.

On appeal, Home Concrete and the taxpayers argue that *Colony* establishes that an overstated tax basis does not constitute an omission from gross income for purposes of extending the limitations period for assessments. We review this question of law *de novo*.

In *Colony*, the IRS alleged that a taxpayer "understated the gross profits on the sales of certain lots of land for residential purposes as a result of having overstated the 'basis' of such lots by erroneously including in their cost certain unallowable items of development expense." 357 U.S. at 30. The IRS further contended that the amount left out of gross income because of the overstated basis exceeded 25% of the amount of gross income stated in the relevant tax returns. The IRS argued that its assessments were therefore timely under the extended five-year statute of limitations in former I.R.C. § 275(c). Id. at 30-31. That section stated that:

> If the taxpayer omits from gross income an amount properly includable therein which is in excess of 25 per centum of the amount of gross income stated in the return, the tax may be assessed, or a proceeding in court for the collection of such tax may be begun without assessment, at any time within 5 years after the return was filed.

26 U.S.C. § 275(c) (1939).

The Supreme Court in *Colony* acknowledged that former § 275(c) was ambiguous and did not clearly answer whether Congress intended an overstated basis to constitute an omission from gross income stated in the return. The Court found in the legislative history "persuasive evidence that Congress was addressing itself to the specific situation where a taxpayer actually omitted some income receipt or accrual in his computation of gross income, and not more generally to errors in that computation arising from other causes." *Id*. at 33. According to the Court, "in enacting [former §] 275(c) Congress manifested no broader purpose than to give the Commissioner an additional two years to investigate tax returns in cases where, because of a taxpayer's omission to report some taxable item, the Commissioner is at a special disadvantage in detecting errors." *Id*. at 37. The Court therefore refused to construe "omits" broadly and instead restricted its applicability to situations where taxpayers actually fail to report income.

Notably, in dicta, the Supreme Court also stated that its conclusion was "in harmony with the *unambiguous* language of section 6501(e)(1)(A)"- the section at issue in this case. *Id*. (emphasis added). In

1954, Congress recodified former § 275(c) at § 6501(e)(1)(A). Congress extended the limitations period from five years to six, and added the following additional subsections:

(i) In the case of a trade or business, the term "gross income" means the total of the amounts received or accrued from the sale of goods or services (if such amounts are required to be shown on the return) prior to diminution by the cost of such sales or services; and

(ii) In determining the amount omitted from gross income, there shall not be taken into account any amount which is omitted from gross income stated in the return if such amount is disclosed in the return, or in a statement attached to the return, in a manner adequate to apprise the Secretary or his delegate of the nature and amount of such item.

Section 6501(e)(1)(A) and former § 275(c) are otherwise essentially identical.

In this case, the district court distinguished *Colony* on the ground that its holding is limited to cases in which the taxpayer is a trade or business selling goods or services. *Home Concrete & Supply*, 599 F.Supp.2d at 685-86; *accord*, e.g., Beard v. Comm'r, No. 09-3741, slip op. at 8-9 (7th Cir. Jan.26, 2011) (holding that *Colony* only applies in the trade or business context); CC & FW. Operations Ltd. P'ship v. Comm'r, 273 F.3d 402, 406 n. 2 (1st Cir.2001) (noting, in dicta, the "arguable implication" that the holding of *Colony* applies only to sales of goods or services by a trade or business). In doing so, the district court relied heavily upon the Court of Federal Claims' decision in Salman Ranch, Ltd. v. United States, 79 Fed.Cl. 189 (2007), which has since been reversed by the Federal Circuit. 573 F.3d 1362 (Fed.Cir.2009). The Federal Circuit expressly refused to limit *Colony*'s application to sales of goods or services by a trade or business because nothing in *Colony* suggests such a limitation. *Salman Ranch*, 573 F.3d at 1373; see also Bakersfield Energy Partners, L.P. v. Comm'r, 568 F.3d 767, 778 (9th Cir.2009) ("There is no ground for suggesting that the [*Colony*] Court intended the same language in § 275(c) to apply differently to taxpayers in a trade or business than to other taxpayers."); Grapevine Imports, Ltd. v. United States, 77 Fed.Cl. 505, 511 (2007) ("[T]his court sees no basis for limiting the Supreme Court's decision [in *Colony*] to sales of goods or services by a trade or business."); UTAM, Ltd. v. Comm'r, 98 T.C.M. (CCH) 422, *3 (2009) (same).

Like the Ninth and Federal Circuits, we hold that the Supreme Court in *Colony* straightforwardly construed the phrase "omits from gross income," unhinged from any dependency on the taxpayer's identity as a trade or business selling goods or services. There is, therefore, no ground to conclude that the holding in *Colony* is limited to cases involving a trade or business selling goods or services. See *Salman Ranch*, 573 F.3d at 1373 ("We are not prepared to conclude-based simply upon the Court's reference to ambiguity in § 275(c) and the lack thereof in § 6501(e)(1)(A)-that the Court's facially unqualified holding nevertheless carries with it a qualification.").

Further, the Supreme Court's discussion of the legislative history behind former § 275(c) is equally compelling with regard to current § 6501(e)(1)(A). The language the Court construed in former § 275(c)-"omits from gross income an amount properly includable therein"-is identical to the language at issue in § 6501(e)(1)(A). Because there has been no material change between former § 275(c) and current § 6501(e)(1)(A), and no change at all to the most pertinent language, we are not free to construe an omission from gross income as something other than a failure to report "some income receipt or accrual." *Colony*, 357 U.S. at 33; see also *Bakersfield Energy Partners, L.P.*, 568 F.3d at 778 (concluding that *Colony* forecloses the argument that an overstated basis can constitute an omission from gross income for purposes of extending the statute of limitations under § 6501(e)(1)(A)); *Salman Ranch*, 573 F.3d at 1377 (same). Thus, we join the Ninth and Federal Circuits and conclude that *Colony* forecloses the argument that Home Concrete's overstated basis in its reporting of the short sale proceeds resulted in an omission from its reported gross income.

III.

The IRS presses another path around *Colony*. After concluding that the IRS's position regarding the meaning of "omits" was barred by *Colony*, the Ninth Circuit commented that the "IRS may have the authority to promulgate a reasonable reinterpretation of an ambiguous provision of the tax code, even if its interpretation runs contrary to the Supreme Court's 'opinion as to the best reading' of the provision." *Bakersfield Energy Partners*, 568 F.3d at 778 (quoting Nat'l Cable & Telecomms. Ass'n v. Brand X Internet Servs., 545 U.S. 967, 982-83, 125 S.Ct. 2688, 162 L.Ed.2d 820 (2005)).

Perhaps in response to the Ninth Circuit's cue, the IRS promulgated a temporary regulation on September 28, 2009, which became final during the pendency of this appeal. Treas. Reg. § 301 .6501(e)-1. The IRS claims that this regulation is entitled to controlling deference under Chevron U.S.A. Inc. v. Natural Resources Defense Council, Inc., 467 U.S. 837, 104 S.Ct. 2778, 81 L.Ed.2d 694 (1984).

The regulation states that:

(iii) For purposes of paragraph (a)(1)(i) of this section, the term gross income, as it relates to any income other than from the sale of goods or services in a trade or business, has the same meaning as provided under section 61(a), and includes the total of the amounts received or accrued, to the extent required to be shown on the return. In the case of amounts received or accrued that relate to the disposition of property, and except as provided in paragraph (a)(1)(ii) of this section, gross income means the excess of the amount realized from the disposition of the property over the unrecovered cost or other basis of the property. Consequently, except as provided in paragraph (a)(1)(ii) of this section, an understated amount of gross income resulting from an overstatement of unrecovered cost or other basis constitutes an omission from gross income for purposes of section 6501(e)(1)(A).

. . .

(e) Effective/applicability date-(1) Income Taxes. Paragraph (a) of this section applies to taxable years with respect to which the period for assessing tax was open on or after September 24, 2009.

Treas. Reg. § 301.6501(e)-1(a)(1)(iii)-1(e)(1) (2010). The IRS asks us to apply the regulation retroactively to produce the result it desires in this case. We decline to do so for several reasons.

First, the 1999 tax year at issue in this case, for which tax returns were due by April 2000, is well beyond the reach of the regulation's express period of applicability. Even assuming *arguendo* that the six-year statute of limitations applied, pursuant to the regulation, the "period for assessing tax" would have expired, according to the district court's unchallenged finding, on September 14, 2006. Thus, the period for assessing tax for the 1999 tax year expired long before September 24, 2009. By its own terms, the regulation does not apply here.[4]

The IRS urges a different interpretation of the regulation's applicability clause in the preamble to Treasury Decision 9511. The preamble suggests that the "six-year period for assessing tax" in § 6501(e)(1) remains open for "all taxable years ... that are the subject of any case pending before any court of competent jurisdiction (including

---

4.   In UTAM, the Tax Court noted that the IRS (curiously) did not rely on the temporary regulation, even though it had been promulgated while that case was still pending. 98 T.C.M. (CCH) at *1 n. 2. We observe that the timeline in this case is virtually identical to the timeline in UTAM: The IRS issued an FPAA on October 13, 2006, alleging that the taxpayer had omitted gross income by overstating basis in its tax return for the 1999 tax year. Id. at *1-2. The IRS did not ask the Tax Court to apply the temporary regulation retroactively in UTAM yet asks this Court to do so in this factually analogous case.

the United States Tax Court and Court of Federal Claims) in which a decision had not become final (within the meaning of [26 U.S.C. §] 7481)." Because this case was not finally resolved as of September 24, 2009, the IRS argues that § 6501(e)(1)'s six-year period for assessing tax remains open and Treasury Regulation § 301.6501(e)-1(e) applies. We cannot agree.

With this logic, the IRS attempts to re-draft I.R.C. § 6501. In the statute, Congress made clear that the window for tax assessments, barring special circumstances, closes after three years. I.R.C. § 6501(a). In the event of an omission, the window closes after six years. I.R.C. § 6501(e). And Congress specifically listed circumstances, such as fraud, in which the assessment window remains open without limitation. *Id.* § 6501(c). Congress unambiguously stated its intent to close the period for assessing tax within six years after a return is filed, except in cases of fraud. Accordingly, the IRS's argument that the period for assessing tax is open-or indeed may be re-opened, as would be the case here-so long as litigation is pending is contrary to the clearly and unambiguously expressed intent of Congress and must fail. United States v. Mead, 533 U.S. 218, 227, 121 S.Ct. 2164, 150 L.Ed.2d 292 (2001) (stating that an agency's interpretation is not binding on courts if it is "manifestly contrary to the statute"). Not surprisingly, the Tax Court rejected the same argument as to the substantially identical applicability clause in the temporary regulation. Intermountain Ins. Serv. of Vail, LLC v. Comm'r, 134 T.C. No. 11, *4-6 (2010) (rejecting the IRS's argument as circular and contrary to the plain language of the regulations).

Second, even putting the applicability clause aside, *Chevron* deference is warranted only when a treasury regulation interprets an ambiguous statute. Mayo Found. for Med. Educ. & Research v. United States, 562 U.S. ----, ----, No. 09-837, slip op. at 6-7 (Jan. 11, 2011); *see also Brand X Internet Servs.*, 545 U.S. at 980; *Chevron*, 467 U.S. at 842-43. While we are aware that lower courts are divided regarding whether an overstated basis constitutes an omission from gross income, the Supreme Court's reference to "the *unambiguous* language of section 6501(e)(1)(A)" cannot be ignored. Colony, 357 U.S. at 37 (emphasis added). Because the regulation here interprets "omits from gross income" under § 6501(e)(1)(A), and the Supreme Court declared that statute unambiguous, we do not believe that the regulation is entitled to controlling deference. See *Chevron*, 467 U.S. at 842-43 ("If the intent of Congress is clear, that is the end of the matter; for the courts, as well as the agency, must give effect to the unambiguously expressed intent of Congress.").

Finally, we are not persuaded by the IRS's argument that the regulation should apply retroactively to this case as a clarification of law established in *Colony* and other cases. The Supreme Court has acknowledged that a subsequent agency interpretation of an ambiguous statute may displace an earlier judicial construction of the same provision. *Brand X Internet Servs.*, 545 U.S. at 982-83. But again, the Supreme Court stated in *Colony* that § 6501(e)(1)(A) is unambiguous as to the very issue to which the regulation purports to speak. The regulation is not, therefore, a mere clarification. Rather, if applied, the regulation would change the law governing the taxpayers' 1999 tax returns and thereby subject the taxpayers to liability to which they would not have been subject under pre-regulation law. See United States v. Capers, 61 F.3d 1100, 1110 (4th Cir.1995) (declining to apply an amendment to the United States Sentencing Guidelines retroactively because the amendment changed Fourth Circuit law so as to deprive the defendant of a benefit to which he would have been entitled under pre-amendment law).

Because *Colony* was established law when the taxpayers filed their returns in April 2000, we refuse to apply Treasury Regulation § 301.6501(e)-1(e), which purports to establish a rule contrary to *Colony* to subject the taxpayers to the extended limitations period ten years later. See Levy v. Sterling Holding Co., 544 F.3d 493, 506 (3d Cir.2008) ("[W]here a new rule constitutes a clarification-rather than a substantive change-of the law as it existed beforehand, the application of that new rule to pre-promulgation conduct necessarily does *not* have an impermissible retroactive effect"); cf. Smiley v. Citibank (South Dakota), N.A., 517 U.S. 735, 744 n. 3, 116 S.Ct. 1730, 135 L.Ed.2d 25 (1996) (stating that an agency interpretation does not have an impermissible retroactive effect where there was previously no clear agency guidance).

IV.

In sum, we conclude that the Supreme Court's holding in *Colony* applies to § 6501(e)(1)(A). An overstated basis in property is not an omission from gross income that extends the limitations period in § 6501(e)(1)(A). Accordingly, Home Concrete's overstated basis in the short sale proceeds did not trigger the six-year statute of limitations. Moreover, Treasury Regulation § 301.6501(e)-1(e), by the plain terms of its applicability clause, does not apply to the tax year at issue in this case and is furthermore not entitled to deference. The general three-year statute of limitations in § 6501(a) applies, making the FPAA here untimely. We reverse the district court's judgment to the contrary.

WILKINSON, CIRCUIT JUDGE, concurring:

I am happy to concur in Judge Wynn's fine opinion in this case. The *Chevron* test is straightforward enough when it comes to post-*Chevron* cases. But it is sometimes difficult to determine whether pre-*Chevron* decisions are based upon "*Chevron* step one" (the plain command of the statute) or upon "*Chevron* step two" (a permissible construction of the statute). *Mayo Found. for Med. Educ. & Research v. United States*, No. 09-837, slip op. at 6-7 (U.S. Jan. 11, 2011). Certainly Justice Harlan in Colony, Inc. v. Commissioner, 357 U.S. 28, 78 S.Ct. 1033, 2 L.Ed.2d 1119 (1958), had no occasion to ponder the permutations of the *Chevron* test, which came down in 1984.

Here, however, I am persuaded that the Supreme Court rested its judgment in *Colony* on the plain language of the statute, which then, as now, stated that the extended statute of limitations for assessing tax liability applies "[i]f the taxpayer *omits* from gross income an amount properly includible therein." 26 U.S.C. § 275(c) (1939) (emphasis added); see 26 U.S.C. § 6501(e)(1)(A) (current version). In other words, I believe that *Colony* was decided under *Chevron* step one.

Lawyers of course are adept at finding ambiguity, and language of course is by its nature imprecise. One need not consult a dictionary, however, to understand that the plain meaning of "omit" is "to leave out" or "to fail to mention." The taxpayers here did not omit, leave out, or fail to mention their transaction. Instead, they provided the details on their returns. To be sure, the IRS asserts that the returns overstated Home Concrete's basis and thus understated the overall tax liability resulting from the sale of its assets. But as the Court noted in *Colony*, if Congress had been concerned with that problem, "it could have chosen another verb such as 'reduces' or 'understates,' either of which would have pointed significantly in the Commissioner's direction." *Colony*, 357 U.S. at 32.

I recognize there is some language in *Colony* suggesting that the Court looked at legislative history or thought that § 275(c) was ambiguous. See *Colony*, 357 U.S. at 33 ("Although we are inclined to think that the statute on its face lends itself more plausibly to the taxpayer's interpretation, it cannot be said that the language is unambiguous. In these circumstances we turn to the legislative history of § 275(c)."). But that language seems to me secondary in importance to the thrust of the opinion and to the Court's argument that "in enacting § 275(c) Congress manifested no broader purpose than to give the Commissioner [additional time] to investigate tax returns in cases where, because of a taxpayer's omission to report some taxable item, the Commissioner is at a special disadvantage in detecting errors." Id. at 36.

More importantly, as Judge Wynn notes, the Court observed that its decision was "in harmony with the *unambiguous* language of" 26 U.S.C. § 6501(e)(1)(A), the successor provision to § 275(c) and the provision at issue here. See id. at 37 (emphasis added).

I appreciate that *Chevron* and National Cable & Telecommunications Ass'n v. Brand X Internet Services, 545 U.S. 967, 125 S.Ct. 2688, 162 L.Ed.2d 820 (2005), afford agencies considerable discretion in their areas of expertise. As *Brand X* put it, "*Chevron* established a presumption that Congress, when it left ambiguity in a statute meant for implementation by an agency, . . . desired the agency (rather than the courts) to possess whatever degree of discretion the ambiguity allows." *Brand X*, 545 U.S. at 982. The Supreme Court's recent decision in *Mayo Foundation* likewise affords full *Chevron* deference to Treasury Regulations, concluding that the Treasury Department's interpretations of ambiguous statutes will stand if they are "a 'reasonable interpretation' of the enacted text." *Mayo Found.*, slip op. at 12 (quoting *Chevron*, 467 U.S. at 844). Given the fact that government today is an enterprise of unprecedented complexity, this makes perfect sense. Nor do judges harbor any desire to impair the mission of the IRS in a day of staggering budget deficits.

Yet it remains the case that agencies are not a law unto themselves. No less than any other organ of government, they operate in a system in which the last words in law belong to Congress and the Supreme Court. What the IRS seeks to do in extending the statutory limitations period goes against what I believe are the plain instructions of Congress, which have not been changed, and the plain words of the Court, which have not been retracted. See *Colony*, 357 U.S. at 37.

This seems to me something of an inversion of the universe and to pass the point where the beneficial application of agency expertise gives way to a lack of accountability and a risk of arbitrariness. We do not stand alone in reaching this determination; other courts have similarly rebuffed the IRS's repeated attempts to adopt the six-year statute of limitations for omissions of gross income so as to cover misleading statements in tax returns that would result in tax deficiencies. See Salman Ranch Ltd. v. United States, 573 F.3d 1362, 1372-74 (Fed.Cir.2009); Bakersfield Energy Partners, L.P. v. Comm'r, 568 F.3d 767, 778 (9th Cir.2009); Grapevine Imports, Ltd. v. United States, 77 Fed.Cl. 505, 511-12 (2007); Intermountain Ins. Serv. of Vail, LLC v. Comm'r, 134 T.C. No. 11, at *6-*8 (2010). These courts have recognized that regardless of whether the IRS's position is sound as a matter of policy, it is simply not the law.

We have been told many times to leave to the Court "the prerogative of overruling its own decisions." See Rodriguez de Quijas v. Shearson/Am. Express, Inc., 490 U.S. 477, 484, 109 S.Ct. 1917, 104 L.Ed.2d 526 (1989). If that injunction has been issued to the circuit courts, it assuredly applies to agencies in situations where the Court has interpreted the plain language of a statutory command. Maybe Congress will conclude at some point that the six-year period should apply to declarations that fall short of omissions or the Court may decide that *Colony* was somehow, after all, a *Chevron* step two case. But those decisions are neither ours nor the agency's to make. *Chevron, Brand X,* and more recently, *Mayo Foundation* rightly leave agencies with a large and beneficial role, but they do not leave courts with no role where the very language of the law is palpably at stake. There is a balance to be struck here, and courts still must play a part in determining where "here" is. The disruption of that balance in this case seems clear and evident.

Notes

The regulations at issue in *Home Concrete* have been criticized on several grounds. First and foremost is the fact that they are a result driven end-run around the adverse judicial decisions such as *Intermountain* and *Salman Ranch.* They represent a serious attempt by the IRS to gain a litigation advantage in tax shelter cases. Second, the regulations would apply retroactively to revive limitations periods that otherwise would have elapsed. Third, the regulations were not properly issued in accordance with the APA notice and comment rulemaking procedure, and there was no qualifying exception to excuse this lapse. Fourth is the lack of a strong tax policy argument to support the regulations.

The Fifth Circuit in Burks v. United States, 2011 WL 438640, reached the same conclusion as the Fourth Circuit that the temporary regulations defining an "omission from gross income" under § 6501(e) to include an understatement of income attributable to an overstatement of basis were "an unreasonable interpretation of settled law," and therefore they did not apply to the taxpayers whom the government alleged had improperly inflated their basis in partnership assets. *Id.* at *12-*13. However, these decisions conflict with the decision of the Seventh Circuit in Beard v. Commissioner, 2011 WL 222249. In *Beard,* the court held that the *Colony* was limited to the 1939 Code and thus was not controlling. The court went to hold that under a plain meaning of § 6501(e)(1)(A), the government was correct that an overstatement of basis constitutes an omission from gross income. Given the clear conflict among the circuits, the Supreme Court granted certiorari in *Home Concrete* to resolve this issue under § 6501(e). 2011 WL 3322358.

B. AMENDED RETURNS

If an amended return is filed on or before the due date of the original return, the amended return is considered the return for the taxable year. Thus the amount of any additional tax shown on the amended return will not constitute a deficiency, and the taxpayer will not be liable for penalties or interest, provided the tax liability is paid by the due date. On the other hand, if a taxpayer files an amended return after the due date of the original return, the Service has the discretion to accept or reject the return, Rev. Rul. 83-36, 1983-1 C.B. 358, although the Service may not abuse this discretion. Under Reg. § 301.6211-1(a), the amount of any tax shown on an amended return filed after the original due date is considered a tax shown on the return. Therefore, it does not constitute a deficiency, and penalties and interest on this amount may be assessed immediately.

BADARACCO v. COMMISSIONER
Supreme Court of the United States, 1984.
464 U.S. 386, 104 S.Ct. 756, 78 L.Ed.2d 549.

MR. JUSTICE BLACKMUN delivered the opinion of the Court.

These cases focus upon § 6501 of the Internal Revenue Code of 1954, 26 U.S.C. § 6501. Subsection (a) of that statute establishes a general 3-year period of limitations "after the return was filed" for the assessment of income and certain other federal taxes. Subsection (c)(1) of § 6501, however, provides an exception to the 3-year period when there is "a false or fraudulent return with the intent to evade tax." The tax then may be assessed "at any time."

The issue before us is the proper application of §§ 6501(a) and (c)(1) to the situation where a taxpayer files a false or fraudulent return but later files a nonfraudulent amended return. May a tax then be assessed more than three years after the filing of the amended return?

II.

Our task here is to determine the proper construction of the statute of limitations Congress has written for tax assessments. This Court long ago pronounced the standard: "Statutes of limitation sought to be applied to bar rights of the Government, must receive a strict construction in favor of the Government." E.I. du Pont de Nemours & Co. v. Davis, 264 U.S. 456, 462 (1924). * * *

We naturally turn first to the language of the statute. Section 6501(a) sets forth the general rule: a 3-year period of limitations on the assessment of tax. Section 6501(e)(1)(A) * * * provides an extended limitations period for the situation where the taxpayer's return nonfraudulently omits more than 25% of his gross income; in a situation of that kind, assessment now is permitted "at any time within 6 years after the return was filed."

Both the 3-year rule and the 6-year rule, however, explicitly are made inapplicable in circumstances covered by § 6501(c). This subsection identifies three situations in which the Commissioner is allowed an unlimited period within which to assess tax. Subsection (c)(1) relates to "a false or fraudulent return with the intent to evade tax" and provides that the tax then may be assessed "at any time." Subsection (c)(3) covers the case of a failure to file a return at all (whether or not due to fraud) and provides that an assessment then also may be made "at any time." Subsection (c)(2) sets forth a similar rule for the case of a "willful attempt in any manner to defeat or evade tax" other than income, estate, and gift taxes.

All these provisions appear to be unambiguous on their face, and it therefore would seem to follow that the present cases are squarely controlled by the clear language of § 6501(c)(1). Petitioners Badaracco concede that they filed initial returns that were "false or fraudulent with the intent to evade tax." * * * Section 6501(c)(1), with its unqualified language, then allows the tax to be assessed "at any time." Nothing is present in the statute that can be construed to suspend its operation in the light of a fraudulent filer's subsequent repentant conduct. Neither is there anything in the wording of § 6501(a) that itself enables a taxpayer to reinstate the section's general 3-year limitations period by filing an amended return. Indeed, as this Court recently has noted, Hillsboro National Bank v. Commissioner, 460 U.S. 370, 378-380, n.10 (1983), the Internal Revenue Code does not explicitly provide either for a taxpayer's filing, or for the Commissioner's acceptance, of an amended return; instead, an amended return is a creature of administrative origin and grace. Thus, when Congress provided for assessment at any time in the case of a false or fraudulent "return," it plainly included by this language a false or fraudulent *original* return. In this connection, we note that until the decision of the Tenth Circuit in Dowell v. Commissioner, 614 F.2d 1263 (1980), courts consistently had held that the operation of § 6501 and its predecessors turned on the nature of the taxpayer's original, and not his amended, return.[8]

The substantive operation of the fraud provisions of the Code itself confirms the conclusion that § 6501(c)(1) permits assessment at any time in fraud cases regardless of a taxpayer's later repentance. It is established that a taxpayer who submits a fraudulent return does not purge the fraud by subsequent voluntary disclosure; the fraud was committed, and the offense completed, when the original return was prepared and filed. See, e.g., United States v. Habig, 390 U.S. 222 (1968); Plunkett v. Commissioner, 465 F.2d 299, 302, 303 (CA& 1972). "Any other result would make sport of the so-called fraud penalty. A taxpayer who had filed a fraudulent return would merely take his chances that the fraud would not be investigated or discovered, and then, if an investigation were made, would simply pay the tax which he owed anyhow and thereby nullify the fraud penalty." George M. Still, Inc. v. Commissioner, 19 T.C. 1072, 1077 (1953), aff'd, 218 F.2d 639 (CA2 1955). In short, once a fraudulent return has been filed, the case remains one "of a false or fraudulent return," regardless of the taxpayer's later revised conduct, for purposes of criminal prosecution and civil fraud liability under § 6653(b). It likewise should remain such a case for purposes of the unlimited assessment period specified by § 6501(c)(3).

We are not persuaded by [eds: the Petitioner's] suggestion that § 6501(c)(1) should be read merely to suspend the commencement of the limitations period while the fraud remains uncorrected. The Tenth Circuit in Dowell v. Commissioner, supra, made an observation to that effect, stating that the 3-year limitations period was "put in limbo" pending further taxpayer action. 614 F.2d, at 1266. The language of the statute, however, is contrary to this suggestion. Section 6501(c)(1) does not "suspend" the operation of § 6501(a) until a fraudulent filer makes a voluntary disclosure. Section 6501(c)(1) makes no reference at all to § 6501(a); it simply provides that the tax may be assessed "at any time." And § 6501(a) itself contains no mechanism for its operation when a

---

8. The significance of the original, and not the amended, return has been stressed in other, but related, contexts. It thus has been held consistently that the filing of an amended return in a nonfraudulent situation does not serve to extend the period within which the Commissioner may assess a deficiency. See, e.g., Zellerbach Paper Co. v. Helvering, 293 U.S. 172 (!934); National Paper Products Co. v. Helvering, 293 U.S. 183 (1934); National Refining Co. v. Commissioner, 1 B.T.A. 236 (1924). It also has been held that the filing of an amended return does not serve to reduce the period within which the Commissioner may assess taxes where the original return omitted enough income to trigger the operation of the extended limitations period provided by § 6501(e) or its predecessors. See, e.g., Houston v. Commissioner, 38 T.C. 486 (1962); Goldring v. Commissioner, 20 T.C. 79 (1953). And the period of limitations for filing a refund claim under the predecessor of § 6501(a) begins to run on the filing of the original, not the amended, return. Kaltreider Construction, Inc. v. United States, 303 F.2d 366, 368 (CA3), cert. denied, 371 U.S. 877 (1962).

fraudulent filer repents. By its very terms, it does not apply to a case, such a one of "a false or fraudulent return," that is "otherwise provided" for in § 6501. When Congress intends only a temporary suspension of the running of a limitations period, it knows how unambiguously to accomplish that result. See, e.g., §§ 6503(a)(1), (a)(2), (b), (c), and (d).

The weakness of petitioners' proposed statutory construction is demonstrated further by its impact on § 6501(e)(1)(A), which provides an extended limitations period whenever a taxpayer's return nonfraudulently omits more than 25% of his gross income.

Under petitioners' reasoning, a taxpayer who *fraudulently* omits 25% of his gross income gains the benefit of the 3-year limitations period by filing an amended return. Yet a taxpayer who *nonfraudulently* omits 25% of his gross income cannot gain that benefit by filing an amended return; instead, he must live with the 6-year period specified in § 6501(e)(1)(A). We agree with the conclusion of the Court of Appeals in the instant cases that Congress could not have intended to "create a situation in which persons who committed willful, deliberate fraud would be in a better position" than those who understated their income inadvertently and without fraud. 693 F.2d, at 302.

We therefore conclude that the plain and unambiguous language of § 6501(c)(1) would permit the Commissioner to assess "at any time" the tax for a year in which the taxpayer has filed "a false or fraudulent return," despite any subsequent disclosure the taxpayer might make. Petitioners attempt to evade the consequences of this language by arguing that their original returns were "nullities." Alternatively, they urge a nonliteral construction of the statute based on considerations of policy and practicality. We now turn successively to those proposals.

III.

Petitioners argue that their original returns, to the extent they were fraudulent, were "nullities" for statues of limitations purposes. Inasmuch as the original return is a nullity, it is said, the amended return is necessarily "the return" referred to in § 6501(a). And if that return is nonfraudulent, § 6501(c)(1) is inoperative and the normal 3-year limitations period applies. This nullity notion does not persuade us, for it is plain that "the return" referred to in § 6501(a) is the original, not the amended, return.

Petitioners do not contend that their fraudulent original returns were nullities for purposes of the Code generally. There are numerous provisions in the Code that relate to civil and criminal penalties for submitting or assisting in the preparation of false or fraudulent returns;

their presence makes clear that a document which on its face plausibly purports to be in compliance, and which is signed by the taxpayer is a return despite its inaccuracies. Neither do petitioners contend that their original returns were nullities for all purposes of § 6501. They contend, instead, that a fraudulent return is a nullity only for the limited purpose of applying § 6501(a). The word "return," however, appears no less than 64 times in § 6501. Surely, Congress cannot rationally be thought to have given that word one meaning in § 6501(a), and a totally different meaning in §§ 6501(b) through (q).

* * *

We conclude, therefore, that nothing in the statutory language, the structure of the Code, or the decided cases supports the contention that a fraudulent return is a nullity for statute of limitations purposes.

IV.

Petitioners contend that a nonliteral reading should be accorded the statute on grounds of equity to the repentant taxpayer and tax policy.

* * *

The cases before us, however, concern the construction of existing statutes. The relevant question is not whether, as an abstract matter, the rule advocated by petitioners accords with good policy. The question we must consider is whether the policy petitioners favor is that which Congress effectuated by its enactment of § 6501. Courts are not authorized to rewrite a statute because they might deem its effects susceptible of improvement. This is especially so when courts construe a statute of limitations, which "must receive strict construction in favor of the Government." E.I. du Pont de Nemours & Co. v. Davis, 264 U.S., at 462.

We conclude that, even were we free to do so, there is no need to twist § 6501(c)(1) beyond the contours of its plain and unambiguous language in order to comport with good policy, for substantial policy considerations support its literal language. First, fraud cases ordinarily are more difficult to investigate than cases marked for routine tax audits. Where fraud had been practiced, there is a distinct possibility that the taxpayer's underlying records will have been falsified or even destroyed. The filing of an amended return, then, may not diminish the amount of effort required to verify the correct tax liability. Even though the amended return proves to be an honest one, its filing does not necessarily "[remove] the Commissioner from the disadvantageous position in which he was originally placed."

Second, the filing of a document styled "amended return" does not fundamentally change the nature of a tax fraud investigation. An amended return, however accurate it ultimately may prove to be, comes with no greater guarantee of trustworthiness than any other submission. It comes carrying no special or significant imprimatur; instead, it comes from a taxpayer who already has made false statements under penalty of perjury. A responsible examiner cannot accept the information furnished on an amended return as a substitute for a thorough investigation into the existence of fraud. We see no "tax policy" justification for holding that an amended return has the singular effect of shortening the unlimited assessment period specified in §§ 6501(c)(1) to the usual three years. Fraud cases differ from other civil tax cases in that it is the Commissioner who has the burden of proof on the issue of fraud. An amended return, of course, may constitute an admission of substantial underpayment, but it will not ordinarily constitute an admission of fraud. And the three years may not be enough time for the Commissioner to prove fraudulent intent.

Third, the difficulties that attend a civil fraud investigation are compounded where * * * the Commissioner's initial findings lead him to conclude that the case should be referred to the Department of Justice for criminal prosecution. The period of limitations for prosecuting criminal tax fraud is generally six years. See § 6531. Once a criminal referral has been made, the Commissioner is under well-known restraints on the civil side and often will find it difficult to complete his civil investigation within the normal 3-year period; the taxpayer's filing of an amended return will not make any difference in this respect. As a practical matter, therefore, the Commissioner frequently is forced to place a civil audit in abeyance where a criminal prosecution is recommended.

* * *

Neither are we persuaded by [the] argument that a literal reading of the statute "punishes" the taxpayer who repentantly files an amended return. * * * The amended return does not change the status of the taxpayer; he is left in precisely the same position he was in before. It might be argued that Congress should provide incentives to taxpayers to disclose their fraud voluntarily. Congress, however, has not done so in § 6501. That legislative judgment is controlling here.

V.

Petitioners contend, finally, that a literal reading of § 6501(c) produces a disparity in treatment between a taxpayer who in the first instance files a fraudulent return and one who fraudulently fails to file any return at all. This, it is said, would elevate one form of tax fraud over another.

The argument centers in § 6501(c)(3), which provides that in a case of failure to file a return, the tax may be assessed "at any time." It is settled that this section ceases to apply once a return has been filed for a particular year, regardless of whether that return is filed late and even though the failure to file a timely return in the first instance was due to fraud. This, however, does not mean that § 6501 should be read to produce the same result in each of the two situations. From the language employed in the respective subsections of § 6501, we conclude that Congress intended different limitations results. Section 6501(c)(3) applies to a "failure to file a return." It makes no reference to a failure to file a timely return (cf. §§ 6651(a)(1) and 7203), nor does it speak of a fraudulent failure to file. The section literally becomes inapplicable once a return has been filed. Section 6501(c)(1), in contrast, applies in the case of "a false or fraudulent return." The fact that a fraudulent filer subsequently submits an amended return does not make the case any less one of a false or fraudulent return. Thus although there may be some initial superficial plausibility to this argument on the part of petitioners, we conclude that the argument cannot prevail. If the result contended for by petitioners is to be the rule, Congress must make it so in clear and unmistakable language.

The judgment of the Court of Appeals in each of these cases is affirmed.

It is so ordered.

JUSTICE STEVENS, dissenting.

The plain language of § 6501(c)(1) * * * conveys a different message to me than it does to the Court. That language is clear enough: "In the case of a false or fraudulent return with the intent to evade tax, the tax may be assessed, or a proceeding in court for collection of such tax may be begun without assessment, at any time." 26 U.S.C. § 6501(c)(1). What is not clear to me is why this is a case of "a false or fraudulent return."

* * * [T]he Commissioner assessed deficiencies based on concededly nonfraudulent returns. The taxpayers' alleged prior fraud was not the basis for the Commissioner's action. Indeed, whether or not the

Commissioner was obligated to accept petitioners' amended returns, he in fact elected to do so and to use them as the basis for his assessment. When the Commissioner initiates a deficiency proceeding on the basis of a nonfraudulent return, I do not believe that the resulting case is one "of a false or fraudulent return."

* * *

In light of the purposes and common law background of the statute, as well as this Court's previous treatment of what a "return" sufficient to commence the running of the limitations period is, it seems apparent that an assessment based on a nonfraudulent amended return does not fall within § 6501(c)(1). Once the amended return is filed the rationale for disregarding the limitations period is absent. The period of concealment is over, and under general common-law principles the limitations period should begin to run. The filing of the return means that the Commissioner is no longer under any disadvantage; full disclosure has been made and there is no reason why he cannot assess a deficiency within the statutory period.

* * *

Under this statute, the filing of a fraudulent return had no greater effect on the limitations period than the filing of no return at all. In either case, since the relevant facts had not been disclosed to the Commissioner, the proper tax could be assessed "at any time." In 1954 the statute was bifurcated; the provisions relating to a failure to file were placed into § 6501(c)(3). The legislative history of this revision indicates that the division was not intended to change the statute's meaning. This history supports petitioners' reading of the statute. Fraudulent returns were treated the same as no return at all since neither gives the Commissioner an adequate basis to attempt an assessment. Once that basis is provided, however, the statute is inapplicable; it is no longer a "case of a false or fraudulent return."

* * *

If anything, considerations of tax policy argue against the result reached by the Court today. In a system based on voluntary compliance, it is crucial that some incentive be given to persons to reveal and correct past fraud. Yet the rule announced by the Court today creates no such incentive; a taxpayer gets no advantage at all by filing an honest return. Not only does the taxpayer fail to gain the benefit of a limitations period, but at the same time he gives the Commissioner additional information which can be used against him at any time. Since the amended return will not give the taxpayer a defense in a criminal or civil fraud action, there is no reason at all for a taxpayer to correct a fraudulent return. Apparently the Court believes that taxpayers should be advised to remain silent, hoping the fraud will go undetected, rather than to make full disclosure in a proper return. I cannot believe that Congress intended such a result.

Questions

1.   Who do you think has the better reasoned argument, the majority or the dissent?

2.   Can an honest amended return ever "cure" a fraudulent original return?

3.   If a taxpayer fraudulently fails to file a return, then subsequently files a delinquent but honest return, can the Commissioner assess a fraud penalty attributable to the initial failure to file? If so, how long does the Commissioner have to assess?

4.   What is a tax advisor's ethical duty, if any, when a client files a fraudulent return? See Circular 230, §§ 10.21 and 10.34, and discussion of Circular 230, Chapter 2.

C.   EXTENSIONS BY AGREEMENT

If there is insufficient time for the Appeals Division to adequately consider a case (usually when there is less than 60 days remaining on the statute of limitations), it will ask the taxpayer to extend the statute of limitations voluntarily. If the taxpayer refuses, the Appeals Division usually will not agree to hear the taxpayer's case.

Section 6501(c)(4) provides that the taxpayer and the Service may agree to extend the period for assessment, provided the agreement is executed before the end of the statutory assessment period. There are two types of extensions, for which the Service uses two different forms: a Form 872 (Consent to Extend the Time to Assess Income Tax), expires at a specific time that has been agreed upon by the taxpayer and the Service, and a Form 872-A (Special Consent Fixing Period of Limitation Upon Assessment of Income Tax), is a long-term, indefinite waiver of the limitations period, although the waiver may be restricted to the specific issues under examination.

1. The Nature of the Agreement

HUBERT v. INTERNAL REVENUE SERVICE
United States Tax Cases, 1996.
96-2 USTC ¶ 50,523.

OPINION BY: STEPHEN V. WILSON, UNITED STATES DISTRICT JUDGE
* * *

Findings of Fact

Plaintiff and his wife filed joint individual tax returns for the years 1982 and 1983. Among other things, the returns claimed tax benefits from the Plaintiff's claimed interest in three tax-shelters, Atolia-WMD Project, Oxford Partners, and Dore.

On or about November 1, 1985, the IRS mailed a package of materials to Plaintiff Hubert. Included in this package were a cover letter, two copies of IRS form 872-A, an envelope, and a copy of IRS publication 1035. The heading of the cover letter read "re: Atolia-WMD Project." The body of the letter indicated that the IRS was examining "the tax return of *an entity* in which you have an interest." (emphasis added). It further stated that "the limitation period prescribed by law for assessing additional tax will expire before *the entity's* examination is completed." (emphasis added). The letter asked Hubert to sign the consent form 872-A to extend the limitations period for assessing additional tax. The letter indicated that, if Hubert did not consent to extend the statute, a "notice of deficiency" would be sent out. Finally, the letter stated that "adjustments may be proposed that could affect your federal income tax return for 1982."

On November 11, 1985, Plaintiff Hubert and his wife executed a form 872-A, Special Consent to Extend the Time to Assess Tax, for their joint individual tax return for 1982. In pertinent part, the form stated that the Huberts were waiving the statute of limitations regarding "the amount(s) of *any* Federal income tax due on *any* return(s) made by or for" the Huberts. (emphasis added). Hubert returned the two copies of the form 872-A to the IRS with a cover letter headed "re: Atolia-WMD Project."

At the time the Huberts signed the form 872-A, the statute of limitations had not yet run on the IRS's ability to assess additional tax for the 1982 return. Except for the signatures of Hubert and his wife, the form 872-A was not altered in any way before it was returned to the IRS. The IRS did not regard the Huberts cover letter as an attempt to limit the scope of the 872-A consent form.

A similar exchange of letters and consent forms occurred in and around November, 1986 with regard to the Huberts' 1983 joint individual return. Again, the heading on the IRS' cover letter read "in re: Atolia-WMD Project: as did the heading on Hubert's return cover letter. The form 872-A consent form had the same language as that quoted above from the first form.

In December, 1988, the Huberts consented to an additional tax assessment of $2,865 on their 1982 income tax return. The additional assessment related to three tax shelters claimed on the 1982 tax return, Atolia-WMD, Oxford Partners, and Dore. Also in December, 1988, the Huberts consented to an additional assessment of $2,639 on their 1983 tax return. The additional assessment related to two tax shelters claimed on the 1983 return, Oxford Partners and Dore. The additional taxes were assessed in February, 1989.

In 1991 and 1992, Hubert complained to the IRS that the additional assessments on the Oxford Partners and Dore tax shelters were improper because the statute of limitations barred such assessments. The IRS rejected these claims. Hubert paid the tax. He then requested adjustment of the tax. His request was disallowed. Hubert then filed this suit for refund.

At trial, Hubert and Mr. Mieszerski, the IRS Group Manager who supervised the unit that processed Hubert's consent forms, were called to testify. Based on their testimony, the Court has made additional findings of fact. First, the Court finds that Hubert did subjectively believe that he was only consenting to an extension of the statute of limitations for assessments relating to the Atolia-WMD Project. Second, the Court finds that neither the IRS nor its agents agreed to restrict the extension of the statute of limitations to the Atolia-WMD Project. Third, the Court finds that Hubert's consenting to an extension of the statute of limitations did not limit the IRS's ability to issue a statutory notice of deficiency even before the full audit was completed.

Findings of Law

Section 6501 of the Internal Revenue Code, Title 26, provides a three year statute of limitations for assessing tax after a return has been filed. However, that statute of limitations can be extended by a written agreement made prior to the expiration of the statutory period. 26 U.S.C. § 6501(c)(4).

Here, Plaintiff and his wife filed their tax returns for 1982 and 1983 on April 15, 1983 and 1984 respectively. Therefore, any assessments would have had to have been made by April 15, 1986 and 1987 respectively. The assessments were not made, however, until February, 1989. Thus, absent any valid extension of the statutory period, the 1989 assessments were barred under § 6501.

The IRS argues that the extensions signed by Hubert extended the assessment period such that the assessments are valid. Hubert argues that the scope of each extension was limited to assessments for the single tax shelter Atolia-WMD Project. The IRS says that the extensions were unrestricted. The Court finds that the extensions were unrestricted.

"An agreement to extend the statute of limitations for assessment and collection [of income tax] is not a contract but a waiver of a defense." Seymour Schulman v. Commissioner, 93 T.C. 623, 639 (November 29, 1989).[2] "Contract principles are significant, however, because section 6501(c)(4) requires a written agreement, and [courts] look to the objective manifestations of mutual assent to determine the terms of such agreement." Id.

The cases reveal that, absent an agreement to alter the terms of the otherwise clear terms of the unilateral waiver embodied in form 872-A, the terms of the waiver control its scope. In order to restrict an otherwise broad consent form, "the restrictive or conditional terms are usually reduced to writing * * * in conjunction with the circumstances surrounding the * * * execution of the consent." Id. In addition, there must be communication and agreement of the terms between the parties. Id.

Here, the form 872-A did not restrict the scope of the extension to the single tax-shelter Atolia-WMD Project. Rather, the form clearly states that the taxpayer is extending the statutory period for assessment on "the amount(s) of any Federal Income tax due on any return(s) made by or for the above taxpayer(s) for the period(s) ended December 21, 1982." Although Hubert believed that he was only extending the statute of limitations as to assessments relating to the Atolia-WMD tax shelter, there is no evidence that the IRS knew or should have known that Hubert intended to so limit the extension or that the IRS objectively manifested an agreement to such a limitation. Rather, as in *Schulman*, the consent form itself was unrestricted.

---

2. At first blush, it is not clear why such an agreement is not a contract. After all, it is a written agreement signed by both parties which appears to bind both parties. At trial, however, it was revealed that the IRS gives up nothing in exchange for a taxpayer's agreement to extend the statute of limitations. When a consent to extend the statute is signed, the IRS has the option of holding off on a notice of deficiency and/or assessment until it completes its audit, but there is nothing in the form 872-A that prohibits the IRS from issuing a notice of deficiency before the audit is complete. In short, the fact that a consent form is signed does not in any way lessen or restrict the IRS's conduct. Thus, there is no consideration and no contract.

The letters exchanged between the IRS and Hubert regarding the execution of the consent do not reveal an agreement to limit that consent form. If anything, the letters are ambiguous on this point and the evidence is that the parties attached materially different meanings to the letters – Hubert thought the letters restricted the consent, the IRS thought they merely explained the circumstances giving rise to the request for a consent. Where parties attach materially different meanings to terms and neither has reason to know of the meaning attached by the other, there is no meeting of the minds and thus no agreement. In short, there was no agreement to restrict the scope of the consent form. Therefore, the terms of the consent form control and the assessments relating to Oxford Partners and Dore were not barred by the statute of limitations.

The Court is not unmindful of the striking unfairness of this case. This entire case would most likely never have arisen had the IRS simply added one sentence to the letter such as "executing the consent waives the statute of limitations for all aspects of your return and our investigation and additional assessments will not necessarily be limited to the claims currently under investigation." As a government agency, the IRS should strive to be as straightforward, open, and fair as possible when dealing with taxpayers who, as in this case, are often unrepresented.

Notes

Congress took the court's message to heart in the IRS Restructuring and Reform Act of 1998, which added new subsection § 6501 (c)(4)(B), which requires the Service as of January 1, 2000, to inform the taxpayer of both the right to refuse to extend the period of limitations and the right to limit any agreed extension to specific issues and specific periods. This notice must be provided each time the taxpayer is asked to waive the limitations period.

2. Termination of an Open-Ended Extension

HOLOF v. COMMISSIONER
United States Court of Appeals, Third Circuit, 1989.
872 F.2d 50.

In this appeal we must decide whether a defective notice of tax deficiency mailed by the Internal Revenue Service terminates taxpayers' Form 872-A consent to waive the statute of limitations on assessment of tax deficiencies. The Commissioner appeals from the Tax Court's decision upholding the termination of the limitations waiver and barring the IRS from assessing the additional taxes owed.

* * *

I.

Taxpayers Harry and Norma Holof filed timely joint federal income tax returns for 1976 and 1977, claiming loss deductions in their partnership interests in two separate tax shelters for each year. The IRS initiated an audit of those returns. Ordinarily, the statute of limitations for assessment of tax deficiencies is three years. I.R.C. § 6501(a). In connection with the audit, however, the Holofs executed a Special consent to Extend the Time for Assessment of Tax (Form 872-A) for 1976 * * * thus extending the limitations period indefinitely.[2]

Form 872-A, commonly known as an "open-ended" waiver because it does not expire at a fixed date, specifies the means by which either the taxpayer or the IRS can terminate the limitations waiver. The IRS can terminate it by mailing to the taxpayer either a Notice of Termination of Special Consent to Extend the Time to Assess Tax (Form 872-T) or a "notice of deficiency." In contrast, the taxpayer effectively terminates the waiver only when the IRS office "considering the case" receives a Form 872-T from the taxpayer. Form 872-A also provides that after termination by either party, the IRS has ninety days within which to "assess" a tax deficiency.

On October 8, 1982, the IRS mailed a notice of deficiency for the taxable years 1976 and 1977, but failed to send it to the Holofs' "last known" address, as required by statute. The Holofs never received the October 1982 notice of deficiency and consequently failed to file a timely petition for redetermination with the Tax Court, a right also secured by statute.[4] The IRS then assessed the tax, and in April 1983 sought to collect it. It was these collection attempts that alerted the Holofs that an assessment had been made. On January 5, 1984, they finally received from the IRS a copy of the October 1982 notice of deficiency. Following a series of petitions, the Tax Court granted the parties' joint motion to dismiss the assessment proceedings on the grounds that the October 1982 notice of deficiency was statutorily defective.

On June 28, 1984, the IRS mailed the Holofs a second notice of deficiency for the years 1976 and 1977, this time to their last known

---

2.   The usual instrument for extending or suspending the statute of limitations is known as a "waiver."

4.   After receiving the notice of deficiency, the taxpayer has ninety days within which to petition the Tax Court to review the assessment. I.R.C. § 6213(a).

address. The Holofs timely filed with the Tax Court a petition asserting that assessment and collection of the deficiencies were now barred by the statute of limitations. The Holofs argued that mailing even an invalid notice of deficiency–in their case the October, 1982 notice–served to terminate the limitations waiver. The Commissioner responded that because the notice of deficiency was defective under the statutory scheme, it was null and void for all purposes.

The Tax Court held that the statute of limitations had expired before the IRS mailed the second notice of deficiency. Holof v. Commissioner, T.C. Memo 1987-540 (1987). In its decision, the Tax Court relied upon Roszkos v. Commissioner, 87 T.C. 1255 (1986), a case with facts similar to *Holof*.

Focusing then on the literal provisions of Form 872-A, and interpreting "doubtful language" against the IRS as the drafting party, the Tax Court in *Roszkos* held that the IRS terminated the waiver by mailing the defective notice of deficiency. Because Form 872-A does not require that the taxpayer receive actual notice of termination, and, in contrast, makes termination by the taxpayer subject to the IRS's receipt of Form 872-T, the Tax Court determined that the Commissioner had drafted Form 872-A to render irrelevant the accuracy of the taxpayer's address. Thus, the Tax Court held that the simple act of mailing on the part of the IRS terminated the agreement.

Next, finding that actual receipt cured defects in a notice of deficiency, the Tax Court in *Roszkos* held that when the taxpayers became aware that the IRS intended to terminate the waiver agreement, the agreement in fact terminated. The court concluded that this result was "conceptually analogous to the case law governing the notices of deficiency."

Applying this reasoning to the Holofs' circumstances, the Tax Court held that "on or about" January 5, 1984–the time the Holofs "became aware" of the October 1982 notice of deficiency–the Form 872-A consent to extend the statute of limitations was terminated. Accordingly, the Tax Court held that the June 28, 1984 notice of deficiency was barred by the statute of limitations because it was not mailed within ninety days after the Holofs became aware of the IRS's intentions to terminate.

Subsequent to the Tax Court's decision in *Holof*, the United States Court of Appeals for the Ninth Circuit reversed the Tax Court's decision in *Roszkos*. Roszkos v. Commissioner, 850 F.2d 514 (9th Cir. 1988). Although we approach the issue somewhat differently, we find persuasive the reasons the Ninth Circuit articulated for reversing the Tax Court.

II.

We review decisions of the Tax Court in the same manner and to the same extent as decisions of the district court in civil actions tried without a jury. 26 U.S.C. § 7482 (a)(1983). Although the Supreme Court has expressly held that a consent to extend the period for assessment of income tax is "not a contract * * * [but is] essentially a unilateral waiver of a defense by the taxpayer,: see Stange v. United States, 282 U.S. 270, 276, 75 L.Ed. 335, 51 S.Ct. 145 (1931) (citing Florsheim Bros. Drygoods Co. v. United States, 280 U.S. 453, 466, 74 L.Ed. 542, 50 S.Ct. 215 (1930)), some courts have analyzed taxpayer consents to waive the statute of limitations defense in contractual terms, see, e.g., Roszkos, 850 F.2d at 516; Pursell v. Commissioner, 38 T.C. 263, 278 aff'd, 315 F.2d 629 (3rd Cir. 1963) (per curiam). We could apply contract principles to this case and reach the same result, but the question before us does not necessarily implicate such principles. At issue here is whether to construe the terms of Form 872-A--a waiver of a statutory defense--in a manner consistent with the statutory framework in which it was designed to operate. This is a question of law, subject to plenary review.

III.

The critical language of a Form 872-A waiver agreement provides:
Taxpayer(s) * * * and the * * * Director of Internal Revenue * * * consent and agree as follows:

(1) The amount(s) of any Federal Income tax due on any return(s) made by or for the above taxpayer(s) for the period(s) ended * * * [on the relevant date], may be assessed on or before the 90th (ninetieth) day after: (a) The Internal Revenue Service office considering the case receives Form 872-T, Notice of Termination of Special Consent to Extend the Time to Assess Tax, from the taxpayer(s); or (b) the Internal Revenue Service mails a Form 872-T to the taxpayer(s); or (c) the Internal Revenue Service mails a notice of deficiency for such period(s). However, if a notice of deficiency is sent to the taxpayer(s), the time for assessing the tax for the period(s) stated in the notice of deficiency will be further extended by the number of days the assessment was previously prohibited, plus 60 days * * *.

Focusing on the literal terms of Form 872-A, the Tax Court found that the act of mailing by the IRS even to an address other than the "last known" one--of either a notice of deficiency or a Form 872-T--would terminate the waiver agreement. The Holofs contend that the issue is not statutory construction but giving "plain meaning" to the written agreement of the parties. The IRS responds that interpreting Form 872-A's termination provisions requires an examination of the statutory framework in which Form 872-A was designed to operate. We agree with the Commissioner. Although Form 872-A appears to enumerate carefully defined procedures for tax assessment, it is not an integrated agreement that encapsulates all rights and obligations of the respective parties. The taxpayer's "plain meaning" argument fails because Form 872-A is an accessory intended to complement a complex statutory scheme.

Form 872-A has legal effect only because the Internal Revenue Code authorizes a waiver of the statute of limitations on assessment, which normally runs three years after the return was filed. I.R.C. §§ 6501(a) & 6501(c)(4). The only function of Form 872-A is to waive the statute of limitations. Its terms cannot abrogate any of the assessment procedures already in place in the Code. "The instruments are nothing more than * * * waivers; and that was all to which the Commissioner was authorized to consent." *Florsheim Bros. Drygoods Co.*, 280 U.S. at 466. Nonetheless, on its face, Form 872-A conflicts with the Code's assessment procedures and overlooks the central role that a notice of deficiency plays in those procedures.

The notice of deficiency is a pivotal feature of the Code's assessment procedures. Unless the IRS first issues the taxpayer an effective notice of deficiency, the Commissioner is precluded by statute from assessing or collecting any taxes. Once the Commissioner issues a notice of deficiency, the taxpayer has ninety days from the mailing of the notice to file a petition with the Tax Court for a redetermination of the deficiency. During this same ninety-day period, the Commissioner is prohibited from assessing or collecting the deficiency.[7] If the taxpayer files a petition with the Tax Court before the ninety-day period expires, the prohibition on assessment continues until the decision of the Tax Court becomes final.[8] This same notice of deficiency suspends the running of the statute of limitations during this period in which the Commissioner is precluded under § 6213 from making the assessment.[9]

---

7.   The Code provides, "no assessment of a deficiency * * * shall be made * * * until the expiration of such 90-day period * * *." I.R.C. § 6213(a).

8.   The Code provides, "no assessment of a deficiency * * * shall be made * * *, if a petition hs been filed with the Tax Court, until the decision of the Tax Court has become final." I.R.C. § 6213(a).

9.   The Code provides, "The running of the period of limitations provided in section 6212 * * * shall (after the mailing of a [deficiency] notice * * *) be suspended for the period during which the Secretary is prohibited from making the assessment * * * and for sixty days thereafter." I.R.C. § 6503(a)(1).

The statute remains suspended for the sixty days after the prohibition on assessment is lifted.[10]

We believe that the terms of the Form 872-A conflict with this statutory scheme. Form 872-A provides that the income tax owed "may be assessed on or before the 90th (ninetieth) day after the mailing or receipt by the IRS of a Form 872-T." Thus, Form 872-A provides that the IRS may simply "assess" the deficiency immediately after the occurrence of one of the three enumerated events. This disregards the Code's requirement that before the IRS can "assess" a deficiency, it must first mail a notice of deficiency to the taxpayer. I.R.C. § 6213(a). Accordingly, if either party sends a Form 872-T to terminate the waiver agreement, the IRS would still be required to send a notice of deficiency before it could "assess" a tax deficiency,[11] and would have to do so within ninety days. In addition, Form 872-A mandates that the IRS "assess" within ninety days of mailing the deficiency notice. The Code in fact prohibits the IRS from assessing the deficiency within that ninety-day period after the deficiency notice is mailed, a period within which the taxpayer may petition the Tax Court for redetermination of the deficiency identified in the deficiency notice. I.R.C. § 6213(a). At the end of that ninety-day period in the case of a default, or after the determination of the Tax Court becomes final, the IRS then has sixty days actually to "assess" the tax.

These discrepancies between Form 872-A and the Code do not permit the parties to ignore established Code procedures. In this case, moreover, the Holofs' own explanations of their rights and obligations acknowledge that Form 872-A operates within the confines of the Codes' procedures. The Holofs agree that the IRS is precluded from assessing any taxes without first issuing the taxpayer a notice of deficiency, and that this notice also serves to prohibit assessment for ninety days. Thus, the meaning of "notice of deficiency" cannot be discerned from the "plain meaning" of Form 872-A. To understand tax assessment procedures for Form 872-A, reference to the statute is required.[12]

---

10. Id.

11. We later note that the IRS sends a Form 872-T only when it determines that the taxpayer owes no additional taxes. Thus, the Commissioner has also referred to the Form 872-A as an "agreement extending the time for issuing a notice of deficiency."

12. We do not suggest that in all instances the language of Form 872-A conflicts with the Code. For example, the distinction between receipt and mailing, clear on the face of Form 872-A and not inconsistent with other statutory provisions, has been given full effect. See, e.g., Brown v. Commissioner, T.C. Memo 1986-239, 51 T.C.M. (CCH) 1171, 1178 (1986).

Furthermore, the Holofs have made no claim that they changed position in justifiable reliance on the language of Form 872-A. While we offer no opinion as to whether there are situations in which

We now examine the significance of a notice of deficiency in the operation of Form 872-A. Viewed within the statutory framework, it is clear that Form 872-A contemplates that only an effective notice of deficiency can terminate the waiver agreement. Given the functions of a notice of deficiency, to say even an effective notice of deficiency was designed to "terminate" the waiver agreement is misleading. Such a characterization suggests that in terminating the waiver agreement in this manner, the IRS has decided to recommence the statute of limitations. In reality, the mailing of an effective notice of deficiency continues to suspend the statute of limitations, while forcing the taxpayer to move forward to protect his rights by filing a petition with the Tax Court within ninety days from the date the notice is mailed. Therefore, when the IRS mails a notice of deficiency, the agency presumes the notice will keep the statute of limitations from running for at least ninety days. In contrast, when the IRS wants to "terminate" not only the limitations waiver but its involvement in the entire matter, it sends a Form 872-T. Thus, the IRS sends a Form 872-T where the agency determines that the taxpayer who signed a limitations waiver owes no additional taxes. We concur with the Ninth Circuit's determination that "Form 872-T exists for a fundamentally different purpose than the notice of deficiency * * * [and] that Form 872-A subjects both to a mailing standard sheds no light on the analysis." Roszkos, 850 F.2d at 518.

Finally, to hold that an ineffective notice of deficiency could terminate the waiver would render unintelligible a crucial provision of Form 872-A. Form 872-A provides that "if a notice of deficiency is sent to the taxpayer(s), the time for assessing the tax * * * will be further extended by the number of days the *assessment was previously prohibited*, plus 60 days" (emphasis added). It appears to us that this sentence refers: (1) to the prohibition on assessment during the ninety-day period after a notice of deficiency is issued, during which the taxpayer may petition the Tax Court for a redetermination of the assessment; and (2) where the taxpayer files a petition for redetermination, to the continued prohibition on assessment until the decision of the Tax Court becomes final. We arrive at this conclusion because the sixty-day extension of the statute of limitations mentioned in Form 872-A corresponds to the Code section providing, "The running of the period of limitations * * * on the making of assessments * * * shall (after the mailing of a notice [of deficiency] * * *) be suspended for the period during which the Secretary is prohibited from making the assessment * * * (and in any event, if a

---

the Commissioner might be estopped by the language of his own forms, the Holofs' acknowledged understanding of the statutory scheme undermines such an argument in this case.

proceeding in respect of the deficiency is placed on the docket of the Tax Court, until the decision of the Tax Court becomes final), and for sixty days thereafter." I.R.C. § 6503(a)(1).

However, a defective notice of deficiency, unless the defect is cured, does not trigger Tax Court jurisdiction. Thus, if the notice of deficiency is defective, the language in Form 872-A cannot refer to the prohibition on assessment during the period the Tax Court may consider, or is considering, the taxpayer's redetermination petition. Were we to apply this provision of Form 872-A to the Holof's situation, we would arrive at a "further extended" period of zero days – because there is no "previously prohibited period" – plus sixty days.[13] Neither party contends that sixty days is the appropriate period of extension following the mailing of a notice of deficiency. This provision in Form 872-A specifying the time period for the limitations extension demonstrates that Form 872-A contemplates only the mailing of an effective deficiency notice. In sum, not only is "notice of deficiency" a "term of art" that must be given its technical meaning, but the entirety of Form 872-A is illogical unless the notice of deficiency has the effects described in the Code.

IV.

We have stated that only an "effective" notice of deficiency will terminate a Form 872-A waiver agreement. A notice of deficiency, however, need not be mailed in strict compliance with § 6212(b) of the Code to be effective. Where the taxpayers receive timely, actual notice that a deficiency is to be assessed, a notice of deficiency that does not comply with § 6212 will nevertheless operate as if it were sent in compliance with that statutory provision. The Holofs argue that the Tax Court properly found that the waiver agreement terminated when the Holofs "became" aware in January, 1984 of the October 1982 notices of deficiency. We believe, however, that precedent governing notices of

---

13. The only alternative meaning of the reference to a "previously prohibited" period would be the prohibition on assessment, which is found in I.R.C. § 6213(a), after a Form 872-A is executed but before the issuance of an effective notice of deficiency. For the purposes of this appeal we need not decide to which prohibition the Tax Court believed this language refers. The improper mailing of a notice of deficiency, unless it falls within certain exceptions, has no effect on either prohibition. Because the notice is defective, the Commissioner remains prohibited from assessing a tax until an effective notice of deficiency is mailed. Consequently, there is no "previously prohibited" period.

In *Holof*, the Tax Court ignored the phrase in Form 872-A that refers to a "previously prohibited" period. Having held that the waiver agreement terminated when the Holofs "became aware" of the October 1982 notice of deficiency, the Tax Court calculated that the statute of limitations was extended for a period of 150 days after that termination, during which time the IRS could issue a valid notice of deficiency. 54 T.C.M. (CCH) at 960.

deficiency – if at all necessary to our analysis – supports the position of the IRS.

The Ninth Circuit, in *Roszkos*, has summarized well this area of law. The court there held that the Tax Court decision giving effect to the misaddressed deficiency notice sent to the Roszkos was "wholly contrary to the clear precedent." Roszkos, 850 F.2d at 517. The court of appeals explained that "a misaddressed notice of deficiency, which is returned to the IRS undelivered, is 'null and void.' The only exception to this scenario * * * is if the taxpayer acknowledges notice by timely petitioning of the Tax Court for a redetermination of deficiency, thereby rendering harmless the IRS's error in mailing." Id. (quoting Mulvania v. Commissioner, 769 F2d 1376, 1380 (9th Cir. 1985)).

This rule comports with our own precedent. In Delman v. Commissioner, 384 F.2d 29 (3d Cir. 1967), we held that a notice of deficiency need not be technically perfect to trigger the jurisdiction of the Tax Court. However, we distinguished the case where a taxpayer learned of a defective deficiency notice in time to file a timely petition with the Tax Court, which cures the defects in the notice, from the situation exemplified by the *Holof* case. Id. at 934. We explained that where "a notice of deficiency * * * [was] mailed to an incorrect address and not received by the taxpayer there would naturally be strong reason for determining that no notice was mailed." Id.; accord Sicker v. Commissioner, 815 F.2d 1400, 1401 (11th Cir. 1987) (an improperly addressed notice of tax deficiency that did not reach taxpayer until at least eighty-three days later, was not received by taxpayer in time to file a petition for redetermination and was therefore not effective when mailed for purposes of determining commencement of ninety-day period for filing redetermination petition).

In this case, the Tax Court found that the Holofs became aware of the October 1982 deficiency notice sometime in January of 1984, well after the ninety-day period for filing a redetermination petition had passed. Because the notice of deficiency was not mailed to the taxpayer at his last known address, see I.R.C. § 6212(b), and no intervening event cured this defect, we treat the October 1982 notice of deficiency as never having been mailed.

V.

In conclusion, the notice of deficiency sent to the Holofs, incorrectly addressed and not actually received in time to petition the Tax Court, could not set into motion any of the statutory assessment procedures.

Consequently, it had no effect upon the statute of limitations waiver. We will reverse the decision of the Tax Court.

Notes and Question

In Silverman v. Commissioner, 86 F.3d 260 (1st Cir. 1996), the taxpayers invested in some tax shelters and were audited. During the course of the audit, they signed a Form 872-A. Subsequently, they entered into a closing agreement with the Service which bound them to the outcome of a similar, so-called "controlling case" that was being heard in the Tax Court. The closing agreement also authorized the IRS to assess a deficiency within one year after the decision in the controlling case became final. The closing agreement made no mention of the Form 872-A. Almost two years after the decision in the controlling case became final, the taxpayers sent Forms 872-T, Notice of Termination of Special Consent to Extend the Time to Assess Tax, to the Service. The Service sent notices of deficiency within 90 days of the receipt of the Form 872-T, with the proposed deficiency calculated according to the outcome in the controlling case. The taxpayers argued that the closing agreement had terminated their indefinite extension because the Service was required to make its assessment within one year of the final decision in the controlling case. The Service responded that the closing agreement had no effect on the Form 872-A extension. The Tax Court held in favor of the government, rejecting the taxpayers' argument that their Form 872-A extensions were superseded by the Form 906 closing agreement. The taxpayers then appealed to the First Circuit, which upheld the Tax Court decision on the ground that the closing agreement was not a valid termination of the Form 872-A under the plain language of the form.

What factors should a taxpayer consider in deciding whether to agree to an extension or a waiver of the assessment period?

CHAPTER 5

OVERPAYMENTS – REFUNDS, CREDITS, ABATEMENTS, AND JUDICIAL DETERMINATIONS

Intaxication: euphoria at getting a refund from the IRS, which lasts until you realize it was your money to start with.

-- Greg Oetjen[1]

I. THE REFUND CLAIM

A taxpayer occasionally may overpay the amount of tax due. If so, the taxpayer may be entitled to a refund, which may be obtained by any of four methods: (1) if the overpayment arises from a mathematical error on the return that is discovered during the processing of the return, the Service will refund the amount of the overpayment voluntarily to the taxpayer, (2) if the overpayment arises from overwithholding from wages, the taxpayer may file a refund claim on the initial return for that taxable year or, if an error is discovered after the return has been filed, a claim for refund may be filed with the Service on an amended return (Form 1040X), (3) if the refund claim is not successful, the taxpayer may file suit and seek a refund through either of the refund fora – i.e., the federal district courts or the United States Court of Federal Claims, and (4) the United States Tax Court, which has deficiency jurisdiction, also has incidental refund jurisdiction if it ultimately determines that a refund is due (provided the overpayment arises in the taxable year that is before the court).

A. OVERPAYMENT

The first step in obtaining a refund is that there must be an overpayment of tax. Although the Internal Revenue Code does not define an overpayment, technically, any amount of tax paid that exceeds the amount owed is an overpayment. An overpayment can arise in several ways: (1) through overwithholding of taxes from wages, (2) through an

---

1. Jeffery L. Yablon, As Certain As Death–Quotations About Taxes (2004 Edition), 102 TAX NOTES 99, 141 (Jan. 5, 2004).

error in the calculation of the tax liability, (3) through carrybacks from other taxable years, (4) through a payment made after the close of the statute of limitations, and (5) through a judicial determination that the tax liability has been overpaid.

INTERNAL REVENUE CODE § 6401

(a) The term "overpayment" includes that part of the amount of the payment of any internal revenue tax which is assessed or collected after the expiration of the period of limitation properly applicable thereto.

INTERNAL REVENUE CODE § 6402

(a)   In the case of any overpayment, the Secretary, within the applicable period of limitations, may credit the amount of such overpayment, including any interest allowed thereon, against any liability in respect of an internal revenue tax on the part of the person who made the overpayment and shall, subject to [certain offsets], refund any balance to such person.

INTERNAL REVENUE CODE § 6514

(a)   A refund of a portion of an internal revenue tax shall be considered erroneous and a credit of any such portion shall be considered void (1) if made after the expiration of the period of limitation for filing a claim therefor, unless within such period the claim was filed; or (2) in the case of a claim filed within the proper time and disallowed by the Secretary, if the credit or refund was made after the expiration of the period of limitation for filing suit, unless within such period suit was begun by the taxpayer.

(b)   Any credit against a liability in respect of any taxable year shall be void if any payment in respect to such liability would be considered an overpayment under § 6401(a).

LEWIS v. REYNOLDS

United States Supreme Court, 1932.
284 U.S. 281, 52 S.Ct. 145, 76 L.Ed. 293.

MR. JUSTICE MCREYNOLDS delivered the opinion of the Court.

Petitioners sued the respondent Collector in the United States District Court for Wyoming, September 20, 1929, to recover $7,297.16 alleged to have been wrongfully exacted as income tax upon the estate of Cooper.

February 18, 1921, the administrator filed a return for the period January 1 to December 12, 1920, the day of final settlement. Among others, he reported deductions for attorney's fees, $20,750, and inheritance taxes paid to the State, $16,870. The amount of tax as indicated by the return was paid.

November 24, 1925, the Commissioner, having audited the return, disallowed all deductions except the one for attorney's fees and assessed a deficiency of $7,297.16. This sum was paid March 21, 1926; and on July 27, 1926, petitioners asked that it be refunded.

A letter from the Commissioner to petitioners, dated May 18, 1929, and introduced in evidence by them, stated that the deduction of $20,750 for attorney's fees had been improperly allowed. He also set out a revised computation wherein he deducted the state inheritance taxes. This showed liability greater than the total sums theretofore exacted. The Commissioner further said: "Since the correct computation results in an additional tax as indicated above which is barred from assessment by the statute of limitations your claim will be rejected on the next schedule to be approved by the commissioner."

The trial court upheld the Commissioner's action and its judgment was affirmed by the Circuit Court of Appeals.

Counsel for petitioners relies upon the five-year statute of limitations (Revenue Act 1926, § 277 (26 USCA § 1057)).[1] He maintains that the Commissioner lacked authority to redetermine and reassess the tax after the statute had run.

After referring to section 284, Revenue Act of 1926, 44 Stat. 66 (26 USCA § 1065) and section 322, Revenue Act of 1928, 45 Stat. 861 (26 USCA § 2322), the Circuit Court of Appeals said:

---

1.   Sec. 277. (a) Except as provided in section 278 (not here important)– * * *

        (3) The amount of income, excess-profits, and war-profits taxes imposed by * * * the Revenue Act of 1918, and by any such Act as amended, shall be assessed within five years after the return was filed, and no proceeding in court without assessment for the collection of such taxes shall be begun after the expiration of such period.

"The above quoted provisions clearly limit refunds to overpayments. It follows that the ultimate question presented for decision, upon a claim for refund, is whether the taxpayer has overpaid his tax. This involves a redetermination of the entire tax liability. While no new assessment can be made, after the bar of the statute has fallen, the taxpayer, nevertheless, is not entitled to a refund unless he has overpaid his tax. The action to recover on a claim for refund is in the nature of an action for money had and received and it is incumbent upon the claimant to show that the United States has money which belongs to him."

We agree with the conclusion reached by the courts below.

While the statutes authorizing refunds do not specifically empower the Commissioner to reaudit a return whenever repayment is claimed, authority therefor is necessarily implied. An overpayment must appear before refund is authorized. Although the statute of limitations may have barred the assessment and collection of any additional sum, it does not obliterate the right of the United States to retain payments already received when they do not exceed the amount which might have been properly assessed and demanded.

* * *

Affirmed.

Notes and Questions

Overpayments commonly arise through overwithholding on wages as a result of a job change during the taxable year. If the taxpayer's wages exceed the base wage amount of FICA tax withholding (Social Security and Medicare taxes), the new employer may calculate withholding based solely on the wages it pays the employee, without a consideration of the amount of wages paid to the employee by the former employer during the taxable year. This can result in an overpayment if the taxpayer/employee does not anticipate the overwithholding and adjust the withholding exemptions accordingly. If such an overpayment occurs, the taxpayer may offset the amount of the overpayment as a credit against the tax liability for the taxable year of the overpayment.

1. Is it possible for the government use a valid refund to offset a barred deficiency without violating § 6514(b)?

2. If the taxpayer in *Lewis v. Reynolds* was entitled to a refund in 1922, and the statute of limitations was open with respect to the 1922 taxable year, could the Commissioner use that refund to offset the 1921 deficiency, if the statute of limitations had run with respect to the 1921 taxable year?

3. If the taxpayer had paid the amount of the 1921 deficiency after the statute of limitations had run with respect to the 1921 taxable year, would the government then be able to use the refund against the 1921 deficiency?

4. Can the principle of *Lewis v. Reynolds* operate in favor of the taxpayer? If so, how? See Union Pacific Railroad v. United States, 389 F.2d 437 (Ct. Cl. 1968).

5. What lesson does *Lewis v. Reynolds* hold for taxpayers filing refund claims?

Does the offset principle of *Lewis v. Reynolds* apply to interest, penalties and other additions to tax? This question is considered in the following case.

PACIFIC GAS AND ELECTRIC CO. v. UNITED STATES
Court of Appeals for the Federal Circuit, 2005
417 F.3d 1375

ARCHER, SENIOR CIRCUIT JUDGE.

* * *

I

This case involves statutory interest erroneously paid to PGE [eds: Pacific Gas and Electric Company and PG & E Corporation are collectively referred to as "PGE"] for tax year 1982. PGE timely filed its 1982 tax return. PGE thereafter filed claims for refund for 1982 . . . . [I]n August 1988, the IRS determined that PGE had overpaid its 1982 tax. In determining the statutory interest under 26 U.S.C. § 6611 to be paid to PGE on this overpayment, the IRS made errors in its calculation resulting in too much interest being paid to PGE.[1]

PGE thereafter filed additional refund claims for tax and interest for the tax year 1982 primarily to claim certain statutorily authorized carryback adjustments from tax year 1984. In reviewing those refund claims, the IRS discovered the interest computation errors it had previously made in the August 1988 refund and determined that it had erroneously overpaid PGE $3,370,535 in statutory interest. The IRS then used the amount of this erroneous interest previously paid to PGE in

---

1. The erroneous interest calculation resulted primarily from the treatment of one installment payment on June 20, 1983, of tax for 1982, in the amount of $63,000,000. In the interest computations, the IRS assumed the due date of the return, March 15, 1983, should commence the running of interest, whereas the correct date was when the installment payment was made. The IRS also double-counted the interest due on a small portion of the overpaid tax.

1988 to offset and reduce the tax and interest for the tax year 1982 that it refunded to PGE in 1992.

PGE filed suit in the Court of Federal Claims, contending it was entitled to the additional amount of $5,037,109 in connection with the 1992 refund.[2] PGE argued that the IRS was not permitted to offset such erroneous interest against its allowable refund of tax and interest in 1992 because it was done after the expiration of the statute of limitations for filing suit to recover an erroneous refund under 26 U.S.C. § 7405. 26 U.S.C. §§ 7405, 6532(b). The government argued that its use of the offset was permissible. Both parties moved for summary judgment.

The Court of Federal Claims held that the IRS's offset action in 1992 was proper. *PGE I*, 55 Fed.Cl. at 277. Although recognizing that a suit under 26 U.S.C. § 7405 for the amount of the erroneously paid interest would have been time-barred, the court said "there is no provision in the [Internal Revenue] Code forbidding the administrative remedy the Service chose here." *Id.* at 276. The court was not persuaded by PGE's efforts to distinguish precedent the court found controlling. Specifically, the court explained:

> The most clearly applicable precedents, *Lewis*, *Dysart*, and *Fisher*, all contemplate the allowance of an offset by the government when, as here, the same tax, taxpayer, and tax year are at issue. Plaintiff has attempted to distinguish the facts of this case from *Lewis* and *Fisher*.
>
> ... The most important fact for the court is that this case involves the same tax, with the same taxpayer, for the same tax year. As the Court of Appeals for the Federal Circuit stated in *Fisher*, "*Lewis* and *Dysart* together stand for the proposition that the government may offset against a tax refund claim any additional amounts the taxpayer owes with respect to the tax shown on the return, even though the statute of limitations would bar assessing the additional amount owed." 80 F.3d at 1579. Here, plaintiff received an amount in overpayment with respect to tax year 1982. By requesting another refund in 1992 with respect to tax year 1982, plaintiff opened the door to the Service's offsetting the 1988 overpayment amount. Therefore, the Service's action in 1992 was legal.

Id. at 277. The court further determined that the offset was implemented correctly.

---

2. The offset, while made in 1992, was effective back to the date the erroneous interest was paid in August 1988. Thus, PGE claims this larger amount because additional interest under section 6611(b)(2) would have accrued on its refund that was paid in 1992.

PGE now appeals the issues of whether the offset was permissible and, if it was, whether the IRS implemented it properly. * * *

III

We must determine whether the IRS was entitled to offset the erroneous interest paid to PGE in 1988 against amounts due and owing PGE on a subsequent refund relating to the same tax year when the government could not have maintained a suit for such erroneous interest due to the expiration of the statute of limitations. See 26 U.S.C. §§ 7405, 6532(b). Surprisingly, this issue appears be one of first impression.[3]

PGE argues that when a taxpayer receives an erroneous refund of statutory interest it is not a tax liability but an ordinary debt obligation to the government. Thus, such erroneous interest mistakenly paid cannot be assessed or collected by the IRS in the same manner as a tax liability. PGE contends that it must be recovered, if at all, only by suit for an erroneous refund under 26 U.S.C § 7405 or by means otherwise afforded to the government for collection of debts (e.g., through a common-law right of offset, provided that the right is exercised within the period of limitations applicable to suits brought under 26 U.S.C. § 7405). PGE also asserts that there is no statutory or regulatory basis for extending the Supreme Court's decision in *Lewis v. Reynolds*, 284 U.S. 281, 52 S.Ct. 145, 76 L.Ed. 293 (1932), and its progeny to non-tax liabilities.

The government responds simply that under *Lewis v. Reynolds* and its progeny the taxpayer's 1992 claim for refund of its 1982 overpayment reopened its entire 1982 liability to redetermination by the IRS. As such, it argues that the remedy of offset was available to the IRS.

---

3. Both parties agree that the general statutory offset provision, 26 U.S.C. § 6402(a), does not apply to this case. Section 6402(a) provides "[i]n the case of any overpayment, the Secretary, within the applicable period of limitations, may credit the amount of such overpayment, including any interest allowed thereon, against any liability in respect of an internal revenue tax on the part of the person who made the overpayment and shall . . . refund any balance to such person." 26 U.S.C. § 6402(a).

Internal documents from the IRS indicate that it has long been the Service's position that unless it can assess the amount to be offset, it may not use its statutory right of offset under 26 U.S.C. § 6402. In Chief Counsel Advice 20014033, the Chief Counsel of the IRS stated "unless the Service can assess the amount erroneously refunded (as in the case of a rebate refund), the Service may not use its statutory right of offset under I.R.C. § 6402 to recover the erroneous refund." IRS CCA 200014033 *9 (2000); see also IRS GCM 36263, 1975 WL 37729 (1975) (stating "[t]he erroneous payment of $900 cannot be recovered by assessment and offset under Code § 6402 or other tax collection procedures, since there is no tax liability"). This may explain why both parties agree that 26 U.S.C. § 6402(a) is inapplicable to the present case, that is, because the erroneous interest at issue here is not assessable.

A

Lewis v. Reynolds was an income tax refund suit in which, in response to the refund claimed, the Commissioner of Internal Revenue determined that a deduction taken on the return, which was previously allowed, had been improperly taken. In determining the amount of the refund, the improper deduction was disallowed by the Commissioner. The limitations period for assessing an additional tax to reflect the disallowance of the deduction had passed when the Commissioner acted. The Supreme Court agreed with the Court of Appeals' conclusion that the relevant statutory provisions "clearly limit refunds to overpayments. It follows that the ultimate question presented for decision, upon a claim for refund, is whether the taxpayer *has overpaid his tax* [and t]his involves a redetermination of the entire tax liability." *Id.* at 283, 52 S.Ct. 145 (quoting *Lewis v. Reynolds*, 48 F.2d 515, 516 (10th Cir.1931) (emphasis added)). Affirming the Commissioner's action, the Court stated:

> While the statutes authorizing refunds do not specifically empower the Commissioner to reaudit a return whenever repayment is claimed, authority therefor is necessarily implied. An overpayment must appear before refund is authorized. Although the statute of limitations may have barred the assessment and collection of any additional sum, it does not obliterate the right of the United States *to retain payments* already received when they do not exceed the amount *which might have been properly assessed and demanded.*

284 U.S. at 283, 52 S.Ct. 145 (emphases added). Thus, the Court simply applied the statutory provisions dealing with refunds[4] which require that an overpayment must be shown by the taxpayer before a refund can be authorized. Accordingly, where the taxpayer has filed a claim for a tax refund, the IRS may offset against the refund claim a tax deficiency for the same tax year that previously had not been assessed, even though the assessment of such tax is barred by the expiration of the applicable

---

4.   The refund statutes at issue in *Lewis v. Reynolds* read as follows:

(a) Where there has been *an overpayment of any income, war-profits, or excess-profits tax imposed by this Act* (Feb. 26, 1926), * * *, or any such Act as amended, the amount of such overpayment shall, except as provided in subdivision (d), be credited against any income, war-profits, or excess-profits tax or installment thereof then due from the taxpayer, and any balance of such excess shall be refunded immediately to the taxpayer.

26 U.S.C. § 284(a) (1926) (emphasis added).

(a) Authorization. Where there has been an *overpayment of any tax* imposed by this title, the amount of such overpayment shall be credited against any income, war-profits, or excess-profits tax or installment thereof then due from the taxpayer, and any balance shall be refunded immediately to the taxpayer.

26 U.S.C. § 322(a) (1928) (emphasis added).

period of limitations. Otherwise, a refund might be made when there was not, in fact, an "overpayment," an event that would be inconsistent with the statute.

This defense of "lack of overpayment," permitting the government to offset a refund claim with a tax deficiency for the same tax year owed by the same taxpayer, was further explored by our predecessor court in *Dysart v. United States*, 169 Ct.Cl. 276, 340 F.2d 624 (1965). In this case, the taxpayer sought a refund of an erroneously assessed and collected penalty for the tax year 1954. The government conceded that the penalty was collected in error but claimed an offset in view of a tax deficiency that exceeded the penalty, despite the fact that the statute of limitations barred the assessment of the tax deficiency.[5] The court ruled that "the tax penalty is an addition to the tax, 26 U.S.C. § 294 (1952), and as such is considered as part of the income tax for the taxable year." *Id.* at 626 n.1.

Another issue before the court was "whether in a suit for refund where both the taxpayers' claim and the government's setoff concern the same tax for the same year by the same taxpayers, the right of the government to assert such a defense is an unconditional right . . . or whether . . . such a right is subject to the court's discretion after evaluating the 'equities' involved in each particular case." *Id.* at 606.[6] The court held that the Supreme Court's language in *Lewis v. Reynolds* laid down an "unqualified rule that 'an overpayment must appear before refund is authorized,' " 340 F.2d at 629 (quoting *Lewis v. Reynolds*, 284 U.S. at 283, 52 S.Ct. 145), and that there was nothing to suggest "limiting the defense of lack of overpayment where the refund claim and the setoff relate to the same tax, for the same year, payable by the same taxpayer," *id.* at 629. The court further commented that when determining whether there was an overpayment, a taxpayer's "entire *tax liability* under the particular tax return was open for redetermination." *Id.* at 628 (emphasis added).

The *Dysart* case, therefore, reiterated the necessity of an overpayment before a refund can be authorized and held that a court may not look to the equities of a case to deny the defense of lack of overpayment to the government. Contrary to the government's assertion, *Dysart* did not open the door wider than *Lewis v. Reynolds* already had for the IRS to offset a refund. At most, it simply clarified that setoff

---

5.   The asserted tax deficiency was used only to reduce the taxpayer's refund to zero.

6.   In reaching the answer to this question, the court discussed the differences between setoff and the doctrine of equitable recoupment (a doctrine which requires a single transaction be at issue and involves attempts to offset tax liability from one year against that for another year or where attempts are made to set off the tax liability of one taxpayer against that of a second taxpayer).

applied to the refund claim for a tax penalty improperly collected, because a tax penalty is an addition to tax and should be considered part of the tax liability.

Our holding in *Fisher v. United States*, 80 F.3d 1576 (Fed.Cir.1996), involved a refund claim against which the government offset deficiency interest owed by the same taxpayer for the same tax year. Our analysis characterized the teachings of *Lewis v. Reynolds* and *Dysart* as permitting the government to offset against a tax refund claim any tax owed for that year: "*Lewis* and *Dysart* together stand for the proposition that the government may offset against a tax refund claim any additional amounts the taxpayer owes with respect to the *tax shown on the return*, even though the statute of limitations would bar assessing the additional amount owed." *Id.* at 1579 (emphasis added). We also emphasized the necessity of the existence of an overpayment before a refund could be authorized.

The crux of our decision in *Fisher*, however, involved the question of whether deficiency interest should be treated any differently than the tax deficiency in *Lewis v. Reynolds* or the tax penalty in *Dysart*. Looking to the Revenue Code and our predecessor court, we held that "for the purposes of offset, interest should [not] be treated any differently than other components of tax liability." *Fisher*, 80 F.3d at 1580; *see* 26 U.S.C. § 6601(e) (1994) (stating that interest on tax underpayments "shall be assessed, collected, and paid in the same manner as taxes" and that any reference "to any tax imposed by this title shall be deemed also to refer to interest imposed by this section on such tax"); Alexander Proudfoot Co. v. United States, 197 Ct.Cl. 219, 454 F.2d 1379, 1382 (1972) (stating "[t]he Code's design for such interest is to assimilate it to the tax itself . . . . For a long time, deficiency interest has been so closely braided to principal that it has been deemed an integral part of the tax").

The common thread in these cases is that the refund statute requires that there be an actual overpayment of tax to support a refund. There cannot be such an overpayment without taking into account any additional amount of assessable tax, interest, or penalty owed by the taxpayer even though such an amount could not be assessed and collected because of the running of the statute of limitations.

B

In the instant case, the amount used to offset the refund claim in 1992 was the erroneously calculated statutory interest, a nonassessable amount. The assessable quantities in *Lewis v. Reynolds* and its progeny (tax deficiency, deficiency interest, and tax penalty) are a part of a taxpayer's tax liability, whereas nonassessable statutory interest is not. Thus, contrary to the government's assertion, *Lewis v. Reynolds* and its progeny are not directly on point with the case before us. We must, however, decide whether to extend this line of cases to cover the situation at issue here. Because the courts have distinguished components of tax liability which are assessable amounts from statutory interest which is not a tax liability component or assessable, we have found no convincing reason the two quantities should be treated the same. We, therefore, decline to extend *Lewis v. Reynolds* and its progeny to reach the facts of this case.

The tax deficiencies (including assessable interest and penalties) asserted as an offset in *Lewis v. Reynolds* and its progeny are very different from the offset at issue here and even treated differently by the Internal Revenue Code. Our case law notes the distinctions. In *Proudfoot*, 197 Ct.Cl. 219, 454 F.2d 1379, for example, our predecessor court explained that statutory interest arises simply because the government had possession of the taxpayer's funds, whereas deficiency interest is additional money due the government that arises from the taxpayer's tax liability:

> [T]he Revenue Code deals quite differently with statutory interest payable by the Government on overpayments. Regulated by §§ 6611-6612, that form of interest is paid by the United States, not as a refund of interest previously paid by the taxpayer on demand of the Service, but simply because the Government has had use of money found to belong to the taxpayer. . . .

Id. at 1384; *see also Fisher*, 80 F.3d at 1580 ("The Internal Revenue Code treats [deficiency] interest as an integral part of the liability itself. Thus, 26 U.S.C. § 6601(e) (1994), provides that interest on tax underpayments 'shall be assessed, collected, and paid in the same manner as taxes' and that any reference 'to any tax imposed by this title shall be deemed also to refer to interest imposed by this section on such tax.' ").

We are not the only court to treat tax monies differently based on the nature or generation of the funds. See O'Bryant v. United States, 49 F.3d 340, 346 (7th Cir.1995); Crocker First Nat'l Bank of S.F. v. United States, 137 F.Supp. 573, 574 (N.D.Cal.1955) (explaining that a suit to recover an erroneous refund is not a suit "in respect of any liability in respect of any tax," because any tax liability was satisfied when the tax was originally paid). In *O'Bryant*, the taxpayers paid their tax and interest liability in advance, which amounts were then assessed. The Service later erroneously sent the taxpayers a refund check. Without reassessing the tax, the Service then instituted collection activities and recovered a portion of the erroneous refund. The taxpayers sued to quiet title and recover the monies they claimed were unlawfully taken by the government. The Seventh Circuit noted that the refund taxpayers received was a nonrebate refund. "Nonrebate refunds are sent to the taxpayer not because the IRS determines that the tax paid is not owing but because of mistakes, typically clerical or computer errors." *O'Bryant*, 49 F.3d at 342. The court stated that there is a fundamental difference between taxpayers' liability for tax and their obligation, if any, to return a refund paid by mistake:

> [The government's proposed] approach would overlook the fundamental difference in character between the money that the O'Bryants now possess (a refund caused by the IRS' error) and the money they originally owed the IRS (their tax liability). The money the O'Bryants have now is not the money that the IRS' original assessment contemplated, since that amount was already paid. Rather, it is a payment the IRS accidentally sent them. They owe it to the government because they have been unjustly enriched by it, not because they have not paid their taxes.

Id. at 346. The court held that because the money the taxpayer received was not a part of the taxpaying transaction, the Service could not recover the funds through post-assessment procedures. *Id.*

A tax deficiency, tax penalty, and deficiency interest, the quantities permitted to offset the taxpayer's claimed refunds in *Lewis v. Reynolds* and its progeny, are all components of a taxpayer's tax liability. *See Dysart*, 340 F.2d at 626 n. 1; *Proudfoot*, 454 F.2d at 1382. Therefore, these components are taken into account in determining whether an overpayment exists and permitting them to offset a claimed tax refund is logical. There is no suggestion, however, that statutory interest is a part of, or even related to, a taxpayer's tax liability. Indeed it cannot be, for in the case of statutory interest mistakenly paid, the taxpayer has no underlying statutory obligation under the tax code to pay the government. As stated in *O'Bryant*, mistaken nonrebate refunds are owed to the government by reason of unjust enrichment. *O'Bryant*, 49 F.3d at 346. Statutory interest is also distinguishable from the components of tax liability because of its nonassessable nature. Given that a nonassessable quantity cannot be determined to be due and collectable, *see* West's Tax Law Dictionary 67 (2004 ed.) (defining "assess" as "[t]he posting of tax, penalty, and interest that has been determined to be due and collectable"), it would be illogical to treat such a quantity as analogous to a taxpayer's tax liability.

The tax code provides an integrated and comprehensive statutory scheme for assessing, collecting, and refunding taxes, deficiency interest, and penalties. *Lewis v. Reynolds* and its progeny did not disturb this framework; they merely applied the refund provision requiring an overpayment. Were we to hold that the IRS is correct in determining that an offset is permissible here, we would be going outside of this well-tailored statutory scheme. We, therefore, decline to extend *Lewis v. Reynolds* to apply to statutory interest improperly paid to PGE.

C

The only case we have found that deals with erroneously refunded statutory interest is factually distinguishable from the instant case. In *Crocker*, 137 F.Supp. 573,[7] the government offset erroneously paid interest for tax year 1942 against a refund for tax year 1945. The court stated that "since it [is] obvious that the offset claimed by the Commissioner must be the equivalent of a cause of action by the Government in a suit to recover the erroneous payment, the parties [do] not dispute that the time limitation for suit applie[d] equally to the offset." *Id.* at 574. The offset in *Crocker* was not made within two years after the payment of the erroneous interest on the 1942 refund. * * * The court determined that the offset had not been timely made and entered judgment for the taxpayer.

As can be seen, *Crocker* dealt with applying the offset to a refund claim for a different tax year, whereas in this the case the offset was applied to a claimed refund in the same tax year. Moreover, the court noted that the government conceded that the statute of limitations pertaining to when the United States may sue to recover erroneous refunds of taxes or erroneous payments of interest on refunds applied, whereas in this case the government makes no such concession. While readily distinguishable on the facts, *Crocker* does equate the ability to offset erroneously or mistakenly paid statutory interest with a cause of action by the government to sue for an erroneous refund under § 7405.

Like the court's determination in *Crocker*, we view the offset claimed by the Service here as akin to a cause of action by the government in a suit to recover the erroneous interest. As noted in *Crocker*, while there is no statute governing the time limit for when such an offset may be made, there is a statute expressly limiting when the government can sue to recover erroneous refunds under 26 U.S.C. § 7405. *Id.* at 574 ("There is no limitation statute specifically fixing the time within which such an offset may be made. There is, however, a statute, limiting to two years, the time within which the United States may sue to recover erroneous refunds of taxes or erroneous payments of interest on refunds."). We see no reason why this statute of limitations should not apply equally to the

---

7. Of course, as a district court decision, this case is non-binding on us.

offset in this case. Thus, we hold that the Service's ability to offset erroneously paid statutory interest against a taxpayer's refund claim in the same tax year is subject to the same statute of limitations that applies to suits by the United States to recover erroneous refunds of taxes or erroneous payments of interest on refunds. *See* 26 U.S.C. §§ 6532(b), 7405.

Recent decisions internal to the IRS are not at odds with our determination today. Indeed, the Chief Counsel of the IRS expressly approved of the *Crocker* decision and further explained "we are of the opinion that as long as the Service is unable to assess nonrebate refunds, the Service may justifiably rely on the common law right of offset to recover these non-tax debts. The applicable statute of limitations for this remedy is the two or five[8] year period set forth in I.R.C. § 6532(b)." IRS CCA 200014033.[9] While not bound by the Service's position, we simply note that our analysis has led us to the position espoused by the Service for at least the last thirty years.

Indeed, *Lewis v. Reynolds* is now over seventy years old. Congress and the IRS have had ample time to provide specific authority that would have broadly allowed the offset the government is seeking in this case. Indeed, if it were intended to allow the government to recover mistaken payments of statutory interest (and other non-tax debts) by way of offset, and not merely tax liabilities used to determine whether there was an overpayment of tax, the tax code or the regulations could have so stated.

---

8.   "[I]f the refund is induced by fraud or misrepresentation of material fact." 26 U.S.C. § 6532(b).

9.   This reasoning dovetails with earlier IRS decisions. In a 1975 General Counsel Memorandum it is stated:

> Suppose for instance, the taxpayer files a return showing no tax liability and claims a refund of tax withheld of $100. The Service erroneously issues a check in the amount of $1000. The erroneous payment of $900 cannot be recovered by assessment and offset under Code § 6402 or other tax collection procedures, since there is no tax liability. A civil suit to recover the refund under Code § 7405 is therefore the Service's sole remedy, except we believe it is proper in this instance for the Service to exercise a common law right of offset by deducting the amount claimed under Code § 7405 from any refund due the taxpayer. Since the amount so claimed is not a tax liability and could never have been collected under the tax recovery provisions of the Code, the procedural safeguards given to the taxpayer by those provisions will not be frustrated by use of common law offset in this situation. We therefore conclude that such offset may be here exercised within the time limitations prescribed by Code § 6532(b).

IRS GCM 36263 *10 (1975).

We do not accord these internal documents *Skidmore* or any other type of deference. *See* Skidmore v. Swift & Co., 323 U.S. 134, 65 S.Ct. 161, 89 L.Ed. 124 (1944); see also IRS GCM 36263 *13 (stating "This document is not to be relied upon or otherwise cited as precedent by taxpayers."). We merely note that the Service has taken the position that offsets of nonassessable quantities against tax refunds must be made within the statute of limitations set forth in 26 U.S.C. § 6532(b).

In the present case the offset occurred after the two-year statute of limitations had expired. As such, the Service's right to offset was time-barred. * * *

IV.

Our decision today results in a windfall for the taxpayer. As the Seventh Circuit has noted in a similar situation, "although it may seem unjust that the IRS cannot recover its erroneous refund in this case, . . . we cannot base our resolution of the issue before us on the equities of a particular factual situation . . . . [T]here are many situations in which permitting the IRS to recover would be just as unfair as barring recovery here." *O'Bryant*, 49 F.3d at 346-47.

We hold that the offset applied to PGE's 1992 refund claim was time-barred. Accordingly, we reverse the trial court's judgment with respect to the offset and remand for further proceedings as necessary.

Notes

The Service issued a nonacquiescence to the *Pacific Gas* case in 2006 because it believes the Federal Circuit's decision is erroneous. The government's position is that not only will it continue to offset erroneously overpaid interest against subsequent refunds for the same taxable year, even if the statute of limitations has elapsed, but it also will continue to litigate this position, even in cases that are appealable to the Federal Circuit. See AOD 200602, available at www.irs.gov/pub/irs-aod/aod200602.

Note that if the Pacific Gas & Electric Co. had lost the case, it would have owed interest on the overpayment from the date the erroneous refund was made. I.R.C. § 6602.

B. FORMAL CLAIMS AND WAIVERS OF CLAIMS

Under §§ 6511(b)(1) and 6514, the Service has no authority to refund or credit the amount of any overpayment (except in the case of a math error on the return) after the tax has been assessed and collected, unless the taxpayer files a refund claim. A claim for refund of income taxes withheld from wages or an overpayment of estimated taxes usually is made on the Form 1040 for that taxable year. If the return has been filed, the refund claim may be made on an amended return (Form 1040X for individuals or Form 1120X for corporations), which, like the Form

1040, must be signed under penalties of perjury. Refund claims for taxes other than income taxes may be made on an IRS Form 843.[2]

The claim must be specific. It must list the amount of the overpayment and must inform the Service whether the amount is be returned to the taxpayer or credited against the taxpayer's tax liability for the year following the year of the overpayment. Also, each ground supporting the refund claim must be set forth in sufficient detail to apprise the Service of the basis of the claim. Reg. § 301.6402-3(a)(5). This latter requirement is critical, because in any subsequent refund suit the taxpayer is limited to the assertions raised in the claim. See § IV, below.

The following case examines the issue of whether a non-specific refund claim may be considered a valid claim.

KIKALOS v. UNITED STATES

United States Court of Appeals, Seventh Circuit, 2007.
479 F.3d 522.

FLAUM, CIRCUIT JUDGE.

The IRS audited the Kikaloses' 1998 tax return and determined that they under-reported their income for that year. The Kikaloses paid additional taxes and penalties and subsequently sought a refund. The IRS denied the refund because the Kikaloses failed to provide the necessary documentation to support their claim. The Kikaloses filed suit, which the district court dismissed for lack of subject matter jurisdiction. For the following reasons, we affirm the district court's ruling.

I. BACKGROUND

On June 1, 1999, Nick and Helen Kikalos filed a timely joint federal income tax return for 1998 with the Internal Revenue Service ("IRS") Center in Cincinnati, Ohio. The Kikaloses paid $504,181 in federal income taxes for that year. On July 28, 1999, the IRS audited the Kikaloses' 1998 return. On July 13, 2001, the Kikaloses filed an amended 1998 federal income tax return and reported an additional $35,982 in income taxes and paid $43,609 to reduce or eliminate penalties in anticipation of the IRS's proposed adjustments.

On March 4, 2002, the IRS issued an examination report proposing over seventeen adjustments that would increase the Kikaloses' tax liability. On March 14, 2002, Nick Kikalos wrote a series of letters to the

---

2. These forms are available at http://www.irs.gov/pub/irs-pdf/f1040X.pdf; http://wwwirs.gov/pub/irs-pdf/f1120Xpdf; http://wwwirs.gov/pub/irs-fill/f843.pdf

IRS that objected to each adjustment. On May 3, 2002, the IRS issued the Kikaloses a statutory notice of deficiency, finding that they had understated their taxes by $81,704. The IRS assessed the Kikaloses an additional $98,044.80 in taxes and penalties, which the Kikaloses paid on May 31, 2002.

On September 18, 2002, the Kikaloses filed an amended federal income tax return that reported a decrease in tax of $81,704 and sought a refund of $141,654.00, which included the $43,609 that the Kikaloses paid on July 13, 2001. The instructions on the tax return form stated, "Enter the line number from page 1 of the form for each item you are changing and give the reasons for each change. . .. If you do not attach the required information, your 1040X may be returned." The Kikaloses wrote, "Income was incorrectly assessed to the above named taxpayer." On December 18, 2002, the IRS rejected the refund claim by letter because the Kikaloses failed to explain or document the decrease in income. The letter stated that "if you want to sue to recover tax, penalties, or other amounts, you may file a lawsuit with the United States District court having jurisdiction or with the United States Court of Federal Claims." The letter also instructed the Kikaloses that they could send in a new claim if they had the missing information. Although the Kikaloses had until May 31, 2004 to file another claim with the necessary information, they did not do so.

On December 13, 2004, the Kikaloses filed a complaint in federal district court in Indiana to recover $141,654 of income tax, penalties, and interest. On September 15, 2005, the government filed a motion to dismiss for lack of subject matter jurisdiction, alleging that the Kikaloses did not file a valid refund claim. The Kikaloses conceded that their refund claim was insufficient, but argued that the IRS waived its formal requirements or, alternatively, that their amended return should be considered an informal refund claim. On March 23, 2006, the district court dismissed the complaint for lack of jurisdiction holding that the Kikaloses failed to submit a valid refund claim. The Kikaloses appeal.

II. ANALYSIS

The Kikaloses argue that the district court erred by holding that it lacked jurisdiction to consider the merits of their claim. * * * Section 7422 of the Internal Revenue Code requires that any taxpayer seeking a refund must first file a valid claim with the Secretary of the Treasury before filing suit in federal court. 26 U.S.C. § 7422(a). Treasury Regulation § 301.6402-2(b)(1) provides that the claim "must set forth in detail each ground upon which a credit or refund is claimed and facts sufficient to apprise the Commissioner of the exact basis thereof." It also states that "[a] claim which does not comply with these requirements will not be considered for any purpose as a claim for refund or credit." 26 C.F.R. § 301.6402-2(b)(1).

The Kikaloses' refund claim stated that "[i]ncome was incorrectly assessed to the above named taxpayer," but did not provide the grounds for their claim. Accordingly, the government contends, the district court did not have subject matter jurisdiction over the merits of their claim. See Martin v. United States, 833 F.2d 655, 658-59 (7th Cir.1987) (holding that "[a] timely sufficient claim for refund is a jurisdictional prerequisite to a refund suit"). The Kikaloses assert that despite the deficiency in their administrative refund claim, the IRS waived its formal requirements, or alternatively, they are excused from the formal requirements pursuant to the informal refund claim doctrine.

A. Waiver

The Supreme Court has held that while the Treasury may not waive the congressionally mandated requirement that a claim be filed, the Treasury can waive its own formal requirements. See Angelus Milling Co. v. Comm'r of Internal Revenue, 325 U.S. 293, 296, 65 S.Ct. 1162, 89 L.Ed. 1619 (1945). The Commissioner may waive the IRS's specificity requirements if 1) the IRS has sufficient knowledge of the claim, and 2) makes a determination on the merits or leads the taxpayer to believe that the IRS treated the claim as formally sufficient. See United States v. Memphis Cotton Oil Co., 288 U.S. 62, 70, 53 S.Ct. 278, 77 L.Ed. 619 (1933); Goulding v. United States, 929 F.2d 329, 332-33 (7th Cir.1991).

In *Goulding*, the IRS issued a deficiency against the taxpayer. After paying the alleged deficiency, the taxpayer filed a refund claim stating that the amount "was neither due, nor properly assessed, and therefore illegally collected." 929 F.2d at 330. The claim did not provide any further details about the taxpayer's grounds for a refund. The IRS rejected the request "per audit determination." The taxpayer filed a complaint, which the district court dismissed for lack of jurisdiction. This Court held that the words "per audit determination" were ambiguous and that the record in the case demonstrated that the IRS had extensive knowledge of the claim because it had litigated the same issues in a suit brought by the taxpayers' son. *Id.* at 333. Accordingly, the Court held that the IRS had waived its defense that the claim was insufficient. *Id.*

The Kikaloses maintain that *Goulding* dictates a finding of waiver in this case. We disagree. Unlike in *Goulding*, where the IRS communication ambiguously stated that refund was rejected "per audit determination," in this case, the IRS explained that it rejected the

Kikaloses' claim because "[n]o documentation was included to verify the amount on line 1 [of the 1998 Refund Claim]." This statement does not indicate that the IRS ruled on the merits of the Kikaloses' claim; to the contrary, the statement indicates that the IRS did not have sufficient information to consider the claim's merits. In order to find waiver, the plaintiffs must unmistakably show "that the Commissioner has in fact seen fit to dispense with his formal requirements and to examine the merits of the claim." Angelus Milling, 325 U.S. at 297, 65 S.Ct. 1162. The Kikaloses have failed to make this showing.

The Kikaloses also argue that, as in *Goulding*, the IRS had extensive knowledge of their claim because of the 1999 audit. They point out that the IRS collected over 5,000 documents from them during the audit and that Nick Kikalos wrote a series of letters on March 14, 2002 objecting to the IRS's proposed adjustments. However, Nick Kikalos's March 14 letters only objected to the IRS's proposed adjustments from March 4, 2002. The letters made no mention of the $43,609.00 that the Kikaloses paid on July 13, 2001, which comprised part of the insufficient refund claim. Thus, the IRS had no information regarding the refund request related to the $43,609.00.

Moreover, the IRS handled the 1999 audit out of its Merrillville, Indiana office, while the Kikaloses sent their refund claim to the Cincinnati, Ohio office. Additionally, the Kikaloses' insufficient refund claim made no reference to the audit or to Nick Kikalos's letters. The Supreme Court has cautioned that "it is not enough that somewhere under the Commissioner's roof is the information which might enable him to pass on a claim for refund . . ." *Angelus Milling Co.*, 325 U.S. at 299, 65 S.Ct. 1162. Consequently, the Kikaloses have not demonstrated that the IRS had sufficient knowledge of their claim and proceeded on the merits.

* * *

III.   Conclusion

For the foregoing reasons, we AFFIRM the district court's ruling.

Notes

In a case in which the taxpayer alleges that the Service waived the specificity requirement, the taxpayer has the burden of establishing that the Service has investigated the facts underlying the claim or otherwise was affirmatively aware of the matters in dispute. In *Angelus Milling Co.*, cited in *Kikalos*, the United States Supreme Court held that the evidence was insufficient to establish that the taxpayer's claim (rather than that of a related party) had been considered by the Service.

A refund claim may be amended after it is filed to add new grounds in support of the alleged overpayment, provided the statute of limitations remains open. But where the taxpayer seeks an untimely amendment of a claim on grounds different from those considered initially by the Service, the taxpayer does not have a sufficient defense of waiver. See United States v. Andrews, 302 U.S. 517 (1938).

C. INFORMAL CLAIMS

Although a formal claim is required, there are some situations in which the taxpayer may be entitled to a refund even though no formal refund claim has been filed.

EBERT v. UNITED STATES
United States Court of Federal Claims, 2005.
66 Fed.Cl. 287

MEROW, SENIOR JUDGE.

* * *

Facts

Plaintiff, a resident of the Philippines, is the widow of a veteran of the U.S. Military. For several years up to and including the first half of 2001, she received compensation under the Survivor Benefit Plan ("SBP"). On July 24, 2001, she received notification from the Department of Veterans Affairs ("DVA") that she was entitled to Dependency and Indemnity Compensation ("DIC"), retroactive to February 1, 1999. Her SBP payments were discontinued as of the end of June 2001, as a result of her award of DIC benefits in a greater amount. SBP benefits are taxable. 26 U.S.C. §§ 72(n), 871(a)(1) (2000). In contrast, DIC payments are exempt from taxation. 38 U.S.C. § 5301(a)(1).

On February 6, 2002, plaintiff wrote to the IRS to request a refund of the taxes withheld from her SBP payments for 1999 and 2000. In her letter to the IRS on this date, plaintiff "solicit[ed] reconsideration determination (sic) on my claim for refund of tax withheld for 12-31-99 and 12-31-00(sic) . . . ." Plaintiff further stated that "DIC VA award dated July 24, 2001, DIC effective 1999, SBP contributions and tax withheld of 1999 and 2000, be refunded (sic)." In support of her claim, she submitted documentation, in the form of IRS Form 1042S,[4] of the amount of tax withheld from her SBP benefits for 1999 and 2000. In a second letter to the IRS, this one dated October 14, 2003, she also requested a refund of

---

4. Form 1042S is entitled "Foreign Person's U.S. Source Income Subject to Withholding." It details the taxpayer's gross income and the amount of U.S. tax withheld.

the taxes withheld during 2001. With this letter, she included a copy of her 2001 income tax return, completed on Form 1040EZ-NR, to substantiate the amount of tax withheld for 2001.

On February 27, 2004, plaintiff, acting pro se, filed a complaint with this court to recover the taxes withheld for the years 1999-2001. In her complaint, plaintiff restates her contention that the conversion of her SBP payments into DIC benefits entitles her to a refund of the taxes withheld. Plaintiff is seeking a refund of $4,887.00 ($1,958.40 for 1999, $1,915.20 for 2000, and $1,013.40 for 2001), plus interest. The government moved for summary judgment on March 22, 2005. Plaintiff responded to the government's motion on May 12, 2005 in a submission that is being treated as a cross-motion for summary judgment.

* * *

Discussion

The SBP program, which is administered by the Defense Finance and Accounting Service ("DFAS"), a division of the Department of Defense ("DOD"), provides compensation to surviving spouses and dependents of U.S. servicemen. Under the program, a portion of the serviceman's retirement pay is set aside to provide an annuity for his or her spouse and dependents after his or her death. Such benefits are taxable once the beneficiary has been paid an amount equal to the contributions made by the serviceman. 26 U.S.C. § 72(n).

DIC benefits are administered by the DVA and are available to any spouse or dependent of a veteran who died of a service-related disability. 38 U.S.C. § 1310(a). As is the case with benefits paid out under any program administered by DVA, DIC benefits are not subject to taxation. § 5301(a)(1). In addition, DIC benefits can be awarded retroactively: DVA is permitted to award DIC benefits retroactive to the date on which it receives the beneficiary's application for such benefits. 38 U.S.C. § 5110(a).

A beneficiary can receive both SBP and DIC payments under certain circumstances. If a beneficiary under the SBP program becomes eligible for DIC payments, then her SBP payment will be reduced by an amount equal to her DIC benefit. 10 USC § 1450(c)(1). If her DIC benefit exceeds her SBP payment, then she is no longer entitled to receive SBP benefits. *Id.* The reduction in SBP payments becomes effective on the day her DIC payments begin. § 1450(c)(2). As discussed below, a retroactive award has the effect of converting any taxable benefits received during the retroactive period into nontaxable DIC benefits.

Plaintiff contends that she is entitled to a refund of the taxes withheld from her SBP payments for the years 1999-2001. She argues that because the SBP payments were converted to DIC benefits retroactive to February 1, 1999, the tax withheld from that date until her payments were discontinued on June 30, 2001, should be refunded to her. In response, the government makes several arguments: First, the government contends that she has not satisfied the requirements for a tax refund claim. * * *

A. Whether Plaintiff Has Satisfied the Requirements for a Tax Refund Claim

In a claim for a tax refund, plaintiff bears the burden of proving that she is entitled to a refund and the exact amount of the refund to which she is entitled. The Code of Federal Regulations states that in order to obtain a refund, plaintiff must "set forth in detail the grounds on which a credit or refund is claimed and facts sufficient to apprise the Commissioner of the exact basis thereof . . . . The statement of the grounds and facts must be verified by a written declaration that it is made under the penalties of perjury." 26 C.F.R. § 301.6402-2(b)(1). The regulations further state that a claim will not be allowed unless these formal requirements are satisfied. *Id.* Nevertheless, courts have not held plaintiffs to these rigorous standards in all cases. Instead, courts have generally recognized "informal claims" where the plaintiff "has adequately apprise[d] the Internal Revenue Service that a refund is sought and for certain years." United States v. Commercial Nat'l Bank of Peoria, 874 F.2d 1165, 1171 (7th Cir.1989); Furst v. United States, 230 Ct.Cl. 375, 678 F.2d 147 (1982); see also United States v. Kales, 314 U.S. 186, 194, 62 S.Ct. 214, 86 L.Ed. 132 (1941). There are three components to an informal claim: 1) it must provide the IRS with notice that plaintiff is asserting a right to a refund; 2) it must present the legal and factual bases for the refund; and 3) it must have some written component. New England Elec. Sys. v. United States, 32 Fed. Cl. 636, 641 (1995). However, the written component is not required to contain the entirety of the plaintiff's case. The court must examine all of the surrounding facts and circumstances to determine whether plaintiff's submissions constitute an adequate informal claim. *Id.* The relevant inquiry is whether the claim is sufficient to notify the IRS that the party is asserting a right to a tax refund, and to enable the IRS to begin an examination of the claim. *Furst*, 678 F.2d at 151. A plaintiff who is claiming a tax refund must prove her case by a preponderance of the evidence. Cook v. United States, 46 Fed. Cl. 110, 116 (2000).

Plaintiff has met her burden here. She provided the IRS with notice that she was claiming the right to a refund, in a form which satisfies the written component requirement. In her letter to the IRS dated February

6, 2002, she specifically requested a tax refund for 1999 and 2000. She also requested a refund for 2001 in her letter to the IRS dated October 14, 2003. In addition, plaintiff apprised the IRS of the factual and legal bases for her claimed refund. She states in her February 6, 2002 letter that she is entitled to a refund as a result of the retroactive conversion of her SBP benefits into DIC payments. She submitted copies of her 1999 and 2000 1042S Forms and a copy of her 2001 income tax return to substantiate the amount of her claimed refund. Plaintiff has thus put the IRS on notice that she is asserting a right to a claim and has provided sufficient supporting documentation to enable the IRS to examine the claim. *Furst*, 678 F.2d at 151. She has therefore submitted a cognizable informal claim showing that she is entitled to a refund, and the exact amount to which she is entitled.

* * *

Conclusion

For the reasons set forth above, plaintiff has established entitlement to a refund of the tax withholdings deducted from the SBP payments made to her, and therefore it is ORDERED that her cross-motion for summary judgment be GRANTED, and defendant's motion for summary judgment be DENIED. Final judgment shall be entered in the amount of $4,727.40, plus interest as provided by law. This value reflects the amount of tax withheld from plaintiff's SBP benefits from February 1, 1999, the effective date of her entitlement to DIC benefits, through the end of June 2001, when her SBP payments were discontinued.

Notes and Questions

The informal claim doctrine is a judicial doctrine that is not likely to be embraced by the IRS. The full opinion of the *Ebert* case illustrates the lengths to which the Service will go to challenge an informal refund claim. In the redacted portion of the *Ebert* opinion, the Service also argued that the substantial variance doctrine applied (see § D., below), that the benefit payments Mrs. Ebert received were from a "closed" transaction that could not be recharacterized for tax purposes, and that Mrs. Ebert had failed to prove that she had not already been reimbursed for the taxes she paid under the SBP. The court, however, easily dispensed with these arguments.

Note that two factors in Mrs. Ebert's favor were that the conversion of the benefit occurred *before* she filed the informal claim and it was an event over which she had no control. Since the conversion of the benefit was the legal basis for her refund claim and it had been mentioned in her letters to the IRS, the substantial variance rule did not apply in her case.

In certain cases a taxpayer who anticipates filing a refund claim in the future, depending on the occurrence of a contingency, may be able to preserve the right to file such a claim after the statute of limitations has run. If the taxpayer has met the requirements for an informal claim, the taxpayer's right to file a claim may be preserved even though he/she has not filed a formal protective claim. It is best, however, to file a formal refund claim rather than rely on the informal claim doctrine.

Informal refund claims have arisen from notations made on the backs of checks, letters attached to signed Forms 870, letters agreeing to the payment of tax in installments, and from letters of protest and other written correspondence between the taxpayer and the Service. The claim, however, must meet the requirements of a valid informal claim. If so, and the claim is deemed sufficient to put the Service on notice that the taxpayer intends to file a refund claim, the informal claim will toll the statute of limitations. See Night Hawk Leasing Co. v. U.S., 84 Ct.Cl. 596 (1937) (notation on back of checks constituted informal refund claims that were perfected by subsequently filed formal claims).

1. Why must the claim be in writing?

2. What is a protective refund claim?

3. Is it possible for a taxpayer to obtain a refund on the basis of a valid claim filed by another taxpayer? See Mills v. United States, 890 F.2d 1133 (11th Cir. 1989).

4. What is the difference between waiver and the informal claim doctrine?

D. SUBSTANTIAL VARIANCE

If the refund claim is denied and the case proceeds to trial, the grounds raised in the suit cannot vary substantially from the grounds set forth in the refund claim.

OTTAWA SILICA CO. v. UNITED STATES
Court of Appeals for the Federal Circuit, 1983.
699 F.2d 1124.

DAVIS, NICHOLS AND NIES, CIRCUIT JUDGES.

PER CURIAM

* * *

In this action, plaintiff, Ottawa Silica Company, seeks to recover federal income taxes and assessed interest for its tax years 1964, 1967, 1969, 1970 and 1971, plus statutory interest. * * *

Ottawa is a family-owned corporation organized and existing under the laws of the State of Delaware and has its principal place of business in Ottawa, Illinois. Ottawa has been engaged in the mining, processing and marketing of industrial sand known as silica since 1900. Silica sand, also known as quartzite, as distinguished from common sand, is a highly refined industrial mineral. It is the basic raw material of the glass and ceramic industry. It is also used in the foundry industry as a core and molding sand. Its industrial uses in chemical markets include: paint, testing sand, and hydrofracing sand for the oil well industry.

* * *

Argument

* * *

The second issue raised by plaintiff concerns the degree to which the court will allow a taxpayer to vary the grounds of its suit from those raised in the claims for refund. Plaintiff has alleged that the IRS failed to allow it the full percentage depletion deduction that it was entitled to and, in so doing also failed to allow plaintiff the full consolidated net operating loss deduction it was entitled to for 1967. The parties have reached an agreement that is dispositive of the substantive aspects of both the percentage depletion and the net operating loss issues. The procedural issue which remains to be resolved is whether the grounds for relief stated in plaintiff's claim for a refund are adequate to confer jurisdiction on this court over an aspect of the percentage depletion deduction not mentioned in the refund claim. It is my opinion that the jurisdiction of this court does not extend to those aspects of the percentage depletion deduction and the 1967 net operating loss that were not adequately raised on plaintiff's claims for refund.

During all times relevant to these proceedings, Ottawa and its subsidiaries sold a form of industrial sand, or quartzite, known as silica, which is a mineral described in section 613(b)(7) of the Internal Revenue Code. The code allows plaintiff a percentage depletion deduction for the silica it removes from each of its mining properties. The allowable deduction is the lesser of: (a) the gross income from the property multiplied by the appropriate percentage depletion rate specified in section 613(b)(7), or (b) 50 percent of the taxable income from the property. 26 U.S.C. § 613(a) (1976). The term "gross income from the property" means the gross income from mining, which is that amount of income "attributable to the processes of extraction of the ores or minerals from the ground and the application of mining processes." Treas.Reg. § 1.613-4(a). Packaging the ore or minerals is a non-mining process. *Id.*

On its federal income tax returns for the tax years 1964 through 1971, plaintiff took percentage depletion deductions for the silica it had mined from its properties. During this time plaintiff sold the silica both in bags and in bulk quantities. In computing the gross income from mining for each type of the silica products, plaintiff's accountants used a bulk sales price. They considered any extra income derived from the sale of bagged products as income attributable to a non-mining process. For that reason, they excluded the extra income from their calculations when determining the gross income from mining figure for the bagged products.

One of the items plaintiff sold was a bagged product known as Ottawa Testing Sand. Plaintiff sold the testing sand only in bags and for a price substantially higher than the bulk price of its other products. Plaintiff's accountants, however, computed the gross income from mining figure for the testing sand by using the bulk sales price. The accountants could have calculated the gross income by using the actual sales price of the testing sand less the costs attributable to the non-mining processes (bagging). Had they done so, the gross income from mining for the testing sand would have been greater than the figure obtained using the bulk price. Thus, the use of the bulk price produced a lower gross income from mining, which in turn yielded a lower percentage depletion deduction for the testing sand when multiplied by the applicable rate. Plaintiff first learned that it had understated the gross income from mining and the depletion deduction for the testing sand in July 1977, during an IRS audit of plaintiff's tax returns for 1972 through 1975.

On its tax returns for the years 1964 through 1972, plaintiff had used rates of 15 percent or 14 percent in calculating its percentage depletion deduction. After examining plaintiff's returns, the IRS reduced the depletion deduction by requiring plaintiff to use a 5 percent rate for some of its products. The reports prepared by the examining agents for the fiscal years ending on January 1, 1967, December 31, 1967, and December 29, 1968, gave the following reasons for reducing the percentage depletion deductions:

> A 15% rate of percentage depletion was claimed on all of the income from the sale of the silica sand and quartzite sold after the application of the ordinary mine treatment processes. A 5% rate of percentage depletion is recommended on the silica sand and quartzite sold for use as strecco stone, plaster, exposed aggregate, golf trap sand and like uses.

In a report dated May 31, 1973, the IRS made similar reductions of the depletion deduction for the fiscal years ending on December 28, 1969, January 3, 1971, and January 2, 1972. That report provided:

> Taxpayer has computed depletion based on 15% in the first year and on 14% in the succeeding two years. Most of the products sold go into use in the glass or foundry industries. Some of the products are

sold to construction industries and some small amounts are sold for such uses as golf trap sand or as playsand, which qualify only for a 5% depletion rate.

The IRS made no other adjustments to the percentage depletion deductions aside from the reduction of the depletion rate for some of plaintiff's products. Accordingly, the IRS reduced plaintiff's depletion deductions by the following amounts for each of the following fiscal years:

FYE		
	1/26/66	$ 5,701.00
	1/1/67	16,977.00
	12/31/67	138,457.15
	12/29/68	24,802.64
	12/28/69	25,180.64
	1/3/71	19,046.37
	1/2/72	20,144.67

Plaintiff subsequently paid the resulting tax deficiencies and filed timely refund claims on or about January 7, 1975, for the tax years 1967, 1969, 1970, and 1971. To each of these refund claims plaintiff attached a statement that provided:

This Statement is being attached to Refund Claims of Ottawa Silica Company and Subsidiary Companies for FYE 12/31/67, FYE 12/28/69, FYE 1/3/71 and FYE 1/2/72. The bases for these Refund Claims are as follows:

1. Pursuant to Revenue Agents Reports dated February 4, 1972, as supplemented by a Conference Report dated August 1, 1972, covering FYE 12/31/62, FYE 12/31/63, FYE 12/31/64, FYE 1/2/66, FYE 1/1/67, FYE 12/31/67 and FYE 12/29/68 and a Revenue Agents Report dated August 27, 1931 (presumably meaning 1973) covering FYE 12/28/69, FYE 1/3/71 and 1/2/72 Ottawa Silica Company and/or certain of its consolidated subsidiaries were erroneously denied deductions for the following items:

(a)   * * *

(b)   Percentage depletion as follows:

FYE		
	1/2/66	$ 5,701.00
	1/1/67	16,977.00
	12/31/67	38,457.15
	12/29/68	24,802.64
	12/28/69	32,333.20
	1/3/71	14,214.37
	1/2/72	12,339.67

(c)   * * *

(d)   The consolidated net operating loss carryback properly deductible in FYE 12/31/67.

At this time plaintiff did not know that it had erred in calculating the depletion deduction for the Ottawa Testing Sand. It was only in July 1977 that plaintiff discovered that it could have taken a greater deduction for the testing sand, but by then the statute of limitations prevented the filing or amending of its refund claims for the tax years 1964 through 1971.

In June 1978 plaintiff petitioned this court for a refund of its income taxes, alleging inter alia, that the IRS had failed to allow it the full depletion deduction it was entitled to. Plaintiff now asks this court to grant it the following deductions for depletion:

Year	Additional Depreciation Allowable
1965	$ 35,000
1966	50,000
1967	174,000
1968	49,000
1969	49,000
1970	48,000
1971	49,000

The conditions under which a taxpayer may sue the United States for the recovery of income taxes are defined by statute and by regulation. The Internal Revenue Code prohibits any taxpayer from maintaining an action to recover taxes from the Government unless a claim for a refund has first been filed with the Internal Revenue Service (IRS). 26 U.S.C. § 7422(a) (1976).[4] The regulations further provide that the claim for a refund "must set forth in detail each ground upon which a credit or a refund is claimed and facts sufficient to apprise the Commissioner of the exact basis thereof." Treas.Reg. § 301.6402-2(b)(1) (1955). Together, the statute and the regulation preclude a taxpayer-plaintiff from substantially varying at trial the factual bases of its arguments from those raised in the refund claims it presented to the IRS.

---

4.   The statute provides:

"No suit or proceeding shall be maintained in any court for the recovery of any internal revenue tax alleged to have been erroneously or illegally assessed or collected, or of any penalty claimed to have been collected without authority, or of any sum alleged to have been excessive or in any manner wrongfully collected, until a claim for refund or credit has been duly filed with the Secretary, according to the provisions of law in that regard, and the regulations of the Secretary established in pursuance thereof."

26 U.S.C. § 7422(a).

This court has on many occasions considered the issue of variance and has adhered to the general rule that a ground for a refund that is neither specifically raised by a timely claim for a refund, nor comprised within the general language of the claim, cannot be considered by a court in a subsequent suit for a refund. Union Pacific Railroad v. United States, 182 Ct.Cl. 103, 108, 389 F.2d 437, 442 (1968); see Forward Communications Corp. v. United States, 221 Ct.Cl. 582, 623, 608 F.2d 485, 508 (1979); John B. Lambert & Associates v. United States, 212 Ct.Cl. 71, 86-87 (1976); Fruehauf Corp. v. United States, 201 Ct.Cl. 366, 378-79, 477 F.2d 568, 575 (1973). The reasons for this rule preventing substantial variance are:

> To prevent surprise and to give adequate notice to the [Internal Revenue] Service of the nature of the claim and the specific facts upon which it is predicated, thereby permitting an administrative investigation and determination. * * * In addition, the Commissioner is provided with an opportunity to correct any errors, and if disagreement remains, to limit the scope of any ensuing litigation to those issues which have been examined and which he is willing to defend.

Union Pacific Railroad v. United States, 182 Ct.Cl. at 109, 389 F.2d at 442.

In the present case, plaintiff's refund claims contained no reference to the error it had made in computing the gross income from mining for the testing sand or to the effect of the error on the deductions for depletion and net operating loss.[5] This issue arose for the first time in the proceedings before this court. The defendant now argues that the court lacks jurisdiction over the testing sand aspect of plaintiff's depletion deduction because that issue is at substantial variance with the issues raised in the refund claims. Plaintiff contends, however, that our jurisdiction, having been properly invoked to consider the appropriate rate for part of the depletion deduction, extends as well to determining the appropriate depletion deduction for the testing sand. As part of this argument, plaintiff asserts that the timely refund claim for the rate issue established its right to sue for a refund on the whole depletion issue and that the testing sand error affects only the amount plaintiff is entitled to recover. This court cannot accept plaintiff's argument.

The statute and the regulations are quite clear. A taxpayer must specify the grounds and the factual bases from which they arise in its claim for a refund if it later wishes to litigate on those grounds. Plaintiff

---

5.   This is necessarily so because the error was not discovered by plaintiff or defendant until 1977, after the claims had been filed.

concedes that it failed to mention the testing sand error in its refund claims, but nonetheless relies on the above-stated argument to bring the testing sand error before this court.

Simply put, plaintiff's argument is without merit-the jurisdiction of this court to hear the dispute over the appropriate depletion rate to be used for some of plaintiff's products does not extend to the effect of the testing sand error on the depletion deduction and net operating loss. The errors plaintiff made in computing the depletion deduction for the Ottawa Testing Sand constitute a separate ground for relief, distinct from the issue of the appropriate rate asserted in the claims for refund. Each issue has a different factual basis and neither is a subsidiary of or integral to the other.[6] That being the case, the rule of substantial variance precludes this court from exercising jurisdiction over the issues arising from the testing sand error because they were not first raised in the claim for a refund.

Essentially, plaintiff is urging this court to embrace an expansive view of our jurisdiction over tax refund suits. To adopt plaintiff's view, however, would fly in the face of the statute and regulations that govern the grounds upon which a taxpayer may sue for a refund of taxes. One reason for requiring a taxpayer to specify the grounds for relief in its claim for a refund is to limit any subsequent litigation to those grounds that the IRS has already had an opportunity to consider and is willing to defend. The case at bar presents precisely this sort of situation. To allow plaintiff to litigate the matter of the depletion deduction allowable for the testing sand would frustrate the purpose of the statute and regulations and would create an exception that would effectively nullify the substantial variance rule.

Plaintiff has attempted to escape the effect of the substantial variance rule by arguing that it established its right to recover on the depletion deduction by timely filing a refund claim in which it challenged the IRS's reduction of its rate of depletion. Plaintiff further asserts that the error made in computing the depletion deduction for the testing sand affects only the amount of recovery, not plaintiff's right to recover, and that the court may properly consider the testing sand error. In support of its position, plaintiff relies on Red River Lumber Co. v. United States, 134 Ct.Cl. 444, 446, 139 F.Supp. 148, 149-50 (1956). Although *Red River Lumber* does state that an error affecting only the amount of recovery may be raised at trial for the first time if the taxpayer has already

---

6.　This case does not present a situation in which the issue raised at the trial stage is derived from or is integral to the ground timely raised in the refund claim and thus may be considered as part of the initial ground. Cf. *Union Pacific Railroad v. United States*, 182 Ct.Cl. at 109-10, 389 F.2d at 443 (citing instances in which subsidiary issues must necessarily have been considered as part of grounds in refund claim).

established its right to recover by timely filing a refund claim, plaintiff's reliance on the case is misplaced.

The *Red River Lumber* case does not allow a taxpayer to introduce new factual bases of another ground for recovery for the first time at trial. This is essentially what plaintiff is attempting to use the case for. The computation of the gross income from mining figure for the testing sand is distinct from the issue concerning the appropriate rate of depletion raised in the refund claim. The erroneous gross income from mining figure constitutes a separate ground upon which plaintiff might have sought a refund had it been timely discovered. Certainly this error affected the amount of the depletion deduction and, in turn, the amount of plaintiff's potential recovery. But it does so only insofar as any separate ground for a refund necessarily affects the amount a litigant may be entitled to recover. The *Red River Lumber* case is distinguishable from the present one. There, the figure allowed to be changed was the sales price-a figure integral to determining gain, which was an issue properly before the court. Here, however, plaintiff wishes to raise the issue of the gross income from mining for the testing sand, which is not at all related to the issue of the rate of depletion that had been properly raised.

There are many distinct tax issues under the general heading of depletion. Plaintiff may not confer on itself the right to litigate on any one of them by the simple expedient of including one depletion issue in its claim for a refund. The purpose of the variance rule is to limit, not expand, the issues subject to litigation in a tax refund suit. Unfortunately for plaintiff, it may not now raise the matter of the testing sand error and its effect on the depletion deduction or net operating loss deduction.

CONCLUSION

It is concluded that * * * the rule of variance precludes plaintiff from raising before this court any issues arising from its failure to properly compute the depletion deduction allowable for the Ottawa Testing Sand for the years here at issue. Accordingly, plaintiff's petition must be dismissed.

Notes and Question

Note that the substantial variance rule does not seem to apply to the government. See Cooper v. United States, 101 AFTR2d 2008-2521, 2523 (5th Cir. 2008) (court noted that it could find no statute limiting its "ability to decide tax refund cases on grounds other than those raised in the administrative process").

A substantial variance may fall under the category of a legal variance or a factual variance, although in some cases the two categories may overlap, as they appear to do in *Ottawa Silica Co.* Courts generally are more inclined to apply the substantial variance rule when the variance is factual. Why?

E. FILING THE CLAIM

1. In General

Refund claims must be filed in a timely manner with the IRS processing center in the district in which the tax was paid. The burden is on the taxpayer to prove the claim was timely filed. This can be done either by hand-delivering the claim to the IRS office where the tax was paid, or by mailing the claim by registered or certified mail. A separate claim must be filed for each type of tax and for each taxable year or taxable period.

2. Proper Parties

a. *Non-Taxpayer Third Parties*

Section 6402(a) provides that the Commissioner "may credit the amount of such overpayment, including any interest allowed thereon, against any liability in respect of an internal revenue tax on the part of the person who made the overpayment and shall subject to subsection (c), refund any balance to such person." But who is entitled to the refund if the person subject to the tax is not the person who made the overpayment and if a non-taxpayer is entitled to a refund, how does that party file the claim?

MUNACO v. UNITED STATES
United States Court of Appeals, Sixth Circuit, 2008.
522 F.3d 651

BOGGS, CHIEF JUDGE.

* * *

I

On January 7, 2005, Salvatore Munaco acquired title to real property in Palm Beach County, Florida, from Stephen and Dana Roncelli. The same day, he recorded a quitclaim deed with the Palm Beach County

Register of Deeds. The Roncellis owed tax liabilities to the United States. On March 17, 2005, the IRS issued a Notice of Federal Tax Lien in the amount of $286,814.24 against the Roncellis. On April 26, the government recorded with the Palm Beach County Register of Deeds a Notice of Federal Tax Lien against the real property that Munaco had purchased in January.

On July 16, 2005, Munaco entered into an agreement to sell the property to a buyer named Copple and was scheduled to transfer title in September 2005. In the course of searching title for the property, Munaco discovered the tax lien. He contacted the IRS and objected to the lien. Munaco says that the IRS informed him that if he conditioned or qualified the lien payment in any way, his title would not be clear and marketable. In order to close his sale, on September 19, 2005, Munaco directed the title company to pay $326,061.34 from the sale proceeds to the United States to discharge the tax lien.[2]

On September 12, 2006, Munaco filed suit in federal court in the Eastern District of Michigan. He alleged that the federal tax lien was not valid because the Roncellis did not own the property at the time that the lien was recorded; therefore, the lien was invalid under 26 U.S.C. § 6323. Accordingly, Munaco sought damages of $326,061.34 (the amount he paid to satisfy the lien) plus interest. He also sued for slander of title and conversion, seeking additional unspecified damages for those claims, plus attorney fees.

On June 1, 2007, the district court granted the government's motion to dismiss on the ground that it lacked subject-matter jurisdiction over the case because the government had not waived sovereign immunity. Munaco appealed. * * *

II

"It is axiomatic that the United States may not be sued without its consent and that the existence of consent is a prerequisite for jurisdiction." United States v. Mitchell, 463 U.S. 206, 212, 103 S.Ct. 2961, 77 L.Ed.2d 580 (1983). When the federal government has waived its immunity and consented to suit, we strictly construe any waiver, and the putative plaintiff must abide the terms of the consent. See Young v. United States, 332 F.3d 893, 895 (6th Cir.2003). As Justice Holmes remarked: "Men must turn square corners when they deal with the Government. If it attaches even purely formal conditions to its consent to be sued those conditions must be complied with." Rock Island, A. &

---

2.   Neither party explains why the actual amount paid exceeded the amount stated in the lien notice by nearly $40,000.

L.R. Co. v. United States, 254 U.S. 141, 142, 41 S.Ct. 55, 65 L.Ed. 188 (1920). This is true even when the square corners constitute a "one-way street" in the government's favor.

In this case, Munaco failed to turn any corners, let alone square ones. Munaco filed suit seeking a refund of the money he paid to clear the tax lien, and he argued that the lien was invalid against him since he had recorded his deed from the Roncellis before the government recorded the tax lien. He alleged that jurisdiction was proper under 28 U.S.C. § 1346(a)(1), which grants district courts jurisdiction over "[a]ny civil action against the United States for the recovery of any internal-revenue tax alleged to have been erroneously or illegally assessed or collected . . . ." Relevant to this appeal, the government argued that it had not waived sovereign immunity because Munaco had ignored the administrative remedies available to him under Sections 6325(b)(4) and 7426(a)(4) of Title 26. The district court agreed and held that sovereign immunity barred Munaco's suit because he had not pursued his administrative remedies.

Notably, if this case had arisen some years ago, Munaco would have been successful because of a then-controlling Supreme Court precedent in his favor. The Supreme Court's 1995 decision in United States v. Williams, 514 U.S. 527, 115 S.Ct. 1611, 131 L.Ed.2d 608 (1995), held that federal courts could hear a similarly-situated plaintiff's claim under § 1346's general grant of jurisdiction over tax cases. However, in 1998, Congress responded to *Williams* and amended the Internal Revenue Code to provide a specific statutory remedy for a person in Munaco's position. The question presented is whether suit under § 1346 is still proper, even though Munaco failed to exhaust the administrative remedies that the 1998 amendments enacted.

In *Williams*, the Supreme Court held that Williams, who had paid a tax under protest to remove a lien on her property, had standing to bring a refund action under 28 U.S.C. § 1346, even though the tax she paid was assessed against a third party. The IRS had placed a lien on the assets of Williams's husband, including his joint interest in their house. Williams's husband deeded his interest in the house to her in contemplation of divorce, and the IRS filed its notice of tax lien several weeks later. Williams contracted to sell the house, the IRS provided actual notice of the lien, and the purchaser threatened to sue if the sale were not completed. Williams had sale proceeds disbursed directly to the IRS to satisfy the lien. She then sued for a refund, claiming that she had taken her husband's interest in the house free of the IRS lien. Like Munaco, Williams invoked § 1346(a)(1). The government insisted that Williams lacked standing because § 1346 supported only actions by the assessed taxpayer. The government also argued that an administrative exhaustion requirement applied, see 26 U.S.C. § 7422, and that Williams was not a "taxpayer" within the meaning of the statutes.

The Court held that Williams could sue under § 1346. *Williams*, 514 U.S. at 529, 115 S.Ct. 1611. In its analysis, the court held that Williams was a "taxpayer" under the statutes because she was subject to the tax, even if she was not the one against whom the tax was assessed. The Court focused heavily on the fact that, if taxpayers in Williams's position could not sue under § 1346, they would be left without a remedy. The Court found that the statutory remedies that existed at the time, including actions for wrongful levy and to quiet title, were pre-deprivation remedies and did not provide any realistic alternative to paying the tax. Williams had paid and needed a post-deprivation remedy, which the Court held that § 1346 supplied. *See id.* at 537-38, 115 S.Ct. 1611.

All else equal, *Williams*'s holding would clearly authorize Munaco's suit under § 1346. Unfortunately for Munaco, all else is not equal because Congress amended the Internal Revenue Code in 1998 to provide the specific remedy that the *Williams* Court had found lacking. In particular, Congress enacted the Internal Revenue Service Restructuring & Reform Act of 1998 (IRRA), Pub.L. No. 105-206, § 3106, 112 Stat. 732, 732-34, to address the problem that the Court faced in *Williams*. See S.Rep. No. 105-174, at 44-55 (1998). Here then, Congress created the square corners around which plaintiffs in Munaco's position must turn.

The amendments added subsection (b)(4) to 26 U.S.C. § 6325 and subsection (a)(4) to 26 U.S.C. § 7426. Under the new statutory scheme, 26 U.S.C. § 6325(b)(4) requires the IRS to issue a certificate of discharge as a matter of right to third parties under specified circumstances.[4] Pursuant to 26 U.S.C. § 6325(b)(4)(A), the third party has the right to obtain a certificate of discharge by applying to the Secretary of the

---

4.   26 U.S.C. § 6325(b)(4) provides:

Right of substitution of value.–

(A) In general.-At the request of the owner of any property subject to any lien imposed by this chapter, the Secretary shall issue a certificate of discharge of such property if such owner-

(i) deposits with the Secretary an amount of money equal to the value of the interest of the United States (as determined by the Secretary) in the property; or

(ii) furnishes a bond acceptable to the Secretary in a like amount.

(B) Refund of deposit with interest and release of bond.-The Secretary shall refund the amount so deposited (and shall pay interest at the overpayment rate under section 6621), and shall release such bond, to the extent that the Secretary determines that-

(i) the unsatisfied liability giving rise to the lien can be satisfied from a source other than such property; or

(ii) the value of the interest of the United States in the property is less than the Secretary's prior determination of such value.

Treasury for such a certificate and either depositing cash or furnishing a bond sufficient to protect the lien interest of the United States. The Secretary does not have the discretion to refuse to issue a certificate of discharge if this procedure is followed. After the property owner follows the procedure under 26 U.S.C. § 6325(b)(4)(A), the Secretary must refund the amount deposited or release the bond, to the extent that the Secretary determines that the taxpayer's unsatisfied liability giving rise to the lien can be satisfied from a source other than property owned by the third party, or the value of the interest of the United States in the property is less than the Secretary's prior determination of its value. 26 U.S.C. § 6325(b)(4)(B).

Section 7426(a)(4) provides a judicial remedy for violations of § 6325(b)(4).[5] The owner of the property has 120 days after the certificate is issued to challenge the Secretary's determination by bringing a civil action against the United States in federal district court. If no action is filed within the 120-day period, the Secretary has 60 days to apply the amount deposited or collected on the bond, to the extent necessary to satisfy the unsatisfied liability secured by the lien and refund any amount which is not used to satisfy the liability. *Id.* § 6325(b)(4)(C). If an action is filed and the court determines that the value of the interest of the United States in the property is less than the value that the Secretary determined, the court will grant a judgment ordering the refund of the amount of the deposit or a release of the bond to the extent that the amount of the deposit or bond exceeds the value determined by the court. *Id.* § 7426(b)(5). The statute states clearly that "[n]o other action may be brought by such person for such a determination." *Id.* § 7426(a)(4). Plaintiffs must exhaust these administrative remedies prior to bringing suit for damages. *See id.* § 7426(h)(2).

In this case, Munaco never requested or received a certificate of discharge, never sought administrative redress, and filed suit approximately one year after he paid the lien. He clearly cannot proceed under §§ 6325 and 7426. The government argues that the 1998 amendments superseded *Williams*, and the IRS has issued a Revenue Ruling to that effect. *See* Rev. Rul. 2005-50, 2005-2 C.B. 124 ("in light of [the 1998 amendments], a person not liable for an underlying tax may not file a refund action under the holding of *United States v. Williams* ").

---

5. 26 U.S.C. § 7426(a)(4) provides: "Substitution of value.-If a certificate of discharge is issued to any person under section 6325(b)(4) with respect to any property, such person may, within 120 days after the day on which such certificate is issued, bring a civil action against the United States in a district court of the United States for a determination of whether the value of the interest of the United States (if any) in such property is less than the value determined by the Secretary. No other action may be brought by such person for such a determination."

The few courts that have addressed this issue have generally ruled in favor of the IRS's position that the 1998 amendments must be followed before one may sue in district court. In the Eastern District of Kentucky, the court confronted a situation very similar to Munaco's and held that the 1998 amendments had indeed superseded *Williams* and that the court lacked jurisdiction because the plaintiff had not exhausted its administrative remedies. See City of Richmond v. United States, 348 F.Supp.2d 807, 812-14 (E.D.Ky. 2004). More recently, the Court of Federal Claims canvassed the relevant authority and concluded that it lacked jurisdiction under § 1346(a)(1) to hear "refund suits brought by third party real property owners who wish to challenge tax lien-related collections by the IRS and who have not pursued the remedy provided to them by §§ 6325(b)(4) and 7426(a)(4)." Four Rivers Invs., Inc. v. United States, 77 Fed.Cl. 592, 603 (Fed.Cl.2007). Only one court has held that § 1346(a)(1) continues to provide jurisdiction for a third-party refund claim. See Crytser v. United States, [eds: 98 A.F.T.R.2d 2006-7723] (E.D.Wash. Nov.2, 2006) (eds: unreported op.). However, in that case, the district court also held that the administrative exhaustion requirement applied and dismissed the suit because the plaintiff had not exhausted her administrative remedies.[7]

The Supreme Court has not decided whether *Williams* remains good law. However, in a recent case, the Court analyzed whether *Williams*'s holding that a third party could challenge a wrongful lien under § 1346 should be extended to cover a third party who was challenging a wrongful levy. See EC Term of Years Trust v. United States, --- U.S. ----, 127 S.Ct. 1763, 1765, 167 L.Ed.2d 729 (2007) (unanimous). In that case, the plaintiff sued under § 7426(a)(1), but missed the nine-month statute of limitations applicable to that subsection. After the district court dismissed the case, the plaintiff sued again, this time under § 1346. The district court dismissed the new case, reasoning that § 7426(a)(1) provided the exclusive remedy, and the Fifth Circuit affirmed. Because the Ninth Circuit had previously held that § 7426(a)(1) was not the exclusive remedy and that a suit could continue under § 1346, see WWSM Invs. v. United States, 64 F.3d 456 (9th Cir.1995), the Supreme Court granted certiorari, affirmed the Fifth Circuit, and rejected the Ninth Circuit precedent.

In *EC Term of Years Trust*, the Court clarified that *Williams*'s holding rested "on the specific understanding that no other remedy . . . was open to the plaintiff in that case." *Id.* at 1768. In *EC Term of Years Trust*, however, the plaintiff "could have made a timely claim under §

---

7.   We also note that the Ninth Circuit has reached the same conclusion that we do in a similar case just decided. See First Am. Title Ins. Co. v. United States, 520 F.3d 1051, 1053-54 (9th Cir. 2008).

7426(a)(1) for the relief it now seeks under § 1346(a)(1)." *Ibid*. The Court applied the general principle that "a precisely drawn, detailed statute pre-empts more general remedies." Brown v. GSA, 425 U.S. 820, 834, 96 S.Ct. 1961, 48 L.Ed.2d 402 (1976) (quoted in *EC Term of Years Trust*, 127 S.Ct. at 1767). Moreover, the Court noted that it "braces the preemption claim when resort to a general remedy would effectively extend the statute of limitations period for the specific one." *EC Term of Years Trust*, 127 S.Ct. at 1767. Accordingly, the Court held that the plaintiff "missed the deadline for challenging a levy under § 7426(a)(1), and may not bring the challenge as a tax refund claim under § 1346(a)(1)." *Id.* at 1769.

Applying that reasoning to this case, we hold that Munaco's failure to follow the statute and to seek a certificate of discharge bars his suit. Thanks to the 1998 amendments, Munaco had access to a post-deprivation administrative remedy under § 6325(b)(4) and a judicial remedy under § 7426(a)(4). Allowing Munaco to sue under § 1346 would ignore the fact that Congress passed a specific statutory remedy for persons in his position and would render meaningless the 120-day limitations period. Congress was quite clear that, other than a suit following receipt of a certificate of discharge, "[n]o other action may be brought by such person" for a review of the value of the United States's interest in a lien. 26 U.S.C. § 7426(a)(4). As the Supreme Court has stated, "[d]espite its spacious terms, § 1346(a)(1) must be read in conformity with other statutory provisions which qualify a taxpayer's right to bring a refund suit upon compliance with certain conditions." United States v. Dalm, 494 U.S. 596, 601, 110 S.Ct. 1361, 108 L.Ed.2d 548 (1990).

The record is not clear about why Munaco failed to apply for a certificate of discharge and exhaust his administrative remedies. Had he done so, the district court presumably would have reached the merits of his claim. With more than $300,000 at stake, Munaco and his counsel had adequate incentive to apprise themselves of the statutory requirements. Unfortunately for Munaco, his argument cannot be heard. Congress enacted a specific statutory scheme to provide a remedy for persons who find themselves precisely in his position. Munaco ignored that scheme at his own peril, and we are not at liberty to dispense with it.

III

Therefore, for the reasons set out above, we AFFIRM the district court's decision to dismiss Munaco's suit against the United States.

Notes and Questions

There must be extenuating circumstances for a third party to obtain a refund because lower courts consistently have held that a person who voluntarily pays the taxes of another lacks standing to file a claim for refund of those taxes. See, e.g., Bruce v. United States, 759 F.2d 755 (9th Cir. 1985); Cindy's Inc. v. United States, 740 F.2d 851 (11th Cir. 1984); Factory Storage Corp. v. United States, 611 F.Supp. 433 (E.D.N.C. 1985). But in *Williams*, as in *Munaco*, the parties had not voluntarily paid the tax of another. The Supreme Court was sympathetic to the plight of Mrs. Williams and under the precedent of the *Williams* case, Munaco probably would have been able to claim a substantial refund. His failure to adhere to the clear requirements of the statute is bewildering.

Who is entitled to file a claim for refund of taxes withheld by an employer from an employee's wages and remitted to the Service? Compare First Nat'l Bank v. United States, 21 Ct.Ct. 479 (1990) with Hotel Conquistador, Inc. v. United States, 597 F.2d 1348 (Ct.Cl. 1979), cert. denied, 444 U.S. 1032 (1980).

b. The Anti-Assignment Statute

Refund claims, as well as other claims against the United States, are non-assignable under 31 U.S.C. § 3727.

R & L REFUNDS, INC. v. UNITED STATES
United States Bankruptcy Court, 1988.
96 B.R. 105

J. Wendell Roberts, Bankruptcy Judge.

* * *

The material facts which give rise to this action are as follows. R & L Refunds, Inc. ("Plaintiff") is in the business of loaning money to individuals by "discounting" the refund due those individuals from their income tax returns and then taking an assignment of the actual refund when it becomes due.

According to the parties' joint stipulation of facts filed on September 22, 1987, a taxpayer would come into the Plaintiff's place of business in order to sell his/her refunds in order to get immediate use of the money. The Plaintiff would pay the taxpayer a portion of his/her anticipated return and, in exchange, the taxpayer would execute a document styled "Contract of Sale/Assignment of Federal Returns" and a document styled "Power of Attorney." The Power of Attorney purported to grant to the President of the Plaintiff, R & L Refunds, the power to receive and sign the income tax refund check and to dispose of the proceeds. In order for the Plaintiff to be assured of receiving the checks, the address of the Plaintiff was placed on the income tax returns. Each federal return then was mailed to the Internal Revenue Service.

As a result of "discounting" operations, such as R & L Refunds, the I.R.S. claims that a variety of problems have arisen including confusion as to the taxpayers last known address and double claiming of tax refunds. In 1984, the I.R.S. commenced what is known as a diversion program whereby the I.R.S. attempted to identify discounted returns. When refunds were identified as having discounting addresses on the returns, the I.R.S. would change the addresses on the returns and send those refunds to the taxpayer's address as it was last known to the I.R.S.

On May 10, 1984, R & L Refunds filed a petition under Chapter 11 of the Bankruptcy Code. On July 5, 1984, the Plaintiff filed this adversary proceeding against the United States Government seeking a turnover of approximately $190,000.00 which was the estimated value of the refund checks which had been assigned to the Plaintiff by the various taxpayers. An additional stipulated fact was that on January 8, 1984, the district director of the Internal Revenue Service in Louisville wrote to Mr. Lowell Hughes, President of R & L Refund, Inc. advising him that the actions being performed by him and R & L Refunds did not violate the Internal Revenue Code of 1954, relative to income tax return preparation. Following a pretrial conference on April 27, 1988, the Court ordered the parties to file cross-motions for summary judgment within thirty days. Identical issues have been raised by both motions for summary judgment. First, we must determine whether the Anti-Assignment Act, 31 U.S.C. § 3727, bars the Plaintiff from bringing this action. If we conclude that the Plaintiff is not barred from bringing this action, we then must determine whether a turnover proceeding is the proper procedure for the recovery of property which is no longer in the possession of the party from whom recovery is sought.

Addressing the first issue, the United States argues that the Anti-Assignment Act bars any relief to the Plaintiff in this particular action. Relevant portions of the Anti-Assignment Act, 31 U.S.C. § 3727 are as follows:

Section 3727. Assignment of Claims.

    (a) In this section, "assignment" means-

        (1) a transfer or assignment of any part of a claim against the United States Government or of an interest in the claim; or

        (2) the authorization to receive payment for any part of the claim.

(b) An assignment may be made only after a claim is allowed, the amount of the claim is decided, and warrant for the payment of the claim has been issued. The assignment shall specify the warrant, must be made freely, and must be attested to by two witnesses. The person making the assignment shall acknowledge it before an official who may acknowledge a deed, and the official shall certify the assignment. The certificate shall state that the official completely explained the assignment when it was acknowledged. An assignment under this section is valid for any purpose.

The government contends that since an assignment may be made only after a claim is allowed, the amount of the claim is decided and a warrant for payment of the claim has been issued pursuant to the Act, then all assignments in this case are rendered "null and void" since all of them were made before the tax returns were ever transmitted to the Internal Revenue Service.

The Plaintiff argues that the Act should not be interpreted literally; but, rather it should be interpreted in light of its sole purpose of protecting the government while continuing to give effect to the contract assignment between the individual parties. Martin v. National Surety Co., 300 U.S. 588, 596, 57 S.Ct. 531, 534, 81 L.Ed. 822, 826 (1936); Segal v. Rochell, 382 U.S. 375, 384, 86 S.Ct. 511, 517, 15 L.Ed.2d 428, 435 (1966).

The Plaintiff also argues the case of A.C. Davenport & Son v. United States, 538 F.Supp. 730 (N.D.Ill.), aff'd, 703 F.2d 266 (7th Cir.1983) wherein the Court dismissed the government's argument that the contract modification violated the Anti-Assignment Act as nothing more than a red herring. However, in the *Davenport* case, the District Court found that the agreement between the parties was not an assignment or, at least, not a valid assignment. Since the Anti-Assignment Act clearly involves valid assignments, it is no surprise that the Court would dismiss the government's argument to apply the Anti-Assignment Act as a red herring.

In Martin v. National Surety Co., *supra*, the Court stated that the provisions of the Anti-Assignment Act voiding certain assignments are primarily for the benefit of the government so that it would be in no danger "of becoming embroiled in conflicting claims, with delay and embarrassment and the chance of multiple liability." Other courts interpreting the statute have explained its purpose to be to "prevent persons of influence from buying up claims against the United States, which might then be improperly urged upon officers of the government and to prevent possible multiple payment of claims, to make unnecessary the investigation of alleged assignments, and to enable the Government to deal only with the original claimant." United States v. Shannon, 342 U.S. 288, 72 S.Ct. 281, 96 L.Ed. 321 (1952) citing United States v. Aetna Surety Co., 338 U.S. 366, 373, 70 S.Ct. 207, 211, 94 L.Ed. 171 (1949). To our knowledge, no court has nullified an assignment as between the individual private parties simply because it failed to comply with the statute.

In light of the foregoing, we are persuaded to rule in favor of the United States. Since the purpose of the Act is to protect the government from multiple litigation with parties other than the original claimant, we can see no better case than the present one where the Act would apply. The Plaintiff has sued the federal government for a turnover of income tax refund checks originally belonging to individual taxpayers and not the Plaintiff. While we find no reason to invalidate the assignments as between the Plaintiff and the individual taxpayers, we conclude that the Anti-Assignment Act bars the Plaintiff from bringing this action against the United States for the recovery of the monies. * * *

Notes and Question

The anti-assignment statute does not cover a third party acting as the agent of the taxpayer. Thus, under certain circumstances, a third party may file a claim for refund on behalf of a taxpayer. These circumstances include claims pursuant to a power of attorney (Form 2848, Power of Attorney and Declaration of Representative), a guardian acting on behalf of a minor, and a common parent of an affiliated group of corporations that files a consolidated income tax return.

There are two general exceptions to the Anti-Assignment provision. One is found within the statute itself when the assignment has been freely made and executed in the presence of at least two attesting witnesses. The other is a judicial exception for transferees who become the owner of the claim by operation of law. Can you think of any examples that would fall within the latter category?

II. STATUTE OF LIMITATIONS

The statute of limitations on refund claims differs slightly from the statute of limitations on assessment, but this difference makes the refund statute of limitations more complicated than the statute of limitations on assessment.

A. INTERNAL REVENUE CODE § 6511

(a) Claim for credit or refund of an overpayment of any tax imposed by this title in respect of which tax the taxpayer is required to file a return shall be filed by the taxpayer within 3 years from the time the return was filed or 2 years from the time the tax was paid, whichever of such periods expires the later, or if no return was filed by the taxpayer, within 2 years from the time the tax was paid. * * *

(b)(1) No credit or refund shall be allowed or made after the expiration of the period of limitation prescribed in subsection (a) for the filing of a claim for credit or refund, unless a claim for credit or refund is filed by the taxpayer within such period.

(2)(A) If the claim was filed by the taxpayer during the 3-year period prescribed in subsection (a), the amount of the credit or refund shall not exceed the portion of tax paid within the period, immediately preceding the filing of the claim, equal to 3 years plus the period of any extension of time for filing the return.* * *

(2)(B) If the claim was not filed within such 3-year period, the amount of the credit or refund shall not exceed the portion of the tax paid during the 2 years immediately preceding the filing of the claim.

(2)(C) If no claim was filed, the credit or refund shall not exceed the amount which would be allowable under subparagraph (A) or (B), as the case may be, if a claim was filed on the date the credit or refund is allowed.

(c) If an agreement under the provisions of § 6501(c)(4) extending the period for assessment of a tax imposed by this title is made within the period prescribed in subsection (a) for the filing of a claim for credit or refund –

(1) The period for filing claim for credit or refund or for making credit or refund if no claim is filed, provided in subsections (a) and (b)(1), shall not expire prior to 6 months after the expiration of the period within which an assessment may be made pursuant to the agreement or any extension thereof under § 6501(c)(4).

(2) If a claim is filed, or a credit or refund is allowed when no claim was filed, after the execution of the agreement and within 6 months after the expiration of the period within which an assessment may be made pursuant to the agreement or any extension thereof, the amount of the credit or refund shall not exceed the portion of the tax paid after the execution of the agreement and before the filing of the claim or the making of the credit or refund, as the case may be plus the portion of the tax paid within the period which would be

applicable under subsection (b)(2) if a claim had been filed on the date the agreement was executed.

(3) This subsection shall not apply in the case of a claim filed, or credit or refund allowed if no claim is filed, either –

     (A)   prior to the execution of the agreement or

     (B)   more than 6 months after the expiration of the period within which an assessment may be made pursuant to the agreement or any extension thereof.

Problem

Annie Scott, a calendar year taxpayer, mailed her federal income tax return for the 2006 taxable year on June 6, 2007, after having obtained an automatic six-month extension of time to file. The return was received by the Service on June 10, 2007. Annie's tax liability was $18,452, of which $15,500 was paid by taxes withheld from her wages and the remaining $2,952 was paid with her return. On May 1, 2010, Annie filed a claim for refund of $3,500. Is her claim timely? Assuming that Annie is entitled to the full amount of the refund on the merits, how much will she receive? Why?

a) Would your answer to question one differ if Annie had neglected to request an extension of time to file her return, but the facts otherwise remained the same?

b) Would your answer to (a) differ if $12,500 of Annie's tax liability had been paid by withholding and the remaining $5,952 had been credited from an overpayment of her 2005 taxes?

c) In the alternative, assume that Annie had received a 30-day letter on March 1, 2010 proposing a deficiency of $2,500. She requested a conference with Appeals and was granted an appeal scheduled for April 1, 2010. At the appeal, she was asked to sign a Form 872 extending the statute of limitations on assessment for six months and she signed the form on April 1. Her appeal was unsuccessful and on July 1, 2010 she received a notice of deficiency and a Form 870. She signed the Form 870 and mailed it on July 1, the day that she received it and she paid the $2,500 on September 20, 2010. How long does Annie have to file a claim for refund and if she is successful on the merits, how much is she entitled to recover? See § 6511(c).

Questions

1. When does the two-year statutory period under § 6511(a) apply?

2. When would a refund claim be considered filed if the initial return is due and filed on April 15, 2008, the refund claim is mailed on April 15, 2011, and is received by the Service on April 18, 2011? See Weisbart v. United States Department of Treasury, 222 F.3d 93 (2d Cir. 2000).

B. PAYMENT

Not all remittances to the government constitute payments of tax. Some are considered deposits made to stop the running of time-sensitive penalties and interest on underpayments of tax. The distinction is important because it may affect Tax Court jurisdiction, the amount of a deficiency, the amount of interest and penalties payable on a deficiency, whether interest is payable to the taxpayer, the procedure the taxpayer must follow to recoup the remittance, the running of the statute of limitations on assessment and collection, and whether the lookback provision of § 6511(b)(2)(A) applies.

A taxpayer is entitled to the return of a deposit at any time, upon written request, whereas a refund of an overpayment requires the taxpayer to follow the specific refund procedures. Also, the date of the payment establishes the beginning point for the statute of limitations, while a deposit has no effect on the statutory period. The taxpayer may not be entitled to interest on all deposits, whereas interest is payable on an overpayment. Finally, a payment of tax will prevent the assessment of a penalty on the corresponding amount of the underpayment, while a deposit may not prevent the assessment.

DEATON v. COMMISSIONER
United States of Appeals, Fifth Circuit, 2006.
440 F.3d 223

DeMoss, Circuit Judge:

Barbara and Ronny Deaton (the "Deatons") appeal a decision of the United States Tax Court (the "Tax Court") sustaining a finding of the Internal Revenue Service Appeals Office (the "Appeals Office") that the Deatons' 1994 remittance of $125,000-which accompanied their Form 4868 application for an extension of time to file their 1993 tax return-was a "payment," not a "deposit," and that as such, it could not be credited against the Deatons' 1994-1996 tax liabilities because it fell outside the "look-back period" of I.R.C. § 6511(b)(2)(A).

I. Facts and Proceedings

On April 15, 1994, the deadline for filing a 1993 U.S. Individual Income Tax Return, the Deatons filed a Form 4868 with the Internal Revenue Service (IRS) to extend the time for filing their return. Form 4868, titled "Application for Automatic Extension of Time to File U.S. Individual Income Tax Return," automatically extends a taxpayer's time to file his return if the taxpayer meets certain conditions; however, it does not extend the time to pay tax. See Treas. Reg. § 1.6081-4(b) (1993) ("[A]ny automatic extension of time for filing an individual income tax return . . . shall not operate to extend the time for payment of any tax due on such return.").[1] To qualify for a Form 4868 automatic extension of time to file, the Deatons had to "[p]roperly estimate [their] 1993 tax liability using the information available to [them], [e]nter [their] tax liability on line 1 of Form 4868, [and] [f]ile Form 4868 by the due date of [their] return." I.R.S. Instructions for Form 4868 (1993); see also Treas. Reg. § 1.6081-4(a)(4) (1993) ("Such application for extension must show the full amount properly estimated as tax for such taxpayer for such taxable year . . . ."). Although the Deatons were not required to remit any amount to the IRS with their form, see I.R.S. Instructions for Form 4868 (1993) ("If you find you can't pay the full amount shown on line 3, you can still get the extension."),[2] the instructions to Form 4868 indicated that a taxpayer would be liable for interest and possibly a late payment penalty if he submitted less than the full amount of estimated taxes with his form, *id.*

To avoid incurring interest and any late payment penalty, the Deatons submitted to the IRS with their Form 4868 a check in the amount of $125,000, which they calculated as the line 3 "balance due" after deducting payments of $13,883 (in the form of withholdings) from their estimated tax liability of $138,883. Following receipt of the form, the IRS extended the Deatons' deadline for filing their 1993 return by six months; however, the Deatons missed the extended deadline and in fact did not file their 1993 return until January 2000, nearly six years after its due date. The Deatons also failed to file timely returns for the tax years 1994, 1995, and 1996.

---

1.   The 1993 version of Form 4868 clearly stated under its title, "This is not an extension of time to pay your tax." I.R.S. Form 4868 (OMB No. 1545-0188) (1993).

2.   Until 1992, full payment was a condition of receiving an extension; however, the IRS removed that condition in 1992 so that taxpayers who were unable to pay the full amount of estimated taxes could nevertheless obtain an automatic four-month filing extension and relief from late-filing penalties. See I.R.S. Notice 92-22, 1993-1 C.B. 305.

On January 10, 2000, the Deatons filed delinquent returns for the tax years 1993 through 1996. On their 1993 return, they reported a tax liability of only $88,662, which indicated that they had overestimated their 1993 tax liability on Form 4868 by $50,221. The Deatons requested that this overpayment be carried forward and credited as a payment toward their tax liabilities for the years following 1993.

Shortly after the IRS received the Deatons' 1993-1996 tax returns, it formally assessed the amounts reported as tax on each of the returns. For 1993, the IRS applied the amount already paid by withholding ($13,883) and the April 1994 remittance ($125,000) to the reported tax liability of $88,662. The IRS then posted the resulting overpayment of $50,221 to an "excess collections" account and did not carry it forward on the Deatons' account as a credit for subsequent tax years as the Deatons requested. According to the IRS, the Deatons' credit request was barred by I.R.C. § 6511(b)(2)(A), which limits the amount of a credit or refund claimed by a taxpayer to the amount paid within the "look-back period" under that subsection, that is, the three years (plus the period of any extension of time for filing the return) immediately preceding the filing of the claim. I.R.C. § 6511(b)(2)(A). The Deatons had paid nothing to the IRS within the applicable look-back period, which dated back to July 10, 1996,[3] so their credit was limited to zero.

This litigation arose out of the IRS's attempt to levy the Deatons' property to satisfy their 1994-1996 tax liabilities, which remained unpaid because of the IRS's refusal to apply the 1993 overpayment as a credit in later years. After the IRS issued a Notice of Intent to Levy, the Deatons timely filed a request for a collection due process hearing with the IRS Appeals Office. In their request for a hearing, the Deatons asserted that the 1994 remittance of $125,000 was a "deposit" rather than a "payment," a status that would have protected the remittance from the look-back period for credits and refunds.[4] The Appeals Office rejected the Deatons' assertion, classified their 1994 remittance as a payment, subject to I.R.C. § 6511(b)(2)(A)'s look-back period, and sustained the IRS's proposed levy.

---

3.   Considering the six-month extension the IRS gave the Deatons to file their 1993 return, the look-back period was the three years and six months immediately preceding the date of their claim for a credit, January 10, 2000.

4.   See I.R.C. § 6511(b)(2)(A) ("[T]he amount of the credit or refund shall not exceed the portion of the tax *paid* within the period . . . ." (emphasis added)). The distinct treatment of deposits and payments first arose in *Rosenman v. United States*, 323 U.S. 658, 65 S.Ct. 536, 89 L.Ed. 535 (1945), in which the Supreme Court recognized that § 6511's predecessor was not applicable to a deposit even though it would have been applicable to a payment. Dantzler v. United States, 183 F.3d 1247, 1249 (11th Cir.1999).

The Deatons were likewise unsuccessful before the Tax Court. Although the Tax Court acknowledged the judicially created distinction between a deposit and a payment, the court also recognized a three-way split of authority regarding the treatment of a Form 4868 remittance. Applying its own precedent in Risman v. Commissioner, 100 T.C. 191, 1993 WL 72856 (1993), which calls for an examination of the facts and circumstances of a case in order to determine whether the taxpayer intended his remittance as a deposit or a payment, the Tax Court reviewed the Deatons' tax records and a letter from their accountant asserting that the $125,000 was a deposit. Finding that the Deatons had failed to demonstrate their contemporaneous intent to treat the remittance as a deposit, the Tax Court sustained the Appeals Office's finding that the Deatons' remittance was a payment made outside the look-back period of § 6511(b)(2)(A) and upheld the Appeals Office's determination that the IRS's proposed levy could proceed. This appeal ensued. Because we agree with the Tax Court that the Deatons' 1994 remittance was a payment, rather than a deposit, we AFFIRM the Tax Court's decision.

II. Discussion
* * *
B. Analysis

The Deaton's argue on appeal that the $125,000 remittance that accompanied their Form 4868 application for an extension of time to file was a deposit and that as such, it is not subject to the look-back period of I.R.C. § 6511(b)(2)(A). They ask this Court to reverse the Tax Court's decision and order the IRS to apply their 1993 overpayment as a credit to their 1994-1996 tax liabilities or refund the overpayment to them. The Deatons concede that if the 1994 remittance is properly classified as a payment, the IRS may keep their overpayment because of § 6511(b)(2)(A)'s look-back period.

In deciding this appeal, we must assess the impact of the Supreme Court's recent decision in Baral v. United States, 528 U.S. 431, 120 S.Ct. 1006, 145 L.Ed.2d 949 (2000), on this Circuit's longstanding rule that remittances made prior to assessment of a tax are deemed deposits rather than payments. See Harden v. United States, 74 F.3d 1237 (5th Cir.1995) (unpublished); Ford v. United States, 618 F.2d 357 (5th Cir.1980); Thomas v. Mercantile Nat'l Bank, 204 F.2d 943 (5th Cir.1953). The Deatons contend that Baral has no effect on their case or on our longstanding rule because it is limited to cases involving remittances governed by the "deemed paid" provision of I.R.C. § 6513(b)[5]-for example, wage withholdings and payments of estimated tax-and they argue that their remittance does not fall under that section. They urge that the proper characterization of their remittance depends on the facts and circumstances associated with it under *Rosenman*, which predates *Baral*. According to the Deatons, the facts and circumstances surrounding their 1994 remittance establish their contemporaneous intent to treat it as a deposit, and they assert that Fifth Circuit law at that time supports such a finding.[6] The Commissioner counters that after *Baral*, we should treat remittances accompanying Form 4868 applications as payments as a matter of law; alternatively, the Commissioner argues that the Tax Court correctly ruled under the facts-and-circumstances test that the Deatons' remittance was a payment, not a deposit. Because we have not previously explicitly addressed *Baral*'s impact on our law,[7] we do so here. And for the reasons stated below, we agree that the Deatons' remittance was a payment, not a deposit. However, we decline to adopt a per se rule to govern remittances accompanying Form 4868 applications as the Commissioner requests.

1.   Origin of the Deposit-Payment Distinction

The distinction between deposits and payments was first established in *Rosenman*. In that case, the Supreme Court considered whether the

---

5. Section 6513(b) states,

Prepaid income tax.–For purposes of section 6511 or 6512-

(1) Any tax actually deducted and withheld at the source during any calendar year under chapter 24 shall, in respect of the recipient of the income, *be deemed to have been paid* by him on the 15th day of the fourth month following the close of his taxable year with respect to which such tax is allowable as a credit under section 31.

(2) Any amount paid as estimated income tax for any taxable year shall *be deemed to have been paid* on the last day prescribed for filing the return under section 6012 for such taxable year (determined without regard to any extension of time for filing such return).

(3) Any tax withheld at the source under chapter 3 shall, in respect of the recipient of the income, *be deemed to have been paid* by such recipient on the last day prescribed for filing the return under section 6012 for the taxable year (determined without regard to any extension of time for filing) with respect to which such tax is allowable as a credit under section 1462. For this purpose, any exemption granted under section 6012 from the requirement of filing a return shall be disregarded.

I.R.C. § 6513(b) (emphasis added).

6.   Because this Circuit treated pre-assessment remittances as deposits at the time the Deatons made their Form 4868 remittance, they argue that it was intended as a deposit under then-current law. This argument fails, as discussed in Part II.B.4.

7.   Although we have decided a deposit-payment case since *Baral*, see Harrigill v. United States, 410 F.3d 786 (5th Cir.2005), we did not discuss *Baral*'s impact on our law in that case because the parties conceded that the *Mercantile National Bank* line of authority, discussed below, was abrogated by *Baral*, see *id*. at 790 n. 6.

predecessor to the current look-back provision barred a claim for refund of estimated estate taxes that the decedent's executors had remitted in response to an absolute deadline, but which they strenuously disputed as erroneous. *Rosenman*, 323 U.S. at 659-61, 65 S.Ct. 536, 89 L.Ed. 535 (1945). The executors had included a transmittal letter with the remittance, emphasizing that "[t]his payment is made under protest and duress, and solely for the purpose of avoiding penalties and interest, since it is contended by the executors that not all of this sum is legally or lawfully due." *Id.* at 660, 65 S.Ct. 536. The IRS credited the remittance to a special suspense account, which was created to hold the funds because no taxes had yet been formally assessed against the estate. After completing an audit of the return nearly three years later, the IRS formally assessed a deficiency. When the executors brought a claim for refund more than three years after the remittance-but within three years of the IRS's formal assessment-the claim was rejected as time barred. *Id.* at 660-61, 65 S.Ct. 536.

In deciding that the taxes were not "paid"-and that the limitations period therefore did not commence-until the tax was actually assessed by the IRS, the Supreme Court specifically considered all of the facts and circumstances surrounding the executors' original remittance, including the executors' intent as stated in the transmittal letter and the IRS's treatment of the remittance once received. The Court determined that when the executors submitted the remittance, they "did not discharge what [they] deemed a liability nor pay one that was asserted. There was merely an interim arrangement to cover whatever contingencies the future might define." *Id.* at 662, 65 S.Ct. 536. Noting the IRS's deposit of the funds into a suspense account, the Court concluded that "[m]oney in these accounts is held not as taxes duly collected are held but as a deposit made in the nature of a cash bond for the payment of taxes thereafter found to be due." *Id.* The Court ruled that considering the specific facts and circumstances of the case, the remittance was a deposit and that the statute of limitations therefore did not bar the executors' claim for refund. Courts have since read *Rosenman* as creating a facts-and-circumstances test for distinguishing between deposits and payments. See, e.g., VanCanagan v. United States, 231 F.3d 1349, 1352-53 (Fed.Cir.2000); Moran v. United States, 63 F.3d 663, 667-68 (7th Cir.1995); Blatt v. United States, 34 F.3d 252, 255 (4th Cir.1994); Ewing v. United States, 914 F.2d 499, 503-04 (4th Cir.1990); Fortugno v. Comm'r, 353 F.2d 429, 435-36 (3d Cir.1965); Risman, 100 T.C. at 197-99. However, this Circuit did not join those courts in their reading of *Rosenman*.

2. Fifth Circuit Law Post-*Rosenman*

Our Circuit first applied *Rosenman* in Thomas v. Mercantile National Bank, 204 F.2d 943 (5th Cir.1953). The *Mercantile National Bank* panel read the *Rosenman* decision as establishing a rule that any amount remitted to the IRS prior to a formal assessment of tax is, as a matter of law, a deposit. *Id.* at 944. Citing *Rosenman*, the Court held a claim for refund timely because

> [u]ntil the Commissioner certified the assessment list . . . there was no deficiency assessment, and no liability on the part of the taxpayer, and consequently nothing to pay. The sum deposited with the Collector . . . was merely an advance deposit to cover additional tax liability expected to arise thereafter. Neither the estate's liability, nor the fact that there was an overpayment could be determined until the deficiency assessment was entered. It would be illogical to hold, as the United States contends, that the statute of limitation began to run against a claim for refund before the deficiency itself came into existence, and before the fact that there was an overpayment, and if so the amount thereof, became ascertainable.

Id. Mercantile National Bank thus took *Rosenman* beyond its narrow facts and circumstances, which the Supreme Court had specifically emphasized in reaching its decision, and adopted a per se rule that pre-assessment remittances are deposits.

Almost thirty years after *Mercantile National Bank* was decided, a panel of this Court begrudgingly applied its per se rule in Ford v. United States, 618 F.2d 357 (5th Cir.1980), but not without making clear its disagreement with *Mercantile National Bank's* holding: "Despite our view of Supreme Court precedent, the course taken by our sister circuits, and appropriate tax policy, we are constrained . . . by the bonds of *Thomas v. Mercantile National Bank at Dallas*." *Id.* at 358. After thoroughly discussing the reasons for abandoning the rule and inviting the Court to reconsider it *en banc*, the panel nevertheless applied *Mercantile National Bank* as binding circuit precedent. The motion for rehearing *en banc* was denied. Ford v. United States, 625 F.2d 1016 (5th Cir.1980).

Fifteen years later, the Fifth Circuit again addressed *Mercantile National Bank* in Harden v. United States, 74 F.3d 1237 (5th Cir.1995) (unpublished).[8] The facts of *Harden* are virtually identical to those of the instant case. The Hardens filed Form 4868 for both the 1984 and 1985

---

8.   Although Harden was unpublished, it is considered precedent because it was issued under our former rule concerning unpublished opinions. See 5th Cir. R. 47.5.3 ("Unpublished opinions issued before January 1, 1996, are precedent.").

tax years, and they submitted remittances with each filing. Several years later, they filed their tax returns for those years, indicating substantially lower tax liabilities than the amounts previously remitted. Like the Deatons, the Hardens sought to apply the overpayments as credits for subsequent tax years, but the IRS denied their request as time-barred. *Id.*

The government argued in *Harden* that *Mercantile National Bank* and *Ford* were distinguishable because they did not address taxpayer remittances accompanying Form 4868. According to the government, 26 U.S.C. § 6513 expressly defined such remittances as "payments" of tax for purposes of the statute of limitations, so the remittances were payments, not deposits, as a matter of law. Although the *Harden* panel appreciated the government's "rational and forceful argument," it concluded that it was "bound to the decisions of this court in [*Mercantile National Bank*] and *Ford*. In those cases we held that as a matter of law a remittance forwarded to the IRS before an assessment of tax is to be considered a deposit rather than a payment." *Id.*

3.   Impact of *Baral v. United States*

We now hold that post-*Baral*, we are no longer bound by the *Mercantile National Bank* line of authority. In *Baral*, the Supreme Court explicitly rejected the taxpayer's argument that a tax cannot be "paid" until tax liability is assessed and thereby abrogated the *Mercantile National Bank* rule that a pre-assessment remittance is a deposit rather than a payment. *Baral*, 528 U.S. at 434, 437, 120 S.Ct. 1006 ("[T]he Code directly contradicts the notion that payment may not occur before assessment.").[9] The unanimous Court construed the plain language of 26 U.S.C. § 6513(b)(1) and (2) as providing unequivocally that two types of remittances, wage withholdings and payments of estimated income tax, are to be "deemed paid" on the due date of the tax return for the tax year in question, not when formal assessment occurs. *Baral*, 528 U.S. at 434-36, 120 S.Ct. 1006. This treatment necessarily precludes the argument that all pre-assessment remittances are deposits, the position that this Court took prior to *Baral* and that the Deatons argue still prevails.

---

9. That the *Baral* Court was specifically addressing the Fifth Circuit's position as compared to those of various other circuits supports a finding of abrogation. *Id.* at 434, 120 S.Ct. 1006 ("In view of an apparent tension between [the Circuits], we granted certiorari."); *see also* Harrigill v. United States, 410 F.3d 786, 790 n. 6 (5th Cir.2005) (not refuting the parties' concession that *Baral* abrogated the Fifth Circuit rule).

According to the Deatons, *Baral* only applies to remittances that fall under 26 U.S.C. § 6513(b), not to transmittals made with Form 4868, and their position is bolstered by the Court's final statement in *Baral*:

> We need not address the proper treatment under § 6511 of remittances that, unlike withholding and estimated income tax, are not governed by a "deemed paid" provision akin to § 6513(b). Such remittances might include remittances of estimated estate tax, as in *Rosenman*, or remittances of any sort of tax by a taxpayer under audit in order to stop the running of interest and penalties. In the latter situation, the taxpayer will often desire treatment of the remittance as a deposit-even if this means forfeiting the right to interest on an overpayment-in order to preserve jurisdiction in the Tax Court, which depends on the existence of a deficiency, a deficiency that would be wiped out by treatment of the remittance as a payment. We note that the Service has promulgated procedures to govern classification of a remittance as a deposit or payment in this context.

Id. at 439 n. 2, 120 S.Ct. 1006. However, this statement does not answer either (1) whether the Deatons' remittance is one that is "governed by a 'deemed paid' provision akin to § 6513(b)" or (2) what the proper treatment is of remittances that are not "governed by a 'deemed paid' provision." The Deatons' position is that a remittance accompanying Form 4868 is not a remittance governed by a deemed paid provision and that remittances not governed by a deemed paid provision are subject to the facts-and-circumstances test established in *Rosenman*.[10] We take up this issue in subpart 4 below.

Post-*Baral*, ours is the only circuit to have addressed the deposit-payment distinction. In Harrigill v. United States, 410 F.3d 786 (5th Cir.2005), we addressed facts similar to the instant facts and held that the pre-assessment remittance at issue was a payment, not a deposit. Harrigill, like the Deatons, had filed a Form 4868 for the 1994 tax year and had submitted it with a remittance of the amount of tax she

---

10. The Deatons also complain that *Baral*'s application to their case should be limited because the *Mercantile National Bank* rule was the law at the time they made their $125,000 remittance. However, we are not free to disregard *Baral* just because it was not decided when the events leading to this appeal occurred:

> When [the Supreme] Court applies a rule of federal law to the parties before it, that rule is the controlling interpretation of federal law and must be given full retroactive effect in all cases still open on direct review and as to all events, regardless of whether such events predate or postdate [the] announcement of the rule.

Harper v. Va. Dep't of Taxation, 509 U.S. 86, 97, 113 S.Ct. 2510, 125 L.Ed.2d 74 (1993). This argument is also foreclosed by our panel decision in Harrigill v. United States, 410 F.3d 786 (5th Cir.2005), which declined to treat a pre-assessment remittance as a deposit even though that remittance would have been treated as a deposit at the time it was made under our pre-*Baral* precedent.

estimated to be due, which was later determined to be overstated. Unlike the Deatons, however, Harrigill filed her tax return for 1994 within the limitations period, and the IRS duly credited her overpayment to her estimated taxes for the 1995 tax year, the return for which she had not yet filed. When Harrigill later filed her 1995 return and found that she had again overestimated her tax liability, she sought to have the overpayment-which resulted from application of the first overpayment to her 1995 taxes-carried over as a credit for 1996. The IRS denied Harrigill's request as time-barred, a decision we upheld. *Id.* at 788, 792.

In upholding the IRS's decision, we did not refute the parties' concession that *Baral* abrogated the *Mercantile National Bank* rule, an abrogation we now expressly recognize, and we used a facts-and-circumstances approach to determine whether the credit applied to Harrigill's estimated taxes for 1995 was an estimated payment of estimated income tax under § 6513(b)(2) subject to *Baral*'s rule that payments of estimated income tax are "deemed paid" on the due date of the return without extension. We did not address whether Harrigill's original remittance accompanying her Form 4868 application was a deposit or a payment as a matter of law because we determined that an application of credit, rather than a Form 4868 remittance, was at issue. The instant case, however, clearly involves a Form 4868 remittance, and we must now address the question left unanswered in *Harrigill*: Is a remittance submitted with a Form 4868 application for an extension of time to file a payment as a matter of law? Or is it subject to the facts-and-circumstances test of *Rosenman*? After *Baral*, this is essentially an issue of first impression in this Circuit; *Harden*, our prior Form 4868 case, which was based on *Mercantile National Bank*, no longer controls.

4. The Deatons' Remittance

The primary issue in this case is the impact of *Baral* and post-*Baral* law on the deposit-payment distinction. As discussed above, *Baral* abrogated the rule established in *Mercantile National Bank*. And the only post-*Baral* case to address the deposit-payment distinction used a facts-and-circumstances test to determine whether the remittance in question was a payment of estimated income tax under § 6513(b)(2) subject to *Baral*'s rule that payments of estimated income tax are deemed paid on the due date of the return without extension. *Harrigill*, 410 F.3d at 791-92. We have been called on here to decide what rule to apply post-*Baral* to characterize a remittance made in conjunction with a Form 4868 application for an extension of time to file. The alternatives offered are (1) a per se rule that all Form 4868 remittances are payments and (2) a facts-and-circumstances inquiry that would require a case-by-case analysis of any Form 4868 remittance made.

Like the *Harrigill* panel, we find it unnecessary to decide whether a Form 4868 remittance is a payment as a matter of law because we find that the Deatons' remittance of $125,000 in conjunction with their Form 4868 application for an extension of time to file constituted a payment of estimated income tax under § 6513(b)(2). We hesitate to adopt a per se rule in a case in which the record clearly indicates that the taxpayers' remittance was a payment, not a deposit, and we therefore decline to do so. We leave for another day the question of whether all Form 4868 remittances should be treated as payments of estimated tax, even though we recognize that several of our sister circuits have already answered this question in the affirmative. See Dantzler v. United States, 183 F.3d 1247, 1251 (11th Cir.1999); Ertman v. United States, 165 F.3d 204, 207 (2d Cir.1999); Ott v. United States, 141 F.3d 1306, 1308-09 (9th Cir.1998); Gabelman v. Comm'r, 86 F.3d 609, 611-12 (6th Cir.1996); Weigand v. United States, 760 F.2d 1072, 1074 (10th Cir.1985). We agree with the Tax Court that even under the facts-and-circumstances approach proposed by the Deatons, their $125,000 remittance must be considered a payment of estimated tax. See VanCanagan v. United States, 231 F.3d 1349, 1352-53 (Fed.Cir.2000). As such, their remittance is "governed by a 'deemed paid' provision" and controlled by *Baral*.

In their 1993 Form 4868, the Deatons indicated that "the amount [they] expect [ed]" to list as their 1993 tax liability was $138,883 and that they had a "balance due" of $125,000. The Deatons remitted that $125,000. The Deatons submitted no contemporaneous evidence supporting their contention that they intended this amount to be a deposit when remitted; there is nothing on the face of the document or on the check submitted with it indicating such an intent. There is no evidence that the Deatons made an attempt to use the IRS procedure for making a deposit. In addition, there is no evidence suggesting that the Deatons were disputing their tax liability as in *Rosenman*. The IRS has always treated their overpayment as an "excess collection." At best, the record suggests that the Deatons had difficulty estimating their tax liability and needed more time to file their 1993 tax return. That they had difficulty estimating their tax liability does not make their remittance of estimated tax a deposit of the kind recognized by *Baral* as retaining legal significance. *Baral*, 528 U.S. at 439 n. 2, 120 S.Ct. 1006.

We reject the Deatons' argument that in light of caselaw prevailing at the time of their remittance, we must presume that they intended to make a deposit. This argument requires that we find that they had actual or presumed knowledge of the prevailing law of this Circuit. They provide no factual evidence to support such a finding. Furthermore, the

Deatons provide no legal authority to support their affirmative use of a presumption that a taxpayer knows the law. Such a presumption is normally reserved to the government in actions against taxpayers. See, e.g., Cheek v. United States, 498 U.S. 192, 199, 111 S.Ct. 604, 112 L.Ed.2d 617 (1991). The Deatons provide no principled reason for allowing the affirmative use of such a presumption against the government, and we refuse to invent such a reason here.

We hold that on the facts and circumstances of this case, the Deatons' remittance of $125,000 was an "amount paid as estimated income tax" under § 6513(b)(2), not a deposit.[11] Under that section, a remittance is deemed paid "on the last day prescribed for filing the return under section 6012 for such taxable year . . . ." I.R.C. § 6513(b)(2). Because the $125,000 was thus paid outside the look-back period of § 6511(b)(2)(A), the Deatons cannot recover their overpayment. I.R.C. § 6511(b)(2)(A).

III. Conclusion

Accordingly, we AFFIRM the Tax Court's decision.

Notes and Questions

Because the Code makes no reference to deposits, it had been up to the courts to determine whether remittances constituted payments or deposits. As you can see from the discussion in *Deaton*, the courts had reached no clear consensus on this issue. The American Jobs Creation Act of 2004, Pub. L. No. 108-357, 118 Stat. 1418, removed many of the payment versus deposit issues from the courts with the enactment of § 6603. This provision offers some clarity by providing that undesignated remittances are considered payments and that a designated § 6603 deposit may be recovered by the taxpayer with interest if it has not been used to pay a tax and it is attributable to a "disputable tax." A disputable tax is defined as "the amount of tax specified at the time of the deposit as the taxpayer's reasonable estimate of the maximum amount of any tax attributable to disputed items." IRC § 6603(d)(2)(A). "Disputable items" are defined as "any item of income, gain, loss, deduction, or credit if the taxpayer – (i) has a reasonable basis for the treatment of such item, and (ii) reasonably believes that the Secretary also has a reasonable basis for disallowing the taxpayer's treatment of such item." Id. If a taxpayer receives a 30-day letter, the items at issue in the 30-day letter are considered disputable and the amount of the disputed tax "shall not be

---

11. Therefore, like the *Baral* Court, we need not address the treatment of remittances not governed by a deemed paid provision. *Baral*, 528 U.S. at 439 n. 2, 120 S.Ct. 1006.

less than the amount of the deficiency proposed in such letter." Id. at § 6603(d)(2)(B). In addition, the taxpayer must attach a statement to the remittance designating the remittance as a § 6603 deposit, identifying the type of tax and taxable year(s) at issue, and identifying the amount of and basis for the disputable tax. Rev. Proc. 2005-18, 2005-1 C.B. 798, § 4.01(1).

Note that once there has been an assessment, or the taxpayer has waived the restrictions on assessment and collection, the tax is no longer disputable and the deposit may be applied against the deficiency. To the extent the deposit is used to pay an assessed tax, it is treated as paid when the deposit is made, so no interest will be payable on this amount and interest on the underpayment will cease as of that date. See further discussion of interest in general and § 6603 in particular in Chapter 6.

In *Deaton*, the payment versus deposit issue arose over a remittance with a Form 4868, request for extension of time to file, but payment issues can arise in other contexts as well. For instance, the Earned Income Tax Credit (EITC) is a refundable credit that applies to working individuals and families with low earned income and a qualifying child. The credit will reduce a qualifying individual's income tax and if there is an excess amount of credit, it will be refunded to the taxpayer. Thus, the EITC is called a "negative income tax." In Israel v. United States, 356 F.3d 221 (2d Cir. 2004), the taxpayers raised the interesting issue of when the refunded amount of the EITC is constructively "paid." This was of concern to them because they had failed to file returns for taxable years 1993 through 1995 until early in 2000. They then attempted to take advantage of the EITC to claim refunds attributable to those taxable years. Their claims were denied by the IRS on the ground that they were barred by the three-year lookback period of § 6511(b)(2)(A). The taxpayers then filed suit in federal district court but the court agreed with the Service and dismissed the suit, agreeing with the IRS that the taxpayers' claims were not timely filed.

On appeal, the taxpayers argued that the EITC is a "unique tax credit" that is a remittance from the federal government to the working poor and is not a refund of taxes that they paid. In fact, in two of the taxable years in question, the taxpayers paid no tax at all. Thus, they argued, § 6511(b)(2)(A) did not apply because there was no payment date from which to calculate the lookback period.

The Second Circuit held for the government while admitting that it was unclear how the Code would apply in this situation (356 F.3d at 222). It reasoned that under the Code, the EITC is an overpayment of tax and it has been similarly characterized by the U.S. Supreme Court. See Sorenson v. Secretary of the Treasury, 475 U.S. 851 (1986). Thus, the deemed paid rule of § 6513(b) applies and the EITC overpayment is deemed to arise on the due date of the return, regardless of whether it arises from a refund of tax liability that the taxpayers' actually paid or not.

The court noted that the purpose of the lookback provision is to prevent the filing of stale claims. A different rule in the case of the EITC would require the government to verify the requirements for eligibility for the EITC many years after the fact. The court thought this would pose too great a hardship for the government.

1. Section 6401(c) states: "An amount paid as tax shall not be considered not to constitute an overpayment solely by reason of the fact that there was no tax liability in respect of which such amount was paid." What does this mean?

2. If the Deatons had written on their check that they were paying the tax "under protest" or to stop the running of interest, and that they intended to file a later claim for refund, would the result in their case have been the same? See New York Life Insurance Co. v. United States, 118 F.3d 1553 (Fed.Cir. 1997); United States v. Dubuque Packing Co., 233 F.2d 453 (8th Cir. 1956); Thomas v. Mercantile National Bank, 204 F.2d 943 (5th Cir. 1953).

3. What effect, if any, would § 6603 have on the Deatons if their case were to arise today?

4. Would an undesignated remittance have any effect on a taxpayer's ability to bring suit in the Tax Court? Compare and contrast your answer before and after the enactment of § 6603.

5. Rev. Proc. 2005-18, 2005-1 C.B. 798 provides procedures for taxpayers to follow under § 6603. It supercedes Rev. Proc. 84-58, which provided procedures for taxpayers to post bonds to stop the running of interest and time-sensitive penalties. Under § 6603, how would the taxpayer stop the running of interest and penalties while preserving Tax Court jurisdiction?

Problem

Susie Taxpayer filed a timely return on April 10, 2008 for the 2007 taxable year. Subsequently, Susie signed a Form 872 on April 1, 2011, extending the statute of limitations for assessment for six months. How long will she have to file a claim for refund attributable to the 2007 taxable year?

C. TIMING OF THE CLAIM

OMOHUNDRO v. UNITED STATES
United States Court of Appeals, Ninth Circuit, 2002.
300 F.3d 1065.

OPINION

PER CURIAM.

Appellant Astrid Omohundro ("Omohundro") appeals an order of the district court dismissing her complaint seeking credit for the overpayment of her 1993 income taxes. Relying on our decision in Miller v. United States, 38 F.3d 473(9th Cir.1994), the district court held it lacked jurisdiction because Omohundro failed to file a timely administrative claim for credit with the Internal Revenue Service ("IRS"). We reverse.

I.

To bring an action for credit or refund of overpaid taxes, a taxpayer must first file an administrative claim with the IRS. See I.R.C. § 7422(a) (2002). The administrative claim must be filed:

> within 3 years from the time the return was filed or 2 years from the time the tax was paid, whichever of such periods expires the later, or if no return was filed by the taxpayer, within 2 years from the time the tax was paid. I.R.C. § 6511(a) (2002). A taxpayer's failure to file an administrative claim within the time periods imposed by statute divests the district court of jurisdiction over an action for a refund or credit.[1] * * *

The issue in this case is whether a taxpayer's claim for credit or refund of overpaid taxes is timely under I.R.C. § 6511(a) if the claim is filed within three years of the date the taxpayer filed his return, regardless of whether the return was filed on or before the date it was due. Omohundro and the United States argue that all claims made

---

1.   Even if a taxpayer files an administrative claim within the applicable limitations period prescribed by I.R.C. § 6511(a), § 6511(b) establishes two "look-back" periods which may limit the amount of refund or credit a taxpayer may recover:

    (A) Limit where claim filed within 3-year period--If the claim was filed by the taxpayer during the 3-year period prescribed in subsection (a), the amount of the credit or refund shall not exceed the portion of the tax paid within the period, immediately preceding the filing of the claim, equal to 3 years plus the period of any extension of time for filing the return * * *.

    (B) Limit where claim not filed within 3-year period--If the claim was not filed within such 3-year period, the amount of the credit or refund shall not exceed the portion of the tax paid during the 2 years immediately preceding the filing of the claim.

within three years of the date of the filing of the return are timely and urge us to overturn *Miller*.

In *Miller*, we held under I.R.C. § 6511(a) that a taxpayer must file a return within two years of payment of the taxes to recover a refund or credit. *Miller*, 38 F.3d at 475. We reasoned that the point at which the court must determine whether a return was filed for purposes of the clause "if no return was filed" is two years after payment of the tax, otherwise no claim could ever be finally barred by the two-year after-payment clause. Id. at 475-476.

We also found our construction of I.R.C. § 6511(a) was necessary to prevent "forum shopping." Id. at 476. Under the 1994 version of § 6512(b)(3), if a taxpayer failed to file a tax return and was issued a deficiency notice, the amount of refund he could recover in tax court was limited to the tax paid during the two-year period immediately preceding the date of the notice. We reasoned if we held that a three-year limitation period applied in district court, taxpayers would improperly derive an advantage by filing a claim there rather than in tax court. Id.

II.

Both Omohundro and the United States contend *Miller* was incorrectly decided and that *Miller* does not bind this panel. We are not bound by the decision of a prior panel if a subsequent en banc decision, Supreme Court decision, or legislation has undermined it.

In deciding *Miller*, we did not consider Revenue Ruling 76-511 which was directly on point and in effect at the time. In 76-511, a taxpayer sought advice on whether he could recover a refund when he filed his 1972 tax return, including a refund claim, on April 30, 1976. The IRS decided the refund claim was timely, stating, "[i]n this case, A [taxpayer] filed a claim for a refund within the 3-year period of limitation prescribed by § 6511(a) of the Code, because, under § 30.6402-3 of the regulations, A's 1972 income tax return was a claim for a refund." Rev. Rul. 76-511, 1976-2 C.B. 428 (1976).

In United States v. Mead Corp., 533 U.S. 218, 121 S.Ct. 2164, 150 L.Ed.2d 292 (2001), the Supreme Court held that an administrative agency's interpretation of a statute contained in an informal rulemaking must be accorded the level of deference set forth in Skidmore v. Swift & Co., 323 U.S. 134, 65 S.Ct. 161, 89 L.Ed.124 (1944). The Court held the deference required depends on the "thoroughness evident in [the agency's] consideration, the validity of its reasoning, its consistency with earlier and later pronouncements, and all those factors which give it the power to persuade * * *." Id. at 228, 121 S.Ct. 2164 (citing *Skidmore*, 323

U.S. at 140, 65 S.Ct. 161). *Mead* involved a Customs Service tariff ruling, which is closely akin to an IRS revenue ruling. Given that the two types of agency rulings are analogous, we are required to apply *Mead's* standard of review to an IRS revenue ruling.

In light of the Supreme Court's intervening holding in *Mead*, we must decide whether Revenue Ruling 76-511 commands deference. We believe it does. First, the IRS's reasoning is valid. Although the IRS's interpretation of I.R.C. § 6511(a) may render the statute's time limitations somewhat "illusory," the look-back provisions of I.R.C. § 6511(b) effectively eliminate any danger of taxpayers recovering on stale claims.[2] Every appellate court that has addressed this issue has reached the same decision as the IRS or has indicated it would do so. See Weisbart v. United States, 222 F.3d 93, 95-96 (2d Cir.2000) (holding a taxpayer has three years from the date his return is actually filed to file a claim for refund or credit); Richards v. C.I.R., 37 F.3d 587, 589 (10th Cir.1994) (noting the "benchmark date" for measuring the triggering events of the relevant limitations period is the date on which taxpayer actually files a return); Oropallo v. United States, 994 F.2d 25, 26-27 (1st Cir.1993) (declining to decide the issue but assuming a three-year limitations period applied when a taxpayer filed a return containing a claim for a refund more than two years after payment of the tax).

Revenue Ruling 76-511 is consistent with later IRS pronouncements. In February of 2001, the Department of the Treasury and the IRS issued a final regulation regarding the application of the "mailbox" rule to late-filed returns including refund claims. The example in the regulation assumes a claim for a refund of overpaid 2001 taxes is timely under I.R.C. § 6511(a) when the claim was included in a return filed on April 15, 2005.

The IRS's interpretation of I.R.C. § 6511(a) is supported by the legislative history of the statute. Under the 1954 version of the statute, the three-year period was intended to run from the date the taxpayer's return was due, not the date it was actually filed. See S.Rep. No. 83-1622 (1954), reprinted in 1954 U.S.C.A.A.N. 4621, 5235. In 1958, Congress amended the statute, expressing concern that taxpayers had to file a timely return in order to benefit from the three-year limitation period while the IRS had three years to complete assessments regardless of whether the return was timely. See S.Rep. No. 85-1983 (1958), reprinted in 1958 U.S.C.A.A.N. 4791, 4887. By amending I.R.C. § 6511(a), Congress intended that "a claim for a refund or credit of any tax

---

2. This is well-illustrated by Revenue Ruling 76-511 in which the IRS found a refund claim was timely under I.R.C. § 6511(a), but was barred by I.R.C. § 6511(b) since the taxpayer did not pay the tax to be refunded within the three-year period immediately preceding the date the return was filed.

may be filed within three years from the time the return was actually filed (or, as under present law, within 2 years from the time of payment, whichever is later)." Id.

Subsequent legislation has also significantly undermined *Miller's* reasoning. The *Miller* court found its holding was necessary to prevent taxpayers who received a deficiency notice from "forum shopping" between district court and tax court. The Taxpayer Relief Act of 1997 eliminated any disparity in deadlines between tax court and district court by amending I.R.C. § 6512(b)(3) to allow a three-year look-back period for a refund claim filed in tax court where no return has been filed and the mailing date of the deficiency notice is during the third year after the return due date. See I.R.C. § 6512(b)(3)(B), (C) (2002). Under the current statute, *Miller* actually creates a disparity since a taxpayer must file a return within two years of payment of the tax in district court, but need not do so in tax court.

In light of the intervening Supreme Court decision in *Mead*, which requires that we accord *Skidmore* deference to revenue rulings, as well as the recent legislation that has obviated the *Miller* court's concern with potential forum-shopping, we conclude we are no longer bound by *Miller*. Accordingly, we hold that under I.R.C. § 6511(a), a taxpayer's claim for credit or a refund is timely if it is filed within three years from the date his income tax return is filed, regardless of when the return is filed.

The district court had jurisdiction over Omohundro's claim for credit for overpaid income taxes because her administrative claim was timely filed. Omohundro's 1993 tax return was considered filed on October 14, 1997, and she had three years from that date to file her claim for credit. Her claim for credit was included in her tax return and was considered filed on the same date. See Treas. Reg. § 301.6402-3(a)(4).

We REVERSE and REMAND to the district court for further proceedings.

Notes and Question

In Baral v. United States, 528 U.S. 431, 120 S.Ct. 1006, 145 L.Ed.2d 949 (2000), discussed in § B. in *Deaton*, the IRS conceded that the three-year lookback period of § 6511(a) applies regardless of when the return is filed.

Is the Ninth Circuit correct in its assertion in *Miller* that applying the three-year lookback period after a delinquent return has been filed will mean that "no claim could ever be finally barred by the two-year after payment clause" of § 6511(a)?

Problems

1. James White failed to file a timely tax return for the taxable year 2007 but $5,500 was withheld from his wages during that year, and was deemed paid on April 15, 2008. On June 10, 2011, he filed a return for the 2007 taxable year in which he claimed a refund of $2,000. Is the refund claim timely? If his claim is valid on the merits, how much will James be entitled to receive? See Allen v. Commissioner, 99 T.C. 475 (1992), aff'd, 23 F.3d 406 (6th Cir. 1994); Galuska v. Commissioner, 98 T.C. 661 (1992), aff'd, 5 F.3d 195 (7th Cir. 1993).

2. Susan J. Scott filed her income tax return on March 5. As it happened, April 15th fell on a Saturday in that particular year, so the deadline for filing individual income tax returns was extended under § 7503 to April 17th. Susan's entire tax liability in that taxable year was paid through wage withholding. Three years later, she filed a claim for refund on April 16th. Is her refund claim timely? See Rev. Rul. 2003-41, 2003-17 I.R.B. 814.

D. TOLLING THE STATUTE OF LIMITATIONS

DOE v. KPMG
United States Court of Appeals, Fifth Circuit, 2005.
398 F.3d 686

EDITH H. JONES, CIRCUIT JUDGE:

This appeal challenges the district court's jurisdiction to apply equitable tolling to the statute of limitations of Internal Revenue Code § 6501, 26 U.S.C. § 6501 (hereafter "I.R.C."). Because we conclude that equitable tolling may not be used to extend this provision's three-year period, we REVERSE the district court.

Background

In September 2000, the Internal Revenue Service ("IRS") published Notice 2000-44,[1] which requires organizers and promoters of certain tax shelters to maintain lists of participants and to provide those lists to the IRS upon request. The Notice also states that these shelter transactions are potentially abusive. In December 2000, John Doe I and John Doe II[2] (collectively "taxpayers") purchased one of these Short Option Strategy

---

1. The IRS issued the notice pursuant to I.R.C. § 6112(b)(2).

2. The district court eventually removed the seal on the case. John Doe I is actually Keith Tucker and John Doe II is Robert Hechler.

("SOS") shelters from KPMG to reduce their federal income tax liabilities for 2000 and 2001.

In 2001, the IRS investigated KPMG's compliance with the registration requirements imposed by Notice 2000-44. As part of the inquiry, the IRS propounded summonses that demanded the names of clients to whom KMPG had sold certain tax shelters, as well as other documentation relating to the transactions. In all, KPMG received twenty-five summonses. In July 2002, the IRS brought an action in the United States District Court for the District of Columbia to enforce nine of the summonses sent to KPMG.[3] In December 2002, the district court ordered KPMG to comply with the summonses and reveal the requested names and transactional information to a special master in charge of the case. The remainder of the case was held in abeyance pending the special master's report.

In August 2003, KPMG first informed the IRS and the taxpayers that the taxpayers' 2000 SOS transaction was responsive to one of the summonses (a summons not involved in the D.C. litigation). This revelation was contrary to KPMG's previous representations to the IRS. KPMG then turned over information about the SOS transactions to the IRS but omitted the taxpayer names from the documents. The taxpayers notified KPMG that they wished to invoke the "tax-practitioner privilege" under I.R.C. (26 U.S.C.) § 7525[4] and instructed KPMG not to take any action that would waive their privilege. KPMG promised the taxpayers that while it would not reveal any information before September 8, 2003, the firm could not entirely refuse to comply with the summonses now that KPMG was aware that the SOS transaction was responsive.

On September 9, 2003, Doe I and Doe II filed the instant suit in federal court against KPMG, seeking declaratory and injunctive relief to prevent KPMG from disclosing their identities to the IRS in response to the summonses. KPMG promptly agreed to the taxpayers' Stipulation and Agreed Order preventing KPMG from disclosing their identities or any relevant documents until the court should enter a final judgment on the merits.[5]

---

3.   See United States v. KPMG, LLP, 237 F.Supp.2d 35, 36 (D.D.C.2002); 316 F.Supp.2d 30 (D.D.C.2004). The IRS did not seek enforcement of the Notice 2000-44 summonses in this suit because KPMG had assured the IRS that it had complied in full with the applicable summons.

4.   I.R.C. § 7525 applies "to a communication between a taxpayer and any federally authorized tax practitioner to the extent the communication would be considered a privileged communication if it were between a taxpayer and an attorney."

5.   Nevertheless, defendant KPMG argued that the taxpayers' identities were not protected by the tax-practitioner privilege.

As of September 8, the IRS learned that KPMG had not fully complied with the Notice 2000-44 summonses.[6] Further, the instant litigation informed the IRS that taxpayers whose identities were not yet known had used these tax shelters. As the litigation continued, the IRS became concerned that the three-year statute of limitations to assess additional taxes would expire while the lawsuit was pending. On March 19, 2004, the IRS requested the taxpayers to sign a consent agreement extending the statute of limitations during litigation. The taxpayers refused. The IRS then filed an emergency motion to intervene under Federal Rule of Civil Procedure 24(a) to protect its interests and the public fisc.

The district court granted the motion and ordered the parties to take all necessary steps to prevent the statute of limitations from expiring. When the taxpayers persisted in their refusal, the IRS sought an order to show cause why they should not be held in contempt. The taxpayers asserted, and the district court agreed, that consent to toll the statute of limitations must be voluntary. See I.R.C. § 6501(a)(4). Nevertheless, the court issued an order equitably tolling the statute of limitations based on I.R.C. § 6503(a)(1) and other equitable principles. That decision is the subject of the instant appeal.[7]

Discussion
* * *

When interpreting a statute, we start with the plain text, and read all parts of the statute together to produce a harmonious whole. Section 6501(a) establishes a three-year statute of limitations "after a return [is] filed" for the assessment of federal income taxes. The statute then lists twenty-six specific exceptions that toll the limitations period.[8] The IRS can use other tools to toll the statute as well. For example, if a taxpayer's identity is unknown to the IRS, the agency may serve a "John Doe" summons pursuant to Section 7609(a), which then tolls the statute pursuant to Section 6501. None of these provisions, however, explicitly permits equitable tolling. Taxpayers thus assert that the district court lacked jurisdiction to apply equitable tolling to Section 6501.

---

6. The taxpayers filed on September 8 but then withdrew an emergency motion to intervene and for protective order in the D.C. litigation.

7. The court also rejected the taxpayers' assertion of privilege under § 7525 and ordered the clerk to remove the seal from all documents relating to the taxpayers' names. The taxpayers do not appeal this aspect of the decision.

8. Tolling provisions are listed in subsections of § 6501, as well as in additional provisions within I.R.C. § 6503.

For other tax disputes, Congress has created exceptions to a statute of limitations following litigation which determined that the statute did not allow tolling. In United States v. Brockamp, for example, the United States Supreme Court held that I.R.C. § 6511, which establishes a three-year (or in some instances two-year) period during which a taxpayer must request a refund for overpayment of taxes, was not subject to equitable tolling. 519 U.S. 347, 117 S.Ct. 849, 136 L.Ed.2d 818 (1997). In that case, the taxpayers suffered from mental disability throughout the statutory period; however, in light of the plain statutory language and existence of numerous tolling provisions, the Supreme Court held that the statute was not subject to general equitable tolling by courts. *Id.* at 352, 117 S.Ct. at 852; *see also id.* ("[C]ongress did not intend courts to read other unmentioned, open-ended 'equitable' exceptions into the statute that it wrote."). In 1998, Congress amended this law to permit tolling when a taxpayer, like those in *Brockamp*, is prevented by a disability from seeking a refund. Congress's decision to specify further exceptions to the statute of limitations-without adding a general equitable tolling provision-further justifies the Supreme Court's reading of the statute in *Brockamp*. Because Congress prefers to provide explicit tolling exceptions to the limitations periods contained in federal tax law, by implication, it does not intend courts to invoke equitable tolling to alter the plain text of the statutes at issue.[9]

As it did following *Brockamp*, Congress recently amended the statute at issue in this case. In Section 814 of the American Jobs Creation Act of 2004, Congress extended the time for assessment of taxes and penalties where the taxpayer fails to include required information on a return or statement regarding a listed transaction. Pub. L. No. 108-357, § 814, 118 Stat. 1418, 1421 (2004). Appellants acknowledge that the amendment is aimed at future taxpayers who, as they did, attempt to shield their identities from the IRS until the statute of limitations expires. The dubious distinction of inspiring the passage of a law to prevent others from following their lead[10] does not, however, detract from the strength of the taxpayers' argument here. "Tax law, after all, is not normally characterized by case-specific exceptions reflecting individualized equities." *Brockamp*, 519 U.S. at 352, 117 S.Ct. at 852.

---

9. In fact, before the Seventh Circuit, the IRS took the position that, pursuant to *Brockamp*, equitable tolling should not apply to any provision in the Internal Revenue Code. See Flight Attendants Against UAL Offset (FAAUO) v. Comm'r, 165 F.3d 572, 577 (7th Cir.1999).

10. See, e.g., H.R. No. 108-548(1), at 267 (June 16, 2004) ("[S]ome taxpayers and their advisors have been employing dilatory tactics and failing to cooperate with the IRS in an attempt to avoid liability because of the expiration of the statute of limitations.").

The Government argues that I.R.C. § 7402(a),[11] broadly read, gives district courts implied authority to use equitable tolling to enforce the revenue code. See United States v. First Nat'l City Bank, 379 U.S. 378, 380, 85 S.Ct. 528, 529, 13 L.Ed.2d 365 (1965); United States v. Raymond, 228 F.3d 804 (7th Cir.2000); United States v. Ernst & Whinney, 735 F.2d 1296, 1300 (11th Cir.1984). But the Government cites no authority in which a court applied Section 7402(a) to Section 6501. Further, several of the authorities cited by the Government stand only for the proposition that district courts have jurisdiction to hear claims made by the IRS in conjunction with its filings of intervention or interpleader; the issue of equitable tolling played no role in these holdings. See, e.g., United States v. Asay, 614 F.2d 655, 662 (9th Cir.1980); Miller & Miller Auctioneers, Inc. v. G.W. Murphy Indus., Inc., 472 F.2d 893, 895 (10th Cir.1973). We are unpersuaded that the general enabling language of Section 7402(a) authorizes a court to inject an equitable tolling provision into a detailed, highly specific provision (Section 6501).

The Government invokes additional broad principles to contravene the plain language of Section 6501. We agree with the Government that, as a general matter, the Internal Revenue Code is to be interpreted broadly in the Government's favor. See Commissioner v. Schleier, 515 U.S. 323, 327-28, 115 S.Ct. 2159, 2162-63, 132 L.Ed.2d 294 (1995). We also agree that statutes diminishing sovereign immunity should be read in the sovereign's favor. See, e.g., Library of Congress v. Shaw, 478 U.S. 310, 106 S.Ct. 2957, 92 L.Ed.2d 250 (1986); Soriano v. United States, 352 U.S. 270, 77 S.Ct. 269, 1 L.Ed.2d 306 (1957). Further, there is some truth in the Government's effort to portray the taxpayers as having less than clean hands in this litigation. None of these general principles and complaints, however, can overcome the specific intent of Congress as demonstrated by the precise language of Section 6501.[12] Even an unsympathetic litigant retains the protection of the statute of limitations unless the Government can toll the statute through one of the congressionally prescribed methods.

---

11. The statute provides:

  The district courts of the United States at the instance of the United States shall have such jurisdiction to make and issue in civil actions, writs and orders of injunction, and of ne exeat republica, orders appointing receivers, and such other orders and processes, and to render such judgments and decrees as may be necessary or appropriate for the enforcement of the internal revenue laws. The remedies hereby provided are in addition to and not exclusive of any and all other remedies of the United States in such courts or otherwise to enforce such laws.

12. To support this contention, the IRS relies heavily on Young v. United States, 535 U.S. 43, 122 S.Ct. 1036, 152 L.Ed.2d 79 (2002). This case, which permitted a bankruptcy court to impose equitable tolling to an aspect of the Bankruptcy Code, is inapposite. Bankruptcy courts are courts of equity by their nature. Id. at 50, 122 S.Ct. at 1041. As discussed *supra*, *Brockamp* is more persuasive and more relevant to the instant tax case.

At oral argument, the IRS attempted to stretch the above issue to embody the district judge's authority to control proceedings in his own courtroom. We disagree. The district court had a panoply of tools available to control the proceedings. Regardless, this argument is beside the point, in that it was the Government's obligation, not the court's, to protect the Government's rights. The true nature of this dispute is whether the district court had statutory authority to use equitable tolling to overcome the statute of limitations. Our reading of the statute answers that question in the negative.

Conclusion

The statute here at issue prohibits the imposition of equitable tolling to prevent expiration of the statute of limitations. The IRS is unable to rely on general equitable principles to protect its right to collect taxes from citizens where the statute does not allow equitable tolling. The IRS had three years to pursue the taxpayers using congressionally approved means. Congress can-and indeed has-remedied the problems posed by the taxpayers' tactics in this case. Since neither retroactive application of the new law nor equitable tolling in the Government's favor is available, the judgment of the district court is REVERSED.

Notes and Question

In Irwin v. Department of Veteran Affairs, 498 US 89 (1990), the Supreme Court held that an untimely lawsuit filed against a government employer under Title VII of the Civil Rights Act of 1964 could be considered timely based on the "rule of equitable tolling," which applies to suits against the Government, in the same way that is applicable" to Title VII suits against private employers.

that the government is arguing in favor the Service has argued that equitable text. While courts have declined Supreme Court in *Brockamp*

fairly simple language, which one taining an implied "equitable tolling" uses language that is not simple. It sets a highly detailed technical manner, that, linguistically speaking, cannot easily be read as containing implicit exceptions. * * *

519 U.S. 347, 350 (1997). The Court went to note that "The nature and potential magnitude of the administrative problem suggest that Congress decided to pay the price of occasional unfairness in individual cases (penalizing a taxpayer whose claim is unavoidably delayed) in order to maintain a more workable tax enforcement system." Id. at 352-535.

What is the administrative problem to which the Court is referring?

E. REMEDIES TO ABSOLVE THE HARSHNESS OF THE STATUTE OF LIMITATIONS

There are some situations in which a year that is closed by the statute of limitations may be reopened to make adjustments to the tax liability. The circumstances under which this may occur are very limited, however.

1. Statutory Mitigation

The mitigation provisions are found at §§ 1311 through 1314 of the Internal Revenue Code. They can operate in favor of either the taxpayer or the government, but the provisions are very narrowly construed. Mitigation is so called because the provisions mitigate the harshness and finality of the statute of limitations. If mitigation applies, it allows an assessment or a refund in a taxable year that is closed by the statute of limitations or some other rule of law, such as res judicata.

The first step in mitigation is that there must have been a determination of the taxpayer's liability. A determination is defined as a court decision, closing agreement, final disposition of a refund claim, and certain written, informal agreements regarding the tax liability. See IRC § 1313(a); Reg. § 1.1313(a)-4(a).

FIRST NATIONAL BANK OF OMAHA v. UNITED STATES
United States Court of Appeals, Eighth Circuit, 1977.
565 F.2d 507.

GIBSON, CHIEF JUDGE.

This is a tax refund suit by trustees of a family trust as successors to the property of the late Margaret H. Doorly, for 1963 income taxes overpaid by Mrs. Doorly. In her 1963 return she recognized the receipt of $10,429,005 from the liquidation of the World Publishing Company (World), publishers of the Omaha World Herald, and paid a tax of $2,332,257.19. It is now conceded that over $1,000,000 should not have been recognized as constructively received for income tax purposes and that she overpaid her taxes for that year in the amount of $267,771.75.

The statute of limitations would normally bar this refund suit. The District Court held that the bar is avoided by application of the mitigation provisions of I.R.C. §§1311-1314[1] and granted judgment for the entire $267,771.75 overpayment plus interest. The Government appeals and argues that the mitigation provisions do not apply and that if they do, the refund was improperly calculated. We affirm in part, reverse in part, and remand.

Factual background

Prior to January 1963, Margaret Doorly owned 23,973 shares of World stock outright and was the remainder beneficiary of the Gilbert M. Hitchcock Trust which owned 32,400 shares. The shareholders of World

---

1. Sections 1311-1313 provide in pertinent part:

§ 1311. Correction of error.

(a) General rule. If a determination (as defined in § 1313) is described in one or more of the paragraphs of § 1312 and, on the date of the determination, correction of the effect of the error referred to in the applicable paragraph of § 1312 is prevented by the operation of any law or rule of law, other than this part and other than § 7122 (relating to compromises), then the effect of the error shall be corrected by an adjustment made in the amount and in the manner specified in § 1314.

(b) Conditions necessary for adjustment. (1) Maintenance of an inconsistent position. * * *(A)djustment shall be made under this part only if (A) in case the amount of the adjustment would be credited or refunded in the same manner as an overpayment under § 1314, there is adopted in the determination a position maintained by the Secretary or his delegate, * * * and the position maintained by the Secretary or his delegate * * * is inconsistent with the erroneous inclusion, exclusion, omission, allowance, disallowance, recognition, or nonrecognition, as the case may be.

§ 1312. Circumstances of adjustment.

The circumstances under which the adjustment provided in § 1311 is authorized are as follows: (1) Double inclusion of an item of gross income. The determination requires the inclusion in gross income of an item which was erroneously included in the gross income of the taxpayer for another taxable year or in the gross income of a related taxpayer.

§ 1313. Definitions.

(b) Taxpayer. Notwithstanding § 7701(a)(14), the term "taxpayer" means any person subject to a tax under the applicable revenue law.

(c) Related taxpayer. For purposes of this part, the term "related taxpayer" means a taxpayer who, with the taxpayer with respect to whom a determination is made, stood, in the taxable year with respect to which the erroneous inclusion, exclusion, omission, allowance, or disallowance was made, in one of the following relationships: (1) husband and wife, (2) grantor and fiduciary, (3) grantor and beneficiary, (4) fiduciary and beneficiary, legatee, or heir, (5) decedent and decedent's estate, (6) partner, or (7) member of an affiliated group of corporations (as defined in § 1504).

* * * Several attempts to explicate these provisions have been made in professional literature. E. g., Cohen, Related Party Provisions of Sections 1311-1315, 22nd Annual N.Y.U. Institute 411 (1964); Coleman, Mitigation of the Statute of Limitations Sections 1311-1315, 31st Annual N.Y.U. Institute 1575 (1973); Knickerbocker, Mysteries of Mitigation: The Opening of Barred Years in Income Tax Cases, 30 Fordham L.Rev. 225 (1961); Maguire, Surrey and Traynor, Section 820 of the Revenue Act of 1938, 48 Yale L.J. 509-32, 719-78 (1939); Plumb, The Problem of Related Taxpayers: A Procedural Study, 66 Harv.L.Rev. 225 (1952).

had, on October 31, 1962, adopted a plan of complete liquidation under § 337 of the Internal Revenue Code.

On December 28, 1962, World was sued for a substantial commission allegedly due a New York broker arising from efforts to sell the newspaper. In order to meet this potential liability and other contingencies, the Board of Directors resolved on January 3, 1963, to retain a fund of four million dollars amounting to $19 per share until all claims were settled. The Board also resolved to pay a liquidating distribution of $166 per share on January 7, 1963.

Under that distribution the Gilbert M. Hitchcock Trust received $5,378,400. In February 1963, the life income beneficiary of that trust died. The corpus of that trust, including 32,400 shares of World, was delivered in August 1963 to the remainderman, Margaret H. Doorly. She immediately transferred those assets by gift to the irrevocable "Margaret H. Doorly Family Trust" of which plaintiffs are trustees. Mrs. Doorly filed a gift tax return listing the value of the remaining proceeds from the 32,400 shares at $17 per share.

Also in the January 7, 1963, distribution, Margaret Doorly received $3,979,518 on the stock she owned in her own name. On her income tax return for the calendar year 1963, Margaret H. Doorly recognized the receipt of $185 per share ($166 actually received plus $19 retained to meet contingent liabilities) on 56,373 World shares held in her name during 1963 (32,400 from the Hitchcock trust and 23,973 in her own right). She reported a capital gain of $10,429,005 from the liquidation and paid a tax of $2,332,257.19, of which $267,771.75 represented the tax on the $19 per share retained by the Board of Directors to meet potential liabilities.

At that time both the taxpayer and the Government thought the retained $19 per share was required to be reported and taxed as constructively received in 1963. The Government continued to contend that the 1963 tax was proper until it filed its brief in this appeal, at which time it conceded that under Nebraska law the reserve should not have been taxed until actually distributed.

The consequences of this error were greatly complicated by the death of Margaret Doorly on May 24, 1964. Under her will, plaintiff Katherine D. Clark was named executrix and plaintiff First National Bank of Omaha was appointed administrator, with will annexed.[4] The right to the final liquidating dividend on the 23,973 shares of World, held in Margaret Doorly's name, was included in her estate for federal estate tax

---

4.   The estate has apparently been closed with the residue poured over into the trust. It is stipulated that plaintiffs are the proper parties to bring this action.

purposes. Eventually a date-of-death fair market value of $17 per share was agreed upon by the Government and the estate.

On August 24, 1965, after all potential liabilities of World were resolved, the final liquidating distribution was paid. It amounted to $18.5525 per share, $0.4475 less than the $19 earlier treated as constructively received. The Margaret H. Doorly Estate income tax return for the fiscal year ending November 30, 1965, claimed a loss of $10,727.92 (23,973 shares X $0.4475) on the liquidating distribution. This return was audited and on March 28, 1967, by written notice, the Government accepted it as filed. Then the audit was reopened on October 19, 1967, and eventually the Government determined that not only was the loss improper but in fact the estate had a capital gain of $37,281.08 (23,973 shares X $1.5525).[5] It assessed a deficiency of $9,489.98 which was paid by the estate. A refund claim was formally disallowed on September 21, 1972.

The income tax returns for the Margaret H. Doorly Family Trust and its subdivisions[6] for the fiscal year ending January 31, 1966, also reported a loss of $0.4475 per share on the final liquidation of the 32,400 shares of World stock owned by the Trust. The total loss claimed amounted to $14,499.00. Upon audit, this loss was disallowed by the Government. The Government took the position that under § 1015 of the Internal Revenue Code neither gain nor loss was reportable.[7] Deficiencies were assessed against the trust which aggregated $509.12. This amount was paid and claims for refund were filed which were disallowed on September 21, 1972.

After a claim for refund of the $267,771.75 overpayment was disallowed on November 14, 1974, plaintiff-trustees instituted this suit for that amount as a refund of the 1963 overpayment. Unquestionably this suit is barred unless the statute of limitations is avoided by either the mitigation provisions of I.R.C. §§ 1311-1315 or equitable estoppel as urged by the trustees.

---

5. The Government relied on the date-of-death fair market value of $17 per share used in the estate tax settlement.

6. The subdivisions were for the benefit of various family members. On this appeal we view them as a single entity.

7. Under I.R.C. § 1015 the basis of gift property is the same as the basis in the hands of the donor, in this case the $19 per share recognized as constructively received. The basis in case of loss is limited to no more than the fair market value at the time of gift, in this case $17 as reported on the gift tax return.

Background of the mitigation provisions

In 1938, the Subcommittee on Internal Revenue Taxation of the House Committee on Ways and Means recommended "that there be prepared suitable provisions under which the statute of limitations should be so adjusted as to insure the taxation of income, and the allowance of deductions, in the year to which properly allocable."[9] The Senate Finance Committee responded to this recommendation by including in the 1938 Revenue Bill provisions which subsequently became §§ 1311-1315 of the Internal Revenue Code of 1954.

The Senate Finance Committee Report stated that legislation was needed "to supplement the equitable principles applied by the courts" and that the proposed legislation was based upon the following principles:

(1) to preserve unimpaired the essential function of the statute of limitations, corrective adjustments should (a) never modify the application of the statute except when the party or parties in whose favor it applies shall have justified such modification by active inconsistency, and (b) under no circumstances affect the tax save with respect to the influence of the particular items involved in the adjustment.

(2) Subject to the foregoing principles, disputes as to the year in which income or deductions belong, or as to the person who should have the tax burden of income or the tax benefit of deductions, should never result in a double tax or a double reduction of tax, or an inequitable avoidance of tax.

(3) Disputes as to the basis of property should not allow the taxpayer or the Commissioner to obtain an unfair tax advantage by taking one position at the time of the acquisition of property and an inconsistent position at the time of its disposition.

(4) Corrective adjustments should produce the effect of attributing income or deductions to the right year and the right taxpayer, and of establishing the proper basis.[10]

In order to appreciate the mitigation provisions and to apply them in light of the above principles it is helpful to understand the state of the law before they were enacted. Long ago the courts recognized that the

---

9. Report of the Subcommittee on Ways and Means on a Proposed Revision of the Revenue Laws, H.Rep.No.79, 75th Cong., 3rd Sess., quoted in 2 Merten's, Law of Federal Income Taxation (Rev.) § 14.01 at 4.

10. Finance Committee Report, S.Rep.No.1567, 75th Cong., 3rd Sess. 48, quoted in 2 Merten's, Law of Federal Income Taxation (Rev.) § 14.02 at 9-10. See also Karpe v. United States, 335 F.2d 454, 460 n. 16, 167 Ct.Cl. 280 (1964), cert. denied, 379 U.S. 964, 85 S.Ct. 655, 13 L.Ed.2d 558 (1965).

statute of limitations could result in severe inequities in the application of the income tax laws in individual cases. This is because the income tax is based on separate and distinct taxpayers paying tax on income in separate and distinct tax years. It is often difficult to decide which taxpayer is chargeable with an item of income or deduction in which tax year. As a result, correction of an error may be barred by the limitations period before the proper treatment is determined and thus either the taxpayer or the public revenues may lose.

The courts responded to the problem by resorting to the doctrines of recoupment and set-off. In a series of cases the Supreme Court approved these methods. Lewis v. Reynolds, 284 U.S. 281, 52 S.Ct. 145, 76 L.Ed. 293 (1932), involved trustees seeking a refund of taxes allegedly overpaid by a decedent's estate. The Collector denied the refund after re-auditing the tax year and determining that other deductions had been improperly allowed. The Supreme Court agreed with the court of appeals that the ultimate question in the refund suit was whether there had been an overpayment. The Court stated:

> Although the statute of limitations may have barred the assessment and collection of any additional sum, it does not obliterate the right of the United States to retain payments already received when they do not exceed the amount which might have been properly assessed and demanded.

284 U.S. at 283, 52 S.Ct. at 146.

Bull v. United States, 295 U.S. 247, 55 S.Ct. 695, 79 L.Ed. 1421 (1935), fleshed out the short *Lewis* opinion and gave relief to a taxpayer against the Government. Simplified, the facts of *Bull* are that a member of a partnership died and the agreement provided that the survivors would continue to operate the business and share profits with the deceased partner's estate for one year unless the estate chose to withdraw within thirty days of the death.

The Government required the estate to include for estate tax purposes the value of the right to continue in the partnership and valued this right at the amount of profits actually received. Thereafter the Government also required the estate to report and pay income tax on the full amount of the profits. The Board of Tax Appeals denied relief from the income tax inclusion. Taxpayer then sued in the court of claims for judgment in the alternative (1) for the income tax paid or (2) for the estate tax paid. The court of claims held the income tax was properly collected and the estate tax issue was not reviewable because of the bar of the statute of limitations.

The Supreme Court reversed in a carefully reasoned opinion. It agreed that the income tax was proper and held the estate tax was improper. The Court noted that the identical money was the basis of two assessments and this was inconsistent in this case.[11] It viewed the timely income tax refund suit as in essence a mechanism for the Government to enforce its claim for taxes. The Court then discussed the estate taxes and stated that while "the money was taken through mistake without any element of fraud, the unjust retention is immoral and amounts in law to a fraud on the taxpayer's rights." 295 U.S. at 261, 55 S.Ct. at 700. Under these circumstances, the Court held the taxpayer was entitled to equitable recoupment[12] and judgment for the amount of the estate tax overpayment plus interest.[13]

The Supreme Court embraced equitable principles where "related" taxpayers were involved in Stone v. White, 301 U.S. 532, 57 S.Ct. 851, 81 L.Ed. 1285 (1937). In that case the Collector relied on decisions of the courts of appeals in assessing a deficiency against trustees for trust income. After the statute of limitations had run on assessing a deficiency against the income beneficiary, the trustees paid the tax. The Supreme Court then decided Helvering v. Butterworth, 290 U.S. 365, 54 S.Ct. 221, 78 L.Ed. 365 (1933), holding that such income should be taxed to the beneficiary. In the refund suit by the trustees, the Court upheld a denial of relief, stating, "No injustice is done to the trustees or the beneficiary by withholding from the trustees money which in equity is the beneficiary's, and which the government received in payment of a tax which was hers to pay." 301 U.S. at 537, 57 S.Ct. at 854.

Recoupment doctrine was clarified in Rothensies v. Electric Storage Battery Co., 329 U.S. 296, 67 S.Ct. 271 (1946), which emphasized that

---

11. The Court suggested a distinction between the facts of *Bull* and a situation where the right to receive an amount and the actual receipt are treated as distinct taxable items. 295 U.S. at 256, 55 S.Ct. 695. Since *Bull* involved estate and income taxes rather than two income taxes, we think the facts of this case come closer to the inconsistency condemned in *Bull*.

12. The Court said, "(R)ecoupment is in the nature of a defense arising out of some feature of the transaction upon which the plaintiff's action is grounded. Such a defense is never barred by the statute of limitations so long as the main action itself is timely." 295 U.S. at 262, 55 S.Ct. at 700.

13. *Bull* has frequently been cited by the Supreme Court in tax and non-tax cases. E. g., United States v. Janis, 428 U.S. 433, 440, 96 S.Ct. 3021, 49 L.Ed.2d 1046 (1976); Perez v. Ledesma, 401 U.S. 82, 127 n. 17, 91 S.Ct. 674, 27 L.Ed.2d 701 (Brennan, J., dissenting in part and concurring in part, 1971); Zenith Corp. v. Hazeltine Research, Inc., 395 U.S. 100, 108 n. 2, 89 S.Ct. 1562, 23 L.Ed.2d 129 (1969); United States v. Vermont, 377 U.S. 351, 359, 84 S.Ct. 1267, 12 L.Ed.2d 370 (1964); Rothensies v. Electric Storage Battery Co., 329 U.S. 296, 299, 303, 67 S.Ct. 271, 91 L.Ed. 296 (1946); Commissioner v. Gooch Milling & Elevator Co., 320 U.S. 418, 421, 64 S.Ct. 184, 88 L.Ed. 139 (1943); United States v. U. S. F. & G., 309 U.S. 506, 511 n. 6, 60 S.Ct. 653, 84 L.Ed. 894 (1940); Guaranty Trust Co. v. Commissioner, 303 U.S. 493, 496, 58 S.Ct. 673, 82 L.Ed. 975 (1938); Stone v. White, 301 U.S. 532, 539, 57 S.Ct. 851, 81 L.Ed.1285 (1937). *Gooch* held that the Board of Tax Appeals lacked jurisdiction to consider recoupment claims. None of these cases, other than *Gooch*, questioned the recoupment doctrine, and *Gooch* explicitly stated that the Court was "not called upon to determine the scope of equitable recoupment when asserted * * * in tribunals possessing general equity jurisdiction." 320 U.S. at 421, 64 S.Ct. at 186.

the various claims must arise from the same "transaction." The Supreme Court refused to permit recoupment of erroneous payments of excise taxes in the years between 1919 and 1922 against income and excess profits taxes paid on a refund in 1935 of excise taxes erroneously paid between 1922 and 1926. The Court refused to expand recoupment beyond *Bull* and *Stone* and said it is "only to permit a transaction which is made the subject of a suit by a plaintiff to be examined in all its aspects, and judgment to be rendered that does justice in view of the one transaction as a whole." 329 U.S. at 299, 67 S.Ct. at 272. *Electric Storage Battery Co.* was decided after the first mitigation provisions were enacted but was not governed by them and did not discuss them.[14]

After reviewing this case law it is easy to see why Congress enacted the mitigation provisions in 1938. First, it was not clear when relief from the statute of limitations would be available. Apparently double payment or complete avoidance of tax was required, although the concepts of inconsistency and mistake were involved. The use of "immoral," "fraud in law" and "equity" added the serious problem of vagueness in the revenue laws and encouraged litigation. The measure to be applied when the remedy was allowed also caused problems. A refund was justified only if an overpayment was shown by a re-audit. However, a refund could be recovered for a year barred by the statute of limitations as long as the same transaction was involved in a year not barred. Finally, recoupment was allowed against related parties but apparently an unspecified identity of interest was required. *Schlemmer v. United States*, 94 F.2d 77, 78 (2d Cir. 1938).

After reviewing the legislative history, the prior case law and, most importantly, the language of the statute, we think the intent of Congress is clear. The mitigation provisions were intended to insure that if certain prerequisites were met either the Government or the taxpayer would be able to secure relief. Second, if relief were allowed it would not be diminished by consideration of any item other than the one that was the subject of the error. Finally, the goal was to leave the parties in as near as possible the position they would have been in if the item had been properly treated through the years.

Application of the mitigation provisions

Internal Revenue Code § 1311 sets out the requirements for avoidance of the normal statute of limitations period by virtue of the mitigation provisions. This is supplemented by I.R.C. § 1312, stating the "circumstances of adjustment," and I.R.C. § 1313, providing additional

---

14. The mitigation statutes only apply to tax years beginning on or after January 1, 1932.

definitions. On this appeal the Government makes three challenges of the applicability of the mitigation provisions: (a) the Commissioner's position adopted in the determination of the 1965 tax liability was not inconsistent with the 1963 error; (b) there was no "item of income" included in the 1965 gross income of the Margaret H. Doorly Family Trust; and (c) Margaret H. Doorly and her estate did not meet the required status of "related taxpayers." We will consider those arguments seriatim.

(a) inconsistency

As applied in this case, I.R.C. § 1311(b)(1)(A) requires that there be "adopted in the determination (i. e., the final 1965 tax treatment) a position maintained by the Secretary or his delegate * * * (which is) * * * inconsistent with the erroneous inclusion" in Margaret Doorly's 1963 income. It is plain that the determination of the 1965 income tax liabilities of the Doorly estate and the Doorly trust adopted positions maintained by the Government. Losses claimed by the estate and trust were disallowed and the estate was required to recognize income from the final liquidation distribution of World. Deficiencies were assessed and paid and the Government urges that these positions are not inconsistent because the 1965 treatment arose from the application of basis rules in I.R.C. §§ 1014 and 1015. According to the Government, those sections resulted in the estate having a date-of-death fair market value basis of $17 per share and thus a gain to be recognized. The trust escaped recognized gain or loss because its gain basis was $19, presumably because the grantor had recognized that amount in 1963; and its loss basis was $17, determined by the fair market value at the time of the gift.

Taxpayers do not refute this reasoning. Neither party has cited authority determining whether such basis determinations avoid the label of inconsistency where income which is realized only once is required to be recognized twice for income tax purposes. Although we are not sure that the Government is accurate in stating that Joyce v. United States, 361 F.2d 602, 606 (3rd Cir. 1966), "held that the Commissioner's subsequent determination must be 'logically inconsistent' with the erroneous treatment of the item in the earlier year in order to adjust such earlier year," we think the correct standard is logical inconsistency. Applying that standard, it is clear that under our system of annual income tax accounting it is inconsistent to require the same money to be recognized and accounted for in income tax returns in two different years. Cf. *Bull v. United States*, supra, 295 U.S. at 256, 55 S.Ct. 695.

Assuming that a literal application of the constructive receipt and basis doctrines would justify the result, it does not change its basic inconsistency and does not prevent the application of the mitigation provisions where the earlier tax treatment was erroneous. We think the District Court correctly held that the Government's positions were inconsistent.

(b) double inclusion of income item

Section 1312 describes the circumstances under which the mitigation provisions apply. The facts of this case are alleged to fall within subsection (1):

> Double inclusion of an item of gross income. The determination requires the inclusion in gross income of an item which was erroneously included in the gross income of the taxpayer for another taxable year or in the gross income of a related taxpayer.

I.R.C. § 1312(1).

The Government does not actively challenge the District Court's holding that this case involves such a double inclusion of income insofar as the estate is concerned. The estate was required to account for, as income, the contingency reserve when it was distributed in 1965. It had already been taxed as constructively received in 1963. Although the stepped-up, date-of-death basis used by the estate reduced the tax liability, we think it evident that there was a double inclusion of an item of income.

The Government vigorously contends that the tax treatment afforded the trust did not amount to a double inclusion of an item of income. It points out that only a loss deduction was disallowed in 1965; nothing new was required to be included. The District Court relied on the broad definition of "item of income" in Gooch Milling & Elevator Co. v. United States, 78 F.Supp. 94, 100, 111 Ct. Cl. 576 (1948), which held, "The term 'item' * * * should be interpreted to include any item or amount which affects gross income in more than one year * * *." The District Court noted that "(t)he unexpended pro rata share of the reserve is an item of income which remains the same item in both years despite the disparity of treatment * * *."

Under our view of the law to be applied in calculating the refund, the question of inclusion of an "item of income" in the trust becomes purely academic. This is because the inclusion of an "item of income" in the estate triggers an analysis and adjustment of the whole transaction.

(c) related parties

The final Government challenge to the applicability of the mitigation provisions is that Margaret Doorly and her estate did not meet the definition of related taxpayers in I.R.C. § 1313(c). Although "decedent and decedent's estate" is listed as an included relationship, the Government argues that the statute literally requires that the relationship exist "in the taxable year with respect to which the erroneous inclusion" occurred. Since the error occurred in 1963 and Mrs. Doorly died in 1964, the Government claims the statutory requirements are not met.

The Government concedes that under its view the Congress corrected only one of two situations that involve the same inequities, i. e. correction is made only when the error is made by the executor. We are not sure that the hypertechnical approach urged by the Government would permit even that application in most cases. We reject the Government's narrow construction, as the statute itself enumerates various relationships involved; when these relationships occur, the ameliorative provisions should apply fully to each party.

The Government argues that this temporal restriction is inherently logical because a related party should recover only when the relationship itself creates the uncertainty of entity to be taxed that results in error. This is not convincing because the Government's own regulations permit adjustments involving tax treatment of related parties where the error is unrelated to the statutory relationship.[15] This circuit has long taken the position that the mitigation provisions should not be so strictly or narrowly interpreted that their purpose is defeated. Taxeraas v. United States, 269 F.2d 283, 289 (8th Cir. 1959); United States v. Rosenberger, 235 F.2d 69, 73 (8th Cir. 1956). We agree with the District Court that the trust and Mrs. Doorly were related parties; we also hold that the estate and Mrs. Doorly were related parties.

In summary, we affirm the District Court's holding that the prerequisites for application of the mitigation provisions were met. The statute of limitations was thus extended one year beyond the date of final determination of the 1965 tax liability, which was September 21, 1974. This action was timely filed on January 27, 1975, but the issue of the proper amount of refund remains.

---

15. Treas.Reg. § 1.1313(c)-1 (1962). This logical argument is also weakened by the Government's position that correction would be allowed when the error occurs in the tax treatment of the estate after the taxpayer's death.

Amount to be refunded

In determining the amount of refund it is necessary to keep in mind Congressional intent and the purposes meant to be served by the mitigation provisions. As we noted above, the mitigation provisions were enacted in response to a House committee recommendation that the statute of limitations be modified to ensure taxation of income in the year to which it is properly allocable. This was carried over in the Senate Finance Committee report as a principle on which the legislation was based. Finally, the mitigation provisions were meant to supplement the equitable doctrines previously developed and applied by the courts.[16] Assuming, without deciding, that the mitigation provisions are the exclusive remedy in the area where they apply, that remedy should be interpreted as consistent with equitable principles unless a contrary intention is manifest in the statute.

Section 1314 provides for the amount and method of adjustment. It provides in pertinent part:

(a) Ascertainment of amount of adjustment. In computing the amount of an adjustment under this part there shall first be ascertained the tax previously determined for the taxable year with respect to which the error was made. The amount of tax previously determined shall be the excess of (1) the sum of (A) the amount shown as the tax by the taxpayer on his return (determined as provided in § 6211(b)(1), (3), and (4), relating to the definition of deficiency), if a return was made by the taxpayer and an amount was shown as the tax by the taxpayer thereon, plus (B) the amounts previously assessed (or collected without assessment) as a deficiency, over (2) the amount of rebates, as defined in § 6211(b)(2), made. There shall then be ascertained the increase or decrease in tax previously determined which results solely from the correct treatment of the item which was the subject of the error (with due regard given to the effect of the item in the computation of gross income, taxable income, and other matters under this subtitle).* * * The amount so ascertained (together with any amounts wrongfully

16. McEachern v. Rose, 302 U.S. 56, 58 S.Ct. 84, 82 L.Ed. 46 (1937), rejected on statutory grounds the application of equitable principles. *McEachern* differs from the present case in that the failure of the Government to assess the appropriate tax in 1928 was not attributable to the erroneous statements made in the returns for the years which were the subject of the refund suit. Id. at 59, 58 S.Ct. 84. *McEachern* approved *Stone v. White*, noting that no statutes precluded equitable relief. *McEachern* did not mention *Bull*. Both *Bull* and *Stone* were later approved as to liabilities arising from a single transaction. Rothensies v. Electric Storage Battery Co., 329 U.S. 296, 67 S.Ct. 271, 91 L.Ed.296 (1946). In enacting the provisions mitigating the statute of limitations, Congress clearly intended to supplement equitable principles except where a contrary intent is shown.

collected as additions to the tax or interest, as a result of such error) for each taxable year shall be the amount of the adjustment for that taxable year.

(b) Method of adjustment. The adjustment authorized in § 1311(a) shall be made by assessing and collecting, or refunding or crediting, the amount thereof in the same manner as if it were a deficiency determined by the Secretary with respect to the taxpayer as to whom the error was made or an overpayment claimed by such taxpayer, as the case may be, for the taxable year or years with respect to which an amount is ascertained under subsection (a), and as if on the date of the determination one year remained before the expiration of the periods of limitation upon assessment or filing claim for refund for such taxable year or years.

(c) Adjustment unaffected by other items. The amount to be assessed and collected in the same manner as a deficiency, or to be refunded or credited in the same manner as an overpayment, under this part, shall not be diminished by any credit or set-off based upon any item other than the one which was the subject of the adjustment. The amount of the adjustment under this part, if paid, shall not be recovered by a claim or suit for refund or suit for erroneous refund based upon any item other than the one which was the subject of the adjustment.

It is obvious from the plain and ordinary meaning of the statute that in this case the computation of the amount of adjustment under subsection (a) is made solely from comparing the correct and erroneous treatment of the liquidation reserve in1963. Subsection (a) depends on the "item which was the subject of the error." Qualitatively that was the 1963 inclusion of the constructive receipt of $19 per share on the total 56,373 shares. The statute plainly prevents our adopting the Government's argument that would define the term retrospectively by the quantitative treatment accorded it in 1965. Even if this were not clear, the Government's position would fail to accomplish the legislative goal of attributing income to the right year and right taxpayer. It would also leave the Government with a sizable undeserved windfall.[19]

Upon a careful review of the statute and the facts as stipulated and conceded by the Government, we think the District Court properly

---

19. The Government's approach would fail to give the estate the benefit of a stepped-up, date-of-death basis. In a footnote in its brief and in oral argument, the Government argued that the 1965 receipt was income in respect to a decedent. This was not fully briefed by the parties and we decline to decide the question based on this record.

determined the adjustment under § 1314(a). However, the determination of the refund to be ordered does not end there.[20]

As we noted above, the Supreme Court had applied equitable principles prior to   adoption of the mitigation provisions. *Lewis* held the Government could conduct a complete re-audit and offset any deficiency, even if barred by the statute of limitations, against refund claims. *Bull* held that recoupment of time-barred estate taxes was available to a taxpayer in a dispute over income taxes properly imposed on the same money when received by the estate. *Stone* held that the Government was entitled to offset time-barred income taxes owing from a beneficiary against a claim for refund of income taxes on the same income erroneously paid by the trustee. The mitigation provisions were meant to supplement this case law development. The only part of the statute that limits this is § 1314(c), providing that the amount refunded shall not be diminished by any "set-off based upon any item *other than the one which was the subject of the adjustment*." [21] (Emphasis added.) The plain import of that language is that re-audits under *Lewis* would not be allowed in refunds under the mitigation provisions. There is no reason to think that Congress intended to limit *Bull* and *Stone* which involved multiple treatment of funds arising from a single transaction.[22]

Our view of the statute and case law carries out the legislative purpose. If a complete re-audit were permitted, the statute of limitations would be weakened and litigation would be encouraged rather than amicable settlement when errors and inconsistencies are pointed out. Similarly, if the principles of *Bull* and *Stone* were not applied, the goal of attributing income to the right year and the right taxpayer could be frustrated. Obviously, where the effect of the same item is involved, the proof problems that would encourage litigation in the re-audit situation are missing. We think it appropriate and in keeping with the statutes involved, now as nearly as possible to place the parties in the same position, tax-wise, that they would have been in had the error of the 1963 tax payment not occurred. No further demand for recoupment of taxes by either party is required. A refund giving consideration to the overpayment of 1963 taxes, and whatever other taxes, income or estate,

---

20. We recognize that, in the vast majority of cases under the mitigation provisions, § 1314(a) will determine the proper refund. Here the splitting of the item after the year of error and the death of Mrs. Doorly calls into play equitable principles not barred by the statute.

21. I.R.C. § 1314(c).

22. The transaction that resulted in all tax liabilities involved in this appeal was the payment of the $19 liquidation distribution reserve.

that may be due the Government, should be calculated according to the principles of our interpretation of §§ 1311 et seq. and *Bull* and *Stone*.[23]

On remand the District Court must examine the Doorly estate tax return[24] and the 1965 income tax returns of the estate and the trust. To the extent that the correct 1963 treatment of the liquidation would have increased these later liabilities, the refund now sought must be reduced. In doing this it must be remembered that the taxpayer is entitled to interest on the amount of overpayment up to the date each (underpaid) amount was due. It must also be kept in mind that any underpayments must be deducted from the overpayment principal.[26]

In other words, the parties should be placed as nearly as possible in the position that they would have been in if the error in the 1963 tax payment had not been made. Neither side is to gain a windfall, nor is any avoidance of taxes that should have been paid on the item in question permitted.

Judgment affirmed in part, reversed in part and remanded for proceedings consistent with this opinion.

Notes and Questions

Since the taxpayer prevailed in *First National Bank of Omaha*, the taxpayer has one year to file a claim for refund. If the Service had prevailed, it would have had a year to mail a notice of deficiency to the taxpayer. The one-year period is suspended during the time the Service is prohibited from assessing the deficiency.

---

23. Cf. United States v. Rosenberger, 235 F.2d 69 (8th Cir. 1956). In *Rosenberger*, a Government counterclaim using the mitigation provisions was the determination that permitted the taxpayer to sue under the mitigation provisions for a refund for a different tax year. If recoupment were not available in this case the Government might be forced to seek a deficiency for 1965 and the estate taxes. Thus, our decision serves the salutary purpose of bringing this litigation to a rapid close and saving the courts, the Government and the taxpayer additional time and expense. Since we hold that the plaintiffs are entitled to recover under the mitigation provisions, we need not consider plaintiffs' alternate argument of estoppel.

24. See Note, "Equitable Recoupment in Tax Law," 42 N.Y.U.L.Rev. 537, 543-44 (1967). We assume the date-of-death fair market value of this refund claim should have been included in the Doorly estate. That value would have been something less than the face value of the overpayment plus interest accrued through the date of Mrs. Doorly's death. Bank of California v. Comm'r., 133 F.2d 428, 432-33 (9th Cir. 1943). The fact that the statute of limitations would now bar a separate suit for the estate tax deficiency does not prevent recoupment in this action. See I.R.C. § 6501(a) and (e)(2); 2 Fed. Est. & Gift Tax Rep. (CCH) P 9860.052. Perhaps on remand the parties will be able to propose a more appropriate method of dealing with the estate tax problem than the method we have suggested. They were unable to do so at oral argument.

26. This is vitally important to insure the proper amount of interest is allowed for later periods and to avoid any need to calculate interest due the Government on underpayments.

The mitigation provisions apparently apply only to income taxes, although there is some question as to whether they apply to excise taxes. See Hall v. United States, 1991 WL 53248 (D. Utah 1991), rev'd by 975 F.2d 722 (10th Cir. 1992); see also Willis, "Correction of Errors via Mitigation and Equitable Recoupment," 52 Tax Notes 1421 (Sept. 16, 1991).

1. Since the mitigation provisions are strictly construed, do you think the court reached the correct decision in *First National Bank of Omaha*?

2. What is the meaning of the statement in the Senate Finance Committee Report that "the party or parties in whose favor [the statute of limitations] applies shall have justified such modification by active inconsistency"?

3. What "circumstance of adjustment" under § 1312 was involved in *First National Bank of Omaha*? Do you think the court was correct in its determination that such a circumstance existed? Why or why not?

2. Equitable Recoupment

After years of debate over whether the Tax Court has jurisdiction to apply equitable doctrines like recoupment, Congress clarified this issue in 2006 by amending § 6214(b) to provide that the court may apply equitable recoupment to the same extent that it may be applied in the federal district courts and the United States Court of Federal Claims. The question considered in the following case is whether the Tax Court may apply the doctrine to taxes over which it otherwise does not have jurisdiction.

MENARD, INC. v. COMMISSIONER
Tax Court of the United States, 2008.
130 T.C. 54.

MARVEL, JUDGE:

* * *

The issue we must decide is whether, under the equitable recoupment doctrine, petitioners are entitled to an offset against their income tax liabilities for TYE 1998 equal to the amount of so-called hospital insurance taxes that they overpaid pursuant to sections 3101(b) and 3111(b) on the portion of petitioner John R. Menard's compensation recharacterized in *Menard I* as a disguised dividend.

BACKGROUND.
* * *

Menard, Inc. (Menards), was incorporated in Wisconsin in 1962 and is engaged primarily in the retail sale of hardware, building supplies, paint, garden equipment, and similar items. As of the trial date, Menards had approximately 160 stores in nine Midwestern States and was one of the nation's top retail home improvement chains.

John R. Menard (Mr. Menard) served as president and chief executive officer of Menards and has been a controlling shareholder of Menards since its incorporation. During the period in question, Mr. Menard owned approximately 89 percent of Menards's voting and nonvoting stock.

Menards is an accrual basis taxpayer and has a fiscal year ending January 31 for tax and financial reporting purposes. On October 15, 1998, Menards timely filed Form 1120, U.S. Corporation Income Tax Return, for TYE 1998. On October 12, 2001, respondent sent to Menards a notice of deficiency with respect to its TYE 1998. Menards timely petitioned this Court seeking a redetermination of the deficiency.

Mr. Menard is a cash basis taxpayer with a taxable year ending December 31. Between March 30 and April 15, 1999, Mr. Menard timely filed Form 1040, U.S. Individual Income Tax Return, for 1998. On October 12, 2001, respondent sent a separate notice of deficiency to Mr. Menard with respect to 1998. Mr. Menard timely petitioned this Court seeking a redetermination of the deficiency.

The two cases were consolidated for trial, briefing, and opinion. Following a trial and the submission of posttrial briefs, we issued our opinion in *Menard I* holding, among other things, that Menards was not entitled to a business expense deduction for a significant portion of the compensation it paid to Mr. Menard for 1998 because the compensation was unreasonable, was not paid entirely for personal services, and was properly characterized as a disguised dividend to Mr. Menard. Separately, we sustained respondent's determination that Mr. Menard was liable for an income tax deficiency to the extent that Menards's payment of certain expenses on Mr. Menard's behalf was unreasonable and constituted a constructive dividend to Mr. Menard.

After we issued our opinions in *Menard I* and *Menard II*, we received and filed respondent's computation for entry of decision pursuant to Rule 155 in each of these consolidated cases. Respondent concluded that (1) Menards owed an income tax deficiency of $5,720,334 and a penalty of $188,295.60, and (2) Mr. Menard owed an income tax deficiency of $921,491 and a penalty of $184,298.20. Petitioners filed a notice of objection to respondent's Rule 155 computations in which they alleged that Menards's correct income tax deficiency and penalty amounts were

$5,523,488.20 and $188,295.60, respectively, and that Mr. Menard's correct income tax deficiency and penalty amounts were $724,645 and $184,298.20, respectively.

The parties' deficiency computations for both Menards and Mr. Menard differ by $196,845.81, which is the amount of hospital insurance tax (hospital tax) that Mr. Menard and Menards contend they overpaid pursuant to sections 3101(b) and 3111(b), respectively. Petitioners contend that, consistent with our holding in *Menard I* recharacterizing a portion of the compensation that Menards paid to Mr. Menard as a constructive dividend, they overpaid so much of the hospital tax that they remitted to the Commissioner during 1998 as was attributable to the constructive dividend. Petitioners argue that, under the doctrine of equitable recoupment, they are entitled to offset the amount of their hospital tax overpayments against their respective income tax deficiencies for TYE 1998 and that they have met all of the requirements necessary to establish their equitable recoupment defense.

Respondent maintains that the Court lacks the authority under the equitable recoupment doctrine to offset petitioners' income tax deficiencies by the amounts of their overpaid hospital taxes because we lack jurisdiction over hospital tax deficiencies and overpayments. Respondent contends that hospital taxes play no role in the determination of a deficiency within the meaning of section 6211 and that neither additional hospital tax liabilities nor hospital tax overpayments are included in a computation for entry of decision because we lack jurisdiction over hospital taxes. According to respondent, applying equitable recoupment in this case "would allow petitioners to slip through a back door to challenge a tax they could not directly petition the Court to review."

Respondent does not dispute the amount by which petitioners contend they overpaid their hospital taxes, nor does respondent dispute that the elements necessary for an equitable recoupment claim are present in this case.[5]

Neither Menards nor Mr. Menard filed a claim for a refund of the hospital taxes that they overpaid. The period of limitations for filing a refund claim has now expired with respect to both petitioners.

* * *

---

5.   Respondent did not raise any specific challenge to Mr. Menard's computations. Respondent does assert, however, that assuming equitable recoupment is available in this case, petitioner Menard, Inc., erred in computing the amount of its income tax deficiency, after accounting for the offset of hospital tax. We shall discuss this issue in greater detail below.

DISCUSSION

These cases present an issue of first impression regarding the scope of our authority to apply the doctrine of equitable recoupment. Specifically, we must decide whether the tax that is the subject of a litigant's equitable recoupment defense must be one over which we have deficiency and overpayment jurisdiction under sections 6211 and 6212.

I. *Jurisdiction of the Tax Court*
A. *Deficiency and Overpayment Jurisdiction*

Like other Federal courts, the Tax Court is a court of limited jurisdiction, and it may exercise its jurisdiction only to the extent authorized by Congress. Section 7442 expressly provides that the Court and its divisions shall have such jurisdiction as is conferred on them by the Internal Revenue Code and by laws enacted after February 26, 1926.

Petitioners each received a notice of deficiency, and they invoked our jurisdiction by filing a petition for redetermination of a deficiency under section 6213(a). Section 6214(a) grants us jurisdiction to redetermine the correct amount of a deficiency and to determine whether any additional amounts or any additions to tax should be assessed. Section 6211(a) in relevant part defines the term "deficiency" as the amount by which the tax imposed by subtitle A (sections 1 through 1563) or subtitle B (sections 2001 through 2704), or chapter 41 (sections 4911 and 4912), chapter 42 (sections 4940 through 4963), chapter 43 (sections 4971 through 4980E), or chapter 44 (sections 4981 and 4982) exceeds the amount shown as the tax by the taxpayer on a return. Section 6212(a), which authorizes the Commissioner to issue a notice of deficiency, likewise is limited to a deficiency in respect of any taxes imposed by subtitle A or B or chapter 41, 42, 43, or 44.

Pursuant to section 6512(b)(1), we also have jurisdiction to determine the amount of an overpayment[6] of tax in limited circumstances. Our jurisdiction to determine whether there has been an overpayment is limited to the same taxable year or years for which the Commissioner has issued a notice of deficiency and with regard to which the taxpayer has timely filed a petition for redetermination of the deficiency. Sec. 6512(b)(1). In addition, our overpayment jurisdiction is limited to determining an overpayment of income, gift, estate, or excise taxes (and related interest) imposed by chapter 41, 42, 43, or 44. Sec. 6512(b)(1) and (2). Once we have determined that there is no deficiency but that the

---

6. An "overpayment" of tax is " 'any payment in excess of that which is properly due.' " See Winn-Dixie Stores, Inc., & Subs. v. Commissioner, 110 T.C. 291, 295 n. 5 (1998) (quoting Jones v. Liberty Glass Co., 332 U.S. 524, 531, 68 S.Ct. 229, 92 L.Ed. 142 (1947)).

taxpayer has made an overpayment of tax, or that there is a deficiency but the taxpayer has made an overpayment of such tax, we have jurisdiction to determine the amount of the overpayment and order a refund of the overpayment, or to credit the overpayment against the deficiency, if the requirements of section 6512(b) are satisfied. Sec. 6512(b)(1) and (2).

B. *Jurisdiction Over Hospital Tax*

Petitioners' equitable recoupment defense pertains to hospital tax imposed by the Federal Insurance Contributions Act, codified as chapter 21 (sections 3101-3128). Section 3101(b) imposes a 1.45-percent hospital tax on the wage income of all employees, which the employer must withhold from the employees' wages and pay to the Secretary. See secs. 3102(a), 3501. In addition, section 3111(b) requires employers to pay to the Secretary a corresponding 1.45-percent hospital tax on all wages paid to employees. See sec. 3501.

Our deficiency and overpayment jurisdiction (described above) does not extend to hospital tax imposed under sections 3101 and 3111. Nevertheless, Congress has recently expanded our jurisdiction with respect to employment tax. In 1997, Congress passed the Taxpayer Relief Act of 1997, Pub.L. 105-34, sec. 1454(a), 111 Stat. 1055, adding section 7436, which confers jurisdiction on the Court to review certain determinations made by the Commissioner regarding employment status (worker classification) and the proper amount of employment tax[7] under such determinations.[8] However, our jurisdiction under section 7436(a) depends upon, and only arises after, a determination of worker classification by the Secretary. *Charlotte's Office Boutique, Inc. v. Commissioner*, [121 T.C. 89, at 103]. The Secretary has not made such a determination in this case, and therefore we do not have original jurisdiction under section 7436 over petitioners' claims for hospital tax offsets against their income tax deficiencies.

Ordinarily, a taxpayer asserting an overpayment of hospital tax must file a claim for refund or credit with the Secretary. See secs. 6402(a), 6413(a); sec. 31.6402(a)-1, Employment Tax Regs. If the Secretary denies

---

7.   Sec. 7436(e) defines the term "employment tax" as any tax imposed by subtit. C, which encompasses secs. 3101 to 3510. Sec. 7436(a) was amended to give the Court authority to determine the proper amount of employment tax by the Consolidated Appropriations Act, 2001, Pub.L. 106-554, app. G, sec. 314(f), 114 Stat. 2763A-643 (2000).

8.   Sec. 7436(d)(1) provides that "The principles of subsections (a), (b), (c), (d), and (f) of section 6213, section 6214(a), section 6215, section 6503(a), section 6512, and section 7481 shall apply to proceedings brought under this section in the same manner as if the Secretary's determination described in subsection (a) were a notice of deficiency."

the taxpayer's claim for refund or credit, the taxpayer may file suit in Federal District Court or the Court of Federal Claims to recover any tax alleged to have been erroneously or illegally assessed or collected. Sec. 7422(a); 28 U.S.C. sec. 1346(a) (2000). In addition, any claim for a refund or credit must be made within 3 years from the time the return was filed or 2 years from the time the tax was paid, whichever of such periods expires later. Sec. 6511(a). No credit or refund shall be allowed or made after the period of limitations for filing such a claim expires. Sec. 6511(b)(1).

II. *The Equitable Recoupment Doctrine*
A. *Generally*

The doctrine of equitable recoupment is a judicially created doctrine that, under certain circumstances, allows a litigant to avoid the bar of an expired statutory limitation period. United States v. Dalm, 494 U.S. 596, 605, 110 S.Ct. 1361, 108 L.Ed.2d 548 (1990); Bull v. United States, 295 U.S. 247, 262, 55 S.Ct. 695, 79 L.Ed. 1421 (1935). The doctrine prevents an inequitable windfall to a taxpayer or to the Government that would otherwise result from the inconsistent tax treatment of a single transaction, item, or event affecting the same taxpayer or a sufficiently related taxpayer. Estate of Mueller v. Commissioner, 101 T.C. 551, 552 (1993) (*Mueller II*);[10] see also *United States v. Dalm, supra* at 605-606 n. 5; *Bull v. United States, supra*. Equitable recoupment operates as a defense that may be asserted by a taxpayer to reduce the Commissioner's timely claim of a deficiency, or by the Commissioner to reduce the taxpayer's timely claim for a refund. O'Brien v. United States, 766 F.2d 1038, 1049 (7th Cir.1985); *Estate of Mueller v. Commissioner, supra* at 552; Estate of Orenstein v. Commissioner, T.C. Memo.2000-150. When applied for the benefit of a taxpayer, the equitable recoupment doctrine allows a taxpayer to recoup the amount of a time-barred tax overpayment by allowing the overpayment to be applied as an offset against a deficiency if certain requirements are met. *Bull v. United States, supra* at 259-263; Crop Associates-1986 v. Commissioner, 113 T.C. 198, 200 (1999).

---

10. In Estate of Mueller v. Commissioner, T.C. Memo.1992-284, we redetermined the increased value of certain shares of stock included in the decedent's gross estate. In Estate of Mueller v. Commissioner, 101 T.C. 551 (1993), we denied the Commissioner's motion to dismiss for lack of jurisdiction in respect of the taxpayer's partial affirmative defense of equitable recoupment. In Estate of Mueller v. Commissioner, 107 T.C. 189 (1996), *affd. on other grounds* 153 F.3d 302 (6th Cir.1998), we rejected the taxpayer's equitable recoupment claim on the ground that equitable recoupment is restricted to use as a defense against an otherwise valid claim for a deficiency and the doctrine may not be used to increase the amount of a tax overpayment where it is determined that no deficiency exists.

As a general rule, the party claiming the benefit of an equitable recoupment defense must establish that it applies. See *Estate of Mueller v. Commissioner, supra* at 556. In order to establish that equitable recoupment applies, a party must prove the following elements: (1) The overpayment or deficiency for which recoupment is sought by way of offset is barred by an expired period of limitation; (2) the time-barred overpayment or deficiency arose out of the same transaction, item, or taxable event as the overpayment or deficiency before the Court; (3) the transaction, item, or taxable event has been inconsistently subjected to two taxes; and (4) if the transaction, item, or taxable event involves two or more taxpayers, there is sufficient identity of interest between the taxpayers subject to the two taxes that the taxpayers should be treated as one. *United States v. Dalm, supra* at 604-605; Estate of Branson v. Commissioner, 113 T.C. 6, 15 (1999), *affd.* 264 F.3d 904 (9th Cir.2001); *Estate of Orenstein v. Commissioner, supra.*

B. *Tax Court Jurisdiction To Apply Equitable Recoupment*

We addressed the question of our authority to consider a claim of equitable recoupment in *Mueller II.* In that case, we held that our authority to apply equitable recoupment was inherent in the jurisdiction conferred on us by statute to redetermine a tax deficiency. *Estate of Mueller v. Commissioner, supra* at 556. We concluded that exercising jurisdiction over the taxpayer's equitable recoupment claim did not require us to exercise jurisdiction that was beyond the scope of the taxpayer's primary claim for redetermination of the deficiency, explaining that "When a taxpayer raises an affirmative defense to a deficiency determination, we need no additional source of jurisdiction to render a decision with respect to the defense. It is part of the entire action over which we have jurisdiction." *Id.*

In several cases following *Mueller II,* we reaffirmed our jurisdiction to consider equitable recoupment as an affirmative defense in resolving a deficiency proceeding. *Estate of Branson v. Commissioner, supra;* Estate of Bartels v. Commissioner, 106 T.C. 430 (1996); *Estate of Orenstein v. Commissioner, supra.*

The Courts of Appeals that considered whether this Court may entertain an equitable recoupment claim split on the question. In *Estate of Mueller v. Commissioner,* 153 F.3d 302 (6th Cir.1998), *affg. on other grounds* 107 T.C. 189 (1996), the Court of Appeals held that this Court lacked jurisdiction to consider a claim of equitable recoupment. In contrast, in *Estate of Branson v. Commissioner,* 264 F.3d 904 (9th Cir.2001), the Court of Appeals reached the opposite conclusion.

For present purposes, any uncertainty regarding the Court's authority to apply the equitable recoupment doctrine was eliminated with the enactment of the Pension Protection Act of 2006(PPA), Pub.L. 109-280, sec. 858(a), 120 Stat. 1020, which amended section 6214(b) by adding a second sentence to the provision. Section 6214(b) now provides as follows:

SEC. 6214(b). Jurisdiction Over Other Years and Quarters.–The Tax Court in redetermining a deficiency of income tax for any taxable year or of gift tax for any calendar year or calendar quarter shall consider such facts with relation to the taxes for other years or calendar quarters as may be necessary correctly to redetermine the amount of such deficiency, but in so doing shall have no jurisdiction to determine whether or not the tax for any other year or calendar quarter has been overpaid or underpaid. Notwithstanding the preceding sentence, the Tax Court may apply the doctrine of equitable recoupment to the same extent that it is available in civil tax cases before the district courts of the United States and the United States Court of Federal Claims.

Section 6214(b), as amended, is effective for any action or proceeding before the Court with respect to which a decision has not become final (as determined under section 7481) as of August 17, 2006. PPA sec. 858(b), 120 Stat. 1020. Because no decisions have been entered in these cases, section 6214(b), as amended, applies in determining the scope of our authority to apply the doctrine of equitable recoupment.

There is very little in the way of legislative history underlying the amendment to section 6214(b). The most complete statement concerning the amendment is contained in S. Rept. 109-336, at 97 (2006), which states in pertinent part:

REASONS FOR CHANGE

The Committee believes that it is important to resolve the conflict among the circuit courts by eliminating the uncertainty or confusion of differing results in differing circuits. The Committee also believes that the provision will provide simplification benefits to both taxpayers and the IRS.

EXPLANATION OF PROVISION

[The bill does not include the provision as approved by the Committee because an identical or substantially similar provision was enacted into law in the Pension Protection Act of 2006 (Pub.L. No. 109-280, sec.858) subsequent to Committee action on the bill. The following discussion described the provision as approved by the Committee.]

The provision confirms that the Tax Court may apply the principle of equitable recoupment to the same extent that it may be applied in Federal civil tax cases by the U.S. District Courts or the U.S. Court of Claims. * * * [11]

III. *Analysis*
A. *The Scope of the Court's Jurisdiction To Consider Equitable Recoupment Claims*

Section 6214(b) provides that this Court "may apply the doctrine of equitable recoupment to the same extent that it is available in civil tax cases before" other Federal trial courts. The limited legislative history underlying the recent amendment to section 6214(b) indicates Congress intended to eliminate confusion over the Court's authority to apply the doctrine created by conflicting Court of Appeals opinions and to provide simplification benefits to both taxpayers and the Commissioner. S. Rept. 109-336, *supra* at 97; see Staff of Joint Comm. on Taxation, Technical Explanation of H.R. 4, The Pension Protection Act of 2006, at 203 (J. Comm. Print 2006).

Respondent acknowledges that section 6214(b) grants the Court authority to apply the doctrine of equitable recoupment in appropriate cases. Nevertheless, respondent asserts that we may not apply the doctrine in this case because our authority is limited to taxes over which we have deficiency or overpayment jurisdiction; i.e ., income, estate, and gift taxes and excise taxes imposed under chapters 41, 42, 43, and 44. In support of his position, respondent attempts to draw parallels between the first and second sentences of section 6214(b). Specifically, while the first sentence of section 6214(b) permits us to consider facts with relation to other taxable years and calendar quarters in determining the correct amounts of the deficiencies for the taxable years properly before us, the provision expressly bars us from exercising jurisdiction to determine whether the tax for those other taxable years or calendar quarters has been overpaid or underpaid. As respondent sees it, just as the first sentence of section 6214(b) limits our jurisdiction, the second sentence of section 6214(b), which grants us authority to apply the doctrine of equitable recoupment, should be narrowly construed so that our

---

11. S. Rept. 109-336 (2006) pertained to S. 1321, 109th Cong., 2d Sess. (2006) (titled "Telephone Excise Tax Repeal and Taxpayer Protection and Assistance Act of 2006"). As explained in the bracketed material contained in the above-quoted portion of the report, after the Senate Finance Committee's action on S. 1321, sec. 6214(b) was amended by the Pension Protection Act of 2006, Pub.L. 109-280, sec. 858, 120 Stat. 1020. Nevertheless, S. Rept. 109-336, supra at 97, correctly describes the substance of the amendment to sec. 6214(b).

jurisdiction is restricted in all events to taxes within our original jurisdiction.

Petitioners assert that respondent is attempting to add words of limitation to the otherwise plain language of section 6214(b). Petitioners maintain that section 6214(b) is broadly worded and clearly expresses Congress's intent to put this Court on equal footing with other Federal trial courts vested with jurisdiction over civil tax disputes. Petitioners argue that to the extent other Federal trial courts with jurisdiction over civil tax cases may apply the doctrine of equitable recoupment in respect of hospital tax, the Tax Court may do so as well.

As explained below, we reject respondent's narrow construction of section 6214(b). Respondent's position regarding our authority to apply the doctrine of equitable recoupment conflicts with the plain language of section 6214(b), its legislative history, and the policies underlying the doctrine.

When Congress recently amended section 6214(b), it confirmed in the broadest of terms our authority to apply the doctrine of equitable recoupment. The plain language of section 6214(b) offers no justification or support for the narrow construction that respondent advocates. Section 6214(b) simply states that the scope of the Court's authority to apply the doctrine of equitable recoupment is equal to that of other Federal trial courts with jurisdiction over civil tax cases. If, as respondent suggests, Congress intended to limit the scope of the Court's equitable recoupment authority to taxes that normally fall within the Court's deficiency and/or overpayment jurisdiction, we are convinced that Congress would have drafted section 6214(b) to say so in clear and unambiguous terms.

Nor does the legislative history underlying the amendment to section 6214(b) provide any support for respondent's position. To the contrary, S. Rept. 109-336, *supra* at 97, indicates that Congress viewed the amendment to section 6214(b) as a means to provide clarity and simplification for taxpayers and the Commissioner alike. The literal interpretation of section 6214(b) that petitioners advocate, under which the Court is authorized to apply the doctrine of equitable recoupment in respect of all internal revenue taxes, offers clarity and a meaningful measure of simplification in that both parties can be confident that the Court may provide a complete remedy for a given taxable year. In contrast, respondent's narrow construction of the provision would add uncertainty to litigation and create a category of cases in which equitable recoupment would not be available in the Tax Court.

Respondent's narrow construction of section 6214(b) is also inconsistent with the central policy underlying the doctrine of equitable recoupment; i.e., to prevent an inequitable windfall to a taxpayer or the

Government that would otherwise result from the inconsistent tax treatment of a single transaction, item, or event. We assume that if the roles were reversed and petitioners had filed timely refund suits in Federal District Court alleging that they overpaid their hospital tax, respondent would assert equitable recoupment and seek to offset some or all of the claimed refunds by the amount of any income tax petitioners might owe in connection with the same transaction. Just as a Federal District Court may apply the doctrine of equitable recoupment in favor of the Commissioner in the scenario described above, fundamental fairness suggests that this Court likewise may apply the doctrine in favor of petitioners under the facts presented in the instant case. Otherwise, respondent will enjoy an inequitable windfall due to the inconsistent tax treatment of a single transaction under two different internal revenue taxes.

As a final matter, we reject respondent's argument that we are allowing petitioners to use the doctrine of equitable recoupment to expand our jurisdiction and introduce hospital tax into the case "through the back door". We have consistently held that " 'While we cannot expand our jurisdiction through equitable principles, we can apply equitable principles in the disposition of cases that come within our jurisdiction.'" Woods v. Commissioner, 92 T.C. 776, 784-785 (1989) (*quoting* Berkery v. Commissioner, 90 T.C. 259, 270 (1988) (Hamblen, J., concurring)); see also *Estate of Branson v. Commissioner*, 113 T.C. at 12; *Estate of Mueller v. Commissioner*, 101 T.C. at 557. In *Mueller II*, and in each of the subsequent cases in which we have applied equitable recoupment, we held that our jurisdiction to redetermine the disputed deficiency provided the basis for the Court to consider affirmative defenses, including equitable recoupment. See *Estate of Branson v. Commissioner*, *supra* at 12; Estate of Bartels v. Commissioner, 106 T.C. 430 (1996); Estate of Orenstein v. Commissioner, T.C. Memo.2000-150. In this light, our authority to consider a claim of equitable recoupment is merely ancillary to our jurisdiction to redetermine a tax deficiency and does not unduly expand upon that jurisdiction.

In sum, we conclude there is no requirement in section 6214(b) that, in applying the doctrine of equitable recoupment, we have original or subject matter jurisdiction over the tax that the Commissioner or the taxpayer seeks to apply as an offset against a claimed deficiency or refund. We hold that, if our jurisdiction is properly invoked upon the filing of a petition for redetermination of a deficiency, we may apply the doctrine in respect of any tax imposed under the Internal Revenue Code so long as the elements necessary to support a claim of equitable recoupment are established.　　* * *

Notes and Questions

Recoupment can be applied in favor of either the taxpayer or the government. See, e.g., IES Industries, Inc. v. United States, 345 F.3d 574 (8th Cir. 2003) (IRS allowed to offset open refund against barred deficiency where both arose from single, tax-driven transaction); United States v. Intrados/International Management Group, 277 F.Supp.2d 55 (D.D.C. 2003) (contractors allowed to use recoupment in counterclaim against government because counterclaim arose from same transaction as government's claims).

1. Many cases in which recoupment arguably could apply also fall under the mitigation provisions. Does mitigation supercede recoupment if both apply?

2. How does equitable recoupment differ from a *Lewis v. Reynolds* set-off?

3. Which is a more advantageous remedy – mitigation or recoupment?

III. ADMINISTRATIVE REVIEW OF THE CLAIM

Service Center personnel scrutinize all requests for refund to determine completeness, validity, and timely filing, and to determine whether the claims involve audit matters, or whether they should be processed at the processing center. Technical personnel then classify the claims according to whether the claim requires examination or is allowable in full with no examination warranted. If an examination is required, the claim is referred to the Examination Division.

Under the Service's operating guidelines, action must be taken on a claim within 30 days of its receipt in the Examination Division. The process begins with the claim being checked to determine whether an examination is permissible or appropriate. In making this determination, IRS personnel look to whether the claim was filed in a timely manner, whether any part of the refund had been waived by the taxpayer as part of a consideration in a previous settlement, whether the claim relates to a return closed on the basis of a final order of a court, or whether the claim raises issues already allowed. If none of these factors operate to warrant rejection of the claim, it is assigned to a revenue agent for examination. The agents generally are instructed that the examination should be completed as quickly as possible. The taxpayer may amend the claim after it is filed to add new grounds for the alleged overpayment, provided the statute of limitations on filing refund claims has not expired.

Because of the *Lewis v. Reynolds* doctrine of set-off, Examination Division personnel are instructed to consider not only the issues stated in the claim, but also any offsetting adjustment that may reduce the refundable amount. When the examination has concluded, the agent will send the taxpayer a report disclosing the allowance or disallowance of the claim and the reasons for any disallowance. If the refundable amount is reduced by an offsetting adjustment, the claim is treated as partially or wholly disallowed, even though the issues stated in the claim may have been allowed in full.

If an additional amount of tax is assessed and paid as a result of an audit, and the taxpayer files a claim for refund of all or part of that additional amount, the claim will be assigned to the same revenue agent or officer who conducted the audit. Such a claim is not likely to be successful unless there are new grounds for claiming a refund, such as a change in the law as a result of a favorable court decision or a discovery of favorable evidence after the examination has been completed. But if the taxpayer decides to bring suit in one of the refund fora, then a refund claim would have to be filed as a prerequisite to jurisdiction in those courts. See § IV, below. Also, if the taxpayer previously had not utilized the informal conference procedure, the filing of the refund claim will provide an opportunity for such a conference with the agent and his supervisor.

A. ABATEMENT

Under certain circumstances, a taxpayer may administratively appeal an assessed tax before paying the assessment. The process is known as abatement, and it is used primarily in cases involving employment and excise taxes. In cases of income, estate, or gift taxes, taxpayers are precluded by statute from filing a claim for abatement. IRC § 6404(b). Thus, abatement of income, estate, and gift taxes is solely within the discretion of the Service.

Under § 6404, the Service is authorized to abate the assessment of a tax that is (1) excessive in amount, (2) assessed after the expiration of the statute of limitations, or (3) is erroneously or illegally assessed. An amount that is too small to warrant the administration and collection costs also may be abated. IRC § 6404(c).

If the Service errs or unreasonably delays in assessing any tax, including income, estate, and gift taxes, the interest attributable to the error or delay may be abated. IRC § 6404(e). Such an abatement is discretionary and is not binding on the Service. Thus, a deficiency may be assessed or redetermined following the abatement, provided the

applicable statute of limitations has not expired.   See Gray v.
Commissioner, 104 F.3d 1226 (10th Cir. 1997). A denial of abatement in
the case of an eligible taxpayer is appealable to the Tax Court, which will
determine whether the denial of the claim is a result of an abuse of the
Service's discretion. If the taxpayer or any party related to the taxpayer
is responsible for the error or delay, that taxpayer will not be eligible to
file a claim for abatement.

The error or delay must be attributable to a ministerial or managerial
act of the Service which occurs after the Service has contacted the
taxpayer in writing with respect to a deficiency or payment.   A
ministerial act is defined under Reg. § 301.6404-2(b)(2) as "a procedural
or mechanical act that does not involve the exercise of judgment or
discretion, and that occurs during the processing of a taxpayer's case
after all prerequisites of the act, such as conferences and reviews by
supervisors, have taken place." The regulation defines a managerial act
as "an administrative act that occurs during the processing of a
taxpayer's case involving the temporary or permanent loss of records or
the exercise of judgment or discretion relating to management of
personnel." Reg. § 301.6404-2(b)(1).

In the case of an erroneous refund under $50,000, the Service must
abate all interest until the date on which a notice and demand for
payment is made. If the taxpayer caused the issuance of the erroneous
refund, the taxpayer is not entitled to an abatement of the interest. IRC
§ 6404(e)(2).

If a taxpayer submits a written request for advice to the Service and
receives erroneous advice in response, which the taxpayer relies upon,
any interest or penalties attributable to the erroneous advice must be
abated. IRC § 6404(f). In order to be eligible for the abatement, the
information furnished by the taxpayer in the written request must be
accurate and complete.

Because interest runs from the original due date of the return to the
date the tax is paid, a considerable amount of interest may accumulate
before the taxpayer becomes aware that an additional tax liability is due.
The resulting tax bill could compromise the financial security of the
taxpayer. In order to address this problem, there is a special rule for
abating interest and penalties that accrue unbeknownst to the taxpayer.
Under this provision, if the taxpayer filed a timely return, the accrual of
interest and penalties is suspended after 36 months (18 months if the
notice was issued before November 26, 2007) from the later of (1) the
original due date of the return (without regard to extensions) or (2) the
date the timely return was filed, unless the Service sends the taxpayer

a notice within that period specifically stating the taxpayer's liability and the basis for that liability. IRC § 6404(g).[3]

B. JOINT COMMITTEE REVIEW

Large refunds and credits in excess of $2 million[4] may not be issued until they have been reviewed by the Joint Committee on Taxation (JCT). The Service is required to submit a report to the JCT stating the name of the taxpayer to whom the refund or credit is to be made, the amount involved, a summary of the facts involved, and the Service's decision on the matter. The Service then must wait at least 30 days before issuing the refund or credit.

Credits or refunds exceeding the threshold amount that arise as a result of tentative carryback adjustments or disaster losses are not subject to advance review by the JCT, but a report must be prepared by the Service and submitted to the JCT after the refund or credit is allowed.

IV. REFUND LITIGATION

The doctrine of sovereign immunity precludes suits against the federal government. In the case of a tax refund, however, the government has waived its immunity under 28 U.S.C. § 1346(a), which authorizes civil suits by taxpayers to obtain refunds of taxes that allegedly have been overpaid. If the Service denies a claim for refund, the taxpayer may bring suit either in the federal district court or in the United States Court of Federal Claims. In order to prevail, the taxpayer must prove that the Service erroneously assessed or collected an excess amount of tax. In addition, the taxpayer must establish the correct amount that the Service has wrongfully retained.

In order to bring a refund suit, however, the taxpayer first must meet the requisite jurisdictional requirements of establishing (1) that full payment of the tax was made and (2) that a timely claim for refund was filed with the Service. IRC § 7422. The suit is limited to the issues raised in the refund claim.

---

3.   This provision was added under the IRS Restructuring and Reform Act of 1998, Pub. L. No. 105-206, and applies to tax years ending after July 22, 1998. Initially, the accrual period was 18 months, but it was reduced to one year for tax years beginning on or after January 1, 2004. This period was extended to extended to 36 months beginning on or after November 26, 2007 under the Small Business and Work Opportunity Act of 2007, Pub. L. No. 110-28.

4.   The threshold amount was raised from $1 million to $2 million under the Community Renewal Tax Relief Act of 2000, and applies to refunds or credits issued pursuant to reports made prior to December 21, 2000.

A. FULL PAYMENT

FLORA v. UNITED STATES
Supreme Court of the United States, 1960.
362 U.S. 145, 80 S.Ct. 630, 4 L.Ed.2d 623, aff'g on rehrg.,
357 U.S. 63, 78 S.Ct. 1079, 2 L.Ed.2d 1165 (1958).

MR. CHIEF JUSTICE WARREN delivered the opinion of the Court.

The question presented is whether a Federal District Court has jurisdiction under 28 U.S.C. § 1346(a)(1), 28 U.S.C.A. § 1346(a)(1), of a suit by a taxpayer for the refund of income tax payments which did not discharge the entire amount of his assessment.

* * *

The Facts

The relevant facts are undisputed and uncomplicated. This litigation had its source in a dispute between petitioner and the Commissioner of Internal Revenue concerning the proper characterization of certain losses which petitioner suffered during 1950. Petitioner reported them as ordinary losses, but the Commissioner treated them as capital losses and levied a deficiency assessment in the amount of $28,908.60, including interest. Petitioner paid $5,058.54 and then filed with the Commissioner a claim for refund of that amount. After the claim was disallowed, petitioner sued for refund in a District Court. The Government moved to dismiss, and the judge decided that the petitioner 'should not maintain' the action because he had not paid the full amount of the assessment. But since there was a conflict among the Courts of Appeals on this jurisdictional question, and since the Tenth Circuit had not yet passed upon it, the judge believed it desirable to determine the merits of the claim. He thereupon concluded that the losses were capital in nature and entered judgment in favor of the Government. 142 F.Supp. 602. The Court of Appeals for the Tenth Circuit agreed with the district judge upon the jurisdictional issue, and consequently remanded with directions to vacate the judgment and dismiss the complaint. 246 F.2d 929. We granted certiorari because the Courts of Appeals were in conflict with respect to a question which is of considerable importance in the administration of the tax laws.

The Statute
* * *

Section 1346(a)(1) provides that the District Courts shall have jurisdiction, concurrent with the Court of Claims, of

"(1) Any civil action against the United States for the recovery of *any internal-revenue tax* alleged to have been erroneously or illegally assessed or collected, or *any penalty* claimed to have been collected without authority or *any sum* alleged to have been excessive or in any manner wrongfully collected under the internal-revenue laws * * *." (Emphasis added.)

It is clear enough that the phrase 'any internal-revenue tax' can readily be construed to refer to payment of the entire amount of an assessment. Such an interpretation is suggested by the nature of the income tax, which is 'A tax * * * imposed for each taxable year,' with the 'amount of *the* tax' determined in accordance with prescribed schedules. (Emphasis added.) But it is argued that this reading of the statute is foreclosed by the presence in § 1346(a)(1) of the phrase 'any sum.' This contention appears to be based upon the notion that 'any sum' is a catchall which confers jurisdiction to adjudicate suits for refund of part of a tax. A catchall the phrase surely is; but to say this is not to define what it catches. The sweeping role which petitioner assigns these words is based upon a conjunctive reading of 'any internal-revenue tax,' any penalty,' and 'any sum.' But we believe that the statute more readily lends itself to the disjunctive reading which is suggested by the connective 'or.' That is, 'any sum,' instead of being related to 'any internal-revenue tax' and 'any penalty,' may refer to amounts which are neither taxes nor penalties. Under this interpretation, the function of the phrase is to permit suit for recovery of items which might not be designated as either 'taxes' or 'penalties' by Congress or the courts. One obvious example of such a 'sum' is interest. And it is significant that many old tax statutes described the amount which was to be assessed under certain circumstances as a 'sum' to be added to the tax, simply as a 'sum,' as a 'percentum,' or as 'costs.' Such a rendition of the statute, which is supported by precedent, frees the phrase 'any internal-revenue tax' from the qualifications imposed upon it by petitioner and permits it to be given what we regard as its more natural reading--the full tax. Moreover, this construction, under which each phrase is assigned a distinct meaning, imputes to Congress a surer grammatical touch than does the alternative interpretation, under which the 'any sum' phrase completely assimilates the other two. Surely a much clearer statute could have been written to authorize suits for refund of any part of a tax merely by use of the phrase 'a tax or any portion thereof,' or simply 'any sum paid under the internal revenue laws.' This Court naturally does not review congressional enactments as a panel of grammarians; but neither do we regard ordinary principles of English prose as irrelevant to a construction of those enactments.

We conclude that the language of § 1346(a)(1) can be more readily construed to require payment of the full tax before suit than to permit suit for recovery of a part payment. But, as we recognized in the prior opinion, the statutory language is not absolutely controlling, and consequently resort must be had to whatever other materials might be relevant.[6]

Legislative History and Historical Background.

Although frequently the legislative history of a statute is the most fruitful source of instruction as to its proper interpretation, in this case that history is barren of any clue to congressional intent.

* * *

It is argued, however, that the puzzle may be solved through consideration of the historical basis of a suit to recover a tax illegally assessed. The argument proceeds as follows: A suit to recover taxes could, before the Tucker Act, be brought only against the Collector. Such a suit was based upon the common-law count of assumpsit for money had and received, and the nature of that count requires the inference that a suit for recovery of part payment of a tax could have been maintained. Neither the Tucker Act nor the 1921 amendment indicates an intent to change the nature of the refund action in any pertinent respect. Consequently, there is no warrant for importing into § 1346(a)(1) a full-payment requirement.

For reasons which will appear later, we believe that the conclusion would not follow even if the premises were clearly sound. But in addition we have substantial doubt about the validity of the premises. As we have already indicated, the language of the 1921 amendment does in fact tend to indicate a congressional purpose to require full payment as a jurisdictional prerequisite to suit for refund. Moreover, we are not satisfied that the suit against the collector was identical to the common-law action of assumpsit for money had and received. One difficulty is that, because of the Act of February 26, 1845, c. 22, 5 Stat. 727, which restored the right of action against the Collector after this Court had held that it had been implicitly eliminated by other

---

6.   In the prior opinion we stated that, were it not for certain countervailing considerations, the statutory language 'might * * * be termed a clear authorization' to sue for the refund of part payment of an assessment. 357 U.S. at page 65, 78 S.Ct. at page 1081. It is quite obvious that we did not regard the language as clear enough to preclude deciding the case on other grounds. Moreover, it could at that time be assumed that the terms of the statute favored the taxpayer, because eight members of the Court considered the extrinsic evidence alone sufficient to decide the case against him. Although we are still of that opinion, we now state our views with regard to the bare words of the statute because the argument that these words are decisively against the Government has been urged so strenuously.

legislation, the Court no longer regarded the suit as a common-law action, but rather as a statutory remedy which 'in its nature (was) a remedy against the Government.' Curtis's Administratrix v. Fiedler, 2 Black 461, 479, 17 L.Ed. 273. On the other hand, it is true that none of the statutes relating to this type of suit clearly indicate a congressional intention to require full payment of the assessed tax before suit. Nevertheless, the opinion of this Court in Cheatham v. United States, 92 U.S. 85, 23 L.Ed. 561, prevents us from accepting the analogy between the statutory action against the Collector and the common-law count. In this 1875 opinion, the Court described the remedies available to taxpayers as follows:

> "So also, in the internal-revenue department, the statute which we have copied allows appeals from the assessor to the commissioner of internal revenue; and, if dissatisfied with his decision, *on paying the tax* the party can sue the collector; and, if the money was wrongfully exacted, the courts will give him relief by a judgment, which the United States pledges herself to pay.

> "* * * While a free course of remonstrance and appeal is allowed within the departments before the money is finally exacted, the general government has wisely made *the payment of the tax claimed*, whether of customs or of internal revenue, a condition precedent to a resort to the courts by the party against whom the tax is assessed. * * * If the compliance with this condition (that appeal must be made to the Commissioner and suit brought within six months of his decision) requires the party aggrieved to pay the money, he must do it. He cannot, after the decision is rendered against him, protract the time within which he can contest that decision in the courts by his own delay in paying the money. It is essential to the honor and orderly conduct of the government that its taxes should be promptly paid, and drawbacks speedily adjusted; and the rule prescribed in this class of cases is neither arbitrary nor unreasonable. * * *

> "The objecting party can take his appeal. He can, if the decision is delayed beyond twelve months, rest his case on that decision; or he can *pay the amount claimed*, and commence his suit at any time within that period. So, after the decision, he can pay at once, and commence suit within the six months * * *." 92 U.S. at pages 88-89, 23 L.Ed. 561. (Emphasis added.)

Reargument has not changed our view that this language reflects an understanding that full payment of the tax was a prerequisite to suit. Of course, * * * the *Cheatham* statement is dictum; but we reiterate that it appears to us to be 'carefully considered dictum.' 357 U.S. at page 68, 78 S.Ct. at page 1083. Equally important is the fact that the Court was construing the claim-for-refund statute from which, as amended, the language of § 1346(a)(1) was presumably taken. Thus it seems that in *Cheatham* the Supreme Court interpreted this language not only to specify which claims for refund must first be presented for administrative reconsideration, but also to constitute an additional qualification upon the statutory right to sue the Collector. It is true that the version of the provision involved in *Cheatham* contained only the phrase 'any tax.' But the phrase 'any penalty' and 'any sum' were added well before the decision in *Cheatham*; the history of these amendments makes it quite clear that they were not designed to effect any change relevant to the *Cheatham* rule; language in opinions of this Court after *Cheatham* is consistent with the *Cheatham* statement; and in any event, as we have indicated, we can see nothing in these additional words which would negate the full-payment requirement.

If this were all the material relevant to a construction of § 1346(a)(1), determination of the issue at bar would be inordinately difficult. Favoring petitioner would be the theory that, in the early nineteenth century, a suit for recovery of part payment of an assessment could be maintained against the Collector, together with the absence of any conclusive evidence that Congress has ever intended to inaugurate a new rule; favoring respondent would be the *Cheatham* statement and the language of the 1921 statute. There are, however, additional factors which are dispositive.

We are not here concerned with a single sentence in an isolated statute, but rather with a jurisdictional provision which is a keystone in a carefully articulated and quite complicated structure of tax laws. From these related statutes, all of which were passed after 1921, it is apparent that Congress has several times acted upon the assumption that § 1346(a)(1) requires full payment before suit. Of course, if the clear purpose of Congress at any time had been to permit suit to recover a part payment, this subsequent legislation would have to be disregarded. But, as we have stated, the evidence pertaining to this intent is extremely weak, and we are convinced that it is entirely too insubstantial to justify destroying the existing harmony of the tax statutes. The laws which we consider especially pertinent are the statute establishing the Board of Tax Appeals (now the Tax Court), the Declaratory Judgment Act, 28 U.S.C.A. § 2201 et seq., and § 7422(e) of the Internal Revenue Code of 1954.

The Board of Tax Appeals.

The Board of Tax Appeals was established by Congress in 1924 to permit taxpayers to secure a determination of tax liability before payment of the deficiency. The Government argues that the Congress which passed this 1924 legislation thought full payment of the tax assessed was a condition for bringing suit in a District Court; that Congress believed this sometimes caused hardship; and that Congress set up the Board to alleviate that hardship. Petitioner denies this, and contends that Congress' sole purpose was to enable taxpayers to prevent the Government from collecting taxes by exercise of its power of distraint.

We believe that the legislative history surrounding both the creation of the Board and the subsequent revisions of the basic statute supports the Government. The House Committee Report, for example, explained the purpose of the bill as follows:

"The committee recommends the establishment of a Board of Tax Appeals to which a taxpayer may appeal *prior to the payment* of an additional assessment of income, excess-profits, war-profits, or estate taxes. *Although a taxpayer may, after payment of his tax, bring suit for the recovery thereof* and thus secure a judicial determination on the questions involved, he can not, in view of section 3224 of the Revised Statutes, which prohibits suits to enjoin the collection of taxes, secure such a determination prior to the payment of the tax. The right of appeal after payment of the tax is an incomplete remedy, and does little to remove the hardship occasioned by an incorrect assessment. The payment of a large additional tax on income received several years previous and which may have, since its receipt, been either wiped out by subsequent losses, invested in nonliquid assets, or spent, sometimes forces taxpayers into bankruptcy, and often causes great financial hardship and sacrifice. These results are not remedied by permitting the taxpayer *to sue for the recovery of the tax after this payment.* He is entitled to an appeal and to a determination of his liability for the tax prior to its payment." (Emphasis added.)

Moreover, throughout the congressional debates are to be found frequent expressions of the principle that payment of the full tax was a precondition to suit * * * .

Petitioner's argument falls under the weight of this evidence. It is true, of course, that the Board of Tax Appeals procedure has the effect of staying collection, and it may well be that Congress so provided in order to alleviate hardships caused by the long-standing bar against suits to enjoin the collection of taxes. But it is a considerable leap to the further conclusion that amelioration of the hardship of prelitigation payment as a jurisdictional requirement was not another important motivation for Congress' action. To reconcile the legislative history with this conclusion seems to require the presumption that all the Congressmen who spoke of payment of the assessment before suit as a hardship understood-- without saying--that suit could be brought for whatever part of the assessment had been paid, but believed that, as a practical matter, hardship would nonetheless arise because the Government would require payment of the balance of the tax by exercising its power of distraint. But if this was in fact the view of these legislators, it is indeed extraordinary that they did not say so. Moreover, if Congress' only concern was to prevent distraint, it is somewhat difficult to understand why Congress did not simply authorize injunction suits. It is interesting to note in this connection that bills to permit the same type of prepayment litigation in the District Courts as is possible in the Tax Court have been introduced several times, but none has ever been adopted.

In sum, even assuming that one purpose of Congress in establishing the Board was to permit taxpayers to avoid distraint, it seems evident that another purpose was to furnish a forum where full payment of the assessment would not be a condition precedent to suit. The result is a system in which there is one tribunal for prepayment litigation and another for post-payment litigation, with no room contemplated for a hybrid of the type proposed by petitioner.

The Declaratory Judgment Act.

The Federal Declaratory Judgment Act of 1934 was amended by § 405 of the Revenue Act of 1935 expressly to except disputes 'with respect to Federal taxes.' The Senate Report explained the purpose of the amendment as follows:

"Your committee has added an amendment making it clear that the Federal Declaratory Judgments Act of June 14, 1934, has no application to Federal taxes. The application of the Declaratory Judgments Act to taxes would constitute a *radical departure* from the long-continued policy of Congress * * * with respect to the determination, assessment, and collection of Federal taxes. Your committee believes that the orderly and prompt determination and collection of Federal taxes should not be interfered with by a procedure designed to facilitate the settlement of private controversies, and that existing procedure both in the Board of Tax

Appeals and the courts affords ample remedies for the correction of tax errors." (Emphasis added.)

It is clear enough that one 'radical departure' which was averted by the amendment was the potential circumvention of the 'pay first and litigate later' rule by way of suits for declaratory judgments in tax cases. Petitioner would have us give this Court's imprimatur to precisely the same type of 'radical departure,' since a suit for recovery of but a part of an assessment would determine the legality of the balance by operation of the principle of collateral estoppel. With respect to this unpaid portion, the taxpayer would be securing what is in effect--even though not technically--a declaratory judgment. The frustration of congressional intent which petitioner asks us to endorse could hardly be more glaring, for he has conceded that his argument leads logically to the conclusion that payment of even $1 on a large assessment entitles the taxpayer to sue--a concession amply warranted by the obvious impracticality of any judicially created jurisdictional standard midway between full payment and any payment.

Section 7422(e) of the 1954 Code.

One distinct possibility which would emerge from a decision in favor of petitioner would be that a taxpayer might be able to split his cause of action, bringing suit for refund of part of the tax in a Federal District Court and litigating in the Tax Court with respect to the remainder. In such a situation the first decision would, of course, control. Thus if for any reason a litigant would prefer a District Court adjudication, he might sue for a small portion of the tax in that tribunal while at the same time protecting the balance from distraint by invoking the protection of the Tax Court procedure. On the other hand, different questions would arise if this device were not employed. For example, would the Government be required to file a compulsory counterclaim for the unpaid balance in District Court under Rule 13 of the Federal Rules of Civil Procedure, 28 U.S.C.A.? If so, which party would have the burden of proof?

Section 7422(e) of the 1954 Internal Revenue Code makes it apparent that Congress has assumed these problems are nonexistent except in the rare case where the taxpayer brings suit in a District Court and the Commissioner then notifies him of an additional deficiency. Under § 7422(e) such a claimant is given the option of pursuing his suit in the District Court or in the Tax Court, but he cannot litigate in both. Moreover, if he decides to remain in the District Court, the Government may--but seemingly is not required to--bring a counterclaim; and if it does, the taxpayer has the burden of proof. If we were to overturn the assumption upon which Congress has acted, we would generate upon a broad scale the very problems Congress believed it had solved.

These, then, are the basic reasons for our decision, and our views would be unaffected by the constancy or inconstancy of administrative practice. However, because the petition for rehearing in this case focused almost exclusively upon a single clause in the prior opinion--'there does not appear to be a single case before 1940 in which a taxpayer attempted a suit for refund of income taxes without paying the full amount the Government alleged to be due,' 357 U.S. at page 69, 78 S.Ct. at page 1083--we feel obliged to comment upon the material introduced upon reargument. The reargument has, if anything, strengthened, rather than weakened, the substance of this statement, which was directed to the question whether there has been a consistent understanding of the 'pay first and litigate later' principle by the interested government agencies and by the bar.

So far as appears, Suhr v. United States, 18 F.2d 81, decided by the Third Circuit in 1927, is the earliest case in which a taxpayer in a refund action sought to contest an assessment without having paid the full amount then due. In holding that the District Court had no jurisdiction of the action, the Court of Appeals said:

"None of the various tax acts provide for recourse to the courts by a taxpayer until he has failed to get relief from the proper administrative body or has paid all the taxes assessed against him. The payment of a part does not confer jurisdiction upon the courts. * * * There is no provision for refund to the taxpayer of any excess payment of any installment or part of his tax, if the whole tax for the year has not been paid." Id., at page 83.

Although the statement by the court might have been dictum, it was in accord with substantially contemporaneous statements by Secretary of the Treasury A. W. Mellon, by Under Secretary of the Treasury Garrard B. Winston, by the first Chairman of the Board of Tax Appeals, Charles D. Hamel, and by legal commentators.

There is strong circumstantial evidence that this view of the jurisdiction of the courts was shared by the bar at least until 1940, when the Second Circuit Court of Appeals rejected the Government's position in Coates v. United States, 111 F.2d 609. Out of the many thousands of refund cases litigated in the pre-1940 period--the Government reports that there have been approximately 40,000 such suits in the past 40 years--exhaustive research has uncovered only nine suits in which the issue was present, in six of which the Government contested jurisdiction on part-payment grounds. The Government's failure to raise the issue in the other three is obviously entirely without significance. Considerations of litigation strategy may have been thought to militate against resting upon such a defense in those cases. Moreover, where only nine lawsuits involving a particular issue arise over a period of many decades, the policy of the Executive Department on that issue can hardly be expected to become familiar to every government attorney. But most important, the number of cases before 1940 in which the issue was present is simply so inconsequential that it reinforces the conclusion of the prior opinion with respect to the uniformity of the pre-1940 belief that full payment had to precede suit.

A word should also be said about the argument that requiring taxpayers to pay the full assessments before bringing suits will subject some of them to great hardship. This contention seems to ignore entirely the right of the taxpayer to appeal the deficiency to the Tax Court without paying a cent. If he permits his time for filing such an appeal to expire, he can hardly complain that he has been unjustly treated, for he is in precisely the same position as any other person who is barred by a statute of limitations. On the other hand, the Government has a substantial interest in protecting the public purse, an interest which would be substantially impaired if a taxpayer could sue in a District Court without paying his tax in full. It is instructive to note that, as of June 30, 1959, tax cases pending in the Tax Court involved $920,046,748, and refund suits in other courts involved $446,673,640. It is quite true that the filing of an appeal to the Tax Court normally precludes the Government from requiring payment of the tax, but a decision in petitioner's favor could be expected to throw a great portion of the Tax Court litigation into the District Courts. Of course, the Government can collect the tax from a District Court suitor by exercising its power of distraint--if he does not split his cause of action--but we cannot believe that compelling resort to this extraordinary procedure is either wise or in accord with congressional intent. Our system of taxation is based upon voluntary assessment and payment, not upon distraint. A full-payment requirement will promote the smooth functioning of this system; a part-payment rule would work at cross-purposes with it.

In sum, if we were to accept petitioner's argument, we would sacrifice the harmony of our carefully structured twentieth century system of tax litigation, and all that would be achieved would be a supposed harmony of § 1346(a)(1) with what might have been the nineteenth century law had the issue ever been raised. Reargument has but fortified our view that § 1346(a)(1), correctly construed, requires full payment of the assessment before an income tax refund suit can be maintained in a Federal District Court.

Affirmed.

Notes and Questions

Although *Flora* involved a refund suit in the federal district court, the full payment requirement applies equally in the United States Court of Federal Claims.

The holding of *Flora* means that only those taxpayers who can afford to pay the full amount of the contested tax will be able to bring suit in a refund forum. There is no hardship exception to the full payment requirement. See Curry v. United States, 774 F.2d 852 (7th Cir. 1985).

In the full *Flora* opinion, four justices dissented. Justice Whittaker, writing for the dissenters, noted that full payment could cause a hardship to taxpayers who had been illegally assessed under a jeopardy or normal assessment and who could not pay the entire amount of the assessment within the statutory period. Justice Whittaker further noted that taxpayers who were paying their tax liability in installments "would be without remedy to recover early installments that were wrongfully collected should the period of limitations run before the last installment is paid." 362 U.S. at 196.

The Supreme Court in *Flora* stated that this should not be much of a problem because the taxpayer could "appeal the deficiency to the Tax Court without paying a cent." But Carlton Smith, in a thoughtful article, lists reasons why this may not be an adequate remedy for many of the poor. Recall that tax court jurisdiction depends upon the receipt of a notice of deficiency and a timely filed petition. Smith notes that many poor people fail to receive timely notice because they move frequently, fail to comprehend the notice because they may not have an adequate grasp of the English language, and fail to respond appropriately to the notice within the 90-day time frame. This problem and a suggested solution is discussed in Carlton M. Smith, "Let the Poor Sue For A Refund Without Full Payment," 125 TAX NOTES 131 (Oct. 5, 2009).

1. What does the Court mean when it states: "A full-payment requirement will promote the smooth functioning of the voluntary compliance system; a part-payment rule would work at cross-purposes with it?"

2. Does full payment include interest and penalties? See Shore v. United States, 9 F.3d 1524 (Fed. Cir. 1993).

Problem

John Brown receives a 30-day letter (Preliminary Notice of Deficiency) proposing a deficiency for an amount of tax that John does not believe he owes. John wants to contest the proposed deficiency, but he is concerned about the running of interest and time-sensitive penalties in the interim if he should lose the contest. What should he do?

B. THE DIVISIBLE TAX PRINCIPLE

STEELE v. UNITED STATES
United States Court of Appeals, Eighth Circuit, 1960.
280 F.2d 89.

PER CURIAM.

Penalties were assessed administratively against the president and the secretary of Davidson-Steele, Inc., in the amount of $5,186.47 as to each officer for willfully failing to pay over to the Internal Revenue Service the withholdings of income taxes and social security taxes made by the corporation from the wages of its employees.

Each officer made a payment of $50 to the Internal Revenue Service on the amount of the assessment against him, and they thereafter brought suit in the District Court for refund of these payments, on the ground that the penalties were erroneously and illegally assessed against them.

The Government moved to dismiss the action, contending that, under the holding in Flora v. United States, 357 U.S. 63, 78 S.Ct. 1079, 2 L.Ed.2d 1165, no right to sue for refund could exist, because the entire penalty had not been paid.

The District Court dismissed the action on this basis, 172 F.Supp. 793, and the plaintiffs have appealed.

The Government now in effect concedes that it was in error in the position which it took in the District Court; that the withholdings involved constituted separate taxes as to the individual employees of the corporation; and that the penalties imposed similarly would be entitled to be regarded as divisible assessments made in relation to the individual withholdings.

A stipulation has been presented to us in which the parties agree that the situation is subject to the recognition made in footnotes 37 and 38 of the Flora opinion, 362 U.S. 145, at pages 171 and 175, that the full-payment rule is not applicable to an assessment of divisible taxes; and that on this basis the judgments herein should be reversed and the case remanded to the District Court for further proceedings on the merits.

We are in accord with and accept the view and implication of the stipulation that the penalties imposed amounted legally, under §§ 6671 and 6672 of the Internal Revenue Code of 1954, 26 U.S.C.A., to divisible assessments or taxes against the officers, in their relationship to and predication upon the separate taxes of the individual employees. Thus, the officers would be legally entitled to make payment of the amount of the penalty applicable to the withheld taxes of any individual employee, to make claim for refund, and to institute suit for recovery, as a means of settling the question of the right of the Government to have made penalty assessment against them personally in the circumstances of the situation.

The judgment as to each appellant is accordingly reversed, and the case is remanded for further proceedings on the merits.

Notes and Question

The divisible tax concept also applies to transactional taxes, so the taxpayer need only pay the tax attributable to a single transaction in order to obtain jurisdiction in a refund forum. However, the underlying transactions must be substantially the same in order for the outcome of the refund suit to determine the liability for the other transactions. Another example of a divisible tax is an excise tax. But the penalty under § 6700 on abusive tax shelter transactions is not a divisible tax, despite the wording of the statute imposing a penalty on "such activity." See Korobkin v. United States 988 F.2d 975 (9th Cir. 1993).

What is the purpose and policy behind the divisible tax principle?

C. LIMITATION PERIODS ON REFUND SUITS

Section 6532(a)(1) provides that no refund suit may be filed before the expiration of six months from the date of filing the refund claim with the Service, unless the Service renders a decision within that time. The provision also states that no refund suit may be filed after the expiration of two years from the date the Service mails a notice of disallowance of the refund claim, although the two-year period may be extended by agreement between the taxpayer and the Service. If the taxpayer files a written waiver of the notice of disallowance with the Service, the two-year period begins to run on the date the waiver is filed. Note that the limitations period for filing refund suits is different from the limitations periods for filing refund claims with the Service.

The Service may send the taxpayer a proposed notice of disallowance that would permit the taxpayer to file an administrative appeal within 30 days. This would allow the taxpayer the opportunity to resolve the case with the Service, instead of pursuing a judicial solution. If the taxpayer's claim for refund involves issues that were contested in a previously examined return, though, an administrative appeal may be futile. If the taxpayer does not wish to pursue an administrative appeal but does wish to accelerate a refund suit, the taxpayer may request in writing that the claim for refund be immediately rejected. The Service then should promptly send a notice of disallowance to the taxpayer. On receipt of the notice, the taxpayer would have two years to file a refund suit in either the federal district court or the U.S. Court of Federal Claims. The six-month waiting period would not apply in that case. Note that unlike the waiver of the notice of disallowance, the request for rejection is not a statutory provision, but rather, is an administrative concession of the Service. Thus, the taxpayer is dependent upon the discretion of the Service and has no right to protest if the Service fails to send such a rejection.

Notes and Questions

A separate six-year statute of limitations applies to suits for the recovery of interest on an overpayment of tax. See 28 U.S.C. § 2401(a) (suits in the U.S. District Court) and § 2501 (suits in the U.S. Court of Federal Claims).

A California district court has held that if the IRS does not issue a notice of disallowance of the refund claim, the six-year limitation period under 28 U.S.C. § 2401 applies instead of a presumed unlimited statutory period under § 6532. The six-year period begins to run after the right of action accrues and under § 6532(a) the right of action accrues six months after the administrative claims is filed. See Wagenet v. United States, 2009 U.S.Dist. LEXIS 115547 (C.D. Cal. 2009).

Section 6330(d) provides a 30-day deadline for a taxpayer to appeal an IRS notice of determination following a collection due process hearing. See discussion of collection due process in Chapter 7. A federal district court has decided that although this deadline is "tangentially related to the refund action," the two-year limitation period under § 6532(a)(1) applies independently of § 6330(d). Killingsworth v. United States, 2003 WL 23112767 (E.D. Tex. 2003) (slip opinion), *aff'd* 110 Fed. Appx. 376 (2004) (unpublished opinion). Thus, the 30-day deadline provided under § 6330(d) does not apply to toll the two-year statutory period for filing refund claims under § 6532(a)(1). In addition, the *Killingsworth* court held that equitable tolling does not apply to the statutory period for filing refund suits. *Id.*

1. What is the earliest period that a refund suit may be filed? What is the latest period? See Rev. Rul. 56-381, 1956-2 C.B. 953; Finkelstein v. United States, 943 F.Supp. 425 (D.N.J. 1996).

2. What is the purpose of a waiver of the notice of disallowance? See Reg. § 301.6532-1(c).

1. Suits on Account Stated

In cases in which the taxpayer has not met the jurisdictional prerequisites to file a refund suit, there are rare instances in which the taxpayer may be able to circumvent the two-year statute of limitations by using a common law contract principle known as a suit on account stated to take advantage of the general six-year statute of limitations on suits against the United States (28 U.S.C. § 2401 in the U.S. District Court and 28 U.S.C. § 2501 in the U.S. Court of Federal Claims). Such a suit is based on an implied contract between the Service and the taxpayer to the extent that the taxpayer has overpaid the tax liability for a given taxable period. In order for this principle to apply, the Service must have proposed to pay the taxpayer a specific sum (as opposed to offsetting the amount of the overpayment by a deficiency for another taxable period) by giving the taxpayer a notice of adjustment (notice of overassessment), and the taxpayer must have accepted the proposal/adjustment in satisfaction of the government's debt to the taxpayer. See Bonwit Teller & Co. v. United States, 283 U.S. 258 (1931). If the principle applies, the six-year period would commence on the date the taxpayer receives the notice of assessment, and no refund claim would be necessary for the taxpayer to recover the amount of the overpayment.

2. Tax Court Claims

The Tax Court has deficiency jurisdiction and thus cannot hear claims for refund. Similarly, a taxpayer who files a petition in the Tax Court loses the ability to bring a refund suit in any of the refund fora. But if the Tax Court determines that there was an overpayment for a taxable year properly before it, it has jurisdiction to determine the amount of the overpayment and to order this amount to be paid or credited to the taxpayer, if the government does not file an appeal. IRC § 6512(b)(1).

Under the general rule, § 6511 limits the amount of overpayment the taxpayer can recover if an administrative refund claim is filed. Since the taxpayer does not have to file a refund claim with the Service in order to assert such a claim in a Tax Court petition, § 6512 limits the amount of overpayment that may be ordered by the Tax Court. There are three rules that apply under § 6512(b)(3). First, under § 6512(b)(3)(A), a taxpayer may obtain a full refund of any overpayment made after the mailing of a notice of deficiency. This may occur where the taxpayer makes a payment to stop the running of interest after the issuance of a notice of deficiency. Second, if the taxpayer files a timely administrative claim for refund before the notice of deficiency is mailed, the Tax Court may hear the refund claim, as well as the deficiency action, in the interest of judicial efficiency. The amount of the overpayment is determined under the normal rules of § 6511, measured from the date the administrative refund claim was filed. If the administrative claim is disallowed prior to the date of the mailing of the notice of deficiency, the Tax Court nevertheless may hear the refund claim if on the date the notice of deficiency was mailed, the taxpayer has brought or could have brought a timely refund suit. IRC § 6512(b)(3)(C)). Third, if the taxpayer has not filed a return or an administrative refund claim prior to the mailing of the notice of deficiency, the date the notice is mailed is the deemed date of the refund claim for purposes of determining the timeliness of the claim. IRC § 6512(b)(3)(B). This provision is the most complex of the three provisions, and requires some explanation of its background.

In 1996, the United States Supreme Court addressed § 6512(b)(3)(B) in the case of Commissioner v. Lundy, 516 U.S. 235, 116 S.Ct. 647, 133 L.Ed.2d 611 (1996), which dealt with a delinquent income tax return. Lundy and his wife overpaid their 1987 tax liability through income taxes withheld from their wages. They neglected to file a return for the 1987 taxable year until December 22, 1990. Prior to that point, on September 26, 1990, the Service mailed a notice of deficiency to the Lundys.

On the return filed on December 22, 1990, the Lundy's claimed a refund of the taxes they alleged had been overpaid. Six days later, Lundy filed a timely petition in the Tax Court seeking a redetermination of the alleged deficiency and a refund of the alleged overpayment.

The Commissioner contended that the Tax Court lacked jurisdiction to award the refund because the notice of deficiency had been mailed before the return was filed. Thus, the Tax Court could only award the taxpayers a refund of taxes paid within two years prior to the date the notice of deficiency was mailed. Since the withheld taxes were deemed paid on April 15, 1988, this was more than two years before the date the notice was mailed.

The Commissioner based her position on § 6512(b)(3)(B), which provides that the Tax Court may award a refund of overpaid taxes only if the taxes were paid:

> within the period which would be applicable under section 6511(b)(2)
> * * * if on the date of the mailing of the notice of deficiency a claim

had been filed (whether or not filed) stating the grounds upon which the Tax Court finds that there is an overpayment.

The Tax Court agreed with the Commissioner and held that if a notice of deficiency is mailed prior to the filing of the return and more than two years after the tax is deemed paid, the look-back period under § 6512(b)(3)(B) is two years and the Tax Court lacks jurisdiction to award the refund. The Court of Appeals for the Fourth Circuit reversed, holding that the applicable period was three years from the date the return was filed and that the Tax Court had jurisdiction to award the refund. The United States Supreme Court granted certiorari to resolve the issue.

The Supreme Court held that the two-year look-back period applied. The Court reasoned:

> "section 6512(b)(3)(B) tolls the limitations period, in that it directs the Tax Court to measure the look-back period from the date on which the notice of deficiency is mailed and not the date on which the taxpayer actually files the claim for refund. But in the case of delinquent filers, § 6512(b)(3)(B) establishes only a two-year look-back period, so the delinquent filer is not assured the opportunity to seek a refund in Tax Court: if the notice of deficiency is mailed more than two years after the taxes were paid, the Tax Court lacks jurisdiction to award the taxpayer a refund."

516 U.S. at 245, 116 S.Ct. at 653. The Court acknowledged that its decision created a disparity between the Tax Court and the refund fora because in either of the refund fora, a three-year look-back period would have applied and the refund would have been granted. It noted, though, that in the Tax Court, unlike in the refund fora, a refund claim is not required. Instead, the taxpayer need only establish that the tax in question was paid during the applicable look-back period. 516 U.S. at 251-252, 116 S.Ct. at 656.

In 1997, Congress reversed the *Lundy* result by amending § 6512(b)(3) to read:

> In a case described in subparagraph (B) where the date of the mailing of the notice of deficiency is during the third year after the due date (with extensions) for filing the return of tax and no return was filed before such date, the applicable period under subsections (a) and (b)(2) of section 6511 shall be 3 years.

Taxpayer Relief Act of 1997, P.L. No. § 105-34, 1282(a).

Questions

1. Does the 1997 amendment to § 6512(b)(3)(B) address the issue of a delinquent return requesting a refund, that is filed more than two years but less than three years after payment?

2. Does the 1997 amendment to § 6512(b)(3)(B) create any further disparities?

3. How, if at all, can a delinquent taxpayer avoid the two-year look-back period?

D. PLEADINGS

1. The Complaint

A refund suit is commenced with the filing of a complaint by the taxpayer. The complaint must be filed with the clerk of the appropriate court and the taxpayer must pay a filing fee. In the district courts, the taxpayer also must serve copies of the complaint on the United States Attorney for the district in which the suit is filed, the IRS director who processed the claim for refund, and the United States Attorney General. Fed. R. Civ. Proc. 4(i)(1). The latter two services may be accomplished by mailing the complaint by registered or certified mail. In the Court of Federal Claims, the clerk will serve the complaint on the defendant.

The complaint must contain: (1) a concise statement of the grounds for jurisdiction, (2) a concise statement of the claim, showing that the plaintiff is entitled to relief, and (3) a demand for judgment for the relief sought. In the Court of Federal Claims, the complaint must contain more specific information, such as a specific cite to any statute or regulation on which the claim is based and the taxpayer identification number of each plaintiff.

In a complaint filed in the district court, the taxpayer also should request a jury trial if the taxpayer wishes to have the case be heard by a jury. If the taxpayer does not request a jury trial, the government may do so. It is possible to have some issues be heard by the jury while other issues may be heard only by the judge. Either party has the right, however, to request that all issues be heard by the jury.

What general grounds for jurisdiction must be stated in the complaint?

2. The Answer

The government has 60 days after service of the complaint to file an answer, although the court may grant extensions of time to file. In its answer, the government may raise any available defenses, such as the statute of limitations, failure of the complaint to conform to the issues raised in the refund claim (variance), and offset of the overpayment. The government also may assert affirmative counterclaims against the taxpayer, and indeed, it is required to do so if the counterclaim arises out of the same transaction or occurrence that is the subject matter of the refund suit.

E. BURDEN OF PROOF

Since the taxpayer is the plaintiff in the refund suit, as well as in Tax Court cases, the taxpayer bears the burden of proving entitlement to the refund. In order to establish this, the taxpayer must show by a preponderance of the evidence that the Service's assessment was erroneous, and that there has been an overpayment of the tax. In establishing that there has been an overpayment, the taxpayer must show the correct amount of tax due. But if the taxpayer meets the requirements of § 7491, the burden of proof may shift to the government, even though the taxpayer is the plaintiff.

KNUDSEN v. COMMISSIONER
United States Tax Court, 2008.
131 T.C. 185.

MARVEL, JUDGE.

On December 19, 2007, pursuant to Rule 161,[1] petitioners filed a timely motion for reconsideration of this Court's Memorandum Opinion in Knudsen v. Commissioner, T.C. Memo.2007-340 (*Knudsen I*). In *Knudsen I* we held that petitioners' exotic animal breeding activity was not an activity engaged in for profit within the meaning of section 183. Petitioners request that we reconsider whether they satisfied the requirements under section 7491(a) to shift the burden of proof to respondent.

* * *

Section 7491(a)(1) provides that, subject to certain limitations, where a taxpayer introduces credible evidence with respect to a factual issue relevant to ascertaining the taxpayer's tax liability, the burden of proof shifts to the Commissioner with respect to such issue. Section 7491(a)(1) applies with respect to a factual issue only if the requirements of section 7491(a)(2) are satisfied. Under section 7491(a)(2), a taxpayer must have

---

1.   All Rule references are to the Tax Court Rules of Practice and Procedure, and all section references are to the Internal Revenue Code in effect at all relevant times.

maintained all records required by the Internal Revenue Code and cooperated with reasonable requests by the Secretary for witnesses, information, documents, meetings, and interviews.

In their motion for reconsideration, petitioners assert that (1) this Court erred in concluding that we did not need to decide whether petitioners met the requirements under·section 7491(a) to shift the burden of proof to respondent, and (2) each factor under section 1.183-2(b), Income Tax Regs., is a separate "factual issue" within the meaning of section 7491(a).

I. Section 7491(a) Burden of Proof Shift

In *Knudsen I* we stated:

We do not need to decide whether petitioners have met all of the requirements under section 7491 to shift the burden of proof to respondent. The outcome of this case is based on a preponderance of the evidence and thus is unaffected by section 7491. * * *

Petitioners contend that "Congress did not intend income tax cases to be 'unaffected' by section 7491" and that we must determine whether petitioners met the requirements under section 7491(a) to shift the burden of proof to respondent. Although this case is appealable, absent a stipulation to the contrary, to the Court of Appeals for the Tenth Circuit, see sec. 7482(b), petitioners rely on Griffin v. Commissioner, 315 F.3d 1017 (8th Cir.2003) (*Griffin II*), vacating and remanding T.C. Memo.2002-6 (*Griffin I*), in support of their argument.

Petitioners argue that the Court of Appeals for the Eighth Circuit in *Griffin II* correctly concluded that section 7491(a) should be applied in all cases. Petitioners' argument applies *Griffin II* too broadly and fails to acknowledge that *Griffin II* is distinguishable from this case.

In *Griffin v. Commissioner*, the taxpayers appealed an unfavorable Tax Court decision and argued that the Tax Court erred in holding that the taxpayers failed to present sufficient evidence to shift the burden of proof to the Commissioner under section 7491(a). The Tax Court in *Griffin I* had concluded that the taxpayers did not introduce credible evidence and thus the burden of proof remained with the taxpayers. Griffin v. Commissioner, T.C. Memo.2002-6.[2] The Court of Appeals disagreed. It concluded that the taxpayers did produce sufficient credible evidence and stated: "It is not sufficient to summarily conclude that the outcome is the

---

2. In a footnote in its opinion, the Tax Court also stated that "Even if the burden of proof were placed on * * * [the Commissioner], we would decide the issue in his favor based on the preponderance of the evidence." Griffin v. Commissioner, T.C. Memo.2002-6, vacated and remanded 315 F.3d 1017 (8th Cir.2003).

same regardless of who bears the burden of proof; if that were the case, § 7491(a) would have no meaning." *Griffin v. Commissioner*, 315 F.3d at 1021-1022.

On remand this Court shifted the burden of proof to the Commissioner in accordance with the decision of the Court of Appeals and revisited the trial record. This Court concluded that the taxpayers were entitled to certain deductions because the Commissioner had not offered sufficient contrary evidence to overcome the taxpayers' evidence, which the Court of Appeals had concluded was credible. See Griffin v. Commissioner, T.C. Memo.2004-64.

The Court of Appeals in *Griffin II* disagreed with this Court's finding regarding the credibility of the taxpayers' evidence, and its opinion is properly read in that context. It is also apparent that once the issue of the credibility of the taxpayers' evidence was resolved, the burden shift did affect the result, as this Court on remand allowed the deductions that it had not allowed in its earlier opinion on the basis of the Commissioner's failure to carry his burden of proof.

Petitioners' argument in their motion for reconsideration reads *Griffin II* too broadly. *Griffin II* does not stand for the proposition that a trial court must decide whether the burden of proof shifts to the Government in all cases where the issue of a burden shift is raised, nor does it stand for the proposition that a trial court's failure to decide a burden shift issue is always reversible error. The Court of Appeals said as much in Polack v. Commissioner, 366 F.3d 608 (8th Cir.2004), affg. T.C. Memo.2002-145.[3]

In *Polack v. Commissioner*, the taxpayer appealed a Tax Court decision arguing, among other things, that the Tax Court erred in not shifting the burden of proof to the Commissioner after the Commissioner abandoned his initial valuation theory in favor of an expert's valuation. The Tax Court had concluded that it did not need to decide whether the burden of proof shifted to the Commissioner because the outcome was on the basis of a preponderance of the evidence. The Court of Appeals agreed with the Tax Court and explained that " 'The shifting of an evidentiary burden of preponderance is of practical consequence only in the rare event of an evidentiary tie'". *Id.* The Court of Appeals did not mention its earlier decision in *Griffin II*.

In 2005, approximately 8 months after it issued its decision in *Polack*, the Court of Appeals for the Eighth Circuit further clarified its position in Blodgett v. Commissioner, 394 F.3d 1030, 1039 (8th Cir.2005), *affg.*

---

3. The taxpayer in Polack v. Commissioner, 366 F.3d 608 (8th Cir.2004), affg. T.C. Memo.2002-145, did not argue for a shift of the burden of proof under sec. 7491(a)(1). Rather, the taxpayer relied on general principles governing shifting the burden of proof.

T.C. Memo.2003-212. The Court of Appeals revisited whether the Tax Court's failure to shift the burden of proof to the Commissioner under section 7491(a) was reversible error and held that, on the record before it, the Tax Court did not commit reversible error by declining to decide the issue. The Court of Appeals explained its holding:

> In a situation in which both parties have satisfied their burden of production by offering some evidence, then the party supported by the weight of the evidence will prevail regardless of which party bore the burden of persuasion, proof or preponderance. * * * Therefore, a shift in the burden of preponderance has real significance only in the rare event of an evidentiary tie. * * * Here, the record is clear, if the tax court did err in failing to shift the burden of proof, any error was harmless because the weight of the evidence supported a decision for the Commissioner. [*Id.*]

At least two other Courts of Appeals have also held that the burden of proof shift under section 7491(a) is relevant only when there is an evidentiary tie. *See* Geiger v. Commissioner, 279 Fed. Appx. 834, 835 (11th Cir.2008) ("any error committed by the tax court by failing to shift the burden was harmless, because the burden of proof is of practical consequence only in the rare event of an evidentiary tie"), *affg.* T.C. Memo.2006-271; FRGC Inv., LLC v. Commissioner, 89 Fed. Appx. 656 (9th Cir.2004) (the Court was not required to determine who had the burden of proof under section 7491(a) when the preponderance of the evidence favored the Commissioner), affg. T.C. Memo.2002-276.

Petitioners argue that *Griffin II* is correct and *Polack* and *Blodgett* are wrong. However, the Court of Appeals for the Eighth Circuit in *Blodgett*, upon revisiting *Griffin II*, held that an allocation of the burden of proof is relevant only when there is equal evidence on both sides. We agree with the analysis of the Court of Appeals in *Blodgett*.[4] In a case where the standard of proof is preponderance of the evidence and the preponderance of the evidence favors one party, we may decide the case on the weight of the evidence and not on an allocation of the burden of proof.[5]

---

4. The Court has often cited Blodgett v. Commissioner, 394 F.3d 1030, 1039 (8th Cir.2005), affg. T.C. Memo.2003-212, for this position. See e.g., Estate of Christiansen v. Commissioner, 130 T.C. 1, 8 n. 7, (2008); Grossman v. Commissioner, T.C. Memo.2005-164; Levine v. Commissioner, T.C. Memo.2005-86.

5. Petitioners also argue that the reliance of the Court of Appeals for the Eighth Circuit on *Polack* is questionable because *Polack* did not involve any argument for a shift of the burden of proof under sec. 7491(a). However, the Court of Appeals in *Blodgett* recognized that its reasoning in *Polack* regarding the shifting of the burden of proof in a case decided on the basis of the preponderance of the evidence was equally applicable to the analysis required by sec. 7491(a). *Blodgett v. Commissioner, supra* at 1039.

In *Knudsen I* the weight of the evidence favored respondent, and consequently, we did not need to decide the allocation of the burden of proof under section 7491(a) with respect to the section 183 issue. We hold, therefore, that in *Knudsen I* we did not err in declining to allocate the burden of proof under section 7491(a).

* * *

Accordingly, we shall deny petitioners' motion for reconsideration. An appropriate order and decision will be entered.

Notes and Questions

There are certain issues on which the government always bears the burden of proof. These include fraud, review of jeopardy levy or assessment procedures, penalties for promoting abusive tax shelters, and status as employees. In addition, the government always bears the burden of proving a penalty, addition to tax or additional amount that applies to an individual taxpayer. IRC § 7491(c). The taxpayer has the burden of proving a credible defense.

1. What effect will the *Knudsen* decision have on taxpayers who bring suit in the Tax Court?

2. In a divisible tax case, the government frequently counterclaims for the unpaid portion of the assessment, which gives the court jurisdiction over the entire assessment. Does this raise any problem with respect to the burden of proof?

3. Discuss the taxpayer's burden of proof in (a) a deficiency suit, (b) a refund suit, and (c) a case in which the government asserts a set-off. See Missouri Pacific Railroad Company v. United States, 338 F.2d 668 (Ct.Cl. 1964).

CHAPTER 6

CIVIL PENALTIES AND INTEREST

The payment of taxes is an obvious and insistent duty, and its sanction is usually punative.

-- Joseph McKenna[1]

Civil penalties provide a backup to the voluntary compliance system. According to the Internal Revenue Manual, "penalties encourage voluntary compliance by defining standards of compliant behavior, defining consequences for noncompliance, and providing monetary sanctions against taxpayers who do not meet the standard." IRM 20.1.1.2.

The Code provides a number of penalties, both civil and criminal, to ensure that taxpayers file their returns and pay their taxes in a timely manner. In some cases, civil penalties may be imposed against third parties, such as return preparers (see discussion, Chapter 2), and the "responsible person" who fails to withhold and remit payroll taxes to the government (see discussion of the "100 percent penalty" in Chapter 7). In other cases, criminal penalties may apply to third parties, as well as to the taxpayer. These are discussed in Chapter 9.

The focus of this chapter is on the delinquency and accuracy-related penalties, as well as the civil fraud penalty, that apply to the taxpayer. In addition to these penalties, interest is required to be paid on underpayments of tax owed by the taxpayer to the government, as well as on overpayments of tax owed by the government to the taxpayer. These penalties, plus the interest on underpayments, constitute additions to tax that are assessed and collected in the same manner as the underlying tax.

I. DELINQUENCY PENALTIES

If the taxpayer fails to file a timely return or pay the tax in a timely manner, the taxpayer may be subject to delinquency penalties under § 6651. These penalties apply to income taxes, estate and gift taxes, and to most excise taxes, and are the most frequently imposed of the civil penalties. Section 6651(a) provides three separate delinquency penal-

---

1. Jeffery L. Yablon, As Certain As Death–Quotations About Taxes (2004 Edition), 102 TAX NOTES 99, 140 (Jan. 5, 2004).

ties: (1) failure to file a return by the prescribed date (determined with regard to extensions of time to file); (2) failure to pay the tax shown on the return by the prescribed date (determined with regard to extensions of time to pay); and (3) failure to pay the tax required to be shown on the return, but not so shown, within 21 days after a notice and demand for payment (10 business days if the amount of the notice and demand equals or exceeds $100,000). These penalties may be avoided if the taxpayer establishes that the failure to timely file or pay was "due to reasonable cause and due not to willful neglect". See § 6651(a). See also § 6664(c) for other instances in which reasonable cause may provide an excuse from penalties under the Code.

A. FAILURE TO FILE

If a return is not filed by the due date, including any extended due date, a penalty for late filing is imposed under § 6651(a)(1). The penalty rate is 5 percent per month (or fraction of a month) of the net amount of tax required to be shown on the return for the first month, with an additional 5 percent per month for each month (or fraction thereof) that the failure to file continues. The rate is capped at a maximum of 25 percent. The net amount of tax is the amount required to be shown on the return, reduced by any allowable credits and any amounts paid on or before the date prescribed for payment. IRC § 6651(a)(1) and (b)(1). The penalty runs from the due date of the return (determined with regard to extensions of time to file) until the date the return is filed. Review the rules in Chapter 3 for determining (1) what constitutes a return and (2) when the return is considered filed.

A civil penalty is assessed and collected in the same manner as the underlying tax. If the penalty is attributable to a deficiency, the taxpayer may petition the Tax Court for a redetermination of the penalty, subject to the jurisdictional requirements discussed in Chapter 4. If the penalty is not attributable to a deficiency, and the taxpayer wishes to contest the penalty in a judicial forum, the taxpayer must pay the amount of the penalty and otherwise meet the jurisdictional requirements for filing a refund suit in the federal district courts or the United States Court of Federal Claims. See Chapter 5 for a discussion of these jurisdictional requirements.

Occasionally, a question may arise as to whether the delinquency penalty itself constitutes a deficiency, entitling the taxpayer to contest the penalty in the Tax Court. This question is likely to arise when the taxpayer concedes or stipulates issues prior to trial.

ESTATE OF FORGEY v. COMMISSIONER
United States Tax Court, 2000.
115 T.C. 142.

VASQUEZ, J.

A Form 706, United States Estate (and Generation-Skipping Transfer) Tax Return, was delinquently filed on behalf of the Estate of Glenn G. Forgey (the estate). Respondent assessed the estate tax reported on the return and a section 6651(a)(1) addition to tax for late filing. Respondent subsequently determined a deficiency in estate tax of $866,434 and an additional section 6651(a)(1) addition to tax of $216,609 based on such deficiency.

The parties reached an agreement as to all issues raised in the notice of deficiency except for the section 6651(a)(1) addition to tax. The agreement, when taken together with the concessions made by respondent in the notice of deficiency, produced an overassessment.

The estate requests the Court to review the late-filing addition to tax assessed by respondent prior to the issuance of the notice of deficiency (the assessed addition to tax). In response to respondent's argument that we lack jurisdiction to do so, the estate contends that, despite the resulting overassessment in tax, a portion of the assessed addition to tax is attributable to a deficiency. Therefore, the issues for decision are whether the Court has jurisdiction to review any portion of the assessed addition to tax, and if so, whether the estate is liable for such addition.

FINDINGS OF FACT

* * *

Glenn G. Forgey (decedent) died testate on October 14, 1993. * * * Decedent's son, Lyle A. Forgey (Mr. Forgey), was appointed as the personal representative of decedent's estate. * * *

The Federal estate tax return for the estate was originally due on July 14, 1994.[3] A day prior to the due date, Mr. Forgey filed a Form 4768, Application for Extension of Time to File a Return and/or Pay U.S. Estate Taxes, requesting an extension of time to file the estate tax return until January 14, 1995, and an extension of time to pay the estate tax until July 14, 1995. The requested extensions were granted by the Commissioner.

The January 14, 1995 extended due date for filing the estate tax return expired with no return having been filed. Following respondent's

---

3.   Form 706, United States Estate (and Generation-Skipping Transfer) Tax Return, must be filed within 9 months of the decedent's date of death. See sec. 6075(a).

written inquiry as to the status of the estate tax return in late May 1995, Mr. Forgey signed the return and mailed it to the Internal Revenue Service Center in Ogden, Utah. The Commissioner received the estate tax return on June 2, 1995. The return reflected an estate tax liability of $2,165,565 and a balance due of $1,683,565.[4]

On July 17, 1995, respondent assessed the estate tax liability and a section 6651(a)(1) addition to tax for late filing in the amount of $378,802.[5] The addition to tax was based on the tax reported as due on the return.

By notice of deficiency dated April 23, 1998, respondent determined a deficiency in estate tax of $866,434. Based on this deficiency, respondent determined an additional section 6651(a)(1) addition to tax in the amount of $216,609.

In the notice of deficiency, respondent determined a $1,580,433 net increase in the amount of the taxable estate. This net adjustment, in turn, was based on the following: (1) A $2,040,249 increase in the value of items included in the gross estate; (2) a $28,373 reduction in the allowable deductions claimed on the estate tax return; and (3) the allowance of a $488,190 deduction for interest accrued on the deferred estate tax obligation (the interest expense deduction).[6]

The parties reached an agreement on the correct amount of the taxable estate, as evidenced by a stipulation of settled issues (the settlement). Apart from the interest expense deduction, the settlement resulted in a $332,352 increase in the taxable estate.[7] However, when the $488,190 interest expense deduction is taken into account, the net adjustment to the taxable estate is negative. Thus, the settlement produced an estate tax liability that was lower than that reported on the

---

4. The estate submitted a payment of $482,000 with the Form 4768, Application for Extension of Time to File a Return and/or Pay U.S. Estate Taxes.

5. Respondent also assessed interest and an addition to tax for late payment under sec. 6651(a)(2). These amounts are not in dispute.

6. The estate made an election under sec. 6166 to pay the estate tax liability on a deferred basis. The estate of a decedent dying prior to 1998 is entitled to deduct interest expense on a deferred estate tax obligation as an administrative expense under sec. 2053(a)(2). See Estate of Bahr v. Commissioner, 68 T.C. 74, 1977 WL 3655 (1977); Rev. Rul. 78-125, 1978-1 C.B. 292. This deduction is expressly disallowed by sec. 2053(c)(1)(D) with respect to estates of decedents dying after 1997.

7. The estate conceded $303,979 of the $2,040,249 valuation increase sought by respondent, and the estate further conceded respondent's $28,373 reduction in allowable deductions claimed on the return.

return.[8] Consequently, any addition to tax under section 6651(a)(1) that remains relates to the amount assessed by respondent prior to the issuance of the notice of deficiency.[9]

OPINION

By way of a motion for entry of decision, respondent contends that this Court does not have jurisdiction to review the assessed addition to tax. The question of the Court's jurisdiction is fundamental and must be addressed when raised by a party or on the Court's own motion.

This Court is a court of limited jurisdiction.* * * We may exercise jurisdiction only to the extent expressly provided by Congress. See sec. 7442; Breman v. Commissioner, 66 T.C. 61, 66 (1976). Section 6213 confers jurisdiction on this Court to redetermine deficiencies in income, estate, gift, and certain excise taxes. The provision which confers jurisdiction on this Court to review an addition to tax for late filing is section 6665.

Section 6665(a) sets forth the general rule that the deficiency procedures applicable to income, estate, gift, and certain excise taxes are equally applicable to additions to tax. See sec. 301.6659-1(a) and (b), Proced. & Admin. Regs. Section 6665(b) excludes from this general rule additions to tax under section 6651. As further provided in paragraph (1) of section 6665(b), however, the exclusion is not applicable "to that portion of such addition which is attributable to a deficiency in tax described in section 6211." Thus, the determination of whether we have jurisdiction over any portion of the assessed addition to tax turns on whether a deficiency within the meaning of section 6211 exists in this case. See Estate of DiRezza v. Commissioner, 78 T.C. 19, 26 (1982); sec. 301.6659-1(c)(1), Proced. & Admin. Regs.

Respondent contends that no statutory deficiency exists, given that the deficiency procedures and the parties' settlement resulted in an overassessment. The estate contends otherwise. The estate's argument is essentially that, but for the "fortuitous accrual of interest", the taxable

---

8. The statement of account dated Feb. 29, 2000, which the parties have stipulated, provides for a revised estate tax liability of $2,003,524. This figure is $162,041 less than the estate tax liability of $2,165,565 shown on the estate tax return.

9. The statement of account provides for a revised sec. 6651(a)(1) addition to tax of $342,343. This figure is $36,459 less than the addition to tax previously assessed by respondent of $378,802.

estate would have increased by $333,919[11] as a result of the deficiency procedures and the parties' settlement. The estate treats the tax attributable to this figure as the deficiency, ignoring the interest expense deduction in this context on grounds that the interest accrual occurred "independent of the deficiency process".

The estate's argument as to the existence of a deficiency must be rejected as it ignores the statutory definition. Section 6211(a) defines a deficiency as:

the amount by which the tax imposed * * * exceeds the excess of–

(1) the sum of

(A) the amount shown as tax by the taxpayer upon his return * * * plus

(B) the amounts previously assessed * * * as a deficiency, over–

(2) the amount of rebates * * * made.

This case involves no rebates. Furthermore, respondent has not previously assessed any amounts as a deficiency. Accordingly, the definition of a deficiency for present purposes is reduced to the excess of the estate tax imposed over the amount of estate tax shown on the return.

The parties' settlement in this case produced an overassessment in tax. This somewhat anomalous result (particularly in light of the concessions made by the estate) is attributable to the interest expense deduction, which the estate was prohibited from claiming prospectively on the estate tax return.[12] Yet, despite the unique circumstances of this case, it remains that the tax imposed on the estate does not exceed the amount of the tax shown on the estate tax return. A deficiency in tax, as defined by section 6211, therefore does not exist.

Having decided that there is no statutory deficiency, it follows that no portion of the assessed addition to tax is attributable to a deficiency. In other words, the requirements of paragraph (1) of section 6665(b) have

---

11. The $333,919 figure ignores an increase of $1,567 in deductions claimed by the estate on the estate tax return that was allowed by respondent in the notice of deficiency. The proper figure therefore should be $332,352.

12. The procedure for claiming a deduction for interest expense attributable to a deferred estate tax obligation is to file a supplemental estate tax return after the interest has accrued and been paid. See Rev. Proc. 81-27, 1981-2 C.B. 548. Therefore, a taxpayer may not take a deduction on the original estate tax return for interest which is estimated to accrue on the deferred estate tax obligation. See Bailly v. Commissioner, 81 T.C. 246 (1983), supplemented by 81 T.C. 949 (1983).

not been met. Accordingly, pursuant to section 6665(b), we lack jurisdiction over the addition to tax at issue.[13] * * *

* * *

Accordingly, respondent's motion for entry of decision will be granted. An appropriate order and decision will be entered.

Notes and Questions

In Estate of DiRezza v. Commissioner, 78 T.C. 19 (1982), cited in *Estate of Forgey*, an estate filed a late estate tax return. The Service determined that the estate owed an additional tax liability, plus a late filing penalty attributable to this amount. The estate conceded the additional tax liability, but contested the penalty. After receiving a notice of deficiency for the amount of the penalty, the estate petitioned the Tax Court for a redetermination. The Tax Court first addressed the issue of whether it had jurisdiction, since technically there was no deficiency when the notice of deficiency was sent because the estate had agreed to the assessment of the additional tax liability. But the court decided that as long as the penalty was attributable to a deficiency, the Tax Court had jurisdiction, even though at the time the notice of deficiency was issued the underlying tax technically did not constitute a deficiency. Can *Estate of DiRezza* be reconciled with *Estate of Forgey*?

In the case of a fraudulent failure to file a return, the amount of the § 6651(a)(1) penalty is increased from 5 percent to 15 percent per month, up to a maximum of 75 percent. IRC § 6651(f). As we saw in Chapter 3, if the return remains unfiled, the Service can prepare the return based on the information available to it. IRC § 6020(b). Such a return will not constitute a filed return for purposes of the late filing penalty under § 6651(a)(1), although it does constitute a return for purposes of the late payment penalty under § 6651(a)(2). IRC § 6651(g); see also § I.B., below.

1. Jennifer Jones is an individual taxpayer who uses the calendar year method of tax accounting. In March 2010, Jennifer requested and received an automatic extension of time to file her individual income tax return for the taxable year 2009 from April 15, 2010, her original due date, to October 15, 2010. She did not file her return, however, until March 15, 2011. On the return, Jennifer showed taxable income of

---

13. That we lack jurisdiction to decide the issue is confined to the facts of this case. We do not hold, for example, that this Court lacks jurisdiction under sec. 6512(b)(1) to decide the same issue in the case of an overpayment. See, e.g., Judge v. Commissioner, 88 T.C. 1175, 1180–1187 (1987). In this regard, the estate does not claim that it overpaid this addition, and we are unable to find that it did.

$86,500, and a tentative tax due of $18,500. Jennifer has tax credits of $14,500 attributable to income taxes withheld by her employer from her wages. She has no reasonable cause defense for her failure to file a timely return. What amount of § 6651(a)(1) penalty, if any, will Jennifer owe?

2. In question one, what amount of § 6651(a)(1) penalty, if any, will Jennifer owe if she remitted $1,000 with her Form 4868 when she requested the automatic filing extension?

3. Would it make any difference to the amount of the penalty in question one if Jennifer instead paid the $1,000 at the time she filed her return, but did not pay the remainder at that time because she could not afford to do so?

4. In question one, what is the amount of the penalty if $20,000 in income taxes had been withheld from Jennifer's wages, instead of $14,500? See Patronik-Holder v. Commissioner, 100 T.C. 374 (1993), acq. 1993-2 C.B. 1.

5. In question one, if Jennifer receives a notice from the Service on April 30, 2011, informing her that there is an additional deficiency of $2,000 attributable to her 2009 return, will this affect the amount of the § 6651(a)(1) penalty? If so, what procedure must the Service follow in assessing the penalty?

B. FAILURE TO PAY TAX SHOWN ON RETURN

If the tax shown on the return is not paid by the prescribed due date, including extensions of time to pay, a late payment penalty applies under § 6651(a)(2). The rate of this penalty is 0.5 percent per month (or fraction of a month) that the tax remains unpaid, up to a maximum of 25 percent. The rate is applied against a base amount equal to the amount of tax shown on the return, reduced by any credits claimed on the return, and further reduced by the amount of any tax paid on or before the beginning of the month in question (i.e., after the prescribed due date of the payment). IRC § 6651(b)(2).

In order for § 6651(a)(2) to apply, a return must be filed. If a taxpayer fails to file a return, a substituted return may be prepared by the Service under § 6020(b). This return will not be considered a return for purposes of the failure to file penalty, although it can be considered a return for purposes of the failure to pay penalty. IRC § 6651(g). The following case addresses the question of when, if ever, a substituted return will not trigger the failure to pay penalty.

CABIRAC v. COMMISSIONER
United States Tax Court, 2003.
120 T.C. 163.

RUWE, J.

* * *

C. *Additions to Tax and Penalty*

* * *

Section 6651(a)(1) provides an addition to tax for a failure to file a return on or before the specified filing date unless it is shown that such failure is due to reasonable cause and not due to willful neglect.[9] Once the Commissioner meets his initial burden of production to show that the addition to tax is appropriate, the taxpayer bears the burden of proving his failure to file timely the required return did not result from willful neglect and that the failure was due to reasonable cause.

Petitioner filed what he claimed to be valid returns for 1997 and 1998. However, those purported returns contain zeros on the relevant lines for computing petitioner's tax liability. Respondent did not accept those returns and treated the documents that petitioner filed as frivolous returns.

The majority of courts, including this Court, have held that, generally, a return that contains only zeros is not a valid return. See Taylor v. United States, 87 AFTR 2d 2001-2518, 2001-2 USTC par. 50,479 (D.C.Cir. 2001); United States v. Mosel, 738 F.2d 157 (6th Cir. 1984); United States v. Moore, 627 F.2d 830 (7th Cir. 1980). For example, in *United States v. Moore*, supra at 835, the Court of Appeals for the Seventh Circuit noted that a tax might conceivably be calculated on the basis of the zero entries; however, "it is not enough for a form to contain some income information; there must also be an honest and reasonable intent to supply the information required by the tax code."[10] In *United States v. Edelson*, 604 F.2d 232, 234 (3d Cir. 1979), the Third Circuit Court of Appeals, to which this case is appealable, stated: "it is now well established that tax forms that do not contain financial

---

9.   The addition to tax is equal to 5 percent of the amount of the tax required to be shown on the return if the failure to file is not for more than 1 month. An additional 5 percent is imposed for each month or fraction thereof in which the failure to file continues, to a maximum of 25 percent of the tax. The addition to tax is imposed on the net amount due. Sec. 6651(a)(1) and (b); Pratt v. Commissioner, T.C. Memo. 2002-279.

10.   See Beard v. Commissioner, 82 T.C. 766, 777, 1984 WL 15573 (1984), affd. 793 F.2d 139 (6th Cir. 1986), to the effect that a document constitutes a "return" for Federal income tax purposes if: (1) It contains sufficient data to calculate tax liability; (2) it purports to be a return; (3) it represents an honest and reasonable attempt to satisfy the requirements of the tax law; and (4) it is executed under penalties of perjury.

information upon which a taxpayer's tax liability can be determined do not constitute returns within the meaning of the Internal Revenue Code".[11]

The Forms 1040 and 1040A that petitioner submitted contain only zero entries, and it is clear from the attachments to those returns that petitioner did not make an honest and reasonable attempt to supply the information required by the Internal Revenue Code. We hold that petitioner did not file valid returns. Petitioner did not establish that his failure to file was due to reasonable cause. We therefore sustain the section 6651(a)(1) additions to tax as determined.

* * *

Section 6651(a)(2) provides for an addition to tax in the case of a failure to pay an amount of tax shown on a return.[12] Section 6651(a)(2) applies only in the case of an amount of tax shown on a return. Petitioner did not file valid returns for 1997 and 1998; however, respondent prepared SFRs [eds.: substitute for return] which he claims should be considered in conjunction with a subsequently prepared notice of proposed adjustments. Respondent argues that when these two documents are considered together, they constitute returns under section 6020(b).[13] Under section 6651(g), a return prepared by the Secretary under section 6020(b) is treated as "the return filed by the taxpayer for purposes of determining the amount of the addition" under section

---

11. In United States v. Long, 618 F.2d 74, 75 (9th Cir. 1980), the Court of Appeals for the Ninth Circuit held that a return containing only zeros was a return for purposes of sec. 7203 since it contained information relating to the taxpayer's income from which the tax could be computed. The holding in United States v. Long, supra, represents the minority view that we do not follow in the present case.

12. The addition to tax is equal to 0.5 percent of the amount shown as tax on the return if the failure to pay is not for more than 1 month, with an additional 0.5 percent for each additional month or fraction thereof during which such failure to pay continues, not exceeding 25 percent in the aggregate. Sec. 6651(a)(2). The addition to tax under sec. 6651(a)(1) is reduced by the amount of the addition under sec. 6651(a)(2) for any month (or fraction thereof) to which an addition to tax under sec. 6651(a)(1) and (2) applies. Sec. 6651(c)(1).

13. Sec. 6020(b) provides:

SEC. 6020(b) Execution of Return by Secretary.–

(1) Authority of secretary to execute return.– If any person fails to make any return required by any internal revenue law or regulation made thereunder at the time prescribed therefor, or makes, willfully or otherwise, a false or fraudulent return, the Secretary shall make such return from his own knowledge and from such information as he can obtain through testimony or otherwise.

(2) Status of returns.– Any return so made and subscribed by the Secretary shall be prima facie good and sufficient for all legal purposes.

6651(a)(2).[14] However, the documents that respondent prepared in this case do not qualify as returns under section 6020(b).

We have previously discussed the requirements of a section 6020(b) return. In *Phillips v. Commissioner*, 86 T.C. 433, 437-438 (1986), affd. in part and revd. in part on another issue 851 F.2d 1492 (D.C.Cir. 1988), we held that a "dummy return", i.e., page 1 of a Form 1040 showing only the taxpayer's name, address, and Social Security number, was not a section 6020(b) return. In *Millsap v. Commissioner*, 91 T.C. 926 (1988), respondent prepared Forms 1040 containing the taxpayer's name, address, Social Security number, and filing status. The Forms 1040 contained no information regarding income or tax and were not subscribed. However, attached to the Forms 1040 was a previously prepared revenue agent's report which contained sufficient information from which to compute the taxpayer's tax liability and was subscribed. We held that the Form 1040 together with the attached revenue agent's report met the requirements for a section 6020(b) return.

The SFRs that the parties stipulated were not subscribed as required by section 6020(b)(2) and show zeros on the relevant lines for computing a tax liability, and do not show any tax due. Indeed, the SFRs contain essentially the same information and entries as the forms petitioner submitted as returns for 1997 and 1998, and we have already held that the forms submitted by petitioner were not valid returns. Moreover, although each of the SFRs contains pages 1 and 2 of a Form 1040, those documents are essentially the same as the "dummy returns" which we held did not constitute section 6020(b) returns in *Phillips v. Commissioner*, supra. The SFRs provide no basis upon which to calculate petitioner's tax liabilities for 1997 and 1998, or, for that matter, the additions to tax under section 6651(a)(2).

* * *

We find that the notice of proposed adjustments and the revenue agent's report cannot be considered to be part of the SFRs that respondent prepared. We cannot agree with respondent's suggestion that the presence of what are essentially "dummy returns" and a revenue agent's report somewhere in the record meets the requirements of section 6020(b). If that were the case, respondent could dispense with any

---

14. Sec. 6651(g) provides:

SEC. 6651(g). Treatment of Returns Prepared by Secretary Under Section 6020(b).–

In the case of any return made by the Secretary under section 6020(b)

(1) such return shall be disregarded for purposes of determining the amount of the addition under paragraph (1) of subsection (a), but

(2) such return shall be treated as the return filed by the taxpayer for purposes of determining the amount of the addition under paragraphs (2) and (3) of subsection (a).

degree of formality in preparing section 6020(b) returns, and sections 6020(b) and 6651(g) would apply in every case that comes before us where a return was not filed and a tax was not paid. Certainly, our decisions in *Phillips* and *Millsap* mandate a greater degree of formality than that suggested by respondent.

The record in the instant case contains essentially the same materials that were involved in *Phillips v. Commissioner*, supra. Notably, in *Phillips*, the Commissioner's file contained a copy of a substitute for return prepared by the Commissioner for 1979 and consisted of page 1 of a Form 1040 that showed only the taxpayer's name, address, and Social Security number. The record did not contain copies of any substitutes for return for 1980 and 1981. However, a certified transcript of account indicated that Forms 1040 were filed as the taxpayer's returns by the Commissioner for 1979, 1980, and 1981. In addition, before the Commissioner mailed the notice of deficiency to the taxpayer, he issued a notice which entitled the taxpayer to an administrative review of the proposed deficiency. We held that those items did not meet the requirements of a section 6020(b) return.[19]

On the basis of the evidentiary record and previously cited cases, we hold that respondent has not met his burden of production with respect to the appropriateness of imposing the section 6651(a)(2) additions to tax.

* * *

Notes and Question

An amended return may affect the amount of the § 6651 penalties. For instance, if the amended return decreases the tax on the original return, this will modify the net amount of tax due and will require a recalculation of the penalties. The period during which the penalties run will not be affected, however. If the amended return shows an additional tax due, this will require a recalculation of the failure of the file penalty,

---

19. However, in Smalldridge v. Commissioner, 804 F.2d 125 (10th Cir. 1986), affg. T.C. Memo.1984-434, in an opinion issued 6 months after our first opinion in *Phillips*, the Tenth Circuit Court of Appeals held that a document signed by the examiner, which included the taxpayer's name, address, Social Security number, wage information for the years in question, a personal exemption where applicable, and indicated married, filing separately status constituted a return filed by the Commissioner pursuant to sec. 6020(b). In our subsequent opinion in *Phillips v. Commissioner*, 88 T.C. at 534 n. 8, concerning a claim under sec. 7430, we distinguished the holding in *Smalldridge* on the basis that the Court of Appeals had concluded that the Commissioner filed valid returns pursuant to sec. 6020(b) in *Smalldridge*, whereas in *Phillips*, "No such returns were filed". But see Phillips v. Commissioner, 88 T.C. at 540 (Swift, J., dissenting) (citing the Court of Appeals opinion in *Smalldridge* as a basis for concluding that there was no justification for a finding that the Commissioner was unreasonable in arguing that certain audit examination documents and a notice of deficiency constituted a "return").

but not a recalculation of the failure to pay penalty. Why? See IRC § 6651(b); IRM 20.1.2.1.2.

The rate of the failure to pay penalty may be increased or decreased in certain cases. For instance, if the Service sends the taxpayer a notice of intent to levy under § 6331(d) (see Chapter 7 for a discussion of the collection process), and the taxpayer fails to pay the tax within ten days of the receipt of the notice, the penalty rate increases to one percent per month for each month afterward during which the tax remains unpaid. IRC § 6651(d). The same increase applies to a failure to pay the tax after the issuance of a notice and demand for immediate payment pursuant to a jeopardy assessment. *Id.* If the taxpayer has entered into an installment agreement with the Service under § 6159, and has timely filed her return pursuant to the agreement but is not able to pay the tax at that time, the failure to pay penalty is limited to half (0.25 percent) the usual rate. IRC § 6651(h).

The § 6651 penalties do not apply to a failure to pay estimated taxes. Instead, separate civil penalties apply to such failures under § 6654 (individuals) and § 6655 (corporations). Section 6651 penalties also do not apply if the taxpayer files a petition in bankruptcy. IRC § 6658(a). If a late payment or nonpayment is due to a willful or intentional failure to pay, the delinquency penalties may be imposed along with criminal penalties under § 7203. See Chapter 8 for a discussion of criminal penalties.

Under § 6651(c), if both the failure to file and failure to pay penalties apply simultaneously, the failure to pay penalty will offset the failure to file penalty during the period the two penalties run together.

Problems

1. In question one of § A, above, if Jennifer had filed her return on August 15, 2010, remitting the remaining tax due of $ 4,000 at that time, would she have been subject to any delinquency penalty under § 6651? See Reg. § 301.6651-1(c)(3).

2. Dick and Jane filed their 2005 joint income tax return on June 15, 2010. The return had been due on April 15, 2006. They had failed to request any extensions of time to file or pay, and their tardiness was not due to reasonable cause. The tax liability shown on their return was $100,000, although they claimed credits on the late return of $75,000 attributable to estimated tax payments made during 2005, and $10,000 attributable to taxes that had been withheld at the source during 2005. They remitted the remaining $15,000 on June 15, 2010, when they filed

their 2005 return. How will their delinquency penalties under § 6651 (a)(1) and (a)(2) be calculated? How many months will these penalties run?

3. In question two, how, if at all, will the delinquency penalties be affected if Dick and Jane subsequently determine that their tax liability for 2005 has been overstated by $5,000?

4. In question two, how, if at all, will the delinquency penalties be affected if, in the alternative, the Service subsequently determines that Dick and Jane's tax liability has been understated by $5,000?

C. FAILURE TO PAY AFTER NOTICE AND DEMAND

Section 6651(a)(2) pertains only to a late payment of the tax shown on the return. But what about a late payment of tax required to be shown on the return but not shown? If the taxpayer receives a notice and demand for payment of a deficiency, and the tax remains unpaid after 21 days from the date of the notice, § 6651(a)(3) provides a 0.5 percent penalty for each month or fraction of a month that the deficiency remains unpaid. (The grace period is ten days if the amount of the deficiency is $100,000 or more). Like the § 6651(a)(2) penalty, the § 6651(a)(3) penalty runs to a maximum rate of 25 percent. If the tax is paid within 21 days of the notice and demand, no § 6651(a)(3) penalty is imposed. Likewise, if the taxpayer demonstrates that the failure to pay within 21 days of the notice and demand is attributable to reasonable cause, the penalty will not apply.

The base amount against which the penalty rate is applied is determined by reducing the amount of the deficiency stated in the notice and demand by any tax paid on or before the beginning of the month in which the addition to tax is determined. While the § 6651(a)(3) penalty is very similar to the § 6651(a)(2) penalty, a difference is that the § 6651(a)(3) penalty will not offset the § 6651(a)(1) penalty when the two penalties are applied together. What is the rationale for this?

D. REASONABLE CAUSE

The delinquency penalties will not be imposed if the failure to file or pay is due to reasonable cause and not to willful neglect.

UNITED STATES v. BOYLE
United States Supreme Court, 1985.
469 U.S. 241, 105 S.Ct. 687, 83 L.Ed.2d 622.

CHIEF JUSTICE BURGER delivered the opinion of the Court.

We granted certiorari to resolve a conflict among the Circuits on whether a taxpayer's reliance on an attorney to prepare and file a tax return constitutes "reasonable cause" under § 6651(a)(1) of the Internal Revenue Code, so as to defeat a statutory penalty incurred because of a late filing.

I.
A.

Respondent, Robert W. Boyle, was appointed executor of the will of his mother, Myra Boyle, who died on September 14, 1978; respondent retained Ronald Keyser to serve as attorney for the estate. Keyser informed respondent that the estate must file a federal estate tax return, but he did not mention the deadline for filing this return. Under 26 U.S.C. § 6075(a), the return was due within nine months of the decedent's death, i.e., not later than June 14, 1979.

Although a businessman, respondent was not experienced in the field of federal estate taxation, other than having been executor of his father's will 20 years earlier. It is undisputed that he relied on Keyser for instruction and guidance. He cooperated fully with his attorney and provided Keyser with all relevant information and records. Respondent and his wife contacted Keyser a number of times during the spring and summer of 1979 to inquire about the progress of the proceedings and the preparation of the tax return; they were assured that they would be notified when the return was due and that the return would be filed "in plenty of time." When respondent called Keyser on September 6, 1979, he learned for the first time that the return was by then overdue. Apparently, Keyser had overlooked the matter because of a clerical oversight in omitting the filing date from Keyser's master calendar. Respondent met with Keyser on September 11, and the return was filed on September 13, three months late.

B.

Acting pursuant to 26 U.S.C. § 6651(a)(1), the Internal Revenue Service assessed against the estate an additional tax of $17,124.45 as a penalty for the late filing, with $1,326.56 in interest. Section 6651(a)(1) reads in pertinent part:

> "In case of failure * * * to file any return ** on the date prescribed therefor * * *, *unless it is shown that such failure is due to reasonable cause and not due to willful neglect*, there shall be added to the amount required to be shown as tax on such return 5 percent of the amount of such tax if the failure is for not more than 1 month, with an additional 5 percent for each additional month or fraction thereof during which such failure continues, not exceeding 25 percent in the aggregate * * *." (Emphasis added.)

A Treasury Regulation provides that, to demonstrate "reasonable cause," a taxpayer filing a late return must show that he "exercised ordinary business care and prudence and was nevertheless unable to file the return within the prescribed time." 26 CFR § 301.6651-1(c)(1) (1984).[1]

Respondent paid the penalty and filed a claim for a refund. He conceded that the assessment for interest was proper, but contended that the penalty was unjustified because his failure to file the return on time was "due to reasonable cause," i.e., reliance on his attorney. Respondent brought suit in the United States District Court, which concluded that the claim was controlled by the Court of Appeals' holding in Rohrabaugh v. United States, 611 F.2d 211 (CA7 1979). In *Rohrabaugh*, the United States Court of Appeals for the Seventh Circuit held that reliance upon counsel constitutes "reasonable cause" under § 6651(a)(1) when: (1) the taxpayer is unfamiliar with the tax law; (2) the taxpayer makes full disclosure of all relevant facts to the attorney that he relies upon, and maintains contact with the attorney from time to time during the administration of the estate; and (3) the taxpayer has otherwise exercised ordinary business care and prudence. 611 F.2d, at 215, 219. The District Court held that, under *Rohrabaugh*, respondent had established "reasonable cause" for the late filing of his tax return;

---

1. The Internal Revenue Service has articulated eight reasons for a late filing that it considers to constitute "reasonable cause." These reasons include unavoidable postal delays, the taxpayer's timely filing of a return with the wrong IRS office, the taxpayer's reliance on the erroneous advice of an IRS officer or employee, the death or serious illness of the taxpayer or a member of his immediate family, the taxpayer's unavoidable absence, destruction by casualty of the taxpayer's records or place of business, failure of the IRS to furnish the taxpayer with the necessary forms in a timely fashion, and the inability of an IRS representative to meet with the taxpayer when the taxpayer makes a timely visit to an IRS office in an attempt to secure information or aid in the preparation of a return. Internal Revenue Manual (CCH) § 4350, (24) ¶ 22.2(2) (Mar. 20, 1980) (Audit Technique Manual for Estate Tax Examiners). If the cause asserted by the taxpayer does not implicate any of these eight reasons, the district director determines whether the asserted cause is reasonable. "A cause for delinquency which appears to a person of ordinary prudence and intelligence as a reasonable cause for delay in filing a return and which clearly negatives willful neglect will be accepted as reasonable." Id., ¶ 22.2(3).

accordingly, it granted summary judgment for respondent and ordered refund of the penalty. A divided panel of the Seventh Circuit, with three opinions, affirmed. 710 F.2d 1251 (1983).

We granted certiorari, 466 U.S. 903, 104 S.Ct. 1676, 80 L.Ed.2d 152 (1984), and we reverse.

II.

A.

Congress' purpose in the prescribed civil penalty was to ensure timely filing of tax returns to the end that tax liability will be ascertained and paid promptly. The relevant statutory deadline provision is clear; it mandates that all federal estate tax returns be filed within nine months from the decedent's death, 26 U.S.C. § 6075(a).[2] Failure to comply incurs a penalty of 5 percent of the ultimately determined tax for each month the return is late, with a maximum of 25 percent of the base tax. To escape the penalty, the taxpayer bears the heavy burden of proving both (1) that the failure did not result from "willful neglect," and (2) that the failure was "due to reasonable cause." 26 U.S.C. § 6651(a)(1).

The meaning of these two standards has become clear over the near-70 years of their presence in the statutes.[3] As used here, the term "willful neglect" may be read as meaning a conscious, intentional failure or reckless indifference. Like "willful neglect," the term "reasonable cause" is not defined in the Code, but the relevant Treasury Regulation calls on the taxpayer to demonstrate that he exercised "ordinary business care and prudence" but nevertheless was "unable to file the return within the prescribed time."[4] 26 CFR § 301.6651(c)(1) (1984). The Commis-

---

2.   Section 6081(a) of the Internal Revenue Code authorizes the IRS to grant "a reasonable extension of time," generally no longer than six months, for filing any return.

3.   Congress added the relevant language to the tax statutes in 1916. For many years before that, § 3176 mandated a 50 percent penalty "in case of a *refusal* or *neglect*, except in cases of sickness or absence, to make a list or return, or to verify the same * * *." Rev. Stat. § 3176 (emphasis added). The Revenue Act of 1916 amended this provision to require the 50 percent penalty for failure to file a return within the prescribed time, "except that, when a return is voluntarily and without notice from the collector filed after such time and it is shown that the failure to file it was *due to a reasonable cause and not due to willful neglect*, no such addition shall be made to the tax." Revenue Act of 1916, ch. 463, § 16, 39 Stat. 756, 775 (emphasis added). No committee reports or congressional hearings or debates discuss the change in language. It would be logical to assume that Congress intended "willful neglect" to replace "refusal"--both expressions implying intentional failure--and "[absence of] reasonable cause" to replace "neglect"--both expressions implying carelessness.

4.   Respondent contends that the statute must be construed to apply a standard of willfulness only, and that the Treasury Regulation is incompatible with this construction of the statute. He argues that the Regulation converts the statute into a test of "ordinary business care," because a taxpayer who demonstrates ordinary business care can never be guilty of "willful neglect." By

sioner does not contend that respondent's failure to file the estate tax return on time was willful or reckless. The question to be resolved is whether, under the statute, reliance on an attorney in the instant circumstances is a "reasonable cause" for failure to meet the deadline.

B.

In affirming the District Court, the Court of Appeals recognized the difficulties presented by its formulation but concluded that it was bound by Rohrabaugh v. United States, 611 F.2d 211 (CA7 1979). The Court of Appeals placed great importance on the fact that respondent engaged the services of an experienced attorney specializing in probate matters and that he duly inquired from time to time as to the progress of the proceedings. As in *Rohrabaugh*, the Court of Appeals in this case emphasized that its holding was narrowly drawn and closely tailored to the facts before it. The court stressed that the question of "reasonable cause" was an issue to be determined on a case-by-case basis.

Other Courts of Appeals have dealt with the issue of "reasonable cause" for a late filing and reached contrary conclusions.[5] In Ferrando v. United States, 245 F.2d 582 (CA9 1957), the court held that taxpayers have a personal and nondelegable duty to file a return on time, and that reliance on an attorney to fulfill this obligation does not constitute "reasonable cause" for a tardy filing. Id., at 589. The Fifth Circuit has similarly held that the responsibility for ensuring a timely filing is the taxpayer's alone, and that the taxpayer's reliance on his tax advisers-- accountants or attorneys--is not a "reasonable cause." Millette & Associates v. Commissioner, 594 F.2d 121, 124-125 (1979) (per curiam); Logan Lumber Co. v. Commissioner, 365 F.2d 846, 854 (1966). The

---

construing "reasonable cause" as the equivalent of "ordinary business care," respondent urges, the IRS has removed from consideration any question of willfulness.

We cannot accept this reasoning. Congress obviously intended to make absence of fault a prerequisite to avoidance of the late-filing penalty. See n. 3, supra. A taxpayer seeking a refund must therefore prove that his failure to file on time was the result neither of carelessness, reckless indifference, nor intentional failure. Thus, the Service's correlation of "reasonable cause" with "ordinary business care and prudence" is consistent with Congress' intent, and over 40 years of case law as well. That interpretation merits deference. See, e.g., Chevron U.S.A. Inc. v. Natural Resources Defense Council, Inc., 467 U.S. 837, 844, and n. 14, 104 S.Ct. 2778, 2782, and n. 14, 81 L.Ed.2d 694 (1984).

5. Although at one point the Court of Appeals for the Sixth Circuit held that reliance on counsel could constitute reasonable cause, see In re Fisk's Estate, 203 F.2d 358, 360 (1953), the Sixth Circuit appears now to be following those courts that have held that the taxpayer has a nondelegable duty to ascertain the deadline for a return and ensure that the return is filed by that deadline. See Estate of Geraci v. Commissioner, 32 TCM 424, 425 (1973), aff'd, 502 F.2d 1148 (CA6 1974), cert. denied, 420 U.S. 992, 95 S.Ct. 1428, 43 L.Ed.2d 673 (1975); Estate of Duttenhofer v. Commissioner, 49 T.C. 200, 205 (1967), aff'd, 410 F.2d 302 (CA6 1969) (per curiam).

Eighth Circuit also has concluded that reliance on counsel does not constitute "reasonable cause." Smith v. United States, 702 F.2d 741, 743 (1983) (per curiam); Boeving v. United States, 650 F.2d 493, 495 (1981); Estate of Lillehei v. Commissioner, 638 F.2d 65, 66 (1981) (per curiam).

III.

We need not dwell on the similarities or differences in the facts presented by the conflicting holdings. The time has come for a rule with as "bright" a line as can be drawn consistent with the statute and implementing regulations.[6] Deadlines are inherently arbitrary; fixed dates, however, are often essential to accomplish necessary results. The Government has millions of taxpayers to monitor, and our system of self-assessment in the initial calculation of a tax simply cannot work on any basis other than one of strict filing standards. Any less rigid standard would risk encouraging a lax attitude toward filing dates.[7]

---

    6. The administrative regulations and practices exempt late filings from the penalty when the tardiness results from postal delays, illness, and other factors largely beyond the taxpayer's control. The principle underlying the IRS regulations and practices--that a taxpayer should not be penalized for circumstances beyond his control--already recognizes a range of exceptions which there is no reason for us to pass on today. This principle might well cover a filing default by a taxpayer who relied on an attorney or accountant because the taxpayer was, for some reason, incapable by objective standards of meeting the criteria of "ordinary business care and prudence." In that situation, however, the disability alone could well be an acceptable excuse for a late filing.

    But this case does not involve the effect of a taxpayer's *disability*; it involves the effect of a taxpayer's *reliance* on an agent employed by the taxpayer, and our holding necessarily is limited to that issue rather than the wide range of issues that might arise in future cases under the statute and regulations. Those potential future cases are purely hypothetical at the moment and simply have no bearing on the issue now before us. The concurring opinion seems to agree in part. After four pages of discussion, it concludes:

        "Because the respondent here was fully capable of meeting the required standard of ordinary business care and prudence, we need not decide the issue of whether and under what circumstances a taxpayer who presents evidence that he was unable to adhere to the required standard might be entitled to relief from the penalty."

This conclusion is unquestionably correct. See also, e.g., Reed v. Ross, 468 U.S. 1, 8, n. 5, 104 S.Ct. 2901, 2906, n. 5, 82 L.Ed.2d 1 (1984); Heckler v. Day, 467 U.S. 104, 119, nn. 33 and 34, 104 S.Ct. 2249, 2257-2258, nn. 33 and 34 (1984); Kosak v. United States, 465 U.S. 848, 853, n. 8, 104 S.Ct. 1519, 1523, n. 8, 79 L.Ed.2d 860 (1984); Bell v. New Jersey, 461 U.S. 773, 779, n. 4, 103 S.Ct. 2187, 2191, n. 4, 76 L.Ed.2d 312 (1983).

    7. Many systems that do not collect taxes on a self-assessment basis have experienced difficulties in administering tax collection. See J. Wagner, France's Soak-the-Rich Tax, Congressional Quarterly (Editorial Research Reports), Oct. 12, 1982; Dodging Taxes in the Old World, Time, Mar. 28, 1983, p. 32.

Prompt payment of taxes is imperative to the Government, which should not have to assume the burden of unnecessary ad hoc determinations.[8]

Congress has placed the burden of prompt filing on the executor, not on some agent or employee of the executor. The duty is fixed and clear; Congress intended to place upon the taxpayer an obligation to ascertain the statutory deadline and then to meet that deadline, except in a very narrow range of situations. Engaging an attorney to assist in the probate proceedings is plainly an exercise of the "ordinary business care and prudence" prescribed by the regulations, but that does not provide an answer to the question we face here. To say that it was "reasonable" for the executor to *assume* that the attorney would comply with the statute may resolve the matter as between them, but not with respect to the executor's obligations under the statute. Congress has charged the executor with an unambiguous, precisely defined duty to file the return within nine months; extensions are granted fairly routinely. That the attorney, as the executor's agent, was expected to attend to the matter does not relieve the principal of his duty to comply with the statute.

This case is not one in which a taxpayer has relied on the erroneous advice of counsel concerning a question of law. Courts have frequently held that "reasonable cause" is established when a taxpayer shows that he reasonably relied on the advice of an accountant or attorney that it was unnecessary to file a return, even when such advice turned out to have been mistaken. See, e.g., United States v. Kroll, 547 F.2d 393, 395-396 (CA7 1977); Commissioner v. American Assn. of Engineers Employment, Inc., 204 F.2d 19, 21 (CA7 1953); Burton Swartz Land Corp. v. Commissioner, 198 F.2d 558, 560 (CA5 1952). This Court also has implied that, in such a situation, reliance on the opinion of a tax adviser may constitute reasonable cause for failure to file a return. See Commissioner v. Lane-Wells Co., 321 U.S. 219, 64 S.Ct. 511, 88 L.Ed. 684 (1944) (remanding for determination whether failure to file return

---

8. A number of courts have indicated that "reasonable cause" is a question of fact, to be determined only from the particular situation presented in each particular case. See, e.g., Estate of Mayer v. Commissioner, 351 F.2d 617 (CA2 1965) (per curiam), cert. denied, 383 U.S. 935, 86 S.Ct. 1065, 15 L.Ed.2d 852 (1966); Coates v. Commissioner, 234 F.2d 459, 462 (CA8 1956). This view is not entirely correct. Whether the elements that constitute "reasonable cause" are *present* in a given situation is a question of fact, but what elements *must* be present to constitute "reasonable cause" is a question of law. See, e.g., Haywood Lumber & Mining Co. v. Commissioner, 178 F.2d 769, 772 (CA2 1950); Daley v. United States, 480 F.Supp. 808, 811 (ND 1979). When faced with a recurring situation, such as that presented by the instant case, the courts of appeals should not be reluctant to formulate a clear rule of law to deal with that situation.

was due to reasonable cause, when taxpayer was advised that filing was not required).[9]

When an accountant or attorney advises a taxpayer on a matter of tax law, such as whether a liability exists, it is reasonable for the taxpayer to rely on that advice. Most taxpayers are not competent to discern error in the substantive advice of an accountant or attorney. To require the taxpayer to challenge the attorney, to seek a "second opinion," or to try to monitor counsel on the provisions of the Code himself would nullify the very purpose of seeking the advice of a presumed expert in the first place. "Ordinary business care and prudence" do not demand such actions.

By contrast, one does not have to be a tax expert to know that tax returns have fixed filing dates and that taxes must be paid when they are due. In short, tax returns imply deadlines. Reliance by a lay person on a lawyer is of course common; but that reliance cannot function as a substitute for compliance with an unambiguous statute. Among the first duties of the representative of a decedent's estate is to identify and assemble the assets of the decedent and to ascertain tax obligations. Although it is common practice for an executor to engage a professional to prepare and file an estate tax return, a person experienced in business matters can perform that task personally. It is not unknown for an executor to prepare tax returns, take inventories, and carry out other significant steps in the probate of an estate. It is even not uncommon for an executor to conduct probate proceedings without counsel.

It requires no special training or effort to ascertain a deadline and make sure that it is met. The failure to make a timely filing of a tax return is not excused by the taxpayer's reliance on an agent, and such reliance is not "reasonable cause" for a late filing under § 6651(a)(1). The judgment of the Court of Appeals is reversed.

It is so ordered.

---

9. Courts have differed over whether a taxpayer demonstrates "reasonable cause" when, in reliance on the advice of his accountant or attorney, the taxpayer files a return after the actual due date but within the time the adviser erroneously told him was available. Compare Sanderling, Inc. v. Commissioner, 571 F.2d 174, 178-179 (CA3 1978) (finding "reasonable cause" in such a situation); Estate of Rapelje v. Commissioner, 73 T.C. 82, 90, n. 9 (1979) (same); Estate of DiPalma v. Commissioner, 71 T.C. 324, 327 (1978) (same), acq., 1979-1 Cum.Bull. 1; Estate of Bradley v. Commissioner, 33 TCM 70, 72-73 (1974) (same), aff'd, 511 F.2d 527 (CA6 1975), with Estate of Kerber v. United States, 717 F.2d 454, 454-455, and n. 1 (CA8 1983) (per curiam) (no "reasonable cause"), cert. pending, No. 83-1038; Smith v. United States, 702 F.2d 741, 742 (CA8 1983) (same); Sarto v. United States, 563 F.Supp. 476, 478 (ND Cal.1983) (same). We need not and do not address ourselves to this issue.

JUSTICE BRENNAN, with whom JUSTICE MARSHALL, JUSTICE POWELL, AND JUSTICE O'CONNOR join, concurring.

I concur that the judgment must be reversed. Although the standard of taxpayer liability found in 26 U.S.C. § 6651(a)(1) might plausibly be characterized as ambiguous,[1] courts and the Internal Revenue Service have for almost 70 years interpreted the statute as imposing a standard of "ordinary business care and prudence." I agree with the Court that we should defer to this long-standing construction. I also agree that taxpayers in the exercise of ordinary business care and prudence must ascertain relevant filing deadlines and ensure that those deadlines are met. As the Court correctly holds, a taxpayer cannot avoid the reach of § 6651(a)(1) merely by delegating this duty to an attorney, accountant, or other individual.[2]

I write separately, however, to underscore the importance of an issue that the Court expressly leaves open. Specifically, I believe there is a substantial argument that the "ordinary business care and prudence" standard is applicable only to the "ordinary person"–namely, one who is physically and mentally capable of knowing, remembering, and complying with a filing deadline. In the instant case, there is no question that the respondent not only failed to exercise ordinary business care in monitoring the progress of his mother's estate, but also made no showing that he was *unable* to exercise the usual care and diligence required of an executor. The outcome could be different if a taxpayer were able to demonstrate that, for reasons of incompetence or infirmity, he understandably was unable to meet the standard of ordinary business care and prudence. In such circumstances, there might well be no good reason for imposing the harsh penalty of § 6651(a)(1) over and above the prescribed statutory interest penalty. See 26 U.S.C. §§ 6601(a), 6621(b).

The Court proclaims the need "for a rule with as 'bright' a line as can be drawn," and it stresses that the Government "should not have to assume the burden of unnecessary ad hoc determinations." On the other hand, it notes that the "bright line" might not cover a taxpayer who is "incapable by objective standards of meeting the criteria of 'ordinary

---

1.   For each month or fraction of a month that a tax return is overdue, 26 U.S.C. § 6651(a)(1) provides for a mandatory penalty of 5% of the tax (up to a maximum of 25%) "unless it is shown that [the failure to file on time] is due to reasonable cause and not due to willful neglect." As Judge Posner observed in his dissent below, "in making 'willful neglect' the opposite of 'reasonable cause' the statute might seem to have modified the ordinary meaning of 'reasonable' * * *." 710 F.2d 1251, 1256 (CA7 1983).

2.   As the Court emphasizes, this principle of non-delegation does not extend to situations in which a taxpayer reasonably relies on expert advice concerning substantive questions of tax law, such as whether a liability exists in the first instance.

business care and prudence,' "reasoning that "the disability alone could well be an acceptable excuse for a late filing."

I share the Court's reservations about the sweep of its "bright line" rule. If the Government were determined to draw a "bright line" and to avoid the "burden" of "ad hoc determinations," it would not provide for any exemptions from the penalty provision. Congress has emphasized, however, that exemptions *must* be made where a taxpayer demonstrates "reasonable cause." 26 U.S.C. § 6651(a)(1). Accordingly, the IRS already allows dispensations where, for example, a taxpayer or a member of his family has been seriously ill, the taxpayer has been unavoidably absent, or the taxpayer's records have been destroyed. Internal Revenue Manual § 4350, (24) ¶ 22.2(2) (Mar. 20, 1980) (Audit Technique Manual for Estate Tax Examiners). Thus the Government itself has eschewed a bright-line rule and committed itself to necessarily case-by-case decision-making. The gravamen of the IRS's exemptions seems to be that a taxpayer will not be penalized where he reasonably was *unable* to exercise ordinary business care and prudence. The IRS does not appear to interpret its enumerated exemptions as being exclusive, see id, ¶ 22.2(3), and it might well act arbitrarily if it purported to do otherwise.[3] Thus a substantial argument can be made that the draconian penalty provision should not apply where a taxpayer convincingly demonstrates that, for whatever reason, he reasonably was unable to exercise ordinary business care.

Many executors are widows or widowers well along in years, and a penalty against the "estate" usually will be a penalty against their inheritance. Moreover, the principles we announce today will apply with full force to the personal income tax returns required of every individual who receives an annual gross income of $1,000 or more. See 26 U.S.C. § 6651(a)(1); see also § 6012. Although the overwhelming majority of taxpayers are fully capable of understanding and complying with the prescribed filing deadlines, exceptional cases necessarily will arise where taxpayers, by virtue of senility, mental retardation, or other causes, are understandably unable to attain society's norm. The Court today properly emphasizes the need for efficient tax collection and stern incentives. But it seems to me that Congress and the IRS already have

---

3. It is difficult to perceive a material distinction, for example, between a filing delay that results from a serious illness in the taxpayer's immediate family or a taxpayer's unavoidable absence--situations in which the IRS excuses the delay--and a filing delay that comes about because the taxpayer is infirm or incompetent. The common thread running through all these unfortunate situations is that the taxpayer, for reasons beyond his control, has been unable to exercise ordinary business care and prudence.

made the decision that efficiency should yield to other values in appropriate circumstances.

Because the respondent here was fully capable of meeting the required standard of ordinary business care and prudence, we need not decide the issue of whether and under what circumstances a taxpayer who presents evidence that he was *unable* to adhere to the required standard might be entitled to relief from the penalty. As the Court has expressly left this issue open for another day, I join the Court's opinion.

Notes and Questions

While the *Boyle* case dealt with a failure to file penalty, reasonable cause also can excuse the taxpayer from a late payment penalty. In determining reasonable cause, the Service will consider whether the taxpayer exercised ordinary business care and prudence in providing for payment of the tax liability, but either was unable to pay the tax or would suffer an undue hardship if forced to pay on the due date. Reg. § 1.6161-1(b). The Service also will consider the facts and circumstances of the taxpayer's financial condition, including the amount and nature of the taxpayer's expenditures in light of the income the taxpayer could reasonably expect to have received prior to the date prescribed for payment of the tax. Reg. § 301.6651-1(c).

There is a split among the circuits, however, as to whether reasonable cause permits an examination of the taxpayer's financial condition with respect to penalties imposed for failure to pay employment taxes. The Sixth Circuit has held that a taxpayer's financial condition can *never* constitute reasonable cause, (see Brewery, Inc. v. United States, 33 F.3d 589 (6th Cir. 1994)), while the Second and Third Circuits have held that all factors that otherwise constitute reasonable cause, including a taxpayer's financial condition, *must* be considered (see Fran Corp. v. United States, 164 F.3d 814 (2d Cir. 1999); East Wind Industries, Inc. v. United States, 196 F.3d 499 (3rd Cir. 1999)).

As Justice Brennan notes, the reasonable cause defense involves a subjective determination of the particular facts and circumstances that apply to the taxpayer's case. In order to constitute a valid reasonable cause defense, however, those facts and circumstances must be attributable directly to the taxpayer's failure to comply with the tax laws.

In addition to the examples of reasonable cause that the Court lists in footnote one, other examples include: lack of records despite the taxpayer's ordinary business care and prudence, and a recent change in the tax law which the taxpayer could not be reasonably expected to know. IRM 20.1.1.3.2.2 (2-22-2008). On the other hand, mistake, forgetfulness, or reliance on a third party to perform a required act generally does not constitute reasonable cause, id. at 20.1.1.3.2 (12-11-2009), and neither does a busy work schedule or heavy work load, see Crittendon v. Commissioner, 85 TCM 1548 (2003). The Internal Revenue Manual is careful to note that when considering a reasonable cause defense, "each case must be judged individually based on the facts and circumstances at hand." IRM 20.1.1.3.2 (12-11-2009). In addition, a taxpayer who believes she is being treated unfairly may avail herself of the services of the National Taxpayer Advocate.

The Internal Revenue Manual anticipates that a taxpayer may have a reasonable cause defense for some months and not for others. But if the factors establishing reasonable cause cease to exist, the taxpayer must comply with the revenue laws within a reasonable period of time. Id.

Under § 6404(f), if a taxpayer makes a written request to the Service for advice, providing adequate and accurate information, and receives erroneous written advice from the Service upon which the taxpayer reasonably relies, the Service must abate any penalty and addition to tax attributable to the erroneous advice. See discussion of abatement, § IV, below.

1. The burden of proving reasonable cause falls on the taxpayer. Can a taxpayer ever establish reasonable cause based on reliance on the advice of a professional? See Swanson v. Commissioner, T.C. Memo. 2009-31.

2. In footnote nine, the Court reserves judgment on whether reasonable cause would be found where a taxpayer relies on the erroneous advice of a professional and files the return after the actual due date but before the erroneous due date. Do you think this would constitute reasonable cause under the rationale of *Boyle*?

II. ACCURACY-RELATED PENALTIES

Prior to 1989, there were more than 150 penalties under the Internal Revenue Code that applied to various errors and omissions on returns. These penalties could be applied independently of each other, resulting in a "stacking" of penalties that could far exceed the original tax liability. In 1989, Congress alleviated the stacking problem by enacting the Improved Penalty Administration and Compliance Tax Act (IMPACT), which repealed several of the most commonly applied penalties under the 1986 Code and consolidated five of them into a single Code provision for which one 20-percent penalty applies. These five penalties are collectively known as the "accuracy-related" penalties or "§ 6662 penalties." Section 6662 imposes a 20-percent penalty against any portion of an underpayment of tax required to be shown on a return that is attributable to: (1) negligence or disregard of rules and regulations (§ 6662(b)(1)), (2) a substantial understatement of income tax (§ 6662(b)(2)), (3) a substantial valuation misstatement (§ 6662(b)(3)), (4) a substantial overstatement of pension liabilities (§ 6662(b)(4)), and (5) a substantial estate or gift tax valuation understatement (§ 6662(b)(5)). In 2010, two other penalties were added to § 6662. These are (1) a 20-percent penalty on the disallowance of claimed tax benefits from a transaction lacking economic substance or failing to meet the requirements of any similar rule of law (§ 6662(b)(6)) and (2) a 40-percent penalty on any undisclosed foreign financial asset understatement (§ 6662(b)(7)). The 20% penalty is increased to 40% for "gross valuation misstatements" under § 6662(h) and for nondisclosure of a transaction lacking economic substance under § 6662(i)(1).

A. NEGLIGENCE OR DISREGARD OF RULES AND REGULATIONS

Prior to the IMPACT legislation of 1989, the negligence penalty was found under § 6653. Section 6653 had undergone several changes prior to IMPACT. It began as a five-percent penalty that applied to the entire understatement on the return if any portion of the liability was attributable to negligence or an intentional disregard of the rules and regulations. In 1982, this was increased by an additional amount equal to 50-percent of the interest attributable to the negligence-tainted portion of the deficiency. This additional amount was time-sensitive because it ran from the due date of the return to the earlier of the date of the assessment or the date the tax was paid. In 1986, the negligence penalty was made applicable to all taxes, so it could apply to the estate tax, as well as the income tax. In 1988, the time-sensitive portion of the penalty was eliminated, but the five-percent penalty continued to apply to the entire underpayment, even if only a small portion of the underpayment was attributable to negligence. Thus, two taxpayers with the same amount of underpayment could be subject to the same amount of negligence penalty, even though one taxpayer may have been much more negligent than the other. This general perception of unfairness was a major impetus behind the IMPACT legislation, which made several major changes to the negligence penalty.

Section 6662 narrowed the base of the penalty so that the 20-percent rate applies only to the underpayment of tax attributable to the negligent conduct. Interest on this amount runs from the due date of the return to the date of payment. IRC § 6601(e)(2)(B). Under § 6662(b)(1), the penalty consists of two parts: (1) negligence and (2) disregard of rules and regulations.

1. The Negligence Penalty

Negligence is defined under § 6662(c) as "any failure to make a reasonable attempt to comply with the provisions of this title; the term 'disregard' includes any careless, reckless or intentional disregard." It also includes any failure to make a reasonable attempt to comply with the provisions of the tax law and any failure to exercise ordinary and reasonable care in the preparation of a return. Reg. § 1.6662-3(b)(1).

A return position that has a reasonable basis is not attributable to negligence. Reg. § 1.6662-3(b)(1). The regulations provide that the reasonable basis standard is "a relatively high standard of tax reporting–significantly higher than not frivolous or not patently improper." Reg. § 1.6662-3(b)(3). The position must be more than merely arguable or colorable. The regulations further provide that the reasonable basis standard is met if the position is "reasonably based" on any of the authorities listed under § 1.6662-4(d)(2) (which include the Code, regulations, cases, rulings, and most of the legislative history), even though such authority may not be considered substantial for purposes of the substantial understatement penalty. See discussion of the substantial understatement penalty below. Notably, the list does not include secondary sources such as treatises and law review articles.

If the Service establishes specific acts of negligence, the assessment of a deficiency attributable to these acts is presumed correct and the taxpayer then has the burden of proving that the imposition of the negligence penalty is erroneous. Under prior law, there was no statutory defense to the penalty. After IMPACT, a negligence penalty may be avoided if the return position is attributable to reasonable cause, provided the taxpayer can establish good faith. IRC § 6664. Thus, even if the return position does not meet the reasonable basis standard, the taxpayer may avoid a negligence or disregard penalty if she can establish that she acted with reasonable cause and in good faith. IRC § 6664. The question is what constitutes reasonable cause for this purpose?

WALLIS v. COMMISSIONER

United States Court of Appeals, Eleventh Circuit, 2010.
391 Fed. Appx. 826; 106 A.F.T.R.2d 2010-5755 (slip opinion)

PER CURIAM:

Donald W. Wallis and his wife Kathryn W. Wallis appeal pro se the Tax Court's order finding an income tax deficiency of $27,305 for 2005 and an accuracy-related penalty of $5,461, pursuant to 26 U.S.C. § 6662. After review, we affirm.

I. BACKGROUND

From 1991 until 2003, Donald Wallis, a tax lawyer, was an equity partner at the law firm of Holland & Knight ("H & K"). The tax deficiency relates to the Wallises' failure to report $80,000 in "Schedule C" payments H & K made to Donald Wallis in 2005. The issue is whether these Schedule C payments were taxable as ordinary income or as long-term capital gains.

In accordance with two partnership agreements Wallis entered with H & K, when he withdrew, he would receive the value of his partnership interest in the firm. The partnership agreement stated that an equity partner's interest was the value of his capital account and the value of his "Schedule C units."

Under Schedule C of the partnership agreement, H & K awarded each equity partner fifty Schedule C units per year, valued at $300 per unit or $15,000 per year. The value of these units generally was payable in quarterly installments after a partner died, became disabled, was expelled or turned 68 years old. H & K did not set aside funds correlating to these Schedule C units.

On March 19, 2003, Wallis withdrew from H & K. At the time, Wallis's capital account balance was $98,161.75 and his Schedule C units were valued at $240,000. Beginning in 2003, Wallis received quarterly payments of $28,180.15, $8,180.15 of which was return of his capital account and $20,000 of which was payment for his Schedule C units. In 2005, H & K made four payments, totaling $80,000, for Wallis's Schedule C units. H & K issued to Wallis, and filed with the IRS, a Form 1099-MISC reflecting the Schedule C payments as "nonemployee compensation" and deducted these amounts from its own income on its partnership return. The Wallises did not report these Schedule C payments as income on their 2005 tax return.

Based on the parties' stipulated facts and the documentary evidence, the Tax Court found that the $80,000 in Schedule C payments were retirement payments paid to Wallis as a withdrawing partner as part of the liquidation of his partnership interest. As such, the Tax Court concluded that the Schedule C payments were "guaranteed payments" under 26 U.S.C. § 736(a)(2) to be taxed as ordinary income pursuant to 26 U.S.C. § 707(c).

II. DISCUSSION

A. Guaranteed Payments v. Partnership Distributions

On appeal, the Wallises argue that the Tax Court wrongly characterized the $80,000 in Schedule C payments as "guaranteed payments" and that they are properly characterized as "partnership distributions" under 26 U.S.C. §§ 731 and 736(b)(1), which are taxed as long-term capital gains pursuant to 26 U.S.C. § 1222(3).

Under § 736 of the tax code, payments made "in liquidation of the interest of a retiring partner" are characterized three different ways. Generally, a payment made in exchange for the interest of a retiring partner are considered: (1) a "distributive share" if it was "determined with regard to the income of the partnership"; or (2) a "guaranteed payment" under § 707(c) if it was "determined without regard to the income of the partnership"; or (3) a "distribution by the partnership and not as a distributive share or guaranteed payment," if it was "made in exchange for the interest of such partner in partnership property." Id. § 736(a)(1)-(2), (b)(1).[2]

The Tax Court found the Schedule C payments were "guaranteed" payments. If the payment is characterized as a "guaranteed payment," then 26 U.S.C. § 707(c) provides that it is taxed as ordinary income to the partner, pursuant to 26 U.S.C. § 61(a), and the partnership may deduct the payment as a trade or business expense, pursuant to 26 U.S.C. § 162(a). 26 U.S.C. §§ 707(c) & 736(a)(2); see also Treas. Reg. § 1.707-1(c) (noting that guaranteed payments are ordinary income to the partner).[3]

---

2.   If the partnership is a personal services partnership and the retiring partner is a general partner, then amounts paid for "unrealized receivables" and "good will" are not considered payments made in exchange for an interest in partnership property. Id. § 736(b)(2).

3.   Section 707 governs the tax consequences of transactions between a partner and his partnership when the partner is not acting in his capacity as a partner. 26 U.S.C. § 707(a). Under § 707(c), if payments to a partner for services or the use of capital are made without regard to the partnership's income, those payments "shall be considered as made to one who is not a member of the partnership" for purposes of 26 U.S.C. § 61(a), governing the recognition of income, and 27 U.S.C. § 162(a), governing deductions for trade or business expenses. Id. § 707(c). Given that the tax code under certain circumstances treats transactions between a partner and the partnership as between a non-partner and the partnership, we reject the Wallises argument that Subchapter K provides the only rules governing the income tax treatment of such transactions.

However, the Wallises claim that the payments were partnership distributions. If a payment is characterized as a partnership distribution, it is treated like a distribution in complete liquidation under 26 U.S.C. §§ 731, 732 and 751. Treas. Reg. § 1.736-1(a)(2). As such, the partner recognizes a taxable gain only to the extent that the amount received exceeds his adjusted basis in the partnership property. 26 U.S.C. § 731(a)(1). Because any gain recognized under § 731 is treated like a gain for the sale or exchange of a partnership interest, it is considered a gain from the sale or exchange of a capital asset. Id. §§ 731(a), 741. Therefore, if the partner holds his partnership interest for more than one year, his gain will be taxed as a long-term capital gain. 26 U.S.C. § 1222(3). Under these circumstances, the remaining partners are not permitted a deduction. Treas. Reg. § 1.736-1(a)(2).

B Schedule C Payments

Here, there was ample evidence in the partnership agreements and stipulated facts to support the Tax Court's finding that Donald Wallis's Schedule C payments were guaranteed payments.[4] Under the H & K partnership agreements, Schedule C units were awarded each year in fixed amounts ($15,000 per year) and ultimately paid to the withdrawing partner without regard to the partnership's income or the partner's particular equity share. H & K considered the Schedule C payments to be additional taxable compensation, as reflected in the 2005 Form 1099-MISC H & K issued to Wallis and filed with the IRS. In addition, H & K deducted the amount of the Schedule C payments (but not the amounts paid for Wallis's capital account) from its own income. See Miller v. Comm'r, 376 F.2d 255, 256-57 (5th Cir. 1967) (noting that a partnership's deduction of payments as expenses was evidence that payments should be characterized as guaranteed payments).[6]

In addition, the Tax Court did not err in concluding that, while Schedule C payments were made in exchange for Wallis's interest in the partnership generally, they were not made in exchange for his interest in "partnership property," and, thus, were not a partnership

---

4. The Wallises' argument that the Tax Court failed to address whether Schedule C payments were "payments made in liquidation of the interest of a retiring partner" is without merit. Because the Tax Court determined that the Schedule C payments were guaranteed payments, it necessarily concluded that those payments were payments made in liquidation of the interest of a retiring partner. See 26 U.S.C. § 736(a)(2) (defining guaranteed payments as a subset of payments made in liquidation of the interest of a retiring or deceased partner).

6. Decisions of the former Fifth Circuit on or before September 30, 1981 are binding precedent in the Eleventh Circuit. Bonner v. City of Prichard, 661 F.2d 1206, 1209 (11th Cir. 1981) (en banc).

distribution.[7] Notably, the parties' stipulation referred to the Schedule C units as a "benefit or entitlement." That benefit could be forfeited if a partner voluntarily left the partnership. Because they could be forfeited, H & K did not consider Schedule C units to be income to the partners in the year they were awarded. Furthermore, H & K did not set aside funds corresponding to future Schedule C payments. Finally, as the Tax Court pointed out, the payments appeared to be designed as a benefit similar to a retirement benefit.

Contrary to the Wallis's assertion, there is sufficient evidence to support the Tax Court's finding that the Schedule C payments, rather than being amounts paid for Wallis's interest in firm property, were essentially a retirement benefit. The H & K partnership agreements provided that (1) eligibility for Schedule C payments was, at least in part, tied to a partner turning 68 years old; (2) Schedule C obligations could be funded through a qualified defined benefit plan that would pay both Schedule C and monthly retirement benefits; (3) if a defined benefit plan was established, funds previously set aside to pay monthly retirement benefits under a discontinued retirement plan could be contributed to the defined benefit plan; and (4) the same monthly payment limits were placed on both retirement benefits and Schedule C payments.

The Wallises counter that there was "sufficient evidence to support the conclusion" that the "actual object" of the transactions was Wallis's interest in partnership property. However, the Wallises do not point to any particular evidence in the record linking the payments to Wallis's interest in any property held by H & K. In any event, even assuming the Wallises were correct, this does not show that the Tax Court's contrary conclusion was clearly erroneous. See Anderson v. Bessemer City, 470 U.S. 564, 574, 105 S.Ct. 1504, 1511, 84 L.Ed.2d 518 (1985) (explaining that a factfinder's choice between two permissible views cannot be clearly erroneous).[8]

---

7. Because the Tax Court determined that the payments were not in exchange for partnership property, it did not need to address the subsidiary question of whether the payments were made in consideration for unrealized receivables or goodwill.

8. The Wallises contend that the Tax Court erred by declining to address whether the Commissioner had the burden of production as to the deficiency, pursuant to 26 U.S.C. § 6201(d), and the burden of proof, pursuant to 26 U.S.C. § 7491(a). Any error in this regard was harmless given that the Commissioner actually satisfied both burdens based on the stipulated facts and the partnership agreements.

C. Accuracy-Related Penalty

The Wallises challenge the Tax Court's imposition of an accuracy-related penalty pursuant to 26 U.S.C. § 6662(a). Section 6662 imposes a twenty percent penalty on the amount of any underpayment that is the result of, inter alia, (1) "[n]egligence or disregard of rules or regulations" or (2) "[a]ny substantial understatement of income tax." 26 U.S.C. § 6662(b)(1)-(2). However, no penalty is imposed on any portion of an underpayment for which the taxpayer has "reasonable cause" and "acted in good faith." 26 U.S.C. § 6664(c)(1). Reasonable cause and good faith may be indicated where the taxpayer has "an honest misunderstanding of fact or law that is reasonable in light of all of the facts and circumstances, including the experience, knowledge, and education of the taxpayer." Treas. Reg. § 1.6664-4(b)(1). Where the underpayment relates to an item reflected on the return of a pass-through entity, such as a partnership, the partnership's treatment of that item is a relevant consideration when determining whether the taxpayer acted with reasonable cause and in good faith. Treas. Reg. § 1.6664-4(e). The Commissioner has the burden of production with respect to a taxpayer's liability for a penalty. 26 U.S.C. § 7491(c).[9]

The Wallises do not challenge the finding that their underpayment was the result of negligence and disregard of the tax code or regulations and was a substantial understatement. Instead, they argue that they had "reasonable cause" and "acted in good faith" pursuant to § 6664(c)(1). We review for clear error the Tax Court's factual finding whether an additional tax is due as a penalty.

Section 6222 provides a means for a partner to inform the IRS when his own treatment of a partnership item "is (or may be) inconsistent with the treatment of the item on the partnership return." 26 U.S.C. § 6222(b)(1). Given that Donald Wallis has 35 years of experience as a tax lawyer, the Tax Court reasonably could conclude that Wallis should have been aware there were inconsistencies between (1) his not reporting the Schedule C payments at all to the IRS and (2) the income Form 1099 he received from H & K. See Treas. Reg. 1.6664-4(b)(1).

The Wallises argue that they had no obligation to report under § 6222 because their inconsistency was with H & K's Form 1099-MISC, not with H & K's 2005 return. Nonetheless, § 6222 requires partners to report even possible inconsistencies to the IRS if they wish to treat partnership

---

9. The Wallises' contention that the Tax Court failed to impose the burden of production upon the Commissioner as to the penalty is without merit. The Tax Court stated in its opinion that the Commissioner had the burden of production and then concluded that the Commissioner had met that burden.

items differently on their own return from the partnership's return. And, Wallis's receipt of the Form 1099-MISC should have alerted him that the Schedule C payments would be reflected as deductions on H & K's partnership return. Rather than alerting the IRS to Wallis's (now-abandoned) theory that the payments did not represent taxable income, the Wallises made no mention of the Schedule C payments when they filed their return. Under the circumstances, the Tax Court did not clearly err in finding that the Wallises did not have reasonable cause for the underpayment or act in good faith with respect to it.

AFFIRMED.

Notes and Questions

As the *Wallis* case illustrates, courts consider the educational background and sophistication of the taxpayer in determining whether there is reasonable cause. In the case of Coleman v. Commissioner, TCM 1990-511, the Tax Court held that an attorney who invested in a tax shelter scheme in reliance on a tax opinion letter prepared by his law firm could not demonstrate reasonable cause. According to the court, "[r]eliance on professional advice, standing alone, is not an absolute defense to negligence, but rather a factor to be considered. First, it must be established that the reliance was reasonable." Id. Reasonableness is determined under the facts and circumstances of each individual case. According to the regulations, the most important factor is the extent of the taxpayer's attempt to determine the proper tax liability. Reg. § 1.6662-4(b)(1).

Many of the negligence cases dealt with taxpayers who had invested in tax shelters which the government later determined lacked economic substance. The taxpayers argued that they had relied on the advice of well-respected professionals (accountants, attorneys, or investment advisors) and, therefore, they met the requirements for reasonable cause. In some of these cases, the taxpayers were successful, see, e.g., Wright v. Commissioner, T.C. Memo 1994-288, but in most they were not. In the latter cases, the courts generally thought the taxpayers knew or should have known that the investment was primarily a tax avoidance device and not a true investment. But in *Wright*, the Tax Court held that the taxpayers had acted reasonably and in good faith in relying on their investment advisor because the taxpayers lacked experience and financial sophistication.

1. Is *Wright* consistent with *Boyle*?

2. Is the *Wright* court likely to reach the same decision if the case were to arise today? Why or why not? See §§ 6662(b)(6) and 7701(o).

3. If a taxpayer neglects to file a return and does not have reasonable cause for the failure to file, can the taxpayer be subject to a negligence penalty as well as a delinquency penalty? If so, under what circumstances?

2. The "Disregard" Penalty

The second portion of the § 6662(b)(1) penalty applies to a careless, reckless or intentional disregard of the rules and regulations.

DRUKER v. COMMISSIONER
United States Court of Appeals, Second Circuit, 1982.
697 F.2d 46.

FRIENDLY, CIRCUIT JUDGE:

* * *

I.

The principal issue on the taxpayers' appeal is the alleged unconstitutionality of the so-called "marriage penalty." The issue relates to the 1975 and 1976 income tax returns of James O. Druker and his wife Joan. During the tax years in question James was employed as a lawyer, first by the United States Attorney for the Eastern District of New York and later by the District Attorney of Nassau County, New York, and Joan was employed as a computer programmer. For each of the two years they filed separate income tax returns, checking the status box entitled "married filing separately." In computing their respective tax liabilities, however, they applied the rates in I.R.C. § 1(c) for "Unmarried individuals" rather than the higher rates prescribed by § 1(d) for "Married individuals filing separate returns." Prior to undertaking this course of action, James consulted with the United States Attorney for the Eastern District and with members of the Intelligence Division of the IRS, explaining that he and his wife wanted to challenge the constitutionality of the "marriage penalty" without incurring liability for fraud or willfulness. Following these conversations they filed their returns as described, attaching to each return a letter explaining that, although married, they were applying the tax tables for single persons because they believed that the "income tax structure unfairly discriminates against working married couples" in violation of the equal protection clause of the fourteenth amendment. The Tax Court rejected this constitutional challenge, sustaining the Commissioner's determination that the Drukers were subject to tax at the rates provided in § 1(d) for married persons filing separately.

Determination of the proper method for federal taxation of the incomes of married and single persons has had a long and stormy history. From the beginning of the income tax in 1913 until 1948 each individual was taxed on his or her own income regardless of marital status. Thus, as a result of the progressive nature of the tax, two married couples with the same aggregate income would often have very different tax liabilities--larger if most of the income belonged to one spouse, smaller as their incomes tended toward equality. The decision in Poe v. Seaborn, 282 U.S. 101, 51 S.Ct. 58, 75 L.Ed. 239 (1930), that a wife was taxable on one half of community income even if this was earned solely by the husband, introduced a further element of geographical inequality, since it gave married couples in community property states a large tax advantage over similarly situated married couples with the same aggregate income in common law states.

After *Poe* the tax status of a married couple in a community property state differed from that of a married couple in a common law state in two significant respects. First, each community property spouse paid the same tax as an unmarried person with one-half the aggregate community income, whereas each common law spouse paid the same tax as an unmarried person with the same individual income. Consequently, marriage usually reduced a couple's tax burden if they resided in a community property state but was a neutral tax event for couples in common law states. Second, in community property states all married couples with the same aggregate income paid the same tax, whereas in common law states a married couple's tax liability depended on the amount of income each spouse earned.

The decision in *Poe* touched off something of a stampede among common law states to introduce community property regimes and thereby qualify their residents for the privilege of income splitting. The Supreme Court's subsequent decision in Commissioner v. Harmon, 323 U.S. 44, 65 S.Ct. 103, 89 L.Ed. 60 (1944), that the income-splitting privileges did not extend to couples in states whose community property systems were elective, slowed but did not halt this movement. The result was considerable confusion and much upsetting of expectations founded on long experience under the common law. Congress responded in 1948 by extending the benefits of "income splitting" to residents of common law as well as community property states. Revenue Act of 1948, ch. 168, 62 Stat. 110. Pursuant to this Act, every married couple was permitted to file a joint return and pay twice the tax that a single individual would pay on one-half of their total income. This in effect taxed a married couple as if they were two single individuals each of whom earned half of the couple's combined income. The Act not only reduced the tax burden on married couples in common law states; it also ensured that all married couples with the same aggregate income paid the same tax regardless of the state in which they lived ("geographical uniformity") and regardless of the relative income contribution of each spouse ("horizontal equity").

While the 1948 Act was good news for married couples, it placed singles at a serious disadvantage. The tax liability of a single person was now sometimes as much as 41% greater than that of a married couple with the same income. Although constitutional challenges to the "singles' penalty" were uniformly rejected, see, e.g., Kellems v. Commissioner, 58 U.C. 556 (1972), aff'd per curiam, 474 F.2d 1399 (2d Cir. 1973); Faraco v. Commissioner, 261 F.2d 387 (4th Cir. 1958), the single taxpayer obtained some relief from Congress. The Tax Reform Act of 1969, Pub.L. No. 91-172, 83 Stat. 487 (1969), increased the number of tax schedules from two to four: § 1(a) for marrieds filing jointly; § 1(b) for unmarried heads of households; § 1(c) for unmarried individuals; and § 1(d) for married individuals filing separately.[1] The schedules were set so that a single person's tax liability under § 1(c) would never be more than 120% that of a married couple with the same income filing jointly under § 1(a).

The 1969 reform spawned a new class of aggrieved taxpayers—the two wage-earner married couple whose combined tax burden, whether they chose to file jointly under § 1(a) or separately under § 1(d), was now greater than it would have been if they had remained single and filed under § 1(c). It is this last phenomenon which has been characterized, in somewhat loaded fashion, as the "marriage penalty" or "marriage tax."[2] * * *

* * *

---

1.   The rates set under § 1(d) were the pre-1969 rates for single taxpayers. So disadvantageous is this schedule that only about 1% of married couples file separately. Staff of the Joint Committee on Taxation, Report on the Income Tax Treatment of Married Couples and Single Persons, 96th Cong., 2d Sess. 48 (1980). As a general rule, married taxpayers file separately only when they are so estranged from one another that they do not wish to sign a joint return or when separate filing enables one spouse to exceed the 3% of income floor for medical deductions. Id. at 9. See Bittker, *supra*, 27 Stan.L.Rev. at 1414.

2.   Not all married couples are so "penalized." For the couple whose income is earned primarily or solely by one partner, marriage still offers significant tax savings. As a general rule of thumb, marriage will increase a couple's tax burden as compared with that of two single persons whenever the lesser-earning spouse earns 20% or more of the couple's total income and decrease its tax burden whenever the lesser-earning spouse earns less than 20%. See Gerzog, The Marriage Penalty: The Working Couple's Dilemma, 47 Fordham L.Rev. 27, 28 (1978).

We do not doubt that the "marriage penalty" has some adverse effect on marriage; indeed, James Druker stated at argument that, having failed thus far in the courts, he and his wife had solved their tax problem by divorcing but continuing to live together. * * *

* * *

IV.

We come finally to the Commissioner's cross-appeal from the Tax Court's refusal to impose a 5% addition for "intentional disregard of rules and regulations" under I..R.C. § 6653(a). This section provides:

> Negligence or intentional disregard of rules and regulations with respect to income or gift taxes.--If any part of any underpayment (as defined in subsection (c)(1)) of any tax imposed by subtitle A or by chapter 12 of subtitle B (relating to income taxes and gift taxes) is due to negligence or intentional disregard of rules and regulations (but without intent to defraud), there shall be added to the tax an amount equal to 5 percent of the underpayment.

See also Treas.Reg. § 301.6653-1(a) (incorporating the statutory language).

In computing their respective tax liabilities the Drukers applied the rates in I.R.C. §1(c) for "Unmarried individuals" instead of the higher rates prescribed by § 1(d) for "Married individuals filing separate returns" as the regulations required. There was, to be sure, nothing furtive or fraudulent in this; they checked the "married filing separately" status box on their returns, cross-referenced the returns by providing each other's Social Security number, and attached to each return a letter explaining what they were doing and why. Nevertheless, the record leaves no doubt that in using rate schedules applicable only to unmarried persons, they intentionally violated Section 1 of the Code and the rules and regulations promulgated thereunder, see Treas.Reg. § 1.1-1(a).

While conceding that the Drukers acted "deliberately and in open disregard of the requirements of the statute", the Tax Court nonetheless disallowed the 5% addition on the ground that the Drukers' "position herein is not so frivolous and meritless as to fall within the ambit of numerous cases involving even sincere taxpayers where the addition to the tax under section 6653(a) has been imposed", that "it is common knowledge that the 'marriage penalty' has been the subject of widespread comment and discussion, including extensive legislative consideration,"[5]

---

5.   We do not grasp the force of this. Many tax issues, e.g., whether capital gains should be taxed and, if so, what the rate and the holding period should be; the alleged "double taxation" of so much of corporate profits as is declared as dividends; indexing of income to avoid "bracket creep"

and that "[a]ccordingly [the Drukers] should not be penalized for seeking to litigate the issue." 77 T.C. at 875. We think the Tax Court took unto itself a dispensing power not granted by Congress.

The statutory language, "there shall be added", could hardly be clearer. The reasonableness of a taxpayer's action may indeed be relevant when he is charged with negligence but not when he admittedly has flouted applicable rules and regulations which he fully understood. Departure from the natural and ordinary meaning of the words, whose literal application does not result in any manifestly absurd or unfair result, could be justified only if there were other evidence that the over-all purpose of Congress would be better served by such a reading. We find no sufficient evidence of this.

* * *

The Commissioner concedes that this suggests that the 1976 Congress believed the 'intentional disregard' language of § 6653(a) to be also subject to a reasonable basis limitation. He seeks to avoid the effect of this, however, on the grounds that, as discussed above, Congress in 1954 specifically declined to adopt such a limitation when it enacted § 6653(a) and that "the views of a subsequent Congress form a hazardous basis for inferring the intent of an earlier one." United States v. Price, 361 U.S. 304, 313, 80 S.Ct. 326, 331, 4 L.Ed.2d 334 (1960). There is force in the Commissioner's argument. The Congressional decision in 1954 not to adopt a "reasonable basis" exception represented the deliberate and considered action of a conference committee with respect to the very provision here at issue. The 1976 episode, apart from being another 22 years down the road, consisted of talk about § 6653(a) incident to enactment of a new section of the tax law in a committee report which few members may have seen. When all is said and done, the most that the 1976 episode could be taken as proving is that some members of the 94th Congress were mistaken as to the long settled construction of what is now § 6653(a) and that the Commissioner in his regulations adopted the statement in the legislative history. Much more than this is needed to overturn a construction settled since 1942.

---

due to inflation, etc., have likewise been and doubtless will continue to be discussed for years. The Tax Court could hardly have meant that persons sincerely entertaining views on such matters differing from the legislators' could resort to self-help without incurring the 5% addition to the tax. If the distinction is thought to be that the Drukers raised constitutional and not mere policy objections, there is no showing of widespread discussion of that. Moreover the generous attitude of the Tax Court presumably would have to carry over to persons who sincerely dispute the legality of their being subjected to income taxation to support activities such as the Vietnam war or nuclear armament of which they strongly disapprove and who make fully disclosed deductions from their taxes on that account.

More important, even if we were to assume for argument's sake only that the reasonable basis limitation of § 6694(a), as expounded in the legislative history and Treas.Reg. § 1.6694-1(a)(4), could properly be read into § 6653(a), this would not help the Drukers. For their position is not that a "rule or regulation does not accurately reflect the Code," § 1.6694-1(a)(4), but rather that Section 1 of the Code is inconsistent with the Constitution. There is nothing in the legislative history of § 6694(a) or in the language of the Treasury regulation promulgated thereunder to suggest that the 1976 Congress believed that a reasonable basis limitation applies in such a case. On the contrary, the House Report and the Joint Committee Explanation of the 1976 Act both clearly stated that a tax return preparer is to enjoy the benefit of the reasonable basis exemption only where the dispute is "about an IRS interpretation of a statute." H.Rep. No. 658, supra, at 278, U.S.Code Cong. & Admin.News 1976, p. 3174; Joint Committee Explanation, supra, at 351. A fortiori, a taxpayer who has intentionally disregarded a rule or regulation can not claim the benefit of any such exemption where, as here, his dispute is with Congress rather than the IRS. We assume that if the Commissioner desires to adopt a regulation under § 6653(a) or to take other action which would exempt persons like the Drukers from the 5% addition to tax, he is free to do so. Absent this, when the Commissioner seeks the additional 5% tax and the facts show such an intentional although honest disregard of the statute as here, the courts have no dispensing power.

On the taxpayers' appeal the judgment against them is affirmed; on the Commissioner's appeal the judgment refusing to assess the additional 5% required by § 6653(a) is reversed and the case is remanded for the making of an additional assessment.

Notes and Questions

Adequate disclosure of a position that is contrary to the rules or regulations may constitute good faith and reasonable cause, provided the taxpayer has a reasonable basis for the position, and has kept adequate books and records. If the position is contrary to a regulation, the position must represent a good faith challenge to the validity of the regulation. In addition, the requisite disclosure must be made by completing a Disclosure Statement (Forms 8275 or 8275-R) and attaching it to the return. Reg. § 1.6662-3(c)(1). Merely filling out the tax return itself is not considered proper disclosure. Reg. § 1.6662-3(c)(2). Note that the disclosure exception may not be used as a defense to the negligence penalty. Reg. § 1.6662-1.

If the position is attributable to a "reportable transaction," the taxpayer will not be able to rely on the reasonable cause defense, but instead must meet special disclosure standards. See § II.B.3, below for a discussion of these standards. Also, if the position is attributable to a transaction that lacks economic substance, neither reasonable cause nor disclosure will absolve the taxpayer of the § 6662(b)(6) penalty although disclosure will reduce the amount of the penalty. If the Drukers had attached a Disclosure Statement to their returns, would this have enabled them to avoid the accuracy-related penalty?

If the position is contrary to an IRS ruling or notice, the taxpayer will not be subject to a disregard penalty if the position has a "realistic possibility of being sustained on its merits." Reg. § 1.6662-3(b)(2). This is the same standard used in determining preparer penalties under § 6694, discussed previously in Chapter 2.

B. SUBSTANTIAL UNDERSTATEMENT OF INCOME TAX

Often, the negligence penalty and the substantial understatement penalty will overlap, so that both penalties may apply to the same conduct. (Remember that the § 6662 penalties cannot be "stacked" so only one penalty will apply in that case). It is possible, however, for a taxpayer to substantially understate tax liability yet not act negligently. The substantial understatement penalty provides an addition to tax of 20-percent of any underpayment of tax that is attributable to a substantial understatement. A substantial understatement is defined as an understatement of income tax that exceeds the greater of (i) 10-percent of the tax required to be shown on the return for the taxable year or (ii) $5,000 ($10,000 in the case of a corporation). IRC § 6662(d).

WOODS, II v. COMMISSIONER
United States Tax Court, 1988.
91 T.C. 88.

OPINION OF THE SPECIAL TRIAL JUDGE

PATE, SPECIAL TRIAL JUDGE:

* * *

William A. Woods, II (petitioner) was single during 1983, the year in issue. He did not file a Federal income tax return despite receiving $32,844 in wages and $53 in interest income during that year. On September 13, 1985, respondent determined a deficiency in petitioner's federal income tax in the amount of $7,152 and additions to tax under section 6651(a)(1) of $834.75, section 6653(a)(1)[2] of $357.60, section 6653(a)(2)[3] of fifty percent of the interest due on the underpayment, and section 6661(a) of $715.20. Petitioner timely filed his petition alleging that respondent erred in asserting all of the additions to tax, and alternatively, that he had not been given credit for withholding taxes of $3,813.77[6] in the calculation of such additions.

Deficiency in Income Tax

In the petition and the various objections filed thereafter, petitioner raised numerous "tax protestor" type arguments. He maintains that his wages do not constitute gross income; that reporting and paying income taxes is strictly voluntary and, therefore, the filing of an income tax return was not required; that the Fifth Amendment to the Constitution of the United States prevents respondent from requiring him to provide the information called for on an income tax return; that the Sixteenth Amendment to the Constitution was not properly ratified; and, at least impliedly, that he was wrongfully denied a jury trial.

All of these arguments have been rejected repeatedly by the courts. There is no doubt that petitioner was required to file an income tax return for the year 1983 and that he was required to pay taxes on his wages and interest income. Moreover, to invoke the Fifth Amendment privilege, petitioner must be faced with substantial hazards of self-incrimination that are real and appreciable and must have reasonable cause to apprehend such danger. Petitioner has shown us no evidence even remotely indicating that petitioner was faced with such a hazard.

* * *

Since no other issues were raised by petitioner with regard to his income tax for 1983, and petitioner bears the burden of proving that respondent's determinations are incorrect, we find that petitioner is liable for the amount of income tax shown on the notice of deficiency.

* * *

---

2. Redesignated as section 6653(a)(1)(A) by section 1503(a) of the Tax Reform Act of 1986, Pub.L. 99-514, 100 Stat. 2742.

3. Redesignated as section 6653(a)(1)(B) by section 1503(a) of the Tax Reform Act of 1986, Pub.L. 99-514, 100 Stat. 2742.

6. In his petition, petitioner alleged that $3,813.77 was withheld from his wages. This amount was not contested by respondent during the course of these proceedings.

Section 6661

Finally, we consider respondent's determination under section 6661.[7]

* * *

We now must decide whether respondent correctly computed the increased addition to tax by applying 25 percent to the entire deficiency of $7,152. He maintains that because petitioner did not file any return for 1983, the percentage is properly applied to the total amount of the income tax determined in the notice of deficiency. On the other hand, petitioner maintains that the percentage applies only to the difference

---

7.   Section 6661 states in its entirety:

SEC. 6661. SUBSTANTIAL UNDERSTATEMENT OF LIABILITY.

   (a) Addition to Tax.–If there is a substantial understatement of income tax for any taxable year, there shall be added to the tax an amount equal to 25 percent [eds: currently 20 percent under § 6662] of the amount of any underpayment attributable to such understatement.

   (b) Definition and Special Rule.--(1) Substantial Understatement.–

      (A) In general.–For purposes of this section, there is a substantial understatement of income tax for any taxable year if the amount of the understatement for the taxable year exceeds the greater of–(i) 10-percent of the tax required to be shown on the return for the taxable year, or (ii) $5,000.

      (B) Special rule for corporations.--In the case of a corporation other than an S corporation or a personal holding company (as defined in section 542), paragraph (1) shall be applied by substituting "$10,000" for "$5,000."

   (2) Understatement.–(A) In general.–For purposes of paragraph (1), the term "understatement" means the excess of–

      (i) the amount of the tax required to be shown on the return for the taxable year, over

      (ii) the amount of the tax imposed which is shown on the return, reduced by any rebate (within the meaning of section 6211(b)(2)).

      (B) Reduction for understatement due to position of taxpayer or disclosed item.–The amount of the understatement under subparagraph (A) shall be reduced by that portion of the understatement which is attributable to–(i) the tax treatment of any item by the taxpayer if there is or was substantial authority for such treatment, or (ii) any item with respect to which the relevant facts affecting the items' tax treatment are adequately disclosed in the return or in a statement attached to the return.

      (C) Special rules in cases involving tax shelters.–(i) In general.–In the case of any item attributable to a tax shelter– (I) subparagraph (B)(ii) shall not apply, and (II) subparagraph (B)(i) shall not apply unless (in addition to meeting the requirements of such subparagraph) the taxpayer reasonably believed that the tax treatment of such item by the taxpayer was more likely than not the proper treatment. (ii) Tax shelter.–For purposes of clause (i), the term "tax shelter" means–(I) a partnership or other entity, (II) any investment plan or arrangement, or (III) any other plan or arrangement, if the principal purpose of such partnership, entity, plan, or arrangement is the avoidance or evasion of Federal income tax.

   (3) Coordination with penalty imposed by section 6659.–For purposes of determining the amount of the addition to tax assessed under subsection (a), there shall not be taken into account that portion of the substantial understatement on which a penalty is imposed under section 6659 (relating to additions to tax in the case of valuation overstatements).

   (c) Authority to Waive.–The Secretary may waive all or any part of the addition to tax provided by this section on a showing by the taxpayer that there was reasonable cause for the understatement (or part thereof) and that the taxpayer acted in good faith.

between the deficiency and the amount of Federal taxes withheld from his wages.[9]

Section 6661(a) provides that:

If there is a substantial *understatement* of income tax for any taxable year, there shall be added to the tax an amount equal to 25 percent of the amount of any *underpayment* attributable to such *understatement*. [Emphasis added.]

Since the statute provides that the 25-percent rate shall be applied to "the amount of any underpayment," our determination turns on the meaning of the term "underpayment" in the context of section 6661.

To put our discussion into perspective, we must first consider the meaning of some of the other terms used in that section. The term "understatement" is expressly defined by section 6661(b)(2) as the excess of the amount of the tax required to be shown on the return over the amount of the tax imposed which is shown on the return. Due to the fact that petitioner failed to report any of his income, the entire amount of the tax required to be shown on the return is equal to the total deficiency of $7,152.[11] Further, since no return was filed by petitioner, the amount of tax which is shown on the return is considered to be zero. Sec. 1.6661-2(d)(2), Income Tax Regs. Therefore, the "understatement" is $7,152.[12]

The term "substantial understatement" is defined in section 6661(b)(1) as an "understatement" which exceeds the greater of 10 percent of the tax required to be shown on the return or $5,000. If a "substantial understatement" is present, it triggers the application of the addition to tax provided for in section 6661(a). We already have determined that the "understatement" is the entire amount of the tax deficiency in this case. Thus, the "understatement" is necessarily greater

---

9.   Respondent asserts that in DuBose v. Commissioner, T.C.Memo. 1986-288, this Court already has found that the section 6661 addition to tax is to be applied to the total deficiency before applying credits for income tax withheld. We have carefully examined that opinion and fail to find any mention of withholding tax or prepayment credits.

11.   Petitioner argues that section 6661 should not be applied in his case since he did not file an income tax return and therefore, could not have had an "understatement" of tax. However, section 1.6661-2(d)(2), Income Tax Regs., provides that "if no return was filed for the taxable year * * * the amount of tax shown on the return is considered to be zero." This regulation is not plainly inconsistent with the statute, and petitioner has not presented any "weighty reasons" why we should invalidate it. Accordingly, his argument fails. Fulman v. United States, 434 U.S. 528, 533 (1978), and cases cited therein. See also Allen v. Commissioner, T.C.Memo.1987-242, where we previously have found this section applicable where no income tax return was filed.

12.   We note that the regulations rightfully disregard withheld taxes in determining "the amount of tax shown on the return" and "the amount of tax required to be shown on the return" in computing the "understatement." Sec. 1.6661-2(d)(5)(i), Income Tax Regs.

than 10 percent of the tax required to be shown. Further, the understatement of $7,152 is greater than $5,000. Therefore, the "understatement" of petitioner's tax is a "substantial understatement" as defined by section 6661(b)(1). Consequently, respondent correctly determined that the addition to tax under section 6661(a) applied in this case.

However, section 6661(a) states the amount of the addition to tax is equal to 25 percent of the "underpayment" attributable to the "understatement." Unlike the terms "understatement" or "substantial understatement," the term "underpayment" is not defined in section 6661. Respondent urges us to construe "underpayment" to be synonymous with "understatement." In fact, that is what the Regulations attempt to do, inasmuch as section 1.6661-2(a), Income Tax Regs., states that:

> If there is a *substantial understatement* of income tax for a taxable year (as defined in paragraph (b) of this section), section 6661 imposes a penalty equal to [25] percent of the *understatement* of tax liability. [Emphasis added.]

In justifying his position, respondent first argues that we should use the definition of the term "underpayment" that is contained in section 6659(g)(1) because section 6661 is coordinated with section 6659.[13] The coordination of these two sections is provided for in section 6661(b)(3) which states:

> Coordination with penalty imposed by section 6659.--For purposes of determining the amount of the addition to tax assessed under subsection (a), there shall not be taken into account that portion of the substantial understatement on which a penalty is imposed under section 6659 (relating to additions to tax in the case of valuation overstatements).

In turn, section 6659(g)(1) defines "underpayment" by reference to section 6653(c)(1).[14] Section 6653(c)(1) defines "underpayment" as a deficiency (as defined in section 6211), except that only the tax shown on a timely filed return is to be used to reduce the amount of the deficiency to arrive at the "underpayment" under section 6653. In other words, where no income tax return is filed, the term "underpayment" under section 6653(c)(1) is equal to the entire amount of the tax that should have been shown on the return if one had been filed.

---

13. Section 6659 provides for an addition to tax in the case of valuation overstatements.

14. Section 6659(g)(1) reads: (1) Underpayment.–The term "underpayment" has the meaning given to such term by section 6653(c)(1).

There is no real merit to this argument. Upon close examination we find that the reason section 6661 is coordinated with section 6659 is to eliminate the overlap which would result when an "underpayment" is caused by a valuation overstatement covered in section 6659 was also a part of the "understatement" covered in section 6661. See section 6661(b)(3). Consequently, the reason for coordinating sections 6659 and 6661 is totally unrelated to the meaning of "underpayment" for purposes of section 6661.[15]

Generally, to glean the meaning of the words used by Congress in a statute, we first look to the ordinary or settled meaning of the words used to convey its intent. In so doing, we find that "pay" means to satisfy a demand or obligation by "transfer of money" and the term "underpayment" means "insufficient payment." As applied to this case, petitioner made *payment* of his *money* to the United States to satisfy his tax liability through payroll deductions. Petitioner's "underpayment" occurred only because he paid less than he was supposed to pay; that is, his *payment was insufficient.*[17] Petitioner's "underpayment" was not caused by his failure to *report* his income on an income tax return as respondent would have us hold, but rather by his failure to *pay* all of the tax that he owed. A reporting error is taken into account only in computing the "understatement" under section 6661. Therefore, the plain reading of the statute clearly means that the 25 percent rate is applied only to the unpaid amount rather than to the entire understatement.[18]

Congress modified the ordinary and regular meaning of the term "underpayment" for purposes of section 6653 and 6659 by including specific definitional sections. Sections 6653(c)(1) and 6659(g)(1). These definitional sections were needed because credits for taxes withheld and

---

15. The term "underpayment" in section 6659 and the term "understatement" in section 6661 are parallel concepts (i.e., differences in tax resulting from adjustments made by the Internal Revenue Service). This is all the more reason that "underpayment" in section 6659 cannot be equated with "underpayment" in section 6661.

17. This interpretation of "underpayment" conforms to the meaning given that term in sections 6654, 6655 and 6656. See sections 6654(b), 6655(b) and 6656(a).

18. Wage earners who file proper W-4 Forms frequently overpay their tax by their withholding, yet many fail to file income tax returns to claim rightful refunds. See Hearings on S. 2198 before the Subcomm. on Oversight of the Internal Revenue Service of the Senate Comm. on Finance, 97th Cong., 2d Sess. 99 (1982). Respondent's interpretation would subject these wage earners to an addition to tax equal to 25% of their entire tax even though it all had been paid. We believe Congress did not intend this result when it enacted section 6661. See 111 Cong.Rec. S. 8791, 8811 (1982) (Remarks by Senator Grassley, cosponsor of S. 2198 Taxpayer Compliance Improvement Act of 1982). See also the minimum addition for extended failure to file a return in section 6651(a) that was enacted concurrently with section 6661.

otherwise paid were not to be taken into account in making computations under those sections. Since there is no such modification in section 6661, it follows that the term "underpayment" takes such credits into account.

Finally, we observe that, if we would construe the terms "understatement" and "underpayment" as basically synonymous, the phrase "of the amount of any underpayment attributable to" in section 6661(a) would be superfluous and totally without meaning or significance. Stated another way, using respondent's interpretation, the statute could merely read "an amount equal to 25 percent of such understatement." In fact, this abbreviated version is essentially what the Regulations say in section 1.6661-2(a), Income Tax Regs.

However, it is a cardinal rule of statutory construction that "effect shall be given to every clause and part of statutes." Ginsberg & Sons v. Popkin, 285 U.S. 204, 208 (1932). Therefore, we find that giving "underpayment" its ordinary meaning in the context of section 6661 is proper, since this gives full effect to every clause and part of the statute and does not ignore the phrase "of the amount of any underpayment attributable to."[19]

To summarize, we do not accept respondent's position (or the regulation) because (1) it would render part of the statutory language of section 6661 superfluous, (2) it ignores the limiting language of the definition of "underpayment" in sections 6653(c)(1) and 6659(g)(1), and (3) it conflicts with the ordinary and settled meaning of "underpayment" (i.e., the amount by which the *payment* was insufficient). For these reasons, we hold that the amount of petitioner's withholding credits must be subtracted from the "understatement" to arrive at the "amount of any underpayment" for the calculation of the addition to tax under section 6661. * * *

---

19. Where, as here, a statute is clear on its face, we require unequivocal evidence of legislative purpose before construing the statute so as to override the plain meaning of the words used therein. Hirasuna v. Commissioner, 89 T.C. 1216 (1987); Huntsberry v. Commissioner, 83 T.C. 742, 747-748 (1984). Section 6661 was enacted on September 3, 1982, as part of the Tax Equity and Fiscal Responsibility Act of 1982, sec. 323, Pub.L. 97-428, 96 Stat. 324, 613 (TEFRA). There is nothing in the legislative history of this bill to refute our definition of "underpayment."

Interestingly, on March 11, 1982, a comparable provision was included in S. 2198 ("Taxpayer Compliance Improvement Act of 1982"), a bill introduced by Senator Dole, then chairman of the Senate Finance Committee. See 128 Cong.Rec. S 8793 and S 8810 (1982) (Senate floor debate of TEFRA, statements of Senators Dole and Grassley, respectively). Section 125 of this bill contained the forerunner of section 6661 which specifically defined "underpayment" by reference to sec. 6653(c). As reported by the Senate Finance Committee on July 12, 1982, section 6661 followed the structure of the S. 2198 provision, except that the reported bill did not include any definition of "underpayment." See generally Staff of J.Comm. on Taxation, General Explanation of the Tax Equity and Fiscal Responsibility Act of 1982, at 217 (J.Comm.Print 1982) (the Bluebook); S.Rept. No. 97-494 to accompany S. 2198, Vol. 1, p. 272-274 (1982). If anything, the deletion of this definitional provision highlights the invalidity of respondent's argument.

Notes and Question

Section 6662(a) is a codification of the *Woods II* holding. The term "understatement" essentially means "deficiency." Thus, a substantial understatement will trigger the accuracy-related penalty, which is applied against an "underpayment." Any carryback of losses from another taxable year will not reduce the amount of the understatement. Reg. § 1.6662-4(c)(2).

Section 6211 defines a deficiency as the amount by which the tax imposed exceeds the excess of the amount shown as tax on the return plus "amounts previously assessed (or collected without assessment) as a deficiency" less the amount of any rebates. Under the regulations, "the amount 'collected without assessment' is the amount by which the total credits allowable under section 31 (relating to tax withheld on wages), * * * estimated tax payments and other payments in satisfaction of tax liability made before the return is filed, exceed the tax shown on the return (provided such excess has not been refunded or allowed as a credit to the taxpayer)." Reg. § 1.6664-2(d). Why do the regulations provide that the amount collected without assessment must exceed the tax shown on the return?

There are two defenses to the substantial understatement penalty under § 6662(d)(2)(B). The understatement is reduced to the extent that (1) it is attributable to a position for which there is substantial authority or (2) there is a reasonable basis for the position and the position is adequately disclosed. In addition, the reasonable cause defense under § 6664 applies.

1. Substantial Authority

If there is substantial authority for a taxpayer's position, the amount of an understatement attributable to that position is reduced and treated as though the items had been properly reported. Thus, the substantial understatement penalty would not apply to this amount. Substantial authority is not defined in the Code, although the regulations list examples of authorities that are considered substantial.

PEERLESS INDUSTRIES, INC. v. UNITED STATES

United States District Court, Eastern District of Pennsylvania, 1994.
1994 WL 13837

OPINION

CAHN, J.

* * *

II.　FACTUAL BACKGROUND

A.　The Parties and The Bond Issuance

The following material facts are not in dispute. Peerless is a Pennsylvania corporation that manufactures hydronic boilers. Eugene C. Fish ("Fish") was, at all times relevant to the instant dispute, a 30% shareholder and the president of Peerless. From the early 1970s though 1981, Fish also sat on the Board of Trustees and Finance Committee of LVC, a small private educational institution in Annville, Pennsylvania. LVC qualifies as a tax-exempt organization under IRC § 501(c)(3).[2]

The long-term financial viability of LVC was a matter of crucial concern to its Board of Trustees during the 1970s. In 1981, Fish learned of a transaction in which J.C. Penney & Co. sold zero-coupon original issue notes to a similar § 501(c)(3) private educational institution. He thought that such an arrangement would be mutually beneficial for Peerless and LVC and, in 1981, proposed that Peerless issue to LVC a zero-coupon original-issue discount bond. Fish prepared the Bond and selected its terms. He proposed the Bond arrangement to Dr. Fredrick P. Sample ("Sample"), then president of LVC, and recommended that LVC enter into the Bond arrangement with Peerless. Fish and Sample then presented the Bond to LVC's Finance Committee, which approved LVC's acquisition of the Bond.

The Bond, which had a term of fifty years, states that Peerless will pay LVC $20,000,000 upon maturity in 2031. The stated purchase price was approximately $23,066, which represents the 1981 present value of $20,000,000, payable in 50 years, discounted semi-annually using a 14% annual interest rate. Under the terms of the Bond, Peerless is to maintain a sinking fund[3] sufficient to retire the Bond at full maturity.

2.　26 U.S.C. §§ 501(a) and 501(c)(3) exempt from taxation "[c]orporations * * * organized and operated exclusively for * * * educational purposes." .

3.　Sinking funds are intended to provide the bond-holder with security. Sinking fund provisions in a bond usually require the debtor/bond-issuer to set aside capital, in a segregated fund, in an amount sufficient to retire the debt. Often, the issuer grants the bond holder a security interest in the fund.

Although Peerless delivered the Bond to LVC in late August, 1981, LVC did not remit the $23,066 upon delivery, nor did it allocate funds for this purpose. Rather, Fish personally arranged for contributions of funds to LVC sufficient to cover the purchase price of the Bond. LVC eventually paid to Peerless the $23,066 in two installments; $12,500 in March, 1982, and $10,566 in July, 1982.

In order to comply with the sinking fund provision, Peerless made an annual accounting entry on its books whereby it shifted $400,000 from an account entitled "Investments" to an account entitled "Sinking Fund". Peerless then deducted $399,539 on its corporate income tax returns in each of the tax years 1985, 1986 and 1987. Peerless claimed that the $399,539 represented interest accrued on indebtedness, which is deductible under IRC §163(a). The IRS audited Peerless, disallowed the deductions, and assessed the following deficiencies and penalties, with interest thereon:

Tax Year	Deficiency	Penalty	Interest
1985	$175,676	$43,919	$135,704.75
1986	183,788	45,947	108,988.44
1987	159,619	39,905	67,513.79
TOTALS:	519,083	129,771	312,206.98

These assessments relate only to the disallowed interest expense deductions for the Bond.

B. Dynamics of the Peerless Bond Transaction

It is important to understand the dynamics of the Peerless Bond transaction. In exchange for $23,066, Peerless sold LVC a sealed promise to pay $20,000,000 in fifty years. The difference, or original issue discount of $19,976,934, represents the total interest that will accrue over the fifty year Bond term.[4] The tax code and regulations in effect in 1981 permitted accrual basis taxpayers such as Peerless to select a straight-line deduction method whereby the taxpayer allocates the original discount ratably over the term of the Bond. 26 C.F.R. § 1.163-4 (1981); IRC § 1232 (1981); 26 C.F.R. § 1.1232-1(a) (1981).

---

4.   26 C.F.R. § 1.163-4(a) (1981) provides that "the amount of original issue discount equals the excess of the amount payable at maturity over the issue price of the bond * * *."

Rather than deducting the interest that would actually accrue on $23,066 at the 14%annual interest rate–approximately $3,500 per year–Peerless deducted one-fiftieth of the $19,976,934 total discount–or $399,538–in each tax year.

An ordinary commercial purchaser of the Peerless Bond would realize the $399,538 accrued interest as taxable gain in the same tax year that Peerless took its deduction, even though the purchaser never actually received the interest in the form of cash. 26 U.S.C. § 1232(a)(3) (1981). However, LVC is a tax-exempt educational institution under IRC § 501(c)(3) and therefore need not recognize the interest as income at all. LVC need only wait fifty years for its $20,000,000.

Peerless reserved for itself an option to retire the Bond at a discount any time after August, 1986. On August 1, 1986, Peerless could have retired the Bond for $45,377. Had it done so, Peerless would have paid only $22,311 ($45,377 less the original $23,066) for about $2,000,000 in tax deductions. Although the IRS presumably could recapture any tax deficiency attributable to Peerless' deductions for interest accrued but not paid, Peerless would have had the use of that money which, if invested at a modest rate of 4.5%, would have yielded a tidy profit.

Thus, it appears that no one could lose in the Peerless Bond transaction. LVC would always come out ahead; it will recognize tax-exempt income on an investment of $23,066 that it never had in the first place. Peerless, of course, receives the interest deduction and could always retire the Bond for an amount well below the effective tax savings. The United States, however, asserts that the loser in this trans-action is the United States Treasury and that the deductions were improper.

II. IRC § 163(a) AND THE "SHAM TRANSACTION" DOCTRINE

* * *

The plaintiff essentially argues that because the debt obligation is real and enforceable under state law, the plain meaning of § 163(a) permits a deduction for interest accrued on the debt and ends the inquiry. In support of this proposition, the plaintiff cites Commissioner v. Park, 113 F.2d 352 (3d Cir. 1940). *Park* involved a husband's gift of a note to his wife under seal. The court noted that

> The obligation in the present case * * * is to pay a sum certain, upon demand, to the holder of the note. "Indebtedness" as used in the revenue acts has been properly defined as something owed in money which one is unconditionally obligated or bound to pay, the payment

of which is enforceable * * *. This is the ordinary meaning of the word and it squarely covers the note here involved.

Id. at 353. Thus, the Peerless Bond falls squarely within the plain meaning of § 163(a).

The defendant argues that *Park*'s "plain meaning" construction of § 163(a) is not dispositive, because courts since *Park* have used a "substance over form" approach to characterizing transactions for the purposes of § 163. It is well-settled that, while state law drives the determination of whether an obligation is binding and enforceable, federal law controls whether such an obligation constitutes "indebtedness" for the purposes of tax treatment. The defendant relies upon what courts have loosely denominated the "sham transaction" doctrine. Under this doctrine, a transaction is recognized for tax purposes only if it has "economic substance which is compelled or encouraged by business or regulatory realities, is imbued with tax-independent considerations, and is not shaped solely by tax-avoidance features that have meaningless labels attached * * *." Frank Lyon Co. v. United States, 435 U.S. 561, 583-84 (1978).

The parties essentially agree that unless the court disregards the form of the Bond transaction, it should allow the § 163 deduction. A review of the cases upon which the parties rely reveals two distinct, yet somewhat interrelated, methods of analysis that courts have used to disregard the taxpayer's characterization of a transaction. First, courts will ignore accounting tricks and other transactional artifices to disregard transactions that exist only on paper and do not occur in fact, or that "were performed in violation of some of the background assumptions of commercial dealing, for example, arms-length dealing at fair market value." Horn v. Commissioner, 968 F.2d 1229, 1236 n. 8 (D.C.Cir. 1992) (citing Lerman v. Commissioner, 939 F.2d 44, 48 n. 6 (3d Cir. 1991)). This "factual sham" rule is the "sham transaction doctrine" in the true sense of the term.

Second, courts have applied what is commonly known as the "economic substance" test or the "economic reality" test. Under this formulation, courts will ignore for tax purposes transactions "that can not with reason be said to have purpose, substance, or utility apart from their anticipated tax consequences." Goldstein v. Commissioner, 364 F.2d 734, 740 (2d Cir. 1966). Accordingly, a transaction will be disregarded if it lacks a purpose other than pure tax avoidance. *Goldstein*, 364 F.2d at 741.

Neither party contends that the Bond transaction never occurred or occurred only on paper. The defendant does not dispute that Peerless issued the Bond to LVC. With respect to the issue of whether the Bond constitutes an "indebtedness" under § 163(a), the parties' arguments address whether the transaction lacked economic substance * * *.

A.   Economic Substance

In Gregory v. Helvering, 293 U.S. 465 (1935), the Supreme Court made clear that:

> The legal right of a taxpayer to decrease the amount of what otherwise would be his taxes, or altogether avoid them, by means which the law permits, cannot be doubted. But the question for determination is whether what was done, apart from the tax motive, was the thing which the statute intended.

Id. at 469 (citations omitted). Accordingly, the question to be decided by this court is whether what was done in this case--the debt transaction--was the type of transaction that Congress intended to treat favorably under § 163. The leading statement of the Congressional purpose behind § 163 suggests that Congress, by allowing taxpayers to deduct from gross income the cost of borrowing money, intended to encourage borrowing as a means of financing "purposive activity." *Goldstein*, 364 F.2d at 74. Accordingly, if a debt transaction is not motivated by concerns other than pure tax avoidance, the transaction is a "sham" for tax purposes and will not be accorded § 163 treatment. As Judge Waterman stated in *Goldstein*:

> In order to fully implement this Congressional policy of encouraging purposive activity to be financed through borrowing, Section 163(a) should be construed to permit the deductibility of interest when a taxpayer has borrowed funds and incurred an obligation to pay interest in order to engage in what with reason can be termed purposive activity, even though he decided to borrow in order to gain an interest deduction rather than to finance to activity in some other way. In other words, the interest deduction should be permitted whenever it can be said that the taxpayer's desire to secure an interest deduction is only one of mixed motives that prompts the taxpayer to borrow funds; or, put a third way, the deduction is proper if there is some substance to the loan arrangement beyond the taxpayer's desire to secure the deduction. After all, we are frequently told that a taxpayer has the right to decrease the amount of what otherwise would be his taxes, or altogether avoid them, by any means the law permits.

Goldstein, 364 F.2d at 741.

In testing transactions for the requisite purposiveness, courts generally have used two devices to determine whether a tax avoidance motive stands alone. First, a court can scrutinize the objective economic substance of a transaction as a whole and, if the transaction lacks economic sense, the court can infer a lack of tax-independent purpose. Second, the fact-finder can inquire subjectively into the actual motives of the taxpayer. These devices, generally denominated the "economic substance" or "economic reality" test, apply in a variety of tax contexts.

The Courts of Appeals have differed on the precise application of these two devices. The majority of courts that have considered the question have rejected a rigid two-step analysis, opting instead to treat the devices as more precise factors in a flexible sham transaction analysis. *Horn*, 968 F.2d at 1237 (D.C.Cir.); *James*, 899 F.2d at 908-09 (10th Cir.); Shriver v. Commissioner, 899 F.2d 724, 726 (8th Cir. 1990); Rose v. Commissioner, 868 F.2d 851, 854 (6th Cir. 1989); Kirchman v. Commissioner, 862 F.2d 1486, 1492 (11th Cir. 1989); Sochin v. Commissioner, 843 F.2d 351, 354 (9th Cir. 1988); Sheldon v. Commissioner, 94 T.C. 738, 759-61 (1990). *But see* Rice's Toyota World v. Commissioner, 752 F.2d 89, 91-92 (4th Cir. 1985) (adopting a two-pronged test). The parties present arguments based upon both devices.

1. Economic Impact

In Knetsch v. United States, 364 U.S. 361, 363 (1960), the Supreme Court disregarded a debt transaction because it did not "appreciably affect [the taxpayer's] beneficial interest except to reduce his tax." Id. at 363. The Court concluded that there was "nothing of substance to be realized" from the transaction other than a § 163(a) interest deduction. Id. In determining whether an obligation constitutes a true "indebtedness" for the purposes of § 163(a), courts have relied on *Knetsch* to test the transaction for real and appreciable economic substance, in the form of some beneficial or detrimental impact, on the taxpayer's financial position. The plaintiff contends that *Knetsch* and other economic impact cases are not determinative of this case because those cases turned upon a finding that no real indebtedness existed. The plaintiff points out, quite correctly, that the leading cases focused on the fact that the transaction(s) at issue, taken as a whole, resulted in a wash.

* * *

In this case, Peerless correctly notes that it will owe LVC $20,000,000 in 2031 unless it retires the Bond early. Whether Peerless waits until 2031 or retires the Bond early, however, Peerless will have to pay more than the $23,060 received to satisfy its obligation under the Bond. Unlike the commodity option straddles, sale/leasebacks, stock/debenture swaps and step transactions that have been exposed by the economic substance test, there is no offsetting transaction or investment that washes out the debt in this case. This court finds that the transaction does not lack economic substance for want of an "appreciable impact" on the taxpayer's beneficial position. Therefore, the court cannot infer from these circumstances alone that the transaction lacked a purpose other than tax avoidance.

2. Purposiveness

The other device courts have used to test a transaction is a subjective evaluation of the taxpayer's motive. Because an inquiry into "motives" is necessarily subjective, disputes about the taxpayer's true motivation are fact issues not normally capable of resolution at the summary judgment stage. However, the undisputed facts concerning Peerless' motives permit the court to make a determination as a matter of law. First, the parties do not dispute that the favorable §163 tax treatment, in conjunction with the straight-line accrual method then available under § 1232, motivated Peerless in part to issue the Bond. At oral argument, Peerless offered one other purpose for engaging in the transaction: the purpose of providing LVC with an investment that would substantially enhance its endowment. No other purpose has been offered.

Thus, the question for this court is whether, as a matter of law, this purpose is "the thing which the statute intended." *Gregory*, 293 U.S. at 469; *Knetsch*, 364 U.S. at 365. Although it is now well-settled that § 163 contemplates purposive activity, there is a split in authority on whether the taxpayer must be motivated by a *business* purpose or a like concern.

* * *

At least two courts have declined to require a business purpose, noting that § 163 does not explicitly require a business purpose or other commercial intent and that it permits individuals to deduct interest as well. See *Goldstein*, 364 F.2d at 741 (2d Cir.) ("there is no requirement that deductible interest serve a business purpose"); *Sheldon*, 94 T.C. at 766-77 ("Unlike sections 162 and 165 which* * * require that claimed deductions and losses be incurred in a trade or business, section 163 does not contain that specific requirement").[9] The Court of Appeals for the

---

9. As enacted, § 163 permitted interest deductions without significant limitation on either individual or corporate taxpayers. See 26 U.S.C. § 163 (1964). In 1986, Congress eliminated individual deductions for interest paid or accrued except where the indebtedness was

Third Circuit, however, has applied *Gregory 's* business purpose rule in the context of what is now § 163. In Weller v. Commissioner, 270 F.2d 294 (3d Cir. 1959), the court affirmed that Tax Court's finding that the

> [T]he principle laid down in the *Gregory* case is not limited to corporate reorganizations, but rather applies to the federal taxing statutes generally. The words of these statutes which describe commercial transactions are to be understood to refer to transactions entered upon for commercial purposes and "not to include transactions entered upon for no other motive but to escape taxation."

Id. at 297 (construing IRC § 23(b)). Even though the *Weller* panel relied upon *Gregory* 's business purpose rule, the Supreme Court in *Knetsch* cited *Weller* with approval despite the fact that the *Knetsch* Court itself did not rely on *Gregory* 's rationale. *Knetsch*, 364 U.S. at 366 n. 4. Although the Court of Appeals for the Third Circuit has not revisited the question, other courts have similarly required a "business purpose" for debt transactions in which the taxpayer sought an interest deduction under § 163. See, e.g., *James*, 899 F.2d at 908-09 (10th Circuit); *Sochin*, 843 F.2d at 354 (9th Circuit); *Rice's Toyota World*, 752 F.2d at 91-92 (4th Circuit). Of course, this court is bound by *Weller*.

Assuming that Peerless' claimed motive is true, this motive is not the type of "purposiveness" required by the rule. Peerless' desire to help LVC enhance its endowment, while admirable, is wholly unlike the economically self-interested purpose that taxpayers must demonstrate under *Weller*.[10] The plaintiff offers no economic, commercial or business purpose for entering into the transaction. There are no other issues of fact with regard to Peerless' motive and, disregarding Peerless' proffered non-business purpose, a tax avoidance purpose stands alone. Based upon the undisputed facts, this court concludes that the Peerless Bond transaction lacked an independent economic purpose. Under *Weller*, the want of such a purpose requires this court to disregard the debt form of the transaction for the purposes of Peerless' claimed deductions under IRC § 163. 270 F.2d at 297. Accordingly, this court will enter judgment for the United States and against Peerless on Peerless' claim for recovery of the deficiency paid and the interest accrued thereon.

* * *

---

business-related, investment-related or related to a residential mortgage/home equity loan. See The Tax Reform Act of 1986, Pub.L. No. 99-514, § 511, 100 Stat.2085, 2244-49 (1986) (codified at 26 U.S.C. § 163(h)). Although *Sheldon* is a 1990 case, the tax court was applying § 163 as it existed in 1981. 94 T.C. at 760.

10. Indeed, Congress has already provided favorable tax treatment for corporations having such disinterested concern for a § 501(c)(3) corporation. See generally IRC § 170.

III. WHETHER PEERLESS WAS PROPERLY PENALIZED

Section 6661 of the Internal Revenue Code imposes a 25 percent penalty on a taxpayer that substantially understates its tax liability. Having determined that Peerless' disallowed deductions created a tax deficiency, the IRS also concluded that Peerless had substantially understated its tax liability. Peerless does not dispute that, if the deductions are disallowed, Peerless' understatement of its tax liability is "substantial" as Congress has defined the term in IRC § 6661(b). Peerless claims, however, that notwithstanding a finding by this court that the IRS properly disallowed the deductions, Peerless is entitled to recover the $129,771 it paid in penalties.

Peerless has the burden of demonstrating that the penalties should not have been   assessed. In support of this proposition, Peerless relies on subsection 6661(b)(2)(B), which provides:

> (B) The Amount of the understatement * * * shall be reduced by that portion of the understatement that is attributable to--(i) the tax treatment of any item by the taxpayer if there is or was substantial authority for such treatment * * *.

26 U.S.C. § 6661(b(2)(B)(i). The "substantial authority" standard is "less stringent than a 'more likely than not' standard * * * but stricter than a reasonable basis standard." 26 C.F.R. § 1.6661-3(a)(2). A taxpayer has substantial authority for a position "only if the weight of the authorities supporting the treatment is substantial in relation to the weight of authorities supporting contrary positions." Id. at § 1.6661-3(b)(1).

The court finds that Peerless had substantial authority to claim the tax treatment at issue here. The court begins by noting that the plain language of IRC §§ 163 and 1232, as they existed in 1981, permitted the treatment that Peerless sought. Indeed, in 1982, Congress amended the law to remove the availability of the straight line deduction method. There is also some caselaw that supports Peerless' plain language interpretation of §163. Commissioner v. Park, 113 F.2d 352 (3d Cir. 1940); Preston v. Commissioner, 132 F.2d 763, 755-56 (2d Cir. 1942). However, since those decisions, the Supreme Court has held that transactions treated as indebtedness under § 163 can be scrutinized for economic substance. Knetsch v. United States, 364 U.S. 361 (1960). The Court of Appeals for the Third Circuit held the same, one year earlier in Weller v. Commissioner, 270 F.2d 294 (3d Cir. 1959).

There is a somewhat confusing mix of authority in the economic substance doctrine. See Bittker & Lokken, supra, ¶ 4.3.3, at 4-34 ("[I]t is almost impossible to distill useful generalizations from the welter of substance-over-form cases"). As discussed above, the courts are split on the precise application of the economic impact and purposiveness devices.

Plaintiff's argument that the Bond transaction had economic substance provided substantial authority for treating the Bond as a genuine "indebtedness" under § 163. First, the plaintiff successfully persuaded this court that *Knetsch* and other economic impact cases were easily distinguishable from the facts of this case. Those cases involved transactions that, when taken as a whole, created a wash and had no appreciable impact on the taxpayer's beneficial interest. Accordingly, this court concluded that the Peerless Bond had an appreciable economic impact.

Rather, this court found that Peerless Bond transaction lacked a tax-independent purpose. The type of purpose required under § 163(a), however, is far from settled. The seminal case on this issue held that § 163 does not require a "business purpose." Goldstein v. Commissioner, 364 F.2d 734, 741 (2d Cir. 1966). Moreover, the Tax Court, per Judge Gerber, has recently reaffirmed *Goldstein 's* interpretation of § 163. Sheldon v. Commissioner, 94 T.C. 738, 777 (1990). Some courts, however, have required an "economic," "commercial" or "business" purpose. The Court of Appeals for the Third Circuit required one in the *Weller* case, and this court is bound by *Weller*. Weller v. Commissioner, 270 F.2d 294 (3d Cir. 1959).

This court finds that, given this split in authority on what type of purposiveness is required, Peerless had substantial authority to treat the Bond as it did. Despite the fact that the *Weller* case is adverse to Peerless' position, the issue is far from settled and substantial authority supports Peerless' position. Because the penalties at issue here were levied solely on Peerless' claimed treatment for the Bond, the court finds that Peerless is entitled to recover the entire $129,771 in penalties paid.

* * *

Notes and Questions

Substantial authority will not serve as a defense against the substantial understatement penalty in the case of a transaction occurring after December 8, 1994 involving corporate tax shelter items. See § II.B.3, below. It also is not a defense to the penalty under § 6662(b)(6) on transactions lacking economic substance.

Under the regulations, the determination of whether a position has substantial authority is made either at the time the return is filed or on the last day of the taxable year to which the return relates. Reg. § 1.6662-4(d)(3)(iv)(C). But, as one commentator has noted, if the authority is substantial, the Service has no right to penalize a taxpayer if the taxpayer's position is supportable, either at the time the return is prepared or at the time the tax is determined. Michael I. Saltzman, IRS PRACTICE AND PROCEDURE ¶ 7B.03[3][c](Revised Second Edition 2002).

The type of authority determines the weight it should be given. Reg. § 1.6662-4(d)(3)(i). Examples of items considered in determining whether a position has substantial authority are: (1) the Internal Code, (2) proposed, temporary and final regulations, (3)revenue rulings and procedures, (4) tax treaties, (5) court cases, (6) congressional intent as reflected in committee reports, joint explanatory explanations of managers included in conference committee reports, and floor statements made prior to enactment by one of a bill's managers, (7) General explanations of tax legislation prepared by the Joint Committee on Taxation (the Blue Book), (8) private letter rulings and technical advice memoranda issued after October 31, 1976, (9) actions on decisions and general counsel memoranda issued after March 12, 1981, (10) Internal Revenue Service information and press releases, and (11) notices, announcements and other administrative pronouncements published by the Service in the Internal Revenue Bulletin. Reg. § 1.6662-4(d)(3)(iii).

Note that substantial authority is an objective standard. Thus, the taxpayer's view on whether the authority is or should be considered substantial is irrelevant.

1. Do you see any problem with the Service's list of substantial authority?

2. The economic substance doctrine was codified under the Health Care and Education Reconciliation Act of 2010. See IRC § 7701(o). Would this have any effect on the *Peerless* decision? See also IRC § 6662(b)(6).

––––––––––––

While it is assumed generally that substantial authority refers to legal precedents, the Tax Court has defined the term to refer to authority "which would support the taxpayer's application of the law to a given fact or set of facts." Antonides v. Commissioner, 91 T.C. 686, 702 (1998). This raises the issue of whether substantial authority can be determined from a factual standpoint or whether it is narrowly confined to the documentary legal authorities listed in the regulations.

ESTATE OF KLUENER v. COMMISSIONER
United States Court of Appeals, Sixth Circuit, 1998.
154 F.3d 630.

OPINION

SILER, CIRCUIT JUDGE.

This case involves the tax consequences of a horse sale. The petitioners are the estate of Robert Kluener and Kluener's widow, Charlotte ("the taxpayers"). In the late 1980's, Robert Kluener ("Kluener") transferred forty-one horses to his closely-held corporation, sold the horses, then transferred the proceeds back to himself tax-free. Respondent, the Commissioner of Internal Revenue ("IRS"), concluded that Kluener himself sold the horses. It issued a notice of deficiency and a penalty for substantial understatement of taxes. The Tax Court upheld the IRS. We AFFIRM the deficiency judgment and REVERSE the penalty.

I. Background

Kluener controlled four separate lines of investment and used them to avoid taxes. This case centers around the American Power Equipment Company ("APECO"). APECO manufactures paint-spraying products in Harrison, Ohio. In 1989, APECO began to develop a series of "turbo airless sprayers" based on a new type of sprayer mechanism. APECO struggled to perfect this series for several years, and these development problems contributed to its serious financial losses. By the middle of 1989, APECO had a net operating loss ("NOL") exceeding $4.4 million and owed a bank over $5.3 million. These losses directly affected Kluener. He owned all of APECO's stock and served as its Chief Executive Officer, and he normally financed APECO through personally guaranteed loans. Kluener, therefore, was personally liable for APECO's entire debt.

Kluener's other investments were also losing money. Through his sole proprietorship, Robert G. Kluener Enterprises, Kluener owned thoroughbred horses worth about $2.5 million. During the first seven months of 1989, however, Kluener Enterprises lost about $400,000. Finally, Kluener and his wife held two related sets of investments involving their bank. They owned over $12.5 million in securities in the bank. They also owned portions of highly leveraged, interest-generating real estate ventures. They had financed the ventures by borrowing $12.2 million from the bank in personal unsecured loans and then repaying the loans using the interest generated by the ventures. Unfortunately, by 1989 real estate values had plummeted, and their loan repayments began to exceed the interest. In other words, they were losing money on real estate, on APECO, and on the horses.

To help stem the losses, Kluener decided to sell his horses. His two tax advisors, however, cautioned against a direct sale. With a direct sale, any gain would have been taxable as ordinary income or a capital gain. Instead, the advisors recommended that Kluener first transfer the horses to APECO, sell them in APECO's name, and use APECO's NOL to shelter any gain. This procedure would result in little or no tax liability. Kluener took the advice. In August 1989, he transferred the horses to APECO and created a separate division of APECO, APECO Equine, to handle them. Over the next several months, APECO Equine sold the horses at open auction for over $2.5 million, resulting in a gain of over $1.2 million. All proceeds went into the accounts of APECO Equine.

Despite the transfer and sale, APECO never used the funds in APECO Equine. APECO Equine never paid any money to APECO, and Kluener continued to finance APECO through loans. At least two reasons explain this forbearance. In part, an unexpected development reduced APECO's need for these funds. In late 1989, APECO collected $1.6 million on a disputed account receivable. This windfall allowed APECO to operate through the middle of 1990.

In addition, Kluener never gave APECO's officers and directors an opportunity to use the funds. Apart from APECO's vice-president for finance, Kluener never told them that APECO Equine contained almost $2.5 million or that APECO Equine even existed. He recorded neither the horses' transfer nor their sale in APECO's monthly financial statements. Indeed, Kluener actively disguised the existence of APECO Equine. For example, in January 1990, Kluener told APECO's Board of Directors that APECO needed between $1.5 and $2.5 million of capital, but that he knew of no funding sources. In a curious charade, he then solicited funding suggestions despite knowing that APECO Equine contained the needed capital.

Kluener's finances came to a head in the summer of 1990. On June 4, his debts to the bank came due. He owed the bank $12.2 million for the real estate loans, and he had personally guaranteed APECO's loans of almost $4.8 million. Furthermore, Kluener's financial statement showed a negative balance of over $3.8 million, mainly due to the collapsing real estate market. Given this bleak financial outlook, the bank refused to renew the loans and instead forced Kluener to renegotiate. He reluctantly agreed. Under the new terms, he agreed to pay $500,000 immediately and $1 million over the next year. The balance would become due by September 1991.

Faced with this new repayment schedule, Kluener decided to use the horse proceeds to repay the loans. Eleven months after first transferring the horses, Kluener dismissed all other APECO directors and distributed the remaining proceeds, $2,176,000, to himself. Kluener used $1 million to repay the bank and $400,000 to repay a loan from his wife. He loaned the remaining funds back to APECO. APECO reported the sale on its federal income tax return but offset the entire gain against its NOL. The Klueners never reported the gain and never paid any taxes on it. Kluener died in 1991, and APECO eventually was sold for $2.5 million.

After Kluener's death, the IRS concluded that Kluener, not APECO, sold the horses. As a result, it assessed the taxpayers a notice of deficiency of $284,247 and an accuracy-related penalty of $56,093 for substantial understatement of taxes. The taxpayers petitioned the Tax Court for relief. They conceded that tax concerns partially motivated the transfer, but contended that Kluener also transferred the horses for a legitimate business purpose, namely, to provide APECO with capital to develop the new sprayers.

At trial, the taxpayers relied heavily on the testimony of Kluener's two tax advisors, both certified public accountants and partners at Deloitte & Touche. Both advisors testified that Kluener first considered removing the horse proceeds in June1990, after the bank refused to renew the loans. In other words, they asserted that Kluener originally transferred the horses to APECO for a legitimate business purpose, and that, at the time he was transferring the horses, he had no plan to remove their proceeds for personal use. The advisors stressed that they never researched or developed such a plan, and that Kluener had consulted them on all tax issues for almost forty years. Kluener himself was not a tax expert.

Despite this testimony, the Tax Court ruled in favor of the IRS. The court concluded that Kluener transferred the horses for his benefit rather than APECO's benefit. It stressed, among other factors, that APECO never used the funds in APECO Equine, that Kluener hid the funds, and that Kluener used most of the proceeds to satisfy his personal debts. With respect to the accuracy-related penalty, the court held that Kluener lacked substantial authority for his acts. It found his legal sources materially distinguishable.

II. The Deficiency

The main issue on appeal is whether Kluener had a valid, non-tax business purpose for transferring the horses to APECO. If Kluener had such a purpose, the law will recognize the transfer and will deem APECO the horses' seller, thereby letting APECO shelter the gain with its NOL. On the other hand, if Kluener had no such purpose, the law will not recognize the transfer and will deem Kluener the seller, thereby forcing the taxpayers to pay personal taxes on the gain.

* * *

B. Discussion

* * *

Here, the Tax Court deemed Kluener, rather than APECO, the horses' seller. It found that *Kluener* had no valid, non-tax business purpose in transferring the horses. Most importantly, APECO never used any of the horse proceeds. Kluener alone ultimately benefitted from the transfer. He distributed the proceeds to himself less than a year after first transferring the horses. He actively hid the horses, the proceeds, and the very existence of APECO Equine from APECO's officers and directors. Furthermore, Kluener's normal business procedures indicate that he transferred the horses solely for tax reasons. Kluener normally funded APECO through loans, and the property transfer broke with his usual practice. After the transfer, Kluener continued to pay his administrative assistant for horse operations out of his personal funds, even though the assistant nominally had become an APECO employee.

While the taxpayers present some valid points, they fail to overcome the strong deference we must afford the trial court. They contend that Kluener transferred the horses so that APECO could develop the new sprayers, and that he never had a prearranged tax-avoidance plan. They point to financial records indicating that APECO needed capital. They argue that APECO would have used the proceeds but for two unexpected events, the windfall on the disputed account receivable and the bank's decision not to renew the loans. Indeed, Kluener's personal notes indicate that he decided to withdraw the proceeds only after meeting with bank officials. His tax advisors testified unequivocally that they never prearranged to withdraw the funds. They also testified that Kluener himself lacked the tax expertise to design such a plan.

Nevertheless, the Tax Court permissibly rejected these explanations. As the trier of fact, it need not have credited any of the taxpayers' witnesses, including Kluener's tax advisors. For example, the court doubted the windfall explanation; APECO, with its finances admittedly teetering on collapse, could have used the proceeds despite the windfall on the account receivable. The court also doubted that Kluener withdrew the proceeds because the bank refused to renew the loans. Kluener withdrew all of the proceeds, about $2.2 million, even though he needed to reduce his debt by only $1.5 million. Moreover, the court permissibly placed little weight on the lack of a prearranged tax-avoidance plan because a market existed for the transferred property, viz., thoroughbred horses.

* * *

In short, the Tax Court must identify the seller. It decided that Kluener sold the horses, and that finding was not clearly erroneous. Therefore, we affirm the deficiency judgment.

III. The Penalty

The Internal Revenue Code imposes a twenty percent tax on the portion of an underpayment attributable to substantial understatement of income taxes. I.R.C. § 6662(b)(2). This penalty deters taxpayers from playing the "audit lottery." Caulfield v. Commissioner, 33 F.3d 991, 994 (8th Cir. 1994). A taxpayer may reduce or eliminate this penalty by establishing that "substantial authority" supported his tax treatment of an item. I.R.C. § 6662(d)(2)(B)(i). Here, the Tax Court penalized the taxpayers $56,093 for substantial understatement of taxes. The taxpayers contest the penalty only on the ground that substantial authority supported Kluener's tax treatment.

A. Standard of Review

The Sixth Circuit has not yet addressed the standard for reviewing substantial understatement penalties. Several circuits have addressed the standard of review in the context of § 6661(a), the predecessor to the current § 6662. See I.R.C. § 6661(a) (repealed 1989). These decisions conflict. The Ninth Circuit adopted de novo review while the Fourth Circuit chose clear error. Compare Norgaard, 939 F.2d at 877-78, with Antonides v. Commissioner, 893 F.2d 656, 660 (4th Cir. 1990). The Fifth and Eleventh Circuits left the standard of review ambiguous. See Streber v. Commissioner, 138 F.3d 216, 223 (5th Cir. 1998); Osteen v. Commissioner, 62 F.3d 356, 359 (11th Cir. 1995). None of these cases addressed § 6662.

In any event, § 6662's regulations countenance de novo review. "The substantial authority standard is an *objective* standard involving an analysis of the law and application of the law to relevant facts." 26 C.F.R. § 1.6662-4(d)(2) (1997) (emphasis added). In contrast, the regulations interpreting the former § 6661 do not emphasize the standard's objective nature. Cf. id. at § 1.6661-3(a)(2). An objective standard accompanies a legal issue, not a factual issue, with no need to defer to a lower court. Therefore, we review de novo a lower court's decision regarding substantial understatement penalties. We review de novo its evaluation of the law and its application of the law to the relevant facts. We review its underlying factual findings only for clear error.

B. Discussion

Substantial authority exists only if the weight of the taxpayer's authorities is substantial in relation to the contrary authorities. 26 C.F.R. § 1.6662-4(d)(3) (1997). "Substantial" means something less than a preponderance, but more than a mere reasonable basis. Id. at § 1.6662-4(d)(2). "Authority" includes several sources of law, such as statutes, court cases, legislative history, and regulations, although none of these is particularly relevant if "materially distinguishable" on its facts. See id. at § 1.6662-4(d)(3)(ii). The taxpayer's subjective belief that there is substantial authority is irrelevant. Id. at § 1.6662- 4(d)(3)(i).

The Sixth Circuit has not yet considered two issues regarding substantial authority. We must consider the precise meaning of "substantial," and whether "authority" includes factual evidence as well as legal sources. A § 6661 case addressed both issues. See Osteen v. Commissioner, 62 F.3d 356, 359 (11th Cir. 1995). In *Osteen*, the taxpayers consistently lost money on their horse breeding operation. The deficiency issue turned on the taxpayers' intent. The Tax Court upheld the deficiency after finding that the taxpayers never intended to earn a profit, and upheld a tax penalty after finding that they lacked substantial authority for their position. On appeal, the Eleventh Circuit criticized the substantial authority standard:

> The application of a substantial authority test is confusing in a case of this kind. If the horse breeding enterprise was carried on for profit, all of the deductions * * * would be allowed. There is no authority to the contrary. If the enterprise was not for profit, none of the deductions would be allowed. There is no authority to the contrary. Nobody argues, however, not even the Government, that because the taxpayers lose on the factual issue, they also must lose on what would seem to be a legal issue.

Id. at 359. In other words, the court criticized the substantial authority test for ignoring factual evidence. Without the facts, the taxpayers could present no authority to support their position, much less substantial authority.

The court then considered the penalty issue from both factual and legal standpoints. It held that substantial factual authority supported the taxpayers' position:

> If the Tax Court was deciding that there was no substantial authority because of the weakness of the taxpayers' evidence to establish a profit motive, we reverse because a review of the record reveals there was evidence both ways. In our judgment, under the clearly erroneous standard of review, the Tax Court would be due to be affirmed [on the deficiency] even if it had decided this case for the taxpayers. With that state of the record, there is substantial authority from a factual standpoint for the taxpayer's position. Only if there was a record upon which the Government could obtain a reversal under the clearly erroneous standard could it be argued that from an evidentiary standpoint, there was not substantial authority for the taxpayer's position.

Id. The court also held that substantial legal authority supported their position:

> If the Tax Court was deciding there was not substantial legal authority for the deductions, we reverse because of the plethora of cases in which the Tax Court has found a profit motive in the horse breeding activities of taxpayers that were similar to those at hand.

Id. Therefore, under *Osteen*, "authority" encompasses factual evidence, particularly in a case that turns on intent; "substantial" authority exists if the taxpayers present sufficient facts to support a judgment in their favor under the clearly erroneous standard of review, looking at the case as if they had won on the deficiency. Id. See also Streber v. Commissioner, 138 F.3d 216, 223 (5th Cir. 1998) (in a § 6661 case that turned on the date of a gift, following *Osteen* and holding that authority includes factual evidence).

Osteen 's analysis applies to § 6662. Under § 6662, "authority" encompasses factual evidence as well as legal sources. Section 6662's regulations direct us to examine relevant facts: "[t]he substantial authority standard * * * involv[es] an analysis of the law and application of the law to relevant facts." 26 C.F.R. § 1.6662-4(d)(2) (1997). Indeed, the regulations demand that we examine the facts: "[t]he weight of authorities is determined in light of the pertinent facts and circumstances." Id. at § 1.6662-4(d)(3)(i). On the other hand, another provision seems to imply that authority consists only of legal sources. After stating that "only the following are authority," the regulations list numerous legal sources of authority, but never refer to factual evidence. Id. at § 1.6662- 4(d)(3)(iii). Nonetheless, we interpret this provision as excluding only certain types of legal sources, not any factual evidence. For example, this provision states that "authority" does not include overruled decisions or the opinions of tax advisors. In any event, to the extent that the regulations may conflict, we reconcile them by noting that two provisions command us to examine relevant facts, whereas nothing explicitly precludes us from examining them.

Moreover, policy concerns indicate that "authority" should include factual evidence. In this case, for example, to ignore the facts is to assess a penalty. Nothing in the regulations supports such a result. Finally, practical jurisprudential factors force courts to examine the facts. A court must examine the facts to evaluate a legal source's relevance. In this sense, a legal source can constitute substantial authority only if its facts resemble those in the current case.

We disagree, however, with *Osteen* 's analysis of "substantial." Under the regulations, "substantial" means more than a reasonable basis. 26 C.F.R. § 1.6662-4(d)(2) (1997). Therefore, "substantial authority" requires a taxpayer to present considerable or ample authority, whereas *Osteen* requires him to present only some evidence. See Streber v. Commissioner, 138 F.3d 216, 228 (5th Cir. 1998) (King, J., dissenting).[2]

Here, the Tax Court found that substantial authority did not support Kluener's position. The court did not examine the factual evidence. In a footnote, it distinguished the taxpayers' legal authority, *Caruth* and *Smalley*, on the ground that the corporations in those cases used the transferred proceeds. This cursory footnote represented the court's entire discussion of an issue that cost the taxpayers $56,093.

We hold that substantial authority supported Kluener's tax treatment of the horse proceeds. Considerable factual evidence indicates that he transferred the horses for a valid, non-tax business purpose. This evidence includes his reference notes, the lack of prior research, his lack of tax expertise, and APECO's genuine need for funds. This evidence is substantial in relation to the contrary evidence. There are

---

2. In appeals from administrative bodies, courts review factual findings under a "substantial evidence" test. See Allentown Mack Sales and Serv., Inc. v. NLRB, 522 U.S. 359, ----, 118 S.Ct. 818, 828, 139 L.Ed.2d 797 (1998). In that context, substantial evidence is the degree of evidence that could satisfy a reasonable factfinder. While "substantial" may mean slightly different things in each context, this formula comports with the text of the regulations and offers a familiar framework. We need not define "substantial" precisely, however, because we would reverse under any of these formulas.

two very strong contrary facts: APECO never used the proceeds, and Kluener actively hid APECO Equine. Neither of these facts, alone or combined with others, overwhelms the taxpayers' evidence. The two unexpected financial developments explain, at least in part, APECO's forbearance. Similarly, Kluener's deceit does not necessarily mean that he never intended to benefit APECO. As APECO's sole shareholder and CEO, Kluener could have controlled the proceeds without deceiving anyone. The taxpayers argue that he wanted APECO personnel to focus on the new sprayers; in light of his total control, this rationale carries at least some weight.

With this factual background, substantial legal authority supported Kluener's tax treatment. In this type of case, the distinctions between valid and invalid transfers are "shadowy and artificial." Several cases support Kluener's tax treatment. In both *Caruth* and *Smalley*, for example, a shareholder transferred property to improve the finances of a legitimate corporation, not a shell. See Caruth v. United States, 688 F.Supp. 1129 (N.D.Tex.1987), aff'd on another issue, 865 F.2d 644 (5th Cir. 1989); Smalley v. Commissioner, 32 T.C.M. (CCH) 373 (1973). In neither case was the transfer essential, and in neither case did the transferee use the funds immediately. Although those transferees ultimately used the funds, those taxpayers never faced an unexpected financial squeeze. As a result, when Kluener prepared his tax returns, *Caruth* and *Smalley* provided substantial authority supporting his tax treatment.

* * *

Therefore, we reverse the imposition of an accuracy-related penalty.[3] AFFIRMED in part, REVERSED in part.

WELLFORD, CIRCUIT JUDGE, concurring in part and dissenting in part.

I concur with my colleagues in affirming the Tax Court with respect to the deficiency judgment of $284,247 against the estate of Robert G. Kluener set out in Parts I and II of the majority opinion. I respectfully dissent, however, from the majority's decision to reverse the penalty against the estate and, therefore, express my disagreement with Part III of the opinion.

* * *

---

3.   Surprisingly, the taxpayers never cite I.R.C. § 6664. Section 6664 precludes penalties under § 6662 if the taxpayer establishes that he underpaid in good faith and based on reasonable cause. Richardson v. Commissioner, 125 F.3d 551, 554 (7th Cir. 1997). See also Betson v. Commissioner, 802 F.2d 365, 372 (9th Cir. 1986); 26 C.F.R. § 1.6664-4, ex. 1 (1997). In *Betson*, for example, the court reversed tax penalties because the taxpayer acted in good faith and in reliance on tax advisors, even though the trial court did not believe his motives. In any event, we need not address § 6664.

Even if the appellants did not waive this issue [eds.: "by failing to cite any compelling authority to support their position except regulatory language"], I would affirm the penalty as assessed by the Tax Court. It appears to this writer that the same standard of review should be applied to a penalty for negligent failure to report as for substantial understatement of tax under 26 U.S.C. § 6661 or § 6662. Without an in-depth analysis of this issue, the court in Norgaard v. Commissioner, 939 F.2d 874 (9th Cir. 1991), simply stated that "[d]e novo review is proper because the existence of 'substantial authority' is a legal question." Id. at 878. The *Norgaard* court went on to hold that " '[s]ubstantial authority' is * * * stricter than a reasonable basis standard." Id. at 880. The court explained that "a taxpayer's position with respect to the tax treatment of an item that is arguable but fairly unlikely to prevail in court would satisfy a reasonable basis standard but *not the substantial authority standard*." Id. (emphasis added). The majority in this case apparently approved of that standard of review, and concluded that we should "review de novo [a lower court's] evaluation of the law and its application of the law to the relevant facts. We review its underlying factual findings only for clear error."

I would affirm the Tax Court's assessment of the penalty in this case under the standard endorsed by the majority. The appellants argue that "substantial authority" existed to support their tax treatment of the horse sales. The legal authority upon which the appellants rely is the same as that relied upon to challenge the deficiency itself. The appellants cite cases which hold "that funding of corporate operations [is] a valid business purpose." I do not disagree with this legal premise. The appellants' argument, however, presupposes that Kluener in fact transferred the proceeds of the horses to APECO to fund corporate operations. We have unanimously found that Kluener had no valid business purpose in the transfer of the horses. In essence, the appellants' entire argument regarding the penalty is a factual one, and it must rise or fall depending on the disposition of the deficiency issue. Because the absence of a valid business purpose undermines the appellants' legal arguments, the argument that "substantial authority" existed for their tax treatment of the horses must fail.

The appellants boldly assert that "it is the policy of the Internal Revenue Service to assess penalties in virtually every situation * * * in the hopes of setting up straw men to use as the basis under which to extract some settlement from a taxpayer." Appellants do not, however, suggest that the assessment of the penalty in this case was merely a "bargaining chip" which the government intended to use against the estate. Conspicuously, they cite no cases to support their argument that the use of the penalty in this case was inappropriate.

Thus, I would find that the Tax Court was not clearly erroneous in its factual findings and was not incorrect in its legal conclusion that the penalty at issue was appropriate. Accordingly, I dissent on that issue and would AFFIRM the Tax Court in its decision on all issues in this appeal.

Notes and Question

Note that Kluener's factual evidence was not sufficient to allow the estate to prevail on the merits, but it was considered sufficient to allow it to avoid a substantial understatement penalty. The substantial authority standard is an uncertain standard, because a position's chance of success is often difficult to quantify, and determining whether the weight of authority is substantial in relation to the weight of contrary authority also is difficult, especially for a taxpayer with no legal training. Therefore, adequate disclosure provides a more certain safe harbor against the substantial understatement penalty.

Judge Siler, in footnote three, finds it surprising that the estate did not raise a reasonable cause defense under § 6664. Reasonable cause focuses on the taxpayer's conduct rather than on the legal and factual authority underlying the taxpayer's position. If the reasonable cause defense had been raised, the court would have had to determine whether Kluener's reliance on his tax advisors constituted reasonable cause and good faith. While this issue was not addressed, the court, in expressing surprise that § 6664 was not raised, implies that such reliance was reasonable. Is the court confusing reasonable cause with substantial authority?

2. Adequate Disclosure

An understatement of tax is reduced to the extent it is attributable to a position that has a reasonable basis and is adequately disclosed on the return or in a statement attached to the return. IRC § 6662(d)(2)(B)(ii); Reg. § 1.6662-4(e)(2)(i).

HENRY v. COMMISSIONER

United States Tax Court, Memorandum Decision, 1997.

1997 WL 14456, rev'd on another issue, 170 F.3d 1217 (9th Cir. 1999).

MEMORANDUM FINDINGS OF FACT AND OPINION

GERBER, JUDGE:

Respondent determined a deficiency in petitioners' 1982 Federal income tax in the amount of $2,099,534 and additions to tax pursuant to sections 6653(a)(1) and 6661 [eds.: now § 6662] in the amounts of $104,976.70 and $524,883.50, respectively.

The issues remaining for our consideration concern whether petitioners are liable for additions to tax under * * * section 6661 for the taxable year 1982. * * *

[Eds: The following facts are taken from Henry v. Commissioner, 170 F.3d 1217, 1218 (9th Cir. 1999): Albert J. Henry was the vice president-finance, chief financial officer and a member of the board of directors of IMED Corporation ("IMED") which provided stock options to him for his services to the corporation. He, along with other officers, filed I.R.C. § 83(b) elections for certain options in which they reported the fair market value of the options as zero. The options were eventually sold to Warner-Lambert Company ("Warner-Lambert") in 1982 and the taxpayers reported long-term capital gain from the sale of these options. In *Cramer* [v. Commissioner, 101 T.C. 225 (1993), affd. 64 F.3d 1406 (9th Cir. 1995)], the Tax Court held that I.R.C. § 83 required the proceeds from these options to be taxable as ordinary income because the options did not have a "readily ascertainable fair market value" as defined in Treas. Reg. § 1.83-7(b)(2). Therefore, the Tax Court in *Cramer* found that the three IMED officers involved in that case, including Richard Cramer, the president and chief executive officer of IMED, understated their income by long-term capital gain treatment of the sale of their options to Warner-Lambert. The petitioners in this case stipulated that they would be bound by the deficiency finding in *Cramer*. Therefore, this issue is not before us on appeal. * * * In *Cramer*, three other officers, Cramer, Warren Boynton, the vice president of IMED, and Kevin Monaghan, the outside general counsel and assistant secretary of the board of directors of IMED, were found liable for intentional disregard of the rules or regulations and assessed additions to tax under § 6653(a). See *Cramer*, 64 F.3d at 1414-15. The basis of this finding was that these three directors knew that long-term capital gain treatment of the 1982 option sale was contrary to Treas. Reg. § 1.83-7(b)(2) and chose to ignore it because they believed there was a valid argument that Treas. Reg. §

1.83-7 was contrary to congressional intent and an invalid interpretation of I.R.C. § 83. Id. The Tax Court disagreed with their interpretation of the regulation, as did this court, when Judge Brunetti observed, "This legislative history does not demonstrate that the Reg. § 1.83-7(b)(2) interpretation of § 83 is unreasonable."[3] *Cramer*, 64 F.3d at 1413. We then concluded that the petitioners in *Cramer* chose to play the "audit lottery" and lost. Id. at 1415.]

* * *

Substantial Understatement Addition to Tax

Next, petitioners contend that respondent erred in determining additions to tax for substantial understatements under section 6661. Section 6661(a) imposes an addition to tax when there is a "substantial understatement of income tax for any taxable year". As applicable here, the addition to tax under section 6661(a) is equal to 25 percent [ed.: now 20 percent under § 6662] of the underpayment attributable to the substantial understatement. Petitioners bear the burden of proving that the addition to tax under section 6661 is not applicable.

Section 6661(b)(2)(A) defines "understatement" as the excess of the amount of tax   required to be shown on the return over the amount of tax actually reported on the return. This understatement will be "substantial" if the amount of such understatement exceeds the greater of 10 percent of the amount of tax required to be shown on the return for the taxable year, or $5,000. Sec. 6661(b)(1)(A).

The section 6661 addition to tax is not applicable, however, if there was substantial authority for the position taken on the taxpayer's return, or adequate disclosure in the return of the relevant facts affecting the treatment of the item. Sec. 6661(b)(2)(B)(i) and (ii).

Petitioners have not contended that there was substantial authority for their reporting position. Petitioners contend that the tax treatment of the proceeds of the sale of IMED's stock options was adequately disclosed in their return as filed. Respondent disputes that petitioners adequately disclosed the item in question.

---

3. This court concluded:

Treasury reasonably concluded that § 83(e)(3) allows restrictions to be considered when determining whether an option has a "readily ascertainable fair market value." Furthermore, Treasury reasonably concluded that certain restrictions, such as those effecting transfer, exercise, and market value, make an option's value not "readily ascertainable," because it is difficult to determine the impact of those restrictions on market value. We therefore reject appellants challenge to Reg. § 1.83- 7(b)(2).

Cramer, 64 F.3d at 1413.

In Schirmer v. Commissioner, 89 T.C. 277, 285-286 (1987), we explained that the regulations provide for two types of adequate disclosure for purposes of section 6661(b)(2)(B)(ii): Disclosure in a statement attached to the return or disclosure on the return pursuant to the Commissioner's revenue procedures. Sec. 1.6661-4(b) and (c), Income Tax Regs. In addition, we noted that a taxpayer may satisfy the adequate disclosure requirement of section 6661(b)(2)(B)(ii) by providing on the return sufficient information to enable the Commissioner to identify the potential controversy involved.

Petitioners' expert witness, John J. Monaco (Monaco), was previously Assistant Commissioner (Examination) for respondent, where he was an employee for 33 years. Monaco opined that the zero basis reported on the return would be adequate disclosure of the relevant facts. Monaco concluded that such disclosure was sufficient to apprise respondent of the facts and the nature of the potential controversy concerning the tax treatment of the item. Monaco decided that the zero basis "would be a clear indication that the options had been awarded to the employee as compensatory stock options and that no value had been reflected in * * * [Henry's] income either at the time the options were received or at any other time prior to the sale of such option." Monaco stated that there was no other likely explanation for a zero basis. Monaco opined that the zero basis reported on petitioners' 1982 return was sufficient to apprise respondent of the tax treatment of the item in question. Based on his experience, Monaco believed that a return with a reported zero basis for employee stock options and claimed capital gain treatment would be selected for examination.

In the present cases, petitioners' 1982 return identified the property in question and clearly distinguished between stocks and options.[5] Furthermore, the return disclosed the dates the shares and options were acquired and sold, sales price, a basis of zero, and the gain involved. It appears likely that the items reported generated respondent's audit. The information reported was sufficient to apprise respondent of and enable respondent to identify the potential controversy involved here; that is, whether petitioners properly treated the stock option proceeds as long-term capital gain.

We hold that petitioners adequately disclosed the information and are not liable for the addition to tax under section 6661.

* * *

---

5.   It should be noted that in Cramer v. Commissioner, 101 T.C. 225, 255-256 (1993), affd. 64 F.3d 1406 (9th Cir. 1995), the returns, unlike petitioners', "contained misrepresentations that actually concealed the true nature of the option proceeds"; i.e., a false claim of basis or, in the Boyntons' case, a mischaracterization of the options as stock. See also 64 F.3d at 1415.

Notes

If an item is recurring, a qualifying disclosure must be made in each taxable year in which the item occurs on a return. See Reg. § 1.6662-4(f)(3). In order to be considered a qualifying disclosure, the disclosure must be made in accordance with Rev. Proc. 99-41, 1999-2 C.B. 566. The taxpayer is required to furnish all required information in accordance with the applicable forms and instructions, and the money amounts must be verifiable. An amount is verifiable if the taxpayer can identify its origin (even if the Service ultimately rejects the numerical amount) and the taxpayer can establish that she acted in good faith in entering that amount on the applicable form.

Problems

1. Carrie filed her federal income tax return for the taxable year 2008 on April 10, 2009. The return showed taxable income of $65,000 and a corresponding tax liability of $18,000, of which $16,000 was paid through wage withholding. Carrie remitted the remaining $2,000 when she filed her return. The return subsequently was audited 16 months later, and the IRS determined that Carrie's taxable income had been understated. Her redetermined taxable income was found to be $78,000, and her recomputed tax liability was determined to be $20,500. Carrie has no substantial authority for her omission of this income and has made no qualifying disclosure. Will she be subject to an accuracy-related penalty? If so, which penalty and how much?

2. In the alternative, assume in question one that the amount of Carrie's redetermined taxable income was $85,000 and the recomputed tax attributable to this amount was $26,000. Will Carrie be subject to an accuracy-related penalty? If so, which penalty and what amount will she have to pay?

3. In question two, assume that Carrie has adequately disclosed the facts behind the omission of $8,000 of taxable income, and her tax liability attributable to that amount is $2,000. Assume further that she has a reasonable basis with respect to this omission. Will she be subject to an accuracy-related penalty? If so, which one and how much?

4. If your client has a substantial understatement of tax on a filed return, what factors might you consider in advising that client whether or not to disclose the understatement?

3. Reasonable Cause

NPR INVESTMENTS, LLC v. UNITED STATES
United States District Court, E.D. Texas, 2010
732 F.Supp.2d 676.

T. JOHN WARD, DISTRICT JUDGE.

* * *

I. BACKGROUND

A. The Participants

Harold W. Nix ("Nix"), Charles C. Patterson ("Patterson"), and Nelson J. Roach ("Roach") (collectively the "Taxpayers") are long-time partners in the law firm of Nix, Patterson & Roach, LLP (the "Law Firm"), located in Daingerfield, Texas. The law firm primarily handles plaintiffs' contingency fee cases and enjoys a reputation for being a premier plaintiffs' trial law firm. Messrs. Nix, Patterson, and Roach are partners in NPR, formed for various investment purposes in August 2001. NPR invested in offsetting foreign currency digital options that created tax losses of approximately $65 million for the Taxpayers by entering into transactions that form the basis of this lawsuit. The IRS has characterized these transactions as "Son of BOSS" transactions, and accordingly, is seeking to recover penalties from the Taxpayers.[3]

B. The Transactions at Issue

In 2001, the Taxpayers expressed to Mr. Sid Cohen ("Cohen"), their personal CPA at Pollans & Cohen, an interest in investing in foreign currencies because investments in foreign currency carried the possibility of returns not achievable in traditional investments.[4] When the Taxpayers expressed their interest in investing in foreign currencies

---

3.   "BOSS" is an acronym for "Bond and Option Sales Strategy" and refers to an abusive tax shelter. Son of BOSS is a variation of the slightly older BOSS tax shelter. A Son of BOSS shelter may take many forms, but common to them all is the transfer to a partnership of assets laden with significant liabilities claimed to be contingent. A Son of BOSS transaction uses a series of contrived steps in a partnership interest to generate artificial tax losses designed to offset income from other transactions. In IRS Notice 2000-44 ("Tax Avoidance Using Artificially High Basis"), which was published on September 5, 2000, the IRS alerted taxpayers that the Son of BOSS scheme had been "listed" as an abusive tax shelter. See generally Kornman & Associates, Inc. v. United States, 527 F.3d 443, 446 n. 2 (5th Cir.2008).

4.   Mr. Cohen had nearly 40 years of experience, much of which was spent at Arthur Andersen in Chicago doing audits, tax work, special consulting, cost studies, and construction audits. (Tr. I at 140-42.) After leaving Arthur Andersen in 1982, Mr. Cohen moved to Beaumont, Texas where he formed the accounting firm Pollans & Cohen. In addition to providing clients with audit and tax work, Pollans & Cohen also evaluated investment opportunities for clients. (Tr. I at 142.)

to Cohen, there was no discussion of tax benefits. Cohen introduced the Taxpayers to the Diversified Group, Inc. ("DGI") in the summer of 2001 because DGI was offering an investment involving options in foreign currencies. Cohen described the foreign currency option investment being offered by DGI as "risky" but also pointed out to the Taxpayers that they had the "potential to make a lot of money on it." On August 28, 2001, Nix and Patterson each set up a single member limited liability company ("SMLLC"). Nix and Patterson each funded their SMLLCs with $625,000. On that same day, August 28, 2010, DGI and Alpha Consultants Inc. ("Alpha") formed NPR and became its co-managers.

At the Taxpayers' direction, Cohen set up a meeting with DGI and R.J. Ruble ("Ruble"), a lawyer with the law firm Sidley, Austin, Brown & Wood LLP ("Sidley Austin"), in New York in October of 2001. The meeting in New York was attended by Cohen, Patterson, Mr. James Haber ("Haber"), and Ruble, among others. Haber explained investments in paired foreign currency options and how they could be profitable. In general with paired options, one can take a long position and/or a short position in a foreign currency. DGI's investment strategy involved both a long and short option in the foreign currency with a certain option period and certain strike prices.[5] The investment strategy could be profitable, excluding any advisement fees, in one of two ways. First, if the reference price for the foreign currency options on the option's expiration date fell between the strike prices on the long and short option positions, the investor would make a substantial profit. Under this scenario, the investor would receive a payment under the long option without having to pay out under the short option. This was coined the "sweet spot." DGI did not provide a stated probability of hitting the "sweet spot" to the Taxpayers.

Second, if the reference price on the expiration date was greater than both strike prices, then the investor would receive a payment under the long position, but would also have to pay out under the short position, resulting in a net profit less than if the reference price settled between the strike prices. If the reference price on the expiration date was less than both strike prices, then the investor would pay nothing and receive nothing.

---

5.   For example, assume that the strike price for the long position was 125.68 in a particular currency and the strike price for the short position was 125.71 for the same currency. (Tr. I at 49.) If, at the end of the option period, the price was 125.68 or greater, then one would be "in the money" with the long position, and, similarly, if it was 125.71 or greater, then one would be "in the money" with the short position. (Id.) If the strike price is between 125.68 and 125.71, then it would be in the "sweet spot." (Id. at 50-51.) The "sweet spot" is the range where the long option pays and the short option does not pay, in other words, a "home run." (Tr. I at 149.)

The same day in New York, Ruble also met with Patterson and Cohen at DGI's office. Ruble brought with him a draft, template tax opinion letter describing a similar transaction to the one proposed to Taxpayers. Ruble went through the opinion with Patterson and Cohen to explain the tax benefits or losses from the transaction and his "legal analysis" of the correct treatment of such benefits. Ruble confirmed that hitting the sweet spot was "a high risk long shot" and that if the options pairs did not "hit all the way" or did not hit the sweet spot, there would be tax losses.

By October 25, 2001, Roach decided to join the investment scheme, formed his own SMLLC, and funded it with $375,000. Like Nix's and Patterson's SMLLCs, Roach's SMLLC was also managed by DGI. On October 30, 2001, each Taxpayer purchased two pairs of offsetting foreign currency options, with each paired option being in the same foreign currency with identical expiration dates and almost identical strike prices, through their respective SMLLCs. The strike prices of the long and short components of each option pair were set apart by only three pips, "a razor thin" margin.[6] The options were European style options and could be exercised only on their respective expiration dates. On November 8, 2001, the Taxpayers each contributed their SMLLCs, and effectively their paired options, to NPR and received partnership interests in NPR. DGI and Alpha were the managers of NPR and on November 1, 2001 each contributed $50,000 to NPR.

Nix and Patterson each paid DGI an "advisory fee" of $750,000 and Roach paid DGI a fee of $450,000. In addition, Nix and Patterson paid Cohen a fee of $250,000 and Roach paid Cohen a fee of $150,000. DGI also directly paid Cohen a fee of $325,000 for referring the Taxpayers as clients, which was unknown to the Taxpayers until after the penalties were assessed. In deciding whether to enter into this transaction, Patterson relied upon the representations of Cohen and DGI. Nix and Roach relied upon the representations of Cohen and Patterson and even appointed Patterson as their agent to investigate the transactions. All three Taxpayers relied on Cohen as their fiduciary agent to DGI and the transactions.

C. Decision to Withdraw from the Partnership and Tax Reporting

On December 18, 2001, all three Taxpayers withdrew from NPR. In exchange for their partnership interests, they received cash and foreign currencies representing the fair market value of their interests in NPR

---

6.   "Pips" are the smallest unit quoted for any given currency. During any 15 minute time span, the prices quoted by different banks for foreign currencies can vary by more than three pips.

as of December 18, 2001. The Taxpayers then contributed their foreign currencies to a different partnership through which they operated their Law Firm. Inside of the Law Firm, all gains or losses on these foreign currencies were to be specially allocated to their respective contributing partners on the Law Firm's books and tax returns such that the Law Firm's other partners did not receive any gain or loss from these foreign currencies. The losses from these foreign currency sales were listed in a "Business Risk Division" on the Law Firm's tax returns. When the foreign currencies were sold in 2001, 2002, and 2003, the Law Firm offset these losses against the income allocated to each Taxpayer to reduce the earned income shown on Schedules K-1 issued to the Taxpayers by the Law Firm. The DGI investment scheme was generally described under IRS Notice 2000-44:

> In another variation, a taxpayer purchases and writes options and purports to create substantial positive basis in a partnership interest by transferring those option positions to a partnership. For example, a taxpayer might purchase call options for a cost of $1,000X and simultaneously write offsetting call options, with a slightly higher strike price but the same expiration date, for a premium of slightly less than $1,000X. Those option positions are then transferred to a partnership which, using additional amounts contributed to the partnership, may engage in investment activities.

> Under the position advanced by the promoters of this arrangement, the taxpayer claims that the basis in the taxpayer's partnership interest is increased by the cost of the purchased call options but is not reduced under § 752 as a result of the partnership's assumption of the taxpayer's obligation with respect to the written call options. Therefore, disregarding additional amounts contributed to the partnership, transaction costs, and any income realized and expenses incurred at the partnership level, the taxpayer purports to have a basis in the partnership interest equal to the cost of the purchased call options ($1,000X in this example), even though the taxpayer's net economic outlay to acquire the partnership interest and the value of the partnership interest are nominal or zero. On the disposition of the partnership interest, the taxpayer claims a tax loss ($1,000X in this example), even though the taxpayer has incurred no corresponding economic loss.

> The purported losses resulting from the transactions described above do not represent bona fide losses reflecting actual economic consequences as required for purposes of § 165. The purported losses from these transactions (and from any similar arrangements designed to produce noneconomic tax losses by artificially overstating

basis in partnership interests) are not allowable as deductions for federal income tax purposes.

See IRS Notice 2000-44, at 3-4. The Taxpayers engaged in similar transactions and tax reporting as described in IRS Notice 2000-44. As stated previously, when the Taxpayers withdrew from NPR, they received cash and foreign currencies representing the fair market value of their interests in NPR as of December 18, 2001. In their tax returns, the Taxpayers claimed that Section 752 allowed them to increase their tax basis in NPR by the premiums on the contributed long options but did not require them to reduce that basis by the amount they might have to pay on the contributed short options. The foreign currencies received by the Taxpayers upon withdrawal from NPR had a basis materially distinct from their value, and the basis was determined by what the Taxpayers paid for the long option position, while ignoring what the Taxpayers were paid for the short option position.

When the Taxpayers resigned from NPR based on Roach's decision to withdraw for personal reasons, the Taxpayers each obtained a thorough, written opinion from Sidley Austin that detailed the proper tax treatment of their investments. In drafting those opinions, Sidley Austin relied on representations made by each of the Taxpayers. Each of the Taxpayers believed these representations to be true at the time they were made, and continued to believe them to be true at the time of trial. Not learned in the area of tax law, the Taxpayers reviewed the Sidley Austin opinions with Cohen. After reviewing the Sidley Austin opinions, Cohen concluded that the opinions "had cited the important areas where there might be potential controversy and had adequately dealt with them to [his] satisfaction that [the Taxpayers] would be okay." Accordingly, Cohen advised the Taxpayers that they could rely on the opinions because Sidley Austin was a "very well known firm," because the opinions were "very, very well reasoned," and because Ruble was an "acknowledged partnership tax expert."

D. The Notice of Final Partnership Administrative Adjustment (FPAA)

NPR's 2001 tax return was prepared by Grant Thornton LLP and filed with the IRS on or about April 1, 2002. On line 2 of Schedule B, the return indicates that one of NPR's partners was a partnership. However, in the same tax return on line 4 of Schedule B, NPR answered "No" to the following question, "Is this partnership subject to the consolidated audit procedures of Sections 6221 through 6223?" Sections 6221 through 6223 refer to TEFRA's audit procedures. In fact, NPR was a partnership subject to the TEFRA audit procedures, and therefore, the answer should have been "Yes."

NPR's return was initially examined by Paul Doerr ("Doerr"), who currently is and was an Internal Revenue Service ("IRS") Agent in 2005. Doerr and his managers did not initiate the standard TEFRA procedures, but instead they applied the normal deficiency procedures set forth in Sections 6211 through 6216 and issued a standard Letter 2205 for notifying non-TEFRA partnerships and other taxpayers that their returns have been selected for examination. The IRS notified NPR on March 25, 2005 that it had completed its audit and had determined that no adjustments would be made to NPR's 2001 tax year. The March 25, 2005 notice stated:

> We've completed the examination of your tax return for the year(s) shown above. We made no changes to your reported tax.
>
> * * *
>
> This letter is the final notice you'll receive regarding your examination unless you are a shareholder in a subchapter S corporation, a beneficiary of a trust, or a partner in a partnership. We may examine the tax return of a subchapter S corporation, trust, or partnership in which you are involved later and find that we have to make changes to the return. Otherwise, this is the final notice you will receive regarding the examination.

Doerr signed the notice on behalf of the IRS. Doerr and his managers initially and mistakenly concluded that there was no need to adjust any of the items on NPR's return. Instead, they intended to deny the losses related to the Taxpayers' participation in NPR by issuing notices of deficiency directly to NPR's partners under the normal audit procedures. While under a belief that NPR was not subject to the TEFRA procedures, Doerr issued the March 2005 no-change letter to NPR indicating that no changes were necessary to its return.

Doerr also prepared deficiency notices denying losses on Patterson's personal tax returns related to both his participation in NPR and losses related to his participation in a separate BLIPS transaction.[7] These normal deficiency notices were reviewed by Robert Gee ("Gee") in his capacity as the group manager for all the BLIPS cases across the

---

7.   BLIPS is an acronym for Bond Linked Issue Premium Structure. It is a type of tax shelter involving investors who take out "illegitimate" bank loans to claim tax losses. Like NPR, Klamath Strategic Investment Fund, LLC ("Klamath") is another company that the Taxpayers used for investment purposes, and Klamath invested in BLIPS transactions. Like NPR, Klamath was involved in a TEFRA partnership proceeding in this Court pursuant to Section 6226. See, generally, Klamath Strategic Investment Fund v. U.S., 568 F.3d 537 (5th Cir.2009), 472 F.Supp.2d 885 (E.D.Tex.2007).

country. Gee's knowledge of how other tax shelters worked caused him to ask several questions of Doerr about whether NPR was subject to the TEFRA audit procedures and whether such procedures had been implemented. Gee concluded that NPR was subject to the TEFRA audit procedures and that it would be necessary for the IRS to issue an FPAA to NPR's partners that contained adjustments to several partnership items on NPR's return. Gee contacted Penny Schupmann ("Schupmann"), a TEFRA technical advisor, who advised Gee that the IRS could still issue the FPAA because the individual partners' statutes of limitations were still open. On August 15, 2005, the IRS issued FPAAs prepared and signed by Schupmann to NPR's partners.

E. Procedural History

On December 6, 2005, NPR filed suit under Section 6226, seeking the redetermination of adjustments made by the IRS to the Form 1065 federal partnership return filed by NPR for its taxable year ending December 31, 2001. The IRS made these adjustments by issuing a Notice of FPAA to NPR on or about August 15, 2005. In the FPAA, the IRS notified NPR of various adjustments made to the Form 1065 partnership tax return and provided various explanations for the adjustments it made. The IRS also determined that NPR was subject to various penalties, including a (i) 40 percent gross valuation misstatement penalty, (ii) 20 percent substantial valuation misstatement penalty, (iii) 20 percent negligence penalty, and (iv) 20 percent substantial understatement penalty. Prior to trial on motion for summary judgment by NPR, the Court ruled that the 40% penalty for gross valuation misstatement and 20% penalty for substantial valuation misstatement do not apply as a matter of law based on the facts of this case. On August 10, 2009, NPR filed its First Amended Petition for Readjustment of Partnership Items Under Internal Revenue Code Section 6226 (the "Amended Petition"). In the Amended Petition, NPR conceded that, if the August 15, 2005 FPAA is valid, NPR did not enter into the transactions at issue with a profit motive, and thus, conceded the adjustments that the IRS made in the FPAA. Thus, the actual adjustments made by the IRS to the tax returns and whether NPR had profit motive are not materially disputed. Rather, the dispute is whether the penalties applied by the IRS are applicable.

II. DISCUSSION

Two primary issues were tried before this Court from March 8 through March 10, 2010. The first issue is whether the notice of final partnership administrative adjustment ("FPAA") issued on August 15, 2005 by the IRS is invalid under Section 6223. [Eds: the court concluded that the FPAA was valid.] The second issue is whether the accuracy-related penalties asserted by the Defendant under Section 6662 are applicable in this case because the Taxpayers allegedly relied reasonably and in good faith on the advice of their tax and legal advisors.

* * *

B.   The Accuracy Related Penalties

This Court has jurisdiction to determine the applicability of any penalty which relates to an adjustment to a partnership issue pursuant to 26 U.S.C. § 6226(f). There are two accuracy-related penalties asserted by the Government that are still in dispute in this case:[9] a 20% penalty for substantial understatement of income tax under Section 6662(b)(2) and (d) and a 20% penalty for negligence or disregard of rules and regulations under Section 6662(b)(1). The Court now addresses the applicability of the penalties.

1.   Substantial Understatement of Income Tax

In the August 15, 2005 FPAA, the IRS imposed a penalty for substantial understatement of income tax. The Court now turns to this penalty.

a.   Legal Principles

Section 6662(b) imposes a 20% penalty to "[a]ny substantial understatement of income tax." 26 U.S.C. § 6662(a), (b)(2). "For purposes of this section, there is a substantial understatement of income tax for any taxable year if the amount of the understatement for the taxable year exceeds the greater of (i) 10 percent of the tax required to be shown on the return for the taxable year, or (ii) $5,000." 26 U.S.C. § 6662(d)(1)(A). The amount of the substantial understatement used to compute the penalty does not include any item for which there was

---

9.   As mentioned previously, the Government originally asserted four accuracy-related penalties, but two of those were resolved by the Court on motion for summary judgment. (See Dkt. No. 109.) Only the 20% negligence and substantial understatement penalties are in dispute.

substantial supporting authority. 26 U.S.C. § 6662(d)(2)(B)(i); Treas. Reg. § 16662-4(a).

> "The substantial authority standard is an objective standard involving an analysis of the law and application of the law to relevant facts. The substantial authority standard is less stringent than the more likely than not standard (the standard that is met when there is a greater than 50-percent likelihood of the position being upheld), but more stringent than the reasonable basis standard." Treas. Reg. § 1.6662-4(d)(2). For substantial authority to exist, "the weight of the authorities supporting the treatment is substantial in relation to the weight of authorities supporting contrary treatment." Treas. Reg. § 1.6662-4(d)(3)(i). Opinions rendered by tax professionals are not authority. Treas. Reg. § 1.6662-4(d)(3)(iii). The authorities underlying such opinions, if applicable to the facts of a particular case, may give rise to substantial authority for the tax treatment of an item. Id. In addition, in a case involving a tax shelter, the "substantial authority" exception does not apply unless the "taxpayer reasonably believed that the tax treatment of such item by the taxpayer was more likely than not the proper treatment." 26 U.S.C. § 6662(d)(2)(C)(i)(II).10 A "tax shelter" includes, among other things, a partnership or an investment plan "if a significant purpose of such . . . is the avoidance or evasion of Federal income tax." 26 U.S.C. § 6662(d)(2)(C)(iii).

b.   Parties' Arguments

The Government argues that the facts satisfy the mathematical test for the penalties because the amount of understatement was greater than 10 percent of the required tax. See 26 U.S.C. § 6662(d)(1)(A). As a result, the Government urges that the penalty applies in this case. The Government argues that the Taxpayers' reliance on the caselaw is misplaced. The Government argues that the Taxpayers knew this was a tax shelter listed in Notice 2000-44, yet decided to enter into the transactions nonetheless. NPR argues that the 20% substantial understatement of income tax penalty does not apply in this instance. NPR argues that there was "substantial authority" for the treatment of the Taxpayers' tax positions. NPR contends that the input and advice of Cohen and Sidley Austin provide substantial authority for the tax treatment at issue. NPR argues that it is not a tax shelter, but even if it were, the substantial-authority exception would still apply. NPR argues that the advice given to the Taxpayers by Cohen and Sidley Austin justifiability relied on the existing case law and strongly supported NPR's position that their tax position was, more likely than not, correct.

c. Analysis

This Court may assume, arguendo, that the NPR partnership was a tax shelter within the definition. The record, however, supports a finding that substantial authority existed. The Taxpayers obtained comprehensive opinions of counsel before they filed their returns. The Sidley Austin opinions relied on the relevant authority at the time. Cohen went over the opinions with the Taxpayers and confirmed that they were reasonable. Further, Mr. Stuart Smith ("Smith") provided expert opinion and testimony that substantial authority supported the tax treatment at issue in this case. Smith's experience includes over 40 years as a tax lawyer, both as Tax Assistant to the Solicitor General in the Department of Justice and now in private practice. After examining the material issues identified in the opinions, Smith concluded that the opinions provided "objectively reasonable tax advice" because they "discussed all of the authorities in an even-handed balanced way, taking into account all possible challenges in a thorough and complete manner." He further concluded that the opinions were the "quality and character upon which a taxpayer could rely in good faith." The Court agrees with Smith's opinions and concludes that the Sidley Austin opinions provided "substantial authority" for the Taxpayers' treatment of their basis in their respective partnerships. The record also supports a finding that the Taxpayers reasonably believed that the tax treatment applied to the transactions was "more likely than not" the proper treatment. Although they are experienced attorneys, the Taxpayers are not tax lawyers. Based on all of the record evidence, the Court finds that the Taxpayers were not aware of any financial agreements between Cohen and DGI when they decided to enter the transactions and when they filed their returns. The Taxpayers believed that Cohen was properly discharging his duties as their fiduciary. The Taxpayers sought advice from Cohen before deciding to enter these transactions and relied heavily upon his advice. The Taxpayers sought to make a profit from the investment plan when they entered the pertinent transactions, even if NPR did not. Accordingly, the Court finds that the substantial understatement penalty does not apply.

2. Negligence

In the August 15, 2005 FPAA, the IRS also imposed a penalty for negligence. The Court now turns to this penalty.

a. Legal Principles

The 20% negligence penalty applies to the extent that an understatement of the tax was attributable to the taxpayer's "negligence or disregard of rules or regulations." 26 U.S.C. § 6662(b)(1). "For purposes of this section, the term negligence' includes any failure to make a reasonable attempt to comply with the provisions of this title, and the term disregard' includes any careless, reckless, or intentional disregard" of the tax laws. 26 U.S.C. § 6662(c). Negligence includes the "failure to make a reasonable attempt to comply with the provisions of the internal revenue laws or to exercise ordinary and reasonable care in the preparation of a tax return." Treas. Reg. § 1.6662-3(b)(1). "Negligence is strongly indicated where . . . [a] taxpayer fails to make a reasonable attempt to ascertain the correctness of a deduction, credit or exclusion on a return which would seem to a reasonable and prudent person to be too good to be true' under the circumstances." Treas. Reg. § 1.6662-3(b)(1)(ii). Disregard for the "rules or regulations is careless' if the taxpayer does not exercise reasonable diligence to determine the correctness of a return position that is contrary to the rule or regulation." Treas. Reg. § 1.6662-3(b)(2). The Fifth Circuit defines negligence as "any failure to reasonably attempt to comply with the tax code, including the lack of due care or the failure to do what a reasonable or ordinarily prudent person would do under the circumstances." Heasley v. Comm'r, 902 F.2d 380, 383 (5th Cir. 1990).

A taxpayer is not negligent where there is a reasonable basis for the position taken. Treas. Reg. § 1.6662-3(b)(1). "Reasonable basis is a relatively high standard of tax reporting, that is, significantly higher than not frivolous or not patently improper. The reasonable basis standard is not satisfied by a return position that is merely arguable or that is merely a colorable claim." Treas. Reg. § 1.6662-3(b)(3). Reasonable basis requires reliance on legal authorities and not on opinions rendered by tax professionals. Id.; Treas. Reg. § 1.6662-4(d)(3)(iii). The Court may, however, examine the authorities relied upon in a tax opinion to determine if a reasonable basis exists. See Treas. Reg. § 1.6662-4(d)(3)(iii). "If a return position is reasonably based on one or more of the authorities set forth in [the substantial authority section] . . . the return position will generally satisfy the reasonable basis standard even though it may not satisfy the substantial authority standard as defined in § 1.6662-4(d)(2)." Treas. Reg. § 1.6662-3(b)(3).

b. Parties' Arguments

The Government argues that entering into a transaction that is "too good to be true" is careless and not what a reasonable person would do. The Government argues that the Taxpayers had full knowledge of their advisors' conflicts of interest. The Government argues that a reasonable, prudent person would not proceed with a transaction that was the subject of an IRS penalty warning without obtaining completely independent advice. NPR argues that case law provided ample support for the Taxpayers' return positions and that the Taxpayers had a reasonable basis for their positions. NPR argues that the Taxpayers' reporting positions were consistent with the IRS' internal position that option positions do not create liabilities within the meaning of Section 752. Thus, NPR argues that they were not negligent.

c. Analysis

The reasonable basis standard is less stringent than the substantial authority standard; if the substantial authority defense is applicable to the substantial understatement penalty, the reasonable cause defense will also be applicable. See Treas. Reg. § 1.6662-4(d)(2); Treas. Reg. § 1.6662-3(b)(3). As discussed above, the Court finds that there was "substantial authority" to rely on the Sidley Austin opinions. Id. Therefore, the "reasonable basis" standard has also been met. Accordingly, a penalty for negligence is not applicable in this case.

C. Reasonable Cause and Good Faith Defense

Finally, the Court turns to the reasonable cause and good faith issues. Notwithstanding the specific requirements of the penalties discussed above, a taxpayer may defeat the imposition of any of those penalties if he demonstrates reasonable cause.

1. Legal Principles

Section 6664(c)(1) provides an absolute defense to any accuracy-related penalty. A taxpayer that would otherwise be subject to a twenty-percent accuracy-related penalty under § 6662(b) is not liable if the taxpayer can demonstrate that the underpayment was made with reasonable cause and the taxpayer acted in good faith. 26 U.S.C. 6664(c)(1); Treas. Reg. § 1.6664-4(a). The plaintiffs bear the burden of production and proof on their reasonable cause defenses. Klamath

Strategic Investment Fund v. U.S., 568 F.3d 537, 548 (5th Cir.2009); see Montgomery v. Commissioner, 127 T.C. 43, 66 (2006). Although each instance requires a case-by-case determination of all pertinent facts and circumstances, generally the most important factor in assessing the applicability of the exception is the amount of effort the taxpayer spent to determine the proper tax liability in light of all the circumstances. Treas. Reg. § 1.6664-4(b). When considering the taxpayer's effort to determine the proper tax liability, the taxpayer's reliance on the advice of a professional tax adviser may not be sufficient to demonstrate reasonable cause and good faith. Treas. Reg. § 1.6664-4(b)(1). Rather, the validity of the reliance turns on "the quality and objectivity of the professional advice which they obtained." Klamath, 568 F.3d at 548, citing Swayze v. U.S., 785 F.2d 715, 719 (9th Cir. 1986). "Reliance on . . . professional advice, or other facts, however, constitutes reasonable cause and good faith if, under all the circumstances, such reliance was reasonable and the taxpayer acted in good faith." Treas. Reg. § 1.6664-4(b)(1). To determine if reliance on a tax professional's advice was reasonable and in good faith, all facts and circumstances must be taken into account. Treas. Reg. § 1.6664-4(c). "For example, the taxpayer's education, sophistication and business experience will be relevant in determining whether the taxpayer's reliance on tax advice was reasonable and made in good faith." Id. "Circumstances that may indicate reasonable cause and good faith include an honest misunderstanding of fact or law that is reasonable in light of all the facts and circumstances, including the experience, knowledge, and education of the taxpayer." Treas. Reg. § 1.6664-4(b)(1). A taxpayer is not required to challenge the advisor's conclusions, seek a second opinion, or check the advice himself. U.S. v. Boyle, 469 U.S. 241, 250-51, 105 S.Ct. 687, 83 L.Ed.2d 622 (1985). "To require the taxpayer to challenge the attorney, to seek a second opinion,' or to try to monitor counsel on the provisions of the Code himself would nullify the very purpose of seeking the advice of a presumed expert in the first place." Id. at 251, 105 S.Ct. 687.

In order to establish reasonable reliance in good faith on the advice of a tax professional, a taxpayer must establish that all facts and circumstances were considered, and no unreasonable assumptions were made. Treas. Reg. § 1.6664-4(c)(1)(i)-(ii). For the advice to be based on "[a]ll the facts and circumstances," it must include all pertinent facts and circumstances, including "the taxpayer's purposes (and the relative weight of such purposes) for entering into a transaction and for structuring a transaction in a particular manner." Treas. Reg. § 1.6664-4(c)(1)(i). Additionally, "[t]he advice must not be based on unreasonable factual or legal assumptions (including assumptions as to future events) and must not unreasonably rely on the representations, statements, findings, or agreements of the taxpayer or any other person." Treas. Reg. § 1.6664-4(c)(1)(ii). "The fact that these requirements are satisfied, however, will not necessarily establish that the taxpayer reasonably relied on the advice (including the opinion of a tax advisor) in good faith." Treas. Reg. § 1.6664-4(c)(1).

2. Parties' Arguments

The Government argues that the Taxpayers' clear objective from the outset was to report these tax shelter transactions in a manner so as to conceal the tax losses and avoid their detection by the IRS. The Government argues that NPR's, the Law Firm's, and the Taxpayer's individual tax returns were replete with false and misleading reporting. The Government argues that the Taxpayers did not exercise reasonable care with these transactions. The Government argues that the Taxpayers sought penalty protection, not independent legal advice, where it was apparent that the advisors were tainted by conflicts of interest. The Government also argues that the Taxpayers were unreasonable in relying upon the obtained advice and opinions. The Government argues that there is no evidence that supports a reasonable belief of a reasonable chance of making a profit with the transactions. The Taxpayers argue that they did not hide the transactions, that they reasonably relied upon their advisors, that any potential conflicts of interest did not make their reliance unreasonable, and that they reasonably believed that they could earn a profit in the transactions.

3. Analysis

Messrs. Nix, Patterson, and Roach are not tax lawyers, and they have no expertise in tax matters. Instead, they rely on qualified, professional advisors for tax advice. Because of the complexity of the tax treatment, it was necessary for the Taxpayers to seek advice from qualified tax attorneys concerning the applicable law to the facts of their investment and the resulting tax effects. The Taxpayers initially relied upon Cohen, their personal CPA at Pollans & Cohen. Cohen introduced them to Ruble, who was a tax expert on partnership matters with the law firm Sidley Austin. Patterson asked Ruble whether there was a conflict of interest and, after a series of questions to Ruble, became assured that there was not a conflict of interest. Based on all of the record evidence, the Court finds that the Taxpayers were not aware of any financial agreements between Cohen and DGI when they decided to enter the transactions and when they filed their returns. The Taxpayers believed that Cohen was properly discharging his duties as their fiduciary. Based in large part on the advice of Cohen, the Taxpayers ultimately decided to invest in the transactions in dispute. The Court finds that the Taxpayers had a reasonable belief that they could make a profit with the transactions. When the Taxpayers resigned from NPR, the Taxpayers each obtained a thorough, written opinion from Sidley Austin that detailed the proper tax treatment of their investments. Not being learned in tax law, the Taxpayers reviewed these opinions with Cohen. The advice given to the Taxpayers by Sidley Austin and Cohen relied on the existing case law and strongly supported NPR's position that the Taxpayers' tax position was "more likely than not" correct. NPR's tax expert Smith also concluded that the opinions complied with standards common to the profession and with administrative standards established by Treasury Circular 230, which addresses conduct of practitioners who provide tax opinions. Smith further concluded that the opinions reached objectively reasonable conclusions. The detailed opinions provided a reasonable interpretation of the law. Based on the opinions they received from Sidley Austin that provided an objectively reasonable explication of the law as it then existed, as confirmed by Smith's trial testimony, the Taxpayers' belief that their tax treatment of their investments in NPR was reasonable. The Court finds that such reliance was reasonable and that the Taxpayers relied upon this advice in good faith. The Court rejects the Government's arguments to the contrary.

In short, the Taxpayers acted reasonably and in good faith in relying on their tax advisors' advice with respect to their investments in the underlying transactions. As aptly stated by Mr. Nix at trial, "at every step, we followed the advice of people we relied on, people who were supposed to have known what they were doing and did know what they were doing. And what else could we have done except follow their advice?" The Court finds that the Taxpayers have proven, by a preponderance of the evidence, their good faith in relying on the advice of qualified tax accountants and tax lawyers. Accordingly, the criteria under the reasonable cause exception of 26 U.S.C. § 6664(c) is satisfied, and the Taxpayers are not liable for accuracy-related penalties.

III. CONCLUSION

The Court finds that the August 15, 2005 notice of FPAA is valid. The Court also finds that no penalties are applicable. The parties are directed to confer and submit, within 15 days, a proposed form of judgment (agreed if possible) consistent with this opinion.

Notes and Question

On December 18, 2008, Raymond J. Ruble was convicted of 10 counts of tax evasion in connection with the marketing of illegal tax shelters.

Five days before the opinion in the *NPR* case was issued, the Tax Court issued its opinion in Canal Corporation v. Commissioner, 135 T.C. No. 9 (2011). *Canal* involved the leveraged sale of a subsidiary corporation through a partnership between an unrelated third party and a newly formed LLC. The subsidiary would contribute its assets and liabilities to the LLC and would receive a distribution of cash. The cash was funded by borrowed money that the new partnership had obtained. This debt was indemnified by the subsidiary. PriceWaterhouseCoopers had issued an opinion stating that the transaction should be upheld as a tax-free transaction and not as a taxable sale. PwC charged a flat fee of $800,000 for its opinion.

The IRS challenged the transaction, claiming that it was a taxable sale and not a contribution/distribution on the formation of a partnership. The Tax Court concluded that the subsidiary's indemnity was illusory and the transaction was a disguised sale. The court then proceeded to penalties and concluded that the company was liable for the accuracy related penalty for a substantial understatement of tax because it had failed to demonstrate reasonable cause. What is the difference between *NPR* and *Canal*? Why do the taxpayers win in *NPR* and lose in *Canal*?

4. Tax Shelters/Reportable Transactions

A tax shelter is defined as a partnership or other entity, investment plan or arrangement, or any other plan or arrangement, if a significant purpose of such partnership, entity, plan, or arrangement is the avoidance or evasion of federal income tax.[1] IRC § 6662(d)(2)(C)(iii). Abusive tax shelter transactions are a problem for the federal government because not only do they cost the Treasury lost revenue, but they also undermine public confidence in the voluntary compliance system in general. The Service is fighting this problem on a number of fronts, including increased accuracy-related penalties that apply to these transactions, early identification of questionable transactions through required disclosure of "reportable or listed transactions" under § 6011,

---

1.   Prior to August 6, 1997, a tax shelter was defined as an entity, plan or arrangement whose *primary* purpose was the avoidance of federal income tax.

and requiring promoters to maintain lists of investors under §§ 6011 and 6012.

Prior to October 22, 2004, noncorporate taxpayers who had items on their returns attributable to tax shelters were able to avoid an accuracy-related penalty if there was substantial authority for the tax treatment of the item and the taxpayer reasonably believed at the time the return was filed that the tax treatment of the item was "more likely than not" proper. The disclosure defense was not available for tax shelter items. IRC § 6662(d)(2)(C)(i); Reg. § 1.6662-4(g)(1)(i) and (iii). Corporate taxpayers could not use the substantial authority or disclosure defenses to mitigate the substantial understatement penalty attributable to a tax shelter item. IRC § 6662(d)(2)(C)(ii). This left only the reasonable cause exception under § 6664(c), under which the corporation was required to demonstrate reasonable cause for its understatement of income and that it acted in good faith.

The regulations provide that the "more likely than not" standard may be met in either of two ways: (1) by demonstrating that the taxpayer reasonably concluded, after analyzing the appropriate facts and authorities, that there was a greater than 50-percent likelihood that the tax treatment of the item would be upheld if challenged by the Service, or (2) by reasonable reliance in good faith on the opinion of a tax professional, where the opinion is based on a reasonable analysis of the pertinent facts and authorities, and which unambiguously states that the professional concludes that there is a greater than 50-percent likelihood that the tax treatment of the item will be upheld if challenged by the Service. Reg. § 1.6662-4(g)(4)(ii). Under the second method, the taxpayer must choose a tax professional who has knowledge of the relevant aspects of the tax law in question in order for the reliance to be considered reasonable and in good faith.

The American Jobs Creation Act of 2004 amended § 6662(d)(2)(C)(i) to provide that for tax years beginning on or after October 22, 2004, no portion of an understatement may be reduced by any amount attributable to a tax shelter item. This amendment applies to both corporate and noncorporate taxpayers. But § 6664(c) provides that the taxpayer may avoid the accuracy-related penalty by demonstrating reasonable cause for the understatement of income and that it acted in good faith. Where the taxpayer relied on professional advice that the substantial authority and more likely than not standards are met, the reasonable cause standard may be met, provided that the professional was reasonable in her legal or factual assumptions, addressed all relevant issues and was not unduly influenced in her decision by representations by or agreements with the taxpayer.

The Health Care and Reconciliation Act of 2010 added new § 6662(b)(6), which provides a 20-percent penalty (40-percent if not disclosed) on any understatement attributable to the disallowance of a tax benefit by reason of a transaction lacking economic substance or failing to meet the requirements of any similar rule of law. Economic substance is defined under § 7701(o). There is no defense or mitigation to this penalty because neither substantial authority, adequate disclosure nor reasonable cause apply. Thus this penalty is a strict liability penalty.

The American Jobs Creation Act of 2004 added a special penalty for understatements arising from reportable transactions. A reportable transaction is a transaction that the Service regards as having a potential for significant tax avoidance or evasion. See IRC § 6111(b)(2). The Service has identified five categories of transactions that it deems reportable: (1) listed transactions (those identified by the Service in published guidance as tax avoidance transactions), (2) transactions marketed under conditions of confidentiality, (3) transactions having contractual protection, (4) transactions that generate tax losses that exceed specified amounts, and (5) transactions of interest (see IRS Notice 2009-55, I.R.B. 2009-31 (July 31, 2009). Reg. § 1.6011-4(b)(2) through (7).

The penalty is 20-percent of an understatement attributable to a reportable transaction, 30-percent if the transaction is not adequately disclosed. See IRC § 6662A(a) and (c). While the reportable transaction penalty can be avoided through a demonstration of reasonable cause and good faith, this is a more stringent standard than under § 6664(c). When a reportable transaction is in issue, there is no reasonable cause defense if the transaction has not been adequately disclosed. Moreover, reasonable cause under this standard requires the taxpayer to establish substantial authority for the position and a reasonable belief that the tax treatment was more likely than not proper. IRC § 6664(d).

The reasonableness of the taxpayer's belief is based upon the facts and law that existed at the time the return was filed, and it must relate solely to the taxpayer's success on the merits of the issue, without consideration of the audit lottery. A taxpayer may rely on the reasonable advice of a qualified tax advisor, but may establish reasonable belief without such reliance. H.R. Conf. Rep. No. 108-755.

Note that § 6707A extends the statute of limitations for unreported listed transactions. Under this provision, if a taxpayer fails to provide any information required by § 6011 on a tax return or statement related to a listed transaction, the statute of limitations with respect to that transaction will not expire before one year from the earlier of: (1) the date the information is furnished to the Service or (2) the date that a material advisor satisfies the list maintenance requirements of § 6112 with respect to the listed transaction.

Notes and Question

On September 13, 2010, the IRS released long-awaited guidance on the codified economic substance doctrine. See IRS Notice 2010-62, 2010 WL 3529402. Practitioners criticized this guidance as "profoundly disappointing" because the Service refused to issue an "angel list" of transactions that would meet the requirement or to provide a list of those that would not. There also is no guidance on how the Service intends to apply the § 6662(b)(6) penalty. One practitioner said of the released guidance "It basically says, 'We're not providing guidance.'" See "Practitioners Blast Economic Substance Guidance," 128 Tax Notes 1212 (Sept. 20, 2010)(quoting Mark Silverman of Steptoe and Johnson LLP).

How, if at all, do the defenses to the accuracy-related penalties differ in the cases of negligence, disregard of rules and regulations, substantial understatements not involving tax shelters, substantial under-statements involving tax shelters or tax avoidance transactions, and substantial understatements involving a listed or reportable transaction?

C. SUBSTANTIAL VALUATION MISSTATEMENTS

A third component of the accuracy-related penalty applies to any underpayment of tax attributable to a substantial valuation misstatement with respect to the value or adjusted basis of property, or with respect to a § 482 (transfer pricing) transaction. IRC § 6662(b)(3). A valuation misstatement is considered substantial if the understatement exceeds a dollar amount of $10,000 for corporations other than S corporations and $5,000 for other entities and (1) the value or adjusted basis of property claimed on a return exceeds 150-percent of the correct value or basis, (2) the price for any property or its use or for services in connection with any transaction between trades or businesses owned or controlled, directly or indirectly, by the same interests (described in § 482) is 200-percent or more (or 50-percent or less) of the amount determined (under § 482) to be the correct price, and (3) the net transfer price adjustment for the year exceeds the lesser of $5 million or 10-percent of the taxpayer's gross receipts. IRC § 6662(e)(2). A penalty of 40-percent of the underpayment applies to a "gross valuation misstatement" under § 6662(h).

1. Determining When An Underpayment Is Attributable to A Valuation Overstatement

Before the substantial valuation misstatement penalty was consolidated into the single accuracy-related penalty provision, it was a separate provision embodied in § 6659, originally enacted as part of the Economic Recovery Tax Act of 1981. The rationale behind the penalty was discussed in Todd v. Commissioner, 862 F.2d 540 (5th Cir. 1988): "[Congress] recognized the large number of property valuation disputes clogging the tax collection system, and added the overvaluation penalty to discourage those taxpayers who would inflate the value of property on their tax returns in hopes of 'dividing the difference' with the IRS. Unfortunately, none of the formal legislative history provides a method for calculating whether a given tax underpayment is attributable to a valuation overstatement."

Questions have arisen as to whether the overvaluation penalty applies when the Service disallows the underlying deduction on other grounds. The following case addresses this problem.

DONAHUE v. COMMISSIONER
United States Court of Appeals, Sixth Circuit, 1992.
959 F.2d 234.

UNPUBLISHED OPINION.

RALPH B. GUY, JR., CIRCUIT JUDGE.

Taxpayer Denise Donahue appeals from a Tax Court determination that, as a result of her investment in a tax shelter which lacked economic substance, she was liable not only for tax deficiencies but also for various penalties. Finding no error, we affirm.

I.

The failed venture at issue was a master-recording leasing program. A limited partnership known as Soul Phonomasters, Ltd., acquired master recordings of songs, from which an album was to be made. The price of the masters was $10,000 upon the signing of the sales agreement, $27,000 upon delivery, and artist royalties. The partnership then leased the masters to Soul Phonomasters Leasing (Soul), a co-tenancy. Under the lease, Soul was to pay $112,500 plus a percentage of gross receipts from record sales for the exclusive right to exploit the masters commercially for three years. The lease also required Soul to hire a co-tenancy operator. Frank Pasternak, a CPA, was selected for this position.

To participate in the leasing program, an investor would sign a two-page offer to the co-tenancy which stated his or her undivided fractional leasehold interest. By signing the offer, the investor also appointed Pasternak as his or her attorney, authorizing him to execute on the investor's behalf the co-tenancy operating agreement, the lease, the marketing agreement, and all requisite IRS documents enabling the investor to take an investment tax credit ("passed through" from the lessor).

Donahue learned about Soul's leasing program from Glenn Crane, one of her close friends. Crane was also a paid agent for the program's promoters. Donahue attended two meetings for investors in 1981. There, she was given general information about the record industry and told of the high-risk nature of the program. The tax consequences of the investment were also explained; the promoters discussed various hypothetical cases in which the tax benefits exceeded the investment. Without asking for or receiving any written sales or cost projections, and without seeking an independent evaluation of the profit potential, Donahue invested $10,000 in the venture. She knew of the risk, but stated that she believed she would at least recoup her investment.

After she paid her money, Donahue paid no further attention to the leasing program other than to attend a 1983 investors' meeting. In 1982, Pasternak, the co-tenancy operator, sent Donahue a statement informing her of her share of the tax benefits. The limited partnership had elected to pass through its investment tax credit to Soul, which claimed that the lessor's basis in the master recording was $3,370,000. Based on Pasternak's information, Donahue claimed a $10,000 business expense deduction on her 1981 tax return, as well as an investment tax credit of $12,000. As Donahue's 1981 gross income was $26,000, these tax benefits completely eliminated her tax liability for that year. Donahue also carried back the unused portion of the tax credit to tax years 1978, 1979, and 1980, and she accordingly sought refunds for those years.

The IRS disallowed these tax benefits on the grounds that the leasing program lacked economic substance and that Donahue's sole reason for participating was to reduce her taxes. It found Donahue liable not only for tax deficiencies but also for various "additions to tax."

In a case consolidated for trial with other Phonomasters investors, the Tax Court sustained the disallowance of Donahue's deduction and investment tax credit as well as the imposition of the penalties.[1] Donahue now appeals.

II.

The Tax Court denied the deduction and investment tax credit after agreeing with the IRS that the leasing transaction lacked economic substance. It based this conclusion on the fact that the price the limited partnership had paid for the master recording vastly exceeded its fair market value, which expert testimony set at $1500 (and there had been no indication that any of the additional payments or artist royalties were ever paid). The court's finding also turned on the manner in which Pasternak managed the operation. He kept no records, carried out no promotion or sales plans, and "provided tax information which can only be described as plain nonsense." According to the court, "[t]he activities were not planned realistically or carried on in a manner which could have resulted in a profit."[2] Donahue does not appeal the denial of the deduction and credits; she challenges only the penalties assessed.

* * *

The court began its section 6653 analysis by observing that the rule prohibiting deductions and credits for activity not conducted with a profit objective "is well established and is not beyond the comprehension of the layman." Despite the investors' insistence that they expected to make a profit due to the involvement of some prominent members of the music industry, their conduct, according to the court, indicated "indifference" to that prospect. Evidence of such indifference included the fact that none of the investors even claimed to have asked for any written projections on sales, costs, and profit margins before tendering their money; none requested copies of the operating agreement, lease, or marketing plan; none sought an independent evaluation of the profit potential, even though they had never heard of the artists performing on the master recordings; and none bothered to determine what remedies might be available if the promoters failed to perform as promised.[4]

1.　　The case is reported at 61 T.C.M. (CCH) 2460 (1991).

2.　　The evidence that the promoters wasted or diverted the investors' funds is undisputed. The "sham" is thus twofold: the promoters bilked the investors, who had participated in what they thought was a scheme to reduce their tax liability rather than make money.

4.　　Donahue points to a 1986 suit filed against Pasternak by Crane, the marketing agent who told Donahue about the leasing program, and who had also invested his own funds in the venture. Such efforts against the delinquent co-tenancy operator do not undermine the above findings of the Tax Court, however, since they occurred after Donahue received her notice of tax deficiency (in 1985). As the court noted, in 1982 Crane proceeded to invest more money in another

The evidence also revealed that the promoters marketed the venture as a tax shelter, informing prospective investors of the tax benefits but providing only minimal information about record production in general. That Donahue invested a substantial amount for her income level, despite her awareness of the venture's risk, suggested a belief that she was "sure to come out ahead because of tax reductions and refunds" even if no profits were ever realized. Indeed, even those investors in the lower brackets claimed tax reductions of $1.50 for every dollar invested. On these facts, it was not fanciful for the Tax Court to find that "[a] reasonably prudent person would have asked a qualified tax advisor if this windfall was not too good to be true."

* * *

Donahue additionally argues that moderate-income investors should not be burdened   with the obligation of performing independent investigations of the ventures in which they invest. This argument would have greater appeal if the facts of the case were different, as they were in the case which Donahue cites. In Heasley v. Commissioner, 902 F.2d 380, 383-84 (5th Cir. 1990), the Fifth Circuit reasoned, "[i]f we require moderate-income investors to independently investigate their investments, the start-up investigation costs may prevent them from investing at all." The taxpayers in *Heasley*, however, did not invest in the subsequently-failing venture to avoid tax liability. They invested to earn a profit. Those taxpayers had also studied the venture's prospectus and its cash flow charts (which showed ever-increasing future profits). They also "monitored their investment," receiving regular reports, and when they received none of the expected income, "they wrote and telephoned the servicing agent to collect their portion* * *." Id. at 384. Unsure how to report their investment on their tax return, the Heasley investors had their accountant review the prospectus and the pertinent legal opinions. As the above account of Donahue's activities indicates, she engaged in no such diligence.

* * *

III.

The Tax Court also sustained the addition to tax under section 6659 for an underpayment attributable to a valuation overstatement–here, an overvaluation of the co-tenancy's asset, the master recording. A valuation overstatement is a valuation exceeding the true value by 150 percent or more. 26 U.S.C. § 6659(c). Donahue does not dispute that the claimed value of the master recording exceeded its fair market value by

---

Pasternak-operated leasing program, despite his claimed dissatisfaction with Pasternak's management.

the requisite amount. Rather, she contends that the underpayment of tax was not attributable to this overstatement, but to the claiming of an improper deduction and tax credit.

Donahue again relies on *Heasley*, a case we find factually distinct from the present one. In *Heasley*, the Fifth Circuit stated:

> [w]henever the I.R.S. totally disallows a deduction or credit, the I.R.S. may not penalize the taxpayer for a valuation overstatement included in that deduction or credit. In such a case, the underpayment is not attributable to a valuation. Instead, it is attributable to claiming an improper deduction or credit.

Heasley, 902 F.2d at 383. The *Heasley* court's decision turned on its observation that the petitioners' tax liability, calculated without the improperly claimed deductions, did not "differ one cent" from the liability calculated with the valuation overstatement included. The valuation overstatement thus failed to change the amount of tax actually owed, according to the court. Id.

Two factors compel us to reject the *Heasley* analysis for resolving the present dispute. First, it was unclear from that opinion why the deductions and credits were disallowed; the taxpayers, unlike Donahue, were found to have operated with a profit motive. Second, *Heasley* relied on that circuit's earlier decision in Todd v. Commissioner, 862 F.2d 540 (5th Cir. 1988), a case whose facts differ significantly from those facts we face here. In *Todd*, the taxpayers claimed depreciation deductions on property found to have an inflated basis. The deductions were denied, however, because the taxpayers had not put the property into service in the tax year for which they claimed the deductions. Id. at 542. The underpayment of tax was correctly attributed to the denial of the (improper) deductions, rather than to the overvaluation of the property. The taxpayers were thus spared the section 6659 penalty.[5] As discussed below, the disallowance of Donahue's deduction and credit was not based on such external reasons.

We find the Second Circuit's approach to this issue more pertinent to our own case. In Gilman v. Commissioner, 933 F.2d 143 (2nd Cir. 1991), the court was faced with a taxpayer whose depreciation deductions were denied because he lacked a business purpose and the computer

---

5.   The same is true of the taxpayers in the other cases Donahue cites. In McCrary v. Commissioner, 92 T.C. 827 (1989), the tax deficiency resulted from the fact that the taxpayers, as licensees of the master recording rather than lessees, were not entitled to the claimed investment tax credit. In that sense, as in *Todd*, the underpayment was not "attributable to" an overvaluation of the property. Similarly, in Gainer v. Commissioner, 893 F.2d 225 (9th Cir. 1990), the taxpayer had overvalued the limited partnership's shipping container, but his claimed deductions and credits were disallowed because the container had not been put into service in the year at issue. Id. at 228.

equipment sale/leaseback transaction in which he participated lacked economic substance. The taxpayer's basis in the computers was also grossly inflated. The taxpayer had argued, as Donahue does here, "that where the underpayment derives from the disallowance of the transaction (i.e., non-recognition of the transaction for tax purposes), then the underpayment is not attributable to an overvaluation." Id. at 151.

There is, of course, some superficial appeal to *Gilman's* and Donahue's argument.[6] It surely is not irrational to attribute the underpayment to the improper deductions--which, as it so happens, were disallowed because of the transaction's lack of economic substance. The Second Circuit, however, delved deeper into this proffered defense, and focused on why the sale/leaseback was found to lack economic substance. "The lack of substance," according to the court, "was due in part to the [computers'] overvaluation." Id. Thus, the court concluded, "'[w]hen an underpayment stems from disallowed depreciation deductions or investment credit[s] due to lack of economic substance, the deficiency is attributable to overstatement of value, and subject to the penalty under section 6659.'" Id. (quoting Massengill v. Commissioner, 876 F.2d 616, 619-20 (8th Cir. 1989)).

In Donahue's case, the overvaluation of the master recording was "an integral part" of the Tax Court's determination that the Soul venture lacked economic substance–which lack prevented Donahue from claiming the deductions and credits. We thus sustain the imposition of the overvaluation penalty.

* * *

The decision of the Tax Court is AFFIRMED.

* * *

Notes

As the *Donahue* court indicated, there is a conflict among the courts over the issue of when a tax understatement is attributable to a valuation overstatement. According to the Fifth and Ninth Circuits, where the Service disallows a taxpayer's entire deduction or credit containing a valuation misstatement, the disallowance is attributable to the improper deduction or credit, and not to the erroneous valuation. These courts have calculated the understatement of tax for purposes of

---

6.   As the Second Circuit noted, it is not "self-evident" that the overvaluation penalty applies to transactions found to lack economic substance. *Gilman*, 933 F.2d at 150. "The statute is most appropriately applied to instances where a taxpayer claims for an asset a value that the Commissioner determines is unduly high. The paradigmatic case is the inflated value claimed for a work of art in order to obtain a large deduction for a charitable donation." Id.

the penalty by comparing the tax liability without the valuation overstatement to the tax liability after proper adjustments have been made. If the two liabilities are the same, the valuation overstatement has not caused the understatement. See Todd v. Commissioner, 862 F.2d 540 (5th Cir. 1988); Heasley v. Commissioner, 902 F.2d 380 (5th Cir. 1990); Gainer v. Commissioner, 893 F.2d 225 (9th Cir. 1990). Other circuits have held in accordance with *Donahue* that if the overvaluation is "an integral part" of the adjustment, the overvaluation penalty applies. See, e.g., Zfass v. Commissioner, 118 F.3d 184 (4th Cir. 1997); Illes v. Commissioner, 982 F.2d 163 (6th Cir. 1993), cert. denied 507 U.S. 984 (1993); Massengill v. Commissioner, 876 F.2d 616 (8th Cir. 1989).

If the property's correct value is determined to be zero, the gross valuation penalty applies because by definition, any overstatement of value is an overvaluation. Id. at § 1.6662-5(g). Note also that disclosure is no defense to the substantial valuation misstatement penalty.

If a substantial valuation misstatement results in a carryover or carryback, the penalty applies to any portion of an underpayment that results in the year to which the loss, deduction, or credit is carried, provided the applicable dollar limitation of § 6662(e) is satisfied in the carryback or carryover year. Reg. § 1.6662-5(c)(1). Thus, a substantial valuation misstatement penalty may apply in both the year in which the carryover or carryback arose, and the year to which the tax benefit was carried, provided that the applicable dollar limitation is met in each year.

The determination of fair market value is not an exact science, and reasonable appraisers may assign different values to the same piece of property. Therefore, the overvaluation must be substantial; minor deviations in valuation will not trigger the overvaluation penalty. But even if a valuation overstatement is not considered substantial, it nevertheless may subject the taxpayer to a negligence penalty or a substantial understatement penalty. Moreover, if the overstatement is attributable to fraud, it does not have to be substantial to trigger the civil fraud penalty. See § III, below.

Problem

Property A has a value of $5,000 but Samantha Smythe claims a value of $7,000 on her return when she contributes the property to charity. Later in the same taxable year, Samantha places two parcels of depreciable real property in service. On her return, she claims valuations for purposes of depreciation deductions of $10,000 for parcel B and $20,000 for parcel C. The correct values are determined to be $6,000 and $5,000 respectively. Has Samantha made a substantial valuation misstatement? If so, what is the consequence? See Reg. § 1. 6662-5(f).

2. Reasonable Cause

Although the reasonable cause defense is in many respects the same defense as that applicable to the other accuracy-related penalties discussed previously, special rules apply in the case of the substantial valuation misstatement penalty.

JACOBSON v. COMMISSIONER
United States Tax Court, Memorandum Decision, 1999.
T.C. Memo. 1999-401

MEMORANDUM FINDINGS OF FACT AND OPINION

COHEN, CHIEF J.

* * *

FINDINGS OF FACT

Some of the facts have been stipulated, and the facts set forth in the stipulation are incorporated in our findings by this reference. At the time the petition in this case was filed, Samuel Jacobson (petitioner) was a resident of New York, New York. He has been in the baked goods distribution business for 30 years and owns Operative Cake Corporation (Operative Cake).

Philately

"Philately" is the collection and study of postage stamps (stamps) and of postal stationery that has passed through the mail. When a new U.S. stamp is issued by the United States Postal Service (Postal Service), it is released on a specific day at a specific location. Stamp collectors refer to that day as the "first day of issue". Since about 1930, a special cancellation bearing the words "FIRST DAY OF ISSUE" along with the date and town of issue has been applied to stamped items furnished to the Postal Service on the first day the stamp is issued. This service is undertaken by the Postal Service at no charge, other than the cost of postage.

One of the modes of collecting first day of issue stamps is the collection of "first day covers". A first day cover is an envelope that bears a stamp postmarked with a first day of issue cancellation. In some instances, the envelope includes a decorative design usually related to the subject matter of the applied stamp. By the 1940's, hundreds of thousands of first day covers were routinely prepared by collectors for every newly issued stamp, and first day covers had become an important part of the hobby of stamp collecting.

There is a primary market and a secondary market for first day covers. The primary market refers to current first day covers (with newly issued stamps) sold directly to customers by the manufacturer. Prices in this market are set by the manufacturer and vary widely depending upon the quality of the products and the method of sale. The secondary market refers to those first day covers sold by traditional stamp dealers, who are not manufacturers or publishers of first day covers. The secondary market operates through local shops, mail-order catalogs, and trade shows. This market can be either at the retail level or wholesale level, and prices are generally determined by the laws of supply and demand.

In addition to first day covers, there are other "first day of issue" collectibles, including first day pages. First day pages are similar to first day covers but vary slightly in size and format. For example, rather than using the envelope format of a first day cover, the format of a first day page might be a photograph, a dinner menu, a diploma reprint, or copies of congressional minutes. Affixed to the first day page is a first day of issue stamp that is typically related to the subject matter of the page.

Charitable Contribution

Petitioner acquired 60,484 first day pages from Rita Ostrer (Ostrer) of the Historic Philatelic Document Company. The first day pages (the Kesslers) were created by Seymour Kessler and included prints, photographs, and other documentary material depicting various events and scenes of historical significance. Theme-appropriate first day of issue stamps were affixed to each page.

Ostrer also owned an art dealership known as Nicolini's that rented art to movie studios. Petitioner acquired from Nicolini's 62 10-volume sets of "Figures of the Bible", a painting entitled "St. Peter as Bishop", a painting entitled "Madonna and Christ Child", and a monstrance. (Hereinafter these articles will be referred to collectively as the religious articles, and the religious articles and the Kesslers will be referred to as the contributed property.)

During the time that he owned the contributed property, which he estimates as 20 to 30 years, petitioner never attempted to obtain insurance on the contributed property. He never attempted to sell the property. He stored the contributed property in boxes on pallets in the Operative Cake bakery warehouse. The warehouse had a rodent problem and was very hot during the summer. Twelve to fifteen people worked in the warehouse. The only security was a guard at the exit of the warehouse.

In 1993, Bishop John Peter Walzer (Walzer) of The Anglican Catholic Church, Diocese of Connecticut, Southern Episcopal Church (diocese) visited petitioner seeking donations. Petitioner met with Walzer several more times to discuss a potential contribution. On November 29, 1993, Gerald Malina (Malina) prepared a document valuing the religious articles for petitioner. Malina, however, provided no methodology or rationale for the values at which he arrived.

Walzer provided to petitioner letters dated December 27, 1993, acknowledging receipt of a $7,000 cash contribution and the religious items. Each letter contained a sentence stating: "We welcome the opportunity to work with you to help maximize your charitable contribution on your Schedule A, form 1040, and thank you again for your generosity to our Diocesan Programs."

In a letter dated April 4, 1994, Walzer acknowledged receipt of the Kesslers, stating that the donation of the Kesslers was made on October 1, 1993. This correspondence also included an inventory of the Kesslers that was prepared by Donald C. Brueggemann (Brueggemann). The Brueggemann inventory placed a value on each Kessler and indicated that the total value of all of the Kesslers was $900,430. The inventory did not contain any valuation methodology, any rationale for the prices quoted, or any reference to comparable sales. It provided only a description of the Kesslers on a lot-by-lot basis.

Petitioner filed Federal income tax returns for 1993 and 1994 on September 30, 1994, and October 17, 1995, respectively. On his 1993 return, petitioner reported adjusted gross income of $1,555,648. He claimed charitable contributions of $13,997 in cash and $949,030 in noncash property to the diocese. Petitioner represented that he purchased the Kesslers on June 1, 1976, at a cost of $135,065. He stated "various" as the acquisition date of each of the religious items and did not state a cost for any of them. Petitioner listed the fair market values of the contributed property on Form 8283 as follows:

Item	Claimed Fair Market Value
Kesslers	$900,430
Biblical books	18,600
St. Peter painting	15,000
Madonna painting	5,000
Monstrance	10,000
Total	$949,030

No appraisal was attached to petitioner's 1993 or 1994 Federal income tax returns substantiating the fair market values claimed by petitioner. The charitable contribution deduction claimed for 1993 was limited to $476,700, with the remaining $486,327 attributable to noncash items being carried forward and deducted on the 1994 Federal income tax return.

In the statutory notice, respondent allowed only $12,973 as the fair market value of the donated noncash property. Thus, respondent disallowed $449,730 of petitioner's charitable contributions for 1993 and all of the $486,327 charitable contribution carryover for 1994.

OPINION

Fair Market Value

Section 170(a)(1) allows a deduction for charitable contributions made to an organization described in section 170(c). In general, the amount of a charitable contribution made in property other than money is the fair market value of the property at the time of the contribution. See sec. 1.170A-1(c)(1), Income Tax Regs. Fair market value is defined as "on the price at which the property would change hands between a willing buyer and a willing seller, neither being under any compulsion to buy or sell and both having reasonable knowledge of relevant facts." Sec. 1.170A-1(c)(2), Income Tax Regs; United States v. Cartwright, 411 U.S. 546 (1973). Fair market value is a question of fact to be determined from the entire record.

Petitioner argues that the cumulative fair market value of the contributed property in 1993 was $949,030. Petitioner bears the burden of proving a higher value than that determined by respondent. See Rule 142(a); Welch v. Helvering, 290 U.S. 111 (1933). Petitioner was unable to produce canceled checks, sales receipts, or other documents that substantiated the price that he paid or the date that he purchased the Kesslers. Petitioner was unable to provide records substantiating the price that he paid or the date that he purchased the religious articles. At trial, petitioner was unable to remember when he purchased the contributed property, how much he paid for it, and when he donated it. Petitioner's recollection of the amounts paid was vague and unreliable. He claimed on his return that he purchased the Kesslers in 1976, but he testified at trial that the correct year was 1981. He asserted in responses to interrogatories that he had purchased the property 20 or 30 years earlier. An employee of the bakery testified that the boxes were in the warehouse for "at least 16 years".

Malina prepared an expert report for trial that purportedly valued the contributed property, and petitioner relies on this report and his own personal experience in valuing the contributed property. Respondent relies on the expert report of Paul T. Schmid (Schmid) to support the fair market values determined in the notice of deficiency.

Opinion testimony of an expert is admissible if and because it will assist the trier of fact to understand evidence that will determine a fact in issue. We evaluate the opinions of experts in light of the demonstrated qualifications of each expert and all other evidence in the record. We are not bound by the opinion of an expert witness, especially when such opinion is contrary to our conclusions. If experts offer divergent estimates of fair market value, we decide the weight to give these estimates by examining the factors they used in arriving at their conclusions. We may reject in its entirety an opinion provided under circumstances that undermine its credibility.

Malina has been a member of the Appraisers Association of America, Inc., since 1964 with a specialty in Oriental art. His investigation of the Kesslers consisted of telephone conversations with Seymour Kessler, a review of trade periodicals offering Kesslers for retail sale, and a review of the Brueggemann inventory. Malina erroneously referred to the Kesslers as "covers"--unaware of or ignoring the distinction between covers and pages. He also claims to have analyzed the market for first day covers. In his report, he listed the Kesslers, assigning a value to each lot. Malina's analysis was limited to an unsupported assertion that respondent's examining agent significantly undervalued the Kesslers and to his contention that the Kesslers were valuable because they were suitable for framing.

With respect to the religious articles, Malina adopted the values set forth in his 1993 valuation. He provided only a limited analysis of his valuation of the "Stories of the Bible" book sets and no analysis of his valuation of the religious articles.

We reject Malina's opinion because he gave no persuasive explanation of his methodology, made no reference to comparable sales or a valuation rationale, and made no reference to any experience he had that would support the values at which he arrived. Without any reasoned analysis, his report is useless. His opinions are so exaggerated that his testimony is not credible. The record is devoid of any evidence of actual sales of any of the Kesslers or other objective evidence supporting the values claimed by Malina and petitioner or any substantial values for the contributed property.

Moreover, the fair market values at which Malina arrived are contradicted by the objective evidence in this case. Petitioner argues that we should rely on his representations of the value of the Kesslers because he examined the market for Kesslers. He recalled no details of his alleged activity in this regard, however. We are not required to accept petitioner's testimony and, under all of the circumstances, conclude that it is unworthy of belief. The contributed property was stored in boxes on pallets for many years in a bakery warehouse that only had limited security. The warehouse had a rodent problem and was described as being extremely hot during the summer. The contributed property was not insured, nor was any special precaution taken to preclude loss due to deterioration, theft, or fire. Petitioner's contemporaneous conduct renders implausible his claim that the property had substantial value. The only evidence of subsequent handling of the contributed property suggests that it had little value. If the contributed property had a value of $949,030 or anything approaching that value, as petitioner claims, petitioner would have treated it with more care.

Respondent's expert, Schmid, has been involved with stamps on a full-time basis for 32 years. His experience includes retail and auction sales, and he has authored two books on the authentication of U.S. stamps. At the time of the trial, Schmid was the owner of Colorano, a major publisher of first day covers in the United States. Schmid provided a careful explanation supporting his opinions of value.

Schmid described the pricing structure of first day covers within the primary and secondary markets and indicated that the prices of first day covers were in the following ranges:

	Primary Market	Secondary Market
Retail	$1.00 – $3.00	$0.35 – $2.00
Wholesale	0.65 – 1.65	0.15 – 0.35

Schmid stated that the drop in price from the primary market to the secondary market is attributable to tremendous oversupply. Schmid indicated, however, that these prices are not necessarily the most accurate picture of fair market value and that many other factors combine to determine fair market value, including sales history and collector demand.

Schmid attempted but was unable to identify documented sales of the Kesslers. Analyzing the demand for Kesslers, Schmid pointed out that the demand for first day pages was much less than the demand for first day covers. Because Schmid was unable to identify a competitive market for Kesslers within which to ascertain an appropriate fair market value, he estimated fair market value using the first day cover market.

In arriving at fair market value, Schmid took into consideration that the Kesslers do not conform to the more popular envelope format, they only span a limited number of years, there is no established collector following, and no past sales history was available. He also considered that the Kesslers are unique first day products and would have some appeal within the overall market for first day collectibles. Accordingly, he stated that the Kesslers would likely trade in secondary markets for first day covers for the same period, thus indicating a range of $1 to $2 on an individual basis and $0.35 to $.59 in larger groups.

He also took into consideration the salability of the Kesslers, noting that some of the pages would not be sold. He proposed the following approach to valuing the Kesslers:

Sales Level	Price	Percent of Lot	Sales
High retail	$2.00	5	$ 6,050
Low retail	0.35	10	2,118
High wholesale	0.35	10	2,118
Low wholesale	0.15	65	5,899
Unsalable	–	10	–
Total			$16,185

Schmid indicated that these estimates are for a competitive market. Schmid stated that a noncompetitive market would have more "high retail" sales but would have fewer opportunities overall for sales at all levels, resulting in a return in the range of $15,000 to $20,000. He suggested that the bottom of this range was more realistic based on his experience with established dealers.

Schmid stated, however, that the most accurate valuation of the Kesslers would be in the wholesale market where the Kesslers would likely sell for $0.07 to $0.15 per page. Under this assumption, the value of the Kesslers would be between $4,200 and $9,000.

Petitioner challenges Schmid's valuation of the Kesslers on a wholesale basis because, he asserts, trade periodicals indicated that a retail market existed for the Kesslers. Petitioner's reliance on trade periodicals to establish a market for the Kesslers is misplaced. There is no evidence that any sales took place at the prices listed in those periodicals. We are convinced that 60,484 Kesslers would likely be sold, if at all, only in a wholesale market.

Based on Schmid's experience in stamp collecting and in the first day cover market, his valuation of the Kesslers is the best evidence we have of fair market value, and it supports respondent's determination.

Respondent presented no expert evidence of fair market value for the religious articles, offering only evidence that they were not treated as valuable by subsequent possessors of the articles. Petitioner, however, failed to establish a fair market value in excess of $12,973 for all of the contributed property. Accordingly, we conclude that petitioner is not entitled to deductions in excess of the amounts allowed by respondent.

* * *

Section 6662(h) Penalty

Respondent determined that petitioner is liable for the accuracy-related penalty under section 6662(h) for 1993 and 1994. Petitioner argues that he reasonably relied on the Brueggemann inventory and Malina's appraisal and that he substantially complied with applicable requirements.

Taxpayers are liable for a penalty equal to 40 percent of the portion of an underpayment of tax attributable to a gross valuation misstatement. Section 6662(h)(2)(A) provides that there is a gross valuation misstatement if the value of any property claimed on a tax return is 400 percent or more of the amount determined to be the correct value. See also sec. 6662(h)(2)(A), (e)(1)(A). In this case, the value of the contributed property that was claimed on petitioner's Federal income tax return, $949,030, exceeds 400 percent of the value determined to be correct, $12,973.

The accuracy-related penalty under section 6662(h) does not apply to any portion of an underpayment if the taxpayer shows that there was reasonable cause for such portion and that the taxpayer acted in good faith. See sec. 6664(c)(1). However, the good faith exception applies only to a section 170 deduction if (1) the claimed value of the property was based on a "qualified appraisal" made by a "qualified appraiser" and (2) in addition to obtaining such an appraisal, the taxpayer made a good faith investigation of the value of the contributed property. See sec. 6664(c)(2) and (3).

Qualified appraisers and qualified appraisals are defined under the regulations in section 170(a)(1). See sec. 6664(c)(3); sec. 1.170A-13(c)(3), Income Tax Regs. Among the items of information to be included on a qualified appraisal is the method of valuation used to determine fair market value and the specific basis for the valuation, such as comparable sales or statistical samples. As we indicated above, neither the Brueggemann inventory nor Malina's 1993 appraisal set forth a methodology or any meaningful analysis of fair market values expressed in each report. Moreover, we are not persuaded that petitioner acted in good faith, because his conduct with respect to the contributed property was not consistent with a belief that it had substantial value. Thus, the reasonable cause exception does not apply, and petitioner is liable for the accuracy-related penalty of section 6662(h) for a gross valuation misstatement.

To reflect the foregoing,

Decision will be entered for respondent.

Notes and Questions

If the taxpayer contributes property to a charity for which the taxpayer claims a charitable deduction of $5,000 or more, the reasonable cause exception does not apply unless the taxpayer meets a two-pronged test: (1) the valuation of the property must be based on a qualified appraisal made by a qualified appraiser, and (2) the taxpayer must have "made a good faith investigation of the contributed property." See IRC § 170(f)(11)(C) and § 6664(c)(3). Do you see any problem with this test?

A qualified appraisal is one that is made by a qualified appraiser, in which the methodology and assumptions underlying the appraisal are stated. In addition, the appraisal must set forth the terms of the agreement between the taxpayer and the donee that relate to the use, sale, or other disposition of the property, as well as the circumstances under which the appraisal was obtained, and the appraiser's relationship to the taxpayer or to the activity in which the property is used. Reg. § 1.6664-4(b). The appraisal must have been made within 60 days of the date of the contribution, and it must provide a physical description of the property, and a description of the fee arrangement between the taxpayer and the appraiser. Reg. § 1.170A-17(a). The fee arrangement must not involve a prohibited type of appraiser fee structure (such as one based on a percentage of the appraised value of the property). Id.

A qualified appraiser is one who holds himself out to the public as an appraiser, is qualified to make appraisals of the type of property being valued, is not related to either the taxpayer or the donee, and understands that an intentionally false or fraudulent valuation overstatement may subject him to penalties. Neither the taxpayer nor the donee nor any party to the transaction in which the donor acquired the property will be considered a qualified appraiser. Reg. § 1.170A-17(b).

For the type of property that was at issue in *Jacobson*, the qualified appraisal must include a complete description of the object; the cost, date and circumstances of acquisition; a provenance of ownership and public exhibitions, including proof of authenticity; the methodology on which the appraisal was based, such as sales or analyses of similar works by the artist on or around the valuation date, the price listing in dealers' catalogs of the artist's works, and the general state of the art market at the time of valuation; and a statement of the interest transferred to the donee and any interest retained by the donor. Reg. §§ 1.170A-17(a) and 1.6664-4(b).

Note that the reasonable cause exception does not apply to gross valuation misstatements of charitable deduction property. Since there is no defense to the accuracy-related penalty in that case, taxpayers should value noncash charitable donations conservatively in claiming charitable deductions.

III. THE CIVIL FRAUD PENALTY

Section 6663 imposes a penalty of 75 percent of any understatement of tax attributable to fraud. In the early United States Supreme Court case, Helvering v. Mitchell, 303 U.S. 391 (1938), the Court characterized the civil fraud penalty as remedial in nature, to compensate the government for its time and expense in investigating the fraud Id. at 401.

The civil fraud penalty may not be "stacked" with the accuracy-related penalties. Thus, if any of the § 6662 penalties apply, the fraud penalty does not apply, and vice versa. The civil fraud penalty applies only to fraud on a filed return; a fraudulent failure to file is covered under § 6651(f). See § I.A., above.

A. RECOGNIZING FRAUD

Although the term "fraud" is not defined under the statute, it involves intentional wrongdoing and bad faith. This is a question of fact to be determined from the facts and circumstances of the entire record. According to the Internal Revenue Manual, fraud generally will involve one or more of the following elements: deception, misrepresentation of material facts, false or altered documents, evasion (i.e., diversion or omission), or conspiracy.

NELON v. COMMISSIONER
United States Tax Court, 1997.
T.C. Memo. 1997-49, 1997 WL 30343.

MEMORANDUM FINDINGS OF FACT AND OPINION

GERBER, JUDGE:

* * *

FINDINGS OF FACT
* * *

Sometime in 1985, petitioner hired Larry R. Melton (Melton) to paint his residence. Melton, who was not a qualified tax adviser, was involved in a tax protester group. The primary precept of members of the protester group was that they were not subject to Federal income taxes. Consonant with that belief, Melton advised that petitioner was not required to pay taxes to the U.S. Government. Petitioner accepted Melton's advice, and he joined the protester group, attended meetings, and paid dues during 1987 and 1988. Beginning with his 1986 taxable year, petitioner did not file a Federal income tax return in accord with his belief that he was not subject to the Federal income tax.

An accountant prepared petitioner's 1985 Federal income tax return. In 1989, respondent audited petitioner's 1985 return. Petitioner represented himself in the audit process and did not agree with the adjustments respondent's agent proposed or that he owed additional tax for his 1985 tax year. Petitioner believed that his income and deductions for 1985 had been correctly reported. Petitioner took no further action, the additional tax was assessed, and respondent seized petitioner's bank account for satisfaction of the assessed deficiency. The results of his 1985 audit during 1989 made petitioner angry and frustrated. Because of that experience and following the seizure of the proceeds of his bank account in 1989, petitioner chose to no longer maintain a bank account.

On June 15, 1992, respondent's agent, David Walden (Walden), advised petitioner by letter that his 1986 through 1991 tax years were being subjected to examination. Brenda Nelon's [eds.: petitioner's wife] 1987 taxable year was also under examination by Walden. By a June 25, 1992, letter, Walden was advised that petitioner was under no obligation to communicate with respondent's agents and that petitioner was not subject to the Federal income tax. The letter also acknowledged that petitioner did not file Federal income tax returns for the years in question. The letter was written by another person but was signed by petitioner. Petitioner did not meet with Walden or produce requested records or documents.

* * *

OPINION

The parties have agreed that petitioner earned income and incurred deductions for the 1986 through 1991 taxable years. The only remaining controversy is whether petitioner is liable for the addition to tax for fraud or, in the alternative, negligence and failure to file. For 1986 and 1987, section 6653(b)(1)(A) and for 1988 section 6653(b)(1) provide for an addition to tax in an amount equal to 75 percent of the underpayment that is attributable to fraud. For 1986 and 1987, section 6653(b)(1)(B) provides for an additional amount equal to 50 percent of the interest due on any part of the underpayment attributable to fraud. Section 6653(b)(2) provides that if any portion of an underpayment is due to fraud, the entire underpayment is treated as fraudulent, unless the taxpayer proves some portion of the underpayment is not due to fraud.

For 1989, 1990, and 1991, section 6651(f) provides for a maximum addition to tax of 75 percent if any failure to file is fraudulent. If the failure to file is not due to reasonable cause and it is not fraudulent, section 6651(a) provides for a maximum addition to tax of 25 percent.

The addition to tax in the case of fraud is a civil sanction provided primarily as a safeguard for the protection of the revenue and to reimburse the Government for the heavy expense of investigation and the loss resulting from the taxpayer's fraud. Helvering v. Mitchell, 303 U.S. 391, 401 (1938).

Respondent bears the burden of proving fraud by clear and convincing evidence. Sec. 7454(a); Rule 142(b). Respondent's burden is met if it is shown that petitioner intended to evade taxes known to be due and owing by conduct intended to conceal, mislead, or otherwise prevent the collection of taxes, and that there is an underpayment of tax.

The existence of fraud is a question of fact to be resolved upon consideration of the entire record. Fraud is never presumed but, rather, must be established by affirmative evidence. Direct evidence of the requisite fraudulent intent is seldom available, but fraud may be proved by circumstantial evidence. Spies v. United States, 317 U.S. 492, 499 (1943); Rowlee v. Commissioner, [eds: 80T.C. 1111, 1123 (1983)]. The taxpayer's entire course of conduct may establish the requisite intent.

Over the years, courts have developed various factors, or "badges", which tend to establish fraud. These include:(1) A pattern of under-statement of income; (2) inadequate books and records; (3) failure to file tax returns; (4) concealment of assets; (5) failure to cooperate with tax authorities; (6) income from illegal activities; (7) implausible or inconsistent explanations of behavior; (8) an intent to mislead which may be inferred from a pattern of conduct; (9) lack of credibility of the taxpayer's testimony; (10) dealings in cash. Laurins v. Commissioner, 889 F.2d 910, 913 (9th Cir. 1989), affg. Norman v. Commissioner, T.C. Memo. 1987-265; Bradford v. Commissioner, 796 F.2d 303, 307 (9th Cir. 1986), affg. T.C. Memo. 1984-601; Petzoldt v. Commissioner, 92 T.C. 661, 699 (1989). These badges of fraud are nonexclusive.

The list of the badges of fraud, however, is illustrative. We consider the totality of the facts and circumstances of each case to determine whether there is fraudulent intent.

Respondent contends that the following facts, taken as a whole, prove that petitioner had the intent to fraudulently evade paying income tax on at least some part of the underpayment for the years in issue: (1) His failure to file income tax returns for the years 1986 through 1991; (2) through that failure to file, a corresponding consistent failure to report substantial amounts of income from the logging business; (3) the failure to maintain books and records of the amounts   derived from the logging business; (4) his failure to pay estimated income taxes for the years in question; and (5) the cashing, rather than depositing, of checks derived from the logging business.

In the instant case, petitioner did not file income tax returns for the taxable years 1986 through 1991. The parties have stipulated this fact. It is also without dispute that petitioner did not report relatively large amounts of income and expenses in connection with his logging business.

An initial analysis reveals that some of the badges of fraud are present. Petitioner earned substantial amounts of income that were not reported, did not keep adequate records, and failed to provide records to or meet with respondent's agent. Due to the 1989 audit of his 1985 Federal income tax return and the seizure of his bank account, petitioner decided to close his bank account and, to some extent, deal in cash. Petitioner, however, did not misrepresent, secrete, or attempt to deceive. Although we do not approve of petitioner's reasons for failing to file returns and failing to submit to respondent's examination, those events, on this record, do not satisfy respondent's burden to clearly and convincingly prove fraud.

On this record, we do not find that petitioner's underpayment was due to an intent to evade taxes known to be due and owing by conduct intended to conceal, mislead, or otherwise prevent the collection of taxes.

Respondent places great emphasis on the fact that petitioner had an accountant for the 1985 taxable year, contending that this reflects a history of filing timely tax returns, and thus petitioner knew of the filing requirements. Petitioner, however, did not set out to evade tax he thought to be due. Instead, he came to believe that he was not obligated to file a Federal tax return and that he had no obligation to pay Federal tax. On this record, we find that his belief was not an intentional attempt to fraudulently evade the payment of tax.

Respondent also argues that petitioner attempted to conceal assets by dealing in cash. Petitioner's resolve to close his bank account and, therefore, use cash was not coupled with his belief that he was not obligated to pay tax. Petitioner, based on his belief, failed to file his 1986 and later years' returns. It was only after his bank account was seized in 1989 in connection with the audit of his 1985 tax return that petitioner closed his bank account. By 1989, petitioner had failed to file several Federal income tax returns. Petitioner believed that he had correctly reported his income and deductions for 1985 by using a professional return preparer (accountant). Petitioner, who is not well educated or versed in business and tax matters, represented himself in the 1985 audit. From his perspective he had properly filed his 1985 return, and the resulting seizure of his bank account caused him to react by closing the bank account. There is no indication that the 1989 audit of petitioner's 1985 return involved the so-called protester arguments or that he failed to cooperate with respondent's agent.

Petitioner did not cooperate with the revenue agent in the determination of his tax liability for 1986 through 1991. On occasion, this has been found to be an indicium of fraud. See Rowlee v. Commissioner, 80 T.C. at 1125; Grosshandler v. Commissioner, 75 T.C. 1, 20 (1980); Gajewski v. Commissioner, 67 T.C. 181, 200 (1976), affd. without published opinion 578 F.2d 1383 (8th Cir. 1978). Here, however, petitioner did not attempt to deceive or mislead the revenue agent. Instead, he acknowledged that he did not file any Federal income tax returns and provided his reasons for not meeting with the agent or filing returns. In this regard, tax protester arguments, even though meritless and frivolous, without more, do not necessarily amount to fraud. Kotmair v. Commissioner, 86 T.C. 1253, 1262 (1986).[7] Petitioner's failure to cooperate here was to his own detriment. Respondent had received Forms 1099 from the company(ies) that had paid petitioner for harvested timber in each year. Petitioner, by his failure to come forward, however, did not obtain the benefit of the deductions to which he was entitled in connection with the harvesting of timber. His failure to cooperate did not keep respondent from being able to determine his income or receipts.

At trial, petitioner admitted that he knew Melton was not an accountant or an attorney experienced in tax matters, but he believed Melton's advice that he did not owe tax. Petitioner is not well versed in tax and financial matters and has only limited formal education. We cannot say that his holding to so-called protester tenets was with intent to defraud or misrepresent. In general, a taxpayer's negligence, whether slight or gross, is not enough to prove fraud.

Respondent maintains that petitioner's failure to file timely income tax returns was part of a pattern of fraud. Although a taxpayer's failure to file is prima facie evidence of negligence for purposes of section 6653(a), see Emmons v. Commissioner, 92 T.C. 342, 350 (1989), affd. 898 F.2d 50 (5th Cir. 1990), it is insufficient in and of itself to prove fraud.

The record here simply does not show any affirmative acts of concealment or misrepresentation so as to constitute fraud, such as filing false information or attempting to mislead respondent. For respondent to sustain her position as to the fraud addition to tax, it is not enough that respondent can show the taxpayer to be devious. The evidence must be clear and convincing. In the instant case, we find that the evidence falls short of being clear and convincing. Accordingly, we find that petitioner is not liable for additions to tax or penalties based on fraud.

* * *

Notes and Questions

Five years prior to the *Nelon* decision, Judge Gerber had decided the case of Niedringhaus v. Commissioner, 99 T.C. 202 (1992), which

---

7. We stated in Kotmair v. Commissioner, 86 T.C. 1253, 1262 (1986) that the taxpayer's protester arguments "may have been meritless, frivolous, wrongheaded, and even stupid, but we cannot hold that they amounted to fraud, without something more. Were we to do so, every failure-to-file protester case would be automatically converted into a fraud case."

involved very similar facts to those of *Nelon*. But in *Niedringhaus*, Judge Gerber held that the taxpayer's actions constituted fraud. Is *Niedringhaus* consistent with *Nelon*?

Other examples of badges of fraud include: (1) a consistent and substantial overstatement of deductions (as well as the consistent understatement of income mentioned in *Nelon*), (2) keeping a double set of books, (3) making false entries or alterations, false invoices or false documents, (4) destroying books or records, (5) covering sources of income (6) handling one's affairs to avoid making records usual in transactions of the kind. Spies v. United States, 317 U.S. 492 (1943); Campfield v. Commissioner, 133 F.3d 906 (2d Cir. 1997)(unpublished opinion).

These badges of fraud overlap with indications of negligence. See Internal Revenue Manual § 20.1.5.7.1. Indeed, there is often a very fine line between negligence and civil fraud on the one hand, and civil fraud and criminal fraud on the other hand. Can you think of any distinguishing factors?

If a married couple files a joint return after having filed separate returns, any fraud on either of the separate returns will be deemed fraud on the joint return. IRM § 20.1.5.12.2. But fraud is not presumed, so if the joint return is considered a fraudulent return, the civil fraud penalty does not apply to the spouse unless the Service can establish by clear and convincing evidence that some portion of the underpayment is due to civil fraud on the part of that spouse. IRC § 6663(c). Note, however, that although the Service has the burden of proving fraud by clear and convincing evidence, once the Service meets this burden, the entire amount of the underpayment is presumed to be attributable to fraud. The burden then shifts to the taxpayer to rebut this presumption by a preponderance of the evidence. IRC § 6663(b).

B. CALCULATING THE FRAUD PENALTY

LEVINSON v. UNITED STATES
United States Court of Appeals, Third Circuit, 1974.
496 F.2d 651.

OPINION OF THE COURT

HUNTER, CIRCUIT JUDGE:

The sole issue on this appeal is the determination of the proper method by which civil tax fraud penalties are to be assessed under 26 U.S.C. § 6653 [eds: now § 6663]. The Internal Revenue Service ('IRS') assessed a 50% [eds: now 75%] Fraud penalty on the difference between taxpayers' true tax liability and the tax liability shown on taxpayers' original tax returns. The district court upheld this method of computation and we affirm.

Taxpayers' returns for 1957 through 1959 were timely filed and the taxes shown thereon timely paid. When the IRS subsequently conducted routine examinations of these returns, adjustments were made resulting in the assessment of additional taxes. Subsequent to this, taxpayers filed amended returns reporting income which had not been included in the original tax returns. The IRS then began an investigation which uncovered further unreported income of taxpayers and which eventually resulted in the bringing of fraud charges against taxpayers. On this appeal taxpayers do not contest their tax liability or the finding of fraud.

Taxpayers do contend, however, that the fraud penalty should not be applied to those deficiencies assessed because of adjustments made to the original tax return at the time routine audits were conducted. The additional taxes assessed at this time resulted from adjustments to inventories and business deductions. These adjustments apparently were not the subject of the subsequent fraud investigation which was based on omitted income. Thus the taxpayers suggest that the fraud penalty should have been computed by the following formula:

50% x (correct tax – (tax shown on original timely filed return minus additional tax assessed because of routine audit on original return))

The fraud penalty was actually computed on the basis of this formula:

50% x (correct tax – tax shown on original timely filed return)

Taxpayers argue that the decisional law and applicable statute supports their view that the fraud penalty should not apply to nonfraudulent deficiencies assessed as a result of routine adjustments made to their original returns. We do not agree.

Under the Internal Revenue Code of 1939, the fraud penalty provision, section 293(b), provided that "if *any part* of any deficiency is *due to fraud* * * * then 50 per centum of the *total amount of the deficiency* * * * shall be so assessed * * *."

"Deficiency" was defined under section 271(a) by the following formula:

deficiency = correct tax – (tax shown on return less amounts previously assessed or collected without assessment – rebates)[1]

---

1.   See Kurtzon v. Commissioner, 17 T.C. 1542, 1548 (1952); Rev.Rul. 60-214, 1960-1 Cum-Bull. 700.

Where there have been several deficiencies, this definition quite logically requires that, in computing the amount of any new deficiency, credit should be given for deficiencies previously assessed or collected.

In computing the fraud penalty under the 1939 Code, however, courts consistently refused to apply the penalty to only this narrowly defined deficiency. E.g., Middleton v. Commissioner, 200 F.2d 94 (5th Cir. 1952); Romm v. Commissioner, 245 F.2d 730 (4th Cir.), cert. denied, 355 U.S. 862, 78 S.Ct. 94, 2 L.Ed.2d 68 (1957). Since the fraud penalty provision referred to 'the total amount of the deficiency,' courts consistently reasoned that where more than one deficiency had been assessed, the penalty applied to all of the deficiencies;[2] thus, the total deficiency was held to be the difference between the correct tax and the tax shown on the original return.

Contrary to what taxpayers suggest, we have found no decision under the 1939 code which deviated from this method of computing the fraud penalty or even suggested that in certain situations a different method of computation would apply. Taxpayers rely heavily on J. S. McDonnell v. Commissioner, 6 B.T.A. 685 (1927) as support for the proposition that in computing the fraud penalty the IRS should allow taxpayers 'legitimate adjustments' to the tax as reported on the original return.

Taxpayers, however, have misread *McDonnell*. The 50% Fraud penalty in that case was applied to the difference between the correct tax and the tax shown on the original return.[4] The court specifically held that no error had been committed in the method of computation of the penalty.[5] What the court did say, which is far different from that contended by the taxpayers, is that in computing the total tax liability and hence the correct deficiency, the IRS had failed to give credit for legitimate deductions and losses. Taxpayers, however, have not contested the final tax liability determined by the IRS and therefore *McDonnell* does not support taxpayers' position. It is also significant that *McDonnell* was specifically cited by the same court in Wilson v. Commissioner, 7 T.C. 395, 398 (1942) when it noted that,

"Since the Revenue Act of 1918, the (IRS) has consistently computed the (fraud) penalty upon the *total amount understated on the return*

---

2.   The effect of this was to refuse to follow the literal definition of deficiency (which would require that credit be given for previously assessed deficiencies) whenever the fraud penalty was imposed. See, e.g., Romm v. Commissioner, supra.

4.   6 B.T.A. at 690-691. See Wilson v. Commissioner, 7 T.C. 395, 398 (1946), wherein the same court explained that in *McDonnell* it had 'held that the penalty was to be computed upon the entire excess of the tax liability over that shown on the return.'

5.   6 B.T.A. at 695.

and in every instance in those cases coming before us of which we are aware, we have approved the computation." (Emphasis added.)

We therefore conclude that under the Internal Revenue Code of 1939, it was the court-sanctioned practice of the IRS to compute fraud penalties on the difference between the correct tax and the tax shown on the original return. The only question remaining then is whether the enactment of the Internal Revenue Code of 1954 affected changes in this substantive policy. We think not.

The present fraud penalty provision, 26 U.S.C. § 6653(b), differs from its predecessor only in its use of the word 'underpayment' rather than deficiency: "If *any part* of any underpayment * * * of tax required to be shown on a return is *due to fraud*, there shall be added to the tax an amount equal to 50 percent of the underpayment." (Emphasis added.)

"Underpayment" is defined in section 6653(c)[6] by reference to the definition of deficiency in 26 U.S.C. § 6211[7] which is virtually identical to its predecessor, section 271(a). Section 6653(c), however, states that for purposes of defining deficiency, only the tax shown on the original timely filed return is to be considered.

On their face these changes appear minor and at most appear to merely clarify what the practice had been under the 1939 Code. That this was the Congressional intent is unquestionably clear from the legislative history.[8] We thus agree with the Second Circuit that the Internal Revenue Code of 1954 did not change the method of computing

---

6. 26 U.S.C. § 6653(c) provides; inter alia:

"For purposes of this section, the term 'underpayment' means–

(1) Income, estate, and gift taxes.– In the case of a tax to which section 6211 (relating to income, estate, and gift taxes) is applicable, a deficiency as defined in that section (except that, for this purpose, the tax shown on a return referred to in section 6211(a)(1)(A) shall be taken into account only if such return was filed on or before the last day prescribed for the filing of such return, determined with regard to any extension of time for such filing) * * *."

7. 26 U.S.C. § 6211 provides, inter alia:

"Definition of a deficiency

"(a) In general.–For purposes of this title in the case of income, estate, and gift taxes, imposed by subtitles A and B, the term 'deficiency' means the amount by which the tax imposed by subtitles A or B exceeds the excess of–

"(1) the sum of

"'(A) the amount shown as the tax by the taxpayer upon his return, if a return was made by the taxpayer and an amount was shown as the tax by the taxpayer thereon, plus

"(B) the amounts previously assessed (or collected without assessment) as a deficiency, over–

"(2) the amount of rebates, as defined in subsection (b)(2), made."

8. For a discussion of the legislative history see Papa v. Commissioner, 464 F.2d 150, 152 (2nd Cir. 1972).

the fraud penalty and that the method by which the IRS has computed the penalty in the present case is proper under 26 U.S.C. § 6653. See Papa v. Commissioner, 464 F.2d 150 (2nd Cir. 1972).

In view of taxpayers' insistence that deficiencies assessed as a result of the routine audit of their returns must be applied as a credit pursuant to 26 U.S.C. § 6211(a)(1)(B), a few further observations appear necessary. First, section 6211(a)(1)(B) is identical to its predecessor under the 1939 Code, section 271(a)(1)(B), and as noted previously, prior deficiencies were never applied under the 1939 Code as a credit in determining the 'total' deficiency subject to the fraud penalty.

Second, taxpayers suggest that previously assessed deficiencies should be applied as credit under section 6211(a)(1)(B) just in some circumstances.[9] Yet, there is no support in the statute, its legislative history or in the case law for applying section 6211(a)(1)(B) selectively.

Third, the inequities of taxpayers' position is manifest. Had there been only one deficiency assessed coupled with a finding that at least a part of the underpayment was due to fraud, then there would not have been any previously assessed deficiency for which taxpayers could claim a credit under section 6211(a)(1)(B). The fraud penalty quite clearly would have been applied to the total underpayment, i.e., the difference between the correct tax and the tax shown on the original timely filed return. It does not seem likely that Congress would have conditioned the severity of the fraud penalty on such a fortuity as whether or not a routine audit had been conducted prior to the assessment giving rise to the fraud charge.

Lastly, if there is ambiguity in the statutory language, we think the clear Congressional purpose must prevail.[10] Since Congress unquestionably did not intend to modify the substantive law under the 1939 Code, we agree with the Second Circuit that the fraud penalty under 26 U.S.C. § 6653 is properly computed on the basis of the difference between the correct tax and the tax shown on the original timely filed return. Accord, Papa v. Commissioner, 464 F.2d 150 (2nd Cir. 1972).

The order of the district court of August 29, 1973 will be affirmed.

---

9. Taxpayers apparently argue that section 6211(a)(1)(B) should be applied just to those deficiencies assessed because of 'legitimate adjustments' made to their original timely filed returns as a result of a routine audit. Presumably, they would add that this previously assessed deficiency was not due to fraud.

10. See, e.g., United States v. American Trucking, 310 U.S. 534, 543-549, 60 S.Ct. 1059, 84 L.Ed. 1345 (1940).

WEIS, CIRCUIT JUDGE (dissenting):

The dreary pages of the Internal Revenue Code contain few passages of any comfort to the taxpayer. The petitioner here has found several provisions which, when read literally and given their common sense meaning, support his position and bring about an equitable result. It is only by reliance upon previous judicial interpretations, written in response to a need which to longer exists, that the Commissioner is able to prevail, thus increasing the government's revenue but diminishing the resources of the taxpayer. Since I believe that the plain wording of the statute should prevail, I must dissent.

As the majority concedes, the fraud penalty is computed on the 'underpayment,'[1] which term is defined as a 'deficiency,'[2] which means the amount by which the correct tax exceeds the sum of (a) the amount shown on the taxpayer's return plus (b) amounts previously assessed.[3]

I agree with the majority's statement of the formula:

deficiency = correct tax − (tax shown on return [less] amounts previously assessed).

Applying the statute literally means that the taxpayer here should pay the penalty of 50 percent only on the amount of tax due because of fraud and not on that portion of the tax which had been paid as a result of a previous assessment based on adjustments for items as to which there was a legitimate basis for difference of opinion. This result is sound and would appear to be eminently reasonable.

The difficulty is that years ago in construing earlier versions of the Internal Revenue Code, the Tax Court found a 'loophole' which it felt obliged to close. The problem was articulated in Still v. Commissioner,

---

1.   Section 6653(b) of the Internal Revenue Code of 1954: 'If any part of any underpayment * * * of tax required to be shown on a return is due to fraud, there shall be added to the tax an amount equal to 50 percent of the underpayment.'

2.   Section 6653(c) of the Internal Revenue Code of 1954.

3.   Section 6211 of the Internal Revenue Code of 1954:
"Definition of a deficiency

    "(a) In general.–For purposes of this title in the case of income, estate, and gift taxes, imposed by subtitles A and B, the term 'deficiency' means the amount by which the tax imposed by subtitles A or B exceeds the excess of–
    "(1) the sum of
        "'(A) the amount shown as the tax by the taxpayer upon his return, if a return was made by the taxpayer and an amount was shown as the tax by the taxpayer thereon, plus
        "(B) the amounts previously assessed (or collected without assessment) as a deficiency, over–
    "(2) the amount of rebates, as defined in subsection (b)(2), made."

19 T.C. 1072, aff'd, 218 F.2d 639 (2d Cir. 1959), where the court said at 1077:

"A taxpayer who had filed a fraudulent return would merely take his chances that the fraud would not be investigated or discovered, and then, if an investigation were made, would simply pay the tax which he owed anyhow, and thereby nullify the fraud penalty."

This rationale was adopted by the Courts of Appeal in Middleton v. Commissioner, 200 F.2d 94 (5th Cir. 1952), and Romm v. Commissioner, 245 F.2d 730 (4th Cir. 1957). These cases involve tax assessments prior to the enactment of the 1954 Code, and in each one all of the deficiencies were based on fraud. While there might be some argument about the court's power to ignore the wording of the statute, nevertheless the equities favor the result.

The 'loophole' about which the courts were concerned was closed through congressional action in 1954 by including in section 6653(c) a provision that the 'amount shown on a taxpayer's return' means a return which is timely filed. Thus, a taxpayer who learns that his tax liability is being questioned and who files a later amended return can secure no reduction of the amount of the penalty due by such action. The calculation of the fraud penalty after 1954 clearly involves only the original return, not an amended one. Therefore, the opportunity to 'make sport of the so-called fraud penalty' which concerned the *Still*, supra, and *Romm*, supra, courts is no longer available.

Papa v. Commissioner, 464 F.2d 150 (2d Cir. 1972), failed to note the pertinent change in the 1954 Code and, adopting the reasoning of the older cases,[4] refused to allow credit for an earlier assessment made by the Internal Revenue Service. However, *Papa*, supra, was in the nature of an ex parte proceeding, the appeal having been taken by the Commissioner and not contested by the taxpayer. Furthermore, the earlier deficiency which the court refused to credit was also fraudulent. Equities, therefore, favor the result in *Papa*, supra, as they did in the earlier cases.

Here, however, fundamental fairness supports the taxpayer's position, and there would seem to be no reason why we should apply decisional law today which was originally developed to remedy a statutory infirmity since cured by legislative revision.

The majority finds fault with petitioner's contention that a deficiency under section 6211(a)(1)(B) should be credited only in circumstances of nonfraudulent assessments, and dismisses the taxpayer's position by

---

4. *Still*, supra, *Romm*, supra, and Wilson v. Commissioner, 7 T.C. 395 (1946).

saying that there is no support in the statute for such an interpretation. We need not reach that point in this case, although to my mind the taxpayer's interpretation is far preferable to the one which the courts have made over the years by completely disregarding credit for all prior assessments paid despite the plain wording of the statute. The petitioner's suggestion requires only a modest construction to promote equity, while the decisional law involves a major interpretation which furthers inequity.

I would give to the petitioner that which the statute requires and reverse the decision of the district court.

Notes and Questions

The fraud is committed when the initial fraudulent return is filed. Thus, the fact of the fraud remains unaffected by subsequent events. For example, if a taxpayer files an amended return and pays the full amount of the deficiency after the return is audited but before an assessment is made, the taxpayer remains subject to the civil fraud penalty. See Stewart v. Commissioner, 66 T.C. 54 (1976); see also Reg. § 1.6664-2(c)(2). Similarly, a subsequent reduction of the amount of tax required to be reported on the fraudulent return due to a carryback or carryover to the year of the fraud, or to the operation of the claim of right doctrine will not reduce the amount of the penalty. See Elmore v. Commissioner, T.C. Memo 1987-72, 1987 WL 40135. On the other hand, if no tax is due when the fraudulent return is filed, no underpayment exists, and no fraud penalty may be assessed. See, e.g., Seebold v. Commissioner, T.C. Memo 1988-183, 1988 WL 39086; Abatti v. Commissioner, T.C. Memo 1078-392, 1978 WL 3065.

Do you agree with the majority's decision or do you think the dissent has the better reasoned argument?

Problems

1. James' 2003 income tax return showed a tax liability of $87,000. No amount of tax previously had been assessed (or collected without assessment) and James had received no rebates. He claimed a credit of income taxes withheld from his wages of $60,000, and a credit of $32,000 for estimated tax payments he had made during that taxable year. He obtained a refund of $5,000. Subsequently, James's 2003 return was audited and the Service determined that the correct amount of tax liability should have been $97,000 and that the additional amount of tax was attributable to a fraudulent understatement of income. The Service

and James agree that the remaining tax liability is not attributable to fraud. Calculate James's fraud penalty.

2. In problem one, assume in the alternative that James' had additional estimated tax payments of $3,000 that he neglected to claim. Will this affect the civil fraud penalty?

3. In problem one, assume in the alternative that James filed an amended return showing an additional tax liability of $3,000. Will this affect the civil fraud penalty?

4. A taxpayer files a federal income tax return that is subject to three adjustments: (1) one for which no penalty is imposed, (2) one for which an accuracy-related penalty is imposed, and (3) one for which a civil fraud penalty is imposed. Subsequently, the taxpayer discovers that he neglected to claim a valid estimated tax credit for that taxable year, which will reduce the underpayment on which these adjustments are based. How should the credit be allocated? See Reg. § 1.6664-3.

C. COLLATERAL ESTOPPEL

It is routine for the Service to impose a civil fraud penalty after a conviction in a criminal tax prosecution, and it is well-established that the principle of double jeopardy does not prevent the relitigation of the civil fraud penalty. See, e.g., Helvering v. Mitchell, 303 U.S. 391 (1938); Trafficant, Jr. v. Commissioner, 884 F.2d 258 (6th Cir. 1989). Since the government's burden of proof in the criminal case is greater than the corresponding burden in the civil case, the taxpayer may be estopped from denying fraud in the civil case after a prior conviction in the criminal case.

WRIGHT v. COMMISSIONER
United States Tax Court, 1985.
84 T.C. 636.

OPINION

TANNENWALD, JUDGE:

* * * After concessions,[2] the sole issue for our decision is whether petitioner John T. Wright's[3] conviction under section 7206(1) collaterally

---

2. Respondent has conceded that the additions to tax as to petitioner Susan L. Wright were erroneously determined; petitioners have conceded the existence and amounts of the understatements of income and underpayments of tax for the years in issue.

3. As this case concerns the addition to tax only as to John T. Wright, see supra note 2, we will hereinafter refer to Mr. Wright as 'petitioner,' and Mr. and Mrs. Wright as 'petitioners.'

estops petitioners from denying, for purposes of section 6653(b), that part of their underpayment for 1978 was due to fraud.

At the time they filed their petition in this case, petitioners maintained their residence in Illiopolis, Illinois. Petitioners filed joint Federal income tax returns for 1976, 1977, and 1978.

Petitioners, in their response to respondent's motion, claim the following: In June 1975, petitioner's father died suddenly, leaving petitioner's mother to run the family farm. Petitioner was asked by his mother to assume responsibility for the farming operation. Prior to June 1975, petitioner had no business or farming experience, and had no training in bookkeeping, accounting, or business management. Petitioner managed the farm through the years in issue, and for purposes of income tax return preparation, turned his records of the farm's receipts and disbursements over to a local accountant skilled in farming bookkeeping methods. Petitioner's wife did not participate in either the farming business or the preparation of petitioners' income tax returns.

On their Federal income tax returns for the years in issue, petitioners understated their taxable income for 1976 by $8,824.46 and their tax table income for 1977 and 1978 by $24,167.18 and $29,904.82, respectively. Petitioners underpaid their Federal income taxes for the years 1976, 1977, and 1978 by $1,487.95, $4,599.72, and $13,810.05, respectively.

Petitioner was indicted in the United States District Court, Central District of Illinois, Springfield Division, on March 22, 1982 on two counts of violation of section 7206(1) and two counts of violation of section 7201, one of each of the counts relating to the taxable year 1977 and one of each of the counts relating to the taxable year 1978. On June 15, 1982, that court, based on petitioner's guilty plea, entered a finding of guilty for 'the offense(s) of subscribing to a false income tax return as charged in Count 3 of the Indictment, in violation of Title 26, USC sec. 7206(1). Counts 1, 2, & 4 dismissed upon Government Motion.'

Count 3 of the indictment charged:

That on or about the 10th day of January 1979, in the Central District of Illinois, John T. Wright a resident of Illiopolis, Illinois, did willfully and knowingly make and subscribe to a United States Individual Tax Return (form 1040) for John T. and Susan L. Wright, which was verified by a written declaration that it was made under the penalties of perjury, and was filed with the Internal Revenue Service, when he did not believe said Income Tax Return to be true and correct as to every material matter in that the Income Tax

Return stated that the grain sale and other income of John T. and Susan L. Wright was $84,665.69 whereas, as he then and there well knew and believed, he had received substantial income in addition to that here before stated.

All in violation of Title 26, United States Code, Section 7206(1).

Respondent issued the deficiency notice on which the instant case is based on September 26, 1983.

* * *

Respondent bases his motion on the allegedly preclusive effect of petitioner's conviction under section 7206(1)[4] upon the issue of fraud under section 6653(b).[5] Respondent contends that our opinions in Goodwin v. Commissioner, 73 T.C. 215 (1979), and Considine v. Commissioner, 68 T.C. 52 (1977), compel the conclusion that petitioner's conviction establishes as a matter of law that the underpayment for 1978 was 'due to fraud,' for purposes of section 6653(b), and thus that respondent's motion should be granted. Petitioners contend that petitioner's lack of business acumen raises a genuine issue as to a material fact, and that respondent's motion should thus be denied. For the reasons hereinafter stated, we agree with petitioners.

The doctrine of collateral estoppel precludes relitigation of any issue of fact or law that is actually litigated and necessarily determined by a valid and final judgment. Montana v. United States, 440 U.S. 147, 153 (1979). Its purpose is to avoid repetitious litigation of issues between the same parties or their privies. The doctrine, however, 'must be confined to situations where the matter raised in the second suit is identical in all respects with that decided in the first proceeding and where the controlling facts and applicable legal rules remain unchanged.' Commissioner v. Sunnen, 333 U.S. 591, 599-600 (1948); see Cromwell v. County of Sac, 94 U.S. 351, 353 (1876). Thus, the question is whether the issue under section 6653(b) is 'identical in all respects' to that decided under section 7206(1).

Under section 6653(b), respondent has the burden of proving, by clear and convincing evidence, that 'any part of any underpayment * * * is due

---

4. Sec. 7206 provides, in relevant part,
Any person who,
(1) DECLARATION UNDER PENALTIES OF PERJURY. Willfully makes and subscribes any return, statement, or other document, which contains or is verified by a written
declaration that it is made under the penalties of perjury, and which he does not believe to be true and correct as to every material matter; * * * shall be guilty of a felony * * *.

5. Sec. 6653(b)(1) provides: 'If any part of any underpayment (as defined in subsection (c)) of tax required to be shown on a return is due to fraud, there shall be added to the tax an amount equal to 50 percent of the underpayment.'

to fraud.' See sec. 7454(a); Rule 142(b). The 'due to fraud' language has been consistently interpreted to require proof of specific intent to evade a tax believed to be owing. See, e.g., Hebrank v. Commissioner, 81 T.C. 640, 642 (1983). Section 7206(1) makes it a crime for one willfully to make and submit any return verified by a written declaration that it is made under the penalties of perjury which he or she does not believe to be true and correct as to every material matter. The indictment on which petitioner's conviction was based charged that he willfully filed a verified return that 'he did not believe * * * to be true and correct as to every material matter' in that petitioner 'well knew and believed (that) he had received substantial income in addition to' that which he reported.

In Considine v. Commissioner, 68 T.C. 52, a case in which the taxpayer had been   convicted under section 7206(1) and was disputing the addition to tax under section 6653(b), we held that 'a conviction under section 7206(1) for 'willfully' making a return which the taxpayer does not believe to be true and correct is proof that the return is fraudulent,' and that the taxpayer was thus 'collaterally estopped to deny that he willfully filed a false and fraudulent return.' *Considine v. Commissioner*, supra at 61, 68.

Our reasoning in *Considine* was as follows: (1) this Court, in Amos v. Commissioner, 43 T.C. 50, 55 (1964), affd. 360 F.2d 358 (4th Cir. 1965), had held that 'the term 'willfully' as used in section 7201[7] has authoritatively been defined in prior judicial decisions to encompass all of the elements of fraud which are envisioned by the civil penalty described in section 6653(b)'; (2) the Supreme Court, in United States v. Bishop, 412 U.S. 346, 356-361 (1973), had held that 'willfully' has the same meaning in each of sections 7201, 7202, 7203, 7204, 7205, 7206, and 7207; therefore, (3) a conviction under section 7206(1) actually and necessarily determined that there was, for purposes of section 6653(b), a specific intention to evade tax. *Considine v. Commissioner*, supra at 59-60. Our opinion in *Considine* and the rationale upon which it was predicated were followed in the Court-reviewed opinion in Goodwin v. Commissioner, 73 T.C. 215, 224 (1979), with six Judges dissenting.

Subsequent to our opinions in *Considine v. Commissioner*, supra, and *Goodwin v. Commissioner*, supra, the Court of Appeals for the Ninth Circuit had occasion, in Considine v. United States, 683 F.2d 1285, 1287 (9th Cir. 1982), to review the imposition of the addition to tax for fraud

---

7.   Sec. 7201 provides, in relevant part, 'Any person who willfully attempts in any manner to evade or defeat any tax imposed by this title or the payment thereof shall, in addition to other penalties provided by law, be guilty of a felony.'

on the Considines for the taxable year 1965[8] by the United States District Court on the ground that Mr. Considine's conviction of a violation of section 7206(1) for that year collaterally estopped him from contesting the fraud element of the addition to tax for that year under section 6653(b). The Ninth Circuit disagreed with the District Court's application of collateral estoppel, and, in so doing, stated flatly that they believed that our opinion in *Considine v. Commissioner*, supra, was incorrect. See 683 F.2d at 1287.[9] Beyond the Ninth Circuit's criticism of our opinion in *Considine v. Commissioner*, supra, it has been held on numerous occasions, both before and after *Considine*, although not in the context of the issue of collateral estoppel, that the intent to evade taxes is not an element of the crime covered by section 7206(1). United States v. Tsanas, 572 F.2d 340, 343 (2d Cir. 1978); United States v. Beasley, 519 F.2d 233, 245 (5th Cir. 1975); United States v. DiVarco, 484 F.2d 670, 673-674 (7th Cir. 1973); Siravo v. United States, 377 F.2d 469, 472 n.4 (1st Cir. 1967); United States v. Hans, 548 F. Supp. 1119, 1124 (S.D. Ohio 1982); United States v. Anderson, 254 F. Supp. 177, 183-185 (W.D. Ark. 1966); see also United States v. Whyte, 699 F.2d 375, 381 (7th Cir. 1983).[10] Against this background, we have reexamined our opinions in *Goodwin v. Commissioner*, supra, and *Considine v. Commissioner*, supra, and have concluded that they should no longer be followed to the extent that they hold that a conviction under section 7206(1) is equated by way of collateral estoppel with the existence of fraud within the meaning of section 6653(b).

---

8.   The interplay between the criminal and civil phases of the Considines' liability for Federal income taxes for the taxable years 1965- 67 and 1969 has had the attention of the courts on several occasions. Mr. Considine was convicted under sec. 7206(1) as to his returns for 1965-67 and 1969, *United States v. Considine*, an unreported case (S.D. Cal. 1973, 34 AFTR 2d 74-5412, 74-2 USTC par. 9639), affd. 502 F.2d 246 (9th Cir. 1973), and brought three separate actions challenging respondent's subsequent imposition of the additions to tax under sec. 6653(b). Considine v. Commissioner, 68 T.C. 52 (1977), concerned the addition for 1969; Considine v. United States, 645 F.2d 925 (Ct.Cl. 1981), concerned the additions for 1966 and 1967; and Considine v. United States, 683 F.2d 1285 (9th Cir. 1982), concerned the addition for 1965.

9.   The District Court was nevertheless affirmed on the ground that the Government had in fact carried its burden of proof on the fraud issue under section 6653(b) with respect to both Mr. and Mrs. Considine. In Considine v. United States, 645 F.2d 925, 928-931 (Ct. Cl. 1981), which involved the Considines' taxable years 1966 and 1967, the Government contended only that the issue of knowing falsification as to the amount of income and deductions should be disposed of on the basis of collateral estoppel, and did not claim that collateral estoppel applied to the issues of intent to evade or existence of an underpayment. See 645 F.2d at 928. The Court of Claims was thus not required to reach the issue which was the fulcrum of our opinions in *Considine* and *Goodwin*. It sustained the Government's limited contention and, like the Court of Appeals for the Ninth Circuit, went on to hold that the Government had in fact carried its burden of proof as to fraud.

10.   We note that respondent has not cited, and our research has not revealed, any authority, other than our opinions in *Considine* and *Goodwin*, that fraud, i.e., intent to evade taxes, is an element of the offense under section 7206(1).

We begin our analysis in support of our conclusion with the word 'willfully,' as used in section 7206(1). In United States v. Pomponio, 429 U.S. 10 (1976), the Supreme Court held that, for purposes of sections 7201-7207, 'willfully' 'simply means a voluntary, intentional violation of a known legal duty.' 429 U.S. at 12; see *United States v. Bishop*, supra at 360. This definition says nothing about fraud, and requires nothing more than a specific intention to violate the law. *United States v. Pomponio*, supra at 11-13, buttressed its conclusion that 'willfully' has this uniform meaning in sections 7201-7207 by noting those statutes' differences from one another, specifically in the express designation of the specific elements of each offense. For example, the Court described the specific element of the offense under section 7201 as the 'attempt to evade.' *United States v. Bishop*, supra at 359. The Court went on explicitly to caution against interpreting the word 'willfully,' as used in sections 7201-7207, to include this section 7201 element. Semantic confusion sometimes has been created when courts discuss the express requirement of an 'attempt to evade' in section 7201 as if it were implicit in the word 'willfully' in that statute. * * * Greater clarity might well result from an analysis that distinguishes the express elements, such as an 'attempt to evade,' prescribed by section 7201, from the uniform requirement of willfulness.

In *Amos v. Commissioner*, supra, we equated the element necessary for conviction under section 7201 (i.e., an 'attempt to evade') with that essential for the imposition of the civil penalty under section 6653(b) (i.e., an 'underpayment * * * due to fraud'). *Amos v. Commissioner*, supra at 55. Because the attempt to evade tax is the gravamen of fraud, we concluded in *Amos* that a taxpayer convicted under section 7201 of having attempted to evade or defeat a tax for a taxable year is collaterally estopped from denying under section 6653(b) that part of his underpayment for the same year was 'due to fraud.' Such identity of criminal tax evasion and civil tax fraud for purposes of collateral estoppel has been repeatedly sustained by the courts. See Gray v. Commissioner, 708 F.2d 243, 246 (6th Cir. 1983), affg. a Memorandum Opinion of this Court, and cases cited thereat; see also Plunkett v. Commissioner, 465 F.2d 299, 305 (7th Cir. 1972), affg. a Memorandum Opinion of this Court. However, to have held, as we did in *Considine v. Commissioner*, supra, and *Goodwin v. Commissioner*, supra, that a conviction for 'willfully' making a false statement in an income tax return within the meaning of section 7206(1) estops a taxpayer from denying that any underpayment made for the year of the return was 'due to fraud' misapplies the principle of collateral estoppel and creates the semantic confusion warned against in *United States v. Bishop*, supra.

In a criminal action under section 7206(1), the issue actually litigated and necessarily determined is whether the taxpayer voluntarily and intentionally violated his or her known legal duty not to make a false statement as to any material matter on a return. The purpose of section 7206(1) is to facilitate the carrying out of respondent's proper functions by punishing those who intentionally falsify their Federal income tax returns, and the penalty for such perjury is imposed irrespective of the tax consequences of the falsification. As noted above, the intent to evade taxes is not an element of the crime charged under section 7206(1). Thus, the crime is complete with the knowing, material falsification, and a conviction under section 7206(1) does not establish as a matter of law that the taxpayer violated the legal duty with an intent, or in an attempt, to evade taxes.

In short, it cannot be said that the combined effect of the Supreme Court's opinions in *United States v. Pomponio*, supra, and *United States v. Bishop*, supra, and our opinion in *Amos v. Commissioner*, supra, is to equate the standards under section 7206(1) with those under section 6653(b); the Supreme Court simply did not engraft the 'attempt to evade' language from section 7201 into section 7206(1) by holding that 'willfully' has a uniform meaning in sections 7201-7207. Thus, to the extent that they give collateral estoppel effect to a conviction under section 7206(1) on the issue of intent to evade tax under section 6653(b), *Considine v. Commissioner*, supra, and *Goodwin v. Commissioner*, supra, are overruled. Of course, a conviction for willful falsification, under section 7206(1), while not dispositive, will be one of the facts to be considered in a trial on the merits.

In the instant case, petitioners argue that we should deny respondent's motion for partial summary judgment because petitioner's lack of business acumen, and not an attempt to evade taxes, was the reason for the underpayments in question, and the factual issue thus raised is a 'genuine issue as to any material fact' under Rule 121(b). We agree. The issue of intent, adequately raised by petitioners herein, is clearly one requiring a trial on the merits. See Oakland Hills Country Club v. Commissioner, 74 T.C. 35, 39-40 (1980); cf. Considine v. United States, supra, 683 F.2d at 1288 (intent to evade is 'natural inference' from willful underpayment by sophisticated, knowledgeable taxpayer).[11] Thus, on the sole issue before us, i.e., the addition to tax for 1978, respondent's motion for partial summary judgment will be denied.

* * *

---

11. We do not have a sufficient factual foundation in the moving papers to determine that no material issue of fact exists as to the fraud, as the Court of Appeals for the Ninth Circuit and the Court of Claims were able to do in the *Considine* cases before them.

KORNER, J., dissenting: I respectfully disagree with the conclusion of the majority in this case that petitioner, John T. Wright, is not estopped by his conviction under section 7206(1) to deny that his Federal income tax return for 1978 was false in that he willfully and knowingly omitted income therefrom which he knew should have been reported. That fact was conclusively established by his guilty plea to the indictment under section 7206(1), which contains the specific allegation of willfully and intentionally failing to report income which petitioner knew he should have done. He is thus collaterally estopped to deny that fact in the instant case. His guilty plea is as much a conviction as a conviction following a jury trial.

For this reason, I would conclude that there is no issue of material fact in this case as to whether petitioner's failure to report all his income on his 1978 return was an innocent mistake due to his lack of business acumen. A conviction under section 7206(1) of filing a false return from which income is omitted does not, standing alone, establish the fraudulent intent to evade tax required to support the addition to tax under section 6653(b). However, here the parties have stipulated that petitioner's willful and knowing omission of income from his 1978 return resulted in an underpayment of tax. In my view, petitioner's willfully and knowingly filing a false return for the year 1978, combined with the stipulation of the parties that the willful omission of income from that return resulted in an underpayment of tax, establishes the intent to evade necessary to a determination of the addition to tax under section 6653(b).

Based on the holdings and discussions in Considine v. United States, 683 F.2d 1285 (9th Cir. 1982); Considine v. United States, 645 F.2d 925 (Ct. Cl. 1981); and Goodwin v. Commissioner, 73 T.C. 215 (1979), I would grant respondent's Motion for Summary Judgment in this case.

Notes and Questions

If collateral estoppel applies, its application is limited to the taxable year(s) of the taxpayer's prior convictions. It also does not extend to any other taxable years or to any person (such as a spouse) other than the convicted taxpayer.

The extent to which collateral estoppel applies depends upon the underlying offense of which the taxpayer was convicted and what was established in the criminal case. For instance, if the taxpayer was convicted of evasion under § 7201, the element of fraud must have been conclusively established by the conviction. So, if the conviction is based on false statements made after the return is filed, the taxpayer may contest the civil fraud penalty because the taxpayer's intent at the time the return was filed was not at issue in the criminal case. Also, the amount of the deficiency often is established by indirect methods of proof (see discussion of these methods, Chapter 9), which may not be precise. Therefore, the taxpayer may contest the amount of the deficiency if the precise amount was not established in the prior criminal prosecution. See Tunnell v. Commissioner, 74 T.C. 44, aff'd. 663 F.2d 527 (5th Cir. 1981).

1. A conviction under § 7203 of willful failure to file a return does not collaterally estop the taxpayer from denying fraudulent intent in a later civil fraud case. Why?

2. Does an acquittal of the criminal charges help the taxpayer in a subsequent suit on civil fraud?

3. If a taxpayer is convicted of criminal tax evasion (§ 7201), does it matter whether the conviction was the result of a plea of guilty rather than a jury verdict after a trial on the merits? What if the conviction was the result of a plea of nolo contendere by the defendant? What if the defendant entered an "Alford plea" in which he pleaded guilty but continued to maintain his innocence?

4. In *Wright*, why did the court hold that collateral estoppel did not apply when the taxpayer had stipulated both to the existence of a willful and knowing omission of income, and to an underpayment of tax?

IV. MISCELLANEOUS PENALTIES

There are a number of other penalties that may apply along with the delinquency penalties, the accuracy-related penalties, and the civil fraud penalty. The most common of these are the frivolous return penalty and the estimated tax penalty.

A. FRIVOLOUS RETURNS

A return must be filed in processable form, which means that it must be filed on a proper form that contains the taxpayer's identifying information, as well as sufficient information from which the Service can verify the tax liability shown on the return, and it must be signed. Failure to conform to any of these requirements will result in a frivolous return penalty under § 6702.

GANZ v. UNITED STATES

United States District Court, Northern District of Illinois, 1985.
1985 WL 3618.

MEMORANDUM OPINION AND ORDER

SUSAN GETZENDANNER, DISTRICT JUDGE:

Plaintiff brings this action to seek a refund of certain administratively assessed penalties. The penalties were assessed pursuant to 26 U.S.C. § 6702 of the Internal Revenue Code which empowers the Secretary of the Treasury to impose a $500 fine on any individual who files a frivolous tax return. * * * Presently before the court is defendant's motion to dismiss or for summary judgment and for an award of costs and attorneys' fees. * * *

[T]he court finds the following facts undisputed or otherwise deemed true for purposes of this motion. The pro se plaintiff, Dennis Ganz, filed an Internal Revenue Service (IRS) Form on April 15, 1983 for the 1982 calendar year. On July 5, 1983, the IRS assessed a penalty of $500 against that return under the authority of 26 U.S.C. § 6702. On September 6, 1983, plaintiff filed a Form 1040X to amend his previously submitted 1040 form for calendar year 1982. No penalty was assessed against this form. On February 26, 1984, plaintiff filed another 1040X Form to further amend his calendar year 1982 return. A $500 penalty was assessed against this second amended return on January 24, 1985 pursuant to § 6702. Finally, on July 8, 1984, plaintiff filed a handwritten 'statement' which purports to be a tax return for the 1983 calendar year. A § 6702 fine of $500 was assessed against this return on January 25, 1985. On February 4, 1985, plaintiff completed a 'regular form' for the calendar year 1983 which he pre-dated to July 8, 1984. No action appears to have been taken against that form.

In this action plaintiff protests only the $500 fine imposed on his second amended 1982 return and his 1983 purported return. He does not contest the fine imposed on the original 1982 return. On both of those returns for which the fine is contested, plaintiff claimed his wages were not income and accordingly failed to include the amount of wages earned in his taxable income.

* * *

Because plaintiff is appearing pro se, the court construes his complaint liberally. Essentially, plaintiff argues that his second amended return of 1984 and his purported tax return of 1984, do not meet the § 6702 statutory prerequisites for the imposition of the $500 penalty. It is the meaning of that statute to which the court now turns.

In 1982 Congress passed the Tax Equity & Fiscal Responsibility Act (TEFRA), Pub.L. No. 97-248. In section 362(a) of TEFRA, now codified at 26 U.S.C. § 6702, Congress provided for a civil penalty to be assessed against frivolous income tax returns:

Sec. 6702. Frivolous Income Tax Return

(a) Civil Penalty.–If–

(1) any individual files what purports to be a return of the tax imposed by subtitle A but which–

(A) does not contain information on which the substantial correctness of the self-assessment may be judged, or

(B) contains information that on its face indicates that the self-assessment is substantially incorrect; and

(2) the conduct referred to in paragraph (1) is due to–

(A) a position which is frivolous, or

(B) desire (which appears on the purported return) to delay or impede the administration of Federal income tax laws, then such individual shall pay a penalty of $500.

(b) Penalty in Addition to Other Penalties.– he penalty imposed by subsection (a) shall be in addition to any other penalty provided by law.

The legislative history to TEFRA reveals that § 6702 was a congressional response to the rapid growth in deliberate defiance of the tax laws by tax protesters. Congress was especially concerned with the lack of any penalty available against tax protesters from whom sufficient tax had already been withheld but who nevertheless filed protest returns demanding refunds. In an effort to help deter the filing of such returns and maintain the integrity of the income tax system, Congress sought to make available an immediately assessable penalty on the filing of a frivolous return.

The facts in this case demonstrate that the second amended 1982 return and the purported 1983 return were properly penalized under § 6702. Specifically, both returns purported to be individual income tax returns and contained 'information that on its face indicate[d] that the self-assessment [was] substantially incorrect' and the incorrect returns were due to 'a position which [was and is] frivolous.' Thus, both parts of § 6702(a) have been satisfied.

In reaching this conclusion, the court first examined the 1982 return. This return is in three parts: the original return, the first amended return filed on September 6, 1983, and the second amended return filed on February 26, 1984. For purposes of administering the tax laws, the treatment of amended returns and their relationship to the original return is within the discretion of the Commissioner of the IRS. Therefore, in determining whether plaintiff's return 'contains information that on its face indicates that [his] self-assessment is substantially incorrect,' the IRS may consider all three parts of the return together. Here, the first amended return for 1982 states in an attached letter that plaintiff did receive wages from an employer, but that these wages are not income. 'I * * * now recognize that wages I recieved [sic] are in fact wages as an employee* * * . However, because I believe wages are not 'gain,' I would be committing [sic] perjury if I listed my wages on line 7 of the 1040 return [for taxable income].' Later in that letter plaintiff states that he did not enter his wages on the 1040 Form 'for fear that the meaning of my signature would be misunderstood as a statement that I believe the receipts identified were in fact 'income." The second amended return, while not so explicitly professing plaintiff's views on the taxability of wages, nevertheless indicates that plaintiff considered that he could not be taxed on the money he had 'labored for.'

If plaintiff's position that wages are not taxable income is wrong, then his admissions, contained in his 1982 amended returns that he did receive wages, clearly indicate that plaintiff's self-assessment of tax liability was 'substantially incorrect,' as required by § 6702(a)(1). The court also notes that if plaintiff's position is so wrong as to be frivolous, then § 6702(a)(2) will also be satisfied, thus establishing that the imposition of the $500 fine on the second amended return complied with the statute.

The court need not belabor the obvious. Plaintiff's position is that because wages are an equal exchange for services they do not represent income. This argument ignores the fundamental legal principle, uniformly embraced, that precisely because wages are compensation for services and therefore gain to the individual, wages are income and subject to taxation. Judge Marshall, in a recent opinion on this very issue wrote:

> Further, plaintiff's conduct * * * was based on a legally frivolous position. The Internal Revenue Code defines gross income as 'all income from whatever source derived, including (but not limited to) the following items: (1) Compensation for services * * *' 26 U.S.C. § 61(a) (1982). In Commissioner v. Glenshaw Co., 348 U.S. 426 (1955), the Supreme Court defined income as 'undeniable accessions to wealth, clearly realized, and over which the taxpayers have complete dominion,' id. at 431, a definition that clearly encompasses wages. In Central Illinois Public Service Co. v. United States, 435 U.S. 21 (1978), the Court restated the obvious, 'Wages are usually income,

but many items qualify as income and yet are clearly not wages.' Id. at 25. Wages are income unless a statute specifically exempts a particular type of wages. Id.

Kalish v. United States, 84-2 U.S.T.C. ¶ 9542 (N.D. Ill. 1984). Other courts have universally rejected plaintiff's position as frivolous. Given the frivolity of his position and the substantial incorrectness of his self-assessment, plaintiff fell squarely within § 6702 and was properly subjected to the $500 penalty. Courts in this district and elsewhere have not been reluctant to uphold imposition of the $500 penalty when a tax protester has advanced the frivolous claim of the non-taxability of wages and the § 6702 requirements have otherwise been met, which is precisely the case here. Kalish v. United States, 84-2 U.S.T.C. § 9542 (N.D. Ill. 1984); Karpowycz v. United States, 586 F.Supp. 48 (N.D. Ill. 1984); Hill v. United States, 599 F.Supp. 118 (M.D. Tenn.1984); Turner v. Secretary of Treasury, 84-2 U.S.T.C. ¶ 9805 (S.D. Ind. 1984).

It is true that there is no evidence as to the amount of plaintiff's 1982 wages. There is only evidence that he did receive wages and he did not include these as taxable income. Although plaintiff does not make the argument, it is possible that one could contend that plaintiff's self-assessment of tax liability is not necessarily 'substantially incorrect' under § 6702(a)(1)(B) because it has not been established that his wages were high enough to substantially increase his self-assessed tax liability. Even if the court were persuaded by this argument--a point which I do not decide because it has not been raised--plaintiff's amended returns would still satisfy § 6702(a)(1) because under the alternative subsection (A) of § 6702(a)(1), liability attaches when the return does not contain information on which the substantial correctness of the self-assessment may be judged. That subsection would certainly apply here where plaintiff has stated he earned wages without specifying the amount and contends that he has no tax liability on them.

Plaintiff appears to raise two further arguments as to why the penalty assessed against his second amended 1982 return was improper, even if the statute was technically complied with. First, plaintiff argues that he subjectively and sincerely believed that wages are not taxable income. Therefore, no fines can be assessed against him because the statute implicitly requires that the tax delinquent have advanced a position in bad faith. This court has previously held that the taxpayer's state of mind is irrelevant to the determination of whether the position he advances is frivolous. Knottnerus v. United States, 582 F.Supp. 1572 (N.D. Ill. 1984) (Getzendanner, J., upholding assessment of $500 penalty under § 6702). This position has been adhered to elsewhere. See, e.g., Vaughn v. United States, 589 F.Supp. 1528 (W.D. La. 1984); Doyle v.

United States, 84-1 U.S.T.C. ¶ 9521 (E.D. Mich. 1984). Thus, plaintiff's good faith belief in the immunity of wages from taxes is no defense to a § 6702 civil penalty when the case law so clearly indicates that wages are indeed taxable income.

Plaintiff's second and final additional argument is that the assessment of a § 6702 fine against his original 1982 return precludes the government from assessing another fine against the second amended 1982 return, all the documents being part of one 'return.' The court rejects this argument. Nothing in the legislative history to § 6702 indicates any congressional intention to differentiate an 'original' return from an 'amended' return. The Senate Report states that § 6702 applies to 'any document which purports to be a return of income tax' and to which the other provisions of the statute apply. S. Rep. No. 494, 97th Cong. 2d Sess. 277, reprinted in 1982 U.S. Code Cong. & Ad. News 781, 1024 (Emphasis added). Furthermore, § 6702(b) provides that the penalties authorized by subsection (a) shall be provided in addition to any others provided by law. Finally, the court observes that it is proper to place a heavy emphasis on the congressional desire to deter the filing of frivolous returns from tax protesters since the penalty is intended to apply even when sufficient taxes have previously been withheld from the protester. See S. Rep. No. 494, 97th Cong., 2d Sess. at 277. Given this background, § 6702 should be applied to each return sent to the IRS, whether it be an amended or an original return. The drain on government   resources and the detriment to the integrity of the tax system are problems that exist regardless of whether the return is labelled 'amended' or is the original return for that calendar year. Therefore, this court is persuaded that the imposition of a § 6702 penalty against an original return for one calendar year does not preclude the imposition of a second § 6702 penalty assessed against the second amended return for that same year.

This brings the court to the 1983 return to determine if the § 6702 penalty imposed there was proper. Plaintiff's purported 1983 return was not filed on an IRS Form 1040. Nevertheless, the 'handmade return' does purport to be a return, as plaintiff so admits. The Form W-2 which plaintiff attached to his purported 1983 return shows that plaintiff had wages of $22,610.39 and miscellaneous income of $1,826.30. Yet, on the purported return, plaintiff claimed only $1,826.30 in 'profit or gain.' The $22,610.30 was characterized only as 'compensation for labor' and was not included in plaintiff's assessment of total income.

These facts clearly make out a § 6702 violation. Plaintiff's admission of compensation for labor in excess of $20,000 alongside his refusal to incorporate that amount as total income is undisputable evidence that plaintiff's purported 1983 return contains information that on its face indicates that the self-assessment is substantially incorrect, as § 6702(a)(1) requires. Further, plaintiff's incorrect self-assessment on the 1983 return is again based on the frivolous position that wages are not taxable, thus satisfying § 6702(a)(2). Given this, the $500 penalty assessed against the 1983 return was proper. As a final note, the court points out that, contrary to plaintiff's suggestion, the penalty was not assessed because plaintiff's return was 'handmade.' The penalty was assessed for the reasons given in § 6702--facial and substantial incorrectness of a return based on a frivolous position.

* * *

Notes and Questions

The § 6702 penalty was increased from $500 to $5,000 under the Tax Relief and Health Care Act of 2006.

In addition to the tactics mentioned in the *Ganz* case, other tactics have included a deliberate use of incorrect tax tables, return information that is inconsistent with information from other sources (such as excess withholding exemptions filed by a taxpayer lists only a few dependents, and consistent understatement of income from forms 1099), use of "gold standard" or "war tax" deductions, and claiming deductions or credits for "slavery reparations." Since 2007, the IRS has issued lists of positions under § 6702(c) that it considers frivolous for purposes of the § 6702 penalty. The current list of 46 positions is found at Notice 2010-33, I.R.B. 2010-17 (Apr. 7, 2010).

1. The § 6702 penalty applies to two general types of conduct. What are they and which was involved in *Ganz*?

2. The *Ganz* case involved several tactics typically employed by tax protestors. What were they?

Ganz was able to be heard in the federal district court by paying 15 percent of the total amount of the penalties and filing a claim for refund, which was denied. This procedure was permitted under former § 6703, which was amended under the Omnibus Budget Reconciliation Act of 1989 to disallow this tactic with respect to the frivolous return penalty. Since this penalty is assessable immediately, it must be challenged through the refund procedure, and suit may be brought only in the district courts or in the Court of Federal Claims.

A taxpayer who files a frivolous return is also at risk of criminal prosecution for willful failure to file a return. See discussion of this penalty, Chapter 9.

B. ESTIMATED TAX PENALTY

As discussed in Chapter 3, the purpose of filing an annual income tax return is to inform the Service of the taxpayer's financial transactions that occurred during the taxable year, sufficient to enable the Service to verify the correct amount of tax liability. When the due date for filing the federal income tax return arrives, the tax liability should have been paid from any or all of three sources: (1) income tax withholding on salary or wages, (2) quarterly estimated tax payments on income not subject to withholding, and (3) a credit for any tax refund applied from the previous year.

Estimated tax payments are due on April 15, June 15, September 15, and on January 15 of the following taxable year. If the due date falls on a Saturday, Sunday or legal holiday, the taxpayer will have until the following business day to file the return and pay the tax. A failure to pay by each quarterly due date is considered a separate infraction of the revenue laws.

A taxpayer whose entire income is derived from salary or wages will not have to worry about underpaying estimated taxes unless her Form W-4 incorrectly reflects her actual number of dependents, so that insufficient tax is withheld. If the wage and salaried taxpayer derives additional income not subject to withholding, such as investment income, she may be required to make estimated tax payments on that income.

Self-employed taxpayers will be subject to estimated taxes on their entire taxable income. These taxpayers will have to discipline themselves to ensure that the required estimated tax payments are made in a timely manner.

Regardless of which category a taxpayer falls into, an estimated tax penalty may be imposed under § 6654 if income tax liability is underpaid. The penalty may be avoided if the taxpayer's total combined annual tax payments (taxes withheld from wages, estimated tax payments, and any refund applied from the previous year) are equal to the lesser of (1) 90 percent of the tax for the current year, or (2) 100 percent of the tax shown on the return for the preceding taxable year (110 percent in taxable year 2003 and after if the taxpayer's adjusted gross income exceeds $150,000 ($75,000 for married taxpayers filing separately)). Note that in 2009, the penalty applied to a qualifying small business taxpayer only if that taxpayer failed to pay at least 90% of the tax shown on the preceding year's return.

No penalty will be imposed if the tax liability, reduced by the amounts withheld from wages and by any other payments made during the taxable year, is less than $1,000. Also, no penalty will be imposed if the taxpayer had no tax liability for the preceding taxable year, provided the taxpayer was a citizen or resident of the United States during that entire year. IRC § 6654(e).

Any amount that is withheld from wages is applied evenly to the four installments unless the taxpayer elects to have the withheld amount applied to the period in which it was actually withheld. In the case of a taxpayer whose income varies throughout the year, the Service authorizes the use of an annualized installment method of payment. This method reflects the income actually derived by the taxpayer during each quarter.

An underpayment of estimated taxes will result in a penalty equal to the amount of interest under § 6621, adjusted quarterly, that would have accrued on the underpayment for the period the tax remains unpaid. The amount of the underpayment is the excess of the required installment over the amount (if any) of the installment paid on or before the due date. IRC § 6654(b)(1). The penalty runs from the payment due date(s) to the earlier of (1) the date on which the payment (or portion of a payment) is received or (2) the 15th day of the fourth month following the close of the taxable year. IRC § 6654(b)(2).

Since the required installments of estimated taxes are based on the tax liability reported on the annual tax return, an amended return adjusting the tax liability filed before the due of the return, including extensions, will result in an adjustment to the amount of the estimated tax penalty. If the ultimate amount of tax on the annual return is adjusted after the due date (including extensions) because of an amended return, or an increase or decrease in tax after an examination of the return, the estimated tax penalty also will be adjusted.

The taxpayer may elect to apply an overpayment of estimated tax against her succeeding year's estimated tax. If this election is made, the overpayment is applied to unpaid installments in the order in which they are required to be paid.

There is no reasonable cause defense to the estimated tax penalty, except for a very narrow exception that applies during the first two years after a taxpayer either retires after reaching age 62 or becomes disabled. I.R.C. § 6654(e)(3). The Service is authorized, however, to grant a waiver if it determines that the failure to make the required payment(s) was due to casualty, disaster or other unusual circumstances under which it would be inequitable to impose the penalty. Examples of the latter include death or serious illness of the taxpayer, a substantial overstatement of tax liability on the return, and destruction of the taxpayer's books and records by a natural disaster. Since there is otherwise no reasonable cause defense, the taxpayer may not avoid the penalty by reliance on the advice of a competent tax professional.

Notes

A similar estimated tax penalty also applies to corporate taxpayers under § 6655.

The penalty applies to each quarterly due date in which the taxpayer fails to pay the estimated tax. Because the penalty applies to each quarterly period, the overpayment of the estimated taxes in a later quarter will not relieve the taxpayer of the penalty attributable to the earlier period, even if the taxpayer ultimately is entitled to a refund. Only an overpayment in the first quarter will relieve the taxpayer of the subsequent penalty. In that case, the amount of the overpayment then will be credited against the succeeding quarters in the order in which the payments are required to be made. The same applies to any refund of tax from the prior year that the taxpayer elects to apply against the estimated tax payments. By applying the refund (and any other overpayment) to the quarters in the order in which the payments are required to be made, the taxpayer may avoid an estimated tax penalty.

V. INTEREST

Interest is a charge for the use of borrowed money and reflects the time value of the use of that money. If a taxpayer underpays her tax liability, she has the use of money that legally belongs to the government. Thus, the taxpayer will owe interest to the government for the use of its money. Conversely, if the taxpayer overpays her tax liability, the government may owe interest to her on the amount of the overpayment. Interest rates are adjusted quarterly and are compounded daily. Prior to the 1998 IRS Restructuring and Reform Act, the interest rate on underpayments was one percent higher than the rate on overpayments. Taxpayers objected to the inequity of the differential rates, and in 1998, Congress equalized the rates of interest on overpayments and underpayments under the IRS Restructuring and Reform Act of 1998, effective after July 23, 1998. Currently, the rate of each is determined by adding three percentage points to the federal short term rate. IRC § 6621(a)(1).

Interest is derivative of the underlying tax. Thus, interest is assessed, collected and paid in the same manner as the underlying tax, and is subject to the same statute of limitations as the underlying tax.

When the statutory period expires, neither the tax liability nor the interest is collectible.

Section 6631, enacted under the IRS Restructuring and Reform Act, provides that for taxable years beginning after June 30, 2000, any notice and demand for payment of taxes sent to an individual taxpayer must state the interest due, show how the computation of interest was made, and provide the statutory authority for interest.

A. UNDERPAYMENTS

Under the general rule, interest on an underpayment runs from the last date prescribed for payment of the tax until the date the tax is paid, regardless of whether or not the statute of limitations is tolled because of a statutory notice of deficiency or a Tax Court review, and regardless of whether collection action is suspended due to uncollectibility. IRC § 6601(a). The date prescribed for payment is generally the due date of the return, without regard to extensions of time to file or pay. Thus, an extension of time to pay will relieve the taxpayer of penalties for late payment, but it will not relieve the taxpayer of the obligation to pay interest from the original due date of the return.

The tax and additions to tax generally are considered paid when they are received by the Service, although the mailbox rule applies to payments of the tax as well as to filing of returns, (§ 7502), as does the extension to the next business day if the due date falls on a Saturday, Sunday or legal holiday (§ 7503).

1. Exceptions to the General Rule of Interest Accrual

a. *Suspension of Interest*

If a taxpayer files a timely return and the Service fails to timely notify the taxpayer of the existence of a deficiency, penalties and interest will be suspended. See further discussion of abatement of penalties and interest at § VI.B., below.

If the taxpayer signs a waiver of restrictions on assessment and collection (Form 870), the Service may assess the deficiency immediately and begin collection action without having to send the taxpayer a notice of deficiency, and without having to wait for the 90-day period to run. If the Service procrastinates and does not send the taxpayer a notice and demand for payment within 30 days of the execution of the waiver, interest stops running after the 30th day and will not resume until a notice and demand is issued. IRC § 6601(c).

After a notice and demand for payment is sent, the taxpayer has a 21-day grace period (10 business days if the total tax bill, including tax, penalties, and interest exceed $100,000) in which interest will not accrue if the payment is received within that time. IRC § 6601(e)(3). Thus, interest runs from the due date of the return to the date of the notice and demand. It stops as of the date of the notice and demand if the tax is paid within the 21-day grace period. If the tax is not paid within this period, the sending of the notice and demand will have no effect on the accrual of interest, which will continue unabated.

b. Deposits Against Interest Accrual

Under § 6603, enacted under the American Jobs Creation Act of 2004, taxpayers may make deposits of tax to stop the running of interest, provided the tax is "disputable" and has not been assessed. A disputable tax is the amount of tax specified at the time of the deposit as attributable to disputable items. A disputable item is any item of income, deduction, or credit for which the taxpayer has a reasonable basis for its treatment on the return and also believes that the Service has a reasonable basis for disallowing the treatment of the item. For this purpose, all items included in a 30-day letter are considered disputable, provided the disputable amount is not less than the amount of the deficiency shown in the 30-day letter..

A § 6603 deposit has all the advantages of the former payment in the nature of a cash bond (see Rev. Proc. 84-58, superceded by Rev. Proc. 2005-18), but the taxpayer is entitled to receive interest for the period of time that the § 6603 deposit is attributable to a disputable tax liability, provided the deposit has not been used to pay a tax liability. The disadvantage of the § 6603 deposit is that the interest rate applicable to these deposits is less than the interest rate payable on overpayments. Interest is payable on a § 6603 deposit at the short-term federal rate, compounded daily, while interest on an overpayment is payable at the short-term federal rate plus three percentage points in the case of noncorporate taxpayers, and the short-term rate plus 0.5 percentage points (two percentage points if the overpayment does not exceed $10,000) in the case of a corporate taxpayer.

If the taxpayer owes an additional amount of tax after the resolution of the dispute, to the extent that the deposit is used to pay the tax, the tax is treated as paid when the deposit was made, so no further interest on that amount will run after the date of the deposit. Since the § 6603 amount is considered a deposit, the taxpayer has the right to request its return provided it has not been used as payment and provided the collection of the tax is not in jeopardy. If the taxpayer requests and receives the return of the deposit, and it is determined subsequently that the taxpayer owes a deficiency, interest runs against the taxpayer from the date prescribed for payment to the date the payment is received, without regard to the period during which the Service retained the deposit.

The procedure for designating a deposit as a § 6603 deposit is found in Rev. Proc. 2005-18, I.R.B. 2005-13. Such a deposit may not be made if a notice of deficiency has been issued. If the deposit is not designated, it is considered an "undesignated remittance." If there is no deficiency or proposed deficiency, the undesignated remittance is treated as a deposit. Otherwise, an undesignated remittance is treated as a payment when received and is applied to the earliest outstanding tax liability, then to penalties and interest, in that order.

If the taxpayer executes a waiver of restrictions on assessment (Form 870) following an examination of the return, the remittance, whether designated or undesignated, becomes a payment and, for purposes of interest, is treated as having been paid at the time the remittance was received by the Service. If the taxpayer does not agree to the proposed deficiency and does not sign the Form 870, the undesignated remittance will be considered a payment and to the extent it covers the proposed deficiency, no notice of deficiency will be issued. A designated deposit, however, will not be considered a payment under those circumstances and a notice of deficiency will be issued. If the taxpayer does not petition the Tax Court within the 90/150-day period, the deposit will become a payment automatically and will be posted to the taxpayer's account. If the taxpayer petitions the Tax Court during the 90/150-day period, the deposit will be treated as a payment at the end of the 90/150-day period unless the taxpayer notifies the Service in writing to continue to treat the deposit as a § 6603 deposit.

Notes and Questions

In the case of a jeopardy assessment, interest does not begin to run until the due date of the return because the jeopardy payment is being demanded in advance of the due date. IRC § 6601(b)(3); Reg. § 1.6601-1(c)(3).

Under Rev. Rul. 87-53, 1987-1 C.B. 348, a payment that is lost by the Service will be regarded as timely received, provided the taxpayer can establish that the payment was made.

The Service has discretion to abate interest in specific situations, such as where the unpaid portion of tax and interest are too small to warrant the administration and collection costs, where the interest is attributable to unreasonable error or delay by the IRS, and where the interest is attributable to erroneous written advice provided upon request of the taxpayer by an IRS officer or employee acting in his official capacity. In addition, the Service must abate interest on any erroneous refund check received by the taxpayer, until the date the Service demands payment. See further discussion of interest abatement at § VI., below.

1. Miranda filed a timely income tax return for 2009 on April 15, 2010. Subsequently, her return was examined and as a result, the Service proposed an additional deficiency of $2,500 because of the disallowance of some deductions Miranda had claimed improperly. On March 25, 2011, she agreed to the deficiency and signed a Form 870 (Waiver of Restrictions on Assessment and Collection). On June 30, 2011, the Service issued a notice and demand for payment, which Miranda paid on August 1, 2011. During what period will interest run on the deficiency?

2. If Miranda instead paid the deficiency on July 15, 2011, would this affect the period of interest accrual?

3. If Miranda had paid the deficiency on March 31, 2011, would this have affected the period of interest accrual?

4. If a taxpayer has made a designated § 6603 deposit and afterward receives a notice of deficiency then petitions the Tax Court, does it matter to the taxpayer at this point whether the remittance becomes a payment or continues as a § 6603 deposit?

2. Effect of Carrybacks

If in a later year, a taxpayer incurs a net operating loss, an excess capital loss, or has excess investment credits, these may be carried back to earlier taxable years to decrease the tax that was owed for that year. This usually entitles the taxpayer to a refund. If, however, there is a deficiency outstanding in the earlier year, the carryback has little effect on the running of interest. Interest continues to accrue from the due date of that year's return to the due date of the return in the later year (excluding extensions) in which the carryback arose. If the carryback is disallowed or does not offset the entire amount of the deficiency, under the general rule interest will not stop with the due date of the return in the later year, but will run until the interest or portion of interest is paid, or until a later carryback arises.

If a net operating loss, capital loss or business credit is carried back to a year that is closed by the statute of limitations, it will offset an unassessed deficiency but not interest attributable to that deficiency. Thus, the carryback, reduced by the unassessed deficiency but not by the interest on the deficiency, will be available to offset tax liability in open years.

Question

Why does a carryback not eliminate interest and why does the interest cease on the due date of the return in the later year of the carryback?

B. OVERPAYMENTS

If a taxpayer overpays her tax liability, she is entitled to file a claim for refund of the amount she overpaid. In the alternative, the taxpayer may credit the overpayment against a prior outstanding underpayment or against estimated taxes for subsequent taxable years. In general, the Service will owe the taxpayer interest on the overpayment at the same rate as that of underpayments, compounded daily. IRC § 6621. But the interest payable on the overpayment may vary according to when the taxpayer filed the return and which of the three alternatives she elects.

1. Claim for Refund

If the taxpayer files a claim for refund, and the claim is granted, the Service generally owes the taxpayer interest from the date of the overpayment to a date that does not precede the refund check by more than 30 days. IRC § 6611(b)(2). However, the Service has a 45-day grace period in which it does not have to pay interest if it refunds the overpayment within 45 days of the later of the due date of the return (determined without regard to extensions) or the date the return is filed. IRC § 6611(e)(1). But if the Service fails to refund the overpayment within the 45-day period, it must pay interest on the overpayment from the due date of the return to the date the refund is made, subject to the 30-day rule under § 6611(b)(2). If the return is delinquent, no interest is payable on any overpayment during the period of the delinquency. IRC § 6611(b)(3).

If the claim for refund is made on an amended return, interest runs from the due date of the original return to the date the amended return is filed, provided the refund is made within the 45-day grace period. If not, interest runs from the due date of the original return to the date of payment, again subject to the 30-day rule under § 6611(b)(2).

An overpayment may be refunded to the taxpayer on the Service's initiative, instead of the taxpayer having to file a claim for refund. This is likely to occur when the overpayment arises because of the failure to report an item on an information return or because of a math error on the return. If the Service initiates the adjustment that results in a refund or a credit, the Service is entitled to obtain the benefit of the 45-day grace period by subtracting 45 days from the number of days interest otherwise would have been allowed. IRC § 6611(e)(3).

In order to calculate the interest on an overpayment, the Service must determine the period for which interest is owed. Thus, it is important to determine whether and when a payment has been made. If the overpayment arises from amounts overpaid as estimated tax or from amounts overwithheld from wages and salary by the taxpayer's employer, the overpayment is deemed made on the original due date of the return for that year. This applies regardless of when the return is filed.

If the carryback of a net operating loss, a net capital loss, an investment tax credit or a foreign tax credit produces an overpayment, for purposes of determining interest, the overpayment is deemed to have arisen on the due date (without regard to extensions) of the return for the year in which the carryback arose. IRC § 6611(f). Thus, no interest will be payable on the overpayment if a refund is made within 45 days after the claim for refund is filed. IRC § 6611(e)(2).

Problems

1. Martha files a timely return for the 2008 taxable year on September 1, 2009, after having obtained an automatic six-month extension of time to file. She files a refund claim on August 10, 2010. The Service determines that the claim is valid, and it mails Martha a check on December 10, 2010. How many months will interest accrue on the overpayment? Are there any other facts you would need to know?

2. In question one, what result if Martha's refund check is lost in the mail, and a replacement check is issued on March 31, 2011? See Rev. Rul. 76-74, 1976 WL 36429 and Godfrey v. United States, 997 F.2d 335 (7th Cir. 1993).

3. What result if Martha received the refund check on December 15, 2010, but she inadvertently threw it away? See Finlen v. United States, 1989 WL 106815 (D. Kan. 1989).

2. Crediting of Overpayments

In general, if an overpayment is credited against a subsequent underpayment, interest on the overpayment runs from the date of the overpayment to the original due date of the return on which the underpayment arose. Interest on the underpayment will cease as of the date of the credit of the overpayment, to the extent the overpayment offsets the underpayment. IRC § 6601(f). If there is an excess amount of underpayment that is not offset by the overpayment, interest runs on this portion of the underpayment from the due date of the return to which it relates, until the date of payment.

a. Earlier Arising Underpayment

If an overpayment is credited against an earlier underpayment, no interest will accrue on the overpayment, and interest on the underpayment will run from the due date of the return on which the underpayment arose to the date of the overpayment credit. If the overpayment is credited against a penalty or other addition to tax, interest will cease to accrue on the overpayment from the earlier of the date of assessment or the date on which interest ordinarily would begin to accrue if the amount of the penalty or addition to tax had not been paid or credited. Reg. § 301.6611-1(h)(2)(vi).

Problems

1. John has an underpayment of tax for the taxable year 2008 in the amount of $1,000. He has overpaid his 2009 taxes by $1,500 because of excess withholding from his wages. John filed a timely return for 2009 and elected to credit $1,000 of his overpayment against his underpayment. On his 2009 tax return, which he filed on March 25, 2010, he claimed a refund of the remainder of the overpayment, and the Service sent him a refund check on May 30, 2010. During what period will interest run on the underpayment? Will interest run on the overpayment? If so, during what period will the interest run on the overpayment?

2. Assume in the alternative in question one that John had an overpayment of $800 in the 2009 taxable year, which he elected to credit against his $1,000 underpayment. Will interest run on either the underpayment or the overpayment (or both) and if so, during what period?

3. In question one, what result if John filed a timely request for an automatic extension of time to file, he then filed his return (with the refund claim) on June 10, 2010, and the date of the refund check is August 15, 2010?

b. Later Arising Underpayment

If an overpayment is credited against estimated taxes for a subsequent year, interest runs from the date of the overpayment to the due date of the amount against which the credit is taken. IRC § 6611(b)(1). Generally, an amount of overpayment that is applied against a subsequent year's estimated taxes will be applied against each estimated tax in the order in which it arises. This prevents the taxpayer from being subject to penalties for failure to pay the estimated taxes. The question, however, is what is the meaning of the phrase in § 6611(b)(1) " * * * amount against which the credit is taken"?

MARSH & McLENNAN COMPANIES, INC. v. UNITED STATES
United States Court of Appeals, Federal Circuit, 2002.
302 F.3d 1369.

DYK, CIRCUIT JUDGE.

* * *

BACKGROUND

The facts of this case are not in dispute. Marsh, a financial services company, overpaid its 1985 federal income taxes by $275,139 ("1985 overpayment") and overpaid its 1986 taxes by $3,412,083 ("1986 overpayment").

Marsh also overpaid the amount of 1987 federal income taxes shown on the return by $12,694,216, and at the time the 1987 return was filed, Marsh elected to apply this overpayment to its 1988 tax liability ("1987 credit elect overpayment"). The Internal Revenue Service ("IRS") permits a corporate taxpayer that has paid more than its liability in one year to claim a credit for the excess against its estimated taxes for the succeeding year. 26 U.S.C. § 6402(b) (2000).[1] The credit is called a "credit elect overpayment." As discussed below, credit elect over-

---

1. Section 6402(b) provides:

The Secretary is authorized to prescribe regulations providing for the crediting against the estimated income tax for any taxable year of the amount determined by the taxpayer or the Secretary to be an overpayment of the income tax for a preceding taxable year.

26 U.S.C. 6402(b) (2000). The pertinent language of the code and regulations has not changed since the relevant time period.

payments do not earn interest. The 1987 credit elect overpayment was transferred by the IRS from Marsh's 1987 tax account into its 1988 tax account on March 15, 1989, the due date of its 1988 tax return.

Marsh also overpaid the amount of 1988 taxes shown on the return by $28,336,308, and at the time the 1988 return was filed, Marsh elected to apply this overpayment to its 1989 tax liability ("1988 credit elect overpayment"). A portion of the 1988 credit elect overpayment was transferred by the IRS from Marsh's 1988 tax account into its 1989 tax account on September 15, 1989, to satisfy its estimated 1989 tax liability, and the remainder of the 1988 credit elect overpayment was transferred from Marsh's 1988 tax account into its 1989 tax account on March 15, 1990, to satisfy its final 1989 tax liability.

Thus, Marsh had made four separate overpayments (if the 1987 and 1988 tax liabilities as shown in the returns were accurate): (1) the 1985 overpayment; (2) the 1986 overpayment; (3) the 1987 credit elect overpayment; and (4) the 1988 credit elect overpayment.

In 1994, the IRS determined that Marsh had in fact underpaid its 1987 taxes by $978,135. This increase in tax was less than the amount of the 1987 credit elect overpayment. The IRS applied Marsh's 1985 overpayment and a portion of its 1986 overpayment to its 1987 tax account on March 15, 1989, the date the 1987 credit elect overpayment was applied to Marsh's 1988 tax account.

Similarly, in 1994, the IRS determined that Marsh had in fact underpaid its 1988 taxes by $2,709,087. This increase in tax was less than the amount of the 1988 credit elect overpayment. The IRS applied the remainder of Marsh's 1986 overpayment to its 1988 tax account. The actual transfers were made on September 15, 1989 (the date the 1988 credit elect overpayment was applied to the estimated tax payment for 1989), and March 15, 1990 (the date the remainder of Marsh's 1988 credit elect overpayment was applied to Marsh's 1989 tax account).

There is no dispute concerning the amount of Marsh's 1985 and 1986 overpayments, the dates that those payments were credited to later years' taxes, the amount of the 1987 and 1988 credit elect overpayments, the dates on which those credit elect overpayments were needed to satisfy later years' obligations, or the amount of Marsh's 1987 and 1988 tax liabilities. The ultimate issue concerns the amount of interest due on the 1985 and 1986 overpayments.

An "overpayment" occurs when a taxpayer "has paid as an installment of the tax more than the amount determined to be the correct amount of such installment." 26 U.S.C. § 6403 (2000). The IRS has authority to either refund or credit the overpayment to any unpaid installment. Unlike credit elect overpayments, overpayments bear interest. See id. § 6611(a). For the 1985 overpayment amount and the portion of the 1986 overpayment amount credited against Marsh's 1987 tax liability, the IRS allowed interest through April 15, 1988, the due date for Marsh's 1987 tax return (plus one month).[2] For the portion of the 1986 overpayment amount credited against Marsh's 1988 tax liability, the IRS allowed interest through April 15, 1989, the due date for Marsh's 1988 tax return (plus one month). The government stopped the running of interest on those dates because it reasoned that overpayment interest runs only until the "due date" of a taxpayer's federal income tax return for the year to which the overpayment was applied.

The governing statute, 26 U.S.C. § 6611 (2000), entitled "Interest on overpayments," provides in relevant part that "[s]uch interest shall be allowed and paid as follows: * * * In the case of a credit, from the date of the overpayment to the due date of the amount against which the credit is taken." Id. § 6611(b)(1). Treasury Regulation § 301.6611-1(h)(1) provides: "General rule. If an overpayment of tax is credited, interest shall be allowed from the date of the overpayment to the due date * * * of the amount against which such overpayment is credited." 26 C.F.R. § 301.6611-1(h)(1) (2001). "Due date" is defined in subsection 301.6611-1(h)(2)(i): "In general. The term 'due date,' as used in this section, means the last day fixed by law or regulations for the payment of the tax (determined without regard to any extension of time) * * *." Id. § 301.6611-1(h)(2)(i). For taxes reported on a return, this payment date is the last unextended date fixed for filing the return. 26 U.S.C. § 6151(a) (2000).

The parties apparently agree that, absent the credit elect overpayments, the two due dates involved here were March 15, 1988, and March 15, 1989 (i.e., the due dates for the 1987 and 1988 tax returns respectively) and that interest on the 1985 and 1986 overpayments would have ceased on those dates. Thus, the issue on appeal is the effect of the credit elect overpayments on the running of interest. It is well established that the taxpayer earns no interest on credit elect overpayments. If a taxpayer elects to credit against its estimated liability for one taxable year an overpayment shown on its return for the preceding year, it collects no interest even though at one point it has paid

---

2. Although the due date of corporate federal income tax returns is March 15 of the following year, 26 U.S.C. § 6072(b) (2000), the IRS computed and paid interest on Marsh's 1985 overpayment until April 15, 1988, rather than March 15, 1988. Similarly, the IRS computed and paid interest on Marsh's 1986 overpayment until April 15, 1989. The government concedes that the statute of limitations bars recovery of the interest attributable to the additional month, so it is not at issue on appeal.

the IRS more than was due. 26 C.F.R. § 301.6611-1(h)(2)(vii) (2001). The question is whether credit elect overpayments must be taken into account in calculating the interest due on other overpayments.

PROCEEDINGS BELOW

Marsh filed a complaint in the Court of Federal Claims seeking $833,522 in overpayment interest for the period between April 15, 1988, and March 15, 1989, for its 1985 overpayment and a portion of its 1986 overpayment; for the period between April 15, 1989, and September 15, 1989, for a portion of its 1986 overpayment; and between April 15, 1989, and March 15, 1990, for the remainder of its 1986 overpayment, the ending dates representing the dates on which the credit elect overpayments were applied to subsequent tax year liabilities. The government filed a motion for summary judgment, and Marsh filed a cross motion for summary judgment.

Marsh argued that 26 U.S.C. § 6611, which provides for the accrual of interest on overpayments "to the due date of the amount against which the credit is taken," should be construed to mean that interest runs until an account actually becomes deficient, that is, "due and unpaid." Marsh argued that its 1987 tax account was not actually deficient until March 15, 1989, when the 1987 credit elect overpayment was applied to its 1988 tax account. Similarly, Marsh argued that its 1988 tax account was not actually deficient until September 15, 1989, when a portion of its 1988 credit elect was applied to its 1989 estimated taxes, and on March 15, 1990, when the remainder of its 1988 credit elect was applied to its 1989 tax account.

The government argued that, under the plain meaning of section 6611 and Treasury Regulation § 301.6611-1(h)(2), the "due date of the amount against which the credit is taken" is the due date of a taxpayer's federal income tax return for the year to which the overpayment is applied. Marsh's 1985 overpayment and a portion of its 1986 overpayment were applied to its 1987 tax account, and the remainder of the 1986 overpayment was applied to Marsh's 1988 tax account. Marsh was required to file its 1987 tax return on March 15, 1988, and its 1988 tax return on March 15, 1989. Therefore, the government argued, Marsh was entitled to interest on its 1985 overpayment and a portion of its 1986 overpayment until March 15, 1988, and on the remainder of its 1986 overpayment until March 15, 1989[3].

---

3. As noted, the government actually paid Marsh interest through April 15, 1988, and April 15, 1989.

The Court of Federal Claims recognized that the case turned on the interpretation of section 6611, and determined that, read in isolation, the statutory language, "which is, at best, not a model of clarity," does not "yield[ ] a satisfactory result." Marsh, 50 Fed. Cl. at 143. Similarly, the court concluded that neither the "use of money" principle, under which overpayments and underpayments are generally netted in calculating interest, nor IRS revenue rulings provided the answer. Id. at 143-45. The court then assessed the relative "predictability" of the parties' competing interpretations. The court noted that Marsh's interpretation would make interest accrual cease on the date an overpayment was actually credited against another tax liability, and, under Marsh's interpretation, "the 'due date' becomes wholly dependent on the IRS's accounting procedures, which have not been shown to be governed by the statutory language of I.R.C. § 6611(b)(1)." Id. at 142. The court rejected Marsh's interpretation in large part because the "due date" would be impossible to predict in advance in that it depended on the "vagaries" of the IRS internal accounting procedures, and accepted the government's interpretation because it "harmonizes with the principle of predictability and comports with the statutory language." Id. at 146. Accordingly, the court granted summary judgment in favor of the government.

Marsh timely appealed. * * *

* * *

DISCUSSION

This case involves the question when interest on tax overpayments ceases to run.

As noted above, the parties apparently agree that, if there had been no credit elect overpayment in 1987 or 1988, the "due date" for the additional tax due for 1987 and 1988 would have been March 15 of the year following the tax year in question, here March 15, 1988, and March 15, 1989. Under either party's interpretation of section 6611, interest on the 1985 and 1986 overpayments would have ceased to run on those dates.

The parties' disagreement arises from the existence of the 1987 and 1988 credit elect overpayments. Marsh argues that because of the credit elect overpayments, there was no outstanding liability in its 1987 account until the 1985 overpayment and a portion of the 1986 overpayment were applied to its 1988 tax account on March 15, 1989, and there was no outstanding liability in its 1988 account until the remainder of the 1986 overpayment was applied to its estimated 1989 tax on September 15, 1989, and its final 1989 tax on March 15, 1990.

Marsh urges that, as a result of its 1987 credit elect overpayment, it overpaid the government between the period of the credit elect overpayment and the due date of the tax return of the year to which the credit elect overpayment was applied, that is, from March 15, 1988, to March 15, 1989. Similarly, Marsh urges that, as a result of its 1988 credit elect overpayment, it overpaid the government from March 15, 1989, to September 15, 1989, and March 15, 1990.

Marsh contends that there was no payment "due" until its 1987 tax account actually became negative on March 15, 1989, i.e., the date that the 1987 credit elect overpayment was applied to its 1988 tax account. Similarly, Marsh contends that there was no payment "due" until its 1988 tax account became negative on September 15, 1989, the date when a portion of its 1988 credit elect overpayment was applied to its 1989 tax account, and again on March 15, 1990, when the remainder of its 1988 credit elect overpayment was applied to its 1989 tax account.

The government urges that the "due date" for purposes of section 6611 is the due date of the returns, and that this date does not change as a result of the 1987 and 1988 credit elect overpayments.

We agree with the government and disagree with Marsh for several reasons.

First, the language of section 6611(b)(1), as interpreted by Treasury Regulation § 301.6611-1(h)(2), requires this result.

Both parties argue from their view of the supposed plain language of section 6611(b)(1). In fact, the statutory language is ambiguous. The "due date" could refer either to the due date of the return (the government's position) or the date on which there is a net deficit in the amount due in the taxpayer's account for the particular year (the taxpayer's position). Under Chevron U.S.A., Inc. v. Natural Resources Defense Council, Inc., 467 U.S. 837, 843-44, 104 S.Ct. 2778, 81 L.Ed.2d 694 (1984), we look to the Treasury regulations to resolve the ambiguity. * * * The Treasury regulations are, we think, quite clear. They provide: "General rule. If an overpayment of tax is credited, interest shall be allowed from the date of the overpayment to the due date * * * of the amount against which such overpayment is credited," 26 C.F.R. § 301.6611-1(h)(1)(2001), and define "due date" as: "In general. The term 'due date,' as used in this section, means the last day fixed by law or regulations for the payment of the tax (determined without regard to any extension of time)," id. § 301.6611-1(h)(2)(i). Marsh notes that because the regulations state that this definition of "due date" will be used "[i]n general," they do not purport to interpret the entire phrase "due date of the amount against which the credit is taken" in section 6611(b)(1). As the government points out, however, Treasury Regulation § 301.6611 is actually keyed to the relevant section of the code, section 6611, indicating that it does in fact relate to section 6611. We agree with the government that the regulation does apply.

Marsh also contends that the regulations are "unreasonable." We cannot agree. For reasons that we discuss below, there is nothing unreasonable in disregarding credit elect overpayments in calculating overpayment interest. And, while an IRS interpretation of its regulation might be entitled to deference where there is an ambiguity, Marsh cites no interpretation of the regulations by the IRS in a context similar to this one that would contradict their plain meaning.

Contrary to Marsh's argument, the legislative history of section 6611 does not support Marsh. Section 6611 as it reads today was enacted in the Technical Amendments Act of 1958, Pub.L. No. 85-866, § 83, 72 Stat. 1606, 1663-64 (1958), reprinted in 1958 U.S.C.C.A.N.1925, 1997, and is identical in relevant part to section 1019 of the Internal Revenue Act of 1924.[5] Marsh urges that the legislative history establishes that the "due date against which the credit is taken" is the date on which the overpayment is economically offset against a liability. Marsh argues that the legislative history reveals that "Congress intended that interest accrue on a credited overpayment until the date on which an overpayment and underpayment simultaneously existed (i.e., on the date on which mutuality of indebtedness' arose)," citing the Senate Finance Committee Report, S.Rep. No.1983, 85th Cong., 2d Sess., 234-35 (1958), reprinted in 1958-3 C.B. 922, 1156. But the legislative history on which Marsh relies does not address the precise issue here or suggest that a credit elect overpayment must be considered in calculating interest. In enacting and amending section 6611 and its predecessor, section 1019, Congress sought to address specific issues, such as: to eliminate the distinction between the running of interest in the situation where an overpayment is credited against a later-arising deficiency and where it is credited against an underpayment of original tax; to eliminate the running of interest where overpayments and underpayments offset each other; to address the anomaly in the transitional situation in which a taxpayer (which owed money to the government on taxes imposed by a prior revenue act) paid no interest but collected interest upon money the government owed it; and to eliminate the requirement of a protest as a

---

5.   That section provided in part:

    Upon the allowance of a credit * * * of any sum which was excessive * * *, interest shall be allowed and paid on the amount of such credit * * * from the date such tax, penalty, or sum was paid * * * to the due date of the amount against which the credit is taken * * *.

Internal Revenue Act of 1924, § 1019, 43 Stat. 253, 346 (1924).

condition precedent for a taxpayer to receive overpayment interest. Thus, the legislative history does not support Marsh's interpretation of the statute.

Second, contrary to Marsh's argument, section 6402(a) of the code does not require a different result. That section provides:

> In the case of any overpayment, the Secretary, within the applicable period of limitations, may credit the amount of such overpayment, including any interest allowed thereon, against any *liability* in respect of an internal revenue tax on the part of the person who made the overpayment and shall, subject to subsections (c), (d), and (e) refund any balance to such person.

26 U.S.C. § 6402(a) (2000) (emphasis added). Marsh argues that there was no "liability" within the meaning of section 6402(a) until the credit elect overpayments were applied to subsequent years' taxes. Marsh points out that the IRS in fact did not apply the 1985 and 1986 overpayments to the 1987 tax account until the 1987 tax account actually became negative, that is, when the 1987 credit elect overpayment was transferred to the 1988 tax account on March 15, 1989. Similarly, the IRS did not apply the 1986 overpayment to the 1988 tax account until the 1988 tax account in fact became negative, that is, when the 1988 credit elect overpayment was transferred to pay 1989 estimated taxes on September 15, 1989, and the final 1989 taxes on March 15, 1990.

Section 6611 makes no reference to section 6402, and whatever limitations section 6402 may impose on the IRS's authority to credit, section 6402 does not define the term "due date" for purposes of section 6611. There is no indication in section 6402 that it was designed to affect the running of overpayment interest.

Third, Marsh argues that we should follow the Second Circuit's decision in Avon Products, Inc. v. United States, 588 F.2d 342 (2d Cir. 1978), which Marsh interprets as holding that there is no tax liability until the credit elect overpayments were in fact credited to later years' taxes. *Avon* is distinguishable and does not stand for the broad proposition attributed to it by Marsh. In *Avon* the taxpayer initially reported an overpayment on its 1967 return, and made a credit elect. 588 F.2d at 343. Thereafter, it filed an amended return showing a 1967 deficiency, and the IRS later assessed an additional 1967 deficiency. The IRS assessed interest on the deficiencies without regard to the credit elect overpayment. The Second Circuit held that this was impermissible, and that the credit elect overpayment could not be disregarded; interest on the deficiencies did not run until the date the credit elect overpayment was applied to the next year's tax. Id. at 344. Marsh argues that the same should be true here, and that the amount of the deficiencies should be offset by the amount of the credit elect overpayments.

However, *Avon* was an underpayment case, interpreting the section of the statutegoverning underpayment interest, section 6601(a). That section provides "If any amount of tax * * * *is not paid* on or before the last date prescribed for payment, interest on such amount * * * shall be paid for the period from such last date to the date paid." 26 U.S.C. § 6601(a) (2000) (emphasis added). Unlike the situation here, the language of the statute contradicted the government's position since the statute focused on the question whether the tax was "paid," and not on the "due date" for the tax. As the Second Circuit noted, "if we were to construe § 6601(a) literally, it would not even be apposite to this case. Avon's full tax was in fact paid 'on or before the last date prescribed for payment,' June 15, and so the premise of the provision is undercut." Avon, 588 F.2d at 344. To avoid a result clearly contrary to the statutory language, the court interpreted section 6601(a) as providing that underpayment interest shall begin running when a tax becomes "both due and unpaid." Id.

As the *Avon* court noted, the tax code differentiates between underpayment and overpayment interest situations. It does not, as Marsh argues, require identical treatment. Underpayment interest ceases to run on "the date paid," 26 U.S.C. § 6601(a) (2000), while overpayment interest ceases to run on "the due date of the amount against which the credit is taken," id. § 6611(b). Thus, cases like *Avon* interpreting the section of the statute governing underpayment interest situations are irrelevant. See also May Dep't Stores Co. v. United States, 36 Fed. Cl. 680, 688 (1996) (holding that the government was not entitled to underpayment interest between the date of payment of the estimated tax and the date of filing of the return where the taxpayer overestimated its overpayment and elected to apply the overpayment to the following year's estimated tax as a credit elect, thereby creating a deficiency); Revenue Ruling 99-40, reprinted in 1999-2 C.B. 441 (analyzing the calculation of underpayment interest in the context of a credit elect overpayment and subsequently determined deficiency). Moreover, the court in *Avon* expressly distinguished the case before it from cases involving overpayment interest, and emphasized that the statutory scheme governing overpayment interest, as well as the policy considerations underlying it, were very different:

> [T]his case is not covered by the cited regulation [Treasury Regulation § 301.6611-1(h)(2)(vii), governing overpayment interest]. Nor do we believe that it provides a helpful analogy. Indeed, the fact that there is a Treasury Regulation explicitly denying the taxpayer

interest in the [credit elect overpayment] situation * * * but nothing comparable suggesting that Avon must pay interest for its later-created deficiency would indicate that the contrary result is compelled.

Avon, 588 F.2d at 345.

* * *

Fourth, Marsh argues that the government had the use of its money and should pay interest. We agree that the IRS had the use of Marsh's money represented by the credit elect overpayments, and that Marsh will not receive interest on those amounts. However, this is not an anomaly. Once the taxpayer designates an overpayment as a credit elect overpayment, the taxpayer loses control over that money. Once the election is made, that election is irrevocable and binding on both the IRS and the taxpayer. The regulations expressly provide that interest shall not be allowed on credit elect overpayments under section 6611(a). 26 C.F.R. § 301.6611- 1(h)(2)(vii) (2001).[8] Marsh does not contest this principle, and admits that "[t]his exception is set forth in Treas. Reg. §§ 301.6402-3(a)(5) and 301.6611-1(h)(2)(vii), and was ratified by Congress."[9] Just as the taxpayer cannot get interest on the credit elect overpayment, the taxpayer cannot use the credit elect overpayment to increase the amount of interest that otherwise would be due on the 1985 and 1986 overpayments.

In any event, the "use of money" cases, on which Marsh so heavily relies, cannot contradict the statutory language as interpreted by the regulation. In general, the "use of money" principle is a tool of statutory construction that supports the payment of interest to compensate one party for the time the other party had the use of its money. The use of money principle has been recognized by the IRS generally,[10] and has

---

8.   Treasury Regulation § 301.6611-1(h)(2)(vii) provides:

Estimated income tax for succeeding year. If the taxpayer elects to have all or part of the overpayment shown by his return applied to his estimated tax for his succeeding taxable year, *no interest shall be allowed on such portion of the overpayment credited* and such amount shall be applied as a payment on account of the estimated tax for such year or the installments thereof. .

26 C.F.R. § 301.6611-1(h)(2)(vii) (2001) (emphasis added).

9.   See H.R.Rep. No. 98-432, pt. 2, at 1490 (1984) ("[T]he taxpayer may elect to credit the overpayment to an estimated tax payment* * *. Where the credit is made to an estimated tax payment arising prior to the election, interest on any overpayment will not be payable* * *." (citing Treas. Reg. § 301.6611-1(h)(2)(vii))).

10.   See Field Serv. Adv. 200149028 (Dec. 7, 2001), available at 2001 WL 1559040 ("Compensation for the use of money is the principal rationale for charging interest with respect to both overpayments and underpayments."); Tech. Adv. Mem. 9730005 (April 7, 1997), available at 1997 WL 415375 (discussing section 905(c) as "a special exception to the general interest rules"

been applied by the statute and the regulations in specific situations.[11] But Marsh has not called our attention to any case in which the use of money principle has been held to override statutory language requiring a contrary result. See MNOPF Trustees, Ltd. v. United States, 123 F.3d 1460, 1465 (Fed.Cir. 1997) (determining the starting date for interest on an overpayment attributable to a refund to be the unextended date by which the banks that withheld the money were required to file returns reporting the withholding, based on the relevant Treasury regulation, rather than from the date that the government actually had "use of" the funds); *May Dep't Stores*, 36 Fed. Cl. at 688 (reaffirming the *Avon* principle that underpayment interest may be imposed only for the period during which a tax is both due and unpaid, based on "the plain language" of section 6601). * * * The use of money principle does not trump the language of the relevant statute and Treasury regulations.

Finally, Marsh argues that if it had sought a refund instead of making the credit elect in 1987, it would have had the use of those funds. This is true enough, but we fail to see how that assists Marsh. There is no principle that requires that the taxpayer be treated the same whether it seeks a refund or a credit elect. Indeed, the statute as interpreted by the regulations provides that, for a refund, interest will be allowed from the date of the overpayment until "a date (to be determined by the Secretary) preceding the date of the refund check by not more than 30 days," 26 U.S.C. § 6611(a)(2) (2000), but denies interest on credit elect overpayments, 26 C.F.R. § 301.6611-1(h)(2)(vii) (2001). The taxpayer could have sought a refund for the excess funds, or left the excess funds as an interest-bearing overpayment. A taxpayer that makes a credit elect has no one to blame but itself for the non-payment of interest on that amount.

---

relating to foreign tax credit: "[t]he Code's interest provisions reflect the economic basis for interest, i.e., use of money * * * [u]nder § 6611, the government pays the taxpayer interest on an overpayment for the time the government has use of the taxpayer's money."); Rev. Proc. 60-17, § 2.01, reprinted in 1960-2 C.B. 942, 943 ("Under the general rule, interest is paid on a tax overpayment for the time the government has the use of the taxpayer's money* * *. The underlying objective is to determine in a given situation whose money it is and for how long the other party had the use of it.").

   11. See 26 U.S.C. § 6601(f) (2000) ("[N]o interest shall be imposed under [the underpayment interest provision] on the portion of the tax [satisfied by credit of an overpayment] for any period during which, if the credit had not been made, interest would have been allowable with respect to such overpayment."); Id. § 6621(d) ("To the extent that, for any period, interest is payable * * * and allowable * * * on equivalent underpayments and overpayments by the same taxpayer * * * the net rate of interest under this section on such amounts shall be zero for such period."); 26 C.F.R. § 301.6611-1(h)(2)(vi) (2001) ("In the case of a credit against an additional   amount, addition to the tax, or assessable penalty, the due date is the earlier of the date of assessment or the date from which such amount would bear interest if not satisfied by payment or credit.").

In essence, Marsh urges that we interpret the statute to achieve what it regards as a more just result. But we cannot revise the language of the statute as interpreted by the Treasury to achieve what might be perceived to be better tax policy, just as we cannot approve the Court of Federal Claims' decision below interpreting the code to achieve greater predictability. The tax code is complex, and we must be careful to enforce the statute as written and interpreted. It is noteworthy that some of the very cases on which Marsh relies recognize that the tax code interest provisions are not to be interpreted, contrary to their language, to require the favorable netting of overpayments and underpayments that Marsh urges is essential to tax equity. See *Seeley Tube*, 338 U.S. at 565-66, 70 S.Ct. 386 (declining to offset deficiency by loss carry-back for interest purposes); N. States Power Co. v. United States, 73 F.3d 764, 768 (8th Cir. 1996) (holding that, in calculating interest, overpayments and underpayments need not be netted to avoid interest rate differential).

* * *

AFFIRMED.

Questions

1. What is the meaning of the term "due date" under § 6611(b)(1) and what was the significance of the term to Marsh and McLellan?

2. What advice would you give Marsh and McLellan the next time it has a substantial overpayment?

3. Erroneous Refunds

If the taxpayer receives a refund with interest, which the Service later determines was erroneous because there was no overpayment for that year but rather, there was a deficiency, the taxpayer will be required to pay interest both on the amount of the refund and on the amount of the interest received. In calculating the amount of the interest due, there are two periods to consider: (1) the period in which the taxpayer was paid interest on the overpayment (generally the period from the due date of the overpayment/deficiency to the date 30 days prior to the date of the refund check), and (2) the period from the date of the refund check to the date the taxpayer repays the amount of the refund plus interest.

During the first period, interest on the underpayment will be charged at the same rate as that of the overpayment. Thus, for the first period, the taxpayer will owe the amount of the deficiency plus the same amount of interest that was paid to her by the government. During the second period, interest will be charged at the underpayment rate on the amount determined from the first period.

Example: Betty makes estimated tax payments of $75,000 for taxable year 2007. On April 1, 2008, she requests and receives an automatic six-month extension of time to file. On August 1, 2008, she files a Form 1040, showing a tax liability of $65,000 and she requests a refund of $10,000. On October 10, 2008, the Service issues her refund, including $370 in interest because the check was issued more than 45 days after the return was received. In March 2009, the Service determines that Betty's tax liability for 2008 was actually $70,000.

Betty owes the government interest on the $5,000 deficiency for the period beginning April 16, 2008 and running until October 10, 2008. Since the overpayment and underpayment rates of interest are the same, she owes the Service the same amount that they owe her on the $5,000. In this case, that amount is $185. From October 10, 2008 until Betty pays the deficiency, she will be charged interest at the underpayment rate on $5,185.

Note

In Pacific Gas and Electric Co. v. United States, 417 F.3d. 1375 (Fed. Cir. 2005) reproduced in Chapter 5, the Court of Federal Claims initially held that the taxpayer was entitled to interest on the taxed portion of an erroneous refund to reflect the "lost time value of [its] money" and that this should have been taken into account by the government when it made its offset. 55 Fed. Cl. 271 (2003). On reconsideration, the court reversed itself on this issue, reasoning that its "equitable approach" was "inappropriate" because there was no statutory provision authorizing interest under these circumstances. 58 Fed. Cl. 1, 2003.

C. NETTING OF OVERPAYMENTS AND UNDERPAYMENTS

If a taxpayer has overpaid tax liability for one taxable period and has underpaid for a different taxable period, the taxpayer and the Service are mutually indebted to each other. To the extent of the interest on equal amounts of overpayment and underpayment that run simultaneously, the net interest rate will be zero. IRC § 6621(d). This applies only if none of the years in question are barred by the statute of limitations. Such a netting, referred to as "global netting," applies to any type of tax, to taxes from different taxable years, and to any type of taxpayer. Thus, an overpayment of excise tax may be netted against an income tax deficiency. Note that a large corporate underpayment that exceeds $100,000 is subject to an increased interest rate under § 6621(c). This is referred to as "hot interest." Conversely, a large corporate overpayment that exceeds $10,000 is subject to a reduced interest rate. IRC § 6621(a)(1). These differential rates do not apply, however, if the amount of an overpayment is netted against the amount of the deficiency. IRC § 6621(d). To the extent that netting applies, the rules under § 6601(f), above, do not apply.

Example: After an examination of its 2009 and 2010 income tax returns in 2011, the Service determines that ABC Co. has overpaid its 2010 taxes by $18,000, and that it has underpaid its 2009 taxes by $12,000. ABC Co. pays the underpayment, plus interest at the underpayment rate on September 15, 2011. The statute of limitations on both taxable years remain open. In determining the amount of ABC Co.'s overpayment, the interest on the underpayment must be netted against the interest on the overpayment for the period that both the underpayment and the overpayment are outstanding. The underpayment interest runs from the due date of the return, March 15, 2010, until it is paid on September 15, 2011. The overpayment interest runs from the due date of the return, March 15, 2011 until a portion is used to offset the underpayment interest on September 15, 2011. Thus, the period of the overlap is from March 15, 2011 to September 15, 2011. The interest rate on the underpayment and overpayment for that period must net out to zero. The interest on the remaining amount of the overpayment, $6,000 is not affected by the netting, so interest on that amount runs from March 15, 2011 until it is paid.

Notes

According to the Conference Report of the American Jobs Creation Act of 2004, a § 6603 deposit is not considered an overpayment for purposes of the interest netting provisions. Thus, if a taxpayer withdraws a § 6603 deposit, the interest allowable on that amount will not be netted against a similar amount of underpayment for the same period. H.R. Conf. Rpt. 108-755.

VI. ABATEMENT OF PENALTIES AND INTEREST

A. ERRONEOUS IRS ADVICE

The Service is required to abate any penalty or addition to tax that is attributable to erroneous written advice furnished by an IRS employee or official acting in his official capacity. IRC § 6404(f). In order to qualify for such an abatement, the taxpayer must have (1) made a specific written request for advice, (2) reasonably relied upon the written advice, and (3) provided adequate and accurate information to the IRS employee or official. Reg. § 301.6404-3(b).

A written request is considered valid if it is made by the taxpayer's representative, provided the representative is a person who is allowed to represent taxpayers before the Service. The representative must be acting under a power of attorney, signed by the taxpayer, that authorizes the representative to represent the taxpayer for purposes of the request. The power of attorney either must accompany the request or be on file with the Service. Reg. § 301.6404-3(b)(3).

The taxpayer is not considered to have reasonably relied on the advice if the advice is received subsequent to the date the return is filed. If an amended return is filed in conformance with the written advice, the reasonable reliance test is met for purposes of the positions taken in the amended return. If the written advice does not relate to an item included on a federal tax return (such as payment of estimated taxes), and such advice is received by the taxpayer subsequent to the act or omission that is the basis for the penalty or addition to tax, then the taxpayer will not be considered to have reasonably relied on the advice. Reg. § 1.6404-3(b)(2)(iv).

If the advice relates to a continuing action or series of actions, it may be relied upon until the taxpayer is placed on notice that the advice no longer represents the Service's position and thus, is no longer valid. Examples of such notice include (1) correspondence from the Service stating that the advice no longer represents the Service's position, (2) enactment of legislation or ratification of a tax treaty setting forth a position inconsistent with the written advice received from the Service, (3) a decision of the United States Supreme Court that is inconsistent with the advice, (4) the issuance of temporary or final regulations expressing a contrary position, or (5) the issuance of a ruling or other statement from the Service expressing a contrary position. Reg. § 301.6404-3(b)(2)(v).

B.　INSUFFICIENT IRS NOTICE

If a taxpayer underpays her tax liability, penalties and interest accrue, regardless of whether or not the taxpayer has knowledge of the deficiency. During the congressional hearings in 1997 that resulted in the 1998 IRS Restructuring and Reform Act, there were numerous taxpayer complaints about the length of time it usually takes the Service to assess deficiencies, and the fact that interest and penalties can quickly increase tax debts during this time to the point that it is virtually impossible for middle-class taxpayers to pay the resulting tax bill without being thrown into bankruptcy or otherwise compromising their lifestyle. In response to these complaints, Congress enacted § 6404(g), providing for an abatement of penalties and interest that accrue unbeknownst to the taxpayer.

Under § 6404(g), if a taxpayer files a timely tax return and the Service does not provide notice to the taxpayer, specifically stating the taxpayer's liability and the basis for the liability, prior to the beginning of the suspension period, then penalties, interest and other additions to tax will be suspended and will not resume until 21 days after the date on which such notice is provided to the taxpayer. The suspension period depends upon the taxable year of the notice. For notices issued after November 25, 2007, the suspension begins 36 months following the filing of a timely return, including extensions of time to file. IRC § 6404(g)(1). For notices issued on or before November 25, 2007, the suspension begins 18 months following the filing of a timely return. The interest and penalty suspension applies to taxable years after July 22, 1998. If the taxpayer files an amended return, the suspension period runs 36 months (or 18 months) after the amended return is filed.

The suspension of interest and penalties is subject to certain exceptions. For instance, it is inapplicable to undisclosed reportable or listed transactions, to cases involving fraud, to any criminal penalty, and to any tax liability shown on the return. See IRC § 6404(g)(2) for a more complete list of exceptions.

The delinquency penalties under § 6651 are excluded from § 6404(g), as are criminal penalties and any interest, penalty or other additions to tax for fraud and for any tax liability shown on the return. IRC § 6404(g)(2). In addition, § 6404(g) applies only to individual taxpayers, and only to penalties and interest imposed under the income tax.

Notes and Problems

One commentator has argued that § 6404 is too narrowly focused because it does not provide a hardship exception for an abatement of interest, nor does it provide an abatement when the Service has unreasonably prolonged an audit or administrative proceeding to the detriment of the taxpayer. See Terri Gutierrez, "Interest Abatement: A Case For Liberalization of the Rules," 100 Tax Notes 809 (2003).

1. Charlotte requested and received an automatic four-month extension of time to file her 2004 federal income tax return that originally was due on April 15, 2005. She timely filed this return on August 1, 2005, but she inadvertently failed to include $2,500 of dividend income. On October 15, 2007, the Service sent her a notice of deficiency proposing a deficiency to her 2004 tax liability, as well as a late payment penalty, a negligence penalty, and interest on the deficiency. How long will each addition to tax run if Charlotte pays the tax liability on December 1, 2007?

2. In question one, what result if the Service sends Charlotte another notice of deficiency on January 20, 2008, proposing an additional deficiency of $1,500 for the taxable year 2004, for which it also proposes to assess the same delinquency and negligence penalties plus interest attributable to this amount?

3. What result in question one if the $2,500 was not omitted from Charlotte's return, but was stated on the return and unpaid as of September 15, 2007, and the Service sends Charlotte a notice and demand for payment on November 5, 2007?

4. What result in question one if the Service sent the notice of deficiency on January 15, 2008 instead of on October 15, 2007 and Charlotte pays the tax on February 15, 2008?

5. After the 2007 revision to § 6404(g) under the Small Business and Work Opportunity Act, which extended the suspension period from 18 months to 36 months, does § 6404(g) retain any vitality for taxpayers?

C. JUDICIAL REVIEW OF ABATEMENT DECISIONS

HINCK v. UNITED STATES
United States Supreme Court, 2007
550 U.S. 501

CHIEF JUSTICE ROBERTS delivered the opinion of the Court.

Bad things happen if you fail to pay federal income taxes when due. One of them is that interest accrues on the unpaid amount. Sometimes it takes a while for the Internal Revenue Service (IRS) to determine that taxes should have been paid that were not. Section 6404(e)(1) of the Internal Revenue Code permits the Secretary of the Treasury to abate interest-to forgive it, partially or in whole-if the assessment of interest on a deficiency is attributable to unreasonable error or delay on the part of the IRS. Section 6404(h) allows for judicial review of the Secretary's decision not to grant such relief. The question presented in this case is whether this review may be obtained only in the Tax Court, or may also be secured in the district courts and the Court of Federal Claims. We hold that the Tax Court provides the exclusive forum for judicial review of a refusal to abate interest under § 6404(e)(1), and affirm.

I.

The Internal Revenue Code provides that if any amount of assessed federal income tax is not paid "on or before the last date prescribed for payment," interest "shall be paid for the period from such last date to the date paid." 26 U.S.C. § 6601(a). Section 6404 of the Code authorizes the Secretary of the Treasury to abate any tax or related liability in certain circumstances. As part of the Tax Reform Act of 1986, Congress amended § 6404 to add subsection (e)(1), which, as enacted, provided in pertinent part:

> "In the case of any assessment of interest on . . . any deficiency attributable in whole or in part to any error or delay by an officer or employee of the Internal Revenue Service (acting in his official capacity) in performing a ministerial act ... the Secretary may abate the assessment of all or any part of such interest for any period."

26 U.S.C. § 6404(e)(1) (1994 ed.).

In the years following passage of § 6404(e)(1), the federal courts uniformly held that the Secretary's decision not to grant an abatement was not subject to judicial review. See, e.g., Argabright v. United States, 35 F.3d 472, 476 (C.A.9 1994); Selman v. United States, 941 F.2d 1060, 1064 (C.A.10 1991); Horton Homes, Inc. v. United States, 936 F.2d 548, 554 (C.A.11 1991); see also Bax v. Commissioner, 13 F.3d 54, 58 (C.A.2 1993). These decisions recognized that § 6404(e)(1) gave the Secretary complete discretion to determine whether to abate interest, "neither indicat[ing] that such authority should be used universally nor provid[ing] any basis for distinguishing between the instances in which abatement should and should not be granted." *Selman, supra,* at 1063. Any decision by the Secretary was accordingly "committed to agency discretion by law" under the Administrative Procedure Act, 5 U.S.C. § 701(a)(2), and thereby insulated from judicial review.

In 1996, as part of the Taxpayer Bill of Rights 2, Congress again amended § 6404, adding what is now subsection (h). As relevant, that provision states:

"Review of denial of request for abatement of interest.–

"(1) In general.–The Tax Court shall have jurisdiction over any action brought by a taxpayer who meets the requirements referred to in section 7430(c)(4)(A)(ii) to determine whether the Secretary's failure to abate interest under this section was an abuse of discretion, and may order an abatement, if such action is brought within 180 days after the date of the mailing of the Secretary's final determination not to abate such interest."

26 U.S.C. § 6404(h)(1) (2000 ed., Supp. IV).

Section 7430(c)(4)(A)(ii) in turn incorporates 28 U.S.C. § 2412(d)(2)(B), which refers to individuals with a net worth not exceeding $2 million and businesses with a net worth not exceeding $7 million. Congress made subsection (h) effective for all requests for abatement submitted to the IRS after July 30, 1996, regardless of the tax year involved. § 302(b), 110 Stat. 1458.[1]

II.

In 1986, petitioner John Hinck was a limited partner in an entity called Agri-Cal Venture Associates (ACVA). Along with his wife, petitioner Pamela Hinck, Hinck filed a joint return for 1986 reporting his share of losses from the partnership. The IRS later examined the tax returns for ACVA and proposed adjustments to deductions that the partnership had claimed for 1984, 1985, and 1986. In 1990, the IRS issued a final notice regarding the partnership's returns, disallowing tens of millions of dollars of deductions. While the partnership sought administrative review of this decision, the Hincks, in May 1996, made an advance remittance of $93,890 to the IRS toward any personal deficiency that might result from a final adjustment of ACVA's returns. In March 1999, the Hincks reached a settlement with the IRS concerning the ACVA partnership adjustments, to the extent they affected the Hincks' return. Shortly thereafter, as a result of the adjustments, the IRS imposed additional liability against the Hincks: $16,409 in tax and

---

1.   The Taxpayer Bill of Rights 2 also modified 26 U.S.C. § 6404(e)(1)(A) to add the word "unreasonable" before the words "error or delay" and to change "ministerial act" to "ministerial or managerial act." § 301(a), 110 Stat. 1457. These changes, however, only apply to interest accruing on deficiencies for tax years beginning after July 30, 1996, see § 301(c), ibid., and thus are not implicated in this case.

$21,669.22 in interest. The IRS applied the Hincks' advance remittance to this amount and refunded them the balance of $55,811.78.

The Hincks filed a claim with the IRS contending that, because of IRS errors and delays, the interest assessed against them for the period from March 21, 1989, to April 1, 1993, should be abated under § 6404(e)(1). The IRS denied the request. The Hincks then filed suit in the United States Court of Federal Claims seeking review of the refusal to abate. That court granted the Government's motion to dismiss, 64 Fed.Cl. 71, 81 (2005), and the United States Court of Appeals for the Federal Circuit affirmed, 446 F.3d 1307, 1313-1314 (2006), holding that § 6404(h) vests exclusive jurisdiction to review interest abatement claims under § 6404(e)(1) in the Tax Court. Because this decision conflicted with the Fifth Circuit's decision in Beall v. United States, 336 F.3d 419, 430 (2003) (holding that § 6404(h) grants concurrent rather than exclusive jurisdiction to the Tax Court), we granted certiorari.

III.

Our analysis is governed by the well-established principle that, in most contexts, " 'a precisely drawn, detailed statute pre-empts more general remedies.' " EC Term of Years Trust v. United States, 550 U.S. 429, ----, 127 S.Ct. 1763, 1764, 167 L.E.2d 729 (2007) (quoting Brown v. GSA, 425 U.S. 820, 834, 96 S.Ct. 1961, 48 L.Ed.2d 402 (1976)). We are also guided by our past recognition that when Congress enacts a specific remedy when no remedy was previously recognized, or when previous remedies were "problematic," the remedy provided is generally regarded as exclusive. *Id.*, at 285, 103 S.Ct. 1811; *Brown, supra*, at 826-829, 96 S.Ct. 1961.

Section 6404(h) fits the bill on both counts. It is a "precisely drawn, detailed statute" that, in a single sentence, provides a forum for adjudication, a limited class of potential plaintiffs, a statute of limitations, a standard of review, and authorization for judicial relief. And Congress enacted this provision against a backdrop of decisions uniformly rejecting the possibility of any review for taxpayers wishing to challenge the Secretary's § 6404(e)(1) determination. Therefore, despite Congress's failure explicitly to define the Tax Court's jurisdiction as exclusive, we think it quite plain that the terms of § 6404(h)-a "precisely drawn, detailed statute" filling a perceived hole in the law-control all requests for review of § 6404(e)(1) determinations. Those terms include the forum for adjudication.

The Hincks' primary argument against exclusive Tax Court jurisdiction is that by providing a standard of review-abuse of discretion-in § 6404(h), Congress eliminated the primary barrier to judicial review that courts had previously recognized; accordingly, they maintain, taxpayers may seek review of § 6404(e)(1) determinations under statutes granting jurisdiction to the district courts and the Court of Federal Claims to review tax refund actions. See 28 U.S.C. §§ 1346(a)(1), 1491(a)(1); 26 U.S.C. § 7422(a). Or, as the Fifth Circuit reasoned: "[T]he federal district courts have always possessed *jurisdiction* over challenges brought to section 6404(e)(1) denials[;] they simply determined that the taxpayers had no *substantive right* whatever to a favorable exercise of the Secretary's discretion . . . .[I]n enacting section 6404(h), Congress indicated that such is no longer the case, and thereby removed any impediment to district court review." Beall, supra, at 428 (emphasis in original).

It is true that by providing an abuse of discretion standard, Congress removed one of the obstacles courts had held foreclosed judicial review of § 6404(e)(1) determinations. But in enacting § 6404(h), Congress did not simply supply this single missing ingredient; rather, it set out a carefully circumscribed, time-limited, plaintiff-specific provision, which also precisely defined the appropriate forum. We cannot accept the Hincks' invitation to isolate one feature of this "precisely drawn, detailed statute"-the portion specifying a standard of review-and use it to permit taxpayers to circumvent the other limiting features Congress placed in the same statute-restrictions such as a shorter statute of limitations than general refund suits, compare § 6404(h) (180-day limitations period) with § 6532(a)(1) (2-year limitations period), or a net-worth ceiling for plaintiffs eligible to bring suit. Taxpayers could "effortlessly evade" these specific limitations by bringing interest abatement claims as tax refund actions in the district courts or the Court of Federal Claims, disaggregating a statute Congress plainly envisioned as a package deal.

The Hincks' other contentions are equally unavailing. First, they claim that reading § 6404(h) to vest exclusive jurisdiction in the Tax Court impliedly repeals the pre-existing jurisdiction of the district courts and Court of Federal Claims, despite our admonition that "repeals by implication are not favored." Morton v. Mancari, 417 U.S. 535, 549, 94 S.Ct. 2474, 41 L.Ed.2d 290 (1974). But the implied-repeal doctrine is not applicable here, for when Congress passed § 6404(h), § 6404(e)(1) had been interpreted not to provide any right of review for taxpayers. There is thus no indication of any "language on the statute books that [Congress] wishe [d] to change," United States v. Fausto, 484 U.S. 439, 453, 108 S.Ct. 668, 98 L.Ed.2d 830 (1988), implicitly or explicitly. Congress simply prescribed a limited form of review where none had previously been found to exist.

Second, the Hincks assert that vesting jurisdiction over § 6404(e)(1) abatement decisions exclusively in the Tax Court runs contrary to the "entire structure of tax controversy jurisdiction,"under which the Tax Court generally hears prepayment challenges to tax liability, see § 6213(a), while postpayment actions are brought in the district courts or Court of Federal Claims. In a related vein, the Hincks point out that the Government's position would force taxpayers seeking postpayment review of their tax liabilities to separate their § 6404(e)(1) abatement claims from their refund claims and bring each in a different court. Even assuming, *arguendo*, that we were inclined to depart from the face of the statute, these arguments are undercut on two fronts. To begin with, by expressly granting to the Tax Court some jurisdiction over § 6404(e)(1) decisions, Congress has already broken with the general scheme the Hincks identify. No one doubts that an action seeking review of a § 6404(e)(1) determination may be maintained in the Tax Court even if the interest has already been paid, and the Hincks point to no case where the Tax Court has refused to exercise jurisdiction under such circumstances.

In addition, an interest abatement claim under § 6404(e)(1) involves no questions of substantive tax law, but rather is premised on issues of bureaucratic administration (whether, for example, there was "error or delay" in the performance of a "ministerial" act, § 6404(e)(1)(A)). Judicial review of decisions not to abate requires an evaluation of the internal processes of the IRS, not the underlying tax liability of the taxpayer. We find nothing tellingly awkward about channeling such discrete and specialized questions of administrative operations to one particular court, even if in some respects it "may not appear to be efficient" as a policy matter to separate refund and interest abatement claims. 446 F.3d, at 1316.[2]

Last, the Hincks contend that Congress would not have intended to vest jurisdiction exclusively in the Tax Court because it would lead to the "unreasonable" result that taxpayers with net worths greater than $2 million (for individuals) or $7 million (for businesses) would be foreclosed from seeking judicial review of § 6404(e)(1) refusals to abate. But we agree with the Federal Circuit that this outcome "was contemplated by Congress." 446 F.3d, at 1316. The net-worth limitation in § 6404(h) reflects Congress's judgment that wealthier taxpayers are more likely to be able to pay a deficiency before contesting it, thereby avoiding accrual of interest during their administrative and legal challenges. In contrast, taxpayers with comparatively fewer resources are more likely to contest their assessed deficiency before first paying it, thus exposing themselves

---

2.   We note that the Hincks sought only interest abatement in the Court of Federal Claims, thus failing to implicate the "claim-splitting" and efficiency concerns they condemn.

to interest charges if their challenge is ultimately unsuccessful. There is nothing "unreasonable" about Congress's decision to grant the possibility of judicial relief only to those taxpayers most likely to be in need of it.

The judgment of the United States Court of Appeals for the Federal Circuit is affirmed.

It is so ordered.

Notes

Section 6404(h) provides that the Tax Court has jurisdiction over any abatement action brought by "a taxpayer who meets the requirements referred to in section 7430(c)(4)(A)(ii)." Section 7430(c)(4)(A)(ii) provides the taxpayer size and net worth requirements for awards of attorneys' fees. In general, an individual's net worth may not exceed $2 million and a business's net worth may not exceed $7 million. Thus, the Hinck's were not eligible for relief and neither is any other individual taxpayer with a net worth over $2 million.

In addition, an action must be brought in the Tax Court within 180 days after the Service mails its final determination denying the abatement.

Note also that an abatement is not a binding action and does not create any taxpayer rights. Thus, it does not prevent the Service from redetermining or reassessing a tax deficiency, as long as it acts before the expiration of the applicable statute of limitations. See Gray v. Commissioner, 104 F.2d 1226 (10th Cir. 1997) (Service not estopped from reasserting a deficiency after an abatement within the statutory period).

CHAPTER 7

THE COLLECTION PROCESS

> Unofficial Motto of the Internal Revenue Service:
> "We have what it takes to take what you have."
>   – – Anonymous[1]

Once a tax deficiency has been assessed, it becomes a liability/debt owed by the taxpayer to the government. The debt also includes any penalties, interest or other additions to tax. If the tax debt is not paid voluntarily, § 6301 of the Code grants the Service the authority to collect the debt through the use of either a summary (administrative) process or a judicial proceeding.

I. THE SUMMARY COLLECTION PROCESS: LIENS, LEVIES, AND DISTRAINT

If the taxpayer fails to pay an assessed tax liability within 10 days after the issuance of a notice of assessment and demand for payment (commonly called a "notice and demand"), a tax lien in favor of the government arises automatically and attaches to "all property and rights to property, whether real or personal, belonging to the taxpayer." IRC § 6321. The Service then may levy upon (i.e., seize) the taxpayer's property, after giving the taxpayer proper notice. Thus the Service may garnish the taxpayer's wages, offset any refund the taxpayer is owed, and perfect its lien on the taxpayer's property (both real and personal) by filing a public notice of its claim. The recording of a notice of tax lien can be potentially devastating to a taxpayer because it can ruin her credit rating, affect pending business transactions, and perhaps force her into bankruptcy. Therefore, the Service must observe certain procedural safeguards before a lien can arise or a levy can occur. Under these safeguards, the Service first must assess a deficiency in accordance with the deficiency assessment procedures discussed in Chapter 4, then it must issue a notice and demand for payment, and finally, it must give the taxpayer a grace period of at least ten days from the notice and demand to make payment. If the Service fails to observe any of these

---

1.   Jeffery L. Yablon, As Certain As Death–Quotations About Taxes (2004 Edition), 102 TAX NOTES 99, 135 (Jan. 5, 2004).

prerequisites the lien is not valid and any levy is subject to challenge. See IRC § 6213(a).

A taxpayer may administratively challenge a lien by requesting a Collection Due Process (CDP) hearing. See IRC § 6320. The IRS must provide notice to the taxpayer within five days of filing a notice of tax lien. The taxpayer then has 30 days to request a CDP hearing before an IRS Appeals Officer to contest the lien filing. At the conclusion of the hearing, the Appeals Officer will issue a Notice of Determination, which is subject to judicial review if the taxpayer files a timely appeal with the Tax Court. The Service also is required to give the taxpayer notice 30 days prior to a levy and the taxpayer at that point also may request a CDP hearing to contest the levy. See IRC § 6330.

A. THE NOTICE AND DEMAND FOR PAYMENT

After a timely assessment, the next step in the collection process generally is the issuance of a notice and demand for payment within 60 days of the assessment, pursuant to § 6303 of the Code. The notice and demand must be mailed to the taxpayer's "last known address" or left at the taxpayer's "dwelling or usual place of business." IRC § 6303(a). (The rules for determining validity of the notice based on the "last known address" are similar to those of the notice of deficiency, discussed in Chapter 4). The taxpayer has 10 days from the receipt of the notice and demand to pay the full amount of the tax liability. IRC § 6331(a). The validity of the collection process is called into question if the notice and demand contains a material error or if the taxpayer does not receive a timely notice.

PLANNED INVESTMENTS, INC. v. UNITED STATES
United States Court of Appeals, Sixth Circuit, 1989.
881 F.2d 340.

MERRITT, CIRCUIT JUDGE.

The issue in this tax case is the adequacy of the notice sent by the Internal Revenue Service ("IRS" or "Government") to inform plaintiff, Planned Investments, Inc. ("PI") that it had been assessed a penalty of $64,000 under § 6700 of the Internal Revenue Code ("Code"), 26 U.S.C. § 6700, for PI's promotion of an abusive tax shelter. The District Court, finding that the notice was inadequate and unfair because it did not clearly specify the time period involved, granted summary judgment to plaintiff and abated the penalty. The Government appeals the grant of summary judgment to PI and the District Court's later denial of its motion for reconsideration of the grant of summary judgment. The notice complied with the applicable statutory form and the unfairness, if any, of the failure to specify correctly the time period was cured by the prior dealings between the parties which show that PI knew exactly what conduct the notice was intended to cover. Accordingly, we reverse.

I.

The facts are not in dispute. PI was incorporated on December 10, 1982, with the stated purpose of evaluating business ventures and finding investors for those ventures. During December, 1982, PI, through an agent, sold 115 interests in a "product" known as the "Children's Classics Series," a master recording tax shelter lease, which was organized, published and produced by Oxford Productions Corporation. As a result of commissions from the sales, PI realized gross income of $64,000. As part of its sales effort, PI furnished investors with promotional materials, prepared by Oxford Publications, which allegedly contained gross overstatements of the value of the master recordings. PI filed a tax return for the tax period December 10, 1982 through November 30, 1983, which reflected the $64,000.

In January, 1983, PI's attorney advised the corporation of potential § 6700 penalties because of its sales of the tax shelter. Shortly thereafter, PI ceased its sales activities. PI has had no income from the sale of any tax shelter since December, 1982. During late 1984, PI became aware that the IRS had conducted an investigation of Oxford and had, in fact, treated the Children's Classics Series as an abusive tax shelter.

Pursuant to an IRS letter dated February 26, 1985, an attorney and an accountant representing PI met with an IRS agent regarding PI's involvement in the Children's Classics Series. On September 10, 1985, PI received a second letter from the IRS which informed PI that the IRS was considering recommending the assessment of a penalty under § 6700 and which invited PI to present any facts or legal arguments before a final decision was made. PI's counsel met with an IRS agent again on September 18, 1985. At this meeting PI's involvement in the Children's Classics Series tax shelter was again discussed.

On March 3, 1986, the IRS sent PI written notification that it was assessing a $64,000 penalty for the promotion of an abusive tax shelter. The notice erroneously stated that the "Tax Period" was December 31, 1985 and incorrectly stated the formula that had been used to calculate the penalty.[1] The notice also outlined the procedures for contesting the assessment but did not contain any description of the specific activity upon which the penalty was based.

On March 28, 1986, PI, pursuant to § 6703 of the Code,[2] paid the IRS $150[3] and filed a claim with the IRS for abatement of the penalty and a refund of the $150. The IRS, by letter, disallowed the claim on September 16, 1986. The letter denying the claim bore the heading: "In Re: Section 6700: Promoting Abusive Tax Shelter Penalty" and correctly stated the amount of the penalty as $64,000. The letter, however, incorrectly stated: "Tax Period Ended: Related to 1985 Form 1040."

On October 6, 1986, PI timely filed its complaint in the District Court, seeking a refund of the $150 payment and an abatement of the penalty. Cross-motions for summary judgment were eventually filed, and the parties entered into a stipulation of the material facts.

The District Court granted summary judgment for PI. Acknowledging that the notice need not take any particular form, the court held that the notice must meet certain minimum "substantial requirements" sufficient to impart the taxpayer with "fair notice." Relying on a line of cases defining the requirement for a notice of deficiency, the court said that a correct statement of the tax period involved must be included in the notice. Concluding that PI did not receive any guidance from the notice of the time period involved, the court ruled that the notice received by PI was invalid.

The District Court further rejected the Government's contention that the December 31, 1985 date on the notice represented the end date of the

---

1. The notice stated that the penalty was "the greater of $1,000 or 20% of the gross income derived or to be derived from the activity." At the time the alleged conduct occurred, however, the penalty for promoting an abusive tax shelter was the greater of $1,000 or 10% of the gross income derived or to be derived from the activity. The "20%" of the gross income language was substituted by a 1984 amendment and did not become effective until July 18, 1984. The 1984 amendment's penalty is concededly inapplicable to PI's 1982 conduct.

2. Section 6703(c)(1) of the Code provides that levy or collection of the penalty may be delayed pending the resolution of the matter by the district court:

[i]f, within 30 days after the day on which notice and demand of any penalty under section 6700 * * * is made against any person, such person pays an amount which is not less than 15 percent of the amount of such penalty and files a claim for refund of the amount so paid * * *. 26 U.S.C. § 6703(c)(1).

Section 6703(c)(2) provides that such levy and collection may be delayed if suit is brought in the district court before the earlier of thirty days after the claim for refund is denied or thirty days after the expiration of six months after the day the claim for refund was filed. 26 U.S.C. § 6703(c)(2).

3. PI arrived at the $150 figure by treating the $64,000 as a divisible assessment and assuming that PI was assessed $1,000 for each of 64 different activities. By treating the assessment as divisible, PI was required to pay only 15% of the penalty ($1,000) assessed for one of the 64 activities, or $150. The government does not contest this manner of treating the penalty.

applicable time period. The court reasoned that PI could not have reasonably been expected to figure out from the 1985 date that it was being penalized for conduct in 1982, especially considering that the notice stated that the statute upon which the penalty amount was premised was passed in 1984.

Finally, the District Court rejected the Government's argument that even if the notice was defective, PI was not prejudiced or misled thereby because it actually knew, from prior dealings with the IRS, exactly what the charged conduct was and when it occurred and had a full opportunity to contest the charge. The court reasoned that it should not allow PI's subjective knowledge to excuse the IRS from its obligation to give fair notice, especially since the IRS's conduct here was "not merely neglectful, but slipshod." Accordingly, the District Court found the notice invalid and unenforceable. The Court further abated the penalty and granted PI a refund of $150 plus interest.

On appeal, the Government contends that the District Court erred (1) in finding that the notice was insufficient because it did not clearly and correctly state the period of time during which the penalized conduct occurred and (2) in rejecting the argument that even if the notice was insufficient the notice should be enforced because PI was not misled or prejudiced by the defect in notice.

II.

Section 6700 of the Code imposes on any person who promotes an abusive tax shelter a penalty calculated with reference to "the gross income derived or to be derived by such person from such activity." 26 U.S.C. § 6700(a). Section 6671 provides that all penalties provided by Subchapter B of Chapter 68 (which includes § 6700) "shall be paid upon notice and demand * * * and shall be assessed and collected as taxes." 26 U.S.C. § 6671(a).

Chapter 63 of the Code, 26 U.S.C. §§ 6201-45, governs assessment of taxes. Accordingly, given the § 6671(a) instruction that an abusive tax shelter penalty be assessed "as taxes," Chapter 63 provides the mechanism for assessment of the abusive tax shelter penalty.

Chapter 63 provides for two modes of assessment–a special deficiency procedure in Subchapter B to be used for assessment of income, estate and gift taxes, and a general procedure in Subchapter A for assessment of other taxes. Section 6703, however, provides that the special deficiency procedures of Subchapter B, established for assessment of income, estate and gift taxes, shall not apply to the assessment or collection of § 6700 penalties. 26 U.S.C. § 6703(b). Section 6700 penalties, therefore, must be assessed under the procedures set forth in Subchapter A.

Section 6203 of Subchapter A provides that assessment be made by recording the liability in accordance with the regulations promulgated by the Secretary. 26 U.S.C.§ 6203. Upon request, a taxpayer may obtain a copy of the assessment. Treasury regulations provide that the assessment be made by signing the summary record of assessment. 26 CFR § 301.6203-1. The summary record, through supporting documents, must contain the following: 1) identification of the taxpayer; 2) character of liability assessed; 3) taxable period, if applicable; and 4) amount of assessment. The regulations further provide that, upon request, the taxpayer may obtain a copy of the "pertinent" parts of the assessment, i.e., those parts which set forth the name of the taxpayer, the date of assessment, the character of the liability, the amount assessed and the taxable period, if applicable.

In accord with the § 6671(a) mandate that § 6700 penalties be assessed and collected as taxes, Chapter 64, which sets forth the rules for collection of taxes, governs the collection of § 6700 penalties. Section 6303 of Chapter 64 provides the general rule for the notice and demand for tax:

> after the making of an assessment of a tax pursuant to section 6203, [the IRS shall] give notice to each person liable for the unpaid tax, stating the amount and demanding payment thereof.

26 U.S.C. § 6303(a). Section 6303 does not prescribe any particular form of notice. Treasury Regulations promulgated under the authority of § 6303 merely parrot the statutory language that the notice shall state the amount of the tax and demand payment thereof. 26 CFR § 301.6303-1(a).

III.

Construing the plain language of the statutes and regulations outlined above, it becomes evident that the form of notice of assessment of a § 6700 penalty requires only a statement of the amount of the penalty and a demand for payment. It is also clear that the notice sent to the plaintiff in this case complied with these requirements as the notice identified the amount assessed and demanded payment.

In holding that the tax period involved should be included in the notice, however, the District Court applied the rules regarding notices of deficiency to the instant notice of assessment. Indeed, all the cases cited by the District Court for the proposition that the tax period involved must be included in the notice were Chapter 63, Subchapter B cases. See, Scar v. Commissioner, 814 F.2d 1363 (9th Cir.1987); Benzvi v. Commissioner, 787 F.2d 1541 (11th Cir.); Abrams v. Commissioner, 787 F.2d 939 (4th Cir.). Such treatment ignores the prohibition of § 6703 that the deficiency procedures of Subchapter B do not apply to § 6700 penalties and also ignores the reality that § 6700 penalties are not assessed for discrete taxable years but for conduct and transactions which may occur over one or many taxable years, not on an annual basis. See 26 U.S.C. § 6700. We conclude, therefore, that such treatment by the District Court was error and that the notice complied with the requirements of the statute.

IV.

Our inquiry, however, does not end here. The notice must meet the general "fairness" requirement of due process. The District Court rejected the Government's argument that the court need not reach the due process question because, notwithstanding any defects in the notice, the notice was "fair" since PI had been informed through its dealings with the IRS of the particular conduct that was being penalized and was, therefore, not prejudiced or misled. The District Court held that in no event could PI's subjective knowledge cure the defect in notice.

Again, the District Court erred. Notices containing technical defects are valid where the taxpayer has not been prejudiced or misled by the error and is afforded a meaningful opportunity to litigate his claims. Marvel v. United States, 719 F.2d 1507 (10th Cir.1983) (notice contained name of corporation rather than names of individual taxpayers); Allan v. United States, 386 F.Supp. 499 (N.D.Tex.), aff'd, 514 F.2d 1070 (5th Cir.1975) (notice contained name of wrong corporation); and Wood Harmon Corp. v. United States, 206 F.Supp. 773 (S.D.N.Y.1962), aff'd, 311 F.2d 918 (2d Cir.1963) (notice did not state correct time period).

In this case it is undisputed that PI was apprised by the IRS long before the formal notice of assessment was issued that the IRS would challenge its activity in 1982 involving the promotion of the Oxford "Children's Classics Series" recording tax shelter. The record reflects that pre-assessment conferences were held with PI and that PI's claim for refund, filed soon after the notice was received, argued not only that PI was not involved in such activity in 1985, but also that its 1982 involvement did not violate § 6700. This record therefore, shows that PI was not misled.

Moreover, PI has been afforded an opportunity to contest the assessment of the penalty. Indeed, this very lawsuit constitutes that opportunity as provided in § 6703(c). PI cannot, therefore, argue that it has been given no opportunity to contest the assessment.

V.

For the foregoing reasons, we reverse the decision of the District Court and remand this case for further proceedings.

ENGEL, CHIEF JUDGE, concurring.

I fully concur in Judge Merritt's concise and well balanced opinion. As he explains, section 6700 penalties for abusive tax shelters are to be assessed and collected "as taxes." 26 U.S.C. § 6671(a). Moreover, the Code and applicable regulations further require only that notices of such assessments include the amount of the penalty and a demand for payment thereof. 26 U.S.C. § 6303(a). Thus, to the extent the district court held that the Code itself requires something more, I agree that the court below erred.

I write only to emphasize that because we believe that the assessee was neither prejudiced nor misled, we do not reach the due process question ultimately raised by this statutory scheme. I, like the district judge, however, entertain some serious reservations concerning the validity if not the wisdom of the bare bones notice apparently required by Congress in these cases. There is in the statutory framework the potential for abuse through mistake or even, perhaps, vindictive purpose because there is no requirement that an assessee be notified of the exact nature and time period of the challenged conduct. Whether, in such a case, the post-assessment remedies or even the pre-assessment notice will be sufficient to satisfy procedural due process can be left, however, to another day for certainly no such evil occurred here. I simply write to make it clear that we do not intend to preclude that kind of constitutional scrutiny at a later date.

Notes and Questions

Section 7524, enacted in 1996, requires the Service to send annual reminder notices to taxpayers with delinquent accounts. The notice must state the amount of the delinquency so that taxpayers will be aware of the amount they owe and the fact that the Service expects payment. The tax liability apparently remains unaffected, however, by the failure to send a timely annual notice.

1. Procedurally, how does a notice and demand differ from a notice of deficiency?

2. Can you think of some examples of when a technically deficient notice and demand will be considered invalid notice? See Bauer v. Foley, 404 F.2d 1215 (2d Cir. 1968); United States v. Lehigh, 201 F.Supp. 224 (W.D. Ark. 1961).

3. In his concurrence in *Planned Investments*, Judge Engel raises a concern about the "wisdom of the bare bones notice" required by Congress. Why do you think Congress requires such minimal notice?

If the court had decided that the notice was invalid, what, if any, remedy would be available to the Service? The next case addresses this issue.

BLACKSTON v. UNITED STATES
United States District Court, District of Maryland, 1991.
778 F. Supp. 244.

GARBIS, DISTRICT JUDGE.

* * *

The issues presented are whether the Internal Revenue Service has complied with § 6303(a) of the Internal Revenue Code by giving notice to the taxpayers stating the amount due and demanding payment within 60 days after the making of the subject assessments and, if not, what is the effect of the Service's failure.

* * *

Noncompliance With Section 6303(a)

Section 6303(a) provides in relevant part that: * * * [The IRS] shall, as soon as practicable, and within 60 days after the making of an assessment of a tax * * * give notice to each person liable for the unpaid tax, stating the amount and demanding payment thereof. Said notice shall * * * be sent by mail to such person's last known address.

The I.R.S. records reflect that a first notice of assessment and demand for payment ("Notice and Demand") was mailed to the taxpayers at their current address on or about January 28, 1985, within 60 days of the assessments. It is stipulated, however, that the first notice which the taxpayers actually received relating to the subject deficiencies was dated May 31, 1985 - more than 60 days after the assessments. The question presented is whether the Service in fact properly mailed a notice and demand on or about January 28, 1985 as reflected in its computer generated records.[2]

It is the Government's position that the mere fact that the Internal Revenue Service is able to present a computer generated printout reflecting that a Notice of Demand had been sent on January 28, 1988 establishes an *irrebuttable presumption* that the notice was in fact sent. This Court rejects this position. A similar contention had been rejected by the district court in the case of United States v. Berman, 825 F.2d 1053, 1056-57 (6th Cir.1987). As found by the trial court in the *Berman* case, and as this Court finds from the evidence presented here, there are sufficient irregularities presented in the IRS computer evidence to cause this Court to doubt its reliability. Therefore, the Court refuses to accept the records as conclusive. In particular, the Court notes that the I.R.S. records reflect the mailing of a first notice on January 28, 1985 and the mailing of a second notice some four months later on May 31, 1985. However, the IRS Service Center computer is programmed to send the second notice five weeks after the first notice. M. Saltzman, IRS Practice and Procedure ¶ 14.03(3) (2nd ed. 1991) and ¶ 14.03 (1st ed. 1981).

This Court was sufficiently concerned about the matter to ask the Government at argument, and in a post trial Order, the following:

> The I.R.S. records reflect the mailing of a first notice on January 28, 1985 and a second notice on May 31, 1985 (a four month period) while the I.R.S. manual allegedly indicates that there would be a much shorter period between a first and second notice. How can this inconsistency be explained without resulting in uncertainty as to the accuracy of either the January or May date, or both?

In response the Government stated:

> [A]fter consultation with the appropriate IRS representative, the United States does not intend to proffer any further evidence on this particular point.

The Court interprets this response to mean that the Government cannot provide any satisfactory answer to the Court's question. Therefore, on the record in this case, which includes the Government's refusal (or inability) to provide an explanation of the inconsistency of its computer generated records as to the date of the first notice,[3] the Court

---

2. The Government, quite correctly, notes that the fact that the taxpayers did not receive the alleged January 28, 1985 first notice is not determinative. So long as the notice was timely mailed to the taxpayers' last known address, the IRS has complied with § 6303(a) even absent receipt.

3. If the first and second notices were, in fact, mailed 5 weeks apart then the computer records are erroneous as to the January 28, 1985 date for the first notice and/or the May 31, 1985 date for the second notice.

finds as a fact that the IRS did not comply with § 6303(a) by sending a Notice and Demand within 60 days of the subject assessments. This finding requires the Court to address the question of the effect of such a failure.

Effect of Noncompliance with Section 6303(a)

Having found that the IRS failed to comply with § 6303(a) by not sending a notice and demand within 60 days of the subject assessments, the Court must determine the effect of such a failure. In this case, the issue arises in both a refund context[4] and in a collection context.[5] In both contexts the issue presented is whether the failure to send a timely notice and demand renders the January 28, 1985 assessment void altogether or whether it leaves the assessment valid but bars the Internal Revenue Service from utilizing its lien and levy collection powers.

There is no Fourth Circuit precedent addressing the issue presented. The decisions in other circuits addressing the absence of a timely notice and demand do not answer all of the questions presented in this case. See United States v. Chila, 871 F.2d 1015 (11th Cir.1989); United States v. Berman, 825 F.2d 1053 (6th Cir.1987); Marvel v. United States, 719 F.2d 1507 (10th Cir.1983). Nevertheless, this Court concludes, consistent with the views expressed in *Berman*, *Marvel*, and *Chila* that the appropriate "sanction" against the I.R.S. for its failure to comply with the § 6303(a) notice and demand requirement is to take away its awesome nonjudicial collection powers. It would be irrational to conclude that an assessment becomes void after 60 days if there is no notice and demand. Such a rule of law would serve only to provide a windfall to permit taxpayers to avoid paying valid assessments of determined tax liabilities because of an I.R.S. clerical error in failing to mail a notice and demand to the taxpayer's last known address.

The Court's decision is in accord with the views of leading publications on federal tax procedures. As stated in M. Saltzman, IRS Practice and Procedure, ¶ 14.05(2) (2nd ed. 1991):

> Under the collection mechanism established by the Code, once tax has been assessed, a taxpayer is subject to the summary nonjudicial procedures (lien and levy) available to the Service to collect the assessed tax. The notice and demand provided by Section 6303 gives

---

4. I.e. for 1979 as to which the taxpayers have made full payment and seek recovery of what they have paid.

5. For 1980 and 1981 the IRS has filed suit to reduce an assessment of judgment.

the taxpayer warning that the taxpayer must take some action to resolve the delinquent account if these summary collection procedures are to be avoided. Thus, preseizure notice serves an important practical, and possibly a due process, purpose in the statutory scheme. A taxpayer's liability is recorded by the official act of assessment, but where no Section 6303 notice is given, or an invalid notice is given, a statutory prerequisite is missing and, absent compliance with the Code, any collection action that follows is invalid. No lien can arise, nor can a levy be effective, absent a notice and demand. Where the government elects to collect tax by a civil suit, the complaint gives the taxpayer notice, and collection cannot be taken without court approval. A Section 6303 notice does not appear to be required where liability is asserted in a judicial proceeding. [Footnotes in original omitted]

And, as stated in Salchow, IRS Practice & Policy, ¶ 1010.A.2.d (1991):

Since the administrative collection remedies require a timely and properly issued notice and demand, it is in the taxpayer's interest initially to determine whether the IRS made such notice and demand. The general rule is that no tax lien arises until the IRS makes a demand for payment. Myrick v. United States, 296 F.2d 312 (5th Cir.1961). Without a valid notice and demand, there can be no tax lien; without a tax lien, the IRS cannot levy against the taxpayer's property. The IRS' failure to serve a timely notice and demand, however, does not prevent the government from instituting a judicial proceeding to collect the tax liability. * * *

The 1979 Refund Claim

As to the year 1979, the outcome depends upon the manner in which the taxes were collected. That is, was collection effected by the illegal use of liens and levies in the absence of a notice and demand. If so, the taxpayers would be entitled to a refund. Here, the 1979 taxes were paid by the taxpayers' check and not through the use of the lien or levy power. Accordingly, there can be no refund for 1979.

The Court has considered the argument that the taxpayers here paid by check only because of the threat of nonjudicial collection action. Hence, it could be argued that the I.R.S., as a practical matter, did utilize its nonjudicial collection powers. However, it is fair to say that many, if not virtually all, tax payments are made because the taxpayer realizes that a failure to pay what is owed will result in I.R.S. collection activity. Accordingly, the effect of the taxpayer's argument would be to provide a windfall to all taxpayers who do not receive a timely notice and demand but pay their tax liability anyhow. Thus, in a not uncommon situation, the I.R.S. might innocently misaddress a notice and demand but the taxpayer would nevertheless become aware of the assessment more than 60 days after it is made. At that point the taxpayer could (and should) pay the I.R.S. (resulting in a closing of the account) without any reason for the IRS to be aware that it had made a clerical error in issuing a notice and demand. It would be strange indeed if this would result in giving the taxpayer the ability to get a refund of the payment and avoid entirely his determined liability.

It should further be noted that a § 6303(a) "violation" occurs 60 days after the assessment. Therefore, if the taxpayer's position were correct, a valid assessment would become invalid on the 61st day after assessment because of the nonoccurrence of an event, i.e. a properly addressed notice and demand. There is nothing to indicate to this Court that such retroactive invalidation was intended or makes any sense at all.

This Court concludes that § 6303(a) was placed in the Code to insure that taxpayers received notice of tax liability so that they could make "voluntary" payment before the I.R.S. could use its lien and levy collection powers. Therefore, the purpose of the statute would be served by preventing the I.R.S. from the exercise of this power where it has not complied with § 6303(a). To go further and eliminate a taxpayer's duly determined liability would be neither consistent with the statutory scheme nor sensible.

The 1980 and 1981 Counterclaim

As to 1980 and 1981, the Government has sued to reduce to judgment the assessments made on January 28, 1985. The taxpayers have defended in reliance on the statute of limitations. In essence, the taxpayers contend that the January 28, 1985 assessments were rendered invalid once 60 days passed without notice and demand. Therefore, they say, the Government could only sue on the underlying tax liability and not on the assessment. Accordingly, since the Counterclaim was filed after the running of limitations for a suit on the liability itself and not the assessment, the taxpayers would be entitled to judgment.[7]

---

7.   § 6502(a)(1). A suit on the tax liability (*sans* assessment) would be timely if brought within three years from the date the return was filed plus the period of time during which the running of limitations was extended by virtue of the Tax Court litigation. § 6503(a). It appears that this period of limitations would have expired prior to the 1988 filing of the Government's counterclaim in this case.

It is the Government's position, with which the Court agrees, that the January 28, 1985 assessment was, and remains, valid and that the Counterclaim was timely filed to reduce the assessment to judgment pursuant to § 6502(a).[8] The Counterclaim is, in effect, a collection suit, which is permitted even though there had been no notice and demand. Thus, the Counterclaim was timely filed and, there being no debate as to the substantive merit of the assessments, the Government is entitled to judgment.

Conclusion

For the foregoing reasons, the Court holds in favor of the Government on the Plaintiff's suit for refund for 1979 and on the Government's Counterclaim to reduce its assessments to judgment for 1980 and 1981.

Notes and Questions

Judge Marvin Garbis, who wrote the *Blackston* opinion, is a leading scholar and commentator on tax procedure. This gives added credence to the *Blackston* decision.

The United States Supreme Court held in Lewis v. United States, 279 U.S. 63, 49 S.Ct. 257, 73 L.Ed. 615 (1929) that "the actions of the IRS enjoy a presumption of official regularity, which establishes that actions taken by the IRS in accordance with its regular procedures occurred in the absence of evidence to the contrary." Since the taxpayer in *Blackston* was able to establish irregularities in the Service's "regular procedures" in sending the requisite notices, the Service lost its presumption of regularity. Note that Certificates of Assessment and Payment are usually presumptive proof that proper notice and demand was made. United States v. Chila, 871 F.2d 1015 (11th Cir. 1989).

Treas. Reg. § 301.6303-1 provides that " * * * failure to give notice within 60 days does not invalidate the notice." Interestingly, this regulation is often ignored by the courts, even though the regulation is one of long-standing. Perhaps this is because the regulation is inconsistent with the statute, which says that the government *shall* give notice within 60 days of an assessment. The question is whether under the regulation, the government could send a late notice and demand, and revive its right to use the summary collection process. Under the *Blackston* case and others taking a similar view, the government is

---

8.   The period of limitations for suit on the January 25, 1985 assessments was originally six years and was, in 1990, extended to ten years. Omnibus Budget Reconciliation Act of 1990, § 11317(a)(1), amending IRC § 6502(a).

precluded from using the summary collection process if the notice is not sent within 60 days of the assessment. Since the majority of courts that have considered the issue have held that the failure to send the notice and demand does not invalidate the assessment, the government must collect by using the judicial process. Note, though, that this issue has not been fully resolved.

In United States v. Associates Commercial Corp., 721 F.2d 1094 (7th Cir. 1983), the Seventh Circuit held that failure to give proper notice and demand barred subsequent civil action. The *Associates Commercial* case involved a third party lender, however, and its holding is highly questionable in light of the Supreme Court's subsequent decision in United States v. Jersey Shore State Bank, 479 U.S. 442, 107 S.Ct. 782, 93 L.Ed.2d 800 (1987), holding that the government is not required to provide notice to third party lenders. For a discussion of the various views on defective notice under § 6303, see Howard W. Gordon, "Failure To Give Notice and Demand: Enjoining the IRS from Administrative Collections," 98 Tax Notes Today 100-100 (May 26, 1998).

What effect, if any, does an invalid notice and demand, or failure to send a notice and demand, have on the § 6651(a)(3) failure to pay penalty? (Review civil penalties, Chapter 6). Does it have any other effect outside of § 6651(a)(3)?

B.　THE TAX LIEN

If the tax is not paid within 10 days of the notice and demand, a lien arises automatically on the taxpayer's real and personal property. Section 6321 provides:

> If any person liable to pay any tax neglects or refuses to pay the same after demand, the amount (including any interest, additional amount, addition to tax, or assessable penalty, together with any costs that may accrue in addition thereto) shall be a lien in favor of the United States upon all property and rights to property, whether real or personal, tangible or intangible, belonging to such person.

Under § 6322, the lien arises at the time the tax is assessed and continues until the assessed amount is paid or becomes unenforceable because of lapse of time. The lien attaches to property owned by the delinquent taxpayer during the life of the lien, including property acquired after the lien arose.

1. Scope of the Lien

UNITED STATES v. CRAFT
Supreme Court of the United States, 2002.
535 U.S. 274, 122 S.Ct. 1414, 152 L.Ed.2d 437.

JUSTICE O'CONNOR delivered the opinion of the Court.

This case raises the question whether a tenant by the entirety possesses "property" or "rights to property" to which a federal tax lien may attach. 26 U.S.C. § 6321. Relying on the state law fiction that a tenant by the entirety has no separate interest in entireties property, the United States Court of Appeals for the Sixth Circuit held that such property is exempt from the tax lien. We conclude that, despite the fiction, each tenant possesses individual rights in the estate sufficient to constitute "property" or "rights to property" for the purposes of the lien, and reverse the judgment of the Court of Appeals.

* * *

II.

Whether the interests of respondent's husband in the property he held as a tenant by the entirety constitutes "property and rights to property" for the purposes of the federal tax lien statute, 26 U.S.C. § 6321, is ultimately a question of federal law. The answer to this federal question, however, largely depends upon state law. The federal tax lien statute itself "creates no property rights but merely attaches consequences, federally defined, to rights created under state law." United States v. Bess, 357 U.S. 51, 55, 78 S.Ct. 1054, 2 L.Ed.2d 1135 (1958); see also United States v. National Bank of Commerce, 472 U.S. 713, 722, 105 S.Ct. 2919, 86 L.Ed.2d 565 (1985). Accordingly, "[w]e look initially to state law to determine what rights the taxpayer has in the property the Government seeks to reach, then to federal law to determine whether the taxpayer's state-delineated rights qualify as 'property' or 'rights to property' within the compass of the federal tax lien legislation." Drye v. United States, 528 U.S. 49, 58, 120 S.Ct. 474, 145 L.Ed.2d 466 (1999).

A common idiom describes property as a "bundle of sticks" – a collection of individual rights which, in certain combinations, constitute property. State law determines only which sticks are in a person's bundle. Whether those sticks qualify as "property" for purposes of the federal tax lien statute is a question of federal law.

In looking to state law, we must be careful to consider the substance of the rights state law provides, not merely the labels the State gives these rights or the conclusions it draws from them. Such state law labels are irrelevant to the federal question of which bundles of rights constitute property that may be attached by a federal tax lien. In *Drye v. United States,* supra, we considered a situation where state law allowed an heir subject to a federal tax lien to disclaim his interest in the estate. The state law also provided that such a disclaimer would "creat[e] the legal fiction" that the heir had predeceased the decedent and would correspondingly be deemed to have had no property interest in the estate. We unanimously held that this state law fiction did not control the federal question and looked instead to the realities of the heir's interest. We concluded that, despite the State's characterization, the heir possessed a "right to property" in the estate–the right to accept the inheritance or pass it along to another–to which the federal lien could attach.

III.

We turn first to the question of what rights respondent's husband had in the entireties property by virtue of state law. In order to understand these rights, the tenancy by the entirety must first be placed in some context.

* * *

A tenancy by the entirety is a unique sort of concurrent ownership that can only exist between married persons. Because of the common-law fiction that the husband and wife were one person at law (that person, practically speaking, was the husband, see J. Cribbet et al., Cases and Materials on Property 329 (6th ed. 1990)), Blackstone did not characterize the tenancy by the entirety as a form of concurrent ownership at all. Instead, he thought that entireties property was a form of single ownership by the marital unity. Neither spouse was considered to own any individual interest in the estate; rather, it belonged to the couple.

Like joint tenants, tenants by the entirety enjoy the right of survivorship. Also like a joint tenancy, unilateral alienation of a spouse's interest in entireties property is typically not possible without severance. Unlike joint tenancies, however, tenancies by the entirety cannot easily be severed unilaterally. Typically, severance requires the consent of both spouses, or the ending of the marriage in divorce. At common law, all of the other rights associated with the entireties property belonged to the husband: as the head of the household, he could control the use of the property and the exclusion of others from it and enjoy all of the income produced from it. The husband's control of the property was so extensive that, despite the rules on alienation, the common law eventually provided that he could unilaterally alienate entireties property without severance subject only to the wife's survivorship interest.

With the passage of the Married Women's Property Acts in the late 19th century granting women distinct rights with respect to marital property, most States either abolished the tenancy by the entirety or altered it significantly. Michigan's version of the estate is typical of the modern tenancy by the entirety. Following Blackstone, Michigan characterizes its tenancy by the entirety as creating no individual rights whatsoever: "It is well settled under the law of this State that one tenant by the entirety has no interest separable from that of the other * * *. Each is vested with an entire title." Long v. Earle, 277 Mich. 505, 517, 269 N.W. 577, 581 (1936). And yet, in Michigan, each tenant by the entirety possesses the right of survivorship. Each spouse–the wife as well as the husband–may also use the property, exclude third parties from it, and receive an equal share of the income produced by it. Neither spouse may unilaterally alienate or encumber the property, although this may be accomplished with mutual consent. Divorce ends the tenancy by the entirety, generally giving each spouse an equal interest in the property as a tenant in common, unless the divorce decree specifies otherwise.

In determining whether respondent's husband possessed "property" or "rights to property" within the meaning of 26 U.S.C. § 6321, we look to the individual rights created by these state law rules. According to Michigan law, respondent's husband had, among other rights, the following rights with respect to the entireties property: the right to use the property, the right to exclude third parties from it, the right to a share of income produced from it, the right of survivorship, the right to become a tenant in common with equal shares upon divorce, the right to sell the property with the respondent's consent and to receive half the proceeds from such a sale, the right to place an encumbrance on the property with the respondent's consent, and the right to block respondent from selling or encumbering the property unilaterally.

IV.

We turn now to the federal question of whether the rights Michigan law granted to respondent's husband as a tenant by the entirety qualify as "property" or "rights to property" under § 6321. The statutory language authorizing the tax lien "is broad and reveals on its face that Congress meant to reach every interest in property that a taxpayer might have." United States v. National Bank of Commerce, 472 U.S., at

719-720, 105 S.Ct. 2919. "Stronger language could hardly have been selected to reveal a purpose to assure the collection of taxes." We conclude that the husband's rights in the entireties property fall within this broad statutory language.

Michigan law grants a tenant by the entirety some of the most essential property rights: the right to use the property, to receive income produced by it, and to exclude others from it. See Dolan v. City of Tigard, 512 U.S. 374, 384, 114 S.Ct. 2309, 129 L.Ed.2d 304 (1994) ("[T]he right to exclude others" is " 'one of the most essential sticks in the bundle of rights that are commonly characterized as property' " (quoting Kaiser Aetna v. United States, 444 U.S. 164, 176, 100 S.Ct. 383, 62 L.Ed.2d 332 (1979)); Loretto v. Teleprompter Manhattan CATV Corp., 458 U.S. 419, 435, 102 S.Ct. 3164, 73 L.Ed.2d 868 (1982) (including "use" as one of the "[p]roperty rights in a physical thing"). These rights alone may be sufficient to subject the husband's interest in the entireties property to the federal tax lien. They gave him a substantial degree of control over the entireties property, and, as we noted in *Drye*, "in determining whether a federal taxpayer's state-law rights constitute 'property' or 'rights to property,' [t]he important consideration is the breadth of the control the [taxpayer] could exercise over the property." 528 U.S., at 61, 120 S.Ct. 474.

The husband's rights in the estate, however, went beyond use, exclusion, and income. He also possessed the right to alienate (or otherwise encumber) the property with the consent of respondent, his wife. It is true, as respondent notes, that he lacked the right to unilaterally alienate the property, a right that is often in the bundle of property rights. There is no reason to believe, however, that this one stick–the right of unilateral alienation–is essential to the category of "property."

This Court has already stated that federal tax liens may attach to property that cannot be unilaterally alienated. In United States v. Rodgers, 461 U.S. 677, 103 S.Ct. 2132, 76 L.Ed.2d 236 (1983), we considered the Federal Government's power to foreclose homestead property attached by a federal tax lien. Texas law provided that " 'the owner or claimant of the property claimed as homestead [may not], if married, sell or abandon the homestead without the consent of the other spouse.' " We nonetheless stated that "[i]n the homestead context * * *, there is no doubt * * * that not only do *both* spouses (rather than neither) have an independent interest in the homestead property, but that a federal tax lien can at least *attach* to each of those interests." 461 U.S., at 703, n. 31, 103 S.Ct. 2132.

Excluding property from a federal tax lien simply because the taxpayer does not have the power to unilaterally alienate it would, moreover, exempt a rather large amount of what is commonly thought of as property. It would exempt not only the type of property discussed in *Rodgers*, but also some community property. Community property states often provide that real community property cannot be alienated without the consent of both spouses. See, e.g., Ariz. Rev. Stat. Ann. § 25-214(C) (2000); Cal. Fam. Code Ann. § 1102 (West 1994); Idaho Code § 32-912 (1996); La. Civ. Code Ann., Art. 2347 (West Supp. 2002); Nev. Rev. Stat. Ann.§ 123.230(3) (Supp. 2001); N. M. Stat. Ann. § 40-3-13 (1999); Wash. Rev. Code § 26.16.030(3) (1994). Accordingly, the fact that respondent's husband could not unilaterally alienate the property does not preclude him from possessing "property and rights to property" for the purposes of § 6321.

Respondent's husband also possessed the right of survivorship--the right to automatically inherit the whole of the estate should his wife predecease him. Respondent argues that this interest was merely an expectancy, which we suggested in *Drye* would not constitute "property" for the purposes of a federal tax lien. 528 U.S., at 60, n. 7, 120 S.Ct. 474 ("[We do not mean to suggest] that an expectancy that has pecuniary value * * * would fall within § 6321 prior to the time it ripens into a present estate"). *Drye* did not decide this question, however, nor do we need to do so here. As we have discussed above, a number of the sticks in respondent's husband's bundle were presently existing. It is therefore not necessary to decide whether the right to survivorship alone would qualify as "property" or "rights to property" under § 6321.

That the rights of respondent's husband in the entireties property constitute "property" or "rights to property" "belonging to" him is further underscored by the fact that, if the conclusion were otherwise, the entireties property would belong to no one for the purposes of § 6321. Respondent had no more interest in the property than her husband; if neither of them had a property interest in the entireties property, who did? This result not only seems absurd, but would also allow spouses to shield their property from federal taxation by classifying it as entireties property, facilitating abuse of the federal tax system.

JUSTICE SCALIA'S and JUSTICE THOMAS' dissents claim that the conclusion that the husband possessed an interest in the entireties property to which the federal tax lien could attach is in conflict with the rules for tax liens relating to partnership property. This is not so. As the authorities cited by Justice THOMAS reflect, the federal tax lien does attach to an individual partner's interest in the partnership, that is, to the fair market value of his or her share in the partnership assets. As a holder of this lien, the Federal Government is entitled to "receive * * * the profits to which the assigning partner would otherwise be entitled," including predissolution distributions and the proceeds from dissolution.

There is, however, a difference between the treatment of entireties property and partnership assets. The Federal Government may not compel the sale of partnership assets (although it may foreclose on the partner's interest). It is this difference that is reflected in JUSTICE SCALIA's assertion that partnership property cannot be encumbered by individual partner's debts. This disparity in treatment between the two forms of ownership, however, arises from our decision in *United States v. Rodgers*, (holding that the Government may foreclose on property even where the co-owners lack the right of unilateral alienation), and not our holding today. In this case, it is instead the dissenters' theory that departs from partnership law, as it would hold that the Federal Government's lien does not attach to the husband's interest in the entireties property at all, whereas the lien may attach to an individual's interest in partnership property.

Respondent argues that, whether or not we would conclude that respondent's husband had an interest in the entireties property, legislative history indicates that Congress did not intend that a federal tax lien should attach to such an interest. In 1954, the Senate rejected a proposed amendment to the tax lien statute that would have provided that the lien attach to "property or rights to property (including the interest of such person as tenant by the entirety)." S. Rep. No. 1622, 83d Cong., 2d Sess., 575 (1954). We have elsewhere held, however, that failed legislative proposals are "a particularly dangerous ground on which to rest an interpretation of a prior statute," Pension Benefit Guaranty Corporation v. LTV Corp., 496 U.S. 633, 650, 110 S.Ct. 2668, 110 L.Ed.2d 579 (1990), reasoning that " '[c]ongressional inaction lacks persuasive significance because several equally tenable inferences may be drawn from such inaction, including the inference that the existing legislation already incorporated the offered change.' " Central Bank of Denver, N.A. v. First Interstate Bank of Denver, N.A., 511 U.S. 164, 187, 114 S.Ct. 1439, 128 L.Ed.2d 119 (1994). This case exemplifies the risk of relying on such legislative history. As we noted in *United States v. Rodgers*, supra, at 704, n. 31, 103 S.Ct. 2132, some legislative history surrounding the 1954 amendment indicates that the House intended the amendment to be nothing more than a "clarification" of existing law, and that the Senate rejected the amendment only because it found it "superfluous." See H. R. Rep. No. 1337, 83d Cong., 2d Sess., A406 (1954) (noting that the amendment would "clarif[y] the term 'property and rights to property' by expressly including therein the interest of the delinquent taxpayer in an estate by the entirety"); S. Rep. No. 1622, 575 ("It is not clear what change in existing law would be made by the parenthetical phrase. The deletion of the phrase is intended to continue the existing law").

The same ambiguity that plagues the legislative history accompanies the common-law background of Congress' enactment of the tax lien statute. Respondent argues that Congress could not have intended the passage of the federal tax lien statute to alter the generally accepted rule that liens could not attach to entireties property. The common-law rule was not so well established with respect to the application of a federal tax lien that we must assume that Congress considered the impact of its enactment on the question now before us. There was not much of a common-law background on the question of the application of federal tax liens, as the first court of appeals cases dealing with the application of such a lien did not arise until the 1950's. United States v. Hutcherson, 188 F.2d 326 (C.A.8 1951); Raffaele v. Granger, 196 F.2d 620 (C.A.3 1952). This background is not sufficient to overcome the broad statutory language Congress did enact, authorizing the lien to attach to "all property and rights to property" a taxpayer might have.

We therefore conclude that respondent's husband's interest in the entireties property constituted "property" or "rights to property" for the purposes of the federal tax lien statute. We recognize that Michigan makes a different choice with respect to state law creditors: "[L]and held by husband and wife as tenants by entirety is not subject to levy under execution on judgment rendered against either husband or wife alone." Sanford v. Bertrau, 204 Mich. 244, 247, 169 N.W. 880, 881 (1918). But that by no means dictates our choice. The interpretation of 26 U.S.C. § 6321 is a federal question, and in answering that question we are in no way bound by state courts' answers to similar questions involving state law. As we elsewhere have held, " 'exempt status under state law does not bind the federal collector.' " Drye v. United States, 528 U.S., at 59, 120 S.Ct. 474.

* * *

The judgment of the United States Court of Appeals for the Sixth Circuit is accordingly reversed, and the case is remanded for proceedings consistent with this opinion.

It is so ordered.

* * *

JUSTICE THOMAS, with whom JUSTICE STEVENS and JUSTICE SCALIA join, dissenting.

The Court today allows the Internal Revenue Service (IRS) to reach proceeds from the sale of real property that did not belong to the taxpayer, respondent's husband, Don Craft,[1] because, in the Court's view, he "possesse[d] individual rights in the [tenancy by the entirety] estate sufficient to constitute 'property' or 'rights to property' for the purposes of the lien" created by 26 U.S.C. § 6321. The Court does not contest that the tax liability the IRS seeks to satisfy is Mr. Craft's alone, and does not claim that, under Michigan law, real property held as a tenancy by the entirety belongs to either spouse individually. Nor does the Court suggest that the federal tax lien attaches to particular "rights to property" held individually by Mr. Craft. Rather, borrowing the metaphor of "property as a 'bundle of sticks'--a collection of individual rights which, in certain combinations constitute property," the Court proposes that so long as sufficient "sticks" in the bundle of "rights to property" "belong to" a delinquent taxpayer, the lien can attach as if the property itself belonged to the taxpayer.

This amorphous construct ignores the primacy of state law in defining property interests, eviscerates the statutory distinction between "property" and "rights to property" drawn by § 6321, and conflicts with an unbroken line of authority from this Court, the lower courts, and the IRS. Its application is all the more unsupportable in this case because, in my view, it is highly unlikely that the limited individual "rights to property" recognized in a tenancy by the entirety under Michigan law are themselves subject to lien. I would affirm the Court of Appeals and hold that Mr. Craft did not have "property" or "rights to property" to which the federal tax lien could attach.

---

1. The Grand Rapids property was tenancy by the entirety property owned by Mr. and Mrs. Craft when the tax lien attached, but was conveyed by the Crafts to Mrs. Craft by quitclaim deed in 1989. That conveyance terminated the entirety estate. The District Court and Court of Appeals both held that the transfer did not constitute a fraudulent conveyance, a ruling the Government has not appealed. The IRS is undoubtedly entitled to any proceeds that Mr. Craft received or to which he was entitled from the *1989 conveyance* of the tenancy by the entirety property for $1; at that point the tenancy by the entirety estate was destroyed and at least half of the proceeds, or 50 cents, was "property" or "rights to property" "belonging to" Mr. Craft. By contrast, the proceeds that the IRS claims here are from *Mrs. Craft's 1992 sale* of the property to a third party. At the time of the sale, she owned the property in fee simple, and accordingly Mr. Craft neither received nor was entitled to these funds.

I.

Title 26 U.S.C. § 6321 provides that a federal tax lien attaches to "all property and rights to property, whether real or personal, belonging to" a delinquent taxpayer. It is uncontested that a federal tax lien itself "creates no property rights but merely attaches consequences, federally defined, to rights created under state law." Consequently, the Government's lien under § 6321 "cannot extend beyond the property interests held by the delinquent taxpayer," United States v. Rodgers, 461 U.S. 677, 690-691, 103 S.Ct. 2132, 76 L.Ed.2d 236 (1983), under state law. Before today, no one disputed that the IRS, by operation of § 6321, "steps into the taxpayer's shoes," and has the same rights as the taxpayer in property or rights to property subject to the lien. I would not expand " 'the nature of the legal interest' " the taxpayer has in the property beyond those interests recognized under state law.

A.

If the Grand Rapids property "belong[ed] to" Mr. Craft under state law prior to the termination of the tenancy by the entirety, the federal tax lien would have attached to the Grand Rapids property. But that is not this case. As the Court recognizes, pursuant to Michigan law, as under English common law, property held as a tenancy by the entirety does not belong to either spouse, but to a single entity composed of the married persons. Neither spouse has "any separate interest in such an estate." Sanford v. Bertrau, 204 Mich. 244, 249, 169 N.W. 880, 882 (1918); see also Long v. Earle, 277 Mich. 505, 517, 269 N.W. 577, 581 (1936) ("Each [spouse] is vested with an entire title and as against the one who attempts alone to convey or incumber such real estate, the other has an absolute title"). An entireties estate constitutes an indivisible "sole tenancy." Because Michigan does not recognize a separate spousal interest in the Grand Rapids property, it did not "belong" to either respondent or her husband individually when the IRS asserted its lien for Mr. Craft's individual tax liability. Thus, the property was not property to which the federal tax lien could attach for Mr. Craft's tax liability.

The Court does not dispute this characterization of Michigan's law with respect to the essential attributes of the tenancy by the entirety estate. However, relying on Drye v. United States, 528 U.S. 49, 59, 120 S.Ct. 474, 145 L.Ed.2d 466 (1999), which in turn relied upon United States v. Irvine, 511 U.S. 224, 114 S.Ct. 1473, 128 L.Ed.2d 168 (1994), and United States v. Mitchell, 403 U.S. 190, 91 S.Ct. 1763, 29 L.Ed.2d

406 (1971), the Court suggests that Michigan's definition of the tenancy by the entirety estate should be overlooked because federal tax law is not controlled by state legal fictions concerning property ownership. But the Court misapprehends the application of *Drye* to this case.

Drye, like *Irvine* and *Mitchell* before it, was concerned not with whether state law recognized "property" as belonging to the taxpayer in the first place, but rather with whether state laws could disclaim or exempt such property from federal tax liability *after* the property interest was created. *Drye* held only that a state-law disclaimer could not retroactively undo a vested right in an estate that the taxpayer already held, and that a federal lien therefore attached to the taxpayer's interest in the estate. 528 U.S., at 61, 120 S.Ct. 474 (recognizing that a disclaimer does not restore the status quo ante because the heir "determines who will receive the property–himself if he does not disclaim, a known other if he does"). Similarly, in *Irvine*, the Court held that a state law allowing an individual to disclaim a gift could not force the Court to be "struck blind" to the fact that the transfer of "property" or "property rights" for which the gift tax was due had already occurred; "*state property transfer rules* do not transfer into federal taxation rules." 511 U.S., at 239–240, 114 S.Ct. 1473 (emphasis added)

Extending this Court's "state law fiction" jurisprudence to determine whether property or rights to property *exist* under state law in the first place works a sea change in the role States have traditionally played in "creating and defining" property interests. By erasing the careful line between state laws that purport to disclaim or exempt property interests after the fact, which the federal tax lien does not respect, and state laws' definition of property and property rights, which the federal tax lien does respect, the Court does not follow *Drye*, but rather creates a new federal common law of property. This contravenes the previously settled rule that the definition and scope of property is left to the States.

B.

That the Grand Rapids property does not belong to Mr. Craft under Michigan law does not end the inquiry, however, since the federal tax lien attaches not only to "property" but also to any "rights to property" belonging to the taxpayer. While the Court concludes that a laundry list of "rights to property" belonged to Mr. Craft as a tenant by the entirety, it does not suggest that the tax lien attached to any of these particular rights.[3] Instead, the Court gathers these rights together and opines that there were sufficient sticks to form a bundle, so that "respondent's husband's interest in the entireties property constituted 'property' or 'rights to property' for the purposes of the federal tax lien statute."

But the Court's "sticks in a bundle" metaphor collapses precisely because of the distinction expressly drawn by the statute, which distinguishes between "property" and "rights to property." The Court refrains from ever stating whether this case involves "property" or "rights to property" even though § 6321 specifically provides that the federal tax lien attaches to "property" and "rights to property" "belonging to" the delinquent taxpayer, and not to an imprecise construct of "individual rights in the estate sufficient to constitute 'property' or 'rights to property' for the purposes of the lien."[4]

Rather than adopt the majority's approach, I would ask specifically, as the statute does, whether Mr. Craft had any particular "rights to property" to which the federal tax lien could attach. He did not.[5] Such

---

3. Nor does the Court explain how such "rights to property" survived the destruction of the tenancy by the entirety, although, for all intents and purposes, it acknowledges that such rights as it identifies exist by virtue of the tenancy by the entirety estate. Even Judge Ryan's concurrence in the Sixth Circuit's first ruling in this matter is best read as making the Federal Government's right to execute its lien dependent upon the factual finding that the conveyance was a fraudulent transaction. See 140 F.3d 638, 648-649 (C.A.6 1998).

4. The Court's reasoning that because a taxpayer has rights to property a federal tax lien can attach not only to those rights but also to the property itself could have far-reaching consequences. As illustration, in the partnership setting as elsewhere, the Government's lien under § 6321 places the Government in no better position than the taxpayer to whom the property belonged: "[F]or example, the lien for a partner's unpaid income taxes attaches to his interest in the firm, not to the firm's assets." Bittker ¶ 44.5[4][a]. Though partnership property currently is "not subject to attachment or execution, except on a claim against the partnership," Rev. Rul. 73-24, 1973-1 Cum. Bull. 602; cf. United States v. Kaufman, 267 U.S. 408, 45 S.Ct. 322, 69 L.Ed. 685 (1925), under the logic of the Court's opinion partnership property could be attached for the tax liability of an individual partner. Like a tenant in a tenancy by the entirety, the partner has significant rights to use, enjoy, and control the partnership property in conjunction with his partners. I see no principled way to distinguish between the propriety of attaching the federal tax lien to partnership property to satisfy the tax liability of a partner, in contravention of current practice, and the propriety of attaching the federal tax lien to tenancy by the entirety property in order to satisfy the tax liability of one spouse, also in contravention of current practice. I do not doubt that a tax lien may attach to a partner's partnership interest to satisfy his individual tax liability, but it is well settled that the lien does not, thereby, attach to property belonging to the partnership. The problem for the IRS in this case is that, unlike a partnership interest, such limited rights that Mr. Craft had in the Grand Rapids property are not the kind of rights to property to which a lien can attach, and the Grand Rapids property itself never "belong[ed] to" him under Michigan law.

5. Even such rights as Mr. Craft arguably had in the Grand Rapids property bear no resemblance to those to which a federal tax lien has ever attached. See W. Elliott, Federal Tax Collections, Liens, and Levies ¶¶ 9.09[3][a]-[f] (2d ed. 1995 and 2000 Cum. Supp.) (hereinafter Elliott) (listing examples of rights to property to which a federal tax lien attaches, such as the right to compel payment; the right to withdraw money from a bank account, or to receive money from accounts receivable; wages earned but not paid; installment payments under a contract of sale of real

"rights to property" that have been subject to the § 6321 lien are valuable and "pecuniary," i.e., they can be attached, and levied upon or sold by the Government.[6] *Drye*, 528 U.S., at 58-60, and n. 7, 120 S.Ct. 474. With such rights subject to lien, the taxpayer's interest has "ripen[ed] into a present estate" of some form and is more than a mere expectancy, and thus the taxpayer has an apparent right "to channel that value to [another]," id., at 61, 120 S.Ct. 474.

In contrast, a tenant in a tenancy by the entirety not only lacks a present divisible vested interest in the property and control with respect to the sale, encumbrance, and transfer of the property, but also does not possess the ability to devise any portion of the property because it is subject to the other's indestructible right of survivorship. This latter fact makes the property significantly different from community property, where each spouse has a present one-half vested interest in the whole, which may be devised by will or otherwise to a person other than the spouse[7].

It is clear that some of the individual rights of a tenant in entireties property are primarily personal, dependent upon the taxpayer's status as a spouse, and similarly not susceptible to a tax lien. For example, the right to use the property in conjunction with one's spouse and to exclude all others appears particularly ill suited to being transferred to another, and to lack "exchangeable value," id., at 56, 120 S.Ct. 474.

Nor do other identified rights rise to the level of "rights to property" to which a § 6321 lien can attach, because they represent, at most, a contingent future interest, or an "expectancy" that has not "ripen[ed] into a present estate." Id., at 60, n. 7, 120 S.Ct. 474. By way of example, the survivorship right wholly depends upon one spouse outliving the other, at which time the survivor gains "substantial rights, in respect of the property, theretofore never enjoyed by [the] survivor." While the Court explains that it is "not necessary to decide whether the right to survivorship alone would qualify as 'property' or 'rights to property' " under § 6321, the facts of this case demonstrate that it would not. Even

---

estate; annuity payments; a beneficiary's rights to payment under a spendthrift trust; a liquor license; an easement; the taxpayer's interest in a timeshare; options; the taxpayer's interest in an employee benefit plan or individual retirement account).

6.   See 26 U.S.C. §§ 6331, 6335-6336.

7.   And it is similarly different from the situation in United States v. Rodgers, 461 U.S. 677, 103 S.Ct. 2132, 76 L.Ed.2d 236 (1983), where the question was not whether a vested property interest in the family home to which the federal tax lien could attach "belong[ed] to" the taxpayer. Rather, in *Rodgers*, the only question was whether the federal tax lien for the husband's tax liability could be *foreclosed* against the property under 26 U.S.C. § 7403, despite his wife's homestead right under state law.

assuming both that the right of survivability continued after the demise of the tenancy estate and that the tax lien could attach to such a contingent future right, creating a lienable interest upon the death of the nonliable spouse, it would not help the IRS here; respondent's husband predeceased her in 1998, and there is no right of survivorship at issue in this case.

Similarly, while one spouse might escape the absolute limitations on individual action with respect to tenancy by the entirety property by obtaining the right to one-half of the property upon divorce, or by agreeing with the other spouse to sever the tenancy by the entirety, neither instance is an event of sufficient certainty to constitute a "right to property" for purposes of § 6321. Finally, while the federal tax lien could arguably have attached to a tenant's right to any "rents, products, income, or profits" of real property held as tenants by the entirety, the Grand Rapids property created no rents, products, income, or profits for the tax lien to attach to.

In any event, all such rights to property, dependent as they are upon the existence of the tenancy by the entirety estate, were likely destroyed by the quitclaim deed that severed the tenancy. Unlike a lien attached to the property itself, which would survive a conveyance, a lien attached to a "right to property" falls squarely within the maxim that "the tax collector not only steps into the taxpayer's shoes but must go barefoot if the shoes wear out." Bittker ¶ 44.5[4][a] (noting that "a state judgment terminating the taxpayer's rights to an asset also extinguishes the federal tax lien attached thereto").

Accordingly, I conclude that Mr. Craft had neither "property" nor "rights to property" to which the federal tax lien could attach.

* * *

Notes and Questions

In Hatchett v. United States, 330 F.3d 875 (6th Cir. 2003), the Sixth Circuit reversed a district court's grant of summary judgment in favor of taxpayers who had filed a wrongful levy suit against the Service under IRC § 7426 to enjoin the tax sale of several properties held by the taxpayers as tenants by the entirety. The district court had based its decision on the Sixth Circuit's decision in Craft v. United States, 140 F.3d 638 (6th Cir. 1998), subsequently overturned by the Supreme Court while *Hatchett* was on appeal. In overturning the district court's decision, the Sixth Circuit quoted Harper v. Virginia Department of Taxation, 509 U.S. 86, 113 S.Ct. 2510, 125 L.Ed.2d 74 (1993), in which the Supreme Court held:

When this Court applies a rule of federal law to the parties before it, that rule is the controlling interpretation of federal law and must be given full retroactive effect in all cases still open on direct review and as to all events, regardless of whether such events predate or postdate our announcement of the rule.

509 U.S. at 97.

Special liens apply to estate and gift taxes under § 6324(a). In the case of the estate tax, the lien arises automatically on the date of death, and continues for ten years or until the lien is either paid in full or becomes unenforceable due to lapse of time. In the case of the gift tax, the lien attaches to the gift and like the estate tax lien, lasts for a ten-year period beginning from the date the gift is made, provided the donor filed a gift tax return.

Note that a money judgment in favor of the United States under 28 U.S.C. § 3201 apparently does not attach to the interest of the spouse in entireties property. This is because 28 U.S.C. § 3201 provides that a judgment "shall create a lien on *all real property* of a judgment creditor." It does not contain the reference under 26 U.S.C. § 6321 to "all property and *rights to* property" that had concerned the Court in *Craft*.

1   Husband and Wife file for divorce, and shortly thereafter the Service assesses a deficiency against Husband. A notice of federal tax lien is filed prior to the entry of the divorce decree. Upon entry of the decree, the court awards certain real property to Wife. The property is subject to the federal tax lien and Wife brings suit to quiet title. Under state statute, all property owned by married persons, whether held individually or in some form of co-ownership, become marital property at the time a divorce action is filed. Under this statute, "Each spouse has a common ownership in marital property which vests at the time of commencement of such action, the extent of the vested interest to be determined and finalized by the court." What result in Wife's suit to quiet title? See Gardner v. United States, 34 F.3d 985 (10th Cir. 1994).

2.   Would it make any difference if the deficiency assessment against Husband had preceded the divorce petition?

2.   Duration of the Lien

The duration of the tax lien is coextensive with the duration of the statutory period for collection. Section 6322 provides that the lien arises when the tax liability is assessed and continues until the liability has been paid or becomes uncollectible because of the lapse of the statute of limitations. Under § 6502, the statute of limitations on collections is 10 years from the date of the assessment (six years for assessments prior to November 5, 1990).

Since the lien does not arise and the collection process does not begin until an assessment has been made, an extension of the limitations period on assessment also will extend the limitations period of the lien and collection. Thus, the suspension of the statute of limitations under § 6503(a) during the 90-day period following the issuance of a notice of deficiency and the further extension during the pendency of a Tax Court proceeding also will extend the statutory period of the lien and collection.

Under § 6503, the statute may be extended under other circumstances as well, such as when the assets of the taxpayer are under the control or custody of a court, when the taxpayer is outside the United States, when the property of a third party has been wrongfully seized or subject to lien, and during the pendency of bankruptcy proceedings.

In order to collect its debt, the government must act within the statutory period either to levy or to proceed in court. Otherwise, the lien will expire at the end of the limitations period. If the Service proceeds in court prior to the expiration of the ten-year statute of limitations on collection and obtains a judgment, either before or after the expiration of that period, will the judgment affect the limitations period of the lien?

Most courts have held that a judgment indefinitely extends the limitations period of the assessment lien, without regard to the limitations period of the judgment. See, e.g., United States v. Jones, 631 F.Supp. 57, 59 (W.D. Mo. 1986) ("When assessment has been reduced to judgment, there is no period of limitations on collection and the lien remains enforceable"); United States v. Colamatteo, 1986 WL 9752 (N.D. Ill) ("Because the tax lien does not merge into the judgment, the tax lien remains enforceable even after the period for bringing suit on the judgment has expired"); United States v. Mandel, 377 F. Supp. 1274, 1277 (S.D. Fla. 1975) (same). Some courts reason that "a state statute of limitation cannot run against the United States unless a federal statute permits." United States v. Overman, 424 F.2d 1142, 1147, n. 7 (9th Cir. 1970).

The Second Circuit in United States v. Hodes, 355 F.2d 746 (2d Cir. 1966) is one of the few courts to hold that the "judgment serves as a measuring rod for the life of the lien." But see Michael I. Saltzman, IRS PRACTICE AND PROCEDURE, ¶ 14.06 (Revised 2d Ed. 2002), noting that while the tax lien does not merge with the judgment, the lien remains enforceable only as long as the judgment is enforceable. The latter view should be the correct one, because as Saltzman notes, "[w]here the judgment arising out of the underlying assessment becomes unenforceable by reason of lapse of time under state law, the extended assessment lien also expires, the purpose for the extension (preserving the government's priority as against other creditors) having been served." Id. This view also is in accordance with the general policy against unlimited statutes of limitation.

Section 6323(g) requires the Service to refile notice of its lien if the lien is extended beyond the ten-year collection period. A failure to refile will result in the loss of priority status for the government with respect to those interests arising after the ten-year period.

Under the 1998 IRS Restructuring and Reform Act, the Service must engage in self-help before seeking a waiver of the limitations period. Thus, the ten-year limitations period on collections may not be extended by agreement if the Service has not levied on the taxpayer's property. An exception applies under an installment agreement. If there has been a levy within the ten-year period, the limitations period may be extended by agreement between the taxpayer and the Service, even though the agreement is made after the ten-year period, if made pursuant to a release of the levy. IRC § 6502(a)(2).

When the Service reduces a tax assessment to judgment, the tax lien is not merged into either the judgment or the judgment lien. Thus, the Service has three methods of collection after a judgement: (1) levy on the tax lien, (2) execute the judgment, or (3) enforce the judgment lien. Both the judgment and the judgment lien are subject to state statutes of limitation.

Questions

1. What is the significance of the nonmerger of the lien and the judgment?

2. Since a judgment often is a more burdensome method of collection, compared with the administrative collection process, why would the government ever consider a judgment instead of an administrative collection action?

3. Priority of Claims

Problems may arise for the government when there are creditors with competing claims. Under the general rule of determining priority of claims, first in time is first in right. Thus, prior claims will take priority over subsequent claims. With respect to federal tax liens, however, there are some exceptions to the general rule.

a) Statutory Priorities and Inchoate Claims

VALLEY BANK OF NEVADA v. CITY OF HENDERSON
United States District Court, District of Nevada, 1981.

528 F.Supp. 907.

CLAIBORNE, CHIEF JUDGE.

* * *

On October 13, 1969, a Water Refunding Agreement dated September 9, 1969, (between the City of Henderson and Bentonite, Inc. * * *) and all proceeds therefrom were pledged and assigned to the Nevada National Bank. The Water Refunding Agreement was based on the City of Henderson Municipal Code which provides that the cost of the water mains installed by a subdivider such as Bentonite, Inc. will be repaid to the subdivider on a quarterly basis upon payment of the connection fees by customers. The Pledge and Assignment provided that the proceeds were to be used as "collateral" to secure a loan. A copy of the Pledge and Assignment was not filed with the Secretary of the State of Nevada.

* * * According to stipulation by the parties, the City of Henderson is currently indebted to Bentonite, Inc. * * * in the sum of $24,828.72, pursuant to the Water and Sewer Refunding Agreements * * *.

On April 16, 1974, Nevada National Bank assigned the Water Refunding Agreement * * * to Valley Bank of Nevada. * * *

On June 24, 1974, the Tax Court entered orders of dismissal in two cases involving Bentonite. In Bentonite, Inc. v. Commissioner, No. 2450-67, the court upheld a deficiency of $61,851.92 against Bentonite, Inc., for the fiscal year ending June 30, 1963. In Bentonite, Inc. v. Commissioner, No. 793-68, the court upheld a deficiency of $12,446.91 for the fiscal year ending June 30, 1964. Pursuant to these decisions, the Commissioner made assessments of $103,232 and $20,005.93 against Bentonite, Inc., for the years 1963 and 1964 on October 25, 1974, and October 29, 1974, respectively. A Notice of Federal Tax Lien covering these assessments was filed with the Secretary of State on March 6, 1975. On July 29, 1980, a Notice of Levy was served upon the City of Henderson demanding the funds being held by the city for the account of Bentonite, Inc.

* * *

* * * [The government's position is] that the tax liens arising as a result of the $103,232 assessment against Bentonite, Inc. on October 25, 1974, and the $20,005.93 assessment against Bentonite Inc. on October 29, 1974, are entitled to priority over the unperfected and inchoate interests of each of the other claimants to the interpleader fund.

* * *

DID THE TAX LIENS * * * GIVE THE UNITED STATES PRIORITY OVER THE OTHER CLAIMANTS TO THE INTERPLEADER FUNDS?

The question of when a federal tax lien has priority over a security interest created under state law must be answered by reference to federal law. Nevada Rock and Sand Co. v. United States, 376 F.Supp. 161, 163 (D. Nev. 1974).

While some have characterized the subject of federal tax liens as being somewhat complex, the complexities of this area of law fade if a step by step analysis is made as to the question of who has priority over the fund in issue.

The initial premise, not challenged by any of the parties to this action, is that the United States acquires a lien against all property and rights to property belonging to a taxpayer upon the assessment of unpaid taxes and notice of demand for payment of same being made upon taxpayer. Section 6321 of the Internal Revenue Code of 1954 provides:

> If any person liable to pay any tax neglects or refuses to pay the same after demand, the amount (including any interest, additional amount, addition to tax, or assessable penalty, together with any costs that may accrue in addition thereto) shall be a lien in favor of the United States upon all property and rights to property, whether real or personal, belonging to such person.

Section 6322 of the Code provides:

> Unless another date is specifically fixed by law, the lien imposed by section 6321 shall arise at the time the assessment is made and shall continue until the liability for the amount so assessed (or a judgment against the taxpayer arising out of such liability) is satisfied or becomes unenforceable by reason of lapse of time.

Here the United States obtained liens against Bentonite, Inc., on October 25, 1974, and October 29, 1974.

These liens immediately attached to all property or rights to property belonging to Bentonite, Inc. However, this lien was not valid against any purchaser, holder of a security interest, mechanic's lienor, or judgment lien creditor until March 6, 1975, when a Notice of Federal Tax Lien was filed with the Secretary of State. See Code § 6323(a) and (f).

DID B. INC. HAVE PROPERTY RIGHTS TO PROPERTY
IN THE REFUNDING AGREEMENT WHEN
THE FEDERAL TAX LIENS ATTACHED?

Valley Bank argues that Bentonite, Inc. had no property or property rights in the refunding agreement at the time the tax liens attached in October, 1974, because it had already assigned its rights to Valley Bank of Nevada. The same factual situation arose in *Nevada Rock and Sand Company v. United States*, supra, where the assignee was to receive the proceeds from the contract rights directly, instead of through the assignor. The same argument was made that there did not exist a property right to which a tax lien could attach since the assignor had assigned its interest. The court firmly rejected this argument and held that there was an interest to which the tax lien could attach.

While the language of the May 24, 1972, "Assignment" could indicate an outright sale, the circumstances surrounding the assignment, the understanding of the parties and the subsequent conduct of the parties manifest the reality of the transaction as a financing arrangement where the agreement was used as collateral.

DID VALLEY BANK QUALIFY AS A "HOLDER OF A SECURITY
INTEREST" UNDER SECTION 6323 OF THE CODE AND NOT
ENTITLED TO PRIORITY OVER THE UNITED STATES?

As noted previously, a tax lien attaches to all property or rights to property of a taxpayer at the moment when an assessment is made. That is not to say, however, that a creditor of the taxpayer cannot obtain priority over the United States after the lien has arisen. The "blueprint" on how to obtain priority is contained in § 6323(a) of the Code which provides:

> The lien imposed by section 6321 shall not be valid as against any purchaser, holder of a security interest, mechanic's lienor, or judgment lien creditor until notice thereof which meets the requirements of subsection (f) has been filed by the Secretary.[2]

---

2.   Prior to 1966, § 6323 provided that mortgages, pledges, purchasers, and judgment creditors were entitled to priority over unfiled federal tax liens. In 1966, Congress amended the section and included holders of security interests, which covers others than mortgagees and pledgees, among the classes of persons entitled to prevail over unfiled federal tax liens. One of the major purposes of the revision was to harmonize the provisions of the Internal Revenue Code with the provisions of the Uniform Commercial Code. As the Senate Committee Report states (S.Rep.No.1708, 89th Cong., 2d Sess., p. 2 (1966-2 Cum.Bull. 876) U.S.Code Cong. & Admin.News, 1966, p. 3722:

> This bill is in part an attempt to conform the lien provisions of the internal revenue laws to the concepts developed in the Uniform Commercial Code. It represents an effort to adjust

Here the Notice of Lien was filed on March 6, 1975. Thus, the question is whether Valley Bank or any of the other parties to this action qualified as a "holder of a security interest" prior to March 6, 1975.[3] A holder of a security interest is defined in § 6323(h) of the Code as follows:

(1) Security Interest.-The term "security interest" means any interest in property acquired by contract for the purpose of securing payment or performance of an obligation or indemnifying against loss or liability. A security interest exists at any time (A) if, at such time, the property is in existence and the interest has become protected under local law against a subsequent judgment lien arising out of an unsecured obligation, and (B) to the extent that, at such time, the holder has parted with money or money's worth.

The Water Refunding Agreement was assigned to Valley Bank on July 16, 1974. The remaining Water and Sewer Refunding Agreements were assigned to Valley Bank on May 24, 1972, (although the bank's security interest in these agreements did not "attach" until January 2, 1973).

The interest obtained by Valley Bank via these assignments, however, was not a security interest within the meaning of § 6323(h)(1), inasmuch as its rights were not protected under local law against a judgment lien arising out of an unsecured obligation.

To obtain a "security interest" sufficient to defeat an unfiled federal tax lien, the creditor must perfect its security interest against a hypothetical judgment lien creditor prior to the time the United States files a Notice of a Federal Tax Lien.[5]

* * *

---

the provisions in the internal revenue laws relating to the collection of taxes of delinquent persons to the more recent developments in commercial practice (permitted and protected under State law) and to deal with a multitude of technical problems which have arisen over the past 50 years.

Congress did not, however, extend priority to all persons asserting security interests under local law, but, rather, limited the class to those persons who had taken steps under local law to protect their interests. United States v. Trigg, 465 F.2d 1264, 1269-1270 (8th Cir. 1972).

3. There is no claim by any of the parties to this action that they should be classified as purchasers, mechanic's lienors, or judgment lien creditors.

5. In addition, it does not matter whether the "hypothetical lien creditor test" or the "subjective knowledge lien creditor test" is used, since there has been no evidence introduced that the Internal Revenue Service had knowledge of Valley Bank's security interests when the liens were acquired on October 25, 1974, and October 29, 1974. Contrary to Valley Bank's assertion at trial, the knowledge of the United States under this test is measured at the time it became a lien creditor against Bentonite, Inc. Such event occurred on October 25, 1974, not on the date of levy on July 29, 1980, as discussed.

ARE EQUITABLE LIENS INCHOATE LIENS AND NOT VALID AGAINST PERFECTED FEDERAL TAX LIENS?

The federal rule "first in time first in right" determines whether a federal tax lien under § 6321, Title 26, United States Code or a competing lien created by state law has priority. United States v. City of New Britain, 347 U.S. 81, 74 S.Ct. 367, 98 L.Ed. 520 (1954).

Under this basic federal priority standard, a federal tax lien takes priority over a state-created lien unless the state lien is specific and perfected in the federal sense.

As part of this rule, the Supreme Court has announced that a state of local lien must be "choate" to defeat the federal lien. This is referred to as the doctrine of choateness. In order for a state of local lien to be "choate" it must meet the three tests of (1) certainty of the lienor, (2) certainty of the property subject to the lien, and (3) certainty of the amount of the lien. In addition, the Supreme Court has indicated that in order to be choate, the state of local lien must also be enforceable summarily without the necessity of a judicial proceeding. United States v. Vermont, 377 U.S. 351, 84 S.Ct. 1267, 12 L.Ed.2d 370 (1964); United States v. Security Trust & Savings Bank, 340 U.S. 47, 71 S.Ct. 111, 95 L.Ed. 53 (1950).

In Bank of Nevada v. United States, 251 F.2d at 823-824, the Ninth Circuit specifically rejected a contention by the appellant bank that an equitable lien held by the bank in the form of a right of set-off could prime a federal tax lien. Thus, in this Circuit, the rule espoused in Morrison Flying Service v. Deming National Bank, 404 F.2d 856 (10th Cir. 1968), and relied upon by Valley Bank is clearly not followed.[6]

* * *

ARE THE LIENS OF THE UNITED STATES AGAINST BENTONITE, INC. VALID?

Both the Valley Bank and Bentonite, Inc. claim that the liens against Bentonite, Inc. arising on October 25, 1974 and October 29, 1974, have lapsed and are therefore invalid. This contention is also untenable.

Section 6502(a) of the Code provides in pertinent part:

Length of Period.-Where the assessment of any tax imposed by this title has been made within the period of limitation properly

---

6. The decision in *Morrison Flying Service* was made without any discussion of the choateness doctrine. Moreover, it appears that the subcontractor in whose favor the decision was entered could not perfect his lien. Such is clearly not the case here, since there is no dispute that Valley Bank could easily have perfected its security interest in this case.

applicable thereto, such tax may be collected by levy or by proceeding in court, but only if the levy is made or the proceeding begun-(1) within 6 years after the assessment of the tax.

On July 29, 1980, within the six year period provided for in the statute, the Internal Revenue Service levied upon the City of Henderson with respect to the tax assessments against Bentonite, Inc.

Both the Valley Bank and Bentonite, Inc. erroneously argue that the levy is somehow to be considered the filing of a lien. This position has absolutely no foundation in law. This Court differentiates between the attachment of the liens (which occurred in October, 1974) and the administrative procedure of levying upon the debtor. The latter event merely permits the Internal Revenue Service to preserve its lien with respect to any funds due from the City of Henderson to Bentonite, Inc., pursuant to any agreements between the City and Bentonite as of the date of the levy. The former event provides the key date for determining priority issues, along with the March 6, 1975 date of the filing of the notice of these tax liens.

Moreover, the institution of this action and the demand that the interpleaded funds be turned over to the United States set forth in the Government's answer served on July 23, 1979, satisfies the requirement in § 6502(a) that the tax may be collected by a proceeding begun within six years [eds: now ten years] after the assessment of the tax.

CONCLUSION

The City of Henderson holds certain sums for the account of Bentonite, Inc. pursuant to the six water and sewer refunding agreements. At trial, the City of Henderson has abandoned its claim to any of the proceeds of the fund in issue. The United States and Valley Bank are not the only two claimants to the fund. However, the only party to have a perfected lien on this fund is the United States. Valley Bank could have perfected its security interest arising from the assignments of the water and sewer refunding agreements. All it had to do was to file a financing statement covering these assignments with the Secretary of State of the State of Nevada prior to March 6, 1975. Failing to have taken this simple step, Valley Bank cannot now claim priority to the interpleaded fund.

* * *

Notes and Questions

Although the *Valley Bank* court held that the pledge and assignment of the Water Refunding Agreement as collateral constituted the transfer of property or a property right, thus permitting the federal tax lien to attach to the interest, not all courts adhere to this view. See In Re Halprin, 280 F.2d 407 (3d Cir. 1960) (assignment of sums to become due under executory contract did not constitute property of the bankrupt taxpayer; thus tax lien could not attach).

1. What is the "doctrine of choateness" and when does it apply? See United States v. Security Trust & Savings Bank, 340 U.S. 47, 71 S.Ct. 111, 95 L.Ed. 53 (1950).

2. What exceptions to the general rule of priority are evident from the *Valley Bank* case?

3. In footnote 2, the court excerpts a portion of the Senate Finance Committee Report which states: "Congress did not, however, extend priority to all persons asserting security interests under local law, but, rather, limited the class to those persons who had taken steps under local law to protect their interests." An exception under § 6323 applies to purchasers of personal property, who are not required to record their interests but who have priority over unfiled federal tax liens. Do purchasers of personal property fit within the category discussed by the Senate Finance Committee? Under what rationale are they included under § 6323?

b. *Superpriorities*

Section 6323(b) lists ten categories of "superpriorities," i.e., creditors whose liens have priority even over a perfected tax lien. These categories are: (1) purchasers and holders of security interests in securities without actual notice or knowledge of the existence of the tax lien, (2) purchasers of motor vehicles without actual notice or knowledge of the tax lien, (3) personal property purchased at retail, (4) personal property of less than $1,000 purchased in casual sale, (5) personal property subject to a possessory lien, provided the holder has been continuously in possession of the property from the time the lien arose, (6) real property tax and special assessment liens, (7) mechanics lien for repairs and improvements made to residential real property, (8) attorney's liens, (9) certain insurance contracts, and (10) deposit secured loans.

UNITED STATES v. RIPA

United States Court of Appeals, Second Circuit, 2003.
323 F.3d 73.

SACK, CIRCUIT JUDGE.

Defendants Glenn H. Ripa and Benedetto Romano appeal from a decision of the United States District Court for the Western District of New York (John T. Curtin, Judge) granting summary judgment to the United States in an interpleader action brought by the United States to determine rights among the parties to a fund in the amount of $491,236.69. The fund comprises $359,500 in United States currency that the United States Customs Service seized from Romano on November 18, 1983, when Romano attempted to carry it across the border into Canada without completing the required currency reporting form, plus interest since paid by the government thereon. Pursuant to the currency reporting statute, the United States sought civil forfeiture of the sum. The suit was suspended while the government brought an unsuccessful criminal prosecution against Romano for tax evasion. Finally, in 1998, some fifteen years after the seizure, Romano prevailed against the government in the civil forfeiture suit. Because of several tax liens against Romano totaling over $1.5 million, including a lien on the taxes assessed on the currency seized in 1983, the district court ordered the $359,500 plus interest deposited with the clerk of the district court. The court permitted the government to bring a suit in the nature of an interpleader to effect the proper distribution of the fund.

The basic principle governing cases assessing the priority of federal tax liens is "first in time, first in right." The government, which created a lien on the sum on the same day it was seized in 1983, therefore asserts a right to first priority in the distribution of the money. Because the interest and penalties on the taxes owed to the government by Romano now exceed the total amount in the fund, the government asserts a claim to the entire fund. Ripa, Romano's attorney, asserts a contrary claim to approximately one-third of the fund, as a contingency-fee payment for his representation of Romano in the forfeiture proceeding. Ripa contends that his attorney's lien has "superpriority" over the government's tax lien under a provision of the Internal Revenue Code (the "Code" or "Tax Code") that allows certain attorneys' liens to take priority over prior government liens. See 26 U.S.C. § 6323(b)(8). In response, the government argues that section 6323(b)(8) does not apply here because the provision contains an exception to attorney's lien superpriority in cases involving a "judgment * * * of a claim or of a cause of action against the United States." Id. Because we agree with the government that that exception applies here, we conclude that section 6323(b)(8) is inapplicable. Ripa therefore has no basis for asserting priority over the prior government tax lien.

Because the government's claim far exceeds the amount deposited by the government in the interpleader action, we affirm the district court's grant of summary judgment to the government and order disbursement of the fund to the government pursuant thereto. * * *

The defendants characterize their travails as "Kafkaesque." Our rehearsal of the facts * * * tends to support that view. The United States Customs Service wrongfully seized a large sum of money from Romano, which he alleges made it impossible for him to pay taxes he owed the IRS on those funds. Although the government paid interest on the seized money, it did so at a rate so low in comparison to the penalties and interest the IRS was charging him on the unpaid taxes that, ultimately, the amount Romano owed the government in taxes and interest on the fund far exceeded the amount in the fund. Meanwhile, the civil proceedings over title to the seized funds were delayed by related criminal prosecutions, which also eventually proved meritless. When Romano finally prevailed in the civil suit over the seized currency, his money had been eaten up by taxes and penalties on it that, he says, he could not have paid because the government had wrongfully seized his money. We conclude, nonetheless, that Romano has not presented us, as an Article III court, with a legal basis upon which to deliver him from these circumstances. We are no more able to relieve Romano of the absurdity of his situation than we are able to relieve Kafka's Joseph K of the absurdity of his. See Franz Kafka, The Trial (Willa & Edwin Muir, trans., Alfred A. Knopf, rev. ed.1992).

* * *

DISCUSSION
* * *

II. The Priority of the Liens

Federal law determines the relative priority of a federal tax lien. Federal law follows the common law rule that a lien "first in time is the first in right." United States v. City of New Britain, 347 U.S. 81, 85,74 S.Ct. 367, 98 L.Ed. 520 (1954). It is undisputed that the IRS "Notice of Federal Tax Lien," filed November 18, 1983, was the first lien filed with respect to the fund at issue in this litigation. The IRS's lien therefore has priority under the first-in-time rule. Unless the defendants can identify an applicable exception or overriding principle, then, the fund must be released to the government.

Ripa asserts that his attorney's lien has priority over the federal tax lien under a statutory exception to the first-in-time rule: the Code's provision for superpriority of some attorneys' liens, 26 U.S.C. § 6323(b)(8).[8] Section 6323(b)(8) was established by the Federal Tax Lien Act of 1966, "the first comprehensive revision and modernization of the provisions of the internal revenue laws concerned with the relationship of Federal tax liens to the interests of other creditors." The Act's amendments to the Code created superpriority for various creditors, such as mechanics, on the theory that the work of these creditors was "likely to add to the value of the property" to the ultimate benefit of the government. Similarly, the Act added a provision establishing super-priority for attorneys' liens under certain circumstances. Specifically, section 6323(b)(8) provides that an existing federal tax lien will not be valid [w]ith respect to a judgment or other amount in settlement of a claim or of a cause of action, as against an attorney who, under local law, holds a lien upon or a contract enforceable against such judgment or amount, to the extent of his reasonable compensation for obtaining such judgment or procuring such settlement * * *. Id. Ripa argues that under this provision he is entitled to superpriority for his reasonable fees accrued during his successful defense of Romano in the forfeiture action.

But section 6323(b)(8) contains an exception to the superpriority of attorneys' liens:

> [T]his paragraph shall not apply to any judgment or amount in settlement of a claim or of a cause of action against the United States to the extent that the United States offsets such judgment or amount against any liability of the taxpayer to the United States.

Id. The question, then, is whether the forfeiture suit resulted in a "judgment * * * of a claim or of a cause of action against the United States" within the meaning of section 6323(b)(8). Ripa argues that, because a federal district court has determined that the money was wrongfully seized from Romano, and the money was at all times Romano's, never belonged to the United States, and the judgment was therefore not "against the United States."

Ripa's argument finds support in a decision by the United States District Court for the District of Massachusetts, United States v. Murray,

---

8.　For the purposes of this discussion, we assume without deciding that Ripa has satisfied the following conditions that courts have identified for the application of section 6323(b)(8): "(1) that a fund was created out of a judgment or settlement of a claim; (2) that local law would recognize the existence of a lien; and (3) that the amount of the lien reflects the extent to which [the lawyer's] efforts 'reasonably contributed to the award.' " See Markham v. Fay, 1993 WL 160604, at *6, (D.Mass. May 5, 1993) (citations omitted). We also need not and do not address the question, raised by the government, whether Ripa has properly assessed the sum that he would be owed from the fund, were section 6323(b)(8) to apply.

963 F.Supp. 52 (D.Mass.1997). The *Murray* court reasoned that a successful defense against a currency forfeiture action by the United States does not result in a judgment "against the United States" within the meaning of section 6323(b)(8) because "[t]he money belonged to [the defendant] all along." Id. at 56. The return of the money thus does not "require the United States to remove any money from its coffers." Id. Two other district courts in addition to the district court in this action, however, have considered the question and held otherwise. See United States v. $319,820.00 in United States Currency, 634 F.Supp. 700, 704 & n. 5 (N.D.Ga.1986); Brooks v. United States, 271 F.Supp. 671, 674 (E.D.Ky.1967).

Statutory analysis begins with the plain meaning of the statute. If the text of a statute is ambiguous, then we must construct an interpretation consistent with the primary purpose of the statute as a whole.

The plain language of section 6323(b)(8) does not supply a clear answer to the question before us. As noted above, we understand the question to be whether a judgment for the defendant in a forfeiture suit brought by the government is a "judgment * * * of a claim or of a cause of action against the United States." This language contains several ambiguities. The phrase "against the United States" could modify "judgment," "claim," "cause of action," or some combination of the three, while each of the terms has more than one possible meaning. The district court interpreted "against the United States" to modify "judgment"– asking whether "the return of the seized funds constitute[s] a 'judgment against the United States,' "– and answered the question in the affirmative. Though we disagree with the district court's construction of the statutory language, we are unable to resolve the ambiguity in the language, and we therefore interpret the statute in accordance with its purpose. We conclude that the statute does not give superpriority to the attorney's lien Ripa asserts.

As noted, the district court's formulation of section 6323(b)(8) implies that the prepositional phrase "against the United States" modifies "judgment." But the phrase "against the United States" must modify "claim or * * * cause of action" because the words "judgment" and "amount" are established as equivalents in the later phrase "offsets such judgment or amount." Thus, "judgment" is opposed to "amount in settlement," and the entire phrase might be aptly punctuated as follows: "this paragraph shall not apply to any judgment [–] or amount in settlement [–] of a claim or of a cause of action against the United States." The key question here is therefore properly framed as whether the suit is one involving an award resulting from a "claim or * * * cause of action against the United States."

Even under our reframing of the provision, the plain language remains ambiguous. On the one hand, a "judgment * * * of a claim or of a cause of action against the United States" could encompass the result in a forfeiture suit, such as Romano's, in which the taxpayer and the government were hostile parties in a lawsuit styled as a proceeding against the money itself. On the other hand, the scope of a "judgment * * * of a claim or of a cause of action against the United States" might be limited to those suits in which a taxpayer brings an action against the United States as the defendant to assert a claim to property owned by the United States. These two readings—and perhaps others—are possible because the terms "claim," "cause of action," and "against" all have multiple meanings. For example, "claim" and "cause of action" have overlapping meanings, including a right to something and a demand or suit filed in pursuit of something.[10] Moreover, if we read "against" as merely hostile or adverse, then the phrase "against the United States" encompasses any action in which the United States is an adverse party. But we could also read "against the United States" to connote an active challenge to governmental action or property, rather than an attempt, as here, simply to reacquire one's own property, by defending against a claim to that property asserted by the government. Because the plain language of the provision is thus ambiguous, we turn to its purpose to try to give the appropriate meaning to its words.

In contrast to its plain language, the purpose of section 6323(b)(8) seems clear. As the district court cogently observed: [T]he primary purpose of the statute was to "collect[ ] taxes, not bestow [ ] benefits on

---

10. The first three definitions of "claim" in Black's Law Dictionary display both meanings:

    1. The aggregate of operative facts giving rise to a right enforceable by a court * * *.

    2. The assertion of an existing right; any right to payment or to an equitable remedy, even if contingent or provisional * * *.

    3. A demand for money or property to which one asserts a right * * *.

    4. An interest or remedy recognized at law; the means by which a person can obtain a privilege, possession, or enjoyment of a right or thing; CAUSE OF ACTION.

Black's Law Dictionary 240 (7th ed.1999).

    The first two definitions of "claim" in Webster's New International Dictionary present two meanings that parallel those offered in Black's. The first definition includes the phrases "an authoritative or challenging request: DEMAND" and "a demand for compensation, benefits, or payment." Webster's New International Dictionary 414 (3d ed.1981). By contrast, the second definition of "claim" is simply "a privilege to something: RIGHT." Id. As apparent from the fourth definition of "claim" in Black's, "cause of action" may be synonymous with "claim"; it also may mean the basis of a lawsuit or the lawsuit itself:

    1. A group of operative facts giving rise to one or more bases for suing; a factual situation that entitles one person to obtain a remedy in court from another person; CLAIM * * *. 2. A legal theory of a lawsuit * * *. 3. Loosely, a lawsuit. Black's Law Dictionary 214 (7th ed.1999).

attorneys." Montavon v. United States, 864 F.Supp. 519, 523 (E.D.Va.1994) (quoting Hill, Christopher, & Phillips, P.C. v. United States Postal Service, 535 F.Supp. 804, 810 (D.D.C.1982)). "Congress intended § 6323(b)(8) to encourage attorneys to bring suits and obtain judgments that would put their clients in a position to be better able to pay their tax liabilities." Consequently, "the attorney receives no protective consideration for his efforts on behalf of a client with a tax liability if the funds to satisfy that liability are going to come from a judgment against the Government." Hill, Christopher, 535 F.Supp. at 809. When a lawyer represents a taxpayer against a party other than the government, the lawyer is working to reach a result that will, if successful, enlarge the amount of funds available to the government to satisfy its tax claim. The lawyer is then probably acting in the government's best interests. If the lawyer cannot be paid out of the amount collected, however, he or she is unlikely to pursue the claim in the first place and the government is, potentially, that much the poorer. If the lawyer represents a taxpayer whose interests are adverse to the government, however, the funds available to the government will not be enhanced by the lawyer's services.

In light of the purpose of section 6323(b)(8), then, we see no reason to read "a judgment * * * of a claim or of a cause of action against the United States" to exclude the monetary award in the forfeiture suit, in which Romano and the United States had adverse claims to the disputed fund. Thus, the exception to superpriority of attorneys' liens in judgments of claims against the United States applies to Ripa's lien for his fees incurred when defending Romano's claim to his money in the forfeiture action.

* * *

We conclude that the district court correctly held that Ripa can assert no priority on behalf of his attorney's lien over the federal tax liens under section 6323(b)(8).

* * *

We conclude, then, that the matter that we may address in this interpleader action is limited to who has the right to the money that has been paid into court. A judgment by a federal district court correctly established Romano's debt to the IRS of $169,981, plus statutory interest, and it is undisputed that that amount, together with penalties, now exceeds the amount of the fund. Because we also agree with the district court that Ripa cannot successfully claim priority over the federal tax lien under section 6323(b)(8), we affirm the district court's judgment that the fund should be released to the United States.

With our conclusion that the government's claim to the fund prevails, our task is complete. We do not doubt that the question of whether it is right and just for the government to obtain the money is an important one. It is, however, a question for the IRS, the Tax Court, and Congress. It is not before us on this appeal.

CONCLUSION

For the foregoing reasons, we affirm the judgment of the district court.

Notes and Questions

Note that superpriority status may be defeated if the claimant has actual notice or knowledge of the tax lien. IRC § 6323(b). This does not apply to the superpriority status of attorneys' fees, however. Thus, actual notice or knowledge of the tax lien will not defeat the superpriority status of a later lien for attorneys' fees.

Where superpriority status applies, the amount of the lien is limited to reasonable attorney's fees, determined in accordance with local law, and under the facts and circumstances of each individual case. Note that the superpriority status of attorneys' liens does not extend to fees and expenses paid to expert witnesses.

The Service takes the position that a superpriority for attorney's fees arises only where the attorney's efforts have created a fund for the client, rather than where the attorney's efforts have merely protected the client's interest or property from the claims of others. This position was rejected by the district court of the District of Columbia, however, in Chicago Title Insurance Co. v. Kern, 81-2 USTC ¶ 9696 where the suit involved a defense in an interpleader action. The court held that the liens of attorneys who "did work to garner taxpayer funds which were the subject of a government lien" were entitled to superpriority status. Id.

1. Should Ripa's one-third contingent fee arrangement cause his claim to be regarded as inchoate?

2. What is the rationale behind superpriority status?

3. Do interest and penalties on the amount secured by a nontax lien assume priority over a federal tax lien if the secured amount assumes such priority? See IRC § 6323(e).

Problem

Blackacre is sold at a foreclosure sale for $50,000 to satisfy the following claims: a $2,500 state property tax lien that was filed six months ago, a $30,000 mortgage lien that arose five years ago when the property was purchased, a $6,000 mechanic's lien for improvements done to the property eight months ago, and a $20,000 federal tax lien that arose from a deficiency assessed ten months ago but which was filed two months ago. How will the $50,000 be distributed?

c. *Claims Arising in Insolvency Outside of Bankruptcy*

If a taxpayer is insolvent but has not declared bankruptcy, special rules may apply to give the government additional priority. Under 31 U.S.C. § 3713, claims of the federal government shall be paid first when (1) an insolvent debtor transfers property in a collective creditor proceeding outside of bankruptcy and (2) when the estate of a deceased debtor does not have sufficient assets to pay all creditors. Section 3713 does not create an additional lien, but exists separate and apart from the lien provisions under Title 26. A fiduciary who transfers assets in contravention of the priority under § 3713 will be personally liable to the government to the extent of the value of the property transferred.

UNITED STATES v. ESTATE OF ROMANI
United States Supreme Court, 1998.
523 U.S. 517, 118 S.Ct. 1478, 140 L.Ed.2d 710.

JUSTICE STEVENS delivered the opinion of the Court.

The federal priority statute, 31 U.S.C. § 3713(a), provides that a claim of the United States Government "shall be paid first" when a decedent's estate cannot pay all of its debts.[1] The question presented is whether that statute requires that a federal tax claim be given

---

1.   § 3713. Priority of Government claims

"(a)(1) A claim of the United States Government shall be paid first when—

"(A) a person indebted to the Government is insolvent and—

"(i) the debtor without enough property to pay all debts makes a voluntary assignment of property;

"(ii) property of the debtor, if absent, is attached; or

"(iii) an act of bankruptcy is committed; or

"(B) the estate of a deceased debtor, in the custody of the executor or administrator, is not enough to pay all debts of the debtor.

"(2) This subsection does not apply to a case under title 11."

31 U.S.C. § 3713. The present statute is the direct descendent of § 3466 of the Revised Statutes, which had been codified in 31 U.S.C. § 191.

preference over a judgment creditor's perfected lien on real property even though such a preference is not authorized by the Federal Tax Lien Act of 1966, 26 U.S.C.§ 6321 et seq.

I.

On January 25, 1985, the Court of Common Pleas of Cambria County, Pennsylvania, entered a judgment for $400,000 in favor of Romani Industries, Inc., and against Francis J. Romani. The judgment was recorded in the clerk's office and therefore, as a matter of Pennsylvania law, it became a lien on all of the defendant's real property in Cambria County. Thereafter, the Internal Revenue Service filed a series of notices of tax liens on Mr. Romani's property. The claims for unpaid taxes, interest, and penalties described in those notices amounted to approximately $490,000.

When Mr. Romani died on January 13, 1992, his entire estate consisted of real estate worth only $53,001. Because the property was encumbered by both the judgment lien and the federal tax liens, the estate's administrator sought permission from the Court of Common Pleas to transfer the property to the judgment creditor, Romani Industries, in lieu of execution. The Federal Government acknowledged that its tax liens were not valid as against the earlier judgment lien; but, giving new meaning to Franklin's aphorism that "in this world nothing can be said to be certain, except death and taxes,"[2] it opposed the transfer on the ground that the priority statute (§ 3713) gave it the right to "be paid first."

The Court of Common Pleas overruled the Government's objection and authorized the conveyance. The Superior Court of Pennsylvania affirmed, and the Supreme Court of the State also affirmed. 547 Pa. 41, 688 A.2d 703 (1997). That court first determined that there was a "plain inconsistency" between § 3713, which appears to give the United States "absolute priority" over all competing claims, and the Tax Lien Act of 1966, which provides that the federal tax lien "shall not be valid" against judgment lien creditors until a prescribed notice has been given. Id., at

---

    2.   Letter of Nov. 13, 1789, to Jean Baptiste Le Roy, in 10 The Writings of Benjamin Franklin 69 (A. Smyth ed.1907). As is often the case, the original meaning of the aphorism is clarified somewhat by its context: "Our new Constitution is now established, and has an appearance that promises permanency; but in this world nothing can be said to be certain, except death and taxes." Ibid.

45, 688 A.2d, at 705.[3] Then, relying on the reasoning in United States v. Kimbell Foods, Inc., 440 U.S. 715, 99 S.Ct. 1448, 59 L.Ed.2d 711(1979), which had noted that the Tax Lien Act of 1966 modified the Federal Government's preferred position in the tax area and recognized the priority of many state claims over federal tax liens, the court concluded that the 1966 Act had the effect of limiting the operation of § 3713 as to tax debts.

The decision of the Pennsylvania Supreme Court conflicts with two federal Court of Appeals decisions, Kentucky ex rel. Luckett v. United States, 383 F.2d 13 (C.A.6 1967), and Nesbitt v. United States, 622 F.2d 433 (C.A.9 1980). Moreover, in its petition for certiorari, the Government submitted that the decision is inconsistent with our holding in Thelusson v. Smith, 2 Wheat. 396, 4 L.Ed. 271 (1817), and with the admonition that " '[o]nly the plainest inconsistency would warrant our finding an implied exception to the operation of so clear a command as that of [31 U.S.C. § 3713],' " United States v. Key, 397 U.S. 322, 324-325, 90 S.Ct. 1049, 1051, 25 L.Ed.2d 340 (1970) (quoting United States v. Emory, 314 U.S. 423, 433, 62 S.Ct. 317, 322-323, 86 L.Ed. 315 (1941)). We granted certiorari to resolve the conflict and to consider whether *Thelusson*, *Key*, or any of our other cases construing the priority statute requires a different result.

II.

There is no dispute about the meaning of two of the three statutes that control the disposition of this case. It is therefore appropriate to comment on the Pennsylvania lien statute and the Federal Tax Lien Act

---

3.   The Federal Tax Lien Act of 1966, 26 U.S.C. § 6321 et seq., provides in pertinent part:
  "§ 6321. Lien for taxes

"If any person liable to pay any tax neglects or refuses to pay the same after demand, the amount (including any interest, additional amount, addition to tax, or assessable penalty, together with any costs that may accrue in addition thereto) shall be a lien in favor of the United States upon all property and rights to property, whether real or personal, belonging to such person."

"§ 6323. Validity and priority against certain persons

  "(a) Purchasers, holders of security interests, mechanic's lienors, and judgment lien creditors

  "The lien imposed by section 6321 shall not be valid as against any purchaser, holder of a security interest, mechanic's lienor, or judgment lien creditor until notice thereof which meets the requirements of subsection (f) has been filed by the Secretary."

Section 6323(f)(1)(A)(i) provides that the required notice "shall be filed[,] * * * [i]n the case of real property, in one office within the State (or the county, or other governmental subdivision), as designated by the laws of such State, in which the property subject to the lien is situated." If the State has not designated such an office, notice is to be filed with the clerk of the federal district court "for the judicial district in which the property subject to the lien is situated." § 6323(f)(1)(B).

before considering the applicability of the priority statute to property encumbered by an antecedent judgment creditor's lien.

The Pennsylvania statute expressly provides that a judgment shall create a lien against real property when it is recorded in the county where the property is located. 42 Pa. Cons.Stat. § 4303(a) (1995). After the judgment has been recorded, the judgment creditor has the same right to notice of a tax sale as a mortgagee.[4] The recording in one county does not, of course, create a lien on property located elsewhere. In this case, however, it is undisputed that the judgment creditor acquired a valid lien on the real property in Cambria County before the judgment debtor's death and before the Government served notice of its tax liens. Romani Industries' lien was "perfected in the sense that there is nothing more to be done to have a choate lien–when the identity of the lienor, the property subject to the lien, and the amount of the lien are established." United States v. City of New Britain, 347 U.S. 81, 84, 74 S.Ct. 367, 369, 98 L.Ed. 520 (1954).

The Federal Government's right to a lien on a delinquent taxpayer's property has been a part of our law at least since 1865. Originally the lien applied, without exception, to all property of the taxpayer immediately upon the neglect or failure to pay the tax upon demand.[6] An unrecorded tax lien against a delinquent taxpayer's property was valid even against a bona fide purchaser who had no notice of the lien. United States v. Snyder, 149 U.S. 210, 213-215, 13 S.Ct. 846, 847-848, 37 L.Ed. 705 (1893). In 1913, Congress amended the statute to provide that the federal tax lien "shall not be valid as against any mortgagee, purchaser,

---

4.   The Pennsylvania Supreme Court has elaborated:

"We must now decide whether judgment creditors are also entitled to personal or general notice by the [County Tax Claim] Bureau as a matter of due process of law.

"Judgment liens are a product of centuries of statutes which authorize a judgment creditor to seize and sell the land of debtors at a judicial sale to satisfy their debts out of the proceeds of the sale. The judgment represents a binding judicial determination of the rights and duties between the parties, and establishes their debtor-creditor relationship for all the world to notice when the judgment is recorded in a Prothonotary's Office. When entered of record, the judgment also operates as a lien upon all real property of the debtor in that county." In re Upset Sale, Tax Claim Bureau of Berks County, 505 Pa. 327, 334, 479 A.2d 940, 943 (1984).

6.   The 1865 revenue Act contained the following sentence: "And if any person, bank, association, company, or corporation, liable to pay any duty, shall neglect or refuse to pay the same after demand, the amount shall be a lien in favor of the United States from the time it was due until paid, with the interests, penalties, and costs that may accrue in addition thereto, upon all property and rights to property; and the collector, after demand, may levy or by warrant may authorize a deputy collector to levy upon all property and rights to property belonging to such person, bank, association, company, or corporation, or on which the said lien exists, for the payment of the sum due as aforesaid, with interest and penalty for non-payment, and also of such further sum as shall be sufficient for the fees, costs, and expenses of such levy." 13 Stat. 470-471. This provision, as amended, became § 3186 of the Revised Statutes.

or judgment creditor" until notice has been filed with the clerk of the federal district court or with the appropriate local authorities in the district or county in which the property subject to the lien is located. Act of Mar. 4, 1913, 37 Stat. 1016. In 1939, Congress broadened the protection against unfiled tax liens to include pledgees and the holders of certain securities. Act of June 29, 1939, § 401, 53 Stat. 882-883. The Federal Tax Lien Act of 1966 again broadened that protection to encompass a variety of additional secured transactions, and also included detailed provisions protecting certain secured interests even when a notice of the federal lien previously has been filed.

In sum, each time Congress revisited the federal tax lien, it ameliorated its original harsh impact on other secured creditors of the delinquent taxpayer.[7] In this case, it is agreed that by the terms of § 6323(a), the Federal Government's liens are not valid as against the lien created by the earlier recording of Romani Industries' judgment.

III.

The text of the priority statute on which the Government places its entire reliance is virtually unchanged since its enactment in 1797.[8] As we pointed out in United States v. Moore, 423 U.S. 77, 96 S.Ct. 310, 46 L.Ed.2d 219 (1975), not only were there earlier versions of the statute,[9]

---

7. For a more thorough description of the early history and of Congress' reactions to this Court's tax lien decisions, see Kennedy, The Relative Priority of the Federal Government: The Pernicious Career of the Inchoate and General Lien, 63 Yale L.J. 905, 919-922 (1954) (hereinafter Kennedy).

8. The Act of Mar. 3, 1797, § 5, 1 Stat. 515, provided:

"*And be it further enacted,* That where any revenue officer, or other person hereafter becoming indebted to the United States, by bond or otherwise, shall become insolvent, or where the estate of any deceased debtor, in the hands of executors or administrators, shall be insufficient to pay all the debts due from the deceased, the debt due to the United States shall be first satisfied; and the priority hereby established shall be deemed to extend, as well to cases in which a debtor, not having sufficient property to pay all his debts, shall make a voluntary assignment thereof, or in which the estate and effects of an absconding, concealed, or absent debtor, shall be attached by process of law, as to cases in which an act of legal bankruptcy shall be committed."

Compare § 3466 of the Revised Statutes, with the present statute quoted in n. 1, supra.

It has long been settled that the federal priority covers the Government's claims for unpaid taxes. Price v. United States, 269 U.S. 492, 499-502, 46 S.Ct. 180, 180-182, 70 L.Ed. 373 (1926); Massachusetts v. United States, 333 U.S. 611, 625-626, and n. 24, 68 S.Ct. 747, 755-756, and n. 24, 92 L.Ed. 968 (1948).

9. "The earliest priority statute was enacted in the Act of July 31, 1789, 1 Stat. 29, which dealt with bonds posted by importers in lieu of payment of duties for release of imported goods. It provided that the 'debt due to the United States' for such duties shall be discharged first 'in all cases of insolvency, or where any estate in the hands of executors or administrators shall be insufficient to pay all the debts due from the deceased* * *.' § 21, 1 Stat. 42. A 1792 enactment broadened the

but "its roots reach back even further into the English common law." The sovereign prerogative that was exercised by the English Crown and by many of the States as "an inherent incident of sovereignty," applied only to unsecured claims. As Justice Brandeis noted in Marshall v. New York, 254 U.S. 380, 384, 41 S.Ct. 143, 145, 65 L.Ed. 315 (1920), the common-law priority "[did] not obtain over a specific lien created by the debtor before the sovereign undertakes to enforce its right." Moreover, the statute itself does not create a lien in favor of the United States. Given this background, respondent argues that the statute should be read as giving the United States a preference over other unsecured creditors but not over secured creditors.

There are dicta in our earlier cases that support this contention as well as dicta that tend to refute it. Perhaps the strongest support is found in Justice Story's statement:

"What then is the nature of the priority, thus limited and established in favour of the United States? Is it a right, which supersedes and overrules the assignment of the debtor, as to any property which the United States may afterwards elect to take in execution, so as to prevent such property from passing by virtue of such assignment to the assignees? Or, is it a mere right of prior payment, out of the general funds of the debtor, in the hands of the assignees? We are of opinion that it clearly falls, within the latter description. The language employed is that which naturally would be employed to express such an intent; and it must be strained from its ordinary import, to speak any other." Conard v. Atlantic Ins. Co. of N.Y., 1 Pet. 386, 439, 7 L.Ed. 189 (1828).

Justice Story's opinion that the language employed in the statute "must be strained" to give it any other meaning is entitled to special respect because he was more familiar with 18th-century usage than judges who view the statute from a 20th-century perspective.

We cannot, however, ignore the Court's earlier judgment in *Thelusson v. Smith*, 2 Wheat., at 426, 4 L.Ed. 271, or the more recent dicta in *United States v. Key*, 397 U.S., at 324-325, 90 S.Ct., at 1051-1052. In *Thelusson*, the Court held that the priority statute gave the United States a preference over the claim of a judgment creditor who had a

Act's coverage by providing that the language 'cases of insolvency' should be taken to include cases in which a debtor makes a voluntary assignment for the benefit of creditors, and the other situations that § 3466, 31 U.S.C. § 191, now covers. 1 Stat. 263." United States v. Moore, 423 U.S., at 81, 96 S.Ct., at 313.

general lien on the debtor's real property. The Court's brief opinion[12] is subject to the interpretation that the statutory priority always accords the Government a preference over judgment creditors. For two reasons, we do not accept that reading of the opinion.

First, as a factual matter, in 1817 when the case was decided, there was no procedure for recording a judgment and thereby creating a choate lien on a specific parcel of real estate. Notwithstanding the judgment, a bona fide purchaser could have acquired the debtor's property free from any claims of the judgment creditor. That is not the case with respect to Romani Industries' choate lien on the property in Cambria County.

Second, and of greater importance, in his opinion for the Court in the *Conard* case, which was joined by Justice Washington, the author of *Thelusson*, Justice Story explained why that holding was fully consistent with his interpretation of the text of the priority statute:

"The real ground of the decision, was, that the judgment creditor had never perfected his title, by any execution and levy on the Sedgely estate; that he had acquired no title to the proceeds as his property, and that if the proceeds were to be deemed general funds of the debtor, the priority of the United States to payment had attached against all other creditors; and that a mere potential lien on land, did not carry a legal title to the proceeds of a sale, made under an adverse execution. This is the manner in which this case has been understood, by the Judges who concurred in the decision; and it is obvious, that it established no such proposition, as that a specific and perfected lien, can be displaced by the mere priority of the United

---

12. The relevant portion of the opinion reads, in full, as follows:

"These [statutory] expressions are as general as any which could have been used, and exclude all debts due to individuals, whatever may be their dignity * * *. The law makes no exception in favour of prior judgment creditors; and no reason has been, or we think can be, shown to warrant this court in making one.

" * * * The United States are to be first satisfied; but then it must be out of the debtor's estate. If, therefore, before the right of preference has accrued to the United States, the debtor has made a bona fide conveyance of his estate to a third person, or has mortgaged the same to secure a debt; or if his property has been seized under a fi. fa., the property is divested out of the debtor, and cannot be made liable to the United States. A judgment gives to the judgment creditor a lien on the debtor's lands, and a preference over all subsequent judgment creditors. But the act of congress defeats this preference in favour of the United States, in the cases specified in the 65th section of the act of 1799." Thelusson v. Smith, 2 Wheat. 396, 425-426, 4 L.Ed. 271 (1817).

In the later *Conard* case, Justice Story apologized for *Thelusson*: "The reasons for that opinion are not, owing to accidental circumstances, as fully given as they are usually given in this Court." Conard v. Atlantic Ins. Co. of N.Y., 1 Pet. 386, 442, 7 L.Ed. 189 (1828).

States; since that priority is not of itself equivalent to a lien." *Conard*, 1 Pet., at 444, 7 L.Ed. 189.[14]

The Government also relies upon dicta from our opinion in *United States v. Key*, 397 U.S., at 324-325, 90 S.Ct., at 1051-1052, which quoted from our earlier opinion in *United States v. Emory*, 314 U.S., at 433, 62 S.Ct., at 322-323: "Only the plainest inconsistency would warrant our finding an implied exception to the operation of so clear a command as that of [§ 3713]." Because both *Key* and *Emory* were cases in which the competing claims were unsecured, the statutory command was perfectly clear even under Justice Story's construction of the statute. The statements made in that context, of course, shed no light on the clarity of the command when the United States relies on the statute as a basis for claiming a preference over a secured creditor. Indeed, the *Key* opinion itself made this specific point: "This case does not raise the question, never decided by this Court, whether § 3466 grants the Government priority over the prior specific liens of secured creditors. See United States v. Gilbert Associates, Inc., 345 U.S. 361, 365-366, 73 S.Ct. 701 [704-705], 97 L.Ed. 1071 (1953)." 397 U.S., at 332, n. 11, 90 S.Ct., at 1056, n. 11.

The *Key* opinion is only one of many in which the Court has noted that despite the age of the statute, and despite the fact that it has been the subject of a great deal of litigation, the question whether it has any application to antecedent perfected liens has never been answered definitively. In his dissent in the United States v. Gilbert Associates, Inc., 345 U.S. 361, 73 S.Ct. 701, 97 L.Ed.2d 1071 (1953), Justice Frankfurter referred to the Court's reluctance to decide the issue "not only today but for almost a century and a half." 345 U.S., at 367, 73 S.Ct., at 705.

The Government's priority as against specific, perfected security interests is, if possible, even less settled with regard to real property. The Court has sometimes concluded that a competing creditor who has not "divested" the debtor of "either title or possession" has only a "general, unperfected lien" that is defeated by the Government's priority. E.g., id., at 366, 73 S.Ct., at 704-705. Assuming the validity of this "title or possession" test for deciding whether a lien on personal property is sufficiently choate for purposes of the priority statute (a question of federal law), we are not aware of any decisions since *Thelusson* applying

---

14. Relying on this and several other cases, in 1857 the Attorney General of the United States issued an opinion concluding that *Thelusson* "has been distinctly overruled" and that the priority of the United States under this statute "will not reach back over any lien, whether it be general or specific." 9 Op. Atty. Gen. 28, 29. See also Kennedy 908-911 (advancing this same interpretation of the early priority Act decisions).

that theory to claims for real property, or of any reason to require a lienor or mortgagee to acquire possession in order to perfect an interest in real estate.

Given the fact that this basic question of interpretation remains unresolved, it does not seem appropriate to view the issue in this case as whether the Tax Lien Act of 1966 has implicitly amended or repealed the priority statute. Instead, we think the proper inquiry is how best to harmonize the impact of the two statutes on the Government's power to collect delinquent taxes.

IV.

In his dissent from a particularly harsh application of the priority statute, Justice Jackson emphasized the importance of considering other relevant federal policies. Joined by three other Justices, he wrote:

> "This decision announces an unnecessarily ruthless interpretation of a statute that at its best is an arbitrary one. The statute by which the Federal Government gives its own claims against an insolvent priority over claims in favor of a state government must be applied by courts, not because federal claims are more meritorious or equitable, but only because that Government has more power. But the priority statute is an assertion of federal supremacy as against any contrary state policy. It is not a limitation on the Federal Government itself, nor an assertion that the priority policy shall prevail over all other federal policies. Its generalities should not lightly be construed to frustrate a specific policy embodied in a later federal statute." Massachusetts v. United States, 333 U.S. 611, 635, 68 S.Ct. 747, 760-761, 92 L.Ed. 968 (1948).

On several prior occasions the Court had followed this approach and concluded that a specific policy embodied in a later federal statute should control our construction of the priority statute, even though it had not been expressly amended. Thus, in Cook County Nat. Bank v. United States, 107 U.S. 445, 448-451, 2 S.Ct. 561, 564-567, 27 L.Ed. 537 (1883), the Court concluded that the priority statute did not apply to federal claims against national banks because the National Bank Act comprehensively regulated banks' obligations and the distribution of insolvent banks' assets. And in United States v. Guaranty Trust Co. of N.Y., 280 U.S. 478, 485, 50 S.Ct. 212, 214, 74 L.Ed. 556 (1930), we determined that the Transportation Act of 1920 had effectively superseded the priority statute with respect to federal claims against the railroads arising under that Act.

The bankruptcy law provides an additional context in which another federal statute was given effect despite the priority statute's literal, unconditional text. The early federal bankruptcy statutes had accorded to " 'all debts due to the United States, and all taxes and assessments under the laws thereof' " a preference that was "coextensive" with that established by the priority statute. As such, the priority Act and the bankruptcy laws "were to be regarded as in pari materia, and both were unqualified; * * * as neither contained any qualification, none could be interpolated." The Bankruptcy Act of 1898, however, subordinated the priority of the Federal Government's claims (except for taxes due) to certain other kinds of debts. This Court resolved the tension between the new bankruptcy provisions and the priority statute by applying the former and thus treating the Government like any other general creditor.[15]

There are sound reasons for treating the Tax Lien Act of 1966 as the governing statute when the Government is claiming a preference in the insolvent estate of a delinquent taxpayer. As was the case with the National Bank Act, the Transportation Act of 1920, and the Bankruptcy Act of 1898, the Tax Lien Act is the later statute, the more specific statute, and its provisions are comprehensive, reflecting an obvious attempt to accommodate the strong policy objections to the enforcement of secret liens. It represents Congress' detailed judgment as to when the Government's claims for unpaid taxes should yield to many different sorts of interests (including, for instance, judgment liens, mechanic's liens, and attorney's liens) in many different types of property (including, for example, real property, securities, and motor vehicles). See 26 U.S.C. § 6323. Indeed, given our unambiguous determination that the federal interest in the collection of taxes is paramount to its interest in enforcing other claims, it would be anomalous to conclude that Congress intended the priority statute to impose greater burdens on the citizen than those specifically crafted for tax collection purposes.

Even before the 1966 amendments to the Tax Lien Act, this Court assumed that the more recent and specific provisions of that Act would apply were they to conflict with the older priority statute. In the *Gilbert Associates* case, which concerned the relative priority of the Federal

---

15. Congress amended the priority statute in 1978 to make it expressly inapplicable to Title 11 bankruptcy cases. Pub.L. 95-598, § 322(b), 92 Stat. 2679, codified in 31 U.S.C. § 3713(a)(2). The differences between the bankruptcy laws and the priority statute have been the subject of criticism: "[As] a result of the continuing discrepancies between the bankruptcy and insolvency rules, some creditors have had a distinct incentive to throw into bankruptcy a debtor whose case might have been handled, with less expense and less burden on the federal courts, in another form of proceeding." Plumb, The Federal Priority in Insolvency: Proposals for Reform, 70 Mich. L.Rev. 3, 8-9 (1971) (hereinafter Plumb).

Government and a New Hampshire town to funds of an insolvent taxpayer, the Court first considered whether the town could qualify as a "judgment creditor" entitled to preference under the Tax Lien Act. Only after deciding that question in the negative did the Court conclude that the United States obtained preference by operation of the priority statute. The Government would now portray *Gilbert Associates* as a deviation from two other relatively recent opinions in which the Court held that the priority statute was not trumped by provisions of other statutes: *United States v. Emory*, 314 U.S., at 429-433, 62 S.Ct., at 320-323 (the National Housing Act), and *United States v. Key*, 397 U.S., at 324-333, 90 S.Ct., at 1051-1056 (Chapter X of the Bankruptcy Act). In each of those cases, however, there was no "plain inconsistency" between the commands of the priority statute and the other federal Act, nor was there reason to believe that application of the priority statute would frustrate Congress' intent. The same cannot be said in the present suit.

The Government emphasizes that when Congress amended the Tax Lien Act in 1966, it declined to enact the American Bar Association's proposal to modify the federal priority statute, and Congress again failed to enact a similar proposal in 1970. Both proposals would have expressly provided that the Government's priority in insolvency does not displace valid liens and security interests, and therefore would have harmonized the priority statute with the Tax Lien Act. But both proposals also would have significantly changed the priority statute in many other respects to follow the priority scheme created by the bankruptcy laws. The earlier proposal may have failed because its wide-ranging subject matter was beyond the House Ways and Means Committee's jurisdiction. The failure of the 1970 proposal in the Senate Judiciary Committee—explained by no reports or hearings—might merely reflect disagreement with the broad changes to the priority statute, or an assumption that the proposal was not needed because, as Justice Story had believed, the priority statute does not apply to prior perfected security interests, or any number of other views. Thus, the Committees' failures to report the proposals to the entire Congress do not necessarily indicate that any legislator thought that the priority statute should supersede the Tax Lien Act in the adjudication of federal tax claims. They provide no support for the hypothesis that both Houses of Congress silently endorsed that position.

The actual measures taken by Congress provide a superior insight regarding its intent. As we have noted, the 1966 amendments to the Tax Lien Act bespeak a strong condemnation of secret liens, which unfairly defeat the expectations of innocent creditors and frustrate "the needs of our citizens for certainty and convenience in the legal rules governing their commercial dealings." 112 Cong. Rec. 22227 (1966) (remarks of

Rep. Byrnes). These policy concerns shed light on how Congress would want the conflicting statutory provisions to be harmonized:

"Liens may be a dry-as-dust part of the law, but they are not without significance in an industrial and commercial community where construction and credit are thought to have importance. One does not readily impute to Congress the intention that many common commercial liens should be congenitally unstable." E. Brown, The Supreme Court, 1957 Term–Foreword: Process of Law, 72 Harv. L.Rev. 77, 87 (1958).

In sum, nothing in the text or the long history of interpreting the federal priority statute justifies the conclusion that it authorizes the equivalent of a secret lien as a substitute for the expressly authorized tax lien that Congress has said "shall not be valid" in a case of this kind.

The judgment of the Pennsylvania Supreme Court is affirmed.

It is so ordered.

Notes and Question

There are some specific exceptions to the government's priority under 31 U.S.C. § 3713 that have been recognized, such as funeral expenses, costs of administering the estate, and widows' allowances. See Rev. Rul. 80-112, 1980-1 C.B. 306 (funeral, administrative expenses and family allowance required to be paid under state law have priority over government's tax claim for which it has no lien) but see PLR 8341018 (choate, perfected assessment lien takes priority over all expenses except administrative expenses necessary for collection and preservation of the estate).

Note that 31 U.S.C. § 3713 also applies to insolvent living taxpayers, and its application in that case differs from that of insolvent estates. In the case of an insolvent living taxpayer, the statute does not apply automatically but instead is triggered by an affirmative event (attachment of the absent debtor's property, an act of bankruptcy by the debtor, and a voluntary assignment for the benefit of creditors).

Once a bankruptcy action has begun, the Bankruptcy Code takes priority over the federal tax provisions. Note that an "act of bankruptcy" does not include a Chapter 11 proceeding because under Chapter 11, creditors have the ability to throw the debtor into bankruptcy involuntarily. See discussion of the bankruptcy provisions in § II, below.

1. After the *Romani* decision, what priority is afforded claims of the Government under 31.S.C. § 3713?

2. What, if any, role does state law play in determining priority status under § 3713?

3. Does a prior perfected state tax lien take priority over a subsequent, unperfected federal tax lien in the case of an insolvent debtor with insufficient assets to satisfy both liens? See Straus v. United States, 196 F.3d 862 (7th Cir. 1999).

4. Releasing the Lien

The Service is not required to give the taxpayer notice of its intent to record its lien. The problem this raises is that if the Notice of Lien is filed in error, an innocent taxpayer could be seriously harmed. Section 6326, enacted in 1988 under the Taxpayer Bill of Rights 2, provides for an administrative appeal of an erroneously recorded lien. The grounds for such appeals are limited to challenges of the erroneous recordings of the liens. Thus, a taxpayer may not challenge the underlying deficiency, although the taxpayer may challenge the validity of the lien itself on the ground that the Service violated the deficiency procedures in assessing the underlying tax liability. Reg. § 301.6326-1(b). Other grounds for appeal include (1) satisfaction of the tax liability prior to the filing of the notice of lien, (2) tax assessment in violation of the provisions of the Bankruptcy Code, and (3) expiration of the statute of limitations on collection prior to the filing of the notice. Id.

If the Service determines that the Notice of Lien was recorded in error, it must issue a Certificate of Release of Lien expeditiously, or to the extent practicable, within 14 days after such determination. IRC § 6326(b). The Certificate must state specifically that the Notice of Lien was filed in error. Id.

If the Service confuses the names of a delinquent taxpayer and a nondelinquent taxpayer, and records a Notice of Lien against the property of the nondelinquent taxpayer, that taxpayer may request that the Service issue a Certificate of Nonattachment of Lien, stating that the federal tax lien never attached to the property of this taxpayer. IRC § 6325(e).

If the Notice of Lien was not filed erroneously, but the taxpayer has satisfied one of the grounds for release of the lien, the Service must release the lien within 30 days of the satisfaction. IRC § 6325(a)(1). Grounds for release include satisfying the tax liability in full, posting a bond for the payment of the assessed amount plus interest, or where the lien has become legally unenforceable. To insure prompt compliance with the 30-day release, the taxpayer may request in writing the issuance of a release of lien. Reg. § 301.6325-1(b)(5).

Even though the underlying tax liability neither has been satisfied nor has become unenforceable, the Service nevertheless may agree to withdraw its notice of lien if it determines that (1) the filing of the Notice of Lien was premature or violated administrative procedures, (2) the taxpayer has entered into an installment agreement with the Service to satisfy the underlying tax liability, (3) the withdrawal of the Notice will facilitate the collection of the tax liability, or (4) the withdrawal of the lien would serve the best interests of the taxpayer (as determined by the National Taxpayer Advocate) and the government. IRC § 6323(j). Such a notice is filed in the office where the notice of tax lien was recorded and it may be sent to creditors, financial institutions, and credit reporting agencies upon written request by the taxpayer. Id. at § 6323(j)(2).

In addition, the Service may agree to discharge its lien with respect to specific property if its interests remain protected. Thus, a Certificate of Discharge may be issued even though the taxpayer has neither paid the underlying tax liability nor entered into an installment settlement. In order for such a discharge to occur, certain conditions must be met: (1) the fair market value of the remaining property subject to the lien must be at least double the amount of the unsatisfied liability secured by the tax lien plus the amount of other liens on the property which have priority over the federal tax lien, (2) the property subject to the lien must have no value or the taxpayer must pay to the government the value of the property to the extent of the lien, (3) the government must agree to substitute the proceeds of sale where it does not lose priority, or (4) the taxpayer must furnish a bond equal to the value of the property being released. IRC § 6325(b).

Finally, the government may agree to subordinate its lien if that will facilitate the ultimate collection of the tax. IRC § 6325(d)(1). This provision is particularly useful where the taxpayer must borrow funds from a lending institution in order to operate her business.

Question

Discuss the effect on the government of (1) the nonattachment of lien, (2) the release of lien, and (3) the withdrawal of lien.

Problems

1. Tom submits a written request to the government to discharge its lien for $20,000 on Blackacre, which Tom owns, and which has a value of $22,000. Tom has other real property, worth $45,000, which will continue to be subject to the federal tax lien. The other property is also

subject to a prior state tax lien of $1,000 for real property taxes that remain unpaid, and a prior mortgage lien of $15,000. Will Tom's request be granted?

2. Assume in question one that the government agrees to issue a Certificate of Discharge of the Lien on Blackacre if Tom agrees to pay the value of the government's interest in Blackacre. The federal tax lien on Blackacre secures an outstanding tax liability of $20,000, but if the lien is foreclosed and the property is sold in order to satisfy the government's claim, the expenses of the sale are likely to be $1,200, and the property is likely to sell for around $18,000, which is less than its listed fair market value of $22,000. What amount should Tom pay to the government?

C. COLLECTION DUE PROCESS

Taxpayers have certain due process rights in the collection process, in specific shortly after the notice of tax lien is filed (§ 6320) and shortly before a levy on the lien (§ 6330), the taxpayer may request a collection due process (CDP) hearing to administratively challenge the action. Section 6320 provides that within five business days of the date the lien is filed, notice must be sent to the taxpayer. This notice must inform the taxpayer of the amount of the outstanding tax and of the taxpayer's right to a hearing to contest the filing. In order to obtain the hearing, the taxpayer must file a request within 30 days of the end of the five-day period following the filing of the notice of federal tax lien. Although the taxpayer may receive several notices of lien filings, the taxpayer is entitled to only one CDP hearing per tax period, although if there are different types of tax in issue (e.g., income and excise), a CDP hearing may be obtained for each type of tax.

Before the Service can levy against the property of the taxpayer, it must send the taxpayer a notice of intent to levy and also must provide notice of the taxpayer's right to a pre-levy collection due process (CDP) hearing with the Appeals Office. IRC § 6330. The government is prohibited from levying on the taxpayer's property for 30 days after the service of the notice of the intent to levy. IRC § 6331(d). If the taxpayer requests a hearing during the 30-day period, the government is further prohibited from levying until the taxpayer has had an opportunity to be heard.

The hearing is informal and will be heard by the IRS Office of Appeals. After the hearing, the Appeals officer will issue findings in a Notice of Determination. While there is no deadline for issuing this Notice, the regulations provide that it should be issued "as expeditiously as possible." Reg. § 301.6320-1(e)(3). The taxpayer then has 30 days from the issuance of the Notice of Determination to seek judicial review of the determination in the Tax Court.

1. Tax Court Review

a. *Abuse of Discretion*

VINATIERI v. COMMISSIONER

United States Tax Court, 2009.
133 T.C. 392

DAWSON, JUDGE.

This matter is before the Court on respondent's motion for summary judgment filed pursuant to Rule 121.[1] Petitioner timely filed a petition pursuant to section 6330(d) appealing respondent's determination to proceed with collection by levy of petitioner's 2002 income tax liability. The issue to be decided is whether respondent's determination was an abuse of discretion.

Background

Petitioner resided in Tennessee when she filed the petition. Her residence is an apartment that she rents for $600 per month.

On September 13, 2007, respondent sent petitioner a Final Notice of Intent to Levy and Notice of Your Right to a Hearing (levy notice). The underlying tax liability was attributable to unpaid self-assessed tax reported on her 2002 return. Petitioner timely requested a hearing on September 24, 2007, and the hearing was conducted through correspondence and by telephone with the settlement officer.

Petitioner first learned of the collection activity when her employer notified her about the proposed levy on her wages. When the settlement officer asked petitioner whether she wanted to enter into an installment agreement, petitioner said "she has nothing."[2] Petitioner told the settlement officer that she has pulmonary fibrosis and is dying. Because of her health she can only find part-time employment.

---

1.   All Rule references are to the Tax Court Rules of Practice and Procedure, and all section references are to the Internal Revenue Code.

2.   Petitioner explained to the settlement officer that she had previously agreed to pay in installments and that she was told she would be sent envelopes for each payment, but she never received the envelopes or monthly bills.

The settlement officer could not find a record that petitioner had filed a return for 2005. Petitioner explained to the settlement officer that the payroll company responsible for completing her 2005 Form W-2, Wage and Tax Statement, was no longer in business. She had attempted to get the tax information from the Internal Revenue Service (IRS), but the IRS had no information regarding her income for 2005.

The settlement officer told petitioner that she might be able to have her account placed in currently not collectible status. The settlement officer asked petitioner to submit a Form 433-A, Collection Information Statement for Wage Earners and Self-Employed Individuals, and a diagnosis regarding her current health condition.

Petitioner sent a completed Form 433-A, indicating she had monthly income of $800 and expenses of $800, had $14 cash on hand, and owned a 1996 Toyota Corolla four-door sedan with 243,000 miles and a value of $300. The Form 433-A reported that petitioner did not own any other assets. Verification received by the settlement officer was consistent with the information petitioner provided in the Form 433-A. Petitioner was unable to obtain a written diagnosis of her medical condition from her physician because her physician would provide a diagnosis only in a claim for worker's compensation.

The settlement officer's log entry dated May 15, 2008, states:

TP [petitioner] meets the criteria to have account placed in CNC [currently not collectible] status per IRM 5.16.[1.] 2.9 Hardship. The balance due is less than 10K and the TP has stated she has a terminal illness. CIS verification is not required. The TP has stated she has nothing and is not able to full pay or make payments. However, the TP is not in compliance. The TP has not filed a 2005 return and there is no record of the 2007 tax return being filed. The TP stated she does not have income information for 2005 and company that did payroll is no longer in business. TP stated she contacted IRS and they advised her they have no income information. There is no information per IRTRL. S/O [the settlement officer] contacted TP regarding filing of the 2007 return. The TP stated the return was filed late. The S/O requested the TP fax a copy of the return with the W-2. TP to fax information by 5-19-08. S/O asked TP if she obtained health diagnosis and the TP stated the doctor would only give her something if she is applying for diability. S/O requested income information for 2005 per IRPTRE.

The settlement officer's log entry dated May 20, 2008, states:

TP did not provide a copy of 2007 return and there is no record that the return has been filed per IDRS research. The TP was employed in 2007 and is currently employed. The 2005 return has not been filed. Since the TP is not in compliance, collection alternative cannot be considered. S/O will issue determination letter. If the 2005 income information is received, the S/O will forward it to the TP.

Respondent issued petitioner a Notice of Determination Concerning Collection Action(s) Under Section 6320 and/or 6330 (notice of determination) dated June 2, 2008, sustaining the proposed levy action and stating that, because petitioner was not in compliance with filing the required tax returns, a collection alternative could not be considered. The notice of determination was reviewed and signed by the Appeals team manager. The attachment to the notice of determination stated:

> The settlement officer inquired about a collection alternative and you stated you could not make payments. You stated you had pulmonary fibrosis and can only work part-time hours due to your heath condition. The Settlement officer [who] advised you of the collection alternative however explained a collection alternative could not be considered because you were not in compliance with filing required tax returns. * * *

The attachment explained the balancing of efficient tax collection with concern regarding intrusiveness as follows:

> Appeals has verified, or received verification, that applicable laws and administrative procedures have been met; has considered the issues raised; and has balanced the proposed collection with the legitimate concern that such action be no more intrusive than necessary by IRC Section 6330(c)(3).
>
> Collection alternatives include full payment, installment agreement, offer in compromise and currently-not-collectible. However, since unfiled tax returns exist, the only alternative at present is to take enforced action by levying your assets. It is Appeals decision that the proposed levy action is appropriate. The proposed levy action balances the need for the efficient collection of the taxes with the legitimate concern that any collection action be no more intrusive than necessary.

Neither the notice of determination nor the attachment reflect any consideration of the fact that the levy would create an economic hardship as stated by the settlement officer in her daily log and supported by the Form 433-A petitioner submitted.

Petitioner timely filed a petition in this Court challenging respondent's determination. Respondent filed the motion for summary judgment, and the Court ordered petitioner to file a response.[3] Petitioner filed a response to respondent's motion for summary judgment but did not file a cross-motion for summary judgment.[4]   In her response petitioner describes her situation as follows:

To Whom It May Concern,

I don't know what you want to know cause I don't understand all the legal stuff you sent me. I can't afford a lawyer. And the closest legal aid is in Knoxville 30 miles away. My poor car will not go that far. So I will start at the beginning of my story and see if you can help me.

I was in an unhealthy relationship for many years. During a great deal of that time my husband was doing alcohol and drugs. I had 2 children plus his 3 to take care of. I had been doing janitorial work at a strip mall * * *. It was the only place that I could work that I could take my [then] 3 year old daughter with me. I could not support my family and pay day care. * * * My husband took care of bills and such cause he demanded that I turn over my money. We even got a divorce during that time cause I was not obeying him. * * *

Now I am not looking for sympathy just understanding. Do you know how hard it is to be a single parent? * * * I have a high school education and nothing else.

It was nearly five years before I was notified of a problem by the I.R.S. Danny [petitioner's former spouse] was suppose to be doing taxes. He even made me sign a form that because he made more money he could claim my kids on his taxes cause we were no longer legally married.

I got all the W-2's from the I.R.S. except 2005 that they still have not sent me. That is why they are not done. I did all those taxes and forfeited the refunds. I do not remember what that total came to. But it was enough to pay I would say most of back taxes. The 2007 taxes were late and I don't know why they didn't arrive. I sent a second

---

3.   In the order we observed that our preliminary review of the record indicated that the proposed levy action involved a hardship situation and that petitioner needed the assistance of an attorney. We urged petitioner to contact the legal aid society or the local bar association pro bono services and provided their addresses and phone numbers.

4.   After petitioner filed her response to respondent's motion for summary judgment, respondent filed a motion to continue the case wherein respondent stated that petitioner was in the process of submitting a collection alternative to the IRS and that, if the alternative is accepted by the IRS, a trial in this case would not be necessary. The Court granted respondent's motion and directed the parties to file a status report on or before July 27, 2009. In a status report filed on July 17, 2009, respondent reported that respondent has not received any communication from petitioner and requested the Court to grant respondent's motion for summary judgment.

copy in as soon as my son gave me my copy. He had my copy for college financial aid and he lost them for a bit of time.

I am not a rich person. I work in a job so I can be home with my daughter. I left my husband in July after he threatened to beat my daughter with a baseball bat. Beating me is one thing but I could not have him beating my girl. So I am a single parent again. Right now we have not had much work in nearly a year. I have rent of 600 a mo. Utilities of 150 and get food stamps or I wouldn't eat. I make about 700-800[per] month. There are no better jobs in our town. My daughter is only 11 so its not like I can leave her alone at night or on weekends. D.H.S. says it's not even legal. She is too young. There is no child care and I have no family here. I have pulmonary fibrosis that makes me sick all the time and the diagnosis says I have about 10 yrs to live. Right now I can work thank God.

I did my taxes this year [for 2008] and you are getting a little over $4,700. I'm not asking for much just a break. You can have my tax returns [refunds ?] I don't care. Well I do that is a tremendous loss but oh well. I don't have any money to send you on a monthly basis. Can we stop all the penalties. They are killing me. I will never be able to pay it off. * * * I let a relationship screw me up. I am truly sorry for that and am begging for a lifeline here. You can come to my home and see for yourself. I don't have fancy t.v.'s or even cable except for internet. I can't afford a phone. My clothes have holes in them. I even cut my own hair. If I could pay this off faster I would just to stop the nightmares it gives me.

Discussion
A. Summary Judgment
* * *

Respondent moves the Court for summary judgment on the ground that the settlement officer did not abuse her discretion in rejecting collection alternatives and determining to proceed with levy because petitioner was not in compliance with the filing requirements. Petitioner asks that the levy not be sustained because, if her wages are taken, she will be unable to pay her basic living expenses; and, if her car is taken, she will not be able to work.

B. Collection of Federal Taxes by Levy

If a taxpayer liable for Federal taxes fails to pay the taxes within 10 days after notice and demand, section 6331 authorizes the Secretary to collect the tax by levy upon all property and rights to property (except any property that is exempt under section 6334) belonging to the taxpayer or on which there is a lien for the payment of the tax.

Section 6343(a)(1) provides that, under regulations prescribed by the Secretary, if the Secretary has determined that the levy is creating an economic hardship due to the financial condition of the taxpayer, the Secretary must release a levy upon all, or part of, a taxpayer's property or rights to property.[5] Sec. 6343(a)(1)(D). The regulations provide that a levy is creating an economic hardship due to the financial condition of an individual taxpayer and must be released "if satisfaction of the levy in whole or in part will cause an individual taxpayer to be unable to pay his or her reasonable basic living expenses." Sec. 301.6343-1(b)(4), Proced. & Admin. Regs.

A taxpayer alleging that collection of the liability would create undue hardship must submit complete and current financial data to enable the Commissioner to evaluate the taxpayer's qualification for collection alternatives or other relief. The regulations provide that, for purposes of determining the taxpayer's reasonable amount of living expenses, any information that is provided by the taxpayer is to be considered, including the following:

(A)   The taxpayer's age, employment status and history, ability to earn, number of dependents, and status as a dependent of someone else;

(B)   The amount reasonably necessary for food, clothing, housing * * *, medical expenses * * *, transportation, current tax payments * * *, alimony, child support, or other court-ordered payments, and expenses necessary to the taxpayer's production of income * * *;

(C)   The cost of living in the geographic area in which the taxpayer resides;

(D)   The amount of property exempt from levy which is available to pay the taxpayer's expenses;

(E)   Any extraordinary circumstances such as special education expenses, a medical catastrophe, or natural disaster; and

---

5.   The regulations provide a method whereby a taxpayer may inform the Secretary that a levy is creating an economic hardship and request that the levy be released. See sec. 301.6343-1(c), Proced. & Admin. Regs. "A taxpayer who wishes to obtain a release of a levy must submit a request for release in writing or by telephone to the district director for the Internal Revenue district in which the levy was made." Id. However, service center directors and compliance center directors (to whom requests by taxpayers are not made) who have determined that a levy is creating an economic hardship must also release the levy and promptly notify the taxpayer of the release pursuant to sec. 301.6343-1(a), Proced. & Admin. Regs.

(F) Any other factor that the taxpayer claims bears on economic hardship and brings to the attention of the director.

Sec. 301.6343-1(b)(4)(ii), Proced. & Admin. Regs.

C. Section 6330 Procedures

Section 6330(a) provides the general rule that no levy may be made on any property or right to property of any taxpayer unless the Secretary has provided 30 days' notice to the taxpayer of the right to an administrative hearing before the levy is carried out. If the taxpayer makes a timely request for an administrative hearing, the hearing is conducted by the IRS Office of Appeals (Appeals Office) before an impartial officer. Sec. 6330(b)(1), (3).

The taxpayer may raise any relevant issue during the hearing, including appropriate spousal defenses and challenges to "the appropriateness of collection actions", and may make "offers of collection alternatives, which may include the posting of a bond, the substitution of other assets, an installment agreement, or an offer-in-compromise." Sec. 6330(c)(2)(A). The taxpayer also may raise challenges to the existence or amount of the underlying tax liability if he/she did not receive a notice of deficiency for that liability or did not otherwise have an opportunity to dispute it. Sec. 6330(c)(2)(B).

During the hearing the Appeals officer must verify that the requirements of applicable law and administrative procedure have been met, consider issues properly raised by the taxpayer, and consider whether any proposed collection action balances the need for the efficient collection of taxes with the taxpayer's legitimate concern that any collection action be no more intrusive than necessary. Sec. 6330(c)(3). The Appeals Office then issues a notice of determination indicating whether the proposed levy may proceed.

Under section 6330(d)(1) the taxpayer may petition this Court to review the determination made by the Appeals Office. See sec. 301.6330-1(f)(1), Proced. & Admin. Regs. Where, as in this case, the underlying tax liability is not at issue, we review the Appeals Office's determinations regarding the collection action for abuse of discretion. Goza v. Commissioner, 114 T.C. 176 (2000). An abuse of discretion occurs if the Appeals Office exercises its discretion "arbitrarily, capriciously, or without sound basis in fact or law." Woodral v. Commissioner, 112 T.C. 19, 23, 1999 WL 9947 (1999).

When a taxpayer establishes in a pre-levy collection hearing under section 6330 that the proposed levy would create an economic hardship, it is unreasonable for the settlement officer to determine to proceed with the levy which section 6343(a)(1)(D) would require the IRS to immediately release. Rather than proceed with the levy, the settlement officer should consider alternatives to the levy.

Respondent argues under the holdings of Rodriguez v. Commissioner, T.C. Memo.2003-153, and McCorkle v. Commissioner, T.C. Memo. 2003-34, that there is no abuse of discretion if a settlement officer rejects collection alternatives because the taxpayer was not in compliance with the filing requirements for all required tax returns.[6]

Generally, we have found the Commissioner's policy requiring individuals seeking collection alternatives to be current with filing their returns to be reasonable.[7] However, taxpayers in those cases have had sufficient income to meet basic living expenses. See, e.g., Speltz v. Commissioner, 124 T.C. 165, 178, 2005 WL 668404 (2005) (taxpayers claimed hardship because the tax liability was disproportionate to the value that they received from initial stock offerings and because they had already been forced to change their lifestyle), affd. 454 F.3d 782 (8th Cir.2006); Peterson v. Commissioner, T.C. Memo.2009-46 (the Court upheld rejection of taxpayers' offer of $20,000 to compromise $70,000 liability where, although they had minimal income from Social Security retirement and disability payments, they had reasonable collection potential of $68,000 from two parcels of real property valued at $80,000); Fangonilo v. Commissioner, T.C. Memo.2008-75 (Commissioner's refusal to treat taxpayer's tax liability as currently not collectible was not an abuse of discretion where although taxpayer's income was not sufficient to meet his stated monthly living expenses, he had a liquid asset worth more than his tax liability); Willis v. Commissioner, T.C. Memo.2003-302 (taxpayers' ability to make some payments toward their cumulative liability made them ineligible to have the cumulative liability classified as currently not collectible); Rodriguez v. Commissioner, T.C. Memo.2003-153 (taxpayer had not filed returns for 12 years and did not submit all of the financial information supporting her

---

6. Generally, the IRS will not grant an installment agreement, accept an offer-in-compromise, or report an account as currently not collectible if any tax return for which the taxpayer has a filing requirement has not been filed. See Internal Revenue Manual pts. 5.14.1.4.1(4)-(6) (Sept. 26, 2008) (installment agreements); 5.8.3.13(1), (2), (4) (Sept. 23, 2008) (offers-in-compromise); 5.16.1.1(5) and (6), 5.16.1.2.9(8) (May 5, 2009) (currently not collectible), 5.1.11.2.3 (June 2, 2004) (general collection procedures).

7. In Estate of Atkinson v. Commissioner, T.C. Memo.2007-89, we found reasonable requirements that an entity seeking collection alternatives to full payment, including reporting an account as currently not collectible, filing any outstanding tax returns and submitting a full financial statement and verification information for analysis. Mandatory release of levy creating an economic hardship applies only to individuals. Sec. 301.6343-1(b)(4), Proced. & Admin. Regs.

offer-in-compromise that the settlement officer requested); Ashley v. Commissioner, T.C. Memo.2002-286 (taxpayer had income in excess of expenses and sufficient equity in his real property to pay his tax liability in full).

We have found no cases addressing the requirement that the taxpayer be current with filing returns in a levy case involving economic hardship under section 6343(a)(1)(D) and section 301.6343-1(b)(4), Proced. & Admin. Regs. Neither section 6343 nor the regulations condition a release of a levy that is creating an economic hardship on the taxpayer's compliance with filing and payment requirements. The purpose of section 6330 is to "afford taxpayers adequate notice of collection activity and a meaningful hearing *before* the IRS deprives them of their property." S. Rept. 105-174, at 67 (1998), 1998-3 C.B. 537, 603 (emphasis added). A determination in a hardship case to proceed with a levy that must immediately be released is unreasonable and undermines public confidence that tax laws are being administered fairly. In a section 6330 pre-levy hearing, if the taxpayer has provided information that establishes the proposed levy will create an economic hardship, the settlement officer cannot go forward with the levy and must consider an alternative.

D. Appeals Office's Determination To Proceed With Levy of Petitioner's Assets

The financial information petitioner submitted on the Form 433-A, which was consistent with other information the settlement officer obtained, showed that if petitioner's wages are levied on, she will be unable to pay her basic living expenses; and, if her car is levied on, she will not be able to work. After analyzing petitioner's financial information, the settlement officer concluded that the levy would create an economic hardship and so stated in her log. However, the settlement officer determined collection alternatives to the levy, including an installment agreement, an offer-in-compromise, and reporting the account as currently not collectible, were not available because petitioner had not filed her 2005 and 2007 returns. The settlement officer's determination to proceed with the levy was reviewed and approved by the Appeals team manager who signed the notice of determination. Although the attachment to the notice of determination shows that the Appeals team manager was aware of petitioner's financial situation and health problems, the Appeals team manager signed the notice of determination to proceed with the levy because petitioner had not filed her 2005 and 2007 returns. Proceeding with the levy would be unreasonable because section 6343 would require its immediate release, and the determination to do so was arbitrary. The determination to proceed with the levy was wrong as a matter of law and, therefore, was an abuse of discretion. Respondent is not entitled to summary judgment, and respondent's motion will be denied.

An order denying respondent's motion will be issued.

Notes

Apparently, the IRS currently is working to revise its CDP procedures in light of *Vinatieri* to forego collection action if a taxpayer can establish economic hardship at the CDP hearing, despite not meeting the tax return filing requirements. In the wake of *Vinatieri*, the IRS was criticized by Nina Olson, the National Taxpayer Advocate, who stated that the IRS was "all about efficiency and consistency" and less about "actual effectiveness." See "Official Describes Likely Revisions To Collection Due Process," 129 Tax Notes 51 (Oct. 4, 2010).

b. Scope of the Record

ROBINETTE v. COMMISSIONER
United States Court of Appeals, Eighth Circuit, 2006.
439 F.3d 455

COLLOTON, CIRCUIT JUDGE.

* * *

I.

Between 1983 and 1991, Robinette failed to pay his federal income taxes. By May 31, 1993, the balance due on his liabilities, including interest and statutory additions, was $989,475.89. At that time, Robinette also was responsible for a liability of $102,030.54 that had accumulated when his medical clinic failed to pay trust fund taxes during portions of 1988, 1989, and 1990. These liabilities combined to leave Robinette owing $1,091,506.43.

On June 1, 1994, Robinette sought to settle his liabilities through an offer-in-compromise. Pursuant to the offer, Robinette submitted $1,000, promised to pay an additional $99,000 within 60 days of receiving notice of the IRS's acceptance of his offer, and agreed to several additional terms and conditions. Among these conditions was a promise that "I/we will comply with all provisions of the Internal Revenue Code relating to filing my/our returns and paying my/our required taxes for five (5) years from the date IRS accepts the offer." The offer also acknowledged that

Robinette understood that he would "remain responsible for the full amount of the tax liability unless and until IRS accepts the offer in writing and I/we have met all the terms and conditions of the offer," and that the tax he was offering to compromise "will remain a tax liability until I/we meet all the terms and conditions of this offer." The offer further recognized the IRS's power, if Robinette failed to meet the terms of the offer, to "file suit or levy to collect the original amount of the tax liability, without further notice of any kind."

Robinette also proposed a collateral agreement, under which he agreed to pay an additional percentage tax on any income over $100,000 for the years 1996 to 2000 and promised to provide a sworn statement of his previous year's income each year by April 15. On October 31, 1995, the IRS accepted this offer-in-compromise, together with the collateral agreement. Robinette filed his tax returns for 1996 and 1997 in a timely manner, after receiving extensions of time to file in October. Except for a delay in providing statements of annual income for 1996, 1997, and 1998, he complied with the terms of his offer-in-compromise. On February 21, 2000, however, the IRS wrote to notify Robinette that it had not received his 1998 tax return and to request that he immediately file the late return. On March 17, 2000, the IRS again notified Robinette by letter that it still had not received his tax return, and that if he failed to send the return within 15 days, the matter would be referred for consideration of whether his offer-in-compromise was in default. A similar letter was sent on April 17, 2000. On July 13, 2000, the IRS sent a letter notifying Robinette that no return had been filed, that the failure to file violated the terms of the agreement, and that the offer was in default.

On September 28, 2000, the IRS sent Robinette a notice of its intent to impose a levy to collect the full original liability (minus the amount already paid under the offer-in-compromise), and of his rights to a hearing before the levy, as required under 26 U.S.C. § 6330. Robinette responded with a timely request for a collection due process hearing, in which he noted that he was disputing whether he owed the amounts being levied. The collection due process proceedings were conducted informally and consisted of a series of telephone calls and correspondence between an IRS appeals officer and Robinette's accountant/attorney, Douglas Coy. During these conversations, Coy claimed that he mailed Robinette's 1998 return on October 15, 1999, which, pursuant to extensions Robinette had received, was the date on which the return was due. Coy provided a copy of the return, which the IRS received and processed as an original return on February 16, 2001.

Despite Coy's insistence that he mailed the 1998 return by first-class mail with several other clients' returns shortly before midnight on October 16, 1999, the appeals officer determined that the return had not been timely filed, and he recommended that the levy be imposed. The appeals officer noted that Robinette had not complied with several requests to file the return before the offer was defaulted, and that Robinette had not proposed a new offer-in-compromise or any other alternative to collection. Consistent with this recommendation, the IRS Office of Appeals issued a determination that the notice of intent to levy was appropriate.

Robinette appealed to the Tax Court pursuant to § 6330(d)(1), arguing that the appeals officer had abused his discretion by proceeding with the collection. The Tax Court held a trial and agreed with Robinette. Robinette v. Comm'r, 123 T.C. 85 (2004). The Tax Court found that Robinette had not filed his 1998 return in a timely manner, but that his failure to do so was not material to his offer-in-compromise. Since the breach was immaterial, the Tax Court reasoned, the offer should not have been defaulted, and the decision to proceed with collection was an abuse of discretion. Id. at 112. The case generated five concurring opinions, a dissenting opinion of two judges, and a third dissenting vote.

II.

Prior to 1998, the IRS was permitted to collect a tax liability by levy against a taxpayer's property, without prior opportunity for a hearing or due process, so long as there were adequate post-deprivation remedies. See Phillips v. Comm'r, 283 U.S. 589, 595-97, 51 S.Ct. 608, 75 L.Ed. 1289 (1931). Apparently concerned about potential abuses of this administrative authority to seize a taxpayer's property, Congress created an administrative proceeding, commonly known as a "collection due process hearing," in the Internal Revenue Service Restructuring and Reform Act of 1998. The applicable statute requires notice to the taxpayer of a right to a hearing before a levy is made, 26 U.S.C. § 6330(a), and guarantees the right to a fair hearing before an impartial officer from the Internal Revenue Service Office of Appeals. Id. § 6330(b). In the hearing, the taxpayer may raise "any relevant issue relating to unpaid tax or the proposed levy," including "challenges to the appropriateness of collection actions," and "offers of collection alternatives, which may include . . . an offer-in-compromise." Id. § 6330(c)(2)(A). The appeals officer then must consider whether any proposed collection action "balances the need for the efficient collection of taxes with the legitimate concern of the person that any collection action be no more intrusive than necessary." 26 U.S.C. § 6330(c)(3)(C).

The statute also affords a right of judicial review of the determination by the impartial hearing officer, in either the Tax Court or a United States District Court, depending on whether the Tax Court has jurisdiction. Id. § 6330(d)(1). Judicial review in this case was available in the Tax Court because the levy related to Robinette's underlying liability for unpaid income tax.

Consistent with the legislative history of the Act, the parties agree that the Tax Court reviews the decision of an IRS hearing officer under an "abuse of discretion" standard of review. See H.R. Conf. Rep. No. 105-599, at 266 (1998) ("Where the validity of the tax liability is not properly part of the appeal, the taxpayer may challenge the determination of the appeals officers for abuse of discretion. In such cases, the appeals officer's determination as to the appropriateness of collection activity will be reviewed using an abuse of discretion standard of review."). Two of our sister circuits have concluded that "in providing for CDP hearings on what is ordinarily a scant record, Congress 'must have been contemplating a more deferential review of these tax appeals than of more formal agency decisions.' " Olsen v. United States, 414 F.3d 144, 150 (1st Cir.2005) (quoting Living Care Alternatives of Utica, Inc., v. United States, 411 F.3d 621, 625 (6th Cir.2005)). We see merit in the observation of these courts that Congress likely contemplated review for " 'a clear abuse of discretion in the sense of clear taxpayer abuse and unfairness by the IRS,' " lest the judiciary become involved on a daily basis with tax enforcement details that Congress intended to leave with the IRS. Id., 414 F.3d at 150 (quoting Living Care, 411 F.3d at 631).[2]

There is a substantial dispute in this case, however, concerning the scope of the record on which this deferential judicial review should take place. Robinette argues, and a majority of the Tax Court held, that the Tax Court may receive new evidence in the course of reviewing whether an appeals officer abused his discretion in denying relief during a collection due process hearing. Indeed, a significant portion of the Tax Court's analysis that the appeals officer abused his discretion in this case was based on evidence not presented during the administrative appeal. The Commissioner contends this was error, and that consistent with

---

2.   Robinette does argue that the Tax Court should have applied de novo review to his case because his challenge to the levy should be construed as a challenge to the underlying liability. His asserted challenge to the underlying liability, however, was merely a claim that his 1998 return was timely filed, such that the original offer-in-compromise should not have been defaulted. The Tax Court disagreed, finding that Robinette "has not proven that he filed his return on October 15, 1999," and that the "return was late filed." 123 T.C. at 106-07. This conclusion accords with the determination of the appeals officer, and Robinette does not now dispute it.

general principles of administrative law and the Administrative Procedure Act ("APA"), judicial review of the agency's decision should be limited to the administrative record developed at the hearing before the appeals officer.

It is a basic principle of administrative law that review of administrative decisions is "ordinarily limited to consideration of the decision of the agency . . . and of the evidence on which it was based." United States v. Carlo Bianchi & Co., 373 U.S. 709, 714-15, 83 S.Ct. 1409, 10 L.Ed.2d 652 (1963). Outside the context of the APA, the Supreme Court has held that where Congress simply provides for judicial review, without setting forth the standards to be used or the procedures to be followed, "consideration is to be confined to the administrative record," and "no de novo proceeding may be held." Id. at 715, 83 S.Ct. 1409. In reviewing agency action under the "abuse of discretion" standard specified in the APA, 5 U.S.C. § 706(2)(A), "the focal point for judicial review should be the administrative record already in existence, not some new record made initially in the reviewing court." Camp v. Pitts, 411 U.S. 138, 142, 93 S.Ct. 1241, 36 L.Ed.2d 106 (1973) (per curiam).

Robinette's contention, therefore, is that the review of decisions by an IRS appeals officer under § 6330 should be exempt from both the statutory framework of the APA and from general principles of administrative law that limit the scope of judicial review to the administrative record.[3] We are not persuaded that Congress endorsed such a departure when it authorized pre-deprivation judicial review of IRS levy activity in the Tax Court and the United States District Courts. The APA itself says that a subsequently enacted statute "may not be held to supersede or modify" the judicial review provisions of 5 U.S.C. § 706, "except to the extent that it does so expressly." 5 U.S.C. § 559. Whether or not the Congress of 1946 may bind the Congress of 1998 to make an "express" statement permitting the Tax Court to consider evidence outside the administrative record, see Lockhart v. United States, 546 U.S. 142, ----, 126 S.Ct. 699, 703, 163 L.Ed.2d 557 (2005) (Scalia, J., concurring), the Supreme Court has discerned in the APA "[a] statutory intent that legislative departure from the norm must be clear," Dickinson v. Zurko, 527 U.S. 150, 155, 119 S.Ct. 1816, 144 L.Ed.2d 143 (1999), and

---

3. Robinette also argues that the Commissioner waived his objection to the consideration of evidence outside the record by failing to object to the introduction of non-record evidence during the trial. In fact, the Tax Court record indicates that the Commissioner raised this argument in a pretrial memorandum, through an objection at the start of the trial, and in a motion to strike on which the court requested written briefs.

held that exemptions from the APA are "not lightly to be presumed." Marcello v. Bonds, 349 U.S. 302, 310, 75 S.Ct. 757, 99 L.Ed. 1107 (1955).

Nothing in the text or history of the Restructuring and Reform Act of 1998 clearly indicates an intent by Congress to permit trials de novo in the Tax Court when that court reviews decisions of IRS appeals officers under § 6330. If anything, the available evidence suggests the opposite. The agreed-upon standard of review itself implies that review is limited to the administrative record, for as the Tax Court seemingly recognized in another case, it would be incongruous to hold that review is limited to determining whether an appeals officer "abused his discretion," but also to conclude that the appeals officer committed such an "abuse" by failing to weigh information that was never even presented to him. See Magana v. Comm'r, 118 T.C. 488, 493 (2002). Congress has employed the abuse of discretion standard of review in various settings, and in each case, judicial review under that standard has been limited to the administrative record. See, e.g., 5 U.S.C. § 706; 8 U.S.C. § 1160(e)(3)(B); 8 U.S.C. § 1252(b)(4). We think it unlikely that Congress meant anything different here.[4]

The Tax Court seemed to believe that because it traditionally has conducted de novo proceedings in deficiency proceedings, and because Congress did not change that practice when it passed the APA in 1946, Congress should likewise be presumed to have intended de novo proceedings in the Tax Court in connection with the review of decisions by an appeals officer under § 6330. We do not think the proposed conclusion follows from the history. Collection due process hearings under § 6330 were newly-created administrative proceedings in 1998, and the statute provided for a corresponding new form of limited judicial review. The nature and purpose of these proceedings are different from deficiency determinations, and it is just as likely that Congress believed judicial review of decisions by appeals officers in this context should be conducted in accordance with traditional principles of administrative law. Indeed, that Congress provided for judicial review in either the Tax

---

4.   That Congress created jurisdiction in the Tax Court for certain appeals under § 6330(d) means that there is not a duplicate cause of action in a United States District Court under the APA. 5 U.S.C. § 704; Bowen v. Massachusetts, 487 U.S. 879, 903, 108 S.Ct. 2722, 101 L.Ed.2d 749 (1988). The availability of an adequate remedy in the Tax Court, rather than the district court, however, does not mean that the judicial review provisions of § 706 of the APA are inapplicable in the Tax Court, just as they are not inapplicable when Congress provides for judicial review in the court of appeals rather than the district court. See Ewing v. Comm'r, 122 T.C. 32, 61 n. 9, 2004 WL 158177 (2004) (Halpern and Holmes, JJ., dissenting), vacated and rev'd on other grounds, Nos. 04-73237, 04-73699, 2006 WL 463788 (9th Cir. Feb.28, 2006); see also, e.g., 15 U.S.C. 78y (placing review of Securities and Exchange Commission orders in the Court of Appeals); D'Alessio v. SEC, 380 F.3d 112, 120 (2d Cir.2004) (noting that the APA's judicial review provisions apply to review of SEC orders); Domestic Sec., Inc. v. SEC, 333 F.3d 239, 248 (D.C.Cir.2003) (same).

Court or a United States District Court, depending on the type of underlying tax liability involved, indicates that traditional principles of administrative law should apply. Every district court to consider an appeal under § 6330 has limited its review to the record created before the agency, see Olsen, 414 F.3d at 154 n. 9, and it would be anomalous to conclude that Congress intended in § 6330(d) to create disparate forms of judicial review depending on which court was reviewing the decision of an IRS appeals officer in a collection due process proceeding.[5]

That the collection due process hearings are informal does not suggest that the scope of judicial review should exceed the record created before the agency. "Agencies typically compile records in the course of informal agency action," and "[t]he APA specifically contemplates judicial review on the basis of the agency record compiled in the course of informal agency action in which a hearing has not occurred." Fla. Power & Light Co. v. Lorion, 470 U.S. 729, 744, 105 S.Ct. 1598, 84 L.Ed.2d 643 (1985). We thus find unpersuasive Robinette's reliance on O'Dwyer v. Commissioner, 266 F.2d 575 (4th Cir.1959), which was premised on a now-outmoded understanding that informal agency action cannot be reviewed based on an administrative record. Of course, where a record created in informal proceedings does not adequately disclose the basis for the agency's decision, then it may be appropriate for the reviewing court to receive evidence concerning what happened during the agency proceedings. The evidentiary proceeding in those circumstances, however, is not a de novo trial, but rather is limited to the receipt of testimony or evidence explaining the reasoning behind the agency's decision. Camp, 411 U.S. at 143, 93 S.Ct. 1241.

Robinette asserts that the record created by the appeals officer here was inadequate to permit judicial review, but he points to no specific deficiencies. The appeals officer examined Robinette's file and obtained relevant documents, including the original compromise and the letters sent by the IRS. He also kept a log detailing the dates and times of contact with the taxpayer's representative, along with brief notes about the subjects discussed in those conversations, and wrote a memorandum explaining his reasons for recommending the levy. The Tax Court supplemented this record with testimony from the appeals officer that further elucidated his rationale. This record is sufficient to permit a determination whether the appeals officer abused his discretion. We will

---

5. Nor are we persuaded by Robinette's reliance on the Tax Court's decision in Nappi v. Commissioner, 58 T.C. 282, 284, 1972 WL 2538 (1972), which held that the APA does not apply to judicial review by the Tax Court because it is not an "agency" of the government. Id. at 284. Nappi focused erroneously on the status of the reviewing court, rather than on the status of the administrative body rendering the decision under review. The Internal Revenue Service, of course, is an agency of the government, and review of its decisions may be governed by the APA.

therefore limit our review to that information which was before the IRS. See Olsen, 414 F.3d at 155 (finding adequate a record that contained, inter alia, an original offer-in-compromise, the IRS's communications and the taxpayer's responses, and the appeal's officer's conclusions).

III.

Basing our review on the information that was before the appeals officer, we next consider whether the IRS abused its discretion in proceeding with collection of Robinette's tax liability. The Tax Court believed that the appeals officer "did not have an open mind" to Robinette's arguments, and that he should have independently analyzed whether the offer-in-compromise had been "materially breached." 123 T.C. at 112. We disagree.

The Tax Court cited Arkansas case law and the Restatement of Contracts for the proposition that a party's obligation to perform under a contract is discharged only by a "material breach." 123 T.C. at 108-09.[6] It is generally true that a material failure to perform excuses the other party's obligations under the contract. It is not true, however, that only material failures to perform excuse the other party's nonperformance. In fact, material failures merely "operate[ ] as the non-occurrence of a condition," the condition being the implied-in-law obligation to perform under the contract. Id. at cmt. a. Where a condition is not a constructive term of the contract, but an express obligation upon which a party's performance depends, performance subject to that condition "cannot become due unless the condition occurs or non-occurrence is excused." Id. § 225(1); see also 13 Williston on Contracts § 38:6 (4th ed.2000). By considering only the "material failure to perform" subset of conditions, therefore, the Tax Court's analysis both reversed and truncated the inquiry: the court should first have inquired whether the requirement that Robinette file a return each year was an express condition on the government's performance, and only reached the materiality of the failure to file, if at all, upon answering the first question in the negative.

It is clear from the text of the offer-in-compromise that Robinette's duty to file a tax return each year was an express condition on the government's agreement to discharge his tax liability. His duty to file, and the consequences of any failure to file, are defined explicitly in the

---

6. Notwithstanding its citation of Arkansas authority, it is not clear that the Tax Court applied or relied upon Arkansas law. To the extent that Arkansas law might differ from the contract principles that derive from federal common law, we agree with the parties that federal law governs this case. See United States v. Kimbell Foods, Inc., 440 U.S. 715, 726, 99 S.Ct. 1448, 59 L.Ed.2d 711 (1979).

portion of his offer-in-compromise describing the offer's "terms and conditions." Robinette agreed to "comply with all provisions of the Internal Revenue Code relating to filing my/our return." He acknowledged that his liability would not be discharged "until I/we have met all the terms of the offer" and that "[i]f I/we fail to meet any of the terms and conditions of the offer, the offer is in default." These words expressly communicate conditions on the IRS's obligation, and since Robinette did not meet the conditions of the offer, it was not an error of law, or an abuse of discretion, for the appeals officer to uphold the decision of the IRS to default the agreement.

Even express conditions may be excused if they are immaterial to the exchange and if enforcement of the condition would cause "disproportionate forfeiture." Restatement (Second) of Contracts § 229 (1981). Robinette, however, did not raise any argument about the excuse of conditions during his collection due process proceedings. Even if we were to consider the issue, it would not have been unreasonable for the appeals officer to conclude that reinstating Robinette's liability would fall short of causing a "disproportionate forfeiture." Default of the agreement does not result in a forfeiture; it results in nothing more than the reinstatement of a liability that Robinette has admitted he owes, with credit for the amounts already paid. We conclude, therefore, that it was not an abuse of discretion for the IRS appeals officer to decline to excuse Robinette's breach of an express condition.

The Tax Court also believed that the appeals officer abused his discretion by not properly weighing the alternatives to collection and failing to "have an open mind regarding reinstatement." 123 T.C. at 112. We disagree. Although it is not at all clear that the IRS's internal regulations and procedures permit reinstatement of an offer that was properly defaulted, the record reflects that the appeals officer independently investigated that possibility. He was aware, for example, that if the offer had been defaulted in error, he could approach the IRS national office and request that the offer be reinstated. Although he found that the Internal Revenue Manual was "silent" on whether an offer could be reinstated during a § 6330 collection due process hearing, the appeals officer acknowledged that if he found that the return had been timely filed, he could have called the national office to "say this is what we've got . . . This is what we need to have done." He also determined through consultation with the national office on March 6, 2001, however, that the original offer-in-compromise could not be reinstated unless there had been an error by the IRS in declaring a default.

Whether or not the appeals officer believed that he personally could reinstate an offer-in-compromise, he clearly was aware that reinstatement was permitted in certain circumstances, and he was prepared to recommend reinstatement to the national office if he thought it was warranted. The record shows, however, that the appeals officer found that reinstatement was not appropriate in this case, given that Robinette's return was not timely filed and there was no error in defaulting the original agreement. This exercise of judgment was not an abuse of discretion.

The record shows that the appeals officer also considered collection alternatives beyond reinstatement of the offer. The notes of the appeals officer reflect that he suggested that Robinette could file a new offer-in-compromise at least three times over the course of the collection due process proceedings, and that Robinette's representative indicated that he was working on that possibility. Robinette twice requested, and twice was granted, an additional 30 days to submit a new offer-in-compromise. It was only after Robinette failed to follow up on these alternatives that the appeals officer issued his recommendation that a levy was appropriate.

Robinette contends that he was dissuaded from filing a new offer because the appeals officer told him such an offer probably could not be based on doubt as to liability for the unpaid taxes. Robinette's theory was that because the 1998 return was timely filed, there was no basis for revocation of the original offer-in-compromise, so the liability already had been eliminated by the original compromise. The appeals officer advised Robinette's representative that he did not think an offer based on doubt as to liability would be accepted. Given that the 1998 return was not timely filed, Robinette's theory for doubt as to liability was without merit, and there was no abuse of discretion in the appeals officer's advice, because it merely dissuaded Robinette from making a meritless proposal. There is no evidence that the appeals officer attempted to dissuade Robinette from submitting a new offer altogether, and the administrative record reveals that Robinette did not file any offer-in-compromise, based either on doubt as to liability or collectibility.

We find no merit in the contention that the appeals officer abused his discretion by refusing to receive evidence that Robinette sought to offer during the collection due process hearing. Much of the new evidence considered by the Tax Court-tax returns for years other than 1998, a postage meter log, cellular telephone records, credit card records, and calendar entries-are documents that Robinette's representative could have transmitted to the appeals officer during the informal hearing process. There was likewise no barrier to Robinette presenting information from other witnesses in written form or through oral statements by his representative. This evidence, moreover, does not establish the proposition for which Robinette sought to offer it-that the 1998 return was timely filed. The Tax Court itself agreed that the return was not timely filed.

We also believe that the appeals officer did reasonably "balance[ ] the need for efficient collection of taxes with the legitimate concern of the person that any collection action be no more intrusive than necessary." 26 U.S.C. § 6330(c)(3)(C). His memorandum specifically referred to this balancing test and noted the absence of any acceptable alternative that would be less intrusive than the levy. Robinette had been relieved by the original offer-in-compromise of his obligation to pay more than $800,000 in taxes that he owed to the Treasury. In exchange, the compromise included an express condition that Robinette file future tax returns in a timely manner. Robinette then elected to follow a practice of seeking multiple extensions of time and filing his return on the last possible day. As an apparent consequence of this practice, the 1998 return was not timely filed. The appeals officer acted within a reasonable range of discretion by concluding that merely reinstating the original offer, despite Robinette's breach of an express condition of the agreement, was not an acceptable alternative.

The Tax Court's decision was based in part on what we conclude was an erroneous application of administrative law and contract law. As to the balancing of considerations identified by § 6330(c)(3)(C), we believe that given the absence in this record of "taxpayer abuse and unfairness by the IRS," Living Care, 411 F.3d at 631, and under the appropriate standard and scope of review, it was inappropriate for the Tax Court to set aside the decision of the IRS appeals officer.

Accordingly, the judgment of the Tax Court is reversed.

Notes

The Pension Protection Act of 2006 provided that the Tax Court has jurisdiction over all appeals of CDP determinations after October 16, 2006, regardless of the type of tax in issue. Prior to October 16, 2006, such appeals had to be filed in the court having jurisdiction over the tax in question. Note that under the Golsen rule (see discussion, Chapter 8), the Tax Court may look outside the administrative record if an appeal in the case is to a court other than the Eighth Circuit.

The regulations provide that the Tax Court may consider:

The case file, including the taxpayer's request for hearing, any other written communications and information from the taxpayer or the taxpayer's authorized representative submitted in connection with the CDP hearing, notes made by an Appeals officer or employee of any oral communications with the taxpayer or the taxpayer's authorized representative, memoranda created by the Appeals officer or employee in connection with the CDP hearing, and any other documents or materials relied upon by the Appeals officer or employee in making the determination under section 6330(c)(3) . . .

Reg. § 301.6320-1(f)(2), Q&A 4.

Although Congress placed time constraints on taxpayers to expedite the CDP proceeding, it neglected to place any such constraints on the Service. While the Service usually tries to process such requests in less than six months, sometimes it takes much longer and this can create problems for taxpayers seeking collection relief. Carlton M. Smith and T. Keith Fogg recommend amending the code to provide that if the Service does not issue a notice of determination within a reasonable time (they suggest six months), the statute of limitations on collection should begin to run and the accrual of interest and time-sensitive penalties should be suspended until the notice is issued. The authors suggest retaining the 90-day protection under § 6330(e)(1) so that the statute would not expire prior to 90 days from the date the notice is issued. See Carlton M. Smith and T. Keith Fogg, "Collection Due Process Hearings Should Be Expedited," Tax Notes 919 (Nov. 23, 2009).

The same authors published a second article noting that CDP cases on the average take significantly longer to resolve than non-CDP cases. They recommended changes in the Tax Court's procedure for handling CDP cases. Carlton M. Smith and T. Keith Fogg "Tax Court Collection Due Process Cases Take Too Long," 130 Tax Notes 403 (Jan. 24, 2011). In response to draft of the article that the authors sent to the court, it apparently took their advice to heart. At the end of 2010, the Tax Court announced proposed changes to its rules that would expedite the CDP process. These include providing half the time required for filing answers in CDP cases (30 days instead of 60 days) and limiting the time for filing summary judgment motions in CDP cases.

2. Statute of Limitations

The statute of limitations on collection (§ 6502), on criminal tax prosecutions (§ 6531) and on refund suits (§ 6532) is tolled during a CDP proceeding. The suspension begins on the date the Service receives the taxpayer's request for a CDP hearing under § 6320 or § 6330 and ends either when the Service receives a written withdrawal of the request for the CDP hearing or after the determination of the CDP hearing becomes final (either by expiration of the period for seeking judicial review or by a final judicial decision). In no event, though, will the statute expire before the 90th day after the Service receives a written withdrawal of the request for the CDP hearing or after the determination of the CDP hearing becomes final. Reg. § 301.6320-1(g)(2); Reg. § 301.6330-1(g)(1). Thus, the statutory periods are tolled while the government is prohibited from levying. IRC § 6330(e)(1).

Problems

1. On September 1, 2001, the IRS assessed an income tax deficiency against Tim Turner. After seven years, a portion of the liability remains unpaid. On October 15, 2008, the IRS filed a notice of federal tax lien against Tim's real property. On October 17, it issued a notice to Tim informing him of his right to request a hearing before the IRS Office of Appeals if he desired to challenge the lien. On November 1, 2008, Tim mailed a request for a hearing and this request was received by the IRS on November 4. On November 21, 2008, Tim was granted a hearing and on January 5, 2009, a Determination was issued in which the Service rejected Tim's rationale. If Tim does not seek judicial review of the determination, how long does the Service have to collect the remaining liability?

2. Assume under the facts of problem one that on February 2, 2009, Tim filed a petition in the Tax Court for review of the Determination and the Tax Court upheld the determination in a decision released on June 15, 2009. Tim does not plan to appeal the decision. How long does the Service have to collect the remaining liability?

3. David Darby had an unpaid tax liability from a deficiency assessed on January 15, 1999. As a result, the IRS had filed liens against his property, both real and personal. On August 1, 2008, he received a notice of intent to levy that stated that the IRS intended to levy against his property on October 1, 2008 and that he was entitled to file a written request for a pre-levy Collection Due Process hearing with the IRS Office of Appeals within 30 days from the date of the notice. David mailed a request on October 20 proposing an offer in compromise. The request was received by the Service on October 23 and David received a hearing on November 15. On December 10, he received a determination from the Appeals Office, dated December 8, rejecting his offer. David does not plan to appeal the determination. How long does the Service have to collect the remaining tax?

3. Equivalent Hearing

If a taxpayer fails to request a CDP hearing within the appropriate 30-day time period, the taxpayer is not entitled to a CDP hearing. In order to give the taxpayer an opportunity to be heard, however, the Service will grant the taxpayer an "equivalent hearing" upon request. This hearing, like the CDP hearing, is before the Appeals Division, which will consider the same issues it would have considered at a CDP hearing. The difference, though, is that the equivalent hearing does not toll the statute of limitations on collections, and any adverse decision is not appealable unless it relates to the denial of innocent spouse relief under § 6015(e), which allows review by the Tax Court if such review is sought within 90 days of the determination. Reg. § 301.6330-1(I), Q&A-15. See discussion of innocent spouse relief, § III.A., below.

CRAIG v. COMMISSIONER
United States Tax Court, 2002.
119 T.C. 252

LARO, JUDGE.

Petitioner, while residing in Scottsdale, Arizona, petitioned the Court under section 6330(d)(1) to review respondent's determination as to his proposed levy upon petitioner's property. Respondent proposed the levy to collect Federal income taxes of approximately $10,656.55 for 1990, $12,192.27 for 1991, $18,437.01 for 1992, and $307.63 for 1995.[1] Currently, the case is before the Court on respondent's motion for summary judgment under Rule 121 and to impose a penalty against petitioner under section 6673(a). Petitioner has filed with the Court a response to respondent's motion.

We decide as a matter of first impression whether the Court has jurisdiction under section 6330(d)(1), given that respondent has never issued to petitioner a notice of determination with respect to a hearing described in section 6330 (Hearing[2]). Respondent acknowledges that petitioner was entitled to and should have been given a Hearing. All the same, respondent argues, the Court has jurisdiction to decide this case. Respondent argues that respondent's failure to grant petitioner's timely

---

1. We use the term "approximately" because these amounts were computed before the present proceeding and have since increased on account of interest.

2. The parties and the Treasury regulations refer to the hearing described in sec. 6330 as a "collection due process hearing" (or a "CDP hearing" for short). That term is not used in either sec. 6330 or the legislative history underlying the promulgation of that section. The legislative history refers to the hearing as a "pre-levy hearing". H. Conf. Rept. 105-599, at 266 (1998); 1998-3 C.B. 747, 1020. We refer to it as a "Hearing".

request for a Hearing was harmless error because petitioner was offered and attended an " equivalent hearing" under section 301.6330-1(i), Proced. & Admin. Regs. (equivalent hearing), and received a decision letter (decision letter) as to the equivalent hearing.

We hold that we have jurisdiction. Also, we shall grant respondent's motion for summary judgment, and we shall impose a $2,500 penalty against petitioner. Unless otherwise noted, section references are to the applicable versions of the Internal Revenue Code. Rule references are to the Tax Court Rules of Practice and Procedure.

Background
A. Income Tax Returns for 1990, 1991, and 1992

Petitioner and his wife, Lorraine Craig (Ms. Craig), did not file timely Federal income tax returns for 1990 and 1991. On February 18, 1993, respondent prepared and filed substitutes for returns for those years under section 6020. In preparing the substitutes for returns, respondent relied on information received from the Bureau of Labor Statistics. On October 27, 1994, and on December 14, 1994, petitioner and Ms. Craig filed joint 1990 and 1991 Federal income tax returns, respectively. Those returns were treated by respondent as amended returns. On February 3, 1995, petitioner and Ms. Craig filed a joint 1992 Federal income tax return.

On October 5, 1995, respondent issued a notice of deficiency to petitioner and Ms. Craig. The notice determined that petitioner and Ms. Craig were liable for deficiencies in their 1990, 1991, and 1992 Federal income taxes as follows:

Additions to Tax

Year	Deficiency	Sec. 6651(a)(1)	Sec. 6654
1990	$6,700	$1,675	$441
1991	50,686	12,672	2,913
1992	6,814	1,704	294

Petitioner and Ms. Craig petitioned the Court with respect to the notice on December 21, 1995. On February 24, 1997, petitioner and Ms. Craig signed a stipulated decision. This decision listed the deficiencies in Federal income tax due from petitioner and Ms. Craig in accordance with the notice of deficiency and provided that "effective upon the entry of the decision by the Court, petitioners [petitioner and Ms. Craig] waive the restriction contained in Internal Revenue Code § 6213(a) prohibiting assessment and collection of the deficiencies and additions to the tax (plus statutory interest) until the decision of the Tax Court has become final." That stipulated decision was entered by the Court on February 27, 1997.

On May 5, 1997, on the basis of the stipulated decision, respondent assessed the 1990, 1991, and 1992 Federal income tax liabilities of petitioner and Ms. Craig.

B.   Income Tax Return for 1995

On December 4, 1997, petitioner filed a 1995 Federal income tax return. On the basis of this return, respondent assessed petitioner's tax liability for 1995 on January 12, 1998.

C.   Request for a Hearing

On February 22, 2001, respondent mailed to petitioner and Ms. Craig a letter, "Final Notice-Notice of Intent to Levy and Notice of Your Right to a Hearing" (final notice), for 1990, 1991, and 1992. On the same day, respondent mailed to petitioner a final notice for 1995. Both final notices were signed by a chief of the IRS Automated Collection Branch in Ogden, Utah. These notices informed petitioner and Ms. Craig of (1) respondent's intent to levy upon their property pursuant to section 6331 and (2) their right under section 6330 to a Hearing with respondent's Office of Appeals (Appeals). Enclosed with the final notices were copies of Forms 12153, Request for a Collection Due Process Hearing. On March 17, 2001, petitioner requested timely the referenced Hearing for 1990, 1991, 1992, and 1995 by mailing to respondent a letter accompanied by two Forms 12153, the first for 1990, 1991, and 1992, and the second for 1995. Petitioner signed the letter, but he did not sign the Forms 12153. In that letter, petitioner requested a Hearing and stated the following disagreement with the proposed levy:

this letter constitutes my request for a Collection Due Process Hearing, as provided for in Code Sections 6320 and 6330, with regards to the Final Notice-Notice of Intent to Levy at issue * * *

Since Section 6330(c)(1) requires that "The appeals officer shall at the hearing obtain verification from the Secretary that the requirements of any applicable law or administrative procedure have been met," I am requesting that the appeals officer have such verification with him at the Collection Due Process Hearing and that he send me a copy such verification within 30 days from the date of this letter. In the absence of any such hearing, and if you fail to send me the requested Treasury Department Regulations and Delegation Orders within 30 days from the date of this letter, then I will consider this entire matter closed. If you do attempt to take any enforcement action against me without according me the hearing requested, and without sending me the documentation requested, you will be violating numerous laws which I will identify in a 7433 lawsuit against you and the government.

On April 12, 2001, the Ogden Service Center returned the requests to petitioner and Ms. Craig because the Forms 12153 were not signed. Two identical letters with respect to 1990, 1991, 1992, and with respect to 1995, sent to petitioner with Forms 12153 stated:

> We are returning your Form 12153, Request for a Collection Due Process Hearing, because you did not sign it. If you have not been able to work out a solution to your tax liability and still want to request a hearing with the IRS Office of Appeals, you need to complete and sign the Form 12153.
>
> If we do not hear from you by May 3, 2001, we may take enforcement action without notifying you further.

On May 6, 2001, the Ogden Service Center received from petitioner two signed Forms 12153 for 1990, 1991, and 1992, and for 1995, respectively, which stated:

> This Form 12153 WAS NOT SIGNED VOLUNTARILY, but UNDER DURESS, not wishing to give the I.R.S. or it's agents any cause to deny or delay the Due Process Hearing guaranteed to me by law as per I.R.C. Section 6330. My signature on this document DOES NOT give even TACIT AGREEMENT that the "statutory period of limitations for collection be suspended during the Collection Due Process Hearing and any subsequent judicial review".

On September 28, 2001, the Appeals officer held with petitioner an equivalent hearing. At the equivalent hearing, the Appeals officer explained to petitioner that it was an equivalent hearing and not a Hearing. The Appeals officer then reviewed and showed to petitioner Forms 4340, Certificate of Assessments, Payments and Other Specified Matters. The Forms 4340 were dated July 17, 2001, and were for 1990, 1991, 1992, and 1995. On September 28, 2001, after the equivalent hearing, the Appeals officer sent the Forms 4340 to petitioner.

On October 27, 2001, the Appeals officer issued to petitioner a "Decision Letter Concerning Equivalent Hearing Under Section 6320 and/or 6330" (i.e., the decision letter) for 1990, 1991, 1992, and 1995. The decision letter sustained the proposed collection action against petitioner. The decision letter stated that petitioner did not have the right to judicial review of the decision set forth in the decision letter. The decision letter stated:

> Your due process hearing request was not filed within the time prescribed under Section 6320 and/or 6330. However, you received a hearing equivalent to a due process hearing except that there is no right to dispute a decision by the Appeals Office in court under IRC Sections 6320 and/or 6330.

Discussion

A. Jurisdiction Under Section 6330(d)(1)

We decide for the first time whether we have jurisdiction under section 6330(d)(1) in the setting at hand. We conclude that we do. * * *

Section 6330(d)(1) is the specific provision that governs our jurisdiction to review a proposed collection action. Our jurisdiction under that section depends upon the issuance of a valid notice of determination and a timely petition for review. E.g., Goza v. Commissioner, 114 T.C. 176, 182 (2000); see also Lunsford v. Commissioner, 117 T.C. 159, 161, (2001). See generally Offiler v. Commissioner, 114 T.C. 492, 498 (2000) ("The notice of determination provided for in section 6330 is, from a jurisdictional perspective, the equivalent of a notice of deficiency."). Here, petitioner has timely filed a petition with this Court.[3] Thus, we are left to decide whether respondent has made a "determination" within the meaning of section 6330(d)(1) which we have jurisdiction to review.

Respondent acknowledges that petitioner did not have the Hearing described in section 6330. All the same, respondent argues, the decision letter issued to petitioner as to the equivalent hearing reflects a "determination" sufficient to invoke the Court's jurisdiction under section 6330(d)(1). We agree. The Treasury Department regulations interpreting section 6330 recognize specifically that there are two types of hearings which may be conducted by Appeals in connection with section 6330; i.e., Hearings and equivalent hearings. As explained below, the Treasury Department regulations state that an Appeals officer will consider at an equivalent hearing the same issues as at a Hearing, and that the contents of the decision letter that results from an equivalent hearing

---

3. The decision letter was sent to petitioner on Oct. 27, 2001, and the petition was postmarked Nov. 21, 2001. Whereas the petition was actually filed by the Court when received on Dec. 28, 2001, the approximately 6-week delivery time was attributable to delays in the receipt of mail experienced by the Court because of anthrax.

will generally be the same as in the notice of determination that results from a Hearing.

As to a Hearing, the statute provides that a taxpayer has a right to a Hearing with an Appeals officer before a levy may be made upon his or her property, if the Hearing is timely requested by the taxpayer. Sec. 6330(a)(1), (a)(2), (a)(3)(B), and (b)(1). The statute provides further that at the Hearing the taxpayer may raise any relevant matter set forth in section 6330(c) and that the Appeals officer shall make a "determination" as to those matters. Sec. 6330(c) and (d)(1); see also sec. 301.6330-1(f), Proced. & Admin. Regs. (regulations interpreting section 6330 provide that the Appeals officer must issue a "Notice of Determination" to any taxpayer who timely requests a Hearing).[4] The statute gives a taxpayer the right to contest the Appeals officer's determination in the appropriate judicial forum, sec. 6330(d)(1), and precludes respondent from proceeding with the proposed levy that is the subject of the Hearing while the Hearing and any appeals thereof are pending, sec. 6330(e)(1). The statute provides that the applicable periods of limitation under sections 6502, 6531, or 6532 are suspended for the same period. Sec. 6330(e)(1).

Whereas the above-stated rules for a Hearing are provided explicitly in the statute, the rules for an equivalent hearing have their genesis in the statute's legislative history and the regulations implementing Congressional intent as gleaned from that history. See H. Conf. Rept. 105-599, at 266 (1998); 1998-3 C.B. 1020 (in the event that a taxpayer does not timely request a Hearing, "The Secretary must provide a hearing equivalent to the hearing if later requested by the taxpayer"); cf. Johnson v. Commissioner, 86 AFTR 2d 2000-5225, 2000-2 USTC par. 50,591 (D.Or.2000) (" 'equivalent hearing' is provided for only by regulation and is not mandated by Section 6330 itself"). The scheme of the regulations as they apply to equivalent hearings generally follows the statutory scheme for Hearings.

---

4.   The regulations provide further that, in general, the notice of determination must set forth the Appeals officer's findings and decisions. Sec. 301.6330-1(e)(3), Q & A-E8, Proced. & Admin. Regs. More specifically, the notice of determination must: (1) State whether respondent met the requirements of any applicable law or administrative procedure; (2) resolve any issue appropriately raised by the taxpayer relating to the unpaid tax; (3) decide any appropriate spousal defenses raised by the taxpayer; (4) decide any challenge made by the taxpayer to the appropriateness of the collection action; (5) respond to any offers by the taxpayer for collection alternatives; (6) address whether the proposed collection action represents a balance between the need for the efficient collection of taxes and the legitimate concern of the taxpayer that any collection action be no more intrusive than necessary; (7) set forth any agreements that Appeals reached with the taxpayer, any relief given the taxpayer, and any actions which the taxpayer or respondent are required to take; and (8) advise the taxpayer of the right to seek judicial review within 30 days of the date of the notice of determination. Id.

Under the regulations, any taxpayer who fails to timely request a Hearing may receive an equivalent hearing. Sec. 301.6330-1(i)(1), Proced. & Admin. Regs. The equivalent hearing (like the Hearing) is held with Appeals, and the Appeals officer considers the same issues which he or she would have considered had the equivalent hearing been a Hearing. Id. The Appeals officer also generally follows the same procedures at an equivalent hearing which he or she would have followed had the equivalent hearing been a Hearing. Id. Although the Appeals officer concludes an equivalent hearing by issuing a decision letter, as opposed to a notice of determination, the different names which are assigned to these documents are merely a distinction without a difference when it comes to our jurisdiction over this case, where a Hearing was timely requested. The decision letter contains all of the information required by section 301.6330-1(e)(3), Q & A-E8, Proced. & Admin. Regs., to be included in a notice of determination but for the fact that the decision letter ordinarily states in regard to most issues that a taxpayer may not (as opposed to may) seek judicial review of the decision.[5] Id.; cf. sec. 301.6330-1(i)(2), Q & A-I5, Proced. & Admin. Regs. (taxpayer may in certain cases contest in court the Appeals officer's decision in an equivalent hearing to deny a claim for relief from joint liability under section 6015).

Under the facts herein, where Appeals issued the decision letter to petitioner in response to his timely request for a Hearing, we conclude that the "decision" reflected in the decision letter issued to petitioner is a "determination" for purposes of section 6330(d)(1). Cf. Moorhous v. Commissioner, 116 T.C. 263, 270 (2001) (decision reflected in a decision letter was not a "determination" under section 6330(d)(1) where the taxpayer's request for a Hearing was untimely); Nelson v. Commissioner, T.C. Memo.2002-264 (same); Lopez v. Commissioner, T.C. Memo.2001-228 (same). The fact that respondent held with petitioner a hearing labeled as an equivalent hearing, rather than a hearing labeled as a Hearing, and that respondent issued to petitioner a document labeled as a decision letter, rather than a document labeled as a notice of determination, does not erase the fact that petitioner received a "determination" within the meaning of section 6330(d)(1). We hold that we have jurisdiction to decide this case.

---

5. Nor do we find a distinction for purposes of our jurisdiction in the fact that the Treasury Department's regulations provide that a taxpayer's request for an equivalent hearing neither automatically suspends the levy actions which are subject of the Hearing nor the running of any period of limitations under secs. 6502, 6531, or 6532. Sec. 301.6330-1(i)(2), Q & A-I1 and 2, Proced. & Admin. Regs.

Notes

In Smith v. Commissioner, T.C. Memo. 2007-221, the taxpayers made a timely request for a CDP hearing which they later withdrew after they entered into a successful installment agreement with the Service. Subsequently, they defaulted on the agreement and in response to a notice of levy, they requested a hearing. They received an equivalent hearing and a decision letter at the conclusion of the hearing. The letter denied the taxpayer's request for another installment agreement and sustained the levy action. The taxpayers then appealed to the Tax Court on the ground that their decision letter was a determination letter because they had made an initial timely request for a CDP hearing. The Tax Court, however, rejected this argument, noting that the taxpayers had withdrawn their initial request and a default on their installment agreement did not revive the request. The court distinguished *Craig* on the ground that the taxpayers in *Craig* had been entitled to a § 6330 hearing but had not received it.

D. ENFORCEMENT OF THE LIEN

A federal tax lien merely establishes the government's claim to property or property rights. The lien is not self-executing, so in order to enforce its claim, the government must take affirmative action within the statutory collection period. There are two general methods, judicial and administrative, available to the government to enforce its claim.

1. Judicial Enforcement

If the government chooses to enforce its claim judicially, it may bring a civil action in the federal district courts under § 7403. All parties having an interest in the property should be given notice of the suit because their rights also will be adjudicated. At the conclusion of the suit, the property subject to the lien will be sold and the proceeds will be used to satisfy the tax lien and any other liens to which the property may be subject.

UNITED STATES v. BARR
United States Court of Appeals, Sixth Circuit, 2010.
617 F.3d 370

ROGERS, CIRCUIT JUDGE.

The Government seeks to foreclose the federal income tax debt owed by Charles Barr against the home that he and his wife Carolyn own as tenants by the entirety. Mrs. Barr argues on appeal, as she did before the district court, that she is entitled to the vast majority of the sale proceeds of any foreclosure sale and that foreclosure is not appropriate based on her dominant interest in the home and other equitable factors. Because spouses owning property as tenants by the entirety are entitled to equal distribution of proceeds under all circumstances contemplated by Michigan law, such an equal division is also proper in this case. In light of this equal division, the district court correctly determined that foreclosure was appropriate.

Charles Barr owed the Government more than three hundred thousand dollars in unpaid income taxes, interest, and other statutory accruals. The Government filed suit seeking to foreclose the federal tax lien created by these debts against the home in Detroit, Michigan, that Mr. Barr and his wife Carolyn Barr own as tenants by the entirety. Mr. Barr did not file a response in the case, and the district court granted default judgment against Mr. Barr in the amount of his tax debt. The Government then filed a motion for summary judgment on its foreclosure claim. Mrs. Barr opposed the motion and asked the district court to exercise its limited equitable discretion to decline to order the sale of the home. She argued in particular that, because she was likely to outlive her husband, her interest in the home was more than fifty percent of the value of the home. She contended that foreclosure was therefore inappropriate because of her larger interest and because only her husband had unpaid federal tax liabilities. The Government argued that an equal division was appropriate under Michigan law and that Mrs. Barr had assisted in shifting properties other than the home out of Mr. Barr's name and into her name. The Government thus urged the conclusion that Mrs. Barr bore some of the responsibility for the fact that the Government could only collect taxes from Mr. Barr by foreclosure. The district court held that an equal division of any proceeds was appropriate, and the court refused to exercise its equitable discretion to prevent the foreclosure sale. Mrs. Barr now appeals, arguing primarily that the district court erred in determining that she was only entitled to half of the proceeds of any foreclosure sale.

Mrs. Barr is entitled to fifty percent of the proceeds of the foreclosure sale of the home. Title 26 U.S.C. § 7403 authorizes federal courts to decree a sale of property to enforce a federal tax lien. When such a foreclosure sale takes place, the proceeds are to be distributed "according to the findings of the court in respect to the interests of the parties and of the United States," thus providing fair compensation both to the Government and to any third parties. Id. § 7403(c). In determining property interests for federal tax law purposes, "the definition of underlying property interests is left to state law, [and] the consequences that attach to those interests is a matter left to federal law." United States v. Rodgers, 461 U.S. 677, 683, 103 S.Ct. 2132, 76 L.Ed.2d 236 (1983). Under Michigan law, Mr. and Mrs. Barr have identical rights to their marital home. Indeed, spouses are entitled to equal interests in entireties property in every situation contemplated by Michigan law. Spouses are "equally entitled to the rents, products, income, or profits . . . of real . . . property held by them as tenants by the entirety." Mich. Comp. Laws § 557.71. If property held by the entirety is sold, each spouse is entitled to half of the proceeds, and upon divorce, state law provides for a default equal division of such property. Id. § 552.102; United States v. Craft, 535 U.S. 274, 282, 122 S.Ct. 1414, 152 L.Ed.2d 437 (2002). Under 26 U.S.C. § 7403(c), the "distribution of the proceeds" of a tax foreclosure sale is made "according to the findings of the court in respect to the interests of the parties and of the United States." Because Mr. and Mrs. Barr have equal interests in their home, division according to their interests results in an equal distribution of the proceeds of the sale of that home. The Third Circuit has reached the same conclusion in the context of distributing the proceeds of the market sale of a federal tax-encumbered home that had been owned by a married couple as tenants by the entirety. Popky v. United States, 419 F.3d 242, 245 (3d Cir.2005). The Third Circuit noted that Pennsylvania entireties law was materially similar to that of Michigan, id. at 244, and reasoned as follows:

> As the District Court correctly observed, "the equal division of assets between spouses . . . parallels the distribution of entireties property when an entireties estate is severed because of a sale with consent of both tenants, divorce or other reasons." Sound policy reinforces the District Court's approach to valuation, as an equal valuation is far simpler and less speculative than the valuation contemplated by the [married couple].

Id. at 245.

Detailed consideration of the component interests of a tenancy by the entirety reinforces this intuitive conclusion. A tenancy by the entirety under Michigan law consists of at least the following rights:

> the right to use the property, the right to exclude third parties from it, the right to a share of income produced from it, the right of survivorship, the right to become a tenant in common with equal shares upon divorce, the right to sell the property with the [the other spouse]'s consent and to receive half the proceeds from such a sale, the right to place an encumbrance on the property with the [the other

spouse]'s consent, and the right to block [the other spouse] from selling or encumbering the property unilaterally.

Craft, 535 U.S. at 282, 122 S.Ct. 1414. Mrs. Barr asserts that her right of survivorship and her right to prevent sale or encumbrance of the property are worth more than her husband's survivorship and sale-prevention rights, but both of these rights generate equal spousal interests.

Michigan law dictates the result that survivorship rights are equal between spouses. If the spouse with the greater life expectancy had a larger interest under Michigan law, then this greater interest would be reflected in the Michigan rules for dividing property upon divorce or consensual sale. However, because Michigan law provides for equal division of property upon divorce or consensual sale, differences in life expectancy do not result in different survivorship interests.

This conclusion is consistent with *Rodgers*. In *Rodgers*, Lucille Rodgers was the widow of Philip Bosco, a tax debtor. 461 U.S. at 687, 103 S.Ct. 2132. Rodgers and her husband had owned and occupied their home as a homestead under Texas law. Id. Texas law provides that, at the death of one spouse, the other spouse "has a vested estate in the [homestead property] of which she cannot be divested during her life except by abandonment or a voluntary conveyance." Id. at 686, 103 S.Ct. 2132 (quoting Paddock v. Siemoneit, 147 Tex. 571, 218 S.W.2d 428, 436 (1949)). Rodgers thus effectively had a life estate in her marital home. See id. at 686, 103 S.Ct. 2132. The *Rodgers* Court held that the Government could force a sale of the home under § 7403 to satisfy Bosco's tax debt. Id. at 703-04, 103 S.Ct. 2132. Recognizing that Rodgers was entitled to a share of the proceeds of that sale corresponding with her interest in the homestead property, the Court offered, "*only for the sake of illustration*," an example of how such property might be valued. Id. at 698-99, 103 S.Ct. 2132 (emphasis in original). The Court suggested that a proper way to value Rodgers's life estate would be to assume an eight percent discount rate, assume that Rodgers would live to her life expectancy, and thus calculate her share of the property's value. Id. This kind of actuarial calculation is not appropriate in the present case. *Rodgers* used actuarial valuation only out of necessity: one cannot determine the value of a life estate-which is effectively what Rodgers possessed-without estimating the length of the measuring life. The Supreme Court thus based its choice of valuation method on the fact that "any calculation of the cash value of a homestead interest must of necessity be based on actuarial statistics." Id. at 704, 103 S.Ct. 2132. No such necessity exists here, and Mrs. Barr presents no compelling reason why this court should not apply the presumption of equal spousal life expectancy implicit in Michigan law.

Mrs. Barr's right to prevent sale also does not support her contention that her interest in the marital home is greater than that of her husband. Mrs. Barr asserts first that her right to prevent sale must have some value, and that this value must increase her interest in the property. This argument overlooks the fact that the ban on unilateral alienation is both a benefit and a detriment to owners of entireties property. Mrs. Barr's sale-prevention right enhances her interest because she can prevent a sale desired only by Mr. Barr. But the same rule detracts from her interest, as she cannot sell or encumber her interest in the property without Mr. Barr's permission. Because these rights are precisely reciprocal between spouses, they have no net effect on the relative interests of spouses who own property as tenants by the entirety.

Relying by analogy on Takings Clause precedents, Mrs. Barr secondly asserts that the fact that she is being deprived of her right to prevent sale distinguishes the present situation from a consensual sale, and thus undermines the conclusion that Michigan law implicitly supports an equal assignment of interests. In upholding § 7403 as consistent with the Fifth Amendment, the Supreme Court in Rodgers noted that, "[t]o the extent that third-party property interests are 'taken' in the process [of a tax foreclosure], § 7403 provides compensation for that 'taking' by requiring that the court distribute the proceeds of the sale 'according to the findings of the court in respect to the interests of the parties and of the United States.' " 461 U.S. at 697-98, 103 S.Ct. 2132. Mrs. Barr is correct that the exercise of the Government's power to force the sale of her home deprives her of her right to refuse a sale, and she is not specifically being compensated for that loss. But this is consistent with the general rule under the Takings Clause that property owners are paid only the fair market value of their property when they are forced to part with it against their will. See Kirby Forest Indus., Inc. v. United States, 467 U.S. 1, 9-10, 104 S.Ct. 2187, 81 L.Ed.2d 1 (1984). " 'Under this standard, the owner is entitled to receive what a willing buyer would pay in cash to a willing seller at the time of the taking.' " Id. at 10, 104 S.Ct. 2187. The Supreme Court has acknowledged that, "[p]articularly when property has some special value to its owner because of its adaptability to his particular use, the fair-market-value measure does not make the owner whole." Id. at 10 n. 15, 104 S.Ct. 2187. But "[w]e are willing to tolerate such occasional inequity because of the difficulty of assessing the value an individual places upon a particular piece of property and because of the need for a clear, easily administrable rule governing the measure of 'just compensation.' " Id. The present situation is distinguishable from a consensual sale only in that Mrs. Barr is being forced to sell the home against her will. Because the Takings Clause does not require compensation for such a loss, Takings Clause jurisprudence supports the conclusion that Mrs. Barr should receive no more here than she would receive after a consensual sale: fifty percent.

Mrs. Barr also asserts that she has an interest in the home greater than half of its value based on a variety of theories that would result in the total of her and her husband's interests in the property's being greater than one hundred percent. Such a result is not possible under § 7403, which requires courts to distribute "the proceeds of such sale according to the findings of the court in respect to the interests of the parties and of the United States." One cannot distribute more than the total value of the sale price, and thus the total of all of the interests in the property-including that of the United States-must be one hundred percent.

The district court therefore correctly determined that Mrs. Barr is entitled to fifty percent of the proceeds of the foreclosure sale. This conclusion renders moot Mrs. Barr's argument that, if this court were to overturn the district court's finding with respect to valuation, remand would be appropriate to determine whether the equities continued to support a sale of the home.

Mrs. Barr also argues that the district court erred in granting summary judgment because it failed to conduct in a proper manner the balancing test described in *Rodgers*. This argument fails because the *Rodgers* Court did not mandate application of the four-factor balancing test before a district court could order a sale under § 7403. To the contrary, the *Rodgers* Court established the balancing test as a requirement only after the district court first determines that a § 7403 sale would cause undue hardship to an innocent third-party; before exercising its limited discretion not to order the sale, a district court must justify that decision by means of the *Rodgers* balancing test. This conclusion is supported by the *Rodgers* Court's declaration that the Government has a "paramount interest" in collecting taxes, 461 U.S. at 711, 103 S.Ct. 2132, and follows established precedent in the Seventh Circuit, United States v. Davenport, 106 F.3d 1333, 1338 (7th Cir.1997) (holding that application of the *Rodgers* factors "is not a prerequisite to a district court's power to decree a sale under § 7403").

Even if the *Rodgers* Court had intended to mandate application of its four-part balancing test prior to any court-ordered foreclosure sale under § 7403, we would still affirm the decision of the district court, as there is no evidence that the district court abused its discretion. In determining that foreclosure was appropriate, the district court applied the four *Rodgers* factors:

> (1) "the extent to which the Government's financial interest would be prejudiced if it were relegated to a forced sale of the partial interest actually liable for the delinquent taxes;" (2) "whether the third party with a non-liable separate interest in the property would, in the normal course of events (leaving aside § 7403 and eminent domain proceedings, of course), have a legally recognized expectation that separate property would not be subject to forced sale by the delinquent taxpayer or his or her creditors;" (3) "the likely prejudice to the third party, both in personal dislocation costs and in . . . practical undercompensation;" and (4) "the relative character and value of the non-liable and liable interests held in the property."

United States v. Barr, No. 07-11717, 2008 WL 4104507, at *2 (E.D.Mich. Sept. 2, 2008) (quoting *Rodgers*, 461 U.S. at 710-11, 103 S.Ct. 2132). The district court determined that the first factor weighed in favor of foreclosure because "the United States cannot look to any other assets of [Mr. Barr] to collect." Id. at *3. The district court noted that, under normal circumstances, the second factor would weigh against foreclosure. Id. The court, however, found that Mrs. Barr had "participated in the conveyance of four properties . . . specifically contemplated to frustrate the United States' tax collection efforts," and thus the court determined that this factor was not entitled to much weight. Id. (citing United States v. Bierbrauer, 936 F.2d 373, 376 (8th Cir.1991)). With respect to the third factor, the district court determined that "[t]he inconvenience of [Mrs. Barr's] relocating is no different from the inconvenience associated with any foreclosure sale and is insufficient to support a denial of such a sale in this case." Id. The court explained that "if 'the inherent indignity and inequity of being removed from one's home' automatically precluded foreclosure, 'the government could never foreclose against a jointly owned residence-a result clearly untenable under § 7403.' " Id. (quoting *Bierbrauer*, 936 F.2d at 375-76). Finally, the district court determined that the fourth factor did not support application of the court's limited equitable discretion not to order foreclosure because Mrs. Barr had only a half interest in the property. Id. at *4. The district court thus found that foreclosure was appropriate and granted summary judgment to the Government. Id. We agree with the district court's resolution of these issues and therefore adopt the district court's thoughtful reasoning with regard to the *Rodgers* factors.

We therefore AFFIRM the judgment of the district court.

ALICE M. BATCHELDER, CHIEF JUDGE, concurring in part and dissenting in part.

I concur with the majority opinion's conclusion that foreclosure of the residence of Charles and Carolyn Barr was appropriate pursuant to 26 U.S.C. § 7403. The majority opinion, however, conflates two distinct issues: (1) whether foreclosure is appropriate, in order to satisfy the tax obligations of her husband, Charles Barr; and (2) the proper distribution of the sales proceeds post-foreclosure. The majority opinion appears to conclude that the district court was correct because it was also correct in determining that Mrs. Barr was entitled to only 50% of the net sales proceeds. While I agree that foreclosure was correct, there is no legal justification for concluding, as the majority opinion does, that the propriety of foreclosure is somehow dependent upon a particular distribution of proceeds. I also strongly reject the majority opinion's surprising conclusion that Michigan law requires us to treat a forced sale for tax purposes as identical to a consensual sale. For these reasons, I respectfully dissent.

A. The District Court's Order of Foreclosure

It is undisputed that the government had the right to request, pursuant to 26 U.S.C. § 7403, that the district court order the sale of the Residence. United States v. Rodgers, 461 U.S. 677, 680, 103 S.Ct. 2132, 76 L.Ed.2d 236 (1983) (holding that § 7403 "grant[s] power to order the sale"); United States v. Craft, 535 U.S. 274, 283, 122 S.Ct. 1414, 152 L.Ed.2d 437 (2002) (holding that, under Michigan law, tenants in the entirety possess sufficient property interests for federal tax liens to attach). The power to order the sale, however, "is limited to some degree by equitable discretion" and, if the property is sold, the non-delinquent spouse is entitled to the portion of the sale proceeds "as represents complete compensation for the loss of the [property interests]." *Rodgers*, 461 U.S. at 680, 103 S.Ct. 2132.

The plain language of § 7403 indicates that a district court may order the sale of property, which allows the district court "limited room . . . for the exercise of reasoned discretion." Id. at 706, 103 S.Ct. 2132. However, the Supreme Court has stated that this discretion is limited and "should be exercised rigorously and sparingly, keeping in mind the Government's paramount interest in prompt and certain collection of delinquent taxes." Id. at 711, 103 S.Ct. 2132. In determining whether to decline to authorize a sale, a district court should consider, among others, the following factors: (1) the extent to which the government's financial interests would be prejudiced if it could sell only a partial interest in the property, rather than the property as a whole; (2) whether the third party with a non-liable separate interest would, in the normal course of events, have a legally recognized expectation that the property would not be subject to a forced sale; (3) the likely prejudice to the third party, both in personal dislocation costs and practical undercompensation; and (4) the relative character and value of the non-liable and liable interests held in the property.[1] Id. at 710-11, 103 S.Ct. 2132.

The majority opinion correctly rejects Mrs. Barr's argument that the *Rodgers* balancing test is mandatory. The majority opinion also correctly concludes that, even if the balancing test was mandatory, foreclosure would still have been required under § 7403. However, although the district court did not err in concluding that foreclosure was appropriate, it did err in its discussion of the second factor and Mrs. Barr's alleged complicity with the transfer of four Saginaw, Michigan properties in order to "frustrate the United States' tax collection efforts."

Mrs. Barr had a legal right to preclude sale of the Residence, and there is no legal justification for concluding that her participation in the transfer of the Saginaw Properties somehow eliminated that "legally recognized expectation" that the Residence could not be sold without her permission. The district court was correct that Mrs. Barr's unclean hands argue against an exercise of discretion in her favor, but that does not justify an incorrect application of the second *Rodgers* factor, especially since the *Rodgers* Court expressly stated that the four factors listed did not comprise a comprehensive list, thus allowing for other considerations. *Rodgers*, 461 U.S. at 710, 103 S.Ct. 2132. The district court should have concluded that the second factor weighed in favor of Mrs. Barr, and discussed Mrs. Barr's participation of the transfers of the Saginaw properties when considering other equitable factors relative to the proposed foreclosure.[2]

B. The District Court's Valuation of Property Interests

The district court is also charged with determining the proper division of sale proceeds between innocent third parties and the

---

1. This factor could be misinterpreted as establishing a correct division of post-foreclosure sale assets as a prerequisite for foreclosure under § 7403. However, the *Rodgers* Court was concerned only with the possibility that the third party interest might be so large as to swamp the interest of the delinquent taxpayer's interest. "[I]f, on the other hand, the third party not only has a possessory interest or fee interest, but that interest is worth 99% of the value of the property, then there might well be virtually no reason to allow the sale to proceed." *Rodgers*, 461 U.S. at 711, 103 S.Ct. 2132.

2. While this may seem hyper-technical, this area of the law has suffered from a lack of clarity for long enough. We ought to clarify the analysis that the district courts should conduct in cases such as these, even at the risk of appearing hyper-technical.

government. The Supreme Court has offered the following instructions to guide that process: (1) distribution of the sale proceeds must consider all the interests held by the parties, *Rodgers*, 461 U.S. at 681, 103 S.Ct. 2132; (2) the district court must look to state law to determine each party's "bundle of sticks-a collection of individual rights which, in certain combinations, constitute property," *Craft*, 535 U.S. at 278, 122 S.Ct. 1414; (3) the district court must ensure that innocent third parties receive "complete compensation" for their interests, *Rodgers*, 461 U.S. at 680, 103 S.Ct. 2132;[3] (4) the district court may not award the government any more of the proceeds than the share to which it is entitled, id. at 699, 103 S.Ct. 2132 (declaring that the provisions of § 7403 "ensur[e] that the Government not receive out of the proceeds of the sale any more than to which it is properly entitled"); and (5) the government's interest is limited to the interest held by the delinquent taxpayer, which interest must be established prior to the § 7403 order of sale, id. at 690-91, 103 S.Ct. 2132. These guidelines make it abundantly clear that Mrs. Barr's proposed valuation method is illogical and unsupportable. However, the majority opinion's simplistic valuation method is similarly flawed.

The majority opinion correctly identifies the property rights Mrs. Barr possesses-a life estate, a survivor interest, and a right to prevent sale, among others-but then loses its way by attempting to infer precisely how a Michigan court would value those property interests in a situation like this. I strongly disagree with the majority opinion's conclusion that a § 7403 forced sale is equivalent to a divorce or consensual sale, for reasons I describe in greater detail below. However, even if Michigan courts would agree with the majority opinion on this point, that conclusion is irrelevant to our consideration of the issues here, because "although the definition of underlying property interests is left to state law, the consequences that attach to those interests is a matter left to federal law." *Rodgers*, 461 U.S. at 683, 103 S.Ct. 2132. We are constrained to recognize the property rights Mrs. Barr possesses under Michigan law, but the issue of how those interests are to be compensated is solely a matter of federal law.

The weight of federal law argues strongly against the majority opinion's conclusion that Mrs. Barr is entitled to a simple fifty percent interest because she is a tenant by the entireties. The district court and the majority opinion rely on Popky v. United States, 419 F.3d 242, 245 (3d Cir.2005), in which the Third Circuit adopted a 50/50 split for tenants

---

3. According to the *Rodgers* Court, it is only through awarding complete compensation to the innocent third party that § 7403 avoids any "difficulties under the Due Process Clause of the Fifth Amendment." *Rodgers*, 461 U.S. at 697, 103 S.Ct. 2132. Therefore, district courts must take care to assure that innocent third parties receive compensation for each property interest they possess.

by the entireties because a 50/50 split was "far simpler and less speculative," and because the Third Circuit viewed a § 7403 sale as equivalent to a consensual sale, id.[4] However, the far greater weight of the cases support a different approach. See Harris v. United States, 764 F.2d 1126, 1131-32 (5th Cir.1985) (valuing the spouses' life estates and contingent survivor interests and determining that, based on her higher life expectancy, the wife had a 50.98% interest.); United States v. Gibbons, 71 F.3d 1496, 1500 (10th Cir.1995) (requiring the valuation of an ex-wife's life estate and survivor interest and concluding that she was entitled to greater than one-half the total value of the property); In re Pletz, 221 F.3d 1114, 1117 (9th Cir.2000) (holding that proper valuation requires consideration of the life expectancies of the joint tenants, and rejecting the proposition that the wife's share was limited to a half interest in the life estate).

Likewise, while this Circuit has never directly addressed this question, our prior decisions in other contexts support a rejection of a blanket 50/50 split. In United States v. 2525 Leroy Lane, 910 F.2d 343 (6th Cir.1990), this court was faced with a criminal forfeiture proceeding in which the property to be sold, via forfeiture, was held as a joint tenancy by the entireties. The court refused to sever the entireties estate and turn it into a tenancy in common because doing so "would not adequately compensate [the wife] for her survivorship interest." Id. at 350. Unquestionably, the wife in *2525 Leroy Lane* would have been entitled to only a one-half share of a tenancy in common, so this court has already determined that an innocent spouse's interest in a tenancy by the entireties must be valued higher than an equivalent interest in a tenancy in common if it is probable that the innocent spouse will outlive the guilty (delinquent) spouse.

Even ignoring the linguistic inconsistency of asserting that a forced sale and a consensual sale should be treated the same, treating a § 7403 forced sale as equivalent to a consensual sale or sale subsequent to a divorce also ignores a fundamental question of timing. When a divorce occurs, and the property is sold, the tenancy by the entirety is severed by the divorce decree first, and only then is the property sold. The divorce decree transforms the tenancy in the entireties into a tenancy in common, so a 50/50 split from a subsequent sale is the natural result. Similarly, when a consensual sale occurs, both parties consent to the

---

4.   There is simply no legal justification for ignoring the vested property rights of litigants in order to avoid complexity and uncertainty and, while I do not believe the majority opinion was adopting that particular rationale in support of its conclusion, I believe we should explicitly reject the Third Circuit's simplicity rationale.

sale, effectively surrendering their survivor interests and their right to prevent sale. Only then is the sale effectuated, and a 50/50 split is, again, the natural result. With a sale pursuant to § 7403, however, the value of the non-delinquent spouse's interests must be determined prior to the § 7403 order, by which the court will extinguish those rights. Valuation of property interests under § 7403 cannot occur as if the non-delinquent spouse had already surrendered her interests. To do so would raise the unsightly specter of a taking without just compensation. See *Rodgers*, 461 U.S. at 697, 103 S.Ct. 2132 (holding that § 7403 requires compensation for every property interest that is "taken" in the process).

Mrs. Barr has legitimate property interests in her residence, and those interests cannot be simply assumed away by pretending that a § 7403 sale is the same as a consensual sale or a sale subsequent to a divorce decree. Supreme Court precedent demands that we protect Mrs. Barr's right to compensation for her property interests during the § 7403 process, something which the majority opinion fails to do. The weight of case law, both from this circuit and our sister circuits, is also strongly in favor of recognizing, and requiring compensation for, Mrs. Barr's survivor interest and right to prevent sale. Because the majority opinion fails to do either of these, I respectfully dissent.

Notes and Questions

In U.S. v. Vogt, 2008 WL 4276241 (N.D. Ind.)(unreported opinion), a district court judge indicated that she might exercise her equitable discretion against ordering an immediate foreclosure of a residence in which the non-liable spouse lived with her children. The spouse had indicated that she was not in good health, that the residence was the only home her children had known, and that it had been built by both her husband and father with their own hands. The judge indicated that she did have enough facts before her to grant summary judgment in the government's favor.

1. How, if at all, does a § 7403 proceeding differ from an in rem proceeding?

2. If there has been a wrongful levy and the property has been sold, how should the proceeds be distributed? See IRC § 6343(b).

3. If the government has a first lien on the property being sold, it is entitled to bid on the property (up to the amount of the lien plus expenses of sale) in order to prevent its sale below full price. In this case, what will happen to any junior liens? What happens in a foreclosure sale if the federal tax lien is the junior lien?

2. Administrative Enforcement

If the government chooses the administrative route, there are several methods of collection available. Section 6331 authorizes enforcement of the lien by administrative levy:

If any person liable to pay any tax neglects or refuses to pay same within 10 days after notice and demand, it shall be lawful for the Secretary to collect such tax (and such further sum as shall be sufficient to cover the expenses of the levy) by levy upon all property and rights to property (except such property as is exempt under § 6334) belonging to such person or on which there is a lien provided in this chapter for the payment of such tax.

26 U.S.C. § 6331(a). The following cases consider the rights of third parties in the collection process and the relationship between liens and levies.

UNITED STATES v. NATIONAL BANK OF COMMERCE
Supreme Court of the United States, 1985.
472 U.S. 713, 105 S.Ct. 2919, 86 L.Ed.2d 565.

JUSTICE BLACKMUN delivered the opinion of the Court.

* * *

The controversy in this case concerns two joint accounts in a bank in Arkansas.[3] The issue is whether the Internal Revenue Service (IRS) has a right to levy on those accounts for delinquent federal income taxes owed by only one of the persons in whose names the joint accounts stand in order that the IRS may obtain provisional control over the amount in question.

* * *

II.

A.

* * *

The Internal Revenue Code provides two principal tools * * * [to enforce collection of the unpaid taxes]. The first is the lien-foreclosure suit. * * * The suit is a plenary action in which the court "shall * * * adjudicate all matters involved therein and finally determine the merits of all claims to and liens upon the property." § 7403(c). The second tool is the collection of the unpaid tax by administrative levy. The levy is a provisional remedy and typically "does not require any judicial intervention." The governing statute is § 6331(a). It authorizes

---

3. "The basic legal conception of a 'joint account' means that it be in two or more names." Harbour v. Harbour, 207 Ark. 551, 555, 181 S.W.2d 805, 807 (1944).

collection of the tax by levy which, by § 6331(b), "includes the power of distraint and seizure by any means."

In the situation where a taxpayer's property is held by another, a notice of levy upon the custodian is customarily served pursuant to § 6332(a). This notice gives the IRS the right to all property levied upon, and creates a custodial relationship between the person holding the property and the IRS so that the property comes into the constructive possession of the Government. If the custodian honors the levy, he is "discharged from any obligation or liability to the delinquent taxpayer with respect to such property or rights to property arising from such surrender or payment." § 6332(d). If, on the other hand, the custodian refuses to honor a levy, he incurs liability to the Government for his refusal. § 6332(c)(1).

The administrative levy has been aptly described as a "provisional remedy." In contrast to the lien-foreclosure suit, the levy does not determine whether the Government's rights to the seized property are superior to those of other claimants; it, however, does protect the Government against diversion or loss while such claims are being resolved. "The underlying principle" justifying the administrative levy is "the need of the government promptly to secure its revenues." "Indeed, one may readily acknowledge that the existence of the levy power is an essential part of our self-assessment tax system," for it "enhances voluntary compliance in the collection of taxes." G.M. Leasing Corp. v. United States, 429 U.S. 338, 350, 97 S.Ct. 619, 627, 50 L.Ed.2d 530 (1977). "Among the advantages of administrative levy is that it is quick and relatively inexpensive." United States v. Rodgers, 461 U.S., at 699, 103 S.Ct., at 2145.

The constitutionality of the levy procedure, of course, "has long been settled." Phillips v. Commissioner, 283 U.S., at 595, 51 S.Ct., at 611.

B.

It is well established that a bank account is a species of property "subject to levy," within the meaning of §§ 6331 and 6332. * * *

The courts uniformly have held that a bank served with an IRS notice of levy "has only two defenses for a failure to comply with the demand." One defense is that the bank, in the words of § 6332(a), is neither "in possession of" nor "obligated with respect to" property or rights to property belonging to the delinquent taxpayer. The other defense, again with reference to § 6332(a), is that the taxpayer's property is "subject to a prior judicial attachment or execution." There is no suggestion here that the Reeves accounts were subject to a prior judicial attachment or execution. Nor is there any doubt that the bank was "obligated with respect to" the accounts because, as it concedes, "Roy Reeves did have a right under Arkansas law to make withdrawals from the bank accounts in question." The bank's only defense, therefore, is that the joint accounts did not constitute "property or rights to property" of Roy J. Reeves. See § 6331(a).

C.

" '[I]n the application of a federal revenue act, state law controls in determining the nature of the legal interest which the taxpayer had in the property.' " Aquilino v. United States, 363 U.S. 509, 513, 80 S.Ct. 1277, 1280, 4 L.Ed.2d 1365 (1960), quoting Morgan v. Commissioner, 309 U.S. 78, 82, 60 S.Ct. 424, 426, 84 L.Ed. 585 (1940). This follows from the fact that the federal statute "creates no property rights but merely attaches consequences, federally defined, to rights created under state law." United States v. Bess, 357 U.S. 51, 55, 78 S.Ct. 1054, 1057, 2 L.Ed.2d 1135 (1958). And those consequences are "a matter left to federal law." United States v. Rodgers, 461 U.S., at 683, 103 S.Ct., at 2137. "[O]nce it has been determined that state law creates sufficient interests in the [taxpayer] to satisfy the requirements of [the statute], state law is inoperative," and the tax consequences thenceforth are dictated by federal law. United States v. Bess, 357 U.S., at 56-57, 78 S.Ct., at 1057-1058.

* * *

[I]t is stipulated that Roy J. Reeves had the unqualified right to withdraw the full amounts on deposit in the joint accounts without notice to his codepositors. In any event, wholly apart from the stipulation, Roy's right of withdrawal is secured by his contract with the bank, as well as by the relevant Arkansas statutory provisions. On its part, the bank was obligated to honor any withdrawal requests Roy might make, even up to the full amounts of the accounts. The Court of Appeals thus correctly concluded that, under Arkansas law, "Roy could have withdrawn any amount he wished from the account and used it to pay his debts, including federal income taxes, and his co-owners would have had no lawful complaint against the bank."

Roy, then, had the absolute right under state law and under his contract with the bank to compel the payment of the outstanding balances in the two accounts. This, it seems to us, should have been an end to the case, for we agree with the Government that such a state-law right constituted "property [or] rights to property * * * belonging to" Roy, within the meaning of § 6331(a). The bank, in its turn, was "obligated with respect to" Roy's right to that property, § 6332(a), since state law required it to honor any withdrawal request he might make. The bank had no basis for refusing to honor the levy.[8]

The overwhelming majority of courts that have considered the issue have held that a delinquent taxpayer's unrestricted right to withdraw constitutes "property" or "rights to property" subject to provisional IRS levy, regardless of the facts that other claims to the funds may exist and that the question of ultimate ownership may be unresolved at the time. And the Eighth Circuit itself has observed that the "unqualified contractual right to receive property is itself a property right subject to seizure by levy." St. Louis Union Trust Co. v. United States, 617 F.2d 1293, 1302 (1980).[9]

Common sense dictates that a right to withdraw qualifies as a right to property for purposes of §§ 6331 and 6332. In a levy proceeding, the IRS "'steps into the taxpayer's shoes,'" United States v. Rodgers, 461 U.S., at 691, n. 16, 103 S.Ct., at 2141, n. 16, quoting 4 Bittker, ¶ 111.5.4, at 111-102. The IRS acquires whatever rights the taxpayer himself possesses. And in such circumstances, where, under state law, a taxpayer has the unrestricted right to withdraw funds from the account, "it is inconceivable that Congress * * * intended to prohibit the Government from levying on that which is plainly accessible to the

---

8. The dissent misunderstands the import of United States v. Bess, 357 U.S. 51, 55, 78 S.Ct. 1054, 1057, 2 L.Ed.2d 1135 (1958). Because state law gives the delinquent the right to withdraw, but puts certain limits on the rights of creditors, and attaches certain consequences to that right as regards the delinquent himself, the dissent asserts that the Government is limited by these same state-law constraints. Thus it urges that the Government's right here is no greater than the rights given under state law, the right to withdraw and nothing else. It therefore erroneously characterizes the Government's authority here as limited to the right to levy on the right to withdraw, and nothing else. But under Bess, state law controls only in determining the nature of the legal interest which the taxpayer has in the property. See also Aquilino v. United States, 363 U.S. 509, 513, 80 S.Ct. 1277, 1280, 4 L.Ed.2d 1365 (1960). Once it is determined that under state law the delinquent has the right to withdraw property in a joint bank account, it is a matter of federal law what consequences attach to this right. And we agree with the Government that as a matter of federal law, the state-law right to withdraw money from a joint bank account is a "right to property" adequate to justify the use of the provisional levy procedure of § 6331. The dissent's references to state cases concerning the state-law implications of the right to withdraw, thus are entirely irrelevant, for such state law is "inoperative" in determining the federal tax consequences of the delinquent's right to withdraw. See Bess, 357 U.S., at 56-57, 78 S.Ct., at 1057-1058.

9. The dissent's suggestion that these cases are "irrelevant," stems from its erroneous assumption that state law dictates the extent of the Government's power to levy. It does not, and these cases all stand for the proposition that a delinquent's state-law right to withdraw funds from the joint bank account is a property interest sufficient for purposes of federal law for the Government to levy the account, notwithstanding the fact that questions as to the ultimate ownership of the funds may be unresolved.

delinquent taxpayer-depositor."[10] The taxpayer's right to withdraw is analogous in this sense to the IRS's right to levy on the property and secure the funds. Both actions are similarly provisional and subject to a later claim by a codepositor that the money in fact belongs to him or her.

III.
* * *

The Court of Appeals' conclusion that Roy did not possess "property [or] rights to property" on which the IRS could levy rested heavily on its understanding of the Arkansas law of creditors' rights, particularly those in garnishment. As we have suggested, this misconceives the role properly played by state law in federal tax-collection matters. The question whether a state-law right constitutes "property" or "rights to property" is a matter of federal law. Thus, the facts that under Arkansas law Roy's creditors, unlike Roy himself, could not exercise his right of withdrawal in their favor and in a garnishment proceeding would have to join his codepositors are irrelevant. The federal statute relates to the taxpayer's rights to property and not to his creditors' rights. The Court of Appeals would remit the IRS to the rights only an ordinary creditor would have under state law. That result "compare[s] the government to a class of creditors to which it is superior."

* * *

In its understandable concern for Ruby's and Neva's property interests, the Court of Appeals has ignored the statutory scheme established by Congress to protect those rights. Crucially, the administrative levy, as has been noted, is only a provisional remedy. "The final judgment in [a levy] action settles no rights in the property subject to seizure." United States v. New England Merchants National Bank, 465 F.Supp. 83, 87 (Mass.1979). Other claimants, if they have rights, may assert them. Congress recognized this when the Code's summary-collection procedures were enacted, and when it provided in § 7426 of the Code that one claiming an interest in property seized for another's taxes may bring a civil action against the United States to have the property or the proceeds of its sale returned.[11] Congress also has

---

10. We stress the narrow nature of our holding. By finding that the right to withdraw funds from a joint bank account is a right to property subject to administrative levy under § 6331, we express no opinion concerning the federal characterization of other kinds of state-law created forms of joint ownership. This case concerns the right to levy only upon joint bank accounts.

11. The dissent would find support in United States v. Stock Yards Bank of Louisville, 231 F.2d 628 (CA6 1956), and Raffaele v. Granger, 196 F.2d 620 (CA3 1952). Both cases are clearly distinguishable. *Stock Yards Bank* concerned an attempted levy upon United States savings bonds,

provided, by § 6343(b), an effective and inexpensive administrative remedy for the return of the property. See Treas.Reg. § 301.6343-1(b)(2)(1984).

Congress thus balanced the interest of the Government in the speedy collection of taxes against the interests of any claimants to the property, and reconciled those interests by permitting the IRS to levy on the assets at once, leaving ownership disputes to be resolved in a post-seizure administrative or judicial proceeding. Its decision that certain property rights must yield provisionally to governmental need should not have been disregarded by the Court of Appeals. Nor would the bank be exposed to double liability were it to honor the IRS levy. The Code provides administrative and judicial remedies for codepositors against the Government, and any attempt to secure payment in this situation from the bank itself would be contrary to the federal enforcement scheme.[13]

The Court of Appeals' final justification for its holding was its belief that an IRS levy "is not normally intended for use as against property in which third parties have an interest" or "as against property bearing on its face the names of third parties, and in which those third parties likely have a property interest." The court acknowledged the existence of § 7426 but felt that that statute was designed to protect only those third parties "whose property has been seized 'inadvertently.' " 726 F.2d, at 1300.

We disagree. The IRS's understanding of the terms of the Code is entitled to considerable deference. Here, moreover, collection provisions plainly contemplate that a taxpayer's interest in property may be less than full ownership. The tax lien attaches not only to "property" but also

---

held in the names of husband and wife, to satisfy the husband's tax liability. Savings bonds, however, are different from joint bank accounts and possess "limitations and conditions * * * which are delineated by the terms of the contract and by federal law." 231 F.2d, at 630. Furthermore, the case was decided prior to the enactment of § 7426, which was added to the Internal Revenue Code by the Federal Tax Lien Act of 1966, § 110(a), 80 Stat. 1142.

Raffaele v. Granger is even less on point. The decision there did not concern the propriety of a provisional remedy, but the final ownership of the property in question. The court held that under Pennsylvania law a husband and wife's joint bank account was held by them together as tenants by the entirety, and that therefore the Government could not use the money in the account to satisfy the tax obligations of one spouse. The fact that either spouse could withdraw the property did not mean that it could be used to satisfy either spouse's tax obligations. 196 F.2d, at 622- 623. The Government here does not claim otherwise; it merely asserts the right to levy on such property and have all third parties who claim to own it come forward and make their claim.

13. As a result, it may well be that any attempt to recover against the bank under state law would be pre-empted. We need not resolve that question, however, for, under Arkansas law, the bank's payment to one depositor was a complete defense against suit on a codepositor's claim. Since the Government stood in Roy's shoes when it levied upon the joint account, the bank's payment to the IRS would likewise insulate the bank from actions by Roy's codepositors.

to "rights to property." Further, we see nothing in the language of § 7426 that distinguishes among various species of third-party claimants. The language of the statute encompasses advertent seizures as well as inadvertent ones.[14] There is nothing express or implied in United States v. Rodgers, 461 U.S. 677, 103 S.Ct. 2132, 76 L.Ed.2d 236 (1983), to the contrary.

[The] *Rodgers* * * * Court contrasted the operation of § 7403 with that of § 6331. The Court noted that § 6331, unlike § 7403, does not "implicate the rights of third parties," because an administrative levy, unlike a judicial lien-foreclosure action, does not determine the ownership rights to the property. Instead, third parties whose property is seized in an administrative levy "are entitled to claim that the property has been 'wrongfully levied upon,' and may apply for its return either through administrative channels * * * or through a civil action." The Court, in other words, recognized what we now make explicit: that § 6331 is a provisional remedy, which does not determine the rights of third parties until after the levy is made, in postseizure administrative or judicial hearings.[15]

---

14. The dissent's central argument apes the decision of the Court of Appeals in suggesting that there is something in the language of § 6331 that, when compared to the language of § 7403, requires that it be read to apply only to the case where the Government has proof that the property levied upon "*completely* belong[s]" to the delinquent. The adverb, however, simply is not part of the statutory language. The dissent bases its reading on the contrast between the language in § 7403, "property * * * in which [the delinquent] has any right, title, or interest," with the language in § 6331, "property and rights to property * * * belonging to the delinquent." While the dissent's reading of the statutes in contrast is plausible, so too is the Government's, especially in light of the fact that § 6331 refers to "rights to property" as well as "property." The legislative history also supports the agency's understanding of the statutory language. Thus when Congress in § 7426 enacted a cause of action for one whose property was wrongfully levied, it explicitly recognized that it was protecting against the situation "where the Government levies on property which, *in part at least*, a third person considers to be his." S.Rep. No. 1708, 89th Cong., 2d Sess., 29 (1966) U.S.Code Cong. & Admin.News 1966, p. 3750 (emphasis added). If Congress intended § 6331 to give the Government the power to levy only upon property it knows to be wholly owned by the delinquent, it never would have felt the need to enact § 7426. When the agency's plausible interpretation of its statute is supported by the plain meaning of the statute, the statutory scheme as a whole, and the legislative history, we shall not reject it because another plausible reading of the statute is possible.

The dissent also is incorrect when it implies that the Court gives the word "wrongful" a strained understanding in finding that a third party's property could be "wrongful[ly]" levied even though the Government properly was following the procedures of § 6331. The legislative history makes clear that the word "wrongful" as it is used in § 7426(a) refers not to intentional wrongdoing on the Government's part, but rather "refers to a proceeding against property which is not the taxpayer's." S.Rep. No. 1708, at 30, U.S.Code Cong. & Admin.News 1966, p. 3751.

15. The dissent's misreading of *Rodgers* is of a piece with its misunderstanding of the Government's use of § 6331 as a provisional remedy to seize property. The reason that § 6331 is not itself "punctilious in protecting the vested rights of third parties caught in the Government's collection effort," *Rodgers*, 461 U.S., at 699, 103 S.Ct., at 2145 is that the levy does not purport to determine any rights to the property. It merely protects the Government's interests so that rights to the property may be determined in a postseizure proceeding. It is in those proceedings that the rights of any who claim an interest to the property are punctiliously protected. In comparing § 6331

The Court of Appeals' result would force the IRS, if it wished to pursue a delinquent taxpayer's interest in a joint bank account, to institute a lien-foreclosure suit under § 7403, joining all codepositors as defendants. The practical effect of this would be to eliminate the alternative procedure for administrative levy under §§ 6331 and 6332. We do not lightly discard this alternative relief that Congress so clearly has provided for the Government. If the IRS were required to bring a lien-foreclosure suit each time it wished to execute a tax lien on funds in a joint bank account, it would be uneconomical, as a practical matter, to do so on small sums of money such as those at issue here. And it would be easy for a delinquent taxpayer to evade, or at least defer, his obligations by placing his funds in joint bank accounts. While one might not be enthusiastic about paying taxes, it is still true that "taxes are the life-blood of government, and their prompt and certain availability an imperious need." Bull v. United States, 295 U.S. 247, 259, 55 S.Ct. 695, 699, 79 L.Ed. 1421 (1935).

The judgment of the Court of Appeals is reversed.

It is so ordered.

JUSTICE POWELL, with whom JUSTICE BRENNAN, JUSTICE MARSHALL, and JUSTICE STEVENS join, dissenting.

* * *

III.

Administrative levy under 26 U.S.C. § 6331 is the more drastic of the Government's two primary collection procedures. By allowing the Government summarily to seize and sell "all property and rights to property * * * belonging to [the delinquent]," 26 U.S.C. § 6331(a), administrative levy permits the IRS to collect unpaid taxes without judicial intervention. It is a "summary, non-judicial process, a method of self-help authorized by statute which provides the Commissioner with a prompt and convenient method for satisfying delinquent tax claims." United States v. Sullivan, 333 F.2d 100, 116 (CA3 1964). It provides no notice to third parties that property in which they may have an interest has been seized. If an individual discovers a levy and believes that it was wrongful, his or her only recourse is to seek administrative review under

---

to § 7403 in this manner, the dissent compares apples and oranges. A more telling comparison to the lien-foreclosure proceeding of § 7403 would be with the administrative and judicial remedies for third parties whose property has been subject to wrongful levy, that is, with §§ 6343(b) and 7426(a)(1). It was just such a comparison that was made in this context by the Court in *Rodgers*. See id., at 696, 103 S.Ct., at 2144. * * *

26 U.S.C. § 6343(b) within nine months[2] or file suit in federal district court under 26 U.S.C. § 7426(a)(1) within the same amount of time.[3]

Section 7403 provides a quite different method for collecting delinquent taxes. Under § 7403, the Attorney General, at the request of the Secretary of the Treasury, institutes a civil action in federal district court "to subject any property * * * in which [the delinquent] has any right, title, or interest, to the payment of such tax." 26 U.S.C. § 7403(a). All persons "claiming any interest in the property" must be joined as parties, § 7403(b), and "duly notified of the action," § 7403(c). Unlike a § 6331 levy, a § 7403 suit is a plenary action in which the court "adjudicate[s] all matters involved" and "finally determine[s] the merits of all claims to and liens upon the property." § 7403(c). The district court may decree the sale of the property and distribution of the proceeds "according to the findings of the court in respect to the interests of the parties and of the United States." Ibid.

The language of these two provisions reveals the central difference between them. While § 6331 applies to "property and rights to property * * * belonging to [the delinquent]," § 6331(a), § 7403 applies to "property * * * in which [the delinquent] has any right, title, or interest * * *," § 7403(a). In other words, § 6331 permits seizure and sale of property or property rights *belonging to* the delinquent, while § 7403 allows the Government to seize and sell any property right in which the delinquent has an interest—even a *partial* interest. In many cases, of course, this difference is unimportant. Both procedures, for example, apply to any property interest that belongs completely to the delinquent, for it is

---

2. Section 6343(b) states in pertinent part:
"If the Secretary determines that property has been wrongfully levied upon, it shall be lawful for the Secretary to return--

    "(1) the specific property levied upon,

    "(2) an amount of money equal to the amount of money levied upon, or

    "(3) an amount of money equal to the amount of money received by the United States from a sale of such property.

"Property may be returned at any time. An amount equal to the amount of money levied upon or received from such sale may be returned at any time before the expiration of 9 months from the date of such levy."

3. Section 7426(a)(1) provides as follows:
"If a levy has been made on property or property has been sold pursuant to a levy, and any person (other than the person against whom is assessed the tax out of which such levy arose) who claims an interest in or lien on such property and that such property was wrongfully levied upon may bring a civil action against the United States in a district court of the United States. Such action may be brought without regard to whether such property has been surrendered to or sold by the Secretary."

26 U.S.C. § 7426(a)(1). Section 6532(c)(1) requires third parties who are not seeking administrative review to file suit within nine months of the levy.

necessarily true that any right to property "belonging to" the delinquent is also property in which he "has a[n] * * * interest."   In general, however, the opposite is not always true. A property right in which the delinquent has only a partial interest does not "belon[g] to" the delinquent and hence is not susceptible to levy.

* * *

In United States v. Rodgers, 461 U.S. 677, 103 S.Ct. 2132, 76 L.Ed.2d 236 (1983), we recently reaffirmed this understanding of the statutory scheme. After noting that § 7403 exhibits "grea[t] solicitude for third parties," id., at 695, 103 S.Ct., at 2143, we discussed how §§ 6331 and 7403 differ:

> "Under * * * § 6331(a), the Government may sell for the collection of unpaid taxes all nonexempt 'property and rights to property * * * *belonging to [the delinquent taxpayer] * * *.'* Section 6331, unlike § 7403, does not require notice and hearing for third parties, *because no rights of third parties are intended to be implicated by § 6331.* Indeed, third parties whose property or interests in property have been seized inadvertently are entitled to claim that the property has been 'wrongfully levied upon,' and may apply for its return either through administrative channels * * * or through a civil action filed in a federal district court * * *. In the absence of such 'wrongful levy,' the entire proceeds of a sale conducted pursuant to administrative levy may be applied, without any prior distribution of the sort required by § 7403, to the expenses of the levy and sale, the specific tax liability on the seized property, and the general tax liability of the delinquent taxpayer." Id., at 696, 103 S.Ct., at 2144 (first emphasis in original, second added).

The Court later described the various advantages of each method of tax collection as follows:

> "Among the advantages of administrative levy is that it is quick and relatively inexpensive. Among the advantages of a § 7403 proceeding is that it gives the Federal Government the opportunity to seek the highest return possible on the forced sale of property interests liable for the payment of federal taxes. The provisions of § 7403 are broad and profound. *Nevertheless, § 7403 is punctilious in protecting the vested rights of third parties caught in the Government's collection effort,* and in ensuring that the Government not receive out of the

proceeds of the sale any more than that to which it is properly entitled." Id., at 699, 103 S.Ct., at 2145 (emphasis added).[6]

* * *

IV.

The narrow question presented, then, is whether the Government levied upon property or rights to property belonging only to Roy Reeves. The Court holds that the Government did so because it levied on Roy Reeves's right under state law to require the bank to pay over to him the outstanding balances in the accounts. This right unquestionably belonged to Roy Reeves, as it did to each of the other codepositors They all had the same right to withdraw. But the right to withdraw funds was no more than that. It was a right accorded parties to joint accounts as a matter of mutual convenience and it was independent of any right *to* or *in* the property. It encompassed no right of possession, use, or ownership over the funds when withdrawn. * * *

The Government, however, is not levying on the mere right to withdraw, which is of little value without any right of ownership. The levy at issue reaches the underlying funds in the accounts--no matter whom they belong to. Roy Reeves could, as the Court argues, have withdrawn all the joint funds, but, if under state law he had no independent right in the property itself, he could not legally possess the funds of the others, let alone use them to pay *his* taxes. That the delinquent might unlawfully convert the money of others to pay his taxes does not give the Government the right to do so. The Government cannot ' "ste[p] into the taxpayer's shoes," ' in this sense. It hardly comports with the "[c]ommon sense" the Court relies on to hold that the

---

6. The Court attempts to minimize the conflict between its holding today and the holding in *Rodgers* by mischaracterizing that case. The Court states that "[t]he [*Rodgers*] Court noted that § 6331, unlike § 7403, does not 'implicate the rights of third parties,' because an administrative levy, unlike a judicial lien-foreclosure action, does not determine the ownership rights to the property." Nothing in *Rodgers*, however, suggests that § 6331 is not intended to implicate third-party rights for this reason. As the first quotation from *Rodgers* in the text above clearly indicates, § 6331 is not meant to implicate such rights because its explicit language limits levies for "unpaid taxes [to] all nonexempt 'property and rights to property * * * *belonging to [the delinquent taxpayer]** * *.' " (emphasis in *Rodgers*).

The Court also argues that comparing § 6331 and § 7403 is like comparing "apples and oranges." It suffices to say that this Court always has relied on comparison of these two provisions. See United States v. Rodgers, 461 U.S., at 695-697, 103 S.Ct., at 2143-2144; Mansfield v. Excelsior Refining Co., 135 U.S., at 341, 10 S.Ct., at 831. Furthermore, the "more telling" comparison that the Court believes *Rodgers* made between § 7403 and a wrongful-levy action, actually works against today's result. By stating that wrongful-levy actions can be pursued when "property ha[s] been seized inadvertently," 461 U.S., at 696, 103 S.Ct., at 2144, the *Rodgers* Court makes clear its assumption that the Government cannot levy on property it knows may belong to third parties. The reasoning of the Court today, however, would allow exactly this result.

Government may seize and sell property belonging only to third parties to pay taxes owed by the delinquent.[8]

The Court nevertheless holds that the right to withdraw all of a joint account is determinative because " 'it is inconceivable that Congress * * * intended to prohibit the Government from levying on that which is plainly *accessible* to the delinquent taxpayer-depositor.' " [9] By holding

---

8.   The Courts of Appeals that have considered whether the IRS can levy on jointly held property to pay a co-owner's taxes have held that it cannot when it does not know how much of the property actually belongs to the delinquent. In United States v. Stock Yards Bank of Louisville, 231 F.2d 628 (CA6 1956), Justice (then Judge) Stewart, writing for the court, held that a joint bondholder's right to present a bond for redemption, receive payment in full, and thereby eliminate completely the other co-owner's interest as far as the issuer was concerned did not give the IRS the right to levy on the entire bond to pay one co-owner's taxes. "Proof of the actual value of the taxpayer's interest was an essential element of the government's case under the statute, and for lack of such proof the case falls." Id., at 631. The Court attempts to distinguish this case on the ground that "[s]avings bonds * * * are different from joint bank accounts* * *." In *Stock Yards Bank*, however, the Court of Appeals expressly analogized savings bonds to joint bank accounts, and the Court today points to no relevant distinguishing feature. It merely creates a distinction without a difference. Likewise, in Raffaele v. Granger, 196 F.2d 620 (CA3 1952), the Court of Appeals rejected the IRS's view that it could levy on joint bank accounts held as tenancies by the entirety when "either spouse may draw upon them." Id., at 622. The court found that the "power of each spouse to withdraw funds," which the IRS argued was determinative, was actually irrelevant because under state law "the ownership of both [spouses] attaches to funds withdrawn by either." "The United States," it held, "has no power to take property from one person, the innocent spouse, to satisfy the obligation of another." Id., at 623. The Court attempts to distinguish this case on the ground that it "did not concern the propriety of a provisional remedy, but the final ownership of the property in question." This is misleading. In *Raffaele*, the Court of Appeals affirmed the District Court's quashing of a warrant of distraint. It thus held that the IRS had no right to seize the property as an initial matter. It did not hold that the IRS had properly seized the property but had to return it.

9.   The Court today states that "[t]he overwhelming majority of courts that have considered the issue have held that a delinquent taxpayer's unrestricted right to withdraw constitutes 'property' or 'rights to property' subject to provisional IRS levy, regardless of the facts that other claims to the funds may exist and that the question of ultimate ownership may be unresolved at the time." Insofar as the Court states that the IRS can levy on the right to withdraw, one can assume, without deciding, that it is correct, because the statement is irrelevant. In the present case, the IRS is not levying on the right to withdraw, but on the underlying right in the property, which may well belong to innocent third parties. On the other hand, insofar as the Court states that "these cases all stand for the proposition that a delinquent's state-law right to withdraw funds from [a] joint bank account is a property interest sufficient for purposes of federal law for the Government to levy the account * * *," it is simply mistaken. *Not one, let alone "all," of these cases stand for this proposition.*

The cases the Court cites from the Courts of Appeals, the District Courts, and the Tax Court either decide a different question or actually support the position taken by the Third and Sixth Circuits. Four of the Court of Appeals cases and one of the District Court cases concern the amount of "property" in an individual's account when the bank has either an unexercised right of setoff or checks still to be drawn against the account at the time of the levy. Citizens & Peoples National Bank v. United States, 570 F.2d 1279 (CA5 1978) (unpaid checks); United States v. Citizens & Southern National Bank, 538 F.2d 1101 (CA5 1976) (unexercised right of setoff); United States v. Sterling National Bank & Trust Co., 494 F.2d 919 (CA2 1974) (same); Bank of Nevada v. United States, 251 F.2d 820 (CA9 1957) (same); United States v. First National Bank of Arizona, 348 F.Supp. 388 (Ariz.1970) (same), aff'd, 458 F.2d 513 (CA9 1972). The fifth Court of Appeals case, the other District Court case, and all the Tax Court cases support a holding opposite to the Court's today. In Babb v. Schmidt, 496 F.2d 957 (CA9 1974), for example, the court allowed the levy against community property only because state law "ha[d] * * * given the [delinquent] rights in that

that mere accessibility controls, the Court simply ignores the plain language of § 6331. It also effectively overrides state law that " 'controls in determining the nature of the legal interest which the taxpayer ha[s] in the property.' "[10] Aquilino v. United States, 363 U.S. 509, 513, 80 S.Ct. 1277, 1280, 4 L.Ed.2d 1365 (1960), quoting Morgan v. Commissioner, 309 U.S. 78, 82, 60 S.Ct. 424, 426, 84 L..Ed. 585 (1940). Under the Court's reasoning, for example, a codepositor's right to withdraw would allow the Government to levy on a joint account even if the Government knew that under state law none of the funds in the joint account "belonged to" the delinquent codepositor, i.e., the delinquent had *no* property interest in

---

property* * *." Id., at 960. And in the other District Court case and all the Tax Court cases the court found that state law gave the delinquent not only a right of withdrawal but also a right of use or possession in the underlying funds themselves. United States v. Third National Bank & Trust Co., 111 F.Supp. 152, 155 (MD Pa.1953) (delinquent was either sole owner of funds or joint tenant); United States v. Equitable Trust Co., 49 AFTR 2d ¶ 82-428, at 82-725 (Md.1982) ("[P]rior to the federal tax levy, both [codepositors] owned the accounts as joint tenants, each having the absolute right to use or withdraw the entire fund* * *. Consequently, [the delinquent codepositor] had property rights in the checking account * * *."); Sebel v. Lytton Savings & Loan Assn., 65-1 USTC ¶ 9343 (SD Cal.1965) (joint tenancy); Tyson v. United States, 63-1 USTC ¶ 9300 (Mass.1962) (holding in the alternative that assessment was jointly against both codepositors or that state law granted any creditor the right to possession of either codepositor's funds).

These cases should also dispel the Court's fear that the IRS will be forced to "bring a lien-foreclosure suit each time it wishe[s] to execute a tax lien on funds in a joint bank account * * *." Nothing in my opinion suggests that under existing federal law the IRS can *never* levy on a joint bank account. As the cited cases make clear, many, if not most, States give codepositors property rights in *all* the funds in a joint account. As long as state law grants such a right--which Arkansas law does not --levy on all the funds to pay a single codepositor's taxes is proper. It is only when state law does not grant such a right that the IRS should not be allowed to levy under § 6331 without first determining that the funds "belong to" the delinquent. The Court's position, however, would permit levies even when the IRS knows that none of the funds in the account belongs to the delinquent taxpayer.

10. At several points, the Court mischaracterizes my reliance on state law. I do not suggest that because state law "puts certain limits on the rights of creditors, and attaches certain consequences to [the right to withdraw] as regards the delinquent himself the Government is limited by these same state-law constraints." Nor do I suggest that "state law dictates the extent of the Government's power to levy." These are strawmen that the Court long ago rejected. United States v. Bess, 357 U.S., at 56-57, 78 S.Ct., at 1057-1058. Like the Court, I would follow the statement in *Bess* that § 6331 "creates no property rights but merely attaches consequences, federally defined, *to rights created under state law* * * *." Id., at 55, 78 S.Ct., at 1057 (emphasis added). As the Court today states, "under *Bess*, state law controls only in determining the nature of the legal interest which the taxpayer has in the property." Here, however, the delinquent taxpayer may have no legal interest in the property. All that is known is that he has a right of withdrawal that is completely independent of the funds themselves. Nevertheless, the Court attaches "federal consequences" sufficient to levy on the accounts. In effect, what the Court holds today is that the delinquent's right against the bank creates "federal consequences" that attach to the completely different right to the funds themselves. By so construing the "federal consequences" of *Bess*, the Court does nothing less than rewrite § 6331, a provision that authorizes levy *only* on "property and rights to property belonging to" the delinquent.

the funds themselves.[11] Cf. Aquilino v. United States, supra, 363 U.S., at 513, n. 3, 80 S.Ct., at 1280 n. 3 ("It would indeed be anomalous to say that the taxpayer's 'property and rights to property' included property in which, under the relevant state law, he had no property interest at all"). Such a position exceeds even the IRS's own interpretation of its levy powers. Rev. Ruling 55-187, 1955-1 Cum.Bull. 1971 ("A joint checking account is subject to levy only to the extent of a taxpayer's interest therein, which will be determined from the facts in each case"). This position, moreover, effectively overrules not only *Mansfield* but also part of *United States v. Bess*, supra, a case in which this Court held that a delinquent could have no "property or right to property" in funds over which he had no right of possession. 357 U.S., at 55-56, 78 S.Ct., at 1057-1058.

The Court also disregards the statutory language and its prior cases when it argues that the levy authorized by § 6331 is only a "provisional" remedy. Third parties who have their property taken may pursue—if they know about the taking—either administrative or judicial relief. But one would hardly characterize as "provisional" the Government's taking of an innocent party's property without notice, especially when, even if the taking is discovered, the burden is then on the innocent party to institute recovery proceedings.[12] Furthermore, absent notice of any kind, the nine months that the administrative, 26 U.S.C. § 6343(b), and judicial, 26 U.S.C. § 6532(c)(1), remedies ordinarily give third parties to contest a levy is a short time indeed. There is no certainty that within this time they will discover that their property has been used to pay someone else's taxes. This may be particularly true as to the owners of joint *savings*

---

11. Moreover, if taken seriously, the Court's reasoning would make any action for wrongful levy fruitless. If the mere right to withdraw payment is indeed the determinative interest, then a levy on a joint account for payment of a codepositor's taxes can never be wrongful. It will always be true that a right to withdraw belonged to the delinquent codepositor. The Court, of course, does not actually take this extreme position. It would apparently allow a third party subsequently to contest a levy on the ground that "the money in fact *belongs to* him or her." (emphasis added). This, however, amounts to recognition that it is the right of ownership, rather than the right to withdraw, that controls. To avoid taking a transparently unreasonable position, the Court switches the basis of its analysis. The relevant property interest, it appears, depends upon whether the Government is trying to seize property or a third party is trying to recoup it. The Court offers no reason for applying this double standard, and the statute itself yields none.

12. The Court also argues that a levy on third-party property may be justified because "[the levy] merely protects the Government's interests so that rights to the property may be determined in a postseizure proceeding." This statement incorrectly states the law. Under the levy statute, the IRS has the power not only to seize but also to sell property. 26 U.S.C. § 6331(b). A co-owner of a house seized and sold to pay a delinquent's taxes would indeed be surprised to discover that the IRS's levy "merely protects the Government's interests * * *." Assuming that the co-owner discovered within nine months that the IRS had levied on the property (for no notice to him is required), he could recover in a wrongful-levy action at most some of the proceeds from the sale. This "remedy" hardly "punctiliously protect[s]" the rights of third parties, as the Court claims.

accounts, owners in common of unimproved real estate, and owners in other situations where there may be little occasion to know that one's property has been seized by an IRS levy. In short, the Court's decision often will place the property rights of third parties in serious jeopardy. * * *

I accordingly dissent, and would affirm the judgment of the Court of Appeals.

Notes and Questions

Section 6331(b) provides that a levy "includes the power of distraint and seizure by any means." If the property or right to property seized is not sufficient to satisfy the delinquent tax liability, the Service may "levy in like manner upon any other property liable to levy of the person against whom such claim exists, until the amount due from him, together with all expenses, is full paid." IRC § 6331(c).

The method of levy may depend upon the property that is the subject of the levy. The usual method of levy is by service of a notice of levy, but tangible personal property such as an automobile may be physically seized, although the Service may not violate a taxpayer's Fourth Amendment rights in seizing the property. See G.M. Leasing Corp. v. United States, 429 U.S. 338, 97 S.Ct. 619, 50 L.Ed.2d 530 (1977). In the case of a going business, the premises may be padlocked and notice posted.

1. What steps must the government take before it can levy? See IRC § 6330.

2. What rights do third-party owners have in the collection process?

3. What does the dissent mean in quoting *Rodgers* that a § 7403 proceeding gives the "* * * Government the opportunity to seek the highest return possible on the forced sale of property interests liable for the payment of federal taxes"?

4. If property is held in joint ownership and a delinquent taxpayer's interest is minuscule, can the government levy against the property?

5. The Anti-Injunction statute (§ 7421) prevents taxpayer suits "to enjoin or restrain the collection of a tax." An exception is made for wrongful levy suits brought by injured third parties. See §§ 7421 and 7426. Also if the property subject to levy is sold by the government, the sale transfers only the "right, title and interest" of the delinquent taxpayer "in and to the property sold." §§ 6329 and 6339. Do these provisions alleviate any of Justice Powell's concerns?

AMERICAN TRUST v. UNITED STATES
United States Court of Appeals, Sixth Circuit (1998)
142 F.3d 920

OPINION

KENNEDY, CIRCUIT JUDGE.

* * *

Although the Code authorizes the IRS to execute an administrative levy without prior judicial approval, it also provides some protection to the taxpayer. Internal Revenue Code § 6334 exempts specific types of property from attachment by levy. Most relevant to the instant case, § 6334(a)(9) provides that the following income is exempt from levy:

> Any amount payable to or received by an individual as wages or salary for personal services, or as income derived from other sources, during any period, to the extent that the total of such amounts payable to or received by him during such period does not exceed the amount determined under subsection (d).

This exemption prevents the IRS from seizing all of a taxpayer's paycheck through a purely administrative proceeding, and allows the taxpayer to retain from his wages or salary an amount that is determined in relation to the sum of the standard personal income tax deduction and the taxpayer's aggregate number of personal income tax exemptions. See 26 U.S.C. § 6334(d).

In the instant case, the IRS first selected the administrative levy from its arsenal of collection tools and demanded that American Community [bank] pay over any of Bradley's property or rights to property that it had in its possession. Instead of complying, American Community filed an interpleader action to resolve the competing claims to the withheld commissions. After removing the interpleader to the District Court, the Government successfully filed a claim for enforcement of its tax lien against the accumulated commissions. Bradley now contends that the judgment in favor of the United States should have been reduced by the amount of money that, pursuant to § 6334(a)(9), he would have been entitled to claim as exempt from the original levy. In response, the United States argues that the judicial enforcement of a lien is independent of and distinct from an administrative levy, and that a valid tax lien may attach property that is exempted from levy.

We have yet to decide whether the Government may enforce a tax lien created by 26 U.S.C. § 6321 against property that § 6334 would exempt from levy. The United States Courts of Appeals that have considered the relationship between administrative levies and tax liens have recognized that a tax lien under § 6321 can attach to property that would be exempt from a § 6331 administrative levy. In United States v. Barbier, 896 F.2d 377 (9th Cir.1990), the Ninth Circuit considered an appeal from a bankruptcy proceeding in which debtor-taxpayers argued that § 6334 prohibited the attachment of a federal tax lien on property that was exempt from an administrative levy. The court rejected the taxpayers' argument, holding that "for the purposes of the Barbiers' Chapter 13 plan, the IRS's claim against the Barbiers for their income tax deficiencies, including interest and penalties, may be secured by a lien on property exempt under § 6334(a)." 896 F.2d at 378. It reasoned that restricting the scope of a tax lien's reach would be inconsistent with both Supreme Court precedent and the statutory purpose of promoting tax collection. It also reasoned that "[t]he IRS's levying power is limited because a levy is an immediate seizure not requiring judicial intervention." Id. at 379. The court, however, confined its opinion to the determination of the scope of a tax lien in a bankruptcy proceeding, stating in a footnote that they "need not consider here whether exempt assets are subject to judicial foreclosure and express no view on that question." Id. at 380 n. 3.

* * *

Finally, the Fifth Circuit has considered this issue, again in the context of bankruptcy proceedings, in Sills v. United States (In re Sills), 82 F.3d 111 (5th Cir.1996). In *Sills*, the taxpayers purchased a house with workers' compensation proceeds. In the bankruptcy proceeding, they sought to insulate that house from a tax lien, arguing that property purchased with workers' compensation benefits is exempt from levy under 26 U.S.C. § 6334(a)(7). The Fifth Circuit rejected their arguments and held that tax liens may reach property exempt from levy. Although the court did not decide if the taxpayers' house actually qualified under § 6334(a)(7), it reasoned as follows:

> Even if the Sills' house were exempt from levy, the tax lien still may be valid and enforceable. For example, the IRS may enforce the lien by foreclosure action under I.R.C. § 7403; it may seek to have its lien satisfied in proceeding brought by third parties, in which the IRS is brought pursuant to 28 U.S.C. § 2410; or it may exercise redemption rights provided by I.R.C. § 7425(d) if another party forecloses on the property.

82 F.3d at 114. This reasoning emphasizes the myriad of mechanisms that the IRS can employ to collect taxes through the enforcement of tax liens that reach property that would be exempt from attachment by levy.

Bradley relies heavily on Don King Productions, Inc. v. Thomas, 749 F.Supp. 79 (S.D.N.Y.1990), rev'd in part, 945 F.2d 529 (2d Cir.1991), a case in which the court reached the opposite conclusion. There, the District Court held, in an interpleader action, that "a lien cannot attach to child support monies that are exempt from levy." 749 F.Supp. at 84. The court based its decision purely on policy grounds, reasoning that "exemption allows the delinquent taxpayer to fulfill his court ordered obligation to support his children." Id.

Although Bradley acknowledges that exemptions under § 6334 would not apply if the United States had sought enforcement of its tax lien by instituting judicial proceedings under § 7403, he argues that this case is different because the United States was responding to an interpleader action that resulted from its levies. He asserts that it is unfair to allow third parties to negate taxpayers' claims to exemptions from levy under § 6334 whenever third parties refuse to surrender property that is the object of an IRS levy and then bring an interpleader action to determine the priority of rights to that property. Appellant's argument can be distilled to the claim that once the IRS files a levy, the taxpayer is entitled to claim exemptions under § 6334, unless it is the IRS that initiates the action for judgment on its lien under § 7403.

Bradley's argument conflicts with the statutory scheme of the Internal Revenue Code, which has created a "number of distinct enforcement tools available to the United States for the collection of delinquent taxes." Rodgers, 461 U.S. at 682, 103 S.Ct. at 2136-37. An administrative levy, one such tool, is a "provisional remedy," without judicial intervention, in which the Government seeks to secure quickly and inexpensively property to satisfy a tax deficiency. Although an administrative recovery may be relatively quick and inexpensive, the IRS's powers to levy are limited by the exceptions in 26 U.S.C. § 6334. These exemptions make sense in an administrative proceeding, where no court has found that taxes are even due. Enforcement of a tax lien is another distinct mechanism for tax collection. Such a proceeding has different characteristics: it requires judicial intervention, but the lien created by 26 U.S.C. § 6321 "is broad and reveals on its face that Congress meant to reach every interest in property that a taxpayer might have." The statute exempts certain property from a levy but not from a lien, and we decline to alter this allocation.

Bradley's argument also relies heavily on the order in which the Government uses its distinct enforcement tools. In this case, although the Government first sought to recover tax deficiencies by administrative levy, the interpleader action changed the nature of the proceedings. The parties were then in court, and the remedy the United States sought was no longer "provisional" in nature. Bradley fails to explain why it should make a difference whether the United States seeks to enforce a tax lien in a proceeding that it initiated or whether it seeks enforcement of the lien in an action that was initiated by another party. The scope of the lien remains the same in either instance. If we were to adopt Bradley's arguments, we would create the odd situation where a tax lien created under § 6321 would reach all of Bradley's commissions if the Government had immediately sought enforcement by filing suit under § 7403, but the same lien would be subject to certain exemptions if the Government sought judicial enforcement of the lien after the quicker and less expensive levy procedure had failed and led to an interpleader. To do so would not only re-write the broad language of § 6321, it would also lessen the incentive of taxpayers to comply with an administrative levy. This would conflict with "the policy inherent in the tax statutes in favor of the prompt and certain collection of delinquent taxes." Id. at 694, 103 S.Ct. at 2142-43.

Notes and Question

Property acquired after the date of the notice of levy generally is not subject to the levy. Thus, a notice of levy served on a bank does not operate to seize deposits made to the taxpayer's account after the date of the notice. Michael I. Saltzman, IRS PRACTICE AND PROCEDURE ¶ 14.12 (Revised 2d Ed. 2002). In order to seize such property, the Code authorizes a continuing levy under § 6331(h) of up to 15% of certain "specified payments" to the taxpayer from the date the levy is made until the date the levy is released. Such a levy must be specifically approved by the Service.

If not for this provision, the Service would have to levy on each continuous payment (such as wages and deposits), because the levy generally extends only to the property or property right held by the taxpayer or a third party at the time of the levy. Section 6331(h) allows the Service to reach a portion of property that otherwise is exempt from levy under § 6334. Although only a minimal amount of wages, salary and other income is exempted under § 6334(a)(9), effective for levies after August 5, 1997, fifteen percent of wages, salary and other income (which may include previously exempted amounts) is subject to continuous levy under §§ 6331(h) and 6334(f) from the date of the levy to the date the levy is released. The continuing levy does not apply to means-tested payments, however, nor does it apply to debtors in bankruptcy or to taxpayers who have filed for innocent spouse relief. See § III.A. of the text for a discussion of innocent spouse relief. As Saltzman notes, this allows taxpayers "to retain a greater portion of their wages and salary then under the previous exemption amount computation, which left delinquent taxpayers with little income that was exempt from levy." Michael I. Saltzman, IRS PRACTICE AND PROCEDURE ¶ 14.14[1] (Revised 2d Ed. 2002).

The 2004 Jobs Act provides for a continuous levy of up to 100 percent of the amount of the payment in the case of a specified payment due to a vendor of goods or services sold or leased to the federal government. Thus, the fifteen percent limit is increased with respect to levies on payments due to a vendor who deals with the federal government. See IRC § 6331(h)(1), as amended by the Jobs Act.

If exempt property is subject to lien and may be seized through a lien-foreclosure suit, what purpose does the exemption provision serve?

a. *Sale of Seized Property*

Section 6335 provides rules for the seizure and sale of property, both real and personal, to satisfy a tax deficiency. After the expiration of the 30-day period following the notice of intent to levy, the government may seize the taxpayer's property and sell it in satisfaction of the unpaid tax liability. If, however, the estimated expenses that would be incurred from the levy and sale of the property are likely to exceed the property's fair market value, no levy can be made. IRC § 6331(f); Reg. § 301.6331-2(b).

Before the Service can sell the seized property, it first must conduct an investigation to (1) verify the taxpayer's liability, (2) determine whether the sale proceeds are likely to exceed the estimated expenses of the levy and sale, (3) determine whether there is sufficient equity in the property to yield net proceeds that can be applied toward the unpaid tax liability, and (4) explore alternative collection methods. IRC § 6331(j).

The Service must send the taxpayer a notice of seizure and a notice of sale as soon as practicable after the seizure. IRC § 6335. The sale must be public and notice of the sale must be published in a newspaper of general circulation in the county where the seizure is made. The sale cannot occur less than 10 days nor more than 40 days from the date of the notice. IRC § 6335(d). The notice of sale must describe the property and the time, place, conditions, and manner of sale. In addition, the notice must state expressly that only the interest of the delinquent taxpayer is to be offered for sale. Reg. § 301.6335-1(b) and (c).

Sales are conducted by public auction with the Service setting a minimum price for which the property will be sold. If no bids meet the minimum price, the government either may purchase the property or may return the property to the taxpayer subject to the tax lien. Otherwise, the property is sold to the highest bidder. When the tax lien has been satisfied and expenses of sale have been paid, any excess proceeds will be returned to the taxpayer.

Since only the interest of the delinquent taxpayer is sold, the property remains subject to the interests of third-party owners, mortgagors and other senior lienholders. The successful bidder takes the property "as is," with no warranty or guaranty of title or fitness for a particular purpose, and without recourse against the government. Reg. § 301.6335-1(c)(5)(iii). The delinquent taxpayer has a right of redemption which she may exercise at any time before the property is sold by paying the tax owed plus the expenses of seizure. If the right of redemption is exercised, the property will be returned to the taxpayer. After the property is sold, the delinquent taxpayer's right of redemption continues for 180 days from the date of sale. This right may be exercised by the taxpayer, her heirs, executor, administrator, anyone acting on her behalf, or by any third party having an interest in or lien on the property. If the right of redemption is exercised, the person exercising the right must pay the successful bidder the amount of the bid price plus 20 percent interest from the date of the sale. If the right of redemption is not exercised within the 180 day period, the successful bidder will receive a quitclaim deed from the government.

The owner has the right to request that the property be sold within 60 days or longer of a written request for sale. The government must comply with the request unless it is determined not to be in the best interest of the government. IRC § 6335(f). If the property is perishable, likely to decline greatly in value, or cannot be kept without great expense, the government may conduct an expedited sale after giving notice to the owner. In such a sale, the government is not required to set a minimum price and the property will be sold to the highest bidder. IRC § 6336.

GRABLE & SONS METAL PRODUCTS, INC. v.
DARUE ENGINEERING CO.
United States United States Court of Appeals, Sixth Circuit, 2004.
377 F.3d 592

BOGGS, CHIEF JUDGE.

* * *

I.

The facts in this case are not disputed. In 1994, the IRS seized property at 601-701 W. Plains Road, in Eaton Rapids, Michigan, to satisfy Grable's tax debt resulting from not paying its corporate income taxes for six years. The IRS served notice of the seizure by certified mail, although 26 U.S.C. § 6335(a), the relevant statute, provides that notice must be "given" personally to the owner of the property. The parties agree that the IRS failed to adhere to the exact provisions of the statute but that Grable nevertheless received actual notice of the seizure. The IRS sold the property to Darue on December 13, 1994, for $44,500. The record before us contains no clear evidence that Grable challenged the sale at the time or attempted to redeem the property at issue in this case. Following its standard procedure, the IRS executed a quitclaim deed to Darue on November 13, 1995.

On December 14, 2000, about six years after Darue bought the property, Grable challenged the sale in Eaton County Circuit Court by filing a quiet-title action. Darue removed the case to the United States Court for the Western District of Michigan under 28 U.S.C. § 1441(b). Grable filed a motion to remand based on lack of subject matter jurisdiction. 28 U.S.C. § 1447(c). The district court held that it had jurisdiction to hear the case because the application of § 6335(a) implicates a substantial federal interest, meaning that Grable's claim was based on a federal question. On March 29, 2002, the district court denied Grable's motion to quiet title and awarded judgment to Darue. Grable appealed to this court in a timely manner.

II.

Federal Question Jurisdiction

* * *

Federal courts also have original jurisdiction over claims "arising under the Constitution, laws, or treaties of the United States." 28 U.S.C. § 1331. Whether a claim presents a federal question "must be determined from what necessarily appears in the plaintiff's statement of his own claim." Taylor v. Anderson, 234 U.S. 74, 75-76, 34 S.Ct. 724, 58 L.Ed.

1218 (1914). In its original complaint to quiet title, Grable alleged that Darue's quitclaim deed was invalid because it "was given with improper notice pursuant to 26 U.S.C. § 6331 et seq. . . . [and] since the tax deed was given pursuant to improper notice as required by 26 U.S.C. § 6335(a), said transfer and claim through the tax deed is null and void and void ab initio." The key question is whether Grable's quiet-title action, based as it is on the faulty process in a tax seizure, "arises under" federal law and thus invokes federal court jurisdiction. We hold that it does.

The statute upon which Grable bases his complaint reads:

As soon as practicable after seizure of property, notice in writing shall be given by the Secretary to the owner of the property . . . *or shall be left at his usual place of abode or business* if he has such within the internal revenue district where the seizure is made. If the owner cannot be readily located, or has no dwelling or place of business within such district, the notice may be mailed to his last known address.

26 U.S.C. § 6335(a) (emphasis added). The parties agree that the IRS failed to "give" or "leave" notification and that therefore the service of notice did not comply with the statute. See Goodwin v. United States, 935 F.2d 1061, 1064 (1991) (noting government concession that the literal meaning of the statute requires personal service); Howard v. Adle, 538 F.Supp. 504, 507 (E.D.Mich.1982) (demonstrating that certified mailing is insufficient for compliance with the statute by quoting 26 C.F.R. § 301.6335-1(b)(1)(1981) and IRS Manual § 5356.1(2)(1980); the latter specifies that the "original notice of sale will be delivered to the taxpayer personally"). Although Grable's complaint hinges on a violation of the Internal Revenue Code, Grable insists that its cause of action does not arise under federal law.

The long history of Supreme Court guidance concerning the meaning of "arising under" the laws of the United States has been synthesized into a three-part test. Although formulations differ slightly among the circuits, a federal question may arise out of a state law case or controversy if the plaintiff asserts a federal right that 1) involves a substantial question of federal law; 2) is framed in terms of state law; and 3) requires interpretation of federal law to resolve the case. Long v. Bando Mfg. of America, 201 F.3d 754, 759 (6th Cir.2000); see e.g., Howery v. Allstate Insurance Co., 243 F.3d 912, 918 (5th Cir.), cert. denied, 534 U.S. 993, 122 S.Ct. 459, 151 L.Ed.2d 377 (2001); Seinfeld v. Austen, 39 F.3d 761, 763 (7th Cir.1994), cert. denied sub nom. Abbott Labs. v. Seinfeld, 514 U.S. 1126, 115 S.Ct. 1998, 131 L.Ed.2d 1000 (1995). The asserted federal right in this case, personal notification of seizure of property as provided by IRS regulations, fulfills these three requirements.

Substantial Federal Interest

To identify a federal question, we must make "a pragmatic assessment of the nature of the federal interest at stake," Howery, 243 F.3d at 917, a simple task in this context. The federal government cannot function without effective tax collection. Society has a strong interest in clear rules for handling delinquent taxpayers. The IRS must have transparent procedures for seizing and selling property so that people will be willing to purchase property at tax sales, allowing the IRS to provide a predictable stream of tax revenue. Determining the scope of the IRS's authority to seize property to satisfy a tax debt undoubtably implicates a substantial federal interest.

Presentation as a state law claim

Grable sued to quiet title, which is generally a state law cause of action. However, the scope of a taxpayer's right to due process in the form of notice of the tax seizure and sale is the essential element of this claim. Grable would not have any cause of action, and Darue would have undisputed title to the property, were it not for the technical notice requirements of § 6335(a). Therefore the Internal Revenue Code, not state property law, lies at the center of this dispute. The state and federal claims are sufficiently entwined to allow us to find that Grable has presented a federal question.

Interpretation of the federal law required

Disposition of all the aspects of this case, including those related to the traditional state law property issues, turn on construction of federal tax law. Both parties agree that the only way to resolve the underlying controversy is to evaluate whether § 6335(a), which mandates notice for IRS seizure of property for non-payment of taxes in person, requires strict, or merely substantial, compliance with its provisions to allow the IRS deed to convey title. If strict compliance is necessary, then Grable is entitled to get his property back because the IRS did not comply with the letter of the statute. If substantial compliance is sufficient, then further analysis and weighing of the equities of the situation is required. Therefore the final requirement is met: interpretation of the federal tax code is necessary to resolve the state law issue.

* * *

III.

Action to Quiet Title

The district court also correctly granted summary judgment to the appellee, Darue. At issue is whether serving notice through a certified letter, which Grable in fact received, constitutes sufficient compliance with the statute to make the resulting quitclaim deed valid. Evaluating whether substantial compliance is applicable is a question of law that is reviewed de novo. In re Eagle-Picher Indus., Inc. 285 F.3d 522, 527 (6th Cir.2002) (applying substantial compliance analysis to notice requirements in a bankruptcy case). However, the rule itself is an equitable doctrine, so that a district court's decision to apply it is reviewed for abuse of discretion. Id. at 529. See Cleveland Newspaper Guild Local 1 v. Plain Dealer Pub. Co., 839 F.2d 1147, 1155 (6th Cir.1988).

The Internal Revenue Code states that:

b) Deed of real property.-In the case of the sale of real property *pursuant to section 6335–*

. . .

(2) Deed as conveyance of title.-If the proceedings of the Secretary as set forth have been *substantially in accordance with the provisions of law*, such deed shall be considered and operate as a conveyance of all the right, title, and interest the party delinquent had in and to the real property thus sold at the time the lien of the United States attached thereto.

26 U.S.C. § 6339(b)(2) (emphasis added). Therefore, if the IRS substantially complied with the provisions of § 6335(a), then the tax sale is valid.

Grable counsels against reading the substantial compliance provision of § 6339(b)(2) as applying to § 6335(a) seizures, in spite of the statutory language to the contrary, since doing so would render the notice provisions "totally ineffective." This argument is not persuasive. Grable is correct that a basic rule of statutory construction mandates that a court should read statutes as a whole and not interpret one provision in a way that would render another meaningless or superfluous.

Allowing substantial compliance does not undermine the purpose of § 6335(a), nor make its provisions superfluous. Should the IRS fail to adhere to the strict statutory notice provisions, it then has the burden of showing it substantially complied with them. Proving that a recalcitrant taxpayer actually received notice of a seizure or sale could be quite difficult. No court would uphold a seizure without notice. Mullane v. Cent. Hanover Bank & Trust Co., 339 U.S. 306, 313, 70 S.Ct. 652, 94 L.Ed. 865 (1950) (stating that "there can be no doubt that at a minimum [the due process clause] require [s] that deprivation of life, liberty or property by adjudication be preceded by notice and opportunity for hearing appropriate to the nature of the case").

Ignoring the provisions of § 6335(a) puts the IRS at risk that a court will find its alternative notification procedures inadequate and invalidate the tax sale. Gauging how much variation will be tolerated puts the IRS in very uncertain territory. For instance, a simple public announcement of a tax sale, as provided for in 26 U.S.C. § 6335(b), is "constitutionally inadequate." Verba v. Ohio Cas. Ins. Co., 851 F.2d 811, 816 (6th Cir.1988). Attempting twice to notify the taxpayer in person of the public sale of his property, and then sending a certified letter, which was returned, and a regular letter, which was not, is insufficient notice to validate the tax sale. Reece v. Scoggins, 506 F.2d 967, 969 (5th Cir.1975). Nor will a court be swayed by the facts that taxpayer received proper notice of the initial property seizure and found out about the auction before the bidding began. Ibid. Adjudication of substantial compliance cases is very fact-specific, and the outcome is uncertain for the litigants. We do not believe that the latitude allowed by § 6339(b)(2) undermines the strong motivation for the IRS to follow the letter of § 6335(a). Only by doing so can it ensure the validity of its tax sales, effectively collect back taxes, and avoid litigation.

The Third Circuit approved the application of the substantial compliance doctrine to § 6335(a) in Kabakjian v. United States, 267 F.3d 208, 213 (2001), a case that is directly on point, and upon which the district court relied. Like Grable, Kabakjian owed the IRS taxes, and his property was seized and sold at auction. He sued the government, claiming that the notices he received pursuant to § 6335(a) were defective because he received them by certified mail, rather than personal delivery. The Third Circuit held that the notices "were not so defective as to void the seizure of property and its transfer to third parties" because § 6339(b)(2) allowed for substantial compliance. Ibid. Because Kabakjian could not demonstrate any prejudice beyond a theoretical deprivation of his right to notice, the court ruled that all his property rights had transferred to a third party, and his claim failed on the merits. Ibid.

Protecting the interests of bona fide purchasers is an important aspect of quiet title analysis. In the one opportunity the Sixth Circuit has had to address the question of substantial compliance in the context of a tax seizure and sale, we too held that procedural irregularities could not void a tax sale. PM Group Inv. Corp. v. PYK Enter., 145 F.3d 1332 (6th Cir.1998) (unpublished opinion) (holding that issuance of a certificate of sale was conclusive evidence of the regularity of the sale). We noted that § 6339(b)(2) was enacted to protect bona fide purchasers, such as Darue in this case. Ibid.

Grable argues that "provisions of law" in § 6339(b)(2) means provisions of state law, citing Fuentes v. United States, 14 Cl.Ct. 157, 167 (1987), and, therefore, that strict adherence to the statute is required. *Fuentes* dealt with a homeowner's suit against the IRS for delivering a quitclaim deed that was invalid under Puerto Rican law. The Court of Claims noted "that a sharp focus must be placed on the distinction between the law applicable to the efficacy of a tax sale and the law applicable to the execution of a deed stemming therefrom. As to the former, we find that federal law is applicable; and as to the latter, local law governs." Id. at 166. This case deals with the efficacy of the tax sale, rather than the validity of the deed, and is thus a question of federal law. See also Reece, 506 F.2d at 970 (holding that faulty notice provisions made the *sale* voidable *ab initio*) (emphasis added). We also adopt the district court's analysis rejecting Grable's reading of Fuentes. The district court correctly pointed out that the substantial compliance language of § 6339(b)(2) does not refer to the execution of the deed, but rather to the *proceedings* by which the Secretary sells real property pursuant to § 6335, and therefore the statute directly contradicts Grable's theory that the substantial compliance provisions only apply to state law. Grable & Sons Metal Products, Inc. v. Darue Engineering & Mfg., 207 F.Supp.2d 694, 697 (W.D.Mich.2002) (emphasis in the original).

Some courts have determined that substantial compliance is not acceptable in the context of a tax seizure. This view follows that of Chief Justice Marshall that "the person invested with such a power [to convey land] must pursue with precision the course prescribed by the law, or his act is invalid. . .." Thatcher v. Powell, 19 U.S. (6 Wheat.) 119, 125, 5 L.Ed. 221 (1821). In *Reece v. Scoggins*, the leading case advocating strict construction, the court voided a tax sale because the IRS "handled this sale of land in a somewhat casual fashion," including failure to comply with notice requirements and irregularities in the subsequent public auction. *Reece*, 506 F.2d at 970. The main rationale behind the court's holding was a recognition of the "Damoclean nature" of the IRS's ability to seize property to satisfy legitimate tax deficiencies and of the importance of strict adherence to the statute to protect the taxpayer.

In this case, however, Grable was amply protected. It received actual notice of the tax sale, which was one of several resulting from a six-year hiatus from paying taxes. It has not alleged any actual prejudice as a result of receiving notice through certified mail, nor did it take any action against Darue for six years. The protections in the statute are designed to prevent the government from seizing property without warning. The district court did not err in refusing to extend these protections to a delinquent taxpayer who knew that its property was being seized but waited years to assert its rights.

Although the statute allows for substantial compliance, the district court also analyzed the case under equitable principles, coming to the same favorable conclusion for Darue. Because we may affirm the district court on any ground supported by the record, we do not have to review the district court's application of equity, but we make two short points. In a case with similar defects in notice, the United States District Court for the Eastern District of Michigan applied equity in holding that substantial compliance was sufficient to validate the sale. *Howard*, 538 F.Supp. at 508 (applying Michigan law to resolve the quiet title action). Secondly, the district court's decision to apply equity to dismiss Grable's quiet title motion does not contradict an earlier Michigan Court of Appeals quiet-title action that was decided in Grable's favor. Village of Dimondale v. Grable, 240 Mich.App. 553, 618 N.W.2d 23 (2000). In defending an action to quiet title to another piece of property that Mr. Grable owned personally, he argued that the tax sale was not valid because of defective IRS notice. The state appeals court held that, as a defendant, he did not have to worry about sleeping on his rights but was entitled to assert any valid defense. *Dimondale*, 618 N.W.2d at 31-32. The court also noted that "equity is a shield, not a sword." Id. at 32. The district court properly relied on that maxim when it held that a delay of approximately six years in pressing a claim provided sufficient basis in equity to deny Grable relief.

IV.

For the reasons set out above, we AFFIRM the decision of the district court to deny Grable summary judgment and to award judgment to Darue.

Question

If the property that is seized and sold by the government is subject to liens in addition to the federal tax lien, what happens to those liens when the purchaser takes the property?

b. *Civil Damages for Wrongful Collection*

Section 7433 is the exclusive remedy for recovering damages against the government for any unauthorized collection activities as a result of a disregard of any of the collection provisions by "any officer or employee of the Internal Revenue Service [either] recklessly or intentionally, or by reason of negligence." IRC§ 7433(a). The amount of damages recoverable is limited to the lesser of $1 million or the sum of the taxpayer's actual economic damages plus costs of the unauthorized collection action. IRC § 7433(b). The taxpayer has a duty to mitigate damages, thus any recovery to which the taxpayer is entitled is reduced by any damages that the taxpayer reasonably could have mitigated. IRC § 7433(d)(2). In addition, § 7433(d)(1) requires the taxpayer to exhaust administrative remedies before bringing an unauthorized collection suit.

There are time constraints on when such a suit may be brought. Under the regulations, the suit may not be brought before the earlier of (1) the date on which a decision is rendered on an administrative claim or (2) six months after the date on which an administrative claim is filed. Treas. Reg. § 301.7433-1(d)(1). Suit may not be brought after the expiration of two years after the date on which the right of action accrued. IRC § 7433(d)(3).

JOHNSON v. UNITED STATES
United States District Court, Northern District of Georgia, Atlanta Division, 1999.
99-1 USTC ¶ 50,463

ORDER
FORRESTER, DISTRICT JUDGE.

* * *

I. Statement of the Case

Plaintiffs William H. Johnson and Linda L. Johnson filed a pro se complaint against the United States Government on July 11, 1996, alleging nineteen causes of action arising from collection of taxes by the Internal Revenue Service ("IRS") and the State of Georgia. Plaintiffs sought refunds, costs, and damages pursuant to 28 U.S.C. § 1346(a), 26 U.S.C. §§ 7422, 7430, 7432, and 7433 for unauthorized tax collection actions for the years 1988, 1989 and 1990.

* * *

Also in their original complaint, Plaintiffs claimed that Defendant had engaged in an unauthorized collection action in violation of 26 U.S.C. § 7433 and had improperly failed to release a tax lien in violation of 26

U.S.C. § 7432. The court read Plaintiffs' pleadings specifically to allege that between 1988 and 1994, six tax liens were filed against them and that these liens were not released until July 29, 1994 and May 10, 1995, even though they were unenforceable. Defendant sought dismissal on the grounds that Plaintiffs had failed to exhaust their administrative remedies as to these claims. The court denied Defendant's motion to dismiss, finding that both parties had provided little more than conclusory allegations as to whether or not Plaintiffs had exhausted their administrative remedies prior to filing in this court.

* * *

II. Discussion

* * *

C. Defendant's Motion for Summary Judgment

* * * The parties agree to the following undisputed facts. The IRS made assessments of federal income taxes, interest, and penalties against Plaintiffs during the years of 1981, 1982, and 1983. In 1988, 1989, and 1990, Plaintiffs filed Form 1040 income tax returns which reported overpayments of $525.00, $630.00 and $186.09, respectively. Plaintiffs' overpayment of 1988 federal income taxes in the amount of $539.43 was applied to the income tax liability assessed by the IRS for 1981. Plaintiffs' overpayment in 1989, in the amount of $652.74 was also applied to Plaintiffs' tax liability as assessed by the IRS for 1981. Plaintiffs' overpayment for 1990 in the amount of $186.09 was applied to a civil penalty assessed by the IRS for the year 1982. The IRS sent a notice of deficiency to Plaintiffs on December 2, 1993 listing the amounts of deficiency assessed for the years 1981, 1982 and 1983. On February 24, 1994, Plaintiffs filed a petition in the United States Tax Court requesting a redetermination of the deficiencies as determined by the IRS and reflected in the December 2, 1993 notice of deficiency. On July 12, 1994, pursuant to an agreement of the parties, the Tax Court entered an order "[t]hat there [we]re no deficiencies in income tax due from, nor overpayment due to, the petitioners for the taxable years 1981, 1982 and 1983 * * *." The activities which form the basis for Plaintiffs' 26 U.S.C. § 7533 [sic] claim for unauthorized collection occurred between September 2, 1988 and March 21, 1994.

* * *

2. 26 U.S.C. § 7433 Claims

Defendant next argues that summary judgment should be granted in its favor because Plaintiffs' 26 U.S.C. § 7433 claim is barred by the statute of limitations. Defendant asserts that § 7433(d)(3) requires that an action be filed within two years after the date a cause of action accrues, and that the acts Plaintiffs allege as the basis for their § 7433 claim occurred earlier than two years prior to the filing of the instant case. Plaintiffs argue in response that their right of action did not accrue until the Tax Court decision was entered, because they did not have all the essential elements of a possible cause of action until that date. The Tax Court order was entered July 12, 1994, and therefore Plaintiffs argue that their filing on July 11, 1996 was timely.

Plaintiffs submitted an amended complaint to amend their § 7453 cause of action to include an itemized list of illegal collection activities. Plaintiffs list 35 acts that they argue occurred without a legally enforceable assessment, all 35 of which occurred on or before March 21, 1994. Section 7433 provides for civil actions for damages arising out of certain unauthorized collection actions. Such an action "may be brought * * * only within 2 years after the date the right of action accrues." 26 U.S.C. § 7433(d)(1). The Treasury Regulations promulgated under § 7433 further provide that "[a] cause of action * * * accrues when the taxpayer has had a reasonable opportunity to discover all essential elements of a possible cause of action." 26 C.F.R. § 301.7433-1(g)(2). In response to Defendant's motion for summary judgment, the court must determine whether, as a matter of law, the statute of limitations provided in § 7433 had already expired when Plaintiffs filed the instant action on July 11, 1996.

The court must first determine which acts of the IRS Plaintiffs are entitled to assert as bases for their § 7433 action. In their amended complaint, they lists various types of acts, including provision of notice of liens, "extortion" of form 1040 returns, seizure of refunds, enforcement of levies, notices of intent to levy, and assessments of tax due. However, not all acts by the IRS are actionable under § 7433. Assessment and determination of an amount of tax cannot form the basis of an action under § 7433. See Shaw v. United States, 20 F.3d 182, 184 (5th Cir.1994). In *Shaw*, the Fifth Circuit explained the distinction between assessment and collection activities in relation to § 7433; that "improper assessment deals with the decision to impose tax liability while improper collection activities involve conduct of an agent trying to collect the taxes owed." Id. at 184. Relying on legislative history, the court stated that because § 7433 created a cause of action for improper *collection* of a tax, that "[a]n action under [§ 7433] may not be based on an alleged reckless or intentional disregard in connection with the *determination* of a tax," and that accordingly "a taxpayer cannot seek damages under § 7433 for an improper assessment of taxes." Id. at 184.

Although actions in connection with assessment and determination are not actionable under § 7433, notice and demand requirements of collection procedures may be. Though not clearly set forth in their complaint, the court reads Plaintiffs' § 7433 cause of action to allege that notice was improper in their case because it was not sent to their last known address and because certain deficiencies were sent out of time. Plaintiffs acknowledge that some activities they assert as wrongful collection activities occurred before the effective date of § 7433, November 10, 1998. In particular, it appears that the notices Plaintiffs complain were improperly not sent to their last known address were issued in September 1987. Accordingly, Plaintiffs' claim that particular notices were not sent to their last known address is not actionable under § 7433.

Plaintiffs also state that notices of deficiencies for years 1981-1983 were filed out of time. As set forth in the undisputed facts, this notice was sent to Plaintiffs on December 2, 1993. Also, Plaintiffs assert that certain notices of tax liens were improperly filed during a period of restriction on January 3, 1994. The court finds these allegedly defective notices of December 2, 1993 and January 3, 1994 actionable under § 7433.[3] The court thus turns to whether the action was timely filed.

A cause of action under § 7433 is generally established when an allegedly unauthorized collection action occurs. The latest date for collection actions Plaintiffs assert as the basis for their § 7433 claim occurred on January 3, 1994. The assumption therefore is that the two-year period of limitations began to run at that time, expiring January 3, 1996.

However, some courts have found the period of limitations to begin running sometime after the collection action, taking into account the language of Treasury Regulation § 301.7433-1(g)(2), which allows a taxpayer a reasonable time to discover the elements of the action. See, e.g., Sylvester, 978 F.Supp. at 1191 (allowing action to proceed on plaintiff's argument that although collection actions occurred outside period of limitations, plaintiff did not receive IRS file until later date and thus could not have discovered information essential to claim); Cunningham v. United States, 165 B.R. 599, 605 (N.D. Tex.1993) (denying summary judgment on basis that statute of limitations had not run as a matter of law because plaintiffs had   received documents

---

3. In Plaintiffs' amended complaint, the acts they set forth as constituting illegal collection activities in violation of § 7433 extended through March 3, 1994. However, the events listed as occurring on that date were assessments, which as discussed above cannot be relied upon for an action under § 7433. The next most recent dates of activities set forth by Plaintiffs are the notices of January 3, 1994.

relating to the challenged assessments more than two years after the date of the assessments).

However, although a taxpayer has a reasonable time to discover the elements of a § 7433 cause of action, where there is evidence that a party was actually aware of a cause of action, some courts consider the statute of limitations to begin running at that time. For example, in Stjernholm v. Peterson, 85 F.3d 641 (10th Cir.1996), a tax liability was established against the plaintiffs in 1991. The Government then seized property from the plaintiffs in April 1992 and sold that property at auction in June 1992. The plaintiffs commenced an action under § 7433 in October 1994. Plaintiffs argued that their cause of action under § 7433 was timely because it was filed within two years of their receipt of final notice from the IRS that their claims for refunds had been disallowed.[4] In rejecting the plaintiffs' argument, the Tenth Circuit relied on the fact that the plaintiffs had published a "public notice" in August 1992 in a newspaper reflecting their opinion that the IRS had committed procedural violations in conducting the sale and seizure of their property and had engaged in illegal activities. Id. The court held that the publication of this public notice "plainly show[ed] that [the plaintiffs] then knew all essential elements of their claim." Id.

Plaintiffs argue that their cause of action did not accrue until the decision of the Tax Court, rendered June 12, 1994, and that thus their period of limitations for their § 7433 action extended until June 12, 1996. The court disagrees. Given the extensive litigation and discovery that had been conducted between Plaintiffs and the IRS prior to June 12, 1994, the court finds that Plaintiffs had a reasonable opportunity to discover the elements of their § 7433 action. Plaintiffs have offered no explanation as to what events on June 12, 1994 allowed them to discover the elements of their action or permitted their action to accrue. The court therefore has no reason to find that Plaintiffs were unable to discover that the notices provided in December 1993 and January 1994 may have given rise to a cause of action for improper collection procedures. Further, there is evidence that Plaintiffs were actually

---

4.   The plaintiffs in that case relied on Gonsalves v. United States, 782 F.Supp. 164 (D.Me. 1992), aff'd, 975 F.2d 13 (1992), where the court held that the two-year statute of limitations for § 7433 claims did not begin to run until the plaintiff had received legal notice from the IRS that his claims for refunds were fully disallowed. In Gonsalves, the collection actions complained of occurred in 1987 and 1988, but the plaintiff did not receive notice that his claims for refunds were fully disallowed until January 1990. Id. at 169. The plaintiff then filed his § 7433 action in March 1991, and the court allowed it to proceed, holding that the two-year period of limitations began to run in January 1990. Id. The Tenth Circuit in Stjernholm rejected the plaintiff's argument that the reasoning of Gonsalves should apply, because C.F.R. § 301.7433-1(g)(2) had been enacted since that decision and indicated that a cause of action under § 7433 was considered to accrue after a reasonable opportunity to discover all elements of the claim. Stjernholm, 1996 WL 238926 at * 2.

aware of the elements of their cause of action under § 7433 prior to June 12, 1994. Plaintiffs filed a petition with the Tax Court on February 22, 1994 stating that the December 2, 1993 notice had been wrongfully sent out of time. Therefore, there is evidence that at least as early as February 22, 1994 Plaintiffs understood and were aware of the elements of their potential § 7433 claims.

In light of the evidence of Plaintiffs' actual knowledge as well as the history of the extensive communication and discovery between the parties in this case, the court finds no reason to extend the time for accrual of Plaintiffs' § 7433 cause of action until June 12, 1994. The court therefore concludes that Plaintiffs' 26 U.S.C. § 7433 action was untimely filed. Defendant's motion for summary judgment as to Plaintiffs' § 7433 claim is GRANTED.

* * *

Notes

Section 7433(e) authorizes an action for civil damages against an officer or employee of the IRS who willfully violates any provision of 11 U.S.C. § 362 (relating to the automatic stay) or 11 U.S.C. § 524 (relating to the effect of discharge) of the Bankruptcy Code. See § II., below. This provision allows an aggrieved taxpayer to bring suit in the Bankruptcy Court to recover up to $1 million in damages against the United States.

c. Restraining Collection

SOKOLOW v. UNITED STATES
United States Court of Appeals, Ninth Circuit, 1999.
169 F.3d 663.

LEAVY, CIRCUIT JUDGE:

* * *

ANALYSIS

Sokolow seeks an injunction to prevent the IRS from continuing its efforts to collect the unpaid balance on his 1988 tax account. The Anti Injunction Act, 26 U.S.C. § 7421, limits actions to enjoin the assessment and collection of taxes. The Act provides, in part, that "no suit for the purpose of restraining the assessment or collection of any tax shall be maintained in any court by any person* * *." I.R.C. § 7421(a). There are, however, several statutory exceptions to the Act, as well as one judicial exception. An action that does not fall within one of the exceptions must be dismissed for lack of subject matter jurisdiction. Id. Thus, ordinarily, once a tax has been assessed, the taxpayer's only recourse is to pay the tax in full and then sue for a refund in district court.

Sokolow concedes that his is a suit to enjoin the collection of taxes and that none of the statutory exceptions is applicable. He seeks an injunction pursuant to the judicial exception to the Act:

> [A]n injunction may be obtained against the collection of any tax if (1) it is "clear that under no circumstances could the government ultimately prevail" and (2) "equity jurisdiction" otherwise exists, i.e., the taxpayer shows that he would otherwise suffer irreparable injury.

Commissioner v. Shapiro, 424 U.S. 614, 627, 96 S.Ct. 1062, 47 L.Ed.2d 278 (1976) (quoting Enochs v. Williams Packing & Navigation Co., 370 U.S. 1, 7, 82 S.Ct. 1125, 8 L.Ed.2d 292 (1962)). The burden is on the taxpayer to establish both prongs of the test. Unless both prongs of the test are met, a suit for injunctive relief must be dismissed.

To meet the second prong of the *Williams Packing* test, the taxpayer must demonstrate entitlement to equitable relief. "[T]he taxpayer must show that he has no adequate remedy at law and that denial of injunctive relief would cause him immediate, irreparable injury." Jensen v. IRS, 835 F.2d 196, 198 (9th Cir.1987).

Sokolow argues that he has no remedy, because he cannot raise his statute of limitations defense in a refund suit. The issue for decision in a refund suit is "whether the taxpayer has overpaid his tax." Lewis v. Reynolds, 284 U.S. 281, 283, 52 S.Ct. 145, 76 L.Ed. 293, as modified, 284 U.S. 599, 52 S.Ct. 264, 76 L.Ed. 514 (1932).

Sokolow correctly points out that *Lewis* effectively prevented a taxpayer from asserting a statute of limitations defense in a refund action. There, the Court held that there is no "overpayment" when the payments already received "do not exceed the amount which might have been properly assessed and demanded." Id.

However, Congress superseded *Lewis*, by statute. Unlike the previous law, which the Court had construed in *Lewis*, the Revenue Act of 1928 "declare[d] that any payment of a tax after expiration of the period of limitations shall be considered an overpayment." McEachern v. Rose, 302 U.S. 56, 60, 58 S.Ct. 84, 82 L.Ed. 46 (1937); 26 U.S.C. § 2607 (1928). After 1928, Congress has continued to use a similar definition of the term "overpayment."

Presently, I.R.C. § 6401(a) provides: "Assessment and collection after limitation period.–The term 'overpayment' includes that part of the amount of the payment of any internal revenue tax which is assessed or collected after the expiration of the period of limitation properly applicable thereto." We have held, based on § 6401(a), that a taxpayer may raise the statute of limitations defense in an action for a refund. Thus, Sokolow fails the second prong of the test, because he does have an adequate remedy at law: to pay the tax and then challenge the validity of the tax liability in a refund suit. Therefore, Sokolow has not established that injunctive relief should be granted under the judicial exception to the Anti-Injunction Act.

CONCLUSION

The district court's dismissal for lack of jurisdiction is AFFIRMED.

Notes and Questions

There are several statutory exceptions to the Anti-Injunction Act, most of which apply when the Service has failed to follow the statutory procedures for assessment and collection, such as making an assessment in violation of § 6212 (notice of deficiency and 90-day waiting period), and initiating collection action in violation of § 6331 (notice and demand for payment, plus 10-day grace period).

In *Commissioner v. Shapiro*, cited in *Sokolow*, the Supreme Court noted that the Government may use affidavits instead of oral testimony and cross-examination to defeat a taxpayer's claim that an assessment has no basis in fact, as long as the affidavits "disclose basic facts from which it appears that the Government may prevail." 424 U.S. at 633.

1. What is the rationale behind the Anti-Injunction Act?

2. Do you think the court's analysis of the judicial exception to the Anti-Injunction Act (*Shapiro* and *Williams Packing*) is correct?

3. Statute of Limitations

Section 6502 provides that where the tax has been assessed, collection action must be taken, either by levy or by proceeding in court, within ten years of the date of the assessment. It further provides:

> If a timely proceeding in court for the collection of a tax is commenced, the period during which such tax may be collected by levy shall be extended and shall not expire until the liability for the tax (or a judgment against the taxpayer arising from such liability) is satisfied or becomes unenforceable.

If a levy has been made within the statutory period, but the property has been transferred to a third party who refuses to honor the levy, what statutory period, if any, applies to collection action against the third party?

UNITED STATES v. WEINTRAUB
United States Court of Appeals, Sixth Circuit, 1979.
613 F.2d 612.

Celebrezze, Circuit Judge.

* * *

I.

The facts involved in this cause are somewhat complicated but can be fairly distilled as follows. Defendant-appellant, Morris Weintraub, is a Kentucky attorney. In 1959 appellant and his brother, Erving Weintraub, obtained interests in two parcels of real estate in Arizona, which they hoped to resell at a profit. They had difficulty making the scheduled payments for this land. Among other means employed to shore up their financing, in 1960 appellant and his brother borrowed $135,000 from Frank Andrews, a client of appellant, and made a required payment.[2]

Loans had previously been received from two other individuals, Messrs. Chalfen and Hecht, who secured their loans by having partial interests in both parcels assigned to them.[3] Despite several extensions of time appellant and his brother were still unable to make the payments on the parcels or otherwise dispose of them, so in 1961 further loans were obtained from Chalfen and Hecht. In exchange Chalfen and Hecht obtained a complete assignment of all interests in both parcels. Other than a payment in 1961 on the note to Andrews,[6] no other payments were made by appellant or his brother. In May 1962 appellant and his brother were sued in Arizona state court by Chalfen and Hecht. Pursuant to the settlement of that lawsuit in November 1962, appellant and his brother executed a deed and assignment of all their interests in

---

2. The loan was evidenced by a note signed by appellant and his brother bearing six percent interest. The note recited that it was secured by the Arizona real estate, but it does not appear that Andrews ever recorded any such "security interest." See note 3, infra.

3. One parcel had been purchased under an Agreement of Trust and the other under an installment contract, with the latter parcel eventually assigned to another trust. Thus, the interests in the real estate were often "assigned" rather than "conveyed." The interests could be redeemed from the trusts by repayment of the loans.

6. This payment reduced the principal balance on the note to $120,760.

the two real estate parcels to Chalfen and Hecht.[7] On May 2, 1963, the Internal Revenue Service (IRS) assessed wagering taxes in the amount of $688,734 against Frank Andrews. On May 3, 1963, the IRS served appellant with a notice of levy on the property of Andrews (and others), pursuant to Internal Revenue Code § 6332,[8] which requires third persons in possession of a taxpayer's property or property rights subject to levy upon which a levy has been made to surrender such to the IRS. Appellant replied in August 1963 to the final demand for surrender of the amount he owed to Andrews by writing on the final demand: "Nothing due or owed by me to any of above at time of service on 5/2/63 or now."

---

7.   The judgment entry provided that "Chalfen is the absolute owner in fee simple, subject only to the equities of * * * Hecht (and others)," of both parcels. Appellant and his brother had an option to repurchase the land until March 10, 1963, which option was never exercised.

8.   I.R.C. § 6332 provides:

(a) Requirement. Except as otherwise provided in subsection (b), any person in possession of (or obligated with respect to) property or rights to property subject to levy upon which a levy has been made shall, upon demand of the Secretary or his delegate, surrender such property or rights (or discharge such obligation) to the Secretary or his delegate, except such part of the property or rights as is, at the time of such demand, subject to an attachment or execution under any judicial process.

* * *

(c) Enforcement of levy.

(1) Extent of personal liability. Any person who fails or refuses to surrender any property or rights to property, subject to levy, upon demand by the Secretary, shall be liable in his own person and estate to the United States in a sum equal to the value of the property or rights not so surrendered, but not exceeding the amount of taxes for the collection of which such levy has been made, together with costs and interest on such sum at an annual rate established under section 6621 from the date of such levy (or, in the case of a levy described in section 6331(d)(3), from the date such person would otherwise have been obligated to pay over such amounts to the taxpayer). Any amount (other than costs) recovered under this paragraph shall be credited against the tax liability for the collection of which such levy was made.

(2) Penalty for violation. In addition to the personal liability imposed by paragraph (1), if any person required to surrender property or rights to property fails or refuses to surrender such property or rights to property without reasonable cause, such person shall be liable for a penalty equal to 50 percent of the amount recoverable under paragraph (1). No part of such penalty shall be credited against the tax liability for the collection of which such levy was made.

(d) Effect of honoring levy. Any person in possession of (or obligated with respect to) property or rights to property subject to levy upon which a levy has been made who, upon demand by the Secretary or his delegate, surrenders such property or rights to property (or discharges such obligation) to the Secretary or his delegate (or who pays a liability under subsection (c)(1) shall be discharged from any obligation or liability to the delinquent taxpayer with respect to such property or rights to property arising from such surrender or payment.
* * *

(e) Person defined. The term "person," as used in subsection (a), includes an officer or employee of a corporation or a member or employee of a partnership, which as such officer, employee, or member is under a duty to surrender the property or rights to property, or to discharge the obligation.

The next action taken against appellant was in April 1964, when appellant was indicted for willfully failing to honor the notice of levy and two counts of making false statements to the IRS. Appellant was acquitted on all three counts after trial in September 1965.

No further action was taken by the IRS vis-a-vis appellant until the filing of the complaint in the instant case in January 1976. This action was brought pursuant to § 6332(c) to enforce the personal liability of appellant for failure to honor the notice of levy served upon him in May 1963. Appellant moved for summary judgment in the district court arguing, inter alia, that the suit was barred by laches and the statute of limitations. This motion was denied without opinion. At trial, the sole issue for the jury to determine was whether appellant was, in fact, indebted to Andrews on May 3, 1963, when he was served with the notice of levy. The jury found that appellant was so indebted and found in favor of the government in the amount of $120,760.

* * *

II.

The principal contention raised by appellant before this court is that this action was time-barred by both laches and the statute of limitations. We find no merit to either branch of this claim.

The rule that the government is exempt from the consequences of its laches and from the operation of statutes of limitations nullum tempus occurrit regi had its genesis in English common law notions of prerogative of the Crown. The principle is well established in this country, but based upon the important public policy of preserving public rights and revenues from the negligence of public officers.

Despite overwhelming authority to the contrary, appellant argues that this is a case in which the sovereign should be barred by laches. He notes the almost eleven year delay between his acquittal on the criminal charges in 1965 and the filing of this action in 1976 and the almost thirteen year delay since service of the notice of levy in 1963. Appellant claims that during this delay he destroyed most of his records concerning this matter. Appellant's brother, who has since died, was in failing health at the time of trial and remembered little of what happened. The IRS special agent who worked on appellant's criminal case, appellant's attorney in the criminal case, appellant's brother's wife and, importantly, Andrews had all died by the time this action was commenced.

* * * "Laches requires proof of (1) lack of diligence by the party against whom the defense is asserted, and (2) prejudice to the party asserting the defense." There is no question that it would have been

preferable, from all viewpoints, for the government to have filed this action sooner than it did. But it cannot be said that there was a lack of diligence by the IRS sufficient for a laches defense inasmuch as the IRS was attempting between 1963 and 1976 to collect from Andrews the taxes he owed, upon which appellant's liability was predicated. Indeed, it was completely reasonable for the IRS to proceed initially against Andrews since collection from him could have obviated this proceeding. And the prejudice appellant argues he has suffered is speculative, at best, and certainly was no greater than the prejudice to the government in trying its case. This case was based almost entirely upon documentary evidence and, to a lesser extent, appellant's credibility, neither of which were greatly affected by the lapse of time. Finally, laches is an equitable defense and, putting to one side the fact that this is a legal action for damages, it can certainly be raised only by one who comes into equity with clean hands.[22] [Eds: The court noted that the appellant sent his brother a letter], containing instructions on defrauding the IRS, [which] was more than enough to soil appellant's hands.

Appellant next argues that this case is barred by the statute of limitations. While the general rule stated above is that the sovereign is exempt from the operation of statutes of limitations, an exception to that general rule exists when the sovereign (through the legislature) expressly imposes a limitation period upon itself. Thus, the issue at hand is whether Congress has imposed a statutory limitation period on suits to enforce the personal liability imposed by § 6332 on persons who refuse to honor a notice of levy. We find no such limitation applicable to § 6332.

The only statute urged by appellant as applicable is Internal Revenue Code § 6502.[24] This section requires that the IRS commence action to

---

22. Laches is purely an equitable doctrine. A venerable equitable maxim is that "He who comes into equity must come with clean hands." The clean hands maxim is typically employed by a defendant against a plaintiff who seeks equitable relief, but it applies equally to a defendant who seeks equitable relief from the chancellor. While it is not normally employed against a defendant merely brought to court by the suit of another, insofar as appellant seeks to invoke the powers of the chancellor to bar the government's claim due to laches, we believe the clean hands maxim should apply to him.

24. I.R.C. § 6502 provides:

(a) Length of period. Where the assessment of any tax imposed by this title has been made within the period of limitation properly applicable thereto, such tax may be collected by levy or by a proceeding in court, but only if the levy is made or the proceeding begun

(1) within 6 years after the assessment of the tax, or

(2) prior to the expiration of any period for collection agreed upon in writing by the Secretary or his delegate and the taxpayer before the expiration of such 6-year period (or, if there is a release of levy under section 6343 after such 6-year period, then before such release). The period so agreed upon may be extended by subsequent agreement in writing made before

collect a tax, either by levy or proceeding in court, within six years after the assessment of the tax. [Eds: now 10 years]. Section 6502 only concerns actions against taxpayers, however, and not actions under § 6332 against third parties in possession of a taxpayer's property or property rights.

Appellant has cited absolutely no authority in support of his contention that the six year limitation of § 6502 applies to § 6332 and we have found none. While we have found no case expressly holding that § 6502 is not applicable to § 6332, there is substantial authority which points to the conclusion that it is not.

First, for a statute of limitations to apply to the sovereign it must be expressly indicated in the statute. There is no express mention of § 6332 in § 6502 nor is the type of action brought under § 6332 even implicitly described in the language of § 6502. By its own terms, the limitation of § 6502 applies only to actions to collect a tax. The instant case, under § 6332, is not to collect a tax (although that is the intended indirect consequence of the suit), but rather is to enforce the personal liability for failure to surrender property after receiving a notice of levy.

Second, this court and others have held that a person served with a notice of levy under § 6332 (or its predecessor) has only two possible defenses: 1) he is not in possession of property or a property right of the taxpayer;[27] or 2) the property is subject to prior judicial attachment or execution.[28] This indicates that the statute of limitations is not a defense to a § 6332 suit.[29] * * *

Third, a review of the cases decided under § 6502 and its predecessor reveals that they uniformly concern actions against taxpayers and not third parties like appellant. And it is significant that these cases consistently hold that the only limitation of § 6502 is that the levy be made or proceeding in court begun against the taxpayer within six years

the expiration of the period previously agreed upon. The period provided by this subsection during which a tax may be collected by levy shall not be extended or curtailed by reason of a judgment against the taxpayer.

(b) Date when levy is considered made. The date on which a levy on property or rights to property is made shall be the date on which the notice of seizure provided in section 6335(a) is given. * * *

27. This defense was resolved adversely to appellant by the jury.

28. This defense was not raised by appellant. Section 6332(a) also contemplates a similar defense that the property is not "subject to levy," which presumably refers to exempt property.

29. It is also no defense that there was no valid levy against the taxpayer. That is a matter for the taxpayer to raise. Commonwealth Bank v. United States, 115 F.2d 327, 329 (6th Cir. 1940). Compare I.R.C. § 7426(c).

of the assessment. There is no time limit whatsoever on an action against the taxpayer to enforce a timely levy or judgment obtained in a timely filed court proceeding.[30] Thus, even if § 6502 could somehow be construed to apply to § 6332, its sole limitation period has been complied with by virtue of the timely levy against Andrews. There is no limitation in § 6502 for enforcement actions, like the instant case, once the liability has been established, which occurred here by service of the notice of levy on appellant.[32]

Fourth, a review of the cases decided under § 6332 demonstrates that the procedures contemplated by § 6332 are consistent with there being no limitation period on actions to enforce a notice of levy. When a third party, like appellant, in possession of the property of a taxpayer is served with a notice of levy on the taxpayer's property, the appropriate procedure is that the third party immediately surrender the property to the IRS. This is in accord with the principle that service of the notice of levy reduces the property or property right (such as the intangible debt in the instant case) to the constructive possession of the United States. * * * Since the notice of levy served on appellant reduced the debt owed to Andrews to the constructive possession of the United States, it would make no sense to impose a time limit upon bringing an action to enforce the notice of levy, which appellant wrongfully failed to honor, to reduce the property right to the actual possession of the United States.

* * *

The judgment of the district court is affirmed.

---

30. Moyer v. Mathas, 458 F.2d 431, 434 (5th Cir. 1972) (foreclosure suit twenty years after timely lien not time-barred); United States v. Overman, 424 F.2d 1142, 1147 (9th Cir. 1970) (foreclosure suit six years after judgment in timely suit not time-barred; tax liens are enforceable at any time); Plisco v. United States, 113 U.S.App.D.C., 177, 179 n. 1, 306 F.2d 784, 786 n. 1 (D.C.Cir.1962) (§ 6502 requires only levy or suit within six years of assessment and does not limit means for enforcing assessment); Hector v. United States, 255 F.2d 84 (5th Cir. 1958) (suit filed within six years of assessment tolls limitation period indefinitely); United States v. Ettelson, 159 F.2d 193, 196 (7th Cir. 1947) (claim filed in probate court within six years of assessment sufficient to toll limitation period and judgment could be enforced anytime thereafter; there is no federal statutory provision as to period of limitation on enforcing judgment); Investment & Securities Co. v. United States, 140 F.2d 894, 896 (9th Cir. 1944)(no federal statutory limitation on enforcing judgment in timely suit; tax can be collected at any time); United States v. Mandel, 377 F.Supp. 1274, 1276-77 (S.D.Fla.1974) (follows Moyer); United States v. American Cas. Co., 238 F.Supp. 36, 38-39 (W.D.Ky.1964) (follows Ettelson); United States v. Caldwell, 74 F.Supp. 114 (M.D.Tenn.1947) (no time limit on enforcing lien acquired in timely suit);* * *.

32. The instant case is to be distinguished from one against a third party pursuant to I.R.C. §§ 6901, et seq., wherein the liability of the third party is based upon being a transferee of the taxpayer. Transferee liability applies to a third party who stands in the shoes of a taxpayer and is imposed in a direct action to collect the tax due. In such a case, the six year limit of § 6502 applies to the transferee-third party. United States v. Updike, 281 U.S. 489, 50 S.Ct. 367, 74 L.Ed. 984 (1930). But the instant case is not an action to collect a tax and does not seek to impose transferee liability on appellant, so *Updike* is inapposite. * * *

KEITH, CIRCUIT JUDGE, concurring.

I concur in part I and most of part II of Judge Celebrezze's well-done opinion.

It is with reluctance that I vote to affirm. There is no reasonable excuse for the government's long delay in proceeding to collect against the defendant. Nonetheless, I must agree that established case law makes laches unavailable here to halt the government's suit.

The statute of limitations question is closer, however. I.R.C. § 6502 provides a six-year statute of limitations from the date of assessment to the levy of "any tax." Judge Celebrezze states that the government action in this case was not to collect a tax, "but rather is to enforce the personal liability for failure to surrender property after receiving a notice of levy." This is literally true. However, I would construe § 6502 as applying to third-party enforcement actions under § 6332. The plain language of § 6502 states that "(any) tax may be collected by levy or by a proceeding in court, but only if the levy is made or the proceeding begun within six years after the assessment of the tax * * *." It should make no difference whether collection of the tax is against the taxpayer himself or against a third-party who has the taxpayer's property. In my view, the situation under § 6502 is analogous to that of a transferee taxpayer. In United States v. Updike, 281 U.S. 489, 494, 50 S.Ct. 367, 74 L.Ed. 984 (1930), the Supreme Court held that the limitations period applied to a transferee taxpayer in language which is fully applicable here:

> It seems plain enough, without stopping to cite authority, that the present suit, though not against the corporation but against its transferees to subject assets in their hands to the payment of the tax, is in every real sense a proceeding in court to collect a tax. The tax imposed upon the corporation is the basis of the liability, whether sought to be enforced directly against the corporation or by suit against its transferees. The aim in the one case, as in the other, is to enforce a tax liability * * *. Indeed, when used to connote payment of a tax, it puts no undue strain upon the word "taxpayer" to bring within its meaning that persons whose property, being impressed with a trust to that end, is subjected to the burden. Certainly it would be hard to convince such a person that he had not paid a tax.

In my view, the six year limitations period should be deemed to run from the date of assessment of the tax against a third party; the IRS should have no more than six years to either seize the property or begin legal proceedings. It is true that this suggested construction results in some anomaly in that if the IRS obtains a judgment against the principle taxpayer, then no statute of limitations bar exists on enforcement of the judgment. The IRS can go after the taxpayer's property, almost wherever it is. This, however, is an anomaly which currently exists regarding transferee liability.

On balance, I think that construing the statute in this manner is a fair way to harmonize the Internal Revenue Code and the multiplicitous fact situations which arise: 1) property is in the hands of the taxpayer the IRS, by the express terms of § 6502 has six years from assessment to seize the taxpayer's property or file suit; 2) property is in the hands of a transferee taxpayer *Updike* mandates compliance with § 6502; 3) property is in the hands of a third party such as the defendant, I don't think that the result should be different; § 6502 should apply as well.

Unfortunately, as Judge Celebrezze notes, this suggested construction does not help the defendant. The reason is that unlike real or personal property, the property in this case was an intangible debt owed by a third party (Weintraub) to the taxpayer. The government served a notice of "demand" upon the defendant third party pursuant to § 6332, requesting that he turn over to the government any money owed to taxpayer Frank J. Andrews. There is no doubt that this "demand" was made within six years of the initial assessment against Andrews. The case law seems clear that the serving of this "demand" was the equivalent of a seizure of the debt and, as Judge Celebrezze says, "reduces the property or property right * * * to the constructive possession of the United States."

Were we writing on a clean slate, I would prefer requiring the government to bring suit within the six year limitations period, at least when dealing with an intangible debt. When dealing with real or personal property, the government can physically seize the property. However, as Judge Hastie said in In re Cherry Valley Homes, Inc., 255 F.2d 706, 707 (3d Cir. 1958), "* * * the possessory concept of 'seizure' is not strictly applicable to a debt * * * ." In such situations, I would hold the mere serving of a notice of "demand" insufficient to operate as a seizure and would require the government to file suit.

The case law, however, clearly establishes that the opposite is true. The serving of the notice of levy operates to reduce property or property rights to the constructive possession of the government. * * *

Although § 6332 uses the term "demand" instead of the term "levy," it is clear that a "demand" upon a third party operates as a levy or seizure so far as property rights are concerned. This has the effect of reducing the property or property rights to the constructive possession of the United States.

Given this authority, all that the government had to do to comply with the six year statute of limitations was to serve a timely levy (demand) upon the defendant debtor. There is no question that this was done. As Judge Celebrezze points out, the government could then wait as long as it wished to bring the instant proceeding, over twelve years later, to enforce the constructive seizure of the debt accomplished by the initial demand. In effect, the government was collecting what it had constructively seized twelve years earlier. Judge Merritt whimsically argues that this construction of the statute is irrational. He is perhaps correct, but that is the law.

MERRITT, CIRCUIT JUDGE, dissenting.

The government's tax collection suit is time-barred and should be dismissed.

The relevant words of the applicable statute of limitations are simple:

Where the assessment of any tax* * * has been made* * * such tax may be collected * * * by a proceeding in court, but only if * * * the proceeding (is) begun * * * within 6 years after the assessment of the tax * * *. 26 U.S.C. § 6502.

The facts are also simple. Weintraub owed a debt to Andrews. Andrews owed money to the IRS. The IRS assessed Andrews. Andrews did not pay the assessment. IRS sought to collect the tax from Weintraub by a process of garnishment or attachment of third party indebtedness allowed under § 6332 of the tax code. Upon receiving the garnishment, Weintraub reported to IRS that he owed no debt to Andrews. Nothing happened for thirteen years. Then, thirteen years later, IRS decided to sue Weintraub to collect on its attachment of Weintraub's debt to Andrews.

The conclusion should be obvious. A tax garnishment attached Weintraub's debt to Andrews thirteen years before suit was filed. No "proceeding" to collect was instituted for thirteen years. Nothing in the statute of limitations excludes collection of garnishments or purports to limit its application only to a "proceeding" to collect the tax directly from the taxpayer who owes the money. The language of the statute says simply the tax may be collected by a proceeding in court "Within 6 years after the assessment." (Emphasis added.)

The consequences of a contrary conclusion are irrational. Under the Court's interpretation, the estate of a garnishee in the hands of his great, great-grandchildren must still pay the IRS 100 years after the six-year federal statute of limitations has run on the original tax bill, 100 years after the garnishment was answered and 100 years after the applicable state statute of limitations has run on the original indebtedness owed by the garnishee to the original creditor. The estate of the original creditor, the taxpayer who owed the money to the government in the first place, is free and clear because the six-year statute ran against him long ago, but the poor garnishee who (let us assume) religiously paid his own taxes all his life remains forever liable for the taxes of another.

The Court reaches this anomalous result by holding that the statute, § 6502, only concerns "actions against taxpayers" and "not actions * * * against third parties in possession of a taxpayer's property or property rights," although it acknowledges that there is "no case expressly holding that § 6502 is not applicable." No attempt is made to discuss the irrational consequences of this conclusion. The Court does not even attempt to parse or analyze the language of the statute in order to justify the conclusion. It simply quotes "the rule nullum tempus occurrit regi " ("time does not run against the king") and combines it with a wonderful legal fiction, the doctrine of "constructive possession" of personal property. The Court says:

> Since the notice of levy served on appellant reduced the debt owed to Andrews to the constructive possession of the United States, it would make no sense to impose a time limit upon bringing an action * * * to reduce the property right to the actual possession of the United States.

Not even the common law during its darkest days of legal formalism and rigid adherence to fiction and abstraction took the doctrine of "constructive possession" this far. In the famous case of Pierson v. Post, 3 Caines 175, 2 Am.Dec. 264 (N.Y.1805), the plaintiff with his hounds was in hot pursuit of a fox, ferae naturae, when the defendant intervened and in the sight of plaintiff shot and carried the fox away. * * *

* * *

After * * * pouring over Justinian, Fleta, Bracton, Puffendorf, Locke, Barbeyrac or Blackstone for enlightenment, the court holds that the doctrine of "constructive possession" does not apply because the "case * * * is one of mere pursuit, and presents no circumstances or acts which can bring it within the definition of occupancy (or control announced) by Puffendorf." The court concludes that "(h)owever uncourteous or unkind the conduct of Pierson towards Post, in this instance, may have been," a contrary holding "would prove a fertile source of quarrels and litigation."

In the instant case, the Court's conclusion means that "quarrels and litigation"over tax claims with an omnipresent government will never end, even if the lifetime of our children's children unto the seventh generation. If the fox in *Pierson v. Post* was not in the constructive possession of the pursuer, I do not see so many years later why we should struggle with Shakespearean imagination to locate the money Mr. Weintraub owed to Mr. Andrews in the "constructive possession" of the government. Mr. Weintraub's fox was invisible, an incorporeal hereditament. If it ever existed, it was killed and skinned long ago. The trail has grown cold. The participants in the hunt who have not already died have grown old and forgotten the facts. After all these years, only the government's appetite for the chase remains.

But in my judgment, they should sound the horn in other fields and send the hounds to follow trails which are not so stale, for lex dilationes semper exhorret ("the law abhors delay"), is a better rule than nullum tempus occurrit regi.

Notes and Questions

Section 6502 was amended in 1990 to extend the statutory period of collection to 10 years from the date of assessment. Section 6322 was extended accordingly to make the lien period consistent with the collection period. Section 6502 was amended further to provide that if a proceeding in court for the collection of the tax has commenced before the end of the 10-year period, the period shall be extended until the tax liability or a judgement arising from such liability has been satisfied or becomes unenforceable. In 1998, § 6502 was amended effective for the taxable year 2000, to provide that the statutory period for collection may be extended only in two limited circumstances: (1) where the taxpayer and the Service enter into an installment agreement before the end of the 10-year period, the Service may collect up to 90 days after the expiration of the installment period the parties have agreed upon, or (2) where before the 10-year period ends, the taxpayer and the Service have agreed in writing to a release of levy the statute may be extended in accordance with the written agreement. IRC § 6502(a)(2).

Although the court in *Weintraub* held that the statutory period is extended after a levy when third parties are involved, apparently the period is not extended with respect to the taxpayer. If it were, there would be no statutory period on collections. Prior to the 1990 amendment of § 6502, if a proceeding in court was instituted before the end of the statutory period, and a judgment was rendered after the expiration of that period, the government's only remedy was to use the process of the court to collect on its judgment. Under the 1990 amendment, the Service may continue to use the administrative levy to collect the tax, (until the judgment becomes unenforceable) provided a suit is brought prior to the expiration of the statutory period.

1. Since the government's right to the property is derivative of the taxpayer's rights (i.e., the Service steps into the shoes of the taxpayer in determining the taxpayer's property or property rights to which the lien attaches), how, if at all, would the state statute of limitations on collectibility of debts affect the decision in *Weintraub*?

2. Do you think the *Weintraub* case was correctly decided?

II. COLLECTION ACTIONS IN BANKRUPTCY PROCEEDINGS

When a debtor files a bankruptcy petition, two important things happen: (1) creditors are automatically stayed or enjoined from taking action to collect on their claims or to enforce their liens and (2) a bankruptcy estate is created which includes "all legal or equitable interests of the debtor in property as of the commencement of the case." 11 U.S.C. §§ 362(a)(6); 541(a)(1).

A. THE AUTOMATIC STAY

The filing of a bankruptcy petition also stays the assessment of pre-petition taxes. The stay applies to judicial and administrative collection proceedings against the debtor, but it does not apply to criminal proceedings or proceedings over which the Bankruptcy Court has jurisdiction. 11 U.S.C. § 362(b). Despite the stay, the Service may (1) audit the debtor's returns, (2) issue a notice of deficiency, (3) demand the debtor's tax returns, and (4) assess a deficiency and issue a notice and demand for payment. 11 U.S.C. § 362(b)(9). If an assessment is made, no lien attaches to the debtor's property unless the assessed tax constitutes a nondischargeable debt, and the property or proceeds have been transferred out of the bankruptcy estate to the debtor. Id.

The stay prevents the commencement of proceedings in the Tax Court during the pendency of the bankruptcy case. 11 U.S.C. § 362(a)(8). Even if a Tax Court petition is filed before the bankruptcy petition, the Bankruptcy Court may decide the tax case, as long as the Tax Court has not adjudicated the case prior to the filing of the bankruptcy petition.

Under Freytag v. Commissioner, 501 U.S. 868, 111 S.Ct. 2631, 115 L.Ed.2d 764 (1991) (see also discussion in Chapter 8), the exercise of jurisdiction by the Bankruptcy Court does not terminate the Tax Court's jurisdiction over the claim. If the stay is not lifted by the Bankruptcy Court, the Tax Court will determine the liability for the non-dischargeable claims at the close of the bankruptcy proceeding. If the taxpayer receives a notice of deficiency prior to filing a bankruptcy petition, § 6213(f) suspends the period for filing a petition in the Tax Court while the taxpayer is prohibited from filing in the Tax Court and for 60 days thereafter.

The Service, the bankruptcy trustee or the debtor/taxpayer may request that the stay be lifted. If the Bankruptcy Court lifts the stay and allows the Tax Court to decide the tax case, the decision of the Tax Court becomes res judicata. If the request is denied, the stay remains effective until the case is closed or dismissed, or the debtor is discharged. A Tax Court proceeding in violation of the stay is invalid.

The following case considers the effect of the automatic stay on the resolution of the tax issues.

IN RE HUNT
United States Bankruptcy Court, 1989.
95 B.R. 442.

MEMORANDUM OPINION

HAROLD C. ABRAMSON, BANKRUPTCY JUDGE.

This case involves the infrequently encountered issue of whether a bankruptcy court should exercise its jurisdiction to determine a debtor's tax liability. The Debtors filed a Motion for Determination of Tax Liability Pursuant to 11 U.S.C. § 505 ("Motion for Determination"). The Internal Revenue Service ("IRS") responded by simultaneously filing both a general response and the United States of America's Motion to Modify Automatic Stay ("IRS MOTION"). Counsel for the Debtors and counsel for the IRS characterize the motions as the "flip side" of one another. The Debtors' Motion for Determination asks this Court to determine numerous and potentially substantial claims asserted by the IRS. The IRS Motion requests modification of the automatic stay to permit the IRS to proceed with liquidation of various tax claims pending in the United States Tax Court.

The IRS figures to be the largest creditor in this proceeding. It anticipates filing a proof of claim in excess of $600,000,000. The anticipated claim is based on the "1974-1978 Sourcing Cases", the "1979 Tax Case", the "1980 Uncollectible Debt/Gift Tax Dispute", the "1981 Claim for Refund", the "1982 Tax Case", the "1983 Tax Case", the Debtors' taxes for 1984, 1985, 1986, 1987 and a 1988 short year return. The parties have agreed to a modification of the automatic stay to enable the United States Tax Court to complete unresolved matters in the 1974-1978 Sourcing Cases, the 1979 Tax Case and the 1980 Uncollectible Debt/Gift Tax Dispute. The parties dispute the proper forum for resolution of the 1982 Tax Case. Following a preliminary hearing on the motions, the Court recommended a procedure whereby the parties would attempt to outline the facts underlying the 1982 Tax Case, the legal contentions involved, an estimate of witnesses and documents, the differences (if any) between the Debtors' case and those of Mr. and Mrs. Lamar Hunt (non-debtors and Mr. N.B. Hunt's brother) and an analysis of a trial in the Tax Court versus the Bankruptcy Court. The parties graciously agreed to the procedure and the Court conducted follow up conferences and hearings on the issue.

FACTUAL BACKGROUND

The forum to resolve the 1982 Tax Case remains for decision. On February 22, 1988 the IRS issued a statutory notice of deficiency (90 day letter) advising the Debtors that a $154,919,798.50 deficiency existed with respect to the Debtors' joint federal income tax return filed for the year ended December 31, 1982 and proposed assessment of such tax liability plus interest of $122,116,353.23. On May 13, 1988 the Debtors filed a Petition in the United States Tax Court contesting the entire amount of the proposed deficiency. The case is styled N.B. and Caroline L. Hunt v. Commissioner of Internal Revenue, ("1982 Tax Court Case"). Mr. N.B. Hunt filed a voluntary petition under Chapter 11 of the United States Bankruptcy Code on September 21, 1988. Ms. Caroline Lewis Hunt, Mr. N.B. Hunt's wife, filed a voluntary petition under Chapter 11 on September 23, 1988. The filing of the bankruptcy petitions automatically stayed the continuation of the 1982 Tax Court Case.[2] Prior to the Debtors' petitions, the parties were in the early stages of preparing for a February 1989 trial of the 1982 Tax Case before the United States Tax Court.

INTRODUCTION

The determination of a debtor's tax liability constitutes a core proceeding under 28 U.S.C. § 157(b)(2)(B) (Supp. IV 1986), and 11 U.S.C. § 505(a)(1) (1982). As a threshold matter, 11 U.S.C. § 505 empowers the bankruptcy court to determine a debtor's tax liability provided that the merits of the tax claim have not been previously adjudicated in a contested proceeding before a court of competent jurisdiction. 11 U.S.C. § 505(a)(1). One policy behind section 505 reflects an intent to protect creditors from a defaulting debtor. "In enacting § 505, Congress was primarily concerned with protecting creditors from the dissipation of the

---

2.   11 U.S.C. § 362(a)(8) (1982).

estate's assets which could result if the creditors were bound by a tax judgment which the debtor, due to his ailing financial condition, did not contest." In re Northwest Beverage, Inc., 46 B.R. 631, 635 (Bankr.N.D. Ill.1985), citing In re Century Vault Co., 416 F.2d 1035, 1041 (3d Cir.1969) and City of Amarillo v. Eakens, 399 F.2d 541, 544 (5th Cir.1968). In the present case, the Debtors have neither defaulted nor evidenced an intent to default. Rather, the Debtors vigorously contest the IRS assessment and recognize the absolute need to resolve the assessment through either settlement or litigation in order to successfully reorganize. Accordingly, the policy concerns voiced by *Northwest Beverage* are not present.

Section 505 also provides a mechanism to ensure prompt and orderly administration of the bankruptcy estate. "* * * [t]he history of this proviso [11 U.S.C. § 505] makes it clear that its purpose was to afford a forum for the ready determination of the legality or amount of the tax claims, which determination if left to other proceedings, might delay conclusion of the administration of the bankruptcy estate." In re Diez, 45 B.R. 137, 139 (Bankr.S.D.Fla.1984), citing Cohen v. United States, 115 F.2d 505 (1st Cir.1940). This Court is vigilant over prompt administration in view of this Circuit's case management directive.[3] If these Debtors are to have a meaningful reorganization plan (if any) that fulfills the reorganization requirements, prompt resolution of the 1982 Tax Case is paramount. Accordingly, this Court has grappled with the question of whether to determine the Debtors' tax liability or yield to the Tax Court. As we stated during the hearings on this issue, good reasons support retention of jurisdiction or deferring to the Tax Court.[4]

While the reported decisions uniformly recognize the Bankruptcy Court's jurisdiction to determine a debtor's tax liability,[5] the same decisions offer little guidance for when the bankruptcy court should exercise its jurisdiction. Our research uncovered only one reported decision after the enactment of the Bankruptcy Reform Act of 1978 which tersely discussed when a Bankruptcy Court should yield to the Tax

---

3. In re Timbers of Inwood Forest Associates, LTD., 808 F.2d 363, 373 (5th Cir.1987), aff'd on other grounds, 484 U.S. 365, 108 S.Ct. 626, 98 L.Ed.2d 740 (1988) ("Early and ongoing judicial management of Chapter 11 cases is essential if the Chapter 11 process is to survive and the goals of reorganizability on the one hand, and creditor protection, on the other, are to be achieved.").

4. While the issue presently before us concerns a clash between the bankruptcy court's jurisdiction and that of the United States Tax Court, it should be remembered that the analysis infra applies equally to a clash with any court of appropriate jurisdiction over tax matters.

5. See generally Bostwick v. United States, 521 F.2d 741, 744 (8th Cir.1975); In re Original Wild West Foods, Inc., 45 B.R. 202 (Bankr.W.D.Tex.1984).

Court.[6] Accordingly, we embark on an attempt to draw a general framework to help analyze the issue.[7]

DISCUSSION

In formulating a decision to exercise his discretion, the bankruptcy judge must examine the issue case by case. The analysis necessarily includes balancing the Bankruptcy Court's need to administer the bankruptcy case in an orderly and efficient manner, the complexity of the tax issues to be decided, the asset and liability structure of the debtor, the length of time required for trial and decision, judicial economy and efficiency, the burden on the Bankruptcy Court's docket, prejudice to the debtor and potential prejudice to the taxing authority responsible for collection from inconsistent assessments. With these general factors in mind, we turn to the present case.

TAX ISSUES INVOLVED AND SPECIALIZED TRIBUNAL

We first consider the complexity of the tax issue involved. Without going into great detail, the IRS contends that the Debtors realized $383,194,502 in income during the 1982 tax year from the dissolution of Placid Investments, LTD ("PIL"). The IRS contention centers upon the realization of income through either one or more of the following theories: discharge from indebtedness income, discharge of guaranty rights income, or a deemed distribution of cash income. Resolution of the IRS claim depends in a large part upon whether PIL may be characterized as a loan vehicle, without any valid business purpose, or as a partnership for federal income tax purposes. The case additionally involves estimating the value of certain properties contributed as capital contributions by the Debtors to PIL at the inception of the transaction. Complex computational adjustments relating to net operating loss carryovers, depreciation, or the like are not involved.

In analyzing the complexity of the issue involved we must not overlook Judge Goldberg's metaphorically elegant opinion in Matter of Gary Aircraft Corp., 698 F.2d 775 (5th Cir.1983). After stimulating analyses (both intellectual and metaphysical) of the Government contract dispute system and the bankruptcy system, the Court held that a

---

6. In re Diez, 45 B.R. 137, 139 (Bankr.S.D.Fla.1984) (Bankruptcy Court abstained from determination of tax claim "where no bankruptcy purpose is served which would outweigh the importance of uniformity of assessment.").

7. Because we cannot predict the potential differences in each case, the factors we analyze are by no means exhaustive or exclusive.

bankruptcy court should defer liquidation of a government contracting dispute to the Armed Services Board of Contract Appeals. The holding is premised on the notion that "[T]he ancillary jurisdiction of a bankruptcy court to liquidate claims, however, involves more nearly the administrative convenience of settling all disputes in a single forum; it is not as vital to the purpose of bankruptcy." Id. at 783.

In reaching the conclusion that the bankruptcy court ought to defer, the *Gary* Court refers to Order of Railway Conductors v. Pitney, 326 U.S. 561, 66 S.Ct. 322, 90 L.Ed. 318 (1946), Smith v. Hoboken Railway Co., 328 U.S. 123, 66 S.Ct. 947, 90 L.Ed. 1123 (1946) and Nathanson v. NLRB, 344 U.S. 25, 73 S.Ct. 80, 97 L.Ed. 23 (1952) "for the general proposition that a bankruptcy court should defer a complicated, technical dispute to a specialized forum." *Gary Aircraft*, at 783. The Court further explains that deferral is proper because "government contracting law tends to be technical and esoteric" and that "there are specialized fora designed specifically to resolve government contract disputes." Id. at 783-784.

We are mindful of the special expertise and jurisdiction that Congress has seen fit to extend to the United States Tax Courts. While a Bankruptcy Court might appear to lack the specialized understanding of certain areas of the Internal Revenue Code, Congress has equally seen fit to grant the Bankruptcy Judge jurisdiction to decide tax matters. Accordingly, we must decide if the facts warrant exercise of this jurisdiction. The IRS suggests without great explanation that the issue of whether PIL may be classified as a partnership for federal income tax purposes is one of the most complicated issues in all tax law. The IRS further argues on a continual basis that the Debtors' argument that the issue is not so complicated is inconsistent with Special Tax Counsel's Application for Employment. Viewing the record, trial of the 1982 case will involve considerable factual analysis rather than the interpretation of obscure tax statutes. "Technical or esoteric" issues that would warrant deferring to the Tax Court are not present. As we stated above, complex computational adjustments relating to net operating loss carries, depreciation, or the like are not involved. Additionally, the estimation of the value of properties is involved, something this Court performs on a regular basis. Finally, the central issue of whether PIL may be characterized as a partnership for federal income tax purposes has a plethora of case law to guide a bankruptcy court. Thus previously undecided areas of tax law would not figure in a trial. Accordingly, the nature of the tax issues to be decided in the present case does not warrant deferring to the Tax Court.

WHIPSAW EFFECT

The starting point of our analysis focuses on the conclusory statement in *Diez* concerning "the importance of uniformity of assessment." In re Diez, supra, at 139. Piecing together the facts in *Diez*, the debtor stood liable for taxes owed by her estranged spouse. After Ms. Diez "failed to avail herself of the opportunity to contest" her liability (as an "innocent spouse") in a tax court proceeding against her husband, Ms. Diez filed a chapter 7 petition to contest the same. Without explaining "the importance of uniformity of assessment" the Bankruptcy Court chose to abstain from determining the debtor's tax liability. Implicit in the abstention was the fact that a determination by the bankruptcy court could possibly conflict with the previous determination (though uncontested by the debtor) by the Tax Court. By abstaining, the Bankruptcy Judge avoided what the tax profession refers to as a "whipsaw" effect.

The Commentators state:

A whipsaw situation occurs in the tax field when two different taxpayers take positions with respect to a particular transaction which are so inconsistent with each other that only one should logically succeed--and yet, because of jurisdictional or procedural reasons, first one and then the other prevails against the government.

Remarks by Phillip R. Miller At Court of Claims Judicial Conference, October 14, 1971 on Whipsaw Problems in Tax Cases, 25 Tax Lawyer 193 (1972). This definition identifies the potential for non-uniform assessment. The public fisc ultimately suffers when a whipsaw occurs causing opposite results.

A whipsaw problem similar to *Diez* and the *Miller* definition exists in the present case. The IRS submits that it would necessarily be prejudiced by this Court's retention of jurisdiction due to a possible whipsaw effect involving the IRS case against Mr. and Mrs. Lamar Hunt over the same transaction. As a part of the procedure this Court recommended to resolve the issue, the parties were to demonstrate differences between the Debtors' case and Mr. and Mrs. Lamar Hunt's case. The significant differences that we glean from the record include computational adjustments. Likewise, the primary issue of whether PIL may be characterized as a partnership for federal income tax purposes should logically succeed or fail in the respective cases. However, due to jurisdictional reasons, different results may occur if Mr. and Mrs. Lamar Hunt's case were tried before the Tax Court on the one hand and the Debtor's case were tried in the Bankruptcy Court on the other. Indeed, the IRS points out that since Mr. and Mrs. Lamar Hunt are non-debtors, "they are not precluded from obtaining a Tax Court judgment which might be inconsistent with the decisions of this Court based on identical issues of fact and law." Accordingly, the whipsaw slices ahead.

An additional factor in the whipsaw problem is the great cost to the IRS of trying the cases in different fora, when the same issues, the same witnesses and the same documents are involved.[8] The IRS concludes that if this Court retains the case "[A]ny inconsistent or unfavorable judgment would certainly be appealed by the dissatisfied party, thereby prolonging the final resolution of these tax cases." A scenario of dual trials would certainly harm the IRS.

While the whipsaw to the IRS is evident from separate trials in the Tax Court and Bankruptcy Court we can envision a reverse whipsaw effect if the cases were all before the Tax Court. For example, if this Court were to yield to the Tax Court and for one reason or another Mr. and Mrs. Lamar Hunt's case was unable to proceed and thereby "delay conclusion of the administration of the bankruptcy estate" a reverse whipsaw effect would occur prejudicing these Debtors' future attempts to culminate plans of reorganization.

On balance, the potential whipsaw effect to the government and the problem of inconsistent assessment weighs in favor of deferring to the Tax Court, because the Tax Court would be in a better position to immunize the IRS against the threat of a whipsaw. This is achieved by trying the Debtors' case along with the related cases against Mr. and Mrs. Lamar Hunt and Mr. & Mrs. W.H. Hunt on a consolidated basis.[9] The potential reverse whipsaw to the Debtors will be prevented by modifying and conditioning the stay as we discuss below.

---

8. In fact, the record reveals the Debtors and Mr. and Mrs. Lamar Hunt each filed virtually identical written protest letters on March 9, 1987, in response to the IRS's February 23, 1987 proposed adjustment letters. Moreover, the Debtors' and Mr. and Mrs. Lamar Hunt's Tax Court Petitions for the 1982 Tax Court Case are virtually identical, with the exception of numerical differences.

9. We would note that under the proper facts the potential whipsaw problem could be avoided by the bankruptcy court's determination of both a debtor's and non-debtor's tax liability. While the parties did not discuss the possibility of having this court decide Mr. and Mrs. Lamar Hunt's tax liability, our jurisdiction to decide the tax liabilities of non-debtor entities remains questionable. See United States v. Huckabee Auto Co., 783 F.2d 1546, 1549 (11th Cir.1986) (Bankruptcy Code section 505 empowers the Bankruptcy Court to determine the tax liabilities of debtors and estates, not the tax liabilities of separate taxpayers who are not debtors under the Bankruptcy Code.); In re Brandt-Airflex Corp., 843 F.2d 90, 96 (2d Cir.1988). But see In re Major Dynamics, Inc., 14 B.R. 969 (Bankr.S.D.Cal.1981).

PROMPT ADMINISTRATION AND BURDEN ON
BANKRUPTCY COURT'S DOCKET

Also involved is the need to ensure that the claims are liquidated in a timely manner to ensure a prompt resolution of the bankruptcy case. The Debtors seek the use of the Bankruptcy Court as the forum for determination because of the Bankruptcy Court's knowledge of the dynamics of this bankruptcy proceeding as well as the ability of the Bankruptcy Court to render a final decision as early as fall 1989 versus winter 1990 for the Tax Court (assuming that the trial commenced summer 1989 and that the Tax Court entertains the matter on a expedited basis). While the first argument is sincere, it lacks practicality. Decision of the 1982 Tax Case rests on its own merits. The timing argument goes to the heart of the issue. Early resolution of the 1982 Tax Case is imperative for the Debtors (and possibly other plan proponents). While this factor weighs in favor of the Bankruptcy Court's hearing the case, the fact that the Tax Court will entertain the matter on an expedited basis lessens the inherent delays ordinarily associated with a trial before the Tax Court.

A factor closely related to the timing argument is the burden on the bankruptcy court's docket. Trial of the 1982 Tax Case will require a minimum of three full weeks of trial according to the parties. The IRS suggests that the Bankruptcy Court's docket would require this Court to conduct the trial in a "sporadic" and "piecemeal" fashion, whereas the Tax Court would be able to conduct the trial without interruption. This Court would undoubtedly afford the parties a full and fair opportunity to try their cases, yet cannot guarantee that some interruptions would not take our attention away from the trial, given the demands of our case docket. On the other hand, deferring to the Tax Court would conserve judicial resources because it would free this Court to consider the other matters in this proceeding as well as the many other cases on our busy docket.

A final consideration is the possible addition or elimination of a level of appeal of the 1982 Tax Case. Because the claims involve such substantial amounts, an adverse decision would negatively impact on both parties litigant. Accordingly, the parties have indicated an intent to appeal this Court's decision or that of the Tax Court before a trial has even occurred. This rationale raises an interesting question as to the respective reviewing courts. The appellate path from a Bankruptcy Court decision leads first to the United States District Court and then to the United States Court of Appeals (if necessary).[10] The appellate path from the Tax Court leads directly to the United States Court of Appeals.[11] Thus, trial before a Bankruptcy Court adds a potential layer of review, extending the time for ultimate resolution. The need for such argument points out a frustrating procedural shortcoming,[12] yet the reality of the situation calls for the Bankruptcy Court to earnestly consider deferring to the Tax Court.

The United States also argues that a trial before the Tax Court is more useful because of the Tax Court's nationwide subpoena power. The Court does not view this as a major problem because the Court can evaluate deposition testimony as well as live testimony in the trial.

CONCLUSION

After reviewing the above factors, we find the potential whipsaw effect and the potential delay in resolution of the 1982 Tax Case most troublesome. To fulfill the goal of providing a forum for prompt resolution to enable the efficient administration of estates and to guard against the whipsaw effect, we will fashion an order conditionally modifying the automatic stay to facilitate the Tax Court in proceeding with the resolution of these issues. Rather than terminating the automatic stay at this juncture, the automatic stay shall remain in effect except as conditionally modified. We modify the automatic stay to the extent that the parties may begin preparing for a trial before the Tax Court in July 1989. The United States may begin all discovery and preparation, file pre-hearing motions, etc. Likewise, we shall monitor the parties between now and the beginning of trial to ensure that meaningful progress occurs towards prompt trial of this case. If this Court discovers that either of the parties are delaying the resolution of these cases without good cause, it will promptly resolve the dispute by conducting a trial as early as October 1, 1989. In the event that the parties progress toward a trial before the Tax Court in a meaningful manner, and upon the parties' announcement of ready for trial before the Tax Court, the automatic stay shall be modified to permit trial and appeal to a final conclusion so as to liquidate the claim of the United States.

---

10. 28 U.S.C. § 158(a) (Supp. IV 1986) and 28 U.S.C. § 158(d) (Supp. IV 1986), respectively.

11. 26 U.S.C. § 7482(a)(1) (Supp. IV 1986).

12. Under section 405(c)(1)(B) of the Transitional and Administrative Provisions of Bankruptcy Acts, the parties to an appeal could agree to a direct appeal to the Court of Appeals. No similar provision exists under the current law which would eliminate this procedural imbalance.

Notes and Questions

If the Service willfully initiates or continues collection against a taxpayer in violation of the automatic stay, the taxpayer may petition the Bankruptcy Court to recover damages under IRC § 7430(a)(1) for reasonable administrative costs incurred in connection with an IRS administrative proceeding, or reasonable litigation costs incurred in a court proceeding. In the alternative, the taxpayer may bring suit under 11 U.S.C. § 362(h) to recover actual damages (costs, attorney's fees and under certain circumstances, punitive damages) for such a willful violation. These two provisions (11 U.S.C. § 362(h) and IRC § 7430), however, are mutually exclusive.

1. If the Service sends the taxpayer a statutory notice of deficiency and more than 150 days later the taxpayer files a bankruptcy petition but does not file a Tax Court petition in response to the notice of deficiency, the Service may assess the deficiency once the 90-day § 6212 restriction lapses. What effect, if any, will the bankruptcy petition have on the assessment?

2. If the taxpayer receives a notice of deficiency and files a timely Tax Court petition, but the Tax Court has not rendered a final decision, what will be the effect, if any, of the bankruptcy petition?

3. When the bankruptcy court exercises jurisdiction over the tax issues, under *Freytag* the Tax Court does not lose its jurisdiction over the case. What is the significance of the retention of jurisdiction by the Tax Court?

B.   THE BANKRUPTCY ESTATE

The filing of a bankruptcy petition creates a bankruptcy estate that will be used to satisfy the claims of creditors. The estate consists of "all legal or equitable interests of the debtor in property as of the commencement of the case," plus "any interest in property that the estate acquires after the commencement of the case." 11 U.S.C. § 541(a). In general, property acquired by the debtor after the bankruptcy petition is filed remains property of the debtor. Complex issues often arise, though, in determining whether property is acquired by the estate or by the debtor, and whether the property is acquired pre-petition or post-petition.

BEGIER v. IRS

Supreme Court of the United States, 1990.
496 U.S. 53, 110 S.Ct. 2258, 110 L.Ed.2d 46.

JUSTICE MARSHALL delivered the opinion of the Court.

This case presents the question whether a trustee in bankruptcy may "avoid" (i.e., recover) from the Internal Revenue Service (IRS) payments of certain withholding and excise taxes that the debtor made before it filed for bankruptcy. We hold that the funds paid here were not the property of the debtor prior to payment; instead, they were held in trust by the debtor for the IRS. We accordingly conclude that the trustee may not recover the funds.

I.

American International Airways, Inc. (AIA), was a commercial airline. As an employer, AIA was required to withhold federal income taxes and to collect Federal Insurance Contributions Act (FICA) taxes from its employees' wages. 26 U.S.C. § 3402(a) (income taxes); § 3102(a) (FICA taxes). As an airline, it was required to collect excise taxes from its customers for payment to the IRS. § 4291. Because the amount of these taxes is "held to be a special fund in trust for the United States," § 7501, they are often called "trust-fund taxes." By early 1984, AIA had fallen behind in its payments of its trust-fund taxes to the Government. In February of that year, the IRS ordered AIA to deposit all trust-fund taxes it collected thereafter into a separate bank account. AIA established the account, but did not deposit funds sufficient to cover the entire amount of its trust-fund tax obligations. It nonetheless remained current on these obligations through June 1984, paying the IRS $695,000 from the separate bank account and $946,434 from its general operating funds. AIA and the IRS agreed that all of these payments would be allocated to specific trust-fund tax obligations.

On July 19, 1984, AIA petitioned for relief from its creditors under Chapter 11 of the Bankruptcy Code, 11 U.S.C. § 1101 et seq. (1982 ed.). AIA unsuccessfully operated as a debtor in possession for three months. Accordingly, on September 19, the Bankruptcy Court appointed petitioner Harry P. Begier, Jr., trustee, and a plan of liquidation in Chapter 11 was confirmed. Among the powers of a trustee is the power under § 547(b)[1] to avoid certain payments made by the debtor that would

---

1.   This case is governed by 11 U.S.C. § 547(b) (1982 ed.), which reads:

"Except as provided in subsection (c) of this section, the trustee may avoid any transfer of property of the debtor-

"enabl[e] a creditor to receive payment of a greater percentage of his claim against the debtor than he would have received if the transfer had not been made and he had participated in the distribution of the assets of the bankrupt estate." H.R.Rep. No. 95-595, p. 177 (1977), U.S.Code Cong. & Admin. News 1978, pp. 5787, 6138. Seeking to exercise his avoidance power, Begier filed an adversary action against the Government to recover the entire amount that AIA had paid the IRS for trust-fund taxes during the 90 days before the bankruptcy filing.

The Bankruptcy Court found for the Government in part and for the trustee in part. In re American International Airways, Inc., 83 B.R. 324 (ED Pa.1988). It refused to permit the trustee to recover any of the money AIA had paid out of the separate account on the theory that AIA had held that money in trust for the IRS. Id., at 327. It allowed the trustee to avoid most of the payments that AIA had made out of its general accounts, however, holding that "only where a tax trust fund is actually established by the debtor and the taxing authority is able to trace funds segregated by the debtor in a trust account established for the purpose of paying the taxes in question would we conclude that such funds are not property of the debtor's estate." Id., at 329. The District Court affirmed. On appeal by the Government, the Third Circuit reversed, holding that any prepetition payment of trust-fund taxes is a payment of funds that are not the debtor's property and that such a payment is therefore not an avoidable preference. 878 F.2d 762 (1989).[2]

"(1) to or for the benefit of a creditor;

"(2) for or on account of an antecedent debt owed by the debtor before such transfer was made;

"(3) made while the debtor was insolvent;

"(4) made-

"(A) on or within 90 days before the date of the filing of the petition; or

"(B) between 90 days and one year before the date of the filing of the petition, if such creditor, at the time of such transfer-

"(i) was an insider; and

"(ii) had reasonable cause to believe the debtor was insolvent at the time of such transfer; and

"(5) that enables such creditor to receive more than such creditor would receive if-

"(A) the case were a case under chapter 7 of this title;

"(B) the transfer had not been made; and

"(C) such creditor received payment of such debt to the extent provided by the provisions of this title."

The statute has been amended to replace "property of the debtor" with "an interest of the debtor in property." See n. 3, infra. The old version of § 547(b) applies to this case, however, because AIA filed its bankruptcy petition before the effective date of the amendment.

2.   No other Court of Appeals has decided a case that presents the precise issue we decide here. The Ninth and District of Columbia Circuits have, however, resolved against the taxing authorities cases presenting related issues. See In re R & T Roofing Structures & Commercial

We granted certiorari, 493 U.S. 1017, 110 S.Ct. 714, 107 L.Ed.2d 734 (1990), and we now affirm.

II.

A.

Equality of distribution among creditors is a central policy of the Bankruptcy Code. According to that policy, creditors of equal priority should receive pro rata shares of the debtor's property. See, e.g., 11 U.S.C. § 726(b) (1982 ed.). Section 547(b) furthers this policy by permitting a trustee in bankruptcy to avoid certain preferential payments made before the debtor files for bankruptcy. This mechanism prevents the debtor from favoring one creditor over others by transferring property shortly before filing for bankruptcy. Of course, if the debtor transfers property that would not have been available for distribution to his creditors in a bankruptcy proceeding, the policy behind the avoidance power is not implicated. The reach of § 547(b)'s avoidance power is therefore limited to transfers of "property of the debtor."

The Bankruptcy Code does not define "property of the debtor." Because the purpose of the avoidance provision is to preserve the property includable within the bankruptcy estate–the property available for distribution to creditors–"property of the debtor" subject to the preferential transfer provision is best understood as that property that would have been part of the estate had it not been transferred before the commencement of bankruptcy proceedings. For guidance, then, we must turn to § 541, which delineates the scope of "property of the estate" and serves as the postpetition analog to § 547(b)'s "property of the debtor."[3]

_____

Framing, Inc., 887 F.2d 981, 987 (CA9 1989) (rejecting the Government's argument that assets the IRS seized from a debtor to satisfy a trust-fund tax obligation before the debtor filed its bankruptcy petition were assets held in trust for the Government under 26 U.S.C. § 7501, and therefore deciding that the transfer effected by the seizure involved "property of the debtor" and was not exempt from avoidance); Drabkin v. District of Columbia, 263 U.S.App. D.C. 122, 125, 824 F.2d 1102, 1105 (1987) (reaching a similar conclusion with respect to a voluntary payment of withheld District of Columbia employee income taxes in a case governed by a provision of local law that "essentially mirror[ed]" § 7501).

3. To the extent the 1984 amendments to § 547(b) are relevant, they confirm our view that § 541 guides our analysis of what property is "property of the debtor" for purposes of § 547(b). Among the changes was the substitution of "an interest of the debtor in property" for "property of the debtor." 11 U.S.C. § 547(b) (1988 ed.). Section 547(b) thus now mirrors § 541's definition of "property of the estate" as certain "interests of the debtor in property." 11 U.S.C. § 541(a)(1) (1988 ed.). The Senate Report introducing a predecessor to the bill that amended § 547(b) described the new language as a "clarifying change." S.Rep. No. 98-65, p. 81 (1983). We therefore read both the older language ("property of the debtor") and the current language ("an interest of the debtor in property") as coextensive with "interests of the debtor in property" as that term is used in 11 U.S.C. § 541(a)(1)

Section 541(a)(1) provides that the "property of the estate" includes "all legal or equitable interests of the debtor in property as of the commencement of the case." Section 541(d) provides:

> "Property in which the debtor holds, as of the commencement of the case, only legal title and not an equitable interest . . . becomes property of the estate under subsection (a) of this section only to the extent of the debtor's legal title to such property, but not to the extent of any equitable interest in such property that the debtor does not hold."

Because the debtor does not own an equitable interest in property he holds in trust for another, that interest is not "property of the estate." Nor is such an equitable interest "property of the debtor" for purposes of § 547(b). As the parties agree, then, the issue in this case is whether the money AIA transferred from its general operating accounts to the IRS was property that AIA had held in trust for the IRS.

B.

We begin with the language of 26 U.S.C. § 7501, the Internal Revenue Code's trust-fund tax provision: "Whenever any person is required to collect or withhold any internal revenue tax from any other person and to pay over such tax to the United States, the amount of tax so collected or withheld shall be held to be a special fund in trust for the United States." The statutory trust extends, then, only to "the amount of tax so collected or withheld." Begier argues that a trust-fund tax is not "collected or withheld" until specific funds are either sent to the IRS with the relevant return or placed in a segregated fund. AIA neither put the funds paid from its general operating accounts in a separate account nor paid them to the IRS before the beginning of the preference period. Begier therefore contends that no trust was ever created with respect to those funds and that the funds paid to the IRS were therefore property of the debtor.

We disagree. The Internal Revenue Code directs "every person receiving any payment for facilities or services" subject to excise taxes to "collect the amount of the tax from the person making such payment." § 4291. It also requires that an employer "collec[t]" FICA taxes from its employees "by deducting the amount of the tax from the wages *as and when paid*." § 3102(a) (emphasis added). Both provisions make clear that the act of "collecting" occurs at the time of payment-the recipient's payment for the service in the case of excise taxes and the employer's

---

(1988 ed.).

payment of wages in the case of FICA taxes. The mere fact that AIA neither placed the taxes it collected in a segregated fund nor paid them to the IRS does not somehow mean that AIA never collected the taxes in the first place.

The same analysis applies to taxes the Internal Revenue Code requires that employers "withhold." Section 3402(a)(1) requires that "every employer making payment of wages shall deduct and withhold *upon such wages* [the employee's federal income tax]." (Emphasis added.) Withholding thus occurs at the time of payment to the employee of his net wages. S.Rep. No. 95-1106, p. 33 (1978) ("[A]ssume that a debtor owes an employee $100 for salary on which there is required withholding of $20. If the debtor paid the employee $80, there has been $20 withheld. If, instead, the debtor paid the employee $85, there has been withholding of $15 (which is not property of the debtor's estate in bankruptcy)"). See Slodov, 436 U.S., at 243, 98 S.Ct. at 1783 (stating that "[t]here is no general requirement that the withheld sums be segregated from the employer's general funds," and thereby necessarily implying that the sums are "withheld" whether or not segregated). The common meaning of "withholding" supports our interpretation. See Webster's Third New International Dictionary 2627 (1981) (defining "withholding" to mean "the act or procedure of deducting a tax payment from income *at the source* ") (emphasis added).

Our reading of § 7501 is reinforced by § 7512, which permits the IRS, upon proper notice, to require a taxpayer who has failed timely "to collect, truthfully account for, or pay over [trust-fund taxes]", or who has failed timely "to make deposits, payments, or returns of such tax," § 7512(a)(1), to "deposit such amount in a separate account in a bank . . . and . . . keep the amount of such taxes in such account until payment over to the United States," § 7512(b). If we were to read § 7501 to mandate segregation as a prerequisite to the creation of the trust, § 7512's requirement that funds be segregated in special and limited circumstances would become superfluous. Moreover, petitioner's suggestion that we read a segregation requirement into § 7501 would mean that an employer could avoid the creation of a trust simply by refusing to segregate. Nothing in § 7501 indicates, however, that Congress wanted the IRS to be protected only insofar as dictated by the debtor's whim. We conclude, therefore, that AIA created a trust within the meaning of § 7501 at the moment the relevant payments (from customers to AIA for excise taxes and from AIA to its employees for FICA and income taxes) were made.

C.

Our holding that a trust for the benefit of the IRS existed is not alone sufficient to answer the question presented by this case: whether the particular dollars that AIA paid to the IRS from its general operating accounts were "property of the debtor." Only if those particular funds were held in trust for the IRS do they escape characterization as "property of the debtor." All § 7501 reveals is that AIA at one point created a trust for the IRS; that section provides no rule by which we can decide whether the assets AIA used to pay the IRS were assets belonging to that trust.

In the absence of specific statutory guidance on how we are to determine whether the assets transferred to the IRS were trust property, we might naturally begin with the common-law rules that have been created to answer such questions about other varieties of trusts. Unfortunately, such rules are of limited utility in the context of the trust created by § 7501. Under common-law principles, a trust is created in property; a trust therefore does not come into existence until the settlor identifies an ascertainable interest in property to be the trust res. A § 7501 trust is radically different from the common-law paradigm, however. That provision states that "the *amount* of [trust-fund] tax . . . collected or withheld shall be held to be a special fund in trust for the United States." (Emphasis added.) Unlike a common-law trust, in which the settlor sets aside particular *property* as the trust res, § 7501 creates a trust in an abstract "amount"-a dollar *figure* not tied to any particular assets-rather than in the actual dollars withheld.[4] Common-law tracing rules, designed for a system in which particular property is identified as the trust res, are thus unhelpful in this special context.

Federal law delineating the nature of the relationship between the § 7501 trust and preferential transfer rules is limited. The only case in which we have explored that topic at any length is United States v. Randall, 401 U.S. 513, 91 S.Ct. 991, 28 L.Ed.2d 273 (1971), a case dealing with a postpetition transfer of property to discharge trust-fund tax obligations that the debtor had accrued prepetition. There, a court had ordered a debtor in possession to maintain a separate account for its withheld federal income and FICA taxes, but the debtor did not comply. When the debtor was subsequently adjudicated a bankrupt, the United States sought to recover from the debtor's general assets the amount of

---

4. The general common-law rule that a trust is not created absent a designation of particular property obviously does not invalidate § 7501's creation of a trust in the "amount" of withheld taxes. The common law of trusts is not binding on Congress.

withheld taxes ahead of the expenses of the bankruptcy proceeding. The Government argued that the debtor held the amount of taxes due in trust for the IRS and that this amount could be traced to the funds the debtor had in its accounts when the bankruptcy petition was filed. The trustee maintained that no trust had been created because the debtor had not segregated the funds. The Court declined directly to address either of these contentions. Rather, the Court simply refused to permit the IRS to recover the taxes ahead of administrative expenses, stating that "the statutory policy of subordinating taxes to costs and expenses of administration would not be served by creating or enforcing trusts which eat up an estate, leaving little or nothing for creditors and court officers whose goods and services created the assets." Id., at 517, 91 S.Ct., at 994.

In 1978, Congress fundamentally restructured bankruptcy law by passing the new Bankruptcy Code. Among the changes Congress decided to make was a modification of the rule this Court had enunciated in Randall under the old Bankruptcy Act. The Senate bill attacked *Randall* directly, providing in § 541 that trust-fund taxes withheld or collected prior to the filing of the bankruptcy petition were not "property of the estate." See S.Rep. No. 95-1106, at 33. The House bill did not deal explicitly with the problem of trust-fund taxes, but the House Report stated that "property of the estate" would not include property held in trust for another. See H.R.Rep. No. 95-595, at 368, U.S.Code Cong. & Admin. News 1978, p. 6324. Congress was unable to hold a conference, so the Senate and House floor managers met to reach compromises on the differences between the two bills. The compromise reached with respect to the relevant portion of § 541, which applies to postpetition transfers, was embodied in the eventually enacted House amendment and explicitly provided that "in the case of property held in trust, the property of the estate includes the legal title, but not the beneficial interest in the property." 124 Cong.Rec., at 32417 (remarks of Rep. Edwards). Accordingly, the Senate language specifying that withheld or collected trust-fund taxes are not part of the bankruptcy estate was deleted as "unnecessary since property of the estate does not include the beneficial interest in property held by the debtor as a trustee. Under [§ 7501], the amounts of withheld taxes are held to be a special fund in trust for the United States." Id., at 32417 (remarks of Rep. Edwards).[5]

---

5.   Because of the absence of a conference and the key roles played by Representative Edwards and his counterpart floor manager Senator DeConcini, we have treated their floor statements on the Bankruptcy Reform Act of 1978 as persuasive evidence of congressional intent. See, e.g., Commodity Futures Trading Comm'n v. Weintraub, 471 U.S. 343, 351, 105 S.Ct. 1986, 1992, 85 L.Ed.2d 372 (1985). Cf. 124 Cong.Rec. 32391 (1978) (remarks of Rep. Rousselot) (expressing view that remarks of floor manager of the Act have "the effect of being a conference report").

Representative Edwards discussed the effects of the House language on the rule established by *Randall*, indicating that the House amendment would supplant that rule:

"[A] serious problem exists where 'trust fund taxes' withheld from others are held to be property of the estate where the withheld amounts are commingled with other assets of the debtor. The courts should permit the use of reasonable assumptions under which the Internal Revenue Service, and other tax authorities, can demonstrate that amounts of withheld taxes are still in the possession of the debtor at the commencement of the case." Ibid.

The context of Representative Edwards' comment makes plain that he was discussing whether a post petition payment of trust-fund taxes involved "property of the estate." This focus is not surprising given that *Randall*, the case Congress was addressing, involved a postpetition demand for payment by the IRS. But Representative Edwards' discussion also applies to the question whether a pre petition payment is made from "property of the debtor." We have explained that "property of the debtor" is that property that would have been part of the estate had it not been transferred before the commencement of bankruptcy proceedings. The same "reasonable assumptions" therefore apply in both contexts.

The strict rule of *Randall* thus did not survive the adoption of the new Bankruptcy Code. But by requiring the IRS to "demonstrate that amounts of taxes withheld are still in the possession of the debtor at the commencement of the case [i.e., at the filing of the petition]," 124 Cong.Rec., at 32417 (remarks of Rep. Edwards), Congress expected that the IRS would have to show some connection between the § 7501 trust and the assets sought to be applied to a debtor's trust-fund tax obligations. See United States v. Whiting Pools, Inc., 462 U.S. 198, 205, n. 10, 103 S.Ct. 2309, 2314, n. 10, 76 L.Ed.2d 515 (1983) (IRS cannot exclude funds from the estate if it cannot trace them to § 7501 trust property). The question in this case is how extensive the required nexus must be. The Bankruptcy Code provides no explicit answer, and Representative Edwards' admonition that courts should "permit the use of reasonable assumptions" does not add much. The House Report does, however, give sufficient guidance regarding those assumptions to permit us to conclude that the nexus requirement is satisfied here. That Report states:

"A payment of withholding taxes constitutes a payment of money held in trust under Internal Revenue Code § 7501(a), and thus will not be a preference because the beneficiary of the trust, the taxing authority, is in a separate class with respect to those taxes, if they have been properly held for payment, as they will have been if the debtor is able to make the payments."

H.R.Rep. No. 95-595, supra, at 373, U.S. Code Cong. & Admin. News 1978, p. 6329.[6]

Under a literal reading of the above passage, the bankruptcy trustee could not avoid any voluntary prepetition payment of trust-fund taxes, regardless of the source of the funds. As the House Report expressly states, the limitation that the funds must "have been properly held for payment" is satisfied "if the debtor is able to make the payments." The debtor's act of voluntarily paying its trust-fund tax obligation therefore is alone sufficient to establish the required nexus between the "amount" held in trust and the funds paid.

We adopt this literal reading. In the absence of any suggestion in the Bankruptcy Code about what tracing rules to apply, we are relegated to the legislative history. The courts are directed to apply "reasonable assumptions" to govern the tracing of funds, and the House Report identifies one such assumption to be that any voluntary prepetition payment of trust-fund taxes out of the debtor's assets is not a transfer of the debtor's property. Nothing in the Bankruptcy Code or its legislative history casts doubt on the reasonableness of that assumption. Other rules might be reasonable, too, but the only evidence we have suggests that Congress preferred this one. We see no reason to disregard that evidence.

III.

We hold that AIA's payments of trust-fund taxes to the IRS from its general accounts were not transfers of "property of the debtor," but were instead transfers of property held in trust for the Government pursuant to § 7501. Such payments therefore cannot be avoided as preferences. The judgment of the Court of Appeals is AFFIRMED.

Notes and Questions

Only the *employee's* share of employment taxes withheld by the employer constitute trust fund taxes. See discussion, § III. C., below.

---

6. Petitioner's claim that this legislative history is irrelevant because the House Bill was not enacted is in error. The exact language to which the quoted portion of the House Report refers was enacted into law. Compare § 547(b) with H.R. 8200, 95th Cong., 1st Sess., § 547(b) (1977). The version of § 541 that was eventually enacted is different from the original House bill, but only in that it makes explicit rather than implicit that "property of the estate" does not include the beneficiary's equitable interest in property held in trust by the debtor. Compare § 541(d) with H.R. 8200, supra, § 541(a)(1).

The amount attributable to the *employer's* share does not constitute trust fund taxes and thus this amount may be avoided as a preferential transfer under 11 U.S.C. § 547(b). See Hoffman v. United States, 208 Bankr. Reps. 788 (BC D. Conn. 1997).

If funds have been commingled in a trust, claimants must be able to identify and trace the funds in order to recover their property. The Supreme Court in *Begier* used the nexus test but the prevailing test under trust law is the "lowest intermediate balance test." This test employs the fiction that when the trustee withdraws funds from an account, the amounts withdrawn are non-trust funds. Thus, if the amount on deposit in the commingled fund has at all times equaled or exceeded the amount of the trust, the claimants will be entitled to the return of the trust funds in their full amount. Conversely, if the commingled fund has been depleted entirely, nothing may be recovered. If, on the other hand, the commingled fund has not been entirely depleted but has been reduced below the level of the trust fund, the claimant is entitled to the lowest intermediate balance in the account. However, the trust may not be replenished by deposits made subsequent to the lowest intermediate balance. See In Re Catholic Diocese of Wilmington, Inc., 435 B.R. 135 (D. Dela. 2010).

Section 522(b) of the Bankruptcy Code provides for the exemption of certain property and amounts of money from the bankruptcy estate. Thus, this property would not be reachable by creditors and the debtor would be able to retain it. However, recall our discussion in § I.D.2, above, of property exempt from levy under § 6334. The property exempted from levy under the Internal Revenue Code is not consistent with the property exempted from collection under the Bankruptcy Code. In general, the Bankruptcy Code allows more property and greater amounts to be exempted than does the Internal Revenue Code, and thus the Bankruptcy Code is more generous to the debtor.

1   How, if at all, can the Bankruptcy Code exemptions and the IRC exemptions be reconciled?

2   What powers does a trustee have to set aside transfers of property by a debtor?

3   What determines whether property is part of the bankruptcy estate?

4   If the Service levies against property of a delinquent taxpayer to enforce its lien, and the taxpayer subsequently files a bankruptcy petition, what is the status of the levy?

1. Priority of Tax Claims in Bankruptcy

The Bankruptcy Code contains nine categories of priority claims under 11 U.S.C. § 507(a). Administrative expenses incurred to preserve the bankruptcy estate and tax liabilities incurred during the administration of the estate are accorded first priority under 11 U.S.C. § 507(a)(1). Since these are expenses of the bankruptcy estate, by definition § 507(a)(1) claims are incurred after the filing of the bankruptcy petition. The second priority taxes are those that accrue in an involuntary bankruptcy action during the ordinary course of business during the "gap period" after the commencement of the bankruptcy case and before the appointment of a trustee. 11 U.S.C. §§ 507(a)(2); 502(f). Third priority is accorded unsecured claims for income taxes withheld on wages, salaries and commissions, as well as unsecured claims for the employees' share of employment taxes on such income, earned within 90 days prior to the filing of the petition. The priority of the remaining tax claims depends upon whether they are secured or unsecured, what type of tax they are, when they arose, and the circumstances under which they arose.

A tax claim is secured to the extent of the value of the property to which the tax lien attaches, provided notice of the tax lien has been filed before the petition date. If such pre-petition notice has not been filed, the Service is treated as an unsecured creditor. Unsecured income tax or gross receipts taxes are entitled to eighth level priority under 11 U.S.C. § 507(a)(8) and are nondischargeable. All other unsecured tax claims (i.e., those not falling under §§ 507(a)(2) or (a)(8)) are considered generally unsecured claims that are dischargeable and are not entitled to priority.

Unsecured tax claims falling under § 507(a)(8) have priority only to the extent they meet certain requirements: (1) if the tax is an income or gross receipts tax, (a) the return for the taxable year must be due (including extensions) within the three-year period immediately preceding the filing of the bankruptcy petition, (b) the taxes must be assessed within the 240-day period prior to the filing of the petition (this period is tolled for the period during which an offer in compromise is pending and for 30 days thereafter, or during the period in which a waiver of the statute of limitations on assessment is in effect), (c) the taxes must be "assessable" but unassessed as of the date the petition is filed and must be unassessed for tax years for which the taxpayer has agreed to an extension of the statute of limitations on assessment, (2) a property tax assessed before the filing of the petition and payable without penalty within one year before the petition is filed, (3) trust fund (withholding) taxes, (4) the employer's share of employment taxes withheld from employees' wages, salaries or commissions, (5) certain excise taxes, (6) certain customs duties, and (7) penalties that compensate the Service for actual pecuniary loss related to a tax claim.

The treatment of secured tax claims is determined under § 724(b) of the Bankruptcy Code, and is somewhat complicated. First, the tax lien must secure an allowed claim for taxes that is not avoidable by the trustee. A trustee has the power to set aside transfers of property by a debtor (see § B, above) and to set aside (avoid) tax liens under §§ 545-549 of the Bankruptcy Code (e.g., fraudulent transfers, pre-petition liens that have not been perfected, and perfected liens that are subordinate to superpriority claims). The property, or proceeds from the sale of the property, is distributed in the following order: (1) to secured claims senior to the tax claim that are not avoidable and that are allowed by the court, (2) to the holders of priority claims in levels one through seven of § 507(a) to the extent of the amount equal to the amount of the tax lien, (3) to the holder of the tax lien to the extent of any excess amount of the distribution in (2), (4) to allowed and unavoidable secured claims that are junior to the tax lien, (5) to the holder of the tax lien, if this claim was not paid in full under (3), and (6) to the estate.

Pre-petition interest is given the same priority as the underlying tax liability to which it relates. Since the Bankruptcy Code must consider fairness to all creditors, it does not authorize the payment of post-petition interest unless the claim is "over-secured." This means that the collateral securing the claim must exceed the amount of the claim. If interest is allowed under the Bankruptcy Code, the rate is determined in accordance with the bankruptcy laws (at the legal rate), and not under the tax laws. If a tax claim is under-secured (so that the collateral is not sufficient to cover the amount of the claim), a distribution from the bankruptcy estate cannot be allocated to the payment of interest unless on the date of the confirmation of the claim, the collateral has increased in value so that the claim is no longer under-secured. An unsecured, general tax claim is not entitled to post-petition interest unless the debtor is solvent.

The priority of penalties depends upon whether they are designed to compensate the government for actual pecuniary loss or whether they are punitive in nature. A compensatory, pecuniary loss penalty is entitled to seventh order priority and is not dischargeable. A punitive, nonpecuniary loss penalty may be allowed, depending on its age. If the penalty was incurred more than three years before the petition filing date, the claim is dischargeable. If it is attributable to fraud, failure to file a return, or filing a delinquent return within two years of the petition, it is not dischargeable, and is entitled to be paid after the priority claims and after the general, unsecured claims. A lien that secures a dischargeable claim may be avoided by the trustee. 11 U.S.C. § 726(a). After the petition is filed, the Bankruptcy Court has control over the debtor's assets, so post-petition penalties are not allowed unless they are pecuniary.

Problems

1   A debtor files a bankruptcy petition in June 2010, and the court allows the following claims: a $5,680 lien for delinquent federal income taxes assessed three months prior to the petition date and attributable to the 2007 and 2008 taxable years; $220 in interest on the tax claims ($85 of which arose post-petition); $92 in late payment penalties on the federal income tax deficiency; a $1500 lien for real property ad valorem taxes attributable to the 2009 taxable year, filed after the federal income tax lien; $1200 of expenses incurred in administering the bankruptcy estate; $950 of federal income taxes arising after the petition was filed and which are now due; and $325 in state income taxes attributable to the 2009 taxable year, for which no lien has been filed, along with $55 of interest ($18 of which arose after the petition was filed) and $35 of late payment fees on that amount. In what order of priority will these claims be considered?

2   If the $5,680 federal tax lien had been filed after the bankruptcy petition, would this affect the payment of the claim?

3   If a debtor has property valued at $12,000 that is subject to an $8,000 lien for unpaid federal income taxes, $ 5,000 in claims attributable to first through seventh priority under § 507 of the Bankruptcy Code, and a $3,000 nontax lien that is junior to the tax lien, in what order of priority will these claims be paid?

4   What is the rationale for the order of priority of the claims in question 3?

2. Discharge of Liabilities

The purpose of bankruptcy is to distribute the debtor's property or reorganize the debtor's debts in a manner that is fair and equitable to creditors, and to provide a fresh start for the debtor. Thus, at the end of the bankruptcy proceeding, the court may discharge some of the debtor's liabilities. A discharge of a claim shields the debtor from personal liability on that claim and operates as an injunction, providing protection from any further collection action. Some claims, however, are not subject to discharge so the debtor will remain personally liable on those claims even after the conclusion of the bankruptcy proceeding. Tax claims granted priority under §§ 507(a)(2) and (a)(8) of the Bankruptcy Code fall into this category. 11 U.S.C. § 523(a)(1). Also, if the taxpayer/debtor files a fraudulent return, or fails to file a return at all, or willfully attempts to evade or defeat the tax, the tax liability is not dischargeable. See In re Sternberg, 229 B.R. 238 (S.D. Fla. 1998)(holding that transfer of attachable assets to a family member without adequate consideration demonstrated fraudulent intent under § 523(a)(1)(C) so that debtor's tax liability was not discharged).

Dischargeability operates in conjunction with the priority provisions. If a claim is dischargeable, the interest and penalties attributable to that claim also are dischargeable. In the *Sternberg* case, the tax liability was determined to be nondischargeable because of the wrongdoing of the debtor. This would mean that the interest on that claim also is nondischargeable, so the debtor would remain personally liable for both the tax and interest following the completion of the bankruptcy proceedings. Thus, the Service will be able to collect its full claim from the debtor's after-acquired property. A pecuniary penalty has eighth level priority and is nondischargeable. A nonpecuniary penalty attributable to a return required to be filed more than three years prior to the filing of the bankruptcy petition ordinarily would be dischargeable. Also, a bankruptcy trustee can avoid a tax lien that secures a claim for a nonpecuniary penalty. Where the penalty is attributable to the failure to file a return, the filing of a fraudulent return, or the filing of a delinquent return within two years of the bankruptcy petition, the penalties are nondischargeable.

Since claims falling within the eighth priority under § 507(a)(8) are not dischargeable, the claim must be examined to determine whether it falls within this section. In order to obtain priority under § 507(a)(8), the return for the taxable year in which the liability arises must be due (including extensions) within the three-year period preceding the filing of the bankruptcy petition. Coordinating § 523(a)(1) with § 507(a)(8), liabilities attributable to returns due within three years of the filing of the bankruptcy petition are not dischargeable. Thus, those falling outside that time period are dischargeable. This presents problems when debtors file bankruptcy petitions under one title of the Bankruptcy Code then later dismiss those petitions and refile under another title after the three-year period has run.

YOUNG v. UNITED STATES

Supreme Court of the United States, 2002.
535 U.S.. 43, 122 S.Ct. 1036, 152 L.Ed.2d 79.

JUSTICE SCALIA delivered the opinion of the Court.

A discharge under the Bankruptcy Code does not extinguish certain tax liabilities for which a return was due within three years before the filing of an individual debtor's petition. 11 U.S.C. §§ 523(a)(1)(A), 507(a)(8)(A)(i). We must decide whether this "three-year lookback period" is tolled during the pendency of a prior bankruptcy petition.

I.

Petitioners Cornelius and Suzanne Young failed to include payment with their 1992 income tax return, due and filed on October 15, 1993 (petitioners had obtained an extension of the April 15 deadline). About $15,000 was owing. The Internal Revenue Service (IRS) assessed the tax liability on January 3, 1994, and petitioners made modest monthly payments ($40 to $300) from April 1994 until November 1995. On May 1, 1996, they sought protection under Chapter 13 of the Bankruptcy Code in the United States Bankruptcy Court for the District of New Hampshire. The bulk of their tax liability (about $13,000, including accrued interest) remained due. Before a reorganization plan was confirmed, however, the Youngs moved on October 23, 1996, to dismiss their Chapter 13 petition, pursuant to 11 U.S.C. § 1307(b). On March 12, 1997, one day before the Bankruptcy Court dismissed their Chapter 13 petition, the Youngs filed a new petition, this time under Chapter 7. This was a "no asset" petition, meaning that the Youngs had no assets available to satisfy unsecured creditors, including the IRS. A discharge was granted June 17, 1997; the case was closed September 22, 1997.

The IRS subsequently demanded payment of the 1992 tax debt. The Youngs refused and petitioned the Bankruptcy Court to reopen their Chapter 7 case and declare the debt discharged. In their view, the debt fell outside the Bankruptcy Code's "three-year lookback period," §§ 523(a)(1)(A), 507(a)(8)(A)(i), and had therefore been discharged, because it pertained to a tax return due on October 15, 1993, more than three years before their Chapter 7 filing on March 12, 1997. The Bankruptcy Court reopened the case but sided with the IRS. Although the Youngs' 1992 income tax return was due more than three years before they filed their Chapter 7 petition, it was due less than three years before they filed their Chapter 13 petition on May 1, 1996. Holding that the "three-year lookback period" is tolled during the pendency of a prior bankruptcy petition, the Bankruptcy Court concluded that the 1992 tax debt had not been discharged. The District Court for the District of New Hampshire and Court of Appeals for the First Circuit agreed. 233 F.3d 56 (2000). We granted certiorari.

II

Section 523(a) of the Bankruptcy Code excepts certain individual debts from discharge, including any tax "of the kind and for the periods specified in section * * * 507(a)(8) of this title, whether or not a claim for such tax was filed or allowed." § 523(a)(1)(A). Section 507(a), in turn, describes the priority of certain claims in the distribution of the debtor's assets. Subsection 507(a)(8)(A)(i) gives eighth priority to "allowed unsecured claims of governmental units, only to the extent that such claims are for– * * * a tax on or measured by income or gross receipts– * * * *for a taxable year ending on or before the date of the filing of the petition for which a return, if required, is last due, including extensions, after three years before the date of the filing of the petition * * * .*" (Emphasis added.) This is commonly known as the "three-year lookback period." If the IRS has a claim for taxes for which the return was due within three years before the bankruptcy petition was filed, the claim enjoys eighth priority under § 507(a)(8)(A)(i) and is nondischargeable in bankruptcy under § 523(a)(1)(A).

The terms of the lookback period appear to create a loophole: Since the Code does not prohibit back-to-back Chapter 13 and Chapter 7 filings (as long as the debtor did not receive a discharge under Chapter 13, see §§ 727(a)(8), (9)), a debtor can render a tax debt dischargeable by first filing a Chapter 13 petition, then voluntarily dismissing the petition when the lookback period for the debt has lapsed, and finally refiling under Chapter 7. During the pendency of the Chapter 13 petition, the automatic stay of § 362(a) will prevent the IRS from taking steps to collect the unpaid taxes, and if the Chapter 7 petition is filed after the lookback period has expired, the taxes remaining due will be dischargeable. Petitioners took advantage of this loophole, which, they believe, is permitted by the Bankruptcy Code.

We disagree. The three-year lookback period is a limitations period subject to traditional principles of equitable tolling. Since nothing in the Bankruptcy Code precludes equitable tolling of the lookback period, we believe the courts below properly excluded from the three-year limitation the period during which the Youngs' Chapter 13 petition was pending.

A.

The lookback period is a limitations period because it prescribes a period within which certain rights (namely, priority and nondischargeability in bankruptcy) may be enforced. Old tax claims–those pertaining to returns due more than three years before the debtor filed the bankruptcy petition–become dischargeable, so that a bankruptcy decree will relieve the debtor of the obligation to pay. The period thus encourages the IRS to protect its rights-- by, say, collecting the debt, 26 U.S.C. §§ 6501, 6502 (1994 ed. and Supp. V), or perfecting a tax lien, §§ 6322, 6323(a), (f) (1994 ed.)--before three years have elapsed. If the IRS sleeps on its rights, its claim loses priority and the debt becomes dischargeable. Thus, as petitioners concede, the lookback period serves the same "basic policies [furthered by] all limitations provisions: repose, elimination of stale claims, and certainty about a plaintiff's opportunity for recovery and a defendant's potential liabilities." Rotella v. Wood, 528 U.S. 549, 555, 120 S.Ct. 1075, 145 L.Ed.2d 1047 (2000). It is true that, unlike most statutes of limitations, the lookback period bars only *some*, and not *all* legal remedies[1] for enforcing the claim (viz., priority and nondischargeability in bankruptcy); that makes it a more limited statute of limitations, but a statute of limitations nonetheless.

Petitioners argue that the lookback period is a substantive component of the Bankruptcy Code, not a procedural limitations period. The lookback period commences on the date the return for the tax debt "is last due," § 507(a)(8)(A)(i), not on the date the IRS discovers or assesses the unpaid tax. Thus, the IRS may have less than three years to protect itself against the risk that a debt will become dischargeable in bankruptcy.

To illustrate, petitioners offer the following variation on this case: Suppose the Youngs filed their 1992 tax return on October 15, 1993, but had not received (as they received here) an extension of the April 15, 1993, due date. Assume the remaining facts of the case are unchanged: The IRS assessed the tax on January 3, 1994; petitioners filed a Chapter 13 petition on May 1, 1996; that petition was voluntarily dismissed and the Youngs filed a new petition under Chapter 7 on March 12, 1997. In

---

1. Equitable remedies may still be available. Traditionally, for example a mortgagee could sue in equity to foreclose mortgaged property even though the underlying debt was time barred. Hardin v. Boyd, 113 U.S. 756, 765-766, 5 S.Ct. 771, 28 L.Ed. 1141 (1885); 2 G. Glenn, Mortgages §§ 141-142, pp. 812-818 (1943); see also Beach v. Owen Fed. Bank, 523 U.S. 410, 415-416, 118 S.Ct. 1408, 140 L.Ed.2d 566 (1998)(recoupment is available after a limitations period has lapsed); United States v. Dalm, 494 U.S. 596, 611, 110 S.Ct. 1361, 108 L.Ed.2d 548 (1990)(same).

this hypothetical, petitioners argue, their tax debt would have been dischargeable in the *first* petition under Chapter 13. Over three years would have elapsed between the due date of their return (April 15, 1993) and their Chapter 13 petition (May 1, 1996). But the IRS–which may not have discovered the debt until petitioners filed a return on October 15, 1993–would have enjoyed less than three years to collect the debt or prevent the debt from becoming dischargeable in bankruptcy (by perfecting a tax lien). The Code even contemplates this possibility, petitioners believe. Section 523(a)(1)(B)(ii) renders a tax debt nondischargeable if it arises from an untimely return filed within two years before a bankruptcy petition. Thus, if petitioners had filed their return on April 30, 1994 (more than two years before their Chapter 13 petition), and if the IRS had been unaware of the debt until the return was filed, the IRS would have had only *two years* to act before the debt became dischargeable in bankruptcy. For these reasons, petitioners believe the lookback period is not a limitations period, but rather a *definition* of dischargeable taxes.

We disagree. In the sense in which petitioners use the term, *all* limitations periods are "substantive": They *define* a subset of claims eligible for certain remedies. And the lookback is not distinctively "substantive" merely because it commences on a date that may precede the date when the IRS discovers its claim. There is nothing unusual about a statute of limitations that commences when the claimant has a complete and present cause of action, whether or not he is aware of it. As for petitioners' reliance on § 523(a)(1)(B)(ii), that section proves, at most, that Congress put different limitations periods on different kinds of tax debts. All tax debts falling within the terms of the three-year lookback period are nondischargeable in bankruptcy. §§ 523(a)(1)(A), 507(a)(8)(A)(i). Even if a tax debt falls outside the terms of the lookback period, it is nonetheless nondischargeable if it pertains to an untimely return filed within two years before the bankruptcy petition. § 523(a)(1)(B)(ii). These provisions are complementary; they do not suggest that the lookback period is something other than a limitations period.

B.

It is hornbook law that limitations periods are "customarily subject to 'equitable tolling,' " Irwin v. Department of Veterans Affairs, 498 U.S. 89, 95, 111 S.Ct. 453, 112 L.Ed.2d 435 (1990), unless tolling would be "inconsistent with the text of the relevant statute," United States v. Beggerly, 524 U.S. 38, 48, 118 S.Ct. 1862, 141 L.Ed.2d 32 (1998).

Congress must be presumed to draft limitations periods in light of this background principle. That is doubly true when it is enacting limitations periods to be applied by bankruptcy courts, which are courts of equity and "appl[y] the principles and rules of equity jurisprudence."

This Court has permitted equitable tolling in situations "where the claimant has actively pursued his judicial remedies by filing a defective pleading during the statutory period, or where the complainant has been induced or tricked by his adversary's misconduct into allowing the filing deadline to pass." *Irwin*, supra, at 96, 111 S.Ct. 453. We have acknowledged, however, that tolling might be appropriate in other cases, see, e.g., Baldwin County Welcome Center v. Brown, 466 U.S. 147, 151, 104 S.Ct. 1723, 80 L.Ed.2d 196 (1984) (per curiam), and this, we believe, is one. The Youngs' Chapter 13 petition erected an automatic stay under § 362, which prevented the IRS from taking steps to protect its claim. When the Youngs filed a petition under Chapter 7, the three-year lookback period therefore excluded time during which their Chapter 13 petition was pending. The Youngs' 1992 tax return was due within that three-year period. Hence the lower courts properly held that the tax debt was not discharged when the Youngs were granted a discharge under Chapter 7.

Tolling is in our view appropriate regardless of petitioners' intentions when filing back-to-back Chapter 13 and Chapter 7 petitions--whether the Chapter 13 petition was filed in good faith or solely to run down the lookback period. In either case, the IRS was disabled from protecting its claim during the pendency of the Chapter 13 petition, and this period of disability tolled the three-year lookback period when the Youngs filed their Chapter 7 petition.

C.

Petitioners invoke several statutory provisions which they claim display an intent to preclude tolling here. First they point to § 523(b), which, they believe, explicitly permits discharge in a Chapter 7 proceeding of certain debts that were nondischargeable (as this tax debt was) in a prior Chapter 13 proceeding. Petitioners misread the provision. Section 523(b) declares that "a debt that was *excepted from discharge* under subsection (a)(1), (a)(3), or (a)(8)

of this section * * * in a prior case concerning the debtor * * * is dischargeable in a case under this title unless, by the terms of subsection (a) of this section, such debt is not dischargeable in the case under this title." (Emphasis added.)

The phrase "excepted from discharge" in this provision is not synonymous (as petitioners would have it) with "nondischargeable." It envisions a prior bankruptcy proceeding that progressed *to the discharge stage*, from which discharge a particular debt was actually "excepted." It thus has no application to the present case; and even if it did, the very same arguments in favor of tolling that we have found persuasive with regard to § 507 would apply to § 523 as well. One might perhaps have expected an explicit tolling provision in § 523(b) if that subsection applied *only* to those debts "excepted from discharge" in the earlier proceeding that were subject to the three-year lookback--but in fact it also applies to excepted debts (see § 523(a)(3)) that were subject to no limitation period. And even the need for tolling as to debts that *were* subject to the three-year lookback is minimal, since a separate provision of the Code, § 727(a)(9), constrains successive discharges under Chapters 13 and 7: Generally speaking, six years must elapse between filing of the two bankruptcy petitions, which would make the need for tolling of the three-year limitation nonexistent. The absence of an explicit tolling provision in § 523 therefore suggests nothing.

Petitioners point to two provisions of the Code, which, in their view, do contain a tolling provision. Its presence there, and its absence in § 507, they argue, displays an intent to preclude equitable tolling of the lookback period. We disagree. Petitioners point first to § 108(c), which reads:

"Except as provided in section 524 of this title, if applicable nonbankruptcy law* * *fixes a period for commencing or continuing a civil action in a court other than a bankruptcy court on a claim against the debtor * * *, and such period has not expired before the date of the filing of the petition, then such period does not expire until the later of--(1) the end of such period, including any suspension of such period occurring on or after the commencement of the case; or (2) 30 days after notice of the termination or expiration of the stay * * * with respect to such claim."

Petitioners believe § 108(c)(1) contains a tolling provision. The lower courts have split over this issue, compare, e.g., Rogers v. Corrosion Products, Inc., 42 F.3d 292, 297 (C.A.5), with Garbe Iron Works, Inc. v. Priester, 99 Ill.2d 84, 75 Ill.Dec. 428, 457 N.E.2d 422 (1983); we need not resolve it here. Even assuming petitioners are correct, we would draw no negative inference from the presence of an express tolling provision in § 108(c)(1) and the absence of one in § 507. It would be quite reasonable for Congress to instruct *nonbankruptcy* courts (including state courts) to toll *nonbankruptcy* limitations periods (including state-law limitations periods) while, at the same time, assuming that bankruptcy courts will use their inherent equitable powers to toll the federal limitations periods within the Code.

Finally, petitioners point to a tolling provision in § 507(a)(8)(A), the same subsection that sets forth the three-year lookback period. Subsection 507(a)(8)(A) grants eighth priority to tax claims pertaining to returns that were *due* within the three-year lookback period, §507(a)(8)(A)(i), and to claims that were *assessed* within 240 days before the debtor's bankruptcy petition, § 507(a)(8)(A)(ii). Whereas the three-year lookback period contains no express tolling provision, the 240-day lookback period is tolled "any time plus 30 days during which an offer in compromise with respect to such tax that was made within 240 days after such assessment was pending." § 507(a)(8)(A)(ii). Petitioners believe this express tolling provision, appearing in the same subsection as the three-year lookback period, demonstrates a statutory intent *not* to toll the

three-year lookback period.

If anything, § 507(a)(8)(A)(ii) demonstrates that the Bankruptcy Code incorporates traditional equitable principles. An "offer in compromise" is a settlement offer submitted by a debtor. When § 507(a)(8)(A)(ii) was enacted, it was IRS practice--though no statutory provision required it--to stay collection efforts (if the Government's interests would not be jeopardized) during the pendency of an "offer in compromise," 26 CFR § 301.7122-1(d)(2) (1978); M. Saltzman, IRS Practice and Procedure ¶ 15.07[1], p. 15-47 (1981).[2] Thus, a court would not have equitably tolled the 240-day lookback period during the pendency of an "offer in compromise," since tolling is inappropriate when a claimant has voluntarily chosen not to protect his rights within the limitations period. Hence the tolling provision in § 507(a)(8)(A)(ii) *supplements* rather than displaces principles of equitable tolling.

* * *

We conclude that the lookback period of 11 U.S.C. § 507(a)(8)(A)(i) is tolled during the pendency of a prior bankruptcy petition. The judgment of the Court of Appeals for the First Circuit is affirmed.

IT IS SO ORDERED.

Notes

The Court's decision in *Young* resolved the conflict among the circuit courts as to whether the three-year period is tolled during the pendency

---

2.   The Code was amended in 1998 to prohibit collection efforts during the pendency of an offer in compomise. See 26 U.S.C. § 6331(k)(1994 ed., Supp. V).

of prior bankruptcy filings. It also closed the loophole that was available to debtors who were able to discharge their tax debts by filing multiple bankruptcy petitions. Prior to the *Young* decision, some courts had concluded that while there was no automatic tolling provision under the Bankruptcy Code, equitable principles could be used to toll the § 507(a)(8) lookback periods if there was evidence of misconduct by the debtor. Without such evidence, however, tolling was not automatic and did not constitute a bar to the discharge of a tax claim. See, e.g., In Re Palmer, 219 F.3d 580 (6th Cir. 2000); United States v. Gilmore, 226 B.R. 567 (E.D. Tex. 1998).

A district court in Maryland has held that equitable tolling does not apply under 11 U.S.C. § 727(a)(8). Section 727(a)(8) provides that a debtor must wait six years from the filing of one Chapter 7 case before she is entitled to discharge of another Chapter 7 case. In Tidewater Finance Co. v. Williams, 341 B.R. 530 (D. Md. 2006), the debtor filed bankruptcy under Chapter 7 then subsequently filed three cases under Chapter 13 before filing a final case under Chapter 7. The time period between the Chapter 7 cases, during the pendency of the Chapter 13 cases was two years and 324 days. The creditor sought equitable tolling of the six-year period for the period that the Chapter 13 cases were pending. The district court affirmed the decision of the Bankruptcy Court, holding that neither the plain text of § 727(a)(8), the statutory framework of § 727 in general, nor the legislative history supported equitable tolling.

III. COLLECTION FROM THIRD PARTIES

Sometimes the collection action is not taken against the taxpayer directly, but against a third party to whom the taxpayer has transferred assets or who, by operation of law, assumes responsibility for the taxpayer's liabilities.

A. INNOCENT SPOUSES

When spouses exercise their privilege to file a joint tax return, they receive the benefit of income splitting, deduction and credit sharing, and lower tax rates. They also assume joint and several liability for all taxes due, regardless of who was at fault. Because of the inequity that often results from joint and several liability, Congress enacted § 6013(e) in 1971 to provide relief to an innocent spouse. The provision proved inadequate, however, because it was difficult to interpret and frequently was applied inconsistently. Under the 1998 IRS Restructuring and

Reform Act, Congress extensively amended the innocent spouse provision, re-enacting it as § 6015.

1. Requirements for Relief

CHESHIRE v. COMMISSIONER
United States Court of Appeals, Fifth Circuit, 2002.
282 F.3d 326.

KING, CHIEF JUDGE:

The Commissioner of Internal Revenue assessed a tax deficiency and associated penalties against Petitioner-Appellant Kathryn Cheshire. In the United States Tax Court, Cheshire asserted claims for innocent spouse relief from the tax deficiency and penalties under § 6015(b), (c), and (f) of the Internal Revenue Code. 26 U.S.C. § 6015 (Supp. 2001). The Tax Court denied Cheshire's request for innocent spouse relief, and Cheshire appeals that denial. For the following reasons, we AFFIRM the judgment of the Tax Court.

I. Factual History

The facts in this case are undisputed. Kathryn Cheshire ("Appellant") married David Cheshire in 1970. More than twenty years later, Mr. Cheshire retired from Southwestern Bell Telephone Company effective January 1, 1992, and received the following retirement distributions in 1992:

Lump sum distribution	$199,771
LESOP for salaried employees	5,919
Savings plan for salaried employees	23,263
ESOP	971
TOTAL	$229,924

Of the $229,924 total distribution, $42,183 was rolled over into a qualified account and is not subject to federal income tax. Mr. Cheshire deposited $184,377 of the retirement distributions into the Cheshires' joint checking account, which earned $1168 in interest for 1992. Appellant knew of Mr. Cheshire's receipt of $229,924 in retirement distributions and of the $1168 in interest earned on the distributions.

The Cheshires made several large disbursements from the retirement distributions in their joint checking account. They withdrew $99,425 from this account to pay off the mortgage on their marital residence, and they withdrew an additional $20,189 to purchase a new family car, a 1992 Ford Explorer. Mr. Cheshire also used the retirement proceeds to provide start-up capital for his new business, to satisfy loans taken out to acquire a family truck and an automobile for the Cheshires' daughter, to pay family expenses, and to establish a college fund for the Cheshires' daughter. Appellant knew of all these expenditures.

Appellant and Mr. Cheshire filed a joint federal income tax return, prepared by Mr. Cheshire, for 1992. On line 17a of this return, they reported the $199,771.05 in retirement distributions[2] but claimed only $56,150.12 of this amount as taxable. Before signing the return, Appellant questioned Mr. Cheshire about the tax consequences of the retirement distributions. Mr. Cheshire replied that John Daniel Mican, a certified public accountant, advised Mr. Cheshire that retirement proceeds used to pay off a mortgage are nontaxable. Appellant accepted this answer and made no further inquiries prior to signing the return on March 14, 1993. In fact, Mr. Cheshire had not consulted Mican, and all retirement proceeds that are not rolled over into a qualified account are taxable. Because of Mr. Cheshire's persistent problems with alcohol, the Cheshires permanently separated on July 13, 1993, and they divorced seventeen months later. The divorce decree awarded Appellant unencumbered title to the marital residence and to the Ford Explorer.

The Commissioner of Internal Revenue (the "Commissioner") audited the Cheshires' 1992 return and determined that Mr. Cheshire had received taxable retirement distributions of $187,741–the difference between the total distributions ($229,924) and the rollover ($42,183). Thus, the Cheshires had understated the amount of their taxable distributions by $131,591. The Commissioner also determined that the Cheshires had underreported the interest income earned on the retirement distributions by $717. Because of these inaccuracies, the Commissioner imposed a penalty under § 6662(a) of the Internal Revenue Code.[3]

II. Procedural History

Appellant commenced this action in the Tax Court. She conceded that $131,591 of the retirement distributions and the corresponding

---

2.   This number corresponds to the amount of the lump sum distribution and excludes the LESOP, ESOP, and savings plan distributions.

3.   Section 6662(a) provides: If this section applies to any portion of an underpayment of tax required to be shown on a return, there shall be added to the tax an amount equal to 20 percent of the portion of the underpayment to which this section applies.
26 U.S.C. § 6662(a) (Supp.2001).

earned interest were improperly excluded from taxable income. She claimed, however, that she was entitled to relief as an innocent spouse under § 6015(b),[4] § 6015(c),[5] or § 6015(f)[6] of the Internal Revenue Code. 26 U.S.C. § 6015. Prior to trial, the Commissioner conceded that Appellant qualified for innocent spouse relief with respect to the LESOP distribution ($5919), the savings plan distribution ($23,262), and the ESOP distribution ($971). Consequently, the taxable income from the retirement distributions and the corresponding earned interest remaining in dispute totaled $101,438 and $691, respectively. These amounts roughly correspond to the improperly deducted amounts that the Cheshires used to pay off their mortgage.

The Tax Court majority, consisting of twelve judges, denied Appellant relief under § 6015(b), (c), and (f). Cheshire v. Comm'r, 115 T.C. 183, 2000 WL 1227132 (2000). The Tax Court found that Appellant failed to establish that she "did not know, and had no reason to know" of the tax understatement as required for relief under § 6015(b)(1)(C). Id. at 193. The Tax Court also found that Appellant was not entitled to relief under § 6015(c) because she had "actual knowledge * * * of any item giving rise

---

4.   Section 6015(b)(1) provides:

[I]f--(A) a joint return has been made for a taxable year; (B) on such return there is an understatement of tax attributable to erroneous items of one individual filing the joint return; (C) the other individual filing the joint return establishes that in signing the return he or she did not know, and had no reason to know, that there was such understatement; (D) taking into account all the facts and circumstances, it is inequitable to hold the other individual liable for the deficiency in tax for such taxable year attributable to such understatement; and (E) the other individual elects * * * the benefits of this subsection not later than the date which is 2 years after the date the Secretary has begun collection activities with respect to the individual making the election, then the other individual shall be relieved of liability for tax (including interest, penalties, and other amounts) for such taxable year to the extent such liability is attributable to such understatement.

26 U.S.C. § 6015(b)(1) (Supp.2001).

5.   Section 6015(c)(1) provides:

[I]f an individual who has made a joint return for any taxable year elects the application of this subsection, the individual's liability for any deficiency which is assessed with respect to the return shall not exceed the portion of such deficiency properly allocable to the individual under subsection (d).

26 U.S.C. § 6015(c)(1) (Supp.2001). The general rule under subsection (d) is that:

[A]ny item giving rise to a deficiency on a joint return shall be allocated to individuals filing the return in the same manner as it would have been allocated if the individuals had filed separate returns for the taxable year.

26 U.S.C. § 6015(d)(3)(A) (Supp.2001).

6.   Section 6015(f) provides:

[I]f—(1) taking into account all the facts and circumstances, it is inequitable to hold the individual liable for any unpaid tax or any deficiency (or any portion of either); and (2) relief is not available to such individual under subsection (b) or (c), the Secretary may relieve such individual of such liability.

26 U.S.C. § 6015(f) (Supp.2001).

to a deficiency" within the meaning of § 6015(c)(3)(C).[7] Id. at 197. Finally, the Tax Court held that the Commissioner did not abuse his discretion in denying Appellant equitable relief under § 6015(f) with respect to the retirement distributions and the interest income, as well as the § 6662(a) penalty associated with the interest income.[8] Id. at 198.

III. The Statutory Scheme

Generally, spouses who choose to file a joint return are subject to joint and several liability for tax deficiencies under the Internal Revenue Code. 26 U.S.C. § 6013(d)(3) (Supp. 2001). Recognizing that joint and several liability may be unjust in certain circumstances, Congress authorized relief from such liability under the "innocent spouse" provision, 26 U.S.C. § 6015. Section 6015 provides three distinct types of relief for taxpayers who file joint returns[9]. First, § 6015(b) provides relief for all joint filers who satisfy the five requirements listed in that section. Second, § 6015(c) allows a spouse who filed a joint tax return to elect to limit her income tax liability for that year to her separate liability amount. Section 6015(c) applies only to taxpayers who are no longer married, are legally separated, or do not reside together over a twelve-month period. 26 U.S.C. § 6015(c)(3)(A)(i). Furthermore, a spouse who had actual knowledge of an item giving rise to a deficiency at the time that spouse signed the return may not seek relief under § 6015(c). 26 U.S.C. § 6015(c)(3)(C).

Finally, a taxpayer may seek relief as an "innocent spouse" under § 6015(f), which authorizes the Secretary of the Treasury (the "Secretary") or his delegate to grant equitable relief from joint and several liability when relief is unavailable under § 6015(b) and (c). Except for the knowledge requirement of § 6015(c)(3)(C) (the provision disallowing election of separate liability to a spouse with actual knowledge of the item giving rise to the deficiency), the taxpayer bears the burden of

---

7.　Section 6015(c)(3)(C) provides:
If the Secretary demonstrates that an individual making an election under this subsection had actual knowledge, at the time such individual signed the return, of any item giving rise to a deficiency (or portion thereof) which is not allocable to such individual under subsection (d), such election shall not apply to such deficiency (or portion).
26 U.S.C. § 6015(c)(3)(C) (Supp.2001).

8.　The Tax Court granted Appellant equitable relief with respect to the portion of the § 6662(a) penalty associated with the retirement distributions, however. Id. at 198-99.

9.　Relief under the former innocent spouse statute, § 6013(e), was difficult to obtain, so Congress repealed § 6013(e) and enacted a new provision, § 6015, in 1998. See S.Rep. No. 105-174, at 55 (1998); H.R.Rep. No. 105-364(I), at 61 (1998). New § 6015(b)(1) provides similar relief to that available under former § 6013(e). New § 6015(c) and (f), however, are new forms of relief.

proving that she has met all the prerequisites for innocent spouse relief. Section 6015(c)(3)(C) explicitly places the burden of proof on the Secretary.

* * *

V. Section 6015(b) Relief

Section 6015(b)(1) provides innocent spouse relief if the taxpayer satisfies all of the five requirements listed in that section. In this case, the parties concede that Appellant satisfied the requirements of subsections (A), (B), and (E) of § 6015(b)(1). Thus, the § 6015(b) issue presented by this case is whether Appellant satisfied the requirements of subsections (C) and (D). We conclude that Appellant has not satisfied the requirement of subsection (C) and thus is not entitled to relief under § 6015(b).

Subsection (C) allows for innocent spouse relief only if the spouse "establishes that in signing the return he or she did not know, and had no reason to know, that there was such understatement."[15] 26 U.S.C. § 6015(b)(1)(C). Originally, the innocent spouse provision (formerly codified at § 6013(e)(1)) granted relief only in cases involving omitted income, i.e., cases in which the tax return failed to report taxable income. Since the enactment of the original provision, courts have agreed that in omitted income cases, the spouse's actual knowledge of the underlying transaction that produced the income is sufficient to preclude innocent spouse relief (the "knowledge-of-the-transaction test").[16] In 1984, the innocent spouse provision was expanded to include relief in erroneous deduction cases, i.e., cases in which an incorrect deduction results in an understatement of taxable income. The Tax Court applies the knowledge-of-the-transaction test to both types of cases, see Bokum v. Comm'r, 94 T.C. 126, 151, 1990 WL 17262 (1990), though some circuits have adopted an alternate test for erroneous deduction cases.[17] See, e.g.,

---

15. Because current subsection (C) of § 6015(b)(1) is virtually identical to former subsection (C) of § 6013(e)(1), we may look to cases construing § 6013(e)(1)(C) for help in construing § 6015(b)(1)(C). See Butler v. Comm'r, 114 T.C. 276, 283, 2000 WL 502841 (2000).

16. The knowledge-of-the-transaction test conflicts with the plain meaning of § 6015(b)(1)(C), which limits relief to spouses with no knowledge of the *understatement*. Along with other courts, this court has concluded that this deviation from plain meaning is justified because it avoids "acceptance of an ignorance of the law defense." Sanders v. United States, 509 F.2d 162, 169 n.14 (5th Cir.1975); see also Price v. Comm'r, 887 F.2d 959, 963 n. 9 (9th Cir.1989).

17. The Tax Court has suggested that if the case is appealable to a circuit that has adopted a different knowledge test for erroneous deduction cases, it will apply that circuit's knowledge test rather than the knowledge-of-the-transaction test. See Bokum, 94 T.C. at 151 (declining to follow the Ninth Circuit's knowledge standard in erroneous deduction cases "except in those instances where appeal lies to that Court of Appeals").

Price v. Comm'r, 887 F.2d 959, 965 (9th Cir.1989); *Reser*, 112 F.3d at 1267 (Fifth Circuit case).

The Ninth Circuit was the first circuit to adopt an alternative knowledge test for erroneous deduction cases. In *Price*, the Ninth Circuit established that a spouse fails to satisfy the § 6015(b)(1)(C) knowledge requirement in erroneous deduction cases if "a reasonably prudent taxpayer in her position at the time she signed the return could be expected to know that the return contained the substantial understatement." 887 F.2d at 965. The Ninth Circuit reasoned that since erroneous deductions are necessarily reported on a tax return, any spouse who signs the joint return is thereby put on notice that an income-producing transaction occurred. Id. at 963 n. 9. Thus, in erroneous deduction cases, it would be illogical to bar recovery for spouses with mere knowledge of the transaction as this would preclude *any* spouse from obtaining relief under § 6015(b). Id. The Ninth Circuit noted that "adoption of such an interpretation would do violence to the intent Congress clearly expressed when it expanded coverage of the provision to include relief for spouses from deficiencies caused by deductions for which there is no basis in fact or law." Id.

Thus, under the *Price* approach, actual knowledge of the underlying transaction, standing alone, is not enough to preclude innocent spouse relief under § 6015(b)(1)(C) in erroneous deduction cases. However, *Price* notes that if the spouse knows "virtually all of the facts pertaining to the transaction which underlies the substantial understatement," then her defense "is premised solely on ignorance of law," and "she is considered *as a matter of law* to have reason to know of the substantial understatement." Id. at 964 (emphasis added).

This court adopted the *Price* approach and reasoning in *Reser*.[18] See 112 F.3d at 1267. Accordingly, in erroneous deduction cases, this court questions whether the spouse "knew or had reason to know that the *deduction* in question would give rise to a substantial understatement of tax on the joint return." Id. (emphasis in original). However, if the spouse knows enough about the underlying transaction that her innocent spouse defense rests entirely upon a mistake of law, she has "reason to know" of the tax understatement as a matter of law. If "reason to know" cannot be determined as a matter of law, the proper factual inquiry is "whether a reasonably prudent taxpayer in the spouse's position at the time she signed the return could be expected to know that the stated

---

18. The Second, Seventh, Eighth, and Eleventh Circuits have also followed the Ninth Circuit's decision in *Price*. See Resser v. Comm'r, 74 F.3d 1528, 1535-36 (7th Cir.1996); Bliss v. Comm'r, 59 F.3d 374, 378 n. 1 (2d Cir.1995); Kistner v. Comm'r, 18 F.3d 1521, 1527 (11th Cir.1994); Erdahl v. Comm'r, 930 F.2d 585, 589 (8th Cir.1991).

liability was erroneous or that further investigation was warranted." *Reser*, 112 F.3d at 1267.

In this case, the Cheshires reported the receipt of $199,771.05 in retirement distributions on line 17a of their joint tax return. On line 17b, they reported $56,150.12 as the taxable amount of those retirement distributions. Mr. Cheshire led Appellant to believe that he calculated this amount of taxable income by properly deducting the money placed in a qualified account ($42,183) and the money used to pay off the mortgage on their home ($99,425). In fact, only the money placed in a qualified account was properly excludable from the Cheshires' taxable income. Appellant argues that these facts present a case of erroneous deduction and that the knowledge-of-the-incorrect-deduction standard is therefore applicable. The Commissioner argues that this is a case of omitted income and that the knowledge-of-the-transaction test is therefore applicable.

This court has not previously determined if such facts present a case of omitted income or of erroneous deduction, and we need not do so here because the outcome under either standard is the same: Appellant knew or had reason to know of the tax understatement.[19] Under the knowledge-of-the-transaction test applied in omitted income cases, Appellant fails to satisfy § 6015(b)(1)(C) because she had actual knowledge of the retirement distributions and of the corresponding earned interest at the time she signed the return.[20] In erroneous deduction cases, this court asks whether Appellant "knew or had reason to know" that the deduction in question would give rise to a tax understatement at the time she signed the return. The parties agree that Appellant did not have actual knowledge that the deduction was improper. However, because Appellant knew all the facts surrounding the transaction that gave rise to the understatement, including the amount of the retirement proceeds, the account where the proceeds were deposited and drawn upon, the amount of interest earned on the proceeds, and the manner in which the proceeds were spent, Appellant had "reason to know" of the improper deduction as a matter of law. Appellant's defense consists only of her mistaken belief that money spent to pay off a mortgage is properly deductible from retirement distributions. Ignorance of the law cannot establish an innocent spouse defense to tax liability.

---

19. This court took the same approach in *Park*. See *Park*, 25 F.3d at 1298-99. Because the result in *Park* was the same under the knowledge-of-the-transaction test and the new erroneous deduction test set forth in the Ninth Circuit's opinion in *Price*, this court declined to determine which test applied. Id.

20. This is the result reached by the Tax Court. Cheshire, 115 T.C. at 193.

Because Appellant "knew or had reason to know" of the understatement under both the omitted income standard and the erroneous deduction standard, she fails to establish the requirement of § 6015(b)(1)(C). This conclusion bars relief under § 6015(b)(1), obviating the need for this court to decide whether Appellant satisfied the requirement of § 6015(b)(1)(D). The Tax Court's determination that Appellant is not entitled to innocent spouse relief under § 6015(b)(1) is not clearly erroneous.

VI. Section 6015(c) Relief

Section 6015(c)(1) allows any divorced (or separated) individual to elect to assume responsibility for only that portion of a joint tax deficiency that is properly allocable to that individual. The parties agree that Appellant falls within the class of taxpayers permitted to make a § 6015(c) election since she and Mr. Cheshire were divorced when she filed her petition with the Tax Court. Moreover, neither party in this case disputes that the deficiency attributable to the retirement distributions is properly allocable to Mr. Cheshire. Thus, if this election is available to Appellant, she can avoid liability for the tax deficiency caused by the retirement distributions. However, the benefit of the § 6015(c) election is not available to an individual with actual knowledge of "any item giving rise to a deficiency." 26 U.S.C. § 6015(c)(3)(C). In order to preclude relief under § 6015(c), the Commissioner must prove by a preponderance of the evidence that Appellant had actual knowledge of "any item giving rise to a deficiency." Culver v. Comm'r, 116 T.C. 189, 196, 2001 WL 314341 (2001). Whether the Commissioner satisfied this burden is the § 6015(c) issue in this appeal.

The debate between the parties focuses on the meaning of the term "item" in § 6015(c)(3)(C). Appellant argues that "item" means "incorrect tax reporting of an item of income, deduction, or credit" so that § 6015(c)(3)(C) only bars relief for spouses with actual knowledge that an entry on the joint tax return is incorrect. The Commissioner argues that "item" means "an item of income, deduction, or credit" so that § 6015(c)(3)(C) bars relief for all spouses with actual knowledge of the income-producing transaction, even if they lacked knowledge of the incorrect tax reporting of that transaction.

The term "item" appears fifteen times in § 6015. Most of these appearances are uninformative, but the uses of the term "item" in § 6015(b)(1)(B) and (d)(4) support the Commissioner's definition. Section 6015(b)(1)(B) refers to "an understatement of tax attributable to erroneous *items* of one individual filing the joint return." If "item" refers to the "incorrect tax reporting of an item," as Appellant asserts, then the reference to an "erroneous item" is redundant. Thus, § 6015(b)(1)(B) suggests that "item" means "an item of income, deduction, or credit," as the Commissioner asserts. Furthermore, § 6015(d)(4) refers to "an *item* of deduction or credit."[24] This use of the term "item" suggests that the term refers to an actual item of income, deduction, or credit, rather than the incorrect reporting of such an item.

Other sections of the Internal Revenue Code define the term "item" without reference to tax consequences. For example, § 61(a) defines "gross income" to include such "items" as compensation for services, interest, rents, and royalties. 26 U.S.C. § 61(a) (1988 & Supp.2001). Thus, in this context, "item" means an item of income. Section 6231(a)(3) defines the term "partnership item" as "any item required to be taken into account for the partnership's taxable year under any provision of subtitle A * * *." 26 U.S.C. § 6231(a)(3) (1989 & Supp.2001). These uses of the term "item," as well as those uses appearing in § 6015, suggest that "item" means "an item of income, deduction, or credit." See Comm'r v. Lundy, 516 U.S. 235, 250, 116 S.Ct. 647, 133 L.Ed.2d 611 (1996) (stating that "identical words used in different parts of the same act are intended to have the same meaning"). This interpretation supports the Commissioner's position that § 6015(c)(3)(C) bars relief for all spouses with actual knowledge of the income-producing transaction, even if they lacked knowledge of the incorrect tax reporting of that transaction.

Furthermore, Appellant's claim that § 6015(c)(3)(C) precludes relief only if the spouse has knowledge of incorrect tax reporting runs afoul of the general rule that ignorance of the tax laws is not a defense to a tax deficiency. In *Sanders*, a case applying the predecessor innocent spouse statute, we noted that the statute "seemingly makes ignorance of the fact that known receipts constitute taxable income a valid justification for not knowing or having reason to know of omissions from gross income." 509 F.2d at 169 n. 14. Rather than establish an ignorance of the law defense, however, in *Sanders* we decided to apply a statutory interpretation that "is difficult to square with a literal reading of the statutory language" because "the practical problems that have always prevented acceptance of an ignorance of the law defense in the criminal law area * * * arguably apply just as forcefully here." Id. Unlike the court in *Sanders*, we need not overlook the literal meaning of the statute at issue in this case. As

---

24. Section 6015(d)(4) provides:

If an item of deduction or credit is disallowed in its entirety solely because a separate return is filed, such disallowance shall be disregarded and the item shall be computed as if a joint return had been filed and then allocated between the spouses appropriately. A similar rule shall apply for purposes of section 86.

26 U.S.C. § 6015(d)(4) (Supp.2001).

the above discussion illustrates, the plain meaning of § 6015(c)(3)(C) suggests that a spouse with actual knowledge of the income-producing transaction cannot receive innocent spouse relief even if she lacks knowledge of the incorrect tax reporting of that transaction. This reading of the plain meaning of § 6015(c)(3)(C) is compelling in light of the general principle that ignorance of the law is not a defense.

* * *

The Tax Court adopted this definition of "item" and indicated that the knowledge standard under § 6015(c)(3)(C) in an omitted income case is "actual and clear awareness" of an item of income.[26] Cheshire, 115 T.C. at 195. Since *Cheshire*, the Tax Court has interpreted the knowledge standard in the context of an erroneous deduction to be "actual knowledge of the factual circumstances which made the item unallowable as a deduction." King v. Comm'r, 116 T.C. 198, 204, 2001 WL 356124 (2001). As Appellant is liable under either standard, we need not determine which standard applies in this case. Appellant had "actual and clear awareness" of Mr. Cheshire's retirement distributions and earned interest. Thus, she satisfies the § 6015(c)(3)(C) knowledge requirement for omitted income cases. Furthermore, Appellant was aware of how the retirement distributions were spent. None of these expenditures qualifies for proper deduction, so Appellant had "actual knowledge of the factual circumstances which made the item unallowable as a deduction." In such circumstances, Appellant satisfies the § 6015(c)(3)(C) knowledge requirement for erroneous deduction cases. Thus, § 6015(c)(3)(C) bars relief under either the omitted income or the erroneous deduction knowledge standard, even though Appellant was unaware of the tax consequences of the deduction. The Tax Court's determination that Appellant is not entitled to innocent spouse relief under § 6015(c) is not clearly erroneous.

VII. Section 6015(f) Relief

Section 6015(f) confers power upon the Secretary and his delegate, the Commissioner, to grant equitable relief where a taxpayer is not entitled to relief under § 6015(b) or (c), but "taking into account all the facts and circumstances, it is inequitable to hold the individual liable for

---

26. Contrary to Appellant's contention, the Tax Court's interpretation of § 6015(c) does not ignore its remedial nature by improperly substituting the knowledge requirement from § 6015(b)(1)(C) (and former § 6013(e)(1)(C)) for the stricter knowledge requirement of § 6015(c)(3)(C). The knowledge standard of § 6015(c)(3)(C) requires "actual knowledge." The Tax Court interpreted this to mean "actual and clear awareness * * * of the existence of an item." Cheshire, 115 T.C. at 195. Unlike former § 6013(e)(1)(C) and current § 6015(b)(1)(C), a mere "reason to know" is not enough to preclude tax relief under § 6015(c).

any unpaid tax or any deficiency (or any portion of either)." In this case, Appellant argues that the Commissioner improperly denied her equitable relief with respect to the retirement distributions and the interest income.[28] This court reviews the Commissioner's decision to deny equitable relief for abuse of discretion.

This court has stated that "[t]he most important factor in determining inequity is whether the spouse seeking relief 'significantly benefitted' from the understatement of tax." *Reser*, 112 F.3d at 1270 (quoting Buchine v. Comm'r, 20 F.3d 173, 181 (5th Cir.1994)). This benefit can be indirect, such as "a spouse's receipt of more than she otherwise would as part of a divorce settlement." *Reser*, 112 F.3d at 1270. In the instant case, Appellant received as part of the divorce settlement the Cheshires' marital residence, the value of which was enhanced by the use of $99,425 in untaxed retirement distributions to pay off the mortgage. Appellant also received the family car, which was purchased with retirement distributions. The Commissioner could have reasonably concluded upon these facts that Appellant received significant benefit from the tax understatement. Thus, the Commissioner's decision to deny equitable relief to Appellant is sufficiently supported and not an abuse of discretion. Accordingly, the Tax Court correctly determined that the Commissioner did not abuse his discretion when he denied equitable relief to Appellant under § 6015(f) with respect to the retirement distributions and the interest income.

* * *

Notes and Questions

In signing a joint return, the parties are expected to have examined the return and to have made reasonable inquiries about items on the return. As the Tax Court notes in *Cheshire*, inquiring about an item or items on the return generally will operate in the taxpayer's favor later if the taxpayer claims innocent spouse status. In determining whether the taxpayer should have delved further, courts have looked to four factors: (1) the taxpayer's level of education, (2) experience and knowledge of the family's business and financial affairs, (3) whether the family's current standard of living was lavish compared to past levels of income and expenditures, and (4) the conduct of the culpable spouse in concealing the true state of the family's finances. Hayman v. Commissioner, 992 F.2d 1256 (2d Cir. 1993).

---

28. The Commissioner also denied Appellant equitable relief with respect to the entire § 6662(a) accuracy-related penalty. The Tax Court affirmed the denial of equitable relief with respect to the § 6662(a) penalty associated with the interest income. Cheshire, 115 T.C. at 198-99. However, the Tax Court granted equitable relief to Appellant for the portion of the § 6662(a) penalty that relates to the retirement distributions. Id. Neither party appeals these findings.

1. Which of these factors operated against Mrs. Cheshire? Are there any other factors that may have operated against her?

2. What distinctions does the court draw between omitted income cases and erroneous deduction cases?

3. Should "ignorance of the law is no excuse" be considered a governing principle in innocent spouse cases? Why or why not?

4. How do §§ 6015(b), (c) and (f) differ?

5. Which taxpayers are eligible to elect proportionate tax treatment under § 6015(c)?

6. What is the policy rationale underlying § 6015(c)?

7. If a divorce decree allocates the tax liability to one particular spouse, is the allocation likely to be respected by the Service?

8. If William marries Kate, and Kate has an outstanding tax deficiency at the time of the marriage, can William be held liable for the deficiency?

2. Tax Court Jurisdiction (Stand Alone Cases)

COMMISSIONER v. NEAL
United States Court of Appeals, Eleventh Circuit, 2009.
557 F.3d 1262

WILSON, CIRCUIT JUDGE:

The Commissioner of the Internal Revenue Service (the "IRS") appeals the decision of the Tax Court granting Ruth E. Neal equitable relief pursuant to the innocent spouse provision of Internal Revenue Code, 26 U.S.C. § 6015(f), for the portion of unpaid federal income taxes attributable to the income of Neal's ex-husband for tax years 1993, 1994, and 1995. The total amount in controversy, exclusive of interest and penalties, is $278,996.

In this case, the Tax Court conducted a trial and granted Neal equitable relief. Both parties agree that the Tax Court appropriately used an abuse of discretion standard of review and that Neal at trial had to establish the Commissioner abused its discretion in denying her relief. They disagree about whether the Tax Court at trial may consider evidence not included in the administrative record or is limited to consideration of the administrative record.

Neal submits that the Tax Court properly followed its precedent in Ewing v. Commissioner, 122 T.C. 32 (2004), rev'd on other grounds, 439 F.3d 1009, 1014 (9th Cir.2006), and Porter v. Commissioner, 130 T.C. No. 10 (2008), wherein the Tax Court held that in § 6015(f) cases it may conduct a "trial de novo" and consider evidence not included in the administrative record before the Commissioner. The Tax Court uses the term "trial de novo" to describe the form of its proceeding and applies an abuse of discretion standard of review in that trial de novo proceeding. However, the Commissioner contends that the Administrative Procedure Act ("APA") governs all agency proceedings and thus, the scope of the Tax Court's inquiry is confined strictly to the administrative record.

This issue has divided the fourteen members of the Tax Court: the twelve judges in the Ewing/Porter majority concluded the Tax Court's determination of equitable relief in § 6015 cases is made in a trial de novo and is not confined to the administrative record. Eleven of these twelve believe that (1) a trial de novo gives effect to the congressional mandate in § 6015(e) that the Tax Court "determine the appropriate relief available to [an] individual" in § 6015 equitable relief cases, (2) the Tax Court's 75-year history of conducting trials de novo under other statutes authorizing the Tax Court to make "determinations" of relief was well established when Congress enacted § 6015(e) using the "determine" language, and (3) the APA's record rule, limiting review to the administrative record, does not apply to the Tax Court's § 6015(e) determinations. Two members dissented and prefer a scope of Tax Court review limited to the administrative record.

* * *

I.

A.

Section 6015, through which Neal seeks relief, was added to the Internal Revenue Code in 1998 to broaden existing innocent spouse relief from joint and several liability. Congress first imposed joint and several liability on joint filers of tax returns in 1938. Until the 1960s, the fairness of this concept was rarely questioned. In 1961, the Supreme Court held that embezzled funds were taxable. James v. United States, 366 U.S. 213, 221, 241, 81 S.Ct. 1052, 1056, 1067, 6 L.Ed.2d 246 (1961). Because many embezzlers were insolvent, the IRS began assessing underpayment of taxes to the joint filers of embezzlers, even if the spouses knew nothing of the embezzlement and had received none of the embezzled funds. See, e.g., Huelsman v. Comm'r, 416 F.2d 477, 478 (6th Cir.1969); Horn v. Comm'r, 387 F.2d 621, 622-23 (5th Cir.1967); Moore v. United States, 360 F.2d 353, 357 (4th Cir.1966). Congress responded by adding to the I.R.C. § 6013(e), which allowed relief from joint liability in certain cases if (1) the underpayment was due to fraud on the part of the taxpayer's spouse; (2) the taxpayer did not know and had no reason to know of the underpayment; and (3) after considering the facts and circumstances, including whether the taxpayer benefitted from the underpayment, it was inequitable to hold the innocent spouse liable for the underpayment. Innocent Spouse Act of 1971, Pub.L. No. 91-679, 84 Stat. 2063, 2063-64 (1971). In 1984, Congress amended § 6013(e) and slightly broadened the grant of relief. Pub.L. No. 98-369, § 424(a), 98 Stat. 494, 801 (1984).

Congress repealed § 6013(e) and enacted § 6015 in the Internal Revenue Service Restructuring and Reform Act of 1998 to make "innocent spouse status easier to obtain." H.R.Rep. No. 105-599, at 249-51 (1998) (Conf. Rep.), reprinted in 1998 U.S.C.C.A.N. 288. Because this case involves § 6015(e) and (f), we quote those two subparts, which provide in pertinent part:

(e) Petition for review by Tax Court.-

(1) In general.-In the case of an individual against whom a deficiency has been asserted and who elects to have subsection (b) or (c) apply, or in the case of an individual who requests equitable relief under subsection (f)-

(A) In general.-In addition to any other remedy provided by law, the individual may petition the Tax Court (and the Tax Court shall have jurisdiction) to determine the appropriate relief available to the individual under this section. . ..

(f) Equitable relief.-Under procedures prescribed by the Secretary, if-

(1) taking into account all the facts and circumstances, it is inequitable to hold the individual liable for any unpaid tax or any deficiency (or any portion of either); and

(2) relief is not available to such individual under subsection (b) or (c),

the Secretary may relieve such individual of such liability.

26 U.S.C. § 6015(e) and (f).

We start with subpart (f) of § 6015, which authorizes the Commissioner to grant equitable relief. Specifically, the Commissioner may grant relief to a taxpayer if, under procedures prescribed by the Commissioner, it would be "inequitable to hold the individual liable for any unpaid tax or any deficiency (or any portion of either)" and relief would not be available under subsection (b) or (c). 26 U.S.C. § 6015(f). The parties agree that relief is not available to Neal under § 6015(b) and (c), and that Neal may properly seek equitable relief under § 6015(f) as an alleged innocent spouse.[1]

In addition, subpart (e) of § 6015 authorizes a taxpayer who has been denied relief pursuant to subparts (b), (c), or (f) to petition the Tax Court for relief. Section 6015(e) expressly grants jurisdiction to the Tax Court to "determine the appropriate relief available to the individual." 26 U.S.C. § 6015(e). Section 6015(e) does not say the taxpayer "may appeal" the Commissioner's § 6015(f) decision to the Tax Court or that the Tax Court may hear an appeal. Rather, § 6015(e) authorizes the taxpayer to seek § 6015(f) relief from the Tax Court.[2] Id. Section 6015(e) also states that a petition for relief from the Tax Court is "[i]n addition to any other remedy provided by law." Id.

B.

Neal and her ex-husband Alimam Neal ("Alimam") married in 1976, resided together until 1996, and divorced in 1998. During the marriage, the couple kept largely separate finances, maintained separate checking accounts, and rarely discussed their financial arrangements. Neal, a radiologist employed by the Medical College of Georgia, paid most of the family expenses, including half of the monthly mortgage payment, groceries, and schooling and activities for the couple's three children. Alimam, a self-employed anesthesiologist, paid the other half of the mortgage, the housekeeper, and the utilities and car payments. Despite

---

1.   Section 6015 provides three distinct types of relief for taxpayers who file joint returns. Subpart (b) of § 6015 provides relief to those taxpayers who can meet certain requirements, such as: (1) an understatement of income attributable to erroneous items; (2) that the taxpayer "did not know, and had no reason to know" of the understatement; and (3) that it would be inequitable to hold the taxpayer liable for the deficiency. 26 U.S.C. § 6015(b). Subpart (c) of § 6015 permits a taxpayer who is no longer married to or is legally separated from his/her spouse to elect to limit liability for any deficiency attributable to the spouse to the taxpayer's separate liability amount in certain situations. 26 U.S.C. § 6015(c).

Subpart (f) applies when relief is not available under § 6015(b) or (c). 26 U.S.C. § 6015(f). Subpart (f) applies to Neal's case because she seeks equitable relief from an unpaid tax, i.e., an underpayment of taxes shown on the return but not paid with the return.

2.   In its Brief to this Court, the Commissioner argued that § 6015(e) did not grant the Tax Court subject matter jurisdiction over § 6015(f) requests. During the briefing stage of this case, Congress amended § 6015(e) to explicitly grant the Tax Court jurisdiction over § 6015(f) cases. Tax Relief and Health Care Act of 2006, Pub.L. No. 109-432, Div. C, § 408, 120 Stat. 2922, 3061-62 (2006). More specifically, in § 6015(e), Congress added, "or in the case of an individual who requests equitable relief under subsection (f)" after "who elects to have subsection (b) or (c) apply." Id. The Commissioner subsequently withdrew this jurisdiction challenge. The Commissioner's remaining claims are: (1) that under § 6015(e) the Tax Court has jurisdiction in innocent spouse cases but its review is confined to consideration of the administrative record, and (2) alternatively, even if the Tax Court appropriately considered evidence outside the administrative record, it nevertheless erred in concluding that the Commissioner's denial of equitable relief was an abuse of discretion.

Neal's requests to Alimam, she was not privy to the financial aspects of Alimam's business.

Neal relied upon Alimam and his accountant to prepare and file the couple's joint federal income tax returns. She merely gave Alimam her W-2 forms and then signed the returns once Alimam received them from the accountant.[4] Neal never spoke to the accountant nor did she examine the completed tax returns. Neal "imagined" that Alimam properly submitted their financial information to the accountant and filed the returns.

In fact, Alimam mailed the completed returns but, unbeknownst to Neal, assiduously failed to include payment of taxes relating to his income. Thus, while Neal's employer appropriately withheld taxes from Neal's salary, the portion of the taxes attributable to Alimam's business went unpaid.

Neal first learned that the couple owed money to the IRS when they sought bankruptcy protection in 1989. Alimam falsely told Neal that the IRS was a creditor because it disallowed certain tax shelters. The bankruptcy hearings revealed that Alimam had purchased in his name, without informing Neal, a boat, a Colorado villa, six or seven cars, and expensive fine art. After the bankruptcy, their home was foreclosed and their cars were repossessed. Over the next several years, Neal's wages were garnished, and she pawned a diamond ring to pay back taxes and a Rolex watch to pay utility bills.

In 1993, the IRS audited the couples' 1990, 1991, and 1992 returns. Though the couple signed the audit report, they did not make any payments toward the back taxes assessed. The couple again filed for bankruptcy in 1995 and the IRS sought underpaid taxes from 1990 to 1993. Alimam falsely claimed to Neal that the IRS had not permitted certain business expenses resulting in the delinquencies.

The second garnishment of Neal's wages in 1996 finally prompted Neal to investigate the reasons underlying the couple's financial turmoil. When questioned, the accountant and bankruptcy attorney disclosed that Alimam had never paid his income taxes. The Commissioner had not contested any of the couple's joint returns, nor had it asserted any deficiencies. Rather, the Commissioner sought to collect $278,996 in unpaid taxes, including interest and penalties. The back taxes due to the

---

4. At the Tax Court trial, Neal presented evidence, not previously presented to the Commissioner, that Alimam forged Neal's signature on the 1993 and 1995 returns.

IRS (without interest and penalties) are as follows: for 1993, $52,689; for 1994, $31,191; and, for 1995, $20,039.[5]

In July 1996, Neal left the marital home with their children and sued for divorce because of Alimam's adulterous relationships and financial mismanagement. Unknown to Neal, Alimam was supporting another woman who bore his child and his share of the tax liability was channeled to his secret life and support of his second family. At the conclusion of the 1998 divorce proceeding, Alimam was ordered to pay all past and future tax liabilities incurred by the couple during their marriage. Alimam made minimal payments to the IRS and the majority of the unpaid taxes are outstanding. Alimam made sporadic child support payments of $3,000 per month until he lost his job in 2001. After the divorce, Neal financially supported herself, one child who lived at home, and two adult children.

C.

On February 8, 2000, Neal petitioned the Commissioner, under § 6015(f), for equitable relief from joint and several liability for the portion of the unpaid taxes attributable to Alimam's income. See 26 U.S.C. § 6015(f). Neal did not contest payment of approximately $5,400, the portion of the underpayment attributable to her income. Neal requested relief because she signed the tax returns "believing that my then-husband was paying any amounts indicated as owed by the tax return."

Neal responded to a written questionnaire sent by the IRS in which she represented that she was not involved with the preparation of tax returns, did not discuss the tax returns with Alimam, and did not review the tax returns. Neal then met with an IRS examining agent and related some of the foregoing facts. Neither a court reporter nor an attorney were

---

5. Neal's employer withheld adequate taxes from Neal's salary, and thus almost all of the underpayments are due to Alimam's salary and his failure to withhold or pay taxes thereon.

	Taxpayer			Alimam			
Year	Earned	Est. sep.	Tax Withheld	Earned	Est. sep.	Tax Withheld	Joint Tax Liability
1993	$110,163	$21,987	$20,302	$154,316	$51,004	0	$72,991
1994	116,759	23,459	21,711	106,180	29,443	0	52,902
1995	122,693	25,194	23,221	78,310	18,066	0	43,260

Neal paid federal income taxes of $173,453 in the years 1999 through 2003. The total amount of state and federal taxes, social security withholding and medicare withholding paid by Neal during the same period totaled $249,752, or 32.83% of her gross income.

present, and no recording was made of this interview. On August 9, 2001, the examining agent denied relief because the agent determined, "[Neal] knew that an underpayment existed when the tax returns were signed; that no economic hardship would exist [if Neal were required to pay the back taxes] and a portion of the tax is attributable to [Neal]."

Neal protested the determination to the IRS Office of Appeals ("Appeals"). Appeals echoed the examining agent's conclusions and issued a notice of determination on April 22, 2003, denying Neal's request for equitable relief. Appeals found that Neal was aware of the underpayment of taxes because the IRS had been a creditor in the 1989 and 1995 bankruptcy actions, the IRS had garnished her salary twice, and Neal had signed the 1994 audit report which indicated the underpaid amounts. Appeals also found that Neal would not suffer economic hardship if relief was withheld because Neal "enjoy[ed] an upper middle income standard of living" based on her salary of $129,000 per year and child support payments of $36,000 per year.

Neal sued in the Tax Court to contest the Commissioner's denial of equitable innocent spouse relief. At a pre-hearing conference with the Tax Court, the Commissioner took the position that the Tax Court's review was limited to the administrative record. The Tax Court disagreed based on its previous decision in *Ewing*, 122 T.C. at 44, and stated that the Tax Court's review and determination was not limited to the administrative record but was de novo. See also *Porter*, 130 T.C. No. 10 (upholding the *Ewing* analysis). Accordingly, the Tax Court agreed to entertain testimony and other evidence the parties wished to introduce. See § 6015(e)(1)(A) (authorizing the Tax Court "to determine the appropriate relief available to [an] individual" under § 6015(f)). As provided in *Ewing*, the Tax Court's longstanding rule and practice has been to hold trials de novo in situations where it makes determination and redeterminations, including § 6015(f) cases. *Ewing*, 122 T.C. at 40-41. To prevail in the trial de novo, the taxpayer petitioner must show that the Commissioner's denial of equitable relief was an abuse of discretion. Id. at 36-37, 39-40; see Mitchell v. Comm'r, 292 F.3d 800, 807 (D.C.Cir.2002).

The Tax Court heard the testimony of two witnesses: Ruth Neal and Gloria Spann. Neal recited the facts summarized above. In addition, to support her position that payment of back taxes would result in an economic hardship, Neal testified that she earned $174,940 in 2003 and had expenses of $158,570.81 for household necessities in that same year. In response, the Commissioner called Spann, a revenue officer (but not the one who initially reviewed Neal's petition for relief). The Commissioner asked Spann to explain the meaning of "economic hardship" according to the Internal Revenue Manual. The Revenue Guidelines specified that individuals with a salary exceeding $5,834 per month were expected to subsist on $2,821 per month. Because Neal spent more than $2,821 per month, Spann testified that requiring Neal to pay the delinquencies would not result in an economic hardship.

After hearing the evidence, the Tax Court issued a Memorandum finding that Neal did not have knowledge of the unpaid taxes because "among other things, the filed tax returns accurately reflected the correct tax liabilities, nonpayment of the balances of the taxes shown to be due on the returns was concealed by Alimam, and [Neal] was not otherwise put on notice of the nonpayment." The Tax Court also found that the facts before it were "inconclusive as to the degree to which [Neal] would suffer economic hardship if she were denied relief from joint liability." Taking into account "all the facts and circumstances," the Tax Court also found that it would be inequitable to hold Neal liable for the tax balances due for 1993, 1994, and 1995 and noted particularly the following:

> Alimam's legal obligation relating to the unpaid taxes, the fact that the taxes in issue are attributable to Alimam's income, Alimam's deception with regard to his investments and nonpayment of the taxes due, the absence of any significant benefit to petitioner from Alimam's failure to pay the taxes, Alimam's exclusion of petitioner from the tax return preparation process and from his financial affairs, petitioner's payment of the majority of the family's expenses and her continued support of the children, and petitioner's payment every year of the Federal income taxes attributable to her income.

The Commissioner timely appealed.

II.

"[W]e review Tax Court decisions 'in the same manner and to the same extent as decisions of the district courts in civil actions tried without a jury.'" L.V. Castle Inv. Group, Inc. v. Comm'r, 465 F.3d 1243, 1245 (11th Cir.2006) (quoting 26 U.S.C. § 7482(a)(1)). Accordingly, we review interpretations of the Internal Revenue Code de novo, and "we review the [tax] court's decision to grant or deny equitable relief for abuse of discretion, reviewing underlying questions of law de novo and findings of fact upon which the decision to grant equitable relief was made under the clearly erroneous standard." Atlanta J. Constitution v. City of Atlanta Dep't of Aviation, 442 F.3d 1283, 1287 (11th Cir.2006); see Cheshire v. Comm'r, 282 F.3d 326, 332, 338 (5th Cir.2002). Whether the Tax Court in a § 6015(e) case may conduct a trial de novo or is confined to considering only the administrative record presents a question of law which this Court reviews de novo.[7]

Joint taxpayers are normally jointly and severally liable for the full amount of federal income taxes due, but may be relieved of joint and several liability under the limited circumstances described in § 6015(b), (c), and (f). As noted earlier, § 6015(f) permits the Commissioner to grant equitable relief to an innocent spouse "for any unpaid tax or any deficiency" if "taking into account all the facts and circumstances, it is inequitable to hold the individual liable" and if "relief is not available to such individual under subsection (b) or (c)." 26 U.S.C. § 6015(f). And as also noted above, § 6015(e), at issue here, expressly grants jurisdiction to the Tax Court "to determine the appropriate relief available to the individual" under § 6015(f).

Although the parties agree that the Commissioner's denial of equitable relief to Neal under § 6015(f) is subject to judicial review by the Tax Court, they disagree as to what the Tax Court may consider in its review. In Ewing, the Tax Court held that in reviewing a denial of § 6015(f) equitable relief, it is not confined to considering only the facts presented in the administrative record below. 122 T.C. at 35-36. The Tax Court reaffirmed that holding in Porter, 2008 WL 2065189, at *2, and applied that holding here to conduct a trial de novo in Neal's case, which resulted in a reversal of the Commissioner's decision to deny her equitable relief. The Commissioner urges us to disapprove the Tax Court's Ewing/Porter reasoning and to restrict the Tax Court's § 6015(e) review in § 6015(f) equitable relief cases to the administrative record.

We first outline the Tax Court's reasoning in Ewing and Porter for its conclusion that it may conduct a trial de novo in § 6015(f) cases. The Ewing/Porter majority focused on the statutory language in § 6015(e)

---

7. By way of background, we review the development of the Tax Court. In 1924, Congress established the Board of Tax Appeals to allow taxpayers to challenge deficiency determinations prior to paying the contested amount. Pub.L. No. 68-176, § 900, 43 Stat. 253, 308, 336-338 (1924); S.Rep. No. 68-398, at 8 (1924). The Board was an independent agency in the executive branch of government. Id. Though not a judicial body, on appeals of such determinations, the Board was authorized to hear cases, administer oaths, and examine and subpoena witnesses. Id.

The Board's jurisdiction was expanded in 1926 to determine overpayment of taxes and again in 1942 to determine refunds of processing taxes. Revenue Act of 1926, Pub.L. No. 69-20, § 284(a), 44 Stat. 9, 66-67 (1926); Revenue Act of 1942, Pub.L. No. 77-753, § 510, 56 Stat. 798, 967 (1942). Congress changed the name of the Board of Tax Appeals to the "Tax Court of the United States" in 1942, but retained the Board's status as an executive agency. Revenue Act of 1942, Pub.L. No. 77-753, § 504, 56 Stat. 798, 957 (1942).

In 1969, the Tax Court took its present form when Congress established an Article I court of record named the "United States Tax Court" to replace the Tax Court of the United States. Pub.L. 91-172, § 951, 83 Stat. 487, 730 (1969). Congress indicated that the change was made to quell questions of propriety of one agency sitting in judgment of another agency and because the Tax Court only had judicial duties. S.Rep. No. 91-552 (1969), reprinted in 1969 U.S.C.C.A.N. 2027, 2341.

and (f). The majority reasoned that, in the Internal Revenue Code, the Tax Court's role in § 6015(f) cases is prescribed by the operative terms of § 6015(e). The *Ewing* majority concluded that a de novo trial gave effect to § 6015(e)'s statutory mandate that the Tax Court "determine the appropriate relief available to the individual," reasoning as follows:

Part of our interpretative responsibility here is to give proper effect to both section 6015(e) and (f). Courts attempt to read statutory provisions harmoniously, so as to give proper effect to all of the words of the statute. . .. Our de novo review of the Commissioner's determinations under section 6015(f) gives effect to the congressional mandate [in section 6015(e)] that we determine whether a taxpayer is entitled to relief under section 6015. The measure of deference provided by the abuse of discretion standard is a proper response to the fact that section 6015(f) authorizes the Secretary to provide procedures under which, based on all the facts and circumstances, the Secretary may relieve a taxpayer from joint liability. That approach (de novo review, applying an abuse of discretion standard) properly implements the statutory provisions at issue here, and has a long history in numerous other areas of Tax Court jurisprudence.

We conclude that our determination whether petitioner is entitled to equitable relief under section 6015(f) is made in a trial de novo and is not limited to matter contained in respondent's administrative record, and that the APA record rule does not apply to section 6015(f) determinations in this Court. 122 T.C. at 43-44 .

As support for its construction of § 6015(e) and (f), the *Ewing/ Porter* majority pointed to the Tax Court's seventy-five year history of conducting trials de novo in other areas where Congress by statute has authorized the Tax Court to make "determinations" or "redeterminations" and reasoned that Congress was well aware of the Tax Court's well-established interpretation of "determine" when it enacted § 6015 in 1998. *Ewing*, 122 T.C. at 37-39; *Porter*, 2008 WL 2065189, at *3. The *Ewing* majority explained, as follows:

Since 1924, the Tax Court (and the predecessor Board of Tax Appeals, see Consol. Cos. v. Commissioner, 15 B.T.A. 645, 652 (1929)) has had jurisdiction to "redetermine" deficiencies and additions to tax, §§ 6213 and 6214(a); and, since 1926, to determine overpayments, § 6512(b). Under section 6213(a) and its predecessors, we (and earlier, the Board of Tax Appeals) have "redetermined" deficiencies de novo, not limited to the Commissioner's administrative record, for more than 75 years.

We can presume that Congress was aware of this long history in 1998 when Congress used the word "determine" in section 6015. If Congress includes language from a prior statute in a new statute, courts can presume that Congress intended the longstanding legal interpretation of that language to be applied to the new statute. Commissioner v. Noel's Estate, 380 U.S. 678, 680-681, 85 S.Ct. 1238, 14 L.Ed.2d 159 (1965); United States v. 101.80 Acres, 716 F.2d 714, 721 (9th Cir.1983).

There are other situations in which this Court makes determinations de novo. For example, section 7436(a) provides that the Tax Court may "determine" whether the Commissioner's determination regarding an individual's employment status is correct. Congress intended that we conduct a trial de novo with respect to our determinations regarding employment status. See H. Rept. 105-148, at 639 (1997)[, 1997 U.S.C.C.A.N. 678], 1997-4 C.B. (Vol. 1) 319, 961; S. Rept. 105-33, at 304 (1997), 1997-4 C.B. (Vol. 2) 1067, 1384; H. Conf. Rept. 105-220, at 734[, 1997 U.S.C.C.A.N. 1129] (1997), 1997-4 C.B. (Vol. 2) 1457, 2204. As another example, section 6404 authorizes this Court to "determine" whether the Secretary's refusal to abate interest was an abuse of discretion. Our practice has been to make our determination after providing an opportunity for a trial de novo. See, e.g., Goettee v. Commissioner, T.C. Memo 2003-43[, 2003 WL 464862 (2003)]; Jean v. Commissioner, T.C. Memo.2002-256[, 2002 WL 31248464 (2002)]; Jacobs v. Commissioner, T.C. Memo.2000-123[, 2000 WL 380216 (2000)].

Our long tradition of providing trials de novo in making our determinations, and Congress's use of the word "determine" in our jurisdictional grant in section 6015(e)(1)(A), suggest that Congress intended that we provide an opportunity for a trial de novo in making our determinations under section 6015(f).

Ewing, 122 T.C. at 38-39.[8]

The Tax Court in *Porter* emphasized that the jurisdiction granted in § 6015(e) "is couched in language similar to that" in §§ 6213, 6214, and 6512(b), where the Tax Court has long conducted trials de novo, and that § 6015 "is part and parcel of the same statutory framework":

---

8. The *Ewing/Porter* majority also cites a longstanding practice of holding trials de novo in many situations where the abuse of discretion standard applies to the Commissioner's conduct. *Ewing*, 122 T.C. at 39; *Porter*, 2008 WL 2065189, at *5. As aptly stated by the Tax Court, "[t]he traditional effect of applying an abuse of discretion standard in this [Tax] Court is to alter the standard of review, not to restrict what evidence we consider in making our determination." *Ewing*, 122 T.C. at 39. Thus, a trial de novo under § 6015 is not incompatible with abuse of discretion review.

The Code has long provided a specific statutory framework for reviewing deficiency determinations of the Internal Revenue Service. Sections 6213 and 6214; Ewing v. Commissioner, 122 T.C. at 52 (Thornton, J., concurring). Section 6015 is part and parcel of the same statutory framework. Our de novo review procedures emanate from that statutory framework.

Our jurisdiction under section 6015 is couched in language similar to that of our deficiency jurisdiction under sections 6213 and 6214. Section 6015(e)(1)(A) authorizes this Court to "determine" the appropriate relief available under section 6015. Section 6213(a) provides that taxpayers who receive a notice of deficiency may petition this Court for a "redetermination" of the deficiency. Section 6214(a) provides this Court jurisdiction to "redetermine" the amount of the deficiency.

Congress first granted the Board of Tax Appeals (the predecessor to the Tax Court) jurisdiction to "redetermine" deficiencies and additions to tax in 1924. Ewing v. Commissioner, 122 T.C. at 38. Since 1926 we have also had jurisdiction to "determine" overpayments. Id. These determinations and redeterminations have always been made de novo. Congress has defined the jurisdiction of this Court using the words "determine" and "redetermination." Ewing v. Commissioner, 122 T.C. at 38. We see no material difference between "determine" in section 6512(b), and "redetermination" in section 6213(a) for purposes of this discussion. Id.

Porter, 2008 WL 2065189, at *3. The Tax Court reasoned that "[w]e can presume that in 1998 when Congress chose to use the word 'determine' in section 6015, it did so in full awareness of our long history of de novo review," and that "[t]he use of the word 'determine' in section 6015(e)(1)(A) suggests that Congress intended that we conduct trials de novo in making our determinations under section 6015(f)." Id.[9]

In both *Ewing* and *Porter*, the Tax Court identified procedural anomalies that further justified its conclusion that trials de novo are appropriate in § 6015 equitable relief cases. *Ewing*, 122 T.C. at 42-44; *Porter*, 2008 WL 2065189, at *6. If the Tax Court were confined to the

---

9. It is also noteworthy that 26 U.S.C. § 7453 provides that, with limited exceptions not relevant here, Tax Court proceedings shall be conducted in accordance with rules prescribed by the Tax Court and rules of evidence in trials without a jury. Further, Congress has mandated in 26 U.S.C. § 7459 that the Tax Court make findings of fact in each report upon "any proceeding instituted before the Tax Court." Id. (quotation marks omitted). Judge Thornton, in a concurring opinion joined by five other members of the Porter majority, emphasized that these "[s]tatutorily mandated standards and procedures contemplate that the Tax Court will generally conduct trials de novo in its proceedings, including actions involving claims for relief from joint and several liability." *Porter*, 2008 WL 2065189, at *12 (Thornton, J., concurring).

administrative record in reviewing stand-alone § 6015(e) petitions (such as Neal's petition), inconsistent procedures would be adopted in equitable spouse relief cases. The Tax Court gave several examples. First, by statute, when a taxpayer files an election for § 6015(f) relief with the Commissioner and the Commissioner fails to render a determination within six months, the Tax Court has jurisdiction under § 6015(e) to make a determination as to the viability of the taxpayer's petition in the absence of an administrative record. 26 U.S.C. § 6015(e)(1)(A)(i)(II).[10] As such, confining the Tax Court to consideration of the administrative record in only those § 6015(f) cases in which the Commissioner has issued a determination would result in inconsistent procedural treatment of essentially identical § 6015(e) petitions. *Ewing*, 122 T.C. at 42; *Porter*, 2008 WL 2065189, at *6.

Second, in deficiency cases, the Tax Court holds a trial de novo even when a taxpayer raises equitable spouse relief under § 6015(f) as an affirmative defense to the deficiency case. *Ewing*, 122 T.C. at 42 (citing Butler v. Comm'r, 114 T.C. 276, 292, 2000 WL 502841 (2000)); *Porter*, 2008 WL 2065189, at *6. Again, without trials de novo under § 6015(e), substantially identical § 6015(f) claims would be treated differently.[11]

Third, under § 6015(e)(4), the non-requesting spouse can intervene "to become a party" when a requesting spouse's petition for equitable relief under § 6015(e) reaches the Tax Court. 26 U.S.C. § 6015(e)(4); *Ewing*, 122 T.C. at 42-43; *Porter*, 2008 WL 2065189, at *6. The Tax Court in *Ewing* and *Porter* concluded that the fact that Congress in § 6015 provided for intervention by a non-requesting spouse as a party directly in the Tax Court also suggests that Congress intended that the Tax Court conduct trials de novo in § 6015 cases in order to permit intervening spouses to offer evidence to challenge the requesting spouse's

---

10. Section 6015(e)(1)(A) provides:

> In addition to any other remedy provided by law, the individual may petition the Tax Court (and the Tax Court shall have jurisdiction) to determine the appropriate relief available to the individual under this section if such petition is filed-
>
> (i) at any time after the earlier of-
>
> > (I) the date the Secretary mails, by certified or registered mail to the taxpayer's last known address, notice of the Secretary's final determination of relief available to the individual, or
> >
> > (II) the date which is 6 months after the date such election is filed or request is made with the Secretary, and
>
> (ii) not later than the close of the 90th day after the date described in clause (i)(I).

26 U.S.C. § 6015(e)(1)(A).

11. In addition, § 6015(e)(1) itself refers to both deficiency cases where the taxpayer elects to have § 6015(b) or (c) apply and other cases where the taxpayer elects to have § 6015(f) apply. The same judicial review should be applicable in § 6015 cases, whether the innocent spouse claim is made in a stand-alone deficiency case or stand-alone unpaid tax case.

entitlement to equitable relief. *Ewing*, 122 T.C. at 43; *Porter*, 2008 WL 2065189, at *6.

In summary, the Tax Court in *Ewing* and *Porter* concluded that Congress intended that taxpayers have the same opportunity for a trial de novo relating to § 6015(f) equitable relief (1) when that relief is raised as an affirmative defense in a deficiency proceeding, (2) in a stand-alone § 6015(e) proceeding where the Commissioner has denied § 6015(f) relief (as in this case), (3) in a stand-alone § 6015(e) proceeding where the Commissioner has failed to rule within six months, and (4) when a non-requesting spouse intervenes in the Tax Court to challenge a requesting spouse's claim to § 6015(f) relief.[12] *Ewing*, 122 T.C. at 42-43; *Porter*, 2008 WL 2065189, at *6. "Identical issues before a single tribunal should receive similar treatment." *Ewing*, 122 T.C. at 43 (quoting Corson v. Comm'r, 114 T.C. 354, 364, 2000 WL 637480 (2000)).

Finally, and of particular import here, the Tax Court explained why the APA's record rule-limiting a reviewing court to the administrative record-does not supplant the Tax Court's own longstanding trial de novo procedures and precedent. APA § 559 "provides that the APA does 'not limit or repeal additional requirements imposed by statute or otherwise recognized by law.' " *Porter*, 2008 WL 2065189, at *4 (quoting 5 U.S.C. § 559). In both *Ewing* and *Porter* the Tax Court specifically discussed how its trial de novo procedures for reviewing IRS decisions were "well-established" and "recognized by law" before the enactment of the APA in 1946. Id.; *Ewing*, 122 T.C. at 52 (Thornton, J., concurring). According to the Tax Court, its trial de novo procedures have remained virtually unchanged since the APA's enactment, supporting its conclusion that the APA did not limit or repeal the Tax Court's de novo review procedures. *Ewing*, 122 T.C. at 38-40.

The fact that the APA (enacted in 1946) predates § 6015 (enacted in 1998) does not change the result because § 6015 is "part and parcel" of the statutory framework for Tax Court review of IRS deficiency determinations. *Ewing*, 122 T.C. at 52-53 (Thornton, J., concurring); *Porter*, 2008 WL 2065189, at **3-4. It is from this framework that the "[Tax Court's] de novo review procedures emanate." *Ewing*, 122 T.C. at 52 (Thornton, J., concurring); *Porter*, 2008 WL 2065189, at *3. Accordingly, when Congress chose to use the same statutory language in § 6015 as it used in establishing the longstanding trial de novo procedure

---

12. The Tax Court noted that intervention by the nonrequesting spouse is available both in deficiency cases in which § 6015(f) relief is requested and in stand-alone § 6015 cases such as this case. *King*, 115 T.C. at 122-23; *Porter*, 2008 WL 2065189, at *6 (both citing Rule 325); King v. Commissioner, 115 T.C. 118, 122-23, 2000 WL 1131914 (2000); and Corson v. Commissioner, 114 T.C. 354, 364-65, 2000 WL 637480 (2000).

for deficiency actions, "it did so in full awareness of [the Tax Court's] long history of de novo review," *Porter*, 2008 WL 2065189, at *3, and did not intend to impose a different procedure. Thus, per § 559, "the APA does not disturb or supersede [the Tax] Court's longstanding de novo judicial review procedures for cases involving spousal relief under section 6015." *Ewing*, 122 T.C. at 54 (Thornton, J., concurring).

The Tax Court also explained that "[a]s a statute of general application, the APA does not supersede specific statutory provisions for judicial review" such as Congress has granted to the Tax Court. *Porter*, 2008 WL 2065189, at *2. The Tax Court pointed out that "nothing in section 6015 or its legislative history indicates that the APA is to apply to section 6015 cases or that we are to restrict our review to the administrative record." Id. at *4.[14] Moreover, the Tax Court emphasized that the legislative history of the APA confirms it does not supersede the Tax Court's adjudication procedures, stating:

> The legislative history of the APA confirms this understanding. See S. Comm. on the Judiciary, 79th Cong., 1st Sess., Administrative Procedure Act (Comm. Print 1945), reprinted in Administrative Procedure Act Legislative History, 1944-46, at 22 (1946) (stating that there are exempted from APA formal adjudication requirements matters that are subject to de novo review of facts and law such "as the tax functions of the Bureau of Internal Revenue (which are triable de novo in The Tax Court)"); S. Rept. 752, 79th Cong., 1st Sess. (1945), reprinted in Administrative Procedure Act Legislative History, 1944-46, at 214 (1946) (explaining that pursuant to APA provisions governing the scope of judicial review, courts establish facts de novo where the agency adjudication is not subject to APA formal adjudication provisions "such as tax assessments * * * not made upon an administrative hearing and record, [where] contests may involve a trial of the facts in the Tax Court"); H. Rept. 1980, 79th Cong., 2d Sess. (1946), reprinted in Administrative Procedure Act Legislative History, 1944-46, at 279 (1946) (same).

---

14. In *Porter*, the Tax Court also contrasted its statutory § 6015 jurisdiction, which has no limitations written into the statute, with its jurisdiction to issue declaratory judgments relating to the status, qualification, valuation, or classification of certain § 501(c)(3) organizations, retirement plans, gifts, and governmental obligations. *Porter*, 2008 WL 2065189, at *4. The Tax Court pointed out (1) that it has adopted rules regarding declaratory judgments that generally require such actions to be disposed of on the basis of the administrative record, and (2) that "[t]he reason for this limited review lies in Congress's legislative directive," discussed in *Porter*, but (3) that Congress did not impose a similar restrictive standard in § 6015. Id.

Ewing, 122 T.C. at 53 (Thornton, J., concurring).[15] That the APA effectively exempted the Tax Court does not mean it exempted the Tax Court only as to tax matters extant in 1946.

We are persuaded by the Tax Court's reasoning. Congress's use of the word "determine" and not "appeal" in § 6015(e)'s jurisdictional grant is significant. And, most importantly, § 6015(e) must be read and considered with the other § 6015 provisions, such as § 6015(e)(4) outlining intervention by the non-requesting spouse and § 6015(e)(1)(A)(i)(II) authorizing a petition to the Tax Court if the Commissioner has not acted in six months. Congress also enacted § 6015 with knowledge of the Tax Court's precedent and history of conducting trials de novo in making its determinations. As the Tax Court noted, § 6015 was enacted "as part and parcel of," and with similar language to, the statutory framework for the Tax Court's review of deficiency determinations, which determinations had been made using trials de novo long before the passage of the APA. The legislative history of the APA contains a clear intent to exempt the Tax Court. At a minimum, the Commissioner has not shown the Tax Court erred in its *Ewing* and *Porter* rulings that it followed in this case.

* * *

For all of these reasons, we agree with Neal that the Commissioner has not shown that the Tax Court erred by refusing to limit its consideration to the administrative record and by conducting a trial de novo in this § 6015(f) case.

III.

The Commissioner alternatively contends that even under trial de novo review, the Tax Court erred in concluding that the Commissioner abused his discretion in denying equitable relief to Neal. We disagree.

Section 6015(f) expressly authorizes the Commissioner to prescribe procedures for determining qualification for equitable relief. Under Revenue Procedure 2000-15, 2000-1 C.B. 447, equitable relief will be granted where (i) the couple has divorced or has not lived together for a year prior to the request for relief; (ii) "[a]t the time the return was signed, the requesting spouse had no knowledge or reason to know that the tax would not be paid"; and (iii) the requesting spouse will suffer

---

15. We quote what the Tax Court said but note that the pertinent legislative history of the APA being referenced states more fully: "[W]here adjudications such as tax assessments are not made upon an administrative hearing and record, contests may involve a trial of the facts in the Tax Court or the United States district courts." S.Rep. No. 79-752, at 214 (1945), reprinted in Administrative Procedure Act Legislative History at 214.

economic hardship if the relief is not granted. Rev. Proc.2000-15, § 4.02, 2000-1 C.B. at 448. If a requesting spouse does not qualify for relief under § 4.02, she may still qualify for relief under § 4.03, which sets forth a partial, non-exhaustive list of factors, no one of which is determinative.[19] Some factors weigh in favor of relief and some weigh against; the Commissioner must take into account all the facts and circumstances, considering and weighing all factors appropriately. Id. at 449. The taxpayer has the burden of demonstrating that relief should be granted. Cheshire v. Comm'r, 282 F.3d 326, 332 (5th Cir.2002); *Ewing*, 122 T.C. at 36-37.

Here, the Commissioner reasoned that Neal was not entitled to relief because (1) when she signed the return, she should have known that the tax was unpaid based on the couple's prior bankruptcy filings, and (2) that no economic hardship would befall her if she had to pay the remaining tax liability. After hearing the evidence at trial, including Neal's testimony, the Tax Court found that the record was "inconclusive" as to the existence of economic hardship. But the Tax Court also found that most of the § 4.03 factors weighed in favor of granting Neal relief. First, Alimam has a legal obligation to pay the unpaid taxes. Next, the couple is divorced. Almost all of the underpayments were attributable only to Alimam. Further, Neal received no significant benefit from the unpaid taxes and has made a good faith effort to comply with federal tax laws with regard to her income throughout her marriage and in subsequent years. Even now, the only two contested factors are whether Neal knew or should have known about Alimam's underpayment, and whether Neal would suffer economic hardship if not granted relief.

In considering "knowledge or reason to know of underpayment," relevant factors include: "(1) the alleged innocent spouse's level of education; (2) the spouse's involvement in the family's business and financial affairs; (3) the presence of expenditures that appear lavish or unusual when compared to the family's past levels of income, standard of income, and spending patterns; and (4) the culpable spouse's evasiveness and deceit concerning the couple's finances." Kistner v. Comm'r, 18 F.3d 1521, 1525 (11th Cir.1994). The Commissioner points

---

19. Under Revenue Procedure 2000-15, § 4.03, factors weighing in favor of relief include (1) if the requesting spouse is separated or divorced from the non-requesting spouse; (2) if the requesting spouse would suffer economic hardship in the absence of relief; (3) if the requesting spouse suffered abuse at the hands of the non-requesting spouse; (4) if the requesting spouse had no knowledge or reason to know that the liability would not be paid; (5) if the non-requesting spouse has a legal obligation to pay the outstanding liability; and (6) if the liability for which relief is sought is attributable solely to the non-requesting spouse.

Further, if the spouse has significantly benefitted, beyond normal support, from the unpaid liability, or the requesting spouse has failed to comply with federal income tax laws, those factors would weigh against granting relief. Rev. Proc.2000-15, § 4.03, 2000-1 C.B. 447, 448-49.

to Neal's knowledge that Alimam filed for bankruptcy in 1989 and 1995 (and the levying of Neal's salary) as evidence that Neal should have known about Alimam's lack of trustworthiness as to tax matters. As the Tax Court noted, however, the couple's filed tax returns accurately reflected their tax liabilities. The couple also maintained separate personal finances, and, although Neal asked, Alimam refused to share information about his business finances. Further, Alimam lied to Neal about the reason the IRS was a creditor in the 1989 bankruptcy, falsely telling her that the IRS had disallowed certain tax shelters, resulting in a tax deficiency. Because Neal knew others who ended up owing large amounts of taxes after investing in tax shelters, she believed Alimam's explanation.[21] Although Neal became aware during the 1989 bankruptcy of some of Alimam's lavish expenses, Neal did not know how much Alimam made in his anesthesiology practice and real estate investments and thus whether his income might support those purchases. Furthermore, Alimam contributed much less than Neal to the family expenses, making it reasonable to assume he had more discretionary income. Given Alimam's general level of deceit, we cannot say that the Tax Court abused its discretion in finding that Neal did not know, nor should she have known, when she signed the 1990-93 tax returns that Alimam would not pay the tax balances shown on them.

With regard to the economic hardship factor, economic hardship is generally defined as the inability to meet "reasonable basic living expenses." See Treas. Reg. § 301.6343-1(b)(4). The Tax Court held that the facts were inconclusive as to the degree to which Neal would suffer economic hardship if she were denied relief. According to the Commissioner, sufficient evidence exists to sketch some picture of Neal's net worth-specifically, the Commissioner points to Neal's substantial salary, which in 1996 was $127,103 and had risen to $174,940 in 2003. Yet Neal testified that she has spent all of her income over time (including supporting her adult children), "just breaks even," and has a poor credit rating. Although an incomplete picture of Neal's "basic living expenses" cuts against relief, economic hardship is only one factor in a non-exhaustive list, and no single factor is determinative of whether equitable relief is appropriate. Rev. Proc.2000-15, § 4.03. Thus, taking into account all of the facts and circumstances and the factors listed in Revenue Procedure 2000-15, § 4.03, we cannot say that the Tax Court

---

21. During the 1995 bankruptcy, Alimam again lied to Neal, falsely explaining that the IRS was a creditor because it had not permitted the deduction of certain business expenses. In any event, the 1995 bankruptcy sheds little light on what Neal should have known between 1990 and 1993 about Alimam's trustworthiness in paying taxes.

abused its discretion in finding that the factors, taken as a whole, weighed in favor of granting relief.

IV.

The Tax Court did not err in conducting a trial de novo in reviewing the Commissioner's decision whether Neal was entitled to equitable relief under § 6015(f). The Tax Court also did not abuse its discretion in granting Neal equitable relief. The judgment of the Tax Court is therefore

AFFIRMED.

Notes

The court refers to the period of time that the petitioner has to seek relief in the Tax Court. Under § 6015(e)(1)(A), the petitioner must file within 90 days of the date the IRS mails a determination in the case. If there is no determination within six months of the request for innocent spouse relief, the taxpayer may file at any time after the close of the six-month period and before the close of the 90th day following the mailing of the determination. Under § 6015(e)(4), the nonclaiming spouse must be given adequate notice and an opportunity to be heard in the case.

B. TRANSFEREE AND FIDUCIARY LIABILITY

Section 6901 addresses the liability of transferees and fiduciaries, i.e., third parties who are not primarily liable for the tax but who nevertheless may be held liable and subject to the collection process. This often occurs when a taxpayer who is facing an IRS collection action transfers assets to a third party in order to avoid paying the federal government. While this smacks of a fraudulent conveyance, transferee liability may arise without fraud. For instance, a corporation may liquidate and distribute assets to its shareholders, or an executor of an estate may innocently transfer assets to beneficiaries without fully satisfying the estate's federal (or state) tax obligations. Thus, transferee liability may be based upon law or equity. Liability at law arises because of a deemed or actual "assumption of liabilities," as in the case of a transfer by a corporation to a shareholder or a purchaser of assets. Liability in equity arises because of actual or constructive fraud.

STANKO v. COMMISSIONER

United States Court of Appeals, Eighth Circuit, 2000.
209 F.3d 1082.

LOKEN, CIRCUIT JUDGE.

This case raises novel and difficult questions concerning transferee liability under the Internal Revenue Code. The transferee, Jean Stanko, appeals the Tax Court's determination that she is liable for $3,442,874 in unpaid taxes owed by Stanko Packing, Inc. ("Stanko Packing"), because she is the successor transferee of an installment note fraudulently conveyed by Stanko Packing to its sole shareholder, Jean's former spouse, Rudy Stanko. We agree Jean is liable as successor transferee, but we conclude the Tax Court miscalculated the amount of her transferee liability under Nebraska law. Accordingly, we reverse and remand.

Rudy Stanko founded Stanko Packing in 1974. At all relevant times, he was its president and sole shareholder. In April 1984, Rudy was indicted for violations of the Federal Meat Inspection Act. As a result of these activities, Stanko Packing faced the revocation of its meat inspection license. In June 1984, Stanko Packing adopted a plan of liquidation, filed a Statement of Intent to Dissolve with the Nebraska Secretary of State, and sold the majority of its assets to Packerland Packing Company for $3,900,000. Stanko Packing received $900,000 in cash and a $3,000,000 five-year installment note bearing 11.5 percent interest ("the Packerland Note").

On September 17, 1984 (three days after Rudy's conviction for Meat Inspection Act violations), Stanko Packing transferred the Packerland Note and other assets to Rudy. Those transfers left Stanko Packing insolvent. On September 19, Rudy transferred the Packerland Note to his wife, Jean. Rudy filed for divorce in July 1985, the same month Jean received her first installment payment on the Packerland Note. The Stankos were divorced in July 1986. The decree awarded Jean no property, maintenance, or child support, and one dollar in alimony. Jean held the Packerland Note until maturity in 1989, receiving installment payments totaling $4,101,779.86. As each installment payment was received, Jean paid the deferred capital gains taxes that Rudy would have paid as a result of Stanko Packing's asset sale and liquidation.

Stanko Packing dissolved in June 1985. It realized substantial taxable income in its final year of operation, primarily deferred taxes on prior export sales. But Stanko Packing did not file the income tax return for this period that was due in September 1985, and it has never paid either the tax deficiency or the substantial additions to tax (penalties and interest) that are now owing. The Commissioner computed the tax and additions to tax and assessed this deficiency against Rudy as transferee of over $6,000,000 of Stanko Packing assets. Rudy petitioned the Tax Court to redetermine this deficiency. When he failed to appear for trial, the Tax Court held him liable by default, and the Ninth Circuit affirmed. See Stanko v. Commissioner, T.C. Mem. 1993-513, 1993 WL 459963 (1993), aff'd per curiam, 42 F.3d 1402 (9th Cir.1994).

In August 1991, the Commissioner sent Jean a notice that she is liable as transferee for Stanko Packing's unpaid deficiency based upon her receipt of the Packerland Note from Rudy in September 1984. Jean, too, petitioned the Tax Court to redetermine the alleged deficiency. Jean's case was tried after Rudy's transferee liability was upheld on appeal. In December 1996, the Tax Court upheld the Commissioner's determination of transferee liability, concluding that Rudy conveyed the note to Jean with actual intent to defraud creditors, that Jean did not give adequate consideration, and that the note had a fair market value of $2,806,979 on the day Jean received it. Almost two years later, the Tax Court adopted the Commissioner's computation of transferee liability and entered judgment against Jean in the amount of $3,442,874. Jean now appeals.

I. Transferee Liability.

In a variety of situations, such as a corporate merger or an individual inheritance, the Commissioner may collect unpaid income taxes from a person to whom the taxpayer transferred assets. Section 6901 of the Code authorizes the Commissioner to assess and collect taxes from a transferee "in the same manner and subject to the same provisions and limitations" as from the taxpayer who initially incurred the tax liability. 26 U.S.C. § 6901(a). However, § 6901 is procedural; state law governs the extent to which a transferee is liable for the transferor's taxes. See Commissioner v. Stern, 357 U.S. 39, 78 S.Ct. 1047, 2 L.Ed.2d 1126 (1958). In this case, the Commissioner asserts that Jean Stanko is liable for Stanko Packing's unpaid income tax liability under the Nebraska law of fraudulent conveyances. Though the Tax Court recognized that this is the governing substantive law, it misapplied this law in a number of respects, errors of law that we review de novo and that complicate our resolution of the issues raised on appeal.

II. Was There a Fraudulent Conveyance?

In general, the law of fraudulent conveyances permits an injured creditor to set aside a transfer of assets by the debtor made with actual or constructive intent to defraud one or more creditors. At the time in question, Nebraska had enacted the Uniform Fraudulent Conveyance Act. See Neb.Rev.Stat. §§ 36-601- 613 (1988). These statutes provided:

> § 36-604. Every conveyance made * * * by a person who is or will be thereby rendered insolvent is fraudulent as to creditors without regard to his or her actual intent if the conveyance is made * * *. without a fair consideration.

> § 36-609(1). Where a conveyance * * * is fraudulent as to a creditor, such creditor, when his or her claim has matured, may, *as against any person except a purchaser for fair consideration without knowledge of the fraud at the time of the purchase* * * * (b) Disregard the conveyance and attach or levy execution upon the property conveyed. (Emphasis added.)

The Tax Court concluded that Jean Stanko is liable as a successor transferee because Rudy transferred the Packerland Note to Jean with actual intent to defraud creditors. Jean attacks that finding of fraudulent intent. We conclude the question is irrelevant. Stanko Packing is the debtor/taxpayer, and the Commissioner is the injured creditor. If the transfer of the Packerland Note *from Stanko Packing to Rudy* was a fraudulent conveyance--and Jean concedes that it was, since Rudy gave no consideration and the plan of liquidation necessarily rendered Stanko Packing insolvent--then § 36-609(1)(b) empowers the Commissioner to levy and execute against this fraudulently conveyed asset in the hands of Jean as successor transferee, unless Jean is "a purchaser for fair consideration without knowledge of the fraud." Thus, the only questions we need address on appeal are whether Jean gave fair consideration for the note, and if not, whether the Tax Court properly calculated her transferee liability.[2]

III. Did Jean Give Fair Consideration?

Jean first argues that she gave fair consideration for the Packerland Note by forgoing claims for alimony, child support, and her share of the

---

2. In our view, there can be no doubt Jean Stanko is a "transferee" for purposes of 26 U.S.C. § 6901. The statute does not define the term except to clarify that it includes a "donee, heir, legatee, devisee, and distributee." § 6901(h). *Stern* held that state law governs. Therefore, the Commissioner may proceed under § 6901 against *any* "transferee" who is liable under state law for the debts of the transferor/taxpayer.

marital property during the Stankos' subsequent divorce proceedings. We disagree. Satisfying an existing or antecedent debt may be fair consideration. See Neb. Rev. Stat. § 36-603 (1988). However, Rudy did not file for divorce for almost a year after conveying the note to Jean, and there is no evidence Jean promised to give up divorce-related claims in exchange for the note. In September 1984, Rudy was facing time in prison and had an obligation to provide support for his children. See Neb. Rev. Stat. § 43- 1402. But there is no evidence Jean undertook to discharge Rudy's financial obligations to their children in exchange for the note, and indeed Jean herself was jointly liable to provide support regardless of the conveyance. Thus, this case bears no resemblance to Bruce v. Dean, 149 Va. 39, 140 S.E. 277 (1927), where a father facing life in prison conveyed all his assets to a school in exchange for its more valuable promise to care for and educate his children.

Jean further argues that she gave fair consideration by assuming Rudy's liability to pay capital gains taxes as payments on the installment note were received. The Packerland Note was an installment obligation. When an installment obligation is transferred between spouses, "the same tax treatment * * * shall apply to the transferee as would have applied to the transferor." 26 U.S.C. § 453B(g)(2). In other words, once the note passed to Jean, she acquired Rudy's capital gains tax liability by operation of law. As we discuss in the next section of this opinion, that liability affected the value of the note in Jean's hands, but it was not fair consideration.

For these reasons, we agree with the Tax Court that Jean Stanko did not give fair consideration when she received the Packerland Note from Rudy in September 1984. Accordingly, the Commissioner may proceed against Jean as successor transferee to recover the value of an asset that was fraudulently conveyed by the taxpayer, Stanko Packing.[3] The remaining question--and the most difficult part of the case--is to determine the proper amount of Jean's transferee liability fifteen years after the conveyances in question.

IV. The Amount of Transferee Liability.

As a general rule in fraudulent conveyance cases, "a creditor may recover judgment for the value of the asset transferred or the amount

---

3. Jean further argues the Commissioner may not proceed against her because there was no reasonable effort to collect the unpaid taxes from her transferor, Rudy. The Commissioner responds that there must be a prior effort to collect from the taxpayer, Stanko Packing, but not from another transferee. As to a successor transferee, this is an open question (whether governed by Nebraska or by federal law). We need not resolve it, because the Commissioner's extensive litigation over Rudy's transferee liability was clearly a reasonable effort to collect from Jean's transferor.

necessary to satisfy the creditor's claim, whichever is less." Eli's, Inc. v. Lemen, 256 Neb. 515, 591 N.W.2d 543, 556 (1999). Accordingly, the starting point in determining Jean Stanko's transferee liability is the fair market value of the Packerland Note on the day it was transferred to Jean, September 19, 1984. Accepting the opinion of the Commissioner's expert, the Tax Court found that the note had a fair market value of $2,806,979 on that day. Jean argues the Tax Court incorrectly valued the note. We agree. The Commissioner's expert valued the note by what a willing buyer would have paid for it on September 19, 1984. That is the proper approach to valuation. But the expert gave no consideration to the deferred capital gains taxes that accompanied the note as a result of Stanko Packing's prior asset sale and liquidation. This has a substantial effect on valuation. Jean Stanko reported on her individual income tax returns the following amounts of taxable "long-term gain from installment sales" over the life of the note:

1985	$ 187,668
1986	$ 488,660
1987	$ 547,920
1988	$ 781,741
1989	$ 499,060

Had Rudy sold the installment note to a third party, then the total deferred capital gain imbedded in the note would have been immediately realized. See 26 U.S.C. § 453B(a). If Rudy as seller paid the resulting capital gains tax, the buyer would no doubt have been willing to pay the fair market value of the note as calculated by the Commissioner's expert. But as we have explained, when an installment obligation is transferred between spouses, the imbedded tax liability continues to be deferred but accompanies the note to the transferee. Obviously, if a third party could purchase the note *on these terms* (which the Code does not allow), he or she would pay only the fair market value of the right to principal and interest reflected by the note, *minus* the capital gains taxes that must be paid when future payments on the note are received. That net amount was the fair market value of the note to Jean as transferee on the date of transfer.[4] The Tax Court erred in concluding otherwise.

---

4. Stated differently, Jean as transferee should not be in a worse position than if she had not been given the note. She paid capital gains tax as she received installment payments on the note. If she now must disgorge the full facial fair-market value of the note, she will have paid more to the Commissioner as creditor than she received from Rudy. That is improper. See United States v. Brown, 86 F.2d 798 (6th Cir.1936); 14 MERTENS § 53.37, at 101-02.

Because the Tax Court seriously overvalued the Packerland Note, we must remand for recalculation of Jean Stanko's transferee liability. Before remanding, there are other valuation questions that deserve a closer look. The Tax Court held Jean liable as transferee for $3,442,874, including interest to August 7, 1991, the date she was sent a notice of transferee liability. The Court did not explain why it assessed transferee liability in excess of $2,806,979, its (erroneous) valuation of the transferred asset. The Commissioner argues that Jean as transferee is liable "for the full amount of Stanko Packing's liability plus interest from September 15, 1985, the due date of Stanko Packing's return," so long as the note was worth more than the tax liability plus additions to tax on September 19, 1984. The Commissioner does not even attempt to justify this proposition under Nebraska fraudulent conveyance law. We conclude the proposition is unsound.

The Commissioner's Computation Statement calculating Jean's transferee tax liability, on which the Tax Court relied without discussion, reflects the following:

Deficiency in income tax	$1,224,726
Penalty for failure to file a return	298,746
5% negligence underpayment penalty	61,236
50% negligence underpayment penalty	335,826[6]
Failure to pay estimated tax penalty	76,747
Interest on tax and penalties, 9/15/85 to 1/20/ 90[7]	839,439
Interest, 1/20/90 to 8/7/91	606,154
Liability to be assessed	$3,442,874

This Statement reveals that much of Stanko Packing's unpaid tax liability was incurred after its fraudulent conveyance of the Packerland Note. It is well settled in Nebraska that, "[a] creditor whose debt did not exist at the date of the voluntary conveyance by the debtor cannot have the conveyance declared fraudulent unless he pleads and proves that the conveyance was made to defraud subsequent creditors whose debts were in contemplation at the time." United States Nat'l Bank v. Rupe, 207

---

6. This penalty under § 6653(a)(2) of the Code was not added to Rudy Stanko's assessed transferee liability. The Commissioner does not explain why Jean Stanko's transferee liability should be greater than her transferor's, which seems grossly unfair as well as contrary to Nebraska law. Cf. Caulfield v. Commissioner, 33 F.3d 991, 994 & n. 4 (8th Cir.1994), cert. denied, 514 U.S. 1016, 115 S.Ct. 1358, 131 L.Ed.2d 216 (1995).

7. The Commissioner does not explain the significance of this date. It appears to be irrelevant under Nebraska law.

Neb. 131, 296 N.W.2d 474, 476 (1980), quoting First Nat'l Bank v. Bunn, 195 Neb. 829, 241 N.W.2d 127, 129 (1976). The Commissioner made no attempt to prove that the transfer of the Packerland Note from Stanko Packing to Rudy (a partial liquidating distribution to the company's only shareholder) was made to defraud subsequent, contemplated creditors. Therefore, the Commissioner's claim against Jean as successor transferee is limited to debts in existence at the time of the fraudulent conveyance.

In general, a transferee is liable under § 6901 for the transferor's unpaid taxes and additions to tax in the year of the transfer. But we are not aware of any case applying this principle to a fraudulent conveyance transferee. Because income taxes are paid annually, some months after the end of the tax year, it is logical to consider unpaid taxes in the year of the transfer part of the transferor's existing tax debt. But penalties for negligent or intentional misconduct by the transferor that occurred many months after the transfer, such as penalties for failure to file a return and for substantial underpayment of the year-end tax liability, are not, by any stretch of the imagination, existing at the time of the transfer. To recover these penalties from a fraudulent conveyance transferee, the Commissioner must prove that the transfer was made with intent to defraud future creditors. (By contrast, the penalty for failure to pay estimated taxes in the year of the transfer is based upon conduct during that year and therefore is part of the taxpayer/transferor's existing debt.) Thus, the penalty for Stanko Packing's failure to file a return and the two negligence penalties (a total of $695,808) are not part of the Commissioner's transferee claim against Jean.

The Commissioner assessed Jean as transferee for all interest owed by Stanko Packing on its unpaid tax liability between September 1985 and August 1991, the day Jean received a notice of transferee liability. This part of the assessment is similarly flawed, for we find nothing in Nebraska fraudulent conveyance law allowing such a recovery of interest. Under the new Uniform Fraudulent Transfer Act, the creditor is limited to recovering "the value of the asset at the time of the transfer, *subject to adjustment as the equities may require*." Neb.Rev.Stat. § 36-709(c) (emphasis added). The prior statute and case law are silent on the issue. Because the delay in recovering from the transferee that occurred before the Commissioner assessed transferee liability is attributable to the Commissioner (absent proof of transferee deceit), we conclude the equities do not require an award of interest for that period. Therefore, Nebraska law does not permit such an award. (On the other hand, the question of prejudgment interest after the date of the Commissioner's notice of transferee liability to Jean may well be a matter of federal law. That issue is not addressed in the Tax Court's judgment, and we do not consider it.)

Conclusion.

The judgment of the Tax Court is reversed. The case is remanded for recalculation of the value of the Packerland Note on September 19, 1984, in accordance with this opinion. Jean Stanko's transferee liability under Nebraska law will then be the lesser of that value or $1,301,473, the amount of the Commissioner's then-existing claim.

Notes and Questions

The court in footnote 3 raises Jean Stanko's argument that the Service cannot collect from her without first attempting to collect from her transferor. While the Service generally is required to exhaust all remedies against the transferor, it may proceed against the transferee without pursuing the transferor if any further proceeding against the transferor would be useless.

In the case of a transfer by one transferor to several transferees, the transferee liability is several, so the Service may proceed against any one of the transferees without proceeding against the rest. If one transferee pays the entire tax liability, or more than that person's proportionate share, that person is entitled to bring a suit for contribution from the other transferees. See Phillips-Jones Corp. v. Parmley, 302 U.S. 233, 58 S.Ct. 197, 82 L.Ed.2d 221 (1937). The issue the court raised without addressing in footnote 3 of the *Stanko* case, however, was whether the Service could proceed against a successor transferee without first proceeding against that person's transferor.

1   The government bears the burden of proving that the third party is liable as a transferee or fiduciary. What elements must the government prove in order to establish transferee liability in equity?

2   Is there a difference in the extent of the transferee liability between cases that arise in law and those that arise in equity? Can a transferee ever be liable for an amount greater than the value of the property on the date of the transfer?

3   What period of limitations applies to Jean Stanko on her transferee liability with respect to the Packerland note? See IRC § 6901(c). Are there any other facts you would need to know?

4   Why do you think Jean did not claim innocent spouse relief?

GRIEB v. COMMISSIONER

Tax Court of the United States, 1961.
36 T.C. 156.

FISHER, JUDGE.

Respondent determined a fiduciary liability against petitioner under [eds: the precursor of I.R.C. § 6901(a)(1)(B)] resulting from the distribution to him of the assets of Victory Builders, Inc., upon its liquidation, and the subsequent payment of some of its debts without first satisfying a liability of that company for unpaid income taxes of $560.37 for the year 1949. Respondent has also determined against petitioner an addition to tax in the amount of $61.88 under section 293(a), I.R.C. 1939, and $177.75 for interest which was also determined against the company.

Petitioner, having failed to contest the propriety of the determination of the tax liability against Victory, either in pleading or on brief, has apparently conceded the corporate liability. The significant question for our determination is whether petitioner is liable as a fiduciary of the company for its tax liability, any transferee liability being barred by limitations.

* * *

OPINION

Pursuant to the provisions of section [§ 6901(a)(1)(B)] which provides for enforcement of Government priority and fiduciary liability imposed under [the precursor of 31 U.S.C. § 3713] the respondent has determined that petitioner was a fiduciary of the company and, as such, is liable for the unpaid balance of the deficiency in income tax determined against the company for the year 1949, additions to tax, and interest.

Section [6901] provides for two separate liabilities, one against a transferee, and another against a fiduciary. A transferee is defined in [§ 6901(h)] as an 'heir, legatee, devisee, and distributee.' The regulation under this section also includes the shareholder of a dissolved corporation, the assignee or donee of an insolvent person, and the successor of a corporation. A transferee may be liable to the full amount which he received from the debtor irrespective of any payments of debts he made on behalf of the debtor transferor. It is a defense, however, if any of the debts so paid, or his own debt, had priority over that of the Government.

Transferee liability covers the situation where one takes complete title to property from an insolvent debtor without full, fair, and adequate consideration to the prejudice of the rights of the creditors of the transferor. The transfer is void against existing creditors. The rights and priorities of the Government, however, as any other creditor, against the transferee is determined under State law. The rationale for this liability is that a transferee, not having priority over the Government, holds the property in trust for the Government.

A fiduciary, on the other hand, is defined in the Code as 'a guardian, trustee, executor, administrator, receiver, conservator, or any person acting in any fiduciary capacity for any person.' [I.R.C. § 7701(a)(6)]. Unlike a transferee, a fiduciary can be liable * * * only to the extent of debts he pays on behalf of the debtor which do not have priority over the Government. Thus, when a fiduciary retains assets for himself absolutely or distributes them to persons for creditors of the transferor, although he may be subject to transferee liability, he is not subject to fiduciary liability * * *.

The basis of fiduciary liability in the Code rests solely upon the provisions of sections 3466 and 3467 of the Revised Statutes. It is not a liability attaching to one receiving funds without fair consideration which is based upon any equitable principles of constructive trust, but rather a liability to enforce the prior claim of the Government to the fund he so received over general creditors of the debtor.

Fiduciary liability has been summarized in Bush v. United States, 14 F.2d 321, 323 (D. Ore. 1882), as follows:

The latter (sec. 3467) is only applicable to cases where the debtor's estate, either by his death, legal bankruptcy, or insolvency, has passed into the hands of an administrator or assignee for the benefit of his creditors, or where the debtor himself has voluntarily made such disposition of it. It does not apply, then, to a conveyance, assignment, or transfer, by whatever means accomplished, to a real or pretended creditor or creditors in payment or satisfaction of a debt or claim. There must be in some way an assignment of the debtor's property to a third person for distribution among his creditors before the statute can be invoked, and then it operates directly upon the assignee by requiring him to pay the claim of the United States first, and making him personally liable therefor if he does not. * * *

The payments made by the fiduciary to creditors not having priority over the Government are not avoided or set aside. Unlike the transferee's liability, which is limited to the value of the property which he has unjustly received, the fiduciary may be liable to the full extent of debts he paid for the transferor, irrespective of any benefit, and notwithstanding that he has received none.

A case illustrating the fine distinction between a fiduciary and a transferee within the meaning of the Code is Bell v. Commissioner, 82 F.2d 499 (C.A. 3, 1936), affirming a Memorandum Opinion of this Court. In that case the executors under a will were also the legatees. It was held that initially, while they held the assets as executors, they could have been liable as fiduciaries, but upon the court order transferring the assets to them under the will, they became transferees, and thus subject to a different liability for the tax owing by the estate.

In another case, Jessie Smith, Executrix, 24 B.T.A. 807 (1931), a wife, upon the death of her husband, received assets as an executrix of her husband's estate and some real estate directly, which was formerly held jointly with her husband. It was held that as to the assets she received as an executrix she would be subject to fiduciary liability if she paid debts of the estate with them before the debt to the Government. But as to the real estate, she was held to be a transferee since she received it absolutely, and thus subject to different liability if said property was burdened with an equitable trust for the payment of taxes.

From the above analysis it is clear that transferee and fiduciary liability attaches to persons holding different interests in property for different purposes, and imposes different standards of liability. While we have seen that one person may hold the same property in both capacities at different times, and one person may hold different properties in both capacities at the same time, from the very nature of the two capacities, one person may not hold the same property in both capacities at the same time.

It has long been established that stockholders receiving the assets of a corporation upon liquidation are liable to the Government for unpaid taxes of the corporation under the broader transferee liability section of the Code, since it is presumed that they received them absolutely for their own benefit. This liability is imposed even in situations when a stockholder in fact subsequently distributes all of the proceeds to liquidate corporate debts. We find no authority for the view that a stockholder, receiving the assets of his liquidated corporation, is liable as a fiduciary rather than a transferee.

* * *

Petitioner, as sole stockholder, received all of the assets of the company at a time when it was liable for income taxes. These facts would indicate liability as a transferee rather than as a fiduciary. The respondent, conceding that the burden lies with him to go forward with the evidence in this respect, maintains that petitioner took the assets of the company under an express trust for the benefit of creditors. If such a trust was, in fact, created, petitioner would be a fiduciary under the Code.

* * *

Respondent has offered no evidence of an express trust created over all of the assets of the company. On the basis of what we have before us, we are unable to find as a fact that any such express trust was ever created between petitioner and the company.

We next must see whether petitioner is included under section 311(a)(2) in a capacity other than an express trustee. From the definition of 'fiduciary' we must eliminate, as not applying to petitioner, a guardian, trustee, executor, administrator, receiver, or conservator. The only remaining position is 'any person acting in any fiduciary capacity for any person.'

The word 'fiduciary' used in the Internal Revenue Code is not mentioned in the Revised Statutes. It is, however, descriptive of the types of persons intended to be covered under the statute. The statute provides that the person covered is executor, administrator, assignee, or other person who pays a debt due by the person 'for whom or for which he acts.'

The mere payment of a debt for another person will not automatically cause one to be included under this section. The crucial test, therefore, looking at both the Internal Revenue Code and the Revised Statutes, is whether the payment of the debts were made by one who is acting for the debtor in a fiduciary or representative capacity.

Petitioner can only be liable as a fiduciary if he, in fact, received the assets from the company as an officer or director for the purpose of liquidating the corporate debts rather than as a stockholder, and that he paid these debts in his capacity as a representative of the company.

* * *

A stockholder receiving all of the assets of a corporation is one of the clearest cases of one receiving assets in his own behalf, and he will be presumed to be acting on his own behalf as a transferee unless there is a clear showing to the contrary. In the absence of such proof, we cannot find that petitioner was acting as a fiduciary upon receipt and distribution of the corporate assets.

* * *

The sole basis for transferee liability is that the recipient of the funds is, under certain circumstances, deemed to hold them in constructive trust for certain creditors. If everyone who is held to hold funds in trust for another is deemed to be fiduciary under the Code, as respondent contends, it would completely eliminate the basis for the distinction between the two liabilities. Respondent has failed to recognize that in order to be a fiduciary, petitioner must have, in fact, acted as such, rather than on his own behalf.

The existence of an actual fiduciary relationship is indispensable in placing one within the provisions of fiduciary liability. This fiduciary capacity must be established from the very nature of the transaction rather than through the equitable 'trust fund' doctrine. This distinction was well illustrated in the case of *Jessie Smith, Executrix*, supra. In this case a wife, upon the death of her husband, received the assets of her husband's estate as executrix, and she received complete title to real estate which was held jointly by her husband and herself. It was held that since the real estate was not a part of the estate she did not receive it as executrix and, therefore, she did not hold it in a fiduciary capacity. Section 3467 was held to relate only to the payment of debts out of the funds or assets coming into her hands as executrix and not to the real estate. It was added that if it were found that the real estate was burdened with the tax liability of the decedent, under the trust fund doctrine, she would be liable as a transferee of the real estate, albeit not as a fiduciary.

The mere finding of a 'trust fund,' then, is insufficient to deem the holder a fiduciary under the statute. If a trust is created out of the nature of the transfer, such as the transfer of assets for the benefit of another, then the holder is a fiduciary. On the other hand, if a trust arises because the person receiving the assets was not rightfully entitled to them, he is a transferee. In the latter situation, the debtor has divested himself completely of the assets to another and this transfer, if prejudicial to other creditors, can be avoided. In the former situation, on the other hand, the debtor by placing his assets with a representative has not divested himself completely of the assets to defraud creditors, inasmuch as his creditors have a beneficial interest in them pursuant to the very nature of the assignment. The transfer to a fiduciary cannot be avoided, and liability attaches to the fiduciary only if he fails to recognize legal priorities in discharging his obligation under the trust.

The distinction between the two different types of trusts was also recognized in Hollins v. Brierfield Coal & Iron Co., 150 U.S. 371, 378 (1893), where it was said (p. 383):

> Becoming insolvent, the equitable interest of the stockholders in the property, together with their conditional liability to the creditors, places the property in a condition of trust, first, for the creditors, and then for the stockholders. Whatever of trust there is arises from the peculiar and diverse equitable rights of the stockholders as against

the corporation in its property and their conditional liability to its creditors. It is rather a trust in the administration of the assets after possession by a court of equity than a trust attaching to the property, as such, for the direct benefit of either creditor or stockholder.

The sole basis for transferee liability is that a trust is created in equity for the benefit of creditors. Wherein would lie the distinction if we were to hold that such equitable trustees were fiduciaries rather than transferees? This would completely nullify the difference between the two liabilities, and, indeed, eliminate transferee liability.

* * *

One of the main objectives of the provisions for transferee liability in the Code is to provide an effective remedy for such a situation as that presented in the instant case. To accept respondent's contention that such persons are fiduciaries rather than transferees would create the anomalous result of providing a statutory remedy only to the extent of the corporate debts they pay with the corporate assets but providing no statutory remedy for recovery of the assets they retain for themselves.

Respondent has failed to show any evidence that petitioner ever received the assets impressed with an express trust or that he received them as a representative or an agent for the corporation. This cannot be presumed from the transfer of assets and the subsequent payment of corporate debts or by the operation of equity.

We have not closed our eyes to the obvious fact that the company was liquidated with the full knowledge on the part of petitioner of the pending tax liability, but this is clearly one of the situations sought to be remedied by proceeding on the basis of transferee liability.

The statute of limitations has obviously barred transferee liability which appears to be the reason why respondent relies solely on a claim of fiduciary liability because, if his contention were well grounded, he would get the benefit of a longer period of limitations. Since we have held that the provisions of section 311(a)(2) relating to fiduciary liability do not apply upon the record before us, we must hold for petitioner.

Decision will be entered for the petitioner.

Notes and Questions

Usually, the crucial test for determining fiduciary liability is whether the person paying the claims was acting in a fiduciary or representative capacity, or whether that person was acting on her own behalf. What are the distinctions between transferee liability and fiduciary liability?

C. TRUST FUND TAXES

There are several provisions in the Code that require third parties to collect taxes from others and remit them to the government. The third party has liability for failure to collect and pay these taxes, and may be subject to a civil penalty or to prosecution by the government. One of the most frequently litigated third-party delinquencies arises when employers fail to remit payroll taxes. Such a failure results in personal liability imposed on the employer and on any "responsible person" for a penalty equal to the total amount of the tax due. IRC § 6672. This penalty often is referred to as "the 100% penalty."

1. The Nature of the Tax

MORTENSON v. NATIONAL UNION FIRE INSURANCE COMPANY
United States Court of Appeals, Seventh Circuit, 2001.
249 F.3d 667.

POSNER, CIRCUIT JUDGE.

This is a diversity suit, governed by Illinois law, seeking the proceeds of a directors' and officers' liability policy. The plaintiff, Lee Mortenson, who was the president of Opelika Manufacturing Company, appeals from the grant of summary judgment to the insurance company. The appeal requires us to determine whether the statutory penalty imposed on responsible persons for willful nonpayment of payroll taxes is a "penalty" within the meaning of an exclusion in the D & O [eds: Directors' and Officers' Liability] policy.

The policy, issued in 1982, covers claims made between August 1982 and August 1985 that resulted in losses to directors or officers by reason of any "wrongful act" committed by them in the course of their corporate duties. But the policy excludes losses consisting of "fines or penalties imposed by law or other matters which may be deemed uninsurable under the law pursuant to which this policy shall be construed." Mortenson became president of Opelika in 1984, at a time when the company was experiencing financial distress as a result of which it had in May of that year, three months before he assumed office, failed to remit more than $100,000 in payroll taxes due the federal government. Mortenson learned about this default in November and told his financial officers that he didn't want to see a repetition of it, but he took no disciplinary steps against the people responsible for the default and he instituted no measures to prevent its recurrence. On the contrary, he participated in efforts by the company to identify creditors whom the company could persuade to allow late payment, though he should have known that by picking and choosing among creditors he was inviting his underlings to put the Internal Revenue Service last (more on that later). And, sure enough, in December of 1984 and the first two months of the following year, Opelika again failed to pay its payroll taxes, while continuing to pay other, more exigent creditors.

The IRS discovered the defaults and in July 1985 hit Mortenson with a proposed assessment of 100 percent of the past-due taxes, pursuant to 26 U.S.C. § 6672(a), which makes any person responsible for collecting, accounting for, and paying over payroll taxes who "willfully" fails to do any of these things "liable to a penalty equal to the total amount of tax evaded, or not collected, or not accounted for and paid over." The government sued Mortenson to collect the penalty, and eventually the parties settled the suit for $900,000--for which loss the insurance company has refused to reimburse him.

The insurance policy does not define "penalties," and Mortenson argues that therefore it is ambiguous and we must interpret the term as favorably to Mortenson as reason allows. So interpreted, the term does not, he continues, encompass the penalty imposed by section 6672(a), because it is not "really" a penalty. He offers a number of reasons why it is not. One is that the aim is to collect taxes rather than to punish the willfully delinquent responsible person, as shown by the fact that it is the policy of the Internal Revenue Service not to use the statute to collect more than the total amount of unpaid tax. So if the unpaid tax were $250,000, which would make each responsible person who had willfully failed in his duty to see to its payment liable for a $250,000 penalty, the total penalties assessed against all those responsible persons would be capped at $250,000. For example, if the IRS was able to collect $100,000 of the $250,000 in unpaid tax from the company itself, the penalties collected from the responsible persons would be capped at $150,000.

Mortenson argues further that a number of cases, though only one involving the interpretation of an insurance policy, St. Paul Fire & Marine Ins. Co. v. Briggs, 464 N.W.2d 535 (Minn.App. 1990), describe the section 6672(a) penalty as not really a penalty. United States v. Sotelo, 436 U.S. 268, 275, 98 S.Ct. 1795, 56 L.Ed.2d 275 (1978); Monday v. United States, 421 F.2d 1210, 1215-16 (7th Cir.1970); Aardema v. Fitch, 291 Ill.App.3d 917, 225 Ill.Dec. 893, 684 N.E.2d 884, 887-89 (1997). Only the last of these cases supports his position. *Briggs* and *Monday* say merely that the section 6672(a) penalty is not a *criminal* penalty, which is correct but irrelevant; and *Briggs* went on to hold that the section 6672(a) penalty was in any event uninsurable as a matter of law, a holding that would do in *Mortenson* as well. The issue in *Sotelo* was not whether the section imposes a penalty, but, as explained in Duncan v. Commissioner, 68 F.3d 315, 318 (9th Cir.1995), which holds that the section does impose a penalty, whether a debt based upon it is dischargeable in bankruptcy--and the Court held that it was not. Aardema v. Fitch, supra, 225 Ill.Dec. 893, 684 N.E.2d at 890, which involved a state statute that allows (as the federal statute now does, 26 U.S.C. § 6672(d)) a responsible person against whom the penalty has been assessed to seek contribution from other responsible persons who may be liable, does state that "section 6672 is merely a collection device for the government and is not meant to punish," though Wynne v. Fischer, 809 S.W.2d 264 (Tex.App.1991), which involves the same issue, is squarely contra. Mortenson adopts the argument of *Aardema* and adds that a penalty is a punishment for deliberate wrongdoing, of which the willfulness required for liability under section 6672(a) is, he contends, only a pale shadow.

Taking the last point first, we point out that penalties are frequently imposed for conduct well short of deliberate wrongdoing. Reckless and negligent homicide are crimes, fines are imposed for speeding even when the driver was unaware that he was exceeding the speed limit, and there are even strict liability crimes, where the defendant's state of mind is irrelevant and even the fact that he could not have prevented the criminal act from occurring is not a defense. Willfulness within the meaning of section 6672(a) "means that the person either knew the taxes were not being turned over to the government and nonetheless opted to pay other creditors, or recklessly disregarded a known risk that the taxes were not being paid over." United States v. Kim, 111 F.3d 1351, 1357-58 (7th Cir.1997); see also Monday v. United States, supra, 421 F.2d at 1215-16. We went further and held in Wright v. United States, 809 F.2d 425, 427-28 (7th Cir.1987), that gross negligence is sufficient to constitute willfulness under the statute.

Although it is true that the Internal Revenue Service caps the penalty at the amount of tax due, this is not a statutory limitation; it is simply an enforcement policy. The fact that the statute now allows contribution does not cap the penalty at the amount of taxes either, or for that matter impose any other ceiling. Contribution is not about total liability, but about its allocation among the wrongdoers. In a case in which the amount of tax due was $250,000, and two responsible persons were each liable for the penalty, the government could if it wanted assess and collect $250,000 from each. The two would be free to seek contribution from other responsible persons, perhaps even to rearrange the liability voluntarily between themselves by means of an indemnity agreement, * * * but their obtaining contribution whether from each other or from others would not change the fact that the government had collected penalties twice as great as the amount of taxes owed. And finally the fact that the IRS uses section 6672(a) as a collection device does not distinguish it from a number of unmistakably criminal penalties, such as those for minor thefts, vandalism, and other minor property crimes, where the police use the threat of prosecution to induce the wrongdoer to make restitution to his victim more often than they actually prosecute.

We conclude that section 6672(a) imposes the civil counterpart of a fine. Monetary penalties for wrongful conduct *are* civil fines, and are encompassed by the "fines or penalties" provision in the insurance policy. Any other conclusion would inject extreme uncertainty into the interpretation of insurance policies. Whether a penalty so designated in the statute creating it, a penalty that on its face was a civil fine, was a penalty within the meaning of the policy exclusion would require a searching and often indeterminate inquiry into the history and function and interpretation and details of the statutory scheme. Alerted to this concern by the court's questions at argument, Mortenson's lawyer suggested that the policy could be rewritten to exclude "penalties that are called penalties in the statutes that create them." That would stop inquiry at the face of the statute. It is a good suggestion, but the possibility of making an insurance policy clearer doesn't imply that it is unclear in its present form. Anyone reading the insurance policy at issue in this case--and remember that a D & O policy is purchased by a firm, not by an individual, and protects business executives, not the average consumer--would think that the term "penalties and fines" covered exactions described as penalties or fines in the statutes imposing them. The reader would not think the exclusion limited to a subset of penalties and fines impossible to identify without a protracted inquiry with an unpredictable outcome.

We have yet to mention the most compelling argument against the interpretation for which Mortenson contends. For obvious reasons, insurance companies try to avoid insuring people against risks that having insurance makes far more likely to occur. The temptation that insurance gives the insured to commit the very act insured against is called by students of insurance "moral hazard" and is the reason that fire insurance companies refuse to insure property for more than it is worth--they don't want to tempt the owner to burn it down. Consider the likely effects of insuring against the section 6672(a) penalty. When a firm gets into financial difficulties and creditors are pressing it for repayment, the firm tries–Opelika tried–to pay the most pressing creditors currently and hold off the others till later. This tendency is one of the reasons for the rules against preferences in bankruptcy, see 11 U.S.C. § 547, preferences being the favoring, often, of the most exigent creditors to the prejudice of the others, as the firm struggles to stay afloat. (When it sinks, the rest of the creditors go down with it.) The temptation to put the IRS at the end of the line is great. The IRS is unlikely to be aware that the firm is in difficulty, and if the firm decides therefore not to remit payroll taxes as they come due, but to favor the creditors who are threatening to seize the firm's assets or petition it into bankruptcy, the IRS is unlikely even to notice for some time that it is being stiffed. By the time it wakes up, the firm will probably be unable to pay the taxes that it failed to remit. It is to prevent firms from yielding to the temptation to put the IRS at the end of the creditor queue that Congress has imposed liability for nonpayment of payroll taxes on the responsible officers of the firm. For those persons to be insured against this liability will tempt them to do just what Opelika did here and what the penalty provision of section 6672(a) is designed to prevent--pay other creditors first, funding the preference by not paying the IRS at all. It would be ironic to use the IRS's policy of lenity in forgoing multiple collection of the statutory penalty to reduce the likelihood of its collecting the taxes for the nonpayment of which the penalty is imposed.

It is strongly arguable, indeed, that insurance against the section 6672(a) penalty, by encouraging the nonpayment of payroll taxes, is against public policy, so falling under the last clause of the policy exclusion and possibly under the rule in Illinois as elsewhere that forbids certain types of insurance as being against public policy because of the acute moral hazard that the insurance creates. A familiar example is taking out a life insurance policy on another person's life without his consent. But closer to this case is the rule that forbids insuring against criminal fines--a rule that Illinois courts have extended to punitive damages, a form of civil penalty and, in one case, Crawford Laboratories, Inc. v. St. Paul Ins. Co., 306 Ill.App.3d 538, 239 Ill.Dec. 899, 715 N.E.2d 653 (1999), to civil penalties explicitly so designated. We need not decide, however, whether insuring against the section 6672(a) penalty falls within this ban. For purposes of interpreting this insurance policy, a penalty is a penalty is a penalty.

AFFIRMED.

Notes and Question

The Ninth Circuit similarly has held that the § 6672 penalty is a true penalty. See Duncan v. Commissioner, 68 F.3d 315 (9th Cir. 1995). In *Duncan,* the taxpayer was liable for the 100% penalty under § 6672, which he paid. He then attempted to deduct this payment on his income tax return as a "non-business bad debt," claiming that the "penalty" was actually a "revenue measure" rather than a penalty. The taxpayer based this assumption on an IRS policy statement that the § 6672 penalty is a "collection device." The court held in favor of the Service, opining that under the rationale of Tank Truck Rentals, Inc. v. Commissioner, 356 U.S. 30, 78 S.Ct. 507, 2 L.Ed.2d 562 (1958) the deduction of a payment levied against a taxpayer as a penal measure frustrates public policy by providing a tax benefit for a payment that was intended as a penalty. Thus, the allowance of the deduction would encourage the behavior the penalty was designed to prevent. In *Duncan,* the court reasoned that the § 6672 tax operates as a penalty.

But other courts, including the U.S. Supreme Court, as well as the IRS itself have viewed the § 6672 assessment not as a true penalty but as a means of collecting the tax owed by the business. See, e.g., U.S. v. Sotelo, 436 U.S. 268, 275, 98 S.Ct. 1795, 1800 (1978)("That the funds due are referred to as a 'penalty' when the Government later seeks to recover them does not alter their essential character as taxes for purposes of the Bankruptcy Act, at least in a case in which, as here, the § 6672 liability is predicated on a failure to pay over, rather than a failure initially to collect, the taxes."); U.S. v. Pepperman, 976 F.2d 123, 126 (3rd Cir. 1992)("Although denominated a "penalty" in the statute, the liability imposed under section 6672 is not penal in nature, but rather is a means of ensuring that withholding taxes are paid"). At the time *Sotelo* was decided, the IRS Handbook provided that under long-standing IRS policy, the government would "retain only one satisfaction of the unpaid trust fund taxes, whether collected in part from each responsible person and the corporate employer, or entirely from one source." 976 F.2d at 127.

Will the filing of a bankruptcy petition affect the amount or nature of the tax?

2. The Responsible Person

DAVIS v. UNITED STATES

United States Court of Appeals, Ninth Circuit, 1992.
961 F.2d 867.

TANG, CIRCUIT JUDGE:

Dan Davis, the president and major shareholder of ITAC Corporation, appeals a jury verdict finding him liable for willfully failing to pay withholding and social security taxes for ITAC's employees for the last quarter of 1981 and the first two quarters of 1982. Davis had argued that he was not a responsible officer and that his subsequent preference of other creditors over the Internal Revenue Service ("IRS") did not evince "willfulness." The district court refused to instruct the jury on Davis's definition of willfulness. The jury subsequently found Davis liable for the employee taxes owed the government. The district court also denied Davis's motion to reduce the assessment for the last quarter of 1981. Davis appeals. We affirm.

BACKGROUND

A. Statutory Framework

The Internal Revenue Code requires employers such as ITAC Corporation ("ITAC") to withhold federal social security and individual income taxes from the wages of their employees. 26 U.S.C. §§ 3102(a), 3402(a). Although an employer collects this money each salary period, payment to the federal government takes place on a quarterly basis. In the interim, the employer holds the collected taxes in trust for the government. 26 U.S.C. § 7501(a). These taxes accordingly are known as "trust fund taxes." Slodov v. United States, 436 U.S. 238, 243, 98 S.Ct. 1778, 1783, 56 L.Ed.2d 251 (1978). Other taxes, such as those directly owed by the business, are referred to as "non-trust fund taxes."

Once net wages are paid to an employee, the government credits that employee with the tax payments, regardless of whether the taxes are ultimately paid over by the employer. In order to protect against revenue losses, the tax code offers the IRS a variety of means of recovering from employers who fail to pay over collected employee taxes. In addition to tax liens, 26 U.S.C. § 6321, and criminal penalties, 26 U.S.C. §§ 7202, 7215, the IRS may assess a civil penalty against responsible corporate officials equal to the amount of delinquent trust fund taxes ("100% penalty"), 26 U.S.C. § 6672. Section 6672 provides, in relevant part:

Any person required to collect, truthfully account for, and pay over any tax imposed by this title who willfully fails to collect such tax, or truthfully account for and pay over such tax, or willfully attempts in any manner to evade or defeat any such tax or the payment thereof, shall, in addition to other penalties provided by law, be liable to a penalty equal to the total amount of the tax evaded, or not collected, or not accounted for and paid over.

A "person," for purposes of section 6672, includes "an officer or employee of a corporation, or a member or employee of a partnership, who as such officer, employee, or member is under a duty to perform the act in respect of which the violation occurs." 26 U.S.C. § 6671(b). The recovery of a penalty under section 6672 entails showing that the individual both was a "responsible person" and acted willfully in failing to collect or pay over the withheld taxes. Maggy v. United States, 560 F.2d 1372, 1374 (9th Cir.1977).

* * *

DISCUSSION

I. The "Willfulness" Instruction

On appeal, Davis does not challenge the jury's conclusion that he was a "responsible person" during the three quarters in which trust fund taxes were not paid over to the IRS. Davis argues only that, as a matter of law, he did not act willfully. Davis insists that, because he lacked knowledge of ITAC's failure to pay the taxes until after they were due, his subsequent use of corporate revenues to compensate other creditors rather than to pay the delinquent taxes does not evince willfulness. Davis contends that he deferred payments to the IRS in an attempt to resuscitate ITAC and thereby maximize the chances that the taxes would be repaid in full over time. To hold otherwise, Davis continues, would encourage management to walk away from the corporation or discontinue business upon learning of a back tax liability, rather than expose themselves to personal liability for the tax debt by continuing to pay the corporation's bills.

* * *

A. Definition of Willfulness

Willfulness, within the meaning of section 6672, has been defined as a " 'voluntary, conscious and intentional act to prefer other creditors over the United States.' " Klotz v. United States, 602 F.2d 920, 923 (9th Cir.1979) (quoting Sorenson v. United States, 521 F.2d 325, 328 (9th Cir.1975)); see also Maggy, 560 F.2d at 1375; Teel v. United States, 529

F.2d 903, 905 (9th Cir.1976). An intent to defraud the government or other bad motive need not be proven. In fact, conduct motivated by a reasonable cause may nonetheless be willful.

Davis's deliberate decision to use corporate revenues received after July 1982 (when Davis first became aware of the delinquency) to pay commercial creditors rather than to diminish ITAC's tax debt falls within the literal terms of this Circuit's definition of willfulness. The payments were a "voluntary, conscious and intentional act to prefer other creditors over the United States." Klotz, 602 F.2d at 923. Indeed, Davis admits that ITAC received sufficient income to satisfy in full its tax delinquency had those funds not been diverted to satisfy other corporate debts.

B. The *Slodov* Decision

Davis argues that his actions fall within the exception to section 6672 liability carved out by the Supreme Court in *Slodov*. The Supreme Court held in *Slodov* that, if new management of a corporation assumes control when a delinquency for trust fund taxes already exists and the withheld taxes have already been dissipated by prior management, the new management's use of after-acquired revenues to satisfy creditors other than the United States does not make it personally liable for a section 6672 penalty. 436 U.S. at 259-60, 98 S.Ct. at 1791-92.

Mr. Slodov purchased the stock and assumed management of three corporations on January 31, 1969. At that time, the corporations owed $250,000 in unpaid withholding taxes. All of the money withheld from the employees' salaries had been spent by prior management before Slodov assumed control. Indeed, when Mr. Slodov came to the helm, the corporations had absolutely no funds, trust or otherwise, with which to pay the tax debt. Under Mr. Slodov's guidance, the companies acquired sufficient revenue to pay the tax liability, but Mr. Slodov used the money to meet other obligations such as wages, rent, and supplies.

The Supreme Court concluded that Mr. Slodov's actions did not incur personal liability under section 6672. [Section] 7501 does not impress a trust on after-acquired funds, and * * * the responsible person consequently does not violate § 6672 by willfully using employer funds for purposes other than satisfaction of the trust-fund tax claims of the United States when at the time [the responsible person] assumed control there were no funds with which to satisfy the tax obligation and the funds thereafter generated are not directly traceable to collected taxes referred to by that statute. Id. at 259-60, 98 S.Ct. at 1791.

Informing the Supreme Court's decision were three considerations. First, the Supreme Court felt that imposing liability under the circumstances would frustrate the statute's purpose. Section 6672 promotes the full collection of taxes. Confronting potential rescuers of a failing institution with the Hobson's Choice of either assuming personal liability for the back taxes or finding the money to satisfy the tax debt in full before conducting any business actually increases the risk of non-collection. Buyers capable of resuscitating the company would be scared off, consigning the business to collapse and the IRS to bankruptcy court to collect its money. Relieving new management from personal liability, on the other hand, would provide the financial breathing room necessary for new officers to get a business back on its feet. Once recovered, the company not only could pay its tax debt, but also could contribute additional tax revenue in the future.

Second, the Supreme Court found the tax code's language and legislative history inconsistent with a penalty theory that imposed "liability without personal fault." Id. at 254, 98 S.Ct. at 1789. After-acquired funds, the Court continued, were not automatically impressed with a trust for the benefit of the government. Rather, some "nexus between the funds collected and the trust created" must be established. Id. at 256, 98 S.Ct. at 1789-80. For new management, no such nexus exists.

Finally, the Court held that a rule automatically requisitioning all after-acquired cash for the federal Treasury would conflict with the priority rules creating a preferred status for some creditors over federal tax liabilities. See 26 U.S.C. § 6323. Responsible persons who paid these preferred creditors before paying back taxes might be deemed liable under section 6672 for diverting funds from the company's trust fund tax repayment obligation. "Surely," the Supreme Court explained, "Congress did not intend § 6672 to hammer the responsible person with the threat of heavy civil and criminal penalties to pay over proceeds in which the [Internal Revenue] Code does not assert a priority interest." 436 U.S. at 259, 98 S.Ct. at 1791.

Davis would have this court extend *Slodov* to hold that the use of after-acquired funds to pay commercial debts by the same persons who were responsible for the failure to collect and pay the withholding taxes in the first instance (as opposed to new management) does not give rise to liability under section 6672. We decline Davis's invitation for three reasons.

1. *Slodov's* language

First, the *Slodov* opinion specifically excludes from its ambit Davis's situation, limiting its holding to cases involving the accession of new management:

> *When the same individual or individuals who caused the delinquency in any tax quarter are also the "responsible persons" at the time the Government's efforts to collect from the [corporate] employer have failed, and it seeks recourse against the "responsible employees," there is no question that § 6672 is applicable to them.* It is the situation that arises when there has been a change of control of the employer enterprise, here corporations, prior to the expiration of a tax quarter, or at a time when a tax delinquency for past quarters already exists that creates the question for our decision.

Id. at 245-46, 98 S.Ct. at 1784 (emphasis added).

While Davis says that he was unaware of ITAC's dereliction until the trust fund taxes were overdue, the district court properly instructed the jury that responsibility is a matter of status, duty, and authority, not knowledge. The jury found that Davis was a responsible person and, as such, his actions or inactions caused ITAC not to pay over the withheld taxes as required by law. Because Davis was responsible both at the time the taxes went unpaid and at the time the government sought to collect under section 6672, "there is no question that § 6672 is applicable to [him]." *Slodov*, 436 U.S. at 246, 98 S.Ct. at 1784.

Davis counters that simply being responsible is not enough. He points out that Mr. Slodov was a corporate officer as of January 31, 1969--the day that payments for the last quarter of 1968 were due. Status as a responsible person, however, does not attach automatically to every officer engaged in fiscal management on the day the tax check must be written. Rather, liability as a responsible person attaches each time salaries are paid during the course of a quarter. "As the employer withholds taxes from the employees, a contingent liability is created. The liability merely becomes fixed on the date when the payments are due." *Teel*, 529 F.2d at 906; see *Maggy*, 560 F.2d at 1375 (holding that Maggy was a responsible person for that portion of the quarter during which he actually exercised control over corporate disbursements; that Maggy was not technically still a responsible officer on the day payment was due did not expunge his liability for the earlier portion of the quarter). Mr. Slodov, unlike Davis, had no role in the corporation at the time the taxes were withheld and salaries disbursed. Nor did the corporation have any funds available with which to pay the tax when Slodov arrived on January 31st.

Davis, by contrast, did not simply appear on the eve of tax payment day. To the contrary, his status and role in the corporation made him a responsible person from the day the first salary was paid in the last quarter of 1981. Moreover, Davis has made no showing that corporate funds did not exist with which to satisfy the tax liability on the payment due date. He contends only that the funds actually withheld had been disbursed by this time. This is insufficient to invoke the protection of *Slodov*.

2. *Slodov's* rationale

Second, the three considerations on which the *Slodov* opinion was predicated do not obtain in this case. Davis claims that, once he learned that ITAC was not paying employees' withholding taxes, he assumed a more active role in supervising corporate disbursements. He contends that the factors animating the *Slodov* decision with respect to new management apply with equal force to the shuffle of duties that took place at ITAC. In other words, Davis would have this court equate transfers of responsibility internal to the corporation with the accession of new management that occurred in *Slodov*. The Supreme Court's analysis, however, will not support such a conclusion.

In *Slodov*, the Supreme Court expressly counseled against interpreting section 6672 in such a manner that "the penalties easily could be evaded by changes in officials' responsibilities prior to the expiration of any quarter." 436 U.S. at 247, 98 S.Ct. at 1785. Davis's theory would encourage corporate roulette. Responsible officers, upon learning that taxes had gone unpaid during their watch, could simply rotate their respective responsibilities and duties. Once theofficers assumed their new duties, they would be relieved from section 6672 personal liability for the use of forthcoming revenues to pay debts other than the back taxes. The corporation could thus delay compensating the federal treasury for the use of its money indefinitely, thereby freeing up corporate income for more self-interested expenses.

Slodov's concern for encouraging new management to salvage failing businesses, thus maximizing the chances for tax recovery, also loses much of its luster in this context. Persons "contemplating assuming control of a financially beleaguered corporation owing back employment taxes," Id. at 252-53, 98 S.Ct. at 1787-88, might be deterred by the risk of personal liability. While Davis suggests that he and other responsible officers, just like potential purchasers, have the option of just walking away when they learn of an accrued withholding tax liability, in reality the choice for existing management is not that simple. Existing management has a vested interest, financial and otherwise, in guiding a business through troubled waters. Legal obligations and duties limit an officer's ability to walk away upon learning of an overdue tax liability. Indeed, for "responsible persons," leaving is no guarantee that liability will still not attach. A jury or judge could disbelieve protestations of ignorance or find that the officer acted recklessly or was willfully ignorant of the failure to pay taxes. Existing management like Davis, in other words, has sufficient incentive to remain and to keep the company afloat and capable of repaying taxes without specifically excepting them from section 6672 liability.

Slodov's insistence on personal fault is also satisfied in this case. Unlike Mr. Slodov, Davis presided over the corporation every day during which taxes were taken from employees' checks and dissipated to satisfy corporate needs, at the expense of the public fisc. The jury found that, throughout these three quarters, Davis had the authority and responsibility to prevent this breach of trust, but failed to do so.[3] While the briefs do not trace the expenditure of the trust funds, Davis at least indirectly benefited from the illicit diversion of the federal government's money. Bills and salaries (including Davis's) were paid and the company kept afloat for three quarters. That might not have been possible without the use of the tax revenues. A much stronger foundation for personal fault thus exists for Davis than for new management like Mr. Slodov.

Concerns about priority rules also have no practical application in this case. Davis has made no showing that any of the creditors he preferred to the IRS held debts given a priority by the tax code. See 26 U.S.C. § 6323. We thus leave for another day the question whether section 6672 liability attaches when existing management uses after-acquired funds to pay only debts having priority over a tax lien. With respect to otherwise unencumbered corporate income, the obligation to repay the taxes remains intact.

Finally, it should be noted that *Slodov* was concerned with the situation where, when new management assumes control, the business has no funds at all available to alleviate its tax debt. While Davis points out that the trust funds were dissipated prior to the time he learned of the delict, he makes no showing that "there were no funds with which to satisfy the tax obligation." 436 U.S. at 259-60, 98 S.Ct. at 1791-92. It is unclear from the Supreme Court's opinion how critical a factor the impoverishment of the business is, other than that the total

---

3. For all the verdict shows, the jury might also have disbelieved Davis's claimed lack of knowledge and found that he was aware of and acquiesced in the failure to pay over withholding taxes throughout the three quarters.

unavailability of cash and liquid assets makes the revival of the business through commercial expenditures much more urgent and the threat that the IRS will be unable to collect due to a bankruptcy much more immediate. To the extent ITAC was in a more solvent financial condition, it had less of an excuse to prefer commercial creditors over the IRS.

3. Circuit court decisions

The third reason we refuse to extend *Slodov* to Davis's situation is that Davis's proposed interpretation of *Slodov* has been implicitly foreclosed by two of our previous decisions and expressly rejected by four other federal courts of appeals. In two decisions pre-dating *Slodov*, we held that the use of after-acquired funds to compensate debtors other than the United States amounts to willfulness. In *Teel*, the responsible corporate officers first learned of the business's failure to pay on October 17, 1966. After October 17th, the same officers knowingly used incoming cash to purchase new merchandise. The Ninth Circuit observed:

> The [purchase] agreement seems sensible and honest. But the trouble is that as the cash went into the cash drawer, it became subject to trust or lien in favor of the federal government for the unpaid withholding taxes. By dissipating the cash for new purchases, of which the taxpayers knew, they unwittingly supplied the necessary willfulness. Because the failure to pay the arrearages and current tax after October 17, 1966, was willful, any factual issue as to ignorance of nonpayment prior to October 17, 1966, is not material.

529 F.2d at 905-06.

Likewise in *Maggy*, we held that a responsible officer's failure to use funds received by the business to repay its tax liability constituted willfulness because "the funds which came into the corporation became immediately subject to a trust or lien in favor of the United States for the unpaid withholding taxes." 560 F.2d at 1375-76.

Davis attempts to distinguish these cases on two grounds. He argues firstly that *Teel's* and *Maggy's* reliance on a trust fund theory is outmoded in light of *Slodov's* admonition that "[n]othing whatever in § 6672 * * * suggests that the effect of the requirement to 'pay over' was to impress a trust on the corporation's after-acquired cash." 436 U.S. at 254, 98 S.Ct. at 1789.

While *Slodov* might quarrel with some of *Teel's* and *Maggy's* phraseology, we nevertheless consider our previous opinions' analyses sound and their bottom-line conclusions consistent with *Slodov*. Applying the appellation "trust" to *Teel's* and *Maggy's* after-acquired funds was simply a shorthand acknowledgment of the obligations section 6672 imposes on persons who (unlike Slodov) are responsible when the taxes are collected, when the funds are dissipated, and when subsequent corporate income is diverted to creditors other than the United States. *Slodov* recognizes this distinction when, at the outset of its opinion, the Supreme Court contrasts Slodov's circumstances with the situation where the same corporate officers who prefer other creditors to the federal treasury were responsible before, during, and after dissipation of the withheld taxes. 436 U.S. at 245-46, 98 S.Ct. at 1784-85. In the latter case, the Supreme Court said "there is no question that § 6672 is applicable to them." Id. at 246, 98 S.Ct. at 1784.

Moreover, the Supreme Court's concern with imposing a trust on all after-acquired funds under all circumstances was that such a theory gave insufficient heed to the necessary nexus between the payment obligation and the after-acquired funds. In Davis's case, his continuing responsibility before, during, and after the tax delinquency creates the requisite linkage between subsequently received cash and a duty to satisfy the trust fund tax delinquency.

Davis also tries to sidestep *Teel* and *Maggy* by pointing out that the responsible officers there learned of the tax delinquency before the actual payment due date and thus were under an absolute obligation to use any and all corporate funds to pay the taxes on time. Davis insists that he remained in the dark until after the money was due. Assuming the jury believed Davis's claim of ignorance, Davis still fails to explain why this timing factor should be critical. What is key in *Teel* and *Maggy* is that (1) the officers were in responsible positions at the time the taxes were or should have been collected and at the time trust moneys were dissipated, and (2) they ignored their obligations as responsible officers, knowingly and willfully diverting after-acquired cash to commercial creditors instead of paying the United States. Like Teel and Maggy, Davis's status and authority throughout the quarters, not his state of mind, made him a responsible person. As in *Maggy* and *Teel*, Davis's actions after he learned of the tax debt are what constituted willfulness. The arrival of a payment date, after all, does not by itself impose liability. It simply marks the fruition of liability--that is, responsibility--accumulated throughout the quarter as salaries were paid and/or trust funds dissipated. Similarly, a person may still be deemed responsible for a quarter's tax payment even if she no longer holds a responsible position when the payment date arrives. See *Slodov*, 436 U.S. at 247, 98 S.Ct. at 1785.

Numerous federal courts of appeals have followed *Teel's* and *Maggy's* holdings in the post-*Slodov* era, specifically rejecting in the process the argument Davis now proffers. In *Mazo*, the Fifth Circuit refused to extend *Slodov* to cases "[w]here there has been no change in [corporate] control." 591 F.2d at 1154. The Fifth Circuit emphasized that the Supreme Court specifically limited *Slodov* to the expenditure of funds acquired after new management's " 'accession to control.' " Id. (quoting *Slodov*, 436 U.S. at 259, 98 S.Ct. at 1791). Concluding that neither *Slodov's* language nor its rationale applied to continuing management, the Fifth Circuit held:

> In the case of individuals who are responsible persons both before and after withholding tax liability accrues, as the appellants were in this case, there is a duty to use unencumbered funds acquired after the withholding obligation becomes payable to satisfy that obligation; failure to do so when there is knowledge of the liability, as was the case here, constitutes willfulness.

591 F.2d at 1157.

All of the other circuits presented with Davis's argument unanimously have limited *Slodov* to changes in management control. [Eds: The court then discusses cases from the Third, Seventh, and Eighth Circuits].

C. The *Johnson* Decision

As an answer to the weight of authority rejecting his position, Davis offers Johnson v. Commissioner, 663 F.Supp. 294 (D.Utah 1987), a case that apparently no other court has followed. In *Johnson*, the district court tracked the argument Davis makes here and extended *Slodov* to corporate officers who, although responsible, did not actually know of the tax diversion until after the fact. [P]enalties cannot be imposed upon [responsible officers] based upon their payment of corporate creditors with cash acquired after they learned of failures to pay tax withholdings, so long as the responsible person did not play a "willful" role in that failure. Id. at 299.

We find *Johnson* unpersuasive. As noted earlier, contrary to the *Johnson* court's holding, neither *Slodov's* language nor its rationale compels excusing continuing management from liability under section 6672.

The *Johnson* approach, moreover, focuses too heavily on corporate officers' actual knowledge, effectively creating two tiers of responsible persons. The first tier consists of corporate officials like Johnson and

Davis who meet all of the traditional criteria for responsible status, but who do not knowingly play a role in the failure to collect, or the dissipation of, withholding taxes. The second tier would be those with responsibility *plus* actual participation in the loss of the trust funds--that is, "a person who was responsible throughout the period [and] *also* acted 'willfully' during that period of time." *Johnson*, 663 F.Supp. at 298. This scheme is inconsistent with our prior articulations of the responsibility test.

Furthermore, *Johnson* ignores the purpose of section 6672, which is to make the federal treasury whole and to encourage diligent compliance with the withholding rules by all those in a position to regulate a corporation's collection and disbursement of money. The *Johnson* approach undercuts this goal by rewarding officers for their ignorance. Davis would be a responsible officer in name only. Although found to have been in a position to prevent ITAC's tax delinquency, Davis would face no sanctions. To the contrary, *Johnson* would permit Davis to continue (as did the officers who actually dissipated the trust funds) to subordinate the public fisc to the corporation's private interests. Despite his responsibility for damage to the federal treasury, *Johnson* would allow Davis to continue to divert funds from the government to other commercial expenses he deems more worthy of the corporate dollar.

In the meantime, the federal government's interest in corporate revenues is held hostage to the continued success of the business. The federal government is in effect subsidizing the corporation's recovery by foregoing collectible tax dollars. Numerous courts have admonished against such interpretations of section 6672. See, e.g., *Thibodeau*, 828 F.2d at 1506 ("[T]he government cannot be made an unwilling partner in a business experiencing financial difficulties."); *Mazo*, 591 F.2d at 1154 ("[T]he United States may not be made an unwilling joint venturer in the corporate enterprise.").

In sum, we eschew adopting the *Johnson* theory of responsibility without consequences. Instead, we join the Third, Fifth, Seventh, and Eighth Circuits in refusing to extend *Slodov* to cases where the responsible officer presided over both the initial loss of the trust funds and the subsequent diversion of after-acquired revenues and hold that the district court properly instructed the jury on willfulness. To hold otherwise would ignore *Slodov's* plain language and analytical foundations, as well as frustrate the remedial and deterrent purposes of section 6672.

* * *

CONCLUSION

We affirm the district court's instructions on willfulness as consistent with *Slodov*. To hold otherwise (i) would be contrary to *Slodov's* language and rationale, (ii) would undermine this circuit's opinions in *Teel* and *Maggy*, (iii) would place this circuit in conflict with at least four other federal courts of appeals, and (iv) would frustrate section 6672's purpose. * * *

AFFIRMED.

Notes and Questions

Payroll taxes consist of two portions: (1) the employer's share of Social Security or FICA (Federal Insurance Contributions Act) taxes under § 3111 and FUTA (Federal Unemployment Tax Act) taxes under § 3301, and (2) the amount the employer is required to withhold from the wages of the employees and to remit quarterly to the government, consisting of income taxes under §§ 3401 and 3402, FICA taxes under § 3102, and RRA (Railroad Retirement Act) taxes under §3202 of the Code. It is the second portion that constitutes the trust fund taxes to which the § 6672 penalty applies. The employer remains liable directly for the first portion.

Section 6672(e), added under the Taxpayer Bill of Rights 2 in 1996, provides that unpaid voluntary board members of tax-exempt organizations are not considered responsible persons unless there is no other person who is considered responsible. In order to fall within this safe harbor, the volunteer must (1) serve solely in an honorary capacity, (2) must not participate in the day-to-day or financial operations of the organization, and (3) must not have actual knowledge of the failure on which the penalty is imposed. IRC § 6672(e).

Note that under the Internal Revenue Manual, trust fund recovery penalty cases are eligible for fast-track mediation (FTM), which allows the case to be completed in 30-40 days. In order to use FTM, though, both the taxpayer/responsible party and the Service must agree to mediate. The taxpayer has a right to appeal an adverse decision to the Appeals Office. I.R.M. 5.7.6.1.3.

1 What is the difference between transferee liability under § 6901 and trust fund liability under § 6672?

2 There can be more than one responsible person, and generally courts take a broad view of who qualifies. What degree of status, control or authority will result in a person being considered a responsible

person? See Gustin v. United States, 876 F.2d 485 (5th Cir. 1989); Wood v. United States, 808 F.2d 411 (5th Cir. 1987); Brown v. United States, 591 F.2d 1136 (5th Cir. 1979); Geiger v. United States, 583 F.Supp. 1166 (D. Ariz. 1984); Cellura v. United States, 245 F.Supp. 379 (N.D. Ohio 1965).

3. Will an individual be considered a responsible person if that person has control of insufficient corporate funds to pay the trust fund tax liability? See Morgan v. United States, 937 F.2d. 281 (5th Cir. 1991).

3. Joint and Several Liability

Although the employment taxes can be collected only once, if there is more than one responsible person, the Service can collect from any or all of them without apportioning the liability. If one responsible person pays more than her fair share of the taxes, that person may seek contribution from the other responsible parties. IRC § 6672(d).

McCRAY v. UNITED STATES
United States Court of Appeals, Fifth Circuit, 1990.
910 F.2d 1289.

Before CLARK, CHIEF JUDGE, REAVLEY and KING, CIRCUIT JUDGES.
PER CURIAM:

I.

Shannon Advertising, a Texas corporation, was owned in equal shares by Louis Scott, Michael McCray, Andrew Martin, and Leonard Raines. Shannon did not pay over its federal employee withholding taxes for the first, second, and third quarters of 1982. Under 26 U.S.C. § 6672 (1954), the Internal Revenue Service (IRS) assessed each of the four owners a penalty of 100% of the payments due. McCray paid $750 and sued for a refund. The IRS counterclaimed, joining the other owners. McCray and the IRS entered a stipulation of dismissal of his refund claim. The district court entered an agreed judgment between the IRS and Martin stating that Martin is jointly and severally liable for 100% of the penalty. The court also granted the motion of the United States for summary judgment against Scott and Raines, holding each liable for 100% of the § 6672 penalty.

II.

Scott raises two issues. He states that he should not be held responsible for paying the penalty because he did not willfully fail to pay over the trust funds as a matter of law. He claims he relied on the other owners, who were in charge of the affairs of the business, and the business's accountants and lawyers to see that the proper taxes were paid. Scott also contends that the district court erred in entering judgment against him for more than the full amount of the penalty now due. He only received credit for the amount which he has paid, yet two of Scott's jointly liable co- defendants have also made partial payments to the IRS. Scott argues that these amounts should have been credited to him in the court's judgment against him.

The summary judgment proof showed Scott is clearly a person responsible for the payment of the withholding tax. Although Scott was not the corporate officer directly in charge of paying federal taxes, he was chairman of the board of directors and a vice president. He admitted knowing as early as June 1982 that the withheld taxes had not been paid over. After that date, he used corporate funds to pay other creditors before paying the delinquent taxes. This makes him a responsible party who willfully withheld tax payments.

As to the amount of the assessment, the IRS states that it is Service policy to collect only 100% of the amount due from any group of jointly liable persons. Because responsible persons are jointly and severally liable under § 6672 for the delinquent taxes, US Life Title Ins. Co. of Dallas v. Harbison, 784 F.2d 1238, 1243 (5th Cir.1986), IRS procedure is to seek a judgment against each party for the full amount due and later abate the total liability by the accumulation of amounts paid by each responsible party. This abatement does not occur, however, until the "expiration of the statutory period for commencement of a refund suit or, if a refund suit is filed, upon final adjudication of the action." Gens v. United States, 615 F.2d 1335, 1340, 222 Ct.Cl. 407 (1980). The IRS argues that in this case the possibility existed at the time of judgment that the owners who had paid portions of the amount due might sue for a refund. The IRS argument here is the same as that accepted by the court in *US Life*:

> Until the limitations period for seeking a refund expires, it cannot be determined with certainty whether the Government will be entitled to retain the funds it has collected. The six-year period for collecting the liabilities assessed against the remaining responsible persons, see 26 U.S.C. § 6502(a), could expire while the first responsible person's refund claim is still pending. In such circumstances, if the

Government were prohibited from pursuing collection activities against the other responsible persons, a successful claim for refund by one of the responsible persons would have the effect of defeating collection of the full amount of the underlying taxes.

784 F.2d at 1244. *US Life*, however, prefaced that explanation of the IRS's prerogative to pursue each responsible party for the full amount of the penalty due by stating:

> It should be noted that the problem involved here is not present when each responsible person has litigated her liability under Section 6672. When a person against whom an assessment has been made contests her liability by instituting a refund suit, the Government joins the other persons against whom Section 6672 assessments have been made. This procedure resolves doubt as to whom the Government may look to for payment of the withholding tax delinquency.

784 F.2d at 1243-44. This passage describes the procedural history of the present case. We are told that each responsible person other than Scott now has either reached a binding settlement with the United States or has had a final and unappealed judgment rendered against him. The United States is no longer in danger of losing its right to collect the full amount due. Since Service policy does not permit recovery of more than the amount due plus interest on the unpaid balance, Scott can secure an administrative adjustment for any amount finally paid by joint debtors plus the proper interest credit.

III.

The judgment of the district court against Scott is affirmed without prejudice to the pursuit by Scott of the administrative remedies the IRS assures us are available to adjust the credit he claims are due him as one jointly and severally liable with joint judgment debtors who have finally paid some portion of the common debt.

AFFIRMED.

Notes

Note that the Service can reach a settlement with one or more responsible persons, yet continue to pursue collection action against other responsible persons. See, e.g., Monday v. United States, 421 F.2d 1210 (7th Cir. 1970); Herzig v. United States, 83-1 USTC ¶ 9232 (N.D. Ohio 1983).

If a responsible person is bankrupt and files a petition with the bankruptcy court, the liability for the trust fund tax is not dischargeable, so the person remains liable. Note also that if an employer corporation files a bankruptcy petition, triggering the automatic stay, the Service may continue to proceed against the responsible persons.

4. Allocation of Partial Payment

If an employer submits a partial payment of employment taxes with no specific instructions, the Service will allocate the payment in a manner that serves the best interest of the government. See Rev. Proc. 2002-26, 2002-1 C.B. 746. Thus, it is the Service's policy to apply voluntary payments on a corporate account first to the non-trust fund portion of the deficiency. See I.R.M. 5.7.7. If the taxpayer wishes to have the payment applied to the trust fund portion, she must specifically designate in writing the payment to be applied to that portion.

If a partial payment is submitted by a responsible person, is this payment considered voluntary, thus enabling that person to direct the payment to the trust fund taxes?

MUNTWYLER v. UNITED STATES
United States Court of Appeals, Seventh Circuit, 1983.
703 F.2d 1030.

PELL, CIRCUIT JUDGE.

The United States appeals from a decision of the district court awarding appellee Fredric C. Muntwyler (taxpayer) a refund of $1288.30 plus interest for overpayment of taxes. The court ruled that the assignee of the assets of the taxpayer's corporation was entitled to direct that the tax payments he made to the Internal Revenue Service (IRS) be applied to trust fund tax liabilities because the payments were voluntary. The Government contends that the payments were involuntary and thus that the IRS was not bound by the assignee's directions and could apply the payments to non-trust fund tax liabilities.

I. FACTS

Fredric C. Muntwyler was the president, treasurer, director, and majority shareholder of Air Mid-America Airlines for the period relevant to this case. Air Mid-America was an Illinois corporation formed in 1968. Beginning in late 1972, the company suffered financial losses and ceased doing business in May 1973. Because of these problems, the company failed to pay certain employees' withholding taxes (trust fund taxes) and excise taxes (non-trust fund taxes).

On June 13, 1973, the company assigned all of its assets to Bernard C. Chaitman, who served as a trustee for the benefit of Air Mid-America's creditors. Chaitman was authorized to collect debts payable to the company, sell the company's interests in the assigned assets, and pay the claims of the company's creditors.

In August 1973, the IRS filed a claim with Chaitman for unpaid corporate taxes totalling $32,242.47, representing both trust fund and non-trust fund liabilities. On August 25, 1973, Chaitman presented three checks to the IRS, totalling $12,132.93, all of which directed that they be applied to the trust fund portion of the tax liabilities. The Service accepted the checks but refused to honor the directions for application of the money to the trust fund liability; instead, it allocated the entire amount to the non-trust fund liability.

On November 3, 1976, the IRS assessed the taxpayer $18,633.21 in trust fund taxes and, on November 15, $1,030.02 in non-trust fund taxes. On April 15, 1977, the IRS credited the taxpayer's $13,526 unrelated 1976 overpayment to the withholding liabilities. On May 5, 1977, the taxpayer paid $1288.30 toward the tax liabilities, and then filed a claim for a refund. On June 6, 1980, after the IRS rejected his claim for refund of the $1288.30, the taxpayer brought this action for refund in the United States District Court for the Northern District of Illinois. On December 22, 1980, the taxpayer filed a second claim for refund with the IRS, seeking to collect the $13,526 credited from his 1976 overpayment. The IRS rejected the claim and the taxpayer amended his complaint to include a claim for a refund of this money.

Both parties filed motions for summary judgment. On February 26, 1982, the district court granted the appellee's motion, holding that the assignee's payment was voluntary and thus that the IRS should have followed his direction as to the payment. The court awarded the taxpayer $1288.30 plus interest in the amount of $550.55. The court ruled that the claim for a refund of the $13,526 in credited overpayments was barred by the statute of limitations, a ruling that the taxpayer does not contest. The Government appealed.

II. VOLUNTARINESS

The Internal Revenue Code directs employers to deduct and withhold a tax upon wages paid. 26 U.S.C. § 3401(a). The withheld taxes are deemed to be held in a special fund in trust for the United States, id. § 7501(a), and accordingly every person required to collect and pay over such a tax (including an officer of the corporation, like the taxpayer here, id. § 6671(b)) is personally liable for the full amount of the tax not paid, id. § 6672. An individual, like the taxpayer, is not personally liable for unpaid non-trust fund taxes. What the taxpayer sought to do in this case was to extinguish his personal liability for unpaid trust fund taxes by having the assignee direct that the payments be credited against the trust fund liability.

When a taxpayer makes voluntary payments to the IRS, he has a right to direct the application of payments to whatever type of liability he chooses. If the taxpayer makes a voluntary payment without directing the application of the funds, the IRS may make whatever allocation it chooses.

When a payment is involuntary, IRS policy is to allocate the payments as it sees fit. This rule has been uniformly followed by the courts. See, e.g., United States v. De Beradinis, 395 F.Supp. 944, 952 (D.Conn.1975), aff'd mem., 538 F.2d 315 (2d Cir.1976). Despite the appellee's objection, we accept this rule as sensible tax policy. The sole question, therefore, is whether the district court correctly held that the assignee's payment was voluntary.

The Government's position is that a payment is involuntary if it is made pursuant to administrative or judicial action. The Government claims that by submitting a claim for unpaid taxes to the assignee, the IRS took administrative action sufficient to make the resulting payment involuntary. The district court, by contrast, held that court involvement or administrative seizure of property was required to make a payment involuntary.

A starting point for ascertaining whether the payments were voluntary is the Tax Court's frequently cited definition of involuntary payments in Amos v. Commissioner, 47 T.C. 65, 69 (1966): "An involuntary payment of Federal taxes means any payment received by agents of the United States as a result of distraint or levy or from a legal proceeding in which the Government is seeking to collect its delinquent taxes or file a claim therefor." The Government contends that this case falls within the *Amos* definition of involuntariness because the claim it filed was an administrative action, just as a levy is an administrative action.

We disagree. The distinction between a voluntary and involuntary payment in *Amos* and all the other cases is not made on the basis of the presence of administrative action alone, but rather the presence of court action or administrative action resulting in an actual *seizure* of property or money as in a levy. No authorities support the proposition that a payment is involuntary whenever an agency takes even the slightest action to collect taxes, such as filing a claim or, as appears to be a logical extension of the Government's position, telephoning or writing the taxpayer to inform him of taxes due.

The strongest indication that our holding is correct is the language of the IRS policy statement on which the Government bases its claim in this case. In discussing 26 U.S.C. § 6672, the section making a corporate officer liable for trust fund taxes, the statement says: "The taxpayer, of course, has no right of designation in the case of collections resulting from *enforced collection measures*." Policy Statement P-5-60, reprinted in Internal Revenue Manual (CCH) 1305-15 (emphasis added). Use of the phrase "enforced collection measures" belies the Government's contention that any administrative action is enough to render payment made in response to that action involuntary. We do not understand how the Government can reasonably argue that merely filing a claim for back taxes is an "enforced collection measure."

Furthermore, the cases uniformly define an involuntary payment as one made pursuant to judicial action or some form of administrative seizure, like a levy. A recent case on the subject is Arnone v. United States, 79-1 U.S. Tax Cas. (CCH) ¶ 9356 (N.D.Ohio 1979). There, the court held that the payment was involuntary because it was pursuant to a levy on a bank account: "[T]he plaintiff had no right to direct the application of funds obtained through enforced collection by administrative seizure." Id. at 86,846. Similarly, the court in United States v. De Beradinis, 395 F.Supp. 944 (D.Conn.1975), aff'd mem., 538 F.2d 315 (2d Cir.1976), held that payments were involuntary where "they resulted from Internal Revenue levies or participation in litigation." Id. at 952.

Cases holding that payments made in bankruptcy are involuntary do not support the Government's position because court action is involved. In First National City Bank v. Kline, 439 F.Supp. 726, 729 (S.D.N.Y.1977), the court held the payments involuntary, saying that "[w]here, as here, moneys are repaid under judicial order, the court has exclusive authority to apply the funds." Likewise, in O'Dell v. United States, 326 F.2d 451, 456 (10th Cir.1964), the court said that a debtor could not direct application of his money to such debts as he chose "where, as here, the payment is made involuntarily as in an execution or judicial sale." In the instant case, there was no levy, judicial order, execution, or judicial sale; rather, there was a mere filing of a claim.

The Government contends that In re Bulk Sale of Inventory, 6 Kan.App.2d 579, 631 P.2d 258 (1981), supports its position that administrative action is sufficient to render a payment involuntary. In that case, the corporation turned over its assets to auctioneers, who sold them. The auctioneers then deposited the sale proceeds into the registry of a state district court and filed an interpleader action requesting that creditors of the corporation be permitted to file their claims in the court, which would determine the amount to which each was entitled. The United States filed a claim with the court for unpaid withholding taxes. The district court directed payments to the Government. 631 P.2d at 259-60.

Although the Government argues that the involvement of the court was irrelevant to the Kansas court's ruling, the language of the case shows that it was precisely the court's involvement that was dispositive. The court said that although the debtor's act of turning over the corporation's assets to auctioneers was voluntary, "when the sums derived from that sale were paid into the district court and creditors were advised to file claims *so that the court could decide the amount and priority to which each was entitled,* the payments *so ordered* were involuntary." 631 P.2d at 262 (emphasis added).

Finally, the Government argues that the situation in the instant case "is in no material respect different than if * * * the Government had seized corporate assets to satisfy the corporate liability or had filed a claim in a bankruptcy[2] or receivership proceeding." This simply is wrong. That the IRS *could have* seized the assets does not mandate that we hold that filing a claim is the same as seizing the property. We will not interpret "involuntary" to mean something completely at odds with the normal understanding of the term and against all authority simply to reach an arguably desirable result or to correct what may have been a mistake in collection tactics by the IRS.

CONCLUSION

For the foregoing reasons, the judgment of the district court is affirmed.

Notes and Question

The Service's policy of applying undesignated partial payments first to non-trust fund taxes has been upheld by the First Circuit in Sotir v.

---

2. The Government might have been correct in its claim if the corporation had been in bankruptcy, which it was not. An assignment for the benefit of creditors is an act of bankruptcy and presumably any creditor, including the Government, could have proceeded to file an involuntary petition for bankruptcy based thereon, but no creditor, including the Government, did so. We do not equate the assignment for the benefit of creditors with a formal bankruptcy proceeding.

United States, 978 F.2d 29 (1st Cir. 1992); see also Begier v. IRS, in § B., above. Why does the Service direct unspecified payments first to the non-trust portion of the liability?

5. Lenders and Sureties

When a business is floundering financially, the lender or surety may try to minimize its losses by advancing only the bare amount necessary for the business to stay afloat. This may mean advancing only the net amount of the wage liability (i.e., without the withholding taxes), knowing that the business will not be able to pay this obligation on its own. Another situation that often arises with financially distressed businesses is where the lender actually takes over the management, or partial management, of the business and either pays the debtor's wage obligations directly, without paying the trust fund taxes, or directs the company not to pay its withholding tax obligations.

If the lender or surety exerts enough control over the payment of the wage claims, it can be considered a responsible party under § 6672 and thus liable for 100% of the unpaid payroll taxes. Under § 3505(a), a lender or surety who pays wages directly to the debtor's employees, without paying the requisite payroll taxes, will be liable for 100% of the unpaid taxes, without regard to willfulness. If the lender or surety advances amounts to a debtor for payment of net-wages and the lender/surety had actual notice or knowledge that the debtor did not intend to pay the trust fund taxes, § 3505(b) imposes liability on the lender/surety for the unpaid taxes, plus interest up to a cap of 25% of the amount loaned to the debtor.

When the lender/surety advances a net amount to the debtor for the payment of wages and the lender/surety directs the debtor to forego paying the trust fund taxes, is the government limited to proceeding against the lender solely under § 3505(b) or may it also proceed under § 6672?

UNITED STATES v. SECURITY PACIFIC BUSINESS CREDIT, INC.
United States Court of Appeals, Seventh Circuit, 1992.
956 F.2d 703.

POSNER, CIRCUIT JUDGE.

We must try to make sense of two overlapping tax statutes that lack any implicit or explicit cross-reference—statutes that exist as it were in a state of mutual oblivion. The earlier enacted one, 26 U.S.C. § 6672(a), imposes "a penalty equal to the total amount of the tax evaded, or not collected, or not accounted for and paid over" on anyone who, being "required to collect, truthfully account for, and pay over any tax," willfully fails to do so. The usual application of this, the "responsible persons" statute, is to employers, or their executives, who fail to remit withholding taxes to the government. The later statute, 26 U.S.C. § 3505(b), provides that if a lender lends money to an employer for the purpose of enabling the employer to pay wages, and knows that the employer will not pay the withholding taxes due on those wages, the lender, even if he does not exert enough control over the employer's affairs to be deemed a responsible person, shall be liable to the government "in a sum equal to the taxes (together with interest) which are not paid over to the United States by such employer with respect to such wages." However, this statute caps the lender's liability at 25 percent of his loan. The responsible-persons statute contains no such cap. It also makes no reference to interest, and this has been assumed to mean that the responsible person has no liability for interest on unpaid taxes that accrues between the date that the employer's tax should have been paid and the date on which the Internal Revenue Service assessed the statutory penalty. So at least the parties to this case assume and they are not alone in this assumption. First National Bank v. United States, 591 F.2d 1143, 1149 (5th Cir.1979); Note, "Taxation: Lender Liability Under I.R.C. § 3505(a)," 39 Okla.L.Rev. 348, 352 n. 27 (1986). Though we have found no analysis of the question, the assumption is reasonable. The penalty is measured by the tax required to be withheld from the employees' paychecks and paid over to the government, and that tax if duly withheld and paid over would include no interest--interest accrues only if the tax is *not* withheld and paid over on time. In contrast, the words "together with interest" in section 3505 have been interpreted--inevitably, we should think--to mean that the net-payroll lender is liable for interest on payroll taxes from the date on which they should have been paid to the government, as well as for the taxes themselves. Treas.Reg. § 31.3505-1(b)(1)(ii).

The net-payroll lender statute provides that payments made under it shall be credited against the tax (and, presumably, interest) due from the employer, the original taxpayer. 26 U.S.C. § 3505(c). There is no counterpart in section 6672 but the policy of the Internal Revenue Service is similar: it tries to collect the tax due only once, thereby treating the section 6672 "penalty" as a tax. It might seem that if the Service had managed to collect the tax owed it by the employer there would be no responsible-person liability in any event and so no need for an administrative policy of lenity. But there could be liability: The responsible person might have caused the taxpayer not to pay the tax, yet the Service might have collected it anyway in enforcement proceedings. Or it might have collected only part of it. Yet the Service's policy is, as we have said, not to pile the penalty atop the tax. If for example the Service were owed $100,000 by the employer, and it managed to squeeze $10,000 out of him, it would assess the responsible person, if there were one, only $90,000. What it would do if the employer owed $90,000 in tax and $10,000 in interest and could pay only $20,000--whether, in other words, the Service would dun the responsible person for $70,000 (thereby ignoring interest) or $80,000--we do not know. We see no statutory obstacle to its collecting the full $80,000. For that matter, there is no apparent statutory obstacle to the Service's collecting the full tax from the taxpayer and the full penalty from the responsible person. Apparently the Service declines to take the penalty route because it fears that if it treated section 6672 as a *real* penalty rather than merely as a device for collecting unpaid taxes the courts would impose too heavy a burden of proof on it.

The overlap between the two statutes has been analyzed extensively, Note, supra; Larry A. Makel & James C. Chadwick, "Lender Liability for a Borrower's Unpaid Payroll Taxes," 43 Bus. Lawyer 507 (1988); Richard A. Kaye, "A Primer on the Defense of Banks Against Liability for Unpaid Withholding Taxes," 2 Compleat Lawyer 37 (1985); Ronald Michael Meneo, "Lender Liability Under Sections 6672 and 3505," 3 Rev. Taxation of Individuals 181 (1989), but the specific question of cumulative liability has not been analyzed at all, so far as we can find; and, as we have said, it also has not been the subject of a reported case.

Security Pacific, the defendant in this case, was a heavy lender to Mystic Tape, Inc., which early in 1983 defaulted. Security Pacific took control of Mystic's finances, telling it what it could and could not spend money on. Over a period of six weeks Security Pacific lent Mystic almost half a million dollars for the purpose of paying Mystic's employees--on condition that none of this money be used to pay withholding taxes, although Security Pacific well knew that Mystic had no other source of funds that it could use to pay those taxes. At the end of the six weeks Mystic filed for bankruptcy, and from then on it paid its withholding taxes when due. But it never paid the withholding taxes due for the six weeks.

In 1987 the Internal Revenue Service slapped an assessment of $241,488.70 on Security Pacific under section 6672 and a further assessment on it of $123,009.50 under section 3505. The first figure represented the amount of withholding taxes that Mystic should have paid but did not pay during the period when its wage bill was financed by Security Pacific. The second figure represented pre-assessment interest (up to 25 percent of Security Pacific's loan) on the $241,488.70 in unpaid withholding taxes. When Security Pacific refused to pay either amount and the government sued, the complaint asked for these sums in the alternative; but five days before the trial the judge permitted the government to change the word "alternative" to "additional." At trial the judge found that Security Pacific had been both a section 6672 responsible person and a section 3505 net-payroll lender, and concluded that since the amount sought by the government under the latter section was for (part of the) preassessment interest, which section 3505 allows, and did not exceed 25 percent of the amount of the loan, the government was entitled to both amounts. 735 F.Supp. 1421 (S.D.Ind.1991). He entered judgment accordingly, from which Security Pacific appeals, complaining only about the cumulation of remedies and not about the judge's finding that it is liable under both sections.

Security Pacific points out correctly that any lender who so far controls his borrower's disbursements as to be adjudged a responsible person will almost certainly violate the net-payroll lender statute as well, and in such a case, it argues, the 25 percent cap will be nugatory if we allow a cumulation of remedies. For the loan to Mystic was for less than $500,000 while the judgment against Security Pacific is for almost $400,000--which is 80 percent of the loan rather than 25 percent. Indeed the preassessment interest alone exceeded the 25 percent cap and had to be cut down accordingly. Security Pacific argues that the government should be content with enforcing full responsible-person liability against it under 6672 and should not use 3505, in violation of the spirit as well as letter of the 25 percent ceiling in that statute, to circumvent Congress's unexplained decision not to allow the collection of preassessment interest from responsible persons.

That is one way to look at this pair of statutes but not the only or the best way. Consider to begin with a case in which the responsible person and the lender are two different persons, rather than one as in this case, and assume the assessments are as in this case, with the principal amount of the tax being assessed against the responsible person and preassessment interest against the lender. The responsible person cannot complain, because he is made to pay no more than he owes. The net-payroll lender cannot complain either, because interest is one of the things he owes, and the amount he is made to pay is under the 25 percent ceiling. The government obtains no windfall, for it merely collects the tax plus interest. It is not as if Congress didn't *want* the government to collect the tax plus interest. That would be an implausible suggestion. The tax is due, and unpaid; the taxpayer therefore owes interest as well as tax, and isn't paying the interest either; so the government has had to turn elsewhere for the money. So long as the government doesn't collect more than it is owed, it can hardly be accused of seeking windfalls.

Section 6672 is silent on preassessment interest, that is true, and it has been assumed, though perhaps prematurely for all we know, that silence in this matter should be construed as a limitation. But no one has given us a *reason* for the omission, and we have not been able to think up one on our own. It appears to have been an oversight. The later statute allows a less culpable entity to be assessed both tax and interest, and while there is the 25 percent cap, often it will be above the sum of tax and preassessment interest, especially if the loan was outstanding for only a short time. So it is not as if Congress had some *aversion* to making persons who are complicit in withholding-tax violations liable for the full cost of the violation to the government, and we are reluctant to truncate section 3505 in order to protect a nonexistent policy.

Security Pacific asks us to impute omniscience to Congress. Congress *must* have had a reason for not making the penalty in section 6672 equal to the sum of the tax due and interest on the tax, and *must* have had a reason when it plugged the net-payroll lender loophole in section 6672 by passing section 3505 for not taking the opportunity to amend the older statute to make responsible persons liable for preassessment interest too. But legislative omniscience is not a realistic assumption. Moreover it belongs to a style of statutory interpretation–the rule-bound style rather than the purposive–that places greater emphasis on the text of statutes than on intentions behind them. In this case the government has the text on its side, while from the standpoint of purposive interpretation we can find no indication that artificially curtailing the government's right to its tax revenues in a case such as this would serve the desires or intentions of Congress.

We have been discussing the hypothetical case in which the responsible person and the lender are two different persons but the analysis is unchanged if they are the same person. Liability for two wrongs that inflict two distinct harms is not generally less just because the two wrongs are committed by one person rather than by two. Why should it be less here? There is no reason to believe that by failing to provide for preassessment interest in section 6672 Congress meant to confer a benefit on a lender who should happen to be a responsible person as well–who should, that is, actually compound his wrongdoing. There is no reason to believe that by placing a 25 percent ceiling on a net-payroll lender's liability Congress intended to benefit a responsible person, for it is only by virtue of the money that it has been ordered to pay as a responsible person that Security Pacific can argue that the ceiling has been pierced. The interest assessment under 3505 didn't pierce it, because the government limited that assessment to 25 percent of the loan.

It is true that if a net-payroll lender were always also a responsible person, the 25 percent ceiling would be a nullity. But this conjunction, at least if we can judge from the absence of reported cases, is unusual. Therefore we do not deprive the ceiling of all practical effect, as Security Pacific argues, by allowing the government to proceed unhindered against the responsible person who happens also to be a lender. And anyway Security Pacific did benefit from the cap in this case, since the preassessment interest exceeded 25 percent of its loan and was therefore cut back.

* * *

AFFIRMED.

Notes and Questions

Section 3505 was enacted in 1966 under the Federal Tax Lien Act. Prior to this time, only "employers" were liable for failure to pay withholding taxes. This caused problems for the government, primarily in dealing with the construction industry where a cash-strapped subcontractor would obtain interim financing, often from the general contractor, who in the interest of keeping costs down would advance only the amount of the net wages. The subcontractor/employer would be liable for the unpaid withholding taxes, but often would be judgement-proof. The government then would have no further recourse to collect the taxes from the contractor, despite the contractor's knowledge and complicity.

Under § 3505(a), a lender who assumes the obligation to pay wages directly to a debtor's employees becomes liable for the entire amount of unpaid withholding taxes, without regard to knowledge or control, and without a 25% limitation.

The Service bears the burden of proving the lender had actual knowledge that the proceeds of the loan were to be used for the payment of wages and that the debtor/employer did not intend to pay the withholding taxes. Note that a lender who advances a working capital loan to a debtor/employer is not obligated to determine the specific use the borrower intends to make of the loan, nor is the lender obligated to specifically determine the ability of the borrower to pay taxes. See

Michael I. Saltzman, IRS PRACTICE AND PROCEDURE ¶ 17.11[3] (Revised 2d Ed. 2002).

1. Who bears the ultimate burden of the payroll taxes when a lender or surety becomes liable?

2. What procedure must the Service follow in collecting the 100% penalty against a lender and what statute of limitations applies?

IV. ALTERNATIVE COLLECTION

A taxpayer who cannot afford to pay her tax liability in full has several alternatives, depending upon the extent of her financial woes. If her circumstances are dire, the taxpayer can consider filing a bankruptcy petition and allow the bankruptcy court to take control of her finances and liabilities. If this is not palatable to the taxpayer or feasible, she can consider making a request to the IRS to suspend collection on the ground of economic hardship. If this request is granted, the Service classifies the case as "currently not collectible" (CNC). The burden is on the taxpayer to prove that the hardship is sufficiently severe to cause her to be unable to pay her tax liability. Examples of such hardship include a terminal illness or excessive medical bills; incarceration; unemployment with no other source of income other than Social Security, unemployment or welfare payments; or where the taxpayer's income does not exceed necessary living expenses. If the Service agrees with the taxpayer that the tax is not collectible, § 6434(e) requires the Service to immediately release any levy on wages or salary. See also I.R.M. 5.16.1. Note, though, that the Service regards the case as *currently* not collectible. The case remains open but inactive; thus, interest continues to run on the tax due. Moreover, if the Service thinks the taxpayer may have the ability to pay at any time within the ten year collection period, it may move the case to collectible or active status.

If the taxpayer's financial woes are less dire, so that she can afford to pay some of the tax liability, she can make an offer in compromise in which she can propose to pay less than the amount she owes. If she is able to pay the entire tax liability but not at the current time, she may enter into an installment arrangement with the Service. She also may request an extension of time to pay. Unlike an extension of time to file, the payment extension is not automatic, but is granted discretionarily by the Service upon a showing of hardship by the taxpayer.

There are other informal collection devices as well, but the most common seem to be installment payment arrangements and offers in compromise.

A. INSTALLMENT PAYMENT ARRANGEMENTS

When a taxpayer is not insolvent but has cash-flow problems to the extent that she cannot afford to pay her tax liability in full when it is due, she may consider an installment arrangement to pay the liability over a period of time in order to avoid enforced collection action. Section 6159(a), enacted under the 1998 IRS Restructuring and Reform Act, authorizes the Service to enter into written agreements with the taxpayer to provide for the payment of tax in installments if the Service "determines that such agreement will facilitate collection" of the tax.

There are three general types of installment payment arrangements (IPAs): (1) a "guaranteed" IPA, (2) a streamlined arrangement, and (3) a general installment arrangement.

Guaranteed IPAs. Although an installment payment arrangement remains largely within the discretion of the Service, § 6159(c) requires the Service to enter into such an agreement when the taxpayer establishes that she is financially unable to pay the tax in full when due (IRC § 6159(c)(3)), the aggregate amount of the tax (determined without regard to penalties and interest) does not exceed $10,000, the agreement provides for payment of the tax in full within three years, and the taxpayer has not within the preceding five taxable years entered into an installment agreement. During the preceding five-year period, the taxpayer also must not have failed to file any tax return or pay any tax required to be shown on the return(s). This guaranteed arrangement otherwise falls under the rules discussed below for general IPAs.

Streamlined Arrangement. If a taxpayer's current tax liability does not exceed $25,000, including penalties and interest, and she demonstrates an inability to pay her current tax liability, she may be entitled to a streamlined installment arrangement, provided her delinquent taxes can be paid fully within 60 months. This arrangement, unlike the general IPA, requires neither a financial statement nor management approval.

General IPA. A general installment payment agreement is not guaranteed, even though the taxpayer establishes an inability to pay. Typically, the Service tries to persuade the taxpayer to pay the full amount due immediately. Only if this tactic fails will the Service consider an IPA. In considering the request for an IPA, the Service may demand a financial statement from the taxpayer, and may reject the taxpayer's request on the ground that the taxpayer has assets that can be liquidated, or that the taxpayer can forego spending on luxury items in order to pay the government. Sometimes the Service may suggest that the taxpayer obtain a loan to pay the tax. Do you see any problem with this suggestion?

In order to obtain an IPA, the taxpayer must not be delinquent in paying any other tax liability. If the taxpayer obtains an IPA, she must take care to pay all installment payments when due and she must supply an updated financial condition statement upon request by the Service. If she fails to do either of these things, the Service may unilaterally alter, modify, or terminate the agreement after giving her 30 days notice of the intended action and an explanation of why the action is being undertaken. If the taxpayer has supplied inaccurate or incomplete information to the Service in order to obtain the IPA, or if the Service believes the collection of the tax is in jeopardy, it may terminate the agreement.

If a request for an IPA is denied, the taxpayer has 30 days to file an appeal with the Service. During this 30-day period, and during the pendency of the appeal, the Service may not levy against the taxpayer. IRC § 6331(k). Similarly, the Service may not levy against the taxpayer's property while an IPA offer is pending, nor during the period an IPA is in effect. IRC § 6331(k)(2). This prohibition does not apply, however, if the Service believes the collection of the tax is in jeopardy. IRC §§ 6331(i)(3) and 6331(k)(3).

A taxpayer may agree to a payroll deduction plan in which the employer withholds the amount of the IPA payments from the employee's wages and remits them directly to the Service. In the alternative, the taxpayer may agree to allow the Service to debit her bank account directly. The advantage of these payment options is that the taxpayer is less likely to default on a payment. The disadvantage is that the taxpayer forfeits some of her right to privacy because the employer must agree to the withholding option. If the taxpayer previously has defaulted on any of the payments under the IPA, the Service may require either of these payment methods as a condition of obtaining or maintaining an IPA.

During the pendency of the arrangement, interest and penalties continue to accrue. Under the 1998 IRS Restructuring and Reform Act, however, the delinquent payment penalty under § 6651(a)(2) is limited to half the usual rate for any month in which an IPA is in effect. IRC § 6651(h). Also under the 1998 Act, the Service is required to provide the taxpayer with an annual statement listing the taxpayer's initial tax balance, all payments made under the IPA during the year, and the balance of the tax liability remaining at the end of the year.

Notes

An IPA prevents the Service from pursuing any further collection action against the taxpayer, but it does not prevent the Service from filing a notice of tax lien against the taxpayer.

If the Service determines that the taxpayer's financial situation has improved, it can unilaterally rescind or modify the agreement. IRC § 6159(b)(3). The taxpayer, on the other hand, cannot unilaterally reduce the amount of the payments if her financial condition worsens. Instead, the taxpayer should attempt to renegotiate the agreement in light of her changed circumstances.

B. OFFERS IN COMPROMISE

An offer in compromise is a binding contractual agreement between the taxpayer and the Service to compromise a civil or criminal tax liability (including penalties, interest, and any other additions to tax) for less than the full amount due, and to determine how that amount will be paid. The offer must be made in writing on a Form 656, Offer in Compromise. The taxpayer must be current on all taxes, and must remain current for at least five years if the offer is accepted. It is important that the Service believe the offer is made in good faith, that it represents a legitimate compromise based on the taxpayer's ability to pay, and that it is not a tactic to delay collection action.

The Service may make a counterproposal to the taxpayer's initial offer. If the Service accepts the taxpayer's offer or the parties reach an agreement, the taxpayer's liability for the stated period is conclusively settled and can be reopened only for fraud (supplying false information or documents, and concealing assets) or for a mutual mistake of material fact. Reg. § 301.7122-1(d)(5). Moreover, the acceptance of the offer in compromise will result in the removal of any Notice of Federal Tax Lien that has been filed against the taxpayer.

An offer cannot be rejected solely on the basis of the amount of the offer, although it can be rejected on the ground that the Service believes it can collect more than the taxpayer is proposing, or that it would not be in the best interests of the government to accept the compromise. I.R.M. 5.8.7.5. An offer will not be accepted if the taxpayer is in bankruptcy or is not current in all filing and payment requirements. A taxpayer may administratively appeal a rejection of an offer if the taxpayer makes a request for an administrative review within 30 days of the date of the letter of rejection.

FOWLER v. COMMISSIONER
United States Tax Court, 2004.
T.C. Memo. 2004-163

MEMORANDUM FINDINGS OF FACT AND OPINION

GERBER, CHIEF J.

Respondent, on February 21, 2002, sent Mark Fowler (petitioner) a Notice of Determination Concerning Collection Action(s) Under Section 63201 and/or 6330, in which respondent sustained the filing of a Federal tax lien for petitioner's 1990-92 tax liabilities. In that same notice respondent also rejected petitioner's offer in compromise. On that same date respondent sent Mark Fowler and Joylyn Souter-Fowler (petitioners) a second Notice of Determination Concerning Collection Action(s) Under Section 6320 and/or 6330. In this notice respondent sustained the filing of a Federal tax lien with respect to petitioners' 1994-96 tax liabilities, and respondent again rejected petitioners' offer in compromise.

Prior to these determinations, petitioners sought and were offered an Appeals hearing, but they did not attend due to personal reasons. One month after the scheduled hearing date, the Appeals officer issued the above determinations sustaining the filing of the Federal tax liens and rejecting petitioners' offers in compromise. With respect to both determinations, petitioners appealed to this Court.

The issue for consideration is whether respondent abused his discretion by rejecting petitioners' offers in compromise and by sustaining the filing of the Federal tax liens.

FINDINGS OF FACT

Petitioners resided in Garden Grove, California, when the petition in this case was filed.

Separate Liabilities

Petitioner filed his 1990 Federal income tax return late on September 6, 1991. On July 21, 1993, respondent mailed a statutory notice of deficiency to petitioner for his 1990 taxable year. Petitioner did not petition this Court to dispute the deficiency. On December 20, 1993, respondent assessed the $399 income tax deficiency and a $98.74 late-filing penalty under section 6651(a)(1). In addition, $104.40 of interest was assessed. Petitioner does not contest the 1990 tax liability.

Petitioner timely filed his 1991 Federal income tax return that contained several mathematical errors. Respondent corrected the mathematical errors in accord with section 6213(b)(1), and assessments were made to correct the errors. Respondent subsequently selected petitioner's 1991 return for an audit examination. On April 5, 1994, respondent mailed petitioner a statutory notice of deficiency for his 1991 taxable year determining a $545 income tax deficiency. Petitioner did not petition this Court with respect to the 1991 notice of deficiency. On September 5, 1994, respondent assessed the $545 deficiency and $103.37 of accrued interest.

Petitioner filed his 1992 Federal income tax return late on July 28, 1993. Respondent selected petitioner's 1992 return for an audit examination. On January 11, 1995, respondent mailed petitioner a statutory notice of deficiency for his 1992 taxable year determining a $1,193 income tax deficiency and a $189 penalty for late filing under section 6651(a)(1). On July 17, 1995, respondent assessed the deficiency, the late-filing penalty, and accrued interest in the amount of $265.92. On the same day, the late-filing penalty was abated leaving an unpaid balance of $1,458.92 for 1992.

Joint Liabilities

Petitioners were married in 1993. Under cover of a letter dated September 15, 1997, petitioners submitted their untimely 1994, 1995, and 1996 joint Federal income tax returns. These returns were filed by respondent on September 29, 1997. Petitioners reported tax due for 1994, 1995, and 1996 on their returns in the amounts of $402.04, $402.03, and $1,480.66, respectively.

On October 27, 1997, respondent assessed the 1994 income tax liability, a late-filing penalty in the amount of $100, a failure to pay tax penalty in the amount of $62.32, and accrued interest in the amount of $128.35, for a total assessment of $692.71. On that same date, respondent assessed the 1995 income tax liability, a late-filing penalty in the amount of $100, a failure to pay tax penalty in the amount of $38.19, and accrued interest in the amount of $73.03, for a total assessment of $613.25. On November 17, 1997, respondent assessed the 1996 income tax liability, a late-filing penalty in the amount of $333.15, a failure to pay tax penalty in the amount of $59.23, and accrued interest in the amount of $99.21, for a total assessment of $1,972.25.

Events Leading to the Issuance of the Notice of Determination

On December 21, 1999, respondent mailed two separate Notices of Intent to Levy and Notice of Your Right to a Hearing to petitioners. The notices reflected petitioners' unpaid Federal income tax liabilities for 1990 through 1992 and 1994 through 1996. On January 26, 2000, petitioners informed respondent of their desire to submit an offer in compromise to resolve all of their individual and joint liabilities. In response, respondent mailed petitioners a package of materials for the submission of offers in compromise for their outstanding individual and joint liabilities.

On April 19, 2000, respondent received petitioners' offer to compromise the 1994 through 1996 joint liabilities for $1,150. On that same date respondent received petitioner's offer to compromise the 1990 through 1992 liabilities for $360. Both offers in compromise were submitted on Form 656, Offer in Compromise. Petitioners' offer was to make monthly payments to satisfy the liabilities. Petitioners planned to pay a portion of the offer amount from their expected tax refund for 1999.

On May 19, 2000, respondent's revenue officer advised petitioners that their offers in compromise could not be processed until petitioners' 1999 Federal income tax return was filed. Under respondent's procedures, offers are not processed while taxpayers are not in compliance with the internal revenue laws.

Petitioners had already filed for an extension of time to file for 1999 because they were awaiting information from third parties to complete the return. On June 15, 2000, respondent filed two Notices of Federal Tax Lien (NFTL) at the county recorder's office in Orange County, California, with respect to the individual and joint tax liabilities. Respondent sent petitioners the filed NFTLs and Notices of Right to a Collection Due Process Hearing. On July 14, 2000, petitioners submitted Form 12153, Request for a Collection Due Process Hearing (administrative hearing), contesting the NFTLs filed by respondent and noting the pending offers in compromise.

Sometime in 2001, petitioners' claims were assigned to respondent's Appeals officer. On June 20, 2001, the Appeals officer and petitioners had a telephone conversation discussing petitioners' desire to compromise all of the liabilities. The Appeals officer requested more information from petitioners, which they timely provided with a copy of their filed 1999 Federal income tax return. At some time in the process, petitioners submitted an amended offer in compromise for $2,400, to be paid in $100-monthly installments. Under those terms, the $2,400-offer could be paid in full in 2 years.

On October 16, 2001, respondent's Appeals officer sent petitioners a letter informing them that he had reviewed the offers in compromise. The Appeals officer determined that the minimum offer to compromise both the individual and joint liabilities should be a total of $2,400. The Appeals officer used petitioners' estimate of their primary vehicle[3] to calculate a quick sale value of $2,400, which was determined to be the minimum acceptable offer. The Appeals officer then attempted to determine whether petitioners would be able to meet the monthly installment offer obligation. In calculating petitioners' financial capability, the Appeals officer used petitioners' submitted monthly gross income figure of $4,608, but did not use petitioners' submitted $3,989 monthly expense figure. Instead of using the $3,989 expense figure provided by petitioners, the Appeals officer used $4,644, an estimated amount based on national statistical averages. Using $4,644 resulted in petitioners' estimated monthly expenses exceeding their monthly income by $36 and rendering petitioners ineligible due to their projected inability to make the $100-monthly payments.

The Appeals officer rejected petitioners' offers in compromise. Petitioners requested an in person hearing, but a hearing was not held due to petitioners' unavailability. On February 21, 2002, respondent issued two separate notices of determination for the individual and joint liabilities sustaining the filing of the notices of Federal tax liens and rejecting petitioners' offers in compromise. Petitioners timely appealed to this Court for review of respondent's determinations.

OPINION

Petitioners contend that the Appeals officer abused his discretion by rejecting their offers in compromise and by sustaining the filing of the Federal tax liens.

Section 6320 provides that a taxpayer shall be notified in writing by the Secretary of the filing of a Federal tax lien and provided with an opportunity for an administrative hearing. Sec. 6320(b). Hearings under section 6320 are conducted in accordance with the procedural requirements set forth in section 6330. Sec. 6320©.

When an Appeals officer issues a determination regarding a disputed collection action, section 6330(d) allows a taxpayer to seek judicial review with the Tax Court or a District Court. Where the validity of the underlying tax liability is properly at issue, the Court will review the

---

3. Petitioners estimated the value of their primary vehicle to be $3,000. Respondent used this figure to calculate the $2,400 quick sale value.

matter on a de novo basis. Sego v. Commissioner, 114 T.C. 604, 610, 2000 WL 889754 (2000). However, when the validity of the underlying tax is not at issue, the Court will review the Commissioner's administrative determination for an abuse of discretion. Id. Petitioners do not dispute the validity of the underlying tax. Accordingly, our review is for an abuse of discretion.

We do not conduct an independent review of what would be acceptable offers in compromise. We review only whether the Appeals officer's refusal to accept the offers in compromise was arbitrary, capricious, or without sound basis in fact or law. See Woodral v. Commissioner, 112 T.C. 19, 23, 1999 WL 9947 (1999). The Court considers whether the Commissioner abused his discretion in rejecting a taxpayer's position with respect to any relevant issues, including challenges to the appropriateness of the collections action, and offers of collection alternatives. See sec. 6330(c)(2)(A). This case involves collection alternatives.

Section 7122(a) authorizes the Secretary to compromise any civil case arising under the internal revenue laws. There are three standards that the Secretary may use to compromise a liability. The first standard is doubt as to liability, the second being doubt as to ability to collect, and the third being promotion of effective tax administration. The record reflects that petitioners' offers are with respect to doubt as to collectibility.[4]

Section 7122(c) provides the standards for evaluation of such offers. Under section 7122(c)(2):

(A) * * * the Secretary shall develop and publish schedules of national and local allowances designed to provide that taxpayers entering into a compromise have an adequate means to provide for basic living expenses.

(B) Use of schedules.–The guidelines shall provide that officers and employees of the Internal Revenue Service shall determine, on the basis of the facts and circumstances of each taxpayer, whether the use of the schedules published under subparagraph (A) is appropriate and *shall not use the schedules to the extent such use would result in the taxpayer not having adequate means to provide for basic living expenses.* [Emphasis added.]

---

4. Doubt as to collectibility exists in any case where the taxpayer's assets and income are less than the full amount of the assessed liability. Sec. 301.7122-1T(b)(3), Temporary Proced. & Admin. Regs., 64 Fed.Reg. 39024 (July 21, 1999).

The Appeals officer chose to use the national averages and that use resulted in petitioners' being categorized as not having adequate means to provide for basic living expenses.

The national average statistics are published by the Internal Revenue Service, but use of the statistics by Appeals officers is not mandatory. The Appeals officer exercised discretion in ignoring petitioners' submitted expense amount and, instead, used the national statistical amount as an estimate of petitioners' expenses. The use of the national averages for petitioners' expenses resulted in petitioners' monthly expenses exceeding their monthly income by $36. Therefore, by using the average expense figure, petitioners' income was $136 short of producing the $100 per month needed to compromise their tax liabilities for $2,400. We note that, percentagewise, the shortfall is less than 3 percent of petitioners' gross income. The Appeals officer chose to use the national statistical averages rather than the expense figures provided by petitioners. If the Appeals officer had used petitioners' submitted expense figure of $3,989, petitioners would have had $619 monthly and would have been financially capable of satisfying the $100 installments.

The Appeals officer is allowed to use the national schedules when considering the facts and circumstances of this case. However, if use of the schedules results in petitioners' not having adequate means to provide for basic living expenses, as here when the Appeals officer determined a negative $36 amount for basic living expenses, an installment offer may not be appropriate. See sec. 7122(c)(2)(B).

Under the regulations for doubt as to collectibility cases:

A determination of doubt as to collectibility will include a determination of ability to pay. In determining ability to pay, the Secretary will permit taxpayers to retain sufficient funds to pay basic living expenses. The determination of the amount of such basic living expenses will be founded upon an evaluation of the individual facts and circumstances presented by the taxpayer's case. To guide this determination, guidelines published by the Secretary on national and local living expense standards will be taken into account. [Sec. 301.7122-1T(b)(3)(ii), Temporary Proced. & Admin. Regs., 64 Fed.Reg. 39024 (July 21, 1999).]

The regulation provides that the guidelines are to be taken into account. When the Appeals officer reviewed petitioners' offers, he decided to use the guidelines because he thought petitioners' actual figures were too low. In that regard, there is no specific explanation why the Appeals officer believed that petitioners' monthly expenses of $3,989 was too low or why the guideline figure of $4,644 was more accurate. The use of the guideline expense figure resulted in a $136 shortfall in petitioners' capability to meet the $100-monthly installment to satisfy the $2,400 compromise. If petitioners' submitted monthly expenses of $3,989 had been used, there would have been a $619 surplus of income over expenses that would have enabled petitioners to meet the $100-monthly installment to satisfy the compromise.

In essence, the Appeals officer decided that petitioners could not live less expensively than the national average (guidelines). We find it curious that the Appeals officer relied on petitioners' figures for their vehicle and for their income, but chose not to use petitioners' figures for their monthly expenses. Petitioners made an estimate of $3,000 for the value of their primary car and the Appeals officer used this figure to calculate the quick sale value of $2,400. Based on this premise, the Appeals officer determined that an offer of $2,400 would be an appropriate amount to settle the outstanding liabilities due for 1990-92 and 1994-96. The Appeals officer requested a lump-sum payment through the sale of petitioners' primary vehicle. Petitioners rejected this approach as this was their primary vehicle and to sell it would have caused great financial harm.

Petitioners submitted an amended offer in compromise for $2,400, to be paid in $100 monthly installments. Under those terms, the $2,400 compromise could be paid in full in 2 years. That offer was rejected due to the Appeals officer's determination that petitioners were financially unable to make the payments. We note that petitioners had cooperated with all requests from the Internal Revenue Service in an attempt to resolve this matter.

Appeals officers, in the consideration of an offer in compromise should verify that the requirements of applicable law and administrative procedures have been met, and "whether any proposed collection action balances the need for the efficient collection of taxes with the legitimate concern of the person that any collection action be no more intrusive than necessary." See sec. 6330(c)(3)(C). The verification of applicable law and administrative procedure was met in this case. However, it is questionable as to whether the proposed collection action balanced the need for efficient collection of taxes with the concern of petitioners that any collection action be no more intrusive than necessary.

Payment plans are one possible option for an offer in compromise. According to the instructions that accompany the Form 656, there are three possible payment plans under the short-term deferred payment offer. One plan requires full payment of the realizable value of assets within 90 days from the date the Internal Revenue Service accepts the offer, and payment, within 2 years of acceptance of the amount that they could collect over 60 months. A second plan permits a cash payment for a portion of the realizable value of petitioners' assets within 90 days of the offer being accepted, and the balance of the realizable value plus the remainder of the amount that could have been collected over 60 months within 2 years. The third plan permits monthly payments of the entire offer amount over a period not to exceed 2 years from the date of acceptance by the Internal Revenue Service. Petitioners offered $100 per month for 2 years or 24 months, which equals the $2,400-compromise amount.[5]

Under the various payment options, respondent would be able to file Federal tax liens to protect his interests until such time as the liability is satisfied. Accordingly, respondent's interest would be protected through the liens while respondent received monthly payments. The result of the Appeals officer's financial analysis, however, was to deny petitioners' offers in compromise. To use the national guidelines rather than actual figures in this instance was arbitrary, capricious, and without a sound basis in fact. Petitioners have stated that they are still willing to compromise their tax liabilities for $2,400, but through monthly payments rather than a lump-sum payment.[6]

Therefore, based on the facts and circumstances of this case, we hold that respondent abused his discretion in denying petitioners' offer to compromise their tax liabilities for $2,400. We further hold that respondent did not abuse his discretion in sustaining the filing of the Notices of Federal Tax Liens.[7]

An appropriate decision will be entered.

Notes and Questions

Most offers in compromise are based on doubt as to collectibility, and in that case, a detailed financial statement (Collection Information Statement) must accompany the Form 656. If the compromise is requested because of doubt as to liability, the taxpayer need not file a

---

5. Although not relevant to the facts of this case, there is also a deferred payment offer that provides for a plan similar to the short-term deferred plan (the third plan described above). The deferred payment plan allows the entire offer amount to be made in monthly payments over the life of the collection statute. The deferred plan could result in a longer payment period than 24 months.

6. Petitioners and respondent agreed on the amount of the compromise. The only disagreement here is the method of payment. Based on the financial information submitted by petitioners, a payment plan is a reasonable option.

7. Petitioners have made no argument of merit from which an abuse of discretion could be found with respect to respondent's determination that the filing of the Notices of Federal Tax Liens was appropriate.

financial statement with the Service, but she must include a detailed affidavit explaining why the liability is in doubt.

The taxpayer should be aware that an offer in compromise may result in the extension of the statute of limitations on collections, even if the offer is rejected, because the regulations provide for a suspension of the statute during the period in which the Service is prohibited from levying. Reg. § 301.7122-1(i)(1). Also, the Service frequently requests that the taxpayer agree to extend the statutes of limitation on assessment and collection for an additional year because the processing of an offer in compromise typically takes between six months and one year. In the past (i.e., prior to January 1, 2000), the Service routinely solicited such extensions. Under the 1998 Act, however, § 6502 was amended to provide that the ten-year statute can be extended only in certain special situations, such as in an installment agreement, a levy against the taxpayer's property, and where a collection action is commenced in court prior to the expiration of the ten-year period. IRC § 6502(a)(2). As a result, the Service no longer routinely requests on the Form 656 that the taxpayer agree to such an extension, but the taxpayer should be prepared for such a request nonetheless. Under § 6501(c)(4)(B), the Service must inform the taxpayer of her right to refuse to extend the statute, or to limit such an extension to particular issues or particular periods of time.

If the taxpayer defaults on the agreement, the Service may rescind the agreement and initiate collection action against the taxpayer for the full amount of the liability. While it is possible to obtain a new offer in compromise, this will involve starting the process anew. In that case, the taxpayer may be subject to an additional extension of the statute of limitations and increased professional expenses.

Prior to the Tax Increase Prevention and Reconciliation Act of 2005 (P.L. 109-222), amounts taxpayers submitted with an offer in compromise or while an offer was pending were considered refundable deposits and would not be applied to the tax liability unless the offer was accepted or the taxpayer authorized in writing that the deposit could be applied to the liability. For offers submitted on or after July 16, 2006, however, taxpayers are required to make nonrefundable partial payments with their offers (Code Sec. 7122(c), as added by P.L. 109-222).

1. What are the advantages and disadvantages of an offer in compromise?

2. How, if at all, does an offer in compromise differ from an installment agreement?

3. Under what circumstances will the Service enter into a compromise to "promote effective tax administration?" See Reg. § 301.7122-1(b)(3).

4. Do you think *Fowler* was correctly decided? See Form 656-B (Offer in Compromise Booklet).

5. The 2004 Jobs Act authorized the Service to enter into partial payment agreements with delinquent taxpayers, effective for agreements entered into on or after October 22, 2004. See IRC § 6159(a) and (d), as added by the Jobs Act. Under such an arrangement, the Service will review the agreement at least every two years to determine whether the taxpayer may be able to pay in full or to pay an increased amount. If the taxpayer's financial condition has deteriorated, the Service then may decide to suspend collection activity. How does a partial payment agreement differ from an offer in compromise?

CHAPTER 8

TAX COURT LITIGATION

There was wisdom as well as wit in the cynical wag's remark that the lawyers had transformed the ancient principle of "no taxation without representation" into a doctrine of "no taxation without litigation."

---- Robert H. Jackson[1]

I. THE TAX COURT

A. TRIBUNAL OR COURT?

Although the Tax Court is a legislatively created tribunal, it exercises judicial power. In the past, this created uncertainty about whether the court was a tribunal or a court of law. This issue was resolved by the U.S. Supreme Court in 1991.

FREYTAG v. COMMISSIONER
United States Supreme Court, 1991.
501 U.S. 868, 111 S.Ct. 2631, 115 L.Ed.2d 764.

JUSTICE BLACKMUN delivered the opinion of the Court.

* * * In this litigation, we must decide whether the authority that Congress has granted the Chief Judge of the United States Tax Court to appoint special trial judges transgresses our structure of separated powers. We answer that inquiry in the negative.

I.

By the Tax Reform Act of 1969, § 951, 83 Stat. 730, 26 U.S.C. § 7441, Congress "established, under article I of the Constitution of the United States, a court of record to be known as the United States Tax Court." It also empowered the Tax Court to appoint commissioners to assist its judges. By the Tax Reform Act of 1984, the title "commissioner" was changed to "special trial judge." By § 463(a) of that Act, 98 Stat. 824, and by § 1556(a) of the Tax Reform Act of 1986, 100 Stat. 2754, Congress authorized the Chief Judge of the Tax Court to appoint and assign these

---

1. Jeffery L. Yablon, As Certain As Death–Quotations About Taxes (2004 Edition), 102 TAX NOTES 99, 136 (Jan. 5, 2004).

special trial judges to hear certain specifically described proceedings and "any other proceeding which the chief judge may designate." 26 U.S.C. §§ 7443A(a) and (b). The Tax Court presently consists of 19 judges appointed to 15-year terms by the President, by and with the advice and consent of the Senate.

II.

This complex litigation began with determinations of federal income tax deficiencies against the several petitioners, who had deducted on their returns approximately $1.5 billion in losses allegedly realized in a tax shelter scheme.[1] When petitioners sought review in the Tax Court in March 1982, their cases were assigned to Tax Court Judge Richard C. Wilbur. Trial began in 1984. Judge Wilbur became ill in November 1985, and the Chief Judge of the Tax Court assigned Special Trial Judge Carleton D. Powell to preside over the trial as evidentiary referee, with the proceedings videotaped. When Judge Wilbur's illness forced his retirement and assumption of senior status effective April 1, 1986, the cases were reassigned, with petitioners' specified consent, to Judge Powell for preparation of written findings and an opinion. The judge concluded that petitioners' tax shelter scheme consisted of sham transactions and that petitioners owed additional taxes. The Chief Judge adopted Judge Powell's opinion as that of the Tax Court. 89 T.C. 849 (1987).

Petitioners took an appeal to the Court of Appeals for the Fifth Circuit. It affirmed. 904 F.2d 1011 (1990). Petitioners did not argue to the Court of Appeals, nor do they argue here, that the Tax Court is not a legitimate body. Rather, they contended that the assignment of cases as complex as theirs to a Special Trial Judge was not authorized by § 7443A, and that this violated the Appointments Clause of the Constitution, Art. II, § 2, cl. 2. The Court of Appeals ruled that because the question of the special trial judge's authority was "in essence, an attack upon the subject matter jurisdiction of the special trial judge, it may be raised for the first time on appeal." 904 F.2d, at 1015. The court

---

1.   At oral argument, counsel for petitioners described the litigation in this way:

"This is a tax case with implications for up to 3,000 taxpayers and a billion and a half in alleged tax deficiencies, and it involved one of the longest trials below in the tax court's history-14 weeks of evidence, complex financial testimony, 9,000 pages of transcripts, 3,000-plus exhibits."

Counsel also stated petitioners' primary position:

"In other words, just to put our point succinctly, Congress did not and could not have intended special trial judges in large, complex, multiparty, multimillion dollar tax shelter cases-alleged tax shelter cases such as this one-Congress did not and could not have intended such cases to be in effect decided by the autonomous actions of a special trial judge."

then went on to reject petitioners' claims on the merits. It concluded that the Code authorized the Chief Judge of the Tax Court to assign a special trial judge to hear petitioners' cases and that petitioners had waived any constitutional challenge to this appointment by consenting to a trial before Judge Powell.

We granted certiorari, 498 U.S. 1066, 111 S.Ct. 781, 112 L.Ed.2d 844 (1991), to resolve the important questions the litigation raises about the Constitution's structural separation of powers.

III.

Section 7443A(b) of the Internal Revenue Code specifically authorizes the Chief Judge of the Tax Court to assign four categories of cases to special trial judges: "(1) any declaratory judgment proceeding," "(2) any proceeding under section 7463," "(3) any proceeding" in which the deficiency or claimed overpayment does not exceed $10,000, and "(4) any other proceeding which the Chief Judge may designate." In the first three categories, the Chief Judge may assign the special trial judge not only to hear and report on a case but also to decide it. § 7443A(c). In the fourth category, the chief judge may authorize the special trial judge only to hear the case and prepare proposed findings and an opinion. The actual decision then is rendered by a regular judge of the Tax Court.

Petitioners argue that adjudication by the Special Trial Judge in this litigation exceeded the bounds of the statutory authority that Congress has conferred upon the Tax Court. Despite what they concede to be the "sweeping language" of subsection (b)(4), petitioners claim that Congress intended special trial judges to preside over only the comparatively narrow and minor matters covered by subsections (b)(1), (2), and (3).

The plain language of § 7443A(b)(4) surely authorizes the Chief Judge's assignment of petitioners' cases to a special trial judge. When we find the terms of a statute unambiguous, judicial inquiry should be complete except in rare and exceptional circumstances. Subsection (b)(4) could not be more clear. It states that the Chief Judge may assign "any other proceeding" to a special trial judge for duties short of "mak[ing] the decision." The subsection's text contains no limiting term that restricts its reach to cases that are minor, simple, or narrow, as petitioners urge. We have stated that courts "are not at liberty to create an exception where Congress has declined to do so." Hallstrom v. Tillamook County, 493 U.S. 20, 27, 110 S.Ct. 304, 309, 107 L.Ed.2d 237 (1989).

Nothing in the legislative history contradicts the broad sweep of subsection (b)(4)'s language. In proposing to authorize the Chief Judge to assign "any other proceeding" to the special trial judges, the

Committee on Ways and Means stated that it intended "to clarify" that any other proceeding could be assigned to special trial judges "so long as a Tax Court judge must enter the decision." H.R.Rep. No. 98-432, pt. 2, p. 1568 (1984), U.S.Code Cong. & Admin.News 1984, pp. 697, 1198. The Report goes on to explain:

> "A technical change is made to allow the Chief Judge of the Tax Court to assign any proceeding to a special trial judge for hearing and to write proposed opinions, subject to review and final decision by a Tax Court judge, regardless of the amount in issue. However, special trial judges will not be authorized to enter decisions in this latter category of cases." Ibid.

The Conference Report "follows the House Bill," and, like the House Report, indicates that Congress knowingly removed the jurisdictional requirement of a maximum amount in dispute in order to expand the authority of special trial judges to hear, but not to decide, cases covered by subsection (b)(4).

* * *

Since the enactment of the Revenue Act of 1943, § 503, 58 Stat. 72, the Tax Court has possessed authority to appoint commissioners to assist it in particular cases. Special trial judges and their predecessors, the commissioners, have been authorized for almost a half century to hear any case before the Tax Court in the discretion of its Chief Judge. In practice, before 1984, special trial judges often heard and reported on large and complex cases. Accordingly, when Congress adopted subsection (b)(4), it codified the Chief Judge's discretion to assign cases like petitioners' to a special trial judge for hearing and preparation of a report. The 1984 amendment was "technical" in light of the historical development of the special trial judges' role; the technical nature of the amendment, however, does not alter the wide-ranging effect of the statutory text's grant of authority to the Chief Judge to assign "any other proceeding" within the Tax Court's jurisdiction to a special trial judge.

Petitioners also argue that the phrase "any other proceeding" is a general grant of authority to fill unintended gaps left by subsections (b)(1), (2), and (3). Reading subsection (b)(4) as a catchall provision, petitioners argue that its meaning must be limited to cases involving a small amount of money because any other interpretation would render the limitations imposed by subsections (b)(1), (2), and (3) a nullity. In support of this argument, petitioners rely on this Court's decision in Gomez v. United States, 490 U.S. 858, 109 S.Ct. 2237, 104 L.Ed.2d 923 (1989).

We held in *Gomez* that the Federal Magistrates Act's general grant of authority allowing magistrates to "be assigned such additional duties as are not inconsistent with the Constitution and laws of the United States," 28 U.S.C. § 636(b)(3), did not permit a magistrate to supervise juror voir dire in a felony trial over a defendant's objection. In so holding, we explained:

> "When a statute creates an office to which it assigns specific duties, those duties outline the attributes of the office. Any additional duties performed pursuant to a general authorization in the statute reasonably should bear some relation to the specified duties." 490 U.S., at 864, 109 S.Ct., at 2241.

In the Magistrates Act, the list of specifically enumerated duties followed the general grant of authority and provided the outlines for the scope of the general grant. Unlike the Magistrates Act, § 7443A explicitly distinguishes between the categories of cases enumerated in subsections (b)(1), (2), and (3), which are declaratory judgment proceedings and cases involving $10,000 or less, and the category of "any other proceeding" found in subsection (b)(4).

The lesser authority exercised by special trial judges in proceedings under subsection (b)(4) also prevents that subsection from serving as a grant of general authority to fill any gaps left in the three preceding subsections. Special trial judges may hear and decide declaratory judgment proceedings and the limited-amount cases. A special trial judge, however, cannot render the final decision of the Tax Court in a case assigned under subsection (b)(4). If the cases that special trial judges may hear, but not decide, under subsection (b)(4) are limited to the same kind of cases they could hear and decide under the three preceding subsections, then subsection (b)(4) would be superfluous. Our cases consistently have expressed "a deep reluctance to interpret a statutory provision so as to render superfluous other provisions in the same enactment." Pennsylvania Dept. of Public Welfare v. Davenport, 495 U.S. 552, 562, 110 S.Ct. 2126, 2133, 109 L.Ed.2d 588 (1990). See also Automobile Workers v. Johnson Controls, Inc., 499 U.S. 187, 201, 111 S.Ct. 1196, 1204, 113 L.Ed.2d 158 (1991). The scope of subsection (b)(4) must be greater than that of subsections (b)(1), (2), and (3).

We conclude that subsection (b)(4) permits the Chief Judge to assign any Tax Court proceeding, regardless of complexity or amount, to a special trial judge for hearing and the preparation of proposed findings and written opinion. The statute's language, structure, and history permit no other conclusion.

IV.

* * *

[Eds: The Appointments Clause, found at Art. II, § 2, cl. 2 of the United States Constitution provides:

> "He [the President] . . . shall nominate, and by and with the Advice and Consent of the Senate, shall appoint Ambassadors, other public Ministers and Consuls, Judges of the Supreme Court, and all other Officers of the United States, whose Appointments are not herein otherwise provided for, and which shall be established by Law; but the Congress may by Law vest the Appointment of such inferior Officers, as they think proper, in the President alone, in the Courts of Law, or in the Heads of Departments."]

* * *

C.

* * *

[W]e repeat petitioners' central challenge: Can the Chief Judge of the Tax Court constitutionally be vested by Congress with the power to appoint? The Appointments Clause names the possible repositories for the appointment power. It is beyond question in this litigation that Congress did not intend to grant to the President the power to appoint special trial judges. We therefore are left with three other possibilities. First, as the Commissioner urges, the Tax Court could be treated as a department with the Chief Judge as its head. Second, as the amicus suggests, the Tax Court could be considered one of "the Courts of Law." Third, we could agree with petitioners that the Tax Court is neither a "Departmen[t]" nor a "Cour[t] of Law." Should we agree with petitioners, it would follow that the appointment power could not be vested in the Chief Judge of the Tax Court.

We first consider the Commissioner's argument. According to the Commissioner, the Tax Court is a department because for 45 years before Congress designated that court as a "court of record" under Article I, see § 7441, the body was an independent agency (the predecessor Board of Tax Appeals) within the Executive Branch. Furthermore, the Commissioner argues that § 7441 simply changed the status of the Tax Court within that branch. It did not remove the body to a different branch or change its substantive duties.

The Commissioner "readily" acknowledges that "the Tax Court's fit within the Executive Branch may not be a perfect one." But he argues that the Tax Court must fall within one of the three branches and that the Executive Branch provides its best home. The reasoning of the Commissioner may be summarized as follows: (1) The Tax Court must fit into one of the three branches; (2) it does not fit into either the Legislative Branch or the Judicial Branch; (3) at one time it was an independent agency and therefore it must fit into the Executive Branch; and (4) every component of the Executive Branch is a department.

We cannot accept the Commissioner's assumption that every part of the Executive Branch is a department, the head of which is eligible to receive the appointment power. The Appointments Clause prevents Congress from distributing power too widely by limiting the actors in whom Congress may vest the power to appoint. The Clause reflects our Framers' conclusion that widely distributed appointment power subverts democratic government. Given the inexorable presence of the administrative state, a holding that every organ in the Executive Branch is a department would multiply indefinitely the number of actors eligible to appoint. The Framers recognized the dangers posed by an excessively diffuse appointment power and rejected efforts to expand that power. So do we. For the Chief Judge of the Tax Court to qualify as a "Hea[d] of [a] Departmen[t]," the Commissioner must demonstrate not only that the Tax Court is a part of the Executive Branch but also that it is a department.

We are not so persuaded. This Court for more than a century has held that the term "Departmen[t]" refers only to " 'a part or division of the executive government, as the Department of State, or of the Treasury,' " expressly "creat [ed]" and "giv[en] . . . the name of a department" by Congress. Accordingly, the term "Heads of Departments" does not embrace "inferior commissioners and bureau officers." [United States v. Germaine, 99 U.S.508, 511, 25 L.Ed. 482 (1879)].

Confining the term "Heads of Departments" in the Appointments Clause to executive divisions like the Cabinet-level departments constrains the distribution of the appointment power just as the Commissioner's interpretation, in contrast, would diffuse it. The Cabinet-level departments are limited in number and easily identified. Their heads are subject to the exercise of political oversight and share the President's accountability to the people.

* * *

Treating the Tax Court as a "Department" and its Chief Judge as its "Hea[d]" would defy the purpose of the Appointments Clause, the meaning of the Constitution's text, and the clear intent of Congress to transform the Tax Court into an Article I legislative court. The Tax Court is not a "Departmen[t]."

Having so concluded, we now must determine whether it is one of the "Courts of Law," as amicus suggests. Petitioners and the Commissioner both take the position that the Tax Court cannot be a "Cour[t] of Law" within the meaning of the Appointments Clause because, they say, that term is limited to Article III courts.[5]

The text of the Clause does not limit the "Courts of Law" to those courts established under Article III of the Constitution. The Appointments Clause does not provide that Congress can vest appointment power only in "one Supreme Court" and other courts established under Article III, or only in tribunals that exercise broad common-law jurisdiction. Petitioners argue that Article II's reference to the "Courts of Law" must be limited to Article III courts because Article III courts are the only courts mentioned in the Constitution. It of course is true that the Constitution "nowhere makes reference to 'legislative courts.' " See Glidden, 370 U.S., at 543, 82 S.Ct., at 1469. But petitioners' argument fails nevertheless. We agree with petitioners that the Constitution's terms are illuminated by their cognate provisions. This analytic method contributed to our conclusion that the Tax Court could not be a department. Petitioners, however, underestimate the importance of this Court's time-honored reading of the Constitution as giving Congress wide discretion to assign the task of adjudication in cases arising under federal law to legislative tribunals. See, e.g., American Insurance Co. v. Canter, 1 Pet. 511, 546, 7 L.Ed. 242 (1828) (the judicial power of the United States is not limited to the judicial power defined under Article III and may be exercised by legislative courts); Williams v. United States, 289 U.S. 553, 565-567, 53 S.Ct. 751, 754-755, 77 L.Ed. 1372 (1933) (same).

Our cases involving non-Article III tribunals have held that these courts exercise the judicial power of the United States. In both *Canter* and *Williams*, this Court rejected arguments similar to the literalistic one now advanced by petitioners, that only Article III courts could exercise the judicial power because the term "judicial Power" appears only in Article III. In *Williams*, this Court explained that the power exercised by some non-Article III tribunals is judicial power:

"The Court of Claims . . . undoubtedly . . . exercises judicial power, but the question still remains—and is the vital question—whether it is the judicial power defined by Art. III of the Constitution.

"That judicial power apart from that article may be conferred by Congress upon legislative courts . . . is plainly apparent from the

---

5. The Commissioner has not been consistent in this position. Indeed, when the present litigation was in the Fifth Circuit, the Government advocated that the Tax Court is one of the "Courts of Law." Brief for Appellee in No. 89-4436 et al., pp. 47-51. It abandoned that position in the later case of Samuels, Kramer & Co. v. Commissioner, 930 F.2d 975 (CA2 1991), and there urged that the Tax Court was a "Department." Brief for Appellee in No. 89-4436 et al., pp. 34-48.

opinion of Chief Justice Marshall in *American Insurance Co. v. Canter* . . . dealing with the territorial courts. . ..[T]he legislative courts possess and exercise judicial power . . . although not conferred in virtue of the third article of the Constitution." 289 U.S., at 565-566, 53 S.Ct., at 754-755.

We cannot hold that an Article I court, such as the Court of Claims in *Williams* or the Territorial Court of Florida in *Canter*, can exercise the judicial power of the United States and yet cannot be one of the "Courts of Law."

* * *

The narrow construction urged by petitioners and the Commissioner also would undermine longstanding practice. "[F]rom the earliest days of the Republic," see Northern Pipeline Constr. Co. v. Marathon Pipe Line Co., 458 U.S. 50, 64, 102 S.Ct. 2858, 2868, 73 L.Ed.2d 598 (1982), Congress provided for the creation of legislative courts and authorized those courts to appoint clerks, who were inferior officers. Congress' consistent interpretation of the Appointments Clause evinces a clear congressional understanding that Article I courts could be given the power to appoint. Because " 'traditional ways of conducting government . . . give meaning' to the Constitution," Mistretta, 488 U.S., at 401, 109 S.Ct., at 669, quoting Youngstown Sheet & Tube Co. v. Sawyer, 343 U.S. 579, 610, 72 S.Ct. 863, 897, 96 L.Ed. 1153 (1952), this longstanding interpretation provides evidence that Article I courts are not precluded from being "Courts of Law" within the meaning of the Appointments Clause.

Having concluded that an Article I court, which exercises judicial power, can be a "Cour[t] of Law" within the meaning of the Appointments Clause, we now examine the Tax Court's functions to define its constitutional status and its role in the constitutional scheme. The Tax Court exercises judicial, rather than executive, legislative, or administrative, power. It was established by Congress to interpret and apply the Internal Revenue Code in disputes between taxpayers and the Government. By resolving these disputes, the court exercises a portion of the judicial power of the United States.

The Tax Court exercises judicial power to the exclusion of any other function. It is neither advocate nor rulemaker. As an adjudicative body, it construes statutes passed by Congress and regulations promulgated by the Internal Revenue Service. It does not make political decisions.

The Tax Court's function and role in the federal judicial scheme closely resemble those of the federal district courts, which indisputably are "Courts of Law." Furthermore, the Tax Court exercises its judicial power in much the same way as the federal district courts exercise theirs. It has authority to punish contempts by fine or imprisonment, 26 U.S.C. § 7456(c); to grant certain injunctive relief, § 6213(a); to order the Secretary of the Treasury to refund an overpayment determined by the court, § 6512(b)(2); and to subpoena and examine witnesses, order production of documents, and administer oaths, § 7456(a). All these powers are quintessentially judicial in nature.

The Tax Court remains independent of the Executive and Legislative Branches. Its decisions are not subject to review by either the Congress or the President. Nor has Congress made Tax Court decisions subject to review in the federal district courts. Rather, like the judgments of the district courts, the decisions of the Tax Court are appealable only to the regional United States courts of appeals, with ultimate review in this Court. The courts of appeals, moreover, review those decisions "in the same manner and to the same extent as decisions of the district courts in civil actions tried without a jury." § 7482(a). This standard of review contrasts with the standard applied to agency rulemaking by the courts of appeals under § 10(e) of the Administrative Procedure Act, 5 U.S.C. § 706(2)(A).

The Tax Court's exclusively judicial role distinguishes it from other non-Article III tribunals that perform multiple functions and provides the limit on the diffusion of appointment power that the Constitution demands. Moreover, since the early 1800's, Congress regularly granted non-Article III territorial courts the authority to appoint their own clerks of court, who, as of at least 1839, were "inferior Officers" within the meaning of the Appointments Clause. Including Article I courts, such as the Tax Court, that exercise judicial power and perform exclusively judicial functions among the "Courts of Law" does not significantly expand the universe of actors eligible to receive the appointment power.

The judgment of the Court of Appeals is affirmed.

It is so ordered.

Notes

The significance of the *Freytag* decision is that the Tax Court is considered a court of law under the U.S. Constitution. Thus, it has full judicial power within the limits of its statutorily defined jurisdiction.

In 2010, the Tax Court decided that an IRS appeals officer, appointed by the IRS Commissioner, who conducts collection due process hearings is not considered an "inferior officer of the United States" for purposes of the Appointments Clause. In Tucker v. Commissioner, 135 T.C. No. 6

(2010), the Tax Court reasoned that such an officer has neither a position "established by law" nor "significant authority"that is required to be considered an officer of the United States within the meaning of the Appointments Clause. This issue is likely to be appealed, however.

B. APPEALS

LAWRENCE v. COMMISSIONER
United States Tax Court, 1957.
27 T.C. 713.

* * *

The Tax Court has always believed that Congress intended it to decide all cases uniformly, regardless of where, in its nationwide jurisdiction, they may arise, and that it could not perform its assigned functions properly were it to decide one case one way and another differently merely because appeals in such cases might go to different Courts of Appeals. Congress, in the case of the Tax Court, 'inverted the triangle' so that from a single national jurisdiction, the Tax Court appeals would spread out among 11 Courts of Appeals, each for a different circuit or portion of the United States. Congress faced the problem in the beginning as to whether the Tax Court jurisdiction and approach was to be local or nationwide and made it nationwide. Congress expected the Tax Court to set precedents for the uniform application of the tax laws, insofar as it would be able to do that.

The Tax Court feels that it is adequately supported in this belief not only by the creating legislation and legislative history but by other circumstances as well. The Tax Court never knows, when it decides a case, where any subsequent appeal from that decision may go, or whether there will be an appeal. It usually, but not always, knows where the return of a taxpayer was filed and, therefore, the circuit to which an appeal could go, but the law permits the parties in all cases to appeal by mutual agreement to any Court of Appeals. Sec. 7482(b)(2), I.R.C. 1954. Furthermore, it frequently happens that a decision of the Tax Court is appealable to two or even more Courts of Appeals. A few examples will illustrate. A corporation, having stockholders scattered over the United States, makes a distribution to all. The Commissioner holds it taxable as a dividend from accumulated earnings. The stockholders join in a trial before the Tax Court which decides the issue as to all petitioning stockholders, contrary to a decision of Court of Appeals A, which reversed a prior Tax Court decision, but perhaps in line with an affirming decision of Court of Appeals B. If it had rendered a separate different decision for those stockholders in Circuit A, what amount of accumulated earnings would remain for future distribution? * * * Or suppose partners live in different circuits. Are the decisions of the Tax Court as to them to vary accordingly? See Choate v. Commissioner, 324 U.S. 1, in which the appeal in the case of Hogan was taken to the Fifth Circuit which affirmed the Tax Court, Hogan v. Commissioner, 141 F.2d 92, and the appeal in the case of Choate was to the Tenth Circuit which reversed the Tax Court, Choate v. Commissioner, 141 F.2d 641, which was then reversed by the Supreme Court, thus affirming the Tax Court. Many more similar examples could be given. There is also the sometimes difficult problem of knowing from prior decisions of the appellate court precisely what its attitude is in relation to the current question before the Tax Court, particularly where it has more than one decision outstanding and each may seem to have a bearing but they are not too easily reconciled. * * *

The Commissioner of Internal Revenue, who has the duty of administering the taxing statutes of the United States throughout the Nation, is required to apply these statutes uniformly, as he construes them. The Tax Court, being a tribunal with national jurisdiction over litigation involving the interpretation of Federal taxing statutes which may come to it from all parts of the country, has a similar obligation to apply with uniformity its interpretation of those statutes. That is the way it has always seen its statutory duty and, with all due respect to the Courts of Appeals, it cannot conscientiously change unless Congress or the Supreme Court so directs.

* * *

GOLSEN v. COMMISSIONER

United States Tax Court, 1970
54 T.C. 742.

* * *

OPINION

RAUM, JUDGE:

* * *

The precise question relating to the deductibility of 'interest' like that involved herein has been adjudicated by two Courts of Appeals. In one case, Campbell v. Cen-Tex., Inc., 377 F.2d 688 (C.A. 5), decision went for the taxpayer; in the other, Goldman v. United States, 403 F.2d 776 (C.A. 10), affirming 273 F.Supp. 137 (W.D. Okla.), the Government prevailed. *Goldman* involved the same insurance company, the same type of policies, and the same financial arrangements as are before us in the present case. *Cen-Tex* involved a different insurance company but dealt with comparable financing arrangements. Despite some rather feeble attempts on the part of each side herein to distinguish the case adverse to it, we think that both cases are in point. It is our view that the Government's position is correct.

Moreover, we think that we are in any event bound by *Goldman* since it was decided by the Court of Appeals for the same circuit within which the present case arises. In thus concluding that we must follow *Goldman*, we recognize the contrary thrust of the oft-criticized case of Arthur L. Lawrence, 27 T.C. 713. Notwithstanding a number of the considerations which originally led us to that decision, it is our best judgment that better judicial administration requires us to follow a Court of Appeals decision which is squarely in point where appeal from our decision lies to that Court of Appeals and to that court alone.[15]

Section 7482(a), I.R.C. 1954,[16] charges the Courts of Appeals with the primary responsibility for review of our decisions, and we think that where the Court of Appeals to which appeal lies has already passed upon the issue before us, efficient and harmonious judicial administration calls for us to follow the decision of that court. Moreover, the practice we are adopting does not jeopardize the Federal interest in uniform application of the internal revenue laws which we emphasized in Lawrence. We shall remain able to foster uniformity by giving effect to our own views in cases appealable to courts whose views have not yet been expressed, and, even where the relevant Court of Appeals has already made its views known, by explaining why we agree or disagree with the precedent that we feel constrained to follow.

To the extent that *Lawrence* is inconsistent with the views expressed herein it is hereby overruled. We note, however, that some of our decisions, because they involve two or more taxpayers, may be appealable to more than one circuit. This case presents no such problem, and accordingly we need not decide now what course to take in the event that we are faced with it. * * *

---

15. Sec. 7482(b)(2), I.R.C. 1954, grants venue in any Court of Appeals designated by both the Government and the taxpayer by written stipulation. However, if the Court of Appeals to which an appeal would otherwise lie has already passed upon the question in issue, it is hardly likely that the party prevailing before the Tax Court would join in such a stipulation.

16. SEC. 7482. COURTS OF REVIEW.

(a) Jurisdiction.—The United States Courts of Appeals shall have exclusive jurisdiction to review the decisions of the Tax Court, except as provided in section 1254 of Title 28 of the United States Code, in the same manner and to the same extent as decisions of the district courts in civil actions tried without a jury; and the judgment of any such court shall be final, except that it shall be subject to review by the Supreme Court of the United States upon certiorari, in the manner provided in section 1254 of Title 28 of the United States Code.

Notes and Questions

Nearly half of the cases filed in the Tax Court are S cases that may not be appealed. Apparently, the Tax Court also applies the *Golsen* rule in these cases, although the rationale for doing so is unclear. For an article proposing that the Tax Court adhere to *Golsen* in small tax cases when it is more favorable to the taxpayer, see Carlton M. Smith, "Does the Tax Court's Use of Its *Golsen* Rule in Unappealable Small Tax Cases Hurt the Poor?", 11 J. Tax Practice & Procedure 35 (Feb.-Mar. 2009).

1. Is it the thrust of the *Golsen* decision that the Tax Court lacks the authority to render a decision inconsistent with the applicable precedent of the court of appeals?

2. What should the Tax Court do if it disagrees with the view of the circuit court?

3. What result if the Tax Court renders a decision in accordance with the precedent of the applicable circuit court and subsequently a similar case appears before the Tax Court in another circuit that has no precedent on the issue in question?

II. DEFICIENCY LITIGATION

A tax litigant has an ability to forum shop (see discussion, Chapter 1) since tax cases may be heard in the United States Tax Court, the federal district courts, or the United States Court of Federal Claims, as well as in the United States Bankruptcy Courts.[2] There are various considerations in determining the choice of forum, but generally one of the most important is the ability to pay the tax. Only the Tax Court offers the ability to litigate before having to pay the proposed deficiency. Because of this ability, the majority of tax cases are brought in the Tax Court.[3]

---

2. A taxpayer who files a petition in bankruptcy may have the deficiency determined in the Bankruptcy Court. Once the bankruptcy petition is filed, however, the taxpayer loses the ability to select the forum.

3. In addition to the Tax Court, a taxpayer who disputes a proposed deficiency, and wishes to contest the deficiency prior to payment may also file an administrative appeal with the Appeals Office of the Service. There are several advantages to this alternative. See Chapter 3 for a discussion of administrative appeals, and § III.A.1 below for a discussion of exhaustion of administrative remedies in the recovery of costs.

If the taxpayer receives a notice of deficiency and has not requested a conference with Appeals previously, the Service generally will allow the taxpayer an opportunity for an Appeals conference in order to try to settle the dispute prior to litigation. Otherwise, if the taxpayer has not received a notice of deficiency, and has not been able to reach an agreement with the Service after an Appeals conference, a notice of deficiency will be sent to the taxpayer.

A. TAX COURT JURISDICTION

The Tax Court is a court of limited jurisdiction. It hears income, estate and gift, and certain excise tax claims involving deficiencies. In general, there are three prerequisites for Tax Court jurisdiction: (1) a determination of a deficiency under § 6211(a), (2) a valid notice of deficiency under § 6212, and (3) a timely filed petition under § 6213(a). Since jurisdiction depends upon a deficiency, the notice of deficiency has been called the taxpayer's "ticket to the Tax Court."

In recent years, however, Congress has expanded the Tax Court's jurisdiction to cases that do not involve deficiencies. Thus, it is possible to be heard in the Tax Court without a notice of deficiency. Examples of such cases include actions for redetermination of employment status, actions for relief from determination of joint and several liability, claims for litigation and administrative costs, and actions to redetermine interest on a deficiency or an overpayment. See IRC §§ 7436; 6015(e); 7430; 7481(c), and Tax Court Rules 290 and 320.

In 2006, Congress resolved the controversy over whether the Tax Court has equity jurisdiction in amending § 6214 to provide that the Tax Court may apply the doctrine of equitable recoupment to the same extent that the doctrine may be applied in the federal district courts or the U.S. Court of Federal Claims. In addition, the court may consider facts with relation to the tax liability for other taxable years to correctly redetermine the amount of deficiency for the taxable year before the court. I.R.C. § 6214(b).

While the Tax Court has deficiency jurisdiction, it also has incidental refund jurisdiction pursuant to § 6512(b). Thus, under certain circumstances, it is possible for the taxpayer to obtain a refund in the Tax Court. See discussion, Chapter 5.

The Tax Court has exclusive jurisdiction over the taxes and taxable period at issue in the notice of deficiency. The question is at what point does this jurisdiction apply?

1. Exclusivity of Tax Court Jurisdiction

WAGNER v. COMMISSIONER

United States Tax Court, 2002.
118 T.C. 330.

OPINION

LARO, J.

Petitioners petitioned the Court under section 6320(c) to review a notice of a Federal tax lien placed upon their property. The lien arose from an assessment of Federal income taxes of $412,787.15 and $844.16 for 1991 and 1996, respectively. Petitioners now, after being served with respondent's answer and respondent's motion for summary judgment, move the Court to dismiss this case without prejudice to their right to seek in Federal District Court a determination that they incurred a net operating loss (NOL) in 1994 that may be carried back to 1991. We shall grant petitioners' motion. Unless otherwise noted, section references are to the Internal Revenue Code in effect for the relevant years, Rule references are to the Tax Court Rules of Practice and Procedure, and rule references are to the Federal Rules of Civil Procedure. * * *

The parties agree that the Court may dismiss this case pursuant to petitioners' request.[3] We distinguish this dismissal from our jurisprudence that holds that taxpayers may not withdraw a petition under section 6213 to redetermine a deficiency. That jurisprudence stems from the seminal case of Estate of Ming v. Commissioner, 62 T.C. 519, 1974 WL 2720 (1974).

In *Estate of Ming*, the taxpayers moved the Court to allow them to withdraw their petition for a redetermination of their 1964, 1965, and 1966 Federal income taxes. Presumably, they made their motion so that they could refile their lawsuit in District Court. We denied the motion. We noted that, whenever this Court dismisses a case on a ground other than lack of jurisdiction, we are generally required by section 7459(d)[4] to enter a decision finding that the deficiency in tax is the amount

---

3. Respondent does not object to dismissal without prejudice to petitioners' filing a refund suit in District Court but takes the position that the dismissal should be with prejudice to their refiling a petition under sec. 6320(c) in our own Court based on the same claim as their existing petition.

4. Sec. 7459(d) provides in relevant part:

SEC. 7459(d). Effect of Decision Dismissing Petition.—If a petition for a redetermination of a deficiency has been filed by the taxpayer, a decision of the Tax Court dismissing the proceeding shall be considered as its decision that the deficiency is the amount determined by the Secretary. * * *

determined in the notice of deficiency. We observed that entering such a decision would serve to preclude the taxpayers from litigating the case on its merits in District Court. Id. at 522-523. We noted that the Commissioner had been prejudiced by the taxpayers' filing of the petition by virtue of the fact that he was precluded from assessing and collecting the taxes which he had determined the taxpayers owed. Id. at 524.

In *Estate of Ming v. Commissioner*, supra at 521-522, we also relied on our opinion in Dorl v. Commissioner, 57 T.C. 720, 1972 WL 2407 (1972), affd. 507 F.2d 406 (2d Cir.1974), which held that a taxpayer may not remove a case from this Court in order to refile it in District Court. We observed in *Dorl* that the filing of a petition in this Court gives us exclusive jurisdiction under section 6512(a), which acts to bar a refund suit in the District Court for the same tax and the same year. We noted that this observation was supported by the legislative history accompanying the enactment of the predecessors of sections 6512(a) and 7459(d). That history states that, when a taxpayer petitions the Board of Tax Appeals, the Board's decision, once final, settles the taxpayer's tax liability for the year in question even if the decision resulted from a dismissal requested by the taxpayer. *Estate of Ming v. Commissioner*, supra at 522.

We believe that our holding in *Estate of Ming* is inapplicable to the setting at hand where petitioners have petitioned this Court under section 6320(c). Section 7459(d) applies specifically to a petition that is filed for a redetermination of a deficiency and makes no mention of a petition that is filed under section 6320(c) to review a collection action. Section 6320 was added to the Code as part of the Internal Revenue Service Restructuring and Reform Act of 1998, Pub.L. 105-206, sec. 3401, 112 Stat. 685, 746, and that act made no amendment to section 7459(d), which finds its roots in section 906(c) of the Revenue Act of 1926, ch. 27, 44 Stat. 107. Nor do we know of any provision in the Code that would require us, upon a dismissal of a collection action filed under section 6320(c), to enter a decision for the Commissioner consistent with the underlying notice of determination. Whereas the relevant legislative history supported our holding in *Dorl v. Commissioner*, supra, we are unaware of any legislative history that would support a holding contrary to that which we reach herein.

Our granting of petitioners' motion is supported by rule 41(a)(2),[5] which we consult given the absence in our Rules of a specific provision as to this matter.[6] See Rule 1. Under rule 41(a)(2), a plaintiff is not entitled as a matter of right to a dismissal after the defendant has served a motion for summary judgment but is allowed such a dismissal in the sound discretion of the court. In general, a court "should" grant a dismissal under rule 41(a)(2) "unless the defendant will suffer clear legal prejudice, other than the mere prospect of a subsequent lawsuit, as a result." McCants v. Ford Motor Co., Inc., 781 F.2d 855, 856-857 (11th Cir.1986). "The crucial question to be determined is, Would the defendant lose any substantial right by the dismissal." Durham v. Fla. E. Coast Ry. Co., 385 F.2d 366, 368 (5th Cir.1967). In making this determination, a court must "weigh the relevant equities and do justice between the parties in each case, imposing such costs and attaching such conditions to the dismissal as are deemed appropriate." *McCants v. Ford Motor Co., Inc.*, supra at 857.

The statutory period in which petitioners could refile their lawsuit in this Court appears to have expired. Section 6330(d)(1) requires that a petition to this Court be filed within 30 days of the determination that is the subject of section 6320. See also sec. 6320(c). The rule is deeply embedded in the jurisprudence of Federal law that the granting of a

---

5. In relevant part, rule 41 provides:

Rule 41. Dismissal of Actions

(a) Voluntary Dismissal: Effect Thereof.

(1) By Plaintiff; by Stipulation. * * * an action may be dismissed by the plaintiff without order of court (i) by filing a notice of dismissal at any time before service by the adverse party of an answer or of a motion for summary judgment, whichever first occurs, or (ii) by filing a stipulation of dismissal signed by all parties who have appeared in the action. Unless otherwise stated in the notice of dismissal or stipulation, the dismissal is without prejudice, except that a notice of dismissal operates as an adjudication upon the merits when filed by a plaintiff who has once dismissed in any court of the United States or of any state an action based on or including the same claim.

(2) By Order of Court. Except as provided in paragraph (1) of this subdivision of this rule, an action shall not be dismissed at the plaintiff's instance save upon order of the court and upon such terms and conditions as the court deems proper. * * * Unless otherwise specified in the order, a dismissal under this paragraph is without prejudice.

* * *

(d) Costs of Previously-Dismissed Action. If a plaintiff who has once dismissed an action in any court commences an action based upon or including the same claim against the same defendant, the court may make such order for the payment of costs of the action previously dismissed as it may deem proper * * *.

6. Our Rule on dismissals, Rule 123(b), relates to dismissals "For failure of a petitioner properly to prosecute or to comply with these Rules or any order of the Court or for other cause which the Court deems sufficient". Pursuant to that Rule, "the Court may dismiss a case at any time and enter a decision against the petitioner." Id. Rule 123(b) does not apply to the setting at hand where petitioners voluntarily move the Court to dismiss their petition filed under sec. 6320(c) to review a notice of Federal tax lien.

motion to dismiss without prejudice is treated as if the underlying lawsuit had never been filed. Monterey Dev. Corp. v. Lawyer's Title Ins. Corp., 4 F.3d 605, 608 (8th Cir.1993); Brown v. Hartshorne Pub. Sch. Dist., 926 F.2d 959, 961 (10th Cir.1991); Robinson v. Willow Glen Acad., 895 F.2d 1168, 1169 (7th Cir.1990). We conclude that respondent is not prejudiced in maintaining the subject collection action against petitioners as if the instant proceeding had never been commenced.

Accordingly, in the exercise of the Court's discretion, and after weighing the relevant equities including the lack of a clear legal prejudice to respondent, we shall grant petitioners' motion. In accordance with the foregoing, An appropriate order of dismissal will be entered granting petitioners' motion to dismiss.

Notes and Question

The subsequent payment of a proposed deficiency after a petition has been filed in the Tax Court does not deprive the Tax Court of jurisdiction. See Estate of Salinitro v. Commissioner, 63 TCM 2994 (1992).

What result if a taxpayer files suit in the Tax Court contesting a proposed deficiency and fails to pay the requisite filing fee? See Bioff v. Commissioner, 47 B.T.A. 942 (1942).

2. Requirements for Jurisdiction

In general, most of the cases heard in the Tax Court involve deficiencies. A typical Tax Court case begins with the filing of a petition with the court within 90 days of the mailing of a notice of deficiency (150 days if the deficiency notice is addressed to a taxpayer outside the United States). Since Tax Court judges travel to different cities to hear cases, the petitioner must designate a location for the trial, and also must remit a $60 filing fee. The petition, with the accompanying fee, must be filed with the clerk of the Tax Court in Washington, D.C., although the petition also may be filed with the judge presiding over the particular session of court.

a. *Sufficiency of the Notice of Deficiency*

In addition to the procedural problem of a notice that is not mailed to the taxpayer's "last known address," discussed in Chapter 4, questions often arise about the validity of the determination of the deficiency itself.

ESTATE OF RICKMAN v. COMMISSIONER

United States Tax Court, Memorandum Decision, 1995.

70 T.C.M. 1335, 1995 WL 679776.

MEMORANDUM OPINION

ARMEN, SPECIAL TRIAL JUDGE:

This case is before the Court on petitioner's Motion to Dismiss for Lack of Jurisdiction, as Amended, and petitioner's Motion to Strike. The issue for decision concerns the validity of the notice of deficiency issued in this case and whether respondent "determined" a deficiency in petitioner's Federal estate tax within the meaning of section 6212(a).

Background

Petitioner is the Estate of Doris L. Rickman. Doris L. Rickman (decedent) died on October 24, 1990, in Franklin, Georgia. Decedent's husband, James R. Rickman, died on October 19, 1990, 5 days before decedent died.

Doris K. Rickman, decedent's daughter, was duly appointed executrix of the decedent's estate under letters testamentary issued by the clerk of the Superior Court of Macon County, North Carolina, on October 30, 1990. Doris K. Rickman is also the duly appointed executrix of the Estate of James R. Rickman. * * *

* * *

On May 20, 1994, respondent issued a notice of deficiency addressed to the Estate of Doris L. Rickman, Deceased, Doris K. Rickman, in care of T. Scott Tufts, petitioner's counsel. The notice of deficiency sets forth respondent's determination of a deficiency in petitioner's Federal estate tax in the amount of $190,785. There is no dispute that the notice of deficiency lists decedent's correct Social Security number and date of death.

The notice of deficiency includes an explanation of adjustments which states:

(a) The decedent and her spouse filed Federal Gift Tax Returns for the period ending December 31, 1990, and elected to split the gifts made by each to third parties. The gift tax returns did not correctly reflect this election. The adjusted taxable gift of the decedent is determined to be $85,711.00, rather than zero as reported at Line 4 of Page 1 of the Federal Estate Tax Return. Exhibits A and B of this notice indicate how the gift tax returns should have been filed. The corrections to the gift tax returns include the determination that all gifts by both donors must be split and that the gifts reported by the decedent's spouse were overstated because a portion of the spouse's gifts were incomplete and should not have been reported. * * *

Accordingly, the taxable estate is increased $85,711.00.

* * *

The parties agree that exhibits A and B referred to in paragraph (a) of the explanation of adjustments were not attached to the notice of deficiency that was sent to petitioner.* * *

* * *

Petitioner's motion to dismiss for lack of jurisdiction is premised on the theory that the notice of deficiency is invalid on the ground that respondent failed to make a valid "determination" as required by Scar v. Commissioner, 814 F.2d 1363 (9th Cir. 1987), revg. 81 T.C. 855 (1983). Petitioner subsequently filed an amendment to its motion to dismiss. Relying primarily on Durkin v. Commissioner, 87 T.C. 1329, 1402 (1986), affd. 872 F.2d 1271 (7th Cir. 1989), and Pearce v. Commissioner, 95 T.C. 250 (1990), revd. without published opinion 946 F.2d 1543 (5th Cir. 1991), petitioner contends that the notice of deficiency should be declared invalid on the grounds that each of the adjustments set forth therein is without merit and reflects the "gross ineptitude" of the persons involved in preparing the notice.

Respondent filed an objection to petitioner's motion to dismiss. Respondent maintains that the adjustments set forth in the notice of deficiency were determined based upon a review of petitioner's estate tax return, and, therefore, the notice of deficiency is valid under Scar v. Commissioner, supra. Attached as exhibits A and B to respondent's objection are the two exhibits (referred to in paragraph (a) of the explanation of adjustments portion of the notice of deficiency) that respondent failed to attach to the notice of deficiency issued to petitioner.[5]

* * *

Discussion

The issue to be decided is whether the notice of deficiency issued in this case is invalid on the ground that respondent failed to make a determination within the meaning of section 6212(a). As explained in greater detail below, we agree with respondent that the notice of deficiency is valid.

---

5. The two exhibits in question are separate Forms 3233 (Report of Gift Tax Examination Changes) prepared by an Internal Revenue Service examiner relating to a review of the previously mentioned gift tax returns filed on behalf of decedent and Mr. Rickman.

This Court's jurisdiction to redetermine a deficiency depends upon the issuance of a valid notice of deficiency and a timely filed petition. Rule 13(a), (c); Levitt v. Commissioner, 97 T.C. 437, 441 (1991). Section 6212(a) expressly authorizes respondent, after determining a deficiency, to send a notice of deficiency to the taxpayer by certified or registered mail.

At a minimum, a notice of deficiency must indicate that respondent has determined a deficiency in tax in a definite amount for a particular taxable year and that respondent intends to assess the tax in due course. Although section 7522(a) provides the general rule that a notice of deficiency shall describe the basis for, and identify the amounts (if any) of tax due, an inadequate description shall not invalidate the notice under that provision.

In *Scar v. Commissioner*, 814 F.2d 1363 (9th Cir. 1987), revg. 81 T.C. 855 (1983), the taxpayers, after receiving a notice of deficiency that disallowed a deduction from a partnership with which the taxpayers had no connection, argued that the Commissioner failed to determine a deficiency as contemplated under section 6212(a). A review of various statements attached to the notice of deficiency revealed that the Commissioner had issued the notice without reviewing the taxpayers' tax return (which admittedly had been filed). Further, the Commissioner admitted to having done so "to protect the government's interest". Scar v. Commissioner, supra at 1365.

After invoking this Court's jurisdiction, the taxpayers filed a motion to dismiss for lack of jurisdiction. We held the notice of deficiency to be valid and denied the taxpayers' motion to dismiss. *Scar v. Commissioner*, 81 T.C. 855 (1983).

In analyzing the issue on appeal, the Court of Appeals for the Ninth Circuit concluded that the Commissioner must consider information relating to a particular taxpayer before it can be said that the Commissioner determined a deficiency with respect to that taxpayer. *Scar v. Commissioner*, 814 F.2d at 1368. With this standard in mind, the court found the notice of deficiency to be invalid under section 6212(a) because the notice on its face revealed that the Commissioner had not reviewed the taxpayers' return or otherwise made a determination respecting the taxpayers' liability for the particular taxable year. *Scar v. Commissioner*, supra at 1370.

Significantly, the courts applying *Scar*, including both this Court and the Court of Appeals for the Ninth Circuit, have limited the rule established in that case to its facts. See *Sealy Power, Ltd. v. Commissioner*, 46 F.3d 382, 387-388 (5th Cir. 1995); *Kantor v.*

Commissioner, 998 F.2d 1514, 1521-1522 (9th Cir. 1993); *Clapp v. Commissioner*, 875 F.2d 1396, 1402 (9th Cir. 1989); *Campbell v. Commissioner*, 90 T.C.110, 114-115 (1988). Simply stated, the rule set forth in *Scar v. Commissioner*, supra, applies in the narrow set of circumstances where the notice of deficiency on its face reveals that respondent failed to make a determination.

The following excerpt from *Kantor v. Commissioner*, supra, reflects the Court of Appeals for the Ninth Circuit's view of the applicability of *Scar*:

> Before issuing a notice of deficiency pursuant to 26 U.S.C. [sec.] 6212(a), the Commissioner must make an actual determination of the taxpayer's liability. *Scar*, 814 F.2d at 1370. As a general rule, however, we will not "look behind a deficiency notice to question the Commissioner's motives and procedures leading to a determination." Id. at 1368. We recognized an exception to this rule in *Scar*, where the notice of deficiency revealed on its face that a determination had not been made using the taxpayer's return. Id. * * * We later emphasized in *Clapp v. Commissioner*, however, that the kind of review exercised in *Scar* is applicable "[o]nly where the notice of deficiency reveals *on its face* that the Commissioner failed to make a determination." 875 F.2d at 1402 (emphasis added). In *Clapp*, we determined that the notices of deficiency were adequate to establish jurisdiction where they indicated various adjustments to income and the fact that these adjustments were based upon the disallowance of deductions. The taxpayers in *Clapp* attempted to show that the Commissioner had not made an actual determination of their deficiency by introducing internal IRS documents which suggested that at the time the notices were issued, the IRS had not decided which legal theory it would rely upon to secure a deficiency judgment. We nevertheless refused to question the Commissioner's determination because there was no indication on the face of the notices that a determination had not been made. Id. at 1400-01. The disallowed deductions did not refer to unrelated entities, nor had the tax rate been arbitrarily set.
>
> After reviewing appellant's 1981 notice of deficiency, we conclude that it was sufficient to establish jurisdiction. The notice clearly indicates that appellants' PCS, Ltd., pass-through deduction of $12,500 was being disallowed, that their tax was being recomputed, and that a negligence penalty was being imposed. There is neither blatant error nor any statement which would suggest that the Commissioner had not made a determination using appellants' tax return.

Kantor v. Commissioner, supra at 1521-1522.

Applying the principles discussed in *Kantor v. Commissioner*, and by this Court in *Campbell v. Commissioner*, supra, to the notice of deficiency issued to petitioner in the present case, we are not convinced, as petitioner contends, that respondent failed to make the requisite determination. There is no dispute that the notice of deficiency relates to the decedent's estate and that respondent correctly listed the decedent's social security number. It is also evident that respondent's determination of a deficiency in petitioner's Federal estate tax derived from a review of both the estate tax and gift tax returns filed on behalf of both petitioner and the Estate of James R. Rickman. Specifically, we need go no further than to point out that the valuation adjustments in respect of the 6 parcels of real estate set forth in the notice of deficiency directly coincide with real estate reported on petitioner's estate tax return. In sum, the evidence is irrefutable that respondent examined petitioner's estate tax return.

Petitioner contends that respondent failed to make a determination as required under section 6212(a) on the grounds: (1) The adjustment described in paragraph (a) of the explanation of adjustments was not adequately supported due to respondent's failure to attach exhibits A and B referred to therein to the notice of deficiency; (2) the valuation adjustments in respect of the real estate listed on petitioner's return are purportedly based on local real estate tax assessments for 1991 (as opposed to 1990); (3) the adjustment described in paragraph (h) of the explanation of adjustments has no basis in law or fact; and (4) the adjustment described in paragraph (I) of the explanation of adjustments contains certain errors in respect of both the date of the transfer in question and the identity of the financial institution involved in the transfer. In short, we are not impressed with any of these contentions. Taking the notice of deficiency as a whole, the errors and flaws that petitioner relies on, while perhaps causing minor confusion, do not demonstrate that respondent failed to make the requisite "determination" contemplated by section 6212(a).

We likewise reject petitioner's invitation to "carve out a narrow extension of *Scar*", to be applied in cases involving so-called "gross ineptitude".[8] In our view, an extension of *Scar* in this manner would, as a general rule, directly conflict with the well-settled rule that, absent extraordinary circumstances, we will not look behind a notice of

---

8. Petitioner's reliance on *Pearce v. Commissioner*, 95 T.C. 250 (1990), revd. without published opinion 946 F.2d 1543 (5th Cir. 1991), is misplaced. For the reasons explained in *Stinnett v. Commissioner*, T.C. Memo. 1993-429, we shall not reconsider our opinion in *Pearce v. Commissioner*, supra, or its reversal by the Fifth Circuit, in deciding this case.

deficiency. Riland v. Commissioner, 79 T.C. 185, 201 (1982); Jackson v. Commissioner, 73 T.C. 394, 400 (1979); Greenberg's Express, Inc. v. Commissioner, 62 T.C. 324, 327-328 (1974). We fail to see any extraordinary circumstances in the present case justifying a probe into respondent's motives and procedures leading to the issuance of the notice of deficiency.

In addition to arguing that the notice of deficiency is invalid under *Scar*, petitioner maintains that the notice of deficiency might be deemed invalid by virtue of respondent's failure to comply with section 7517. Section 7517, enacted as section 2008(a)(1) of the Tax Reform Act of 1976, Pub. L. 94-455, 90 Stat. 1520, 1891, provides in pertinent part:

> (a) General Rule.–If the Secretary makes a determination or a proposed determination of the value of an item of property for purposes of the tax imposed under chapter 11, 12, or 13, he shall furnish, on the written request of the executor, donor, or the person required to make the return of the tax imposed by chapter 13 (as the case may be), to such executor, donor, or person a written statement containing the material required by subsection (b). Such statement shall be furnished not later than 45 days after the later of the date of such request or the date of such determination or proposed determination.
>
> (b) Contents of Statement.–A statement required to be furnished under subsection (a) with respect to the value of an item of property shall–(1) explain the basis on which the valuation was determined or proposed, (2) set forth any computation used in arriving at such value, and (3) contain a copy of any expert appraisal made by or for the Secretary.

Initially, we find it significant that section 7517 does not include an enforcement mechanism. Although petitioner has suggested that respondent's failure to comply with section 7517 may provide grounds for holding the notice of deficiency invalid, petitioner has failed to cite any authority for this proposition and we are aware of none. In the absence of express language declaring that a notice of deficiency will be deemed invalid as a consequence of respondent's failure to comply with a written request under section 7517, we will not graft such an extreme remedy onto the provision.[9]

---

9. On the whole, petitioner's reliance on sec. 7517 seems superficial. Although the District Director may not have responded to petitioner's request pursuant to sec. 7517, we note that petitioner's counsel was apparently provided with a copy of the revenue agent's report on or about July 27, 1995. Moreover, our Rules provide the means for petitioner to obtain such information either through the required informal exchange of information contemplated under Rule 70(a) or later through formal discovery requests such as a request for production of documents.

Finally, we observe that Congress has provided adequate remedies for taxpayers confronted with an inaccurate deficiency determination. In light of remedies such as shifting the burden of proof to respondent and/or awarding litigation costs, petitioner's call for an expanded substantive review of the matters leading to respondent's determination is unwarranted.

Consistent with the foregoing, we shall deny petitioner's motion to dismiss for lack of jurisdiction.

* * *

Notes

There are two conflicting views regarding the sufficiency of a notice of deficiency. One is that since § 6212 is not specific about what the notice should contain, the contents are not important. Instead, it is the notice to the taxpayer that the "Commissioner means to assess him" that is important. See Olsen v. Helvering, 88 F.2d 650, 651 (2d Cir. 1937). The other view is that the notice must contain enough information to establish that the Service has made a "determination" of deficiency. See Scar v. Commissioner, 814 F.2d 136 (9th Cir. 1987); see also Michael I. Saltzman, IRS PRACTICE & PROCEDURE ¶ 10.93[3][b] (Revised 2d Ed. 2002).

The notice of deficiency is required to include a notice of the taxpayer's right to contact the local office of the National Taxpayer Advocate (see § 6212(a)), and it must specify the last date on which the taxpayer can file a petition in the Tax Court (see § 6213(a)). See also Chapter 4.

b. Proper Parties

The taxpayer is always the plaintiff/petitioner in the Tax Court, while the Commissioner is always the respondent. Under the Tax Court Rules, the case must be brought by the person against whom the deficiency or liability was determined, although a fiduciary may bring suit on behalf of such person. Tax Court Rule 60. If the suit is not brought by the proper party, the court will not dismiss the suit immediately, but instead will give the proper party a reasonable time to ratify the suit. If the party ratifies, the case will be considered to have brought by that party.

If the case involves more than one party, any of the parties may bring suit and if one party brings the action, only that party's claim will be heard. If the proper party is an infant or incompetent person, the representative of that person may bring the case on behalf of the party.

If there is no authorized representative, a next friend or guardian ad litem may be appointed to act on behalf of that person.

If a proper party dies or becomes incompetent after the commencement of the suit, the court, either on its own motion or upon motion of the successor or representative of the party, may order substitution of the proper parties. Frequently, problems arise where the taxpayer is a corporation that has merged or dissolved.

FLETCHER PLASTICS, INC. v. COMMISSIONER
Tax Court of the United States, 1975.
64 T.C. 35.

DAWSON, CHIEF JUDGE:

This matter is before the Court on respondent's motion to dismiss for lack of jurisdiction on the ground that the petition in this case was not filed by a proper party.

In a notice of deficiency dated June 20, 1974, respondent determined * * * Federal income tax deficiencies* * *.

* * *

This notice of deficiency was addressed to 'Atlas Tool Co. Inc., Successor to Fletcher Plastics, Inc.' The petition filed herein on September 13, 1974, was captioned 'Fletcher Plastics, Inc., Stephan Schaffan, Transferee, Petitioner.' It alleged that Fletcher Plastics was a corporation organized under the laws of New Jersey but dissolved more than 3 years before the mailing of the notice of deficiency, and that Stephan Schaffan was its sole shareholder.

On October 25, 1974, respondent filed a motion to dismiss this case for lack of jurisdiction on the ground that the petition had not been filed by a proper party. On November 12, 1974, counsel for Atlas Tool filed a memorandum objecting to respondent's motion to dismiss and a motion to amend the caption together with a motion to amend its petition pursuant to Rules 41(a) and 60(a), Tax Court Rules of Practice and Procedure. At the same time it also filed an amended petition in which the caption was the same as that set forth in the statutory notice of deficiency. * * *

There is no dispute that the petition captioned 'Fletcher Plastics, Inc., Stephan Schaffan, Transferee, Petitioner' was timely filed. However, respondent asserts in his motion that neither Fletcher Plastics, Inc., nor Stephan Schaffan is the party to whom a notice of deficiency was sent nor are they legally entitled to institute a case on behalf of Atlas Tool

Co., Successor to Fletcher Plastics, Inc., based on the notice of deficiency mailed in this case.

The only issue for our decision is whether Atlas Tool Co., Inc., the taxpayer to whom the notice of deficiency was sent, can ratify and amend, after the 90-day statutory period has expired, a petition filed on its behalf and signed by its counsel which was intended to contest the deficiencies determined in that notice, but incorrectly captioned.

The jurisdiction of the Tax Court is specifically limited by statute, section 7442, and the statutory requirements must be satisfied for us to acquire jurisdiction.

To invoke our jurisdiction, section 6213(a) requires that 'the taxpayer' to whom a notice of deficiency is addressed must file a timely petition with this Court for a redetermination of the deficiency determined in such notice.

A review of the cases decided prior to the adoption of our new Rules of Practice and Procedure on January 1, 1974, indicates that the general rule is that a petition must be filed by the taxpayer against whom the deficiency was determined or his duly authorized representative, except in cases of transferee liability, and except where a party is permitted to ratify an imperfect petition, after proving that the original filing was made on his behalf by one authorized to do so.

* * *

Respondent notes that Rule 60(a) provides that a petition should be filed by and in the name of the person against whom the Commissioner determined a deficiency. He contends that since that was not done here, Rule 41(a) bars amendment of the petition. The pertinent part of that Rule reads as follows:

> No amendment shall be allowed after expiration of the time for filing the petition, however, which would involve conferring jurisdiction on the Court over a matter which otherwise would not come within its jurisdiction under the petition as then on file * * *

In support of this position, respondent stresses the Note following this Rule which reads:

> The rule of liberal amendment provided here applies to all pleadings, except for certain areas relating to the petition which concern the jurisdiction of the Court. The Court's jurisdiction is limited with respect to (a) the taxpayers whose tax deficiency or liability may be redetermined; (b) the years for which such redetermination may pertain. In these respects, a case is fixed by the petition as originally filed or as amended within the statutory period

for filing the petition, and thereafter may not be altered by amendment as to any of these areas.

* * *

To the contrary, petitioner argues that this is a procedural, not a jurisdictional, problem. After noting that Rules 23(a)(1) and 32(a) require that a proper caption[3] be placed on all pleadings filed with this Court, petitioner cites Rule 41(a) which provides in relevant part, that a party may amend his pleadings either 'by leave of court or by written consent of the adverse party; *and leave shall be given freely when justice so requires.*' (Emphasis added.) Petitioner argues that this reflects a liberal attitude toward amendment of pleadings.

In further support of this position, petitioner refers to Rule 60(a) which provides, in relevant part, that:

A case timely brought shall not be dismissed on the ground that it is not properly brought on behalf of a party until a reasonable time has been allowed after objection for ratification by such party of the bringing of the case; and such ratification shall have the same effect as if the case had been properly brought by such party. * * *

The Note following this Rule further shows a liberal attitude toward amendment and/or correction of pleadings in a case like that presently before us:

Where the intention is to file a petition on behalf of a party, the scope of this provision permits correction of errors as to the proper party or his identity made in a petition otherwise timely and correct. * * *

After careful examination of the record and the law, we will deny respondent's motion to dismiss and grant petitioner's motion to amend the caption and the pleadings. Atlas Tool clearly intended to file a petition to contest the deficiencies determined in a notice of deficiency sent to it and this petition was signed by its duly authorized counsel, as permitted by Rule 34(b)(7). Rule 60(a) expressly permits a party to timely ratify a defective petition filed on its behalf. The Note states that this Rule permits the correction of errors as to the proper party to be made where there was an intent to file a petition on behalf of a party.

Our holding here is consistent with Rule 34(a) which provides that 'Failure of the　petition to satisfy applicable requirements *may* be ground for dismissal of the case.' (Emphasis added.) The Note to this Rule explains the emphasized language as follows:

---

3. The practitioner can easily satisfy this requirement by using the name of the party to whom the notice of deficiency was sent, as it appears on the statutory notice, in the caption of the petition.

The dismissal of a petition, for failure to satisfy applicable requirements, depends on the nature of the defect, and therefore is put in the contingent 'may' rather than the mandatory 'shall' of present T.C. Rule 7(a)(2). * * *

In so acting, we are not taking jurisdiction of a matter which is outside our jurisdiction as determined by the petition originally filed. See Rule 41(a). A review of the cases cited in the Note to that Rule shows that most deal with untimely amendments relating to taxable years or categories of taxes different than those contained in the original petition. * * *

The remaining case cited in the Note, Percy N. Powers, 20 B.T.A. 753 (1930), is not on point, but does illustrate that our policy on amendments involving parties is more liberal. In that case a joint petition was filed on behalf of 10 petitioners, but not signed by all of them. We refused to permit an untimely amendment to add the nonsigning petitioners because counsel had not signed the original petition and, furthermore, there was no showing of his authority to act on their behalf.

However, we noted in *Powers* at page 757, that we had permitted amendments to petitions signed by taxpayer's counsel upon a showing that the person who signed the original petition had been duly authorized to do so. * * *

The instant case is clearly distinguishable from *Powers* because the petition here was signed by counsel for Atlas Tool who had authority to sign the petition on its behalf, and Atlas Tool timely ratified that act. Since the petition was filed on behalf of a party who has timely ratified the act of its authorized agent, this is not a case where the administrative problems noted in [*Powers*] * * * would arise.

This situation is also distinguishable from those cases where a petition has been brought by a nonexistent party, see Great Falls Bonding Agency, Inc., 63 T.C. 304 (1974), since Atlas Tool was in existence when the petition and amendment were filed. Finally, this case is to be distinguished from [those cases in which] a party to whom a statutory notice of deficiency was not sent attempts to join as a party-petitioner, the taxpayer to whom the notice of deficiency was sent. Here the statutory notice was sent to Atlas Tool on whose behalf a petition was filed. Atlas Tool has ratified that filing and seeks to amend that petition here.

Accordingly, we conclude that although the original defective petition was not filed in the name of a proper party as required by Rule 60, and did not have a proper caption as required by Rules 23(a)(1) and 32(a), the clear language of Rule 60(a) bars dismissal under these particular facts. We hold that this is a proper case for amendment of the pleadings under Rule 41(a); and under Rule 41(d) the amendment will relate back to the date of the filing of the original petition.

An appropriate order will be entered.

Notes

Generally, the party or parties named in the notice of deficiency will be considered the proper parties for bringing suit in the Tax Court. If there is a variance between the names listed in the notice of deficiency and the proper parties, however, Tax Court Rule 34(b)(1) requires the parties to provide a statement of the reasons for such variance in the petition. Note that the Tax Court has determined that a corporation whose status was suspended under state law for nonpayment of state income taxes lacked capacity to bring suit in the Tax Court, even though the taxpayer was named in the notice of deficiency. See Le v. Commissioner, 114 T.C. 268 (2000).

Problems

1. Sylvia is a 21-year old college student. In 2002, her father gave her a one-third interest in some timber land that he owned. In 2007, the timber was cut and Sylvia received $45,000. Sylvia's father had his accountant prepare Sylvia's tax return, along with his own, and Sylvia's father paid the accountant for preparing the return. It was determined that Sylvia owed $10,800 in income taxes for 2007. Sylvia had spent her timber income on a new car, a trip to Europe, and on living expenses. Therefore, she had no money with which to pay the tax, so her father paid it for her. Two years later, both Sylvia's return and her father's return were audited and as a result, both received notices of deficiency. The Service asserted a deficiency of $20,500 attributable to her father's return, and $8,000 attributable to Sylvia's return. The Service argued that $2,000 of Sylvia's $8,000 alleged deficiency was attributable to the economic benefit she had received when her father paid her taxes. Since her father had not filed a gift tax return, his payment of Sylvia's taxes constituted additional income to her. Can Sylvia's father file a single petition in Tax Court and argue that he intended the tax payment to be a gift? See Duberstein v. Commissioner, 363 U.S. 278 (1960).

2. Jack and Jill were husband and wife in 2007, and they filed a joint federal income tax return for 2007. In 2009, they divorced, and shortly afterward, they received a notice of deficiency attributable to the 2007 return. Jack filed a timely petition in the Tax Court but Jill did

not. It is now well past the 90-day filing period from the mailing of the notice of deficiency. Can Jill's case be heard by the court? See Abeles v. Commissioner, 90 T.C. 103 (1988).

c. Timely Petition

CORREIA v. COMMISSIONER
United States Court of Appeals, Ninth Circuit, 1995.
58 F.3d 468.

PER CURIAM:

Taxpayers Vernon L. Correia and Charlotte M. Correia timely appeal the Tax Court's dismissal of their petition for redetermination of deficiency. The Tax Court dismissed the petition for lack of jurisdiction. We review de novo and affirm.

I. BACKGROUND

The Commissioner of Internal Revenue issued a statutory notice of deficiency to Taxpayers on April 9, 1993. See 26 U.S.C. § 6211. Pursuant to 26 U.S.C. § 6213(a), Taxpayers had 90 days–until July 8, 1993–to file their petition for redetermination. On July 8 Taxpayers delivered their petition to Federal Express for delivery to the Tax Court. The petition was not delivered to the Tax Court until July 9. The Tax Court dismissed the petition as untimely.

II. DISCUSSION

The timely filing of a petition for redetermination is a jurisdictional requirement. Shipley v. Commissioner, 572 F.2d 212, 213 (9th Cir.1977). It is undisputed that Taxpayers' petition was not timely received by the Tax Court. However, Taxpayers contend that their otherwise untimely petition is saved by the timely-mailing-as-timely-filing provision of 26 U.S.C. § 7502. Under § 7502, for a document "delivered by United States mail * * *, the date of the United States postmark * * * shall be deemed to be the date of delivery." § 7502(a).

Section 7502 by its plain and unambiguous language applies to documents delivered by the United States Postal Service. It does not apply to documents delivered by private companies such as Federal Express. See Treas. Reg. § 301.7502-1(c). Nonetheless, Taxpayers contend that because § 7502 and its corresponding regulations reflect outdated notions of reliable delivery methods, we should "adopt a new rule" extending the scope of § 7502 to private delivery services. Although

Taxpayers put forth what may be a legitimate policy rationale for extending the rule to private delivery services, it is for Congress, not the courts, to make such a change.

Taxpayers also argue that the Tax Court violated their due process rights by sua sponte notifying the Commissioner of the late filing. Subject matter jurisdiction in the Tax Court cannot be conferred by the parties' consent or waiver. Clapp v. Commissioner, 875 F.2d 1396, 1398 (9th Cir.1989). The Tax Court properly examined its own jurisdiction. See id. at 1399 (jurisdiction of Tax Court reviewed in same manner as jurisdiction of Article III courts); FW/PBS, Inc. v. Dallas, 493 U.S. 215, 231, 110 S.Ct. 596, 607, 107 L.Ed.2d 603 (1990) ("federal courts are under an independent obligation to examine their own jurisdiction"). Its conduct did not violate due process.

AFFIRMED.

Notes

If the notice of deficiency is addressed to a person outside the United States, the period to file the petition is extended to 150 days. IRC § 6213. Whether the 90-day period or the 150-day period applies, the first day of the filing period is the calendar day after the notice was mailed. See Tax Court Rule 25(a)(1). If the last day falls on a Saturday, Sunday, or legal holiday in the District of Columbia, the deadline is extended to the next business day.

B. CASE DESIGNATION

In a case in which the amount in controversy, including penalties but excluding interest, does not exceed $50,000 ($10,000 prior to July 22, 1998) for one taxable year, the taxpayer has the option of having the case heard under expedited and simplified procedures. IRC § 7463(a)(1). If a small tax case procedure option is elected, the case is referred to as an "S" case, and is conducted more informally than a regular case. For instance, strict rules of evidence are not applied, and no briefs or oral arguments are required, although they may be permitted upon request of either party or by the court on its own motion. It is anticipated that most taxpayers will choose to represent themselves (pro se) in a small tax case, which is why S cases are conducted with less formality, but a taxpayer may be represented by anyone authorized to practice before the Tax Court if the taxpayer so chooses. A decision entered in an S case is neither precedent for future cases nor reviewable upon appeal by either party. IRC § 7463(b).

While the taxpayer must opt for S case status, the status must be approved by the Tax Court. After the trial has begun, the court may order a discontinuance of the small tax case procedure and instead order that the case be tried under the regular rules. Such a discontinuance is likely to occur if (1) the court finds that there are reasonable grounds to believe that the amount of deficiency in dispute, or the amount of an overpayment, will exceed the applicable jurisdictional amount and (2) the amount of the excess is large enough to justify discontinuance. IRC § 7463(d).

DRESSLER v. COMMISSIONER
United States Tax Court, 1971.
56 T.C. 210.

OPINION

SCOTT, JUDGE:

On January 4, 1971, the petition in the above-entitled case was filed. The deficiency in dispute was stated to be for the year 1967 and in the amount of $498.20, the entire amount of deficiency for the year 1967 as shown by the notice of deficiency attached to the petition.

The petition was served on respondent on January 14, 1971, and on that same date there was served on petitioners, with a copy to respondent, a Notice to Petitioners Having a Small Tax Case, which stated in part as follows:

> In small tax cases such as yours, Rule 36 provides that you may make a request to have the proceedings conducted under the provisions of Section 7463, Code of 1954. A Request Form for this purpose is enclosed with this notice. Unless the Commissioner of Internal Revenue objects to your request–in which case you will be notified–your request will ordinarily be granted by the Court.

On February 5, 1971, petitioners filed a Request to Have Proceedings Conducted Under Section 7463.

Respondent on February 9, 1971, filed his answer, generally denying the allegations in the petition and on the same date, in accordance with the provisions of Rule 36(c)(2) of the Rules of Practice of this Court, filed his Motion to Deny Petitioners' Request for Conduct of Proceedings Under Section 7463. Respondent in support of his motion stated that he did not know of a case in which the precise issue involved in the instant case had been decided. Respondent stated that he had issued a revenue ruling, Rev. Rul. 59-270, 1959-2 C.B. 44, stating his position on the issue involved in this case.

Both parties state the issue involved in the above-entitled case to be whether petitioner John Dressler, a 'minister of music' in the Methodist Church, is a 'minister of the gospel' within the intendment of section 107, I.R.C. 1954, so as to be entitled under that section to exclude from his taxable income the amount of $2,599.92 which he received as a housing allowance during the year 1967.

The allegations contained in the petition state that petitioner John Dressler holds a degree in church and school music from the Academy of Music in Vienna and a master's degree in music from Birmingham Southern College in Birmingham, Ala.; that he has held the position of 'minister of music' in the Methodist Church for 26 years and from 1963 to the present time has held that position with the Peachtree Road Methodist Church in Atlanta, Ga.; that he has attended special leadership training courses which led to his being certified as a 'minister of music' in the Methodist Church; and that in January 1959 he was consecrated as a 'minister of music' by a bishop of the Methodist Church in a special laying on of hands ceremony. The petition further alleges that petitioner John Dressler as a 'minister of music' in the Methodist Church, performs duties of a sacerdotal nature and takes part in the conducting of the worship services of his congregation, including, but not by way of limitation, direction of the choir and congregational singing, selection of appropriate music for the choir and congregational signing, training of the choirs in the theology of hymns, as well as in vocal presentation, preparation, and conducting of the musical portion of the Lord's Supper services and baptismal services, counseling with congregation members about their personal problems, and visiting the sick at the local hospitals.

This Court held in Abraham A. Salkov, 46 T.C. 190 (1966), that a full-time cantor of the Jewish faith who was commissioned by the Cantors Assembly of America and installed by a congregation is a 'minister of the gospel' within the meaning of section 107 of the 1954 Code. In Robert D. Lawrence, 50 T.C. 494 (1968), we held that a 'minister of education' in the Baptist Church who was not an ordained minister but served a church that had a regular paster who was an ordained minister was not a 'minister of the gospel' within the meaning of section 107 and in W. Astor Kirk, 51 T.C. 66 (1968), affd. 425 F.2d 492 (C.A.D.C. 1970), held that a professional employee of the General Board of Christian Social Concerns of the Methodist Church who was not ordained, licensed, or commissioned as a minister and performed no functions of a sacerdotal character was not a 'minister of the gospel' within the meaning of section 107 even though 9 of the 11 professional employees of the Board of Christian Social Concerns of the Methodist

Church who did work similar to that done by the taxpayer were ordained ministers of the Methodist Church.

Respondent's Rev. Rul. 59-270, supra, concludes that a 'minister of music' may not exclude from his gross income the rental value of a dwelling provided to him since he was not ordained, commissioned or licensed as a 'minister of the gospel.'

Respondent contends that the precise issue in the instant case has not been decided by this Court or other courts and states that he believes the issue is of sufficient legal importance to be tried as a regular case.

Petitioners in their memorandum in opposition to respondent's motion filed February 22, 1971, and through their counsel at the hearing on respondent's motion, argue that respondent has failed to present as a ground for his motion the only statutory basis for discontinuance of a case as a small tax case, which petitioners state is the basis provided in section 7463(d) that the Court concludes that there are reasonable grounds for believing that the amount of the deficiency placed in dispute exceeds or may exceed the applicable jurisdictional amount of $1,000 for any 1 year. Petitioners further argue that if they are incorrect in their interpretation of the only basis on which a request for the case to be heard in accordance with section 7463 may be denied, this case is not of sufficient legal or factual importance to warrant the amount which petitioners would be required to expend to try the case under other than the provisions of section 7463. Petitioners argue that section 7463 was intended to permit an economical trial for a taxpayer who contests a small amount of deficiency and that their request to try this case under the provisions of section 7463 should be granted since the issue here is primarily one of fact. Petitioners contend that previously decided cases have clarified the law with respect to the necessary requisites of a 'minister of the gospel' under section 107. Petitioners state that a decision in the instant case will not determine whether all 'ministers of music' in the Methodist Church or of all Protestant churches are entitled to the benefits of section 107, but rather will determine whether the petitioner John Dressler with his particular qualifications and the particular services he rendered to his church should be classed as a 'minister of the gospel.'

In our view respondent's motion is properly filed under the provisions of rule 36(c)(2) of the Rules of Practice of this Court. The provisions of section 7463(d) to which petitioners refer in their argument concern discontinuance of a case as a small tax case after this Court has concurred in the taxpayer's request as provided by section 7463(a) which generally would be when trial of the case commenced. This situation is covered by Rule 36(d) of the Rules of Practice of this Court. However, we agree with petitioners that a taxpayer should be entitled to have his case tried as a small tax case where the jurisdictional amount of the deficiency brings it within the provisions of section 7463 unless respondent shows that the issue involved is an issue of importance which will establish a principle of law applicable to other tax cases. In the instant case respondent has made no such showing. In previous cases this Court has concluded that in order to be a 'minister of the gospel' a taxpayer must be ordained, commissioned, or licensed as such or must perform sacerdotal duties.

From the allegations contained in the petition, the issue here appears to be primarily one of fact. Whether the certificate which petitioner John Dressler obtained and his consecration by the bishop amount in substance to his being commissioned, ordained, or licensed as a 'minister of the gospel' is a factual question. Whether the duties he performed are of a sacerdotal nature is also a factual question.

Respondent's counsel at the trial argued that because there are subsequent years in which the issue here involved will again arise with respect to this same petitioner, his motion should be granted. In our view this fact alone is not sufficient ground for refusing the request of a petitioner that his case be tried as a small tax case. It might be to a petitioner's advantage not to have a case involving a continuing issue heard under section 7463 so he could obtain a decision which would be a precedent for future years. However, in our view this is not a sufficient ground for the Court to grant a motion by respondent to deny a petitioner's request for a hearing under section 7463.

We therefore hold that respondent has not shown adequate reasons to support his Motion to Deny Petitioners' Request for Conduct of Proceedings under Section 7463, filed February 9, 1971. An order will be entered denying respondent's motion.

Notes and Questions

The jurisdictional amount for small tax cases previously was raised from $5,000 to $10,000 under the Deficit Reduction Act of 1984, P.L. No. 98-369. In 1998, the IRS Restructuring and Reform Act raised the amount to $50,000. Pub. L. No. 105-206. Because of the relatively large increase, Congress was concerned that some cases newly eligible for S status might have precedential value. Accordingly, the Tax Court is expected to consider carefully a taxpayer's request for S status, giving particular attention to the issue of precedential value of the case.

1. What effect might the denial of S status have on a taxpayer?

2. What factors should the court consider in determining whether a case has precedental value?

3. Is a taxpayer eligible to request S status if the taxpayer receives a notice of deficiency that proposes a deficiency of $48,000, along with penalties of $5,000, and the taxpayer concedes $5,000 of the deficiency? See Kallich v. Commissioner, 89 T.C. 676 (1987).

C. PLEADINGS

The purpose of the pleadings, according to the Tax Court Rules, is to give both the parties and the Court "fair notice of the matters in controversy and the basis for their respective positions." Tax Court Rule 31(a). Although no technical form of pleading is required, the Tax Court rules provide that pleadings must be "simple, concise, and direct." Id. at Rule 31(b). The pleadings also must be signed by the taxpayer if the taxpayer is appearing pro se, or by counsel if the taxpayer is represented. The signature certifies that the signer has read the pleading, and that to the best of the signer's "knowledge, information, and belief," the pleading is "well grounded in fact" and "warranted by existing law or a good faith argument for the extension, modification, or reversal of existing law." Id. at Rule 33(b). The signature further certifies that the taxpayer's counsel is duly authorized to represent the taxpayer on whose behalf the pleading is filed. If the pleading is "interposed for any improper purpose, such as to harass or to cause unnecessary delay or needless increase in the cost of litigation," a sanction may be imposed that may include court costs and reasonable expenses, including reasonable counsel's fees. Id.

When the petition is received by the Clerk of Court, the case will be docketed with an assigned number, and the parties will be notified. The Clerk then will serve the pleading upon the Commissioner, who will have 60 days from the date of the service to file an Answer, or 45 days from the date of service to file a motion with respect to the petition. If the motion is denied, the Commissioner will have to file an Answer. The Answer must contain a specific admission or denial of each material element of the petition. Any material element not so expressly admitted or denied is deemed admitted. Id. at Rule 36(a) and (b).

After receiving the Answer, the Clerk will serve it on the petitioner, who will have 45 days from the date of service to file a Reply, or 30 days from that date to file a motion with respect to the Answer. The Reply should contain a specific admission or denial as to each material allegation in the Answer on which the government bears the burden of proof, such as res judicata, collateral estoppel, equitable estoppel, waiver, duress, fraud, or the statute of limitations. These must be specifically raised in the pleadings. Id. at Rule 39. If the petitioner is "without knowledge or information sufficient to form a belief as to the truth of an allegation," the petitioner should so state, and the statement will have the effect of a denial. Otherwise, any affirmative allegation in the Answer that is not specifically admitted or denied in the Reply is deemed admitted. If no Reply is filed, the affirmative allegations in the Answer will be deemed denied unless within 45 days of the expiration of the date for filing a Reply, the Commissioner moves that specified allegations be admitted. Id. at Rule 37.

The court will allow one amendment of a pleading before a responsive pleading is served, or if no responsive pleading is permitted and the case has not been placed on the trial calendar, the pleading may be amended within 30 days after it is served. If the pleading is not amended within this time frame, it may be amended only with leave of the court or upon written consent of the opposing party. After the expiration of the period for filing the petition, the pleading may not be amended to accommodate any matter that would involve conferring jurisdiction on the Court. Any amendment that is made will relate back to the time of the filing of the pleading, unless the court orders otherwise.

The Court will allow a party to file supplemental pleadings, upon motion, to reflect a transaction, occurrence, or event that has happened since the filing of the original pleading, and which will have a bearing on the case.

D. DISCOVERY

Discovery is available in the Tax Court through written interrogatories, requests for production of documents or things, depositions with or without consent of the parties, and depositions of expert witnesses. See Tax Court Rules 70 through 76. Since the Tax Court is a more informal forum than either the federal district court or the Court of Federal Claims, the court expects the parties to utilize informal consultation or communication before resorting to the discovery procedures.

1. The Informal Discovery Process

THE BRANERTON CORPORATION v. COMMISSIONER
United States Tax Court, 1974.
61 T.C. 691.

OPINION

Dawson, Judge:

This matter is before the Court on respondent's motion for a protective order, pursuant to Rule 103(a)(2), Tax Court Rules of Practice and Procedure, that respondent at this time need not answer written interrogatories served upon him by petitioners in these cases. Oral arguments on the motion were heard on February 20,1974, and, in addition, a written statement in opposition to respondent's motion was filed by the petitioners.

The sequence of events in these cases may be highlighted as follows: The statutory notices of deficiencies were mailed to the respective petitioners on April 20, 1973. As to the corporate petitioner, the adjustments relate to (1) additions to a reserve for bad debts, (2) travel, entertainment, and miscellaneous expenses, (3) taxes, and (4) depreciation. As to the individual petitioners, the adjustments relate to (1) charitable contributions, (2) entertainment expenses, (3) dividend income, and (4) medical expenses. Petitions in both cases were filed on July 2, 1973, and, after an extension of time for answering, respondent filed his answers on September 26, 1973. This Court's new Rules of Practice and Procedure became effective January 1, 1974. The next day petitioners' counsel served on respondent rather detailed and extensive written interrogatories pursuant to Rule 71. On January 11, 1974, respondent filed his motion for a protective order. The cases have not yet been scheduled for trial.

Petitioners' counsel has never requested an informal conference with respondent's counsel in these cases, although respondent's counsel states that he is willing to have such discussions at any mutually convenient time.   Consequently, in seeking a protective order, respondent specifically cites the second sentence of Rule 70(a)(1) which provides: 'However, the Court expects the parties to attempt to attain the objectives of discovery through informal consultation or communication before utilizing the discovery procedures provided in these Rules.'

It is plain that this provision in Rule 70(a)(1) means exactly what it says. The discovery procedures should be used only after the parties have made reasonable informal efforts to obtain needed information voluntarily. For many years the bedrock of Tax Court practice has been the stipulation process, now embodied in Rule 91. Essential to that process is the voluntary exchange of necessary facts, documents, and other data between the parties as an aid to the more expeditious trial of cases as well as for settlement purposes.[1] The recently adopted discovery procedures were not intended in any way to weaken the stipulation process. See Rule 91(a)(2).

Contrary to petitioners' assertion that there is no 'practical and substantial reason' for granting a protective order in these circumstances, we find good cause for doing so. Petitioners have failed to comply with the letter and spirit of the discovery rules. The attempted use of written interrogatories at this stage of the proceedings sharply conflicts with the intent and purpose of Rule 70(a)(1) and constitutes an abuse of the Court's procedures.

Accordingly, we conclude that respondent's motion for a protective order should be granted and he is relieved from taking any action with respect to these written interrogatories. The parties will be directed to have informal conferences during the next 90 days for the purpose of making good faith efforts to exchange facts, documents, and other information. Since the cases have not been scheduled for trial, there is sufficient time for the parties to confer and try informally to secure the evidence before resorting to formal discovery procedures. If such process does not meet the needs of the parties, they may then proceed with discovery to the extent permitted by the rules.

An appropriate order will be entered.

Notes and Question

Usually, the Service initiates the discovery process, because the taxpayer (who is the plaintiff in the Tax Court) is generally aware of the facts and has copies of most of the relevant material in the government's files. Tax Court Rule 103 provides that a protective order from discovery may be requested upon a showing of good cause by a party or non-party against whom discovery is sought. Annoyance, embarrassment, oppression or undue burden or expense all constitute good cause.

The discovery process often commences when one party, usually the government, sends the other a *Branerton* letter requesting a conference and a voluntary production of "facts, documents, and other information." Discovery in S cases usually is handled entirely through *Branerton*

---

1. Part of the explanatory note to Rule 91 (60 T.C. 1118) states that—"The stipulation process is more flexible, based on conference and negotiation between parties, adaptable to statements on matters in varying degrees of dispute, susceptible of defining and narrowing areas of dispute, and offering an active medium for settlement."

conferences, simply because these cases are heard through an expedited process, and thus there is insufficient time for the government to use the more formal discovery procedure. Discovery generally must commence 30 days after the filing of an answer (or 30 days after a reply to the answer if a reply is required), and must conclude no less than 45 days prior to the trial date.

Why does the court prefer the informal discovery process?

2. Methods of Discovery

After the parties have availed themselves of the informal consultation and communication process, if there are questions remaining that may be resolved through discovery, the parties may use the formal discovery process. There are several methods through which formal discovery may be obtained. These include written interrogatories, request for production of documents or things, and depositions.

a. Interrogatories

Interrogatories are written questions to be answered by the opposing party. The party on whom the interrogatories are served must answer each question separately and fully under oath, and must serve the answers on the propounding party within 30 days after service of the interrogatories. Tax Court Rule 71(c).

PLEIER v. COMMISSIONER
United States Tax Court, 1989.
92 T.C. 499.

PARR, JUDGE:

On February 13, 1989, respondent filed a motion to compel responses to his first set of interrogatories and, upon failure to provide responses, to impose sanctions under Rule 104. Petitioner objected, and on March 3, 1989, petitioner filed a motion for protective order pursuant to Rule 103(a). Petitioner objects to the interrogatories on the ground that respondent has not asked any questions. We agree.

Respondent's interrogatories are set forth below:

Please provide answers to each of the questions below:

1. Prepare the blank 1040 tax forms (Exhibits A through C) showing each item that you contend is relevant or might be relevant in determining your correct income tax liability for each year. Technical assistance and additional forms are available from respondent's counsel,

if requested in sufficient time to allow your timely response to these questions.

2. With respect to determining the correctness of each item on Exhibit A through C:

(a) List on Form A (documents list) all documents relating to each item.

(b) Explain on Form B (document relationship) the extent to which each document, listed on Form A, relates to each item.

(c) Describe on Form C (personally known facts) all personally known facts relating to each item (including your testimony).

(d) Describe on Form D (third person facts) all facts known by persons other than yourself, relating to each item and the name, address and telephone number of such persons.

Respondent attached a blank Form 1040 for each of the three years in issue. Respondent also attached four sheets of paper. The first was labeled 'FORM A DOCUMENTS LIST.' The form had four columns headed 'line,' 'page' and 'exhibit,' on which petitioner was requested to provide a list of documents supporting the items. Form B was entitled 'DOCUMENT RELATIONSHIP.' It had the same first three columns as Form A, but column four was titled 'EXPLAIN.' Forms C and D were entitled 'PERSONALLY KNOWN FACTS' and 'THIRD PARTY FACTS' respectively. The first three columns were identical to the preceding two forms, but column four was entitled 'DESCRIBE.'

Rule 103 authorizes the Court to issue protective orders upon a motion of a party or other affected person, and for good cause shown, which justice requires to protect a party or other person from annoyance, embarrassment, oppression, or undue burden or expense. The Court has countless times issued protective orders to protect taxpayers and the government from having to answer inappropriate interrogatories, or we have simply denied a party's motion to compel responses. See, e.g., Penn-Field Industries, Inc. v. Commissioner, 74 T.C. 720 (1980).

Rule 71 sets forth the parameters and requirements of interrogatories. Nowhere in the text of Rule 71 are 'interrogatories' defined. The official Tax Court note following revisions made to Rule 71 in 1974 states:

As a method of discovery, *interrogatories consist of written questions* submitted by a party, to which the other side files written answers. * * * [60 T.C. 1057, 1099 (1974).] [Emphasis added.]

A majority of Rule 71 was modeled after Rule 33 of the Federal Rules of Civil Procedure. The Federal Rules of Civil Procedure also do not define 'interrogatories.' However, interrogatories should be simple, concise and concerning only matters relevant to the action. A request to sign a form authorizing release of medical records is not an interrogatory within the meaning of Rule 33. McNight v. Blanchard, 667 F.2d 477 (5th Cir. 1982). It has also been said that:

> Interrogatories should be framed, as near as may be, as single, definite questions. * * * Interrogatories should be as simple and definite as the subject matter permits, so that it will be clear what it is the interrogated party is called upon to answer. [4A J. Moore, Federal practice, par. 33.08 (2d ed. 1948).]

A request to fill out Forms 1040 or other forms is not a single, definite question. If respondent wishes to obtain information contained in a Form 1040, respondent must serve petitioner separately numbered, written questions soliciting specific information. Respondent's interrogatories do not comply with Rule 71.

To reflect the foregoing,

An order will be entered denying respondent's motion to compel and granting petitioner's motion for protective order.

Notes

The party responding to interrogatories may opt to produce business records where an examination or inspection of the business records addresses the question, and the burden of deriving the information from the records is substantially the same for the party serving the interrogatories as it is for the party served. Tax Court Rule 71(e).

Interrogatories may be served only upon an adverse party. A limited exception is made, however, if a party intends to call an expert witness. If so, the opposing party may serve interrogatories requiring the identification of each expert witness whom the party intends to call. Such identification includes the witness' name, address, vocation or occupation, and a statement of the qualifications that entitles the witness to testify as an expert. In addition, the expert witness may be required to state the subject matter of her testimony, as well as the facts and opinions underlying that testimony. The expert also may be required to give a summary of the grounds for each opinion or to present such information in an expert witness report. Tax Court Rule 71(d).

b. *Requests for Productions of Documents*

Either party may request the other to produce or allow the requesting party to inspect or copy "any designated documents (including writings, drawings, graphs, charts, photographs, phono-records, and other data compilations * * *)" or to permit the requesting party "to inspect and copy, test, or sample any tangible thing," that is relevant to the case and is in the "possession, custody, or control of the party on whom the request is served." Tax Court Rule 72(a)(1). Such requests may be served only on an adverse party, and not on non-party witnesses, except to the extent that the designated document or thing is in the possession, custody or control of a transferee of the party. Tax Court Rules 72 and 73.

The party served has 30 days after service of the request for production to respond in writing, either permitting the request with respect to each item, or objecting in whole or in part. The requesting party may seek a ruling on the objection or on a failure of the opposing party to respond, and may file a motion to compel production. If the material requested is subject to a protective order issued by another court, what weight should the Tax Court give to the determination by the other court?

MELEA LIMITED v. COMMISSIONER
United States Tax Court, 2002.
118 T.C. 218.

GERBER, J.

* * *

Background

Melea Limited is a Gibraltar corporation with a business address in Geneva, Switzerland. Michael Ladney (Ladney), who is the petitioner in a related case pending in this Court, is a U.S. citizen who was the prior owner of several patents associated with petitioner's business activity, as it relates to plastic injection molding. Ladney is the principal shareholder of several U.S. corporations involved in the manufacture of plastic parts. At some time, Ladney transferred patents and other assets to offshore entities, including petitioner.

* * *

Respondent seeks copies of deposition transcripts taken in connection with litigation in the U.S. District Court for the Middle District of Florida. Petitioner was a defendant in litigation styled Cinpres Ltd. v. Hendry, Case No. 96-752-CIV-T-24B (M.D.Fla., Dec. 12, 1998) (*Cinpres* case). That case involved a patent infringement action brought by Cinpres, a British company, against petitioner and a competitor of petitioner. Petitioner, a foreign corporation, questioned the U.S. District Court's jurisdiction over it, and depositions were taken, in part, to discern the relationship between petitioner and two of Ladney's U.S. entities (the same ones that respondent determined were petitioner's dependent agents).

Pursuant to stipulation and agreement of the parties in the *Cinpres* case, the District Court entered a protective order on June 10, 1997, in order to "expedite the flow of discovery material, facilitate the prompt resolution of disputes over confidentially, adequately protect material entitled to be kept confidential, and insure that protection is afforded only to material so entitled".

Although there had been disagreement between the parties as to the content of the order, the parties, after assistance from the District Court, stipulated and agreed to an order, which the District Court approved. Under the protective order, any party, without court approval, could designate documents as either "confidential" or "attorney's eyes only" by stamping same on the document. Only documents containing "highly sensitive business or technical information" could be stamped for "attorney's eyes only". The *Cinpres* case was closed on December 12, 1998, without a trial and following a settlement reached by the parties.

In pertinent part, the *Cinpres* protective order contained the following prohibition on the use of documents classified as confidential by the parties: (1) Other than use by the parties to the *Cinpres* litigation and their counsel, disclosure of a classified document was not permitted without prior written consent of the party that had classified the document as confidential; (2) parties could apply to the court for declassification of a document; (3) confidential information in depositions could be classified as confidential by underlining the confidential portion and designating that portion as under the protective order; (4) if a classified document was subpoenaed or ordered produced by another court, the party that classified the document was to be advised; (5) classified documents were to be used only for preparation and trial in the *Cinpres* case; (6) the protective order provisions did not terminate at the conclusion of the *Cinpres* case; and (7) within 120 days of the termination of the *Cinpres* case the parties' counsel were permitted to maintain one set of protected matter, and all other copies were to be returned to originating party or destroyed, at the option of the originating party.

Initially, petitioner refused to produce any of the depositions but now has produced redacted versions to respondent. The redacted versions reflect that the redacted portions had been classified as confidential under the protective order.[2] Respondent contends he is entitled to the redacted portions. Petitioner contends that to the extent it has not produced documents or provided the redacted portions, it is unable to do so because of the protective order entered in the *Cinpres* case.

Discussion

Petitioner urges this Court to respect the terms of the protective order, which prohibits disclosure without modification of the order and/or approval of the District Court that issued the order. Petitioner suggests that respondent should first attempt to request the District Court that issued the order to modify it in order to accommodate the disclosure. Petitioner further postulates that this Court should not entertain respondent's discovery request until after respondent has shown that he was unable to obtain the materials from the District Court. Petitioner, however, also argues that respondent is not entitled to the protected material. We note that petitioner, who was a party in the *Cinpres* case and would have standing under the terms of the protective order, has not offered to approach the District Court to facilitate respondent's access to the protected material.[3] Petitioner is vigorously attempting to keep from respondent the redacted portions of the deposition transcripts.

The material sought by respondent is relevant to the issues we consider. As stated in Rosenfeld v. Commissioner, 82 T.C. 105, 112, 1984 WL 15524 (1984):

> Rule 70(b) limits discovery to information or responses which are relevant to the *subject matter* of the pending litigation and which are not otherwise protected from discovery on the ground of privilege or other limitation. The standard of relevancy in a discovery action is liberal. Zaentz v. Commissioner, 73 T.C. 469, 471-472, 1979 WL 3860 (1979). The burden of establishing that the documents or responses sought are not relevant or otherwise not discoverable is on the party

---

2. There is no indication who classified the redacted portions as protected. We assume that the deponent classified the redacted portions. The deponents were generally either parties or their agents.

3. We observe that petitioner has resisted the production of the depositions. Petitioner appears to be using another court's protective order as a shield or bar to compliance with respondent's discovery request. Petitioner has not suggested any alternatives and has displayed an aversion to seeking modification of the protective order under consideration. Petitioner does not contend that any portion of the deposition transcripts it has withheld contains proprietary business information that would be in need of protection.

opposing production. Rutter v. Commissioner, 81 T.C. 937, 1983 WL 14902 (1983); *Branerton II*, supra at 193.

Petitioner has not shown that the material sought by respondent is not relevant. Petitioner, however, has raised the question of whether the protective order issued in the *Cinpres* case is a limitation on production in this proceeding.

This is our first occasion to consider whether this Court should order the production of material which was subject to another court's protective order in a case which has been closed. Under the District Court's protective order, a party or "aggrieved entity" was permitted to intervene to declassify a document. Clearly, petitioner would have been entitled to seek to declassify the redacted portions of the deposition. To the extent petitioner is the classifying party, it may have been entitled to disclose without declassification. Respondent, possibly as an "aggrieved entity", would have been able to seek declassification of the materials sought here.[4]

There appears to be no question about whether the protective order survived the *Cinpres* litigation and continues to have full force and effect on the parties subject to it or about the issuing District Court's ability/authority to modify or revoke the order.

Matters of comity influence courts' decisions whether to issue orders that affect or modify protective orders issued by other courts. These principles, while unquestionably important, are not absolute, and courts asked to issue discovery orders in litigation pending before them also have not shied away from doing so, even when it would modify or circumvent a discovery order by another court". Tucker v. Ohtsu Tire & Rubber Co., 191 F.R.D. 495, 499-500 (D.Md.2000).

Respondent did not have the opportunity to intervene in the *Cinpres* case to seek access to the materials, and we are not certain that respondent has standing to currently seek modification of the protective order that was entered. The materials in question go to the heart of the merits of the tax controversy in this case; i.e., the relationship between petitioner and certain U.S. corporations. Under similar circumstances, courts have recognized that a practical solution may be needed. In that regard, the *Cinpres* case is closed, and considerable delay and expense would be occasioned by the reopening of that case or the filing of a new action to seek modification of a protective order.

---

4.   We must assume from petitioner's argument that respondent should first attempt to obtain the documents by seeking them from the District Court that petitioner believes that respondent had standing under the protective order to seek declassification of a document.

One pivotal consideration is whether the court issuing the order merely sanctioned the agreement of the parties or whether the terms of the order instead reflect the issuing court's deliberative process. Where the issuing court has merely sanctioned the parties' agreement, those circumstances have been considered to be more like a private "contract" between the parties than a holding of a court. Id.

The circumstances of the case before us appear to fit within the guidelines that have been established by other courts for compelling discovery of material that was specifically or generally under a protective order of another court. We proceed with caution and employ a pragmatic approach to a difficult procedural problem. In doing so we follow the direction of several other Federal courts.[5] The court in *Tucker v. Ohtsu Tire & Rubber Co.*, supra, formulated guidelines, which it distilled from various court holdings, to assist in deciding whether it is appropriate to enter a discovery order that would have the effect of modifying an order issued by another court. We find that formulation helpful in our consideration of respondent's motion to compel petitioner's production of the deposition transcripts in question.

The first area of inquiry is the nature of the other court's protective order. This inquiry focuses on whether the order was issued by a court as its resolution of a controversy or whether the court simply approved the parties' agreement. Courts have afforded less deference to orders based on an agreement of the parties and merely approved by the court. Conversely, more deference has been afforded in situations where a court's order resulted from a holding that is based on the court's deliberative process.

Concerning this aspect, petitioner contends that the protective order in the *Cinpres* case was entered after an extended period of disagreement by the parties, hearings by the District Court, and assistance/ involvement of the judge. Petitioner also points out that the protective order that was finally entered was different in some respects from those originally proposed by each party. Petitioner contends that the order we consider did not merely represent a ministerial act by the District Court, and, accordingly, more deference should be afforded the order.

Respondent points out that the parties stipulated and agreed to the protective order entered by the District Court. In that regard, the order

---

5.   Cases where one court compelled production of material from a prior proceeding subject to a protective order: Morton Intl., Inc. v. Atochem N. Am., Inc., 18 U.S.P.Q.2d 1411 (D.Del.1990); LeBlanc v. Broyhill, 123 F.R.D. 527 (W.D.N.C.1988); and Carter-Wallace Inc. v. Hartz Mountain Indus., Inc., 92 F.R.D. 67 (S.D.N.Y.1981). Cases where production was denied: Dushkin Publg. Group, Inc. v. Kinko's Serv. Corp., 136 F.R.D. 334, 335 (D.D.C.1991); Deford v. Schmid Prods. Co., 120 F.R.D. 648, 650, 655 (D.Md.1987); and Puerto Rico Aqueduct & Sewer Auth. v. Clow Corp., 111 F.R.D. 65, 67-68 (D.P.R.1986).

and the matters it covers were not subjected to deliberation by the District Court. Although the District Court played a role (mediator or monitor) in resolving the parties' disagreement/negotiations regarding the content of the proposed protective order, the District Court did not deliberate or decide the controversy. Ultimately, the District Court entered a protective order which had been stipulated and agreed to by the parties. Under those circumstances, less deference need be afforded the protective order on the theory that it is essentially an agreement of the parties. Although we pay less deference to the order conceptually, we defer to its substance and intent to protect the confidential materials that may be contained in the deposition transcripts.

The second *Tucker* factor concerns the identity of the party from whom discovery is sought. This factor focuses on whether the document sought is from a person originally entitled to have it. As a party to the *Cinpres* case, petitioner was entitled to the transcript of depositions, and, therefore, petitioner was an original holder of this document.

Petitioner points out that the *Tucker* case involved a one-sided order; i.e., the protected materials flowed from one source. Petitioner contends that the circumstances of this case are different because it was not a one-sided (sole source) order. Respondent counters that the documents sought (depositions) could have been designated as protected by any of the parties in the *Cinpres* case. In effect, the deposition transcripts are the rightful property of each litigant and could have been treated by any as confidential. In that regard, petitioner has not shown or contended that the redacted portions of the deposition testimony were exclusively sourced in another party in the *Cinpres* case.[6] Additionally, petitioner does not contend that the redacted portions of the deposition transcripts contained material that, in substance, requires protection, such as proprietary business information.

The third *Tucker* factor concerns whether the case in which the order was issued is still pending, and if not, the court is to consider the burden and expense that will be incurred in order to seek modification of the order. The District Court proceeding was settled by the parties and is no longer pending. On this aspect, petitioner recognizes that expense and delay would be occasioned by an action to reopen the infringement proceeding simply to seek modification of the protective order. Petitioner, however, contends that it is the only avenue by which the protective order should be approached and that this Court should not "circumvent" the District Court's order.

6.　If petitioner had shown that the protected material was exclusively sourced in another, the protective order provides for notice to that party before production of a protected document pursuant to another court's order.

Respondent contends that he is not a party to the *Cinpres* case. In addition, intervention in the *Cinpres* case would require the involvement of the U.S. Department of Justice, which would further complicate this matter and increase the expenditure of public resources. Respondent also contends that it would be an imposition on the District Court to interject it into a discovery dispute in the U.S. Tax Court.

We agree with respondent. The District Court would have to be asked, for the first time, to interpret and/or to modify an order negotiated by the parties in a case that is now closed and final. The additional cost in expense, time, and inconvenience of the courts and the parties to seek review by the court that issued the order is not warranted in this setting.

The final factor concerns whether this Court, by incorporating similar terms and protections in our order, could continue the protections originally approved in the District Court's order. On that point, petitioner argues that neither petitioner nor respondent has moved this Court for such a protective order. Petitioner's concern is that the *Cinpres* case involved patent infringement and the possible need to protect any proprietary business information. In that regard, the District Court's protective order appears to adequately provide for protection of any proprietary business information. If we incorporate the terms of the District Court's protective order into an order compelling the production of the requested deposition materials, the same obligations and restrictions will be imposed, with the exception that they will now be imposed on respondent. We see no reason why the terms of the District Court's protective order cannot be incorporated into this Court's order compelling any production of materials from the *Cinpres* case.

As explained, the information respondent seeks is relevant to the issues we consider. It would be unjust to permit petitioner continued access to this type of information with no access to respondent. Another approach to remedying this situation would have been to order petitioner to produce the materials without addressing the protective order. To simply order such production would, however, place petitioner in the position of having to seek modification of the *Cinpres* order and to bear the expense of same. As a practical matter, petitioner has not shown why the approach we have chosen (order production with continued protection under the terms of the protective order) is not appropriate under the conditions we consider.

To reflect the foregoing,

An order will be issued granting respondent's motion to compel and providing for continued protection of the materials to be produced.

Notes and Question

A protective order is issued in the interests of justice "to protect a party or other person from annoyance, embarrassment, oppression, or undue burden or expense * * *." Tax Court Rule 103. Can you think of any other factors that may have affected the court's decision?

c. *Depositions*

A deposition generally is an oral examination of a party or non-party under oath for purposes of discovery or to preserve the testimony of the deponent for use at trial. Under special circumstances, the deposition may be taken through written questions, but such a method is not favored by the court. Tax Court Rule 74(e).

A deposition of a party may be taken only if the party consents. Depositions of non-parties may be taken without the consent of the other party, upon service of notice to the non-party. Such a non-consensual deposition is regarded as an "extraordinary method of discovery" that should be used "only where a nonparty witness can give testimony or possesses documents or things which are discoverable * * * and where such testimony, documents, or things practicably cannot be obtained through informal consultation or communication or by a deposition taken with the consent of the parties." Tax Court Rule 75(b). Either the opposing party or the nonparty witness may object to the nonconsensual deposition, but such an objection must occur within 15 days of the service of the notice of deposition. The burden then is on the party seeking the deposition to move for an order to compel compliance. A nonconsensual deposition may be taken only after a notice of trial has been issued or the case has been assigned to a judge.

A deposition to perpetrate evidence (evidentiary deposition) may be taken in a pending case, prior to the commencement of the case, or during the trial. Such depositions may be taken only for the purpose of preserving testimony, or any document or thing, as evidence to be used at trial. In a pending case, the court generally will allow the evidentiary deposition where the testimony, document, or thing is not privileged and is material to a matter in controversy, and where there is a substantial risk that the person, document, or thing will not be available at trial. Tax Court Rule 81.

If an application to the court is made for a deposition prior to the filing of the petition, the court generally will grant the application if the party requesting the deposition establishes (1) that the applicant expects to be a party before the court but is currently unable to bring the action,

(2) the subject matter of the expected action and the applicant's interest in the action, and (3) that the content of the application conforms to that of the application in a pending case under Tax Court Rule 81(b)(1). This includes giving a reason for deposing the witness now rather than waiting for the action to be brought, establishing the substance of the testimony that the applicant expects to elicit from the deponents, and a statement of how the testimony (or document or thing) is material to a matter in controversy. Id.

The rules regarding deposition of an expert witness are similar to the general rules on depositions, but if the deposition is nonconsensual, the party seeking the deposition must obtain approval of the court. Such a motion may be made only after a notice of trial has been issued or the case has been assigned to a judge. Tax Court Rule 76.

The scope of the deposition is limited to (1) the knowledge, skill, experience, training, or education that qualifies the witness to testify as an expert, (2) the expert's opinion on the matter in dispute, (3) the facts or data that underlie the opinion, and (4) the expert's analysis, based on the facts and data, of how the conclusion that supports the opinion was derived. This information also is required to be submitted to the court as an expert witness report before the expert can testify. Tax Court Rule 143(f). Rule 76(e) permits the deposition transcript to be submitted as the expert witness report. The report must be submitted to the court and to the opposing party no later than 30 days prior to the commencement of the trial.

The expert witness report is very important because after it is submitted, it serves as the direct testimony of the expert, subject to certain narrow exceptions such as clarification of matters in the report, coverage of matters arising after the preparation of the report, or otherwise in the discretion of the court. Tax Court Rule 143(f)(1). The expert may not testify to legal conclusions, and if the report relies on such conclusions, the court is likely to disregard the report. See further discussion of expert witnesses, § F.2, below.

3. Sanctions for Failure to Comply

If a discovery request causes annoyance, embarrassment, oppression, or undue burden or expense to a party or non-party, a Motion for a Protective Order may be made. The movant must establish good cause for the issuance of such an order. The court is likely to grant such a motion where justice requires protection of the moving party. A protective order may take several forms, such as an order to forbid the disclosure of a trade secret or other information, that certain methods or procedures be conducted to insure secrecy and confidentiality, that a particular method or procedure not be used, and that sealed depositions or other written materials be opened only by order of the court. Tax Court Rule 103(a).

If a party, or a non-party, fails to respond to a request for discovery, various sanctions are available, including contempt of court. It is no defense that the person failing to comply with the discovery request considers the request objectionable, unless the person has raised the objection or has applied for a protective order at the proper time and in the proper manner, and the court either has ruled in the person's favor or has not yet ruled on the objection. Tax Court Rule 104. Generally, if a person refuses to comply with a discovery request, the requesting party may make a Motion to Compel Discovery. If such a motion is granted, the court will issue a discovery order compelling compliance.

There are other sanctions available as well. These include:

1) an order that the designated facts and matters in issue will be treated as established, for purposes of the case, in accordance with the claims of the party obtaining the order;

2) an order prohibiting the disobedient party from introducing designated matters into evidence, and from supporting or opposing designated claims or defenses;

3) an order striking pleadings or portions of pleadings, staying further proceedings until the order is obeyed, dismissing the case, or rendering a judgment by default against the disobedient party;

4) the court may treat the failure as contempt of court and may require the disobedient party to comply with the request or order, and to pay reasonable expenses, including attorney's fees caused by the failure, unless the court finds that the failure to comply was substantially justified or that other circumstances make an award of expenses unjust.

Tax Court Rule 104(c). Under § 6673, similar sanctions may be imposed against attorneys who unreasonably and vexatiously delay the proceedings.

JOHNSON v. COMMISSIONER
United States Court of Appeals, Seventh Circuit, 2002.
289 F.3d 452.

POSNER, CIRCUIT JUDGE.

Attorney Joe Alfred Izen, Jr., has appeared in the United States Tax Court in many cases since the early 1980s. A number of them, including the recently decided Muhich v. Commissioner, 238 F.3d 860 (7th Cir.2001), involve the same script: the IRS determines a deficiency arising from the use of sham trusts established for the taxpayer by a promoter; the taxpayer petitions for redetermination of the deficiency; Izen appears for the taxpayer; the case drags on, with the taxpayer sometimes resisting discovery; the court usually finds the taxpayer's arguments frivolous and either threatens or imposes sanctions.

The present case follows this pattern except that instead of sanctioning the taxpayer the court sanctioned Izen under 26 U.S.C. § 6673(a)(2) by ordering him to pay the attorneys' fees that the IRS had incurred as a consequence of his discovery abuses. Izen appeals, arguing that section 6673(a)(2) is a denial of equal protection; that the Tax Court's sanction was impermissible because really the court disciplined him not for discovery abuses as it said but for representing "disfavored" litigants who promote or utilize sham trusts to avoid taxes, and for allowing his client to invoke the Fifth Amendment in response to the IRS's discovery demands; and that the Tax Court overstated the amount of attorneys' fees that the IRS had incurred as a consequence of his discovery abuses.

In April 1999, Shirley Johnson, an Indiana resident whose severe diabetes hinders her ability to travel, filed in the Tax Court two *pro se* petitions challenging a notice of deficiency. Then, hiring Izen, a Texas lawyer, to represent her, she–realistically, Izen–took advantage of the Tax Court's liberal rule on venue, Tax Ct. R. 140, to designate Houston as the place for trial. And then the stonewalling began. At first Johnson simply ignored discovery demands. In September 1999 the Tax Court ordered her to respond to those demands and threatened her with sanctions if she did not.   Her response was to answer 27 of 34 interrogatories and 37 of 51 document requests with the words "Fifth Amendment." The IRS requested sanctions, and though declining that relief the court conducted a hearing and ruled that the Fifth Amendment defense was baseless. The court ordered Johnson to cooperate fully in discovery, and scheduled trial for May 3, 2000.

In December 1999 the IRS issued a second set of interrogatories and document requests, but again had to resort to filing a motion to compel. The Tax Court granted the motion and ordered, under an express threat of sanctions, that Johnson comply fully by April 7, 2000. Johnson did not. Instead she gave notice that she would be physically unable to participate in a May trial. The court continued the trial to December 2000 but maintained the May 3 date for hearing the IRS's renewed motion for sanctions.

Izen did not appear on May 3 but instead sent his associate and sister, Jane Afton Izen. The IRS explained to the court what interrogatories remained unanswered and also noted Johnson's failure to comply with a demand for copies of checks from 1996 and 1997. Expressing skepticism that Johnson had made "a good faith effort to comply with the court's orders," the court again threatened sanctions unless she answered the interrogatories by May 17 and the document requests by July 5. The court also expressed annoyance that Joe Izen had failed to appear. Jane Izen promised to provide the delinquent discovery by the court's deadlines.

May 17 came and went with no response from Johnson. Instead, on May 22 the court received a motion dated May 15 seeking postponement of the now-expired deadline. As grounds Izen offered his busy schedule and Johnson's poor health. The court responded that his workload did not excuse his disobeying the court's orders and this time it promised sanctions if the interrogatories were not answered by June 1. On that day the IRS received partial responses. Later, after missing the July 5 deadline to produce checks from 1996 and 1997, Izen tendered checks from the wrong bank and for the wrong years. These were the same checks Izen had produced twice before; the IRS had repeatedly told him the checks were noncomplying.

On August 21, 2000, the court's patience ran out. After listening to Izen's explanations that he had "inadvertently" failed to answer one of the interrogatories and that Johnson's poor health hampered compliance with discovery orders, the court ruled that Izen had unreasonably and vexatiously multiplied the proceedings within the meaning of 26 U.S.C. § 6673(a)(2) and in a subsequent order it sanctioned him in the amount of $9,394 to cover the attorneys' fees incurred by the IRS in trying to obtain compliance with its second set of discovery requests. The court also dismissed Johnson's case for failure to prosecute, a ruling she has not appealed.

Izen contends that section 6673(a)(2) denies equal protection of the laws (actionable under the due process clause of the Fifth Amendment by virtue of the Supreme Court's decision in Bolling v. Sharpe, 347 U.S. 497, 74 S.Ct. 693, 98 L.Ed. 884 (1954)), because it exempts government attorneys, and only government attorneys, from personal liability for unreasonably and vexatiously multiplying Tax Court proceedings. Izen waived the argument by first including it in a motion under Tax Court Rule 162, the analog to Fed.R.Civ.P. 60(b).

Anyway the argument is frivolous. Section 6673(a)(2) states:

Counsel's liability for excessive costs.--Whenever it appears to the Tax Court that any attorney or other person admitted to practice before the Tax Court has multiplied the proceedings unreasonably and vexatiously, the Tax Court may require--

(A) that such attorney or other person pay personally the excess costs, expenses, and attorneys' fees reasonably incurred because of such conduct, or

(B) if such attorney is appearing on behalf of the Commissioner of Internal Revenue, that the United States pay such excess costs, expenses, and attorneys' fees in the same manner as such an award by a district court.

This language authorizes the Tax Court to sanction government attorneys personally or to require the United States to pay for their misconduct. Izen's contrary argument rests on a misreading. The equal protection claim would be frivolous in any event, as it is easy to imagine a rational basis for treating public lawyers in this respect different from private ones.

The next issue is Izen's bad faith. We hold (it is a question of first impression at the appellate level) that a finding of "bad faith" is indeed required before an attorney may be sanctioned under section 6673(a)(2). The language of that statute is materially identical to that of 28 U.S.C. § 1927, which has been held to require a finding of bad faith, IDS Life Ins. Co. v. Royal Alliance Associates Inc., 266 F.3d 645, 654 (7th Cir.2001); Fox Valley Construction Workers Fringe Benefit Funds v. Pride of the Fox Masonry & Expert Restorations, 140 F.3d 661, 666 (7th Cir.1998); In re Prudential Ins. Co. America Sales Practice Litigation Actions, 278 F.3d 175, 188 (3d Cir.2002), and the two statutes serve the same purpose, just in different but similar forums, and should therefore be interpreted similarly. See Harper v. Commissioner, 99 T.C. 533, 545 (1992).

Bad faith under section 1927 of the Judicial Code (and hence, we hold, under section 6673(a)(2) of the Internal Revenue Code) is not a subjective concept, as the words "who so multiplies the proceedings in any case unreasonably *and vexatiously*" (emphasis added) might be thought to imply; "reckless" or "extremely negligent" conduct will satisfy it. And appellate review of the decision to impose sanctions is for abuse of discretion, as is normally the case with respect to decisions imposing sanctions, and is therefore consistent with the general principle that the standards for appellate review of Tax Court decisions are identical to those for appellate review of district court decisions. E.g., Freytag v. Commissioner, 501 U.S. 868, 891, 111 S.Ct. 2631, 115 L.Ed.2d 764

(1991); Estate of Kunze v. Commissioner, 233 F.3d 948, 950 (7th Cir.2000); 26 U.S.C. § 7482(a)(1).

Izen's complaint that the Tax Court based its finding of bad faith on his conduct in other cases is off the mark in two respects. The court placed primary reliance on his conduct in the present case; our recital of the facts showing that Izen recklessly, and in all likelihood intentionally, obstructed discovery was drawn from the Tax Court's opinion. The court further noted that Johnson's trial memorandum, due on November 17, 2000, was postmarked November 27 yet certified by Izen as having been served on November 22, and that Izen had deposed Johnson without adequate notice to the IRS yet persisted in offering her deposition as evidence despite the court's denying him permission to do so. Izen's repeated flouting of discovery orders even after being threatened with sanctions and promising to comply established his bad faith all by itself.

The Tax Court was not required to ignore Izen's bad conduct in other cases; indeed it would have been remiss not to consider it. In prior litigation, Izen's clients were sometimes sanctioned because he employed tactics like those in this case; and dogged good-faith persistence in bad conduct becomes sanctionable once an attorney learns or should have learned that it is sanctionable.

Izen argues that the court penalized him for Johnson's frivolous assertion of her right against self-incrimination. It did not, as a matter of fact; but in any event "if a competent attorney would find no basis for a legal argument, then it does not interfere with zealous advocacy to penalize the repetitious assertion of that argument." [In Re TCI, Ltd., 769 F.2d 441, 447 (7th Cir. 1985)]. Johnson had the burden of proving that the IRS should have allowed deductions for certain business expenses. Competent counsel would have recognized that burden as incompatible with asserting a Fifth Amendment privilege covering the entirety of Johnson's business affairs, and so would have declined to make such a claim.

As for Izen's challenge to the amount of the sanction, it is waived because he delayed presenting it to the Tax Court until his Rule 162 motion.

If anything, the Tax Court treated Izen too gently. But his travails are not over. As his appeal is frivolous, we are issuing an order to show cause why he should not be sanctioned for his antics in this court.

AFFIRMED.

Notes

The *Johnson* case was heard by the Tax Court in Houston, Texas, in the Fifth Circuit. Note, however, that the appeal was heard by the Seventh Circuit. This is because § 7482(b)(2) allows an appeal to any United States Court of Appeals if agreed to in writing by the Secretary and the taxpayer. The Service probably agreed to have the appeal be heard in the Seventh Circuit because Mrs. Johnson resided in that circuit. Perhaps Izen also thought that he might receive better treatment in a circuit in which the courts were not as familiar with his antics.

E. PRE-TRIAL PROCEEDINGS

Although the parties are expected to develop the case to the extent possible before trial through use of *Branerton* conferences and stipulations, occasionally the parties are unable to reach an agreement on one or more issues. In such cases, the court may order a pretrial conference for purposes of narrowing the issues, stipulating facts, simplifying the presentation of evidence, or otherwise assisting in the preparation of the case for trial or possible disposition without trial. Tax Court Rule 110(a). If the case has been calendared for trial (i.e., listed on the trial calendar), either the court on its own motion or at the request of either party may order a pretrial conference. If the case has not been calendared, the Chief Judge has discretion to order a pretrial conference, either on his own motion or upon motion of either party. Tax Court Rule 110(b) and (c).

A request or motion for pretrial conference by the parties must include a written statement of the reasons for the request. The party requesting the pretrial conference must have made a good faith, but unsuccessful attempt to obtain stipulation from the opposing party. The court will not permit the pretrial conference to substitute for the stipulation process. Also, no request for a pretrial conference will be granted where the court determines that the request is frivolous or made for purposes of delay. Tax Court Rule 110(d).

1. Settlement Procedures

Relatively few tax cases proceed to trial. As we saw in Chapter 3, during the administrative audit process (prior to the filing of a Tax Court petition), there is an opportunity for the taxpayer to reach a settlement or compromise with the Service through the Appeals Office. After the

Tax Court petition is filed, there is further opportunity for settlement, either through the Appeals Office or with the District Counsel. Thus, most tax cases are settled or compromised without judicial involvement. Indeed, IRS Chief Counsel attorneys are directed specifically to conduct the settlement negotiations without the involvement of the judge to whom the case has been assigned, although any final settlement must be presented to the Tax Court for approval as a stipulated settlement.

District Counsel has exclusive settlement authority over the case once it has been docketed in the Tax Court. If the case is docketed prior to any conference with the Appeals Division, the case will be transferred by the District Counsel to the Appeals Division for a settlement conference. District Counsel will act in an advisory capacity if the case involves a large deficiency or significant issues, or if Appeals requests assistance.

The petitioner will be notified that the case has been transferred to Appeals, and Appeals usually will schedule a conference within 45 days of the transfer. Although Appeals has exclusive settlement authority over most cases, only the District Counsel may execute the settlement stipulation before the Tax Court.

The case will be transferred automatically from Appeals to the District Counsel within a month of the date on which the case is calendared for trial, or sooner if Appeals is making no progress toward settlement. A case also may be transferred upon the request of the District Counsel in order to prepare the case for trial. When a case is transferred, the District Counsel has exclusive authority to dispose of the case, either by settlement or by proceeding to trial, unless the District Counsel and Appeals agree that settlement authority over some or all of the issues will be retained by Appeals. If this happens, the District Counsel will prepare the case for trial while Appeals simultaneously will conduct settlement negotiations. See Rev. Proc. 87-24, 1987-1 C.B. 720.

In an "S" case, Appeals will retain jurisdiction for a period of six months, unless the case is calendared for trial. If so, the case will be transferred automatically to the District Counsel within 15 days of the calendar call, although the transfer may be delayed or the case may be returned to Appeals if the District Counsel and the Appeals officer agree that a settlement seems likely. Id.

If the case is transferred from Appeals to the District Counsel, the District Counsel will have exclusive settlement authority and the taxpayer will be notified of the transfer. The Service will actively prepare the case for trial after the transfer, using the discovery process to obtain records and documents that are not provided within a reasonable period of time after a request has been made. After the facts have been fully developed, the District Counsel will evaluate the Service's litigation position to determine whether further settlement negotiations should be entertained. Although the District Counsel is not bound by any prior settlement offers or counteroffers made by Appeals, as a practical matter prior settlement offers generally will be honored unless the factual development of the case reveals additional litigation hazards.

Question

What factors should the taxpayer consider before entering into the settlement process?

2. Admissions and Stipulations

Both the taxpayer and the government are required to stipulate fully to all matters that are relevant to the case and are not privileged, regardless of whether such matters involve fact, opinion, or law. Tax Court Rule 91(a). All facts, documents, papers, and evidence not in dispute are included within the matters to which the parties are required to stipulate. Matters relevant to the case that are not privileged and are not stipulated are typically litigated. The requirement of stipulations streamlines both the discovery process and the introduction of documents, since no foundation or authentication needs to be made if the document has been stipulated.

Stipulations must be made in writing, signed by the parties or their counsel, and filed with the court in duplicate. They also must be clear and concise. Tax Court Rule 91(b). Stipulations are considered binding admissions by the parties, unless the parties agree otherwise or the court permits the stipulation to have nonbinding effect. Stipulations apply only to the pending case, however, and cannot be used against either party in any other case or proceeding. Tax Court Rule 91(c). If all relevant facts are stipulated, the parties may submit the case for decision without trial. Tax Court Rule 122.

BAKARE v. COMMISSIONER

United States Tax Court, 1994.
1994 WL 52378.

MEMORANDUM OPINION

NAMEROFF, SPECIAL TRIAL JUDGE:

This case, originally involving 34 petitioners, is before the Court on petitioner Norman Katz' motion to be relieved of his stipulation of settlement filed with the Court on June 26, 1987.

This case was part of a litigation project regarding a shelter entitled Midas International or "Uranium For Tax $". Petitioner, as well as many other investors, was represented by Attorney Gregory Alohawiwoole Altman (Altman). Nine docketed cases involving Midas International were selected by Altman and respondent as test cases and consolidated for trial. A stipulation of settlement was signed on petitioner's behalf by Altman and filed with the Court on June 26, 1987. In the stipulation of settlement, petitioner agreed to be bound by the results of the test case. By notice of deficiency dated January 30, 1986, respondent determined a deficiency in Federal income tax due from petitioner of $4,740, plus additions to tax under section 6653(a)(1) and (2).

In the test case, Howard v. Commissioner, T.C.Memo. 1988-531, affd. 931 F.2d 578 (9th Cir.1991), we held that the Midas International transactions were utterly devoid of economic substance and must be ignored for Federal income tax purposes. As a result, we determined that the taxpayers therein were not entitled to deductions for mining development expenditures under the provisions of section 616[1] or mining exploration costs under the provisions of section 617. We also sustained respondent's determinations as to the additions to tax under section 6653(a)(1) and (2) for negligence. Finally, we held that the taxpayers therein were liable for the increased interest under section 6621(c) with regard to underpayments attributable to disallowed deductions incurred in connection with the Midas International program for 1980 and 1981. The Court of Appeals for the Ninth Circuit affirmed our decision, stating:

> In a case such as this where the taxpayers have been found to have entered into sham transactions without primary profit motivation, they have failed to meet their burden of showing due care. No reasonably prudent person would have acted as they did. * * * [931 F.2d at 582.]

---

1. All section references are to the Internal Revenue Code in effect for the years at issue. All Rule references are to the Tax Court Rules of Practice and Procedure.

In petitioner's motion to set aside the stipulation of settlement, petitioner alleges that Altman was unable to render competent legal representation as he had been diagnosed as a manic depressive and was taking lithium to control his medical condition, but the medication had become ineffective due to a kidney infection.

By order dated October 22, 1993, the Court, in considering petitioner's motion, ordered petitioner to file a supplement to his motion outlining (1) the issues which would be tried in the event his motion were granted, (2) the documents which he intended to offer in evidence, (3) the names and addresses of the witnesses which he intended to call, including a brief summary as to what they would testify to, and (4) a statement as to how his case differs from *Howard v. Commissioner*, supra. In petitioner's supplement to his motion, he stated that he would be the sole witness and that his testimony would prove that he had the requisite profit motive, used due care, and was reasonably prudent. No additional relevant documentation was attached to petitioner's supplement.

At the hearing on petitioner's motion, petitioner submitted a letter dated June 1, 1990, from Altman addressed to "Uranium For Tax $" clients indicating that he has an adverse health condition stemming from a brain disorder which is life threatening, and, is, therefore, terminating his law practice. No additional documentation as to Altman's health was offered by petitioner nor was any additional relevant documentation offered to support any of petitioner's allegations of Altman's incompetence prior to June 1, 1990. However, petitioner did state that while in attendance at the trial of the test cases, he observed some disturbing signs in Altman's behavior.[2]

As to the merits of the income tax case, petitioner urged the Court to trace the money invested in the program, and that such tracing would indicate that actual drilling was commenced, thereby proving that the project was not a sham. However, petitioner neither has any of the bank records nor has attempted to obtain them. At this late date, we believe that it is extremely unlikely that he would be able to obtain bank records dating back to 1980 and 1981.

Moreover, we note that in *Howard* we found that there was no evidence to establish that Power Resources, Inc., the New Mexico drilling company which was hired as a contractor, ever received any of the $23 million allegedly obtained from purported option sales. We further found that the evidence indicated that only a fraction of the initial cash

---

2. Petitioner, a certified public accountant who had advised many of his own clients to invest in the Uranium For Tax Dollars program, attended the trial as a consultant to Altman.

payments made by investors was actually expended by Power Resources for drilling on the mining claims involved in the Uranium For Tax Dollars program. Thus, the Court has already considered the cash flow and the extent of the drilling in reaching its conclusion that the investment was a sham. Accordingly, we are not convinced of any need to revisit this issue.

With regard to the additions to tax for negligence, petitioner contends that he relied upon the representations of Altman who allegedly visited the mining site, and that he, as a knowledgeable certified public accountant, had a bona fide profit-making objective. In *Howard v. Commissioner*, supra, we stated, as follows:

> With the exception of Mr. Bambeck and Mr. Grosvenor, all of the petitioners were college graduates actively pursuing careers in, inter alia, medicine, dentistry, financial planning, insurance and banking. Mr. Bambeck has been a general constructor for some 25 years and Mr. Grosvenor has been a mason contractor for some 20 years. The petitioners, for the most part, displayed a marked indifference to the economic plausibility of the Uranium For Tax Dollars programs upon which they embarked in 1980 and 1981. * * * We find it inconceivable that any prudent individual would really believe that their agent, chosen by the promoter, could assuredly and routinely sell a uranium option to acquire each and every mining claims lease in the Uranium For Tax Dollars programs within seven days for $20,000 (in 1980) or $15,000 (in 1981), with the assurance that the investor's check would be returned in the event a uranium option sale could not be arranged.

> Nor does it appear that any of the investors in the Uranium For Tax Dollars programs questioned the authenticity of the transaction which gave them a drilling expense deduction which included the full amount of their initial payment of $5,000 with no allowances whatever for fees or commissions normally paid to the seller of such packaged, tax-advantaged deals. In short, we deem it highly unlikely that any of the petitioners here involved actually believed that the transactions did in fact occur as heralded by the promoters. The commercial surrealism of these transactions should have alerted a reasonable person to the chimerical nature of the uranium mining venture in New Mexico. * * *

Rule 91(e) provides that a stipulation, to the extent of its terms, shall be treated as a conclusive admission by the parties to the stipulation. This Court will not permit a party to qualify, change, or contradict a stipulation, except where justice requires. We will enforce a settlement of stipulation, whether written or orally stipulated into the record, unless for reasons of justice a party should be relieved from the stipulation. We have also enforced stipulations to be bound where the parties have agreed to be bound by the outcome of a test case. Hillman v. Commissioner, 687 F.2d 164, 165 (6th Cir.1982), affg. T.C.Memo. 1982-468. Here, the stipulation was entered into fairly and freely by both parties and was entirely in accordance with their intentions. There is nothing in the record to indicate that Altman, in 1987, was not a competent attorney of record for petitioner. The stipulation of settlement to be bound by the results of *Howard* was beneficial to petitioner in that his case was not scheduled for trial and he was not required to put on extensive proof of his case. It was not until several years had passed after the trial, the opinion of the Court was issued, and the Court's decision was affirmed on appeal and became final that petitioner decided to have the settlement set aside and to retry the entire case. We find no compelling circumstances that indicate an injustice is being done in upholding the stipulation of settlement, and, therefore, will not permit the stipulation of settlement to be set aside. Accordingly, we deny petitioner's motion to have the settlement stipulation set aside.

An appropriate order denying petitioner's motion will be issued.

Notes and Question

In order to be binding, a stipulation first must be filed or presented to the court at trial. Until that point, either party can unilaterally repudiate the stipulation. In the case of a settlement agreement, however, where the parties have agreed to an entry of judgment after discovery, admission, and stipulations procedures, the parties waive their right to appeal, except on very narrow grounds of lack of consent or lack of subject matter jurisdiction by the court. A higher standard applies to settlement stipulations because the court has invested more time in them and often may have suspended trial proceedings in an effort to encourage the settlement.

If a party refuses to stipulate or fails to confer with the opposing party, the party proposing to stipulate may file a motion to compel stipulation. Such a motion must be filed no later than 45 days prior to trial. Once filed, the court will issue an order directing the delinquent party to show cause why the matters covered in the motion should not be admitted. Tax Court Rule 91(f). The delinquent party then has 20 days from the service of the order to file a response. If no response is filed within this period, or if the response is evasive or otherwise insufficient, the matter(s) will be deemed stipulated and an order to that effect will be issued. If a response is filed that contains opposing claims of evidence, such claims will not be the subject of stipulation under the motion unless such evidence is "patently incredible." Tax Court Rule 91(f)(4). If there is a genuinely controverted or doubtful issue of fact raised (and this is ultimately for the court to determine), such issues will not be the subject of stipulation but instead will be raised at trial.

1. If a taxpayer stipulates to a settlement, and subsequently a judicial opinion upholding the taxpayer's position is rendered by a court in the taxpayer's circuit, will the taxpayer prevail if he asks to have the settlement set aside? Compare Brast v. Winding Gulf Colliery Co., 94 F.2d 179 (4th Cir. 1938) with Guterman v. Scanlon, 222 F. Supp. 1007 (D.C.N.Y. 1963).

2. What result if a taxpayer requests that a stipulation be set aside because his attorney stipulated without his knowledge and consent? See Hillman v. Commissioner, 687 F.2d 164 (6th Cir. 1982).

3. Test Case Procedures

If there are docketed cases that involve similar issues, the court may encourage the parties in the pending cases to enter into stipulations agreeing to be bound by the decision or settlement in a test case. The Service has developed a standardized agreement for multiple taxpayer litigation, referred to as a "piggyback agreement." If a taxpayer signs the agreement, the taxpayer agrees to be bound by the decision of the court or the settlement in the test case. After the conclusion of the test case, the court will enter the decision in the piggybacked taxpayer's case as if it had been independently resolved. From that point on, the taxpayer's rights are the same as they would have been if the Tax Court had actually heard the case. For instance, the taxpayer has a right to appeal the decision, but generally does not have the right to appeal a stipulated settlement that has been approved by the court

4. Alternative Dispute Resolution (ADR)

Tax Court Rule 124 provides that at any time after a case is at issue and prior to trial, the parties may agree to submit any factual issue in controversy to voluntary binding arbitration. Upon appropriate motion by the parties, the Chief Judge will assign the case to a judge or special trial judge, who will appoint the arbitrator and supervise the arbitration. The parties must attach to the motion a joint stipulation containing:

1) a statement of the issues to be resolved by the arbitration;

2) the parties' agreement to be bound by the determination of the arbitrator;

3) the name of the arbitrator or the procedure to be used to select the arbitrator;

4) the method in which all costs, including fees, expenses, and the arbitrator's compensation, is to be allocated between the parties;

5) a statement that any ex parte communication with the arbitrator is prohibited;

6) such other provisions as the parties may deem appropriate.

Tax Court Rule 124(b)(5) provides "Nothing contained in this Rule shall be construed to exclude use by the parties of other forms of voluntary disposition of cases, including mediation." This opens the door to other forms of dispute resolution, including mediation. Unlike arbitration, mediation is nonbinding and the mediator cannot force the parties to settle. Mediation merely provides another avenue for the parties to attempt to reach a settlement prior to trial.

Notes and Question

Section 7123 prescribes the use of ADR procedures during the Appeals process. If the taxpayer takes advantage of these procedures, but the case, nevertheless, proceeds to trial, the ADR techniques at the Tax Court level, particularly mediation, are not likely to be successful.

What considerations are there in choosing to use the ADR process?

5. Protective Orders

In general, official records of all courts, including the Tax Court, are open and available to the public. Often, considerations of public disclosure enter into a taxpayer's decision whether to bring suit or to settle in secret. Tax Court Rule 103 gives the court broad discretion to control and seal records and files in its possession, and it may do so on motion by a party or other affected person who shows good cause.

ANONYMOUS v. COMMISSIONER
United States Tax Court, 2006.
127 T.C. 89

KROUPA, JUDGE.

This matter is before the Court on petitioner's motion to seal court records. Petitioner requests us to seal the record in this case and permit petitioner to proceed anonymously. Petitioner has demonstrated a significant risk of physical harm to petitioner and petitioner's family members if the record were to remain open. We conclude that it is appropriate to seal the record and permit petitioner to proceed anonymously.

* * *

Background

Petitioner is a foreign national. At the time petitioner filed the petition, petitioner resided outside the United States. A member of petitioner's family was kidnapped and held for ransom several years ago. Kidnappings are a rampant problem in the country where petitioner and most of petitioner's family reside. Petitioner fears that petitioner or other members of petitioner's family might also be kidnapped and their lives placed in jeopardy if petitioner's identity or petitioner's financial circumstances were made public in this case. Petitioner filed the motion to seal court records at the same time petitioner filed the petition.

Discussion

We shall begin by describing the general presumption of openness that attaches to judicial proceedings. Generally, official records of all courts shall be open and available to the public for inspection and copying. Hearings and the evidentiary record of proceedings before this Court shall be open to the public. Secs. 7458, 7461(a). Common law, statutory law, and the U.S. Constitution all support this important principle. Willie Nelson Music Co. v. Commissioner, 85 T.C. 914, 918, 1985 WL 15420 (1985); In re Coordinated Pretrial Proceedings in Petroleum Prods. Antitrust Litig., [101 F.R.D. 34, 38 (C.D. Cal. 1984)]. The right to inspect and copy judicial records, however, is not absolute. Nixon v. Warner Commcns., Inc., [435 U.S. 589, 598 (1978)]. Courts have supervisory power over their own records and files, and access to records has been denied where the court files might become a vehicle for improper purposes. Id.

Sealing the Record

This Court has broad discretionary power to control and seal, if necessary, records and files in our possession. *Willie Nelson Music Co. v. Commissioner*, supra. We may, in our discretion, seal the record or portions of the record if justice so requires and the party seeking such relief demonstrates good cause. Sec. 7461(b)(1); Rule 103(a); AT & T Co. v. Grady, 594 F.2d 594, 596 (7th Cir.1978); *Willie Nelson Music Co. v. Commissioner*, supra at 920; Tavano v. Commissioner, T.C. Memo.1991-237, affd. 986 F.2d 1389 (11th Cir.1993). To determine whether sealing the record is appropriate, we must weigh the presumption, however gauged, in favor of public access to judicial records against the interests advanced by the parties. *Nixon v. Warner Commcns., Inc.*, supra at 602; *AT & T Co. v. Grady*, supra at 598; *Willie Nelson Music Co. v. Commissioner*, supra at 919.

Taxpayers seeking to seal court records must come forward with appropriate testimony and factual data to show good cause. *Willie Nelson Music Co. v. Commissioner*, supra at 920 (citing Wyatt v. Kaplan, 686 F.2d 276, 283 (5th Cir.1982); *Tavano v. Commissioner*, supra. Taxpayers may not rely on conclusory or unsupported statements to establish claims of harm that would result from disclosure. *Willie Nelson Music Co. v. Commissioner*, supra at 920; *In re Coordinated Pretrial Proceedings in Petroleum Prods. Antitrust Litig.*, supra at 44.

Good cause has been demonstrated and records sealed where patents, trade secrets, or confidential information are involved or where an individual's business reputation will be hurt. See In re Smith, 656 F.2d 1101 (5th Cir.1981) (striking an individual's name from factual resumes on due process grounds as resumes were prepared in criminal proceeding where the individual was not indicted); Crystal Grower's Corp. v. Dobbins, 616 F.2d 458 (10th Cir.1980) (sealing portions of record involving documents alleged to be subject to attorney-client privilege or work product doctrine); In re Sarkar, 575 F.2d 870 (C.C.P.A.1978) (sealing record involving patent application proceeding so that the information would remain a trade secret in the event of an adverse decision); Sendi v. Prudential-Bache Sec., 100 F.R.D. 21 (D.D.C.1983) (sealing parties' tax returns to protect confidentiality and privacy interests). Merely asserting annoyance, embarrassment, or harm to a person's personal reputation, however, is generally insufficient to demonstrate good cause and overcome the strong common law presumption in favor of access to court records. *Willie Nelson Music Co. v. Commissioner*, supra at 921, 925 (record not sealed where nationally known entertainer sought to avoid public scrutiny or news coverage of case); *Tavano v. Commissioner*, supra (record not sealed where taxpayer had civil suit pending against employer and did not want employer to learn facts of case).

Petitioner submitted affidavits together with supporting documentation that demonstrate the severe degree of harm petitioner and petitioner's family members would risk if we did not seal the record. These affidavits and documentation show that a member of petitioner's family was kidnapped several years ago and that kidnapping is rampant in the country where petitioner and most of petitioner's family reside. Petitioner fears that publicizing petitioner's identity and financial circumstances will increase the risk that either petitioner or a member of petitioner's family will be the target of another kidnapping and that petitioner's life or the lives of petitioner's family will be placed in jeopardy. We find these facts compelling. Petitioner has demonstrated through these affidavits that physical harm has actually been inflicted against a member of petitioner's family, and there is a risk that the same type of physical harm may be inflicted upon petitioner or another member of petitioner's family.

We must evaluate this risk of physical harm against the public interest in access to judicial records. See *Nixon v. Warner Commcns., Inc.*, supra at 602; Does I Thru XXIII v. Advanced Textile Corp., 214 F.3d 1058, 1069 (9th Cir.2000); *AT & T Co. v. Grady*, supra at 596; *Willie Nelson Music Co. v. Commissioner*, supra at 919. After careful consideration of the facts of this case, we find that the balance favors petitioner. The risk of extreme physical harm to petitioner and petitioner's family outweighs the countervailing public interest favoring open judicial proceedings.

Permission To Proceed Anonymously

Petitioner also requests permission to proceed anonymously. There is no provision in our Rules that permits a taxpayer to proceed anonymously.[1] The Rules generally require taxpayers' names to be included on pleadings and other papers filed with the Court. See Rules 32(a) (requiring a party's name to be set forth on pleadings), 23(a) (requiring all papers filed to contain the full name and surname of each petitioner), 60(a) (requiring a case be brought by and in the name of a person against whom the Commissioner determined the deficiency in the case of a deficiency notice).

When there is no applicable Rule, we may prescribe the procedure, giving particular weight to the Federal Rules of Civil Procedure to the extent adaptable to the matter at hand. Rule 1(a). Where our Rules are silent, we have looked to the Federal Rules of Civil Procedure and cases in other Federal courts interpreting the Federal Rules of Civil Procedure for guidance. See *Willie Nelson Music Co. v. Commissioner*, 85 T.C. at 917 (looking to decisions interpreting rule 26(c) of the Federal Rules of

---

1. Written determinations of the Commissioner such as rulings, determination letters, technical advice memoranda or Chief Counsel Advice and background file documents are generally made public with certain deletions of names, addresses, and other identifying information. Sec. 6110(a), (c). A person may act to restrain disclosure of these materials, however, under the procedures set forth in sec. 6110(f).

Civil Procedure for guidance in interpreting Rule 103(a)); Allen v. Commissioner, 71 T.C. 577, 579, 1979 WL 3722 (1979).

Several U.S. Courts of Appeals have permitted litigation to proceed anonymously. See, e.g., *Does I Thru XXIII v. Advanced Textile Corp.*, supra at 1067; James v. Jacobson, 6 F.3d 233, 238 (4th Cir.1993); Doe v. Stegall, 653 F.2d 180, 185-186 (5th Cir.1981). The Supreme Court and the U.S. Court of Appeals for the District of Columbia Circuit have occasionally permitted anonymous litigation to proceed. Qualls v. Rumsfeld, 228 F.R.D. 8, 10 (D.D.C.2005) (citing Roe v. Wade, 410 U.S. 113, 93 S.Ct. 705, 35 L.Ed.2d 147 (1973), and Doe v. Sullivan, 938 F.2d 1370, 1374 (D.C.Cir.1991)).

The decision whether to allow parties to proceed anonymously is in the discretion of the trial court. A party may generally proceed anonymously when the trial court reasonably determines that the need for anonymity outweighs the prejudice to the opposing party and the general presumption that the parties' identities are public information. Some factors to be considered in deciding whether a party may proceed anonymously include whether the party challenges governmental activity, whether the party is required to disclose information of the utmost intimacy, and whether the party is compelled to admit his or her intention to engage in illegal conduct. *Doe v. Stegall*, supra at 185.

Petitioner has a unique need for anonymity in this case. Petitioner fears that physical harm may come to petitioner or petitioner's family and their lives placed in jeopardy if petitioner's identity or financial circumstances were made public in this case. We weigh this risk of physical harm against the risk of prejudice to respondent and the public interest in knowing the parties' identities. We hold that petitioner may preserve anonymity in the special circumstances of this proceeding because petitioner's need for anonymity outweighs prejudice to the opposing party and the public interest in knowing the identities of parties to judicial proceedings. There is little risk of prejudice to respondent here. Petitioner wants only to keep the information from public view. Petitioner is willing to provide sealed copies of documents to respondent. Further, the risk of severe physical harm to petitioner and petitioner's family outweighs the general public interest in knowing the parties' identities. Accordingly, we conclude that the balance is in petitioner's favor, and petitioner may therefore proceed anonymously.

Prior Public Disclosure of Information

Respondent objects to sealing the record here because some of the information has already been disclosed in a different judicial forum, and the records of that forum have not yet been sealed. Respondent argues that we therefore cannot maintain or protect petitioner's privacy due to the previous disclosure. We disagree. The public availability of some facts in another forum should not bar protection against the risk of future harm caused by disclosure in this Court. The prior disclosure of some information does not preclude our decision to seal the record in this Court and permit petitioner to proceed anonymously.

Conclusion

After a careful review of the facts and circumstances of this case, we find that the demonstrated risk of severe physical harm to petitioner and petitioner's family outweighs the public interest in access to judicial records and to the identity of the parties. There is little prejudice to respondent in permitting petitioner to proceed anonymously. Accordingly, we shall grant petitioner's motion to seal the entire record and permit petitioner to proceed anonymously. We do not address whether or to what extent any later opinions in this case will be sealed.

F. TRIAL

The Tax Court is based in Washington, D.C., and its judges travel around the country to various designated cities to hear cases. In the petition, the taxpayer must designate a location for the trial, although the location may be changed subsequently for "good cause." After a petition has been filed (i.e., the case is "at issue"), it will be placed on a trial calendar for the location designated by the taxpayer. The Clerk then will contact the parties to notify them of the time and place of the trial calendar setting. Tax Court Rule 131. The Clerk also should provide the parties with a copy of the Pretrial Order, advising the parties of how the particular judge expects the pretrial proceedings, and in some cases, the trial itself, to be conducted. Failure to adhere closely to the Pretrial Order may result in the imposition of sanctions against the party. In some cases, the sanctions could affect the outcome of the case.

Under exceptional circumstances, the Tax Court may grant a motion for continuance, or it may continue a case on its own initiative. Tax Court Rule 133 specifically provides that conflicting engagements of counsel or employment of new counsel do not constitute grounds for a continuance. Also, a motion filed within 30 days or less of the date to which it is directed ordinarily will be regarded as "dilatory" and will be denied unless the ground for the motion arose during that period or there was other good reason for not making the motion sooner.

ESTATE OF SELS v. COMMISSIONER

United States Tax Court, 1984.
82 T.C. 64.

OPINION

HAMBLEN, JUDGE:

This matter is before the Court on petitioners' Motion for Continuance under Rule 134 [eds: now Rule 133][1] filed on November 9, 1983, * * *. Respondent opposes [the motion].

Pursuant to notice, a hearing on both motions was held on November 30, 1983, in Washington, D.C. Counsel for both parties appeared at the hearing and presented argument. In addition, various memoranda have been filed by each party setting forth their respective positions as to each motion.

The main case involves respondent's determination of a deficiency in the amount of $2,446,096.00 in petitioners' estate tax. The central dispute therein is the value of various undivided minority interests in certain timberlands in California as of February 10, 1983, the date of decedent's death. The large amount of money and the complex valuation issues involved require the use of expert witnesses by both parties.

* * *

We turn now to consideration of petitioners' motion for continuance of trial under Rule 134. Rule 134 permits the Court to grant a continuance where a motion for same is timely, sets forth good and sufficient cause, and complies with all applicable rules. Petitioners request a continuance on grounds including that the focusing on the matter of valuation methodology as a central issue in the case has occurred only relatively recently, i.e., as of the mid-1983 exchange of conflicting initial reports prepared by expert witnesses for each party. Petitioners believe that more time is needed, in light of the conflict between experts, to consult with additional experts and potential witnesses. Furthermore, because of other commitments by appraisers for both parties, current information as to the timber volumes involved in this case is not yet available. Petitioners expect, as does this Court, that such information can be shortly forthcoming and can provide a basis for stipulation as to the issue of timber volume.

We have considered respondent's objections to a continuance. However, in light of the facts that no prior continuances have been

---

1. Unless otherwise indicated, all rule references are to the Tax Court Rules of Practice and Procedure.

requested and a bona fide need for the current continuance has been demonstrated to our satisfaction, we find respondent's arguments unpersuasive. Therefore, petitioners' motion for continuance of trial has been granted.

To reflect the foregoing, An appropriate order has been issued.

Notes

The Service usually will object to a motion for continuance. If there are compelling grounds for granting the motion, however, the Court will do so. Such grounds include documented illness of the petitioner, the counsel or a key witness; the pendency of a related case, provided the motion includes the name and docket number of the related case, the names of the counsels for the parties, the status of the case, and an identification of the common related issues in the case; and where the continuance would conserve the Court's resources and prevent multiple trials that could lead to inconsistent determinations involving related parties. As the *Sels* court indicates, the motion for continuance may be more favorably regarded if the Court expects the continuance to result in stipulations by the parties.

1. Burden of Proof

Since the taxpayer is the plaintiff (petitioner) in the Tax Court, the taxpayer generally bears the burden of proof by a preponderance of the evidence. See Tax Court Rule 142(a). The burden is on the Service, however, if so provided by statute or determined by the Court, and with respect to any new matter or additional deficiency raised by the Service, or any affirmative defenses pleaded in the answer. Id.

There are several situations in which the statute provides that the Service has the burden of proof. These include cases involving fraud, in which the Service must establish fraud by clear and convincing evidence (§ 7454(a)); cases in which the Service alleges that the petitioner is liable as a transferee of property–the Service must prove the petitioner's liability as a transferee (§ 6902(a)); review of jeopardy levy or assessment procedures (§ 7429(g)(1)); illegal bribes, kickbacks and other payments (§ 162(c)(1) and (2)); penalties for promoting abusive tax shelters (§ 6703(a)); and the return preparer's penalty (§ 7427).

a. Shift of the Burden to the Service under § 7491

In an effort to increase the Service's accountability to taxpayers, the IRS Restructuring and Reform Act of 1998 provides that the burden of proof in a court proceeding may be shifted to the Service if the taxpayer presents credible evidence with respect to the factual issues in question. IRC §7491. But under § 7491(c), the Service has the burden of production with respect to penalties, additions to tax, or additional amounts imposed upon an individual taxpayer. The question is what constitutes "credible evidence" and what does the phrase "burden of production" mean?

HIGBEE v. COMMISSIONER
United States Tax Court, 2001.
116 T.C. 438.

OPINION

VASQUEZ, J.

* * *

Discussion

I. Disallowed Deductions

Deductions are a matter of legislative grace, and a taxpayer bears the burden of proving that he is entitled to the deductions claimed. See Rule 142(a). The taxpayer is required to maintain records that are sufficient to enable the Commissioner to determine his correct tax liability. See sec. 6001; sec.1.6001-1(a), Income Tax Regs. In addition, the taxpayer bears the burden of substantiating the amount and purpose of the claimed deduction.

Section 7491(a), a new provision created by Internal Revenue Service Restructuring and Reform Act of 1998 (RRA 1998), Pub.L. 105-206, sec. 3001, 112 Stat. 685, 726, places the burden of proof on respondent with regard to certain factual issues. Section 7491 applies to examinations commenced after July 22, 1998. See RRA 1998 sec. 3001(c), 112 Stat. 727. The examination in the instant case commenced after July 22, 1998; accordingly, we evaluate whether respondent bears the burden of proof pursuant to section 7491(a).

Section 7491(a)(1) provides that if, in any court proceeding, the taxpayer introduces credible evidence with respect to factual issues relevant to ascertaining the taxpayer's liability for a tax (under subtitle A or B), the burden of proof with respect to such factual issues will be placed on the Commissioner. For the burden to be placed on the

Commissioner, however, the taxpayer must comply with the substantiation and record-keeping requirements of the Internal Revenue Code. See sec. 7491(a)(2)(A) and (B). In addition, section 7491(a) requires that the taxpayer cooperate with reasonable requests by the Commissioner for "witnesses, information, documents, meetings, and interviews". Sec. 7491(a)(2)(B). Finally, the benefits of section 7491(a) are unavailable in the cases of partnerships, corporations, and trusts unless the taxpayer meets the net worth requirements of section 7430(c)(4)(A)(ii). See sec. 7491(a)(2)(C).

Respondent argues that because petitioners have failed to meet the requirements of section 7491(a)(1) and (2), the burden of proof should remain with petitioners as to the remaining issue associated with respondent's determination of petitioners' 1996 tax liability. We therefore examine the evidence to establish whether petitioners have presented credible evidence and have met the other requirements of section 7491(a)(1) and (2) so as to place the burden of proof on respondent.

A. Casualty Losses

Pursuant to section 165(a) and (c)(3), a taxpayer is allowed a deduction for an uncompensated loss that arises from fire, storm, shipwreck, or other casualty. Section 165(h), however, states that any "loss * * * shall be allowed only to the extent that the amount of the loss to such individual arising from each casualty * * * exceeds $100" and only to the extent that the net casualty loss "exceeds 10 percent of the adjusted gross income".

When property is damaged rather than totally destroyed by casualty, the proper measure of the amount of the loss sustained is the difference between the fair market value of the property immediately before and after the casualty, not to exceed the property's adjusted basis. See sec. 1.165-7(b)(1), Income Tax Regs. The fair market values required by the Treasury regulations must generally be ascertained by competent appraisal. See sec. 1.165-7(a)(2)(I), Income Tax Regs. As an alternative, the Treasury regulations provide that if the taxpayer has repaired the property damage resulting from the casualty, the taxpayer may use the cost of repairs to prove the casualty loss. See sec. 1.165-7(a)(2)(ii), Income Tax Regs. In general, estimates of the cost of repairs are not evidence of the actual costs of repairs unless the repairs are actually made. See Lamphere v. Commissioner, 70 T.C. 391, 396, 1978 WL 3307 (1978); Farber v. Commissioner, 57 T.C. 714, 719 (1972).

Petitioners claim a casualty loss deduction in the amount of $1,328 on account of alleged damage to their home and personal property which was not deducted on their tax return. Mr. Higbee testified that the $1,328 represents the damage to petitioners' property which was not reimbursed by their insurance company but awarded by a small claims court.[3] In support, petitioners provided a form document entitled "Small Claims Complaint/Summons/Answer" which appears to be issued by the Glendale Justice Court in Glendale, Arizona, but which does not bear any type of notation or certification by a governmental official.

In order for section 7491(a) to place the burden of proof on respondent, the taxpayer must first provide credible evidence. The statute itself does not state what constitutes credible evidence. The conference committee's report states as follows:

> Credible evidence is the quality of evidence which, after critical analysis, the court would find sufficient upon which to base a decision on the issue if no contrary evidence were submitted (without regard to the judicial presumption of IRS correctness). A taxpayer has not produced credible evidence for these purposes if the taxpayer merely makes implausible factual assertions, frivolous claims, or tax protestor-type arguments. The introduction of evidence will not meet this standard if the court is not convinced that it is worthy of belief. If after evidence from both sides, the court believes that the evidence is equally balanced, the court shall find that the Secretary has not sustained his burden of proof. [H. Conf. Rept. 105-599, at 240-241 (1998), 1998-3 C.B. 747, 994-995 .]

Further, the conference report explains the purpose of the limitations set forth in section 7491(a)(2):

> Nothing in the provision shall be construed to override any requirement under the Code or regulations to substantiate any item. Accordingly, taxpayers must meet applicable substantiation requirements, whether generally imposed[10] or imposed with respect to specific items, such as charitable contributions or meals, entertainment, travel, and certain other expenses. Substantiation requirements include any requirement of the Code or regulations that the taxpayer establish an item to the satisfaction of the Secretary. Taxpayers who fail to substantiate any item in accordance with the legal requirement of substantiation will not have satisfied

---

3. Petitioners assert that the judgment remains unpaid.

10. See e.g., Sec. 6001 and Treas. Reg. sec. 1.6001-1 requiring every person liable for any tax imposed by this Title to keep such records as the Secretary may from time to time prescribe, * * *. [Id. at 241, 1998-3 C.B. at 995; certain fn. refs. omitted.]

the legal conditions that are prerequisite to claiming the item on the taxpayer's tax return and will accordingly be unable to avail themselves of this provision regarding the burden of proof. Thus, if a taxpayer required to substantiate an item fails to do so in the manner required (or destroys the substantiation), this burden of proof provision is inapplicable.

* * *

Petitioners' evidence does not meet the requirements of section 7491(a). Besides the fact that the form document entitled "Small Claims Complaint/Summons/Answer" does not actually indicate whether litigation in small claims court was commenced or completed, the document itself does not qualify as a competent appraisal or reliable estimate of the cost of any repairs. Because petitioners have failed to provide credible evidence of a casualty loss, the burden of proof as to this issue is not placed on respondent. Further, for similar reasons regarding our discussion of petitioners' evidence for purposes of section 7491, we conclude that petitioners have not met their burden of proof. See Rule 142(a). Consequently, we reject petitioners' claimed casualty loss deduction.

B. Charitable Contributions

Section 170(a)(1) provides that a taxpayer may deduct "any charitable contribution* * * payment of which is made within the taxable year. A charitable contribution shall be allowable as a deduction only if verified under regulations prescribed by the Secretary." Pursuant to the Treasury regulations, contributions of money are required to be substantiated by canceled checks, receipts from the donee organizations showing the date and amount of the contributions, or other reliable written records showing the name of the donee, date, and amount of the contributions. See sec. 1.170A- 13(a)(1), Income Tax Regs. Similarly, contributions of property other than money must be substantiated, at a minimum, by a receipt from the donee showing the name and address of the donee, the date and location of the contribution, and a description of the property in detail reasonably sufficient under the circumstances. See sec. 1.170A-13(b)(1), Income Tax Regs. Where it is unrealistic to obtain a receipt, taxpayers must maintain reliable written records of their contributions.

To substantiate additional charitable contributions of $6,937.20 for 1996 not previously claimed on their return for that year, petitioners offered several documents to the Court. Some of the documents do not have any indication of being provided by a donee organization but instead appear to have been generated by petitioners. Other documents consist of preprinted forms issued by alleged charitable organizations which petitioners filled in with the type and number of items donated and the estimated value of the donation. In addition, petitioners submitted checks and receipts which appear to be for the purchase of goods and services. Lastly, at trial, petitioners attempted to buttress their claims by describing the types of goods allegedly donated.

While the preprinted forms appear authentic, we nevertheless conclude that petitioners' self-generated receipts and other documents are not credible evidence of the order necessary to substantiate the deductions claimed in the instant case. Further, we do not find petitioners' testimony credible. We hold that petitioners have failed to introduce credible evidence to substantiate the actual items contributed and their fair market values.[4] See sec. 7491(a)(1) and (2)(A). Consequently, the burden of proof is not placed on respondent. Because petitioners have failed to present us with any credible evidence, they have not met their burden of proof pursuant to Rule 142(a) to support their claimed deductions. We therefore hold that petitioners are not entitled to a deduction for charitable contributions in excess of the $1,500 that respondent has already allowed.

* * *

II. Addition to Tax and Accuracy-Related Penalty

Under RRA 1998, Congress also enacted a provision, section 7491(c), requiring the Commissioner to carry the "burden of production" in any court proceeding with respect to the liability of any individual for any penalty, addition to tax, or additional amount (penalties). Although the statute does not provide a definition of the phrase "burden of production", we conclude that Congress' intent as to the meaning of the burden of production is evident from the legislative history. The legislative history of section 7491(c) sets forth:

> [i]n any court proceeding, the Secretary must–initially come forward with evidence that it is appropriate to apply a particular penalty to the taxpayer before the court can impose the penalty. This provision is not intended to require the Secretary to introduce evidence of elements such as reasonable cause or substantial authority. Rather, the Secretary must come forward initially with evidence regarding

---

4. For instance, on one of the preprinted forms, petitioners listed a charitable contribution of $700 for "cribs" and $200 for "baby clothes". Because petitioners have failed to establish how they arrived at those fair market values, we are unable to allow such deductions. Further, petitioners have not produced any other independent and credible evidence indicating that those donations were actually made.

the appropriateness of applying a particular penalty to the taxpayer; if the taxpayer believes that, because of reasonable cause, substantial authority, or a similar provision, it is inappropriate to impose the penalty, it is the taxpayer's responsibility (and not the Secretary's obligation) to raise those issues. [H. Conf. Rept. 105-599, supra at 241, 1998-3 C.B. at 995.]

Therefore, with regard to section 7491(c), we conclude that for the Commissioner to meet his burden of production, the Commissioner must come forward with sufficient evidence indicating that it is appropriate to impose the relevant penalty.

The legislative history to section 7491(c), however, also discloses that the Commissioner need not introduce evidence regarding reasonable cause, substantial authority, or similar provisions. In addition, the legislative history indicates that it is the taxpayer's responsibility to raise those issues. We therefore conclude that the taxpayer bears the burden of proof with regard to those issues.

Finally, we note that Congress placed only the burden of production on the Commissioner pursuant to section 7491(c). Congress' use of the phrase "burden of production" and not the more general phrase "burden of proof" as used in section 7491(a) indicates to us that Congress did not desire that the burden of proof be placed on the Commissioner with regard to penalties.[6] See sec. 7491(c). Therefore, once the Commissioner meets his burden of production, the taxpayer must come forward with evidence sufficient to persuade a Court that the Commissioner's determination is incorrect.

Having described the framework of section 7491(c), we evaluate whether respondent has met his burden of production with regard to the section 6651(a)(1) addition to tax and the section 6662 accuracy-related penalty. We also discuss whether petitioners have presented any evidence which would cause us not to sustain respondent's determinations with regard to the addition to tax and the accuracy-related penalty.

Section 6651(a)(1) imposes an addition to tax for a taxpayer's failure to file a required return on or before the specified filing date, including extensions. The amount of the liability is based upon a percentage of the tax required to be shown on the return. See sec. 6651(a)(1). The addition

---

6. We note that sec. 6665(a)(2) provides that any reference to tax shall be deemed also to refer to penalties. However, the application of sec. 6665(a)(2) is limited by the language "Except as otherwise provided in this title". Considering that limiting language of sec. 6665(a)(2), the reference in sec. 7491(a) to tax liabilities imposed by subtitle A or B (whereas penalties are imposed by subtitle F), and the structure of sec. 7491 as a whole, we believe that Congress intended for sec. 7491(c) (and not sec. 7491(a)) to apply to penalties.

to tax is inapplicable, however, if the taxpayer's failure to file the return was due to reasonable cause and not to willful neglect. See sec. 6651(a)(1). Under section 7491(c), as noted above, the Commissioner bears the burden of production with regard to whether the section 6651(a)(1) addition to tax is appropriate, but he does not bear the burden of proof with regard to the "reasonable cause" exception of section 6651(a).

Respondent determined that petitioners are liable for a section 6651(a)(1) addition to tax with regard to their 1996 tax return. The parties have stipulated that petitioners filed their 1996 return on April 18, 1998, approximately 1 year after it was due. Accordingly, we conclude that respondent has produced sufficient evidence to show that the section 6651(a)(1) addition to tax is appropriate, unless petitioners prove that their failure to file was due to reasonable cause.

Petitioners have not provided any evidence indicating that their failure to file was due to reasonable cause. Therefore, an addition to tax of 25 percent of the amount required to be shown as tax on the return is sustained in the instant case. Because the parties have made several concessions, respondent's original section 6651(a)(1) addition to tax computation must be adjusted to reflect such changes. * * *

Pursuant to section 6662(a), a taxpayer may be liable for a penalty of 20 percent on the portion of an underpayment of tax (1) attributable to a substantial understatement of tax or (2) due to negligence or disregard of rules or regulations. See sec. 6662(b). A substantial understatement of tax is defined as an understatement of tax that exceeds the greater of 10 percent of the tax required to be shown on the tax return or $5,000. See sec. 6662(d)(1)(A). The understatement is reduced to the extent that the taxpayer has (1) adequately disclosed his or her position and has a reasonable basis for such position or (2) has substantial authority for the tax treatment of the item. See sec. 6662(d)(2)(B). In addition, section 6662(c) defines "negligence" as any failure to make a reasonable attempt to comply with the provisions of the Internal Revenue Code, and "disregard" means any careless, reckless, or intentional disregard.

Whether applied because of a substantial understatement of tax or negligence or disregard of the rules or regulations, the accuracy-related penalty is not imposed with respect to any portion of the understatement as to which the taxpayer acted with reasonable cause and in good faith. See sec. 6664(c)(1). The decision as to whether the taxpayer acted with reasonable cause and in good faith depends upon all the pertinent facts and circumstances. See sec. 1.6664-4(b)(1), Income Tax Regs. Relevant factors include the taxpayer's efforts to assess his proper tax liability, including the taxpayer's reasonable and good faith reliance on the advice of a professional such as an accountant. See id. Further, an honest misunderstanding of fact or law that is reasonable in light of the experience, knowledge, and education of the taxpayer may indicate reasonable cause and good faith. See Remy v. Commissioner, T.C. Memo.1997-72.

For the 1997 tax year, respondent determined that petitioners are liable for an accuracy-related penalty attributable to a substantial understatement of tax or, in the alternative, due to negligence or disregard of rules or regulations. Petitioners have conceded that they are not entitled to $30,245 in itemized deductions relating to NOL carryovers ($28,036) and certain taxes ($2,209) claimed on Schedule A of their 1997 tax return. With regard to respondent's determination that petitioners were negligent and disregarded rules and regulations, respondent argues that he has met his burden of production under section 7491(c) through petitioners' above concessions, along with evidence in the record indicating that petitioners were experienced in business affairs. Further, respondent contends that because petitioners have failed to introduce any evidence to indicate that they were not negligent, petitioners have failed to meet their burden of proof, which they retain despite the application of section 7491(c).

Respondent has shown that petitioners have failed to keep adequate books and records or to substantiate properly the items in question. Such a failure in the instant case is evidence of negligence. See sec. 1.6662-3(b), Income Tax Regs. Consequently, we conclude that respondent has met his burden of production for his determination of the accuracy-related penalty based on negligence or disregard of rules or regulations. Additionally, with regard to that determination, petitioners have failed to meet their burden of proving that they acted with reasonable cause and in good faith. We therefore sustain respondent's determination that petitioners are liable for the accuracy-related penalty on the underpayment associated with the disallowed itemized deductions conceded by petitioners.[9]

In reaching our holdings herein, we have considered all arguments made, and to the extent not mentioned above, we find them to be moot, irrelevant, or without merit.

* * *

---

9. Because of respondent's concessions * * *, we conclude that the accuracy-related penalty based on a substantial understatement of tax is not applicable as the understatement does not exceed the greater of 10 percent of tax required to be shown on the return or $5,000. See sec. 6662(d)(1).

Notes and Questions

Because of the conditions placed on the taxpayer under § 7491 before the burden of proof will shift, it was speculated initially that the shift in burden to the Service would be of little consequence. See Jerome Borison, Effectively Representing Your Client Before the "New" IRS, ¶ 7A.6.2 (2000). But an interesting empirical study conducted by John R. Gardner and Benjamin R. Norman shows a significant decrease in the number of Tax Court cases in the wake of the burden shifting provision of the RRA '98, although the study also shows relatively little change in the case settlement rate, the taxpayers' success rate, and the amount of the Service's recovery. The authors conclude that the decrease in the number of Tax Court cases indicates that the shift in the burden of proof has caused a corresponding shift in the Service's view of the litigation potential of the cases. Some of the cases that it previously may have litigated are now settled, and some of the cases that previously may have been settled are not pursued. The authors conclude that this explains both the decline in the number of cases brought and the fact that the settlement rate remains relatively unchanged. John R. Gardner and Benjamin R. Norman, Effects Of The Shift In The Burden Of Proof In The Disposition Of Tax Cases, 38 Wake Forest L. Rev. 1357 (2003).

1. Explain the difference, if any, among "burden of proof," "burden of persuasion," and the "burden of going forward with the evidence." Who bears the burden in the Tax Court in each case? What is the "presumption of correctness" and when does it apply? What changes, if any, have occurred in the burdens and the presumption as a result of § 7491?

2. Under what circumstances might taxpayers find it easier to shift the burden to the Service (other than complying with the conditions of § 7491(a)(2)?

3. What constitutes "credible evidence?" Is the taxpayer's own testimony ever sufficient? See Griffin v. Commissioner, 315 F.3d 1017 (8th Cir. 2003).

b. New Matters

As we discussed in Chapter 4, the statute of limitations for assessment is stayed during the 90-day period after the notice of deficiency is mailed, and if the taxpayer files a petition in the Tax Court during that period the statute is tolled further until the decision of the Tax Court becomes final. The taxpayer should be aware that the Service can raise new issues, increasing the amount of the deficiency, at any time prior to the decision of the court. The other side of the coin, however, is that any issues that could have been raised with respect to the taxable year or years before the court, are res judicata once the court renders its decision, even if the issues were not raised. Thus, the Service has an incentive to raise all the issues it feasibly can raise with respect to the taxable year(s) before the court.

The Service has the burden of proof with respect to any new matter, increase in deficiency, and affirmative defense. Tax Court Rule 142(a).

ABATTI v. COMMISSIONER

United States Court of Appeals, Ninth Circuit, 1981.
644 F.2d 1385.

SOLOMON, JUDGE:

The tax court disallowed $2,356,381 in deficiencies assessed against Ben and Tony Abatti and their wives for the tax years 1971, 1972, and 1973. The Commissioner of Internal Revenue (the Commissioner) appeals. We reverse.

Ben and Tony Abatti are farmers. They conduct their farming operations through three entities. Abatti Brothers (B&T) is a partnership which owns or leases land. It has a calendar year. Abatti Farms (Farms) is a subchapter S corporation which grows crops for B&T and others. It has a May 31 fiscal year end. Abatti Produce (Produce) is a subchapter S corporation which harvests, packages and markets crops for B&T and others. It has a January 31 fiscal year end. All these entities use the cash method of accounting.

There were many intercompany transfers of funds for services rendered, disbursements of sales proceeds and intercompany loans. They kept no records to reflect the reasons for these transfers and there were no billings or invoices. At each entity's year end, the intercompany accounts were closed by payments to the other entities for amounts due. These intercompany transactions were the subject of the Commissioner's audit.

The 1971-1972 year end transactions illustrate the transactions which the Commissioner examined. On December 31, 1971, B&T obtained a one month loan of $861,127.36 from Security Pacific National Bank. On the same day B&T distributed $660,000 of the loan proceeds to Produce and the other $201,127.36 to Farms. These entities bought Time Certificates of Deposit (TCD's) in those amounts which they pledged to the bank as collateral for B&T's loan. On January 31, 1972, the certificates matured and the bank deposited the proceeds in B&T's account. On the same day B&T repaid the loan.

Frank Hatfield, an Internal Revenue Agent, was assigned to conduct an audit of Produce for its fiscal year ending January 31, 1971. He called Produce and asked to speak with Ben Abatti. Hatfield gave his name and told Ben that he was going to conduct an examination of Produce's 1971 tax return but Ben testified that Hatfield did not identify himself as an IRS agent. Ben told Hatfield to contact his accountant, Mickey Macklin, to make arrangements for the audit. Macklin had been the Abattis' accountant since 1959 and was responsible for making the entities' accounting decisions.

Because of the many intercompany transfers, Hatfield expanded the audit to all three entities for 1971, 1972, and 1973. Hatfield questioned Ben about these transactions and Ben referred him to Macklin, because as Ben later testified, he knew nothing about the record keeping and he relied on Macklin to do all the accounting work. Thereafter, Hatfield made his requests for information to Macklin. Macklin was not enrolled to practice before the IRS. In July, 1974, Macklin told Hatfield that the Abattis had retained Charles A. Pinney, Jr. as their attorney in this matter. Pinney was enrolled to practice before the IRS.

On October 9, 1974, Pinney, Macklin, and Hatfield met at Pinney's office. A ring binder prepared by Macklin, which contained accounting schedules and other data principally prepared by Macklin and by Mrs. Poloni, the Abattis' sister and bookkeeper, was delivered to Hatfield. The binder showed how the intercompany transactions were reported and how they should have been reported.

On April 15, 1976, the Commissioner sent revenue agent's reports for 1971 and 1972 to the three Abatti entities and to Pinney. The reports proposed adjustments to each entity's income and deductions on the ground that under Section 482 of the Internal Revenue Code, as amended, 26 U.S.C. s 482 (Section 482),[1] the intercompany transactions did not clearly reflect income. On the same day, the Commissioner mailed statutory notices of deficiency to the taxpayers. These notices contained the same explanation of the adjustments to income and deductions:

> It is determined from the books and records of the partnership (or subchapter S corporation) that you have income of * * * dollars for the taxable year * * * in lieu of * * * dollars reported on your return.

---

1. Section 482 provides: "In any case of two or more organizations, trades, or businesses (whether or not incorporated, whether or not organized in the United States, and whether or not affiliated) owned or controlled directly or indirectly by the same interests, the Secretary or his delegate may distribute, apportion or allocate gross income, deductions, or credits, or allowances between or among such organizations, trades, or business, if he determines that such distribution, apportionment, or allocation is necessary in order to prevent evasion of taxes or clearly to reflect the income of any of such organizations, trades or businesses."

The taxpayers petitioned the United States Tax Court for a redetermination of the deficiencies. The Commissioner, in his answer, admitted or denied the various allegations and affirmatively alleged fraud.

On June 29, 1976, Pinney, Macklin, Hatfield, and Revenue Agents Kellogg and Herstedt met at Pinney's office. A second binder containing additional schedules relating to 1974 and new summaries and other information was delivered to Hatfield. Herstedt reconciled the books and records of each of the entities with its tax return.

On March 30, 1977, the Commissioner issued notices of deficiency for 1973 to the taxpayers with the same explanation as those sent in 1976 but no revenue agent's report was mailed.

On March 27, 1978, at a tax court calender call, Pinney made a settlement offer but these was no settlement. The tax court set the trial for June 26, 1978.

On June 1, 1978, the court was informed that the taxpayers had discharged Pinney and had retained James O. Hewitt, an experienced tax attorney. The Commissioner moved to postpone the trial because Hewitt refused to stipulate to the deficiencies. The court denied the postponement and advanced the trial from June 26 to June 21.

On June 7, 1978, Hewitt asked the Commissioner's counsel what legal theories he planned to use. Counsel told him that he would be unable to answer until the following week. On June 16, 1978, counsel informed Hewitt that the Commissioner would rely on Section 482.

At the beginning of the trial Hewitt moved: (1) to exclude reliance on Section 482 and evidence related thereto; (2) to shift the burden of proof to respondent; (3) to limit reliance of respondent to issues properly raised.

The tax court granted all three of these motions.

The tax court, because it found that the deficiency notices contained no valid grounds, permitted the Commissioner to amend his answers to allege that the deficiencies were based on fraud. This required the Commissioner to assume the burden of proof under Rule 142(a) of the Rules of Practice and Procedure of the United States Tax Court (Rule 142(a)).[2]

The Commissioner's counsel called Ben Abatti; four bank officials; Mrs. Poloni; Pinney; Macklin, who refused to testify on the ground of

---

2.   Rule 142(a) Provides: "The burden of proof shall be upon the petitioner, except as otherwise provided by statute or determined by the Court; and except that, in respect of any new matter, increases in deficiency, and affirmative defenses, pleaded in his answer, it shall be upon the respondent."

self-incrimination; and Hatfield. During direct examination of Hatfield, counsel sought to introduce the binders. The court held that the binders were inadmissible. The Commissioner's counsel stated that he was precluded from presenting his case based on fraud and rested. The tax court then announced from the bench that it would hold for the taxpayers.

In this appeal, the Commissioner contends that the tax court erred when it precluded him from relying on Section 482, when it shifted the burden of proof, and when it held that the binders were not admissible in evidence.

The Commissioner does not appeal the tax court's disallowance of the fraud penalties.

SECTION 482

The tax court held that the taxpayers did not have fair warning that the Commissioner intended to invoke Section 482 when the statutory deficiency notices and the pleadings did not expressly mention that section.

The Commissioner may not rely on Section 482 when its use would surprise the taxpayer at the trial. The Commissioner may, however, use Section 482 when the taxpayer has reason to believe that the Commissioner intends to invoke that section. In Rubin v. CIR, 56 T.C. 1155 (1971), aff'd per curiam, 460 F.2d 1216 (2d Cir. 1972), the court allowed the Commissioner to rely on Section 482 because the taxpayers conceded that the Commissioner had informed them of his intent to use that section during a conference well before trial.

* * *

The agent's reports contained a full statement on Section 482. The taxpayers and Pinney, who was their attorney at that time and who had represented them in these cases for three years, received them. Pinney thereafter filed petitions for the taxpayers that contained numbers and other information showing that he referred to the revenue agent's report. It appears incredible that Pinney was unaware of the Commissioner's theory or the basis for the Commissioner's determinations.

It likewise appears incredible that James O. Hewitt, the taxpayers' new counsel, who had access to all of Pinney's files, did not know of the basis for the deficiencies. Hewitt's argument to the tax court, and the court's holding, was based solely on a stupid remark made two weeks before trial by the Commissioner's counsel. Five days before trial, the Commissioner's counsel did inform Mr. Hewitt of the basis of the

Commissioner's case. The delay in telling Hewitt what he must have already known is not an adequate basis for the tax court to rule that the taxpayer did not have fair warning. We hold that the taxpayers had fair warning of the Commissioner's intent to rely on Section 482.

THE BURDEN OF PROOF

The tax court interpreted the deficiency notices to mean that the Commissioner was alleging a difference between the entities' books and records and the taxpayers' individual tax returns. It therefore shifted the burden of proof to the Commissioner because the Commissioner had never argued that there was a difference. The Commissioner did not make that argument because he was contending that the intercompany accounts did not clearly reflect income.

The tax court's reading of the notices is a finding of fact which can be overturned only if clearly erroneous. Clark v. CIR, 266 F.2d 698 (9th Cir. 1959). We find that the tax court's interpretation was arbitrary because it gave an interpretation which the Commissioner did not intend and which the taxpayers could not reasonably have believed that the Commissioner intended. In our view a more reasonable interpretation of the notices is that they informed the taxpayers that there were deficiencies and the amount of them but contained no explanation. This type of notice is sufficient to raise the presumption of correctness and to place the burden of proof on the taxpayer. Judge Hand, in *Olsen v. Helvering, supra*, stated, "the notice is only to advise the person who is to pay the deficiency that the Commissioner means to assess him; anything that does this unequivocally is good enough." Id. at 651.

Based on its interpretation of the deficiency notices, the tax court found that the Commissioner's amended answer and proposed use of Section 482 were "new matter.' Rule 142(a) states that statutory notices of deficiency are presumptively correct unless the Commissioner introduces "new matter." This determination depends on whether the basis for the deficiency advanced at trial or in an amended answer is "inconsistent with some position necessarily implicit in the determination itself. . .. "Arthur Sorin, 29 T.C. 959, aff'd per curiam, 271 F.2d 741 (2d Cir. 1959). In fact, if a deficiency notice is broadly worded and the Commissioner later advances a theory not inconsistent with that language, the theory does not constitute new matter, and the burden of proof remains with the taxpayer.

We hold that the wording of the deficiency notices was broad enough to include Section 482 and that the Commissioner's reliance on that section does not constitute new matter.

* * *

REVERSED AND REMANDED.

Notes and Questions

In 1988, Congress enacted § 7522, which provides:

(a) General Rule.–Any notice to which this section applies shall describe the basis for, and identify the amounts (if any) of, the tax due, interest, additional amounts, additions to the tax, and assessable penalties included in such notice. An inadequate description under the preceding sentence shall not invalidate such notice.

(b) Notices to Which Section Applies.–This section shall apply to–(1) any tax due notice or deficiency notice described in section 6155, 6212, or 6303, * * *

1. Does § 7522 change the result in *Abatti*? See Shea v. Commissioner, 112 T.C. 183 (1999).

2. Does the § 7491 shift in the burden of proof to the Service have any effect on the *Abatti* decision?

2. Evidence

Trials before the Tax Court will be conducted in accordance with the Federal Rules of Evidence applicable to nonjury trials. Tax Court Rule 143; IRC § 7453. Ex parte affidavits, statements made in briefs, and unadmitted allegations in the pleadings do not constitute evidence and may not be admitted. Tax Court Rule 143(b). Depositions also are not considered evidence until they are offered and received in evidence by the Court. If there is an error in the deposition, it may be corrected by agreement of the parties, or by the Court upon proof by either party that the error exists. Tax Court Rule 143(c).

Under the Federal Rules of Evidence, the original of a document must be offered in evidence. The Tax Court Rules provide, however, that a copy generally is admissible unless the authenticity of the original is questioned or if the Court determines that it would be unfair to admit the copy in lieu of the original. Tax Court Rule 143(d). If the original is admitted, a clearly legible copy may be substituted later in the discretion of the Court.

Exhibits in the case will be destroyed by the Court, unless the party who submitted the exhibit wants it returned. If so, the party must make a written request to the clerk within 90 days after the decision in the case has become final and must pay the costs of returning the exhibits.

Rule 702 of the Federal Rules of Evidence authorizes the admissibility of expert testimony. Expert witnesses are expected to submit a written report setting forth the expert's qualifications, opinion, the facts or data on which that opinion is based, and the reasons for the expert's conclusion. If the court determines that the witness is qualified as an expert, the report will be admitted into evidence and will constitute the direct testimony of the expert. The court may allow additional direct testimony with respect to the report if needed to clarify or emphasize matters in the report, to cover matters arising after the preparation of the report, or otherwise in the court's discretion. Tax Court Rule 143(f). Usually, after the case is calendared for trial or assigned to a judge, the party who intends to call an expert witness must submit a report to both the court and the opposing party not later than 30 days prior to the call of the trial calendar on which the case appears. Failure to comply will result in the testimony of the expert witness being excluded. In order to encourage settlements, however, some judges may require the submission of reports 90 to 120 days prior to the calendar call, with the submission of rebuttal reports within 30 to 45 days.[4] Where the expert's testimony is offered to rebut the testimony of the opposing party's expert, or where the expert testifies only to the industry practice, the court may allow the expert to testify without the submission of a written report. The court also may excuse the failure to submit an expert witness report where the failure is due to good cause and where the opposing party is not unduly prejudiced by significantly impairing that party's ability to cross-examine the witness or by denying the party the reasonable opportunity to obtain rebuttal evidence. Id.

Expert testimony is limited to assisting the court in understanding the evidence or determining a fact in issue. Testimony that expresses a legal conclusion is not admissible. See FPL Group, Inc. v. Commissioner, 83 T.C.M. 1463 (2002). The Tax Court has discretion to accept or reject the testimony of the expert in whole or in part, and to determine what weight to give the testimony if it is admitted.

---

4.   See Gerald A. Kafka, LITIGATION OF FEDERAL CIVIL TAX CONTROVERSIES ¶ 8.02[4] (1997 and Supplement 2000).

LUKENS v. COMMISSIONER
United States Court of Appeals, Fifth Circuit, 1991.
945 F.2d 92

KING, CIRCUIT JUDGE:

* * *

I. FACTS AND PROCEDURAL HISTORY

On December 21, 1981, Lukens and seventeen other individuals formed Univestors in Utah, a Utah partnership ("Univestors" or "partnership"). The purpose of Univestors, in which Lukens had a 4.6% interest, was to purchase timeshare units in vacation homes in Park City, Utah. On December 29, 1981, Univestors purchased twenty-seven timeshare units in a tri-level house, identified as Lot # 1033, Jeremy Ranch Plat B ("House # 30"). The purchase price of each timeshare unit was $3,600. For each unit, the partnership paid a down payment of $800, which left an unpaid principal balance of $2,800. The partnership was to pay $570 per unit per year for ten years, which payments were to be applied to interest. No further principal or interest payments were required until thirty years from the purchase date. At that time, because the debt was nonrecourse, the partnership could either forfeit its interest in the unit or make a balloon payment of approximately $86,700 to become the owner.

On his federal income tax return for 1981, Lukens claimed a $7,179.54 deduction, as his proportional share of the partnership's loss, for his $993.60 (4.6% of the $21,600 total down payment for the 27 units) expenditure on December 29, 1981. On June 17, 1985, the Commissioner issued a statutory deficiency notice to Lukens determining a $2,953 deficiency in Lukens' federal income taxes for 1981 and completely disallowing the deduction. The Commissioner determined also that Lukens was liable for an increased rate of interest under 26 U.S.C. § 6621(c).

On September 19, 1985, October 15, 1985, and January 23, 1986, Lukens filed a petition, amended petition, and second amended petition, respectively, in the tax court challenging the Commissioner's findings. He argued that the timeshare units were worth the purchase price, and because the value of the units would appreciate during the life of the contract, purchase of them was a sound business investment. At trial, the parties proffered the testimony of experts to aid the tax court in its determination of the fair market value of the timeshare units purchased by Univestors. Lukens elicited the testimony of two expert witnesses: Clyde E. Williams concluded that the appraised value for each timeshare unit in House # 30 was $3,950; Kathleen Conroy appraised each unit at $2,920. The Commissioner's expert, Michael Greene, testified that the value of each timeshare unit in House # 30 was $1,200.[5] At trial, Lukens also sought to elicit the testimony of Francis Longstaff as an expert witness. Longstaff was to testify as to the expected appreciation in value of each timeshare unit. The tax court, however, concluded that Longstaff did not qualify as an expert, but allowed him to testify as a fact witness and admitted his written reports into evidence.

The tax court, after hearing the expert testimony, selected from the various methods of valuing the timeshare units proffered by all of the experts to arrive at its conclusion that each timeshare unit in House # 30 had a fair market value of $919, far lower than the purchase price of $3,600. The tax court further found each unit would not appreciate to the point where its market value would equal or exceed the balloon payment due in the thirtieth year after purchase, and that, because the financing was nonrecourse, Lukens would forfeit his interest in each unit in lieu of making the balloon payment.

Based on these findings, the tax court determined that the nonrecourse debt incurred by the partnership in the acquisition of the units did not constitute genuine debt and, consequently, did not give rise to interest deductions. The court also imposed an increased rate of interest, with respect to the transaction, under section 6621(c) of the Internal Revenue Code based on Lukens' "substantial underpayment" of tax attributable to a tax motivated transaction. 26 U.S.C. § 6621(c).

II. DISCUSSION

Lukens contends that the tax court erred by (I) valuing the timeshare units lower than any of the three expert witnesses; (ii) refusing to allow, or disregarding, all expert witness testimony as to likely appreciation rates; (iii) finding that the nonrecourse debt lacked economic substance; (iv) completely disallowing the claimed interest deduction; and (v) imposing an increased rate of interest under 26 U.S.C. § 6621(c). We will address these issues seriatim.

---

5. Greene first determined the value of a one-day timeshare as of 1986, and then adjusted the 1986 value to reflect the 1981 purchase date of the property. Greene made this adjustment by reducing the value in an amount equal to the change in the consumer price index over the same period of time. We agree with the tax court that this method is "incredible" and not worthy of consideration by the court.

A. Expert Testimony as to Value of Timeshare Units

Lukens contends that the tax court improperly ignored all expert testimony proffered by both parties in valuing the timeshare units. The valuation of the units by the tax court, complains Lukens, was lower than expert valuations, including that of the Commissioner's expert.

The tax court's determination of the fair market value of the timeshare units is a finding of fact reviewable under the clearly erroneous standard. The court is free either to accept or reject expert testimony in accordance with its own judgment. See Helvering v. National Grocery Co., 304 U.S. 282, 295, 58 S.Ct. 932, 938, 82 L.Ed. 1346 (1938); Tripp v. Commissioner, 337 F.2d 432 (7th Cir.1964); Parker v. Commissioner, 86 T.C. 547, 562 (1986) (the tax court need not accept any expert testimony that does not withstand careful analysis). In fact, the court is not in any way bound by the opinions or formulas proffered by experts, and may reach a determination of value based upon its own evaluation of the evidence in the record. Silverman v. Commissioner, 538 F.2d 927, 933 (2d Cir.1976); In re Williams' Estate, 256 F.2d 217, 219 (9th Cir.1958) ("the trier of fact * * * may disregard [expert opinion] altogether in decision"). As this court has noted, "[v]aluation is * * * necessarily an approximation * * *. It is not necessary that the value arrived at by the trial court be a figure as to which there is specific testimony, if it is within the range of figures that may properly be deduced from the evidence." Anderson v. Commissioner, 250 F.2d 242, 249 (5th Cir.1957).

The tax court had the opportunity to hear and evaluate the credibility of both parties' expert witnesses. The tax court devoted a considerable portion of its opinion to in-depth discussion of each expert's valuation methods. The tax court found most of the testimony suspect, and fashioned its own valuation from what credible testimony was proffered. The tax court's valuation of $919 for each timeshare unit was "within the range of figures that may properly be deduced from the evidence," *Anderson*, 250 F.2d at 249, and was therefore not clearly erroneous.

B. Expert Testimony as to Appreciation

Lukens also contends that the tax court erred in refusing to allow expert testimony from Longstaff regarding appreciation. This contention is without merit. Longstaff was allowed to testify as a fact witness, and two reports he prepared concerning appreciation of the timeshare units were admitted into evidence. Inasmuch as Longstaff was pursuing a B.A. in accounting and studying for his C.P.A. examination during the time he was writing the two reports, the tax court did not abuse its discretion in refusing to admit his testimony as expert.

Lukens also argues that the tax court erred in disregarding "admissions" by the government's expert witness, Dr. Hoag, regarding the inflation rate, when it found that the timeshares would never appreciate to a value comparable to the final balloon payment. As we noted above, the tax court is free to accept or reject expert testimony in accordance with its own judgment. The tax court committed no clear error in disregarding Dr. Hoag's testimony.

C. "Sham" Transaction

The tax court's determination that the transaction was a "sham" is a finding of fact, and therefore reviewable under the clearly erroneous standard. According to the tax court, "[t]he motivating factor in th[is] case[ ] was the extravagant tax write-off petitioners received as compared to their cash outlay. Without the tax write-offs, petitioners would have received no benefit from the purchase of the timeshares." *Ames [v. Commissioner]*, 58 T.C.M. [1470 (1990)] at 1491. The court also noted that Lukens would have received a deduction of $8 for each $1 actually invested. The tax court found further that each timeshare unit would not have appreciated enough in value over thirty years to induce Lukens to pay the final $89,600 balloon payment.

We find that the tax court did not clearly err in finding that the transaction in question lacked economic substance and constituted a "sham."

* * *

III. CONCLUSION

The judgment of the tax court is, in all respects, AFFIRMED.

Notes

In addition to possessing the proper credentials, the expert must be credible. The testimony is likely to be disregarded if the court determines that the expert is merely acting as an advocate for the party for whom the expire was hired to testify. Thus, an expert opinion must be independent and objective. As Judge Hamblen has stated:

> Judge Cohen has said, and I agree, that too often it seems experts tend to think a judge will be overwhelmed by their credentials and by the complexity of the subject matter and will simply accept their conclusion as the gospel, but Judge Cohen and I

can assure you that judges are resistant to evidence that is counter-intuitive, contrary to common sense, and inconsistent with the judge's real world business background.

Hamblen, The Changing Tide of Tax Court Litigation: Large Case Management, 14 Va. Tax Rev. 1, 10 (1994).

G. POST-TRIAL PROCEEDINGS

When the Tax Court has heard a case, the case will be decided by the judge, sitting without a jury. The judge must make a report and render a decision "as quickly as practicable." IRC § 7459. The judge's findings of fact and opinion in the case are written as a draft report, which is then forwarded to the Chief Judge for review. The Chief Judge reviews the report for consistency with other Tax Court opinions and to determine whether the report adheres to the *Golsen* rule. See § I.B.of this Chapter. The Chief Judge also determines whether to adopt the report as a decision of the court, or to submit it to the full court for review. Factors that may influence the Chief Judge's decision to submit a case for review include (1) whether the case involves an issue of first impression, (2) whether the case presents issues of fact that may be likely to recur in other cases, (3) whether the trial judge proposes to declare a regulation invalid or to overrule a prior Tax Court decision, (4) whether the decision conflicts with a court of appeals decision, (5) whether the Chief Judge has doubts about the grounds on which the proposed opinion attempts to distinguish a prior decision of the Tax Court or a decision of the district court or the Court of Federal Claims or (6) whether the Chief Judge questions the legal approach adopted by the trial judge in deciding the case. See Theodore Tannewald, Jr., Tax Court Trials: An Updated View From the Bench, 47 Tax Law. 587, 600-601 (1994).

The Tax Court meets in conference to review the draft report that the Chief Judge has selected for review. The conference must consist of a quorum (at least half) of the regular judges. The draft is submitted in advance to the judges, who can independently investigate and evaluate the report. If a judge thinks he will dissent or concur in the result, he can prepare an opinion and circulate it in advance of the conference. Failure to issue an advance dissenting or concurring opinion does not preclude a judge from submitting a dissenting or concurring opinion later if the draft report is adopted.

If the draft opinion is not adopted, the trial judge may elect to re-write the opinion and resubmit it for another vote. In the alternative, the trial judge may request that the case be reassigned to another judge, who will re-write and re-submit the opinion.

If the Chief Judge decides that a report is satisfactory as is, it will be adopted as the final report of the court within 30 days. IRC § 7460. The Chief Judge then decides whether the case should be designated "regular" or "memorandum." A third category, "Special Reports" , is reserved exclusively for S cases. Regular cases are published in the Tax Court Reports. They have greater precedential value than the other two categories of cases. This category usually is reserved for cases of first impression or for those that present more complex issues of law. Those cases that merely apply a well-established legal principle usually are issued as memorandum decisions. These opinions are published by private publishers (as opposed to the Government Printing Office) and do not have the precedential value of the regular opinions. Special reports are not published and have no precedential value. But see Leandra Lederman, Transparency and Obfuscation in Tax Court Procedure, 102 Tax Notes 1539 (March 22, 2004) (arguing that the reports of special trial judges should be disclosed, at least to reviewing courts of appeal, because otherwise meaningful appellate review is precluded).

If the Tax Court dismisses a proceeding for lack of jurisdiction, an order to that effect may be entered in the records of the court, and the order shall constitute the entry of decision in the case. Otherwise, a Tax Court decision is an order entered in the records of the court that specifies a dollar amount of deficiency, liability or overpayment determined by the court. IRC § 7459(c). If the court finds entirely in favor of the Commissioner, upholding the amount of the proposed deficiency, or entirely in favor of the taxpayer, that no deficiency is due, a decision may be entered immediately in the Tax Court records after the report is accepted by the court. Many cases, however, do not fall into these categories. Indeed, there are cases that involve multiple issues, only some of which may be settled while others may not. Some cases also require a computation, consistent with the findings of fact and opinion of the court, to determine the amount of the deficiency, liability, or overpayment. This computation is referred to as a "Rule 155 computation," and frequently Tax Court cases will conclude with the phrase "Decision will be entered under Rule 155."

Rule 155 computations are either agreed or unagreed. If the parties are in agreement about the amount of deficiency or overpayment, they will file an original and two copies of the computation with the court, showing the amount of the deficiency, liability, or overpayment, and stating that there is no disagreement that the figures shown are in accordance with the findings and conclusions of the court. If the computation involves an overpayment, it also must include the amount and date of each payment made by the petitioner. The court will then enter its decision based on this agreement. Tax Court Rule 155(a).

If the parties are not in agreement as to the amount of the deficiency, liability, or overpayment, either of them may file with the court a computation of the amount believed to be in accordance with the findings and conclusions of the court. The clerk then will serve a notice of the filing and a copy of the computation on the opposing party. If the opposing party fails to file an objection, accompanied or preceded by an alternative computation by the date specified in the clerk's notice, the court may enter a decision in accordance with the computation already submitted. If differing computations are submitted by the parties, the court, at its discretion, may afford the parties an opportunity for oral argument. Any argument permitted by the court under Rule 155 will be limited to the issue of the correct computation of the dollar amount of the deficiency, liability, or overpayment; no new issues may be raised. A Rule 155 proceeding is not an opportunity to reargue the case. After the argument, the court will decide the correct amount of deficiency, liability, or overpayment and will enter its decision accordingly. The date of the entry of decision is important in determining the period during which an appeal may be made.

1. Appellate Review

A party may appeal an adverse decision of the Tax Court, except in a stipulated decision or an S case. The appellate route of a Tax Court case is the same as that of a federal district court case: jurisdiction lies exclusively with the federal circuit court (the United States court of appeals) for the judicial circuit in which the taxpayer resides. In the case of a corporate taxpayer, the proper venue is in the judicial circuit in which the taxpayer has its principle place of business or principle office at the time the petition is filed. IRC § 7482. If the corporate taxpayer has no principle place of business or principle office in the United States, venue lies in the circuit in which the taxpayer files its tax return. The parties may agree to any venue by written stipulation. IRC § 7482(b)(1).

Appealable decisions include not only those involving a determination of the amount of a deficiency, liability, or overpayment, but also those involving a dismissal for lack of jurisdiction and those granting summary judgment motions, as well as those denying a motion to amend the petition.

a. Interlocutory Appeals

Since 1986, interlocutory orders of the Tax Court have been appealable, provided certain requirements are met.

KOVENS v. COMMISSIONER
United States Tax Court, 1988.
91 T.C. 74.

OPINION

GERBER, JUDGE:

Petitioners, by a motion dated April 6, 1988, seek an interlocutory appeal pursuant to section 7482(a)(2) and Rule 193. In a recent opinion, Kovens v. Commissioner, 90 T.C. 452 (1988), we denied petitioners' Motion to Dismiss for Lack of Jurisdiction. In that motion, petitioners maintained that respondent's notice of deficiency was untimely. Petitioners argued that the Form 872-A agreement extending the assessment period should be considered terminated when petitioners mailed their Form 872-T. The terms of the Form 872- A required that respondent receive the Form 872-T to terminate the Form 872-A agreement. Petitioners argued they were entitled to this extraordinary relief because respondent 'intentionally or negligently' made the Form 872-T unavailable to them. The Form 872-T is the only means through which taxpayers can terminate an outstanding Form 872-A agreement. The other means of termination are solely within respondent's control.

In their motion, petitioners argued that respondent had a contractual obligation to timely provide them with a Form 872-T to terminate the Form 872-A agreement. Petitioners contended, further, that because respondent breached this obligation they were relieved of their contractual obligation to provide respondent with a Form 872-T before the Form 872-A agreement could be considered terminated. After consideration of petitioners' argument, based on the record before us, we held that the facts did not support the finding that respondent breached an obligation to provide petitioners with a Form 872-T. Consequently, petitioner's Motion to Dismiss for Lack of Jurisdiction was denied. It is with reference to this opinion that petitioners seek an appeal pursuant to section 7482(a)(2).

Section 7482(a)(2) provides as follows:

(A) IN GENERAL.–When any judge of the Tax Court includes in an interlocutory order a statement that a controlling question of law is involved with respect to which there is a substantial ground for difference of opinion and that an immediate appeal from that order may materially advance the ultimate termination of the litigation, the United States Court of Appeals may, in its discretion, permit an appeal to be taken from such order, if application is made to it within 10 days after the entry of such order. Neither the application for nor the granting of an appeal under this paragraph shall stay proceedings in the Tax Court, unless a stay is ordered by a judge of the Tax Court or by the United States Court of Appeals which has jurisdiction of the appeal or a judge of that court.

(B) ORDER TREATED AS TAX COURT DECISION.–For purposes of subsections (b) and (c), an order described in this paragraph shall be treated as a decision of the Tax Court.

(C) VENUE FOR REVIEW OF SUBSEQUENT PROCEEDING.– If a United States Court of Appeals permits an appeal to be taken from an order described in subparagraph (A), except as provided in subsection (b)(2), any subsequent review of the decision of the Tax Court in the proceeding shall be made by such Court of Appeals.

Prior to 1986, this Court did not have the authority to issue an interlocutory order; such authority was possessed by the United States district courts. To remedy this situation Congress enacted section 7482(a)(2).[2]

Section 7482(a)(2) permits this Court to certify for appeal orders that involve a controlling question of law as to which there is substantial ground for difference of opinion and where an immediate appeal from the order may materially advance the ultimate termination of the litigation.[3] This procedure is an exception to the 'final judgment rule.'

The 'final judgment rule' was the rule prior to the statutory creation of interlocutory appeals. Under this rule an appeal lies only from a final decision of the district courts, except when direct appeal to the Supreme Court of the United States is provided.[4] 28 U.S.C. sec. 1291 (1948). To

---

2.   In the opinion of the staff of the Joint Committee on Taxation, Congress believed it was appropriate that a party be able to pursue an appeal from an interlocutory order in Tax Court litigation, parallel to the procedure available for district court litigation. Staff of Joint Comm. on Taxation, General Explanation of the Tax Reform Act of 1986, at 1305. (J. Comm. Print 1987). We have no reason to challenge this conclusion.

3.   After certification of an interlocutory order is granted by the trial court, the court of appeals determines if the appeal will be granted. Denial or grant of the appeal is within the court of appeals' discretion and denial can be for reasons such as a congested appellate docket or the desire to have a full record before considering the disputed legal issue. See Hearings on H.R. 6238 and H.R.7260 Before Subcomm. of the House Comm. on the Judiciary, 85th Cong., 2d Sess. 21 (1958).

4.   The final judgment rule is believed to eliminate wasteful delay at the trial court level and provide a more complete record for a consolidated review. The effect of this rule is to disallow appeal from any decision which is tentative, informal or incomplete.

modify the undesirable results sometimes experienced through the application of the 'final judgment rule' some limited exceptions were provided. Such modification of the 'final judgment rule' resulted from the recognition that in some situations the traditional view of efficiency which forms the basis of the 'final judgment rule' must yield to other goals of appellate review. The exceptions to this rule are set forth in 28 U.S.C. secs. 1292(a) (1986)[5] and 1292(b) (1986), and section 7482(a)(2). The exceptions permit the review of orders other than final judgments when the orders have a final and irreparable effect on the rights of the parties. The primary goals sought to be achieved through these exceptions are (1) to alleviate hardship by providing an opportunity to review orders of the trial court before they irreparably modify the rights of litigants; (2) to provide supervision of the development of the law by providing a mechanism for resolving conflicts among trial courts on issues not normally open on final appeal; and (3) to avoid waste of trial time at the trial court level through an opportunity to review orders before fruitless litigation and wasted expense. See Note, 'Interlocutory Appeals in the Federal Courts Under 28 U.S.C. Sec. 1292(b), ' 88 Harv. L. Rev. 607, 609 (1975).

Our focus here is centered on 28 U.S.C. sec. 1292(b) (1986), and its companion section 7482(a)(2). Because section 7482(a)(2) contains identical language to 28 U.S.C. sec. 1292(a) (1986) and sec. 1292(b) (1986) has an established history, we look to cases and commentary under 28 U.S.C. sec. 1292(b) (1958) for guidance in interpreting section 7482(a)(2). In 28 U.S.C. sec. 1292(b) (1958), authority is granted to the district courts to certify for interlocutory appeal orders that involve a controlling question of law, as to which there is substantial ground for difference of opinion, and where an immediate appeal from the order may materially advance the ultimate termination of the litigation. The enactment of this section resulted from dissatisfaction with the prolongation of litigation and the resulting harm to the litigants sometimes uncorrectable on appeal. This resulted on occasion from the strict application of the 'final judgment rule.'

An interlocutory appeal order permits the petitioning party to appeal from such order concerning an intermediate matter rather than a final matter. Congress, aware of the need to avoid fruitless litigation in exceptional cases and the countervailing need of discouraging frivolous or dilatory appeals, has entrusted the use of 28 U.S.C. sec.1292(b) (1986) to the wisdom of the judges of the trial courts. The trial court's

---

5.　The three exceptions to the final judgment rule provided in 28 U.S.C. sec.1292(a) (1951), allow for appeal from interlocutory decisions: (1) Granting or denying preliminary injunctions; (2) creating or continuing receiverships; and (3) determining rights and liabilities in admiralty cases.

familiarity with the record and the original order places that court in an advantageous position for certifying whether the order meets the criteria for an interlocutory appeal.   Before certifying an order pursuant to section 7482(a)(2) or 28 U.S.C. sec. 1292(b) (1986) the trial judge must verify that the order (1) involves a 'controlling question of law,' (2) offers 'substantial ground for difference of opinion' as to its correctness, and (3) be able, if immediately appealed, to 'materially advance the ultimate termination of the litigation.'   Failure to meet any one of the three requirements is grounds for denial of certification.

Orders qualifying under 28 U.S.C. sec. 1292(b) (1986) and section 7482(a)(2) embrace a small class which finally determine claims of right separable from, and collateral to, rights asserted in the action, too important to be denied review and too independent of the cause itself to require that appellate consideration be deferred until the whole case is adjudicated.   Cohen v. Beneficial Loan Corp., 337 U.S. 541, 546 (1949). In determining whether the instant situation under consideration fits within this class the key consideration is whether the opinion truly implicates the policies which favor such an appeal. Through the creation of interlocutory orders Congress sought to achieve the avoidance of wasted trial and harm to litigants. Whether the opinion being appealed involves the exercise of discretion is not to be considered during the certification process. In reaching its determination the court also must weigh the policies favoring the 'final judgment rule,' i.e., the avoidance of piecemeal litigation and dilatory and harassing appeals. If the avoidance of wasted trials is taken as the sole guide, a multitude of interlocutory opinions will become appealable. This is contrary to the intent of the draftsmen and proponents of 28 U.S.C. sec. 1292(b) (1958) and section 7482(a)(2), who were of the view that interlocutory orders should be granted only in exceptional cases. See 3 U.S. Code Cong. & Admin. News, at 5255, 5259, 5260-5261 (1958). Such a desire to limit availability of this process to exceptional cases reflects a strong policy in favor of avoiding piecemeal review and its attendant delay and waste of time.

Petitioners contend that our opinion as set forth in Kovens v. Commissioner, 90 T.C. 452 (1988), satisfies the requirements necessary for certification of an interlocutory order. For the reasons set forth below we disagree with petitioners.

An opinion is not appealable on the mere ground that it may be erroneous, it must be final. Firestone Tire & Rubber Co. v. Risjord, 449 U.S. 368 (1981). An interlocutory appeal is not to be used as a device to second guess the application of facts, as found by the trial court, to the appropriate law.   In the present case petitioners seek to obtain certification of an interlocutory order for purposes of appealing our decision set forth in *Kovens*.

In *Kovens*, we recognized that the Forms 872-T could be obtained only with some effort on the part of the person seeking to obtain them. We cautioned respondent that steps should be taken to make these forms more readily available. However, we made a factual determination that the record before us did not support a finding that respondent breached an obligation to provide petitioners with Forms 872-T. While we are cognizant of the fact that the procedural argument advanced by petitioners in *Kovens*, if accepted by this Court, would have given petitioners the opportunity to avoid litigation of this case on the merits, we were bound in our findings by the record. The record before us did not support petitioners' claim. The opinion petitioners seek to have certified for an interlocutory appeal does not meet the requirements set forth in section 7482(a)(2).

The requirement that the order contain a 'controlling question of law' has been interpreted to mean more than a question which if decided erroneously would lead to a reversal on repeal but entails a question of law which is serious to the conduct of the litigation. See Hearings on H.R. 6238 and H.R. 7260 Before Subcomm. of the House Comm. on the Judiciary, 85th Cong., 2d Sess. 21 (1958). Petitioners have erroneously interpreted this to include decisions of the trial court which are contrary to their desired results which would terminate any possible litigation. We feel compelled to make the distinction here between a clear legal issue and an issue that requires the application of findings of fact to existing law. Petitioners maintain that this Court's interpretation of the Form 872-A agreement and the rights and duties of the parties thereto constitutes a controlling question of law. As set forth in *Kovens*, it is settled law that even though contract principles are significant to understanding the Form 872-A agreement, the agreement is not a contract. Rather, it constitutes a unilateral waiver of the taxpayer's defense. Moreover, we found as a matter of fact that even if we should hold that respondent was contractually obligated to provide petitioners with the Form 872- T, that the facts of this case did not support a finding that respondent 'intentionally or negligently' breached his obligation.

The 'substantial ground for difference of opinion' test has been interpreted by the courts to involve questions that present serious and unsettled legal issues. See Cohen v. Beneficial Loan Corp., 337 U.S. 541, 547 (1949); Shapiro v. Commissioner, 73 T.C. 313 (1979). The situation in this case does not meet this requirement. As we have already stated, the issue of whether contract principles govern the interpretation of a

Form 872-A agreement has been settled by the Supreme Court of the United States, this Court, and others.

The final requirement that 'an immediate appeal from the order may materially advance the termination of the litigation' is petitioner's strongest argument. The present case involves substantial amounts of money and could result in a lengthy trial.[6] While these facts are factors in petitioners' favor, considered alone they do not justify the dismissal of a case that should be tried on the merits. Petitioners seek to use the appeal of an interlocutory order as a procedural mechanism to avoid having to prove their case on the merits. This is outside the intended purpose of interlocutory orders. When Congress sought to develop a procedure that would avoid unnecessarily long trials it was intended for those cases where it could be determined at an early stage that liability would not be ascertained, even after a lengthy trial. Petitioners' case does not fit within this class. Appeal of an interlocutory order was intended to resolve a legal issue, not

to be used as a procedural maneuver.

Petitioners argue that an interlocutory order should be granted because should the reviewing court of appeals disagree with our holding as set forth in *Kovens*, the very purpose for permitting interlocutory appeals would be accomplished, i.e., avoiding wasted time and expense litigating the merits of the case. This argument ignores the very reason Congress granted the trial courts the power to determine whether the opinion should be certified as an interlocutory order. The trial court generally is better able to assess the future course of the litigation and is familiar with the record.

After consideration of petitioners' arguments in favor of our certifying an interlocutory order and evaluation of the logic and policy supporting both the granting of an interlocutory order and the 'final judgment rule,' we hold that the opinion under consideration does not meet the requirements of an interlocutory order as set forth in section 7482(a)(2).

To reflect the foregoing, an appropriate order will be issued.

Notes

Neither the application of a motion for interlocutory appeal nor the granting of such a motion will automatically stay the Tax Court proceedings. IRC § 7482(a)(2)(A).

---

6. The notice of deficiency involved herein consists of 74 pages, includes taxable years 1971 through 1978, asserts deficiencies in excess of $6,000,000, and includes 89 adjustments.

The venue for appeal of an interlocutory order lies with the circuit court of appeals to which a final decision of the Tax Court is appealable. If an interlocutory appeal is made, any subsequent review of the Tax Court decision must occur in the same court of appeals. IRC § 7482(a)(2)(C).

b. Appeals Procedure

A party that wishes to appeal a decision of the Tax Court must file a notice of appeal with the clerk of the Tax Court within 90 days of the entry of the decision. Where the case involves multiple issues, some of which may have been decided in favor of the Commissioner and others of which may have been decided in favor of the taxpayer, both parties may appeal. If one party files a timely notice of appeal, the other may cross appeal by filing a notice of appeal within 120 days after the entry of the decision. Tax Court Rule 190(a); IRC § 7483. Note that the mailbox rule of § 7502 also applies for purposes of determining timeliness of the appeal.

In some cases, the Commissioner may file a protective appeal to prevent being whipsawed by related parties or pending suits involving similar issues. For example, if the Service allows a dependency exemption to a taxpayer, a subsequent suit on this issue may result in the exemption being given to the ex-spouse of the taxpayer. Since both parties cannot claim the dependency exemption for the same child, the Service may file an appeal to protect itself from being whipsawed if its subsequent attempt to recharacterize the taxpayer's exemption is not upheld or if the statute of limitations prevents it from assessing a deficiency against the taxpayer. Other examples of actions in which the Commissioner may file a protective appeal are when the disposition of an item has a correlative effect on a related tax or causes a correlative change in another taxable year, when the dispute involves the timing of when an item should be taxed and the tax years involved are not included in the same docket, and when the Commissioner presents alternative theories to support a deficiency and the court sustains the deficiency based on one theory but rejects the other. See Gerald A. Kafka and Rita A. Cavanagh, Litigation of Federal Civil Tax Controversies, ¶ 11.13[2] (2000).

c. Venue

Under § 7482(b)(1) appeals from Tax Court decisions for "a redetermination of tax liability" in the case of a taxpayer other than a corporation are properly heard in the circuit court of appeals in which the taxpayer resides, and if the taxpayer is a corporation the appeal may be filed in the circuit in which the taxpayer's principal place of business, principal office or agency is located. If there is no principal place of business, office or agency, the appeal is proper in the circuit in which the company's tax return is filed. The default place of venue is the District of Columbia. Notwithstanding § 7482(b)(1), the taxpayer and the government may agree in writing for the appeal to be heard in a different court of appeals.

The problem is that § 7482(b)(1) was drafted in 1966 when the Tax Court's jurisdiction was much more limited than it is at present. Since that time, the court has acquired jurisdiction to hear collection due process issues under § 6330, innocent spouse cases under § 6015(e), interest abatement cases under § 6404, whistleblower cases under § 7623, and cases reviewing the denial of awards for administrative costs under § 7430. Although these cases may not involve a "redetermination of tax liability," the parties generally appeal to the circuit of residence instead of to the D.C. Circuit. The Tax Court, also applies *Golsen* in these cases according to the precedent of the circuit of residence and not the D.C. Circuit. For a discussion of this issue see James Bamberg, "A Different Point of Venue: The Plainer Meaning of Section 7482(b)(1)," 61 Tax Lawyer 445 (Winter 2008)(concluding that both the litigants and the courts have wrongly ignored the flush language of § 7482(b)(1)).

2. Finality of Tax Court Decisions and Restrictions on Assessment and Collection

As we saw in Chapter 4, filing a Tax Court petition stays the statute of limitations on assessment and collection until the decision of the Tax Court becomes final. IRC § 6213(a). Although the finality of Tax Court decisions generally is determined under § 7481, for purposes of the restrictions on assessment and collection, § 7481 must be read in conjunction with § 7485. Under § 7481, the decision of the Tax Court becomes final at the end of the 90-day period for filing an appeal, provided no notice of appeal is filed within that time. If a notice of appeal is filed, the decision of the Tax Court becomes final when the period for filing a writ of certiorari to the Supreme Court expires.

An adverse decision of the court of appeals is reviewable by the United States Supreme Court upon the granting of a writ of certiorari, which must be filed within 90 days after the entry of judgment by the appellate court. Very few writs of certiorari are granted by the Court. Those cases heard by the Supreme Court generally are those that involve issues in which the circuits are in conflict or issues that are considered of substantial importance in the administration of the tax laws.

If a writ of certiorari is filed, the decision becomes final when the writ is denied or if the writ is granted, 30 days after the Court issues its decision. If the Court remands the case, the decision of the Tax Court becomes final 30 days after the entry of its re-decision.

For purposes of the restrictions on assessment and collection, however, § 7485 provides "notwithstanding any other provision of law imposing restrictions on assessment and collection of deficiencies * * * ", the automatic stay of assessment and collection will expire at the end of the 90-day period following the entry of the Tax Court decision. If the taxpayer wishes to appeal an adverse decision without first paying the amount of the deficiency and additions to tax, the taxpayer must file a timely notice of appeal and post an adequate appeal bond with the Tax Court. If the taxpayer files the notice of appeal but fails to post the bond, the taxpayer may appeal the decision, but the Service can assess and collect the amount of the deficiency unless the taxpayer pays the deficiency prior to any collection action.

III. RECOVERY OF COSTS

If a taxpayer prevails against the government in a civil suit in any of the fora having jurisdiction over tax claims (including the United States Courts of Appeals and the United States Supreme Court), § 7430 allows the taxpayer to recover reasonable litigation costs, including attorneys' fees. In addition, § 7430 allows the taxpayer to recover reasonable administrative costs if the taxpayer prevails in an administrative proceeding before the Service. The purpose of § 7430 is "to enable taxpayers to vindicate rights regardless of economic circumstances and to prevent overreaching by the IRS in tax disputes." Powell v. Commissioner, 791 F.2d 385, 392 (5th Cir.1986). In order to recover such costs, though, the taxpayer first must meet certain requirements under § 7430. Even if these requirements are met, the taxpayer may not be able to recover costs if the government establishes that its position in the proceeding was substantially justified.

A. LIMITATIONS ON THE RIGHT TO RECOVER COSTS

The prevailing party may recover costs in connection with the determination, collection or refund of any tax, penalty, or interest incurred in an administrative or court proceeding, including the expenses of litigating the right to recover costs under § 7430. There are certain limitations imposed upon the taxpayer under § 7430 before the right to recover costs arises. For each of these limitations, the burden of proof is on the taxpayer.

1. Exhaustion of Administrative Remedies

The prevailing party first must exhaust available administrative remedies in order to recover costs. This means that the taxpayer must request an administrative Appeals conference prior to filing suit, and file a protest, if required. If an Appeals conference is granted, either the taxpayer or the taxpayer's representative must participate in the conference.

ALLEN v. COMMISSIONER
United States Tax Court, 2002.
84 T.C.M. 636

MEMORANDUM FINDINGS OF FACT AND OPINION

GERBER, J.

In this opinion, the third one issued in this case,[1] we consider whether petitioners exhausted their administrative remedies so as to be entitled to recover costs and fees under section 7430.

Prior History

In our first opinion, Allen v. Commissioner, T.C. Memo.1998-406, we found that a payment received by petitioners was not paid by the insurance company to settle petitioners' claim for punitive damages. We also held that petitioners were entitled to nonrecognition treatment under section 1033 with respect to any gain realized in connection with the settlement payment. After their success in litigation, petitioners filed a motion seeking to recover $46,419.11 of administrative and litigation costs under section 7430.[4] In the second opinion, Allen v. Commissioner, T.C. Memo.1999-118, we decided that respondent's position was substantially justified under the facts and circumstances of this case. Accordingly, petitioners' motion for litigation costs (attorney's fees) was denied.

1.　See Allen v. Comm'r, T.C. Memo. 1998-406; Allen v. Comm'r, T.C. Memo. 1999-118.

4.　Petitioners were also seeking additional attorney's fees incurred to pursue the motion.

Petitioners appealed the denial of their motion, and the Court of Appeals for the Ninth Circuit, in an unpublished opinion, held as follows:

> We affirm that part of the tax court's determination that the respondent was reasonably justifiable in believing that the award was taxable, and accordingly that attorney fees incurred by the taxpayer through the pretrial discovery and negotiating period were not reimbursable. It was, however, an abuse of discretion to deny reimbursement of attorney fees actually incurred by the trial, which should have been abandoned by the Commissioner when all parties knew, three days before trial, that the Commissioner's witness had recanted and that the [C]ommissioner could not reasonably expect to prevail in the ensuing trial.
>
> Accordingly, the order appealed from is vacated and the cause is remanded to the Tax Court to determine, (1) whether the taxpayers have otherwise satisfied the requirements of section 7430 with respect to exhaustion, and not unreasonably protracting the litigation, and (2) if the parties do not agree on the amount due for the costs of trial, to fix and award a reasonable sum. [Allen v. Commissioner, 246 F.3d 672 (9th Cir.2000).]

The holding of the Court of Appeals for the Ninth Circuit limits any recovery of costs by petitioners to those incurred during the period that began 3 days before trial. Because this Court decided that respondent's position was substantially justified, we did not have to consider the other prerequisites to recovery of litigation costs under section 7430.[5] The only requirement of section 7430 that remains in controversy[6] is whether petitioners exhausted their administrative remedies as required by section 7430(b)(1). See also sec. 301.7430-1(b)(2), Proced. & Admin. Regs.

FINDINGS OF FACT

Petitioners' residence was damaged by a neighbor's removal of soil supporting the foundation under petitioners' residence. Petitioners' insurance claim ended in disagreement, and suit was filed against the insurance company. In their pleading, petitioners sought recovery on several grounds, including the claim that the insurance company had acted in bad faith (punitive damages).

---

5. A taxpayer's failure to meet any of the requirements of sec. 7430 is fatal to their claim for litigation costs.

6. There is no remaining controversy with respect to the amount of fees petitioners are entitled to if we decide that they did exhaust their administrative remedies.

After an arbitrator appraised the damage at $128,084, the insurance company paid petitioners $102,000 during 1990. Following negotiations, a global settlement was reached, and the parties' settlement agreement contained the statement that all of petitioners' claims, including the one for "bad faith", were being settled. As part of that 1991 settlement, the insurance company paid petitioners an additional $130,000, which was intended to be in full settlement of petitioners' claims against the insurance company. Following the final settlement, petitioners amended their 1991 joint income tax return in order to claim a $37,852 casualty loss and seek a $5,821 refund. In support of their refund claim, petitioners' relied on the casualty loss provisions of section 165.

Petitioners' 1991 tax return was examined by the Internal Revenue Service. The sole focus of the examination was the $130,000 payment received during 1991. Petitioners' representative, an enrolled agent, argued that the cost to repair the residence exceeded the total amount received from the insurance company, so that no portion of petitioners' settlement recovery could have been a payment for punitive damages.

During the examination, the enrolled agent presented a March 28, 1995, letter, to the examining agent. The letter was from the attorney who represented petitioners in the suit against the insurance company. The letter contained a list of checks paid to petitioners in the total amount of $269,467.20 and the attorney's conclusion that "The appraiser's award was $128,084. Therefore $25,616.80 of the $130,000 could logically be for damages due to the removal of the berm with the remainder ($104,383.20) being bad faith".

In a January 23, 1996, letter, to the examining agent, petitioners' attorney in the insurance case attempted to recant his earlier letter, stating that, notwithstanding his March 28, 1995, letter, the settlement payment was for neither bad faith damages nor punitive damages. In addition, the enrolled agent wrote to the examining agent reiterating that the attorney's "bad faith" characterization was a mistake. Despite the attempts to correct the attorney's statement, the examining agent concluded that $104,000 of the $130,000 payment from the insurance company was for punitive damages and was therefore income taxable to petitioners for 1991.

Further, although petitioners' claim for refund of 1991 tax relied on the casualty loss provisions of section 165, during the examination petitioners argued that some injury or sickness was caused by the insurance company's actions. Under this argument, petitioners contended that the $130,000 was excludable as payment for physical injury under section 104.

Following the examination, petitioners hired a tax lawyer to represent them and to proceed to Appeals for further consideration of the examining agent's findings. The lawyer engaged by petitioners was qualified in litigation and tax issues, and he assigned a law clerk to represent petitioners' interests before Appeals.

The law clerk and the Appeals officer focused upon the examining agent's findings; i.e., the question of whether the settlement was for punitive damages. The law clerk argued that no portion of the $130,000 settlement was attributable to punitive damages. As support for this argument, the law clerk attempted to show that the total amount received from the insurance company was needed to repair petitioners' residence. The documents shown to the Appeals officer included receipts for repair to petitioners' residence and the insurance settlement documents. During consideration by Appeals, petitioners conceded that they were not entitled to exclude any portion of the settlement recovery under section 104.

The Appeals officer concluded that petitioners had not shown that the $130,000 recovery was not attributable to taxable punitive damages. The Appeals officer's conclusion was based on the examiner's report, the underlying documents indicating that petitioners were seeking punitive damages, and the insurance settlement document referencing punitive damages. The Appeals officer was also aware of the initial letter from the attorney who represented petitioners against the insurance company containing the statement that $104,000 of the $130,000 was for "bad faith". Although the primary focus was the question of punitive damages, the Appeals officer's report also contained some discussion of section 1033.

Following the Appeals conference, petitioners wrote to the Appeals officer explaining, a second time, that they spent more on repairing their residence than was received from the insurance company. In that same letter, petitioners cited section 165 and sections 1.165-7(a)(2)(ii) and 1.123-1, Income Tax Regs. In response to petitioners' letter, the Appeals officer explained that the issue in controversy was whether any portion of the $130,000 received represented taxable punitive damages. In that same letter, the Appeals officer acknowledged that the cost of repairs could be used to determine a decrease in fair market value. The Appeals officer restated the conclusion that the $130,000 was paid for punitive damages and that petitioners' pleading and the insurance settlement agreement contained statements to the effect that petitioners were seeking and/or settling punitive damage claims.

Petitioners, in response to the Appeals officer, requested that a notice of deficiency be issued so that the matter would be considered by respondent's attorneys. A notice of deficiency issued, and a petition was filed with this Court during January 1997. In the pretrial setting, petitioners' attorney advanced the same argument-that the settlement payment was not for punitive damages because the total amount of the payments was insufficient to cover the cost to repair the damage to the residence.

A substantial portion of the trial preparation by petitioners' attorneys occurred approximately 1 year after the Appeals conference and during the 3-month period immediately preceding the trial. During their preparation for trial, petitioners' attorneys obtained the insurance company's files, and they contacted the attorney who represented the insurance company. Based on the information procured in preparation for trial, petitioners developed evidence showing that the insurance company did not intend any part of the $130,000 as payment for petitioners' claim that the company had acted in bad faith.

Petitioners' attorney's billable time [is] divided into three periods representing the time in Appeals, the pretrial period before extensive preparation, and the 3 months preceding trial * * *.

OPINION

We consider here, on remand from the Court of Appeals for the Ninth Circuit, whether petitioners meet the requirements of section 7430 so as to be entitled to recover a portion of their litigation costs. In an earlier opinion, Allen v. Commissioner, T.C. Memo.1999-118, we held that respondent's position in the proceeding was substantially justified. Under our holding, petitioners were not entitled to administrative or litigation costs, and, accordingly, there was no need to decide whether the remaining section 7430 requisites for recovery had been met. The Court of Appeals for the Ninth Circuit reversed our holding to the extent that the Court of Appeals held that respondent's position in the proceeding ceased to be substantially justified beginning 3 days before the trial. The parties have resolved all but one of the requirements necessary for the recovery of litigation costs.[8]

The question that remains in dispute is whether petitioners exhausted their administrative remedies within the Internal Revenue

---

8. Sec. 7430(b) and (c) provides that prevailing parties, to recover litigation costs, must establish that: (1) They exhausted available administrative remedies; (2) they substantially prevailed in the controversy; (3) the position of the United States in the proceeding was not substantially justified; (4) they meet certain net worth requirements; (5) they did not unreasonably protract the proceeding; and (6) the amount of costs is reasonable. Failure to meet any of the requirements will defeat some part or all of a taxpayer's recovery of litigation costs.

Service. Sec. 7430(b)(1). In order to exhaust administrative remedies, section 301.7430- 1(b)(2), Proced.& Admin. Regs., requires "participation" in an Appeals conference. The parties dispute whether petitioners' representative "participated" in an Appeals conference within the meaning of the statute and regulations. The question of what constitutes "participation" under section 7430 is one of first impression in the context of an Appeals conference held prior to the issuance of a notice of deficiency.

Section 7430(b)(1) contains the general requirement that "the court * * * [must decide] that the prevailing party has exhausted the administrative remedies available to such party within the Internal Revenue Service." The Secretary has explained and interpreted the "exhaustion" requirement, as follows:

Exhaustion of administrative remedies. (a) In general. Section 7430(b)(1) provides that a court shall not award reasonable litigation costs in any civil tax proceeding under section 7430(a) unless the court determines that the prevailing party has exhausted the administrative remedies available to the party within the Internal Revenue Service. This section sets forth the circumstances in which such administrative remedies shall be deemed to have been exhausted.

(b) Requirements. (1) In general. A party has not exhausted the administrative remedies available within the Internal Revenue Service with respect to any tax matter for which an Appeals office conference is available under §§ 601.105 and 601.106 of this chapter (other than a tax matter described in paragraph (c) of this section) unless–(I) The party, prior to filing a petition in the Tax Court or a civil action for refund in a court of the United States (including the Court of Federal Claims), participates, either in person or through a qualified representative described in § 601.502 of this chapter, in an Appeals office conference; or

    * * *

(2) *Participates.* For purposes of this section, a party or qualified representative of the party * * * participates in an Appeals office conference if the party or qualified representative *discloses to the Appeals office all relevant information regarding the party's tax matter to the extent such information and its relevance were known or should have been known to the party or qualified representative at the time of such conference.* [Emphasis supplied.]

Sec. 301.7430-1(a) and (b), Proced. & Admin. Regs.

In this case, the question of whether petitioners' administrative remedies were exhausted depends upon whether they "participated" in an Appeals conference. In common parlance, petitioners, through their representatives, participated in an Appeals office conference.[9] Respondent, however, relying on the above-quoted definition of "participates" in section 301.7430-1(b)(2), Proced. & Admin. Regs., contends that petitioners did not exhaust their administrative remedies. Therefore, the narrower question we must decide is whether petitioners disclosed "to the Appeals office all relevant information * * * to the extent such information and its relevance were known or should have been known * * * at the time of such conference." Id.

In an earlier case, concerning whether a taxpayer participated in an Appeals conference, we held that the requisite participation was present even though the taxpayer "failed to answer all of the questions and to supply all of the * * * documents [requested by the Appeals officer]." Rogers v. Commissioner, T.C. Memo.1987-374. The taxpayer's attorney in that case had provided some answers to the Appeals officer's questions, and, in order to avoid further costs, made an offer of settlement, to which the Appeals officer made a counteroffer.

The definition of the term "participates", as set forth in section 301.7430-1(b)(2), Proced. & Admin. Regs., was avoided in *Rogers* because the Appeals conference took place after the issuance of the notice of deficiency. In *Rogers v. Commissioner*, supra, the Court looked to section 301.7430-1(f), Proced. & Admin. Regs.,[10] which contains exceptions to the requirement that a taxpayer exhaust administrative remedies. That subsection provided that if no Appeals conference is made available to a taxpayer prior to issuance of a notice of deficiency and the taxpayer does not refuse to participate in an Appeals conference during docketed status, the taxpayer will be treated as having exhausted administrative remedies. Accordingly, *Rogers* was not based on the regulatory definition of the term "participates" as contained in sec. 301.7430-1(b)(2), Proced. & Admin. Regs.

---

9. The term "participate" generally means to take part in some activity with others. Webster's Third New International Dictionary 1646 (1986).

10. At the time relevant to Rogers v. Commissioner, T.C. Memo.1987-374, the requirement was set forth in paragraph (f) of sec. 301.7430-1 Proced. & Admin. Regs. Under the regulation at that time, the definition of "participates" was "For the purposes of this paragraph," which was limited to pre-petition Appeals conferences. Accordingly, the Court in *Rogers v. Commissioner*, supra, distinguished situations where the conference occurred after the issuance of a notice of deficiency and filing of a petition. The revised version of that regulation is currently in sec. 301.7430-1(b)(2) and uses the phrase "For purposes of this section". Accordingly, the pre- or post-petition distinction of *Rogers v. Commissioner*, supra, may no longer pertain.

The definition of the term "participates" in the (b)(2) paragraph of the regulation requires that a taxpayer provide the Appeals officer with information that is relevant at the time of the conference. Accordingly, the question of whether a taxpayer has supplied relevant information depends upon the parties' positions and the factual development of the case at the time of the Appeals conference. Our decision as to whether there was "participation" must therefore focus on what information may be relevant at the time and in the context of an Appeals conference. In that regard, theories or evidence subsequently developed by the parties are not necessarily relevant to the controversy as it existed at the time of the Appeals conference.

To better understand what information may be relevant at an Appeals conference, we consider the overall purpose or goal of section 7430 and the specific purpose of an Appeals conference.

Section 7430 was enacted to permit taxpayers to recover their litigation costs if they prevail in the litigation. To some extent, the enactment of section 7430 was intended to encourage the Internal Revenue Service to take a reasonable approach to settlement and/or litigation. The House report for section 7430, which was enacted as part of the Tax Equity and Fiscal Responsibility Act of 1982, Pub.L. 97-248, 96 Stat. 324, contains the following explanation:

> The committee believes that taxpayers who prevail in civil tax actions should be entitled to awards for litigation costs and attorneys' fees up to $50,000 when the United States has acted unreasonably in pursuing the case. *Fee awards in such tax cases will deter abusive actions or overreaching by the Internal Revenue Service and will enable individual taxpayers to vindicate their rights regardless of their economic circumstances.* [Emphasis supplied.]

H. Rept. 97-404, at 11 (1981).

Interrelated with and complementary to that goal, Congress required that taxpayers exhaust their administrative remedies. The exhaustion of taxpayers' administrative remedies is intended to ensure that the Commissioner will have an opportunity to evaluate the quality of taxpayers' positions. In addition, the exhaustion requirement is intended to prevent taxpayers from intentionally presenting superficial information merely to enable the recovery of costs under section 7430(b)(1). Accordingly, the exhaustion requirement is integrally tied to the question of whether the Commissioner's position is justified.

The legislative history for the initial enactment of section 7430 contains the explanation that the exhaustion of the administrative remedies provision was intended to preserve the role that the administrative appeals process plays in the resolution of tax disputes by requiring taxpayers to pursue such remedies prior to litigation. A taxpayer who actively participates in and discloses all relevant information during the administrative stages of the case will be considered to have exhausted the available administrative remedies. Failure to so participate and disclose information may be sufficient grounds for determining that the taxpayer has not exhausted administrative remedies and, therefore, is ineligible for an award of litigation costs.

H. Rept. 97-404, supra at 13. Finally, section 7430 was not intended "to permit awards for litigation costs which the taxpayer could have reduced or avoided through full disclosure of all relevant facts." Id. at 15.

Accordingly, section 7430 was intended to motivate respondent to consider and react reasonably to taxpayers' evidence and arguments. Consistent with that purpose is the regulatory requirement that taxpayers provide respondent with relevant information supporting their position. Obviously, if the theories and/or information presented to Appeals is irrelevant, without substance, or unsupportable, the taxpayer will not have exhausted administrative remedies and will not likely be a prevailing party within the meaning of section 7430. As a result, such a taxpayer will not be entitled to recover litigation costs. Additionally, in such situations, respondent's position in the proceeding will likely be reasonable or justified so as to preclude the recovery of administrative or litigation costs.

The purpose or goal of Appeals has been generally described in the following global statement of the Appeals mission:

> The Appeals mission is to resolve tax controversies, without litigation, on a basis which is fair and impartial to both the Government and the taxpayer and in a manner that will enhance voluntary compliance and public confidence in the integrity and efficiency of the Service. * * *

4 Administration, Internal Revenue Manual (CCH), sec. 8.1.3.2, at 27, 037.[11]

In this context, we consider the facts in the case before us. The parties' positions and the information available to them in this case

---

11. The same perspective is shared by legal commentators, as reflected in following commentary about the Appeals process:

> The Service encourages taxpayers who disagree with actions by district offices, such as adjustments in their tax liability, to resolve their disagreements through administrative appeal. The use of negotiation and settlement, rather than court litigation, is intended to minimize expenditures of time and money by the government and taxpayers alike. * * *

Saltzman, IRS Practice and Procedure, ¶. 9.01, at 2 (2d ed.1991).

continued to develop throughout the administrative process and until trial. Petitioners were examined concerning whether the $130,000 payment they received was paid to settle claims for punitive damages. Petitioners, through their representative, an enrolled agent, contended that the entire insurance recovery was used to repair their residence, so that no part was attributable to punitive damages. Petitioners, in their amended return, had taken the position that the amount received was a casualty loss under section 165. It also appears that, at the examination, petitioners argued that the $130,000 was not taxable because it was due to personal injury within the meaning of section 104. Ultimately, the examiner concluded that $104,000 of the $130,000 payment was received in settlement of petitioners' claim for punitive damages.

After the examination was complete, petitioners hired a law firm to seek consideration of the examiner's findings by Appeals and to attempt settlement of the controversy. They attempted to show that the cost of repairing their residence exceeded the total payments received from the insurance company. Petitioners, by using this approach, hoped to convince the Appeals officer that no part of the settlement payment could have been for punitive damages. Petitioners chose this approach after evaluating the available evidence and balancing the viability of their position at the Appeals conference with the much larger cost of obtaining information from third parties. Petitioners' approach to settlement did not result in an agreement with the Appeals officer. The Appeals officer concluded that the $130,000 was received in settlement of petitioners' claim for punitive damages. The Appeals officer also considered the application of section 1033 to the circumstances of petitioners' facts.

Accordingly, petitioners were forced to decide whether to proceed to trial. Approximately 3 months prior to trial, petitioners proceeded to procure information from third parties that would show that the insurance company's payment was not intended to settle petitioners' claim for punitive damages.[12] A few days before trial, respondent's attorney became aware that the insurance company's lawyer would testify that the $130,000 payment was not for "bad faith" or punitive damages. Respondent's attorney had expected that the insurance company's lawyer would testify otherwise. In spite of that newly discovered information, respondent proceeded to trial, and, ultimately, respondent's position in the litigation was held to be unjustified, beginning 3 days before trial.

---

12. Subsequent to the Appeals conference, petitioners' pretrial cost to develop third party information was $34,031. By comparison, the amount of the income tax deficiency was $39,697.

Respondent, relying on sec. 301.7430-1(b)(2), Proced. & Admin. Regs., contends that there was more information available to petitioners at the time of the Appeals conference and that petitioners' failure to seek out and/or present that information to the Appeals officer should result in a failure to exhaust administrative remedies. On the other hand, petitioners contend that they provided the Appeals officer with relevant information in an attempt to settle the case in Appeals. Petitioners' contention is based on their understanding of the controversy and the factual development of the case at the time of the Appeals conference. Petitioners argue that they made a good faith effort to settle and thereby exhausted their administrative remedies.

Respondent's contentions that petitioner should have provided Appeals with more information can be divided into two general categories: (1) Information already in petitioners' possession concerning the damage to their residence, and (2) information concerning the insurance company's intent not to pay petitioners for punitive damages. Initially, we consider the first category of information available to petitioners that was not provided to the Appeals officer.

In connection with their claim against the insurance company, petitioners obtained two engineering reports concerning the damage to the subsoil and to petitioners' residence. Those reports were not provided to the Appeals officer, but they were presented at trial in order to support petitioners' position regarding the repairs to the residence. Although the reports provided some support for petitioners' contention that the repairs exceeded the insurance recovery, the reports would not have resolved the issue being considered by Appeals; i.e., whether the settlement payment was paid to petitioners in satisfaction of their claim for punitive damages.

Significantly, if respondent had been made aware of the expert reports, that information would not have caused respondent's position in the deficiency notice or in the litigation to be unreasonable or unjustified. The evidence already available to the Appeals officer sufficiently showed that the cost to repair the residence exceeded the amount of the insurance recovery. In addition, the Appeals officer was in possession of probative evidence supporting her conclusion that the payment may have been made in satisfaction of the punitive damages claim. In that setting, additional evidence bolstering petitioners' argument regarding the cost of repairs was cumulative. Therefore, petitioners' failure to provide the expert reports did not result in a failure to exhaust their administrative remedies.

Respondent also contends that under the language of the regulation–specifically "all relevant information that is known or should have been known", petitioners were required to seek out and present evidence of the intent behind the insurance company's settlement payment. We reject respondent's contention. It appears that respondent is employing the "known or should have been known" phrase out of context. The regulation requires disclosure of information, the relevance of which was "known or should have been known to the party or qualified representative *at the time of * * * [the Appeals] conference*." Sec. 301.7430-1(b)(2), Proced. & Admin. Regs. (Emphasis supplied.) At the time of the Appeals conference, petitioners were not aware of the insurance company's intent in making the settlement payment. That information was discovered from third-party sources shortly before trial and almost 1 year after the Appeals conference.

The regulation requires disclosure of relevant information "to the extent such information and its relevance were known or should have been known to the party or qualified representative at the time of such conference." Id. In the context of the settlement conference with Appeals, that requirement was met by petitioners, who made a reasonable and good faith effort to provide the Appeals officer with relevant facts and law in the context and development of the case at the time of the conference.

In addition, under respondent's view, taxpayers might be required to seek out every possible piece of relevant evidence and/or to postulate every plausible theory in order to exhaust administrative remedies and to recover administrative or litigation costs. Respondent's approach also disregards the relative cost of developing all relevant information that is known or should have been known. Under respondent's approach to the regulation, few, if any, taxpayers might be able to present all relevant evidence that could have been developed.

The regulation does not require that petitioners present to the Appeals officer all evidence later adduced at trial. Instead, we are to consider whether petitioners exhausted their administrative remedies by providing relevant information in an attempt to settle the case in the context of the case development at the time of the Appeals conference.

At all pertinent times, petitioners were represented by tax professionals. They participated in the Appeals conference in a manner that provided relevant information in an attempt to resolve the case without litigation. The standard with respect to exhaustion of administrative remedies was intended to preserve the important role that the administrative Appeals process plays in the resolution of tax disputes. It was not intended to require taxpayers to adduce all possible arguments or evidence. Petitioners' approach to settlement was a reasonable attempt to convince the Appeals officer that the examiner's finding was in error.

In the circumstances of this case, we hold that petitioners exhausted their administrative remedies and are entitled to their litigation costs for the period commencing 3 days before trial, as decided by the Court of Appeals for the Ninth Circuit.

Notes

Under the Taxpayer Bill of Rights 2, enacted in 1996, a taxpayer's failure to agree to extend the statute of limitations as a condition of obtaining an Appeals conference should not be taken into account in determining whether the taxpayer has exhausted available administrative remedies. See IRC § 7430(b)(1); Prop. Treas. Reg. § 301.7430-1(b)(4).

If the action involves summonses, liens, levies, or jeopardy and termination assessments, in order to exhaust administrative remedies, the taxpayer is required to submit a written claim for relief to the district director of the district having jurisdiction over the matter prior to filing suit in any of the fora having jurisdiction over tax claims (whether deficiencies or refunds). The written claim must provide sufficient facts and circumstances to establish the nature of the relief requested and why the taxpayer is entitled to such relief. The claim must be denied in writing or the district director must have failed to act on the claim within a reasonable period after having received the claim. Reg. § 301.7430-1(d)(1). Under the regulations, a reasonable period is (1) the five-day period prior to the filing of a petition to quash an administrative summons issued under § 7609 (special procedures for third-party summons), (2) the five-day period prior to the filing of a wrongful levy action in which a demand is made for the return of the property, (3) the period provided for administrative review of the taxpayer's claim (such as the 16-day period provided under § 7429(b)(1)(B) for review of jeopardy assessments), or (4) the 60-day period following the receipt of the taxpayer's claim in all other cases. Reg. § 301.7430-1(d)(2).

The regulations provide several exceptions to the exhaustion requirement: (1) where the Service sends the taxpayer written notice that the taxpayer does not have to exhaust administrative remedies; (2) where a Tax Court petition is filed and the taxpayer (a) did not receive a notice of proposed deficiency (30-day letter), (b) the failure to send such a notice was not due to the taxpayer's actions (such as failing to supply a current mailing address), and (c) the taxpayer does not refuse to participate in an Appeals conference while the case is in docketed status; (3) in the case of a refund suit, (a) where the taxpayer already has participated in an Appeals Office conference prior to the issuance of a notice of deficiency, or (b) the taxpayer did not receive notice that an Appeals Office conference was available prior to the issuance of the notice of disallowance, and the failure to receive such notice was not due to the taxpayer's actions, or (c) the taxpayer did not receive notice that an Appeals Office conference had been granted within six months of the date of filing of the refund claim and the failure to receive such notice was not due to the taxpayer's actions. Reg. § 301.7430-1(f). Additional rules apply in the case of refund suits for penalties under § 6703 and § 6694. See Reg. § 301.7430-1(f)(4).

2. No Unreasonable Protraction of the Proceedings

NORDVIK v. COMMISSIONER
United States Court of Appeals, Ninth Circuit, 1995.
67 F.3d 1489.

MICHAEL DALY HAWKINS, CIRCUIT JUDGE:

We consider here the circumstances under which private parties may recover post-settlement litigation costs incurred in the tax court. Tax-payers Claire and William Nordvik ("the Nordviks") appeal the denial of their motion for such costs, which the tax court based on its finding that the Nordviks had unreasonably protracted the litigation and its conclusion that the government's position was substantially justified. We have jurisdiction under 26 U.S.C. § 7430 and we affirm.

I. Background

In early 1982 and again in 1984-85, the Nordviks invested in certain energy-producing wind turbines. In October 1989, the Internal Revenue Service ("IRS") mailed the Nordviks a Notice of Deficiency for the years 1983 through 1986, assessed for the total amount that the Nordviks claimed as tax credits for investments in the turbines and as deductions for business expenses incurred with respect to the turbines, including interest, taxes and depreciation. The deficiencies totaled $127,136 and the additions to tax assessed for negligence and valuation overstatement totaled another $44,497. The Nordviks filed a petition for redetermination and the case was set for trial.

Prior to trial, the parties agreed to settle the case. The IRS decided to allow the Nordviks a tax basis (i.e. a value for tax purposes) equal to the amount the Nordviks actually paid "out of pocket" for each turbine. The Nordviks agreed to (and did) provide the IRS with documentation substantiating the amounts actually paid. The IRS agreed not to assess penalties for any deficiencies.

When the IRS contacted the Nordviks regarding the revised calculations, it proposed a $21,004 deficiency for 1984, no deficiencies for 1983, 1985 and 1986, and no penalties. The Nordviks agreed to stipulate that they owed this amount, even though they had not reviewed how the IRS had computed the proposed deficiency.[1] Pursuant to a formal, written stipulation, the tax court entered an order and decision on April 10, 1991 establishing the result agreed to by the parties.

After the tax court entered an order based on the parties' agreement, the IRS sent its computations to the Nordviks. When the Nordviks finally did review the figures, they concluded that the calculations contained several errors and sent the IRS a set of revised calculations along with an explanation of the errors they believed that the IRS had made. The Nordviks requested that the IRS explain these perceived errors.

The Nordviks thereafter sought and obtained permission to file an untimely motion to vacate or revise the April 10, 1991 decision and asked that it be revised after the parties agreed on the correct calculations.

The Nordviks and the IRS then attempted to come to an agreement on the Nordviks' tax liability. Although the parties resolved some issues, they still could not agree on the Nordviks' liability, so the Nordviks filed a motion to vacate or revise to which the IRS responded. These documents indicate that the Nordviks and the IRS disputed several calculations. The Nordviks thereafter filed a status report stating that no progress had been made in resolving the key issues. The tax court informed the parties that if they could not settle the matter by March 27, 1992, the court would rule on the motion to vacate or revise.

Following this, the Nordviks set forth their analysis of the disputed calculations and proposed a settlement agreement providing for no deficiencies and an adjustment on a credit owed to the Nordviks in a separate matter, the latter to avoid having to make precise calculations on minor issues. The IRS accepted this settlement offer and on May 12, 1992, the tax court entered a decision and order pursuant to this agreement.

The Nordviks filed a contemporaneous motion requesting that they be awarded litigation costs from the point at which they initially agreed to settle the case (March, 1991) through the tax court's approval of the

---

1.   The Nordviks did not make their acceptance conditional upon their review of the IRS calculations. At argument, their counsel conceded that any delay in reviewing these calculations was not the fault of the government, but his own busy schedule.

second settlement (May 12, 1992). The tax court denied the motion for litigation costs in a memorandum decision filed December 29, 1992 and a formal order of denial entered on January 19,1993. The Nordviks filed a motion for reconsideration on February 1, 1993, which the tax court denied on April 23, 1993. The Nordviks filed the present appeal on May 6, 1993.

* * *

IV. Attorney's Fees

We next consider whether the tax court erred in denying the Nordviks' motion for attorney's fees. In an administrative proceeding or court proceeding involving determination of taxes, the "prevailing party" may be awarded a judgment for reasonable administrative costs and reasonable litigation costs, including attorney's fees. 26 U.S.C. § 7430(a)(1)-(2), (c)(1). However, fees will be denied for any portion of the court proceedings during which the prevailing party "unreasonably protracted" the proceedings. 26 U.S.C. § 7430(b)(4).

The tax court concluded that the Nordviks had unreasonably protracted the proceedings. The court reasoned that the Nordviks did not question the deficiencies in the first settlement until they received the IRS calculations, after the court order was entered. In addition, the tax court noted that the Nordviks did not file a motion for leave to file an untimely motion to vacate or revise until eighty-six days after the original order was entered, well past the thirty-day deadline for such motions. The tax court decision is reviewed for abuse of discretion.

The Nordviks stipulated to a settlement figure of a $21,004 deficiency without reviewing the IRS calculations. Although the Nordviks and the IRS had reached a general understanding, the only specific number that the Nordviks agreed on was this final deficiency figure. The Nordviks were unaware of how the IRS had arrived at this figure. They assumed that the IRS would allow various deductions and credits, but did not know whether the IRS had actually done so. Given the plethora of rules involved in calculating tax liability, it is not surprising that the Nordviks had several disagreements with the IRS once they did review the calculations. By this

time, however, the tax court had long since entered judgment pursuant to the stipulation.

Because the Nordviks failed to review the calculations before settling, they ultimately spent several months quarreling with the IRS about the correct interpretation of the initial agreement. Had they agreed on a set of calculations initially, rather than a final figure, the later proceedings would have been unnecessary.[6]

The Nordviks compounded their problems by failing to review the IRS calculations promptly upon receipt on April 22, 1991. Had they done so, the Nordviks could have entered a timely motion to vacate or revise within 30 days of the tax court's April 10 decision. However, the Nordviks delayed their review until the ninety day finality period was almost at an end. They had to file an untimely motion for reconsideration. Considering both the Nordviks' failure to review IRS calculations before stipulating to a deficiency figure, and the failure to promptly review the IRS's calculations upon receipt after judgment, the district court's conclusion that the Nordviks unreasonably protracted the proceedings was not an abuse of discretion.

* * *

The decision of the tax court is AFFIRMED.

Notes and Questions

The regulations define an administrative proceeding as "any procedure or other action before the Internal Revenue Service" except (1) proceedings involving matters of general application, including hearings on regulations, comments on forms, or proceedings involving revenue rulings or revenue procedures; (2) proceedings involving requests for private letter rulings or similar determinations; (3) proceedings involving technical advice memoranda, except those submitted after the "administrative proceeding date" (defined as the date of the taxpayer's receipt of the notice of the Appeals Office decision or the date of the notice of deficiency); and (4) proceedings involving collection actions. Reg. § 301.7430-3(a).

1. John Doe, an individual, calendar-year taxpayer, filed a timely income tax return for the 2008 taxable year. On May 15, 2010, John received a notice from the Service questioning several items of deductions on the return and asking for supporting documentation. John duly complied by supplying the requested documentation within the requested time frame. On June 30, he received a statutory notice of deficiency proposing a deficiency attributable to the disallowance of the questioned items of deduction. On July 25, 2010, John received a no-

---

6. The fact that the settlement was provided to the tax court shortly before the trial date does not excuse the Nordviks' failure to review the IRS's calculations before stipulating to a final deficiency figure. The tax court likely would have given more time to the parties in the midst of settlement negotiations, as the tax court liberally granted the parties additional time later in the proceedings.

change letter, informing him that his items of deduction had been accepted and advising him to disregard the notice of deficiency. John sought the advice of an attorney, who advised John to file a protective petition in the Tax Court. The Service filed an answer to the petition, conceding that there was no deficiency, and attaching the no-change letter. On December 3, 2010, the Tax Court entered a decision in favor of John. On January 14, 2011, John filed a Motion for Award of Reasonable Administrative and Litigation Costs, requesting an award in the amount of $2,500. The Service opposed the Motion on the grounds of unreasonable protraction of the proceedings because John pursued the Tax Court suit after the Service had conceded the deficiency. What result? See Nguyen v. Commissioner, T.C. Memo 2001-41; Culpepper-Smith v. United States, 50 F.Supp.2d 425 (DC Pa. 1999), reproduced in § 4, below.

2. If a taxpayer unreasonably protracts a portion of an administrative proceeding but does not protract other portions, can the taxpayer recover a portion of the costs? See Reg. § 301.7430-2(d).

3. Jenny Smith received a notice of proposed deficiency (30-day letter) and in response, she requested and was granted an Appeals office conference. Appeals requested that Jenny submit certain documents as substantiation for the tax matters in question, and Jenny complied with the request. The documentation, however, was misdirected and was not considered by Appeals. Appeals then issued a notice of deficiency. Jenny did not file a petition with the Tax Court. After sending the notice of deficiency, Appeals located the misdirected documentation and determined that the notice of deficiency was incorrect and that Jenny owed no tax. Appeals then closed the case showing a zero deficiency and mailed Jenny a notice to this effect. Assuming that Jenny has met the other requirements of § 7430, may she recover reasonable administrative costs? If so, what costs may she recover?

4. Assume the same facts as in question 3, except that after receipt of the notice of deficiency, Jenny met with an Appeals officer, but no agreement was reached on the issues in question. Jenny then filed a petition with the Tax Court and prevailed. Can Jenny recover her reasonable administrative costs?

3. Reasonable Costs

Both reasonable administrative costs and reasonable litigation costs that are actually paid or incurred are recoverable under § 7430. The burden of proof is on the taxpayer, so the taxpayer must present accurate and detailed records to the court. No interest accrues on the award, and the taxpayer may only recover fees attributable to the period during which the government's position was unjustified.

a. Administrative Costs

Section 7430(c) provides that reasonable administrative costs are those expenses, costs, and fees imposed by the Service and reasonable expenses of expert witnesses; reasonable attorneys' fees; and the reasonable costs of any study, analysis, engineering report, test, or project which the court finds necessary for the preparation of the taxpayer's case. IRC § 7430(c)(2). These costs must be incurred on or before the earlier of (1) the date the taxpayer receives the notice of the decision of the Appeals Office, (2) the date of the notice of deficiency, or (3) the date of the first notice of proposed deficiency (30-day letter) which allows the taxpayer an opportunity for an Appeals Office review. Id. The latter provision was added by the Taxpayer Bill of Rights 3, effective for costs incurred more than 180 days after July 22, 1998.

b. Litigation Costs

Reasonable litigation costs include reasonable court costs; reasonable expenses of expert witnesses; reasonable costs of any study, analysis, engineering report, test or project that is necessary for the party's case; reasonable attorneys' fees; and other reasonable miscellaneous expenses.

c. Attorneys' Fees

Section 7430(c)(3)(A) defines attorneys' fees as fees for the services of an individual (whether or not an attorney) who is authorized to practice before the Tax Court or before the Service. See Chapter 2 for a discussion of who may practice before the Service.

Section 7430(c)(1)(B) provides a cap of $125 per hour on the rate at which attorneys' fees may be awarded, although such fees may be awarded at a higher rate if the attorney establishes the existence of a "special factor." Special factors include limited availability of qualified attorneys for such proceeding, difficulty of issues presented in the case, and the local availability of tax expertise. Id. The regulations provide other special factors, including the novelty and difficulty of the issues, the undesirability of the case, the work and ability of counsel, the result obtained, and customary fees and awards in other cases. Reg. § 301.7430-4(b)(3)(iii)(B).

ACTION ON DECISION
AOD-2002-06

Issue: Does an LL.M. in Taxation qualify as a "special factor" justifying an award of attorneys' fees to plaintiff's counsel in excess of the statutory rate under I.R.C. section 7430?

Discussion: Taxpayers filed a delinquent return claiming a refund. At the time they filed their return, the Service took the position that the "timely mailed is timely filed" rule of I.R.C. section 7502(a) did not apply to claims for refund on delinquent original returns. The Service disallowed the claim as untimely because, although the taxpayers mailed the return within the 3 year claim period of I.R.C. section 6511(b)(2)(A), the return was not delivered until after the 3 year period expired. After the taxpayers filed suit, the Government changed its position. See Weisbart v. United States, 222 F.3d 93 (2(d) Cir. 2000), acq. 2000-2 C.B. xiii; AOD CC-2000-09. In light of the acquiescence in *Weisbart*, the Government conceded this case prior to trial.

In a motion for attorneys' fees, the taxpayers argued for a higher rate because their attorney had "specialized expertise in tax matters" and an LL.M. in Taxation. The *Curell* court [eds: Currell v. United States, 2001 WL 1480294] awarded attorneys' fees, finding the Service's position was not substantially justified. In doing so, the court allowed an increase over the hourly rate allowed by section 7430(c)(1)(B)(iii) for the period in question.

The increased rate is only permitted if the court determines that a "special factor" justifies a higher rate. The statute lists, as non-exclusive examples of special factors, the limited availability of qualified attorneys, the difficulty of the issues presented in the case, and the local availability of tax expertise. The example in Treas. Reg. section 301.7430- 4(b)(3)(iii)(D) is specifically on point as to what constitutes a special factor for adjustment.

In the example, the taxpayer's attorney has an LL.M. in Taxation with Highest Honors and regularly deals with TEFRA partnership matters. The regulation concludes that "even extraordinary knowledge of the tax laws does not constitute distinctive knowledge or a unique and specialized skill constituting a special factor." See also Regimbal v. United States, 2001- 2 U.S.T.C. 50,583; 2001-2 U.S.T.C. 60,414; 88 A.F.T.R.2d 5330 (E.D. Wash. 2001) (no special factors, including attorney's LL.M. in Taxation, to justify increased fee under I.R.C. section 7430); Cozean v. Commissioner, 109 T.C. 227(1997) (same); Tinsley v. Commissioner, T.C. Memo 1992-195 (1992) (same). Although *Cozean* and *Tinsley* were decided before the 1998 amendment to section

7430(c)(1)(B)(iii), the outcome of these cases would not change due to the amendment which essentially incorporated the factors considered in those cases into the Code.

When Congress creates a statutory cap for attorneys' fees, only truly extraordinary circumstances justify an increase, lest the exception swallow the rule. Pierce v. Underwood, 487 U.S. 552 (1988) (arising under the Equal Access to Justice Act (EAJA), 28 U.S.C. sec. 2412(d) (1994), but relevant to section 7430 as well, e.g. Cozean v. Commissioner, 109 T.C. at 233, n9; Powers v. Commissioner, 43 F.3d 172, 183 (5(th) Cir. 1995)). The tax expertise of a taxpayer's lawyer alone is not a special factor under section 7430(c)(1)(B)(iii). Cassuto v. Commissioner, 936 F.2d 736, 743 (2(d) Cir.1991); Bode v. United States, 919 F.2d 1044, 1050 (5th Cir. 1990). Litigating this case did not require extraordinary skill or ability. Instead, the case presented a straightforward legal question where the Service's position was clear from prior litigation and subsequent announcement of position, as well as readily ascertainable by taxpayers' counsel through ordinary legal research. The lower court's award of attorney's fees in excess of the statutory cap under section 7430, in the absence of special factors, as set forth in the applicable Treasury Regulation, was incorrect as a matter of law.

Recommendation: Nonacquiescence.

Notes and Questions

Once it is determined that a special factor exists, the court will award an increase over the statutory cap for attorneys' fees. However, if the case involves work to which the special factor does not apply (i.e., specialized knowledge), the statutory cap may apply to that portion of the fees. See Pietro v. Commissioner, T.C. Memo. 1999-383

1. If the fees charged are less than the hourly cap, the court generally will award fees on the basis of the amount actually charged. Can you think of any circumstance in which an exception to this rule might apply?

2. What happens if the attorney represents the taxpayer on a contingency fee basis instead of on an hourly rate? See Marre v. United States, 117 F.3d 297 (5th Cir. 1997).

3. Joe has an LL.M. in taxation and is admitted to practice before both the Service and the Tax Court. He receives a notice of deficiency attributable to his 2003 taxable year. Joe files a petition and represents himself (pro se) before the Tax Court. He prevails. What result on his

Motion to Recover Reasonable Attorneys' Fees? See United States v. McPherson, 840 F.2d 244 (4th Cir. 1988).

4.　The Taxpayer Must Be the Prevailing Party

A prevailing party is defined as any party other than the United States or any creditor of the taxpayer who substantially prevails with respect to the amount in controversy or with respect to the most significant issue or set of issues presented. IRC § 7430(c)(4).

CULPEPPER-SMITH v. UNITED STATES
United States District Court, E.D. Pennsylvania, 1999.
50 F. Supp 2d 425.

MEMORANDUM

O'NEILL, DISTRICT JUDGE.

Having obtained the agreement of the Internal Revenue Service to abate an assessment of $150,000, including interest and penalties, dating from an alleged underpayment on her 1980 tax return, plaintiff requests $40,912.50 in attorney fees and costs as the "prevailing party" pursuant to § 7430 of the Internal Revenue Code. 26 U.S.C. § 7430. The government tacitly concedes that plaintiff is entitled to fees as a prevailing party insofar as she avoided the 1980 tax assessment, but contends that plaintiff is not entitled to recover legal costs incurred in pursuing several other issues on which she was not successful. The government also contends that certain other fees and costs sought by plaintiff are not recoverable under § 7430. For the reasons set forth below, I will reduce the requested fee award but not by as much as sought by the government.

BACKGROUND

As set forth in a previous opinion by the late Judge McGlynn, the facts giving rise to this litigation are as follows: In 1980, plaintiff invested as a sole proprietor in the lease of certain audio recordings for a 7 ½ year period. The following year, plaintiff filed a timely federal income tax return for 1980 claiming no taxes were owed for that year because her claimed deductions and investment credit eliminated any tax liability. Ten years later, sometime in 1991, the IRS began sending plaintiff notices of its intent to levy on her for failure to pay taxes for 1980. On March 6, 1991, the IRS assessed plaintiff for unpaid federal income tax, interest and possible penalties for the 1980 tax year. Plaintiff claims the assessment was illegal because the IRS did not send her a notice of deficiency as required by 26 U.S.C. § 6212. On April 15, 1994, the IRS credited plaintiff's 1993 tax refund of $2,618 against the 1980 tax liability. It did the same with her 1995 tax refund of $2,640 on May 13, 1996. Plaintiff brought this lawsuit to enjoin the Government's collection of the assessment amount and recover her 1993 and 1995 tax refunds, along with damages and litigation costs. The Government now concedes the IRS never sent plaintiff a statutorily-required notice of deficiency, and that the assessment for tax year 1980 was therefore illegal. It has agreed to abate the assessment, but refuses to return plaintiff's 1993 and 1995 tax refunds which were applied to the 1980 tax deficiency. Culpepper-Smith v. United States, 1998 WL 544964, at *1 (E.D.Pa. Aug.24, 1998).

The government made its concession on June 2, 1998, at which time it also represented that it would abate the 1980 assessment and asked plaintiff to stipulate to dismissal of the case.[1] Plaintiff refused to sign the proposed stipulation for reasons that are not altogether clear, but appear to have included the facts that the government did not concede that the assessment was untimely (and therefore in theory could have issued another notice of deficiency and again sought assessment), and that the proposed stipulation would have waived plaintiff's claim for attorney fees and costs. At any rate, so far as the record shows there were no addition proposals or even negotiations for a stipulated dismissal, and on June 29, 1998 the government filed a motion to dismiss the case. The government argued that plaintiff's claims were mooted by its concession and that the court lacked authority to enter an injunction in plaintiff's favor. On July 15 and 21, plaintiff filed three cross-motions: (1) a motion for summary judgment as to plaintiff's right to a permanent injunction, attorney fees and costs, and damages; (2) a motion to amend her complaint to specifically assert claims for return of the 1993 and 1995 tax overpayments; and (3) a motion to enforce the IRS's concession and order the levies against her removed and to prohibit any future attempt by the IRS to collect on the 1980 assessment.　　On August 24, 1998, Judge McGlynn granted defendant's motion to dismiss plaintiff's claim for an injunction against the 1980 assessment "subject to the IRS' abatement of the assessment and removal of all levies against plaintiff's property and/or funds." Id. at *11. The Court also dismissed plaintiff's claim for an injunction returning to her the 1993 and 1995 tax overpayments for lack of subject jurisdiction, finding that plaintiff had failed to demonstrate that she exhausted administrative remedies available to her

---

1.　　The Stipulation of Dismissal proposed by the IRS provided: "The parties hereto * * * stipulate and agree that this action be dismissed with prejudice, the parties to bear their own costs and expenses, including attorney fees."

on these claims. As to plaintiff's cross motions, the Court (1) denied as futile the motion to amend to add the refund claims; (2) denied the motion to enforce the IRS' concession as moot, again subject to the IRS removing any liens and levies against the plaintiff's property; and (3) denied the motion for summary judgment as to a permanent injunction and as to plaintiff's claims for damages for wrongful collection of taxes pursuant to 26 U.S.C. § 7433(a) and denied without prejudice to renewal plaintiff's motion for litigation expenses. Id. at *7-*11. On March 23, 1999, the parties stipulated to dismissal of plaintiff's remaining claim under § 7433(a) for damages for wrongful tax collection.

In opposing plaintiff's fee petition, the government's main contention is that while plaintiff was successful in opposing the 1980 assessment, she should not have continued the litigation after the government's June 2, 1998 concession. Having lost on all issues litigated thereafter, the government contends, plaintiff is not entitled to fees and costs for her litigation of the government's motion to dismiss and her summary judgment motion.

In addition, the government contends that plaintiff may not recover fees incurred prior to early August, 1996 (i.e., prior to preparation of the complaint). According to the government, a taxpayer can recover only those attorney fees incurred in court proceedings. Finally, the government argues that pursuant to § 7430(c)(2) plaintiff is not entitled to recover costs incurred prior to her receipt on August 16, 1996 of the IRS' Problem Resolution Office's final response to her inquiry concerning the 1980 assessment.

In support of its various contentions, the government cites provisions of the statute but no case law whatsoever. Nor has the government set forth how much of plaintiff's claimed fees and costs should be subtracted as to each of its three contentions should the Court agree with any of them.

DISCUSSION

The central issue here is whether plaintiff is entitled to fees and expenses incurred in litigating the government's motion to dismiss and her responsive cross-motions after the government's June 2, 1998 concession that plaintiff had not received the required notice of deficiency. The government contends that plaintiff cannot be considered a "prevailing party" pursuant to § 7430(a) after the government's June 2, 1998 concession because she lost all issues she continued to press after that date. In the alternative, the government argues that plaintiff "unreasonably protracted" the litigation after the government's concession and therefore is not entitled to fees and costs for that period pursuant to § 7430(b)(3).

The relevant portions of the statute provide:

§ 7430. Awarding of costs and certain fees

(a) In general.–In any administrative or court proceeding which is brought by or against the United States in connection with the determination, collection, or refund of any tax, interest, or penalty under this title, the prevailing party may be awarded a judgment or a settlement for–(1) reasonable administrative costs incurred in connection with such administrative proceeding within the Internal Revenue Service, and (2) reasonable litigation costs incurred in connection with such court proceeding.

(b) Limitations.–(1) Requirement that administrative remedies be exhausted.–A judgment for reasonable litigation costs shall not be awarded under subsection (a) in any court proceeding unless the court determines that the prevailing party has exhausted the administrative remedies available to such party within the Internal Revenue Service. Any failure to agree to an extension of the time for the assessment of any tax shall not be taken into account for purposes of determining whether the prevailing party meets the requirements of the preceding sentence. * * * (3) Costs denied where party prevailing protracts proceedings.–No award for reasonable litigation and administrative costs may be made under subsection (a) with respect to any portion of the administrative or court proceeding during which the prevailing party has unreasonably protracted such proceeding.

A "prevailing party" is defined as follows, in pertinent part. See § 7430(c)(4):

(4) Prevailing party.–(A) In general.–The term "prevailing party" means any party in any proceeding to which subsection (a) applies (other than the United States or any creditor of the taxpayer involved)–(I) which–(I) has substantially prevailed with respect to the amount in controversy, or (II) has substantially prevailed with respect to the most significant issue or set of issues presented[.]* * *

(B) Exception if United States establishes that its position was substantially justified.–(I) General rule.–A party shall not be treated as the prevailing party in a proceeding to which subsection (a) applies if the United States establishes that the position of the United States in the proceeding was substantially justified.

* * *

It is not immediately clear from the definition of "prevailing party" whether a court is authorized to divide up proceedings in stages for which there are different "prevailing parties" and award attorney fees accordingly. The statute seems to require that the prevailing party be determined with respect to the entire litigation, defining the prevailing party as the party that has "substantially prevailed with respect to the amount in controversy" or "with respect to the most significant issue or set of issues presented." Looking at the entire litigation in these terms, plaintiff is clearly the prevailing party.

On the other hand, it also seems obvious that a plaintiff cannot prevail on the main issue of the litigation and then seek to pursue additional claims for which the government will have to pick up the litigation expenses–regardless of the outcome–on the mere strength of the plaintiff's initial victory. The perverse effects of a contrary rule are obvious. The government would have a reduced incentive to resolve tax disputes by concession as quickly as possible to avoid litigation expenses, because as soon it made a concession on the major subject of the litigation it would become liable for litigation expenses at the whim of the adverse (now "prevailing") party. Conversely, the taxpayer (and/or his or her counsel) would have an incentive to engage in protracted, essentially risk-free litigation at the expense of the government.

Moreover, when considered all together, the many qualifications and limitations on fee awards imposed by § 7430 suggest that Congress intended that courts consider awards carefully and on a fact-intensive basis that would frequently necessitate an issue-by-issue analysis. Thus, a court must consider not only whether the taxpayer "substantially prevailed," but also whether the government's position was "substantially justified," whether the taxpayer exhausted all of his or her administrative remedies, whether the taxpayer unreasonably protracted the proceedings, and whether the legal expenses sought are "reasonable." In cases involving more than one tax issue, these inquiries may not make sense or be possible without issue-by-issue analysis. In this case, for example, the taxpayer exhausted her administrative remedies so far as was possible with regard to the 1980 assessment, but failed to exhaust her remedies with regard to the refund claims. Similarly, different issues may require separate analysis as to the reasonableness of the government's position and whether the proceedings were unreasonably protracted by the taxpayer.

For these reasons, it appears clear to me, as it has to others, that courts deciding fee petitions under § 7430 may consider different phases and/or issues of the litigation discretely. Compare, e.g., Ragan v. Commissioner of Internal Revenue, 135 F.3d 329, 334 (5th Cir.1998) (taxpayer entitled to expenses incurred in defending against meritless claim by IRS for repayment of one-half of refund on her joint return that IRS had paid to her husband's bankruptcy estate, but was not entitled to expenses incurred pursuing her meritless claim against IRS for one-half of same refund); Kenagy v. United States, 942 F.2d 459, 465-467 (8th Cir.1991) (considering justifiability of government's position separately as to each of four fiscal-year quarters for which taxpayer allegedly underpaid payroll taxes); Boatmen's First National Bank v. United States, 723 F.Supp. 163, 170-171(W.D.Mo.1989) (finding support in statutory framework of § 7430 and from considerations of fairness and good policy for proposition that court could consider different issues in single action separately for purposes of fee and cost award determination).

Here, there are a number of different issues that are easily distinguished in analysis of the fee and costs petition. First, there is plaintiff's challenge to the 1980 assessment. It is undisputed that this claim was the most substantial one in the litigation, that plaintiff prevailed on it, that the government's position was not substantially justified, and that plaintiff exhausted her administrative remedies. Thus, plaintiff is entitled to fees and costs incurred in challenging the assessment at least until the government's concession.

The litigation that followed the government's concession involved plaintiff's claims for the 1993 and 1995 refunds, for injunctive relief to enforce the government's concession and for judgment as a matter of law on the assessment issue, and for damages under § 7433. As to the refund claim, plaintiff is not entitled to fees and costs for these claims because she has not established that she exhausted administrative remedies for them, see § 7430(b)(1); to the contrary, Judge McGlynn expressly determined that the claims had to be dismissed for failure to exhaust administrative remedies. As to the § 7433 claim, Judge McGlynn's opinion denying summary judgment on this claim, which has since been dismissed by stipulation of the parties, is sufficient to establish that the government's position in opposing the claim was justified.

The litigation concerning plaintiff's motion to enforce the abatement of the 1980 assessment and the government's motion to dismiss presents a more difficult question. Here, Judge McGlynn denied the plaintiff's motion as moot and granted defendant's, but in both instances did so subject to the IRS' abatement of the assessment and/or removal of all liens or levies against plaintiff's property. The government appears to argue that plaintiff should have simply terminated the litigation voluntarily after she received the government's concession. But the government offers no argument for why the plaintiff should have been satisfied merely with the concession letter, and there is no evidence that the government took any concrete action to provide more solid assurance to her, such as immediately removing the liens against her, or officially renouncing any future assessment on the alleged 1980 deficiency, or moving to have judgment entered against itself. The government did offer to stipulate to dismissal, but the proposed stipulation included language waiving plaintiff's right to seek fees under § 7430. The government has presented no evidence that it subsequently offered better terms or even attempted to negotiate different dismissal language. The government cannot avoid subsequent litigation expenses caused by its own unjustified position merely by conceding the position and then offering to stipulate to dismissal under terms that reasonably are viewed as unacceptable by the other party.

In light of these circumstances, it seems to me that plaintiff's attempts to enforce the government's concession and to obtain judgment in her favor on the abatement issue and her opposition to defendant's motion to dismiss are best considered part of her overall effort to defend against the 1980 assessment--an effort on which she substantially prevailed and for which she is therefore entitled to fees. In addition, in light of the government's failure to offer evidence that plaintiff had any alternative to continued litigation other than the proposed stipulation of dismissal, which a reasonable litigant in plaintiff's shoes could well find unacceptable, I cannot conclude that plaintiff unreasonably protracted the litigation by continuing her litigation efforts after the government's concession letter.

Insofar as she reasonably continued to pursue the litigation, I also cannot find that plaintiff was unreasonable in continuing to press her claims for the 1993 and 1995 refunds and for damages under § 7433, even if she was ultimately unsuccessful on these issues. However, as established by Judge McGlynn's decision in its favor, the government clearly was substantially justified in opposing these claims. Accordingly, plaintiff is not entitled to fees and costs attributable to her unsuccessful claims for the 1993 and 1995 refunds and for damages under § 7433. Because it is not possible to discern from counsel's records precisely what time was spent on these issues and what was not, I will simply subtract one-third of the fees incurred between June 30, 1998 (when the government filed its motion to dismiss) and August 24, 1998, when the Court entered its opinion rejecting these claims. The total fees incurred during this period was ($12,647.41), so I will subtract $4,215.80 from the fee request.

2.

The government next contends that plaintiff is not entitled to legal fees incurred prior to "early" August 1996, when plaintiff filed her complaint, because such fees were not incurred "in connection" with a court proceeding as is required, according to the government, for them to be recovered under § 7430. The government also contends that plaintiff is not entitled to any "costs" incurred prior to August 16, 1996, when she received the final response from the IRS' Problem Resolution office.[3]

The government is incorrect in contending that attorney fees cannot be recovered for administrative as opposed to court proceedings. Section § 7430(c)(2) defines "reasonable administrative costs" to include "expenses, costs, and fees described in paragraph [(c)](1)(B)." § 7430(c)(2)(B).[4] Section (c)(1)(B) defines "reasonable litigation costs" to include attorney fees.[5] Thus, "reasonable administrative costs" includes all of the same expenses, including attorney fees, covered by "reasonable litigation costs." The only differences between "administrative costs" and "litigation costs" are (1) in situations where all the proceedings are administrative, the IRS rather than the court determines what, if any, "reasonable administrative costs" should be recovered by the taxpayer;

---

3. The government has not set forth how much it seeks to avoid on these grounds, but it appears that plaintiff seeks fees and costs incurred prior to August 1996 in the amount of $ 3395.48.

4. Section 7430(c) provides: (2) Reasonable administrative costs.–The term "reasonable administrative costs" means–(A) any administrative fees or similar charges imposed by the Internal Revenue Service, and (B) expenses, costs, and fees described in paragraph (1)(B), except that any determination made by the court under clause (ii) or (iii) thereof shall be made by the Internal Revenue Service in cases where the determination under paragraph (4)(C) of the awarding of reasonable administrative costs is made by the Internal Revenue Service. Such term shall only include costs incurred on or after whichever of the following is the earliest: (I) the date of the receipt by the taxpayer of the notice of the decision of the Internal Revenue Service Office of Appeals; (ii) the date of the notice of deficiency; or (iii) the date on which the first letter of proposed deficiency which allows the taxpayer an opportunity for administrative review in the Internal Revenue Service Office of Appeals is sent.

5. Section 7430(c) provides: (1) Reasonable litigation costs.–The term "reasonable litigation costs" includes– (A) reasonable court costs, and (B) based upon prevailing market rates for the kind or quality of services furnished– (I) the reasonable expenses of expert witnesses in connection with a court proceeding, except that no expert witness shall be compensated at a rate in excess of the highest rate of compensation for expert witnesses paid by the United States, (ii) the reasonable cost of any study, analysis, engineering report, test, or project which is found by the court to be necessary for the preparation of the party's case, and (iii) reasonable fees paid or incurred for the services of attorneys in connection with the court proceeding, except that such fees shall not be in excess of $125 per hour unless the court determines that a special factor, such as the limited availability of qualified attorneys for such proceeding, the difficulty of the issues presented in the case, or the local availability of tax expertise, justifies a higher rate. * * *

"Court proceeding" is defined as "any civil action brought in a court of the United States * * *." § 7430(c)(6).

and (2) administrative costs may only be awarded after certain defined dates, which are the earliest of the date when the taxpayer received the notice of deficiency; the date when the taxpayer could first obtain administrative review of a proposed tax deficiency notice; or the date of the decision of the IRS Appeals Office. § 7430(c)(2)

Based on my examination of counsel's time records, I find that as of the beginning of August 1996 counsel's services were clearly "in connection with the court proceeding." The question, then, is whether the modest services rendered by plaintiff's counsel between April and July 1996 were connected with either administrative proceedings or the court proceeding within the meaning of § 7430(a) and (c).

I think these expenses can be fairly characterized as either litigation costs or administrative costs and are therefore recoverable. Most of the attorney services, amounting to $ 3248.02 in fees, involved communications with the IRS. Since plaintiff apparently never received either a proposed or actual notice of deficiency, she never had access to normal administrative review processes, including review by the Appeals Office. Thus, counsel's communications with the IRS might be considered attempts to obtain administrative redress through "administrative proceedings" despite the fact that normal avenues of redress were blocked. Considered in this manner, counsel's fees were "administrative costs" within the meaning of § 7430.[6] In the alternative, counsel's services and other expenses may be considered to have been incurred "in connection with the court proceeding" because (1) plaintiff was never given the opportunity to proceed through normal administrative channels for lack of notice and (2) counsel's services involved communications with the IRS and other preparatory work that would normally (and laudably) precede the filing of a complaint. In either event, plaintiff is entitled to attorney fees and costs incurred between April and July 1996.

---

6. The government contends that plaintiff is not entitled to any "administrative costs" incurred before August 16, 1996, when she received the final response of the IRS Problem Resolution Office. Presumably, the government contends that that response should be considered a substitute for the decision of the Appeals Office which, had plaintiff ever obtained it, would have marked a date after which her fees and other expenses would have been recoverable. See § 7430(c)(2). On the facts of this case, the government's position is absurd. As plaintiff has insisted and the government now concedes, plaintiff never got a proposed or actual deficiency notice, and therefore did not have the chance to seek review of a proposed deficiency before the Appeals Office. Accordingly, the triggering events of § 7430(c)(2) have no application to this case. According to the government's original position, moreover, plaintiff's "administrative costs" would have become recoverable by 1991 at the latest, when the IRS began to send her levy notices, having purportedly already sent her a deficiency notice.

CONCLUSION

I find, as the government tacitly concedes, that plaintiff was the "prevailing party" in this litigation and therefore is entitled to attorney fees. I also find that plaintiff did not unreasonably protract the proceedings by continuing to press the litigation after the government's "concession." On the other hand, the government was substantially justified in opposing several of the claims plaintiff continued to press and plaintiff may not recover fees incurred in pursuing these claims. In sum, I will award plaintiff all but $4,215.80 of the $ 40,912.50 in fees and costs that she has requested, for a total of $36,696.70.

* * *

Notes and Question

Occasionally, questions may arise as to whether the taxpayer actually was the prevailing party. Section 7430(c)(4)(A) provides three methods of making this determination: (1) by agreement between the parties, (2) in an administrative proceeding, by final determination of the Service, and (3) in a court case, by final determination of the court.

In a recovery of attorneys' fees under § 7430, to whom are the fees paid? See Stephens ex rel. R.E. v. Astrue, 565 F.3d 131 (4th Cir. 2009).

a. Substantial Justification

Despite meeting the requirements discussed above, a taxpayer will not be considered a prevailing party if the Service establishes that its position was substantially justified. IRC § 7430(c)(4)(B).

CLEVELAND GOLDEN GLOVES ASSOC. v. UNITED STATES

United States District Court, Northern District of Ohio, Eastern Division, 2000.
2000 WL 1727776.

MEMORANDUM & ORDER

OMALLEY, DISTRICT J.

* * *

The Internal Revenue Service ["IRS"] issued a third-party summons to the petitioner's attorneys without sending notice to the petitioner, as the IRS is required to do under its own rules. On March 24, 2000, the petitioner filed a Motion to Quash the summons. On June 2, 2000, the IRS sent a letter to the petitioner stating that it had withdrawn the summons. The petitioner, however, did not withdraw its Motion to

Quash. On June 26, 2000, the IRS filed a Motion to Dismiss based on the fact that the action was now moot as there was nothing to quash. The Court granted that Motion and dismissed the case on July 5, 2000. The petitioner now asks the Court to grant its attorneys fees because, as the IRS withdrew the summons, it was the prevailing party in the above case.

Under 26 U.S.C. § 7430, a taxpayer who prevails against the government may recover reasonable litigation costs, including reasonable attorney fees and costs, unless the government can prove its position was substantially justified. It is the government's burden to prove that its position was substantially justified. See 26 U.S.C. § 7430(c)(4)(B)(I). To prove it was substantially justified, the government must show its position was (1) "justified in substance or in the main," (2) "justified to a degree that could satisfy a reasonable person," or, (3) had "a reasonable basis both in law and fact." See Pierce v. Underwood, 487 U.S. 552, 565 (1988); William L. Comer Family Equity Pure Trust v. Commissioner, 958 F.2d 136, 139-40 (6th Cir.1992) (applying the *Pierce* definition to the "substantially justified" inquiry under 26 U.S.C. § 7430). The *Pierce* court explicitly rejected the "Justified to a high degree" test, a more demanding standard. In determining whether the government's position is substantially justified, the Court considers "all the facts and circumstances and the government's position as a whole." See Fouts v. U.S., 107 F.Supp.2d 815, 816 (2000).

Here, the United States conceded and withdrew the summons within a relatively short period after being served with the complaint, and prior to answering it. The United States argues that a concession prior to answering a complaint should be deemed reasonable for purposes of determining whether its position was substantially justified. See St. John v. U.S., 1999 WL 744104, 3 (W.D.Mich.1999); W & S Distributing, Inc., v. United States, 1996 WL 636119 (E.D.Mich.1996). Although the Court may consider pre-litigation conduct when determining reasonableness, See Comer v. Commissioner of Internal Revenue, 856 F.2d 775, 780 (6th Cir.1988) ("the relevant inquiry extends to the reasonableness of the behavior which forced the taxpayer to incur the expenses related to the filing of a petition"), the Court does not believe the failure to notify the party of the summons, a procedural mistake rather than a substantive position, is unreasonable when the United States withdrew the summons upon becoming aware of its mistake.[1] As

---

1. Petitioner argues that unreasonableness must be presumed because the United States did not follow its regulations which require notice of third-party summons be given. This presumption only applies if the Internal Revenue Service did not follow its published guidance in "administrative proceedings." See 26 U.S.C. § 7430(c)(4)(B)(ii). The presumption does not apply here because this

the United States' litigation position was not unreasonable, petitioner is not entitled to attorneys fees.

The United States asks for sanctions in the form of costs it incurred in answering the petitioner's motion for attorney fees, because it contends the motion was frivolous. The Court finds that petitioner's motion, though not well-taken, is also not frivolous. The United States failed to point to Sixth Circuit precedent which allows the Court to take into account IRS actions which provoke a suit. See, e.g., *Comer*, 856 F.2d at 780. Although the Court does not find that the IRS's action in issuing the summons was "unreasonable," the Motion for Attorneys Fees in this case was not without some basis. Accordingly, the United States' Motion for Sanctions is also denied.

For the reasons stated, the petitioner's Motion for Attorneys Fees and Costs is DENIED. The United States' Motion for Sanctions is also DENIED.

IT IS SO ORDERED.

Notes and Questions

Prior to the Taxpayer Bill of Rights 2 in 1996, the burden was on the taxpayer to prove that the Service's position was not substantially justified. After July 30, 1996, the burden of proving substantial justification shifted to the Service. The position of the United States is the position taken in the judicial proceeding for purposes of litigation costs, and the position taken in the notice of deficiency for purposes of administrative costs. IRC § 7430(c)(7). There is some conflict among the courts as to the point at which the Service's position becomes fixed in a judicial proceeding. Some view the Service's position in the answer as the determinating position (see Rosario v. Commissioner, T.C. Memo 2002-247), while others view the notice of deficiency as the defining position (see Weiss v. Commissioner, 850 F.2d 111 (2d Cir. 1988), rev'g 89 T.C. 779 (1987)).

For purposes of an administrative proceeding, § 7430(c)(7)(B) provides that the Service's position shall be determined at the earlier of (1) the date the taxpayer receives the notice of Appeals' final determination or (2) the date of the notice of deficiency.

What other factors should be considered in determining whether the Service's position is substantially justified?

---

is a judicial, not an administrative, proceeding as defined within the statute. See § 7430(c)(5) & (6).

b. *Qualified Offers*

Despite the justification of the Service's position, if the taxpayer makes a qualified offer to the Service which the Service declines, and subsequently, the Service obtains a judgment against the taxpayer in an amount equal to or less than the offer, the taxpayer may recover costs. IRC §7430(c)(4)(E). A qualified offer is a written offer that is made by the taxpayer to the government during the "qualified offer period," defined as the period beginning on the date the 30-day letter is mailed and ending 30 days before the date the case is set for trial. IRC § 7430(g)(2). The offer must specify the amount the taxpayer is offering to settle the liability (without regard to interest); it must be designated as a qualified offer; and it must remain open until the earlier of (1) the date the offer is rejected, (2) the date the trial begins, or (3) the 90th day after the date the offer is made. Id. at § 7430(g)(1).

The qualified offer exception does not apply to proceedings in which the amount of tax liability is not at issue, such as declaratory judgment proceedings or any action to restrain disclosure under § 6110(f). The exception also does not apply to judgments issued pursuant to settlements between the taxpayer and the government. IRC § 7430(c)(4)(E).

GLADDEN v. COMMISSIONER
United States Tax Court, 2003.
120 T.C. 446.

SUPPLEMENTAL OPINION

Swift, J.

* * *

This matter is before us on petitioners' motion for partial summary judgment as to the applicability of the qualified offer provision of section 7430(c)(4)(E). Petitioners seek a recovery of litigation costs relating to a Federal income tax deficiency adjustment determined by respondent with respect to income to be charged to petitioners on termination of water rights (water rights adjustment).

* * *

Under the qualified offer provision of section 7430(c)(4)(E), petitioners seek to obtain an award of litigation costs that they incurred after May 12, 1999, the date on which petitioners made a qualified offer to respondent to settle the water rights adjustment.

Relying on the "settlement limitation" set forth in section 7430(c)(4)(E)(ii)(I), respondent argues that the ultimate settlement by the parties, on remand to us from the Court of Appeals for the Ninth Circuit, of factual issues relating to the water rights adjustment precludes the application of the qualified offer provision.

In our prior Opinion in this case, Gladden v. Commissioner, 112 T.C. 209, 217-226 (1999), also involving the water rights adjustment and the parties' cross-motions for partial summary judgment, we held in favor of petitioners that, as a matter of law, the water rights owned by petitioners constituted capital assets and the relinquishment thereof by petitioners in exchange for monetary distributions constituted a taxable sale or exchange (capital asset issues).

In the same opinion and in the context of the same cross-motions for partial summary judgment, we held in favor of respondent that, as a matter of law, petitioners were not entitled to allocate any portion of their cost basis in the underlying land (which petitioners had acquired prior to acquiring the water rights) to their tax basis in the water rights (legal allocation issue). Id. at 226-230.[2]

Because of our determinations on cross-motions for partial summary judgment of the capital asset issues and of the legal allocation issue, each of which related to the water rights adjustment, in our prior opinion we did not address the related factual issue as to what amount of petitioners' cost basis in the land might be allocable to petitioners' tax basis in the water rights.

On May 12, 1999, after our above opinion was filed in April of 1999, petitioners made a "qualified offer" to respondent to settle the water rights adjustment, which offer respondent did not accept. On October 20, 1999, a decision was entered in this case in which we redetermined petitioners' tax deficiency based on our prior opinion on summary judgment and on a stipulation filed by the parties settling remaining issues.

On January 5, 2000, petitioners filed an appeal with the Court of Appeals for the Ninth Circuit with regard to our partial summary judgment in favor of respondent on the legal allocation issue. Respondent did not appeal our partial summary judgment in favor of petitioners on the capital asset issues.

On August 20, 2001, the Court of Appeals for the Ninth Circuit in Gladden v. Commissioner, 262 F.3d 851 (9th Cir.2001), reversed our partial summary judgment in favor of respondent on the legal allocation issue and concluded that petitioners may be entitled to allocate some

---

2. The water rights and the land actually were owned by a partnership in which petitioners had an interest. For convenience herein, we refer to the water rights and the land as if owned by petitioners.

portion of their cost basis in the land to their tax basis in the water rights. Because the trial record had not been developed on aspects of that factual allocation issue, the Court of Appeals remanded the case to us for a determination of that factual issue. Id. at 856.

Upon remand, petitioners and respondent entered into renewed settlement negotiations of the water rights adjustment, and on September 12, 2002, petitioners and respondent agreed to a final settlement of all aspects of the water rights adjustment under which petitioners' Federal income tax liability relating to the sale of their water rights will be less than what it would have been under petitioners' qualified offer that petitioners made in May of 1999.

For a discussion of aspects of the qualified offer provision of section 7430(c)(4)(E), see Haas & Associates Accountancy Corp. v. Commissioner, 117 T.C. 48, 54-63 (2001), affd. 55 Fed. Appx. 476 (9th Cir.2003).

Respondent now claims that, as a matter of law, the settlement limitation reflected in section 7430(c)(4)(E)(ii)(I) is applicable to petitioners' May12, 1999, qualified offer. Generally, under the settlement limitation of section 7430(c)(4)(E)(ii)(I), where the parties settle a tax adjustment rather than litigate and obtain a court determination of the adjustment, the qualified offer provision will not apply.

The specific statutory language in section 7430(c)(4)(E) reflecting the settlement limitation to the qualified offer provision provides as follows:

(ii). Exceptions.–This subparagraph shall not apply to–

(I) any judgment issued pursuant to a settlement;

Respondent argues that this statutory language means that the ultimate resolution of a disputed tax adjustment pursuant to "any" settlement disqualifies a taxpayer's qualified offer from being treated as such.

Petitioners contend that the above settlement limitation on qualified offers should not apply where, as in the instant case, a disputed tax adjustment is involved in litigation and is resolved by settlement between the parties only after a court has decided arguments and issues relating to the adjustment. Here, petitioners emphasize that the water rights adjustment was resolved by the parties by settlement only after this Court has rendered its opinion on the capital asset issues and on the legal allocation issue and only after the Court of Appeals for the Ninth Circuit had rendered an opinion on the legal allocation issue, each of which was part and parcel of respondent's water rights adjustment.

In support of their position, petitioners cite the policy underlying the qualified offer provision and respondent's temporary regulations under section 7430(c)(4)(E). With regard to the policy argument, petitioners quote from the Senate report associated with section 7430(c)(4)(E) as follows:

The Committee believes that settlement of tax cases should be encouraged whenever possible. Accordingly, the Committee believes that the application of a rule similar to FRCP 68 is appropriate to provide an incentive for the IRS to settle taxpayers' cases for appropriate amounts, by requiring reimbursement of taxpayer's costs when the IRS fails to do so. [S. Rept. 105-174, at 48 (1998), 1998-3 C.B. 537, 584.]

Petitioners emphasize the purpose underlying rule 68 of the Federal Rules of Civil Procedure, namely, to encourage settlements and to reduce litigation. Fed.R.Civ.P. 68, Advisory Committee's Note, 1946 Amendment, 28 U.S.C. app. at 801-802 (2000).

Although technically applicable only to qualified offers made in administrative and court proceedings after January 3, 2001, petitioners emphasize that the temporary regulations promulgated under section 7430 support their interpretation of section 7430(c)(4)(E)(ii)(I) because the temporary regulations provide that the settlement limitation will apply only where the settlement occurs and the judgment is entered "exclusively" pursuant to a settlement. Section 301.7430-7T(a), Temporary Proced. & Admin. Regs., 66 Fed.Reg. 726 (Jan. 4, 2001), provides, in part, as follows:

The provisions of the qualified offer rule do not apply if the taxpayer's liability under the judgment * * * is determined *exclusively* pursuant to a settlement * * * [Emphasis supplied.]

We agree with petitioners. The purpose underlying the qualified offer provision of section 7430(c)(4)(E), like that of rule 68 of the Federal Rules of Civil Procedure, is to encourage settlements by imposing litigation costs on the party not willing to settle. Herein, legal issues integral to the water rights adjustment were litigated and decided by this Court and by the Court of Appeals for the Ninth Circuit. Only after those legal issues were litigated and decided was the bottom-line substantive tax adjustment resolved by way of settlement between the parties. The ultimate settlement entered into by the parties herein can in no way be viewed as entered into exclusively pursuant to a settlement.

To treat the instant water rights adjustment as resolved pursuant to the parties' settlement would require us to ignore the threshold legal issues relating thereto that were resolved by way of litigation, not settlement, and would require us to treat the related factual allocation issue eventually settled by the parties as controlling for purposes of the settlement limitation of section 7430(c)(4)(E)(ii)(I). Further, it would require us to isolate the factual allocation issue that was settled and to treat it as distinct from the legal issues relating to the water rights that were litigated and that were not settled and each of which involved the same underlying substantive tax adjustment.

The decision to be entered in this case on the water rights adjustment will be entered not simply "pursuant to" a settlement, but also "pursuant to" our holdings on the capital asset issues (decided in favor of petitioners and not appealed) and "pursuant to" the Court of Appeals's holding on the legal allocation issue that was appealed and resolved in favor of petitioners. In particular, we note that the appellate litigation and the Court of Appeals for the Ninth Circuit's holding relating to the legal allocation issue occurred after petitioners' qualified offer was made to respondent on May 12, 1999.[3]

Herein, because legal arguments and issues relating to the water rights adjustment were litigated and decided by a court, not by settlement, the judgment to be entered herein with regard to the water rights adjustment is not to be regarded as issued merely pursuant to a settlement, and petitioners' qualified offer with regard to the water rights adjustment is not limited by the settlement limitation on qualified offers that is set forth in section 7430(c)(4)(E)(ii)(I). Petitioners qualify as a prevailing party under section 7430(c)(4) by reason of section 7430(c)(4)(E).

To reflect the foregoing, An appropriate order will be issued.

Notes

The qualified offer, once accepted, is regarded as a contract to settle docketed cases. Thus, the taxpayer cannot unilaterally reduce the amount stated in the qualified offer. See, e.g., Johnston v. Commissioner, 2004 WL 244282 (where taxpayer unsuccessfully tried to reduce the amount of the deficiency agreed to in the qualified offer by offsetting subsequently arising net operating losses). The lesson to be learned is that when making a qualified offer, the taxpayer should be careful to consider any offsets that may arise with the passage of time and that otherwise would have been allowed. See Burgess J.W. Raby

---

3.   We do not have before us the situation where no court determinations were made on any issues relating to a substantive tax adjustment after a qualified offer was made and where the pending issues and related tax adjustment were all settled without any court determinations being obtained after the qualified offer was made.

and William L. Raby, *Second Thoughts After Settling Tax Controversies*, 102 Tax Notes 1117 (March 1, 2004).

A taxpayer may make multiple qualified offers during the offer period. A qualified offer supercedes any previously made qualified offer, and only the last offer, made most closely to the end of the qualified offer period will be considered the valid qualified offer that will be compared to the taxpayer's liability under the judgment. Reg. § 301.7430-7(c)(6).

c. Net Worth Requirement

Finally, in order to prevail under § 7430, the taxpayer must establish a net worth of not more than $2 million when the action was filed.

CHRISTOPH v. UNITED STATES
United States District Court, S.D. Georgia, Savannah Division, 1996.
931 F. Supp. 1564.

ORDER

MOORE, DISTRICT JUDGE.

* * *

Mrs. Christoph timely filed this motion subsequent to this Court's determination that she and her husband Dieter Christoph were entitled to judgment as a matter of law on the issue of the deductibility of a $250,000 lump sum alimony payment made by Mr. Christoph to his ex-wife, Jutta Duse. Mrs. Christoph moved this Court to award her $11,185 (one-half of $22,370 legal bill) in attorneys' fees under the authority of 26 U.S.C. § 7430(a)(2).

In order for Mrs. Christoph to be awarded fees under § 7430(a)(2), she must show that three basic requirements have been satisfied. First, she must have exhausted all of the administrative remedies available to her within the structure of the Internal Revenue Service. 26 U.S.C. § 7430(b)(1). Next, she must show that she is a "prevailing party"--a term of art which possesses many internal qualifiers. 26 U.S.C. § 7430(c)(4)(A). She must also show that the award she seeks equals the amount of "reasonable fees" she has "paid or incurred" in connection with the court proceeding. 26 U.S.C. § 7430(c)(1). Mrs. Christoph must establish all of the above elements in order to recover an award for attorney fees under § 7430.

Defendant concedes that Mrs. Christoph exhausted all her available administrative remedies. Thus, the first requirement is satisfied. Defendant argues, however, that Mrs. Christoph failed to satisfy the next two requirements. Looking first to the third requirement as listed in §

7430(c)(1), this Court patently disagrees with Defendant's position that Mrs. Christoph has not yet paid or incurred fees. Defendant argues: Plaintiff Barbara Christoph has not produced any documentation that she has actually paid any attorney's fees in the present action. Further, she has not provided any proof that she, and not her husband Dieter Christoph, would "have to pay" any attorney's fee in this case. Also, based upon plaintiff Barbara Christoph's statement in her affidavit that her net worth was "less than $30,000 when this action was filed and remains less than $30,000 today," it is very unlikely that Mrs. Christoph could actually pay an attorney's fee in this case. As a result, she has not established that she has "paid or incurred" an attorney's fee in the present case and is thus not entitled to an award of such fee.

This argument is a bit too fanciful and attenuated to merit the serious consideration of this Court. While this Court agrees that it has not been shown that Mrs. Christoph has paid any attorney's fee, it appears abundantly clear that she has incurred an attorney's fee even though she incurred it in concert with her husband. To "incur" means "to meet or fall in with (as an inconvenience); become liable or subject to; bring down upon oneself." WEBSTER'S THIRD NEW INTERNATIONAL DICTIONARY OF THE ENGLISH LANGUAGE, UNABRIDGED, 1971. The documentation produced in this case satisfies this Court that Mrs. Christoph has rendered herself liable and subject to payment of attorney's fees for the services rendered in this case. Thus, Mrs. Christoph and Mr. Christoph have incurred a legal and contractual obligation to pay their attorneys' fees. If, for example, Mr. Christoph were to somehow escape his responsibility to pay those fees by moving to a small island off the coast of Bolivia, then Mrs. Christoph would remain responsible for their payment. She has incurred a debt to her attorneys; Defendant has not adequately refuted that fact.

A more difficult question is raised regarding Mrs. Christoph's status as a "prevailing party" under 26 U.S.C. § 7430(c)(4)(A). To satisfy the "prevailing party" requirement, three sub-requirements must be met. First, the Court must find that the "position of the United States in the proceeding was not substantially justified." 26 U.S.C. § 7430(c)(4)(A)(I). Second, the Court must find that Mrs. Christoph "substantially prevailed" as to the amount or matter in controversy. 26 U.S.C. § 7430(c)(4)(A)(ii). Finally, the Court must find that Mrs. Christoph's net worth did not exceed $2,000,000 at the time this civil action was filed. 26 U.S.C. § 7430(c)(4)(A)(iii) (citing 28 U.S.C. § 2412(d)(2)(B)).

By winning this case, along with her husband, on the Motion for Summary Judgment, Mrs. Christoph substantially prevailed as to the amount or matter in controversy; she has satisfied the § 7430(c)(4)(A)(ii) requirement. Regarding the lack of substantial justification criterion of § 7430(c)(4)(A)(I), this Court indeed has serious questions and reservations concerning whether or not the position of the government was "substantially justified." An IRS "position that is 'substantially justified' is one that is 'justified to a degree that could satisfy a reasonable person' or that has a 'reasonable basis both in law and fact.' " In re Rasbury, 24 F.3d 159, 168 (11th Cir.1994) (quoting Pierce v. Underwood, 487 U.S. 552, 565, 108 S.Ct. 2541, 2550, 101 L.Ed.2d 490 (1988)); see also Estate of Johnson v. C.I.R., 985 F.2d 1315, 1318 (5th Cir.1993). While the law pertaining to the $250,000 lump sum deductibility may have been a bit murky, this Court cannot conclude that the actions of the Internal Revenue Service were justified in light of the facts of this case: namely, that it knowingly and intentionally tried to effect a double recovery from Mr. Christoph and Ms. Duse. Such an action constitutes sheer opportunism and cannot, in the opinion of the Court, amount to substantial justification; taxpayers have a clear right to more civilized and responsible conduct from public officials, including tax collectors.

Despite all of the above findings favorable to Mrs. Christoph, this Court was a bit reluctant to grant her request for legal fees because it had doubts regarding whether she satisfied the net worth requirement. Mrs. Christoph has submitted an affidavit averring that she has no liabilities and that her assets amount to less than $30,000. Defendant asserts that this affidavit is insufficient to prove the amount of her net worth for purposes of § 7430. Mrs. Christoph has subsequently submitted a balance sheet which clearly shows that her liabilities are $0 but that her assets are well below $30,000. The affidavit and the balance sheet are sufficient to establish that her net worth falls below the $2,000,000 threshold.

It is uncontested that Mr. Christoph's net worth exceeds $2,000,000 and that Mr. Christoph and Mrs. Christoph filed a joint tax return in 1989 which later became the subject matter of this civil action. The question before this Court then is whether it should consider Mrs. Christoph's net worth independently of Mr. Christoph's or whether, because they filed a joint tax return, the net worths of Mr. Christoph and Mrs. Christoph are to be considered as one combined net worth of the constructive individual created by the filing of the joint tax return.

Mrs. Christoph cites one case which, standing alone, would seem to indicate that this Court should rule in her favor on the net worth issue. In Hong v. C.I.R., the Tax Court ruled that the net worths of married petitioners are to be considered independently: [T]he language of 28 U.S.C. § 2412(d)(2)(B)(I) refers to "an individual", not to "the plaintiffs", "the petitioners", or "the complainants". The words refer to separate individuals, not to the marital community. We find nothing ambiguous in the statutory language and accordingly feel controlled by the clear language. Neither do we find that our interpretation of the statute arrives at a result that is absurd or futile. Lastly, there is nothing in the legislative history of [26 U.S.C.] § 7430 or 28 U.S.C. § 2412 which leads us to conclude that our result is an unreasonable one at variance with the policy of the legislation. In fact, the legislative history of the latter statute confirms that "an individual whose net worth did not exceed $2,000,000 at the time the adjudication was initiated" meets the requirement. The legislative history adds: "As used in this section the term 'individual' means a natural person." H.Rept. 99-120 (Part I), at 14 (1985). *We accordingly look to the net worth of each individual petitioner.* 100 T.C. 88, 91 (1993) (emphasis added). Defendant has offered three cases, only one of which was reported in hardcopy format, to counter the *Hong* court's reasoning. See Sierra Club v. United States Army Corps of Engineers, 590 F.Supp. 1509 (S.D.N.Y.1984); Sneller v. United States, 1993 WL 109769 (Bankr.M.D.Ala.1993); Papson v. United States, 1982 WL 11261 (Ct.Cl.1992). This Court does not find any of these cases as clearly reasoned and straight-forward as the *Hong* decision which, relying upon Congressional intent, finds that the legal term "individual" actually matches the lay meaning of the term: an "individual" is one natural person.

Defendant has cited to 26 C.F.R. § 301.7430-5(f) which states, for purposes of attorney's fees, "individuals filing a joint return shall be treated as 1 taxpayer * * *." Defendant essentially argues that this treasury regulation, adopted in June 1994, emasculates the *Hong* court ruling. This Court cannot agree. Defendant, in referring to the language quoted at the beginning of this paragraph, fails to mention that this regulation, on its face, applies only to administrative proceedings and not judicial proceedings such as that which has been conducted in this Court. If an agency of the executive branch desires to regulate how it will administer attorney fee awards in cases which are disposed of at the administrative level then it is free to do so. That same regulation, however, does not serve to trump the *Hong* court ruling which applied to attorney fee awards in judicial proceedings. If an administrative agency could simply adopt regulations which would serve to override judicial decisions, then the independence and integrity of the third branch of government would be greatly undermined.

This reading of the application of 26 C.F.R. § 301.7430-5(f) is supported by the *Prager* court's decision. That opinion, issued after the adoption of the treasury regulation, followed the *Hong* court's understanding of "individual" and did not even cite to the treasury regulation. *Prager*, 68 T.C.M. at 524. As a result, this Court follows the approach of the *Hong* and *Prager* decisions and rules that Mrs. Christoph has satisfied the net worth requirement of 26 U.S.C. § 7430(c)(4)(A)(iii) and 28 U.S.C. § 2412(d)(2)(B). In having so ruled, this Court determines that Mrs. Christoph has satisfied all the requirements and subrequirements of § 7430.

This, however, does not mean that she is entitled to all the attorneys' fees which she seeks.

* * *

It is clear, however, that Mrs. Christoph is not entitled to the total allowable fee since both she and her husband were clients of Attorney Painter and Attorney Stansfield. There is really no system of calculation which this Court can employ to fix the attorney's fee award. Both the *Prager* and *Hong* decisions stop short of fixing a rate by which the attorney fee determination can be made when a co-plaintiff spouse files a motion for award of attorney's fee individually. Mrs. Christoph has suggested that the Court simply divide the allowable fee into two halves and award her one half in attorney fees. This the Court will not do. It is clear to anyone familiar with this case that this case is, in blood and treasure, Mr. Christoph's battle with the Internal Revenue Service.[2] This Court, however, recognizes that Mrs. Christoph is, in some sense, connected to the subject matter of the controversy, if only tangentially, and had an interest in seeing this litigation through to a successful conclusion. This interest amounts to no more than one-half of a one-half interest and so Mrs. Christoph is entitled to 25% of the allowable attorney fees in this case. Therefore, pursuant to 26 U.S.C. § 7430, the total attorney fee award which Defendant must pay to Mrs. Christoph amounts to $16,299.45 x 25% = $4,074.86.

So Ordered.

Notes

The net worth limitations also apply to estates, trusts, and unincorporated businesses. In the case of an estate, the $2 million net worth limitation is determined as of the date of the decedent's death, and in the case of a trust, the limitation is determined as of the last day of the taxable year involved in the proceeding. IRC § 7430(c)(4)(D). An

---

2. Indeed, this Court is somewhat puzzled that Congress has not yet amended the net worth requirement to prevent a wife of a millionaire from recovering attorney's fee but, as has been stated above, this Court will neither critically reexamine nor dilute the Congressional intent as discussed in the *Hong* and *Prager* decisions.

unincorporated business meets the net worth requirement if on the administrative proceeding date, the net worth of the business does not exceed $ 7 million and the business does not have more than 500 employees. Reg. § 301.7430-5(f)(2). The net worth requirement does not apply to § 501(c)(3) organizations, although the employee limitation does apply.

In general, the taxpayer may establish net worth by filing an affidavit with the court. If the Service challenges the taxpayer's statement, the taxpayer may be required to submit additional evidence. Also, the court is not compelled to accept the taxpayer's affidavit, but may require additional evidence on its own motion.

B. APPEALING A DENIAL OF COSTS

An order granting or denying an award of reasonable costs may be incorporated as part of the decision in a court proceeding, and is appealable in the same manner as the decision. IRC § 7430(f)(1). In the case of a denial of costs, in whole or in part, in an administrative proceeding, the denial may be appealed to the Tax Court. Id. at § 7430(f)(2). The taxpayer has 90 days from the date of the notice of denial to file suit in the Tax Court.

Notes

Since the denial of reasonable costs is incorporated into the decision or judgment of the court, the appeal becomes subject to the same appellate rules as the initial decision. Thus, an appellate court has held that it lacked jurisdiction to consider a denial of reasonable litigation costs incurred in connection with the judicial review of a termination assessment, because § 7429(f) provides that the determination of a district court in reviewing a termination assessment is final and not reviewable by any other court. The appellate court then held that it did not have jurisdiction to hear the taxpayer's appeal. See Randazzo v. U.S. Dept. of Treasury, 581 F. Supp. 1235 (W.D. Pa. 1984), appeal dismissed by 751 F.2d 145 (3d Cir. 1984).

CHAPTER 9

FEDERAL TAX CRIMES

It took an IRS accountant to catch Al Capone.
— — IRS Recruiting Poster[1]

Criminal penalties and prosecutions are the ultimate weapons in the government's arsenal to ensure compliance with the reporting and payment provisions of the Internal Revenue Code. A criminal investigation can be stigmatizing, emotionally trying, and financially devastating to the person being investigated because it can result in a prosecution. If so, the end result could be a prison term and/or a very stiff monetary penalty.

In addition to the criminal offenses under Title 26 of the United States Code (the IRC), a tax offender may be charged with and prosecuted for non-tax crimes such as conspiracy, mail fraud, aiding and abetting, RICO offenses, and perjury under Title 18 of the United States Code. These offenses offer prosecutors several distinct advantages over the IRC offenses. A tax offender also may be charged with one or more of the currency transaction offenses under the IRC and Titles 11 and 31 of the United States Code.

Moreover, the civil tax penalties, including the civil fraud penalty, may run concurrently with the criminal tax penalties. The Tax Court has jurisdiction over civil tax penalties because these penalties are assessed under the deficiency procedures, discussed in Chapter 4. Criminal tax cases are prosecuted in the same manner as non-tax criminal cases. Thus, the federal district courts have jurisdiction over these offenses, and the defendants are entitled to the same constitutional guarantees and protections as the defendants in non-tax criminal cases. (See discussions of some of these protections in Chapter 10).

Under the United States Sentencing Commission Guidelines, alternative maximum penalties apply to federal crimes committed on or after November 1, 1987. In the case of tax crimes, the offense level depends upon the tax loss involved, the presence of specific offense characteristics (such as the use of "sophisticated means" to hide the existence of the crime), the presence of aggravating and mitigating

---

1. Jeffery L. Yablon, As Certain As Death–Quotations About Taxes 99, 139 (Jan. 5, 2004).

factors (such as the defendant's playing a major role in a criminal activity, or accepting responsibility for her actions), and the criminal history of the defendant. The overall effect of the Guidelines for the majority of tax offenders is to increase both the probability and extent of incarceration, as well as to increase the monetary penalty for the offenses.

I. CRIMINAL OFFENSES UNDER THE INTERNAL REVENUE CODE

A. MOST COMMONLY PROSECUTED OFFENSES

There are a variety of criminal offenses under the IRC. The most commonly prosecuted of these are (1) the attempt to evade or defeat tax under § 7201, (2) the willful failure to file a return, supply information, or pay the tax under § 7203, (3) fraud and false statements under § 7206, and (4) the delivery or disclosure of fraudulent returns, statements, or other documents under § 7207.

1. Evasion – § 7201

Evasion is a felony attempt offense, and the most serious of the criminal tax offenses. It applies both to an attempt to avoid reporting the proper amount of tax liability, as well as to an attempt to defeat or evade collection of a tax. Under the IRC, evasion is punishable by a fine of not more than $100,000 ($500,000 in the case of a corporation) and/or imprisonment for not more than five years, together with the costs of prosecution.

In order to obtain a conviction under § 7201, the Government must prove beyond a reasonable doubt that (1) there was a tax deficiency due and owing, (2) there was an attempt to evade or defeat the tax, and (3) the taxpayer acted willfully.

a. Deficiency Due and Owing

BOULWARE v. UNITED STATES

United States Supreme Court, 2008.
552 U.S. 421

JUSTICE SOUTER delivered the opinion of the Court.

Sections 301 and 316(a) of the Internal Revenue Code set the conditions for treating certain corporate distributions as returns of capital, nontaxable to the recipient. 26 U.S.C. §§ 301, 316(a) (2000 ed. and Supp. V.). The question here is whether a distributee accused of criminal tax evasion may claim return-of-capital treatment without producing evidence that either he or the corporation intended a capital return when the distribution occurred. We hold that no such showing is required.

I.

"[T]he capstone of [the] system of sanctions . . . calculated to induce . . . fulfillment of every duty under the income tax law," Spies v. United States, 317 U.S. 492, 497, 63 S.Ct. 364, 87 L.Ed. 418 (1943), is 26 U.S.C. § 7201, making it a felony willfully to "attemp[t] in any manner to evade or defeat any tax imposed by" the Code.[1] One element of tax evasion under § 7201 is "the existence of a tax deficiency," Sansone v. United States, 380 U.S. 343, 351, 85 S.Ct. 1004, 13 L.Ed.2d 882 (1965)[2] which the Government must prove beyond a reasonable doubt * * *.

Any deficiency determination in this case will turn on §§ 301 and 316(a) of the Code. According to § 301(a), unless another provision of the Code requires otherwise, a "distribution of property" that is "made by a corporation to a shareholder with respect to its stock shall be treated in the manner provided in [§ 301(c)]." Under § 301(c), the portion of the distribution that is a "dividend," as defined by § 316(a), must be included in the recipient's gross income; and the portion that is not a dividend is, depending on the shareholder's basis for his stock, either a nontaxable return of capital or a gain on the sale or exchange of stock, ordinarily

---

1. A related provision, 26 U.S.C. § 7206(1), criminalizes the willful filing of a tax return believed to be materially false.

2. "[T]he elements of § 7201 are willfulness[,] the existence of a tax deficiency, . . . and an affirmative act constituting an evasion or attempted evasion of the tax." Sansone v. United States, 380 U.S. 343, 351, 85 S.Ct. 1004, 13 L.Ed.2d 882 (1965). The Courts of Appeals have divided over whether the Government must prove the tax deficiency is "substantial," see United States v. Daniels, 387 F.3d 636, 640-641, and n. 2 (C.A.7 2004) (collecting cases); we do not address that issue here.

taxable to the shareholder as a capital gain. Finally, § 316(a) defines "dividend" as

"any distribution of property made by a corporation to its shareholders–

"(1) out of its earnings and profits accumulated after February 28, 1913, or

"(2) out of its earnings and profits of the taxable year (computed as of the close of the taxable year without diminution by reason of any distributions made during the taxable year), without regard to the amount of the earnings and profits at the time the distribution was made."

Sections 301 and 316(a) together thus make the existence of "earnings and profits"[3] the decisive fact in determining the tax consequences of distributions from a corporation to a shareholder with respect to his stock. This requirement of "relating the tax status of corporate distributions to earnings and profits is responsive to a felt need for protecting returns of capital from tax." 4 Bittker & Lokken ¶ 92.1.1, p. 92-3.

II.

In this criminal tax proceeding, petitioner Michael Boulware was charged with several counts of tax evasion and filing a false income tax return, stemming from his diversion of funds from Hawaiian Isles Enterprises (HIE), a closely held corporation of which he was the president, founder, and controlling (though not sole) shareholder. At trial,[4] the United States sought to establish that Boulware had received taxable income by "systematically divert [ing] funds from HIE in order to support a lavish lifestyle." 384 F.3d 794, 799 (C.A.9 2004). The Government's evidence showed that "[Boulware] gave millions of dollars of HIE money to his girlfriend . . . and millions of dollars to his wife . . . without reporting any of this money on his personal income tax returns. . . . [H]e siphoned off this money primarily by writing checks to employees and friends and having them return the cash to him, by diverting payments by HIE customers, by submitting fraudulent invoices

---

3.   Although the Code does not "comprehensively define 'earnings and profits,' " 4 B. Bittker & L. Lokken, Federal Taxation of Income, Estates and Gifts ¶ 92.1.3, p. 92-6 (3d ed.2003) (hereinafter Bittker & Lokken), the "[p]rovisions of the Code and regulations relating to earnings and profits ordinarily take taxable income as the point of departure," id., at 92-9.

4.   The trial at issue in this case was actually Boulware's second trial on §§ 7201 and 7206(1) charges, his convictions on those counts in an earlier trial having been vacated by the Ninth Circuit for reasons not at issue here, see 384 F.3d 794 (2004). * * *

to HIE, and by laundering HIE money through companies in the Kingdom of Tonga and Hong Kong." Ibid.

In defense, Boulware sought to introduce evidence that HIE had no retained or current earnings and profits in the relevant taxable years, with the consequence (he argued) that he in effect received distributions of property that must have been returns of capital, up to his basis in his stock. See § 301(c)(2). Because the return of capital was nontaxable, the argument went, the Government could not establish the tax deficiency required to convict him.

The Government moved in limine to bar evidence in support of Boulware's return-of-capital theory, on the grounds of "irrelevan[ce] in [this] criminal tax case." The Government relied on the Ninth Circuit's decision in United States v. Miller, 545 F.2d 1204 (1976), in which that court held that in a criminal tax evasion case, a diversion of funds may be deemed a return of capital only after "some demonstration on the part of the taxpayer and/or the corporation that such [a distribution was] intended to be such a return," id., at 1215. Boulware, the Government argued, had offered to make no such demonstration.

The District Court granted the Government's motion, and when Boulware sought "to present evidence of [HIE's] alleged over-reporting of income, and an offer of proof relating to the issue of . . . dividends," the District Court denied his request. The court said that "[n]ot only would much of [his proffered] evidence be excludable as expert legal opinion, it is plainly insufficient under the *Miller* case," id., at 138, and accordingly declined to instruct the jury on Boulware's return-of-capital theory. The jury rejected his alternative defenses (that the diverted funds were nontaxable corporate advances or loans, or that he used the moneys for corporate purposes), and found him guilty on nine counts, four of tax evasion and five of filing a false return.

The Ninth Circuit affirmed. 470 F.3d 931 (2006). It acknowledged that "imposing an intent requirement creates a disconnect between civil and criminal liability," but thought that under *Miller*, "the characterization of diverted corporate funds for civil tax purposes does not dictate their characterization for purposes of a criminal tax evasion charge." 470 F.3d, at 934. The court held the test in a criminal case to be "whether the defendant has willfully attempted to evade the payment or assessment of a tax." Ibid. Because Boulware " 'presented no concrete proof that the amounts were considered, intended, or recorded on the corporate records as a return of capital at the time they were made,' " id., at 935 (quoting *Miller*, *supra*, at 1215), the Ninth Circuit held that Boulware's proffer was "properly rejected . . . as inadequate," 470 F.3d, at 935.

Judge Thomas concurred because the panel was bound by *Miller*, but noted that " *Miller*-and now the majority opinion-hold that a defendant may be criminally sanctioned for tax evasion without owing a penny in taxes to the government." 470 F.3d, at 938. That, he said, not only "indicate[s] a logical fallacy, but is in flat contradiction with the tax evasion statute's requirement . . . of a tax deficiency." Ibid.[5]

We granted certiorari, 551 U.S. ----, 128 S.Ct. 32, 168 L.Ed.2d 808 (2007), to resolve a split among the Courts of Appeals over the application of §§ 301 and 316(a) to informally transferred or diverted corporate funds in criminal tax proceedings.[6] We now vacate and remand.

III.

A.

The colorful behavior described in the allegations requires a reminder that tax classifications like "dividend" and "return of capital" turn on "the objective economic realities of a transaction rather than . . . the particular form the parties employed," Frank Lyon Co. v. United States, 435 U.S. 561, 573, 98 S.Ct. 1291, 55 L.Ed.2d 550 (1978); a "given result at the end of a straight path is not made a different result . . . by following a devious path," Minnesota Tea Co. v. Helvering, 302 U.S. 609, 613, 58 S.Ct. 393, 82 L.Ed. 474 (1938).[7] As for distributions with respect

---

5.　　Judge Thomas went on to say that the Government would prevail even without *Miller*'s rule because, in his view, Boulware's diversions were "unlawful," and the return-of-capital rules would not apply to diversions made for unlawful purposes. See 470 F.3d, at 938-939.

6.　　As noted, the Ninth Circuit holds that §§ 301 and 316(a) are not to be consulted in a criminal tax evasion case until the defendant produces evidence of an intent to treat diverted funds as a return of capital at the time it was made. See 470 F.3d 931 (2006). By contrast, the Second Circuit allows a criminal defendant to invoke §§ 301 and 316(a) without evidence of a contemporaneous intent to treat such moneys as returns of capital. See United States v. Bok, 156 F.3d 157, 162 (1998) ("[I]n return of capital cases, a taxpayer's intent is not determinative in defining the taxpayer's conduct"). Meanwhile, the Third, Sixth, and Eleventh Circuits arguably have taken the position that §§ 301 and 316(a) are altogether inapplicable in criminal tax cases involving informal distributions. See United States v. Williams, 875 F.2d 846, 850-852 (C.A.11 1989); United States v. Goldberg, 330 F.2d 30, 38 (C.A.3 1964); Davis v. United States, 226 F.2d 331, 334-335 (C.A.6 1955); but see Brief for Petitioner 16 ("[T]hese cases can be read to address the allocation of the burden of proof on the return of capital issue, rather than the applicable substantive principles").

7.　　We have also recognized that "[t]he legal right of a taxpayer to decrease the amount of what otherwise would be his taxes, or altogether avoid them, by means which the law permits, cannot be doubted." Gregory v. Helvering, 293 U.S. 465, 469, 55 S.Ct. 266, 79 L.Ed. 596 (1935). The rule is a two-way street: "while a taxpayer is free to organize his affairs as he chooses, nevertheless, once having done so, he must accept the tax consequences of his choice, whether contemplated or not, . . . and may not enjoy the benefit of some other route he might have chosen to follow but did not," Commissioner v. National Alfalfa Dehydrating & Milling Co., 417 U.S. 134, 149, 94 S.Ct. 2129, 40 L.Ed.2d 717 (1974); see also id., at 148, 94 S.Ct. 2129 (referring to "the established tax principle that

to stock, in economic reality a shareholder's informal receipt of corporate property "may be as effective a means of distributing profits among stockholders as the formal declaration of a dividend," Palmer v. Commissioner, 302 U.S. 63, 69, 58 S.Ct. 67, 82 L.Ed. 50 (1937), or as effective a means of returning a shareholder's capital, see ibid. Accordingly, "[a] distribution to a shareholder in his capacity as such . . . is subject to § 301 even though it is not declared in formal fashion." B. Bittker & J. Eustice, Federal Income Taxation of Corporations and Shareholders ¶ 8.05[1], pp. 8-36 to 8-37 (6th ed. 1999) (hereinafter Bittker & Eustice).

There is no reason to doubt that economic substance remains the right touchstone for characterizing funds received when a shareholder diverts them before they can be recorded on the corporation's books. While they "never even pass through the corporation's hands," Bittker & Eustice ¶ 8.05[9], p. 8-51, even diverted funds may be seen as dividends or capital distributions for purposes of §§ 301 and 316(a), see Truesdell v. Commissioner, 89 T.C. 1280, 1987 WL 258105 (1987) (treating diverted funds as "constructive" distributions in civil tax proceedings). The point, again, is that "taxation is not so much concerned with the refinements of title as it is with actual command over the property taxed-the actual benefit for which the tax is paid." Corliss v. Bowers, 281 U.S. 376, 378, 50 S.Ct. 336, 74 L.Ed. 916 (1930); see also Griffiths v. Commissioner, 308 U.S. 355, 358, 60 S.Ct. 277, 84 L.Ed. 319 (1939).[8]

B.

Miller's view that a criminal defendant may not treat a distribution as a return of capital without evidence of a corresponding contemporaneous intent sits uncomfortably not only with the tax law's

---

a transaction is to be given its tax effect in accord with what actually occurred and not in accord with what might have occurred"); Founders Gen. Corp. v. Hoey, 300 U.S. 268, 275, 57 S.Ct. 457, 81 L.Ed. 639 (1937) ("To make the taxability of the transaction depend upon the determination whether there existed an alternative form which the statute did not tax would create burden and uncertainty"). The question here, of course, is not whether alternative routes may have offered better or worse tax consequences, see generally Isenbergh, Review: Musings on Form and Substance in Taxation, 49 U. Chi. L.Rev. 859 (1982); rather, it is "whether what was done . . . was the thing which the statute[, here §§ 301 and 316(a),] intended," *Gregory, supra,* at 469, 55 S.Ct. 266.

8.   Thus in the period between this Court's decisions in Commissioner v. Wilcox, 327 U.S. 404, 66 S.Ct. 546, 90 L.Ed. 752 (1946) (holding embezzled funds to be nontaxable to the embezzler) and James v. United States, 366 U.S. 213, 81 S.Ct. 1052, 6 L.Ed.2d 246 (1961) (overruling *Wilcox,* holding embezzled funds to be taxable income), the Government routinely argued that diverted funds were "constructive distributions," taxable to the recipient as dividends. See generally Gardner 237 ("While *Wilcox* was good law, the safest way to insure that both the corporation and the shareholder would be taxed on their respective gain from the diverted funds was to label them dividends"); 4 Bittker & Lokken ¶ 92.2(7), p. 92-23, n. 37.

economic realism, but with the particular wording of §§ 301 and 316(a), as well. As those sections are written, the tax consequences of a "distribution by a corporation with respect to its stock" depend, not on anyone's purpose to return capital or to get it back, but on facts wholly independent of intent: whether the corporation had earnings and profits, and the amount of the taxpayer's basis for his stock.

When the *Miller* court went the other way, needless to say, it could claim no textual hook for the contemporaneous intent requirement, but argued for it as the way to avoid two supposed anomalies. First, the court thought that applying §§ 301 and 316(a) in criminal cases unnecessarily emphasizes the exact amount of deficiency while "completely ignor[ing] one essential element of the crime charged: the willful intent to evade taxes. . .." 545 F.2d, at 1214. But there is an analytical mistake here. Willfulness is an element of the crimes charged because the substantive provisions defining tax evasion and filing a false return expressly require it, see § 7201 ("Any person who willfully attempts . . ."); § 7206(1) ("Willfully makes and subscribes . . . "). The element of willfulness is addressed at trial by requiring the Government to prove it. Nothing in §§ 301 and 316(a) as written (that is, without an intent requirement) relieves the Government of this burden of proving willfulness or impedes it from doing so if evidence of willfulness is there. Those two sections as written simply address a different element of criminal evasion, the existence of a tax deficiency, and both deficiency and willfulness can be addressed straightforwardly (in jury instructions or bench findings) without tacking an intent requirement onto the rule distinguishing dividends from capital returns.

Second, the *Miller* court worried that if a defendant could claim capital treatment without showing a corresponding and contemporaneous intent,

> "[a] taxpayer who diverted funds from his close corporation when it was in the midst of a financial difficulty and had no earnings and profits would be immune from punishment (to the extent of his basis in the stock) for failure to report such sums as income; while that very same taxpayer would be convicted if the corporation had experienced a successful year and had earnings and profits." 545 F.2d, at 1214.

"Such a result," said the court, "would constitute an extreme example of form over substance." Ibid. The Circuit thus assumed that a taxpayer like Boulware could be convicted of evasion with no showing of deficiency from an unreported dividend or capital gain.

But the acquittal that the author of *Miller* called form trumping substance would in fact result from the Government's failure to prove an element of the crime. There is no criminal tax evasion without a tax deficiency, [9] and there is no deficiency owing to a distribution (received with respect to a corporation's stock) if a corporation has no earnings and profits and the value distributed does not exceed the taxpayer-shareholder's basis for his stock. Thus the fact that a shareholder distributee of a successful corporation may have different tax liability from a shareholder of a corporation without earnings and profits merely follows from the way §§ 301 and 316(a) are written (to distinguish dividend from capital return), and from the requirement of tax deficiency for a § 7201 crime. Without the deficiency there is nothing but some act expressing the will to evade, and, under § 7201, acting on "bad intentions, alone, [is] not punishable," United States v. D'Agostino, 145 F.3d 69, 73 (C.A.2 1998).

It is neither here nor there whether the *Miller* court was justified in thinking it would improve things to convict more of the evasively inclined by dropping the deficiency requirement and finding some other device to exempt returns of capital. [10] Even if there were compelling reasons to extend § 7201 to cases in which no taxes are owed, it bears repeating that "[t]he spirit of the doctrine which denies to the federal judiciary power to create crimes forthrightly admonishes that we should not enlarge the reach of enacted crimes by constituting them from anything less than the

---

9.   Boulware was also convicted of violating § 7206(1), which makes it a felony "[w]illfully [to] mak[e] and subscrib[e] any return, statement, or other document, which contains or is verified by a written declaration that it is made under the penalties of perjury, and which [the taxpayer] does not believe to be true and correct as to every material matter." He argues that if the Ninth Circuit erred, its error calls into question not only his § 7201 conviction, but his § 7206(1) conviction as well. Brief for Petitioner 15-16. Although the Courts of Appeals are unanimous in holding that § 7206(1) "does not require the prosecution to prove the existence of a tax deficiency," United States v. Tarwater, 308 F.3d 494, 504 (C.A.6 2002); see also United States v. Peters, 153 F.3d 445, 461 (C.A.7 1998) (collecting cases), it is arguable that "the nature and character of the funds received can be critical in determining whether . . . § 7206(1) has been violated, [even if] proof of a tax deficiency is unnecessary," 1 I. Comisky, L. Feld, & S. Harris, Tax Fraud & Evasion ¶ 2.03[5], p. 21 (2007); see also Brief for Petitioner 15-16. The Government does not argue that Boulware's §§ 7201 and 7206(1) convictions should be treated differently at this stage of the proceedings, however, and we will accede to the Government's working assumption here that the §§ 7201 and 7206(1) convictions stand or fall together.

10.   "A better [method of exempting returns of capital from taxation] could no doubt be devised." 4 Bittker & Lokken ¶ 92.1.1, p. 92-3; see ibid. (suggesting, for example, that "all receipts from a corporation could be treated as taxable income, and a correction for any resulting overtaxation could be made in computing gain or loss when stock is sold, exchanged, or becomes worthless"); see also Andrews, "Out of its Earnings and Profits": Some Reflections on the Taxation of Dividends, 69 Harv. L.Rev. 1403, 1439 (1956) (criticizing the earnings and profits concept "[a]s a device for separating income from return of capital," and suggesting that "[d]istributions which ought to be treated as return of capital [could] be brought within the concept of a partial liquidation by special provision").

incriminating components contemplated by the words used in the statute," Morissette v. United States, 342 U.S. 246, 263, 72 S.Ct. 240, 96 L.Ed. 288 (1952) (opinion for the Court by Jackson, J.). If § 301, § 316(a), or § 7201 could stand amending, Congress will have to do the rewriting.

C.

Not only is *Miller* devoid of the support claimed for it, but it suffers the demerit of some anomalies of its own. First and most obviously, §§ 301 and 316 are odd stalks for grafting a contemporaneous intent requirement, given the fact that the correct application of their rules will often become known only at the end of the corporation's tax year, regardless of the shareholder's or corporation's understanding months earlier when a particular distribution may have been made. Section 316(a)(2) conditions treating a distribution as a constructive dividend by reference to earnings and profits, and earnings and profits are to be "computed as of the close of the taxable year . . . without regard to the amount of the earnings and profits at the time the distribution was made." A corporation may make a deliberate distribution to a shareholder, with everyone expecting a profitable year and considering the distribution to be a dividend, only to have the shareholder end up liable for no tax if the company closes out its tax year in the red (so long as the shareholder's basis covers the distribution); when such facts are clear at the time the reporting forms and returns are filed, the shareholder does not violate § 7201 by paying no tax on the moneys received, intent being beside the point. And since intent to make a distribution a taxable one cannot control, it would be odd to condition nontaxable return-of-capital treatment on contemporaneous intent, when the statute says nothing about intent at all.

The intent interpretation is strange for another reason, too (a reason in some tension with the Ninth Circuit's assumption that an unreported distribution without contemporaneous intent to return capital will support a conviction for evasion). The text of § 301(a) ostensibly provides for all variations of tax treatment of distributions received with respect to a corporation's stock unless a separate provision of the Code requires otherwise. Yet *Miller* effectively converts the section into one of merely partial coverage, with the result of leaving one class of distributions in a tax status limbo in criminal cases. That is, while § 301(a) expressly provides that distributions made by a corporation to a shareholder with respect to its stock "shall be treated in the manner provided in [§ 301(c)]," under *Miller*, a distribution from a corporation without earnings and profits would fail to be a return of capital for lack of contemporaneous intent to treat it that way; but to the extent that distribution did not exceed the taxpayer's basis for the stock (and thus become a capital gain), § 301(a) would leave the distribution unaccounted for.

It is no answer to say that § 61(a) of the Code would step in where § 301(a) has been pushed out. Although § 61(a) defines gross income, "[e]xcept as otherwise provided," as "all income from whatever source derived," the plain text of § 301(a) does provide otherwise for distributions made with respect to stock. So using § 61(a) as a stopgap would only sanction yet another eccentricity: § 301(a) would be held not to cover what its text says it "shall" (the class of distributions made with respect to stock for which no other more specific provision is made), while § 61(a) would need to be applied to what by its terms it should not be (a receipt of funds for which tax treatment is "otherwise provided" in § 301(a)).

The implausibility of a statutory reading that either creates a tax limbo or forces resort to an atextual stopgap is all the clearer from the Ninth Circuit's discussion in this case of its own understanding of the consequences of *Miller'*s rule: the court openly acknowledged that "imposing an intent requirement creates a disconnect between civil and criminal liability," 470 F.3d, at 934. In construing distribution rules that draw no distinction in terms of criminal or civil consequences, the disparity of treatment assumed by the Court of Appeals counts heavily against its contemporaneous intent construction (quite apart from the Circuit's understanding that its interpretation entails criminal liability for evasion without any showing of a tax deficiency).

Miller erred in requiring a contemporaneous intent to treat the receipt of corporate funds as a return of capital, and the judgment of the Court of Appeals here, relying on *Miller*, is likewise erroneous.

IV.

The Government has raised nothing that calls for affirmance in the face of the Court of Appeals's reliance on *Miller*. The United States does not defend differential treatment of criminal and civil cases, and it thus stops short of fully defending the Ninth Circuit's treatment. The Government's argument, instead, is that we should affirm under the rule that before any distribution may be treated as a return of capital (or, by a parity of reasoning, a dividend), it must first be distributed to the shareholder "with respect to . . . stock." The taxpayer's intent, the Government says, may be relevant to this limiting condition, and Boulware never expressly claimed any such intent.

The Government is of course correct that "with respect to . . . stock" is a limiting condition in § 301(a).[11] As the Government variously says, it requires that "the distribution of property by the corporation be made to a shareholder because of his ownership of its stock," and that " 'an amount paid by a corporation to a shareholder [be] paid to the shareholder in his capacity as such.' "

This, however, is not the time or place to home in on the "with respect to . . . stock" condition. Facts with a bearing on it may range from the distribution of stock ownership[12] to conditions of corporate employment (whether, for example, a shareholder's efforts on behalf of a corporation amount to a good reason to treat a payment of property as salary). The facts in this case have yet to be raked over with the stock ownership condition in mind, since *Miller* seems to have pretermitted a full consideration of the defensive proffer, and if consideration is to be given to that condition now, the canvas of evidence and Boulware's proffer should be made by a court familiar with the whole evidentiary record.[13]

---

11.   Another limiting condition is that the diversion of funds must be a "distribution" in the first place (regardless of the "with respect to stock" limitation), see supra, at 1175 - 1177, though the Government is content to assume that § 301(a)'s "distribution" language is capacious enough to cover the diversions involved here, and that if Boulware bears the burden of production in going forward with the defense that the funds he received constituted a "distribution" within the meaning of § 301(a), see n. 14, infra, that burden has been met. Nor does the Government dispute that Boulware offered sufficient evidence of his basis and HIE's lack of earnings and profits. See Brief for United States 34, n. 11.

12.   See, e.g., Truesdell v. Commissioner, IRS Non Docketed Service Advice Review, 1989 WL 1172952 (Mar. 15, 1989) ("We believe a corporation and its shareholders have a common objective-to earn a profit for the corporation to pass onto its shareholders. Especially where the corporation is wholly owned by one shareholder, the corporation becomes the alter ego of the shareholder in his profit making capacity. . . . [B]y passing corporate funds to himself as shareholder, a sole shareholder is acting in pursuit of these common objectives"). We note, however, that although Boulware was not a sole shareholder, the Tax Court has taken it as "well settled that a distribution of corporate earnings to shareholders may constitute a dividend," and so a return of capital as well, "notwithstanding that it is not in proportion to stockholdings." Dellinger v. Commissioner, 32 T.C. 1178, 1183, 1959 WL 1087 (1959); see ibid. (noting that because other stockholders did not complain when a taxpayer received unequal property, "under the circumstances they must be deemed to have ratified the distribution"). (Remaining citations omitted).

13.   Boulware does not dispute that he bears the burden of producing some evidence to support his return-of-capital theory, including evidence that the corporation lacked earnings and profits and that he had sufficient basis in his stock to cover the distribution. See Tr. of Oral Arg. 53. He instead argues that, as to the "with respect to . . . stock" requirement, it suffices to show "[t]hat he is a stockholder, and that he did not receive this money in any nonstockholder capacity." Id., at 57. The Government, for its part, on the authority of Holland v. United States, 348 U.S. 121, 75 S.Ct. 127, 99 L.Ed. 150 (1954) and Bok, 156 F.3d, at 163-164, argues that Boulware must offer more evidence than that. We express no view on that issue here, just as we decline to consider the more general question whether the Second Circuit's rule in Bok, which places on the criminal defendant the burden to produce evidence in support of a return-of-capital theory, is authorized by Holland and consistent with Sandstrom v. Montana, 442 U.S. 510, 99 S.Ct. 2450, 61 L.Ed.2d 39 (1979), and related cases.

As a more specific version of its "with respect to . . . stock" position, the Government says that the diversions of corporate funds to Boulware were in fact unlawful, and it argues that §§ 301 and 316(a) are inapplicable to illegal transfers, see D'Agostino, 145 F.3d, at 73 ("[T]he 'no earnings and profits, no income' rule would not necessarily apply in a case of *unlawful* diversion, such as embezzlement, theft, a violation of corporate law, or an attempt to defraud third party creditors" (emphasis in original)); see also n. 8, *supra*. The Government goes so far as to claim that "[t]he only rational basis for the jury's judgment was a conclusion that [Boulware] unlawfully diverted the funds."

But we decline to take up the question whether an unlawful diversion may ever be deemed a "distribution . . . with respect to [a corporation's] stock," a question which was not considered by the Ninth Circuit. We do, however, reject the Government's current characterization of the jury verdict in Boulware's case. True, the jurors were not moved by Boulware's suggestion that the diversions were corporate advances or loans, or that he was using the funds for corporate purposes. But the jury was not asked, and cannot be said to have answered, whether Boulware breached any fiduciary duty as a controlling shareholder, unlawfully diverted corporate funds to defraud his wife, or embezzled HIE's funds outright.

V.

Sections §§ 301 and 316(a) govern the tax consequences of constructive distributions made by a corporation to a shareholder with respect to its stock. A defendant in a criminal tax case does not need to show a contemporaneous intent to treat diversions as returns of capital before relying on those sections to demonstrate no taxes are owed. The judgment of the Court of Appeals is vacated, and the case is remanded for further proceedings consistent with this opinion.

It is so ordered.

Notes and Questions

On remand, the Ninth Circuit found Boulware's evidence insufficient to support his return of capital theory and it declined to give Boulware a third trial. Thus, the decision of the district court was affirmed.

In *United States v. Helmsley*, 941 F.2d 71 (2d Cir. 1991), hotelier Leona ("only the little people pay taxes") Helmsley appealed her conviction on various charges, including tax evasion and filing false returns, arising from a scheme in which she and her husband charged personal expenditures to various enterprises that they controlled. She argued on appeal that her conviction of tax evasion should be overturned because she had overpaid her taxes and this refuted the government's proof of a tax deficiency. Helmsley based this argument on the fact that her accountants had failed to segregate depreciable personal property from depreciable real property. Under the Accelerated Cost Recovery System in effect when the Helmsleys filed their tax returns, the personal property was depreciable using a shorter useful life than was available for the real property. This would have resulted in greater depreciation deductions in the years in question.

The Second Circuit denied Mrs. Helmsley's claim on the ground that once she had selected a depreciation method, the doctrine of election prevented her 'from abandoning that choice" simply because she realized later that her tax liability would be reduced further if she had elected another method of depreciation. Mrs Helmsley argued that the method selected was not allowed under the Code, and therefore the doctrine of election could not apply. But the court reasoned that "[c]ommon sense dictates that, if recalculation is denied to tax cheats who have selected valid depreciation periods, it must a fortiori be denied to tax cheats like Mrs Helmsley who further enhanced tax benefits by selecting impermissible methods."

Section 6211 of the IRC defines a deficiency as the amount by which the tax exceeds the amount reported on the return, plus the amounts previously assessed as a deficiency. Section 6601(e) specifically excludes interest from being treated as tax for purposes of deficiency procedures. Both interest and penalties also are excluded under the Federal Sentencing Guidelines in assessing the penalty for tax evasion. See U.S. SENTENCING GUIDELINES MANUAL § 2T1.1 & App. Notes; see also United States v. Wright, 211 F.3d 233, 236 (5th Cir. 2000) (declining to apply a different definition to § 7201).

In *Wright*, the taxpayer claimed that § 7201 could not apply because there was no deficiency since his total payments exceeded the tax owed. The court noted that while this was true to some extent, nevertheless some of the tax had been collected through seizure and those amounts typically are applied first against the liability (tax, interest, and penalties) for the earliest year owed. Under those circumstances, the court held there was a deficiency in the later year. Thus, despite the fact that the taxpayer technically had paid more than the amount of the deficiency, the amounts collected by seizure could be applied against the interest and penalties in the earlier years, leaving a deficiency in the later year.

1. Would it have made any difference if Boulware had executed a loan agreement with the company prior to diverting the funds?

2. In footnote 2, the Court notes that lower courts are divided "over whether the Government must prove the deficiency is 'substantial.' Why would a court require the deficiency to be substantial?

3. Can a conviction for tax evasion be avoided if there is a loss realized in a year following the year charged in the indictment that if carried back to the year in question ordinarily would reduce the amount of tax due and owing?

4. Would the *Boulware* case help or hurt Mrs. Helmsley if her case were being tried today?

1) *Methods of Proof*

How does the Government establish that the taxpayer evaded tax liability? Simply issuing a notice of deficiency is self-serving and insufficient. Instead, the Government must be able to prove that the taxpayer underpaid the tax and that there is an additional amount due and owing. In order to meet its burden, the Government may use either a direct method or an indirect method of proof. The direct method requires proof of the existence of specific items that affected taxable income which were not reported on the return, or that specific deductions were inflated or fictitious. Under this method, the Government may examine the taxpayer's books and records, bank statements, customer invoices, or Forms 1099 to establish the amount of income that was under-reported (or deductions or credits that were overstated). The indirect or circumstantial method of proof involves establishing that the taxpayer's wealth in a particular taxable year grew beyond the amount reported on the return, thereby raising the specter of unreported income. The government can establish such unreported income through the use (either singularly or in combination) of three methods: (1) net worth, (2) cash expenditures, and (3) bank deposits.

2) *Contrasting the Direct and Indirect Methods of Proof*

UNITED STATES v. BLACK

United States Court of Appeals, District of Columbia, 1988.
843 F.2d 1456.

SILBERMAN, CIRCUIT JUDGE.

* * *

Black was indicted and prosecuted on numerous counts including
* * * four counts of tax evasion. After a forty day trial, Black was
convicted on three counts of tax evasion. The Government charged that
although Black received $65,827 of taxable income in 1978, $109,251 of
taxable income in 1979, and $174,755 of taxable income in 1981, he failed
to file a return for any of those years.

I.

The resolution of Black's claims concerning sufficiency of evidence
and adequacy of the jury charge turns entirely upon the proper
characterization of the actual method used by the Government to prove
Black's tax evasion. The Government contends it employed the "specific
items" method of proof, a direct method of demonstrating tax evasion in
which the Government "produce[s] evidence of the receipt of specific
items of reportable income by the defendant that do not appear on his
income tax return." Black claims, however, that the Government used
the "bank deposits/cash expenditures" method. When using that indirect
method of proof, the Government shows, either through increases in net
worth, increases in bank deposits, or the presence of cash expenditures,
that the taxpayer's wealth grew during a tax year beyond what could be
attributed to the taxpayer's reported income, thereby raising the
inference of unreported income.

In any indirect method case, the Government must prove that the
increased wealth did not come from non-taxable sources. Otherwise the
evidence will be insufficient, for there is always the possibility that the
taxpayer deposited cash that he received from a non-taxable source or
from income taxed in a prior year but kept on hand as cash or even from
unreported income from a prior year kept on hand in cash. Such events
are common human occurrences, and this possibility may of itself create
reasonable doubt. Therefore, the government must establish in some
fashion the amount of cash the taxpayer had on hand at the start of the
period. This is part of the government's duty to negate the possibility
that bank deposits or cash expenditures in the year under investigation

originated from non-taxable sources. United States v. Boulet, 577 F.2d 1165, 1168 (5th Cir. 1978).

On the other hand, where the Government's case is based on evidence showing *specific items* of unreported income, the safeguards required for indirect methods of proof are not necessary, as the possibility that the defendant may be convicted because non-taxable income is mistakenly presumed to be taxable income, or because cash expenditures are mistakenly assumed to be made from taxable income, is not present.[2] See United States v. Lewis, 759 F.2d 1316, 1328 (8th Cir. 1985) (Proof of opening net worth not required in case involving both net worth and specific-item methods); Conford v. United States, 336 F.2d 285, 287 (10th Cir. 1964) (rule of Holland v. United States, 348 U.S. 121, 99 L.Ed. 150, 75 S.Ct. 127 (1954), requiring proof of net worth, not applicable where expenditures evidence used only to corroborate specific items proof).

Black claims that the Government relied on a bank deposits/cash expenditures method of proof, but utterly failed to rebut the possibility that his expenditures originated from non-taxable sources, and therefore the evidence was insufficient to sustain a conviction. In particular, Black maintains that the Government was obliged to negate the possibility that his bank deposits and cash expenditures were from non-income sources, and to establish his opening net worth for the years in question. Black, moreover, argues that the jury instructions omitted necessary explanations of the assumptions inherent in indirect methods of proof, and of the inferences that may properly be made by the jury, all in violation of the Supreme Court's clear guidance in Holland v. United States, 348 U.S. 121, 99 L.Ed. 150, 75 S.Ct. 127 (1954). In short, Black claims the Government tried to convict him of tax evasion "by simply showing that he spent money and did not file a tax return during the tax years in question."

The Government's response is that since it introduced evidence of *specific items* of *income* received by Black, it was not required to disprove the likelihood of a cash hoard or a non-taxable source of income. From approximately 1975 to the time of the trial, Black was subject to an IRS lien of approximately three million dollars. During this time, Black created two corporations, Dunbar and Machine-A-Rama, portrayed by the Government as dummy corporations which had neither paid employees nor offices. At trial, Black disputed the bogus nature of these entities, claiming the corporations were involved in developing a casino in Atlantic City – a project which never materialized – and he also

---

2. There remains, of course, the possibility that legitimate deductions would cancel out the unreported income, but no such claim is made in this case.

insisted that any money he took from these corporations was in the form of loans which he felt obligated to repay. Nevertheless, it was uncontroverted that during the period covered by the indictment Black had no personal bank accounts and that many of Black's personal expenses were paid by checks drawn on accounts of these two corporations. Black further conceded that he created Dunbar because he did not want to put property in his own name and because he wished to conceal from the IRS money he was spending.

In the Government's view, Black received taxable income each time he wrote a check on the accounts of Dunbar and Machine-A-Rama to cover his personal expenses. Evidence that Black paid for personal expenses with checks drawn on corporate accounts and that Black never truly considered the checks to be loans would be sufficient for conviction, for "all the law requires is that there be proof sufficient to establish that there has been a receipt of taxable income by the accused and a willful evasion of the tax thereon." United States v. Nunan, 236 F.2d 576, 586 (2d Cir. 1956).[3]

Black, by focusing on isolated remarks at trial, argues that the Government presented only a cash expenditures case against him. We disagree. If the statements by the prosecutor, the testimony of the Government's tax witness, and the trial judge's instructions to the jury, are each considered in light of the evidence actually submitted, it is clear that the Government presented direct proof that Black received specific items of taxable income and did not pay tax on that income.

In the brief part of his opening statement devoted to the tax charge, the prosecutor told the jury the Government would show that, during the years in question, Black had personal expenditures of $538,000, that the Government would prove this by evidence of checks made out for personal expenses, and that the expenditures were taxable income, as distinguished from non-taxable expenses.[4] The prosecutor then proceeded to list some of the expenditures, which included rent for an apartment at the Watergate complex in Washington, D.C., purchases of jewelry, payments to restaurants, and then reiterated that these expenditures were personal – not business related. And at the close of the trial, the prosecutor summed up the tax case by describing it as based on Black's expenditures for "personal purposes, as against any so-

----

3. Black did not suggest that the checks represented a non-income producing distribution of corporate funds, such as a return of capital; his defense was that the checks were personal loans.

4. The Government asserted only that clearly personal expenditures made out of the corporate accounts were income to Black, giving Black the benefit of the doubt on expenditures that could arguably have been business related. And Black does not argue on appeal that the Government wrongly classified any expenditures as personal rather than business related.

called business purpose." While the prosecutor did in fact refer to personal expenditures, he did so to distinguish checks Black wrote that could arguably have been to cover business expenses related to Machine-A-Rama and Dunbar (and so did not result in specific items of income to Black), from checks Black wrote to cover personal expenses, which on the prosecutor's theory did result in income.

The Government's tax case against Black was presented largely through the testimony of James May, an IRS agent. Explaining how he arrived at a figure for Black's taxable income for 1979, the witness said:

> basically, I did an analysis of all expenditures from the [checking] account of Dunbar and Machine-A-Rama for the year 1979. I broke those into categories of personal expenditures for the benefit of Mr. Black or his family members, and then those which could be classified as business in nature, and all of those checks to cash. And I used those personal expenditures to arrive at a gross income figure.

Later, the witness again explained his method of calculating Black's income as "a[n] expenditures method based on expenditures or disbursements from the accounts of Dunbar and Machine-A-Rama." Just as did the prosecutor, May referred to personal expenditures and the expenditures method, but he was using that term merely to distinguish business from personal expenditures. The personal expenditures Black paid for by corporate checks were not circumstantial evidence of income from some hidden source; on the Government's theory the checks were themselves the specific items of income.

Similarly, in his charge to the jury, the trial judge also referred to the purposes for which these checks were written:

> in order to prove the defendant received substantial additional income which was not disclosed to the Internal Revenue Service, the prosecution relies upon proof by the "Bank Deposit/Expenditures Method" – that is, the Government has examined the sources of the funds deposited into the bank accounts of Dunbar and Machine-A-Rama for the tax years in question. The Government has also examined all of the checks written by Mr. Black on the Dunbar management and Machine-A-Rama accounts, as well as the purpose for those expenditures. As you will recall from the evidence presented during the case, there were numerous stipulations agreed to by the Government and Mr. Black describing checks written by him or at his direction to various payees for Mr. Black's own personal use and benefit.

While there were several explicit references to the "personal expenditures method" by the prosecutor, the Government's witness, and the trial judge in his instructions, at no point in the trial was it suggested to the jury that evidence of personal expenditures, without more, would be sufficient to convict Black of tax evasion. Evidence of personal expenditures was relevant only because the Government contended that the very writing of the checks created income to Black. Thus, the danger encountered in a classic "cash expenditure" case – that the defendant could be convicted for spending non-taxable income – is not at all present here. See United States v. Meriwether, 486 F.2d 498, 505 (5th Cir. 1973) (failure to include figures for net worth or cash on hand at beginning of taxable years cannot prejudice defendant in a specific items case). In this case, the use of the phrase "personal expenditures method" was not associated at all with the "cash expenditures method" of proving tax evasion; the phrase was used solely to distinguish Black's business expenditures from his personal expenditures.

During the trial, moreover, Black's counsel undoubtedly understood the Government was not presenting a cash expenditures case, for no objection was made to the jury instructions given by the trial judge, and yet those instructions would have been inadequate had the Government relied on a cash expenditures method of proof.

Black's defense to the tax charge was not that the expenditures were made from a source of non-taxable income unknown to the Government, for example an inheritance or a sum of cash squirreled away in previous years, yet that would be a typical defense in a cash expenditures case.[5]

The claim, however, the jury was entitled to reject, as their verdict indicates they did. Viewing the evidence most favorably to the Government, the Government established that Black received substantial taxable income that he did not report to the IRS. We thus decline to reverse Black's conviction on the grounds of insufficient evidence.

Black also challenges the adequacy of the trial judge's instructions. But because no objection was made to the instructions at trial, we may reverse only if we find plain error. FED. R. CRIM. P. 30, 52(b). It is true that the trial judge's reference to the "bank deposits/expenditures method" was misconceived, but nevertheless the instructions did direct the jury to that part of the Government's case concerning the checks written by Black on the accounts of Dunbar and Machine-A-Rama, and the stipulations that the checks were written for Black's personal use

---

5.   Of course the burden is initially on the Government to investigate and make a reasonable attempt to negate the possibility that the expenditures are from a non-taxable source. See United States v. Bianco, 534 F.2d 501, 504-06 (2d Cir. 1976). But "once the Government has established its case, the defendant remains quiet at his peril." *Holland*, 348 U.S. at 138-39.

and benefit. In addition, Black's counsel, in his closing argument, reiterated Black's claim that these checks were actually loans. We think, therefore, the jury was properly apprised of the issue to be resolved. Considering the strength of the Government's evidence against Black, the uncontested personal nature of the expenditures, and the incredibility of Black's claim that he considered the transactions to be loans, we do not believe any shortcomings in the instructions rose to the level of plain error affecting substantial rights.

We thus reject Black's argument that under the reasoning of United States v. Meriwether, 440 F.2d 753 (5th Cir. 1971), we should reverse because the jury might have convicted Black merely because he spent money. In *Meriwether* the jury was instructed on both a specific items and net worth method of proof, with the emphasis placed on the net worth method. The court of appeals reversed because the instructions on the net worth method were flawed and there was "no way to be certain upon which method of proof the jury based its verdict of guilty." Id. at 757. In this case, however, the jury was never instructed on the cash expenditures method, nor was it ever argued to the jury that Black could be convicted on the theory that cash expenditures were circumstantial evidence of taxable income. Ironically, a tax lawyer sitting in the courtroom could perhaps have been confused by the use of the phrase "personal expenditures method," for it might well have suggested the cash expenditures method, but the slight possibility that a jury never instructed on the cash expenditures method would have been confused is so insignificant that it cannot justify a reversal on grounds of plain error.

Appellant's conviction is therefore *affirmed*.

Notes and Questions

One of the most common defenses to the allegation that the taxpayer had unreported income is the existence of a cash horde or savings attributable to previous taxable years. Since this is difficult for the government to refute, once the government establishes the existence of an unreported increase in net worth and that there is a likely source for this increase, the burden shifts to the taxpayer to explain the existence of the horde. In the case of Holland v. United States, 348 U.S. 121, 75 S.Ct. 127, 99 L.Ed. 150 (1954), cited in *Black*, the Supreme Court stated: "Any other rule would burden the Government with investigating the many possible nontaxable sources of income, each of which is as unlikely as it is difficult to prove. This is not to say that the Government may disregard explanations of the defendant reasonably susceptible of being checked. But where relevant leads are not forthcoming, the Government is not required to negate every possible source of nontaxable income, a matter peculiarly within the knowledge of the defendant." Id. at 138, 75 S.Ct. at 137.

1. Under what circumstances is the government most likely to use the net worth method? The cash expenditures method? The bank deposits method?

2. How does the government establish the amount of cash the taxpayer had on hand (or the net worth of the taxpayer) at the start of the taxable period?

3. The indirect methods of proof generally are effective only where the underpayment is a large one. Why?

b) Attempt to Evade

1) Distinction Between Misdemeanor and Felony Offenses

SPIES v. UNITED STATES
Supreme Court of the United States, 1943.
317 U.S. 492, 63 S.Ct. 364, 87 L.Ed. 418.

MR. JUSTICE JACKSON delivered the opinion of the Court.

Petitioner has been convicted of attempting to defeat and evade income tax, in violation of § 145(b) of the * * * Internal Revenue Code. [Eds.: Section 145(b) of the Internal Revenue Code of 1939 is the precursor of § 7201 of the Internal Revenue Code of 1986, while § 145(a) is the precursor of current § 7203].

* * *

Petitioner admitted at the opening of the trial that he had sufficient income during the year in question to place him under a statutory duty to file a return and to pay a tax, and that he failed to do either. The evidence during nearly two weeks of trial was directed principally toward establishing the exact amount of the tax and the manner of receiving and handling income and accounting, which the Government contends shows an intent to evade or defeat the tax. * * *

Section 145(a) makes, among other things, willful failure to pay a tax or make a return by one having petitioner's income at the time or times required by law a misdemeanor.[1] Section 145(b) makes a willful attempt in any manner to evade or defeat any tax such as his a felony.[2]

The petitioner requested an instruction that "You may not find the defendant guilty of a willful attempt to defeat and evade the income tax, if you find only that he had willfully failed to make a return of taxable income and has willfully failed to pay the tax on that income." This was refused, and the Court charged that "If you find that the defendant had a net income for 1936 upon which some income tax was due, and I believe that is conceded, if you find that the defendant willfully failed to file an income tax return for that year, if you find that the defendant willfully failed to pay the tax due on his income for that year, you may, if you find that the facts and circumstances warrant it find that the defendant willfully attempted to evade or defeat the tax." The Court refused a request to instruct that an affirmative act was necessary to constitute a willful attempt, and charged that "Attempt means to try to do or accomplish. In order to find an attempt it is not necessary to find affirmative steps to accomplish the prohibited purpose. An attempt may be found on the basis of inactivity or on refraining to act, as well."

It is the Government's contention that a willful failure to file a return, together with a willful failure to pay the tax, may, without more, constitute an attempt to defeat or evade a tax within § 145(b). Petitioner claims that such proof establishes only two misdemeanors under § 145(b). The legislative history of the section contains nothing helpful on the question here at issue, and we must find the answer from the section itself and its context in the revenue laws.

* * *

The penalties imposed by Congress to enforce the tax laws embrace both civil and criminal sanctions. The former consist of additions to the tax upon determinations of fact made by an administrative agency and with no burden on the Government to prove its case beyond a reasonable

---

1.   "Any person required under this title to pay any tax, or required by law or regulations made under authority thereof to make a return, keep any records, or supply any information, for the purposes of the computation, assessment, or collection of any tax imposed by this title, who willfully fails to pay such tax, make such return, keep such records, or supply such information, at the time or times required by law or regulations, shall, in addition to other penalties provided by law, be guilty of a misdemeanor and, upon conviction thereof, be fined not more than $10,000, or imprisoned for not more than one year, or both, together with the costs of prosecution."

2.   "Any person required under this title to collect, account for, and pay over any tax imposed by this title, who willfully fails to collect or truthfully account for and pay over such tax, and any person who willfully attempts in any manner to evade or defeat any tax imposed by this title or the payment thereof, shall, in addition to other penalties provided by law, be guilty of a felony and, upon conviction thereof, be fined not more than $10,000, or imprisoned for not more than five years, or both, together with the costs of prosecution."

doubt. The latter consist of penal offenses enforced by the criminal process in the familiar manner. Invocation of one does not exclude resort to the other. Helvering v. Mitchell, 303 U.S. 391.

The failure in a duty to make a timely return, unless it is shown that such failure is due to reasonable cause and not due to willful neglect, is punishable by an addition to the tax of 5 to 25 per cent thereof, depending on the duration of the default. But a duty may exist even when there is no tax liability to serve as a base for application of a percentage delinquency penalty; the default may relate to matters not identifiable with tax for a particular period; and the offense may be more grievous than a case for civil penalty. Hence the willful failure to make a return, keep records, or supply information when required, is made a misdemeanor, without regard to existence of a tax liability. Punctuality is important to the fiscal system, and these are sanctions to assure punctual as well as faithful performance of these duties.

Sanctions to insure payment of the tax are even more varied to meet the variety of causes of default. It is the right as well as the interest of the taxpayer to limit his admission of liability to the amount he actually owes. But the law is complicated, accounting treatment of various items raises problems of great complexity, and innocent errors are numerous, as appears from the number who make overpayments. It is not the purpose of the law to penalize frank difference of opinion or innocent errors made despite the exercise of reasonable care. Such errors are corrected by the assessment of the deficiency of tax and its collection with interest for the delay. If any part of the deficiency is due to negligence or intentional disregard of rules and regulations, but without intent to defraud, five per cent of such deficiency is added thereto; and if any part of any deficiency is due to fraud with intent to evade tax, the addition is 50 per cent thereof. Willful failure to pay the tax when due is punishable as a misdemeanor. The climax of this variety of sanctions is the serious and inclusive felony defined to consist of willful attempt in any manner to evade or defeat the tax. The question here is whether there is a distinction between the acts necessary to make out the felony and those which may make out the misdemeanor.

A felony may, and frequently does, include lesser offenses in combination either with each other or with other elements. We think it clear that this felony may include one or several of the other offenses against the revenue laws. But it would be unusual and we would not readily assume that Congress by the felony defined in § 145(b) meant no more than the same derelictions it had just defined in § 145(a) as a misdemeanor. Such an interpretation becomes even more difficult to accept when we consider this felony as the capstone of a system of sanctions which singly or in combination were calculated to include prompt and forthright fulfillment of every duty under the income tax law and to provide a penalty suitable to every degree of delinquency.

The difference between willful failure to pay a tax when due, which is made a misdemeanor, and willful attempt to defeat and evade one, which is made a felony, is not easy to detect or define. Both must be willful. And willful, as we have said, is a word of many meanings, its construction often being influenced by its context. United States v. Murdock, 290 U.S. 389. It may well mean something more as applied to nonpayment of a tax than when applied to failure to make a return. Mere voluntary and purposeful, as distinguished from accidental, omission to make a timely return might meet the test of willfulness. But in view of our traditional aversion to imprisonment for debt, we would not without the clearest manifestation of Congressional intent assume that mere knowing and intentional default in payment of a tax, where there had been no willful failure to disclose the liability, is intended to constitute a criminal offense of any degree. We would expect willfulness in such a case to include some element of evil motive and want of justification in view of all the financial circumstances of the taxpayer.

* * *

The difference between the two offenses, it seems to us, is found in the affirmative action implied from the term "attempt," as used in the felony subsection. It is not necessary to involve this subject with the complexities of the common-law "attempt." The attempt made criminal by this statute does not consist of conduct that would culminate in a more serious crime but for some impossibility of completion or interruption or frustration. This is an independent crime, complete in its most serious form when the attempt is complete, and nothing is added to its criminality by success or consummation, as would be the case, say, of attempted murder. Although the attempt succeeds in evading tax, there is no criminal offense of that kind, and the prosecution can be only for the attempt. We think that in employing the terminology of attempt to embrace the gravest of offenses against the revenues, Congress intended some willful commission in addition to the willful omissions that make up the list of misdemeanors. Willful but passive neglect of the statutory duty may constitute the lesser offense, but to combine with it a willful and positive attempt to evade tax in any manner or to defeat it by any means lifts the offense to the degree of felony.

Congress did not define or limit the methods by which a willful attempt to defeat and evade might be accomplished and perhaps did not define lest its effort to do so result in some unexpected limitation. Nor would we by definition constrict the scope of the Congressional provision that it may be accomplished "in any manner." By way of illustration, and not by way of limitation, we would think affirmative willful attempt may be inferred from conduct such as keeping a double set of books, making false entries or alterations, or false invoices or documents, destruction of books or records, concealment of assets or covering up sources of income, handling of one's affairs to avoid making the records usual in transactions of the kind, and any conduct, the likely effect of which would be to mislead or to conceal. If the tax-evasion motive plays any part in such conduct the offense may be made out even though the conduct may also serve other purposes such as concealment of other crime.

In this case there are several items of evidence apart from the default in filing the return and paying the tax which the Government claims will support an inference of willful attempt to evade or defeat the tax. These go to establish that petitioner insisted that certain income be paid to him in cash, transferred it to his own bank by armored car, deposited it, not in his own name but in the names of others of his family, and kept inadequate and misleading records. Petitioner claims other motives animated him in these matters. We intimate no opinion. Such inferences are for the jury. If on proper submission the jury found these acts, taken together with willful failure to file a return and willful failure to pay the tax, to constitute a willful attempt to evade or defeat the tax, we would consider conviction of a felony sustainable. But we think a defendant is entitled to a charge which will point out the necessity for such an inference of willful attempt to defeat or evade the tax from some proof in the case other than that necessary to make out the misdemeanors; and if the evidence fails to afford such an inference, the defendant should be acquitted.

The Government argues against this construction, contending that the milder punishment of misdemeanor and the benefits of a short statute of limitation should not be extended to violators of the income tax laws such as political grafters, gamblers, racketeers, and gangsters. We doubt that this construction will handicap prosecution for felony of such flagrant violators. Few of them, we think, in their efforts to escape tax, stop with the mere omission of the duties put upon them by the statute, but if such there be, they are entitled to be convicted only of the offense which they have committed.

Reversed.

Notes and Question

The evasion statute applies to "any person" who willfully attempts to evade or defeat any tax. IRC § 7201. The tax code defines "person" under § 7701(a)(1) as an individual, a trust, estate, partnership, association, company, or corporation. Thus, the evasion provision may apply to the preparer, attorney, accountant, corporate officer, or other professional who attempts to evade or defeat a tax liability. If the professional gives advice that enables a taxpayer to evade tax, the professional also may be prosecuted as a principal under the aiding and abetting statute, 18 U.S.C. § 2, and under the conspiracy statute, 18 U.S.C. § 371, if there is an agreement to evade tax liability. See §§ I.A.3(b) and II.A., below.

If a taxpayer has willfully failed to file a federal tax return or pay a tax, or has filed a false and fraudulent federal tax return, the chances are that the individual has committed the same offense at the state level. If so, does the constitutional principle of double jeopardy apply, or can both the state and federal governments prosecute the individual for the same offense? See United States v. Wheeler, 435 U.S. 313, 98 S.Ct. 1079, 55 L.Ed2d 303 (1978); Abbate v. United States, 359 U.S. 187, 79 S.Ct. 666, 3 L.Ed.2d 729 (1959); Bartkus v. United States, 359 U.S. 121, 79 S.Ct. 676, 3 L.Ed.2d 684 (1959).

2) Acts of Evasion

UNITED STATES v. McGILL
United States Court of Appeals, Third Circuit, 1992.
964 F.2d 222.

ROTH, CIRCUIT JUDGE.

I.
* * *

B. Facts
* * *

McGill is a self-employed attorney in Philadelphia. During the decade 1980 through 1990, he received income from three sources: private criminal defense work, for which he was paid in cash and by personal check; court appointments to represent indigent criminal defendants, for which he was paid, upon submitting vouchers, by the City of Philadelphia (the City); and service as an appointed member of a Pennsylvania commission[7] for which he received a stipend from the Commonwealth.

For each of the years 1980 through 1987, McGill filed federal income tax returns indicating taxes due. There is no dispute as to the accuracy

---

7. McGill served as a representative to the Commissioner of the Pennsylvania Human Relations Commission, a position which he resigned in February of 1990.

of McGill's tax forms. However, he failed to include with his returns payment of any of the tax which he admittedly owed.

In 1983 the Internal Revenue Service (IRS) directed McGill to pay his 1978 taxes and file returns for the years 1979-1982. He submitted the overdue returns, and acknowledged amounts due, but remitted no payment. The IRS then in 1984 issued levies against McGill's two personal bank accounts. The banks informed the IRS that no funds were available in these accounts. In May 1985, the IRS again issued levies against McGill's two personal bank accounts, and also against McGill's fees from the Commonwealth and the City. McGill was aware of the levies from the time they were imposed, as he acknowledged in a meeting with the IRS in late May 1985.

After the 1985 levies were imposed, McGill ceased using his personal bank accounts. Those accounts were later closed by the Banks. McGill deposited and wrote checks on an account in his wife's name[9] (the Lillie account) and on a joint account which he and several other lawyers had established for the purpose of handling common expenses for office space they shared (the McGill & Seay account). The IRS had no record of the Lillie and the McGill & Seay accounts. McGill testified that he used the family and the business accounts because he thought his two personal accounts had been closed. At the same time, he admitted at trial that he used the business account "thinking that the IRS wouldn't bother the money."

McGill made one attempt in 1986 to settle his debts with the IRS: he hired an attorney and prepared an Offer in Compromise (OIC) of his tax liability. He filed financial disclosure forms in connection with the OIC in late May 1986. The record contains conflicting information about the adequacy of the disclosure forms, none of which is before us. IRS Agent Kroll assured the trial court that McGill had provided him with information about all bank accounts, but the Government alleged in oral argument that McGill failed to include the McGill & Seay account with the filing. The OIC was finally withdrawn after the IRS suggested that the proposed level of payment was too low.[12] The IRS further noted that McGill had made no effort to pay his current year's (1986) estimated taxes, a prerequisite for a good faith OIC. McGill asserted that he could not pay his 1986 taxes because most of his earnings–his income from the Commonwealth and the City–were subject to IRS levies.

---

   9. McGill's wife is also an attorney who has held positions with the federal government and with the City of Philadelphia.

   12. McGill proposed paying $16,000 on a debt then amounting with penalties and interest to approximately $70,000.

During the period from January 1986 until January 1987, when the OIC was being negotiated, McGill on the advice of counsel did not submit expense vouchers to the City. Thus, the IRS received no levy payments from the City in that year. McGill submitted the entire year's vouchers–worth approximately $5,000–after he withdrew his Offer In Compromise. Of this amount, approximately $3,700 went to the IRS.

In 1987, McGill sent a $3,000 check to the IRS. He was seeking election to a local judgeship at the time. This was the only non-levy payment McGill made to the IRS between April 1985 and March 1990, the period relevant to the indictment.[13]

In March 1988, the Government instituted a criminal tax investigation of McGill. McGill continued to accept court appointments from the City. The IRS kept the income levied from these City appointments in a "suspense account" while pursuing the criminal charges. At the time of trial, the suspense account contained nearly $30,000. None of these funds was allocated toward McGill's liability for the tax years charged in the indictment (1980 through 1987).[15]

In about August 1988, five months after the Government initiated its criminal investigation, McGill opened a checking account in his own name at the Philadelphia Savings Fund Society (the PSFS account). He testified at trial that he opened the account "because my attorney advised me that questions were being raised about my use of the McGill & Seay account." The IRS was not initially aware of the PSFS account.[16]

At about the same time, approximately $9,000 of McGill's fees from the City were not captured by the IRS levy but were sent directly to him. McGill contacted the City Comptroller's Office to inquire about his receipt of these funds. As a result, the remaining $1,000 then due to him from the City was sent directly to the IRS. It appears that McGill deposited the $9,000 in one of his accounts and did not forward any part

---

13. In fact, the $3,000 was the only voluntary payment McGill made to the IRS during the decade 1980-1990.

15. The IRS has a policy of holding levied income in a separate account until criminal investigations are concluded. During the criminal investigation, the IRS applied approximately $22,000 of McGill's ongoing levy receipts to his delinquent 1978 and 1979 taxes. These years were not part of the indictment. The 1978 taxes, plus penalties and interest, were paid off in 1987, and the 1979 tax liability was finally discharged in 1989.

16. The IRS claims that they should have been notified of the PSFS account. At trial, however, a former IRS employee testified that a taxpayer does not have an obligation to volunteer information to the IRS, even where the information contained in a previously-filed financial statement has changed. As noted infra, we decline to impose an affirmative reporting duty as opposed to a duty to respond truthfully, upon taxpayers who are in arrears in their payments.

of it to the IRS.[17] He did, however, claim that he declared the money as income on his income tax return for that year.

In the fall of 1989, McGill took a part-time job as a law clerk to a Philadelphia judge, at a salary of about $25,000. He has also continued to take court appointments from the City.

The total amount of moneys which the IRS levied from McGill during the period up to his trial is in dispute. The IRS contends that a total of $57,746.88 was levied. McGill claims that the total levy was over $75,000. The main part of the discrepancy apparently lies in certain fees which the City has indicated were sent to the IRS but which at the time of McGill's trial had not been recorded as received by the IRS.

II.

McGill was charged under 26 U.S.C. § 7201 with five counts of attempted evasion of payment of tax. He was convicted of three counts of felony evasion and of two counts of the lesser offense of willful failure to pay taxes under 26 U.S.C. § 7203.

The elements of the felony of attempted evasion of payment of tax under § 7201 are three: 1) the existence of a tax deficiency, 2) an affirmative act constituting an attempt to evade or defeat payment of the tax, and 3) willfulness. Sansone v. United States, 380 U.S. 343, 351 (1965). Willful failure to pay tax under § 7203 contains two elements: 1) failure to pay a tax when due, and 2) willfulness.

A. Tax Deficiency

The first element in a § 7201 offense is a tax due and owing. *Sansone,* 380 U.S. at 351. There is no dispute that McGill owes taxes in the amount of $46,910. He has contemporaneously satisfied the first element of § 7203, by failing to pay the amounts owed according to the returns he has filed.

B. Affirmative Acts

Section 7201 further requires proof of an affirmative act of evasion. One act will suffice. McGill argues that the Government did not prove that he committed affirmative acts of evasion during each time period charged. The Government asserts that McGill met the threshold for

---

17. The record does not in fact contain evidence of the fate of the $9,000. See text of footnote 24, infra.

felony evasion under § 7201 when 1) after learning that the IRS had placed a levy on his assets to recover unpaid taxes, he ceased using the personal bank accounts and instead deposited and withdrew money from the Lillie and the McGill & Seay accounts; and 2) he opened the PSFS account without informing the IRS and deposited $9,000 in fee checks from the City. Additionally, the Government maintains that the jury could have inferred affirmative acts of evasion from the consistent pattern of cash withdrawals from the Lillie account, even after deposits attributable to McGill had ceased.

Our review of the sufficiency of the evidence is "governed by strict principles of deference to a jury's findings." When a motion for judgment of acquittal brought on a claim of insufficient evidence to support a conviction is denied, this court must sustain the verdict if "any rational trier of fact could have found the essential elements of the crime beyond a reasonable doubt." The reviewing court must simply determine whether "the conclusion chosen by the factfinders was permissible."

1. Evasiveness

McGill alleges that the charged acts–the use of the Lillie and the McGill & Seay accounts, and the opening of the PSFS account–are not affirmative acts of evasion within the meaning of 26 U.S.C. § 7201.

An affirmative act is anything done to mislead the government or conceal funds to avoid payment of an admitted and accurate deficiency. The offense is complete when a single willful act of evasion has occurred. Section 7201 explicitly refers to "attempts [to evade] in any manner." 26 U.S.C. § 7201. Generally, affirmative acts associated with evasion of payment involve some type of concealment of the taxpayer's ability to pay his or her taxes or the removal of assets from the reach of the Internal Revenue Service. Thus, "any conduct, the likely effect of which would be to mislead or to conceal" is sufficient to establish an affirmative act of evasion. Spies v. United States, 317 U.S. 492, 499 (1943).

Section 7201 encompasses two kinds of affirmative behavior: the evasion of assessment and the evasion of payment. Evasion of assessment cases are far more common. The affirmative act requirement in such a case is satisfied, *inter alia*, with the filing of a false return. See, e.g., *Sansone*, 380 U.S. at 351-52. If the false filing is shown to be willful, the offense is complete with the filing. Evasion of payment cases are rare, and the required affirmative act generally occurs after the filing, if there is a filing at all. United States v. Mal, 942 F.2d 682, 687 (9th Cir. 1991)(evasion of payment "involves conduct designed to place assets beyond the government's reach *after* a tax liability has been assessed")(emphasis added).　　McGill was charged with evasion of payment.

Affirmative acts of evasion of *payment* include: placing assets in the name of others; dealing in currency; causing receipts to be paid through and in the name of others and causing debts to be paid through and in the name of others. For example, in *Spies*, the petitioner "insisted that certain income be paid to him in cash, transferred it to his own bank by armored car, deposited it, not in his own name but in the names of *others of his family,* and kept inadequate and misleading records." The Supreme Court found this evidence sufficient to sustain a finding of attempted evasion. *Spies*, 317 U.S. at 499 (emphasis added). In *Conley,* the Court of Appeals for the Seventh Circuit affirmed a § 7201 conviction where the defendant placed assets in his sons' names, deposited his assets with others, dealt in currency, and paid creditors but not the government. *Conley*, 826 F.2d at 557. See United States v. Voorhies, 658 F.2d 710, 714 (9th Cir. 1981)(affirming § 7201 conviction where defendant traveled out of country on three occasions in one year, carrying over $80,000 in negotiable assets, did not declare these amounts to customs, and was later unable to account for use of large amount of cash and gold coins); United States v. Hook, 781 F.2d 1166 (6th Cir. 1986)(affirming § 7201 conviction where the defendant did most of his business in cash, used credit cards belonging to others, and bought a house in his girlfriend's name).

Merely failing to pay assessed taxes, without more, however, does not constitute evasion of payment, though it may satisfy the requirements for the willful failure to pay taxes under § 7203. *Sansone*, 380 U.S. at 351; United States v. Romano, 938 F.2d 1569, 1573 (2d Cir. 1991). Only affirmatively evasive acts–acts intending to conceal–are punishable under § 7201.[18]

* * *

3. Acts of Evasion: Count 6

For Count 6, the alleged act of evasion is McGill's use of certain bank accounts beginning on April 15, 1986. After the IRS issued levies on both of McGill's personal bank accounts in 1985, he ceased using those accounts and instead deposited funds into and drew checks on the Lillie account and the McGill & Seay account.

18.　The government advises its attorneys that "obstinately refusing to pay taxes due, possession of the funds needed to pay the taxes, or even the open assignment of the income, without more, merely constitute a willful failure to pay taxes * * *. They do not meet the requirement of the affirmative act necessary for an evasion charge." U.S. Dept. of Justice, Criminal Tax Manual, § 8.04 at 8-7, 8-8 (6th Ed. 1985).

IRS Special Agent Isabella performed a detailed analysis of the Lillie and the McGill & Seay accounts. * * * McGill's use of the Lillie account decreased between 1985 and 1988, in both absolute dollars and as a percentage of total deposits. His use of the McGill & Seay account is more sporadic. Agent Isabella testified that McGill used the accounts "as you and I would use our own personal checking accounts."

McGill testified that he knew once the levies took effect that any money he put into an account in his own name "would be taken." He put funds into the McGill & Seay account "thinking that the IRS wouldn't bother the money." He admitted that he saw income taxes as "another bill that I didn't have the money to pay."

On the other hand, he also testified that he thought this two personal bank accounts had been closed by the banks after the levies were imposed:

Thinking that [one of the personal accounts] was closed and that the Provident Bank account was closed, I still had bills to pay. I had office expenses, as well as expenses at home that had to be paid an so I began using the McGill [& Seay] account to pay business expenses and the account—my wife's account to pay bills at home.

* * * Agent Isabella admitted that there were no luxury items on the list of expenses paid from the Lillie account on behalf of McGill. McGill himself commented that he did not lead a luxurious lifestyle, and that he "wasn't trying to escape anything."

The Government alleges that McGill's shift in bank accounts constituted an affirmative act of evasion of payment. McGill did not tell the IRS of the existence of the Lillie and the McGill & Seay accounts.[22] The Government argues that it could not have discovered the accounts because his wife's name was "different from his, " and "that the McGill & Seay account bore McGill's surname made it no more identifiable as his than would be the case for any other account bearing that not-uncommon name."

McGill counters that the use of these accounts cannot be an affirmative act because he did not act with evasive intent. He argues that it is unlikely one could "conceal" assets in an account partially in one's own name (McGill & Seay) or in an account bearing the name of one's spouse, especially when these accounts were fully reachable by the IRS. At trial, IRS Special Agent Kroll, who reviewed McGill's OIC,

---

22. There is evidence that McGill was asked and failed to disclose the existence of a "business account" to the IRS, either under the name McGill & Seay or Clark, McGill & Seay. While on the facts of this case an "omission" of this sort cannot amount to an affirmative "act" of evasion under § 7201, the information is relevant to a determination of willfulness.

testified that he did not believe that McGill was concealing any information about the money he was receiving. Further, Kroll admitted that he did not ask McGill where he banked, instead "assuming" that McGill was using his "attorney's" account.

We are not presented here with evasion of the magnitude of *Spies, Voorhies,* or *Conley,* supra. However, in *Spies,* the Supreme Court specifically included as an affirmative act of evasion deposits into an account registered to a family member. The *Conley* court found similar conduct objectionable. *Conley,* 826 F.2d at 557 (defendant used his son's name on a bank account he opened for personal use). Banking under the name of one's spouse satisfies the affirmative act requirement under § 7201. By analogy, banking though a business account containing the names of others also suffices as an affirmative act.

Thus, based on the rationale of *Spies* and *Conley,* the evidence is sufficient for the jury to find an act of evasion for, at minimum, Count 6. Any evasive behavior after April 15, 1986, satisfies the affirmative act requirement for this charge. McGill's substitute use of the Lillie and the McGill & Seay accounts began in mid-1985 and continued through to early 1988. While McGill's argument concerning a lack of evasive intent is perhaps plausible, a jury could have found evasive intent from his testimony ('I thought the IRS wouldn't bother the money') and his failure simply to set up another account in his own name. McGill's challenge to the sufficiency of the evidence of an act of evasion for Count 6 will be denied.

4. Acts of Evasion: Counts 7 & 8

McGill also disputes the Government's evidence of affirmative acts after May 15, 1988, the crucial period for Counts 7 and 8. The Government alleges that McGill opened the PSFS account in August of 1988, five months after the criminal investigation into his tax affairs had begun, and failed to report this account to the IRS. McGill allegedly deposited $9,000 of levied City fees into this account without forwarding any of the money to the IRS.

We find that, unless a taxpayer is in the situation of giving voluntary admissions during an investigation or a forced response to a subpoena, the failure of the taxpayer to report the opening of an account in his or her own name in his or her own locale cannot amount to an affirmative act of evasion. Omissions, including failures to report, do not satisfy the requirements of § 7201; the Government must prove a specific act to mislead or conceal. See *Spies,* 317 U.S. at 499; *Romano,* 938 F.2d at 1572-73 (failure to report income is not by itself an affirmative act of evasion). McGill testified that he opened the account on the advice of counsel in response to IRS criticism for banking under the names of others. There is no evidence that McGill concealed this new account from the IRS apart from the fact that he did not inform the IRS of its existence.

The Government also cites as an affirmative act of evasion McGill's retention, allegedly in 1988, of $9,000 in City checks subject to levy. This action, if it occurred, does not suffice as an affirmative act under § 7201. Supposedly, McGill received the funds and deposited them into the PSFS account, an act necessarily occurring after August 1988 when the account was opened. By extension of our holding above, however, the deposit of funds into an account in one's own name cannot be an affirmative act of evasion. Thus, on the facts presented by the Government, there was no evidence that McGill attempted to conceal these funds.[23]

In fact, McGill inquired as to why the City had sent the $9,000 to him; the City replied that it should not have done so and it forwarded the remaining $1,000 due McGill directly to the IRS.[24] Moreover, McGill apparently reported the money as income on his tax returns. Though he

---

23. We note that there is not clear proof in the record of the date McGill received the $9,000. IRS Agent Dollard noted in a letter to defense counsel, without mentioning the source of his information, that McGill deposited $9,200 in the PSFS account, which was not opened until 1988. During oral argument to this court, however, defense counsel asserted that the $9,000 was received in 1987 and most likely deposited in either the Lillie or the McGill & Seay account. In any case, McGill admits receiving $9,000 in levied City fees, and depositing the checks in a checking account.

Unlike the Lillie and the McGill & Seay accounts, we have no deposit analysis for the PSFS account, so we cannot know which party's assertions are correct. McGill's testimony refers only to $9,000 mistakenly received in "one year," without a specific date. He stated that, during this time, $9,000 went to him and "the rest of the money, another $1,000 or so, went to the IRS." Though McGill testified that he filed the $9,000 in his 1099 tax return that unknown year, the record does not contain such a return. We do not know the source of Agent Dollard's assertion to defense counsel that McGill deposited $9,200 in the (1988) PSFS account. McGill's W-2 form from the *Commonwealth* for 1988 discloses income totalling $10,200, but the Government had maintained throughout, and McGill himself testified, that the mistakenly-received funds were payments from the *City,* not from the Commonwealth.

The burden of proving an evasive act is on the Government. In regard to the $9,000 payment, the Government has not demonstrated that the $9,000 was ever deposited into the Lillie or the McGill & Seay accounts–either as proof of the offenses charged in Count 6 or of the offenses charged in Counts 7 or 8. Nor has the Government presented evidence that the $9,000 was deposited into or otherwise handled by McGill after May 15, 1988, in such a fashion as to constitute an act by him to mislead the Government or conceal the funds.

In the absence of any such proof of an evasive act, we decline to assume that the jury could have reasonably found McGill's treatment of the $9,000 to be affirmatively evasive

24. In fact, the 1985 levy issued on McGill's fees from the City was supposed to catch only those funds due McGill at that time. The levy was designed, not as an ongoing wage levy, but as an accounts receivable instrument. Revenue Officer Kroll acknowledged that the City was not technically required to remit future sums to the IRS, and that McGill had never told the City to stop sending payments.

did not surrender the money, he was not ordered to do so, and it appears that he had no affirmative obligation to report its receipt, albeit he did have an obligation to pay his taxes.[25]

* * *

On the facts of this case, McGill's use of the Lillie account becomes affirmative evasion only when he uses it to conceal his own funds. The jury could not conclude beyond a reasonable doubt that there were deposits of McGill's funds into the Lillie and McGill & Seay accounts after May 15, 1988. Nor could it conclude beyond a reasonable doubt that any of the funds in these accounts on and after that date were funds of McGill. The jury therefore could not find an affirmative act of evasion even if funds were disbursed from those accounts for the sole benefit of McGill. IRS Agent Isabella testified that the last deposit in the Lillie account of an item payable to McGill occurred on February 16, 1988. Moreover, we have no evidence that McGill took in any cash payments from private clients after May 15, 1988. If such payments existed, the evidence should have been easy to produce, as McGill's secretary testified that she issued a receipt for each cash payment received. Finally, there were cash transactions through the Lillie account during 1988, but there is no indication how many, if any, occurred after May 15. Assuming there was activity beyond May, none of the transactions has been affirmatively linked to McGill. The record contains only total deposit and withdrawal figures for all users in 1988.

Thus, the record contains no evidence that identifiable McGill transactions continued with respect to the alternative accounts after May 15, 1988.[26] No jury could have found beyond a reasonable doubt that the evidence after May 15, 1988 sufficed to prove evasion under § 7201.

The Government did not meet its burden of proving evasive acts for Counts 7 and 8. We will, therefore, reverse McGill's convictions on Counts 7 and 8, for insufficient evidence of affirmative acts of evasion during the relevant period.

5. Jury Instructions on Affirmative Acts

Alternatively, McGill argues that the jury instructions on affirmative acts were faulty on several grounds, and for this reason he requests that

---

25. McGill's failure to turn over the $9,000 to the IRS might, if willful, be a violation of § 7203. Without an affirmative act to mislead the government or to conceal the funds, however, such a failure to turn over the money would not be a violation of § 7201.

26. Evidence relating to the McGill & Seay account ends on March 4, 1988, making this account irrelevant to proof of affirmative acts under Counts 7 and 8.

we grant him a new trial. He contends, first, that the initial instructions were misleading–they suggested to the jury that a mere failure to pay taxes could constitute an affirmative act of evasion. Subsequent "amplification" by the court allegedly did not cure this fault. Second, McGill asserts that the charge did not include any affirmative acts of evasion relating to Counts 7 and 8 (1986 and 1987 tax years). The 1986 and 1987 taxes were delinquent as of May 15, 1988, the day the returns for both years were filed, and the only evasive behavior mentioned in the *charge* occurred prior to that date. Third, the judge instructed the jury that evasion of payment of tax was complete at the time a tax return is filed, while the Government's case focused on behavior subsequent to each filing.

* * *

a.

The jury was instructed twice on the tax charges. After the jury returned from a deadlock with questions, the trial judge repeated his initial instructions with modifications. Regarding affirmative acts, he stated:

> The first element of the offense which the Government must prove is an affirmative act constituting an attempt to evade or defeat taxes. A tax deficiency exists from the date a return is due to be filed, April 15th following each taxable year, for the calendar years up to and including 1983 through 1987 as named in the indictment.

> If you find that the defendant furnished information to his accountant showing the amount of income received for each year, signed and mailed or delivered a return for each year to the Internal Revenue Service Center showing the amount of taxes due; *and secondly, that there was an affirmative act to attempt to evade or defeat the payment of taxes,* yet willfully failed and refused to pay the taxes shown thereon to be due, the offense is complete for each year when the return is filed on or about April 15th and the taxes are not paid. *The affirmative act alleged by the Government was the diversion of the defendant's income from accounts in his name only to other accounts; specifically, the McGill and Seay account, and the Charisse Lillie account.*

The italicized portions were added after complaints by the defense and queries by the jury. Specifically, after the initial instructions the jury returned with two questions, 1) "Should we consider failing to file a return evasion of taxes as it applies to count four?" [tax years 1980-83, filed in 1985] and 2) "Is failing to include a check with your filed taxes simple evasion?" The court answered both questions "clearly no." Id.

Without proof of willfulness and, for § 7201, proof of an affirmative act of evasion, a taxpayer cannot be convicted of violating §§ 7201 or 7203. See *Spies, supra*; United States v. Masat, 896 F.2d 88, 98-99 (5th Cir. 1990) (reversal of conviction required where jury was left with the impression that failure to file plus willfulness would be sufficient to convict under § 7201). The jury's confusion on this very fundamental issue indicates that the initial instructions were inadequate in making this clear.

We conclude that any inadequacy was cured by the subsequent reinstruction, however. The judge's reinstruction emphasized that to convict of a felony there must be "an affirmative act to attempt to evade or defeat the payment of taxes." The judge also told the jury before he reread the instructions that a failure to pay was not enough. The need for an affirmative act was adequately stressed.

* * *

[Eds.: The court reversed the tax evasion conviction. See § c., below].

SCIRICA, CIRCUIT JUDGE, concurring.
* * *

The majority holds that, "unless a taxpayer is in the situation of giving voluntary admissions during an investigation or a forced response to a subpoena, the failure of the taxpayer to report the opening of an account in his or her own name in his or her own locale cannot amount to an affirmative act of evasion." Extending this holding to the facts here, the majority concludes that, even assuming McGill deposited the $9,000 in City legal fees subject to levy in his PSFS account, there is insufficient evidence to support the jury's convictions on Counts 7 and 8. I cannot agree.

In Spies v. United States, 317 U.S. 492, 499, 87 L.Ed. 418, 63 S.Ct. 364 (1943), the Supreme Court said that an "affirmative willful attempt [of tax evasion] may be inferred from * * * any conduct, the likely effect of which would be to mislead or to conceal." This is an expansive definition, one which takes into account that not all tax payment evaders approach their problem in the same way." United States v. Conley, 826 F.2d 551, 557 (7th Cir. 1987). See also United States v. Hook, 781 F.2d 1166, 1169 (6th Cir.1986). Where there is sufficient evidence, the question whether conduct supports a legitimate inference of willful attempt to evade taxes is for the jury, see *Spies*, 317 U.S. at 500, whose findings we must accord deference.

At the time McGill opened the PSFS account in August 1988, he was the target of a criminal investigation for tax evasion and had been the subject of five years of civil collection efforts by the IRS. The $9,000 the Government alleges he deposited in the PSFS account consisted of City legal fees which had escaped an IRS levy. Although McGill was aware these funds were subject to levy, he admitted expending them on personal and business items. Nevertheless, he claims to have reported them on his income tax return for that year.

I agree that, in the ordinary case, opening a personal banking account and depositing funds in it will not by itself amount to an affirmative act of tax evasion. But it seems to me that under the proper circumstances, this conduct may support a legitimate inference that a taxpayer has attempted to evade payment of federal tax liabilities. Cf. United States v. White, 417 F.2d 89, 92 (2d Cir. 1969) (allowing jury to infer affirmative act of tax evasion from fact that defendant had "maintained a separate personal banking account in a neighboring town in which he deposited large amounts of [unreported] currency from unidentified sources").

Assuming McGill deposited the $9,000 in City legal fees subject to levy in the PSFS account, I would find these circumstances present here. Even though McGill claims to have reported the $9,000 on his tax return, because he was aware these funds were subject to levy and was the target of a criminal investigation for tax evasion at the time, I would hold that his deposit and expenditure of the $9,000 without first notifying the IRS supports a legitimate inference that he committed an affirmative act of tax evasion under § 7201. See United States v. Eley, 314 F.2d 127, 132 (7th Cir. 1963) (upholding jury instruction which listed as an "affirmative, willful attempt" to evade taxes the "failure during the course of an investigation to supply any information for purposes of a computation, assessment or collection of income tax when such failure is found * * * to be unjustified").

However, because I agree with the majority that the Government has failed to meet its burden in establishing that McGill in fact deposited the $9,000 which had escaped the IRS levy in the PSFS account in August 1988, I concur in the results on Counts 7 and 8.

Notes and Questions

An omission may constitute an affirmative act of evasion where the taxpayer is under a legal duty to act and fails to do so. In United States v. Williams, 928 F.2d 145 (5th Cir. 1991), the taxpayer filed a fraudulent Form W-4 withholding statement with his employer, claiming many more withholding exemptions than he was entitled to claim. This reduced to a negligible amount the tax withheld from his salary. The taxpayer then failed to file returns for several years. While admitting that filing the fraudulent Form W-4 constituted an affirmative act, the taxpayer argued that in subsequent years there was no affirmative act of evasion. The Fifth Circuit affirmed the taxpayer's conviction of tax evasion, holding that the taxpayer had a "continuing obligation to correct his misrepresentations" and his failure to do so constituted an affirmative act of evasion in each subsequent year in which the misrepresentation remained uncorrected. But see United States v. Payne, 978 F.2d 1177, 1180 (10th Cir. 1992)("The continuing offense doctrine 'should be applied in only limited circumstances' * * * [in which] the explicit language of the substantive criminal statute compels such a conclusion, or the nature of the crime involved is such that Congress must assuredly have intended that it be treated as a continuing one."), citing Toussie v. United States, 397 U.S. 112, 115, 90 S.Ct. 858, 25 L.Ed. 2d 156 (1970).

Timing of affirmative acts. An issue raised by the court in *McGill* but not decided was whether affirmative acts of evasion can pre-date the tax deficiency in an evasion of payment case. The court notes that under certain circumstances, a prior act may suffice to prove evasion. 964 F.2d at 231. For instance, where the defendant's acts evidence a "continuous course of conduct" in which "each affirmative act of tax evasion was intended to evade payment of all taxes owed, or which [the defendant] expected to owe at the time of the affirmative act," United States v. Shorter, 809 F.2d 54, 57 (D.C. Cir. 1987). The *McGill* court also noted that in United States v. Mal, 942 F.2d 682 (9th Cir. 1991), the Ninth Circuit held that where a defendant commits acts of evasion prior to assessment, he does so to evade assessment; where he commits affirmative acts *after* assessment, he does so to evade payment. 964 F.2d at 231.

1. Why are evasion of payment cases not as common as evasion of assessment cases?

2. How, if at all, does the court distinguish McGill's use of the PSFS account from his use of the Lillie and the McGill & Seay accounts?

c. *Willfulness*

CHEEK v. UNITED STATES
United States Supreme Court, 1991.
498 U.S. 192, 111 S.Ct. 604, 112 L.Ed.2d 617.

MR. JUSTICE WHITE delivered the opinion of the Court.

Title 26, § 7201 of the United States Code provides that any person "who willfully attempts in any manner to evade or defeat any tax imposed by this title or the payment thereof" shall be guilty of a felony. Under 26 U.S.C. § 7203, "any person required under this title * * * or by regulations made under authority thereof to make a return * * * who willfully fails to * * * make such return' shall be guilty of a misdemeanor. This case turns on the meaning of the word "willfully" as used in §§ 7201 and 7203.

I.

Petitioner John L. Cheek has been a pilot for American Airlines since 1973. He filed federal income tax returns through 1979 but thereafter ceased to file returns.[1] He also claimed an increasing number of with-holding allowances–eventually claiming 60 allowances by mid-1980–and for the years 1981 to 1984 indicated on his W-4 forms that he was exempt from federal income taxes. In 1983, petitioner unsuccessfully sought a refund of all tax withheld by his employer in 1982. Petitioner's income during this period at all times far exceeded the minimum necessary to trigger the statutory filing requirement.

As a result of his activities, petitioner was indicted for 10 violations of federal law. He was charged with six counts of willfully failing to file a federal income tax return for the years 1980, 1981, and 1983 through 1986, in violation of 26 U.S.C. § 7203. He was further charged with three counts of willfully attempting to evade his income taxes for the years 1980, 1981, and 1983 in violation of § 7201. In those years, American Airlines withheld substantially less than the amount of tax petitioner owed because of the numerous allowances and exempt status he claimed on his W-4 forms.[2]

At trial, the evidence established that between 1982 and 1986, petitioner was involved in at least four civil cases that challenged various aspects of the federal income tax system.[3] In all four of those cases, the

---

1. Cheek did file what the Court of Appeals described as a frivolous return in 1982.

2. Because petitioner filed a refund claim for the entire amount withheld by his employer in 1982, petitioner was also charged under 18 U.S.C. § 287 with one count of presenting a claim to an agency of the United States knowing the claim to be false and fraudulent.

3. In March 1982, Cheek and another employee of the company sued American Airlines to challenge the withholding of federal income taxes. In April 1982, Cheek sued the Internal Revenue Service (IRS) in the United States Tax Court, asserting that he was not a taxpayer or a person for purposes of the Internal Revenue Code and that his wages were not income, and making several other related claims. Cheek and four others also filed an action against the United States and the Commissioner of Internal Revenue in Federal District Court, claiming that withholding taxes from their wages violated the Sixteenth Amendment. Finally, in 1985 Cheek filed claims with the IRS seeking to have refunded the taxes withheld from his wages in 1983 and 1984. When these claims

plaintiffs were informed by the courts that many of their arguments, including that they were not taxpayers within the meaning of the tax laws, that wages are not income, that the Sixteenth Amendment does not authorize the imposition of an income tax on individuals, and that the Sixteenth Amendment is unenforceable, were frivolous or had been repeatedly rejected by the courts. During this time period, petitioner also attended at least two criminal trials of persons charged with tax offenses. In addition, there was evidence that in 1980 or 1981 an attorney had advised Cheek that the courts had rejected as frivolous the claim that wages are not income.[4]

Cheek represented himself at trial and testified in his defense. He admitted that he had not filed personal income tax returns during the years in question. He testified that as early as 1978, he had begun attending seminars sponsored by, and following the advice of, a group that believes, among other things, that the federal tax system is unconstitutional. Some of the speakers at these meetings were lawyers who purported to give professional opinions about the invalidity of the federal income tax laws. Cheek produced a letter from an attorney stating that the Sixteenth Amendment did not authorize a tax on wages and salaries but only on gain or profit. Petitioner's defense was that, based on the indoctrination he received from this group and from his own study, he sincerely believed that the tax laws were being unconstitutionally enforced and that his actions during the 1980-1986 period were lawful. He therefore argued that he had acted without the willfulness required for conviction of the various offenses with which he was charged.

In the course of its instructions, the trial court advised the jury that to prove "willfulness" the Government must prove the voluntary and intentional violation of a known legal duty, a burden that could not be proved by showing mistake, ignorance, or negligence. The court further advised the jury that an objectively reasonable good-faith misunderstanding of the law would negate willfulness, but mere disagreement with the law would not. The court described Cheek's

---

were not allowed, he brought suit in the District Court claiming that the withholding was an unconstitutional taking of his property and that his wages were not income. In dismissing this action as frivolous, the District Court imposed costs and attorneys fees of $1,500 and a sanction under Federal Rule of Civil Procedure 11 in the amount of $10,000. The Court of Appeals agreed that Cheek's claims were frivolous, reduced the District Court sanction to $5,000, and imposed an additional sanction of $1,500 for bringing a frivolous appeal.

4.   The attorney also advised that despite the Fifth Amendment, the filing of a tax return was required and that a person could challenge the constitutionality of the system by suing for a refund after the taxes had been withheld, or by putting himself "at risk of criminal prosecution."

beliefs about the income tax system[5] and instructed the jury that if it found that Cheek "honestly and reasonably believed that he was not required to pay income taxes or to file tax returns," a not guilty verdict should be returned.

After several hours of deliberation, the jury sent a note to the judge that stated in part:

> "We have a basic disagreement between some of us as to if Mr. Cheek honestly & reasonably believed that he was not required to pay income taxes.

* * *

> "'Page 32 [the relevant jury instruction] discusses good faith misunderstanding & disagreement. Is there any additional clarification you can give us on this point?'" Id., at 85.

The District Judge responded with a supplemental instruction containing the following statements:

> "[A] person's opinion that the tax laws violate his constitutional rights does not constitute a good faith misunderstanding of the law. Furthermore, a person's disagreement with the government's tax collection systems and policies does not constitute a good faith misunderstanding of the law." Id., at 86.

At the end of the first day of deliberation, the jury sent out another note saying that it still could not reach a verdict because "we are divided on the issue as to if Mr. Cheek honestly & reasonably believed that he was not required to pay income tax." Id., at 87. When the jury resumed its deliberations, the District Judge gave the jury an additional instruction. This instruction stated in part that "an honest but unreasonable belief is not a defense and does not negate willfulness," id., at 88, and that "advice or research resulting in the conclusion that wages of a privately employed person are not income or that the tax laws are unconstitutional is not objectively reasonable and cannot serve as the basis for a good faith misunderstanding of the law defense." The court also instructed the jury that "persistent refusal to acknowledge the law

---

5.   "The defendant has testified as to what he states are his interpretations of the United States Constitution, court opinions, common law and other materials he has reviewed * * *. He has also introduced materials which contain references to quotations from the United States Constitution, court opinions, statutes, and other sources.

"He testified he relied on his interpretations and on these materials in concluding that he was not a person required to file income tax returns for the year or years charged, was not required to pay income taxes and that he could claim exempt status on his W-4 forms, and that he could claim refunds of all moneys withheld."

"Among other things, Mr. Cheek contends that his wages from a private employer, American Airlines, does [sic] not constitute income under the Internal Revenue Service laws." Id., at 81.

does not constitute a good faith misunderstanding of the law." Approximately two hours later, the jury returned a verdict finding petitioner guilty on all counts.[6]

Petitioner appealed his convictions, arguing that the District Court erred by instructing the jury that only an objectively reasonable misunderstanding of the law negates the statutory willfulness requirement. The United States Court of Appeals for the Seventh Circuit rejected that contention and affirmed the convictions. 882 F.2d 1263 (1989). In prior cases, the Seventh Circuit had made clear that good-faith misunderstanding of the law negates willfulness only if the defendant's beliefs are objectively reasonable; in the Seventh Circuit, even actual ignorance is not a defense unless the defendant's ignorance was itself objectively reasonable. See, e.g., United States v. Buckner, 830 F.2d 102 (1987). In its opinion in this case, the court noted that several specified beliefs, including the beliefs that the tax laws are unconstitutional and that wages are not income, would not be objectively reasonable.[7] Because the Seventh Circuit's interpretation of "willfully" as used in these statutes conflicts with the decisions of several other Courts of Appeals, see e.g., United States v. Whiteside, 810 F.2d 1306, 1310-1311 (CA5 1987); United States v. Phillips, 775 F.2d 262, 263-264 (CA10 1985); United States v. Aitken, 755 F.2d 188, 191-193 (CA1 1985), we granted certiorari, 493 U.S. 1068 (1990).

---

6. A note signed by all 12 jurors also informed the judge that although the jury found petitioner guilty, several jurors wanted to express their personal opinions of the case and that notes from these individual jurors to the court were "a complaint against the narrow & hard expression under the constraints of the law." Id., at 90. At least two notes from individual jurors expressed the opinion that petitioner sincerely believed in his cause even though his beliefs might have been unreasonable.

7. The opinion states, 882 F.2d 1263, 1268-1269, n.2 (CA7 1989), as follows:

"For the record, we note that the following beliefs, which are stock arguments of the tax protester movement, have not been, nor ever will be, considered 'objectively reasonable' in this circuit:

"(1) the belief that the sixteenth amendment to the constitution was improperly ratified and therefore never came into being;

"(2) the belief that the sixteenth amendment is unconstitutional generally;

"(3) the belief that the income tax violates the takings clause of the fifth amendment;

"(4) the belief that the tax laws are unconstitutional;

"(5) the belief that wages are not income and therefore are not subject to federal income tax laws:

"(6) the belief that filing a tax return violates the privilege against self-incrimination; and

"(7) the belief that Federal Reserve Notes do not constitute cash or income.

"Miller v. United States, 868 F.2d 236, 239-41 (7th Cir. 1989); Buckner, 830 F.2d at 102; United States v. Dube, 820 F.2d 886, 891 (7th Cir. 1987); Coleman v. Comm'r., 791 F.2d 68, 70-71 (7th Cir. 1986); Moore, 627 F.2d 830 at 833. We have no doubt that this list will increase with time."

II.

The general rule that ignorance of the law or a mistake of law is no defense to criminal prosecution is deeply rooted in the American legal system. Based on the notion that the law is definite and knowable the common law presumed that every person knew the law. This common law rule has been applied by the Court in numerous cases construing criminal statutes.

The proliferation of statutes and regulations has sometimes made it difficult for the average citizen to know and comprehend the extent of the duties and obligations imposed by the tax laws. Congress has accordingly softened the impact of the common-law presumption by making specific intent to violate the law an element of certain federal criminal tax offenses. Thus, the Court almost 60 years ago interpreted the statutory term "willfully" as used in the federal criminal tax statutes as carving out an exception to the traditional rule. This special treatment of criminal tax offenses is largely due to the complexity of the tax laws. In United States v. Murdock, 290 U.S. 389, 78 L.Ed. 381, 54 S.Ct. 223 (1933), the Court recognized that:

> "Congress did not intend that a person, by reason of a bona fide misunderstanding as to his liability for the tax, as to his duty to make a return, or as to the adequacy of the records he maintained, should become a criminal by his mere failure to measure up to the prescribed standard of conduct." Id., at 396.

The Court held that the defendant was entitled to an instruction with respect to whether he acted in good faith based on his actual belief. In *Murdock*, the Court interpreted the term "willfully" as used in the criminal tax statutes generally to mean "an act done with a bad purpose," id., at 394, or with "an evil motive," id., at 395.

Subsequent decisions have refined this proposition. In United States v. Bishop, 412 U.S. 346, 35 L.Ed.2d 941, 93 S.Ct. 2008 (1973), we described the term "willfully" as connoting "a voluntary, intentional violation of a known legal duty," id., at 360, and did so with specific reference to the "bad faith or evil intent" language employed in *Murdock*. Still later, United States v. Pomponio, 429 U.S. 10, 50 L.Ed.2d 12, 97 S.Ct. 22 (1976) (per curiam), addressed a situation in which several defendants had been charged with willfully filing false tax returns. The jury was given an instruction on willfulness similar to the standard set forth in *Bishop*. In addition, it was instructed that "good motive alone is never a defense where the act done or omitted is a crime." Id., at 11. The defendants were convicted but the Court of Appeals reversed, concluding that the latter instruction was improper because the statute required a finding of bad purpose or evil motive.

We reversed the Court of Appeals, stating that "the Court of Appeals incorrectly assumed that the reference to an 'evil motive' in *United States v. Bishop*, supra, and prior cases," ibid., "requires proof of any motive other than an intentional violation of a known legal duty." Id., at 12. As "the other Courts of Appeals that have considered the question have recognized, willfulness in this context simply means a voluntary, intentional violation of a known legal duty." Ibid. We concluded that after instructing the jury on willfulness, "an additional instruction on good faith was unnecessary." Id., at 13. Taken together, *Bishop* and *Pomponio* conclusively establish that the standard for the statutory willfulness requirement is the "voluntary, intentional violation of a known legal duty."

III.

Cheek accepts the *Pomponio* definition of willfulness, but asserts that the District Court's instructions and the Court of Appeals' opinion departed from that definition. In particular, he challenges the ruling that a good-faith misunderstanding of the law or a good-faith belief that one is not violating the law, if it is to negate willfulness, must be objectively reasonable. We agree that the Court of Appeals and the District Court erred in this respect.

A.

Willfulness, as construed by our prior decisions in criminal tax cases, requires the Government to prove that the law imposed a duty on the defendant, that the defendant knew of this duty and that he voluntarily and intentionally violated that duty. We deal first with the case where the issue is whether the defendant knew of the duty purportedly imposed by the provision of the statute or regulation he is accused of violating, a case in which there is no claim that the provision at issue is invalid. In such a case, if the Government proves actual knowledge of the pertinent legal duty, the prosecution, without more, has satisfied the knowledge component of the willfulness requirement. But carrying this burden requires negating a defendant's claim of ignorance of the law or a claim that because of a misunderstanding of the law, he had a good-faith belief that he was not violating any of the provisions of the tax laws. This is so because one cannot be aware that the law imposes a duty upon him and yet be ignorant of it, misunderstand the law, or believe that the duty does not exist. In the end, the issue is whether, based on all the evidence, the Government has proved that the defendant was aware of the duty at issue, which cannot be true if the jury credits a good-faith misunderstanding and belief submission, whether or not the claimed belief or misunderstanding is objectively reasonable.

In this case, if Cheek asserted that he truly believed that the Internal Revenue Code did not purport to treat wages as income, and the jury believed him, the Government would not have carried its burden to prove willfulness, however unreasonable a court might deem such a belief. Of course, in deciding whether to credit Cheek's good-faith belief claim, the jury would be free to consider any admissible evidence from any source showing that Cheek was aware of his duty to file a return and to treat wages as income, including evidence showing his awareness of the relevant provisions of the Code or regulations, of court decisions rejecting his interpretation of the tax law, of authoritative rulings of the Internal Revenue Service, or of any contents of the personal income tax return forms and accompanying instructions that made it plain that wages should be returned as income.[8]

We thus disagree with the Court of Appeals' requirement that a claimed good-faith belief must be objectively reasonable if it is to be considered as possibly negating the Government's evidence purporting to show a defendant's awareness of the legal duty at issue. Knowledge and belief are characteristically questions for the factfinder, in this case the jury. Characterizing a particular belief as not objectively reasonable transforms the inquiry into a legal one and would prevent the jury from considering it. It would of course be proper to exclude evidence having no relevance or probative value with respect to willfulness; but it is not contrary to common sense, let alone impossible, for a defendant to be ignorant of his duty based on an irrational belief that he has no duty, and forbidding the jury to consider evidence that might negate willfulness would raise a serious question under the Sixth Amendment's jury trial provision. It is common ground that this Court, where possible, interprets congressional enactments so as to avoid raising serious constitutional questions.

It was therefore error to instruct the jury to disregard evidence of Cheek's understanding that, within the meaning of the tax laws, he was

---

8.   Cheek recognizes that a "defendant who knows what the law is and who disagrees with it * * * does not have a bona fide misunderstanding defense," but asserts that "a defendant who has a bona fide misunderstanding of [the law] does not 'know' his legal duty and lacks willfulness." The Reply Brief for Petitioner, at 13, states: "We are in no way suggesting that Cheek or anyone else is immune from criminal prosecution if he knows what the law is, but believes it should be otherwise, and therefore violates it."

not a person required to file a return or to pay income taxes and that wages are not taxable income, as incredible as such misunderstandings of and beliefs about the law might be. Of course, the more unreasonable the asserted beliefs or misunderstandings are, the more likely the jury will consider them to be nothing more than simple disagreement with known legal duties imposed by the tax laws and will find that the Government has carried its burden of proving knowledge.

B.

Cheek asserted in the trial court that he should be acquitted because he believed in good faith that the income tax law is unconstitutional as applied to him and thus could not legally impose any duty upon him of which he should have been aware.[9] Such a submission is unsound, not because Cheek's constitutional arguments are not objectively reasonable or frivolous, which they surely are, but because the *Murdock-Pomponio* line of cases does not support such a position. Those cases construed the willfulness requirement in the criminal provisions of the Internal Revenue Code to require proof of knowledge of the law. This was because in "our complex tax system, uncertainty often arises even among taxpayers who earnestly wish to follow the law," and "it is not the purpose of the law to penalize frank difference of opinion or innocent errors made despite the exercise of reasonable care." United States v. Bishop, 412 U.S. 346, 360-361, 36 L.Ed.2d 941, 93 S.Ct. 2008 (1973)

---

9.   In his opening and reply briefs and at oral argument, Cheek asserts that this case does not present the issue whether a claim of unconstitutionality would serve to negate willfulness and that we need not address the issue. Cheek testified at trial, however, that "it is my belief that the law is being enforced unconstitutionally." He also produced a letter from counsel advising him that "'Finally you make a valid contention * * * that Congress' power to tax comes from Article I, Section 8, Clause 1 of the U.S. Constitution, and not from the Sixteenth Amendment and that the [latter], construed with Article I, Section 2, Clause 3, never authorized a tax on wages and salaries, but only on gain and profit." We note also that the jury asked for "the portion [of the transcript] wherein Mr. Cheek stated he was attempting to test the constitutionality of the income tax laws," and that the trial judge later instructed the jury that an opinion that the tax laws violate a person's constitutional rights does not constitute a good-faith misunderstanding of the law. We also note that at oral argument Cheek's counsel observed that "personal belief that a known statute is unconstitutional smacks of knowledge with existing law, but disagreement with it." Tr. Of Oral Arg. 5. He also opined:

"If the person believes as a personal belief that known—law known to them [sic] is unconstitutional, I submit that that would not be a defense, because what the person is really saying is I know what the law is, for constitutional reasons I have made by own determination that it is invalid. I am not suggesting that that is a defense.

"However, if the person was told by a lawyer or by an accountant erroneously that the statute is unconstitutional, and it's my professional advice to you that you don't have to follow it, then you have got a little different situation. This is not that case." Id., at 6.

Given this posture of the case, we perceive no reason not to address the significance of Cheek's constitutional claims to the issue of willfulness.

(quoting Spies v. United States, 317 U.S. 492, 496, 87 L.Ed. 418, 63 S.Ct. 364 (1943)).

Claims that some of the provisions of the tax code are unconstitutional are submissions of a different order.[10] They do not arise from innocent mistakes caused by the complexity of the Internal Revenue Code. Rather, they reveal full knowledge of the provisions at issue and a studied conclusion, however wrong, that those provisions are invalid and unenforceable. Thus in this case, Cheek paid his taxes for years, but after attending various seminars and based on his own study, he concluded that the income tax laws could not constitutionally require him to pay a tax.

We do not believe that Congress contemplated that such a taxpayer, without risking criminal prosecution, could ignore the duties imposed upon him by the Internal Revenue Code and refuse to utilize the mechanisms provided by Congress to present his claims of invalidity to the courts and to abide by their decisions. There is no doubt that Cheek, from year to year, was free to pay the tax that the law purported to require, file for a refund, and, if denied, present his claims of invalidity, constitutional or otherwise, to the courts. See 26 U.S.C. § 7422. Also, without paying the tax, he could have challenged claims of tax deficiencies in the Tax Court, § 6213, with the right to appeal to a higher court if unsuccessful. § 7482(a)(1). Cheek took neither course in some years, and when he did was unwilling to accept the outcome. As we see it, he is in no position to claim that his good-faith belief about the validity of the Internal Revenue Code negates willfulness or provides a defense to criminal prosecution under §§ 7201 and 7203. Of course, Cheek was free in this very case to present his claims of invalidity and have them adjudicated, but like defendants in criminal cases in other contexts, who "willfully" refuse to comply with the duties placed upon them by the law, he must take the risk of being wrong.

We thus hold that in a case like this, a defendant's views about the validity of the tax statutes are irrelevant to the issue of willfulness and

---

10. In United States v. Murdock, 290 U.S. 389, 78 L.Ed. 381, 54 S.Ct. 223 (1933), the defendant Murdock was summoned to appear before a revenue agent for examination. Questions were put to him, which he refused to answer for fear of self-incrimination under state law. He was indicted for refusing to give testimony and supply information contrary to the pertinent provisions of the Internal Revenue Code. This Court affirmed the reversal of Murdock's conviction, holding that the trial court erred in refusing to give an instruction directing the jury to consider Murdock's asserted claim of a good-faith, actual belief that because of the Fifth Amendment he was privileged not to answer the questions put to him. It is thus the case that Murdock's asserted belief was grounded in the Constitution, but it was a claim of privilege not to answer, not a claim that any provision of the tax laws were unconstitutional, and not a claim for which the tax laws provided procedures to entertain and resolve. Cheek's position at trial, in contrast, was that the tax laws were unconstitutional as applied to him.

need not be heard by the jury, and, if they are, an instruction to disregard them would be proper. For this purpose, it makes no difference whether the claims of invalidity are frivolous or have substance. It was therefore not error in this case for the District Judge to instruct the jury not to consider Cheek's claims that the tax laws were unconstitutional. However, it was error for the court to instruct the jury that petitioner's asserted beliefs that wages are not income and that he was not a taxpayer within the meaning of the Internal Revenue Code should not be considered by the jury in determining whether Cheek had acted willfully.

IV.

For the reasons set forth in the opinion above, the judgment of the Court of Appeals is vacated, and the case is remanded for further proceedings consistent with this opinion.

It is so ordered.

MR. JUSTICE SCALIA, concurring in the judgment.

I concur in the judgment of the Court because our cases have consistently held that the failure to pay a tax in the good-faith belief that it is not legally owing is not "willful." I do not join the Court's opinion because I do not agree with the test for willfulness that it directs the Court of Appeals to apply on remand.

As the Court acknowledges, our opinions from the 1930's to the 1970's have interpreted the word "willfully" in the criminal tax statutes as requiring the "bad purpose" or "evil motive" of "intentionally violating a known legal duty." See, e.g., United States v. Pomponio, 429 U.S. 10, 12, 50 L.Ed.2d 12, 97 S.Ct. 22 (1976); United States v. Murdock, 290 U.S. 389, 394-395, 78 L.Ed. 381, 54 S.Ct. 223 (1933). It seems to me that today's opinion squarely reverses that long-established statutory construction when it says that a good-faith erroneous belief in the unconstitutionality of a tax law is no defense. It is quite impossible to say that a statute which one believes unconstitutional represents a "known legal duty." See Marbury v. Madison, 5 U.S. 137, 1 Cranch 137, 177-178, 2 L.Ed. 60 (1803).

Although the facts of the present case involve erroneous reliance upon the Constitution in ignoring the otherwise "known legal duty" imposed by the tax statutes, the Court's new interpretation applies also to erroneous reliance upon a tax statute in ignoring the otherwise "known legal duty" of a regulation, and to erroneous reliance upon a regulation in ignoring the otherwise "known legal duty" of a tax assessment. These situations as well meet the opinion's crucial test of "revealing full knowledge of the provisions at issue and a studied conclusion, however, wrong, that those provisions are invalid and unenforceable[.]" There is, moreover, no rational basis for saying that a "willful" violation is established by full knowledge of a statutory requirement, but is not established by full knowledge of a requirement explicitly imposed by regulation or order. Thus, today's opinion works a revolution in past practice, subjecting to criminal penalties taxpayers who do not comply with Treasury Regulations that are in their view contrary to the Internal Revenue Code, Treasury Rulings that are in their view contrary to the regulations, and even IRS auditor pronouncements that are in their view contrary to Treasury Rulings. The law already provides considerable incentive for taxpayers to be careful in ignoring any official assertion of tax liability, since it contains civil penalties that apply even in the event of a good-faith mistake, see e.g., 26 U.S.C. §§ 6651, 6653. To impose in addition *criminal* penalties for misinterpretation of such a complex body of law is a startling innovation indeed.

I find it impossible to understand how one can derive from the lonesome word "willfully" the proposition that belief in the nonexistence of a textual prohibition excuses liability, but belief in the invalidity (*i.e.*, the legal nonexistence) of a textual prohibition does not. One may say, as the law does in many contexts, that "willfully" refers to consciousness of the act but not to consciousness that the act is unlawful. Or alternatively, one may say, as we have said until today with respect to the tax statutes, that "willfully" refers to consciousness of both the act *and* its illegality. But it seems to me impossible to say that the word refers to consciousness that some legal text exists, without consciousness that that legal text is binding, i.e., with the good-faith belief that it is not a valid law. Perhaps such a test for criminal liability would make sense (though in a field as complicated as federal tax law, I doubt it), but some text other than the mere word "willfully" would have to be employed to describe it–and that text is not ours to write.

Because today's opinion abandons clear and longstanding precedent to impose criminal liability where taxpayers have had no reason to expect it, because the new contours of criminal liability have no basis in the statutory text, and because I strongly suspect that those new contours make no sense even as a policy matter, I concur only in the judgment of the Court.

* * *

Notes and Questions

Cheek is the first of a trilogy of United States Supreme Court cases interpreting the term "willfully" in the criminal context. A few years after the *Cheek* decision, the Supreme Court again required subjective knowledge of illegality (i.e., the prosecution must prove that the defendant knew that his conduct was unlawful) in a case involving a violation of the currency transaction reporting requirements under 31 U.S.C. §§ 5322-5324. See Ratzlaf v. United States, 510 U.S. 135 (1994). Congress, however, wasted no time in overturning the decision by eliminating the "willfulness" requirement in the currency transaction laws. See Pub. L. No. 103-325 (1994). For further discussion, see § III.C., below.

In a third case, Bryan v. United States, 524 U.S. 184 (1998), the Supreme Court addressed the question of whether willfulness required knowledge of the specific law that allegedly had been violated. In *Bryan*, the petitioner appealed his conviction of "willfully" dealing in firearms without a federal license in violation of 18 U.S.C. § 924(a)(1)(D). The question presented to the Court was whether the term "willfully" requires proof only that the petitioner knew that his conduct in general was unlawful, or whether it also requires proof that the petitioner knew of the federal licensing requirement. In upholding the decisions of both of the lower courts, the Supreme Court stated:

> The word "willfully" is sometimes said to be "a word of many meanings" whose construction is often dependent on the context in which it appears. Most obviously it differentiates between deliberate and unwitting conduct, but in the criminal law it also typically refers to a culpable state of mind. As a general matter, when used in the criminal context, a "willful" act is one undertaken with a "bad purpose." In other words, in order to establish a "willful" violation of a statute, "the Government must prove that the defendant acted with knowledge that his conduct was unlawful." Ratzlaf v. United States, 510 U.S. 135 (1994).

524 U.S. at 191. The Court also distinguished *Cheek* and *Ratzlaf*:

> Both the tax cases and *Ratzlaf* involved highly technical statutes that presented the danger of ensnaring individuals engaged in apparently innocent conduct. As a result, we held that these statutes "carv[e] out an exception to the traditional rule" that ignorance of the law is no excuse and require that the defendant have knowledge of the law. The danger of convicting individuals engaged in apparently innocent activity that motivated our decisions in the tax cases and *Ratzlsaf* is

not present here because the jury found that his petitioner knew that his conduct was unlawful.

Id., at 194-95.

One effect of the *Cheek* decision is to allow more readily the use of expert testimony concerning the reasonableness of the defendant's belief, particularly where expert testimony is admitted on behalf of the government. See United States v. Lankford, 955 F.2d 1545, 1550 (11th Cir. 1992) ("any evidence concerning the reasonableness of [the defendant's] * * * belief * * * is relevant to the determination of whether [he] willfully violated the tax laws").

1. What effect, if any, is the *Cheek* decision likely to have in criminal cases involving a defense of mistake or ignorance of the law?

2. Do you think Justice Scalia has a valid point in his concurrence when he questions how a statute one believes unconstitutional can be considered the violation of "a known legal duty?"

3. Do you think Justice Scalia is correct when he opines that the majority's decision will result in the imposition of criminal liability when taxpayers have no reason to expect it?

UNITED STATES v. McGILL
United States Court of Appeals, Third Circuit, 1992.
964 F.2d 222.

* * *

C. Willfulness

Finally, conviction of evasion of payment under § 7201 requires proof that the defendant's behavior was willful. "Willfulness" is the voluntary, intentional violation of a known legal duty. United States v. Pomponio, 429 U.S. 10,12, 50L.Ed. 2d 12, 97 S.Ct. 22 (1976). The definition of willfulness is the same under both felony (§7201) and misdemeanor (§ 7203) tax charges. United States v. Bishop, 412 U.S. 346, 359-61, 36 L.Ed. 2d 941, 93 S.Ct. 2008 (1973). See *Sansone*, 380 U.S. at 353-54. Under § 7201, the defendant has the duty not to act to evade his tax obligation. Under § 7203, the duty is simply to pay one's taxes. In both cases, willfulness may be inferred from a pattern of conduct, "the likely effect of which would be to mislead or to conceal." Spies v. United States, 317 U.S. 492, 499, 87 L.Ed. 418, 63 S.Ct. 364 (1943).

Willfulness is "closely connected" to the affirmative act element of § 7201. See United States v. Romano, 938 F.2d 1569, 1572 (2d Cir. 1991). "Evidence of affirmative acts may be used to show willfulness, and the defendant must commit the affirmative acts willfully to be convicted of tax evasion." Id. Under § 7201, "if the affirmative act element is satisfied, there is no question that willfulness is also present." Id. Because we have determined that the Government did not prove an affirmative act for Counts 7 and 8, we do not reach the willfulness inquiry for those charges. We do reach the issue for Counts 4, 5 and 6, and find that the jury could reasonably have concluded that McGill acted willfully.

McGill also challenges the definition of willfulness in the jury instructions. He contends that his proposed instruction on willfulness would have focused the jury's attention on the necessary issue of whether he had specific knowledge that "his cessation of the use of the levied accounts and use of the other accounts constituted a violation of the tax laws." He argues that the instruction given on willfulness–"voluntary intentional violation of a known legal duty," – did not satisfy the requirement that a tax defendant is entitled to a particularized instruction concerning his actual knowledge of the tax laws. Cheek v. United States, 112 L.Ed. 2d 617, 111 S.Ct. 604 (1991).

McGill misreads *Cheek*. The Court in *Cheek* held that it is error to require, in order to negate willfulness, that "a good-faith misunderstanding of the law or a good-faith belief that one is not violating the law" must also be objectively reasonable. Id. at 610-611. The Court, in making its finding, elaborated on the application of this standard to the customary "voluntary intentional violation of a known legal duty" definition of willfulness. In a situation in which the issue is whether the defendant knew of the duty purportedly imposed by the statute in question, the Government must prove actual knowledge of the pertinent legal duty, but this requires negating a defendant's claim of ignorance of the law or a claim that because of a misunderstanding of the law, he had a good faith belief that he was not violating any of the provisions of the tax laws.

The District Court here did not give the erroneous instruction, given by the District Court in *Cheek*, that only an objectively reasonable misunderstanding of the law negates the statutory willfulness requirement. Rather, as noted above, the judge gave the jury the customary definition of willfulness: the voluntary intentional violation of a known legal duty. Moreover, the jury heard evidence from which it could consider whether McGill did in fact realize that he was violating the law, e.g., McGill's use of the Lillie and the McGill & Seay account because he thought "the IRS wouldn't bother the money[;]" his "overlooking" of his IRS debt on twelve financial disclosure forms filed with the Pennsylvania Ethics Committee, an arm of the state bar, from 1981 through 1987; and his alleged failure to disclose the existence of a business account to the Collections Division of the IRS.[29] The jury could thus properly assess the good-faith of McGill's belief as to the legality of what he was doing, and could reasonably have found that McGill acted willfully as to Counts 4, 5 and 6.[30]

* * *

Notes

If a taxpayer's conduct establishes willfulness sufficient to support a conviction for tax evasion under § 7201, it makes little difference that the conduct was intended to conceal another crime. For example, a lawyer who embezzled money from an estate and took steps not only to conceal his embezzlement from the estate, but also to conceal his receipt of the embezzled funds from the Service, committed an act sufficient for a

---

29. McGill submitted Forms 433-A (Collection Information Statement for Individuals) and 433-B (Collection Information Statement for Businesses) to the Collections Division on May 22, 1985. He made no mention of the shared-expense account on either form. While we know that the McGill & Seay account did not exist under that name when McGill filed Form 433-B, we do not know whether the McGill & Seay precursor–the Clark, McGill & Seay account–was still open on May 22, 1985. However, if the jury were to believe McGill's testimony that the McGill & Seay account was simply renamed in May 1985, and not conveniently opened two days after the disclosure forms were signed, then they could infer some willfulness from that omission.

30. McGill further challenges the trial judge's exclusion of certain evidence from the jury's consideration of willfulness. Specifically, the court instructed the jury that McGill's levy payments and his 1986 OIC were irrelevant to whether he knowingly violated his tax obligations. Even assuming that evidence of both the levies and the OIC might tend to prove that McGill did not act willfully, and that the trial judge's exclusion on these points was in error, we conclude that McGill did not suffer prejudice from the omission because of the considerable evidence which does support willfulness as to these counts.

The jury had evidence before it that McGill had negotiated with the IRS over a long period of time; clearly he was interested in solving his tax problems. The jury also knew that McGill made one voluntary payment of $3,000 near the time of the OIC. The jury knew as well that McGill voluntarily continued to take indigent cases after the IRS lien was in place. In addition, McGill testified at length to his intent to cooperate with the government to the fullest extent possible. If the $3,000 voluntary payment and the voluntary work for the City did not corroborate McGill's testimony about his state of mind for the jury, it is hard to believe that the same jury would have been impressed by an offer to pay a fraction of his tax liability and his failure to pay voluntarily *anything* on that tax liability in a year when he could presumably raise $16,000 to settle his tax obligations.

Further, the judge told the jury that McGill's inability to pay his taxes had no bearing on willfulness. McGill vehemently asserts that he never raised inability to pay as a defense to the evasion of payment charge, though he did assert inability to pay as a defense to the charge of willful failure to pay. We decline to resolve the apparent split of authority as to whether a taxpayer's inability to pay should bear on the willfulness of his violations. Compare United States v. Poll, 521 F.2d 329, 332-33 (9th Cir. 1975); United States v. Andros, 484 F.2d 531 (9th Cir. 1973); United States v. Harper, 397 F. Supp. 983, 990 (E.D. Pa. 1975); United States v. Goodman, 190 F. Supp. 847, 854 (N.D. Ill. 1961) with United States v. Ausmus, 774 F.2d 722 (6th Cir. 1985); United States v. Tucker, 686 F.2d 230 (5th Cir.1982); United States v. Lewis, 671 F.2d 1025, 1028 (7th Cir. 1982). Even if the inability to pay were relevant, the defense is unavailing to McGill, who could have altered his lifestyle and thus freed the money required to pay his tax obligations.

conviction of felony tax evasion. See United States v. Eaken, 17 F.3d 203 (7th Cir. 1994).

In footnote 30, the court refers to the inability to pay as having no bearing on willfulness. For further discussion of the financial inability to pay the taxes as a defense to willfulness, see the next section.

2. Willful Failure to Collect or Pay Over Tax – § 7202

Section 7202 is a felony provision, punishable by fine of not more than $10,000 and imprisonment for not more than five years. It is most often invoked for a failure to pay withholding taxes and the most common defense to the charge is a financial inability to pay.

UNITED STATES v. EASTERDAY
United States Court of Appeals, Ninth Circuit, 2009
564 F.3d 1004

SCHROEDER, CIRCUIT JUDGE:

* * *

Background

Easterday operated a chain of nursing homes in Northern California through a parent corporation, Employee Equity Administration ("EEA"), and its subsidiaries. Between 1998 and 2005, the total payroll tax liability for EEA and its subsidiaries for the period from the fourth quarter of 1998 through the fourth quarter of 2005 was $44,864,162, of which $26,018,869 was paid. Although the companies' tax filings accurately stated its tax liabilities, Easterday, through the corporation, repeatedly failed to pay over to the Internal Revenue Service ("IRS") the full amount of payroll taxes due.

The IRS sent Easterday's companies numerous notices requesting payment of the delinquent taxes. When those notices did not result in payment, the IRS sent notices informing Easterday's companies of an intent to levy against each company's assets. Although Easterday was cooperative with the IRS and took full responsibility for the tax delinquency, his pattern of nonpayment continued. The IRS assessed liens against corporate accounts, but when payment was still not forthcoming, it eventually filed criminal charges. In 2005, the government charged Easterday with 109 counts of failure to pay over taxes in violation of 26 U.S.C. § 7202, with each count representing a different quarter in which the taxes of EEA and its subsidiaries were deficient.

Easterday did not dispute that he failed to pay the taxes when due. His defense was simply that he lacked the financial ability to comply with his tax obligations. Although the district court ruled that ability to pay was not relevant, Easterday was able to put on testimony that the nursing homes were struggling financially and he had trouble paying the bills, with losses of more than $20,000,000 between 1996 and 2005.

Easterday's witnesses testified, in essence, that Easterday did not pay the payroll taxes because he used the money to pay other company bills in order to keep the nursing homes operational. Easterday asked the court to instruct the jury that the government, in order to prove a willful failure to pay taxes, must prove that at the time the taxes were due, the taxpayer had the funds, and hence the ability to pay the obligation. Easterday's proposed instruction was drawn in part from the opinion in *United States v. Poll*, and provided as follows:

> The word "willfully" means a voluntary, intentional violation of a known legal duty, and not through ignorance, mistake, negligence, even gross negligence, or accident. In other words, the defendant must have acted voluntarily and intentionally and with the specific intent to do something he knew the law prohibited; that is to say, with the intent either to disobey or disregard the law.

> In the context of this case, in order for the government to meet its burden of willfulness beyond a reasonable doubt, it must prove that on the dates the taxes were due the taxpayer possessed sufficient funds to be able to meet his legal obligations to the government or that the lack of sufficient funds on such date was created by (or was the result of) a voluntary and intentional act, without justification in light of the financial circumstances of the taxpayer.

The district court declined to give this instruction, but did instruct the jury that the government had the burden of proving that the defendant did not have a good faith belief that he was complying with the tax laws, and that a defendant's belief could be in good faith even if it was unreasonable. The court also instructed the jury that "[t]he tax laws do not permit an employer to choose to use the monies held in trust for the United States for other purposes, such as to pay business expenses."

Following a six-day jury trial, Easterday was found guilty on 107 of 109 counts. The district court denied Easterday's motion for a judgment of acquittal or a new trial and sentenced him to 30 months imprisonment, followed by three years supervised release. Easterday now appeals from the judgment and sentence.

Easterday's principal contention on appeal is that pursuant to *United States v. Poll*, he was entitled to a jury instruction on the ability to pay "element" of 26 U.S.C. § 7202, and he was entitled to present evidence to negate that "element." Accordingly, Easterday argues that the district court erred in declining to give a Poll instruction and that it abused its discretion by limiting the testimony Easterday could offer concerning the financial situation of, and burdens on, his companies.

Discussion

The statute under which Easterday was found guilty is 26 U.S.C. § 7202, a fairly rarely invoked provision that criminalizes a willful failure to pay over employees' federal income withholding taxes on wages. Section 7202 provides that "[a]ny person required . . . to collect, account for, and pay over any tax imposed by this title who willfully fails to collect or truthfully account for and pay over such tax shall . . . be guilty of a felony."

The main issue in this appeal, as well as a subject of considerable debate before the district court, pertains to the status of *Poll*, and to what constitutes "willfulness" under the Tax Code. Specifically, the parties disagree as to whether "willfulness" requires an affirmative showing by the government that a defendant had an ability to pay his tax obligations and whether it can be negated by a showing that a defendant was financially unable to satisfy his tax debt. This court has not meaningfully revisited this issue since the 1970s.

In United States v. Andros, 484 F.2d 531, 533-34 (9th Cir.1973), we said that to establish the "wilful failure to pay the taxes assessed," the government must prove that, on the date the taxes were due, the taxpayer possessed "sufficient funds" to pay the taxes, and that the taxpayer voluntarily and intentionally did not pay them. We went on to say: "the requirement of wilfulness connotes 'bad faith or evil intent' or 'evil motive and want of justification in view of all the financial circumstances of the taxpayer.' " Id. at 534 (quoting United States v. Bishop, 412 U.S. 346, 93 S.Ct. 2008, 36 L.Ed.2d 941 (1973)).

Two years later, in *United States v. Poll*, this court apparently found plausible.the taxpayer's contention that the failure to pay over the taxes could not be considered "willful" because he had offered to prove "that the corporation lacked the liquid resources to pay the full amounts due and that he intended to make up the deficiencies later." 521 F.2d at 330-31. Citing to *Andros* and Spies v. United States, 317 U.S. 492, 497-98, 63 S.Ct. 364, 87 L.Ed. 418 (1943), we held that Poll's offer of proof regarding the liquid resources of the corporation was relevant to the determination of whether the failure to pay over taxes was willful. 521 F.2d at 332. In the language that Easterday sought to include as part of the charge to the jury in this case, we said:

> [T]o establish willfulness the Government must establish beyond a reasonable doubt that at the time payment was due the taxpayer possessed sufficient funds to enable him to meet his obligation or that the lack of sufficient funds on such date was created by (or was the result of) a voluntary and intentional act without justification in view of all the financial circumstances of the taxpayer.

Id. at 333.

This holding in *Poll* regarding ability to pay relied upon a definition of willfulness, taken from *Spies* and *Andros*, that included an element of "evil motive." 521 F.2d at 333 (citing *Spies*, 317 U.S. at 498, 63 S.Ct. 364). We recognized this in Sorenson v. United States, 521 F.2d 325, 328 n. 3 (9th Cir.1975) (quoting *Spies*, 317 U.S. at 498, 63 S.Ct. 364), where we said: "The *Poll* holding is only applicable to the criminal test of willfulness which requires 'some element of evil motive and want of justification in view of all the financial circumstances of the taxpayer.' "

The year after this court decided *Poll*, the United States Supreme Court decided United States v. Pomponio, 429 U.S. 10, 97 S.Ct. 22, 50 L.Ed.2d 12 (1976) (per curiam), in which it repudiated this formulation of willfulness. In *Pomponio*, the Court examined the various formulations that had been used for the definition of "willfully" in the Tax Code. See id. at 12, 97 S.Ct. 22. The Court attempted to dissipate the confusion that had arisen from its decision in United States v. Bishop, 412 U.S. 346, 93 S.Ct. 2008, 36 L.Ed.2d 941 (1973), in which the Court referred to a number of formulations of the standard, including the formulation it used in Spies, of "evil motive and want of justification in view of all the financial circumstances of the taxpayer."

The troublesome paragraph in *Bishop* was the following:

> The Court, in fact, has recognized that the word 'willfully' in these statutes generally connotes a voluntary, intentional violation of a known legal duty. It has formulated the requirement of willfulness as 'bad faith or evil intent,' United States v. Murdock, 290 U.S. 389, 398, 54 S.Ct. 223, 78 L.Ed. 381, or 'evil motive and want of justification in view of all the financial circumstances of the taxpayer,' Spies v. United States, 317 U.S. 492, 498, 63 S.Ct. 364, 87 L.Ed. 418, or knowledge that the taxpayer 'should have reported more income than he did.' Sansone v. United States, 380 U.S. 343, 353, 85 S.Ct. 1004, 13 L.Ed.2d 882. See James v. United States, 366 U.S. 213, 221, 81 S.Ct. 1052, 6 L.Ed.2d 246; McCarthy v. United States, 394 U.S. 459, 471, 89 S.Ct. 1166, 22 L.Ed.2d 418.

412 U.S. at 360, 93 S.Ct. 2008.

The court in *Pomponio* endeavored to erase the misconception that such different formulations, including the "evil motive" formulation of *Spies*, actually established different standards. The Court clarified that "willfulness" means a voluntary, intentional violation of a known legal duty, and does not "require[ ] proof of any [other] motivative." 429 U.S. at 12, 97 S.Ct. 22. The Court said, "Our references to other formulations of the standard did not modify [that] standard." Id. The Court explained that *Bishop* "did not . . . hold that the term requires proof of any motive other than an intentional violation of a known legal duty." Id.

Accordingly, the portion of our decision in *Poll* which created an additional requirement of proving ability to pay has been undermined by the Supreme Court's subsequent decision in *Pomponio*. *Poll* is not consistent with the intervening authority of the United States Supreme Court that must control our decision here.

In support of his contention that *Poll* nevertheless remains good law, Easterday argues that *Pomponio* is "coextensive" with this court's earlier determination in United States v. Hawk, 497 F.2d 365, 368 (9th Cir.1974), that neither bad purpose nor evil motive is an independent element of willfulness. Easterday reasons that because *Poll* stated that it was consistent with *Hawk*, and *Pomponio* approved *Hawk*, then *Poll* is still good law.

This argument does not withstand close analysis. *Poll* involved a charge of willful failure to collect or pay over tax. *Poll* distinguished *Hawk* on the basis that the offense charged in *Hawk* "was a *willful failure to file federal income tax returns.*" *Poll*, 521 F.2d at 332 (emphasis in original). Therefore, instead of following *Hawk*, *Poll* followed our earlier decision in *Andros* because *Andros* involved prosecution of a willful failure to pay a tax. Id. *Andros*, in turn, had followed the Supreme Court's decision in *Spies*. In *Poll*, we quoted at length from *Spies*, highlighting its statement with respect to a charge of willful failure to pay a tax, that " *[w]e would expect willfulness in such a case to include some element of evil motive and want of justification in view of all the financial circumstances of the taxpayer.*" *Poll*, 521 F.2d at 333 (citing *Spies*, 317 U.S. at 498, 63 S.Ct. 364) (emphasis in original). Because *Poll* applied the *Spies* "evil motive" formulation of willfulness, and expressly distinguished *Hawk*, *Poll* held that financial circumstances were relevant to proof of willfulness under 26 U.S.C. § 7202.

Later, in *Pomponio*, the Supreme Court approved the willfulness formulation of *Hawk*, but disapproved the "evil motive" formulation of *Spies*, holding that the standard is the same in all tax contexts. It approved the standard iterated in *Bishop*: "a voluntary, intentional violation of a known legal duty," and continued, "[o]ur references to other formulations of the standard did not modify the standard set forth in [*Bishop*]." *Pomponio*, 429 U.S. at 12-13, 97 S.Ct. 22. *Pomponio* thus undermines the heart of *Poll*'s holding that financial circumstances are relevant to a determination of willfulness under § 7202, failure to collect or pay over tax. This is because *Pomponio* expressly repudiates *Spies*' "evil motive" formulation on which *Poll* relied. 429 U.S. at 11-12, 97 S.Ct. 22.

The dissent, however, insists that the basis for *Poll*'s requirement of proving an "ability to pay" has not been undermined. It does so because it fails to recognize that the *Poll* requirement was founded upon the *Spies* formulation of willfulness that the Supreme Court rejected in *Pomponio*. Although the dissent agrees that *Pomponio* intended to do away with the misconception that the "evil motive" formulation of *Spies* established a different standard of willfulness, the dissent fails to recognize that *Poll*'s holding rested on just such a misconception.

This court, in *Poll*, thus held that the ability to pay was relevant to the charge of willful failure to collect or pay over tax because of *Spies'* incorporation of an element of "evil motive" into the requirement of willfulness in such tax cases. After *Pomponio*, we must hold that there is no longer any requirement of evil motive, upon which *Poll*'s holding rested.

We therefore hold that insofar as *Poll* may be interpreted as requiring the government, in a failure to pay case under § 7202, to prove that defendant had the money to pay the taxes when due, and allowing the defendant to defend on the ground that he had spent the money for other expenses, *Poll* is inconsistent with *Pomponio*. It is also inconsistent with common sense, for we think it unlikely that even under *Poll* and *Spies*, a defendant could succeed in arguing that he did not willfully fail to pay because he spent the money on something else. Cf. United States v. Gilbert, 266 F.3d 1180, 1185 (9th Cir.2001) (concluding that defendant's "act of paying wages to his employees, instead of remitting withholding taxes to the IRS, shows that he voluntarily and intentionally violated § 7202").

Indeed, in rejecting *Andros* and *Poll*, two of our sister circuits have made that very point. In United States v. Tucker, 686 F.2d 230 (5th Cir.1982), a prosecution for willfully failing to pay income taxes, under 26 U.S.C. § 7203, the defendant argued that he could not pay the taxes when they were due because he had no assets to satisfy the debt and that his failure to pay was not willful. The Fifth Circuit said that "[t]his argument borders on the ridiculous. . . .. [A] financial ability to pay the tax when it comes due is not a prerequisite to criminal liability under § 7203. Otherwise, a recalcitrant taxpayer could simply dissipate his liquid assets at or near the time when his taxes come due and thereby evade criminal liability." Id. at 233. In United States v. Ausmus, 774 F.2d 722, 725 (6th Cir.1985), the Sixth Circuit "rejected" the language in *Andros* that suggested financial ability to pay was relevant to criminal liability. The court said, "[o]therwise, a recalcitrant taxpayer could spend his money as fast as he earns it and evade criminal liability while not paying taxes as long as his bank balance is zero when the taxpayer's taxes are due." Id. Despite what we consider to be the unassailable logic presented by our sister circuits here, Easterday asks us to follow the contrary reasoning of *Andros* and *Poll* essentially because we have never formally repudiated it before now.

While we may not have explicitly overruled *Poll* or *Andros* in the more than three decades since we issued those opinions, neither have we cited them for the proposition that Easterday asserts here. *Poll* is not completely dead, for it has been used as a shorthand term describing the standard of "willful failure" to pay that has been discussed in the context of child support. See United States v. Ballek, 170 F.3d 871, 874 (9th Cir.1999); H.R.Rep. No. 102-771, at 6 (1992). In the tax field, however, it now exists only as a nearly completely buried obstacle to traffic that generally has run over it or passed it by for more than thirty years.

The only remaining question is whether we are nevertheless bound by *Poll* because it has not been overruled by an en banc court. Generally, a panel opinion is binding on subsequent panels unless and until overruled by an en banc decision of this circuit. See, e.g., Ross Island Sand & Gravel v. Matson, 226 F.3d 1015, 1018 (9th Cir.2000) (per curiam) ("[A]bsent a rehearing en banc, we are without authority to overrule [controlling circuit precedent].").

In Miller v. Gammie, 335 F.3d 889 (9th Cir.2003), we convened an en banc court to consider the question of when a panel decision may be overruled by intervening higher authority that, while not on an identical issue or expressly repudiating the panel decision, is inconsistent with its reasoning. We held that en banc review is not required to overturn a case where "intervening Supreme Court authority is clearly irreconcilable with our prior circuit authority." Id. at 900. We explained that we must avoid inconsistencies between our decisions and the decisions of a court of last resort. We said:

> We must recognize that we are an intermediate appellate court. A goal of our circuit's decisions, including panel and en banc decisions, must be to preserve the consistency of circuit law. The goal is codified

in procedures governing en banc review. See 28 U.S.C. § 46; Fed. R.App. P. 35. That objective, however, must not be pursued at the expense of creating an inconsistency between our circuit decisions and the reasoning of state or federal authority embodied in a decision of a court of last resort.

We hold that the issues decided by the higher court need not be identical in order to be controlling. Rather, the relevant court of last resort must have undercut the theory or reasoning underlying the prior circuit precedent in such a way that the cases are clearly irreconcilable.

335 F.3d at 900.

Pursuant to *Miller*, we conclude that it is not necessary to convene an en banc court in order to hold that *Poll*, and its antecedent *Andros*, are no longer binding authority for the proposition that a defendant's ability to pay his tax liability is relevant to the determination of willfulness under 26 U.S.C. § 7202. In keeping with *Pomponio*, 429 U.S. at 12, 97 S.Ct. 22, and *Cheek*, 498 U.S. at 201-02, 111 S.Ct. 604, we hold that willfulness does not require the government to prove that a defendant had the ability to meet his tax obligations. The district court's refusal to give a *Poll* instruction to the jury and the instruction it did give on willfulness were thus proper.

For similar reasons, the district court did not abuse its discretion in refusing to admit evidence proffered by Easterday in order to show how and why he spent money owed to the IRS to pay other business expenses. Such evidence would have been relevant only if a defendant were entitled to defend on the ground that he had spent the tax money for other needs. Because the financial circumstances of a defendant do not bear on the determination of willfulness under § 7202, Easterday's proffered evidence was irrelevant, and the district court did not abuse its discretion by excluding it. See Fed.R.Evid. 401.

Easterday's remaining contentions are without merit.

AFFIRMED.

N.R. SMITH, CIRCUIT JUDGE, dissenting:

In this case, I find myself between "the proverbial rock and a hard place." I can either adhere to precedent (with which I do not agree) or I can join the majority and try to overrule bad circuit precedent. Although I agree that United States v. Poll, 521 F.2d 329 (9th Cir.1975) is bad law, *Poll* is the controlling law of this circuit and I understand a three-judge panel is not able to undo precedent set forth by another three-judge panel. See Hulteen v. AT & T Corp., 498 F.3d 1001, 1009 (9th Cir.2007)

("A three-judge panel must follow a prior circuit decision unless a subsequent decision by a relevant court of last resort either effectively overrules the decision in a case 'closely on point' or undercuts the reasoning underlying the circuit precedent rendering the cases 'clearly irreconcilable.' "). In my view, because *Poll* is not irreconcilable with United States v. Pomponio, 429 U.S. 10, 97 S.Ct. 22, 50 L.Ed.2d 12 (1976) (per curiam), we are required to either follow *Poll* or make a sua sponte en banc call. See In re Complaint of Ross Island Sand & Gravel, 226 F.3d 1015, 1018 (9th Cir.2000) (per curiam) ("[A]bsent a rehearing en banc, we are without authority to overrule [controlling circuit precedent].").

The majority, however, has chosen to write around circuit precedent in order to avoid a result that they do not like. I therefore respectfully dissent for the following reasons. First, the majority legally errs by finding that *Poll* is no longer good law. Second, because of its error in finding that *Poll* was overruled by *Pomponio*, the majority incorrectly affirms the district court in its refusal to instruct the jury that the government must prove that Easterday had the financial ability to meet his tax obligations. Thus, I would reverse and remand for a new trial, because Easterday's ability to pay was an element of the crime the government needed to prove beyond a reasonable doubt.

I. Discussion

Poll discusses two separate questions: (a) willfulness, and (b) the relevance of evidence demonstrating an inability to pay in order to rebut the willfulness of a failure to pay over employee payroll taxes. See 521 F.2d at 331 ("These actions raise two questions: Viz. whether the foregoing definition of 'willfully' is correct and whether the evidence offered to rebut the presence of willfulness was irrelevant and inadmissible."). In *Poll*, we held that the willfulness definition was correct, and that the evidence of inability to pay was relevant to rebut the presence of willfulness. See id.

The majority, however, incorrectly concludes that " *Poll*'s requirement that the government prove that the taxpayer had sufficient funds to pay the tax was premised on a definition of willfulness that included some element of evil motive." In *Poll*, we based our holding, in part, on Supreme Court precedent found in Spies v. United States, 317 U.S. 492, 498, 63 S.Ct. 364, 87 L.Ed. 418 (1943), which states that "[w]e would expect willfulness . . . to include some element of evil motive and want of justification in view of all the financial circumstances of the taxpayer." *Poll*, 521 F.2d at 333. We also, however, relied on United States v. Hawk, 497 F.2d 365 (9th Cir.1974) to recognize that it is "not error to fail to include the words 'and/or evil motive' " when determining the "willfully" standard. *Poll,* 521 F.2d at 332.

The majority correctly recognizes that the Supreme Court "in *Pomponio* endeavored to erase the misconception that such different formulations, including the 'evil motive' formulation of *Spies,* actually established different standards." In *Pomponio,* the Court held that the term "willfully" does not require "proof of any motive other than an intentional violation of a known legal duty." 429 U.S. at 12, 97 S.Ct. 22. The Court explained the meaning of willfulness by stating that

> The Court, in fact, has recognized that the word "willfully" . . . generally connotes a voluntary, intentional violation of a known legal duty. It has formulated the requirement of willfulness as "bad faith or evil intent," or "evil motive and want of justification in view of all the financial circumstances of the taxpayer," or knowledge that the taxpayer "should have reported more income than he did."

> Our references to other formulations of the standard did not modify the standard [that the word 'willfully' . . . generally connotes a voluntary, intentional violation of a known legal duty].

Id.

Thus, even when the formulation of "evil motive" or "bad purpose" is used in explaining the standard for willfulness, the standard is not modified. Willfulness, in the context of tax laws, "simply means a *voluntary, intentional* violation of a known legal duty." Id. at 12-13, 97 S.Ct. 22 (emphasis added) (citing *Hawk,* 497 F.2d at 368); see also Cheek v. United States, 498 U.S. 192, 201-02, 111 S.Ct. 604, 112 L.Ed.2d 617 (1991). There is no requirement the government prove bad purpose or evil motive and want of justification. See *Pomponio,* 429 U.S. at 12-13, 97 S.Ct. 22; *Hawk,* 497 F.2d at 368. The holding in *Poll* is therefore consistent with the *Pomponio* definition of willfulness.

In *Poll,* we held that "to establish willfulness the Government must establish beyond a reasonable doubt that at the time payment was due the taxpayer possessed sufficient funds to enable him to meet his obligation or that the lack of sufficient funds on such date was created by (or was the result of) a *voluntary* and *intentional* act without justification in view of all the financial circumstances of the taxpayer." 521 F.2d at 333 (emphasis added). Our holding in *Poll* therefore relied on the same definition of willfulness as determined in *Pomponio* ("a *voluntary, intentional* violation of a known legal duty"). In fact, *Pomponio* actually supports that idea that *Poll* used the correct definition of willfulness. See 429 U.S. at 12-13, 97 S.Ct. 22 (noting that "as the other Courts of Appeals that have considered the question have recognized, willfulness in this context simply means a voluntary, intentional violation of a known legal duty" (citing *Hawk*, 497 F.2d at 366-69)).

As discussed, our determination of willfulness in *Poll* relied, in part, on *Hawk*, which the Supreme Court approved in *Pomponio*. In *Hawk*, we noted that the Supreme Court, in United States v. Murdock, 290 U.S. 389, 54 S.Ct. 223, 78 L.Ed. 381 (1933), held that

> [W]illfulness requires proof that the act was done with knowledge it was wrongful. The Court discussed a number of ways of expressing this type of specific intent, and among the terms mentioned were "bad purpose" and "evil motive."
>
> However, neither bad purpose nor evil motive is an independent element of a willful failure to file under § 7203. The term "evil motive" is merely a "convenient shorthand expression to distinguish liability based on conscious wrongdoing from liability based on mere carelessness or mistake." Thus the term expresses, in a brief way, the more cumbersomely stated concept of specific intent in *Murdock*, a concept the instructions must ultimately convey. This, we think, was all that *Murdock*- and *Bishop*-meant by the use of that term.

Hawk, 497 F.2d at 368.

Thus, although *Poll* quoted Supreme Court precedent regarding the inclusion of "evil motive and want of justification" to determine willfulness, we were referencing the "voluntary, intentional violation of a known legal duty" formulation discussed in *Pomponio*. Even though the wording was different, Supreme Court precedent dictates that the meaning underlying the term "willfulness" in *Poll* was the same as used in *Hawk* and *Pomponio*. *Poll*'s definition of willfulness was not premised on a belief that willfulness requires an evil motive or bad purpose. *Poll*, therefore, still holds that the ability to pay is relevant to demonstrate willfulness, and *Pomponio* did not state otherwise. Although *Pomponio* did discuss the willfulness question, see 429 U.S. at 12-13, 97 S.Ct. 22, the portion of our decision in *Poll* that created an additional requirement of proving ability to pay was not undermined by *Pomponio*. The basis for *Poll*'s requirement of proving ability to pay has therefore not been eliminated. No subsequent decision from this circuit or from a relevant court of last resort has overruled the requirement presented in *Poll* that evidence regarding inability to pay is relevant to rebut the presence of willfulness. See *Poll*, 521 F.2d at 332 ("We believe, and so hold, that the defendant's offer of proof regarding the liquid resources of the corporation and his intention to make up the deficiencies later was relevant and admissible in his effort to refute the willfulness of the failure to pay over.").

Pomponio also did not overrule *Poll* because *Pomponio* and *Poll* address different issues. In *Pomponio*, the Supreme Court, affirming this court's holding in *Hawk*, held that evil motive is not an independent element of filing false income tax returns under 26 U.S.C. § 7206 and that instructions regarding evil motive are thus unnecessary. 429 U.S. at 12-13, 97 S.Ct. 22. In *Poll*, by contrast, this court considered whether the government must prove that a defendant was capable of meeting his tax obligations. 521 F.2d at 333. We specifically noted that the ability to pay rule was not contrary to *Hawk* because *Hawk* addressed "a [w]illful failure to file [a] federal income tax return[ ]," not a crime "involving a failure to pay." 521 F.2d at 332. Because *Pomponio* affirmed *Hawk*, and because this court held, in *Poll*, that the ability to pay rule is consistent with *Hawk*, *Poll* is consistent with *Pomponio*. Thus, *Pomponio* is not "clearly irreconcilable" with *Poll*, and *Poll* remains good law. See *Hulteen*, 498 F.3d at 1009. We are therefore bound by *Poll* because it has not been overruled by an en banc court. See *In re Complaint of Ross Island Sand & Gravel*, 226 F.3d at 1018.

The majority also references this court's decision in United States v. Gilbert, 266 F.3d 1180 (9th Cir.2001), for the proposition that *Poll* is inconsistent with both *Pomponio* and common sense. In *Gilbert*, the defendant argued "that his failure to pay over the withholding tax was not willful because [his business] did not have the funds to pay the taxes." 266 F.3d at 1185. The government responded "that it presented sufficient evidence at trial that Gilbert voluntarily and intentionally paid net wages to his employees with knowledge that withholding taxes were not being remitted to the IRS." Id. This court affirmed on the basis that the evidence was sufficient. See Id. This court, however, did not explicitly or implicitly overrule the ability to pay rule. The district court in *Gilbert* had given a *Poll* instruction, and this court did not criticize the district court for having done so. In fact, this court did not reference the ability to pay rule or *Pomponio*. This court instead discussed how *Poll* did not concern "whether § 7202 required the failure [to both account for and pay over withholding tax], but instead addressed the issue of how to define willfulness under § 7202." Id. at 1183. This court held that "whether § 7202 required the failure to both account for and pay over the tax, were dicta." Id. That holding, however, does not address whether the ability to pay can be used as a defense. *Gilbert* therefore merely discusses whether § 7202 requires the failure to both account for and pay over withholding tax. Thus, there is no basis in *Gilbert* for the proposition that *Pomponio* overruled *Poll*.

To the extent the district court excluded evidence regarding the financial situation of Easterday's companies and his inability to pay (based on its flawed interpretation of *Pomponio*), the district court abused its discretion. See United States v. Gallagher, 99 F.3d 329, 331-32 (9th Cir.1996). Moreover, the district court's failure to instruct the jury that the government must prove that Easterday had the ability to meet his tax obligations is a constitutional error "because the jury did not have the opportunity to find each element of the crime beyond a reasonable doubt." Martinez v. Borg, 937 F.2d 422, 423 (9th Cir.1991). The district court rejected a large amount of evidence regarding Easterday's nursing homes' financial difficulties. Because this evidence "could rationally lead to a contrary finding with respect to the omitted element," the district court's error was not harmless and Easterday is entitled to a new trial. Neder v. United States, 527 U.S. 1, 19, 119 S.Ct. 1827, 144 L.Ed.2d 35 (1999).

Notes and Questions

Although the court refers to § 7202 as a "fairly rarely invoked provision," there have more frequent prosecutions under this provision in recent years. See Steve R. Johnson, "*Easterday* and the 'Inability to Pay' Defense For Tax Crimes," 124 Tax Notes 787, 788 n.7 (Aug. 24, 2009). In addition, financial inability to pay has been raised as a defense to the willfulness element in evasion cases as well as in § 7203 cases. See next section, below.

Does the financial inability to pay defense retain any vitality? See the Johnson article cited above.

3. Willful Failure to File, Supply Information or Pay the Tax – § 7203

Section 7203 is the misdemeanor counterpart of § 7201, carrying a fine of $25,000 ($100,000 in the case of a corporation), and/or imprisonment for not more than one year, plus the costs of prosecution. It punishes the willful failure to (1) file a tax return (including an estimated tax return), (2) pay any tax (including an estimated tax) due and owing, (3) maintain records and (4) supply information. The most commonly prosecuted of these offenses is the willful failure to file a return.

UNITED STATES v. KIMBALL

United States Court of Appeals, Ninth Circuit, 1991.
925 F.2d 356 (en banc).

[Eds.: Kimball filed IRS Forms 1040 for the years 1979 through 1982 in which he supplied asterisks in the spaces provided, with the notation: "This means that specific objection is made under the 5th Amendment, U.S. Constitution. Similar objection is made to the question under the 1st, 4th, 7th, 8th, 9th, 10th, 13th, 14th, and 16th Amendments for civil issues." He signed his name "Ted Kimball" at the bottom of the form. The Service sent him warning letters by registered mail advising him that if he did not file his income tax returns, he would be subject to prosecution for failure to file.]

PER CURIAM.

Kimball appeals from his conviction on three counts of willful failure to file an income tax return in violation of 26 U.S.C. § 7203. A panel of this court reversed Kimball's conviction, holding that he had filed returns. See United States v. Kimball, 896 F.2d 1218 (9th Cir. 1990) (Kimball). We then granted rehearing en banc. See United States v. Kimball, 914 F.2d 1386 (9th Cir. 1990). Now in our *en banc* capacity, we vacate the original opinion in part and remand the appeal to the original panel.

* * *

Kimball contends that his 1040 forms constitute returns as a matter of law. As a general rule, a document "which does not contain any information relating to the taxpayer's income from which the tax owed can be computed" is not a return within the meaning of section 7203. United States v. Klee, 494 F.2d 394, 397 (9th Cir. 1974) (*Klee*) (quoting United States v. Porth, 426 F.2d 519, 523 (10th Cir.1970)). Here, Kimball's 1040 forms contain no financial information whatsoever, and therefore, appear squarely within the rule of *Klee*. Other circuits considering documents similar to Kimball's have held they do not constitute returns.

The three-judge panel, however, held that the 1040 forms filed by Mr. Kimball did constitute "returns" on the basis of United States v. Long, 618 F.2d 74, 75-76 (9th Cir. 1980) (*Long*) (a form containing only zeros entered in the spaces provided for exemptions, income, tax, and tax withheld constitutes a return under § 7203), and Fuller v. United States, 786 F.2d 1437, 1439 (9th Cir. 1986) (taxpayers filing blank tax forms or forms containing only asterisks or the word "object" in the spaces provided for financial information had filed purported returns under §

6702). See *Kimball*, 896 F.2d at 1220. We conclude *Long* and *Fuller* do not control.

Turning first to *Fuller*, we point out that the questions presented by § 7203 in this appeal and § 6702 in *Fuller* are distinct. Section 7203 asks whether the taxpayer has filed a return. See 26 U.S.C. § 7203 ("Any person * * * who willfully fails to *.* * make such return"). Section 6702 raises a different issue: whether the taxpayer has filed a *purported* return. See 26 U.S.C. § 6702 ("any individual [who] files what purports to be a return"). We have previously observed this distinction in Bradley v. United States, 817 F.2d 1400, 1403 (9th Cir. 1987), where we held that "§ 6702 requires only that the document filed *purport* to be a tax return, not that it actually be a tax return." We should not rely on any superficial similarity between §§ 6702 and 7203. It is not incongruous to hold that an individual has failed to file a tax return under § 7203 and, nonetheless, has filed a frivolous purported return under § 6702. One can submit a document which purports to be a tax return, but which fails to meet the requirements for filing.

Nor does *Long* assist Kimball because its reasoning excludes the facts of his case:

> The zeros entered on Long's tax forms constitute "information relating to the taxpayer's income from which the tax can be computed." The I.R.S. could calculate assessments from Long's strings of zeros, just as it could if Long had entered other numbers. The resulting assessments might not reflect Long's actual tax liability, but some computation was possible.

Long, 618 F.2d at 75, quoting *Klee,* 494 F.2d at 397. *Long* properly turns on the presence or absence of financial information, in keeping with *Klee.* "Nothing can be calculated from a blank, but a zero, like other figures, has significance. A return containing false or misleading figures is still a return." Id. at 76. Here, as with Long's hypothetical blank form, nothing can be calculated from Kimball's asterisks. A proper reading of *Long* demonstrates that Kimball did not file a return.

Long's distinction is admittedly formalistic. It may be that whether a form contains zeros, asterisks, or nothing at all, it makes essentially the same point: the taxpayer refuses to report income. We nevertheless reaffirm *Long's* analysis. A line must be drawn somewhere, and given the need for clear law on an arcane point, it should be as bright as possible. *Long* accomplishes that, consistent with *Klee.*

We hold that the district court correctly ruled that Kimball's 1040 forms do not constitute returns. * * *

Notes and Questions

The *Long* decision has been rejected by several courts. See, e.g., United States v. Mosel, 738 F.2d 157 (6th Cir. 1984); United States v. Rickman, 638 F.2d 182 (10th Cir. 1980); United States v. Moore, 627 F.2d 830 (7th Cir. 1980).

In *Kimball*, the district court reviewed *en banc* the decision of a United States Magistrate. Under the Federal Rules of Criminal Procedure, a defendant who is indicted for a "minor offense" may elect in writing to have the case heard by a magistrate instead of by a federal district court judge. A defendant might choose this route because often the case will be heard more quickly by a magistrate than by a judge. If such an election is made, the defendant cannot object subsequently that the case was heard by a magistrate. Since the federal courts of appeal have no jurisdiction over the findings of a magistrate, appeals from a magistrate's decision are to the federal district court for the district in which the magistrate's court sits. There is no trial de novo when the district court hears the appeal. Instead, the scope of review is the same as that of an appeal to a federal circuit court of appeals. The magistrate's conclusions of law, however, are subject to de novo review. See United States v. Bronx Reptiles, 26 F. Supp. 2d 481 (E.D. NY 1998).

Section 7203 requires only a willful failure to file a return or pay a tax; it does not require an affirmative act to establish the offense. If the government fails to meet its burden of proof under § 7201 by proving an affirmative act of evasion, it often will have met the burden of proof for a misdemeanor conviction under § 7203.

If the offense is a willful failure to file a return required under the currency transaction reporting provision, § 6050I of the Code, the crime is elevated under § 7203 to a felony, punishable by up to five years in prison. (See discussion of § 6050I in § III.B., below). Each year that the taxpayer willfully fails to file a return constitutes a separate offense under § 7203 that can compound the potential sentence under the Federal Sentencing Commission Guidelines.

Section 6702, to which the *Kimball* court refers, is a civil penalty provision known as the "tax protestor penalty," under which a $500 fine is imposed for the filing of a frivolous return. Kimball's return fits squarely within the definition of "frivolous return" because his returns were not in processable form. Thus, under *Fuller,* cited in *Kimball,* the return "does not contain information from which the *substantial accuracy of* [taxpayer's] assessment [of tax liability] can be judged." By its terms, § 6702 applies in addition to any other penalty, whether civil or criminal. See § 6702(b). Since the penalty applies automatically when a frivolous return is filed, it does not fall within the assessment procedures discussed in Chapter 4. Thus, it is immediately due and payable, and the taxpayer may contest the penalty only after it has been paid in full. Since the taxpayer then would be claiming a refund, the Tax Court does not have jurisdiction over such suits.

1. After the Ninth Circuit's decision in *Kimball* had been rendered, could the government impose a § 6702 penalty on Kimball?

2. What elements must the government prove in order to obtain a conviction under § 7203?

3. Kimball's argument was that he had attended a tax shelter seminar offered by the American Law Association where he was told that if he funneled his income through a series of foreign trusts, he would not be required to file a more complete return. This was similar to Cheek's claim. Would the *Cheek* decision have been useful to Kimball if it had been available at the time?

4. Fraud and False Statements – § 7206

Section 7206 is a felony provision encompassing five separate offenses: (1) false declarations made under penalty of perjury, (2) willfully aiding or assisting in the preparation of a false or fraudulent document, (3) simulating or fraudulently executing any bond, permit or other document required by the internal revenue laws, (4) removing or concealing property with the intent to evade the assessment or collection of tax, and (5) concealing property, making false statements, or destroying records in connection with any offer in compromise or closing agreement.

Under the IRC, the penalty for violating § 7206 is a fine of not more than $100,000 ($500,000 in the case of a corporation) or imprisonment for not more than three years, or both, together with costs of prosecution. Greater maximum penalties may apply under the Federal Sentencing Commission Guidelines.

The most commonly prosecuted of these offenses are the false statements (perjury) offense under § 7206(1) and the preparer offense under § 7206(2).

a. *False Statements – § 7206(1)*

UNITED STATES v. BORMAN
United States Court of Appeals, Seventh Circuit, 1993.
992 F.2d 124.

FAIRCHILD, SENIOR CIRCUIT JUDGE.

The government appeals from an order granting Richard K. Borman's and Betty L. White's motion to dismiss the indictment. * * * The indictment charged Borman and White with willfully making and subscribing joint U.S. Individual Income Tax Returns, made under the penalties of perjury, which he/she did not believe to be correct as to every material matter, in violation of 26 U.S.C. § 7206(1). The returns referenced in the indictment were for the 1985, 1986 and 1987 tax years, one count for each defendant for each year. Each count alleged that Borman and White represented that, for each year, they received only wages, salaries, tips and interest in specified amounts, although they knew and believed that they also received gross receipts in specified amounts from the manufacture and sale of seasonal wreaths, which by law were required to be disclosed. Borman and White were husband and wife at the time of the alleged offenses.

Borman and White filed motions to dismiss the indictment. They asserted that the return involved in each count was IRS Form 1040A, which inquires about total wages, salaries, tips, interest income, and two other types of income not relevant in this case. The form does not inquire about income of other types nor about the amount of receipts from a business. Defendants did not insert any representation concerning other income. Thus, they argued that each return was true and correct, and therefore there was no violation of 26 U.S.C. § 7206(1), as held in United States v. Reynolds, 919 F.2d 435 (7th Cir. 1990). The government conceded that the defendants filed Forms 1040A and took the position that "the defendants' motions raise only a question of law and the court should rule on them at this time. Such a ruling will be time-saving and serve the interests of judicial economy."

The motions were referred to a magistrate judge, and on April 21, 1992, he issued a Report recommending that the motions to dismiss be granted. The district court adopted the Report, relying principally on *Reynolds*, 919 F.2d 434, in which we held that § 7206(1) is a perjury statute and literal truth is a defense to perjury, even if the answer is highly misleading. Id. at 437. Although Borman and White had a duty to file a different form, which called for disclosure of their receipts from business, the government makes no claim that the answers on the Forms

1040A for the years at issue were untrue. The court ruled that the defendants' filing of the wrong form could not constitute a violation of § 7206(1). We affirm.

DISCUSSION

The indictment alleges that Borman and White did not believe their returns to be correct as to every material matter in that the said return represented that they received only wages, salaries, tips and interest. The government's theory must be that the filing of Form 1040A implicitly represented that they received no income of a type or amount which would require the use of a different form. The issue before us is whether an indictment, limited to that theory, charges an offense.

To establish a violation of § 7206(1), the government must prove that (1) the defendant made or subscribed a return which he verified as true; (2) the return contained a written declaration that it was made under penalty of perjury; (3) the defendant signed the return willfully, believing that it was not true and correct as to every material matter; and (4) the return was false as to a material matter. 26 U.S.C. § 7206(1).

In *Reynolds*, we reversed a conviction under § 7206(1) where the taxpayer filed a Form 1040EZ and the statements thereon were literally correct, but the taxpayer had received income of a type which he had a duty to report on a different form. The facts differ in that the *Reynolds* indictment did not allege a representation that the taxpayer received only income of particular types, and instead alleged that Reynolds represented his taxable income as the amount he had reported on line 7 of the form. These differences are insignificant for our present purpose, however, notwithstanding a remark in *Reynolds* that an "argument that by filing Form 1040EZ a taxpayer implicitly represents that he has no additional income has more substance." Id. at 437.

Thus, under the *Reynolds* rationale, the untruth must be found in a statement of some material information called for by the form itself, and any implication drawn from the filing of a particular form–that the taxpayer had received no income requiring the use of a different form–is simply not enough. As the *Reynolds* opinion put it, "using the wrong form does not violate § 7206(1)." Id.

There is no question that if Borman and White had income of other types, they had a legal obligation to file Form 1040, not 1040A. However, the parties assume for present purposes that the statements made on the Forms 1040A for the years at issue are literally true. The Form 1040A does not call for the taxpayer to declare that he or she has no income of a type other than that required to be disclosed on the form. Although in

Reynolds we noted that the IRS's implicit representation theory has "more substance" than a theory that line 7 of the Form 1040EZ called for a representation of total taxable income, we expressly held that § 7206(1) is not violated by filing the wrong form. Id. at 437. A charge that the taxpayer makes an implicit representation when filing the wrong form adds nothing beyond a charge of filing the wrong form. Therefore, dismissal of the indictment was appropriate.

The government additionally argues that such a ruling would unduly diminish its ability to protect the integrity of the federal tax system. We are not persuaded. As we noted in *Reynolds,* the government may seek an indictment for tax evasion, 26 U.S.C. § 7201, or failure to supply information required by law, 26 U.S.C. § 7203. Moreover, the present problem is easily remedied without abandoning the use of simplified forms. The IRS need only add a single question to its Form 1040A–e.g., "did you receive income of any type not reported on this return?" If the taxpayer willfully fails to answer this question correctly, the government could prosecute under § 7206(1). See United States v. Mattox, 689 F.2d 531, 533 (5th Cir. 1982) (leaving a question unanswered constitutes making a false statement if in fact the question should have been answered).

For the foregoing reasons, we AFFIRM the district court's dismissal of the indictment.

Notes and Question

The current form 1040A requires the taxpayer to sign, and thus swear under penalties of perjury that the form "accurately lists all amounts and sources of income [the taxpayer] received during the taxable year."

Section 7206(1) applies not only to false statements made on returns, but also to false statements made to IRS agents.

Can you think of any reason(s) why the government would prefer to charge a taxpayer with perjury under § 7206(1) instead of evasion under § 7201 or willful failure to supply information under § 7203?

1) Materiality

UNITED STATES v. LUIZ BEN ZVI
United States Court of Appeals, Second Circuit, 1999
168 F.3d 49

* * *

BACKGROUND

Roz Ben Zvi was the owner of Josi Jewelry, a gold chain manufacturing business in New York City. Luiz Ben Zvi was an employee of Josi Jewelry. On February 26, 1988, police responded to cries for help at Josi Jewelry and found the Zvis bound together in a back room. The Zvis falsely told the police that unidentified assailants had overtaken them, bound them, and stolen millions of dollars worth of gold chain. In actuality, a co-conspirator tied them up after they had created the appearance of a struggle; he then struck Roz Ben Zvi for added "realism" and left them locked in the back room. The Zvis subsequently filed an insurance claim with Lloyd's of London for $3,995,000. On August 15, 1988, Lloyd's made an electronic funds transfer from London, England, to Josi Jewelry's account at Chemical Bank in New York as full payment on the claim.

In the spring of 1993, the government informed the Zvis that they were under investigation by a grand jury for possible violations of federal law. * * *

* * *

On August 11, 1993, the grand jury indicted Luiz Ben Zvi, alleging her participation in a conspiracy to stage the February 26, 1988 robbery in order to defraud Lloyd's. * * *

On March 9, 1994, a second superseding indictment was filed alleging that: (1) prior to the staged robbery of February 26, 1988, the Zvis had surreptitiously sold all of the gold they later claimed was stolen; (2) the Zvis allegedly laundered the proceeds of the wire fraud through six additional international funds transfers, dated May 17, 1988, July 28, 1988, September 1, 1988, September 23, 1988, November 11, 1988, and March 3, 1989; (3) Roz Ben Zvi had also engaged in three counts of laundering proceeds from narcotics trafficking and two counts of filing false tax returns; (4) international and domestic money laundering and filing false tax returns were additional objects of the conspiracy charged in count one * * *.

* * *

* * * Defendants were found guilty on the [false tax return charges]. This appeal followed.

DISCUSSION

The defendants challenge their convictions on numerous grounds. Specifically, they contend that: * * * (5) the district court's failure to instruct the jury on the element of materiality in the false tax return claims was plain error; * * *.

* * *

E.   Omission of Element of Materiality in Tax Count Charge

Roz Ben Zvi claims that his convictions for filing false tax returns, in violation of 26 U.S.C. § 7206(1),[3] must be reversed because the district court did not instruct the jury that the false statements at issue must be material. The instruction read:

> In order to sustain its burden of proof . . . the government must prove the following four essential elements beyond a reasonable doubt.
> * * *

> 3. That the defendant Roz Ben Zvi did not believe the returns to be true and correct as to the gross sales and receipts of Josi Jewelry Corporation or as to the personal income of himself.

Because defendants failed to object to the instruction, we review the district court's instruction for plain error * * *.

The omission of materiality from the jury charge was probably not error at all; and, in any event, it was not plain error. This circuit has held that the issue of materiality on false tax returns is a matter for the court to decide. See United States v. Klausner, 80 F.3d 55, 60-61 (2d Cir.1996); United States v. Greenberg, 735 F.2d 29, 31 (2d Cir.1984). But see United States v. Neder, 136 F.3d 1459, 1464 (11th Cir.1998) (noting that every other circuit addressing the question has held that materiality under § 7206(1) is a question for the jury). Here the jury heard the district court read the indictment and the statute, both of which recite the element of materiality. The district court further instructed the jury that it could find Roz Ben Zvi guilty only if it found the particular misrepresentations   contained   in   the   indictment;   all   of   those

---

3.   Section 7206(1) provides that a person commits a felong if he "willfully makes and subscribes any return, statement, or other document, which contains or is verified by a written declaration that it is made under the penalties of perjury, and which he does not believe to be true and correct as to every *material* matter." 26 U.S.C. § 7206(1) (emphasis added).

misrepresentations entailed the failure to report substantial amounts of income and were therefore material as a matter of law. See *Klausner*, 80 F.3d at 60 (test for materiality is whether particular item must be reported in order for taxpayer to assess tax liability correctly).

In *Johnson* [eds: Johnson v. United States, 520 U.S. 461, 117 Sup. Ct. 1544, 137 L.Ed.2d 718 (1997)] * * * there was no plain error in the trial court's failure to charge the jury on materiality because the materiality was apparent from the evidence, even though under the statute at issue in those cases materiality is a jury issue. See *Johnson*, at 469-70, 117 S.Ct. at 1550. In light of these decisions, a fortiori, we cannot find plain error for lack of a materiality charge when materiality is both an issue for the court and apparent from the evidence.

The better practice in false tax return cases is for the district court to make a determination of materiality, and then inform the jury that the alleged misrepresentation, if found, is material under the statute as a matter of law. Such a charge ensures that the question is not left to the jury by implication. The failure of a district court to give such an instruction could result in a wrongful acquittal if the jury decided materiality in the defendant's favor. In the face of a conviction, such a failure could never be prejudicial to a defendant even if the defendant had objected; under the law of this circuit, the jury in a false tax return case is not empowered to resolve the question of materiality in a defendant's favor.

Materiality was an issue for the court, and materiality was apparent because the tax return at issue involved the under-reporting of income by thousands of dollars. Accordingly, we affirm Roz Ben Zvi's convictions for filing false tax returns.

* * *

Notes and Questions

As the court in *Ben Zvi* indicates, there has been some conflict about whether materiality is a question of fact for the jury or a question of law for the court to resolve. This issue appeared to have been resolved by the United States Supreme Court in United States v. Gaudin, 515 U.S. 506, 115 S.Ct. 2310, 132 L.Ed.2d 444 (1995), a case involving false statements on a loan document filed with the Department of Housing and Urban Development. The Court held that when materiality is an element of the offense, the defendant has a constitutional right to have that issue submitted to the jury. While many courts interpret *Gaudin* to mean that the issue of materiality is an issue to be decided by the jury, (see, e.g., United States v. DiRico, 78 F.3d 732 (1st Cir. 1995); United States v.

McGuire, 79 F.3d 1396 (5th Cir. 1996) (*en banc*)), the Second Circuit takes a more restrictive view, at least in prosecutions involving § 7206.

In United States v. Klausner, 80 F.3d 55 (2d Cir. 1996), cited in *Ben Zvi,* the defendant was convicted of assisting in the preparation of false tax returns under § 7206(2) by advising his clients to take false deductions. On appeal, the court held that the question of whether the deductions were false was a question of fact for the jury, but the issue of whether the false deductions were material was an issue of law for the court.

Subsequently, the United States Supreme Court considered the case of Neder v. United States, 527 U.S. 1, 119 S.Ct. 1827, 144 L.Ed.2d 35 (1997) (which is reproduced in § II.D, below) in which the defendant had been convicted of tax fraud under § 7206(1), as well as mail fraud, wire fraud and bank fraud. The lower court had failed to instruct the jury on materiality of the false statements in the tax fraud charge. The Supreme Court held this was error, citing *Gaudin,* but that the error was harmless because under the provision in question, the jury must find that the defendant submitted a return that he did not believe to be true and correct as to every material matter. The Court noted that "several courts [had] determined 'that any failure to report income is material.'" In *Neder,* however, the defendant had omitted a "substantial" amount of income, therefore "no jury could reasonably find that Neder's failure to report substantial amounts of income on his tax returns was not 'a material matter.'" Id., at 16. Justice Stevens, in his concurrence in *Neder,* cites *Klausner* in defining the term "material matter" as "any information necessary to a determination of a taxpayer's income tax liability." Id., at 26 (Stevens, J., concurring).

The Ninth Circuit in United States v. Uchimura, 107 F.3d 1321 (9th Cir. 1997) held that materiality is a question for the jury. Subsequently, however, the Ninth Circuit withdrew its decision and reissued it. In its substituted opinion, the court followed its earlier opinion in United States v. Knapp, 120 F.3d 928 (9th Cir. 1997), holding that the question of materiality was an issue for the jury, but where the defendant did not object at trial, the decision should be reviewed only for plain error. Where the defendant grossly understated taxable income, the lower court's error did not seriously affect the fairness, integrity or public reputation of the judicial proceedings. United States v. Uchimura, 125 F.3d 1282 (9th Cir. 1997) (substituted opinion). The question of whether materiality is an issue for the jury or an issue for the court remains unresolved.

The Second Circuit also refers to materiality in terms of the "under-reporting of income by thousands of dollars." But previously, it had determined that a misstatement is material if it has the potential to "impede the IRS's performance of its responsibilities," regardless of the amount of the underpayment. See United States v. Greenberg, 735 F.2d 29 (2d Cir. 1984).

1. In *Klausner*, there were two types of false deductions at issue -- one type was entirely fictitious while the other type was grossly overstated. The amount of the deductions was in question in both types. If the issue is not the amount of the deductions, but whether the item constitutes a deductible expenditure, would this be considered an issue of fact for the jury or an issue of law for the court? What if the issue is a novel one? See United States v. Garber, 607 F.2d 92 (5th Cir. 1979) (involving a novel question of income); but see United States v. DiRico, 78 F.3d 732 (1st Cir. 1996)(holding that materiality is a question for the jury and that "harmless error is not applicable where the jury is prevented from determining an essential element of the crime").

2. What standard of review should the appellate court employ if the judge fails to properly instruct the jury on materiality? See Neder v. United States, 527 U.S. 1 (1997).

3. If the Supreme Court had granted certiorari in the *Ben Zvi* case, how do you think the Court would have decided the case? Why?

2) *Willfulness*

Willfulness is an element of all the § 7206 offenses, and it has the same meaning as in the felony evasion provision discussed earlier. See § A.1.(a) 3, above.

b. *Aiding and Assisting – § 7206(2)*

The aiding and assisting provision is often called the preparer's penalty because many of the cases prosecuted under § 7206(2) have involved return preparers. The provision may apply more broadly, however, as you will see in the following case.

UNITED STATES v. HOOKS

United States Court of Appeals, Seventh Circuit, 1988.
848 F.2d 785.

GRANT, SENIOR DISTRICT JUDGE.

* * *

Facts

This case concerns the unreported, untaxed assets of a decedent's estate. The underlying facts are not in dispute. Appellant Hooks' father-in-law, Floyd Loge, died in Evansville, Indiana, on September 26, 1978, leaving an $8 million estate. Loge's widow, Celia May Loge, and the Citizens National Bank of Evansville were co-executors under the will; the bank administered the estate.

Mrs. Loge and her daughter, Patricia Susan Hooks, turned over to the bank a box of stock certificates and bonds to be included in Loge's estate. When the bank asked Loge's personal broker to determine the market value of those assets, the broker discovered that he was not given ten issues of bearer bonds that had previously been a part of Loge's portfolio. The face value of those bonds was approximately $375,000.00.

The bank questioned Mrs. Loge about this discrepancy, and was told that the missing bonds could not be found. On the assurance that all of Floyd Loge's assets had been turned over, therefore, the bank prepared the federal estate tax return without including those ten bearer bonds in the estate. The return was filed on March 20, 1980.

In 1978, appellant William Hooks was a vice president of the Plasti-Drum Corporation. He asked his employer, Walter Craig, to store some bearer bonds in Craig's safe deposit box because he did not want anyone to know of his connection with the bonds. According to Craig, Hooks said that "the girls" (Mrs. Loge and Patricia Hooks) told Hooks to take the bonds from under Mr. Loge's bed. When Hooks and Craig went to the bank to put the bonds in Craig's box, they chatted with the loan officer of the bank, Patrick Richter. Hooks showed Richter the bonds. Richter told him he could convert the bonds to cash; Hooks responded that the cashing of the bonds would have to be done in such a manner that it could not be connected or traced to him.

Craig placed the bonds in his safe deposit box on October 31, 1978, and removed them, at Hooks' request, on December 1, 1978. Hooks then handed the bonds to Richter and told him to proceed with their plan for cashing them.

Richter approached bond broker Harold Finley with seven bond issues to be negotiated, and asked whether the bond proceeds could be paid by check payable to bearer or to cash. Both Finley and his office manager answered that, because the IRS required records of such transactions, payment had to be made by check to the owner of the bonds. Richter responded, "Well, we are trying to keep them out of a ten million dollar estate."

Although Finley refused to sell the bonds under those conditions, Richter eventually did sell them through Paul Gantzert, a trust officer of Union National Bank in Joliet, Illinois. All the bonds were cashed between December 1978 and March 1979. The proceeds of the bond sales were transmitted payable to the Union National Bank; Gantzert then issued checks and money orders to Richter and others. One money order for $45,000 was made payable to Green Bay Aviation Corporation as a down payment on the purchase of a corporate airplane for Plasti-Drum. The proceeds were also used to set up a new bank account and to purchase such items as two pieces of art by Chagall and a condominium.

It is undisputed that the bonds given to Richter for sale by Hooks were the ones missing from Loge's estate, and that their value was not included in that estate or reported on the estate tax return. As a result, $96,564.58 in estate tax was avoided.

Although the government considered Mrs. Loge and Mrs. Hooks to be unindicted co-conspirators who were a part of the plan to defraud the government, Hooks and Richter were the only members of the conspiracy who were indicted. The trial began August 26, 1986, and lasted thirteen days. On September 15, 1986, a jury found Hooks and Richter[1] guilty of conspiracy to defraud the government (18 U.S.C. § 371) and of aiding in the preparation of a materially false federal estate tax return (26 U.S.C. § 7206(2)).[2]

Hooks has appealed, contending that (1) the evidence at trial was insufficient to support either count of the conviction; * * *

II. *Sufficiency of the Evidence*

A. 26 U.S.C. § 7206(2): "Aiding and Abetting"

Section 7206(2) of the Internal Revenue Code imposes criminal sanctions against one who willfully aids or assists in, or procures, counsels, or advises the preparation or presentation under, or in

---

1. Co-defendant Patrick Richter does not appeal his conviction.

2. The court sentenced Hooks to eighteen months in the custody of the Attorney General and fined him $5,000 on the conspiracy count. It placed him on probation for five years following his imprisonment and fined him $5,000 on the aiding and abetting charge.

connection with any matter arising under, the internal revenue laws, of a return, affidavit, claim, or other document, which is fraudulent or is false as to any material matter, whether or not such falsity or fraud is with the knowledge or consent of the person authorized or required to present such return, affidavit, claim, or document. 26 U.S.C. § 7206(2).

Appellant Hooks asserts that the government's proof showed only that he concealed and cashed the bonds, and not that he aided or assisted in the filing of a false tax return. Claiming that this prosecution involved a "rare and novel application" of 26 U.S.C. § 7206(2), Hooks insists that one who is not the taxpayer, tax preparer, or supplier of information for the return cannot be charged with aiding and abetting a false estate tax filing.

* * *

The essential elements of an offense under section 7206(2) are (1) that defendant aided, assisted, procured, counseled, advised or caused the preparation and presentation of a return; (2) that the return was fraudulent or false as to a material matter; and (3) that the act of the defendant was willful. No challenge to the second criterion has been raised.

To establish the first element of the offense, aiding and abetting the filing of a false tax return, "there must exist some affirmative participation which at least encourages the perpetrator."

It is well engrained in the law that one who aids or abets the commission of an act is as responsible for that act as if he committed it directly. Nye & Nissen v. United States, 336 U.S. 613, 618, 69 S.Ct. 766, 93 L.Ed. 919 (1949).

> In order to aid and abet another to commit a crime it is necessary that a defendant "in some sort associate himself with the venture, that he participate in it as in something that he wishes to bring about, that he seek by his action to make it succeed." L. Hand, J., in United States v. Peoni, 100 F.2d 401, 402 (2nd Cir. 1938).

Id. at 619.

The government showed that Hooks engaged in affirmative participation to make the common goal successful: He both concealed and liquidated the bearer bonds which were purportedly assets of the Loge estate. The evidence established that Hooks received from Celia Loge the ten bonds that should have been turned over to the tax preparer; that he hid those bonds in his employer's safe deposit box; and that he later cashed the bonds with the aid of his co-defendant Patrick Richter in such a way that they could not be traced back to him or to the estate. As a result, the estate did not include those bonds, Hooks and Richter were the beneficiaries of the proceeds from the bonds, and the Loge estate tax return, which did not report approximately $375,000 in assets, was false.

It is true that there was no direct evidence tying Hooks to the false tax return involved in the substantive count. Yet, as was the case in *Nye & Nissen,* there is circumstantial evidence wholly adequate to support the finding of the jury that he aided and abetted in the commission of that offense. Clearly the government has been defrauded within the meaning of § 7206(2) when the scheme is calculated to defeat government collection of tax. The scheme herein to defraud the government included both the nondisclosure of estate assets, which resulted in the false tax return and loss of revenue to the United States, and the subsequent cashing of the secreted bonds, which resulted in a gain of revenue to Hooks and Richter. The evidence presented, and the reasonable inferences drawn therefrom, were sufficient for the jury to decide that the defendants' activities constituted aiding and abetting the filing of the false tax return.

To establish the third element of the offense under § 7206(2), the government must also prove that the defendant's act was willful. The Eighth Circuit has recently examined what constitutes a "willful act" under this provision in United States v. Kouba, 822 F.2d 768 (8th Cir. 1987):

> The Supreme Court has defined the term "willfully" under § 7206 and related statutes to mean a voluntary intentional violation of a known legal duty. United States v. Pomponio, 429 U.S. 10, 12, 97 S.Ct. 22, 23, 50 L.Ed. 2d 12 (1976). See also United States v. Pohlman, 522 F.2d 974 (8th Cir. 1975). "Willful" requires "proof of a specific intent to do something which the law forbids; more than a showing of careless disregard for the truth is required." United States v. Dahlstrom, 713 F.2d at 1427; see also United States v. Pohlman, 522 F.2d at 976.

Kouba, 822 F.2d at 773. Therefore there must be sufficient evidence that Hooks knowingly concealed the bonds with the expectation that Mrs. Loge, by denying the existence of those hidden assets, could cause a false estate tax return to be filed.

The court finds ample evidence from the record of the scheme to conceal the estate assets from the IRS. Hooks knew that the bonds had belonged to Loge; he intentionally hid them in a safe deposit box that was not his own; he deliberately made several unsuccessful attempts, through his co-defendant Richter, to cash the bonds without identifying himself or Loge; he succeeded in negotiating the bonds only after they were taken from Indiana to an Illinois bank, which disposed of the bonds without divulging the recipient of the proceeds and without disclosing the transactions to the tax preparer who would have included them in the estate. These activities were deliberate, willful efforts to keep the bonds out of the taxable estate of Floyd Loge. The evidence is clear support for the jury's finding of Hooks' willfulness on the aiding counts.

Appellant Hooks makes essentially the same argument in a different light: He asserts that the aiding and abetting statute is intended to prosecute those who supply false information to the tax preparer, or those who are under a duty to provide information; therefore, the violation of § 7206(2) actually occurred when Celia Loge decided neither to turn over nor to report the bonds to the tax preparer as part of her husband's gross estate. Under this interpretation of the offense, Hooks' later concealment and liquidation of the bonds was subsequent to, rather than part of, the conspiracy to cause the filing of a false estate tax return and immaterial to that violation.

This theory is similar to the argument presented by the defendant in United States v. Collazo, 815 F.2d 1138 (7th Cir. 1987). Collazo had been convicted of aiding and abetting the unlawful possession of stolen checks. On appeal, he asserted, unsuccessfully, that the evidence of aiding and abetting was insufficient because it had demonstrated that he dealt with the checks only after the act of unlawful possession was completed. 815 F.2d at 1144. In both cases, however, the defendants were willing recipients of the illegally possessed evidence which had been passed to them by other conspirators, and the scheme was furthered by their subsequent actions. See 815 F.2d at 1144-45.

The Supreme Court has made clear that the crime of aiding in the fraudulent preparation of a tax return is "committed at the time the return is filed." United States v. Habig, 390 U.S. 222, 223, 88 S.Ct. 926, 927, 19 L.Ed. 2d 1055 (1968). The fraudulent return for the Loge estate was filed March 20, 1980; the bonds were concealed and sold by March 1979.

Moreover, Hooks' attempt to narrow his own involvement to the mere liquidation of assets while Mrs. Loge actually conceptualized the scheme and performed the illegal act of assisting in the preparation of a false tax return must fail. There is substantial evidence in the record that establishes a common scheme to withhold the bonds from the tax preparer, whether the purpose for that nondisclosure and concealment was to obtain less estate tax liability or more personal profit. Hooks' deliberate concealment of the existence and sale of the bonds, the true owner of the bonds, the amount of the proceeds from the secret sales, and the recipient of those proceeds did in fact keep those amounts out of Loge's estate, thereby reducing the collection of tax revenue on that estate. Mrs. Loge and Mrs. Hooks furthered the scheme by denying the existence of the bonds when questioned about them. Together their efforts succeeded in evading the payment of federal estate tax. It is not significant that different fraudulent practices occurred at different periods. The circumvention of the federal taxation system by the presentation of false information about the estate assets and by the carefully manipulated selling of estate assets "were part and parcel of the same conspiracy as charged and proved." Nye & Nissen v. United States, 336 U.S. at 617. The jury had sufficient evidence reasonably to conclude that Hooks had been a willful and knowing participant in a criminal violation of § 7206(2). That is all the government had to prove.

The court finds the government's application of § 7206(2) in these circumstances to be appropriate rather than "rare and novel."[3] Section 7206(2) has a broad sweep, making all forms of willful assistance in preparing a false return an offense. United States v. Shortt Accountancy Corp., 785 F.2d 1448, 1454 (9th Cir.1986). One may be guilty of aiding the preparation or filing of a false return under § 7206(2) whether or not the tax preparer knew of such falsity or fraud. "The scope of the statute extends to all participants of a scheme which results in the filing of a false return, whether or not those parties actually prepare it." The evidence adduced by the government showed Hooks to be a knowing and willful participant in the scheme which resulted in the filing of a false return. The court thus holds that a reasonable jury could have found the essential elements of an offense under § 7206(2) beyond a reasonable doubt.

* * *

---

3.   To challenge appellant's assertion that the prosecution's application of § 7206(2) was "rare and novel," the government cited six aiding and abetting cases that found liability because of the defendant's concealing actions: United States v. Johnson, 319 U.S. 503, 87 L.Ed. 1546, 63 S.Ct. 1233 (1943); United States v. Graham, 758 F.2d 879 (3d Cir.1985); United States v. Guthartz, 573 F.2d 225 (5th Cir.1978); United States v. Crum, 529 F.2d 1380 (9th Cir. 1976); Baker v. United States, 131 U.S. App. D.C. 7, 401 F.2d 958 (D.C. Cir. 1968); United States v. Frazier, 365 F.2d 316, 318 (6th Cir. 1966). Hooks claims that some of the cases are inapposite because they involve prosecutions under 26 U.S.C. § 7201 rather than under § 7206. However, § 7206 is simply a lesser-included offense of § 7201, which has been described as "the capstone of a system of sanctions which singly or in combination were calculated to induce prompt and forthright fulfillment of every duty under the income tax law." Spies v. United States, 317 U.S. 492, 497, 63 S.Ct. 364, 367, 87 L.Ed. 418 (1943). A charge is a lesser-included offense when "it is composed of fewer than all of the elements of the [greater] offense charged, and if all of its elements are elements of the [greater] offense charged." United States v. Citron, 783 F.2d 307, 312 (2d Cir. 1986), citing United States v. LoRusso, 695 F.2d 45, 52 n.3 (2d Cir. 1982). Therefore, the cases listed by the government are not inappropriate simply because they fall under section 7201 rather than section 7206. Section 7201 proscribes willfully attempting in any manner to evade or defeat any tax imposed by the Internal Revenue Code. Sansone v. United States, 380 U.S. 343, 350, 85 S.Ct. 1004, 13 L.Ed. 2d 882 (1965).

V. Conclusion

Based on a thorough review of the record and reviewing the evidence in the light most favorable to the prosecution, we hold that any rational trier of fact could have found beyond a reasonable doubt the elements of the offenses of 26 U.S.C. § 7206(2) * * *. Accordingly, we affirm the conviction of the appellant.

Notes and Questions

As the *Hooks* case demonstrates, § 7206(2) is not limited to preparers. It also may apply to attorneys and others who prepare false or fraudulent documents, knowing that they will be used in the preparation of a tax return. See United States v. Crum, 529 F.2d 1380 (9th Cir. 1976) (beaver breeder participated in fraudulent tax shelter scheme involving backdated documents).

Section 7206(2) overlaps with 18 U.S.C. § 2, which provides that a person who aids and abets another in committing an offense against the United States is liable as a principal. This provision applies to (1) an individual who engages indirectly in the commission of a federal offense and (2) an individual who does not engage in the proscribed activity at all, but who aids those who do. The offense is derivative, thus in order for § 2 to apply, the government must establish that a substantive crime was committed. The punishment then is determined by the underlying substantive offense.

An accomplice who aids or abets another in the commission of a substantive federal offense may be punished as a principal. At common law, an accessory could not be convicted unless the principal also was convicted. That rule no longer applies and the accessory is liable regardless of whether the principal is prosecuted and regardless of whether the principal's identity is known. See Standefer v. United States, 447 U.S. 10 (1980).

When the underlying offense is aiding and abetting the preparation of a false tax return, what is the relationship between 26 U.S.C. § 7206(2) and 18 U.S.C. § 2? In United States v. Searan, 259 F.3d 434 (6th Cir. 2001) the court noted:

This court long ago recognized that the "willfully aiding, assisting, procuring, counseling, advising, or causing" language of § 7206(2) effectively incorporates into this statute the theory behind accomplice liability. In [United States v. Sassak, 881 F.2d 276 (6th Cir. 1989)] this court observed that, "theoretically, anyone who causes a false return to be filed or furnishes information that leads to the filing of a false return could be guilty of violating 26 USC § 7206(2)." *Sassak*, 881 F.2d at 277. In order to avoid the harsh and probably unintended consequences of such strict liability, *Sassak* followed the Third Circuit in holding that one must engage in 'some affirmative participation which at least encourages the perpetrator' in order to be guilty of aiding in the preparation and presentation of false tax returns." Ibid. (quoting United States v. Graham, 758 F.2d 879, 885 (3d Cir. 1985)). *Sassak* explained: courts should "analyze violation of 26 U.S.C. § 7206(2) in terms of an actor's actual willfulness and knowledge of the falsity of the return that is prepared." *Sassak*, 881 F.2d at 278. *Sassak* thus interpreted § 7206(2) as incorporating the complicity theory of criminal liability set forth more fully in 18 U.S.C. § 2 and its interpretive jurisprudence. We reaffirm that principle today and look to 18 U.S.C. § 2 caselaw for an understanding of what Congress criminalized with the inclusion of the 'aiding, assisting, procuring' language in 26 U.S.C. § 7206(2).

The recognition that the first element of a § 7206(2) charge effectively incorporates "aiding and abetting" complicity liability means that charging a defendant with "aiding and abetting," under 18 U.S.C.§ 2, the "aiding, assisting, procuring * * *" of false tax returns, under 26 U.S.C. § 7206(2), is a redundancy. Conceptually, a complicitous defendant * * * could "aid and abet" a principal * * * in her endeavor to "aid, assist, procure * * *." Yet the latter language, adapted from § 7206(2), contains no limitations on whom the defendant aids, assists, or procures. Accordingly, we hold that the broad language of § 7206(2) reaches far enough to cover the acts of a defendant who aids, assists, or procures another person to aid, assist, or procure the filing of a false return. That is, § 7206(2) treats [a defendant's] activities in aiding or assisting [a principal] as merged with [the principal's], which obviates the need for a grand jury to add 18 U.S.C. § 2 to an indictment. Of course, Congress's incorporation of traditional complicity liability into § 7206(2) means that the principles underlying aiding and abetting liability also underlie § 7206(2) charges, and trial courts should turn to 18 U.S.C. § 2 jurisprudence in explaining § 7206(2) charges to defendants and juries. Id. at 443-444.

1. As we saw in *Hooks*, a conspiracy charge under 18 U.S.C. § 371 often accompanies a § 7206(2) charge. Why?

2. Compare and contrast § 7206(2) and 18 U.S.C. § 2.

3. A person charged with aiding and abetting the filing of a false or fraudulent return may also be charged with and convicted of evasion under § 7201. Compare and contrast § 7206(2) and § 7201.

5. Delivery or Disclosure of Fraudulent Statements and Returns – § 7207

Section 7207 is a misdemeanor provision that punishes the willful delivery or disclosure of a fraudulent return, account, statement or other document. The statute imposes a fine of not more than $10,000 ($50,000 for corporations) or imprisonment for not more than one year or both. Section 7207 offenses are prosecuted less often than the other tax offenses discussed to this point. Section 7207 is used primarily in the case of fraudulently altered documents submitted to IRS agents in order to enable the taxpayers to gain an undeserved tax benefit. For instance, the provision has applied to those who have filed false 1099's, altered checks or invoices that were presented to an IRS agent, and to others who have supplied false information to the IRS.

The elements of § 7207 are (1) delivery or disclosure of a list, return, account, statement or other document to the IRS, (2) that is known to be fraudulent or false as to any material matter, and (3) willfulness.

Section 7207 can be a lesser included offense to an evasion (§ 7201) charge or to a fraud and false statements (§ 7206(1)) charge. The following case examines the extent to which a lesser included instruction is required to be given.

SANSONE v. UNITED STATES
United States Supreme Court, 1965.
380 U.S. 343, 85 S.Ct. 1004, 13 L.Ed.2d 882.

MR. JUSTICE GOLDBERG delivered the opinion of the Court.

Petitioner Sansone was indicted for willfully attempting to evade federal income taxes for the year 1957 in violation of § 7201 of the Internal Revenue Code of 1954. Section 7201 provides:

> "Any person who willfully attempts in any manner to evade or defeat any tax imposed by this title or the payment thereof shall, in addition to other penalties provided by law, be guilty of a felony and, upon conviction thereof, shall be fined not more than $10,000, or imprisoned not more than 5 years, or both, together with the costs of prosecution."

The following facts were established at trial. In March 1956 petitioner and his wife purchased a tract of land for $22,500 and simultaneously sold a portion of the tract for $20,000. In August 1957 petitioner sold another portion of the tract for $27,000. He did not report the gain on either the 1956 or 1957 sale in his income tax returns for those years.[1] Petitioner conceded that the 1957 transaction was reportable and that, in not reporting it, he understated his tax liability for that year by $2,456.48. He contended, however, that this understatement was not willful since he believed at the time that extensive repairs on a creek adjoining a portion of the tract he retained might be necessary and that the cost of these repairs might wipe out his profit on the 1957 sale.

To counter this defense, the Government introduced the following signed statement made by petitioner during the Treasury investigation of his tax return:

"I did not report the 1957 sale in our joint income tax return for 1957 because I was burdened with a number of financial obligations and did not feel I could raise the money to pay any tax due. It was my intention to report all sales in a future year and pay the tax due. I knew that I should have reported the 1957 sale, but my wife did not know that it should have been reported. It was not my intention to evade the payment of our proper taxes and I intended to pay any additional taxes due when I was financially able to do so."

At the conclusion of the trial, petitioner requested that the jury be instructed that it could acquit him of the charged offense of willfully attempting to evade or defeat taxes in violation of § 7201, but still convict him of either or both of the asserted lesser-included offenses of willfully filing a fraudulent or false return, in violation of § 7207[2] or willfully failing to pay his taxes at the time required by law, in violation of § 7203.[3] Section 7201 is a felony providing for a maximum fine of $10,000 and imprisonment for five years. Both §§ 7203 and 7207 are misdemeanors with maximum prison sentences of one year under each

---

1.   Petitioner was charged with a violation of § 7201 for 1956 in addition to the charge for 1957. The jury acquitted him with respect to the 1956 charge, which is consequently not involved in this case.

2.   Section 7207 of the Internal Revenue Code of 1954 provides:

"Any person who willfully delivers or discloses to the Secretary or his delegate any list, return, account, statement, or other document, known by him to be fraudulent or to be false as to any material matter, shall be fined not more than $1,000, or imprisoned not more than 1 year, or both."

3.   Section 7203 of the Internal Revenue Code of 1954 provides:

"Any person required under this title to pay any estimated tax or tax, or required by this title or by regulations made under authority thereof to make a return, * * * keep any records, or supply any information, who willfully fails to pay such estimated tax or tax, make such return, keep such records, or supply such information, at the time or times required by law or regulations, shall, in addition to other penalties provided by law, be guilty of a misdemeanor and, upon conviction thereof, shall be fined not more than $10,000, or imprisoned not more than 1 year, or both, together with the costs of prosecution."

section, and maximum fines of $10,000 under § 7203 and $1,000 under § 7207.

The requested instructions were denied.[4]

We are faced with the threshold question as to whether or not § 7207, which proscribes the willful filing with a Treasury official of any known false or fraudulent "return," applies to the filing of an income tax return.[5] If § 7207 does not apply to income tax returns, it is obvious that the

---

4.   The full instructions requested by petitioner were as follows:

No. 1.   "Under the law you may find a defendant guilty of a lesser crime than the crimes charged in the indictment.

     'A statute upon which a lesser crime is based (§ 7203 of the Internal Revenue Code of 1954), omitting that part of the Act which does not apply in this case, reads as follows:

"Any person required under this title to pay any * * * tax, * * * who willfully fails to pay such tax, * * * at the time or times required by law or regulations, shall, in addition to other penalties provided by law, be guilty of a misdemeanor.'

'and then the statute provides for the penalty.

     'Therefore, if you find beyond a reasonable doubt that (with respect to either or both of the counts in this indictment) the defendant willfully failed to pay the correct tax to the United States at the time of the filing of his return, but you further find that the defendant did not willfully attempt to defeat and evade his income taxes by the filing of a false and fraudulent return, you will in your verdict say 'Guilty of violating a lesser-included offense.'

     'If you have a reasonable doubt as to whether defendant willfully failed to pay the correct tax when filing his income tax return or returns under any count or counts of this indictment, you will resolve the doubt in favor of the defendant and acquit him of the lesser-included offense as to such count or counts.'

No. 2.   'As I have said previously, the law permits the jury to find a defendant guilty of any lesser offense which is necessarily included in the crime charged.   The offense charged in the indictment here necessarily includes a lesser offense based upon the following statute (Section 7207 of the Internal Revenue Code of 1954), omitting that part of the Act which does not apply in this case; it reads as follows:

     "'Any person who willfully delivers or discloses to the Secretary [of the Treasury] or his delegate any * * * return, * * * or other document known by him to be fraudulent or to be false as to any material matter,'

'and then the statute provides for the penalty.

     'Therefore, if you find beyond a reasonable doubt that (with respect to either or both of the counts in this indictment) the defendant willfully delivered to the District Director of Internal Revenue at St. Louis, Missouri his and his wife's federal joint income tax return or returns for the years 1956 and 1957 which were known by him to be fraudulent or false as to any material matter, but you further find that the defendant did not willfully attempt to defeat and evade his income tax by the filing of a false and fraudulent return, you will in your verdict say 'Guilty of violating a lesser-included offense.'

     'If you have a reasonable doubt as to whether defendant willfully so delivered under any count or counts of this indictment his and his wife's federal joint income tax return or returns which were known by him to be fraudulent or false as to a material matter, you will resolve the doubt in favor of the defendant and acquit him of the lesser-included offense as to such count or counts.'

5.   This issue divided the Court of Appeals, with two judges holding that § 7207 does not apply to false income tax returns and one judge, concurring in result, dissenting on this point.

defendant was not here entitled to a lesser-included offense charge based on that section.

* * *

We conclude, * * * that § 7207 applies to income tax violations. Since there is no doubt that §§ 7201 and 7203 also apply to income tax violations, with obvious overlapping among them, there can be no doubt that the lesser-included offense doctrine applies to these statutes in an appropriate case. See Spies v. United States, 317 U.S. 492, 495.

II.

The basic principles controlling whether or not a lesser-included offense charge should be given in a particular case have been settled by this Court. Rule 31(c) of the Federal Rules of Criminal Procedure provides, in relevant part, that the "defendant may be found guilty of an offense necessarily included in the offense charged." Thus, "in a case where some of the elements of the crime charged themselves constitute a lesser crime, the defendant, if the evidence justifie[s] it * * * [is] entitled to an instruction which would permit a finding of guilt of the lesser offense." But a lesser-offense charge is not proper where, on the evidence presented, the factual issues to be resolved by the judge are the same as to both the lesser and greater offenses. In other words, the lesser offense must be included within but not, on the facts of the case, be completely encompassed by the greater. A lesser-included offense instruction is only proper where the charged greater offense requires the jury to find a disputed factual element which is not required for conviction of the lesser-included offense.[6] We now apply the principles declared in these cases to the instant case.

III.

The offense here charged was a violation of § 7201, which proscribes willfully attempting in any manner to evade or defeat any tax imposed by the Internal Revenue Code. As this Court has recognized, this felony

---

6. This Court has long recognized that to hold otherwise would only invite the jury to pick between the felony and the misdemeanor so as to determine the punishment to be imposed, a duty Congress has traditionally left to the judge. This general principle is particularly applicable in this area. In commenting on § 7201, the House Ways and Means Committee expressly stated that minimum penalties were omitted from § 7201 in order to make it "possible for the judges to better fix the penalties to fit the circumstances." H.R. Rep. No. 1337, 83d Cong., 2d Sess., 108. The lack of minimum penalties also, of course, denies to the prosecutor an unbridled discretion as to the penalty to be imposed upon particular defendants by deciding whether, on the same facts, to charge a felony or a misdemeanor.

provision is "the capstone of a system of sanctions which singly or in combination were calculated to induce prompt and forthright fulfillment of every duty under the income tax law and to provide a penalty suitable to every degree of delinquency." *Spies v. United States*, supra, at 497. As such a capstone, § 7201 necessarily includes among its elements actions which, if isolated from the others, constitute lesser offenses in this hierarchical system of sanctions. Therefore, if on the facts of a given case there are disputed issues of fact which would enable the jury rationally to find that, although all the elements of § 7201 have not been proved, all the elements of one or more lesser offenses have been, it is clear that the defendant is entitled to a lesser-included offense charge as to such lesser offenses.

As has been held by this Court, the elements of § 7201 are willfulness; the existence of a tax deficiency, and an affirmative act constituting an evasion or attempted evasion of the tax, *Spies v. United States*, supra [at 496]. In comparison, § 7203 makes it a misdemeanor willfully to fail to perform a number of specified acts at the time required by law – the one here relevant being the failure to pay a tax when due. This misdemeanor requires only willfulness and the omission of the required act – here the payment of the tax when due. As recognized by this Court in *Spies v. United States*, supra, at 499, the difference between a mere willful failure to pay a tax (or perform other enumerated actions) when due under § 7203 and a willful attempt to evade or defeat taxes under § 7201 is that the latter felony involves "some willful commission in addition to the willful omissions that make up the list of misdemeanors." Where there is, in a § 7201 prosecution, a disputed issue of fact as to the existence of the requisite affirmative commission in the addition to the § 7203 omission, a defendant would, of course, be entitled to a lesser-included offense charge based on § 7203. In this case, however it is undisputed that petitioner filed a tax return and that the petitioner's filing of a false tax return constituted a sufficient affirmative commission to satisfy that requirement of § 7201. The only issue at trial was whether petitioner's act was wilful. Given this affirmative commission and the conceded tax deficiency, if petitioner's act was willful, that is, if the jury believed, as it obviously did, that he knew that the capital gain on the sale of the property was reportable in 1957, he was guilty of violating both §§ 7201 and 7203. If his act was not willful, he was not guilty of violating either § 7201 or § 7203. Thus on the facts of this case, §§ 7201 and 7203 "covered precisely the same ground." This being so, on the authorities cited, it is clear that petitioner was not entitled to a lesser-included offense charge based on § 7203.

Section 7207 requires the willful filing of a document known to be false or fraudulent in any material manner. The elements here involved are willfulness and the commission of the prohibited act. Section 7207 does not, however, require that the act be done as an attempt to evade or defeat taxes. Conduct could therefore violate § 7207 without violating § 7201 where the false statement, though material, does not constitute an attempt to evade or defeat taxation because it does not have the requisite effect of reducing the stated tax liability. This may be the case, for example, where a taxpayer understates his gross receipts and he offsets this by also understating his deductible expenses. In this example, if the Government in a § 7201 case charged tax evasion on the grounds that the defendant had understated his tax by understating his gross receipts, and the defendant contended that this was not so, as the misstatement of gross receipts had been offset by an understatement of deductible expenses, the defendant would be entitled to a lesser-included offense charge based on § 7207, there being this relevant disputed issue of fact. This would be so, for in such a case, if the jury believed that an understatement of deductible expenses had offset the understatement of gross receipts, while the defendant would have violated § 7207 by willfully making a material false and fraudulent statement on his return, he would not have violated § 7201 as there would not have been the requisite § 7201 element of a tax deficiency. Here, however, there is no dispute that petitioner's material misstatement resulted in a tax deficiency. Thus there is no disputed issue of fact concerning the existence of an element required for conviction of § 7201 but not required for conviction of § 7207. Given petitioner's material misstatement which resulted in a tax deficiency if, as the jury obviously found, petitioner's act was willful in the sense that he knew that he should have reported more income than he did for the year 1957, he was guilty of violating both §§ 7201 and 7207. If his action was not willful, he was guilty of violating neither. As was true with § 7203, on the facts of this case §§ 7201 and 7207 "covered precisely the same ground," and thus petitioner was not entitled to a lesser-included offense charge based on § 7207.

Petitioner makes one final contention. He argues that he could have been acquitted of attempting to evade or defeat his 1957 taxes, in violation of § 7201, but still have been convicted for willfully failing to pay his tax when due in violation of § 7203 or willfully filing a fraudulent return in violation of § 7207, if the jury believed his statement contained in the government-introduced affidavit, that, although he knew that profit on the sale in question was reportable for 1957 and that tax was due thereon, he intended to report the sale and pay the 1957 tax at some unspecified future date. The basic premise of this argument is that, although all three sections require willfulness, on the facts here, the contents of these wilfulness requirements differ. The argument is made that while an intent to report and pay the tax in the future does not vitiate the willfulness requirements of §§ 7203 and 7207, it does constitute a defense to a willful attempt "in any manner to evade or defeat any tax imposed by" the Internal Revenue Code, in violation of § 7201. While we agree that the intent to report the income and pay the tax sometime in the future does not vitiate the willfulness required by §§ 7203 and 7207, we cannot agree that it vitiates the willfulness requirement of § 7201.

No defense to a § 7201 evasion charge is made out by showing that the defendant willfully and fraudulently understated his tax liability for the year involved but intended to report the income and pay the tax at some later time. As this Court has recognized, § 7201 includes the offense of willfully attempting to evade or defeat the *assessment* of a tax as well as the offense of willfully attempting to evade or defeat the *payment* of a tax. The indictment here charged an attempt to evade income taxes by defeating the assessment for 1957. The fact that petitioner stated to a revenue agent that he intended to report his 1957 income in some later year, even if taken at face value, would not detract from the criminality of his willful act defeating the 1957 assessment. That crime was complete as soon as the false and fraudulent understatement of taxes (assuming, of course, that there was in fact a deficiency) was filed. See United States v. Beacon Brass Co., 344 U.S. 43, 46. See also Spies v. United States, supra at 498-499.

In sum, it is clear here that there were no disputed issues of fact which would justify instructing the jury that it could find that petitioner had committed all the elements of either or both of the §§ 7203 and 7207 misdemeanors without having committed a violation of the § 7201 felony. This being the case, the petitioner was not entitled to a lesser-included offense charge and the judgment of the Court of Appeals is

Affirmed.

Notes and Questions

In the *McGill* case, discussed above, the defendant objected to the trial judge's instruction to the jury that it could find him guilty of a lesser-included offense if it acquitted him of felony evasion. The defendant was concerned about the jury reaching a "compromise verdict" if this instruction was given. In considering the objection, the appellate court stated:

McGill argues that § 7203 is not necessarily a lesser included offense within § 7201 because one element of the misdemeanor–failure to pay a tax–requires different proof than the parallel affirmative act of evasion under § 7201 which as the Court held in *Spies* cannot be the mere failure to pay. McGill argues that "failure to pay a tax" and "an affirmative act of evasion of payment" are not identical. However, McGill's argument overlooks the fact that it is exactly in the situation where proof of the affirmative act to evade payment fails, that the lesser included offense of willful failure to pay may become relevant.
964 F.2d at 239.

1. Based on the facts of the *McGill* case, why do you think the court concluded that the lesser-included offense instruction was proper?

2. Why do you think false statement offenses under § 7207 are prosecuted less often than any of the other offenses previously discussed?

B. MISCELLANEOUS OFFENSES

There are other criminal provisions under the tax code, but they are more limited in scope than the provisions discussed above. Thus, they will be mentioned only briefly.

1. Fraudulent Withholding Information – § 7205

Section 7205 applies to two types of conduct: (1) furnishing false withholding information to an employer and (2) filing false certifications under the backup withholding system for interest, dividends and certain other payments. This is a misdemeanor provision that is not an exclusive penalty. Thus, an offender may be convicted of both evasion and filing a false withholding form. Moreover, a taxpayer charged with filing false W-4 forms can be charged under § 7206(2) for aiding and assisting in the preparation of a false or fraudulent return. Since bad motive is not required for willfulness, it is no defense that the taxpayer filed the false W-4 in order to protest government policies. See United States v. Malinowski, 472 F.2d 850 (3rd Cir. 1973), cert. denied, 411 U.S. 970 (1973).

2. Interference With the Administration of the Internal Revenue Laws – § 7212(a)

Section 7212 makes it a felony to intimidate or impede government officers or employees acting in an official capacity. This provision applies to those who use corrupt means, force or threats of force (including threatening letters or communication) against government officers, employees, or their family members. This provision punishes two types of conduct: (1) attempts to intimidate or impede an officer or employee of the United States, corruptly or by force of threat, and (2) attempts to obstruct or impede the due administration of the internal revenue laws. The latter is an omnibus, or catchall clause that greatly expands the scope of § 7212. Thus, the prohibited act need not be an effort to intimidate or impede, nor must it be an act that is itself illegal. An element of the offense, though, is that the defendant must have been aware of a pending IRS action (i.e., audit, investigation or proceeding) that was underway. See United States v. Kassouf, 144 F.3d 952, 957 (6th Cir. 1998); but see United States v. Armstrong, 974 F. Supp. 528 (E.D. Va. 1997) (holding that pending investigation is not required under § 7212).

The omnibus clause may result in an overlap between § 7212(a) and several of the provisions already discussed. For example, filing false withholding exemption certificates could result in a conviction under both § 7205 and § 7212(a). Similarly, supplying false information to the IRS in violation of §§ 7201 and 7203 may result in convictions under those provisions, as well as under § 7212(a).

Under the IRC, if actual force is used against an officer or employee of the government, or against any member of their families, the penalty under § 7212 increases from one year imprisonment and $3,000 in fines, to three years imprisonment and $5,000 in fines.

3. Unauthorized Disclosure and Unauthorized Browsing – §§ 7213 and 7213A

Section 7213 makes it a felony for a current or former employee of the federal government (and in some cases, the state government) to disclose tax return information unless such disclosure is authorized. This provision also may apply to members of the news media who disseminate information with knowledge that the disclosure is prohibited. This provision does not prohibit disclosure of return information to a grand jury, however, nor does it prevent an accountant from disclosing financial data in a court proceeding, even though the data may have been used to prepare a tax return.

Willfulness is a material element of this offense. Thus, where tax return information is released in the reasonable belief that the disclosure is authorized, the felony provision should not apply. Note that this provision may overlap with the Privacy Act (see Chapter 2), which provides a civil cause of action for disclosure of confidential return information.

Unauthorized inspection of tax returns also is a very serious offense. Section 7213A makes it a misdemeanor to browse through taxpayers' confidential returns and other documents unless it is in the course of official duty. This provision applies to federal officers and employees, as well as to state officers and employees who acquire federal tax information in the course of their duties. It also applies to IRS contractors, who may be involved in processing returns, programming computers, or repairing equipment.

In addition to the criminal sanctions, a federal officer or employee who is convicted under this provision will be dismissed from office or discharged from employment under § 7213A(b)(2), and an action for civil damages may be brought under § 7431. Since § 7213A applies to unauthorized inspections, and willfulness is not an element of this offense, the fact that the offender did not disclose the information to third parties will not constitute a defense. There is no liability under this provision, however, if the inspection or disclosure is requested by the taxpayer, or if it results from a good faith, but erroneous interpretation of the confidentiality provision under § 6103.

4. Preparer Disclosure of Unauthorized Return Information – § 7216

A paid preparer who violates a client's confidence by knowingly and recklessly releasing tax return information without the client's consent, or who uses the information for a purpose other than to prepare the return, will be guilty of a misdemeanor. The term "tax return" includes both an amended return and an estimated tax return. The penalty will not apply if the release of the information is required under the IRC or by a court order, or is made to report the commission of a crime. Also, return information can be released pursuant to a quality or peer review without the client's consent, but only to the extent necessary to conduct the review. Since this is a federal provision, it does not apply to the disclosure of information from state and local tax returns.

C. DEFENSES

There are a variety of defenses that taxpayers have used in attempting to avoid being convicted of a tax crime. Since willfulness is an element that is common to most of the tax offenses, a defense based on lack of willfulness is seen frequently.

1. Third Party Reliance

UNITED STATES v. CHEEK
United States Court of Appeals, Third Circuit, 1993.
3 F.3d 1057, cert. denied 510 U.S. 1112, 114 S.Ct. 1055, 127 L.Ed.2d 376 (1994).

ALDISERT, SENIOR CIRCUIT JUDGE.

Like most of us, John Cheek does not like to pay taxes. Unlike most of us, however, he has refused to pay them. As a result of his refusal to pay federal income taxes, Mr. Cheek has been a frequent visitor to our courts.

On several occasions, Mr. Cheek has attempted to persuade the district courts of this Circuit and, on one occasion, this court to declare federal income taxes and the withholding of Social Security and tax contributions unconstitutional. Not only were his attempts unsuccessful, but he was required to pay $1,500 in attorney's fees, $5,000 in sanctions under Rule 11, Federal Rules of Civil Procedure, for filing a frivolous lawsuit and $1,500 as sanctions under Rule 28, Federal Rules of Appellate Procedure, for filing a frivolous appeal.

Mr. Cheek has been party to criminal proceedings before us as well. In 1987, Cheek was charged in a superseding indictment with six counts of willfully failing to file a federal income tax return for the years 1980, 1981, and 1983 through 1986, in violation of 26 U.S.C. § 7203. He was further charged with three counts of willfully attempting to evade his income taxes for the years 1980, 1981 and 1983 in violation of 26 U.S.C. § 7201. On November 12, 1987, Cheek was convicted by a jury on all counts and sentenced to jail for a year and a day. On appeal, we affirmed his conviction, United States v. Cheek, 882 F.2d 1263 (7th Cir. 1989), but the Supreme Court reversed it on the basis of erroneous jury instructions, Cheek v. United States, 498 U.S. 192, 112 L.Ed. 2d 617, 111 S.Ct. 604 (1991), the Court holding that a good-faith misunderstanding of the law or a good-faith belief that one is not violating the law negates willfulness, irrespective of whether the claimed belief is objectively reasonable.

In 1992, following a second jury trial before another district judge, who instructed the jury in strict accordance with the Supreme Court's new formulation of willfulness, Cheek was again convicted on all counts, was sentenced to jail for a year and a day, and was fined $62,000. It is from the conviction upon retrial and sentence that he now appeals.

Other questions are presented, but essentially Cheek argues that the district court erred by refusing to instruct the jury on a reliance of counsel defense, * * *. We will affirm the judgment of the district court in all respects.

I.

* * *

Cheek described his various lawsuits as an attempt to prove his belief that the law did not require him to pay tax on what he described as his right to work. In addition to pursuing his own lawsuits, Cheek also attended the criminal tax trials of various friends and associates. All of these trials resulted in convictions.

Cheek testified that many of his actions were based on legal advice. Throughout the time period covered in the indictment, Cheek claims to have conferred with several attorneys regarding his research, beliefs and lawsuits.

On March 13, 1992, after his second trial, Cheek was sentenced by Judge Zagel to one year and one day imprisonment, and he was placed on five years probation. The conditions of probation were that he cooperate with the IRS in a civil determination of his tax liabilities, that he pay all back taxes, interest and penalties, and that he file current tax returns. Finally, Cheek was ordered to pay a fine of $62,000 immediately, a fine that included costs of incarceration and supervision.

* * *

III.

Cheek first argues that the district court erred in its jury instructions in * * * refusing to give an instruction based on an advice of counsel defense * * *.

A.

At trial Cheek testified that his actions after 1982 were the result of "bum legal advice." He argues that three different attorneys advised him that the tax system was based on voluntary compliance and that his many previous lawsuits were dismissed for procedural rather than substantive reasons.[3] Under these circumstances, he contends that he was entitled to a jury instruction on the advice of counsel defense.

According to the government, the evidence presented by Cheek fell short of satisfying the requirements of the defense. It contends that

---

3.   In Cheek v. Doe, 110 F.R.D. at 421, the district court specifically stated that regardless of its procedural inadequacies, "this case is frivolous on the merits. The constitutionality of the income tax laws, enacted pursuant to the Sixteenth Amendment, has long been established."

Cheek sought confirmation of his own view of the tax laws rather than independent legal advice, that he sought such opinions after he had already chosen his course of conduct, that several attorneys told him that his conduct could lead to criminal sanctions, and that the majority of the testimony undermined rather than supported the advice of counsel defense.

In order to establish an advice of counsel defense, a defendant must establish that: (1) before taking action, (2) he in good faith sought the advice of an attorney whom he considered competent, (3) for the purpose of securing advice on the lawfulness of his possible future conduct, (4) and made a full and accurate report to his attorney of all material facts which the defendant knew, (5) and acted strictly in accordance with the advice of his attorney who had been given a full report. Liss v. United States, 915 F.2d 287, 291 (7th Cir. 1990). A crucial element in this defense is that "defendant secured the advice on the lawfulness of his possible future conduct." United States v. Polytarides, 584 F.2d 1350, 1352 (4th Cir. 1978).

Cheek testified that he received the advice of at least three competent attorneys on the status of the tax laws, but we are not satisfied that he sought or received advice on "possible future conduct." He did not seek any advice until after 1980, when he first failed to file proper tax returns. Furthermore, Cheek had been told by the IRS, American Airlines personnel and by at least one court that his contentions were without merit prior to his discussions with counsel. Reduced to its essence, the record indicates that Cheek merely continued a course of illegal conduct begun prior to contacting counsel. See *Polytarides,* 584 F.2d at 1353 (good faith reliance on advice of counsel defense was not available when defendant had taken significant steps toward the illegal activity and had been warned of its illegality prior to seeking advice of an attorney). In addition, at least one attorney, Robert L. Collins, testified that Cheek sought his opinion solely for the purpose of protecting himself in the event he was indicted.

Nowhere does Mr. Cheek contend either that he made a full and accurate report as to his tax status to any attorney or that he "acted strictly in accordance with the advice of his attorney." In United States v. Becker, 965 F.2d 383, 388 (7th Cir. 1992), we held that an advice of counsel instruction was unwarranted where there was no evidence that the defendant fully disclosed his position to his lawyer or that he followed the specific advice of his attorney. Defendant Becker attempted to rely on a legal memorandum from attorney Collins discussing the constitutionality and voluntary nature of the current tax system, the same exact memorandum Cheek relies on here.

Moreover, attorney Susan Keegan testified that she discussed with Cheek "more or less" that he was required to obey the law until he was told by a court that the law in question was not valid. He admittedly did not follow this advice. Attorney Andrew Spiegel testified that he told Cheek that the courts were interpreting the tax laws as requiring the filing of income tax returns, that wages were considered income subject to taxation and that it was possible that Cheek would be prosecuted criminally for not filing a tax return. Attorney Adrian Flipse told Cheek that she could not prove his theory of taxation one way or the other.

None of these attorneys advised him not to file tax returns. To the contrary, each advised him that he might be criminally prosecuted if he failed to file. Accordingly, on the basis of the evidence presented, the district court did not err in refusing to give a jury instruction on the advice of counsel defense.

B.

The government contents also that even if the evidence could be construed to support the theory of good faith reliance on counsel, the jury instructions as a whole were sufficient to encompass that theory. It is well settled that a criminal defendant is entitled to have the jury "'consider any theory of the defense which is supported by law and which has some foundation in the evidence, however tenuous.'" United States v. Kelley, 864 F.2d 569, 572 (7th Cir. 1989) (quoting United States v. Grimes, 413 F.2d 1376, 1378 (7th Cir. 1969). He is not entitled, however, to a particular instruction on that theory. "The defendant is entitled only to have his theory, if supported by the evidence, considered by the jury." Id.

The tax offenses with which Cheek was charged are specific intent crimes that require the defendant to have acted willfully. Thus, the district court instructed the jury that, in order to find him guilty, they had to find that the defendant acted knowingly and willfully. The court defined "willfully" as meaning the "voluntary and intentional violation of a known legal duty or the purposeful omission to do what the law requires." The jury was further instructed that a "defendant does not act willfully if he believes in good faith that he is acting within the law or that his actions comply with the law." According to the government, this instruction on willfulness necessarily encompassed Cheek's theory of good faith reliance on counsel's advice.

In United States v. Kelley, 864 F.2d at 573, we determined that the district court's instructions on willfulness encompassed the defendant's theory of good faith reliance on counsel's advice, thus obviating the need for an additional instruction. In *Kelley*, the district court had defined willfully as "voluntarily and intentionally with the purpose of avoiding a known legal duty." Id.

We are satisfied that on the basis of the trial record the court's instructions did "treat the issues fairly and accurately," and, therefore, they should not be disturbed on appeal.

* * *

Questions

Why do third party reliance defenses seldom seem to succeed? See Boyle v. United States, 469 U.S. 241 (1985). When is the defense most likely to be successful?

2. Lack of Notice of Illegality

UNITED STATES v. HARRIS
United States Court of Appeals, Seventh Circuit, 1991.
942 F.2d 1125.

ESCHBACH, SENIOR CIRCUIT JUDGE.

David Kritzik, now deceased, was a wealthy widower partial to the company of young women. Two of these women were Leigh Ann Conley and Lynnette Harris, twin sisters. Directly or indirectly, Kritzik gave Conley and Harris each more than half a million dollars over the course of several years. For our purposes, either Kritzik had to pay gift tax on this money or Harris and Conley had to pay income tax. The United States alleges that, beyond reasonable doubt, the obligation was Harris and Conley's. In separate criminal trials, Harris and Conley were convicted of willfully evading their income tax obligations regarding the money, and they now appeal.

Under Commissioner v. Duberstein, 363 U.S. 278, 285, 4 L.Ed. 2d 1218, 80 S.Ct. 1190 (1960), the donor's intent is the "critical consideration" in distinguishing between gifts and income. We reverse Conley's conviction and remand with instructions to dismiss the indictment against her because the government failed to present sufficient evidence of Kritzik's intent regarding the money he gave her. We also reverse Harris' conviction. The district court excluded as hearsay letters in which Kritzik wrote that he loved Harris and enjoyed giving things to her. These letters were central to Harris' defense that she believed in good faith that the money he received was a nontaxable gift, and they were not hearsay for this purpose.

We do not remand Harris' case for retrial, however, because Harris had no fair warning that her conduct might subject her to criminal tax liability. Neither the tax code, the Treasury Regulations, or Supreme Court or appellate cases provide a clear answer to whether Harris owed any taxes or not. The closest authority lies in a series of Tax Court decisions–but these cases *favor* Harris' position that the money she received was not income to her. Under this state of the law, Harris could not have formed a "willful" intent to violate the statutes at issue. For this reason, we remand with instructions that the indictment against Harris be dismissed. The same conclusion applies to Conley, and provides an alternative basis for reversing her conviction and remanding with instructions to dismiss the indictment.

Insufficiency of the Evidence as to Conley

Conley was convicted on each of four counts for violating 26 U.S.C. § 7203, which provides,

> Any person * * * required * * * to make a [tax] return * * * who willfully fails to * * * make such return * * * shall, in addition to other penalties provided by law, be guilty of a misdemeanor * * *.

Conley was "required * * * to make a return" only if the money that she received from Kritzik was income to her rather than a gift. Assuming that the money was income, she acted "willfully," and so is subject to criminal prosecution, only if she knew of her duty to pay taxes and "voluntarily and intentionally violated that duty." Cheek v. United States, 498 U.S. 192, 111 S.Ct. 604, 610, 112 L.Ed. 2d 617 (1991). The government met its burden of proof if the jury could have found these elements beyond a reasonable doubt, viewing the evidence in the light most favorable to the government.

The government's evidence was insufficient to show either that the money Conley received was income or that she acted in knowing disregard of her obligations. "Gross income" for tax purposes does not include gifts, which are taxable to the donor rather than the recipient. In Commissioner v. Duberstein, 363 U.S. 278, 285, 4 L.Ed. 2d 1218, 80 S.Ct. 1190 (1960), the Supreme Court stated that in distinguishing between income and gifts the "critical consideration * * * is the transferor's intention." A transfer of property is a gift if the transferor acted out of a "detached and disinterested generosity, * * * out of affection, respect, admiration, charity, or like impulses." Id. By contrast, a transfer of property is income if it is the result of "the constraining force of any moral or legal duty, constitutes a reward for services rendered, or proceeds from the incentive of anticipated benefit of an economic nature."

Regarding the "critical consideration" of the donor's intent, the only direct evidence that the government presented was Kritzik's gift tax returns. On those returns, Kritzik identified gifts to Conley of $24,000, $30,000, and $36,000 for the years 1984-6, respectively, substantially less than the total amount of money that Kritzik transferred to Conley. This leaves the question whether Kritzik's other payments were taxable to Conley or whether Kritzik just underreported his gifts. The gift tax returns raise the question, they do not resolve it.[3]

This failure to show Kritzik's intent is fatal to the government's case. Without establishing Kritzik's intent, the government cannot establish that Conley had any obligation to pay income taxes. Further , Conley could not have "willfully" failed to pay her taxes unless she knew of Kritzik's intent. Even if Kritzik's gift tax returns proved anything, the government presented no evidence that Conley knew the amounts that Kritzik had listed on those returns. Absent proof of Kritzik's intent, and Conley's knowledge of that intent, the government has no case.

The government's remaining evidence consisted of a bank card that Conley signed listing Kritzik in a space marked "employer" and testimony regarding the form of the payments that Conley received. The bank card is no evidence of Kritzik's intent and even as to Conley is open to conflicting interpretations–she contends that she listed Kritzik as a reference and no more. As to the form of the payments, the government showed that Conley would pick up a regular check at Kritzik's office every week to ten days, either from Kritzik personally or, when he was not in, from his secretary. According to the government, this form of payment is that of an employee picking up regular wages, but it could just as easily be that of a dependent picking up regular support checks.

---

3.   Our discussion assumes that the gift tax returns were admissible as evidence because the parties have not raised the issue. We note, however, that the returns appear on their face to be hearsay. The government used the returns (out of court statements) to prove that Kritzik's gifts were the amount that he reported (that is, to prove the truth of the matter asserted). Nor does the public records exception to the hearsay rule in Fed. R. Evid. 803(8) appear to apply, given that the information on the return reflects neither "the activities of [an] office or agency" nor "matters observed [by the office or agency] pursuant to duty imposed by law."

Along these lines, the United States tried to present direct evidence of Kritzik's intent in the form of an affidavit that he provided IRS investigators before his death. In the affidavit, Kritzik states that he regarded both Harris and Conley as prostitutes. But Kritzik had an obvious motive to lie to the investigators–he could have been subject to civil or criminal penalties for failure to pay gift taxes if he failed to shift the tax burden to the sisters. The District Court was correct to exclude this affidavit under the hearsay rule and under the confrontation clause. In general, evidentiary difficulties such as this will often be insurmountable in trying to prove a willful tax violation that hinges on the intent of a dead person. The civil remedies available to the IRS will almost always lead to surer justice in such cases than a criminal prosecution.

We will "not permit a verdict based solely upon the piling of inference upon inference." United States v. Balzano, 916 F.2d 1273, 1284 (7th Cir. 1990). In this regard, we emphasize the indirect, inconclusive nature of the evidence in establishing Kritzik's intent. We further emphasize that the gift tax returns and the bank card speak for themselves–the jury heard no testimony that would enable them to make a credibility determination based on information that is unavailable to the Court. Similarly, the fact that Conley received checks at fairly regular intervals was not in dispute, and the presentation of that evidence through the testimony of Kritzik's former secretary could not have provided the jury with additional insight.

* * *

* * * [T]he bare facts of Kritzik's gift tax return, the bank card, and the form of the payments are as consistent with an inference of innocence as one of guilt. The evidence does not support a finding of guilt beyond a reasonable doubt, and we reverse Conley's conviction and remand with instructions to dismiss the indictment against her.

The Admissibility of Kritzik's Letters

Harris was convicted of two counts of willfully failing to file federal income tax returns under 26 U.S.C. § 7203 (the same offense for which Conley was convicted) and two counts of willful tax evasion under 26 U.S.C. § 7201. At trial, Harris tried to introduce as evidence three letters that Kritzik wrote, but the District Court excluded the letters as hearsay. The District Court also suggested that the letters would be inadmissible under Fed. R. Evid. 403 because the possible prejudice from the letters exceeded their probative value. We hold that the letters were not hearsay because they were offered to prove Harris' lack of willfulness, not for the truth of the matters asserted. We further hold that the critical nature of the letters to Harris' defense precludes their exclusion under Rule 403, and so reverse her conviction.

The first of the letters at issue was a four page, handwritten letter from Kritzik to Harris, dated April 4, 1981. In it, Kritzik wrote that he loved and trusted Harris and that, "so far as the things I give you are concerned–let me say that I get as great if not even greater pleasure in giving than you get in receiving." He continued, "I love giving things to you and to see you happy and enjoying them." In a second letter to Harris of the same date, Kritzik again wrote, "I * * * love you very much and will do all that I can to make you happy," and said that he would arrange for Harris' financial security. In a third letter, dated some six years later on May 28, 1987, Kritzik wrote to this insurance company regarding the value of certain jewelry that he had "given to Ms. Lynette Harris as a gift." Kritzik forwarded a copy of the letter to Harris.

These letters were hearsay if offered for the truth of the matters asserted—that Kritzik did in fact love Harris, enjoyed giving her things, wanted to take care of her financial security, and gave her the jewelry at issue as a gift. But the letters were not hearsay for the purpose of showing what Harris believed, because her belief does not depend on the actual truth of the matters asserted in the letters. Even if Kritzik were lying, the letters could have caused Harris to believe in good faith that the things he gave her were intended as gifts. This good faith belief, in turn, would preclude any finding of willfulness on her part.

In general, hearsay problems like this—evidence being admissible for one purpose but not for another—still leave the District Court discretion. Jurors are not robots, after all, and can rarely consider evidence strictly for a single purpose to the exclusion of other, often more obvious purposes. For this reason, we will usually defer to a trial judge's conclusion that, * * * otherwise admissible evidence is likely to do more harm than good.

In this case, however, the letters were too important to Harris' defense to be excluded. Her belief about Kritzik's intent decides the issue of willfulness, which is an element of the offense, and she had no other objective means of proving that belief. True, admitting the letters would probably lead to some prejudice to the government's case. The jury would be hard pressed to consider the letters only for the permissible issue of what Harris thought of Kritzik's intent, and not for the impermissible issue of what Kritzik actually intended. The alternative, however, is to strip Harris of evidence that we believe was essential to a fair trial. In these circumstances, we hold that the District Court abused its discretion in excluding the letters and so reverse Harris' conviction.

The Tax Treatment of Payments to Mistress

Our conclusion that Harris should have been allowed to present the letters at issue as evidence would ordinarily lead us to remand her case for retrial. We further conclude, however, that current law on the tax treatment of payments to mistresses provided Harris no fair warning that her conduct was criminal. Indeed, current authorities favor Harris' position that the money she received from Kritzik was a gift. We emphasize that we do not necessarily agree with these authorities, and that the government is free to urge departure from them in a noncriminal context. But new points of tax law may not be the basis of criminal convictions. For this reason, we remand with instructions that the indictment against Harris be dismissed. Although we discuss only Harris' case in this section, the same reasoning applies to Conley and provides an alternative basis for dismissal of the indictment against her.

Again, the definitive statement of the distinction between gifts and income is in the Supreme Court's *Duberstein* decision, which applies and interprets the definition of income contained in 26 U.S.C. § 61. But as the Supreme Court described, the *Duberstein* principles are "necessarily general." It stated, "'One struggles in vain for any verbal formula that will supply a ready touchstone. The standard set up * * * is not a rule of law; it is rather a way of life. Life in all its fullness must supply the answer to the riddle.'" Id., quoting *Welch v. Helvering*, 290 U.S. 111 (1933). Along these lines, Judge Flaum's concurrence properly characterizes *Duberstein* as "eschew[ing] * * * [any] categorical, rule-bound analysis" in favor of a "case-by-case" approach.

Duberstein was a civil case, and its approach is appropriate for civil cases. But criminal prosecutions are a different story. These must rest on a violation of a clear rule of law, not on conflict with a "way of life." If "defendants [in a tax case] * * * could not have ascertained the legal standards applicable to their conduct, criminal proceedings may not be used to define and punish an alleged failure to conform to those standards." *United States v. Mallas*, 762 F.2d 361, 361 (4th Cir. 1985). This rule is based on the Constitution's requirement of due process and its prohibition on *ex post facto* laws; the government must provide reasonable notice of what conduct is subject to criminal punishment. The rule is also statutory in tax cases, because only "willful" violations are subject to criminal punishment. In the tax area, "willful" wrongdoing means the "voluntary, intentional violation of a known"–and therefore knowable–"legal duty." *Cheek*, 111 S.Ct. at 610, quoting *United States v. Bishop*, 412 U.S. 346, 36 L.Ed. 2d 941, 93 S.Ct. 2008 (1973). If the obligation to pay a tax is sufficiently in doubt, willfulness is impossible as a matter of law, and the "defendant's actual intent is irrelevant." *United States v. Garber*, 607 F.2d 92, 98 (5th Cir. 1979) (en banc), quoting *United States v. Critzer*, 498 F.2d 1160, 1162 (4th Cir. 1974).[6]

---

6.   See also *James v. United States*, 366 U.S. 213, 221-22, 6 L.Ed. 2d 246, 81 S.Ct. 1052 (1961). In *James*, the Supreme Court held that embezzled funds are income to the recipient, formally overruling its prior decision in Commissioner v. Wilcox, 327 U.S. 404, 90 L.Ed. 752, 66 S.Ct. 546 (1946), a case that had been all but overruled in Rutkin v. United States, 343 U.S. 130, 96 L.Ed. 833, 72 S.Ct. 571 (1952). A plurality of the *James* Court decided that its new holding would only apply prospectively, and reversed the defendant's conviction because "the element of willfulness *could not* be proven in a criminal prosecution" given the unsettled state of the case law, apparently regardless of the defendant's actual reliance on that case law. Id., 366 U.S. at 221-22 (emphasis added). On this point, the plurality was joined by Justices Black and Douglas, forming a majority. Id., at 224; see United States v. Garber, 607 F.2d 92, 98-9 & n.4 (5th Cir. 1979)(en banc)(discussing

We do not doubt that *Duberstein's* principles, though general, provide a clear anser to many cases involving the gift versus income distinction and can be the basis for civil as well as criminal prosecutions in such cases. We are equally certain, however, that *Duberstein* provides no ready answer to the taxability of transfers of money to a mistress in the context of long term relationship. The motivations of the parties in such cases will always be mixed. The relationship would not be long term were it not for some respect or affection. Yet, it may be equally clear that the relationship would not continue were it not for financial support or payments.

Usually, a tax decision by the Supreme Court does not stand by itself. Treasury Regulations add specifics to broad principles, and federal cases apply the broad principles and prevailing regulations to the facts of particular cases. But these usual sources of authority are silent when it comes to the tax treatment of money transferred in the course of long term, personal relationships. No regulations cover the subject, and we have found no appellate or district court cases on the issue.

* * *

The Tax Court did find that payments were income to the women who received them in Blevins v. Commissioner, T.C. Memo 1955-211, and in Jones v. Commissioner, T.C. Memo 1977-329. But in *Blevins,* the taxpayer was a woman who practiced prostitution and "used her home to operate a house of prostitution" in which six other women worked. Nothing suggested that the money at issue in that case was anything other than payments in the normal course of her business. Similarly in

---

James).

We further note that the *Garber* decision cited above and in the text raises an issue regarding the role of the jury in determining whether a principle of tax law is doubtful or not. In our view, the doubtfulness of a tax law can influence a criminal trial in two ways. The law can be objectively ambiguous, as in the present case, so that it fails to provide fair notice as a matter of law. A claim of objective ambiguity requires that the court examine all of the relevant precedents and dismiss the indictment if it concludes that the tax obligation is ambiguous as a matter of law. Alternatively, the defendant or the defendant's tax advisors may have subjectively, but wrongly, seen an ambiguity. In such a case, the defendant may present evidence to the jury showing the basis for the defendant's allegedly good faith belief. Necessarily, this evidence may include expert testimony about case law, to the extent that the defendant claims actual reliance on that case law. Case law on which the defendant did not in fact rely is irrelevant because only the defendant's subjective belief is at issue.

Both the objective and subjective elements were discussed in *Garber*, with some overlap. Certain language in the opinion suggests that expert testimony about tax law was appropriate in that case if the testimony "supported Garber's [subjective] feelings," without any express requirement that Garber actually have relied on this advice. 607 F.2d at 99. Subsequent courts, including a panel of the Fifth Circuit, have declined to follow this language in *Garber,* and have instead taken positions regarding the role of the jury that are consistent with our analysis. See United States v. Herzog, 632 F.2d 469, 473 (5th Cir. 1980); see also United States v. Curtis, 782 F.2d 593, 598-600 (6th Cir. 1986); United States v. Mallas, 762 F.2d 361, 364 n.4 (4th Cir. 1985); United States v. Ingredient Technology Corp., 698 F.2d 88, 96-7 (2d Cir. 1983).

Jones, a woman had frequent hotel meetings with a married man, and on "*each* occasion" he gave her cash. (Emphasis added). Here too, the Tax Court found that the relationship was one of prostitution, a point that was supported by the woman's similar relationships with other men.

If these cases make a rule of law, it is that a person is entitled to treat cash and property received from a lover as gifts, as long as the relationship consists of something more than specific payments for specific sessions of sex. What's more, even in *Blevins*, in which the relationship was one of raw prostitution, the Tax Court rejected the IRS' claim that a civil fraud penalty should be imposed. Nor was a fraud penalty applied in *Jones,* the other prostitution case, although there the issue apparently was not raised. The United States does not allege that Harris received specific payments for specific sessions of sex, so [these cases] support Harris' position.

Judge Flaum argues in his concurrence that these cases turn on their particular facts and do not make a rule of law. We need not decide this issue. We only conclude that a reasonably diligent taxpayer is entitled to look at the reported cases with the most closely analogous fact patterns when trying to determine his or her liability. When, as here, a series of such cases favors the taxpayer's position, the taxpayer has not been put on notice that he or she is in danger of crossing the line into criminality by adhering to that position. These Tax Court cases can turn entirely on their facts, yet together show that the law provided no warning to Harris that she was committing a criminal act in failing to report the money that she received. * * *

Besides Harris' prior suit, the United States also presented evidence regarding the overall relationship between Harris and Kritzik. Testimony showed that Harris described her relationship with Kritzik as "a job" and "just making a living." She reportedly complained that she "was laying on her back and her sister was getting all money," described how she disliked when Kritzik fondles her naked, and made other derogatory statements about sex with Kritzik.

This evidence still leaves Harris on the favorable side of the Tax Court's cases. Further, this evidence tells us only what Harris thought of the relationship. Again, the Supreme Court in *Duberstein* held that the *donor's* intent is the "critical consideration" in determining whether a transfer of money is a gift or income. Commissioner v. Duberstein, 363 U.S. 278, 285, 4 l.Ed. 2d 1218, 80 S.Ct. 1190 (1960). If Kritzik viewed the money he gave Harris as a gift, or if the dearth of contrary evidence leaves doubt on the subject, does it matter how mercenary Harris' motives were? *Duberstein* suggests that Harris' motives may not matter, but the ultimate answer makes no difference here. As long as the answer is at least a close call, and we are confident that it is, the prevailing law is too uncertain to support Harris' criminal conviction.

Finally, the evidence showed Harris to be a thief and to have evaded her tax obligations regarding *other* money. The thievery occurred when Kritzik offered to pay for extensive remodelling of a house that he had bought for Harris. Harris inflated the bills that she submitted to him for payment by more than a hundred thousand dollars, and funneled her "profit" through a paper corporation that she had set up. The law is clear that embezzled or fraudulently obtained funds are income to the recipient. But the government has relied on Harris' theft only to illustrate the nature of Harris' relationship with Kritzik, not as an independent criminal act. Along these lines, the government failed to request a jury instruction on point and failed to refer to any embezzled or misappropriated amounts in the indictment. The issue is waived. Similarly, the government presented evidence that, even apart from the money that she received from Kritzik, Harris willfully failed to file retuns in 1984. Again, however, the government has not argued this point as an alternative basis for affirming the relevant count of Harris' conviction. The government based its case on the gift/income distinction, and its case must stand or fall on that distinction.

In short, criminal prosecutions are no place for the government to try out "pioneering interpretations of tax law." United States v. Garber, 607 F.2d 92, 100 (5th Cir. 1979) (en banc). The United States has not shown us, and we have not found, a single case finding tax liability for payments that a mistress received from her lover, absent proof of specific payments for specific sex acts. Even when such specific proof is present, the cases have not applied penalties for civil fraud, much less criminal sanctions. The broad principles contained in *Duberstein* do not fill this gap. Before she met Kritzik, Harris starred as a sorceress in an action/adventure film. She would have had to be a real life sorceress to predict her tax obligations under the current state of the law.

Conclusion

For the reasons stated, we REVERSE Harris and Conley's convictions and remand with instructions to DISMISS the indictments against them.

Questions

1. Consider the court's statement that "criminal prosecutions are no place for the government to try out 'pioneering interpretations of tax

law.'" Why do you think this case involved a criminal prosecution instead of a civil penalty?

2. What does the court mean when it states in footnote 3 that "the civil remedies available to the IRS will almost always lead to surer justice in such cases than a criminal prosecution?"

3. Note the court's acknowledgment in footnote six that there is a split among the circuits as to whether expert testimony or other evidence may be admitted to establish that the law may be ambiguous or susceptible to more than one reasonable interpretation, where the defendant did not in fact rely upon that law. In your opinion, should such evidence be admissable?

4. Is there any similarity between the third party reliance defense and the lack of notice defense? Explain.

3. Mental Incompetence

UNITED STATES v. McCAFFREY
United States Court of Appeals, Seventh Circuit, 1999.
181 F.3d 854.

DIANE P. WOOD, CIRCUIT JUDGE.

Michael McCaffrey makes his living computing and filing income tax returns for others as a tax accountant, but he was not so industrious when it came to his own tax responsibilities. McCaffrey was convicted of four counts of willful failure to file his tax returns, in violation of 26 U.S.C. § 7203. McCaffrey now urges us to conclude his failure was not willful and reverse his conviction; he also presses an objection to an evidentiary ruling. Because there is enough evidence to support the court's finding that he acted willfully and because the court did not err in admitting the contested evidence, we affirm.

I.

McCaffrey suffers from a neurological disorder as a result of contracting encephalitis in 1961 while he was a student at Notre Dame University. This disorder causes him to sleep for all but four hours each day. McCaffrey also suffers from chronic depression as a result of his disability.

Still, McCaffrey has not been wholly debilitated. Since earning his degree in business administration and accounting in 1966, he has worked as an accountant, first rising to the level of senior accountant at the accounting firm of Haskins & Sells, then leaving to go into business for himself. As a sole practitioner, McCaffrey has prepared personal, corporate, and employment-related tax returns and reports for his clients. He has maintained an Illinois accounting license, which has required him to complete 40 hours of continuing education each year. His personal life has been as robust as his professional life: McCaffrey has married and raised three children, and he has successfully pursued a second-degree blackbelt in one of the martial arts. Throughout the years, he has remained financially secure and has consistently paid his mortgage and his bills on time.

In the beginning, McCaffrey also filed his tax returns on time. But he did not file his and his wife Sharon's joint personal income tax returns for the tax years 1980 through 1992. Only when, in early 1994, one of his clients (who is also a relative) told him that the IRS had recently visited him and revealed that McCaffrey was under investigation did McCaffrey act: a mere eight days later he filed all 13 delinquent federal returns. A few months later, he filed his 13 delinquent state returns for the same years.

On July 30, 1996, McCaffrey was charged with four counts of willful failure to file his federal tax returns for the years 1989 through 1992 (the statute of limitations barred criminal penalties for the remaining years). He consented to a trial before United States Magistrate Judge Arlander Keys. In a two-day bench trial held April 21 and 22, 1997, the government offered evidence of the facts recited above. In defense, McCaffrey called two expert witnesses to testify to his neurological condition and mental state. Dr. Jean Tracy, a personal friend who began treating McCaffrey for depression in October 1994, opined that McCaffrey's chronic depression could have detrimentally affected his ability to file his taxes. The second expert, Dr. John Collins, testified about the severity of McCaffrey's sleep disorder, but concluded that the disorder would not make him incapable of filing his tax returns. In rebuttal, the government offered the testimony of Dr. Neil Pliskin, who had conducted a seven-hour neuropsychological evaluation of McCaffrey in 1997. Dr. Pliskin, like Dr. Collins, concluded that McCaffrey's impairments would not have precluded him from filing his tax returns.

On May 7, 1997, the magistrate judge found McCaffrey guilty on all counts. On October 17, 1997, he sentenced McCaffrey to six months' imprisonment, a $2,500 fine, and a $100 assessment. The judge also ordered McCaffrey to file tax returns for the years 1993 through 1996, which he had remarkably failed to do despite a civil audit and the criminal charges against him. McCaffrey appealed his conviction and sentence to the district court as was his right under 18 U.S.C. § 3402 and

Federal Rule of Criminal Procedure 58(g)(2). On June 10, 1998, that court affirmed. This appeal followed.

II.

McCaffrey offers two arguments for our consideration. He urges that the government did not present enough evidence that his failure to file his tax returns was willful to sustain a conviction. He also claims that the court wrongfully admitted evidence that he failed to file income tax returns for the uncharged years, 1980 through 1988.

* * *

McCaffrey concedes that he failed to file his income tax returns for the years charged in the indictment, but he claims his failure was not willful, as 26 U.S.C. § 7203 requires it to be. The Supreme Court has defined willfulness in this context as a "voluntary, intentional violation of a known legal duty." Cheek v. United States, 498 U.S. 192, 201, 112 L.Ed. 2d 617, 111 S.Ct. 604 (1991). Thus the government had to prove that McCaffrey deliberately intended not to file tax returns he knew he had a duty to file.

The United States provided ample evidence of such willfulness. As a tax accountant, there can be no doubt that McCaffrey was aware of his duty to file. From the scope of McCaffrey's professional and personal accomplishments during those years, the court was entitled to infer that he had the ability to file, making his failure to do so voluntary. See In re Carlson, 126 F.3d 915, 923 (7th Cir. 1997) (finding the ability to carry on day-to-day affairs the best indication that an illness did not account for non-payment of taxes). The expert medical testimony of Dr. Collins and Dr. Pliskin, each of whom was of the opinion that McCaffrey's conditions did not keep him from filing his taxes, buttressed this conclusion. Moreover, throughout the time that McCaffrey was ignoring his own personal income tax returns, he was filing timely returns on his clients' behalf. This selective non-filing of only his own returns allowed the court to infer that McCaffrey's omissions were deliberate. It makes no difference that this amounted to circumstantial evidence of willfulness, as "the general rule in the majority of criminal cases that intent may be inferred from circumstantial evidence is no different in tax evasion prosecutions." United States v. King, 126 F.3d 987, 993 (7th Cir. 1997).

McCaffrey also attacks the finding of willfulness by presenting an alternative theory of the case. He suggests that his pervasive need to sleep and his depression made his failure to file his taxes innocently inadvertent, rather than criminally willful. Simply recasting his trial defense in this way does nothing to help his case, however, because the fact that some of the evidence might have supported his defense has no bearing on the question whether the prosecution submitted sufficient evidence to support its contrary theory. The court chose to credit the government's explanation rather than McCaffrey's, noting that "it would strain credulity to believe that Defendant's excessive need for sleep and his depression were so severe that they precluded filing his own personal income tax returns, yet they were not so severe as to preclude his timely filing of the returns of his clients." As long as there is sufficient evidence to support a finding of willfulness—and there is—we will not interfere with the court's conclusion that McCaffrey's intent was culpable.

We therefore Affirm McCaffrey's conviction.

Notes and Questions

Cases in which the mental infirmity defense is likely to be successful also are likely to be settled administratively. If a mental infirmity case proceeds to trial, an important issue usually is the admission of expert testimony. Often, such evidence is necessary for the defendant to establish the existence of the disorder, but the testimony is properly excluded if the defendant fails to establish a connection between the mental condition and the failure to pay taxes or file returns. See United States v. Shorter, 809 F.2d 54 (D.C. 1987). For a discussion of a novel mental condition, see Ryan Cochran, "Failure to File" Syndrome; Lawyers, Accountants and Specific Intent, 30 Cumb. L. Rev. 507 (2000).

1. How does the mental incompetence defense differ from the defenses previously discussed?

2. Usually, a defendant who pleads mental incompetence is pleading a mental disability short of insanity. How, if at all, does the mental incompetency defense differ from the insanity defense?

4. Statute of Limitations

The expiration of the statute of limitations is an absolute defense. A taxpayer cannot be prosecuted if the statute of limitations has run. The general limitations period is three years, but § 6531 provides a six-year period for certain offenses, including those offenses under §§ 7201, 7202, 7203, 7206, and 7212(a). The indictment must be found or an information must be instituted within the appropriate period "after the commission of the offense." IRC § 6531.

UNITED STATES v. HABIG

United States Supreme Court, 1968.
390 U.S. 222, 88 S.Ct. 926, 19 L.Ed.2d 1055.

MR. JUSTICE FORTAS delivered the opinion of the Court.

Appellees were indicted for crimes relating to allegedly false income tax returns. The District Court dismissed Counts 4 and 6 of the indictment, charging an attempt to evade taxes by filing of a false return (26 U.S.C. § 7201) and aiding in the preparation and presentation of a false return (26 U.S.C. § 7206(2)), on the ground that the six-year statute of limitations, 26 U.S.C. § 6531, barred prosecution under those counts. * * *

The question presented is the construction of §§ 6531 and 6513(a) of the Internal Revenue Code of 1954. It is squarely raised by the facts of this case. The indictment was filed on August 12, 1966. The income tax returns involved in Counts 4 and 6 were filed on August 12 and 15, 1960. Section 6531 limits the time when indictments may be filed for the charged offenses to six years "next after the commission of the offense."

The offenses involved in Counts 4 and 6 are committed at the time the return is filed. Six years had not quite elapsed from the commission of the crimes in the present case to the filing of the indictment. Appellees do not contest the chronological calculation. But because of § 6513(a) of the Code, they say that the critical date here is not the date when the returns were actually filed but the date when they were initially due to be filed, *viz.*, May 15, and not August 15, 1960.

The basis for this contention is as follows: Section 6531, which prescribes the six-year period of limitations, also says that "for the purpose of determining [such] periods of limitation * * * the rules of § 6513 shall be applicable." Instead of filing on the due date of May 15, 1960, the corporations obtained extensions of time to August 15, 1960. Accordingly, if the six-year period of limitations runs not from the date of actual filing (August 12 and 15, 1960) but from the original due date of the returns (May 15, 1960), the indictment, having been filed on August 12, 1966, was several months too late.

Section 6513(a) reads as follows:

"SECTION 6513. TIME RETURN DEEMED FILED AND TAX CONSIDERED PAID.

"(a) *Early Return or Advance Payment of Tax.* – For purposes of § 6511 [relating to claims for credit or refund], any return filed before the last day prescribed for the filing thereof shall be considered as filed on such last day. For purposes of § 6511(b)(2) and (c) and § 6512 [relating to suits in the Tax Court], payment of any portion of the tax made before the last day prescribed for the payment of the tax shall be considered made on such last day. For purposes of this subsection, the last day prescribed for filing the return or paying the tax shall be determined without regard to any extension of time granted the taxpayer and without regard to any election to pay the tax in installments."

Appellees' argument is that by reason of the third sentence of § 6513(a), the starting date for computing the six-year limitations period is to be determined by the original due date of the return, May 15, 1960, "without regard to any extension of time granted the taxpyer." The District Court agreed. * * *

On the other hand, the Government argues that appellees' contention, despite its support in the decisions of several courts, is necessarily based upon the surprising assertion that Congress intended the limitations period to begin to run before appellees committed the acts upon which the crimes were based. It argues that this result cannot be squared with the language of the Code or the intent of Congress. We perforce agree with the Government's analysis.

Section 6513(a), as its title clearly indicates, was designed to apply when a return is filed or a tax is paid before the statutory deadline. The first two sentences provide that the limitations periods on claims for refunds and tax suits, when the return has been filed or payment made in advance of the date "prescribed" therefor, shall not begin to run on the early date, but on the "prescribed" date. The third sentence states that, for "purposes of [the] subsection," the date "prescribed" for filing or payment shall be determined on the basis fixed by statute or regulations, without regard to any extension of time. The net effect of the language is to prolong the limitations period when, and only when, a return is filed or tax paid in advance of the statutory deadline.

There is no reason to believe that § 6531, by reference to the "rules of § 6513" expands the effect and operation of the latter beyond its own terms so as to make it applicable to situations other than those involving early filing or advance payment. The reference to § 6513 in § 6531 extends the period within which criminal prosecution may be begun only when the limitations period would also be extended for the refunds and tax suits expressly dealt with in § 6513 – only when there has been early filing or advance payment. In other words, if a taxpayer anticipates the April 15 filing date by filing his return on January 15, the six-year limitations period for prosecutions under § 6531 commences to run on April 15. Practically, the effect of the reference to § 6513 in § 6531 is to give the Government the administrative assistance, for purposes of its criminal tax investigations, of a uniform expiration date for most taxpayers, despite variations in the dates of actual filing.

The legislative history supports this reading. The first predecessor of § 6513(a) was enacted in 1942. See § 332(b)(4) of the 1939 Code, added by Act of October 21, 1942, c. 619, § 169(a), 56 Stat. 877. This section applied only to civil income tax refund proceedings. The Report of the House Ways and Means Committee (H.R. Rep. No. 2333, 77th Cong., 2d Sess., 119) states:

> "If the taxpayer files his return before the last day on which it is due, the period in which he can file a claim for refund under the provisions of § 322(b)(1), measured from the date the return was filed, will expire sooner than would be the case if he waited until such last day. Section 150 of the bill adds paragraph (4) to § 322(b) to provide that the period of limitations with respect to credit or refund is measured from the last day prescribed for the filing of the return in cases where the return is filed before such last day. *This provision does not apply to taxpayers who are given the benefit of an extension of time in which to file their returns, and file the return before the last day of the extended period * * *."* (Emphasis added.)

Then, in adopting the 1954 Code, the contested reference to § 6513 was added to § 6531. The House and Senate Reports expressly confirmed that § 6513 still encompassed "the existing * * * rule *as to early returns and advance payment."* H.R. Rep. No. 1337, 83d Cong., 2d Sess., A 416; S. Rep. No. 1622, 83d Cong., 2d Sess., 587. (Emphasis added.)

The language of § 6513(a) does not purport to apply when a return is filed during an extension of time. The legislative history is to the same effect. Accordingly, although we reiterate the principle that criminal limitations statutes are "to be liberally interpreted in favor of repose," we cannot read the statute as appellees urge.

The judgment of the District Court is reversed, and the case is remanded for further proceedings.

Notes and Questions

If the taxpayer is a fugitive from justice or is outside the United States, the statute of limitations is tolled during this period. IRC § 6531.

1. When does the statute begin to run in a tax evasion case? When would the statute commence in a willful failure to file case? See United States v. Creamer, 370 F.Supp.2d 715 (N.D. Ill. 2005); United States v. Mousley, 194 F. Supp. 119 (E.D. Pa. 1961); United States v. Feldman, 731 F.Supp. 1189 (SDNY 1990).

2. If a fraudulent tax return is filed after the due date of the return, when is it considered filed for purposes of the statute of limitations?

3. If the taxpayer fails to raise the statute of limitations as a bar to prosecution, is the defense waived? See United States v. Akmakjian, 647 F.2d 12 (9th Cir. 1981); United States v. Fuchs, 218 F.3d 957 (9th Cir. 2000); Walters v. United States, 328 F.2d 739 (10th Cir. 1964); Benes v. United States, 276 F.2d 99 (6th Cir. 1960).

4. If the limitations period is nearing a close, so that time is of the essence for the government, and the grand jury is not in session and will not reconvene until after the statute of limitations has run, what (if anything) should the government do? See Jaben v. United States, 381 U.S. 214 (1965).

II. GENERAL CRIMINAL OFFENSES UNDER TITLE 18 OF THE U.S. CODE

An offender may be subject to prosecution under both the Internal Revenue Code (Title 26) and Title 18 of the U.S. Code for the same conduct. There are several offenses under the non-tax criminal provisions under Title 18 that may overlap with the criminal tax offenses under Title 26. These include conspiracy, false statements, wire fraud, mail fraud, bank fraud, money laundering, and RICO.

A. CRIMINAL CONSPIRACY – 18 U.S.C. § 371

Section 371 provides:

If two or more persons conspire either to commit any offense against the United States or to defraud the United States, or any agency thereof in any manner or for any purpose, and one or more of such persons do any act to effect the object of the conspiracy, each shall be fined under this title or imprisoned not more than five years, or both.

18 U.S.C. § 371 (1994).

1. *Klein* Conspiracy

UNITED STATES v. GRICCO
United States Court of Appeals, Third Circuit, 2002.
277 F.3d 339.

ALITO, CIRCUIT JUDGE.

Appellants Anthony Gricco and Michael McCardell were convicted of conspiracy to defraud the United States, tax evasion, and making false tax returns. All of the charges related to the conspirators' failure to report on their personal income tax returns money that had been stolen from airport parking facilities. We affirm the appellants' convictions, but we vacate their sentences and remand for further sentencing proceedings and resentencing.

I.

From 1990 to 1994, Anthony Gricco was the regional manager for private companies that contracted with the Philadelphia Parking Authority to operate the parking facilities at the Philadelphia International Airport. Gricco was responsible for the general operation of the facilities, including the hiring of employees and the collection of parking fees. Michael McCardell, Gricco's brother-in-law, was Gricco's chief assistant. McCardell oversaw the day-to-day activities of the tollbooths and picked up money from the cashiers at the end of their shifts.

The parking facilities at the airport used automated ticket machines as well as cashiers. Upon entering a lot, a customer would take a ticket from a machine. The date and time would be printed on the ticket and encoded in the magnetic strip on the back. To leave the lot, the customer would drive to a tollbooth and the ticket would be put into another machine. This machine would read the date and time of issuance, calculate the length of time that the customer had parked in the lot, and display the parking fee owed. The customer would then pay the cashier in the tollbooth. At the end of a shift, each cashier would bundle together the tickets and cash received and put them in a brown bag labeled with the cashier's name and the number of the tollbooth. Each cashier would also place in the bag a tape from the ticket-reading machine that provided a record of the tickets that the machine had processed. The supervisors then would forward the bags to Gricco's assistants.

In early 1990, Gricco, McCardell, and others made a plan to steal money by substituting customers' real tickets with replacement tickets showing false dates and times of entry. A customer who had parked in the lot for a long period of time would have a real ticket reflecting a high parking fee. On leaving the lot, the customer would pay this fee to the cashier. However, instead of inserting the real ticket into the ticket-reading machine, a cashier participating in the scheme would insert a replacement ticket, and the machine would calculate the parking fee based on the false date and time stamped on the replacement ticket. This replacement ticket would indicate that the customer had parked for only a short period of time, and thus the parking fee would be much lower. The thieves would pocket the difference between the amount paid by the customer and the amount of the fee shown on the replacement tickets.

Michael Flannery, a technician for the company responsible for maintaining the ticket machines, provided the replacement tickets. Flannery also disabled the fare displays on the ticket-reading machines so that customers could not see that the parking fees that they were paying were higher than the fees recorded by the machines.

Flannery initially supplied Gricco with replacement tickets by removing tickets from the ticket-issuing machines and then resetting the counters on those machines. In the beginning, Flannery obtained 30 tickets a day using this method, and one cashier, enlisted by Gricco, used the replacement tickets to steal cash. Gricco scheduled either McCardell or David Million, another supervisor, to oversee the tollbooth plaza at which this cashier worked. Gradually, more corrupt cashiers were enlisted, and eventually Flannery began printing counterfeit tickets.

Gricco, McCardell, Million, and Flannery expanded their scheme over the next four years. At first, Gricco enlisted cashiers who had engaged in a similar but smaller scheme in 1988. Eventually Gricco recruited about 15 other cashiers to participate. Flannery delivered the counterfeit tickets that he manufactured to Gricco, McCardell, or McCardell's wife. McCardell then distributed the replacement tickets to the corrupt cashiers, and at the end of their shifts, McCardell picked up the stolen money and forwarded it to Gricco, who distributed the money among the participants. The cashiers received a portion of the proceeds stolen during their shifts, and the rest was divided into four equal shares for Gricco, McCardell, Million, and Flannery.

The leading participants in the scheme did not report their unlawful income on their federal income tax returns. Gricco kept his money in a safe, loaned cash to others and received repayments in the form of checks or money orders, gave cash to family members, and placed real estate under his family members' names. Through a real estate broker named Ludwig Cappozi, Gricco purchased several properties for cash. Capozzi also engaged in real estate transactions with McCardell's wife, who used cash to purchase properties under both her own and McCardell's name.

The cashiers involved in the scheme also failed to report their unlawful income on their income tax returns. They did not deposit their embezzled funds into banks for fear of being detected by the Internal Revenue Service. Gricco cautioned some cashiers not to put their money in banks, and he advised Flannery and Million to invest in real estate through Capozzi.

The scheme ended in September 1994, when the Philadelphia District Attorney's Office executed search warrants at the airport. In July 1996, the Commonwealth of Pennsylvania brought state charges of theft, forgery, and unlawful use of a computer against Gricco, McCardell, Flannery, Million, and numerous cashiers. The cashiers waived their right to a jury trial and were convicted in the Philadelphia Court of Common Pleas. After a three-day jury trial, Gricco, McCardell, and Million were acquitted, and the judge dismissed Flannery's case.

In April 1999, a federal grand jury returned an indictment against Gricco, McCardell, Million, and Flannery for conspiracy to defraud the United States by obstructing the lawful function of the Internal Revenue Service in the collection of federal income taxes, in violation of 18 U.S.C. § 371; tax evasion, in violation of 26 U.S.C. § 7201; and making false federal income tax returns, in violation of 26 U.S.C. § 7206(1). Prior to trial, Million and Flannery pleaded guilty and agreed to testify for the prosecution. Gricco and McCardell proceeded to trial.

The jury found Gricco and McCardell guilty on all counts. The government submitted a sentencing memorandum asserting that the total amount stolen between 1990 and 1994 was $ 3.4 million and that the tax loss was $ 952,000 (i.e., 28% of $ 3.4 million). * * *

* * *

The district court sentenced Gricco to 120 months of imprisonment and McCardell to 108 months of imprisonment. The court also sentenced each defendant to three years of supervised release, a $ 75,000 fine, and $ 700 in special assessments. Gricco and McCardell appealed.

II.

The appellants contend that their convictions for conspiracy are not supported by sufficient evidence. The appellants were convicted for a so-called "*Klein*" conspiracy[1] – a conspiracy to defraud the United States by obstructing the lawful function of the Internal Revenue Service in assessing and collecting federal income taxes.

In order for a *Klein* conspiracy to exist, an agreed-upon objective must be to impede the IRS. This need not be the sole or even a major objective of the conspiracy. In addition, impeding the IRS need not be an objective that is sought as an end in itself: an intent to hide unlawful income from the IRS in order to conceal an underlying crime is enough. Moreover, in a *Klein* conspiracy case, as in other conspiracy prosecutions, the objectives of the conspiracy may sometimes be inferred from the conduct of the participants. In the end, however, the evidence must be sufficient to prove beyond a reasonable doubt that impeding the IRS was one of the conspiracy's objects and not merely a foreseeable consequence or collateral effect. See United States v. Goldberg, 105 F.3d 770, 774 (1st Cir. 1997) ("Mere collateral effects of jointly agreed-to activity, even if generally foreseeable, are not mechanically to be treated as an object of the conspiracy."); United States v. Adkinson, 158 F.3rd 1147, 1154 (11th Cir. 1998) (The government must "prove that there was an agreement whose purpose was to impede the IRS (the conspiracy), and that each defendant knowingly participated in that conspiracy"). In determining whether the evidence is sufficient, we must of course view the proof in the light most favorable to the verdict and ask whether any rational jury could have found that the government met its burden. In this case, the government contends that the evidence is sufficient to meet this standard and relies chiefly on three categories of circumstantial proof.

First, the government relies on evidence that Gricco, McCardell, and other participants in the scheme did not report their illicit income. This evidence of parallel individual conduct has some probative value for present purposes, but it is plainly not enough by itself to show an agreed-upon objective to impede the IRS. It would not be at all surprising if all of these participants independently reached the conclusion that it would be best not to report their illicit income—either because they feared attracting investigative attention or because they simply wanted to keep the money that they would have been required to pay in taxes if the extra income had been reported. Accordingly, the mere fact that participants in the scheme did not report the income in question cannot reasonably be viewed as giving rise to a strong inference that the participants agreed upon this course of action.

Second, the government points to evidence that Gricco and Capozzi, the real estate broker who assisted him in purchasing property,

---

1. See United States v. Klein, 247 F.2d 908 (2d Cir. 1957).

structured various financial transactions so as to avoid the filing of currency transaction reports.[2] In addition, the government notes that on one occasion Gricco told Million never to "put any large sums of money in the bank, to be careful with that, especially anything over $ 10,000 because that would generate a report the bank would send to the IRS." This proof has some probative significance for present purposes because Gricco's desire to avoid the filing of currency transaction reports could have stemmed from a fear that such reports would interfere with his plan to evade the payment of taxes on the illicit income. We recognize, however, that the value of this evidence is limited. The appellants were not convicted of conspiring to violate the anti-structuring statutes, see 31 U.S.C. § 5322-23, but with conspiring to obstruct the IRS in the assessment and collection of taxes, and structuring does not necessarily result in the evasion of taxes.

The government's best evidence against Gricco is testimony that he told various participants not to deposit their illicit income in a bank but instead to purchase safes for their homes. These individuals testified that they followed this advice because they did not want to attract the attention of the IRS. It is likely that a person who acquires illegal cash and places that cash in a home safe, rather than a bank, will not report the cash as income on his or her tax returns. Accordingly, a rational jury could infer that Gricco knew that the participants to whom he gave this advice would, in all likelihood, not pay tax on their illicit income.

The difficult question is whether a rational jury could go further and find that Gricco not only foresaw that this would occur but actually intended for it to occur. Although the question is close, we conclude that the evidence, viewed as a whole, could persuade a rational jury to make such a finding. A rational jury could conclude that, if participants in the embezzlement scheme had reported their illicit income, this might have sparked an investigation that might have ultimately led to Gricco. Thus, not only did Gricco have strong grounds to foresee that the participants he advised would not report their illegal income, but a rational jury could conclude that he had also a reason to desire this result and that the result was something that he specifically intended. Viewing all of the evidence against Gricco together, we hold that it is sufficient to support his conspiracy conviction.

We reach the same conclusion respecting McCardell. McCardell admitted that Gricco told him to purchase a safe and that he did so. A rational jury could infer that McCardell agreed upon the objective of not

---

2. Under 31 U.S.C. § 5313(a) and 31 C.F.R. § 103.22(b)(1), financial institutions must file a currency transaction report when they engage in a cash transaction in excess of $10,000.

reporting or paying taxes on the illicit income because to do so would have created a risk of discovery. We cannot say that the evidence against McCardell is insufficient as a matter of law.

* * *

VII.

McCardell argues that the district court erred in admitting out-of-court statements under the co-conspirator exception to the hearsay rule. In making this argument, McCardell's brief cites a passage in the trial transcript in which McCardell's counsel objected when a cashier began to relate certain statements made to her by Gricco. McCardell's attorney objected on the ground that there had been no evidence of Gricco's participation in a conspiracy and that Gricco's out-of-court statements were therefore inadmissible hearsay. The district court overruled the objection after the government assured the court that it would establish the existence of a conspiracy.

We hold that Gricco's statements were properly admitted against McCardell under Rule 801(d)(2)(E), which governs statements by "a co-conspirator of a party during the course and in furtherance of the conspiracy." To admit statements under this rule, it must be shown by a preponderance of the evidence that "(1) a conspiracy existed; (2) the declarant and the party against whom the statement is offered were members of the conspiracy; (3) the statement was made in the course of the conspiracy; and (4) the statement was made in furtherance of the conspiracy." United States v. Ellis, 156 F.3d 493, 496 (3d Cir. 1998). In this case, as we have held, the evidence sufficed to show that McCardell and Gricco both were members of a conspiracy having as one of its objectives the impeding of the IRS. In addition, the evidence very clearly showed that they were both members of a conspiracy to steal money from the airport. This latter conspiracy provided an additional basis for admitting co-conspirator statements even though this theft conspiracy was not charged in the indictment. See id. at 497 (statements are admissible pursuant to Rule 801(d)(2)(E) even if the basis for admission is a conspiracy different from the one charged). Thus, the district court did not err in admitting Gricco's statements.

* * *

IX.

In sum, we affirm the appellants' convictions, * * *.

MCKEE, CIRCUIT JUDGE, concurring in part and dissenting in part.

I concur with the majority in all aspects of its opinion except for my colleagues' conclusion that there was sufficient evidence to convict McCardell of a *Klein* conspiracy. In United States v. Alston, 77 F.3d 713 (3d Cir. 1995) we held:

> A *Klein* conspiracy is comprised of three elements: (1) the existence of an agreement, (2) an overt act by one of the conspirators in furtherance of the agreement's objectives, and (3) an intent on the part of the conspirators to agree, as well as to defraud the United States.

Id. at 720 n.17. Although a defendant's failure to report income can be an overt act in furtherance of a *Klein* conspiracy, the government must "still prove there was an *agreement* whose purpose was to impede the IRS (the conspiracy), and that each defendant knowingly participated in that conspiracy." United States v. Adkinson, 158 F.3d 1147, 1154 (11th Cir. 1998)(emphasis added). Of course, where there is no direct evidence "of an agreement by all for each to evade his income taxes," the government can rely on circumstantial proof. Id.

However, "the failure to disclose income is, without more, generally insufficient to establish a *Klein* conspiracy." Id. "To be sufficient, the evidence must establish an agreement among the conspirators with the intent to obstruct the government's knowledge and collection of the revenue due." Id. "When the government relies upon circumstantial evidence to establish a tax conspiracy the circumstances must be such as to warrant a jury's finding that the alleged conspirators had some common design with unity of purpose to impede the IRS." Id. A *Klein* conspiracy is not established if the evidence implies only separate purposes to evade taxes. Id. at 1155. Rather, the evidence must "support an inference that each alleged tax evader * * * knew of the others' tax evasion" and that "they agreed to [evade taxes]." Id. "Although each defendant does not have to know every act taken in furtherance of the conspiracy, each defendant * * * must know that there is a conspiracy and demonstrate a specific intent to join it." Id.

McCardell argues that the government never produced any evidence that he spoke to, or agreed with, anyone about evading federal income taxes. Significantly, the government appears to concede that point. Its recitation of the evidence that McCardell was a *Klein* conspirator amounts to the following: (1) he told Million that he was concerned about alerting the IRS by exchanging large quantities of old $ 100 bills for new ones at a bank; (2) he did not report the stolen money on his federal tax returns; (3) he deposited small sums of cash to avoid generating a currency transaction report ("CTR"); (4) he purchased real estate; (5) he used Capozzi to purchase real estate and to launder the stolen money, and (6) he purchased a safe at Gricco's direction.

I agree that the evidence is sufficient to allow a rational jury to conclude that McCardell did all of these things to avoid paying taxes, and to avoid detection; and not just to hide the proceeds of the theft. However, as noted, a *Klein* conspiracy requires more. That crime is not established if the evidence implies only separate purposes to evade taxes. Adkinson, at 1155. On the contrary, the evidence must "support an inference that each alleged tax evader * * * knew of the others' tax evasion" and "that they agreed to do so." Id. I do not believe that a jury could reasonably conclude that this evidence proves that McCardell knew of anyone else's tax evasion, much less that he agreed with anyone else to evade the payment of income taxes.

Essentially, the government's case against McCardell is that "the jury could infer that Gricco spoke to McCardell, his brother-in-law and chief assistant, at least that he spoke to his lower level thieves, and Million and Flannery, about impeding the IRS," because his conduct paralleled Gricco's conduct and the other *Klein* co-conspirators' conduct. Therefore, claims the government, there is sufficient evidence to support McCardell's conviction as a *Klein* conspirator.

Although there is authority for the proposition that a defendant's connection to a *Klein* conspiracy need only be "slight," Adkinson, at 1152, the reference to "slight" refers to the "extent of the defendant's connection to the conspiracy, not to the quantum of evidence required to prove that connection." Id., at 1152 n.10. Obviously, the government must still meet its constitutional burden of proof beyond a reasonable doubt, and "slight" proof that a defendant committed a crime simply can not support a criminal conviction. At best, the government's evidence of McCardell's guilt of a *Klein* conspiracy was "slight." At worst, it was pure speculation. Far from resting upon substantial evidence, the government's case against McCardell boils down to the bare-bones contention that because Gricco, Flannery, Million and the cashiers were *Klein* conspirators; McCardell must also have been one. That is nothing more than an attempt to boot strap McCardell's conduct in the theft scheme into a *Klein* conspiracy by suggesting that it paralleled the conduct of Gricco and the other *Klein* conspirators. However, the majority correctly concedes that parallel conduct is not, by itself, enough to prove a *Klein* conspiracy. Yet, that is the only "proof" of McCardell's guilt of that offense.

Accordingly, I respectfully dissent from the majority's decision insofar as it affirms McCardell's conviction for a *Klein* conspiracy.

Notes and Questions

The elements of a conspiracy are an agreement between two or more persons to commit an illegal act, plus an act in furtherance of the agreement. Note that the act in furtherance can be a legal act, such as purchasing a safe.

Prosecutorial advantages to a conspiracy charge. Conspiracy is a frequently charged offense because it offers prosecutors distinct advantages. For instance, it is much easier to admit evidence that otherwise might be excluded under the hearsay rule; prosecutors often are given greater latitude in the introduction of circumstantial evidence; wider venue opportunities may be available; and because conspiracy is a separate offense, the offender may be punished for both the conspiracy and the substantive offense. The prospect of the latter advantage may make it easier for the prosecution to obtain a plea bargain.

Vicarious Liability. Under the rule of Pinkerton v. United States, 328 U.S. 640 (1946), conspirators are vicariously liable for the substantive crimes committed by their co-conspirators, as long as the crimes are in furtherance of the conspiracy and reasonably foreseeable. This gives the government a powerful weapon in its arsenal.

1. There are two types of conspiracies encompassed within a *Klein* conspiracy under § 371: (1) a conspiracy to commit a substantive offense proscribed by another statute (the "offense conspiracy") and (2) a conspiracy to defraud the United States (the "defraud conspiracy"). Can a defendant be acquitted of the substantive tax offense and convicted of a *Klein* conspiracy?

2. Do you think Judge McKee, in his dissent, is correct in his view that the government did not prove beyond a reasonable doubt that McCardell had been involved in the *Klein* conspiracy? Why or why not?

2. Defenses

A general defense to a conspiracy charge is that the government failed to establish one or more elements of the offense. There are more specific defenses available, however. Two of the most common are withdrawal from the conspiracy and the running of the statute of limitations. While there is no express statute of limitations found within § 371, most conspiracies are subject to the general five-year limitations period that applies to non-capital offenses under Title 18, although a six-year statute of limitations governs *Klein* conspiracies. Regardless of its length, however, the limitations period runs from the last overt act in furtherance of the conspiracy. Grunewald v. United States, 353 U.S. 391, 396 (1957).

UNITED STATES v. MANN
Unites States Court of Appeals, Fifth Circuit, 1998.
161 F.3d 840.

REAVLEY, CIRCUIT JUDGE.

Appellants James Mann and William Moore were convicted on numerous counts relating to their dealings with Jefferson Savings and Loan Association, McAllen, Texas (Jefferson), and its successor institutions. They challenge the sufficiency of the evidence and raise numerous other grounds for reversal. We affirm.

A. Sufficiency of the Evidence
1. Count 1 and Related Counts

Mann and Moore challenge the sufficiency of the evidence on count 1 and related counts of the superseding indictment on which they were tried. These counts concern Jefferson's purchase of oil and gas properties known as the Tartan properties in late 1982. Count 1 charged Peter Gallaher, Moore, Julian Alsup, Charles Christensen (GMAC),[3] and Mann with conspiracy in violation of 18 U.S.C. § 371. Generally, "[t]o establish guilt for conspiracy, the government must prove beyond a reasonable doubt that two or more people agreed to pursue an unlawful objective together, that the defendant voluntarily agreed to join the conspiracy, and that one of the members of the conspiracy performed an overt act to further the conspiracy." By its terms, § 371 provides that the unlawful objective of the conspiracy may be "to commit any offense against the United States," i.e. to commit a federal crime, or "to defraud the United States."

In order to convict a defendant of conspiracy, the prosecution must offer substantial evidence that the defendant was a member of the conspiracy. However, each element of a conspiracy may be inferred from circumstantial evidence.6 An agreement may be inferred from a "concert of action." A conspiracy may exist by tacit agreement; an express or explicit agreement is not required.

Count 1 charged that GMAC and Mann conspired:

---

3. Alsup died before trial. Gallaher was severed from the case because his lawyer was injured shortly before trial, and later pleaded guilty to a single count. Christensen went to trial with Mann and Moore and was acquitted on all counts against him.

(a) to defraud the United States by impeding, impairing, obstructing and defeating the lawful governmental functions of the Federal Home Loan Bank Board (FHLBB) in the regulation, supervision, and examination of the affairs of Jefferson;

(b) to willfully misapply monies, funds, assets, and credits of Jefferson in violation of 18 U.S.C. § 657;

(c) to make false entries in the records, reports, and statements of Jefferson, in violation of 18 U.S.C. § 1006;

(d) to defraud the United States by impeding, impairing, obstructing and defeating the lawful governmental functions of the Internal Revenue Service in the ascertainment, computation, assessment, and collection of revenue, namely, income taxes; and

(e) to make and file with the Internal Revenue Service false income tax returns in violation of 26 U.S.C. § 7206(1).

* * *

[Eds: Through a complicated series of transactions in the span of a few days, Mann and GMAC transferred millions of dollars in cash, land, and notes through companies, joint ventures, and partnerships that they controlled. Ultimately, the GMAC partnership bought Jefferson, a financially troubled institution, with funds that had been loaned by Jefferson, and the partners executed a promissory note to a company, Parkway South Development Corporation (PSDC), which Moore and Gallagher controlled. No payments were made on this note, but for years after the transfer of the note, PSDC identified the note on its books as a "loan from stockholders," rather than income to Moore and Gallagher].

* * *

A rational jury could find that the price Jefferson paid for the Tartan properties was grossly inflated. First, the very nature of the transactions support such a finding. Mann and Gordon, on behalf of the sellers, reached an arms-length price that was $4.2 million less than the price Jefferson paid. The incentive on the part of those who controlled Jefferson to cause Jefferson to overpay is manifest: GMAC were thereby able to use Jefferson's own federally insured deposits to acquire Jefferson; Mann personally profited by over $1 million; and Cartaya was able to unload his troubled institution and walk away with approximately $5 million in cash and real estate. The rank self-dealing, by itself, is compelling evidence that Jefferson paid too much. The complex nature of the transactions and appellants' efforts to conceal them from federal regulators (discussed further below) casts further doubt on the legitimacy of the price Jefferson paid.

* * *

In summary, a rational jury could find that Mann and Moore participated in a conspiracy whereby: (1) Mann sold the Tartan properties to Jefferson at an inflated price; (2) Mann, for personal financial gain, and GMAC used the profits from the sale of the Tartan properties to transfer ownership of Jefferson to GMAC, in effect misapplying Jefferson's own assets to acquire Jefferson, at a time when the institution was already in poor financial shape; and (3) the conspirators concealed the true nature of the acquisition scheme from federal banking authorities; (4) overstated the assets of the institution to perpetuate GMAC's control of it; and (5) filed false returns with the IRS to conceal the nature of their transactions and avoid taxes. The evidence is sufficient on count 1.

* * *

2. Count 30 and Related Counts

Mann and Moore challenge the sufficiency of the evidence on count 30. This count alleged a conspiracy whereby GMAC and Mann caused Northwest, the successor institution of Jefferson, to swap the stock in the subsidiary holding the Tartan properties for a piece of real estate owned by Mann. The property swap was part of an alleged conspiracy to "willfully misapply money, funds, assets, and credits of Northwest Savings," and "to fraudulently make and cause false entries in the records, statements, and reports of Northwest Savings." The alleged objectives of the conspiracy were "to fraudulently maintain the inflated net worth of Northwest Savings Association and to prevent regulatory intervention by the Federal Home Loan Bank Board," and "to transfer ownership and control of Northwest Savings to Defendant Mann by fraudulent means."

A rational jury could find the following. In 1984, Northwest still owned the Tartan properties and was still controlled by GMAC. Northwest was a financially troubled institution. In October 1984, the FHLBB informed Northwest that it was insolvent and that the directors should make efforts to infuse capital or otherwise increase the institution's net worth. GMAC responded with a letter to the FHLBB, informing it that it intended to increase its net worth by swapping its oil and gas properties for a tract of land known as Bridgepoint. The letter states that the real estate to be acquired "would have an appraised value equal to or greater than the present book value of" the oil and gas investment. Bridgepoint was part of a larger tract Mann had purchased through Camco from Pinnacle/Affiliated Joint Venture (Pinnacle). For business reasons unrelated to this case, Pinnacle had released its vendor's lien on the rest of the tract, leaving Bridgepoint saddled with $7.1 million in debt. Mann, by way of a guaranty, was personally liable for $1 million of this debt.

Mann told Dick Matz, who had helped Mann with financing on the Bridgepoint property, that he was purchasing Northwest and that the swap was part of the consideration. In December 1984, Northwest, through GMAC, swapped the Tartan properties (through a transfer of stock in Northwest's energy subsidiary) for Bridgepoint. Northwest assumed Mann's personal guaranty and Camco's $7.1 million debt on the Bridgepoint property. Northwest paid $1.1 million in principal and interest due to Pinnacle on December 30.

A rational jury could find that while the Tartan properties were worth millions of dollars, Bridgepoint had a negative net worth, due to the $7.1 million debt on the property. In late 1983, Patrick McClusky, an MAI appraiser, had appraised Bridgepoint at $3.2 million if it was sold separately. Eve Williams, another MAI appraiser, worked for First Franklin Appraisal Company, a subsidiary of Franklin Savings, which was controlled by GMAC. In early 1985 she appraised the property at $4.5 million. These appraisals did not consider debt on the property. Williams' boss asked her to "to keep looking at the lot values and the absorption to make sure that [she] had taken into consideration how good, how nice this piece of property was." Frustrated and confused, she asked her boss, "you know, what's the magic number?" Her boss, "who didn't look like he was real serious about it," said the magic number was $19 million. Williams testified there wasn't any way she could come up with that evaluation.

In 1986, the FHLBB conducted an examination that included an investigation of the Bridgepoint swap. One examiner was concerned that the swap "didn't make any sense," and another, Steven Taylor, "couldn't understand the economic justification for Northwest's part of the deal." An appraisal for the Bridgepoint property could not be located in the institution's records. Written inquiries were sent to Northwest's directors and Mann. A response from GMAC claimed that they had reviewed a December 9, 1983 appraisal, and that they had placed a value of $4 million on the oil and gas properties. The appraisal, however, placed a $3.2 million market value on Bridgepoint. GMAC conceded that Bridgepoint was encumbered with $7.1 million in debt and that Northwest had had to pay $781,000 in accrued interest. Based on these figures, Taylor concluded that Northwest had swapped a property worth $4 million for a property with a negative worth of approximately $5 million, resulting in a loss to the institution of approximately $9 million.

An accountant and acting controller of Northwest, on instructions from Moore or Plotkin, booked Bridgepoint on Northwest's books at $18.8 million. This figure was the sum of the overstated value of the Tartan properties and the outstanding debt on Bridgepoint Northwest had assumed. Northwest had not had an appraisal done on the property prior to the swap. In 1985 FHLBB reports, Northwest reported that Bridgepoint was worth $19.18 million in March, and $19.354 million in April. The accountant testified that when she showed Moore the Eve Williams appraisal, he "threw it across the room." Audie Pete, a CPA with Ernst and Whinney, became Northwest's controller in May 1985. He was concerned about accounting for the Bridgepoint property because it was such a large part of Northwest's total assets. He asked for an appraisal on more than one occasion. Eventually he ordered an appraisal. Marcella Pardo, another MAI appraiser with First Franklin Appraisal Company, appraised the market value of the property, as of December 31, 1984, at $4.8 million.

In 1985 Mann acquired Northwest Savings from GMAC. He merged it with Equitable Savings and created CreditBanc Savings and Loan Association (CreditBanc). At first he had proposed using Northwest's own money to buy out his partner in Equitable. After this proposal was rejected, the FHLBB reluctantly accepted a later proposal, in part because the FHLBB was of the view that "Northwest is insolvent and we have no other option currently available." At the time federal takeovers of insolvent institutions were limited to those institutions that were "desperately insolvent," according to the official who reviewed the proposed merger. The merger application included a pro forma balance sheet for Northwest, Equitable and the proposed merged institution. The line item for Northwest's real estate owned reflected a value of $18-19 million for the Bridgepoint property.

Prior to the merger Audie Pete * * * received an oral preliminary appraisal of $5-6 million for the Bridgepoint property. He adjusted the value of Bridgepoint on Northwest's books downward by $14.8 million, an adjustment he believed "would have a very significant impact on the operations." Mann instructed Pete to cancel the appraisal. Pete then "whited-out" the $14.8 million adjustment.

In summary, a rational jury could find that GMAC and Mann swapped the Tartan properties for the Bridgepoint property in an effort to falsely inflate the reported assets of Northwest. This effort forestalled the FHLBB from declaring Northwest insolvent, allowed Mann to personally unload a property with a negative net worth for valuable oil and gas properties, and allowed for the planned transfer of Northwest to Mann. The swap also removed the oil and gas properties from the books of Jefferson, and the jury could reasonably find this swap as a further effort to delay or hinder regulatory investigation of the earlier transaction made the basis of count 1. * * *

The evidence was also sufficient to convict Moore and Mann on related counts 31 and 32. Count 31 charged that GMAC and Mann with the substantive count of misapplying Northwest's funds in connection with the land swap. A rational jury could find that Moore, as a director of Northwest, grossly misapplied the institution's funds in connection with the swap, and that Mann aided and abetted this misapplication. Count 32 alleged that GMAC, aided and abetted by Mann, made a false entry by booking the Bridgepoint property at almost $19 million. As explained above, a rational jury could conclude that this value was grossly overstated.

Appellants again argue that, under *Beuttenmuller* [eds: United States v. Beuttenmuller, 29 F.3d 973 (5th Cir. 1994)], the Bridgepoint swap cannot be criminal because it was a value-for-value transaction. Under *Beuttenmuller*, the property swap is considered value-for-value unless the property acquired had no value, or had "a value so low that the transaction was essentially a sham to cover the fact that" the institution was providing "the down payment money for the purchase of" the institution's real estate. Again, we think the conspiracy here went far beyond a mere subterfuge to avoid regulations requiring a down payment. Further, even under the Beuttenmuller test, the jury could easily find that the Bridgepoint property was burdened with so much debt that it had a negative net worth.

* * *

B. Limitations

Mann and Moore argue that the count 1 conspiracy count was barred by limitations, and that allowing evidence on this time-barred count prejudiced the jury's consideration of the other counts. The limitations period runs from the last overt act of the conspiracy alleged in the indictment and proved at trial.[26]

As explained above, count 1 alleged a conspiracy (1) to defraud the United States by impairing the functions of the FHLBB, (2) to violate 18 U.S.C. § 657 (misapplication of bank funds); (3) to violate 18 U.S.C. § 1006 (false entry in bank records); (4) to defraud the United States by impeding the lawful governmental functions of the Internal Revenue Service; and (5) to file false income tax returns in violation of 26 U.S.C. § 7206.

---

26. Grunewald v. United States, 353 U.S. 391, 396 (1957).

Three different limitations periods apply to count 1. The general criminal limitations statute of five years applies to the first object.[27] The fourth and fifth objects, alleging a conspiracy to commit tax fraud and to defraud the IRS, are subject to a six-year limitations period.[28] Conspiracies to violate §§ 657 or 1006 are governed by a ten-year limitations period, 18 U.S.C. § 3293, but this statute applies to offenses occurring prior to its passage only if the previous limitations period (5 years) had not run on the date of enactment of the statute, August 9, 1989. The indictment issued on June 30, 1993. So to fall within the applicable limitations periods, the last act in furtherance of a conspiracy to impede the FHLBB had to occur after June 30, 1988, the last act in furtherance of a conspiracy to impede the IRS or violate the tax laws had to occur after June 30, 1987, and the last act in furtherance of a conspiracy to violate §§ 657 and 1006 had to occur after August 9, 1984.

Moore argues that if any one of the alleged objectives of the conspiracy is barred by limitations, the conviction on count 1 must be reversed. We cannot agree. If any one of the five alleged violations was proven, then the government proved a violation of § 371. "The general rule is that when a jury returns a guilty verdict on an indictment charging several acts in the conjunctive . . . the verdict stands if the evidence is sufficient with respect to any one of the acts charged."[30] Moore relies on *Yates v. United States*.[31] In *Yates*, the defendant was convicted on a conspiracy count alleging two objectives. The Court held that one of the objectives was barred by limitations, and that the conviction therefore required reversal, since "it is impossible to tell which ground the jury selected."[32]

However, in Griffin v. United States[33] the Court restricted the holding of *Yates* to cases where one of the alleged objects of the conspiracy is *legally* defective. "Legal error" is not insufficiency of evidence, but "means a mistake about the law, as opposed to a mistake

---

27. 8 U.S.C. § 3282.

28. 26 U.S.C. § 6531.

30. Turner v. United States, 396 U.S. 398, 420, 24 L.Ed.2d 610, 90 S.Ct. 642 (1970).

31. 354 U.S. 298, 77 S.Ct. 1064, 1 L.Ed.2d 1356 (1957).

32. Id. at 312.

33. 502 U.S. 46, 112 S.Ct. 466, 116 L.Ed.2d 371 (1991).

concerning the weight or factual import of the evidence."[34] In cases where the evidence of one of the alleged objectives of the conspiracy is factually insufficient, the Court in *Griffin* held that the verdict should stand so long as there is sufficient evidence on another alleged object of the conspiracy. Moore does not demonstrate that one of the alleged objects of the conspiracy was "legally defective," in the *Griffin* sense; he argues only that there was insufficient evidence of acts committed within the limitations period as to some of the alleged objects of the conspiracy.

Moore alternatively argues that the government failed to prove any act in furtherance of any objective of the conspiracy within the applicable limitations period. We agree with the government that there was sufficient evidence of numerous overt acts in furtherance of the alleged conspiracy occurring within the limitations periods. There was evidence that in 1987, 1988, 1989 and 1990, Moore caused the filing of corporate tax returns for PSDC, showing a $4 million "loan" from stockholders. A rational jury could find that this loan * * * was a sham, and that the tax filings allowed the GMAC partners to avoid taxes and conceal the fact that Mann and GMAC had used Jefferson's own funds to acquire Jefferson.[36] A rational jury could find that these filings were acts in furtherance of concealing the first, fourth and fifth objects of the conspiracy.[37] As to the third object of the conspiracy-the making of false

---

34. Id. at 59.

36. Mann argues that the jury could not have found the 1989 and 1990 tax filings to be in furtherance of the conspiracy, because the jury acquitted Moore on counts 28 and 29, the substantive counts for filing a false tax return. The verdict is not necessarily inconsistent in this regard. The jury might have found that the later filings were not "material" since they simply restated past filings. While materiality is an element for tax fraud, see 26 U.S.C. § 7206(1), there is no requirement that an act in furtherance of a conspiracy must be "material." More likely, the jury simply decided that convicting Moore on two counts relating to the PSDC tax return (counts 26 and 27) was sufficient, and that additional convictions would amount to overkill. Even if the verdict is inconsistent, the conviction on count 1 should stand, as long as the evidence is sufficient to support a conviction on that count. United States v. Powell, 469 U.S. 57, 67-69, 105 S.Ct. 471, 83 L.Ed.2d 461 (1984). Given "the Government's inability to invoke review, the general reluctance to inquire into the workings of the jury, and the possible exercise of lenity . . . the best course to take is simply to insulate jury verdicts from review on this ground." Id. at 68-69, 105 S.Ct. 471.

37. Moore argues that the tax filings could not have furthered the first object of the conspiracy-impeding the lawful governmental functions of the FHLBB in the regulation, supervision, and examination of the affairs of Jefferson Savings-because there was no evidence that the FHLBB and the IRS shared information. However, in the course of the 1985 IRS examination of GMAC and their companies, agent Burns requested "documents that the GMAC group filed with any regulatory agency regarding the acquisition of Jefferson Savings and Loan," and received some documents. A dispute with the IRS over the treatment of the "loan" became a matter of public record when the GMAC partners filed a tax court action in 1988. A rational jury could find that Moore and Mann, from the outset, recognized that the means employed to acquire Jefferson required concealment from and misrepresentations to the IRS as well as the FHLBB. Moore also argues that all efforts to impede the IRS ended in April 1987, when Mann disclosed key aspects of the acquisition of Jefferson

records and reports of Jefferson-there was evidence that Northwest continued to overstate the value of the Tartan properties to the FHLBB until the time of the swap of these properties for the Bridgepoint Residential property in late 1984. A rational jury could find that these filings were in furtherance of the conspiracy to make false statements. Moore argues that filings with the FHLBB in 1984 could not have related to Jefferson, since Jefferson did not even exist at the time. However, Jefferson's successor entity, Northwest, continued to operate after Jefferson was merged into Northwest. Examination of the affairs of Jefferson by the FHLBB, including examinations that might, and did, lead to the pursuit of criminal sanctions, did not end with the merger.[38]

Relying on *Grunewald v. United States*, [39] Mann and Moore argue that the overt acts on which the government relied were at most acts to conceal an already completed conspiracy, and that such acts are not acts in furtherance of the conspiracy for limitations purposes. The conspiracy count in *Grunewald* concerned efforts by the defendants to obtain "no prosecution" rulings in two tax cases by bribing an IRS official. The Court reversed the conspiracy conviction on limitations grounds, reasoning that "after the central criminal purposes of a conspiracy have been attained, a subsidiary conspiracy to conceal may not be implied from circumstantial evidence showing merely that the conspiracy was kept a secret and that the conspirators took care to cover up their crime in order to escape detection and punishment."[40] The Court's concern was that holding otherwise "would for all practical purposes wipe out the statute of limitations in conspiracy cases, as well as extend indefinitely

---

to IRS agent Burns. According to Burns, Mann disclosed that he had received a $1 million fee as agent or broker for the sale of the Tartan properties to Jefferson, that via the $4 million loan from Camco to PSDC, "the funds had been loaned or transferred to [GMAC]," and that the PSDC note had been repurchased by Alsup and Christensen at a discount. This testimony does not establish that all efforts by the conspirators ceased after these disclosures. First, Mann continued to characterize the $4 million transfer to GMAC as a "loan." Second, the jury could find that later efforts by the conspirators, including the filing of the PSDC tax returns, and the prosecution of the tax court action, were efforts to impede the IRS.

38. Regarding the second object of the alleged conspiracy-misapplication of Jefferson's funds-the government conceded to the jury and the district judge that limitations had run on the original misapplication of Jefferson's funds in the purchase of the Tartan properties. However, it argues on appeal that later "misapplications occurred when the conspirators, on a month by month basis, caused and approved the payment of interest necessary to carry the oil and gas properties in Jefferson's asset portfolio at the inflated $13 million-plus value." It made a similar argument to the district court. Without deciding the merit of this argument, we hold that limitations had not run on the other objects of the conspiracy.

39. 353 U.S. 391 (1957).

40. Id. at 401-01.

the time within which hearsay declarations will bind co-conspirators."[41] Appellants argue that under *Grunewald* all of the alleged acts in furtherance of the conspiracy within the limitations periods were no more than efforts to conceal the alleged central purpose of the conspiracy-the 1982-83 purchase of the oil and gas properties and takeover of Jefferson by GMAC.

We cannot agree with appellants that the count 1 conspiracy convictions must be reversed under *Grunewald*. As quoted above, the Court held that the limitations period runs where, after the "central criminal purposes of a conspiracy have been attained," the only acts occurring within the limitations period are acts of concealment from which a "subsidiary conspiracy to conceal may not be implied." *Grunewald* recognized, however, that "a vital distinction must be made between acts of concealment done in furtherance of the main criminal objectives of the conspiracy, and acts of concealment done after these central objectives have been attained."[42] It recognized that in some cases "the successful accomplishment of the crime necessitates concealment."[43] Later cases have recognized that acts of concealment are in furtherance of the conspiracy for limitations purposes where the nature of the conspiracy is such that concealment is part of or in furtherance of the main objectives of the conspiracy. We have recognized that acts of concealment are "part of the central conspiracy itself" where "the purpose of the main conspiracy . . . by its very nature, called for concealment."[44] "[C]oncealment is sometimes a necessary part of a conspiracy, so that statements made solely to aid the concealment are in fact made during and in furtherance of the charged conspiracy."[45] In *Forman v. United States*,[46] the Court held that an indictment alleged and the evidence supported a conspiracy to evade taxes extending from 1942 to 1953, even though the last fraudulent return was for 1945, because concealment had to continue if the evasion was to succeed.[47]

---

41. Id. at 402.

42. Id. at 405.

43. Id.

44. United States v. Diez, 515 F.2d 892, 897-98 (5th Cir. 1975).

45. United States v. Del Valle, 587 F.2d 699, 704 (5th Cir. 1979).

46. 361 U.S. 416, 80 S.Ct. 481, 4 L.Ed.2d 412 (1960).

47. Id. at 423-24.

In the pending case, the count 1 conspiracy was not limited to a conspiracy to misapply the assets of Jefferson, and obtain control of Jefferson through that fraudulent transaction. The central aim of the conspiracy extended to concealing the fraudulent nature of the transaction, in order to evade taxes and maintain control of the institution in the face of continual regulatory oversight. Frustration of investigatory efforts by the FHLBB and the IRS in a highly regulated environment was central to the conspiracy. The evidence supported a conspiracy, as alleged in the indictment, not only to defraud Jefferson and obtain control of the institution, but "to hide and keep concealed from the [FHLBB] the true facts and circumstances surrounding the acquisition, financing, operation, and management of Jefferson Savings;" "to hinder and defeat the [IRS] in the ascertainment, assessment, collection, and payment of income tax on the $4.2 million fraudulently obtained from Jefferson Savings;" and "to defraud the United States by impeding, impairing, obstructing and defeating the lawful governmental functions of the [FHLBB] in the regulation, supervision, and examination of the affairs of Jefferson Savings."

Mann argues that, irrespective of evidence of overt acts in furtherance of the conspiracy committed by others, *his* participation in the conspiracy ended no later than September 1983, when he sold the PSDC note to Alsup and Christensen and received, in the government's words, his $1 million "payoff" for his efforts to transfer control and ownership of Jefferson to GMAC. We cannot agree that Mann's role in the conspiracy ended on this date. Ordinarily, a defendant is presumed to continue his involvement in a conspiracy unless he makes a substantial affirmative showing of " 'withdrawal, abandonment, or defeat of the conspiratorial purpose.' . . . Indeed, '[a] member of a conspiracy continues to be responsible for acts committed by coconspirators even after the former's arrest unless he has withdrawn from the conspiracy.' " To demonstrate withdrawal from the conspiracy, the defendant must show that he has committed affirmative acts inconsistent with the object of the conspiracy that are communicated in a manner reasonably calculated to reach conspirators. Mann does not meet this burden.

* * *

AFFIRMED.

Notes and Questions

In United States v. Upton, 559 F.3d 3 (5th Cir. 2009), the Fifth Circuit analyzed *Grunewald* from the context of 18 U.S.C. §§ 1956 and 1957. In *Upton*, the defendant stole money and attempted to conceal the theft by comingling the stolen funds with his business funds, purchasing property in the name of a trust with a sham mortgage, failing to file a tax return in one taxable year and filing a false return in another taxable year. He subsequently was charged with conspiracy to commit money laundering in violation of 18 U.S.C.§§ 1956 and 1957, failure to file a tax return under § 7203, and filing a false return under § 7206(1). The defendant argued that his failure to file a tax return and his filing a false tax return were attempts to cover up completed financial transactions, and thus the two tax offenses could not extend the statute of limitations on the conspiracy. The court noted that if the sole charge against the defendant had been the § 1957 charge, which prohibits monetary transactions in criminally derived property, the argument would have merit because § 1957 "does not contain an element of concealment or disguise." 559 F.3d at 13. But § 1956(a)(1)(B) "prohibits engaging in financial transactions involving proceeds of unlawful activities, knowing that the transaction is designed in whole or in part to conceal or disguise the nature, location source, ownership, or control of the proceeds of specified unlawful activity." According to the court, where intent to conceal is an element of the substantive crime, any "additional acts of concealment that facilitate the central aim of the conspiracy are in furtherance of the conspiracy." Id.

1. What "affirmative acts" would Mann have had to prove in order to establish that he had withdrawn from the conspiracy?

2. What are the advantages and disadvantages of such a defense?

B. FALSE STATEMENTS – TITLE 18 U.S.C. § 1001

The false statements statute provides:

whoever, in any matter within the jurisdiction of the executive, legislative, or judicial branch of the Government of the United States, knowingly and willfully–(1) falsifies, conceals, or covers up by any trick, scheme, or device a material fact; (2) makes any materially false, fictitious or fraudulent statement or representation; or (3) makes or uses any false writing or document knowing the same to contain any materially false, fictitious, or fraudulent statement or entry; shall be fined under this title or imprisoned not more than 5 years, or both * * *.

18 U.S.C. § 1001(a).

In order to be convicted of this offense, the government must prove that the defendant (1) made a statement (2) that was false, (3) material,

(4) made knowingly and willfully, and (5) made in a matter within the jurisdiction of a federal agency.

UNITED STATES v. FERN
United States Court of Appeals, Ninth Circuit, 1983.
696 F.2d 1269.

DYER, SENIOR CIRCUIT JUDGE.

Fern appeals his jury conviction for violating 18 U.S.C.§ 1001[1] by making a materially false statement to an Internal Revenue Service Tax Auditor.[2] He asserts that § 1001 is inapplicable within the parameters of this case; that it was error for the Court to hold that his statement was material; that the evidence was insufficient to sustain a conviction; and that Fern was never identified as the person who made the false statement. We disagree and affirm.

When the evidence is viewed in the light most favorable to the Government, it shows the following facts:

Fern was a practicing accountant. On April 19, 1974 he and an investment partner executed an agreement to provide the New Testament Baptist Church with $125,000 in gifts. On April 25, 1974 Fern and his partner purchased property from Dade Christian School, a sister organization of the church. On that date $50,000 was paid to the church.

In late December 1974, Fern asked his client Brumer if he would make a $25,000 contribution to the church which would be tax deductible. He told Brumer that the money would be used to pay off pledges to the church in place of a mortgage, and that the money would be paid off at the time of the sale of the property. Brumer made out his check to the church for $25,000 and gave it to Fern, who delivered it to the church. The church treated the check as a contribution, and cancelled the $75,000 indebtedness of Fern in exchange for the Brumer check.

In January 1975, Brumer decided not to claim his $25,000 payment as a charitable deduction and asked Fern for repayment. On Fern's

---

1. Section 1001 provides in pertinent part:

Whoever, in any matter within the jurisdiction of any department or agency of the United States knowingly and willfully * * * makes any false, fictitious or fraudulent statements or representations . . . shall be fined not more than $10,000 or imprisoned not more than five years, or both.

2. Count 2 of the Indictment returned against Fern charged him with submitting a document which falsely stated that a $25,000 payment made by his client Brumer was a charitable contribution. The jury deadlocked on Count 2 and a mistrial was declared.

partnership tax return the $25,000 was listed as a liability. When Fern sold the property he had acquired from the church on April 1, 1975, Fern gave Brumer a check for $25,000, which included a notation that it was for repayment of a loan.

In March 1975 (before the repayment of $25,000 from Fern to Brumer), Fern suggested that Brumer take the $25,000 as a charitable deduction. Brumer told Fern that he did not want to take it as a tax deduction and that it was not to be claimed on his 1974 tax return.

In the spring of 1976, the Internal Revenue Service notified Brumer that it would audit his 1974 return, having challenged deductions claimed by Brumer for air conditioning repair and a part of his daughter's wedding expense. Fern attended the audit interview on May 17, 1976 with Tax Auditor Wilson. After Wilson indicated that she would disallow the challenged deductions, Fern stated that Brumer had found a deduction that he had not claimed on his tax return and that he, Fern, would like to submit it to her. He said that it was a contribution, and handed Wilson a copy of a cancelled check made out to the New Testament Baptist Church in the amount of $25,000. Wilson examined the check, marked it into her worksheet, checked a rough copy of Brumer's 1975 return given to her by Fern to ascertain whether the payment had been claimed for that year, and then told Fern she would accept it as a charitable contribution.

After this interview Wilson telephoned and wrote Fern requesting further verification of the contribution. By mail she received a copy of a letter from the church to Brumer thanking him for the $25,000 gift and a letter directly from the church erroneously indicating that no contribution had been received from Brumer.

As a result of the conflicting letters from the church, Internal Revenue Service Auditor Eddins called Fern and asked if there was a contribution made by Brumer. Fern told him there was a contribution made to the church but that Brumer was uncertain whether or not he would take credit for it. Later Fern told Eddins that after discussing the matter further with Brumer they had decided not to claim a deduction. However, such a conversation between Fern and Brumer had not taken place after the audit.

Fern first urges that he could not be prosecuted under § 1001 because the application of the statute in this case would reach a patently absurd result. In any event, it is argued, the Government should be required to proceed under the more specific, tax-related misdemeanor statute, 26 U.S.C. § 7207. We find no merit to these contentions.

Fern's absurdity-result argument rests upon Sorrells v. United States, 287 U.S. 435, 53 S.Ct. 210, 77 L.Ed. 413 (1932). There the Court held that even though there was a violation of the literal terms of the National Prohibition Act, the conviction could not be upheld in the light of admitted entrapment, saying "[t]o construe statutes so as to avoid absurd or glaringly unjust results, foreign to the legislative purpose, is, as we have seen, a traditional and appropriate function of the courts." Id. at 450.

Lifting this sentence out of context, Fern argues that to apply §1001 here creates the absurd result of swallowing up the perjury statute contrary to Congressional intent.[3] We disagree.

Sorrells was careful to point out that "the case lies outside of the purview of the Act" and that "its general words should not be construed to demand a proceeding * * * abhorrent to the sense of justice." Quite unlike *Sorrells* the opposite is true here. The purpose of § 1001 is clearly to protect the Government from fraud and deceit. The reach of the statute covers all materially false statements, including non-monetary fraud, made to any branch of the Government. Moreover, the term "jurisdiction" should not be given a narrow or technical meaning for purposes of § 1001. As we said in United States v. Lichenstein, 610 F.2d 1272, 1278 (5th Cir. 1980) the statute prohibits a false statement that is *capable* of affecting or influencing the exercise of a government function. That, as here, the government is not actually influenced by the statement is immaterial. The potential effect on the Government need not involve pecuniary loss. The false statement must simply have the capacity to impair or pervert the functioning of a governmental agency.

Clearly, the Internal Revenue Service is a "department or agency" of the United States. A false material oral statement made to a tax auditor falls within the purview of § 1001.

Fern made an affirmative, unsolicited, false statement which caused a tax auditor to initially conclude that an additional charitable deduction was due the taxpayer. If it was material, the statute applies for "[p]erversion of a governmental body's function is the hallmark of a § 1001 offense." United States v. Lambert, 501 F.2d 943, 946 (5th Cir. 1974)(en banc).

---

3. Fern also relies on Friedman v. United States, 374 F.2d 363 (8th Cir. 1967), to bolster his absurdity-result argument. There the defendant made a voluntary statement to the F.B.I. complaining of mistreatment by a highway patrolman. The statement was false and he was prosecuted under § 1001. The Court of Appeals reversed his conviction. However, the Fifth Circuit, sitting en banc in United States v. Lambert, 501 F.2d 943 (5th Cir. 1974), explicitly refused to adopt the *Friedman* holding. The Court held that a false statement concerning possible criminal conduct was within the jurisdiction of the F.B.I. and amenable to § 1001.

Relying on United States v. Beer, 518 F.2d 168 (5th Cir. 1975), Fern argues that Congress never intended that 18 U.S.C. § 1001 should be used to prosecute false statements made to the Internal Revenue Service since a specific statute, 26 U.S.C. § 7207[4] is applicable, and a specific statute controls a more general one.[5] Fern's reliance on *Beer* is misplaced. While it is true that we expressed a preference for prosecution under specific statutes, we expressly declined to reverse a § 1001 prosecution on that ground despite the presence of a more specific statute, § 1005, and despite the fact that the § 1001 penalty was twice as severe as the penalty provided in §1005. In commenting on *Beer,* we said in United States v. Carter, 526 F.2d 1276, 1278 (5th Cir. 1976):

> "Many statutes in the Criminal Code overlap, and the Government may elect the provision under which it wishes to proceed. Although we recently indicated a preference for prosecution under specific false statements statutes, we declined to reverse the conviction on grounds that 18 U.S.C. § 1001 had been chosen for prosecution."

The Supreme Court has long recognized that when an act violates more than one criminal statute, the Government may prosecute under either so long as it does not discriminate against any class of defendants * * *. Whether to prosecute and what charge to file or bring before a grand jury are decisions that generally rest in the prosecutor's discretion * * *.

There is no appreciable difference between the discretion a prosecutor exercises when deciding whether to charge under one of two statutes with different elements and the discretion he exercises when choosing one of two statutes with identical elements. United States v. Batchelder, 442 U.S. 114, 123-125, 99 S.Ct. 2198, 60 L.Ed. 2d 755 (1979).

Fern's argument is categorically foreclosed by the Ninth Circuit in United States v. Schmoker, 564 F.2d 289 (9th Cir. 1977)(concurring opinion) in which the Court said, "the Government [may] choose to prosecute a taxpayer who makes a false statement to an Internal Revenue agent for a felony, under the general false statement statute, 18 U.S.C. § 1001, rather than for a misdemeanor, under 25 U.S.C. § 7207,

---

4.   26 U.S.C. § 7207 provides:
Any person who willfully delivers or discloses to the Secretary or his delegate any list, return, account, statement, or other document, known by him to be fraudulent or to be false as to any material matter, shall be fined not more than $1,000 or imprisoned not more than one year, or both* * *.

5.   We are not called upon to determine whether 26 U.S.C. § 7207 applies to oral statements or only to written statements. Fern argues it, even though he concedes that there is no case law to support the application of that section to an oral statement. We adopt Fern's argument for the purposes of discussion only.

a statute specifically directed to persons who made false statements to the Internal Revenue Service."

Fern next questions the materiality of the statements made by him to Wilson. He argues that the court was misled by the Government in describing the audit procedure because no claim was made in the manner required by the Internal Service regulations,[6] and consequently the statement made by Fern, that his client Brumer had made a charitable contribution, was not material since there was nothing to investigate. Materiality is a question of law, United States v. Krause, 507 F.2d 113 (5th Cir. 1975); thus we are concerned only with the correctness of the district court's ruling and not the reasons underlying it.

We start with the premise that "[a] material false statement under this rule is one that is *capable* of affecting or influencing the exercise of a government function* * *. The statement must have been made with an intent to deceive, a design to induce belief in the falsity or to mislead, but § 1001 does not require an intent to defraud--that is, the intent to deprive someone of something by means of deceit." United States v. Lichenstein, supra, at 1277-1278.

Fern's contention that his statements could not have been material because all claims for refunds must be in writing misses the point. Statements such as that given by Fern to Wilson falsely stating that his taxpayer had found a deduction that he had not claimed, i.e., a charitable contribution of $25,000, and that he would like to submit it, led Wilson to add it to her worksheet as an item opened by the Service. She was prepared to execute a report including the charitable deduction, which would have resulted in an offer of an agreement regarding Brumer's tax liability[7] until her supervisor required her to obtain further verification. Clearly this was a material false statement which perverted the agency's function, and the fact that it did not actually influence the Government is immaterial. *United States v. Beer,* supra, is not to the contrary as argued by Fern. There the false statement made to the Federal Deposit Insurance Corporation could not have influenced that agency when the loan had already been repaid before the agency learned about the

---

6.   Fern cites 26 C.F.R. § 301.6402-2 (1982) which sets forth the procedure for filing claims for refunds and which requires, among other things, that the claim must set forth in detail the ground upon which the credit is claimed, contain supporting evidence, and be verified by a written declaration that it is made under the penalties of perjury.

7.   If a taxpayer agrees to a written proposed assessment prepared by a tax auditor, 26 C.F.R. § 601.105(b)(4)(1982), it operates as a formal claim for a refund. Bauer v. United States, 594 F.2d 44, 46 (5th Cir. 1974).

statement. Nor are we persuaded by Fern's assertion that, assuming for the sake of argument, his statement of a claim was false and material, he subsequently orally recanted it and under United States v. Cowden, 677 F.2d 417 (8th Cir. 1982) there can be no criminal liability. In *Cowden* the defendant made a false declaration on a customs form, but amended his claim *before* the official indicated that he had found undeclared currency. The court held that even if the official had found the currency in the defendant's luggage before he orally amended his declaration it would be "manifestly unfair that a customs officer should make every effort to conceal his discovery of an item and then, once a passenger has requested to amend his declaration [pursuant to 18 C.F.R. § 148.16], to forbid amendment." Id. at 421. Obviously this case is inapposite to the case sub judice where Fern apparently changed his story only after the Internal Revenue Service became suspicious.

Fern next asserts error in the court's holding that there was sufficient proof of a violation of § 1001 to submit the case to the jury. Relying on United States v. Poutre, 646 F.2d 685 (1st Cir. 1980); United States v. Clifford, 426 F.Supp. 696 (E.D.N.Y. 1976), and United States v. Ehrlichman, 379 F.Supp. 291 (D.D.C. 1974), Fern argues that since Wilson's testimony as to what Fern said to her was ambiguous and uncorroborated, and since the statements of Fern were susceptible to an interpretation that was literally true, the evidence was insufficient to take the case to the jury. Evaluating these contentions in the light of the evidence most favorable to the Government, we disagree.

Fern would have us take twelve sentences of Wilson's testimony and construct a reading of them to mean that rather than making an actual claim to the Internal Revenue Service, Fern was only speculating out loud as to what he might do, and in effect told Wilson that he could claim a deduction if he wished. We are unwilling to isolate a statement from context and give it a meaning entirely different from that which it has when the entire evidence is considered. We need not iterate the evidence we have previously related. Suffice it to say that it established that the audit was open for both the Service and Brumer; that Wilson examined a copy of the check to the church and asked Fern for the rough return for 1975. She told Fern that she thought the deduction was acceptable and she added it to her worksheet as an item approved by the Service.

Moreover, while no corroboration is necessary to sustain a conviction for making a false statement under § 1001, Wilson's testimony was corroborated. The Service requested verification of the alleged donation to the church and Fern answered this request. Fern told Agent Eddins that Brumer was entitled to the $25,000 contribution deduction. Fern questioned Agent Mastin whether the Service was trying to make a case out of the contribution. All of this testimony would have made no sense without the occurrence of the conversation between Wilson and Fern as related by Wilson. *Poutre* is clearly distinguishable. The Court there held that a verbatim transcript or written statement is not required per se in a prosecution under § 1001, but when a transcript of some answers was taken and two or three of the allegedly false answers are not included in the transcript, and only one prosecution witness testified as to one of the statements, the evidence was "too fragile" to support a conviction. 646 F.2d at 688. In contrast, Fern's statements were unambiguous and corroborated by witnesses and documents.

In *Ehrlichman* the Court applied the "literal truth test" enunciated in Bronston v. United States, 409 U.S. 352, 93 S.Ct. 595, 34 L.Ed. 2d 568 (1972), to allegedly false representations under § 1001 and found that the defendant was too disadvantaged in attempting to argue that his statements to the F.B.I. were literally true on the sole basis of the agents' sketchy notes. The Court concluded, therefore, that § 1001 was improperly invoked.[8] But we discern no parallelism between *Ehrlichman* and the case at bar. Quite properly the Court found insufficient proof of the underlying statements in *Ehrlichman,* as opposed to our findings here.

In *Clifford,* the Court referring to *Bronston,* found that in the absence of a transcript of what was said Clifford was in the same untenable position as was Ehrlichman in trying to argue that his statements were literally true because "* * * there was no basis, other than pure speculation upon which a reasonable juror could determine what question was asked and what response was given." 426 F.Supp. at 703. It seems clear that in each of these cases the truthfulness of the statement was left in doubt because there was a deficiency in the proof of the underlying facts, while here the falsity of the statement depends on the unambiguous testimony that Fern referred to the check as a contribution.

In *Bronston* the Court held that non-responsive, misleading answers, which were nevertheless literally true, could not support a perjury conviction. 409 U.S. at 362, 93 S.Ct. at 601. There the defendant's statements were not contested as being untruthful. Not so here. Fern did not base his defense on the basis that his statements to Wilson were literally truthful, nor did he raise this issue at trial. On the contrary, he

---

8.   The Court also premised its holding in *Ehrlichman* on the exculpatory "no" answer doctrine which applies a limiting principle to § 1001 to prevent its broad language from being used to prosecute a person who answers an exculpatory "no" when he is asked by the F.B.I. if he had committed a crime, since Congress did not intend to add a felony conviction to compel potential defendants to confess guilt to governmental investigators. This doctrine is inapplicable to this case.

flatly denied that he made the statements as related by Wilson and presented his own version. Thus the jury was presented with a clear choice of who was telling the truth, and it obviously disbelieved Fern.

Finally, Fern contends that since Wilson never identified Fern as the person who made the false statements, Fern's motion for a judgment of acquittal should have been granted. This argument gives us little pause. Courtroom identification is not necessary when the evidence is sufficient to permit the inference that the defendant on trial is the person who made the statements in question. The inference here was overwhelming. Agent Mastin identified Fern as the person who told him he had met with Wilson, and Brumer identified Fern as having represented him at the audit. Fern could not have denied making the statements to Wilson in his various conversations with the Internal Revenue Service agents unless he had been at the meeting in question.

AFFIRMED.

Notes and Questions

In 1995, the United States Supreme Court decided United States v. Gaudin, 515 U.S. 506 (1995), which held that the issue of materiality is a question of fact for the jury to decide. Subsequently, in United States v. Bok, 156 F.3d 157 (2d Cir. 1998), the Second Circuit, upheld a jury instruction in a § 7206 case, in which the trial judge charged the jury that : "* * * the test of materiality * * * is whether the information required to be reported on the tax return in question was necessary for the proper evaluation of the accuracy of the tax return * * *." 156 F.3d at 165. See also Neder v. United States, § C., below.

1. What differences, if any, are there between the false statements provisions under 26 U.S.C. § 7207 and 18 U.S.C. § 1001? Can a defendant be prosecuted under both provisions?

2. Is there any other Title 26 offense that might overlap with § 1001?

3. What lessons can be learned from *Fern* about how to represent a taxpayer at a routine audit?

4. Formerly, some courts distinguished the making of an affirmatively false statement from a mere denial or "exculpatory no" response to accusations or questions raised during an investigation. *Fern* refers to the "exclupatory no" doctrine in footnote 8. An "exculpatory no" was not considered a false statement and thus the defendant could not be subject to criminal liability under § 1001 simply for answering "no" to an incriminating question. The Supreme Court rejected this doctrine, however, in Brogan v. United States, 522 U.S. 398

(1998), holding that the statute does not distinguish between types of false statements. Do you think this holding might present Fifth Amendment problems? See U.S. v. Ballard, 2008 WL 214797 (E.D. Calif.).

C. MAIL FRAUD, WIRE FRAUD AND BANK FRAUD

NEDER v. UNITED STATES
United States Supreme Court, 1999.
527 U.S. 1, 119 S.Ct. 1827, 144 1.Ed.2d 3.

REHNQUIST, CHIEF JUSTICE delivered the opinion of the Court.

* * *

I.

In the mid-1980's, petitioner Ellis E. Neder, Jr., an attorney and real estate developer in Jacksonville, Florida, engaged in a number of real estate transactions financed by fraudulently obtained bank loans. Between 1984 and 1986, Neder purchased 12 parcels of land using shell corporations set up by his attorneys and then immediately resold the land at much higher prices to limited partnerships that he controlled. Using inflated appraisals, Neder secured bank loans that typically amounted to 70% to 75% of the inflated resale price of the land. In so doing, he concealed from lenders that he controlled the shell corporations, that he had purchased the land at prices substantially lower than the inflated resale prices, and that the limited partnerships had not made substantial down payments as represented. In several cases, Neder agreed to sign affidavits falsely stating that he had no relationship to the shell corporations and that he was not sharing in the profits from the inflated land sales. By keeping for himself the amount by which the loan proceeds exceeded the original purchase price of the land, Neder was able to obtain more than $7 million. He failed to report nearly all of this money on his personal income tax returns. He eventually defaulted on the loans.

Neder also engaged in a number of schemes involving land development fraud. * * *

Neder was indicted on, among other things, 9 counts of mail fraud, in violation of 18 U.S.C. § 1341; 9 counts of wire fraud, in violation of § 1343; 12 counts of bank fraud, in violation of § 1344; and 2 counts of filing a false income tax return, in violation of 26 U.S.C. § 7206(1). The fraud counts charged Neder with devising and executing various schemes to defraud lenders in connection with the land acquisition and development loans, totaling over $40 million. The tax counts charged Neder with filing false statements of income on his tax returns. According to the Government, Neder failed to report more than $1 million in income for 1985 and more than $4 million in income for 1986, both amounts reflecting profits Neder obtained from the fraudulent real estate loans.

In accordance with then-extant Circuit precedent and over Neder's objection, the District Court instructed the jury that, to convict on the tax offenses, it "need not consider" the materiality of any false statements "even though that language is used in the indictment." The question of materiality, the court instructed, "is not a question for the jury to decide." The court gave a similar instruction on bank fraud, and subsequently found, outside the presence of the jury, that the evidence established the materiality of all the false statements at issue. In instructing the jury on mail fraud and wire fraud, the District Court did not include materiality as an element of either offense. Neder again objected to the instruction. The jury convicted Neder of the fraud and tax offenses, and he was sentenced to 147 months' imprisonment, 5 years' supervised release, and $25 million in restitution.

The Court of Appeals for the Eleventh Circuit affirmed the conviction. It held that the District Court erred under our intervening decision in United States v. Gaudin, 515 U.S. 506, 115 S.Ct. 2310, 132 L.Ed. 2d 444 (1995), in failing to submit the materiality element of the tax offense to the jury. It concluded, however, that the error was subject to harmless-error analysis and, further, that the error was harmless because "materiality was not in dispute," 136 F.3d, at 1465, and thus the error " 'did not contribute to the verdict obtained,' " ibid. (quoting Yates v. Evatt, 500 U.S. 391, 403, 111 S.Ct. 1884, 114 l.Ed. 2d 432 (1991)). The Court of Appeals also held that materiality is not an element of the mail fraud, wire fraud, and bank fraud statutes, and thus the District Court did not err in failing to submit the question of materiality to the jury.

We granted certiorari to resolve a conflict in the Courts of Appeals on two questions: (1) whether, and under what circumstances, the omission of an element from the judge's charge to the jury can be harmless error, and (2) whether materiality is an element of the federal mail fraud, wire fraud, and bank fraud statutes.

* * *

III.

We also granted certiorari in this case to decide whether materiality is an element of a "scheme or artifice to defraud" under the federal mail fraud (18 U.S.C. § 1341), wire fraud (§ 1343), and bank fraud (§ 1344) statutes. The Court of Appeals concluded that the failure to submit materiality to the jury was not error because the fraud statutes do not require that a "scheme to defraud" employ *material* falsehoods. We disagree.

Under the framework set forth in United States v. Wells, 519 U.S. 482, 117 S.Ct. 921, 137 L.Ed. 2d 107 (1997), we first look to the text of the statutes at issue to discern whether they require a showing of materiality. In this case, we need not dwell long on the text because, as the parties agree, none of the fraud statutes defines the phrase "scheme or artifice to defraud," or even mentions materiality. Although the mail fraud and wire fraud statutes contain different jurisdictional elements (§ 1341 requires use of the mails while § 1343 requires use of interstate wire facilities), they both prohibit, in pertinent part, "any scheme or artifice to defraud" or to obtain money or property "by means of false or fraudulent pretenses, representations, or promises."[3] The bank fraud statute, which was modeled on the mail and wire fraud statutes, similarly prohibits any "scheme or artifice to defraud a financial institution" or to obtain any property of a financial institution "by false or fraudulent pretenses, representations, or promises."[4] Thus, based

---

3. Section 1341 provides in pertinent part:

"Whoever, having devised or intending to devise any scheme or artifice to defraud, or for obtaining money or property by means of false or fraudulent pretenses, representations, or promises, * * * for the purpose of executing such scheme or artifice or attempting so to do, places in any post office or authorized depository for mail matter, any matter or thing whatever to be sent or delivered by the Postal Service, or deposits or causes to be deposited any matter or thing whatever to be sent or delivered by any private or commercial interstate carrier, or takes or receives therefrom, any such matter or thing, or knowingly causes to be delivered by mail or such carrier according to the direction thereon, or at the place at which it is directed to be delivered by the person to whom it is addressed, any such matter or thing, shall be fined under this title or imprisoned not more than five years, or both. If the violation affects a financial institution, such person shall be fined not more than $1,000,000 or imprisoned not more than 30 years, or both."

Section 1343 provides:

"Whoever, having devised or intending to devise any scheme or artifice to defraud, or for obtaining money or property by means of false or fraudulent pretenses, representations, or promises, transmits or causes to be transmitted by means of wire, radio, or television communication in interstate or foreign commerce, any writings, signs, signals, pictures, or sounds for the purpose of executing such scheme or artifice, shall be fined under this title or imprisoned not more than five years, or both. If the violation affects a financial institution, such person shall be fined not more than $1,000,000 or imprisoned not more than 30 years, or both."

4. Section 1344 provides:

"Whoever knowingly executes, or attempts to execute, a scheme or artifice—
"(1) to defraud a financial institution; or
"(2) to obtain any of the moneys, funds, credits, assets, securities, or other property owned by, or under the custody or control of, a financial institution, by means of false or fraudulent pretenses, representations, or promises;
"shall be fined not more than $1,000,000 or imprisoned not more than 30 years, or both."

solely on a "natural reading of the full text," id., at 490, 117 S.Ct. 921, materiality would not be an element of the fraud statutes.

That does not end our inquiry, however, because in interpreting statutory language there is a necessary second step. It is a well-established rule of construction that " '[w]here Congress uses terms that have accumulated settled meaning under * * * the common law, a court must infer, unless the statute otherwise dictates, that Congress means to incorporate the established meaning of these terms.' " Nationwide Mut. Ins. Co. v. Darden, 503 U.S. 318, 322, 112 S.Ct. 1344, 117 L.Ed. 2d 581 (1992) (quoting Community for Creative non-Violence v. Reid, 490 U.S. 730, 739, 109 S.Ct. 2166, 104 L.Ed. 2d 811 (1989)). Neder contends that "defraud" is just such a term, and that Congress implicitly incorporated its common-law meaning, including its requirement of materiality,[5] into the statutes at issue.

The Government does not dispute that both at the time of the mail fraud statute's original enactment in 1872, and later when Congress enacted the wire fraud and bank fraud statutes, actionable "fraud" had a well-settled meaning at common law. Nor does it dispute that the well-settled meaning of "fraud" required a misrepresentation or concealment of *material* fact. Indeed, as the sources we are aware of demonstrate, the common law could not have conceived of "fraud" without proof of materiality. See BMW of North America, Inc. v. Gore, 517 U.S. 559, 579, 116 S.Ct. 1589, 134 L.Ed. 2d 809 (1996)("[A]ctionable fraud requires a *material* misrepresentation or omission" (citing Restatement (Second) of Torts § 538 (1977). Thus, under the rule that Congress intends to incorporate the well-settled meaning of the common-law terms it uses, we cannot infer from the absence of an express reference to materiality that Congress intended to drop that element from the fraud statutes.[6] On the contrary, we must *presume* that Congress intended to incorporate materiality " 'unless the statute

---

5. The Restatement instructs that a matter is material if:

"(a) a reasonable man would attach importance to its existence or nonexistence in determining his choice of action in the transaction in question; or

"(b) the maker of the representation knows or has reason to know that its recipient regards or is likely to regard the matter as important in determining his choice of action, although a reasonable man would not so regard it." Restatement (Second) of Torts § 538 (1977).

6. We concluded as much in Field v. Mans, 516 U.S. 59, 69, 116 S.Ct. 437, 133 l.Ed. 2d 351 (1995):

" '[F]alse pretenses, a false representation, or actual frau[d]' carry the acquired meaning of terms of art. They are common-law terms, and * * * they imply elements that the common law has defined them to include * * *. Congress could have enumerated their elements, but Congress's contrary drafting choice did not deprive them of a significance richer than the bare statement of their terms."

otherwise dictates.' " *Nationwide Mut. Ins.,* supra, at 322, 112 S.Ct. 1344.[7]

The Government attempts to rebut this presumption by arguing that the term "defraud" would bear its common-law meaning only if the fraud statutes "indicated that Congress had codified the crime of false pretenses or one of the common-law torts sounding in fraud." Instead, the Government argues, Congress chose to unmoor the mail fraud statute from its common-law analogs by punishing, not the completed fraud, but rather any person "having devised or intending to devise any scheme or artifice to defraud." Read in this light, the Government contends, there is no basis to infer that Congress intended to limit criminal liability to conduct that would constitute "fraud" at common law, and in particular, to *material* misrepresentations or omissions. Rather, criminal liability would exist so long as the defendant *intended* to deceive the victim, even if the particular means chosen turn out to be immaterial, *i.e.,* incapable of influencing the intended victim. See n. 3, supra.

The Government relies heavily on Durland v. United States, 161 U.S. 306, 16 S.Ct. 508, 400 L.Ed. 709 (1896), our first decision construing the mail fraud statute, to support its argument that the fraud statutes sweep more broadly than common-law fraud. But *Durland* was different from this case. There, the defendant, who had used the mails to sell bonds he did not intend to honor, argued that he could not be held criminally liable because his conduct did not fall within the scope of the common-law crime of "false pretenses." We rejected the argument that "the statute reaches only such cases as, at common law, would come within the definition of 'false pretenses,' in order to make out which there must be a misrepresentation as to some existing fact and not a mere promise as to the future." Id., at 312, 16 S.Ct. 508. Instead, we construed the statute to "includ[e] everything designed to defraud by representations as to the past or present, or suggestions and promises as to the future."

---

7. The Government argues that because Congress has provided express materiality requirements in other statutes prohibiting fraudulent conduct, the absence of such an express reference in the fraud statutes at issue " 'speaks volumes.' " Brief for United States 35 (citing 21 U.S.C. § 843(a)(4)(A))(prohibiting the furnishing of "false or fraudulent material information" in documents required under federal drug laws); 26 U.S.C. § 6700(a)(2)(A)(criminalizing the making of a statement regarding investment tax benefits that an individual "knows or has reason to kno[w] is false or fraudulent as to any material matter"). These later enacted statutes, however, differ from the fraud statutes here in that they prohibit both "false" and "fraudulent" statements or information. Because the term "false statement" does not imply a materiality requirement, United States v. Wells, 519 U.S. 482, 491, 117 S.Ct. 921, 137 L.Ed. 2d 107 (1997), the word "material" limits the statutes' scope to material falsehoods. Moreover, these statutes cannot rebut the presumption that Congress intended to incorporate the common-law meaning of the term "fraud" in the mail fraud, wire fraud, and bank fraud statutes. That rebuttal can only come from the text or structure of the fraud statutes themselves. *See Nationwide Mut. Ins.,* 503 U.S. at 322, 112 S.Ct. 1344.

Id., at 313, 16 S.Ct. 508. Although *Durlan* held that the mail fraud statute reaches conduct that would not have constituted "false pretenses" at common law, it did not hold, as the Government argues, that the statute encompasses more than common-law fraud.

In one sense, the Government is correct that the fraud statutes did not incorporate *all* the elements of common-law fraud. The common-law requirements of "justifiable reliance" and "damages," for example, plainly have no place in the federal fraud statutes. By prohibiting the "scheme to defraud," rather than the completed fraud, the elements of reliance and damage would clearly be inconsistent with the statutes Congress enacted. But while the language of the fraud statutes is incompatible with these requirements, the Government has failed to show that this language is inconsistent with a materiality requirement.

Accordingly, we hold that materiality of falsehood is an element of the federal mail fraud, wire fraud, and bank fraud statutes. Consistent with our normal practice where the court below has not yet passed on the harmlessness of any error, we remand this case to the Court of Appeals for it to consider in the first instance whether the jury-instruction error was harmless.

IV.

The judgment of the Court of Appeals respecting the tax fraud counts is affirmed. The judgment of the Court of Appeals on the remaining counts is reversed, and the case is remanded for further proceedings consistent with this opinion.

It is so ordered.

Notes and Questions

Scope of Mail Fraud. In McNally v. United States, 483 U.S. 350, 107 S.Ct., 2875, 97 L.Ed.2d 292 (1987), the Supreme Court held that the mail fraud statute "is limited in scope to the protection of property rights," and was not intended to apply to "schemes to defraud citizens of their intangible rights to honest and impartial government." Id., at 355. There have been various arguments based on the property rights holding, that tax revenues prior to assessment do not constitute a "tangible property right," but these arguments have been uniformly rejected by the courts. See United States v. Bucey, 876 F.2d 1297 (7th Cir. 1989); United States v. Regan, 713 F.Supp. 629 (S.D.N.Y. 1989).

Pyramiding Charges. In United States v. Henderson, 386 F.Supp. 1048 (S.D.N.Y. 1974), the district court held that Congress had not intended the mail fraud statute to apply to an offense that was properly addressed under the attempted tax evasion statute. The court opined that this constituted improper pyramiding of sentences because the mail fraud statute simply addressed the mailing of the fraudulent return. This decision has been rejected or distinguished, however, in virtually all the courts that have cited it, including the Second Circuit where *Henderson* was decided, although *Henderson* has not been overruled in that circuit. See Fountain v. U.S., 357 F.3d 250, 258 (2d Cir. 2004)("*Henderson*-which other circuits have rejected-provides weak authority for the proposition that schemes aimed at defrauding the government of taxes do not fall within the scope of the mail and wire fraud statutes"). See also United States v. Miller, 26 F. Supp 2d. 415 (N.D.N.Y. 1998); United States v. Weatherspoon, 581 F.2d 585 (7th Cir. 1978);

The Tax Division of the Department of Justice takes the position, espoused in *Henderson*, that when the offense arises essentially out of a violation of the tax statutes, Congress intended the tax statutes to provide the basis of the prosecution. Thus, the authorization of the Tax Division is required before a mail fraud charge can be brought in a tax case. Such authorization is required regardless of whether the mail fraud charge is an independent count or a predicate act to a RICO charge. Authorization will be granted, however, only in exceptional circumstances. See further discussion, § D., below.

1. What are the elements of mail fraud, wire fraud and bank fraud?

2. In what way(s) does a charge of mail fraud transform a tax evasion charge? Does a charge of mail fraud also transform a charge under § 7207 (delivering or disclosing false or fraudulent returns or documents)?

D. RICO – TITLE 18 U.S.C. §§ 1961-1968

The Racketeering Influenced and Corrupt Organizations Act (RICO) was enacted in 1970 as a part of the Organized Crime Control Act, which in turn was enacted in a congressional effort to combat organized crime. The RICO statute applies broadly, however, to reach far beyond its initial scope.

In order to secure a conviction under RICO, the government must prove both the existence of an "enterprise" and a connected "pattern of racketeering activity." 18 U.S.C. §§ 1961 and 1962. "An 'enterprise' includes any individual, partnership, corporation, association, or other legal entity, and any union or group of individuals associated in fact although not a legal entity* * *." Id., at § 1961(4). Thus, RICO can be used against both legitimate and illegitimate enterprises. In order to meet this element, the government must establish (1) the existence of an ongoing organization or association, (2) that various associates function as a continuing unit for a common purpose, and (3) an existence separate and apart from the pattern of activity in which it is engaged.

A "pattern of racketeering activity" requires at least two acts of racketeering activity that demonstrate a pattern. Thus, the existence of two or more predicate acts does not mean that RICO will be available automatically. The United States Supreme Court has stated that a pattern is produced by a "continuity plus relationship." H.J. Inc. v. Northwestern Bell Telephone Co., 492 U.S. 229, 239 (1989). The Court noted that this is established by showing that the "racketeering predicates are related and that they amount to or pose a threat of continued criminal activity." Id.

Although RICO is charged as a discrete offense, it is dependent upon predicate acts of "racketeering activity" which include mail fraud, wire fraud, and bank fraud. While Title 26 offenses are not listed as predicate acts, nevertheless, they are drawn into the net through the Title 18 predicates.

UNITED STATES v. ZICHETTELLO

United States Court of Appeals, Second Circuit, 2000.
208 F.3d 72.

WINTER, CHIEF JUDGE.

Following a three and one-half month jury trial, * * * Ronald Reale, the former President of the New York City Transit Police Benevolent Association ("TPBA"), Richard Hartman, a disbarred lawyer who was the TPBA's former labor negotiator and insurance broker, and James J. Lysaght and Peter Kramer, partners in the law firm Lysaght, Lysaght and Kramer ("LL & K"), who received millions of dollars in legal fees from the TPBA in return for kickbacks, appeal from their convictions and sentences. These appellants were convicted of conspiracy to violate the Racketeer Influenced and Corrupt Organizations Act ("RICO") 18 U.S.C. § 1962, for their role in corrupting the TPBA and transforming it into a RICO enterprise through bribery and other illegal acts. Reale and Hartman were also convicted of various substantive offenses. Frank Richardone, a former Treasurer of the TPBA, pleaded guilty to mail fraud and related crimes. Richardone appeals only from his sentence. (For convenience purposes, "appellants" will refer only to the defendants who went to trial unless otherwise specified.) This appeal involves a unique set of circumstances. Appellants' opening briefs advanced substantial claims of error based on instructions to the jury concerning aiding and abetting that were found in the official trial transcript. In its brief, the government responded by arguing that the instructions were not error or at least not reversible error. * * * We conclude that the trial court committed no reversible error in the unusually lengthy, difficult and complex RICO conspiracy trial that is the subject of this appeal, * * *. For the reasons set forth below, the government's motion is granted. Because we reject appellants' remaining arguments on appeal, we affirm.

* * *

a) *The Charges*

* * * On September 15, 1997, the government filed a thirty-nine count indictment, against Reale, Hartman, Lysaght, and Kramer.[1] Counts One and Two charged them with participating and conspiring to participate in the affairs of the TPBA through a pattern of racketeering in violation of 18 U.S.C. §§ 1962(c) & (d). These counts also alleged that the appellants had committed eleven racketeering acts in furtherance of the charged enterprise, including bribery, mail fraud, wire fraud, money laundering, and witness tampering.

[Eds: Counts three through thirty-nine charged the appellants with various other crimes relating to the alleged racketeering acts including tax evasion in violation of 26 U.S.C. § 7201, conspiracy to commit tax evasion in violation of 18 U.S.C. § 371, and other substantive tax offenses in violation of § 7206].

* * *

1) RICO Conspiracy Convictions

Hartman, Lysaght, and Kramer attack their RICO conspiracy convictions for violating 18 U.S.C. § 1962(d) on several grounds.

A. Co-Conspirator Liability

Hartman, Lysaght, and Kramer first contend that their convictions for RICO conspiracy must be reversed because of the Supreme Court's decision in Reves v. Ernst & Young, 507 U.S. 170, 113 S.Ct. 1163, 122

---

1. The original indictment was charged against Richardone and Thomas Zichettello. [Eds: Zichetello was a former vice-president of the TPBA]. Thereafter, Zichettello entered into a cooperation agreement with the government pursuant to which he pleaded guilty to charges of participating in a RICO enterprise and committing tax evasion. Richardone also pleaded guilty but did not enter into a cooperation agreement with the government.

L.Ed. 2d 525 (1993), and our decision in United States v. Viola, 35 F.2d 37 (2d Cir. 1994). Relying upon the district court's statement that they "did not operate or manage, directly or indirectly, the enterprise" in dismissing the substantive RICO violation charged in the indictment, appellants contend that *Reves* precludes a RICO conspiracy conviction for "outsiders" not involved in the operation or management of the enterprise. Alternatively, they contend that a conviction for RICO conspiracy requires a showing that such outsiders knew about and agreed to all the racketeering activity of the enterprise, including racketeering acts in which they were not personally involved. Appellants thus argue that because they did not know the TPBA Officers were accepting bribes from other vendors, they cannot be guilty of RICO conspiracy. We disagree.

Appellants' reading of *Reves* is simply incorrect. *Reves* ruled only that for a defendant to be convicted of a substantive RICO violation under § 1962(c), the defendant must have taken some part in directing the enterprise's affairs. See *Reves,* 507 U.S. at 179, 113 S.Ct. 1163. No such requirement exists under § 1962(d), however. See *Salinas,* 118 S.Ct. at 477 ("A person * * * may be liable for conspiracy even though he was incapable of committing the substantive offense."); Napoli v. United States, 45 F.3d 680, 683-84 (2d Cir. 1995) ("[Defendant] was convicted only on the RICO conspiracy charge, and that conviction is unaffected by the *Reves* error."); *Viola,* 35 F.3d at 43; see also Goren v. New Vision Int's, Inc. 156 F.3d 721, 731 (7th Cir. 1998) ("[W]e have held that a defendant can be charged under § 1962(d) even if he cannot be characterized as an operator or manager of a RICO enterprise under *Reves* * * *.").

To argue that *Reves* controls the instant case confuses substantive RICO crimes with conspiracy. "A defendant can be guilty of conspiring to violate a law, even if he is not among the class of persons who could commit the crime directly." *Viola,* 35 F.3d at 43. The "straightforward language of § 1962(d) provides: 'It shall be unlawful for any person to conspire to violate any of the provisions of subsection (a), (b), or (c) of this section.'" Id. (quoting 18 U.S.C. § 1962(d)). A RICO conspiracy charge "is proven if the defendant 'embraced the objective of the alleged conspiracy,' and agreed to commit * * * predicate acts in furtherance thereof." Id. (quoting United States v. Neapolitan, 791 F.2d 489, 495 (7th Cir. 1986)). Assuming that a RICO enterprise exists, the government must prove only "that the defendant[s] * * * know the general nature of the conspiracy and that the conspiracy extends beyond [their] individual role[s]." United States v. Rastelli, 870 F.2d 822, 828 (2d Cir. 1989). In applying this analysis, we need inquire only whether an alleged conspirator knew what the other conspirators "were up to" or whether the situation would logically lead an alleged conspirator "to suspect he was part of a larger enterprise." *Viola,* 35 F.3d at 44-45; see also *Salinas,* 118 S.Ct. at 478 (upholding conviction under § 1962(d) where defendant "knew about and agreed to facilitate the scheme").[13]

We turn then to appellants' argument that, because the district court, in dismissing the substantive RICO count, stated that appellants did not know of certain acts of the RICO enterprise, reversal of their conspiracy convictions is necessary. However, there is no rule requiring the government to prove that a conspirator knew of all criminal acts by insiders in furtherance of the conspiracy.

No theory requires co-conspirators to have such knowledge. To be convicted as a conspirator, one must be shown to have possessed knowledge of only the general contours of the conspiracy. See, e.g., *Rastelli,* 870 F.2d at 828 ("[T]he government need not prove that a [RICO] conspirator-defendant agreed with every other conspirator, or knew all the other conspirators, or had full knowledge of all the details of the conspiracy."). Accordingly, the district court properly instructed the jury that the government did not have to prove "full knowledge of all the details of the conspiracy" but only that each defendant "was aware of the general nature of the conspiracy and that the conspiracy extended beyond the defendant's individual role." While we have held that too little knowledge may undermine a conspiracy conviction, see, e.g., *Viola,* 35 F.3d at 44-45, there is no requirement that a defendant must have been omniscient.

---

13. When this trial began, it was governed by our ruling in *Viola. Viola* held that to prove a violation of 18 U.S.C. § 1962(d), the government must prove that "the defendant 'embraced the objective of the alleged conspiracy,' and agreed to commit two predicate acts in furtherance thereof." 35 F.3d at 43 (quoting *Neapolitan,* 791 F.2d at 495). Accordingly, the indictment thus alleged that each appellant knowingly agreed to join the conspiracy and agreed to commit at least two predicate acts.

During the trial, the Supreme Court ruled in *Salinas* that § 1962(d) does not require proof that each co-conspirator agreed to commit two predicate acts. See 118 S.Ct. at 478. Nevertheless, the district court instructed the jury on the pre-*Salinas* standard, thus heightening

the government's burden beyond what the statute required. The government argues that in addressing appellants' various challenges to their conspiracy conviction, we should follow *Salinas.* We generally agree. We note that doing so does not raise any due process concerns. Because circuits were divided on the proper interpretation of § 1962(d), the Supreme Court's decision in *Salinas* was sufficiently foreseeable to defeat any due process challenge to its retroactive application. See United States v. Rodgers, 466 U.S. 475, 484, 104 S.Ct. 1942, 80 L.Ed. 2d 492 (1984)("[A]ny argument * * * against retroactive application * * * of our present decision * * * would be unavailing since the existence of conflicting cases from other Courts of Appeals made review of that issue by this Court * * * reasonably foreseeable."); United States v. Seregos, 655 F.2d 33, 36 (2d Cir. 1981).

However, we also note that because this case was tried as though *Viola* were still the law, the jury's consideration of whether appellants were guilty of conspiring to commit two predicate acts may have been inseparable from its determination that they were guilty of RICO conspiracy. * * *

The evidence easily suffices to support the jury's finding that the appellants were aware of the general nature of the conspiracy. Hartman, Lysaght, and Kramer each knew that the kickback schemes extended beyond themselves individually and involved at least each other, Reale, Zichettello, Montoro, and A & G.

* * *

We therefore affirm.

Notes

RICO offers prosecutors a number of discrete advantages. If convicted, a defendant may face enhanced penalties, as well as forfeiture "of any interest the person has acquired or maintained in violation of section 1962." 18 U.S.C. § 1963 (a)(3). Because of the seriousness of a RICO conviction, a RICO charge may increase the government's chances of obtaining a plea bargain.

Although the government recently has been more aggressive in its use of fraud statutes to prosecute tax offenses, it has announced that it will not use the RICO or other fraud provisions to prosecute routine tax offenses. However, it is likely to use such provisions in cases in which there is a large fraud loss, a substantial pattern of conduct or a where the government obtains a significant benefit in bringing charges under these provisions instead of under the Title 26 provisions.

UNITED STATES v. BUSHER
United States Court of Appeals, Ninth Circuit, 1987.
817 F.2d 1409.

KOZINSKI, CIRCUIT JUDGE.

We review the conviction and order of forfeiture entered against appellant, James E. Busher, for violating the Racketeer Influenced and Corrupt Organizations Act, 18 U.S.C. §§ 1961 et seq. (1982) (RICO).

Facts

Busher owns 92 percent of ATL, Inc., a Hawaii corporation engaged in the construction business. ATL's principal client was the U.S. Department of Defense. Busher used a Nevada corporation, J.W. Contracting Co., as a fictitious subcontractor, receiving purported subcontracting payments from ATL. This and similar practices got Busher into trouble. In January 1984, Busher was advised that he was under investigation for submitting false claims to the government, conspiracy to defraud the government and mail fraud, all in connection with ATL's contracts with the Department of Defense. In February and March, Busher testified on these matters before the grand jury, which later expanded its investigation to include income tax evasion and submission of false tax returns.

Busher was indicted in September 1984 and, after a jury trial, was convicted of violating RICO; submitting false statements to the government, 18 U.S.C. § 1001 (1982); presenting false claims to the government, 18 U.S.C. § 287 (1982); mail fraud, 18 U.S.C. § 1341 (1982); tax evasion; 26 U.S.C. § 7201 (1982), and submitting false income tax returns, 26 U.S.C. § 7206(1)(1982). As a result of his RICO conviction, Busher forfeited to the United States his entire interest in ATL, J.W. Contracting and certain Nevada real estate purchased through J.W. Contracting. In addition, Busher was sentenced to four years imprisonment on the RICO counts, to run concurrently with two years on the tax charges and two years on the false statements, false claims and mail fraud charges.

Issues

Busher levels [eds: several] challenges against his conviction and forfeiture. * * * Second, he contends that RICO may not be used to convert simple Internal Revenue Code violations into racketeering charges. Finally, he argues that forfeiture of his entire interest in ATL, J.W. Contracting and the Nevada real estate is so disproportionate to the criminal conduct for which he was convicted as to violate the eighth amendment.

Discussion
* * *
2.   Propriety of RICO Charges

Busher argues that RICO charges based on the mailing of two fraudulent federal income tax returns were improper because Congress deliberately omitted tax fraud from the list of predicate acts that may give rise to RICO violations. 18 U.S.C. § 1961 (1982). However, "any act which is indictable under" 18 U.S.C. § 1341 may serve as a predicate act for purposes of RICO. 18 U.S.C. § 1961 (1982). We have previously held that mailing fraudulent tax returns is indictable as mail fraud under § 1341. United States v. Miller, 545 F.2d 1204, 1216 n. 17 (9th Cir. 1976); see United States v. Condo, 741 F.2d 238, 239 (9th Cir. 1984). It follows that such violations can serve as predicate acts of racketeering under RICO.

3. Forfeiture

The jury found that Busher's interests in ATL, J.W. Contracting and the Nevada real estate were subject to forfeiture. Busher does not challenge the jury's finding that these interests were forfeitable under RICO. 18 U.S.C. § 1963 (1982). Rather, he contends that forfeiture of his entire interest in these properties is so grossly disproportionate to the crimes for which he was convicted that it violates the eighth amendment's prohibition against "excessive fines * * * [and] cruel and unusual punishments." U.S. Const., amend. VIII.

In United States v. Marubeni America Corp., 611 F.2d 763, 769 n. 12 (9th Cir. 1980) we noted that § 1963 could "be read to produce penalties shockingly disproportionate to the offense" committed.[14] In *Marubeni,* we left to another day consideration of the statutory and constitutional issues raised by a potentially disproportionate forfeiture under RICO. Id. That day is here.[15]

---

14. The holding of *Marubeni*--that criminal forfeiture under RICO was limited to racketeering income invested "in an enterprise"--was rejected in Russello v. United States, 464 U.S. 16, 22, 29, 104 S.Ct. 296, 303, 78 L.Ed. 2d 17 (1983). The Supreme Court's decision did not, however, bear on our observation that § 1963 could produce disproportionate penalties.

15. Courts have traditionally exercised an important role in preventing unduly harsh applications of forfeiture statutes. Judicial construction of statutes providing for forfeiture of land used to operate illegal stills is a notable example. One such statute requires forfeiture of "all the right, title, and interest of [a] person [operating an illegal still] in the lot or tract of land on which the distillery is situated." 26 U.S.C. § 5615(3)(C)(1982). In interpreting this and predecessor still forfeiture statutes, the courts have consistently avoided excessively and fortuitously harsh results by limiting forfeiture to land and structures actually used for the distillery or in connection with the use of the distillery. In United States v. Certain Piece of Land, 25 Fed. Cas. 366 (D.Cal. 1870), the court refused to order forfeiture of the entire tract of land stating:

> The operation of such a law would not only be harsh but unequal--for it would make the amount of the forfeiture depend, not on the value of the distillery establishment and the presumed magnitude of its operations, but upon the accidental circumstance that the illicit distiller happened to own a large tract, on the corner of which a still, perhaps of insignificant proportions, was erected.

Id. at 366; see United States v. Elliott Hall Farm, 42 F.Supp. 235, 239 (D.N.J. 1941).

A. Section 1963

Section 1963 is purposely broad.[16] At the time Busher committed the acts for which he was convicted, § 1963(a) provided that a person convicted under § 1962--the substantive provision of RICO--"shall forfeit to the United States (1) any interest he has acquired or maintained in violation of § 1962, and (2) any interest in * * * any enterprise which he has established, operated, controlled, conducted, or participated in the conduct of, in violation of § 1962." 18 U.S.C. § 1963(a)(1982).[17] Section 1963 was designed to totally separate a racketeer from the enterprise he operates. Thus, forfeiture is not limited to those assets of a RICO enterprise that are tainted by use in connection with racketeering activity, but rather extends to the convicted person's entire interest in the enterprise.

Moreover, the substantive provisions of RICO, to which section 1963 is keyed, cover an extraordinarily broad range of activities. Forfeiture under RICO can thus result from very serious, as well as from more trivial, violations of the law.[18] At one end of the spectrum is the paradigmatic racketeering enterprise: an organization deriving almost all its income from serious criminal conduct. At the other end of the

---

16. The purpose of RICO was "to provide new weapons of unprecedented scope for an assault upon organized crime and its economic roots." *Russello,* 464 U.S. at 26, 104 S.Ct. at 302 (1983); see also id. at 27 (citing S.Rep. No. 617, 91st Cong., 1st Sess. 76 (1969); 116 Cong. Rec. 819 (1969) (remarks of Senator Scott); id. at 591-92 (Section 1963 is the first modern statute to impose forfeiture as a criminal sanction directly upon an individual defendant rather than through a separate in rem proceeding against property involved in criminal conduct. (remarks of Senator McClellan)).

17. Section 1963(a) was amended on October 12, 1984 as part of the Comprehensive Crime Control Act of 1984, Publ. L. No. 98-473, tit.II, § 302, 1984 U.S. Code Cong. & Admin. News (98 Stat.) 2040. The purpose of this amendment was to clarify that the term "any interest" used in section 1963 extended to proceeds, income, or profits derived from a pattern of racketeering activity. H.R.Rep. No. 1030, 98th Cong., 2d Sess., 194-95, 199-200, reprinted in 1984 U.S. Code Cong. & Admin. News 3182, 3377-78, 3382-83. The amendment reaffirmed the Supreme Court's earlier holding that the prior version of section 1963 extended to profits and proceeds of racketeering activity. *Russello,* 464 U.S. at 22. In *Russello,* the Court rejected the position of this circuit that forfeiture under section 1963(a)(1) was limited to interests in a RICO enterprise. See United States v. Marubeni America Corp., 611 F.2d 763, 766-67 (9th Cir. 1980). Therefore, we will assume that, both at the time of Busher's illegal conduct and at the time of his conviction, forfeiture under section 1963 extended to profits and proceeds derived from a pattern of racketeering activity.

18. Section 1962, containing RICO's substantive prohibitions, is violated by the investment in, acquisition or maintenance of, or the conducting of or participating in, an enterprise through a pattern of racketeering activity. 18 U.S.C. § 1962(a)-(c)(1982). Violation of section 1962 can result from the commission of two predicate acts of racketeering within a ten year period. These predicate acts of racketeering include not only such traditionally heinous acts of organized crime such as murder, kidnaping, arson, bribery and extortion, but also simple mail or wire fraud. 18 U.S.C. § 1961(1)(1982).

spectrum is conduct by an otherwise legitimate business, consisting of as few as two isolated predicate acts of relatively minor consequence, but which nevertheless amount to a RICO violation. Forfeiture of the enterprise where the conduct in question falls close to this end of the spectrum may well take more than the constitution allows.[19]

B. The Eighth Amendment

Forfeiture under section 1963(a) is clearly "punishment" as that term is used in the eighth amendment. Moreover, the Supreme Court has held that the eighth amendment "prohibits not only barbaric punishments, but also sentences that are disproportionate to the crime committed." Solem v. Helm, 463 U.S. 277, 284, 103 S.Ct. 3001, 3006, 77 L.Ed. 2d 637 (1983). *Solem* noted that the prohibition against disproportionate punishment is firmly rooted in both our common law and constitutional history: "When the Framers of the Eighth Amendment adopted the language of the English Bill of Rights, they also adopted the English principle of proportionality." Id. at 285-86, 103 S.Ct. at 3007. The Supreme Court has consistently applied this principle "for almost a century." Id. at 286, 103 S.Ct. 3008.[20]

Busher claims that the forfeiture of his entire interests in ATL, J.W. Contracting and the Nevada real estate is grossly disproportionate to the offenses for which he was convicted. He contends that, by and large, the scope of ATL's business activity was legitimate. Busher points out that

---

19. The problem of forfeiture of an entire enterprise is essentially limited to the situation where the convicted defendant owns substantially all of the stock of a corporation, or where the enterprise is a sole proprietorship. This is so because under section 1963 only the *defendant's interest* in the enterprise is forfeitable, not the enterprise itself. At the same time, it is the law of this circuit that the enterprise may not also be the defendant in an action brought under section 1962(c)--*i.e.,* where the claim is that the defendant has conducted the affairs of the enterprise through a pattern of racketeering activity. Schreiber Distributing Co. v. Serv-Well Furniture Co., 806 F.2d 1393, 1398 (9th Cir. 1986). Thus, only where the culpable person owns the entire enterprise will it be subject to complete forfeiture for violation of RICO.

20. The Court first endorsed the principle of proportionality as a constitutional limitation on punishment in Weems v. United States, 217 U.S. 349, 30 S.Ct. 544, 54 L.Ed. 793 (1910). In *Weems,* the defendant had been sentenced to 15 years at hard labor with permanent civil disabilities for falsifying a public document. The Court held that the punishment was "cruel in its excess of imprisonment," id. at 377, 30 S.Ct. at 553, as well as in its nature and restrictions. More than fifty years later, in Robinson v. California, 370 U.S. 660, 82 S.Ct. 1417, 8 L.Ed. 2d 758 (1962), the Court reaffirmed the principle of proportionality and added the requirement that the excessiveness of a punishment be determined not in the abstract, but in light of the specific nature of the crime for which the defendant was convicted. *Robinson* invalidated a ninety-day sentence for the crime of being addicted to narcotics. The Court observed that although "imprisonment for ninety days is not, in the abstract, a punishment which is either cruel or unusual * * * the question cannot be considered in the abstract. Even one day in prison would be a cruel and unusual punishment for the 'crime' of having a common cold." Id. at 667, 82 S.Ct. at 1421.

ATL performed 14 defense contracts totaling approximately $27 million. Only 3 of those contracts were the subject of the indictment brought against defendants, and appellant claims the total dollar amount of the fraudulent conduct for which he was convicted–including tax evasion–amounted to only $335,000. Thus, he argues, forfeiture of his entire 92 percent interest in ATL–a corporation worth approximately $3 million–plus all of J.W. Contracting and the Nevada real estate, is so excessive as to violate the eighth amendment.

Our review of the relevant Supreme Court cases, particularly *Solem,* convinces us that Busher has raised legitimate concerns as to the constitutionality of the forfeiture ordered in this case. RICO's forfeiture provision affords the trial court no discretion. Once the jury determines that property was acquired, maintained or operated in violation of § 1962, it must find forfeitable the defendant's entire interest in that property. 18 U.S.C. § 1963(a). Moreover, the statute gives the district judge no authority to exclude from the forfeiture order any of the property the jury finds is covered by the liberal language of § 1963(a). But RICO's breadth and inflexibility counsels caution, for "no penalty is per se constitutional." *Solem,* 463 U.S. at 290, 103 S.Ct. at 3009-10. Since RICO's forfeiture provision is quite literally without limitation, it may well exceed constitutional bounds in any particular case.[21]

We believe the Fourth Circuit misapplied the eighth amendment's requirement of proportionality. That the statute ties the amount forfeited to a defendant's stake in an enterprise that violated the law merely states the issue. As we have previously noted, RICO's impressive breadth, and the interplay of its substantive and punitive provisions, may result in forfeitures of vast amounts of property as a result of relatively minor offenses. In any one case the amount forfeited may have no relationship whatsoever to the severity of the wrong committed.

Even though the statute provides no discretion, the district court must avoid unconstitutional results by fashioning forfeiture orders that stay within constitutional bounds. We therefore hold that where, as here, plaintiff makes a prima facie showing that the forfeiture may be excessive, the district court must make a determination, based upon appropriate findings, that the interest ordered forfeited is not so grossly disproportionate to the offense committed as to violate the eighth amendment.

---

21. In United States v. Grande, 620 F.2d 1026 (4th Cir. 1980), the Fourth Circuit held that forfeiture under RICO is "not cruel and unusual in the constitutional sense." Id. at 1039. The court appears to have concluded that forfeiture under § 1963 is per se proportional because "the magnitude of [RICO] forfeiture is directly keyed to the magnitude of defendant's interest in the enterprise conducted in violation of law." Id.

The district court in this case did not take these constitutional considerations into account in fashioning its forfeiture order, and we therefore remand for it to do so. Because the eighth amendment, as interpreted in *Solem,* embodies fluid concepts that vary in application with the circumstances of each case, there is relatively little guidance we can give the district court in making its determination. We do, however, offer the following observations.

The district court must, consistent with *Solem,* consider (1) the harshness of the penalty[22] in light of the gravity of the offense; (2) sentences imposed for other offenses in the federal system; and (3) sentences imposed for the same or similar offenses in other jurisdictions. 463 U.S. at 292, 103 S.Ct. at 3010. In comparing the penalty imposed to the gravity of the offense, the district court may consider the circumstances surrounding the defendant's criminal conduct. More particularly, *Solem* noted that, in considering the gravity of the offense, a court should look both at the harm suffered by the victim and the defendant's culpability. 463 U.S. at 292, 103 S.Ct. at 3010.

In considering the harm caused by defendant's conduct, it is certainly appropriate to take into account its magnitude: the dollar volume of the loss caused, whether physical harm to persons was inflicted, threatened or risked, or whether the crime has severe collateral consequences, e.g., drug addiction. In addition, the court may consider the benefit reaped by the convicted defendant. However, the forfeiture is not rendered unconstitutional because it exceeds the harm to the victims or the benefit to the defendant. After all, RICO's forfeiture provisions are intended to be punitive. The eighth amendment prohibits only those forfeitures that, in light of all the relevant circumstances, are *grossly* disproportionate to the offense committed.

With regard to the defendant's culpability, *Solem* observed that, among other things, the defendant's state of mind and his motive in committing the crime should be considered.[23] 463 U.S. at 293, 103 S.Ct. at 3011. In the context of RICO, the court may consider the degree to which the enterprise operated by the defendant is infected by criminal conduct.   The court should be reluctant to order forfeiture of a

---

22. The penalty to be considered is the total punishment imposed for the offense, which would include not only the forfeiture but any incarceration, fines or probation imposed by the district court.

23. In considering a challenge to the imposition of the death penalty to a murder accomplice, the Court defined the degree of culpability in terms of the defendant's "intentions, expectations, and actions." *Enmund,* 458 U.S. at 800, 102 S.Ct. at 3378. Perhaps the most elegant disproportionality formula was offered by Justice Powell in Rummel v. Estelle, 445 U.S. 263, 100 S.Ct. 1133, 63 L.Ed.2d 382 (1980): "The inquiry focuses on whether a person deserves such punishment, not simply on whether punishment would serve a utilitarian goal." Id. at 288, 100 S.Ct. at 1146 (dissent).

defendant's entire interest in an enterprise that is essentially legitimate where he has committed relatively minor RICO violations not central to the conduct of the business and resulting in relatively little illegal gain in proportion to its size and legitimate income. Conversely, if illegal activity accounts for all or almost all of an enterprise's activity, or an interest in an enterprise was acquired entirely or almost entirely with ill-gotten funds, it would not normally violate the eighth amendment to order forfeiture of all of defendant's interest in that enterprise.[24]

Consideration of these factors, reviewed for abuse of discretion, should ensure that no forfeiture is so disproportionate to the offense committed as to violate the eighth amendment. If, on remand in this case, the court finds to the contrary, it must limit the forfeiture to such portion of the interest as it deems consistent with these principles; or it may condition the forfeiture upon payment of such sum or relinquishment of such other property as seems just under the circumstances;[25] or it may limit or eliminate other punishment it would otherwise impose so as to bring the total sanction within constitutional boundaries.

This is, admittedly, not an easy line to draw; the eighth amendment does not provide a bright line separating punishment that is permissible from that which is not. But a court may not turn its back on a constitutional constraint simply because it is difficult to apply. When all is said and done, the district court may well conclude that its original forfeiture order was proper; we express no view on that score. We hold only that when the defendant raises a legitimate claim that the full force of permissible forfeiture under RICO may be grossly disproportionate to the offense committed, potentially violating the eighth amendment, the district court must discharge its constitutional function by giving the matter careful scrutiny. Here the district court did not. We remand that it may do so.

---

24. The factors listed are not exclusive. For example, one commentator has suggested that "settled principle[s] of Anglo-American justice" prohibit monetary penalties that "threaten the defendant's economic viability." Jeffries, A Comment on the Constitutionality of Punitive Damages, 72 Va. L.Rev. 139, 154 (1986). The district court may consider this and other factors it deems appropriate for purposes of determining proportionality.

25. In *Huber,* the Second Circuit approved an order of conditional forfeiture, giving the convicted defendant the option to redeem his corporations by payment of cash or other property worth $100,000. 603 F.2d at 391.

Conclusion

We affirm defendant's conviction but remand for a determination by the district court whether the forfeiture order was so grossly disproportionate to the offense committed as to violate the eighth amendment and, if so, for such action as the district court deems appropriate to avoid such constitutional infirmity.

Notes

On remand, the court held that the forfeiture of the appellant's entire interest did not violate the Eighth Amendment. United States v. Busher, 872 F.2d 431 (9th Cir. 1989). Conviction of the predicate acts together with the RICO offense does not violate the principal of double jeopardy. Although the Ninth Circuit rejected, with very little discussion, the appellant's argument that RICO specifically excludes tax offenses, the Justice Department (DOJ) has found the argument meritorious. In its 1999 U.S. Attorney's Manual, the DOJ clarified that "tax offenses are not predicates for RICO offenses—a deliberate Congressional decision—and charging a tax offense as a mail fraud charge could be viewed as circumventing Congressional intent unless unique circumstances are present justifying the use of a mail fraud charge." U.S. Atty's Manual § 6-4.210 (1999). However, in the more recent Manual, a more aggressive tone is struck. The cautionary language of the former Manual has been deleted. Instead, the recent Manual provides that "absent unusual circumstances, * * * the Tax Division will not approve mail or wire fraud charges if a case involves only one person's tax liability or when all submissions to the IRS were truthful." It does not describe what circumstances will be considered sufficiently unusual to warrant a RICO prosecution. The Tax Division of the Department of Justice must approve any charges brought under the Internal Revenue law, including mail fraud, wire fraud and bank fraud charges brought either alone or as predicate offenses to a RICO charge. US Attorney's Manual § 6-4.210. If a RICO charge is brought, the U.S. Attorney must also obtain the approval of the Criminal Division's Organized Crime and Racketeering Section. Id.

As *Busher* illustrates, courts have taken the position that a tax violation/mail fraud charge can serve as a predicate offense to a RICO charge. For more recent examples of a tax violation coupled with mail fraud used as a predicate offense in a RICO case, see Minneapolis Community Development Agency v. Buchanan, 268 F.3d 562 (8th 2001) and United States v. Swan, 250 F.3d 495 (7th Cir. 2001). For a general discussion of the background of the RICO provision and its use in tax crimes, see Donald Crump, "Criminals Don't Pay: Using Tax Fraud To Prohibit Organized Crime," 9 Houston Bus. & Tax L.J. 386 (2009).

III.   CURRENCY TRANSACTION OFFENSES

A.   MONEY LAUNDERING –
TITLE 18 U.S.C. §§ 1956 and 1957

Money laundering is the process of cleansing or disguising the sources of income from illegal activities to make them appear legitimate, thus enabling a criminal to avoid prosecution or evade tax liability. Money laundering became a criminal offense in 1986, under the Money Laundering Control Act, enacted during the Reagan Administration's war on drugs and organized crime. More recently, it has been used, and continues to be used, to combat suspected terrorist activity.

There are two general forms of money laundering: (1) changing bulk quantity small bills into larger bills in order to make transportation of the money easier, and (2) concealing the ownership of the proceeds of illicit activity.

There are two statutory provisions under Title 18 that address this offense. Section 1956 criminalizes the act of laundering money, and thus it prohibits financial transactions undertaken with the intent to further the criminal enterprise or conceal the proceeds of the "specified unlawful activity." Section 1957 is a broader provision designed to discourage third parties from engaging in even ordinary commercial transactions with someone suspected of involvement in criminal activity.   This provision makes it a crime to knowingly engage or attempt to engage in a monetary transaction in criminally derived property with a value greater than $10,000, and that is derived from specified unlawful activity. Thus this provision makes it a crime to knowingly accept funds from a money launderer and to make a "deposit, transfer, withdrawal or exchange" of those funds.   Under § 1957, the offender commits an additional felony when he deposits the proceeds of a specified illegal activity in a bank.

1. Commingled Funds

The elements of the offense of money laundering under § 1956 are: (1) knowledge, (2) proceeds derived from a specified unlawful activity, (3) a financial transaction, and (4) intent.   The next case addresses the question of whether the government must trace proceeds to a particular offense or unlawful activity to support a money laundering conviction under § 1956.

UNITED STATES v. BRAXTONBROWN-SMITH

United States Court of Appeals, District of Columbia Circuit, 2002.
278 F.3d 1348.

ROGERS, CIRCUIT JUDGE.

Denise Braxtonbrown-Smith appeals her conviction and sentence on numerous fraud and money laundering charges. Her principal contention is that the government failed to prove, by tracing or otherwise, that any of the funds used in the alleged money laundering transactions represented the proceeds of unlawful activity. In turn, she contends, this failure to trace necessarily tainted other counts of the judgment of conviction. * * * We affirm the judgment of conviction * * *.

I.

Viewing the evidence, as we must, in the light most favorable to the government, the evidence showed that Braxtonbrown-Smith used Medicaid reimbursements paid to her company, Psychological Development Associates ("PDA"), for personal purposes, did not pay taxes on that money, and attempted to obtain loans through the submission of false documents. In early 1994, PDA began a day-treatment program for mentally retarded adults called Better Treatment Centers ("BTC") that enabled it to obtain a provider number for billing Medicaid for services provided to its Medicaid eligible clients. PDA began receiving its first clients in February 1994 for its day-treatment program, who were assigned to the centers by the Mental Retardation and Developmentally Disabled Administration ("MRDDA") of the D.C. Department of Human Services, at an approved rate of $175.44 per client, per day. Prior to this time, PDA had been in desperate financial shape, missing payrolls on occasion throughout 1994 and failing to pay its debts. Its financial condition changed by the end of 1994 by which time Medicaid had reimbursed PDA for over $400,000. The BTC program accounted for nearly all of the income that PDA was receiving and by 1995, Braxtonbrown-Smith and Kenneth A. Strachan, the PDA controller, were able to skim funds from PDA for personal purposes. For example, numerous checks were drawn on the PDA operating account at NationsBank, ranging from $6000 to $8000, for Braxtonbrown-Smith's personal benefit.

In May 1995, PDA obtained a second Medicaid provider number for services it was to provide through a "free-standing" mental health clinic.

Braxtonbrown- Smith's efforts over the next two years to set up the clinic in accord with Medicaid rules for staffing never proved fruitful. Notwithstanding the fact that PDA had failed to set up and operate the clinic, Braxtonbrown-Smith, through PDA's controller Kenneth Strachan, used the provider number to bill Medicaid for services that PDA never actually provided. This billing scheme continued for several years, surviving Strachan's dismissal in October 1996 and continuing under Braxtonbrown-Smith's direction until 1998.

By early 1996, Braxtonbrown-Smith's personal financial needs were becoming more pronounced, as she had contracted to purchase a $400,000 house and needed to show cash in her personal account to support a down payment. She also needed funds for her wedding, honeymoon, improvements on the new house, and to support an expensive lifestyle. She would later generate and submit false income tax statements for this time period to Provident Mortgage Corporation in order to obtain a mortgage, and to Mellon Bank in order to obtain a line of credit. By the Spring of 1996, the false billings escalated. For example, in April 1996 in response to Braxtonbrown-Smith's growing personal financial needs, Strachan began submitting false claims to Medicaid representing that BTC clients were receiving psychotherapy from a psychiatrist every day, despite the fact that the clinic was not yet operational and many of BTC's clients were non-communicative and could not speak. Although alerted to billing irregularities by Arnett Smith, an employee of PDA and a former MRDDA employee, Braxtonbrown-Smith took no steps to stop the submission of false bills to Medicaid.

Braxtonbrown-Smith and Strachan together diverted over $400,000 of funds from PDA accounts for their personal use. All told, PDA's false claims totaled $1,693,708, representing approximately 30% of PDA's total Medicaid billings. Additionally, Braxtonbrown-Smith drew down her line of credit with Mellon Bank to the point that when PDA went out of business in the summer of 1998, she owed Mellon approximately $440,000.

In 1997 Braxtonbrown-Smith was indicted for conspiracy, 18 U.S.C. § 371 (Count 1); mail fraud, 18 U.S.C. § 1341 (Counts 2 & 3); tax evasion, 26 U.S.C. § 7201 (Counts 4-6); money laundering, 18 U.S.C. §§ 1956(a)(1)(A)(ii) & 1956(a)(1)(B)(i) (Counts 7-12); bank fraud, 18 U.S.C. § 1344 (Counts 13 & 14); and wire fraud, 18 U.S.C. § 1343 (Count 15). At trial, Braxtonbrown-Smith's evidence was confined to six character witnesses who testified regarding her reputation for truthfulness and honesty in the community. The jury convicted her on all counts except one count of mail fraud. * * *

II.

On appeal, Braxtonbrown-Smith contends that instead of proving that any of the funds used in the alleged money laundering transactions represented the proceeds of unlawful activity, the government relied on a judicially-created presumption that any withdrawal of funds from a commingled account involves unlawful proceeds, even when the amount of legitimately earned money in the account exceeds the amount withdrawn. Because the presumption relieved the government of its burden of proof under the plain language of 18 U.S.C. § 1956(a)(1)(A), she contends that the money laundering counts must be dismissed for insufficient evidence. Failing that, she contends the jury was erroneously instructed on the unconstitutional commingling presumption, and those counts must be remanded for a new trial. Likewise, she contends that she must be granted a new trial on the conspiracy count because the jury was instructed on three alternative conspiracy objects, including money laundering, and it is impossible to determine from the general conspiracy verdict that it is not tainted by the allegedly improper money laundering instruction. * * *

A.

Section 1956 provides, in relevant part,

(a)(1) Whoever, knowing that the property involved in a financial transaction represents the proceeds of some form of unlawful activity, conducts or attempts to conduct such a financial transaction which in fact involves the proceeds of specified unlawful activity–

(A)(i) with the intent to promote the carrying on of specified unlawful activity; or (ii) with intent to engage in conduct constituting a violation of section 7201 or 7206 of the Internal Revenue Code of 1986; * * * shall be [subject to fine and imprisonment].

18 U.S.C. § 1956(a)(1) (2000).

Braxtonbrown-Smith focuses on the phrase "property involved" and the word "represents" in contending that the government failed to meet its burden to prove that each of her withdrawals from the PDA account at NationsBank for her personal use included funds that were diverted from Medicaid reimbursements to PDA. In other words, Braxtonbrown-Smith contends that the plain language of § 1956(a)(1) requires the government to demonstrate affirmatively that the particular illegitimate dollars were laundered and urges adoption of a presumption, based on the rule of lenity, that withdrawals from a commingled account are withdrawals of any "clean" money in the account. Although acknowledging "substantial" circuit precedent contrary to a complete tracing requirement, she maintains that the statutory language does not permit the government to rely on evidence that she personally spent money she withdrew from an account in which illegal and legitimate funds were commingled. This is because millions of dollars from legitimate Medicaid billing were in the PDA account, and hence there was a sufficient amount of legal funds in the account to cover the alleged unlawful transactions under § 1956. As an issue of statutory construction, our review is de novo.

In construing a statute, the court begins with the plain language of the statute. Where the language is clear, that is the end of judicial inquiry "in all but the most extraordinary circumstances." Id. Where the language is subject to more than one interpretation and the meaning of Congress is not apparent from the language itself, the court may be forced to look to the general purpose of Congress in enacting the statute and to its legislative history for helpful clues. In addressing Braxtonbrown-Smith's interpretation of §1956(a)(1), it is helpful to keep in mind the Supreme Court's observation in United States v. American Trucking Ass'ns, Inc., 310 U.S. 534, 60 S.Ct. 1059, 84 L.Ed. 1345 (1940), that "even when the plain meaning did not produce absurd results but merely an unreasonable one 'plainly at variance with the policy of the legislation as a whole' this Court has followed that purpose, rather than the literal words." Id. at 543, 60 S.Ct. at 1064 (quoting Ozawa v. United States, 260 U.S. 178, 194, 43 S.Ct. 65, 67-68, 67 L.Ed. 199 (1922)). Thus, the court must avoid an interpretation that undermines congressional purpose considered as a whole when alternative interpretations consistent with the legislative purpose are available.

Contrary to Braxtonbrown-Smith's contention, a no-tracing rule is consistent with the plain language of the statute. The broad language of the statute suffices to reach transactions that "involve[ ]" illegal proceeds. As the Seventh Circuit observed, "money need not be derived from crime to be 'involved' in it; perhaps a particular sum is used as the bankroll facilitating the fraud." United States v. $448,342.85, 969 F.2d 474, 476 (7th Cir.1992). Although "involve" might also be read to mean that the individual transaction must include illegal proceeds in some amount, no circuit to consider this issue has held that complete tracing of the sort that Braxtonbrown-Smith urges is required under §1956(a)(1)(A).[1] This is a necessary result of the fungibility of money, a

---

1. The circuits have taken various approaches with regard to the amount of tracing that is required. First, some courts have held that any transaction out of a commingled account constitutes laundering. See, e.g. United States v. Ward, 197 F.3d 1076, 1083 (11th Cir.1999). Second, some courts have suggested that defendants will be responsible only for those transactions from a

factor of which Congress was undoubtedly aware when it enacted §
1956(a)(1) as part of the Money Laundering Control Act, the purpose of
which was to "punish transactions that are undertaken with the proceeds
of crimes or that are designed to launder the proceeds of crime." H.R.
Rep. No. 99-855, pt. 1, at 7 (1986); United States v. Sperry Corp., 493
U.S. 52, 62 n. 9, 110 S.Ct. 387, 395, 107 L.Ed.2d 290 (1989). The tracing
of dollars emanating from a bank account (as distinct from the tracing of
actual bills used in a particular cash transaction) to specific dollars
deposited into a bank account is no less than "a mathematical
impossibility" where, as in the instant case, "the amount of the transfer
was less than the amount of untainted funds in the account." *Voigt*, 89
F.3d [1050] at 1081 [3RD Cir. 1996]. To create a presumption, based on
the rule of lenity, as Braxtonbrown- Smith urges that withdrawals from
a commingled account are withdrawals of any "clean" money therein
would come close to rendering money laundering invulnerable; a person
who deposits $10,000 of dirty money in a $100,000 account could later
withdraw $10,000 repeatedly without penalty so long as there were
sufficient clean money in the account to cover the withdrawals. Were
such a presumption required under § 1956(a)(1), Congress' purpose
would be undermined because such a requirement would allow
"participants in unlawful activities [to] prevent their own convictions
under the money laundering statute simply by commingling funds
derived from both 'specified unlawful activities' and other activities."
Jackson, 935 F.2d [832] at 840 [7th Cir. 1996]. This would be a
nonsensical outcome in light of the fact that "[i]t is precisely the
commingling of tainted funds with legitimate money that facilitates the
laundering and enables it to continue." *Tencer*, 107 F.3d [1120] at 1135
[5th Cir. 1997].

In contending that the plain language of § 1956(a)(1) requires the
government to show complete tracing, Braxtonbrown-Smith downplays
these realities about the nature of money as a fungible commodity and
the unreasonable, if not absurd, results her approach would produce.
Her reliance on United States v. Wynn, 61 F.3d 921 (D.C.Cir. 1995), is
misplaced, for the holding in that case did not rely on a circumstantial
inference that the funds at issue represented illegal proceeds as opposed
to legitimate income. In *Wynn*, the defendant maintained there was
insufficient evidence that the cash used to purchase cashiers' checks used
to purchase a car constituted　illegal proceeds because the source

---

commingled account that do not exceed the total amount of illegitimate funds. See, e.g. United
States v. Wilkinson, 137 F.3d 214, 222 (4th Cir.1998). Finally, other courts have decided to treat
spending from commingled accounts as involving "proportional fractions of clean and dirty money."
United States v. Loe, 248 F.3d 449, 467 n. 81 (5th Cir.2001).

laundering the funds had won $150,000 in the Maryland lottery and could have used those funds to make the purchase. *Wynn*, 61 F.3d at 926. The court did not resolve the issue of whether tracing was required to be proven by the government, although it did characterize the argument as "an uncertain legal proposition." Id. Instead, and fatal to Braxtonbrown-Smith's position, notwithstanding evidence of lottery proceeds, the court held that the government presented sufficient evidence from which a reasonable juror could find that the money used to purchase the cashiers' checks totaling nearly $9000 flowed directly from the major narcotics trafficking operation of the source of the funds. Braxtonbrown-Smith's reliance on United States v. Rutgard, 116 F.3d 1270 (9th Cir. 1997), is likewise misplaced; *Rutgard* involved a prosecution under §1957, which the Ninth Circuit explicitly distinguished from § 1956, and its holding that tracing is required under § 1957 is a minority view.

The risk of unduly harsh consequences that Braxtonbrown-Smith maintains could occur in the absence of a tracing requirement is mitigated by the statute. Under § 1956(a)(1)(A), the government must prove that the defendant, first, knew that the transaction "represents the proceeds" of unlawful activity, and, second, intended either to promote the "carrying on of a specified unlawful activity" or "to conceal or disguise the nature, the location, the source, the ownership, or the control of the proceeds of specified unlawful activity." After multiple transactions, then, the government will have a difficult burden to prove the second intent for recent transactions based on proof of a single unlawful dollar deposited long ago.

Furthermore, there is no such harsh result in the instant case. Braxtonbrown-Smith states in her brief that the government's evidence "was simply that the challenged transactions, totaling approximately $500,000, were conducted using funds from the PDA operating account at NationsBank and that of the millions of dollars that went into that account, less than 30%--approximately $1.6 million--was from illegal Medicaid billings." The amount of money that the government's evidence showed was involved in the money laundering scheme is hardly minuscule. In view of the government's evidence, a reasonable juror could conclude that the bilking engaged in by Braxtonbrown-Smith was facilitated by her multitude of false Medicaid claims, which provided an influx of surplus funds in the PDA account and that these funds were "involved" in the charged transactions. See United States v. Harrison, 204 F.3d 236, 239 (D.C.Cir.2000). That is all the statute requires.

Accordingly, we need not decide among the various possible tracing rules, see supra n. 1, because it suffices for this appeal to join our sister circuits in declining to "read Congress's use of the word 'involve' as imposing the requirement that the government trace the origin of all funds deposited into a bank account to determine exactly which funds were used for what transaction." *Jackson*, 935 F.2d at 840. Allowing the mere commingling of legitimate funds to defeat a money laundering conviction so easily would wholly undermine Congress's intent and effectively nullify the offense.

* * *

Notes and Questions

Under § 1957, there is a conflict among the circuits as to whether tracing is required. Some courts have held that under § 1957, a tracing requirement is implied. See United States v. Rutgard, 116 F.3d 1270 (9th Cir. 1997) (holding that since § 1957 criminalizes the "deposit, transfer, withdrawal, or exchange" of funds, if tainted money is deposited in an account with clean money and an amount equal to or less than the amount of clean money is withdrawn, the presumption is that the withdrawn amount represents a withdrawal of clean money). Other circuits have held that since money is fungible, the actual dollars derived from the illegal activity cannot be traced once they are deposited into an account with untainted dollars. See United States v. Davis, 226 F.3d 346 (5th Cir. 2000); accord U.S. v. Haddad, 462 F.3d 783 (7th Cir. 2006). Thus, all funds from a commingled account are presumed tainted and no further tracing is required. See United States v. Sokolow, 91 F.3d 396 (3rd Cir. 1996); United States v. Moore, 27 F.3d 969 (4th Cir. 1994).

In 1977, the DOJ issued guidelines on the use of the money laundering statutes. Under the guidelines, prior authorization is required from both the Tax Division and the Criminal Division's Asset Forfeiture and Money Laundering Section before an indictment can be sought under the money laundering statutes for tax related offenses.

1. What is the "rule of lenity" to which the defense refers in *Braxtonbrown-Smith*?

2. What, if anything, must the government establish with respect to the proceeds of the unlawful activity element of the offense in order to support a money laundering conviction?

3. How, if at all, does § 1956 differ from § 1957?

2. Criminal Forfeiture

The advantage to the government of a money laundering charge is two-fold. First, the statute applies very broadly to cover many tax offenses. Second, the penalties under the money laundering provisions are diverse and more severe than under Title 26. In addition to prison terms and both civil and criminal fines, there is also the possibility of civil and criminal forfeiture under Title 18, §§ 981 and 982. Because the penalties are so severe, the government may use the threat of a money laundering charge to force a plea bargain. See Charles W. Blau, Money Laundering and Currency Violations: The Prosecutor's "Financial Crime" of Choice, ABA Center for Continuing Legal Education, Criminal Justice Section (1997).

a. Burden of Proof and Tracing of Forfeitable Funds

UNITED STATES v. VOIGHT
United States Court of Appeals, Third Circuit, 1996.
89 F.3d 1050, *cert. denied* 519 U.S. 1047.

COWEN, CIRCUIT JUDGE.

John Voigt appeals from a judgment of conviction and sentence entered by the District Court for the District of New Jersey. The conviction arises from Voigt's role as the mastermind of a pernicious "advance fee" scheme whereby Voigt, operating under the auspices of the Euro-American Money Fund Trust, would obtain substantial fees in advance from, respectively, unsuspecting loan applicants and potential investors for various loans and investments that never materialized. Over a three-year period the Trust took in a total of 18.5 million dollars.

We also confront several questions of first impression in this Circuit pertaining to the money laundering statute, 18 U.S.C. § 1956(a)(1), and its forfeiture counterpart. Id. § 982. We must decide whether those statutes require formal "tracing" where laundered funds have been commingled in a bank account with untainted funds. We also must determine what is the proper burden of persuasion for forfeiture proceedings under 18 U.S.C. § 982, a question we have addressed previously in two other contexts. * * *

* * *

VI.

THE FORFEITURE ORDER

In connection with the four money laundering counts charged in the superseding indictment, the government brought separate criminal forfeiture allegations under 18 U.S.C. § 982 seeking forfeiture of certain vehicles and pieces of jewelry either as "involved in" or "traceable to"

Voigt's money laundering activity, id. § 982(a)(1),[16] or as substitute assets under 21 U.S.C.§ 853(p)(5),[17] the CCE [ed: the Continuing Criminal Enterprise] criminal forfeiture provision, which is incorporated in 18 U.S.C. § 982(b)(1).[18] At a nonjury proceeding conducted prior to sentencing, the district court determined that Voigt's money laundering convictions rendered him liable to the government for $1,661,960 in criminal forfeiture. In satisfaction of that amount, the court ordered forfeiture of, *inter alia*, two pieces of jewelry, finding "by a preponderance of the evidence" that they were "items of personal property * * * traceable to the money involved in the [money-laundering] violations." The jewelry had been purchased with funds from an account in which money laundering proceeds had been commingled with other funds--numerous deposits and withdrawals having intervened between the deposit of the laundered funds and the purchase of the jewelry.

Voigt raises two assignments of error. First, he contends that the district court applied the wrong burden of persuasion. He maintains that our decision in United States v. Pelullo, 14 F.3d 881 (3d Cir.1994), requires the government to prove its forfeiture allegations beyond a reasonable doubt. Second, Voigt asserts that the government failed to prove that the jewelry it sought was "traceable to" the proceeds of his money laundering activity, since it had been purchased with commingled funds from an account subject to numerous intervening deposits and withdrawals after the original deposit of the laundered funds.

* * *

---

16. The court, in imposing sentence on a person convicted of an offense in violation of section * * * 1956 * * * of this title, shall order that the person forfeit to the United States any property, real or personal, involved in such offense, or any property traceable to such property* * *. 18 U.S.C.§ 982(a)(1).

17. Forfeiture of Substitute Property

(p) If any of the property described in subsection (a) of this section, as a result of any act or omission of the defendant--

· * * *

    (5) has been commingled with other property which cannot be divided without difficulty; the court shall order the forfeiture of any other property of the defendant up to the value of any property described in paragraph[ ] * * * (5).

21 U.S.C.§ 853(p)(5).

18. (b)(1) Property subject to forfeiture under this section, any seizure and disposition thereof, and any administrative or judicial proceeding in relation thereto, shall be governed-- (A) in the case of a forfeiture under subsection (a)(1) of this section, by subsections (c) and (e) through (p) of the Comprehensive Drug Abuse Prevention and Control Act of 1970 (21 U.S.C. § 853)[.]

18 U.S.C. § 982(b)(1).

A.

The forfeiture provision upon which the court's order was based, 18 U.S.C. § 982, provides that a district court sentencing a person convicted of, *inter alia*, money laundering in violation of 18 U.S.C. § 1956, "shall order that the person forfeit to the United States any property, real or personal, involved in such offense, or any property traceable to such property." 18 U.S.C. § 982(a)(1). Voigt first contends that the government's burden of persuasion for criminal forfeiture under 18 U.S.C. § 982(a)(1) is proof beyond a reasonable doubt. We have not yet had occasion to address the burden-of-proof issue with respect to § 982(a)(1), and to date only one other court of appeals has considered it, concluding that preponderance-of-the-evidence standard applies. United States v. Myers, 21 F.3d 826, 829 (8th Cir.1994). We have, however, addressed this issue twice previously in the context of other criminal forfeiture provisions. *Pelullo*, 14 F.3d at 881 (RICO, reasonable doubt); United States v. Sandini, 816 F.2d 869 (3d Cir.1987) (CCE; preponderance). A description of the *Sandini, Pelullo* and *Myers* decisions is in order.

1.

In *Sandini*, 816 F.2d at 869, we addressed the appropriate burden of persuasion under 21 U.S.C. § 853, the CCE criminal forfeiture provision. The defendant there argued that § 853(d)'s inclusion of a rebuttable presumption of forfeitability if the government could demonstrate two factors by a preponderance of the evidence was unconstitutional to the extent it failed to require proof beyond a reasonable doubt. After discussing the history of and distinction between civil in rem and criminal in personam forfeiture, we concluded that criminal forfeiture under CCE constitutes punishment for a crime, and not a separate element of the offense * * *. Because other federal statutes providing for enhanced penalties have established the government's burden of proof as a preponderance of the evidence, we concluded that § 853(d) withstands constitutional scrutiny as long as the forfeiture proceeding follows a conviction by proof beyond a reasonable doubt.

Seven years later we confronted the same question in the context of 18 U.S.C. § 1963, the RICO statute's criminal forfeiture provision. *Pelullo*, 14 F.3d at 881. We held that the beyond-a-reasonable-doubt standard governs such forfeitures. Our conclusion was premised mainly on Congress' simultaneous amendments to the RICO and CCE forfeiture statutes in 1984, and its decision not to add a rebuttable presumption provision to § 1963(a) when it added such a provision to the CCE statute. See 21 U.S.C. § 853(d) (discussed in *Sandini*, 816 F.2d at 874-75). We concluded that the omission was deliberate and, hence, dispositive: "This indicates that Congress intended the higher beyond a reasonable doubt standard to control in a § 1963(a) proceeding. If Congress wanted a preponderance standard for § 1963(a), it would have so stated as it specifically did for CCE." *Pelullo*, 14 F.3d at 905. See id. at 903 ("Most important, the CCE rebuttable presumption * * * does not exist in the RICO forfeiture provisions.") We distinguished our decision in *Sandini* on the basis that it pertained only to CCE and could not bind a future panel of this court considering a different forfeiture provision. See id.

In *Myers*, 21 F.3d at 826, the Court of Appeals for the Eighth Circuit concluded that the government's burden of proof under § 982(a)(1) was the preponderance standard. Noting that it had decided in a different case handed down the same day that the preponderance standard governed forfeitures under CCE, the court reasoned that [t]he language of the money laundering forfeiture statute is very similar to the language of section 853(a). By stating that "the court, in imposing sentence on a person convicted" of a money laundering offense, shall forfeit property involved in the offense, Congress indicates that forfeiture under the money laundering provision is also a sentencing sanction, not an offense or element of an offense. Id. at 829.

2.

While *Sandini* and *Pelullo* are useful guides, we begin by observing that prior decisions of this court interpreting different criminal forfeiture provisions do not constitute binding precedent on the issue before us. Similarly, the reasoning underlying those decisions is not binding, although to the extent that the statutes are analogous it may be persuasive. We must begin the task afresh and determine which burden of proof Congress intended to apply to § 982(a)(1).

Perhaps the most striking feature of the forfeiture provision is that it requires the district court to order forfeiture "in imposing sentence on a person [already] *convicted* of an offense in violation of * * * section 1957 * * * of this title* * *." 18 U.S.C. § 982(a)(1) (emphasis added). As the *Myers* court observed, the plain language of the statute reveals that forfeiture is a form of sentence enhancement that follows a previous finding of personal guilt. *Myers*, 21 F.3d at 829. As a result, we conclude that the preponderance, not the reasonable doubt, standard governs forfeiture under § 982(a)(1).

Voigt's most forceful argument to the contrary is that when Congress enacted the money laundering forfeiture statute, it specifically incorporated in § 982(b)(1), the statute's procedural component, virtually all of the subsections of 21 U.S.C. § 853, the procedural provisions of the CCE forfeiture statute, yet it omitted § 853(d), the rebuttable presumption provision we found dispositive in *Sandini*. Relying on *Pelullo*, where we attached much significance to Congress' failure to add a provision like § 853(d) to RICO's forfeiture provision, Voigt argues that Congress' decision not to include § 853(d) as one of the subsections incorporated via § 982(b)(1) evinces an intent to require application of the reasonable doubt standard. We think Voigt's argument proves too much. At most, Congress may have decided it did not want the rebuttable presumption to apply in money laundering cases. But that by no means compels us to conclude that the reasonable doubt standard should apply in such cases.

Furthermore, acknowledging that the burden of proof is simply a means of expressing our tolerance for erroneous outcomes, there are good reasons for employing the reasonable doubt standard in the RICO context but not in the money laundering context. The RICO forfeiture provision is by far the most far reaching, requiring the district court to order forfeiture of "any interest the person has acquired or maintained in violation of section 1962," 18 U.S.C. § 1963(a)(1), as well as any "interest in," "security of," "claim against," or "property or contractual right of any kind affording a source of influence over [ ] any enterprise which the person has established, operated, controlled, conducted, or participated in the conduct of in violation of section 1962." Id. § 1963(a)(2). The statute further requires forfeiture of "any property constituting, or derived from, any proceeds which the person obtained, directly or indirectly, from racketeering activity * * * in violation of section 1962." Id. § 1963(a)(3). Section 1963(a)'s coverage, to say the least, is extremely broad and sweeping. Indeed, § 1963(a) sweeps far more broadly than the elements of the substantive RICO offense itself. See 18 U.S.C. § 1962. Accordingly, since the identity and extent of property subject to forfeiture will not have been addressed in the course of proving the substantive RICO charge, a reasonable doubt burden of persuasion ensures greater accuracy in determining the scope of property subject to forfeiture.

In the money laundering context, by contrast, the forfeiture provision makes clear that the government is entitled only to property "involved in" or "traceable to" money laundering activity. See generally United States v. $448,342.85, 969 F.2d 474, 476 (7th Cir.1992) (government entitled only to "funds" used in offense, not whole account into which such funds had been deposited). Furthermore, "property involved in a financial transaction" is part of an element of the money laundering offense, see 18 U.S.C. § 1956(a)(1), and the term "transaction" is defined in the statute. See id. § 1956(c)(3). Unlike the RICO context, we have no reason to doubt that the amount of the transaction that forms the basis of a substantive money laundering offense will be identified in the indictment and, thus, that its connection to money laundering activity will have been proved beyond a reasonable doubt at trial. As the government has observed, in many cases the only factual issues left for resolution after trial will be whether particular items bought with tainted funds are "traceable to" money laundering activity. Applying a beyond-a-reasonable-doubt standard to that issue appears unnecessary. Accordingly, we agree with the Eighth Circuit's decision in *Myers* that the government's burden for forfeiture under § 982(a)(1) is the preponderance standard.

B.

Voigt next argues that the government failed to prove that the money used to purchase the jewelry in question was "traceable to" money laundering proceeds, as required by 18 U.S.C. § 982(a)(1). His argument is based on the fact that the jewelry was purchased with funds drawn from an account in which money laundering proceeds had been commingled with other funds, and that those funds were further "diluted" by numerous intervening deposits and withdrawals. Voigt asserts that if the jewelry was subject to forfeiture, it was under 21 U.S.C. § 853(p)(5), the CCE substitute asset provision incorporated into the money laundering forfeiture scheme via 18 U.S.C. § 982(b)(1). The government counters by observing that criminal forfeiture is an *in personam* punishment, which obviates the need for strict tracing, especially where tainted and untainted funds are commingled in a bank account, making tracing a virtual impossibility.

1.

The government's observation concerning the in personam nature of criminal forfeiture is helpful to a certain extent: the amount of forfeiture to which the government is entitled under 18 U.S.C. § 982 is not dictated by whether the government can prove that certain of the defendant's property is in fact property "traceable to" money laundering activity. When a defendant has been convicted of committing $1.6 million in money laundering offenses (as Voigt was here), the government has proved beyond a reasonable doubt that it is entitled to $1.6 million in criminal forfeiture; that amount represents property "involved in" money laundering activity for purposes of § 982(a)(1). What is at issue here is the question of how the government may go about seizing property in satisfaction of that $1.6 million amount.[19]

The government's principal contention is that money is fungible, making it impossible to differentiate between "tainted" and "untainted" dollars in a bank account. The government also advances what is clearly a policy argument, contending that interpreting the term "traceable to" to require even some tracing "would perversely permit money launderers to escape with all of their proceeds intact simply by commingling such tainted proceeds with untainted sums—a result Congress could not have intended."

To support its arguments, the Government has cited a number of cases dealing with the tracing issue in the context of 18 U.S.C. § 1963(a), the RICO statute's criminal forfeiture provision. These cases hold that where crime proceeds have been commingled in a bank account with untainted funds, tracing is not required. The reasoning supporting those holdings is (1) the *in personam* nature of criminal forfeiture, and (2) the courts' conclusion that when Congress used the term "traceable to," it could not have intended to require the government to demonstrate some nexus between the criminal activity and the property sought--at least not where cash has been deposited into a bank account.

Regardless of whether these cases were correct on their merits, however, they were decided before the President signed into law the Anti-Drug Abuse Act of 1988. Pub.L. No. 100-690, 102 Stat. 4374-75 (1988). With that act Congress added subsection (b) to § 982, which incorporates the CCE forfeiture statute's "substitute asset" provision:

> [i]f any of the property described in subsection (a) of this section, as a result of any act or omission of the defendant * * * has been commingled with other property which cannot be divided without difficulty; the court shall order the forfeiture of any other property of the defendant up to the value of any property described in paragraph [ ] * * * (5).

21 U.S.C. § 853(p)(5). The inclusion of the substitute asset provision in the money laundering forfeiture scheme represents Congress' express recognition that property subject to criminal forfeiture can be commingled with "untainted" property. It may also be an acknowledge-

---

19. Indeed, Voigt does not allege on appeal that the district court erroneously determined that the government is entitled to $1.6 million in criminal forfeiture. He argues only that the jewelry in question is not directly forfeitable under § 982(a)(1).

ment by Congress that its earlier-enacted criminal forfeiture provisions, such as RICO and CCE, were unartfully drafted to the extent that they failed to address the problem posed by commingled property.

In our view the specific inclusion in § 982 of a substitute asset provision precludes us from interpreting the term "traceable to," as did the courts in the RICO context, to avoid a perceived bad policy result. See United States v. Spinsky, 20 F.3d 359, 365 n. 8 (9th Cir.1994) (" § 982 * * * defines forfeitable assets to be only those associated with the underlying offense or traceable to the offense and distinguishes between 'forfeitable' and 'substitute' assets."). Because Congress has made the determination not to "perversely permit money launderers to escape with all of their proceeds intact simply by commingling such tainted proceeds with untainted sums* * *," we should not be in the business of overlooking the plain terms of a statute in order to implement what we, as federal judges, believe might be better policy.[20]

Accordingly, the government's policy arguments, along with the cases supporting them, are inapposite.

Seeking to avoid our conclusion that cases decided prior to the enactment of the money laundering forfeiture statute are not controlling, the government observes that in 1986 Congress added a substitute asset provision to RICO's forfeiture scheme. Relying on In re Billman, 915 F.2d 916, 920 (4th Cir.1990), the government contends that the addition of a substitute asset provision to the RICO statute could not affirmatively undo the settled judicial determination that the words "traceable to" in the RICO forfeiture statute do not require tracing of commingled funds. The government therefore suggests that in the money laundering forfeiture context it can seek forfeiture of items purchased with commingled funds either as "traceable to" or as substitute assets. We disagree.

As the Ninth Circuit's decision in *Ripinsky* [20 F.3d 359 (9th Cir. 1994)] makes clear, the government's position is internally inconsistent. The substitute asset provision comes into play only when forfeitable property cannot be identified as directly "involved in" or "traceable to" money laundering activity. Clearly, if funds commingled in a bank account are sufficiently identifiable as to be considered "traceable to" money laundering activity, then the substitute asset provision should have no applicability whatsoever. Accordingly, the government's

---

20. To put it bluntly, even if the *in personam* nature of criminal forfeiture were sufficient, in and of itself, to obviate the need for tracing as a policy matter, that still does not explain why federal courts should be free to ignore the fact that prior to the enactment of the substitute asset provisions, Congress, by using the terms "involved in" and "traceable to," clearly required that there be a connection between the criminal activity and the property sought in criminal forfeiture.

contention that the "traceable to" and substitute asset theories merely create alternative paths to forfeiture, which the government may choose at its option, is illogical.

We also do not understand why an amendment to a statute cannot affirmatively reverse, or at least cast substantial doubt on, prior court decisions interpreting earlier versions of that statute. This is especially true where, in undertaking to discern the plain meaning, those decisions essentially held (for policy reasons) that Congress simply could not have meant what it said. Indeed, if the legitimacy of the courts' interpretation of the RICO statute had been beyond doubt, then the addition of a substitute asset provision to the RICO, CCE and money laundering criminal forfeiture schemes would seem superfluous.

Furthermore, we think the government's interpretation of *Billman* proves too much. In *Billman* the Fourth Circuit cited to the prior case law holding that the *in personam* nature of criminal forfeiture makes tracing under the RICO statute's forfeiture provision unnecessary. It then made the unremarkable observation, which the government apparently finds significant, that "[t]hese principles are embodied in an amendment to the act, which makes provision for the forfeiture of substitute assets." 915 F.2d at 920. Contrary to the government's interpretation, however, that observation may signal the Fourth Circuit's view (which we expressed above) that Congress recognized its unartfulness in using the term "traceable to" in its forfeiture statutes. Moreover, the Fourth Circuit may have recognized that in amending forfeiture statutes to include a substitute asset provision, Congress may have appreciated that courts had been stretching to avoid the result of applying the plain meaning of the term "traceable to" to commingled property.[21]

Even if *Billman* can be read to suggest that the addition of a substitute asset provision to RICO's criminal forfeiture scheme cannot

---

21. We also reject the government's suggestion that references to the *in personam* nature of criminal forfeiture in the legislative history surrounding the enactment of § 982(b)(1) somehow authorize a federal court to interpret the words "traceable to" out of the statute. If anything, Congress' reference to the *in personam* nature of criminal forfeiture was offered as a justification for including in § 982 a substitute asset provision that allows the government to seize property having no connection to money laundering activity:

> Because criminal forfeitures are *in personam* * * * the substitute assets provision also gives the government the ability to receive, in essence, a general judgment against the defendant. When a certain sum is alleged in the indictment as amount of criminal proceeds and those proceeds can not be found after the jury enters a special verdict against that sum, the government can then execute against any other property belonging to the defendant.

Arthur W. Leach & John G. Malcolm, Criminal Forfeiture: An Appropriate Solution to the Civil Forfeiture Debate, 10 Ga. St. U.L.Rev. 241, 295 n. 164 (1994) (so concluding in the RICO forfeiture context).

undo prior judicial interpretations of the words "traceable to" in the RICO context, we simply cannot ignore the plain fact that the money laundering criminal forfeiture provision contains a substitute asset provision that appears to be addressed directly to the situation confronting us in this case. We are unaware of any decision that has imported the restrictive definition of "traceable to" prevalent in the RICO context into the money laundering forfeiture scheme.

In sum, to accept the government's argument that "traceable to" does not mean what it says for purposes of commingled property, in effect would render the substitute asset provision a nullity, in contravention of a well-settled canon of statutory construction that "courts should disfavor interpretations of statutes that render language superfluous." Connecticut Nat'l Bank v. Germain, 503 U.S. 249, 253, 112 S.Ct. 1146, 1149, 117 L.Ed.2d 391 (1992).

2.

We hold that the term "traceable to" means exactly what it says.[22] In light of our holding on the burden of proof, this means that the government must prove by a preponderance of the evidence that the property it seeks under § 982(a)(1) in satisfaction of the amount of criminal forfeiture to which it is entitled has some nexus to the property "involved in" the money laundering offense. For example, if the defendant receives $500,000 cash in a money laundering transaction and hides the cash in his house, the government may seize that money as property "involved in" the money laundering offense. If the defendant purchased a $250,000 item with that money, the government may seek the remaining cash as "involved in" the offense, whereas the item purchased is subject to forfeiture as property "traceable to" property involved in the money laundering offense.

Where the property involved in a money laundering transaction is commingled in an account with untainted property, however, the government's burden of showing that money in the account or an item purchased with cash withdrawn therefrom is "traceable to" money laundering activity will be difficult, if not impossible, to satisfy. While we can envision a situation where $500,000 is added to an account containing only $500, such that one might argue that the probability of

---

22. Interpreting the word "traceable to" to mean exactly what it says is no doubt salutary. We avoid the problems plaguing other courts that have attempted to devise a workable tracing analysis for tainted property that has been commingled in a bank account with untainted property. See United States v. Banco Cafetero Panama, 797 F.2d 1154 (2d Cir.1986) (exploring various tracing options); see also $448,342.85, 969 F.2d at 477 ("It is easy to imagine difficult problems in associating proceeds with crime").

seizing "tainted" funds is far greater than the government's preponderance burden (50.1%), such an approach is ultimately unworkable. As the Seventh Circuit, speaking through Judge Easterbrook, has observed, a bank account is simply a number on a piece of paper:

> Bank accounts do not commit crimes; people do. It makes no sense to confiscate whatever balance happens to be in an account bearing a particular number, just because proceeds of crime once passed through that account* * *. An "account" is a name, a routing device like the address of a building; the money is the "property" [for purposes of the forfeiture statute]. Once we distinguish the money from its container, it also follows that the presence of one illegal dollar in an account does not taint the rest--as if the dollar obtained from [money laundering activity] were like a drop of ink falling into a glass of water.

U.S. v. $448,342.85, 969 F.2d 474, 476 (7th Cir.1992).[23]

The solution, we think, is to give effect to the substitute asset provision. See 18 U.S.C. § 982(b)(1) (incorporating 21 U.S.C. § 853(p)(5)). Thus, once a defendant has commingled laundered funds with untainted funds–whether in a bank account or in a tattered suitcase–such that they "cannot be divided without difficulty," 21 U.S.C. § 853(p)(5),[24] the government must satisfy its forfeiture judgment through the substitute asset provision. Once property subject to forfeiture under § 982(a)(1) is no longer identifiable due to some act of the defendant, the government may seek any property, cash or merchandise, in satisfaction of the amount of criminal forfeiture to which it is entitled.

---

23. The Seventh Circuit's opinion in United States v. $448,342.85 dealt with the money laundering civil forfeiture statute, 18 U.S.C. § 981, which also contains the terms "involved in" and "traceable to." The decision was handed down prior to Congress' enactment of 18 U.S.C. § 984, a substitute asset provision applicable to civil forfeiture under § 981. It is significant that in the absence of such a provision, the court refused to countenance the government's argument that the terms "involved in" and "traceable to" need not be given their ordinary meaning. *$448,342.85*, 969 F.2d at 477 ("Only property used in or traceable to the 'specified unlawful activity' is forfeit.").

24. We do not understand the phrase "cannot be divided without difficulty" in § 853(p)(5) as meaning simply that the amount of crime proceeds cannot be separated out (e.g., where tainted and untainted funds are pooled together to purchase a piece of real property). We think the substitute asset provision applies equally to commingling of cash, which makes it impossible to distinguish between tainted and untainted dollars, although one readily could separate out the amount subject to forfeiture.

3.

In light of our analysis, the district court's forfeiture order, which is incorporated into Voigt's judgment of conviction and sentence, cannot stand. Even under the preponderance standard, the items of jewelry cannot be considered "traceable to" the proceeds of money laundering activity; the jewelry was purchased with funds from an account into which money laundering proceeds had been commingled with other funds, and after numerous intervening deposits and withdrawals. We therefore cannot say that, more probably than not, the jewelry is "traceable to" money laundering activity.

Notwithstanding our conclusion, the government continues to be entitled to $1.6 million in criminal forfeiture. But to the extent that the forfeiture order incorporated in the judgment required Voigt to hand jewelry over to the government under an erroneous legal determination, the government is improperly in possession of that jewelry. We do not envision that the district court will have to conduct a *de novo* forfeiture proceeding on remand. Since all that is at issue is the process by which the government may seize property in satisfaction of the $1.6 million to which it is lawfully entitled, on remand the government should be permitted to move to amend the judgment to reflect that the jewelry is forfeitable as a substitute asset. Cf. United States v. Hurley, 63 F.3d 1, 23 (1st Cir.1995) (no error where, after notice of appeal from conviction was filed, government moved for and received from district court permission to seize certain property as "substitute assets"); Todd Barnet & Ivan Fox, Trampling on the Sixth Amendment: The Continued Threat of Attorney Fee Forfeiture, 22 Ohio N.U.L.Rev. 1, 55 (1995) ("The substitute assets provisions constitute a procedural alternative for collecting a forfeiture judgment and are not a form of punishment in their own right* * *.").

X.

CONCLUSION

We will affirm Voigt's conspiracy, money laundering and tax evasion convictions, as well as the district court's order of restitution. We will vacate the forfeiture order, which is incorporated into the judgment of conviction and sentence, and remand for further proceedings consistent with this opinion.

Notes and Questions

Eighth Amendment claims. The *Voigt* court notes that the criminal forfeiture provision involves an *in personam* proceeding. Such proceedings are subject to Eighth Amendment challenges under the Excessive Fines Clause. The United States Supreme Court has held that where the forfeiture is punitive in nature it constitutes a "fine" that may be considered unconstitutionally excessive when it is "grossly disproportional to the gravity of the offense." See United States v. Bajakajian, 524 U.S. 321 (1998) (where government tried to seize over $357,000 when the defendant attempted to leave the country without completing a customs form declaring that he was transporting more than $10,000 in currency). See further discussion in § C, below.

1. How may assets subject to forfeiture under the money laundering provisions be identified?

2. When and how does the "substitute asset" provision apply? Should it make any difference to the government which forfeiture provision applies?

b. *Third Party Transferees*

A wrongdoer cannot avoid the forfeiture provisions by transferring the proceeds to a third party, unless that party is a bona fide purchaser for value without reason to believe the property was subject to forfeiture. Thus, the proceeds generally may be traced to and recovered from the third party. But what if the proceeds were used to pay the offender's attorney and the attorney no longer has the proceeds? Are those proceeds recoverable from the attorney?

UNITED STATES v. SACCOCCIA
United States Court of Appeals, First Circuit, 2003.
354 F.3d 9

CYR, SENIOR CIRCUIT JUDGE.

Three attorneys who represented Stephen A. Saccoccia-a convicted drug dealer and money launderer-appeal from a district court order directing that they forfeit some of their attorney fees to the government.

I

BACKGROUND

The grand jury returned an indictment against Stephen A. Saccoccia in November 1991, charging him with one count of conspiracy under the Racketeering Influenced and Corrupt Organizations Act, 18 U.S.C. § 1963(d) (RICO), as well as several counts of laundering proceeds from an illegal drug trafficking operation. See United States v. Saccoccia, 58 F.3d 754 (1st Cir.1995). The government also sought the forfeiture of all the business and personal property directly or indirectly derived from Saccoccia's racketeering activities, explicitly including almost $137,000,000 in currency, and, in the alternative, sought the surrender of all non-tainted property of equivalent value (if any) should Saccoccia's tainted property have become unavailable. See 18 U.S.C. § 1963(a), (m). The district court promptly enjoined the transfer of the forfeitable property designated in the indictment. See id. § 1963(d)(1)(A).

Saccoccia retained Jack Hill, Esquire, and Kenneth O'Donnell, Esquire, to defend him in the RICO prosecution; he retained Stephen Finta, Esquire, to defend him against money laundering charges pending in California. We turn now to a more detailed description of the district court proceedings below.

Beginning in March 1992, under rather suspicious circumstances, Saccoccia caused $504,985 to be delivered to Hill, $410,000 to O'Donnell, and $469,200 to Finta, all for legal fees. Approximately one year later, Saccoccia was convicted and ordered to forfeit the $137,000,000 in currency specified in the indictment. We subsequently affirmed both the conviction and the forfeiture. *Saccoccia*, 58 F.3d at 754; see also United States v. Hurley, 63 F.3d 1 (1st Cir.1995). Once the government discovered that Saccoccia had paid large legal fees to Hill, O'Donnell, and Finta, it submitted a motion to compel them to turn over the fees as property subject to forfeiture.

The district court granted the motion to compel, United States v. Saccoccia, 165 F.Supp.2d 103 (D.R.I.2001), holding that (i) the government established that the legal fees paid to the appellants must have derived from Saccoccia's racketeering activity, given that Saccoccia had no legitimate sources of income, and the legal fees were paid "under especially suspicious circumstances" (viz., by "covert deliveries of large quantities of cash, made by anonymous intermediaries"), id. at 111-12; (ii) appellants met their burden of proving that they had no reasonable cause to believe that the monies Saccoccia used to pay their fees, prior to Saccoccia's conviction, were subject to forfeiture, given that an Assistant United States Attorney's pre-conviction assurances to appellants-that the government would not seek forfeiture of their legal fees-implied some government uncertainty regarding whether Saccoccia might possess sufficient non-tainted assets with which to pay his attorneys, id. at 112 (citing 18 U.S.C. § 1963(c)); (iii) following the trial at which Saccoccia was convicted, appellants could not have held a reasonable belief that Saccoccia's assets were not subject to forfeiture, given that the trial record made it clear that virtually all of Saccoccia's assets had been derived through illegitimate means, id. at 112-13; (iv) appellants were ordered to turn over only the portion of their legal fees received following Saccoccia's conviction, id. at 113; and (v) the government could not reach their pre-conviction legal fees by means of the district court's contempt power due to the fact that the government had initiated no such proceeding and the district court had already determined that appellants lacked reasonable cause to believe that the pre-conviction legal fees were subject to forfeiture, hence appellants could not have violated the post-indictment injunction willfully, id. at 113-14.

Appellants now challenge the district court order which determined that their post-conviction legal fees are subject to forfeiture.[1]

II

DISCUSSION

Appellants Hill and O'Donnell contend, as they did in opposing the government's motion to compel below, that the forfeiture statute does not permit the government to reach the legal fees they received from Saccoccia, due to the fact that those fees have been expended. We subject statutory interpretations to plenary review. See Bryson v. Shumway, 308 F.3d 79, 84 (1st Cir.2002).[2]

The operative statutory language requires that a defendant forfeit "tainted" property, viz., property (i) acquired by committing the offense, and (ii) "constituting, or derived from, any proceeds . . . obtained, directly or indirectly" from its commission. 18 U.S.C. § 1963(a)(1),(3).[3] Once an

---

1.   For its part, the government has not cross-appealed from the district court ruling that the legal fees appellants received prior to the Saccoccia conviction are not subject to forfeiture.

2.   As the forfeiture provisions prescribed by RICO are substantially similar to the criminal forfeiture provisions in 21 U.S.C § 853, we cite cases interpreting § 853 as persuasive analogous authority. See United States v. Hooper, 229 F.3d 818, 821 n. 7 (1st Cir.2000).

3.   For instance, the profits Saccoccia derived from the drug conspiracy would be subject to forfeiture under subsection (1). Were Saccoccia to use some of the drug profits to purchase a boat for $50,000, the boat would be forfeitable, under subsection (3), as property "derived from" tainted proceeds, even though not utilized in the conspiracy.

indictment issues, the district court may enjoin the transfer of all property "subject to forfeiture under [section 1963]." Id. § 1963(d)(1). In the event that tainted property is unavailable for forfeiture (as when it has been transferred to a third party),[4] the government may recover "substitute" property, viz., defendant's other untainted property of equivalent value. See id. § 1963(m); United States v. Lester, 85 F.3d 1409, 1411 n. 3 (9th Cir.1996) (" '[S]ubstitute property,' . . . by its very nature is 'not connected to the underlying crime.' ").[5]

The operative statute enables the government to recover from the defendant "tainted" or "substitute" property in a defendant's possession, or "tainted" property held by a third party by virtue of a voidable fraudulent transfer. Id. § 1963(c). A third party may petition the court for a hearing to determine the validity of its legal interest in tainted property, id. § 1963(l)(2), and may defeat a forfeiture petition by establishing, inter alia, that it is a bona fide purchaser for value, "reasonably without cause to believe" that the property was subject to forfeiture at the time it was purchased, id. § 1963(l)(6)(B).

Nonetheless, the "substitute property" provision is exclusively applicable to "any other property of the *defendant*." Id. § 1963(m) (emphasis added). The statutory language plainly does not afford an avenue through which the government may reach a third party's untainted assets as a substitute for tainted assets which the third party had already transferred prior to the date of forfeiture. See Bryson, 308 F.3d at 84 ("If the meaning of a statute is clear, we enforce that meaning."); United States v. Meade, 175 F.3d 215, 219 (1st Cir.1999) (noting that when "the plain language of a statute unambiguously reveals its meaning, and the revealed meaning is not eccentric, courts need not consult other aids to statutory construction."); see also Lohnes v. Level 3 Communications, Inc., 272 F.3d 49, 61 (1st Cir.2001) ("[T]he maxim expressio unius est exclusio alterius instructs that, 'when parties list specific items in a document, any item not so listed is typically thought to be excluded.' ").[7]

---

4. Tainted property may be unreachable if it "(1) cannot be located upon the exercise of due diligence; (2) has been transferred or sold to, or deposited with, a third party; (3) has been placed beyond the jurisdiction of the court; (4) has been substantially diminished in value; or (5) has been commingled with other property which cannot be divided without difficulty." 18 U.S.C. § 1963(m).

5. The original district court forfeiture order against Saccoccia was amended to include his substitute assets based on evidence that Saccoccia was in the process of transferring tainted assets. See Saccoccia, 58 F.3d at 783.

7. The government's contrary argument relies primarily upon one unpublished decision as "persuasive authority." United States v. McCorkle, No. 6:98-CR-52-ORL-19C, 2000 WL 133759 (M.D.Fla. Jan.14, 2000) (holding that government could recoup attorney's other property where he

The government does not contend that it can recover the "tainted" property already transferred to Hill and O'Donnell by Saccoccia (i.e., the in-cash legal fees), nor does it maintain that either Hill or O'Donnell presently holds any property fairly traceable to, or acquired with the proceeds of, their legal fees. Rather, it argues that its right to recover derives from the knowing violations, by Hill and O'Donnell, of the post-indictment injunction entered pursuant to § 1963(d)(1), which constrained Saccoccia and his counsel from transferring any funds subject to forfeiture under subsection 1963(a). Cf. In re Moffitt, Zwerling & Kemler, 864 F.Supp. 527, 530-31 (E.D.Va.1994) (finding assets non-forfeitable where transfers to counsel occurred prior to injunction); id. at 544 n. 46 ("Where an attorney accepts payment in violation of such a restraining order, the government can recover regardless of the fact that the attorney has dissipated the funds."), rev'd on other grounds, 83 F.3d 660 (4th Cir.1996).

The absence of language in subsection 1963(m), relating to the forfeitability vel non of a third party's substitute assets, simply forecloses one form of remedy, not all. Relief from a willful violation of a subsection 1963(d)(1) injunction may be obtained in a contempt proceeding. See United States v. Kirschenbaum, 156 F.3d 784, 795 (7th Cir.1998). On the other hand, the government's initiation of contempt proceedings would significantly alter its burden in litigation. Whereas subsections 1963(c) and (l)(6) require the third party to establish that it was without reasonable cause to believe that the transferred property was subject to forfeiture under subsection 1963(a), in a criminal or civil contempt proceeding the government would bear the burden of persuasion on that issue. In a criminal contempt proceeding, moreover, the government's burden of proof would be beyond-a-reasonable-doubt, see Fed.R.Crim.P. 42; United States v. Mourad, 289 F.3d 174, 180 (1st Cir.), cert. denied, 537 U.S. 933, 123 S.Ct. 337, 154 L.Ed.2d 232 (2002); and in a civil contempt proceeding, clear and convincing evidence would be required, see AccuSoft Corp. v. Palo, 237 F.3d 31, 47 (1st Cir.2001). The district court noted, however, that "the government is not seeking to hold the attorneys in contempt." Saccoccia, 165 F.Supp.2d at 114.

---

had already dissipated the tainted legal fees); see also 1st Cir. Local R. 32.3(b). However, McCorkle contains neither an analysis of the pertinent statutory provisions, nor any other authority supporting its conclusory holding. Indeed, McCorkle erroneously cites In re Moffitt, Zwerling & Kemler, 83 F.3d 660, 667-70 (4th Cir.1996), for the proposition that the forfeiture statute "does not abrogate the government's right to recover attorneys' fees that have been dissipated by a third party law firm," McCorkle, 2000 WL 133759, at *3 (citing Moffitt, 83 F.3d at 666-69), even though Moffitt found the basis for the government's potential recovery not in the forfeiture statute's "substitute asset" provision, but in an extra-statutory claim for common-law conversion, see infra.

Additionally, subsection 1963(m) would not preempt various remedies otherwise available to the government outside the forfeiture statute, which would maximize its monetary recovery from the substitute assets of culpable third parties. See United States v. Moffitt, Zwerling & Kemler, 83 F.3d 660, 667-70 (4th Cir.1996) (holding that § 1963(m) does not preempt state common-law claims that enable the government to reach a third-party transferee's substitute assets). For instance, since the government's right, title, and interest in all tainted property "relates back" to the date Saccoccia committed the relevant acts, see 18 U.S.C. § 1963(c) ("All right, title, and interest in property described in subsection (a) vests in the United States upon the commission of the act giving rise to the forfeiture."), presumably it could initiate a state-law proceeding against Hill and O'Donnell for conversion of such property, and recover compensatory damages from their non-tainted assets. See Fuscellaro v. Indus. Nat'l Corp., 117 R.I. 558, 368 A.2d 1227, 1230 (R.I.1997) ("[T]he gravamen of an action for conversion lies in the defendant's taking the plaintiff's personalty without consent and exercising dominion over it inconsistent with the plaintiff's right of possession."). However, had the government brought such a tort claim in the district court, the claim presumably would be adjudicated under substantially different standards than a claim under subsection 1963(a) or (m), since the government would bear the burden of proof, and appellants might be entitled to additional procedural safeguards under state law, such as a right to jury trial. See, e.g., Ross v. Bernhard, 396 U.S. 531, 533, 90 S.Ct. 733, 24 L.Ed.2d 729 (1970); Evergreen Marine Corp. v. Six Consignments of Frozen Scallops, 4 F.3d 90, 95 (1st Cir.1993); Russell v. City of Bryan, 919 S.W.2d 698, 704 (Tx.App.1996); Meyers Way Dev. Ltd. P'ship v. Univ. Sav. Bank, 80 Wash.App. 655, 910 P.2d 1308, 1320 (Wash.Ct.App.1996).

At first blush, the present holding may appear to diverge from the stated legislative intent to accord the government extremely aggressive forfeiture remedies so as to preclude criminals from realizing the monetary benefits of their crimes. See Caplin & Drysdale, Chartered v. United States, 491 U.S. 617, 631, 109 S.Ct. 2646, 105 L.Ed.2d 528 (1989). On the other hand, the very potency of the forfeiture power demands that it be reasonably contained within ascertainable limits. Thus, for example, Congress provided that a non-defendant third party with rights in forfeitable property may redeem its interest by establishing either (i) that it predated the defendant's crime, see United States v. Lester, 85 F.3d 1409, 1414 (9th Cir.1996) (holding that non-defendant spouse had non-forfeitable pre-existing interest in jointly-held property), or (ii) that it subsequently acquired a non-forfeitable interest under a bona fide purchase for value, see 18 U.S.C. § 1963(l)(6).

The implicit limitation in § 1963(m)-the "substitute assets" provision-that the government may reach only the defendant's substitute assets and not those of a third party-is similar in nature. Forfeiture is an in personam criminal remedy, targeted primarily at the defendant who committed the criminal offense. See Lester, 85 F.3d at 1414 n. 8 (noting crucial distinction between in personam judgment in criminal forfeiture proceeding and in rem judgment in civil forfeiture proceeding).

Finally, the implicit limitation in § 1963(m) does not trammel the basic statutory policy by foreclosing all other remedies available to the government, nor does it enable culpable attorneys to dissipate tainted fees with impunity. Rather, the government may utilize its enforcement powers under subsection 1963(k) to "trace" tainted funds, thereby disproving the contention that appellants' cash-on-hand is neither the tainted fees, nor other property directly or indirectly derived from the tainted fees. Furthermore, absent such evidence, the government may reach other non-tainted cash of the attorneys by sustaining the somewhat weightier, though not insurmountable, burden of establishing the elements of either contempt or conversion.

As our construction of the language utilized in the forfeiture statute is one of first impression, the forfeiture award against Hill and O'Donnell must be vacated and the case must be remanded to the district court for further proceedings consistent with this opinion. Upon remand, the government is to be accorded a reasonable opportunity to determine whether it intends to institute contempt proceedings or submit conversion claims against appellants.

Accordingly, the district court order directing appellants Hill and O'Donnell to surrender their post-conviction legal fees is hereby vacated, and the case is remanded for further proceedings consistent with this opinion. The order to compel appellant Finta to surrender $242,000 in post-conviction legal fees is hereby affirmed. SO ORDERED

Notes and Questions

Note that the government is not powerless to prevent an attorney or any other third party from dissipating assets that may be subject to forfeiture. Under 21 U.S.C. § 853(e)(1), the government may petition a court to "enter a restraining order or injunction, require the execution of a satisfactory performance bond, or take any other action to preserve the availability of property" subject to forfeiture under the statute. A restraining order may be obtain even before indictment if the government demonstrates (i) "a substantial probability that [it] will prevail on the issue of forfeiture and that failure to enter the order will result in the property being . . . unavailable for forfeiture" and (ii) that "the need to preserve the availability of the property . . . outweighs the hardship on any party against whom the order is to be entered". If it has probable cause, it also could obtain a warrant authorizing the seizure of the property.

Section 982 (a)(6)(B) provides that criminal forfeiture shall be governed by the provisions of 21 U.S.C. § 853, pertaining to drug law violations. Section 853(c) provides that "[a]ll right, title, and interest in property * * * vests in the United States upon the commission of the act giving rise to forfeiture * * *." This is referred to as the "relation-back doctrine" and it serves to reach all property transferred by the defendant to third parties after the commission of the offense, unless the transferee proves that she is a bona fide purchaser for value and was reasonably without cause to believe that the property was subject to the forfeiture provisions.

According to the majority opinion in *Caplin & Drysdale:*

> As soon as [the possessor of the forfeitable asset committed the violation] of the internal revenue laws, the forfeiture under those laws took effect, and (though needing judicial condemnation to perfect it) operated from that time as a statutory conveyance to the United States of all the right, title, and interest then remaining in the [possessor]; and was as valid and effectual, against all the world, as a recorded deed. The right so vested in the United States could not be defeated or impaired by any subsequent dealings of the * * * [possessor].

491 U.S. at 627 (quoting United States v. Stowell, 133 U.S. 1, 19 (1890)).

The dissent in *Caplin & Drysdale* notes the distinction between civil forfeiture and criminal forfeiture, as well as the distinction between § 853(a) and § 853(c). Section 853(a) provides that any person convicted of a violation of the drug laws *shall forfeit* proceeds or property derived from or used in a continuing criminal enterprise or used in the commission of the offense. Section 853(c), on the other hand, provides that the property transferred to third parties "may be the subject of a special verdict of forfeiture and thereafter shall be ordered forfeited to the United States * * *." Id.

The dissent argues that under a civil forfeiture provision, the property is tainted by virtue of having been used in or derived from the commission of an offense. Thus, the defendant forfeits the property regardless of whether the defendant is ultimately convicted of the offense. Since the criminal forfeiture provisions are penal in nature, they hinge upon the adjudicated guilt of the defendant. Where the rights of a third party are affected, the "Government's penal interests are weakest * * *." 491 U.S. at 638, n.5 (Blackmun, J., dissenting).

Under § 853(c), the third party is entitled to a special verdict of forfeiture in which the court has considerable discretion in determining which property, if any, should be forfeited. The dissent further argues that the effect of the majority decision will be to punish the defendant before he has been convicted and that this was not the purpose of the pre-conviction forfeiture provisions. According to the legislative history of § 853, the pre-conviction forfeiture provisions were designed to prevent the transfer of tainted property, but property does not become tainted until the defendant has been convicted of the offense. 491 U.S. at 637-38.

1. If forfeiture applies to an attorney, does this present a Sixth Amendment problem? See Caplin & Drysdale, Chartered v. United States, 491 U.S. 617 (1989).

2. What arguments are available to third parties who wish to contest a forfeiture? Which of these, if any, are more likely to prevail in the case of an attorney who is arguing against the forfeiture of funds transferred in payment of legal fees?

B. CURRENCY TRANSACTION REPORTING – TITLE 26 U.S.C. § 6050I

Section 6050I(a) provides: "Any person (1) who is engaged in a trade or business, and (2) who, in the course of such trade or business, receives more than $10,000 in cash in 1 transaction (or 2 or more related transactions), shall [file a Form 8300] with respect to such transaction (or related transactions) at such time as the Secretary may be regulations prescribe."

Section 6050I(f) provides that "No person shall for the purpose of evading the return requirements of this section–(A) cause or attempt to cause a trade or business to fail to file a return required under this section, (B) cause or attempt to cause a trade or business to file a return required under this section that contains a material omission or misstatement of fact, or (C) structure or assist in structuring, or attempt to structure or assist in structuring, any transaction with one or more trades or businesses."

UNITED STATES v. McLAMB

United States Court of Appeals, Fourth Circuit, 1993.
985 F.2d 1284.

PHILLIPS, CIRCUIT JUDGE.

* * *

I.

In early July 1990 Harry Godwin contacted a salesman, M.L. "Bill" Stallings, at the Smithfield Ford-Lincoln-Mercury car dealership in Smithfield, North Carolina ("Smithfield Ford"), seeking to purchase a new Ford van for his girlfriend, Margie Jenkins. Godwin told Stallings he would pay cash for the van because both he and Jenkins had poor credit. Stallings selected a Ford Aerostar van for Jenkins and told McLamb, who owned the dealership, about the deal.

Jenkins purchased the van on July 5. She paid Stallings $13,927.79 in cash, which he took, together with the completed buyer's order, to McLamb. McLamb told Stallings the deal couldn't be done that way, wrote one receipt for $9,900 in cash and one for a $4,027.79 check, then told Stallings to make out a personal check to Smithfield Ford for $4,027.79. Stallings wrote the check, and McLamb gave him $4,028 in cash, which Stallings deposited in his checking account. McLamb then deposited Stallings's check and the $9,900 cash in the Smithfield Ford account. Jenkins later picked up the van, following its delivery from another dealership. No Form 8300 (reporting cash transactions exceeding $10,000) was filed with the IRS.

Somewhat later the IRS became aware that McLamb might be involved in money laundering activities, and on August 1 IRS Special Agent Anthony Asbridge, using a   pseudonym and wearing a hidden tape recorder, negotiated the purchase of a Lincoln Towncar with McLamb. Discussing during the course of their negotiations Asbridge's professed desire to pay in cash, McLamb noted that he ran a "straight up business" but that "there are ways to do that, that don't get anybody in trouble." "[I]t can be quite a serious problem," he said, "if you don't do it right." Asbridge then explained to McLamb that his brother-in-law wanted to buy a Lincoln Towncar, but he just is in a situation right now where he can't buy it himself. He * * * has problems * * * with the drug people * * *. [T]he money's not clean money * * * [H]e can't have a car in his name * * * [W]e're dealing with green money, * * * and * * * one of the problems is all the reporting stuff * * *."

McLamb told him that the "easy way," "the clean way" to work the transaction would be to pay roughly $9,000 in cash and finance the balance or purchase separate cashier's checks in amounts under $10,000 sufficient to cover the balance. Discussing his belief that this would enable him to avoid reporting the transaction, McLamb warned Asbridge that "if the IRS had ever questioned me, [sic] * * * this conversation never existed!" But he agreed to proceed with the transaction, noting that although he was also obligated to report a transaction he knew was broken up to evade the reporting requirements, "you can't live by the letter of the law."

Asbridge and McLamb then moved on to a discussion of the car's particulars. Asbridge deferred decision on the actual purchase, saying he needed to consult his brother-in-law.

On August 2 Asbridge phoned McLamb and agreed to purchase a new Lincoln Towncar for $31,374.51, to be titled in the name of Bobbie Jeane Melton. While discussing the method of payment Asbridge would use, McLamb reminded him that purchases of cashier's checks for over $10,000 get recorded. The next day Asbridge brought about $7,000 cash and three sub-$10,000 cashier's checks to the dealership. After discussing the sale with McLamb, Asbridge helped the dealership's financial officer complete some paperwork, turning over the checks and telling him to title the car in the name of Bobbie Jean [sic] Melton. When the financial officer told Asbridge the cash balance owed, Asbridge left the office, ostensibly to get the cash from his car. This signalled other IRS agents to execute a search warrant, which they did, entering the premises and seizing the dealership's records, including documentation of the transaction negotiated by Asbridge.[1]

McLamb was subsequently indicted on multiple charges arising out of these two transactions. The jury ultimately returned guilty verdicts on two of them, structuring the Ford van sale to Margie Jenkins for the purpose of evading the IRS reporting requirement in violation of 26 U.S.C. § 6050I(f)(1) and money laundering arising out of the sham transaction McLamb negotiated with Asbridge in violation of 18 U.S.C. § 1956(a)(3), on the basis of which the district judge sentenced McLamb to concurrent terms of 71 months and 60 months, respectively.

. McLamb appealed.

---

1.   This seizure led to the information used to prosecute McLamb for the Ford van transaction described earlier.

II.

McLamb contests his conviction for structuring the van sale on three grounds, alleging insufficiency of the evidence, erroneous jury instructions, and improperly admitted evidence.

A.

McLamb argues that the government's evidence, which showed that he substituted Stallings's personal check for $4,027.79 of the Godwin-Jenkins cash, was insufficient to convict him under 26 U.S.C. § 6050I(f)(1) because it demonstrated that McLamb acted after the obligation to file a return had already arisen (with Jenkins's payment to Stallings) and therefore could not have "structured" the transaction to avoid the filing of a Form 8300. This misinterprets the statute's requirements.

Section 6050I(a) requires business persons receiving more than $10,000 in one or more related transactions in the course of their business to file a return with the IRS. But McLamb was not charged with violating § 6050I(a); he was charged with violating § 6050I(f)(1). That section forbids individuals to "structure or assist in structuring" a business transaction or transactions "for the purpose of evading" the return requirement of § 6050I(a). The evidence was unquestionably sufficient for a reasonable jury to conclude beyond a reasonable doubt that McLamb did so, by assisting in structuring the transaction between Jenkins and McLamb's Smithfield dealership for the purpose of evading the obligation to file a Form 8300 return. The statute requires nothing more.

McLamb's contention that the obligation to report arose before he acted and applied to another individual is, even if correct, irrelevant to our determination that his conduct violated § 6050I(f)(1)(C). The statute's plain language indicates that the structuring prohibition's applicability is not limited to those on whom the duty to file falls and that a person's ability to structure a transaction for the purpose of evading the reporting obligation does not turn on when that obligation arises. That being so, we must reject McLamb's challenge to the sufficiency of the evidence used to convict him of structuring a transaction to evade IRS return requirements in violation of 26 U.S.C. § 6050I(f)(1)(C).

B.

McLamb also presses [an] objection[] to the district court's jury instructions on the structuring charge. * * *

McLamb * * * argues * * * that the district court's explanation of the obligation to file a return imposed by § 6050I(a) left unclear whether that obligation rested with McLamb or with the dealership. We need not address that contention directly, because the district court's instructions were flawed in a different way—one entirely favorable to McLamb—which rendered the instruction on the filing obligation altogether superfluous and any error in its formulation therefore harmless.

Count Four of the indictment charged McLamb with assisting in the structuring of a financial transaction with Smithfield Ford for the purpose of evading the transaction reporting requirement and with causing or attempting to cause the dealership to fail to file a required return, all in violation of § 6050I(f). The district judge outlined all this for the jury. Before detailing the elements of the offense, he explained that the return in question was required by § 6050I(a), which obligated persons engaged in business to report certain business-related transactions. He then discussed § 6050I(f), which McLamb was charged with violating. In doing so, he failed to reiterate at first that which he had outlined earlier in discussing the indictment, that § 6050I(f) forbade structuring a transaction to evade the reporting requirement as well as causing a business not to file a return, mentioning only the latter.

In summing up, the district judge did include the structuring possibility, but he made a further mistake in charging the jury that the government had to prove both the elements of the structuring offense and those related to causing a failure to file in order to convict McLamb. In reality, the portion of § 6050I(f)(1) under which McLamb was charged makes it clear that, while they require the same specific intent, proof of either structuring or causing a failure to file will do; both are not required:

> [n]o person shall for the purpose of evading the return requirements of this section—(A) cause or attempt to cause a trade or business to fail to file a return required under this section, * * * *or* (C) structure or assist in structuring, or attempt to structure or assist in structuring, any transaction with one or more trades or businesses. (emphasis added).

It should be obvious from the text of the statute and the analysis in Part II.A that the question whether the district court properly instructed the jury with respect to the party on whom the filing obligation fell is relevant only to violation of § 6050I(f)(1)(A) and not to violation of § 6050I(f)(1)(C). Read in light of the district court's overly generous instructions, the jury's verdict demonstrates that it found all the elements for a violation of both provisions. Since McLamb's objection concerns an element relevant only to the offense of causing or attempting to cause a failure to file a required return under § 6050I(f)(1)(A), an erroneous instruction on that element would not impeach the jury's conclusion that the government proved each element of the structuring offense defined by § 6050I(f)(1)(C) beyond a reasonable doubt. Any error in the court's instruction on the filing obligation therefore was not of the "plain" variety, was indeed harmless, and McLamb's objection to the instruction cannot prevail.

C.

In his final attack on the structuring conviction, McLamb contends that the district court violated Fed.R.Evid. 404(b) by admitting similar acts evidence tending to show three vehicle purchases for which no transaction return was filed, each of which involved cash amounts under $10,000 coupled with personal checks and/or other bank instruments, also in denominations under $10,000. * * *

While Fed.R.Evid. 404(b) prohibits the introduction of evidence of other crimes, wrongs, or acts to show bad character or action in conformity with it, it permits the introduction of such evidence to show--among other things--knowledge or intent. The evidence in question must be relevant, necessary, and reliable, but we have otherwise endorsed an inclusionary view of the rule which admits all similar acts evidence except that which proves nothing but criminal disposition. United States v. Masters, 622 F.2d 83, 85 (4th Cir.1980). In this case McLamb's plea of not guilty placed his state of mind directly in issue. If he in fact committed or ratified the similar acts, there can be little doubt that they are both relevant and necessary to the government's effort to demonstrate that McLamb had the necessary specific intent for the structuring and money laundering offenses.

In order to introduce this similar acts evidence, however, the government must demonstrate both that the acts occurred and that McLamb was the actor. In this case, the government undoubtedly proved the former, but its proof of the latter is more attenuated, and the admission of similar acts evidence where no such proof exists may constitute plain error. Here there was no direct evidence demonstrating that McLamb structured the three additional transactions introduced into evidence. There was, however, considerable circumstantial evidence that made his participation in and ratification of the other structured transactions plausible. First, he played a documented role in two of the three similar transactions. Second, he told special Agent Asbridge that he had structured other sales. And finally, there was substantial testimony that McLamb personally participated in an abnormally large number of dealership sales for an owner and frequently handled the proceeds from them personally. While none of this is conclusive, the role of the district court in these cases is limited to determining from all the evidence whether the jury could reasonably find that the defendant committed the similar acts by a preponderance of the evidence. On the record presented here the district court's implicit conclusion that a jury could reasonably do so here was not plainly erroneous.

* * *

IV.

None of McLamb's objections warrants a reversal of his convictions. For the foregoing reasons the district court's judgment is AFFIRMED.

Notes and Question

Section 7203, discussed previously, increases the failure to file penalty from one year to five years in the case of a willful violation of § 6050I.

The regulations describe a "transaction" as "the underlying event precipitating the payer's transfer of cash to the recipient. Transactions include (but are not limited to) [sales and rentals], an exchange of cash for other cash; the establishment or maintenance of or contribution to a custodial, trust, or escrow arrangement; a payment of a preexisting debt; a conversion of cash to a negotiable instrument; a reimbursement of expenses paid; for the making or repayment of a loan. A transaction may not be divided into multiple transactions in order to avoid reporting under this section." Reg. § 1.6050I-1(c)(7)(i).

A "related transaction" is described as a transaction conducted within a 24-hour period, but transactions extending beyond that period are considered related if the "recipient knows or has reason to know that each transaction is one of a series of connected transactions." Reg. § 1.6050I-1(c)(7(ii).

Does the *McLamb* decision raise any direct problems for attorneys?

C. THE BANK SECRECY ACT

The Bank Secrecy Act[2] predates § 6050I and contains some parallel provisions. For instance, a financial institution must file a currency transaction report (CTR) with the IRS for all currency transactions involving more than $10,000. The CTR must be filed within fifteen days of the transaction. Similarly, any person who transports more than $10,000 into or out of the United States must file a declaration with the U.S. Customs Office. Multiple transactions totaling more than $10,000 and occurring within a 24-hour period are considered a single transaction and must be reported. Finally, each person subject to United States jurisdiction who has an interest in a foreign financial account with a value over $10,000 is required to file a report.

Like § 6050I, willful violations of the Bank Secrecy Act carry both civil and criminal penalties. The criminal penalties provide for of up to five years imprisonment plus a fine, although both can be increased if other federal laws are violated as well.

A defense to the criminal penalty is good faith reliance on the advice of counsel.

UNITED STATES v. EISENSTEIN
United States Court of Appeals, Eleventh Circuit, 1984.
731 F.2d 1540.

HILL, CIRCUIT JUDGE.

A jury convicted appellants of conspiracy to defraud the United States, in violation of 18 U.S.C. § 371 (1976), and felonious failure to file currency transaction reports (CTRs) with the Internal Revenue Service, as required by 31 U.S.C. §§ 1059, 1081, 1082 (1976),[1] and regulations promulgated under those provisions. Ample evidence supported the convictions. Neither appellant asserted that the CTRs were actually filed. Nevertheless, we must reverse the convictions because appellants were prohibited from establishing their one plausible line of defense, good faith reliance on advice of counsel.

---

2. The Bank Secrecy Act contains two titles: Title I, codified at Title 12 of the U.S. Code, requires financial institutions to maintain certain records for up to five years; Title II, codified at Title 31 of the U.S. Code, requires financial institutions to report certain foreign and domestic transactions to the government.

1. The applicable provisions of the Currency and Foreign Transactions Reporting Act were originally codified at 31 U.S.C. §§ 1051-83 (1976). After revision and recodification, those provisions now appear at 31 U.S.C. §§ 5301-22 (1982).

I. BACKGROUND

Appellant Ghitis owned and operated a currency exchange business in Cali, Colombia. Ghitis testified that the major thrust of his business concerned buying American dollars and exchanging them for Colombian pesos or for checks or money orders. According to Ghitis, a typical exchange transaction involved four steps: (1) Ghitis agreed to buy American dollars from a seller in Colombia; (2) the seller directed his agent in the United States to deposit the dollars in Ghitis' U.S. bank account; (3) Ghitis verified the deposit; and (4) Ghitis gave the seller pesos or checks to cover the amount deposited. Later, Ghitis hired Appellant Eisenstein to run a branch office for the currency exchange in Miami, enabling Eisenstein, rather than the seller's agent, to make the deposits and report the transactions to Ghitis.

The Government introduced Ghitis' business records for the first eight months of 1981 to show that the exchange business took in more than $240 million during that period. Bank officials in Miami, no doubt alerted by the staggering amounts of money flowing into Ghitis' account, told Eisenstein in January of 1981 that he was required to file CTRs for the currency exchange for any transaction that exceeds $10,000. Eisenstein promised to ask Ghitis about the CTRs. Eisenstein later assured bank officials that he had mentioned the CTRs to Ghitis.

However, no CTRs were filed by Ghitis or Eisenstein. They were thus indicted for failing to report a $1 million transaction that occurred in late February of 1981 and a $1.5 million transaction that occurred in March of 1981. In addition, the indictment alleged a conspiracy to violate the reporting laws and a pattern of illegal activity involving currency transactions in excess of $100,000 in a twelve-month period. Both appellants were convicted on all counts.

II. DISCUSSION

Ghitis and Eisenstein appeal their convictions on several grounds. In light of our decision to reverse, we reach only two of the issues raised by appellants' arguments: (1) whether appellants' currency exchange business was a "domestic financial institution" covered by 31 U.S.C. § 1081; and (2) whether the district court erroneously excluded evidence that appellants relied in good faith on the advice of counsel in refusing to file the CTRs. We conclude that the   statute covers Ghitis' business but that the erroneous exclusion of highly relevant evidence requires reversal.

A.   Domestic Financial Institutions.

By enacting the Currency and Foreign Transactions Reporting Act, Congress authorized the Secretary of the Treasury to require certain types of financial institutions to report currency transactions. See 31 U.S.C. § 1051 (1976)(revised version at 31 U.S.C.§ 5311 (1982)). Under the Act, "domestic financial institutions" must report any exchange of United States currency exceeding the amount prescribed by the Treasury Secretary. See 31 U.S.C. § 1081 (1976) (revised version at 31 U.S.C. § 5313 (1982)). The Secretary has promulgated regulations that require such institutions to report exchanges involving more than $10,000. See 31 C.F.R. § 103.22(a).

Appellants concede that on at least two occasions they completed currency exchange transactions involving more than $10,000. They argue, however, that they were not required to file reports on the transactions because their currency exchange business is not a domestic financial institution within the meaning of the Act. Appellants base their argument on the testimony of Ghitis that all transactions were negotiated and completed in Colombia, leaving nothing for Eisenstein to do in Miami except deposit the money and report to Ghitis in Colombia.

We find appellants' reasoning unpersuasive. The statutory definition of "domestic" is clear: The term "domestic" used in reference to institutions or agencies, limits the applicability of the provision wherein it appears to the performance by such institutions or agencies of functions within the United States. 31 U.S.C. § 1052(f) (1976) (revised version at 31 U.S.C.§ 5312(b) (1982)).[2]

Appellants' currency exchange business performs "functions within the United States" by receiving dollars in the United States, by depositing the money in a U.S. bank, and by relaying information about each transaction from Miami to headquarters in Colombia. Therefore, the business was a "domestic financial institution" under the Act.

B.   Reliance on Advice of Counsel.

Only willful failures to file CTRs are subject to criminal penalties under the Act. See 31 U.S.C. § 1058 (1976) (revised version at 31 U.S.C.§ 5322 (1982)). The law of this circuit is well established that, as it is used in the currency reporting statute, the term "willful require[s] proof of the defendant's knowledge of the reporting requirement and his specific

---

2.   As revised, the statute reads: "[D]omestic financial agency" and "domestic financial institution" apply to an action in the United States of a financial agency or institution. 31 U.S.C. § 5312(b)(1) (1982).

intent to commit the crime." United States v. Granda, 565 F.2d 922, 926 (5th Cir.1978). Congress no doubt made the failure to file CTRs a specific intent crime because, without knowledge of the reporting requirement, a would-be violator cannot be expected to recognize the illegality of his otherwise innocent act.

A defendant charged with violating the reporting statute can attempt to negate proof of specific intent by establishing the defense of good faith reliance on advice of counsel. In order to take advantage of this defense, the defendant must show that he relied in good faith after first making a full disclosure of all facts that are relevant to the advice for which he consulted the attorney. When the defendant presents evidence that he disclosed all relevant facts to his attorney and relied on the attorney's advice based on the disclosure, the trial court must instruct the jury on the defense of good faith reliance on counsel.

Here, the trial court gave appellants' requested instruction on the advice of counsel defense. The jury was told: Among their defenses, the defendants claim that they are not guilty of willful wrongdoing because they acted on the basis of advice from an attorney. If a defendant, before taking any action, sought the advice of an attorney whom he considered competent, in good faith and for the purpose of securing advice on the lawfulness of his possible future conduct, and made a full and accurate report to his attorney of all material facts of which he has the means of knowledge concerning, in this case, the necessity of filing a currency transaction report, that is, IRS Form 4789, and acted strictly in accordance with the advice of his attorney, given following his full report, then the defendant would not be willfully doing wrong in omitting something the law requires, as that term is used in these instructions.

Whether a defendant acted in good faith for the purpose of seeking guidance as to the questions about which he is in doubt, and whether he made a full and complete report to his attorney concerning the necessity of filing a currency transaction report[,] IRS Form 4789, and whether he acted strictly in accordance with the advice received are questions for you to determine.

Clearly, the instructions emphasized the importance of the "full disclosure" requirement. The jury, however, was deprived of evidence that was relevant, indeed crucial, to its determination of whether Ghitis and Eisenstein made a "full and complete report" to their attorney. After defense counsel established that Ghitis and Eisenstein met with their attorney on at least one occasion prior to the acts charged in the indictment, the following colloquy occurred between defense counsel and the attorney on whose advice appellants allegedly relied:

BY MR. TAKIFF (Attorney for Ghitis):

Q. When Mr. Ghitis met with you, did he then indicate to you the type of business he was involved in?

A. Yes, he did.

Q. Mr. Fernandez, on behalf of Mr. Ghitis, as his counsel now, he waives all privilege that might exist with respect to attorney-client. Did Mr. Ghitis discuss with you in any depth the kind of work that he was doing in particular?

MR. SHAPOS (the Prosecuting Attorney):

Objection, your Honor. That would be hearsay.

THE COURT:

The objection is sustained.

BY MR. TAKIFF:

Q. Did you speak with Mr. Ghitis about the kind of work he did?

A. Yes, I did.

Q. Did Mr. Ghitis indicate to you whether or not he was in the currency exchange business?

MR. SAPHOS:

Objection, your Honor; hearsay.

THE COURT:

The objection is sustained.

BY MR. TAKIFF:

Q. How long was your first meeting with Mr. Ghitis?

A. An hour, hour and a half.

Q. Subsequent to that meeting or during that meeting, did there come a time when Mr. Ghitis asked you your advice in terms of his requirement to file certain governmental forms

* * *

A. Well, in the manner that he explained to me the procedures that he was following, how he was operating and the type of business that he was in, I expressed an opinion that I didn't feel that he had to file.

Q. Did he indicate to you, sir, that he was making deposits in a local bank?

A. Yes, he did.

Q. Did he indicate to you, sir, that--

THE COURT:

Counsel, please don't lead this witness. It's a lawyer; you don't have to lead him.

MR. SAPHOS:

Objection as to hearsay.

MR. TAKIFF:

Your Honor, if the Court please, this is, of course, a statement of the defendant.

THE COURT:

I don't care. You can't lead this witness. He is a lawyer; he doesn't have to be led.

MR. TAKIFF:

Yes, Your Honor.

Q. Please go on in your own words and tell the Court and jury what it is that Mr. Ghitis indicated to you his business was.

MR. SAPHOS:

Objection, your Honor; hearsay.

THE COURT:

The objection is sustained.

MR. TAKIFF:

Your Honor, would the Court hear me on that, sir?

THE COURT:

No.

BY MR. TAKIFF:

Q. What, if anything, did Mr. Ghitis tell you concerning currency exchange?

MR. SAPHOS:

Objection, your Honor, hearsay.

THE COURT:

The objection is sustained.

MR. TAKIFF:

Your Honor, if the Court please. Would you hear me on this?

THE COURT

No. [3]

---

3. The trial court missed its best opportunity to avoid its erroneous exclusion of the lawyer's testimony on hearsay grounds when it refused to permit defense counsel to explain this line of questioning. Had the judge heard counsel's explanation, the testimony might have come in and we would not today be required to reverse otherwise valid convictions.

* * *

The Government now concedes that the trial court erred by sustaining the prosecutor's hearsay objections to defense counsel's questions about Ghitis' disclosure to his attorney. The lawyer's testimony was not offered as proof of the matter asserted–i.e., that Ghitis and Eisenstein operated a currency exchange–but as evidence that Ghitis fully disclosed the nature of his business to his attorney.

The testimony was admissible to show the attorney's knowledge and to show Ghitis'compliance with the "full disclosure" requirement of his advice of counsel defense. See Fed.R.Evid. 803(3); cf. United States v. McLennan, 563 F.2d 943, 945-47 (9th Cir.1977) ("When the defense is advice of counsel, the advice given, whether correct or not, and whether recitals in it are true or not, is always admissible.").

Perhaps it is unrealistic to suggest that the operators of a business exchanging nearly a quarter of a billion dollars in one eight-month period could be unaware of, or uncertain about, these reporting requirements. Nevertheless, in our system of American justice, a defendant must be allowed the opportunity to try to establish the suggested unrealism. The lawyer's testimony might not have been credible. Ghitis and Eisenstein might have been fanciful to argue their lack of knowledge about the reporting requirements. Still, the issue was one for the jury to decide on the presentation of all relevant evidence.

While it may stretch credulity to believe that anyone engaged in a business such as appellants' might not know of these reporting requirements, it is equally difficult to believe that the Government's prosecuting attorney was unaware of the relevance of the testimony sought to be elicited from Ghitis' attorney. In order for appellants to establish their good faith reliance on advice of counsel, it was necessarily relevant for the lawyer to tell the jury the nature of the enterprise presented to him by Ghitis and Eisenstein and upon which he gave his advice. It was of scant relevance that the lawyer might have told appellants that they were not required to file CTRs unless it also appeared that the lawyer had been fully advised of the operations of their business. Appellants were required to show that, as to this particular enterprise, the lawyer advised them not to be concerned about the CTRs.

The Government, although conceding that the lawyer's testimony should have been admitted, argues that any error was harmless because Ghitis testified as to the substance of his conversations with the lawyer and, in any case, because the attorneys for both sides argued to the jury as if Ghitis actually made a full disclosure. Hence, the government urges that the lawyer's testimony was merely cumulative of evidence already before the jury and that appellants can show no harm resulting from the trial judge's ruling.

We are not convinced by the Government's "harmless error" argument.[4] As we have said, it might have been unrealistic to suggest that Ghitis and Eisenstein, operators of a business of this magnitude, relied in good faith on the advice of their attorney that they were not required to file these reports. However, even though it might be true that appellants would have been convicted for the lack of credibility of their only defense, the harm in having been denied such a defense is

highlighted by the fact that, weak as it might have been, reliance on advice of counsel was appellants' only defense. The evidence of full disclosure, consisting entirely of Ghitis' unsupported testimony, could have been corroborated by his lawyer. The trial judge's failure to permit this highly relevant testimony cannot be dismissed as harmless error. Therefore, we reverse.

REVERSED.

Notes and Question

Under the Bank Secrecy Act, a "financial institution" includes "any person doing business, whether or not on a regular basis or as an organized business concern, in one or more of the [various capacities] listed * * *." 31 C.F.R. § 103.11(g). One of the capacities listed is "a currency dealer or exchange * * * " which has been defined as "a person who engages as a business in dealing or exchanging currency." See United States v. Cuevas, 847 F.2d 1417 (9th Cir. 1988), cert. denied, 489 U.S. 1012 (1989).

If a small business owner structures cash deposits in order to avoid a tax audit, will that person be guilty of violating the antistructuring provision of the Bank Secrecy Act?

The Supreme Court subsequently decided in Ratzlaf v. United States, 510 U.S. 135 (1994) that term "willfully" in the antistructuring provision (31 U.S.C. § 5324) meant that the Government was required to prove that "the defendant acted with knowledge that his conduct was

---

4. If anything, the Government's "harmless error" theory illustrates how unwise it might have been for the prosecutor to have misled the judge into making this error. By keeping the lawyer's testimony from the jury, the prosecutor excluded evidence tending to support his theory that Ghitis and Eisenstein must have known about the reporting requirements. If the lawyer's testimony agreed with that of Ghitis, then from the extent of the disclosure made by Ghitis to the lawyer the prosecutor might have argued, and the jury might well have agreed, that appellants knew about the CTRs and realized that they were required to file such reports.

unlawful." Congress reversed this decision in the Riegle Community Development and Regulatory and Improvement Act of 1994, which modified § 5324 to omit the term "willfully" and to make structuring a separate offense under § 5324(c). This means that the Government now must establish only that the defendant had the intent to evade the reporting requirement in order to obtain a structuring conviction.

The question is how far does *Ratzlaf* extend? The next case addresses this issue.

UNITED STATES v. REGUER

United States District Court, Eastern District of New York 1995.
901 F. Supp. 515.

MEMORANDUM AND ORDER

SIFTON, CHIEF JUDGE.

Gabriel Reguer ("Reguer"), after pleading guilty to a charge of causing his bank to fail to file currency transaction reports in violation of 31 U.S.C. §§ 5313 and 5322(a), now moves, *pro se*, to expunge his conviction and recover amounts paid for fines and restitution in light of the Supreme Court's decision in Ratzlaf v. United States, 510 U.S. 135, 114 S.Ct. 655, 126 L.Ed.2d 615 (1994). The government opposes Reguer's motion, contending that *Ratzlaf* does not apply to Reguer's conviction and that, even if it did, Reguer would only be entitled to a trial on the underlying information. For the reasons discussed below, Reguer's application is granted. His plea and conviction are vacated* * *.

BACKGROUND

The following facts are drawn from a stipulation signed at the time of sentencing by Reguer and the government setting forth facts to be considered by the Court in sentencing Reguer. In 1986 Reguer sold a counterfeit version of a rare Passover Haggadah to an unsuspecting buyer. The Haggadah recounts the story of the exodus of the Jews from Egypt and is used during the Passover services. Reguer received $59,800 in cash for the Haggadah.

Reguer then went to a bank to deposit the money and was informed that a single deposit of that size would be reported to the federal government. Reguer then "structured" his deposits into smaller amounts so that no individual deposit would trigger the reporting requirements. Reguer contends that he was concerned that a report of the deposits would lead the government to believe that he was a drug dealer.

Subsequently, Reguer made two unsuccessful attempts to sell a counterfeit Haggadah to other buyers.

In 1988 a grand jury indicted Reguer and his brother-in-law for mail fraud. After a jury was selected and the government had made its opening statement, Reguer decided to plead guilty to an information charging him with violating 31 U.S.C. §§ 5313, 5322(a) and 18 U.S.C. § 2 by causing The First National Savings Bank to fail to file a currency transaction report. Reguer maintained, however, that he was merely acting for his brother-in-law and did not know that he was dealing in counterfeits. In addition, Reguer admitted that he "structured" his transaction to avoid the reporting requirements, but contended that he was never aware that it was a crime to do so. Reguer was sentenced to three years of probation and a fine of $150,000. Reguer was also ordered to pay restitution to the victims, but that aspect of the sentence was vacated upon consent of the government because Reguer's offense did not cause direct loss to the victims.

Reguer subsequently sent a letter to the Court seeking to expunge his conviction and recover amounts paid in restitution and towards the fine. Reguer contends that his conviction must be overturned in light of the Supreme Court's holding in *Ratzlaf v. United States* that a defendant is not guilty of structuring under 31 U.S.C. § 5324(3)[1] unless he knew that his actions were illegal. Reguer continues to maintain, as he did at sentencing, that, although he structured his deposits to avoid the reporting requirements, he did not know that he was committing a crime.

Upon receipt of Reguer's letter, the Court directed the government to show cause why the relief requested should not be granted. The government contends that the *Ratzlaf* decision does not apply to Reguer because he was not convicted under 31 U.S.C. § 5324(3) but under 31 U.S.C. § 5313. The government argues that a defendant need only be shown to have been aware of and intended to avoid the reporting requirement in order to prove a willful violation of § 5313. The government asserts that Reguer's conviction may be distinguished from that of the petitioner in *Ratzlaf* because the conduct prohibited by § 5324(3), the section at issue in *Ratzlaf*, is the structuring of transactions and not, as under § 5313, causing a bank to fail to file the required reports. Finally, the government contends that, even if the *Ratzlaf* decision adds the element of knowledge to the crime to which Reguer pleaded guilty, Reguer's relief would be limited to allowing him to

---

1.   Sections 5324(1)-(3) have been recodified as 5324(a)(1)- (3). See *Ratzlaf*, 510 U.S. at ---- n. 5, 114 S.Ct. at 659 n. 5.

withdraw his guilty plea and proceed to trial on the underlying information.

The government states that Reguer would then be entitled to a jury instruction that the government had to prove that Reguer knew that the structuring of his transactions was illegal.

DISCUSSION
* * *

Despite the government's argument to the contrary, *Ratzlaf* has indeed added an element of knowledge to the crime to which Reguer pleaded guilty. In *Ratzlaf*, the Supreme Court held that by virtue of 31 U.S.C. § 5322(a), the enforcement provision of the Currency and Foreign Transactions Reporting Act, a violation of the antistructuring provision of the Money Laundering Control Act of 1986, 31 U.S.C. § 5324(3), occurs only when a defendant has "willfully violated" that section. Section 5322(a) provides:

> A person willfully violating this subchapter [31 U.S.C. §§ 5311 et seq.] or a regulation prescribed under this subchapter (except section 5315 of this title or a regulation prescribed under section 5315) shall be fined not more than $250,000 or imprisoned for not more than five years or both.

The Court held that the willfulness requirement of § 5322(a) requires that the government show an intent to do the illegal act with the knowledge that the act itself was illegal. Thus the Court held that the petitioner in *Ratzlaf* could not have been found guilty of the structuring crime with which he was charged without a showing that he not only knew that he was evading the reporting requirements but that he knew it was a crime to do so.

In reaching its decision, the Court relied upon the fact that various Courts of Appeals had construed the willfulness requirement of §5322(a) to mean that the defendant had to have both knowledge of the reporting requirement and a specific intent to commit the crime, *i.e.*, "a purpose to disobey the law." *Ratzlaf*, 510 U.S. at ----, 114 S.Ct. at 659. In particular, the Court cited approvingly *United States v. Eisenstein*, in which the Eleventh Circuit held that a willful violation of § 5313's reporting requirement for cash transactions requires " 'proof of the defendant's knowledge of the reporting requirement and his specific intent to commit the crime,'" 731 F.2d 1540, 1543 (11th Cir.1984) (quoting United States v. Granda, 565 F.2d 922, 926 (5th Cir.1978)), and United States v. Dichne, 612 F.2d 632, 636 (2d Cir.1979), in which the Second Circuit held that a violation of currency reporting requirements of 31 U.S.C. § 5316 (concerning transporting money into or out of the

United States) was shown only with proof that the defendant knew of the reporting requirement and intended to commit the crime. The Supreme Court held that the "willfulness" requirement of § 5322(a) should be read consistently throughout the statute, rejecting the contention that structuring itself is so inherently evil that the very act of engaging in structuring satisfied the willfulness requirement.

In light of these decisions and, in particular, the decision in *Eisenstein*, the government's argument that the decision in *Ratzlaf* applies only to 31 U.S.C. § 5324 is unpersuasive. Section 5322, the enforcement provision on which the Supreme Court based its decision in *Ratzlaf*, is the same enforcement provision used against Reguer to make his actions a crime. The *Ratzlaf* analysis extends the willfulness requirement to all the subchapters of the Currency and Foreign Transactions Reporting Act, including § 5313.

* * *

Since no evidence was elicited by the Court about petitioner's state of mind (and, in fact, the only information was volunteered by petitioner who stated that he did not know that his conduct was illegal), the retroactive application of *Ratzlaf* to petitioner must be considered. When, as here, the Supreme Court resolves a conflict among circuits as to the interpretation of a statute, the decision is deemed to not be creating new law, but rather as interpreting the law as it should have been interpreted from its inception. See Strauss v. United States, 516 F.2d 980   (7th Cir.1975); see also Gates v. United States, 515 F.2d 73 at 75 (7th Cir.1975) ("A statute does not mean one thing prior to the Supreme Court's interpretation and something entirely different afterwards."). Because knowledge of illegality was, under the Court's holding in *Ratzlaf*, always an element of structuring as a crime, Reguer was convicted without any proof of one of the elements of the crime.

That fact alone, however, does not necessarily render Reguer's conviction invalid. In Sunal v. Large, 332 U.S. 174, 67 S.Ct. 1588, 91 L.Ed. 1982 (1947), the Supreme Court addressed the issue of whether a change in the law can be used as the basis for a collateral attack on a conviction. At trial, petitioners Sunal and Kulick had been denied the opportunity to raise a specific defense. They were convicted and did not appeal. Approximately nine months after their convictions, the Supreme Court held in a case with comparable facts that the petitioners were entitled to defend themselves on the same grounds which were denied to Sunal and Kulick. When the new rule of law was announced, Sunal and Kulick immediately filed writs of habeas corpus, one of which was denied in both the district court and the Court of Appeals. The Supreme Court granted both writs of certiorari. While the Court conceded that the new rule of law would have applied to the petitioners had their cases been on appeal at the time the new rule was announced, the Court denied the petitions, reiterating the general rule that "the writ of habeas corpus will not be allowed to do service for an appeal." *Sunal*, 332 U.S. at 178, 67 S.Ct. at 1590 (quoting Adams v. United States ex re. McCann, 317 U.S. 269, 274, 63 S.Ct. 236, 240, 87 L.Ed. 268 (1942)). While the Court stated that there were exceptional circumstances where a writ should be issued even when the appellate route was not fully pursued, the Court found that Sunal and Kulick's situation was not exceptional. The Supreme Court ruled that, "if [petitioners] had pursued the appellate course and failed, their cases would be quite different. But since they chose not to pursue the remedy which they had * * * they should not be allowed to justify their failure by saying they deemed any appeal futile." *Sunal*, 332 U.S. at 181, 67 S.Ct. at 1592.

In Davis v. United States, 417 U.S. 333, 94 S.Ct. 2298, 41 L.Ed.2d 109 (1974), the Court did apply a change in substantive law retroactively on collateral attack in a case where the petitioner raised the issue on direct appeal. The Court held that *Sunal* cannot be read to stand for the broad proposition that nonconstitutional claims can never be asserted in collateral attacks upon criminal convictions. Rather, the implication would seem to be that, absent the particular considerations regarded as dispositive in that case, the fact that a contention is grounded not in the Constitution, but in the 'laws of the United States' would not preclude its assertion in a § 2255 proceeding. *Davis,* 417 U.S. at 346, 94 S.Ct. at 2305. The Court reasoned that, if due to a novel decision by the Supreme Court a conviction and punishment are for an act that the law does not make criminal, "[t]here can be no room for doubt that such a circumstance 'inherently results in a complete miscarriage of justice' and 'present[s] exceptional circumstances' that justify collateral relief." *Davis*, 417 U.S. at 346-347, 94 S.Ct. at 2305. It has been held that the "logic of the *Davis* opinion applies with equal force to petitions for writ of error *coram nobis* based on non-constitutional changes in the law after trial and appeal." United States v. Mandel, 672 F.Supp. 864 (D.Md.1987); see *Travers*, 514 F.2d at 1173 n. 1 ("Although the *Davis* case arose under 28 U.S.C. § 2255 the standards applied in federal *coram nobis* are similar.")

In *Travers,* the Second Circuit applied a non-constitutional change in the law retroactively to a petitioner who filed a writ of error *coram nobis.* The petitioner was convicted under § 1341, a mail fraud statute, in 1969. Five years later, in United States v. Maze, 414 U.S. 395, 94 S.Ct. 645, 38 L.Ed.2d 603 (1974), the Supreme Court interpreted the statute as only applying to certain types of credit card schemes. Under the interpretation of § 1341 in *Maze*, Travers' act was no longer criminal. He then filed a writ of *coram nobis* seeking to vacate his conviction. The motion was denied, and Travers appealed the decision. The Second Circuit found that, because of the Supreme Court's decision in *Maze*, Travers had been convicted for an act that was not a crime. The Court granted the motion, stating that "the *Davis* holding has been encapsulated as being 'that fundamental notions of fairness are implicated by continued incarceration after a change in judicial interpretation of a statute makes the punished conduct free from sanctions.' " *Travers*, 514 F.2d at 1176.

However, in light of the Court's holding in *Sunal*, the Court of Appeals limited its decision "to defendants who, like Travers, had gone through the full appellate process." *Travers*, 514 F.2d at 1177. The court decided to "leave to another day the determination of the proper result when less has been done." Id. Reguer, unlike Travers, did not make any effort to appeal his conviction. Thus the question is still open whether he can now, having failed to previously pursue his appellate remedies, benefit from the retroactive application of *Ratzlaf*.

In certain circumstances, the Court of Appeals has declined to impose an exhaustion requirement on petitioners who sought the retroactive application of a change in the substantive law despite a failure to pursue the issue on direct appeal.

In Ingber v. Enzor, 841 F.2d 450 (2d Cir.1988), Ingber had been convicted of mail fraud. Two of the counts for which he was convicted involved the deprivation of intangible rights and were not connected to property. However, the Supreme Court in McNally v. United States, 483 U.S. 350, 107 S.Ct. 2875, 97 L.Ed.2d 292 (1987), limited the statute under which he was convicted to the protection of property rights and overruled established Second Circuit precedent to the contrary. Immediately after the *McNally* decision, Ingber filed a habeas petition attacking his mail fraud convictions on the ground that two of the counts for which he was convicted were not connected to property rights. This was an issue which Ingber did not bring up on direct appeal. Noting that by the time of Ingber's trial nearly every appellate decision for in the prior decade had determined that Ingber's conduct was made illegal by the mail fraud statute, the court chose not to penalize him "for failing to challenge such entrenched precedent." *Ingber*, 841 F.2d at 455. The court saw "no value in imposing a responsibility to pursue such a 'patently futile' course," particularly since it would encourage appeals on even well-settled law. Id.

* * *

At the time of petitioner's conviction, the Second Circuit had decided United States v. Heyman, 794 F.2d 788 (2d Cir.1986) two years earlier. In *Heyman*, the court held a person who willfully caused a financial institution to fail to file a currency transaction report was criminally liable. The court held that "willful" required only that the defendant know of the reporting requirement:

> [T]he requirement of § 2(b) that a defendant's acts be 'willful' provides adequate protection for individuals who might unwittingly stumble into a violation of federal law. Village of Hoffman Estates v. The Flipside, Hoffman Estates, Inc., 455 U.S. 489, 499 [102 S.Ct. 1186, 1193, 71 L.Ed.2d 362] (1982)(a scienter requirement may mitigate a law's vagueness with respect to adequacy of notice that specified conduct is proscribed); Boyce Motor Lines v. United States, 342 U.S. 337, 342 [72 S.Ct. 329, 331, 96 L.Ed. 367] (1952) ('requirement of the presence of culpable intent as a necessary element of the offense does much to destroy any force in the argument that application of the Regulation would be so unfair that it must be held invalid').

Id. at 792. The court then said that "[w]e believe this lends persuasive support to the large number of cases holding that any individual, including a customer, may be held criminally liable for willfully causing a financial institution to fail to file CTRs"* * *. The court specifically distinguished other decisions holding that bank customers could not be liable under § 2(b) on the ground that in those cases the banks were never under any obligation to file reports because the customers made only single deposits at each bank for less than $10,000. Id. at 791-92. In particular, the Court distinguished United States v. Anzalone, 766 F.2d 676, 681 (1st Cir.1985), a decision in which the First Circuit noted that the reporting requirements did not specifically prohibit breaking transactions down into smaller amounts to avoid triggering a bank's duty to report. Thus the petitioner was faced with a Court of Appeals precedent holding that a defendant who was aware of the reporting requirement could be found guilty under § 2(b). As the court said in *Loschiavo*, and later in *Ingber*, "To say that in such circumstances the system of justice can provide no remedy because of a court-made rule that failure to take a direct appeal on the specific issue bars all later motions for collateral attack * * * indicates a lack of due process in the judicial system." *Ingber*, 841 F.2d at 455 (quoting *Loschiavo*, 531 F.2d at 666).

Accordingly, for the reasons stated above, the petition is granted; petitioner's conviction and plea of guilty are vacated; * * *.

So Ordered.

Notes and Question

Reguer initially had been indicted on three counts of wire fraud and one count of conspiracy to commit wire fraud. Before the trial began, however, he accepted a plea bargain and pleaded guilty to the lesser offense of failure to file a CTR in violation of §§ 5313 and 5322(a). After Reguer's conviction was vacated in the above case, the government moved to reinstate the original indictment. Reguer then moved to dismiss the indictment as time barred, but this motion was denied. United States v. Reguer, 901 F. Supp. 525 (E.D.N.Y. 1995). In the second trial Reguer was found guilty and a judgment of conviction was entered against him. He appealed on the grounds that the reinstatement of the indictment violated the Double Jeopardy clause of the U.S. Constitution and should have been time-barred because the indictment had been reinstated after the statute of limitations had expired.

The Second Circuit held that the reinstatement of the indictment did not violate the principle of Double Jeopardy because the trial following the reinstatement of the indictment was the result of a voluntary action by Reguer (i.e., the withdrawal of the guilty plea). On the issue of the timeliness of the suit, the court held in favor of Reguer, reasoning that the statute of limitations had expired four years before the reinstatement of the indictment. The court suggested that the government could have avoided this problem by getting a waiver of the statute of limitations as part of the plea agreement. See United States v. Podde, 105 F.3d 813 (2d Cir. 1997).

Dual Liability. The same conduct may be prosecuted under both the false statements provision under 18 U.S.C. § 1001 and the currency transaction provisions. See United States v. Bucey, 876 F.2d 1297 (7th Cir. 1989).

Whistle Blower Protection. The currency transaction provisions contain a protection for whistle blowers who inform on financial institutions. The remedies available to the whistle blower include job reinstatement and the right to bring a civil action in the federal district court. See 31 U.S.C. § 5328.

Can a person who does not have a legal duty to file a CTR nevertheless be held liable for another party's failure to file? See United States v. Tota, 847 F.2d 836 (2d Cir.), cert. denied 488 U.S. 888 (1987).

IV. FEDERAL SENTENCING GUIDELINES IN TAX OFFENSES

In 1984, Congress created the U.S. Sentencing Commission and charged it with drafting sentencing guidelines that would provide greater uniformity, proportionality, and fairness in sentencing. The resulting guidelines apply to all federal prosecutions of crimes committed on or after November 1, 1987. The guidelines provide a sentencing range (expressed in months of imprisonment) based on both the crime for which the offender has been convicted and the criminal history of the offender. In recognition of the seriousness of the tax offenses and the need for greater deterrence, the effect of the Guidelines is to insure that tax offenders are likely to be incarcerated and to serve most of their sentences.

In 2000, the United States Supreme Court held in the case of Apprendi v. New Jersey, 530 U.S. 466, that in order for a sentence to exceed the maximum of the Guideline range, the aggravating factor must be alleged in the indictment and based on a finding by the jury beyond a reasonable doubt, unless the defendant admitted the factor. Four years later, the Court decided Blakely v. Washington, 542 U.S. 296 (2004), which held the Washington State sentencing system unconstitutional on the ground that it was a violation of the Sixth Amendment to increase a criminal sentence by considering factors that had not been admitted by the defendant or proved to a jury. This, of course, raised doubts about the constitutionality of the federal sentencing guidelines.

The following year, the Court resolved those doubts in United States v. Booker, 543 U.S. 220 (2005), when it held that the Guidelines are advisory rather than mandatory and it clarified that appellate review of sentencing decisions is limited to an abuse of discretion standard rather than the de novo standard that previously had applied.

A. DETERMINATION OF TAX LOSS

The first step in computing the sentence is to determine the guideline applicable to the offense (tax offenses are listed in Part T), then to match the conviction to the base offense levels specified in the guideline. Some base levels also take into account certain facts or conduct, referred to as "specific offense characteristics." For instance, most of the tax offenses involve a consideration of the amount of the "tax loss." The higher the tax loss, the greater or more serious the offense level. The judge then applies the permissible aggravating or mitigating adjustments, which consider "all relevant conduct" in the commission of the offense. When the adjusted offense level is determined, the judge then uses a sentencing table in which the 43 offense levels are found on the vertical axis. The horizontal axis contains six criminal history categories. The category into which an offender falls depends on the number and length of prior sentences of imprisonment. The intersection of the two axes produces a sentence range expressed in months of imprisonment.

UNITED STATES v. DELFINO
United States Court of Appeals, Fourth Circuit, 2007.
510 F.3d 468

SHEDD, CIRCUIT JUDGE:

James and Jeaniene Delfino appeal their convictions for tax evasion, mail fraud, and conspiracy to defraud the United States, alleging trial and sentencing errors. Finding no error, we affirm.

I.

A grand jury returned a four-count superseding indictment charging the Delfinos with one count of conspiracy to defraud the United States in violation of 18 U.S.C. § 371; two counts of attempted evasion of payment of income tax in violation of 26 U.S.C. § 7201 and 18 U.S.C. § 2; and one count of mail fraud in violation of 18 U.S.C. § 1341. The case was tried to a jury.

At trial, the evidence tended to show that during the 1990s and 2000s, the Delfinos owned and operated several computer consulting firms which generated their personal income. However, for the years 1993 through 2004, the Delfinos did not file income tax returns. Instead, the Delfinos established several trusts in which they placed their incomes. These trusts likewise failed to file income tax returns or pay income taxes, and the Government alleged that the trusts were formed for the purpose of avoiding the payment of income taxes.

In 1997, the Internal Revenue Service ("IRS") began an audit of the Delfinos and their trusts, but the Delfinos refused to cooperate. As a result, the IRS calculated the Delfinos' income from bank records and prepared the Delfinos' tax returns for the years they had failed to do so. The IRS then assessed tax on the Delfinos' total income for those years without allowing any deductions which they could have claimed. This assessment formed the basis for the tax evasion and the conspiracy-to-defraud counts against the Delfinos.

The Delfinos sought to prove that they had relied in good faith on the advice of Royce McCarley, a trust promoter and self-described tax consultant. The Delfinos presented evidence that McCarley advised them how to structure their trusts, that their trusts could be used to shift liability for income taxes, and that the use of these trusts was legal. Based on this testimony, the district court instructed the jury that it could consider the Delfinos' good-faith defense.

The jury found the Delfinos guilty on all counts. At sentencing, the Delfinos argued that the tax loss contained in the presentence report was erroneous because it did not credit them with the deductions which they could have claimed had they filed their tax returns. The district court rejected this argument and sentenced the Delfinos based on the tax loss calculated in the presentence report.

The Delfinos now appeal, arguing * * * the district court incorrectly calculated their tax loss.

* * *

IV.

Finally, the Delfinos assert that the district court erred in calculating their tax loss for purposes of sentencing by not subtracting from the amount of the loss any deductions they could have claimed for the years in question but did not claim due to their failure to file returns. We review de novo the legal question of whether the tax loss includes deductions. United States v. Moreland, 437 F.3d 424, 433 (4th Cir.2006).

The sentencing guidelines define "tax loss" as: "the total amount of loss that was the object of the offense (i.e., the loss that would have resulted had the offense been successfully completed)." U.S.S.G. § 2T1.1(c)(1). In arguing that the district court erred in its interpretation of this provision, the Delfinos rely on United States v. Schmidt, 935 F.2d 1440 (4th Cir.1991), where we held that it was error to disallow deductions a defendant could have taken under U.S.S.G. § 2T1.3(a) (1989), the then-applicable guideline for conspiracy to impair, impede, or defeat tax defined tax loss. We concluded that "a fair reading of § 2T1.3(a) supports . . . punishing a crime whose gravity is represented by the *actual* loss of tax revenue to the IRS." 935 F.2d at 1451 (emphasis added).

We believe we can no longer rely on *Schmidt*'s interpretation of "tax loss" under the sentencing guidelines. When we decided *Schmidt*, the guidelines defined tax loss as "the greater of: (A) the total amount of tax that the taxpayer evaded or attempted to evade; and (B) the 'tax loss' defined in § 2T1.3." U.S.S.G. § 2T1.1(a) (1989). Section 2T1.3, in turn, defined tax loss as "28% of the amount by which the greater of gross income and taxable income was understated, plus 100% of the total amount of any false credits claimed." U.S.S.G. § 2T1.3(a) (1989).

However, the Sentencing Commission amended the guidelines in 1993 by replacing the definition of "tax loss" on which we relied in *Schmidt* with the current definition found in § 2T1.1(c)(1). The current guideline refers to the "total amount of the loss that was the object of the offense (i.e., the loss that would have resulted had the offense been successfully completed)" rather than "the total amount of the tax that the taxpayer evaded or attempted to evade." The Sentencing Commission explained that it adopted this amendment so that a uniform definition of tax loss would "eliminate[ ] the anomaly of using actual tax loss in some cases and an amount that differs from actual tax loss in others." U.S.S.G.App. C, Amend. 491 (1993). By altering the language which *Schmidt* interpreted and on which it rested, this change in the sentencing guidelines supersedes our holding in *Schmidt*.

With *Schmidt* no longer binding on this point, we conclude that the phrase "object of the offense" means "the *attempted*, or *intended* loss, rather than the *actual* loss to the [G]overnment." United States v. Chavin, 316 F.3d 666, 677 (7th Cir.2002) (emphasis in original). In other words, "the object of the offense" means the loss that would have resulted had a defendant been successful in his scheme to evade payment of tax. Thus, if the Delfinos' scheme had succeeded, the Government would have been deprived of the tax on the amount by which they underreported (or failed to report) their taxable income. This unpaid tax represents the intended loss to the Government. It was this amount which the district court properly used to calculate the tax loss for purposes of sentencing.

The Delfinos next look to U.S.S.G. § 2T1.1(c)(2)(A) for relief.[1] Section 2T1.1(c)(2)(A) provides: If the offense involved failure to file a tax return, the tax loss shall be treated as equal to 20% of the gross income . . . less any tax withheld or otherwise paid, unless a more accurate determination of the tax loss can be made.

The Delfinos claim that the phrase "a more accurate determination of the tax loss" mandates the calculation of deductions before tax loss is determined. The three courts of appeals which have considered this issue have split, with a majority rejecting the position advanced by the Delfinos. Compare *Chavin*, 316 F.3d at 679 (rejecting the inclusion of deductions) and United States v. Spencer, 178 F.3d 1365, 1368 (10th Cir.1999) (same) with United States v. Gordon, 291 F.3d 181, 187 (2d

---

1.   The Government asserts that the Delfinos' reliance on § 2T1.1(c)(2)(A) is misplaced because the Delfinos were sentenced under § 2T1.1(c)(1) (tax evasion) rather than § 2T1.1(c)(2)(A) (failure to file a tax return). While that the Delfinos were, indeed, convicted of tax evasion, § 2T1.1(c)(2)(A) at least arguably applies because the Delfinos' conduct did include "failure to file a tax return." We therefore consider the Delfinos' argument that § 2T1.1(c)(2)(A) entitles them to resentencing.

Cir.2002) (concluding that § 2T1.1(c)(1)(A) requires the calculation of deductions). We agree with and adopt the majority view.

In *Spencer*, the Tenth Circuit stated:

> The sentencing guidelines simply authorize a court to avoid the presumptive tax *rates* if a "more accurate determination of the tax loss can be made." We do not interpret this provision as giving taxpayers a second opportunity to claim deductions after having been convicted of tax fraud. It must be remembered that, in tax loss calculations under the sentencing guidelines, we are not computing an individual's tax liability as is done in a traditional audit. Rather, we are merely assessing the tax loss resulting from the manner in which the defendant chose to complete his income tax returns.

178 F.3d at 1368 (emphasis added). We find this reasoning persuasive. The Delfinos chose not to file their income tax returns. They also chose not to cooperate with the initial IRS audit, at which time they could have claimed deductions to which they were entitled. By doing so, they forfeited the opportunity to claim these deductions. Were the district court now to attempt to reconstruct the Delfinos' income tax returns post hoc, it would be forced to speculate as to what deductions they would have claimed and what deductions would have been allowed. This would place the court in a position of considering the many "hypothetical ways" that the Delfinos could have completed their tax returns. *Chavin*, 316 F.3d at 678. The law simply does not require the district court to engage in this speculation, nor does it entitle the Delfinos to the benefit of deductions they might have claimed now that they stand convicted of tax evasion.

V.

Based on the foregoing, we affirm the Delfinos' convictions and sentences.

AFFIRMED.

Notes and Question

In U.S. v. Mercer, 2010 WL 2104262, the defendant was a tax preparer who had prepared 23 false returns for clients claiming bogus deductions. In addition, he tried to persuade his former clients to lie for him when he learned that the IRS was investigating him. Consequently, he was indicted on 23 counts of aiding and assisting the filing of a false tax return under 26 U.S.C. § 7206(2), and seven counts of obstruction of the due administration of the revenue laws under 26 U.S.C. § 7212(a).

Upon conviction, he was sentenced to 86 months in prison followed by a year of supervised release based on a tax loss of $331,478. He argued that the tax loss had been incorrectly calculated because the government had recovered some of the amounts claimed as deductions by his clients and that these recoveries should have been offset against the amount of the tax loss calculated by the Court. The court noted that § 2T.1. provides special rules for calculating the tax loss and these rules vary according to the offense. Section 2T1.1 provides in part:

(1) If the offense involved tax evasion or a fraudulent or false return, statement, or other document, the tax loss is the total amount of loss that was the object of the offense (i.e., the loss that would have resulted had the offense been successfully completed).

* * * *

(4) If the offense involved improperly claiming a refund to which the claimant was not entitled, the tax loss is the amount of the claimed refund to which the claimant was not entitled.

(5) The tax loss is not reduced by any payment of the tax subsequent to the commission of the offense.

U.S.S.G. § 2T1.1(c). The court held that the provision is clear that any subsequent payment or recovery does not reduce the amount of the tax loss.

1. Review the *Badarracco* case in Chapter 4. Does § 2T1.1 have any implications for *Badarracco?*

2. As the *Delfino* opinion notes, there currently is a split among the circuits as to whether convicted tax offenders should benefit from their unclaimed deductions to reduce their sentences. What are the arguments for and against the allowance of such deductions in the determination of the sentence? See United States v. Hoskins, 2011 WL 3528735 (10th Cir.).

B. SENTENCING UNDER THE GUIDELINES

UNITED STATES v. SEDORE
United States Court of Appeals, Sixth Circuit, 2008.
512 F.3d 819

Sᴇᴀɴ F. Cox, Dɪsᴛʀɪᴄᴛ Jᴜᴅɢᴇ.

* * *

I. BACKGROUND

This action arises out of the sentencing of Defendant for one count of conspiracy to defraud the Internal Revenue Service ("IRS") in violation of 18 U.S.C. § 286; and one count of identity theft in violation of 18 U.S.C. § 1028(a)(7). From 1999 through 2002, Defendant engaged in a scheme to defraud the IRS by preparing false tax returns using stolen names and social security numbers. Defendant's aunt, Katherine King, also participated in the scheme. Some of the names and social security numbers used for the false tax returns were obtained from legitimate tax returns Defendant prepared for friends and acquaintances. One such instance involved an individual named Thaddeus Taylor ("Taylor") who Defendant met while in a rehabilitation facility. Defendant prepared a legitimate tax return for Taylor. However, Defendant filed false tax returns using the names and social security numbers of Taylor's children, which he obtained while preparing Taylor's tax return. Taylor was not a participant in the scheme. Other names and social security numbers were allegedly taken from a local newspaper that published such information in regard to child guardianship matters.

Defendant was incarcerated for most of the conspiracy. Defendant, along with his aunt, claimed approximately $155,869.39 in refunds, and received $51,950.33 from the IRS.

A federal grand jury returned an indictment on December 18, 2003 charging Defendant with: (1) conspiring to defraud the IRS in violation of 18 U.S.C. § 286; (2) making false tax returns to the IRS in violation of 18 U.S.C. § 287; and (3) identity theft in violation of 18 U.S.C. § 1028(a)(7). On March 30, 2004, Defendant pled guilty to Counts I and III, conspiracy to defraud the IRS and identity theft.

Defendant filed four objections to the initial pre-sentence report. He objected to: (1) an enhancement for abuse of trust pursuant to U.S.S.G. § 3B1.3; (2) failure to award a three-level reduction for acceptance of responsibility pursuant to U.S.S.G. § 3E1.1; (3) an enhancement for obstruction of justice pursuant to U.S.S.G. § 3C1.1; and (4) the finding that his crime included 50-250 victims, rather than 10-50 victims pursuant to U.S.S.G. § 2B1.1(b)(2)(A). The district court held a sentencing hearing on July 13, 2004, however the hearing was continued to August 3, 2004, to allow supplemental briefing regarding the applicability of the United States Sentencing Guidelines. At the August 3, 2004 sentencing hearing, the district court accepted Defendant's argument with respect to his objections regarding acceptance of responsibility and agreed with Defendant's argument that there were only 31 victims. The sentencing enhancement for number of victims was calculated based on 31 victims, rather than 50-250 victims. The district court did not find in Defendant's favor on his objections to the obstruction of justice and abuse of trust enhancements. Additionally, the court found Defendant's criminal history was underrepresented and departed upwards. The district court determined that Defendant's offense level was 22 with a criminal history category of VI, resulting in a guideline range of 84 to 105 months. On August 3, 2004, the district court sentenced Defendant to 84 months.

Defendant appealed his sentence, arguing that the district court erred when it: (1) found he has a special skill for purposes of the abuse of trust enhancement; (2) found he obstructed justice; (3) enhanced his base offense level on facts found by a preponderance of the evidence contrary to United States v. Booker, 543 U.S. 220, 125 S.Ct. 738, 160 L.Ed.2d 621 (2005); and (4) departed upward based on his past criminal history. On April 13, 2006, this Court vacated the sentence and remanded the case for re-sentencing pursuant to *Booker*. In addition, we stated that, for guidance, the district court should consider the Tenth Circuit case United States v. Guidry, 199 F.3d 1150, 1160 (10th Cir.1999), with respect to whether Defendant occupied a position of trust. United States v. Sedore, 175 Fed.Appx. 714 (6th Cir.2006).

Defendant's re-sentencing hearing was held on September 5, 2006. In his sentencing memorandum for re-sentencing, Defendant argued, in addition to his previous arguments, that the district court erred when it found at his first sentencing that there were more than ten victims. At the re-sentencing hearing, the district court addressed the abuse of trust enhancement and stated that the enhancement was applied with respect to the identity theft charge, based on Defendant's use of Taylor's children's information. The district court also reaffirmed its finding with respect to the obstruction of justice enhancement. However, the number of victims argument was not addressed at the hearing and Defendant did not raise it. The district court found that Defendant's offense level was 21, including a two point upward departure, and extrapolated a criminal history category of VIII. The advisory sentencing guideline range was 77-96. The district court sentenced Defendant to a term of 84 months.

Defendant filed the instant appeal on September 11, 2006. Defendant argues that the district court misapplied U.S.S.G. § 3B1.3 when it enhanced his sentence based on an abuse of a position of trust. According to. Defendant, the district court erred by imputing the relationship between Taylor and Defendant to Taylor's children and Defendant. Defendant argues that under *Guidry, supra,* the position of trust must be found in relation to the victim of the offense, and there must be pecuniary loss. According to Defendant, the victims of the offense of identity theft are Taylor's children, with whom Defendant did not have a position of trust and who suffered no pecuniary loss. Defendant concludes that because the § 3B1.3 enhancement was predicated on Defendant's relationship with Taylor, whose identity was not stolen, the enhancement is improper. Defendant further contends that the district court misapplied § 2B1.1(B)(2) when it found that the number of victims was between 10-50. Defendant asserts that, consistent with *Guidry*, only the IRS suffered pecuniary loss and is, therefore, the only "victim."

Finally, Defendant asks the Court to order that on remand the re-sentencing range is limited to 51 to 63 months, assuming the Court finds for Defendant on his arguments. In the alternative, Defendant asks that if this Court declines to issue a limited remand, that it require the district court to explain in detail its reasons for the sentence it imposes. Specifically, Defendant is concerned that the district court will choose to further increase the offense level, above the two points added under the previous re-sentencing, out of vindictiveness.

II. STANDARD OF REVIEW

We review a district court's sentencing determination for reasonableness. United States v. Wilms, 495 F.3d 277, 280 (6th Cir.2007). Reasonableness has both substantive and procedural components. United States v. Liou, 491 F.3d 334, 337 (6th Cir.2007). "As to procedural reasonableness, we have held that 'a sentence may be procedurally unreasonable if the district judge fails to consider the applicable Guidelines range or neglects to consider the other factors listed in 18 U.S.C. § 3553(a), and instead simply selects what the judge deems an appropriate sentence without such required consideration.' " Id. "In considering substantive reasonableness, we have held that 'a sentence may be substantively unreasonable where the district court selects the sentence arbitrarily, bases the sentence on impermissible factors, fails to consider pertinent § 3553(a) factors, or gives an unreasonable amount of weight to any pertinent factor.' " *Liou*, 491 F.3d at 337. A rebuttable presumption of substantive reasonableness applies for sentences that fall within the applicable sentencing guideline range. Id. See also Rita v. United States, --- U.S. ----, 127 S.Ct. 2456, 2459, 168 L.Ed.2d 203 (2007)(holding that the courts of appeals may apply a presumption of reasonableness for sentences within the advisory Guidelines range).

III. ANALYSIS

On appeal, Defendant raises three arguments: (1) the district court erred by enhancing Defendant's sentence pursuant to U.S.S.G. § 3B1.3; (2) the district court erred by enhancing Defendant's sentence pursuant to U.S.S.G. § 2B1.1(b)(2)(A); and (3) Defendant's sentence was substantively unreasonable.

A. Sentencing Enhancement Under U.S.S.G. § 3B1.3

Defendant contends that the district court erred by applying a two level enhancement to his offense level pursuant to U.S.S.G. § 3B1.3, which provides in pertinent part, "[i]f the defendant abused a position of public or private trust, or used a special skill, in a manner that significantly facilitated the commission or concealment of the offense, increase by 2 levels."

The district court applied the position of trust enhancement specifically with respect to Thaddeus Taylor:

> I overrule the objection under 3B1.3. Based on the testimony, Thaddeus Taylor was a victim. He gave the names and Social Security numbers of his children based on his trust that Mr. Sedore would be, if not a certified tax preparer, certainly a trusted tax preparer to file tax returns for his children. And Mr. Sedore violated that trust by using the names and Social Security numbers of his children for his own purposes. And, as I said, therefore, the objection is overruled.

[J.A. at 184]. In the initial appeal, we remanded for re-sentencing in light of Booker, and did not address whether the enhancement under § 3B1.3 was proper. However, we did note that:

> [I]n determining whether Sedore abused a position of trust under U.S.S.G. § 3B1.3, the district court may reevaluate whether Sedore occupied a position of trust, reassessing who qualifies as a victim within the meaning of U.S.S.G. § 2B1.1 cmt n. 1-the IRS and/or the individuals whose personal information Sedore used for his scheme. See United States v. Guidry, 199 F.3d 1150, 1160 (10th Cir.1999)(holding that a "position of trust must be found in relation

to the victim of the offense" and concluding that, although the government was the victim of the defendant's false tax-return filings, the defendant did not occupy a position of trust with the government).

Sedore, 175 Fed. Appx. at 174

At the re-sentencing, the parties debated the intent of this Court in directing the district court to consider *Guidry* and the commentary following § 2B1.1.[1] After hearing argument, the district court held:

> I reconsidered it, and I'm going to rule the same way for the same reasons. And that is, if you take a look at Count 4, the theft is of the identity of one or more persons who he used without lawful authority with the intent to commit and aid and abet a violation of federal law. Forget all of the people whose names were in the newspapers where he got the information. Focus simply on Thaddeus Taylor and his family. That was an abuse of a position of trust for Thaddeus Taylor and his family, where he got the information by preparing income tax returns for Taylor at Mr. Taylor's request and then utilized the information using the names of the children in the Taylor family to line his own pockets. And in my judgment, that's exactly what identity theft is. It might not be a pecuniary loss, but 3B1.1, as pointed out by the government, doesn't require it for that particular enhancement. So that's the ruling.

[J.A. at 210-211].

The district court held that the requirement of pecuniary loss in U.S.S.G. § 2B1.1 does not apply to U.S.S.G. § 3B1.3. The district court also found *Guidry* inapplicable because in the instant case, the § 3B1.3 enhancement applied based on the identity theft count, not the false claims count. Thus, the district court held that Defendant used his position of trust with Taylor to steal the identities of Taylor's children, for use in filing false tax returns. Regardless of whether the children suffered a pecuniary loss, the district court found they were victims, justifying application of the enhancement.

In the instant appeal, Defendant contends the enhancement should not apply because he did not hold a position of trust with Taylor's children, and they are the only victims of the charged offense. The plain language of § 3B1.3 states that "[i]f the defendant abused a position of public or private trust . . . in a manner that significantly facilitated the

---

1.   Section 2B1.1 cmt n. 1 provides that for purposes of that section, "victim" means "(A) any person who sustained any part of the actual loss determined under subsection (b)(1); or (B) any individual who sustained bodily injury as a result of the offense." Note 3 of the same commentary defines "actual loss" as "the reasonably foreseeable pecuniary harm that resulted from the offense." U.S.S.G. § 2B1.1 cmt n. 3.

commission or concealment of the offense," the enhancement applies. Defendant does not deny that he held a position of trust with Taylor, or that he stole Taylor's children's personal information. Under the plain language of § 3B1.3, Defendant abused his position of trust with Taylor in a manner that significantly facilitated the offense of identity theft with respect to Taylor's children-and the enhancement should apply. However, there is a line of cases that seemingly narrows the broad application of this enhancement. This Circuit has held that "[i]n order for the abuse of a position of trust enhancement to be applied to a defendant, the evidence must show that the defendant's position with the *victim of the offense* significantly facilitated the commission of the offense." United States v. Moored, 997 F.2d 139, 145 (6th Cir.1993)(emphasis added). See also United States v. White, 270 F.3d 356, 371 (6th Cir.2001)(citing *Moored*)("The abuse-of-trust enhancement may only be applied where the defendant abused a position of trust *with the victim of his charged conduct*.")(emphasis added); and United States v. Duerson, 25 F.3d 376, 383 (6th Cir.1994)("We held in *Moored* that a defendant's offense level could not be increased for abuse of a position of trust unless *the person or entity with which the defendant held such a position was a victim or intended victim of the offense*.")(emphasis added).

It is on *Moored, supra,* and its progeny, that Defendant relies for his argument that the enhancement should not apply. In *Moored,* the defendant used his position as a trustee at a local college to bolster his credibility with lenders and fraudulently obtain a loan. The defendant pled guilty to fraud charges. The district court applied a two-level enhancement for abuse of a position of trust pursuant to § 3B1.3. The district court held "Mr. Moored's affiliation with Jordan College as an officer, trustee, and/or affiliate was used to facilitate the commission of the fraudulent documents that were sent through the wire, and therefore, the two point addition under 3B1.3 is clearly in order in this particular matter." *Moored,* 997 F.2d at 142.

This Court agreed that in the commission of the offense, the defendant abused his position of trust with the college. However, this Court disagreed that the abuse was sufficient to warrant application of the enhancement for abuse of a position of trust. The defendant argued that his position was "no different from any other loan applicant's" and that finding his crime worthy of the abuse of trust enhancement "would permit an enhancement for any defrauding borrower who, in the course of loan negotiations, discloses a position of trust, even if that position had nothing to do with the loan decision." Id. at 144. The *Moored* court noted that the situation in which a defendant abused a position of trust with someone other than the victim of the charged conduct was novel. The

Moored court found that the district court's approach was "overly broad." Id. at 145. The court held:

> Applying the standard that the lower court applied, a sentencing court would enhance the sentence of virtually every defendant who occupied any position of trust with anyone, victim or otherwise. An argument could be made in virtually every case that the position of trust, though not directly a part of the offense conduct, had some remote connection with the defendant's crime.
>
> In order for the abuse of a position of trust enhancement to be applied to a defendant, the evidence must show that the defendant's position with the victim of the offense significantly facilitated the commission of the offense. In this case, the Defendant held no position of trust with the intended victims of his offense. Accordingly, we find that the district court incorrectly enhanced Defendant's offense level.

Moored, 997 F.2d at 145.

In this case, the district court stated that it applied the § 3B1.3 enhancement based on an abuse of Defendant's position of trust with Taylor, specifically in regards to the identity theft of Taylor's children's information. The first issue is whether Defendant held a position of trust with the victims of the charged offense of identity theft, i.e. Taylor's children. The government argues that the relationship between Defendant and Taylor should be imputed to Taylor's children, who relied upon their father's relationship with his tax preparer to protect their confidential information.

We agree with the government's argument under these particular circumstances. It is undisputed for purposes of this appeal, that Defendant held a position of trust with Taylor. Defendant, in the course of preparing legitimate tax returns for Taylor, obtained Taylor's children's personal information and used that information to file false tax returns. Where a parent provides the personal information of his children for the purpose of tax preparation, it is reasonable that any trust relationship between the parent and the preparer extends to the children and the preparer. This is different than the situation addressed in *Moored*. In *Moored*, this Court was concerned with application of § 3B1.3 where the position of trust relied on to support the enhancement had nothing to do with the conduct that was the substance of the charged offense. This Court sought to prevent application of the enhancement where the relied on position of trust had only "some remote connection with the defendant's crime." *Moored*, 997 F.2d at 145. Such is not the case here. Defendant's position of trust with Taylor was his sole means of gaining Taylor's children's personal information. Further, Taylor only provided his children's information to facilitate legitimate tax return preparation. Under these circumstances, the district court was correct in extending the position of trust Defendant held with Taylor to Taylor's children.

In his Reply, Defendant also appears to argue that Taylor's children cannot be considered victims for purposes of § 3B1.3 because they did not suffer pecuniary loss. Nothing in the language of U.S.S.G. § 3B1.3, or the commentary following it, indicates that pecuniary loss is a necessary element for application of the enhancement. The definition of "victim" provided in the commentary following § 2B1.1, cited by Defendant, specifically states the definition is for purposes of that guideline. U.S.S.G. § 2B1.1 cmt n. 1.

In this case, Defendant does not offer any basis for imposing a requirement that the victim for purposes of a § 3B1.3 enhancement must suffer pecuniary loss, and we do not find any.

Accordingly, application of the two point enhancement pursuant to U.S.S.G. § 3B1.3 was proper.

B. Sentencing Enhancement Under U.S.S.G. § 2B1.1(b)(2)(A)

Defendant contends the district court erred by applying a two level enhancement under U.S.S.G. § 2B1.1(b)(2)(A). Section 2B1.1(b)(2)(A) provides that when 10 or more victims are involved, the offense level is increased by 2 levels. For purposes of § 2B1.1, "victim" is defined as "(A) any person who sustained any part of the actual loss determined under subsection (b)(1); or (B) any individual who sustained bodily injury as a result of the offense." U.S.S.G. § 2B1.1 cmt n. 1. "Actual loss" is defined as "the reasonably foreseeable pecuniary harm that resulted from the offense." Id. at cmt n. 3. At the initial sentencing on August 3, 2004, counsel for Defendant stated that it is his position "and Mr. Sedore's position that when we totaled up the information submitted from the Probation Department, that there were thirty-one actual victims . . . [s]o it was our position that the actual number of victims itself was thirty-one.". The court accepted Defendant's admission that the number of victims was 31 and applied a two level enhancement.

Following this Court's ruling in Defendant's first appeal, as outlined above, the case was remanded for re-sentencing. In his re-sentencing memorandum, filed June 30, 2006, Defendant asserted that this Court suggested that the IRS was the victim, rather than the individual taxpayers. Based on Defendant's interpretation of this Court's "suggestion," Defendant contends that the number of victims is one.

However, Defendant did not raise the issue at the re-sentencing hearing and it was not addressed by the district court.

The government argues that Defendant waived any argument that the IRS was the only victim because he did not raise the issue in his first appeal to this Court and because Defendant is bound by his admission at his initial sentencing that there were 31 victims.

We agree that Defendant is bound by his admission. It would be unreasonable to allow a defendant to admit to a particular fact during sentencing, and then argue against the existence of that fact on appeal. Further, Defendant did not present any evidence to this Court that he argued in his initial appeal that the enhancement pursuant to § 2B1.1(b)(2)(A) was improper because the IRS was the only victim. If Defendant did not raise the argument in his first appeal, he is now foreclosed from making such a claim. Generally, "on remand following a direct appeal, a district court can consider de novo any arguments regarding sentencing if the remand order does not limit its review." United States v. Saikaly, 207 F.3d 363, 369 (6th Cir.2000). However, "when a party fails to seek review of a district court's final order, it is barred from reasserting that issue in any subsequent appeals occurring in that case." United States v. McKinley, 227 F.3d 716, 718 (6th Cir.2000). In *McKinley*, the Court ruled that the government waived its argument for application of a sentence enhancement that was available in the first appeal but not pursued. Id. at 718-719. "While the district court may entertain any issues it feels are relevant to the overall sentencing decision (following a general remand), this does not give the parties license to re-assert issues that they should have raised during an earlier appeal." Id. at 718. The court noted that the waiver doctrine "exists to forestall this kind of perpetual litigation by notifying parties that they will forfeit their claims if they fail to seek review in the first appeal." Id. at 719. Accordingly, because Defendant admitted at his initial sentencing on August 3, 2004 that the number of victims was 31, and does not offer evidence that an argument to the contrary was raised on his appeal of that sentence, Defendant is bound by his admission and any argument to the contrary is waived.

C. Substantive Reasonableness

Defendant argues that his sentence is substantively unreasonable because Defendant's "conduct does not warrant a sentence of this length . . .". However, Defendant's brief was submitted before the Supreme Court decided *Rita, supra,* and Gall v. United States, --- U.S. ----, 128 S.Ct. 586, 169 L.Ed.2d 445 (2007). In *Rita* and *Gall*, the Supreme Court upheld the application of a presumption of reasonableness to sentences that fall within the applicable Sentencing Guidelines range. *Liou*, 491 F.3d at 338 (citing *Rita*, 127 S.Ct. at 2459). Defendant does not convince us that this presumption of reasonableness does not apply to his case simply by stating that his sentence was too long. See United States v. Crowell, 493 F.3d 744, 751 (6th Cir.2007)("[The defendant] contends the sentence is longer than it need be, but the 'mere allegation that the sentence imposed is greater than necessary to achieve the goals of punishment in § 3553(a) is insufficient to rebut the presumption of reasonableness.' "). Defendant fails to offer any explanation as to why 84 months is an unreasonably lengthy sentence. Accordingly, we find that the sentence imposed by the district court was not unreasonable.

IV. CONCLUSION

For the foregoing reasons, we AFFIRM the decision of the district court.

CLAY, CIRCUIT JUDGE, concurring.

* * *

I [f]ind Judge Merritt's explanation of the ideal sentencing procedure to be inconsistent with the Supreme Court's most recent sentencing pronouncements. Contrary to what Judge Merritt suggests, the Supreme Court in *Gall* did not direct district court judges to start only with the Guidelines base offense level and then make adjustments to that level based upon his or her own sentencing discretion. See Merritt, J., dissenting at 833. Rather, the Supreme Court directed district judges to "begin all sentencing proceedings by correctly calculating the applicable Guidelines range" which would then serve as the "starting point and the initial benchmark" for sentencing. *Gall*, 128 S.Ct. at 596. This "applicable Guidelines range" includes not only the base offense level recommended by the Guidelines, but also any applicable adjustments to that level which the Sentencing Commission has recommended in the Guidelines. Thus, contrary to what Judge Merritt claims, post-*Booker*, sentencing judges must begin their sentencing deliberations by properly calculating the entire recommended Guidelines sentencing range, including any sentencing enhancements, not just the Guidelines-recommended base offense level. However, Judge Merritt is correct in emphasizing that after judges have determined this advisory Guidelines range, they must "then consider all of [the other] § 3553(a) factors" and "make an individualized assessment based on the facts presented." Id. at 596-97. In this process, judges must use their discretion and should not unreflectively impose a within-Guidelines sentence. During this "individualized assessment" process, sentencing judges should not permit the Guidelines to be a strait-jacket which compel a particular sentence, but rather, as their name suggests, a helpful "guide" for crafting a sentence which is "sufficient but not greater than necessary to comply with the purposes" of sentencing set forth in § 3553(a).

Inasmuch as the judge in this case engaged in such an "individualized assessment" after properly calculating the advisory Guidelines range, including the applicable sentencing enhancements under the Guidelines, I am not persuaded that he committed a reversible sentencing error and, accordingly, I join Judge Cox in affirming Defendant's sentence.

MERRITT, CIRCUIT JUDGE, dissenting.

Except for those judges and lawyers who prefer to continue routine conformity to the old pre-*Blakely-Booker* process of guideline sentencing, there is widespread disapproval of the present muddled system. This is because, in the main, the old system is just continuing on as though nothing had happened-continuing under the pretext that the guidelines are only "advisory" instead of being considered only as a starting point against the backdrop of the more sensible and humane penalogical goals set out in § 3553(a), Title 18. This case is one more example of the continuing problem, the problem of guidelineism, or "guidelinitis," the inability of most federal courts to break their habit of mechanically relying just on the guidelines alone.

By ratcheting up the sentence, as is typical under the guidelines, piling aggravator on aggravator, the District Court (as though *Booker* had never been decided), went from a base offense level of 6 with criminal history Category VI (corresponding to defendant's guilty plea)-carrying a penalty of 12-18 months-to offense level 22. It then sentenced him to 7 years-5 times more than the base offense level corresponding to the facts of the guilty plea.

Such harsh sentences are par for the course under the guidelines. The sentencing court imposed a harsh sentence without seriously considering mitigating family and personal factors or rehabilitation possibilities-all in line with the U.S. Sentencing Commission rules against the consideration of such individual factors in Chapters 5H and 5K of the Guidelines.[1] This refusal to seriously consider individual factors,

---

1.   The Commission's "not relevant" rule against consideration of a host of mitigating factors such as age, physical condition, education, employment, military, public service, good works, disadvantaged upbringing, addiction, mental illness, family ties, and rehabilitation possibilities are directly contrary to the Supreme Court's interpretation of the Eighth Amendment in Lockett v. Ohio,

including rehabilitation, has been the most important characteristic of the work of the Sentencing Commission. From the beginning, the guidelines have emphasized collectives, not individuals; and individualized sentencing by federal judges, the weighing of aggravators and mitigators through a process of dialectic reflection and reconciliation, has become a relic of the past. The creation of these guidelines involved the breakdown of behavior into smaller and smaller parts and categories of aggravators or enhancements without consideration of other important individual factors.

The ratcheting-up process in the instant case was all based upon judicial findings of fact.[2] It is obvious to anyone who has watched this disingenuous process develop that the present system is completely inconsistent with the *Blakely* and *Booker* opinions, which confine judicial fact finding to those facts carrying out a jury verdict or plea of guilty. As the Court said in *Cunningham*, "under the Sixth Amendment, any fact that *exposes* a defendant to a greater *potential* sentence must be found by a jury, not a judge." Cunningham v. California, --- U.S. ----, 127 S.Ct. 856, 863-64, 166 L.Ed.2d 856 (2007) (emphasis added). This statement of the Sixth Amendment rule was first stated in *Blakely* even more clearly and then repeated in *Booker* and *Rita*. It is still unclear, however, whether the Supreme Court is going to abide by or erode and then reject the clear holding of *Blakely*:

---

438 U.S. 586, 98 S.Ct. 2954, 57 L.Ed.2d 973 (1978), and Eddings v. Oklahoma, 455 U.S. 104, 102 S.Ct. 869, 71 L.Ed.2d 1 (1982), requiring states in sentencing to consider such mitigating factors. The Sentencing Commission, and now the federal courts at its direction, refuse to take into account the mitigating and humanizing factors that Lockett and Eddings require. There is no indication that any such factors were considered or influenced the sentence in this case.

2. It is significant that in the recent cases, Rita v. United States, --- U.S. ----, 127 S.Ct. 2456, 168 L.Ed.2d 203 (2007), Gall v. United States, --- U.S. ----, 128 S.Ct. 586, 169 L.Ed.2d 445 (2007), and Kimbrough v. United States, --- U.S. ----, 128 S.Ct. 558, 169 L.Ed. 481 (2007), in which the Supreme Court upheld the district court sentences, the sentence was within or below the guideline range corresponding to the jury verdict or guilty plea. There was no ratcheting up of the sentence by enhancements outside of the initial sentencing range. There were no judicial fact findings that raised the sentence, and there is no Supreme Court case that allows a court to use guideline enhancements to raise a sentence above the guideline range corresponding to the jury verdict or plea. So when the Supreme Court uses the phrase "within the guidelines," as it does frequently in these cases, it is not yet clear what precisely it means or that it means enhanced sentences based on findings of facts by the judge over and above the facts found by the jury verdict or the guilty plea.

The Supreme Court did not say in *Gall* or *Rita* that the sentencing judge should "start" the sentencing process by enhancing the sentence aggravator by aggravator, as happened in the instant case. The Court said that the sentencing judge should begin with the "applicable Guidelines range" which in *Gall* was the initial base offense level corresponding to facts admitted by the guilty plea, which carried a range of 30 to 37 months. There is no language in *Gall* or *Rita* that requires appellate or district judges to "begin" with the enhancement process. That process is directly contrary to the language quoted below in *Blakely* that a "judge exceeds his proper authority" by basing a higher sentence on judicial findings outside the jury verdict.

[T]he *'statutory maximum' for Apprendi purposes* is the maximum sentence a judge may impose *solely on the basis of the facts reflected in the jury verdict or admitted by the defendant*. In other words, the relevant 'statutory maximum' is not the maximum sentence a judge may impose after finding additional facts, but the maximum he may impose without any additional findings. When a judge inflicts punishment that the jury's verdict alone does not allow, the jury has not found all the facts 'which the law makes essential to the punishment,' and the judge exceeds his proper authority.

Blakely v. Washington, 542 U.S. 296, 303-04, 124 S.Ct. 2531, 159 L.Ed.2d 403 (2004) (emphasis added). What is clear is that the district courts and the courts of appeals, as the majority in this case expressly acknowledges, are not applying this rule and do not believe the Supreme Court actually intends to enforce it. The view seems to be that the remedial opinion in *Booker* is inconsistent with this rule, and so the rule may be simply disregarded in practice.[3] Justice Scalia predicted such a result in *Booker*, noting that the Court's remedial scheme risked preserving "de facto mandatory guidelines by discouraging district courts from sentencing outside Guidelines ranges." United States v. Booker, 543 U.S. 220, 313, 125 S.Ct. 738, 160 L.Ed.2d 621 (2005) (Scalia, J., dissenting). Indeed, this de facto, mandatory application of the guidelines runs afoul of the Supreme Court's admonition that "*Booker*'s remedy for the Federal Guidelines . . . is not a recipe for rendering our Sixth Amendment case law toothless." Cunningham v. California, --- U.S. ----, 127 S.Ct. 856, 870, 166 L.Ed.2d 856 (2007). Many of the members of the Supreme Court have recognized in opinions at one time or another the unprincipled, inconsistent nature of the sentencing game in which we are now engaged.[4]

---

3. The empirical data on this point are clear. From 1990-2003, 90.6% of offenders received sentences adhering to the Guidelines range. In 2006, after *Booker* purportedly made the Guidelines "advisory," 86.3% of offenders still received sentences in the Guidelines range, a range including judicial enhancements. Furthermore, appellate review of these within-Guidelines sentences has not changed post-*Booker*, as circuit courts have affirmed 99.9% of within-Guidelines sentences. Conversely, Circuit courts reversed below Guidelines sentences almost 85% of the time, while only reversing above-Guidelines sentences in less than 5% of the cases. See James Bilsborrow, Note, Sentencing Acquitted Conduct to the Post-*Booker* Dustbin, 49 Wm. & Mary L.Rev. 289, 314-15 (2007).

4. See, for example, the separate opinions of Justice Stevens ("I am not blind to the fact" that "many federal judges continue to treat the Guidelines as virtually mandatory"); Justices Scalia and Thomas, ("no one knows-and perhaps no one is meant to know-how advisory Guidelines . . . will function in practice"); Justice Souter ("consistency began to falter," the "gravitational pull to now-discretionary Guidelines . . . preserve the very feature . . . that threaten to trivialize the jury right" so that it is "fair to ask just what has been accomplished"). See *Rita*, --- U.S. ----, 127 S.Ct. 2456, 2474, 2475, 2487-88, 168 L.Ed.2d 203.

The only way to begin to return the process to something consistent with the Sixth Amendment and with the concept of individualized sentencing is to recognize and insist that we adhere to two overriding principles: First, that judicial fact finding and the length of a sentence be limited somewhere within the base-offense-level, guideline range corresponding to the jury verdict or the plea, unless the sentencing judge explains why the concepts of general and individual deterrence should require a longer sentence for the particular individual and outweigh the mitigating circumstances of the case (including factors like age, addiction, and family responsibility deemed irrelevant by the Sentencing Commission in Chapters 5H and 5K), as well as the likelihood of successful rehabilitation. Second, that the sentencing judge explain the weighing process outlined above (taking into account moral culpability, general and special deterrence, mitigating circumstances and rehabilitation) so that the sentence and its explanation comply with the "overarching provision instructing district courts to 'impose a sentence . . . not greater than necessary' to accomplish the goals of sentencing," Kimbrough v. United States, --- U.S. ----, 128 S.Ct. 558, 570, 169 L.Ed.2d 481 (2007) (quoting 18 U.S.C. § 3553(a)). This "overarching provision," enacted by Congress in § 3553(a), sets a humane, balancing standard that the sentencing judge should keep as the Golden Mean governing the judicial reflection necessary in each sentencing case to reconcile contrary factors and arguments in the weighing process in order to arrive at a fair sentence.

In other words, the sentencing judge should start with the base offense level corresponding to the facts found by the jury verdict or admitted by the guilty plea. The sentencing judge should not go up or down from that point unless in his or her own mind the weighing process of the two overriding principles stated above requires it. The judge should not engage in guidelineism, adjusting the sentence up or down just because the guidelines say so, as occurred in the instant case, but rather because the judge's own sense of justice, upon reflection, leads to a different result than the beginning, base-offense level. This allows the guidelines to play a pivotal role to begin with but requires the judge to use his or her own mental faculties and best judgment, just as judges did in the days of indeterminate sentencing before the mandatory federal sentencing guideline era.

The job of the Court of Appeals should be only to see that the federal sentencing judge (1) starts at the right place in the reasoning process (at the base offense level corresponding to the jury verdict or guilty plea), as required by the Sixth Amendment as interpreted by *Blakely* and *Booker*, and (2) engages in a general process of serious dialectical reflection and reconciliation, as evidenced by the reasons given for deviating from the starting point established under Sixth Amendment constraints. This process should put an end to the rote, ratcheting-up process that now characterizes the sentencing process, a process based on the Commission's rule that mitigating factors are "not relevant."

This modified system based on these two principles is, more or less, what the system would have looked like in the beginning if the Guidelines were truly "guidelines" rather than mandatory rules. If the Commission, in the beginning, as many judges and lawyers recommended, had adopted guidelines to assist judges rather than to discipline and correct judges this modified system would have perhaps provided a workable system. I myself testified before the Commission advising it not to saddle the judiciary with mandatory rules that are constitutionally suspect because such rules would most likely eliminate individualized sentencing and full consideration of mitigating factors. The Commission, however, believed that federal judges could not be trusted to exercise discretion properly and that harsher sentencing rules must be imposed on judges in order to insure longer sentences and collective uniformity. The current Guidelines that ratchet up sentences without considering mitigating factors or rehabilitation are the result.

The modified system described above is a different process of sentencing from either pure indeterminate sentencing, as it operated before the guidelines, or the mandatory, rote guideline process that prevailed before the Sixth Amendment was recognized as a limitation on fact finding. Hopefully, such a modified system would begin to provide a balance between the collectivized, sentencing process of lock-step, upward adjustments heretofore required by the Commission, and the thoughtful individual sentencing by federal judges that was the ideal behind the federal sentencing system used so effectively (in my opinion) for 200 years since the first Congress enacted the first sentencing law, 1 Stat. 112, ch. 9 (1790).[5] Further, a system that incorporates facets of indeterminate sentencing preserves the historical role of judges as sentencing experts and the jury as fact finder. Sentencing procedures based on these roles were never challenged as undermining the Sixth

---

    5.   The system of jury fact finding and individualized sentencing by judges enacted by the First Congress was the system developed to reconcile justice with mercy by our judicial forebearers as the English system of criminal law-developed particularly after the demise of the prerogative courts of Star Chamber and High Commission following the English civil war, the Glorious revolution of 1688, the English Bill of Rights of 1689, and the creation of an independent judiciary in the Judges' Bills of 1692 and 1701. See Harold J. Berman, Law and Revolution II, The Impact of the Protestant Reformation on the Western Legal Tradition, 226-28, 306-29 (Harvard Univ. Press 2003); Blackstone, Commentaries on the Laws of England, Book IV, Chap. 29, 368-82 (Legal Classics Library Ed. 1983). The Sentencing Guidelines removed individualized sentencing by judges that had existed in Anglo-American law for more than three centuries.

Amendment's right to a jury trial because judges did not function as objective fact finders and judge-found facts did not carry determinate consequences.

Such a modified system includes an element of democratic, legislative control over sentencing while keeping elements of individualized sentencing from the old system. Such a modified system may be strongly resisted by prosecutors and the Department of Justice officials who have now become accustomed to controlling sentencing through the charging process, the release of enhancement information to probation officers and plea bargaining. Back in my day as U.S. Attorney 40 years ago, prosecutors were viewed solely as parties to the case and not entitled to control the length of the sentence. Removing control of sentencing from the prosecutorial arm of the government should be viewed as a step forward, although it is really a step back in history to restore the benefits of individualized sentencing practiced by English and American judges since the beginning of the 18th Century.

The modified scheme proposed above squares with the most recent Supreme Court decision, Gall v. United States, --- U.S. ----, 128 S.Ct. 586, 597, 169 L.Ed.2d 445 (2007), in which the Court instructed district court judges to "make an individualized assessment based on the facts presented" with the Guidelines operating as the "initial benchmark" but "not the only consideration." In *Gall*, the Supreme Court affirmed the district court's sentence of thirty-six months probation, a punishment based upon the district judge's individualized evaluation of the factors under 18 U.S.C. § 3553(a)-particularly rehabilitation-and rejected the appellate court's rote application of the Guidelines. Moreover, this approach lessens the likelihood of as-applied Sixth Amendment challenges, which, as Justice Scalia points out, are still available. Id. at 603 (Scalia, J., concurring).

Unfortunately, the sentencing process in this case was just a repeat of guidelinitis, the system of rote sentencing in which the sentencing judge ratchets up the sentence instead of engaging in anything close to the deliberative or reflective process outlined by the two overriding principles stated above. Hence, I would reverse and remand the case for resentencing in compliance with the two overriding principles stated above. The sentencing court should start with the guideline sentence corresponding to the guilty plea, take a look at how the guidelines would operate from that point and then engage in the weighing and explanatory process outlined above without feeling an obligation to reach a result consistent with the Commission's guideline structure or policies. After finding the beginning guideline sentence, it is up to the judge to act like a common law judge of old engaged in the same process that prevailed in the federal system after 1790 but before the failed, 20-year experiment in mandatory guideline sentencing.

Notes

Under 18 U.S.C. § 3553(a), a sentencing court is required to consider consider:

(1) the nature and circumstances of the offense and the history and characteristics of the defendant;

(2) the need for the sentence imposed-

(A) to reflect the seriousness of the offense, to promote respect for the law, and to provide just punishment for the offense;

(B) to afford adequate deterrence to criminal conduct;

(C) to protect the public from further crimes of the defendant; and

(D) to provide the defendant with needed educational or vocational training, medical care, or other correctional treatment in the most effective manner;. . ..

18 U.S.C. § 3553(a)(1)-(2).

In United States v. Saac, 2011 WL 414995 (2011), the Eleventh Circuit noted that it used a two-prong test to determine whether a sentence is procedurally and substantively unreasonable.

First, we "ensure that the district court committed no significant procedural error, such as failing to calculate (or improperly calculating) the Guidelines range, treating the Guidelines as mandatory, failing to consider the § 3553(a) factors, selecting a sentence based on clearly erroneous facts, or failing to adequately explain the chosen sentence-including an explanation for any deviation from the Guidelines range." [United States v. Shaw, 560 F.3d 1230, 1237 (11th Cir. 2009)] (quoting *Gall*, 552 U.S. at 51, 128 S.Ct. at 597). "[T]he second step is to review the sentence's 'substantive reasonableness' under the totality of the circumstances, including 'the extent of any variance from the Guidelines range.' " Id. (quoting *Gall*, 552 U.S. at 51, 128 S.Ct. at 597). "[T]he party who challenges the sentence bears the burden of establishing that the sentence is unreasonable in the light of both th[e] record and the factors in section 3553(a)."

2011 WL 414995 at *7.

Chapter 10

CRIMINAL TAX INVESTIGATION AND PROSECUTION

> As a cop, the IRS has to balance customer service and law enforcement. Stated another way, the agency's motto could be: "We're your friend. But if you push that friendship too far, we'll ruin your life and then throw you in jail."
>
> — Christopher Bergin[1]

I. INITIATION OF A CRIMINAL INVESTIGATION

In most nontax criminal cases the authorities initially are presented with a crime and their efforts then are spent discovering who committed the offense and why. In a criminal tax investigation, however, the initial focus usually is on the taxpayer and the authorities' efforts are spent determining whether the taxpayer committed a crime. When the taxpayer is suspected of committing a tax offense, the investigation is conducted by special agents of the Criminal Investigation Division of the IRS (CID). If the special agents determine that the case warrants a criminal prosecution, it is referred to the IRS Division Counsel (formerly District Counsel) for review. If the Division Counsel concurs, the case is forwarded to the Criminal Tax Section of the Justice Department, which determines whether the case has litigation potential. If the case is recommended for prosecution, it is forwarded to the United States Attorney's office for trial preparation.

---

1. Jeffery L. Yablon, As Certain As Death–Quotations About Taxes (2004 Edition), 102 TAX NOTES 99, 140 (Jan. 5, 2004).

A. THE INTERFACE OF CIVIL AND CRIMINAL INVESTIGATIONS

UNITED STATES v. RUTHERFORD
United States Court of Appeals, Sixth Circuit, 2009.
555 F.3d 190.

BOGGS, CHIEF JUDGE.

Defendants Jon Rutherford and Judith Bugaiski were charged with numerous tax violations and conspiracy to defraud investigators from the Internal Revenue Service (IRS). The United States appeals the district court's suppression of certain statements and documents obtained pursuant to an allegedly improper civil investigation. The IRS civil examiners who interviewed Rutherford and Bugaiski were required under an IRS manual to suspend their investigation when a "firm indication of fraud on the part of the taxpayer[s]" surfaced and refer the case to the criminal division. Internal Revenue Manual § 4565.21(1). Despite the fact such indications had emerged, civil examiners continued their investigation, conducting further interviews with the defendants and requesting additional documents.

In the criminal proceedings that followed, the IRS sought admission of their incriminating statements. The district court held the statements had to be suppressed, initially citing United States v. McKee, 192 F.3d 535 (6th Cir.1999), for the proposition that any continuation of discussions under a civil audit after firm indications of fraud have emerged would violate the Due Process Clause of the Fifth Amendment. At a later hearing, the court narrowed its explanation orally, remarking that not every "violation of the [IRS] manual [creates] a per se constitutional violation," but that this case did establish a violation. The United States now appeals, contending that the district court misread the Sixth Circuit's precedent and that the defendants' statements were improperly suppressed.

Because the defendants' constitutional rights were not violated by the IRS's negligent violation of its manual, we reverse the district court. Despite the district court's reliance on *McKee*, in that case the Sixth Circuit explicitly reserved the issue now before us. Whether the government violates a person's due process rights in the course of taking his statement is assessed under a voluntariness standard, and the Constitution does not demand a bright-line rule whereby every breach of federal administrative policy also violates the Due Process Clause. The Fifth Amendment is implicated only when a federal agent's conduct actually compels a person to speak against his will. With respect to

Rutherford and Bugaiski, there is no credible basis for concluding that their statements were coerced.

Although the civil examiners may have been negligent in failing to refer the case to the IRS's Criminal Division, the district court found no evidence that they deliberately disregarded the manual in order to mislead the defendants. Nor is there evidence in the record that suggests Rutherford and Bugaiski were familiar with the manual, or that they were lulled into a false sense of security about the nature of the charges they might face. In short, their statements were given voluntarily and may be properly admitted into evidence without infringing upon their constitutional rights.

I.

Rutherford and Bugaiski were both officers of Metro Emergency Services (MES), a non-profit tax exempt organization operating a homeless shelter for women in Highland Park, Michigan. Rutherford served as the organization's president, and Bugaiski served as its controller. The IRS first became interested in MES when a newspaper article reported on political contributions made by the group. As a non-profit organization, such disbursements could affect the group's tax status. In the course of reviewing the IRS filings, agent Wesley Tagami of the Tax Exempt and Government Entities Division discovered that MES had not filed several forms related to tax withholding from employee salaries. At this point, no direct evidence of fraud had surfaced, as there was no indication that Rutherford or any other employee had not reported all income. But Tagami's findings suggested there was the potential for fraud and, noting the irregularity, he referred the case to a fraud specialist. Soon thereafter, several other agents were assigned to work on this case, including Suzanne Carene, a revenue agent, who was tasked with examining the organization's tax returns, and another agent who was charged with collecting any unpaid taxes from MES.

Some indications of fraud began to emerge. Agents discovered that Rutherford's personal tax return showed that taxes had been withheld from his pay, even though MES never remitted the money to the IRS. Still, agents believed no firm indications of fraud were yet apparent, because certain elements of criminal fraud remained unsupported by the records. As the government notes, "there could be innocent explanations for the problem with the returns, such as Rutherford's lack of knowledge about the non-filings of 941s or the fact that the funds had not been remitted to the IRS." Since a taxpayer's intent is crucial to the distinction between criminal and civil fraud, agents could not determine whether there was an innocent explanation for the discrepancy or if the omission was intentional and therefore potentially criminal until they interviewed Rutherford and Bugaiski.

Agent Carene met with the defendants and their CPA for the first time on December 16, 2003. Rutherford and Bugaiski stated that their failure to remit taxes was unintentional, and that funds owed to them had come in late. Rutherford thereafter abruptly ended the interview. Agent Carene attempted to continue the interview, but the defendants refused to answer any more questions. She then made several requests to meet with the defendants again for further questioning, and when they declined, she caused a summons to be served on the defendants. Pursuant to the summons, Carene met with defendants on June 17, 2004. At that time, Bugaiski turned over various documents, but no interviews were conducted. On June 21 and June 25, 2004, Carene interviewed Rutherford for a second and third time. In the course of these interviews, he answered some questions and declined to answer others. On June 23, 2004, she interviewed Bugaiski.

IRS agents involved in the case held a conference call on July 20, 2004, and finally determined that a criminal referral should be made. Explaining the decision later, one investigator said, "I believe we had enough, or we had affirmative acts that showed intent and willfulness by the taxpayer to fail to collect and turn over the employment taxes, not report substantial amounts of income, not file tax returns. . .." On April 21, 2006, defendants were charged in a 22-count indictment alleging various violations of the tax code, including tax evasion, failure to pay taxes that were withheld from employees, making false returns, and conspiracy to defraud IRS investigators. In a pretrial motion to suppress evidence and dismiss the indictment, the defendants claimed that the IRS agents improperly continued the civil examination after firm indications of fraud had emerged. By doing so, the defendants argued, their rights under the Due Process Clause had been violated. The district court agreed that statements made in the later stage of the investigation had to be suppressed as violating the Constitution.

II.

The district court found that firm indications had emerged by the time the IRS conducted its second round of interviews in June 2004. Although the United States did not concede this point on appeal, the government paid little attention to this issue in its brief and at oral argument-perhaps in recognition of the standard of review. Whether firm indications of fraud had emerged is a question of fact, and this court reviews such findings for clear error. *McKee*, 192 F.3d at 543. Nothing in the record suggests the district court's finding was clearly erroneous, and therefore we proceed on the assumption that the IRS civil investigation was improperly continued.

The Sixth Circuit has once before considered the issue now before this court, and this case has proven a source of some confusion. In *United States v. McKee*, the defendant asked this court to suppress statements made to the IRS because the statements had purportedly been made pursuant to an improper investigation. 192 F.3d 535. In an opinion for the court, Judge Jones first set forth the traditional rule for determining whether a statement should be suppressed:

> [I]t is incumbent upon [the defendant] to show by clear and convincing evidence that (1) [the revenue agent] made affirmative misrepresentations in the course of her investigation, and (2) because of those misrepresentations, [the defendant] disclosed incriminating evidence to the prejudice of her constitutional rights.

Id. at 542. In this respect, the opinion is wholly conventional. Although defendant's motions to exclude statements she made to the IRS were based on an allegation that the revenue agent had failed to refer the case to the Criminal Division after firm indications of fraud surfaced, the district court found that the manual had not been violated and therefore denied her motions. Id. at 540-41. The Sixth Circuit affirmed this decision, again relying on the fact that the manual had not been violated. Id. at 543 ("Far from disregarding the Manual's provisions, [the IRS] acted in complete conformance with them by contacting the McKees and offering them the chance to account for the improprieties alleged by Pique and the other anonymous source.").

Only in dicta did the lead opinion in *McKee* touch on the issue we are now asked to resolve. After affirming the district court's finding that the IRS manual had not been violated, the opinion departed from the well-established rule, elaborating, "[The defendant] can satisfy her burden, as a practical matter, by showing that [the revenue agent] knowingly failed to comply with the Manual's suspension-of-investigation rules." 192 F.3d at 542. Judge Jones also added a footnote, explicitly stating: "If the revenue agent continues the civil audit even after she has developed 'firm indications of fraud,' then she is, in fact, making affirmative misrepresentations to the constitutional detriment of the taxpayer because she is gathering criminal evidence against the taxpayer under the guise of a civil proceeding." Id. at 542 n. 5.

Although Judge Jones's analysis may serve as a persuasive authority, it does not bind this panel in resolving this issue today. See Williams v.

Anderson, 460 F.3d 789, 796 (6th Cir.2006) (holding that dicta is not binding precedent). Further undercutting the district court's reliance on *McKee* is the fact that the two other judges on that panel explicitly stated that this issue was not being decided. Writing separately, Judge Nelson observed,

> Because we conclude that agent Loges was not shown to have violated the Internal Revenue Manual in failing to turn the investigation over to the Criminal Investigation Division sooner than she did, I am not sure that we need to express an opinion as to what the constitution implications would have been had we concluded that Agent Loges did violate the manual. . . . I do not mean to suggest that I think the rule is wrong; I simply see no reason for us to decide the question at this juncture.

McKee, 192 F.3d at 545 (Nelson, J. concurring). Judge Norris joined Judge Nelson's concurring opinion, so Judge Jones's discussion of the Due Process Clause would not be controlling even if it were not dicta. For these reasons, the trial court's reliance on *McKee* is problematic. Now that the issue is before us, we are free to reach a contrary conclusion. And a different result is warranted, because merely failing to refer a case to the Criminal Division pursuant to the IRS's internal policy is not alone sufficient to establish a violation of the defendants' right to due process.

The Due Process Clause of the Fifth Amendment provides that "No person shall . . . be deprived of life, liberty, or property, without due process of law. . . ." Violating this right entails government conduct that "shocks the sensibilities of civilized society." Moran v. Burbine, 475 U.S. 412, 433-34, 106 S.Ct. 1135, 89 L.Ed.2d 410 (1986). The sort of conduct at issue may be proscribed by internal government policy, or in certain cases, the government may even have a policy of engaging in the objectionable behavior. Whether a person's due process rights were violated in the course of taking his statement hinges on the voluntariness of the statement. Colorado v. Connelly, 479 U.S. 157, 166, 107 S.Ct. 515, 93 L.Ed.2d 473 (1986); United States v. Johnson, 351 F.3d 254, 260 (6th Cir.2003). So the effect of the government misconduct on the defendants, not its mere existence, is what must guide our analysis. Consequently, the IRS's failure to refer a case cannot of its own force violate the Due Process Clause, and to find otherwise would radically overstate the protections afforded by the Fifth Amendment. In this case, the district court said that the IRS agents were "perhaps" negligent in failing to refer the matter to the Criminal Division, but that there was insufficient evidence of intentionality to find that the failure to refer was deliberate. The record reveals that the agents knew of the manual and were sensitive to its requirements well before their first interview with the defendants. But whether the agents were acting deliberately or merely negligently, the failure to refer a case, standing alone, does not demonstrate a lack of voluntariness in the defendants' statements, absent evidence that the defendants were in fact compelled to talk by the government's affirmative misrepresentations.

There is no bright-line rule for determining whether a suspect's statements were given voluntarily. Voluntariness is instead judged by the "totality of the circumstances" in which the person made the statement. United States v. Greene, 250 F.3d 471, 479 (6th Cir.2001). To frame this analysis, the Sixth Circuit has set forth three factors for courts to consider: "(i) the police activity was objectively coercive; (ii) the coercion in question was sufficient to overbear the defendant's will; and (iii) the alleged police misconduct was the crucial motivating factor in the defendant's decision to offer the statement." United States v. Mahan, 190 F.3d 416, 422 (6th Cir.1999). Nothing in the record of this case suggests that IRS agents made affirmative misrepresentations to Rutherford and Bugaiski, or that defendants' will was overcome by the circumstances of these interviews. That a summons was issued cannot on its own mean that their later statements were involuntarily given, because the statements of persons who are subpoenaed by grand juries are routinely admitted in criminal proceedings against them.[2]

The tenor of the IRS's interviews does not in any way suggest that the suspects were either in custody or that their statements were compelled. The trial court's review of the record uncovered no indicia of coercion. "[The IRS agent] did not threaten, force, or trick the defendants." Indeed, the defendants declined to answer questions on numerous occasions, suggesting they felt free when they answered those questions that they did. At one point, Rutherford even laughed in explaining one of the deductions he was asked about. There is no evidence that the suspects relied on, or even knew of, the provisions of the manual in making the incriminating statements, which strongly suggests they were made voluntarily. Although defendants could argue the improper use of a civil examiner acted as a silent misrepresentation, lulling them into a false sense of security such that their statements were compelled, this argument is not persuasive for two reasons. First, the defendants bear the burden of proof here, and they do not claim, let alone put forward any evidence indicating, that the use of a civil

---

2.   Indeed, the district court properly recognized the authority of grand juries to gather evidence, noting that if a grand jury separately gathered the documents handed over to civil examiners, there would be no need to suppress them. In this appeal, neither party has focused on the documents produced by the defendants after firm indications of fraud emerged. For the sake of clarity, we note explicitly that we reach the same result with respect to them as we do with respect to the defendant's statements.

examiner played a "crucial motivating factor" in their decision to answer questions in June 2004. Second, even if the defendants had believed there was only a civil investigation underway, the regulation does not stipulate that a civil investigation cannot later become a criminal investigation. As a result, the potential repercussions of making incriminating statements remained the same, and the defendants had no basis for concluding that a criminal investigation would not be undertaken in the future. Perhaps the defendants could argue they would have exercised greater caution if the agents questioning them had represented the investigation as criminal in nature, but notes of the conversations suggest the defendants were already guarded in their dealings with the IRS.

Our holding today is consistent with our caselaw prior to *McKee*. In *United States v. Nuth*, we stressed that evidence collected in the course of an improperly continued investigation will be suppressed only upon a "clear showing that the taxpayer was tricked or deceived." 605 F.2d 229, 234 (6th Cir.1979); see also United States v. Allen, 522 F.2d 1229, 1233 (6th Cir.1975) ("In the absence of a clear showing that the taxpayer has been tricked or deceived by the government agents into providing incriminating information, the documents and statements obtained by the Internal Revenue agents are admissible."). In these decisions, this court has emphasized the effect of the government's action on the individual in determining whether suppression was constitutionally mandated, and observed that even certain affirmative misrepresentations will not give rise to a constitutional violation if the individual is not misled. Nuth, 605 F.2d at 234 (holding that the failure of an IRS agent to give certain warnings, as required by internal policy, did not require suppression, because the defendant was "an attorney who practiced to some extent and is an experienced businessman, and that as such he must have been aware of the 'potential criminal aspects' of an audit").

Nearly every other federal court to address this issue has held the IRS's violation of internal policy does not of its own force infringe upon a person's constitutional rights, thus requiring suppression of evidence.[3] In United States v. Caceres, the Supreme Court held that when the

---

3. In *McKee*, Judge Jones correctly observed that the First Circuit once suggested in dicta that the courts can enforce an overinclusive exclusionary rule when it comes to misconduct by the executive agencies. 192 F.3d at 541. The First Circuit said courts may exclude evidence collected in violation of agency rules that are designed to protect constitutional rights "even though these [agency] standards may go somewhat further than the Constitution requires." United States v. Leahey, 434 F.2d 7, 10 (1st Cir.1970). Despite Judge Jones's comments to the contrary, this contention in *Leahey* is at odds with the Supreme Court's later decision in United States v. Caceres. See 440 U.S. at 751, 99 S.Ct. 1465.

Constitution does not mandate a particular regulation, there is no need to exclude evidence improperly collected in violation of executive policy. 440 U.S. 741, 754-55, 99 S.Ct. 1465, 59 L.Ed.2d 733 (1979) ("In view of our conclusion that none of respondent's constitutional rights has been violated here, . . . our precedents enforcing the exclusionary rule to deter constitutional violations provide no support for the rule's application in this case."). Explaining this decision, the Court cited two reasons for its rule. First, there was a separation-of-powers issue. If the courts could simply exclude evidence whenever federal agents violated executive regulation, then it "would take away from the Executive Department the primary responsibility for fashioning the appropriate remedy for the violation of its regulations." Id. at 756, 99 S.Ct. 1465. Second, and equally significant, the court noted, if the judiciary applied the exclusionary rule in an overinclusive manner, it would discourage agencies from adopting "protective regulations." Ibid. ("In the long run, it is far better to have rules like those contained in the IRS Manual, and to tolerate occasional erroneous administration of the kind displayed by this record, than either to have no rules except those mandated by statute, or to have them framed in a mere precatory form.").

The United States Courts of Appeals have been equally reluctant to impose the exclusionary rule when the Constitution has not been violated by executive misconduct. In a case involving the same IRS provision, the Eighth Circuit held that failure to a refer a case to the Criminal Division must be accompanied by "clear and convincing evidence that the IRS affirmatively and intentionally misled the defendant" to violate the defendant's constitutional rights. United States v. Grunewald, 987 F.2d 531, 534 (8th Cir.1993). Likewise, the Seventh Circuit has held that "courts must remember that the 'firm indications of fraud' rule is but a tool for courts to utilize in determining whether the revenue agents made an *affirmative misrepresentation* to the a defendant or her representatives concerning the nature of their investigation." United States v. Peters, 153 F.3d 445, 453 (7th Cir.1998) (emphasis in original); see also Crystal v. United States, 172 F.3d 1141, 1149 (9th Cir.1999) (admitting evidence when the IRS agent's conduct "was totally innocent, albeit incorrect, and was in no sense a 'sneaky deliberate deception.' "). The Fifth Circuit has not addressed the specific provision of the IRS manual at issue in this case, but it has reached the same result in interpreting the effect of an agent's violation of another provision. United States v. Tweel, 550 F.2d 297, 299-300 (5th Cir.1977) (suppressing evidence when the IRS conducted a criminal investigation through civil examiners and lied to the taxpayer's accountant about whether a "special agent" was involved, which would have indicated the inquiry was criminal).

If anything, these courts may have been too generous in defining the sort of conduct that rises to the level of a due process violation. Even when the police are conducting a custodial interrogation, the Supreme Court has held that mere deception will not violate a person's due process rights. *Moran*, 475 U.S. at 423, 106 S.Ct. 1135. In the same vein, the Sixth Circuit has held: "Coercive police activity is a necessary predicate to a finding that a confession is not 'voluntary' within the meaning of the Due Process Clause of the Fourteenth Amendment." Colorado v. Connelly, 479 U.S. 157, 166, 107 S.Ct. 515, 93 L.Ed.2d 473 (1986). This is a high standard to overcome, which is not itself satisfied by showing that a police officer lied. When "promises of leniency, coupled with threats of immediate imprisonment, have a coercive effect on a suspect," due process rights are violated. Williams v. Withrow, 944 F.2d 284, 289 (6th Cir.1991), modified on other grounds, 507 U.S. 680, 113 S.Ct. 1745, 123 L.Ed.2d 407 (1993). But the same conduct does not violate the Constitution when it does not have a "coercive effect." Ibid. In other words, even demonstrating that an affirmative misrepresentation was made in the course of taking a statement is insufficient to establish a violation of the Due Process Clause, requiring the suppression of evidence. See *Moran*, 475 U.S. at 423, 106 S.Ct. 1135 ("[E]ven deliberate deception of an attorney could not possibly affect a suspect's decision to waive his *Miranda* rights unless he were at least aware of the incident."). The misrepresentation at issue must in fact overbear the will of the accused. See *Johnson*, 351 F.3d at 261 ("Police promises of leniency and threats of prosecution can be objectively coercive.").

To affirm the district court's decision notwithstanding this record would be to embrace openly a double standard for the incriminating statements of white-collar criminals, making it much more likely their statements will be considered involuntary and thus excluded from criminal proceedings. Such a rule would not only be hypocritical, it would be contrary to the Supreme Court's Fifth Amendment jurisprudence, which recognizes that statements made while under arrest, during a custodial interrogation with the prospect of imprisonment, are much more likely to involve coercion. See Miranda v. Arizona, 384 U.S. 436, 468, 86 S.Ct. 1602, 16 L.Ed.2d 694 (1966) ("[A Miranda] warning is an absolute prerequisite in overcoming the inherent pressures of the interrogation atmosphere."). To increase the standard for voluntariness in a noncustodial context moves in the exact opposite direction of recent Supreme Court cases.

III.

The Due Process Clause is not violated here where there was no deception or trickery and where defendants' statements were clearly voluntary. IRS agents did not engage in any affirmative misrepresentation, and to the extent that the very use of civil examiners silently misrepresented the nature of the government's investigation, the defendants have presented no evidence indicating that they relied upon the regulation so that their statements were not voluntary. In short, though government misconduct is regrettable, whether engaged in deliberately or, as here, merely negligently, the misconduct at issue in this case simply does not "shock[ ] the conscience." Rochin v. California, 342 U.S. 165, 172, 72 S.Ct. 205, 96 L.Ed. 183 (1952). If a remedy does exist, it is not one this court may impose by application of the exclusionary rule. We therefore REVERSE the district court's pre-trial motion suppressing statements and documents and REMAND for further proceedings consistent with this opinion.

COLE, CIRCUIT JUDGE, concurring.

I join the majority's decision to reverse the district court's suppression of the defendants' post-June 17, 2004 statements, but I write separately to emphasize my belief that United States v. Caceres left the door open for courts to consider the IRS's violation of its internal policies as one aspect of the two-prong voluntariness analysis. See 440 U.S. 741, 754-55, 99 S.Ct. 1465, 59 L.Ed.2d 733 (1979). In short, though I agree that the IRS's failure to comply with its internal policy does not amount to a per se violation of a defendant's constitutional rights, a court is entitled to consider (and, in fact, should consider) such non-compliance in analyzing whether the IRS made affirmative misrepresentations to a taxpayer about the nature of its investigation. Thus, I conclude that the IRS's failure to refer a case is a crucial consideration in evaluating whether the IRS made affirmative misrepresentations to a defendant about the nature of its investigation.

As the Seventh Circuit has accurately noted:

On the one side, courts face the Scylla of judicial micro-management of the inner functionings of an administrative agency, a peril recognized by many of the courts that have addressed this issue. Yet, on the other side, courts face the Charybdis of judicial abdication of their Article III duty to protect the constitutional rights of criminal defendants. . . . [T]his latter peril will be realized if the courts are forced to rely solely on the afterthe-fact assessments of revenue agents who may have an incentive to use the discretionary nature of the 'firm indications' rule to shield their actions from judicial scrutiny. . .. In navigating the narrow course necessitated by these two perils, courts must remember that the 'firm indications of fraud' rule is but a tool for courts to utilize in determining whether the revenue agents made an affirmative misrepresentation to a defendant or her representatives concerning the nature of their investigation.United States v. Peters, 153 F.3d 445, 453 (7th Cir.1998). Further, there is certainly risk that the public's trust in the IRS will be undermined should the IRS's "internal operating procedures afford anything less than faithful adherence to constitutional guarantees." See United States v. McKee, 192 F.3d 535, 544 (6th Cir.1999).

Therefore, although the IRS's failure to timely refer its investigation of defendants to its criminal unit amounts to mere negligence in this case, I can certainly foresee a situation in which the IRS intentionally pursues a criminal investigation under the auspices of a civil investigation. See United States v. Tweel, 550 F.2d 297, 299 (5th Cir.1977) (suppressing evidence where IRS agent falsely stated that the audit was routine though he knew that a special investigator was involved); United States v. Kontny, 238 F.3d 815, 819 (7th Cir.2001) (an affirmative misrepresentation could occur where an agent "pretend[s] to be a U.S. Attorney and assure[s defendants] that they would not be prosecuted if they cooperated with him. . ..."). Moreover, although I agree with the majority that the issuance of a summons on its own will not make a defendant's statements in response to thereto involuntary, a scenario of intentional government misrepresentation becomes even more probable given that the IRS is statutorily entitled to issue a civil summons to a taxpayer for a purely criminal investigation. See, e.g., Scotty's Contracting & Stone, Inc. v. United States, 326 F.3d 785, 788 (6th Cir.2003) (the IRS's authority to issue a summons for the purpose of investigating any offense relating to the tax code, be it civil or criminal, is extinguished only when the investigation is referred to the Department of Justice) (citing 26 U.S.C. § 7602 (IRS civil summons power)).

In conclusion, given the substantial likelihood that the IRS may intentionally blend its civil and criminal arms in conducting an investigation, we must strongly encourage the agency to observe and protect the public's constitutional rights when exercising its power. Allowing courts to consider the impact of the IRS's violations of internal policies on a defendant's constitutional rights helps to achieve this goal.

Notes And Questions

In the past, when the IRS conducted a civil examination that veered into a criminal investigation, its policy was to cease the civil examination until the conclusion of the criminal case. But today, the new policy of the IRS is to conduct parallel civil and criminal investigations, at least under certain circumstances. For a discussion of the hazards of this policy, see George B. Abney, "The Perils of 'Parallel' IRS Strategies," 85 Pract. Tax Strategies 148 (2010).

In United States v. Kontny, 238 F.3d 815 (7th Cir. 2001), the Kontny's appealed their conviction of evasion of employment taxes. Judge Posner, writing for the majority, held that the taxpayers must prove that the Service's conduct prejudiced their constitutional rights. Where the taxpayer can show that the Service induced reasonable reliance then "pulled the rug out from under [her]," she has established a sound ground for exclusion. But where the taxpayer is not in custody and is interviewed by a civil investigator under nonthreatening conditions in which she is not being pressured to respond to questions, her answers are considered voluntary unless the government has made threats or false promises to her. Id. at 818.

Judge Posner also noted in *Kontny* that the fact that a revenue agent does not terminate the examination when she has a firm indication of fraud is "merely a factor to be considered in evaluating the defendant's constitutional claim." Id. at 819. He adds that "[t]rickery, deceit, even impersonation do not render a confession inadmissible, certainly in noncustodial situations and usually in custodial ones as well, unless government agents makes threats or promises." Id. at 817.

In an older version of the Internal Revenue Manual, the Service advised special agents not to use "trickery, misrepresentation, or deception in obtaining any evidence or information." IRM 9.4.5.11.3.1.1 (Nov. 17, 2000). The newer version has deleted this advice and instead cautions special agents "to avoid making statements of any kind in discussion with the subject or his/her representative that might be construed to compromise any criminal components of the investigation." IRM 9.4.5.6.4.3 (May 15, 2008).

Origins of a Criminal Tax Case. There are four general ways in which a criminal investigation can arise. One is through an informant. Generally, disgruntled employees, jealous colleagues, and ex-spouses rank high on the list of potential informants. The Tax Relief and Health Care Act of 2006 (Pub. L. No. 109-432) created a new Whistleblower Office within the IRS, to process tips received from individuals who spot tax problems in their workplace while conducting day-to-day personal business or anywhere else they may be encountered. The tipster may receive a reward of 15-30 % of the total proceeds collected as a result of the tip, provided the tax is collected because of the information provided. A second way in which a criminal investigation may arise is through revenue agents, who may stumble across evidence of criminal activity in the course of a routine audit and recommend that the case be transferred to the CID, as we saw in *Rutherford*. A third way is through special agents, who may develop information through projects targeting noncompliance in particular geographic locales or among particularly troublesome groups, such as taxpayers who are likely to have income from illegal sources. Special agents also may develop leads through newspaper articles and other media links, including internet databases, which can provide important information about a taxpayer, such as club memberships, business customers, society memberships, professional licenses, etc. Through the legal research databases, such as Westlaw, agents can research legal decisions, property ownership records, and newspapers, magazines, and journal articles. See IRM § 9.4 (Apr. 26, 1999). In addition, special agents may obtain information from other federal, state and local criminal investigative agencies which often share information with the IRS. Finally, a criminal investigation may arise through the action of the taxpayer in filing an incomplete currency transaction report or a false or fraudulent tax return.

While relatively few examinations become criminal investigations, nevertheless, the consequences to the taxpayer of a criminal investigation can be dire. Thus, the tax practitioner is well advised to consider the criminal potential in any audit. It may not be evident to the taxpayer in the early stages of an investigation that the revenue agent suspects that the case has criminal potential, but there are certain warning signs that may signal that the revenue agent thinks the case may have fraud potential. Can you think of any of these signs?

B. METHODS OF INVESTIGATION

In a criminal tax investigation, the special agent frequently must obtain and examine numerous documents in order to reconstruct the taxpayer's financial and tax history over a period of several years. These documents may be in the possession of (1) the taxpayer, (2) a third party, such as a business associate, and/or (3) a third-party record keeper, such as a bank or CPA. In addition, some of the documents or transactions underlying the documents may need further explanation that can only be supplied by witnesses. Some or all of these parties may not be willing to cooperate with the agents absent compulsion.

There are two general methods available to the special agents to assist them in gathering evidence: the use of an administrative summons and grand jury investigations.

1. Administrative Summons

The Service has broad authority under § 7602 to examine books and compel the testimony of witnesses to ensure proper compliance with the internal revenue laws. This authority is referred to as "summons power," because it is initiated through the service of a summons, enforceable by the federal district court. IRC § 7604. There is debate, however, as to whether this authority extends to investigations that are solely criminal in nature, as opposed to investigations that have mixed civil and criminal motives.

JONES v. UNITED STATES

United States District Court, Eastern District of Arkansas, 1992.
791 F.Supp. 760.

ORDER DISMISSING PETITION

Wright, District Judge.

* * *

Petitioners claim that the Internal Revenue Service seeks to use its civil summons power for the purpose of uncovering information to be used in criminal proceedings. Consequently, petitioners claim, the IRS issued the summonses here in bad faith with the purpose, inter alia, of violating petitioners' Fourth and Fifth Amendment rights under the United States Constitution. Petitioners cite United States v. LaSalle, 437 U.S. 298, 98 S.Ct. 2357, 57 L.Ed.2d 221 (1978), in support of their petition claiming the summonses should be quashed.

Petitioners' grounds to quash the summonses are insufficient. Petitioners claim that an IRS agent has determined that he will recommend a criminal prosecution involving petitioners' tax returns for the relevant tax years. Assuming, arguendo, for petitioners' benefit that it is still valid, *LaSalle* does not give petitioners any grounds to quash the summonses here. The *LaSalle* Court held that complainants could only quash an IRS summons by showing that the matter had been referred to the Department of Justice for a criminal prosecution. "Only at that point do civil and criminal aspects of a tax fraud case begin to diverge." *LaSalle*, 437 U.S. at 311, 98 S.Ct. at 2365. The mere assertion of a criminal aspect to the investigation by the investigating agent was not a sufficient basis to quash the summonses in *LaSalle*.

The *LaSalle* Court stated: In this case, respondents submit that such a departure [from a mixed civil and criminal fraud investigation into a purely criminal investigation] did indeed occur because [the IRS investigating agent] was interested only in gathering evidence for a criminal prosecution. We disagree. The institutional responsibility of the Service to calculate and to collect civil fraud penalties and fraudulently reported or unreported taxes is not necessarily overturned by a single agent who attempts to build a criminal case. The review process over and above his conclusions is multilayered and thorough. Apart from the control of his immediate supervisor, the agent's final recommendation is reviewed by the district chief of the Intelligence Division, 26 C.F.R. §§ 601.107(b) and (c) (1977) * * *. The Office of Regional Counsel also reviews the case before it is forwarded to the National Office of the Service or to the Justice Department * * *. If the Regional Counsel and the Assistant Regional Commissioner for Intelligence disagree about the disposition of a case, another complete review occurs at the national level centered in the Criminal Tax Division of the Office of General Counsel * * *. Only after the officials of at least two layers of review have concurred in the conclusion of the special agent does the referral to the Department of Justice take place. At any of the various stages, the Service can abandon the criminal prosecution, can decide instead to assert a civil penalty, or can pursue both goals. While the special agent is an important actor in the process, his motivation is hardly dispositive * * *.

* * * Furthermore, the inquiry into the criminal enforcement objectives of the agent would delay summons enforcement proceedings while the parties clash over, and judges grapple with, the thought processes of each investigator * * *. This obviously is undesirable and unrewarding. As a result, the question whether an investigation has solely criminal purposes must be answered only by an examination of the institutional posture of the IRS. Contrary to the assertions of respondents, this means that those opposing enforcement of a summons do bear the burden to disprove the actual existence of a valid civil tax determination or collection purpose by the Service * * *. *LaSalle*, 437 U.S. at 314-16, 98 S.Ct. at 2366-67.

The Court finds that there is not a sufficient factual basis in the petition to merit petitioners' conclusion that the IRS has referred the matter to the Department of Justice for the commencement of criminal proceedings. Such a finding is required in order to quash a summons. 26 U.S.C. § 7602(c); *LaSalle*, 437 U.S. at 314-16, 98 S.Ct. at 2366-67. Petitioners' contention that an IRS agent has determined to pursue a criminal investigation is not alone sufficient grounds on which to quash the summonses.

Moreover, petitioners' reliance on *LaSalle* is misplaced. The courts have virtually unanimously held that the Supreme Court's holding in *LaSalle* has been superseded by the 1982 recodification of the Internal Revenue statutes. See, e.g., United States v. Millman, 822 F.2d 305 (2d Cir.1987); United States v. Cahill, 920 F.2d 421 (7th Cir.1990). This Court agrees.

The Second Circuit succinctly explained the matter this way: * * * At one time, the Internal Revenue Code allowed IRS summonses to be enforced only when the purpose of the investigation was to determine potential civil tax liability; courts then uniformly held that 26 U.S.C. § 7602 did not authorize the issuance of an IRS summons "for the improper purpose of obtaining evidence for use in a criminal prosecution," Reisman v. Caplin, 375 U.S. 440, 449 [84 S.Ct. 508, 513, 11 L.Ed.2d 459] (1964); LaSalle National Bank, 437 U.S. at 316 [98 S.Ct. at 2367]. * * * In 1982, however, congress [sic] amended § 7602 to permit the issuance of a summons for "the purpose of inquiring into any offense connected with the administration or enforcement of the internal revenue laws." 26 U.S.C. § 7602(b).

The Court concludes, as a matter of law, that the IRS may simultaneously pursue civil and criminal investigations of the petitioners prior to referring the matter to the Department of Justice. Congress contemplated dual civil and criminal investigations such as the instant investigation when it revised the statute, 26 U.S.C. § 7602. The Supreme Court has held that such investigations do not violate petitioners' constitutional rights. *LaSalle*, 437 U.S. at 316 [98 S.Ct. at 2367].

IT IS THEREFORE ORDERED that petitioners' petition to quash three Internal Revenue Service summonses be, and it is hereby, DENIED.

* * *

Notes And Questions

The Sixth Circuit has joined the Second, Third, Eighth, Tenth, and Eleventh Circuits in concluding that the 1982 amendment to § 7602 permits the Service to validly issue a summons for the sole purpose of a criminal investigation, provided the case has not been transferred to the Department of Justice. See Scotty's Contracting and Stone, Inc. v. United States, 326 F.3d 785 (6th Cir. 2003).

The procedure for challenging the enforcement of a summons depends upon whether the summons was issued to the taxpayer or to a third party. If the summons was issued to the taxpayer, it may not be challenged until the Service initiates enforcement proceedings in the federal district court under § 7602. If a third-party summons is issued, the procedure for challenging the summons is determined under § 7609, which provides that the taxpayer has 20 days from the receipt of the notice of issuance of the summons to bring suit in federal district court.[2]

If a summons is contested, the government must establish a prima facie case that the summons was issued for a proper purpose. This must be done in accordance with the standard set out by the Supreme Court in United States v. Powell, 379 U.S. 48 (1964). Under this standard, the government must show that (1) the investigation is being conducted pursuant to a legitimate purpose; (2) the inquiry may be relevant to that purpose; (3) the information sought is not already within the government's possession; and (4) the administrative steps required by the Code have been followed. Id., at 57-58. Under *Powell,* the administrative steps require the Service to notify the taxpayer in writing that further examination of books and records is necessary. Once the government establishes this prima facie case, the burden shifts to the taxpayer to disprove the "existence of a valid civil tax determination or collection purpose," as the *Jones* court noted, above. See Chapter 3, § II.B; see also U.S. v. Bernhoft, 666 F.Supp. 2d 943 (E.D. Wis. 2009) (petition to enforce administrative summons against law firm's founder in connection with an IRS investigation into firm's alleged involvement in the promotion of abusive tax schemes).

John Doe summons. In some cases, the identity of the individual taxpayer(s) may not be known to the Service, as for instance, in the case of a tax shelter with many individual investors. Under § 7609(f), the Service can launch an ex parte investigation through the use of a John Doe summons. The Service may not use the John Doe summons, however, to investigate taxpayers that it otherwise would have been prohibited from investigating. See United States v. Ritchie, 15 F.3d 592, 600 (6th Cir. 1994) (where John Doe summons was issued to determine whether law firm's clients had complied with the currency transaction reporting requirements, court noted that summons to determine the identity of firm's clients was not a legitimate purpose).

Good faith enforcement. In Anaya v. United States, 815 F.2d 1373 (10th Cir. 1987), the governor of New Mexico had been investigated by both the FBI and the IRS for allegedly taking and failing to report

---

2.   Note that the 20-day period is a jurisdictional requirement under § 7609(b). This period commences on the date of the mailing of the notice of issuance of the summons. Stringer v. U.S., 776 F.2d 274 (11th Cir. 1985). Thus, the district court does not have jurisdiction if the taxpayer fails to challenge the summons within this period of time. Ponsford v. U.S., 771 F.2d 1305 (9th Cir. 1985).

"payoffs" on the award of state contracts. After he was convicted, Anaya appealed on the ground that the district court erred in enforcing the IRS summons because the summons was based on improperly received grand jury information and thus had been issued in violation of Fed. Rule of Crim. Proc. 6(e). The defense argued that this constituted "institutional bad faith" on the part of the IRS. In addressing this issue, the Tenth Circuit stated:

> Institutional good faith on the part of the Internal Revenue Service is essential to insure honest pursuit of the goals of 26 U.S.C. § 7602 in the issuance of the summons. *LaSalle*, 437 U.S. at 313, 98 S.Ct. at 2365. In *LaSalle*, the IRS agent began his investigation of the taxpayer with information he received from the FBI, the local United States Attorney, and other federal agencies. To aid in this investigation, he issued two administrative summons which were subsequently made the subject of an enforcement hearing in the district court. The district court refused enforcement of the summons upon a finding that they were issued "solely for the purpose of unearthing evidence of criminal conduct" by the taxpayer. *LaSalle*, 437 U.S. at 304, 98 S.Ct. at 2361. That order was affirmed by the Seventh Circuit with the admonition that the use of an administrative summons "solely for criminal purposes is a quintessential example of bad faith." United States v. LaSalle National Bank, 554 F.2d 302, 309 (7th Cir. 1977), rev'd, 437 U.S. 298, 98 S.Ct. 2357, 57 L.Ed.2d 221 (1978). In reversing, the Supreme Court concluded that the coincidence between a taxpayer's civil and criminal liability was such that the two could not be untwined prior to referral by the IRS to the Department of Justice for prosecution. Thus, until referral occurs, the pendency of a criminal investigation against the taxpayer does not inhibit the authority of the IRS to conduct investigations pursuant to § 7609. Moreover, the Court continued, the government does not lose its interest in collecting unpaid taxes just because a taxpayer has become the subject of a criminal investigation. Yet, prohibiting the use of administrative summons after referral "is a prophylactic measure intended to safeguard * * * the role of the grand jury as a principal tool of criminal accusation." 437 U.S. at 312, 98 S.Ct. at 2365. Although pre-referral use of the administrative summons is restricted to the good faith limitations of *Powell,* good faith is not abandoned when a summons is used to gather evidence for a criminal investigation. *LaSalle*, 437 U.S. at 314, 98 S.Ct. at 2366.

Contrary to the position taken by the taxpayers here, the good faith that is to be considered in the enforcement proceeding is that of the IRS as an institution. *LaSalle*, 437 U.S. at 314, 98 S.Ct. at 2366. Indeed, the Court pointed out, the acts of one person are only a part of the disposition of any case within the Service, and to that extent cannot be used as the sole criterion of the good faith test.[7]

815 F.2d at 1377.

1. Would a summons be valid if it is issued after the IRS has decided to forward the case to the Justice Department but before the case is actually transferred? What if the summons is issued after the case is transferred, but the Justice Department ultimately decides not to prosecute? See United States v. Scholbe, 664 F.2d 1163 (10th Cir. 1981).

2. Would an informant's improper motive be grounds for invalidating a summons? See Cortese v. United States, 614 F.2d 914 (3rd Cir. 1980).

3. In practice, an administrative summons generally is used only as a last resort to get documents or information which the taxpayer refuses to turn over to the government. Why is the summons seldom used?

2. Grand Jury Investigations

The principal role of the grand jury is to accuse. The government may prosecute a felony charge only when the grand jury has returned an indictment, unless the defendant waives this right. The grand jury also may serve as an investigative body, and in fact, an increasing number of criminal tax investigations are conducted by grand juries, primarily because of the increasing number of mail fraud, wire fraud, bank fraud, and RICO cases. Grand jury investigations generally are conducted under the aegis of the U.S. Attorney (or Assistant U.S. Attorney) who will prosecute the case, although the IRS also may become involved in the investigation. This can happen in either of two ways. The U.S. Attorney may request the Service's assistance whenever there is a possibility that a tax crime may have been committed, or the Service may initiate a request for a grand jury either before, during, or after conducting an administrative investigation. The Service is likely to initiate such a request when the facts cannot be developed within a

---

7.   The Court stated:
To do so would unnecessarily frustrate the enforcement of the tax laws by restricting the use of the summons according to the motivation of a single agent without regard to the enforcement policy of the Service as an institution. Furthermore, the inquiry into the criminal enforcement objectives of the agent would delay summons enforcement proceedings while parties clash over, and judges grapple with, the thought processes of each investigator * * *. As a result, the question whether an investigation has solely criminal purposes [lacks good faith] must be answered only by an examination of the institutional posture of the IRS.
437 U.S. at 316, 98 S.Ct. at 2367.

reasonable time through an administrative investigation, or when the prosecution potential of the case would be strengthened by the grand jury process. IRM § 9.5.2.2 (Nov. 5, 2004).

a. Exculpatory Evidence

UNITED STATES v. WILLIAMS
Supreme Court of the United States, 1992.
504 U.S. 36, 112 S.Ct. 1735, 118 L.Ed.2d 352.

JUSTICE SCALIA delivered the opinion of the Court.

The question presented in this case is whether a district court may dismiss an otherwise valid indictment because the Government failed to disclose to the grand jury "substantial exculpatory evidence" in its possession.

* * *

A.

"[R]ooted in long centuries of Anglo-American history," the grand jury is mentioned in the Bill of Rights, but not in the body of the Constitution. It has not been textually assigned, therefore, to any of the branches described in the first three Articles. It "'is a constitutional fixture in its own right.'" In fact the whole theory of its function is that it belongs to no branch of the institutional Government, serving as a kind of buffer or referee between the Government and the people. Although the grand jury normally operates, of course, in the courthouse and under judicial auspices, its institutional relationship with the Judicial Branch has traditionally been, so to speak, at arm's length. Judges' direct involvement in the functioning of the grand jury has generally been confined to the constitutive one of calling the grand jurors together and administering their oaths of office.

The grand jury's functional independence from the Judicial Branch is evident both in the scope of its power to investigate criminal wrongdoing and in the manner in which that power is exercised. "Unlike [a] [c]ourt, whose jurisdiction is predicated upon a specific case or controversy, the grand jury 'can investigate merely on suspicion that the law is being violated, or even because it wants assurance that it is not.'" It need not identify the offender it suspects, or even "the precise nature of the offense" it is investigating. The grand jury requires no authorization from its constituting court to initiate an investigation, nor does the prosecutor require leave of court to seek a grand jury indictment. And in its day-to-day functioning, the grand jury generally operates without the interference of a presiding judge. It swears in its own witnesses, and deliberates in total secrecy.

True, the grand jury cannot compel the appearance of witnesses and the production of evidence, and must appeal to the court when such compulsion is required. And the court will refuse to lend its assistance when the compulsion the grand jury seeks would override rights accorded by the Constitution, or even testimonial privileges recognized by the common law. Even in this setting, however, we have insisted that the grand jury remain "free to pursue its investigations unhindered by external influence or supervision so long as it does not trench upon the legitimate rights of any witness called before it." Recognizing this tradition of independence, we have said that the Fifth Amendment's "constitutional guarantee presupposes an investigative body 'acting independently of either prosecuting attorney or judge' * * *."

No doubt in view of the grand jury proceeding's status as other than a constituent element of a "criminal prosecutio[n]," U.S. Const., Amdt. 6, we have said that certain constitutional protections afforded defendants in criminal proceedings have no application before that body. The Double Jeopardy Clause of the Fifth Amendment does not bar a grand jury from returning an indictment when a prior grand jury has refused to do so. We have twice suggested, though not held, that the Sixth Amendment right to counsel does not attach when an individual is summoned to appear before a grand jury, even if he is the subject of the investigation. And although "the grand jury may not force a witness to answer questions in violation of [the Fifth Amendment's] constitutional guarantee" against self-incrimination, our cases suggest that an indictment obtained through the use of evidence previously obtained in violation of the privilege against self-incrimination "is nevertheless valid."

Given the grand jury's operational separateness from its constituting court, it should come as no surprise that we have been reluctant to invoke the judicial supervisory power as a basis for prescribing modes of grand jury procedure. Over the years, we have received many requests to exercise supervision over the grand jury's evidence-taking process, but we have refused them all, including some more appealing than the one presented today. In United States v. Calandra, [414 U.S. 338, 94 S.Ct. 613, 38 L.Ed.2d 561 (1974)], a grand jury witness faced questions that were allegedly based upon physical evidence the Government had obtained through a violation of the Fourth Amendment; we rejected the proposal that the exclusionary rule be extended to grand jury proceedings, because of "the potential injury to the historic role and functions of the grand jury." 414 U.S., at 349, 94 S.Ct., at 620. In

Costello v. United States, 350 U.S. 359, 76 S.Ct. 406, 100 L.Ed. 397 (1956), we declined to enforce the hearsay rule in grand jury proceedings, since that "would run counter to the whole history of the grand jury institution, in which laymen conduct their inquiries unfettered by technical rules." Id., at 364, 76 S.Ct., at 409.

These authorities suggest that any power federal courts may have to fashion, on their own initiative, rules of grand jury procedure is a very limited one, not remotely comparable to the power they maintain over their own proceedings. It certainly would not permit judicial reshaping of the grand jury institution, substantially altering the traditional relationships between the prosecutor, the constituting court, and the grand jury itself. As we proceed to discuss, that would be the consequence of the proposed rule here.

B.

Respondent argues that the Court of Appeals' rule can be justified as a sort of Fifth Amendment "common law," a necessary means of assuring the constitutional right to the judgment "of an independent and informed grand jury," Wood v. Georgia, 370 U.S. 375, 390, 82 S.Ct. 1364, 1373, 8 L.Ed.2d 569 (1962). Respondent makes a generalized appeal to functional notions: Judicial supervision of the quantity and quality of the evidence relied upon by the grand jury plainly facilitates, he says, the grand jury's performance of its twin historical responsibilities, i.e., bringing to trial those who may be justly accused and shielding the innocent from unfounded accusation and prosecution. We do not agree. The rule would neither preserve nor enhance the traditional functioning of the institution that the Fifth Amendment demands. To the contrary, requiring the prosecutor to present exculpatory as well as inculpatory evidence would alter the grand jury's historical role, transforming it from an accusatory to an adjudicatory body.

It is axiomatic that the grand jury sits not to determine guilt or innocence, but to assess whether there is adequate basis for bringing a criminal charge. That has always been so; and to make the assessment it has always been thought sufficient to hear only the prosecutor's side. As Blackstone described the prevailing practice in 18th-century England, the grand jury was "only to hear evidence on behalf of the prosecution[,] for the finding of an indictment is only in the nature of an enquiry or accusation, which is afterwards to be tried and determined." 4 W. Blackstone, Commentaries 300 (1769); see also 2 M. Hale, Pleas of the Crown 157 (1st Am. ed. 1847). So also in the United States. According to the description of an early American court, three years before the Fifth

Amendment was ratified, it is the grand jury's function not "to enquire * * * upon what foundation [the charge may be] denied," or otherwise to try the suspect's defenses, but only to examine "upon what foundation [the charge] is made" by the prosecutor. As a consequence, neither in this country nor in England has the suspect under investigation by the grand jury ever been thought to have a right to testify or to have exculpatory evidence presented.

Imposing upon the prosecutor a legal obligation to present exculpatory evidence in his possession would be incompatible with this system. If a "balanced" assessment of the entire matter is the objective, surely the first thing to be done–rather than requiring the prosecutor to say what he knows in defense of the target of the investigation–is to entitle the target to tender his own defense. To require the former while denying (as we do) the latter would be quite absurd. It would also be quite pointless, since it would merely invite the target to circumnavigate the system by delivering his exculpatory evidence to the prosecutor, whereupon it would have to be passed on to the grand jury–unless the prosecutor is willing to take the chance that a court will not deem the evidence important enough to qualify for mandatory disclosure.

Respondent acknowledges (as he must) that the "common law" of the grand jury is not violated if the grand jury itself chooses to hear no more evidence than that which suffices to convince it an indictment is proper. Thus, had the Government offered to familiarize the grand jury in this case with the five boxes of financial statements and deposition testimony alleged to contain exculpatory information, and had the grand jury rejected the offer as pointless, respondent would presumably agree that the resulting indictment would have been valid. Respondent insists, however, that courts must require the modern prosecutor to alert the grand jury to the nature and extent of the available exculpatory evidence, because otherwise the grand jury "merely functions as an arm of the prosecution." We reject the attempt to convert a nonexistent duty of the grand jury itself into an obligation of the prosecutor.

The authority of the prosecutor to seek an indictment has long been understood to be "coterminous with the authority of the grand jury to entertain [the prosecutor's] charges." United States v. Thompson, 251 U.S., at 414, 40 S.Ct., at 292. If the grand jury has no obligation to consider all "substantial exculpatory" evidence, we do not understand how the prosecutor can be said to have a binding obligation to present it.

There is yet another respect in which respondent's proposal not only fails to comport with, but positively contradicts, the "common law" of the Fifth Amendment grand jury. Motions to quash indictments based upon the sufficiency of the evidence relied upon by the grand jury were unheard of at common law in England. And the traditional American practice was described by Justice Nelson, riding circuit in 1852, as follows:

> "No case has been cited, nor have we been able to find any, furnishing an authority for looking into and revising the judgment of the grand jury upon the evidence, for the purpose of determining whether or not the finding was founded upon sufficient proof, or whether there was a deficiency in respect to any part of the complaint * * * ." United States v. Reed, 27 F.Cas. 727, 738 (No. 16,134) (CCNDNY 1852).

We accepted Justice Nelson's description in *Costello v. United States*, where we held that "[i]t would run counter to the whole history of the grand jury institution" to permit an indictment to be challenged "on the ground that there was inadequate or incompetent evidence before the grand jury." 350 U.S., at 363-364, 76 S.Ct., at 409. And we reaffirmed this principle recently in *Bank of Nova Scotia*, where we held that "the mere fact that evidence itself is unreliable is not sufficient to require a dismissal of the indictment," and that "a challenge to the reliability or competence of the evidence presented to the grand jury" will not be heard. 487 U.S., at 261, 108 S.Ct., at 2377. It would make little sense, we think, to abstain from reviewing the evidentiary support for the grand jury's judgment while scrutinizing the sufficiency of the prosecutor's presentation. A complaint about the quality or adequacy of the evidence can always be recast as a complaint that the prosecutor's presentation was "incomplete" or "misleading."[8] Our words in *Costello* bear repeating: Review of facially valid indictments on such grounds "would run counter to the whole history of the grand jury institution[,] [and] [n]either justice nor the concept of a fair trial requires [it]." 350 U.S., at 364, 76 S.Ct., at 409.

* * *

Echoing the reasoning of the Tenth Circuit in United States v. Page, 808 F.2d, at 728, respondent argues that a rule requiring the prosecutor to disclose exculpatory evidence to the grand jury would, by removing from the docket unjustified prosecutions, save valuable judicial time. That depends, we suppose, upon what the ratio would turn out to be between unjustified prosecutions eliminated and grand jury indictments

---

8. In *Costello*, for example, instead of complaining about the grand jury's reliance upon hearsay evidence the petitioner could have complained about the prosecutor's introduction of it. See, e.g., United States v. Estepa, 471 F.2d 1132, 1136-1137 (CA2 1972) (prosecutor should not introduce hearsay evidence before grand jury when direct evidence is available); see also Arenella, Reforming the Federal Grand Jury and the State Preliminary Hearing to Prevent Conviction Without Adjudication, 78 Mich.L.Rev. 463, 540 (1980) ("[S]ome federal courts have cautiously begun to * * * us[e] a revitalized prosecutorial misconduct doctrine to circumvent *Costello's* prohibition against directly evaluating the sufficiency of the evidence presented to the grand jury").

challenged–for the latter as well as the former consume "valuable judicial time." We need not pursue the matter; if there is an advantage to the proposal, Congress is free to prescribe it. For the reasons set forth above, however, we conclude that courts have no authority to prescribe such a duty pursuant to their inherent supervisory authority over their own proceedings. The judgment of the Court of Appeals is accordingly reversed, and the cause is remanded for further proceedings consistent with this opinion.

So ordered.

JUSTICE STEVENS, with whom JUSTICE BLACKMUN and JUSTICE O'CONNOR join, and with whom JUSTICE THOMAS joins as to Parts II and III, dissenting.

* * *

II.

Like the Hydra slain by Hercules, prosecutorial misconduct has many heads. * * *

Nor has prosecutorial misconduct been limited to judicial proceedings: The reported cases indicate that it has sometimes infected grand jury proceedings as well. The cases contain examples of prosecutors presenting perjured testimony, questioning a witness outside the presence of the grand jury and then failing to inform the grand jury that the testimony was exculpatory, failing to inform the grand jury of its authority to subpoena witnesses, operating under a conflict of interest, misstating the law,[8] and misstating the facts on cross-examination of a witness.

Justice Sutherland's identification of the basic reason why that sort of misconduct is intolerable merits repetition: "The United States Attorney is the representative not of an ordinary party to a controversy, but of a sovereignty whose obligation to govern impartially is as compelling as its obligation to govern at all; and whose interest, therefore, in a criminal prosecution is not that it shall win a case, but that justice shall be done. As such, he is in a peculiar and very definite sense the servant of the law, the twofold aim of which is that guilt shall not escape or innocence suffer. He may prosecute with earnestness and vigor--indeed, he should do so. But, while he may strike hard blows, he

---

8.   The court found the Government guilty of prosecutorial misconduct because it "fail[ed] to provide the polygraph evidence to the Grand Jury despite the prosecutor's guarantee to Judge Pregerson that all exculpatory evidence would be presented to the Grand Jury, and compound[ed] this indiscretion by erroneously but unequivocally telling the Grand Jury that the polygraph evidence was inadmissible." United States v. Roberts, 481 F.Supp.[1385,] 1389 [C.D. Calif. 1980)].

is not at liberty to strike foul ones. It is as much his duty to refrain from improper methods calculated to produce a wrongful conviction as it is to use every legitimate means to bring about a just one." Berger v. United States, 295 U.S., at 88, 55 S.Ct. at 633.

It is equally clear that the prosecutor has the same duty to refrain from improper methods calculated to produce a wrongful indictment. Indeed, the prosecutor's duty to protect the fundamental fairness of judicial proceedings assumes special importance when he is presenting evidence to a grand jury. As the Court of Appeals for the Third Circuit recognized, "the costs of continued unchecked prosecutorial misconduct" before the grand jury are particularly substantial because there "the prosecutor operates without the check of a judge or a trained legal adversary, and virtually immune from public scrutiny. The prosecutor's abuse of his special relationship to the grand jury poses an enormous risk to defendants as well. For while in theory a trial provides the defendant with a full opportunity to contest and disprove the charges against him, in practice, the handing up of an indictment will often have a devastating personal and professional impact that a later dismissal or acquittal can never undo. Where the potential for abuse is so great, and the consequences of a mistaken indictment so serious, the ethical responsibilities of the prosecutor, and the obligation of the judiciary to protect against even the appearance of unfairness, are correspondingly heightened." United States v. Serubo, 604 F.2d 807, 817 (CA3 1979).

* * * Before the grand jury the prosecutor has the dual role of pressing for an indictment and of being the grand jury adviser. In case of conflict, the latter duty must take precedence. "The *ex parte* character of grand jury proceedings makes it peculiarly important for a federal prosecutor to remember that, in the familiar phrase, the interest of the United States 'in a criminal prosecution is not that it shall win a case, but that justice shall be done.' Berger v. United States, 295 U.S. 78, 88 [55 S.Ct. 629, 633, 79 L.Ed. 1314] * * * (1935)." Id., at 628-629.[9]

---

9. Although the majority in *Ciambrone* [eds: U.S. v. Ciambrone, 601 F.2d 616 (2d Cir. 1979)] did not agree with Judge Friendly's appraisal of the prejudicial impact of the misconduct in that case, it also recognized the prosecutor's duty to avoid fundamentally unfair tactics during the grand jury proceedings. Judge Mansfield explained: "On the other hand, the prosecutor's right to exercise some discretion and selectivity in the presentation of evidence to a grand jury does not entitle him to mislead it or to engage in fundamentally unfair tactics before it. The prosecutor, for instance, may not obtain an indictment on the basis of evidence known to him to be perjurious, United States v. Basurto, 497 F.2d 781, 785-86 (9th Cir.1974), or by leading it to believe that it has received eyewitness rather than hearsay testimony, United States v. Estepa, 471 F.2d 1132, 1136-37 (2d Cir.1972). We would add that where a prosecutor is aware of any substantial evidence negating guilt he should, in the interest of justice, make it known to the grand jury, at least where it might reasonably be expected to lead the jury not to indict.

The standard for judging the consequences of prosecutorial misconduct during grand jury proceedings is essentially the same as the standard applicable to trials. In United States v. Mechanik, 475 U.S. 66, 106 S.Ct. 938, 89 L.Ed.2d 50 (1986), we held that there was "no reason not to apply [the harmless error rule] to 'errors, defects, irregularities, or variances' occurring before a grand jury just as we have applied it to such error occurring in the criminal trial itself," id., at 71-72, 106 S.Ct., at 942. We repeated that holding in Bank of Nova Scotia v. United States, 487 U.S. 250, 108 S.Ct. 2369, 101 L.Ed.2d 228 (1988), when we rejected a defendant's argument that an indictment should be dismissed because of prosecutorial misconduct and irregularities in proceedings before the grand jury. Referring to the prosecutor's misconduct before the grand jury, we "concluded that our customary harmless-error inquiry is applicable where, as in the cases before us, a court is asked to dismiss an indictment prior to the conclusion of the trial." Id., at 256, 108 S.Ct., at 2374. Moreover, in reviewing the instances of misconduct in that case, we applied precisely the same standard to the prosecutor's violations of Rule 6 of the Federal Rules of Criminal Procedure and to his violations of the general duty of fairness that applies to all judicial proceedings. This point is illustrated by the Court's comments on the prosecutor's abuse of a witness: "The District Court found that a prosecutor was abusive to an expert defense witness during a recess and in the hearing of some grand jurors. Although the Government concedes that the treatment of the expert tax witness was improper, the witness himself testified that his testimony was unaffected by this misconduct. The prosecutors instructed the grand jury to disregard anything they may have heard in conversations between a prosecutor and a witness, and explained to the grand jury that such conversations should have no influence on its deliberations. In light of these ameliorative measures, there is nothing to indicate that the prosecutor's conduct toward this witness substantially affected the grand jury's evaluation of the testimony or its decision to indict." 487 U.S., at 261, 108 S.Ct., at 2377.

Unquestionably, the plain implication of that discussion is that if the misconduct, even though not expressly forbidden by any written rule, had played a critical role in persuading the jury to return the indictment, dismissal would have been required.

In an opinion that I find difficult to comprehend, the Court today repudiates the assumptions underlying these cases and seems to suggest that the court has no authority to supervise the conduct of the prosecutor in grand jury proceedings so long as he follows the dictates of the Constitution, applicable statutes, and Rule 6 of the Federal Rules of Criminal Procedure. The Court purports to support this conclusion by invoking the doctrine of separation of powers and citing a string of cases in which we have declined to impose categorical restraints on the grand jury. Needless to say, the Court's reasoning is unpersuasive.

Although the grand jury has not been "textually assigned" to "any of the branches described in the first three Articles" of the Constitution, it is not an autonomous body completely beyond the reach of the other branches. Throughout its life, from the moment it is convened until it is discharged, the grand jury is subject to the control of the court. As Judge Learned Hand recognized over 60 years ago, "a grand jury is neither an officer nor an agent of the United States, but a part of the court." Falter v. United States, 23 F.2d 420, 425 (CA2 1928). This Court has similarly characterized the grand jury: "A grand jury is clothed with great independence in many areas, but it remains an appendage of the court, powerless to perform its investigative function without the court's aid, because powerless itself to compel the testimony of witnesses. It is the court's process which summons the witness to attend and give testimony, and it is the court which must compel a witness to testify if, after appearing, he refuses to do so." Brown v. United States, 359 U.S. 41, 49, 79 S.Ct. 539, 546, 3 L.Ed.2d 609 (1959).

This Court has, of course, long recognized that the grand jury has wide latitude to investigate violations of federal law as it deems appropriate and need not obtain permission from either the court or the prosecutor. Correspondingly, we have acknowledged that "its operation generally is unrestrained by the technical procedural and evidentiary rules governing the conduct of criminal trials." *Calandra,* 414 U.S., at 343, 94 S.Ct., at 617. But this is because Congress and the Court have generally thought it best not to impose procedural restraints on the grand jury; it is not because they lack all power to do so.[10]

To the contrary, the Court has recognized that it has the authority to create and enforce limited rules applicable in grand jury proceedings. Thus, for example, the Court has said that the grand jury "may not itself violate a valid privilege, whether established by the Constitution, statutes, or the common law." Id., at 346, 94 S.Ct., at 619. And the Court may prevent a grand jury from violating such a privilege by quashing or modifying a subpoena, or issuing a protective order forbidding questions in violation of the privilege. Moreover, there are, as the Court notes, a series of cases in which we declined to impose

---

10. Indeed, even the Court acknowledges that Congress has the power to regulate the grand jury, for it concedes that Congress "is free to prescribe" a rule requiring the prosecutor to disclose substantial exculpatory evidence to the grand jury.

categorical restraints on the grand jury. In none of those cases, however, did we question our power to reach a contrary result.[11]

Although the Court recognizes that it may invoke its supervisory authority to fashion and enforce privilege rules applicable in grand jury proceedings, and suggests that it may also invoke its supervisory authority to fashion other limited rules of grand jury procedure, it concludes that it has no authority to prescribe "standards of prosecutorial conduct before the grand jury," because that would alter the grand jury's historic role as an independent, inquisitorial institution. I disagree.

We do not protect the integrity and independence of the grand jury by closing our eyes to the countless forms of prosecutorial misconduct that may occur inside the secrecy of the grand jury room. After all, the grand jury is not merely an investigatory body; it also serves as a "protector of citizens against arbitrary and oppressive governmental action." United States v. Calandra, 414 U.S., at 343, 94 S.Ct., at 617. Explaining why the grand jury must be both "independent" and "informed," the Court wrote in Wood v. Georgia, 370 U.S. 375, 82 S.Ct. 1364, 8 L.Ed.2d 569 (1962): "Historically, this body has been regarded as a primary security to the innocent against hasty, malicious and oppressive persecution; it serves the invaluable function in our society of standing between the accuser and the accused, whether the latter be an individual, minority group, or other, to determine whether a charge is founded upon reason or was dictated by an intimidating power or by malice and personal ill will." Id., at 390, 82 S.Ct., at 1373. It blinks reality to say that the grand jury can adequately perform this important historic role if it is intentionally misled by the prosecutor-- on whose knowledge of the law and facts of the underlying criminal investigation the jurors will, of necessity, rely.

Unlike the Court, I am unwilling to hold that countless forms of prosecutorial misconduct must be tolerated – no matter how prejudicial they may be, or how seriously they may distort the legitimate function of the grand jury– simply because they are not proscribed by Rule 6 of the Federal Rules of Criminal Procedure or a statute that is applicable

---

11. In Costello v. United States, 350 U.S. 359, 363, 76 S.Ct. 406, 408, 100 L.Ed. 397 (1956), for example, the Court held that an indictment based solely on hearsay evidence is not invalid under the Grand Jury Clause of the Fifth Amendment. The Court then rejected the petitioner's argument that it should invoke "its power to supervise the administration of justice in federal courts" to create a rule permitting defendants to challenge indictments based on unreliable hearsay evidence. The Court declined to exercise its power in this way because "[n]o persuasive reasons are advanced for establishing such a rule. It would run counter to the whole history of the grand jury institution, in which laymen conduct their inquiries unfettered by technical rules. Neither justice nor the concept of a fair trial requires such a change." Id., at 364, 76 S.Ct., at 409.

in grand jury proceedings. Such a sharp break with the traditional role of the federal judiciary is unprecedented, unwarranted, and unwise. Unrestrained prosecutorial misconduct in grand jury proceedings is inconsistent with the administration of justice in the federal courts and should be redressed in appropriate cases by the dismissal of indictments obtained by improper methods.[12]

III.

What, then, is the proper disposition of this case? I agree with the Government that the prosecutor is not required to place all exculpatory evidence before the grand jury. A grand jury proceeding is an ex parte investigatory proceeding to determine whether there is probable cause to believe a violation of the criminal laws has occurred, not a trial. Requiring the prosecutor to ferret out and present all evidence that could be used at trial to create a reasonable doubt as to the defendant's guilt would be inconsistent with the purpose of the grand jury proceeding and would place significant burdens on the investigation. But that does not mean that the prosecutor may mislead the grand jury into believing that there is probable cause to indict by withholding clear evidence to the contrary. I thus agree with the Department of Justice that "when a prosecutor conducting a grand jury inquiry is personally aware of substantial evidence which directly negates the guilt of a subject of the investigation, the prosecutor must present or otherwise disclose such evidence to the grand jury before seeking an indictment against such a person." U.S. Dept. of Justice, United States Attorneys' Manual ¶ 9-11.233, p. 88 (1988).

Although I question whether the evidence withheld in this case directly negates respondent's guilt,[13] I need not resolve my doubts because the Solicitor General did not ask the Court to review the nature of the evidence withheld. Instead, he asked us to decide the legal question whether an indictment may be dismissed because the prosecutor failed to present exculpatory evidence. Unlike the Court and

---

12. Although the Court's opinion barely mentions the fact that the grand jury was intended to serve the invaluable function of standing between the accuser and the accused, I must assume that in a proper case it will acknowledge--as even the Solicitor General does – that unrestrained prosecutorial misconduct in grand jury proceedings "could so subvert the integrity of the grand jury process as to justify judicial intervention.

13. I am reluctant to rely on the lower courts' judgment in this regard, as they apparently applied a more lenient legal standard. The District Court dismissed the indictment because the "information withheld raises reasonable doubt about the Defendant's intent to defraud," and thus "renders the grand jury's decision to indict gravely suspect." The Court of Appeals affirmed this decision because it was not "clearly erroneous." 899 F.2d 898, 902-904 (CA10 1990).

the Solicitor General, I believe the answer to that question is yes, if the withheld evidence would plainly preclude a finding of probable cause. I therefore cannot endorse the Court's opinion.

* * *

Question

What are the differences between an administrative investigation and a grand jury investigation?

b. Grand Jury Secrecy

Rule 6(e) of the Federal Rules of Criminal Procedure prohibits the disclosure of grand jury material or information except as authorized under Rule 6(e). Thus, evidence obtained in a grand jury investigation may not be used by the government in a civil case unless the evidence is obtained independently of the grand jury or a district court has decided that there is a "particularized need" for such evidence and has issued an order pursuant to Rule 6(e). In making such a determination, the court will consider all relevant facts and circumstances, including any alternate means of obtaining the evidence.

UNITED STATES v. DYNAVAC

United States Court of Appeals, Ninth Circuit, 1993.
6 F.3d 1407.

SUHRHEINRICH, CIRCUIT JUDGE.

* * *

I.

The Internal Revenue Service is presently investigating the federal income tax liability of Dynavac, Inc. (formerly Allied Tank Cleaning, Inc.), for the taxable years ending September 30, 1979, September 30, 1980, September 30, 1981, and September 30, 1982. As part of this investigation, IRS Agent Ronald Sheresh issued administrative summonses to Corn, and to Helmer and Wright, the current owners of Dynavac, and to Dynavac, seeking that company's business books and records for the years in question. Respondents resisted, contending that the requested materials were "matters occurring before the grand jury" not subject to disclosure because they had been previously disclosed to the grand jury during a 1983 criminal investigation of Corn.

In the criminal investigation, the books and records of three corporations in which Corn was the sole or majority shareholder, Transambient Corporation, Commercial Cleaning Corp. and Allied Tank

Cleaning, Inc. (now known as Dynavac, Inc.), were turned over to the grand jury. Corn was later indicted on twenty-three counts of conspiracy, income tax evasion, and the filing of fraudulent claims with the United States Navy, and eventually pled guilty to three of the counts. At the plea hearing Corn also purportedly agreed to waive his rights (but not those of any other individual or entity) under Rule 6(e) and agreed to let the IRS have any and all information by the grand jury in the criminal case for the purpose of its making a "tax assessment" against Corn. Corn's criminal attorney later transmitted to the United States Attorney the special agent's report ("SAR") prepared as part of the criminal tax investigation of Corn, which included a number of references to the substance and results of the grand jury's inquiry.

After Corn pled guilty, Revenue Agent Reginald Curtis ("Curtis"), took over the federal civil tax audits of Corn and the three corporations. Curtis reviewed Corn's criminal file which contained the indictment, the transcript of the guilty plea, and the sentencing report; requested documents; and made a preliminary determination of the taxpayers' (Corn and his companies) tax deficiencies.

Curtis and his group manager Jim Thibault received word from the United States Attorney's office in San Diego, which had been involved in the grand jury investigation, that the SAR could be used in the civil tax audit so long as it was received from the taxpayer. Sometime after receiving the SAR, Curtis issued a summons for the books and records of Dynavac. The district court refused to enforce the summons, however, because of Curtis's use of the report, and the government withdrew its enforcement petition. Thibault thereafter directed Curtis to purge all references of the SAR from Curtis's papers, which Curtis did. Thibault physically took the Dynavac files away from Curtis and sent them to the chief of the examinations branch for reassignment to a group that was outside of Thibault's branch. Curtis eventually finished the audit of Corn and the other two corporations, excluding Dynavac, Inc.

The Dynavac civil tax audit was reassigned to Sheresh, who issued the administrative summonses which are the subject of the current enforcement proceeding. Sheresh is an agent in the general program of the IRS examination division. The file which he received contained only Dynavac's tax returns for the years 1979 through 1982, Corn's indictment, the transcript of Corn's plea, and portions of an Internal Revenue manual. No one contends that Sheresh has had any improper contact with Curtis or Thibault concerning the SAR.

* * *

The government filed petitions in the district court to enforce the internal revenue summonses issued by Sheresh. After conducting an evidentiary hearing, the district court concluded that the materials, Dynavac's books and records, were not "grand jury material," because they existed prior to the issuance of the grand jury subpoena. The court also found that there was a violation of Rule 6(e) when Curtis obtained the SAR, but that it was subsequently cured after the file was purged and the case transferred to Sheresh. The district court therefore declined respondents' request to quash the summonses. This appeal followed.

II.
A.

With certain exceptions, Rule 6(e) imposes a general rule against disclosure of "matters occurring before the grand jury" on government attorneys. Fed.R.Crim.P. 6(e)(2).[1] This long-established policy of nondisclosure seeks to: (1) prevent the escape of prospective indictees, (2) insure the grand jury of unfettered freedom in its deliberations, (3) impede the subornation of perjury and tampering of witnesses by targets of the investigation, (4) encourage forthrightness in witnesses without fear of retaliation, and (5) act as a shield for those who are exonerated by the grand jury. When government attorneys seek grand jury information for use in related civil proceedings, the concerns are that disclosure will increase the risk of inadvertent or illegal further release of the information to unauthorized persons, the integrity of the grand jury process itself will be compromised, and possible subversion of the limits otherwise placed on the government's investigative and discovery powers in the civil context. However, Rule 6(e) "is intended only to protect

---

1.   Rule 6(e) provides in relevant part:

(e) Recording and Disclosure of Proceedings.

* * *

(2) General Rule of Secrecy. A grand juror, an interpreter, a stenographer, an operator of a recording device, a typist who transcribes recorded testimony, an attorney for the government, or any person to whom disclosure is made under paragraph (3)(A)(ii) of this subdivision shall not disclose matters occurring before the grand jury, except as otherwise provided for in these rules. No obligation of secrecy may be imposed on any person except in accordance with this rule. A knowing violation of Rule 6 may be punished as a contempt of court.* * *

(3) Exceptions. * * * (C) Disclosure otherwise prohibited by this rule of matters occurring before the grand jury may also be made—(i) when so directed by a court preliminarily to or in connection with a judicial proceeding; (i) when permitted by a court at the request of the defendant, upon a showing that grounds may exist for a motion to dismiss the indictment because of matters occurring before the grand jury; (iii) when the disclosure is made by an attorney for the government to another federal grand jury; or (iv) when permitted by a court at the request of an attorney for the government, upon a showing that such matters may disclose a violation of state criminal law, to an appropriate official of a state or subdivision of a state for the purpose of enforcing such law. If the court orders disclosure of matters occurring before the grand jury, the disclosure shall be made in such manner, at such time, and under such conditions as the court may direct.

against disclosure of what is said or takes place in the grand jury room * * * it is not the purpose of the Rule to foreclose from all future revelation to proper authorities the same information or documents which were presented to the grand jury." United States v. Interstate Dress Carriers, Inc., 280 F.2d 52, 54 (2d Cir.1960). Thus, if a document is sought for its own sake rather than to learn what took place before the grand jury, and if its disclosure will not compromise the integrity of the grand jury process, Rule 6(e) does not prohibit its release. Id.

When the grand jury investigation is already terminated and an indictment has been issued, only "institutional" concerns are implicated by the documentary disclosure. See generally Nervi, *FRCrP 6(e) and the Disclosure of Documents Reviewed by a Grand Jury,* 57 U.Chi.L.Rev. 221, 230 (1990). The fear of compromising future grand jury proceedings is further reduced when the request is for business records created for purposes independent of grand jury investigations, which have legitimate uses unrelated to the substance of the grand jury proceedings. In sum, we think that the disclosure of business records independently generated and sought for legitimate purposes, would not "seriously compromise the secrecy of the grand jury's deliberations." *DiLeo,* 959 F.2d at 19 (quoting In re Special March 1981 Grand Jury (Almond Pharmacy), 753 F.2d 575, 578 (7th Cir.1985)).[2]

Various different tests have been utilized by other circuits. See generally, Nervi, *FRCrP and Disclosure of Documents;* In re Grand Jury Proceedings, 851 F.2d at 860 (recognizing four approaches, citing In re John Doe Grand Jury Proceedings, 537 F.Supp. 1038 (D.R.I.1982), and creating a fifth approach). In re John Doe Grand Jury Proceedings, 537 F.Supp. 1038 (D.R.I.1982) (classifying four distinct approaches). The per se approach, which never classifies documents as "matters occurring before the grand jury," see, e.g., United States v. Weinstein, 511 F.2d 622, 627 n. 5 (2d Cir. 1975) ("[i]n any event it is questionable whether Rule 6(e) applies to documents"); In re Grand Jury Investigation of

---

2.   We are not unaware of criticisms of this approach. See, e.g., Nervi, *FRCrP and Disclosure of Documents,* 57 U.Chi.L.Rev. at 235-36 (purpose test "focuses on an issue–the party's motive in seeking disclosure–ultimately unrelated to the question of whether grand jury secrecy is violated through release of the document"); In re Grand Jury Proceedings, 851 F.2d at 865 ("Even documents 'sought for their own sake' may, when considered in the aggregate and in their relationship to one another, make possible inferences about the nature and direction of the grand jury inquiry."); In re Special February, 1975 Grand Jury, 662 F.2d 1232, 1243-44 (7th Cir.1981) ("If that is all there is to the test, grand jury secrecy should be seriously eroded by being sacrificed to the alleged need for the documents by someone else and the power of the grand jury could be misused."); In re John Doe Grand Jury Proceedings, 537 F.Supp. 1038, 1046 (D.R.I.1982) (agreeing with In re Special February). We think these concerns a bit exaggerated in the case of business records created for purposes other than furthering a grand jury investigation. However, we allow for the possibility in a rare and unusual case of making a showing that learning which documents were subpoenaed by the grand jury may disclose the grand jury's deliberative process.

Ven-Fuel, 441 F.Supp. 1299, 1303 (M.D.Fla.1977) ("it is doubtful whether mere documentary information was ever included within the scope of Rule 6(e)"), and the opposite per se approach, which treats documents as always protected from disclosure under Rule 6(e), see, e.g., Texas v. United States Steel, 546 F.2d 626 (5th Cir. 1977); In re Grand Jury Proceedings (Kluger), 827 F.2d 868 (2d Cir.1987); see also In re Grand Jury Matter (Garden Court), 697 F.2d 511, 512 (3rd Cir.1982) (dicta) ("[w]ere we writing on a clean slate, we might well hold that disclosure of any material generated in connection with a grand jury proceeding is governed by Rule 6(e)(2)"), offer bright line rules, but suffer by their over-and under-inclusiveness. Nervi, *FRCrP 6(e) and the Disclosure of Documents*, at 237-39. The per se rule has been criticized as being inattentive to " 'the important privacy and confidentiality purposes embodied in Rule 6(e) and to the need for judicial supervision of the release of material obtained by coercion with the promise of secrecy.' " Id. at 238 & n. 70 (quoting In re Grand Jury Proceedings, 851 F.2d at 864-65). See also In re Doe, 537 F.Supp. at 1044 ("an examination of all documents subpoenaed and reviewed by the grand jury can reveal a great deal about the nature, scope, and purpose of a secret grand jury investigation * * * [a]nd it is clear that such things as scope and direction of the grand jury investigation constitute 'matters occurring before the grand jury' and are therefore protected from disclosure by the provisions of Rule 6(e)"). The opposite per se approach ("per se subject to Rule 6(e)"), may unduly hinder discovery, because every specific document request that coincided with a grand jury inquiry must be denied unless the civil litigant makes a showing of particularized need under Rule 6(e)(3)(C)(i). Furthermore, a savvy party under grand jury investigation could effectively insulate documents from anticipated civil discovery simply by turning over incriminating documents to the grand jury.

The "effect" test determines whether disclosure of a particular requested item will reveal some secret aspect of the inner workings of the grand jury. This approach has been adopted by the Third, see, e.g., In re Grand Jury Matter (Catania), 682 F.2d 61, 63 (3d Cir.1982) ("Rule 6(e) applies * * * to anything which may reveal what occurred before the grand jury"); Fourth, In re Grand Jury Subpoena (United States v. Under Seal), 920 F.2d 235, 241 (4th Cir.1990) ("The substantive content of 'matters occurring before the grand jury' can be anything that may reveal what has transpired before the grand jury."); Seventh, see, e.g., *Almond Pharmacy*, 753 F.2d at 578 ("[i]f a document is sought for its own sake rather than to learn what took place before the grand jury, and if its release will not seriously compromise the secrecy of the grand jury's deliberations, Rule 6(e) does not forbid its release") (and cases cited therein); Eighth, see, e.g., In re Grand Jury Proceedings Relative to Perl, 838 F.2d 304, 306 (8th Cir.1988) ("[u]nless a document reveals something about the intricate workings of the grand jury itself, the documents are not intrinsically secret just because they were examined by a grand jury"); Tenth, see, e.g., Anaya v. United States, 815 F.2d 1373, 1379 (10th Cir.1987) ("the test of whether disclosure of information will violate Rule 6(e) depends upon 'whether revelation in the particular context would in fact reveal what was before the grand jury' ") and D.C., see, e.g., Senate of Puerto Rico v. United States Dept. of Justice, 823 F.2d 574, 582 (D.C. Cir.1987) ("there is no per se rule against disclosure of any and all information which has reached the grand jury chambers * * * the touchstone is whether disclosure would 'tend to reveal some secret aspect of the grand jury's investigation' "), Circuits. The strength of the effect test is its mandate that the court make a factual inquiry on a document-by-document basis, thereby offering greater assurance of grand jury secrecy. In its strength lies its weakness however, because, as pointed out by Nervi, its application requires considerable judicial time and resources, and the ad hoc nature of the test limits the value of precedent for both litigants and courts. Id. at 234-35.

Finally, there is the Sixth Circuit's rebuttable presumption approach, which presumes that documents are "matters occurring before the grand jury," but permits the moving party to rebut that presumption by showing that "the information is public or was not obtained through coercive means or that disclosure would be otherwise available by civil discovery and would not reveal the nature, scope, or direction of the grand jury inquiry." *In re Grand Jury Proceedings*, 851 F.2d at 867. Although the rebuttable presumption approach offers a compromise between the per se rules and the case-by-case approach, it has been criticized because the rebuttal factors proposed "fail to distinguish between critical and unimportant disclosures." Nervi, *FRCrP and Disclosure of Documents*, at 242-43. The first showing, that the information sought is public, overlooks the fact that most of the items commonly considered can be obtained even without resort to discovery. The second factor, that the information was not obtained by coercion, creates a distinction between documents that are subpoenaed and those that are voluntarily submitted, and in doing so, discourages voluntary production of documents and doesn't necessarily prevent civil litigants from misusing the grand jury's broad investigative powers to advance their cause. Finally, the third rebuttal factor, which requires the moving party to demonstrate that disclosure would otherwise be available through civil discovery and would not reveal the direction of the grand jury's inquiry, defeats the purpose of a rebuttable presumption approach by introducing what is essentially an "effect" analysis. This in turn undermines the advantages of a rebuttable presumption. Id.

Here, the business records of Dynavac predated the grand jury investigation. Although the SAR was a "matter occurring before the grand jury" such that its disclosure to Curtis was a violation of Rule 6(e), the district court found as a matter of fact, that any taint was cured by the purging of Curtis's file and the transferring the case to Sheresh. Further, the IRS has a legitimate interest in the documents as part of its authority to assess civil tax liabilities, see, 26 U.S.C. §§ 7601-7602 (West 1989); and the records were subpoenaed directly from respondents, without mention of the grand jury. We are therefore satisfied that the integrity of the grand jury's deliberative process would not be compromised by their disclosure.

* * *

For all the foregoing reasons, the judgment of the district court is AFFIRMED.

Notes And Questions

Exceptions to Rule 6(e)'s prohibition on disclosure of grand jury matters are made only in cases of compelling necessity – i.e., "where there is proof that without access to the grand jury materials, a litigant's position would be 'greatly prejudiced' or 'an injustice would be done.' " United States v. Procter & Gamble, 356 U.S. 677, 681-82, 78 S.Ct 983, 986, 2 L.Ed.2d 1077 (1958).

A private party seeking disclosure of grand jury material has the burden of demonstrating a compelling necessity or particularized need for that material before a determination is made about disclosure. This is established by showing that "(a) the material sought will prevent a possible injustice, (b) the need for disclosure outweighs the need for secrecy, and (c) the request is narrowly tailored to provide only material so needed." FDIC v. Ernst & Whinney, 921 F.2d 83, 86 (6th Cir. 1990), citing Douglas Oil Co. v. Petrol Stops Northwest, 441 U.S. 211, 222-23 (1979).

According to the court in *Ernst & Whinney*, the fact that the grand jury documents are relevant or that production of them by the Federal Bureau of Investigation would expedite civil discovery or reduce expenses for the parties is insufficient to show particularized need when the evidence can be obtained through ordinary discovery, *i.e.,* subpoenaing the documents from other sources, or pursuing other routine avenues of investigation. Id. at 86-87.

Grand Jury Secrecy. Note that the grand jury proceeding at issue in *Dynavac* had terminated. Where the grand jury investigation is ongoing, the need for secrecy is difficult to overcome by a litigant seeking grand jury materials. Any grand jury evidence or information used at trial, however, is no longer protected under Rule 6(e) and may be used in a subsequent civil investigation.

Because of the secrecy of the grand jury proceedings, the special agent must determine whether a civil action is being considered or is currently underway, and if so, the agent must coordinate any request for a grand jury investigation with the local IRS representative, who must notify the appropriate civil unit. The civil investigation then must cease unless permission has been obtained to continue the investigation during the course of the grand jury investigation.

1. Which test does the Ninth Circuit adopt for determining whether documents constitute "matters occurring before the grand jury"?

2. Testimony of witnesses is always presumed to be "matters occurring before the grand jury." Why?

3. Under what circumstances may business records created independently of the grand jury investigation be protected from disclosure under Rule 6(e)?

C. VOLUNTARY DISCLOSURE

Occasionally, a taxpayer who has fraudulently failed to file a return or who has filed a fraudulent return may repent and consider filing an honest return. If such a person seeks your counsel, what advice would you give?

UNITED STATES v. HEBEL
United States Court of Appeals, Eighth Circuit, 1982.
668 F.2d 995.

PER CURIAM.

Carlyle Merritt and Richard Hebel appeal from single-count convictions for criminal violation of the income tax laws. In a bench trial on stipulated facts the district court found Merritt guilty of knowingly and willfully subscribing his 1975 income tax return which failed to report his true income. The court convicted Merritt of violating 26 U.S.C. § 7206(1), and fined him $5,000. At the same bench trial, the district court found Hebel guilty of income tax evasion for calendar year 1975, in violation of 26 U.S.C. § 7201, and fined him $10,000. We affirm.

Merritt and Hebel do not dispute these violations on appeal. Each taxpayer voluntarily disclosed his filing of a false return to the Internal Revenue Service, corrected the tax discrepancies in an amended return, and paid the appropriate tax due. They contend, however, that an IRS practice of not prosecuting persons who make such voluntary disclosures bars their prosecution.

Based on this alleged practice of the IRS, appellants assert the following issues on appeal:

1) That the trial court erred in finding that defendants had not established a governmental practice not to prosecute voluntary disclosure tax cases and therefore erred in denying the motions to enjoin their indictments, and motions to dismiss and suppress; 2) That the trial court erred in denying dismissal on grounds of selective prosecution; and 3) That these prosecutions violated due process and denied taxpayers effective assistance of counsel because their attorneys counseled them to make disclosure of the facts concerning their tax delinquencies in reliance upon the policy and practice of the Government not to prosecute taxpayers who voluntarily disclose tax falsifications.

The district court initially referred these matters to Magistrate James D. Hodges, Jr., to hear and make recommendations concerning defendants' motions to suppress evidence and to dismiss the prosecutions. After an evidentiary hearing, the magistrate made the following findings:

8. Messrs. Smith and Brown (experienced tax lawyers) advised defendants that based upon their experience in the tax area that while the Internal Revenue Service and Justice Department had publicly stated in 1952 that they would no longer assure taxpayers of nonprosecution where a voluntary disclosure of previous tax errors was made, that it had been counsels' experience that prosecution would not result where a true voluntary disclosure was made.

9. Based upon this advice defendants requested counsel to disclose to the Internal Revenue Service that apparently errors existed in their income tax returns. Pursuant to these instructions counsel informed the Internal Revenue Service on December 2, 1976 of the defendants' identities and that there appeared to be substantial tax deficiencies on defendants' individual returns as well as those of Hebel Fertilizer & Chemical, Inc. for the years at issue. At this time neither defendants nor counsel was aware of any pending investigations involving defendants.

10. At the time the disclosure was made to Robert J. Moeller, acting Chief of the Internal Revenue Service Audit Division, and Jack L. Schroeder, Chief of Internal Revenue Service Branch I counsel were advised that defendants' returns had previously been referred to a Revenue Agent for audit.

11. Defendants provided a complete and absolute disclosure of any and all transactions which may have had tax ramifications for the years at issue to his counsel and to the CPAs engaged by counsel. At the conclusion of the independent audit defendants caused amended individual and corporate tax returns to be prepared. These amended returns were filed on December 27, 1976 and the tax due of approximately $ 200,000 was paid.

12. Subsequent to filing the amended returns, defendants supplied the IRS with detailed identification of the location, amounts, time periods and occasions of the then determined inaccuracies in defendants' tax returns by allowing the IRS to examine and make copies of extensive accounting workpapers and produced by the accounting firm working for defendants' counsel. Defendants also provided access to their original records and were interviewed by the IRS regarding their tax returns.

13. Defendants were indicted on February 24, 1981.

15. Defendants' disclosures were voluntarily made in reliance upon the advice of counsel but with knowledge that, while it was counsel's belief that they would not be prosecuted, there was no absolute grant of immunity from prosecution.

In considering the motions to suppress and dismiss, Magistrate Hodges reviewed the same factual matters asserted in this appeal. His opinion stated in part:

> In light of the fact that the IRS publicly abandoned its voluntary disclosure policy in 1952 and defendants and their counsel were aware of this, the court is of the view that defendants' disclosures were knowingly and voluntarily made and accordingly all motions should be denied, alternatively, if a voluntary disclosure policy should be found to exist there appears to be a serious question as to whether defendants' disclosure was in fact a true voluntary disclosure.

> Specifically, defendants have moved to dismiss the indictment against them under the due process clause of the fifth amendment to the United States Constitution based upon lack of notice, failure to comply with the Administrative Procedure Act, equitable estoppel and selective prosecution. The record appears to be relatively clear

that the IRS and Department of Justice followed a written policy of not prosecuting criminally, taxpayers who made voluntary disclosures of irregularities in their tax returns during the period between 1934 and 1952. However, this policy was abandoned in 1952 and from that time until the present it has been the announced policy of the IRS that a voluntary disclosure would be considered along with all other facts and circumstance of a case in determining whether or not criminal charges would be filed. See generally, United States v. Shotwell Mfg. Co., 355 U.S. 233, 235 n.2, 78 S.Ct. 245, 248, 2 L.Ed. 2d 234 (1957); United States v. Choate, 619 F.2d 21 (9th Cir. 1980). Since counsel was aware of this change in policy and advised defendants of the change, defendants' arguments based upon lack of notice and under the APA must fail. In this regard, defendants argue that while no written policy existed there was an unwritten practice of not prosecuting taxpayers who made a voluntary disclosure. The simple answer to this is defendants have failed to establish the existence of such a practice. While there appears to have been few, if any, prosecutions of true voluntary disclosures the IRS has consistently reserved the right to do so. Indeed, the position is recognized by the legal publications submitted by the government and at best there appears to be disagreement among the bar as to the possibility of prosecution.

Further, defendants' motion based upon selection (sic) prosecution is without merit. To prevail on this motion defendants must show both that he was singled out for prosecution and that the prosecution was based upon impermissible grounds. Here, defendants have failed to meet either prong of the test. In light of the amount of tax due and the status of the IRS's investigation at the time of disclosure, the record shows ample reason for prosecuting defendants. Further, defendants have been unable to raise any colorable claim of improper motive.

Finally, defendants' motion to suppress must likewise be denied. It is well recognized that the government must establish guilt by evidence independently secured and not by evidence obtained as a result of trickery or coercion from defendants. Further, this principal clearly includes evidence induced from a person under a governmental promise, either direct or implied, of immunity. Here, however, the record does not support a finding that defendants' disclosures were brought about as a result of any government conduct. Rather, it does support a finding that all disclosures were freely made by defendants in hope that they would not be prosecuted rather than in reliance upon any governmental promise of immunity.

Indeed, as noted above, the government has withdrawn its policy of non-prosecution of voluntary disclosures and this fact was known to counsel and related to defendants. Further, there is no evidence of any acts on the part of the government which could be considered calculated to lead defendants to believe that the practice was any different from the stated policy. Indeed, this record reveals that the IRS and its officials have consistently maintained that prosecution was a possibility in voluntary disclosure cases. Finally, defendants have produced no evidence of direct promises or inducements made to defendants or counsel during the proceedings.

United States v. Hebel and Merritt, at 4-7 (magistrate's report and recommendation).

The magistrate recommended denial of the motions, and the district court accepted that recommendation. Thereafter, the trial proceeded before the district court upon facts stipulated by the parties subject to reserved objections. The district court found each defendant guilty on one count of a multiple indictment. On appeal, the defendants attack the findings and rulings denying dismissal of the indictments and suppression of the evidence.

We agree with the district court. The magistrate's findings, which are supported by the evidence, demonstrate that no governmental policy or practice on voluntary disclosure relating to false tax returns necessarily relieves taxpayers who file false tax returns from criminal prosecution. The prior existence of that policy and its abandonment came to the attention of the Supreme Court in United States v. Shotwell Manufacturing Co., 355 U.S. 233, 78 S.Ct. 245, 2 L.Ed. 2d 234 (1957). The Court noted:

> Under that policy, first announced by the Treasury Department in 1945, the Department did not refer to the Department of Justice for prosecution cases of intentional income tax evasion where the taxpayers had made a clean breast of things to the Treasury before any investigation had been initiated by the Revenue Service. This policy was set forth in various informal announcements by Treasury officials, but was never formalized by statute or regulation. The policy was abandoned in January 1952.

As of 1973, the Treasury Department's "voluntary disclosure policy" read as follows:

> The Treasury Department on January 10, 1952, formally abandoned its long-standing "voluntary disclosure policy". It is, therefore, no longer an administrative basis for declining prosecution in the Revenue Service that a prospective defendant voluntarily

revealed his tax fraud to an appropriate official of that Service before any investigation of his affairs had begun. * * * Now the fact that a taxpayer seeks voluntarily to rectify a false return without prodding by investigators or the threat of investigation is given some weight in determining whether to prosecute but is not conclusive of the issue. (U.S. Department of Justice Manual for Criminal Tax Trials, Ch. 1, p. 5.)

In an earlier civil case brought by Hebel to enjoin his prosecution, the same district court noted the Treasury Department's 1973 position.

In this case, taxpayers Hebel and Merritt received a substantial benefit from disclosing and rectifying past errors. The indictment consisted of seven counts, three counts each charging Hebel and Merritt individually, and one count charging them both. Each defendant was convicted on only one count, and neither received a sentence of imprisonment.

Regardless of whether a taxpayer actually benefits or suffers detriment from voluntarily disclosing and rectifying faulty tax returns, that disclosure itself does not insulate the taxpayer from prosecution under any administrative policy or practice recognized by this court. Taxpayers and their attorneys cannot rely on a long-since abandoned policy of non-prosecution when a taxpayer voluntarily discloses violation of the tax laws. Accordingly, we affirm the convictions of Hebel and Merritt on the basis of the magistrate's findings and opinion, adopted by the district court.

Notes And Questions

Although the government's voluntary disclosure policy was withdrawn in 1952, as the *Hebel* opinion states, the fact is there have been very few reported cases of prosecution after a voluntary disclosure, and those few cases have involved extenuating circumstances. One such case was Crystal v. United States, 172 F.3d 1141 (9th Cir. 1999), in which the taxpayers were mistakenly informed by the IRS that there was no investigation underway and based on that information, they made what they thought was a voluntary disclosure. When the government served third party summonses, the taxpayers moved to quash arguing that the government had acted in bad faith and that their disclosure should be viewed as voluntary. The Ninth Circuit held there was no bad faith and thus the summonses were valid. Id. at 1152-53.

In 2009, the government resurrected the voluntary disclosure program for offshore accounts. While the government expected approximately 1,000 voluntary disclosures, it received about 15,000. The program was so successful that in 2011 the IRS initiated a new voluntary disclosure program for offshore accounts in 2011. This program, which expired on August 31, 2011, provided a higher penalty than the 2009 program, although like the 2009 program, it offered participants the opportunity to avoid a criminal prosecution.

1. What constitutes a voluntary disclosure? Was the disclosure in *Hebel* voluntary?

2. If the government no longer takes the position that a voluntary disclosure will insulate a taxpayer from criminal liability, why do you think there have been so few criminal prosecutions after a voluntary disclosure?

3. How would you go about making a voluntary disclosure while ensuring that your client is fully protected? Should your advice to the client differ depending upon whether or not a return had been filed initially? Why or why not? Will it make any difference if your client has unreported illegal source income?

4. Prior to 2009, the voluntary disclosure program did not impose civil penalties. During the 2009 voluntary disclosure program for offshore accounts the IRS required those taking advantage of the program to pay a civil penalty of 20% and this penalty was increased to 25% in the 2011 program. Why has the government decided to impose civil penalties in the voluntary disclosure program and is this a good policy?

5. Mr. Big travels widely on business and has considerable assets. In 1995, he opened an account in Zurich with $2 million. He chose Zurich because of Switzerland's bank secrecy laws and its low tax rate. He opened the account in the name of himself and his son but he requested that no statements be sent. Mr. Big knew about the U.S. reporting laws for foreign accounts but purposely did not report the account to avoid paying U.S. taxes. In 2011, Mr. Big died and his son inherited the account. Although the son had known about the account, he had never withdrawn any money from it. Son seeks your advice as to his liability and what, if anything, he should do.

D. INVESTIGATIVE TECHNIQUES

In investigating a potential criminal case, special agents may find it necessary to search a premises for documents, books, records, property, contraband, etc. If there is sufficient probable cause to believe a crime has been committed, and that the property subject to seizure is on the premises to be searched, a search warrant may be issued. But it is the policy of the IRS and the Department of Justice that search warrants must be utilized with restraint. IRM § 9.4.9.2 (6-19-2008). The request for a search warrant must be made in writing and approved by the District Counsel as well as by the Justice Department. In addition, a search warrant will not be issued unless the case is significant. The significance of a case is determined by considering such factors as the amount of taxes owed, the nature of the offense, the need for the evidence to be seized, and the deterrent impact of the case. In addition, the warrant will not be issued where there is an ongoing grand jury investigation or where it is anticipated that such an investigation will commence during the time the warrant will be executed. Id.

Where a request is made to search the premises of a practicing attorney, special considerations apply to avoid violating the attorney-client privilege. Thus, the warrant must be specific in order to reduce the likelihood of privileged material being searched and reviewed. Generally, a privilege team should accompany the investigating agents. The team should view any material that may be subject to the privilege in order to determine what may be viewed by the agents conducting the investigation.

A warrantless search is permissible in two cases: (1) where the taxpayer/occupant of the premises consents and (2) where the search is for weapons and the search is made pursuant to an arrest. In the latter case, the search area is confined to the person of the arrestee and the immediate area within reach of the arrestee if the investigating agents have reason to suspect that a weapon might be located there. In the former case, only the person whose rights are being affected can give consent. Thus, a landlord cannot give permission for a tenant. Similarly, an employee cannot waive the rights of an employer unless the employee is authorized to act as agent for the employer.

The Supreme Court held in California v. Greenwood, 486 U.S. 35, 108 S.Ct. 1625, 100 L.Ed.2d 30 (1988), that there is no expectation of privacy in garbage left on the curtilage outside the home for pickup by a trash collector. Thus, special agents legally can conduct a warrantless search and seizure of a taxpayer's trash.

In a felony investigation, special agents may monitor the taxpayer's use of the mails to locate a fugitive, determine whether a tax offense has been committed, or identify property or assets subject to forfeiture. A request for a mail cover must be made to the Chief of the Criminal Investigation unit with a separate request for each post office that must conduct the mail cover. The request must be specific and may not be made for fishing or exploratory purposes. If the request is granted, a record is made of any data appearing on the outside of sealed or unsealed mail, and of the contents of any unsealed mail.

The Service is prohibited from using wiretaps or similar recording devices to investigate potential tax offenses without the consent of the parties involved. If only one of two or more parties consents, the permission of the chief of the CID or the National Office must be obtained. Under 18 USC § 2517(l), a federal or state agency may share information obtained in a lawful wiretap with "another investigative or law enforcement officer" to the extent that such disclosure is "appropriate to the proper performance of the official duties of the officer making or receiving the disclosure." The Fifth Circuit has held that § 2517(l) permits disclosure of wiretap information to agents of the Internal Revenue Service. See Fleming v. United States, 547 F.2d 872 (5th Cir.1977), cert. denied, 434 U.S. 831, 98 S.Ct. 113, 54 L.Ed.2d 90 (1978).

Seizures of books, records, documents or other property are susceptible to challenges under Fourth Amendment, and sometimes Fifth Amendment, grounds. For a discussion of these constitutional challenges, see discussion, § II.B., below.

II. PROSECUTION OF A CRIMINAL TAX CASE

A. VENUE

UNITED STATES v. MELVAN
United States District Court for the Central District of California, 1987.
676 F.Supp. 997.

MEMORANDUM OPINION

RAFEEDIE, DISTRICT JUDGE.

Defendant John Melvan, one of 11 alleged co-conspirators charged in this case, moves for a change of venue as a matter of right. Melvan is accused of defrauding a federally insured financial institution along with other co-conspirators, and of personal income tax evasion. He moves for a change of venue to the district of his residence, the Southern District of California pursuant to 18 U.S.C. § 3237(b), which provides for change of venue as a matter of right in some circumstances to the home district of a defendant charged with tax evasion. Section 3237(b) was amended in 1984, and the application of the new language presents a case of first impression. While it appears the motion for change of venue would be well taken under the old statute and the case law interpreting it, the new language and Legislative history of the amendment require denying Melvan's motion for change of venue.

FACTUAL BACKGROUND

John Melvan is charged, along with 10 other alleged co-conspirators, in a 40 count indictment. The charges include defrauding federally insured financial institutions by obtaining loans on various pieces of property which had been fraudulently inflated in value by the use of multiple escrows and straw buyers. Melvan is accused of acting as a straw buyer for a piece of property in Bel Air, California, a wealthy suburb of Los Angeles. Melvan allegedly allowed his name and background to be used through a double escrow to falsely inflate the value of the Property. A loan was then allegedly obtained by other co-conspirators at the inflated value from Progressive Savings and Loan in Alhambra, California.

Melvan is also charged with personal income tax evasion. He allegedly received a payment for allowing the use of his name in the double escrow from the other co-conspirators. According to the indictment, however, he failed to report the payment as income on his 1982 federal income tax return.

Melvan is a resident of Vista, California, in the Southern District of California. The property allegedly used in the fraud is located in the Central District, as is the Savings and Loan which was the alleged victim. Other property allegedly used by others in the conspiracy is also located in the Central District, as are other financial institutions that were allegedly victimized by the scheme. Most of the other defendants in the indictment reside in the Central District. Most of the evidence and witnesses also are here in the Central District. The Internal Revenue Service Processing Center which received Melvan's 1982 tax return for processing is located in the Eastern District of California.

LEGAL DISCUSSION

The United States Constitution provides that venue for a criminal trial shall be in the state and district where the offense was committed. U.S. Const.Amend.VI. The venue statute and the Federal Rules of Criminal Procedure likewise guarantee that the prosecution of a crime will take place within the state and district which was also the location of the charged crimes. 18 U.S.C. § 3232; Fed.R.Crim.Proc. Rule 18.

When an offense occurs in more than one district, or is completed in a district other than the district in which the crime began, the

Government has the option of prosecuting the offense in any district in which criminal activity took place. 18 U.S.C. § 3237. That statute provides that any offense which was begun in one district and completed in another may be "prosecuted in any district in which such offense was begun, continued or completed." 18 U.S.C. § 3237(a). In addition, any offense which "involves the use of the mails or interstate transportation" may be prosecuted "in any district from, through, or into which such commerce, mail matter, or imported object moves." Id.

Some tax offenses are exempted from this broad discretion concerning choice of venue for an offense involving the use of the mails. Charges of tax evasion, willful failure to file a return and falsifying documents associated with a tax return must be prosecuted in the district of residence of the defendant when venue outside that district is chosen "based solely on a mailing to the Internal Revenue Service * * *." 18 U.S.C. § 3237(b).

The language of § 3237(b) is the result of attempts by Congress to prevent the IRS from requiring a taxpayer to travel a great distance to the district of the IRS collection office which receives his tax return for processing when the taxpayer is charged with an enumerated tax offense. Without the limitations imposed by § 3237(b), § 3237(a) would allow the IRS to compel a taxpayer charged with tax evasion to face the charges hundreds of miles from his home, far from the evidence and witnesses necessary to the case.

The attempt to limit the venue choices of the IRS in these tax cases led to the original language of § 3237(b). That text, written in 1958, mirrored the language of § 3237(a):

"[W]here an offense involves the use of the mails and is an offense [of tax evasion or falsifying tax-related documents, a defendant may] elect to be tried in the district in which he was residing at the time the alleged offense was committed * * *."

The legislative history of this 1958 amendment indicated that the authors intended to address the problem of a taxpayer forced to defend a tax evasion charge far from home merely because the IRS had received his tax return at a location a great distance from the taxpayer. The legislative history is described in detail in In re United States (Clemente), 608 F.2d 76 (2nd Cir.1979). Congressman Prince H. Preston, the principal author of the bill, stated in legislative hearings that he felt it was unfair to force a resident of, for example, Savannah, Georgia to travel to Atlanta to defend against a tax evasion charge merely because the IRS collection office was in Atlanta. Id. at 79. The statute was aimed at preventing the imposition of the burden of traveling a great distance to defend against a criminal charge, on the notion that the mere receipt by the IRS of an allegedly false tax return should not be sufficient to establish venue for a criminal prosecution far from the taxpayer's home.

The broad language of § 3237(b), "involves the use of the mails," presented problems in applying the law. Criminal prosecutions which included tax evasion charges were split up by courts, moving the tax evasion charges to the home district of a defendant, while maintaining other charges in the district in which the prosecution was originally brought. In addition, a split developed between the circuits over whether the mailing referred to by the statute must be a mailing to the IRS.

In United States v. Wortman, 26 F.R.D. 183 (E.D.Ill.1960), rev'd on other grounds, 326 F.2d 717 (7th Cir.1964), six defendants were charged with conspiracy and with tax evasion. Two of the defendants moved to transfer venue of the tax evasion charges to their home districts, one to the Eastern District of Missouri, and one to the Southern District of Illinois. Id. at 193. Their motions were granted for the tax evasion charges, but the conspiracy charge was retained in the Eastern District of Illinois, as were the charges against the other four defendants. Id. The Government wound up pursuing the prosecution of a single conspiracy in three different districts as a result of this ruling. One can well imagine the costly duplication of effort necessary to perform such a feat, where the same evidence of a single conspiracy would be presented to three different juries at three different times and in three different places.

In United States v. Dalitz, 248 F.Supp. 238 (S.D.Cal.1965), the court was faced with a similar tax evasion and conspiracy indictment. The court ruled that one defendant, a resident of Las Vegas, was entitled to have venue transferred to his home district of Nevada. Id. at 239. This was necessary even though the indictment did not allege the mailing as part of the conspiracy. Id. A transfer was required because the defendant had mailed his tax return to the IRS. Moreover, the court also transferred the conspiracy count to Las Vegas, despite the fact that the other co-defendant was a resident of Los Angeles. Id. at 241-42.

Transfer of venue under § 3237(b) has been ordered regardless of the distance to the home district of the defendant. In *Wortman, supra,* the courthouses in the home districts of the defendants were farther away from their homes than the courthouse where the action was originally brought. Id. at 192-93. In United States v. DeMarco, 394 F.Supp. 611 (D.D.C.1975), an indictment for conspiracy and tax evasion was brought by the Watergate Special Prosecutor against two men involved in appraising the papers of then-President Richard Nixon for the purposes of a tax deduction. One of the defendants was a resident of Los Angeles, and the other lived in Chicago. Each defendant's motion for a transfer of venue to his home district was granted, despite the recognition by the court that this meant sending part of the case from the District of Columbia to the Central District of California and part to the Northern District of Illinois. Id. at 618. The conspiracy count against one defendant was also moved to California. Id. This case, the simplest of conspiracy prosecutions, involving only two conspirators, was split up and moved to two different locations, one over 1,000 miles away, and one over 3,000 miles away. Again, there was a substantial duplication of effort in presenting the evidence of one conspiracy to two different juries in two different locations.

A complicated splitting of a large tax fraud prosecution was upheld in United States v. United States District Court, 693 F.2d 68 (9th Cir.1982). A large tax fraud scheme, organized and run from San Diego, resulted in an 89-count indictment against five defendants in the Southern District of California. Two defendants, charged with tax evasion, were residents of the Northern District of California, and had mailed their tax returns to the IRS in the Eastern District of California. The district court ruled that since the tax returns had been mailed, the tax evasion charges must be moved to the Northern District. Id.[at 69]. The court retained the conspiracy charges in the Southern District, along with the other charges against other defendants. The Court of Appeals agreed that the statute required the transfer, despite the costly result of two lengthy trials in two separate locations. Id. at 70-71. The court noted, however, that this result did not seem to be intended by Congress. Id. at 69-70. The court felt constrained to read the statute as written, however, and transfer the case, stating that Congress had the power to change the statute, but the Court did not. Id. Again, a complex and lengthy trial involving several defendants was split up by the old language of § 3237(b), requiring enormous duplication of effort and cost.

This Ninth Circuit decision conflicted with rulings from the Second Circuit and the Fourth Circuit. *In re United States (Clemente), supra,* held that a defendant charged with racketeering and tax evasion was not entitled to a change of venue under § 3237(b). Id. at 81. The Appeals Court read the statute narrowly, and relied on the legislative history to prevent the change. A strong dissent argued that the transfer was required by the language of the statute, regardless of any narrow intent discovered from the legislative history. Id. at 81-87 (Kearse, J., dissenting). This decision stood alone amongst the case authority against transferring venue.

The reasoning of the Second Circuit was later adopted by the Fourth Circuit in In re United States (Nardone), 706 F.2d 494 (4th Cir.1983). In this case, a defendant was charged, not with evading personal income taxes himself, but with selling fraudulent tax shelters which enabled others to evade taxes. The request to transfer venue was denied, in part because the transfer would have taken the case to the Southern District of New York, where *Clemente* controlled, and the district court there had refused to docket the case. Id. at 495-96.

In 1984, Congress stepped into this confusion with an effort to narrow the statute to reflect its original intent of assisting a taxpayer who could be forced to travel a great distance simply because he lived a great distance from an IRS collection office. Using the vehicle of the Deficit Reduction Act of 1984, P.L. 98-369, 98 Stat. 697, § 3237(b) was amended. The phrase "use of the mails" was eliminated, and the right to have venue of criminal charges in one's home district was limited to cases where the Government had chosen venue "based solely on a mailing to the Internal Revenue Service * * *." 98 Stat. 697.

In the accompanying House Conference Report, the authors of the amendment set forth their intention with regard to this amendment. H.R.Conf.Rep. No. 861, 98th Cong., 2d Sess. 757 (1984), U.S.Code Cong. & Admin.News 1984, pp. 697, 1445. The conflict between the circuits as to the application of the phrase "use of the mails" is noted, and the intended result of the amendment is described:

> Thus, defendants will not be able to force transfer of venue solely because the mails were used as part of the alleged offense. The conferees note that the Internal Revenue Service and the Department of Justice generally attempt to establish venue for a criminal tax prosecution in the judicial district of the taxpayer's residence or principal place of business, because prosecution in that judicial district usually has the most significant deterrent effect. The conferees do not intend a change in that general policy. The conferees also note, however, that the Service and the Department may have valid reasons for bringing a prosecution in another district. Examples of this are multiple defendant cases or cases where venue for non-tax charges is established in a district other than the place of residence or business. The conferees do not intend to restrict the Service and the Department in instances such as these.

Id. at 1002-03, U.S.Code Cong. & Admin.News 1984, pp. 1690, 1691. The phrase which had caused so much confusion, and led to anamolous and costly splitting of cases involving tax evasion was eliminated, while the effort to protect a taxpayer from prosecution at an unreasonable location was preserved. The transfer was still available to a taxpayer as a matter of right, when venue outside his home district was based "solely on a mailing to the Internal Revenue Service."

Only one reported case has considered the amended 18 U.S.C. § 3237(b). In United States v. Benjamin, 623 F.Supp. 1204 (D.D.C.1985), the district court considered a motion to transfer venue from the District of Columbia to California. The motion was made under both § 3237(b) and Fed.R.Crim.P. 21(b). The court ruled that the offenses with which the defendants were charged were not among the tax offenses to which § 3237(b) applied. Id. at 1211. The court nonetheless transferred the case under rule 21(b), for the convenience of the parties and witnesses. Id. at 1215–16.

Defendant Melvan's motion for change of venue thus presents a case of first impression as to application of the new language of 18 U.S.C. § 3237(b). Under the previous version of § 3237(b), this court would have been forced to transfer venue of the tax evasion charge against Melvan to the Southern District of California. The old statute granted Melvan the right to transfer the case, as he had used the mails to send his allegedly false tax return to the IRS in Fresno. This would have resulted in splitting up of a very large and complex criminal prosecution involving 11 co-defendants and 40 charges. Evidence and witnesses, located in the Central District, would have been forced into court on two occasions, the second time over 100 miles away. In addition, the single conspiracy case would have to be proven twice, as the tax evasion here arises from alleged unreported income that was the fruit of the conspiracy. This court would also have had to choose between transferring the conspiracy count to the Southern District along with the tax evasion charge, as was done in *DeMarco, supra,* or keeping the conspiracy charge here, as was done in *Wortman, supra.*

The new language of § 3237(b) does not require so costly and complex a result. The new law does not grant the right to a change of venue for tax evasion to the defendant's home district unless venue outside the home district is "based solely on a mailing to the Internal Revenue Service." This is not the case here. Melvan mailed his tax return to the IRS office in Fresno, California, which is in the Eastern District of California. The Government does not rely on the receipt of the tax return in any fashion to establish venue here in the Central District. The new statute therefore does not apply to Melvan's situation, and no change of venue is required.

This result is also consistent with the expressed intent of Congress in a case such as Melvan's. The legislative history states that Congress intends to allow venue outside the home district of a defendant in "multiple defendant cases or cases where venue for non-tax charges is established in a district other than the place of residence." This case involves 11 defendants, charged with a total of 40 counts of violating federal law, including defrauding a federally insured financial institution and tax evasion. Venue for the non-tax charges is established in the Central District by the location of the property involved, and the location of the acts alleged in the indictment. The intent of Congress is clearly that venue for Melvan's single tax evasion charge should not be transferred.

* * *

The motion of defendant John Melvan to change venue of the tax evasion charge against him is therefore denied.

Notes and Question

In United States v. Nathanson, 813 F.Supp.1433 (E.D. Calif. 1993), the court considered whether severance and transfer were required where tax counts had been properly joined with non-tax criminal counts in a case in which the non-tax counts had determined the venue. The court noted that "[t]he premise of the Government's argument is that joinder trumps venue. The argument cannot prevail because although joinder is governed by the federal rules, venue in criminal cases is colored by the Constitution." Id. at 1435. The court goes on to disagree with *Melvan's* characterization of 18 U.S.C. § 3237(b) as perhaps changing the prior rule that "nontax counts venued in a particular district w[ere] irrelevant to the question of whether the defendant had a right to sever and transfer." Id., citing *Melvan,* 676 F.Supp. at 999-1000. *Nathanson* notes, however, that *Melvan's* characterization is dictum because that particular issue was not before the court. Id. at 1436. The *Nathanson* court went on to hold that the statute was clear and unambiguous, and thus the defendant had an absolute right to have the tax counts severed and transferred to the district in which he resided. Id. at 1438.

Why was the *Melvan* case heard in the Central District of California?

B. THIRD PARTY WITNESSES

In determining whether the taxpayer has properly complied with the internal revenue laws, it may be necessary to examine the books and records, or compel the testimony of third parties with whom the taxpayer may have had business or financial dealings. If so, a third-party summons may be issued under the authority of § 7602. Since the third party often has little interest in protecting the rights and privileges of the taxpayer, § 7609 requires the Service to provide the taxpayer with notice that a third-party summons has been issued. The taxpayer then may challenge the summons, and if successful, the third-party may not divulge the information sought by the Service. In the case of a criminal investigation, however, the Service is not required to give such notice to the taxpayer if there is reasonable cause to believe that doing so would lead to the concealment, destruction or alteration of records, flight by the taxpayer, or the taxpayer's intimidating, bribing or colluding with the third party in order to prevent that person from testifying or producing records. IRC § 7609(c)(2).

1. Expert Testimony

Frequently, the parties may use an expert witness to assist the court in understanding the complexities of the evidence. Rule 702 of the Federal Rules of Evidence permits such testimony "if scientific, technical or other specialized knowledge will assist the trier of fact to understand the evidence or to determine a fact in issue, a witness qualified as an expert by knowledge, skill, experience, training or education, may testify thereto in the form of an opinion or otherwise, if (1) the testimony is based upon sufficient facts or data, (2) the testimony is the product of reliable principals and methods, and (3) the witness has applied the principals and methods reliably to the facts of the case." FED. R. EVID. 702.

UNITED STATES v. MONUS
United States Court of Appeals, Sixth Circuit, 1997.
128 F.3d 376, cert.denied 525 U.S. 823, 119 S.Ct. 67, 142 L.Ed.2d 58 (1998).

KENNEDY, CIRCUIT JUDGE.

* * *

B. Convictions for Filing False Tax Returns
(Counts 107 and 108)

Defendant was convicted, under 26 U.S.C. § 7206(1), of filing false personal income tax returns for 1990 and 1991. These charges resulted from defendant's failure to report as income the money that he embezzled from Phar-Mor through checks paid to the WBL [eds: World Basketball League], checks paid to himself, and checks paid to third parties for his benefit. He argues that [eds: his conviction should be reversed because] the expert testimony of I.R.S. Agent Kurzweil invaded the province of the jury to decide the facts underlying the charge* * *.

* * *

2. Ultimate Issue Testimony

IRS Revenue Agent Bradley Kurzweil testified at trial as an expert witness for the government regarding the two tax counts. Defendant argues that Kurzweil intruded on the province of the jury by testifying to underlying factual issues and offered impermissible opinions on a legal question. Defendant objects to the following trial testimony:

> Q: If you assume that funds have been taken from Phar-Mor, which are not authorized, if you assume that those funds have been diverted to the World Basketball League, and assuming that is an entity owned by Mr. Monus, and you assume a specific amount of funds that have been diverted, what is the impact of those funds on Mr. Monus' tax liabilities for 1990 and 1991?

> A: The dollar amount would be taxable to him in each year.

This testimony did not usurp the function of the jury. Kurzweil did not give his opinion about whether or not defendant was guilty; he merely gave his opinion that the events assumed in the question would trigger tax liability. Such testimony is permissible as an expert opinion to help the jury determine a fact in issue. See United States v. DeClue, 899 F.2d 1465, 1473 (6th Cir.1990) (finding that expert testimony of IRS agent regarding tax liability did not usurp function of jury because agent did not give her opinion about guilt of defendant).

Defendant's arguments that Kurzweil's testimony was an impermissible opinion on a legal question are also without merit. Defendant relies on United States v. Zipkin, 729 F.2d 384 (6th Cir.1984), where we held that it was impermissible for a judge to delegate the responsibility of deciding the law of the case "to a jury through the submission of testimony on controlling legal principles." Id. at 387. That did not occur in this case. Kurzweil did not give a legal opinion that necessarily determined the guilt of defendant or instructed the jury on controlling legal principles. He merely gave his opinion as to whether particular payments under assumed circumstances would be taxable. The jury still had to decide whether the defendant actually stole funds from Phar-Mor and knowingly failed to report them as income before it could conclude that defendant was guilty.

Notes

The Sixth Circuit in United States v. Green, 548 F.2d 1261 (6th Cir. 1977), held that the court further must determine the extent of the potential prejudicial impact of the testimony on the substantial rights of the accused. The court then postulated a 4-pronged test: (1) a qualified expert, (2) must testify on a proper subject, (3) in conformity to a generally accepted explanatory theory, and (4) the probative value of the testimony must outweigh the prejudicial effect. Id. at 1268.

2. Conflicts in Representation

When the third party witness is represented by an attorney, certified public accountant or other person who also represents the taxpayer, the dual representation may create a potential conflict of interest. There are several ways in which such a conflict could arise: (1) when the attorney represents multiple targets of an investigation, (2) when the attorney represents the target and a non-target witness, and (3) when the attorney may be called as a witness.

WHEAT v. UNITED STATES
Supreme Court of the United States, 1988.
486 U.S. 153, 108 S.Ct. 1692, 100 L.Ed.2d 140.

CHIEF JUSTICE REHNQUIST delivered the opinion of the Court.

* * *

I.

Petitioner Mark Wheat, along with numerous codefendants, was charged with participating in a far-flung drug distribution conspiracy. Over a period of several years, many thousands of pounds of marijuana were transported from Mexico and other locations to southern California. Petitioner acted primarily as an intermediary in the distribution ring; he received and stored large shipments of marijuana at his home, then distributed the marijuana to customers in the region.

Also charged in the conspiracy were Juvenal Gomez-Barajas and Javier Bravo, who were represented in their criminal proceedings by attorney Eugene Iredale. Gomez-Barajas was tried first and was acquitted on drug charges overlapping with those against petitioner. To avoid a second trial on other charges, however, Gomez-Barajas offered to plead guilty to tax evasion and illegal importation of merchandise. At the commencement of petitioner's trial, the District Court had not accepted the plea; Gomez-Barajas was thus free to withdraw his guilty plea and proceed to trial.

Bravo, evidently a lesser player in the conspiracy, decided to forgo trial and plead guilty to one count of transporting approximately 2,400 pounds of marijuana from Los Angeles to a residence controlled by Victor Vidal. At the conclusion of Bravo's guilty plea proceedings on August 22, 1985, Iredale notified the District Court that he had been contacted by petitioner and had been asked to try petitioner's case as well. In response, the Government registered substantial concern about the possibility of conflict in the representation. After entertaining some initial discussion of the substitution of counsel, the District Court instructed the parties to present more detailed arguments the following Monday, just one day before the scheduled start of petitioner's trial.

At the Monday hearing, the Government objected to petitioner's proposed substitution on the ground that Iredale's representation of Gomez-Barajas and Bravo created a serious conflict of interest. The Government's position was premised on two possible conflicts. First, the District Court had not yet accepted the plea and sentencing arrangement negotiated between Gomez-Barajas and the Government; in the event that arrangement were rejected by the court, Gomez-Barajas would be free to withdraw the plea and stand trial. He would then be faced with the prospect of representation by Iredale, who in the meantime would have acted as petitioner's attorney. Petitioner, through his participation in the drug distribution scheme, was familiar with the sources and size of Gomez-Barajas' income, and was thus likely to be called as a witness for the Government at any subsequent trial of Gomez-Barajas. This scenario would pose a conflict of interest for Iredale, who would be prevented from cross-examining petitioner and thereby from effectively representing Gomez-Barajas.

Second, and of more immediate concern, Iredale's representation of Bravo would directly affect his ability to act as counsel for petitioner. The Government believed that a portion of the marijuana delivered by Bravo to Vidal's residence eventually was transferred to petitioner. In this regard, the Government contacted Iredale and asked that Bravo be made available as a witness to testify against petitioner, and agreed in exchange to modify its position at the time of Bravo's sentencing. In the likely event that Bravo were called to testify, Iredale's position in representing both men would become untenable, for ethical proscriptions would forbid him to cross-examine Bravo in any meaningful way. By failing to do so, he would also fail to provide petitioner with effective assistance of counsel. Thus, because of Iredale's prior representation of Gomez-Barajas and Bravo and the potential for serious conflict of interest, the Government urged the District Court to reject the substitution of attorneys.

In response, petitioner emphasized his right to have counsel of his own choosing and the willingness of Gomez-Barajas, Bravo, and petitioner to waive the right to conflict-free counsel. Petitioner argued that the circumstances posited by the Government that would create a conflict for Iredale were highly speculative and bore no connection to the true relationship between the co-conspirators. If called to testify, Bravo would simply say that he did not know petitioner and had no dealings with him; no attempt by Iredale to impeach Bravo would be necessary. Further, in the unlikely event that Gomez-Barajas went to trial on the charges of tax evasion and illegal importation, petitioner's lack of involvement in those alleged crimes made his appearance as a witness highly improbable. Finally, and most importantly, all three defendants agreed to allow Iredale to represent petitioner and to waive any future claims of conflict of interest. In petitioner's view, the Government was manufacturing implausible conflicts in an attempt to disqualify Iredale, who had already proved extremely effective in representing Gomez-Barajas and Bravo.

After hearing argument from each side, the District Court noted that it was unfortunate that petitioner had not suggested the substitution sooner, rather than two court days before the commencement of trial. The court then ruled: "[B]ased upon the representation of the Government in [its] memorandum that the Court really has no choice at this point other than to find that an irreconcilable conflict of interest exists. I don't think it can be waived, and accordingly, Mr. Wheat's request to substitute Mr. Iredale in as attorney of record is denied."

Petitioner proceeded to trial with his original counsel and was convicted of conspiracy to possess more than 1,000 pounds of marijuana with intent to distribute, and five counts of possessing marijuana with intent to distribute.

The Court of Appeals for the Ninth Circuit affirmed petitioner's convictions, 813 F.2d 1399 (1987), finding that, within the limits prescribed by the Sixth Amendment, the District Court has considerable discretion in allowing substitution of counsel. The Court of Appeals found that the District Court had correctly balanced two Sixth Amendment rights: (1) the qualified right to be represented by counsel of one's choice, and (2) the right to a defense conducted by an attorney who is free of conflicts of interest. Denial of either of these rights threatened the District Court with an appeal assigning the ruling as reversible error, and the Court of Appeals concluded that the District Court did not abuse its discretion in declining to allow the substitution or addition of Iredale as trial counsel for petitioner.

Because the Courts of Appeals have expressed substantial disagreement about when a district court may override a defendant's waiver of his attorney's conflict of interest,[2] we granted certiorari.

II.

The Sixth Amendment to the Constitution guarantees that "[i]n all criminal prosecutions, the accused shall enjoy the right * * * to have the Assistance of Counsel for his defence." In United States v. Morrison, 449 U.S. 361, 364, 101 S.Ct. 665, 667, 66 L.Ed.2d 564 (1981), we observed that this right was designed to assure fairness in the adversary criminal process. Realizing that an unaided layman may have little skill in arguing the law or in coping with an intricate procedural system, we have held that the Sixth Amendment secures the right to the assistance of counsel, by appointment if necessary, in a trial for any serious crime. Gideon v. Wainwright, 372 U.S. 335, 83 S.Ct. 792, 9 L.Ed.2d 799 (1963). We have further recognized that the purpose of providing assistance of counsel is simply to ensure that criminal defendants receive a fair trial," Strickland v. Washington, 466 U.S. 668, 689, 104 S.Ct. 2052, 2065, 80 L.Ed.2d 674 (1984), and that in evaluating Sixth Amendment claims, "the appropriate inquiry focuses on the adversarial process, not on the accused's relationship with his lawyer as such." United States v. Cronic, 466 U.S. 648, 657, n. 21, 104 S.Ct. 2039, 2046 n. 21, 80 L.Ed.2d 657 (1984). Thus, while the right to select and be represented by one's preferred attorney is comprehended by the Sixth Amendment, the essential aim of the Amendment is to guarantee an effective advocate for each criminal defendant rather than to ensure that a defendant will inexorably be represented by the lawyer whom he prefers.

The Sixth Amendment right to choose one's own counsel is circumscribed in several important respects. Regardless of his persuasive powers, an advocate who is not a member of the bar may not

---

2.   See, e.g., In re Paradyne Corp., 803 F.2d 604, 611, n. 16 (CA11 1986) (the right of counsel "does not override the broader societal interests in the effective administration of justice * * * or in the maintenance of 'public confidence in the integrity of our legal system'"); In re Grand Jury Subpoena Served Upon Doe, 781 F.2d 238, 250-251 (CA2), cert. denied sub nom. Roe v. United States, 475 U.S. 1108, 106 S.Ct. 1515, 89 L.Ed.2d 914 (1986) ("[C]ourts have the power and duty to disqualify counsel where the public interest in maintaining the integrity of the judicial system outweighs the accused's constitutional right"); United States v. Reese, 699 F.2d 803, 805 (CA6 1983) (a trial court should override a defendant's knowing waiver only in "compelling circumstances"); United States v. Flanagan, 679 F.2d 1072, 1076 (CA3 1982) (a trial court may refuse a waiver when an actual conflict is "very likely"), rev'd on other grounds, 465 U.S. 259, 104 S.Ct.1051, 79 L.Ed.2d 288 (1984).

represent clients (other than himself) in court.[3] Similarly, a defendant may not insist on representation by an attorney he cannot afford or who for other reasons declines to represent the defendant. Nor may a defendant insist on the counsel of an attorney who has a previous or ongoing relationship with an opposing party, even when the opposing party is the Government. The question raised in this case is the extent to which a criminal defendant's right under the Sixth Amendment to his chosen attorney is qualified by the fact that the attorney has represented other defendants charged in the same criminal conspiracy.

In previous cases, we have recognized that multiple representation of criminal defendants engenders special dangers of which a court must be aware. While "permitting a single attorney to represent codefendants * * * is not per se violative of constitutional guarantees of effective assistance of counsel," Holloway v. Arkansas, 435 U.S. 475, 482, 98 S.Ct. 1173, 1178, 55 L.Ed.2d 426 (1978), a court confronted with and alerted to possible conflicts of interest must take adequate steps to ascertain whether the conflicts warrant separate counsel. As we said in *Holloway*:

> "Joint representation of conflicting interests is suspect because of what it tends to prevent the attorney from doing * * *. [A] conflict may * * * prevent an attorney from challenging the admission of evidence prejudicial to one client but perhaps favorable to another, or from arguing at the sentencing hearing the relative involvement and culpability of his clients in order to minimize the culpability of one by emphasizing that of another."

435 U.S., at 489-490, 98 S.Ct. at 1181.

Petitioner insists that the provision of waivers by all affected defendants cures any problems created by the multiple representation. But no such flat rule can be deduced from the Sixth Amendment presumption in favor of counsel of choice. Federal courts have an independent interest in ensuring that criminal trials are conducted within the ethical standards of the profession and that legal proceedings appear fair to all who observe them. Both the American Bar Association's Model Code of Professional Responsibility and its Model Rules of Professional Conduct, as well as the rules of the California Bar Association (which governed the attorneys in this case), impose limitations on multiple representation of clients. Not only the interest of a criminal defendant but the institutional interest in the rendition of

---

3.   Our holding in Faretta v. California, 422 U.S. 806, 95 S.Ct. 2525, 45 L.Ed.2d 562 (1975), that a criminal defendant has a Sixth Amendment right to represent himself if he voluntarily elects to do so, does not encompass the right to choose any advocate if the defendant wishes to be represented by counsel.

just verdicts in criminal cases may be jeopardized by unregulated multiple representation.

* * *

To be sure, this need to investigate potential conflicts arises in part from the legitimate wish of district courts that their judgments remain intact on appeal. As the Court of Appeals accurately pointed out, trial courts confronted with multiple representations face the prospect of being "whip-sawed" by assertions of error no matter which way they rule. If a district court agrees to the multiple representation, and the advocacy of counsel is thereafter impaired as a result, the defendant may well claim that he did not receive effective assistance. On the other hand, a district court's refusal to accede to the multiple representation may result in a challenge such as petitioner's in this case. Nor does a waiver by the defendant necessarily solve the problem, for we note, without passing judgment on, the apparent willingness of Courts of Appeals to entertain ineffective-assistance claims from defendants who have specifically waived the right to conflict-free counsel.

Thus, where a court justifiably finds an actual conflict of interest, there can be no doubt that it may decline a proffer of waiver, and insist that defendants be separately represented. * * *

Unfortunately for all concerned, a district court must pass on the issue whether or not to allow a waiver of a conflict of interest by a criminal defendant not with the wisdom of hindsight after the trial has taken place, but in the murkier pre-trial context when relationships between parties are seen through a glass, darkly. The likelihood and dimensions of nascent conflicts of interest are notoriously hard to predict, even for those thoroughly familiar with criminal trials. It is a rare attorney who will be fortunate enough to learn the entire truth from his own client, much less be fully apprised before trial of what each of the Government's witnesses will say on the stand. A few bits of unforeseen testimony or a single previously unknown or unnoticed document may significantly shift the relationship between multiple defendants. These imponderables are difficult enough for a lawyer to assess, and even more difficult to convey by way of explanation to a criminal defendant untutored in the niceties of legal ethics. Nor is it amiss to observe that the willingness of an attorney to obtain such waivers from his clients may bear an inverse relation to the care with which he conveys all the necessary information to them.

For these reasons we think the district court must be allowed substantial latitude in refusing waivers of conflicts of interest not only in those rare cases where an actual conflict may be demonstrated before trial, but in the more common cases where a potential for conflict exists which may or may not burgeon into an actual conflict as the trial progresses. In the circumstances of this case, with the motion for substitution of counsel made so close to the time of trial, the District Court relied on instinct and judgment based on experience in making its decision. We do not think it can be said that the court exceeded the broad latitude which must be accorded it in making this decision. Petitioner of course rightly points out that the Government may seek to "manufacture" a conflict in order to prevent a defendant from having a particularly able defense counsel at his side; but trial courts are undoubtedly aware of this possibility, and must take it into consideration along with all of the other factors which inform this sort of a decision.

Here the District Court was confronted not simply with an attorney who wished to represent two coequal defendants in a straightforward criminal prosecution; rather, Iredale proposed to defend three conspirators of varying stature in a complex drug distribution scheme. The Government intended to call Bravo as a witness for the prosecution at petitioner's trial.[4] The Government might readily have tied certain deliveries of marijuana by Bravo to petitioner, necessitating vigorous cross-examination of Bravo by petitioner's counsel. Iredale, because of his prior representation of Bravo, would have been unable ethically to provide that cross-examination.

Iredale had also represented Gomez-Barajas, one of the alleged kingpins of the distribution ring, and had succeeded in obtaining a verdict of acquittal for him. Gomez-Barajas had agreed with the Government to plead guilty to other charges, but the District Court had not yet accepted the plea arrangement. If the agreement were rejected, petitioner's probable testimony at the resulting trial of Gomez-Barajas would create an ethical dilemma for Iredale from which one or the other of his clients would likely suffer.

Viewing the situation as it did before trial, we hold that the District Court's refusal to permit the substitution of counsel in this case was within its discretion and did not violate petitioner's Sixth Amendment rights. Other district courts might have reached differing or opposite conclusions with equal justification, but that does not mean that one conclusion was "right" and the other "wrong". The District Court must recognize a presumption in favor of petitioner's counsel of choice, but that presumption may be overcome not only by a demonstration of actual conflict but by a showing of a serious potential for conflict. The evaluation of the facts and circumstances of each case under this

---

4. Bravo was in fact called as a witness at petitioner's trial. His testimony was elicited to demonstrate the transportation of drugs that the prosecution hoped to link to petitioner.

standard must be left primarily to the informed judgment of the trial court.

The judgment of the Court of Appeals is accordingly

Affirmed.

JUSTICE MARSHALL, with whom JUSTICE BRENNAN joins, dissenting.
* * *

This Court long has recognized, and today reaffirms, that the Sixth Amendment provides protection for a criminal defendant's choice of counsel. More than 50 years ago, we stated that "[i]t is hardly necessary to say that, the right to counsel being conceded, a defendant should be afforded a fair opportunity to secure counsel of his own choice." Powell v. Alabama, 287 U.S. 45, 53, 53 S.Ct. 55, 58, 77 L.Ed. 158 (1932). This Court has reiterated this principle on frequent occasions. Our statements on this score stem largely from an appreciation that a primary purpose of the Sixth Amendment is to grant a criminal defendant effective control over the conduct of his defense. As this Court previously has stated, the Sixth Amendment "grants to the accused personally the right to make his defense," because "it is he who suffers the consequences if the defense fails." Faretta v.California, 422 U.S. 806, 819-820, 95 S.Ct. 2525, 2533, 45 L.Ed.2d 562 (1975). An obviously critical aspect of making a defense is choosing a person to serve as an assistant and representative. In addition, lodging the selection of counsel with the defendant generally will promote the fairness and integrity of criminal trials.

The right to counsel of choice, as the Court notes, is not absolute. When a defendant's selection of counsel, under the particular facts and circumstances of a case, gravely imperils the prospect of a fair trial, a trial court may justifiably refuse to accede to the choice. Thus, a trial court may in certain situations reject a defendant's choice of counsel on the ground of a potential conflict of interest, because a serious conflict may indeed destroy the integrity of the trial process. As the Court states, however, the trial court must recognize a presumption in favor of a defendant's counsel of choice. This presumption means that a trial court may not reject a defendant's chosen counsel on the ground of a potential conflict of interest absent a showing that both the likelihood and the dimensions of the feared conflict are substantial.[1] Unsupported or dubious speculation as to a conflict will not suffice. The Government

_____

1.   In stating this principle, I mean to address only cases in which all parties to the potential conflict have made a fully informed waiver of their right to conflict-free representation. It is undisputed in this case that petitioner, as well as Juvenal Gomez-Barajas and Javier Bravo, had agreed to waive this right.

must show a substantial potential for the kind of conflict that would undermine the fairness of the trial process. In these respects, I do not believe my position differs significantly, if at all, from that expressed in the opinion of the Court. I do disagree, however, with the Court's suggestion that the trial court's decision as to whether a potential conflict justifies rejection of a defendant's chosen counsel is entitled to some kind of special deference on appeal. The Court grants trial courts "broad latitude" over the decision to accept or reject a defendant's choice of counsel, although never explicitly endorsing a standard of appellate review, the Court appears to limit such review to determining whether an abuse of discretion has occurred. This approach, which the Court supports solely by noting the difficulty of evaluating the likelihood and magnitude of a conflict, accords neither with the nature of the trial court's decision nor with the importance of the interest at stake.

The trial court's decision as to whether the circumstances of a given case constitute grounds for rejecting a defendant's chosen counsel – that is, as to whether these circumstances present a substantial potential for a serious conflict of interest – is a mixed determination of law and fact. The decision is properly described in this way because it requires and results from the application of a legal standard to the established facts of a case. Appellate courts traditionally do not defer to such determinations. For this reason, the Court in Cuyler v. Sullivan, 446 U.S. 335, 100 S.Ct. 1708, 64 L.Ed.2d 333 (1980), held that a trial court's determination as to whether an attorney had represented conflicting interests at trial was not entitled to any deference. The determination at issue here, which focuses on the potential for a conflict of interest, is not different in any relevant respect.[2]

The inappropriateness of deferring to this determination becomes even more apparent when its constitutional significance is taken into account. The interest at stake in this kind of decision is nothing less than a criminal defendant's Sixth Amendment right to counsel of his choice. The trial court simply does not have "broad latitude," to vitiate this right. In my view, a trial court that rejects a criminal defendant's chosen counsel on the ground of a potential conflict should make findings on the record to facilitate review, and an appellate court should

---

2. It is true that a trial court, in making a determination regarding the potential for a conflict of interest, must make a prediction as to future events, which frequently is a difficult task. This aspect of the decision, however, does not call for a lax standard of review. The question on review is whether the trial court was correct in holding that the facts and circumstances apparent at the time of its decision demonstrated a substantial potential for a serious conflict of interest. Appellate courts are fully capable of posing and resolving this question. A deferential standard of review therefore is not necessary to generate appellate decisions that take into account and appropriately reflect the uncertainties existing at the time of the trial court's ruling.

scrutinize closely the basis for the trial court's decision. Only in this way can a criminal defendant's right to counsel of his choice be appropriately protected.

The Court's resolution of the instant case flows from its deferential approach to the District Court's denial of petitioner's motion to add or substitute counsel; absent deference, a decision upholding the District Court's ruling would be inconceivable. Indeed, I believe that even under the Court's deferential standard, reversal is in order. The mere fact of multiple representation, as the Court concedes, will not support an order preventing a criminal defendant from retaining counsel of his choice. As this Court has stated on prior occasions, such representation will not invariably pose a substantial risk of a serious conflict of interest and thus will not invariably imperil the prospect of a fair trial. See *Cuyler v. Sullivan, supra,* 446 U.S., at 346-348, 100 S.Ct., at 1717-1718; Holloway v. Arkansas, 435 U.S. 475, 482-483, 98 S.Ct. 1173, 1177-1178, 55 L.Ed.2d 426 (1978). The propriety of the District Court's order thus depends on whether the Government showed that the particular facts and circumstances of the multiple representation proposed in this case were such as to overcome the presumption in favor of petitioner's choice of counsel. I believe it is clear that the Government failed to make this showing. Neither Eugene Iredale's representation of Juvenal Gomez-Barajas nor Iredale's representation of Javier Bravo posed any threat of causing a conflict of interest.

At the time of petitioner's trial, Iredale's representation of Gomez-Barajas was effectively completed. As the Court notes, Iredale had obtained an acquittal for Gomez-Barajas on charges relating to a conspiracy to distribute marijuana. Iredale also had negotiated an agreement with the Government under which Gomez-Barajas would plead guilty to charges of tax evasion and illegal importation of merchandise, although the trial court had not yet accepted this plea arrangement. Gomez- Barajas was not scheduled to appear as a witness at petitioner's trial; thus, Iredale's conduct of that trial would not require him to question his former client. The only possible conflict this Court can divine from Iredale's representation of both petitioner and Gomez-Barajas rests on the premise that the trial court would reject the negotiated plea agreement and that Gomez-Barajas then would decide to go to trial. In this event, the Court tells us, "petitioner's probable testimony at the resulting trial of Gomez-Barajas would create an ethical dilemma for Iredale."

This argument rests on speculation of the most dubious kind. The Court offers no reason to think that the trial court would have rejected Gomez-Barajas' plea agreement; neither did the Government posit any such reason in its argument or brief before this Court. The most likely occurrence at the time petitioner moved to retain Iredale as his defense counsel was that the trial court would accept Gomez-Barajas' plea agreement, as the court in fact later did. Moreover, even if Gomez-Barajas had gone to trial, petitioner probably would not have testified. The record contains no indication that petitioner had any involvement in or information about crimes for which Gomez-Barajas might yet have stood trial. The only alleged connection between petitioner and Gomez-Barajas sprang from the conspiracy to distribute marijuana, and a jury already had acquitted Gomez-Barajas of that charge. It is therefore disingenuous to say that representation of both petitioner and Gomez-Barajas posed a serious potential for a conflict of interest.

Similarly, Iredale's prior representation of Bravo was not a cause for concern. The Court notes that the prosecution intended to call Bravo to the stand at petitioner's trial and asserts that Bravo's testimony could well have "necessitat[ed] vigorous cross-examination * * * by petitioner's counsel." The facts, however, belie the claim that Bravo's anticipated testimony created a serious potential for conflict. Contrary to the Court's inference, Bravo could not have testified about petitioner's involvement in the alleged marijuana distribution scheme. As all parties were aware at the time, Bravo did not know and could not identify petitioner; indeed, prior to the commencement of legal proceedings, the two men never had heard of each other. Bravo's eventual testimony at petitioner's trial related to a shipment of marijuana in which petitioner was not involved; the testimony contained not a single reference to petitioner. Petitioner's counsel did not cross-examine Bravo, and neither petitioner's counsel nor the prosecutor mentioned Bravo's testimony in closing argument. All of these developments were predictable when the District Court ruled on petitioner's request that Iredale serve as trial counsel; the contours of Bravo's testimony were clear at that time. Given the insignificance of this testimony to any matter that petitioner's counsel would dispute, the proposed joint representation of petitioner and Bravo did not threaten a conflict of interest.[3]

---

3. The very insignificance of Bravo's testimony, combined with the timing of the prosecutor's decision to call Bravo as a witness, raises a serious concern that the prosecutor attempted to manufacture a conflict in this case. The prosecutor's decision to use Bravo as a witness was an 11th-hour development. Throughout the course of plea negotiations with Bravo, the prosecutor never had suggested that Bravo testify at petitioner's trial. At Bravo's guilty-plea proceedings, when Iredale notified the District Court of petitioner's substitution motion, the prosecutor conceded that he had made no plans to call Bravo as a witness. Only after the prosecutor learned of the substitution motion and decided to oppose it did he arrange for Bravo's testimony by agreeing to recommend to the trial court a reduction in Bravo's sentence. Especially in light of the scarce value of Bravo's testimony, this prosecutorial behavior very plausibly may be viewed as a maneuver to

Moreover, even assuming that Bravo's testimony might have "necessitat[ed] vigorous cross-examination," the District Court could have insured against the possibility of any conflict of interest without wholly depriving petitioner of his constitutional right to the counsel of his choice. Petitioner's motion requested that Iredale either be substituted for petitioner's current counsel or be added to petitioner's defense team. Had the District Court allowed the addition of Iredale and then ordered that he take no part in the cross-examination of Bravo, any possibility of a conflict would have been removed. Especially in light of the availability of this precautionary measure, the notion that Iredale's prior representation of Bravo might well have caused a conflict of interest at petitioner's trial is nothing short of ludicrous.[4]

The Court gives short shrift to the actual circumstances of this case in upholding the decision below. These circumstances show that the District Court erred in denying petitioner's motion to substitute or add Iredale as defense counsel. The proposed representation did not pose a substantial risk of a serious conflict of interest. The District Court therefore had no authority to deny petitioner's Sixth Amendment right to retain counsel of his choice. This constitutional error demands that petitioner's conviction be reversed. I accordingly dissent.

* * *

Notes and Question

Wheat applies in the federal courts. At the state level, however, the defendant may waive a conflict of interest if the waiver is knowingly made. According to a California court, "In the face of a knowing and intelligent waiver, the possibility that the defendant will later raise the

---

prevent Iredale from representing petitioner at trial. Iredale had proved to be a formidable adversary; he previously had gained an acquittal for the alleged kingpin of the marijuana distribution scheme. As the District Court stated in considering petitioner's motion: "Were I in [petitioner's] position I'm sure I would want Mr. Iredale representing me, too. He did a fantastic job in that [Gomez-Barajas] trial * * *." App. 124-125. The prosecutor's decision to call Bravo as a witness may well have stemmed from a concern that Iredale would do an equally fantastic job at petitioner's trial. As the Court notes, governmental maneuvering of this kind is relevant to a trial court's decision as to whether to accept a criminal defendant's chosen counsel. The significant possibility that the prosecutor was engaging in such bad-faith conduct provides yet another reason to dispute the Court's resolution of this case.

4.   The Court somewhat obliquely suggests that the timing of the motion to substitute or add Iredale as trial counsel helps to justify the District Court's ruling. I cannot agree. Iredale made clear to the District Court that notwithstanding the proximity of the scheduled trial date, he would neither need nor request a continuance of the trial were he substituted or added as defense counsel. The timing of petitioner's motion is therefore relevant only insofar as it affected the ability of the District Court to consider the issues that the motion raised. The District Court itself believed that it had sufficient time to consider these issues. Far from denying the motion because of its timing, the District Court issued a decision on the merits after full briefing and oral argument.

conflict as a basis for reversal is insufficient to outweigh the defendant's right to continue with counsel." See Alcocer v. Superior Court, 206 Cal.App.3d 951, 958-959, 254 Cal.Rptr. 72 (1988).

What limitations on the right to be represented by one's counsel of choice does the Court recognize?

C. DEFENSE CHALLENGES

1. Fourth Amendment

During the course of a criminal investigation, special agents may find it necessary to search the taxpayer's premises and seize certain documents or other evidence. Unless the taxpayer consents to such a search and seizure, or evidence is uncovered pursuant to a search for weapons immediately prior to an arrest, a search warrant must be obtained. The IRS and the Department of Justice have a policy that search warrants will be used with restraint and only in significant tax cases. IRM § 9.4.9.2 (6-19-2008). The factors to be considered in determining the significance of a case include (1) the amount of taxes due, (2) the nature of the alleged fraud, (3) whether the evidence is available through other means, and (4) the impact of the case on voluntary compliance. Id.

If evidence is obtained in violation of the Fourth Amendment, the remedy generally is to exclude the evidence from being used at any stage of a criminal tax prosecution.

a. *Standing*

UNITED STATES v. PAYNER
Supreme Court of the United States, 1980.
447 U.S. 727, 100 S.Ct. 2439, 65 L.Ed.2d 468.

MR. JUSTICE POWELL delivered the opinion of the Court.

I.

Respondent Jack Payner was indicted in September 1976 on a charge of falsifying his 1972 federal income tax return in violation of 18 U.S.C. § 1001.[1] The indictment alleged that respondent denied maintaining a

---

1.   Title 18 U.S.C. § 1001 provides in relevant part:

"Whoever, in any matter within the jurisdiction of any department or agency of the United States knowingly and willfully * * * makes any false, fictitious or fraudulent statements or representations, * * * shall be fined not more than $10,000 or imprisoned not more than five

foreign bank account at a time when he knew that he had such an account at the Castle Bank and Trust Company of Nassau, Bahama Islands. The Government's case rested heavily on a loan guarantee agreement dated April 28, 1972, in which respondent pledged the funds in his Castle Bank account as security for a $100,000 loan.

Respondent waived his right to jury trial and moved to suppress the guarantee agreement. With the consent of the parties, the United States District Court for the Northern District of Ohio took evidence on the motion at a hearing consolidated with the trial on the merits. The court found respondent guilty as charged on the basis of all the evidence. The court also found, however, that the Government discovered the guarantee agreement by exploiting a flagrantly illegal search that occurred on January 15, 1973. The court therefore suppressed "all evidence introduced in the case by the Government with the exception of Jack Payner's 1972 tax return * * * and the related testimony." 434 F.Supp. 113, 136 (D.C.Ohio 1977). As the tax return alone was insufficient to demonstrate knowing falsification, the District Court set aside respondent's conviction.

The events leading up to the 1973 search are not in dispute. In 1965, the Internal Revenue Service launched an investigation into the financial activities of American citizens in the Bahamas. The project, known as "Operation Trade Winds," was headquartered in Jacksonville, Fla. Suspicion focused on the Castle Bank in 1972, when investigators learned that a suspected narcotics trafficker had an account there. Special Agent Richard Jaffe of the Jacksonville office asked Norman Casper, a private investigator and occasional informant, to learn what he could about the Castle Bank and its depositors. To that end, Casper cultivated his friendship with Castle Bank vice president Michael Wolstencroft. Casper introduced Wolstencroft to Sybol Kennedy, a private investigator and former employee. When Casper discovered that the banker intended to spend a few days in Miami in January 1973, he devised a scheme to gain access to the bank records he knew Wolstencroft would be carrying in his briefcase. Agent Jaffe approved the basic outline of the plan.

Wolstencroft arrived in Miami on January 15 and went directly to Kennedy's apartment. At about 7:30 p. m., the two left for dinner at a Key Biscayne restaurant. Shortly thereafter, Casper entered the apartment using a key supplied by Kennedy. He removed the briefcase and delivered it to Jaffe. While the agent supervised the copying of approximately 400 documents taken from the briefcase, a "lookout"

---

years, or both."

observed Kennedy and Wolstencroft at dinner. The observer notified Casper when the pair left the restaurant, and the briefcase was replaced. The documents photographed that evening included papers evidencing a close working relationship between the Castle Bank and the Bank of Perrine, Fla. Subpoenas issued to the Bank of Perrine ultimately uncovered the loan guarantee agreement at issue in this case.

The District Court found that the United States, acting through Jaffe, "knowingly and willfully participated in the unlawful seizure of Michael Wolstencroft's briefcase * * *." Id., at 120. According to that court, "the Government affirmatively counsels its agents that the Fourth Amendment standing limitation permits them to purposefully conduct an unconstitutional search and seizure of one individual in order to obtain evidence against third parties * * *." Id., at 132-133. The District Court also found that the documents seized from Wolstencroft provided the leads that ultimately led to the discovery of the critical loan guarantee agreement. Id., at 123.[3] Although the search did not impinge upon the respondent's Fourth Amendment rights, the District Court believed that the Due Process Clause of the Fifth Amendment and the inherent supervisory power of the federal courts required it to exclude evidence tainted by the Government's "knowing and purposeful bad faith hostility to any person's fundamental constitutional rights." Id., at 129; see id., at 133, 134-135.

* * *

II.

This Court discussed the doctrine of "standing to invoke the [Fourth Amendment] exclusionary rule" in some detail last Term. Rakas v. Illinois, 439 U.S. 128, 138, 99 S.Ct. 421, 427-28, 58 L.Ed.2d 387 (1978). We reaffirmed the established rule that a court may not exclude evidence under the Fourth Amendment unless it finds that an unlawful search or seizure violated the defendant's own constitutional rights. Id., at 133-140, 99 S.Ct., at 425-429. And the defendant's Fourth Amendment rights are violated only when the challenged conduct invaded his legitimate expectation of privacy rather than that of a third party.

The foregoing authorities establish, as the District Court recognized, that respondent lacks standing under the Fourth Amendment to suppress the documents illegally seized from Wolstencroft. The Court of

---

3. The United States argued in the District Court and the Court of Appeals that the guarantee agreement was discovered through an independent investigation untainted by the briefcase search. The Government also denied that its agents willfully encouraged Casper's illegal behavior. For purposes of this opinion, we need not question the District Court's contrary findings on either point.

Appeals did not disturb the District Court's conclusion that "Jack Payner possessed no privacy interest in the Castle Bank documents that were seized from Wolstencroft." Ibid.; see 590 F.2d, at 207. Nor do we. United States v. Miller, 425 U.S. 435, 96 S.Ct. 1619, 48 L.Ed.2d 71 (1976), established that a depositor has no expectation of privacy and thus no "protectable Fourth Amendment interest" in copies of checks and deposit slips retained by his bank. Nothing in the record supports a contrary conclusion in this case.

The District Court and the Court of Appeals believed, however, that a federal court should use its supervisory power to suppress evidence tainted by gross illegalities that did not infringe the defendant's constitutional rights. The United States contends that this approach–as applied in this case–upsets the careful balance of interests embodied in the Fourth Amendment decisions of this Court. In the Government's view, such an extension of the supervisory power would enable federal courts to exercise a standardless discretion in their application of the exclusionary rule to enforce the Fourth Amendment. We agree with the Government.

III.

We certainly can understand the District Court's commendable desire to deter deliberate intrusions into the privacy of persons who are unlikely to become defendants in a criminal prosecution. No court should condone the unconstitutional and possibly criminal behavior of those who planned and executed this "briefcase caper."[5] Indeed, the decisions of this Court are replete with denunciations of willfully lawless activities undertaken in the name of law enforcement. But our cases also show that these unexceptional principles do not command the exclusion of evidence in every case of illegality. Instead, they must be weighed

---

5. "The security of persons and property remains a fundamental value which law enforcement officers must respect. Nor should those who flout the rules escape unscathed." Alderman v. United States, 394 U.S. 165, 175, 89 S.Ct. 961, 967, 22 L.Ed.2d 176 (1969). We note that in 1976 Congress investigated the improprieties revealed in this record. See Oversight Hearings into the Operations of the IRS before a Subcommittee of the House Committee on Government Operations (Operation Tradewinds, Project Haven, and Narcotics Traffickers Tax Program), 94th Cong., 1st Sess. (1975). As a result, the Commissioner of Internal Revenue "called off" Operation Trade Winds. The Commissioner also adopted guidelines that require agents to instruct informants on the requirements of the law and to report known illegalities to a supervisory officer, who is in turn directed to notify appropriate state authorities. IR Manual §§ 9373.3(3), 9373.4 (Manual Transmittal 9-21, Dec. 27, 1977). Although these measures appear on their face to be less positive than one might expect from an agency charged with upholding the law, they do indicate disapproval of the practices found to have been implemented in this case. We cannot assume that similar lawless conduct, if brought to the attention of responsible officials, would not be dealt with appropriately. To require in addition the suppression of highly probative evidence in a trial against a third party would penalize society unnecessarily.

against the considerable harm that would flow from indiscriminate application of an exclusionary rule.

Thus, the exclusionary rule "has been restricted to those areas where its remedial objectives are most efficaciously served." United States v. Calandra, 414 U.S. 338, 348, 94 S.Ct. 613, 620, 38 L.Ed.2d 561 (1974). The Court has acknowledged that the suppression of probative but tainted evidence exacts a costly toll upon the ability of courts to ascertain the truth in a criminal case. Our cases have consistently recognized that unbending application of the exclusionary sanction to enforce ideals of governmental rectitude would impede unacceptably the truth-finding functions of judge and jury. After all, it is the defendant, and not the constable, who stands trial.

The same societal interests are at risk when a criminal defendant invokes the supervisory power to suppress evidence seized in violation of a third party's constitutional rights. The supervisory power is applied with some caution even when the defendant asserts a violation of his own rights.[7]

* * *

We conclude that the supervisory power does not authorize a federal court to suppress otherwise admissible evidence on the ground that it was seized unlawfully from a third party not before the court. Our Fourth Amendment decisions have established beyond any doubt that the interest in deterring illegal searches does not justify the exclusion of tainted evidence at the instance of a party who was not the victim of the challenged practices. *Rakas v. Illinois,* supra, 439 U.S., at 137, 99 S.Ct., at 427; *Alderman v. United States*, 394 U.S., at 174-175, 89 S.Ct., at 966-67.[8] The values assigned to the competing interests do not change

---

7. Federal courts may use their supervisory power in some circumstances to exclude evidence taken from the defendant by "willful disobedience of law." McNabb v. United States, 318 U.S. 332, 345, 63 S.Ct. 608, 615, 87 L.Ed. 819 (1943); see Elkins v. United States, 364 U.S. 206, 223, 80 S.Ct. 1437, 1447, 4 L.Ed.2d 1669 (1960); Rea v. United States, 350 U.S. 214, 216-217, 76 S.Ct. 292, 293-294, 100 L.Ed. 233 (1956); cf. Hampton v. United States, 425 U.S. 484, 495, 96 S.Ct. 1646, 1652, 48 L.Ed.2d 113 (1976) (POWELL, J., concurring in judgment). This Court has never held, however, that the supervisory power authorizes suppression of evidence obtained from third parties in violation of Constitution, statute, or rule. The supervisory power merely permits federal courts to supervise "the administration of criminal justice" among the parties before the bar. *McNabb v. United States, supra*, 318 U.S., at 340, 63 S.Ct. 612.

8. "The deterrent values of preventing the incrimination of those whose rights the police have violated have been considered sufficient to justify the suppression of probative evidence even though the case against the defendant is weakened or destroyed. We adhere to that judgment. But we are not convinced that the additional benefits of extending the exclusionary rule to other defendants would justify further encroachment upon the public interest in prosecuting those accused of crime and having them acquitted or convicted on the basis of all the evidence which exposes the truth." *Alderman v. United States*, 394 U.S., at 174-175, 89 S.Ct., at 967.

The dissent post, urges that the balance of interests under the supervisory power differs from

because a court has elected to analyze the question under the supervisory power instead of the Fourth Amendment. In either case, the need to deter the underlying conduct and the detrimental impact of excluding the evidence remain precisely the same.

The District Court erred, therefore, when it concluded that "society's interest in deterring [bad faith] conduct by exclusion outweigh[s] society's interest in furnishing the trier of fact with all relevant evidence." 434 F.Supp., at 135. This reasoning, which the Court of Appeals affirmed, amounts to a substitution of individual judgment for the controlling decisions of this Court.[9] Were we to accept this use of the supervisory power, we would confer on the judiciary discretionary power to disregard the considered limitations of the law it is charged with enforcing. We hold that the supervisory power does not extend so far.

The judgment of the Court of Appeals is

Reversed.

MR. JUSTICE MARSHALL, with whom MR. JUSTICE BRENNAN and MR. JUSTICE BLACKMUN join, dissenting.

The Court today holds that a federal court is unable to exercise its supervisory powers to prevent the use of evidence in a criminal prosecution in that court, even though that evidence was obtained through intentional illegal and unconstitutional conduct by agents of the

---

that considered in *Alderman* and like cases, because the supervisory power focuses upon the "need to protect the integrity of the federal courts." Although the District Court in this case relied upon a deterrent rationale, we agree that the supervisory power serves the "twofold" purpose of deterring illegality and protecting judicial integrity. As the dissent recognizes, however, the Fourth Amendment exclusionary rule serves precisely the same purposes. Thus, the Fourth Amendment exclusionary rule, like the supervisory power, is applied in part "to protect the integrity of the court, rather than to vindicate the constitutional rights of the defendant * * *." See generally *Stone v. Powell,* supra, at 486, 96 S.Ct., at 3048; *United States v. Calandra,* supra, at 348, 94 S.Ct., at 620.

In this case, where the illegal conduct did not violate the respondent's rights, the interest in preserving judicial integrity and in deterring such conduct is outweighed by the societal interest in presenting probative evidence to the trier of fact. None of the cases cited by the dissent, supports a contrary view, since none of those cases involved criminal defendants who were not themselves the victims of the challenged practices. Thus, our decision today does not limit the traditional scope of the supervisory power in any way; nor does it render that power "superfluous." We merely reject its use as a substitute for established Fourth Amendment doctrine.

9. The same difficulty attends respondent's claim to the protections of the Due Process Clause of the Fifth Amendment. The Court of Appeals expressly declined to consider the Due Process Clause. But even if we assume that the unlawful briefcase search was so outrageous as to offend fundamental " 'canons of decency and fairness,' " Rochin v. California, 342 U.S. 165, 169, 72 S.Ct. 205, 208, 96 L.Ed. 183 (1952), quoting Malinski v. New York, 324 U.S. 401, 417, 65 S.Ct. 781, 789, 89 L.Ed. 1029 (1945) (opinion of Frankfurter, J.), the fact remains that "[t]he limitations of the Due Process Clause * * * come into play only when the Government activity in question violates some protected right of the *defendant,*" Hampton v. United States, supra, 425 U.S., at 490, 96 S.Ct., at 1650 (plurality opinion).

United States, because the defendant does not satisfy the standing requirement of the Fourth Amendment. That holding effectively turns the standing rules created by this Court for assertions of Fourth Amendment violations into a sword to be used by the Government to permit it deliberately to invade one person's Fourth Amendment rights in order to obtain evidence against another person. Unlike the Court, I do not believe that the federal courts are unable to protect the integrity of the judicial system from such gross Government misconduct.

I.

The facts as found by the District Court need to be more fully stated in order to establish the level of purposeful misconduct to which agents of the United States have sunk in this case. Operation Trade Winds was initiated by the Internal Revenue Service (IRS) in 1965 to gather information about the financial activities of American citizens in the Bahamas. The investigation was supervised by Special Agent Richard Jaffe in the Jacksonville, Fla., office. It was not until June 1972 that the investigation focused on the Castle Bank and Trust Company of the Bahamas. In late October 1972 Jaffe asked one of his informants, Norman Casper, to obtain the names and addresses of the individuals holding accounts with the Castle Bank. Casper set to work soon thereafter. He was already an acquaintance of Michael Wolstencroft, vice president and trust officer of the Castle Bank. Casper knew that Wolstencroft frequently visited the United States carrying a briefcase with documents from the Castle Bank. Casper therefore introduced Wolstencroft to Sybol Kennedy, a private detective who worked for Casper. In early January 1973, Casper learned that Wolstencroft planned a business trip to the United States on January 15, 1973, and that he would have Castle Bank records with him on that trip. Plans for the "briefcase caper," as Casper called it, began in earnest.

As found by the District Court, Casper discussed the details of the plan with Jaffe on several occasions during the week before Wolstencroft's trip.[1] Casper told Jaffe that he could get the needed documents from Wolstencroft, but that Jaffe would have to supply photographic services. On January 11, Casper specifically informed Jaffe that he planned to enter an apartment and take Wolstencroft's briefcase.

---

1. The Court rather blandly states that "Agent Jaffe approved the basic outline of the plan[.]" Such a characterization is misleading in light of the findings of the District Court. As is noted in the text infra, Jaffe knew explicit details of the operation in advance and helped to make the arrangements by recommending a locksmith who could be "trusted," by providing a safe and convenient location for the photographing of the documents, and by providing a photographer from the IRS.

Jaffe then stated that he would have to clear the operation with his superior, Troy Register, Jr., Chief of the IRS Intelligence Division in Jacksonville. Clearance was obtained, and Jaffe told Casper to proceed with the plan.[2] Casper called Jaffe the following day and asked if the IRS could refer him to a locksmith who could be "trusted." Jaffe gave him such a referral.[3]

The plans were finalized by the time of Wolstencroft's arrival on January 15. Wolstencroft went directly to Sybol Kennedy's apartment. The couple eventually went to a restaurant for dinner. Using a key provided by Kennedy,[5] Casper entered the apartment and stole Wolstencroft's briefcase. Casper then rendezvoused with the IRS-recommended locksmith in a parking lot five blocks from the apartment; the locksmith made a key to fit the lock on the case. Casper took the briefcase and newly made key to the home of an IRS agent. Jaffe had selected that location for the photographing because it was only eight blocks from the parking lot where Casper met the locksmith and Jaffe knew there was a need to act with haste. The briefcase was opened in Jaffe's presence. Jaffe, Casper, and an IRS photography expert then

---

2. Jaffe testified in the District Court that "[w]hatever I knew, he [Register] knew." See 434 F.Supp. 113, 121, n. 40.

3. It was clear why Casper needed a locksmith who could be "trusted." Casper testified as follows in the District Court:

"Q. Isn't it a fact, Mr. Casper, you knew you were committing an illegal act, and you wanted somebody who could be trusted to keep his mouth shut about it?

"A. There is that possibility, yes.

"Q. Isn't that the fact?

* * *

"A. Yes."

434 F.Supp., at 119, n. 20.

It is interesting to note that even the locksmith who could be "trusted" refused to enter Kennedy's apartment with Casper.

The Government contends that when Agent Jaffe made the referral he did not know what use Casper intended to make of such a locksmith. Brief for United States 6, n. 4. The District Court found, however, that Jaffe already knew at the time of the referral that Casper intended to enter Kennedy's apartment and to take and open Wolstencroft's briefcase. There were, then, only two logical alternatives why Casper would want such a locksmith: to make a key to enter the briefcase, or to make a key to enter the apartment. Either way, Jaffe must have known that Casper's conduct was improper, and yet Jaffe made the referral anyway.

5. The District Court, after hearing the testimony of both Casper and Jaffe, disbelieved Jaffe's assertion that Casper had informed him beforehand that Kennedy had given Casper a key with which to enter the apartment. See id., at 119, n. 15, 121, n. 40. See also n. 3, supra.

photographed over 400 documents.[7] Casper had arranged for Kennedy and Wolstencroft to be watched on their date, and this lookout called Casper at the IRS agent's home when the couple finished their dinner. After all the documents had been copied, Casper relocked the briefcase and returned it to Kennedy's apartment. The entire "caper" lasted approximately one and one-half hours.

The illegalities of agents of the United States did not stop even at that point, however. During the following two weeks, Jaffe told Casper that the IRS needed additional information. Casper therefore sent Kennedy to visit Wolstencroft in the Bahamas. While there, acting pursuant to Casper's instructions, Kennedy stole a rolodex file from Wolstencroft's office. This file was turned over to Jaffe, who testified in the District Court that he had not cared how the rolodex file had been obtained.[8]

The IRS paid Casper $8,000 in cash for the services he rendered in obtaining the information about Castle Bank. Casper in turn paid approximately $1,000 of this money to Kennedy for her role in the "briefcase caper" and the theft of the rolodex file.

The "briefcase caper" revealed papers which showed a close relationship between the Castle Bank and a Florida bank. Subpoenas issued to that Florida bank resulted in the uncovering of the loan guarantee agreement which was the principal piece of evidence against respondent at trial. It is that loan agreement and the evidence discovered as a result of it that the District Court reluctantly[9] suppressed under the Due Process Clause of the Fifth Amendment and under its supervisory powers.

The District Court made several key findings concerning the level of misconduct of agents of the United States in these activities. The District Court found that "the United States, through its agents, Richard Jaffe, and others, knowingly and willfully participated in the unlawful seizure of Michael Wolstencroft's briefcase, and encouraged its informant, Norman Casper, to arrange the theft of a rolodex from the offices of Castle Bank." 434 F.Supp. 113, 120-121 (ND Ohio 1977). The

---

7. As noted previously, Casper had told Jaffe to provide the photographic equipment. Jaffe testified that one of the cameras used was a "microfilmer" which was "much quicker" than a regular camera. This camera had been brought by the IRS because "Casper had to get the documents and the briefcase back to the apartment prior to the return of the owner." Id., at 493-495. This testimony again shows that Jaffe was fully aware in advance that the activities of the evening were improper.

8. See 434 F.Supp., at 120, and n. 34.

9. See 434 F.Supp., at 124, 129, 134, n. 74.

District Court concluded that "the United States was an active participant in the admittedly criminal conduct in which Casper engaged * * *." Id., at 121. The District Court found that "the illegal conduct of the government officials involved in this case compels the conclusion that they knowingly and purposefully obtained the briefcase materials with *bad faith hostility* toward the strictures imposed on their activities by the Constitution." Id., at 130 (emphasis in original). The District Court considered the actions of Jaffe and Casper "outrageous," because they "plotted, schemed and ultimately acted in contravention of the United States Constitution and laws of Florida, knowing that their conduct was illegal." Ibid.

The most disturbing finding by the District Court, however, related to the intentional manipulation of the standing requirements of the Fourth Amendment by agents of the United States, who are, of course, supposed to uphold and enforce the Constitution and laws of this country. The District Court found: "It is evident that the Government and its agents, including Richard Jaffe, were, and are, well aware that under the standing requirement of the Fourth Amendment, evidence obtained from a party pursuant to an unconstitutional search is admissible against third parties who's [sic] own privacy expectations are not subject to the search, even though the cause for the unconstitutional search was to obtain evidence incriminating those third parties. This Court finds that, in its desire to apprehend tax evaders, a desire the Court fully shares, the Government affirmatively counsels its agents that the Fourth Amendment standing limitation permits them to purposefully conduct an unconstitutional search and seizure of one individual in order to obtain evidence against third parties, who are the real targets of the governmental intrusion, and that the IRS agents in this case acted, and will act in the future, according to that counsel. Such governmental conduct compels the conclusion that Jaffe and Casper transacted the 'briefcase caper' with a purposeful, bad faith hostility toward the Fourth Amendment rights of Wolstencroft in order to obtain evidence against persons like Payner." Id., at 131-133.

The Court of Appeals did not disturb any of these findings. 590 F.2d 206 (CA6 1979) (*per curiam*). Nor does the Court today purport to set them aside. It is in the context of these findings – intentional illegal actions by Government agents taken in bad-faith hostility toward the constitutional rights of Wolstencroft for the purpose of obtaining evidence against persons such as the respondent through manipulation of the standing requirements of the Fourth Amendment – that the suppression issue must be considered.

II.

This Court has on several occasions exercised its supervisory powers over the federal judicial system in order to suppress evidence that the Government obtained through misconduct. The rationale for such suppression of evidence is twofold: to deter illegal conduct by Government officials, and to protect the integrity of the federal courts. The Court has particularly stressed the need to use supervisory powers to prevent the federal courts from becoming accomplices to such misconduct.

The need to use the Court's supervisory powers to suppress evidence obtained through governmental misconduct was perhaps best expressed by Mr. Justice Brandeis in his famous dissenting opinion in Olmstead v. United States, 277 U.S. 438, 471-485, 48 S.Ct. 564, 570-575, 72 L.Ed. 944 (1928): "Decency, security and liberty alike demand that government officials shall be subjected to the same rules of conduct that are commands to the citizen. In a government of laws, existence of the government will be imperilled if it fails to observe the law scrupulously. Our Government is the potent, the omnipresent teacher. For good or for ill, it teaches the whole people by its example. Crime is contagious. If the Government becomes a lawbreaker, it breeds contempt for law; it invites every man to become a law unto himself; it invites anarchy. To declare that in the administration of the criminal law the end justifies the means—to declare that the Government may commit crimes in order to secure the conviction of a private criminal—would bring terrible retribution. Against that pernicious doctrine this Court should resolutely set its face." Id., at 485, 48 S.Ct., at 575. Mr. Justice Brandeis noted that "a court will not redress a wrong when he who invokes its aid has unclean hands," id., at 483, 48 S.Ct., at 574, and that in keeping with that principle the court should not lend its aid in the enforcement of the criminal law when the government itself was guilty of misconduct. "Then aid is denied despite the defendant's wrong. It is denied in order to maintain respect for law; in order to promote confidence in the administration of justice; in order to preserve the judicial process from contamination." Id., at 484, 48 S.Ct., at 574-575. See also id., at 469-471, 48 S.Ct. at 569-70 (HOLMES, J., dissenting).[10]

The reason for this emphasis on the need to protect the integrity of the federal courts through the use of supervisory powers can be derived

---

10. The Court's opinion inexplicably ignores this basic thrust of our prior supervisory powers cases, and instead implies that the only value served by suppression is deterrence of future misconduct. Deterrence is one purpose behind the suppression of evidence in such situations, but it is by no means the only one.

from the factual contexts in which supervisory powers have been exercised. In large part when supervisory powers have been invoked the Court has been faced with intentional illegal conduct. It has not been the case that "[t]he criminal is to go free because the constable has blundered," People v. Defore, 242 N.Y. 13, 21, 150 N.E. 585, 587 (1926). In these cases there has been no "blunder" by the Government agent at all; rather, the agent has intentionally violated the law for the explicit purpose of obtaining the evidence in question. If the federal court permits such evidence, the intended product of deliberately illegal Government action, to be used to obtain a conviction, it places its imprimatur upon such lawlessness and thereby taints its own integrity.

The present case falls within that category. The District Court found, and the record establishes, a deliberate decision by Government agents to violate the constitutional rights of Wolstencroft for the explicit purpose of obtaining evidence against persons such as Payner. The actions of the Government agents – stealing the briefcase, opening it, and photographing all the documents inside – were both patently in violation of the Fourth Amendment rights of Wolstencroft and plainly in violation of the criminal law.[12] The Government knew exactly what information it wanted, and it was that information which was stolen from Wolstencroft. Similarly, the Government knew that it wanted to prosecute persons such as Payner, and it made a conscious decision to forgo any opportunity to prosecute Wolstencroft in order to obtain illegally the evidence against Payner and others.

Wolstencroft in fact was indicted for aiding and abetting Payner. However, Wolstencroft is a Bahamian resident, and did not return to the United States to answer the indictment. The mere fact that the Government went through the steps of indicting Wolstencroft does not in any way undermine the District Court's finding, based on substantial evidence in the record, that Wolstencroft was never the target of the IRS investigation. In light of the Government's concession that Wolstencroft's Fourth Amendment rights were violated, it is hard to see how the banker could be successfully prosecuted on the aiding and abetting charge.

Since the supervisory powers are exercised to protect the integrity of the court, rather than to vindicate the constitutional rights of the

---

12. The Court characterizes the actions of Jaffe and Casper in the briefcase incident as "possibly criminal behavior," ibid. The District Court concluded that the actions of the IRS appeared to constitute a prima facie case of criminal larceny under Florida law, and possibly violated other criminal laws of that State as well. 434 F.Supp., at 130, n. 66. Casper admitted in the District Court that he knew he was committing an illegal act. The stealing of the rolodex file from Wolstencroft's office was also both unconstitutional and criminal. That theft, however, produced no additional evidence against Payner. See 434 F.Supp., at 123, n. 56.

defendant, it is hard to see why the Court today bases its analysis entirely on Fourth Amendment standing rules. The point is that the federal judiciary should not be made accomplices to the crimes of Casper, Jaffe, and others. The only way the IRS can benefit from the evidence it chose to obtain illegally is if the evidence is admitted at trial against persons such as Payner; that was the very point of the criminal exercise in the first place. If the IRS is permitted to obtain a conviction in federal court based almost entirely on that illegally obtained evidence and its fruits, then the judiciary has given full effect to the deliberate wrong-doings of the Government. The federal court does indeed become the accomplice of the Government lawbreaker, an accessory after the fact, for without judicial use of the evidence the "caper" would have been for nought. Such a pollution of the federal courts should not be permitted.[14]

It is particularly disturbing that the Court today chooses to allow the IRS deliberately to manipulate the standing rules of the Fourth Amendment to achieve its ends. As previously noted, the District Court found that "the Government affirmatively counsels its agents that the Fourth Amendment standing limitation permits them to purposefully conduct an unconstitutional search and seizure of one individual in order to obtain evidence against third parties, who are the real targets of the governmental intrusion, and that the IRS agents in this case acted, *and will act in the future*, according to that counsel." 434 F.Supp., at 132-133 (emphasis supplied). Whatever role those standing limitations may play, it is clear that they were never intended to be a sword to be used by the Government in its deliberate choice to sacrifice the constitutional rights of one person in order to prosecute another.

The Court's decision to engraft the standing limitations of the Fourth Amendment onto the exercise of supervisory powers is puzzling not only because it runs contrary to the major purpose behind the exercise of the supervisory powers – to protect the integrity of the court – but also because it appears to render the supervisory powers superfluous. In order to establish that suppression of evidence under the supervisory powers would be proper, the Court would also require Payner to establish a violation of his Fourth or Fifth Amendment rights,[15] in which case

---

14. It is simply not a sufficient cure for the Court to denounce the actions of the IRS, while at the same time rewarding the Government for this conduct by permitting the IRS to use the evidence in the very manner which was the purpose of the illegal and unconstitutional activities.

15. The Court appears to suggest that there can be no suppression of evidence based on a violation of the Due Process Clause in this case because it was not Payner who was the immediate victim of the Government's outrageous conduct. Although the District Court concluded that the evidence should be suppressed under the Due Process Clause as well as under its supervisory powers, the Court of Appeals specifically did not reach that issue, 590 F.2d 206 (CA6 1979) (*per*

suppression would flow directly from the Constitution. This approach is totally unfaithful to our prior supervisory power cases, which, contrary to the Court's suggestion, are not constitutional cases in disguise.

I also do not understand the basis for the Court's assertion that this is not a case in which the District Court was supervising the administration of justice "among the parties before the bar," and therefore supervisory powers are inapplicable. Clearly the Government is before the bar. Equally clearly, the Government embarked on this deliberate pattern of lawless behavior for the express purpose of gaining evidence against persons such as Payner, so there can be no legitimate claim that the illegal actions are only tangentially related to the present prosecution. Instead, the Government misconduct is at the very heart of this case; without the evidence produced by the illegal conduct, there would have been no case at all, and Payner would never have been brought before the bar. This is simply not a case in which a federal court has attempted to exercise "general supervisory authority over operations of the Executive Branch." Rather, this is a case where the District Court refused to be made an accomplice to illegal conduct by the IRS by permitting the agency to use the proceeds of its crimes for the very purpose for which they were committed – to convict persons such as Payner.

Contrary to the Court's characterization, this is also not a case in which there has been "indiscriminate" or "unbending" application of the exclusionary rule. The District Court noted that "exclusion on the basis of supervisory power is only done as a last resort," 434 F.Supp., at 134, n. 74. That court concluded that suppression was proper only where there had been "purposefully illegal" conduct by the Government to obtain the evidence or where the Government's conduct was "motivated by an intentional bad faith hostility to a constitutional right." Id., at 134-135. In this case, both those threshold requirements were met, and the District Court in addition concluded that absent suppression there

---

curiam), and the Government purposely did not raise the issue in this Court. The Court therefore should not reach out to address the issue in a footnote.

In addition, the only authority cited by the Court for its suggestion is Hampton v. United States, 425 U.S. 484, 490, 96 S.Ct. 1646, 1650, 48 L.Ed.2d 113 (1976) (plurality opinion). *Hampton* was only a plurality opinion, and the issue for which the Court purports to cite it was not raised by the facts of that case. Similarly, in the Court of Appeals below the United States was able to cite only Sims v. Georgia, 389 U.S. 404, 407, 88 S.Ct. 523, 525, 19 L.Ed.2d 634 (1967), a case plainly not on point, and the sentence from the *Hampton* plurality opinion quoted by the Court, n. 9, for the proposition that Payner lacked standing to raise a due process argument. The issue whether the standing limitations this Court has imposed for challenging Fourth Amendment violations also apply for violations of the Due Process Clause based on outrageous Government conduct has not yet been settled by this Court. Cf. 434 F.Supp., at 129, n. 65, and authorities discussed therein. The due process issue should be left for consideration in the first instance by the Court of Appeals on remand.

was no deterrent to continued lawless conduct undertaken by the IRS to facilitate these types of prosecutions.[16] This is not "a 'chancellor's foot' veto [by the District Court] over law enforcement practices of which it did not approve," United States v. Russell, 411 U.S. 423, 435, 93 S.Ct. 1637, 36 L.Ed.2d 366 (1973); Hampton v. United States, 425 U.S. 484, 490, 96 S.Ct. 1646, 1650, 48 L.Ed.2d 113 (1976)˙ (plurality opinion). As my Brother POWELL noted on a prior occasion: "The fact that there is sometimes no sharply defined standard against which to make these judgments [of fundamental fairness] is not itself a sufficient reason to deny the federal judiciary's power to make them when warranted by the circumstances * * *. Nor do I despair of our ability in an appropriate case to identify appropriate standards for police practices without relying on the 'chancellor's' 'fastidious squeamishness or private sentimentalism.' " *Hampton v. United States, supra,* at 495, n. 6, 96 S.Ct., at 1652 (concurring in judgment). That appropriate case has arrived, and the Court should prevent the Government from profiting by use in the federal courts of evidence deliberately obtained by illegal actions taken in bad-faith hostility to constitutional rights.

I would affirm the judgment of the Court of Appeals and suppress the fruits of the Government's illegal action under the Court's supervisory powers.

Accordingly, I dissent.

Notes and Question

Prior to the *Payner* decision, it was thought that federal courts had the authority under its general supervisory power to suppress illegally obtained evidence where such evidence was not excludable under the Fourth Amendment–for instance where the taxpayer lacked standing because the victim of the unconstitutional search and /or seizure was a third party. The *Payner* decision clarified that standing issues with respect to the federal court's supervisory power are coextensive with those of the exclusionary rule.

In footnote 8, the majority provides further justification for its decision by quoting *Stone v. Powell* for the proposition that "the interest in preserving judicial integrity and in deterring such conduct is

---

16. There is no suggestion by the Government that any action has been taken against Casper, Jaffe, or others for the conduct exposed in this case. The Court admits that the corrective measures taken by the IRS "appear on their face to be less positive than one might expect from an agency charged with upholding the law," *ante,* at n. 5. The District Court specifically found that the Government agents knew they were violating the Constitution at the time, 434 F.Supp., at 135, n. 79, and that continued manipulation of the standing limitations of the Fourth Amendment by the IRS could be deterred only by suppression of the evidence, id., at 133.

outweighed by the societal interest in presenting probative evidence to the trier of fact." Do you agree that this justifies the majority's decision?

Some states reject the view of *Payner*. New Jersey, for instance, recognizes a right of privacy in bank records and places limits on the government's power to obtain these records. Under New Jersey law, bank records can be obtained only upon an order by a court of competent jurisdiction. This is to preserve the public's confidence in the banking system. State v. McAllister, 184 N.J. 17, 875 A.2d 866 (2005).

b. *Particularity*

In addition to being based on probable cause, a search warrant also must describe with particularity the objects of the search in order to prevent "the seizure of one thing under a warrant describing another." Andresen v. Maryland, 427 U.S. 463, 480 (1976).

VONDERAHE v. HOWLAND
United States Court of Appeals, Ninth Circuit, 1975.
508 F.2d 364.

MOORE, CIRCUIT JUDGE.

Just after 8:00 A.M., on the morning of June 16, 1970, a group of four Special Agents of the Internal Revenue Service (IRS) arrived at the office of Dr. Donn VonderAhe, a dentist practicing in Fremont, California. Simultaneously, a second group of three agents arrived at the home of the doctor and his wife, Barbara, in Newark, California. Each group was armed with a search warrant issued by a United States Commissioner. The Agents then proceeded to search or, more accurately, to ransack both office and home and to asport practically every piece of paper they could lay their hands on.

The background to this rather extraordinary procedure is best portrayed somewhat chronologically.

Dr. VonderAhe (usually referred to herein as the 'doctor') apparently has a successful dental practice. On June 16th his office consisted of eight rooms and a hallway. He had one or more employees who kept his patients' records and recorded bills and payments.

The doctor and his wife, Barbara, filed joint income tax returns. In the early part of 1969, i.e., between early January and late March, an IRS Agent (Holmes) made an audit of their 1966 and 1967 income tax returns. There were made available to him six sets of records for the years in question:

(1) combined cash-receipts-cash-disbursements journal; (2) bank

statements and cancelled checks; (3) savings account passbooks; (4) daily patient appointments book with amounts charged and amounts collected; (5) patient cards containing dental information together with charges and collections; and (6) cash receipts books. Agent Holmes found that the books and records examined accurately reflected the income reported, and recommended acceptance of the taxpayers' returns as filed.

This recommendation was not long to endure because a telephone call from a former employee, Lynette Bush, to IRS revealed that the doctor during her period of employment had maintained two sets of records. This former employee was most specific concerning the records and the location thereof. She stated that the records of 'regular' patients were recorded on white 'Banco' cards; those of 'emergency' patients on yellow sheets – subsequently green cards. She further disclosed that checks received for services from patients listed on the yellow sheets or green cards were hand endorsed by the doctor and cashed by another employee.

In the office, according to Mrs. Bush and Mrs. Van Order, another former employee of Dr. VonderAhe, the 'emergency' cards were kept in a portable file cabinet maintained in the 'opratory' room, separate and apart from the other file cabinets or, during Van Order's regime, in the third drawer of the cabinets on the right side of the office.

There were four 'emergency receipt books' during the period of employee Bush's employment, and three during employee Van Order's tenure, which were relevant to VonderAhe's allegedly unreported income. The books in question were described as 'approximately one inch thick with six receipts per page.' When filled, they were taken to the doctor's home.

Agent Romano was assigned to investigate further. To him it was obvious that if only the white card income had been disclosed to Agent Holmes, the doctor's income would have been understated by the amount of the yellow sheet/green card 'emergency' income. At least an investigation was in order to ascertain whether it had been reported. This suspicion was strengthened by remarks made by another employee, a Mrs. Comegys, who told the Agent that she and the doctor had removed the yellow sheets and green cards from the files when the 1969 audit was pending; that the doctor had taken these records to his home so that they would not be available to the Examining Agent; and that the doctor had instructed her to remain at home on the day of the audit so that she would not give any 'wrong' answers. In addition to information about the cards and books, Mrs. Comegys stated that she had, in 1968, arranged the opening of a Swiss bank account for her employer and had deposited a check for $6,050 therein.

The Search Warrant

Having received this information, IRS was alerted to the fact that there existed previously unexamined yellow sheets and green cards and books in which entries therefrom had been made. There were various ways by which these records could have been obtained. The doctor had voluntarily made available to Agent Holmes all records of income received from his 'regular' patients. Confronted with the knowledge that IRS knew of the withheld records, the doctor was scarcely in a position to place the undisclosed records in a different category from the disclosed. The Agents could have asked for them; they could have subpoenaed them; or, if they thought that there was danger of destruction, they could have sought a warrant. The Service chose this last course of action.

In spite of the fact that the 'things' to be seized and the places to be searched were known to the Service with a high degree of specificity, the warrants as they were requested and issued were, for all practical purposes, 'general warrants.' The property allegedly concealed was described as: 'Fiscal records relating to the income and expenses of Dr. Donn VonderAhe from his dental practice and other sources since January 1, 1966, to date, including, but not limited to dental patient cards, appointment books, combined appointment-cash receipts books, combined cash receipts and cash disbursements journals, business ledgers, expense records, bank ledger sheets and statements, cancelled checks, bank savings account pass books, records and correspondence relating to the opening of and deposits and withdrawals from a bank account maintained by said Doctor at the Banaue Romande in Geneva, Switzerland, plus copies of invoices and bills sent to patients of the aforesaid Doctor.'

The grounds for search and seizure were stated as: 'now and have been used as a means of committing and constitute evidence of offenses in violation of the provisions of the Internal Revenue laws; particularly §§ 7201 and 7206(1) of Title 26 United States Code; and which further comprise and constitute evidence of offenses committed in violation of the laws of the United States within the meaning of § 1001 of Title 18, United States Code.'

There was no allegation in the supporting affidavit of Agent Holmes that he sought to re-audit the material listed by him as already audited and reconciled. In the principal affidavit of Agent Romano, he states that he has 'reason to believe that the amount of fees collected from patients during the years 1966 and 1967 whose names appeared on yellow information sheets were intentionally segregated by Dr. VonderAhe and Mrs. Comegys and not made available to Revenue Agent Holmes for the audit examination of early 1969.' Thus, what had been revealed and what had been concealed had already been made abundantly clear.

The Execution of the Warrants
The Office

According to Dr. VonderAhe, at about 8:15 A.M., on June 16, 1970, three (elsewhere stated as four or five) Treasury Agents forced their way into his inner office. They apparently took over the premises, and continued their search until 1:15 P.M. The search necessitated cancellations of patient appointments because the Agents seized patient cards and records and virtually were in charge of the office. The doctor alleges that he was unable to resume his practice for approximately two weeks when most of the original records were returned.

The extent of the seizure may be judged by the list ('Document Receipt') made by the Agents, which consisted of thirty-two pages of papers and records which were carted away in cartons in a small truck. By way of brief illustration, the Agents took the contents of the drawers of the doctor's desk in his private office, including correspondence relating to the purchase of property in Bull River, Montana, a U-Haul rental contract, an application for insurance, personal letters, notes relating to the VonderAhe's planned new home, and correspondence with an investment advisory service. Hundreds of patient record cards were taken. The receptionist's desk was also searched.

The Home

The warrant enforcement technique employed by the Agents at the home was quite similar to that used at the office. They forced their way in, made a room by room search of the premises, searched the contents of Mrs. VonderAhe's purse and even that of a Mrs. Perez, a visiting friend.   Items were seized in an unused bedroom involving the VonderAhe's real estate and records labeled 'New House.' Again, over objection, an IRS Agent forced his way into the VonderAhe's car which was parked in their garage and searched it. Papers taken from the garage included many folders of patients' records, 'lab slips,' etc. Several cartons of seized material were loaded into a truck and taken away.

The oral protests of the VonderAhes were quickly followed by legal protests. From a procedural point of view, Rule 41(e) of the Federal

Rules of Criminal Procedure was unavailable to the doctor because neither he nor his wife had been indicted and there was no criminal case in being against them. However, they were well aware of potential civil and criminal consequences of the alleged concealment of records. They quite naturally desired to cause these records to be unavailable for use by the Commissioner or by a Grand Jury. Accordingly, they brought 'an independent civil action prior to indictment pursuant to the Court's inherent equity power seeking return of property seized and its suppression as evidence in any subsequent criminal proceedings.' By this 'independent equitable action' they sought to avoid the appealability question which might have otherwise arisen. Thus, having invoked the equity powers of the court, they must abide by this standard. In their complaint, filed July 7, 1970, they sought (1) the return of their books and records; (2) an injunction against the use of their property, allegedly illegally seized, in any investigation and prosecution against them; (3) an injunction against the use of copies or notes made from the material seized for prosecution purposes; (4) an injunction against contacting persons or businesses, the names of which were disclosed in the seized material; (5) the suppression of the property seized as evidence in any 'criminal proceeding' and in any proceeding to determine the tax liability of the VonderAhes; and (6) a hearing to be held by the court, prior to the presentation of the evidence to a Grand Jury or a Commissioner, at which the defendants 'shall prove that said evidence was not illegally obtained.' By leave of court, the complaint was amended to assert damages suffered by the disruption to the doctor's dental practice caused by the Agent's action in the amount of $15,000.

The government moved to dismiss the complaint on the grounds that (1) the United States had not consented to be sued; (2) the court lacked jurisdiction over the subject matter; and (3) that the complaint failed to state a claim upon which relief could be granted.

In the meantime, the government had photocopied the seized records and returned the originals.

The District Court denied the VonderAhes' motion for a preliminary injunction and granted the government's motion to dismiss. The doctor and his wife appealed.

* * *

The Fourth Amendment

Initially, the search and seizure must be considered within the confines of the Fourth Amendment. In fact, limitation to consideration of this appeal within the confines of the Fourth Amendment is suggested by the taxpayers themselves in arguing that 'assuming the Court finds probable cause for a search warrant to exist, the government's showing of probable cause did not justify the extent of the searches and seizures at bar,' and that 'the affidavits only justified the search for the records which the taxpayers allegedly had withheld, the location of which an employee of the VonderAhes had described to the Treasury Agents.'

The Fourth Amendment declares the 'right of the people to be secure in their persons, houses, papers and effects' but only against 'unreasonable searches and seizures'. Any warrant therefor shall issue 'upon probable cause' and shall describe 'the place to be searched, and the persons or things to be seized.' As to 'probable cause,' the district court found that 'the affidavits submitted were more than sufficient to provide probable cause to believe that plaintiffs were violating the income tax laws.'

But the words 'probable cause' are not self-defining – 'probable cause' for what? The supporting affidavits were quite specific in describing the allegedly concealed property, namely, yellow sheets and green cards. No facts were alleged which showed probable cause for the issuance of a general warrant. No charge was made that the books and records submitted to Agent Holmes were false and that they should be subjected to a re-audit. To proceed by the 'warrant' method without first seeking the desired papers by request or subpoena should be based upon the strongest showing of necessity but if such drastic procedure is to be availed of, it should be strictly limited as constitutionally required. Therefore, although there may have been 'probable cause' to search for and seize the yellow sheets and green cards for 1966 and 1967, there was no probable cause shown for a seizure of all the doctor's dental books and records, or his personal and private papers.

In seeking and executing such a general warrant, the agents themselves must assume the responsibility for its breadth. They could have restricted it to the concealed items and thus have avoided the ransacking procedure in which they, in executing the warrant, indulged.

There remain for consideration specificity and unreasonableness, issues which are subject to a similar analysis. Although the District Court noted that 'general warrants which fail to adequately specify the area to be searched or the items to be seized have historically met with judicial disapproval,' it held that 'the warrants were as specific as practical' and while recognizing their 'broad scope,' they were 'not overly broad in a constitutional sense.'

What is 'overly broad' cannot be resolved in an abstract or academic manner but only in relation to the facts, circumstances under, and the purpose for, which the warrants were issued. The warrants here were, in effect, general warrants. They sought all fiscal records of the doctor from January 1, 1966 to date (June 1970) relating to his income and expenses 'but not limited to (books and records enumerated) * * *.' In short, except for the yellow sheets and green cards, this was the identical material which had been delivered to and examined by Agent Holmes.

The Supreme Court has stated that there are certain permissible standards to be applied in connection with the issuance of search warrants. Thus in Berger v. New York, 388 U.S. 41, 58, 87 S.Ct. 1873, 1883, 18 L.Ed.2d 1040 (1967), the Court said:

> 'The proceeding by search warrant is a drastic one,' Sgro v. United States, 287 U.S. 206, 210, 53 S.Ct. 138, 140, 77 L.Ed. 260 (1932), and must be carefully circumscribed so as to prevent unauthorized invasions of 'the sanctity of a man's home and privacies of life.' Boyd v. United States, supra, 116 U.S. 616, 630, 6 S.Ct. 524, 532, (29 L.Ed. 746).

And in Coolidge v. New Hampshire, 403 U.S. 443, 91 S.Ct. 2022, 29 L.Ed.2d 564 (1971), the Court said:

> The second, distinct objective is that those searches deemed necessary should be as limited as possible. Here, the specific evil is the 'general warrant' abhorred by the colonists, and the problem is not that of intrusion *per se*, but of a general, exploratory rummaging in a person's belongings. The warrant accomplishes this second objective by requiring a 'particular description' of the things to be seized.

Upon the information available to it, the government knew exactly what it needed and wanted and where the records were located. There was no necessity for a massive re-examination of all records bearing on income and expenses. Were this the law, the Commissioner, upon finding any suspicious deficiency, could order a seizure of every such taxpayer's records upon the mere allegation that the omission or an inaccurate statement of one item might bespeak inaccuracies as to others which, in his opinion, necessitates a seizure of all records, at office and home. Important as it is to enable the government to obtain information to assure itself of the correct reporting of taxes, it is difficult to believe that the draftsmen of the Fourth Amendment did not insert 'unreasonable' to avoid just such an in terrorem state as the Agents created and wreaked here.

Moreover, just as 'unreasonable' can be applied to the breadth of the warrant, so much the more can it be applied to the manner of execution because it is the 'manner' which, as vividly illustrated by the facts of this case, can create and constitute the prohibited invasion. As previously mentioned, the Agents could have sought the allegedly concealed records by other means. If they had desired to question the accuracy of patient payments, they could have made a patient check. All this could have occurred in an orderly way without the sudden assault causing not only damage to the doctor's finances and prestige but undoubtedly inconvenience and possibly pain and suffering to the many patients who could not be treated for weeks due to the disruption.

* * *

Conclusion

The problem here is one of resolving the equities. The government should not be benefitted in any forthcoming actions against the VonderAhes, civil or criminal, by using books and records illegally seized. On the other hand, the VonderAhes should not benefit from their own acts of concealment and thus avoid the payment of taxes legally due and also the possible consequences of illegal concealment. Our equitable powers would be much distorted were we to hold that the allegedly concealed records (yellow sheets and green cards) were improperly seized.

The VonderAhes have asked us to invoke in their favor what has become known as the 'exclusionary rule,' *i.e.*, to decree at this time that all records seized, including yellow sheets and green cards and any leads therefrom cannot be introduced in any proceeding, civil or criminal against them. However, if the facts are, as represented, that the taxpayers by their own wrong, deliberately concealed income and failed to pay taxes thereon, it would seem to be the height of inequity for the courts to enable them to profit thereby. Using equity as the standard, the warrants as issued restricted to the yellow sheets and green cards would have been reasonable; beyond these records they were too broad. Although the manner of execution was quite unjustified, the penalty of exclusion which the taxpayers would impose is equally unjustified. Our present task is to place the government's allegedly unlawful procedure in obtaining and executing the warrants and the VonderAhes' allegedly unlawful concealment on the mythical scales of justice, and observe the balance. Observing this balance (or possibly imbalance), we believe that justice can best be achieved by reversing the order of the District Court dismissing the complaint and, upon remand, directing the District Court to grant the injunctive relief sought by appellants except as to the yellow sheets and green cards, copies of which the government may retain and use subject, however, to any and all objections thereto, including objections based on the Fifth Amendment, in any proceeding, civil or criminal, which may be raised by the VonderAhes.

Insofar as the complaint seeks money damages because of the Agents' acts, the serious pecuniary loss caused thereby would appear to bring this case within the *Bivens* doctrine. In Bivens v. Six Unknown Fed. Narcotics Agents, 403 U.S. 388, 91 S.Ct. 1999, 29 L.Ed.2d 619 (1971), the Supreme Court upheld federal jurisdiction over such a suit and held that money damages may be recovered for any injuries consequent upon a violation of the Fourth Amendment by federal officials. Mr. Justice Harlan in his concurring opinion pointed to the judiciary's 'particular responsibility to assure the vindication of constitutional interests such as are embraced by the Fourth Amendment.' *Bivens, supra*, at 407, 91 S.Ct. at 2010.

The amended complaint seeks damages of $15,000 for the disruption of the doctor's practice. Upon the facts set forth, appellants are entitled to have these issues adjudicated. Therefore, the complaint as amended should not have been dismissed.

Order affirmed in part, reversed in part.

* * *

Notes And Questions

The Supreme Court held in United States v. Janis, 428 U.S. 433, 96 S.Ct. 3021, 49 L.Ed.2d 1046 (1976), that illegally obtained evidence may be used in a federal civil tax case if the evidence was obtained by state officers acting on their own without collusion or encouragement from federal officers. This is known as the "silver platter doctrine." It does not apply to criminal trials, however, so the exclusionary rule will render such evidence inadmissible regardless of whether it was obtained by state or federal officers. Cf. United States v. Leon, 468 U.S. 897, 104 S.Ct. 3430, 82 L.Ed.2d 677 (1984), holding that "suppression is appropriate only if the officers were dishonest or reckless in preparing their affidavit or could not have harbored an objectively reasonable belief in the existence of probable cause." Id. at 926.

The Second Circuit held in Tirado v. Commissioner, 689 F.2d 307 (2d Cir. 1982) that *Janis* extends to an intra-sovereign use of illegally obtained evidence. In *Tirado*, evidence seized by federal narcotics agents under an invalid warrant was used in a federal civil tax proceeding.

The exclusionary rule also does not apply to parole revocation hearings or to grand jury proceedings because "those proceedings play a special role in the law enforcement process and * * * the traditionally flexible, nonadversarial nature of those proceedings would be jeopardized by the application of the rule." Pennsylvania Board of Probation and

Parole v. Scott, 524 U.S. 357, 118 S.Ct. 2014, 141 L.Ed.2d 344 (1998), citing United States v. Calandra, 414 U.S. 338, 343-346 (1974).

Plain View Doctrine. An exception to the particularity requirement is where the seized evidence was in plain view. Thus, such evidence may be admissible at trial even though it was not listed in the warrant, provided certain requirements are met. For instance, the law enforcement agents must have been lawfully present on the premises, the discovery of the evidence must have been inadvertent, and the incriminating nature of the evidence must have been "immediately apparent." United States v Blakeney, 942 F.2d 1001, 1028 (6th Cir. 1991).

1. Why did the court think the warrant in *Vonder Ahe* was overly broad?

2. Do you see any problem with the court's decision?

c. *Reasonableness*

UNITED STATES v. CACERES
Supreme Court of the United States, 1979.
440 U.S. 741, 99 S.Ct. 1465, 59 L.Ed.2d 733.

MR. JUSTICE STEVENS delivered the opinion of the Court.

The question we granted certiorari to decide is whether evidence obtained in violation of Internal Revenue Service (IRS) regulations may be admitted at the criminal trial of a taxpayer accused of bribing an IRS agent.

* * *

I.

Neither the Constitution nor any Act of Congress requires that official approval be secured before conversations are overheard or recorded by Government agents with the consent of one of the conversants. Such "consensual electronic surveillance" between taxpayers and IRS agents is, however, prohibited by IRS regulations unless appropriate prior authorization is obtained.[3]

---

3.   The IRS regulations were drafted to conform to the requirements of the Attorney General's October 16, 1972, Memorandum to the Heads of Executive Departments and Agencies. The memorandum mandates Justice Department approval for all consensual monitoring of nontelephone conversations by federal departments and agencies. The only exceptions are if less than 48 hours is available to secure approval or if exigent circumstances preclude requests for advance authorization from the Justice Department; in such cases, monitoring may be instituted under the authorization of the head of the department or agency, or other officials designated by him.

The IRS Manual sets forth in detail the procedures to be followed in obtaining such approvals.[4]   For all types of requests the regulations require an explanation of the reasons for the proposal, the type of equipment to be used, the names of the persons involved, and the duration of the proposed monitoring.

* * *

II.

On March 14, 1974, Agent Yee met with respondent and his wife in connection with an audit of their 1971 income tax returns. After Mrs. Caceres left the meeting, respondent offered Yee a "personal settlement" of $500 in exchange for a favorable resolution of the audit. When he returned to the IRS office, Yee reported the offer to his superiors and prepared an affidavit describing it.

The record reflects no further discussion of the offer until January 1975. It does indicate, however, that one telephone conversation between Yee and respondent, on March 21, 1974, was recorded with authorization, and that authority was also obtained to monitor

---

4.   Paragraph 652.22 of the IRS Manual (in effect Sept. 1975) provides in pertinent part:

"(1) The monitoring of non-telephone conversations with the consent of one party requires the advance authorization of the Attorney General or any designated Assistant Attorney General. Requests for such authority may be signed by the Director, Internal Security Division, or, in his/her absence, the Acting Director. This authority cannot be redelegated. These same officials may authorize temporary emergency monitoring when exigent circumstances preclude requesting the authorization of the Attorney General in advance. If the Director, Internal Security Division, cannot be reached the Assistant Commissioner (Inspection) may grant emergency approval. This authority cannot be redelegated.

"(2) Written approval of the Attorney General must be requested 48 hours prior to the use of mechanical, electronic or other devices to overhear, transmit or record a non-telephone private conversation with the permission of one party to the conversation. * * * Any requests being telefaxed into the National Office should be submitted four days prior to the anticipated equipment use. * * *

"(3) [A request] must be signed and submitted by the Regional Inspector or Chief, Investigations Branch, to the Director, Internal Security Division. Such requests will contain [reason for such proposed use; type of equipment to be used; names of persons involved; proposed location of equipment; duration of proposed use (limited to 30 days from proposed beginning date); and manner or method of installation] * * *.

* * *

"(6) When emergency situations occur, the Director or Acting Director, Internal Security Division, or the Assistant Commissioner (Inspection) will be contacted to grant emergency approval to monitor. This emergency approval authority cannot be redelegated. * * * Emergency authorization pursuant to this exception will not be given where the requesting official has in excess of 48 hours to obtain written advance approval from the Attorney General.

"(7) If, at the time the emergency approval request is submitted, it is desired that approval for use of electronic equipment be given for an extended period, this should be indicated on the [appropriate form]. The Director, in addition to reporting his authorization for emergency use to the Attorney General, will also request approval for the Use of Electronic Equipment for the duration of that period specified by the requestor."

face-to-face conversations with respondent from time to time during the period between March and September 1974. Yee continued to work on the audit of respondent's records throughout this period, but his meetings, until January 1975, were with Mrs. Caceres and the Caceres' accountant.[8]

On January 27, 1975, Yee had a meeting with respondent that was not recorded. According to Yee's affidavit, the meeting proceeded in two stages. First, he discussed his calculations with respondent, Mrs. Caceres, and their accountant. When respondent and his wife asked for an additional week to check their records, Yee told them it would be necessary to sign an extension because the statute of limitations would otherwise expire soon. Respondent stated that he would have to consult his attorney before signing any extension, and would call Yee with his decision later that day.

Yee then left the office to return to his car. He was followed by respondent, who revived the subject of a "personal settlement." This time, respondent indicated that he had $500 that he would give Yee immediately, with an additional $500 to be paid when the matter was finally settled. Yee refused the offer, but at respondent's insistence, eventually stated that he might consider it.

In subsequent conversations initiated by Agent Yee, all of which were monitored, respondent indicated that he was not prepared for another meeting with Yee. Finally, in a conversation on January 30 at 5:15 p. m., respondent agreed to a meeting the following day at 2 p. m. At 8:15 a. m. on the 31st, the Regional Inspector in San Francisco telephoned the Director of Internal Security in Washington and obtained emergency approval for the use of electronic equipment to monitor the meeting that afternoon. On the same day, a written request for authority to monitor face-to-face conversations for a period of 30 days was initiated and, in due course, forwarded to Washington for submission to the Department of Justice.

At the meeting on the 31st, respondent gave Yee $500 and promised to give him an additional $500 when he received a notice from IRS showing his deficiency at an amount upon which he and Yee had agreed. As in all his future meetings with respondent, Yee wore a concealed radio transmitter which allowed other agents to monitor and record their conversation.

Yee next called respondent on February 5 and arranged a meeting for the next day to review the audit agreement. Because the Department of

---

8.   Yee had one follow-up conversation with respondent later in March, which was not monitored. From that point until January 1975, he had no further contact with respondent.

Justice had not yet acted on, or perhaps even received, the request for a 30-day authorization, the Regional Inspector again requested and obtained emergency approval to monitor the meeting with respondent. At the February 6 meeting, respondent renewed his promise to pay an additional $500 in connection with the 1971 return, and also offered Yee another $2,000 for help in settling his 1973 and 1974 returns.

On February 11, a Deputy Assistant Attorney General approved the request for authority to monitor Yee's conversations with respondent for 30 days. The approval was received in time to cover a meeting held that day at which Yee was paid the additional $500. Because the 30-day period did not commence until February 11, however, no approval from the Department of Justice was ever obtained for the earlier monitorings of January 31 and February 6.

The District Court and the Court of Appeals both held that the two earlier meetings had not been monitored in accordance with IRS regulations, since Justice Department approval had not been secured. The courts recognized that such approval is not required, by the terms of the regulations, in "emergency situations" when less than 48 hours is available to secure authorization. They recognized, too, that in each instance, less than 48 hours did exist between the time the IRS initiated its request for monitoring approval and the time of the scheduled meeting with Yee. But the courts concluded that neither meeting fell within the emergency provision of the regulations because the exigencies were the product of "government-created scheduling problems."

The Government does not challenge that conclusion. We are therefore presented with the question whether the tape recordings, and the testimony of the agents who monitored the January 31 and February 6 conversations, should be excluded because of the violation of the IRS regulations.

III.

A court's duty to enforce an agency regulation is most evident when compliance with the regulation is mandated by the Constitution or federal law. In this case, however, * * * the agency was not required by the Constitution or by statute to adopt any particular procedures or rules before engaging in consensual monitoring and recording. While Title III of the Omnibus Crime Control and Safe Streets Act of 1968, 18 U.S.C. § 2510 et seq., regulates electronic surveillance conducted without the consent of either party to a conversation, federal statutes impose no restrictions on recording a conversation with the consent of one of the conversants.

Nor does the Constitution protect the privacy of individuals in respondent's position. In Lopez v. United States, 373 U.S. 427, 439, 83 S.Ct. 1381, 1388, 10 L.Ed.2d 462, we held that the Fourth Amendment provided no protection to an individual against the recording of his statements by the IRS agent to whom he was speaking. In doing so, we repudiated any suggestion that the defendant had a "constitutional right to rely on possible flaws in the agent's memory, or to challenge the agent's credibility without being beset by corroborating evidence that is not susceptible of impeachment," concluding instead that "the risk that petitioner took in offering a bribe to [the IRS agent] fairly included the risk that the offer would be accurately reproduced in court, whether by faultless memory or mechanical recording." The same analysis was applied in United States v. White, 401 U.S. 745, 91 S.Ct. 1122, 28 L.Ed.2d 453, to consensual monitoring and recording by means of a transmitter concealed on an informant's person, even though the defendant did not know that he was speaking with a Government agent[.] * * *

* * *

Our decisions in *Lopez* and *White* demonstrate that the IRS was not required by the Constitution to adopt these regulations.[14] It is equally clear that the violations of agency regulations disclosed by this record do not raise any constitutional questions.

It is true, of course, that respondent's conversations were monitored without the approval of the Department of Justice, whereas the conversations of others in a similar position would, assuming the IRS generally follows its regulations, be recorded only with Justice Department approval. But this difference does not even arguably amount to a denial of equal protection. No claim is, or reasonably could be, made that if the IRS had more promptly addressed this request to the Department of Justice, it would have been denied. As a result, any

---

14. It does not necessarily follow, however, as a matter of either logic or law, that the agency had no duty to obey them. "Where the rights of individuals are affected, it is incumbent upon agencies to follow their own procedures. This is so even where the internal procedures are possibly more rigorous than otherwise would be required." Morton v. Ruiz, 415 U.S. 199, 235, 94 S.Ct. 1055, 1074, 39 L.Ed.2d 270. See, e. g., United States ex rel. Accardi v. Shaughnessy, 347 U.S. 260, 74 S.Ct. 499, 98 L.Ed. 681 (holding habeas corpus relief proper where Government regulations "with the force and effect of law" governing the procedure to be followed in processing and passing upon an alien's application for suspension of deportation were not followed); Service v. Dulles, 354 U.S. 363, 77 S.Ct. 1152, 1 L.Ed.2d 1403 (invalidating Secretary of State's dismissal of an employee where regulations requiring approval of the Deputy Undersecretary and consultation of full record were not satisfied); Vitarelli v. Seaton, 359 U.S. 535, 79 S.Ct. 968, 3 L.Ed.2d 1012 (invalidating dismissal of Interior Department employee where regulations governing hearing procedures for national security dismissals were not followed). See also Yellin v. United States, 374 U.S. 109, 83 S.Ct. 1828, 10 L.Ed.2d 778 (reversing contempt conviction where congressional committee had not complied with its rules requiring it to consider a witness' request to be heard in executive session).

inconsistency of which respondent might complain is purely one of form, with no discernible effect in this case on the action taken by the agency and its treatment of respondent.

Moreover, the failure to secure Justice Department authorization, while conceded here to be a violation of the IRS regulations, was attributable to the fact that the IRS officials responsible for administration of the relevant regulations, both in San Francisco and Washington, construed the situation as an emergency within the meaning of those regulations. Their construction of their own regulations, even if erroneous, was not obviously so. That kind of error by an executive agency in interpreting its own regulations surely does not raise any constitutional questions.

Nor is this a case in which the Due Process Clause is implicated because an individual has reasonably relied on agency regulations promulgated for his guidance or benefit and has suffered substantially because of their violation by the agency.[15] Respondent cannot reasonably contend that he relied on the regulation, or that its breach had any effect on his conduct. He did not know that his conversations with Yee were being recorded without proper authority. He was, of course, prejudiced in the sense that he would be better off if all monitoring had been postponed until after the Deputy Assistant Attorney General's approval was obtained on February 11, 1975, but precisely the same prejudice would have ensued if the approval had been issued more promptly. For the record makes it perfectly clear that a delay in processing the request, rather than any doubt about its propriety or sufficiency, was the sole reason why advance authorization was not obtained before February 11.

* * *

IV.

Respondent argues that the regulations concerning electronic eavesdropping, even though not required by the Constitution or by

---

15. In Raley v. Ohio, 360 U.S. 423, 437-438, 79 S.Ct. 1257, 1265-1266, 3 L.Ed.2d 1344, we held that due process precluded the conviction of individuals for refusing to answer questions asked by a state investigating commission which itself had erroneously provided assurances, express or implied, that the defendants had a privilege under state law to refuse to answer. And in Cox v. Louisiana, 379 U.S. 559, 85 S.Ct. 476, 13 L.Ed.2d 487, the Court held that an individual could not be punished for demonstrating "near" a courthouse where the highest police officials of the city had advised the demonstrators that they could meet where they did without violating the statutory proscription against demonstrations "near" the courthouse. Cf. Arizona Grocery Co. v. Atchison, T. & S. F. R. Co., 284 U.S. 370, 52 S.Ct. 183, 76 L.Ed. 348 (holding invalid Interstate Commerce Commission's retroactive application of new rate); Columbia Broadcasting System, Inc. v. United States, 316 U.S. 407, 422, 62 S.Ct. 1194, 1202, 86 L.Ed. 1563 (agency regulations on which individuals are "entitled to rely" bind agency and are therefore ripe for judicial review). The underlying rationale of the foregoing cases is plainly inapplicable here.

statute, are of such importance in safeguarding the privacy of the citizenry that a rigid exclusionary rule should be applied to all evidence obtained in violation of any of their provisions. We do not doubt the importance of these rules. Nevertheless, without pausing to evaluate the Government's challenge to our power to do so, we decline to adopt any rigid rule requiring federal courts to exclude any evidence obtained as a result of a violation of these rules.

* * *

Nor can we accept respondent's further argument that even without a rigid rule of exclusion, his is a case in which evidence secured in violation of the agency regulation should be excluded on the basis of a more limited, individualized approach. Quite the contrary, this case exemplifies those situations in which evidence would not be excluded if a case-by-case approach were applied. The two conversations at issue here were recorded with the approval of the IRS officials in San Francisco and Washington. In an emergency situation, which the agents thought was present, this approval would have been sufficient. The agency action, while later found to be in violation of the regulations, nonetheless reflected a reasonable, good-faith attempt to comply in a situation in which no one questions that monitoring was appropriate and would have certainly received Justice Department authorization, had the request been received more promptly. In these circumstances, there is simply no reason why a court should exercise whatever discretion it may have to exclude evidence obtained in violation of the regulations.

The judgment of the Court of Appeals is Reversed.

Notes And Questions

For a criticism of the *Caceres* decision, see Amanda A. Cochran, Evidence Handed to the IRS Criminal Division On A 'Civil" Platter: Constitutional Infringements on Taxpayers, 91 J. Crim. L. & Criminology 699 (2001).

Under what circumstances might evidence obtained in violation of a regulation be suppressed? What factors should the courts consider?

2. Fifth Amendment

a. *Privilege Against Self-Incrimination*

1) *Failure to File*

GARNER v. UNITED STATES
Supreme Court of the United States, 1976.
424 U.S. 648, 96 S.Ct. 1178, 47 L.Ed.2d 370.

MR. JUSTICE POWELL delivered the opinion of the Court.

This case involves a nontax criminal prosecution in which the Government introduced petitioner's income tax returns to prove the offense against him. The question is whether the introduction of this evidence, over petitioner's Fifth Amendment objection, violated the privilege against compulsory self-incrimination when petitioner made the incriminating disclosures on his returns instead of then claiming the privilege.

I.

Petitioner, Roy Garner, was indicted for a conspiracy involving the use of interstate transportation and communication facilities to "fix" sporting contests, to transmit bets and information assisting in the placing of bets, and to distribute the resultant illegal proceeds. The Government's case was that conspirators bet on horse races either having fixed them or while in possession of other information unavailable to the general public. Garner's role in this scheme was the furnishing of inside information. The case against him included the testimony of other conspirators and telephone toll records that showed calls from Garner to other conspirators before various bets were placed.

The Government also introduced, over Garner's Fifth Amendment objection, the Form 1040 income tax returns that Garner had filed for 1965, 1966, and 1967. In the 1965 return Garner had reported his occupation as "professional gambler," and in each return he reported substantial income from "gambling" or "wagering." The prosecution relied on Garner's familiarity with "the business of wagering and gambling," as reflected in his returns, to help rebut his claim that his relationships with other conspirators were innocent ones.

The jury returned a guilty verdict. Garner appealed to the Court of Appeals for the Ninth Circuit, contending that the privilege against compulsory self-incrimination entitled him to exclude the tax returns despite his failure to claim the privilege on the returns instead of making disclosures. Sitting en banc the Court of Appeals held that Garner's failure to assert the privilege on his returns defeated his Fifth Amendment claim. We agree.

II.

In United States v. Sullivan, 274 U.S. 259, 47 S.Ct. 607, 71 L.Ed. 1037 (1927), the Court held that the privilege against compulsory self-incrimination is not a defense to prosecution for failing to file a return at all. But the Court indicated that the privilege could be claimed against specific disclosures sought on a return* * *.

* * *

Had Garner invoked the privilege against compulsory self-incrimination on his tax returns in lieu of supplying the information used against him, the Internal Revenue Service could have proceeded in either or both of two ways. First, the Service could have sought to have Garner criminally prosecuted under § 7203 of the Internal Revenue Code of 1954 (Code), 26 U.S.C. § 7203, which proscribes, among other things, the willful failure to make a return. Second, the Service could have sought to complete Garner's returns administratively "from (its) own knowledge and from such information as (it could) obtain through testimony or otherwise." 26 U.S.C. § 6020(b)(1). Section 7602(2) of the Code authorizes the Service in such circumstances to summon the taxpayer to appear and to produce records or give testimony. 26 U.S.C. § 7602(2).[5] If Garner had persisted in his claim when summoned, the Service could have sued for enforcement in district court, subjecting Garner to the threat of the court's contempt power. 26 U.S.C. § 7604.

Given *Sullivan*, it cannot fairly be said that taxpayers are "volunteers" when they file their tax returns. The Government compels the filing of a return much as it compels, for example, the appearance of

---

5.   Title 26 U.S.C. § 7602 reads in part:

"For the purpose of ascertaining the correctness of any return, making a return where none has been made, determining the liability of any person for any internal revenue tax * * *, or collecting any such liability, the Secretary or his delegate is authorized

"(2) To summon the person liable for tax or required to perform the act, or any officer or employee of such person, or any person having possession, custody, or care of books of account containing entries relating to the business of the person liable for tax or required to perform the act, or any other person the Secretary or his delegate may deem proper, to appear before the Secretary or his delegate at a time and place named in the summons and to produce such books, papers, records, or other data, and to give such testimony, under oath, as may be relevant or material to such inquiry * * *."

a "witness"[7] before a grand jury. The availability to the Service of § 7203 prosecutions and the summons procedure also induces taxpayers to disclose unprivileged information on their returns. The question, however, is whether the Government can be said to have compelled Garner to incriminate himself with regard to specific disclosures made on his return when he could have claimed the Fifth Amendment privilege instead.

III.

We start from the fundamental proposition:

"(A) witness protected by the privilege may rightfully refuse to answer unless and until he is protected at least against the use of his compelled answers and evidence derived therefrom in any subsequent criminal case in which he is a defendant. Kastigar v. United States, 406 U.S. 441, 92 S.Ct. 1653, 32 L.Ed.2d 212 (1972). Absent such protection, if he is nevertheless compelled to answer, his answers are inadmissible against him in a later criminal prosecution. * * *

Lefkowitz v. Turley, 414 U.S. 70, 78, 94 S.Ct. 316, 322, 38 L.Ed.2d 274, 282 (1973).

Because the privilege protects against the use of compelled statements as well as guarantees the right to remain silent absent immunity, the inquiry in a Fifth Amendment case is not ended when an incriminating statement is made in lieu of a claim of privilege. Nor, however, is failure to claim the privilege irrelevant.

The Court has held that an individual under compulsion to make disclosures as a witness who revealed information instead of claiming the privilege lost the benefit of the privilege. United States v. Kordel, 397 U.S. 1, 7-10, 90 S.Ct. 763, 766-769, 25 L.Ed.2d 1, 7-9 (1970). Although *Kordel* appears to be the only square holding to this effect, the Court frequently has recognized the principle in dictum. Maness v. Meyers, 419 U.S. 449, 466, 95 S.Ct. 584, 42 L.Ed.2d 574, 587 (1975); Rogers v. United States, 340 U.S.67, 370-371, 71 S.Ct. 438, 440-441, 95 L.Ed. 344, 347- 348 (1951); Smith v. United States, 337 U.S. 137, 150, 69 S.Ct. 1000,

---

7.   The term "witness" is used herein to identify one who, at the time disclosures are sought from him, is not a defendant in a criminal proceeding. The more frequent situations in which a witness' disclosures are compelled, subject to Fifth Amendment rights, include testimony before a grand jury, in a civil or criminal case or proceeding, or before a legislative or administrative body possessing subpoena power.

1007, 93 L.Ed.1264, 1273 (1949.[8]   These decisions stand for the proposition that, in the ordinary case, if a witness under compulsion to testify makes disclosures instead of claiming the privilege, the government has not "compelled" him to incriminate himself.

* * *

* * * Despite its cherished position, the Fifth Amendment addresses only a relatively narrow scope of inquiries. Unless the government seeks testimony that will subject its giver to criminal liability, the constitutional right to remain silent absent immunity does not arise. An individual therefore properly may be compelled to give testimony, for example, in a noncriminal investigation of himself. See, e. g., Gardner v. Broderick, 392 U.S. 273, 278, 88 S.Ct. 1913, 1916, 20 L.Ed.2d 1082, 1086 (1968). Unless a witness objects, a government ordinarily may assume that its compulsory processes are not eliciting testimony that he deems to be incriminating. Only the witness knows whether the apparently innocent disclosure sought may incriminate him, and the burden appropriately lies with him to make a timely assertion of the privilege. If, instead, he discloses the information sought, any incriminations properly are viewed as not compelled. * * *

IV.

The information revealed in the preparation and filing of an income tax return is, for purposes of Fifth Amendment analysis, the testimony of a "witness," as that term is used herein. Since Garner disclosed information on his returns instead of objecting, his Fifth Amendment claim would be defeated by an application of the general requirement that witnesses must claim the privilege. Garner, however, resists the application of that requirement, arguing that incriminating disclosures made in lieu of objection are "compelled" in the tax-return context. He relies specifically on three situations in which incriminatory disclosures have been considered compelled despite a failure to claim the privilege. But in each of these narrowly defined situations, some factor not present here made inappropriate the general rule that the privilege must be claimed. In each situation the relevant factor was held to deny the individual a "free choice to admit, to deny, or to refuse to answer." Lisenba v. California, 314 U.S. 219, 241, 62 S.Ct. 280, 292, 86 L.Ed. 166,

---

8.   The Court also has held, analogously, that a witness loses the privilege by failing to claim it promptly even though the information being sought remains undisclosed when the privilege is claimed. United States v. Murdock, 284 U.S. 141, 148, 52 S.Ct. 63, 64, 76 L.Ed. 210, 212 (1931), disapproved on other grounds, Murphy v. Waterfront Comm'n, 378 U.S. 52, 84 S.Ct. 1594, 12 L.Ed.2d 678 (1964); see Rogers v. United States, 340 U.S., at 371, 71 S.Ct., at 440, 95 L.Ed., at 348.

182 (1941). For the reasons stated below, we conclude that no such factor deprived Garner of that free choice.

A.

Garner relies first on cases dealing with coerced confessions, e. g., Miranda v. Arizona, 384 U.S. 436, 86 S.Ct. 1602, 16 L.Ed.2d 694 (1966), where the Court has required the exclusion of incriminating statements unless there has been a knowing and intelligent waiver of the privilege regardless of whether the privilege has been claimed.* * *

It is evident that these cases have little to do with disclosures on a tax return. The coerced-confession cases present the entirely different situation of custodial interrogation. It is presumed that without proper safeguards the circumstances of custodial interrogation deny an individual the ability freely to choose to remain silent. At the same time, the inquiring government is acutely aware of the potentially incriminatory nature of the disclosures sought. Thus, any pressures inherent in custodial interrogation are compulsions to incriminate, not merely compulsions to make unprivileged disclosures. Because of the danger that custodial interrogation posed to the adversary system favored by the privilege, the Court in *Miranda* was impelled to adopt the extraordinary safeguard of excluding statements made without a knowing and intelligent waiver of the privilege. Id., at 467, 475-476, 86 S.Ct., at 1624, 1628-1629, 16 L.Ed.2d at 719, 724-725. Nothing in this case suggests the need for a similar presumption that a taxpayer makes disclosures on his return rather than claims the privilege because his will is overborne. In fact, a taxpayer, who can complete his return at leisure and with legal assistance, is even less subject to the psychological pressures at issue in *Miranda* than a witness who has been called to testify in judicial proceedings.

B.

Garner relies next on Mackey v. United States, 401 U.S. 667, 91 S.Ct. 1160, 28 L.Ed.2d 404 (1971), the relevance of which can be understood only in light of Marchetti v. United States, 390 U.S. 39, 88 S.Ct. 697, 19 L.Ed.2d 889 (1968), and Grosso v. United States, 390 U.S. 62, 88 S.Ct. 709, 19 L.Ed.2d 906 (1968). In the latter cases the Court considered whether the Fifth Amendment was a defense in prosecutions for failure to file the returns required of gamblers in connection with the federal occupational and excise taxes on gambling. The Court found that any disclosures made in connection with the payment of those taxes tended to incriminate because of the pervasive criminal regulation of gambling activities. *Marchetti,* supra, 390 U.S., at 48-49, 88 S.Ct. at 702-703, 19 L.Ed.2d at 897-898; *Grosso,* supra, 390 U.S., at 66-67, 88 S.Ct. at 712-713, 19 L.Ed.2d at 911-912. Since submitting a claim of privilege in lieu of the returns also would incriminate, the Court held that the privilege could be exercised by simply failing to file.[11]

In *Mackey*, the disclosures required in connection with the gambling excise tax had been made before *Marchetti* and *Grosso* were decided. Mackey's returns were introduced in a criminal prosecution for income tax evasion. Although a majority of the Court considered the disclosures on the returns to have been compelled incriminations, 401 U.S., at 672, 91 S.Ct., at 1163, 28 L.Ed.2d, at 408 (plurality opinion), Mackey was not immunized against their use because *Marchetti* and *Grosso* were held nonretroactive. Garner assumes that if Mackey had made his disclosures after *Marchetti* and *Grosso*, they could not have been used against him. He then concludes that since Mackey would have been privileged to file no returns at all, *Mackey* stands for the proposition that an objection at trial always suffices to preserve the privilege even if disclosures have been made previously.

---

11. As we have noted, the privilege is an exception to the general principle that the Government has the right to everyone's testimony. A corollary to that principle is that the claim of privilege ordinarily must be presented to a "tribunal" for evaluation at the time disclosures are initially sought. See Albertson v. SACB, 382 U.S. 70, 78-79, 86 S.Ct. 194, 198-199, 15 L.Ed.2d 165, (1965); *United States ex rel. Vajtauer v. Commissioner of Immigration,* 273 U.S., at 113, 47 S.Ct., at 306, 71 L.Ed., at 566; Mason v. United States, 244 U.S. 362, 364-365, 37 S.Ct. 621, 622, 61 L.Ed. 1198, 1199-1200 (1917). This early evaluation of claims allows the Government to compel evidence if the claim is invalid or if immunity is granted and therefore assures that the Government obtains all the information to which it is entitled. In the gambling tax cases, however, making a claim of privilege when the disclosures were requested, i. e., when the returns were due, would have identified the claimant as a gambler. The Court therefore forgave the usual requirement that the claim of privilege be presented for evaluation in favor of a "claim" by silence. See *Marchetti,* supra, 390 U.S., at 50, 88 S.Ct., at 703, 19 L.Ed.2d at 898. Nonetheless, it was recognized that one who "claimed" the privilege by refusing to file could be required subsequently to justify his claim of privilege. See id., at 61, 88 S.Ct., at 709, 19 L.Ed.2d at 905. If a particular gambler would not have incriminated himself by filing the tax returns, the privilege would not justify a failure to file.

Assuming that Garner otherwise reads *Mackey* correctly,[13] we do not think that case should be applied in this context. The basis for the holdings in *Marchetti* and *Grosso* was that the occupational and excise taxes on gambling required disclosures only of gamblers, the great majority of whom were likely to incriminate themselves by responding. Therefore, as in the coerced-confession cases, any compulsion to disclose was likely to compel self-incrimination.[14]

Garner is differently situated. Although he disclosed himself to be a gambler, federal income tax returns are not directed at those " 'inherently suspect of criminal activities.' " *Marchetti*, supra, 390 U.S. at 52, 88 S.Ct., at 704, 19 L.Ed.2d, at 900. As noted in Albertson v. SACB, 382 U.S. 70, 79, 86 S.Ct. 194, 199, 15 L.Ed.2d 165, 172 (1965), "the questions in (an) income tax return (are) neutral on their face and directed at the public at large." The great majority of persons who file income tax returns do not incriminate themselves by disclosing their occupation. The requirement that such returns be completed and filed simply does not involve the compulsion to incriminate considered in *Mackey*.

C.

Garner's final argument relies on Garrity v. New Jersey, 385 U.S. 493, 87 S.Ct. 616, 17 L.Ed.2d 562 (1967). There policemen summoned during an investigation of police corruption were informed that they

---

13. It does not follow necessarily that a taxpayer would be immunized against use of disclosures made on gambling tax returns when the Fifth Amendment would have justified a failure to file at all. If *Marchetti* and *Grosso* had been held retroactive, immunization might have been appropriate in Mackey's case. But at the time Mackey filed there was in fact no privilege not to file. Not only had *Marchetti* and *Grosso* not yet been decided, but United States v. Kahriger, 345 U.S. 22, 73 S.Ct. 510, 97 L.Ed. 754 (1953), and Lewis v. United States, 348 U.S. 419, 75 S.Ct. 415, 99 L.Ed. 475 (1955), previously had held that the privilege was not a defense to prosecution for failure to file the occupational tax returns. Mackey therefore was compelled to file his returns, thereby necessarily identifying himself as a gambler and thus risking self-incrimination. Accordingly, there were two related reasons to view the disclosures made in *Mackey* as compelled incriminations. The first was the inherently incriminating nature of the information demanded by the Government. The second was the gambler's inability to claim the privilege by refusing to file at the time Mackey's disclosures were required. Cf. *Mackey*, supra, 401 U.S., at 704, 91 S.Ct., at 1165, 28 L.Ed.2d, at 427 (Brennan, J., concurring in judgment); Leary v. United States, 395 U.S. 6, 27-28, 89 S.Ct. 1532, 1543-1544, 23 L.Ed.2d 57, 76-77 (1969); *Grosso*, supra, 390 U.S., at 70-71, 88 S.Ct. at 714-715, 19 L.Ed.2d at 913-914. In the case of gambling tax returns filed after *Marchetti* and *Grosso*, the second factor would not be present.

14. *Marchetti* and *Grosso*, of course, removed the threat of a criminal conviction when one validly claims the privilege by failing to file gambling tax returns. We do not pause here to consider whether there may be circumstances that would deprive a gambler of the free choice to claim the privilege by failing to file such returns, and therefore allow him to exclude a completed gambling tax return by claiming the privilege at trial. Cf. n. 13, supra.

could claim the privilege but that they would be discharged for doing so. The disclosures they made were introduced against them in subsequent criminal prosecutions. The Court held that the penalty of discharge for reliance on the privilege foreclosed a free choice to remain silent, and therefore had the effect of compelling the incriminating testimony given by the policemen. Garner notes that a taxpayer who claims the privilege on his return faces the possibility of a criminal prosecution under § 7203 for failure to make a return. He argues that the possibility of prosecution, like the threat of discharge in *Garrity*, compels a taxpayer to make incriminating disclosures rather than claim the privilege. This contention is not entirely without force, but we find it unpersuasive.

The policemen in *Garrity* were threatened with punishment for a concededly valid exercise of the privilege, but one in Garner's situation is at no such disadvantage. A § 7203 conviction cannot be based on a valid exercise of the privilege. This is implicit in the dictum of United States v. Sullivan, 274 U.S. 259, 47 S.Ct. 607, 71 L.Ed. 1037 (1927), that the privilege may be claimed on a return. Furthermore, the Court has held that an individual summoned by the Service to provide documents or testimony can rely on the privilege to defend against a § 7203 prosecution for failure to "supply any information." See United States v. Murdock, 290 U.S. 389, 54 S.Ct. 223, 78 L.Ed. 381 (1933) (*Murdock II*); United States v. Murdock, 284 U.S. 141, 52 S.Ct. 63, 76 L.Ed. 210 (1931) (*Murdock I*), disapproved on other grounds, Murphy v. Waterfront Comm'n, 378 U.S. 52, 84 S.Ct.1594, 12 L.Ed.2d 678 (1964). The Fifth Amendment itself guarantees the taxpayer's insulation against liability imposed on the basis of a valid and timely claim of privilege, a protection broadened by § 7203's statutory standard of "willfulness."[18]

Since a valid claim of privilege cannot be the basis for a § 7203 conviction, Garner can prevail only if the possibility that a claim made on the return will be tested in a criminal prosecution suffices in itself to deny him freedom to claim the privilege. He argues that it does so, noting that because of the threat of prosecution under § 7203 a taxpayer contemplating a claim of privilege on his return faces a more difficult choice than does a witness contemplating a claim of privilege in a judicial proceeding. If the latter claims the protection of the Fifth Amendment,

---

18. Because § 7203 proscribes "willful" failures to make returns, a taxpayer is not at peril for every erroneous claim of privilege. The Government recognizes that a defendant could not properly be convicted for an erroneous claim of privilege asserted in good faith. * * * See United States v. Bishop, 412 U.S. 346, 93 S.Ct. 2008, 36 L.Ed.2d 941 (1973). In this respect, the protection for the taxpayer in a § 7203 prosecution is broader than that for a witness who risks contempt to challenge a judicial order to disclose. In the latter case, a mere erroneous refusal to disclose warrants a sanction. See Maness v. Meyers, 419 U.S. 449, 460-461, 95 S.Ct. 584, 592-593, 42 L.Ed.2d 574, 584-585 (1975).

he receives a judicial ruling at that time on the validity of his claim, and he has an opportunity to reconsider it before being held in contempt for refusal to answer. * * * A § 7203 prosecution, however, may be brought without a preliminary judicial ruling on a claim of privilege that would allow the taxpayer to reconsider.

In essence, Garner contends that the Fifth Amendment guarantee requires such a preliminary-ruling procedure for testing the validity of an asserted privilege. It may be that such a procedure would serve the best interests of the Government as well as of the taxpayer, but we certainly cannot say that the Constitution requires it. The Court previously has considered Fifth Amendment claims in the context of a criminal prosecution where the defendant did not have the benefit of a preliminary judicial ruling on a claim of privilege. It has never intimated that such a procedure is other than permissible. Indeed, the Court has given some measure of endorsement to it. In *Murdock I*, supra, an individual was prosecuted under predecessors of § 7203 for refusing to make disclosures after being summoned by the Bureau of Internal Revenue. In this Court he contended, apparently on statutory grounds, that there could be no prosecution without a prior judicial enforcement suit to allow presentation of his claim of privilege to a court for a preliminary ruling. The Court said:

> "While undoubtedly the right of a witness to refuse to answer lest he incriminate himself may be tested in proceedings to compel answer, there is no support for the contention that there must be such a determination of that question before prosecution for the willful failure so denounced." 284 U.S., at 148, 52 S.Ct., at 64, 76 L.Ed., at 213.

We are satisfied that *Murdock I* states the constitutional standard. What is at issue here is principally a matter of timing and procedure. As long as a valid and timely claim of privilege is available as a defense to a taxpayer prosecuted for failure to make a return, the taxpayer has not been denied a free choice to remain silent merely because of the absence of a preliminary judicial ruling on his claim. We therefore do not agree that Garner was deterred from claiming the privilege in the sense that was true of the policemen in *Garrity*.

V.

In summary, we conclude that since Garner made disclosures instead of claiming the privilege on his tax returns his disclosures were not compelled incriminations.[21] He therefore was foreclosed from invoking the privilege when such information was later introduced as evidence against him in a criminal prosecution.

The judgment is Affirmed.

MR. JUSTICE MARSHALL, with whom MR. JUSTICE BRENNAN joins, concurring in the judgment.

* * *

This case ultimately turns on a simple question whether the possibility of being prosecuted under 26 U.S.C. § 7203 for failure to make a return compels a taxpayer to make an incriminating disclosure rather than claim the privilege against self-incrimination on his return. In discussing this question, the Court notes that only a "willful" failure to make a return is punishable under § 7203, and that "a defendant could not properly be convicted for an erroneous claim of privilege asserted in good faith." Since a good-faith erroneous assertion of the privilege does not expose a taxpayer to criminal liability, I would hold that the threat of prosecution does not compel incriminating disclosures in violation of the Fifth Amendment. The protection accorded a good-faith assertion of the privilege effectively preserves the taxpayer's freedom to choose between making incriminating disclosures and claiming his Fifth Amendment privilege, and I would affirm the judgment of the Court of Appeals for that reason.

Not content to rest its decision on that ground, the Court decides that even if a good-faith erroneous assertion of the privilege could form the basis for criminal liability, the threat of prosecution does not amount to compulsion. It is constitutionally sufficient, according to the Court, that a valid claim of privilege is a defense to a § 7203 prosecution. In so holding, the Court answers a question that by its own admission is not presented by the facts of this case. And, contrary to the implication contained in the Court's opinion, the question is one of first impression in this Court.

Citing, United States v. Murdock, 284 U.S. 141, 52 S.Ct. 63, 76 L.Ed. 210 (1931) (*Murdock I*), the Court observes that a taxpayer who claims the privilege on his return can be convicted of a § 7203 violation without

---

21. No language in this opinion is to be read as allowing a taxpayer desiring the protection of the privilege to make disclosures concurrently with a claim of privilege and thereby to immunize himself against the use of such disclosures. If a taxpayer desires the protection of the privilege, he must claim it instead of making disclosures. Any other rule would deprive the Government of its choice between compelling the evidence from the claimant in exchange for immunity and avoiding the burdens of immunization by obtaining the evidence elsewhere. See *Mackey v. United States*, 401 U.S., at 711-713, 91 S.Ct., at 1169-1171, 28 L.Ed.2d, at 431-433 (Brennan, J., concurring in judgment).

having been given a preliminary ruling on the validity of his claim and a "second chance" to complete his return after his claim is rejected. The Court then leaps to the conclusion that the Fifth Amendment is satisfied as long as a valid claim of privilege is a defense to a § 7203 prosecution.

I accept the proposition that a preliminary ruling is not a prerequisite to a § 7203 prosecution. But it does not follow, and *Murdock I* does not hold, that the absence of a preliminary ruling is of no import in considering whether a defense of good-faith assertion of the privilege is constitutionally required. It is one thing to deny a good-faith defense to a witness who is given a prompt ruling on the validity of his claim of privilege and an opportunity to reconsider his refusal to testify before subjecting himself to possible punishment for contempt. It would be quite another to deny a good-faith defense to someone like petitioner, who may be denied a ruling on the validity of his claim of privilege until his criminal prosecution, when it is too late to reconsider. If, contrary to the undisputed fact, a taxpayer had no assurance of either a preliminary ruling or a defense of good-faith assertion of the privilege, he could claim the privilege only at the risk that an erroneous assessment of the law of self-incrimination would subject him to criminal liability. In that event, I would consider the taxpayer to have been denied the free choice to claim the privilege, and would view any incriminating disclosures on his tax return as "compelled" within the meaning of the Fifth Amendment. Only because a good-faith erroneous claim of privilege entitles a taxpayer to acquittal under § 7203 can I conclude that petitioner's disclosures are admissible against him.

Notes And Question

Does a taxpayer waive the privilege against self-incrimination in its entirety by reporting income on her return?

The *Garner* decision expressly limited its reach to "only those (claims of privilege) justified by a fear of self-incrimination other than under the tax laws." 424 U.S. at 650, n. 3. *Garner* thus left open the extent to which the Fifth Amendment prevents compelled self-incrimination in tax returns for past criminal violations of the tax laws. This issue is examined in the *Carlson* case.

UNITED STATES v. CARLSON

United States Court of Appeals, Ninth Circuit, 1980.
617 F.2d 518.

WALLACE, CIRCUIT JUDGE.

Carlson was convicted of willful failure to file income tax returns in violation of 26 U.S.C. § 7203. On appeal he seeks reversal by claiming that his failure to file proper returns constituted a valid exercise of his Fifth Amendment privilege against self-incrimination. We affirm the conviction.

I.

Carlson, a factory worker, earned $9,346.21 in 1974 and $13,053.53 in 1975. Although he had filed complete tax returns for previous years, Carlson did not do so for 1974 and 1975. Instead, as part of a tax protest movement, he utilized the following tax-evasion scheme for each of those years. In 1974, Carlson claimed 99 withholding exemptions on the withholding tax form (form W- 4) that he submitted to his employer, although he was not married and had no dependents. This form W-4 remained effective through 1975, and resulted in no federal income taxes being withheld from Carlson's wages in either 1974 or 1975. Carlson thereafter asserted the Fifth Amendment on his 1974 and 1975 year-end tax returns (form 1040) in lieu of providing any information from which his tax liability could be calculated. He appended to the 1974 return tax protest material claiming that federal reserve notes were unconstitutional, that he therefore had not received enough constitutionally valid money to require filing a tax return, and that all rules promulgated by the Secretary of the Treasury were also unconstitutional.

The result of Carlson's submission of the false withholding form and his subsequent assertion of the Fifth Amendment in his year-end returns was that Carlson paid no federal income taxes for 1974 or 1975. Carlson claims that he validly asserted the Fifth Amendment to avoid incriminating himself for having previously filed the false withholding forms. After hearing all of the evidence, however, the district judge, sitting without a jury, found that Carlson "did not have a good-faith claim or reasonable ground for (asserting the) privilege, as he was a tax protestor and his activities and his actions and methods of submitting his returns were those of a tax protestor only." He held, therefore, that Carlson's Fifth Amendment claim did not constitute a defense to his prosecution, pursuant to § 7203, for failure to file a tax return.

II.

This case presents a question of first impression: can the privilege against self-incrimination constitute a defense to a § 7203 prosecution when it is asserted to avoid incrimination for a past violation of income tax laws? * * *

An examination of the facts of this case reveals that Carlson did assert the privilege at the time he filed his return, and did so while facing a real and appreciable hazard of prosecution for having previously filed a false withholding form. In addition, there is little doubt that a truthfully completed tax return, stating his gross income, the lack of federal income taxes actually withheld, and the true number of available deductions would have provided " 'a lead or clue' to evidence having a tendency to incriminate" Carlson. It is equally certain that a trial judge examining these facts would find a substantial threat of incrimination. Thus, it appears that Carlson satisfies those indicia of validity previously considered by us in cases where the privilege has been asserted to avoid self-incrimination other than under the tax laws.   When the privilege is asserted to avoid incrimination for past tax crimes, however, additional complications arise. If Carlson's assertion of the privilege were valid, it would license a form of conduct that would undermine the entire system of personal income tax collection. The essence of Carlson's plan was to claim 99 withholding exemptions so that no federal income tax would be withheld by his employer, and then to assert the Fifth Amendment privilege in lieu of a properly completed tax return, thus attempting to avoid both prosecution for the false withholding claim and payment of required income taxes. The widespread use of such a scheme would emasculate the present system of revenue collection which, by virtue of its scope alone, necessarily depends upon personal reporting by wage earners. We are thus confronted with the collision of two critical interests: the privilege against self-incrimination, and the need for public revenue collection by a process necessarily reliant on self-reporting.

To decide which of these two interests prevails, we follow Supreme Court guidance:

> Tension between the State's demand for disclosures and the protection of the right against self-incrimination is likely to give rise to serious questions. Inevitably these must be resolved in terms of balancing the public need on the one hand, and the individual claim to constitutional protections on the other; neither interest can be treated lightly.

California v. Byers, 402 U.S. 424, 427, 91 S.Ct. 1535, 1537, 29 L.Ed.2d 9 (1971). * * *

* * *

The history of the privilege against self-incrimination predates its enshrinement within the Bill of Rights. It initially arose in response to procedures whereby the ecclesiastical courts of England would compel one against whom no charge had been made to incriminate himself in response to broad, incrimination-seeking questions. The privilege, which had been recognized to some extent in colonial America, and which had been incorporated into the constitutions of several states prior to ratification of the federal Constitution, was adopted by the drafters of the Bill of Rights "not only (as) an answer to numerous instances of colonial misrule but (as) a shield against 'the evils that lurk(ed) in the shadows of a new and untried sovereignty.' "

As history illustrates, the primary purpose of the privilege is protective. The ancient privilege of a witness against being compelled to incriminate himself is precious to free men as a shield against high-handed and arrogant inquisitorial practices. It has survived centuries of controversies, periodically kindled by popular impatience that its protection sometimes allows the guilty to escape punishment. But it has endured as a wise and necessary protection of the individual against arbitrary power, and the price of occasional failures of justice is paid in the larger interest of general personal security.

* * *

In the case before us, Carlson has attempted to take advantage of the privilege's protective capacity to further a calculated effort to avoid the payment of taxes. Although it is true that Carlson actually seeks protection against self-incrimination for his prior tax crime, he does so only as part of an overall plan to evade taxes. The first step of that plan–submitting a false withholding form to his employer–was concealed from the Service by assertion of the Fifth Amendment on Carlson's year-end returns; and the very act of asserting the Fifth Amendment also effectuated the second step of the plan–failing to file meaningful returns that would divulge both his prior misstatement and his overall year-end tax liabilities. In other words, the Fifth Amendment was the linchpin of Carlson's plan to evade the payment of taxes. He used the privilege more as a sword than as a shield. The history and purpose of the privilege do not, in light of such circumstances, weigh heavily in favor of extending its coverage to Carlson.

At the same time, the character and urgency of the public interest in raising revenue through self-reporting weighs heavily against affording the privilege to Carlson. The federal government's power to raise revenue is its lifeblood. Were taxpayers permitted to employ Carlson's scheme, they could avoid filing completed tax returns and thereby severely impair the government's ability to determine tax liability.* * *

Another factor in our weighing process is that the requirement of filing an annual income tax return is primarily designed to facilitate revenue collection, not criminal prosecution. "(T)he questions in the income tax return (are) neutral on their face and directed at the public at large." For this reason, refusal to file any return at all has never been protectable by a taxpayer's privilege against self-incrimination. United States v. Sullivan, 274 U.S. 259, 263-64, 47 S.Ct. 607, 607-08, 71 L.Ed. 1037 (1927). We think the policies that justify the Court's continued adherence to the rule in *Sullivan* are equally applicable here.

After weighing the appropriate factors, we conclude that the purpose and history of the privilege against self-incrimination do not compel protection of Carlson's actions, and that the character and urgency of the opposing revenue interests require that his scheme not be permitted. We therefore hold that an individual who seeks to frustrate the tax laws by claiming too many withholding exemptions, with an eye to covering that crime and evading the tax return requirement by assertion of the Fifth Amendment, is not entitled to the amendment's protection.

III.

In spite of our holding that Carlson is not entitled to protection of the Fifth Amendment, we still must review the district court's finding that Carlson did not assert his claim in "good faith." * * * In prosecutions of the kind before us, * * * a defendant's assertion of even an invalid Fifth Amendment claim in "good faith" would defeat the § 7203 requirement that a failure to file income tax returns be "willful." Someone who thinks he is complying with the law cannot be said to be "willfully" violating it. Therefore, we must review the trial court's finding that Carlson did not make his claim in good faith.

The trial judge's determination was a finding of fact. "(U)pon appeal of a conviction in a criminal case the evidence must be considered in a light most favorable to the government and the findings of fact of a trial judge (or jury) may not be set aside unless clearly erroneous." United States v. Glover, 514 F.2d 390, 391 (9th Cir.1975). The record clearly discloses that Carlson was a tax protestor who attempted to frustrate the tax laws by use of the Fifth Amendment. We cannot say that the trial judge's conclusion that Carlson failed to assert the privilege in good faith was clearly erroneous.

AFFIRMED.

Note and Question

According to one commentator, while the *Carlson* decision has been criticized, "it reflects a general antagonism to claims of privilege on tax returns." Jeremy H. Temkin, Privilege Against Self-Incrimination and Income Tax Filings," 242 N.Y.Law J. (July 6, 2009).

Review the *Cheek* case in Chapter 9. Would the *Cheek* decision have had any effect on the *Carlson* case if it had been applicable at the time?

UNITED STATES v. NEFF
United States Court of Appeals, Ninth Circuit, 1980.
615 F.2d 1235.

WALLACE, CIRCUIT JUDGE.

* * *

During 1974 and 1975, Neff was employed as a police officer and received wages from the City of San Jose, California. During 1974 he also received capital gains from dealings in gold and silver coins. His community property share of income from employment and investments exceeded $14,000 in 1974 and $8,500 in 1975. During each of these years, Neff, who had previously filed proper returns, submitted to the IRS a standard individual income tax return form (form 1040) on which Neff provided no financial information from which his tax liabilities could be calculated. As returned by Neff, the forms contained only essential identification information and Neff's signature. In response to more than 25 questions about his financial and tax status, Neff had printed the words "Object: Self-Incrimination." Remaining questions had been answered either "None" or "Unknown." Neff also appended to the forms, in each of these years, over 100 pages of general protest material challenging, among other things, the national monetary system, government spending, and federal reserve notes.

The Internal Revenue Service (IRS) responded by letter to Neff, explaining that the forms as he filled them out were not acceptable tax returns and providing additional blank forms for proper completion. Neff refused to comply, claiming that by doing so he would waive his Fifth Amendment privilege against self-incrimination. The government filed an information charging Neff with two counts of willful failure to file income tax returns, and a jury found him guilty of both counts.* * *

II.

We are here faced with a case in which the taxpayer did assert his privilege in response to specific questions in the tax return form, but did so on such a wholesale basis as to deny the IRS any useful financial or tax information. Other circuits, faced with similar wholesale assertions of the privilege against self-incrimination, have concluded that a tax return form which contains no information from which tax liability can be calculated does not constitute a tax return within the meaning of the IRS laws. Once these courts determine that the taxpayer has filed no return, simple application of the *Sullivan* precedent, which states that the Fifth Amendment will never justify a complete failure to file a return, invalidates the Fifth Amendment defense.

Although we recognize the ease with which the logic used in these cases would resolve the issue before us, we conclude that such reliance upon the definition of a tax return is inappropriate, because it lacks independent Fifth Amendment analysis. Moreover, the usefulness of this definitional approach is too limited because it is confined to facts such as those presented here: the wholesale assertion, albeit in response to specific questions, of the privilege against self-incrimination. In settings in which the Fifth Amendment right has been more discretely asserted, it would be difficult to conclude that no return has been filed, and, therefore, inappropriate to apply this definitional analysis.[3] We therefore choose not to follow the lead of the cited cases. We believe that the better approach to this and future Fifth Amendment tax return cases is to apply more traditional Fifth Amendment analysis.[4]

The requirement that citizens file a yearly income tax return does not, of itself, violate their privilege against self-incrimination. This conclusion is implicit in the Supreme Court ruling that taxpayers cannot rely upon the Fifth Amendment to justify a complete failure to file. Other statutory reporting requirements have been found to violate the privilege, but the reporting schemes in these cases were "directed at a highly selective group inherently suspect of criminal activities * * * in an area permeated with criminal statutes * * *." Albertson v. SACB, 382 U.S. 70, 79, 86 S.Ct. 194, 199, 15 L.Ed.2d 165 (1965). Questions on

---

3. Moreover, we are not certain that these circuit court decisions comport with Supreme Court precedent. The cases indicate that the taxpayer may never assert his privilege against self-incrimination in lieu of tax form responses essential to the calculation of tax liability. This rule, which limits the tax form questions to which a Fifth Amendment response is proper to those questions not essential to tax liability calculation, necessarily limits perhaps too much the scope of the Supreme Court's declaration in *Garner* that the Fifth Amendment may be asserted on a tax return. 424 U.S. at 662, 96 S.Ct. at 1186.

4. This is not to say that we reject the previous decision by this court that tax return forms devoid of financial information are not tax returns within the meaning of 26 U.S.C. § 7203. United States v. Klee, 494 F.2d 394, 397 (9th Cir. 1974). Such precedent has value in determining when § 7203 has been violated. We simply conclude that it does not have value as a means to determine the validity of Neff's assertion of the privilege against self-incrimination.

income tax returns, in contrast, are "neutral on their face and directed at the public at large * * *." Id. Therefore, in order for Neff to escape prosecution under § 7203, there must be something peculiarly incriminating about his circumstances that justifies his reliance on the Fifth Amendment. Before examining that circumstance, we will set forth pertinent Fifth Amendment principles.

To claim the privilege validly a defendant must be faced with "'substantial hazards of self incrimination,' " *California v. Byers,* supra, 402 U.S. at 429, 90 S.Ct. at 1538, that are " 'real and appreciable' and not merely 'imaginary and unsubstantial.' " *Marchetti v. United States,* supra, 390 U.S. at 48, 88 S.Ct. at 702, quoting in part Rogers v. United States, 340 U.S. 367, 374-75, 71 S.Ct. 438, 442, 95 L.Ed. 344 (1951). Moreover, he must have "reasonable cause to apprehend (such) danger from a direct answer" to questions posed to him. Hoffman v. United States, 341 U.S. 479, 486, 71 S.Ct. 814, 818, 95 L.Ed. 1118 (1951). The information that would be revealed by direct answer need not be such as would itself support a criminal conviction, however, but must simply "furnish a link in the chain of evidence needed to prosecute the claimant for a federal crime." Id. Indeed, it is enough if the responses would merely "provide a lead or clue" to evidence having a tendency to incriminate. Id. at 348.

In determining whether such a real and appreciable danger of incrimination exists, a trial judge must examine the "implications of the question(s) in the setting in which (they are) asked * * *." *Hoffman v. United States,* supra, 341 U.S. at 486, 71 S.Ct. at 818. He " '(m)ust be governed as much by his personal perception of the peculiarities of the case as by the facts actually in evidence.' " *Hoffman v. United States,* supra, 341 U.S. at 487, 71 S.Ct. at 818, quoting Ex parte Irvine, 74 F. 954, 960 (C.C.Ohio, 1896). If the trial judge decides from this examination of the questions, their setting, and the peculiarities of the case, that no threat of self-incrimination exists, it then becomes incumbent "upon the defendant to show that answers to (the questions) might incriminate him." United States v. Weisman, 111 F.2d 260, 261 (2d Cir. 1940). This does not mean that the defendant must confess the crime he has sought to conceal by asserting the privilege. The law does not require him " 'to prove guilt to avoid admitting it.' " *Marchetti v. United States,* supra, 390 U.S. at 50, 88 S.Ct. at 754, quoting United States v. Kahriger, 345 U.S. 22, 34, 73 S.Ct. 510, 516, 97 L.Ed. 754 (1953) (Jackson, J., concurring). But neither does the law permit the defendant to be the final arbiter of his own assertion's validity. "The witness is not exonerated from answering merely because he declares that in so doing he would incriminate himself–his say-so does not of itself establish the hazard of incrimination. It is for the court to decide whether his silence is justified * * *." *Hoffman v. United States,* supra, 341 U.S. at 486, 71 S.Ct. at 818.

* * *

Applying these principles to the facts before us, we conclude that the trial judge correctly decided that Neff had no valid Fifth Amendment defense to the § 7203 prosecution. The questions asked of Neff on the income tax form did not, of themselves, suggest that the response would be incriminating; nor did the setting in which they were asked–a general inquiry about Neff's financial and tax status, to be completed in the privacy of his own home–alter the non-incriminatory nature of those questions. Moreover, the peculiarities of the case did not strengthen Neff's claim.   If anything, the tax protest nature of defense witness Holmes' testimony and of the materials that Neff appended to his returns suggest that Neff's refusal to complete the forms was motivated by a desire to protest taxes, rather than a fear of self-incrimination. In short, the whole circumstance was "innocuous and thus unprotected absent some positive disclosure by the witness of its hidden dangers * * *." *Hashagen v. United States,* supra, 283 F.2d at 350.

Neff made no such disclosure. At no point during the trial, including when Neff testified, was the district judge presented with any indicia of potential incrimination. On the contrary, Neff's counsel argued that Neff's sincerity of belief was sufficient to validate his assertion of the privilege, and that Neff alone should be the final arbiter of the assertion's validity.[6] As we have seen, that is not the law. Neff did not show that his response to the tax form questions would have been self-incriminating.   He cannot, therefore, prevail on his Fifth Amendment claim.

* * *

Affirmed.

---

6.   Counsel for Neff stated in his closing argument:
There's only one test that's important, whether or not Mr. Neff, in good faith, believed that he might be incriminated if he gave information * * *. If you find that his belief was erroneously held, but was held in good faith, then he had a right to use it, even if it's erroneous, as long as he's sincere. That has to be the test in this country, otherwise every man, when he asserted his right to privacy, would be subject to some other person's test for whether or not he was really a criminal. * * * He may raise the objection in the (tax) return and if he believed it in good faith, it was right. And that's the whole issue.

Questions

1. Why was there no willfulness inquiry in *Neff*, as there had been in *Carlson*?

2. When, if ever, may a defendant validly claim a Fifth Amendment privilege on a tax return? See United States v. Nipper, 210 F.Supp.2d 1259 (N.D. Okla. 2002).

2)   *Document Production*

UNITED STATES v. HUBBELL
Supreme Court of the United States, 2000.
530 U.S. 27, 120 S.Ct. 2037, 147 L.Ed.2d 24.

JUSTICE STEVENS delivered the opinion of the Court.

I.

This proceeding arises out of the second prosecution of respondent, Webster Hubbell, commenced by the Independent Counsel appointed in August 1994 to investigate possible violations of federal law relating to the Whitewater Development Corporation. The first prosecution was terminated pursuant to a plea bargain. In December 1994, respondent pleaded guilty to charges of mail fraud and tax evasion arising out of his billing practices as a member of an Arkansas law firm from 1989 to 1992, and was sentenced to 21 months in prison. In the plea agreement, respondent promised to provide the Independent Counsel with "full, complete, accurate, and truthful information" about matters relating to the Whitewater investigation.

The second prosecution resulted from the Independent Counsel's attempt to determine whether respondent had violated that promise. In October 1996, while respondent was incarcerated, the Independent Counsel served him with a subpoena duces tecum calling for the production of 11 categories of documents before a grand jury sitting in Little Rock, Arkansas. On November 19, he appeared before the grand jury and invoked his Fifth Amendment privilege against self-incrimination. In response to questioning by the prosecutor, respondent initially refused "to state whether there are documents within my possession, custody, or control responsive to the Subpoena." Thereafter, the prosecutor produced an order, which had previously been obtained from the District Court pursuant to 18 U.S.C. § 6003(a),[3] directing him to respond to the subpoena and granting him immunity "to the extent allowed by law." Respondent then produced 13,120 pages of documents and records and responded to a series of questions that established that those were all of the documents in his custody or control that were responsive to the commands in the subpoena, with the exception of a few documents he claimed were shielded by the attorney-client and attorney work-product privileges.

The contents of the documents produced by respondent provided the Independent Counsel with the information that led to this second prosecution. On April 30, 1998, a grand jury in the District of Columbia returned a 10-count indictment charging respondent with various tax-related crimes and mail and wire fraud. The District Court dismissed the indictment relying, in part, on the ground that the Independent Counsel's use of the subpoenaed documents violated § 6002 because all of the evidence he would offer against respondent at trial derived either directly or indirectly from the testimonial aspects of respondent's immunized act of producing those documents. Noting that the Independent Counsel had admitted that he was not investigating tax-related issues when he issued the subpoena, and that he had " 'learned about the unreported income and other crimes from studying the records' contents,' " the District Court characterized the subpoena as "the quintessential fishing expedition."

The Court of Appeals vacated the judgment and remanded for further proceedings. The majority concluded that the District Court had incorrectly relied on the fact that the Independent Counsel did not have prior knowledge of the contents of the subpoenaed documents. The question the District Court should have addressed was the extent of the Government's independent knowledge of the documents' existence and authenticity, and of respondent's possession or control of them. It explained:

> "On remand, the district court should hold a hearing in which it seeks to establish the extent and detail of the [G]overnment's knowledge of Hubbell's financial affairs (or of the paperwork documenting it) on the day the subpoena issued. It is only then that the court will be in a position to assess the testimonial value of Hubbell's response to the subpoena. Should the Independent Counsel prove capable of demonstrating with reasonable particularity a prior awareness that the exhaustive litany of documents sought in the subpoena existed

---

3. Section 6003(a) authorizes a district court to issue an order requiring an "individual to give testimony or provide other information which he refuses to give or provide on the basis of his privilege against self-incrimination." The effect of such an order is covered by § 6002 * * *.

and were in Hubbell's possession, then the wide distance evidently traveled from the subpoena to the substantive allegations contained in the indictment would be based upon legitimate intermediate steps. To the extent that the information conveyed through Hubbell's compelled act of production provides the necessary linkage, however, the indictment deriving therefrom is tainted." Id., at 581.

* * *

On remand, the Independent Counsel acknowledged that he could not satisfy the "reasonable particularity" standard prescribed by the Court of Appeals and entered into a conditional plea agreement with respondent. In essence, the agreement provides for the dismissal of the charges unless this Court's disposition of the case makes it reasonably likely that respondent's "act [of] production immunity" would not pose a significant bar to his prosecution. The case is not moot, however, because the agreement also provides for the entry of a guilty plea and a sentence that will not include incarceration if we should reverse and issue an opinion that is sufficiently favorable to the Government to satisfy that condition. Despite that agreement, we granted the Independent Counsel's petition for a writ of certiorari in order to determine the precise scope of a grant of immunity with respect to the production of documents in response to a subpoena. We now affirm.

II.

It is useful to preface our analysis of the constitutional issue with a restatement of certain propositions that are not in dispute. The term "privilege against self-incrimination" is not an entirely accurate description of a person's constitutional protection against being "compelled in any criminal case to be a witness against himself."

The word "witness" in the constitutional text limits the relevant category of compelled incriminating communications to those that are "testimonial" in character. As Justice Holmes observed, there is a significant difference between the use of compulsion to extort communications from a defendant and compelling a person to engage in conduct that may be incriminating.[9] Thus, even though the act may

---

9.   "A question arose as to whether a blouse belonged to the prisoner. A witness testified that the prisoner put it on and it fitted him. It is objected that he did this under the same duress that made his statements inadmissible, and that it should be excluded for the same reasons. But the prohibition of compelling a man in a criminal court to be witness against himself is a prohibition of the use of physical or moral compulsion to extort communications from him, not an exclusion of his body as evidence when it may be material. The objection in principle would forbid a jury to look at a prisoner and compare his features with a photograph in proof." Holt v. United States, 218 U.S. 245, 252-253, 31 S.Ct. 2, 54 L.Ed. 1021 (1910).

provide incriminating evidence, a criminal suspect may be compelled to put on a shirt, to provide a blood sample or handwriting exemplar, or to make a recording of his voice. The act of exhibiting such physical characteristics is not the same as a sworn communication by a witness that relates either express or implied assertions of fact or belief. Similarly, the fact that incriminating evidence may be the byproduct of obedience to a regulatory requirement, such as filing an income tax return, maintaining required records, or reporting an accident, does not clothe such required conduct with the testimonial privilege.

More relevant to this case is the settled proposition that a person may be required to produce specific documents even though they contain incriminating assertions of fact or belief because the creation of those documents was not "compelled" within the meaning of the privilege. Our decision in Fisher v. United States, 425 U.S. 391, 96 S.Ct. 1569, 48 L.Ed.2d 39 (1976), dealt with summonses issued by the Internal Revenue Service (IRS) seeking working papers used in the preparation of tax returns. Because the papers had been voluntarily prepared prior to the issuance of the summonses, they could not be "said to contain compelled testimonial evidence, either of the taxpayers or of anyone else." Accordingly, the taxpayer could not "avoid compliance with the subpoena merely by asserting that the item of evidence which he is required to produce contains incriminating writing, whether his own or that of someone else." Id., at 409-410, 96 S.Ct. 1569.[18] It is clear, therefore, that respondent Hubbell could not avoid compliance with the subpoena served on him merely because the demanded documents contained incriminating evidence, whether written by others or voluntarily prepared by himself.

On the other hand, we have also made it clear that the act of producing documents in response to a subpoena may have a compelled testimonial aspect. We have held that "the act of production" itself may implicitly communicate "statements of fact." By "producing documents in compliance with a subpoena, the witness would admit that the papers existed, were in his possession or control, and were authentic."[19]

---

18. "Respondent does not contend that he prepared the documents involuntarily or that the subpoena would force him to restate, repeat, or affirm the truth of their contents. The fact that the records are in respondent's possession is irrelevant to the determination of whether the creation of the records was compelled. We therefore hold that the contents of those records are not privileged." United States v. Doe, 465 U.S., at 611-612, 104 S.Ct. 1237.

19. "The issue presented in those cases was whether the act of producing subpoenaed documents, not itself the making of a statement, might nonetheless have some protected testimonial aspects. The Court concluded that the act of production could constitute protected testimonial communication because it might entail implicit statements of fact: by producing documents in compliance with a subpoena, the witness would admit that the papers existed, were in his possession

Moreover, as was true in this case, when the custodian of documents responds to a subpoena, he may be compelled to take the witness stand and answer questions designed to determine whether he has produced everything demanded by the subpoena. The answers to those questions, as well as the act of production itself, may certainly communicate information about the existence, custody, and authenticity of the documents. Whether the constitutional privilege protects the answers to such questions, or protects the act of production itself, is a question that is distinct from the question whether the unprotected contents of the documents themselves are incriminating.

Finally, the phrase "in any criminal case" in the text of the Fifth Amendment might have been read to limit its coverage to compelled testimony that is used against the defendant in the trial itself. It has, however, long been settled that its protection encompasses compelled statements that lead to the discovery of incriminating evidence even though the statements themselves are not incriminating and are not introduced into evidence. Thus, a half century ago we held that a trial judge had erroneously rejected a defendant's claim of privilege on the ground that his answer to the pending question would not itself constitute evidence of the charged offense. As we explained:

"The privilege afforded not only extends to answers that would in themselves support a conviction under a federal criminal statute but likewise embraces those which would furnish a link in the chain of evidence needed to prosecute the claimant for a federal crime." Hoffman v. United States, 341 U.S. 479, 486, 71 S.Ct. 814, 95 L.Ed. 1118 (1951).

Compelled testimony that communicates information that may "lead to incriminating evidence" is privileged even if the information itself is not inculpatory. Doe v. United States, 487 U.S. 201, 208, n. 6, 108 S.Ct. 2341, 101 L.Ed.2d 184 (1988). It is the Fifth Amendment's protection against the prosecutor's use of incriminating information derived directly or indirectly from the compelled testimony of the respondent that is of primary relevance in this case.

* * *

The "compelled testimony" that is relevant in this case is not to be found in the contents of the documents produced in response to the

---

or control, and were authentic. Thus, the Court made clear that the Fifth Amendment privilege against self-incrimination applies to acts that imply assertions of fact.

* * * An examination of the Court's application of these principles in other cases indicates the Court's recognition that, in order to be testimonial, an accused's communication must itself, explicitly or implicitly, relate a factual assertion or disclose information. Only then is a person compelled to be a 'witness' against himself." Doe v. United States, 487 U.S., at 209-210, 108 S.Ct. 2341.

subpoena. It is, rather, the testimony inherent in the act of producing those documents. The disagreement between the parties focuses entirely on the significance of that testimonial aspect.

IV.

The Government correctly emphasizes that the testimonial aspect of a response to a subpoena duces tecum does nothing more than establish the existence, authenticity, and custody of items that are produced. We assume that the Government is also entirely correct in its submission that it would not have to advert to respondent's act of production in order to prove the existence, authenticity, or custody of any documents that it might offer in evidence at a criminal trial; indeed, the Government disclaims any need to introduce any of the documents produced by respondent into evidence in order to prove the charges against him. It follows, according to the Government, that it has no intention of making improper "use" of respondent's compelled testimony.

The question, however, is not whether the response to the subpoena may be introduced into evidence at his criminal trial. That would surely be a prohibited "use" of the immunized act of production. But the fact that the Government intends no such use of the act of production leaves open the separate question whether it has already made "derivative use" of the testimonial aspect of that act in obtaining the indictment against respondent and in preparing its case for trial. It clearly has.

It is apparent from the text of the subpoena itself that the prosecutor needed respondent's assistance both to identify potential sources of information and to produce those sources. Given the breadth of the description of the 11 categories of documents called for by the subpoena, the collection and production of the materials demanded was tantamount to answering a series of interrogatories asking a witness to disclose the existence and location of particular documents fitting certain broad descriptions. The assembly of literally hundreds of pages of material in response to a request for "any and all documents reflecting, referring, or relating to any direct or indirect sources of money or other things of value received by or provided to" an individual or members of his family during a 3-year period, is the functional equivalent of the preparation of an answer to either a detailed written interrogatory or a series of oral questions at a discovery deposition. Entirely apart from the contents of the 13,120 pages of materials that respondent produced in this case, it is undeniable that providing a catalog of existing documents fitting within any of the 11 broadly worded subpoena categories could provide a prosecutor with a "lead to incriminating evidence," or "a link in the chain of evidence needed to prosecute."

Indeed, the record makes it clear that that is what happened in this case. The documents were produced before a grand jury sitting in the Eastern District of Arkansas in aid of the Independent Counsel's attempt to determine whether respondent had violated a commitment in his first plea agreement. The use of those sources of information eventually led to the return of an indictment by a grand jury sitting in the District of Columbia for offenses that apparently are unrelated to that plea agreement. What the District Court characterized as a "fishing expedition" did produce a fish, but not the one that the Independent Counsel expected to hook. It is abundantly clear that the testimonial aspect of respondent's act of producing subpoenaed documents was the first step in a chain of evidence that led to this prosecution. The documents did not magically appear in the prosecutor's office like "manna from heaven." They arrived there only after respondent asserted his constitutional privilege, received a grant of immunity, and – under the compulsion of the District Court's order – took the mental and physical steps necessary to provide the prosecutor with an accurate inventory of the many sources of potentially incriminating evidence sought by the subpoena. It was only through respondent's truthful reply to the subpoena that the Government received the incriminating documents of which it made "substantial use * * * in the investigation that led to the indictment."

For these reasons, we cannot accept the Government's submission that respondent's immunity did not preclude its derivative use of the produced documents because its "possession of the documents [was] the fruit only of a simple physical act – the act of producing the documents." Id., at 29. It was unquestionably necessary for respondent to make extensive use of "the contents of his own mind" in identifying the hundreds of documents responsive to the requests in the subpoena. The assembly of those documents was like telling an inquisitor the combination to a wall safe, not like being forced to surrender the key to a strongbox. The Government's anemic view of respondent's act of production as a mere physical act that is principally nontestimonial in character and can be entirely divorced from its "implicit" testimonial aspect so as to constitute a "legitimate, wholly independent source" (as required by *Kastigar*) for the documents produced simply fails to account for these realities.

In sum, we have no doubt that the constitutional privilege against self-incrimination protects the target of a grand jury investigation from being compelled to answer questions designed to elicit information about the existence of sources of potentially incriminating evidence. That constitutional privilege has the same application to the testimonial aspect of a response to a subpoena seeking discovery of those sources. Before the District Court, the Government arguably conceded that respondent's act of production in this case had a testimonial aspect that entitled him to respond to the subpoena by asserting his privilege against self-incrimination. See 167 F.3d, at 580 (noting District Court's finding that "Hubbell's compelled act of production required him to make communications as to the existence, possession, and authenticity of the subpoenaed documents"). On appeal and again before this Court, however, the Government has argued that the communicative aspect of respondent's act of producing ordinary business records is insufficiently "testimonial" to support a claim of privilege because the existence and possession of such records by any businessman is a "foregone conclusion" under our decision in Fisher v. United States, 425 U.S., at 411, 96 S.Ct. 1569. This argument both misreads *Fisher* and ignores our subsequent decision in United States v. Doe, 465 U.S. 605, 104 S.Ct. 1237, 79 L.Ed.2d 552 (1984).

[F]isher involved summonses seeking production of working papers prepared by the taxpayers' accountants that the IRS knew were in the possession of the taxpayers' attorneys. 425 U.S., at 394, 96 S.Ct. 1569. In rejecting the taxpayers' claim that these documents were protected by the Fifth Amendment privilege, we stated:

> "It is doubtful that implicitly admitting the existence and possession of the papers rises to the level of testimony within the protection of the Fifth Amendment. The papers belong to the *accountant,* were prepared by him, and are the kind usually prepared by an accountant working on the tax returns of his client. Surely the Government is in no way relying on the 'truthtelling' of the *taxpayer* to prove the existence of or his access to the documents * * *. The existence and location of the papers are a foregone conclusion and the taxpayer adds little or nothing to the sum total of the Government's information by conceding that he in fact has the papers." Id., at 411, 96 S.Ct. 1569 (emphases added).

Whatever the scope of this "foregone conclusion" rationale, the facts of this case plainly fall outside of it. While in *Fisher* the Government already knew that the documents were in the attorneys' possession and could independently confirm their existence and authenticity through the accountants who created them, here the Government has not shown that it had any prior knowledge of either the existence or the whereabouts of the 13,120 pages of documents ultimately produced by respondent. The Government cannot cure this deficiency through the overbroad argument that a businessman such as respondent will always possess general business and tax records that fall within the broad categories described in this subpoena.   The *Doe* subpoenas also sought several broad categories of general business records, yet we upheld the District Court's finding that the act of producing those records would involve testimonial self-incrimination.

Given our conclusion that respondent's act of production had a testimonial aspect, at least with respect to the existence and location of the documents sought by the Government's subpoena, respondent could not be compelled to produce those documents without first receiving a grant of immunity under § 6003. As we construed § 6002 in *Kastigar,* such immunity is coextensive with the constitutional privilege. *Kastigar* requires that respondent's motion to dismiss the indictment on immunity grounds be granted unless the Government proves that the evidence it used in obtaining the indictment and proposed to use at trial was derived from legitimate sources "wholly independent" of the testimonial aspect of respondent's immunized conduct in assembling and producing the documents described in the subpoena. The Government, however, does not claim that it could make such a showing. Rather, it contends that its prosecution of respondent must be considered proper unless someone–presumably respondent–shows that "there is some substantial relation between the compelled testimonial communications implicit in the act of production (as opposed to the act of production standing alone) and some aspect of the information used in the investigation or the evidence presented at trial."   We could not accept this submission without repudiating the basis for our conclusion in *Kastigar* that the statutory guarantee of use and derivative-use immunity is as broad as the constitutional privilege itself. This we are not prepared to do.

Accordingly, the indictment against respondent must be dismissed. The judgment of the Court of Appeals is affirmed.

It is so ordered.

JUSTICE THOMAS, with whom JUSTICE SCALIA joins, concurring.

Our decision today involves the application of the act-of-production doctrine, which provides that persons compelled to turn over incriminating papers or other physical evidence pursuant to a subpoena duces tecum or a summons may invoke the Fifth Amendment privilege against self-incrimination as a bar to production only where the act of producing the evidence would contain "testimonial" features. I join the opinion of the Court because it properly applies this doctrine, but I write separately to note that this doctrine may be inconsistent with the original meaning of the Fifth Amendment's Self-Incrimination Clause.

A substantial body of evidence suggests that the Fifth Amendment privilege protects against the compelled production not just of incriminating testimony, but of any incriminating evidence. In a future case, I would be willing to reconsider the scope and meaning of the Self-Incrimination Clause.

I.

The Fifth Amendment provides that "[n]o person * * * shall be compelled in any criminal case to be a witness against himself." The key word at issue in this case is "witness." The Court's opinion, relying on prior cases, essentially defines "witness" as a person who provides testimony, and thus restricts the Fifth Amendment's ban to only those communications " that are 'testimonial' in character." None of this Court's cases, however, has undertaken an analysis of the meaning of the term at the time of the founding. A review of that period reveals substantial support for the view that the term "witness" meant a person who gives or furnishes evidence, a broader meaning than that which our case law currently ascribes to the term. If this is so, a person who responds to a subpoena duces tecum would be just as much a "witness" as a person who responds to a subpoena ad testificandum.[1]

Dictionaries published around the time of the founding included definitions of the term "witness" as a person who gives or furnishes evidence. Legal dictionaries of that period defined "witness" as someone who "gives evidence in a cause." 2 G. Jacob, A New Law-Dictionary (8th ed. 1762); 2 T. Cunningham, New and Complete Law-Dictionary (2d ed. 1771). And a general dictionary published earlier in the century similarly defined "witness" as "a giver of evidence." J. Kersey, A New English Dictionary (1702). The term "witness" apparently continued to have this meaning at least until the first edition of Noah Webster's dictionary, which defined it as "[t]hat which furnishes evidence or proof." An American Dictionary of the English Language (1828).[2]

---

1.   Even if the term "witness" in the Fifth Amendment referred to someone who provides testimony, as this Court's recent cases suggest without historical analysis, it may well be that at the time of the founding a person who turned over documents would be described as providing testimony. See Amey v. Long, 9 East. 472, 484, 103 Eng. Rep. 653, 658 (K.B.1808) (referring to documents requested by subpoenas duces tecum as "written * * * testimony").

2.   Further, it appears that the phrases "gives evidence" and "furnishes evidence" were not simply descriptions of the act of providing testimony. For example, in King v. Purnell, 1 Black. 37, 96 Eng. Rep. 20 (K.B.1748), the phrase "furnish evidence" is repeatedly used to refer to the compelled production of books, records, and archives in response to a government request. Id., at 40, 41, 42, 96 Eng. Rep., at 21, 22, 23.

Such a meaning of "witness" is consistent with, and may help explain, the history and framing of the Fifth Amendment. The 18th-century common-law privilege against incrimination protected against the compelled production of incriminating physical evidence such as papers and documents. And this Court has noted that, for generations before the framing, "one cardinal rule of the court of chancery [wa]s never to decree a discovery which might tend to convict the party of a crime." Boyd v. United States, 116 U.S. 616, 631, 6 S.Ct. 524, 29 L.Ed. 746 (1886). See also Counselman v. Hitchcock, 142 U.S. 547, 563-564, 12 S.Ct. 195, 35 L.Ed. 1110 (1892) ("It is an ancient principle of the law of evidence, that a witness shall not be compelled, in any proceeding, to make disclosures or to give testimony which will tend to criminate him or subject him to fines, penalties or forfeitures").

* * *

II.

This Court has not always taken the approach to the Fifth Amendment that we follow today. The first case interpreting the Self-Incrimination Clause—*Boyd v. United States*—was decided, though not explicitly, in accordance with the understanding that "witness" means one who gives evidence. In *Boyd*, this Court unanimously held that the Fifth Amendment protects a defendant against compelled production of books and papers. And the Court linked its interpretation of the Fifth Amendment to the common-law understanding of the self-incrimination privilege. Id., at 631-632, 6 S.Ct. 524.

But this Court's decision in Fisher v. United States, 425 U.S. 391, 96 S.Ct. 1569, 48 L.Ed.2d 39 (1976), rejected this understanding, permitting the Government to force a person to furnish incriminating physical evidence and protecting only the "testimonial" aspects of that transfer. Id., at 408, 96 S.Ct. 1569. In so doing, *Fisher* not only failed to examine the historical backdrop to the Fifth Amendment, it also required—as illustrated by extended discussion in the opinions below in this case—a difficult parsing of the act of responding to a subpoena duces tecum.

None of the parties in this case has asked us to depart from *Fisher*, but in light of the historical evidence that the Self-Incrimination Clause may have a broader reach than *Fisher* holds, I remain open to a reconsideration of that decision and its progeny in a proper case.

Notes And Question

In some cases, a witness who claims the Fifth Amendment privilege can receive immunity from government prosecution under 18 U.S.C. §§

6001-6005. There are two types of immunity that can be obtained: use immunity and transactional immunity. Transactional immunity protects the witness against prosecution for the offense or offenses involved; use immunity provides protection from the government's use of the immunized statement to prosecute the witness, although the witness may be prosecuted if the government obtains the information independently of the immunized statement. Transactional immunity is not available from the court, but may be obtained only through negotiation with the government.

1. Why do you think the Independent Counsel tried to prosecute Hubbell on these new grounds in light of his earlier promise of immunity from prosecution?

2. What "testimony" does the Court say is inherent in the act of producing documents?

b. *Double Jeopardy*

In addition to establishing a privilege against self-incrimination, the Fifth Amendment also provides that "no person [shall] be subject for the same offense to be twice put in jeopardy of life or limb * * *." U.S. CONST. amend. V.

LOUIS v. COMMISSIONER
United States Court of Appeals, Ninth Circuit, 1999.
170 F.3d 1232.

PER CURIAM.

After conviction and punishment for tax fraud during the years 1977 and 1978, John R. Louis ("Louis") challenges the IRS's imposition under 26 U.S.C. § 6653(b) of additions to tax for fraud for the years 1976, 1977 and 1978 as violative of: (1) the Double Jeopardy Clause; (2) the Eighth Amendment; and (3) the Fifth and Sixth Amendments. We review the tax court's rejection of Louis's challenges de novo and affirm.

I.

This court recently held additions to tax for fraud to be a civil remedy, not a criminal punishment, and therefore beyond the scope of the Double Jeopardy Clause, which prohibits only multiple criminal punishments for the same offense. See I & O Publishing Co., Inc. v. Commissioner of Internal Revenue Serv., 131 F.3d 1314, 1316 (9th Cir.1997). Shortly before *I & O Publishing* was filed, the Supreme Court decided Hudson v. United States, 522 U.S. 93, 118 S.Ct. 488, 139 L.Ed.2d 450 (1997), which considered the nature of monetary penalties imposed on bank officers previously convicted of misapplying bank funds. *Hudson* laid out a two- step analysis to determine whether a penalty is civil or criminal. See id. at 493, 118 S.Ct. 488. Apparently *Hudson* was not called to the attention of the *I & O Publishing* panel, which concluded that additions to tax for fraud are not punishment but did not explicitly employ the two-step *Hudson* test. We now apply that test and affirm.

According to *Hudson*, determining whether a particular punishment is criminal or civil involves a two-step process: (1) statutory construction to determine whether Congress indicated an express or implied preference for one label or the other; and if Congress intended to establish a civil penalty, (2) an evaluation of "'whether the statutory scheme [is] so punitive either in purpose or effect'" as to transform the intended civil sanction into a criminal penalty. The following factors are "useful guideposts" in determining whether the second step is satisfied:

> (1) "[w]hether the sanction involves an affirmative disability or restraint"; (2) "whether it has historically been regarded as a punishment"; (3) "whether it comes into play only on a finding of scienter "; (4) "whether its operation will promote the traditional aims of punishment-retribution and deterrence"; (5) "whether the behavior to which it applies is already a crime"; (6) "whether an alternative purpose to which it may rationally be connected is assignable for it"; and (7) "whether it appears excessive in relation to the alternative purpose assigned." Id. at 493, 118 S.Ct. 488 (quoting Kennedy v. Mendoza-Martinez, 372 U.S. 144, 168-69, 83 S.Ct. 554, 9 L.Ed.2d 644 (1963)). These factors are to be considered in relation to the "statute on its face," and "only the clearest proof" will suffice to override legislative intent that a remedy be civil in nature. Id. at 493, 118 S.Ct. 488 (citing *Ward*, 448 U.S. at 249, 100 S.Ct. 2636).

A.

There is no double jeopardy problem with the addition to tax for fraud imposed for 1976, since Louis was not criminally prosecuted for that year. Turning to 1977 and 1978, it is clear Congress intended additions to tax for fraud to be "a civil, not a criminal, sanction." [Eds: Helvering v. Mitchell, 303 U.S. 391, 402, 58 S.Ct. 630.] *Mitchell's* conclusion that Congress intended additions to tax for fraud to be a civil sanction is not limited to cases in which the taxpayer has previously been acquitted, rather than convicted, of criminal tax fraud. See *Mitchell*, 303 U.S. at 401-05, 58 S.Ct. 630.

B.

Considering the "guidepost" factors laid out in *Hudson*, Louis has produced   little evidence, much less the "clearest proof," that the additions to tax for fraud imposed in his case are so punitive as to overcome clear congressional intent that they be civil rather than criminal in nature. Additions to tax for fraud do not amount to an affirmative disability or restraint, nor have they historically been regarded as punishment. Their purpose is remedial; they "are provided primarily as a safeguard for the protection of the revenue and to reimburse the Government for the heavy expense of investigation and the loss resulting from the taxpayer's fraud." *Mitchell*, 303 U.S. at 401, 58 S.Ct. 630.   Even if deterrence is an additional purpose for the additions, the Supreme Court has recognized that monetary penalties may deter others without being criminal in nature. See *Hudson*, 522 U.S. at ----, 118 S.Ct. at 496 ("[T]he mere presence of this purpose is insufficient to render a sanction criminal.").

Several of the guidepost factors are present to some degree, but they are insufficient to render the additions to tax criminal. Although it is certainly true that fraud, and therefore fraudulent intent, are prerequisites to the imposition of an addition to tax for fraud, punishing fraudulent intent is not the central focus of these additions to tax. The fraud requirement is designed to ensure that the additions are imposed only on taxpayers who engage in the type of deceptive behavior that is difficult and costly for the IRS to detect. To the extent this factor may favor a finding that the addition to tax is punitive, it does so only to a very limited degree.

It is clear that Congress intended tax fraud to be subject to both criminal sanctions and additions to tax for fraud. This factor alone, however, "is insufficient to render the money penalties * * * criminally punitive." Congress may impose both civil and criminal penalties in connection with the same proscribed behavior without violating the Double Jeopardy Clause.

Finally, while it is true that the magnitude of the addition will fluctuate somewhat over time as tax rates rise and fall, the addition achieves "rough justice" and is not "so divorced from the reality of what the government suffered in damages and expenses as to constitute punishment."[2] Moreover, even if we agreed with Louis that this final guidepost factor may suggest the additions to tax for fraud were punitive, it would be improper to elevate this factor to dispositive status, as the Court did in *Halper* [United States v. Halper, 490 U.S. 435, 109 S.Ct. 1892, 104 L.Ed.2d 487 (1989)].

II.

The Excessive Fines Clause of the Eighth Amendment prohibits the government from imposing excessive fines as punishment. U.S. Const. amend. VIII. Even a civil sanction may be punitive for Eighth Amendment purposes. A civil sanction is punitive if "it can only be explained as serving in part to punish." Id.; see also United States v. Bajakajian, 524 U.S. 321, ----, 118 S.Ct. 2028, 2034 n. 4, 141 L.Ed.2d 314 (1998). In making this determination, the court considers factors such as the language of the statute creating the sanction, the sanction's purpose(s), the circumstances in which the sanction can be imposed, and the historical understanding of the sanction.

Although § 6653(b)(3) provides an "innocent spouse exception" similar to the "innocent owner defense" of the forfeiture statute considered punitive in *Austin*, 509 U.S. at 619, 113 S.Ct. 2801, the statutory language provides no other indication of punitive intent. Furthermore, as we noted in Part II, the purposes of additions to tax for fraud are primarily remedial: to protect the revenue and to reimburse the government for the expense of investigating fraud. Moreover, unlike the forfeiture at issue in *Bajakajian*, additions to tax for fraud can be imposed regardless of whether the taxpayer has been convicted of a felony, and are not imposed as part of a criminal sentence. See *Mitchell*, 303 U.S. at 406, 58 S.Ct. 630 (taxpayer liable for additions to tax for fraud even though he was acquitted of the criminal charges).

---

2.   Louis argues that under United States v. United States Shoe Corp., 523 U.S. 360, 118 S.Ct. 1290, 140 L.Ed.2d 453 (1998), charges assessed on an ad valorem basis can never be a valid method of reimbursing the government for its expenses. *United States Shoe Corp.* analyzed a "Harbor Maintenance Tax" (HMT) under the Exports Clause, which prohibits federal taxation of exports, but allows the government to charge user fees "as compensation for government-supplied services." The Court concluded that the HMT, an ad valorem assessment based on the amount of cargo a ship is carrying, did not "correlate reliably with the federal harbor services used," and was therefore a tax rather than a user fee. Louis relies on this language to argue that because additions to tax for fraud are an ad valorem assessment based on the amount of the underpayment of taxes, they do not "correlate reliably" with the government's costs. However, *United States Shoe Corp.'s* analysis was limited to the context of the Exports Clause.

The Court noted that in other contexts, it has upheld ad valorem charges as a valid method of reimbursing the government. See id. at ---- - ----, 118 S.Ct. at 1294-95. Contrary to Louis' argument, *United States Shoe Corp.* does not hold that ad valorem assessments are never sufficiently related to the government's costs to serve a remedial purpose.

The eighteenth-century predecessors to § 6653(b) which Louis cites do not support his argument that additions to tax for fraud have historically been understood as punitive. The statutes merely provide that a person who did not pay his taxes was subject to a fine equal to a stipulated percentage of the underpayment. Louis has not shown that § 6653(b)'s many predecessors were considered punitive rather than remedial.

We therefore conclude that additions to tax for fraud are "properly * * * characterized as remedial," *Austin*, 509 U.S. at 608 n. 4, 113 S.Ct. 2801, and as such, are not subject to review under the Excessive Fines Clause.

III.

Louis' argument that the Fifth and Sixth Amendments were violated by the administrative assessment of additions to tax for fraud fails for the same reason as his Double Jeopardy challenge-the additions are civil, not criminal, in nature.

AFFIRMED.

Notes And Questions

The Double Jeopardy Clause of the Fifth Amendment prohibits "a second prosecution for the same offense after acquittal, a second prosecution for the same offense after conviction, and multiple punishments for the same offense." North Carolina v. Pearce, 395 U.S. 711, 717 (1969).

A defendant will be considered placed in double jeopardy only if "every violation of one statute entails a violation of another." United States v. Benton, 852 F.2d 1456, 1465 (6th Cir.1988). The test for determining whether double jeopardy applies is the "same elements" test espoused by the United States Supreme Court in Blockburger v. United States, 284 U.S. 299 (1932). In *Blockburger*, the Court stated: " * * * where the same act or transaction constitutes a violation of two distinct statutory provisions, the test to be applied to determine whether there are two offenses or only one is whether each provision requires proof of an additional fact which the other does not." Id. at 304. Thus, if each offense requires proof of a fact or element that the other does not, the *Blockburger* test is satisfied and the act or transaction will be considered two separate offenses, even though there may be "a substantial overlap in the proof offered to establish the crimes." State v. Verive, 128 Ariz. 70, 627 A.2d 721 (1981).

If the evidence needed to convict the defendant in the first trial is the same as the evidence needed to obtain a conviction in the second trial, the second prosecution is barred by double jeopardy, regardless of whether the convictions are obtained under statutes that satisfy *Blockburger*'s "same elements" test.

The United States Supreme Court has held that under certain circumstances, a civil penalty may constitute punishment for purposes of the Double Jeopardy Clause. See United States v. Halper, 490 U.S. 435 (1989). In reaching its decision, the Court noted that "it is the purposes actually served by the sanction in question, not the underlying nature of the proceeding giving rise to the sanction, that must be evaluated." Id. at 447. The Court further notes that civil penalties "may advance punitive as well as remedial goals" while criminal penalties may have both a "punitive and remedial" aim. Id.

How can a court distinguish between punishment and remediation? Under what circumstances may a civil penalty be considered punitive for purposes of the Double Jeopardy Clause? See United States v. Halper, 490 U.S. 435, 109 S.Ct. 1892, 104 L.Ed.2d 487 (1989); Desimone v. State of Nevada, 996 P.2d 405 (2002).

3. Sixth Amendment Right to Counsel

UNITED STATES v. JEFFREY STEIN
United States Court of Appeals, Second Circuit, 2008.
541 F.3d 130

JACOBS, CHIEF JUDGE:

The United States appeals from an order of the United States District Court for the Southern District of New York (Kaplan, J.), dismissing an indictment against thirteen former partners and employees of the accounting firm KPMG, LLP. Judge Kaplan found that, absent pressure from the government, KPMG would have paid defendants' legal fees and expenses without regard to cost. Based on this and other findings of fact, Judge Kaplan ruled that the government deprived defendants of their right to counsel under the Sixth Amendment by causing KPMG to impose conditions on the advancement of legal fees to defendants, to cap the fees, and ultimately to end payment. See United States v. Stein, 435 F.Supp.2d 330, 367-73 (S.D.N.Y.2006) (" Stein I "). Judge Kaplan also ruled that the government deprived defendants of their right to substantive due process under the Fifth Amendment. Id. at 360-65.

We hold that KPMG's adoption and enforcement of a policy under which it conditioned, capped and ultimately ceased advancing legal fees to defendants followed as a direct consequence of the government's overwhelming influence, and that KPMG's conduct therefore amounted to state action. We further hold that the government thus unjustifiably interfered with defendants' relationship with counsel and their ability to mount a defense, in violation of the Sixth Amendment, and that the government did not cure the violation. Because no other remedy will return defendants to the status quo ante, we affirm the dismissal of the indictment as to all thirteen defendants. * * *

BACKGROUND
The Thompson Memorandum

In January 2003, then-United States Deputy Attorney General Larry D. Thompson promulgated a policy statement, Principles of Federal Prosecution of Business Organizations (the "Thompson Memorandum"), which articulated "principles" to govern the Department's discretion in bringing prosecutions against business organizations. The Thompson Memorandum was closely based on a predecessor document issued in 1999 by then-U.S. Deputy Attorney General Eric Holder, Federal Prosecution of Corporations. Along with the familiar factors governing charging decisions, the Thompson Memorandum identifies nine additional considerations, including the company's "timely and voluntary disclosure of wrongdoing and its willingness to cooperate in the investigation of its agents." Mem. from Larry D. Thompson, Deputy Att'y Gen., U.S. Dep't of Justice, Principles of Federal Prosecution of Business Organizations (Jan. 20, 2003), at II. The Memorandum explains that prosecutors should inquire

> whether the corporation appears to be protecting its culpable employees and agents [and that] a corporation's promise of support to culpable employees and agents, either through the advancing of attorneys fees, through retaining the employees without sanction for their misconduct, or through providing information to the employees about the government's investigation pursuant to a joint defense agreement, may be considered by the prosecutor in weighing the extent and value of a corporation's cooperation.

Id. at VI. A footnote appended to the highlighted phrase explains that because certain states require companies to advance legal fees for their officers, "a corporation's compliance with governing law should not be considered a failure to cooperate." Id. at VI n. 4. In December 2006-after the events in this prosecution had transpired-the Department of Justice replaced the Thompson Memorandum with the McNulty Memorandum, under which prosecutors may consider a company's fee advancement policy only where the circumstances indicate that it is "intended to impede a criminal investigation," and even then only with the approval of the Deputy Attorney General.

Commencement of the Federal Investigation

After Senate subcommittee hearings in 2002 concerning KPMG's possible involvement in creating and marketing fraudulent tax shelters, KPMG retained Robert S. Bennett of the law firm Skadden, Arps, Slate, Meagher & Flom LLP ("Skadden") to formulate a "cooperative approach" for KPMG to use in dealing with federal authorities. Stein I, 435 F.Supp.2d at 339. Bennett's strategy included "a decision to 'clean house'-a determination to ask Jeffrey Stein, Richard Smith, and Jeffrey Eischeid, all senior KPMG partners who had testified before the Senate and all now [Defendants-Appellees] here-to leave their positions as deputy chair and chief operating officer of the firm, vice chair-tax services, and a partner in personal financial planning, respectively." Id. Smith was transferred and Eischeid was put on administrative leave. Stein resigned with arrangements for a three-year $100,000-per-month consultancy, and an agreement that KPMG would pay for Stein's representation in any actions brought against Stein arising from his activities at the firm. KPMG negotiated a contract with Smith that included a similar clause; but that agreement was never executed.

In February 2004, KPMG officials learned that the firm and 20 to 30 of its top partners and employees were subjects of a grand jury investigation of fraudulent tax shelters. Stein I, 435 F.Supp.2d at 341. On February 18, 2004, KPMG's CEO announced to all partners that the firm was aware of the United States Attorney's Office's ("USAO") investigation and that "[a]ny present or former members of the firm asked to appear will be represented by competent coun[sel] at the firm's expense." Stein IV, 495 F.Supp.2d at 407.

The February 25, 2004 Meeting

In preparation for a meeting with Skadden on February 25, 2004, the prosecutors-including Assistant United States Attorneys ("AUSAs") Shirah Neiman and Justin Weddle-decided to ask whether KPMG would advance legal fees to employees under investigation. Bennett started the meeting by announcing that KPMG had resolved to "clean house," that KPMG "would cooperate fully with the government's investigation," and that its goal was not to protect individual employees but rather to save the firm from being indicted. AUSA Weddle inquired about the firm's plans for advancing fees and about any legal obligation to do so. Later on, AUSA Neiman added that the government would "take into account" the firm's legal obligations to advance fees, but that "the Thompson Memorandum [w]as a point that had to be considered." Id. Bennett then advised that although KPMG was still investigating its legal obligations to advance fees, its "common practice" was to do so. Id. at 342. However, Bennett explained, KPMG would not pay legal fees for any partner who refused to cooperate or "took the Fifth," so long as KPMG had the legal authority to do so. Id.

Later in the meeting, AUSA Weddle asked Bennett to ascertain KPMG's legal obligations to advance attorneys' fees. AUSA Neiman added that "misconduct" should not or cannot "be rewarded" under "federal guidelines." Id. One Skadden attorney's notes attributed to AUSA Weddle the prediction that, if KPMG had discretion regarding fees, the government would "look at that under a microscope." Id. at 344.

Skadden then reported back to KPMG. In notes of the meeting, a KPMG executive wrote the words "[p]aying legal fees" and "[s]everance" next to "not a sign of cooperation." Stein IV, 495 F.Supp.2d at 408.

Communications Between the Prosecutors and KPMG

On March 2, 2004, Bennett told AUSA Weddle that although KPMG believed it had no legal obligation to advance fees, "it would be a big problem" for the firm not to do so given its partnership structure. Stein I, 435 F.Supp.2d at 345. But Bennett disclosed KPMG's tentative decision to limit the amount of fees and condition them on employees' cooperation with prosecutors. Id.

Two days later, a Skadden lawyer advised counsel for Defendant-Appellee Carol G. Warley (a former KPMG tax partner) that KPMG would advance legal fees if Warley cooperated with the government and declined to invoke her Fifth Amendment privilege against self-incrimination. Id.

On a March 11 conference call with Skadden, AUSA Weddle recommended that KPMG tell employees that they should be "totally open" with the USAO, "even if that [meant admitting] criminal wrongdoing," explaining that this would give him good material for cross-examination. Id. That same day, Skadden wrote to counsel for the KPMG employees who had been identified as subjects of the investigation. Id. The letter set forth KPMG's new fees policy ("Fees Policy"), pursuant to which advancement of fees and expenses would be

[i] capped at $400,000 per employee;

[ii] conditioned on the employee's cooperation with the government; and

[iii] terminated when an employee was indicted.

Id. at 345-46. The government was copied on this correspondence. Id. at 345.

On March 12, KPMG sent a memorandum to certain other employees who had not been identified as subjects, urging them to cooperate with the government, advising them that it might be advantageous for them to exercise their right to counsel, and advising that KPMG would cover employees' "reasonable fees." Id. at 346 n. 62.

The prosecutors expressed by letter their "disappoint[ment] with [the] tone" of this memorandum and its "one-sided presentation of potential issues," and "demanded that KPMG send out a supplemental memorandum in a form they proposed." Id. at 346. The government's alternative language, premised on the "assum[ption] that KPMG truly is committed to fully cooperating with the Government's investigation," Letter of David N. Kelley, United States Attorney, Southern District of New York, March 17, 2004, advised employees that they could "meet with investigators without the assistance of counsel," Stein I, 435 F.Supp.2d at 346. KPMG complied, and circulated a memo advising that employees "may deal directly with government representatives without counsel." Id.

At a meeting in late March, Skadden asked the prosecutors to notify Skadden in the event any KPMG employee refused to cooperate. Over the following year, the prosecutors regularly informed Skadden whenever a KPMG employee refused to cooperate fully, such as by refusing to proffer or by proffering incompletely (in the government's view). Skadden, in turn, informed the employees' lawyers that fee advancement would cease unless the employees cooperated. The employees either knuckled under and submitted to interviews, or they were fired and KPMG ceased advancing their fees. For example, Watson and Smith attended proffer sessions after receiving KPMG's March 11 letter announcing the Fees Policy, and after Skadden reiterated to them that fees would be terminated absent cooperation. They did so because (they said, and the district court found) they feared that KPMG would stop advancing attorneys fees-although Watson concedes he attended a first session voluntarily. See United States v. Stein, 440 F.Supp.2d 315, 330-33 (S.D.N.Y.2006) (" Stein II "). As Bennett later assured AUSA Weddle: "Whenever your Office has notified us that individuals have not . . . cooperat [ed], KPMG has promptly and without question encouraged them to cooperate and threatened to cease payment of their attorney fees and . . . to take personnel action, including termination." Letter of Robert Bennett to United States Attorney's Office, November 2, 2004; see, e.g., Stein II, 440 F.Supp.2d at 323 (describing KPMG's termination of Defendant-Appellant Warley after she invoked her Fifth Amendment privilege against self-incrimination).

KPMG Avoids Indictment

In an early-March 2005 meeting, then-U.S. Attorney David Kelley told Skadden and top KPMG executives that a non-prosecution agreement was unlikely and that he had reservations about KPMG's level of cooperation: "I've seen a lot better from big companies." Bennett reminded Kelley how KPMG had capped and conditioned its advancement of legal fees. Kelley remained unconvinced.

KPMG moved up the Justice Department's chain of command. At a June 13, 2005 meeting with U.S. Deputy Attorney General James Comey, Bennett stressed KPMG's pressure on employees to cooperate by conditioning legal fees on cooperation; it was, he said, "precedent[ ]setting." Stein I, 435 F.Supp.2d at 349. KPMG's entreaties were ultimately successful: on August 29, 2005, the firm entered into a deferred prosecution agreement (the "DPA") under which KPMG admitted extensive wrongdoing, paid a $456 million fine, and committed itself to cooperation in any future government investigation or prosecution. Id. at 349-50.

Indictment of Individual Employees

On August 29, 2005-the same day KPMG executed the DPA-the government indicted six of the Defendants-Appellees (along with three other KPMG employees): Jeffrey Stein; Richard Smith; Jeffrey Eischeid; John Lanning, Vice Chairman of Tax Services; Philip Wiesner, a former tax partner; and Mark Watson, a tax partner. A superseding indictment filed on October 17, 2005 named ten additional employees, including seven of the Defendants-Appellees: Larry DeLap, a former tax partner in charge of professional practice; Steven Gremminger, a former partner and associate general counsel; former tax partners Gregg Ritchie, Randy Bickham and Carl Hasting; Carol G. Warley; and Richard Rosenthal, a former tax partner and Chief Financial Officer of KPMG.[4] Pursuant to

---

4. The superseding indictment filed on October 17, 2005 charged 19 defendants in 46 counts for conspiring to defraud the United States and the IRS, tax evasion and obstruction of the internal revenue laws (although not every individual was charged with every offense).

the Fees Policy, KPMG promptly stopped advancing legal fees to the indicted employees who were still receiving them. Id. at 350.

Procedural History

On January 12, 2006, the thirteen defendants (among others) moved to dismiss the indictment based on the government's interference with KPMG's advancement of fees. In a submission to the district court, KPMG represented that the Thompson memorandum in conjunction with the government's statements relating to payment of legal fees affected KPMG's determination(s) with respect to the advancement of legal fees and other defense costs to present or former partners and employees . . .. In fact, KPMG is prepared to state that the Thompson memorandum substantially influenced KPMG's decisions with respect to legal fees. . ..Stein IV, 495 F.Supp.2d at 405.

* * *

Stein I

Judge Kaplan's opinion and order of June 26, 2006 noted, as the parties had stipulated, that KPMG's past practice was to advance legal fees for employees facing regulatory, civil and criminal investigations without condition or cap. Starting from that baseline, Judge Kaplan made the following findings of fact. At the February 25, 2004 meeting, Bennett began by "test[ing] the waters to see whether KPMG could adhere to its practice of paying its employees' legal expenses when litigation loomed [by asking] for [the] government's view on the subject." Id. at 341. It is not clear what AUSA Neiman intended to convey when she said that "misconduct" should not or cannot "be rewarded" under "federal guidelines"; but her statement "was understood by both KPMG and government representatives as a reminder that payment of legal fees by KPMG, beyond any that it might legally be obligated to pay, could well count against KPMG in the government's decision whether to indict the firm." Id. at 344. "[W]hile the USAO did not say in so many words that it did not want KPMG to pay legal fees, no one at the meeting could have failed to draw that conclusion." Id.

Based on those findings, Judge Kaplan arrived at the following ultimate findings of fact, all of which the government contests on appeal:
[1] "the Thompson Memorandum caused KPMG to consider departing from its long-standing policy of paying legal fees and expenses of its personnel in all cases and investigations even before it first met with the USAO" and induced KPMG to seek "an indication from the USAO

that payment of fees in accordance with its settled practice would not be held against it";

[2] the government made repeated references to the Thompson Memo in an effort to "reinforce[ ] the threat inherent in the Thompson Memorandum";

[3] "the government conducted itself in a manner that evidenced a desire to minimize the involvement of defense attorneys"; and

[4] but for the Thompson Memorandum and the prosecutors' conduct, KPMG would have paid defendants' legal fees and expenses without consideration of cost.

Id. at 352-53.

Against that background, Judge Kaplan ruled that a defendant has a fundamental right under the Fifth Amendment to fairness in the criminal process, including the ability to get and deploy in defense all "resources lawfully available to him or her, free of knowing or reckless government interference," id. at 361, and that the government's reasons for infringing that right in this case could not withstand strict scrutiny. Judge Kaplan also ruled that the same conduct deprived each defendant of the Sixth Amendment right "to choose the lawyer or lawyers he or she desires and to use one's own funds to mount the defense that one wishes to present." Id. at 366. He reasoned that "the government's law enforcement interests in taking the specific actions in question [do not] sufficiently outweigh the interests of the KPMG Defendants in having the resources needed to defend as they think proper against these charges." Id. at 368. "[T]he fact that advancement of legal fees occasionally might be part of an obstruction scheme or indicate a lack of full cooperation by a prospective defendant is insufficient to justify the government's interference with the right of individual criminal defendants to obtain resources lawfully available to them in order to defend themselves. . .." Id. at 369.

Judge Kaplan rejected the government's position that defendants have no right to spend "other people's money" on high-priced defense counsel: "[T]he KPMG Defendants had at least an expectation that their expenses in defending any claims or charges brought against them by reason of their employment by KPMG would be paid by the firm," and "any benefits that would have flowed from that expectation-the legal fees at issue now-were, in every material sense, their property, not that of a third party." Id. at 367. He further determined that defendants need not show how their defense was impaired: the government's interference with their Sixth Amendment "right to be represented as they choose," "like a deprivation of the right to counsel of their choice, is complete irrespective of the quality of the representation they receive." Id. at 369.

* * *

Stein IV

Judge Kaplan dismissed the indictment against the thirteen defendants on July 16, 2007. Stein IV, 495 F.Supp.2d at 427. He reinforced the ruling in Stein I that the government violated defendants' right to substantive due process by holding that the prosecutors' conduct also "independently shock[s] the conscience." Id. at 412-15. Judge Kaplan concluded that no remedy other than dismissal of the indictment would put defendants in the position they would have occupied absent the government's misconduct. Id. at 419-28.

The government appeals the dismissal of the indictment.

DISCUSSION

We review first [I] the government's challenges to the district court's factual findings, including its finding that but for the Thompson Memorandum and the prosecutors' conduct KPMG would have paid employees' legal fees-pre-indictment and post-indictment-without regard to cost. Next, because we are hesitant to resolve constitutional questions unnecessarily, [II] we inquire whether the government cured the purported Sixth Amendment violation by the AUSA's in-court statement on March 30, 2006 that KPMG was free to decide whether to advance fees. Since we conclude that this statement did not return defendants to the status quo ante, [III] we decide whether the promulgation and enforcement of KPMG's Fees Policy amounted to state action under the Constitution and [IV] whether the government deprived defendants of their Sixth Amendment right to counsel.

I.

* * *

The government points out that the Thompson Memorandum lists "fees advancement" as just one of many considerations in a complex charging decision, and thus argues that Judge Kaplan overread the Thompson Memorandum as a threat that KPMG would be indicted unless it ceased advancing legal fees to its employees.

Judge Kaplan's finding withstands scrutiny. KPMG was faced with the fatal prospect of indictment; it could be expected to do all it could, assisted by sophisticated counsel, to placate and appease the government. As Judge Kaplan noted, KPMG's chief legal officer, Sven Erik Holmes, testified that he considered it crucial "to be able to say at the right time with the right audience, we're in full compliance with the Thompson Memorandum." Stein I, 435 F.Supp.2d at 364. Moreover, KPMG's management and counsel had reason to consider the impact of the firm's indictment on the interests of the firm's partners, employees, clients, creditors and retirees.

The government reads the Thompson Memorandum to say that fees advancement is to be considered as a negative factor only when it is part of a campaign to "circle the wagons," i.e., to protect culpable employees and obstruct investigators. And it is true that the Thompson Memorandum instructs a prosecutor to ask "whether the corporation appears to be protecting its culpable employees and agents." But even if the government's reading is plausible, the wording nevertheless empowers prosecutors to determine which employees will be deprived of company-sponsored counsel: prosecutors may reasonably foresee that employees they identify as "culpable" will be cut off from fees.

The government also takes issue with Judge Kaplan's finding that the prosecutors (acting under DOJ policy) deliberately reinforced the threat inherent in the Thompson Memorandum. It protests that KPMG considered conditioning legal fees on cooperation even before the February 25, 2004 meeting and that KPMG adopted its Fees Policy free from government influence. However, Judge Kaplan's interpretation of the meeting is supported by the following record evidence. Because withholding of fees would be problematic for a partnership like KPMG, Bennett began by attempting to "sound out" the government's position on the issue. Stein IV, 495 F.Supp.2d at 402. The prosecutors declined to sign off on KPMG's prior arrangement. Instead they asked KPMG to ascertain whether it had a legal obligation to advance fees. KPMG responded with its fallback position: conditioning fees on cooperation. Id. In Judge Kaplan's view, this was not an official policy announcement, but rather a proposal: Skadden lawyers repeatedly emphasized to the prosecutors that no final decision had been made. One available inference from all this is that the prosecutors' inquiry about KPMG's legal obligations was a routine check for conflicts of interest; but on this record, Judge Kaplan was entitled to see things differently.[6]

Nor can we disturb Judge Kaplan's finding that "the government conducted itself in a manner that evidenced a desire to minimize the

---

6. It is unnecessary for us to determine the import of AUSA Neiman's statement that misconduct should not or cannot be rewarded or to decide whether AUSA Weddle actually said that the government would look at discretionary fee advancement "under a microscope." Stein I, 435 F.Supp.2d at 344.

involvement of defense attorneys." Stein I, 435 F.Supp.2d at 353. During the March 11 phone call between the prosecutors and Skadden, AUSA Weddle demanded that KPMG tell its employees to be "totally open" with the USAO, "even if that [meant admitting] criminal wrongdoing," so that he could gather material for cross-examination. Id. at 345. On March 12, the prosecutors prevailed upon KPMG to supplement its first advisory letter with another, which clarified that employees could meet with the government without counsel. In addition, prosecutors repeatedly used Skadden to threaten to withhold legal fees from employees who refused to proffer-even if defense counsel had recommended that an employee invoke the Fifth Amendment privilege. Judge Kaplan could reasonably reject the government's version of these events.

Finally, we cannot say that the district court's ultimate finding of fact-that absent the Thompson Memorandum and the prosecutors' conduct KPMG would have advanced fees without condition or cap-was clearly erroneous. The government itself stipulated in Stein I that KPMG had a "longstanding voluntary practice" of advancing and paying employees' legal fees "without regard to economic costs or considerations" and "without a preset cap or condition of cooperation with the government . . . in any civil, criminal or regulatory proceeding" arising from activities within the scope of employment. Id. at 340. Although it "is far from certain" that KPMG is legally obligated to advance defendants' legal fees, a firm may have potent incentives to advance fees, such as the ability to recruit and retain skilled professionals in a profession fraught with legal risk. Also, there is evidence that, before the prosecutors' intervention, KPMG executed an agreement under which it would advance Stein's legal fees without cap or condition (and negotiated toward an identical agreement with Smith). And while the government maintains that the civil, criminal and regulatory investigations confronting KPMG constituted an unprecedented state of affairs that might have caused KPMG to adopt new and different policies, Judge Kaplan was not required to agree. Indeed, KPMG itself represented to the court that the Thompson Memorandum and the prosecutors' conduct "substantially influenced [its] determination(s) with respect to the advancement of legal fees."

For the foregoing reasons, we cannot disturb Judge Kaplan's factual findings, including his finding that, but for the Thompson Memorandum and the prosecutors' conduct, KPMG would have advanced legal fees without condition or cap.

II.

We now consider the government's claim of cure. If the government is correct, the "taint" of the purported Sixth Amendment violation would be "neutralize[d]," dismissal of the indictment would be inappropriate, and we could avoid deciding the constitutional question.

"Cases involving Sixth Amendment deprivations are subject to the general rule that remedies should be tailored to the injury suffered from the constitutional violation and should not unnecessarily infringe on competing interests." Id. at 364, 101 S.Ct. 665. Therefore, we must "identify and then neutralize the taint by tailoring relief appropriate in the circumstances to assure the defendant the effective assistance of counsel and a fair trial." Id. at 365, 101 S.Ct. 665. Dismissal of an indictment is a remedy of last resort, id., and is appropriate only where necessary to "restore [ ] the defendant to the circumstances that would have existed had there been no constitutional error," United States v. Carmichael, 216 F.3d 224, 227 (2d Cir.2000).

In *Stein IV*, Judge Kaplan concluded that dismissal of the indictment as to the thirteen defendants was warranted because no other remedy would restore them to the position they would have enjoyed but for the government's unconstitutional conduct. *Stein IV*, 495 F.Supp.2d at 419-28. Specifically, Judge Kaplan found that the government deprived four defendants-Gremminger, Hasting, Ritchie and Watson-of counsel of their choice. Id. at 421 ("[T]hey simply lack the resources to engage the lawyers of their choice, lawyers who had represented them as long as KPMG was paying the bills." Judge Kaplan also found that all thirteen defendants-even those who were still represented by their counsel of choice-were forced by KPMG's withholding of post-indictment legal fees "to limit their defenses . . . for economic reasons and that they would not have been so constrained if KPMG paid their expenses." Id. at 419. After reviewing defendants' finances and determining the estimated cost of legal representation, Judge Kaplan concluded: "[N]one of the thirteen KPMG Defendants . . . has the resources to defend this case as he or she would have defended it had KPMG been paying the cost, even if he or she liquidated all property owned by the defendant." Id. at 425.

The government argues that it cured any Sixth Amendment violation on March 30, 2006, when it told the district court that KPMG was free to "exercise [its] business judgment." Therefore, the government contends, the appropriate remedy for any constitutional violation would be to allow defendants to retain their counsel of choice using whatever funds KPMG is willing to provide now. At most, the government claims, all that would be warranted is an adjournment of trial to afford defendants additional time to review documents and consult with counsel and expert witnesses; and since 16 months passed between the government's March 30, 2006 in-court statement and the July 16, 2007 dismissal of the indictment, defendants have already enjoyed this remedy.

Judge Kaplan was unpersuaded. In his view, KPMG is unlikely to pay defendants' legal fees as if the government had never exerted any pressure: KPMG might prefer not to be seen as reversing course and implicitly "admitting that it caved in to government pressure"; the defendants have been "indicted on charges the full scope of which may not previously have been foreseeable to KPMG"-so that defense costs may be larger than expected; and KPMG has since paid a $456 million fine under the DPA, reducing the firm's available resources. *Stein I*, 435 F.Supp.2d at 374.

We agree with the district court. The prosecutor's isolated and ambiguous statement in a proceeding to which KPMG was not a party (and the nearly 16-month period of legal limbo that ensued) did not restore defendants to the status quo ante.

Judge Kaplan asked whether the government would represent that [i] it has no objection to "KPMG exercising its free and independent business judgment as to whether to advance defense costs" and [ii] "if it were to elect to do so the government would not in any way consider that in determining whether it had complied with the DPA." The AUSA affirmed only the first proposition. And as to that, the AUSA stated that the government's position had not changed: so the import of that statement depends on what position one thinks the government had previously adopted.

Furthermore, it was unrealistic to expect KPMG to exercise uncoerced judgment in March 2006 as if it had never experienced the government's pressure in the first place. The government's intervention, coupled with the menace inherent in the Thompson Memorandum, altered the decisional dynamic in a way that the district court could find irreparable. Having assumed a supine position in the DPA-under which KPMG must continue to cooperate fully with the government-it is not all that likely that the firm would feel free to reverse course.

True, even if KPMG had decided initially to advance legal fees, it might always have changed course later: it is undisputed that KPMG's longstanding fees policy was voluntary and subject to revision. (In fact, in the civil suit KPMG represented that it would not have obligated itself to pay millions of dollars in fees on behalf of an unknown number of employees without regard to the charges ultimately lodged against them.) So, the government argues, even absent government pressure

KPMG would not have advanced legal fees indefinitely and without condition.

This is certainly plausible; but it directly contradicts the district court's central finding-which is not clearly erroneous-that "[a]bsent the Thompson Memorandum and the actions of the USAO, KPMG would have paid the legal fees and expenses of all of its partners and employees both prior to and after indictment, without regard to cost." Id. at 353. Because we cannot disturb this finding, we cannot accept the government's claim of cure on this score.

* * *

The appropriate remedy for a constitutional violation is "one that as much as possible restores the defendant to the circumstances that would have existed had there been no constitutional error." Carmichael, 216 F.3d at 227. Since it has been found that, absent governmental interference, KPMG would have advanced unlimited legal fees unconditionally, only the unconditional, unlimited advancement of legal fees would restore defendants to the status quo ante. The government's in-court statement and the ensuing 16-month delay were not enough. If there was a Sixth Amendment violation, dismissal of the indictment is required.

III.

Judge Kaplan found that "KPMG's decision to cut off all payments of legal fees and expenses to anyone who was indicted and to limit and to condition such payments prior to indictment upon cooperation with the government was the direct consequence of the pressure applied by the Thompson Memorandum and the USAO." Stein I, 435 F.Supp.2d at 353; see also Stein II, 440 F.Supp.2d at 334. The government protests that KPMG's adoption and enforcement of its Fees Policy was private action, outside the ambit of the Sixth Amendment.

* * *

Actions of a private entity are attributable to the State if "there is a sufficiently close nexus between the State and the challenged action of the . . . entity so that the action of the latter may be fairly treated as that of the State itself." Jackson v. Metro. Edison Co., 419 U.S. 345, 351, 95 S.Ct. 449, 42 L.Ed.2d 477 (1974). The "close nexus" test is not satisfied when the state "[m]ere[ly] approv[es] of or acquiesce[s] in the initiatives" of the private entity, or when an entity is merely subject to governmental regulation. "The purpose of the [close-nexus requirement] is to assure that constitutional standards are invoked only when it can be said that the State is responsible for the specific conduct of which the plaintiff complains." Blum v. Yaretsky, 457 U.S. 991, 1004, 102 S.Ct. 2777, 73 L.Ed.2d 534 (1982). Such responsibility is normally found when the State "has exercised coercive power or has provided such significant encouragement, either overt or covert, that the choice must in law be deemed to be that of the State." Id.

Although Supreme Court cases on this issue "have not been a model of consistency," some principles emerge. "A nexus of state action exists between a private entity and the state when the state exercises coercive power, is entwined in the management or control of the private actor, or provides the private actor with significant encouragement, either overt or covert, or when the private actor operates as a willful participant in joint activity with the State or its agents, is controlled by an agency of the State, has been delegated a public function by the state, or is entwined with governmental policies." Flagg v. Yonkers Sav. & Loan Ass'n, 396 F.3d 178, 187 (2d Cir.2005).

The government argues: KPMG simply took actions in the shadow of an internal DOJ advisory document (the Thompson Memorandum) containing multiple factors and caveats; the government's approval of KPMG's Fees Policy did not render the government responsible for KPMG's actions enforcing it; even if the government had specifically required KPMG to adopt a policy that penalized non-cooperation, state action would still have been lacking because KPMG would have retained the power to apply the policy; and although the prosecutors repeatedly informed KPMG when employees were not cooperating, they did so at KPMG's behest, without knowing how KPMG would react. We disagree.

KPMG's adoption and enforcement of the Fees Policy amounted to "state action" because KPMG "operate[d] as a willful participant in joint activity" with the government, and because the USAO "significant[ly] encourage[d]" KPMG to withhold legal fees from defendants upon indictment. The government brought home to KPMG that its survival depended on its role in a joint project with the government to advance government prosecutions. The government is therefore legally "responsible for the specific conduct of which the [criminal defendants] complain[ ]." Blum, 457 U.S. at 1004, 102 S.Ct. 2777.

The government argues that "KPMG's decision to condition legal fee payments on cooperation, while undoubtedly influenced by the Thompson Memorandum, was not coerced or directed by the Government." But that argument runs up against the district court's factual finding (which we do not disturb) that the fees decision "was the direct consequence" of the Memorandum and the prosecutors' conduct. Stein I, 435 F.Supp.2d at 353. Nevertheless, it remains a question of law whether the facts as found by the district court establish state action.

State action is established here as a matter of law because the government forced KPMG to adopt its constricted Fees Policy. The Thompson Memorandum itself-which prosecutors stated would be considered in deciding whether to indict KPMG-emphasizes that cooperation will be assessed in part based upon whether, in advancing counsel fees, "the corporation appears to be protecting its culpable employees and agents." Since defense counsel's objective in a criminal investigation will virtually always be to protect the client, KPMG's risk was that fees for defense counsel would be advanced to someone the government considered culpable. So the only safe course was to allow the government to become (in effect) paymaster.

The prosecutors reinforced this message by inquiring into KPMG's fees obligations, referring to the Thompson Memorandum as "a point that had to be considered," and warning that "misconduct" should not or cannot "be rewarded" under "federal guidelines." Stein I, 435 F.Supp.2d at 341-42. The government had KPMG's full attention. It is hardly surprising, then, that KPMG decided to condition payment of fees on employees' cooperation with the government and to terminate fees upon indictment: only that policy would allow KPMG to continue advancing fees while minimizing the risk that prosecutors would view such advancement as obstructive.

To ensure that KPMG's new Fees Policy was enforced, prosecutors became "entwined in the . . . control" of KPMG. They intervened in KPMG's decisionmaking, expressing their "disappoint[ment] with [the] tone" of KPMG's first advisory memorandum, Stein I, 435 F.Supp.2d at 346, and declaring that "[t]hese problems must be remedied" by a proposed supplemental memorandum specifying that employees could meet with the government without being burdened by counsel. Prosecutors also "made plain" their "strong preference" as to what the firm should do, and their "desire to share the fruits of such intrusions." Skinner, 489 U.S. at 615, 109 S.Ct. 1402. They did so by regularly "reporting to KPMG the identities of employees who refused to make statements in circumstances in which the USAO knew full well that KPMG would pressure them to talk to prosecutors." Stein II, 440 F.Supp.2d at 337. (The government's argument that it could not have known how KPMG would react when informed that certain employees were not cooperating is at best plausible only vis-à-vis the first few employees.) The prosecutors thus steered KPMG toward their preferred fee advancement policy and then supervised its application in individual cases. Such "overt" and "significant encouragement" supports the conclusion that KPMG's conduct is properly attributed to the State.[9]

* * *

Here, however, [1] KPMG was never "free to define" cooperation independently: AUSA Weddle told Bennett that he had "had a bad experience in the past with a company conditioning payments on a person's cooperation, where the company did not define cooperation as 'tell the truth' the[ ] way we [the prosecutors] define it." KPMG's fees advancement decisions in individual cases thus depended largely on state-influenced standards. In addition, [2] the prosecution designated particular employees for deprivation of fees (and, in some cases, termination of employment) by demanding that KPMG threaten and penalize those employees for non-cooperation. As Bennett later reported to the Deputy Attorney General, "[w]henever your Office has notified us that individuals have not . . . cooperat[ed], KPMG has promptly and without question encouraged them to cooperate and threatened to cease payment of their attorneys fees and . . . to take personnel action, including termination." Furthermore, by indicting the thirteen defendants after inspiring and shaping KPMG's Fees Policy and after exacting KPMG's compliance with it, prosecutors effectively selected which employees would be deprived of attorneys' fees. Having forced the constriction of KPMG's longstanding policy of advancing fees, the government then compelled KPMG to apply the Fees Policy to particular employees both pre- and post-indictment. * * *

* * * (as the district court found), absent the prosecutors' involvement and the Thompson Memorandum, KPMG would not have changed its longstanding fee advancement policy or withheld legal fees from defendants upon indictment. *See Stein I*, 435 F.Supp.2d at 353.

The government responds: Solomon declined to find state action even though it involved a private entity compelling interviews with one of its members, backed by the explicit threat of expulsion, in the context of continuous coordination between the NYSE and the SEC on the same side. So how can KPMG, an adversary of the government, also be its partner?

An adversarial relationship does not normally bespeak partnership. But KPMG faced ruin by indictment and reasonably believed it must do

---

9. Because the Sixth Amendment attaches only upon indictment, the KPMG conduct attributable to the government is relevant only insofar as it contributed to KPMG's decision to withhold legal fees upon defendants' indictment. Many of KPMG's actions occurred prior to the August and October 2005 indictments. Nevertheless, when the defendants were indicted, KPMG had been so schooled by the government in the necessity of enforcing a particular fee advancement policy that KPMG understood what was expected of it once the indictments came down.

everything in its power to avoid it. The government's threat of indictment was easily sufficient to convert its adversary into its agent. KPMG was not in a position to consider coolly the risk of indictment, weigh the potential significance of the other enumerated factors in the Thompson Memorandum, and decide for itself how to proceed.

We therefore conclude that KPMG's adoption and enforcement of the Fees Policy (both before and upon defendants' indictment) amounted to state action. The government may properly be held "responsible for the specific conduct of which the [criminal defendants] complain[ ]," Blum, 457 U.S. at 1004, 102 S.Ct. 2777, i.e., the deprivation of their Sixth Amendment right to counsel, if the violation is established.

IV.

The district court's ruling on the Sixth Amendment was based on the following analysis (set out here in précis). The Sixth Amendment protects "an individual's right to choose the lawyer or lawyers he or she desires," Stein I, 435 F.Supp.2d at 366 (citing Wheat v. United States, 486 U.S. 153, 164, 108 S.Ct. 1692, 100 L.Ed.2d 140 (1988)), and "to use one's own funds to mount the defense that one wishes to present," id. (citing Caplin & Drysdale, Chartered v. United States, 491 U.S. 617, 624, 109 S.Ct. 2646, 105 L.Ed.2d 528 (1989)). The goal is to secure "a defendant's right to spend his own money on a defense." Id. at 367. Because defendants reasonably expected to receive legal fees from KPMG, the fees "were, in every material sense, their property." Id. The government's interest in retaining discretion to treat as obstruction a company's advancement of legal fees "is insufficient to justify the government's interference with the right of individual criminal defendants to obtain resources lawfully available to them in order to defend themselves." Id. at 369. Defendants need not make a "particularized showing" of how their defense was impaired, id. at 372, because "[v]irtually everything the defendants do in this case may be influenced by the extent of the resources available to them," such as selection of counsel and "what the KPMG Defendants can pay their lawyers to do," id. at 371-72. Therefore, the Sixth Amendment violation "is complete irrespective of the quality of the representation they receive." Id. at 369.[10]

---

10. In Stein IV, Judge Kaplan nevertheless expanded his findings as to Sixth Amendment harms suffered by particular defendants: defendants Gremminger, Hasting and Watson were deprived of their chosen counsel, "lawyers who had represented them as long as KPMG was paying the bills"; and defendant Ritchie was deprived of the services of Cadwalader Wickersham & Taft, "which was to have played an integral role in his defense." 495 F.Supp.2d at 421. In addition:

All of the [present] KPMG Defendants . . . say that KPMG's refusal to pay their post-indictment legal fees has caused them to restrict the activities of their counsel, limited or precluded their

A.

Most of the state action relevant here-the promulgation of the Thompson Memorandum, the prosecutors' communications with KPMG regarding the advancement of fees, KPMG's adoption of a Fees Policy with caps and conditions, and KPMG's repeated threats to employees identified by prosecutors as being uncooperative-pre-dated the indictments of August and October 2005. . (Of course, after the indictments were filed KPMG ceased advancing fees to all thirteen of the present defendants who were still receiving fees up to that point. * * * So we must determine how this pre-indictment conduct may bear on defendants' Sixth Amendment claim.

"The Sixth Amendment right of the 'accused' to assistance of counsel in 'all criminal prosecutions' is limited by its terms: it does not attach until a prosecution is commenced." Rothgery v. Gillespie County, 554 U.S. ----, 128 S.Ct. 2578, 2583, 171 L.Ed.2d 366 (2008) (quoting U.S. Const. amend. VI). "Attachment" refers to " when the [Sixth Amendment] right may be asserted"; it does not concern the separate question of " what the right guarantees," i.e., "what the substantive guarantee of the Sixth Amendment" is at that stage of the prosecution. Id. at 2592, 2594 (Alito, J., concurring). The Supreme Court has "pegged commencement [of a prosecution] to 'the initiation of adversary judicial criminal proceedings-whether by way of formal charge, preliminary hearing, indictment, information, or arraignment.' " Id. at 2583 (majority opinion). "The rule is not 'mere formalism,' but a recognition of the point at which 'the government has committed itself to prosecute,' 'the adverse positions of government and defendant have solidified,' and the accused 'finds himself faced with the prosecutorial forces of organized society, and immersed in the intricacies of substantive and procedural criminal law.' " Id. (quoting Kirby v. Illinois, 406 U.S. 682, 689, 92 S.Ct. 1877, 32 L.Ed.2d 411 (1972) (plurality opinion)).

Judge Kaplan focused on KPMG's decision to withhold fees upon indictment: "[T]he constitutional violation pertinent to possible dismissal

---

attorneys' review of the documents produced by the government in discovery, prevented them from interviewing witnesses, caused them to refrain from retaining expert witnesses, and/or left them without information technology assistance necessary for dealing with the mountains of electronic discovery. The government has not contested these assertions. The Court therefore has no reason to doubt, and hence finds, that all of them have been forced to limit their defenses in the respects claimed for economic reasons and that they would not have been so constrained if KPMG paid their expenses subject only to the usual sort of administrative requirements typically imposed by corporate law departments on outside counsel fees.

Id. at 418-19. Judge Kaplan explained that even though many defendants had net assets ranging from $1 million to $5 million, their resources were inadequate "to defend this case as they would have defended it absent the government's actions." Id. at 423.

of the indictment was the government's role in KPMG's action in cutting off payment of legal fees for those who were indicted as distinct from the limitations on payment of legal fees during the investigative stage." Stein IV, 495 F.Supp.2d at 404 n. 54 (citing Stein I, 435 F.Supp.2d at 373). Therefore, Judge Kaplan explained, "[a]ctions by the government that affected only the payment of legal fees and defense costs for services rendered prior to the indictment . . . do not implicate the Sixth Amendment." Stein I, 435 F.Supp.2d at 373.

By the same token, state action that also (or only) affected the advancement of legal fees for services rendered post-indictment does implicate defendants' Sixth Amendment rights, regardless of when the conduct took place:

> It is true, of course, that the Sixth Amendment right to counsel typically attaches at the initiation of adversarial proceedings-at an arraignment, indictment, preliminary hearing, and so on. But the analysis can not end there. The Thompson Memorandum on its face and the USAO's actions were parts of an effort to limit defendants' access to funds for their defense. Even if this was not among the conscious motives, the Memorandum was adopted and the USAO acted in circumstances in which that result was known to be exceptionally likely. The fact that events were set in motion prior to indictment with the object of having, or with knowledge that they were likely to have, an unconstitutional effect upon indictment cannot save the government. This conduct, unless justified, violated the Sixth Amendment. Id. at 366. In other words, the government's pre-indictment conduct was of a kind that would have post-indictment effects of Sixth Amendment significance, and did.

We endorse this analysis. Although defendants' Sixth Amendment rights attached only upon indictment, the district court properly considered pre-indictment state action that affected defendants post-indictment. When the government acts prior to indictment so as to impair the suspect's relationship with counsel post-indictment, the pre-indictment actions ripen into cognizable Sixth Amendment deprivations upon indictment.[12] As Judge Ellis explained in United States v. Rosen, 487 F.Supp.2d 721 (E.D.Va.2007), "it is entirely plausible that pernicious effects of the pre-indictment interference continued into the post-indictment period, effectively hobbling defendants' Sixth Amendment rights to retain counsel of choice with funds to which they had a right. . . .. [I]f, as alleged, the government coerced [the employer] into halting fee advances on defendants' behalf

---

12. As Judge Kaplan recognized, the pre-indictment conduct is separately constrained by the Fifth Amendment.

and the government did so for the purpose of undermining defendants' relationship with counsel once the indictment issued, the government violated defendants' right to expend their own resources towards counsel once the right attached." Id. at 734.

Since the government forced KPMG to adopt the constricted Fees Policy-including the provision for terminating fee advancement upon indictment-and then compelled KPMG to enforce it, it was virtually certain that KPMG would terminate defendants' fees upon indictment. We therefore reject the government's argument that its actions (virtually all pre-indictment) are immune from scrutiny under the Sixth Amendment.

B.

We now consider " what the [Sixth Amendment] right guarantees." Rothgery, 128 S.Ct. at 2592 (Alito, J., concurring).

The Sixth Amendment ensures that "[i]n all criminal prosecutions, the accused shall enjoy the right . . . to have the Assistance of Counsel for his defence." U.S. Const. amend. VI. Thus "the Sixth Amendment guarantees the defendant the right to be represented by an otherwise qualified attorney whom that defendant can afford to hire, or who is willing to represent the defendant even though he is without funds." Caplin & Drysdale, Chartered v. United States, 491 U.S. 617, 624-25, 109 S.Ct. 2646, 105 L.Ed.2d 528 (1989). "[A]n element of this right is the right of a defendant who does not require appointed counsel to choose who will represent him." United States v. Gonzalez-Lopez, 548 U.S. 140, 144, 126 S.Ct. 2557, 165 L.Ed.2d 409 (2006).[14]

The government must "honor" a defendant's Sixth Amendment right to counsel:

> This means more than simply that the State cannot prevent the accused from obtaining the assistance of counsel. The Sixth Amendment also imposes on the State an affirmative obligation to respect and preserve the accused's choice to seek this assistance. . . .. [A]t the very least, the prosecutor and police have an affirmative obligation not to act in a manner that circumvents and thereby dilutes the protection afforded by the right to counsel.

---

14. Although the Sixth Amendment right to counsel of choice "has been regarded as the root meaning of the constitutional guarantee," id. at 147-48, 126 S.Ct. 2557, the right is qualified: the attorney must be admitted to the bar, willing to represent the defendant, free from certain conflicts of interest, compliant with the rules of the court, and so on, see Wheat v. United States, 486 U.S. 153, 159-60, 108 S.Ct. 1692, 100 L.Ed.2d 140 (1988).

Maine v. Moulton, 474 U.S. 159, 170-71, 106 S.Ct. 477, 88 L.Ed.2d 481 (1985). This is intuitive: the right to counsel in an adversarial legal system would mean little if defense counsel could be controlled by the government or vetoed without good reason.

Consistent with this principle of non-interference, courts have identified violations of the Sixth Amendment right to counsel where the government obtains incriminating statements from a defendant outside the presence of counsel and then introduces those statements at trial. See, e.g., id. at 176, 106 S.Ct. 477; Massiah v. United States, 377 U.S. 201, 206, 84 S.Ct. 1199, 12 L.Ed.2d 246 (1964). Likewise, the government violates the Sixth Amendment when it intrudes on the attorney-client relationship, preventing defense counsel from "participat[ing] fully and fairly in the adversary factfinding process." Herring v. New York, 422 U.S. 853, 858, 95 S.Ct. 2550, 45 L.Ed.2d 593 (1975); (remaining citations omitted).

Defendants-Appellees do not say that they were deprived of constitutionally effective counsel. Their claim is that the government unjustifiably interfered with their relationship with counsel and their ability to mount the best defense they could muster.

The government, relying on Caplin & Drysdale, Chartered v. United States, 491 U.S. 617, 109 S.Ct. 2646, 105 L.Ed.2d 528 (1989), contends that a defendant has no Sixth Amendment right to a defense funded by someone else's money. In that case, the Supreme Court ruled that a defendant's Sixth Amendment right to retain counsel of choice was not violated when the funds he earmarked for defense were seized under a federal forfeiture statute, because title to the forfeitable assets had vested in the United States. Id. at 628, 109 S.Ct. 2646.

The government focuses on the following passage from Caplin & Drysdale:

> Whatever the full extent of the Sixth Amendment's protection of one's right to retain counsel of his choosing, that protection does not go beyond 'the individual's right to spend his own money to obtain the advice and assistance of . . . counsel.' Walters v. National Assn. of Radiation Survivors, 473 U.S. 305, 370, 105 S.Ct. 3180, 87 L.Ed.2d 220 (1985) (Stevens, J., dissenting). A defendant has no Sixth Amendment right to spend another person's money for services rendered by an attorney, even if those funds are the only way that that defendant will be able to retain the attorney of his choice. A robbery suspect, for example, has no Sixth Amendment right to use funds he has stolen from a bank to retain an attorney to defend him if he is apprehended. The money, though in his possession, is not rightfully his . . ..

Caplin & Drysdale, 491 U.S. at 626, 109 S.Ct. 2646. The holding of Caplin & Drysdale is narrow: the Sixth Amendment does not prevent the government from reclaiming its property from a defendant even though the defendant had planned to fund his legal defense with it. It is easy to distinguish the case of an employee who reasonably expects to receive attorneys' fees as a benefit or perquisite of employment, whether or not the expectation arises from a legal entitlement. As has been found here as a matter of fact, these defendants would have received fees from KPMG but for the government's interference. Although "there is no Sixth Amendment right for a defendant to obtain counsel using tainted funds, [a defendant] still possesses a qualified Sixth Amendment right to use wholly legitimate funds to hire the attorney of his choice." United States v. Farmer, 274 F.3d 800, 804 (4th Cir.2001).

It is axiomatic that if defendants had already received fee advances from KPMG, the government could not (absent justification) deliberately interfere with the use of that money to fuel their defenses. And the government concedes that it could not prevent a lawyer from furnishing a defense gratis. See Caplin & Drysdale, 491 U.S. at 624-25, 109 S.Ct. 2646 ("[T]he Sixth Amendment guarantees a defendant the right to be represented by an otherwise qualified attorney . . . who is willing to represent the defendant even though he is without funds."). Presumably, such a lawyer could pay another lawyer to represent the defendant (subject, of course, to ethical rules governing third-party payments to counsel. And if the Sixth Amendment prohibits the government from interfering with such arrangements, then surely it also prohibits the government from interfering with financial donations by others, such as family members and neighbors-and employers. In a nutshell, the Sixth Amendment protects against unjustified governmental interference with the right to defend oneself using whatever assets one has or might reasonably and lawfully obtain.

The government points out that KPMG's past fee practice was voluntary and subject to change, and that defendants therefore could have had no reasonable expectation of the ongoing advancement of fees. But this argument simply quarrels with Judge Kaplan's finding that absent any state action, KPMG would have paid defendants' legal fees and expenses without regard to cost. See Stein I, 435 F.Supp.2d at 353. Defendants were not necessarily entitled to fee advancement as a matter of law, see Stein v. KPMG, LLP, 486 F.3d 753, 762 n. 3 (2d Cir.2007) (commenting that defendants' likelihood of success in obtaining a judgment against KPMG for legal fees is "far from certain"); but the Sixth Amendment prohibits the government from impeding the supply of defense resources (even if voluntary or gratis), absent justification.

Therefore, unless the government's interference was justified, it violated the Sixth Amendment.

The government is sometimes allowed to interfere with defendants' choice or relationship with counsel, such as to prevent certain conflicts of interest. See, e.g., United States v. Curcio, 680 F.2d 881 (2d Cir.1982). However, the government has failed to establish a legitimate justification for interfering with KPMG's advancement of legal fees.

The government argues that it may inquire into third-party payment of legal fees in certain circumstances. For example, in United States v. Locascio, we affirmed the disqualification of defendant's counsel based in part on defendant's "benefactor payments" to the attorney to serve as "house counsel" to members of the Gambino organized crime family. Locascio, 6 F.3d at 932. We explained that "the acceptance of such 'benefactor payments' . . . raises an ethical question as to whether the attorney's loyalties are with the client or the payor," id., and that "proof of house counsel can be used by the government to help establish the existence of the criminal enterprise under RICO, by showing the connections among the participants," id. at 932-33.

The government's reliance on *Locascio* is misplaced. There, the attorney's status as "house counsel" "was potentially part of the proof of the Gambino criminal enterprise," id. at 933, i.e., it was evidence going to an element of the crime itself, and it was relevant to ascertaining and preventing potential conflicts of interest, id. at 932. But here, the government claims no such compelling justifications.

It is also urged that a company may pretend cooperation while "circling the wagons," that payment of legal fees can advance such a strategy, and that the government has a legitimate interest in being able to assess cooperation using the payment of fees as one factor. Even if that can be a legitimate justification, it would not be in play here: prosecutors testified before the district court that they were never concerned that KPMG was "circling the wagons." Moreover, it is unclear how the circling of wagons is much different from the legitimate melding of a joint defense.

The government conceded at oral argument that it is in the government's interest that every defendant receive the best possible representation he or she can obtain. A company that advances legal fees to employees may stymie prosecutors by affording culpable employees with high-quality representation. But if it is in the government's interest that every defendant receive the best possible representation, it cannot also be in the government's interest to leave defendants naked to their enemies.

* * * Defendants were indicted based on a fairly novel theory of criminal liability; they faced substantial penalties; the relevant facts are scattered throughout over 22 million documents regarding the doings of scores of people, id. at 417; the subject matter is "extremely complex," id. at 418; technical expertise is needed to figure out and explain what happened; and trial was expected to last between six and eight months, id. As Judge Kaplan found, these defendants "have been forced to limit their defenses . . . for economic reasons and . . . they would not have been so constrained if KPMG paid their expenses." Id. at 419. We therefore hold that these defendants were also deprived of their right to counsel under the Sixth Amendment.

CONCLUSION

For the foregoing reasons, we Affirm the judgment of the district court dismissing defendants' indictment.

Notes and Questions

Of the remaining defendants whose indictments were not dismissed, three were convicted of various charges, one other KPMG partner and two investment advisors pled guilty, and one was acquitted of all charges.

Coincidentally, on the same day that the Second Circuit upheld the decision of Judge Kaplan, Deputy U.S. Attorney General Mark Filip announced new prosecution rules aimed at avoiding penalizing companies as noncooperative for protecting attorney-client material or paying for their employees' attorneys.

Another interesting Sixth Amendment case is Baxter v. U.S., 634 F.Supp.2d 897 (N.D. Ill. 2009). In this case, Laura Baxter, a CPA, was accused of submitting a false document to a revenue agent. She ultimately was convicted of obstruction of justice under 26 U.S.C. § 7212(a) and sentenced to two years in prison. She filed a motion to set aside or correct her sentence on the ground that her Sixth Amendment right had been violated because her attorneys had refused to retain an expert who could advise them on whether the government's tax loss compilation and calculation, used in determining her sentence, were correct. In granting her motion, the court noted that her attorneys had failed to object to the government's tax-loss amount and instead, had accepted it outright. If they had calculated the correct amount or hired an expert to do this, their client's sentence would have been significantly reduced. The court noted that Ms. Baxter had been "prejudiced by her criminal defense attorneys' constitutionally deficient performance." 634 F.Supp.2d at 911.

The court also stated that "defense counsel in criminal tax cases need not always retain a tax expert to assist." Id., at 908. But, Professor Steve R. Johnson notes that there are three aspects of the *Baxter* opinion worth considering: (1) the two attorneys representing Ms. Baxter were not "rank neophytes"; they were "experienced, skillful attorneys," (2) *Baxter* did not involve a "complicated sentencing puzzle." According to Professor Johnson, it was, among criminal tax cases, "at most, [of] middling complexity", (3) *Baxter* involved an abusive trust scheme of a type that has "been around for generations." Professor Johnson concludes by noting " if experienced counsel in a case of roughly average sentencing complexity involving a rather well-known class of issues needs to retain tax experts to satisfy the Sixth Amendment, *Baxter* and similar cases could mean that those experts will continue to be in demand." Steve R. Johnson, "The Sixth Amendment and Expert Witnesses In Criminal Tax Cases," 2009 TNT 171-9.

1. Why would KPMG have agreed in the first place to pay its employees' legal fees?

2. What practical effect would a decision to stop paying legal fees have on the KPMG defendants?

3. Why did Judge Kaplan continue to think there was a Sixth Amendment problem after the AUSA's statement that KPMG was "free to decide whether to advance legal fees"(statement of March 30, 2006)?

INDEX

References are to Pages

A

ABATEMENT
See Assessment; Interest; Penalties

ADMINISTRATIVE APPEALS PROCESS
234, 309, 311-318
Appeals conference, 312, 313, 314, 963 n.3,
1056, 1068, 1069, 1073
Appeals office waiver
See offer to waive restrictions on
assessment and collection
Burden of proof, 300
Collateral agreement, 317, 318
Closing agreement, 316, 317, 337, 344, 345,
387, 456
Docketed cases, 312, 314-315, 1089
Exhaustion of remedies, 963 n.3, 1068
Nondocketed cases, 312
Closing agreements, 60
Collateral agreement, 318
Offer in compromise, rejection of, 939
Offer to waive restrictions on assessment and
collection (Form 870-AD), 317, 337, 344,
345
Protest, 311, 312, 313-314, 1056
Recovery of costs, 312
Refund claims, 483, 499
Request for technical advice, 315
Settlements, 309, 312, 315, 316-318
Small case procedure, 313

ADMINISTRATIVE PROCEDURE ACT
Generally, 11, 12, 23, 26
Notice and comment, 11, 23, 25, 49, 365
Public disclosure, 155

ADMINISTRATIVE SUMMONS
See also Criminal Investigation
In general, 308, 347, 1068, 1356-1361
John Doe summons, 1359

ALTERNATIVE DISPUTE RESOLUTION
309, 316
Binding arbitration, 316
Fast track mediation, 921
Mediation, 316
Nonbinding arbitration, 316
Tax Court cases, 1015-1016

AMERICAN BAR ASSOCIATION (ABA)
Formal Opinions, 123, 124-139, 140, 143
Model Rules, 79, 123, 124, 139

**AMERICAN INSTITUTE OF CERTIFIED
PUBLIC ACCOUNTANTS (AICPA)**
139
Statements on Standards for Tax Services,
123, 139

**AMERICAN JOBS CREATION ACT OF
2004**
251-252, 443, 598, 599, 650, 669,
799, 949

ANTI-BROWSING PROVISION
195

ANTI-INJUNCTION ACT
815

ASSESSMENT
64, 68, 299, 319, 649, 678, 679, 827
Abatement, 483
Jeopardy and termination, 60, 346-347, 651,
938, 1068
Burden of proof, 508, 1023
Notice and demand for immediate
payment, 346, 521
Notice of appeal rights, 346
Post-assessment hearing, 346
Stay, 346
Offer to waive restrictions (Form 870-AD)
See Administrative Appeals Process
Penalties, 509, 510, 535
Restrictions, 470, 1054-1055
Waiver of restrictions (Form 870), 308-309,
310, 317, 334-345, 347, 444, 649, 651

**ASSISTANT TREASURY SECRETARY
FOR TAX POLICY**
2, 6, 10, 11, 26

AUDITS
See Examination of Returns and Civil
Investigations

B

BANKRUPTCY
See also Bankruptcy Court
Appellate panel, 69
Discharge of liabilities, 241, 850-859
    Penalties, 851
    Tolling of lookback periods, 858-859
    Trust fund taxes, 925
Estate, 68, 69, 827, 837-859
    Exemptions, 847
Petition, 68, 827, 837, 848, 850, 851, 909, 925, 936
Priority of claims, 848-850
    Penalties, 849-850, 851
    Post-petition interest, 849
    Pre-petition interest, 849
    Secured tax claims, 848, 849
    Unsecured tax claims, 848
    Stay, 68, 827-837, 925
    Damages for violation, 837

BANKRUPTCY CODE
848, 849, 851, 859

BANK SECRECY ACT
1303, 1310-1318
Antistructuring provision, 1310
Currency dealer or exchange, 1310
Financial institution, 1310

BLUE BOOK
See Legislation

BOOKS AND RECORDS
Access, 262-276
Duty to make and keep, 270
Third party contacts, 271
Prohibition against subsequent inspections, 271-276

BURDEN OF PROOF
See Administrative Appeals Process;
    Deficiency; Tax Court; Penalties

C

CERTIFICATE OF ASSESSMENT AND PAYMENT
692

CERTIFIED PUBLIC ACCOUNTANTS
71, 72, 195, 300

CIRCULAR 230
70-72, 79, 129, 139, 143-154
Disbarment, 144-149, 154

CIVIL INVESTIGATIONS
60, 1380

CLOSING AGREEMENTS
See Administrative Appeals Process

COLLATERAL AGREEMENTS
See Administrative Appeals Process

COLLATERAL ESTOPPEL
See Fraud

COLLECTIONS
Alternative collection, 936-949
Bankruptcy proceedings, 735, 736, 827-859
    See also Bankruptcy
Distraint, 679
Due process, 316, 738
Due process hearing, 680, 738, 760, 761, 768, 959
    Determination, 889
    Equivalent hearing, 761-768
Extension of time to pay, 936
Fiduciary liability
    See Third parties
Foreclosure suit, 768-779
Installment payment arrangements, 254, 316, 521, 709, 737, 768, 826, 936, 937-939, 948
Levy, 346, 679, 680, 708, 709, 738, 936, 948, 1068
    Continuous, 798-799
    Distraint, 794
    Exemptions, 798, 799
    Prohibition on levy, 760, 948
    Release of levy, 826
Liens, 679, 680, 693-738, 1068
    Discharge, 736
    Duration, 707-709
    Enforcement, 768-827
    Erroneous recording, 736
    Nonattachment, 735
    Release, 736-738
    Scope, 694-707
    Subordination, 737
Notice and demand, 105, 253, 299, 522, 649, 650, 679, 680-693, 815, 827
Notice and due process, 738
Notice of determination, 499, 680, 738-739, 759
Notice of intent to levy, 521, 738, 760, 768, 794, 798, 799

Notice of lien, 679, 680, 709, 736, 737, 738, 760, 939
Notice of sale, 799
Notice of seizure, 799
Offers in compromise, 254, 316, 318, 760, 936, 939-949
Priority of claims, 709-736
    Inchoate claims, 710-716
    Insolvency outside of bankruptcy, 724-736
    Superpriorities, 716-724
Restraining collection, 813-815
Sale of seized property, 768, 799-807
    Expedited sale, 800
    Right of redemption, 800
Statute of limitations
    See heading Statutes of Limitation
    CDP proceeding, 759-760
    Collection against third parties, 816-827
    Effect of judgment, 707-708
    Extensions, 948
    General, 707, 736, 759, 815-827
    Tolling, 759-760, 761
Tax Court review
    See U.S. Tax Court
Third parties, 859-903
    Fiduciary liability, 889, 897-903
    Innocent spouses, 859-889
    Third party rights, 800
    Transferee liability, 889-903
    Trust fund taxes, 846-847, 904-936
        Joint and several liability, 922-925
        Lenders and sureties, 930-936
        Partial payment, 925-930
        Responsible person, 910-922, 924-925, 930
Wrongful collection
    Civil damages, 808-813

COMMUNITY RENEWAL TAX ACT OF 2000
    485 n.4

COSTS, RECOVERY OF
    1055-1099
Administrative costs, 1055, 1073, 1074, 1088
Appealing a denial, 1099
Attorneys' fees, 1055, 1074-1077
Burden of proof, 1056, 1073, 1088
Exhaustion of remedies, 1056-1069
Interest, 1055, 1073
Litigation costs, 1055, 1074
Net worth requirement, 1094-1099
Prevailing party, 1055, 1056, 1077-1086
Qualified offers, 1089-1094

CRIMINAL INVESTIGATIONS
    60, 258, 301, 307, 1100, 1342-1388
Administrative summons, 262-271
Exclusionary rule, 1424, 1433-1434
    Silver platter doctrine, 1433
Exculpatory evidence, 1362-1373
Fraud, 301-302
Grand jury investigations, 1361-1380, 1387
    Secrecy, 1373-1380
Informants, 1354-1355
Investigative techniques, 1386-1388
    Mail cover, 1387-1388
    Wiretaps, 1388
Search warrants, 1386-1388, 1410
    Particularity, 1425-1434
    Plain view doctrine, 1434
    Warrantless searches, 1387
Summons, 301, 1356-1361
    John Doe Summons
        See Administrative Summons
    Third party, 1259, 1396
    Third party recordkeeper, 1355
Voluntary disclosure, 1380-1386
    Offshore accounts, 1385-1386

CRIMINAL OFFENSES
Aiding and assisting, 1100, 1126, 1179, 1186-1187, 1195, 1323
Bank fraud, 1178, 1218, 1248, 1254, 1361
Conspiracy, 1100, 1126, 1187, 1218-1239, 1318
    Defenses, 1227-1239
    Klein conspiracy, 1219, 1227
    Prosecutorial advantages, 1227
    Statute of limitations, 1227
    Vicarious liability, 1227
Currency transactions, 1100, 1296-1302
    See also Bank Secrecy Act
    Currency transaction report, 1296, 1303, 1318, 1355, 1359
    Related transactions, 1302
    Money laundering, 1218, 1268-1296
        Commingled funds, 1268-1275
        Forfeiture, 1275-1296
        Third party transferees, 1288-1296
        Tracing of forfeitable funds, 1276-1288
    Structuring, 1296, 1310, 1311
    Whistle blower protection, 1318
Defenses, 1197-1218
    Financial inability to pay, 1155-1167
    Lack of notice, 1202-1211
    Mental incompetence, 1211-1214
    Statute of limitations, 1214-1218
    Third party reliance, 1198-1202, 1211, 1303

Delivery of fraudulent statements and
    returns, 1101, 1188
Evasion, 851, 1101-1155, 1174, 1179, 1187,
    1195, 1217, 1254, 1324
        Acts of evasion, 1126-1139, 1154-
           1155, 1170, 1195
        Deficiency due, 1102-1121
        Methods of proof, 1114-1121
False and fraudulent return, 1126, 1239,
    1324, 1355, 1380
False statements (Title 18), 1239-1248 , 1318
Fraud and false statements, 1101, 1171-1187,
    1188, 1218
        Materiality, 1175-1179, 1247
Fraudulent withholding information, 1195
Lesser included offenses, 1188-1195
Mail fraud, 1100, 1178, 1218, 1248, 1253-
    1254, 1267, 1361
Obstruction or interference with
    administration of internal revenue laws,
    1195-1196, 1323
Perjury, 1100, 1174
Preparer disclosure, 1197
Preparers' penalty, 1179
RICO, 1100, 1218, 1254, 1361
Unauthorized disclosure and browsing, 1196-
    1197
Willful failure to collect or pay withholding
    tax, 1155-1167
Willful failure to file, pay or supply
    information, 1101, 1126, 1167-1171,
    1174, 1217, 1239, 1302
Willfulness, 1101, 1139-1155, 1167, 1179-
    1188, 1195, 1196, 1197, 1310-1311
Wire fraud, 1178, 1218, 1248, 1254, 1267,
    1318, 1361

CRIMINAL PROSECUTIONS
    1100, 1388-1501
Defenses
    Fifth amendment, 1441-1476
        Document production, 1460-1471
        Double jeopardy, 1471-1476
        Privilege against self-incrimination,
           1441-1460
    Fourth amendment, 1410-1440
        Particularity, 1425-1434
        Reasonableness, 1434-1440
        Standing, 1410-1425
    Sixth amendment, 1476-1501
Representation,
    Conflicts, 1398
Venue, 1388-1395
Witnesses
    Experts, 1396-1398
    Third party, 1395-1410

CUMULATIVE BULLETIN
    27-28, 58

D

DEFICIENCY
    See Assessment
Burden of proof, 333
Generally, 64, 240, 241, 254, 315, 319, 366,
    432, 510, 535, 555, 652, 963, 964, 1055,
    1113
Indirect methods of proof, 639,
Notice of, 64, 68, 278, 288, 309, 310, 314, 319,
    346, 347, 387, 470, 501, 502, 515, 649,
    651, 680, 708, 815, 827, 837, 963 n.3, 964,
    968, 975, 980, 982, 987, 1032, 1069, 1072,
    1073, 1074, 1088
Last known address, 319-32, 680, 968
Validity, 319-333, 680, 968-975
Preliminary notice of deficiency (30-day letter)
        See Preliminary Notice of Deficiency

DEFICIT REDUCTION ACT OF 1984
    986

DEPARTMENT OF JUSTICE
    See Justice Department

DOUBLE JEOPARDY
    631, 1126, 1267, 1318

E

**ECONOMIC RECOVERY TAX ACT OF
1981**
    601

**ECONOMIC SUBSTANCE DOCTRINE
(SEE ALSO PENALTIES)**
    566, 600

**EMERGENCY ECONOMIC
STABILIZATION ACT OF 2008**
    79

EMPLOYMENT TAXES
    64, 69, 848, 849, 921-936
        Trust fund taxes, 847, 848-849, 904-
          936

ENROLLED ACTUARIES
    71, 72, 195, 300

ENROLLED AGENTS
    1, 64, 71, 72, 195, 300

EQUITABLE REMEDIES
Equitable recoupment
    See Recoupment
Estoppel, 345
Tolling, 450-456

EVASION
    See Criminal Penalties

EXAMINATION OF RETURNS
Agreed cases, 308-309
Fraud and false statements, 253, 301
Generally, 255-311
Methods of examination, 259-260
    Correspondence audits, 259, 306, 309
    Field audits, 259-260, 300, 306, 307, 309,
        311
    Office audits, 259, 260, 300, 306, 307,
        309, 311
Methods of selection, 256
    Discriminant information function, 256,
        259
    Economic reality audit, 258
    Information reporting program, 256, 261
    Market segment specialization program,
        258-259
    Rational research program, 257
    Return preparer program, 256
    Taxpayer compliance measurement
        program, 256-257
Non-filer program, 261
Production of books and records, 262-263, 302
    Information document request, 301, 302
Prohibition against subsequent inspections,
    271-276
Revenue agent's report (RAR), 309, 310
Settlement, 307
Specialized audit procedures, 276-299
    Coordinated examination program, 276,
        297-299
    Employment tax examination program,
        276, 290-297
    Industry Sspecialization Program, 299,
        316
    TEFRA partnership audit procedure,
        277-290
Third party contacts, 271
Unagreed cases, 309-311

EXPERT WITNESSES
    See U.S. Tax Court; Criminal
        Prosecutions

F

**FEDERALLY AUTHORIZED TAX
    PRACTITIONERS**
    195, 302

**FEDERAL RULES OF CIVIL
    PROCEDURE**
    66

**FEDERAL RULES OF CRIMINAL
    PROCEDURE**
    207, 503, 1170, 1360, 1373

FEDERAL RULES OF EVIDENCE
    66, 311, 1038, 1039, 1396

FEDERAL TAX LIEN ACT
    935

**FIFTH AMENDMENT PRIVILEGE
    AGAINST SELF-INCRIMINATION**
    253

**FOURTH AMENDMENT PROHIBITION
    AGAINST COMPULSORY SEARCHES**
    270, 794

FRAUD
    See also Penalties, Civil and Criminal,
        262, 307, 851
Badges of fraud, 623
Burden of proof, 508, 623, 631, 1023
Collateral estoppel, 631-639

FREEDOM OF INFORMATION ACT
    50, 59, 60, 62, 155-170, 172, 173

G

GRAND JURY
Investigations, 1356
Proceedings, 1433

H

**HEALTH CARE AND EDUCATION
    RECONCILIATION ACT OF 2010**
    566, 599

HOUSE LEGISLATIVE COUNSEL
    3

**HOUSE WAYS AND MEANS
COMMITTEE**
See Legislation

I

**IMPROVED PENALTY
ADMINISTRATION AND
COMPLIANCE TAX ACT OF 1989
(IMPACT)**
87, 104, 105, 533, 534, 535

INFORMATION DOCUMENT REQUEST
301, 302

INNOCENT SPOUSE
64, 761, 798, 1054

INSTALLMENT AGREEMENTS
See Collections, Installment Payment
Arrangements

INTEREST
244, 253, 254, 309, 366, 402, 419, 432,
445, 501, 648-669, 723, 851, 936,
939, 1113
Abatement, 483-484, 533, 649-650, 651-652,
670-678, 1054
Accrual, 653-667, 759, 938
Alternative collection, 936, 938
Bankruptcy proceedings, 68
Carrybacks, 652-653
Deposits against accrual, 444, 650-653
Erroneous refunds, 484, 652, 667-668
Jeopardy assessments, 651
Overpayments, 650, 653-668, 655
Netting, 668-669
Global netting, 668
"Hot interest", 669
Payment, 651, 655
Underpayments, 444, 509, 535, 647, 649-653,
655
Waiver of restrictions on assessment, 444

INTERNAL REVENUE BULLETIN
26, 57, 566

INTERNAL REVENUE CODE
1, 9

INTERNAL REVENUE MANUAL
58, 63, 155, 308, 346, 509, 533, 618, 921,
1354

INTERNAL REVENUE SERVICE (IRS)
Appeals division, 7, 64, 299, 308, 309, 311, 313,
315, 374, 761, 1009, 1010
Appeals office, 59, 312, 315, 316, 738, 760, 963,
1008, 1009, 1072, 1074
Appeals officer, 59, 309, 313, 315, 316, 680,
738, 759, 959-960, 1073
Area director, 61
Assistant Commissioner (Technical), 62
Associate Chief Counsel, 26, 62
Case manager, 298
Chief Counsel, 7, 10, 50, 59, 60, 61, 62, 346,
1009
Commissioner, 6, 7, 8, 10, 11, 12, 26, 27, 32, 33,
62, 70, 959, 975, 987, 1053
Computing centers, 8-9
Criminal investigation division/unit, 7, 301,
1342, 1387, 1388
Customer service sites, 9
Director of practice, 70
District counsel, 315, 1009, 1010, 1342, 1387
District director, 59, 314, 1068
District offices, 6
Division counsel, 1342
Examination division, 59, 259, 301, 312, 482,
483
Examination officer, 315
Functional divisions, 7
National office, 6, 7, 26, 59, 61, 62, 256, 298,
315, 1388
National Taxpayer Advocate, 8, 9, 325, 533,
737, 748, 975
Office of Professional Responsibility, 144, 148,
149
Operating divisions, 7-8, 61
Oversight board, 8-9
Revenue agents, 63, 259, 260, 298, 299–300,
301, 307, 308, 310, 314, 482, 1354, 1355
Service centers (campuses), 8-9, 242, 253, 256,
482
Special agents, 1342, 1354, 1355, 1356, 1380,
1386, 1387, 1410
"Ten deadly sins", 9
Whistleblower office, 1354-1355

**IRS RESTRUCTURING AND REFORM
ACT OF 1998**
6-9, 59, 243, 281 n.21, 311, 316, 333,
346, 378, 485 n.3, 648, 649, 671,
709, 859-860, 937, 938, 948, 986,
1024, 1032

J

JEOPARDY AND TERMINATION ASSESSMENTS
See Assessments

JOINT BOARD FOR ENROLLMENT OF ACTUARIES
71

JOINT COMMITTEE ON TAXATION
See Legislation

JUDICIAL DEFERENCE
See Treasury Regulations, Judicial Review

JUSTICE DEPARTMENT
Criminal Tax Section, 1275, 1342
Tax Division, 66, 1254, 1267, 1275, 1387
Division Counsel, 64, 66
U.S. Attorney, 1342, 1361

L

LEGISLATION
Blue Book, 2 n.3, 89, 566
Conference Committee, 4, 5
Conference Report, 4
Effective date, 4
House Ways and Means Committee, 2, 3, 4
Hearings, 3
House Ways and Means Committee Report, 3
Joint Committee on Taxation, 2, 3, 89, 485, 566
Joint Committee Report, 3
Revenue neutrality, 5
Senate Finance Committee, 2, 3, 4
Senate Finance Committee Report, 3

LIENS
See Collection

LISTED TRANSACTIONS
See Tax Shelters; Reportable Transactions

LEVY
See Collections

M

MAGNETIC MEDIA
See Returns

MAILBOX RULE
See also Returns; Payment

MITIGATION (STATUTORY)
See also Statutes of Limitation

MODEL RULES OF PROFESSIONAL CONDUCT (ABA)
See American Bar Association

MONEY LAUNDERING CONTROL ACT,
1268

N

NOTICE AND DEMAND
See Collection

NOTICE OF DEFICIENCY
See Deficiency

NOTICE OF LIEN
See Collections

O

OFFERS IN COMPROMISE
See Collection

OMNIBUS BUDGET RECONCILIATION TAX ACT OF 1989
645

ORGANIZED CRIME CONTROL ACT
1254

P

PAYMENT
432-445
Cash bond, 650
Deemed paid rule, 444
Deposits, 432, 443-445
Disputable items, 443
Disputable tax, 443, 444
Due date, 649
Electronic federal tax payment system, 255
Electronic returns, 243-244
Extensions, 244, 253, 649, 936
Interest
See also Interest (separate heading)
Mailbox rule, 649

PENALTIES - CIVIL
79, 432, 445, 509-648, 851, 938, 939

Abatement, 306, 533

Adequate disclosure, 547, 548, 555, 577-581, 598, 599, 607

Aiding and abetting understatement, 106-112

Accuracy related, 56, 533-617, 639
    Disregard of rules and regulations, 254, 534, 542-548, 600
    Negligence, 254, 534-542, 547, 548, 600, 607, 623
    Substantial estate or gift tax valuation understatement, 534
    Substantial overstatement of pension liabilities, 534
    Substantial understatement, 89, 139, 534, 535, 548-600, 607
    Substantial valuation misstatement, 534, 600-617
    Transaction lacking economic substance, 534
    Undisclosed foreign financial asset understatement, 534

Assessment, 366

Bankruptcy petition, effect of, 521

Burden of production, 1024-1032

Burden of proof, 508, 623

Delinquency, 242, 509-533, 542, 639, 671
    Late filing, 241, 255, 510-516, 520, 521, 522, 532, 851
    Late payment, 254, 255, 510, 515, 516-522, 532, 693, 938
    Late payment after notice and demand, 510, 522

Estimated taxes, 521, 639, 646-648

Failure to file information returns, 347

Failure to produce books and records, 262

Financial inability to pay, 532

Fraud, 254, 301, 607, 617-631, 639, 671, 1100

Fraudulent failure to file, 515, 851

Frivolous returns, 639-645, 1170

100% penalty, 509, 904, 909, 930, 936

Listed transactions, 671

Promoting abusive shelters, 93-105
    Burden of proof, 105, 1023
    Gross valuation overstatement, 105
    Injunctions, 105

Realistic possibility standard, 548

Reasonable basis standard, 535, 547, 555, 577

Reasonable cause, 151, 254, 510, 522-533, 535-548, 555, 577, 582-597, 608-617, 647-648

Reportable transactions, 89, 92, 547, 599, 671

Return preparer penalties, 79, 144, 1023
    Adequate disclosure, 89, 90, 90-91, 92, 143
    Aggressive return positions, 143-144
    Burden of proof, 1023
    Failure to sign return, 92-93

Frivolous positions, 143

Injunctions, 115-123

Negligence, 87, 88

Realistic possibility, 139, 143

Reasonable basis, 90, 91, 92, 139, 143

Reasonable cause, 91-92

Reckless or intentional disregard of IRS rules and regulations, 92

Substantial authority, 89-90, 91, 92, 139

Substantial understatement, 92

Unauthorized disclosure, 115

Unreasonable position, 79, 89

Willful disregard, 92

Willfulness, 87, 88, 92, 144

Substantial authority, 52, 535, 555-577, 598, 599

Tax protestors, 1170

Tax shelters
    See Tax Shelters

Transactions lacking economic substance, 548, 565, 599

PENALTIES - CRIMINAL
    79, 939

Aiding and abetting, 112-114

Defenses
    See Criminal Offenses

Evasion, 638, 639

Failure to file, 241, 639, 645
    Information returns, 347

Failure to pay, 521

Fraud, 623

Unauthorized disclosure, 114, 193

PENSION PROTECTION ACT OF 2006
    758

POWER OF ATTORNEY (FORM 2848)
    71 n.4, 300, 313, 429, 670

PRIVACY ACT
    171-173, 193, 300, 1196

PRELIMINARY NOTICE OF DEFICIENCY (30-DAY LETTER)
    309-311, 314, 443, 650, 1068, 1073, 1074

PRIVILEGE

Attorney-client, 60, 195-207, 233, 1387

Federally authorized tax practitioners
    See separate heading, above

Log, 303

PROTEST
    See Administrative Appeals Process

R

RECOUPMENT
See Statutes of Limitation
REFUND ANTICIPATION LOANS
243

REFUND CLAIMS
70, 307, 308, 309, 310, 344, 345, 388-429,
500, 502, 653-654
Amended returns, 653-654
Amended claims, 482
Anti-assignment, 426
Bankruptcy court, 68
Disallowance, 483
Erroneous refunds, 483, 667-668
Filing, 419-450, 470
Formal claims, 402-407
Informal claims, 407-411
Joint Committee review, 485
Lookback rule, 444, 449, 501-502
Notice of disallowance, 498, 499, 500
Overpayment, 388-402, 445, 652-653
Setoff, 483, 504
Substantial variance, 410, 411-419, 504

REFUND LITIGATION
307, 309, 310, 345, 485-508, 1069
Burden of proof, 504-508
Divisible tax principle, 497-498, 508
Full payment rule, 485, 486-497
Interest, 499
Pleadings, 503-504
Statute of limitations, 498-503
Suits on account stated, 500

REGULATIONS
See Treasury Regulations

REPORTABLE TRANSACTIONS
See Tax Shelters

RETURNS
Amended returns, 249-253, 366-374, 388, 520,
630, 670, 671, 1197
Effect on estimated tax penalty, 647
Confidentiality, 60, 157, 173-194, 1197
Filing, 242-249
Certified/registered mail, 248
Due date, 242, 510
Electronic filing, 243-244
Extensions, 244-249, 254, 444
Magnetic media, 243
Mailbox rule, 242, 245, 249
Generally, 234-253
Nonfilers, 260-262

Processing, 9
Substantial preparation, 87
Substitute return, 241, 261, 516-520

RETURN PREPARERS
79, 80-87, 88
See also Penalties

REVENUE ACT OF 1913
171

REVENUE ACT OF 1924
64

REVENUE ACT OF 1978
292

REVENUE AGENT'S REPORT (RAR)
309, 310

**RIEGLE COMMUNITY DEVELOPMENT
AND REGULATORY IMPROVEMENT
ACT OF 1994**
1311

RULINGS
Acquiescences, 62
Actions on decisions, 62, 566
Chief counsel advice, 59, 60, 61
Closing agreements
See Administrative Appeals Process
Consistency, 51-57, 61
Determination letters, 61, 170
Disclosure, 60, 61
Field service advice, 59, 60
General counsel memoranda, 566
Generally, 1, 6, 7, 26-63
Information letters, 61
Judicial deference, 1-2, 33-49
Precedent, 27, 50, 56, 59
Private letter rulings, 26, 50-57, 60, 89, 155,
566, 1072
Retroactivity, 27-33
Revenue procedures, 57-58, 89, 566, 1072
Revenue rulings, 26-49, 60, 89, 170, 566, 1072
Revenue rulings program, 26-27
Substantial authority, 56
Technical advice memoranda, 7, 59, 89, 155,
170, 315, 566, 1072
User fees, 56

S

SET-OFF
66

SMALL BUSINESS JOBS PROTECTION ACT OF 1996
277 n.8, 297

SMALL BUSINESS AND WORK OPPORTUNITY TAX ACT OF 2007
79, 485 n.3, 672

STANDARDS OF TAX PRACTICE
70, 79-154
Administrative standards, 143-154
Certified public accountants, 139
Professional standards, 123-143
Statutory standards, 79-123

STATUTES OF LIMITATION
Amended returns, 366-374
Assessment, 64-65, 66, 68, 240, 241, 242, 245, 262, 286, 300, 345, 347-348, 432, 678, 708, 1032, 1054
Bankruptcy petition (effect of), 68, 708
Collection, 240, 241, 432, 707-709, 759
Criminal offenses, 759
Extensions, 347, 708
    By agreement, 347-348, 373-387, 948, 1068
Fraud, 300, 345, 347, 1218
Interest, 648-649, 668
Listed transactions, 351, 599-600
Notice of deficiency (effect of), 347
Refund claims, 242, 429-482
Refund suits, 485-508, 759
Remedies
    Equitable tolling, 69, 319, 325, 450-456, 499
    Mitigation, 297, 456-471, 482
    Recoupment, 471-482
Substantial omissions of income, 345, 347, 348-366
Tolling, 649, 759, 1032
Waiver, 1318

STATUTORY NOTICE OF DEFICIENCY
See Deficiency, Notice of

SUITS ON ACCOUNT STATED
See Statutes of Limitation

SUMMONS POWER
See Administrative Summons; Criminal Investigation

T

TAX EQUITY AND FISCAL RESPONSIBILITY ACT OF 1982 (TEFRA)
277-278, 287-289

TAX INCREASE PREVENTION AND RECONCILIATION ACT OF 2005
948

TAX LEGISLATIVE COUNSEL
10

TAX MATTERS PARTNER
280-282

TAXPAYER ASSISTANCE ORDERS
9

TAXPAYER BILL OF RIGHTS
TBOR 1 (1988), 300, 302, 306
TBOR 2 (1996), 12, 302, 736, 921, 1068, 1088
TBOR 3 (1998), 302 n.85, 1074

TAXPAYER RELIEF ACT OF 1997
278, 279, 287, 502

TAX RELIEF AND HEALTHCARE ACT OF 2006
645, 1354

TAX REFORM ACT OF 1986
10

TAX SHELTERS
89, 92, 195, 351, 565, 597-600
Abusive, 149-151, 498, 597
    Promoting, 93, 508, 1023
Corporate taxpayers, 151, 598
Definition, 150, n.7, 151-152, 597
Listed transaction, 151, 152, 233, 597, 599-600
"More likely than not" standard, 89, 139, 150-151, 152, 598, 599
Noncorporate taxpayers, 598
Opinions, 129-139, 148, 150, 151, 541
    Covered opinion, 151-153, 154
    Limited scope opinion, 153
    Marketed opinion, 152
    Negative opinions, 129-130, 139, 150
    Reliance opinion, 152
    Standards of professional conduct, 93-106
Other written advice, 153-154
Reportable transactions, 89, 92, 547, 597, 599, 600
Standard settlement policy, 307, 308

"TEN DEADLY SINS"
See Internal Revenue Service

TERMINATION ASSESSMENT
63

TREASURY REGULATIONS
Effective dates, 12
Generally, 1, 6, 10-25, 566
Interpretive regulations, 10, 13, 25
Judicial review (deference), 1, 12-25
Legislative regulations, 10, 13, 25
Procedural regulations, 10, 25
Promulgation, 10-12
Proposed regulations, 11, 89, 566
Retroactivity, 12, 25, 89
Temporary regulations, 11-12, 24, 566

U

U.S. BANKRUPTCY COURT
63, 67-69, 813, 828, 850, 963
See also Bankruptcy
Appeals, 69
Jurisdiction, 68-69, 827
Petition, 347, 827, 837, 963 n.2

U.S. COURT OF FEDERAL CLAIMS
63, 66, 67, 171, 285, 388, 471, 499, 510,
645, 963, 964, 988
Appeals, 67
Pleadings
Answer, 503-504
Complaint, 503
Jurisdiction, 68, 485, 496
Precedent, 67

U.S. CIRCUIT COURT OF APPEALS
60, 1046, 1053, 1054, 1170

U.S. DISTRICT COURTS
62, 65-67, 105, 115, 157, 285, 388, 471,
499, 510, 645, 963, 964, 988, 1170
Appeals, 67, 1046
Burden of proof, 66
Criminal penalties, 1100
Discovery, 66
Jurisdiction, 65, 66, 67, 485, 496, 1100
Lien enforcement, 768
Pleadings
Answer, 503-504
Complaint, 66, 503
Precedent, 66
Settlement potential, 66
Summons enforcement, 1356, 1358, 1359
Whistleblower suits, 1318

U.S. SENTENCING COMMISSION GUIDELINES
1100-1101, 1113, 1170, 1171, 1319-
1341
Sentencing under the Guidelines, 1324-1341
Tax loss, 1319-1324, 1500

U.S. TAX COURT
Alternative dispute resolution, 309, 1015
Appeals, 65, 314-315, 960-963, 1046-1054
Bond, 1055
Interlocutory, 1047-1053
Protective, 1053
Venue, 1053-1054
Bankruptcy, 68-69, 827
Burden of proof, 66, 1023-1038, 1056
Chief judge, 65, 1044, 1045
Collection due process, 1054
Continuance, 1021-1023
Costs
See Recovery of Costs
Decision, 1045
Finality, 65, 828, 1054-1055
Discovery, 988-1008
Entry of decision, 1045, 1046, 1053
Evidence, 64, 1038-1044
Expert witnesses, 988, 993, 1002, 1039, 1043-
1044, 1074
Filing fee, 968
Generally, 7, 62, 63-65, 66, 67, 649, 963
Golsen rule, 758, 960-963, 1044, 1054
Judge, 315, 1021, 1044
Judgment, 313-314
Jurisdiction, 66, 67, 310, 388, 432, 471, 496,
500, 501, 502, 515, 678, 827, 837, 964-982,
1054
Equity jurisdiction, 964
Exclusivity, 965-968
Expanded, 1054
Refund jurisdiction, 964
New issues, 1046
Opinions, 65, 1044
Penalties, 510, 515, 1100
Petition, 64, 68, 278, 285-286, 288, 312, 314,
319, 333, 500, 827, 828, 837, 964, 968,
981-982, 1009, 1021, 1054
Last date for filing, 975, 982
Statute of limitations, 69, 708, 1032
Pleadings, 987-988
Pre-trial conferences, 1008
Proper parties, 975
Protective orders, 1016-1021
Recovery of costs, 1055-1099
Remedies,
Equity, 471-482
Refunds, 388, 500-503
Reports, 1039, 1044, 1045

Review of determination (collection due process), 739-759, 760
S cases, 65, 963, 982, 983, 1009, 1045, 1046
Settlements, 66, 1008-1010
Special trial judges, 65, 1045
Standards of professional conduct, 123
Stipulations, 66, 1008, 1009, 1010-1015, 1023
Stipulated decision, 1010, 1046
Test cases, 1015
Whistleblower actions, 65, 1054

W

WAIVER OF RESTRICTIONS ON ASSESSMENT
    See Assessment

WITNESSES
    See Expert Witnesses

WORK PRODUCT DOCTRINE
    60, 207-233

*